Honoring America

For Americans, the flag has always had a special meaning. It is a symbol of our nation's freedom and democracy.

Flag Etiquette

Over the years, Americans have developed rules and customs concerning the use and display of the flag. One of the most important things every American should remember is to treat the flag with respect.

- The flag should be raised and lowered by hand and displayed only from sunrise to sunset. On special occasions, the flag may be displayed at night, but it should be illuminated.
- The flag may be displayed on all days, weather permitting, particularly on national and state holidays and on historic and special occasions.
- No flag may be flown above the American flag or to the right of it at the same height.
- The flag should never touch the ground or floor beneath it.

- The flag may be flown at half-staff by order of the president, usually to mourn the death of a public official.
- The flag may be flown upside down only to signal distress.
- The flag should never be carried flat or horizontally, but always carried aloft and free.
- When the flag becomes old and tattered, it should be destroyed by burning. According to an approved custom, the Union (stars on blue field) is first cut from the flag; then the two pieces, which no longer form a flag, are burned.

The American's Creed

I believe in the United States of America as a Government of the people, by the people, for the people, whose just powers are derived from the consent of the governed; a democracy in a republic; a sovereign Nation of many sovereign States; a perfect union, one and inseparable; established upon those principles of freedom, equality, justice, and humanity for which American patriots sacrificed their lives and fortunes.

I therefore believe it is my duty to my Country to love it; to support its Constitution; to obey its laws; to respect its flag, and to defend it against all enemies.

The Pledge of Allegiance

I pledge allegiance to the Flag of the United States of America and to the Republic for which it stands, one Nation under God, indivisible, with liberty and justice for all.

The Star-Spangled Banner

O! say, can you see, by the dawn's early light,
What so proudly we hail'd at the twilight's last gleaming?
Whose broad stripes and bright stars, thro' the perilous fight,
O'er the ramparts we watched were so gallantly streaming?
And the rockets' red glare, the bombs bursting in air,
Gave proof thro' the night, that our flag was still there.
O! say, does that Star-Spangled Banner yet wave
O'er the land of the free and the home of the brave?

On the shore, dimly seen thro' the mist of the deep,
Where the foe's haughty host in dread silence reposes,
What is that which the breeze, o'er the towering steep,
As it fitfully blows, half conceals, half discloses?
Now it catches the gleam of the morning's first beam,
In full glory reflected now shines on the stream.
'Tis the Star-Spangled Banner. O long may it wave
O'er the land of the free and the home of the brave.

And where is that band who so vauntingly swore,
That the havoc of war and the battle's confusion
A home and a country should leave us no more?
Their blood has wash'd out their foul footstep's pollution.
No refuge could save the hireling and slave
From the terror of flight or the gloom of the grave,
And the Star-Spangled Banner in triumph doth wave
O'er the land of the free and the home of the brave.

O thus be it e'er when free men shall stand
Between their lov'd home and war's desolation,
Blest with vict'ry and peace, may the Heav'n-rescued land
Praise the pow'r that hath made and preserv'd us a nation.
Then conquer we must, when our cause it is just,
And this be our motto, "In God is our Trust."
And the Star-Spangled Banner in triumph shall wave
O'er the land of the free and the home of the brave.

Teacher Wraparound Edition

Glencoe

WORLD HISTORY

Modern Times

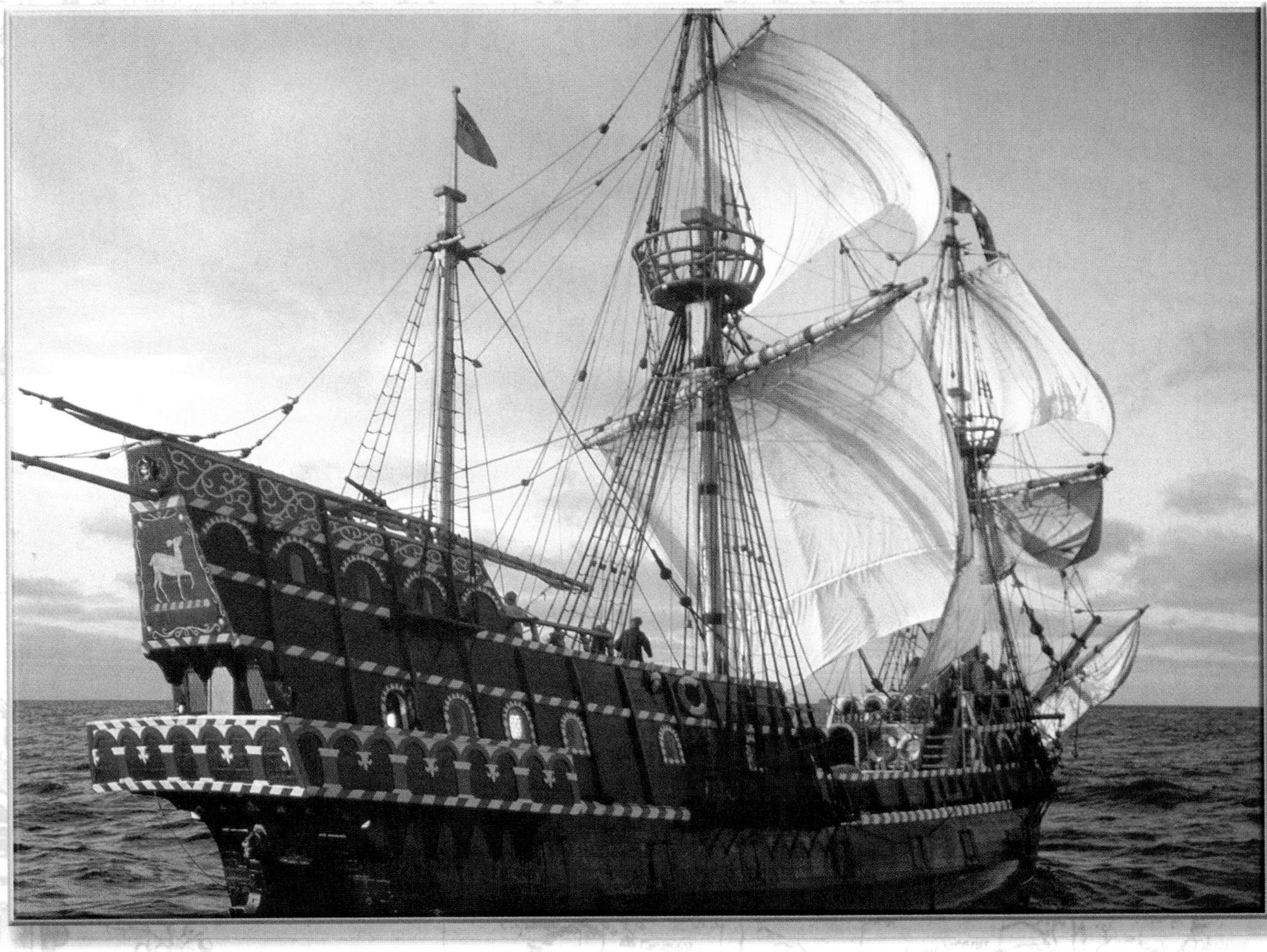

JACKSON J. SPIELVOGEL, Ph.D.

New York, New York Columbus, Ohio Chicago, Illinois Peoria, Illinois Woodland Hills, California

Authors

Jackson J. Spielvogel

Jackson J. Spielvogel is associate professor emeritus of history at The Pennsylvania State University. He received his Ph.D. from The Ohio State University, where he specialized in Reformation history under Harold J. Grimm. His articles and reviews have appeared in such journals as *Moreana, Journal of General Education, Archiv für Reformationsgeschichte,* and *American Historical Review.* He has also contributed chapters or articles to *The Social History of the Reformation, The Holy Roman Empire: A Dictionary Handbook, Simon Wiesenthal Center Annual of Holocaust Studies,* and *Utopian Studies.* His book *Hitler and Nazi Germany* was published in 1987 (fourth edition, 2001). His book *Western Civilization* was published in 1991 (fourth edition, 2000). He is the co-author (with William Duiker) of *World History,* published in 1994 (third edition, 2001). Professor Spielvogel has won five major university-wide teaching awards, and in 1997, he became the first winner of the Schreyer Institute's Student Choice Award for innovative and inspiring teaching.

The National Geographic Society, founded in 1888 for the increase and diffusion of geographic knowledge, is the world's largest nonprofit scientific and educational organization. Since its earliest days, the Society has used sophisticated communication technologies, from color photography to holography, to convey geographic knowledge to a worldwide membership. The School Publishing Division supports the Society's mission by developing innovative educational programs—ranging from traditional print materials to multimedia programs including CD-ROMs, videos, and software.

Glencoe/McGraw-Hill
A Division of The McGraw-Hill Companies

Printed in the United States of America.
Send all inquiries to:
Glencoe/McGraw-Hill
8787 Orion Place
Columbus, Ohio 43240-4027

ISBN 0-07-829944-6 (Student Edition)
ISBN 0-07-829945-4 (Teacher Wraparound Edition)

1 2 3 4 5 6 7 8 9   071/055   05 04 03 02 01

Consultants & Reviewers

Academic Consultants

W. Lindsay Adams, Ph.D.
Department of History
University of Utah
Salt Lake City, Utah

Frank de Varona, Ph.D.
College of Education
Florida International University
Miami, Florida

Anthony Florek, Ph.D.
School of Behavioral
and Social Sciences
St. Edwards University
Austin, Texas

Richard Golden, Ph.D.
Department of History
University of North Texas
Denton, Texas

Jonathan Grant, Ph.D.
Department of History
Florida State University
Tallahassee, Florida

Robert E. Herzstein, Ph.D.
Department of History
University of South Carolina
Columbia, South Carolina

Marilynn J. Hitchens, Ph.D.
College of Liberal Arts and Sciences
University of Colorado
Denver, Colorado

Farid Mahdavi, Ph.D.
College of Arts and Letters
San Diego State University
San Diego, California

Frances Malino, Ph.D.
Department of History
Wellesley College
Wellesley, Massachusetts

Shabbir Mansuri
Founding Director
Susan Douglass
Affiliated Scholar
Council on Islamic Education
Fountain Valley, California

The Reverend Marvin O'Dell
Faith Baptist Church
Thousand Oaks, California

Rabbi Joseph Rosenbloom, Ph.D.
Temple Emmanuel
St. Louis, Missouri

Eric C. Rust, Ph.D.
Department of History
Baylor University
Waco, Texas

Teacher Reviewers

Larayne Anderson
Hudson's Bay High School
Vancouver, Washington

Joan Arno
George Washington High School
Philadelphia, Pennsylvania

Michele Austin
La Reina High School
Thousand Oaks, California

Linda Clark
Padua Franciscan High School
Parma, Ohio

Candee Collins
Pine Tree High School
Longview, Texas

Timothy Connell
Laurel School
Shaker Heights, Ohio

W. Dean Eastman
Beverly High School
Beverly, Massachusetts

William Everdell
St. Ann's School
Brooklyn, New York

Sam Gellens, Ph.D.
Horace Mann School
Riverdale, New York

Helen Grady
Springfield High School
Philadelphia, Pennsylvania

Anthony Hammontree
H. Grady Spruce High School
Dallas, Texas

Robert Hastings
H. Grady Spruce High School
Dallas, Texas

Mel Maskin, Ph.D.
The Bronx High School of Science
Bronx, New York

Ronald Romancheck
H. Grady Spruce High School
Dallas, Texas

David Seiter
Northridge High School
Layton, Utah

Bonnie Sussman
Bishop O'Dowd High School
Oakland, California

Andrew Turay
Evander Childs High School
Bronx, New York

Jeff Wright
John Marshall High School
Rochester, Minnesota

Contents

Alternative Course Outlines ... T18
NCSS Thematic Strands ... T19
Scope and Sequence ... T26
Classroom Solutions: Teacher Professional Handbook ... T30
What Is History? ... xviii
Reading for Information ... xxii
Geography's Impact on History ... xxiv

NATIONAL GEOGRAPHIC Reference Atlas

World: Political ... RA2
World: Physical ... RA4
North America: Political ... RA6
North America: Physical ... RA7
South America: Political ... RA8
South America: Physical ... RA9
Europe: Political ... RA10
Europe: Physical ... RA12
Africa: Political ... RA14
Africa: Physical ... RA15
Asia: Political ... RA16
Asia: Physical ... RA18
Middle East: Physical/Political ... RA20
Pacific Rim: Physical/Political ... RA22
World Land Use ... RA24
World Population Cartogram ... RA26
World Gross Domestic Product Cartogram ... RA28
World's People ... RA30
World Historical Eras ... RA32
Polar Regions ... RA34

NATIONAL GEOGRAPHIC Geography Handbook

How Do I Study Geography? ... 2
Globes and Maps ... 4
Common Map Projections ... 6
Understanding Latitude and Longitude ... 8
Types of Maps ... 9
Geographic Dictionary ... 10

UNIT 1

The World Before Modern Times, 12
Prehistory–A.D. 1500

CHAPTER 1
The First Civilizations and Empires, Prehistory–A.D. 500 ... **16**
1 The First Humans ... 19
2 Western Asia and Egypt ... 24
3 India and China ... 36

CHAPTER 2
Ancient Greece and Rome, 1900 B.C.–A.D. 500 ... **48**
1 Ancient Greece ... 51
2 Rome and the Rise of Christianity ... 66

SPECIAL FEATURE
World Religions ... 80–85

CHAPTER 3
Regional Civilizations, 400–1500 ... **86**
1 The World of Islam ... 89
2 Early African Civilizations ... 97
3 The Asian World ... 103
4 Emerging Europe and the Byzantine Empire ... 116

CHAPTER 4
Toward a New World, 1000–1500 ... **126**
1 Europe in the Middle Ages ... 129
2 The Americas ... 140

UNIT 2

The Early Modern World, *1400–1800* 150

CHAPTER 5
Renaissance and Reformation, 1350–1600 . . . . . **154**
1 The Renaissance 157
2 The Intellectual and Artistic Renaissance 164
3 The Protestant Reformation 171
4 The Spread of Protestantism and the Catholic Response 177

CHAPTER 6
The Age of Exploration, 1500–1800 . . . **186**
1 Exploration and Expansion 189
2 Africa in an Age of Transition 197
3 Southeast Asia in the Era of the Spice Trade 201

CHAPTER 7
Crisis and Absolutism in Europe, 1550–1715 . . . . . **208**
1 Europe in Crisis: The Wars of Religion 211
2 Social Crises, War, and Revolution 216
3 Response to Crisis: Absolutism 223
4 The World of European Culture 230

CHAPTER 8
The Muslim Empires, 1450–1800 . . . . . **236**
1 The Ottoman Empire 239
2 The Rule of the Safavids 250
3 The Grandeur of the Moguls 255

CHAPTER 9
The East Asian World, 1400–1800 . . . . **264**
1 China at Its Height 267
2 Chinese Society and Culture 273
3 Tokugawa Japan and Korea 278

SPECIAL FEATURE
World Languages 286–289

CHAPTER 10
Revolution and Enlightenment, 1550–1800 . . . . . **290**
1 The Scientific Revolution 293
2 The Enlightenment 300
3 The Impact of the Enlightenment 308
4 Colonial Empires and the American Revolution 318

CHAPTER 11
The French Revolution and Napoleon, 1789–1815 . . . . . **326**
1 The French Revolution Begins 329
2 Radical Revolution and Reaction 337
3 The Age of Napoleon 345

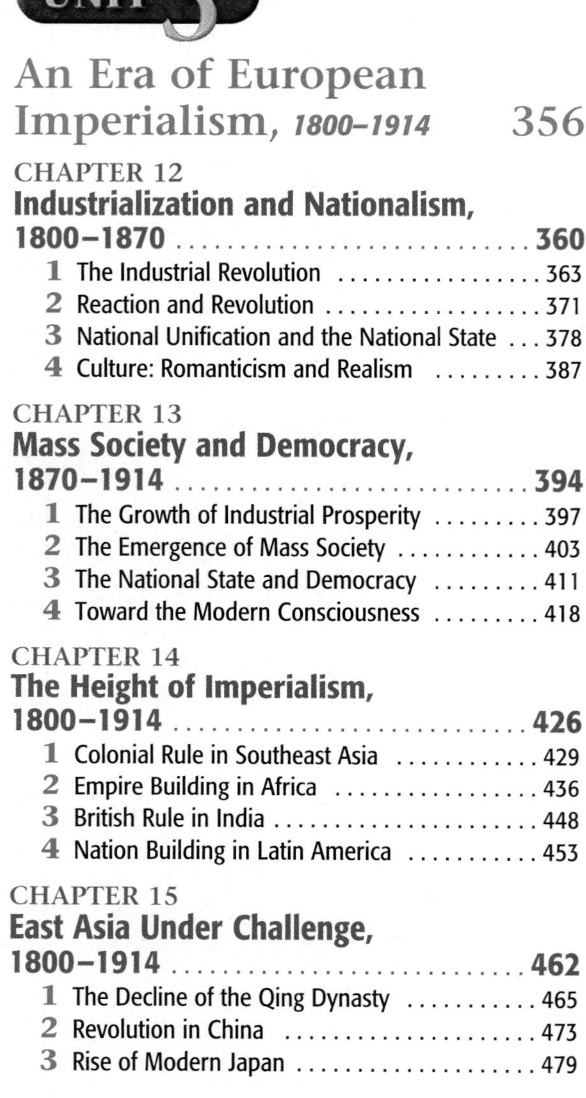

UNIT 3

An Era of European Imperialism, *1800–1914* 356

CHAPTER 12
Industrialization and Nationalism, 1800–1870 ... 360
1 The Industrial Revolution ... 363
2 Reaction and Revolution ... 371
3 National Unification and the National State ... 378
4 Culture: Romanticism and Realism ... 387

CHAPTER 13
Mass Society and Democracy, 1870–1914 ... 394
1 The Growth of Industrial Prosperity ... 397
2 The Emergence of Mass Society ... 403
3 The National State and Democracy ... 411
4 Toward the Modern Consciousness ... 418

CHAPTER 14
The Height of Imperialism, 1800–1914 ... 426
1 Colonial Rule in Southeast Asia ... 429
2 Empire Building in Africa ... 436
3 British Rule in India ... 448
4 Nation Building in Latin America ... 453

CHAPTER 15
East Asia Under Challenge, 1800–1914 ... 462
1 The Decline of the Qing Dynasty ... 465
2 Revolution in China ... 473
3 Rise of Modern Japan ... 479

UNIT 4

The Twentieth-Century Crisis, *1914–1945* 492

CHAPTER 16
War and Revolution, 1914–1919 ... 496
1 The Road to World War I ... 499
2 The War ... 503
3 The Russian Revolution ... 514
4 End of the War ... 521

CHAPTER 17
The West Between the Wars, 1919–1939 ... 530
1 The Futile Search for Stability ... 533
2 The Rise of Dictatorial Regimes ... 540
3 Hitler and Nazi Germany ... 548
4 Cultural and Intellectual Trends ... 554

CHAPTER 18
Nationalism Around the World, 1919–1939 ... 560
1 Nationalism in the Middle East ... 563
2 Nationalism in Africa and Asia ... 568
3 Revolutionary Chaos in China ... 575
4 Nationalism in Latin America ... 581

CHAPTER 19
World War II, 1939–1945 ... 588
1 Paths to War ... 591
2 The Course of World War II ... 596
3 The New Order and the Holocaust ... 606
4 The Home Front and the Aftermath of the War ... 612

UNIT 5

Toward a Global Civilization, *1945–Present* 624

CHAPTER 20
Cold War and Postwar Changes, 1945–1970 .... **628**
1 Development of the Cold War 631
2 The Soviet Union and Eastern Europe 637
3 Western Europe and North America 642

CHAPTER 21
The Contemporary Western World, 1970–Present **654**
1 Decline of the Soviet Union 657
2 Eastern Europe 661
3 Europe and North America 666
4 Western Society and Culture 671

CHAPTER 22
Latin America, 1945–Present **680**
1 General Trends in Latin America 683
2 Mexico, Cuba, and Central America 688
3 The Nations of South America 693

CHAPTER 23
Africa and the Middle East, 1945–Present **700**
1 Independence in Africa 703
2 Conflict in the Middle East 711

CHAPTER 24
Asia and the Pacific, 1945–Present **720**
1 Communist China 723
2 Independent States in South and Southeast Asia 734
3 Japan and the Pacific 739

CHAPTER 25
Challenges and Hopes for the Future **748**
1 The Challenges of Our World 751
2 Global Visions 756

Appendix

Mini Almanac 765
Primary Sources Library 770
Honoring America 782
Glossary 783
Spanish Glossary 790
Index 798
Acknowledgements 828

Features

Primary Sources Library

Unit 1
An Egyptian Father's Advice to His Son 772
A Woman May Need to Have the Heart of a Man 773
The Buddha's Sermon 773

Unit 2
A Reformation Debate 774
The Silk Industry in China 775
Declaration of the Rights of Woman and the Female Citizen 775

Unit 3
Imperial Decree to Free the Serfs 776
The Unfortunate Situation of Working Women 777
The Impact of British Rule in India 777

Unit 4
Over the Top—World War I 778
Gandhi Takes the Path of Civil Disobedience 779
The Holocaust—The Camp Victims 779

Unit 5
Progress Never Stops 780
An Ideal for Which I Am Prepared to Die 781
China's Gilded Age 781

SCIENCE, TECHNOLOGY & SOCIETY

Papermaking in Han China 44
Harnessing the Power of Water and Wind 130
The Impact of Printing 162
Sea Travel in an Age of Exploration 191
The Changing Face of War 218
The Automobile 398
The Atomic Bomb 616

THE WAY IT WAS

Young People In . . .
Greece 56
The Ottoman Empire 242
Revolutionary France 340
The Industrial Revolution 368
China 476
Nazi Germany 550

Sports & Contests
The Deadly Games of Central America 142
The Martial Arts in China 270
The New Team Sports 408

Focus on Everyday Life
The Castles of the Aristocrats 118
At the Court of Versailles 224
British Official's Home in India 450
Trench Warfare 504
Youth Protest in the 1960s 646

FACT FICTION FOLKLORE

The First Razor 22
Robin Hood 131
Cyclones in India 257
The Hitokiri Battousai 481
"Tears, Sweat, and Blood"? 603
Electronic Road Pricing 743

Opposing Viewpoints

How Did the Arab Empire Succeed? 92
What Was the Impact of Columbus on the Americas? 192
Who Benefited from the New Imperialism? 440
Who Caused World War I? 522

Features

CONNECTIONS

Around the World

Rulers and Gods 55
Gunpowder and Gunpowder Empires 202
Natural Disasters in History 220
A Population Explosion 274
A National Holiday 333
The Role of Quinine 439
The Great Flu Epidemic 534
Paths to Modernization 571
Women as Spies in World War II 601
Economic Miracles: Germany and Japan 644
Global Terrorism 673
International Women's Conferences 686
Global Migrations 712
Cities and Cars 742

Past to Present

Conflict in Palestine 31
From African Rhythms to Rock and Roll 100
From Saint Nicholas to Santa Claus 135
The Descendants of the Anabaptists 180
Conflict in Yugoslavia 240
Magazines, Then and Now 305
Russian Troops in Hungary 375
May Day 400
The Return of Hong Kong to China 467
The Mystery of Anastasia 516

Eyewitness to History

Hammurabi's Code 35
Cincinnatus Saves Rome 77
The Salt Mines 102
The *Quipu* 145
The Genius of Leonardo da Vinci 170
Columbus Lands in the Americas 196
Queen Elizabeth's Golden Speech 215
An Elephant Fight for the King's Entertainment 261
The Japanese Discover Firearms 283
The Mission 323
Declaration of the Rights of Man and the Citizen 336
Revolutionary Excitement 377
Marx and Engels Proclaim the Classless Society 402
A Call to Arms 435
A Letter to the Emperor 487
Ten Days That Shook the World 520
The Formation of Collective Farms 547
The Path to Liberation 574
A German Soldier at Stalingrad 605
"I Have a Dream" 651
Václav Havel—The Call for a New Politics 665
Student Revolt in Mexico 692
The Suez Canal Belongs to Egypt 717
School Regulations, Japanese Style 745

What If...

Roman legions had defeated the Germanic tribes? 68
Britain's East India Company had been a financial disaster? 259
Napoleon had won at Waterloo? 351
Trotsky had succeeded Lenin? 545
Quebec had seceded from Canada? 670
Salvador Allende had lost the Chilean election? 695
Mao Zedong had died on the Long March? 726

World Literature

Li Bo, Five Poems 148
Voltaire, from *Candide* 354
George Orwell, from *Shooting an Elephant* 490
Virginia Woolf, from *A Room of One's Own* 622
Chinua Achebe, "Civil Peace," from *Girls and War and Other Stories* 762

Features

NATIONAL GEOGRAPHIC Special Report

More Than Myth to the *Iliad* 62
Lord of the Mongols, Genghis Khan 112
The World of Süleyman 246
Stanley and Livingstone in Africa 444
The *Lusitania* 510
Transforming Beijing 730

A Story That Matters

The Cradle of the Human Race .... .18
Pericles Addresses Athens .... .50
Japan Faces Kublai Khan .... .88
Two Cultures Collide .... .128
Painting the Sistine Chapel .... .156
Magellan Sails Around the World .... .188
The Majesty of Louis XIV .... .210
The Conquests of Babur .... .238
Mission to China .... .266
Galileo on Trial .... .292
Fall of the Bastille .... .328
The Congress of Vienna .... .362
The New Leisure .... .396
Livingstone in Africa .... .428
Looting of the Summer Palace .... .464
The Battle of the Somme .... .498
The Great Depression .... .532
Gandhi's March to the Sea .... .562
Hitler's Vision .... .590
A Sober Victory .... .630
"Tear Down This Wall" .... .656
The Castro Brothers .... .682
Revolution in Iran .... .702
A Movement for Democracy .... .722
A Time for Heroes .... .750

People In History

Hatshepsut 29
Hannibal 67
Sundiata Keita 98
Hildegard of Bingen 133
King Afonso I 200
Peter the Great 229
Matsuo Basho 281
Mary Wollstonecraft 304
Frederick II
(Frederick the Great) 311
Sor Juana Inés de la Cruz 320
Jean-Paul Marat 338
Maximilien Robespierre 338
Anne-Louise-Germaine de Staël 348
Klemens von Metternich 373
Berthe Morisot 421
Ci Xi 470
Sun Yat-sen 474
Edith Cavell 509
Georges Clemenceau 524
Benito Mussolini 542
Joseph Stalin 543
Mao Zedong 579
Chiang Kai-shek 579
Winston Churchill 603
Anne Frank 607
Nikita Khrushchev 639
Charles de Gaulle 643
Simone de Beauvoir 649
Jackson Pollock 675
Gabriela Mistral 687
Rigoberta Menchú 691
Eva Perón 694
Nelson Mandela 705
Desmond Tutu 705
Deng Xiaoping 725
Mother Teresa of Calcutta 736

SKILLBUILDER

Social Studies

Finding Exact Location on a Map 277
Interpreting Graphs 344
Understanding World Time Zones 641
Interpreting Statistics 710

Critical Thinking

Understanding Cause and Effect 23
Making Comparisons 61
Distinguishing Between Fact and Opinion 96
Analyzing Primary and Secondary Sources 139
Making Inferences and Drawing Conclusions 205
Making Generalizations 222
Identifying an Argument 386
Detecting Bias 417
Interpreting Military Movements on Maps 527
Analyzing Political Cartoons 539
Synthesizing Information 619
Reading a Cartogram 729

Technology

Evaluating a Web Site 443
Using an Electronic Spreadsheet 580
Developing a Database 697
Developing Multimedia Presentations 759

Study & Writing

Summarizing Information 176
Using Library Resources 254
Outlining 317
Writing a Report 472
Preparing a Bibliography 677

Looking Back...to See Ahead

Systems of Law 14
Revolution 152
Industrialization 358
International Peacekeeping 494
Communication 626

Primary Source Quotes

Unit 1

The World Before Modern Times

Socrates . . . 13

CHAPTER 1 • The First Civilizations and Empires

Spanish girl, on discovering Stone Age cave paintings . . . 19
Early Arab traveler, praising the Nile . . . 24
Hammurabi's Code . . . 35
Confucius, on good government . . . 36

CHAPTER 2 • Ancient Greece and Rome

Thucydides, on the Peloponnesian War . . . 51
Plutarch, on education of boys in Sparta . . . 56
Plato, on money and virtue, from *The Apology of Socrates* . . . 58
Virgil, on Roman art of governing . . . 66
Livy, *The Early History of Rome* . . . 77

CHAPTER 3 • Regional Civilizations

Ibn Sina, describing his early training . . . 89
Herbert J. Muller, from *The Loom of History* . . . 92
Albert Hourani, from *A History of the Arab Peoples* . . . 92
Ibn Battuta, on an African king and his subjects . . . 97
Ibn Battuta, describing work in the salt mines . . . 102
John of Plano Carpini, on the Mongols . . . 103
Bishop Fulbert of Chartres, on lords and vassals . . . 116

CHAPTER 4 • Toward a New World

Pope Gregory VII, a decree . . . 129
Sioux sacred woman, on the sacredness of all creation . . . 140
Description of the *Quipu* . . . 145

Unit 2

The Early Modern World

Immanuel Kant . . . 151

CHAPTER 5 • Renaissance and Reformation

Machiavelli, from *The Prince,* on political power . . . 157
Pico della Mirandola, from *Oration on the Dignity of Man* . . . 164
Giorgio Vasari, describing Leonardo da Vinci . . . 170
Martin Luther, refusing to renounce his religious views . . . 171
Ignatius Loyola, on principles of Catholicism . . . 177

CHAPTER 6 • The Age of Exploration

Christopher Columbus, reporting on his first journey . . . 189
Samuel Eliot Morrison, from *Admiral of the Ocean Sea: A Life of Christopher Columbus* . . . 192
David E. Stannard, from *American Holocaust: Columbus and the Conquest of the New World* . . . 192
George P. Horse Capture, from "An American Indian Perspective," *Seeds of Change* . . . 193
Christopher Columbus, describing his arrival on the island of Hispaniola . . . 196
Dutch trader, on the slave trade . . . 197
Observer, on unhealthiness of Batavia for Dutch settlers . . . 201

CHAPTER 7 • Crisis and Absolutism in Europe

Description of conflict during French Wars of Religion . . . 211
Queen Elizabeth I, *The Golden Speech* . . . 215
Survivor of Thirty Years' War, a report . . . 216
French bishop Jacques Bossuet, on sacredness of kings . . . 228
Shakespeare, patriotic passage from *Richard II* . . . 230

CHAPTER 8 • The Muslim Empires

Greek writer, describing Ottoman Turk conquest of Constantinople . . . 239
English traveler, on beauty of Persian capital Isfahan . . 250
English traveler, on lavish lifestyle of Mogul ruler . . . 255
A French traveler, describing an Indian festival for the emperor . . . 261

CHAPTER 9 • The East Asian World

Ferdinand Verbiest, on Chinese emperor Kangxi . . . 267
Italian Matteo Ricci, admiring Chinese printing . . . 273
Japanese government edict for peasants . . . 278
Daimyo, describing how to use a firearm . . . 283

Primary Source Quotes

CHAPTER 10 • Revolution and Enlightenment

Galileo, describing observations with telescope 293
Voltaire, on religious intolerance 300
Prussian king Frederick II, on duties of a monarch . . . 308
Declaration of Independence 318
Félix de Azara, describing a Jesuit mission in Paraguay 323

CHAPTER 11 • The French Revolution and Napoleon

Newspaper correspondent, on French Revolution 329
Declaration of the Rights of Man and the Citizen . . . 336
Henry de Firmont, on execution of King Louis XVI 337
Napoleon, on the greatness of great men 345

Unit 3

An Era of European Imperialism

Cecil John Rhodes 357

CHAPTER 12 • Industrialization and Nationalism

Berlin factory rules for workers in 1844 363
Prince von Metternich, on political stability 371
Carl Schurz, *Reminiscences* 377
London *Times*, report on Giuseppe Garibaldi 378
Otto von Bismarck, on military force. 381
Charles Dickens, description of old mill town 387

CHAPTER 13 • Mass Society and Democracy

Marconi, reporting discovery of radio waves 397
Karl Marx and Friedrich Engels, *The Communist Manifesto* 402
Sylvia Pankhurst, on efforts of women to vote 403
Description of massacre of petitioners of Czar Nicholas II 411
Camille Pissarro, on his philosophy of painting 418

CHAPTER 14 • The Height of Imperialism

Douwes Dekker, on the Dutch colonial system 429
An appeal to Vietnamese citizens to resist the French 435
King Lo Bengula, letter to Queen Victoria 436
Rudyard Kipling, from *The White Man's Burden* 440
Edward Morel, from *The Black Man's Burden* 440
Thomas Macaulay, on the English language 448
Simón Bolívar, proclamation to people of New Granada 453

CHAPTER 15 • East Asia Under Challenge

Zhang Zhidong, arguing against political reforms 465
Sun Yat-sen, arguing for reforms 473
Wang Tao, on the need for reform in China 475
Japanese imperial decree for schoolchildren 479
President Millard Fillmore, letter to the emperor of Japan 487

Unit 4

The Twentieth-Century Crisis

Winston Churchill 493

CHAPTER 16 • War and Revolution

Conspirator, on assassination of Archduke Ferdinand. . 499
Emperor William II of Germany, on the power of the sword 501
Stefan Zweig, describing Austrians going to war 503
John Reed, describing beginning of Bolshevik revolution 514
John Reed, *Ten Days That Shook the World* 520
Description of first tanks used in World War I. 521
Treaty of Versailles, Article 231, 1919. 522
Sidney Bradshaw Fay, from *Origins of the World War* 522
Harry Elmer Barnes, from the *Genesis of the World War* 523
Fritz Fischer, from *Germany's Aims in the First World War* 523

CHAPTER 17 • The West Between the Wars

Description of workers protesting government policies 533
Mussolini, on the principles of fascism. 540
Max Belov, *The History of a Collective Farm* 547
Adolf Hitler, from speech appealing to the German people. 548
Adolf Hitler, on lying to the masses. 553
Poet Tristan Tzara, on the artistic movement dadaism 554

CHAPTER 18 • Nationalism Around the World

Hayyim Bialik, at opening of the Hebrew University of Palestine 563
Jomo Kenyatta, advocating independence in Kenya . . . 568
Ho Chi Minh, on becoming a Communist 574
Mao Zedong, calling for massive peasant revolt 575
Getúlio Vargas, explaining his New State. 581

Primary Source Quotes

CHAPTER 19 • World War II

Winston Churchill, on failure to support Czechoslovakia 591
Adolf Hitler, demanding allegiance of all Germans 596
German soldier, on the Battle of Stalingrad. 605
Rudolf Höss, on arrival of Jews at Auschwitz 606
German civilian, on an Allied bombing raid 612

Unit 5

Toward a Global Civilization

Nelson R. Mandela 625

CHAPTER 20 • Cold War and Postwar Changes

Winston Churchill, defining the "iron curtain" 631
Soviet Union, explaining takeover of Hungary 637
Student graffiti on walls of University of Paris in 1968 . . 642
Martin Luther King, Jr., *I Have a Dream*. 651

CHAPTER 21 • The Contemporary Western World

Mikhail Gorbachev, on restructuring world thinking. . . 657
Roy Gutman, on "ethnic cleansing" in Bosnia 661
Václav Havel, a speech to the U.S. Congress 665
German reporter, describing attacks against foreigners 666
Economist E.F. Schumacher, on evolving lifestyle 671

CHAPTER 22 • Latin America

Observer, on U.S. intervention in Panama in 1989 683
Catholic missionary, on an encounter with the contras. . 688
Account of the clash between the government and students in Mexico, October 2, 1968 692
Catholic priest, on the economic "miracle" in Brazil . . . 693

CHAPTER 23 • Africa and the Middle East

Humphrey Taylor, on massacre of black demonstrators in South Africa 703
David Ben-Gurion, announcing formation of the State of Israel in 1948. 711
Gamal Abdel Nasser, speech nationalizing the Suez Canal Company 717

CHAPTER 24 • Asia and the Pacific

Widow in Chiang Kai-shek's regime, on the Red Guards. 723
Maneka Gandhi, from article "Why India Doesn't Need Fast Food" 734
Kumiko Fujimura-Fanselow, from introduction to book, *Japanese Women* 739
School regulations, Japanese style. 745

CHAPTER 25 • Challenges and Hopes for the Future

Rachel Carson, on use of pesticides, from *Silent Spring* 751
The United Nations, from the *Universal Declaration of Human Rights* 756

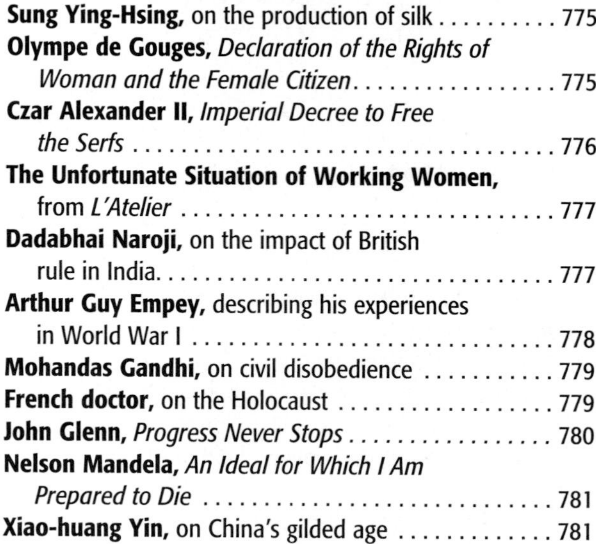

Primary Sources Library

Vizier Ptah-hotep, giving instructions to his son 772
Christine de Pizan, *The Treasure of the City of Ladies* 773
The Buddha's Sermon 773
Martin Luther and Huldrych Zwingli, debating the sacrament of the Lord's Supper 774
Sung Ying-Hsing, on the production of silk 775
Olympe de Gouges, *Declaration of the Rights of Woman and the Female Citizen*. 775
Czar Alexander II, *Imperial Decree to Free the Serfs* 776
The Unfortunate Situation of Working Women, from *L'Atelier* 777
Dadabhai Naroji, on the impact of British rule in India. 777
Arthur Guy Empey, describing his experiences in World War I 778
Mohandas Gandhi, on civil disobedience 779
French doctor, on the Holocaust 779
John Glenn, *Progress Never Stops* 780
Nelson Mandela, *An Ideal for Which I Am Prepared to Die* 781
Xiao-huang Yin, on China's gilded age 781

Charts, Graphs, & Tables

Unit 1

Comparing Life in Mesopotamia and Egypt 30
The Ten Commandments 32
Major World Religions 80
Dynasties of China, 581–1279 104
Economic Changes in the Middle Ages 147

Unit 2

Ottoman and Safavid Empires 252
Expansion of the Ottoman Empire, 1451–1566 263
World Languages 286
"How Are You?"—Language Comparisons 288
Reading Chinese Characters 288
Ptolemaic Universe 294
Copernican Universe 295
The Three Estates in Pre-Revolutionary France 330

Unit 3

Comparing Britain and the United States 366
Revolution in the Arts and Sciences 420
Forms of Government, 1900 425
Height of European Imperialism 430
Meiji Restoration: Birth of Modern Japan 482

Unit 4

Paris Peace Conference: The Big Three 529
Treaty of Versailles 529
Three Dictators: Mussolini, Stalin, and Hitler 552
Selected Nationalist Movements in the Early Twentieth Century 584
Battle Deaths in World War II 599
World War II: Attack and Counterattack 600

Unit 5

Economic Spectrum 668
Population of Latin America, 1950–2020 685
Democratic Reforms in Latin America 690
2001 Index of Economic Freedom 710
Foundations of Postwar Japan 741

Mini Almanac

World Population, A.D. 1–2001 766
Population by Continent, 2001 766
Life Expectancy 766
Infant Mortality 766
Most Populous Countries 766
World's Richest Countries 767
World's Poorest Countries 767
Highest Inflation Rates 767
Lowest Inflation Rates 767
World's Ten Largest Companies, 2000 767
Most Livable Countries 768
Highest Adult Literacy Rates 768
Lowest Adult Literacy Rates 768
Years, by Country, in which Women Gained the Right to Vote 768
World Adult Illiteracy by Gender 768
Highest Military Expenditures 769
Nuclear Weapons Capability 769
Communication around the World 769

Three Dictators: Mussolini, Stalin, and Hitler

	Benito Mussolini (1883–1945)	Joseph Stalin (1879–1953)	Adolf Hitler (1889–1945)
Country	Italy	USSR	Germany
Political Title	Prime Minister	General Secretary	Chancellor
Date in Power	1922	1929	1933
Political Party	Fascist Party	Communist Party	National Socialist German Workers' Party (NSDAP, or Nazi)
Type of Government	Fascist	Communist	Fascist
Source(s) of Support	Middle-class industrialists and large land owners	Party officials	Industrial leaders, landed aristocrats, military, and bureaucracy
Methods of Controlling Opposition	Secret police (OVRA), imprisonment, outlawing other parties, propaganda, censorship of the press	Purges, prison camps, secret police, state-run press, forced labor camps, executions	*Schutzstaffeln* (SS) police force, propaganda, state-run press, terror, repression, racial laws, concentration and death camps
Other Characteristics	Support for Catholic Church, nationalism, antisocialism, anticommunism	Five-Year Plans for rapid industrialization, collectivization of farms	Enabling Act, rearmament, public projects to put people to work, anti-Semitism, racism, social Darwinism, extreme nationalism

NATIONAL GEOGRAPHIC Maps

NATIONAL GEOGRAPHIC Reference Atlas

World: Political RA2
World: Physical RA4
North America: Political RA6
North America: Physical RA7
South America: Political RA8
South America: Physical RA9
Europe: Political RA10
Europe: Physical RA12
Africa: Political RA14
Africa: Physical RA15
Asia: Political RA16
Asia: Physical RA18
Middle East: Physical/Political RA20
Pacific Rim: Physical/Political RA22
World Land Use RA24
World Population Cartogram RA26
World Gross Domestic Product Cartogram RA28
World's People RA30
World Historical Eras RA32
Polar Regions RA34

Unit 1

Spread of Farming to 1 B.C. 21
Ancient Mesopotamia 26
Persian Empire, 500 B.C. 33
Aryan Migration, 2000–500 B.C. 38
Trade Routes of the Ancient World 41
Han Empire, 202 B.C.–A.D. 221 43
Early Asian Civilizations 47
Greece, 1400 B.C. 52
Empire of Alexander the Great, 323 B.C. 59
Roman Empire: Trade and Expansion 69
Invasions into the Roman Empire, A.D. 200–500 75
Greek Colonies, 750–550 B.C. 79
World Religions 80
Spread of Islam, 632–750 91
Trading for Salt and Gold in West Africa, A.D. 800–1500 99
Sui, Tang, and Song Empires in China, 581–1279 104
Early Japan 107
Southeast Asia, 1200 110
Europe, 1160 120
Crusades, 1096–1204 122
Agriculture of West Africa 125
Cultures of Mesoamerica, 900 B.C.–A.D. 1500 141

Unit 2

Renaissance Italy, 1500 159
Artists of the Renaissance 167
Political Europe, 1555 174
Major European Religions, 1600 181
Holy Roman Empire, 1400 185
European Voyages of Discovery 190
Atlantic Slave Trade, 1500s–1600s 198
European Trade in Southeast Asia, 1700 203
Height of Spanish Power, c. 1560 213
Defeat of the Spanish Armada, 1588 214
Thirty Years' War, 1618–1648 217
Europe after the Peace of Westphalia, 1648 219
Expansion of Prussia, 1618–1720 227
Expansion of Austria, 1525–1720 227
Expansion of Russia, 1462–1796 228
Growth of France under Louis XIV, 1643–1715 235
Expansion of the Ottoman Empire, c. 1300–1699 241
Safavid Empire, c. 1700 251
Expansion of the Mogul Empire, 1530–1707 256
British in India, c. 1700 258
Voyages of Zheng He, 1405–1433 268
Ming and Qing Empires, 1368–1911 269
Early Japan 277
Tokugawa Japan, 1603–1868 280
Japan, 1572 285
World Languages 286
Europe in the Age of Enlightenment 306
Dominant Religions (during the Enlightenment) 306
Europe, 1795 313
Seven Years' War, 1756–1763 314
French and Indian War 315
Seven Years' War in Europe 315
Seven Years' War in India 315
Colonial Latin America to 1750 319
Seven Years' War in the West Indies 325
Spread of the Great Fear, 1789 334
Napoleonic Europe, 1799–1815 349
Reign of Terror, 1793–1794 353

Unit 3

Industrialization of Europe by 1870 . . . 367
Europe after the Congress of Vienna, 1815 . . . 372
Revolutions in Europe, 1848–1849 . . . 376
Unification of Italy, 1859–1870 . . . 379
Unification of Germany, 1866–1871 . . . 380
Slaveholders, 1860 . . . 384
Industrialization of Europe by 1914 . . . 399
European Population Growth and Relocation, 1820–1900 . . . 404–405
Europe, 1871 . . . 412
Imperialism in Southeast Asia, 1900 . . . 431
Imperialism in Africa, 1914 . . . 437
Imperialism in Africa, 1880 . . . 437
Panama Canal . . . 456
Travel Distance (and the Panama Canal) . . . 456
Suez Canal . . . 461
Qing Empire, 1911 . . . 466
Spheres of Influence in China, 1900 . . . 469
Japanese Expansion, 1870–1918 . . . 484

Unit 4

Alliances in Europe, 1914 . . . 500
World War I in Europe, 1914–1918 . . . 507
Russian Revolution and Civil War, 1917–1922 . . . 517
Europe and the Middle East after World War I . . . 525
Middle East in World War I, 1914–1918 . . . 527
Europe, 1923 . . . 535
Politics of Europe, 1930s . . . 541
Soviet Union, 1914–1938 . . . 544
Spanish Civil War, 1936–1939 . . . 559
Middle East, 1919–1935 . . . 565
Africa, 1919–1939 . . . 569
Japanese Expansion, 1910–1933 . . . 572
China, 1926–1937 . . . 577
Latin America, 1939 . . . 582
Geography of China and Japan, c. 1920 . . . 587
German and Italian Expansion, 1935–1939 . . . 593
Japanese Expansion, 1933–1941 . . . 594
World War II in Europe and North Africa, 1939–1945 . . . 598
Axis Offensives, 1939–1941 . . . 599
Allied Offensives, 1942–1945 . . . 599
World War II in Asia and the Pacific, 1941–1945 . . . 602
Major Nazi Camps . . . 608
Europe after World War II . . . 617

Unit 5

Divided Germany and the Berlin Air Lift . . . 633
Balance of Power after World War II . . . 634
Time Zones of the World . . . 641
European Economic Community, 1957 . . . 645
Cuban Missile Crisis, 1962 . . . 653
Breakup of the Soviet Union, 1991 . . . 659
Former Yugoslavia, 1991–1999 . . . 663
Expansion of the European Union, 1957–1995 . . . 667
Caucasus Region, 1991 . . . 679
U.S. Involvement in Latin America since 1945 . . . 684
Per Capita Income, 1960s (Latin America) . . . 685
Main Exports, 1990s (Latin America) . . . 685
Population of Latin America, 2000 . . . 699
Independent Africa . . . 704
Modern Middle East and Palestinian Conflict . . . 713
China, 1949–1989 . . . 724
Korean War, 1950–1953 . . . 727
Relative Exports of Asian Nations, 1999 (cartogram) . . . 729
Partition of India, 1947 . . . 735
Vietnam War, 1968–1975 . . . 737
Modern Japan . . . 740
Indochina, 1946–1954 . . . 747
Global Deforestation . . . 752
Radioactive Fallout from Chernobyl, 1986 . . . 761

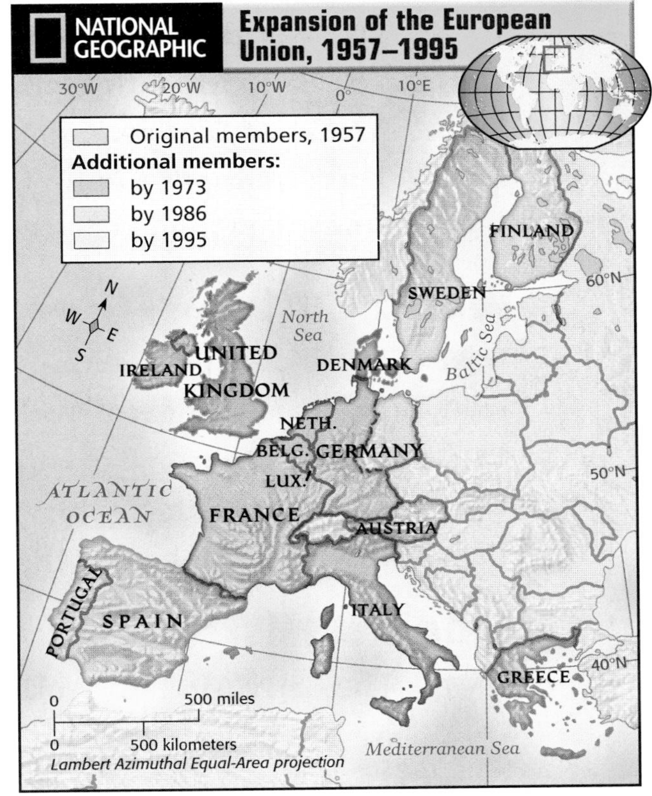

Five Alternative Course Outlines

Glencoe World History—Modern Times may be used in a variety of courses. Listed below are five examples.

OUTLINE 1 — World History Survey

UNIT 1 The World Before Modern Times .... *Chapters 1, 2, 3, 4*
UNIT 2 The Early Modern World .... *Chapters 5, 6, 7, 8, 9, 10, 11*
UNIT 3 An Era of European Imperialism .... *Chapters 12, 13, 14, 15*
UNIT 4 The Twentieth-Century Crisis .... *Chapters 16, 17, 18, 19*
UNIT 5 Toward a Global Civilization .... *Chapters 20, 21, 22, 23, 24, 25*

OUTLINE 2 — Western Civilization

UNIT 1 The World Before Modern Times .... *Chapters 1, 2, 4*
UNIT 2 The Early Modern World .... *Chapters 5, 6, 7, 10, 11*
UNIT 3 An Era of European Imperialism .... *Chapters 12, 13, 14*
UNIT 4 The Twentieth-Century Crisis .... *Chapters 16, 17, 19*
UNIT 5 Toward a Global Civilization .... *Chapters 20, 21, 25*

OUTLINE 3 — Non-Western Civilization

UNIT 1 The World Before Modern Times .... *Chapters 1, 3*
UNIT 2 The Early Modern World .... *Chapters 6, 8, 9*
UNIT 3 An Era of European Imperialism .... *Chapters 14, 15*
UNIT 4 The Twentieth-Century Crisis .... *Chapters 16, 18, 19*
UNIT 5 Toward a Global Civilization .... *Chapters 22, 23, 24, 25*

OUTLINE 4 — World Cultures/Global Studies

UNIT 1 The World Before Modern Times .... *Chapters 1, 2, 3, 4*
UNIT 2 The Early Modern World .... *Chapters 5, 6, 7, 8, 9, 10, 11*
UNIT 3 An Era of European Imperialism .... *Chapters 12, 13, 14, 15*
UNIT 4 The Twentieth-Century Crisis .... *Chapters 17, 18*
UNIT 5 Toward a Global Civilization .... *Chapters 20, 21, 22, 23, 24, 25*

OUTLINE 5 — Modern History

UNIT 2 The Early Modern World .... *Chapters 5, 6, 7, 8, 9, 10, 11*
UNIT 3 An Era of European Imperialism .... *Chapters 12, 13, 14, 15*
UNIT 4 The Twentieth-Century Crisis .... *Chapters 16, 17, 18, 19*
UNIT 5 Toward a Global Civilization .... *Chapters 20, 21, 22, 23, 24, 25*

Correlation to

NCSS Ten Thematic Strands

In *Curriculum Standards for Social Studies: Expectations of Excellence,* the National Council for the Social Studies (NCSS) identified 10 themes that serve as organizing strands for the social studies curriculum at every school level. These themes are interrelated and draw from all of the social science disciplines. Each theme provides student performance expectations in the areas of knowledge, processes, and attitudes. The 10 NCSS themes were the basis for the themes used in *Glencoe World History—Modern Times.*

Theme and Performance Expectation	Student Pages
I. *Culture* The study of culture helps students understand similarities and differences within groups of people. By studying a culture's beliefs, values, and traditions, students begin to gain a perspective that helps them relate to different groups. In high school, students can understand and use complex cultural concepts such as adaptation, assimilation and acculturation to explain how culture and cultural systems function. *Glencoe World History—Modern TImes* Related Theme: The Importance of Cultural Development/Religion in History	
A. Analyze and explain the ways groups, societies, and cultures address human needs and concerns.	21, 26–27, 30, 32, 35, 37–39, 43–45, 47, 50, 55, 57, 60, 61, 68, 70–72, 74, 78–79, 88, 94–95, 98–101, 102, 105, 106, 108–109, 111, 118–119, 123, 124–125, 128, 131–132, 135, 138, 144, 145, 146–147, 172, 271, 323, 370, 391, 646, 656, 671
B. Predict how data and experiences may be interpreted by people from diverse cultural perspectives and frames of reference.	30, 32, 35, 37–39, 45, 46, 55, 57, 60, 65, 68, 92–93, 95, 96, 111, 125, 128, 135, 139, 261, 272, 284, 234
C. Apply an understanding of culture as an integrated whole that explains the functions and interactions of language, literature, the arts, traditions, beliefs and values, and behavior patterns.	22, 25–27, 29–30, 31–33, 38–45, 46, 50, 53, 54, 55, 59, 60, 72, 78–79, 88, 94–95, 100, 101, 105, 106, 108–109, 111, 124, 128, 134, 144, 145, 146, 156, 197, 230, 253, 260, 281, 309, 310, 387, 388, 421, 450, 485, 556, 674, 687
D. Compare and analyze societal patterns for preserving and transmitting culture while adapting to environmental or social change.	27–30, 31–32, 38–39, 43–45, 46–47, 50, 55, 58, 60, 71, 72, 74, 76, 78–79, 94–95, 99, 100, 106, 110, 111, 124–125, 135, 138, 144, 145, 146–147, 171, 201, 223, 259, 282, 328, 408, 409, 410, 646, 647
E. Demonstrate the value of cultural diversity, as well as cohesion, within and across groups.	26–27, 29–30, 31–33, 36, 38, 41–42, 43–45, 54, 59, 60, 61, 67, 69, 71, 94, 95, 100, 105, 107, 109, 128, 131, 270, 464, 471, 486
F. Interpret patterns of behavior reflecting values and attitudes that contribute or pose obstacles to cross-cultural understanding.	31, 33–34, 37–38, 47, 53, 58, 70, 71, 73–74, 79, 88, 91, 101, 106, 109–110, 121, 124–125, 134, 138, 139, 143, 146, 193, 196, 198, 266, 269, 275, 294, 420, 430, 672
G. Construct reasoned judgments about specific cultural responses to persistent human issues.	22, 23, 30, 31, 34, 35, 45, 47, 71, 76, 92–93, 95, 101, 102, 105, 109, 111, 119, 124, 135, 138, 144, 145, 146–147, 216, 243, 276, 376, 389, 184, 420, 647
H. Explain and apply ideas, theories, and modes of inquiry drawn from anthropology and sociology in the examination of persistent issues and social problems.	22, 23, 28, 31, 34, 45, 47, 50, 53, 60, 70, 71, 78–79, 92–93, 95, 101, 102, 119, 125, 135, 138, 143, 144, 145, 146–147, 216, 274, 430, 461, 471, 648, 672
II. *Time, Continuity, and Change* Understanding time, continuity, and change involves being knowledgeable about what things were like in the past and how things change and develop over time. Knowing how to read and reconstruct the past helps students gain a historical perspective. In high school, students examine the past's relationship with the present while extrapolating into the future. They also integrate individual stories about people, events, and situations to form a more complete conception, in which continuity and change persist in time and across cultures. Students will use their knowledge of history to make informed choices and decisions in the present. *Glencoe World History—Modern TImes* Related Theme: The Role of Ideas	
A. Demonstrate that historical knowledge and the concept of time are socially influenced constructions that lead historians to be selective in the questions they seek to answer and the evidence they use.	14–15, 18, 20–22, 27, 30, 34, 47, 62–65, 79, 92–93, 95, 100, 101, 117, 122, 124, 128, 135, 136–138, 139, 141, 144, 145, 146–147, 154, 186, 202, 284, 441, 672

Theme and Performance Expectation	Student Pages
B. Apply key concepts such as time, chronology, causality, change, conflict, and complexity to explain, analyze, and show connections among patterns of historical change and continuity.	14–15, 22, 23, 27, 30, 31, 33, 34, 35, 45, 46–47, 50, 52, 55, 57, 58–59, 60, 67, 68, 70, 71, 72, 75, 78–79, 88, 91, 94, 100, 105, 109, 119, 123, 124–125, 129–130, 131–132, 135, 136–138, 141, 144, 145, 146–147, 162, 170, 202, 218, 274, 292, 315, 339, 364, 399, 413, 415, 449, 475, 656, 669, 461, 694
C. Identify and describe significant historical periods and patterns of change within and across cultures, such as the development of ancient cultures and civilizations, the rise of nation-states, and social, economic, and political revolutions.	19–22, 24–34, 36–45, 46–47, 51–60, 66–76, 78–79, 88, 92–93, 94, 97–99, 101, 105–106, 111, 116–117, 118–123, 124–125, 129–133, 136–138, 140–144, 146–147, 157, 179, 196, 213, 238–245, 250–253, 255–261, 266–276, 278–285, 328–335, 337–343, 345–351, 362–385, 397–418, 429–442, 448–459, 464–471, 473–486, 498–526, 532–557, 562–579, 591–618, 656–676, 682–696
D. Systematically employ processes of critical historical inquiry to reconstruct and reinterpret the past, such as using a variety of sources and checking their credibility, validating and weighing evidence for claims, and searching for causality.	18, 21, 22, 23, 35, 37, 45, 47, 50, 55, 57, 60, 61, 65, 73, 76, 91, 92–93, 95, 96, 101, 102, 111, 115, 123, 124–125, 128, 131, 134, 135, 138, 139, 141, 146–147, 149, 163, 205, 233, 245, 266, 305, 401, 499, 595
E. Investigate, interpret, and analyze multiple historical and contemporary viewpoints within and across cultures related to important events, recurring dilemmas, and persistent issues, while employing empathy, skepticism, and critical judgement.	22, 31, 45, 47, 50, 55, 57, 58, 60, 77, 79, 80–85, 91, 92–93, 95, 101, 102, 110, 124–125, 128, 134, 138, 139, 147, 189, 232, 328, 375, 437, 441, 498, 604
F. Apply ideas, theories, and modes of historical inquiry to analyze historical and contemporary developments, and to inform and evaluate actions concerning public policy issues.	50, 55, 60, 76, 78–79, 92–93, 123, 125, 130, 139, 173, 197, 217, 274, 301, 353, 386, 402, 410, 417, 442, 611
III. *People, Places, and Environments* The study of people, places, and environments will help students as they create their spatial views and geographic perspectives of the world. Students begin to make informed and critical decisions about the relationship between humans and their environment. In high school, geographic concepts become central to students' comprehension of global connections as they expand their knowledge of diverse cultures, both historical and contemporary. *Glencoe World History—Modern Times* Related Theme: The Environment and History	
A. Refine mental maps of locales, regions, and the world that demonstrate understanding of relative locations, direction, size, and shape.	21, 26, 33, 38, 41, 43, 47, 52, 59, 63, 69, 75, 79, 91, 99, 104, 107, 110, 115, 120, 122, 137, 141, 167, 190, 213, 633, 634, 693
B. Create, interpret, use, and synthesize information from various representations of the earth, such as maps, globes, and photographs.	21, 26, 33, 38, 41, 43, 47, 52, 59, 64, 75, 79, 91, 99, 102, 104, 109, 120, 125, 141,167, 198, 219, 241, 251, 256, 258, 280, 313, 314, 372, 399, 404, 405, 431, 437, 469, 507, 517, 535, 569, 617, 685, 699
C. Use appropriate resources, data sources, and geographic tools such as aerial photographs, satellite images, geographic information systems (GIS), map projections, and cartography to generate, manipulate, and interpret information such as atlases, data bases, grid systems, charts, graphs, and maps.	26, 33, 37, 38, 41, 43, 59, 64, 69, 75, 79, 91, 99, 104, 107, 120, 125, 159, 203, 269, 285, 325, 544, 565, 599, 685, 697, 699
D. Calculate distance, scale, area, and density, and distinguish spatial distribution patterns.	21, 41, 43, 52, 59, 75, 79, 99, 104, 107, 110, 120, 125, 141, 167, 203, 214, 268, 280, 353, 456, 461, 577, 653
E. Describe, differentiate, and explain the relationships among various regional and global patterns of geographic phenomena such as landforms, soils, climate, vegetation, natural resources, and population.	18, 21, 24, 26, 31, 38, 41, 47, 51–52, 69, 78, 79, 89, 97–98, 107, 110, 129–131, 141, 146–147, 158, 228, 320, 367, 404, 405, 455, 466, 484, 500, 572, 582, 602
F. Use knowledge of physical system changes such as seasons, climate and weather, and the water cycle to explain geographic phenomena.	18, 21, 23, 26, 124–125, 129–131, 141, 147, 196, 598

Theme and Performance Expectation	Student Pages
G. Describe and compare how people create places that reflect culture, human needs, government policy, and current values and ideals as they design and build specialized buildings, neighborhoods, shopping centers, urban centers, industrial parks, and the like.	18, 22, 25, 28, 37, 42, 45, 47, 53, 54, 57–58, 60, 64, 70, 71–72, 76, 79, 90, 95, 100, 109, 111, 118–119, 128, 136, 137, 138, 141, 143, 144, 146–147, 157, 196, 228, 396, 451
H. Examine, interpret, and analyze physical and cultural patterns and their interactions, such as land use, settlement patterns, cultural transmission of customs and ideas, and ecosystem changes.	18, 21, 22, 23, 24, 27, 30, 31, 33, 38, 41, 43, 52, 53, 66, 67, 69, 73–74, 78–79, 88, 89, 91, 94, 95, 99, 100, 101, 106, 108, 111, 117, 119, 122, 125, 129–131, 135, 138, 140–141, 145, 146–147, 177, 198, 228, 306, 185, 404, 659, 686, 687
I. Describe and assess ways that historical events have been influenced by, and have influenced, physical and human geographic factors in local, regional, national, and global settings.	18, 20–22, 28–29, 31, 33–34, 36–38, 41, 43, 51, 52, 53, 54, 59, 65, 67, 69, 75, 78–79, 88, 94, 95, 98–99, 102, 107, 115, 122, 125, 129–131, 136–137, 138, 141, 146–147, 175, 198, 228, 331, 349, 412, 593, 687
J. Analyze and evaluate social and economic effects of environmental changes and crises resulting from phenomena such as floods, storms, and drought.	20, 23, 24, 30, 37, 129–130, 142, 194, 217, 220, 257, 534
K. Propose, compare, and evaluate alternative policies for the use of land and other resources in communities, regions, nations, and the world.	24, 30, 43, 130, 147, 180, 196

IV. *Individual Development and Identity*

People and culture influence a person's identity. Examining the different forms of human behavior improves one's understanding of social relationships and the development of personal identity. The study of human behavior helps students become aware of how social processes influence a person's identity. In high school, students use methods from the behavioral sciences to examine individuals, societies, and cultures.

***Glencoe World History—Modern Times* Related Theme: The Role of Individuals**

Theme and Performance Expectation	Student Pages
A. Articulate personal connections to time, place, and social/cultural systems.	22, 23, 26–27, 31, 32, 35, 38–39, 44–45, 47, 56–57, 60, 79, 93, 95, 100, 111, 123, 125, 135, 139, 144, 147, 149, 301, 341, 377, 452, 559, 664, 679
B. Identify, describe, and express appreciation for the influence of various historical and contemporary cultures on an individual's daily life.	16–17, 22, 23, 27, 29, 32, 34, 37–39, 42–43, 45, 47, 50, 57, 60, 76, 95, 100, 110, 111, 119, 125, 130, 135, 138, 149, 320, 405, 477, 585, 644, 675, 676, 687
C. Describe the ways family, religion, gender, ethnicity, nationality, socioeconomic status, and other group and cultural influences contribute to the development of a sense of self.	22, 26–27, 29, 31–33, 35, 37–40, 42, 43–45, 53, 54, 55, 56, 57, 58, 68, 71, 73–74, 80–85, 91, 94, 98, 100, 101, 106, 109, 115, 118–119, 125, 134, 144, 146, 147, 163, 259, 281, 405, 483, 587, 649, 672, 686, 690
D. Apply concepts, methods, and theories about the study of human growth and development, such as physical endowment, learning, motivation, behavior, perception, and personality.	19–20, 22, 27, 29, 32, 34, 37–38, 42, 45, 54, 56–57, 58–59, 61, 115, 125, 133–134, 147, 298, 385, 419, 516, 660, 663, 665
E. Examine the interaction of ethnic, national, or cultural influences in specific situations or events.	14–15, 22, 30, 31, 37, 40, 44, 45, 47, 55, 56, 58, 60, 67, 72, 76, 78–79, 91, 95, 99, 100, 109, 110, 111, 123, 124–125, 128, 131, 133–135, 138, 139, 143, 144, 147, 274, 330, 505, 545, 566, 609, 666, 675, 679
F. Analyze the role of perceptions, attitudes, values, and beliefs in the development of personal identity.	22, 26–27, 31–32, 34, 39–40, 43–45, 47, 54, 55, 56–57, 58, 73–74, 80–85, 91, 100, 115, 133–134, 147, 300, 418, 491, 508, 509
G. Compare and evaluate the impact of stereotyping, conformity, acts of altruism, and other behaviors on individuals and groups.	26–27, 32, 34, 35, 36, 38–40, 43–45, 58, 67, 70, 71, 78, 79, 92–93, 95, 111, 131–132, 134, 146–147, 197, 217, 420, 421, 549, 392, 621
H. Work independently and cooperatively within groups and institutions to accomplish goals.	47
I. Examine factors that contribute to and damage one's mental health and analyze issues related to mental health and behavioral disorders in contemporary society.	419

Theme and Performance Expectation	Student Pages
V. *Individuals, Groups, and Institutions* **Institutions, such as schools, governments, and churches, influence people and often reflect a society's values. Because of the vital role that institutions play in people's lives, it is important that students know how institutions develop, what controls and influences them, and how humans react to them. High school students must understand the traditions and theories that support social and political traditions.** ***Glencoe World History—Modern Times* Related Theme: Social Life**	
A. Apply concepts such as role, status and social class in describing the connections and interactions of individuals, groups, and institutions in society.	22, 26–27, 29–30, 31, 34, 35, 37–38, 41–42, 45, 46, 50, 53, 54, 55, 58, 66, 67, 68, 70, 71, 72, 73, 77, 78–79, 94, 101, 108, 111, 117–119, 123, 131–133, 134, 135, 138, 139, 141, 144, 146, 162, 181, 244, 405, 406, 690
B. Analyze group and institutional influences on people, events, and elements of culture in both historical and contemporary settings.	21–22, 24–25, 30, 31, 34, 37–38, 43–44, 45, 47, 50, 55, 57–59, 60, 61, 67, 68, 70–72, 73–74, 76, 78–79, 80–85, 94, 95, 101, 109, 111, 117, 123, 124–125, 131–132, 133–134, 135, 137–138, 141, 143–144, 146–147, 157, 192, 228, 245, 274, 307, 407, 324, 551, 566, 607, 674, 682, 694
C. Describe the various forms institutions take, and explain how they develop and change over time.	22, 34, 35, 43–44, 45, 47, 50, 53, 55, 68, 69–70, 71, 73–74, 76, 79, 90–91, 106, 108, 117, 118–119, 124, 132–136, 137–138, 146–147, 165, 197, 218, 252, 662, 668
D. Identify and analyze examples of tensions between expressions of individuality and efforts used to promote social conformity by groups and institutions.	26–27, 29, 37–38, 41–42, 45, 50, 54, 58, 67, 68, 71, 74, 79, 90, 110, 132, 134, 138, 146, 173, 192, 217, 278, 515, 650, 661, 672, 692
E. Describe and examine belief systems basic to specific traditions and laws in contemporary and historical movements.	32, 34, 35, 37–40, 44–45, 47, 50, 54, 55, 58, 60, 66, 70, 71, 73–74, 76, 78, 80–85, 90–91, 94, 95, 101, 106, 109, 111, 117, 124, 133–135, 138, 140, 143–144, 146, 174, 180, 204, 212, 251, 311, 553, 668
F. Evaluate the role of institutions in furthering both continuity and change.	31, 34, 35, 38–40, 43–44, 45, 50, 53, 55, 68, 69–70, 71, 73–74, 76, 79, 90–91, 106, 108, 117, 118–119, 124, 132, 133, 137–138, 144, 146, 174, 200, 220, 296, 406, 408, 660, 664
G. Analyze the extent to which groups and institutions meet individual needs and promote the common good in contemporary and historical settings.	31, 34, 35, 45, 47, 50, 53, 54, 58–59, 60, 66, 67–68, 70, 71, 72, 74, 75, 76, 94, 101, 117, 118–119, 128, 132, 134, 135, 138, 144, 145, 146, 147, 161, 334, 401, 412, 664, 688
H. Explain and apply ideas and modes of inquiry drawn from behavioral science and social theory in the examination of persistent issues and social problems.	22, 31, 34, 35, 56–57, 58, 79, 115, 147, 161, 419, 557
VI. *Power, Authority, and Governance* **Studying structures of power, authority, and governance and their functions in the United States and around the world is important for developing a notion of civic responsibility. Students will identify the purpose and characteristics of various types of government and how people try to resolve conflicts. Students will also examine the relationship between individual rights and responsibilities. High school students study the various systems that have been developed over time to allocate and employ power and authority in the governing process.** ***Glencoe World History—Modern Times* Related Theme: Politics and History**	
A. Examine persistent issues involving the rights, roles, and status of the individual in relation to the general welfare.	22, 26–27, 29–30, 35, 37–38, 39, 43–44, 45, 50, 53, 54, 55, 58, 66, 67, 68, 70, 71, 72, 73, 76, 77, 78–79, 94, 101, 108, 111, 117–119, 123, 131, 132, 133–134, 138, 144, 146, 161, 233, 244, 336, 373, 384, 413, 583, 601, 692
B. Explain the purpose of government and analyze how its powers are acquired, used, and justified.	22, 30, 34, 47, 50, 53, 58–59, 60, 66, 67–68, 71, 77, 93, 105, 108, 114–115, 117, 119–122, 123, 124, 132–133, 137–138, 141, 142, 144, 146, 160, 191, 212, 302, 304, 308, 371
C. Analyze and explain ideas and mechanisms to meet needs and wants of citizens, regulate territory, manage conflict, establish order and security, and balance competing conceptions of a just society.	22, 25, 26–27, 29–30, 33–34, 35, 40–43, 46–47, 50, 53, 54, 58–59, 60, 66, 67–68, 70, 71, 72, 74, 75, 76, 95, 98, 100, 101, 103–105, 107, 117, 120–121, 123, 124–125, 128, 131–133, 143–144, 145, 146, 147, 175, 256, 267, 325, 345, 347, 348, 382, 412, 461, 541, 578, 670, 694

Theme and Performance Expectation	Student Pages
D. Compare and analyze the ways nations and organizations respond to conflicts between forces of unity and forces of diversity.	25, 26–27, 29, 31, 37–38, 42, 51, 54, 55–56, 59, 67, 68, 70, 73, 76, 78, 91–93, 103–105, 106, 108, 110, 112–115, 117–118, 120–121, 123, 124, 132–134, 138, 144, 174, 194, 220, 243, 252, 258, 278, 279, 313, 338, 343, 374, 381, 414, 416, 518, 524, 550, 576, 579, 600, 635, 660, 669, 689, 691
E. Compare different political systems (their ideologies, structure, institutions, processes, and political cultures) with that of the United States, and identify representative political leaders from selected historical and contemporary settings.	26–27, 34, 35, 47, 50, 53, 59, 60, 67, 68, 71, 75, 78, 115, 117–118, 119–121, 158, 194, 220, 311, 312, 316, 332, 400, 411, 470, 526, 546, 552
F. Analyze and evaluate conditions, actions, and motivations that contribute to conflict and cooperation within and among nations.	22, 25, 26–27, 33–34, 35, 46–47, 50, 53, 54, 58–59, 60, 66, 67–68, 70, 71, 72, 74, 75, 76, 95, 98, 100, 101, 103–105, 107, 117, 120–121, 124, 132–134, 138, 144, 146, 178, 194, 228, 239, 241, 251, 257, 268, 281, 316, 320, 331, 340, 342, 434, 467, 478, 595, 640, 645, 673, 674, 682, 688
G. Evaluate the role of technology in communications, transportation, information-processing, weapons development, or other areas as it contributes to or helps resolve conflicts.	22, 23, 29, 34, 42, 70, 72, 76, 105, 106–107, 124, 144, 145, 146–147, 162, 191, 218, 238, 240, 242, 597, 689
H. Explain and apply ideas, theories, and modes of inquiry drawn from political science to the examination of persistent ideas and social problems.	23, 31, 34, 35, 47, 50, 53, 55, 58–59, 60, 68, 70–71, 76, 77, 78–79, 92–93, 119, 124, 138, 139, 144, 146, 176, 205, 222, 304, 482, 529, 660, 669, 670, 690
I. Evaluate the extent to which governments achieve their stated ideals and policies at home and abroad.	46–47, 50, 56, 58–59, 60, 67, 68, 69, 71, 72, 76, 78, 93, 105, 108, 111, 115, 123, 124–125, 128, 138, 144, 146–147, 172, 188, 229, 313, 343, 481, 571, 670
J. Prepare a public policy paper and present and defend it before an appropriate forum in school or community.	163, 200, 229, 393
VII. *Production, Distribution, and Consumption* Societies try to meet people's needs and wants by trying to answer the basic economic questions: What is to be produced? How should goods be produced? How should goods and services be distributed? How should land, labor, capital, and management be allocated? By studying how needs and wants are met, students learn how trade and government economic policies develop. In high school, students develop economic perspectives and deeper understanding of key economic concepts and processes. *Glencoe World History—Modern Times* Related Theme: Economics and History	
A. Explain how the scarcity of productive resources (human, capital, technological, and natural) requires the development of economic systems to make decisions about how goods and services are to be produced and distributed.	22, 23, 46–47, 54, 58, 69, 70, 71–72, 78, 94, 95, 98–99, 102, 104, 105, 110–111, 118–119, 124, 130–132, 137, 138, 146–147, 195, 197, 536, 547
B. Analyze the role that supply and demand, prices, incentives, and profits play in determining what is produced and distributed in a competitive market system.	46, 69, 70, 94, 95, 99–100, 101, 102, 125, 130–132, 137, 146, 147, 191, 217, 226, 273, 430, 683, 689
C. Consider the costs and benefits to society of allocating goods and services through private and public sectors.	22, 70, 72, 105, 117, 118–119, 125, 130–132, 195, 217, 330, 669, 694
D. Describe the relationships among the various economic institutions that comprise economic systems such as households, business firms, banks, government agencies, labor unions, and corporations.	55, 68, 70, 78, 102, 108, 118–119, 125, 131, 132, 161, 195, 258, 280, 480, 489, 613, 667, 691, 694
E. Analyze the role of specialization and exchange in economic processes.	22, 40, 44, 46, 69, 70, 94, 98–99, 101, 105, 124–125, 130–132, 191, 292, 470
F. Compare how values and beliefs influence economic decisions in different societies.	26, 35, 37, 45, 50, 54, 58, 68, 69, 70, 71, 72, 78, 105, 108, 161, 195, 217, 269, 274, 432, 567, 667
G. Compare basic economic systems according to how rules and procedures deal with demand, supply, prices, the role of government, banks, labor and labor unions, savings and investments, and capital.	29–30, 161, 195, 217, 253, 285, 573, 670, 699

Theme and Performance Expectation	Student Pages
H. Apply economic concepts and reasoning when evaluating historical and contemporary social developments and issues.	22, 23, 46–47, 54, 58, 68, 69, 70, 71, 72, 78, 90, 95, 99, 102, 105, 129–132, 138, 146, 191, 195, 216, 259, 476, 669, 696
I. Distinguish between the domestic and global economic systems, and explain how the two interact.	191, 433, 425
J. Apply knowledge of production, distribution, and consumption in the analysis of a public issue such as the allocation of health care or the consumption of energy, and devise an economic plan for accomplishing a socially desirable outcome related to that issue.	216
K. Distinguish between economics as a field of inquiry and the economy.	303
VIII. *Science, Technology, and Society* **The study of science, technology, and society is ever changing. It raises questions about who will benefit from it and how fundamental values and beliefs can be preserved in a technology-driven society. In high school, students will confront issues that balance the benefits of science and technology against the accompanying social consequences.** ***Glencoe World History—Modern Times* Related Theme: The Impact of Science and Technology**	
A. Identify and describe both current and historical examples of the interaction and interdependence of science, technology, and society in a variety of cultural settings.	21–22, 23, 27, 28, 30, 34, 44, 46–47, 55, 57–58, 72, 78–79, 95, 98, 105, 106–107, 108, 124, 128, 129–130, 136, 137, 138, 142, 144, 145, 146–147, 162, 191, 202, 218, 269, 294, 368, 390, 398, 419
B. Make judgments about how science and technology have transformed the physical world and human society and our understanding of time, space, place, and human-environment interactions.	20, 21, 22, 23, 46–47, 55, 72, 79, 95, 105, 107, 124, 128, 130, 144, 145, 146–147, 162, 191, 202, 218, 300, 297, 362, 364, 506, 506, 673
C. Analyze how science and technology influence the core values, beliefs, and attitudes of society, and how core values, beliefs, and attitudes of society shape scientific and technological change.	22, 30, 33, 34, 40, 53, 55, 56–58, 79, 95, 106, 124, 136, 137, 145, 146–147, 162, 191, 202, 218, 292, 296, 396, 554, 555, 557, 644, 673
D. Evaluate various policies that have been proposed as ways of dealing with social changes resulting from new technologies, such as genetically engineered plants and animals.	162, 191, 218, 674
E. Recognize and interpret varied perspectives about human societies and the physical world using scientific knowledge, ethical standards, and technologies from diverse world cultures.	22, 23, 34, 35, 50, 51, 53, 54, 55–58, 66, 68, 71, 73, 78–79, 95, 100, 158, 191, 218, 295, 299
F. Formulate strategies and develop policies for influencing public discussions associated with technology-society issues, such as the greenhouse effect.	22, 162, 638, 674
IX. *Global Connections* **As countries grow more interdependent, understanding global connections among world societies becomes important. Students will analyze emerging global issues in many different fields. They will also investigate relationships among the different cultures of the world. High school students will address critical issues such as peace, human rights, trade, and global ecology.** ***Glencoe World History—Modern Times* Related Theme: Global Connections**	
A. Explain how language, art, music, belief systems, and other cultural elements can facilitate global understanding or cause misunderstanding.	22, 31, 34, 38–39, 44–45, 48, 50, 53, 55, 57–59, 60, 62–65, 70, 71, 72–73, 100, 101, 111, 133–134, 135, 138, 144, 145, 146, 157, 188, 232, 279, 350, 436, 448, 642, 673, 674, 675, 676, 686, 695
B. Explain conditions and motivations that contribute to conflict, cooperation, and interdependence among groups, societies, and nations.	26, 31, 51, 54, 55–56, 59, 62, 65, 67, 68, 70–71, 75–76, 79, 81–85, 95, 98, 100, 101, 103–105, 107, 117, 120–121, 124, 132–134, 138, 144, 157, 193, 219, 269, 349, 400, 413, 480, 519, 537, 614, 617, 673, 690, 691, 698

Theme and Performance Expectation	Student Pages
C. Analyze and evaluate the effects of changing technologies on the global community.	22, 27, 47, 55, 72, 76, 95, 105, 107, 124, 130, 162, 191, 218, 283, 366, 399, 400, 673
D. Analyze the causes, consequences, and possible solutions to persistent, contemporary, and emerging global issues, such as health, security, resource allocation, economic development, and environmental quality.	165, 335, 370, 574, 686
E. Analyze the relationships and tensions between national sovereignty and global interests, in such matters as territory, economic development, nuclear and other weapons, use of natural resources, and human rights concerns.	31, 56, 59–60, 67, 69, 70, 71, 75–76, 79, 173, 203, 217, 257, 268, 272, 314, 351, 487, 523, 570, 590, 616, 653, 663, 686
F. Analyze or formulate policy statements demonstrating an understanding of concerns, standards, issues, and conflicts related to universal human rights.	35, 50, 58–59, 68, 70, 78, 181, 197, 489, 636, 663
G. Describe and evaluate the role of international and multinational organizations in the global arena.	31, 173, 194, 212, 455, 459, 570, 582
H. Illustrate how individual behaviors and decisions connect with global systems.	31, 55–56, 59–60, 70, 73, 78, 82, 160, 173, 193, 213, 477, 501
X. *Civic Ideals and Practices* Understanding civic ideals and practices is crucial to complete participation in society and is the main purpose of social studies. Students will learn about civic participation and the role of the citizen within his or her community, country, and world. High school students learn, through experience, to identify social needs, setting directions for public policy, and working to support both individual dignity and the common good. ***Glencoe World History—Modern Times*** **Related Themes: Politics and History, The Role of Individuals**	
A. Explain the origins and interpret the continuing influence of key ideals of the democratic republican form of government, such as individual human dignity, liberty, justice, equality, and the rule of law.	26–27, 35, 50, 53, 55–56, 58, 60, 67–68, 70–71, 76, 119–121, 233, 300, 302, 305, 310, 321, 322, 348, 413, 562, 584, 695, 699
B. Identify, analyze, interpret, and evaluate sources and examples of citizens' rights and responsibilities.	26–27, 35, 50, 53, 55, 56, 58, 60, 67, 68, 71, 77, 78, 221
C. Locate, access, analyze, organize, synthesize, evaluate, and apply information about selected public issues—identifying, describing, and evaluating multiple points of view.	22, 47, 61, 79, 233, 376, 441, 621
D. Practice forms of civic discussion and participation consistent with the ideals of citizens in a democratic republic.	79, 579, 618, 679
E. Analyze and evaluate the influence of various forms of citizen action on public policy.	50, 77, 79, 281, 333, 408, 473, 569
F. Analyze a variety of public policies and issues from the perspective of formal and informal political actors.	60, 61, 70, 79, 160, 179, 194, 219, 233, 369, 538, 653, 695
G. Evaluate the effectiveness of public opinion in influencing and shaping public policy developments and decision-making.	58–59, 68, 175, 233, 468, 650, 656, 666
H. Evaluate the degree to which public policies and citizen behaviors reflect or foster the stated ideals of a democratic republican form of government.	50, 56, 58–59, 60, 66, 68, 71–72, 233, 435, 474, 502, 632, 636
I. Construct a policy statement and an action plan to achieve one or more goals related to an issue of public concern.	325, 461, 478, 651
J. Participate in activities to strengthen the "common good" based upon careful evaluation of possible options for citizen action.	759, 761

Scope and Sequence

Themes and Concepts

Each section of *Glencoe World History—Modern Times* focuses on one central theme, although related themes also appear in each section. The section numbers highlighted here in **red** indicate the central theme that is key to that section. Related themes are listed in black.

Chapter	1	2	3	4	5
Politics and History	Section 1, 2, 3	Section 1, 2	Section 1, 2, 3, 4	Section 1, 2	Section 1, 3, 4
The Role of Ideas	Section 1, 2, 3	Section 1, 2	Section 1, 2, 3, 4	Section 1, 2	Section 1, 2, 3, 4
Economics and History	Section 1, 2, 3	Section 1, 2	Section 1, 2, 3, 4	Section 2	Section 1
The Importance of Cultural Development	Section 1, 2, 3	Section 1, 2	Section 1, 2, 3, 4	Section 1, 2	Section 1, 2, 4
Religion in History	Section 1, 2, 3	Section 1, 2	Section 1, 2, 3, 4	Section 1	Section 3, 4
The Role of Individuals	Section 1, 2, 3	Section 1, 2	Section 1, 2, 3, 4	Section 1	Section 1, 2, 3, 4
The Impact of Science and Technology	Section 1, 2, 3	Section 1, 2	Section 1, 2, 3, 4	Section 1, 2	Section 1, 2
The Environment and History	Section 1, 2, 3	Section 1, 2	Section 1, 2, 3, 4	Section 2	

Skills

These skills are taught in the Chapter SKILLBUILDERS and reinforced in the Chapter Assessment Activities, **Chapter Skills Activities** in the Unit Resource books, and **Glencoe's Skillbuilder Interactive Workbook CD-ROM**.

Chapter	1	2	3	4	5
Skill Category	*Critical Thinking Skill*	*Critical Thinking Skill*	*Critical Thinking Skill*	*Critical Thinking Skill*	*Study and Writing Skill*
Specific Skill	Understanding Cause and Effect	Making Comparisons	Distinguishing Between Fact and Opinion	Analyzing Primary and Secondary Sources	Summarizing Information

6	7	8	9	10	11	12
Section 1, 2, 3	Section 1, 2, 3, 4	Section 1, 2, 3	Section 1, 3	Section 2, 3, 4	Section 1, 2, 3	Section 2, 3
	Section 2, 3, 4	Section 2	Section 1, 2	Section 1, 2, 3	Section 1, 2, 3	Section 1, 2, 4
Section 1, 2, 3	Section 1, 2, 3	Section 1, 2, 3	Section 1, 2, 3	Section 2, 3, 4	Section 1, 2, 3	Section 1, 2, 3, 4
Section 2, 3	Section 1, 3, 4	Section 1, 2, 3	Section 1, 2, 3	Section 1, 2, 3, 4	Section 1	Section 1, 4
Section 3	Section 1, 2, 3	Section 1, 2, 3		Section 4	Section 2	
Section 1, 2	Section 1, 2, 3, 4	Section 1, 3	Section 1, 3	Section 1, 2, 3	Section 1, 3	Section 3, 4
Section 1	Section 2, 3	Section 1, 2	Section 2	Section 1, 4		Section 1, 2, 3, 4
Section 1, 2, 3	Section 2	Section 1, 3	Section 1, 3	Section 4	Section 2	Section 1, 2, 4
Critical Thinking Skill	*Critical Thinking Skill*	*Study and Writing Skill*	*Social Studies Skill*	*Study and Writing Skill*	*Social Studies Skill*	*Critical Thinking Skill*
Making Inferences and Drawing Conclusions	Making Generalizations	Using Library Resources	Finding Exact Location on a Map	Outlining	Interpreting Graphs	Identifying an Argument

Chapter	13	14	15	16	17	18
Themes and Concepts						
Politics and History	Section 1, 2, 3	Section 1, 2, 3, 4	Section 1, 2, 3	Section 1, 2, 3, 4	Section 1, 2, 3	Section 2, 3, 4
The Role of Ideas	Section 1, 2, 3, 4	Section 1, 3	Section 3	Section 1, 3, 4	Section 1, 2, 3	Section 1, 2, 3
Economics and History	Section 1, 2, 3	Section 1, 2, 3, 4	Section 1, 2, 3	Section 1, 2, 3, 4	Section 1, 2, 3	Section 2, 4
The Importance of Cultural Development	Section 2, 4	Section 3, 4	Section 1, 2, 3	Section 3, 4	Section 2, 3, 4	Section 1, 3, 4
Religion in History	Section 4	Section 1			Section 4	Section 1, 2
The Role of Individuals	Section 1, 2, 3, 4	Section 1, 2, 3	Section 1, 2, 3	Section 1	Section 1, 2, 3	Section 2, 3, 4
The Impact of Science and Technology	Section 1, 4	Section 2, 4	Section 3	Section 2	Section 1, 4	Section 1, 4
The Environment and History	Section 3, 4	Section 1, 2, 4	Section 1, 3	Section 1, 2, 3		Section 2, 3
Skills						
Skill Category	*Critical Thinking Skill*	*Technology Skill*	*Study and Writing Skill*	*Critical Thinking Skill*	*Critical Thinking Skill*	*Technology Skill*
Specific Skill	Detecting Bias	Evaluating a Web Site	Writing a Report	Interpreting Military Movements on Maps	Analyzing Political Cartoons	Using an Electronic Spreadsheet

19	20	21	22	23	24	25
Section 1, 3	Section 1, 2	Section 1, 2, 3	Section 1, 2, 3	Section 1, 2	Section 1, 2, 3	Section 1, 2
Section 1, 3	Section 1, 2	Section 1, 2, 3, 4	Section 1, 2, 3	Section 1, 2	Section 1, 2, 3	Section 1, 2
Section 4	Section 1, 3	Section 1, 3	Section 1, 2, 3	Section 1, 2	Section 1, 2, 3	Section 1, 2
Section 4	Section 2, 3	Section 3, 4	Section 1, 2, 3	Section 1	Section 1, 2, 3	Section 1, 2
		Section 4		Section 2	Section 2	
Section 1, 2, 3, 4	Section 1, 3	Section 1, 2	Section 3			Section 1
Section 1, 2, 3, 4	Section 1	Section 1, 4	Section 3		Section 3	Section 1
Section 1, 3	Section 2	Section 1, 2, 4	Section 2	Section 1		Section 1
Critical Thinking Skill	*Social Studies Skill*	*Study and Writing Skill*	*Technology Skill*	*Social Studies Skill*	*Critical Thinking Skill*	*Technology Skill*
Synthesizing Information	Understanding World Time Zones	Preparing a Bibliography	Developing a Database	Interpreting Statistics	Reading a Cartogram	Developing a Multimedia Presentation

Classroom Solutions

Reading Strategies

How Can I Help My Students Read and Understand the Textbook?

Social studies teachers do not have to be reading teachers to help students read and understand their textbooks. Often poor readers lack interest in the topic, have trouble concentrating, cannot understand a word or sentence, or are confused as to how the information fits together. These problems can frustrate the student and the teacher, but there are strategies that can be used to improve comprehension and retention of information. Using these reading strategies not only helps poor readers, but also strengthens the reading skills of strong readers.

Activate Prior Knowledge

Activating prior knowledge provides opportunities for students to discover and articulate what they already know about key concepts and ideas. It stimulates student interest and prepares students to incorporate new information into a larger picture. In addition, it helps the teacher to determine a starting place for instruction.

- ✔ Write the topic on the board and have students brainstorm what they know about it. Record their responses on the board.
- ✔ Ask general or specific questions about the topic and see how students respond to them.
- ✔ Present an anticipation guide. An anticipation guide provides a series of statements about an idea or topic. Students read each statement and tell whether they agree or disagree, based on their prior understandings and experiences.
- ✔ Use a K-W-L-H or K-W-L chart to activate prior knowledge and set reading purposes. Students identify what they already **know** (or think they know) and what they **want** to find out about the topic. After reading, students complete the chart.

K	W	L	H
What I **Know**	What I **Want** to Find Out	What I **Learned**	**How** I Can Learn More

Set Reading Purposes

Reading is a purposeful activity. We read to find answers to specific questions, to satisfy curiosity, and to be entertained.

- ✔ Have students preview the reading selection. Tell students to read the title, headings, and subheadings. Draw students' attention to diagrams, tables, and other visuals and their captions. Discuss how these will help comprehension.
- ✔ Prompt students to predict what they might learn in the selection, based on their preview. Invite them to list additional questions they hope to answer through the reading. Have them identify possible problems, such as unfamiliar words or ideas, to watch for as they read.
- ✔ Discuss the need to "shift gears" in reading speed and attention when reading. Support students as they plan how best to read a selection—slowly to watch for new vocabulary and ideas or quickly to review previously learned ideas. They can also discuss new information with a buddy as they read.

Vocabulary Development

Vocabulary knowledge and reading comprehension are closely related.

- ✔ Before students read, preteach vocabulary that is crucial for understanding key topics and concepts.
- ✔ Relate new vocabulary to known words and ideas. After introducing a word and its definition, have students name synonyms or related words they know.
- ✔ If a student encounters an unfamiliar word while reading, have him or her try to pronounce it aloud. Sometimes saying the word will trigger one's memory of its meaning.
- ✔ As students read, help them use prefixes (word parts added to the beginning of base words), suffixes (word parts added to the end of base words), and roots (word elements from which other words are formed) as clues to decipher the meaning of words.
- ✔ Encourage students to use the context of surrounding words and sentences to determine a word's meaning.
- ✔ If context clues and structural analysis fail to help a student understand an important word as

Tom & DeeAnn McCarthy/CORBIS STOCK MARKET

Common Prefixes	Meanings	Examples
un-, dis-, non-, im- and il-	"not" or "the opposite of"	unwrapped, dishonest, nonprofit, immortal, illogical
re-	"again" or "back"	reheat
post-	"after"	postwar
uni-	"one"	unicycle

Common Suffixes	Meanings	Examples
-ship, -hood	"state of" or "condition of"	friendship, neighborhood
-ment	"act of" or "state of"	management
-ish	"like"	childish
-ous	"full of" or "like"	joyous

they read, have students find the definition in a glossary or dictionary. If the word is not critical for understanding, have students note the word and read on. Later, have students reread the word in context. If the meaning is still unclear, have students consult the dictionary.

Taking Notes

Taking notes challenges readers to determine what is most important and to organize information in a way that makes sense. Note-taking can also help students stay focused as they read. Reviewing notes can build students' retention of important information.

✔ Have students take notes after they have read long paragraphs in the section rather than the entire chapter. This helps them focus on important ideas and details and prevents them from losing track of the flow of information.

✔ Remind students that as they take notes on the section, they should not take a long time to do it. Students should read, think, write, and move on.

✔ Have students take notes using note cards. Notes should be recorded in the students' own words and labeled with the page number where the entire text appears.

✔ To use notes to review a passage, have students read through the notes, highlighting the most important information. As they review, encourage students to annotate their notes, making connections between related ideas and clarifying difficult concepts.

Summarizing

Summarizing demands that students identify the most important ideas and details to create a streamlined version of the text.

✔ After reading the section, have students recall as much of the information as possible. If the main idea and its supporting details are presented in a certain order, make sure students can recall that organization.

✔ As they summarize, students should try to answer as many of the following questions as possible: *who, what, where, when, why,* and *how.*

✔ If the section does not have a main idea that is clearly stated, have students create one that is concise but comprehensive. Have students state the main idea in a topic sentence at the beginning of their summaries.

✔ Sometimes summaries seem disconnected when details are left out. Students should use connector words such as "and" or "because," along with introductory or closing statements, to make ideas more connected.✦

Reading Comprehension: Be Aware, Reread, and Connect (BARC)

Advice from Dr. Elizabeth Pryor, Ph.D.
Research Center for Educational Technology
Kent State University, Kent, Ohio

Many students think silent reading means just looking at words and saying them in their heads. They do not make the connection that reading is supposed to make sense! Have you ever read a paragraph or a page and then said to yourself, "What was that?" As a good reader, you were aware of your lack of understanding. Poor readers, on the other hand, just keep on reading the words, unaware that they do not understand them.

What strategies do good readers use when this happens? Most reread the text they did not understand. Before rereading I study key words I might have missed. When I reread, sometimes I "whisper read" so I can hear the text as well as read it. As I reread, I try to connect what I am reading with something I already know. If I reread and still don't understand, I read it a third (or fourth) time. Each rereading increases comprehension.

In summary, **Be aware** of understanding as you read, **reread,** and **connect** the reading to what you already know. **BARC!**

Classroom Solutions

Test-Taking Strategies

How Can I Help My Students Succeed on Tests?

It's not enough for students to learn social studies facts and concepts—they must be able to show what they know in a variety of test-taking situations.

How Can I Help My Students Do Well On Objective Tests?

Objective tests may include multiple choice, true/false, and matching questions. Applying the following strategies can help students do their best on objective tests.

Multiple Choice Questions

- ✔ Students should read the directions carefully to learn what answer the test requires—the best answer or the right answer. This is especially important when answer choices include "all of the above" or "none of the above."
- ✔ Advise students to watch for negative words in the questions, such as *not, except, unless, never,* and so forth. If the question contains a negative, the correct answer choice is the one that does not fit.
- ✔ Students should try to mentally answer the question before reading the answer choices.
- ✔ Students should read all the answer choices and cross out those that are obviously wrong. Then they should choose an answer from those that remain.

True/False Questions

- ✔ It is important that students read the entire question before answering. For an answer to be true, the entire statement must be true. If one part of a statement is false, the answer should be marked *False.*
- ✔ Remind students to watch for words like *all, never, every,* and *always.* Statements containing these words are often false.

Matching Questions

- ✔ Students should read through both lists before they mark any answers.
- ✔ Unless an answer can be used more than once, students should cross out each choice as they use it.
- ✔ Using what they know about grammar can help students find the right answer. For instance, when matching a word with its definition, the definition is often the same part of speech (noun, verb, adjective, and so forth) as the word.

How Can I Help My Students Do Well On Essay Tests?

Essay tests require students to provide thorough and well-organized written responses, in addition to telling what they know. Help students use the following strategies on essay tests.

Analyze:	To **analyze** means to systematically and critically examine all parts of an issue or event.
Classify or Categorize:	To **classify** or **categorize** means to put people, things, or ideas into groups, based on a common set of characteristics.
Compare and Contrast:	To **compare** is to show how things are similar, or alike. To **contrast** is to show how things are different.
Describe:	To **describe** means to present a sketch or impression. Rich details, especially details that appeal to the senses, flesh out a description.
Discuss:	To **discuss** means to systematically write about all sides of an issue or event.
Evaluate:	To **evaluate** means to make a judgment and support it with evidence.
Explain:	To **explain** means to clarify or make plain.
Illustrate:	To **illustrate** means to provide examples or to show with a picture or other graphic.
Infer:	To **infer** means to read between the lines or to use knowledge and experience to draw conclusions, make a generalization, or form a prediction.
Justify:	To **justify** means to prove or to support a position with specific facts and reasons.
Predict:	To **predict** means to tell what will happen in the future, based on an understanding of prior events and behaviors.
State:	To **state** means to briefly and concisely present information.
Summarize:	To **summarize** means to give a brief overview of the main points of an issue or event.
Trace:	To **trace** means to present the steps or stages in a process or event in sequential or chronological order.

Read the Question

The key to writing successful essay responses lies in reading and interpreting questions correctly. Teach students to identify and underline key words in the questions, and to use these words to guide them in understanding what the question asks. Help students understand the meaning of some of the most common key words, listed in the chart on page T32.

Plan and Write the Essay

After students understand the question, they should follow the writing process to develop their answers. Encourage students to follow the steps below to plan and write their essays.

1. Map out an answer. Make lists, webs, or an outline to plan the response.

2. Decide on an order in which to present the main points.

3. Write an opening statement that directly responds to the essay question.

4. Write the essay. Expand on the opening statement. Support key points with specific facts, details, and reasons.

5. Write a closing statement that brings the main points together.

6. Proofread to check for spelling, grammar, and punctuation.

How Can I Help My Students Prepare for Standardized Tests?

Students can follow the steps below to prepare for a test.

✔ **Read About the Test** Students can familiarize themselves with the format of the test, the types of questions that will be asked, and the amount of time they will have to complete the test.

✔ **Review the Content** Consistent study throughout the school year will help students build social studies knowledge and understanding. If there are specific objectives or standards that are tested on the exam, help students review these facts or skills to be sure they are proficient.

✔ **Practice** Provide practice, ideally with real released tests, to build students' familiarity with the content, format, and timing of the real exam. Students should practice all the types of questions they will encounter on the test—multiple choice, short answer, and extended response.

Jose L. Pelaez/CORBIS STOCK MARKET

✔ **Analyze Practice Results** Help students improve test-taking performance by analyzing their test-taking strengths and weaknesses. Spend time discussing students' completed practice tests, explaining why particular answers are right or wrong. Help students identify what kinds of questions they had the most difficulty with. Look for patterns in errors and then tailor instruction to review the appropriate test-taking skills or social studies content.✦

Help Students Learn by Reviewing Graded Tests

Advice from Tara Musslewhite
Humble Independent School District
Humble, Texas

Frequently reviewing graded tests is a great way for students to assess their test-taking skills. It also gives teachers the opportunity to teach test-taking strategies and review content. As the class rereads each test question, guide students to think logically about their answer choices. Show students how to:

1. Read each question carefully to determine its meaning.
2. Look for key words in the question to support their answers.
3. Recognize synonyms in the answer choices that may match phrases in the question.
4. Narrow down answer choices by eliminating ones that don't make sense.
5. Anticipate the answer before looking at the answer choices.
6. Circle questions of which they are unsure and go back to them later. Sometimes a clue will be found in another question on the test.

Classroom Solutions

Alternative Assessment Strategies

How Can I Go Beyond Tests to Assess Students' Understanding of Social Studies Facts and Concepts?

In response to the growing demand for accountability in the classroom, educators must use multiple assessment measures to accurately gauge student performance. In addition to quizzes, tests, essay exams, and standardized tests, assessment today incorporates a variety of performance-based measures and portfolio opportunities.

What Are Some Typical Performance-Based Assessments?

There are many kinds of performance-based assessments. They all share one common characteristic—they challenge students to create products that demonstrate what they know. One good way to present a performance assessment is in the form of an open-ended question.

Writing

Performance-based writing assessments challenge students to apply their knowledge of social studies concepts and information in a variety of written ways. Writing activities are most often completed by one student, rather than by a group.

- ✔ **Journals** Students write from the perspective of a historical character or a citizen of a particular historical era.
- ✔ **Letters** Students write a letter from one historical figure to another or from a historical figure to a family member or other audience.
- ✔ **Position Paper or Editorial** Students explain a controversial issue and present their own opinion and recommendations, supported with strong evidence and convincing reasons.
- ✔ **Newspaper** Students write a variety of stories from the perspective of a reporter living in a particular historical time period.
- ✔ **Biographies and Autobiographies** Students write about historical figures either from the third person point of view (biography) or from the first person (autobiography).
- ✔ **Creative Stories** Students integrate historical events into a piece of fiction, incorporating the customs, language, and geography of the period.
- ✔ **Poems and Songs** Students follow the conventions of a particular type of song or poem as they tell about a historical event or person.
- ✔ **Research Reports** Students synthesize information from a variety of sources into a well-developed research report.

Oral Presentations

Oral presentations allow students to demonstrate their social studies literacy before an audience. Oral presentations are often group efforts, although this need not be the case.

- ✔ **Simulations** Students hold simulations, or reenactments, of actual events, such as trials, acts of civil disobedience, battles, speeches, and so forth.
- ✔ **Debates** Students debate two or more sides to a historical policy or issue. Students can debate from a contemporary perspective or in a role play in which they assume a viewpoint held by a historical character.
- ✔ **Interview** Students conduct a mock interview of a historical character or bystander.
- ✔ **Oral Reports** Students present the results of research efforts in a lively oral report.
- ✔ **Skits and Plays** Students use historical events as the basis for a play or skit. Details should accurately reflect customs, language, and the setting of the period.

Visual Presentations

Visual presentations allow students to demonstrate their social studies understandings in a variety of visual formats. Visual presentations can be either group or individual projects.

- ✔ **Model** Students make a model to demonstrate or represent a process, place, event, battle, artifact, or custom.
- ✔ **Museum Exhibit** Students create a rich display of materials around a topic. Typical displays might include models, illustrations, photographs, videos, writings, and audiotaped explanations.
- ✔ **Graph or Chart** Students analyze and represent historical data in a line graph, bar graph, table, or other chart format.
- ✔ **Drawing** Students represent or interpret a historical event or period through illustration, including political cartoons.
- ✔ **Posters and Murals** Posters and murals may include maps, time lines, diagrams, illustrations, photographs, and written explanations that reflect students' understandings of historical information.

to the model, using a scoring rubric, and writing their own goals and then evaluating how well they have met the goals they set for themselves. Regardless of which method or methods students use, they should be encouraged to evaluate their behaviors and processes, as well as the finished product.

- ✔ **Quilt** Students sew or draw a design for a patchwork quilt that shows a variety of perspectives, events, or issues related to a key topic.
- ✔ **Videotapes** Students film a video to show historical fiction or to preserve a simulation of a historical event.
- ✔ **Multimedia Presentation or Slide Show** Students create a computer-generated multimedia presentation containing historical information and analysis.

How Are Performance Assessments Scored?

There are a variety of means used to evaluate performance tasks. Some or all of the following methods may be used.

- ✔ **Scoring Rubrics** A scoring rubric is a set of guidelines for assessing the quality of a process and/or product. It sets out criteria used to distinguish acceptable responses from unacceptable ones, generally along a scale from excellent to poor.
- ✔ **Models of Excellent Work** Teacher-selected models of excellent work concretely illustrate expectations and help students set goals for their own projects.
- ✔ **Student Self-Assessment** Common methods of self-assessment include ranking work in relation to the model, using a scoring rubric, and writing their own goals and then evaluating how well they have met the goals they set for themselves. Regardless of which method or methods students use, they should be encouraged to evaluate their behaviors and processes, as well as the finished product.
- ✔ **Peer or Audience Assessment** Many of the performance tasks target an audience other than the classroom teacher. If possible, the audience of peers should give the student feedback. Have the class create rubrics for specific projects together.
- ✔ **Observation** As students carry out their performance tasks, you may want to formally observe students at work. Start by developing a checklist, identifying all the specific behaviors and understandings you expect students to demonstrate. Then observe students as they carry out performance tasks and check off the behaviors as you observe them.
- ✔ **Interviews** As a form of ongoing assessment, you may want to conduct interviews with students, asking them to analyze, explain, and assess their participation in performance tasks. When projects take place over an extended period of time, you can hold periodic interviews as well as exit interviews. In this way the interview process allows you to gauge the status of the project and to guide students' efforts along the way.✦

Targeting Multiple Intelligences

Advice from John Cartaina
Consultant, New Jersey Council of Social Studies

Authentic performance assessment provides students with different learning styles opportunities to demonstrate their successful learning. The table below list types of learning styles.

Learning Style	Characteristics of Students
Linguistic	Read regularly, write clearly, and easily understand the written word
Logical-Mathematical	Use numbers, logic, and critical thinking skills
Visual-Spatial	Think in terms of pictures and images
Auditory-Musical	Remember spoken words and produce rhythms and melodies
Kinesthetic	Learn from touch, movement, and manipulating objects
Interpersonal	Understand and work well with other people
Intrapersonal	Have a realistic understanding of their strengths and weaknesses
Naturalist	Can distinguish among, classify, and use features of the environment

You may want to assign activities to students that accommodate their strongest learning styles, but frequently ask them to use their weakest learning styles.

Classroom Solutions

Cooperative Group Strategies

How Can I Use Cooperative Learning to Teach Social Studies?

Today's social and economic climate requires flexibility. Workers must be able to function independently, work well with groups, and engage in fair-minded competition. For this reason, most educators recommend a healthy balance of instructional strategies to foster cooperative, competitive, and individualistic styles of problem solving and learning. Cooperative learning requires students to work together—each with a specific task—to pursue a common goal. Because part of each student's evaluation is determined by the overall quality of the group's work, students help one another accomplish the group goal.

How Do I Form Cooperative Groups?

- ✔ **Composition** Most experts recommend that cooperative groups be heterogeneous, reflecting a range of student abilities, backgrounds, and learning styles. However, this does not necessarily mean that students should be assigned to groups on a random basis.
- ✔ **Group Size** The size of cooperative groups can change, depending upon the task. Some cooperative tasks are best accomplished in pairs. For most projects, groups of three to five students are ideal.
- ✔ **Abilities** Consider the tasks and projects the groups will undertake as you make group assignments. You may want to make sure each group has a strong manager, a strong writer, a strong artist, a good listener, and so forth.
- ✔ **Balance** Some teachers use a "family-of-five" approach to grouping. A strong leader heads each group. Two pairs of students with opposing styles or strengths complete the "family." Paired students might exhibit traits such as outgoing and shy, creative and conventional, spontaneous and methodical, and so on. Each group continues to work together throughout the semester or year, with the goal that students develop greater flexibility in their own problem-solving abilities and greater respect for the contributions of others.
- ✔ **Roles** In most instances, you will want to assign a specific role for each student to play in a group, such as designer, moderator, recorder, researcher, presenter, graphic artist, actor, and so forth. Roles should be interdependent, requiring students to rely upon one another in order to successfully carry out their individual responsibilities. As students gain experience in working in cooperative groups, turn over more of the responsibility for establishing individual roles and responsibilities to the group.

How Do I Help Groups Run Smoothly?

- ✔ **Seating Arrangements** Explain how and where groups should sit. Pairs can sit with desks or chairs face-to-face. Larger groups do well with desks or chairs gathered in a circle or with students seated around a table.
- ✔ **Warm-Ups** Provide an introductory activity for new groups. Even when students know one another, they can benefit by making formal introductions and sharing their thoughts on a sentence starter, such as "If I could go anywhere in the world, I would go to . . ." or "If I could have lived at any period in history, I would choose. . ."
- ✔ **Rules** Set clear expectations and rules for groups. Typical rules include addressing group members by name, making eye contact, listening politely, expressing disagreement with respect, welcoming others' questions, valuing others' contributions, providing positive feedback, and assisting others when asked.

How Do I Use Cooperative Groups in My Classroom?

- ✔ **Share and Tell** Have students form groups of four. Assign each group member a number between one and four. Ask a factual recall question. Have group members discuss the question and come up with an answer. Call out a number between one and four. The student with that number who is first to raise his or her hand answers the question. The group earns a point for a correct answer.
- ✔ **Circle Partners** Have the class separate into two equal groups and form two circles, with one circle inside the other. Each student faces a partner in the

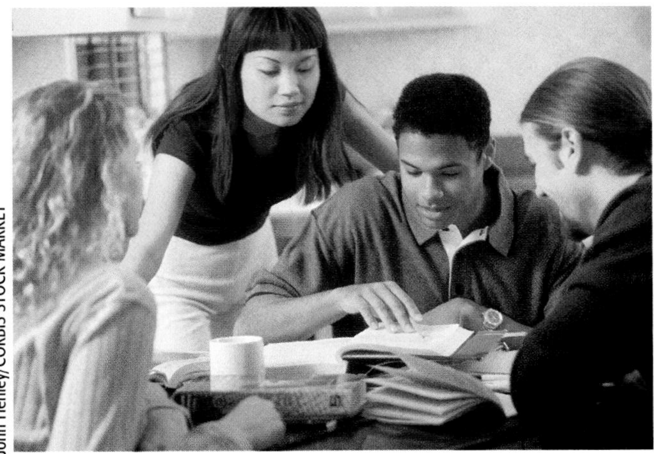

John Henley/CORBIS STOCK MARKET

opposing circle. Ask a question and have partners discuss the answer. If partners do not know the answer they can ask another pair for help. Then, call on students in the inside circle, the outside circle, or all students to say the answer aloud together.

- ✔ **In the Know** Provide students with a set of end-of-chapter questions or other questions covering content you want students to master. Tell students to circulate around the room to find someone who can answer a question on the worksheet. After listening to the answer, the student paraphrases it, writes the answer on the worksheet, and asks the "expert" to read and sign off on the answer if it is correct. Students move on to find a student to answer the next question. The process continues until students have completed their worksheets.
- ✔ **Open-Ended Projects** The best long-term projects for cooperative groups are those that are open-ended and multidimensional. That is, the task or question should have many possible answers and should lend itself to many different presentation possibilities.

  Multiple intelligences Appropriate projects should challenge students and allow students of various abilities and backgrounds to contribute significantly to solving the problem and executing the project. One way to assess the validity of a potential project is to see whether it requires the use of many different strengths or "intelligences."

  Assigning roles Because of the complexity of long-term projects, it is essential that students have clearly assigned roles and responsibilities. Once cooperative groups are established and successful in your classroom, be sure to vary the assignments given to each student from project to project.

  Deadlines Define interim and final deadlines to encourage students to pace their efforts appropriately.

How Do I Assess Group and Individual Efforts?

- ✔ **Expectations** As with any assignment, set clear guidelines and high expectations for projects. Show models of excellent past projects, if possible, and define what criteria projects must meet to earn the highest grade.
- ✔ **Group and Individual Grades** Before students begin, define what percentage of the grade will be based on group work and how much will be based on individual effort. Many teachers give two equally weighted grades: a group grade—the same for each team member—and an individual grade.
- ✔ **Self-Assessment** Provide a checklist or rating scale for each group member. Have students evaluate their own contribution to the group, as well as the contributions of other group members. In addition to assessing the quality of the finished product, have students evaluate the processes they used within the group, such as showing respect for others' ideas. Provide space on the evaluation sheet for students to explain why they rated themselves and group members as they did.✦

Troubleshooting

Advice from Carey Boswell, M.Ed.
Humble Independent School District
Humble, Texas

Modern research overwhelmingly suggests that student learning is enhanced when cooperative groups are used in the classroom. Like many other teachers, I was uncertain of how much learning was taking place when I set up cooperative groups. I struggled with noise and control issues and off-task behavior by some students. I found a solution, though.

A cooperative group activity occurs whenever a student works with another student. Cooperative groups do not have to be large groups. Smaller groups ensure that all students are engaged and contribute to the group effort. Smaller groups also guarantee that members perform multiple tasks so that real learning occurs. I often combine two or more small groups into a larger group for short comparative tasks. After making this small adjustment, I am able to assign cooperative group tasks to students at least once a week and student performance, comprehension, and learning has increased in my classroom.

Classroom Solutions

Web Strategies

How Can I Use the Internet to Teach Social Studies?

Aaron Haupt

From the Internet to round-the-clock live newscasts, teachers and students have never before had so much information at their fingertips. Yet never before has it been so confusing to determine where to turn for reliable content and what to do with it once you have found it. In today's world, social studies teachers must not only use the Internet as a source of up-to-the-minute information for students; they must teach students how to find and evaluate sources on their own.

What's Available On the Internet?

- ✔ **Teacher-Focused Web Sites** These Web sites provide teaching tips, detailed lesson plans, and links to other sites of interest to teachers and students.
- ✔ **Historical Documents** Thousands of primary source documents have now been cataloged and placed on the Web. Some sites provide text-only versions. Others provide photographs of actual documents and artifacts as well as insightful commentary and analysis.
- ✔ **Geographical Information** The Web holds a variety of geographical resources, from historical, physical, and political maps; to interactive mapping programs; to information about people and places around the world.
- ✔ **Statistics** Government Web sites are rich depositories for statistics of all kinds, including census data and information about climate, education, the economy, and political processes and patterns.
- ✔ **Reference Sources** Students can access full-text versions of encyclopedias, dictionaries, atlases, and other reference books, as well as databases containing millions of journal and newspaper articles.
- ✔ **News** Traditional media sources, including television, radio, newspapers, and newsmagazines, sponsor Internet sites that provide almost instantaneous news updates, as well as in-depth news coverage and analysis. Extensive archives facilitate research on past news stories.
- ✔ **Topical Information** Among the most numerous Web sites are those organized around a particular topic or issue, such as the Civil War or the stock market. These Internet pages may contain essays, analyses, and other commentaries, as well as primary source documents, maps, photographs, video and audio clips, bibliographies, and links to related online resources.
- ✔ **Organizations** Many organizations such as museums post Web pages that provide online exhibits, archives, and other information.

Glencoe Online

Glencoe provides an integrated Web curriculum for your textbook. The **Chapter Overview** Web link provides previews and reviews to help students better understand each chapter's organization and content. Engaging **Student Web Activities** challenge students to apply what they've learned. **Self-Check Quizzes** at the end of each chapter let you and your students assess their knowledge. You can also access additional resources, including links relevant to your state.

Finding Things on the Internet

The greatest asset of the Internet—its vast array of materials—is also its greatest deterrent. Many excellent social studies-specific sites provide links to relevant content. Using Internet search engines can also help you find what you need.

- ✔ A search engine is an Internet search tool. You type in a keyword, name, or phrase, and the search engine lists the URLs for Web sites that match your search. However, a search engine may find things that are not at all related or may miss sites that you would consider of interest. The key is to find ways to define your search.
- ✔ Not all search engines are the same. Each seeks out information a little bit differently. Different search engines use different criteria to determine what constitutes a "match" for your search topic. The Internet holds numerous articles

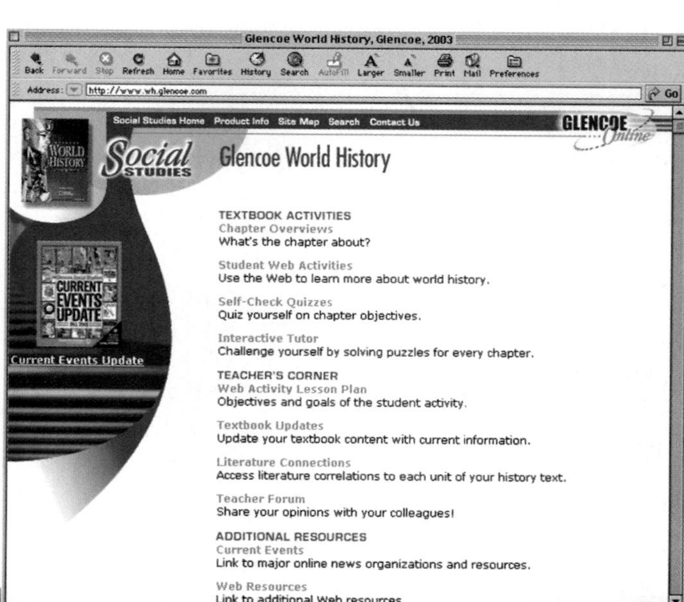

that compare search engines and offer guidelines for choosing those that best meet your needs.

- ✔ An advanced search allows you to refine the search by using a phrase or a combination of words. The way to conduct an advanced search varies from search engine to engine; check the search engine's Help feature for information. Encourage students to review this information regularly for each of the search engines they use.

How Do I Teach Students to Evaluate Web Sites?

Anyone can put up a Web site. Web content is easy to change, too, so Webmasters constantly update their Web sites by adding, modifying, and removing content. These characteristics make evaluating Web sites both more challenging and more important than traditional print resources. Teach students to critically evaluate Web resources, using the questions and criteria below.

1 **Purpose:** What is the purpose of the Web site or Web page? Is it an informational Web page, a news site, a business site, an advocacy site, or a personal Web page? Many sites serve more than one purpose. For instance, a news site may provide current events accompanied by banner ads that market the products advertisers think readers might want.

2 **URL:** What is the URL, or Web address? Where does the site originate? That can sometimes tell you about the group or business behind the Web page. For example, URLs with .edu and .gov domain names indicate that the site is connected to an educational institution or a government agency, respectively. A .com suffix usually means that a commercial or business interest hosts the Web site, but may also indicate a personal Web page. A nonprofit organization's Web address may end with .org.

3 **Authority:** Who wrote the material or created the Web site? What qualifications does this person or group have? Who has ultimate responsibility for the site? If the site is sponsored by an organization, are the organization's goals clearly stated?

4 **Accuracy:** How reliable is the information? Are sources listed so that they can be verified? Is the Web page free from surface errors in spelling and grammar? How does it compare with other sources you've found on the Web and in print?

5 **Objectivity:** If the site presents itself as an informational site, is the material free from bias? If there is advertising, is it easy to tell the difference between the ads and other features? If the site mixes factual information with opinion, can you spot the difference between the two? If the site advocates an opinion or viewpoint, is the opinion clearly stated and logically defended?

6 **Currency:** When was the information first placed on the Web? Is the site updated on a regular basis? When was the last revision? If the information is time-sensitive, are the updates frequent enough?

7 **Coverage:** What topics are covered on the Web site? What is the depth of coverage? Are all sides of an issue presented? How does the coverage compare with other Web and print sources? ✦

See the *Glencoe Social Studies Guide to Using the Internet* for additional information and teaching strategies.

Avoiding Online Pitfalls

Advice from Jim Matiya
Carl Sandburg High School
Orland Park, Illinois

Integrating technology into your social studies curriculum can have its pitfalls. Because something often goes wrong when you least expect it, here is some advice about technology, computers, and students.

1. Make sure the hyperlinks work—check them yourself.
2. Design assignments that go from easy to complex. Students have varying degrees of success with computers so start with simple, concrete assignments and move to complex, abstract assignments.
3. Vary the selection of sites for students. You can use a search engine and a museum site for one assignment and then use a historical document page and a statistical site for another assignment. Varying the sites negates predictability and breaks the routine.
4. Make sure you have given students enough information to find what you want. Do not give them a question that can lead to thousands of different answers on different sites.
5. Design Web assignments so that students with less Internet experience can achieve some degree of success. Have computer-literate students become mentors for their classmates.
6. Have alternative assignments in case the Internet is temporarily down, the computers are locked inside a closet, or lightning has wiped out a bank of computers.

Classroom Solutions

Primary Source Strategies

How Do I Use Primary Sources in My Classroom?

PhotoDisc

A primary source is direct evidence of an event, idea, period, or development. It is an oral or written account obtained from actual participants in an event. Examples of primary sources include the following:

- ✔ official documents (records, statistics)
- ✔ political declarations, laws, and rules for governance
- ✔ speeches and interviews
- ✔ diaries, memoirs, and oral histories
- ✔ autobiographies
- ✔ recipes and cookbooks
- ✔ advertisements and posters
- ✔ letters

Physical objects, such as tools and dishes, can be primary sources; so can visual evidence in the form of fine art, photographs, maps, films, and videotapes. Primary sources can also include songs and audio recordings.

Why Use Primary Sources in Your Classroom?

Using primary sources to teach transforms the study of social studies from a passive process to an active one. Students become investigators—finding clues, formulating hypotheses and drawing inferences, making judgments, and reaching conclusions. Bringing primary sources into the classroom stimulates students to think critically about events, issues, and concepts rather than just memorizing dates, names, and generalizations reached by others.

Choosing Primary Sources

- ✔ Provide exposure to a variety of source types, including historic photographs, folk or popular music, financial records or household accounts, as well as letters, journals, and historic documents.
- ✔ When choosing print sources, consider the interests and reading levels of your students. Many texts contain challenging vocabulary and unfamiliar sentence structure. You may need to create a reader's guide that defines key vocabulary and paraphrases the main points of the reading.
- ✔ Some documents may be too long. Decide whether using an excerpt will provide enough information for students to draw conclusions.
- ✔ Depending upon the topic and your instructional objectives, you may need to provide several different primary sources to expose students to a variety of perspectives.
- ✔ Decide how students will access the primary sources: through the Internet, the library, a museum, or other print resources. Consider the possibility of an Internet virtual field trip for students. Moving from URL to URL, students can visit museum sites and other Web pages to view artifacts; interpret economic or census data; and read journals, letters, and official documents.

Anthony Redpath/CORBIS STOCK MARKET

How Do I Introduce Students to Primary Sources?

Carefully explain the nature of primary sources when you introduce them to students. Although primary sources contain valuable clues, be sure to alert students that primary sources contain biases and prejudices, and must be approached with caution. Every primary source reflects the creator's point of view to some degree.

Using Primary Sources in the Classroom

Primary sources provide a rich source of inspiration for a variety of instructional strategies. They can be used to spark interest in a new topic, foster deeper exploration into a historical era, or assess students' understanding of social studies concepts and facts.

- ✔ **Pre-Reading Activities** Present a primary source for students to study at the beginning of a new chapter or topic. Have students analyze the source, using the questions and guidelines presented on the next page. Then have students make

We the People of the
insure domestic Tranquility, provide for the common defence,
and our Posterity, do ordain and establish this Constitution
Article. I.
Section. 1. All legislative Powers herein granted shall be vested in a Congress of the United States, which shall consist of a Senate and House of Representatives.

Aaron Haupt

Interpreting a Primary Source

Before students interpret a primary source, they need to know the context into which the source fits. Then they can use questions and guidelines, such as those below, to help them analyze and interpret the primary source.

Print Sources

- Who created the source, and what was the purpose for doing so?
- Did the writer personally experience or witness the event(s)?
- At what point did the writer record the information—as it happened or afterward? How long after?
- Who was the intended audience?
- Was the writer trying to record facts, express an opinion, or persuade others to take action?
- What is the author's main message?
- What values does the document convey?
- What bias does it reflect?
- What information about the topic can you gather from this document?
- Compare this document with what you know about the topic. Does it confirm those ideas or introduce a new perspective?
- How might other accounts about this topic support or modify the message this source delivers?

Visual Sources

- Who created the source, and what was the purpose for doing so?
- What does the image show?
- What mood does the image convey?
- Who or what dominates the image or catches your eye?
- How does the view impact the message?
- What details can you learn from the image?
- What is excluded from view?
- What bias does the visual reflect?
- What information about the topic can you gather from this visual?
- How might other visuals about this topic support or modify the message this one delivers?

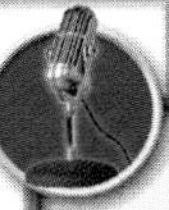

Audio Sources

- Who created the source? What was the purpose for creating this source?
- What is the main idea of the audio?
- What mood does the recorder's voice convey?
- What bias does the audio text reflect?
- What information about the topic can you gather from this audio source?
- Compare the information in this source with what you already know about the topic. Does it confirm those ideas or introduce a new perspective?
- How might other sources about this topic support or modify the message that this one delivers?

predictions about what they might learn in the upcoming lessons.

✔ **Exploring Information** Provide a variety of primary sources related to a topic or time period. Have students compare and contrast the items, analyzing the information, making inferences, and drawing conclusions about the period.

✔ **Evaluation Activities** Have students evaluate a primary source and tell how it supports or refutes what they learned in the textbook or have students read a primary source document that provides one perspective on a topic, and have students write their own account, presenting another perspective or opinion.✦

How to Use the Declaration of Independence in Your Classroom

Advice from Susan Hirsch
East Wake High School
Wendell, North Carolina

Divide students into groups of three or four. Tell students that it is 1777, and one member of their group has been arrested for joining the revolutionary struggle against Great Britain. This person will be sent to London to be tried on charges of treason. Hanging is the punishment for those found guilty of treason. Each group must prepare a defense using only one source—the Declaration of Independence. One person from each group will speak to the class, acting as either the defendant or the defendant's attorney. After all the presentations, the class will vote to determine which person did the best job of defending himself or herself or the client.

Classroom Solutions

Using Maps, Graphs, and Charts

How Can I Use Visuals to Improve Students' Reading Comprehension?

Maps, graphs, and charts are visual tools. By using images rather than words, these tools present complex information in an easy-to-understand format. Teach students the following generalized viewing strategies, and encourage them to apply these strategies as they study each chapter.

- ✔ **Asking Questions** Students should start by looking over the graphic and asking themselves questions, such as "What is my purpose for looking at this image?" Then students can identify questions they hope to answer, such as "What is being compared?" or "What are the most important features?"
- ✔ **Finding Answers** Next, students should use the graphic's structural features, such as the title, labels, colors, and symbols, to help them find the answers to their questions. If the source of the graphic is available, students should also determine its reliability.
- ✔ **Drawing Conclusions** After studying the visual, students should summarize its main points and draw conclusions.
- ✔ **Connecting** Before moving on, students should relate what they learned from the visual with what they gained from reading the text selection. Students can examine how the visual supports or extends the meaning of the text.

Maps

Maps show the relative size and location of specific geographic areas. There are as many different kinds of maps as there are uses for them. Two of the most common general purpose maps are political maps and physical maps. Political maps show human-made boundaries, such as state and country borders. Physical maps show physical features, such as mountains and lakes. Special purpose maps might show historical change, cultural features, population, land use, or climate.

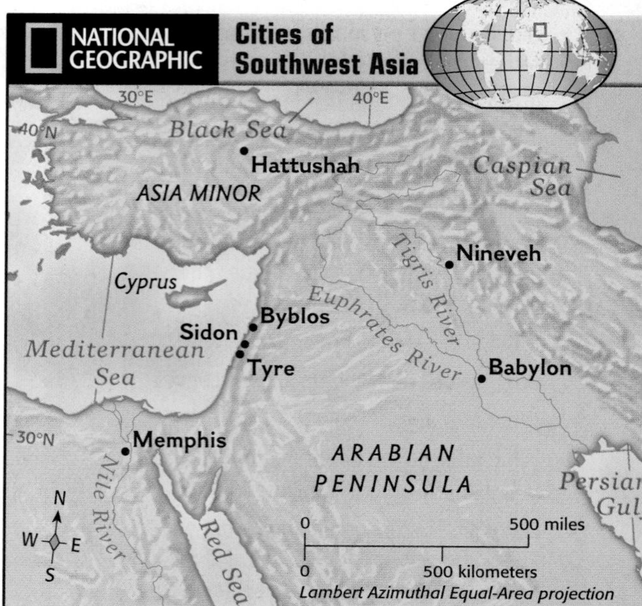

Parts of Maps

All maps contain parts that assist in interpreting the information. Help students learn to identify the following map parts.

- ✔ **Title** The map title identifies the area shown on the visual. The title can also identify a map's special focus.
- ✔ **Map Key** The map key, or legend, explains the symbols presented on the map, thus unlocking the map's information.
- ✔ **Compass Rose** A compass rose is a direction marker. It is a symbol that points out where the cardinal directions—north, south, east, and west—are positioned.
- ✔ **Scale** A measuring line, often called a scale bar, indicates the relationship between the distances on the map and the actual distances on Earth. Distance on a map can be determined by measuring the distance between points, then multiplying that measure by the number of miles or kilometers specified in the map scale ratio.
- ✔ **Latitude and Longitude** Mapmakers use lines of latitude and longitude to pinpoint exact locations on maps and globes. The imaginary horizontal lines that circle the globe from east to west are lines of latitude, also called parallels. The imaginary vertical lines are lines of longitude, also called meridians. Both parallels and meridians are measured in degrees.

Graphs

Graphs are a way of showing numbers or statistics in a clear, easy-to-read way. Because graphs summarize and present information visually, readers have an easier time understanding the data and drawing conclusions. The most common types of graphs are bar graphs, line graphs, circle graphs, and pictographs.

NATIONAL GEOGRAPHIC **GRAPH STUDY**

Populations: Selected Countries

Morocco

Libya

Algeria

Tunisia

Egypt

= 5,000,000

Source: National Geographic Atlas of the World, 7th edition

✔ **Bar Graphs** A bar graph shows how two or more subjects or statistics compare. It provides information along two sides or axes. The horizontal axis is the line across the bottom of the graph. The vertical axis is the line along the side. The bars may be either vertical or horizontal. In most cases the labels on one axis show quantity, while the labels on the opposite axis show the categories of data being compared.

✔ **Line Graphs** A line graph shows change over time. Like a bar graph, it organizes information along the horizontal and vertical axes. The horizontal axis usually shows passing time, such as months, years, or decades. The vertical axis usually shows quantity or amount. Sometimes more than one set of data is shown in a line graph. A double-line graph, for instance, plots data for two related quantities, which may be represented in different colors or patterns.

✔ **Circle Graphs** A circle graph, also called a pie graph, shows how each part or percentage relates to the whole. A circle graph enables a viewer to make comparisons between parts and to analyze the relationship of each part to the whole.

✔ **Pictograph** A pictograph uses rows of small symbols or pictures, each representing a particular amount. Like a bar graph, a pictograph is useful for making comparisons.

Charts

While all charts present information or data in a visual way, the type of chart is often dictated by the nature of the information and by the chart-maker's purposes.

✔ **Tables** Tables show information, including numerical data, in columns and rows. This organized arrangement facilitates comparisons between categories of information. Labels are usually located at the top of each column and on the left-hand side of the table.

✔ **Diagrams** Diagrams are specialized drawings. They can show steps in a process; point out parts of an object, organization, or idea; or explain how something works. Arrows or lines may join parts of a figure and can show relationships between parts or the flow of steps.✦

Classroom Activity: Create a Graph

Advice from Faith Vautour
Camden Hills Regional High School
Rockport, Maine

Graphs can be difficult to interpret and understand. Help students by having them create their own graph. To help students begin thinking about graphs, separate students into small groups. Then explain that each group should take a quick survey of classmates and make a graph to show their survey results. Suggest that students make either a bar graph, line graph, circle graph, or pictograph to show their data. To prompt students' thinking, ask the following questions.

- *Do you play on a sports team? Which sport(s)?*
- *What do you plan to do after high school?*
- *About how much time do you spend watching TV each day? About how much time did you spend on TV when you were 10 years old? When you were five years old?*

After students are done graphing their data, invite each group to share its work. Discuss the types of graphs students made and their reasons for choosing them. Each group should then take the graph that another group has prepared and transfer the information into another type of graph.

Classroom Solutions

Addressing the Needs of Special Students

How Can I Help ALL my Students Learn Social Studies?

Today's classroom contains students from a variety of backgrounds and with a variety of learning styles, strengths, and challenges. With careful planning, you can address the needs of all students in the social studies classroom. The following tips for instruction can assist your efforts to help all students reach their maximum potential.

- ✔ Survey students to discover their individual differences. Use interest inventories of their unique talents so you can encourage contributions in the classroom.
- ✔ Model respect of others. Adolescents crave social acceptance. The student with learning differences is especially sensitive to correction and criticism—particularly when it comes from a teacher. Your behavior will set the tone for how students treat one another.
- ✔ Expand opportunities for success. Provide a variety of instructional activities that reinforce skills and concepts.
- ✔ Establish measurable objectives and decide how you can best help students meet them.
- ✔ Celebrate successes and praise "work in progress."
- ✔ Keep it simple. Point out problem areas—if doing so can help a student affect change. Avoid overwhelming students with too many goals at one time.
- ✔ Assign cooperative group projects that challenge all students to contribute to solving a problem or creating a product.

How Do I Reach Students with Learning Disabilities?

- ✔ Provide support and structure. Clearly specify rules, assignments, and responsibilities.
- ✔ Practice skills frequently. Use games and drills to help maintain student interest.
- ✔ Incorporate many modalities into the learning process. Provide opportunities to say, hear, write, read, and act out important concepts and information.
- ✔ Link new skills and concepts to those already mastered.
- ✔ Allow students to record answers on audiotape.
- ✔ Allow extra time to complete tests and assignments.
- ✔ Let students demonstrate proficiency with alternative presentations, including oral reports, role plays, art projects, and with music.
- ✔ Provide outlines, notes, or tape recordings of lecture material.
- ✔ Pair students with peer helpers, and provide class time for pair interaction.

Michael Newman/PhotoEdit

How Do I Reach Students with Behavioral Disorders?

- ✔ Provide a structured environment with clear-cut schedules, rules, seat assignments, and safety procedures.
- ✔ Reinforce appropriate behavior and model it for students.
- ✔ Cue distracted students back to the task through verbal signals and teacher proximity.
- ✔ Set very small goals that can be achieved in the short term. Work for long-term improvement in the big areas.

How Do I Reach Students with Physical Challenges?

- ✔ Openly discuss with the student any uncertainties you have about when to offer aid.
- ✔ Ask parents or therapists and students what special devices or procedures are needed, and whether any special safety precautions need to be taken.
- ✔ Welcome students with physical challenges into all activities, including field trips, special events, and projects.

Jose L. Pelaez/CORBIS STOCK MARKET

- ✔ Provide information to help able-bodied students and adults understand other students' physical challenges.

How Do I Reach Students with Visual Impairments?

- ✔ Facilitate independence. Modify assignments as needed.
- ✔ Teach classmates how and when to serve as guides.
- ✔ Limit unnecessary noise in the classroom if it distracts the student with visual impairments.
- ✔ Provide tactile models whenever possible.
- ✔ Foster a spirit of inclusion. Describe people and events as they occur in the classroom. Remind classmates that the student with visual impairments cannot interpret gestures and other forms of nonverbal communication.
- ✔ Provide taped lectures and reading assignments.
- ✔ Team the student with a sighted peer for written work.

How Do I Reach Students with Hearing Impairments?

- ✔ Seat students where they can see your lip movements easily and where they can avoid visual distractions.
- ✔ Avoid standing with your back to the window or light source.
- ✔ Use an overhead projector to maintain eye contact while writing.
- ✔ Seat students where they can see speakers.
- ✔ Write all assignments on the board, or hand out written instructions.
- ✔ If the student has a manual interpreter, allow both student and interpreter to select the most favorable seating arrangements.
- ✔ Teach students to look directly at each other when they speak.

How Do I Reach English Language Learners?

- ✔ Remember, students' ability to speak English does not reflect their academic abilities.
- ✔ Try to incorporate the students' cultural experience into your instruction. The help of a bilingual aide may be effective.
- ✔ Avoid cultural stereotypes.
- ✔ Pre-teach important vocabulary and concepts.
- ✔ Encourage students to preview text before they begin reading, noting headings, graphic organizers, photographs, and maps.

How Do I Reach Gifted Students?

- ✔ Make arrangements for students to take selected subjects early and to work on independent projects.
- ✔ Ask "what if" questions to develop high-level thinking skills. Establish an environment safe for risk taking.
- ✔ Emphasize concepts, theories, ideas, relationships, and generalizations.
- ✔ Promote interest in the past by inviting students to make connections to the present.
- ✔ Let students express themselves in alternate ways, such as creative writing, acting, debate, simulations, drawing, or music.
- ✔ Provide students with a catalog of helpful resources, listing such things as agencies that provide free and inexpensive materials, appropriate community services and programs, and community experts.
- ✔ Assign extension projects that allow students to solve real-life problems related to their communities.✦

Customize Your Classroom!

Advice from Marilyn Gerken
Pickerington Local Schools
Pickerington, Ohio

Provide individualized activities and assignments for a variety of student ability levels. Develop learning packets for chapters and units of study with varying formats, levels, and types of assignments. Assign points and contract students based on their selection of activities to be completed. The activities in the Student Edition can be used for many of the learning activities and assignments.

What Is History?

World history is more than just a series of dramatic events. It is the story of the human community—how people lived on a daily basis, how they shared ideas, how they ruled and were ruled, and how they fought. World history includes big subjects like economics, politics, and social change, but it is also the story of dreams fulfilled or unfulfilled, personal creativity, and philosophical and religious inspiration.

You may think of history as a boring list of names and dates, an irrelevant record of revolutions and battles, or the meaningless stories of kings, queens, and other rulers. History is not, however, just what happens to famous and infamous people. History includes everything that happens to everyone, including you.

A Record of the Past

The most common definition of history is "a record of the past." To create this record, historians use documents (what has been recorded or written); artifacts, such as pottery, tools, and weapons; and even artworks. History in this sense really began five thousand to six thousand years ago, when people first began to write and keep records. The period before written records we call *prehistory.*

Herodotus, a Greek who lived in the fifth century B.C., was one of the first historians. In his history of the Greek and Persian wars, he used evidence, tried to tell a good story, and showed concern for the causes and effects of events. Today's historians still try to discover what happened (the factual evidence), but

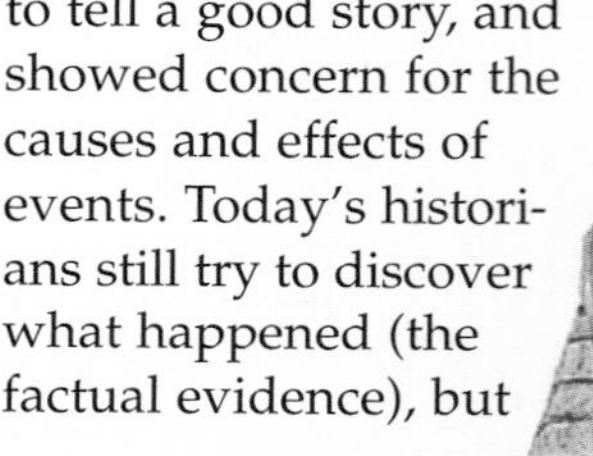

African statue

Ramses II

Roman coin, Alexander the Great

they also want to know why it happened. They use critical thinking and detailed investigation to explain the cause-and-effect relationships that exist among facts, and they look for new discoveries that might change our view of the past.

All of us are involved in the making of history. Alex Haley, the editor of *The Autobiography of Malcolm X*, grew up in Tennessee listening to his grandmother tell stories of Kunta Kinte, a family ancestor kidnapped in Africa during the 1700s and taken to America as a slave. Haley's search for his family's history led to his famous book, *Roots: The Saga of an American Family*. The book was turned into one of the most watched television miniseries of all time. Although Haley's family was a small part of larger historical events, the personal family history had universal appeal.

You will find, with some investigation, that history has been made by your own family and by the families of your friends. You are who you are because of the choices and experiences of your ancestors. Their experiences guide your choices and actions, just as yours will guide your children's and grandchildren's. You are an important link in a chain that stretches back into your ancestors' history and forward into your descendants' future.

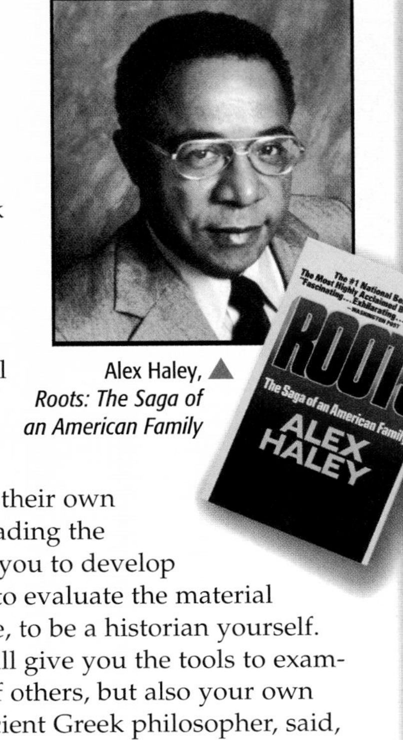

Alex Haley, ▲ *Roots: The Saga of an American Family*

In this book, you will read one account of the history of the world, as well as documents that historians use to create their own pictures of the past. Reading the documents will enable you to develop your critical skills and to evaluate the material in this book—in a sense, to be a historian yourself. The study of history will give you the tools to examine not only the lives of others, but also your own life. As Socrates, an ancient Greek philosopher, said, "The unexamined life is not worth living."

Themes for Understanding World History

To examine the past, historians often organize their material according to themes. This enables them to ask and then try to answer basic questions about the past. The following nine themes are especially important, and you will find them again and again in our story.

1 Politics and History

Historians study politics to answer certain basic questions about the structure of a society. How were people governed? What was the relationship between the ruler and the ruled? What people or groups of people held political power? What rights and liberties did the people have? What actions did people take to change their forms of government?

The study of politics also includes the role of conflict. Historians examine the causes and results of wars in order to understand the impact of war on human development.

2 The Role of Ideas

Ideas have great power to move people to action. For example, the idea of nationalism, which is based on a belief in loyalty to one's nation, has led to numerous wars and the deaths of millions of people. At the same time, nationalism has also motivated people to work together to benefit the lives of a nation's citizens. The spread of ideas from one society to another has also played an important role in world history.

3 Economics and History

A society's existence depends on meeting certain basic needs. How did the society grow its food? How did it make its goods? How did it provide the services people needed? How did individual people and governments use their limited resources? Did they spend more money on hospitals or military forces? By answering these questions, historians examine the different economic systems that have played a role in history.

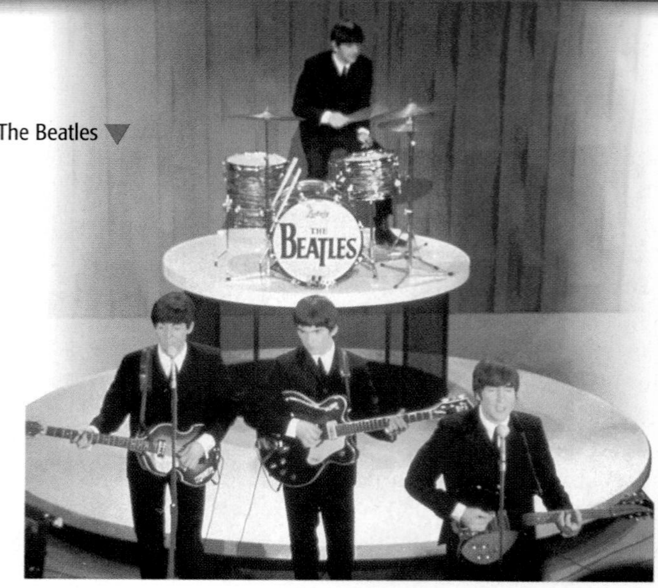

The Beatles

 The Importance of Cultural Development

We cannot understand a society without looking at its culture, or the common ideas, beliefs, and patterns of behavior that are passed on from one generation to another. Culture includes both high culture and popular culture. High culture consists of the writings of a society's thinkers and the works of its artists. Many of these people were illiterate and so passed on their culture orally. Today the term *popular culture* describes current trends and fashions such as popular television programs, movies, and music.

 Religion in History

Throughout history, people have sought to find a deeper meaning to human life. How have the world's great religions—such as Hinduism, Buddhism, Judaism, Christianity, and Islam—influenced people's lives? How have those religions spread to create new patterns of culture?

 The Role of Individuals

Julius Caesar, Queen Elizabeth I, Mohandas Gandhi, and Adolf Hitler remind us of the role of individuals in history. Decisive actions by powerful individuals have played a crucial role in the course of history. So, too, have the decisions of ordinary men and women who must figure out every day how to survive, protect their families, and carry on their ways of life.

 The Impact of Science and Technology

For thousands of years, people around the world have made scientific discoveries and technological innovations that have changed our world. From the creation of stone tools that made farming easier to the advanced computers that guide our airplanes, science and technology have altered how humans have related to their world.

8 The Environment and History

Throughout history, peoples and societies have been affected by the physical world in which they live. In turn, human activities have had a profound impact on the world. From slash-and-burn farming to industrial pollution, people have affected the environment and even endangered the existence of entire societies.

9 Social Life

From a study of social life and customs, we learn about the different social classes that make up a society, the nature of family life, and how knowledge is passed on from one generation to the next. We also examine how people in history dressed, where they lived, how and what they ate, and what they did for fun.

These nine themes should be looked at in connection to each other, rather than individually. They help us to understand the forces that create civilizations and cause them to fall. At the same time, world history consists of more than just the study of individual civilizations. It should be seen in a broad comparative and global framework, as people and countries come into contact—and often into conflict—with one another.

In our time, the concept of contact between societies has changed. Computers, television, and multinational corporations have, to a certain extent, turned the world into a single community or global village.

Historians and the Dating of Time

In recording the past, historians try to determine the exact time when events occurred. World War II in Europe, for example, began on September 1, 1939, when Adolf Hitler sent German troops into Poland. The war in Europe ended on May 7, 1945, when Germany surrendered. By using dates, historians can place events in the order they occurred and try to determine the development of patterns over periods of time.

The dating system most commonly used in the Western world (Europe and the Western Hemisphere) is based on the assumed date of the birth of Jesus Christ (the year 1). An event that took place 400 years before the birth of Jesus would be dated 400 B.C. ("before Christ"). Dates after the birth of Jesus are labeled A.D. These letters stand for the Latin words *anno Domini*, which mean "in the year of the Lord." An event that took place 250 years after the birth of Jesus is written A.D. 250. It can also be written as 250.

Because B.C. and A.D. are so Western and Christian-oriented, some historians now prefer to use the abbreviations B.C.E. ("before the common era") and C.E. ("common era"). Thus, 1850 B.C. could be written as 1850 B.C.E.

Historians use other terms to refer to time. A decade is 10 years, a century is 100 years, and a millennium is 1,000 years. The fourth century B.C. is the fourth period of 100 counting backward from 1, the assumed date of the birth of Jesus. The first century B.C. encompasses the years 100 to 1 B.C. Therefore, the fourth century B.C. refers to the years 400 to 301 B.C. We say, then, that an event in 650 B.C. took place in the seventh century B.C.

The fourth century A.D. is the fourth period of 100 years after the birth of Jesus. The first period of 100 years includes the years 1 to 100, so the fourth hundred-year period, or the fourth century, encompasses the years 301 to 400. For example, we say that an event in 750 took place in the eighth century. Just as the first millennium B.C. span the years 1000 to 1 B.C., the first millennium A.D. span the years 1 to 1000.

General Dwight D. Eisenhower ▶ speaks to his troops just before the invasion of France in June 1944.

Reading for Information

When you read this textbook, you are reading for information, but you are also gaining insights into the world around you, the how and why of events that have happened. History is nonfiction writing—it describes real-life events, people, ideas, and places. Here is a menu of reading strategies that will help you become a better textbook reader. As you come to passages in your textbook that you do not understand, refer to these reading strategies for help.

Before You Read

Set a Purpose

- Why are you reading the textbook?
- How does the subject relate to your life?
- How might you be able to use what you learn in your own life?

Preview

- Read the chapter title to find what the topic will be.
- Read the chapter key events and section titles to see what you will learn about the topic.
- Skim the photos, charts, graphs, or maps. How do they support the topic?
- Look for key terms that are in color and boldfaced. How are they defined?

Draw from Your Own Background

- What have you read or heard about concerning new information on the topic?
- How is the new information different from what you already know?
- How will the information that you already know help you understand the new information?

As You Read

Question

- What is the main idea?
- How do the photos, charts, graphs, and maps support the main idea?

Connect

- Think about people, places, and events in your own life. Are there any similarities with those in your textbook?
- Can you relate the textbook information to other areas of your life?

Predict

- Predict events or outcomes by using clues and information that you already know.
- Change your predictions as you read and gather new information.

Visualize

- Pay careful attention to details.
- Create graphic organizers to show relationships in the reading. Use the graphic organizer in the Guide to Reading to help organize the information in each section.

Look for Clues

Compare and Contrast Sentences

- Look for clue words and phrases that signal comparison, such as *similarity, just as, both, in common, also,* and *too.*
- Look for clue words and phrases that signal contrast, such as *on the other hand, in contrast to, however, different, instead of, rather than, but,* and *unlike.*

Cause-and-Effect Sentences

- Look for clue words and phrases such as *because, as a result, therefore, that is why, since, so, for this reason,* and *consequently.*

Chronological Sentences

- Look for clue words and phrases such as *after, before, first, next, last, during, finally, earlier, later, since,* and *then.*

After You Read

Summarize

- Describe the main idea and how the details support it.
- Use your own words to explain what you have read.

Assess

- What was the main idea?
- Did you learn anything new from the material?
- Can you use this new information in other school subjects or at home?
- What other sources could you use to find more information about the topic?

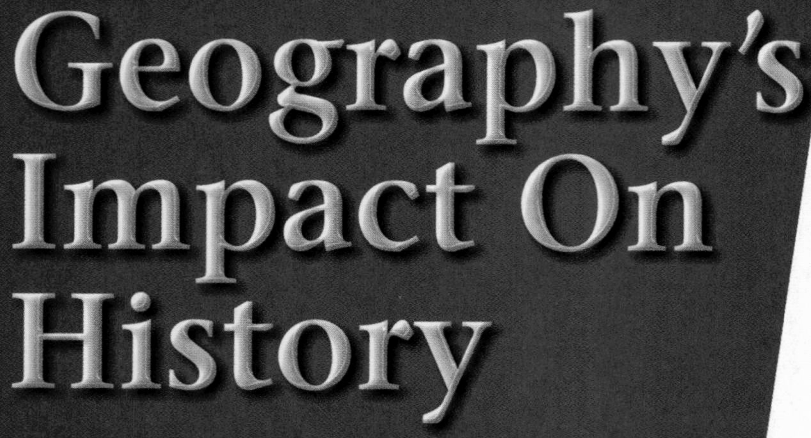

Geography's Impact On History

Throughout this text, you will discover how geography has shaped the course of events in world history. Landforms, waterways, climate, and natural resources all have helped or hindered human activities. Usually people have learned either to adapt to their environment or to transform it to meet their needs. Here are some examples of the role that geographic factors have played in the story of humanity.

Great Sphinx, Giza, Egypt

Unit 1: The World Before Modern Times

Rivers contributed to the rise of many of the world's early civilizations. By 3000 B.C., the Sumerians of Southwest Asia had set up 12 prosperous city-states in the Tigris-Euphrates River valley. The area is often called the Fertile Crescent because of its relatively rich topsoil and its curved shape.

Fertile land produced abundant food supplies and led to population growth. The river valleys of Mesopotamia, Egypt, India, and China became some of the great food-producing areas of the ancient world.

Landforms and waterways also affected the political relationship of the world's developing civilizations. For example, the rugged landscape of Greece divided the ancient Greeks into separate city-states instead of uniting them into a single nation. Furthermore, closeness to the sea allowed the Greeks to expand their trade, culture, and sense of civic pride to other parts of the Mediterranean world. In Southeast Asia, the unique geography of the region led to the development of separate, distinctive cultures.

Singapore skyline

Climatic changes had an important impact as well. The early inhabitants of the Americas are believed to have traveled from Asia across a land bridge produced by the Ice Age. In Europe during the Middle Ages, improving climates resulted in better agricultural conditions and increased food production, resulting in a growth in population.

Civilizations also developed at trade crossroads. From about A.D. 400 to A.D. 1500, the city of Makkah (Mecca) in the Arabian Peninsula was a crossroads for caravans from North Africa, Palestine, and the Persian Gulf.

At the dawn of the modern era, Asians and Europeans came into contact with one another partly because Europeans wanted Asia's spices and silks.

When the Asiatic people known as the Mongols could no longer guarantee safe passage for traders on overland routes, Europeans were forced to consider new water routes to Asia. This began a new global age that brought people of Europe, Asia, Africa, and the Americas into closer contact with each other.

Unit 2: The Early Modern World

Climate often affects the way a country interacts with its neighbors. For example, many of Russia's harbors stay frozen during the long winter months. In the past, Russia has gone to war to capture land for warmer ports.

Climate was one reason the Russians were able to stop the invasions of the French ruler Napoleon Bonaparte in 1812 and the German dictator Adolf Hitler in 1941. The Russians were used to the cold and snow of their country's winter. The invaders were not equipped for months of battle in frigid conditions.

Unit 3: An Era of European Imperialism

Utilizing natural resources, such as coal and iron, was an important factor in the growth of the Industrial Revolution. Modern industry started in Great Britain, which had large amounts of coal and iron ore for making steel. Throughout Europe and North America, the rise of factories that turned raw materials into finished goods prompted people eager for employment to move from rural areas to urban centers.

Also, the availability of land and the discovery of minerals in the Americas, Australia, and South Africa caused hundreds of thousands of Europeans to move to these areas in hopes of improving their lives. These mass migrations were possible because of improvements in industrial technology and transportation that enabled people to overcome geographic barriers.

Unit 4: The Twentieth-Century Crisis

Environmental disasters during the first part of the 1900s affected national economies in various parts of the world. For example, during the 1930s, winds blew away so much of the soil in the Great Plains of central North America that the area became known as the Dust Bowl. It took many years of normal rainfall and improved farming techniques to transform the Great Plains from a Dust Bowl into productive land once again.

Unit 5: Toward a Global Civilization

The world's peoples have become more aware of the growing scarcity of nonrenewable resources. Oil takes millions of years to form and the earth's supply is limited. Industrialized countries like the United States consume far more oil than they produce and must import large amounts. Many experts agree that consumption must be limited and alternative energy sources found.

Environmental problems are no longer limited to a single nation or region. For example, deforestation in one area and pollution in another area may be responsible for climate changes that cause floods and droughts all over the world. Global problems require global solutions, and nations are beginning to work together to ensure solutions that will work for all.

Reference Atlas

World: Political RA2

World: Physical RA4

North America: Political RA6

North America: Physical RA7

South America: Political RA8

South America: Physical RA9

Europe: Political RA10

Europe: Physical RA12

Africa: Political RA14

Africa: Physical RA15

Asia: Political RA16

Asia: Physical RA18

Middle East: Physical/Political RA20

Pacific Rim: Physical/Political RA22

World Land Use RA24

World Population Cartogram RA26

World Gross Domestic Product Cartogram RA28

World's People RA30

World Historical Eras RA32

Polar Regions RA34

ATLAS KEY

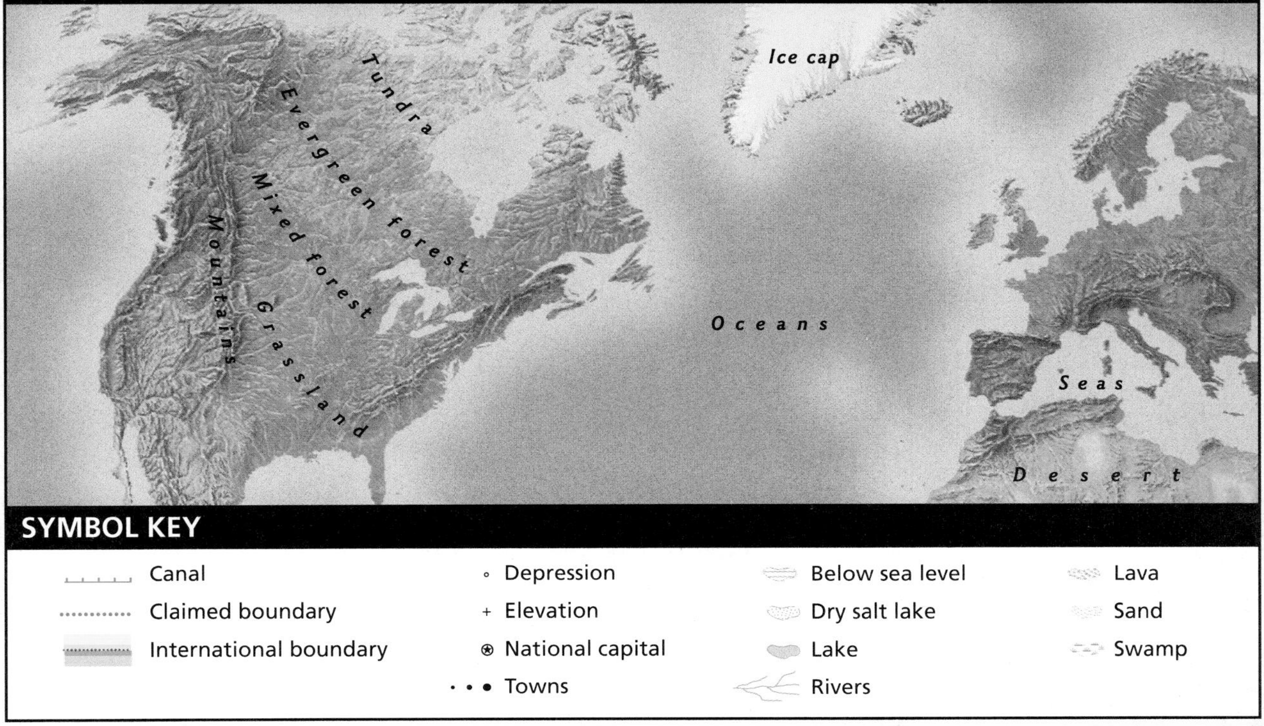

Tundra

Evergreen forest

Mixed forest

Mountains

Grassland

Ice cap

Oceans

Seas

Desert

SYMBOL KEY

Canal

Claimed boundary

International boundary

Depression

Elevation

National capital

Towns

Below sea level

Dry salt lake

Lake

Rivers

Lava

Sand

Swamp

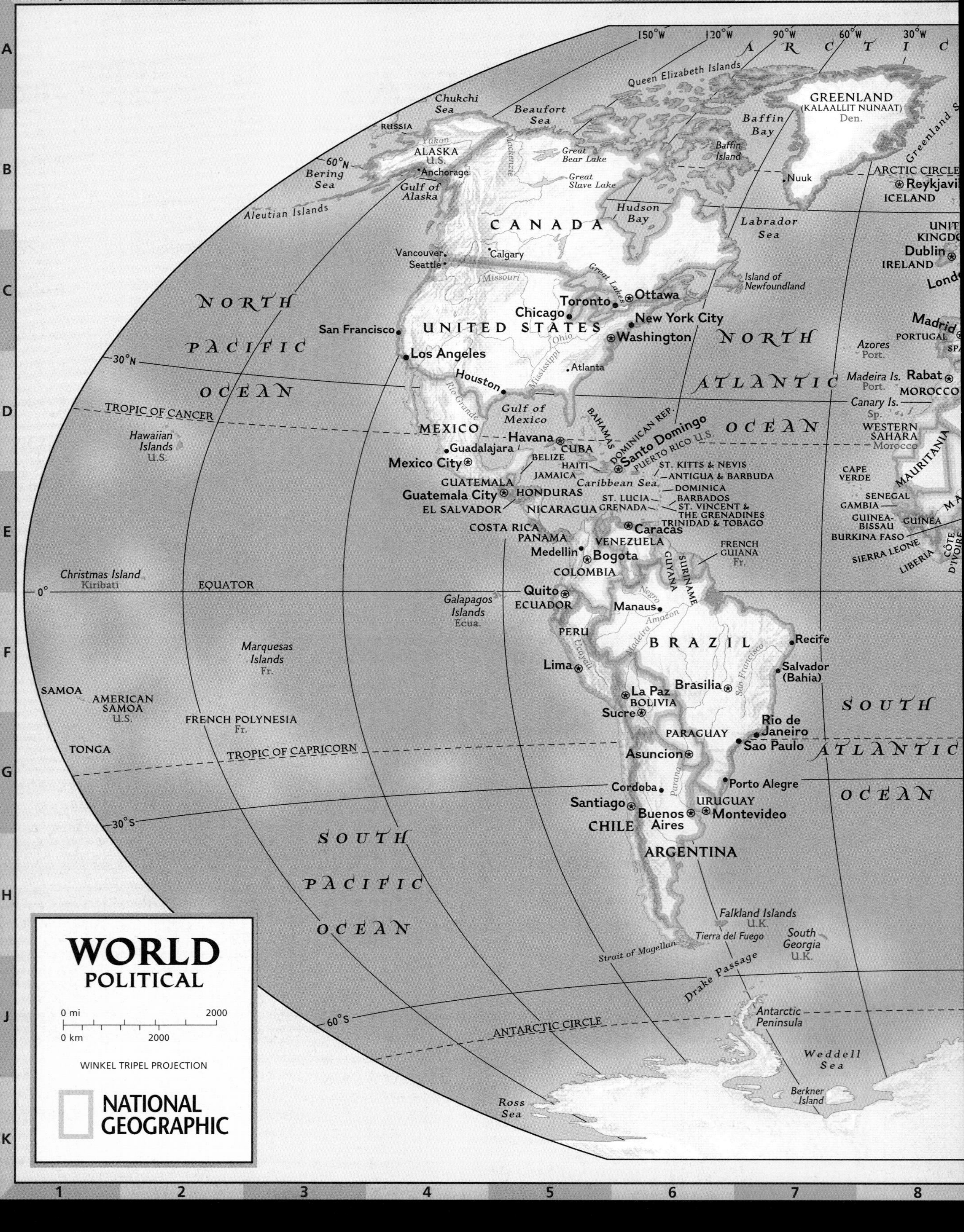
WORLD
POLITICAL
0 mi 2000
0 km 2000
WINKEL TRIPEL PROJECTION
NATIONAL GEOGRAPHIC
NORTH PACIFIC OCEAN
NORTH ATLANTIC OCEAN
SOUTH PACIFIC OCEAN
SOUTH ATLANTIC OCEAN
CANADA
UNITED STATES
MEXICO
BRAZIL
GREENLAND (KALAALLIT NUNAAT) Den.
ALASKA U.S.
RUSSIA
ICELAND
IRELAND
Washington
Ottawa
Mexico City
Havana
Santo Domingo
Guatemala City
Caracas
Bogota
Quito
Lima
La Paz
Sucre
Brasilia
Asuncion
Santiago
Buenos Aires
Montevideo
ARGENTINA
CHILE
URUGUAY
PARAGUAY
BOLIVIA
PERU
ECUADOR
COLOMBIA
VENEZUELA
GUYANA
SURINAME
FRENCH GUIANA Fr.
Tropic of Cancer
Tropic of Capricorn
Equator
Arctic Circle
Antarctic Circle

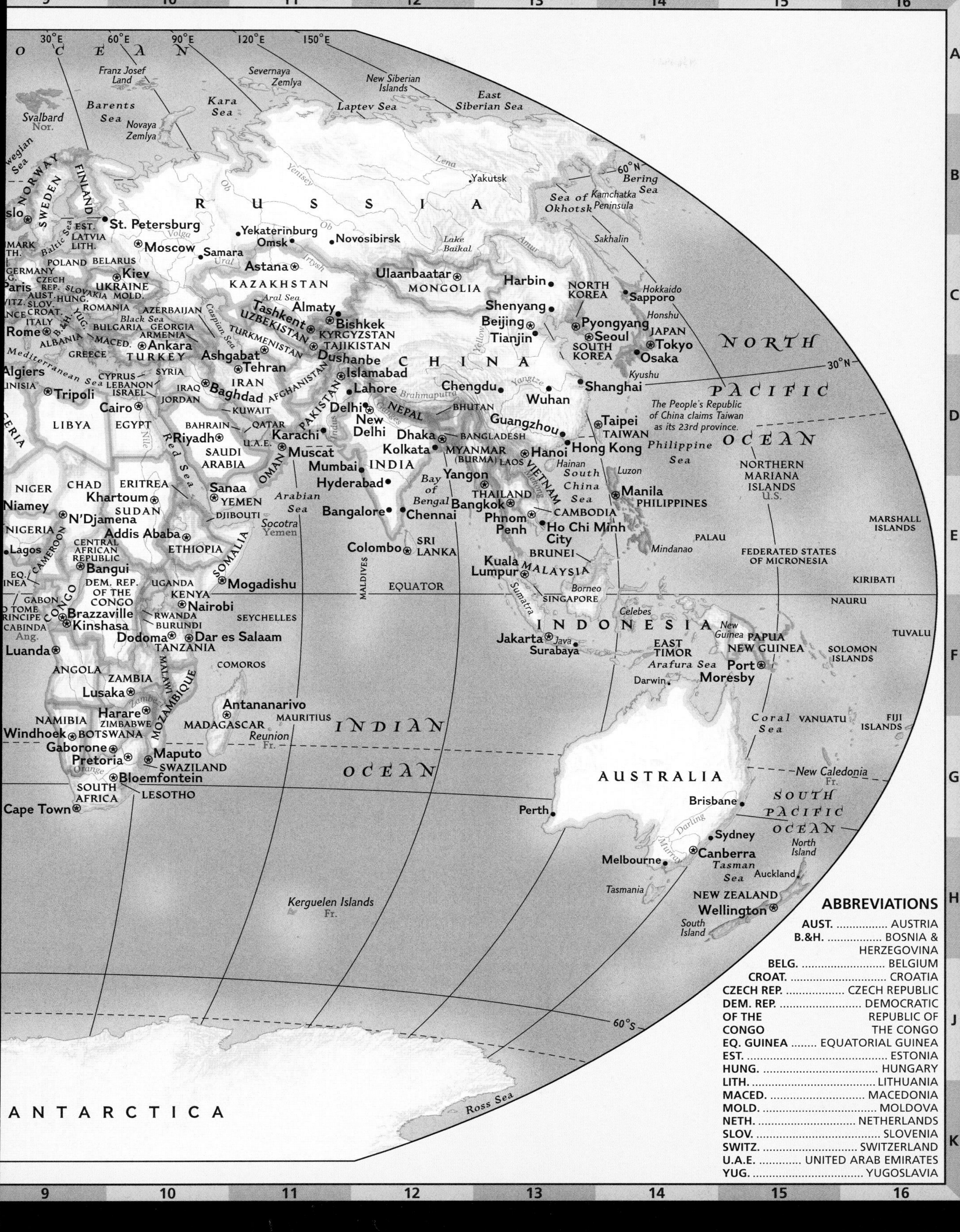

9
10
11
12
13
14
15
16
A
B
C
D
E
F
G
H
J
K
30°E
60°E
90°E
120°E
150°E
O C E A N
Franz Josef Land
Severnaya Zemlya
New Siberian Islands
East Siberian Sea
Laptev Sea
Kara Sea
Barents Sea
Novaya Zemlya
Svalbard
Nor.
NORWAY
SWEDEN
FINLAND
R U S S I A
Yakutsk
60°N
Bering Sea
Sea of Okhotsk
Kamchatka Peninsula
St. Petersburg
EST.
LATVIA
LITH.
Baltic Sea
Moscow
Samara
Yekaterinburg
Omsk
Novosibirsk
Lake Baikal
Sakhalin
Amur
Lena
Yenisey
Ob
Volga
Ural
Irtysh
POLAND
BELARUS
GERMANY
CZECH REP.
SLOVAKIA
UKRAINE
Kiev
MOLD.
Paris
AUST.
HUNG.
SLOV.
CROAT.
ROMANIA
ITALY
B.&H.
YUG.
BULGARIA
Rome
ALBANIA
MACED.
GREECE
Astana
KAZAKHSTAN
Aral Sea
Almaty
Ulaanbaatar
MONGOLIA
Harbin
NORTH KOREA
Hokkaido
Sapporo
AZERBAIJAN
Black Sea
GEORGIA
ARMENIA
Caspian Sea
Tashkent
UZBEKISTAN
Bishkek
KYRGYZSTAN
TURKMENISTAN
TAJIKISTAN
Shenyang
Beijing
Tianjin
Pyongyang
Seoul
SOUTH KOREA
Honshu
JAPAN
Tokyo
Osaka
Kyushu
NORTH
TURKEY
Ankara
Ashgabat
Dushanbe
C H I N A
Yellow
Mediterranean Sea
Algiers
CYPRUS
SYRIA
Tehran
IRAN
Islamabad
LEBANON
ISRAEL
IRAQ
Baghdad
AFGHANISTAN
Lahore
Chengdu
Wuhan
Yangtze
Shanghai
30°N
PACIFIC
Tripoli
Cairo
JORDAN
KUWAIT
PAKISTAN
Brahmaputra
Delhi
New Delhi
NEPAL
BHUTAN
Guangzhou
Taipei
TAIWAN
The People's Republic of China claims Taiwan as its 23rd province.
LIBYA
EGYPT
BAHRAIN
QATAR
Karachi
Indus
Ganges
Dhaka
BANGLADESH
Hong Kong
OCEAN
Nile
Riyadh
U.A.E.
Muscat
Kolkata
MYANMAR (BURMA)
LAOS
Hanoi
Philippine Sea
SAUDI ARABIA
OMAN
Mumbai
INDIA
Hainan
VIETNAM
Luzon
NORTHERN MARIANA ISLANDS
U.S.
Red Sea
NIGER
CHAD
ERITREA
Sanaa
YEMEN
Hyderabad
Bay of Bengal
Yangon
THAILAND
South China Sea
Mekong
Manila
PHILIPPINES
Niamey
Khartoum
SUDAN
N'Djamena
DJIBOUTI
Arabian Sea
Bangalore
Chennai
Bangkok
Phnom Penh
CAMBODIA
Ho Chi Minh City
MARSHALL ISLANDS
NIGERIA
Addis Ababa
ETHIOPIA
Socotra
Yemen
SOMALIA
SRI LANKA
Colombo
BRUNEI
PALAU
Mindanao
Lagos
CAMEROON
CENTRAL AFRICAN REPUBLIC
Bangui
Kuala Lumpur
MALAYSIA
FEDERATED STATES OF MICRONESIA
EQ. GUINEA
DEM. REP. OF THE CONGO
UGANDA
KENYA
Mogadishu
MALDIVES
EQUATOR
Sumatra
SINGAPORE
Borneo
KIRIBATI
GABON
CONGO
Brazzaville
Kinshasa
CABINDA
Ang.
Nairobi
RWANDA
BURUNDI
SEYCHELLES
Celebes
NAURU
Dodoma
Dar es Salaam
TANZANIA
I N D O N E S I A
Jakarta
Java
Surabaya
New Guinea
PAPUA NEW GUINEA
EAST TIMOR
TUVALU
Luanda
ANGOLA
COMOROS
Arafura Sea
Port Moresby
SOLOMON ISLANDS
ZAMBIA
Lusaka
MALAWI
MOZAMBIQUE
Zambezi
Darwin
Harare
ZIMBABWE
Antananarivo
MADAGASCAR
MAURITIUS
INDIAN
Coral Sea
VANUATU
FIJI ISLANDS
NAMIBIA
Windhoek
BOTSWANA
Gaborone
Reunion
Fr.
Pretoria
Maputo
SWAZILAND
OCEAN
Orange
Bloemfontein
AUSTRALIA
New Caledonia
Fr.
SOUTH AFRICA
LESOTHO
Cape Town
Perth
Brisbane
SOUTH PACIFIC OCEAN
Darling
Sydney
Murray
Canberra
North Island
Melbourne
Tasman Sea
Auckland
Tasmania
Kerguelen Islands
Fr.
NEW ZEALAND
Wellington
South Island
60°S
Ross Sea
A N T A R C T I C A
ABBREVIATIONS
AUST. .... AUSTRIA
B.&H. .... BOSNIA & HERZEGOVINA
BELG. .... BELGIUM
CROAT. .... CROATIA
CZECH REP. .... CZECH REPUBLIC
DEM. REP. OF THE CONGO .... DEMOCRATIC REPUBLIC OF THE CONGO
EQ. GUINEA .... EQUATORIAL GUINEA
EST. .... ESTONIA
HUNG. .... HUNGARY
LITH. .... LITHUANIA
MACED. .... MACEDONIA
MOLD. .... MOLDOVA
NETH. .... NETHERLANDS
SLOV. .... SLOVENIA
SWITZ. .... SWITZERLAND
U.A.E. .... UNITED ARAB EMIRATES
YUG. .... YUGOSLAVIA

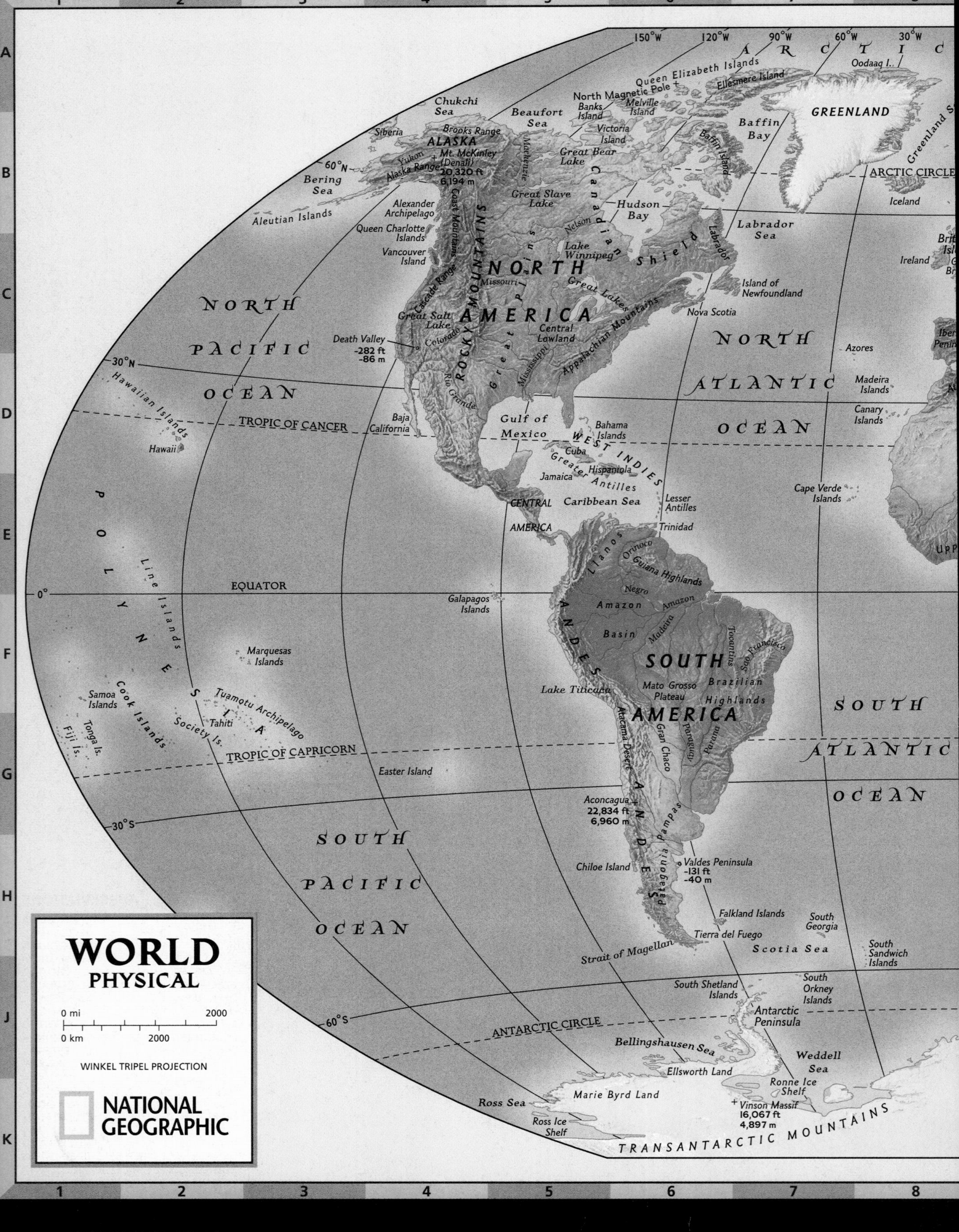

WORLD
PHYSICAL
0 mi 2000
0 km 2000
WINKEL TRIPEL PROJECTION
NATIONAL GEOGRAPHIC
ARCTIC
Queen Elizabeth Islands
Ellesmere Island
Oodaaq I.
North Magnetic Pole
GREENLAND
Chukchi Sea
Beaufort Sea
Banks Island
Melville Island
Victoria Island
Siberia
Brooks Range
ALASKA
Mt. McKinley (Denali) 20,320 ft 6,194 m
Yukon
Alaska Range
Bering Sea
Aleutian Islands
Great Bear Lake
Great Slave Lake
Mackenzie
Baffin Bay
Baffin Island
Greenland Sea
ARCTIC CIRCLE
Iceland
Hudson Bay
Labrador Sea
Labrador
Alexander Archipelago
Queen Charlotte Islands
Vancouver Island
Coast Mountains
Canadian Shield
Nelson
Lake Winnipeg
Ireland
NORTH AMERICA
Missouri
Great Lakes
Island of Newfoundland
Nova Scotia
Cascade Range
ROCKY MOUNTAINS
Great Salt Lake
Colorado
Great Plains
Central Lowland
Appalachian Mountains
Mississippi
Death Valley -282 ft -86 m
NORTH PACIFIC OCEAN
NORTH ATLANTIC OCEAN
Azores
Madeira Islands
Canary Islands
Rio Grande
Hawaiian Islands
Hawaii
TROPIC OF CANCER
Baja California
Gulf of Mexico
Bahama Islands
WEST INDIES
Cuba
Hispaniola
Greater Antilles
Jamaica
Caribbean Sea
Lesser Antilles
Trinidad
CENTRAL AMERICA
Cape Verde Islands
POLYNESIA
Line Islands
EQUATOR
Llanos
Orinoco
Guiana Highlands
Negro
Amazon
Amazon Basin
Madeira
Tocantins
São Francisco
Galapagos Islands
ANDES
Marquesas Islands
SOUTH AMERICA
Mato Grosso Plateau
Brazilian Highlands
Lake Titicaca
Samoa Islands
Cook Islands
Tuamotu Archipelago
Tahiti
Society Is.
Tonga Is.
Fiji Is.
Atacama Desert
Gran Chaco
Paraguay
Paraná
SOUTH ATLANTIC OCEAN
TROPIC OF CAPRICORN
Easter Island
Aconcagua 22,834 ft 6,960 m
Pampas
SOUTH PACIFIC OCEAN
Chiloe Island
Patagonia
Valdes Peninsula -131 ft -40 m
Falkland Islands
South Georgia
Tierra del Fuego
Scotia Sea
South Sandwich Islands
Strait of Magellan
South Shetland Islands
South Orkney Islands
Antarctic Peninsula
ANTARCTIC CIRCLE
Bellingshausen Sea
Weddell Sea
Ellsworth Land
Marie Byrd Land
Ronne Ice Shelf
Ross Sea
Vinson Massif 16,067 ft 4,897 m
Ross Ice Shelf
TRANSANTARCTIC MOUNTAINS
150°W 120°W 90°W 60°W 30°W
60°N 30°N 0° 30°S 60°S

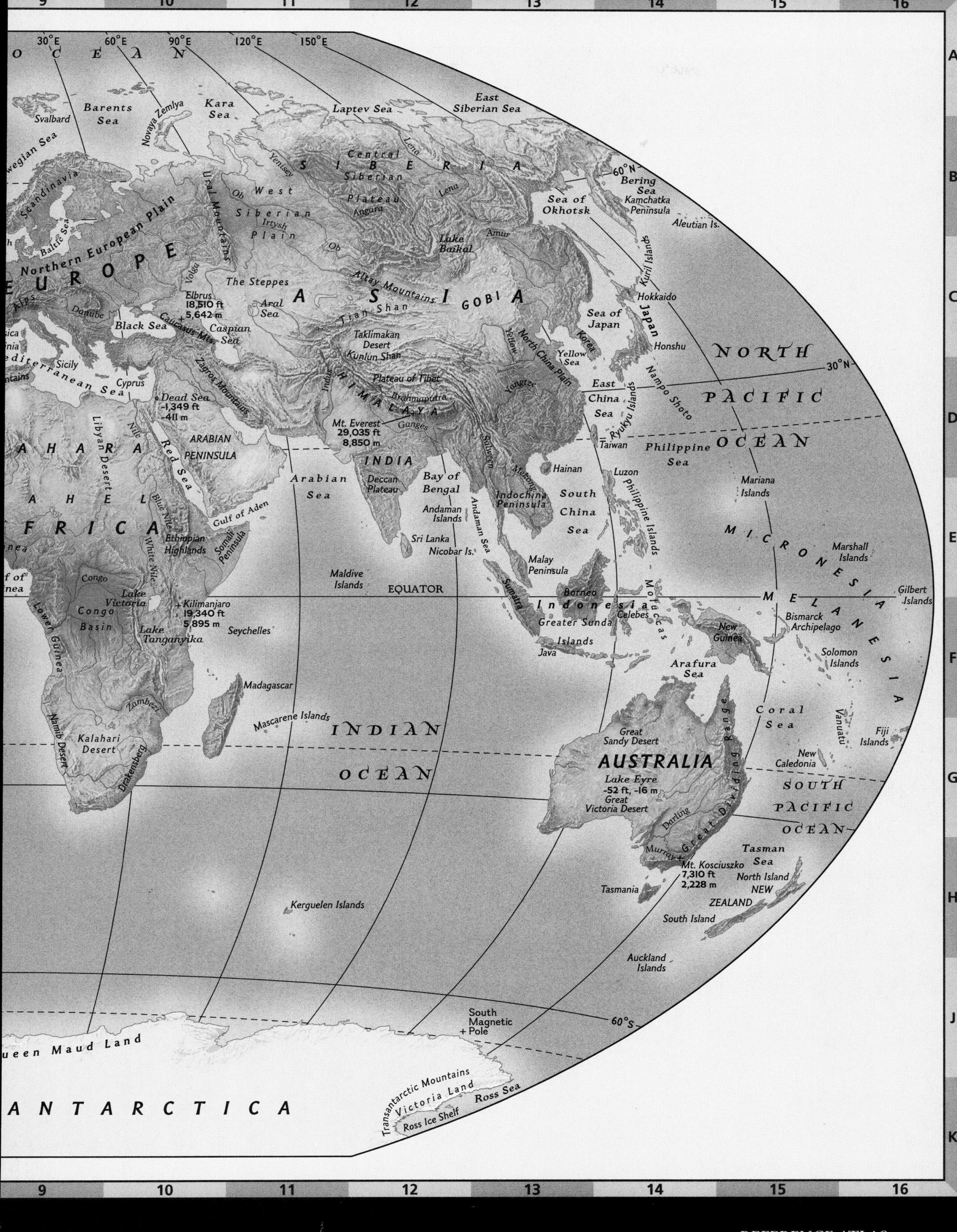

9
10
11
12
13
14
15
16
A
B
C
D
E
F
G
H
J
K
30°E
60°E
90°E
120°E
150°E
O C E A N
Barents Sea
Svalbard
Novaya Zemlya
Kara Sea
Laptev Sea
East Siberian Sea
Norwegian Sea
Scandinavia
Baltic Sea
Northern European Plain
EUROPE
Ural Mountains
Ob
West Siberian Plain
Irtysh
Yenisey
Lena
Central Siberian Plateau
Angara
S I B E R I A
60°N
Bering Sea
Sea of Okhotsk
Kamchatka Peninsula
Aleutian Is.
Amur
Lake Baikal
Kuril Islands
Hokkaido
Volga
Alps
Danube
Elbrus
18,510 ft
5,642 m
Caucasus Mts.
Black Sea
Caspian Sea
The Steppes
Aral Sea
A S I A
Altay Mountains
GOBI
Tian Shan
Taklimakan Desert
Kunlun Shan
Plateau of Tibet
Sea of Japan
Japan
Honshu
Korea
Yellow
Yellow Sea
North China Plain
NORTH PACIFIC OCEAN
30°N
Nampo Shoto
Sicily
Mediterranean Sea
Cyprus
Zagros Mountains
Indus
HIMALAYA
Brahmaputra
Yangtze
East China Sea
Ryukyu Islands
Dead Sea
-1,349 ft
-411 m
Mt. Everest
29,035 ft
8,850 m
Ganges
Taiwan
Philippine Sea
Nile
Libyan Desert
SAHARA
ARABIAN PENINSULA
Red Sea
INDIA
Arabian Sea
Deccan Plateau
Bay of Bengal
Salween
Mekong
Hainan
Luzon
Philippine Islands
Mariana Islands
SAHEL
AFRICA
Blue Nile
Gulf of Aden
Ethiopian Highlands
Somali Peninsula
White Nile
Andaman Islands
Andaman Sea
Indochina Peninsula
South China Sea
Sri Lanka
Nicobar Is.
MICRONESIA
Marshall Islands
Malay Peninsula
Maldive Islands
Congo
Lake Victoria
Congo Basin
EQUATOR
Sumatra
Borneo
Indonesia
Moluccas
Celebes
MELANESIA
Gilbert Islands
Kilimanjaro
19,340 ft
5,895 m
Seychelles
Lake Tanganyika
Lower Guinea
Greater Sunda Islands
Java
New Guinea
Bismarck Archipelago
Solomon Islands
Arafura Sea
Madagascar
Zambezi
Mascarene Islands
INDIAN OCEAN
Namib Desert
Kalahari Desert
Drakensberg
Great Sandy Desert
AUSTRALIA
Great Dividing Range
Coral Sea
Vanuatu
Fiji Islands
New Caledonia
Lake Eyre
-52 ft, -16 m
Great Victoria Desert
Darling
Murray
SOUTH PACIFIC OCEAN
Tasman Sea
Mt. Kosciuszko
7,310 ft
2,228 m
Tasmania
North Island
NEW ZEALAND
South Island
Kerguelen Islands
Auckland Islands
South Magnetic Pole
60°S
Queen Maud Land
ANTARCTICA
Transantarctic Mountains
Victoria Land
Ross Ice Shelf
Ross Sea

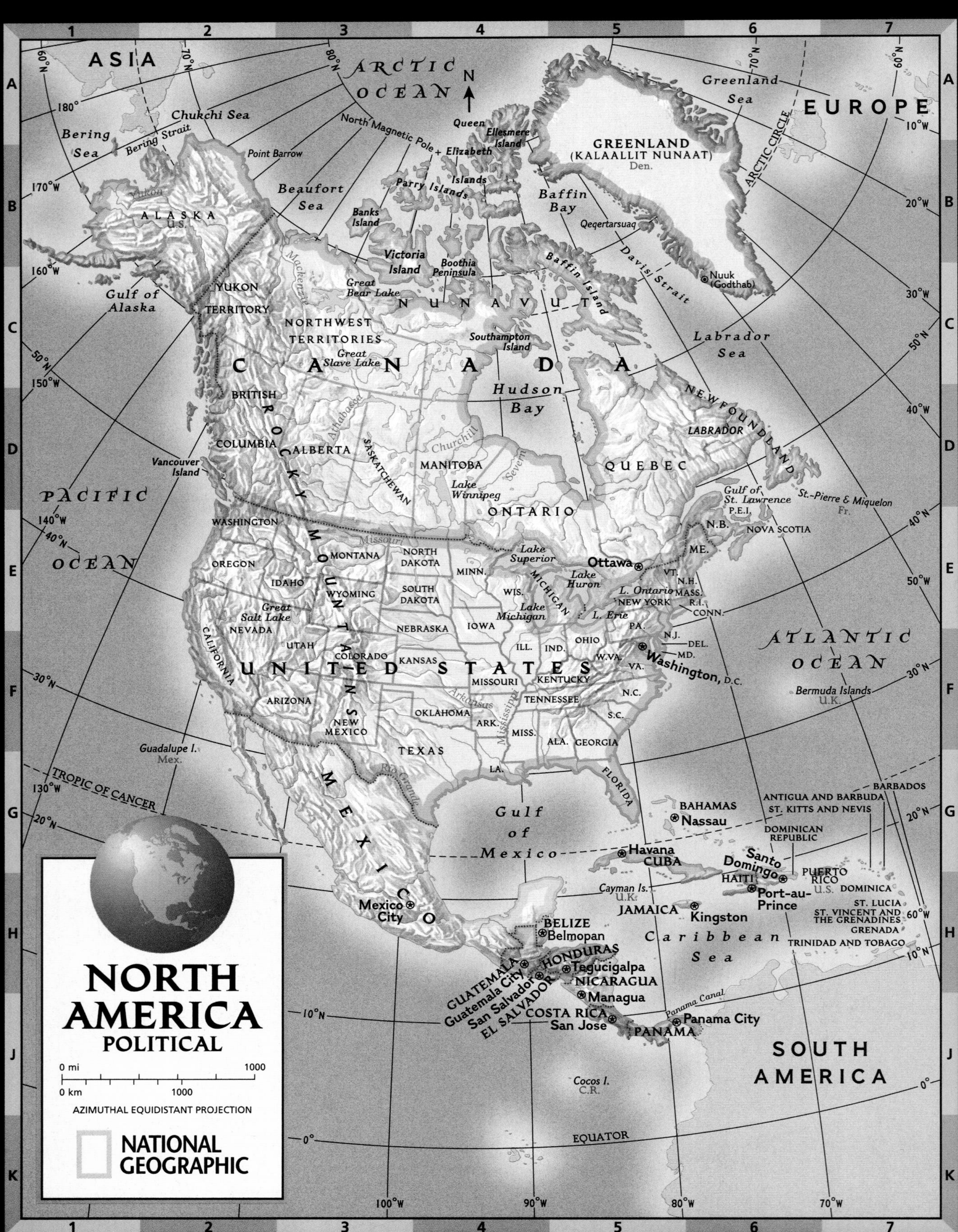
NORTH
AMERICA
POLITICAL
0 mi
1000
0 km
1000
AZIMUTHAL EQUIDISTANT PROJECTION
NATIONAL
GEOGRAPHIC
ASIA
ARCTIC OCEAN
EUROPE
GREENLAND
(KALAALLIT NUNAAT)
Den.
CANADA
UNITED STATES
MEXICO
PACIFIC OCEAN
ATLANTIC OCEAN
SOUTH AMERICA
Gulf of Mexico
Caribbean Sea
Hudson Bay
Ottawa
Washington, D.C.
Mexico City
TROPIC OF CANCER
ARCTIC CIRCLE
EQUATOR

NORTH AMERICA
PHYSICAL
0 mi
1000
0 km
1000
AZIMUTHAL EQUIDISTANT PROJECTION
NATIONAL GEOGRAPHIC
ASIA
ARCTIC OCEAN
N
Oodaaq Island
Lincoln Sea
Greenland Sea
EUROPE
Chukchi Sea
Bering Sea
St. Lawrence Island
Seward Peninsula
Point Barrow
North Slope
Brooks Range
North Magnetic Pole
Queen Elizabeth Islands
Ellesmere Island
Hayes Peninsula
GREENLAND
Gunnbjorn
12,139 ft
3,700 m
ARCTIC CIRCLE
Nunivak Island
Yukon
ALASKA
Beaufort Sea
Melville Island
Banks Island
Devon I.
Baffin Bay
Kuskokwim
Mt. McKinley (Denali)
20,320 ft
6,194 m
Bristol Bay
Aleutian Range
Alaska Range
Prince of Wales I.
Somerset I.
Victoria Island
Boothia Peninsula
Kodiak I.
Kenai Peninsula
Gulf of Alaska
19,551 ft
5,959 m
Mt. Logan
Yukon Plateau
Mackenzie Mts.
Mackenzie
Great Bear Lake
Melville Peninsula
Baffin Island
Davis Strait
Nuuk (Godthab)
Cape Farewell
Foxe Basin
Labrador Sea
Southampton Island
Hudson Strait
Great Slave Lake
CANADA
Ungava Bay
Alexander Archipelago
Slave
Peace
Lake Athabasca
Hudson Bay
Queen Charlotte Islands
Coast Mountains
ROCKY MOUNTAINS
CANADIAN SHIELD
Athabasca
Churchill
Nelson
Belcher Islands
LABRADOR
Fraser Plateau
Columbia Mts.
Saskatchewan
GREAT PLAINS
James Bay
Island of Newfoundland
Avalon Peninsula
Vancouver Island
PACIFIC OCEAN
Lake Winnipeg
Laurentian Mountains
Gulf of St. Lawrence
Gaspe Pen.
Olympic Peninsula
Cascade Range
Cape Breton Island
Prince Edward Island
Nova Scotia
Missouri
Lake Superior
St. Lawrence
Bay of Fundy
Columbia Plateau
Ottawa
Lake Michigan
Lake Huron
L. Ontario
Gulf of Maine
Cape Mendocino
Snake
Coast Ranges
Cape Cod
Great Basin
Great Salt Lake
L. Erie
APPALACHIAN MOUNTAINS
Sierra Nevada
Mt. Whitney
14,494 ft
4,418 m
High Plains
Platte
CENTRAL LOWLAND
Long Island
Washington
ATLANTIC OCEAN
Colorado Plateau
UNITED STATES
Ohio
Chesapeake Bay
Death Valley
-282 ft
-86 m
Grand Canyon
Ozark Plateau
Arkansas
Cape Hatteras
Bermuda Islands
Channel Islands
Sonoran Desert
Red
Mississippi
COASTAL PLAIN
Baja California
Gulf of California
Rio Grande
Sierra Madre Occidental
Sierra Madre Oriental
MEXICO
Florida
TROPIC OF CANCER
BAHAMAS
Gulf of Mexico
Florida Keys
Havana
CUBA
WEST INDIES
Virgin Islands
Puerto Rico
Hispaniola
HAITI
DOMINICAN REPUBLIC
Guadeloupe
Martinique
Lesser Antilles
Orizaba
18,855 ft
5,747 m
Yucatan Peninsula
Cozumel Island
Cayman Islands
Greater Antilles
Mexico City
JAMAICA
Kingston
Isthmus of Tehuantepec
BELIZE
Belmopan
Caribbean Sea
Trinidad
Gulf of Tehuantepec
HONDURAS
Tegucigalpa
GUATEMALA
Guatemala City
San Salvador
EL SALVADOR
NICARAGUA
Managua
Lake Nicaragua
COSTA RICA
San Jose
Isthmus of Panama
Panama City
PANAMA
CENTRAL AMERICA
SOUTH AMERICA
EQUATOR
180°
170°W
160°W
150°W
140°W
130°W
100°W
90°W
80°W
70°W
60°N
70°N
80°N
50°N
40°N
30°N
20°N
10°N
0°
10°W
20°W
30°W
40°W
50°W

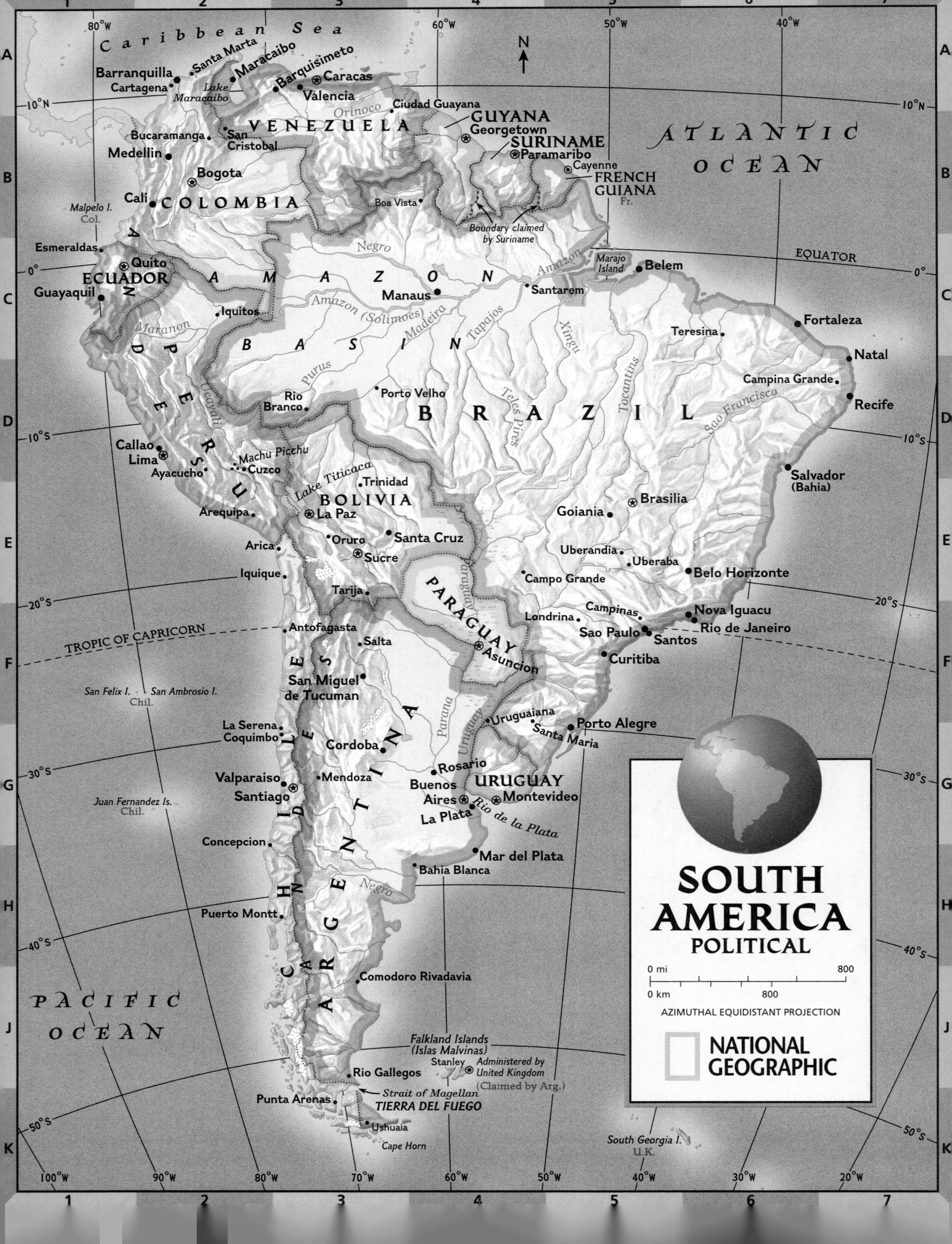
SOUTH AMERICA
POLITICAL
Caribbean Sea
ATLANTIC OCEAN
PACIFIC OCEAN
VENEZUELA
GUYANA
SURINAME
FRENCH GUIANA
Fr.
COLOMBIA
ECUADOR
PERU
BRAZIL
BOLIVIA
PARAGUAY
CHILE
ARGENTINA
URUGUAY
AMAZON BASIN
ANDES
Barranquilla
Santa Marta
Cartagena
Maracaibo
Lake Maracaibo
Barquisimeto
Caracas
Valencia
Ciudad Guayana
Orinoco
Georgetown
Paramaribo
Cayenne
Bucaramanga
San Cristobal
Medellin
Bogota
Cali
Malpelo I.
Col.
Boa Vista
Boundary claimed by Suriname
Esmeraldas
Quito
Guayaquil
Iquitos
Maranon
Negro
Amazon
Amazon (Solimoes)
Manaus
Santarem
Marajo Island
Belem
EQUATOR
Madeira
Tapajos
Xingu
Purus
Teresina
Fortaleza
Natal
Campina Grande
Recife
Sao Francisco
Tocantins
Teles Pires
Ucayali
Rio Branco
Porto Velho
Callao
Lima
Machu Picchu
Cuzco
Ayacucho
Lake Titicaca
Trinidad
La Paz
Arequipa
Salvador (Bahia)
Brasilia
Goiania
Oruro
Santa Cruz
Sucre
Arica
Uberandia
Uberaba
Belo Horizonte
Iquique
Campo Grande
Tarija
Paraguay
Campinas
Nova Iguacu
Rio de Janeiro
Londrina
Sao Paulo
Santos
Antofagasta
Salta
TROPIC OF CAPRICORN
Asuncion
Curitiba
San Felix I.
San Ambrosio I.
Chil.
San Miguel de Tucuman
Parana
Uruguay
Uruguaiana
Santa Maria
Porto Alegre
La Serena
Coquimbo
Cordoba
Rosario
Valparaiso
Mendoza
Santiago
Buenos Aires
Montevideo
La Plata
Rio de la Plata
Juan Fernandez Is.
Chil.
Concepcion
Mar del Plata
Bahia Blanca
Negro
Puerto Montt
Comodoro Rivadavia
Falkland Islands (Islas Malvinas)
Stanley
Administered by United Kingdom
(Claimed by Arg.)
Rio Gallegos
Strait of Magellan
Punta Arenas
TIERRA DEL FUEGO
Ushuaia
Cape Horn
South Georgia I.
U.K.
0 mi
800
0 km
800
AZIMUTHAL EQUIDISTANT PROJECTION
NATIONAL GEOGRAPHIC
N
80°W
60°W
50°W
40°W
10°N
0°
10°S
20°S
30°S
40°S
50°S
100°W
90°W
80°W
70°W
60°W
50°W
40°W
30°W
20°W
1
2
3
4
5
6
7
A
B
C
D
E
F
G
H
J
K

SOUTH AMERICA
PHYSICAL
0 mi 800
0 km 800
AZIMUTHAL EQUIDISTANT PROJECTION
NATIONAL GEOGRAPHIC
Caribbean Sea
ATLANTIC OCEAN
PACIFIC OCEAN
Caracas
Lake Maracaibo
Orinoco
VENEZUELA
LLANOS
Angel Falls Total drop 3,212 ft 979 m
GUYANA
Georgetown
SURINAME
Paramaribo
Cayenne
FRENCH GUIANA
GUIANA HIGHLANDS
Boundary claimed by Suriname
Bogota
COLOMBIA
Malpelo I.
Quito
ECUADOR
EQUATOR
Marajo Island
Amazon
Negro
AMAZON
Selvas
BASIN
Madeira
Tapajos
Xingu
Purus
Ucayali
Teles Pires
Tocantins
Sao Francisco
BRAZIL
ANDES
PERU
Lima
Machu Picchu
Lake Titicaca
BOLIVIA
La Paz
Altiplano
Sucre
Salar de Uyuni
MATO GROSSO PLATEAU
BRAZILIAN HIGHLANDS
Brasilia
Paraguay
PARAGUAY
Asuncion
Iguazu Falls
GRAN CHACO
Parana
Uruguay
TROPIC OF CAPRICORN
San Felix I.
San Ambrosio I.
Aconcagua 22,834 ft 6,960 m
Santiago
CHILE
Juan Fernandez Is.
ARGENTINA
PAMPAS
Buenos Aires
URUGUAY
Montevideo
Rio de la Plata
Negro
PATAGONIA
-131 ft -40 m
Valdes Peninsula
Chiloe Island
Gulf of San Jorge
Taitao Peninsula
Wellington I.
Falkland Islands (Islas Malvinas)
Stanley
Strait of Magellan
Tierra del Fuego
Cape Horn
South Georgia I.

EUROPE
POLITICAL
0 mi 400
0 km 400
AZIMUTHAL EQUIDISTANT PROJECTION
NATIONAL GEOGRAPHIC
ICELAND
Reykjavik
Akureyri
ARCTIC CIRCLE
Norwegian Sea
Faroe Islands Den.
Torshavn
Shetland Islands
Lerwick
Orkney Islands
Rockall U.K.
Isle of Lewis
MERIDIAN OF GREENWICH (LONDON)
Inverness
UNITED KINGDOM
SCOTLAND
Aberdeen
Glasgow
Edinburgh
NORTHERN IRELAND
Belfast
IRELAND
Dublin
Cork
Irish Sea
Liverpool
Manchester
WALES
Birmingham
ENGLAND
Cardiff
London
Celtic Sea
Land's End
Southampton
English Channel
North Sea
ATLANTIC OCEAN
NORWAY
SWEDEN
Trondheim
Are
Alesund
Sundsvall
Bergen
Oslo
Stavanger
Uppsala
Stockholm
Skagerrak
Goteborg
Gotland
DENMARK
Arhus
Copenhagen
Malmo
Kiel
Hamburg
Gdansk
NETH.
The Hague
Amsterdam
Berlin
Bydgoszcz
GERMANY
POLAND
Brussels
BELGIUM
Bonn
Rhine
Frankfurt
Wroclaw
LUX.
Prague
CZECH REP.
Le Havre
Brest
Rennes
Paris
Strasbourg
Nantes
FRANCE
La Rochelle
Bay of Biscay
Limoges
Bordeaux
Munich
Bratislava
Vienna
Zurich
LIECH.
Bern
SWITZERLAND
AUSTRIA
ALPS
Geneva
Lyon
Budapest
SLOVENIA
HUNGARY
Ljubljana
Zagreb
CROATIA
Milan
Turin
Venice
Genoa
BOSNIA HERZEGOVINA
Sarajevo
MONACO
Nice
Marseille
SAN MARINO
ITALY
Adriatic Sea
MONTENEGRO
Corsica Fr.
VATICAN CITY
Rome
Tirana
ALBANIA
Naples
Sardinia It.
Cagliari
Tyrrhenian Sea
Ionian Sea
Palermo
Sicily
Messina
Catania
Valletta
MALTA
A Coruna
Vigo
Porto
Coimbra
PORTUGAL
Lisbon
Bilbao
Donostia-San Sebastian
Pyrenees
Toulouse
Valladolid
ANDORRA
Zaragoza
Madrid
SPAIN
Barcelona
Valencia
Palma
Balearic Islands Sp.
Cordoba
Seville
Murcia
Cartagena
Cadiz
Malaga
GIBRALTAR U.K.
Strait of Gibraltar
Cape St. Vincent
Mediterranean Sea
AFRICA

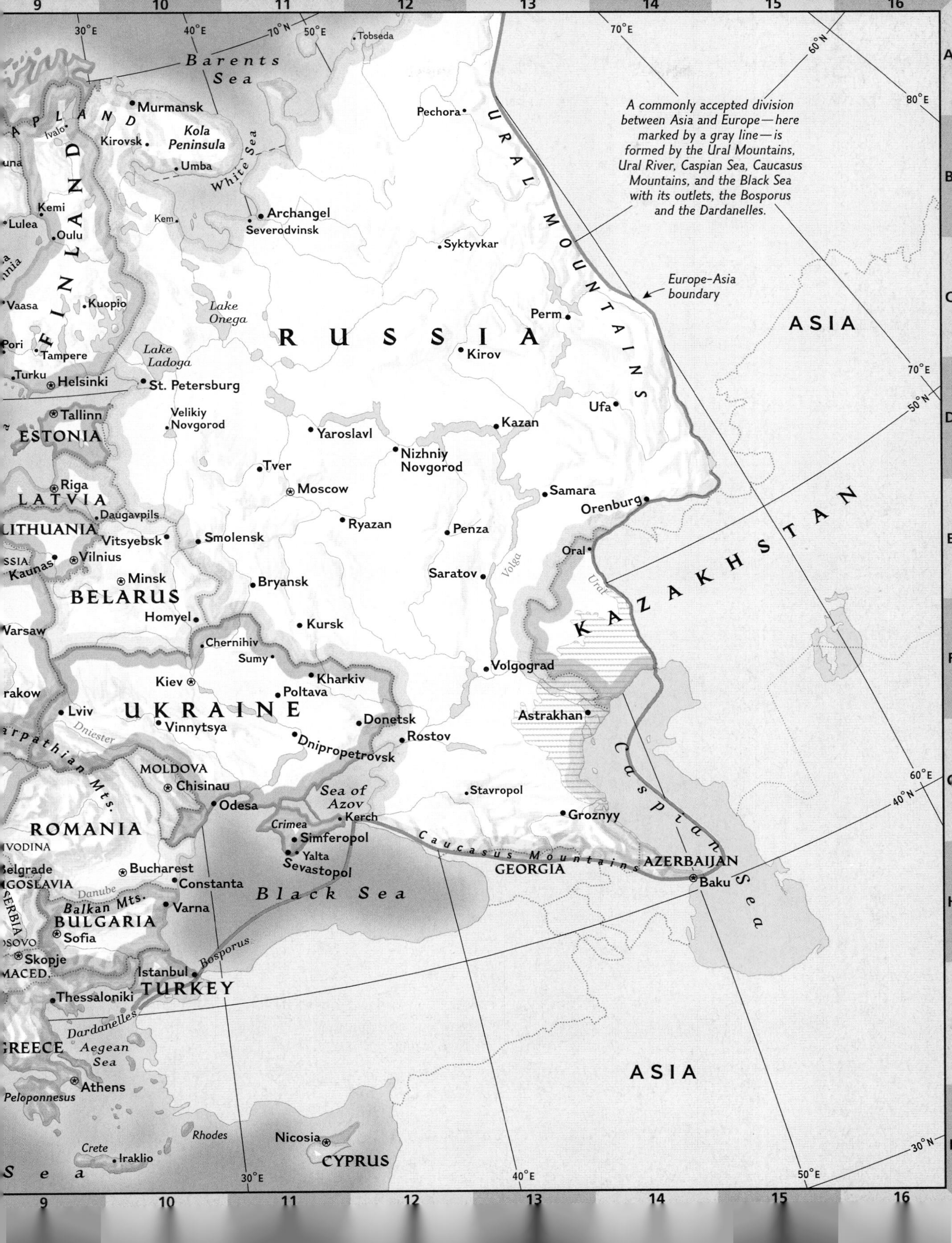
A commonly accepted division between Asia and Europe—here marked by a gray line—is formed by the Ural Mountains, Ural River, Caspian Sea, Caucasus Mountains, and the Black Sea with its outlets, the Bosporus and the Dardanelles.
Europe-Asia boundary
ASIA
RUSSIA
URAL MOUNTAINS
KAZAKHSTAN
UKRAINE
BELARUS
ESTONIA
LATVIA
LITHUANIA
FINLAND
LAPLAND
MOLDOVA
ROMANIA
BULGARIA
GEORGIA
AZERBAIJAN
TURKEY
GREECE
CYPRUS
Barents Sea
White Sea
Kola Peninsula
Black Sea
Sea of Azov
Caspian Sea
Aegean Sea
Caucasus Mountains
Carpathian Mts.
Balkan Mts.
Lake Onega
Lake Ladoga
Crimea
Bosporus
Dardanelles
Peloponnesus
Crete
Rhodes
Volga
Ural
Danube
Dniester
Murmansk
Kirovsk
Umba
Kem
Archangel
Severodvinsk
Pechora
Tobseda
Syktyvkar
Perm
Kirov
Ufa
Kazan
Samara
Orenburg
Oral
Saratov
Penza
Volgograd
Astrakhan
Stavropol
Groznyy
Baku
St. Petersburg
Velikiy Novgorod
Yaroslavl
Nizhniy Novgorod
Tver
Moscow
Ryazan
Smolensk
Bryansk
Kursk
Vitsyebsk
Minsk
Homyel
Chernihiv
Sumy
Kharkiv
Kiev
Poltava
Lviv
Vinnytsya
Donetsk
Rostov
Dnipropetrovsk
Chisinau
Odesa
Kerch
Simferopol
Yalta
Sevastopol
Bucharest
Constanta
Varna
Sofia
Skopje
Istanbul
Thessaloniki
Athens
Iraklio
Nicosia
Helsinki
Tallinn
Riga
Daugavpils
Vilnius
Kaunas
Turku
Tampere
Pori
Vaasa
Kuopio
Oulu
Kemi
Lulea
Ivalo
30°E
40°E
50°E
60°E
70°E
80°E
30°N
40°N
50°N
60°N
70°N

EUROPE
PHYSICAL
0 mi
400
0 km
400
AZIMUTHAL EQUIDISTANT PROJECTION
NATIONAL GEOGRAPHIC
ATLANTIC OCEAN
Reykjavik
ICELAND
ARCTIC CIRCLE
Norwegian Sea
Faroe Islands
Shetland Islands
Orkney Islands
MERIDIAN OF GREENWICH (LONDON)
Outer Hebrides
Highlands
British Isles
Edinburgh
Belfast
UNITED KINGDOM
IRELAND
Dublin
Irish Sea
Great Britain
Cardiff
London
North Sea
Jutland
DENMARK
Copenhagen
Zealand
Oslo
Stockholm
NORWAY
SWEDEN
SCANDINAVIA
Amsterdam
NETH.
BELGIUM
Brussels
LUX.
Rhine
GERMANY
Berlin
POLAND
Oder
Elbe
Prague
CZECH REP.
English Channel
Brittany
Seine
Paris
Loire
FRANCE
Bay of Biscay
Mont Blanc
15,771 ft
4,807 m
Massif Central
Rhone
Bern
SWITZ.
LIECH.
ALPS
Danube
AUSTRIA
Bratislava
Vienna
Budapest
HUNGARY
SLOVENIA
Ljubljana
Zagreb
CROATIA
Drava
Sava
BOSNIA & HERZEGOVINA
Sarajevo
Po
MONACO
Riviera
SAN MARINO
Apennines
Adriatic Sea
Cantabrian Mountains
Pyrenees
Douro
PORTUGAL
IBERIAN PENINSULA
Madrid
SPAIN
Ebro
Tagus
Lisbon
ANDORRA
Corsica
ITALY
VATICAN CITY
Rome
Tirana
ALBANIA
Sardinia
Tyrrhenian Sea
Balearic Islands
GIBRALTAR
Baetic Mountains
Strait of Gibraltar
Mediterranean
Ionian Sea
Sicily
Etna
10,902 ft
3,323 m
Valletta
MALTA
AFRICA
30°W
20°W
10°W
0°
10°E
60°N
70°N

Barents Sea
North Cape
Kola Peninsula
White Sea
Pechora
URAL MOUNTAINS
FINLAND
Lake Region
Lake Onega
Lake Ladoga
Northern Dvina
RUSSIA
EUROPEAN PLAIN
Europe-Asia boundary
ASIA
Helsinki
Gulf of Finland
Tallinn
ESTONIA
Kama
Volga
Ural
Riga
LATVIA
Moscow
LITHUANIA
Vilnius
Oka
CENTRAL RUSSIAN UPLAND
Minsk
BELARUS
Dnieper
Don
Warsaw
KAZAKHSTAN
Caspian Depression
Kiev
UKRAINE
Dniester
Carpathian Mountains
MOLDOVA
Chisinau
Sea of Azov
Crimea
Elbrus 18,510 ft 5,642 m
Caucasus Mountains
ROMANIA
Bucharest
Danube
Belgrade
BALKAN PENINSULA
BULGARIA
Balkan Mountains
Sofia
Skopje
Black Sea
GEORGIA
AZERBAIJAN
Baku
Caspian Sea
Bosporus
TURKEY
Dardanelles
GREECE
Aegean Sea
Athens
Peloponnesus
Rhodes
Crete
Nicosia
CYPRUS
ASIA
30°E
40°E
50°E
60°E
70°E
80°E
30°N
40°N
50°N
60°N
70°N

AFRICA
POLITICAL
AZIMUTHAL EQUIDISTANT PROJECTION
0 mi
1000
0 km
1000
NATIONAL GEOGRAPHIC
EUROPE
ASIA
ATLANTIC OCEAN
INDIAN OCEAN
Mediterranean Sea
Red Sea
Gulf of Aden
Mozambique Channel
Strait of Gibraltar
Suez Canal
Sinai
TROPIC OF CANCER
TROPIC OF CAPRICORN
SAHARA
ATLAS MOUNTAINS
Libyan Desert
KALAHARI DESERT
Cape of Good Hope
MOROCCO
Rabat
Casablanca
Fes
Marrakech
Oran
Algiers
Constantine
ALGERIA
TUNISIA
Tunis
LIBYA
Tripoli
EGYPT
Alexandria
Cairo
Port Said
Suez
Lake Nasser
Aswan High Dam
Laayoune
WESTERN SAHARA
Mor.
MAURITANIA
MALI
Tombouctou (Timbuktu)
Bamako
NIGER
Niamey
CHAD
N'Djamena
Lake Chad
AOZOU STRIP
SUDAN
Omdurman
Khartoum
ERITREA
Asmara
DJIBOUTI
Djibouti
ETHIOPIA
Addis Ababa
SOMALIA
Mogadishu
Boundary in dispute
Nile
White Nile
BURKINA FASO
Ouagadougou
GUINEA
Bissau
Freetown
LIBERIA
CÔTE D'IVOIRE
Yamoussoukro
Abidjan
GHANA
Accra
TOGO
Lome
BENIN
Porto-Novo
NIGERIA
Abuja
Ibadan
Lagos
CAMEROON
Yaounde
Douala
Malabo
EQUATORIAL GUINEA
SAO TOME & PRINCIPE
Sao Tome
RIO MUNI
GABON
Libreville
CONGO
Brazzaville
Kinshasa
CABINDA
Ang.
CENTRAL AFRICAN REPUBLIC
Bangui
Congo
DEMOCRATIC REPUBLIC OF THE CONGO
UGANDA
Kampala
Lake Victoria
Lake Turkana
KENYA
Nairobi
Mombasa
Kigali
RWANDA
BURUNDI
Bujumbura
Lake Tanganyika
TANZANIA
Dodoma
Dar es Salaam
SEYCHELLES
COMOROS
Moroni
Ascension
U.K.
ANGOLA
Luanda
Kolwezi
Lubumbashi
ZAMBIA
Kitwe
Lusaka
Zambezi
MALAWI
Lake Malawi
Lilongwe
MOZAMBIQUE
Maputo
Harare
ZIMBABWE
MADAGASCAR
Antananarivo
NAMIBIA
Windhoek
BOTSWANA
Gaborone
Pretoria
Johannesburg
Mbabane
SWAZILAND
SOUTH AFRICA
Orange
Bloemfontein
Maseru
LESOTHO
Durban
Cape Town
Port Elizabeth
EQUATOR
Senegal
Niger

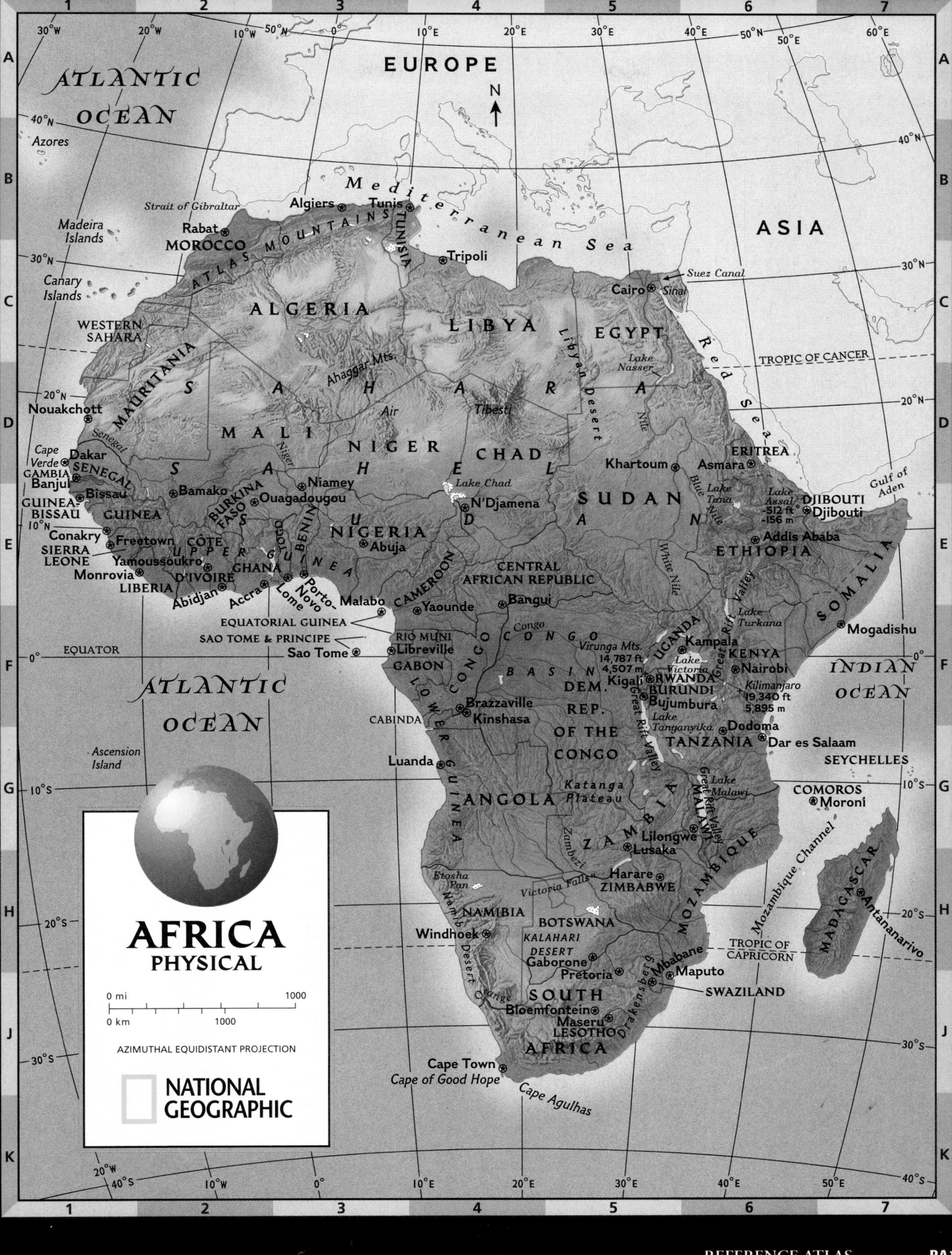
AFRICA
PHYSICAL
EUROPE
ASIA
ATLANTIC OCEAN
INDIAN OCEAN
Mediterranean Sea
Red Sea
Gulf of Aden
Mozambique Channel
ATLAS MOUNTAINS
SAHARA
SAHEL
UPPER GUINEA
LOWER GUINEA
CONGO BASIN
Ahaggar Mts.
Tibesti
Air
Libyan Desert
Katanga Plateau
KALAHARI DESERT
Namib Desert
Drakensberg
Great Rift Valley
Virunga Mts. 14,787 ft 4,507 m
Kilimanjaro 19,340 ft 5,895 m
Lake Assal -512 ft -156 m
Lake Chad
Lake Nasser
Lake Tana
Lake Turkana
Lake Victoria
Lake Tanganyika
Lake Malawi
Etosha Pan
Victoria Falls
Nile
Blue Nile
White Nile
Niger
Senegal
Congo
Zambezi
Orange
Strait of Gibraltar
Suez Canal
Sinai
Azores
Madeira Islands
Canary Islands
Cape Verde
Ascension Island
Cape of Good Hope
Cape Agulhas
TROPIC OF CANCER
EQUATOR
TROPIC OF CAPRICORN
MOROCCO
Rabat
ALGERIA
Algiers
TUNISIA
Tunis
LIBYA
Tripoli
EGYPT
Cairo
WESTERN SAHARA
MAURITANIA
Nouakchott
MALI
Bamako
NIGER
Niamey
CHAD
N'Djamena
SUDAN
Khartoum
ERITREA
Asmara
DJIBOUTI
Djibouti
ETHIOPIA
Addis Ababa
SOMALIA
Mogadishu
SENEGAL
Dakar
GAMBIA
Banjul
GUINEA-BISSAU
Bissau
GUINEA
Conakry
SIERRA LEONE
Freetown
LIBERIA
Monrovia
CÔTE D'IVOIRE
Yamoussoukro
Abidjan
BURKINA FASO
Ouagadougou
GHANA
Accra
TOGO
Lome
BENIN
Porto-Novo
NIGERIA
Abuja
CAMEROON
Yaounde
CENTRAL AFRICAN REPUBLIC
Bangui
EQUATORIAL GUINEA
Malabo
RIO MUNI
SAO TOME & PRINCIPE
Sao Tome
GABON
Libreville
CONGO
Brazzaville
CABINDA
DEM. REP. OF THE CONGO
Kinshasa
UGANDA
Kampala
KENYA
Nairobi
RWANDA
Kigali
BURUNDI
Bujumbura
TANZANIA
Dodoma
Dar es Salaam
SEYCHELLES
COMOROS
Moroni
ANGOLA
Luanda
ZAMBIA
Lusaka
MALAWI
Lilongwe
MOZAMBIQUE
Maputo
ZIMBABWE
Harare
NAMIBIA
Windhoek
BOTSWANA
Gaborone
SOUTH AFRICA
Pretoria
Bloemfontein
Cape Town
LESOTHO
Maseru
SWAZILAND
Mbabane
MADAGASCAR
Antananarivo
0 mi 1000
0 km 1000
AZIMUTHAL EQUIDISTANT PROJECTION
NATIONAL GEOGRAPHIC

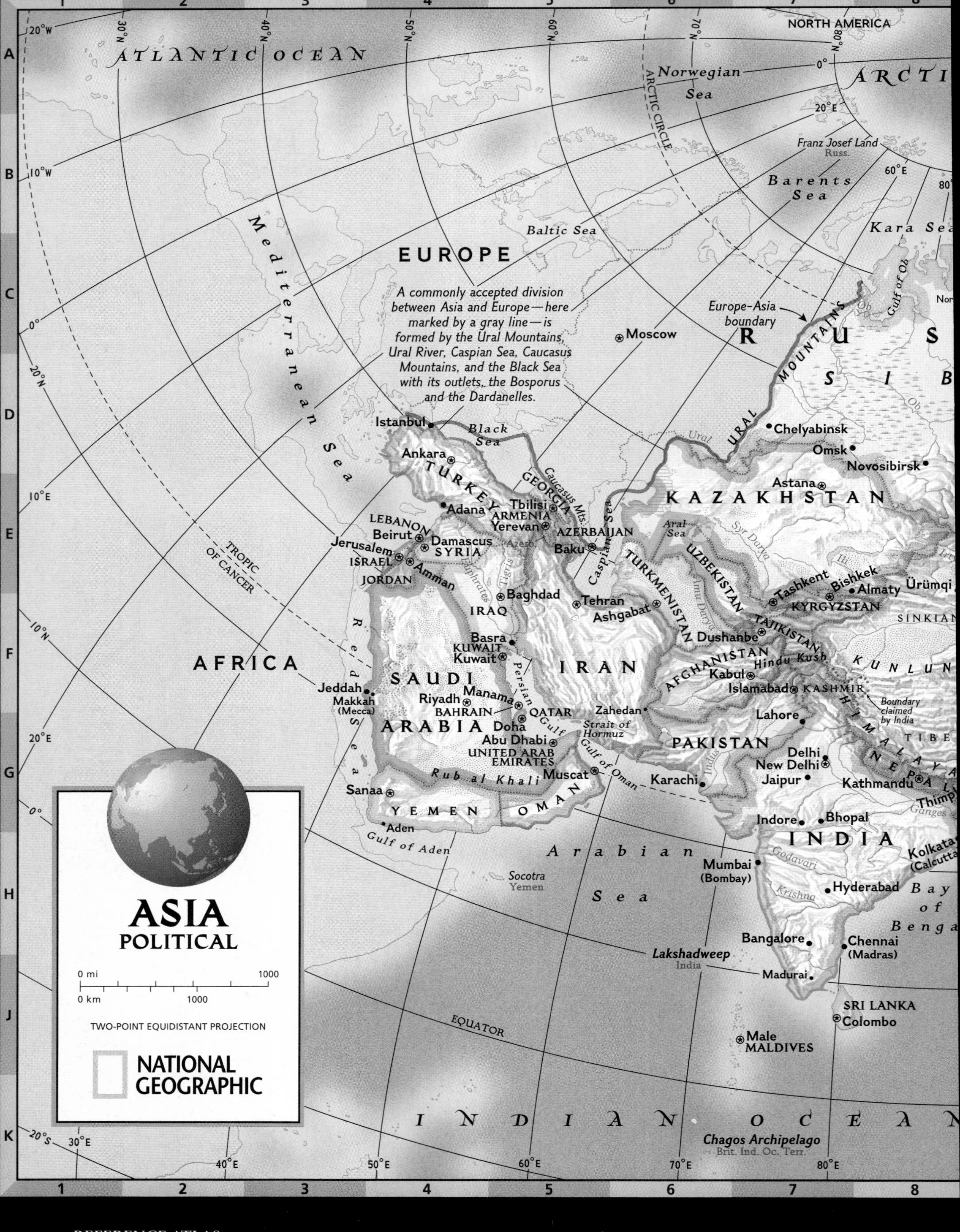
ASIA
POLITICAL
TWO-POINT EQUIDISTANT PROJECTION
NATIONAL GEOGRAPHIC
0 mi 1000
0 km 1000
ATLANTIC OCEAN
NORTH AMERICA
ARCTI
Norwegian Sea
ARCTIC CIRCLE
Franz Josef Land Russ.
Barents Sea
Kara Sea
Baltic Sea
EUROPE
Mediterranean Sea
A commonly accepted division between Asia and Europe—here marked by a gray line—is formed by the Ural Mountains, Ural River, Caspian Sea, Caucasus Mountains, and the Black Sea with its outlets, the Bosporus and the Dardanelles.
Europe-Asia boundary
URAL MOUNTAINS
Gulf of Ob
Moscow
RUSSIA
SIBERIA
Istanbul
Black Sea
Ankara
TURKEY
GEORGIA
Caucasus Mts.
Tbilisi
ARMENIA
Yerevan
AZERBAIJAN
Baku
Caspian Sea
Adana
LEBANON
Beirut
Damascus
SYRIA
Jerusalem
ISRAEL
Amman
JORDAN
Euphrates
Tigris
Baghdad
IRAQ
Tehran
Chelyabinsk
Omsk
Novosibirsk
Astana
KAZAKHSTAN
Aral Sea
Syr Darya
UZBEKISTAN
TURKMENISTAN
Amu Darya
Ashgabat
Tashkent
Bishkek
Almaty
Ürümqi
KYRGYZSTAN
SINKIANG
TAJIKISTAN
Dushanbe
AFGHANISTAN
Hindu Kush
Kabul
Islamabad
KASHMIR
Boundary claimed by India
KUNLUN
HIMALAYA
TROPIC OF CANCER
AFRICA
Red Sea
Basra
KUWAIT
Kuwait
SAUDI ARABIA
Jeddah
Makkah (Mecca)
Riyadh
Manama
BAHRAIN
QATAR
Doha
Persian Gulf
IRAN
Zahedan
Strait of Hormuz
Abu Dhabi
UNITED ARAB EMIRATES
Gulf of Oman
Muscat
Rub al Khali
Sanaa
YEMEN
OMAN
Aden
Gulf of Aden
Socotra Yemen
PAKISTAN
Indus
Lahore
Karachi
Delhi
New Delhi
Jaipur
Kathmandu
NEPAL
Thimphu
Ganges
Indore
Bhopal
INDIA
Kolkata (Calcutta)
Godavari
Mumbai (Bombay)
Krishna
Hyderabad
Bay of Bengal
Arabian Sea
Bangalore
Chennai (Madras)
Lakshadweep India
Madurai
SRI LANKA
Colombo
Male
MALDIVES
EQUATOR
INDIAN OCEAN
Chagos Archipelago Brit. Ind. Oc. Terr.

NORTH AMERICA
Bering Strait
Chukchi Sea
Wrangel I.
Gulf of Anadyr
Anadyr
Bering Sea
East Siberian Sea
New Siberian Islands
Laptev Sea
Kolyma Range
Commander Is.
Kamchatka Peninsula
Cherskiy Range
Magadan
Verkhoyansk Range
Sea of Okhotsk
Yakutsk
Sakhalin
Kuril Islands
Hokkaido
Sapporo
Lake Baikal
Irkutsk
MANCHURIA
Sea of Japan
Vladivostok
Ulaanbaatar
Changchun
JAPAN
Tokyo
MONGOLIA
Marcus I. Jap.
TROPIC OF CANCER
Shenyang
Honshu
NORTH KOREA
Kyoto
GOBI
Pyongyang
Seoul
Osaka
SOUTH KOREA
Hiroshima
Beijing
Shijiazhuang
Qingdao
Yellow Sea
Kyushu
Bonin Is. Jap.
Volcano Is. Jap.
Lanzhou
Xuzhou
Xi'an
Nanjing
Shanghai
East China Sea
Ryukyu Islands
Okinawa
CHINA
Chengdu
Nanchang
Parece Vela Jap.
Fuzhou
Taipei
Boundary claimed by China
Changsha
TAIWAN
Guiyang
The People's Republic of China claims Taiwan as its 23rd province.
Guangzhou
Kunming
Hong Kong
Macau
PACIFIC OCEAN
Philippine Sea
MYANMAR (BURMA)
Hanoi
Haiphong
Luzon
LAOS
South China Sea
Hainan
Quezon City
Manila
Samar
Vientiane
Yangon (Rangoon)
Da Nang
Mindoro
PHILIPPINES
THAILAND
Leyte
Panay
Negros
EQUATOR
Bangkok
CAMBODIA
VIETNAM
Palawan
Andaman Islands India
Phnom Penh
Ho Chi Minh City
Mindanao
Andaman Sea
Gulf of Thailand
Bandar Seri Begawan
BRUNEI
SABAH
Morotai
Biak
Jayapura
Halmahera
New Guinea
MALAYSIA
SARAWAK
Moluccas
Kuala Lumpur
Medan
Borneo
Kepi
Aru Is.
Merauke
Ceram
Buru
Dolak
SINGAPORE
Celebes
INDONESIA
Tanimbar Is.
Sumatra
Jambi
GREATER SUNDA ISLANDS
Mentawai Islands
Dili
EAST TIMOR
Timor Sea
Java Sea
AUSTRALIA
Jakarta
Java
Kupang

ASIA
PHYSICAL
0 mi
1000
0 km
1000
TWO-POINT EQUIDISTANT PROJECTION
NATIONAL GEOGRAPHIC
ATLANTIC OCEAN
NORTH AMERICA
ARCTIC CIRCLE
Norwegian Sea
Barents Sea
Kara Sea
Baltic Sea
RUSSIA
EUROPE
Moscow
Europe-Asia boundary
URAL MOUNTAINS
WEST SIBERIAN PLAIN
Mediterranean Sea
Aegean Sea
Black Sea
ANATOLIA
Ankara
TURKEY
Caucasus Mts.
GEORGIA
Tbilisi
ARMENIA
Yerevan
AZERBAIJAN
Baku
Caspian Depression
Caspian Sea
THE STEPPES
Astana
KAZAKHSTAN
Aral Sea
Syr Darya
L. Balkhash
LEBANON
Beirut
SYRIA
Damascus
Syrian Desert
Jerusalem
ISRAEL
Sinai
JORDAN
Amman
Dead Sea -1,349 ft -411 m
Mesopotamia
Tigris
Euphrates
IRAQ
Baghdad
Zagros Mountains
Elburz Mts.
Tehran
TURKMENISTAN
Ashgabat
UZBEKISTAN
Amu Darya
Tashkent
Bishkek
Almaty
KYRGYZSTAN
TIAN SHAN
TAJIKISTAN
Dushanbe
TAKLIMAKAN DESERT
AFGHANISTAN
HINDU KUSH
Kabul
Islamabad
Kunlun Shan
PLATEAU OF TIBET
Mt. Everest 29,035 8,850
HIMALAYA
KUWAIT
Kuwait
IRAN
Persian Gulf
BAHRAIN
QATAR
Riyadh
SAUDI ARABIA
Arabian Peninsula
Rub al Khali
Strait of Hormuz
UNITED ARAB EMIRATES
Gulf of Oman
Muscat
OMAN
YEMEN
Sanaa
Gulf of Aden
Red Sea
AFRICA
TROPIC OF CANCER
PAKISTAN
Indus
Great Indian Desert
New Delhi
Kathmandu
Ganges
INDIA
DECCAN PLATEAU
Western Ghats
Eastern Ghats
Arabian Sea
Bay of Bengal
Laccadive Sea
SRI LANKA
Colombo
Maldive Islands
Male
MALDIVES
EQUATOR
INDIAN OCEAN
Irtysh
Ob
Gulf of Ob
Ural

NORTH AMERICA
Bering Strait
Chukchi Sea
Chukchi Peninsula
Gulf of Anadyr
Wrangel Island
East Siberian Sea
New Siberian Islands
Laptev Sea
Bering Sea
Aleutian Islands
Commander Islands
Kamchatka Peninsula
Kolyma
Kolyma Range
Cherskiy Range
Verkhoyansk Range
Lena
Aldan
CENTRAL SIBERIAN PLATEAU
SIBERIA
ASIA
Sea of Okhotsk
Sakhalin
Kuril Islands
Hokkaido
Amur
Sikhote Alin Range
Lake Baikal
Yablonovyy Range
Greater Khingan Range
Manchurian Plain
Yenisey
Ulaanbaatar
MONGOLIA
GOBI
Sea of Japan
JAPAN
Tokyo
Honshu
NORTH KOREA
Pyongyang
Seoul
SOUTH KOREA
Beijing
North China Plain
Yellow
Shikoku
Kyushu
Yellow Sea
East China Sea
Ryukyu Islands
Nampo Shoto
PACIFIC OCEAN
TROPIC OF CANCER
Qaidam Basin
CHINA
Yangtze
Mekong
Salween
Sichuan Basin
Gongga Shan
24,790 ft
7,556 m
Taipei
TAIWAN
Philippine Sea
Mariana Islands
MYANMAR (BURMA)
Hanoi
LAOS
Vientiane
Yangon (Rangoon)
THAILAND
Bangkok
CAMBODIA
VIETNAM
Phnom Penh
Andaman Islands
Andaman Sea
Gulf of Thailand
Hainan
South China Sea
Luzon
Manila
PHILIPPINES
PHILIPPINE ISLANDS
Caroline Islands
EQUATOR
Sulu Sea
Mindanao
Celebes Sea
Bandar Seri Begawan
BRUNEI
MALAYSIA
Malay Peninsula
Kuala Lumpur
SINGAPORE
Borneo
Celebes
Moluccas
New Guinea
INDONESIA
Sumatra
Mentawai Islands
GREATER SUNDA ISLANDS
Java Sea
Java
Jakarta
Dili
EAST TIMOR
Timor Sea
Arafura Sea
AUSTRALIA

EUROPE
Black Sea
Istanbul
ANATOLIA
Ankara
TURKEY
Tunis
TUNISIA
Mediterranean Sea
Tripoli
Taurus Mountains
CYPRUS
LEBANON
Beirut
ISRAEL
Jerusalem
Alexandria
Cairo
El Giza
Sinai Pen.
See inset below
LIBYA
EGYPT
Nile R.
Aswan High Dam
SAHARA
AFRICA
10 E
20 E
30 E
Eastern Mediterranean Area
30 E
TURKEY
N
Aleppo
CYPRUS
SYRIA
LEBANON
Mediterranean Sea
Beirut
Damascus
Sea of Galilee
Golan Heights
Jordan River
Tel Aviv–Yafo
West Bank
Jerusalem
Amman
Gaza Strip
Dead Sea
ISRAEL
JORDAN
El Giza
Cairo
30 N
EGYPT
SAUDI ARABIA
Nile River
Gulf of Suez
Gulf of Aqaba
0 mi 100
0 km 100
Red Sea

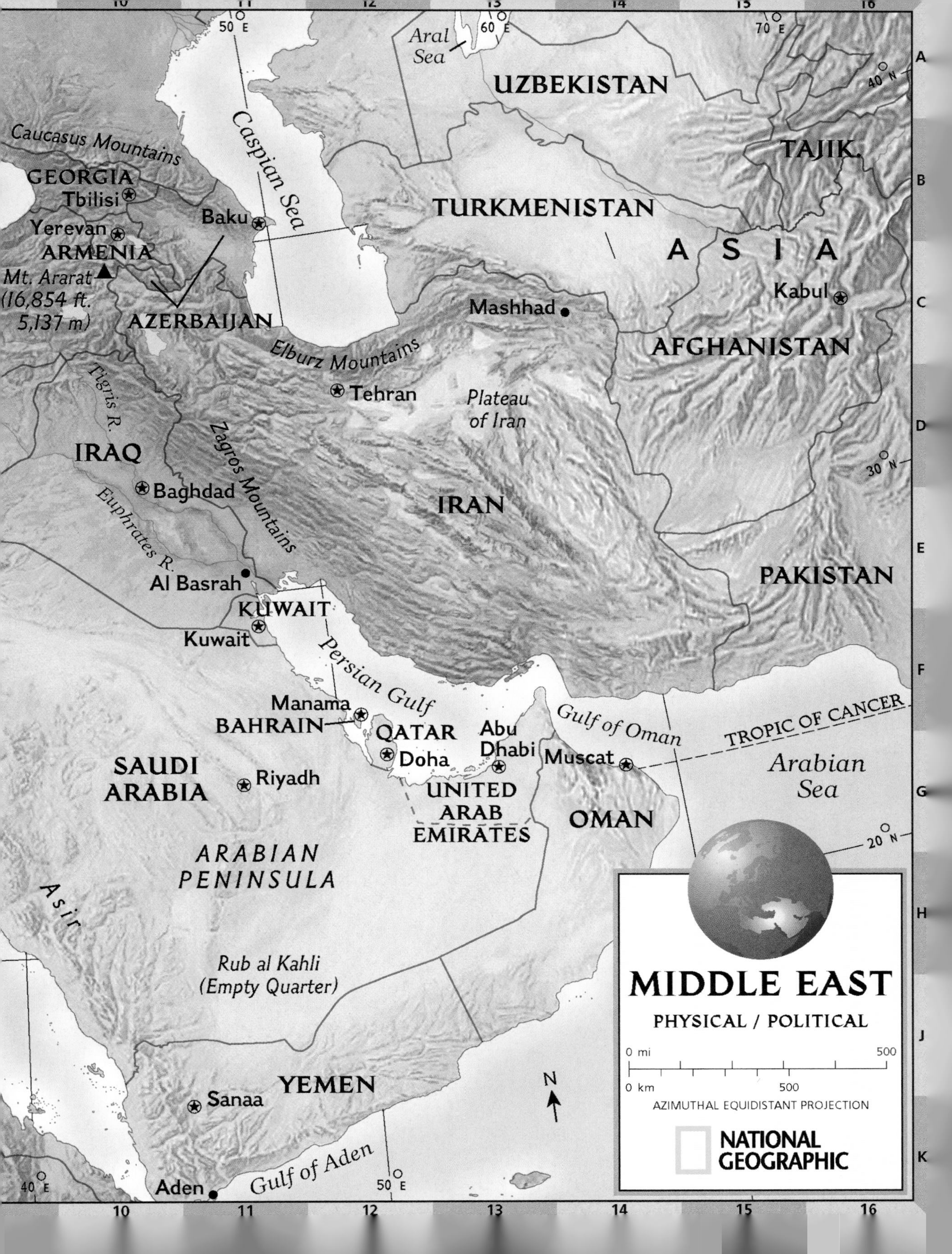
MIDDLE EAST
PHYSICAL / POLITICAL
0 mi 500
0 km 500
AZIMUTHAL EQUIDISTANT PROJECTION
NATIONAL GEOGRAPHIC
Aral Sea
UZBEKISTAN
TAJIK.
Caucasus Mountains
GEORGIA
Tbilisi
Caspian Sea
Baku
Yerevan
ARMENIA
Mt. Ararat (16,854 ft. 5,137 m)
AZERBAIJAN
TURKMENISTAN
A S I A
Kabul
Mashhad
AFGHANISTAN
Elburz Mountains
Tehran
Plateau of Iran
Tigris R.
IRAQ
Zagros Mountains
Baghdad
Euphrates R.
IRAN
Al Basrah
PAKISTAN
KUWAIT
Kuwait
Persian Gulf
Manama
BAHRAIN
QATAR
Doha
Abu Dhabi
Gulf of Oman
Muscat
TROPIC OF CANCER
Arabian Sea
SAUDI ARABIA
Riyadh
UNITED ARAB EMIRATES
OMAN
ARABIAN PENINSULA
Asir
Rub al Kahli (Empty Quarter)
YEMEN
Sanaa
Gulf of Aden
Aden
N
50 E
60 E
70 E
40 N
30 N
20 N
40 E

RUSSIA
MONGOLIA
CHINA
NORTH KOREA
SOUTH KOREA
JAPAN
NORTH PACI
INDIAN OCEAN
AUSTRALIA
INDONESIA
MALAYSIA
PHILIPPINES
NEW ZEALAND
PAPUA NEW GUINEA
MICRONESIA
MELANESIA
Beijing
Tokyo
Canberra
Wellington
Sea of Okhotsk
Sea of Japan
Yellow Sea
East China Sea
South China Sea
Philippine Sea
Coral Sea
Tasman Sea
TROPIC OF CAPRICORN
105°E
120°E
135°E
150°E
165°E
180°

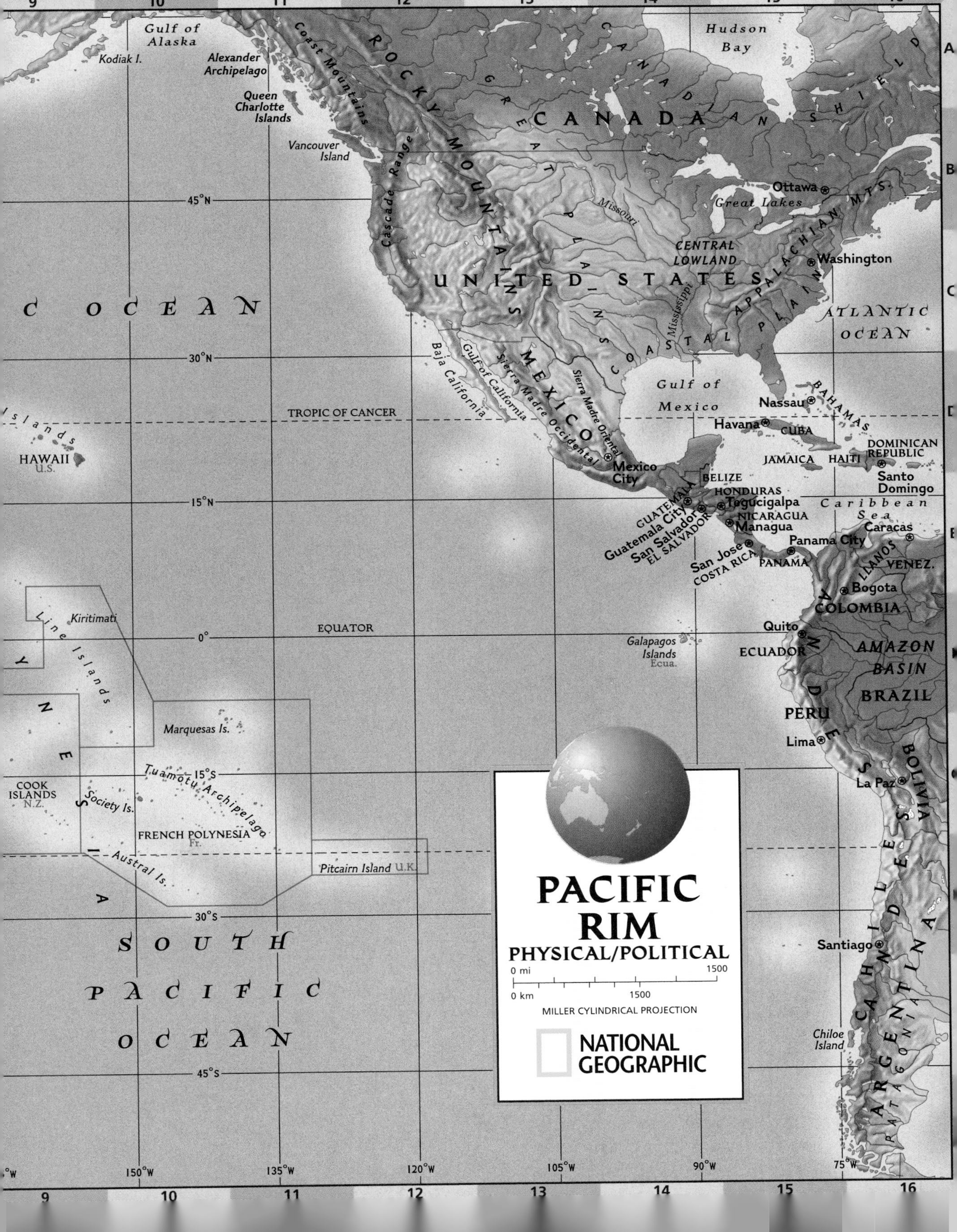

PACIFIC RIM
PHYSICAL/POLITICAL
0 mi 1500
0 km 1500
MILLER CYLINDRICAL PROJECTION
NATIONAL GEOGRAPHIC
Gulf of Alaska
Kodiak I.
Alexander Archipelago
Queen Charlotte Islands
Vancouver Island
Coast Mountains
ROCKY MOUNTAINS
GREAT PLAINS
CANADA
CANADIAN SHIELD
Hudson Bay
Cascade Range
Missouri
Great Lakes
Ottawa
CENTRAL LOWLAND
APPALACHIAN MTS.
Washington
UNITED STATES
Mississippi
COASTAL PLAIN
ATLANTIC OCEAN
OCEAN
Baja California
Gulf of California
Sierra Madre Occidental
Sierra Madre Oriental
MEXICO
Gulf of Mexico
Nassau
BAHAMAS
TROPIC OF CANCER
Havana
CUBA
DOMINICAN REPUBLIC
JAMAICA
HAITI
Santo Domingo
HAWAII U.S.
Mexico City
BELIZE
HONDURAS
Tegucigalpa
GUATEMALA
Guatemala City
San Salvador
EL SALVADOR
NICARAGUA
Managua
Caribbean Sea
Caracas
Panama City
San Jose
COSTA RICA
PANAMA
LLANOS
VENEZ.
Bogota
COLOMBIA
Kiritimati
Line Islands
EQUATOR
Quito
Galapagos Islands Ecua.
ECUADOR
AMAZON BASIN
BRAZIL
PERU
ANDES
Lima
Marquesas Is.
Tuamotu Archipelago
COOK ISLANDS N.Z.
Society Is.
FRENCH POLYNESIA Fr.
POLYNESIA
Austral Is.
Pitcairn Island U.K.
BOLIVIA
La Paz
SOUTH PACIFIC OCEAN
Santiago
CHILE
ARGENTINA
PATAGONIA
Chiloe Island
45°N
30°N
15°N
0°
15°S
30°S
45°S
150°W
135°W
120°W
105°W
90°W
75°W
9
10
11
12
13
14
15
16
A
B
C
D
E

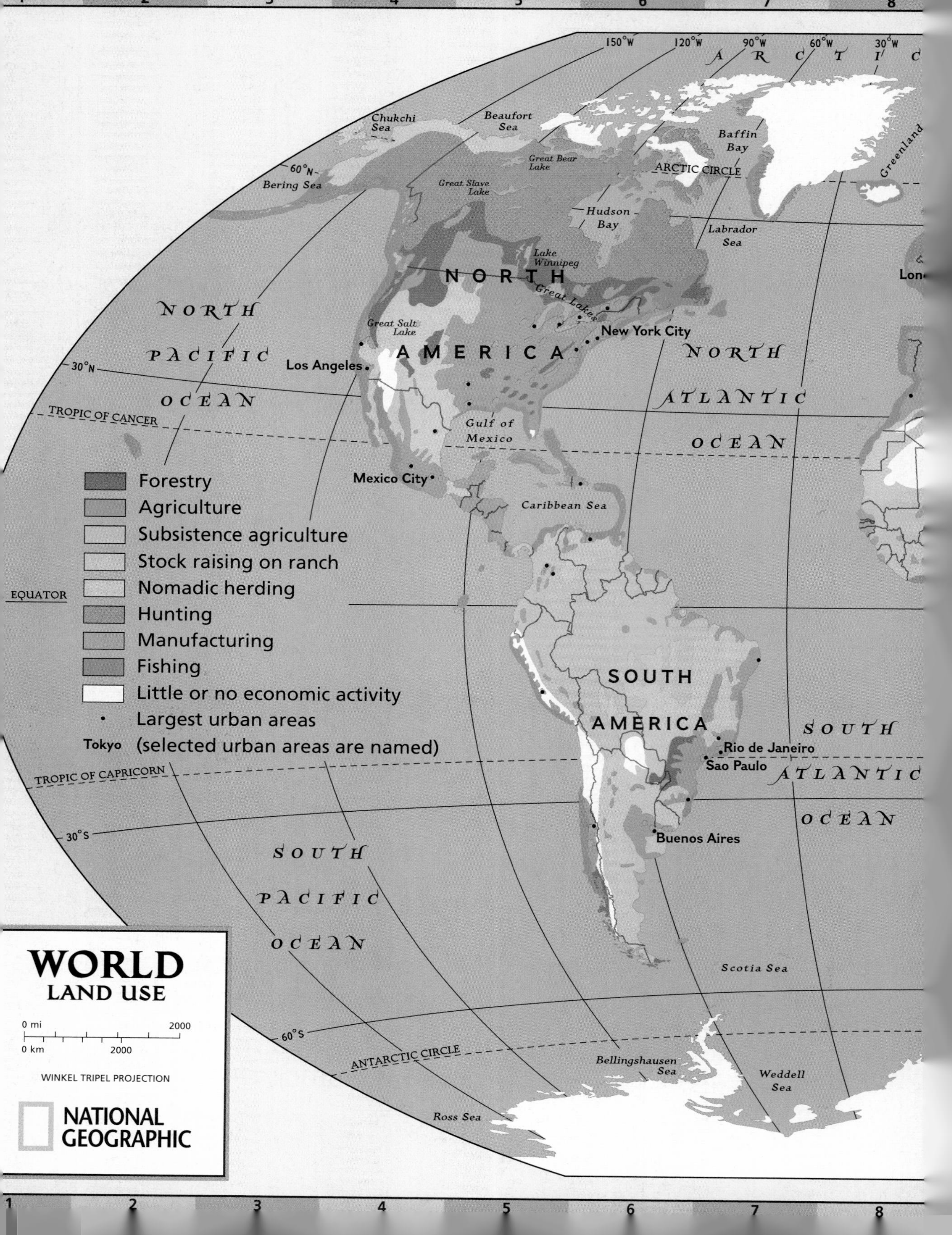

WORLD
LAND USE
0 mi
2000
0 km
2000
WINKEL TRIPEL PROJECTION
NATIONAL GEOGRAPHIC
Forestry
Agriculture
Subsistence agriculture
Stock raising on ranch
Nomadic herding
Hunting
Manufacturing
Fishing
Little or no economic activity
Largest urban areas
Tokyo
(selected urban areas are named)
150°W
120°W
90°W
60°W
30°W
ARCTIC
Chukchi Sea
Beaufort Sea
Baffin Bay
Greenland
60°N
Bering Sea
Great Bear Lake
Great Slave Lake
ARCTIC CIRCLE
Hudson Bay
Labrador Sea
Lake Winnipeg
NORTH AMERICA
Great Lakes
Great Salt Lake
New York City
Los Angeles
NORTH PACIFIC OCEAN
NORTH ATLANTIC OCEAN
30°N
TROPIC OF CANCER
Gulf of Mexico
Mexico City
Caribbean Sea
EQUATOR
SOUTH AMERICA
Rio de Janeiro
Sao Paulo
SOUTH ATLANTIC OCEAN
TROPIC OF CAPRICORN
30°S
Buenos Aires
SOUTH PACIFIC OCEAN
Scotia Sea
60°S
ANTARCTIC CIRCLE
Bellingshausen Sea
Weddell Sea
Ross Sea
1
2
3
4
5
6
7
8

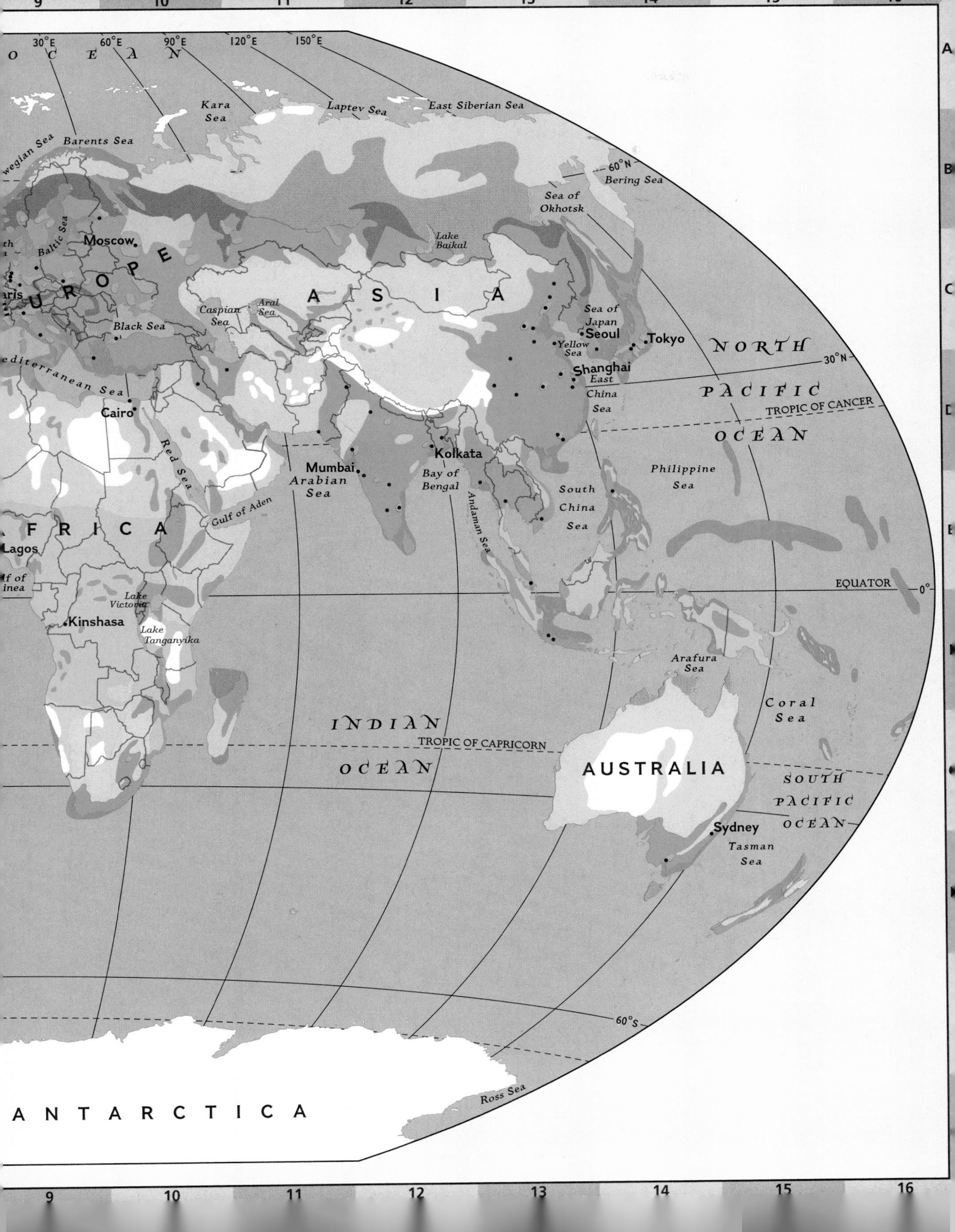

9
10
11
12
13
14
15
16
30°E
60°E
90°E
120°E
150°E
O C E A N
Kara Sea
Laptev Sea
East Siberian Sea
Barents Sea
Norwegian Sea
60°N
Bering Sea
Sea of Okhotsk
Baltic Sea
Moscow
Lake Baikal
EUROPE
Paris
ASIA
Caspian Sea
Aral Sea
Sea of Japan
Seoul
Tokyo
Black Sea
Yellow Sea
NORTH
30°N
Mediterranean Sea
Shanghai
East China Sea
PACIFIC
Cairo
TROPIC OF CANCER
OCEAN
Red Sea
Kolkata
Philippine Sea
Mumbai
Arabian Sea
Bay of Bengal
South China Sea
Andaman Sea
Gulf of Aden
AFRICA
Lagos
Gulf of Guinea
EQUATOR
0°
Lake Victoria
Kinshasa
Lake Tanganyika
Arafura Sea
Coral Sea
INDIAN
TROPIC OF CAPRICORN
OCEAN
AUSTRALIA
SOUTH
PACIFIC
OCEAN
Sydney
Tasman Sea
60°S
Ross Sea
ANTARCTICA
A
B
C
D
E

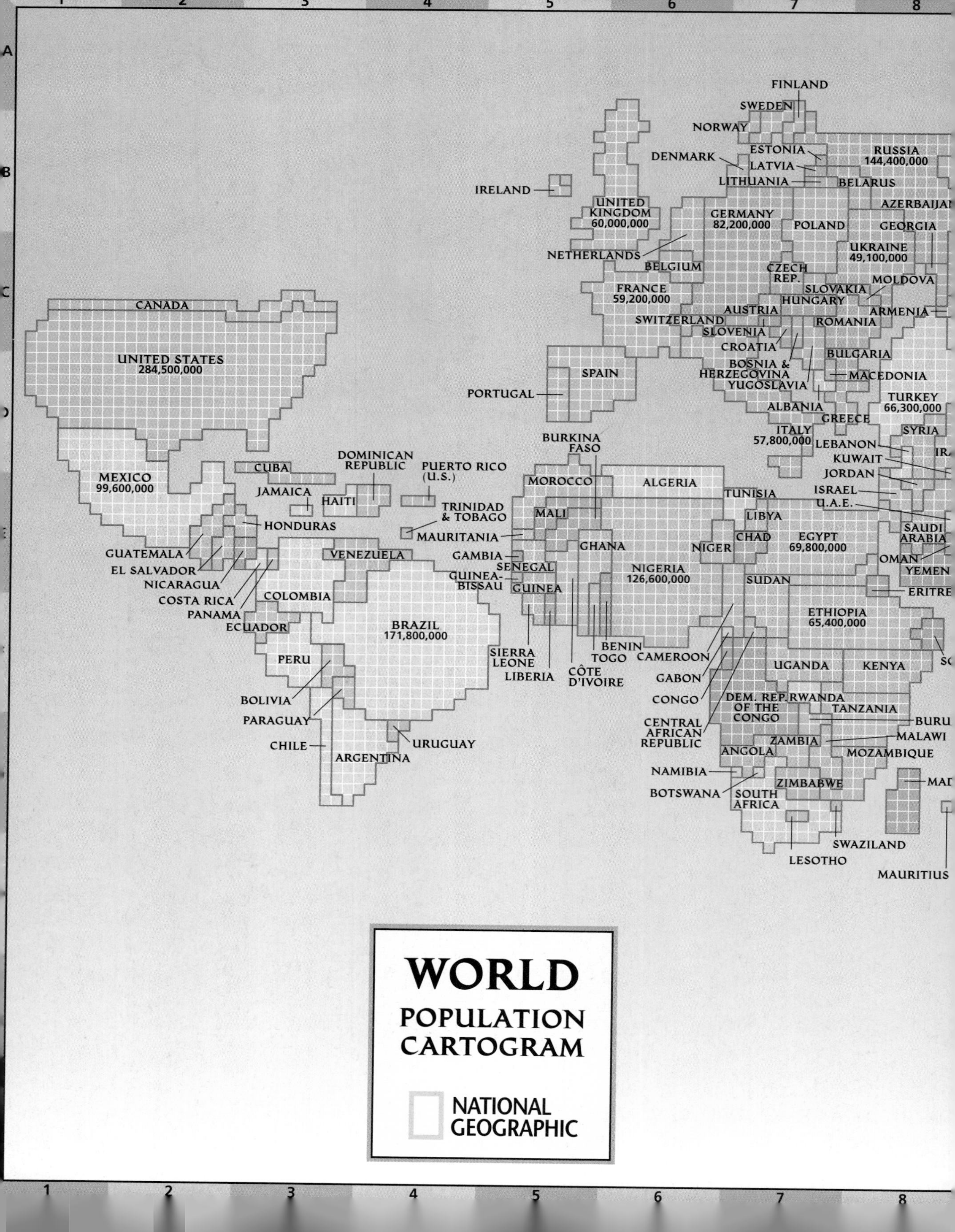

CANADA
UNITED STATES
284,500,000
MEXICO
99,600,000
CUBA
JAMAICA
HAITI
DOMINICAN REPUBLIC
PUERTO RICO (U.S.)
TRINIDAD & TOBAGO
HONDURAS
GUATEMALA
EL SALVADOR
NICARAGUA
COSTA RICA
PANAMA
VENEZUELA
COLOMBIA
ECUADOR
PERU
BRAZIL
171,800,000
BOLIVIA
PARAGUAY
CHILE
ARGENTINA
URUGUAY
IRELAND
UNITED KINGDOM
60,000,000
NETHERLANDS
BELGIUM
FRANCE
59,200,000
SPAIN
PORTUGAL
SWITZERLAND
GERMANY
82,200,000
DENMARK
NORWAY
SWEDEN
FINLAND
ESTONIA
LATVIA
LITHUANIA
RUSSIA
144,400,000
BELARUS
POLAND
CZECH REP.
SLOVAKIA
HUNGARY
AUSTRIA
SLOVENIA
CROATIA
BOSNIA & HERZEGOVINA
YUGOSLAVIA
ROMANIA
BULGARIA
MACEDONIA
ALBANIA
GREECE
ITALY
57,800,000
UKRAINE
49,100,000
MOLDOVA
AZERBAIJAN
GEORGIA
ARMENIA
TURKEY
66,300,000
SYRIA
LEBANON
KUWAIT
JORDAN
ISRAEL
U.A.E.
SAUDI ARABIA
OMAN
YEMEN
ERITREA
MOROCCO
ALGERIA
TUNISIA
LIBYA
EGYPT
69,800,000
BURKINA FASO
MALI
MAURITANIA
GAMBIA
SENEGAL
GUINEA-BISSAU
GUINEA
SIERRA LEONE
LIBERIA
CÔTE D'IVOIRE
GHANA
TOGO
BENIN
NIGER
CHAD
NIGERIA
126,600,000
SUDAN
CAMEROON
GABON
CONGO
CENTRAL AFRICAN REPUBLIC
DEM. REP. OF THE CONGO
ETHIOPIA
65,400,000
UGANDA
KENYA
RWANDA
TANZANIA
BURUNDI
MALAWI
ZAMBIA
ANGOLA
MOZAMBIQUE
NAMIBIA
BOTSWANA
ZIMBABWE
SOUTH AFRICA
SWAZILAND
LESOTHO
MADAGASCAR
MAURITIUS
WORLD
POPULATION CARTOGRAM
NATIONAL GEOGRAPHIC

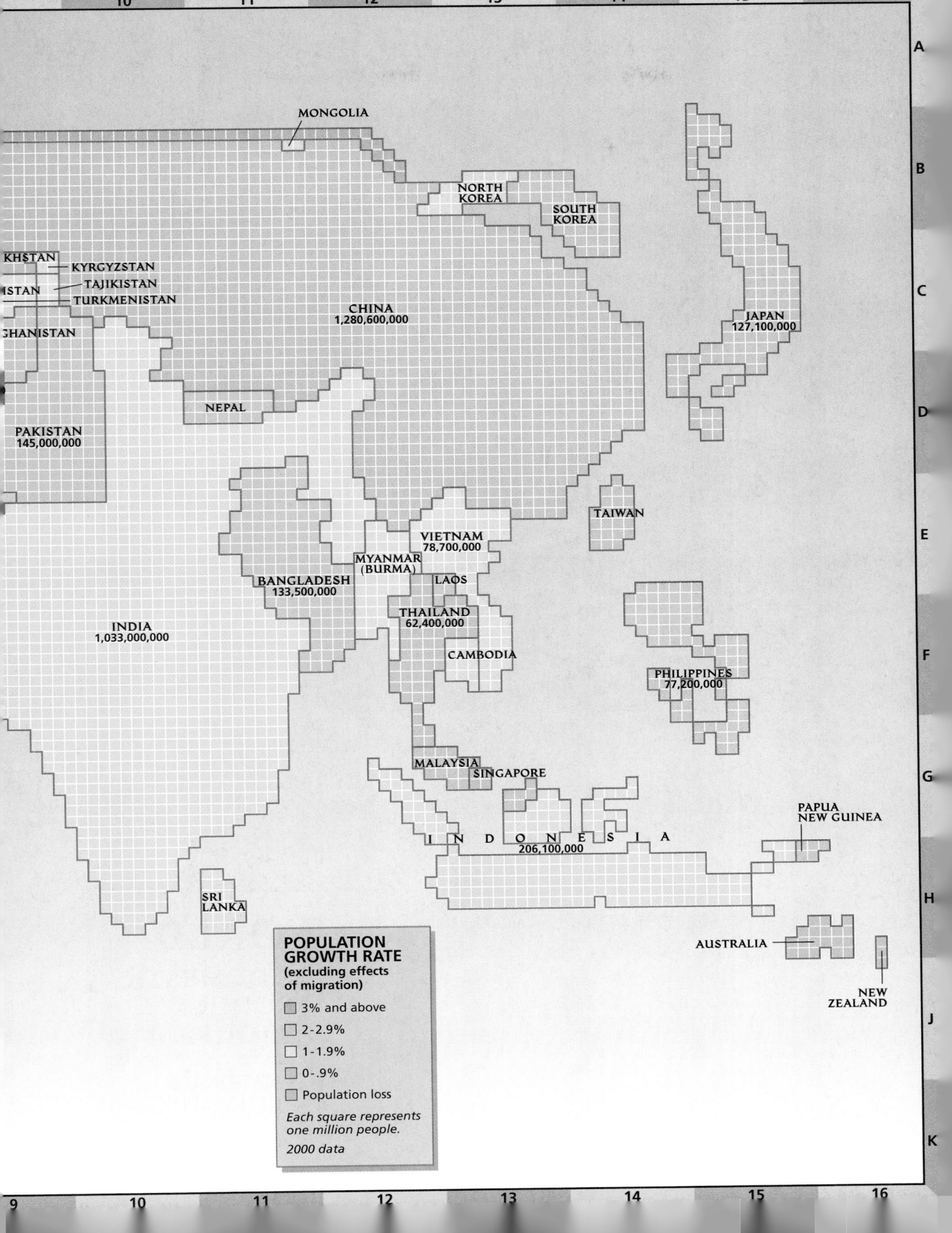

MONGOLIA
NORTH KOREA
SOUTH KOREA
KHSTAN
KYRGYZSTAN
TAJIKISTAN
ISTAN
TURKMENISTAN
GHANISTAN
CHINA 1,280,600,000
JAPAN 127,100,000
NEPAL
PAKISTAN 145,000,000
TAIWAN
VIETNAM 78,700,000
MYANMAR (BURMA)
BANGLADESH 133,500,000
LAOS
THAILAND 62,400,000
INDIA 1,033,000,000
CAMBODIA
PHILIPPINES 77,200,000
MALAYSIA
SINGAPORE
PAPUA NEW GUINEA
I N D O N E S I A 206,100,000
SRI LANKA
AUSTRALIA
NEW ZEALAND
POPULATION GROWTH RATE (excluding effects of migration)
3% and above
2-2.9%
1-1.9%
0-.9%
Population loss
Each square represents one million people.
2000 data

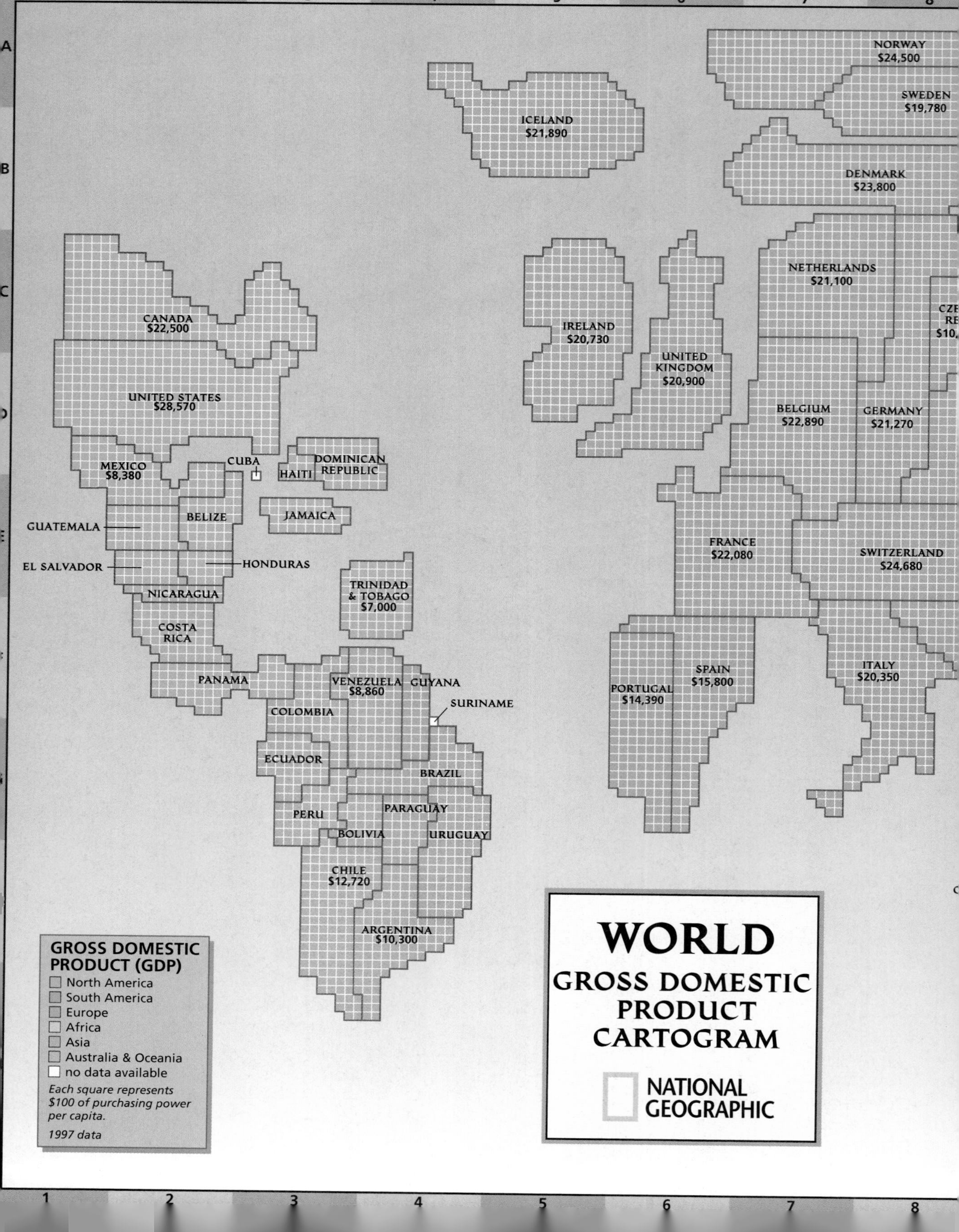

NORWAY
$24,500
SWEDEN
$19,780
ICELAND
$21,890
DENMARK
$23,800
NETHERLANDS
$21,100
IRELAND
$20,730
UNITED
KINGDOM
$20,900
CANADA
$22,500
UNITED STATES
$28,570
BELGIUM
$22,890
GERMANY
$21,270
MEXICO
$8,380
CUBA
HAITI
DOMINICAN
REPUBLIC
JAMAICA
BELIZE
GUATEMALA
EL SALVADOR
HONDURAS
NICARAGUA
FRANCE
$22,080
SWITZERLAND
$24,680
TRINIDAD
& TOBAGO
$7,000
COSTA
RICA
PANAMA
VENEZUELA
$8,860
GUYANA
SURINAME
COLOMBIA
ECUADOR
BRAZIL
PERU
PARAGUAY
BOLIVIA
URUGUAY
CHILE
$12,720
ARGENTINA
$10,300
PORTUGAL
$14,390
SPAIN
$15,800
ITALY
$20,350
GROSS DOMESTIC
PRODUCT (GDP)
North America
South America
Europe
Africa
Asia
Australia & Oceania
no data available
Each square represents
$100 of purchasing power
per capita.
1997 data
WORLD
GROSS DOMESTIC
PRODUCT
CARTOGRAM
NATIONAL
GEOGRAPHIC

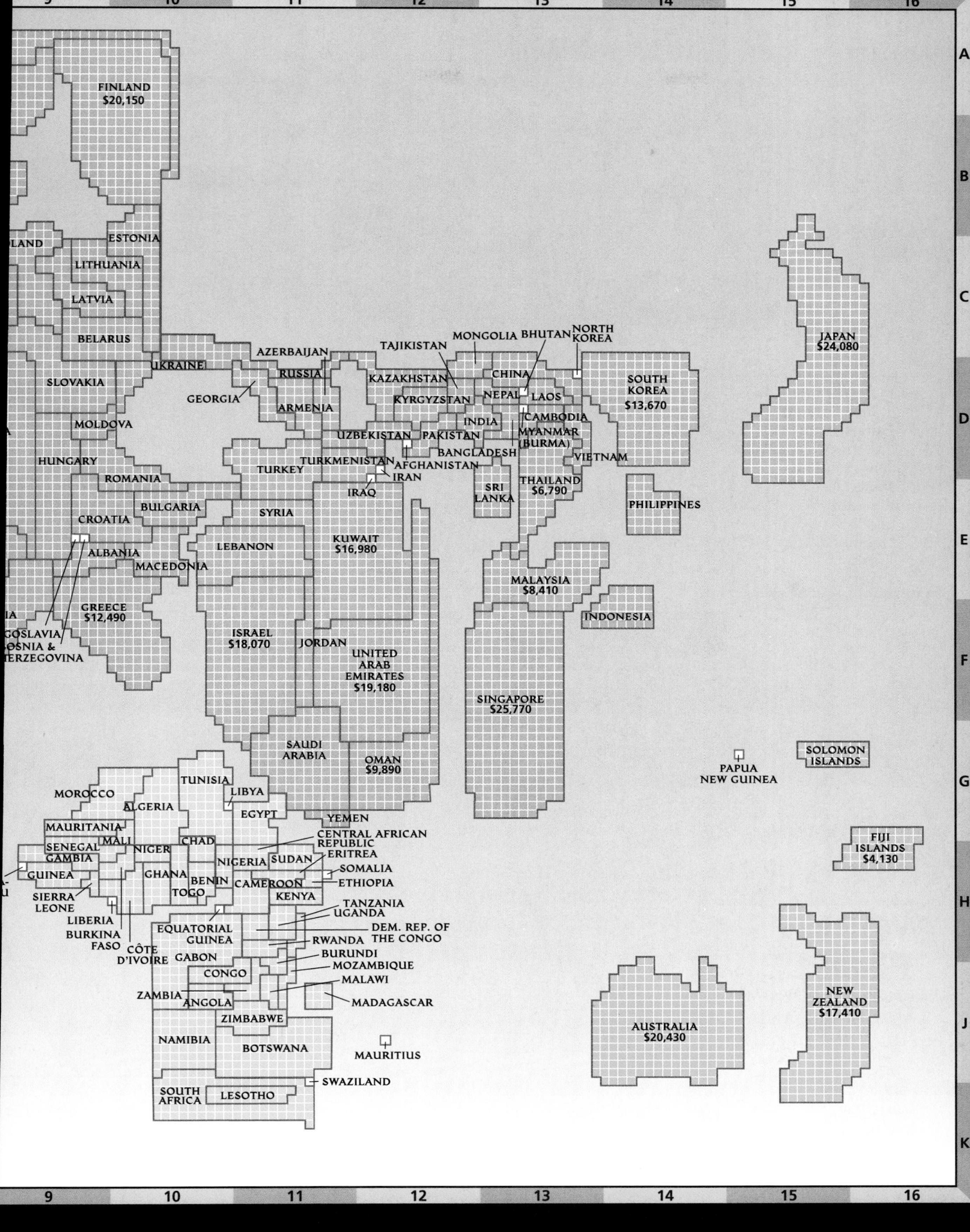
9
10
11
12
13
14
15
16
A
B
C
D
E
F
G
H
J
K
FINLAND
$20,150
ESTONIA
LITHUANIA
LATVIA
BELARUS
UKRAINE
SLOVAKIA
MOLDOVA
HUNGARY
ROMANIA
BULGARIA
CROATIA
ALBANIA
MACEDONIA
GREECE
$12,490
BOSNIA &
HERZEGOVINA
AZERBAIJAN
RUSSIA
GEORGIA
ARMENIA
TURKEY
SYRIA
LEBANON
ISRAEL
$18,070
JORDAN
KUWAIT
$16,980
UNITED
ARAB
EMIRATES
$19,180
SAUDI
ARABIA
OMAN
$9,890
YEMEN
TAJIKISTAN
KAZAKHSTAN
KYRGYZSTAN
UZBEKISTAN
TURKMENISTAN
AFGHANISTAN
IRAN
IRAQ
PAKISTAN
MONGOLIA
BHUTAN
NORTH
KOREA
CHINA
NEPAL
LAOS
INDIA
CAMBODIA
MYANMAR
(BURMA)
BANGLADESH
VIETNAM
SRI
LANKA
THAILAND
$6,790
SOUTH
KOREA
$13,670
JAPAN
$24,080
PHILIPPINES
MALAYSIA
$8,410
INDONESIA
SINGAPORE
$25,770
PAPUA
NEW GUINEA
SOLOMON
ISLANDS
FIJI
ISLANDS
$4,130
AUSTRALIA
$20,430
NEW
ZEALAND
$17,410
MOROCCO
TUNISIA
LIBYA
ALGERIA
EGYPT
MAURITANIA
MALI
SENEGAL
GAMBIA
NIGER
CHAD
GUINEA
SIERRA
LEONE
LIBERIA
BURKINA
FASO
CÔTE
D'IVOIRE
GHANA
BENIN
TOGO
NIGERIA
SUDAN
CAMEROON
CENTRAL AFRICAN
REPUBLIC
ERITREA
SOMALIA
ETHIOPIA
KENYA
TANZANIA
UGANDA
DEM. REP. OF
THE CONGO
RWANDA
BURUNDI
MOZAMBIQUE
EQUATORIAL
GUINEA
GABON
CONGO
MALAWI
ZAMBIA
ANGOLA
MADAGASCAR
ZIMBABWE
NAMIBIA
BOTSWANA
MAURITIUS
SWAZILAND
SOUTH
AFRICA
LESOTHO

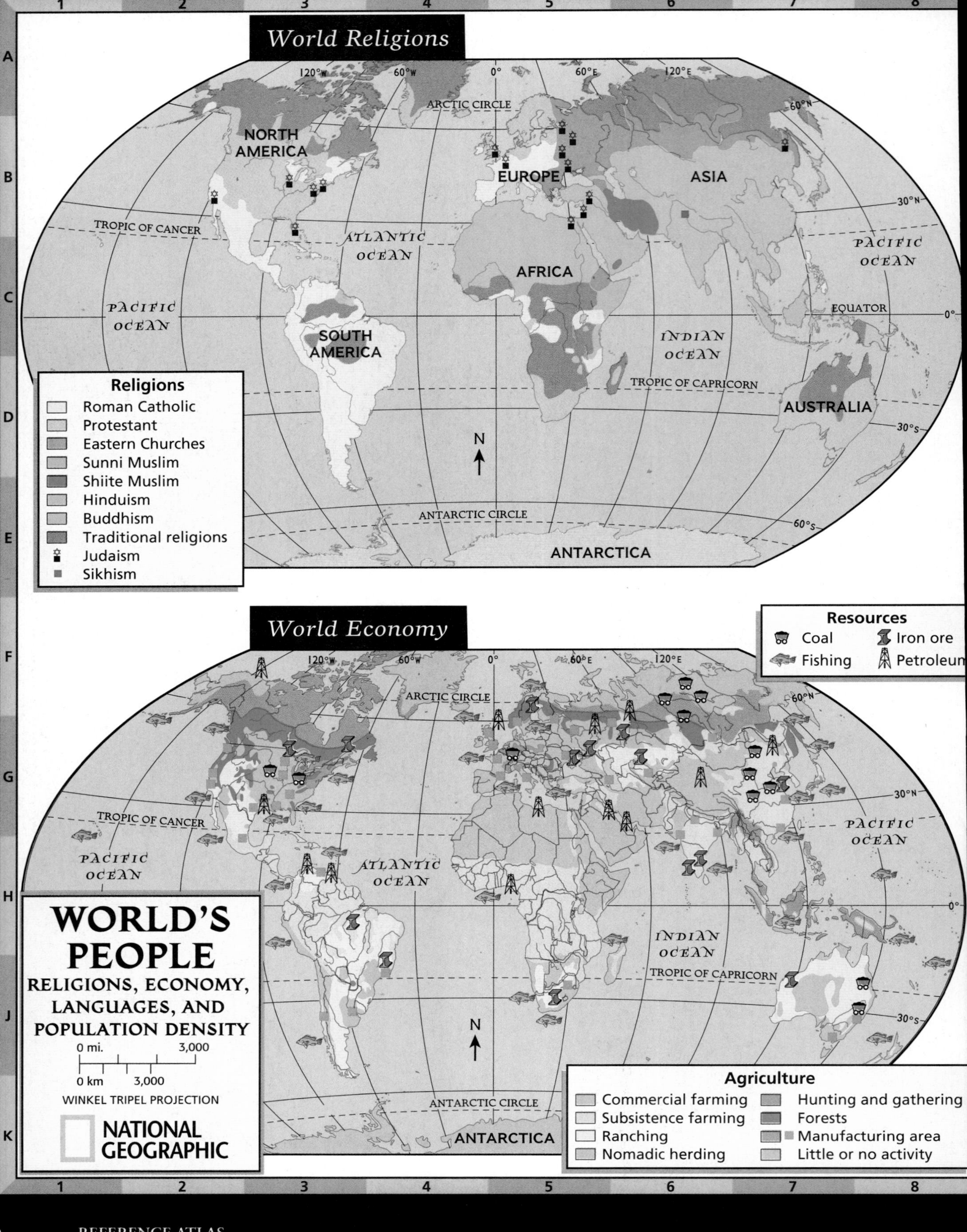
World Religions
NORTH AMERICA
EUROPE
ASIA
AFRICA
SOUTH AMERICA
AUSTRALIA
ANTARCTICA
ATLANTIC OCEAN
PACIFIC OCEAN
INDIAN OCEAN
ARCTIC CIRCLE
TROPIC OF CANCER
EQUATOR
TROPIC OF CAPRICORN
ANTARCTIC CIRCLE
Religions
Roman Catholic
Protestant
Eastern Churches
Sunni Muslim
Shiite Muslim
Hinduism
Buddhism
Traditional religions
Judaism
Sikhism
World Economy
Resources
Coal
Iron ore
Fishing
Petroleum
Agriculture
Commercial farming
Subsistence farming
Ranching
Nomadic herding
Hunting and gathering
Forests
Manufacturing area
Little or no activity
WORLD'S PEOPLE
RELIGIONS, ECONOMY, LANGUAGES, AND POPULATION DENSITY
0 mi. 3,000
0 km 3,000
WINKEL TRIPEL PROJECTION
NATIONAL GEOGRAPHIC

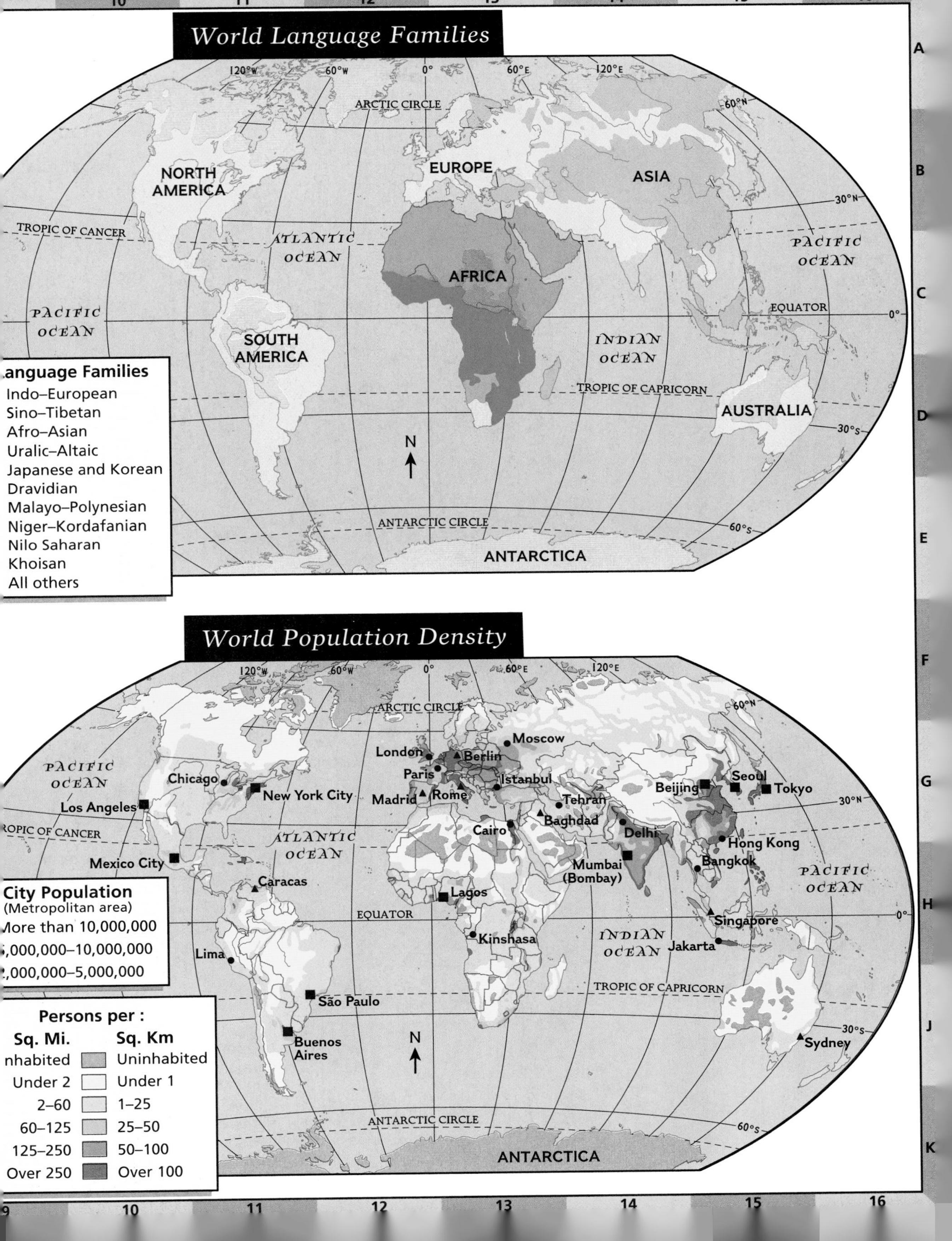

World Language Families
NORTH AMERICA
SOUTH AMERICA
EUROPE
ASIA
AFRICA
AUSTRALIA
ANTARCTICA
ATLANTIC OCEAN
PACIFIC OCEAN
INDIAN OCEAN
ARCTIC CIRCLE
TROPIC OF CANCER
EQUATOR
TROPIC OF CAPRICORN
ANTARCTIC CIRCLE
anguage Families
Indo–European
Sino–Tibetan
Afro–Asian
Uralic–Altaic
Japanese and Korean
Dravidian
Malayo–Polynesian
Niger–Kordafanian
Nilo Saharan
Khoisan
All others
World Population Density
London
Berlin
Moscow
Paris
Madrid
Rome
Istanbul
Tehran
Baghdad
Cairo
Delhi
Mumbai (Bombay)
Beijing
Seoul
Tokyo
Hong Kong
Bangkok
Singapore
Jakarta
Sydney
Chicago
New York City
Los Angeles
Mexico City
Caracas
Lima
São Paulo
Buenos Aires
Lagos
Kinshasa
City Population
(Metropolitan area)
More than 10,000,000
5,000,000–10,000,000
2,000,000–5,000,000
Persons per :
Sq. Mi. | Sq. Km
Uninhabited | Uninhabited
Under 2 | Under 1
2–60 | 1–25
60–125 | 25–50
125–250 | 50–100
Over 250 | Over 100

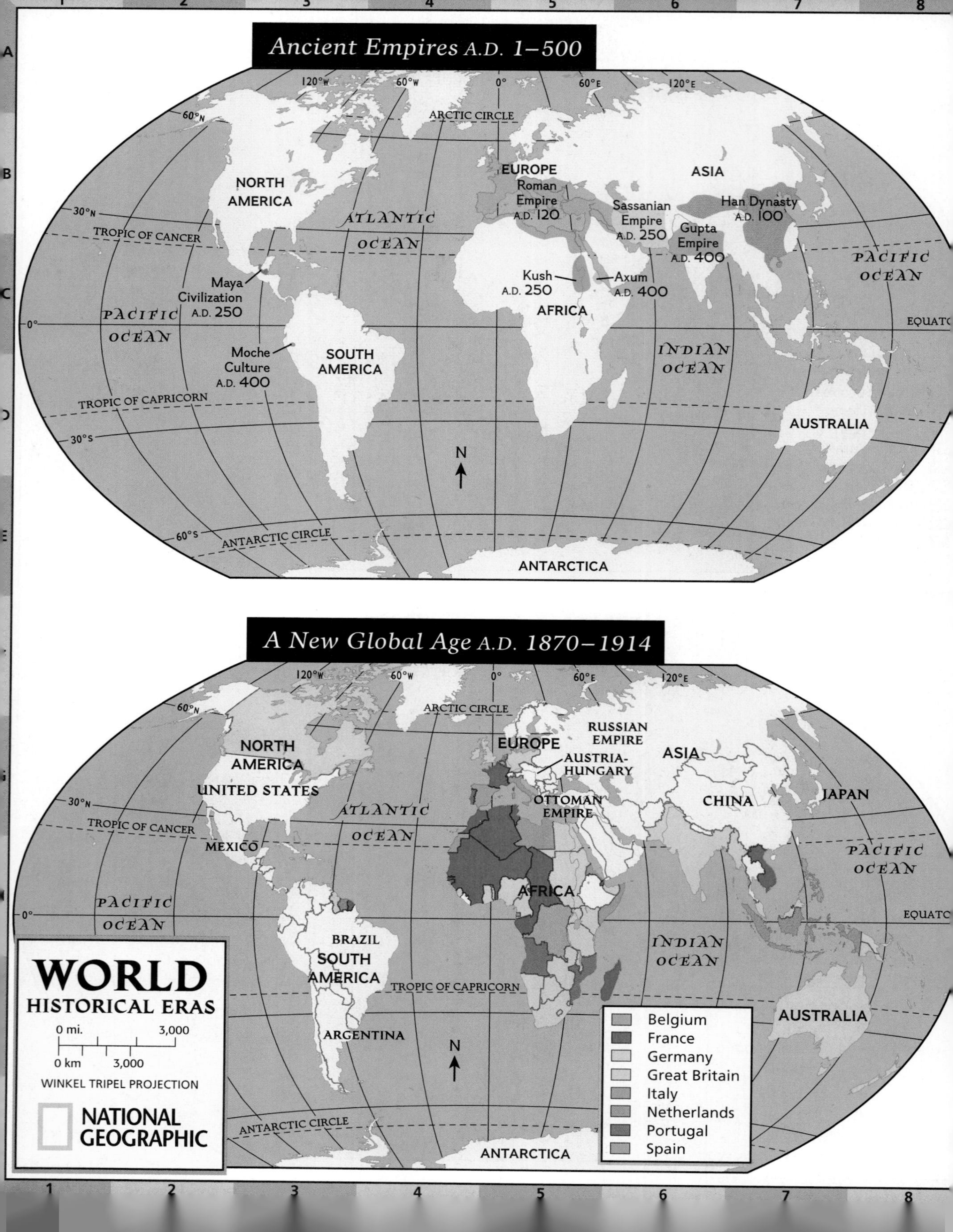

Ancient Empires A.D. 1–500
ARCTIC CIRCLE
EUROPE
Roman Empire A.D. 120
ASIA
NORTH AMERICA
Sassanian Empire A.D. 250
Han Dynasty A.D. 100
ATLANTIC OCEAN
TROPIC OF CANCER
Gupta Empire A.D. 400
PACIFIC OCEAN
Kush A.D. 250
Axum A.D. 400
Maya Civilization A.D. 250
AFRICA
PACIFIC OCEAN
EQUATOR
Moche Culture A.D. 400
SOUTH AMERICA
INDIAN OCEAN
TROPIC OF CAPRICORN
AUSTRALIA
N
ANTARCTIC CIRCLE
ANTARCTICA
A New Global Age A.D. 1870–1914
ARCTIC CIRCLE
NORTH AMERICA
EUROPE
RUSSIAN EMPIRE
AUSTRIA-HUNGARY
ASIA
UNITED STATES
OTTOMAN EMPIRE
CHINA
JAPAN
ATLANTIC OCEAN
TROPIC OF CANCER
MEXICO
PACIFIC OCEAN
AFRICA
PACIFIC OCEAN
EQUATOR
BRAZIL
SOUTH AMERICA
INDIAN OCEAN
TROPIC OF CAPRICORN
ARGENTINA
AUSTRALIA
N
ANTARCTIC CIRCLE
ANTARCTICA
Belgium
France
Germany
Great Britain
Italy
Netherlands
Portugal
Spain
WORLD HISTORICAL ERAS
0 mi. 3,000
0 km 3,000
WINKEL TRIPEL PROJECTION
NATIONAL GEOGRAPHIC

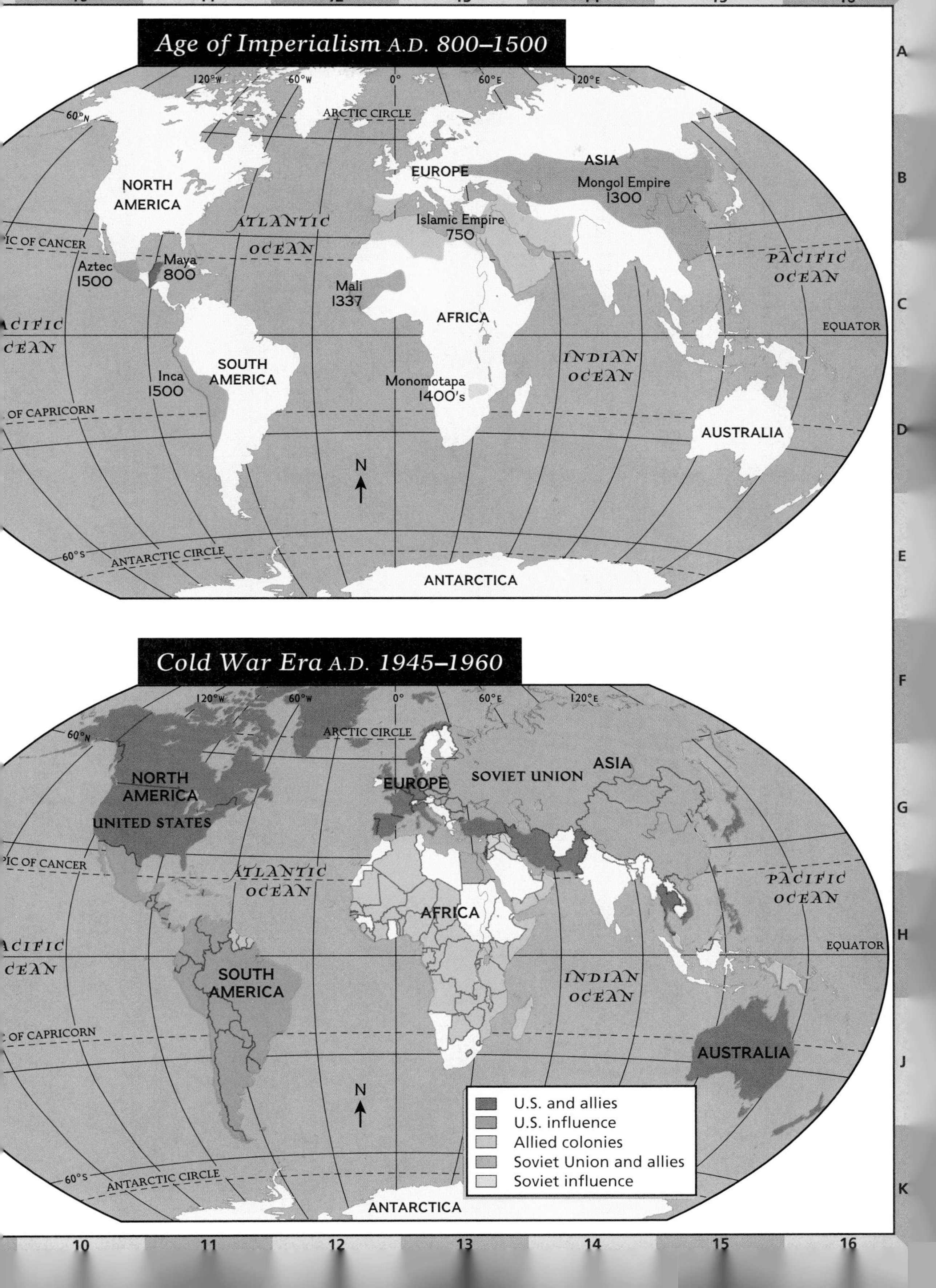

Age of Imperialism A.D. 800–1500
120°W
60°W
0°
60°E
120°E
60°N
ARCTIC CIRCLE
NORTH AMERICA
EUROPE
ASIA
Mongol Empire 1300
ATLANTIC OCEAN
Islamic Empire 750
TROPIC OF CANCER
Aztec 1500
Maya 800
PACIFIC OCEAN
Mali 1337
AFRICA
EQUATOR
PACIFIC OCEAN
SOUTH AMERICA
Inca 1500
Monomotapa 1400's
INDIAN OCEAN
TROPIC OF CAPRICORN
AUSTRALIA
N
60°S
ANTARCTIC CIRCLE
ANTARCTICA
Cold War Era A.D. 1945–1960
120°W
60°W
0°
60°E
120°E
60°N
ARCTIC CIRCLE
NORTH AMERICA
EUROPE
SOVIET UNION
ASIA
UNITED STATES
TROPIC OF CANCER
ATLANTIC OCEAN
PACIFIC OCEAN
AFRICA
PACIFIC OCEAN
EQUATOR
SOUTH AMERICA
INDIAN OCEAN
TROPIC OF CAPRICORN
AUSTRALIA
N
U.S. and allies
U.S. influence
Allied colonies
Soviet Union and allies
Soviet influence
60°S
ANTARCTIC CIRCLE
ANTARCTICA
A
B
C
D
E
F
G
H
J
K
10
11
12
13
14
15
16

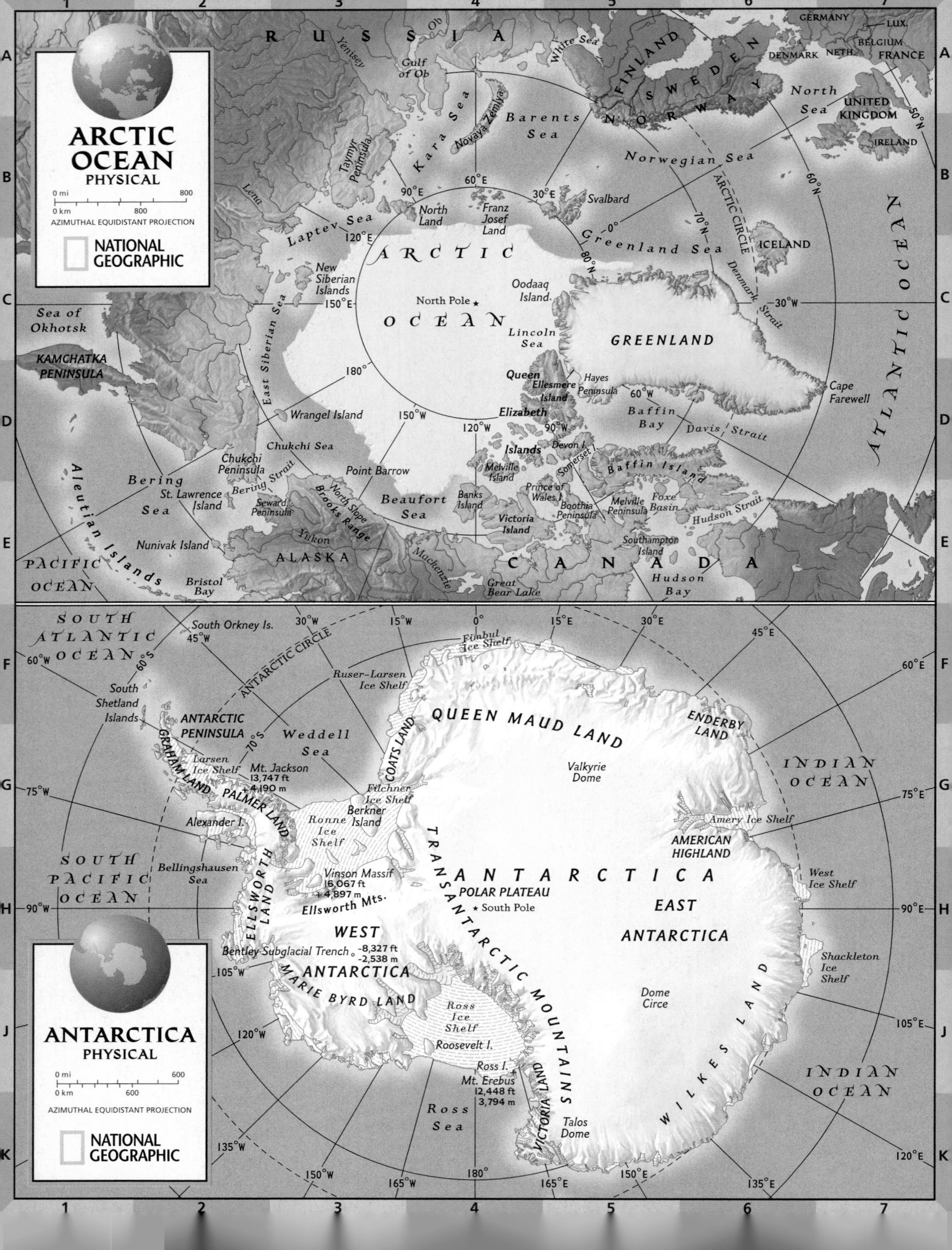

ARCTIC OCEAN
PHYSICAL
AZIMUTHAL EQUIDISTANT PROJECTION
NATIONAL GEOGRAPHIC
RUSSIA
Gulf of Ob
Kara Sea
Barents Sea
Laptev Sea
ARCTIC OCEAN
North Pole
GREENLAND
Greenland Sea
Norwegian Sea
ICELAND
Svalbard
Franz Josef Land
North Land
New Siberian Islands
East Siberian Sea
Sea of Okhotsk
KAMCHATKA PENINSULA
Wrangel Island
Chukchi Sea
Bering Sea
Bering Strait
Aleutian Islands
PACIFIC OCEAN
ALASKA
Beaufort Sea
Point Barrow
Brooks Range
Queen Elizabeth Islands
Ellesmere Island
Baffin Bay
Baffin Island
Davis Strait
Hudson Strait
Hudson Bay
CANADA
Victoria Island
Banks Island
Great Bear Lake
ATLANTIC OCEAN
FINLAND
SWEDEN
NORWAY
North Sea
UNITED KINGDOM
IRELAND
ANTARCTICA
PHYSICAL
AZIMUTHAL EQUIDISTANT PROJECTION
NATIONAL GEOGRAPHIC
SOUTH ATLANTIC OCEAN
South Orkney Is.
ANTARCTIC CIRCLE
South Shetland Islands
ANTARCTIC PENINSULA
Weddell Sea
Larsen Ice Shelf
Mt. Jackson 13,747 ft 4,190 m
GRAHAM LAND
PALMER LAND
Alexander I.
Ronne Ice Shelf
Berkner Island
Filchner Ice Shelf
COATS LAND
QUEEN MAUD LAND
Fimbul Ice Shelf
Ruser-Larsen Ice Shelf
Valkyrie Dome
ENDERBY LAND
INDIAN OCEAN
Amery Ice Shelf
AMERICAN HIGHLAND
West Ice Shelf
ANTARCTICA
POLAR PLATEAU
South Pole
EAST ANTARCTICA
Vinson Massif 16,067 ft 4,897 m
Ellsworth Mts.
ELLSWORTH LAND
SOUTH PACIFIC OCEAN
Bellingshausen Sea
WEST ANTARCTICA
Bentley Subglacial Trench -8,327 ft -2,538 m
MARIE BYRD LAND
TRANSANTARCTIC MOUNTAINS
Ross Ice Shelf
Roosevelt I.
Ross I.
Mt. Erebus 12,448 ft 3,794 m
Ross Sea
VICTORIA LAND
Talos Dome
Dome Circe
WILKES LAND
Shackleton Ice Shelf

Geography Handbook

The story of the world begins with geography—the study of the earth in all of its variety. Geography describes the earth's land, water, and plant and animal life. It is the study of places and the complex relationships between people and their environment.

The resources in this handbook will help you get the most out of your textbook—and provide you with skills you will use for the rest of your life.

The Gui River, Guilin, China ▼

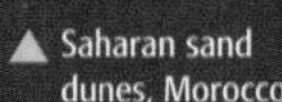

▲ Saharan sand dunes, Morocco

The Amazon, Brazil ▶

GEOGRAPHY HANDBOOK RESOURCES

Reproducible Masters
- Glencoe Social Studies Outline Map Resource Book
- Building Skills in Geography Workbook

Transparencies
- NGS PicturePack Transparancies: Physical Geography of the World

Multimedia
- **Student Desk Map**
- **Zip! Zap! Map! World**
- **Picture Atlas of the World**
- **STV: World Geography:**
  - **Vol. 1: Asia and Australia**
  - **Vol. 2: Africa and Europe**
  - **Vol. 3: South America and Antarctica**
- **STV: North America**

Introducing the National Geographic Geography Handbook

Handbook Objectives

After studying this handbook, students should be able to:

1. understand the themes and elements associated with the study of geography;
2. understand the purpose and uses of globes and map projections;
3. identify the most commonly used geographic terms;
4. analyze geographic factors that have shaped the course of historic events.

Vocabulary Pre-check

Survey the students' knowledge of geographic terms. Create three columns on the chalkboard with the headings *landforms, map elements*, and *bodies of water.*

List one term that fits each column, such as "canyon," "meridian," and "bay." Ask students to volunteer as many other terms for each column as they can. Then have students turn to the geographic dictionary and identify additional terms for each column. Write the terms on the chalkboard in the appropriate columns of the chart.

TEACH

PICTURE ATLAS OF THE WORLD
You and your students can see the challenges and solutions involved in making maps by viewing the Mapping Our World animation "Round Earth on Flat Paper."

Writing Activity

Ask students to write definitions for the five themes of geography and the six essential elements. Have the students share their definitions with the class. **L1**

Critical Thinking

Ask students to identify the physical and human characteristics of place. *(Each place has distinctive landforms, bodies of water, climate, soils, vegetation, people with a particular language and political beliefs.)* Have students describe the characteristics of place that distinguish their neighborhood, city, or town from others nearby. **L1**

Critical Thinking

Have students keep a geography journal in which they can record significant geographical information as they read this textbook. Ask students to select and record in their journals three major events in world history. Once they have made their selections, ask students to write an essay in which they analyze the effects of physical and human geographic factors on each of these three major events. As part of their analysis, have students locate historical and contemporary maps related to the events they have selected. Ask students to interpret these maps to identify and explain geographic factors that influenced the people and events in their analysis. Have students convey their findings to the class in an oral and visual presentation. **L1**

I Study Geography?

To understand how our world is connected, some geographers have divided the study of geography into five themes. ***The Five Themes of Geography are*** *(1) location, (2) place, (3) human/environmental interaction, (4) movement, and (5) regions.*

Six Essential Elements

Recently geographers have broken down the study of geography into **Six Essential Elements.** Being aware of these elements will help you better understand and organize what you are learning about geography.

Element 1

The World in Spatial Terms

Geographers first take a look at where a place is located. **Location** serves as a starting point by defining where a place is. Knowing the location of places helps you develop an awareness of the world around you.

Element 2

Places and Regions

Place has a special meaning in geography. It means more than where a place is. It also describes what a place is like. Physical characteristics such as landforms, climate, and plant or animal life help geographers distinguish different kinds of places. Human characteristics, including language and way of life, also describe places.

Geographers often group places or areas into regions. **Regions** are united by one or more common characteristics.

Element 3

Physical Systems

When studying places and regions, geographers analyze how **physical systems**—such as hurricanes, volcanoes, and glaciers—shape the earth's surface. As part of their study of physical systems, geographers look at communities of plants and animals that depend upon one another and their surroundings for survival.

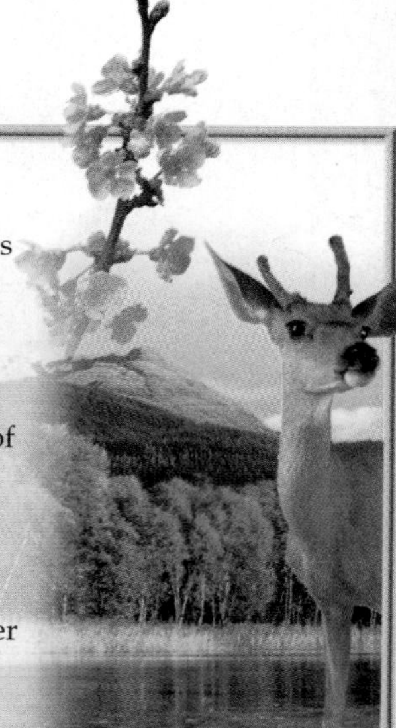

Teacher's Notes

Element 4

Human Systems
Geographers also examine **human systems,** or how people have shaped our world. Geographers look at how boundary lines are determined and analyze why people settle in certain places and not in others. A key theme in geography is the continual **movement** of people, ideas, and goods.

Element 5

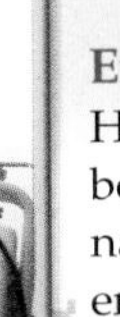

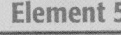

Environment and Society
How does the relationship between people and their natural surroundings influence the way people live? Geographers study how people use the **environment** and how their actions affect the environment.

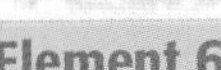

Element 6

The Uses of Geography
How does a war in the Middle East affect the economy of the United States? Knowing **how to use geography** helps people understand the relationships between people, places, and environments over time. Learning how to study geography also prepares you for life in our modern society.

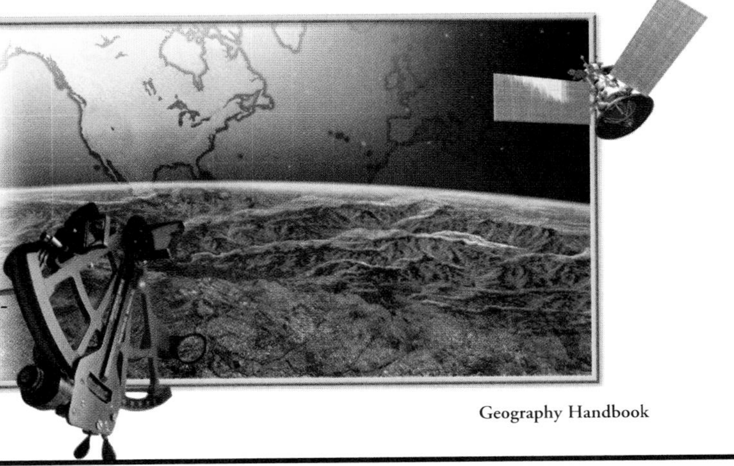

Connecting Across Time

People both adapt to and change their environments. Pioneers pushed into Native American hunting grounds, killed the bison, and destroyed the means of life for the Plains Indians. Gradually, generations of people transformed the Great Plains into a carefully managed human landscape of ranches and farms.

Critical Thinking

Ask students why people modify environments. During the class discussion, have the class identify human factors that determine how people change their environment. *(people modify environments to make them more productive and more comfortable; human factors are beliefs, ideas, technology, economy, social organization)* Have students give examples from their neighborhood as well as global examples of how humans have modified environments. **L1**

Reteaching Activity

Have students review the five themes of geography by having them write each theme and list at least two characteristics describing each theme. It might be beneficial to have students work in pairs to complete the lists. **L1**

EXTENDING THE CONTENT

James Cook British sea captain James Cook was the greatest explorer and cartographer of the eighteenth century. In the three voyages that he undertook between 1769 and 1779, Cook surveyed and charted huge areas of the Pacific Ocean. He also verified the existence of the continent of Antarctica and provided a wealth of information about the south Atlantic, south Indian, and Arctic Oceans. Using the latest scientific developments, Cook created incredibly accurate charts of his journeys. These charts revolutionized cartographic knowledge and practices.

Enrich

The following exercises will help students understand the difficulty of transferring information about the earth's surface to a map.

Have students bring an orange to class. Ask students to draw a face on the orange. Then have students peel the orange so that the peel lies flat. Ask students to describe what happened to the face.

Give students a copy of a world map and ask them to draw a line connecting San Francisco, California, to Istanbul, Turkey, by the most direct route. Give two students a piece of string and, using a classroom globe, ask them to connect those same two cities by the most direct route. Ask all students to note the location of the string on the globe and trace its course on their maps. Discuss with students how both these exercises illustrate the difficulty of projecting the earth's curved surface on a flat map. **L1**

Who?What?Where?When?

Antarctica covers about 3.2 million square miles (8.3 million sq km) of landmass. Including the islands and shelf ice, it is about 5.4 million square miles (14 million sq km). No nation owns this territory. The Antarctica Treaty, signed by 16 nations, allows only the exploration of the continent.

Globes and Maps

*Photographs from space show Earth in its true form—a great ball spinning around the Sun. The most accurate way to depict the earth is as a **globe,** a spherical scale model of the earth. A globe gives a true picture of the continents' relative sizes and the shapes of landmasses and bodies of water. Globes are proportionately correct, accurately representing distance and direction.*

*A **map** is a flat drawing of all or part of the earth's surface. Unlike globes, maps can show small areas in great detail. People use maps to locate places, plot routes, and judge distances. Maps can also display useful information, such as political boundaries, population densities, or even voting returns.*

From Globes to Maps

Maps, however, do have their limitations. As you can imagine, drawing a round object on a flat surface is very difficult. Think about the surface of the earth as the peel of an orange. To flatten the peel, you might have to cut it like the globe shown here. **Cartographers,** or mapmakers, use mathematical formulas to transfer information from the three-dimensional globe to a two-dimensional map. However, when the curves of a globe become straight lines on a map, distortion of size, shape, distance, or area occurs.

How Map Projections Work

To create maps, cartographers *project* the round earth onto a flat surface—making a **map projection.** There are more than a hundred kinds of map projections, each with some advantages and some degrees of accuracy. The purpose of the map usually dictates which projection is used. Three of the basic categories of projections used are shown here: **planar, cylindrical,** and **conic.**

Planar Projection

Planar projections show the earth centered in such a way that a straight line going from the center to any other point on the map represents the shortest distance. Since they are most accurate at the center, they are often used for maps of the Poles.

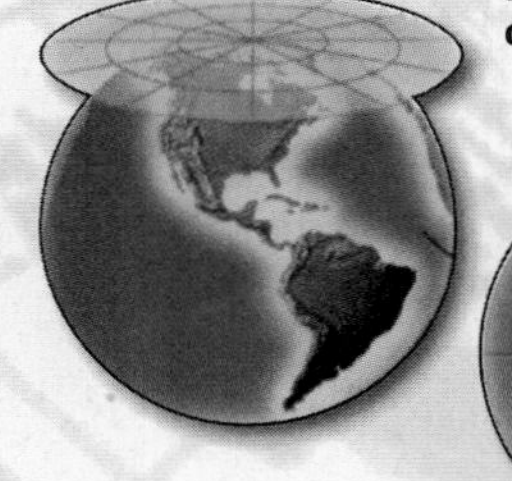

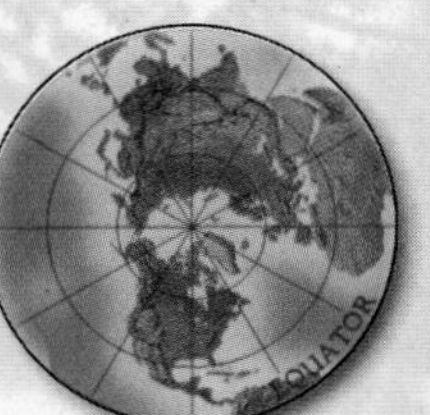

COOPERATIVE LEARNING ACTIVITY

Creating a Presentation Divide the class into two groups. Assign one group to research the National Geographic Society, and the other group to research the United States Geological Survey. Have each group prepare a presentation on what the organization does, what research and resources it provides, how it is funded, and career opportunities. Encourage students to contact their assigned organization and, if possible, arrange for a speaker to come before the class to discuss the organization's purpose and goals. **L2**

Great Circle Routes

A *great circle* is an imaginary line that follows the curve of the earth. A line drawn along the Equator is an example of a great circle. Traveling along a great circle is called following a **great circle route.** Airplane pilots use great circle routes because they represent the shortest distances from one city to the next.

The idea of a great circle shows one important difference between a globe and a map. Because a globe is round, it accurately shows great circles. On a flat map, however, the great circle route between two points may not appear to be the shortest distance. For example, on map A the great circle distance (dotted line) between Tokyo and Los Angeles appears to be far longer than the true direction distance (solid line). In fact, the great circle distance is 345 miles (555 km) shorter, which is evident on map B.

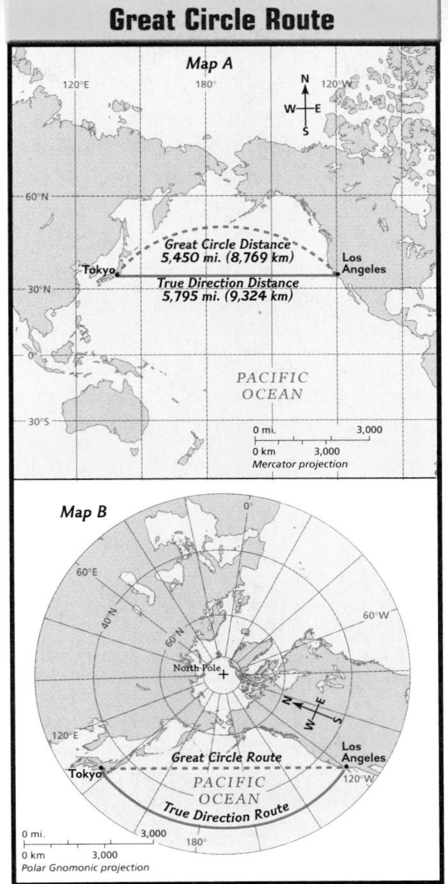

Geographic Information Systems

Technology has changed the way maps are made. Most cartographers use software programs called **geographic information systems (GIS).** A GIS uses data from maps, satellite images, printed text, and statistics. Cartographers can program the GIS to produce the maps they need, and it allows them to make changes quickly and easily.

Cylindrical Projection

Cylindrical projections are based on the projection of the globe onto a cylinder. They are most accurate near the Equator, but shapes and distances are distorted near the Poles.

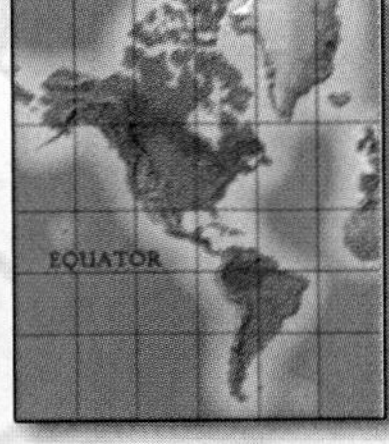

Conic Projection

Conic projections are made by placing a cone over part of the globe. They are best suited for showing east-west areas that are not too far from the Equator. For these uses, a conic projection can indicate distances and directions fairly accurately.

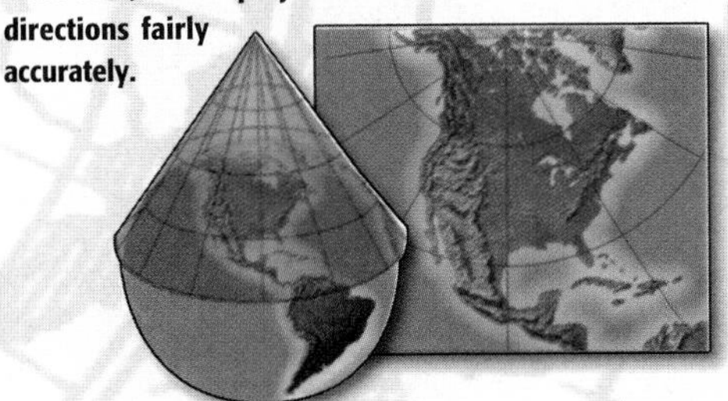

CURRICULUM CONNECTION

Computer Literacy Computers have revolutionized cartography. They reduce distortions and calculate changes at incredible speeds. They gather, process, and store data about contour reliefs, ethnicities, economics, waterways, and much more. They even produce animated "flow maps," such as those that show storm movement.

Enrich

The following exercise will help students understand the different map projections. You will need a glass bowl, tracing paper, a flashlight, and a marking pen. Draw lines of latitude and longitude inside the bowl. For a planar projection, place the bowl on a piece of tracing paper. Holding the flashlight above, shine it into the bowl. Ask students to trace the lines of latitude and longitude projected onto the tracing paper. For a cylindrical projection, place the bowl on its side and roll the tracing paper into a cylinder around the outside of the bowl. Shine the flashlight into the bowl and trace. For a conical projection, make a cone out of the tracing paper and rest it on top of the upside-down bowl. Shine the flashlight into the bowl and trace the projected lines onto the paper. **L2**

EXTENDING THE CONTENT

Geographic Information Systems (GIS) are computer hardware and software systems that can store, display, analyze, and map information. Geographers, urban planners, engineers, and utility companies use these systems. GIS are vital to planning because they enable geographers, scientists, and other technicians to combine data and look at layers of information at the same time. One GIS, for example, may begin with a digitized base map. A retailer wishing to make an informed decision about where to build a store may need to consider a combination of data such as population distribution, traffic movement, land availability, and real estate prices. Using the GIS, the retailer can input and analyze all this information at the same time.

CURRICULUM CONNECTION

Cartography Ask students to flip through their textbooks and look at the maps. Ask students what map projections were used for this book. Why? Have students read the section on these two pages titled *Reading a Map.* Ask students to look at two or three maps in the book and locate the compass rose, key, cities and capitals, relative location, absolute location, boundary lines, and scale bar. Ask students if each map they looked at had all of these features. **L1**

Who?What?Where?When?

Gerardus Mercator Flemish mathematician, geographer, and cartographer Gerardus Mercator created his well-known projection in 1568. The Mercator projection exaggerates areas as they increase in distance from the Equator, and has been favored by sailors for more than 400 years.

Connecting Across Time

The early Greeks established a classification of climate based only on what they knew of differences between where they lived and lands to the north and south of Greece. They called their own climate *temperate* because it posed few problems regarding shelter or clothing. They believed that the area south of the Mediterranean became increasingly hotter, so they called these lands *torrid*. Stories told by travelers from the north and the cold winter winds that came from that direction, led the Greeks to call the northern area *frigid*.

Map Projections

Four of the most popular map projections are named for the cartographers who developed them. These are the ***Winkel Tripel*** *projection, the* ***Robinson*** *projection,* ***Goode's Interrupted Equal-Area*** *projection, and the* ***Mercator*** *projection. Remember, all map projections have some degree of inaccuracy in distance, shape, or size because the curved surface of the earth cannot be shown accurately on a flat map. Every map projection stretches or breaks the curved surface of the earth in some way.*

Winkel Tripel Projection

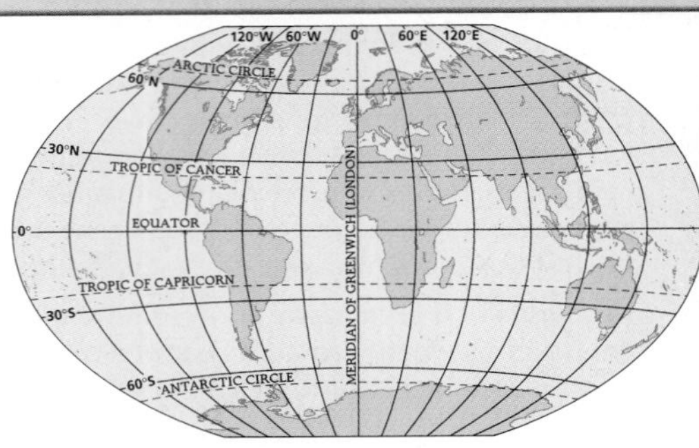

▲ Most reference world maps use the Winkel Tripel projection. Adopted by the National Geographic Society in 1998 for use in most maps, this projection provides a better balance between the size and shape of land areas as they are shown on the map. Even the polar areas are depicted with little distortion of size and shape.

Reading a Map

Maps include several important tools to help you interpret the information contained on a particular map. Learning to use these map tools will help you read the symbolic language of maps more easily.

Compass Rose A compass rose is a marker that indicates directions. The four cardinal directions—north, south, east, and west—are usually indicated with arrows or points of a star. Sometimes a compass rose may point in only one direction because the other directions can be determined in relation to the given direction. The compass rose on this map indicates all four cardinal directions.

Key Cartographers use a variety of symbols to represent map information. Because these symbols are graphic and commonly used, most maps can be read and understood by people around the world. To be sure that the symbols are clear, however, every map contains a key—a list that explains what the symbols stand for. This key shows symbols used for a battle map. It indicates troop movements, supply lines, and U.S. bases.

December 1972 Giant B-52 bombers, powered by jet engines, were among the aircraft used to fly more than 2,000 missions against North Vietnam in the "Christmas" bombing. It was the most concentrated bombing of the war—and in history.

Major U.S. and South Vietnamese troop movements
Major North Vietnamese supply lines
■ U.S. bases

Miller Cylindrical projection

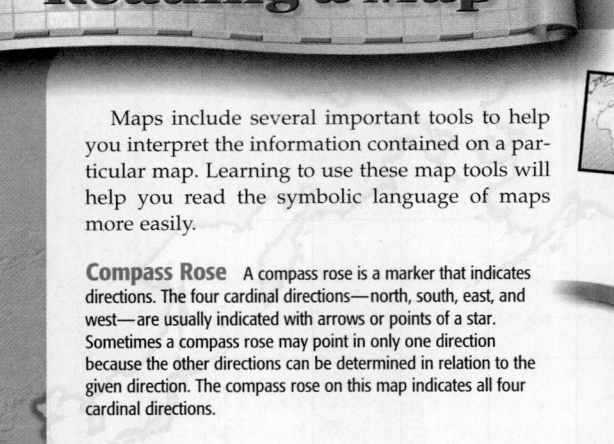

COOPERATIVE LEARNING ACTIVITY

Planning a Survival Strategy Organize students into four or more groups. Assign each group a climate type: tropical, high latitude, mid-latitude, or dry. Encourage group members to imagine that they will be stranded for one year in a remote area that has their assigned climate type. Have groups plan a survival strategy to live in that climate. Each group should identify at least the following: 1) the type of shelter they will need and will be able to make or obtain; 2) the type of clothing that they will need and will be able to make; and 3) the way they will obtain food and water. Have each group present their survival plan to the class, and have the class challenge each plan with situations or conditions likely to arise in the climate region. **L3**

Robinson Projection

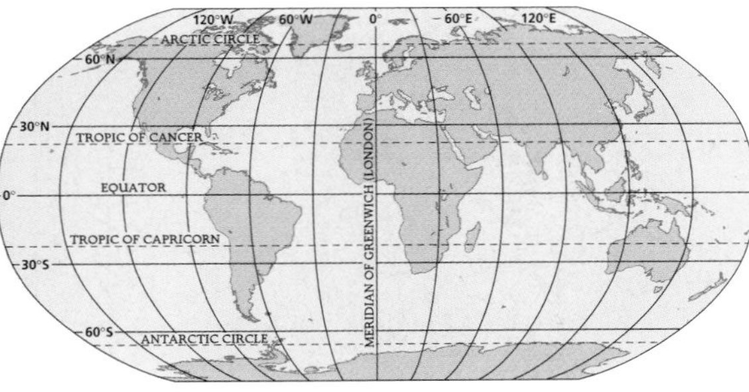

▲ The Robinson projection has minor distortions. The sizes and shapes near the eastern and western edges of the map are accurate, and the outlines of the continents appear much as they do on the globe. However, the shapes of the polar areas appear somewhat flat.

Goode's Interrupted Equal-Area Projection

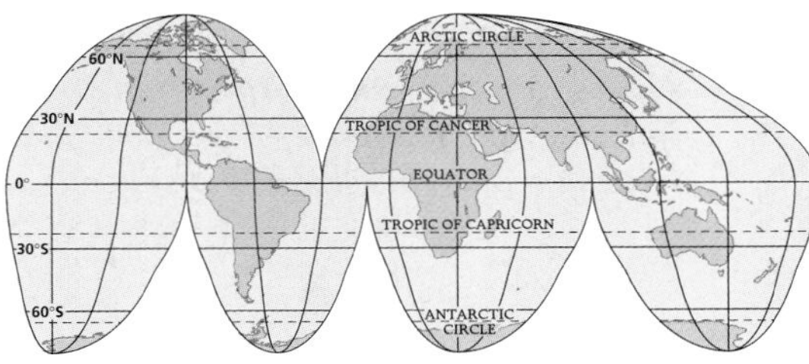

▲ An interrupted projection looks something like a globe that has been cut apart and laid flat. Goode's Interrupted Equal-Area projection shows the true size and shape of the earth's landmasses, but distances are distorted.

Cities and Capitals Cities are symbolized by a solid circle. Sometimes the relative sizes of cities are shown with circles of different sizes. Capitals are represented by a star within a circle.

Relative Location People use relative direction to indicate location. You may be told, for example, to look for a street that is "two blocks north" of another street. Relative location is the location of one place in relation to another place, while absolute location indicates the exact position of a place on the earth's surface. On this map, the relative position of where the Vietnam War took place is given in relation to the rest of the world.

Boundary Lines On political maps of large areas, boundary lines highlight the borders between different countries, states, provinces, or counties.

Scale Bar Every map is a representation of a part of the earth. The scale bar shows the relationship between map measurements and actual distance. Scale can be measured with a ruler to calculate actual distances in standard or metric measurements. On this map, three-fourths inch represents 200 miles (322 km).

Mercator Projection

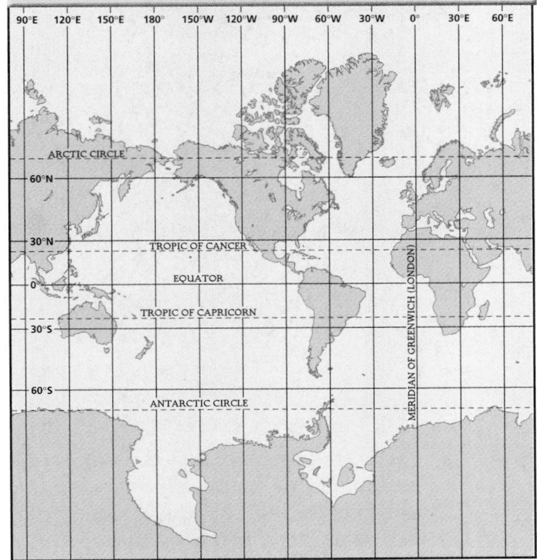

▲ The Mercator projection, once the most commonly used projection, increasingly distorts size and distance as it moves away from the Equator. This makes areas such as Greenland and Antarctica look much larger than they would appear on a globe. However, Mercator projections do accurately show true directions and the shapes of landmasses, making these maps useful for sea travel.

Critical Thinking

Types of maps and map projections are as varied as the purpose of the map. Ask students to research map projections not mentioned in this National Geographic Geography Handbook and create a chart that lists them and explains how they are used. Have each student create a display of one of the researched map projections. **L2**

Writing Activity

The National Geographic Society is renowned for the quality and accuracy of its maps. The Society changed from the Robinson projection to the Winkel Tripel projection in 1998. Ask students to research why the Society made the change. Students should write a brief paper with the results of their research. **L3**

Enrich

Geography has had an impact on the major historic events discussed in this text. As they read the text, have students locate places and regions of historical significance and describe their physical and human characteristics. **L3**

EXTENDING THE CONTENT

Geographers Geographers work for the federal government in the Defense Mapping Agency, United States Geological Survey, Central Intelligence Agency, Army Corps of Engineers, National Science Foundation, Smithsonian Institution, and Office of the Geographer in the Department of State. State environmental and transportation agencies hire geographers and analysts, planners, and cartographers. In the private sector, geographers work as professors, researchers, and cartographers for high-tech computer mapmakers. Businesses as varied as fast-food chains and ski resorts consult geographers about optimal locations for new restaurants and effects of pollution on the ski slopes.

NATIONAL GEOGRAPHIC

PICTURE ATLAS OF THE WORLD
Have students view the Mapping Our World animation "Where in the World," which introduces the concepts of latitude and longitude.

CURRICULUM CONNECTION

English Language Arts The word *longitude* comes from the Latin word for "length," and the word *latitude* comes from the Latin word for "breadth."

Who?What?Where?When?

Prime Meridian There is a point on Earth that is considered to have no latitude and no longitude. This point is at 0° N-S, 0° E-W—the absolute location where the Prime Meridian and the Equator intersect off the African coast in the Atlantic Ocean.

Critical Thinking

After students read this page, check their comprehension by asking them the following questions: What line is at 0° latitude? *(Equator)* What is the latitude of the North Pole? *(90° N)* Through which continents does the Prime Meridian pass? *(Africa, Europe)* **L1**

Understanding Latitude and Longitude

*Lines on globes and maps provide information that can help you easily locate places on the earth. These lines—called **latitude** and **longitude**—cross one another, forming a pattern called a grid system.*

Latitude

Lines of latitude, or **parallels,** circle the earth parallel to the **Equator** and measure the distance north or south of the Equator in degrees. The Equator is at 0° latitude, while the Poles lie at latitudes 90°N (north) and 90°S (south).

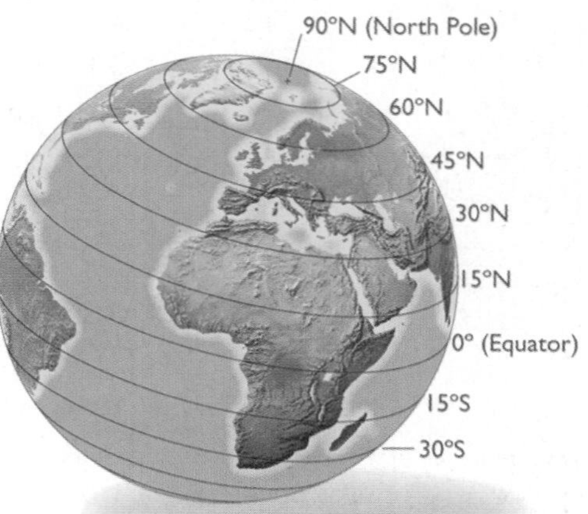

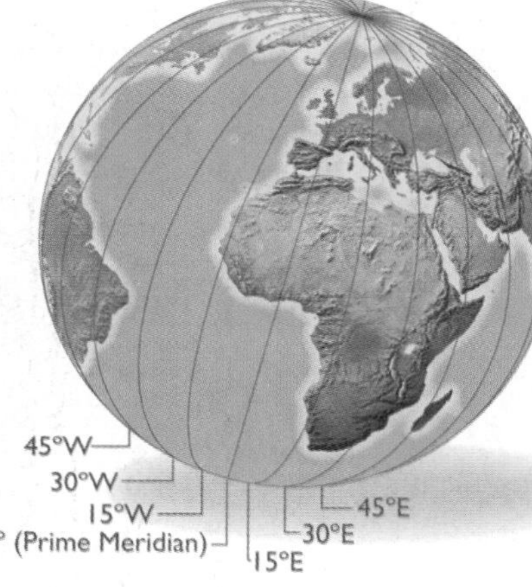

Longitude

Lines of longitude, or **meridians,** circle the earth from Pole to Pole. These lines measure distances east or west of the starting line, which is at 0° longitude and is called the **Prime Meridian.** The Prime Meridian runs through the Royal Observatory in Greenwich, England.

Absolute Location

The grid system formed by lines of latitude and longitude makes it possible to find the absolute location of a place. Many places can be found along a line of latitude, but only one place can be found at the point where a certain line of latitude crosses a certain line of longitude. By using degrees and minutes (points between degrees), people can pinpoint the precise spot where one line of latitude crosses one line of longitude—an absolute location.

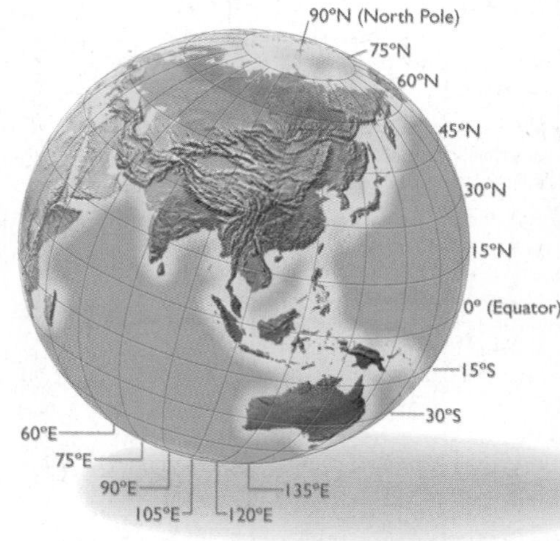

COOPERATIVE LEARNING ACTIVITY

Playing a Game Have students prepare a game called "My Grid Address." Students should write out grid address question cards, with each card containing one multiple-choice question regarding the grid address of a well-known location—a city, lake, mountain, and so on. A sample question format is "My grid address is 36° north latitude and 140° east longitude. What city am I? a) Madrid; b) Tokyo; c) New York; d) Cairo." After students have completed at least 30 to 40 cards, organize the class into teams and play "My Grid Address." Allow five points for each correct answer. **L1**

Maps are prepared for many uses. The information depicted in the map depends on how the map will be used. Learning to recognize a map's purpose will help you make the best use of its content.

General-Purpose Maps

Maps that show a wide range of general information about an area are called **general-purpose** maps. Two of the most common general-purpose maps are physical maps and political maps.

Physical maps show the location and the topography, or shape, of the earth's physical features. They use colors or patterns to indicate relief—the differences in elevation, or height, of landforms.

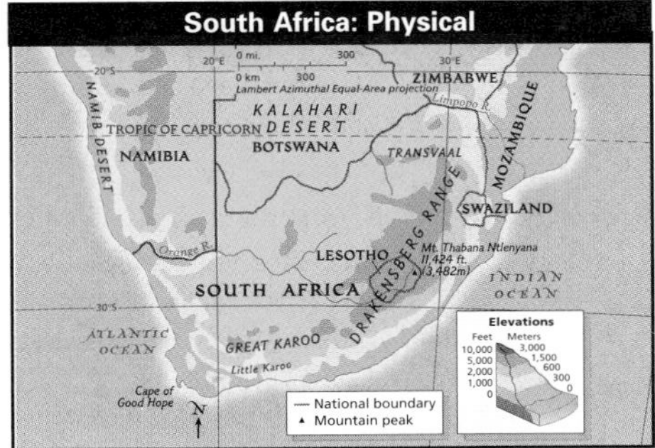

Political maps show the boundaries between countries. Smaller internal divisions, such as states or counties, may also be indicated by different symbols. Political maps usually feature capitals and other cities.

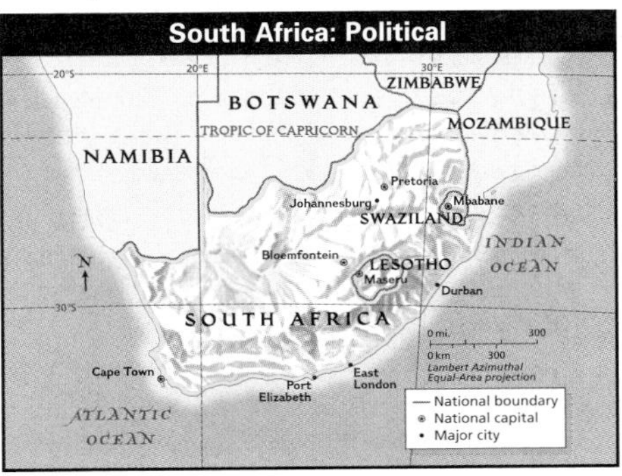

Special-Purpose Maps

Special-purpose maps show information on specific topics, such as climate, land use, or vegetation. Human activities, such as exploration routes, territorial expansion, or battle sites, also appear on special-purpose maps. Colors and map key symbols are especially important on this type of map.

LANDSAT Maps

LANDSAT maps are made from photographs by camera-carrying LANDSAT satellites in space. The cameras record millions of energy waves invisible to the human eye. Computers then change this information into pictures of the earth's surface. With LANDSAT images, scientists can study whole mountain ranges, oceans, and geographic regions. Changes to the earth's environment can also be tracked using the satellite information.

LANDSAT image, Mt. St. Helens, Washington ▼

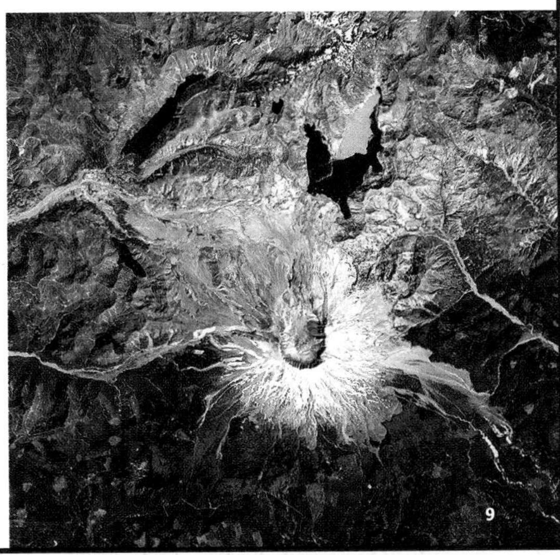

CURRICULUM CONNECTION

Cartography Explain that general-purpose maps may include both physical and political information. Students should always carefully read the map title and key to determine the purpose and the date of the map. Because of changes that occur in history, political maps should always identify the time period that they represent. If a political map does not identify a date, we usually assume that it is a current map.

Enrich

Ask students to glance through the text and find examples of physical, political, and special-purpose maps. Have students write down the page numbers of one of each to share with the class. **L1**

Who?What?Where?When?

Tactile Maps As high technology enters more and more aspects of everyday life, mapmakers are struggling to keep up with the ways that maps are used. One very special need is in the area of maps for the visually or hearing impaired. The Americans with Disabilities Act is opening the door to the production of tactile maps—maps that can be accessed with senses other than sight. Examples include a tactile subway map and a three-dimensional talking map. These maps are, by necessity, much simpler and handle less data since the sense of touch distinguishes less information than the eye. Cartographers are convinced, however, that with increased computer capabilities and innovations in technology, tactile maps will soon be as detailed and informative as any visual maps currently being produced.

COOPERATIVE LEARNING ACTIVITY

Creating Maps and Models Ask students to create a map and a model based on a topic discussed in this textbook. Students can, for example, create a map of a particular war and then create a model based on one aspect of that war, such as a specific battle. Students should transfer information from one medium to another, including written to visual and statistical to written or visual, using computer software as appropriate. Then have students interpret their information by posing and answering questions about geographic distributions and patterns in world history shown on both their map and model. Make sure that students use appropriate mathematical skills to interpret the information contained on their map. **L2**

Writing Activity

Assign students to create a travel brochure for the destination of their choice. The brochure should contain information about absolute and relative location, place and region, physical and human systems, environment, and society. Encourage students to review pages 2 and 3 of this National Geographic Geography Handbook before they begin writing. **L2**

CURRICULUM CONNECTION

History Ask students to discuss the following statement: Historians must understand geography and its themes in order to understand history. Put key points from the classroom discussion on the board in outline form. **L3**

Enrich

Encourage students to keep a geography journal as they begin their study of world history. An easy format would be a notebook with two columns. For each chapter, the student could list in the first column one or more events that were affected by specific geography. In the second column, the student could write a sentence explaining how geography shaped history. **L2**

GEOGRAPHIC

Geographic Dictionary

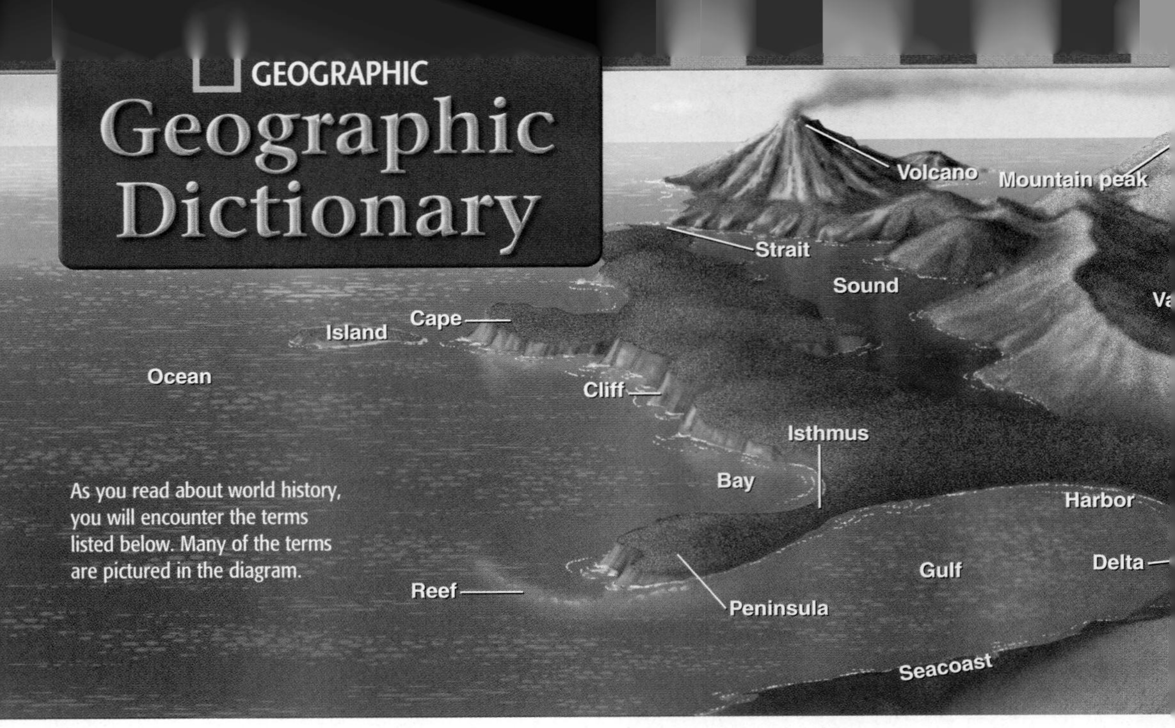

As you read about world history, you will encounter the terms listed below. Many of the terms are pictured in the diagram.

absolute location exact location of a place on the earth described by global coordinates

basin area of land drained by a given river and its branches; area of land surrounded by lands of higher elevation

bay part of a large body of water that extends into a shoreline, generally smaller than a gulf

canyon deep and narrow valley with steep walls

cape point of land that extends into a river, lake, or ocean

channel wide strait or waterway between two landmasses that lie close to each other; deep part of a river or other waterway

cliff steep, high wall of rock, earth, or ice

continent one of the seven large landmasses on the earth

cultural feature characteristic that humans have created in a place, such as language, religion, housing, and settlement pattern

delta flat, low-lying land built up from soil carried downstream by a river and deposited at its mouth

divide stretch of high land that separates river systems

downstream direction in which a river or stream flows from its source to its mouth

elevation height of land above sea level

Equator imaginary line that runs around the earth halfway between the North and South Poles; used as the starting point to measure degrees of north and south latitude

glacier large, thick body of slowly moving ice

gulf part of a large body of water that extends into a shoreline, generally larger and more deeply indented than a bay

harbor a sheltered place along a shoreline where ships can anchor safely

highland elevated land area such as a hill, mountain, or plateau

hill elevated land with sloping sides and rounded summit; generally smaller than a mountain

island land area, smaller than a continent, completely surrounded by water

isthmus narrow stretch of land connecting two larger land areas

lake a sizable inland body of water

latitude distance north or south of the Equator, measured in degrees

longitude distance east or west of the Prime Meridian, measured in degrees

lowland land, usually level, at a low elevation

map drawing of the earth shown on a flat surface

meridian one of many lines on the global grid running from the North Pole to the South Pole; used to measure degrees of longitude

mesa broad, flat-topped landform with steep sides; smaller than a plateau

mountain land with steep sides that rises sharply (1,000 feet

COOPERATIVE LEARNING ACTIVITY

Creating a Map Assign students to groups of three or four. Each group is to make a large map of the school. The map should include a title, a compass rose, a scale bar, and a key. Have students attach to the map six index cards. On each card students should list one of the six essential elements for the study of geography. Have students refer to pages 2 and 3 of this National Geographic Geography Handbook to review these elements. Then have students fill out each card with information that pertains to their school. **L2**

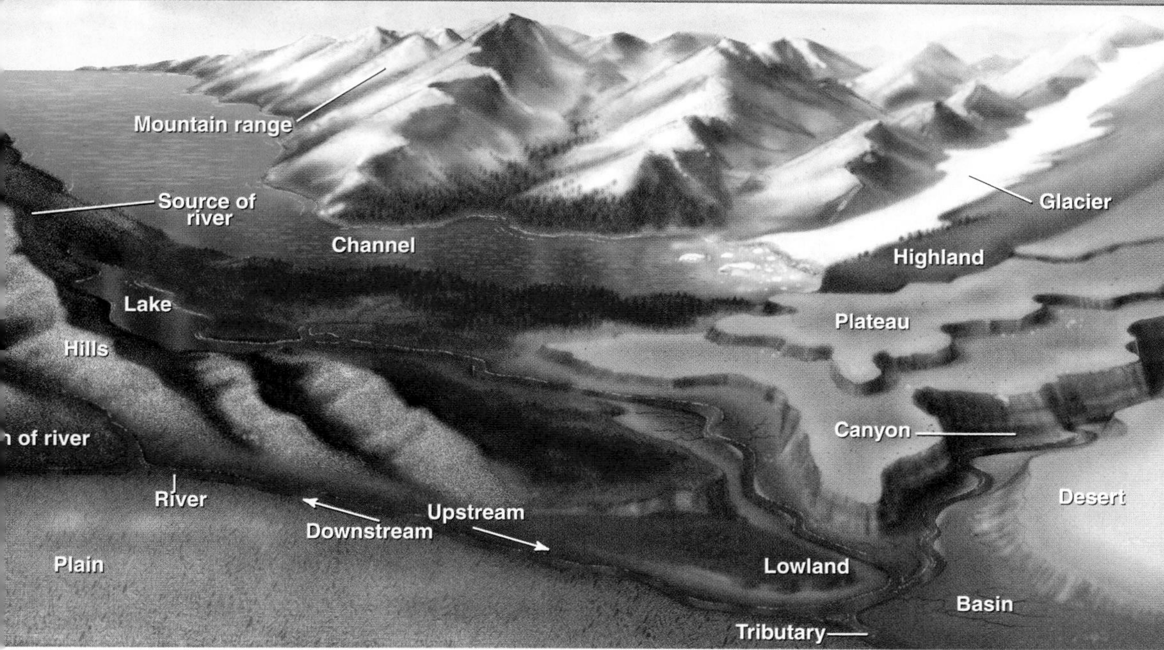

[305 m] or more) from surrounding land; generally larger and more rugged than a hill

mountain peak pointed top of a mountain

mountain range a series of connected mountains

mouth (of a river) place where a stream or river flows into a larger body of water

ocean one of the four major bodies of salt water that surround the continents

ocean current stream of either cold or warm water that moves in a definite direction through an ocean

parallel one of many lines on the global grid that circle the earth north or south of the Equator; used to measure degrees of latitude

peninsula body of land jutting into a lake or ocean, surrounded on three sides by water

physical feature characteristic of a place occurring naturally, such as a landform, body of water, climate pattern, or resource

plain area of level land, usually at a low elevation and often covered with grasses

plateau area of flat or rolling land at a high elevation, about 300–3,000 feet (91–914 m) high

Prime Meridian line of the global grid running from the North Pole to the South Pole at Greenwich, England; starting point for measuring degrees of east and west longitude

relief changes in elevation over a given area of land

river large natural stream of water that runs through the land

sea large body of water completely or partly surrounded by land

seacoast land lying next to a sea or ocean

sea level position on land level with surface of nearby ocean or sea

sound body of water between a coastline and one or more islands off the coast

source (of a river) place where a river or stream begins, often in highlands

strait narrow stretch of water joining two larger bodies of water

tributary small river or stream that flows into a larger river or stream; a branch of a river

upstream direction opposite the flow of a river; toward the source of a river or stream

valley area of low land between hills or mountains

volcano mountain created as liquid rock or ash erupts from inside the earth

CURRICULUM CONNECTION

Civics Geographic knowledge and perspectives help people become responsible citizens, especially when they must make decisions that affect their community, region, country, and world.

Who? What? Where? When?

Krakatau One of the most violent volcanic eruptions in history occurred in 1883 on the island of Krakatau in Indonesia. The volcano collapsed from a height of 2,640 feet (692 m) to 1,000 feet (300 m) below sea level. Its collapse triggered a tidal wave that killed 36,000 people in nearby Java and Sumatra.

Enrich

To help give students a sense of appreciation for the complexities of map making, conduct the following activity. Students will need drawing paper and no more than five different colored crayons or markers. Their assignment is to "draw" a map of their shoe, designing a projection or system that would indicate the shoe's three-dimensional, or curved, characteristics.

Allow students to attempt to draw a cross-section, top view, or other perspective that they choose. Some students may become frustrated, but others will create beautifully illustrated "shoe maps."

Remind students that they will need a key and a scale bar on their completed maps. **L3**

EXTENDING THE CONTENT

Terminology To promote communication, geographers all over the world use the same terminology. The terms they use come from many different languages. For example, *tsunami* is a Japanese word meaning "overflowing wave," and *fjord* is a Norwegian word meaning "long, narrow bay."

The grid system also provides a kind of universal language. Citizens of all countries, no matter how different their cultures, speak the same language of latitude and longitude. This common language is essential in moments of emergency when people and places must be located without the danger of miscommunication.

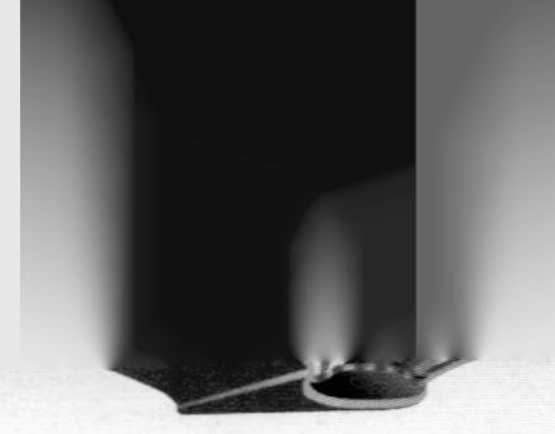

SUGGESTED PACING CHART

Unit 1 (1 day)	Chapter 1 (5 days)	Chapter 2 (4 days)	Chapter 3 (6 days)	Chapter 4 (4 days)	Unit 1 (1 day)
Day 1 Introduction	**Day 1** Chapter 1 Intro, Section 1 **Day 2** Section 2 **Day 3** Section 3 **Day 4** Chapter 1 Review **Day 5** Chapter 1 Assessment	**Day 1** Chapter 2 Intro, Section 1 **Day 2** Section 2 **Day 3** Chapter 2 Review **Day 4** Chapter 2 Assessment	**Day 1** Chapter 3 Intro, Section 1 **Day 2** Section 2 **Day 3** Section 3 **Day 4** Section 4 **Day 5** Chapter 3 Review **Day 6** Chapter 3 Assessment	**Day 1** Chapter 4 Intro, Section 1 **Day 2** Section 2 **Day 3** Chapter 4 Review **Day 4** Chapter 4 Assessment	**Day 1** Wrap-Up/ Projects/Unit 1 Assessment

Use the following tools to easily assess student learning in a variety of ways:

- Performance Assessment Activities and Rubrics
- Chapter Tests
- Section Quizzes
- Standardized Test Skills Practice Workbook
- SAT I/II Test Practice
- www.wh.mt.glencoe.com
- Interactive Tutor Self-Assessment CD-ROM
- MindJogger Videoquiz
- ExamView® Pro Testmaker CD-ROM

TEACHING TRANSPARENCIES

Unit Time Line Transparency 1

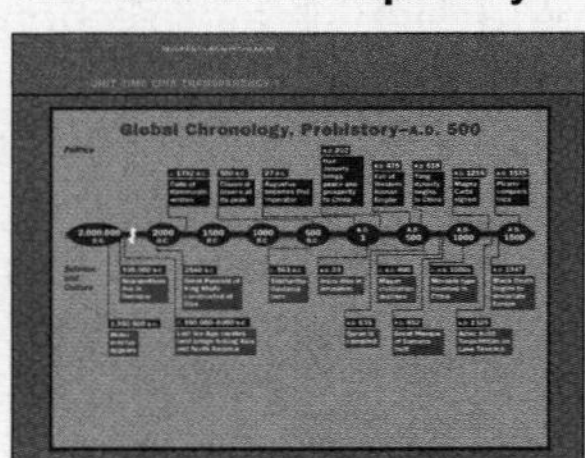

Cause-and-Effect Transparency 1

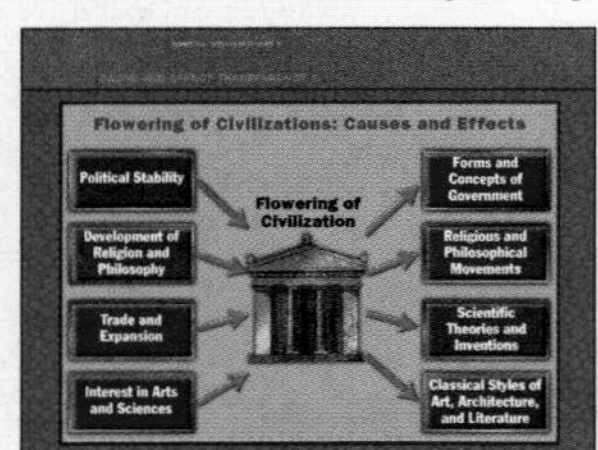

interNET RESOURCES

- www.wh.mt.glencoe.com

Glencoe World History—Modern Times
Visit the *Glencoe World History—Modern Times* Web site for history overviews, activities, assessments, and updated charts and graphs.

- www.socialstudies.glencoe.com

Glencoe Social Studies
Visit the Glencoe Web site for social studies activities, updates, and links to other sites.

- www.teachingtoday.glencoe.com

Glencoe Teaching Today
Visit the new Glencoe Web site for teacher development information, teaching tips, Web resources, and educational news.

- www.time.com

TIME Online
Visit the TIME Web site for up-to-date news and special reports.

Assessment

Unit 1 Tests Forms A and B

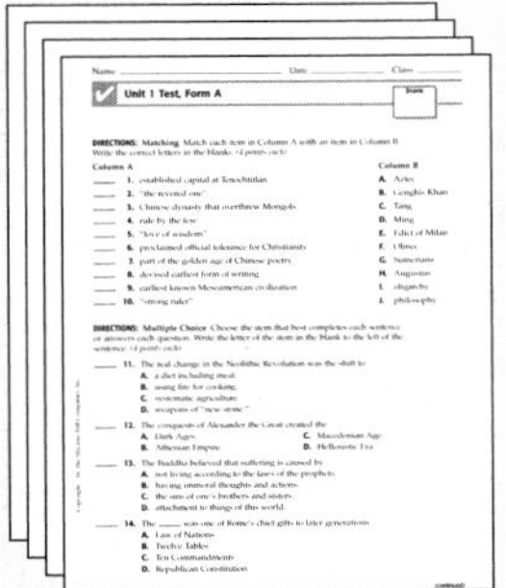

ExamView® Pro Testmaker CD-ROM

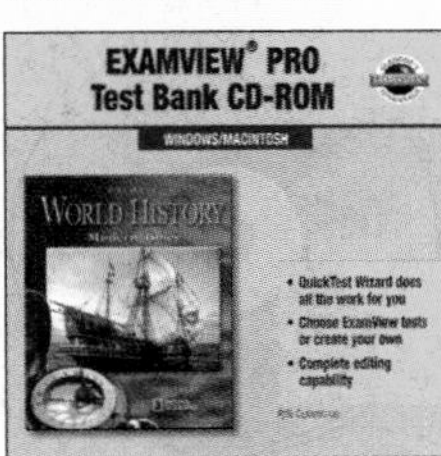

Interdisciplinary Activities

World Literature Reading 1

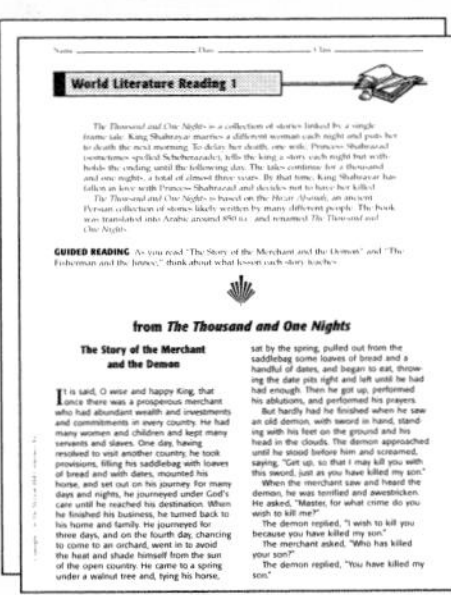

Economics and History Activity 1

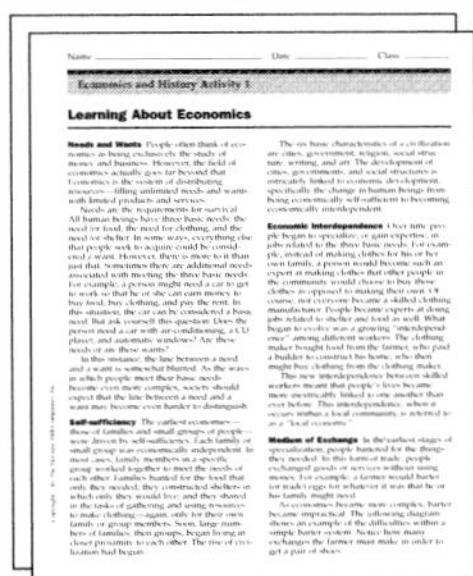

Application and Enrichment

Charting and Graphing Activity 1

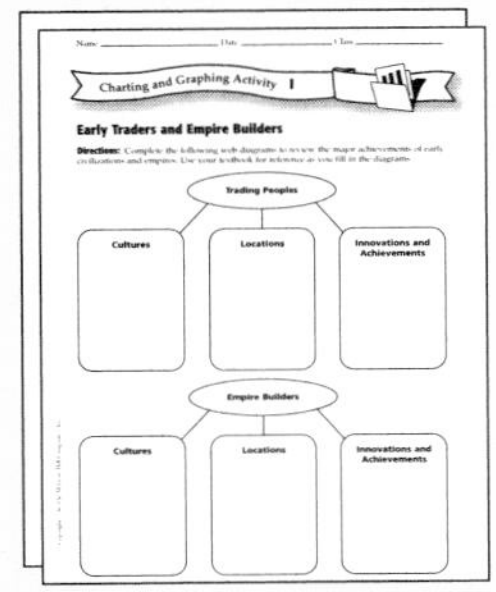

Geographic Literacy

NGS Focus on Geographic Literacy

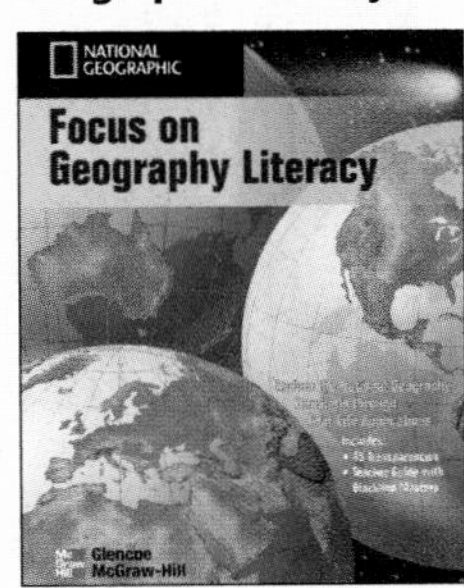

Building Geography Skills for Life

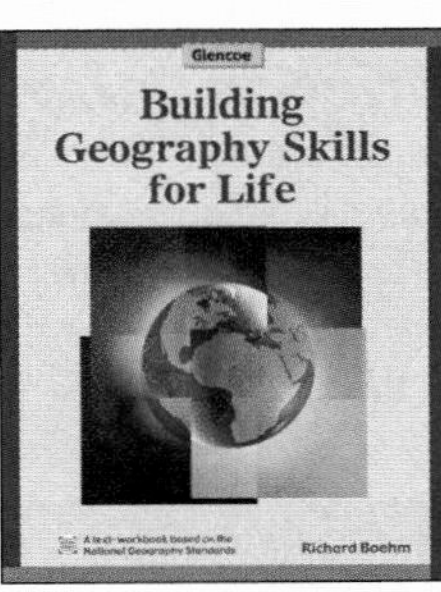

Bibliography

Readings for the Student

Chisholm, Jane, Anne Millard, and A. Milard. ***Early Civilizations (Usborne Illustrated World History).*** E D C Publications, 1992. The rise and development of human culture as revealed by archaeological finds.

Newman, Paul B. ***Daily Life in the Middle Ages.*** McFarland and Company, 2001. Examines many aspects of life in medieval times.

Riley, Judith Merkle. ***In Pursuit of the Green Lion.*** Publishing Mills, 1991. A fictional story that takes place during the Crusades.

Gordon, Matthew S. ***Islam.*** Facts on File, 1991. The history, religious practices, and political influence of Islamic sects.

Readings for the Teacher

Gowlett, John. ***Ascent to Civilization: The Archaeology of Early Man.*** New York: Knopf, 1984.

Multimedia Resources

Software. ***Age of Empires: Gold Edition.*** Microsoft.

CD-ROM. ***Culture 3.0: The Contextual Guide to Western Civilization.*** Cultural Resources, 30 Iroquois Road, Cranford, NJ 07016, 908–709–1574. A resource guide to 3,800 years of Western civilization containing a multitude of visuals.

Additional Glencoe Resources for this Unit:

- Glencoe Skillbuilder Interactive Workbook CD-ROM, Level 2
- Glencoe World History Primary Source Document Library
- World Art Prints
- World Biography: People in History
- Outline Map Resource Book
- World Desk Map
- World Art and Architecture Transparencies
- World Music: Cultural Traditions
- World Music: A Cultural Legacy
- Glencoe World Literature Library
- Reading in the Content Area
- Teaching Strategies for the World History Classroom (Including Block Scheduling Pacing Guides)
- Inclusion for the High School Social Studies Classroom Strategies and Activities

0:00 Out of Time?

If time does not permit teaching each chapter in this unit, you may use the **Reading Essentials and Study Guide** summaries.

Unit Objectives

After studying this unit, students should be able to:

1. explain how the first civilizations emerged;
2. list and explain contributions of the Greeks and Romans to Western civilization;
3. identify how Arab, African, and Asian empires spread;
4. summarize the development of civilizations in the Americas.

The Period in Perspective

Have students contrast modern and ancient civilizations. For example, farming is essential to survival, and governments ensure safety and human services, just as they did in the past.

NATIONAL GEOGRAPHIC

Use these materials to enrich student understanding of the rise and development of civilizations around the world.

NGS Pictureshow™ CD-ROM
Egypt and the Fertile Crescent
China and India
Greece and Rome

NGS Picturepack Transparency Sets
Ancient Civilizations, Parts 1 & 2
Africa

Ancient Civilizations Poster Sets
The Fertile Crescent
Egypt
Greece
Rome

UNIT

1 The World Before Modern Times

Prehistory–1500

The Period in Perspective

Around 3000 B.C., civilizations began to emerge in four different areas of the world—Western Asia, Egypt, India, and China—and give rise to the great empires of the ancient world. By the beginning of the first millennium A.D., however, the great states of the ancient world were mostly in decline or at the point of collapse. On the ruins of the ancient empires, new patterns of civilization began to take shape.

At the same time, between 400 and 1500, new civilizations were beginning to appear in a number of other parts of the world—Japan, Southeast Asia, Africa, and across the Atlantic Ocean in the Americas. All of these states were increasingly linked by trade into the first "global civilization."

Primary Sources Library

See pages 772–773 for primary source readings to accompany Unit 1.

Use The World History ***Primary Source Document Library CD-Rom*** *to find additional primary sources about The World Before Modern Times.*

▲ Grecian urns and pottery were often used to portray mythological scenes.

▶ The temple at Delphi was built to honor the Greek god Apollo.

12

TEAM TEACHING ACTIVITY

Science What we know about early man comes from ongoing excavations and scientific explorations in various archaeological sites around the world. Work with the science teacher to coordinate a study of recent findings of both human and animal life. For example, in 2001, researchers in Kenya found an almost complete skull of a new human species dating from 3.5 million years ago. In China, new dinosaur remains are being unearthed. With students, explore how these remains are located and identified, and how dating is done. L3

"...let no day pass without discussing goodness..."

—Socrates, *The Apology*

13

SERVICE-LEARNING PROJECT

Have students develop a list of questions to ask senior citizens about life when they were young. Arrange an after-school visit to a senior citizens' activity center. During the visit, students should ask their questions and try to discover how people depended on each other and helped each other. Follow up this visit by discussing ways students could be helpful to senior citizens. Encourage students to volunteer to help senior citizens with household tasks such as changing light bulbs, mowing lawns, delivering groceries, reading to them, or playing a musical instrument for them. You might also discuss ways the seniors could help the students. **L1** ELL

Refer to ***Building Bridges: Connecting Classroom and Community through Service in Social Studies*** from the National Council for the Social Studies for information about service-learning.

GLENCOE TECHNOLOGY

CD-ROM
World History Primary Source Document Library CD-ROM

Use the World History Primary Source Document Library CD-ROM to access primary source documents related to the first civilizations and empires.

More About the Photo

According to Greek myth, Delphi was the center of the world. A sacred site since the Bronze Age, Delphi held a unique position in Greek culture. The most important shrine was that of the Delphic oracle, housed in the Temple of Apollo, but there was also a theatre, a site for games, and several treasuries.

History *and the* Humanities

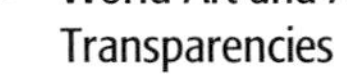

World Art and Architecture Transparencies
- 1 *Woman's Head*
- 2 *Standard of Ur: Peace*
- 3 *Tutankhamen's Throne*
- 4 *Amphora from Vulci*
- 6 *Terra-cotta Warriors*
- 9 *Pantheon*
- 10 *Gold Pendant Mask*
- 13 *Cover of the Lindau Gospels*
- 15 *Angkor Wat*
- 16 *Siva Nataraja*
- 18 *Great Mosque of Djenné*
- 19 *Buddha*
- 20 *Court of the Lions, Alhambra*
- 21 *Mirhab*

World Music: Cultural Traditions, Lessons 1, 2, 5, 6, 7, 8, 9

Looking Back to See Ahead

TEACH

Introduction

This feature focuses on the influence of Roman law and government on the development of legal and political systems in the West. Although the Greeks pioneered the idea of democratic government, it was Roman law, spread across Europe by Roman armies, that shaped the legal systems of most of the West.

Background Notes

Linking Past and Present

Roman history and law were common areas of study and discussion for educated American colonists. At the Constitutional Convention of 1787, delegates cited the fall of the Roman Republic as proof that a government allowing too much direct participation could not survive. Alexander Hamilton reminded delegates that when the Roman tribunes "levelled the boundary between the *patricians and the plebeians,*" disaster followed. The United States Constitution's limits on direct democracy reflect the fears of the founders that, as in Rome, too much democracy would destroy the new nation. Remind students that just as American law continues to evolve and change, the Justinian Code also evolved. The final part, known as the *Novellae,* was not finished until 545. Also remind students that legal systems are closely tied to political systems. The Justinian Code thus had both a legal and a political impact.

UNIT 1

Looking Back...

Systems of Law

Law is a code of conduct and rights recognized by a society. It provides social control, order, and justice, and it enables people to know their rights and responsibilities. Law is also the cornerstone of a constitutional government, helping to ensure justice and fair treatment of all citizens. "Where law ends, tyranny begins," said William Pitt, an English leader in 1770.

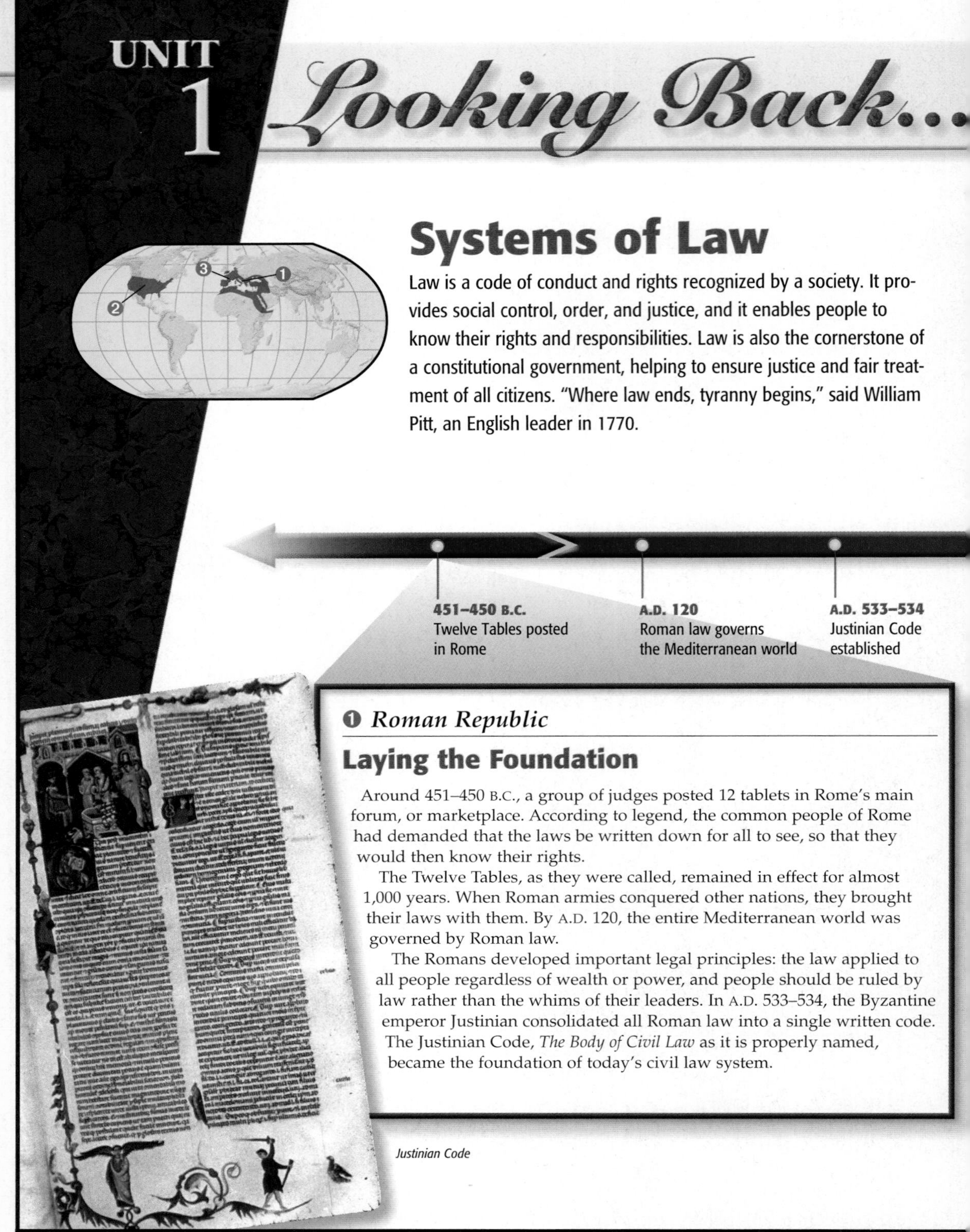

3
1
2
451–450 B.C.
Twelve Tables posted in Rome
A.D. 120
Roman law governs the Mediterranean world
A.D. 533–534
Justinian Code established

❶ *Roman Republic*

Laying the Foundation

Around 451–450 B.C., a group of judges posted 12 tablets in Rome's main forum, or marketplace. According to legend, the common people of Rome had demanded that the laws be written down for all to see, so that they would then know their rights.

The Twelve Tables, as they were called, remained in effect for almost 1,000 years. When Roman armies conquered other nations, they brought their laws with them. By A.D. 120, the entire Mediterranean world was governed by Roman law.

The Romans developed important legal principles: the law applied to all people regardless of wealth or power, and people should be ruled by law rather than the whims of their leaders. In A.D. 533–534, the Byzantine emperor Justinian consolidated all Roman law into a single written code. The Justinian Code, *The Body of Civil Law* as it is properly named, became the foundation of today's civil law system.

Justinian Code

COOPERATIVE LEARNING ACTIVITY

Writing a Constitution Ask students to imagine what school would be like if there were no rules for administrators, teachers, or students. Guide students in a discussion of the importance of rules for both nations and organizations, from community civic groups to the United Nations. Then have students develop a list of the most important rules that govern behavior at their school. Based on the list, have groups of students write a "Constitution" that embodies the school's fundamental principles and the goals these laws seek to accomplish. After groups have written their own constitutions, ask students to identify the impact of political and legal ideas contained in significant historic documents. L3

to See Ahead

Preamble to the United States Constitution

❷ The United States

A Model for Constitutional Government

The founders of the United States knew about and admired the Romans and their belief in limiting the power of government. When it came time to draw up a plan of government, the Framers wrote a constitution that balanced the powers of government among three branches.

To ensure that elected leaders did not place themselves above the law, the Framers included a provision that made the Constitution "the supreme law of the land." The Constitution was adopted on September 17, 1787.

A.D. 1787
United States Constitution adopted

A.D. 1804
Napoleonic Code established in France

❸ France

Unifying the Law

In 1799, a French general named Napoleon Bonaparte set out to build an empire even larger than Rome's. To rule this empire, Napoleon followed the Roman example. He appointed a commission to write a uniform code of laws. This code, known as the Napoleonic Code, was completed in 1804.

Although Napoleon ruled as emperor, he drew upon many of the legal precedents first introduced by the Romans. This included the principle that the same laws should be used to govern all people. Under Napoleon, this code was adopted in areas across the globe, such as present-day Belgium, Spain, and Latin America.

Napoleon Bonaparte

Why It Matters

The Romans developed the principle that people should be ruled by law rather than by the whims of leaders. How did the United States ensure that leaders would not place themselves above the law?

Looking Back to See Ahead

Geography

Movement Have students look at the small map on page 14 and identify the areas that are highlighted. (*Roman Empire, France, United States*) How did Roman law spread through Europe? (*Roman armies carried the law with them to conquered regions.*) How did the influence of Roman law and government cross the Atlantic to the United States? (*The Founders were familiar with Justinian's code,* The Body of Civil Law, *and admired the Roman Republic.*)

Cultural Diffusion

Roman Influence The influence of Roman law is evident today in American law schools and courthouses. The familiar vocabulary of the legal world, including *court, judge, jury, crime, verdict,* and *punish,* are all from Latin, the language of Rome. Lawyers often use terms taken directly from Latin, such as *stare decisis*, which means to follow precedent.

Despite the influence of Roman law, the U.S. legal system is based largely on the English common law tradition. The previous decisions of judges, together known as "case law," rather than legislative enactments or administrative codes, guide the decisions of the courts.

Why It Matters

ANSWER: The United States Constitution was adopted as the supreme law of the land, and all citizens, legislators, and the president are legally bound to uphold the Constitution. The Supreme Court is charged with the duty of enforcing and interpreting the Constitution. The system of checks and balances also ensures that leaders will not place themselves above the law.

Chapter 1 Resources

Timesaving Tools

TeacherWorks™ All-In-One Planner and Resource Center

- **Interactive Teacher Edition** Access your Teacher Wraparound Edition and your classroom resources with a few easy clicks.
- **Interactive Lesson Planner** Planning has never been easier! Organize your week, month, semester, or year with all the lesson helps you need to make teaching creative, timely, and relevant.

Use Glencoe's **Presentation Plus!** multimedia teacher tool to easily present dynamic lessons that visually excite your students. Using Microsoft PowerPoint® you can customize the presentations to create your own personalized lessons.

TEACHING TRANSPARENCIES

Graphic Organizer Student Activity 1 Transparency

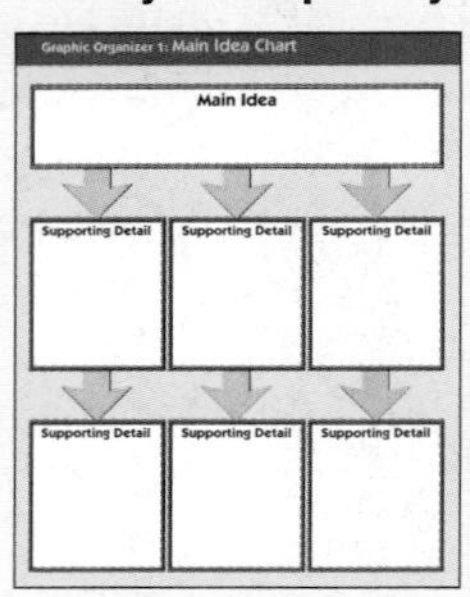

Chapter Transparency 1

Map Overlay Transparency 1

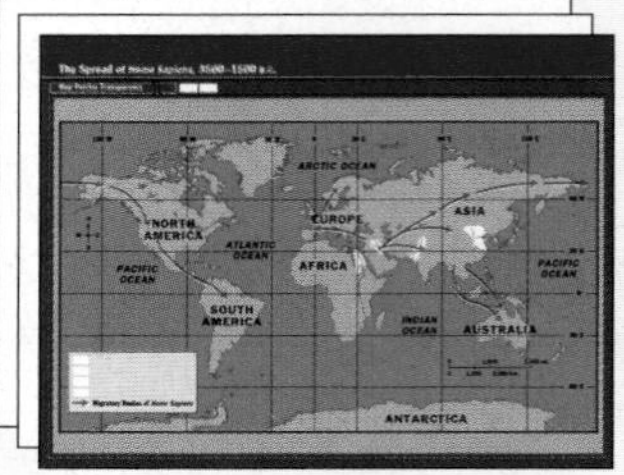

APPLICATION AND ENRICHMENT

Enrichment Activity 1

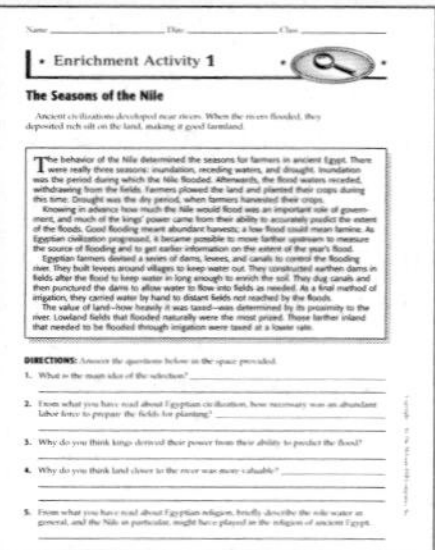

Primary Source Reading 1

History Simulation Activity 1

Historical Significance Activity 1

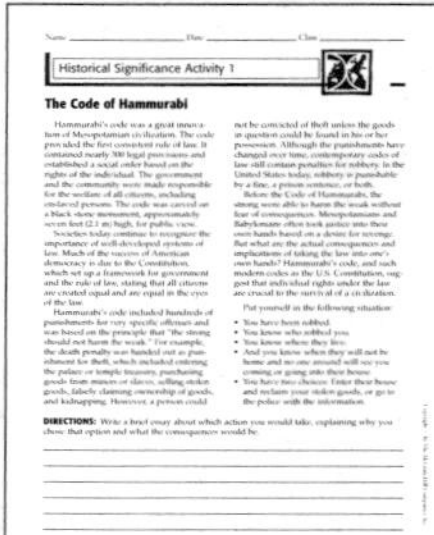

Cooperative Learning Activity 1

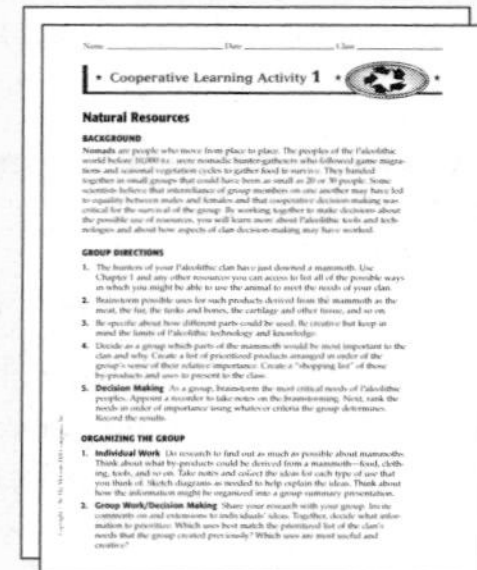

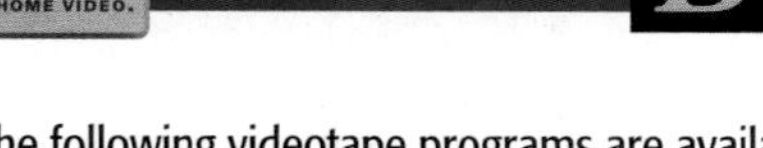

The following videotape programs are available from Glencoe as supplements to Chapter 1:

- **Mummies and Wonders of Ancient Egypt** (ISBN 1–56501–773–0)
- **Seven Wonders of the Ancient World** (ISBN 0–7670–0401–9)
- **Cleopatra: Destiny's Queen** (ISBN 1–56501–454-5)
- **King Tut** (Volumes 1 and 2) (ISBN 1–56501–236-4)
- **Confucius: Words of Wisdom** (ISBN 0–7670–0407–8)
- **The Great Wall of China** (ISBN 0–7670–0361–6)

To order, call Glencoe at 1–800–334–7344. To find classroom resources to accompany many of these videos, check the following home pages:
A&E Television: www.aande.com
The History Channel: www.historychannel.com

Chapter 1 Resources

Review and Reinforcement

Linking Past and Present Activity 1

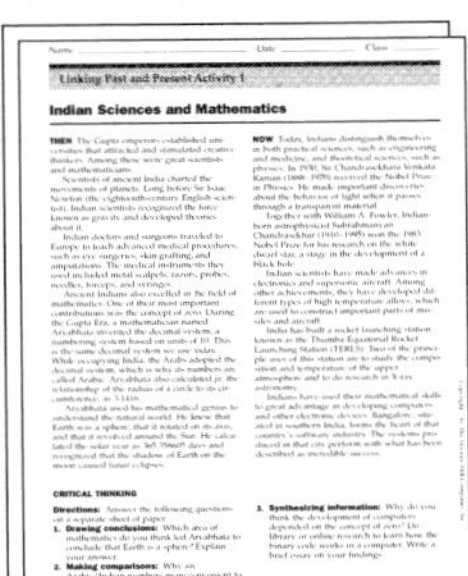

Time Line Activity 1

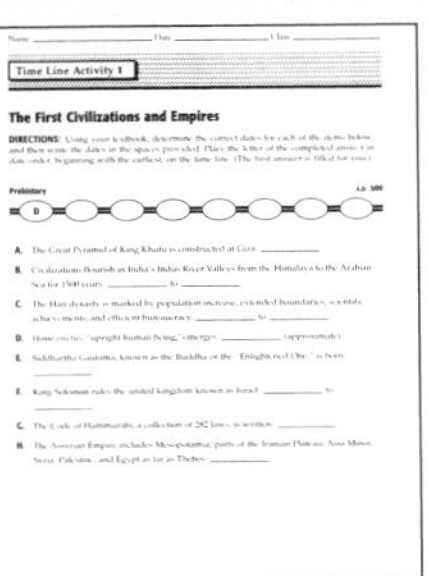

Reteaching Activity 1

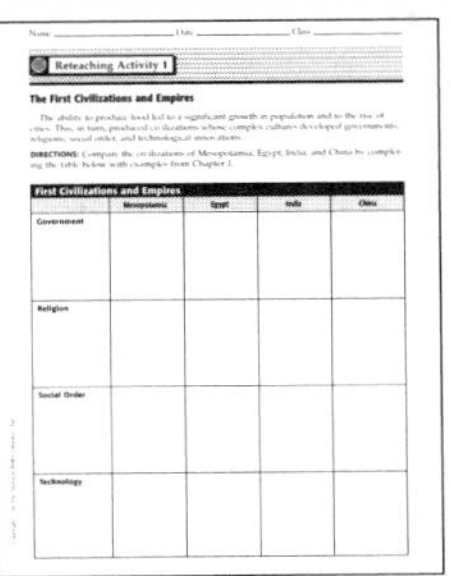

Vocabulary Activity 1

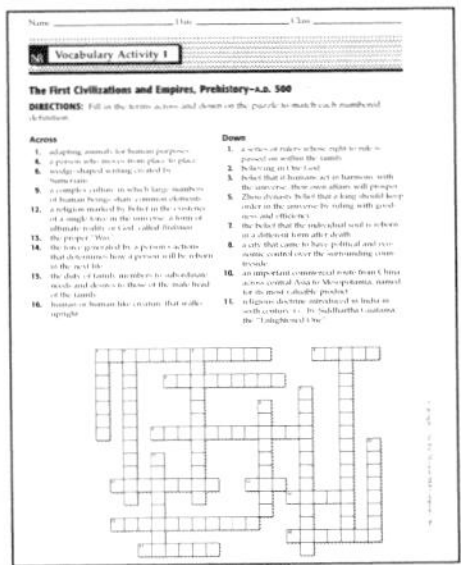

Critical Thinking Skills Activity 1

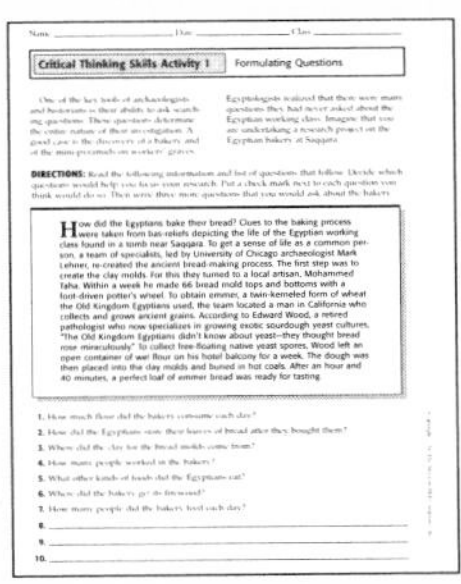

Assessment and Evaluation

Chapter 1 Test Form A

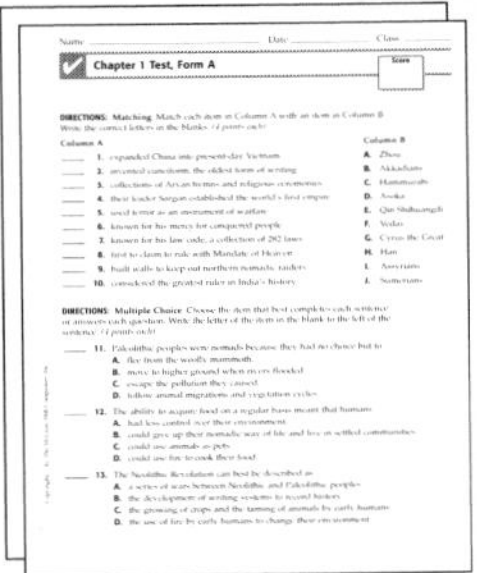

Chapter 1 Test Form B

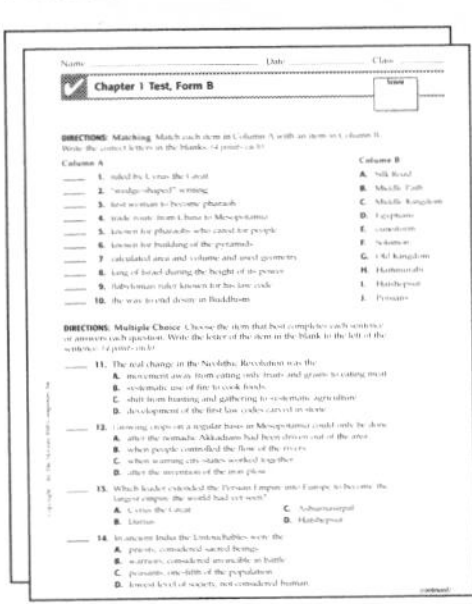

Performance Assessment Activity 1

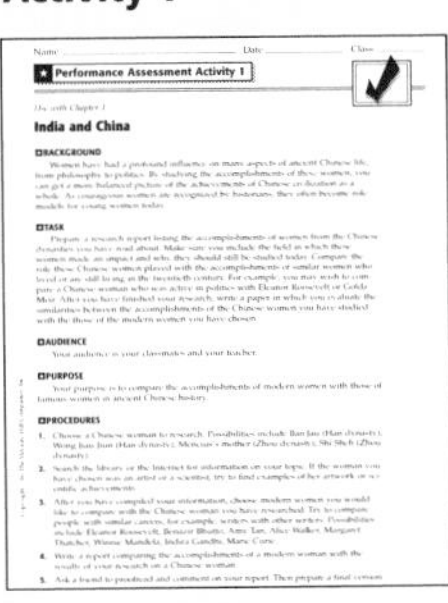

ExamView® Pro Testmaker CD-ROM

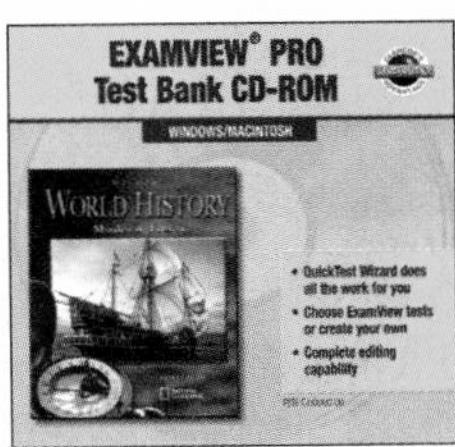

Standardized Test Skills Practice Workbook Activity 1

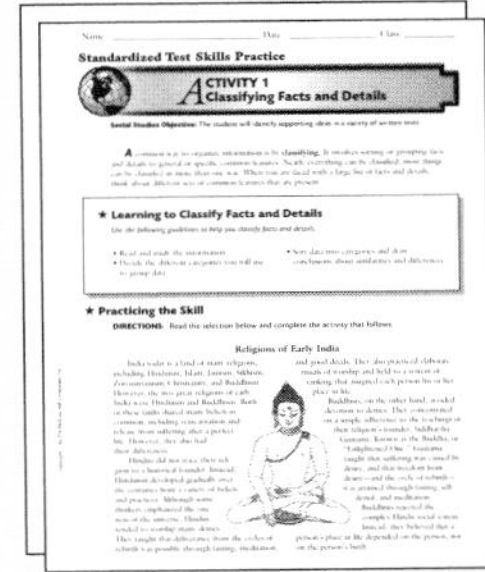

Interdisciplinary Activities

Mapping History Activity 1

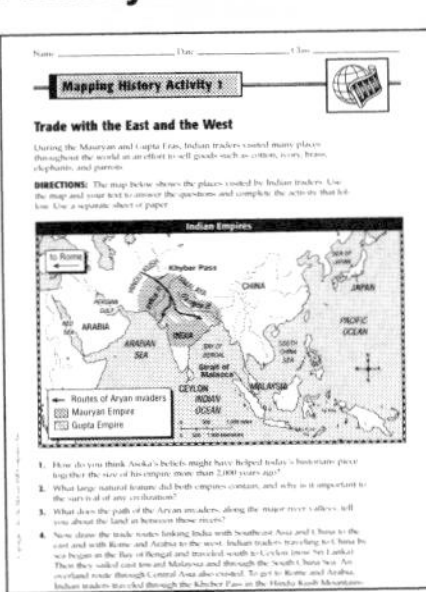

World Art and Music Activity 1

History and Geography Activity 1

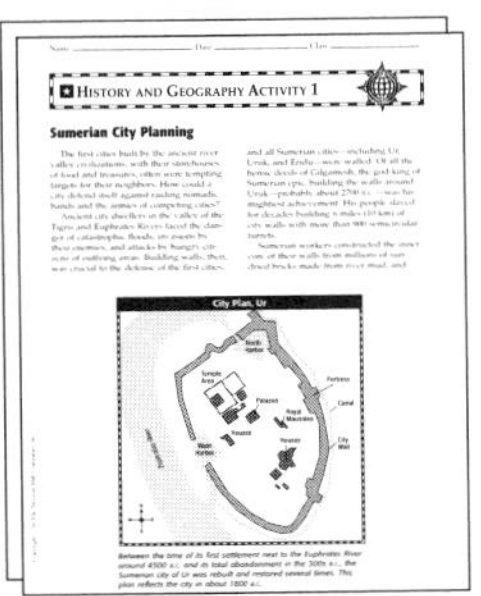

People in World History Activity 1

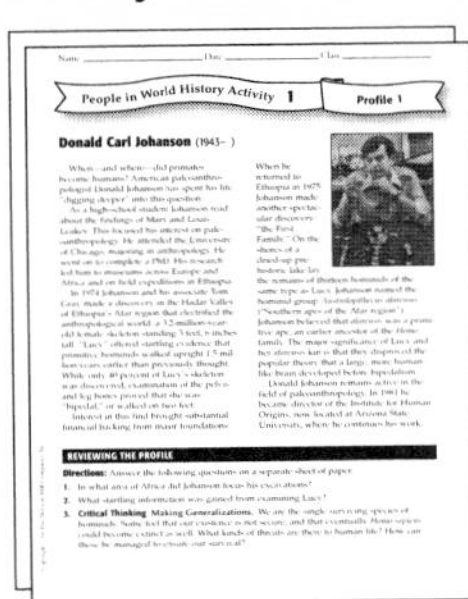

Multimedia

- Vocabulary PuzzleMaker CD-ROM
- Interactive Tutor Self-Assessment CD-ROM
- ExamView® Pro Testmaker CD-ROM
- Audio Program
- World History Primary Source Document Library CD-ROM
- MindJogger Videoquiz
- Presentation Plus! CD-ROM
- TeacherWorks CD-ROM
- Interactive Student Edition CD-ROM
- The World History—Modern Times Video Program

Spanish Resources

The following Spanish language materials are available in the Spanish Resources Binder:

- Spanish Guided Reading Activities
- Spanish Reteaching Activities
- Spanish Quizzes and Tests
- Spanish Vocabulary Activities
- Spanish Summaries

Chapter 1 Resources

SECTION RESOURCES

Daily Objectives	Reproducible Resources	Multimedia Resources
SECTION 1 **The First Humans** 1. Describe the stages of development of the earliest humans. 2. Discuss the changes that occurred during the Neolithic Revolution that made the development of cities possible.	Reproducible Lesson Plan 1–1 Daily Lecture and Discussion Notes 1–1 Guided Reading Activity 1–1* Section Quiz 1–1* Reading Essentials and Study Guide 1–1	Daily Focus Skills Transparency 1–1 Interactive Tutor Self-Assessment CD-ROM ExamView® Pro Testmaker CD-ROM Presentation Plus! CD-ROM
SECTION 2 **Western Asia and Egypt** 1. Explain how geography affected the rise of civilizations in Western Asia and Egypt. 2. Discuss the world religion of Judaism, which influenced the religions of Christianity and Islam.	Reproducible Lesson Plan 1–2 Daily Lecture and Discussion Notes 1–2 Guided Reading Activity 1–2* Section Quiz 1–2* Reading Essentials and Study Guide 1–2	Daily Focus Skills Transparency 1–2 Interactive Tutor Self-Assessment CD-ROM ExamView® Pro Testmaker CD-ROM Presentation Plus! CD-ROM
SECTION 3 **India and China** 1. Examine the caste system—a set of rigid social categories in Indian society. 2. Characterize the rise and fall pattern of Chinese dynasties.	Reproducible Lesson Plan 1–3 Daily Lecture and Discussion Notes 1–3 Guided Reading Activity 1–3* Section Quiz 1–3* Reteaching Activity 1* Reading Essentials and Study Guide 1–3	Daily Focus Skills Transparency 1–3 Interactive Tutor Self-Assessment CD-ROM ExamView® Pro Testmaker CD-ROM Presentation Plus! CD-ROM

0:00 **OUT OF TIME?**
Assign the Chapter 1 **Reading Essentials and Study Guide.** 

*Also Available in Spanish

 Blackline Master
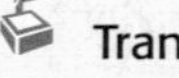 Transparency
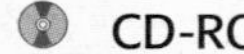 CD-ROM
 DVD
 Poster
Music Program
Audio Program
Videocassette

Chapter 1 Resources

NATIONAL GEOGRAPHIC Teacher's Corner

INDEX TO NATIONAL GEOGRAPHIC MAGAZINE

The following articles relate to this chapter:

- "The Dawn of Humans," by Rick Gore, September 1997.
- "Face-to-Face with Lucy's Family," by Donald C. Johanson, March 1996.
- "The Imperiled Nile Delta," by Peter Theroux, January 1997.
- "New Views of the Holy Land," by Richard Cleave and Technion-Israel Institute of Technology, June 1995.
- "China's Terra-Cotta Warriors," by O. Louis Mazzatenta, October 1996.
- "Pilgrimage to Buddhist Caves," by Reza, April 1996.

NATIONAL GEOGRAPHIC SOCIETY PRODUCTS AVAILABLE FROM GLENCOE

To order the following products call Glencoe at 1-800-334-7344:

- *Picture Atlas of the World* (CD-ROM)
- *STV: World Geography* (Videodisc)
- *PictureShow: Egypt and the Fertile Crescent* (CD-ROM)
- *PictureShow: Ancient Civilizations: India and China* (CD-ROM)

ADDITIONAL NATIONAL GEOGRAPHIC SOCIETY PRODUCTS

To order the following, call National Geographic at 1-800-368-2728:

- *Mysteries of Mankind* (Video)
- *Wonders of the Ancient World: National Geographic Atlas of Archaeology* (Book)
- *Mr. Mummy* (Video)
- *Who Built the Pyramids?* (Video)

NGS ONLINE

Access National Geographic's new dynamic MapMachine Web site and other geography resources at:
www.nationalgeographic.com
www.nationalgeographic.com/maps

KEY TO ABILITY LEVELS

Teaching strategies have been coded.

L1 BASIC activities for all students
L2 AVERAGE activities for average to above-average students
L3 CHALLENGING activities for above-average students
ELL ENGLISH LANGUAGE LEARNER activities

WORLD HISTORY Online

Use our Web site for additional resources. All essential content is covered in the Student Edition.

You and your students can visit www.wh.mt.glencoe.com, the Web site companion to *Glencoe World History—Modern Times.* This innovative integration of electronic and print media offers your students a wealth of opportunities. The student text directs students to the Web site for the following options:

- **Chapter Overviews**
- **Self-Check Quizzes**
- **Student Web Activities**
- **Textbook Updates**

Answers to the Student Web Activities are provided for you in the **Web Activity Lesson Plans.** Additional Web resources and Interactive Tutor Puzzles are also available.

From the Classroom of...

Lee Reay
International Studies Academy
Glendale, Arizona

Stone Age Survival Guide

Explain how early humans survived by using what they could find in their surroundings. Discuss what might have been available in your area—plants, animals, rock shelters, and so on. Then organize students into groups of four or five and ask each group to write a "Stone Age Survival Guide." The guide should provide practical advice for acquiring sufficient food, water, and shelter for a group of 15 to 40 people. Further, it should provide useful information on locally available materials that could be used to make tools and clothing. It might also contain travel tips including suggestions for transporting all the group's belongings. A section on first aid would be helpful. Students may even want to discuss forms of social organization for achieving goals.

When the survival guides are completed and published in a usable form, the student groups should exchange their guides for peer review and evaluation.

Block Schedule

Activities that are suited to use within the block scheduling framework are identified by:

Refer to Activity 1 in the Performance Assessment Activities and Rubrics booklet.

The Impact Today

Since the time of the Paleolithic peoples, humans have continued to develop new technologies that allow them to better control their physical environment. As a result, populations and societies have grown in size and complexity. The great advances made during this early period laid the foundation for future civilizations. Early systems of law and government influenced later civilizations, and writing systems developed during early times are still in use today. The religions that developed during early times also continue to influence people around the globe.

GLENCOE TECHNOLOGY

The World History—Modern Times Video Program

To learn more about early humans, students can view the Chapter 1 video, "Before History," from **The World History—Modern Times Video Program.**

MindJogger Videoquiz

Use the **MindJogger Videoquiz** to preview Chapter 1 content.

 Available in VHS.

CHAPTER 1

The First Civilizations and Empires

Prehistory–A.D. 500

Key Events

As you read, look for the key events in the history of the first civilizations and empires.

- *The agricultural revolution of the Neolithic Age gave rise to more complex human societies that became known as the first civilizations.*
- *The Sumerians in Mesopotamia were among the first groups to build a civilization.*
- *Under the Shang, Zhou, Qin, and Han dynasties, China developed into a flourishing empire and produced numerous cultural, scientific, and technological achievements.*

The Impact Today

The events that occurred during this time period still impact our lives today.

- *Paleolithic peoples used technological inventions to change their physical environment, just as humans do today.*
- *Judaism, Hinduism, Buddhism, and Confucianism continue to have a major impact on people and events around the world.*

World History—Modern Times Video *The Chapter 1 video, "Before History," chronicles the emergence of the first civilizations and empires.*

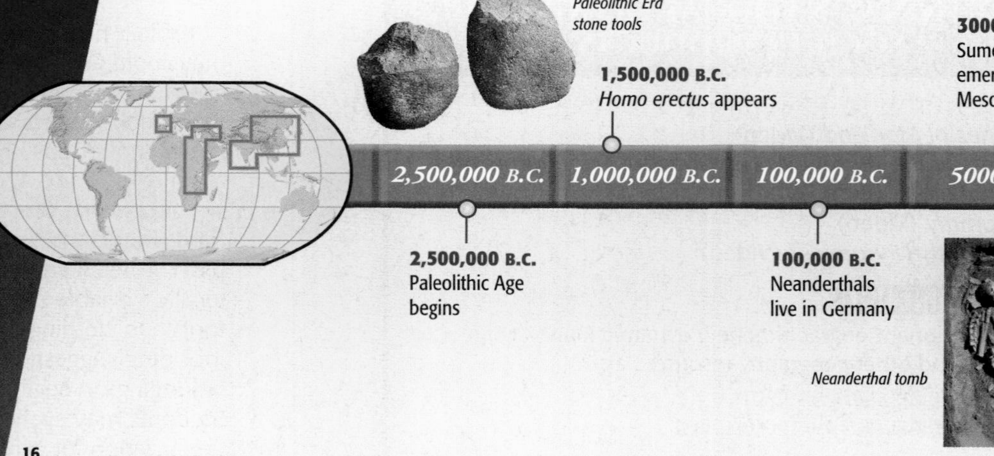

Paleolithic Era stone tools

1,500,000 B.C. *Homo erectus* appears

3000 B.C. Sumerian cities emerge in southern Mesopotamia

2,500,000 B.C. Paleolithic Age begins

100,000 B.C. Neanderthals live in Germany

Neanderthal tomb

16

TWO-MINUTE LESSON LAUNCHER

Archaeologists learn about ancient civilizations by conducting digs. The objects they find help them learn who ancient people were and how they lived. Bring a backpack to class containing items that your students would normally bring to school. Remove each item from the backpack and lay it out on a table in front of the class. As you remove an item, ask students to describe that item's defining characteristics. **Ask:** **What can you tell about the owner of this backpack from the items contained in it?** *(Answers will vary but may include: the owner must wear eyeglasses; likes tuna fish; has allergies; loves to read.)* **L1 L2**

The Great Sphinx and the Great Pyramids at Giza, Egypt, symbolize the power and longevity of Egyptian kingdoms.

Death mask of King Tutankhamen of Egypt

Han burial suit of jade

1500 B.C.	1000 B.C.	500 B.C.	A.D. 1	A.D. 500

1567 B.C. New Kingdom begins

1333 B.C. King Tutankhamen rules Egypt

563 B.C. Siddhartha Gautama, founder of Buddhism, is born

221 B.C. Qin dynasty begins

A.D. 221 Han dynasty ends

The Buddha

HISTORY Online

Chapter Overview
Visit the *Glencoe World History—Modern Times* Web site at wh.mt.glencoe.com and click on **Chapter 1–Chapter Overview** to preview chapter information.

17

Chapter Objectives

After studying this chapter, students should be able to:

1. compare and contrast the nature of human life during the Old Stone Age with that of the New Stone Age;
2. define *civilization* and identify the characteristics of a civilization;
3. explain how geography influenced the development of the early civilizations;
4. name the first empires and explain their transitory natures;
5. list characteristics of life in these societies;
6. list the contributions of each civilization.

Chapter Overview
Introduce students to chapter content and key terms by having them access **Chapter Overview 1** at wh.mt.glencoe.com.

Time Line Activity

As students read the chapter, have them review the time line on pages 16 and 17. Then, have students create their own time lines showing the relative chronology of the emergence of the first civilizations and empires.

MORE ABOUT THE ART

The Great Pyramid at Giza Pyramids were built as repositories for the bodies of the pharaohs. The body of the pharaoh would remain in the tomb awaiting reunification with its soul, or *ka*. The pyramid of King Khufu was built at Giza around 2540 B.C. and covers 13 acres (5.3 ha). The pyramid measures 756 feet (230 m) at each side of its base and stands 481 feet (147 m) high. Its four sides are almost precisely oriented to the four points of the compass. The pyramid contains more than 2 million stone blocks that weigh an average of 2 1/2 short tons (2.3 t) each. It may have taken 100,000 Egyptians 20 years to build the Great Pyramid.

CHAPTER PREVIEW

Introducing

A Story That Matters

Depending upon the ability levels of your students, select from the following questions to reinforce the reading of *A Story That Matters*.

- How long ago does this story take place? *(approximately 150 years ago)*
- How hot was it? *(120° Fahrenheit)* Have students ever experienced temperatures this high? *(Answers will vary.)*
- What metaphors are used to indicate that the region Loftus was in was where civilization began? *(roots, cradle)* **L1 L3**

About the Art

One of the most noticeable features of the remains at Uruk is the ziggurat, a stepped tower. The ziggurat functioned as a religious temple and supported a shrine on its top. The number of tiers on Mesopotamian ziggurats varies from two to seven. Access to the shrine at the top was provided by a series of ramps on one side or by a continuous spiral ramp from base to summit. The sloping sides and terraces of ziggurats were often landscaped with trees and bushes. The Hanging Gardens of Babylon, for example, were roof gardens that were laid out on a series of ziggurat terraces.

CHAPTER PREVIEW

A Story That Matters

Sumerian ruins at Uruk

The Cradle of the Human Race

In the winter of 1849, a daring young Englishman made a difficult journey into the deserts and swamps of southern Iraq. He moved south down the banks of the river Euphrates while braving high winds and temperatures that reached 120 degrees Fahrenheit (48.9° C). The man, William Loftus, led a small expedition in search of the roots of civilization. As he said, "From our childhood we have been led to regard this place as the cradle of the human race."

Guided by native Arabs into the southernmost reaches of Iraq, Loftus and his small group of explorers were soon overwhelmed by what they saw. He wrote, "I know of nothing more exciting or impressive than the first sight of one of these great piles, looming in solitary grandeur from the surrounding plains and marshes."

One of these "piles" was known to the natives as the mound of Warka. The mound contained the ruins of the ancient city of Uruk, one of the first real cities in the world and part of one of the world's first civilizations. Southern Iraq, known to ancient peoples as Mesopotamia, was one of four areas in the world where civilization began.

Why It Matters

In the fertile river valleys of Mesopotamia, Egypt, India, and China, intensive farming made it possible to support large groups of people. The people in these regions were able to develop the organized societies that we associate with civilization. The beginnings of Western civilization lie in the early civilizations of Southwest Asia and Egypt.

History and You Make a list of ancient cities mentioned in this chapter. Using the Internet or library, research what current archaeological work is being conducted at those sites. Select one site and prepare a brief report on what types of artifacts are being recovered from that area.

18

HISTORY AND YOU

Systematic agriculture was one of the most significant accomplishments of early civilizations, making it possible for people to have dependable food supplies and enabling them to live in communities, towns, and, eventually, cities. Students should use primary and secondary sources to evaluate the importance of systematic agriculture and to trace the development of crops that were grown in each of the regions discussed in this chapter. Students may wish to compare ancient crops with those produced in their area today. **L2**

SECTION 1 Early Humans

Guide to Reading

Main Ideas
- By 10,000 B.C., *Homo sapiens sapiens* had spread throughout the world.
- Systematic agriculture brought about major economic, political, and social changes for early humans.

Key Terms
hominid, nomad, Neolithic Revolution, systematic agriculture, domestication, civilization

People to Identify
Neanderthals, *Homo sapiens sapiens*

Places to Locate
Africa, Europe

Preview Questions
1. What important developments took place during the Paleolithic Age?
2. What changes occurred during the Neolithic Revolution that made the development of cities possible?

Reading Strategy
Summarizing Information As you read this section, fill in a chart like the one below listing six characteristics of a civilization.

1.	4.
2.	5.
3.	6.

Preview of Events

3,000,000 B.C.	100,000 B.C.	30,000 B.C.	10,000 B.C.	8000 B.C.	3000 B.C.
3,000,000 B.C. Australopithecines make simple stone tools	**100,000 B.C.** Neanderthals appear	**30,000 B.C.** Neanderthals are extinct	**10,000 B.C.** Neolithic Age begins	**8000 B.C.** Systematic agriculture develops	**3000 B.C.** River valley civilizations develop

Voices from the Past

In 1879, a Spanish landowner, who was an amateur archaeologist, took his 12-year-old daughter Maria with him to examine a cave on their farm in northern Spain. While her father busied himself digging for artifacts at the entrance to the cave, Maria wandered inside, holding a lantern. She was startled by what she discovered:

> ❝Ahead was a big dark hole like a doorway. Beyond it was a huge long room. I held my lantern high for a better look. Then, suddenly, I saw big red-and-black animals all over the ceiling. I stood amazed, looking at them.❞
>
> —***Secrets from the Past,*** **Gene S. Stuart, 1979**

Cave painting of a bison in Altamira, Spain

Today, the simple cave paintings made by Stone Age artists provide historians with clues to the lives of early humans.

Before History

Historians rely mostly on documents, or written records, to create their pictures of the past. However, an account of prehistory—the period before written records—depends on the work of archaeologists and anthropologists. These scientists rely on the analysis of artifacts and human fossils to construct theories about the development of early human beings.

Early Stages of Development The earliest humanlike creatures lived in **Africa** as long as three to four million years ago. Called australopithecines (aw•STRAY•loh•PIH•thuh•SYNS), or "southern apes," they flourished in eastern and southern Africa. They were the first **hominids** (humans and other humanlike creatures that walk upright) to make simple stone tools.

CHAPTER 1
Section 1, 19–22

1 FOCUS

Section Overview
This section describes the development of the earliest humans and the changes that took place during the Neolithic Age and the rise of civilizations.

BELLRINGER
Skillbuilder Activity

Project transparency and have students answer questions.

Available as a blackline master.

Daily Focus Skills Transparency 1-1

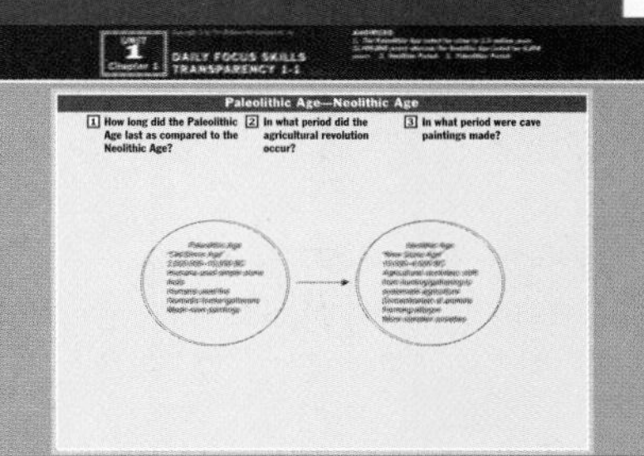

Guide to Reading

Answers to Graphic:
1. cities
2. government
3. religion
4. social structure
5. writing
6. art

Preteaching Vocabulary: Have students explain the Neolithic Revolution and how it made the development of cities possible.

SECTION RESOURCES

Reproducible Masters
- Reproducible Lesson Plan 1–1
- Daily Lecture and Discussion Notes 1–1
- Guided Reading Activity 1–1
- Section Quiz 1–1
- Reading Essentials and Study Guide 1–1

Transparencies
- Daily Focus Skills Transparency 1–1

Multimedia
- Interactive Tutor Self-Assessment CD-ROM
- ExamView® Pro Testmaker CD-ROM
- Presentation Plus! CD-ROM

2 TEACH

Daily Lecture and Discussion Notes 1–1

Daily Lecture and Discussion Notes

Chapter 1, Section 1

Did You Know? Early hominids called australopithecines were primarily herbivores. However, the development of stone tools, which allowed early hominids to remove flesh from animal carcasses, meant that later hominids, such as *Homo habilis*, could eat meat regularly.

I. **Before History** *(pages 19–20)*

A. The period before history—prehistory—is the period for which we have no written records. Archaeologists and anthropologists use the scientific analysis of human remains to study the development of early human beings.

B. The earliest human-like beings—australopithecines—lived in **Africa** three to four million years ago. They were the first **hominids** (humans and other creatures that walk upright) to make stone tools.

C. *Homo erectus* ("upright human being") marks the next stage of human development. This species dates from about 1.5 million years ago and used larger and more varied tools than the first hominids.

D. The emergence of *Homo sapiens* ("wise human being") around 250,000 years ago marked the third, most crucial, stage in human development. Two subgroups developed from *Homo sapiens:* **Neanderthals** and ***Homo sapiens sapiens.*** The Neanderthals

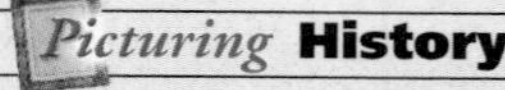

Picturing History

Answer: the shift from hunting and gathering to systematic agriculture

Reading Check

Answer: Australopithecines were the first humanlike creatures to walk upright and to make simple stone tools. *Homo erectus* used larger and more varied tools. *Homo sapiens* relied on a variety of stone tools and seem to be the first early people to bury their dead.

TURNING POINT

To reinforce this turning point in history, ask students to research and report on how Paleolithic people used technological discoveries and innovations to change their physical environment. *(Answers may include that Paleolithic people used tools to build new shelters and used fire to scare away wild animals and to keep warm during the Ice Ages.)*

Reading Check

Answer: the making of tools and the use of fire

A second stage in early human development occurred with the appearance of *Homo erectus* ("upright human being"), a species that emerged around 1.5 million years ago. *Homo erectus* made use of larger and more varied tools.

Around 250,000 years ago, a third—and crucial—stage in human development began with the emergence of a new species, *Homo sapiens* ("wise human being"). Two distinct subgroups, Neanderthals and *Homo sapiens sapiens,* both developed from *Homo sapiens.*

Neanderthals were first found in the Neander Valley in Germany. Their remains have been dated between 100,000 and 30,000 B.C. and have been found in **Europe** and Southwest Asia. Neanderthals relied on a variety of stone tools and seem to be the first early people to bury their dead.

The first anatomically modern humans (people who looked like us), known as ***Homo sapiens sapiens*** ("wise, wise human being"), appeared in Africa between 150,000 and 200,000 years ago. Recent evidence indicates that they began to spread outside Africa around 100,000 years ago.

The Spread of *Homo Sapiens Sapiens* By 30,000 B.C., *Homo sapiens sapiens* had replaced the Neanderthals, who had largely died out, possibly as a result of conflict between the two groups.

The spread of these first modern humans was a slow process, but by 10,000 B.C., members of the *Homo sapiens sapiens* subspecies of the species *Homo sapiens* could be found throughout the world. All humans today, whether they are Europeans, Australian Aborigines (A•buh•RIJ•NEES), or Africans, belong to the same subspecies of human being.

Reading Check **Summarizing** Identify and describe the three stages of early human development.

The Hunter-Gatherers of the Old Stone Age

TURNING POINT **Just as people do today, Paleolithic peoples used technological innovations, including stone tools, to change their physical environment.**

The term *Paleolithic Age* is used to designate the early period of human history from approximately 2,500,000 to 10,000 B.C. in which humans used simple stone tools. *Paleolithic* is Greek for "old stone," and the Paleolithic Age is sometimes called the Old Stone Age.

For hundreds of thousands of years, human beings lived in small communities, seeking to survive by hunting, fishing, and gathering in an often hostile environment. Over a long period of time, Paleolithic peoples learned how to create more sophisticated tools; how to use fire; and how to adapt to, and even change, their physical environment. Paleolithic peoples were primarily **nomads** (people who moved from place to place) who hunted animals and gathered wild plants for survival. They also created a human culture that included sophisticated cave paintings.

Reading Check **Identifying** What are the two most important technological innovations of Paleolithic peoples?

Picturing History

Although he was found in a glacier in the Alps, this Iceman actually died 5,000 years after the Ice Age. Recent discoveries prove that he was killed by an arrow. The cold mummified his remains. After the end of the last Ice Age (c. 8000 B.C.), what important change occurred that altered the pattern of human living?

INTERDISCIPLINARY CONNECTIONS ACTIVITY

Science, Technology, and Society For many years people thought the remains of a vast river system lay hidden under the Sahara. When scientists studied the radar scan of the Sahara taken by the space shuttle Columbia in 1981, they saw a network of waterways, floodplains, and broad river valleys throughout southern Egypt and northern Sudan. Prompted by these images, an Egyptian-American team excavated along the banks of an ancient river in 1982. They found tools and other artifacts believed to have been used by *Homo erectus,* who lived and hunted in the fertile Sahara 200,000 years ago. Ask students to locate other areas in which the climate has changed markedly in the past 200,000 years. **L3**

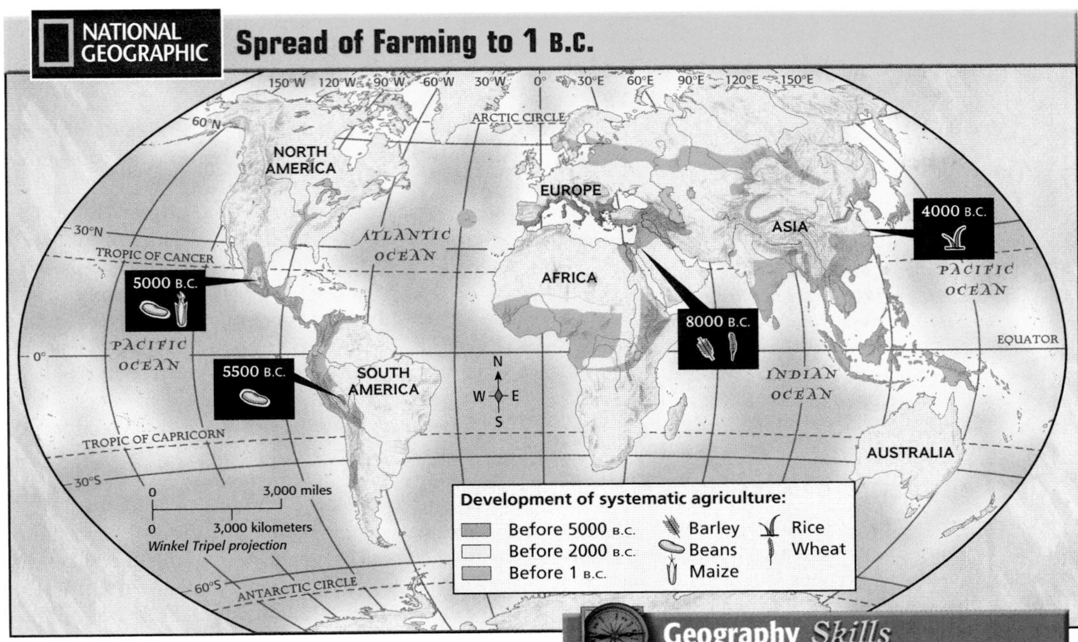

Geography *Skills*

Agriculture developed independently in different regions of the world.

1. **Interpreting Maps** Between what latitudes did the earliest farming develop?
2. **Applying Geography Skills** What geologic, geographic, and climatic factors influenced the development of farming?

The Neolithic Revolution

TURNING POINT **Despite all of our technological progress, human survival still depends on the systematic growing and storing of food, an accomplishment of people in the Neolithic Age.**

The end of the last Ice Age, around 8000 B.C., was followed by what is called the **Neolithic Revolution**—that is, the revolution that occurred in the Neolithic Age, the period of human history from 10,000 to 4000 B.C. The word *neolithic* is Greek for "new stone." The name *New Stone Age* is somewhat misleading, however. The real change in the Neolithic Revolution was the shift from the hunting of animals and the gathering of food to the keeping of animals and the growing of food on a regular basis—what we call **systematic agriculture.**

The planting of grains and vegetables provided a regular supply of food. The **domestication** (adaptation for human use) of animals added a steady source of meat, milk, and wool. Animals could also be used to do work. The growing of crops and the taming of food-producing animals created what historians call an agricultural revolution. Some believe this revolution was the single most important development in human history.

The growing of crops on a regular basis gave rise to more permanent settlements, which historians call Neolithic farming villages. Once people began settling in villages or towns, they saw the need to build houses for protection and other structures for storage. Organized communities stored food and other material goods, which encouraged the development of trade.

As village inhabitants mastered the art of farming, they gradually began to develop more complex societies. As their wealth increased, these societies began to create armies and to build walled cities. By 3000 B.C., large numbers of people were concentrated in the river valleys of Mesopotamia, Egypt, India, and China. This would lead to a whole new pattern for human life.

Reading Check **Identifying** What changes resulted from the development of systematic agriculture?

CRITICAL THINKING ACTIVITY

The Domestication of Animals One of the unfortunate side effects of civilization and the domestication of animals has been an increase in the number of diseases that afflict humans. Many diseases are the result of humans living in close proximity to animals. Once humans began to domesticate animals, they began to have close daily interaction with animals they had previously only hunted. Influenza is known to originate from pigs and ducks, measles is closely related to canine distemper, and cattle are responsible for anthrax, smallpox, and tuberculosis. Several hundred diseases that now afflict humans come from other species. Have students research the medical responses to these diseases and then have them describe changes produced by these discoveries and innovations. **L2**

Geography *Skills*

Answers:

1. between 45° North and 25° South
2. answers could include: the availability of water; moderate climate; level ground; native plants suitable for agriculture

Guided Reading Activity 1–1

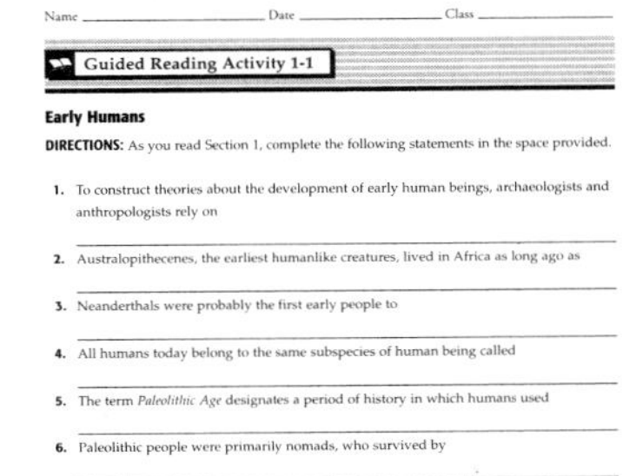

Name ______ Date ______ Class ______

Guided Reading Activity 1-1

Early Humans

DIRECTIONS: As you read Section 1, complete the following statements in the space provided.

1. To construct theories about the development of early human beings, archaeologists and anthropologists rely on ______
2. Australopithecenes, the earliest humanlike creatures, lived in Africa as long ago as ______
3. Neanderthals were probably the first early people to ______
4. All humans today belong to the same subspecies of human being called ______
5. The term *Paleolithic Age* designates a period of history in which humans used ______
6. Paleolithic people were primarily nomads, who survived by ______
7. The end of the last Ice Age was followed by what is called the ______

TURNING POINT

Ask students to identify important changes in human life caused by the Neolithic agricultural revolution. *(The practice of farming and the domestication of animals enabled people to have a steady food supply and to settle in villages, as they no longer had to travel to hunt and gather food.)* **L1**

Reading Check

Answer: domestication of animals for food and to help with work; development of villages with permanent buildings for housing and storage; development of trade; creation of armies and walled cities

3 ASSESS

Assign Section 1 Assessment as homework or as an in-class activity.

Have students use **Interactive Tutor Self-Assessment CD-ROM.**

Section Quiz 1-1

Name ______ Date ______ Class ______

Chapter 1 — Score

Section Quiz 1-1

DIRECTIONS: Matching Match each item in Column A with an item in Column B. Write the correct letters in the blanks. *(10 points each)*

Column A	Column B
____ 1. period before writing was developed	A. nomads
____ 2. humans and other creatures that walk upright	B. systematic agriculture
____ 3. "new stone" in Greek	C. prehistory
____ 4. the keeping of animals and the growing of food	D. neolithic
____ 5. people who move from place to place	E. hominids

Reading Check

Answer: An increase in food production led to significant population growth and the rise of cities. Growing numbers of people, the need to maintain the food supply, and the need to build walls for defense soon led to the growth of governments.

Reading Essentials and Study Guide 1-1

Name ______ Date ______ Class ______

Reading Essentials and Study Guide

Chapter 1, Section 1

For use with textbook pages 19-22

THE FIRST HUMANS

KEY TERMS

hominids humans and other humanlike creatures that walk upright *(page 19)*

nomads people who move from place to place in search of food *(page 20)*

Neolithic Revolution the shift from hunting of animals and gathering of food to the keeping of animals and the growing of food on a regular basis that occurred around 8000 B.C. *(page 21)*

systematic agriculture the keeping of animals and the growing of food on a regular basis *(page 21)*

ABCNEWS INTERACTIVE™

Turning Points in World History
The ABC News videotape includes a segment on the rise of cities.

4 CLOSE

Have students write four topic sentences that express main ideas about the development of human life from the Paleolithic Age to the rise of civilizations. Have students read and discuss their sentences in class. **L2**

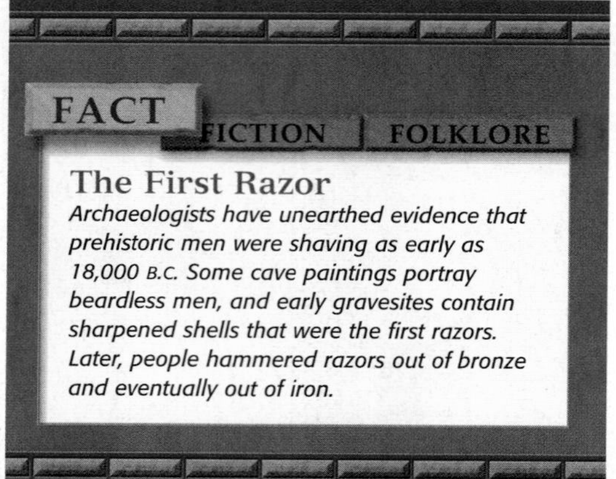

FACT
FICTION
FOLKLORE
The First Razor
Archaeologists have unearthed evidence that prehistoric men were shaving as early as 18,000 B.C. Some cave paintings portray beardless men, and early gravesites contain sharpened shells that were the first razors. Later, people hammered razors out of bronze and eventually out of iron.

The Emergence of Civilization

In general terms, the culture of a people is the way of life that they follow. As we have seen, early human beings formed small groups that developed a simple culture that enabled them to survive. As human societies grew and became more complex, a new form of human existence—called civilization—came into being.

A civilization is a complex culture in which large numbers of human beings share a number of common elements. Historians have identified the basic characteristics of civilizations. Six of the most important characteristics are cities, government, religion, social structure, writing, and art.

An increase in food production in the river valleys of Mesopotamia, Egypt, India, and China led to a significant growth in human population and the rise of cities. Growing numbers of people, the need to maintain the food supply, and the need to build walls for defense soon led to the growth of governments in these new urban civilizations.

All of the new urban civilizations developed religions to explain the workings of the forces of nature and the fact of their own existence. Rituals were developed to please the gods and goddesses. A new social structure based on economic power also arose. Rulers and an upper class of priests, government officials, and warriors dominated society.

Abundant food supplies created new opportunities, enabling some people to work in occupations other than farming. The demand of the upper class for luxury items encouraged artisans and craftspeople to create new products.

Writing was an important feature in the life of these new civilizations. Above all, rulers, priests, merchants, and artisans used writing to keep accurate records. Significant artistic activity was another feature of the new civilizations. Temples and pyramids were built as places for worship or sacrifice, or for the burial of kings and other important people. The emergence of civilizations was a dramatic new stage in the story of world history.

Reading Check **Describing** Describe the relationship between an increase in food production and the rise of cities and governments.

SECTION 1 ASSESSMENT

Checking for Understanding

1. **Define** hominid, nomad, Neolithic Revolution, systematic agriculture, domestication, civilization.
2. **Identify** Neanderthals, *Homo sapiens sapiens.*
3. **Locate** Africa, Europe.
4. **Contrast** the evidence that archaeologists and anthropologists use to understand the past to that used by historians.
5. **List** the species that emerged during the different stages of human development.

Critical Thinking

6. **Analyze** Does the development of systematic agriculture by Neolithic peoples after the end of the last Ice Age deserve to be called a revolution? Why was the shift to systematic agriculture important to the development of civilization?
7. **Sequencing Information** Create a diagram like the one below to show how changes during the Neolithic Revolution led to the emergence of civilization. In the last box, write where the first civilizations appeared.

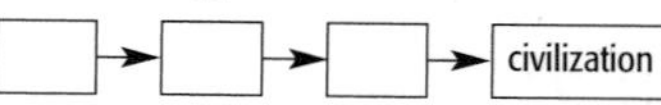

Analyzing Visuals

8. **Examine** the cave painting of a bison shown on page 19. Many cave paintings from the prehistoric period depict similar subjects. What do these paintings tell us about the lifestyles of prehistoric peoples?

Writing About History

9. **Expository Writing** Much disagreement exists about the interpretation of available data on the origins of humankind. Discuss and document at least two different points of view besides the one presented in the text.

SECTION 1 ASSESSMENT

1. Key terms are in blue.
2. Neanderthals *(p. 20); Homo sapiens sapiens (p. 20)*
3. See chapter maps.
4. While historians use written records, archaeologists and anthropologists must analyze human remains to understand the period before written records were kept.
5. first stage: australopithecines; second stage: *Homo erectus;* third stage: *Homo sapiens* with subgroups Neanderthals and *Homo sapiens sapiens*
6. Answers will vary. A regular food supply allowed humans to give up their nomadic existence and live in settled communities. As communities became more complex, government became necessary.
7. regular food supply; rise of permanent villages; trading of goods; civilization: Mesopotamia, Egypt, India, China
8. the importance of hunting and animals to nomadic societies
9. Answers may include creationism; no real evidence that humans are descended from australopithecines.

CRITICAL THINKING SKILLBUILDER

Understanding Cause and Effect

Why Learn This Skill?

It is important to understand how or why an event occurred. What action or situation caused a particular event? What were the effects or consequences of that particular action or situation?

Learning the Skill

Understanding cause and effect involves considering how or why an event occurred. A cause is the action or situation that produces an event. An effect is the result or consequence of an action or situation. To identify cause-and-effect relationships, follow these steps:

- Identify two or more events or developments.
- Decide whether or not one event caused the other. Look for "clue words" such as *because, led to, brought about, produced, as a result of, so that, since,* and *therefore.*
- Identify the outcomes of events.

Making a graphic organizer can help you understand cause and effect. Read the passage below and examine the graphic organizer:

Unlike the floods on Mesopotamia's rivers, the flooding of the Nile was gradual and predictable. The river was seen as life-giving, not life-threatening. Whereas massive, state-controlled irrigation and flood control were needed in Mesopotamia, the small villages along the Nile easily managed small irrigation systems that required no state assistance. As a result, Egyptian civilization tended to remain more rural. Many small villages were gathered along a narrow band of land on both sides of the Nile.

Cause and Effect

Cause
- The flooding of the Nile was gradual and predictable.

Effects
- Villages used small irrigation systems that required no state assistance.
- Egyptian civilization tended to remain rural, with many small villages gathered along the Nile.

Practicing the Skill

On a separate piece of paper, make a cause-and-effect diagram for each of the following statements. Some of the statements may have more than one cause and effect.

1. Irrigation and drainage ditches made it possible to grow crops on a regular basis. The resulting abundance of food supplies enabled large numbers of people to live together in cities.
2. Under Hammurabi's code, a son found guilty of striking his father had his hand cut off.
3. The Hyksos invaded Egypt and defeated the Egyptian soldiers. Their new rulers taught the conquered Egyptians how to use bronze to make tools and weapons.

Applying the Skill

Read an account of a current event in your community as reported in a local newspaper. Determine at least one cause and one effect of that event. Show the cause-and-effect relationship in a chart.

GO TO Glencoe's **Skillbuilder Interactive Workbook, Level 2,** provides instruction and practice in key social studies skills.

23

ANSWERS TO PRACTICING THE SKILL

1. Cause: irrigation and drainage ditches built; Effects: crops can be grown on regular basis→abundant food supplies→large numbers of people can live together in cities
2. Cause: son strikes father; Effect: son's hand cut off
3. Cause: Hyksos invade Egypt; Effects: Egyptians conquered→Egyptians learn to use bronze→Egyptian soldiers have more advanced weapons

Applying the Skill: Students will determine a cause and effect of a local event and create a chart showing the cause-and-effect relationship.

CRITICAL THINKING SKILLBUILDER

TEACH

Understanding Cause and Effect To demonstrate cause and effect, use examples from biology. Have students explain how or why the following diseases occur in human beings: malaria *(bite of infected mosquito)*, rickets *(lack of vitamin D)*, beriberi *(lack of thiamine)*, typhoid *(contaminated food or water)*, rabies *(bite of infected animal)*, scurvy *(lack of vitamin C)*. Ask how the causes of these diseases were discovered. *(observation, experimentation, logic)* Emphasize that cause-and-effect relationships in history may be less certain than those in science and medicine.

Additional Practice

Skills Reinforcement Activity 1

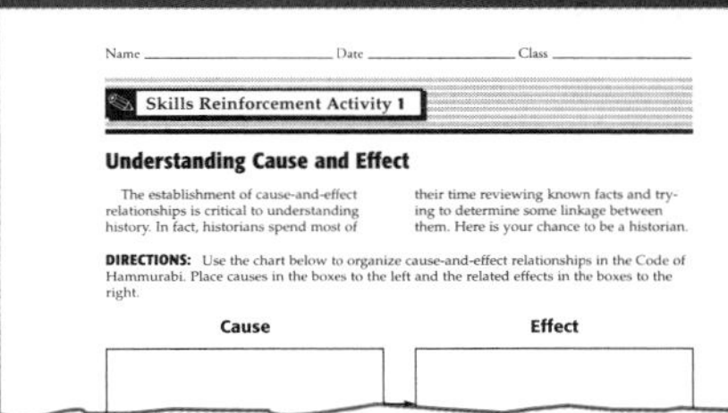

Name ______ Date ______ Class ______

Skills Reinforcement Activity 1

Understanding Cause and Effect

The establishment of cause-and-effect relationships is critical to understanding history. In fact, historians spend most of their time reviewing known facts and trying to determine some linkage between them. Here is your chance to be a historian.

DIRECTIONS: Use the chart below to organize cause-and-effect relationships in the Code of Hammurabi. Place causes in the boxes to the left and the related effects in the boxes to the right.

Cause	Effect

GLENCOE TECHNOLOGY

CD-ROM

Glencoe Skillbuilder Interactive Workbook CD-ROM, Level 2

This interactive CD-ROM reinforces student mastery of essential social studies skills.

1 FOCUS

Section Overview

This section describes the key developments in the civilizations of Mesopotamia and ancient Egypt. It also traces the early history of the Israelites, discusses Assyrian contributions, and reviews the significance of the Persian Empire.

BELLRINGER
Skillbuilder Activity

 Project transparency and have students answer questions.

 Available as a blackline master.

Daily Focus Skills Transparency 1–2

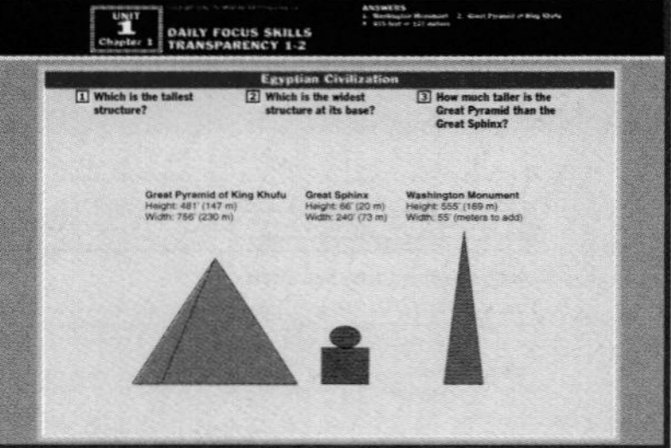

Guide to Reading

Answers to Graphic: Western Asia includes Sumer, Akkad, Babylon, Israel, Assyria, and Persia. Egypt includes the Three Kingdoms. Assyria and Persia extended into Egypt.

Preteaching Vocabulary: Discuss the meaning of *city-states* and their importance to the development of government in Mesopotamia *(cities with political and economic control over the surrounding countryside; basic units of Sumerian civilization).*

SECTION 2 Western Asia and Egypt

Guide to Reading

Main Ideas
- The civilizations of western Asia and Egypt contributed technology and beliefs that affect our lives today.
- The rise and fall of empires is an important part of history.

Key Terms
city-state, empire, patriarchal, cuneiform, dynasty, hieroglyphics, Judaism, monotheistic

People to Identify
Sargon, Hammurabi, Menes, King Solomon, Cyrus

Places to Locate
Tigris River, Euphrates River, Fertile Crescent, Nile River, Lower Egypt, Upper Egypt, Jerusalem, Royal Road

Preview Question
1. How did geography affect the civilizations of western Asia and Egypt?

Reading Strategy
Organizing Information As you read this section complete a chart like the one below listing the geographic locations of the civilizations of western Asia and Egypt.

Western Asia	Egypt

Preview of Events

3500 B.C. — 3000 B.C. — 2500 B.C. — 2000 B.C. — 1500 B.C. — 1000 B.C. — 500 B.C.

- **3100 B.C.** King Menes unites Upper and Lower Egypt
- **c. 3000 B.C.** Sumerians establish independent city-states
- **1792 B.C.** Hammurabi comes to power
- **1200 B.C.** Israelites emerge as a distinct group of people
- **559 B.C.** Cyrus rules Persian Empire

Voices from the Past

Shepherd and his sheep on the banks of the Nile River

The Nile was crucial to the development of Egyptian civilization.

“The Egyptian Nile,” wrote one Arab traveler, “surpasses all the rivers of the world in sweetness of taste, in length of course and usefulness. No other river in the world can show such a continuous series of towns and villages along its banks.” In their “Hymn to the Nile,” Egyptians wrote of their reliance on the river: “The bringer of food, rich in provisions, creator of all good, lord of majesty, sweet of fragrance. . . . [The Nile] makes the granaries wide, and gives things to the poor. He who makes every beloved tree to grow.”

—*Ancient Near Eastern Texts,* James B. Pritchard, 1969

Egypt, like Mesopotamia, was one of the first river valley civilizations. Like the people of Mesopotamia, the Egyptians left records of their developing civilization.

The City-States of Ancient Mesopotamia

The ancient Greeks spoke of the valley between the **Tigris** and **Euphrates Rivers** as Mesopotamia, the land “between the rivers.” Mesopotamia was at the eastern end of an area known as the **Fertile Crescent,** an arc of land from the Mediterranean Sea to the Persian Gulf. Because this land had rich soil and abundant crops, it was able to sustain an early civilization.

Farming in ancient Mesopotamia could be done only when people controlled the flow of the rivers. Irrigation and drainage ditches—part of a large-scale system of water control—made it possible to grow crops on a regular basis. The resulting abundance of food enabled large numbers of people to live together in cities.

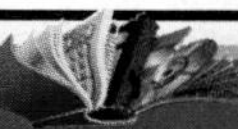

SECTION RESOURCES

Reproducible Masters
- Reproducible Lesson Plan 1–2
- Daily Lecture and Discussion Notes 1–2
- Guided Reading Activity 1–2
- Section Quiz 1–2
- Reading Essentials and Study Guide 1–2

Transparencies
- Daily Focus Skills Transparency 1–2

Multimedia
- Interactive Tutor Self-Assessment CD-ROM
- ExamView® Pro Testmaker CD-ROM
- Presentation Plus! CD-ROM

The first states in Mesopotamia were **city-states** (cities that came to have political and economic control over the surrounding countryside). They were created by the Sumerians, a people whose origin remains a mystery. By 3000 B.C., the Sumerians had established a number of independent city-states in southern Mesopotamia, including Eridu, Ur, and Uruk.

The most prominent building in a Sumerian city was the temple dedicated to the chief god or goddess of the city. The Sumerians believed that gods and goddesses owned the cities. The people devoted much of their wealth to building temples, as well as elaborate houses for the priests and priestesses who served the gods.

Priests and priestesses, who supervised the temples and their property, had a great deal of power. Eventually, however, ruling power passed into the hands of kings. Kings led armies and organized workers for the irrigation projects on which Mesopotamian farming depended.

Reading Check **Explaining** What role did geography play in the development of Mesopotamian civilization?

Empires in Ancient Mesopotamia

As the number of Sumerian city-states grew and the city-states expanded, new conflicts arose. City-state fought city-state for control of land and water. Located on the flat land of Mesopotamia, the Sumerian city-states were also open to invasion by other groups.

To the north of the Sumerian city-states were the Akkadians (uh•KAY•dee•uhnz). Around 2340 B.C., **Sargon,** leader of the Akkadians, overran the Sumerian city-states and set up the first empire in world history. An **empire** is a large political unit or state, usually under a single leader, that controls many peoples or territories. Empires are often easy to create but difficult to maintain. The rise and fall of empires is an important part of history.

Attacks from neighboring hill peoples eventually caused the Akkadian Empire to fall. Its end by 2100 B.C. brought a return to warring city-states. Not until 1792 B.C. did a new empire come to control much of Mesopotamia. Leadership came from Babylon, a city-state south of Akkad, where **Hammurabi** (HA•muh•RAH•bee) came to power. He gained control of Sumer and Akkad, thus creating a new Mesopotamian kingdom. As ruler, Hammurabi built temples, encouraged trade, and brought an economic revival to his land. After his death in 1750 B.C., however, Hammurabi's empire fell to new invaders.

Reading Check **Evaluating** Why was it so easy for Sargon and his army to invade the Sumerian city-states?

The Royal Standard of Ur is a box, created about 2700 B.C., that depicts different Sumerian scenes. This panel shows a royal celebration following a military victory.

2 TEACH

Reading Check

Answer: The land between the two rivers was filled with rich soil, which made growing abundant crops and sustaining a civilization possible.

Daily Lecture and Discussion Notes 1–2

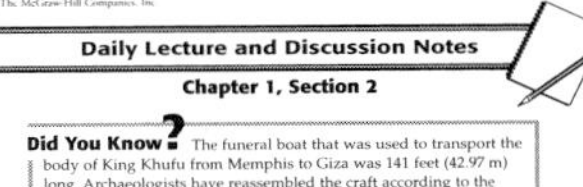

Daily Lecture and Discussion Notes

Chapter 1, Section 2

Did You Know? The funeral boat that was used to transport the body of King Khufu from Memphis to Giza was 141 feet (42.97 m) long. Archaeologists have reassembled the craft according to the shipwright's original instructions, which were discovered with the craft's pieces next to Khufu's tomb.

I. The City-States of Ancient Mesopotamia *(pages 24–25)*

A. The valley between the **Tigris** and **Euphrates Rivers** is part of the **Fertile Crescent,** an arc of land extending from the Mediterranean Sea to the Persian Gulf.

B. Through a large-scale system of water control, crops could be grown on a regular basis, enabling large numbers of people to live together in cities.

C. The first **city-states** in Mesopotamia were created by the Sumerians. These states controlled the surrounding countryside politically and economically.

D. The most prominent building in a Sumerian city was the temple. The people devoted much of their wealth to building temples and providing elaborate houses for the priests and priestesses.

E. Power passed from religious leaders to kings. Kings led armies and organized the water control projects necessary to sustain farming.

Discussion Question

The prominent temples and the money devoted to religious concerns suggest that religion was an important part of Sumerian life. What does today's architecture suggest is important to life in the United States. *(Schools and universities are prominent in some communities. In other communities, sports and entertainment venues dominate.)*

II. Empires in Ancient Mesopotamia *(page 25)*

A. City-states fought for control of land and water. The flat land of Mesopotamia encouraged invasion by outside groups.

B. **Sargon,** leader of the Akkadians, overran the Sumerian city-states in 2340 B.C. and set up the first empire in history.

C. An **empire** is a large political unit that controls many peoples and territories.

D. In 1792 B.C., **Hammurabi** of Babylon established a new empire over much of Akkad and Sumeria.

turn

4

Reading Check

Answer: land was flat, providing no geographical barriers against invasion

Enrich

Have students research more details about Sumerian cities and then list the differences between Sumerian cities and contemporary cities. *(Differences might include: today's cities have no outer walls, few buildings are made of mud bricks, religious buildings are not necessarily the most prominent in the city, and religious officials are not the political leaders.)* Ask students to explain why these differences exist. **L2**

EXTENDING THE CONTENT

Sumerian Achievements Our modern system of mathematics comes directly from developments in mathematics in ancient Mesopotamia. Mathematics grew out of the need for record keeping for administrative and trade purposes. Four thousand years ago, Babylonians were using multiplication tables, square roots, reciprocals, and linear and quadratic equations like those used in our modern system of mathematics. The Babylonians also developed a number system based upon sixty that we still use today for telling time.

CHAPTER 1
Section 2, 24–34

Geography Skills

Answers:
1. Zagros Mountains
2. southeast; north

TURNING POINT

The Code of Hammurabi is the most complete law code known from ancient civilization.

ABCNEWS INTERACTIVE™

Turning Points in World History
The ABC News videotape includes a segment on the Code of Hammurabi.

Guided Reading Activity 1–2

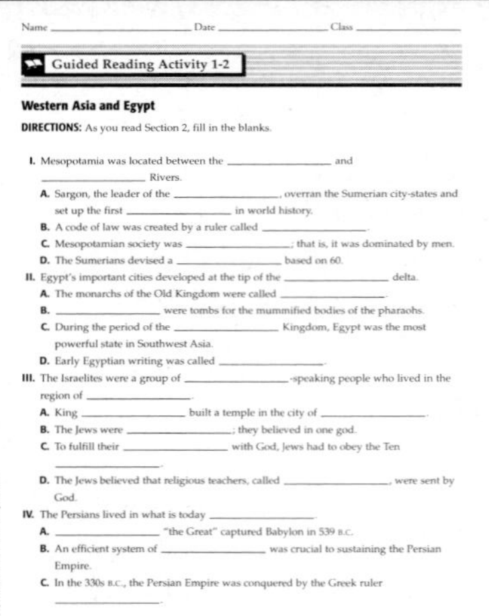
Name ______ Date ______ Class ______

Guided Reading Activity 1-2

Western Asia and Egypt

DIRECTIONS: As you read Section 2, fill in the blanks.

I. Mesopotamia was located between the ______ and ______ Rivers.
   - A. Sargon, the leader of the ______, overran the Sumerian city-states and set up the first ______ in world history.
   - B. A code of law was created by a ruler called ______.
   - C. Mesopotamian society was ______; that is, it was dominated by men.
   - D. The Sumerians devised a ______ based on 60.

II. Egypt's important cities developed at the tip of the ______ delta.
   - A. The monarchs of the Old Kingdom were called ______.
   - B. ______ were tombs for the mummified bodies of the pharaohs.
   - C. During the period of the ______ Kingdom, Egypt was the most powerful state in Southwest Asia.
   - D. Early Egyptian writing was called ______.

III. The Israelites were a group of ______-speaking people who lived in the region of ______.
   - A. King ______ built a temple in the city of ______.
   - B. The Jews were ______; they believed in one god.
   - C. To fulfill their ______ with God, Jews had to obey the Ten ______.
   - D. The Jews believed that religious teachers, called ______, were sent by God.

IV. The Persians lived in what is today ______.
   - A. ______ "the Great" captured Babylon in 539 B.C.
   - B. An efficient system of ______ was crucial to sustaining the Persian Empire.
   - C. In the 330s B.C., the Persian Empire was conquered by the Greek ruler ______.

NATIONAL GEOGRAPHIC Ancient Mesopotamia

Fertile Crescent
Direction of flow

Lambert Azimuthal Equal-Area projection

Geography Skills

Several important cultures and civilizations developed in Mesopotamia.

1. **Interpreting Maps** Identify the mountain range closest to where the Tigris and Euphrates Rivers originate.
2. **Applying Geography Skills** In which direction do the Tigris and Euphrates Rivers flow? In which direction does the Nile flow?

The Code of Hammurabi

TURNING POINT **Hammurabi is remembered for his law code, a collection of 282 laws. Many of the code's ideas found their way into Israelite civilization.**

The **Code of Hammurabi** was based on a system of strict justice. Penalties for criminal offenses were severe, and they varied according to the social class of the victim. A crime against a member of the upper class (a noble) by a member of the lower class (a commoner) was punished more severely than the same offense against a member of the lower class. The principle of retaliation ("an eye for an eye, tooth for a tooth") was a fundamental part of this system of justice.

The law code encouraged the proper performance of work with what could be called consumer protection laws. Builders were held responsible for the buildings they constructed. If a house collapsed and caused the death of the owner, the builder was put to death. If the collapse caused the death of the son of the owner, the son of the builder was put to death. If goods were destroyed, they had to be replaced and the house rebuilt at the builder's expense.

The largest category of laws in the Code of Hammurabi focused on marriage and the family. Parents

COOPERATIVE LEARNING ACTIVITY

Facilitating a Discussion Divide students into groups of two. Ask them to rewrite (in modern English) the laws from the Code of Hammurabi printed on page 35. Then ask students to consider present-day American laws regarding similar crimes. Ask students to identify the American punishments for similar crimes. Choose student groups to share their English translations and their lists of punishments in a class discussion. Compare and contrast Hammurabi's laws and punishments with present-day laws and punishments. For further discussion, ask the class to consider the ways that Hammurabi's laws assign value to human beings. Do such distinctions occur in American laws? **L1**

arranged marriages for their children. After marriage, the two parties signed a marriage contract. Without a contract, no one was considered legally married.

Society in ancient Mesopotamia was **patriarchal**—that is, Mesopotamian society was dominated by men. Hammurabi's code makes it clear that women had far fewer privileges and rights in marriage than did men.

A woman's place was in the home. If she failed to fulfill her duties, her husband had legal grounds for divorce. If a wife was not able to bear children or tried to leave home to engage in business, her husband could divorce her. A wife who was a "gadabout . . . neglecting her house [and] humiliating her husband," could be drowned.

Fathers ruled their children as well as their wives. Obedience was expected: "If a son has struck his father, he shall cut off his hand." If a son committed a serious enough offense, his father could disinherit him. Obviously, Hammurabi's law code covered almost every aspect of people's lives.

Reading Check **Identifying** Identify at least three aspects of Mesopotamian society as revealed by the Code of Hammurabi.

The Creativity of the Sumerians

The Sumerians invented the oldest writing system. Historians also credit them with many technological innovations.

Writing Around 3000 B.C., the Sumerians created a **cuneiform** ("wedge-shaped") system of writing. Using a reed stylus (a tool for writing), they made wedge-shaped impressions on clay tablets, which were then baked or dried in the sun. Once dried, these tablets lasted a very long time. Several hundred thousand tablets have been found. They have been a valuable source of information for modern scholars.

Writing was important because it allowed a society to keep records and to pass along knowledge from person to person and generation to generation. Writing also made it possible for people to communicate ideas in new ways. This is especially evident in *The Epic of Gilgamesh*, a Mesopotamian poem that records the exploits of a legendary king named Gilgamesh.

Technology The Sumerians also invented several tools and devices that made daily life easier and more productive. They developed the wagon wheel, for example, to help transport people and goods from place to place. The potter's wheel to shape containers, the sundial to keep time, and the arch used in construction are other examples of Sumerian technology. The Sumerians were the first to make bronze out of copper and tin, creating finely crafted metalwork.

The Sumerians also made outstanding achievements in mathematics and astronomy. In math, they devised a number system based on 60. Geometry was used to measure fields and to erect buildings. In astronomy, the Sumerians charted the heavenly constellations. A quick glance at your watch and its division into 60 minutes in an hour should remind you of our debt to the Sumerians.

Reading Check **Identifying** Name two major inventions of the Sumerians and tell how those inventions affect our lives today.

The Course of Egyptian History

The **Nile** is a unique river, beginning in the heart of Africa and coursing northward for more than 4,000 miles (6,436 km). It is the longest river in the world. Before it empties into the Mediterranean, the Nile splits into two major branches. This split forms a triangular territory, the delta. The Nile Delta is called **Lower Egypt;** the land upstream, to the south, is called **Upper Egypt.** Egypt's important cities developed at the tip of the delta, the point at which the Nile divides.

Egyptian history can be divided into three major periods: the Old Kingdom, the Middle Kingdom, and the New Kingdom. These were periods of long-term stability marked by strong leadership, freedom from invasion, the building of temples and pyramids, and considerable intellectual and cultural activity. Between the periods of stability were ages of political chaos and invasion, known as the Intermediate periods.

The history of Egypt begins around 3100 B.C., when **Menes** (MEE•NEEZ) the king united the villages of Upper and Lower Egypt into a single kingdom and created the first Egyptian royal dynasty. A **dynasty** is a family of rulers whose right to rule is passed on within the family.

The Old Kingdom The Old Kingdom, which lasted from around 2700 to 2200 B.C., was an age of prosperity and splendor. Like the kings of the Sumerian city-states, the monarchs of the Old Kingdom were powerful rulers over a unified state. Among the various titles of Egyptian monarchs, that of pharaoh (originally meaning "great house" or "palace") eventually became the most common.

Kingship was a divine institution in ancient Egypt and formed part of a universal cosmic order: "What

Reading Check

Answer: Answers may include: severe penalties for criminal offenses; different social classes not treated the same under the law; consumers protected against shoddy workmanship; regulated marriage; patriarchal society; women had few rights and privileges.

Writing Activity

Poetry has long been used to express human emotion and to describe landscapes as well as events. Write the following poem on the chalkboard. Have students read the poem and rewrite it in their own words. Ask students to capture the emotions expressed by the Mesopotamian writer. Finally, have students illustrate their poems and ask volunteers to share their poems and illustrations with the class. **L2**

"The rampant flood which no man can oppose,
Which shakes the heavens and causes earth to tremble,
In an appalling blanket folds mother and child,
And drowns the harvest in its time of ripeness."

Reading Check

Answer: Answers may include: writing—we still use writing as a major means of communication; the wagon wheel—much of our transportation is still dependent upon vehicles with wheels; a number system based on 60—we still use this system for minutes and seconds.

CRITICAL THINKING ACTIVITY

Explaining Ask students to explain why writing was so important to the development of civilization. Point out that because writing was held in high esteem, scribes—those who recorded information by writing—were elevated to important government positions. Scribes were usually children of the wealthy and privileged class, and they were the only ones given the opportunity to learn how to read and write. These skills were unique and ensured that scribes would be indispensable to the government. Remind students that the craft of the scribe—writing on clay tablets and papyrus—was not easy, but that scribes were able to perfect this craft. **L2**

 **History**

Answer: Medical investigators might be able to learn about elements of Egyptian life such as the quality of medical and dental care at the time and the diets of the day. Artifacts found with the mummy might indicate what Egyptians thought was important in the afterlife, as well as what types of skills and craftsmanship were practiced at the time.

CURRICULUM CONNECTION

Technology In 1987, scientists from Egypt and the United States used advanced technology to view the remains of an ancient Egyptian boat that had been sealed inside a chamber for 4,600 years. To see inside without excavating and damaging the chamber, the scientists employed a special drill with technology invented for moon exploration. After drilling through the outer rock, they inserted a miniature video camera.

Have students research other techniques used to handle and explore ancient Egyptian remains and report them to the class. **L2**

Enrich

Have students research the Great Pyramid built for King Khufu. Many pyramids had two temples that were connected by a long stone passageway. Funeral ceremonies were performed in these temples. **Ask: Why did the Egyptians build pyramids for their kings?** *(They built the pyramids to honor the kings, believed to be gods, and to provide them with an eternal place of rest.)*

Picturing **History**

The mummy of Ramses the Great has remained intact for 3,000 years. Ramses, who ruled Egypt from 1279 to 1213 B.C., was nearly 90 when he died. What might medical investigators discover about Egyptian life from this mummy?

is the king of Upper and Lower Egypt? He is a god by whose dealings one lives, the father and mother of all men, alone by himself, without an equal." In obeying their pharaoh, subjects believed that they were helping to maintain a stable world order.

The Pyramids One of the great achievements of Egyptian civilization, the building of pyramids, occurred in the time of the Old Kingdom. Pyramids were built as part of a larger complex of buildings dedicated to the dead—in effect, a city of the dead. The area included several structures: a large pyramid for the pharaoh's burial; smaller pyramids for his family; and several mastabas, rectangular structures with flat roofs used as tombs for the pharaoh's officials.

To preserve the physical body after death, the Egyptians practiced mummification, a process of slowly drying a dead body to prevent it from rotting. This process took place in workshops run by priests, primarily for the wealthy families who could afford it. Workers first removed the liver, lungs, stomach, and intestines and placed them in four special jars that were put in the tomb with the mummy. The priests also removed the brain by extracting it through the nose. They then covered the corpse with a natural salt that absorbed the body's water. Later, they filled the body with spices and wrapped it with layers of linen soaked in resin. At the end of the process, which took about 70 days, a lifelike mask was placed over the head and shoulders of the mummy. The mummy was then sealed in a case and placed in its tomb.

Pyramids were tombs for the mummified bodies of pharaohs and their families. The largest and most magnificent of all the pyramids was built under King Khufu (KOO•FOO). Constructed at Giza around 2540 B.C., the famous Great Pyramid of King Khufu covers 13 acres (5.3 ha), measures 756 feet (230 m) at each side of its base, and stands 481 feet (147 m) high.

Guarding the Great Pyramid at Giza is a huge statue carved from rock, known as the Great Sphinx. This colossal statue is 240 feet (73 m) long and 66 feet (20 m) high. It has the body of a lion and a human head. The head is believed by many to be a likeness of Khufu's son Khafre, who ordered the statue's construction.

The Middle Kingdom The Old Kingdom's collapse was followed by a period of chaos that lasted about 150 years. Eventually, a new royal dynasty gained control of all Egypt and began the Middle Kingdom, a period of stability lasting from about 2050 to 1652 B.C. Egyptians later portrayed the Middle Kingdom as a golden age—an age of stability.

One feature of the Middle Kingdom was a new concern of the pharaohs for the people. Pharaohs of the Middle Kingdom undertook a number of helpful projects. The draining of swampland in the Nile Delta provided thousands of acres of new farmland.

EXTENDING THE CONTENT

The Pyramids The mystery of the pyramids has intrigued historians throughout the ages. Some archaeologists contend that, given the technology of the ancient Egyptians, they could not have moved the blocks required to build the Great Pyramids in one person's lifetime. One intriguing theory about the building of the pyramids is that the giant blocks of stone were not carved at all, but rather were poured from a very sophisticated concrete-like, limestone substance. This would explain the amazing similarity among all of the blocks and their incredibly close fit, and would more realistically fit the ancient Greek historian Herodotus's statement that it took twenty years to complete the pyramids.

The digging of a canal to connect the Nile to the Red Sea aided trade and transportation.

The New Kingdom The Middle Kingdom came to an end around 1652 B.C. with the invasion of Egypt by a group of people from western Asia known to the Egyptians as the Hyksos (HIK•SAHS). The Hyksos used horse-drawn war chariots and overwhelmed the Egyptian soldiers, who fought from donkey carts.

For almost a hundred years, the Hyksos ruled much of Egypt. The conquered Egyptians learned a great deal, however, from their conquerors. From the Hyksos, the Egyptians learned to use bronze in the making of their farming tools and their weapons. The Egyptians also mastered many of the military skills of the Hyksos, especially the use of horse-drawn war chariots.

Eventually, a new dynasty of pharaohs used the new weapons to drive out the Hyksos and reunite Egypt. The New Kingdom was established and lasted from approximately 1567 to 1085 B.C. This reunification launched the Egyptians along a new militaristic path. During the period of the New Kingdom, Egypt created an empire and became the most powerful state in Southwest Asia.

Massive wealth boosted the power of the New Kingdom pharaohs. The Egyptian rulers showed their wealth by building new temples. Hatshepsut—the first woman to become pharaoh—built a great temple at Deir el Bahri, near Thebes.

The New Kingdom was not without troubles, however. New invasions in the thirteenth century B.C. by the "Sea Peoples," as Egyptians called them, drove the Egyptians back within their old frontiers and ended the Egyptian Empire. The New Kingdom itself collapsed in 1085 B.C.

The Egyptians learned much, including the use of war chariots, from the Hyksos.

People In History

Hatshepsut
Ruled 1503–1482 B.C.
Egyptian pharaoh

Hatshepsut was the daughter of the pharaoh Thutmose I. She married her half-brother, who became the pharaoh Thutmose II. When he died, Hatshepsut assumed the full power of pharaoh. Statues show Hatshepsut clothed and bearded as a king would be. She was addressed as "His Majesty."

Hatshepsut's reign was a prosperous one. She is best known for the temple dedicated to herself at Deir el Bahri on the west bank of the Nile at Thebes. One of the inscriptions she had placed there reads: "Now my heart turns to and fro, in thinking what will the people say, they who shall see my monument in later years, and shall speak of what I have done."

For the next thousand years, Egypt was dominated by Libyans, Nubians, Persians, and finally Macedonians after the conquest of Alexander the Great (see Chapter 2). In the first century B.C., the pharaoh Cleopatra VII tried to reestablish Egypt's independence. However, her involvement with Rome led to her defeat and suicide, and Egypt became a province in Rome's mighty empire.

Reading Check **Contrasting** What were the major differences between the Old Kingdom, the Middle Kingdom, and the New Kingdom?

Society in Ancient Egypt

Over a period of thousands of years, Egyptian society maintained a simple structure. It was organized like a pyramid, with the god-king at the top. The pharaoh was surrounded by an upper class of nobles and priests, who joined in the elaborate rituals of the pharaoh's life. The members of this ruling class ran the government and managed their own landed estates. *(See page 772 to read excerpts from Vizier Ptahhotep's* An Egyptian Father's Advice to His Son *in the Primary Sources Library.)*

Below the upper class were merchants, artisans, scribes, and tax collectors. Merchants carried on an active trade up and down the Nile, as well as in town and village markets. Egyptian artisans made an

3 ASSESS

Assign Section 2 Assessment as homework or as an in-class activity.

Have students use **Interactive Tutor Self-Assessment CD-ROM.**

Who?What?Where?When?

Abu Simbel One of the impressive temple sites of Ramses II is Abu Simbel, located near the Nile River about 762 miles (1,226 km) south of Cairo. In the 1960s, the High Dam at Aswan would have flooded the site, but 51 countries contributed funds to move the temples block by block to higher ground further inland.

Enrich

Write this quotation from the Persian poet Sadi on the chalkboard. "(A King) requires a prudent and able man." Discuss the meaning of this quotation and how it applies to the pharaohs. Lead the class in a discussion to consider how choosing wise people to help govern can ensure good government. **L1**

Reading Check

Answer: Old Kingdom: age of prosperity and splendor, built pyramids; Middle Kingdom: golden age of stability, pharaohs concerned about people; New Kingdom: militaristic, created an empire, built temples

COOPERATIVE LEARNING ACTIVITY

Researching a Report Just as the pharaohs built pyramids to symbolize their greatness and power, other rulers, both secular and religious, have built shrines to honor themselves. Divide students into groups. Have individual students complete a portion of the following research. Each group will be responsible for a two-page paper compiling the results of the group's research. Have students identify shrines or monuments that other rulers have built. Ask students to compare these monuments and their purposes to the pyramids. Then have students identify monuments in their own towns. Are there any local historical monuments that pay homage to certain Americans? If so, have students compare them with the pyramids. **L3**

For grading this activity, refer to the ***Performance Assessment Activities*** booklet.

Chart *Skills*

Answers:
1. Students will create maps comparing Mesopotamia and Egypt.
2. Mesopotamian city-states had no natural defenses; Egypt had natural defenses in every direction.

Reading Check

Answer: At the top was the ruling class of pharaohs, nobles, and priests. This class ran the government and managed landed estates, providing much of Egypt's wealth. Below this class was a middle class of merchants, artisans, scribes, and tax collectors. These people obtained products through trade or created goods. At the bottom was a large peasant class. They farmed the land and provided military service and forced labor for building projects.

Enrich

Ask students to give examples of major mathematical and scientific discoveries and technological innovations that occurred in Mesopotamian and Egyptian civilizations. Have students describe the changes produced by these discoveries and innovations. **L2**

Reading Check

Answer: hieroglyphics: complex, used both pictures and more abstract forms for writing on temple walls and in tombs; hieratic: highly simplified version of hieroglyphics, used for the general needs of everyday life

Comparing Life in Mesopotamia and Egypt

	Mesopotamia	Egypt
Geography	Fertile Crescent (Southwest Asia)	Africa
Rivers	Tigris and Euphrates	Nile
Natural Barriers	Flat plains	Deserts, seas, cataracts
Religion	Polytheistic	Polytheistic
Government	City-states; theocracy; large bureaucracy; kings ruled	Rural villages; dynasties; divine kings ruled
Social Structure	Nobles, commoners, slaves	Upper classes, merchants, artisans, peasants
Economy	Farming and trade	Farming and trade
Written Language	Cuneiform	Hieroglyphics

Chart *Skills*

Ancient civilizations thrived in both Mesopotamia and Egypt.

1. **Making Comparisons** Create a map of Mesopotamia and Egypt. Develop icons to illustrate the differences and similarities in the cultures.
2. **Evaluating** How did geographical differences influence the development of these cultures?

incredible variety of well-built, beautiful goods: stone dishes; painted boxes; wooden furniture; gold, silver, and copper tools and containers; and linen clothes.

By far, the largest number of people in Egypt simply worked the land. In theory, the pharaoh owned all the land but granted portions of it to the subjects. Most of the lower classes were peasants who farmed the land of these estates. They paid taxes in the form of crops to the pharaoh, nobles, and priests; lived in small villages or towns; and provided military service and forced labor for building projects.

Reading Check **Summarizing** List the social classes of ancient Egypt and identify their roles.

Writing, Art, and Science

Writing in Egypt emerged around 3000 B.C. The Greeks later called this earliest Egyptian writing **hieroglyphics**, meaning "priest-carvings" or "sacred writings." The hieroglyphic system of writing, which used both pictures and more abstract forms, was complex. Learning and practicing it took much time and skill. Hieroglyphic script was used for writing on temple walls and in tombs. A highly simplified version of hieroglyphics, known as hieratic script, came into being. It used the same principles as hieroglyphic writing, but the drawings were simplified by using dashes, strokes, and curves to represent them. Hieratic script was used for business transactions, record keeping, and the general needs of daily life. Egyptian hieroglyphs were at first carved in stone. Later, hieratic script was written on papyrus, a paper made from the papyrus reed that grew along the Nile.

Pyramids, temples, and other monuments bear witness to the architectural and artistic achievements of the Egyptians. Artists and sculptors were expected to follow particular formulas in style. This gave Egyptian art a distinctive look for thousands of years. For example, the human body was often portrayed as a combination of profile, semiprofile, and frontal view to accurately represent each part.

Egyptians also made advances in mathematics and science. Mathematics helped them in building their massive monuments. Egyptians were able to calculate area and volume and used geometry to survey flooded land. The Egyptians developed an accurate 365-day calendar by basing their year not only on the movements of the moon, but also the bright star Sirius. Egyptians also had medical expertise. Archaeologists have recovered directions from Egyptian doctors for treating wounds and diseases.

Reading Check **Contrasting** What are the differences between hieroglyphics and hieratic script?

New Centers of Civilization: The Israelites

By 1500 B.C., much of the creative impulse of the Mesopotamian and Egyptian civilizations was beginning to decline. By 1200 B.C., a power vacuum had emerged in western Asia that allowed a number of small states to emerge and flourish. The Israelites were one of these peoples. Though the Israelites did not create an empire, their religion, **Judaism**, flourished as a world religion and later influenced the religions of Christianity and Islam.

EXTENDING THE CONTENT

The Rosetta Stone For centuries, scholars were unable to understand ancient Egyptian hieroglyphics. Then, in A.D. 1799, a stone slab dating to the 200s B.C. was found near the town of Rosetta in Egypt. The stone contained both Greek and ancient Egyptian writing. In 1822, Jean-François Champollion realized that the Greek and Egyptian writing on the stone matched. By using his knowledge of Greek, Champollion was able to decipher the Egyptian hieroglyphics and read the entire stone. The Rosetta Stone can be seen today at the British Museum in London.

The "Children of Israel" The Israelites were a group of Semitic-speaking people. Much of the history and the religious beliefs of the Israelites were eventually recorded in written form in the Hebrew Bible, parts of which are known to Christians as the Old Testament. According to their history, the Israelites migrated from Mesopotamia to the land that they referred to as Canaan. They followed a lifestyle based on grazing flocks and herds rather than on farming. Then, because of drought, the Israelites migrated to Egypt, where they were enslaved until a leader named Moses led them out of Egypt. They wandered for many years in the desert of the Sinai Peninsula until they returned to Canaan.

Recent interpretations of archaeological evidence sometimes contradict the details of the biblical account. What is generally agreed, however, is that between 1200 and 1000 B.C., the Israelites emerged as a distinct group of people, organized in tribes, who established a united kingdom known as Israel.

By the time of **King Solomon,** who ruled from about 970 to 930 B.C., the Israelites had established control over much of Canaan and had made **Jerusalem** into the capital of Israel. Solomon greatly strengthened royal power. He expanded the government and army and encouraged trade. Solomon is best known for building a temple in the city of Jerusalem. The Israelites viewed the temple as the symbolic center of their religion and of the Israelite kingdom itself. Under Solomon, ancient Israel was at the height of its power.

King Solomon

After Solomon's death, tension between the northern and southern Israelite tribes led to the creation of two separate kingdoms—a northern kingdom of Israel and a southern kingdom of Judah. Both kingdoms eventually fell to the large empires of the Assyrians and Babylonians. However, the people of Judah survived, eventually becoming known as the Jews and giving their name to Judaism. It became a stateless religion based on the belief that God was not fixed to one particular land but instead was creator and lord of the whole world.

CONNECTIONS Past To Present

Conflict in Palestine

Conflict in Southwest Asia has a long history. When the Israelites entered Canaan, around 1220 B.C., other peoples were already settled there. One of these peoples was the Philistines. For over two centuries, Israelites and Philistines fought for control.

By 1020 B.C., the Israelites found themselves on the verge of being conquered by the Philistines. The Israelites decided to give up their loose tribal organization, choosing to unite behind one of their members—Saul—as king.

At first, Saul and the small army he organized were successful. Around 1000 B.C., however, when they dared to meet the Philistines on an open plain, Saul and his army were defeated.

David, the next king of the Israelites, defeated the Philistines and established control over much of Canaan. Although the Israelites eventually would be conquered and scattered, Canaan (later called Palestine) remained the Promised Land in the minds of many Jews.

In 1948, the independent Jewish state of Israel was established in part of Palestine. About 90 percent of the people in Palestine were Arabs who were not eager to be governed by the Israelis. Arab neighbors of the new state were outraged. In 1964, an Arab organization called the Palestine Liberation Organization was founded to bring about an independent Arab state of Palestine. Conflict between Arabs and Israelis over Palestine continues to this day.

▲ ***Conflict in the Middle East***

Comparing Past and Present

Research the steps that have been taken to reach a settlement between the Israelis and Palestinian Arabs over the past five years. What actions have been the most successful? What are the most significant reasons that a lasting peace still does not exist?

Answers: Answers will vary depending on current events.

CURRICULUM CONNECTION

Geography Have students look at a map of Canaan. The Canaanites settled in Canaan about 3000 B.C. Before the Israelites conquered them in about 1200 B.C., some Canaanites settled along the coast and became known as Phoenicians. **Ask: Where was Canaan in relation to Egypt and Babylon?** *(Canaan lay northeast of Egypt and west of Babylon.)* **L1**

Enrich

Ask students to write descriptions of both *nomadic* and *nonnomadic* people. Have volunteers share their descriptions aloud. During a class discussion, determine the best descriptions and work with the class to develop them further. Once you have a final description for each term, ask students to write a one-page essay about which type of skills were most influential in the development of ancient civilizations. Ask students to support their opinions with logic and reason. **L2**

MEETING INDIVIDUAL NEEDS

English Language Learners Organize students with limited English proficiency into two groups. Have one group prepare a poster on King David and the other a poster on King Solomon. Explain that each poster should summarize information about the king. Have students work together to choose the information and then decide on a format for presenting it on the poster. Encourage the students to include copies of art depicting "their" king. Pair students from the two groups and have them describe their posters. **L1** ELL

Refer to ***Inclusion for the High School Social Studies Classroom Strategies and Activities*** in the TCR.

Critical Thinking

Jewish rulers did not claim divine right nor did they ever claim to be descended from God. Ask students how this made the Jewish kingdom and kings different from civilizations that believed their rulers to be divine. Ask students to describe and contrast the different civic roles of people living in cultures where rulers are divine and in cultures where rulers are not divine. **L2**

Section Quiz 1–2

Name ______________ Date ________ Class ______

Chapter 1 Score

Section Quiz 1-2

DIRECTIONS: Matching Match each item in Column A with an item in Column B. Write the correct letters in the blanks. *(10 points each)*

Column A	Column B
____ 1. Sumerian writing system	A. hieroglyphics
____ 2. family of rulers whose right to rule is passed on within the family	B. communication system
____ 3. early Egyptian writing that means "priest-carvings"	C. dynasty
____ 4. belief in one god	D. cuneiform
____ 5. sustained the Persian Empire	E. monotheism

DIRECTIONS: Multiple Choice In the blank, write the letter of the choice that best completes the statement or answers the question. *(10 points each)*

____ 6. The most famous piece of Mesopotamian literature is
A. *The Scribe.* C. *The Epic of Gilgamesh.*
B. *The Code of Hammurabi.* D. *The Ziggurat.*

____ 7. The Egyptians learned about making bronze tools and using chariots from the
A. Hyksos. C. "Sea Peoples."
B. Sumerians. D. Assyrians.

____ 8. The Nile Delta is called
A. the Cradle of Civilization.
B. Lower Egypt.
C. Upper Egypt.
D. the Fertile Crescent.

____ 9. The people known as the Israelites
A. were a major factor in the politics of the Mediterranean area.
B. used iron weapons to establish an empire.
C. invented an alphabet of 22 characters representing sounds.
D. were a distinct group of tribes who established a united kingdom.

____ 10. The Persian ruler Cyrus was called "the Great" because he
A. showed no mercy to enemies.
B. thought Persian culture was superior to others.
C. was a large man.
D. showed wisdom and compassion.

2 *Glencoe World History—Modern Times*

Enrich

Have students compare the Ten Commandments that God gave the Jewish people, listed on this page, with the laws from Hammurabi's code on page 35. Ask students how they are similar. In what ways are they different? **L2**

The Spiritual Dimensions of Israel According to Jewish beliefs, there is but one God, called Yahweh (YAH•WAY), the creator of the world and everything in it. In the Jewish view, God ruled the world; all peoples were his servants, whether they knew it or not. God had created nature but was not in nature. The stars, moon, rivers, wind, and other natural phenomena were not gods, as other ancient peoples believed, but God's handiwork. All of God's creations could be admired for their awesome beauty, but not worshipped as gods.

This powerful creator, however, was not removed from the life he had created. God was just and good, and he expected goodness from his people. If they did not obey his will, they would be punished. However, God was also full of mercy and love: "The Lord is gracious and compassionate, slow to anger and rich in love. The Lord is good to all; he has compassion on all he has made." Each person could have a personal relationship with this powerful being.

The Jews were **monotheistic;** they believed in one God. The covenant, law, and prophets were three aspects of the Jewish religious tradition. The Jews believed that during their exodus from Egypt, when Moses led his people out of bondage into the promised land, God made a covenant, or contract, with them. In the covenant, Yahweh promised guidance in return for the people's obedience to God's will stated in the Ten Commandments. Yahweh revealed these laws to Moses on Mount Sinai.

The Jews believed that certain religious teachers, called prophets, were sent by God to serve as his voice to his people. Isaiah, one of the prophets, made clear the prophets' belief that unjust actions by the people would bring God's punishment:

> "The Lord enters into judgment against the elders and leaders of his people: 'It is you who have ruined my vineyard; the plunder from the poor is in your houses. What do you mean by crushing my people and grinding the faces of the poor?' declares the Lord, the Lord Almighty. The Lord says, 'The women of Zion are haughty . . . with ornaments jingling on their ankles. Therefore the Lord will bring sores on the heads of the women of Zion; the Lord will make their scalps bald. . . . Instead of fragrance there will be a stench; . . . instead of fine clothing, sackcloth; instead of beauty, branding. Your men will fall by the sword, your warriors in battle. The gates of Zion will lament and mourn; destitute, she will sit on the ground.'"

The age of prophecy lasted from the eleventh to the fifth centuries B.C. during the time when the people of Judah and Israel faced threats or endured conquests by powerful neighbors. The prophets declared that faithlessness to God would bring punishment and catastrophe, but that turning from evil would brings God's mercy.

From the prophets came new concepts that enriched the Jewish tradition. The prophets embraced a concern for all humanity. All nations would someday come to the God of Israel. This vision included the end of war and the establishment of peace for all the nations of the world. In the words of the prophet Isaiah:

> "He will judge between the nations and will settle disputes for many people. They will beat their swords into plowshares and their spears into pruning hooks. Nation will not take up sword against nation, nor will they train for war anymore."

The prophets also cried out against social injustice. They condemned the rich for causing the poor to suffer. They denounced luxuries as worthless, and they threatened Israel with prophecies of dire punishments for these sins. They said that God's command was to live justly, share with one's neighbors, care for the poor and the unfortunate, and act with compassion.

Judaism was unique among the religions of western Asia and Egypt. The most dramatic difference was the Jewish belief that there is only one God for all

The Ten Commandments

1. I am the Lord thy God . . . . Thou shalt have no other gods before me.
2. Thou shalt not make unto thee any graven image . . . .
3. Thou shalt not take the name of the Lord thy God in vain . . . .
4. Remember the Sabbath day, to keep it holy.
5. Honor thy father and thy mother . . . .
6. Thou shalt not kill.
7. Thou shalt not commit adultery.
8. Thou shalt not steal.
9. Thou shalt not bear false witness against thy neighbor.
10. Thou shalt not covet . . . anything that is thy neighbor's.

Source: Exodus 20:1–17

INTERDISCIPLINARY CONNECTIONS ACTIVITY

Religion Many of the customs and beliefs we have today have filtered into our lives from early civilizations. This is true of our religious heritage. For example, Judaism, which developed from Hebrew monotheism, influenced both Christianity and Islam. Ask students to summarize the historical origins and central ideas of Judaism. Then ask students to research and summarize the spread of Judaism from its beginnings through modern times. Also have students identify examples of the ways in which Judaism has influenced historic and contemporary world events. **L2**

NATIONAL GEOGRAPHIC **Persian Empire, 500 B.C.**

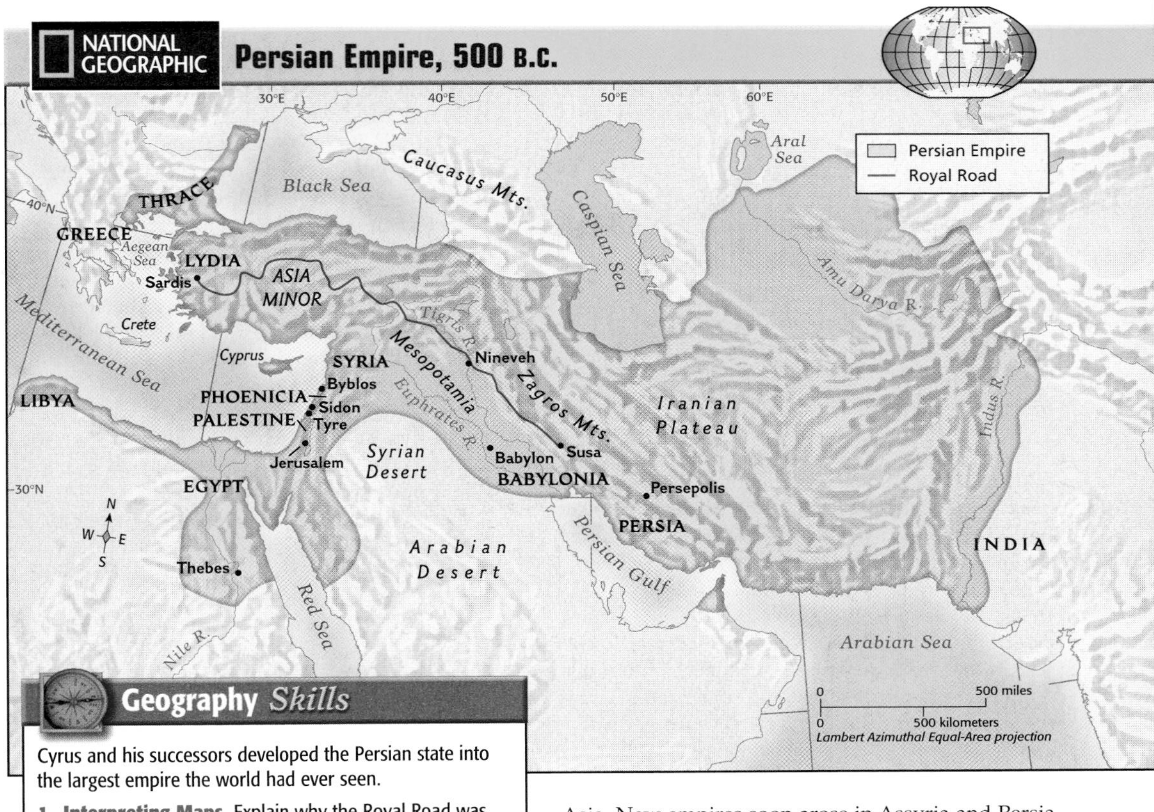

Geography *Skills*

Cyrus and his successors developed the Persian state into the largest empire the world had ever seen.

1. **Interpreting Maps** Explain why the Royal Road was constructed and why it was constructed where it was.
2. **Applying Geography Skills** Using your text, identify the areas added to the empire by Cyrus, Cambyses, and Darius. What problems might these rulers have encountered as the empire grew?

peoples (monotheism). In all other religions at that time, only priests (and some rulers) had access to the gods. In the Jewish tradition, God's wishes, though communicated to the people through prophets, had all been written down. No Jewish spiritual leader could claim that he alone knew God's will. This knowledge was open to anyone who could read the Hebrew Bible.

Reading Check **Identifying** Which aspect of the Israelite culture had the greatest impact on Western civilization?

The Rise of New Empires

A small and independent Israelite state could exist only as long as no larger state dominated western Asia. New empires soon arose in Assyria and Persia, however, that conquered vast stretches of the ancient world.

The Assyrian Empire The first of the new empires was formed in Assyria, located on the upper Tigris River. The Assyrians were a Semitic-speaking people who exploited the use of iron weapons to establish an empire by 700 B.C. The Assyrian Empire included Mesopotamia, parts of the Iranian Plateau, sections of Asia Minor, Syria, Palestine, and Egypt down to Thebes. Within less than a hundred years, however, internal strife and resentment of Assyrian kings began to tear the Assyrian Empire apart. In 605 B.C., the empire fell to a coalition of Chaldeans and Medes (people who lived in the East), and was divided between those two powers.

The Assyrians used terror as an instrument of warfare. They regularly laid waste the land in which they were fighting. They smashed dams; looted and destroyed towns; set crops on fire; and cut down trees, particularly fruit trees. The Assyrians were especially known for committing atrocities on their

Geography *Skills*

Answers:

1. Answers should include that the road ended at Susa because Susa was the capital. The road may have moved west toward the coastal areas because most likely those were the more significant commerce centers. They were probably more populated than inland settlements.
2. Cyrus: Bablyon; Cambyses: Egypt; Darius: area in western India to Indus River, Thrace; Royal Road ended at Susa so rulers may have had trouble communicating with and administrating empire east to Indus River

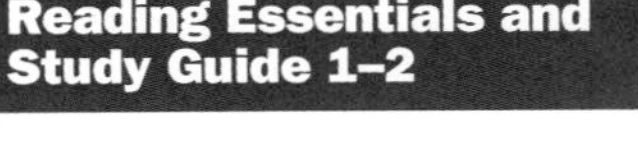
Reading Essentials and Study Guide 1–2

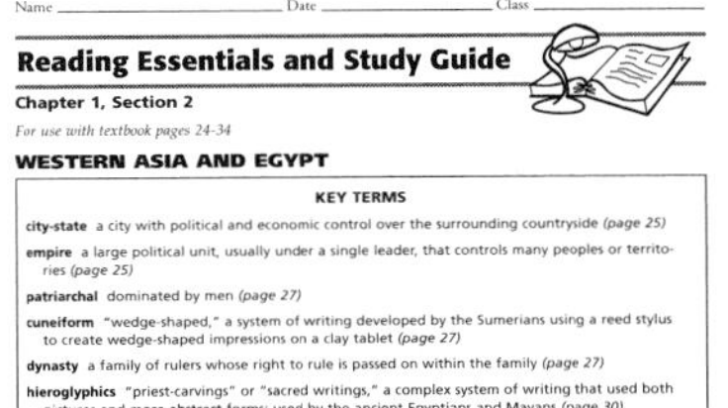
Name ______ Date ______ Class ______

Reading Essentials and Study Guide

Chapter 1, Section 2

For use with textbook pages 24-34

WESTERN ASIA AND EGYPT

KEY TERMS

city-state a city with political and economic control over the surrounding countryside *(page 25)*

empire a large political unit, usually under a single leader, that controls many peoples or territories *(page 25)*

patriarchal dominated by men *(page 27)*

cuneiform "wedge-shaped," a system of writing developed by the Sumerians using a reed stylus to create wedge-shaped impressions on a clay tablet *(page 27)*

dynasty a family of rulers whose right to rule is passed on within the family *(page 27)*

hieroglyphics "priest-carvings" or "sacred writings," a complex system of writing that used both pictures and more abstract forms; used by the ancient Egyptians and Mayans *(page 30)*

Judaism monotheistic religion developed among the Israelites *(page 30)*

monotheistic having one God *(page 32)*

Reading Check

Answer: their religion, Judaism

Connecting Across Time

To reinforce the impact of Israelite culture on Western civilization, ask students to name three ways in which the history or religion of the ancient Israelites still affects life today. *(Answers may include: laws; roots of Christianity; Middle East political situation; commonly quoted proverbs and psalms; concept of monotheism; creation story of Genesis.)* **L2**

CRITICAL THINKING ACTIVITY

Problem Solving Have students look at the map of the Persian Empire on this page. The Persians operated a postal system along the Royal Road much like the American Pony Express. Postal stations were set up along the road a day's ride apart. At each station, a fresh rider and horse would wait to take the mail from the incoming rider. **Ask:** **What was the distance a message traveled between Susa and Nineveh?** *(About 400 miles or 644 km)* **L1**

CHAPTER 1
Section 2, 24–34

Enrich
Discuss why Cyrus's policies toward other religious and cultural groups were considered enlightened. Have students identify other rulers who have followed similar policies and the advantages of these practices. **L2**

Reading Check

Answer: After Darius, kings became more and more isolated at their courts and increased taxes to pay for more luxuries, causing loyalty to the empire to decline. Struggles over the throne weakened the monarchy.

Reteaching Activity
Have students reread this section and take notes of each time a river is mentioned. Ask students to summarize the impact of rivers on the development of early civilizations. **L1**

4 CLOSE

Ask students to write a paragraph about each of the civilizations and empires discussed in this section. The paragraph should begin with this sentence: *We influenced the course of human history.* Then ask students to summarize the contributions of each of these civilizations in their paragraphs. Request volunteers to read their paragraphs aloud in class. **L2**

captives. King Ashurnasirpal recorded this account of his treatment of prisoners: "3,000 of their combat troops I felled with weapons. . . . Many I took alive; from some of these I cut off their hands to the wrist, from others I cut off their noses, ears and fingers; I put out the eyes of many of the soldiers. . . . I burned their young men and women to death."

The Persian Empire The Persians were an Indo-European people who lived in what is today southwestern Iran. Primarily nomadic, the Persians were organized in groups until one family managed to unify them. One of the family's members, **Cyrus,** created a powerful Persian state that stretched from Asia Minor to western India.

Cyrus ruled from 559 to 530 B.C. In 539 B.C., he entered Mesopotamia and captured Babylon. His treatment of Babylonia showed remarkable restraint and wisdom. Cyrus also issued an edict permitting the Jews, who had been brought to Babylon earlier in the century, to return to Jerusalem.

The people of his time called Cyrus "the Great." Indeed, he must have been an unusual ruler for his time, a man who demonstrated much wisdom and compassion in the conquest and organization of his empire. Unlike the Assyrian rulers, Cyrus had a reputation for mercy. Cyrus had a genuine respect for other civilizations. In building his palaces, for example, he made use of Assyrian, Babylonian, and Egyptian designs and building methods.

Cyrus's successors extended the territory of the Persian Empire. His son Cambyses (kam•BY•SEEZ) successfully invaded Egypt. Darius, who ruled from 521 to 486 B.C., added a new Persian province in western India that extended to the Indus River. He then moved into Europe, conquering Thrace and creating the largest empire the world had yet seen.

An efficient system of communication was crucial to sustaining the Persian Empire. Well-maintained roads made it easy for officials to travel throughout the entire kingdom. The **Royal Road** stretched from Lydia to Susa, the chief capital of the empire. Like the Assyrians, the Persians set up way stations that provided food and shelter, as well as fresh horses, for the king's messengers.

In this vast system, the Persian king—the "Great King"—occupied an exalted position. The Great King held the power of life and death.

After Darius, the Persian kings became more and more isolated at their courts, surrounded by luxuries provided by the immense quantities of gold and silver that flowed into their treasuries. As the Persian kings increased taxes to gain more wealth, loyalty to the empire declined. Struggles over the throne weakened the monarchy (rule by a king or queen). Over a period of time, this bloody struggle for the throne weakened the empire and led to its conquest by the Greek ruler Alexander the Great during the 330s B.C.

Reading Check **Examining** What caused the Persian Empire to decline after the death of Darius?

SECTION 2 ASSESSMENT

Checking for Understanding

1. **Define** city-state, empire, patriarchal, cuneiform, dynasty, hieroglyphics, Judaism, monotheistic.
2. **Identify** Sargon, Hammurabi, Code of Hammurabi, Menes, King Solomon, Cyrus.
3. **Locate** Tigris River, Euphrates River, Fertile Crescent, Nile River, Lower Egypt, Upper Egypt, Jerusalem, Royal Road.
4. **Explain** why Cyrus was called "the Great."
5. **List** the technological achievements of the civilizations of western Asia and Egypt.

Critical Thinking

6. **Describe** What were the unique aspects of the Jewish religion compared to the other religions of western Asia and Egypt? Include the impact of Judaism on the development of Islam and Christianity.
7. **Organizing Information** Use a chart like the one below to compare the Old Kingdom, Middle Kingdom, and New Kingdom of Egypt.

	Dates	Achievements
Old Kingdom		
Middle Kingdom		
New Kingdom		

Analyzing Visuals

8. **Compare** the Royal Standard of Ur on page 25 with the photo of the war chariot on page 29. What can historians learn about the cultures of the Sumerians and the Egyptians from these two pieces of art? What technologies and cultural values are evident?

Writing About History

9. **Expository Writing** Explain why Hammurabi's code was a significant development. Develop a set of laws based on the Code of Hammurabi that would apply to your community today. Explain why your code differs from that developed by Hammurabi, or why it is similar.

SECTION 2 ASSESSMENT

1. Key terms are in blue.
2. Sargon *(p. 25);* Hammurabi *(p. 25);* Code of Hammurabi *(p. 26);* Menes *(p. 27);* King Solomon *(p. 31);* Cyrus *(p. 34)*
3. See chapter maps.
4. He extended and organized the empire, ruled with wisdom and compassion, and respected the contributions of other cultures.
5. Answers include law code, writing, the wheel, the arch, geometry, 365-day calendar.
6. belief in only one God (monotheism), beliefs recorded in writing; Islam and Christianity also monotheisic, and their beliefs are written
7. Old Kingdom: 2700–2200 B.C.; pyramids, mastabas, mummification; Middle Kingdom: 2050–1652 B.C.; stability, public works; New Kingdom: 1567–1085 B.C.; massive wealth, power
8. Both cultures valued war, both had the wheel. Egyptian art shows bow and arrow, writing, and wheel with spokes.
9. Students will develop a law code and explain similarities and differences with Hammurabi's code.

EYEWITNESS TO HISTORY

Hammurabi's Code

ALTHOUGH THERE WERE EARLIER Mesopotamian legal codes, the Code of Hammurabi is the most complete. The law code emphasizes the principle of retribution ("an eye for an eye") and punishments that vary according to social status. Punishments could be severe, as these examples show.

22: If a man has committed highway robbery and has been caught, that man should be put to death.

23: If the highwayman has not been caught, the man that has been robbed shall state on oath what he has lost and the city or district governor in whose territory or district the robbery took place shall restore to him what he has lost.

25: If fire broke out in a free man's house and a free man, who went to extinguish it, cast his eye on the goods of the owner of the house and has appropriated the goods of the owner of the house, that free man shall be thrown into that fire.

196: If a free man has destroyed the eye of a member of the aristocracy, they shall destroy his eye.

198: If he has destroyed the eye of a commoner or broken the bone of a commoner, he shall pay one mina of silver.

199: If he has destroyed the eye of a free man's slave or broken the bone of a free man's slave, he shall pay one-half his value.

229: If a builder constructed a house for a nobleman but did not make his work strong, with the result that the house which he built collapsed and so has caused the death of the owner of the house, that builder shall be put to death.

232: If it has destroyed goods, he shall make good whatever it destroyed; also, because he did not make the house strong that he built and it collapsed, he shall reconstruct the house that collapsed at his own expense.

—***The Code of Hammurabi***

Hammurabi's code was written on a stone monument, approximately seven feet (2.1 m) tall, called a stele. The upper section of the stele shows Hammurabi standing in front of the seated sun god.

Analyzing Primary Sources

1. Explain the principle of retribution.
2. According to the Code of Hammurabi, what was most highly valued in Mesopotamian society? What was the least valued? Explain your answers.
3. What is the guiding principle in the American criminal justice system? How does this compare with Hammurabi's justice?

ANSWERS TO ANALYZING PRIMARY SOURCES

1. Retribution means repayment. It is the consequence that results from one's actions.
2. social status; penalties were harshest when the injured party was a noble and least harsh when the injured party was a slave, which suggests that nobles were more highly valued than slaves
3. The guiding principle in the American criminal justice system is equality under the law. Under Hammurabi's code, penalties for crimes varied with social class, and laws favored members of the higher social classes.

EYEWITNESS TO HISTORY

TEACH

Ask students to identify differences between ancient Mesopotamian society and their own society as indicated by these laws. *(Mesopotamians practiced slavery; punished theft with death; penalties varied depending on social class.)* Bring in a newspaper and select a story for the students to analyze. Ask students to identify elements in a contemporary situation described in the selected story that parallel a historical situation. Then, ask the students to evaluate how the story might have been different if Hammurabi's code were the current law of the land. **L2**

Who?What?Where?When?

Stelae The first known stelae were tall stones upended and carved. The stele that contained the Code of Hammurabi was approximately seven feet (2.13 m) tall. It is now located in the Louvre Museum, Paris.

Discuss the advantages and disadvantages of a government being able to state its entire body of law on a stele.

Critical Thinking

Ask students to identify the impact of the political and legal ideas contained in the Code of Hummurabi. **L1**

CHAPTER 1
Section 3, 36–45

1 FOCUS

Section Overview

This section focuses on the early civilizations of India and China and explores the schools of religious thought that emerged there.

BELLRINGER
Skillbuilder Activity

Project transparency and have students answer questions.

Available as a blackline master.

Daily Focus Skills Transparency 1–3

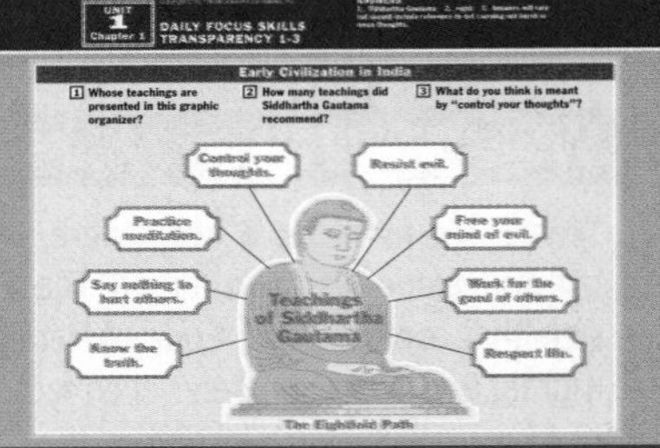

Guide to Reading

Answers to Graphic: Hinduism: karma, yoga, many gods; Buddhism: Four Noble Truths, Eightfold Path, all people can achieve nirvana; Both: a single force governs universe; reincarnation; humans can merge with universal force

Preteaching Vocabulary: Discuss the relationship between the Hindu belief in *reincarnation* and the idea of karma. **L2**

SECTION 3 India and China

Guide to Reading

Main Ideas
- The caste system was a set of rigid social categories in Indian society.
- Like other empires, Chinese dynasties followed a rise-and-fall pattern.

Key Terms
caste system, Hinduism, reincarnation, Buddhism, Mandate of Heaven, Dao, filial piety, Confucianism

People to Identify
Aryans, Siddhartha Gautama, Asoka, Qin Shihuangdi, Confucius

Places to Locate
India, Indus River, Hindu Kush, Deccan Plateau, China, Gobi

Preview Questions
1. How did the caste system influence the lives of people in ancient India?
2. Why was the Mandate of Heaven important to Chinese rulers?

Reading Strategy
Compare and Contrast As you read this section, prepare a Venn diagram like the one below to show the similarities and differences between Hinduism and Buddhism.

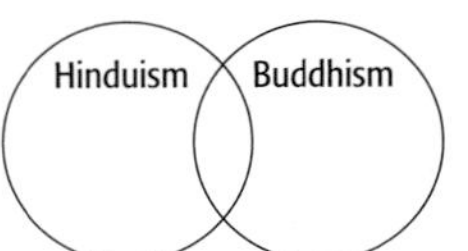

Preview of Events

500 B.C. — 400 B.C. — 300 B.C. — 200 B.C. — 100 B.C. — A.D. 1 — A.D. 100

- **c. 500 B.C.** Buddhism develops
- **480 B.C.** Gautama (the Buddha) dies
- **232 B.C.** Asoka dies
- **202 B.C.** Han dynasty begins
- **c. A.D.100** Silk Road connects China and Mesopotamia

Confucius

Voices from the Past

Confucius wanted to promote good government in China. Confucius said:

> ❝If the people be led by laws, and uniformity be imposed on them by punishments, they will try to avoid the punishment, but will have no sense of shame. If they be led by virtue, and uniformity be provided for them by the rules of propriety, they will have the sense of shame, and will become good." He also said, "Let the ruler be filial and kind to all people; then they will be faithful to him. Let him advance the good and teach the incompetent; then they will eagerly seek to be virtuous.❞
>
> —***The Chinese Classics,*** **James Legge, 1893**

Confucianism, an ancient Chinese philosophy, sought to spell out the principles that would create stability and order in society.

Early Civilization in India

India is a land of diversity. As of the year 2000, people in India spoke 18 languages, with hundreds of dialects (varieties of a language). Diversity is also apparent in India's geography. The Indian subcontinent, shaped like a triangle hanging from the southern ridge of Asia, is composed of a number of core regions, including mountain ranges, river valleys, a dry interior plateau, and fertile coastal plains.

As in Mesopotamia and Egypt, early civilization in India emerged in river valleys. Between 3000 B.C. and 1500 B.C., the valleys of the **Indus River** supported a flourishing civilization. It extended hundreds of miles from the Himalaya, the highest mountains in the world, to the coast of the Arabian Sea. Archaeologists have found the remains of more than a thousand settlements in this region. Two

SECTION RESOURCES

Reproducible Masters
- Reproducible Lesson Plan 1–3
- Daily Lecture and Discussion Notes 1–3
- Guided Reading Activity 1–3
- Section Quiz 1–3
- Reading Essentials and Study Guide 1–3

Transparencies
- Daily Focus Skills Transparency 1–3

Multimedia
- Interactive Tutor Self-Assessment CD-ROM
- ExamView® Pro Testmaker CD-ROM
- Presentation Plus! CD-ROM

of the ruins, about 400 miles (643.6 km) apart, were sites of what once were the major cities of Harappa (huh•RA•puh) and Mohenjo-Daro (moh•HEHN•joh DAHR•oh). An advanced civilization—known as Harappan or Indus civilization—flourished in these cities for hundreds of years.

The Arrival of the Aryans Eventually, floods, an earthquake, changes in climate, and even a change in the course of the Indus River weakened the once-flourishing civilization in the Indus River valley. Invaders brought its final end.

Around 1500 B.C., a group of Indo-European nomadic peoples began to move out of their original homeland in central Asia. Known as the **Aryans,** they moved south across the **Hindu Kush** mountain range into the plains of northern India. They invaded and conquered the Harappans and created a new Indian society based on Aryan culture and institutions.

Like other nomadic peoples, the Aryans excelled at the art of war. Between 1500 and 1000 B.C., the Aryan peoples gradually advanced eastward from the Indus Valley, across the fertile plain of the Ganges River. Later they moved southward into the **Deccan Plateau.** Eventually they extended their control throughout all of India.

Society in Ancient India The conquest by the Aryans had a lasting impact on Indian society. Out of the clash between conqueror and conquered came a set of social institutions and class divisions that has lasted in India, with only minor changes, to the present day.

The caste system of ancient India was a set of rigid social categories that determined not only a person's occupation and economic potential, but also his or her position in society. There were five major divisions of Indian classes (known as castes in English) in ancient times.

The priestly class, whose members were known as the Brahmans, was usually considered to be at the top of the social scale. They were in charge of the religious ceremonies that were so important in Indian society. The second caste was the Kshatriyas (KSHA•tree•uhz), or warriors. The third-ranked caste in Indian society was the Vaisyas (VYSH•yuhz), or commoners. The Vaisyas were usually the merchants who engaged in commerce.

Below these three castes were the Sudras (SOO•druhz), who made up the great bulk of the Indian population. Most Sudras were peasants, artisans, or people who worked at other forms of manual labor. They had only limited rights in society.

At the lowest level of Indian society—and in fact not even considered a real part of the caste system—

Picturing **History**

A priest-king and the restored city of Mohenjo-Daro are pictured. What elements of an advanced civilization can you find in these photos?

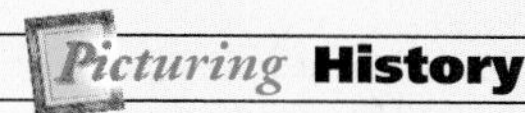

2 TEACH

Picturing **History**

Answer: Intricate carvings on the statue; symbols adorning the priest-king; and extensive, well-organized brick buildings indicate an advanced civilization.

Writing Activity

Have students write a paragraph explaining how India's geography affected its settlements. *(Answers may include the following: India is a land of diverse geography in a massive area. Its high mountains, lush river valleys, dry interior plateau, and fertile coastal plains separate the population and support different ways of life.)* **L1** ELL

CURRICULUM CONNECTION

Architecture The city of Mohenjo-Daro seems to have been carefully planned. Its architecture reveals the remains of an advanced civilization that had a public water supply and sophisticated drainage and trash disposal systems. Historians theorize that the city government must have been well organized to support such services.

COOPERATIVE LEARNING ACTIVITY

Creating a Visual Display Organize the class into groups of five or six students. Have each group choose a topic from this list of suggestions: religion, architecture, city planning, farming, textiles, arts and crafts, commerce, and geography. Have groups research their topics as they pertain to Harappan civilization. Each group should then create simple drawings depicting what it has learned about its topic. The items may be labeled, but the emphasis should be on a visual presentation. Each group should decide what task its members will perform. Provide space for each group to display its work. The class discussion of the displays should allow time for questions and answers. **L2** ELL

For grading this activity, refer to the ***Performance Assessment Activities*** booklet.

Geography Skills

Answers:

1. the Ganges River
2. They moved toward the coast and followed it toward the Deccan Plateau. There would have been more to eat on the coasts, and vegetation was probably lush.

Reading Check

Answer: Brahmans (priests), Kshatriyas (warriors), Vaisyas (commoners, usually merchants), Sudras (peasants, artisans, manual laborers); at the lowest level of Indian society, the Untouchables are actually outside the caste system as they are not considered human

Writing Activity

During a class discussion, ask students to explain the caste system and write their descriptions on the chalkboard. Then divide the class into five groups, and assign each group a caste. Members of each caste must write a one-page paper on what it's like to be a member of their caste. Have one volunteer from each group read the brief essay to the class. **Ask: Is society in the United States organized by social status? What is the main difference between the Indian caste system and American social structure?** *(Answers will vary, but students should note that in the United States people can move between social classes.)* **L2**

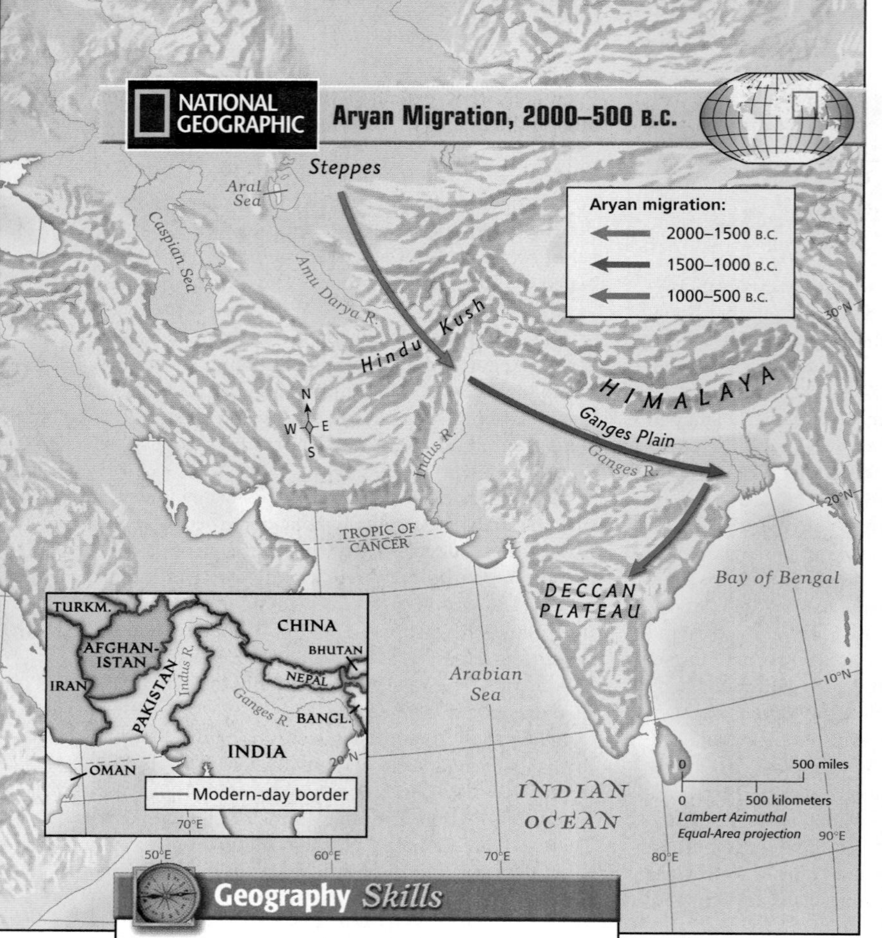

Geography Skills

The Aryans were nomadic peoples who moved through India. Eventually, they controlled most of India.

1. **Interpreting Maps** What geographical feature enabled the Aryans to end their nomadic lifestyle?
2. **Applying Geography Skills** Examine the pattern of Aryan migration. Why do you think the Aryans followed such a route?

were the Untouchables. The Untouchables probably made up about 5 percent of the total population of ancient India. The Untouchables were given menial, degrading tasks that other Indians would not accept, such as collecting trash and handling dead bodies. They were not considered human, and their very presence was considered harmful to members of the other classes.

Reading Check **Summarizing** What are the names of the castes in Indian society?

Hinduism

Two of the world's great religions, Hinduism and Buddhism, began in India. **Hinduism** had its origins in the religious beliefs of the Aryan peoples who settled in India after 1500 B.C. Evidence about the religious beliefs of the Aryan peoples comes from the Vedas, collections of hymns and religious ceremonies that were passed down orally through the centuries by Aryan priests and then eventually written down.

Early Hindus believed in the existence of a single force in the universe, a form of ultimate reality or God, called *Brahman*. It was the duty of the individual self—called the *atman*—to seek to know this ultimate reality. By doing so, the self would merge with Brahman after death.

By the sixth century B.C., the idea of reincarnation had appeared in Hinduism. **Reincarnation** is the belief that the individual soul is reborn in a different form after death. After a number of existences in the earthly world, the soul reaches its final goal in a union with Brahman.

Important to this process is the idea of karma, the force generated by a person's actions that determines how the person will be reborn in the next life. According to this idea, what people do in their current lives determines what they will be in their next lives. In the same way, a person's current status is not simply an accident. It is a result of the person's actions in a past existence.

The system of reincarnation provided a religious basis for the rigid class divisions in Indian society. It justified the privileges of those on the higher end of the scale. After all, they would not have these privileges if they were not deserving. At the same time, the concept of reincarnation gave hope to those lower on the ladder of life. The poor, for example, could

MEETING INDIVIDUAL NEEDS

Visual/Spatial Have students contribute to a class chart with the following terms across the top: Religious Terms, Places, and Peoples/Groups. Ask the students to place the following words under the corresponding category, and have students share the definitions or importance of the words with the class. The words include *Hinduism, Vaisyas, yoga, Hindu Kush, Ganges, karma, Aryans, Brahmans, Sudras, Untouchables, Buddhism, reincarnation, Siddhartha, nirvana,* and *Asoka.* The resulting chart will help students who learn better visually or have limited reading ability to organize and understand the major terms in the chapter. **L2**

Refer to ***Inclusion for the High School Social Studies Classroom Strategies and Activities*** in the TCR.

hope that if they behaved properly in this life, they would improve their condition in the next.

How does one achieve oneness with God? Hindus developed the practice of yoga, a method of training designed to lead to such union. (In fact, yoga means "union.") The final goal of yoga was to leave behind the cycle of earthly life and achieve union with Brahman, seen as a kind of dreamless sleep.

Most ordinary Indians, however, could not easily relate to this ideal and needed a more concrete form of heavenly salvation. It was probably for this reason that the Hindu religion came to have a number of humanlike gods and goddesses, including three chief ones: Brahma the Creator, Vishnu the Preserver, and Siva (SIH•vuh) the Destroyer. Many Hindus regard the multitude of gods as simply different expressions of the one ultimate reality, Brahman. However, the various gods and goddesses give ordinary Indians a way to express their religious feelings. Hinduism is the religion of the vast majority of the Indian people.

Reading Check **Comparing** How do karma and yoga relate to reincarnation?

Buddhism

In the sixth century B.C., a new doctrine, called **Buddhism,** appeared in northern India and soon became a rival of Hinduism. Buddhism was the product of one man, **Siddhartha Gautama** (sih•DAHR•tuh GOW•tuh•muh). Born around 563 B.C., Siddhartha Gautama is better known as the Buddha, or "Enlightened One."

In his lifetime, Siddhartha gained thousands of devoted followers. People would come to him seeking to know more about him. They asked, "Are you a god?"

"No," he answered.

"Are you an angel?"

"No."

"Are you a saint?"

"No."

"Then what are you?"

The Buddha replied, "I am awake."

The religion of Buddhism began with a man who claimed that he had awakened and seen the world in a new way.

Siddhartha denied the reality of the material world. The physical surroundings of humans, he believed, were simply illusions. The pain, poverty, and sorrow that afflict human beings are caused by their attachment to things of this world. Once people let go of their worldly cares, pain and sorrow can be forgotten. Then comes *bodhi,* or wisdom. (The word *bodhi* is the root of the word *Buddhism* and of Siddhartha's usual name—Gautama Buddha.) Achieving wisdom is a key step to achieving nirvana, or ultimate reality—the end of the self and a reunion with the Great World Soul.

Siddhartha preached this message in a sermon to his followers in the Deer Park at Sarnath (outside India's holy city of Banaras). It is a simple message based on the Four Noble Truths:

1. Ordinary life is full of suffering.
2. This suffering is caused by our desire to satisfy ourselves.
3. The way to end suffering is to end desire for selfish goals and to see others as extensions of ourselves.
4. The way to end desire is to follow the Middle Path.

This Middle Path is also known as the Eightfold Path, because it consists of eight steps:

1. *Right view* We need to know the Four Noble Truths.
2. *Right intention* We need to decide what we really want.
3. *Right speech* We must seek to speak truth and to speak well of others.

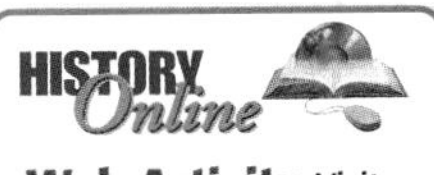

Web Activity Visit the *Glencoe World History—Modern Times* Web site at wh.mt.glencoe.com and click on **Chapter 1–Student Web Activity** to learn more about Buddhism.

The Buddha

Who?What?Where?When?

Yoga The word *yoga* means "union" in Sanskrit. This system of physical and mental exercises was developed to achieve isolation of the soul from the mind and body and union with the universal spirit. Today many people outside India practice yoga for exercise and relaxation.

Reading Check

Answer: Karma is the force that determines how a person will be reborn in the next life, and yoga is the way through which a person achieves union with Brahman and leaves the earthly life. These both lead to rebirth after death.

Enrich

Ask students to research how the Hindu concept of time differs from the Western idea of time. *(The Hindu concept of time, introduced by India's Aryan invaders, sees time as a revolving, endless circle. To Hindus, everything that happens today has happened before and will happen again. Westerners view time as a linear progression.)* **L2**

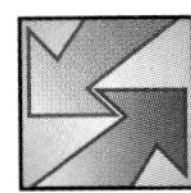

CURRICULUM CONNECTION

Religion Considered by many to be the world's oldest religion, Hinduism is not identified with the teachings of a single individual, unlike Christianity, Buddhism, and Islam. The Hindu religion has evolved over many centuries, and today it has about 800 million followers, most of whom live in India.

CRITICAL THINKING ACTIVITY

Examining Primary Sources Divide the class into two groups. One group will study quotations from the sacred texts of Hinduism; the other will study quotations from the sacred texts of Buddhism. Ask students to read the texts as if the students were historians. How do the texts increase understanding of the time period? Each group should compile a list of twenty quotations. When the lists are compiled, members of each group will read their quotes. The class will then compile the quotes into a combined booklet to enhance the study of this chapter. **L2**

Daily Lecture and Discussion Notes 1–3

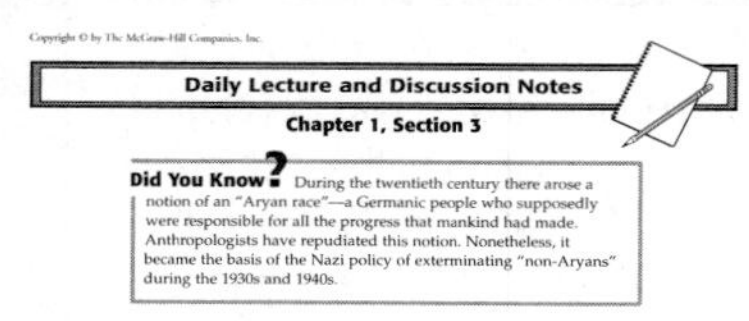

Daily Lecture and Discussion Notes

Chapter 1, Section 3

Did You Know? During the twentieth century there arose a notion of an "Aryan race"—a Germanic people who supposedly were responsible for all the progress that mankind had made. Anthropologists have repudiated this notion. Nonetheless, it became the basis of the Nazi policy of exterminating "non-Aryans" during the 1930s and 1940s.

I. **Early Civilizations in India** *(pages 36–38)*

A. The geography of **India** is very diverse. Its many core regions include mountain ranges, river valleys, a dry interior plateau, and fertile coastal plains.

B. Early civilization in India developed in the **Indus River** valley. A civilization flourished there from 3000 to 1500 B.C. Archaeologists have found remains of over a thousand settlements in this area.

C. Two sites have ruins of the major cities of Harappa and Mohenjo-Daro. The advanced civilization that flourished for hundred of years in these cities is called the Harappan or Indus civilization.

D. The **Aryans** were a nomadic Indo-European people living in central Asia. Around 1500 B.C., they moved south across the **Hindu Kush** mountain range into northern India. The Aryan invaders conquered the Harappans and ended the civilization of the Indus River valley.

E. The Aryans created a new Indian society. Like other nomadic people, the Aryans excelled at war. They advanced eastward and then southward into the **Deccan Plateau.** By 1000 B.C. they had extended their control throughout India.

F. The Aryan conquest had a lasting effect on India. The meeting of conquered and conqueror created a set of social institutions and class divisions that last to this day.

G. The **caste system** was one of the most important Indian social creations. It set up a rigid hierarchy of classes that determined a person's occupation, economic potential, and social status.

H. There were five major classes, or castes, in ancient India. At the top of the social scale were the Brahmans, or members of the priestly class. The second caste was the Kshatriyas, or warriors. The third caste consisted of Vaisyas, or commoners. Many members of this caste were merchants. Below these three castes were the Sudras, who made up most of the ... population. Most Sudras were peasants, artisans, or peo-

Reading Check

Answer: Buddhism more simplistic than Hinduism, rejects caste system and multiple gods of Hinduism, says people can reach nirvana as a result of their own behavior

CURRICULUM CONNECTION

Literature Hermann Hesse's novel *Siddhartha*, published in 1922, is a poetic expression of Indian philosophy. Hesse, a German, narrates how his young hero, the Brahman Siddhartha, after encountering the Buddha, sets off in search of self-fulfillment. His goal is to conquer suffering and fear, to attain serene contentment, and to see the unity in seeming contrasts— in short, to reach nirvana.

Reading Check

Answer: Asoka set up hospitals for people and animals, sent missionaries to China and other parts of Asia, and expanded trade so India prospered.

4. *Right action* The Buddha gave five precepts: "Do not kill. Do not steal. Do not lie. Do not be unchaste. Do not take drugs or drink alcohol."
5. *Right livelihood* We must do work that uplifts our being.
6. *Right effort* The Buddha said, "Those who follow the Way might well follow the example of an ox that arches through the deep mud carrying a heavy load. He is tired, but his forward-looking gaze will not relax until he comes out of the mud."
7. *Right mindfulness* We must keep our minds in control of our senses.
8. *Right concentration* We must meditate to see the world in a new way.

Siddhartha accepted the idea of reincarnation, but he rejected the Hindu division of human beings into rigidly defined castes based on previous reincarnations. He taught instead that all human beings could reach nirvana as a result of their behavior in this life.

Reading Check **Contrasting** How does Buddhism differ from Hinduism?

New Empires in India

For most of the time between 325 B.C. and A.D. 500, India was a land of many different states. Two major empires, however, were able to create large, unified Indian states.

The first of these empires, the Mauryan Empire in northern India, lasted from 324 to 183 B.C. The Mauryan Empire flourished during the reign of **Asoka** (uh•SHOH•kuh), who ruled from 269 until 232 B.C. Asoka is generally considered to be the greatest ruler in the history of India.

After his conversion to Buddhism, Asoka used Buddhist ideals to guide his rule. He set up hospitals for both people and animals. He sent missionaries to **China** and other parts of Asia, thus introducing Buddhism to those areas.

Asoka was more than a kind ruler, however. His kingdom prospered as India's role in regional trade began to expand. India became a major crossroads in a vast commercial network.

One of the most important parts of that network was the route known as the **Silk Road,** so called because silk was China's most valuable product. The Silk Road reached from the city of Changan in China across central Asia to Mesopotamia, covering a distance of about 4,000 miles (6,436 km). People used camels to transport goods through the mountains and deserts of the Silk Road, winding up at Antioch, a port city on the Mediterranean Sea. At Antioch, luxury goods from the West were traded for luxury goods from the East, which were then shipped across the Mediterranean to Greece and Rome.

After Asoka's death in 232 B.C., the Mauryan Empire began to decline, and in 183 B.C., it collapsed. India then fell back into disunity until a new empire arose. This new empire, the Gupta Empire, flourished from A.D. 320 until the late fifth century when the invasion of the Huns reduced its power.

Reading Check **Evaluating** Why was Asoka considered a great ruler?

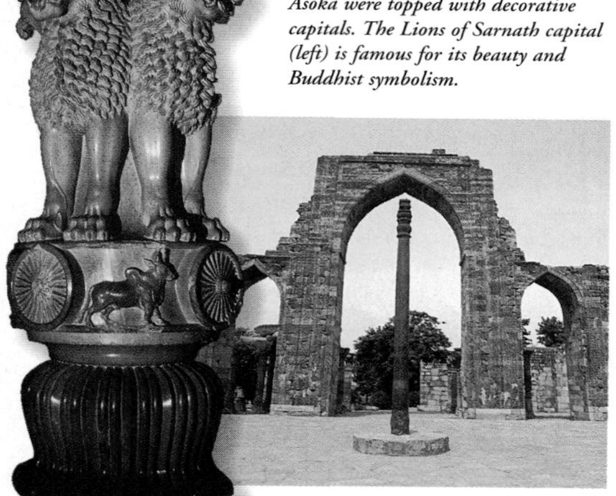

Stone pillars built during the rule of Asoka were topped with decorative capitals. The Lions of Sarnath capital (left) is famous for its beauty and Buddhist symbolism.

Early Chinese Civilizations

Of the great civilizations discussed so far, China was the last to come into full flower. By the time the first Chinese dynasty began to emerge as an organized state, the societies in Mesopotamia, Egypt, and India had already reached an advanced level of civilization. One likely reason for China's late arrival was its isolation from the emerging centers of culture elsewhere in the world. Basically, China was forced to develop on its own.

The Shang Dynasty The Shang dynasty (about 1750 to 1122 B.C.) created the first flourishing Chinese civilization. Under the Shang, China developed organized government, a system of writing, and advanced skills in the making of bronze vessels.

EXTENDING THE CONTENT

Pepper and the Indian Economy One of the primary exports of southern India was pepper. In the ancient world, spices, especially peppercorns, were an important commodity because of the difficulty in preserving food. Pepper was often used to cover the flavor of meat that had become rancid. Once ancient Europeans discovered this flavor enhancer, they were willing to pay its weight in gold. Indians received so many gold coins from the Roman Empire that emperor Nero banned the importation of peppercorns in order to stop the drain on the Roman economy. This same condiment would later play a role in history as the enticement for European traders and explorers of the fifteenth and sixteenth centuries.

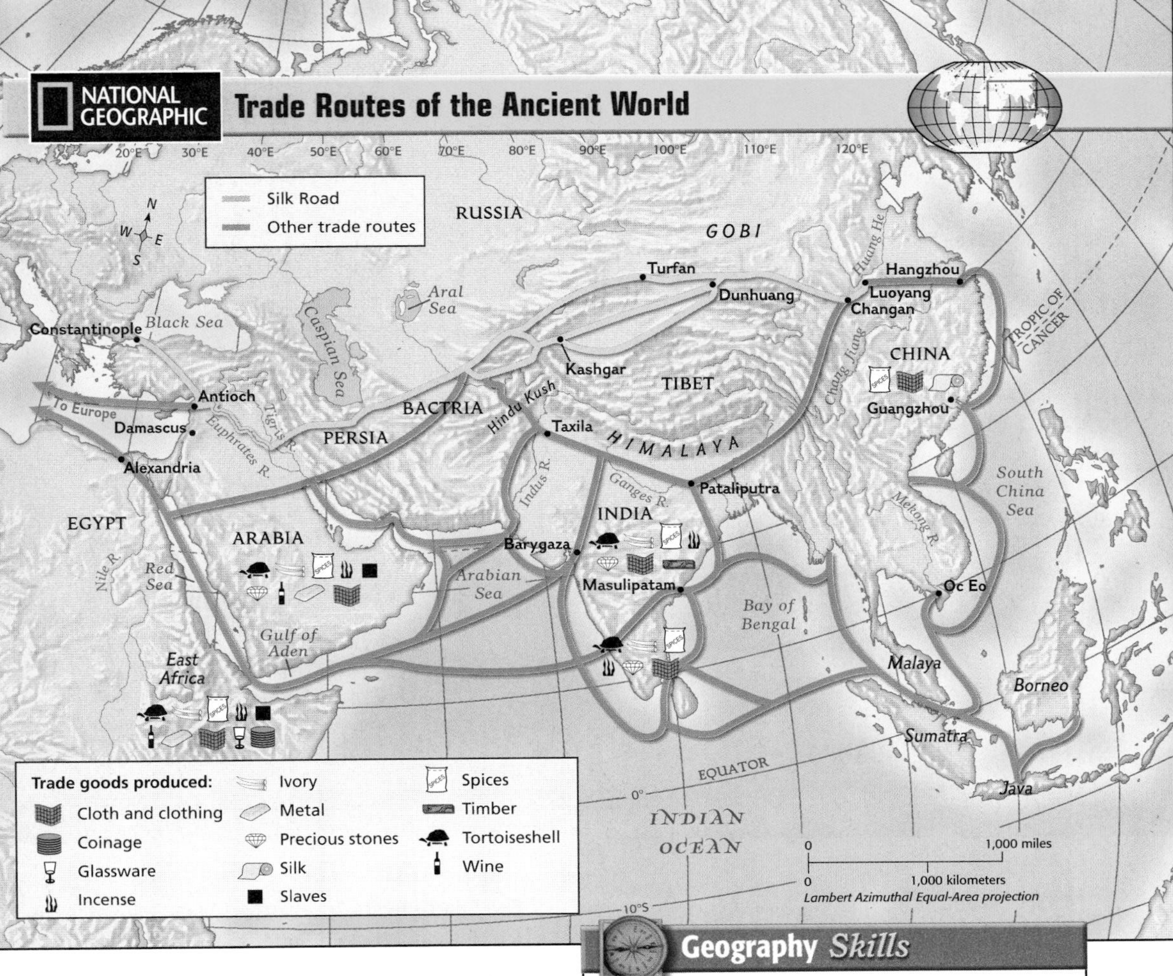

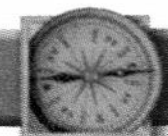

Geography Skills

Trade in the ancient world brought many cultures and kingdoms together. The Silk Road was one of the main routes of trade, allowing people and camels to move goods across 4,000 miles (6,436 km).

1. **Interpreting Maps** How was the Silk Road different from the other trade routes of the ancient world?
2. **Applying Geography Skills** What pattern do you see behind the location of the ancient trade routes?

The Chinese believed they could communicate with supernatural forces to obtain help in worldly affairs. To do so, they made use of oracle bones. These were bones on which priests scratched questions asked by the rulers, such as: Will the king be victorious in battle? Will the king recover from his illness? Heated metal rods were then stuck into the bones, causing them to crack. The priests interpreted the shapes of the cracks as answers from the gods. The priests wrote down the answers, then the bones were stored. The inscriptions on the bones have become a valuable source of information about the Shang period.

The Zhou Dynasty During the Zhou dynasty (1122 to 256 B.C.), China began to adopt many of the features that characterized Chinese civilization for centuries. Especially important politically was the Mandate of Heaven.

The Zhou dynasty claimed that it ruled China because it possessed the **Mandate of Heaven.** The Zhou believed that Heaven—which was an impersonal law of nature—kept order in the universe through the Zhou king. Thus, he ruled over all humanity by a mandate, or authority to command, from Heaven. The king, who was chosen to rule because of his talent and virtue, was then responsible for ruling the people with goodness and efficiency.

Geography Skills

Answers:

1. The Silk Road went through the mountains, was inland, and directly connected China to Antioch and Constantinople, which would have been a much more convoluted journey prior to the Silk Road.
2. Many of them followed or went across bodies of water, which would have made transportation easier.

Guided Reading Activity 1–3

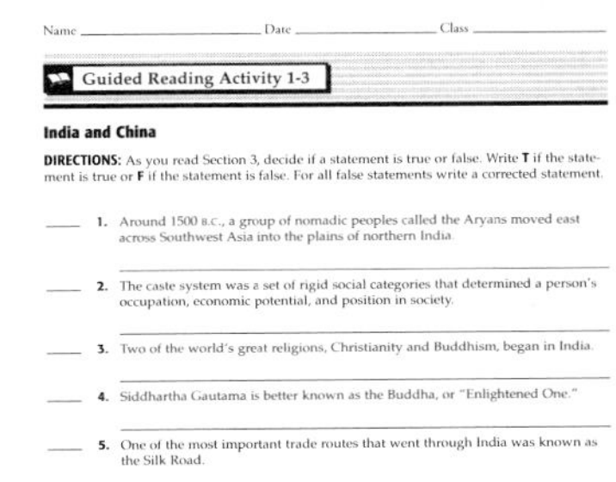
Name ______ Date ______ Class ______

Guided Reading Activity 1-3

India and China

DIRECTIONS: As you read Section 3, decide if a statement is true or false. Write **T** if the statement is true or **F** if the statement is false. For all false statements write a corrected statement.

____ 1. Around 1500 B.C., a group of nomadic peoples called the Aryans moved east across Southwest Asia into the plains of northern India.

____ 2. The caste system was a set of rigid social categories that determined a person's occupation, economic potential, and position in society.

____ 3. Two of the world's great religions, Christianity and Buddhism, began in India.

____ 4. Siddhartha Gautama is better known as the Buddha, or "Enlightened One."

____ 5. One of the most important trade routes that went through India was known as the Silk Road.

Who?What?Where?When?

The Silk Road For more than 2,000 years the Silk Road and its westward extensions into Roman territory formed the world's longest road. The road extended from China's Pacific coast to the Mediterranean Sea. In addition to being a route for transporting luxury items, the Silk Road provided the means for spreading the concepts of Christianity and Buddhism. Recently, historians have begun comparing the impact of the Silk Road on ancient cultures to the impact of the Internet on modern cultures. Silk Road travelers encountered and then spread different beliefs, cultures, languages, and technologies.

INTERDISCIPLINARY CONNECTIONS ACTIVITY

Religion Leaders of the Shang and Zhou dynasties used the Chinese belief in supernatural forces to help them govern. Ask students to review the religious beliefs of the civilizations studied in Section 2. Then ask students whether any of these civilizations relied on supernatural forces to govern? *(Yes)* If so, which societies? *(Sumerians, Egyptians)* Take this exercise one step further by asking students to research and report on present-day governments that rely on people's religious beliefs to help them govern. *(Answers may include Iran, Iraq, Israel, Bosnia, Kosovo, Macedonia, Singapore.)* **L3**

CHAPTER 1
Section 3, 36–45

Who?What?Where?When?

Zhou Technology The Zhou dynasty made many technological advances: building roads, riding horses, inventing the crossbow, creating an improved writing system, and using iron plows, irrigation systems, and flood control channels. Did these advances lead to increased population? *(yes)* If so, how? *(Irrigation systems allowed farmers to control rivers and to distribute water evenly to their crops; iron plows let them use more land to plant crops. Population increased when more food was available.)* **L2**

Writing Activity

During the Qin dynasty, Li Su, a chief minister of the First Qin Emperor, ordered the burning of all books, except the memoirs of Qin. The idea of destroying books to try to destroy ideas or knowledge is not unique to China.

Today people want to limit the types of material that can be sent over the Internet. Ask students to write a paragraph explaining why they support or oppose the position of Li Su. **L2**

3 ASSESS

Assign Section 3 Assessment as homework or as an in-class activity.

Have students use **Interactive Tutor Self-Assessment CD-ROM.**

The Great Wall of China

The Mandate of Heaven, however, was double-edged. The king was expected to rule according to the proper "Way," called the **Dao** (DOW). It was his duty to keep the gods pleased in order to protect the people from natural disaster or a bad harvest. If the king failed to rule effectively, he could be overthrown and replaced by a new ruler.

The Mandate of Heaven was closely tied to the pattern of dynastic cycles. From the beginning of Chinese history to A.D. 1912, China was ruled by a series of dynasties. The Zhou dynasty, as we have seen, lasted for almost nine hundred years. Others did not last as long, but the king of each dynasty ruled with the Mandate of Heaven.

No matter how long the dynasties lasted, all went through a cycle of change. A new dynasty established its power, ruled successfully for many years, and then began to decline. The power of the central government would begin to collapse, giving rise to rebellions or invasion. Finally, the dynasty collapsed and a new dynasty took over, beginning another dynastic cycle.

The Qin Dynasty The collapse of the Zhou dynasty was followed by two hundred years of civil war. A new dynasty, known as the Qin, then created an era of Chinese unity. The Qin dynasty was founded by **Qin Shihuangdi** (CHIN SHUR•HWONG•DEE), meaning "the First Qin Emperor."

Qin Shihuangdi, a person of much ambition, unified the Chinese world, but his major foreign concern was in the north. In the vicinity of the **Gobi** resided a nomadic people known to the Chinese as the Xiongnu (SYEN•NOO), who often made raids into Chinese territory. Qin Shihuangdi's answer to this problem was to strengthen the existing system of walls to keep the nomads out.

Today we know Qin Shihuangdi's project as the Great Wall of China. However, the Great Wall that we know today from films and photographs was built 1,500 years after the rule of Qin Shihuangdi. Some of the walls built by Qin Shihuangdi do remain standing, but many of them were constructed of loose stone, sand, or piled rubble, and disappeared long ago.

EXTENDING THE CONTENT

Mandate of Heaven The Chinese political philosophy of the Mandate of Heaven provided an ethical foundation for the right to rule: a ruler was selected by Heaven to rule for the benefit of his people. If he did not rule properly, a would-be ruler could overthrow him. During the Zhou dynasty, no other civilization in the world had a more advanced ethical foundation. More than two thousand years later, Niccolò Machiavelli (see pages 161–162) proposed a different ethic: morality plays no role in governing; if it works, do it. Have students speculate on whether or not more modern governments are guided by Machiavelli's ideas or ethical ideas similar to those of the Zhou.

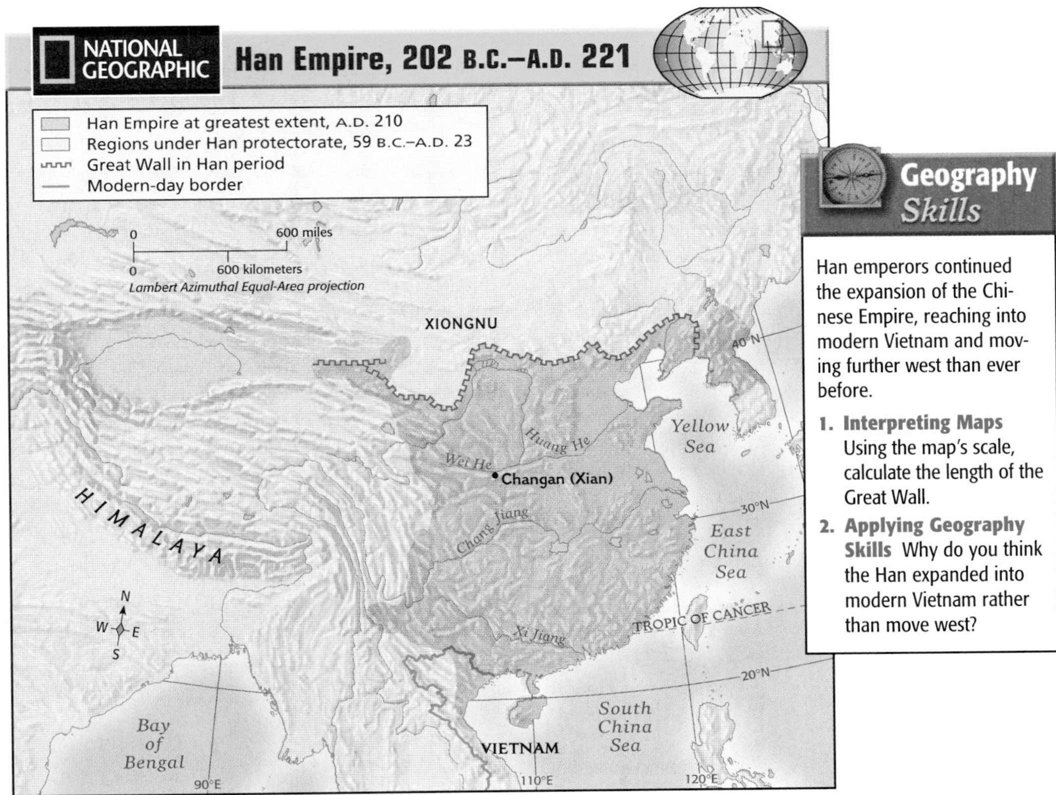

Geography Skills

Han emperors continued the expansion of the Chinese Empire, reaching into modern Vietnam and moving further west than ever before.

1. **Interpreting Maps** Using the map's scale, calculate the length of the Great Wall.
2. **Applying Geography Skills** Why do you think the Han expanded into modern Vietnam rather than move west?

This is not to say, of course, that Qin Shihuangdi's wall was not a massive project. It required the efforts of thousands of laborers. Many of them died while working there and, according to legend, are now buried within the wall. The wall enabled the First Qin Emperor to enjoy some success in fighting off the threat of the nomads, but the victory was only temporary.

The Han Dynasty The First Qin Emperor was also the last of his dynasty. A new dynasty—the Han—then established an empire that lasted over four hundred years (202 B.C. to A.D. 221).

China under the Han dynasty was a vast empire. The population increased rapidly—by some estimates rising from about twenty million to over sixty million at the height of the dynasty. The large population created a growing need for a bigger and more efficient bureaucracy to keep the state in proper working order.

During the glory years of the Han dynasty, China extended the boundaries of its empire far into the sands of central Asia and southward along the coast of the South China Sea into what is modern-day Vietnam. Chinese culture appeared to be unrivaled, and its scientific and technological achievements were unsurpassed.

Reading Check **Explaining** Why did the First Qin Emperor build walls across northern China?

The Family in Ancient China

Few social institutions have been as closely identified with China as the family. As in most agricultural societies, in ancient China the family served as the basic economic and social unit. However, the Chinese family took on an almost sacred quality as a symbol of the entire social order.

At the heart of the concept of family in China was the idea of filial piety. The word *filial* refers to a son or daughter. *Filial piety,* then, refers to the duty of members of the family to subordinate their needs and desires to those of the male head of the family.

MEETING INDIVIDUAL NEEDS

Visual/Spatial Bring to class items that are examples of China's influence on the world: paper, silk, tea, a compass, porcelain, rice, and pasta. Discuss the importance of these items in the development of trade, the importance of these items in Chinese lives and in our society, and the role that rice played in China. Discuss trade in China during ancient times and today. Divide the class into two groups. One group will make a poster displaying China's imports and exports during the Qin and Han dynasties. The second group will make a poster showing China's imports and exports today. Display the posters and discuss the similarities and differences. **L2**

Refer to ***Inclusion for the High School Social Studies Classroom Strategies and Activities*** in the TCR.

Geography Skills

Answers:

1. Approximately 1,500 miles (2,400 km)
2. Western expansion would have meant moving into desert and mountain areas.

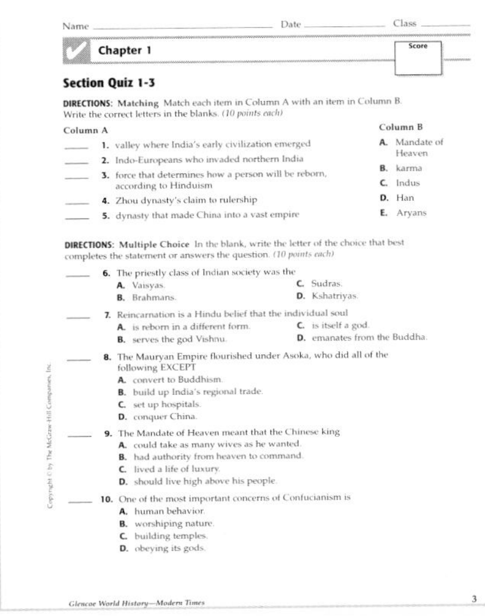

Section Quiz 1–3

Name ____ Date ____ Class ____

Chapter 1 Score

Section Quiz 1-3

DIRECTIONS: Matching Match each item in Column A with an item in Column B. Write the correct letters in the blanks. *(10 points each)*

Column A

____ 1. valley where India's early civilization emerged
____ 2. Indo-Europeans who invaded northern India
____ 3. force that determines how a person will be reborn, according to Hinduism
____ 4. Zhou dynasty's claim to rulership
____ 5. dynasty that made China into a vast empire

Column B

A. Mandate of Heaven
B. karma
C. Indus
D. Han
E. Aryans

DIRECTIONS: Multiple Choice In the blank, write the letter of the choice that best completes the statement or answers the question. *(10 points each)*

____ 6. The priestly class of Indian society was the
A. Vaisyas.
B. Brahmans.
C. Sudras.
D. Kshatriyas.

____ 7. Reincarnation is a Hindu belief that the individual soul
A. is reborn in a different form.
B. serves the god Vishnu.
C. is itself a god.
D. emanates from the Buddha.

____ 8. The Mauryan Empire flourished under Asoka, who did all of the following EXCEPT
A. convert to Buddhism.
B. build up India's regional trade.
C. set up hospitals.
D. conquer China.

____ 9. The Mandate of Heaven meant that the Chinese king
A. could take as many wives as he wanted.
B. had authority from heaven to command.
C. lived a life of luxury.
D. should live high above his people.

____ 10. One of the most important concerns of Confucianism is
A. human behavior.
B. worshiping nature.
C. building temples.
D. obeying its gods.

Glencoe World History—Modern Times 3

Reading Check

Answer: to protect against invaders from the north

Connecting Across Time

Officials in the Qin and Han dynasties were chosen for their abilities, similar to the American civil service system for government employees. Have students research the U.S. civil service system and write a paragraph explaining how it works. **L2**

CHAPTER 1
Section 3, 36–45

Critical Thinking

Discuss the meaning of *filial piety* with your students. Ask them how much influence they expect their parents or guardians to have over their eventual career choice. How would they react if they were told that they must pursue a career that was against their personal wishes? Why did (do) young people in many parts of the world tolerate being told what to do by their parents? L1

Reading Check

Answer: Males were responsible for providing food for their family.

CURRICULUM CONNECTION

Politics Most ancient Chinese would have agreed that being loyal to family should always come first. The family was the most important social unit in China, not only supplying basic human needs, but also serving as the focus of religious practice through ancestor worship. Confucius was once asked why he did not take part in government. In response, he quoted from an ancient classic, the *Shu Jhing* (Classic of History): "Simply by being a good son and friendly to his brothers a man can exert an influence upon government!" He thus made clear his belief that the public good is served by the practice of family ethics. Ask students to write a paragraph about someone they know who exemplifies this quote. L2

SCIENCE, TECHNOLOGY & SOCIETY

Answer: hemp or linen rags soaked in water, then mixed with potash

Thus, the term describes a system in which every family member had his or her place. The concept is important in Confucianism, as you will see later in this section.

What explains the importance of the family in ancient China? The need to work together on the land was a significant factor. In ancient times, as today, farming in China required the work of many people. Children, too, were essential to the family's needs. They worked in the fields during their early years. Later, sons were expected to take over the burden of physical labor on the family plots and provide for the well-being of their parents.

Male supremacy was a key element in the social system of ancient China, as it was in the other civilizations that we have examined. The male was considered so important because he was responsible for providing food for his family. In ancient China, men worked in the fields. They also governed society and were the warriors, scholars, and government ministers. Women raised the children and worked in the home.

Reading Check **Explaining** Why were males considered to be superior to females in Chinese families?

The Importance of Confucius

The civilization of China is closely tied to **Confucius** (in pinyin, Kongfuzi), a philosopher who lived in the sixth century B.C. Confucius traveled the length of China observing events and seeking employment as a political counselor. He had little success in his job search and instead became a teacher to hundreds of students who sought his wise advice. Some of his students became ardent disciples of their teacher and recorded his sayings. Until the twentieth century, almost every Chinese pupil studied his sayings. This made Confucianism, or the

SCIENCE, TECHNOLOGY & SOCIETY

Papermaking in Han China

The ancient Chinese were responsible for four remarkable inventions that were crucial to the development of modern technology: the magnetic compass, paper, printing, and gunpowder. How to make paper was one of their early discoveries.

The oldest piece of paper found in China dates from the first century B.C. Made from hemp fibers, it was thick, rough, and useless for writing. That was not a problem for the ancient Chinese, however, because they preferred to write on bamboo or silk.

Paper with writing on it dates from around A.D. 100. By this time, the Chinese had figured out how to make paper of better quality. After hemp or linen rags were soaked in water, they were mixed with potash and mashed into a pulp. A frame with a fine bamboo mesh was lowered into this vat of pulp. When the frame was removed, it held a thin sheet of pulp. Any extra water was removed before the sheets of paper were hung up to dry.

The art of papermaking spread westward from China beginning in the seventh century A.D. First India and then the Arab world developed the technique. The Arab cities of Baghdad, Damascus, and Cairo all had large papermaking industries. Paper was shipped from these centers to the West, but Europeans did not begin their production of paper until the twelfth century.

Describing ***What did the Chinese use to make paper?***

Bamboo is lifte out of China's Mekong River.

A contemporary artisan demonstrates ancient papermaking techniques.

COOPERATIVE LEARNING ACTIVITY

Creating an Interview Divide the class into two groups. Assign both groups of students the task of preparing a press conference interview with Confucius. Remind students that each group member must contribute to the research effort. One member of each group should play Confucius, and the other group members should act as reporters. All group members should prepare a list of questions, and the group should meet to compile a single list of questions before the interview. After the interview each group should compile its answers and present them to the class. L1

system of Confucian ideas, an important part of Chinese history.

Confucius believed that the universe was made in such a way that if humans would act in harmony with its purposes, their own affairs would prosper. Much of his concern was with human behavior. The key to proper behavior was to behave in accordance with the Dao (Way).

Two elements stand out in the Confucian view of the Dao: duty and humanity. The concept of duty meant that all people had to subordinate their own interests to the broader needs of the family and the community. Everyone should be governed by the Five Constant Relationships: parent and child, husband and wife, older sibling and younger sibling, older friend and younger friend, and ruler and subject. Each person in the relationship had a duty to the other. Parents should be loving, and children should revere their parents. Husbands should fulfill their duties, and wives should be obedient. The elder sibling should be kind, and the younger sibling respectful. The older friend should be considerate, and the younger friend deferential. Rulers should be benevolent, and subjects loyal.

The Confucian concept of duty is often expressed in the form of a "work ethic." If each individual worked hard to fulfill his or her duties, then the affairs of society as a whole would prosper as well.

An army of life-sized terra-cotta soldiers was found in Qin Shihuangdi's tomb.

Above all, the ruler must set a good example. If the king followed the path of goodness and the common good, then subjects would respect him, and society would prosper.

The second key element in the Confucian view of the Dao is the idea of humanity. This consists of a sense of compassion and empathy for others. It is similar in some ways to Christian ideas but with a twist. Christians are taught, "Do unto others as you would have others do unto you." Confucius would say, "Do not do unto others what you would not wish done to yourself." Confucius urged people to "measure the feelings of others by one's own."

✓Reading Check **Describing** Describe the meaning of duty and humanity in the Confucian view of the Dao.

SECTION 3 ASSESSMENT

Checking for Understanding

1. **Define** caste system, Hinduism, reincarnation, Buddhism, Mandate of Heaven, Dao, filial piety, Confucianism.
2. **Identify** Aryans, Siddhartha Gautama, Asoka, Silk Road, Qin Shihuangdi, Confucius.
3. **Locate** India, Indus River, Hindu Kush, Deccan Plateau, China, Gobi.
4. **Explain** the importance of filial piety to the Chinese. How does the concept of filial piety relate to the Confucian view of how society should function?
5. **List** the five major classes in Indian society and describe the role each class played in Indian society.

Critical Thinking

6. **Analyze** how the Hindu system of reincarnation supported the Indian caste system.
7. **Taking Notes** Using an outline format, describe the Confucian ideas of the Five Constant Relationships.

I. The Five Constant Relationships
  A. Parent and Child
    1. parents should be loving; children should revere their parents
  B.
  C. Older Sibling and Younger Sibling
  D.
  E. Ruler and Subject
    1. rulers should be benevolent; subjects loyal

Analyzing Visuals

8. **Examine** the photo of Qin Shihuangdi's tomb shown above. These soldiers were to accompany the emperor to the next world. What does this burial site tell us about what people valued and believed during the Qin dynasty?

Writing About History

9. **Expository Writing** Write an essay in which you compare and contrast the influence of the caste system on Indian society to the influence of filial piety on Chinese society. How do both the caste system and filial piety help to organize relationships between individuals? How are the two systems the same and how are they different?

✓Reading Check

Answer: *duty* meant subordinating one's own interests to the needs of the family and community; *humanity* meant having compassion and empathy for others

Reading Essentials and Study Guide 1–3

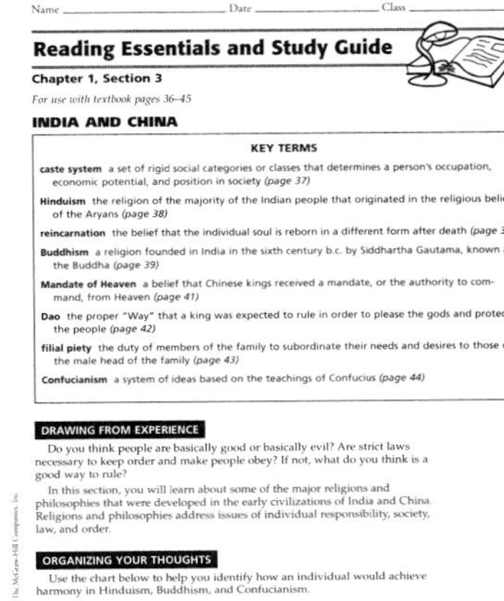

Name ______ Date ______ Class ______

Reading Essentials and Study Guide

Chapter 1, Section 3

For use with textbook pages 36–45

INDIA AND CHINA

KEY TERMS

caste system a set of rigid social categories or classes that determines a person's occupation, economic potential, and position in society *(page 37)*

Hinduism the religion of the majority of the Indian people that originated in the religious beliefs of the Aryans *(page 38)*

reincarnation the belief that the individual soul is reborn in a different form after death *(page 38)*

Buddhism a religion founded in India in the sixth century b.c. by Siddhartha Gautama, known as the Buddha *(page 39)*

Mandate of Heaven a belief that Chinese kings received a mandate, or the authority to command, from Heaven *(page 41)*

Dao the proper "Way" that a king was expected to rule in order to please the gods and protect the people *(page 42)*

filial piety the duty of members of the family to subordinate their needs and desires to those of the male head of the family *(page 43)*

Confucianism a system of ideas based on the teachings of Confucius *(page 44)*

DRAWING FROM EXPERIENCE

Do you think people are basically good or basically evil? Are strict laws necessary to keep order and make people obey? If not, what do you think is a good way to rule?

In this section, you will learn about some of the major religions and philosophies that were developed in the early civilizations of India and China. Religions and philosophies address issues of individual responsibility, society, law, and order.

ORGANIZING YOUR THOUGHTS

Use the chart below to help you identify how an individual would achieve harmony in Hinduism, Buddhism, and Confucianism.

	How To Achieve Harmony
1. Hinduism	
2. Buddhism	
3. Confucianism	

Reteaching Activity

Have students work in pairs to make charts summarizing the contributions of the early civilizations of India and China. **L1** **ELL**

4 CLOSE

Organize the class into two teams. Appoint one person as scorekeeper. Have the teams take turns challenging each other by giving specific names or occurrences from this section and having the other team identify one fact about the person or event. **L2**

SECTION 3 ASSESSMENT

1. Key terms are in blue.
2. Aryans *(p. 37);* Siddhartha Gautama *(p. 39);* Asoka *(p. 40);* Silk Road *(p. 40);* Qin Shihuangdi *(p. 42);* Confucius *(p. 44)*
3. See chapter maps.
4. family members are subordinate to male head of the family
5. priests (Brahmans), performed religious ceremonies; warriors (Kshatriyas), fought; commoners (Vaisyas), usually merchants; peasants, artisans (Sudras), performed manual labor; Untouchables not considered part of caste system, performed tasks no others would do
6. justified privileges of upper classes and gave hope of future rewards to lower classes
7. B. Husband and Wife; 1. husbands fulfill duties, wives obedient; C.1. older kind, younger respectful; D. Older/Younger Friend; 1. older considerate, younger deferential
8. shows importance of army to emperor, belief in life after death
9. Both: rigid, hierarchical, define relationships; Filial piety: defines family relationships

CHAPTER 1
Assessment and Activities

GLENCOE TECHNOLOGY

MindJogger Videoquiz
Use the **MindJogger Videoquiz** to review Chapter 1 content.

 Available in VHS.

Using Key Terms
1. nomads **2.** empire **3.** Mandate of Heaven **4.** domestication **5.** Filial piety **6.** Neolithic Revolution **7.** monotheistic **8.** Hinduism **9.** cuneiform **10.** Confucianism **11.** systematic agriculture **12.** Buddhism **13.** civilization

Reviewing Key Facts
14. The social categories determined a person's occupation, economic potential, and position in society.

15. nomadic, created tools, used fire, made cave paintings

16. systematic agriculture led to the development of civilization

17. cities, government, religion, social structure, writing

18. They developed near rivers.

19. keep accurate records, for law codes, epic poems, sacred writings, to record history

20. top: pharaoh; below pharaoh: upper class of nobles and priests; below them: larger group of merchants, artisans, scribes, tax collectors; bottom: farmers and peasants

21. communication system based on well-maintained roads and way stations for the king's messengers

22. Brahma the Creator, Vishnu the Preserver, Siva the Destroyer

23. His kingdom prospered; he used Buddhist ideals to govern.

24. It prospered as trade expanded.

25. Confucianism emphasized the duty of the subject to work hard so that society would prosper and for the ruler to set an example to encourage his subjects' respect.

26. The mandate said that the king ruled with the authority of Heaven. Natural disasters or bad harvests

CHAPTER 1 ASSESSMENT and ACTIVITIES

Using Key Terms
1. People who move from place to place for survival are called _____.
2. An _____ is a large political unit or state, usually under a single leader, that controls many peoples or territories.
3. The Zhou dynasty claimed that it ruled China because it possessed the _____.
4. The _____ of animals provided a steady source of meat, milk, and wool.
5. _____ refers to the duty of members of the family to be subordinate to the male head.
6. The _____ was the shift from hunting and gathering to systematic agriculture.
7. Since the Israelites worshipped one god, they are called _____.
8. _____ had its origins in the religious beliefs of the Aryans.
9. The Sumerians created a wedge-shaped system of writing known as _____.
10. Two elements stand out in _____: duty and humanity.
11. Keeping animals and growing food on a regular basis is called _____.
12. The religion of _____ began with Siddhartha Gautama.
13. The rise of cities, growth of governments, and development of religion are characteristics of _____.

Reviewing Key Facts
14. **Culture** Explain the social divisions in the caste system of India.
15. **Culture** Describe the lifestyle of Paleolithic peoples.
16. **History** What was the consequence of the most significant development of the Neolithic Age?
17. **Culture** List at least four characteristics of civilization.
18. **Geography** What geographic feature do the civilizations of the Fertile Crescent, Egypt, and India have in common?
19. **Science and Technology** Use examples from this chapter to show the different ways writing was used in early civilizations.
20. **Culture** Describe the pyramid-like structure of Egyptian society.
21. **Government** What did the Persian and Assyrian Empires use to maintain communication in their vast empires?
22. **Culture** Name three important Hindu deities.
23. **History** Why is Asoka considered to be the greatest ruler in the history of India?
24. **Economy** How did India benefit from the Silk Road?
25. **Citizenship** How did Confucianism impact the relationship between king and subject?
26. **Government** Explain how the Mandate of Heaven was closely tied to the pattern of dynastic cycles in China.

Chapter Summary
The chart below features some of the key people and achievements of early civilizations.

Civilization	Religion/ Philosophy	Key People	Achievements	Government/ Society
Mesopotamian	Gods and goddesses	Sargon Hammurabi	Cuneiform writing Wagon wheel Bronze	City-states Code of Hammurabi
Egyptian	Priests Divine kingship	Menes Hatshepsut	Pyramids 365-day calendar	Old, Middle, and New Kingdoms Pyramid-shaped social structure
Israelite	Judaism Monotheistic	Solomon	Hebrew Bible	Ten Commandments Israelite tribes divided
Indian	Hinduism Buddhism	Siddhartha Gautama Asoka	Built hospitals	Caste system Wealth from Silk Road
Chinese	Confucianism	Confucius Qin Shihuangdi	Great Wall Paper	Mandate of Heaven Cyclical dynasties Family central to society

meant that the gods were displeased and the king could be overthrown, leading to a new dynastic cycle.

Critical Thinking
27. For a ruler a city-state is easier to govern, but the ruler would have fewer resources at his disposal. A subject might have greater access to a ruler in a city-state, perhaps have fewer taxes to pay, but a city-state could be overrun by an empire.

28. Empires had the authority, bureaucracy, and military strength to collect taxes, to hire or use forced labor, and to locate building materials. The Great Wall was needed for defense, while the pyramids enhanced the prestige of the pharaohs.

29. Answers may include: Judaism: monotheism, concern for humanity, relationship with God; Hinduism: reincarnation, karma; Buddhism: the world is an illusion, nirvana; Confucianism: duty, compassion, and empathy for others.

Self-Check Quiz

Visit the *Glencoe World History—Modern Times* Web site at wh.mt.glencoe.com and click on **Chapter 1–Self-Check Quiz** to prepare for the Chapter Test.

Critical Thinking

27. Comparing and Contrasting What are the advantages and disadvantages of a city-state and an empire as governing systems? Consider the question from the point of view of a ruler and of a subject.

28. Drawing Conclusions To build the Great Wall of China or the pyramids of Egypt required tremendous amounts of material, finances, and labor. Describe how and why empires were able to devote vast resources to these projects.

29. Analyzing Identify at least two beliefs associated with each of the following religions/philosophies: Judaism, Hinduism, Buddhism, and Confucianism.

Writing About History

30. Descriptive Writing The Silk Road was important to trade, and the road provided economic benefits to the people who used it. However, ideas and information could also travel along the road. Write an article comparing the Silk Road to the Internet as vehicles to share information. Describe the impact of each on the cultures they benefited.

Analyzing Sources

Read the following decree of Asoka, one of India's greatest rulers.

> “By order of the Beloved of the Gods [Asoka] to the officers in charge: Let us win the affection of all people. All people are my children, and as I wish all welfare and happiness in this world and the rest for my own children, so do I wish it for all men. . . . For that purpose many officials are employed among the people to instruct them in righteousness and to explain it to them.”

31. What does the title “Beloved of the Gods” imply?

32. How does this quote reflect the Buddhist beliefs that were adopted by Asoka?

Applying Technology Skills

33. Using the Internet Search the Internet for the e-mail address of an Egyptologist from an international museum or university. Compose a letter requesting information about aspects of ancient Egyptian culture such as architecture, religion, or hieroglyphics.

NATIONAL GEOGRAPHIC **Early Asian Civilizations**

0 — 1,000 miles
0 — 1,000 kilometers
Two-Point Equidistant projection

Hindu Kush · Harappa · Mohenjo-Daro · Indus R. · Kunlun Shan · Plateau of Tibet · Brahmaputra R. · HIMALAYA · Ganges R. · Vindhya Mts. · Deccan Plateau · Western Ghats · Arabian Sea · Bay of Bengal · GOBI · Huang He · Anyang · Yellow Sea · Chang Jiang · Xi Jiang · Yunnan Plateau · South China Sea · 40°N · 30°N · 20°N · 70°E · 80°E · 90°E

Indus River valley civilization, 2500–1700 B.C.
Shang Empire, 1700–1000 B.C.

Analyzing Maps and Charts

Study the map above to answer the following questions.

34. In what mountain range does the Indus River originate?

35. Identify the two rivers found within the Shang Empire.

36. Name the river valley civilizations studied thus far.

Making Decisions

37. Each of the cultures studied so far had unique characteristics and faced unique challenges. Which culture would you prefer to live in as an ordinary citizen? Support your decision with reasons why you chose that civilization and reasons why you did not choose the other civilizations.

The Princeton Review — Standardized Test Practice

Directions: Choose the best answer to the following question.

The Neolithic Revolution, which occurred between 10,000 and 4000 B.C., led to all of the following EXCEPT

A an increase in human population.
B the cultivation of grains.
C the domestication of animals.
D an increase in the importance of hunting.

Test-Taking Tip: Be careful with questions that contain the key words EXCEPT or NOT. With these questions, you need to find an answer choice that is *false.* In this question, you want something that did *not* result from the Neolithic Revolution.

HISTORY Online

Have students visit the Web site at wh.mt.glencoe.com to review Chapter 1 and take the Self-Check Quiz.

Making Decisions

37. Answers will vary but should demonstrate knowledge of the various civilizations.

Standardized Test Practice

Answer: D

Answer Explanation: Have students consider the results of the Neolithic Revolution. The statement that is not a result is the correct answer.

Bonus Question ?

Ask: What factors can lead to the decline or fall of a civilization or dynasty? *(weak rulers, foreign invasion, natural disasters, climate changes)* **L3**

Writing About History

30. Answers will vary. Students may describe positive or negative results.

Analyzing Sources

31. It implies a special relationship between Asoka and the gods.

32. Buddhism sees others as an extension of ourselves.

Applying Technology Skills

33. Students will compose a letter based on their Internet search.

Analyzing Maps and Charts

34. Hindu Kush

35. Huang He and Chang Jiang

36. Mesopotamia, Egypt, India, China

Chapter 2 Resources

Timesaving Tools

TeacherWorks™ All-In-One Planner and Resource Center

- **Interactive Teacher Edition** Access your Teacher Wraparound Edition and your classroom resources with a few easy clicks.
- **Interactive Lesson Planner** Planning has never been easier! Organize your week, month, semester, or year with all the lesson helps you need to make teaching creative, timely, and relevant.

Use Glencoe's **Presentation Plus!** multimedia teacher tool to easily present dynamic lessons that visually excite your students. Using Microsoft PowerPoint® you can customize the presentations to create your own personalized lessons.

TEACHING TRANSPARENCIES

Graphic Organizer Student Activity 2 Transparency

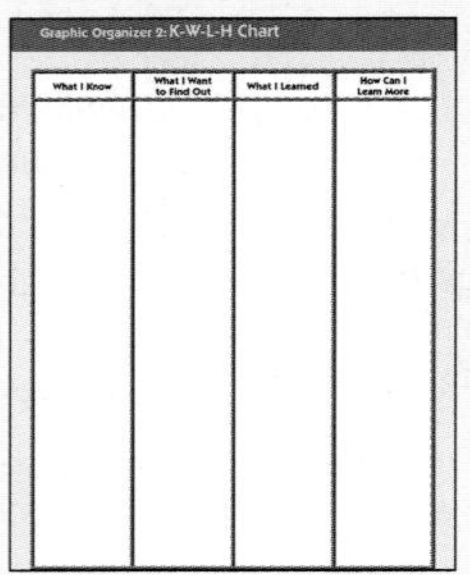

Chapter Transparency 2

Map Overlay Transparency 2

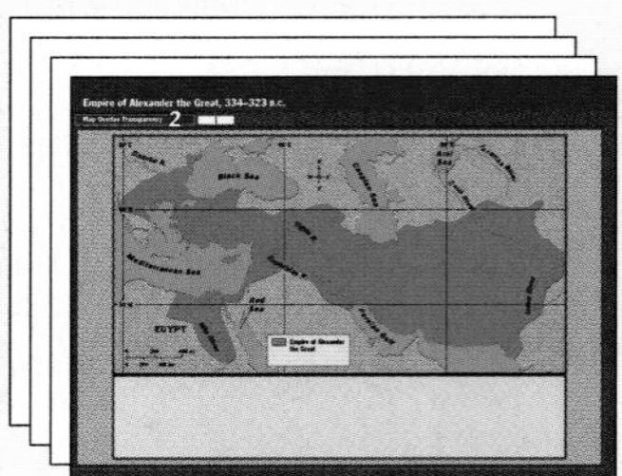

APPLICATION AND ENRICHMENT

Enrichment Activity 2

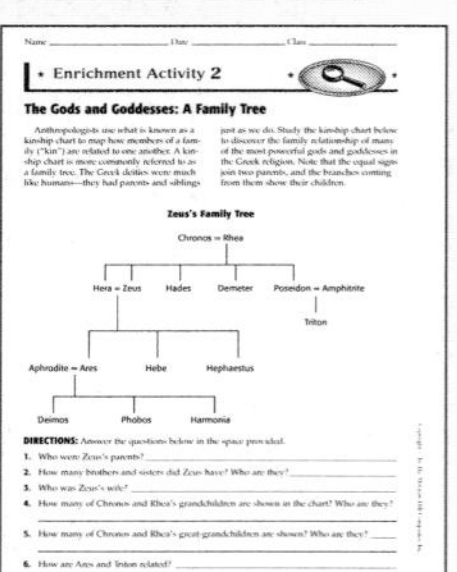

Primary Source Reading 2

History Simulation Activity 2

Historical Significance Activity 2

Cooperative Learning Activity 2

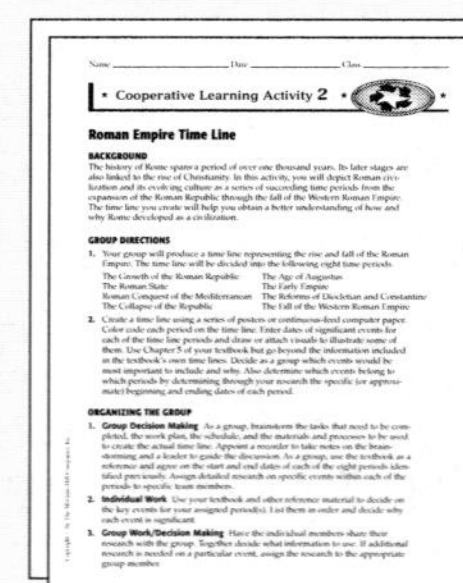

The following videotape programs are available from Glencoe as supplements to Chapter 2:

- **Hercules: Power of the Gods** (ISBN 0-56501-659-9)
- **Mystical Monuments of Ancient Rome** (ISBN 0-7670-0012-9)
- **Powerful Gods of Mt. Olympus** (ISBN 0-56501-927-X)
- **Ancient Rome** (ISBN 0-7670-1263-1)
- **Julius Caesar: Master of the Romans** (ISBN 0-7670-0572-4)

To order, call Glencoe at 1–800–334–7344. To find classroom resources to accompany many of these videos, check the following home pages:
A&E Television: www.aande.com
The History Channel: www.historychannel.com

Chapter 2 Resources

Review and Reinforcement

Linking Past and Present Activity 2

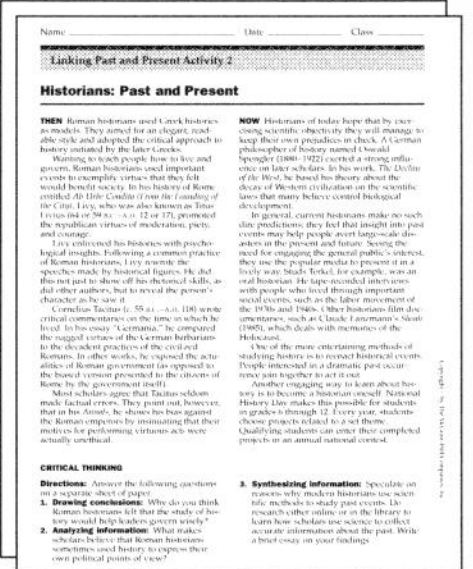

Time Line Activity 2

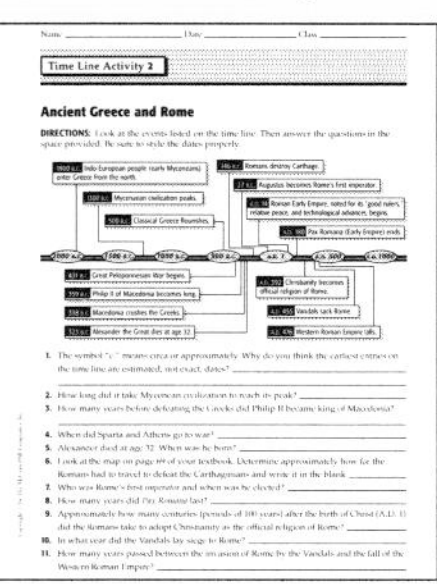

Reteaching Activity 2

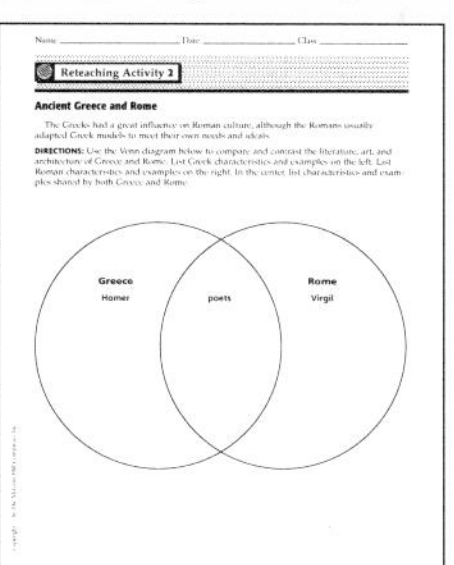

Vocabulary Activity 2

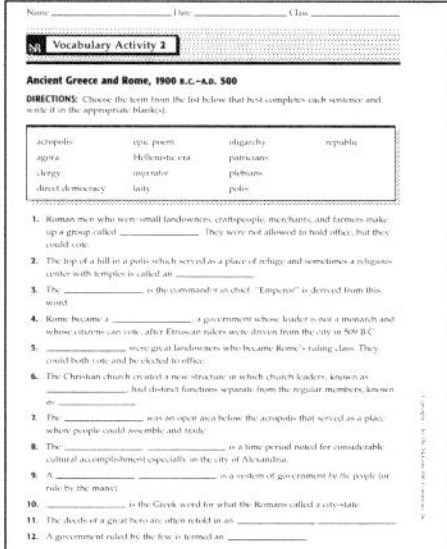

Critical Thinking Skills Activity 2

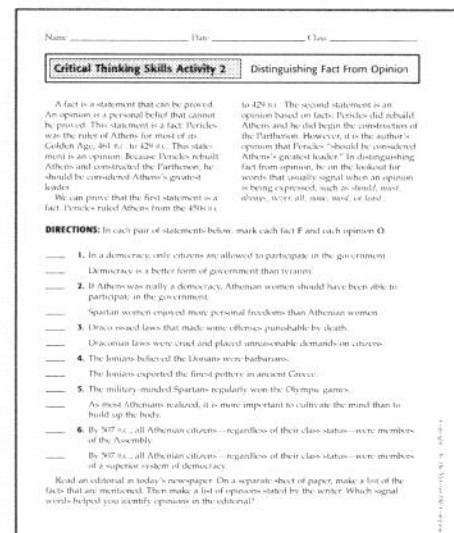

Assessment and Evaluation

Chapter 2 Test Form A

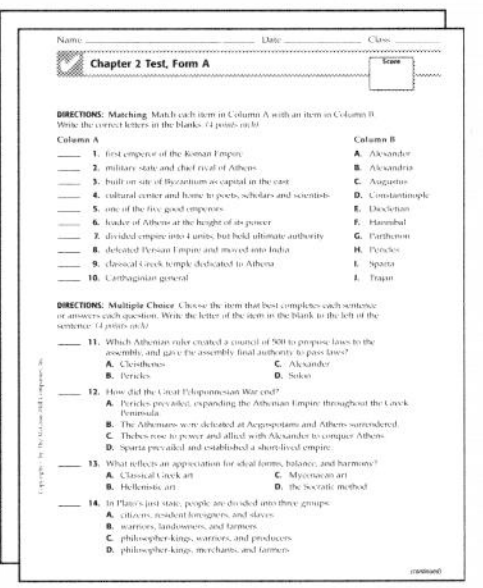

Chapter 2 Test Form B

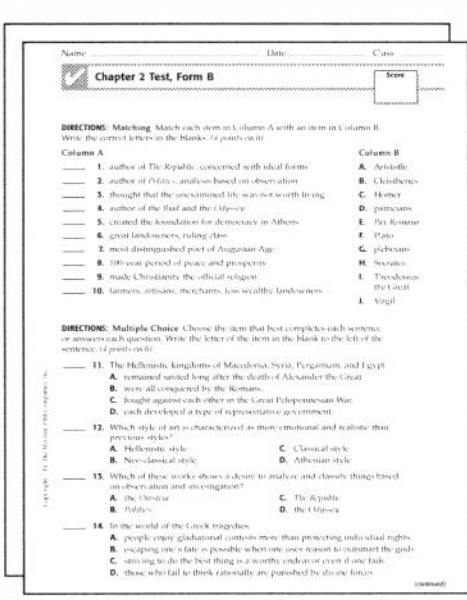

Performance Assessment Activity 2

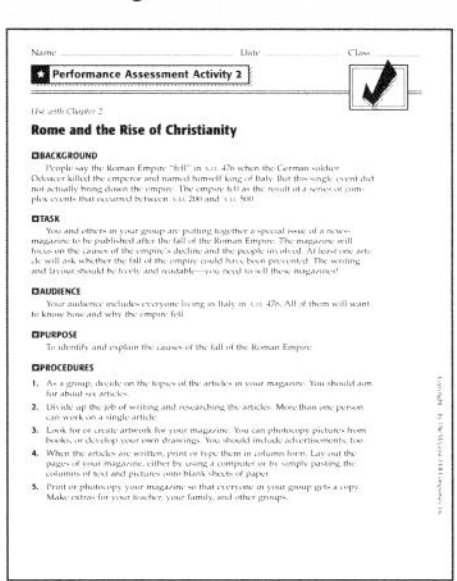

ExamView® Pro Testmaker CD-ROM

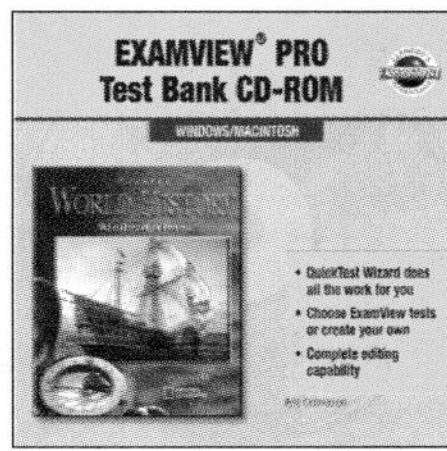

Standardized Test Skills Practice Workbook Activity 2

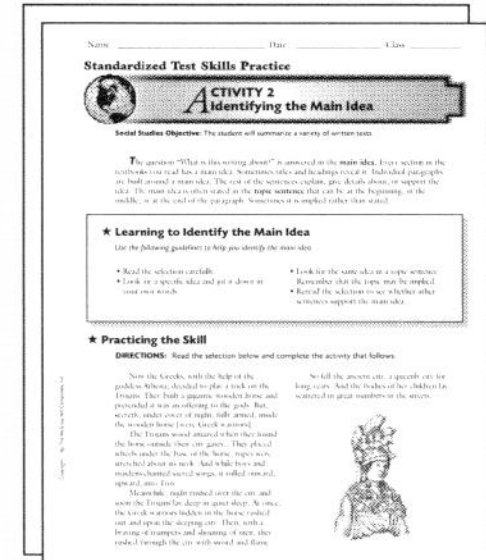

Interdisciplinary Activities

Mapping History Activity 2

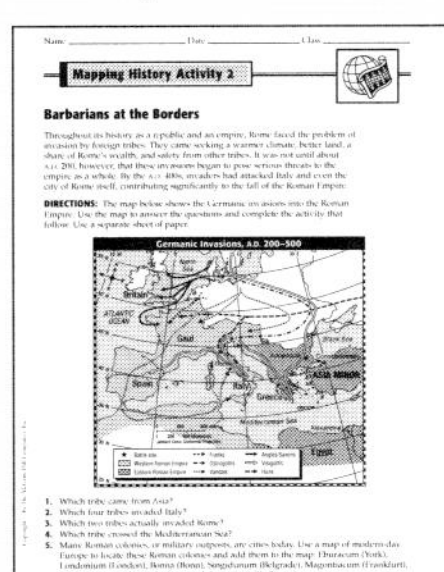

World Art and Music Activity 2

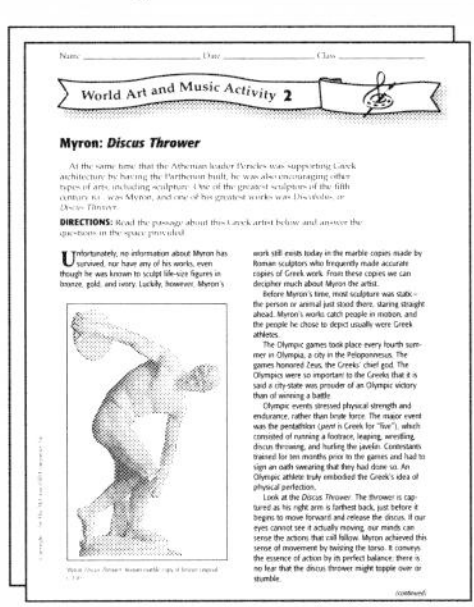

History and Geography Activity 2

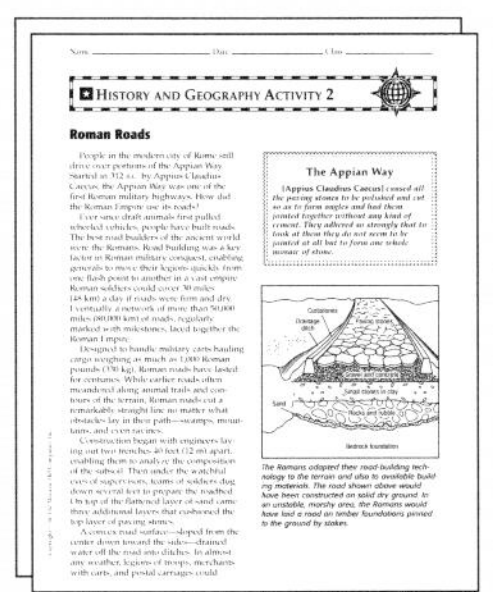

People in World History Activity 2

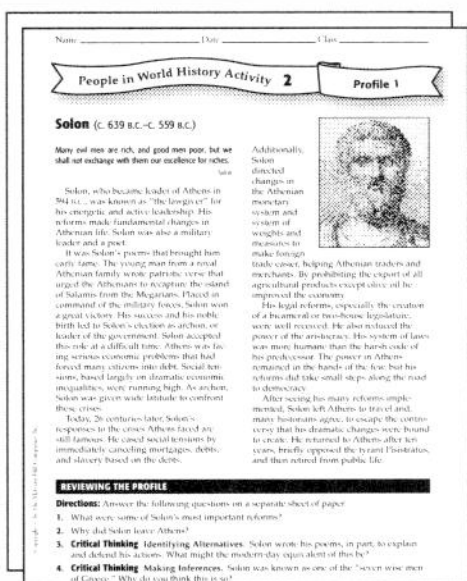

Multimedia

- Vocabulary PuzzleMaker CD-ROM
- Interactive Tutor Self-Assessment CD-ROM
- ExamView® Pro Testmaker CD-ROM
- Audio Program
- World History Primary Source Document Library CD-ROM
- MindJogger Videoquiz
- Presentation Plus! CD-ROM
- TeacherWorks CD-ROM
- Interactive Student Edition CD-ROM
- The World History—Modern Times Video Program

Spanish Resources

The following Spanish language materials are available in the Spanish Resources Binder:

- Spanish Guided Reading Activities
- Spanish Reteaching Activities
- Spanish Quizzes and Tests
- Spanish Vocabulary Activities
- Spanish Summaries

Chapter 2 Resources

SECTION RESOURCES

Daily Objectives	Reproducible Resources	Multimedia Resources
SECTION 1 **Ancient Greece** 1. Trace the history of early Greece—from the first Greek state of Mycenae, through the era of Classical Greece, to the Hellenistic period of Alexander the Great. 2. Discuss the contributions of early Greece to Western civilization.	Reproducible Lesson Plan 2–1 Daily Lecture and Discussion Notes 2–1 Guided Reading Activity 2–1* Section Quiz 2–1* Reading Essentials and Study Guide 2–1	Daily Focus Skills Transparency 2–1 Interactive Tutor Self-Assessment CD-ROM ExamView® Pro Testmaker CD-ROM Presentation Plus! CD-ROM
SECTION 2 **Rome and the Rise of Christianity** 1. Discuss how Roman culture and society were heavily influenced by the Greeks. 2. Summarize how Christianity spread throughout the empire and eventually became the state religion of Rome.	Reproducible Lesson Plan 2–2 Daily Lecture and Discussion Notes 2–2 Guided Reading Activity 2–2* Section Quiz 2–2* Reteaching Activity 2* Reading Essentials and Study Guide 2–2	Daily Focus Skills Transparency 2–2 Interactive Tutor Self-Assessment CD-ROM ExamView® Pro Testmaker CD-ROM Presentation Plus! CD-ROM

0:00 **OUT OF TIME?**
Assign the Chapter 2 **Reading Essentials and Study Guide.**

*Also Available in Spanish

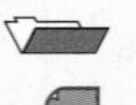 Blackline Master  Transparency  CD-ROM  DVD

 Poster  Music Program  Audio Program  Videocassette

Chapter 2 Resources

NATIONAL GEOGRAPHIC Teacher's Corner

INDEX TO NATIONAL GEOGRAPHIC MAGAZINE

The following articles relate to this chapter:

- "The Quest for Ulysses," by Tim Severin, August 1986.
- "Let the Games Begin," by Frank Deford, July 1996.
- "Warriors From a Watery Grave: Glorious Bronzes of Ancient Greece," by Joseph Alsop, June 1983.
- "Roman Legacy," by T.R. Reid, August 1997.
- "Brindisi Bronzes," by O. Louis Mazzatenta, April 1995.
- "The Eternal Etruscans," by Rick Gore, June 1998.

NATIONAL GEOGRAPHIC SOCIETY PRODUCTS AVAILABLE FROM GLENCOE

To order the following products, call Glencoe at 1-800-334-7344:

- *PictureShow: Greece and Rome* (CD-ROM)
- *Ancient Greece* (Transparencies, Poster Set)
- *Ancient Rome* (Transparencies, Poster Set)

ADDITIONAL NATIONAL GEOGRAPHIC SOCIETY PRODUCTS

To order the following, call National Geographic at 1-800-368-2728:

- *PictureShow: Ancient Civilizations Library* (CD-ROMs)
- *PicturePack: Ancient Civilizations Library, Part I* (Transparencies)

NGS ONLINE

Access National Geographic's new dynamic MapMachine Web site and other geography resources at:
www.nationalgeographic.com
www.nationalgeographic.com/maps

KEY TO ABILITY LEVELS

Teaching strategies have been coded.

L1 BASIC activities for all students
L2 AVERAGE activities for average to above-average students
L3 CHALLENGING activities for above-average students
ELL ENGLISH LANGUAGE LEARNER activities

Block Schedule

Activities that are suited to use within the block scheduling framework are identified by:

Use our Web site for additional resources. All essential content is covered in the Student Edition.

You and your students can visit www.wh.mt.glencoe.com, the Web site companion to *Glencoe World History—Modern Times.* This innovative integration of electronic and print media offers your students a wealth of opportunities. The student text directs students to the Web site for the following options:

- **Chapter Overviews**
- **Self-Check Quizzes**
- **Student Web Activities**
- **Textbook Updates**

Answers to the Student Web Activities are provided for you in the **Web Activity Lesson Plans.** Additional Web resources and Interactive Tutor Puzzles are also available.

From the Classroom of...

Ray Barron
Heritage High School
Littleton, Colorado

Comparing Pericles' *Funeral Oration* and Lincoln's *Gettysburg Address*

The purpose of this activity is to enable students to see the similarities among all civil wars and realize that there are connections between the American Civil War and that of the ancient Greeks.

Have students read both Pericles' *Funeral Oration* and Abraham Lincoln's *Gettysburg Address.* As they read each, have them list the qualities of individuals, government, and war that are mentioned. Next have them list those qualities of individuals, government, and war that seem to be mentioned in both orations. A Venn diagram is a helpful graphic organizer for this part of the activity. After they have done this, organize students into small groups and have each group reach a consensus as to which qualities are present in both orations and why this is so.

Have students write a paragraph explaining why these two speeches were made to the people of Greece and the United States, respectively, and summarize what we can learn about civil war from the speeches.

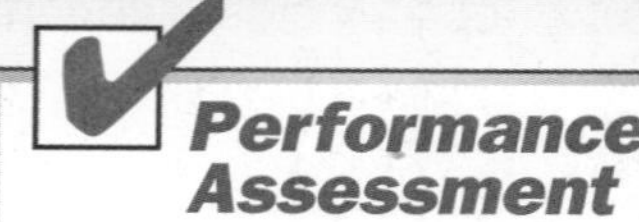

Performance Assessment

Refer to Activity 2 in the Performance Assessment Activities and Rubrics booklet.

The Impact Today

Have students explain how they think the Greeks and Romans contributed to Western civilization. Students should evaluate their answers before they have completed the chapter. Discuss student responses before and after students have read the chapter.

GLENCOE TECHNOLOGY

The World History—Modern Times Video Program

To learn more about ancient Greece, students can view the Chapter 2 video, "The Early Olympics," from **The World History—Modern Times Video Program.**

MindJogger Videoquiz

Use the **MindJogger Videoquiz** to preview Chapter 2 content.

Available in VHS.

CHAPTER 2 Ancient Greece and Rome

1900 B.C.–A.D. 500

Key Events

As you read, look for the key events in the history of Greece and Rome.

- *Greek philosophers established the foundations of Western philosophy.*
- *The Peloponnesian War weakened Athens and Sparta.*
- *Rome's republican government was eventually replaced by the rule of an emperor.*
- *Christianity became the official religion of the Roman Empire.*

The Impact Today

The events that occurred during this time period still impact our lives today.

- *Much of Western culture was influenced by the artistic ideals of Classical Greece.*
- *Current democratic systems of government are based on ideas originally developed by the Greeks.*
- *Roman achievements in law, government, language, and engineering influenced Western civilization.*

World History—Modern Times Video The Chapter 2 video, "The Early Olympics," *chronicles the origins of the Olympic games.*

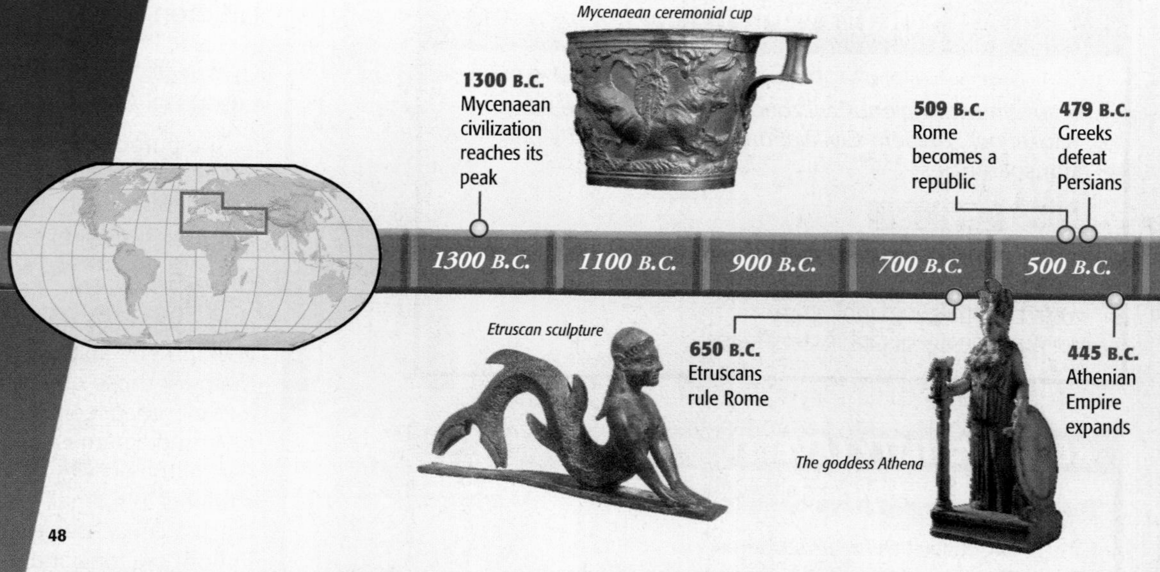
1300 B.C. Mycenaean civilization reaches its peak
509 B.C. Rome becomes a republic
479 B.C. Greeks defeat Persians
1300 B.C.
1100 B.C.
900 B.C.
700 B.C.
500 B.C.
650 B.C. Etruscans rule Rome
445 B.C. Athenian Empire expands

Mycenaean ceremonial cup

Etruscan sculpture

The goddess Athena

48

TWO-MINUTE LESSON LAUNCHER

Have students use the Reference Atlas in the front of their textbooks to locate the eastern Mediterranean region, including the Balkan Peninsula, the Aegean Sea, Asia Minor, and Crete. **Ask:** **How did geography affect the life of the ancient Greeks?** *(Mountains protected the people from foreign attack but limited communication within the region. Numerous harbors and the proximity of the sea led many people to take up fishing, trading, and piracy. Because of the mild climate, many activities were carried on outdoors.)* Have students locate Europe, the Mediterranean Sea, Asia Minor, North Africa, and Southwest Asia—the regions controlled by the Roman Empire by A.D. 130. **Ask:** **What problems might arise in governing such a vast area?** *(Answers will vary but may include delays in communications, the need to provide defense against invaders and rebellions, tax collection.)* **L1**

The Pont du Gard, a Roman aqueduct in southern France

Assassination of Julius Caesar

c. 350 B.C. Plato teaches at the Academy in Athens

44 B.C. Julius Caesar is assassinated

300 B.C. | *100 B.C.* | *A.D. 100* | *A.D. 300* | *A.D. 500*

338 B.C. Macedonia crushes the Greeks

312 B.C. Appian Way built

c. A.D. 33 Jesus dies in Jerusalem

A.D. 476 Fall of the Roman Empire

Ruins of the Appian Way

HISTORY Online

Chapter Overview
Visit the *Glencoe World History—Modern Times* Web site at wh.mt.glencoe.com and click on **Chapter 2–Chapter Overview** to preview chapter information.

49

Introducing CHAPTER 2

Chapter Objectives

After studying this chapter, students should be able to:

1. define *city-state* and tell how the city-states of Athens and Sparta differed;
2. list the cultural contributions of the Greeks to Western civilization;
3. explain how Alexander the Great created his empire;
4. tell how and why the Roman Republic developed and collapsed;
5. describe the major aspects of Roman culture and society;
6. list the major steps in the development of Christianity;
7. describe the decline and fall of the Roman Empire.

Chapter Overview
Introduce students to chapter content and key terms by having them access **Chapter Overview 2** at wh.mt.glencoe.com.

Time Line Activity

As students read the chapter, have them review the time line on pages 48 and 49. Ask students to explain the significance of the dates 509 B.C. and 338 B.C. *(In 509 B.C. Romans overthrew the last Etruscan king and established the Roman Republic. This new form of government had a leader elected by a select group of citizens. In 338 B.C. Philip II of Macedonia conquered and united Greece, setting the stage for Alexander the Great to spread Greek culture and ideas to the non-Greek world.)*

MORE ABOUT THE ART

The Pont du Gard is an ancient Roman aqueduct that spans a broad valley in Nîmes, a city in southern France. Aqueducts are structures or bridges built to carry water across great distances. Constructed in the early first century A.D., the Pont du Gard contains a series of arched openings framed by columns built using concrete faced with stone. This method of construction was used in other renowned Roman edifices like the Colosseum in Rome. The Pont du Gard's rugged, clean lines are a tribute to the high quality of Roman engineering and the sense of order and permanence that inspired its construction. It endures as a monument to the grandeur of ancient Rome. After students have read this chapter, ask them to identify significant examples of architecture that demonstrate a visual principle and an artistic ideal from Roman culture. L2

Introducing

A Story That Matters

Depending on the ability level of your students, select from the following questions to reinforce the reading of *A Story That Matters*.

- How long ago did this story take place? *(approximately 2,430 years ago)*
- What was the purpose of the ceremony? *(a public funeral to honor the Athenians who had died in the war between Sparta and Athens)*
- According to Pericles, why is Athens called a democracy? *(Power is in the hands of all the people.)* **L1 L2**

About the Art

In the illustration on this page, Pericles stands above the Athenian crowd as he delivers his famous *Funeral Oration*. Pericles was a dominant figure in Athenian politics between 461 and 429 B.C., a period that historians call the Age of Pericles. As leader, Pericles encouraged all citizens to participate in the government of Athens. During his rule, Athens became a great center for art and literature, and magnificent buildings were built, including the Parthenon.

CHAPTER PREVIEW

A Story That Matters

Pericles giving his famous Funeral Oration

Pericles Addresses Athens

In 431 B.C., war erupted in Greece as two very different Greek states—Athens and Sparta—fought for domination of the Greek world. Strengthened by its democratic ideals, Athens felt secure behind its walls.

In the first winter of the war, the Athenians held a public funeral to honor those who had died in combat. On the day of the ceremony, the citizens of Athens joined in a procession. The relatives of the dead mourned their loved ones.

As was the custom in Athens, one leading citizen was asked to address the crowd. On this day it was Pericles who spoke to the people. He talked about the greatness of Athens and reminded the Athenians of the strength of their political system.

"Our constitution," Pericles said, "is called a democracy because power is in the hands not of a minority but of the whole people. When it is a question of settling private disputes, everyone is equal before the law; when it is a question of putting one person before another in positions of public responsibility, what counts is not membership in a particular class, but the actual ability which the man possesses. No one . . . is kept in political obscurity because of poverty. And, just as our political life is free and open, so is our day-to-day life in our relations with each other. . . . Here each individual is interested not only in his own affairs but in the affairs of the state as well."

Why It Matters

In his famous speech, called the Funeral Oration, Pericles describes the Greek ideal of democracy and the importance of the individual. This is but one example of how the Greeks laid the intellectual foundations of Western civilization. They asked basic questions about the purpose of life, divine forces, and truth. The Greeks not only strove to answer these questions, they also created a system of logical thought for answering such questions. This system of thought remains worthwhile today.

History and You Reread the quote by Pericles. What portions of Athenian democracy described in this passage are found in the Constitution of the United States? Prepare a written report explaining and supporting your position with examples from the United States Constitution.

HISTORY AND YOU

The Greeks contributed two very important ideas to the Western world. First is the idea that the individual has the ability to use rational thought to gain true wisdom. Second is the idea that citizens should make the decisions concerning how they are to be governed. This second point is the democratic ideal that is embodied in the United States Constitution, and it is the idea behind universal suffrage. Discuss the significance of universal suffrage with students. You might wish to review the struggle for the vote in this nation, beginning with the Fifteenth Amendment, the Nineteenth Amendment, the Twenty-fourth Amendment, and the Voting Rights Acts of the 1960s and 1970s.

SECTION 1 Ancient Greece

Guide to Reading

Main Ideas
- The polis was the central focus of Greek life.
- During the Age of Pericles, Athens became the center of Greek culture.
- Hellenistic cities became centers for the spread of Greek culture.

Key Terms
epic poem, polis, acropolis, democracy, oligarchy, direct democracy

People to Identify
Homer, Solon, Cleisthenes, Pericles, Socrates, Plato, Aristotle, Alexander the Great

Places to Locate
Mycenae, Troy, Sparta, Athens, Macedonia, Alexandria

Preview Questions
1. Who lived in the polis?
2. How did Athens and Sparta differ?

Reading Strategy
Organizing Information Use a concept map like the one below to show the elements that contributed to the Classical Age of Greece.

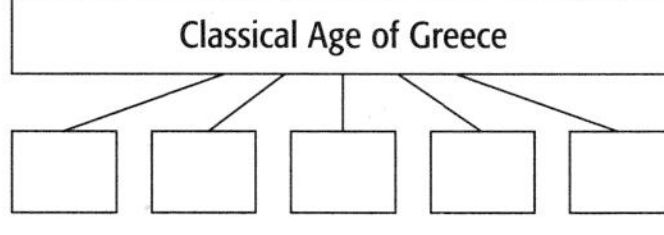

Preview of Events

1300 B.C. | 1250 B.C. | 500 B.C. | 450 B.C. | 400 B.C. | 350 B.C. | 300 B.C.

- **1300 B.C.** Mycenaean civilization peaks
- **500 B.C.** Classical Age begins
- **461 B.C.** Pericles comes to power
- **405 B.C.** Peloponnesian War ends
- **331 B.C.** Alexander takes possession of the Persian Empire

Voices from the Past

Thucydides

Classical Greece is the name given to the period of Greek history from around 500 B.C. to the conquest of Greece by the Macedonian king Philip II in 338 B.C. This period was marked not only by a brilliant culture but also by a disastrous war among the Greeks, the Peloponnesian War, described here by the Greek historian Thucydides:

“The Peloponnesian War not only lasted for a long time, but throughout its course brought with it unprecedented suffering for Greece. Never before had so many cities been captured and then devastated, whether by foreign armies or by the Greek powers themselves; never had there been so many exiles; never such loss of life—both in the actual warfare and in internal revolutions.”

— ***The History of the Peloponnesian War,*** **Thucydides, R. Warner, trans., 1954**

For all their accomplishments, the Greeks were unable to rise above the divisions and rivalries that caused them to fight one another and undermine their own civilization.

Early Greek Civilization

Geography played an important role in the development of Greek civilization. Compared with Mesopotamia and Egypt, Greece occupies a small area. It is a mountainous peninsula about the size of the state of Louisiana. Much of Greece consists of small plains and river valleys surrounded by high mountain ranges. The mountains isolated Greeks from one another, causing different Greek communities to develop their own ways of life.

The sea also influenced the evolution of Greek society. Greece has a long seacoast dotted by bays and inlets that provided many harbors. The Greeks lived on

1 FOCUS

Section Overview

This section explores early Greek history and discusses the influence of Greek culture on Western civilization.

BELLRINGER
Skillbuilder Activity

 Project transparency and have students answer questions.

 Available as a blackline master.

Daily Focus Skills Transparency 2–1

Guide to Reading

Answers to Graphic: democracy, classical ideals expressed in art and architecture, drama, philosophy

Preteaching Vocabulary: Explain the influence of *epic poems* on early Greeks. **L2**

SECTION RESOURCES

Reproducible Masters
- Reproducible Lesson Plan 2–1
- Daily Lecture and Discussion Notes 2–1
- Guided Reading Activity 2–1
- Section Quiz 2–1
- Reading Essentials and Study Guide 2–1

Transparencies
- Daily Focus Skills Transparency 2–1

Multimedia
- Interactive Tutor Self-Assessment CD-ROM
- ExamView® Pro Testmaker CD-ROM
- Presentation Plus! CD-ROM

2 TEACH

Geography Skills

Answers:

1. about 230 miles (370 km)
2. inlets provided natural harbors, many islands encouraged seafaring, mountains isolated Greeks from one another

Enrich

According to Homer, the Trojan War started when Paris was asked to judge who was the most beautiful goddess—Aphrodite, Hera, or Athena. Paris chose Aphrodite, after she promised him the love of the world's most beautiful woman, Helen of Troy.

Ask students to locate Troy on the map of classical Greece on page 63. After noting Troy's location, ask students to speculate on a more likely explanation for the war. *(Mycenae was jealous of the power of Troy to control trade in and out of the Propontis, the Sea of Marmara.)* **L1**

Writing Activity

Have students write paragraphs or short essays in which they explain the term *monarchy.* Have students cite differences between Mycenaean monarchies and modern-day monarchies.

Greece's geography helped shape Greek civilization.

a number of islands to the west, south, and east of the Greek mainland. It was no accident that the Greeks became seafarers.

The First Greek State: Mycenae **Mycenae** (my•SEE•nee) was a fortified site in Greece that was first discovered by the German archaeologist Heinrich Schliemann. Mycenae was one of a number of centers in an early Greek civilization that flourished between 1600 and 1100 B.C.

The Mycenaean Greeks were part of the Indo-European family of peoples who spread into southern and western Europe, India, and Iran. One of these groups entered Greece from the north around 1900 B.C. Over a period of time, this group managed to gain control of the Greek mainland and develop a civilization.

Mycenaean civilization, which reached its high point between 1400 and 1200 B.C., was made up of powerful monarchies. Each resided in a fortified palace center. Like Mycenae, these centers were built on hills and surrounded by gigantic stone walls.

Archaeological evidence indicates that the Mycenaean monarchies developed an extensive commercial network. Some historians believe that the Mycenaeans also spread outward militarily, conquering Crete and making it part of the Mycenaean world. The story of the most famous of all their supposed military adventures, the sacking of the city of **Troy,** is told in the *Iliad,* written by the great Greek poet **Homer.**

The Dark Age and Homer When Mycenaean civilization collapsed around 1100 B.C., Greece entered a difficult period in which the population declined and food production dropped. Historians call the period from approximately 1100 to 750 B.C. the Dark Age, because few records of what happened exist. At the same time, the basis for a new Greece was forming.

NATIONAL GEOGRAPHIC **Greece, 1400 B.C.**

Geography Skills

The physical geography of Greece had a major impact on the development of Greek civilization.

1. **Interpreting Maps** How many miles apart are Mycenae and Troy?
2. **Applying Geography Skills** Using the map, give examples of how Greece's geography affected Greek civilization.

CRITICAL THINKING ACTIVITY

Making Generalizations Assign students two-page essays on one of the following topics: (1) a comparison of the *Iliad* and the *Odyssey* with the Roman *Aeneid,* pointing out the portions of the Roman work that have been influenced by the Greek epics; (2) the three possible causes of the decline of the Mycenaean civilization *(internal: fighting between states; external: invaders; natural: earthquakes)* and an evaluation of which of the three causes seems most critical in the decline of Mycenaean Greece; (3) a comparison of one aspect of Mycenaean civilization with an aspect of civilizations that students have already studied. **L3**

Near the very end of the Dark Age, the work of Homer appeared.

The *Iliad* and the *Odyssey* were the first great epic poems of early Greece. An **epic poem** is a long poem that tells the deeds of a great hero. The *Iliad* and the *Odyssey* were based on stories that had been passed down from generation to generation.

Specifically, Homer used stories of the Trojan War to compose his epic poems. The war is caused by Paris, a prince of Troy. By kidnapping Helen, the wife of the king of the Greek state of Sparta, Paris outrages all the Greeks. Under the leadership of the Spartan king's brother, King Agamemnon of Mycenae, the Greeks attack Troy and capture it ten years later.

The *Odyssey* recounts the journeys of one of the Greek heroes, Odysseus, after the fall of Troy, and his ultimate return to his wife. The *Odyssey* has long been considered Homer's other masterpiece.

Homer did not so much record history; he created it. The Greeks looked on the *Iliad* and the *Odyssey* as true history and as the works of one poet, Homer. These masterpieces gave the Greeks an ideal past with a cast of heroes. The epics came to be used as basic texts for the education of generations of Greek males. Homer gave to later generations of Greek males a model of heroism and honor. The *Iliad* taught students to be proud of their Greek heritage and their heroic ancestors.

Reading Check **Summarizing** Why is Homer thought to have created, rather than to have recorded, Greek history?

Golden Mask of Agamemnon, c. 1500 B.C.
This gold mask was found by Heinrich Schliemann at a royal grave circle at Mycenae. Who was Agamemnon? What was his role in Greek history?

The Polis: Center of Greek Life

By 750 B.C., the city-state—or what the Greeks called a **polis**—became the central focus of Greek life. Our word *politics* is derived from the Greek word *polis*. In a physical sense, the polis was a town, a city, or even a village, along with its surrounding countryside. The town, city, or village served as the central point where people could meet for political, social, and religious activities.

The main gathering place in the polis was usually a hill. At the top of the hill was a fortified area called an **acropolis**. The acropolis served as a place of refuge during an attack and sometimes came to be a religious center on which temples and public buildings were built. Below the acropolis was an agora, an open area that served both as a place where people could assemble and as a market.

City-states varied greatly in size, from a few square miles to a few hundred square miles. They also varied in population. Athens had a population of more than three hundred thousand by the fifth century B.C., but most city-states were much smaller, consisting of only a few hundred to several thousand people.

The polis was, above all, a community of people who shared a common identity and common goals. As a community, the polis consisted of citizens with political rights (adult males), citizens with no political rights (women and children), and noncitizens (slaves and resident aliens).

Citizens of a polis had rights, but these rights were coupled with responsibilities. The Greek philosopher Aristotle argued that a citizen did not belong just to himself or herself: "We must rather regard every citizen as belonging to the state."

Greek states had different forms of government. In some Greek city-states, there emerged **democracy**, which is government by the people or rule of the many. Other city-states remained committed to government by an **oligarchy**, rule by the few. The differences in how Greek city-states were governed is especially evident in the two most famous and most powerful Greek city-states, **Sparta** and **Athens**.

Reading Check **Identifying** Who had political rights in a Greek polis? Who did not?

CHAPTER 2
Section 1, 51–60

Reading Check

Answer: While the stories that inspired the *Iliad* and the *Odyssey* had some historical basis, they also gave Greece an ideal past to serve as a model for future generations.

Answer: king of Mycenae and brother to Spartan king; led Greek forces against Troy

Daily Lecture and Discussion Notes 2–1

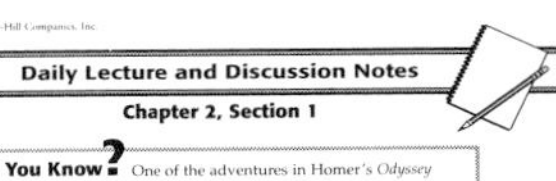

Daily Lecture and Discussion Notes

Chapter 2, Section 1

Did You Know? One of the adventures in Homer's *Odyssey* involved a one-eyed giant called a Cyclops. He shut Odysseus in a cave and blocked the entrance with a gigantic boulder. To escape, Odysseus made the Cyclops drunk, blinded him while he slept, and escaped while clinging to the belly of a sheep let out to pasture. Odysseus was known for being clever.

I. **Early Greek Civilization** *(pages 51–53)*

A. The mountains and the seas were important geographic influences on Greece. The many mountain ranges separated the small, independent Greek communities, causing them to develop different ways of life.

B. The presence of a long seacoast with bays, inlets, and harbors encouraged sea trade.

C. Mycenaean civilization was named for the fortified site, **Mycenae,** first discovered by Heinrich Schliemann. The Mycenaean civilization flourished between 1600 and 1100 B.C.

D. The high point of the civilization was 1400–1200 B.C. Powerful monarchs lived in fortified palaces on hills surrounded by stone walls.

E. Hundreds of years later, Homer recorded the military adventures of the Mycenaeans in his epic poems, the *Iliad* and *Odyssey*.

F. Mycenaean civilization collapsed around 1100 B.C. Greece then entered a Dark Age when population declined and there was less food. Few records remain from this period, which lasted from 1100 to 750 B.C.

G. The works of **Homer** appeared at the end of the Dark Age. The *Iliad* and *Odyssey* are **epic poems.** They tell the story of the kings of **Troy** and Mycenae, the Trojan War, and several Greek heroes.

Reading Check

Answer: Adult males were citizens and had political rights. Women and children were citizens but did not have political rights. Slaves and resident aliens were considered noncitizens and did not have political rights.

Enrich

After students have read the description of a Greek polis, have them list similarities between the Greek polis and a town in colonial America. *(Similarities might include the town serving as a meeting point for social and religious activities, an open space for meeting and markets [town square], town surrounded by agricultural lands, citizens had defined rights.)* **L3**

COOPERATIVE LEARNING ACTIVITY

Conducting Mock Interviews Organize the class into groups of seven or eight to do mock interviews before the class. Have four or five in each group play the roles of typical residents of Athens and the remaining group members play newspaper reporters who ask them questions about their lives and times. Before the interviews, have each group research the lives of the following people: an Athenian merchant, a tyrant, an upper-class woman, a priestess of Athena, or an enslaved person. Ask the group to compose their questions so that the answers describe the different roles of the residents of Athens, especially as the roles pertain to civic participation. **L1**

For grading this activity, refer to the ***Performance Assessment Activities*** booklet.

CHAPTER 2
Section 1, 51–60

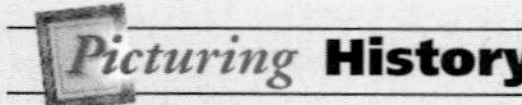

Picturing History

Answer: The acropolis was a place of refuge during an attack and was sometimes a religious center.

Reading Check

Answer: The restrictions placed on the male population of Sparta made Spartan warriors tough, skilled in fighting, and obedient to authority.

Guided Reading Activity 2-1

Name ______ Date ______ Class ______

Guided Reading Activity 2-1

Ancient Greece

DIRECTIONS: Answer the following questions as you read Section 1.

1. What geographic features played especially significant roles in the development of Greek history?
2. What happened to Greece after the collapse of the Mycenaean civilization?
3. According to Homer's writings, Troy was captured by the Greeks under whose leadership?
4. What is the physical definition of a polis?
5. What kind of government did Sparta have?
6. How did Cleisthenes change Athenian government?
7. How did the Great Peloponnesian War lead to the conquest of Greece by Macedonia?
8. What was the main subject matter of classical Greek art?
9. What did Socrates consider the real task of philosophy?
10. What were the three basic groups that Plato describes in *The Republic?*
11. Why wasn't Philip II of Macedonia able to undertake an invasion of Asia?
12. What were the four Hellenistic kingdoms that emerged after Alexander the Great?

64

Writing Activity

After they have read this section, have students describe in a brief essay life in Sparta, including the different roles of men and women.

Sparta

Between 800 and 600 B.C., the lives of Spartans were rigidly organized and tightly controlled (thus, our word *spartan*, meaning "highly self-disciplined"). Males spent their childhood learning military discipline. Then they enrolled in the army for regular military service at age 20. Although allowed to marry, they continued to live in the military barracks until age 30. At 30, Spartan males were allowed to vote in the assembly and live at home, but they stayed in the army until the age of 60.

While their husbands lived in the barracks, Spartan women lived at home. Because of this separation, Spartan women had greater freedom of movement and greater power in the household than was common elsewhere in Greece. Many Spartan women upheld the strict Spartan values, expecting their husbands and sons to be brave in war. The story is told of a Spartan woman who, as she was handing her son his shield, told him to come back carrying his shield or being carried on it.

The Spartan government was an oligarchy headed by two kings, who led the Spartan army on its campaigns. A group of five men, known as the ephors (EH•fuhrs), were elected each year and were responsible for the education of youth and the conduct of all citizens. A council of elders, composed of the two kings and 28 citizens over the age of 60, decided on the issues that would be presented to an assembly made up of male citizens. This assembly did not debate; it only voted on the issues.

To make their new military state secure, the Spartans turned their backs on the outside world. Foreigners, who might have brought in new ideas, were discouraged from visiting. Except for military reasons, Spartans were not allowed to travel abroad, where they might encounter ideas dangerous to the stability of the state. Likewise, Spartan citizens were discouraged from studying philosophy, literature, or the arts—subjects that might encourage new thoughts. The art of war was the Spartan ideal.

Reading Check **Summarizing** How did the restrictions placed on Spartan males affect their lives?

Athens

By 700 B.C., Athens had become a unified polis on the peninsula of Attica. Early Athens was ruled by a king. By the seventh century B.C., however, Athens had become an oligarchy under the control of its aristocrats. These aristocrats owned the best land and controlled political life. There was an assembly of all the citizens, but it had few powers.

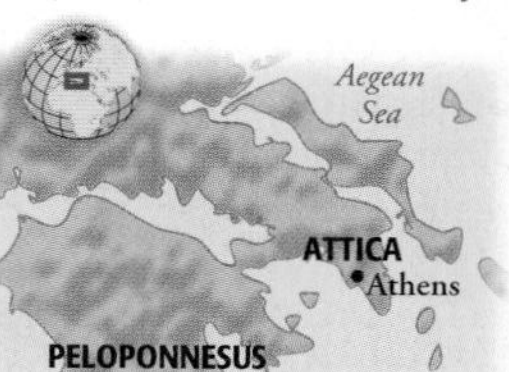

Near the end of the seventh century B.C., Athens faced political turmoil because of serious economic problems. Many Athenian farmers were sold into slavery when they were unable to repay their debts to their aristocratic neighbors. Over and over, there were cries to cancel the debts and give land to the poor. Athens seemed on the verge of civil war.

The ruling Athenian aristocrats reacted to this crisis in 594 B.C., by giving full power to **Solon,** a reform-minded aristocrat. Solon canceled all land debts and freed people who had fallen into slavery for debts. He refused, however, to take land from the rich and give it to the poor.

Solon's reforms, though popular, did not solve the problems of Athens. Aristocrats were still powerful, and poor peasants could not obtain land. It was not until 508 B.C. that **Cleisthenes** (KLYS•thuh•neez), another reformer, gained the upper hand.

Picturing History

The Acropolis in Athens is crowned by the Parthenon. What function(s) did the area of the acropolis play in the ancient Greek city-states?

MEETING INDIVIDUAL NEEDS

English Language Learners Ask students who find it hard to use large words to search for difficult words in the text. Assign partners to work with these students to define each word. Once the words are defined, divide the class into groups of ten. Ask each group to form two teams of five players each. Each group member on the team takes a turn giving a definition to the opposing team whose members must say the word that has been defined. If the opposing team answers correctly, it takes a turn giving a definition. If it does not supply the correct answer, the other team continues giving definitions until one of their opponents supplies the correct word. **L1**

Refer to ***Inclusion for the High School Social Studies Classroom Strategies and Activities*** in the TCR.

Vases such as this one are an excellent source of information about everyday life in ancient Greece.

Cleisthenes created a new council of five hundred that supervised foreign affairs, oversaw the treasury, and proposed the laws that would be voted on by the assembly. The Athenian assembly, composed of male citizens, was given final authority to pass laws after free and open debate. Because the assembly of citizens now had the central role in the Athenian political system, the reforms of Cleisthenes created the foundations for Athenian democracy.

Reading Check **Explaining** How did Cleisthenes create the foundation for democracy in Athens?

Classical Greece

TURNING POINT **Pericles expanded the involvement of Athenians in their democracy. By creating a direct democracy, he enabled every male citizen to play a role in government.**

Classical Greece is the name given to the period of Greek history from around 500 B.C. to the conquest of Greece in 338 B.C. This period was marked by two wars. In the first one, fought between 499 B.C. and 479 B.C., the Greeks worked together to defeat two invasions by the Persians.

After the defeat of the Persians, Athens took over the leadership of the Greek world. Under **Pericles,** who was a dominant figure in Athenian politics between 461 and 429 B.C., Athens expanded its new

CONNECTIONS Around The World

Rulers and Gods

All of the world's earliest civilizations believed that there was a close connection between rulers and gods. In Egypt, pharaohs were considered gods whose role was to maintain the order and harmony of the universe in their own kingdoms. In Mesopotamia, India, and China, rulers were thought to rule with divine assistance. Kings were often seen as rulers who derived their power from the gods and who were the agents or representatives of the gods. Many Romans certainly believed that their success in creating an empire was a visible sign of divine favor. As one Roman stated, "We have overcome all the nations of the world, because we have realized that the world is directed and governed by the gods."

The rulers' supposed connection to the divine also caused them to seek divine aid in the affairs of the world. This led to the art of *divination*—an organized method to figure out the intentions of the gods. In Mesopotamian and Roman society, divination took the form of examining the livers of sacrificed animals or the flights of birds to determine the will of the gods. The Chinese used oracle bones to receive advice from the gods. The Greeks consulted oracles.

Underlying all of these practices was a belief in a supernatural universe—a world in which divine forces were in charge and human well-being depended on those divine forces. It was not until the scientific revolution of the 1600s that many people began to believe in a natural world that was not governed by spiritual forces.

▲ *An Athenian king consults the oracle at Delphi.*

Comparing Cultures

Why were rulers of early civilizations considered to have divine powers? How did this affect their systems of government?

Answer: Everything that happened was believed to have happened because the gods wanted it to happen, so rulers must either be gods themselves or rule with assistance of the gods. Kings ruled by divine right, which lent authority to their governments and allowed the kings to do as they wished.

Reading Check

Answer: Cleisthenes created a new council of 500 that supervised foreign affairs and the treasury and proposed the laws that would be voted on by an assembly composed of male citizens. Because the assembly now had a central role in the political system, these reforms created the foundation for Athenian democracy.

TURNING POINT

The development of direct democracy in Athens was an important step toward the creation of our modern democratic system. Have students create a time line to be displayed in class that traces the process by which democratic-republican government evolved from its beginings in Classical Greece. Have students add to the time line as they continue their study of world history. **L2**

3 ASSESS

Assign Section 1 Assessment as homework or as an in-class activity.

Have students use **Interactive Tutor Self-Assessment CD-ROM.**

INTERDISCIPLINARY CONNECTIONS ACTIVITY

Government Athens taught the West that democracy was the most desirable form of government. Yet Athens itself adopted democracy only for roughly 100 years. After the Age of Pericles and Athens's defeat by Sparta in the Great Peloponnesian War, Athens lost confidence in its democratic system. After all, the authoritarian Spartans, the same people whom Pericles disdained in his famous *Funeral Oration,* had defeated it! None of the great Greek philosophers who taught in Athens—Socrates, Plato, Aristotle—were believers in the virtues of democracy. Although Athens turned its back on democracy, this form of government survived and is the backbone of many nations today. Have students work in pairs to compile a list of the democratic governments throughout the world today.

Reading Check

Answer: After the war, Sparta, Athens, and Thebes continued petty wars, ignoring the growing threat of Macedonia to their north.

Enrich

During a class discussion, ask students to identify developments from the Age of Pericles that have had an important impact on the United States. **L1**

Section Quiz 2–1

Name ______ Date ______ Class ______

Chapter 2 Score

Section Quiz 2-1

DIRECTIONS: Matching Match each item in Column A with an item in Column B. Write the correct letters in the blanks. *(10 points each)*

Column A	Column B
____ 1. poet who wrote the *Iliad*	A. ephor
____ 2. fortified area on a hilltop	B. Aristotle
____ 3. elected member of Sparta's oligarchy	C. acropolis
____ 4. Athenian ruler at the height of Athenian power	D. Homer
____ 5. Plato's student	E. Pericles

DIRECTIONS: Multiple Choice In the blank, write the letter of the choice that best completes the statement or answers the question. *(10 points each)*

____ 6. The *Iliad* describes the sacking of Troy by the
A. Athenians. C. Cretans.
B. Mycenaeans. D. Romans.

____ 7. A Spartan warrior was told to return from war
A. after he married.
B. after he turned 20.
C. with his shield or on it.
D. to repay his debts.

____ 8. The war between Sparta and Athens is called the
A. Trojan War.
B. Battle of Sparta.
C. Persian War.
D. Great Peloponnesian War.

____ 9. Plato believed that
A. individuals should live in a just and rational state.
B. an ideal government should be ruled by dictators.
C. democracy was the best form of government.
D. men and women should not have the same education.

____ 10. After the death of Alexander the Great, all of the following happened EXCEPT
A. four Hellenistic kingdoms emerged.
B. his united empire continued.
C. Macedonian generals struggled for power.
D. Greek culture spread through Southwest Asia.

Glencoe World History—Modern Times 9

Connecting Across Time

Give students a research assignment to write an essay in which they describe either the democratic system practiced in Athens, the economic system used in Athens, or the responsibilities of women in an Athenian household. When students have completed their essays, ask volunteers to read their essays aloud to the class. Discuss how each of these—democracy, economic systems, and the role of women—has evolved, and compare them with contemporary conditions in the United States and in other countries. **L2**

empire abroad. At the same time, democracy flourished at home. This period of Athenian and Greek history, which historians have called the Age of Pericles, saw the height of Athenian power and brilliance.

In the Age of Pericles, the Athenians became deeply attached to their democratic system, which was a direct democracy. In a **direct democracy,** the people participate directly in government decision making through mass meetings. In Athens, every male who was a citizen participated in the governing assembly and voted on all major issues.

The growth of an Athenian Empire, however, left the Greek world divided into two major camps: the Athenian Empire and Sparta. Athens and Sparta had built two very different kinds of societies, and neither state was able to tolerate the other's system. Sparta and its allies feared the growing Athenian Empire, and a series of disputes finally led to the outbreak of the Great Peloponnesian War in 431 B.C.

This disastrous civil war lasted until 405 B.C., when the Athenian fleet was destroyed at Aegospotami (EE•guh•SPAH•tuh•MEE). Within the next year, Athens surrendered. Its walls were torn down, the navy disbanded, and the Athenian Empire destroyed.

The Great Peloponnesian War weakened the major Greek states and ruined any possibility of cooperation among them. During the next 70 years, Sparta, Athens, and Thebes (a new Greek power) struggled to dominate Greek affairs. In continuing their petty wars, the Greeks ignored the growing power of Macedonia to their north.

Reading Check **Explaining** How did the Great Peloponnesian War weaken the Greek states?

The Culture of Classical Greece

Classical Greece, especially Athens under the rule of Pericles, witnessed a period of remarkable intellec-

THE WAY IT WAS

YOUNG PEOPLE IN . . .

Greece

In Sparta, boys were trained to be soldiers. At birth, each child was examined by state officials, who decided whether the child was fit to live. Those who were judged unfit were left on a mountainside to die. Boys judged fit were taken from their mothers at the age of seven and put under control of the state.

These boys lived in military-style barracks, where they were subjected to harsh discipline to make them tough and mean. Their education stressed military training and obedience to authority. The Greek historian Plutarch described the handling of young Spartans:

> "After they were twelve years old, they were no longer allowed to wear any undergarments, they had one coat to serve them a year; their bodies were hard and dry, with but little acquaintance of baths; these human indulgences they were allowed only on some few particular days in the year. They lodged together in little bands upon beds made of the rushes which grew by the banks of the river Eurotas, which they were to break off with their hands with a knife."

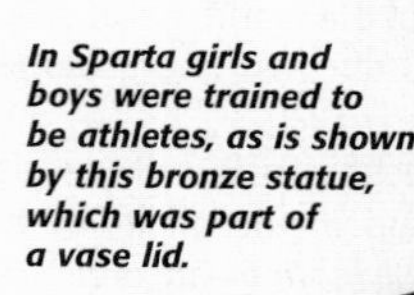

In Sparta girls and boys were trained to be athletes, as is shown by this bronze statue, which was part of a vase lid.

EXTENDING THE CONTENT

Common Identity of Athenians It seems that humans have traditionally placed more emphasis on what makes them different from one another than on what makes them alike. If you had stopped a person on the Acropolis and asked her what she was, her answer would have been, "I am an Athenian." Only secondly would she have answered, "I am a Hellene" (a descendant of the goddess Helen from whom the Greeks believed they came). This provincial self-perception contributed much to the frequent state of warfare that existed among the inhabitants of Hellas (Ancient Greece). This same provincialism often exists in today's world. Ask students to identify a contemporary situation that parallels this historic situation.

Discobolos, *a famous Greek statue, pays tribute to athletes and the Greek ideals of sound mind and sound body.*

tual and cultural growth. The developments of this period became the main source of Western culture.

The Classical Ideals of Greek Art The arts of the Western world have been largely dominated by the standards set by the Greeks of the classical period. Classical Greek art was concerned with expressing eternal ideals—reason, moderation, balance, and harmony in all things. The subject matter of this art was the human being, presented as an object of great beauty. The classic style was meant to civilize the emotions.

In architecture, the most important form was the temple dedicated to a god or goddess. At the center of Greek temples were walled rooms that housed both the statues of deities and treasuries in which gifts to the gods and goddesses were safeguarded. These central rooms were surrounded by a screen of columns that made Greek temples open structures rather than closed ones.

Some of the finest examples of Greek classical architecture were built in Athens in the fifth century B.C. The most famous building, regarded as the greatest example of the classical Greek temple, was the

Basically, the Spartan system worked. Spartan males were known for their toughness and their meanness. They were also known as the best soldiers in all of Greece.

Spartan girls received an education similar to that of the boys. Girls, too, underwent physical training, including running, wrestling, and throwing the javelin. The purpose was clear: to strengthen the girls for their roles as healthy mothers.

Well-to-do Athenian citizens raised their children very differently. Athenian children were nurtured by their mothers until the age of seven. At seven, a boy of the upper class was turned over to a male servant, known as a *pedagogue*. The pedagogue, who was usually a slave, accompanied the child to school. He was also responsible for teaching his charge good manners. He could punish the child with a birch rod to impose discipline.

The purpose of an education for upper-class Athenian boys was to create a well-rounded person. To that end, a boy had three teachers. One taught him reading, writing, and arithmetic. Another taught physical education, a necessity to achieve the ideal of a sound mind in a sound body. A third taught him music, which consisted of playing the lyre (a stringed instrument) and singing. Education ended at 18, when an Athenian male formally became a citizen.

Girls of all classes remained at home, as their mothers did. Their mothers taught them how to run a home, which included how to spin and weave—activities expected of a good wife. Only in some wealthy families did girls learn to read, write, and perhaps play the lyre.

CONNECTING TO THE PAST

1. **Summarizing Information** Describe a Spartan upbringing. How does this differ from the childhood of an American child?
2. **Compare and Contrast** Compare a well-educated Spartan boy with a well-educated Athenian and a well-educated American. What are the differences?
3. **Writing about History** Does your education today incorporate any Spartan or Athenian ideas? If so, give specific examples.

THE WAY IT WAS

Answers:

1. Spartan children were taken away from their mothers at age 7 and placed in military barracks, where they were subjected to harsh discipline. They were allowed no luxuries or comforts. Many American children stay at home until they reach adulthood.
2. A well-educated Spartan boy would know only how to fight and how to obey orders. A well-educated Athenian boy would be a well-rounded citizen. He would have studied reading, writing, arithmetic, music, and physical education until age 18. A well-educated American would have an education similar to that of the Athenian, but would probably have studied sciences, foreign languages, and computers. Education does not necessarily end at 18.
3. Answers will vary but should incorporate more Athenian ideas than Spartan ones.

Enrich

Ask students to use outside resources to identify significant examples of art and architecture that demonstrate an artistic ideal or visual principle from ancient Greece. Have students share their findings with the class, and ask students to explain how their examples relate to ancient Greece.

COOPERATIVE LEARNING ACTIVITY

Producing a Skit Divide the class into groups and ask the class to research daily life in Classical Athens in order to write and produce a skit that shows typical activity in an ancient Greek marketplace. Assign groups to handle various activities: scriptwriting; designing and producing a simple set, costumes, program, and promotional materials; acting; and directing. Ask students to include a variety of people in the skit: women, slaves, children, aristocrats, artisans, and merchants. The skit should clearly convey the operation of democracy in the polis through action and words. After the presentation, have students assess the skit to determine if this goal was accomplished. L1

CURRICULUM CONNECTION

English Arrange with an English teacher to discuss Greek theater with the class, especially Greek tragedy, focusing on the playwrights mentioned in this section. If available, you may wish to show part of a videotape of one of the more famous plays, such as *Antigone* or *Oedipus Rex.* **L2**

Who?What?Where?When?

Theaters in Greece were built in naturally occurring amphitheaters. The action took place within a level circle called the *orchestra.* The audience sat in naturally tiered seats set into the hillside. On the opposite side of the orchestra, a façade (false front) was erected that served two purposes: a changing room for the actors and a backdrop for scenery.

Critical Thinking

In this two-part critical thinking activity, ask students to use print or Internet resources to analyze examples of Greek art, architecture, literature, music, and drama. Then, assign students to write essays demonstrating what they have learned. In the first part of their essays have students identify how the examples reflect Greek history and culture. In the second part of their essays, ask students to identify how Greek art, architecture, literature, music, and drama have transcended the culture, how they convey universal themes, and how they have influenced contemporary culture. **L3**

"I tell you that virtue does not come from money, but that money comes from virtue, as does every other good of man, public and private."

—The Apology of Socrates, *Plato*

Socrates

Parthenon. It was built between 447 and 432 B.C. Dedicated to Athena, the patron goddess of Athens, and to the glory of Athens itself, the Parthenon was an expression of Athenian pride in their city-state. The Parthenon shows the principles of classical architecture: the search for calmness, clarity, and freedom from unnecessary detail.

Greek sculpture also developed a classical style. Lifelike statues of the male nude, the favorite subject of Greek sculptors, showed relaxed attitudes. Their faces were self-assured, their bodies flexible and smooth muscled. Greek sculptors sought to achieve a standard of ideal beauty rather than realism.

Greek Drama Drama as we know it in Western culture was created by the Greeks. Plays were presented in outdoor theaters as part of religious festivals. The first Greek dramas were tragedies, which were presented in a trilogy (a set of three plays) built around a common theme. The only complete trilogy we possess today, called the *Oresteia,* was composed by Aeschylus. This set of three plays relates the fate of Agamemnon, a hero in the Trojan War, and his family after his return from the war.

Greek tragedies dealt with universal themes still relevant today. They examined such problems as the nature of good and evil, the rights of the individual, the nature of divine forces, and the nature of human beings. In the world of the Greek tragedies, striving to do the best thing may not always lead to success, but the attempt is a worthy endeavor. Greek pride in accomplishment and independence was real. As the chorus chanted in Sophocles' *Antigone,* "Is there anything more wonderful on earth, our marvelous planet, than the miracle of man?"

Greek Philosophy The term *philosophy* comes from a Greek word that means "love of wisdom." Early Greek philosophers were concerned with the development of critical or rational thought about the nature of the universe. Socrates, Plato, and Aristotle remain to this day three of the greatest philosophers of the Western world.

Socrates was a stonemason, but his true love was philosophy. He taught many pupils, but he accepted no pay. He believed that the goal of education was only to improve the individual.

Socrates used a teaching method that is still known by his name. The Socratic method of teaching uses a question-and-answer format to lead pupils to see things for themselves by using their own reason. Socrates believed that all real knowledge is already present within each person. Only critical examination is needed to call it forth. This was the real task of philosophy, because, as Socrates said, "the unexamined life is not worth living." This belief in the individual's ability to reason was an important contribution of the Greeks.

One of Socrates' students was **Plato,** considered by many to be the greatest philosopher of Western civilization. Unlike his master Socrates, who did not write down his thoughts, Plato wrote a great deal. He was particularly fascinated with the question of how we know what is real.

Plato's ideas about government were explained in a work entitled *The Republic.* Based on his experiences in Athens, Plato had come to distrust the workings of democracy. To him, individuals could not achieve a good life unless they lived in a just (fair) and rational state.

Plato's search for the just state led him to construct an ideal state in which people were divided into three basic groups. At the top was an upper class of philosopher-kings. The second group in Plato's ideal state were warriors who protected society. The third group contained all the rest, the masses, people driven not by wisdom or courage but by desire. They would be the producers of society—artisans, tradespeople, and farmers. Contrary to Greek custom, Plato also believed that men and women should have the same education and equal access to all positions.

Plato established a school in Athens known as the Academy. One of his pupils, who studied at the Academy for 20 years, was **Aristotle.** Aristotle's interests lay in analyzing and classifying things based on observation and investigation. He wrote about many subjects, including ethics, logic, politics, poetry, astronomy, geology, biology, and physics.

CRITICAL THINKING ACTIVITY

Analyzing Information Drama played a major role in Greek culture, as it conveyed values, portrayed real-life situations, and focused on universal themes. It also satirized society, using humor to criticize certain aspects of life. Drama followed very strict rules. One rule limited all speaking parts to three actors. Another rule insisted the actors wear masks. During a class discussion, ask: 1. Why do you think Greek drama had such strict rules? 2. What reasons could it have for limiting the number of actors? 3. Why do you think the actors were required to wear masks? *(Answers may include: 1. plays easier to write if the form restricted; 2. difficult to find actors; 3. masks suspended reality, males could play female characters.)* **L3**

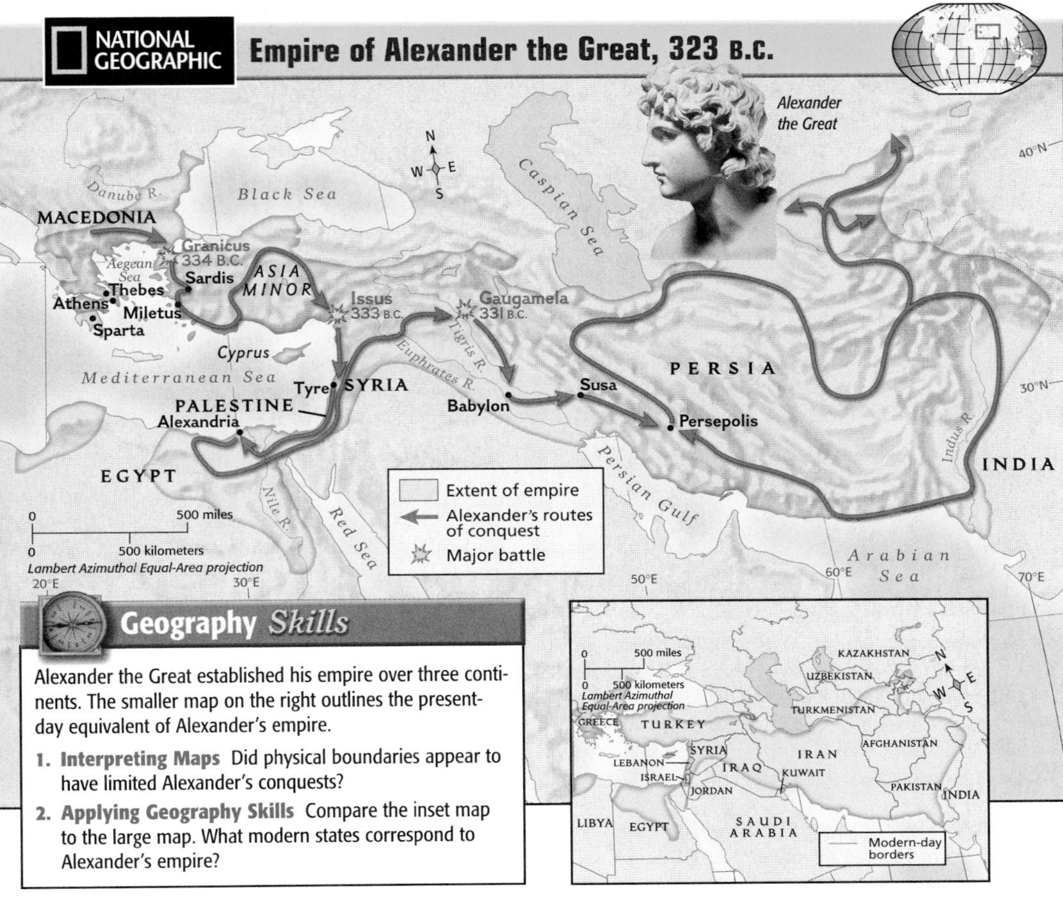

Geography Skills

Alexander the Great established his empire over three continents. The smaller map on the right outlines the present-day equivalent of Alexander's empire.

1. **Interpreting Maps** Did physical boundaries appear to have limited Alexander's conquests?
2. **Applying Geography Skills** Compare the inset map to the large map. What modern states correspond to Alexander's empire?

Like Plato, Aristotle wanted an effective form of government that would rationally direct human affairs. Unlike Plato, he did not seek an ideal state but tried to find the best form of government by analyzing existing governments. For his *Politics,* Aristotle looked at the constitutions of 158 states and found three good forms of government: monarchy, aristocracy, and constitutional government. He favored constitutional government as the best form for most people.

Reading Check **Summarizing** What ideals were expressed in classical Greek art, architecture, and drama?

Alexander the Great

TURNING POINT **As a result of Alexander's conquests, Greek language, art, architecture, and literature spread throughout Southwest Asia.**

The Greeks viewed their northern neighbors, the Macedonians, as barbarians, but in 359 B.C., Philip II came to the Macedonian throne. A great admirer of Greek culture, he longed to unite all of Greece under **Macedonia.** He finally did so in 338 B.C. at the Battle of Chaeronea (KEHR•uh•NEE•uh), near Thebes. The Macedonian army crushed the Greeks.

Philip insisted that the Greek states form a league and then cooperate with him in a war against Persia. Before Philip could undertake his invasion of Asia, however, he was assassinated, leaving the task to his son Alexander.

Alexander the Great was only 20 when he became king of Macedonia. After his father's death, Alexander moved quickly to fulfill his father's dream of invading the Persian Empire. In the spring of 334 B.C., Alexander entered Asia Minor with an army of some thirty-seven thousand men, both Macedonians and Greeks. By 331 B.C., Alexander had taken possession of the Persian Empire. However, he was not content.

Over the next three years, Alexander moved east and northeast, as far as modern-day Pakistan. By the

CHAPTER 2
Section 1, 51–60

Geography Skills

Answers:

1. not really, except that his empire seems to have been bounded by rivers such as the Euphrates or Indus
2. Turkey, Syria, Iraq, Iran, Egypt, Afghanistan, Pakistan, Lebanon, Israel

Reading Check

Answer: reason, moderation, balance, and harmony in all things

TURNING POINT

Greek culture had a tremendous impact upon the development of art and ideas in Western society.

Reading Essentials and Study Guide 2–1

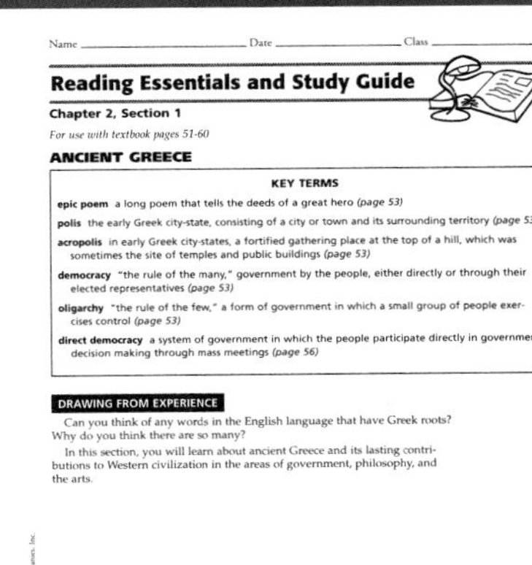

Name ______ Date ______ Class ______

Reading Essentials and Study Guide

Chapter 2, Section 1

For use with textbook pages 51-60

ANCIENT GREECE

KEY TERMS

epic poem a long poem that tells the deeds of a great hero *(page 53)*

polis the early Greek city-state, consisting of a city or town and its surrounding territory *(page 53)*

acropolis in early Greek city-states, a fortified gathering place at the top of a hill, which was sometimes the site of temples and public buildings *(page 53)*

democracy "the rule of the many," government by the people, either directly or through their elected representatives *(page 53)*

oligarchy "the rule of the few," a form of government in which a small group of people exercises control *(page 53)*

direct democracy a system of government in which the people participate directly in government decision making through mass meetings *(page 56)*

DRAWING FROM EXPERIENCE

Can you think of any words in the English language that have Greek roots? Why do you think there are so many?

In this section, you will learn about ancient Greece and its lasting contributions to Western civilization in the areas of government, philosophy, and the arts.

EXTENDING THE CONTENT

The Education of Alexander the Great As a boy, Alexander the Great was tutored by the great philosopher Aristotle. Alexander developed a love of philosophy and philosophers because of this experience. One day Alexander visited the cynic Diogenes, made famous by his search for an honest man. Diogenes was sitting beside a barrel enjoying the sun. The emperor asked the poor man if there was anything he could do for him or anything he desired. "Yes," replied Diogenes, "You can stand to one side. You are blocking my sun." Alexander obliged him. It is said he learned something about riches and power that day.

CHAPTER 2
Section 1, 51–60

Reading Check

Answer: The Greek states lost their freedom as they were united under Philip II. They formed a league and then cooperated with Philip in a war against Persia.

Enrich

To help students consider the impact one individual can have on history, ask them to consider Alexander the Great. During a class discussion, ask them to list three ways in which he changed the world in which he lived. **L2**

Reading Check

Answer: Macedonia, Syria, Pergamum, Egypt

Reteaching Activity

Ask students to discuss why the form of government that Pericles introduced was so popular with citizens of ancient Athens. **L1** ELL

4 CLOSE

The pursuit of wisdom, support for the arts, and the endorsement of athletic prowess all played prominent roles in classical Greece. Ask students to state which of these areas was most important and why. **L1**

HISTORY Online

Web Activity Visit the *Glencoe World History—Modern Times* Web site at wh.mt.glencoe.com and click on **Chapter 2–Student Web Activity** to learn more about Alexander the Great and his conquests.

summer of 327 B.C., he had entered India, where he experienced a number of difficult campaigns. Weary of fighting year after year, his soldiers refused to go farther.

Alexander returned to Babylon, where he planned more campaigns. However, in June 323 B.C., exhausted from wounds, fever, and too much alcohol, he died at the age of 32.

Reading Check **Identifying** What changes in the Greek states resulted from the Greeks' defeat at the Battle of Chaeronea?

The Hellenistic Era

Alexander created a new age, the Hellenistic Era. The word *Hellenistic* is derived from a Greek word meaning "to imitate Greeks." It is an appropriate way, then, to describe an age that saw the expansion of the Greek language and ideas to the non-Greek world of Southwest Asia and beyond.

The Hellenistic Kingdoms The united empire that Alexander created by his conquests fell apart soon after his death as the most important Macedonian generals engaged in a struggle for power. By 300 B.C., any hope of unity was dead. Eventually, four Hellenistic kingdoms emerged as the successors to Alexander: Macedonia, Syria in the east, the kingdom of Pergamum in western Asia Minor, and Egypt. All were eventually conquered by the Romans.

Hellenistic rulers encouraged a massive spread of Greek colonists to Southwest Asia. Greeks (and Macedonians) provided not only new recruits for the army but also a pool of civilian administrators and workers. Architects, engineers, dramatists, and actors were all in demand in the new Greek cities. The Greek cities of the Hellenistic Era became the chief agents in the spread of Greek culture in Southwest Asia—as far, in fact, as modern-day Afghanistan and India.

Hellenistic Culture The Hellenistic Era was a period of considerable cultural accomplishment in many areas. Certain centers—especially the great Hellenistic city of **Alexandria**—stood out. Alexandria became home to poets, writers, philosophers, and scientists—scholars of all kinds.

The founding of new cities and the rebuilding of old ones presented many opportunities for Greek architects and sculptors. Both Hellenistic kings and rich citizens patronized sculptors. Thousands of statues were erected in towns and cities all over the Hellenistic world. Hellenistic sculptors moved away from the idealism of earlier classicism to a more emotional and realistic art. This is especially evident in the numerous statues of women and children.

Reading Check **Identifying** Which four kingdoms emerged following Alexander's death?

SECTION 1 ASSESSMENT

Checking for Understanding

1. **Define** epic poem, polis, acropolis, democracy, oligarchy, direct democracy.
2. **Identify** Homer, Solon, Cleisthenes, Pericles, Socrates, Plato, Aristotle, Alexander the Great.
3. **Locate** Mycenae, Troy, Sparta, Athens, Macedonia, Alexandria.
4. **Describe** the importance of the *Iliad* and the *Odyssey* to Greek culture.
5. **Identify** the values and standards exemplified by Greek art and architecture.

Critical Thinking

6. **Contrast** How were the governments favored by Plato and Aristotle different? Which view makes more sense to you? Why?
7. **Organizing Information** Using a table like the one below, identify the reforms that led to democracy in Athens and the leaders who initiated them.

Leader	Reforms
Solon	
Cleisthenes	
Pericles	

Analyzing Visuals

8. **Examine** the photo of the Parthenon shown on page 54. Where is the Parthenon located? When was it built? How does this famous temple demonstrate the principles of classical architecture?

Writing About History

9. **Descriptive Writing** Imagine that you are a 25-year-old male living in Sparta in 700 B.C. Create a diary in which you record your activities for one week. Write one diary page for each day.

SECTION 1 ASSESSMENT

1. Key terms are in blue.
2. Homer *(p. 52);* Solon *(p. 54);* Cleisthenes *(p. 54);* Pericles *(p. 55);* Socrates *(p. 58);* Plato *(p. 58);* Aristotle *(p. 58);* Alexander the Great *(p. 59)*
3. See chapter maps.
4. They were used in education, as models of heroism and honor, and as a source of Greek pride.
5. Sculptors sought an ideal of beauty; art and architecture reflected calmness, clarity, reason, harmony, moderation, and balance.
6. Plato distrusted democracy, favored a philosopher-king ruling a three-tiered state; Aristotle favored a constitutional government. Both looked to government to guide people's lives rationally.
7. Solon: canceled land debt, freed debtors from slavery; Cleisthenes: created council of 500, gave Athenian assembly central role; Pericles: created direct democracy
8. Athens; between 447 and 432 B.C.; it reflects search for calmness, clarity, and harmony
9. Students will create diary entries.

CRITICAL THINKING SKILLBUILDER

Making Comparisons

Why Learn This Skill?

When making comparisons, you identify the similarities and differences among two or more ideas, objects, or events.

Learning the Skill

Follow these steps to make comparisons:

- Find two subjects that can be compared. They should be similar enough to have characteristics that are common to both. For example, it would be more appropriate to compare a Greek statue to an Egyptian statue than to an abstract modern painting.
- Determine which features the subjects have in common that are suitable for comparison.
- Look for similarities and differences within these areas.
- If possible, find information that explains the similarities and differences.

Practicing the Skill

The following excerpts from the text discuss Spartan and Athenian models for raising children. Read both excerpts, then answer the questions that follow.

Athena

Passage A

In Sparta, boys were trained to be soldiers. State officials examined all children at birth and decided whether or not they were fit to live. Those who were judged unfit were left in the open on a mountainside to die. Boys judged fit were put under control of the state at age seven. They lived in military-style barracks and were subjected to harsh discipline to make them tough. Their education stressed military training and obedience to authority.

Passage B

Athenian children were nurtured by their mothers until the age of seven, when boys of the upper class were turned over to a male servant, known as a pedagogue. The pedagogue accompanied the child to school and was responsible for teaching his charge good manners. He could punish the child with a birch rod to impose discipline.

The purpose of an education for upper-class Athenian boys was to create a well-rounded person. A boy had three teachers. One taught reading, writing, and arithmetic; a second taught physical education; and a third taught music. Education ended at eighteen, when an Athenian male formally became a citizen.

1. Make a chart with one column labeled Sparta and one labeled Athens. List the similarities in how the two states raised children, then list the differences.
2. How did the similarities and differences in raising children suit the needs of each city-state?

Applying the Skill

Survey your classmates about an issue in the news. Summarize their opinions and compare the different results in a paragraph.

Glencoe's **Skillbuilder Interactive Workbook, Level 2,** provides instruction and practice in key social studies skills.

CRITICAL THINKING SKILLBUILDER

TEACH

Making Comparisons Many television ads are based on comparisons. Have two volunteers with different preferences in morning cereal bring in the cereal box or a copy of the nutrition information, net weight, and price each box displays. Other students can transfer the nutritional data to the chalkboard. Then write the price per ounce of each cereal on the chalkboard. Ask students to draw conclusions from the comparison. **L2**

Additional Practice

Skills Reinforcement Activity 2

Name ______ Date ______ Class ______

Skills Reinforcement Activity 2

Making Comparisons

Making comparisons means finding differences as well as similarities.

DIRECTIONS: Read the two passages below, which provide information about the Greek and Egyptian approaches to religion. Make a diagram like the one below on a separate sheet of paper. Complete the diagram to record what is unique to Greek religion and what is unique to Egyptian religion (differences), as well as what is common to both religions (similarities). Questions have been provided to help you start to organize the information on the chart.

Egyptian Religion

It is difficult to speak of Egyptian beliefs as religion, if "religion" means a unified system of belief. Although the most popular god was Re, the god of the sun, every temple in Egypt worshiped its own local deities. The Egyptian gods and goddesses were pictured with human bodies and either animal or human heads. For example, Re had a human body with the head of a hawk; like the hawk, the sun made its way swiftly across the sky. Anubis, a god connected with the dead, was given the head of a jackal because jackals were often

Greek Religion

By the time Homer composed the *Iliad* and the *Odyssey* in the 700s B.C., the major gods and goddesses of the Greeks had been well established, although each polis worshiped its own particular deity. The Greek deities were presented in an entirely human form but were given superhuman powers. For example, Poseidon controlled the seas and could cause violent storms at will. Like humans, the deities were subject to a force considered so powerful that not even Zeus could turn it back. This force was presented in the form of a goddess called Moira (Fate)

GLENCOE TECHNOLOGY

CD-ROM

Glencoe Skillbuilder Interactive Workbook CD-ROM, Level 2

This interactive CD-ROM reinforces student mastery of essential social studies skills.

ANSWERS TO PRACTICING THE SKILL

1. Similarities: boys stayed home until age 7, harsh punishment used to impose discipline; Differences: Sparta: children deemed unfit to live were left to die, at age 7 boys put under control of state, lived in military-style barracks, education stressed military training and obedience; Athens: children nurtured by their mothers, after age 7 boys taught good manners by a pedagogue, purpose of education to create a well-rounded individual, at 18 formally became a citizen

2. Sparta wanted to create tough, single-minded soldiers to maintain control over their conquered territories; Athens wanted to create well-rounded citizens.

Applying the Skill: Answers will vary depending on current events.

SPECIAL REPORT SUMMARY

The *Iliad* is not a true, historical account, but a poem written by Homer that is based on the story of the Trojan Wars.

■

The *Iliad* does record many accurate facts about Mycenaean civilization, Troy, and the Greek Bronze Age.

■

Heinrich Schliemann, a wealthy German amateur archaeologist, carried out excavations in the late 1800s that uncovered the sites of Troy and Mycenae. Ongoing excavations have uncovered the entire site of Troy, nine levels ranging from 3000 B.C. to the early sixth century A.D.

■

These findings contribute to the belief that wars between Troy and Mycenae may well have occurred as recorded in the *Iliad.*

TEACH

Points to Discuss

After students have read this selection, discuss the following: **Why was (and is) oral tradition an important part of literature?** *(In the earliest civilizations, writing was nonexistent, and so stories were passed down from one generation to another. This oral tradition was carried on into later civilizations, and it still exists in many cultures; students will learn about the importance of the griot to African culture later in this text.)* **Why was Heinrich Schliemann determined to conduct archaeological digs in Greece?** *(As students have read in the text and in this article, Schliemann believed that Homer's account was based on historical fact,*

MORE THAN MYTH TO THE *ILIAD*

1

In Homer's epic poem the *Iliad*, the rich and powerful city-state of Mycenae headed a united Greek attack against "windy Ilion"—the wealthy city of Troy—to avenge the kidnapping of "love[ly-] haired Helen," wife of Sparta's king Menelaus. F[or] centuries, the fabled treasures of these legendary cities were thought to exist—like the Trojan Wa[r] itself—in imagination only. But modern archaeol[-] ogy suggests there may be more than myth to Homer's classic tale.

Greeks in antiquity considered the *Iliad* to be a historical account of their past. Alexander the Great, for example, traced his mother's family back to the hero Achilles. We know today that the poem is not a true story of a war in Greece's late Bronze Age (about 1600 to 1100 B.C.). For one thing, the *Iliad* was not written during this period. It is the result of more than 500 years of oral tradition, handed down by generations of professional poets. Credit for the final masterpiece went to someone the Greeks called "divine Homer," but they knew nothing more about this person than his supposed name—and neither do we.

Still, myths often spring from a kernel of historical truth, and in the late nineteenth century, the Trojan War's mythic rival cities entered the real world of history. Between 1870 and 1890 German businessman and amateur archaeologist Heinrich Schliemann carried out archaeological digs that put Troy and Mycenae on the map. Since then, archaeologists and scholars have uncovered numerous details suggesting that Homer's *Iliad* records many aspects of the Greek Bronze Age (known to historians as the Mycenaean Age, for the city that dominated the period). The giant walls of Mycenae and its fabulous treasure, for example, and the geography around Troy itself in northwestern Turkey, all support descriptions you can find in the poem's stirring rhythms.

Descendants of Greek-speaking peoples who appeared on the Greek mainland around 1900 B.C., the Mycenaeans eventually developed societies that revolved around a central palace. In addition to Mycenae itself, Schliemann and later archaeologists have discovered major Mycenaean centers whose names appear in the *Iliad:* "sacred" Pylos, Tiryns "of the huge walls," and "thirsty" Argos, to list only a few of them. Researchers have also discovered hundreds of settlements and tombs—all with a shared culture.

The historical Mycenae dominated the plain of Argos, a wealthy region that controlled much of the trade

Teacher's Notes

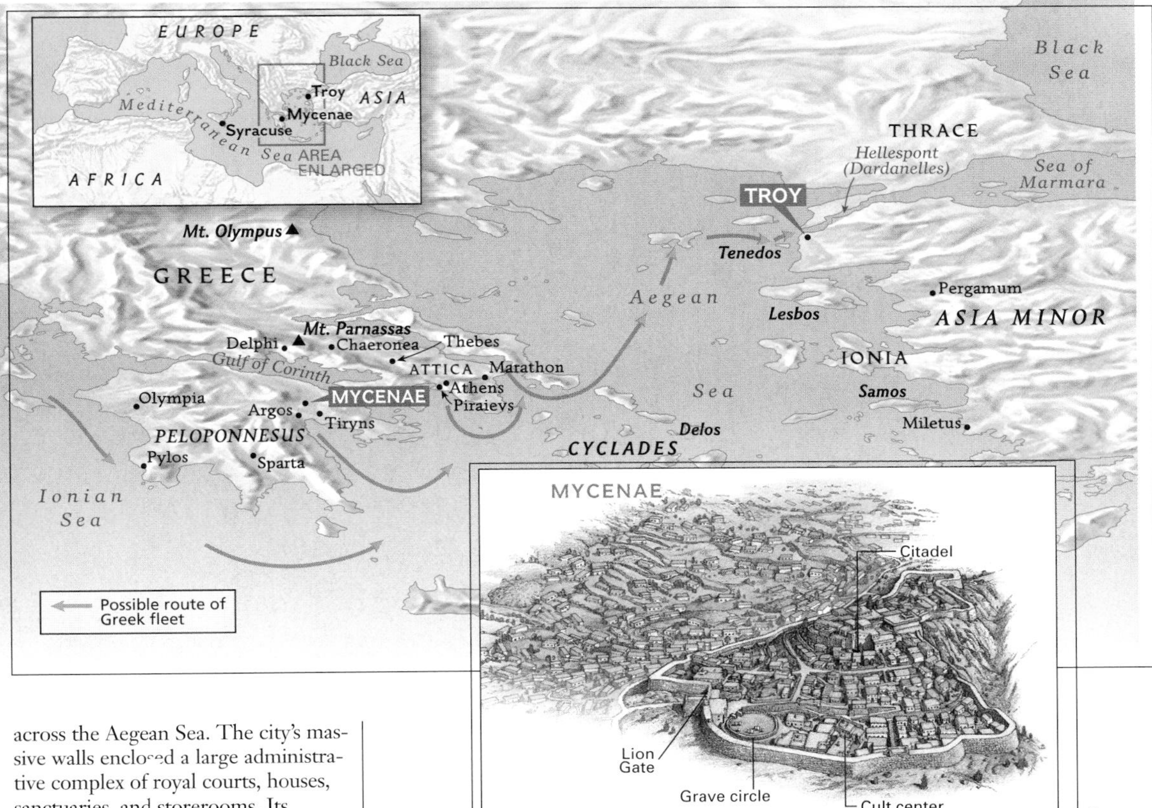

across the Aegean Sea. The city's massive walls enclosed a large administrative complex of royal courts, houses, sanctuaries, and storerooms. Its famous grave circle, unearthed by Schliemann in 1876, revealed rich treasures suggesting that as early as the sixteenth century B.C. the Mycenaean ruling class possessed a treasure trove of silver, gold, and ivory.

From archaeological digs at both Mycenae and Troy came signs that Homer's *Iliad* told of real things in the ancient world. Among the items found at Mycenae, for example, was a small gold ring. Carved on its face is a miniature battle scene showing a man protecting his entire body behind a huge shield, the kind that Homer describes the Greek hero Ajax holding in front of him "like a wall." The *Iliad's* heroes were known across the sea in Asia as well. Tomb art found in Turkey and dating from the fourth century B.C. depicts a scene from the Trojan siege (opposite page).

■

Troy's location at the mouth of the Dardanelles, the strait that Homer called the Hellespont, gave it command of the water route into central Asia. From this vantage point, the historical Trojans traded skillfully throughout central Asia. What remains of Troy's walls still overlooks a plain crossed by willow-lined rivers mentioned in the *Iliad*.

Heinrich Schliemann's excavation of Troy was crude and impatient. He sank trenches straight to bedrock, believing Homer's "windy Ilion" would lie at the bottom, thus destroy-

1 A scene etched in stone on a fourth century B.C. tomb found in Turkey suggests the *Iliad's* tragic final battle, between Hector of Troy and Achilles, hero of the Greeks.

2 Prosperous Mycenae traded throughout the Aegean. The reconstruction above shows the city's fortress in the late thirteenth century B.C., at the peak of its power. Some 250 miles (402 km) away, its rival Troy commanded the strait called the Dardanelles (Homer's Hellespont), a key link to the Black Sea. Today Troy's ruins lie 3 miles (4.8 km) inland, but in the late Bronze Age, the city sat on the edge of a bay that opened directly onto the Hellespont.

and he was determined to prove that Troy and Mycenae existed as recorded in the poem.) **What evidence did Schliemann find to support his theory that Mycenae was a rich, flourishing city?** *(Schliemann's excavations revealed royal courts, houses with lavish furnishing, gold, silver, and ivory.)* **Ask students to point out ways in which the current archaeological team inferred that at least 6,000 people lived in Troy.** *(While student answers will vary, students should discuss the finding of a trench that revealed the lower town of wooden houses.)* **Why do some archaeologists and historians believe that trade was the source of the Trojan War?** *(Troy stood at the entrance to the Dardanelles, a key point in the trading route. Have students examine the map of Greece and then discuss the strategic position of both Mycenae and Troy.)* **L1 L2**

FUN FACTS

- The terms *Achilles' heel* and *Achilles tendon* come from Homer's *Iliad.* Achilles, who slayed Hektor in the *Iliad,* was considered to be vulnerable only at the heel, the part of his body that his mother failed to dip in the River Styx. The Achilles tendon is the strong tendon that joins the muscles in the calf of the leg to the bone of the heel.
- The Trojan Horse, the large, hollow wooden horse in which the soldiers of Mycenae supposedly hid in order to invade Troy, is not mentioned in either the *Iliad* or the *Odyssey*. It was reported in the *Aeneid,* which was written by the Roman poet Virgil.
- The character of Odysseus, the king of Ithaca and the Greek leader during the Trojan Wars, was originally portrayed as courageous, honest, and heroic. Later interpretations portray the king as crafty and sly.

NATIONAL GEOGRAPHIC

Critical Thinking

Have students refer to the map of Greece and Mycenae that appears on page 63. Have students identify the various bodies of water that surround Greece. Ask them why access to the Black Sea through the Dardanelles was of such importance and why control of the Dardanelles was critical to the prosperity and stability of Troy. *(Ionian Sea, Aegean Sea, Mediterranean Sea; the quickest and easiest route to countries and peoples that border the Black Sea was through the Dardanelles. Controlling the entrance provided Troy with a means of extracting tolls and controlling who went through this narrow water passage.)* **L2**

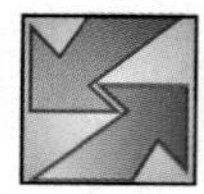

CURRICULUM CONNECTION

Art Ask students to research and identify works of art from ancient Greece that depict stories and heroes from the *Iliad* or the *Odyssey*.

Critical Thinking

The landscape of Greece has changed a great deal since Troy was a powerful city. The city itself fell to ruin. Ask students to identify the ways archaeologists, anthropologists, historians, and geographers analyzed the limited evidence available and developed a theory of the role of Troy in the ancient world. **L3**

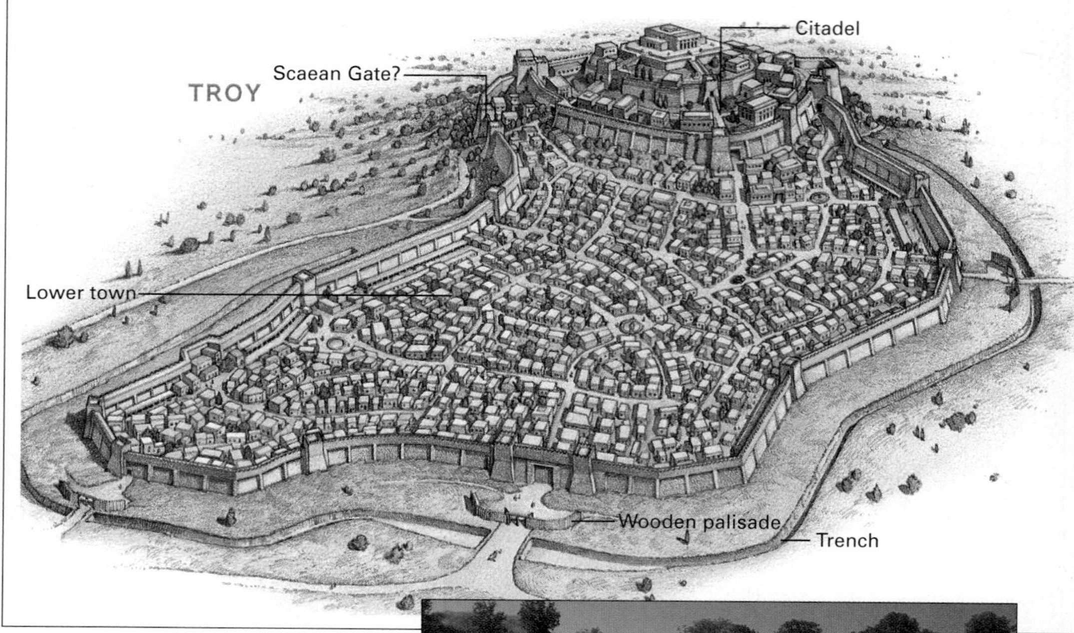

3

ing several layers of history. Today an international team of archaeologists directed by Manfred Korfmann of Germany's Tubingen University is reexcavating the entire site—nine levels ranging from 3000 B.C. to the Roman city of New Ilium in the early sixth century A.D. The sixth and seventh levels straddle the years 1250 to 1150 B.C., the era of Homer's war.

Whether or not the Greeks actually launched an invasion or entered Troy by means of the famous Trojan horse ruse (opposite page), evidence shows that the two peoples were in trading contact. Mycenaean pottery found at Troy dates back to 1500 B.C.

Some 1,300 feet (396 m) beyond the citadel first uncovered by Schliemann, Korfmann's team of archaeologists has made a most exciting find. They uncovered an extensive trench 8 feet (2.4 m) deep and 10 feet (3 m) wide encircling an entire lower town of wooden houses. The reconfigured city (reconstruction above)—which increases the known area of the sixth level of Troy by as much as 50 acres (20.25 ha)— is almost ten times as large as the citadel and held a population of at least 6,000. This finding makes Troy an opponent more equal to the mighty Mycenae than Schliemann's hilltop fortress.

Farther afield, in a nearby sand cove, lies evidence to support speculation that the Trojans took advantage of their commanding position at this crossroads of trade between Europe and Asia. Because of prevailing northeasterly winds, shallow-keeled Bronze Age merchant ships would have been forced to wait at Troy for a favorable breeze before proceeding north of the Dardanelles to the Black Sea.

Korfmann's team has located burials in the cove that reflect different cultural influences, suggesting that

Teacher's Notes

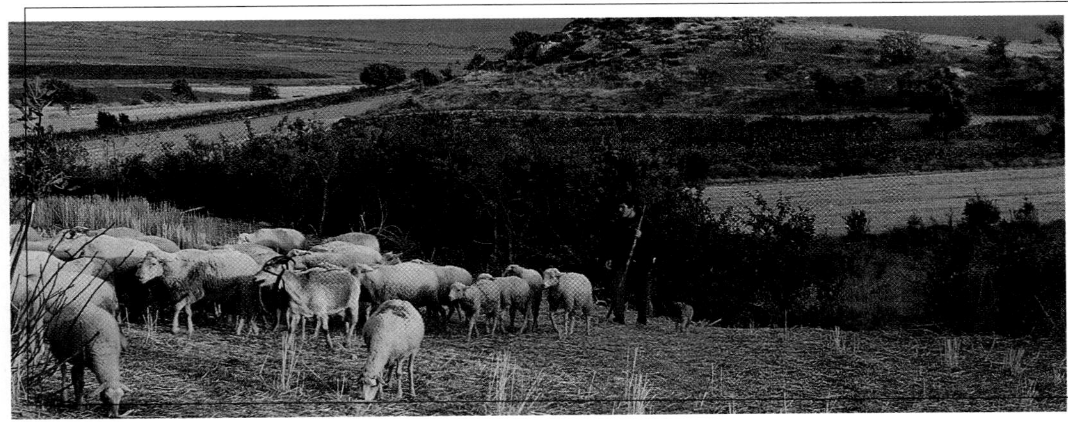

4

the crews of stranded vessels may have died while waiting for the wind to change. Korfmann says later texts confirm that "occupants of the region exacted tolls from incoming vessels." If Troy grew rich with this practice, it would have made bitter enemies of merchants like the Mycenaeans.

Indeed, some historians speculate that conflict over trade routes, rather than Helen's legendary beauty, may have sparked the Trojan War. As Korfmann sees it, "It is possible that Troy experienced several commercial skirmishes, if not one Trojan War."

5

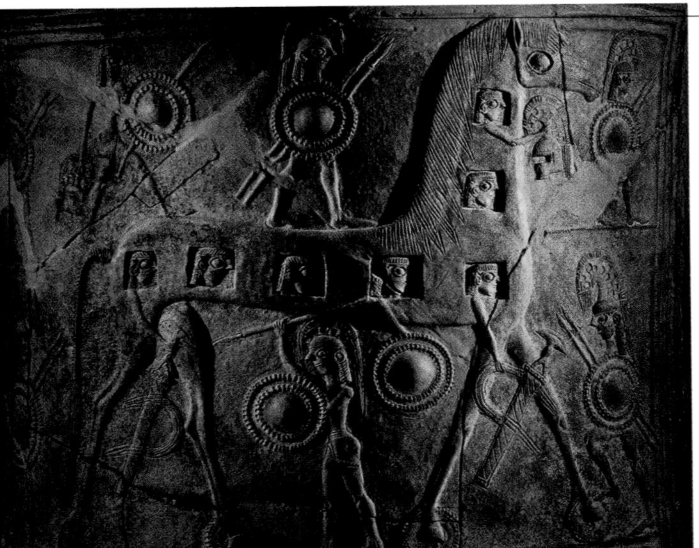

3 Stone walls believed to be the citadel of Troy were first unearthed in the 1870s. Troy holds the remains of at least nine settlements spanning 3,500 years. In the early 1990s, archaeologists discovered several wooden palisades and a 10-foot (3 m) trench encircling a lower town (reconstruction). Earlier only the hilltop citadel was known.

4 The Tumulus of Ajax is one of more than 40 mounds on the plain of Troy said to honor fallen heroes of the Trojan War.

5 A seventh-century B.C. amphora from Mykonos shows the earliest known depiction of the wooden horse that bore "death and doom for the Trojans."

INTERPRETING THE PAST

1. Was there a Trojan War? If so, what was its likely cause?

2. What is significant about the strait called the Dardanelles?

Who?What?Where?When?

Heinrich Schliemann Heinrich Schliemann was an archaeologist from Germany. Schliemann had always been fascinated by the story of the Greek siege of Troy, a city in Asia Minor. Most people, including Schliemann's father, believed that the writer of the story, an ancient Greek poet named Homer, had made up his account. Schliemann, though, believed Homer's story was true. He told his father: "If such walls once existed, they cannot possibly have been completely destroyed: vast ruins of them must still remain." Schliemann became a wealthy businessman, learned Greek, and went to Asia Minor. After years of digging, he found his beloved Troy and proved that Homer's account was true. Students might be interested to know that Schliemann is buried in Athens, in a mausoleum he had built for himself. The inscription at its entrance reads "For the hero Schliemann."

INTERPRETING THE PAST

Answers:

1. Historians and archaeologists disagree on whether or not the Trojan War or Wars actually occurred. Recent excavations suggest the possibility that wars over trade routes and control of the Dardanelles by Troy may have indeed occurred. However, there is no conclusive evidence to support this view.
2. The Dardanelles are the quickest route between the Mediterranean and the Black Sea. As such, they are strategically, politically, and economically very important to all countries in the region.

1 FOCUS

Section Overview

This section describes the key events in the history of Rome and early Christianity.

BELLRINGER
Skillbuilder Activity

 Project transparency and have students answer questions.

 Available as a blackline master.

Daily Focus Skills Transparency 2–2

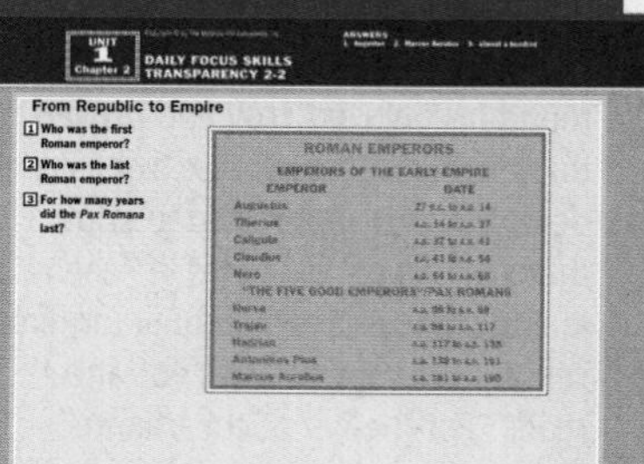
UNIT 1 Chapter 2 DAILY FOCUS SKILLS TRANSPARENCY 2-2

From Republic to Empire

1. Who was the first Roman emperor?
2. Who was the last Roman emperor?
3. For how many years did the *Pax Romana* last?

ROMAN EMPERORS

EMPEROR	DATE
EMPERORS OF THE EARLY EMPIRE	
Augustus	27 B.C. to A.D. 14
Tiberius	A.D. 14 to A.D. 37
Caligula	A.D. 37 to A.D. 41
Claudius	A.D. 41 to A.D. 54
Nero	A.D. 54 to A.D. 68
"THE FIVE GOOD EMPERORS"/PAX ROMANA	
Nerva	A.D. 96 to A.D. 98
Trajan	A.D. 98 to A.D. 117
Hadrian	A.D. 117 to A.D. 138
Antoninus Pius	A.D. 138 to A.D. 161
Marcus Aurelius	A.D. 161 to A.D. 180

Guide to Reading

Answers to Graphic: Officials: consuls, praetors, tribunes of the plebs; Legislative Bodies: Senate, centuriate assembly, council of the plebs

Preteaching Vocabulary: Explain the establishment of the Roman *republic.* **L2**

SECTION 2 Rome and the Rise of Christianity

Guide to Reading

Main Ideas
- Octavian, titled Caesar Augustus, was the first emperor of the Roman Empire.
- Christianity spread throughout the empire and eventually became the state religion of Rome.

Key Terms
republic, patrician, plebeian, imperator, Christianity, clergy, laity

People to Identify
Hannibal, Julius Caesar, Augustus, Virgil, Jesus, Constantine

Places to Locate
Rome, Carthage, Mediterranean Sea, Asia Minor, Constantinople

Preview Questions
1. Why did Rome become an empire?
2. Why did Christianity grow so quickly?

Reading Strategy
Categorizing Information As you read this section, complete a chart like the one shown below listing the government officials and the legislative bodies of the Roman Republic.

Officials	Legislative Bodies

Preview of Events

500 B.C. · A.D. 1 · A.D. 100 · A.D. 200 · A.D. 300 · A.D. 400 · A.D. 500

- **509 B.C.** Romans overthrow Etruscans
- **27 B.C** Octavian is named emperor
- **A.D. 180** *Pax Romana* ends
- **A.D. 313** Constantine proclaims official tolerance of Christianity
- **A.D. 410** The Visigoths sack Rome

Voices from the Past

Virgil

Virgil's masterpiece, the *Aeneid,* was an epic poem clearly meant to rival the work of Homer. It was also meant to express that the art of ruling was Rome's gift, as seen here:

❝Let others fashion from bronze more lifelike, breathing images—
For so they shall—and evoke living faces from marble;
Others excel as orators, others track with their instruments
The planets circling in heaven and predict when stars will appear.
But, Romans, never forget that government is your medium!
Be this your art: to practise men in the habit of peace,
Generosity to the conquered, and firmness against aggressors.❞

—***Aeneid,* C. Day Lewis, trans., 1952**

One of the most noticeable characteristics of Roman culture and society is the impact of the Greeks.

The Emergence of Rome

Indo-European peoples moved into Italy during the period from about 1500 to 1000 B.C. The Latins were one such group. These people spoke Latin, which, like Greek, is an Indo-European language. The Latins were herders and farmers who lived in settlements consisting of huts on the tops of Italy's hills. After 800 B.C.,

SECTION RESOURCES

Reproducible Masters
- Reproducible Lesson Plan 2–2
- Daily Lecture and Discussion Notes 2–2
- Guided Reading Activity 2–2
- Section Quiz 2–2
- Reading Essentials and Study Guide 2–2

Transparencies
- Daily Focus Skills Transparency 2–2

Multimedia
- Interactive Tutor Self-Assessment CD-ROM
- ExamView® Pro Testmaker CD-ROM
- Presentation Plus! CD-ROM

other people also began settling in Italy—most notably, the Greeks and the Etruscans.

Roman tradition maintains that early **Rome** (753–509 B.C.) was under the control of seven kings and that two of the last three kings were Etruscans. Historians know for certain that Rome did fall under Etruscan influence during this time. In 509 B.C., the Romans overthrew the last Etruscan king and established a republic, a form of government in which the leader is not a monarch and certain citizens have the right to vote. This was the beginning of a new era in Rome's history.

Rome's Conquest of Italy At the beginning of the republic, Rome was surrounded by enemies. For the next two hundred years, the city was engaged in almost continuous warfare. By 267 B.C., the Romans had overcome the Greeks and completed their conquest of southern Italy. After defeating the remaining Etruscan states to the north over the next three years, Rome had conquered virtually all of Italy.

To rule Italy, the Romans devised the Roman Confederation. Under this system, Rome allowed some peoples—especially Latins—to have full Roman citizenship. Most of the remaining communities were made allies. They remained free to run their own local affairs but were required to provide soldiers for Rome. The Romans made it clear that loyal allies could improve their status and even become Roman citizens. The Romans made the conquered peoples feel they had a real stake in Rome's success.

Rome Conquers the Mediterranean After their conquest of Italy, the Romans found themselves face to face with a strong power in the Mediterranean—the state of **Carthage.** Carthage had been founded around 800 B.C. on the coast of North Africa. The state had created an enormous trading empire in the western Mediterranean. By the third century B.C., the Carthaginian Empire included the coast of northern Africa, southern Spain, Sardinia, Corsica, and western Sicily.

The presence of the Carthaginians in Sicily, an island close to the Italian coast, made the Romans fearful. The Romans fought three wars with Carthage, beginning in 264 B.C. During the second war, Rome came close to disaster as a result of the victories of **Hannibal,** Carthage's greatest general. Despite their losses, the Romans refused to give up and created new armies and a navy to carry on the struggle. In 202 B.C., the Romans crushed Hannibal's forces, ending the second war. Carthage lost Spain, which became a Roman province. Rome had become the dominant power in the western Mediterranean. Fifty years later, the Romans fought their third and final war with Carthage, completely destroying Carthage in 146 B.C.

During its wars with Carthage, Rome also battled the Hellenistic states in the eastern Mediterranean. In 148 B.C., Macedonia was made a Roman province. Two years later, Greece was placed under the control of the Roman governor of Macedonia. In 133 B.C., Pergamum became Rome's first province in Asia. Rome was now master of the **Mediterranean Sea.**

Reading Check **Summarizing** What is the sequence of events that led Rome to become master of the Mediterranean Sea by 133 B.C.?

People In History

Hannibal
247–183 B.C.
Carthaginian general

When Hannibal was only nine years old, his father, a Carthaginian general, took him to a temple in Carthage and made him swear that he would always hate the Romans. Hannibal later inflicted terrible losses on the Romans—his army killed or captured 170,000 Romans and allied soldiers in Italy. Unable to win the war, Hannibal eventually sought refuge with Rome's enemies.

The Romans never forgave Hannibal. They pursued him for years and finally caught up with him in Bithynia. To avoid capture, Hannibal took poison after remarking, "Let us relieve the Romans of the fear which has so long afflicted them, since it seems to tax their patience too hard to wait for an old man's death."

The Roman State

The Romans had been ruled by kings under the Etruscans. As a result, they distrusted kingship and devised a very different system of government.

Early Rome was divided into two groups or orders—the patricians and the plebeians (plih•BEE•uhns).

2 TEACH

CURRICULUM CONNECTION

Geography Have the class create a chart comparing the climates, physical features, landforms, and agriculture of the Italian peninsula and the region where class members live. Discuss with students how environmental factors have made their lives similar to or different from the lives of the people of Italy. **L2** ELL

Reading Check

Answer: Beginning in 264 B.C. Rome fought three wars with rival Carthage, winning Spain in the second war and destroying Carthage in the third. In 148 B.C. Rome gained Macedonia. In 133 B.C. Pergamum in Asia became a Roman province.

Enrich

Have students research various aspects of Carthage and its history and present short oral reports to the class. Suggest the following topics: the legend of Dido (legendary queen) and Aeneas; the city's founding as a Phoenician colony; the extent of the Carthaginian Empire; the type of trade, culture, and religion; styles of art and architecture; famous leaders and rulers. **L3**

COOPERATIVE LEARNING ACTIVITY

Staging a Debate Divide the class into two groups—Greeks and Etruscans. Ask each group to research and compile a list of Greek or Etruscan cultural contributions to Roman culture and civilization. Groups should consider law, language, literature, art, architecture, religion, and so forth. After the lists have been made, choose volunteers from each group to debate the question: "Which culture contributed more to the development of Roman civilization—the Etruscan or the Greek?" Remind students to give concrete examples when they speak. Complete the debate with a class vote. **L2**

Daily Lecture and Discussion Notes 2–2

Daily Lecture and Discussion Notes

Chapter 2, Section 2

Did You Know? A Yugoslavian man traveling through Europe in the nineteenth century discovered the longest-known Etruscan inscription. Originally a roll of linen cloth, the 1,300-word inscription—which included a calendar and instructions for sacrifice—had been cut into strips to be wrapped around a mummy.

I. The Emergence of Rome *(pages 66–67)*

A. Indo-European peoples moved into Italy from about 1500 to 1000 B.C. One people spoke Latin, an Indo-European language, and lived as herders and farmers on Rome's hills. After 800 B.C., other people, including the Greeks and Etruscans, settled in Italy.

B. Early **Rome** was ruled by kings, some of whom were Etruscan. In 509 B.C. the Romans overthrew the last Etruscan king and established a **republic.** In a republic the leader is not a king and certain citizens have the right to vote.

C. Enemies surrounded Rome, and so the young republic began a long period of continuous warfare. By 267 B.C., Rome had defeated the Greeks and remaining Etruscan states and controlled almost all of Italy.

D. To rule, the Romans devised the Roman Confederation. Some people had full Roman citizenship. Other groups were allies who controlled their local affairs but gave soldiers to Rome. Such people could become Roman citizens. Thus many of the conquered peoples felt invested in Rome's success.

E. Rome faced a strong power in the Mediterranean—**Carthage,** which was founded around 800 B.C. on the coast of North Africa. Carthage had a large trading empire in the western Mediterranean.

F. The Romans fought three wars with Carthage. During the second war, the victories of Carthage's greatest general, **Hannibal,** almost brought Rome to disaster. After creating new armies and a navy, the Romans defeated Hannibal's forces. Spain became a Roman province, and Rome controlled the western Mediterranean. Rome completely destroyed Carthage in 146 B.C.

G. In the second century B.C. Rome also conquered Macedonia and Greece. In 133 B.C. Pergamum became Rome's first province in Asia. Rome was now master of the **Mediterranean Sea.**

Discussion Question

Why did extending Roman citizenship to conquered peoples help Rome expand its empire? *(Granting conquered people citizenship gave them a stake in Rome's growth and success. They were much less likely to revolt, therefore, and more likely to contribute to the empire.)*

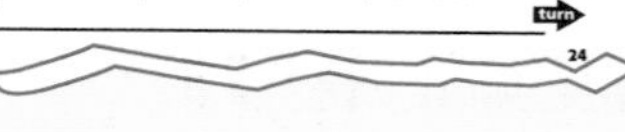
turn

24

What If...

Answers may include that all of Europe might have become Roman territory, with Latin replacing local languages and Roman law providing a unified legal code.

Reading Check

Answer: Originally, only patricians could be elected to government office, and only patricians could serve in the Senate. The centuriate assembly, which elected the chief officials, was organized by classes based on wealth, and the wealthiest citizens always had a majority.

TURNING POINT

The Roman Empire spread Roman culture, law, and ideas to over 50 million people.

The **patricians** were great landowners, who became Rome's ruling class. Less wealthy landholders, craftspeople, merchants, and small farmers were part of a larger group called **plebeians.** Men in both groups were citizens and could vote, but only the patricians could be elected to governmental offices.

The Government of Rome The chief executive officers of the Roman Republic were the consuls and praetors (PREE•tuhrs). Two consuls, chosen every year, ran the government and led the Roman army into battle. The praetor was in charge of civil law—law as it applied to Roman citizens. As the Romans' territory expanded, another praetor was added to judge cases in which people were noncitizens. The Romans also had a number of officials who had special duties, such as supervising the treasury.

The Roman Senate came to hold an especially important position in the Roman Republic. It was a select group of about three hundred patricians who served for life. At first, the Senate's only role was to advise government officials. However, the advice of the Senate carried a great deal of weight. By the third century B.C., it had the force of law.

The Roman Republic had several people's assemblies in addition to the Senate. By far the most important of these was the centuriate assembly. The centuriate assembly elected the chief officials, such as consuls and praetors, and passed laws. Because it was organized by classes based on wealth, the wealthiest citizens always had a majority. The council of the plebs was the assembly for plebeians only, and it came into being as a result of the struggle between the two social orders in Rome.

The Struggle of the Orders There was often conflict between the patricians and the plebeians in the early Roman Republic. Children of patricians and plebeians were forbidden to marry each other. Plebeians resented this situation, especially since they served in the Roman army that protected the Republic. They thought that they deserved both political and social equality with the patricians.

The struggle between the patricians and plebeians dragged on for hundreds of years. Ultimately, it led to success for the plebeians, and the council of the plebs was created in 471 B.C. New officials, known as tribunes of the plebs, were given the power to protect the plebeians. In the fourth century B.C., plebeians were permitted to become consuls. Finally, in 287 B.C., the council of the plebs received the right to pass laws for all Romans.

By 287 B.C., all male Roman citizens were supposedly equal under the law. In reality, however, a few wealthy patrician and plebeian families formed a new senatorial ruling class that came to dominate the political offices. The Roman Republic had not become a democracy.

Reading Check **Explaining** How did the differences between plebeians and patricians prevent Rome from becoming a true democracy?

What If...

Roman legions had defeated the Germanic tribes?

The Roman Empire was near its height during the first century A.D. However, in A.D. 9, three Roman legions, approximately 15,000 men, were wiped out by Germanic tribesmen led by Arminius in the Teutoburg Forest. From that point on, Rome made no serious attempts to conquer what we know today as Germany.

Consider the Consequences Identify and explain at least two ways in which European history might have been different if the Romans had defeated the German warriors in the Teutoburg Forest.

From Republic to Empire

TURNING POINT **After the collapse of Rome's republican institutions and a series of brutal civil wars, Augustus created a new order that began the Roman Empire.**

Between 509 and 264 B.C., most of what is modern-day Italy was unified under Rome's control. Even more dramatic is that by 133 B.C., Rome stood supreme over the Mediterranean Sea.

Rome's republican institutions, however, proved inadequate for ruling an empire. By the second century B.C., the Senate had become the real governing body of the Roman state. Within the Senate, rival factions of wealthy families began to compete for power, creating disorder.

In addition, in the first century B.C. Roman leaders began to recruit armies that swore an oath of loyalty to the general, not to the Roman state. For 50 years

INTERDISCIPLINARY CONNECTIONS ACTIVITY

Culture To give students a better understanding of the importance of cultural developments during this period of Roman history, ask students to research and find an "artifact" that reflects some aspect of Rome's past. Students should consider Rome's law, government, language, architectural, and engineering achievements. Ask the students to select a building, bas-relief, mosaic, statue, or other pictorial symbol and explain its importance to the legacy of Rome in a one-page essay that includes a graphic. Students will present their essays in class, and some will be posted on class bulletin boards. **L3**

NATIONAL GEOGRAPHIC

Roman Empire: Trade and Expansion

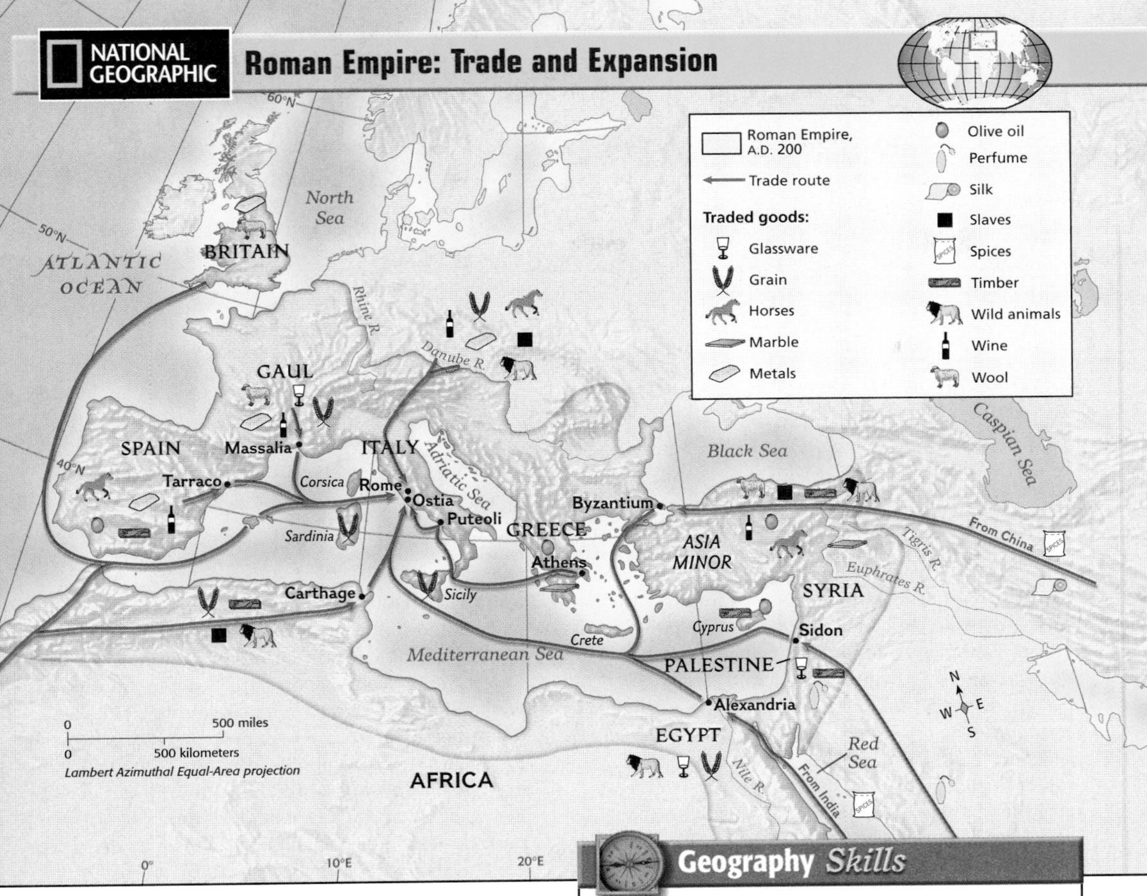

(82–31 B.C.), Roman history was characterized by civil wars as a number of individuals competed for power. In one of these struggles, **Julius Caesar** defeated the forces led by Pompey. After Caesar was assassinated, Octavian, Caesar's heir and grand-nephew, defeated Mark Antony and took control of the Roman world.

The period beginning in 31 B.C. and lasting until A.D. 14 came to be known as the Age of Augustus. (In 27 B.C., the Senate had awarded Octavian the title of **Augustus**—"the revered one.") Augustus proved to be highly popular, but his continuing control of the army was the chief source of his power. The Senate named Augustus imperator, or commander in chief. Our word *emperor* comes from the word *imperator.* Augustus thus became the first emperor of the Roman Empire.

Reading Check **Summarizing** What factors contributed to disorder and civil war in the Roman Republic during the second and first centuries B.C.?

Geography Skills

In about 350 years, the Romans conquered an area four times the size of the present-day United States. Exchange and communication through trade was extensive throughout the vast Roman Empire.

1. **Interpreting Maps** Explain how the trading routes indicated on this map allowed for the areas in the furthest reaches of the Roman Empire to trade with one another.
2. **Applying Geography Skills** Why would control of the Mediterranean region benefit Rome's economy? What are the names of the two chief Italian port cities of the Roman Empire?

The Early Empire

Beginning in A.D. 14, a series of new emperors ruled Rome. This period, ending in A.D. 180, is called the Early Empire.

The Five Good Emperors The first four emperors after Augustus grew increasingly more powerful and

CRITICAL THINKING ACTIVITY

Compare and Contrast Octavian was awarded many titles during his reign in Rome. He became *Augustus*—the revered one, *imperator*—commander in chief, *princeps*—first citizen, and *pontifex maximus*—chief pontiff, head of the official state religion. During a class discussion, ask students whether they think it is unusual for a ruler to have so many titles. Then tell students that the president of the United States also has several titles attached to the office. List all the president's titles on the chalkboard. (*chief executive, commander in chief, chief of state, chief diplomat, chief legislator*). Have students discuss similarities and differences in the titles of Octavian and the president of the United States. **L2**

Geography Skills

Answers:

1. All the trading routes converged in Rome, so the traders could bring goods, meet in the capital of the empire, and trade with one another.
2. Stability allowed the five emperors to concentrate on constructive projects rather than on constant fighting, and the wealth generated by trade gave them the money to pay for those projects; Ostia and Puteoli

Reading Check

Answer: Rival factions of wealthy families within the Senate began to compete for power, creating disorder. Civil wars occurred as Roman leaders created their own armies and fought each other for control.

Guided Reading Activity 2–2

Name ______ Date ______ Class ______

Guided Reading Activity 2-2

Rome and the Rise of Christianity

DIRECTIONS: Fill in the blanks below as you read Section 2.

In 509 B.C. the Romans overthrew the last Etruscan king and established a **(1)** ______. To rule Italy, the Romans devised the Roman **(2)** ______, under which some peoples could become Roman citizens. In 202 B.C., Rome crushed Carthage and became the dominant power in the western **(3)** ______.

Early Rome was divided into two types of citizens: the **(4)** ______, landowners who were the ruling class, and the **(5)** ______, who were merchants, craftspeople, and small farmers. Two **(6)** ______, chosen every year, ran the government and led the army into battle. The **(7)** ______ was in charge of civil law. By the second century B.C., the **(8)** ______ had become the real governing body of the Roman state. However, in 27 B.C., **(9)** ______ became the first emperor of the Roman Empire. During the second century, the five "good emperors" created a period of peace and prosperity called the **(10)** ______.

Rome is remembered for many achievements. One of Rome's chief gifts to the world was its system of **(11)** ______. During the Augustan Age, the poet Virgil wrote his great work, the **(12)** ______. Romans excelled in architecture. They were the first people in antiquity to use **(13)** ______ on a massive scale. In Rome, almost a dozen **(14)** ______ kept a population of one million supplied with water.

By A.D. 6, Judea had been made a Roman province under a Roman official called a **(15)** ______. During this period of conflict, Jesus of Nazareth began to preach. After Jesus was crucified, a religious movement began called **(16)** ______. In the fourth century, **(17)** ______ became the first Christian emperor. Under **(18)** ______, the Romans adopted Christianity as the official religion of the Roman Empire. After Constantine, the Roman empire was divided into a Western Roman Empire, with its capital in **(19)** ______, and an Eastern Roman Empire, with the capital in **(20)** ______.

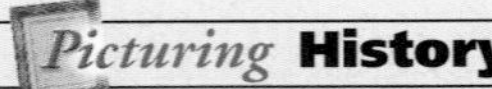

Answer: They had servants, enjoyed a life of ease, and valued art and music.

Reading Check

Answer: The five good emperors maintained peace, gave assistance to the poor, and completed many building programs that improved transportation and increased trade, bringing greater prosperity to the empire.

Connecting Across Time

Have students outline the economic and social problems that ended the Roman Republic. Then ask them to compare their outlines to problems that exist in the present-day United States. How are the outlines similar? How do they differ? **L1** ELL

Enrich

Rome could be described as a "consumption-oriented society." Discuss the meaning of the phrase with students. *(The phrase refers to the desired luxuries that were wanted rather than needed, which the wealthy Romans could afford.)* Have students compare Rome's consumption-oriented society with societies such as the Native American civilizations and cultures that flourished in the early history of the United States. Then compare Rome's society to present-day U.S. society. **L3**

Picturing **History**

A detail from the Villa of the Mysteries in Pompeii shows that life for many in the city offered several comforts and pleasures. The city of Pompeii was buried in a single day when the volcano Vesuvius erupted in A.D. 79. What does this surviving wall painting from Pompeii tell us about the lifestyles of upper-class Romans?

corrupt. At the beginning of the second century, a series of five so-called good emperors—Nerva, Trajan, Hadrian, Antoninus Pius, and Marcus Aurelius—came to power. These emperors created a period of peace and prosperity known as the ***Pax Romana***—the "Roman Peace." The *Pax Romana* lasted for almost a hundred years (96–180). These rulers treated the ruling classes with respect, ended arbitrary executions, maintained peace in the empire, and supported domestic policies that were generally helpful to the empire.

Under the five good emperors, the powers of the emperor continued to expand at the expense of the Senate. Officials who were appointed and directed by the emperor took over the running of the government.

The good emperors also created new programs to help the people. Trajan, for example, created a program that provided state funds to assist poor parents in the raising and education of their children. The good emperors were widely praised for their building programs. Trajan and Hadrian were especially active in building public works—aqueducts, bridges, roads, and harbor facilities—throughout the provinces and in Rome.

Prosperity and Trade At its height in the second century, the Roman Empire was one of the greatest states the world had ever seen. It covered about three and a half million square miles (about 9.1 million square km) and had a population that has been estimated at more than fifty million.

The Early Empire was also a period of much prosperity, with internal peace leading to high levels of trade. Merchants from all over the empire came to the chief Italian ports of Puteoli (pyuh•TEE•uh•LY) on the Bay of Naples and Ostia at the mouth of the Tiber River. Trade went beyond the Roman frontiers as well and included even silk goods from China. Large quantities of grain were imported, especially from Egypt, to feed the people of Rome. Luxury items poured in to satisfy the wealthy upper classes. Despite the active trade and commerce, however, farming remained the chief occupation of most people and the underlying basis of Roman prosperity.

Reading Check **Explaining** How did the policies and programs of the five good emperors benefit the Early Empire and its people?

Roman Law

One of Rome's chief gifts to the Mediterranean world of its day and to later generations was its system of law. Rome's first code of laws was the **Twelve Tables,** which was adopted in 450 B.C. This code was a product of a simple farming society and proved inadequate for later Roman needs. From the Twelve Tables, the Romans developed a more sophisticated system of civil law. This system applied only to Roman citizens, however.

As Rome expanded, legal questions arose that involved both Romans and non-Romans. The Romans found that although some of their rules of civil law could be used in these cases, special rules were often needed. These rules gave rise to a body of law known as the **Law of Nations.** The Romans came to identify the Law of Nations with natural law, or universal law

MEETING INDIVIDUAL NEEDS

Visual/Spatial Divide the class into small groups to create a pictorial history of events in this section. The history might include drawings of events or objects, illustrated maps, diagrams, charts, and political cartoons. Each image must include a caption that explains the picture. The pictures can be compiled into a class notebook that students can use as a classroom resource. You might also wish to create a classroom bulletin board with these images. **L1**

Refer to ***Inclusion for the High School Social Studies Classroom Strategies and Activities*** in the TCR.

based on reason. This enabled them to establish standards of justice that applied to all people.

These standards of justice included principles still recognized today. A person was regarded as innocent until proved otherwise. People accused of wrongdoing were allowed to defend themselves before a judge. A judge, in turn, was expected to weigh evidence carefully before arriving at a decision. These principles lived on long after the fall of the Roman Empire.

✓Reading Check **Identifying** Name at least two principles in the Law of Nations that are still recognized today.

Slavery in the Roman Empire

Slavery was common throughout the ancient world, but no people had more slaves or relied so much on slave labor as the Romans did. Before the third century B.C., slaves used in Rome were usually from Italy and were often regarded as part of the family household.

The Roman conquest of the Mediterranean brought a drastic change in the use of slaves. Large numbers of foreign peoples who had been captured in different wars were brought back to Italy as slaves. Greek slaves were in much demand as tutors, musicians, doctors, and artists. Roman businessmen would employ them as shop assistants or craftspeople. Many slaves of all nationalities were used as household workers, such as cooks, valets, waiters, cleaners, and gardeners.

Slaves built roads and public buildings, and farmed the large estates of the wealthy. The conditions under which these slaves lived were often pitiful. One Roman writer argued that it was cheaper to work slaves to death and then replace them than to treat them well.

Some slaves revolted. The most famous slave revolt in Italy occurred in 73 B.C. Led by the gladiator Spartacus, the revolt broke out in southern Italy and involved seventy thousand slaves. Spartacus managed to defeat several Roman armies before being trapped and killed in 71 B.C. Six thousand followers of Spartacus were crucified (put to death by nailing to a cross).

✓Reading Check **Describing** How did the Roman conquest of the Mediterranean change slavery in the Roman world?

Daily Life in the City of Rome

At the center of the colossal Roman Empire was the ancient city of Rome. Truly a capital city, Rome had the largest population of any city in the empire—close to one million by the time of Augustus. For anyone with ambitions, Rome was the place to be. People from all over the empire resided there.

Living Conditions Rome was an overcrowded and noisy city. Because of the congestion, cart and wagon traffic was banned from the streets during the day.

An enormous gulf existed between rich and poor. The rich had comfortable villas, while the poor lived in apartment blocks called *insulae,* which could be six stories high. Constructed of concrete walls with wooden beam floors, these buildings were usually poorly built and often collapsed.

Fire was a constant threat in the *insulae* because of the use of movable stoves, torches, candles, and lamps within the rooms for heat and light. Once started, fires were extremely difficult to put out. High rents forced entire families to live in one room. There was no plumbing or central heating. As a result, many poor Romans spent most of their time outdoors in the streets.

Public Programs Rome boasted public buildings unequaled anywhere in the empire. Its temples, markets, baths, theaters, governmental buildings, and amphitheaters gave parts of the city an appearance of grandeur and magnificence.

Although it was the center of a great empire, Rome had serious problems. Beginning with Augustus, the emperors provided food for the city's poor. About

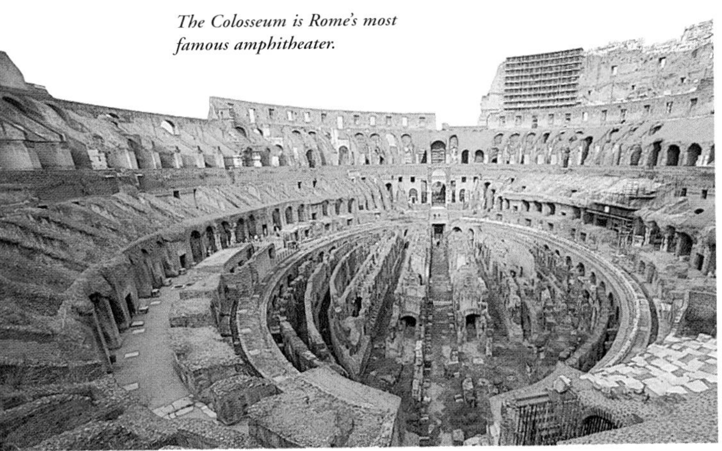

The Colosseum is Rome's most famous amphitheater.

CHAPTER 2
Section 2, 66–76

✓Reading Check

Answer: Answers may include: a person was recognized as innocent until proven otherwise; people accused of wrongdoing were permitted to defend themselves in front of a judge; a judge was expected to weigh evidence before making a decision.

Enrich

The Colosseum was built as an arena for gladiator fights. The dedication ceremonies in A.D. 80 included 100 days of games and competition. The Colosseum measures 620 by 530 feet (190 by 155 meters) and could seat 50,000 spectators. Ask students to name and compare some arenas used for public events today with the Roman Colosseum. *(Answers may include sports stadiums, convention centers, and concert auditoriums.)*

✓Reading Check

Answer: Rome's conquests increased the use of slaves. Large numbers of the conquered foreign peoples were enslaved and put to work in Rome.

Connecting Across Time

Lead students in a class discussion that compares and contrasts slavery in the early United States with slavery in ancient Rome. Which slaves were better off? Why do students feel the way they do? **L2**

INTERDISCIPLINARY CONNECTIONS ACTIVITY

Math, Science, and Technology While the Romans admired and adopted many aspects of Greek culture, they gave it a distinctly Roman stamp. Romans were also innovative and practical. Shorthand, the pontoon bridge, and central heating are among the many Roman innovations that have been passed down to us. Ask students to research and identify the new ideas in mathematics, science, and technology that occurred during Roman civilization. Then have students trace the spread of these ideas to other civilizations. Have students write a report based on their research. **L2**

Answer: Answers may include overcrowding, noise, poverty, and fire.

Then and Now

Answer: Greek: colonnade; Roman: dome and rounded lines

✓ Reading Check

Answer: The Romans built with concrete and used new architectural forms such as the arch, vault, and dome.

CURRICULUM CONNECTION

Architecture Take your students on a visual tour of the public buildings of Washington, D.C. You might use photos in books, slides, videos, or a DVD. Point out the Roman influence seen in the buildings to students. Ask if any have visited Washington, D.C., and if they would like to share their impressions of the city's buildings. Then invite a local architect or historian to talk to your class about Roman influence on local construction. **L2**

3 ASSESS

Assign Section 2 Assessment as homework or as an in-class activity.

Have students use **Interactive Tutor Self-Assessment CD-ROM.**

two hundred thousand people received free grain. Even so, conditions remained grim for the poor.

Entertainment was provided on a grand scale for the inhabitants of Rome. Public spectacles were provided by the emperor as part of the great religious festivals celebrated by the state. The festivals included three major types of entertainment. At the Circus Maximus, horse and chariot races attracted hundreds of thousands. Dramatic performances were held in theaters. The most famous of all the public spectacles, however, were the gladiatorial shows.

✓ Reading Check **Summarizing** What problems did people face in the ancient city of Rome?

Roman Culture

The high point of Latin literature was reached in the Age of Augustus. The Augustan Age has been called the golden age of Latin literature.

The most distinguished poet of the Augustan Age was **Virgil.** The son of a small landholder in northern Italy near Mantua, he welcomed the rule of Augustus and wrote his greatest work, the *Aeneid* (ih•NEE•uhd), in honor of the ruler. In the poem, the character of Aeneas is portrayed as the ideal Roman—his virtues are duty, piety, and faithfulness. Virgil's overall purpose was to show that Aeneas had fulfilled his mission to establish the Romans in Italy and thereby start Rome on its divine mission to rule the world.

During the third and second centuries B.C., the Romans adopted many features of the Greek style of art. They developed a taste for Greek statues, which they placed not only in public buildings but also in their private houses. While Greek sculptors aimed for an ideal appearance in their figures, Roman sculptors produced realistic statues that included even unpleasant physical details.

The Romans excelled in architecture, a highly practical art. Although they continued to use Greek styles such as colonnades and rectangular buildings, the Romans also used forms based on curved lines: the arch, vault, and dome. The Romans were the first people in antiquity to use concrete on a massive scale. Using concrete along with the new architectural forms made it possible for the Romans to construct huge buildings undreamed of by the Greeks.

The remarkable engineering skills of the Romans were also used to construct bridges, aqueducts, and roads such as the Appian Way. The Romans built a network of some 50,000 miles (80,450 km) of roads throughout the empire. In Rome, almost a dozen aqueducts kept a population of one million supplied with water. The Romans were superb builders.

✓ Reading Check **Contrasting** Why were the Romans able to construct buildings larger than those of the Greeks?

Then and Now

Thomas Jefferson copied Roman temples in his designs for the buildings of the University of Virginia at Charlottesville. How do the two buildings illustrate Roman architectural innovations and the ideas the Romans borrowed from the Greeks?

Rotunda at the University of Virginia

Hadrian's Pantheon in Rome

The Emergence of Christianity

In Hellenistic times, the Jewish people had been given considerable independence. By A.D. 6, however, Judaea, which embraced the lands of the old Jewish kingdom of Judah, had been made a Roman province and had been placed under the direction of a Roman official called a procurator. Unrest was widespread in Judaea because many Jews wanted freedom from the Romans. It was in the midst of the confusion and conflict in Judaea that a Jew named **Jesus** began his public preaching.

Jesus proclaimed that through him God was completing the salvation long promised to Israel: "Do not think that I have come to abolish the Law or the Prophets; I have not come to abolish them but to fulfill them." According to Jesus, what was important was not strict adherence to the letter of the law but the transformation of the inner person: "So in everything, do to others what you would have them do to you, for this sums up the Law and the Prophets."

COOPERATIVE LEARNING ACTIVITY

Creating a Diagram The Romans borrowed extensively from other cultures, adapting Etruscan rituals, Etruscan and Greek deities, Greek styles of architecture and sculpture, and Greek medicine and science. Provide students with a wall-sized sheet of paper to create a wall diagram that shows a composite of items Romans borrowed from other cultures. Assign students to small groups and have each group research one major topic to include on the wall diagram. Within each group, members should be assigned different tasks, including research, illustration or photo acquisition, caption composition, and presentation of the group's work to the class. **L1**

Saint Matthew

God's command was to love God and one another. Jesus said, "Love the Lord your God with all your heart and with all your soul and with all your mind and with all your strength. This is the first commandment. The second is this: Love your neighbor as yourself." Jesus voiced the ethical concepts—humility, charity, and love toward others—that would form much of the value system of Western civilization.

To some political and religious leaders in Judaea, Jesus was a potential revolutionary. His opponents turned him over to the Roman authorities. The procurator Pontius Pilate ordered his crucifixion.

Soon after Jesus' death, his loyal followers claimed that Jesus had overcome death and had revealed himself to them. They believed Jesus to be the Messiah (anointed one), the long expected deliverer of Israel.

Reading Check **Explaining** Why was Jesus turned over to the Roman authorities?

The Spread of Christianity

Christianity began as a religious movement within Judaism. After the reports that Jesus had overcome death, Christianity spread quickly. According to early Christian accounts, within 60 days there were approximately ten thousand converts to Christianity in the city of Jerusalem alone.

Prominent leaders arose in early Christianity. One of these was Simon Peter, a Jewish fisherman who had become a follower of Jesus during Jesus' lifetime. Peter was recognized as the spokesperson for the disciples, or followers, of Jesus. Another leader was Paul, a highly educated Jewish Roman citizen who joined the movement later. Paul took the message of Jesus to Gentiles (non-Jews) as well as to Jews. He founded Christian communities, or churches, throughout **Asia Minor** and along the shores of the Aegean Sea.

At the center of Paul's message was the belief that Jesus was the Savior, the Son of God who had come to Earth to save humanity. Paul taught that Jesus' death made up for the sins of all people. By accepting Jesus as Christ (from *Christos,* the Greek term for Messiah) and Savior, people could be saved from sin and reconciled with God.

The life of Jesus and his teachings at first were passed on orally to the earliest Christian communities scattered throughout the Mediterranean world. In time, written materials appeared, primarily in the form of letters written by disciples to Christian churches or individuals. Later, between A.D. 70 and 100, the oral accounts about Jesus became the basis of

Picturing **History**

Early Christians buried their dead in catacombs, underground chambers that sometimes had multiple rooms and levels. This catacomb was built in Rome in the second century. Why might early Christians have wanted an underground sanctuary for their dead?

Reading Check

Answer: The Judaean authorities viewed him as a potential revolutionary.

Picturing **History**

Answer: The catacombs may have provided a more secure burial place and a place for early Christians to hold their religious services.

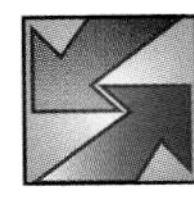

CURRICULUM CONNECTION

Religion Discuss with students the impact religion can have on a country. Remind students of the religious heritage of the United States. Ask students to describe events in history that were directly related to religion. **L2**

Who?What?Where?When?

The Apostles The word *apostle* comes from the Greek for "one who is sent out." Jesus sent his original followers out into the world to preach the *gospel,* which literally means "good news." The apostles formed churches for worship, fellowship, and instruction.

MEETING INDIVIDUAL NEEDS

Visual/Spatial Many movies have been made about the life of Jesus and about the impact of Christianity on the people of imperial Rome. Since some students learn better visually, show a videotape of one of the following: *The Robe, Ben Hur, The Silver Chalice,* or *The Greatest Story Ever Told.* Ask students to write a report that includes details of life under the *Pax Romana.* Call on students to read their reports aloud in class, and allow time for students to ask questions after each presentation. **L1**

Refer to ***Inclusion for the High School Social Studies Classroom Strategies and Activities*** in the TCR.

Section Quiz 2–2

Name ______ Date ______ Class ______

Chapter 2 Score

Section Quiz 2-2

DIRECTIONS: Matching Match each item in Column A with an item in Column B. Write the correct letters in the blanks. *(10 points each)*

Column A	Column B
____ 1. landowners who were the ruling class	A. Augustus
____ 2. it means "the revered one"	B. Trajan
____ 3. apartments for the poor	C. Constantine
____ 4. created a program to assist poor parents	D. *insulae*
____ 5. called his capital "New Rome"	E. patricians

DIRECTIONS: Multiple Choice In the blank, write the letter of the choice that best completes the statement or answers the question. *(10 points each)*

____ 6. During the early Roman Republic, plebeians were allowed to
A. marry patricians.
B. serve in the Roman army.
C. serve in the Senate.
D. pass laws for all Romans.

____ 7. Rome's first code of law was the
A. Law of Nations.
B. Council of the Plebs.
C. Twelve Tables.
D. Centuriate Assembly.

____ 8. In 73 B.C., the gladiator Spartacus
A. wrote a history of Rome.
B. led a slave revolt.
C. became a Roman senator.
D. overthrew the emperor.

____ 9. The Gospels were all of the following EXCEPT
A. some of the sayings of Jesus in writing.
B. a record of Jesus' life.
C. the core of the New Testament.
D. written during Jesus' lifetime.

____ 10. Diocletian divided the empire
A. into four units.
B. into north and south.
C. into provinces.
D. among his sons.

Reading Check

Answer: The teachings of Jesus were first passed on orally and were later written in what is known as the Gospels.

TURNING POINT

Christianity began with a single person who attracted many followers. During the fourth century A.D., the number of Christians greatly increased. What led to this increase? *(adoption and support by Constantine, Edict of Milan, increased government support)* **L1**

Reading Check

Answer: Christianity offered salvation and eternal life, gave meaning and purpose to life, fulfilled the human need to belong and express love, created community, and stressed a sense of spiritual equality for all people.

the written Gospels—the "good news" concerning Jesus. These writings, along with the disciples' letters and recorded teachings, became the basis of the **New Testament,** the second part of the Christian Bible.

By 100, Christian churches had been established in most of the major cities of the eastern empire and in some places in the western part of the empire. Most early Christians came from the Jews and the Greek-speaking populations of the east. In the second and third centuries, however, an increasing number of followers were Latin-speaking people.

Many Romans came to view Christians as harmful to the Roman state because Christians refused to worship the state gods and emperors. The Romans saw the Christians' refusal to do so as an act of treason, punishable by death. The Christians, however, believed there was only one God. To them, the worship of state gods and the emperors meant worshiping false gods and endangering their own salvation.

The Roman government began persecuting (harassing to cause suffering) Christians during the reign of Nero (A.D. 54–68). The emperor blamed the Christians for the fire that destroyed much of Rome and subjected them to cruel deaths. In contrast, in the second century, persecution of Christians diminished. By the end of the reigns of the five good emperors, Christians still represented a small minority, though it was one of considerable strength.

Reading Check **Summarizing** How were the teachings of Jesus preserved and passed on?

The Triumph of Christianity

TURNING POINT **Under Theodosius the Great, who ruled from 378 to 395, the Romans adopted Christianity as the official religion of the Roman Empire.**

Though the Romans persecuted Christians in the first and second centuries, this did nothing to stop the growth of Christianity. In fact, it did just the opposite, strengthening Christianity in the second and third centuries by forcing it to become more organized.

Crucial to this change was the emerging role of the bishops, who began to assume more control over church communities. The Christian church was creating a new structure in which the clergy (the church leaders) had distinct functions separate from the laity (the regular church members).

Christianity grew quickly in the first century, took root in the second, and by the third had spread widely. Why was Christianity able to attract so many followers?

First, the Christian message had much to offer the Roman world. Christianity was personal and offered salvation and eternal life to individuals. Christianity gave meaning and purpose to life.

Christianity also fulfilled the human need to belong. Christians formed communities bound to one another. In these communities, people could express their love by helping one another and offering assistance to the poor and the sick. Christianity satisfied the need to belong in a way that the huge Roman Empire could never provide.

Christianity proved attractive to all classes, but especially to the poor and powerless. Eternal life was promised to all—rich, poor, aristocrats, slaves, men, and women. Christianity stressed a sense of spiritual equality for all people.

In the fourth century, Christianity prospered as never before when **Constantine** became the first Christian emperor. Although he was not baptized until the end of his life, in 313 Constantine issued the Edict of Milan, which proclaimed official tolerance of Christianity. Then, under Theodosius the Great, the Romans adopted Christianity as their official religion.

Reading Check **Evaluating** What benefits did Christianity offer to individuals and Roman society as a whole?

The Decline

Marcus Aurelius, the last of the five good emperors, died in A.D. 180. For the next hundred years a period of civil wars, political disorder, and economic decline almost brought the Roman Empire to its end.

At the end of the third and the beginning of the fourth centuries, the Roman Empire gained a new lease on life through the efforts of two emperors, Diocletian and Constantine. The empire was changed into a new state: the Late Roman Empire. It included a new governmental structure, a rigid economic and social system, and a new state religion—Christianity.

Believing that the empire had grown too large for a single ruler, Diocletian, who ruled from 284 to 305, divided it into four units, each with its own ruler. Diocletian's military power still enabled him to claim a higher status and to hold the ultimate authority. Constantine, who ruled from 306 to 337, continued and expanded the policies of Diocletian.

Both rulers greatly strengthened and enlarged the administrative bureaucracies of the Roman Empire. A hierarchy of officials exercised control at the various levels of government. The army was enlarged to five hundred thousand men, including German troops.

CRITICAL THINKING ACTIVITY

Summarizing It is important that students realize how much of our culture, institutions, and values were shaped by previous civilizations. The civilizations of Greece and Rome were among the most influential for the Western world. After reading this section and utilizing outside sources, students should write an essay in which they identify, summarize, and describe the fundamental ideas and institutions of Western civilization that originated in Rome. Then have students select the two ideas or institutions that they feel have been the most influential on Western civilization. Students should explain how their chosen ideas or institutions have been the most influential or most important. **L2**

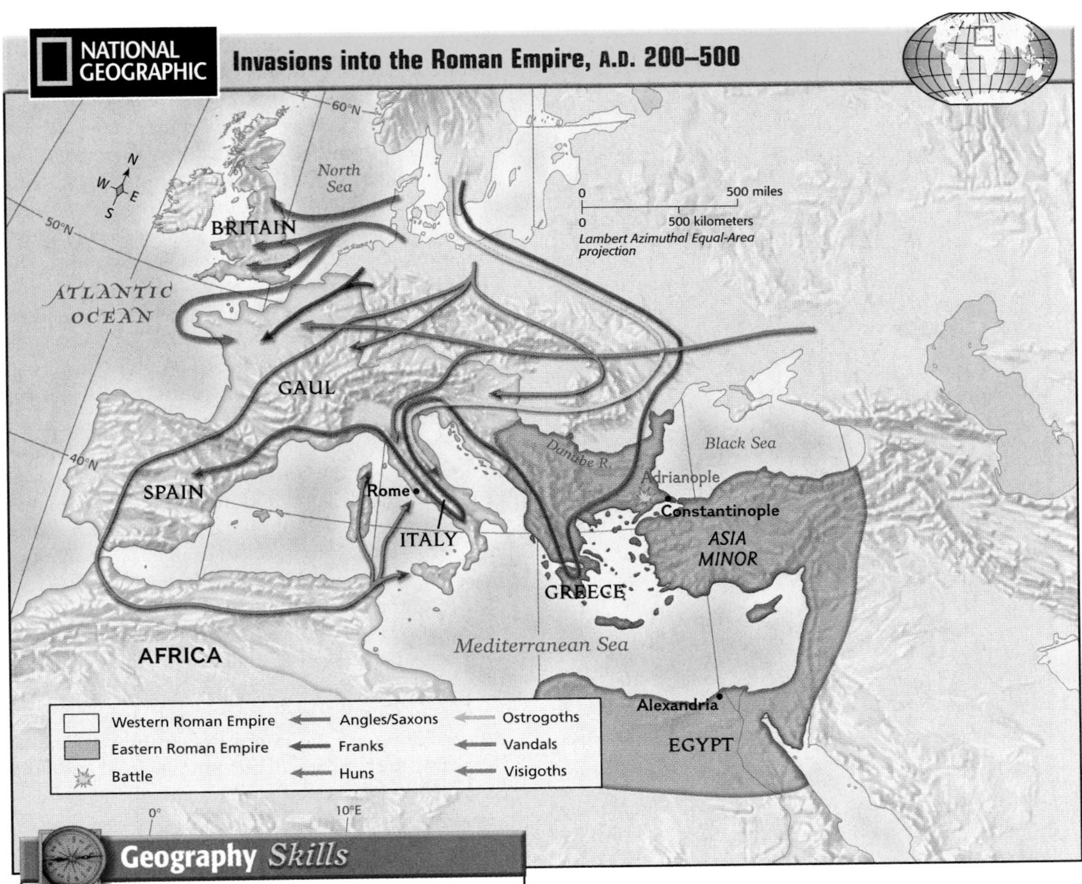

Geography Skills

Contributing to the fall of the Western Roman Empire were invasions that pressed in on all sides of the empire.

1. **Interpreting Maps** Which group of invaders made the most limited incursions?
2. **Applying Geography Skills** Which parts of the Roman Empire seem to have been more secure from the invasion? Why do you think this was?

The political and military reforms of Diocletian and Constantine greatly enlarged two institutions—the army and civil service—which drained most of the public funds. More revenues were needed to pay for the army and bureaucracy. The population was not growing, however, so the tax base could not be increased. To ensure the tax base and keep the empire going despite the shortage of labor, the emperors issued edicts that forced people to remain in their designated vocations. Basic jobs, such as bakers and shippers, became hereditary.

By 324, Constantine had emerged as the sole ruler of the empire. Constantine's biggest project was the construction of a new capital city in the east, on the site of the Greek city of Byzantium on the shores of the Bosporus. Calling it his "New Rome," Constantine enriched the city with a forum, large palaces, and a vast amphitheater. Eventually renamed **Constantinople,** the city would become the center of the Eastern Roman Empire and one of the great cities of the world.

In general, the economic and social policies of Diocletian and Constantine were based on control and coercion. Although temporarily successful, such policies in the long run stifled the very vitality the Late Empire needed to revive its sagging fortunes.

Reading Check **Evaluating** Identify two reforms of Diocletian and Constantine. What were the short-term effects of those policies?

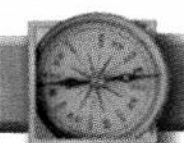

Geography Skills

Answers:

1. the Franks
2. the Eastern Roman Empire (Asia Minor and Egypt); it was farthest away and would have required crossing water at the closest points of contact

Reading Essentials and Study Guide 2–2

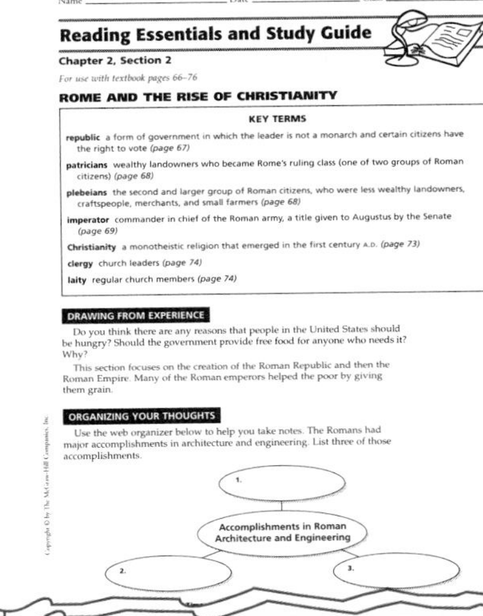

Name ____ Date ____ Class ____

Reading Essentials and Study Guide

Chapter 2, Section 2

For use with textbook pages 66–76

ROME AND THE RISE OF CHRISTIANITY

KEY TERMS

republic a form of government in which the leader is not a monarch and certain citizens have the right to vote *(page 67)*

patricians wealthy landowners who became Rome's ruling class (one of two groups of Roman citizens) *(page 68)*

plebeians the second and larger group of Roman citizens, who were less wealthy landowners, craftspeople, merchants, and small farmers *(page 68)*

imperator commander in chief of the Roman army, a title given to Augustus by the Senate *(page 69)*

Christianity a monotheistic religion that emerged in the first century A.D. *(page 73)*

clergy church leaders *(page 74)*

laity regular church members *(page 74)*

DRAWING FROM EXPERIENCE

Do you think there are any reasons that people in the United States should be hungry? Should the government provide free food for anyone who needs it? Why?

This section focuses on the creation of the Roman Republic and then the Roman Empire. Many of the Roman emperors helped the poor by giving them grain.

ORGANIZING YOUR THOUGHTS

Use the web organizer below to help you take notes. The Romans had major accomplishments in architecture and engineering. List three of those accomplishments.

1.
Accomplishments in Roman Architecture and Engineering
2.
3.

Reading Check

Answer: They enlarged the army and civil service, which drained public funds. As a short-term result, people were forced to remain in their designated vocations with jobs becoming hereditary.

Enrich

Have students work in pairs or groups of three to list both the positive and negative contributions of the Roman Empire. **L1**

COOPERATIVE LEARNING ACTIVITY

Creating Oral Presentations Organize the class into several groups, and assign each group to research one of the religions practiced in the Roman Empire: the official religion of Rome, Judaism, Christianity, Mithraism (a Persian religion), and the cult of Isis (an Egyptian religion). Each group member should have an assignment: research, compiling information, providing illustrations, preparing answers to possible questions, or presenting results to the class. After one member presents the group's report to the class, the group should act as a panel to answer additional questions. **L2**

For grading this activity, refer to the ***Performance Assessment Activities*** booklet.

Enrich

Many theories have been proposed to explain the decline and fall of the Roman Empire. Discuss with the class the following popular explanations: 1) Christianity's emphasis on a spiritual kingdom weakened Roman military virtues. 2) Traditional Roman values declined as non-Italians gained prominence in the empire. 3) Lead poisoning through leaden water pipes and cups caused a mental decline in the population. 4) Plague wiped out one-tenth of the population. 5) Rome failed to advance technologically because of slavery. 6) Rome was unable to put together a workable political system.

Reading Check

Answer: Germanic tribes—the Visigoths and Vandals

Reteaching Activity

Have students list two facts about the ancient Romans in each of the following areas: literature, art, architecture, law, living conditions, slavery, and entertainment. **L1** ELL

4 CLOSE

Work with students to prepare a chronology of events and issues that traces the rise and fall of the Roman Empire. Have students choose two or three events or issues that they think were most significant and explain their impact. **L1**

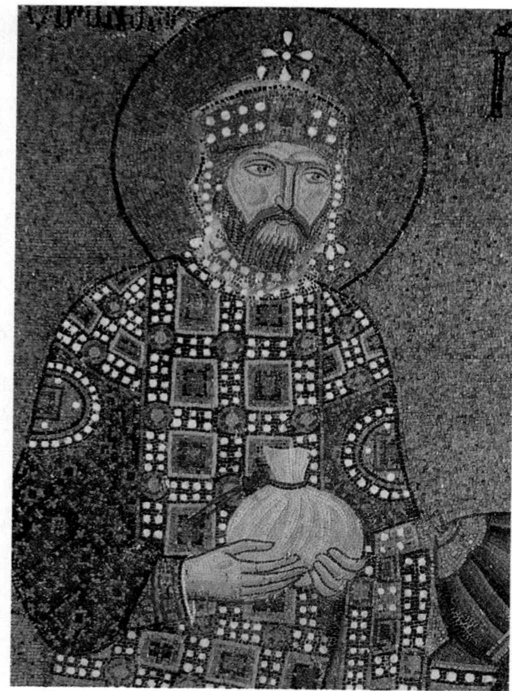

Emperor Constantine

The Fall

The restored empire of Diocletian and Constantine limped along for more than a century. After Constantine, the empire continued to be divided into western and eastern parts. The capital of the Western Roman Empire remained in Rome. Constantinople remained the capital of the Eastern Roman Empire.

The Western Roman Empire came under increasing pressure from the invading Germanic tribes. The major breakthrough of invaders into the west came in the second half of the fourth century. The Huns, who came from Asia, moved into eastern Europe and put pressure on the Germanic Visigoths. The Visigoths, in turn, moved south and west, crossed the Danube River into Roman territory, and settled down as Roman allies. However, the Visigoths soon revolted. The Romans' attempt to stop the revolt at Adrianople in 378 led to a crushing defeat for the Romans.

Increasing numbers of Germans now crossed the frontiers. In 410, the Visigoths sacked Rome. Another group, the Vandals, poured into southern Spain and Africa. They crossed into Italy from northern Africa and, in 455, they too sacked Rome. (Our modern word *vandal* is taken from this tribe.)

In 476, the Western emperor, Romulus Augustulus, was deposed by the Germanic head of the army. This is usually taken as the date of the fall of the Western Roman Empire. As we shall see in Chapter 3, a series of German kingdoms replaced the Western Roman Empire. The Eastern Roman Empire, or the Byzantine Empire, however, continued to thrive with its center at Constantinople.

Reading Check **Identifying** Which groups invaded the Western Roman Empire?

SECTION 2 ASSESSMENT

Checking for Understanding

1. **Define** republic, patrician, plebeian, imperator, Christianity, clergy, laity.
2. **Identify** Hannibal, Julius Caesar, Augustus, *Pax Romana,* Twelve Tables, Law of Nations, Virgil, Jesus, New Testament, Constantine.
3. **Locate** Rome, Carthage, Mediterranean Sea, Asia Minor, Constantinople.
4. **Describe** the significance of the Twelve Tables and the Law of Nations.
5. **List** the ethical concepts voiced by Jesus.

Critical Thinking

6. **Explain** How were the Romans able to obtain large numbers of slaves? How were slaves utilized in ancient Rome?
7. **Summarizing Information** Create a table like the one below describing the contributions of the Greeks and the contributions of the Romans to Western civilization.

Greek contributions	Roman contributions

Analyzing Visuals

8. **Examine** the photograph of the Colosseum on page 71. What types of entertainments were performed in Roman amphitheaters and other public buildings?

Writing About History

9. **Expository Writing** Use the Internet or library sources to research the theories about why the Roman Empire fell. Summarize the theories in a brief essay and explain why some theories seem more convincing than others.

SECTION 2 ASSESSMENT

1. Key terms are in blue.
2. Hannibal *(p. 67);* Julius Caesar *(p. 69);* Augustus *(p. 69); Pax Romana (p. 70);* Twelve Tables *(p. 70);* Law of Nations *(p. 70);* Virgil *(p. 72);* Jesus *(p. 72);* New Testament *(p. 74);* Constantine *(p. 74)*
3. See chapter maps.
4. Twelve Tables provided law codes; Law of Nations provided standards of justice for all people.
5. humility, charity, love
6. captured foreigners in war; used as tutors, musicians, doctors, household workers; built roads and public buildings; farmed
7. Greeks: democracy, philosophy, art, architecture; Romans: government, law, engineering
8. horse and chariot races, dramatic performances, gladiatorial shows
9. Answers will vary. Some theories include: traditional Roman values declined as non-Italians gained power; Christianity weakened military values; lead poisoning and plague weakened population; slavery hindered Roman technological progress.

Eyewitness to History

Cincinnatus Saves Rome

THERE IS PERHAPS NO BETTER account of how the virtues of duty and simplicity enabled good Roman citizens to succeed during the difficulties of the fifth century B.C. than Livy's account of Cincinnatus.

Lucius Quinctius Cincinnatus, Roman statesman and dictator, is shown here receiving his dictatorship.

❝The city was thrown into a state of turmoil, and the general alarm was as great as if Rome herself were surrounded. The situation evidently called for a dictator [the position of dictator was a temporary one used only in emergencies], and, with no dissenting voice, Lucius Quinctius Cincinnatus was named for the post.

Now I would solicit the particular attention of those numerous people who imagine that money is everything in this world, and that rank and ability are inseparable from wealth: let them observe that Cincinnatus, the one man in whom Rome reposed all her hope of survival, was at that moment working a little three-acre farm west of the Tiber. A delegation from the city found him at work on his land—digging a ditch, maybe, or ploughing. Greetings were exchanged, and he was asked—with a prayer for divine blessing on himself and his country—to put on his toga and hear the Senate's instructions. This naturally surprised him, and, asking if all were well, he told his wife to run to their cottage and fetch his toga. The toga was brought, and wiping the grimy sweat from his hands and face he put it on; at once the envoys from the city saluted him, with congratulations, as Dictator, invited him to enter Rome, and informed him of the terrible danger of the enemy's army. . . .

[Cincinnatus proceeded to raise an army, marched out, and defeated the enemy.]

In Rome the Senate was convened, and a decree was passed inviting Cincinnatus to enter in triumph with his troops. The chariot he rode in was preceded by the enemy commanders and the military flags, and followed by his army loaded with its spoils. . . . Cincinnatus finally resigned after holding office for fifteen days, having originally accepted it for a period of six months. He returned to his farm.❞

—Livy, ***The Early History of Rome***

Analyzing Primary Sources

1. How did Cincinnatus embody the characteristics of an ideal Roman citizen?
2. What lesson(s) did Livy hope to teach his readers?
3. Compare the position of dictator in this account with present-day dictators.

77

TEACH

Analyzing Primary Sources
Cincinnatus was chosen dictator of Rome to defend the city against the Aequi. During this time in Rome, a dictator could be chosen to rule temporarily. The consuls would resign from their positions, and the dictator would have unlimited power for up to six months. However, not all of the people liked this idea. The common people were not pleased when a dictator was chosen because they feared his excessive power and how it might be used.

Ask students to discuss how the United States government is organized. Is it possible for one person to control the country? *(No. Students might discuss the separation of powers in the United States government.)* **L1** ELL

Government Cincinnatus was an unusual ruler with regard to succession. He remained leader as long as he was needed, and then returned to his farm allowing for an orderly change of power. Later, during the Roman Empire, the lack of orderly succession brought political instability and gave the military greater control of the government. Ask students how power is passed on in the United States. What ensures that this process is orderly? **L2**

ANSWERS TO ANALYZING PRIMARY SOURCES

1. He was loyal and dutiful, he abandoned work on his own land to go to Rome, placing the needs of Rome before his own needs.
2. He hoped to inspire Romans with the example of a humble citizen who became a great leader for unselfish reasons. Cincinnatus put the needs of the state before his own, did what needed to be done, and relinquished power as soon as he had accomplished what he was asked to do.
3. Rather than being asked to serve, most modern dictators seize power, and rather than relinquishing it voluntarily when they have accomplished what they set out to do, modern dictators usually cling to power until they die or are deposed.

GLENCOE TECHNOLOGY

MindJogger Videoquiz

Use the **MindJogger Videoquiz** to review Chapter 2 content.

 Available in VHS.

Using Key Terms

1. imperator **2.** polis **3.** patricians **4.** democracy, oligarchy **5.** Plebeians **6.** republic **7.** acropolis **8.** direct democracy **9.** epic poem **10.** clergy, laity

Reviewing Key Facts

11. Mountains isolated Greek communities from one another. The many harbors and islands caused Greeks to become seafarers.

12. Adult males were citizens with political rights; women and children were citizens without political rights.

13. the Persian Wars and the Great Peloponnesian War

14. Tragedies explore good and evil, the rights of individuals, the nature of divine forces, and the nature of human beings.

15. It is a teaching method that uses a question-and-answer format. Socrates believed that all real knowledge was already inside a person.

16. A power struggle between generals resulted in the empire's being divided into four kingdoms.

17. Patricians had more wealth, political power, and prestige than plebeians, who resented the inequality. After hundreds of years a council of the plebs, tribunes, and consul positions was created. Eventually the council of the plebs could pass laws that affected all Romans.

18. The poor lived in overcrowded, unsafe apartments called *insulae.* The empire provided food and entertainment.

19. They were superb builders. Utilizing concrete, the arch, the dome, and the vault, they constructed huge buildings. They also built roads, aqueducts, and bridges.

20. primarily farming, also trade

Critical Thinking

21. The weakened city-states were overcome by Philip of Macedonia. His son Alexander the Great later spread Greek culture throughout his empire. The Romans admired Greek culture and continued to spread a mixture of Greek and Roman ideas throughout their empire.

22. Answers will vary but should include the person's leadership qualities, governmental policies, wealth, and ability to influence armies.

Writing About History

23. Answers should show evidence of careful research.

Analyzing Sources

24. Livy says that we can learn from the positive and negative examples in history.

CHAPTER 2 ASSESSMENT and ACTIVITIES

Chapter Summary

A series of causes and effects shaped the history of ancient Greece and Rome.

Cause	Effect
Cleisthenes gives the Athenian assembly the final authority to pass laws.	Male citizens play a central role in politics, creating the foundation for Athenian democracy.
Disputes among city-states lead to the Great Peloponnesian War in 431 B.C.	Philip II of Macedonia defeats the weakened Greek city-states in 338 B.C.
Alexander the Great becomes king of Macedonia and creates an expansive empire.	Greek ideas and culture are spread to the non-Greek world of Southwest Asia and beyond.
The expansion of Rome weakens its republican rule and leads to civil wars.	Octavian gains control of the state and becomes the first emperor of the Roman Empire.
Christianity attracts many followers and quickly spreads throughout the Roman Empire.	Theodosius the Great makes Christianity the official religion of the Roman Empire.
Economic and social policies of Diocletian and Constantine are based on coercion.	The policies of these two emperors contribute to the empire's eventual collapse.

Using Key Terms

1. The English word *emperor* comes from the Latin word _____.
2. The focus of Greek life was the _____, or city-state.
3. The _____ were great landowners, who became Rome's ruling class.
4. Some Greek city-states were committed to government by the many, called _____, while others were ruled by _____, which means rule by the few.
5. _____ were Roman citizens and could vote, but they could not hold government office.
6. Romans established a _____ when they overthrew the last Etruscan king.
7. The _____ served as a place of refuge and sometimes came to be a religious center.
8. In a _____, the people participate directly in government decision making.
9. The *Odyssey,* an _____, tells the story of the Greek hero Odysseus.
10. During the Roman Empire, the Christian church developed a new structure in which church leaders, or _____, had distinct functions separate from church members, or _____.

Reviewing Key Facts

11. **Geography** How did the geography of Greece affect Greek history?
12. **Citizenship** Contrast the rights of male and female citizens in the Greek polis.
13. **History** Identify the wars that Greece fought during the Classical Age.
14. **Culture** Describe the themes of Greek tragedies.
15. **Culture** What is the Socratic method?
16. **History** What became of Alexander's empire after his death?
17. **Culture** What was the political and social standing of the patricians and plebeians? How was the struggle between the orders resolved?
18. **Culture** Describe the living conditions of a poor family in Rome. What services did the empire provide?
19. **Science and Technology** How did the Romans utilize their engineering skills?
20. **Economics** What was the economic base of the Roman Empire?

Critical Thinking

21. **Understanding Cause and Effect** The Peloponnesian War weakened Greek states, yet later, Greek culture was spread farther than ever. How did this happen?
22. **Analyzing** Choose four influential men from Greece and Rome and describe their impact on the government and politics of the time.

Self-Check Quiz
Visit the *Glencoe World History—Modern Times* Web site at wh.mt.glencoe.com and click on **Chapter 2–Self-Check Quiz** to prepare for the Chapter Test.

Writing About History

23. Expository Writing Research reasons why Romans thought Christianity was dangerous to their empire. Compare these arguments to actual Christian doctrine and practices. Present your findings in a carefully prepared essay. Show that your sources corroborate your position.

Analyzing Sources

In his book *The Early History of Rome,* the Roman historian Livy traced the development of Rome from its beginnings to 9 B.C.

> "The study of history is the best medicine for a sick mind; for in history you have a record of the infinite variety of human experience plainly set out for all to see; and in that record you can find for yourself and your country both examples and warnings: fine things to take as models, base things, rotten through and through, to avoid."

24. According to Livy, what is the benefit of studying history? Do you agree with Livy? Why or why not?
25. Why might modern-day historians find Livy to be an important resource ?

Applying Technology Skills

26. **Creating a Multimedia Presentation** Using the Internet and traditional print sources, conduct further research on Greek architecture, especially the design and building of temples. Then, design and construct a small three-dimensional temple, using the type of column best suited to your building. Attach the following information: the location of the temple, the god or goddess it serves, and the approximate dates a temple like this would have been constructed in Greece.

Making Decisions

27. In groups of two, have one person take the role of a plebeian, and the other, the role of a patrician. Discuss the extent to which the gulf between patricians and plebeians is straining the Roman Republic. Together, decide on measures that could end the struggle and benefit the republic as a whole.

NATIONAL GEOGRAPHIC **Greek Colonies, 750–550 B.C.**

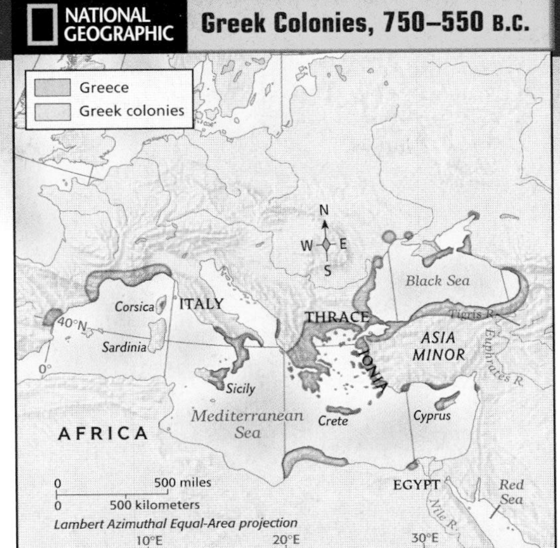

Analyzing Maps and Charts

Study the map above to answer the following questions.

28. Between 750 and 550 B.C., large numbers of Greeks left their homeland to settle in distant lands. Analyze the location of the Greek colonies. What generalizations can you make about their locations?
29. What is the approximate maximum distance that a Greek citizen would have to travel to reach the sea?
30. Based on this map and others in the chapter, how important was a navy to the Athenian Empire?

Standardized Test Practice

Directions: Choose the best answer to the following question.

One lasting contribution of the Roman Empire was

A the *Pax Romana.*
B the Christian church.
C the gladiatorial shows.
D its system of law.

Test-Taking Tip: Do not pick an answer just because it sounds good. Sometimes a choice is deliberately meant to sound correct but is not. Read all of the answer choices very carefully before you select the best one and avoid making any hasty decisions.

CHAPTER 2
Assessment and Activities

Have students visit the Web site at wh.mt.glencoe.com to review Chapter 2 and take the Self-Check Quiz.

Standardized Test Practice

Answer: D
Answer Explanation: While the Christian Church began during the empire, it was not directly created by the Roman Empire.

Bonus Question ?

Ask: Which of the philosophical outlooks discussed in this chapter do you think is most relevant to today's world? Why? *(Answers should include the basic tenets of the philosopher.)* **L1**

25. Modern-day historians can discover a particular point of view from reading Livy.

Applying Technology Skills

26. Students will create a model that reflects accurate research.

Making Decisions

27. Solutions should take into account the points of view of both patricians and plebeians.

Analyzing Maps and Charts

28. located near water, chief means of transportation would be ship
29. approximately 80 miles (129 km)
30. A navy was important for defense against Persia and Sparta.

Introducing World Religions

Travel, the media, the Internet, immigration, and interactions with classmates are just a few ways that students have been exposed to religion. In your classroom there may be students of various beliefs and religious affiliations. Despite the availability of information, many people remain ignorant about world religions. Before students read the World Religions feature, ask them to identify as many major religions as they can and list the facts they know about each religion. What areas of religion would students like to learn more about? *(Answers may include Baha'i, Buddhism, Christianity, Confucianism, Hinduism, Jainism, Judaism, Islam, Sikhism, Shintoism; students may also list the Church of Jesus Christ of Latter-day Saints, Unification Church, Theosophy, International Society for Krishna Consciousness.)* **L1**

Critical Thinking

During your class discussions, it is important that students demonstrate the proper respect for views and beliefs that may differ from their own. Therefore, you may want to ask the class to develop guidelines for discussing religion. Guidelines might include not judging the validity of a religion; showing respect and understanding for all ideas presented, and being receptive to the interpretations offered; not accepting or rejecting views as right or wrong, better or worse. Post guidelines on the chalkboard or on an overhead transparency.

WORLD RELIGIONS

How was the universe created? What happens when we die? How do we become good people? These are some of the questions that religions attempt to answer. By creating an organized system of worship, religions help us make sense of our lives and our world.

Religion can be an individual belief. In some nations, religion is also state policy. Throughout history, religions have had both the power to unite people and to create terrible conflict. Today, there are thousands of religions practiced by about 6 billion people around the world.

Major World Religions

Religion	Number of Followers
Christianity	1,974,181,000
Islam	1,155,109,000
Hinduism	799,028,000
Buddhism	356,270,000
Confucianism	154,080,000
Judaism	14,313,000

Source: *Encyclopedia Britannica Book of the Year.*
Note: The figure for Confucianism includes Chinese followers.

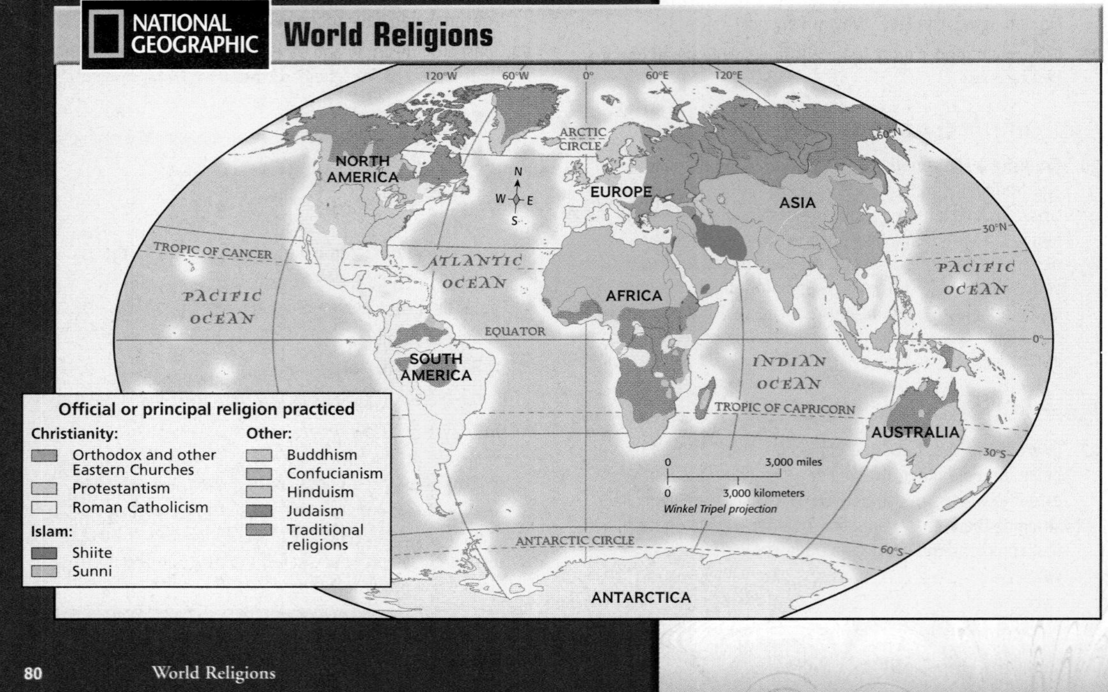

INTERDISCIPLINARY CONNECTIONS ACTIVITY

English Language Arts As in any field of study, religion has developed its own specialized vocabulary. In a class discussion, ask students to identify unfamiliar words that they have been introduced to by the World Religions feature and that they have come across in their research for the various exercises. Have students work in groups to create a glossary of twenty-five religious terms. Encourage students to illustrate their glossaries. Have students include definition, pronunciation, syllable divisions, and etymology where possible. **ELL L1**

Local Religions

Although some religions have spread worldwide, many people still practice religions that originated and developed in their own area.

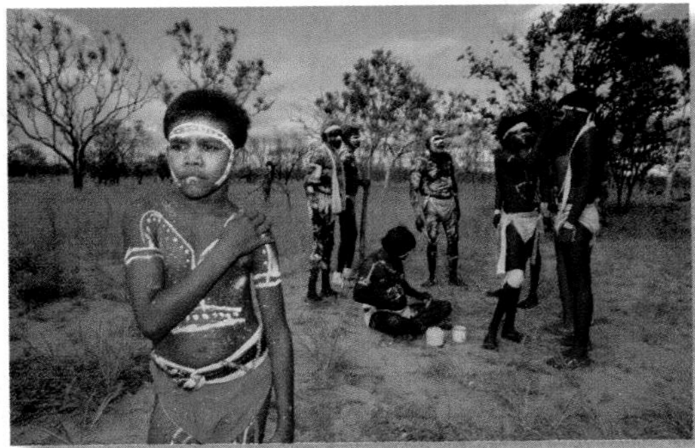

Australia

There are no deities in the traditional beliefs of the aborigines of Australia. Their lives revolve around a belief known as the Dreamtime. According to aboriginal mythology, ancestor heroes created the world and all it contains during the Dreamtime. The aborigines also believe in spirits that inhabit the natural world and can be reborn or return to the earth many times.

Africa

Many Africans south of the Sahara continue traditional religious practices. Because Africa has many ethnic groups, languages, customs, and beliefs, it is not surprising that local religions are just as diverse. Despite the differences, however, most Africans recognize one god whom they consider to be a supreme creator.

Japan

In Japan there are over 80,000 Shinto shrines, such as the one shown to the left. Shintoism, which goes back to prehistoric times, has no formal doctrine. Believers worship *kami,* which are sacred spirits that take on natural forms such as trees or mountains. Followers also worship ancestors or protectors of families.

North America

The Navajo religion is distinct in that it must be practiced in a particular geographical area. Navajo people believe that the Creator instructed them never to leave the land between four sacred mountains located in Colorado, New Mexico, and Arizona. Navajo dwellings, called hogans (at right), are sacred and constructed to symbolize their land: the four posts represent the sacred mountains, the floor is Mother Earth, and the dome-like roof is Father Sky.

WORLD RELIGIONS

Critical Thinking

Students today may be most familiar with religions based on sacred text. For example, the Bible, Quran, and Torah are essential to adherents of Christianity, Islam, and Judaism, respectively. Practitioners of those faiths are sometimes referred to as "people of the Book." Non-literate societies throughout history, however, have also been deeply religious. Ask students to identify and analyze ways non-literate people pass on their faith to future generations, worship, and express their beliefs. *(myth, ritual, drawing, sculpture, magic, song, dreams, prayer)* **L2**

Connecting Across Time

Ask students to select one of their responses to the question in the Critical Thinking activity, and have them conduct further research on this issue. Is the means they selected in use today? Is it common to all religions or exclusive to a particular religion? Ask students to write a paragraph with their research results. **L2**

Enrich

Invite clergy from different faiths to come to your class. Tell the clergy in advance how much time they will have, who the other guests will be, and what you would like them to speak about. Before they come, have students prepare a list of interview questions. If possible, allow the clergy to see the lists ahead of time.

COOPERATIVE LEARNING ACTIVITY

Creating an Oral Presentation Divide students into small groups. Have each group select one of the geographic areas featured on this page. Each group will prepare a presentation for the class on a local religion associated with the geographic area they selected. The presentation should include political and thematic maps, a brief history, a description of the beliefs and practices associated with the local religion, and photos or artifacts if possible. Encourage the students to discover how the local religion meets the needs of that particular culture. Each group should prepare a short quiz that students will take after the presentation. The quiz should contain three or four fact-based questions and one critical thinking question. **L1**

Connecting Across Time

Ask students to define religious liberty, religious toleration, separation of church and state, and state-based religion. Using an atlas and other sources, ask students to identify countries that practice each of these policies. Encourage students to examine the historical basis behind the practice. Assign students to identify examples of religious influence in both historic and contemporary world events. Compile a class list and use it as a basis for discussion throughout the year.

Who?What?Where?When?

Clergy Most religions are guided or led by clergy. Clergy are religious leaders who may be paid staff or volunteers. Some religious denominations require clergy to obtain advanced education; others do not. Some clergy are appointed by the religious administration, others are selected from within the religious community they serve. Procedures and requirements for becoming a member of the clergy vary from religion to religion and also among denominations within religions. Titles of clergy members also vary. Depending upon the religion, a member of the clergy could be called rabbi, priest, mullah, pastor, mujtahid, or chaplain, to name just a few.

Major Religions → History and Beliefs

Buddhism

Buddhism began in India around the sixth century B.C. and today is practiced by over 350 million people throughout Asia. It is based on the teachings of Siddhartha Gautama, known as the Buddha, or Enlightened One. The Buddha taught that to escape the suffering caused by worldly desires, people must follow the Eightfold Path, which prescribes a life of morality, wisdom, and contemplation. The Wheel of Law (at left) is an important Buddhist symbol, representing the endless cycle of life.

Christianity

Christians believe in one God and that Jesus Christ is the Savior, the Son of God, who was sent to Earth and died on the cross to save humanity. Christians believe that faith in Jesus saves believers from God's penalty for sin and bestows eternal life. The cross remains a very potent symbol of the religion. For Christians, the Bible is the inspired word of God. Christianity began approximately 2,000 years ago. It is practiced by almost 2 billion people in nearly all parts of the world.

Confucianism

Although many people consider Confucianism a religion, it is actually a philosophy based on the teachings of Confucius, a Chinese scholar who lived about 500 B.C. He believed that moral character and social responsibility were the way to lead a fulfilling life. Confucianism has been an important influence on Chinese life since its founding, and Confucius is often honored as a spiritual teacher.

MEETING INDIVIDUAL NEEDS

Visual Symbols are associated with almost every religion. Religious symbols serve many functions. The symbol may communicate a truth or doctrine about the faith. For Protestants, for example, the empty cross communicates God's power over death. Symbols also give a sense of identity to participants of a religion. Sikhs wear a ceremonial sword as a sign of dignity and as a sign of their struggle against injustice. Ask students to identify the symbols associated with the six religions on this page and the next. Have students bring six index cards to class. On one side of the index card students should draw the symbol associated with one of the religions. On the other side students should describe what the symbol represents. Give extra credit to students who research additional religious symbols. **L2**

WORLD RELIGIONS

Major Religions — History and Beliefs

Hinduism

Hinduism is the world's oldest organized religion, starting in India about 1500 B.C. It has influenced and absorbed many other religions. This has led to a wide variety of beliefs and practices among its followers, who number about 800 million and still live principally in India. Although Hindus worship a number of gods, today they primarily worship Siva and Vishnu (shown at left). Siva represents both the destructive and creative forces of the universe. Vishnu is considered the preserver of the universe.

Islam

The followers of Islam, known as Muslims, believe in one God, *Allah.* They also accept all the prophets of Judaism and Christianity. Muslims follow the practices and teachings of the Quran, which the prophet Muhammad said was revealed to him by Allah beginning in A.D. 610. In 2000, there were about 1.1 billion Muslims, living mainly in Asia and Africa. Islam is often symbolized by a crescent moon, an important element of Muslim rituals, which depend on the lunar calendar.

Judaism

Jews believe in only one God; in fact, their faith, Judaism, was the first monotheistic religion. Today, about 14 million people throughout the world practice Judaism, with most Jews living in Israel and the United States. The main laws and practices of Judaism are contained in the Torah, the first five books of the Hebrew Bible (the *Pentateuch*). The six-pointed star, known as the Star of David (see the Torah mantle at left), has often been a controversial symbol of Judaism, but today it is widely accepted and appears on the Israeli flag.

Critical Thinking

Ask students to imagine that they are members of the local city council. For years the city has decorated city hall with a nativity scene and a menorah. A city resident complained that the display violated the separation of church and state clause of the U.S. Constitution, and the resident has threatened a lawsuit. The city immediately banned all holiday displays. Long-time residents are angry that a harmless tradition that they have long enjoyed is now gone. They are threatening to vote the city council out of office. In their roles as council members, ask students to use a problem-solving process to identify the problems associated with this issue, gather information, list and consider options, consider advantages and disadvantages, and then to develop guidelines for public displays that meet local ordinances and federal laws, as well as reflect the community's beliefs and wishes. Students should also evaluate the effectiveness of their proposed solution. **L3**

Connecting Across Time

Religious, cultural, and national identities are often intertwined. Ask students to identify places where religious, cultural, and national identity have been combined. Then assign students to watch televised news programs and read the front-page section of the newspaper for three days. Have students report on the local, national, or international events where religion has played a role. **L1**

CRITICAL THINKING ACTIVITY

Using Primary and Secondary Sources Have students select one of the religions that is practiced in their community as a basis for a research project. Have the class develop questions that students will use to research the religion they selected. Include: What does the religion say about God or gods? Is there life after death? How was the world created? Does belief solve the problem of sin, suffering, and how to live in harmony with others? What moral values are associated with the religion? Have students conduct their research using primary and secondary sources. Remind students that they must evaluate the validity of their sources, and that they should also identify biases within their research material. After students have completed their research projects, set aside time for a class discussion. **L3**

Connecting Across Time

Places of worship have been designed to evoke a sense of awe or perhaps a deeper understanding of God or the deity worshiped. The architecture of these buildings reflects an artistic ideal of the culture. Decorations and architectural embellishments illustrate scenes from sacred text or from history, or reflect the tradition or laws concerning worship. Ask students to identify places of worship in their community today. Is the actual building as important today to the practice of worship as it was in past times? You might wish to have students refer to Chapter 4 in their text, which features Gothic church architecture and to Chapter 3, which has illustrations of mosques. Ask students to analyze how the architecture transcends the cultures that produced these masterpieces. **L1** ELL

Connecting Across Time

Mohandas Gandhi and Martin Luther King, Jr., were inspired by Henry David Thoreau, a New England transcendentalist. Ask students to analyze the influence of significant religious leaders such as Pope John Paul II, Mother Teresa, and Archbishop Desmond Tutu on events in the twentieth century. Have students create an oral or visual presentation in which they describe the ways those individuals influence others today. **L2**

Major Religions → Worship and Celebrations

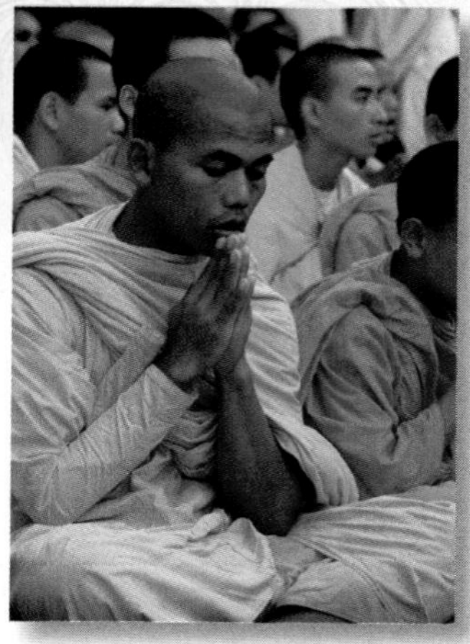

Buddhism

The ultimate goal of Buddhism is to reach nirvana, an enlightened state that frees an individual from the suffering that is found in life. Anyone might reach nirvana, but it is considered most attainable by Buddhist monks. These devout believers usually live in monasteries, leading a disciplined life of poverty, meditation, and study. Those who are not monks pursue enlightenment by making offerings and performing rituals such as walking clockwise around sacred domes, called *stupas*.

Christianity

Christians gather weekly to worship God and pray. Christians also observe important and joyful holidays such as Easter, which celebrates the resurrection of Jesus Christ. Christians believe that his resurrection was the evidence of God's power over sin and death. Holy Week, the week before Easter, begins with Palm Sunday, which celebrates Jesus' arrival into Jerusalem. Maundy Thursday, or Holy Thursday, commemorates Jesus' last meal with his disciples. Good Friday is a somber day in remembrance of Jesus' death.

Confucianism

Confucianism does not have a god or clergy and does not concern itself with what could be considered religious issues. It is more of a guide to ethical behavior and good government. Despite this, Confucius is venerated as a spiritual leader, and there are many temples dedicated to him. His teachings were recorded by his students in a book called the *Analects*, which have influenced Chinese people for generations.

COOPERATIVE LEARNING ACTIVITY

Visual Presentation Celebrations and holy days are often the most memorable activities associated with religion. Celebrations can be joyous or somber, open to the entire community or to a small group. Have students work in small groups to examine a religious celebration such as Purim, *Eid ul-Fitr,* Kwanzaa, Easter, or a Passover seder. Ask students to bring in food items, clothing, gifts, or decorations associated with that celebration and to explain their history and symbolism. Remind students of the guidelines they developed in an earlier exercise for discussing religion. **L1**

Major Religions ⟶ Worship and Celebrations

Hinduism

Hindus believe that after death the soul leaves the body and is reborn in another person, animal, vegetable, or mineral. Where a soul is reborn depends upon its karma, or the accumulated merits or faults of its past lives. One of the ways Hindus increase "good" karma is through rituals such as washing away their sins. The Ganges is considered a sacred river to Hindus, and each year thousands come to bathe in the water to purify themselves.

Islam

Ramadan is the ninth month of the Muslim calendar, commemorating the time during which Muhammad received the Quran from Allah. During Ramadan, Muslims read from the Quran and fast from dawn until sunset. Fasting helps believers focus on spiritual rather than bodily matters. The daily fast is broken with prayers and a meal called the *iftar.* People celebrate the end of Ramadan with the Feast of the Fast, *Eid-ul-Fitr.*

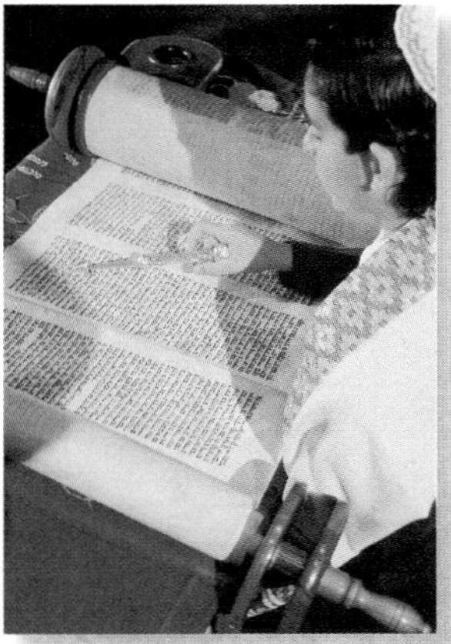

Judaism

Observant Jews follow many strict laws that guide their daily lives and the ways in which they worship. They recite their prayers standing up and often wear a prayer shawl. Their heads are covered as a sign of respect for God. Every synagogue (place of worship) has a Torah, handwritten on a parchment scroll. During services, the Torah is read to the congregation, and the entire text is read in the course of a year.

CURRICULUM CONNECTION

Philosophy Based on the information in the text, the exercises students have completed, and their personal experiences, guide students in a discussion of the ways in which religion gives value and meaning to life. Have students refer to information presented in the first chapters of the text, as well as to current events. **L3**

Connecting Across Time

Religious persecution is an unfortunate fact. Ask students to identify periods of religious persecution in the chapters they have already read and to name other major examples of religious persecution, such as the Holocaust. In many countries today, adherents of a minority or unofficial religion face persecution. Despite persistent persecution, many believers would rather lose their jobs, homes, and even their lives rather than deny their faith. Ask students what conclusions about faith they can draw from this statement. **L2**

CRITICAL THINKING ACTIVITY

Compare and Contrast After students study the information in this feature and the following chapters, ask students to write essays in which they compare and contrast the historical origins, central ideas, and the spread of major religions and philosophical traditions, focusing on the six discussed in this feature. Students should use the process of historical inquiry to research, interpret, and use multiple sources of evidence. Assign students the task of evaluating the validity of sources they use based on language, corroboration with other sources, and information about the authors. Students should also be expected to identify bias in written, oral, and visual materials used in their research. **L2**

Chapter 3 Resources

Timesaving Tools

TeacherWorks™ All-In-One Planner and Resource Center

- **Interactive Teacher Edition** Access your Teacher Wraparound Edition and your classroom resources with a few easy clicks.
- **Interactive Lesson Planner** Planning has never been easier! Organize your week, month, semester, or year with all the lesson helps you need to make teaching creative, timely, and relevant.

Use Glencoe's **Presentation Plus!** multimedia teacher tool to easily present dynamic lessons that visually excite your students. Using Microsoft PowerPoint® you can customize the presentations to create your own personalized lessons.

Teaching Transparencies

Graphic Organizer Student Activity 3 Transparency

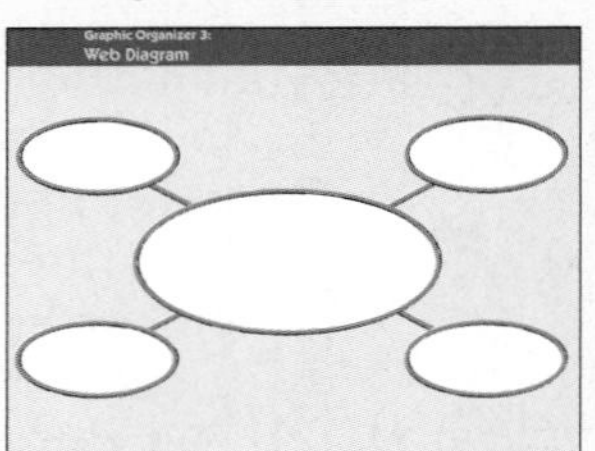

Chapter Transparency 3

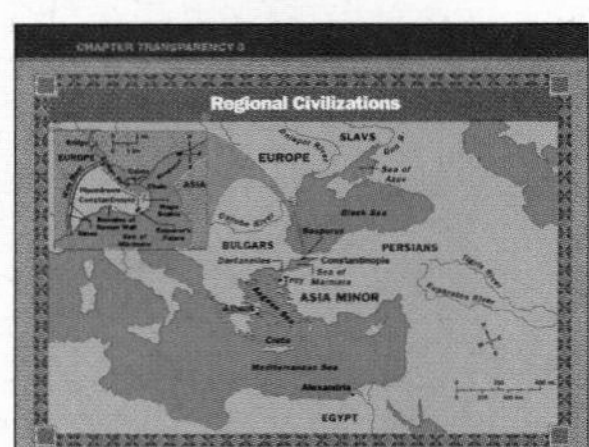

Map Overlay Transparency 3

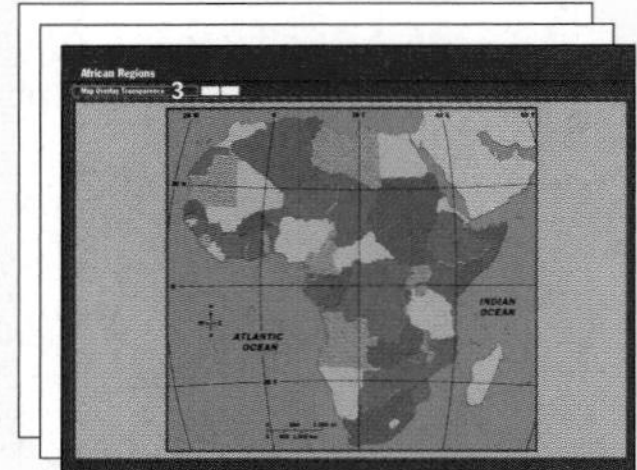

Application and Enrichment

Enrichment Activity 3

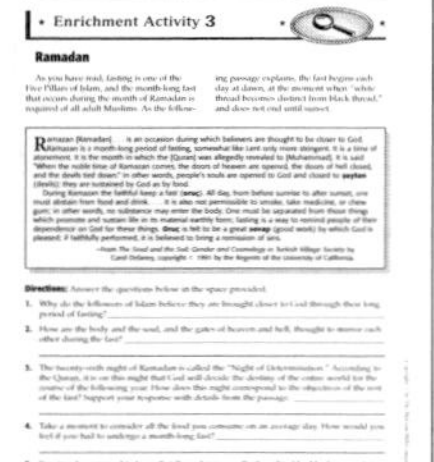

Primary Source Reading 3

History Simulation Activity 3

Historical Significance Activity 3

Cooperative Learning Activity 3

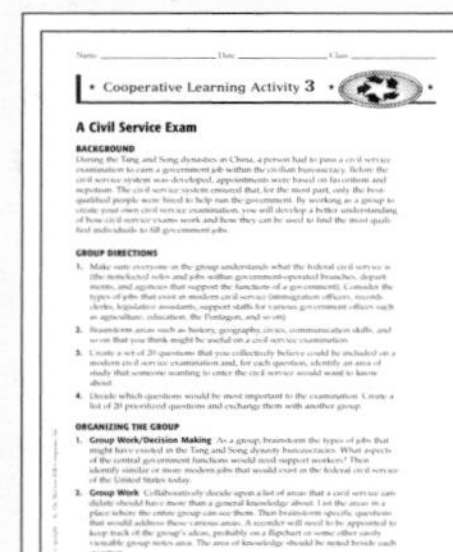

A&E HOME VIDEO. Biography® THE HISTORY CHANNEL.

The following videotape programs are available from Glencoe as supplements to Chapter 3:

- **Legends of the Arabian Nights** (ISBN 0–7670–0232–6)
- **Seven Wonders of the Ancient World** (ISBN 0–7670–0401–9)
- **Marco Polo: Journey to the East** (ISBN 0–56501–668–8)
- **Genghis Khan: Terror and Conquest** (ISBN 0–56501–578–9)
- **Knights and Armor** (ISBN 0–56501–443–X)

To order, call Glencoe at 1–800–334–7344. To find classroom resources to accompany many of these videos, check the following home pages:
A&E Television: www.aande.com
The History Channel: www.historychannel.com

Chapter 3 Resources

Review and Reinforcement

Linking Past and Present Activity 3

Time Line Activity 3

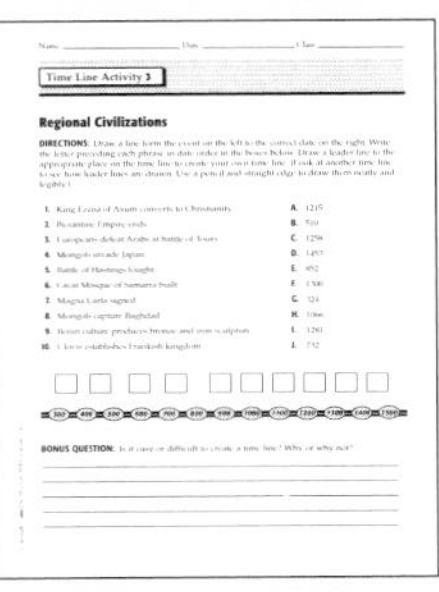

Reteaching Activity 3

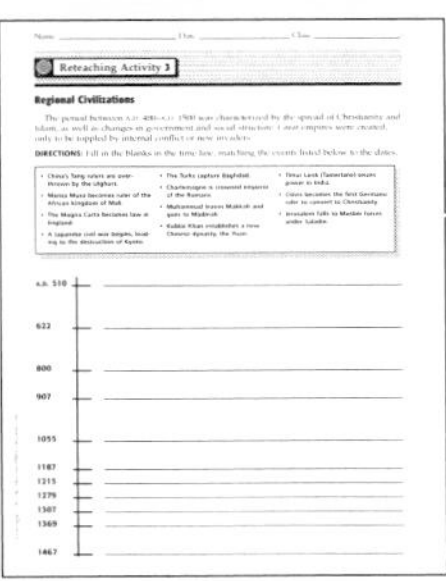

Vocabulary Activity 3

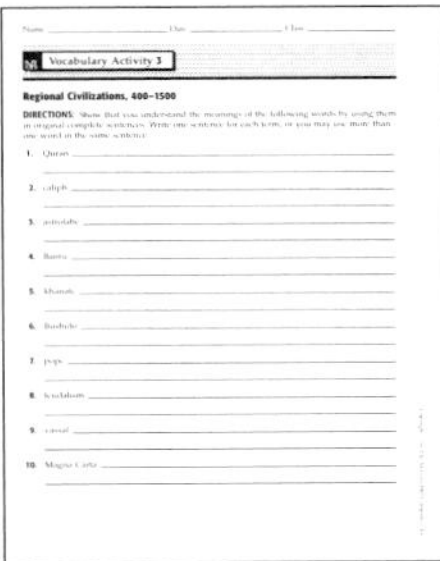

Critical Thinking Skills Activity 3

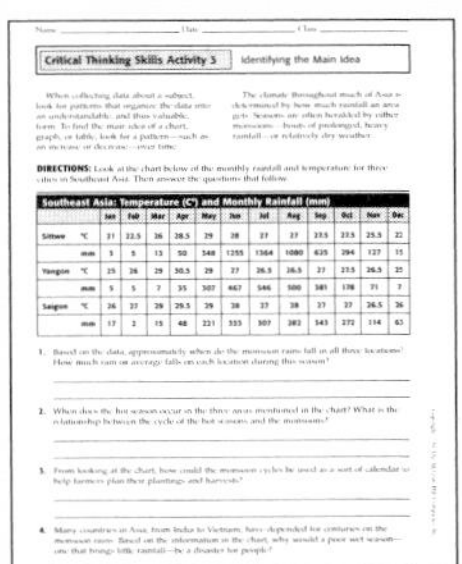

Assessment and Evaluation

Chapter 3 Test Form A

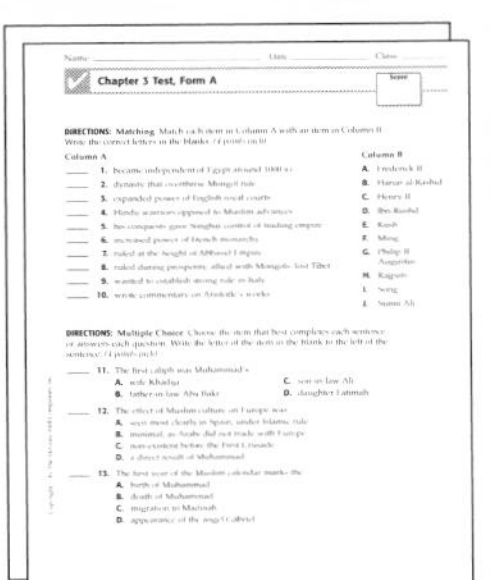

Chapter 3 Test Form B

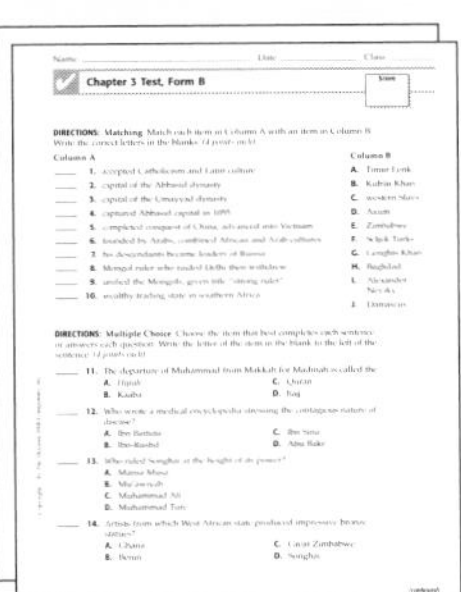

Performance Assessment Activity 3

ExamView® Pro Testmaker CD-ROM

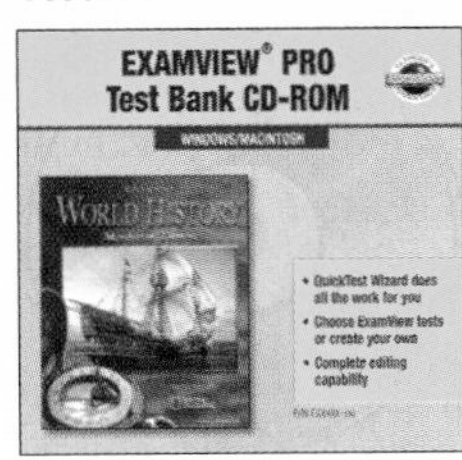

Standardized Test Skills Practice Workbook Activity 3

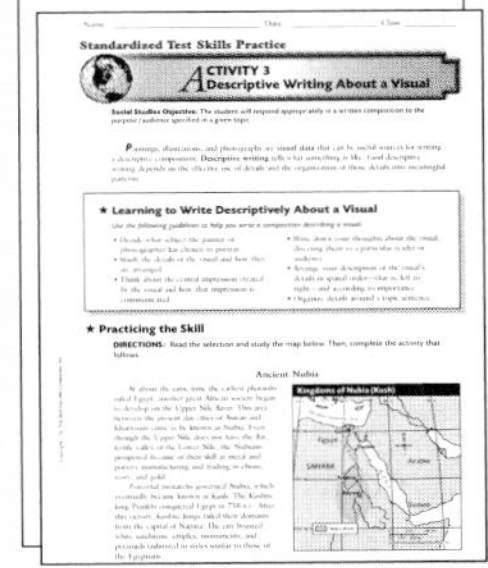

Interdisciplinary Activities

Mapping History Activity 3

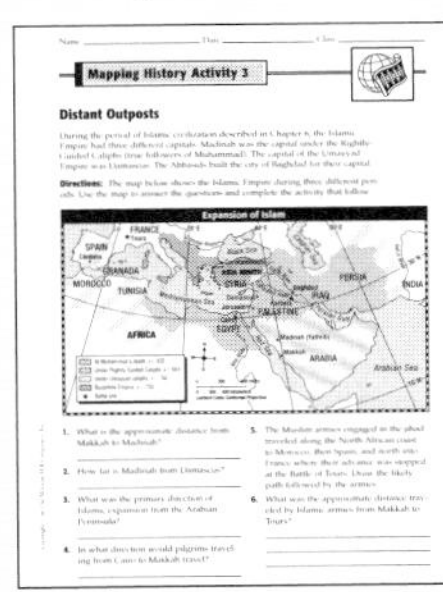

World Art and Music Activity 3

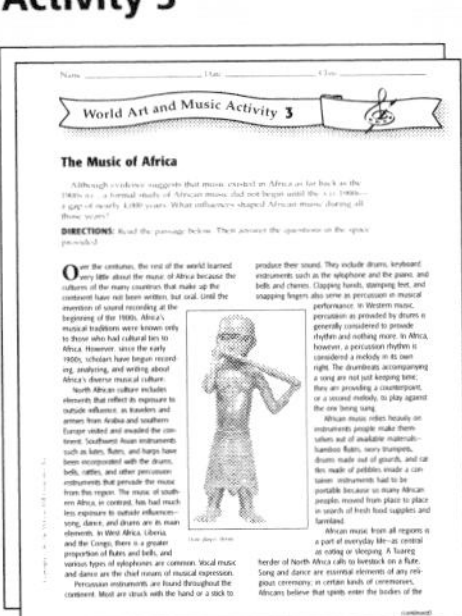

History and Geography Activity 3

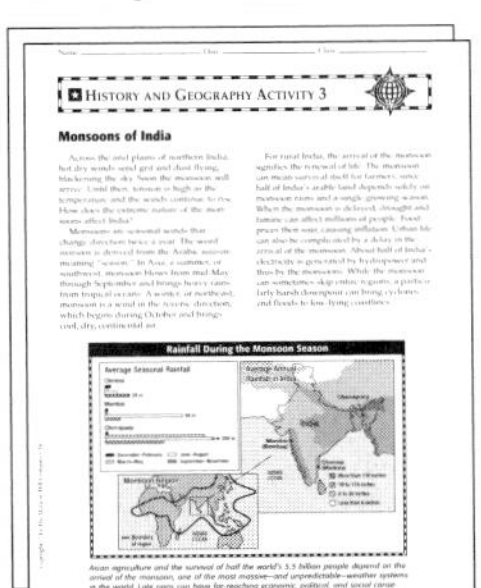

People in World History Activity 3

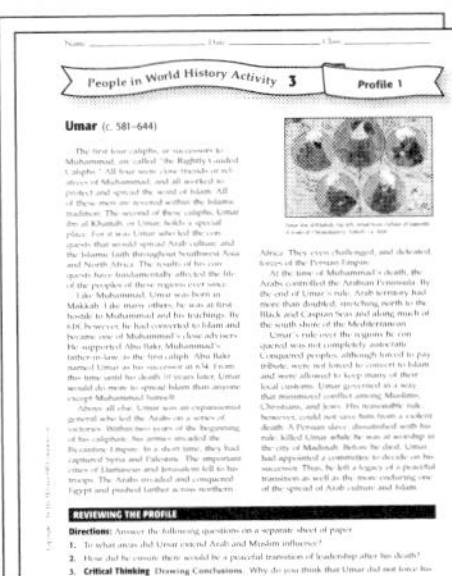

Multimedia

- Vocabulary PuzzleMaker CD-ROM
- Interactive Tutor Self-Assessment CD-ROM
- ExamView® Pro Testmaker CD-ROM
- Audio Program
- World History Primary Source Document Library CD-ROM
- MindJogger Videoquiz
- Presentation Plus! CD-ROM
- TeacherWorks CD-ROM
- Interactive Student Edition CD-ROM
- The World History—Modern Times Video Program

Spanish Resources

The following Spanish language materials are available in the Spanish Resources Binder:

- Spanish Guided Reading Activities
- Spanish Reteaching Activities
- Spanish Quizzes and Tests
- Spanish Vocabulary Activities
- Spanish Summaries

Chapter 3 Resources

SECTION RESOURCES

Daily Objectives	Reproducible Resources	Multimedia Resources
SECTION 1 **The World of Islam** 1. Describe the life of Muhammad and the basic tenets of Islam. 2. Explain the growth of Islam and its expansion to other parts of the world.	Reproducible Lesson Plan 3–1 Daily Lecture and Discussion Notes 3–1 Guided Reading Activity 3–1* Section Quiz 3–1* Reading Essentials and Study Guide 3–1	Daily Focus Skills Transparency 3–1 Interactive Tutor Self-Assessment CD-ROM ExamView® Pro Testmaker CD-ROM Presentation Plus! CD-ROM
SECTION 2 **Early African Civilizations** 1. Analyze how the expansion of trade led to the growth of new kingdoms. 2. Characterize the extended family units that formed the basis of African villages.	Reproducible Lesson Plan 3–2 Daily Lecture and Discussion Notes 3–2 Guided Reading Activity 3–2* Section Quiz 3–2* Reading Essentials and Study Guide 3–2	Daily Focus Skills Transparency 3–2 Interactive Tutor Self-Assessment CD-ROM ExamView® Pro Testmaker CD-ROM Presentation Plus! CD-ROM
SECTION 3 **The Asian World** 1. Characterize the Sui, Tang, Song, and Mongol dynasties. 2. Analyze how geography affected the development of Japan.	Reproducible Lesson Plan 3–3 Daily Lecture and Discussion Notes 3–3 Guided Reading Activity 3–3* Section Quiz 3–3* Reading Essentials and Study Guide 3–3	Daily Focus Skills Transparency 3–3 Interactive Tutor Self-Assessment CD-ROM ExamView® Pro Testmaker CD-ROM Presentation Plus! CD-ROM
SECTION 4 **Emerging Europe and the Byzantine Empire** 1. Describe the rise of the Germanic and Frankish kingdoms, the influence of Christianity, and the importance of Charlemagne. 2. Explain the Norman Conquest, Magna Carta, French kingdoms, and the growth of the Slavic states.	Reproducible Lesson Plan 3–4 Daily Lecture and Discussion Notes 3–4 Guided Reading Activity 3–4* Section Quiz 3–4* Reteaching Activity 3* Reading Essentials and Study Guide 3–4	Daily Focus Skills Transparency 3–4 Interactive Tutor Self-Assessment CD-ROM ExamView® Pro Testmaker CD-ROM Presentation Plus! CD-ROM

0:00 **OUT OF TIME?**
Assign the Chapter 3 **Reading Essentials and Study Guide.**

*Also Available in Spanish

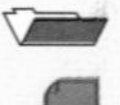 Blackline Master  Transparency  CD-ROM  DVD
 Poster   Music Program  Audio Program 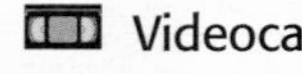 Videocassette

Chapter 3 Resources

NATIONAL GEOGRAPHIC **Teacher's Corner**

INDEX TO NATIONAL GEOGRAPHIC MAGAZINE

The following articles relate to this chapter:

- "The Three Faces of Jerusalem," by Alan Mairson, April 1996.
- "When the Moors Ruled Spain," by Thomas J. Abercrombie, July 1988.
- "Kingdom of Kush," by Timothy Kendall, November 1990.
- "The Cruelest Commerce: African Slave Trade," by Colin Palmer, September 1992.
- "India," by Geoffrey C. Ward, May 1997.
- "Sumo," by T.R. Reid, July 1997.
- "The Temples of Angkor: Ancient Glory in Stone," by Peter T. White, May 1982.
- "Rome of the East: The Byzantine Empire," by Merle Severy, December 1983.

NATIONAL GEOGRAPHIC SOCIETY PRODUCTS AVAILABLE FROM GLENCOE

To order the following products call Glencoe at 1-800-334-7344:

- *STV: World Geography* (Videodisc)
- *Picture Atlas of the World* (CD-ROM)
- *Physical Geography of the World* (Transparencies)

ADDITIONAL NATIONAL GEOGRAPHIC SOCIETY PRODUCTS

To order the following, call National Geographic at 1-800-368-2728:

- *PicturePack: Ancient Africa* (Transparencies)
- *Physical Geography of the Continents Series: Asia* (Video)
- *PictureShow: The Middle Ages* (CD-ROM)

NGS ONLINE

Access National Geographic's new dynamic MapMachine Web site and other geography resources at:
www.nationalgeographic.com
www.nationalgeographic.com/maps

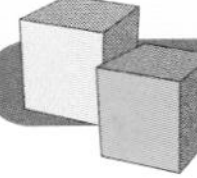

Block Schedule

Activities that are suited to use within the block scheduling framework are identified by:

Use our Web site for additional resources. All essential content is covered in the Student Edition.

You and your students can visit www.wh.mt.glencoe.com, the Web site companion to *Glencoe World History—Modern Times.* This innovative integration of electronic and print media offers your students a wealth of opportunities. The student text directs students to the Web site for the following options:

- **Chapter Overviews**
- **Self-Check Quizzes**
- **Student Web Activities**
- **Textbook Updates**

Answers to the Student Web Activities are provided for you in the **Web Activity Lesson Plans.** Additional Web resources and Interactive Tutor Puzzles are also available.

From the Classroom of...

Pride Adami
Dr. Michael M. Krop High School
Miami, Florida

Creating a Comic Strip

Divide students into groups of four. Have each group create a comic strip depicting a trip from the Mediterranean coast to a West African kingdom for the purpose of trading goods as well as ideas and technological innovations. The strip, of at least six panels, should illustrate the stages of the journey, including descriptions of the trade goods, animals, landscape, and hardships that fifth-century caravans would have encountered.

Students who are unsure of their drawing skills may write detailed descriptions of each panel. One student from each group may present the finished work to the class, after which strips may be displayed around the room for close examination.

KEY TO ABILITY LEVELS

Teaching strategies have been coded.

- **L1** BASIC activities for all students
- **L2** AVERAGE activities for average to above-average students
- **L3** CHALLENGING activities for above-average students
- **ELL** ENGLISH LANGUAGE LEARNER activities

Performance Assessment

Refer to Activity 3 in the Performance Assessment Activities and Rubrics booklet.

The Impact Today

Discuss with students the ways in which trade acted as a means of exchange for knowledge and culture, as well as for goods. Emphasize that trade greatly enriched the lives and cultures of the civilizations that students will study in this chapter. Conclude by guiding students in a discussion of the importance of trade, both import and export trade, to their own lives.

GLENCOE TECHNOLOGY

The World History—Modern Times Video Program

To learn more about the contributions of Islam, students can view the Chapter 3 video, "Islamic Scientific Advances," from **The World History—Modern Times Video Program.**

MindJogger Videoquiz

Use the **MindJogger Videoquiz** to preview Chapter 3 content.

Available in VHS.

CHAPTER 3 Regional Civilizations

400–1500

Key Events

As you read this chapter, look for the key events in the history of early regional civilizations.

- *Muhammad and his followers established the beliefs and practices of Islam.*
- *The development of trade throughout Asia, Africa, and Europe led to the exchange of goods and cultural ideas.*
- *In the 1100s, European monarchs began to build strong states.*

The Impact Today

The events that occurred during this time period still impact our lives today.

- *More than 1 billion people around the world are devout Muslims who follow the teachings of the Quran, and Islam is one of the world's leading faiths.*
- *The expansion of trade continues to create a global society, allowing people to exchange goods, services, and ideas throughout the world.*
- *The codification of Roman law, the emergence of common law, and the signing of the Magna Carta continue to influence our American legal system.*

World History—Modern Times Video *The Chapter 3 video, "Islamic Scientific Advances," chronicles the many contributions of Islamic culture to our world.*

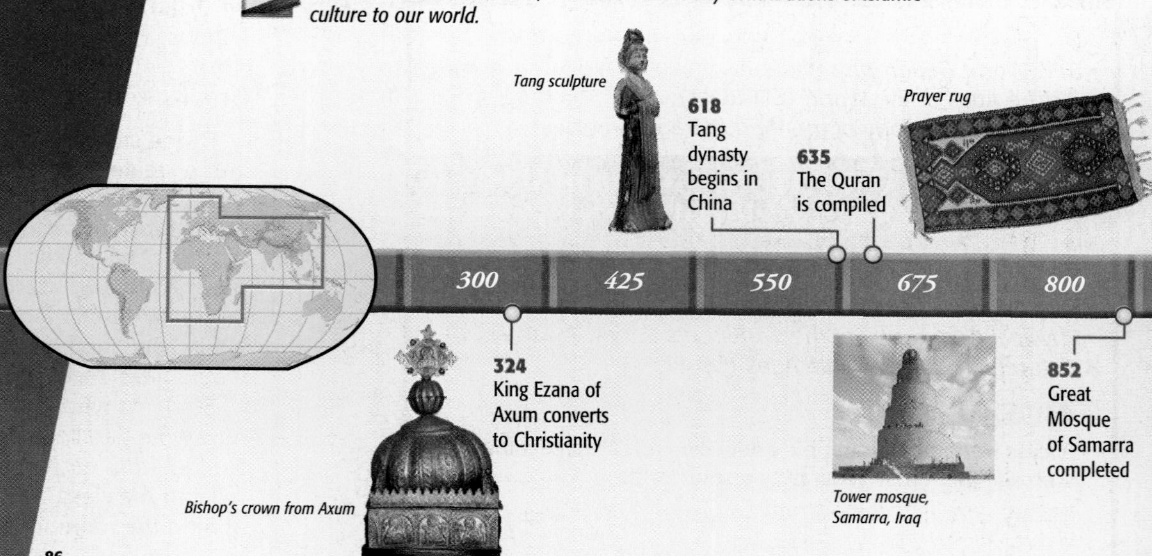

300
425
550
675
800
324 King Ezana of Axum converts to Christianity
618 Tang dynasty begins in China
635 The Quran is compiled
852 Great Mosque of Samarra completed

Tang sculpture

Prayer rug

Bishop's crown from Axum

Tower mosque, Samarra, Iraq

86

TWO-MINUTE LESSON LAUNCHER

Ask students to speculate about the effects a region's geography has on its history and development. Encourage students to consider such factors as the abundance or scarcity of lakes and rivers, whether a region is flat or mountainous, whether it is subject to climatic extremes such as floods or earthquakes, whether it has land suitable for farming, whether it is landlocked or next to a body of water, and who its neighbors are. After various effects on history have been suggested, have students rank the list in order of importance, justifying their ranking. L1

Heiji Scroll (detail) This scroll depicts one of the first samurai battles, the Heiji Insurrection of 1159.

A returning crusader

Medieval knight

Leopard from Benin

- 925
- **1000s** Movable type improves printing
- 1050
- **c. 1050** Feudalism spreads throughout western Europe
- **1096** Crusades begin
- 1175
- 1300
- **c. 1300** Artists in Ife and Benin produce bronze sculptures
- 1425
- **1453** Byzantine Empire ends

HISTORY Online

Chapter Overview
Visit the *Glencoe World History—Modern Times* Web site at wh.mt.glencoe.com and click on **Chapter 3–Chapter Overview** to preview chapter information.

87

Introducing CHAPTER 3

Chapter Objectives

After studying this chapter, students should be able to:

1. identify how Arab, African, and Asian empires spread;
2. list the basic tenets of Islam;
3. list the accomplishments of the early African kingdoms;
4. explain the influence of Buddhism, Hinduism, Islam, and Confucianism on the development of Asian civilizations;
5. compare medieval Europe with earlier civilizations;
6. summarize feudalism;
7. examine the unique civilization of the Byzantine Empire in the eastern Mediterranean.

Chapter Overview
Introduce students to chapter content and key terms by having them access **Chapter Overview 3** at wh.mt.glencoe.com.

Time Line Activity

As students read the chapter, have them review the time line on these pages. Ask them to explain the significance of A.D. 635. *(The Quran was compiled.)* **L1**

MORE ABOUT THE ART

The Heiji Scroll This scene from *Tales of the Heiji Insurrection,* which hangs in Boston's Museum of Fine Arts, is called "The Burning of the Palace." The battle it depicts took place during the Heiji Insurrection in Japan, one of many episodes that occurred during centuries of civil war. This scene depicts the burning of a retired emperor's palace, the Sanjo Palace in Kyoto, in the middle of the night. Servants and ladies of the court try in vain to flee the massive flames. Confusion and violence are vividly portrayed. The Heiji Scroll was produced in the thirteenth century, during the Kamakura period, a time when Japan was governed by the military. It shows superb skill and imagination. The art form of the scroll focuses on the affairs of people, whether the subject is religious or secular.

CHAPTER PREVIEW

Introducing

A Story That Matters

Depending upon the ability level of your students, select from the following questions to reinforce the reading of *A Story That Matters.*

- What reasons might the leaders of China have had to invade the much less developed state of Japan? *(Answers may include: to show the might of China, to force the Japanese to pay tribute.)*
- Why did Kublai Khan wait seven years before trying to invade Japan a second time? *(Answers may include: that he was distracted with other campaigns, needed to rebuild or strengthen naval fleet, or needed time to recruit and train 120,000 more warriors.)*
- How could the relatively poor and weak states in Japan maintain their independence from foreign domination for many years? *(Japan's island geography kept it isolated.)* **L1**

About the Art

This painting of Kublai Khan, by an unknown artist, presents a calm image of the leader. The nineteenth-century painting of the Mongol fleet's destruction shows the Japanese summoning the divine wind, the *kamikaze,* to help them in their fight.

CHAPTER PREVIEW

A Story That Matters

Kublai Khan, grandson of Genghis Khan

Destruction of the Mongol fleet attacking Japan

Japan Faces Kublai Khan

In 1274, the Mongol emperor of China, Kublai Khan, demanded that the Japanese pay tribute to China or face invasion. When the Japanese refused, the khan sent a force of 30,000 warriors to teach the Japanese a lesson. Bad weather forced the emperor's forces to retreat, however.

Not until 1281 was the Great Khan prepared to try again. This time he sent a force of two fleets, consisting of 4,400 ships carrying almost 150,000 warriors. The Japanese appeared to be doomed. The emperor ordered prayers to be offered everywhere in Japan.

Then, on August 15, just as the khan's forces were preparing to land, the sky darkened. For two days, massive typhoons struck, uprooting trees and raising waves that battered the Mongol fleet and killed tens of thousands. One Korean observer wrote, "The bodies of men and broken timbers of the vessels were heaped together in a solid mass so that a person could walk across from one point of land to another on the mass of wreckage." Those warriors who made it to shore were cut down by the Japanese defenders.

To the Japanese, this victory over the Mongols was a sign of supernatural aid. They called the storm a "divine wind," or *kamikaze,* and became convinced that they would always be protected from foreign invasion.

Why It Matters

This great confrontation between the ancient and well-established civilization of China and the newly-emerged Japanese state was a turning point in Asia during this period. Chinese civilization continued to build on the achievements of previous dynasties, making it one of the greatest civilizations in the world. Other societies were emerging along the fringes of China, as well as in other parts of the world.

History and You Many important civilizations developed between 400 and 1500. As you read this chapter, create a database containing each civilization's name (specify empire, trading state, dynasty, or kingdom); dates (if noted); ruler(s); religion(s); significant people, events, or accomplishments; and the reason it ended.

HISTORY AND YOU

Although China influenced Japan, Japan was able to develop its own unique civilization. The contrast between China and Japan remains one of the most complex and fascinating issues in the study of East Asian society today. These two cultures are expected to play a dominant role in the politics and economy of the twenty-first-century world in which students will live. An understanding of these cultures will help students thrive in that world. Discuss how recent events, such as the return of Hong Kong to Chinese control, will extend the role of China in the twenty-first century. Ask students what other signs they see of the growing prominence of other East Asian nations. **L2**

SECTION 1 The World of Islam

Guide to Reading

Main Ideas
- The religion of Islam arose in the Arabian Peninsula in the 600s.
- Muhammad's successor organized the Arabs and set in motion a great expansion.
- An extensive trade network brought prosperity to the Islamic world.

Key Terms
Islam, *Hijrah,* caliph, sultan, astrolabe, mosque

People to Identify
Muhammad, Abu Bakr, Ibn Sina

Places to Locate
Arabian Peninsula, Makkah, Madinah, Damascus, Baghdad

Preview Questions
1. What are the major beliefs and principles of Islam?
2. What major developments occurred under the Umayyads and Abbasids?

Reading Strategy
Summarizing Information Use a chart like the one below to identify the achievements of Islamic civilization.

Achievements of Islam

Preview of Events

600 · 700 · 800 · 900 · 1000 · 1100 · 1200

- **610** Muhammad receives first message
- **632** Abu Bakr becomes first caliph
- **661** Umayyads establish Islamic Empire
- **732** Europeans defeat Arabs at Battle of Tours
- **750** The Abbasid dynasty comes to power
- **1258** Mongols capture Baghdad

Voices from the Past

In his *Autobiography*, the eleventh-century Islamic scholar Ibn Sina, known in the West as Avicenna, described his early training:

> ❝By the time I was [10] I had mastered the Quran and a great deal of literature. There followed training in philosophy . . . then I took to reading texts by myself . . . mastering logic, geometry and astronomy. I now occupied myself with mastering the various texts and commentaries on natural science and metaphysics, until all the gates of knowledge were open to me. Next I desired to study medicine, and proceeded to read all the books that have been written on this subject. At the same time I continued to study and dispute on law, being now sixteen years of age.❞
>
> —***Autobiography,* Ibn Sina**

An Arabic manuscript

Ibn Sina was one of the Islamic world's greatest scholars.

The Arabs

Like the Israelites and the Assyrians, the Arabs were a Semitic-speaking people who lived in the **Arabian Peninsula,** a desert land sorely lacking in rivers and lakes. The Arabs were nomads who, because of their hostile surroundings, moved constantly to find water and food for their animals. Survival in such a harsh environment was not easy, and the Arabs organized into tribes to help one another.

The Arabs lived as farmers and sheepherders on the oases and rain-fed areas of the Arabian Peninsula. After the camel was domesticated in the first millennium B.C., the Arabs populated more of the desert and expanded the caravan trade. Towns developed along the routes as the Arabs became major carriers of goods between the Indian Ocean and the Mediterranean, where the Silk Road ended.

1 FOCUS

Section Overview

This section explores the early history of Islam and discusses the influence of Islamic cultural, artistic, and scientific contributions on the world.

BELLRINGER
Skillbuilder Activity

Project transparency and have students answer questions.

Available as a blackline master.

Daily Focus Skills Transparency 3–1

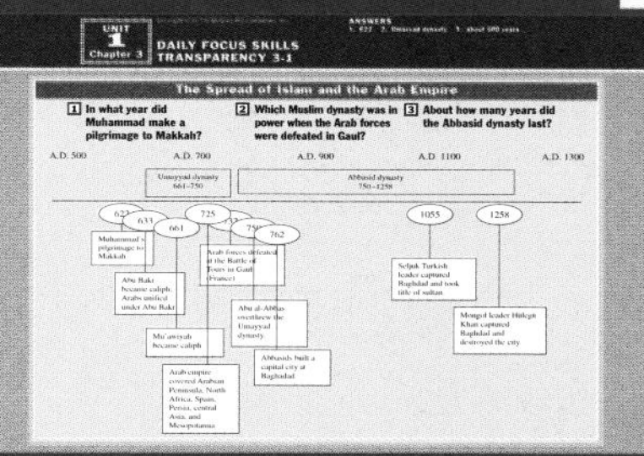

Guide to Reading

Answers to Graphic: translations of Plato and Aristotle with commentaries by Arabic philosophers; contributions to mathematics; perfected the astrolabe; developed medicine as a field of scientific study; Islamic art and architecture including Great Mosque of Samarra

Preteaching Vocabulary: Explain the *Hijrah. (The* Hijrah *is the journey of Muhammad and his followers to what is now the city of Madinah in order to gain acceptance for his teachings. The* Hijrah *occurred in* A.D. *622, which became the year 1 in the Islamic calendar.)* **L2**

SECTION RESOURCES

Reproducible Masters
- Reproducible Lesson Plan 3–1
- Daily Lecture and Discussion Notes 3–1
- Guided Reading Activity 3–1
- Section Quiz 3–1
- Reading Essentials and Study Guide 3–1

Transparencies
- Daily Focus Skills Transparency 3–1

Multimedia
- Interactive Tutor Self-Assessment CD-ROM
- ExamView® Pro Testmaker CD-ROM
- Presentation Plus! CD-ROM

2 TEACH

Reading Check

Answer: The domestication of the camel led to larger populations of people in the desert and expanded the caravan trade. Towns grew along the major trade routes.

Daily Lecture and Discussion Notes 3–1

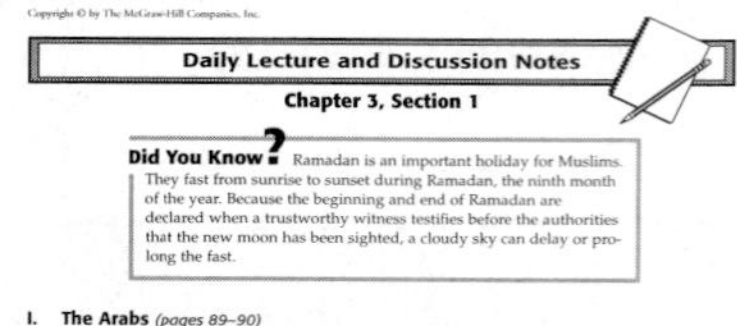

Daily Lecture and Discussion Notes

Chapter 3, Section 1

Did You Know? Ramadan is an important holiday for Muslims. They fast from sunrise to sunset during Ramadan, the ninth month of the year. Because the beginning and end of Ramadan are declared when a trustworthy witness testifies before the authorities that the new moon has been sighted, a cloudy sky can delay or prolong the fast.

I. **The Arabs** *(pages 89–90)*

A. The Arabs were a nomadic, Semitic-speaking people who lived in the **Arabian Peninsula,** a harsh desert with little water. The hostile surroundings made the Arabs move continually to water and feed their animals.

B. Early Arabs herded sheep and farmed on the oases of the Arabian Peninsula. Caravan trade expanded into Arab regions and towns developed as the Arabs carried goods between the Indian Ocean and the Mediterranean, the end of the Silk Road.

C. The Arabs trace their ancestors to Abraham and his son Ishmael, who were believed to have built a shrine at **Makkah** (Mecca) called the Kaaba, whose cornerstone was a sacred stone called the Black Stone. The Arabs recognized a supreme god named Allah (Arabic for "God") but also believed in other tribal gods.

Discussion Question

Tensions arose early in the Arab Empire between the rich and the poor classes. What are some examples of similar tensions in the history of the United States? *(Answers will vary. Numerous examples come from the history of the relations between industrial and manufacturing workers—miners and factory workers, for example—and their employers.)*

II. **The Life of Muhammad** *(pages 90–91)*

A. Muhammad was born into a merchant family in Makkah. He became a caravan manager and married his boss, a rich widow named Khadija.

B. Muslims believe that Muhammad received revelations from God while meditating in the hills. Muhammad came to believe that Allah had revealed himself partially through Moses (Judaism) and Jesus (Christianity) and that Allah's final revelations were to him.

turn

34

Reading Check

Answer: It is considered to be the final revelations of Allah, out of which came the Quran.

Writing Activity

Ask students to write a paragraph stating how they feel they would have reacted to the teachings of Muhammed had they lived during his time.

The Dome of the Rock in Jerusalem was built by Muslims in the seventh century. Muslims believe that Muhammad ascended into Paradise from this site.

Arabs trace their ancestors to Abraham and his son Ishmael, who were believed to have built at **Makkah** (Mecca) the Kaaba (KAH• buh), a house of worship whose cornerstone was a sacred stone called the Black Stone. The Arabs recognized a supreme god named Allah (*Allah* is Arabic for "God"), but they also believed in other tribal gods.

Reading Check **Explaining** What factors contributed to the development of towns on the Arabian Peninsula?

The Life of Muhammad

Born in Makkah to a merchant family, **Muhammad** grew up to become a caravan manager and married a rich widow named Khadija, who was also his employer. Troubled by problems in society, Muhammad often visited the nearby hills to pray and meditate.

During one of his visits, Muslims believe, Muhammad received revelations from God. According to Islamic teachings, the messages were given by the angel Gabriel.

Muhammad came to believe that Allah had already revealed himself in part through Moses and Jesus—and thus through the Hebrew and Christian traditions. He believed, however, that the final revelations of Allah were now being given to him.

Out of these revelations, which were eventually written down, came the **Quran,** the holy book of the religion of Islam. (The word *Islam* means "peace through submission to the will of Allah.") The Quran contains the ethical guidelines and laws by which the followers of Allah are to live. Those who practice the religion of Islam are called **Muslims.** Islam has only one God, Allah, and Muhammad is God's prophet.

After receiving the revelations, Muhammad set out to convince the people of Makkah of the truth of his revelations. After three years of preaching, he had only 30 followers.

Muhammad became discouraged by persecution of his followers, as well as by the failure of the Makkans to accept his message. He and some of his closest supporters left Makkah and moved north to Yathrib, later renamed **Madinah** (Medina; "city of the prophet"). The journey of Muhammad and his followers to Madinah is known as the *Hijrah* (HIH• jruh). The year the journey occurred, 622, became year 1 in the official calendar of Islam.

Muhammad soon began to win support from people in Madinah, as well as from Bedouin tribes in the surrounding countryside. From these groups, he formed the first community of practicing Muslims.

Muhammad became both a religious and a political leader. He assembled a military force to defend himself and his followers and began to attract large numbers of supporters.

In 630, Muhammad returned to Makkah with a force of ten thousand men. The city quickly surrendered, and most of the townspeople converted to the new faith. During a visit to the Kaaba, Muhammad declared it a sacred shrine of Islam. Two years after his triumphal return to Makkah, Muhammad died, just as Islam was beginning to spread throughout the Arabian Peninsula. All Muslims are encouraged to make a pilgrimage to Makkah, known as the hajj (HAJ), if possible.

Reading Check **Identifying** What was the significance of the message given to Muhammad by Gabriel?

The Teachings of Muhammad

Like Judaism and Christianity, Islam is monotheistic. Allah is the all-powerful being who created the universe and everything in it. Islam emphasizes salvation and offers the hope of an afterlife.

COOPERATIVE LEARNING ACTIVITY

Creating a Map Southwest Asia is the birthplace of three major world religions—Judaism, Christianity, and Islam. Each of these religions has its respective holy place in Jerusalem—the Western Wall, the Church of the Holy Sepulchre, and the Dome of the Rock. Organize the class into three groups, and assign each group to research and report on one of these holy places. Ask students to provide a diagram of the city of Jerusalem and show the location of their assigned holy place. Encourage students to show drawings or copies of photographs as well. After the reports and maps have been presented, **Ask:** **Why is it significant that these sites are all in the same city? What problems have their locations created? L2**

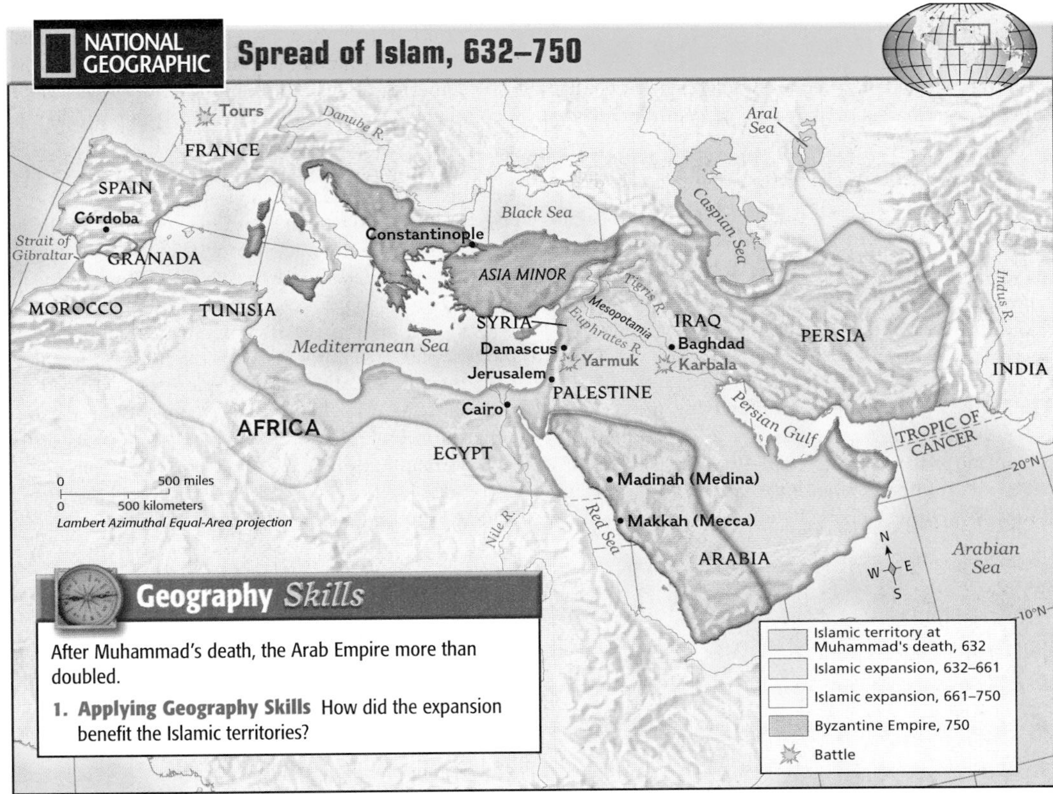

Geography Skills

After Muhammad's death, the Arab Empire more than doubled.

1. **Applying Geography Skills** How did the expansion benefit the Islamic territories?

Unlike Christianity, Islam does not believe that its first preacher was divine. Muhammad is considered a prophet, similar to Moses, but he was also a man like other men. Muslims believe that because human beings rejected Allah's earlier messengers, Allah sent his final revelation through Muhammad.

Islam is a direct and simple faith, stressing the need to obey the will of Allah. This means practicing acts of worship known as the Five Pillars of Islam: belief, prayer, charity, fasting, and pilgrimage. Muslims believe there is no deity but the One God, and Muhammad is his messenger (belief). They perform prescribed prayers five times a day (prayer) and give part of their wealth to the poor (charity). During the month of Ramadan, Muslims refrain from food and drink from dawn to sunset (fasting). Finally, believers are expected to make a pilgrimage to Makkah at least once in their lifetime (pilgrimage). The faithful who follow the law are guaranteed a place in an eternal paradise.

Reading Check **Comparing** How is Islam similar to Judaism and Christianity?

Creation of an Arab Empire

Muhammad had been accepted as both the political and religious leader of the Islamic community. The death of Muhammad left his followers with a problem: Muhammad had never named a successor. Shortly after Muhammad's death, some of his closest followers chose **Abu Bakr** (uh•BOO BA•kuhr), a wealthy merchant and Muhammad's father-in-law, to be their leader. He was named **caliph** (KAY•luhf), or successor to Muhammad.

Under Abu Bakr's leadership, the Islamic movement began to grow. As the Romans had slowly conquered Italy, so also the Muslims expanded over Arabia, and beyond.

At Yarmuk in 636, the Arabs, unified under Abu Bakr, defeated the Byzantine army in the midst of a dust storm that enabled the Arabs to take their enemy by surprise. Four years later, they took control of the Byzantine province of Syria. By 642, Egypt and other areas of northern Africa had been added to the new Arab Empire. To the east, the Arabs had conquered the entire Persian Empire by 650.

Geography Skills

Answer:

1. The expansion provided Islamic territories better access to trade—in expanding almost out to India, they would have much better access to Indian and Chinese goods; larger empires are more secure.

Guided Reading Activity 3–1

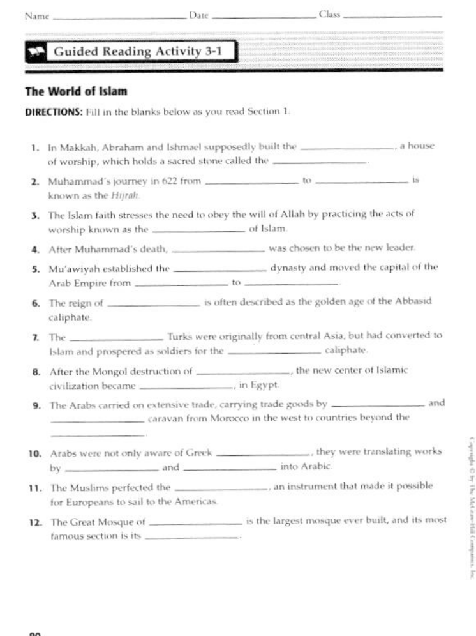

Name ______ Date ______ Class ______

Guided Reading Activity 3-1

The World of Islam

DIRECTIONS: Fill in the blanks below as you read Section 1.

1. In Makkah, Abraham and Ishmael supposedly built the ______, a house of worship, which holds a sacred stone called the ______.
2. Muhammad's journey in 622 from ______ to ______ is known as the *Hijrah*.
3. The Islam faith stresses the need to obey the will of Allah by practicing the acts of worship known as the ______ of Islam.
4. After Muhammad's death, ______ was chosen to be the new leader.
5. Mu'awiyah established the ______ dynasty and moved the capital of the Arab Empire from ______ to ______.
6. The reign of ______ is often described as the golden age of the Abbasid caliphate.
7. The ______ Turks were originally from central Asia, but had converted to Islam and prospered as soldiers for the ______ caliphate.
8. After the Mongol destruction of ______, the new center of Islamic civilization became ______, in Egypt.
9. The Arabs carried on extensive trade, carrying trade goods by ______ and ______ caravan from Morocco in the west to countries beyond the ______.
10. Arabs were not only aware of Greek ______, they were translating works by ______ and ______ into Arabic.
11. The Muslims perfected the ______, an instrument that made it possible for Europeans to sail to the Americas.
12. The Great Mosque of ______ is the largest mosque ever built, and its most famous section is its ______.

90

Reading Check

Answer: All three are monotheistic; all three have prophets; all three have laws that believers must obey (the Ten Commandments of Judaism and Christianity, the Five Pillars of Islam). Like Christianity, Islam offers the hope of salvation and an afterlife.

CRITICAL THINKING ACTIVITY

Explaining A serious weakness of any system of government or rule based upon a single person is the transfer of authority upon the death or incapacity of that person—whether it be a dictator, emperor, monarch, or general. The tendency is always toward civil war and an internal power struggle, which often invites attack from outside. Constitutional governments, in theory, offer protection against this, since they create distinct rules of succession. In constitutional governments power must be transferred at fixed intervals according to clearly defined rules. As a current events project, have students explain the impact of constitutional systems of government on significant world political developments. **L2**

Reading Check

Answer: Abu Bakr was the first caliph to unify the Arabs and begin an expansionist movement.

Opposing Viewpoints

Answers:

1. Each of these viewpoints has some validity. The fact that the Arabs did not try to force their religion on conquered peoples may have influenced their success.
2. Answers will vary. Most of the conquered peoples were merely exchanging one imperial master for another—for example, Persian for Arab or Byzantine for Arab. They probably saw it as their lot in life. Rebellion against a well-armed, disciplined army was usually not a viable option.

Critical Thinking

The teachings of the Quran and the Arabic language were the unifying, common bonds of the Islamic world. Ask students to write a position paper stating whether these two factors alone are sufficient to maintain political and religious institutions. Conduct a class discussion and ask student volunteers to debate this issue in class. **L1**

The Arabs, led by a series of brilliant generals, had put together a large, dedicated army. The courage of the Arab soldiers was enhanced by the belief that Muslim warriors were assured a place in Paradise if they died in battle.

Reading Check **Identifying** Who was the first caliph to unify the Arabs and begin an expansionist movement?

Successors of the Arab Empire

After Abu Bakr died, problems arose over who should become the next caliph. There were no clear successors to Abu Bakr.

The Umayyads In 661, Mu'awiyah (moo•UH•wee•uh), the governor of Syria, became caliph. Mu'awiyah moved quickly to make the office of caliph, called the caliphate, hereditary in his own family. In doing this, he established the Umayyad (oo•MY•uhd) dynasty. He then moved the capital of the Arab Empire from Madinah to **Damascus,** in Syria.

At the beginning of the eighth century, Arab armies conquered and converted the Berbers, a pastoral people living along the Mediterranean coast of North Africa. Around 710, combined Berber and Arab forces crossed the Strait of Gibraltar and occupied southern Spain. By 725, most of Spain had become a Muslim state with its center at Córdoba. In 732, however, Arab forces were defeated at the Battle of Tours in Gaul (now France), halting Arab expansion in Europe.

In 717, another Muslim force had launched an attack on Constantinople with the hope of defeating the Byzantine Empire. The Byzantines destroyed the Muslim fleet. The Arab advance ended, but not before the southern and eastern Mediterranean parts of the old Roman Empire had been conquered. Arab power also extended to the east in Mesopotamia and Persia and northward into central Asia.

Opposing Viewpoints

How Did the Arab Empire Succeed?

During the early eighth century, the Muslims vastly extended their empire. Their swift conquest of Southwest Asia has intrigued many historians. Was their success due to religious fervor or military strength, or were there other reasons for their military victories that are not so obvious?

"They were aided by the weakness of the two contemporary empires, the Sassanian (Persian) and the Byzantine, which had largely exhausted themselves by their wars on one another. . . . Nor were these Arabs simply zealots fired by the ideal of a Holy War. They were by long tradition tough fighters, accustomed to raiding out of hunger and want; many or perhaps even most of them were not ardent followers of Mohammed. Yet there can be little question that what got the Arabs started, and kept them going, was mainly the personality and the teaching of the Prophet."

—**Herbert J. Muller, 1958**
The Loom of History

"Perhaps . . . another kind of explanation can be given for the acceptance of Arab rule by the population of the conquered countries. To most of them it did not much matter whether they were ruled by Iranians, Greeks or Arabs. Government impinged for the most part on the life of cities and . . . city-dwellers might not care much who ruled them,

MEETING INDIVIDUAL NEEDS

Visual/Kinesthetic Assign students to design and draw the floor plan of a place of worship or to design and create a segment of a decorative wall in either a Byzantine church or a Muslim mosque. Ask students to list the materials they would use to construct their projects if they were real. Display the resulting pieces in class, and ask each student to explain the inspiration and thinking that led to the development of the design. Ask how religious beliefs of a group can inspire artistic expression and how religous restraints can affect its artistic expression. **L2**

Refer to ***Inclusion for the High School Social Studies Classroom Strategies and Activities*** in the TCR.

The Abbasid Dynasty In 750, Abu al-Abbas, a descendant of Muhammad's uncle, overthrew the Umayyad dynasty and set up the **Abbasid** (uh•BA•suhd) **dynasty,** which lasted until 1258.

In 762, the Abbasids built a new capital city at **Baghdad,** on the Tigris River, far to the east of the Umayyad capital at Damascus. The new capital was well placed. It was located on the caravan route from the Mediterranean Sea to central Asia.

The Abbasid dynasty experienced a period of splendid rule during the ninth century. Best known of the caliphs of the time was Harun al-Rashid (ha•ROON ahl•rah•SHEED), whose reign is often described as the golden age of the Abbasid caliphate. Harun al-Rashid was known for his charity, and he also lavished support on artists and writers.

This was also a period of growing prosperity. The Arabs had conquered many of the richest provinces of the Roman Empire, and they now controlled the trade routes to the East. Baghdad became the center of an enormous trade empire that extended into Asia, Africa, and Europe, greatly adding to the riches of the Islamic world.

Eventually, rulers of the provinces of the Abbasid Empire began to break away from the central authority and establish independent dynasties. A new dynasty under the Fatimids was established in Egypt with its capital at Cairo, in 973.

The Seljuk Turks The Fatimid dynasty soon became the center of Islamic civilization. The Fatimids played a major role in the trade passing from the Mediterranean to the Red Sea and beyond. They created a strong army by hiring non-native soldiers to fight for them. One such group was the Seljuk (SEHL•JOOK) Turks.

The Seljuk Turks were a nomadic people from central Asia. They had converted to Islam and prospered as soldiers for the Abbasid caliphate. As the Abbasids grew weaker, the Seljuk Turks grew stronger, moving gradually into Iran and Armenia. By the eleventh century, they had taken over the eastern provinces of the Abbasid Empire.

In 1055, a Turkish leader captured Baghdad and took command of the empire. His title was **sultan**—or "holder of power." The Abbasid caliph was still the chief religious authority, but, after they captured Baghdad, the Seljuk Turks held the real military and political power of the state.

The Mongols The **Mongols** were a pastoral people who swept out of the Gobi in the early thirteenth century to seize control over much of the world.

Beginning with the advances led by Genghis Khan in North China, Mongol armies spread across central Asia. In 1258, under the leadership of Hülegü (hoo•LAY•GOO), brother of the more famous Kublai (KOO•BLUH) Khan, the Mongols seized Persia and Mesopotamia. The Abbasid caliphate at Baghdad ended. Hülegü had a strong hatred of Islam. After his forces captured Baghdad in 1258, he decided to destroy the city.

Over time, the Mongol rulers converted to Islam and intermarried with local peoples. They began to rebuild the cities. By the fourteenth century, the Mongol Empire had begun to split into separate kingdoms. The old Islamic Empire established by the Arabs in the seventh and eighth centuries had come to an end. As a result of the Mongol destruction of Baghdad, the new center of Islamic civilization became Cairo, in Egypt.

Reading Check **Describing** How did the Mongols bring about the end of the old Islamic Empire?

rovided they were secure, at peace and reasonbly taxed. The people of the countryside . . . ved under their own chiefs and . . . with their wn customs, and it made little difference to 1em who ruled the cities. For some, the replace1ent of Greeks and Iranians by Arabs even ffered advantages.”

—**Albert Hourani, 1991**
A History of the Arab Peoples

You Decide

- Review the information presented in this section carefully. Using the material from the text and information obtained from your own outside research, explain why both of these viewpoints can be considered valid.
- Compare the information given in the second excerpt to attitudes of other conquered peoples that you have read about. Do you believe that most people easily accept outside rule? What factors lead to acceptance and what factors lead to rebellion against outside rule?

3 ASSESS

Assign Section 1 Assessment as homework or as an in-class activity.

Have students use **Interactive Tutor Self-Assessment CD-ROM.**

Enrich

During a class discussion, ask students to list some of the reasons for the rise of the Abbasids. Then ask students to choose the one reason they consider most important to the dynasty's rise and defend it in a written paragraph.

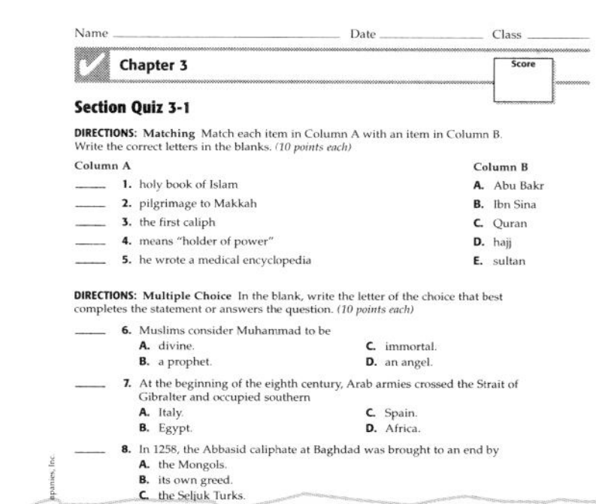

Section Quiz 3–1

Name ______ Date ______ Class ______

Chapter 3 Score

Section Quiz 3-1

DIRECTIONS: Matching Match each item in Column A with an item in Column B. Write the correct letters in the blanks. *(10 points each)*

Column A	Column B
____ 1. holy book of Islam	A. Abu Bakr
____ 2. pilgrimage to Makkah	B. Ibn Sina
____ 3. the first caliph	C. Quran
____ 4. means "holder of power"	D. hajj
____ 5. he wrote a medical encyclopedia	E. sultan

DIRECTIONS: Multiple Choice In the blank, write the letter of the choice that best completes the statement or answers the question. *(10 points each)*

____ 6. Muslims consider Muhammad to be
A. divine. C. immortal.
B. a prophet. D. an angel.

____ 7. At the beginning of the eighth century, Arab armies crossed the Strait of Gibralter and occupied southern
A. Italy. C. Spain.
B. Egypt. D. Africa.

____ 8. In 1258, the Abbasid caliphate at Baghdad was brought to an end by
A. the Mongols.
B. its own greed.
C. the Seljuk Turks.

Reading Check

Answer: The Mongols seized Persia and Mesopotamia, bringing the Abbasid caliphate to an end. After their forces captured Baghdad, they destroyed the city, which had been the center of the old Islamic world.

CRITICAL THINKING ACTIVITY

Analyzing Information Imperialism has existed as long as there have been empires. Ask students to analyze the Mongol Empire by comparing it to the Arab Empire. Factors to consider in the comparison include origins of the empire, methods of war, conquests, assimilation of conquered peoples, methods of administration, and influence on subsequent cultures. Have students research both empires and write a report with the results of their research. Remind students to include important changes that occurred in world history due to the influence of both empires. Have students locate and use primary and secondary sources such as computer software, databases, media and news services, biographies, interviews, and artifacts to acquire information. L3

Critical Thinking

Prior to a class discussion on Islamic culture, have students research and identify new ideas in mathematics, science, and technology that occurred during Islamic civilization. During class, have students give examples of mathematical and scientific discoveries, as well as technological innovations. Ask students to describe the changes in the culture that developed due to these discoveries and to trace the spread of these ideas and innovations to other civilizations. Ask each student to choose the contribution that he or she feels is most significant and to write a one-page paper explaining why this contribution is so important. **L2**

Reading Check

Answer: the teachings of the Quran

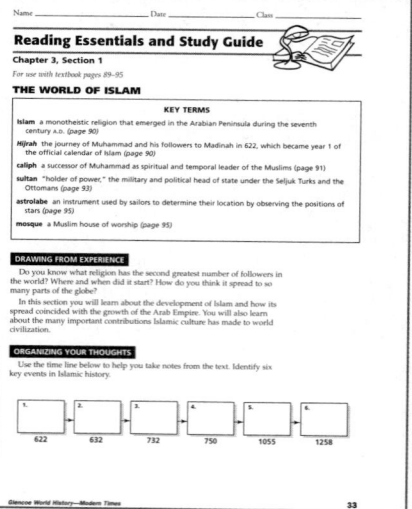

Reading Essentials and Study Guide 3–1

Name ______ Date ______ Class ______

Reading Essentials and Study Guide

Chapter 3, Section 1

For use with textbook pages 89–95

THE WORLD OF ISLAM

KEY TERMS

Islam a monotheistic religion that emerged in the Arabian Peninsula during the seventh century A.D. *(page 90)*

Hijrah the journey of Muhammad and his followers to Madinah in 622, which became year 1 of the official calendar of Islam *(page 90)*

caliph a successor of Muhammad as spiritual and temporal leader of the Muslims (page 91)

sultan "holder of power," the military and political head of state under the Seljuk Turks and the Ottomans *(page 93)*

astrolabe an instrument used by sailors to determine their location by observing the positions of stars *(page 95)*

mosque a Muslim house of worship *(page 95)*

DRAWING FROM EXPERIENCE

Do you know what religion has the second greatest number of followers in the world? Where and when did it start? How do you think it spread to so many parts of the globe?

In this section you will learn about the development of Islam and how its spread coincided with the growth of the Arab Empire. You will also learn about the many important contributions Islamic culture has made to world civilization.

ORGANIZING YOUR THOUGHTS

Use the time line below to help you take notes from the text. Identify six key events in Islamic history.

1.	2.	3.	4.	5.	6.
622	632	732	750	1055	1258

Economy and Social Structure

Overall, the period of the Arab Empire was prosperous. The Arabs carried on extensive trade, not only within the Islamic world but also with China, the Byzantine Empire, India, and Southeast Asia. Trade was carried both by ship and by camel caravans, which traveled from Morocco in the west to the countries beyond the Caspian Sea.

Starting around 750, trade flourished under the Abbasid dynasty. From south of the Sahara came gold and slaves; from China, silk and porcelain; from eastern Africa, gold and ivory; and from the lands of Southeast Asia and India, sandalwood and spices. Within the empire, Egypt contributed grain; Iraq provided linens, dates, and precious stones; and western India supplied textiles.

With flourishing trade came prosperous cities. While the Abbasids were in power, Baghdad was probably the greatest city in the empire and one of the greatest cities in the world. After the rise of the Fatimids, the focus of trade shifted to Cairo.

To be a Muslim is not simply to worship Allah but also to live one's life according to Allah's teachings as revealed in the Quran. As Allah has decreed, so must humans live. Questions concerning politics and social life are answered by following Islamic teachings.

The minaret of the Samarra mosque

According to Islam, all people are equal in the eyes of Allah. In reality, however, this was not strictly the case in the Arab Empire. There was a fairly well defined upper class that consisted of ruling families, senior officials, nomadic elites, and the wealthiest merchants. Even ordinary merchants, however, enjoyed a degree of respect that merchants did not receive in Europe, China, or India.

The Quran granted women spiritual and social equality with men. Women had the right to the fruits of their work and to own and inherit property. Islamic teachings did account for differences between men and women in the family and social order. Both had duties and responsibilities. As in most societies of the time, however, men were dominant in Muslim society.

Reading Check **Summarizing** On what ideas was society in the Arab Empire built?

The Brilliance of Islamic Culture

During the first few centuries of the Arab Empire, the ancient Greek philosophers were largely unknown in Europe. The Arabs, however, were not only aware of Greek philosophy, they were translating works by Plato and Aristotle into Arabic. The process of translating works and making them available to scholars was aided by the making of paper, which was introduced from China in the eighth century.

It was through the Muslim world that Europeans recovered the works of Aristotle and other Greek philosophers. In the twelfth century, the Arabic translations were in turn translated into Latin, making them available to the West. The brilliant Islamic civilization contributed more intellectually to the West than translations, however.

Philosophy and Science When Aristotle's works arrived in Europe in the twelfth century, they were accompanied by commentaries written by outstanding Arabic philosophers. One such philosopher was Ibn-Rushd (IH•buhn-RUSHT). He lived in Córdoba and wrote a commentary on virtually all of Aristotle's surviving works.

Islamic scholars also made contributions to mathematics and the natural sciences that were passed on to the West. The Muslims adopted and passed on the numerical system of India, including the use of the zero. In Europe, it became known as the "Arabic" system.

In astronomy, Muslims set up an observatory at Baghdad to study the position of the stars. They were aware that Earth was round, and they named

EXTENDING THE CONTENT

Literature Omar Khayyám was a famous scholar who excelled in the arts and the sciences. One of his best-known compositions was a collection of poetry known as the *Rubaiyat,* with poems written in four-line stanzas, called quatrains. Although the *Rubaiyat* was not popular in Persia during Omar Khayyám's lifetime, it gained popularity during the nineteenth century after Edward Fitzgerald translated it into English. The most famous quatrain follows:

"A Book of Verses underneath the Bough,
A Jug of Wine, a Loaf of Bread—and Thou
Beside me singing in the Wilderness—
Oh, Wilderness were Paradise now!"

many stars. They also perfected the astrolabe, an instrument used by sailors to determine their location by observing the positions of stars and planets. The astrolabe enabled Europeans to sail to the Americas.

Muslim scholars developed medicine as a field of scientific study. Especially well known was the philosopher and scientist **Ibn Sina** (IH•buhn SEE•nuh). He wrote a medical encyclopedia that, among other things, stressed the contagious nature of certain diseases. After it was translated into Latin, Ibn Sina's work became a basic medical textbook for university students in medieval Europe.

History *through Architecture*

The Mosque of Córdoba This mosque in Spain is famous for the symmetry of its arches. Intricate arabesque patterns highlight the interior of this mosque and others. When did Arab armies cross into Spain?

Art and Architecture Islamic art is a blend of Arab, Turkish, and Persian traditions. The best expression of Islamic art is found in the magnificent Muslim mosques (houses of worship). The mosque represents the spirit of Islam.

Constructed between 848 and 852, the Great Mosque of Samarra in present-day Iraq is the largest mosque ever built. It covers 10 acres (more than 40,000 square m). The most famous section of the Samarra mosque is its minaret. This is the tower from which the muezzin (moo•EH•zuhn), or crier, calls the faithful to prayer five times a day. The minaret of Samarra, nearly 90 feet (around 27 m) in height, was unusual because of its outside spiral staircase.

One of the most famous mosques is the ninth-century mosque at Córdoba in southern Spain. It is still in remarkable condition today. Its 514 columns, which support double-horseshoe arches, transform this building into a unique "forest of trees."

Reading Check **Identifying** Name two cultural achievements of the Arab Empire after 700.

SECTION 1 ASSESSMENT

Checking for Understanding

1. **Define** Islam, *Hijrah*, caliph, sultan, astrolabe, mosque.
2. **Identify** Muhammad, Quran, Muslims, Abu Bakr, Abbasid dynasty, Mongols, Ibn Sina.
3. **Locate** Arabian Peninsula, Makkah, Madinah, Damascus, Baghdad.
4. **Describe** how the Arabs created a trade empire. Identify the items traded in the empire and where they came from.
5. **List** the Five Pillars of Islam.

Critical Thinking

6. **Explain** How did the Muslims transmit ancient literature to other cultures? Argue against the viewpoint that Islamic civilization was mainly a preserver and transmitter of culture, rather than a creator of culture.
7. **Summarizing Information** Create a diagram to list the main characteristics of the Islamic religion. Your diagram can list more characteristics than this example.

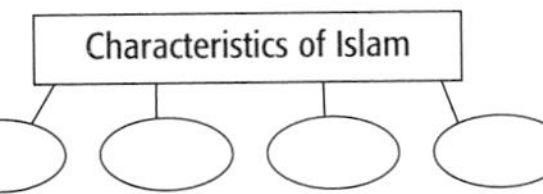

Analyzing Visuals

8. **Examine** the photograph of the Mosque of Córdoba shown above. What architectural influences from other cultures do you see reflected in this Islamic mosque? What elements are unique to Islamic architecture?

Writing About History

9. **Descriptive Writing** Imagine that you are a young Muslim Arab corresponding with a European friend. In one or two brief paragraphs, describe Islamic accomplishments in philosophy, mathematics, science, medicine, art, and architecture to your friend.

History *through Architecture*

Answer: in the beginning of the eighth century

Reading Check

Answer: Answers may include they translated and wrote commentary on the works of the great Greek philosophers, perfected the astrolabe, developed medicine as a field of study, created new style of architecture in mosques.

Who?What?Where?When?

Mosques Mosques fulfill numerous functions. They contain schools, libraries, and hospitals. Have students research the role of the mosque in Muslim daily life and prepare oral reports focusing on one of a mosque's functions. **L3**

Reteaching Activity

Ask students to summarize the origins of Islam, its central ideas, and the reasons for its expansion. **L2**

4 CLOSE

Have students create a chart comparing the major features of Islamic civilization with those of another civilization they have studied, such as Egyptian, Greek, or Roman. **L2**

SECTION 1 ASSESSMENT

1. Key terms are in blue.
2. Muhammad *(p. 90);* Quran *(p. 90);* Muslims *(p. 90);* Abu Bakr *(p. 91);* Abbasid dynasty *(p. 93);* Mongols *(p. 93);* Ibn Sina *(p. 95)*
3. See chapter maps.
4. Arabs conquered richest provinces of Roman Empire, controlled eastern trade routes, and made Baghdad center of great trade empire. Arabs traded gold and slaves from south of Sahara; silk and porcelain from China; gold and ivory from eastern Africa; sandalwood and spices from India; grain from Egypt; linens, dates, and precious stones from Iraq.
5. belief, prayer, charity, fasting, pilgrimage
6. They translated works from earlier cultures. Islamic commentaries influenced Western scholars; many of their advances were imitated by Europeans.
7. monotheistic, belief in afterlife, must obey the will of Allah, Five Pillars of Islam, hajj
8. Greek column, Roman arch
9. Answers will vary.

CRITICAL THINKING SKILLBUILDER

TEACH

Distinguishing Between Fact and Opinion Point out to students that they are confronted with facts and opinions every day in newspapers and magazines. Ask where they would look for opinions in newspapers. *(editorial pages, book and movie reviews)* Where would they find solid facts? *(news stories, sports scores, weather reports from day before)* Have students consider how headlines can offer clues as to whether a piece of writing is fact or opinion. Ask them to bring in samples of fact and opinion headlines to discuss and display in class. **L1**

Additional Practice

Skills Reinforcement Activity 3

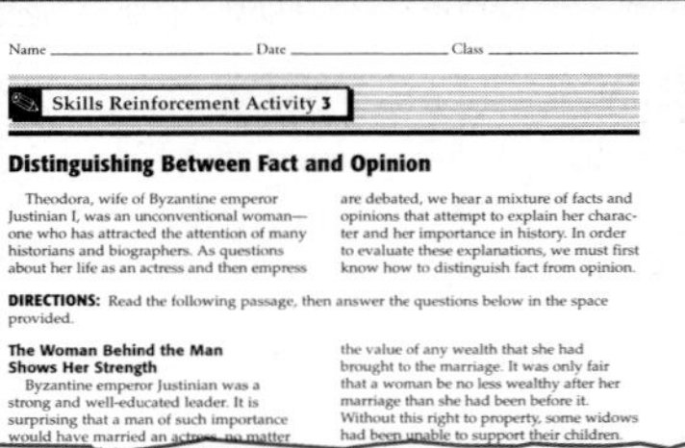

Name __________ Date __________ Class __________

Skills Reinforcement Activity 3

Distinguishing Between Fact and Opinion

Theodora, wife of Byzantine emperor Justinian I, was an unconventional woman—one who has attracted the attention of many historians and biographers. As questions about her life as an actress and then empress are debated, we hear a mixture of facts and opinions that attempt to explain her character and her importance in history. In order to evaluate these explanations, we must first know how to distinguish fact from opinion.

DIRECTIONS: Read the following passage, then answer the questions below in the space provided.

The Woman Behind the Man Shows Her Strength

Byzantine emperor Justinian was a strong and well-educated leader. It is surprising that a man of such importance would have married an actress, no matter the value of any wealth that she had brought to the marriage. It was only fair that a woman be no less wealthy after her marriage than she had been before it. Without this right to property, some widows had been unable to support their children.

GLENCOE TECHNOLOGY

CD-ROM
Glencoe Skillbuilder Interactive Workbook CD-ROM, Level 2

This interactive CD-ROM reinforces student mastery of essential social studies skills.

CRITICAL THINKING SKILLBUILDER

Distinguishing Between Fact and Opinion

Why Learn This Skill?

Imagine that you are watching two candidates for president debate the merits of the college loan program. One says, "In my view, the college loan program must be reformed. Sixty percent of students do not repay their loans on time."

The other replies, "College costs are skyrocketing, but only 30 percent of students default on their loans for more than one year. I believe we should spend more on this worthy program."

How can you tell who or what to believe? You must learn to distinguish fact from opinion in order to effectively evaluate and analyze information acquired from a variety of sources such as books, television, and the Internet.

Learning the Skill

A fact is a statement that can be proved to be true. In the example above, the statement "Sixty percent of students do not repay their loans on time" is a fact. By reviewing statistics on the number of student loan recipients who repay their loans, we can determine whether it is true or false. To identify facts, look for words and phrases indicating specific people, places, events, dates, and times.

An opinion, on the other hand, expresses a personal belief, viewpoint, or emotion. Because opinions are subjective, we cannot prove or disprove them. In the opening example, one statement from each candidate appears to be fact, and one statement appears to be opinion.

Opinions often include qualifying words and phrases such as *I think, I believe, probably, seems to be, may, might, could, ought, in my judgment,* or *in my view.* Also, look for expressions of approval or disapproval such as *good, bad, poor,* and *satisfactory.* Be aware of superlatives such as *greatest, worst, finest,* and *best.* Notice words with negative meanings and implications such as *squander, contemptible,* and *disgrace.* Also, identify generalizations such as *none, every, always,* and *never.*

Practicing the Skill

For each pair of statements below, determine which is fact and which is opinion. Give a reason for each choice.

1. a The Byzantine Empire came to a pitiful end at the hands of the savage Turks.
   b The Byzantine Empire ended when Constantine XI died while defending Constantinople in 1453.
2. a The alliance with the Byzantine Empire made Kiev a major trading link between Europe and Asia and between Scandinavia and Southwest Asia.
   b In the 900s, Kiev was the most isolated, uncivilized place and it possessed little in the way of culture.
3. a The Byzantine culture was more advanced than any other of its day.
   b Vladimir's conversion to Eastern Orthodoxy brought Byzantine culture to Kievan Rus.

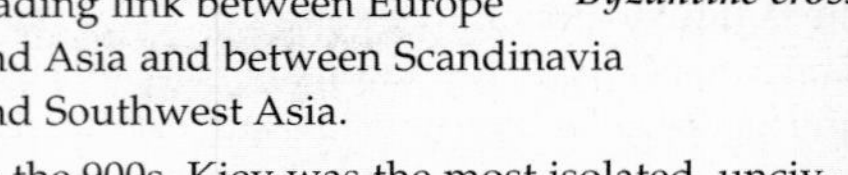

Byzantine cross

Applying the Skill

Find a news article and an editorial pertaining to the same subject in your local newspaper. Identify three facts and three opinions from these sources.

GO TO Glencoe's **Skillbuilder Interactive Workbook, Level 2,** provides instruction and practice in key social studies skills.

ANSWERS TO PRACTICING THE SKILL

1. a: opinion; b: fact; the first statement contains words with negative implications *(pitiful, savage)*, while the second statement contains facts (specific name, date, and event)
2. a: fact; b: opinion; the first statement includes specific names, while the second has superlatives (*most isolated, uncivilized*) and a phrase with negative implications (*little in the way of culture*)
3. a: opinion; b: fact; the first statement includes an expression of personal viewpoint (*more advanced than any other*) that is not backed up by specifics, while the second includes specific names

Applying the Skill: Answers will vary. Point out to students the advantages of knowing how to distinguish between fact and opinion. Mention the importance of the skill for living as an informed citizen in a free society.

SECTION 2

Early African Civilizations

Guide to Reading

Main Ideas
- The mastery of farming gave rise to the first civilizations in Africa: Egypt, Kush, and Axum.
- The expansion of trade led to migration and the growth of new kingdoms.
- Extended family units formed the basis of African villages.

Key Terms
savanna, Bantu, lineage group

People to Identify
King Ezana, Sundiata Keita, Mansa Musa, Sunni Ali, Muhammad Ture

Places to Locate
Sahara, Ghana, Mali, Songhai, Benin

Preview Questions
1. What are the four distinct climate zones of Africa and where are they located?
2. What factors led to the spread of Islam in Africa?

Reading Strategy
Using a chart like the one below, list the African kingdoms discussed in this chapter and whether they were in north, south, east, or west Africa.

Kingdom	Location

Preview of Events

100 · 325 · 550 · 775 · 1000 · 1225 · 1450

- **150** Kush declines as Axum emerges
- **324** King Ezana converts to Christianity
- **400s** Ghana emerges as a trading state
- **1240** Sundiata defeats Ghanaians
- **1307** Mansa Musa begins reign
- **1493** Muhammad Ture expands Songhai

Benin brass casting honoring the king (top, center)

Voices from the Past

The Arab traveler Ibn Battuta once described an audience between an African king and his subjects:

> ❝When [the king] calls one of [his subjects] while he is in session the man invited takes off his clothes and wears patched clothes, takes off his turban, puts on a dirty cap, and goes in raising his clothes and trousers up his legs half-way to his knees. He advances with humility looking like a beggar. He hits the ground with his elbows, he hits it hard. He stands bowed, listening to what the king says. When one of them speaks to the king and he gives him an answer, he removes his clothes from his back and throws dust on his head and back, as a person does when bathing with water. I used to wonder how they do not blind their eyes.❞
>
> —***Ibn Battuta in Black Africa,*** **Said Hamdun and Noel King, eds., 1975**

Because most African societies did not have written languages, much of what we know about these societies comes from descriptions recorded by foreign visitors, like Ibn Battuta.

The Emergence of Civilization

After Asia, Africa is the largest of the continents. It stretches nearly five thousand miles (around eight thousand km) and is almost completely surrounded by two oceans and two seas.

CHAPTER 3
Section 2, 97–101

1 FOCUS

Section Overview

This section explores how trade and the introduction of Christianity and Islam affected the way the early African civilizations developed and interacted.

BELLRINGER
Skillbuilder Activity

Project transparency and have students answer questions.

Available as a blackline master.

Daily Focus Skills Transparency 3–2

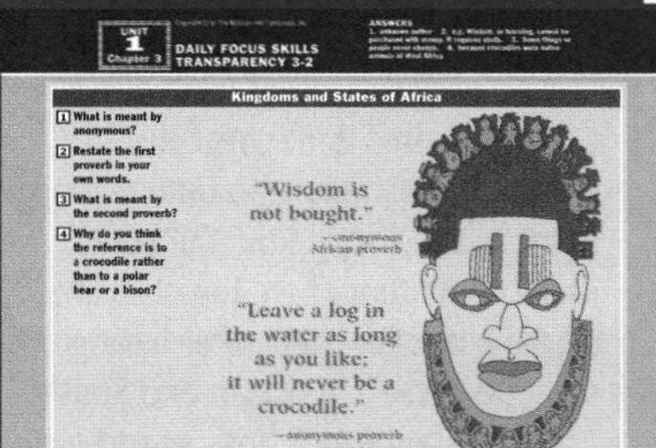

Guide to Reading

Answers to Graphic: Kush: north; Axum: northeast; Ghana: west; Mali: west; Songhai: west; Zimbabwe: south

Preteaching Vocabulary: Discuss *savanna* and ask students to speculate on the effects of unreliable rainfall on farming. **L1**

SECTION RESOURCES

Reproducible Masters
- Reproducible Lesson Plan 3–2
- Daily Lecture and Discussion Notes 3–2
- Guided Reading Activity 3–2
- Section Quiz 3–2
- Reading Essentials and Study Guide 3–2

Transparencies
- Daily Focus Skills Transparency 3–2

Multimedia
- Interactive Tutor Self-Assessment CD-ROM
- ExamView® Pro Testmaker CD-ROM
- Presentation Plus! CD-ROM

2 TEACH

Reading Check

Answer: The first three civilizations in Africa were Egypt, Kush, and Axum.

CURRICULUM CONNECTION

Geology When the first reliable world maps were made, several scientists noted the remarkable fit between the west coast of Africa and the east coast of South America. The suggestion was made that the two continents might once have been joined but had broken apart and moved to their present locations. Guide students to discover this for themselves by taking an outline map of the world, cutting out the continents, and fitting them together like a jigsaw puzzle. Then, after having students research African and South American landforms, fossils, and natural resources, have them present evidence other than shape that might confirm the idea that the continents were once joined. Students should support their points of view on this social studies issue using both examples and logical arguments. **L2**

Daily Lecture and Discussion Notes 3–2

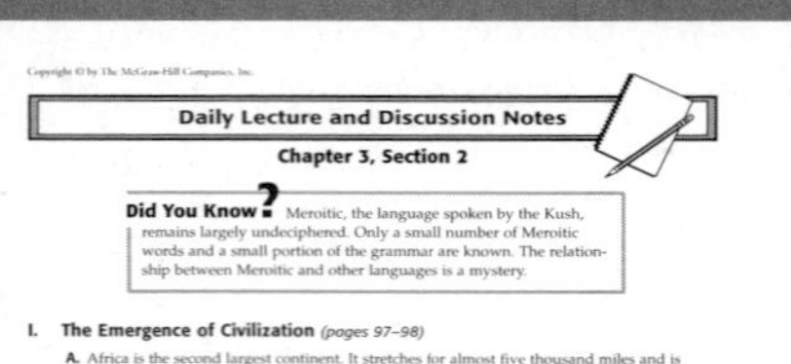

Copyright © by The McGraw-Hill Companies, Inc.

Daily Lecture and Discussion Notes

Chapter 3, Section 2

Did You Know? Meroitic, the language spoken by the Kush, remains largely undeciphered. Only a small number of Meroitic words and a small portion of the grammar are known. The relationship between Meroitic and other languages is a mystery.

I. **The Emergence of Civilization** *(pages 97–98)*

A. Africa is the second largest continent. It stretches for almost five thousand miles and is surrounded by two seas and two oceans.

B. Africa has four distinct climate zones: a mild zone across the northern coast and the southern tip; deserts in the north (the **Sahara**) and the south (Kalahari); the rain forest along the equator; and **savannas** (broad grasslands) that stretch across Africa both north and south of the rain forest. The four different climate zones have affected the way Africans live.

Africa includes four distinct climate zones: a mild zone across the northern coast and southern tip; deserts in the north (the **Sahara**) and south (the Kalahari); the rain forest along the Equator; and savannas (broad grasslands) that stretch across Africa both north and south of the rain forest. These four climate zones have affected the way the peoples of Africa live.

The mastery of farming gave rise to the first civilizations in Africa: Egypt (discussed in Chapter 1), Kush, and Axum. Much later, Islam became an important factor in the development of African empires.

Kush By 2000 B.C., a busy trade had grown between Egypt and the area to the south known as Nubia. Although subject to Egyptian control for many centuries, Nubia freed itself around 1000 B.C. and became the independent state of Kush.

Kush soon emerged as one of the major trading states in the region. Kush flourished from about 250 B.C. to about A.D. 150 but declined because of the rise of a new power in the region known as Axum.

Axum Axum was located in the highlands of what is now Ethiopia. Axum was founded as a colony by Arabs from the southern tip of the Arabian Peninsula. Eventually, Axum emerged as an independent state that combined Arab and African cultures.

Perhaps the most distinctive feature of Axumite civilization was its religion. In A.D. 324, **King Ezana** converted to Christianity and made it the official religion of Axum.

The rise of Islam in the Arabian Peninsula also had an impact on Africa. In 641, Arab forces took control of Egypt. By the early eighth century, the entire coastal region of North Africa as far west as the Strait of Gibraltar was under Arab rule. Several Muslim trading states were established on the African coast of the Red Sea.

Until the twelfth century, relations between Christian Axum and its Muslim neighbors were relatively peaceful. Then conflict arose when the Muslim states along the coast moved inland to gain control over the trade that Axum had dominated for hundreds of years.

Reading Check **Identifying** What were the first three civilizations in Africa?

The Royal Kingdoms of West Africa

During the eighth century, a number of major trading states emerged in the area south of the Sahara in West Africa. Eventually, these states—Ghana, Mali, and Songhai—made the Sahara into one of the leading avenues of world trade.

The Kingdom of Ghana **Ghana,** the first great trading state in West Africa, emerged in the fifth century A.D. in the upper Niger River valley. (The modern state of Ghana takes its name from this early state but is located in the forest region to the south.)

The kings of Ghana were strong rulers who governed without any laws. Their wealth was vast. To protect their kingdom and enforce their wishes, Ghanaian kings relied on a well-trained regular army of thousands of men.

Ghana had an abundance of gold. The heartland of the state was located near one of the richest gold-producing areas in all of Africa. Ghana's gold made it the center of an enormous trade empire.

Muslim merchants from North Africa brought to Ghana metal goods, textiles, horses, and salt. Salt was especially desirable. Used to preserve food, salt was also important because people needed extra salt to replace what their bodies lost in the hot climate. Ghanaians traded their abundant gold for salt and other products brought from North Africa.

Much of the trade across the desert was carried by the **Berbers,** nomadic peoples whose camel caravans became known as the "fleets of the desert." Camels became a crucial factor in trade across the Sahara.

People In History

Sundiata Keita
c. 1210–1260—Malian ruler

The name *Sundiata* means the "lion prince." The lion was the symbol of the Keita clan, of which Sundiata was a member.

Sundiata belonged to a family that had ruled Mali for about two centuries. Born with a disability, he still could not walk when he was seven years old. With the aid of a blacksmith who made braces for his legs, however, Sundiata gradually and painfully learned to walk.

Although he became a Muslim, Sundiata kept his traditional African religion as well. This enabled him to maintain the support of the common people, who believed that the king had magical powers. As a powerful warrior-king and the creator of the kingdom of Mali, Sundiata Keita became revered as the father of his country.

COOPERATIVE LEARNING ACTIVITY

Creating a Historical Journal Organize the class into groups of three to four students. Have each group select either of the two civilizations covered in this section—Kush or Axum—for further study. The members of each group should work together to write a journal of an imaginary archaeological expedition that has uncovered artifacts from the selected culture. Each member of the group should participate in collecting and recording the information, drawing pictures of the artifacts, and drawing the location of the finds on maps of the site. Have each group share the results of their work with the class. **L2** ELL

For grading this activity, refer to the ***Performance Assessment Activities*** booklet.

NATIONAL GEOGRAPHIC **Trading for Salt and Gold in West Africa, A.D. 800–1500**

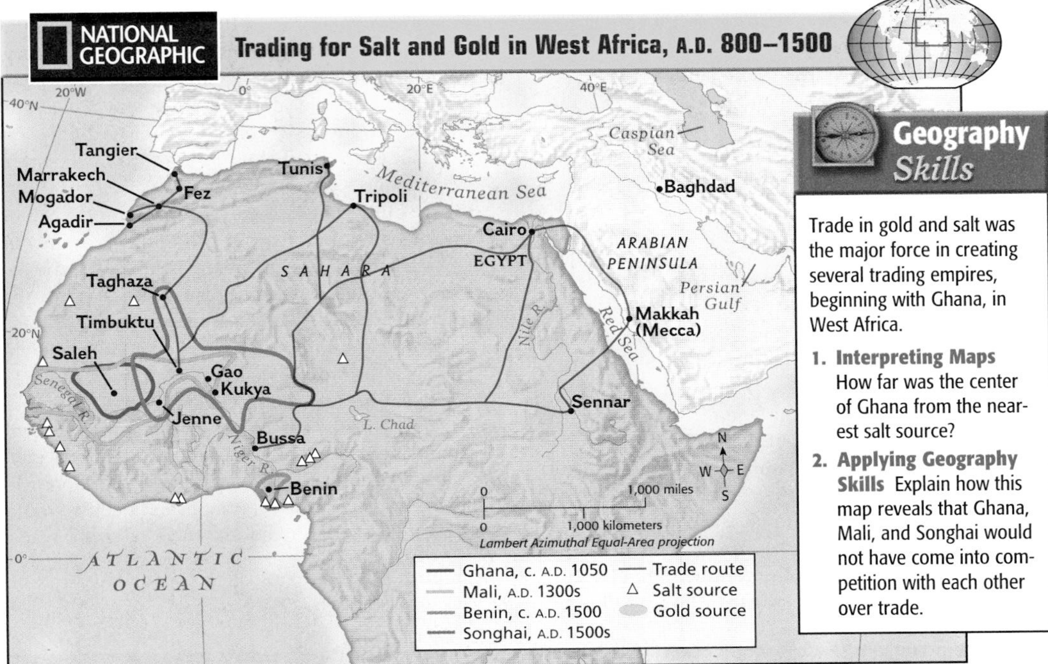

Geography Skills

Trade in gold and salt was the major force in creating several trading empires, beginning with Ghana, in West Africa.

1. **Interpreting Maps** How far was the center of Ghana from the nearest salt source?
2. **Applying Geography Skills** Explain how this map reveals that Ghana, Mali, and Songhai would not have come into competition with each other over trade.

They were well adapted to conditions in the desert, since they could drink enormous quantities of water at one time and needed little food for days.

The Kingdom of Mali The state of Ghana flourished for several hundred years. Eventually, it was weakened by wars, and it collapsed around 1200. In its place rose a number of new trading societies in West Africa. The greatest of these states was **Mali,** established in the mid-thirteenth century by **Sundiata Keita.**

Like George Washington in the United States, Sundiata is considered the founder of his nation. Sundiata defeated the Ghanaians and captured their capital in 1240. He united the people of Mali and created a strong government. Mali built its wealth and power on the gold and salt trade. Most of its people, however, were farmers who grew grains such as sorghum, millet, and rice.

One of the richest and most powerful kings was **Mansa Musa,** who ruled from 1307 to 1337 (*mansa* means "king"). Mansa Musa doubled the size of the kingdom of Mali. He created a strong central government and divided the kingdom into provinces. Once he felt secure, Mansa Musa decided—as a devout Muslim—to make a pilgrimage to Makkah.

A king, of course, was no ordinary pilgrim. Mansa Musa was joined by thousands of servants and soldiers. Accompanying the people were hundreds of camels carrying gold, as well as food, clothing, and other supplies.

Mansa Musa's pilgrimage caused people to view the king as a great ruler of a powerful and prosperous kingdom. Mansa Musa left another legacy. Earlier rulers of Mali had already converted to Islam, but Mansa Musa strongly encouraged the building of mosques, such as the famous Sankore mosque in Timbuktu, as well as the study of the Quran in his kingdom.

The Kingdom of Songhai By the fifteenth century, a new kingdom—**Songhai**—was beginning to surpass Mali. Under the leadership of **Sunni Ali,** who created the Sunni dynasty in 1464, Songhai began to expand. Sunni Ali spent much of his reign on horseback and on the march as he led his army in one military campaign after another. His conquests gave Songhai control of the trading empire—especially trade in salt and gold—that had made Ghana and Mali so prosperous.

The Songhai Empire reached the height of its power during the reign of **Muhammad Ture.** He

Geography Skills

Answers:

1. 500–700 miles (800–1,100 km)
2. Legend indicates that these kingdoms existed at different times.

Who?What?Where?When?

Sundiata Keita Ask students why Sundiata Keita, who might be called "the George Washington of Mali," might also be called "the Franklin Roosevelt of Mali." *(Both Sundiata and Roosevelt had disabilities that impeded walking; both were from famous families.)* **L1**

Guided Reading Activity 3-2

Name ____________ Date ________ Class ________

Guided Reading Activity 3-2

Early African Civilizations

DIRECTIONS: As you are reading the section, decide if a statement is true or false. Write **T** if the statement is true or **F** if the statement is false. For all false statements write a corrected statement.

____ 1. The first civilizations in Africa arose in Egypt, Kush, and Axum.

____ 2. By the early eighth century, the entire inland area of North Africa as far west as the Strait of Gibraltar was under Arab rule.

____ 3. The first of the great trading states to emerge in West Africa, south of the Sahara, was Axum.

____ 4. The kingdom of Ghana prospered from its possession of both ivory and diamonds.

____ 5. Salt was especially desirable because it was used to preserve food and improve food's flavor.

____ 6. Sundiata Keita defeated the Ghanaians and established the nation of Mali.

____ 7. Once Mansa Musa felt secure in his rule, he decided as a devout Christian to make a pilgrimage to Makkah.

____ 8. The Songhai Empire reached its height during the reign of Sunni Ali.

____ 9. On the eastern fringe of the continent, Bantu-speaking peoples gradually began

Enrich

Ask students to examine the map on this page and identify and explain the geographic factors that influenced the peoples and events of the early African civilizations. **L1**

EXTENDING THE CONTENT

Salt Essential to human body chemistry, salt is widely used for the preservation and flavoring of food. As a result, salt mining has always been a lucrative trade, and salt has been called "white gold." The Tang dynasty of China derived a large portion of its tax revenues from a salt monopoly. Salt was as important to the economy of central Africa as copper and textiles. As with the Tang, African rulers often tried to control the trade in salt. Another important location for salt mining is Salzburg, Austria (Salzburg means "salt mountain"), where salt has been mined since prehistoric times. In Salzburg, archaeologists have gotten valuable insight into earlier times from prehistoric workers who died in the mines and were preserved in the salt.

Reading Check

Answer: Mansa Musa created a strong central government; imported scholars and books to encourage the study of the Quran; and brought architects to build mosques.

Answer: Answers will vary. Students should identify the pieces being compared, and student work should reflect careful consideration.

Reading Check

Answer: The walls illustrate the kingdom's power and influence. The size of the area enclosed in the walls shows that ten thousand people would have been able to live in the kingdom.

3 ASSESS

Assign Section 2 Assessment as homework or as an in-class activity.

Have students use **Interactive Tutor Self-Assessment CD-ROM.**

Section Quiz 3–2

Name ______ Date ______ Class ______

Chapter 3 Score

Section Quiz 3-2

DIRECTIONS: Matching Match each item in Column A with an item in Column B. Write the correct letters in the blanks. *(10 points each)*

Column A	Column B
____ 1. Axum king who converted to Christianity	A. Bantu
____ 2. the founder of Mali	B. Ezana
____ 3. created a Songhai dynasty	C. Sundiata Keita
____ 4. dialect that came from the Niger River region	D. Ife
____ 5. the capital of the Yoruba people	E. Sunni Ali

DIRECTIONS: Multiple Choice In the blank, write the letter of the choice that best completes the statement or answers the question. *(10 points each)*

____ 6. Ghana traded its gold for all of the following EXCEPT

continued Sunni Ali's policy of expansion, creating an empire that stretched a thousand miles along the Niger River. The chief cities of the empire prospered as never before from the salt and gold trade until the end of the sixteenth century.

Reading Check **Summarizing** What were Mansa Musa's accomplishments?

Societies in East and South Africa

In eastern Africa, a variety of states and small societies took root. Islam strongly influenced many of them. Some became extremely wealthy as a result of trade.

Beginning in the first millennium B.C., farming peoples who spoke dialects of the **Bantu** (BAN•TOO) family of languages began to move from the region of the Niger River into East Africa and the Congo River basin. They moved slowly, not as invading hordes but as small communities.

On the eastern fringe of the continent, the Bantu-speaking peoples gradually began to take part in the regional trade that moved by sea up and down the East African coast. Beginning in the eighth century, Muslims from the Arabian Peninsula and the Persian Gulf began to settle at ports along the coast. The result was the formation of a string of trading ports that included Mogadishu (MAH•guh•DIH•shoo), Mombasa, and Kilwa in the south.

In the southern half of the African continent, states formed more slowly than in the north. From about 1300 to about 1450, Zimbabwe (zihm•BAH•bwee) was the wealthiest and most powerful state in the region. It prospered from the gold trade with the trading communities on the eastern coast of the continent.

The ruins of Zimbabwe's capital, known as Great Zimbabwe, illustrate the kingdom's power and influence. The town sits on a hill overlooking the Zambezi River and is surrounded by stone walls. The local people stacked granite blocks together without mortar to build the massive walls. Ten thousand people would have been able to live in the area enclosed by the walls.

Reading Check **Evaluating** What do the walled enclosures tell us about Great Zimbabwe?

CONNECTIONS Past To Present

From African Rhythms to Rock and Roll

Beginning in the 1500s, Africans were brought as slaves to the Western Hemisphere. Their music came with them and became an important ingredient in the development of musical styles in the Americas.

A strong rhythmic pattern was an important feature of African music, an effect achieved through a wide variety of instruments, including drums, bells, harps, gourds, pots, sticks beaten together, and hand clapping. Another important feature of African music was the coming together of voice and instrument. A call and response pattern was common: a leader would sing a short piece and people would repeat it back to the beat of a drum.

As slaves in North America, Africans would use work songs, sung to rhythmic patterns, to make their long work days less burdensome. At rest, others sang folk songs known as spirituals to lament the loss of their homeland and their freedom. Over the years, these African musical forms developed into new forms known as blues, gospel, jazz, and ragtime. In the twentieth century, African American artists inspired new forms of music known as rock and roll and rap.

In Latin America, the beat of African drums was combined with European instruments, such as the Spanish guitar, and Native American instruments, such as the maraca and wooden rhythm sticks. From the combination of these elements came such styles as reggae, calypso, and salsa music.

▼ *Burundi drummers*

▲ *Jazz saxophonist*

Comparing Past and Present

Listen to blues, gospel, jazz, and ragtime music. Describe the similarities and the differences between these types of music. Compare these musical types to contemporary, popular music.

EXTENDING THE CONTENT

Economics By the late 1100s, thriving Swahili port cities, such as Kilwa, Malindi, and Mombasa, served as trading links between the gold and ivory producers of East Africa's interior and traders from India, Ceylon (Sri Lanka), and China. Cotton, porcelain, and pottery were the major imports. By the 1500s, China's withdrawal from foreign trade and the coming of European rule to East Africa contributed to a serious decline in East Africa's international trade. Today, the East African coast has become an important link in the global trading network. East African agricultural products are exported from Mombasa, as are petroleum products produced from the foreign oil refined at Mombasa's refinery.

African Society and Culture

The relationship between king and subjects was often less rigid in African society than in other civilizations. Frequently, the ruler would allow people to voice their complaints to him. Still, the king was held in a position high above all others.

Few Africans, of course, ever met with their kings. Most people lived in small villages. Their sense of identity was determined by their membership in an extended family and a lineage group. **Lineage groups,** which were communities of extended family units, were the basis of African society.

Early African religious beliefs varied from place to place. Most African societies shared some common religious ideas. These ideas included belief in various gods, the power of diviners (people who believe they can foretell events), and the importance of ancestors.

In early Africa, as in much of the rest of the world at the time, the arts—whether painting, literature, or music—were a means of serving religion. In the thirteenth and fourteenth centuries, metalworkers at Ife (EE•feh), in what is now southern Nigeria, produced handsome bronze and iron statues. The Ife sculptures may have influenced artists in **Benin** in West Africa, who produced equally impressive works in bronze during the same period. The Benin sculptures include bronze heads, many of kings, and figures of various types of animals.

Reading Check **Summarizing** Describe the role of lineage groups on African society.

▲ *Benin bronze figures*

▲ *Ife king, bronze*

Delicately carved bronze head of Benin, queen mother, from 1500s ▲

SECTION 2 ASSESSMENT

Checking for Understanding

1. **Define** savanna, Bantu, lineage group.
2. **Identify** King Ezana, Berbers, Sundiata Keita, Mansa Musa, Sunni Ali, Muhammad Ture.
3. **Locate** Sahara, Ghana, Mali, Songhai, Benin.
4. **Describe** the most distinctive feature of Axumite civilization. How did this affect Axum's relations with its neighbors?
5. **List** the trading commodities that made the African kingdoms wealthy. How were camels a crucial factor in African trade?

Critical Thinking

6. **Analyze** How did the indigenous religious beliefs of Africans differ from Islam and Christianity?
7. **Sequencing Information** Using a diagram like the one below, put the royal kingdoms of West Africa in chronological order (include dates) along the top row of boxes. In the second row, add details about the accomplishments of each kingdom.

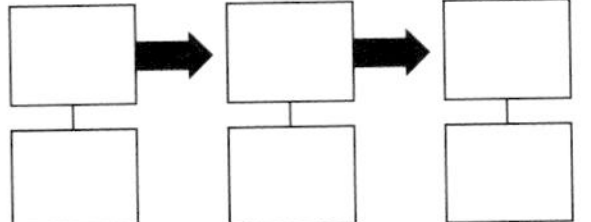

Analyzing Visuals

8. **Examine** the art works shown on this page and on page 97. Approaching the task as if you were an anthropologist, what can you learn about African art, culture, society, and technology from these figures?

Writing About History

9. **Expository Writing** Music, dance, and storytelling do not leave a physical archaeological record in the same way as buildings or roads. Describe how historians have been able to determine the significance of the performing arts in African society.

SECTION 2 ASSESSMENT

1. Key terms are in blue.
2. King Ezana *(p. 98);* Berbers *(p. 98);* Sundiata Keita *(p. 99);* Mansa Musa *(p. 99);* Sunni Ali *(p. 99);* Muhammad Ture *(p. 99)*
3. See chapter maps.
4. Christianity was the official religion. Conflicts arose when the Muslim states along the coast moved inland to gain control of Axum's trade.
5. gold and salt; camels were well adapted to the harsh conditions of the desert
6. African beliefs: various gods; Islam and Christianity: monotheistic.
7. Ghana: ended c. 1200; was center of vast trade empire. Mali: began c. 1240; built great mosques and strengthened Islam. Songhai: created 1464; expanded empire significantly and gained control of African salt and gold trade.
8. the technological and artistic skills; valued the decorative arts
9. Answers should include that historians rely on contemporary African cultures for insights into the past.

Reading Check

Answer: They were the basis of African society. Africans' sense of identity came from their membership in a lineage group.

Reading Essentials and Study Guide 3–2

Name ________ Date ________ Class ________

Reading Essentials and Study Guide

Chapter 3, Section 2

For use with textbook pages 97–101

EARLY AFRICAN CIVILIZATIONS

KEY TERMS

savanna a broad grassland dotted with small trees and shrubs *(page 98)*

Bantu a family of languages spoken by peoples who migrated from the Niger River region to East Africa and the Congo River basin *(page 100)*

lineage group a community whose members trace their lineage (descent) from a common ancestor *(page 101)*

DRAWING FROM EXPERIENCE

What are some of the largest buildings in your town or city? What is the function of these buildings? What do these buildings reflect about society?

In this section, you will read about early kingdoms and societies in Africa. One of these kingdoms was Mali. A Mali ruler, Mansa Musa, built the Sankore mosque in the city of Timbuktu to encourage scholarly study and the spread of Islam. The mosque still stands today.

ORGANIZING YOUR THOUGHTS

Use the chart below to help you take notes. Describe the location, government and economy of each of the kingdoms in this chart.

Kingdom	Location	Government	Economy
Ghana	1.	2.	3.
Mali	4.	5.	6.
Songhai	7.	8.	9.

Reteaching Activity

Ask students to create a visual that illustrates the way African kings conveyed grandeur and importance. **L1**

4 CLOSE

Ask students to create a chart comparing the East African empires, Kush and Axum, with the West African empires, Ghana, Mali, and Songhai. **L1**

TEACH

Analyzing Primary Sources
Review with students the importance of salt as a trade item. Next, ask for a list of words to describe life at Taghaza, based on this account. Why do students think Ibn Battuta says that Taghaza is "a village with no good in it"? Ask students to discuss what the following part of Ibn Battuta's account suggests about life and thought during this time, in this place: "Nobody lives in the village except slaves. . . ." **L2**

Enrich

Ask if anyone knows what truffles are. *(a kind of edible fungi)* Ask students to find out more about truffles. Ask them to explain the irony of truffles being mentioned in the context of Ibn Battuta's description of Taghaza. *(truffles considered a delicacy; Taghaza is a "miserable" place)* **L2**

CURRICULUM CONNECTION

Art Interested students might like to draw, paint, or create a mural depicting the village of Taghaza as Ibn Battuta describes it. **L2**

Writing Activity

Ask students to write a diary entry or a poem in the voice of a modern worker in an African salt mine. **L2**

EYEWITNESS TO HISTORY

The Salt Mines

IBN BATTUTA WAS BORN IN MOROCCO in 1304. When he was 21 years old, he went on a pilgrimage to Makkah. He spent the next 24 years wandering throughout Africa and Asia. In writing an account of his travels, he provided modern readers with an accurate description of conditions in the fourteenth century.

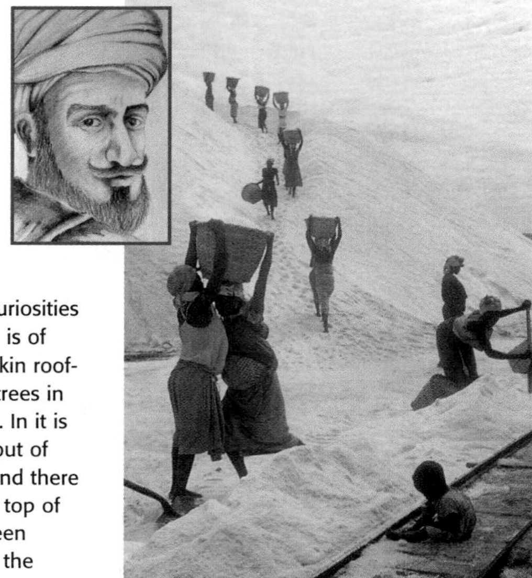

African salt mines were described by Ibn Battuta (inset photo) in the 1300s and still exist today.

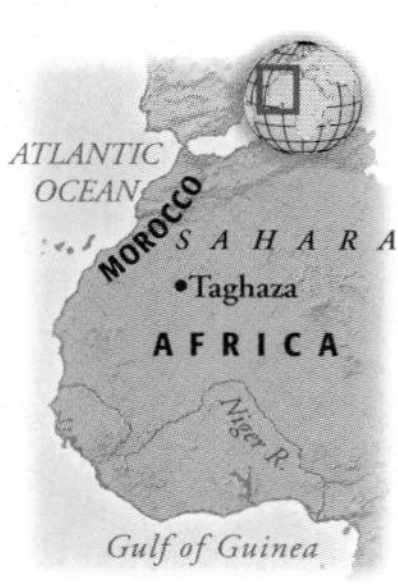

"We arrived after 25 days at Taghaza. It is a village with no good in it. Among its curiosities is the fact that the construction of its houses is of rock salt with camel skin roofing and there are no trees in it, the soil is just sand. In it is a salt mine. It is dug out of the ground and is found there in huge slabs, one on top of another as if it had been carved and put under the ground. A camel can carry two slabs of salt. Nobody lives in the village except slaves who dig for the salt and live on dates and on the meat of camels that is brought from the land of the blacks. The blacks arrive from their country and carry away the salt from there. The blacks exchange the salt as money as one would exchange gold and silver. They cut it up and trade with it in pieces. In spite of the insignificance of the village of Taghaza, much trading goes on in it. We stayed in it 10 days in miserable conditions, because its water is bitter and it is of all places the most full of flies. In it water is drawn for the entry into the desert which comes after it. This desert is a traveling distance of 10 days and there is no water in it except rarely. But we found much water in it in pools left behind by the rains. One day we found a pool of sweet water between two hillocks of rocks. We quenched our thirsts from it and washed our clothes. In that desert truffles are abundant. There are also so many lice in it that people put strings around their necks in which there is mercury which kills the lice. In those days we used to go ahead in front of the caravan. When we found a place suitable for pasture we would let the animals pasture."

—**Ibn Battuta, *Ibn Battuta in Black Africa***

Analyzing Primary Sources

1. Why did Ibn Battuta write that the village of Taghaza was a village "with no good in it"?
2. Explain the economic value of Taghaza.

102

ANSWERS TO ANALYZING PRIMARY SOURCES

1. Ibn Battuta identified many aspects of Taghaza that were disagreeable to him. Among those mentioned are the fact that no one lived there but slaves, the land was just sand, there were no trees, houses were built of rock salt with camel skin roofing, the water was bitter, and the place was full of flies.
2. It provided salt, which is necessary for life and was important in African trade. Besides being the site of salt mines, Taghaza served also as a major center of trade.

SECTION 3 The Asian World

Guide to Reading

Main Ideas
- The Mongols created a vast land empire.
- Rulers and powerful families struggled for control in Japan.
- Muslim power grew in India.
- New Southeast Asian states adapted Chinese and Indian models.

Key Terms
khanate, samurai, Bushido, shogun, daimyo, Shinto, archipelago

People to Identify
Genghis Khan, Kublai Khan, Li Bo, Shotoku Taishi, Timur Lenk

Places to Locate
Tibet, Mongolia, Beijing, Nara, Kyoto, Angkor Thom, Malay Peninsula

Preview Questions
1. Why did Japan not develop a centralized government like China's?
2. What impact did Muslim rule have on India?

Reading Strategy
Using a diagram like the one below, identify all the civilizations that were affected by Mongol expansion.

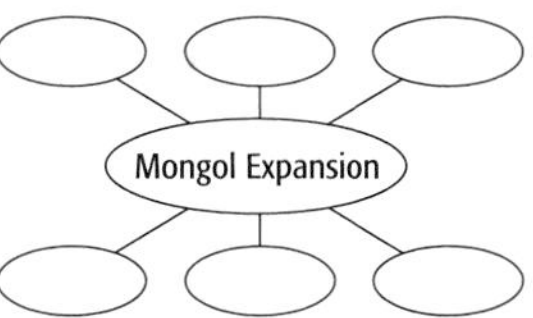

Preview of Events

600 · 750 · 900 · 1050 · 1200 · 1350 · 1500

- **581** Sui dynasty begins
- **794** Heian period begins in Japan
- **1279** Kublai Khan defeats the Song and establishes the Yuan dynasty
- **1369** Timur Lenk begins conquests
- **1432** Thai set up capital at Ayutthaya

Voices from the Past

Mongol horseman

The Mongols were masters of military tactics. John of Plano Carpini, a Franciscan friar, wrote:

❝As soon as they discover the enemy they charge and each one unleashes three or four arrows. If they see that they can't break him, they retreat in order to entice the enemy to pursue, thus luring him into an ambush prepared in advance. If they conclude that the enemy army is stronger, they retire for a day or two and ravage neighboring areas. Or they [set up] camp in a well chosen position, and when the enemy army begins to pass by, they appear unexpectedly.❞

—*L'Empire des Steppes,* Rene Grousset, 1939

Due in large part to their military prowess, the Mongols rose to power in Asia with stunning speed.

China Reunified

The Han dynasty came to an end in 220, and China fell into chaos. For the next three hundred years, the Chinese suffered through disorder and civil war. Then, in 581, a new Chinese empire was set up under a dynasty known as the Sui (SWAY). The Sui dynasty (581–618) did not last long, but it managed to unify China once again under the emperor's authority.

The Tang Dynasty A new dynasty, the Tang (TONG), soon emerged. It would last for almost three hundred years, from 618 until 907. The early Tang rulers began their reigns by instituting reforms, as rulers often did in the early days of new dynasties. They restored the civil service examination started by the Qin

1 FOCUS

Section Overview

This section describes the Sui, Tang, Song, and Mongol dynasties of early China. It also discusses the rise of Japan, the influence of Islam on India, and the formation of the states of Southeast Asia.

BELLRINGER
Skillbuilder Activity

Project transparency and have students answer questions.

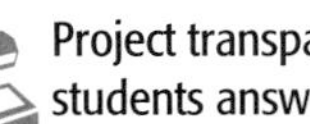
Available as a blackline master.

Daily Focus Skills Transparency 3-3

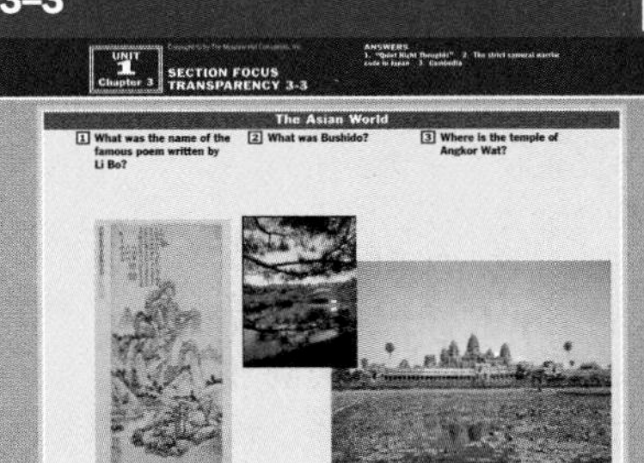

Guide to Reading

Answers to Graphic: Song dynasty, Vietnam, Java, Sumatra, India

Preteaching Vocabulary: Ask students to discuss the relationship between *samurai* and *Bushido.*

SECTION RESOURCES

Reproducible Masters
- Reproducible Lesson Plan 3–3
- Daily Lecture and Discussion Notes 3–3
- Guided Reading Activity 3–3
- Section Quiz 3–3
- Reading Essentials and Study Guide 3–3

Transparencies
- Daily Focus Skills Transparency 3–3

Multimedia
- Interactive Tutor Self-Assessment CD-ROM
- ExamView® Pro Testmaker CD-ROM
- Presentation Plus! CD-ROM

2 TEACH

Geography Skills

Answers:

1. about 800 miles (1,330 km)—the equivalent of about half the length of China running north/south
2. border changes reflect dynasty's relationship with Tibet and surrounding states

Critical Thinking

The Tang dynasty fell after the people they had hired to fight for them, the Uighurs, turned on them instead and overthrew their government. Soldiers hired into foreign service are called *mercenaries.* Discuss common associations with the word *(only interested in money, greedy).* Ask students to discuss why states that rely on hired mercenaries to fight for them are often destroyed or are, at the least, unsuccessful. One example from a later time is the Hessian soldiers who were hired by the British to fight in the American Revolution. Ask students to imagine that they are leading a state that is at war. If necessary, would they hire mercenaries to help their state fight? Why or why not? **L2**

Enrich

Ask students to prepare a chart comparing the Sui, Tang, and Song dynasties in terms of founders, time periods covered, and cultural contributions. **L1**

ELL

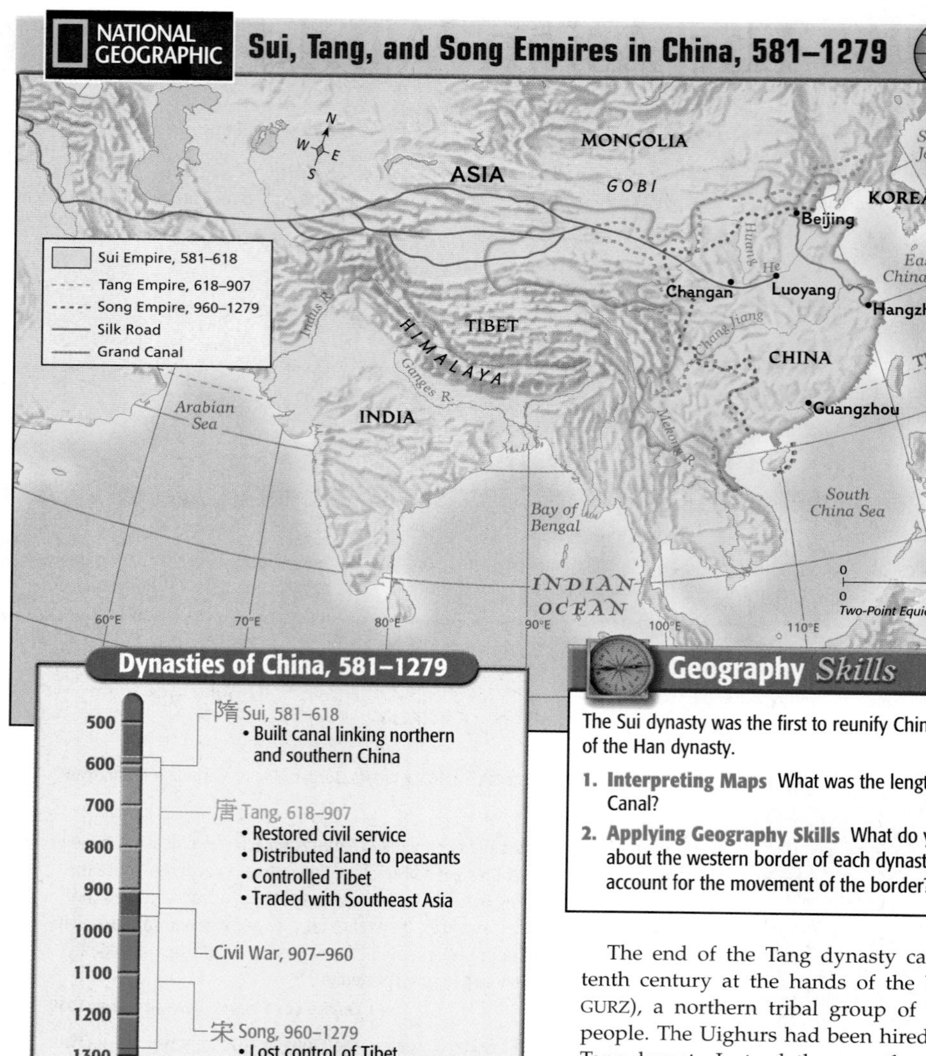

Geography Skills

The Sui dynasty was the first to reunify China after the fall of the Han dynasty.

1. **Interpreting Maps** What was the length of the Grand Canal?
2. **Applying Geography Skills** What do you notice about the western border of each dynasty? What would account for the movement of the border?

dynasty, to serve as the chief method of recruiting officials for the civilian bureaucracy. They also tried to create a more stable economy by giving land to the peasants and breaking up the power of large landowners.

Tang rulers worked hard to restore the power of China in East Asia. They brought peace to northwestern China and expanded China's control into the area north of the Himalaya—known as **Tibet.** China claimed to be the greatest power in East Asia.

The end of the Tang dynasty came in the early tenth century at the hands of the Uighurs (WEE• GURZ), a northern tribal group of Turkic-speaking people. The Uighurs had been hired to fight for the Tang dynasty. Instead, they overthrew the Tang ruler in 907. China again slipped into civil war.

The Song Dynasty In 960, a new dynasty known as the Song (SOONG) rose to power. The Song ruled during a period of economic prosperity and cultural achievement, from 960 to 1279. From the start, however, the Song also experienced problems, especially from the Uighurs in northern China. The Song also lost control over Tibet.

The Song dynasty could never overcome the challenge from the north. During the 1200s, the Mongols—a nomadic people from the Gobi—carried out wars of conquest and built a vast empire. Within 70 years, they

COOPERATIVE LEARNING ACTIVITY

Creating a Group Presentation Organize the class into four groups. Ask each group to choose one of the following technological advances of the Tang and Song dynasties: block printing, steel, or gunpowder. Have each group research its topic to learn more about when and how the invention came about, how it was used, and how knowledge of it spread. If possible, each group should find illustrations of its subject. Then have the groups present their findings to the class. **L2**

For grading this activity, refer to the ***Performance Assessment Activities*** booklet.

controlled all of China. The Mongols overthrew the Song and created a new Mongol dynasty.

Government, Economy, and Society The era from the beginning of the Sui dynasty to the end of the Song dynasty lasted nearly seven hundred years. During that period, a mature political system based on principles first put into practice during the Qin and Han dynasties gradually emerged in China. As in the Han Era, China was a monarchy that employed a relatively large bureaucracy. Beyond the capital, government was centered around provinces, districts, and villages. Confucian ideals were the cement that held the system together.

During the long period between the Sui and Song dynasties, the Chinese economy grew in size and complexity. Agriculture flourished, and manufacturing and trade grew dramatically. In Chinese cities, technological developments added new products and stimulated trade. During the Tang dynasty, for example, the Chinese began to make steel for swords and sickles and invented gunpowder, used for explosives and a flamethrower called a fire-lance.

Long-distance trade had declined between the fourth and sixth centuries as a result of the collapse of both the Han dynasty and the Roman Empire. Trade revived under the Tang dynasty, in part because of the unification of much of Southwest Asia under the Arabs. The Silk Road was renewed and thrived as caravans carried goods between China and the countries of Southwest and South Asia.

Economic changes had an impact on Chinese society. For wealthier city dwellers, the Tang and Song Eras were times of prosperity. The Song capital of Hangzhou, for example, flourished. In the late thirteenth century the Italian merchant Marco Polo described the city to European readers as one of the largest and wealthiest cities on Earth. "So many pleasures may be found," he said, "that one fancies himself to be in Paradise."

The vast majority of the Chinese people still lived off the land in villages. Most peasants never left their villages except for an occasional visit to a nearby market town. Changes were taking place in the countryside, however. Before, there had been a great gulf between wealthy landowners and poor peasants. A more complex mixture of landowners, free peasants, sharecroppers, and landless laborers now emerged.

Reading Check **Describing** Identify one of the broad goals of the Tang dynasty and describe how Tang rulers worked to reach it.

The Mongol Empire

The Mongols were a pastoral people from the region of modern-day **Mongolia** who were organized loosely into clans. Temujin (teh•MOO•juhn), born during the 1160s, gradually unified the Mongols. In 1206, he was elected **Genghis Khan** ("strong ruler") at a massive meeting somewhere in the Gobi. From that time on, he devoted himself to conquest.

The Mongols brought much of the Eurasian landmass under a single rule, creating the largest land empire in history. To rule the new Mongol Empire, Genghis Khan set up a capital city at Karakorum. Mongol armies traveled both to the west and to the east. Some went as far as central Europe.

After the death of Genghis Khan in 1227, the empire began to change. Following Mongol custom, upon the death of the ruling khan, his heirs divided the territory. The once-united empire of Genghis Khan was thus split into several separate territories called khanates, each under the rule of one of his sons.

In 1231, the Mongols attacked Persia and then defeated the Abbasids at Baghdad in 1258. In the 1260s, a new wave of invasion began when Mongol forces attacked the Song in China. In their attack on the Chinese, the Mongols encountered the use of gunpowder and the firelance. By the early fourteenth century, foreigners employed by the Mongol rulers of China had introduced gunpowder and firearms into Europe.

This silk watercolor shows students taking a civil service examination during the Song dynasty.

Reading Check

Answer: Tang rulers worked hard to restore the power of China in East Asia. They restored the civil service examination in China, redistributed land to peasants, gained control of Tibet, and traded with Southeast Asia.

Daily Lecture and Discussion Notes 3–3

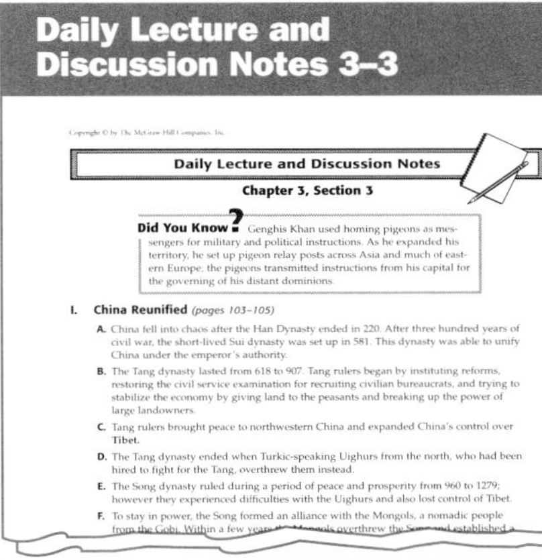

Daily Lecture and Discussion Notes

Chapter 3, Section 3

Did You Know? Genghis Khan used homing pigeons as messengers for military and political instructions. As he expanded his territory, he set up pigeon relay posts across Asia and much of eastern Europe; the pigeons transmitted instructions from his capital for the governing of his distant dominions.

I. **China Reunified** *(pages 103–105)*

A. China fell into chaos after the Han Dynasty ended in 220. After three hundred years of civil war, the short-lived Sui dynasty was set up in 581. This dynasty was able to unify China under the emperor's authority.

B. The Tang dynasty lasted from 618 to 907. Tang rulers began by instituting reforms, restoring the civil service examination for recruiting civilian bureaucrats, and trying to stabilize the economy by giving land to the peasants and breaking up the power of large landowners.

C. Tang rulers brought peace to northwestern China and expanded China's control over **Tibet.**

D. The Tang dynasty ended when Turkic-speaking Uighurs from the north, who had been hired to fight for the Tang, overthrew them instead.

E. The Song dynasty ruled during a period of peace and prosperity from 960 to 1279; however they experienced difficulties with the Uighurs and also lost control of Tibet.

F. To stay in power, the Song formed an alliance with the Mongols, a nomadic people from the Gobi. Within a few years [illegible]

Connecting Across Time

Ask students to write an essay explaining why they believe young men in China were willing to complete the work and follow the rules of their society to prepare to take the civil service examination. Do they think young people today would be willing to make the same effort? Why or why not? Students should be able to provide support for their point of view. After students have completed their essays, lead the class in a discussion on their views. **L2**

EXTENDING THE CONTENT

Marco Polo (1254–1324), who grew up in Venice, is probably the most famous Westerner who ever traveled on the Silk Road. He surpassed all other travelers in his determination, his writing, and his influence. His journey through Asia lasted 24 years. He traveled farther than any of his predecessors, beyond Mongolia to China. A gifted linguist and master of four languages, he became a confidant of Kublai Khan. He traveled the whole of China. However, after Marco Polo returned to Italy, he was captured and imprisoned by the Genoese, who were archrivals of the Venetians. While in prison, he dictated his book, known in English as the *Travels of Marco Polo,* to a fellow prisoner. It was instantly popular and soon known all over Europe.

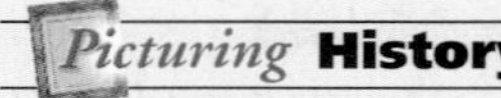

Picturing History

Answer: Song dynasty

Enrich

After students have read this section, have them identify changes that resulted from the Mongol invasions. **L1**

Who?What?Where?When?

Chinese Classical Writing Chinese writing dates back over 2,500 years and is an intricate system of characters that used to be written with a paintbrush. A Chinese typewriter contains a tray of over 2,000 characters, with several thousand more available on other trays.

Critical Thinking

Help students understand that important advancements can be made by civilizations in which most people are peasant farmers who never leave the immediate vicinity of their farms. This was the case in China and in most other ancient civilizations. Take a poll of students to find how far they have traveled from their homes. Ask them if they have traveled further than their parents have traveled, and if their parents have traveled further than their own parents. Discuss how people who never travel can still contribute to advancements in civilizations. **L1** ELL

Picturing **History**

In the thirteenth-century battle shown above, Mongol troops storm across the Chang Jiang on a bridge made of boats. Which Chinese dynasty do you think the Mongols were attempting to conquer in this battle?

The Mongol Dynasty in China In 1279, one of Genghis Khan's grandsons, named **Kublai Khan,** completed the conquest of the Song and established a new Chinese dynasty, the Yuan (YOO•AHN). Kublai Khan, who ruled China until his death in 1294, established his capital at Khanbaliq ("the city of the Khan") in northern China. Later the city would be known by the Chinese name **Beijing.**

Under the leadership of the talented Kublai Khan, the Yuan, or Mongol, dynasty continued to expand the empire. Mongol armies advanced into Vietnam, and Mongol fleets were launched against Java and Sumatra and twice against the islands of Japan. Only Vietnam was conquered, however—and then only for a while.

The Mongols had more success in ruling China. Mongol rulers adapted to the Chinese political system. Over time, the Mongols won the support of many Chinese people. Some came to respect the stability and economic prosperity that the Mongols at first brought to China. The capital at Khanbaliq reflected Mongol prosperity. It was a magnificent city, and foreign visitors were impressed by its splendor.

The Mongol dynasty eventually fell victim to the same problems that had plagued other dynasties. In 1368, Zhu Yuanzhang (JOO YOO•AHN•JAHNG), the son of a peasant, raised an army, ended the Mongol dynasty, and set up a new dynasty, the Ming dynasty.

Religion By the time the Mongols established their dynasty in China, religious preferences in the Chinese court had undergone a number of changes. Confucian principles became the basis for Chinese government during the Han dynasty (202 B.C.–A.D. 220). By the time of the Sui and Tang dynasties, Buddhism and Daoism rivaled the influence of Confucianism. During the last half of the Tang dynasty, however, Confucianism became dominant at court, a position it retained until the early twentieth century. *(See page 773 to read excerpts from* The Buddha's Sermon *in the Primary Sources Library.)*

A Golden Age in Art and Literature The period between the Tang and Ming dynasties was in many ways the great age of Chinese art and literature. During the Song and Mongol dynasties, landscape painting reached its high point. Influenced by Daoism, Chinese artists went into the mountains to paint and find the Dao, or Way, in nature. This practice explains in part the emphasis on nature in traditional Chinese painting. The word for landscape in Chinese means "mountain-water" and reflects the Daoist search for balance between the earth and water.

Chinese artists tried to reveal the hidden forms of the landscape. Rather than depicting the realistic shape of a specific mountain, for example, they tried to portray the idea of "mountain." Empty spaces were left in the paintings because Daoists believe one cannot know the whole truth.

Song ink and watercolor drawing on silk

The invention of printing during the Tang dynasty helped to make literature more readily available and more popular. It was in poetry, above all, that the Chinese of this time best expressed their

COOPERATIVE LEARNING ACTIVITY

Creating Biographies Genghis Khan and his grandson Kublai Khan were both warriors, but both also had many other accomplishments. For example, Genghis Khan worked to fuse many tribes into a single people. He built an army, imposed uniform laws, and established a written language. Kublai Khan completed the unification of China, promoted economic prosperity, and fostered Chinese scholarship and arts. Divide students into two groups, assigning Genghis Khan to one and Kublai Khan to the other. Ask students to research the life and accomplishments of their assigned figure and to work together on a class presentation that includes visuals (posters, time lines, illustrations, transparencies) and oral reports. **L1**

literary talents. Chinese poems celebrated the beauty of nature, the changes of the seasons, and the joys of friendship. They expressed sadness at the shortness of life and the necessity of parting.

Li Bo (LEE BWAW) was one of the most popular poets during the Tang Era. Li Bo was a free spirit whose writing often centered on nature. The following is probably the best-known poem in China and has been memorized by schoolchildren for centuries. It is entitled "Quiet Night Thoughts":

> ❝Beside my bed the bright moonbeams bound
> Almost as if there were frost on the ground.
> Raising up, I gaze at the Mountain moon;
> Lying back, I think of my old home town.❞

Reading Check **Summarizing** What invention helped make literature both more available and more popular?

The Rise of the Japanese State

Chinese and Japanese societies have historically been very different. One of the reasons for these differences is geography. Whereas China is on a vast continent, Japan is a chain of many islands. The population is concentrated on four main islands: Hokkaido, the main island of Honshu, and the two smaller islands of Kyushu and Shikoku. Japan's total land area is approximately 146,000 square miles (378,000 sq km)—about the size of the state of Montana.

In the early seventh century, **Shotoku Taishi,** a prince of the Yamato clan, tried to unify the various Japanese clans in order to more effectively resist an invasion by the Chinese. He began to create a new centralized system of government in Japan, based roughly on the structure of the Chinese government.

Prince Shotoku wanted a centralized government under a supreme ruler. His objective was to limit the powers of the small class of aristocrats and enhance the Yamato ruler's (his own) authority. As a result, the ruler was portrayed as a divine figure and the symbol of the Japanese nation.

The Nara Period After Shotoku Taishi's death in 622, political power fell into the hands of the Fujiwara clan. A Yamato ruler was still emperor, but he was strongly influenced by the Fujiwara family. In 710, a new capital was established at **Nara.** The emperor began to use the title "son of Heaven."

Though the reforms begun by Prince Shotoku continued during this period, Japan's central government could not overcome the power of the aristocrats. These powerful families were able to keep the taxes from the lands for themselves. Unable to gain tax revenues, the central government steadily lost power and influence.

NATIONAL GEOGRAPHIC **Early Japan**

Geography Skills

The geography of Japan influenced the development of Japanese culture.

1. **Interpreting Maps** List, from north to south, the four major islands that make up Japan. On which island are the major cities of early Japan located?
2. **Applying Geography Skills** Heian (Kyoto) and Osaka were important cities in early Japan. Today Tokyo is a major city. What geographic features contributed to Tokyo's importance?

The Heian Period In 794, the emperor moved the capital from Nara to nearby Heian, on the site of present-day **Kyoto.** At Heian, the emperor continued to rule in name, but actual power remained in the hands of the Fujiwara clan.

In fact, the government was returning to the decentralized system that had existed before the time of Shotoku Taishi. Powerful families whose wealth was based on the ownership of tax-exempt farmland dominated the rural areas. With the decline of central power, local aristocrats tended to take justice into their own hands. They turned increasingly to military force as a means of protecting their interests. A new class of military servants emerged whose purpose was to protect the security and property of their employers.

Called the **samurai** ("those who serve"), these warriors resembled the knights of medieval Europe.

CHAPTER 3
Section 3, 103–111

Reading Check

Answer: The invention of printing made literature more available and more popular.

Geography Skills

Answers:

1. Hokkaido, Honshu, Shikoku, Kyushu; Honshu
2. large flat plain, protected by a peninsula, located on a bay

Guided Reading Activity 3–3

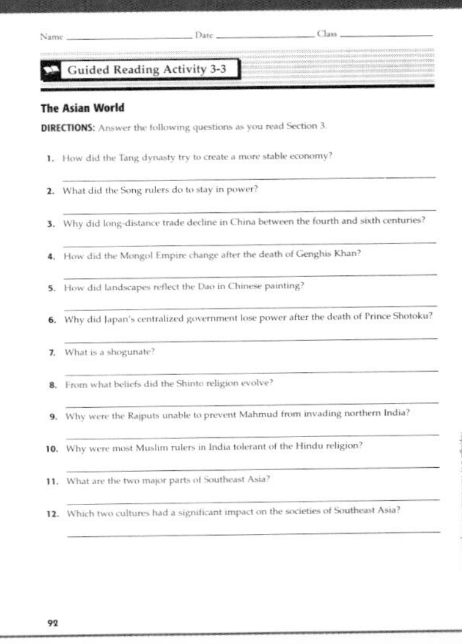

Name ______ Date ______ Class ______

Guided Reading Activity 3-3

The Asian World

DIRECTIONS: Answer the following questions as you read Section 3.

1. How did the Tang dynasty try to create a more stable economy?
2. What did the Song rulers do to stay in power?
3. Why did long-distance trade decline in China between the fourth and sixth centuries?
4. How did the Mongol Empire change after the death of Genghis Khan?
5. How did landscapes reflect the Dao in Chinese painting?
6. Why did Japan's centralized government lose power after the death of Prince Shotoku?
7. What is a shogunate?
8. From what beliefs did the Shinto religion evolve?
9. Why were the Rajputs unable to prevent Mahmud from invading northern India?
10. Why were most Muslim rulers in India tolerant of the Hindu religion?
11. What are the two major parts of Southeast Asia?
12. Which two cultures had a significant impact on the societies of Southeast Asia?

92

Enrich

Ask students to compare the idea that the Japanese sovereign was considered divine with the Mandate of Heaven enjoyed by rulers in China's Zhou and Shang dynasties. Why is this connection between rulers and divine power common throughout history? **L2**

EXTENDING THE CONTENT

The Ainu Because of Japan's geographic isolation, the country today has very few minorities. There is, however, one group that may have descended from Japan's very first inhabitants—the Ainu people. Most now live on the northernmost main island, Hokkaido. Although many Ainu have intermarried with other Japanese, a few still live in isolated villages where they follow their traditional way of life. The Ainu people have a long history of discrimination and forced assimilation in Japan. Ask students to discuss how a small ethnic minority can best preserve its culture and identity, particularly in a homogeneous nation like Japan. Interested students may want to investigate the current status of the Ainu people in Japan. **L2**

Picturing **History**

Answer: Both suits of armor provide padding and cover vital areas. Armor worn by samurai warriors was not made of metal but heavy quilting. The face is exposed and the horse is not covered.

Who?What?Where?When?

Kamikaze The *kamikaze,* or "divine wind," that saved Japan from Mongol defeat in 1281 never lost its importance for the Japanese. During World War II, Japanese suicide pilots who dived their planes into Allied aircraft carriers were known as *kamikaze* pilots.

Reading Check

Answer: The power of local aristocrats grew during this time. Japanese rulers could not contain the small group of powerful aristocratic families who were vying for control.

CURRICULUM CONNECTION

Government Lead students in a discussion about Japan's government. Ask the class to speculate about how limited trade, mountainous land, and an agrarian economy would have contributed to the lack of a central government in Japan. **L2**

Like knights, the samurai fought on horseback, clad in helmet and armor, although a samurai carried a sword and a bow and arrow rather than a lance and shield. Like knights, the samurai were supposed to live by a strict warrior code, known in Japan as **Bushido** ("the way of the warrior"). Above all, the samurai's code was based on loyalty to his lord.

The Kamakura Shogunate By the end of the twelfth century, rivalries among Japanese aristocratic families had led to almost constant civil war. Finally, a powerful noble named Minamoto Yoritomo defeated several rivals and set up his power near the modern city of Tokyo.

To strengthen the state, he created a more centralized government under a powerful military leader known as the **shogun** (general). In this new system—called the shogunate—the emperor remained ruler in name only, and the shogun exercised the actual power. The Kamakura shogunate, founded by Yoritomo, lasted from 1192 to 1333.

At first the system worked well. The Japanese were fortunate that it did, because the government soon faced its most serious challenge yet from the Mongols. In 1281, Kublai Khan sent nearly 150,000 warriors to invade Japan. Fortunately for the Japanese, most of the Mongol ships were destroyed by a typhoon (violent storm) before the forces could land. Japan would not again face a foreign invader until American troops landed in the summer of 1945. Fighting the Mongols put a heavy strain on the political system. In 1333, the Kamakura shogunate was overthrown by a group of powerful families led by the Ashikaga family.

The power of the local aristocrats grew during the fourteenth and fifteenth centuries. Heads of noble families, now called **daimyo** (DY•mee•OH), "great names," controlled vast landed estates that owed no taxes to the government. By 1500, Japan was close to chaos. A disastrous civil war, which lasted from 1467 to 1477, led to the virtual destruction of the capital city of Kyoto. Armies passed back and forth through the city, burning temples and palaces. Central authority disappeared.

Reading Check **Describing** What difficulties did Japanese rulers encounter in establishing a strong central government?

Life and Culture in Early Japan

Early Japan was mostly a farming society. Its people took advantage of the limited amount of farmland and abundant rainfall to grow wet rice (rice grown in flooded fields). As we have seen, noble families were able to maintain control over most of the land.

Trade and manufacturing began to develop during the Kamakura period. Markets appeared in the larger towns, and industries such as paper, iron casting, and porcelain emerged. Trade between regions also grew. Foreign trade, mainly with Korea and China, began during the eleventh century. Japan shipped raw materials, paintings, swords, and other manufactured items in return for silk, porcelain, books, and copper coins.

Early Japanese people worshiped spirits, called *kami,* whom the Japanese believed resided in trees, rivers, streams, and mountains. The Japanese also believed that the spirits of their ancestors were present in the air around them. In Japan, these beliefs evolved into a kind of state religion called **Shinto** ("the Sacred Way" or "the Way of the Gods"), which is still practiced today.

Picturing **History**

The suit of armor (above) was worn by samurai warriors, such as the warrior in the painting at left. Compare this type of armor to the armor shown on the chapter time line (page 87). What similarities and differences do you see?

INTERDISCIPLINARY CONNECTIONS ACTIVITY

Government Ask students to write the text of a fictional debate that takes place between two leaders in Japan. One leader wants to maintain the independence and power of local nobles. The other wants a strong central government. Tell students to emphasize logic and reason as they write statements for the two fictitious leaders. This debate has some similarity to questions of states' rights versus federal government jurisdiction in the United States. Ask students to list the advantages of local control and rule and the advantages of a powerful central government. Also have students list the disadvantages of each. After students have completed their assignment, hold a class debate on the issue. **L3**

In Japanese art and architecture, landscape serves as an important means of expression. The landscape surrounding the fourteenth-century Golden Pavilion in Kyoto displays a harmony of garden, water, and architecture that makes it one of the treasures of the world.

Reading Check **Identifying** What industries emerged in Japan during the Kamakura period?

India after the Guptas

In the early eighth century, Islam became popular in the northwestern corner of the Indian subcontinent. The new religion had a major impact on Indian civilization. This impact is still evident today in the division of the Indian subcontinent into mostly Hindu India and the two Islamic states of Bangladesh and Pakistan.

One reason for Islam's success in South Asia is that it arrived at a time when India was in a state of great political disunity. The Gupta Empire had collapsed, and no central authority had replaced it. India was divided into about seventy states, which fought each other constantly.

When the Arab armies reached India in the early eighth century, they did little more than move into the frontier regions. At the end of the tenth century, however, a new phase of Islamic expansion took place when rebellious Turkish slaves founded a new Islamic state known as Ghazni, located in present-day Afghanistan.

When the founder of the new state died in 997, his son, Mahmud of Ghazni, succeeded him. Mahmud, an ambitious man, began to attack neighboring Hindu kingdoms to the southeast. Before his death in 1030, he was able to extend his rule throughout the upper Indus Valley and as far south as the Indian Ocean.

Resistance against the advances of Mahmud and his successors into northern India was led by the **Rajputs,** who were Hindu warriors. They fought bravely, but their military tactics, based on infantry supported by elephants, were no match for the cavalry of the invaders. Mahmud's successors continued their advances. By 1200, Muslim power had reached over the entire plain of northern India, creating a new Muslim state known as the Sultanate of Delhi. In the fourteenth century, this state extended its power into the Deccan Plateau.

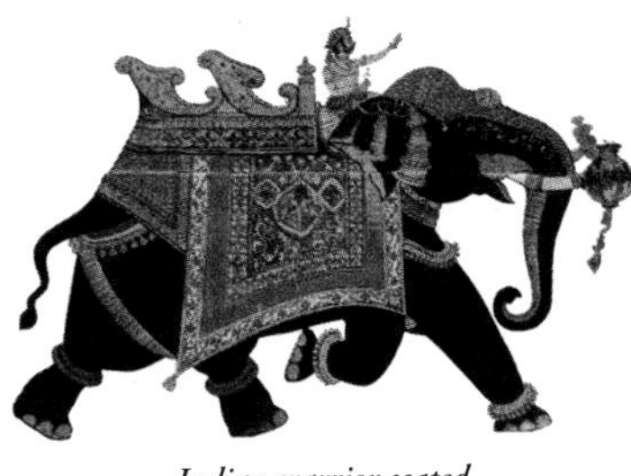

Indian warrior seated on his elephant

The Impact of Timur Lenk During the latter half of the fourteenth century, the Sultanate of Delhi began to decline. Near the end of the century, a new military force crossed the Indus River from the northwest, raided the capital of Delhi, and then withdrew. As many as 100,000 Hindu prisoners were massacred before the gates of the city. It was India's first meeting with **Timur Lenk** (Tamerlane).

Timur Lenk was the ruler of a Mongol state based in Samarkand, to the north of the Pamir Mountains. Born sometime during the 1330s in Samarkand, Timur Lenk seized power in 1369 and immediately launched a program of conquest. During the 1380s, he placed the entire region east of the Caspian Sea under his authority and then occupied Mesopotamia. After his brief foray into northern India, he turned to the west. He died in 1405 in the midst of a military campaign.

The death of Timur Lenk removed a menace from the various states of the Indian subcontinent, but the calm did not last long. By the early sixteenth century, two new challenges had appeared from beyond the horizon. One came from the north in the form of the Moguls, a newly emerging nomadic power. The other came from Europe, from Portuguese traders arriving by sea in search of gold and spices.

Islam and Indian Society The Muslim rulers in India viewed themselves as foreign conquerors. As a result, they maintained a strict separation between the Muslim ruling class and the mass of the Hindu population.

Many Muslim rulers in India were tolerant of other faiths. They used peaceful means, if any, to encourage people to convert to Islam. Most Muslim rulers realized that there were simply too many Hindus to convert them all. They accepted the need to tolerate what to them was an alien religion. Nevertheless, Muslim rulers did impose many Islamic customs on Hindu society. Overall, the relationship between Muslim and Hindu was that of conqueror and conquered, a relationship marked

Reading Check

Answer: During the Kamakura period, industries such as paper, iron casting, and porcelain emerged.

3 ASSESS

Assign Section 3 Assessment as homework or as an in-class activity.

Have students use **Interactive Tutor Self-Assessment CD-ROM.**

Section Quiz 3–3

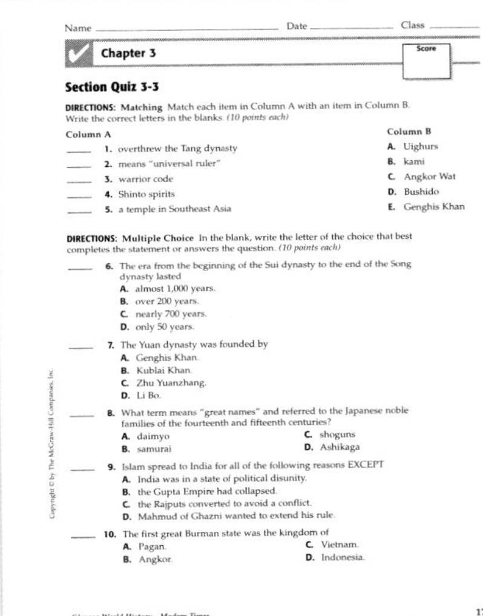

Name ______ Date ______ Class ______

Chapter 3 Score

Section Quiz 3-3

DIRECTIONS: Matching Match each item in Column A with an item in Column B. Write the correct letters in the blanks. *(10 points each)*

Column A	Column B
____ 1. overthrew the Tang dynasty	A. Uighurs
____ 2. means "universal ruler"	B. kami
____ 3. warrior code	C. Angkor Wat
____ 4. Shinto spirits	D. Bushido
____ 5. a temple in Southeast Asia	E. Genghis Khan

DIRECTIONS: Multiple Choice In the blank, write the letter of the choice that best completes the statement or answers the question. *(10 points each)*

____ 6. The era from the beginning of the Sui dynasty to the end of the Song dynasty lasted
A. almost 1,000 years.
B. over 200 years.
C. nearly 700 years.
D. only 50 years.

____ 7. The Yuan dynasty was founded by
A. Genghis Khan.
B. Kublai Khan.
C. Zhu Yuanzhang.
D. Li Bo.

____ 8. What term means "great names" and referred to the Japanese noble families of the fourteenth and fifteenth centuries?
A. daimyo
B. samurai
C. shoguns
D. Ashikaga

____ 9. Islam spread to India for all of the following reasons EXCEPT
A. India was in a state of political disunity.
B. the Gupta Empire had collapsed.
C. the Rajputs converted to avoid a conflict.
D. Mahmud of Ghazni wanted to extend his rule.

____ 10. The first great Burman state was the kingdom of
A. Pagan.
B. Angkor.
C. Vietnam.
D. Indonesia.

Glencoe World History—Modern Times 17

Writing Activity

After students have read this section, have them write an essay in which they summarize the major political, economic, and cultural developments of early Japanese civilizations. **L1**

CRITICAL THINKING ACTIVITY

Analyzing Information Ask students to consider why wars are fought in the name of religion. Assign them to investigate religious conflicts other than those between Islam and Hinduism. Examples would be conflicts between Protestants and Catholics in Europe at the time of the Reformation or in Northern Ireland today. In other cases, people have been willing to leave their homes to achieve religious freedom. This was the case when the Puritans colonized Massachusetts. Do students believe India would be a more peaceful land today if there had been greater religious toleration in the past? Why have people throughout history fought or emigrated in the name of religious freedom? **L2**

Geography Skills

Answer:

1. It is located north of the Equator.

Reading Check

Answer: The Muslim ruling class viewed themselves as foreign conquerors and kept themselves separate from the mass of the Hindu population. Most Muslim rulers were tolerant of the Hindu faith but did impose many Islamic customs on Hindu society.

Reading Essentials and Study Guide 3–3

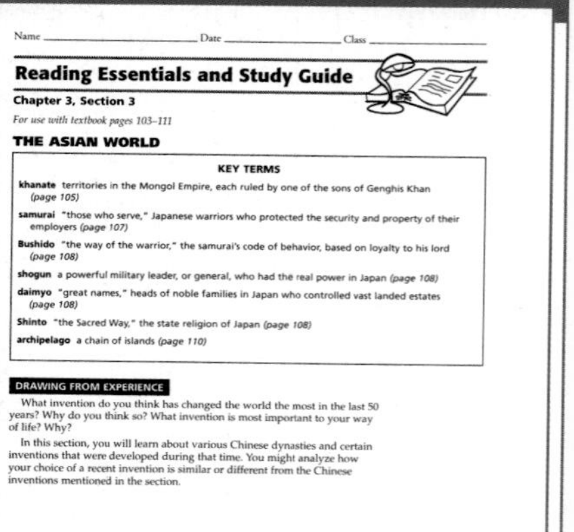

Name ________ Date ________ Class ________

Reading Essentials and Study Guide

Chapter 3, Section 3

For use with textbook pages 103–111

THE ASIAN WORLD

KEY TERMS

khanate territories in the Mongol Empire, each ruled by one of the sons of Genghis Khan *(page 105)*

samurai "those who serve," Japanese warriors who protected the security and property of their employers *(page 107)*

Bushido "the way of the warrior," the samurai's code of behavior, based on loyalty to his lord *(page 108)*

shogun a powerful military leader, or general, who had the real power in Japan *(page 108)*

daimyo "great names," heads of noble families in Japan who controlled vast landed estates *(page 108)*

Shinto "the Sacred Way," the state religion of Japan *(page 108)*

archipelago a chain of islands *(page 110)*

DRAWING FROM EXPERIENCE

What invention do you think has changed the world the most in the last 50 years? Why do you think so? What invention is most important to your way of life? Why?

In this section, you will learn about various Chinese dynasties and certain inventions that were developed during that time. You might analyze how your choice of a recent invention is similar or different from the Chinese inventions mentioned in the section.

CURRICULUM CONNECTION

Geography Using a wall map if possible, have students locate the water routes by which cultural elements from India and China were transported to the countries of Southeast Asia. *(Bay of Bengal, South China Sea, Mekong River)* **L1**

by suspicion and dislike rather than friendship and understanding.

Reading Check **Evaluating** What was the relationship between the Muslims and Hindus in India?

Civilization in Southeast Asia

Between China and India lies the region that today is called Southeast Asia. It has two major parts. One is the mainland region, extending southward from the Chinese border down to the tip of the Malay Peninsula. The other is an extensive archipelago, or chain of islands, most of which is part of present-day Indonesia and the Philippines. Located between India and China—two highly advanced and densely populated regions of the world—Southeast Asia is a melting pot of peoples.

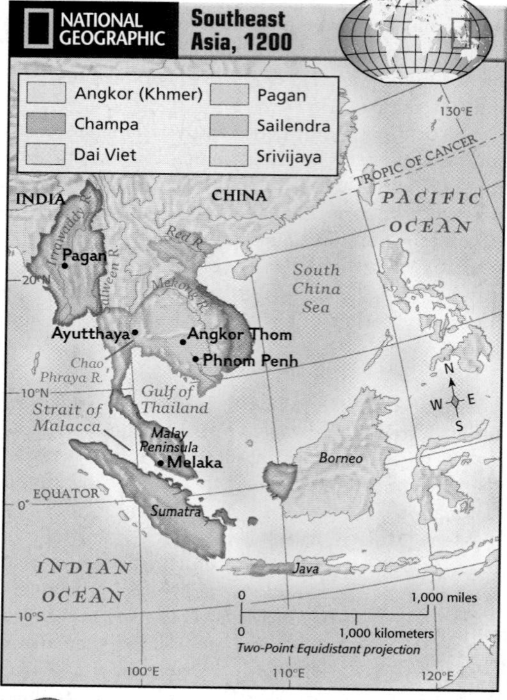

Geography Skills

Southeast Asia is a diverse area, largely due to the region's geographical barriers.

1. **Interpreting Maps** Is the mainland region of Southeast Asia located north or south of the Equator?

The Formation of States Between 500 and 1500, a number of organized states developed throughout Southeast Asia. When the peoples of the region began to form states, they used models from China and India. At the same time, they adapted these models to their own needs and created their own unique states.

The Chinese conquered Vietnam in 111 B.C., but the Vietnamese overthrew Chinese rule in the tenth century. Chinese influence remained, though. Vietnamese rulers followed the Chinese model of centralized government, calling themselves emperors and practicing Chinese court rituals. The new Vietnamese state, which called itself Dai Viet (Great Viet), also adopted state Confucianism.

In the ninth century, the kingdom of Angkor arose in the region that is present-day Cambodia. A powerful figure named Jayavarman united the Khmer (kuh•MEHR) people and established a capital at **Angkor Thom.** For several hundred years, Angkor—or the Khmer Empire—was the most powerful state in mainland Southeast Asia.

In 1432, the Thai from the north destroyed the Angkor capital. They set up their own capital at Ayutthaya (ah•YU•tuh•yuh) on the Chao Phraya (chau PRY•uh) River, where they remained as a major force for the next four hundred years.

The Thai were threatened from the west by the Burman peoples, who had formed their own society in the valleys of the Salween and Irrawaddy (IHR•uh•WAH•dee) Rivers. In the eleventh century, they founded the first great Burman state, the kingdom of Pagan. Like the Thai, they adopted Indian political institutions and culture.

In the **Malay Peninsula** and the Indonesian Archipelago, a different pattern emerged. For centuries, this area had been tied to the trade that passed from East Asia into the Indian Ocean. The area had never been united under a single state, however. The vast majority of the people of the region were of Malay background, but the peoples were divided into numerous separate communities.

Society and Culture At the top of the social ladder in most Southeast Asian societies were the hereditary aristocrats. They held both political power and economic wealth. Most aristocrats lived in the major cities. Angkor Thom, for example, was a city with royal palaces, parks, and numerous temples.

Beyond the major cities lived the rest of the population, which consisted of farmers, fishers, artisans, and merchants. In most Southeast Asian societies, the

EXTENDING THE CONTENT

Vietnamese Legend Kublai Khan, the Mongol leader of thirteenth-century China, sent an army to conquer Vietnam. The Mongols smashed the Vietnamese capital but were repulsed by a Vietnamese guerrilla counter-offensive. A second Mongol invasion followed that consisted of 500,000 soldiers. The Mongols were met by a Vietnamese force of 200,000 men led by Tran Hung Dao, who is today considered to be Vietnam's greatest national hero. According to a legend that reminds us of England's King Arthur story, a magical turtle arose from a lake and gave Tran an enchanted sword. He used this sword to again defeat the Mongols and then returned it to the turtle in the lake.

Angkor Wat, which is encircled by a three-mile (4.8-km) moat, is located in northern Cambodia at the site of the ruins of the old capital city of Angkor Thom.

majority of people were probably rice farmers who lived at a bare level of subsistence and paid heavy rents or taxes to a landlord or local ruler.

Chinese culture made an impact on Vietnam. In many other areas of Southeast Asia, Indian cultural influence prevailed. The most visible example of this influence was in architecture. Of all the existing structures at Angkor Thom, the temple of **Angkor Wat** is the most famous and most beautiful. It combines Indian architectural techniques with native inspiration in a structure of impressive grace. The construction of Angkor Wat, which took 40 years to complete, required an enormous quantity of stone—as much as it took to build Egypt's Great Pyramid.

Reading Check **Contrasting** How did the development of the Malay Peninsula and the Indonesian Archipelago differ from development elsewhere in Southeast Asia?

SECTION 3 ASSESSMENT

Checking for Understanding

Define khanate, samurai, Bushido, shogun, daimyo, Shinto, archipelago.

Identify Genghis Khan, Kublai Khan, Li Bo, Shotoku Taishi, Rajputs, Timur Lenk, Angkor Wat.

Locate Tibet, Mongolia, Beijing, Nara, Kyoto, Angkor Thom, Malay Peninsula.

Describe the golden age of literature and art in China.

List the religious and philosophical influences on the civilizations mentioned in this section.

Critical Thinking

6. **Explain** How did the samurai and shogun affect the government of early Japan?
7. **Organizing Information** Use a table like the one below to list the achievements of the Sui, Tang, Song, and Mongol dynasties.

Dynasty	Achievements
Sui	
Tang	
Song	
Mongol	

Analyzing Visuals

8. **Describe** what you see in the Song landscape drawing shown on page 106 of your text. How do you think the painting reflects the culture in which it was painted? What artistic, philosophical, or cultural ideals are expressed by the artist?

Writing About History

9. **Descriptive Writing** Imagine that you are a samurai living in Japan during the fourteenth century. Describe your role and your daily duties.

Who?What?Where?When?

Borobudur Another magnificent religious complex in Southeast Asia, Borobudur, is located on the island of Java. Built about 800 A.D., it is not only a temple but also a representation of Buddhist doctrine. As visitors climb its five terraces, they pass from sculptural depictions of the ordinary world to those suggesting the profound truths of Buddhist enlightenment.

Reading Check

Answer: They were divided into numerous separate communities, not united under a single state.

Enrich

Have students research the city of Angkor Thom and its magnificent temple, Angkor Wat. Then, ask students to compare Angkor Thom with major cities they have learned about in India or China. How were they similar? What were their differences? **L1**

Reteaching Activity

From the descriptions of each of the cultures mentioned in this section, ask students to find one sentence that provides an important fact or insight about the culture. **L1** ELL

4 CLOSE

Lead students in a discussion of the importance of the physical geography of Asia on the development of cultures in its history. **L2**

SECTION 3 ASSESSMENT

1. Key terms are in blue.
2. Genghis Khan *(p. 105);* Kublai Khan *(p. 106);* Li Bo *(p. 107);* Shotoku Taishi *(p. 107);* Timur Lenk *(p. 109)*
3. See chapter maps.
4. landscape painting flourished, printing invented, poetry popular
5. Confucianism, Buddhism, and Daoism influenced China. Shinto influenced Japan. Hinduism and Islam influenced India. Vietnam adopted state Confucianism.
6. Samurai were warriors who served the interests of the shogun. The power of the shoguns kept Japan from developing a strong centralized government.
7. Sui: unified China under the authority of the emperor; Tang: restored civil service exams, created a more stable economy, gunpowder invented; Song: capital of Huangzhou, landscape paintings, economic prosperity; Mongol: stability and prosperity
8. love of nature, balance between earth and sky, influence of Daoism
9. Answers will vary.

SPECIAL REPORT SUMMARY

Mongolians today view Genghis Khan as the father of their country.

■

Even as a young man, Genghis Khan was known for leadership and for vengeance.

■

Genghis Khan's troops were highly disciplined and highly skilled. In just five years and in three major campaigns, they were able to conquer China.

■

Later conquests took Genghis Khan and his forces through Northern India and into Europe.

TEACH

Points to Discuss

What is the significance of Mongol superiority on horseback? *(The Mongols were able to fight quickly from horseback, were avid riders, and were equipped to literally mow down their enemies with their fierce war-trained ponies. Students may also note that the horses provided sustenance to Genghis Khan and his troops during long, arduous treks.)* **Why did Genghis Khan give command to those who had already proven themselves in military battle?** *(Those who survived battles would be expected to be loyal to Genghis Khan, and their troops would also be loyal to their leader, Genghis Khan. Further, some leaders would have been killed in battle,*

LORD OF THE MONGOLS
GENGHIS KHAN

1

Samarkand, Bukhara, Urgench, Balkh, Merv, Nishapur, Herat, Ghazni: The glorious cities of central Asia toppled like dominoes before fierce horsemen who burst from the Mongolian steppe in the thirteenth century. According to one survivor of a Mongol raid, "They came, they sapped, they burnt, they slew, they plundered, and they departed." The leader of this ruthless horde was called Genghis Khan—"strong ruler." But was Genghis Khan only a merciless killer and looter? The answer, say modern historians, is yes—and no.

There is no question that the Mongols blazed a trail of destruction. Some historians think that Genghis Khan stifled development in parts of Asia for centuries. Other scholars point out that Genghis was simply a major player in one of the most war-torn centuries in history. While Crusaders attacked in the Holy Land, and dynasties fought one another in China, central Asia suffered a number of wars even before Genghis invaded.

Whatever opinions historians may hold, present-day Mongolians regard Genghis Khan as a national hero. After more than six decades of Soviet domination—during which Mongolia's own history was suppressed to destroy any trace of national pride—Mongolians have reclaimed Genghis Khan as the father of their country. In the capital, Ulaanbataar, the former Lenin Avenue is now Genghis Khan Avenue, and Genghis's face is stamped on the currency.

■

The boy who would grow up to be the great khan was born in the 1160s some 200 miles (321.8 km) northeast of Ulaanbataar near the Onon River. It is said that the baby, named Temujin ("blacksmith"), was born with a clot of blood in his hand—a sign of good fortune.

Teacher's Notes

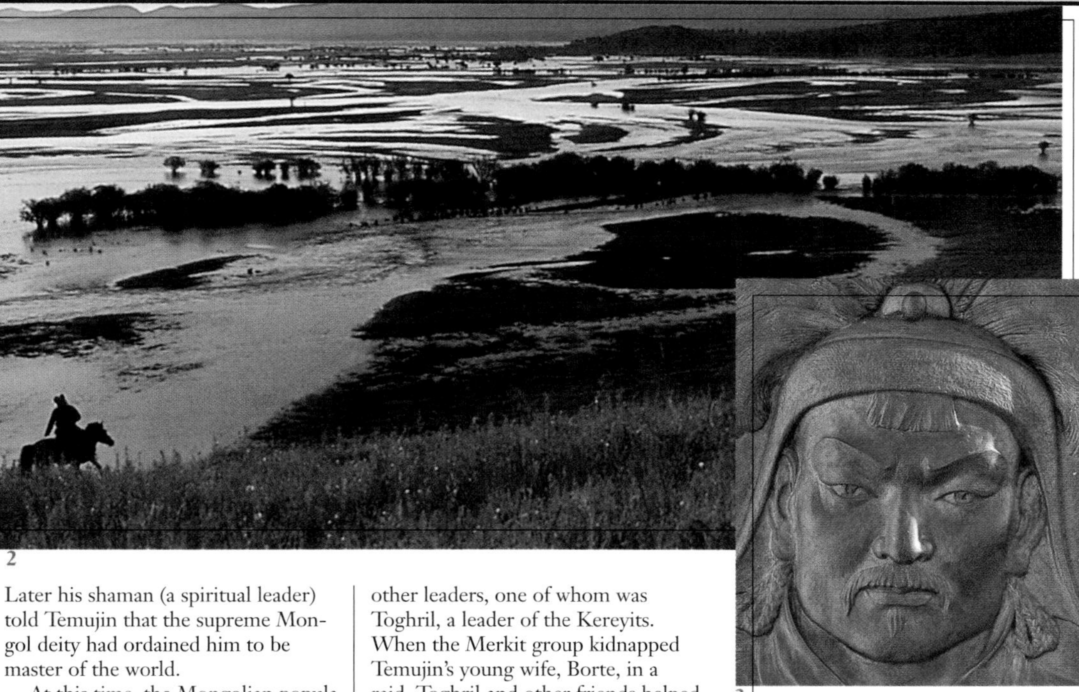

2

Later his shaman (a spiritual leader) told Temujin that the supreme Mongol deity had ordained him to be master of the world.

At this time, the Mongolian population included some 30 nomadic groups that had long vied with one another for power. When Temujin was nine, Tatars poisoned his father, a minor chieftain. To help the family survive, Temujin and his brothers caught fish and snared small animals called marmots. Like other Mongol children, Temujin grew up on horseback, probably learning to ride at age four or five.

In his youth Temujin began to demonstrate the leadership that would make him famous. He made allies with other leaders, one of whom was Toghril, a leader of the Kereyits. When the Merkit group kidnapped Temujin's young wife, Borte, in a raid, Toghril and other friends helped Temujin rescue her. Later, through conquest or bestowal of gifts, Temujin steadily built a confederation of groups. He did not include the Tatars, who had killed his father. When he defeated them he left only the smallest males alive and enslaved the women and children. This act of vengeance effectively erased the Tatars from the face of the earth. (One of the ironies of history is that Europeans for centuries used a variation of the name "Tartars" to refer to the Mongols.)

Eventually, some of Temujin's former friends began to oppose his growing power, but he crushed them. When he was about 40, the Mongols named him Genghis Khan.

Some historians suggest Genghis did not consciously set out to conquer the world. He acted because he needed to feed his people and supply them with horses, although he may at times have been out for revenge.

Whatever the Mongol leader's

4

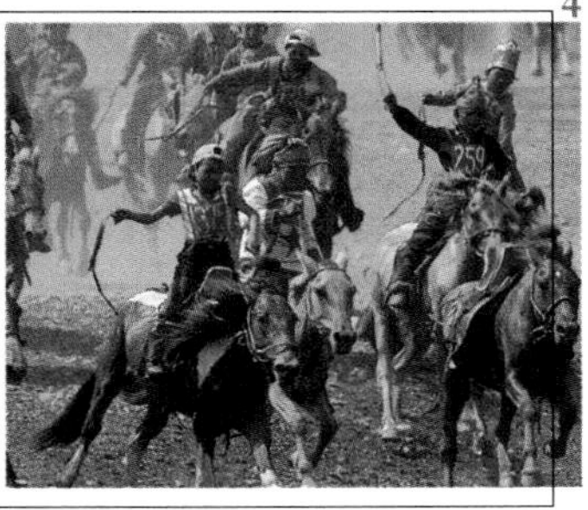

3

1 A Mongol cavalryman, lightly armored in leather, was much more agile than the knights of Europe in their heavy chain mail. He carried a small leather shield that he could raise to protect his face, and under a loose robe he wore a tightly woven silk tunic to blunt enemy arrows. Braced on disk-shaped stirrups he could maneuver easily during battle, firing arrows either forward or backward.

2 A lone horseman rides on the floodplain of the Onon River in northeastern Mongolia, where a boy named Temujin was born in the 1160s.

3 Bronze plaque of Genghis Khan.

4 Mongol youngsters, like these children racing at a summer festival, learn to ride by the time they are about five—just as their ancestors did eight centuries ago.

lessening the number of leaders fighting for power.) **Why did Genghis Khan return to Mongolia after each major campaign?** *(Students should recognize the need to return to one's homeland, rest, recruit new troops as needed, and most importantly shore up the government and make sure that all was in order before leaving on the next campaign.)* **What reasons might have led Genghis Khan to invade Europe?** *(Student answers will vary, but students should recognize the determination of Genghis to conquer new lands and to explore new areas.)* **Why would the forces of Genghis Khan have obliterated his burial site so that its location has been a mystery for centuries?** *(It is possible that Genghis Khan himself ordered this; it might be that his troops realized that the site could be plundered and the body desecrated by those who had been conquered by Genghis.)*

FUN FACTS

- In the summer of 2001, an archaeological team searching for the grave site of Genghis Khan reported that the site had finally been found 200 miles northeast of the Mongolian capital of Ulan Bator. The burial site is near the site where Genghis Khan is thought to have been born and may be near the site where he was proclaimed emperor of all Mongols in 1206.
- The Mongolian wild horse, the takhi, is better known to Westerners as the *Przewalski horse.* A Russian explorer, Nikolai Przhevalsky discovered these horses in 1870 and then introduced the Mongolian takhi to western Europe where it is now bred in zoos. A newborn takhi can stand upon its legs immediately and can run soon after birth.

CURRICULUM CONNECTION

Science The Gobi is known as a vast zone of desert, occupying about 30 percent of Mongolia. However, the Gobi also features semi-arid grasslands. The western part of the Gobi has high mountains, forests, and steppes. The Gobi is home to wild horses, whose ancestors were used by Genghis Khan. It is also home to snow leopards, mountain sheep, ibex, lynx, gazelles, the Gobi bear, and the khavtagi, a wild camel that is the ancestor of the bactrian camel. Summer temperatures in the Gobi often reach 104° F, and winter temperatures can drop as low as –40° F.

Critical Thinking

The Mongolian people are sometimes stereotyped as having a simplistic or unfriendly culture, as might fit the ancestors of Genghis Khan. However, living in a harsh desert fosters cooperation and hospitality, and Mongolians are known for these two characteristics. Ask students why stereotypes evolve, especially those about people who live far from the United States. Further, ask students why cooperation and hospitality are necessary for survival in harsh climates.

motivation, however, warfare was an old tradition among these nomads, and soon Genghis's army was on the move. According to modern researchers, his troops never numbered more than 110,000, but they were molded into a disciplined force. Genghis was a canny judge of men who had survived power struggles. To prevent other leaders from gaining too much influence, Genghis gave command only to those who had proven themselves in campaigns.

Genghis's army moved against two kingdoms in quick succession. His first campaign outside Mongolia was in 1209 against Xi Xia. Xi Xia was a kingdom in northern China that controlled oases along the Silk Road and exacted heavy taxes from Mongol caravans. To reach Ningxia, the capital (now the Chinese city of Yinchuan), Genghis's army had to cross the Gobi, a harsh desert that had discouraged invasions. Crossing was relatively easy for Mongol nomads, however, who could survive on mare's milk and blood drawn from a cut in a horse's hide. After a defeat by Genghis's forces, the emperor of Xi Xia opted for peace in 1210, offering tribute and giving Genghis one of his daughters to marry.

This pattern was repeated with the vastly richer kingdom east of Xi Xia, ruled by the Jin dynasty, which had controlled northern China for more than a century. With much of the 600,000-man Jin army bogged down in a war in the south, Genghis's 70,000 troops slaughtered the remnant force blocking their way into northern China. Chinese texts say disheartened Jin troops changed sides and swore allegiance to the invader. 5

When the Mongols surrounded the Jin capital of Zhongdu (present-day Beijing) in 1214, the emperor offered gold, silver, and other tribute—including one of his daughters—if Genghis would withdraw his troops.

Returning to Mongolia as he would after each campaign, Genghis began to build a capital at Karakorum. Not one to waste talented artisans, he marched some 30,000 of them back from Xi Xia to put them to work raising his citadel. Genghis also borrowed from other cultures to develop Mongol society. He used a scholar in China to advise him on building a government and recruited Uighurs, his advanced Turkic neighbors, as accountants and scribes. Soon a school was turning out Mongol tax collectors and record keepers.

In 1218, Genghis sent one of his trusted generals, Jebe, to preemp[t] a possible attack by the prince [of] Kara-Khitai, at Mongolia's western border. The mostly Muslim people rejoiced to be freed of their ruler, wh[o] had forbidden them to practice their religion an[d] had crucified a religious leader. Genghis took Kara-Khitai into his protection.

With success in that quarter, Genghis's territory now touched that of the wealthy Khwarizm Empire, ruled by Shah Muhammad in Samarkand. Genghis attempted to establish friendly trade relations with the shah, but the Khwarizm would not cooperate. A caravan of 450 Mongol merchants were murdered by the governor of one of Khwarizm's outlying regions. When Genghis sent an ambassador to the shah to demand the governor be handed over, the sha[h] had the ambassador killed and his head sent back to Genghis. Thus, Genghis aimed to punish his enemies although the possibility of enormous plunder was surely an added incentive for his campaign. Although the shah's army was much larger than that of th[e] Mongols, he proved a weak adversary. When Genghis appeared outside Samarkand, the shah fled. City nobles opened the gates and begged for mercy, but some of the shah's soldiers refused to surrender. About a thousand took refuge in the mosque hoping for Allah's protection, but flaming Mongol arrows rained on the building. When archaeologists excavated the site centuries later, they found burned bones.

More destruction was to come. In Bukhara, Genghis rode his horse into the courtyard of the Friday Mosque, ordered the nobles to bring him their riches, then turned his troops loose to

6

Teacher's Notes

Who?What?Where?When?

Karakorum The Mongolian capital of Karakorum was founded in 1220 in the Orkhon Valley, at the crossroads of the Silk Road. The city was visited by a papal mission led by Giovanni Carpini in 1267. Karakorum still has ruins of the first Buddhist monastery built in Mongolia, which was built in 1586, more than three hundred years after Kublai Khan had moved his capital to Beijing in 1267. The monastery was surrounded by majestic walls, approximately 400 meters long, and the ruins are still visible. The ruins of Karakorum were found in 1889 by a Russian explorer, N. M. Yadrinstev.

7

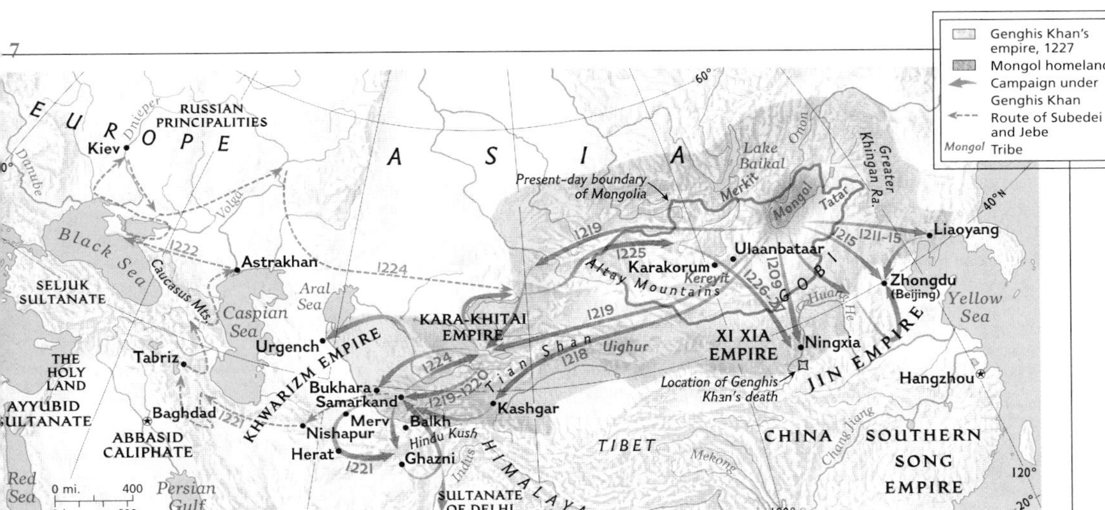

pillage, rape, and burn the city to the ground. Next came the Silk Road cities of Urgench and Merv. By one account, a Muslim holy man and his helpers spent 13 days in Merv counting corpses—tallying 1.3 million in all—"taking into account only those that were plain to see."

Although Muslim accounts of Mongol butchery also report enormous numbers, historians doubt these cities had such large populations. Some cities might have been decimated to frighten others.

While Genghis pursued Muhammad's son Jalal, who had escaped, he sent his generals Jebe and Subedai after the shah. The pair chased Muhammad to the Caspian Sea, where the exhausted shah died. Having now entered new territory, the two generals took 20,000 troops on a reconnaissance of Europe. Living off the land over the next three years and vanquishing every opposing army, they rode 8,000 miles (12,872 km), circling the Caspian in one of the greatest cavalry exploits of all time.

Upon rejoining Genghis in the central Asian steppe, the warriors headed for home. Genghis had a last score to settle. Just before the campaign against the Khwarizm Empire, the Xi Xia had insulted him and they had since been trying to revolt. In 1226 he decided it was time to teach them a lesson. As fate would have it, the lesson would be taught by someone else. One account says that Genghis had an accident and fell when his horse shied, another that he was ill, perhaps with typhus. In any case, the great khan delivered his final orders from his deathbed: the extermination of the Xi Xia people. His army is said to have killed "mothers and fathers down to the offspring of their offspring." Finally, in August 1227, Genghis Khan died. His body is supposed to be buried near a mountain called Burkhan Khaldun. It is said that a thousand horsemen trampled the site so the grave could not be found. Its location is still a mystery.

5 **Many Mongol cavalrymen wore elaborately designed helmets inlaid with silver.**

6 **One of the Mongols' great advantages in warfare was the mobility of its armies. To help sustain the army, the Mongols traveled with their *gers*, or felt tent homes, their families, and thousands of animals. The large *ger* in the center is the khan's, which functioned as his portable court.**

7 **Between 1206 and his death in 1227, Genghis Khan unified Mongolia and conquered kingdoms across central Asia.**

INTERPRETING THE PAST

1. How did Genghis Khan's experiences in his youth prepare him for his later military and political success?

2. What made Mongol armies so much stronger than their enemies?

3. What region suffered the most at the hands of the Mongols? Why was this region so harshly ravaged?

INTERPRETING THE PAST

Answers:

1. Genghis learned to catch food, to ride and control horses, and how to forge political friendships and allies.
2. Mongol armies were trained to fight from horseback. They fired arrows forward and backward from their horses. They wore leather and their silk tunics were designed to blunt enemy arrows.
3. The Khwarizm Empire was ravaged because Shah Muhammad refused to establish friendly trade relations with Genghis Khan; the governor of one of the provinces had a caravan of Mongol trade merchants murdered, and an ambassador sent by Genghis Khan to meet the shah was murdered.

1 FOCUS

Section Overview

This section describes the key events in the history of early Europe and the Byzantine Empire.

BELLRINGER
Skillbuilder Activity

Project transparency and have students answer questions.

Available as a blackline master.

Daily Focus Skills Transparency 3–4

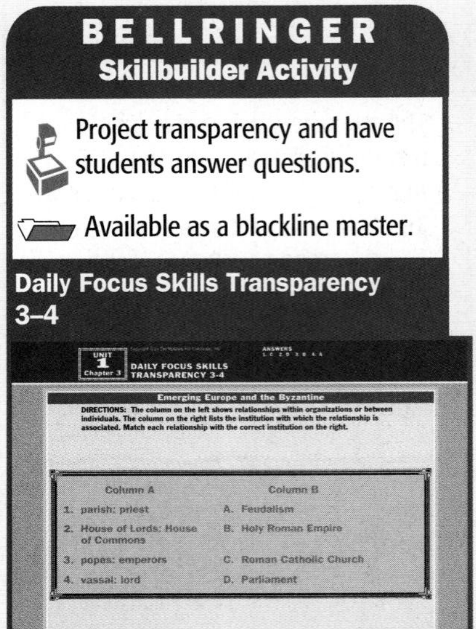
UNIT 1 Chapter 3 DAILY FOCUS SKILLS TRANSPARENCY 3-4

ANSWERS 1. C 2. D 3. B 4. A

Emerging Europe and the Byzantine

DIRECTIONS: The column on the left shows relationships within organizations or between individuals. The column on the right lists the institution with which the relationship is associated. Match each relationship with the correct institution on the right.

Column A	Column B
1. parish: priest	A. Feudalism
2. House of Lords: House of Commons	B. Holy Roman Empire
3. popes: emperors	C. Roman Catholic Church
4. vassal: lord	D. Parliament

Guide to Reading

Answers to Graphic: Feudalism: local, voluntary relationship based on feudal contract, many people responsible for keeping order; Empires: large political unit, control usually obtained through military conquest, control is usually centralized

Preteaching Vocabulary: Discuss *common law.* Ask students if they think we have common law in the United States. **L1**

SECTION 4 Emerging Europe and the Byzantine Empire

Guide to Reading

Main Ideas
- The new European civilization was formed by the Germanic peoples, the legacy of the Romans, and the Church.
- While European monarchs began to build strong states, Byzantine rulers created an empire in the East.

Key Terms
pope, monk, feudalism, vassal, fief, common law, Magna Carta, Crusades

People to Identify
Clovis, Charlemagne, William of Normandy, Justinian, Pope Urban II

Places to Locate
England, Runnymeade, Holy Roman Empire, Kiev, Jerusalem

Preview Questions
1. What led to the development of feudalism?
2. What was the impact of the Crusades?

Reading Strategy
Contrasting Information Use a table like the one below to list the differences between the systems of feudalism and empires.

Feudalism	Empires

Preview of Events

500 — 650 — 800 — 950 — 1100 — 1250

- **c. 510** Clovis establishes Frankish kingdom
- **529** Justinian codifies Roman law
- **800** Charlemagne crowned Roman emperor
- **1066** Battle of Hastings fought
- **1215** Magna Carta is signed

A medieval lord and his vassals

Voices from the Past

In 1020, Bishop Fulbert of Chartres wrote about the mutual obligations between lord and vassals:

❝[The vassal] who swears loyalty to his lord ought always to have these six things in memory: what is harmless, safe, honorable, useful, easy, practicable. *Harmless*, that is to say, that he should not injure his lord in his body; *safe*, that he should not injure him by betraying his secrets; *honorable*, that he should not injure him in his justice; *useful*, that he should not injure him in his possessions; *easy* and *practicable*, that that good which his lord is able to do easily he make not difficult, nor that which is practicable he make not impossible to him.❞

—***Readings in European History,*** **James Harvey Robinson, 1934**

A system of lords and vassals spread over Europe after the collapse of the Carolingian Empire.

The New Germanic Kingdoms

A new European civilization came into being in western Europe after the collapse of the Western Roman Empire. This new civilization was formed by the coming together of three major elements: the Germanic peoples who moved in and settled the Western Roman Empire, the legacy of the Romans, and the Christian church. By 800, this new European civilization was taking shape. Increasingly, Europe would become the center of what we call Western civilization.

SECTION RESOURCES

Reproducible Masters
- Reproducible Lesson Plan 3–4
- Daily Lecture and Discussion Notes 3–4
- Guided Reading Activity 3–4
- Section Quiz 3–4
- Reading Essentials and Study Guide 3–4

Transparencies
- Daily Focus Skills Transparency 3–4

Multimedia
- Interactive Tutor Self-Assessment CD-ROM
- ExamView® Pro Testmaker CD-ROM
- Presentation Plus! CD-ROM

European civilization emerged and developed during a period called the Middle Ages or the medieval period. It lasted from about 500 to 1500. To historians who first used the title, the Middle Ages was a middle period between the ancient world and the modern world.

By 500, the Western Roman Empire had been replaced by a number of states ruled by German kings. Only one of the German states on the European continent proved long lasting—the kingdom of the Franks. The Frankish kingdom was established by **Clovis,** a strong military leader who around 500 became the first Germanic ruler to convert to Christianity. By 510, Clovis had established a powerful Frankish kingdom that stretched from the Pyrenees in the southwest to German lands in the east (modern-day France and western Germany).

Reading Check **Identifying** What is the name of the period during which European civilization developed?

The Role of the Church

By the end of the fourth century, Christianity had become the supreme religion of the Roman Empire. As the official Roman state fell apart, the Christian church played an increasingly important role in the growth of the new European civilization.

By the fourth century, the Christian church had developed a system of organization. Local Christian communities called parishes were led by priests. A group of parishes was headed by a bishop, whose area of authority was known as a bishopric, or diocese.

Over time, one bishop—the bishop of Rome—began to claim that he was the leader of what was now called the Roman Catholic Church. Later bishops of Rome came to be known as **popes** (from the Latin word *papa,* "father") of the Catholic Church.

The Catholic Church developed a body of doctrine. Especially important was the church council, a meeting of representatives from the entire Christian community. Church councils defined church teachings.

Also important to the early Christian church was the role of monks. A **monk** is a man who pursues a life of total dedication to God. The practice of living the life of a monk is known as monasticism. In the sixth century, Saint Benedict founded a community of monks for which he wrote a set of rules. The Benedictine rule came to be used by other monastic groups. Monks were the social workers of their communities, providing schools for the young, hospitals for the sick, and hospitality for travelers. They became the new heroes of Christian civilization.

Reading Check **Describing** How was the Christian church organized?

Charlemagne and the Carolingians

In 768, a new ruler came to the throne of the Frankish kingdom. This new king was the dynamic and powerful ruler Charles the Great, or **Charlemagne.**

A medieval depiction of the crowning of Charlemagne

CRITICAL THINKING ACTIVITY

Drawing Conclusions Discuss with students why religious and political leaders often cooperate with each other. This cooperation can be seen in the conversion of Clovis to Christianity and the support he then received from the Church. Another example was the crowning of Charlemagne by the pope. In this exchange, the Church gained the support of the strongest king in western Europe and Charlemagne gained the official sanction of the leader of the prevalent religion for his rule. Ask students to identify other examples of religious and political cooperation. What value for society do students see in this cooperation? What are the dangers or disadvantages of close ties between religious and political leaders? L2

2 TEACH

Reading Check

Answer: the Middle Ages

Enrich

As a result of the collapse of the Western Roman Empire, new political, economic, and social systems evolved to create a new civilization in western Europe. After they have read this section, have students write an essay in which they compare medieval Europe with previous civilizations that they have studied. L2

Reading Check

Answer: Local Christian communities, called parishes, were led by priests. A group of parishes was headed by a bishop. Over time, popes became leaders over the whole Roman Catholic Church.

Writing Activity

Tell students that Clovis was the first Germanic ruler to convert to Christianity. Ask students to write several paragraphs about how the history of western Europe and the Christian religion might have been different if he had not converted. L2

Critical Thinking

In this section, students will read about Charlemagne. Have students use outside resources to research this leader. Then have students compare and contrast Charlemagne to other emperors they studied in earlier chapters. How did Charlemagne's military successes compare to those of the Arabs or the Mongols? L2

Reading Check

Answer: It symbolized the coming together of Roman, Christian, and Germanic elements; a new civilization had emerged.

Daily Lecture and Discussion Notes 3–4

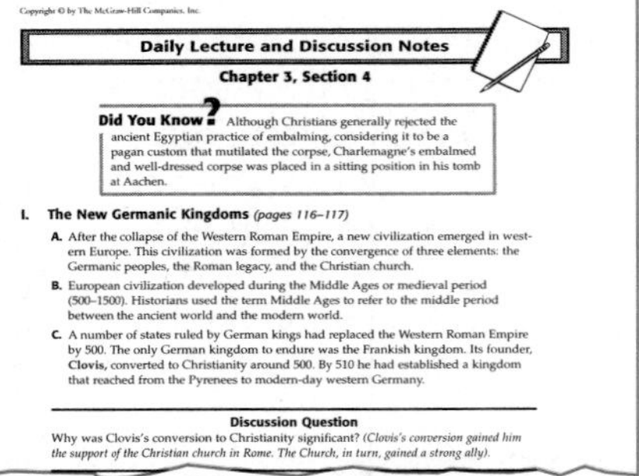

Daily Lecture and Discussion Notes

Chapter 3, Section 4

Did You Know? Although Christians generally rejected the ancient Egyptian practice of embalming, considering it to be a pagan custom that mutilated the corpse, Charlemagne's embalmed and well-dressed corpse was placed in a sitting position in his tomb at Aachen.

I. **The New Germanic Kingdoms** *(pages 116–117)*

A. After the collapse of the Western Roman Empire, a new civilization emerged in western Europe. This civilization was formed by the convergence of three elements: the Germanic peoples, the Roman legacy, and the Christian church.

B. European civilization developed during the Middle Ages or medieval period (500–1500). Historians used the term Middle Ages to refer to the middle period between the ancient world and the modern world.

C. A number of states ruled by German kings had replaced the Western Roman Empire by 500. The only German kingdom to endure was the Frankish kingdom. Its founder, **Clovis,** converted to Christianity around 500. By 510 he had established a kingdom that reached from the Pyrenees to modern-day western Germany.

Discussion Question

Why was Clovis's conversion to Christianity significant? *(Clovis's conversion gained him the support of the Christian church in Rome. The Church, in turn, gained a strong ally).*

Writing Activity

Ask students to write a poem of similar length to the one below that expresses their personal feelings toward war. Have them also write a paragraph comparing the messages and feelings evoked by the two poems. **L2**

"And well I like to hear the call of
'Help' and see the wounded fall,
Loudly for mercy praying,
And see the dead, both great and
small,
Pierced by sharp spearheads one
and all."

Who? What? Where? When?

Armor Early medieval armor, called chain mail, consisted of small metal rings linked closely together. With the development of more deadly weaponry—crossbows, maces, and axes—heavier protection was needed. By the 1300s, most knights wore plate armor.

Charlemagne was a determined and decisive man who was highly intelligent and curious. He was a strong statesman and a pious Christian. Although unable to read or write, he was a wise patron of learning.

During his lengthy rule from 768 to 814, Charlemagne greatly expanded the territory of the Frankish kingdom and created what came to be known as the Carolingian (KAR•uh•LIN•jee•uhn) Empire. At its height, Charlemagne's empire covered much of western and central Europe. Not until the time of Napoleon Bonaparte in the nineteenth century would an empire its size be seen again in Europe.

As Charlemagne's power grew, so too did his prestige as the most powerful Christian ruler. One monk even described Charlemagne's empire as the "kingdom of Europe." In 800, Charlemagne was crowned emperor of the Romans by the pope.

Charlemagne's coronation as Roman emperor symbolized the coming together of Roman, Christian, and Germanic elements. A Germanic king had been crowned emperor of the Romans by the pope, the spiritual leader of western Christendom. A new civilization had emerged.

Reading Check **Analyzing** What was the significance of Charlemagne's coronation as Roman emperor?

Feudalism

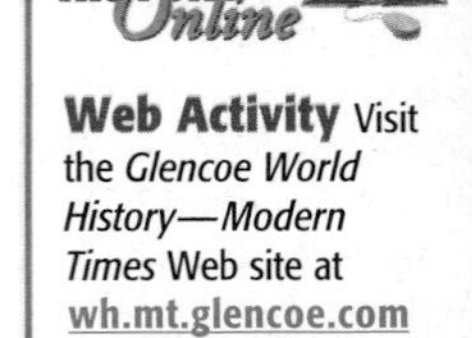

Web Activity Visit the *Glencoe World History—Modern Times* Web site at wh.mt.glencoe.com and click on **Chapter 3–Student Web Activity** to learn more about medieval Europe.

After the death of Charlemagne in 814, the Carolingian Empire that he had established began to fall apart. Rulers found it more and more difficult to defend their subjects from invaders such as the Vikings, a Germanic people from Scandinavia. Thus, people began to turn to local landed aristocrats, or nobles, to protect them. It became important to find a powerful lord who could offer protection in return for service. This led to a new political and social system called **feudalism.**

Knights and Vassals At the heart of feudalism was the idea of vassalage. In Germanic society, warriors swore an oath of loyalty to their leaders and fought for them. The leaders, in turn, took care of the warriors' needs. By the eighth century, a man who served a lord in a military capacity was known as a **vassal.**

In the eighth century, warriors on horseback were armored in coats of mail (armor made of metal links

THE WAY IT WAS

FOCUS ON EVERYDAY LIFE

The Castles of the Aristocrats

The growth of the European nobility in the High Middle Ages (1000 to 1300) was made visible by a growing number of castles scattered across the landscape. Castles varied considerably but possessed two common features: they were permanent residences for the noble family, its retainers, and servants, and they were defensible fortifications.

The earliest castles were made of wood. However, by the eleventh century, castles of stone were being built. At first, the basic castle plan had two parts. The *motte* was a man-made or natural steep-sided hill. The *bailey* was an open space next to the motte. Both motte and bailey were encircled by large stone walls. The *keep*, the central building of the castle, was built on the motte.

The keep was a large building with a number of stories constructed of thick stone walls. On the ground floor were the kitchens and stables. The basement housed storerooms for equipment and foodstuffs. Above the ground floor was the great hall. This very large room served a number of purposes.

Bodiam Castle, England

INTERDISCIPLINARY CONNECTIONS ACTIVITY

Music The best-known music to come down to us from the Middle Ages is the Gregorian chant. A Gregorian chant consists of a single melodic line that is sung in unison without a set rhythm. The timelessness of this music was demonstrated in 1994 when a recording of Church hymns by the Benedictine monks of Santo Domingo de Silos became a best seller. Ask interested students to bring in recordings of Gregorian chants. Students might, in particular, look into the discography of Hildegard of Bingen (1098–1179), a German nun who wrote beautiful chants that have become quite popular in recent years. Have students explain the history, form, and rhythm of Gregorian chants. **L2**

or plates). They wielded long lances that enabled them to act as battering rams. For almost five hundred years, warfare in Europe was dominated by heavily armored cavalry, or knights, as they came to be called. The knights had great social prestige and formed the backbone of the European nobility.

It was expensive to have a horse, armor, and weapons. With the breakdown of royal governments, the more powerful nobles took control of large areas of land. When these lords wanted men to fight for them, they granted each vassal a piece of land that supported the vassal and his family. Land was the most important gift a lord could give to a vassal.

The Feudal Contract By the ninth century, the grant of land made to a vassal had become known as a fief (FEEF). Vassals who held fiefs came to hold political authority within them. As the Carolingian world fell apart, the number of separate powerful lords and vassals increased. Instead of a single government, many different people were now responsible for keeping order.

Feudalism came to be characterized by a set of unwritten rules—known as the feudal contract—that determined the relationship between a lord and his vassal. The major obligation of a vassal to his lord was to perform military service, usually about 40 days a year.

Reading Check **Describing** What social and political conditions led to the establishment of feudalism?

The Growth of European Kingdoms

TURNING POINT **When King John of England was forced to put his seal on the Magna Carta in 1215, John recognized the rights of his nobles. This act affirmed that English monarchs had to obey the law of the land.**

The feudal system put power into the hands of many different lords. Gradually, however, kings began to extend their own powers. Their actions laid the foundations for the European kingdoms that have dominated Europe ever since. One of these kingdoms—**England**—created political institutions that later influenced the formation of the democratic political system of the United States.

England in the High Middle Ages On October 14, 1066, an army of heavily armed knights under **William of Normandy** landed on the coast of England and defeated King Harold and his soldiers at the **Battle of Hastings.** William was then crowned

THE WAY IT WAS

Answers:

1. The keep provided a residence for the noble family, retainers, and servants; the moat, walls, gatehouse, and towers provided for defense.
2. Growing wealth made it possible for them to buy luxury goods such as jewelry and exotic spices, as well as to build elaborate castles with rooms that were well furnished and elaborately decorated.
3. Yes, several countries in Europe and elsewhere still have nobility. Probably the best-known example is the United Kingdom.

Here, the lord of the castle held court and received visitors. Here, too, the inhabitants of the castle ate and even slept. Smaller rooms might open off the great hall, including bedrooms with huge curtained beds with straw mattresses, latrines, and possibly a chapel.

The growing wealth of the High Middle Ages made it possible for European nobles to improve their standard of living. Nobles sought to buy more luxury goods, such as jewelry, better clothes, and exotic spices. They also built more elaborate castles with thicker walls and more buildings and towers. Rooms became better furnished and more elaborately decorated.

Medieval Castle

The basic architecture of a medieval castle

CONNECTING TO THE PAST

1. **Explaining** What architectural and design features supported the two basic functions of castles?
2. **Describing** What was the lifestyle of the European nobility in the High Middle Ages?
3. **Writing about History** Does a nobility exist today? Where?

119

Reading Check

Answer: The threat of invasion by peoples such as the Vikings created a need for protection. People turned to their local landed aristocrats, who had land to offer warriors, who in turn would protect the lord's subjects.

TURNING POINT

Unlike the United States, the United Kingdom has no single written constitution. Instead, it is governed according to a series of laws and charters. The oldest of them is the Magna Carta. Ask students how the Magna Carta changed the balance of power in government. *(placed clear limits on royal power and bound the king to law)* **L1**

COOPERATIVE LEARNING ACTIVITY

Building Castles Have the class work in small groups to create plans for a medieval castle like those described in the text. Students may wish to refer to David Macaulay's book *Castle* and the videocassette that accompanies it. Tasks may be divided in several ways: researching medieval architecture, organizing data, writing plans, and illustrating the finished design by blueprint and sketch on poster board. Special attention should be paid to the outer wall, the turrets, surrounding fields, the drawbridge, the keep and well, the chapel, and the great hall. Conclude the activity with a class presentation. **L1** ELL

For grading this activity, refer to the ***Performance Assessment Activities*** booklet.

Geography Skills

Answers:

1. Magna Carta signed; it strengthened the idea that a monarch's power was limited, not absolute
2. Small to large might be Wales, Venetian Territories, Papal States, Navarre, Prussia, Ireland, Aragon, Denmark, Scotland, Sicily, Leon, Castille, Poland, Norway, France, Hungary, England, Sweden, Byzantine, Holy Roman Empire, Kievan Rus.

Guided Reading Activity 3–4

Name ______ Date ______ Class ______

Guided Reading Activity 3-4

Emerging Europe and the Byzantine Empire

DIRECTIONS: Fill in the blanks below as you read Section 4.

I. European civilization emerged during a period called the ______.
  A. By 500, the Western Roman Empire had been replace by states ruled by ______ kings.
  B. The Catholic Church developed a body of ______, defined by church ______ meetings held by representatives of the Christian community.
  C. In 768, ______ came to the throne of the Frankish kingdom, and in 800 he was crowned ______ of the Romans.
II. When the Carolingian Empire fell apart, a new political and social system called ______ was established.
  A. A man who served a lord in a military capacity was known as a ______.
  B. A set of unwritten rules, known as the ______, determined the relationship between a lord and his vassal.
III. The power of the British monarch was greatly enlarged during the reign of

CURRICULUM CONNECTION

Language Arts For years after the Norman Conquest, two languages were spoken in England—Norman French by the upper classes and Anglo-Saxon English by the lower classes. This double heritage is preserved in the English language today. For example, the words for animals in the field (in the Middle Ages, tended by the lower classes) are Anglo-Saxon: *ox, pig, sheep.* The words for cooked meat (served to the upper classes) are derived from French: *beef, pork, mutton.* Ask students to research other examples of the influence of Norman French on English. Suggest that they look at vocabulary, pronunciation, and spelling. Have them create posters, charts, or transparencies illustrating their findings to be used in a class presentation. **L2**

Geography Skills

Strong monarchies developed in France and England, while Germany and Italy consisted of independent states.

1. **Interpreting Maps** Locate Runnymeade. What event occurred there and why was it significant?
2. **Applying Geography Skills** Create a bar graph comparing the physical sizes of the kingdoms shown on this map.

king of England. He began combining Anglo-Saxon and Norman institutions to create a new England.

The power of the English monarchy was greatly enlarged under Henry II, who reigned from 1154 to 1189. Henry increased the number of criminal cases tried in the king's court and devised means for taking property cases from local courts to the royal courts. By expanding the power of the royal courts, Henry expanded the power of the king. In addition, because the royal courts were now found throughout England, a body of **common law**—law that was common to the whole kingdom—began to replace law codes that varied from place to place.

Many English nobles resented the ongoing growth of the king's power and rose in rebellion during the reign of King John. At **Runnymeade** in 1215, John was forced to put his seal on a document of rights called the **Magna Carta,** or the Great Charter.

Feudal custom had always recognized that the relationship between king and vassals was based on mutual rights and obligations. The Magna Carta gave written recognition to that fact and was used in later years to strengthen the idea that a monarch's power was limited, not absolute.

Some provisions of the Magna Carta came to have greater significance because of the way they were later interpreted. For example, Chapter 39 reads: "No free man shall be taken or imprisoned or dispossessed, or outlawed, or banished, or in any way destroyed, . . . except by the legal judgment of his peers or by the law of the land." In 1215, the label of "free man" applied to less than half of the English population. Later this statement was applied to all. In the fourteenth century, it gave rise to trial by jury.

In the thirteenth century, during the reign of Edward I, an important institution in the development of representative government—the English Parliament—also emerged. The Parliament came to be composed of two knights from every county, two

EXTENDING THE CONTENT

Magna Carta King John's cruelty and greed united the powerful feudal nobles, church officials, and townspeople against him. While he was waging a disastrous war in France, the leading nobles met secretly and swore to compel him to respect his subjects' rights. When John returned, they presented him with a series of demands. John tried to gather support, but almost all his followers deserted him. Finally, on June 15, 1215, he met with the nobles and bishops along the south bank of the Thames in a meadow called Runnymeade and affixed his seal to the Magna Carta. The Magna Carta proclaims rights that have become a part of English law and are now the foundation of the constitution of every English-speaking nation.

people from every town, and all of the nobles and bishops from throughout England. Eventually, nobles and church lords formed the House of Lords; knights and townspeople, the House of Commons. The Parliament imposed taxes and passed laws.

The French Kingdom In 843, the Carolingian Empire was divided into three sections. One, the west Frankish lands, formed the core of what would become the kingdom of France. In 987, after the death of the last Carolingian king, the west Frankish nobles chose Hugh Capet as the new king, thus establishing the Capetian (kuh•PEE•shuhn) dynasty of French kings. The Capetians had little power and controlled only the area around Paris.

The reign of King Philip II Augustus, who ruled from 1180 to 1223, was a turning point in the growth of the French monarchy. Philip waged war against the rulers of England, who also ruled a number of French territories. Philip gained control of most of these territories. In doing so, he expanded the income of the French monarchy and greatly increased its power. By 1300, France was the largest and best-governed monarchical state in Europe.

The Holy Roman Empire In the tenth century, the powerful dukes of the Saxons became kings of the eastern Frankish kingdom (another section of the Carolingian Empire), which came to be known as Germany. The best-known Saxon king of Germany was Otto I. In return for protecting the pope, Otto I was crowned emperor of the Romans in 962. The title had not been used since the time of Charlemagne.

As leaders of a new Roman Empire, the German kings attempted to rule both German and Italian lands. Kings Frederick I and Frederick II, instead of building a strong German kingdom, tried to create a new kind of empire. Frederick I planned to get his chief revenues from Italy. He considered Italy the center of a "holy empire"—hence the name ***Holy Roman Empire.*** Frederick's attempt to conquer northern Italy was opposed by the pope and the cities of northern Italy, which were unwilling to become his subjects. The main goal of Frederick II was to establish a centralized state in Italy. However, he also became involved in a losing struggle with the popes and the northern Italian cities.

The pope crowning Frederick II

By spending their time fighting in Italy, the German emperors left Germany in the hands of powerful German lords. These nobles created their own independent kingdoms. This made the German monarchy weak and incapable of maintaining a strong monarchical state. As a result, the German Holy Roman Emperor had no real power over either Germany or Italy.

Central and Eastern Europe The Slavic peoples were originally a single people in central Europe. Gradually, they divided into three major groups: the western, southern, and eastern Slavs.

The western Slavs eventually formed the Polish and Bohemian kingdoms. The Poles and Czechs, along with the non-Slavic Hungarians, all accepted western Christianity and became part of the Roman Catholic Church and its Latin culture.

The southern Slavic peoples included the Croats, the Serbs, and the Bulgarians. The Croats remained Catholic. The other southern Slavs, as well as the eastern Slavic peoples, embraced Eastern Orthodoxy, the faith of the neighboring Byzantine Empire.

Russia Eastern Slavic peoples had also settled in the territory of present-day Ukraine and Russia. There, beginning in the late eighth century, they began to encounter Swedish Vikings. The Vikings eventually came to dominate the native peoples. The native peoples called the Viking rulers the Rus, from which the name *Russia* is derived.

One Viking leader, Oleg, settled in **Kiev** at the beginning of the tenth century and created the Rus state known as the principality of Kiev. His successors extended their control over the eastern Slavs and expanded Kiev until it included the territory between the Baltic and Black Seas and the Danube and Volga Rivers.

Civil wars and invasions brought an end to the first Russian state in 1169. In the thirteenth century, the Mongols conquered Russia. They occupied Russian lands and required tribute from Russian princes.

One prince emerged as more powerful than the others—Alexander Nevsky, prince of Novgorod. The khan, leader of the western Mongol Empire, awarded Nevsky the title of grand-prince. Nevsky's descendants eventually became leaders of all Russia.

Reading Check **Analyzing** Why is 1066 considered an important date in history?

3 ASSESS

Assign Section 4 Assessment as homework or as an in-class activity.

Have students use **Interactive Tutor Self-Assessment CD-ROM.**

Section Quiz 3–4

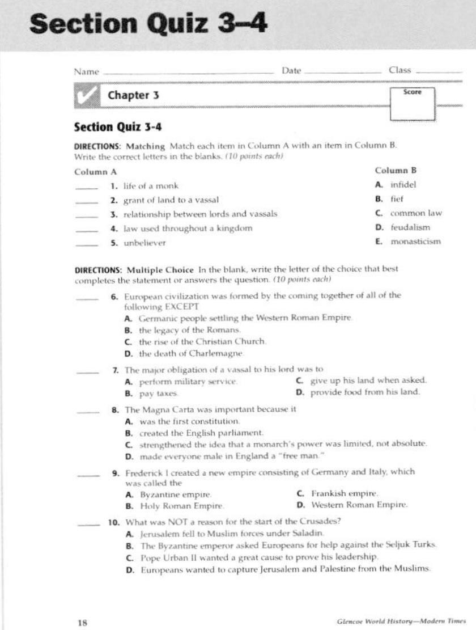
Name ______ Date ______ Class ______

Chapter 3 Score

Section Quiz 3-4

DIRECTIONS: Matching Match each item in Column A with an item in Column B. Write the correct letters in the blanks. *(10 points each)*

Column A	Column B
____ 1. life of a monk	A. infidel
____ 2. grant of land to a vassal	B. fief
____ 3. relationship between lords and vassals	C. common law
____ 4. law used throughout a kingdom	D. feudalism
____ 5. unbeliever	E. monasticism

DIRECTIONS: Multiple Choice In the blank, write the letter of the choice that best completes the statement or answers the question. *(10 points each)*

____ 6. European civilization was formed by the coming together of all of the following EXCEPT
A. Germanic people settling the Western Roman Empire.
B. the legacy of the Romans.
C. the rise of the Christian Church.
D. the death of Charlemagne.

____ 7. The major obligation of a vassal to his lord was to
A. perform military service.
B. pay taxes.
C. give up his land when asked.
D. provide food from his land.

____ 8. The Magna Carta was important because it
A. was the first constitution.
B. created the English parliament.
C. strengthened the idea that a monarch's power was limited, not absolute.
D. made everyone male in England a "free man."

____ 9. Frederick I created a new empire consisting of Germany and Italy, which was called the
A. Byzantine empire.
B. Holy Roman Empire.
C. Frankish empire.
D. Western Roman Empire.

____ 10. What was NOT a reason for the start of the Crusades?
A. Jerusalem fell to Muslim forces under Saladin.
B. The Byzantine emperor asked Europeans for help against the Seljuk Turks.
C. Pope Urban II wanted a great cause to prove his leadership.
D. Europeans wanted to capture Jerusalem and Palestine from the Muslims.

Who?What?Where?When?

Louis IX Much of the thirteenth century in France was dominated by the reign of saintly Louis IX. Louis advised his son: "[Have] a tender pitiful heart for the poor . . . [and] hold yourself loyal toward your subjects and your vassals . . . if a poor man have a quarrel with a rich man, sustain the poor until the truth is made clear, and when you know the truth, do justice to them."

Reading Check

Answer: date of William of Normandy's victory at Hastings, and the beginning of a reorganization of English government

COOPERATIVE LEARNING ACTIVITY

Exploring Ethnic Heritage Organize the class into three groups—one representing the West Slavs, the second representing the South Slavs, and the third representing the Eastern Slavs. Group members are to work together to research and prepare a family chronicle that reveals the cultural and religious influences on their group, and then present the results of their work to the class. All members should participate in gathering and recording information, preparing the chronicle, finding appropriate illustrations, and presenting the oral report. Conclude with a discussion of similarities, differences, and any conflicts that divided the three groups. **L2**

CHAPTER 3
Section 4, 116–123

Geography *Skills*

Answers:

1. First: Cologne, Paris, Clermont; Jerusalem; Second: Paris; Antioch, Acre; Third: England, Paris, Holy Roman Empire; Marseille, Antioch, Tyre, Acre; Fourth: Venice, Constantinople
2. new trading opportunities, Crusaders passed through cities

Reading Essentials and Study Guide 3–4

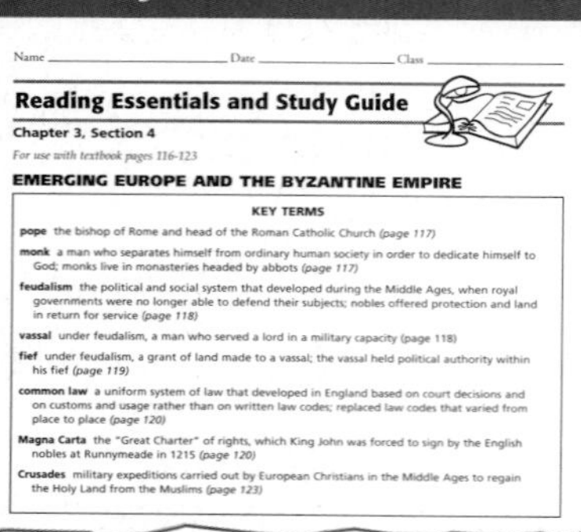

Name ______ Date ______ Class ______

Reading Essentials and Study Guide

Chapter 3, Section 4

For use with textbook pages 116-123

EMERGING EUROPE AND THE BYZANTINE EMPIRE

KEY TERMS

pope the bishop of Rome and head of the Roman Catholic Church *(page 117)*

monk a man who separates himself from ordinary human society in order to dedicate himself to God; monks live in monasteries headed by abbots *(page 117)*

feudalism the political and social system that developed during the Middle Ages, when royal governments were no longer able to defend their subjects; nobles offered protection and land in return for service *(page 118)*

vassal under feudalism, a man who served a lord in a military capacity (page 118)

fief under feudalism, a grant of land made to a vassal; the vassal held political authority within his fief *(page 119)*

common law a uniform system of law that developed in England based on court decisions and on customs and usage rather than on written law codes; replaced law codes that varied from place to place *(page 120)*

Magna Carta the "Great Charter" of rights, which King John was forced to sign by the English nobles at Runnymeade in 1215 *(page 120)*

Crusades military expeditions carried out by European Christians in the Middle Ages to regain the Holy Land from the Muslims *(page 123)*

Enrich

The reestablishment of the Roman Empire ended soon after the death of Justinian. Ask students to identify and compare the fates of other empires they have studied that apparently relied on the personal leadership of one man for their existence. Examples are the empires of Alexander the Great and of Timur Lenk. Ask interested students to share their work with the class. **L2**

The Byzantine Empire

During the fifth century, Germanic tribes moved into the western part of the Roman Empire and established their states. In contrast, the Roman Empire in the East, centered in Constantinople, continued to exist, although pressured by powerful Islamic forces.

The Reign of Justinian When **Justinian** became emperor of the Eastern Roman Empire in 527, he was determined to reestablish the Roman Empire in the entire Mediterranean world. By 552, he appeared to have achieved his goals. However, only three years after Justinian's death in 565, the Lombards had conquered much of Italy, and other areas were soon lost.

Justinian's most important contribution was his codification of Roman law. The Eastern Roman Empire had inherited a vast quantity of legal materials, which Justinian wished to simplify. The result was ***The Body of Civil Law.*** This code of Roman laws was also used in the West and became the basis for much of the legal system of Europe.

From Eastern Roman Empire to Byzantine Empire A serious challenge to the Eastern Roman Empire came from the rise of Islam, which unified Arab groups and created a powerful new force that swept through the Eastern Roman Empire. Islamic forces defeated an army of the Eastern Roman

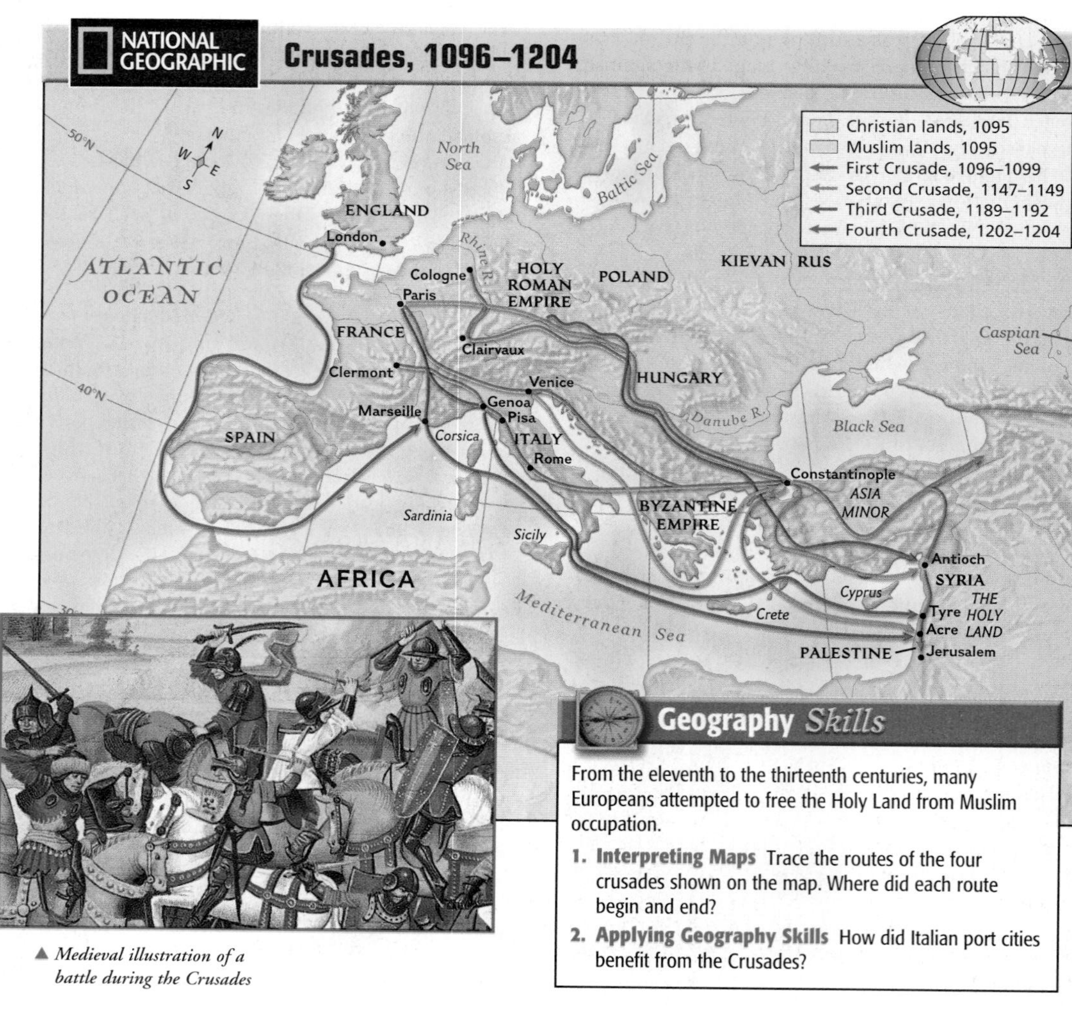

▲ *Medieval illustration of a battle during the Crusades*

Geography *Skills*

From the eleventh to the thirteenth centuries, many Europeans attempted to free the Holy Land from Muslim occupation.

1. **Interpreting Maps** Trace the routes of the four crusades shown on the map. Where did each route begin and end?
2. **Applying Geography Skills** How did Italian port cities benefit from the Crusades?

COOPERATIVE LEARNING ACTIVITY

Staging a Mock Trial Shortly after becoming emperor, Justinian appointed a commission of ten scholars and a legal expert to codify the empire's Roman laws. For more than six years, the commission collected, simplified, and organized vast numbers of laws. The commission's work was recorded in a collection of books, *The Body of Civil Law,* or the Justinian Code. Have students research a section of the Justinian law code that interests them and have them work in small groups to prepare a mock court session in which someone is tried for breaking the chosen law. Afterwards, have students identify and discuss the impact of the political and legal ideas contained in the Justinian Code of Laws. **L2**

Empire at Yarmuk in 636. Problems arose along the northern frontier as well, especially in the Balkans.

By the beginning of the eighth century, the Eastern Roman Empire was much smaller, consisting only of the eastern Balkans and Asia Minor. Historians call this smaller Eastern Roman Empire the **Byzantine Empire,** a unique civilization that lasted until 1453.

The Byzantine Empire was both a Greek and a Christian state. Greek, the common language, replaced Latin as the official language of the empire. At the same time, the empire was built on a Christian faith that was shared by many citizens. The Christian church of the Byzantine Empire came to be known as the Eastern Orthodox Church.

New Heights and New Problems The Byzantine Empire recovered and even expanded, due to the efforts of a new dynasty of emperors known as the Macedonians, who ruled from 867 to 1081. By 1025, the Byzantine Empire was the largest it had been since the beginning of the seventh century.

The Byzantine Empire continued to face threats from abroad, however. The greatest challenge came from the advance of the Seljuk Turks, who had moved into Asia Minor. In 1071, a Turkish army defeated Byzantine forces at Manzikert. Lacking the resources to undertake new campaigns against the Turks, Emperor Alexius I turned to Europe for military aid.

Reading Check **Evaluating** How did the rise of Islam affect the Eastern Roman Empire?

The Crusades

From the eleventh to the thirteenth centuries, European Christians carried out a series of military expeditions known as the **Crusades.** The push for the Crusades came when the Byzantine emperor Alexius I asked the Europeans for help against the Seljuk Turks, who were Muslims. **Pope Urban II,** who responded to the request, saw an opportunity to provide papal leadership for a great cause. That cause was rallying the warriors of Europe for the liberation of **Jerusalem** and the Holy Land (Palestine) from the infidels or unbelievers—the Muslims.

The First Crusade was the only successful one. The crusaders captured Jerusalem in June 1099. After further conquests, the crusaders organized four Latin crusader states. Surrounded by Muslims, these crusader kingdoms depended on Italian cities for supplies from Europe.

It was not easy for the crusader kingdoms to maintain themselves. By the 1120s, the Muslims had begun to strike back. In 1187, the Holy City of Jerusalem fell to Muslim forces under Saladin.

Did the Crusades have much effect on European civilization? Historians disagree. The Crusades certainly benefited some Italian port cities, especially Genoa, Pisa, and Venice. Even without the Crusades, however, Italian merchants would have pursued new trade contacts with the Eastern world.

Reading Check **Describing** What was the purpose of the Crusades in the view of European Christians?

SECTION 4 ASSESSMENT

Checking for Understanding

Define pope, monk, feudalism, vassal, fief, common law, Magna Carta, Crusades.

Identify Clovis, Charlemagne, William of Normandy, Battle of Hastings, Justinian, *The Body of Civil Law,* Byzantine Empire, Pope Urban II.

Locate England, Runnymeade, Holy Roman Empire, Kiev, Jerusalem.

Describe the role of monks in the Christian church.

List Justinian's accomplishments.

Critical Thinking

6. **Explain** What is vassalage and what is its place in the system of feudalism?
7. **Organizing Information** Use a chart to identify key achievements of monarchs in England and France.

Monarch/ Country	Achievements
1.	
2.	
3.	
4.	

Analyzing Visuals

8. **Examine** the painting of the pope crowning Frederick II on page 121. How did the struggle between German emperors and the popes impact the Holy Roman Empire?

Writing About History

9. **Informative Writing** Imagine that you are a journalist attending a meeting of the first English Parliament. What questions would you ask? Write a newsletter for people of your town explaining what happened.

CHAPTER 3
Section 4, 116–123

Reading Check

Answer: It diminished the size of the Eastern Roman Empire.

Enrich

Ask students to follow on the map on page 122 the routes of the Crusaders from western Europe to Palestine. Ask how far the Crusaders on the First Crusade traveled before reaching Jerusalem. *(about 2,000 miles [3,218 km])* the Second Crusade? *(about 1,875 miles [3,017 km])* What geographic reality made it virtually impossible for the Crusaders to maintain control of Jerusalem? *(distance between Jerusalem and Rome too great to maintain communication or supply lines; westerners not used to desert-like climate)* **L1** ELL

Reading Check

Answer: The European Christians viewed the Crusades as a method of liberating Jerusalem and the Holy Land from the Muslims.

Reteaching Activity

Ask students to review the key terms in this section. Have them use each term in a sentence that demonstrates their understanding of its meaning. **L1** ELL

4 CLOSE

Have students work in small groups to list the important events that shaped Europe during the Middle Ages. **L1** ELL

SECTION 4 ASSESSMENT

1. Key terms are in blue.
2. Clovis *(p. 117);* Charlemagne *(p. 118);* William of Normandy *(p. 119);* Battle of Hastings *(p. 119);* Justinian *(p. 122); The Body of Civil Law (p. 122);* Urban II *(p. 123)*
3. See chapter maps.
4. social workers of communities, educators, cared for the sick
5. restored Roman Empire in Mediterranean, codified Roman law
6. Vassalage is the system of vassals swearing an oath and fighting for their lords and lords taking care of their vassals' needs. It was the heart of feudalism.
7. England: Henry II: strengthened royal courts; John: signed Magna Carta; Edward I: development of English Parliament; France: Hugh Capet: established Capetian dynasty; Philip II Augustus: regained territory from England
8. German emperors focused on conflicts in Italy, left Germany under control of lords, strong monarchy never developed.
9. Answers will vary.

GLENCOE TECHNOLOGY

MindJogger Videoquiz

Use the **MindJogger Videoquiz** to review Chapter 3 content.

 Available in VHS.

Using Key Terms

1. sultan **2.** astrolabe **3.** khanate **4.** mosques **5.** caliph **6.** Islam **7.** lineage groups **8.** pope **9.** common law **10.** savanna **11.** Bushido **12.** feudalism **13.** Bantu **14.** monk

Reviewing Key Facts

15. salt

16. 640-Syria, 642-Egypt, 650-Persian Empire, 725-Spain

17. Berbers took camel caravans across the Sahara, carrying on trade between Muslim North Africa and Africa south of the Sahara.

18. Mansa Musa doubled the size of Mali and created a strong central government.

19. It destroyed the Mongol fleet that was attempting to invade Japan.

20. Printing made literature more popular and affordable. This invention created the great age of poetry in China.

21. He expanded the king's power and helped to create common law.

22. Parliament

23. It provided a hierarchical organization of people with a common interest, military service, and taxation.

24. He created a centralized government. He limited the powers of the aristocrats and increased the ruler's authority.

CHAPTER 3 ASSESSMENT and ACTIVITIES

Using Key Terms

1. The leader of the Seljuk Turks was called a _____, or "holder of power."
2. Muslims perfected the _____, an instrument used by sailors to determine location.
3. The sons of Genghis Khan divided his empire into separate territories called _____.
4. _____ are Muslim houses of worship.
5. Abu Bakr was named _____, or successor to Muhammad.
6. The word _____ means "peace through submission to the will of Allah."
7. Larger communities formed from extended families are known as _____.
8. The bishop of Rome became known as _____ of the Catholic Church.
9. Royal courts created a body of _____, rather than laws that varied from place to place.
10. A _____ is an area of broad grassland.
11. The way of the warrior, or _____, strictly governed the behavior of the Japanese military class.
12. _____ was a political and social system in the Middle Ages.
13. Farming peoples who spoke dialects of the _____ family of languages migrated into East Africa and the Congo Basin.
14. A _____ is a man who pursues a life of total dedication to God.

Reviewing Key Facts

15. **Economics** What was the highly desired item that Arab traders brought to Ghana from North Africa?
16. **Geography** Trace the expansionist movement of the Arabs from 632 to 1055.
17. **Economics** What role did Berbers play in African trade?
18. **Culture** How did Mansa Musa carry on the advances begun by Sundiata Keita?
19. **History** Discuss the importance of the *kamikaze,* the "divine wind," in early Japanese history.
20. **Science and Technology** Discuss the importance of printing, which was invented during the Tang dynasty.
21. **Government** Explain what Henry II accomplished when he expanded the power of the royal courts in England.
22. **History** What important English political institution emerged during the reign of Edward I?
23. **Government** How is feudalism a political system?
24. **History** What reforms in government did Shotoku Taishi initiate in Japan?

Critical Thinking

25. **Compare and Contrast** Compare and contrast the Islamic religion to Christianity.
26. **Drawing Conclusions** Evaluate the significance in world history of the Battle of Tours in 732.

Chapter Summary

This chart shows some of the defining characteristics of regional civilizations between 400 and 1500.

Economics	Religion	Government	Culture
• Baghdad is the center of the Islamic trade empire. • African trading states prosper from the trade of gold and salt. • The Silk Road revives and flourishes under the Arab and Chinese Empires. • Italian port cities benefit from the Crusades.	• Islam spreads throughout Asia and Africa. • Confucianism gains prominence at court under the Tang dynasty. • The Japanese state religion of Shinto evolves. • Monasticism helps spread Christianity throughout Europe.	• Abu Bakr establishes the Islamic caliphate. • The shogunate creates more centralized government in Japan. • Muslim rulers establish the Sultanate of Delhi in Hindu India. • Lack of central authority in Europe leads to the rise of feudalism.	• Arab scholars translate ancient texts. • Artists in Ife and Benin create African sculptures. • Li Bo writes Chinese poetry celebrating nature. • Byzantine emperor Justinian codifies Roman law.

Critical Thinking

25. Both are monotheistic; both have prophets; both have laws; both offer the hope of salvation and an afterlife. Muhammad was not considered divine. Christians believe Jesus was divine. Muslims view Muhammad as the last and greatest prophet and the Quran as the final scriptural revelation.

26. Islamic expansion into Europe was stopped.

Writing About History

27. Student essays will examine the connections between the regional civilizations studied in this chapter.

Self-Check Quiz

Visit the *Glencoe World History—Modern Times* Web site at wh.mt.glencoe.com and click on **Chapter 3–Self-Check Quiz** to prepare for the Chapter Test.

Writing About History

27. Although the civilizations studied in this chapter are separated geographically, they came into contact with each other through trade, expansion, or war. Write an essay explaining the various ways these civilizations were connected and in what ways they influenced each other.

Analyzing Sources

In the feudal system, lords and vassals had responsibilities to each other. The following is a description of the vow of loyalty both parties took.

> ❝The man should put his hands together as a sign of humility, and place them between the two hands of his lord as a token that he vows everything to him and promises faith to him; and the lord should receive him and promise to keep faith with him. Then the man should say: 'Sir, I enter your homage and faith and become your man by mouth and hands (that is, by taking the oath and placing his hands between those of the lord), and I swear and promise to keep faith and loyalty to you against all others.'❞

28. Why is it significant that the vow was given to a particular person rather than a nation, written constitution, or religion?

29. What is meant by the phrase "and the lord should receive him and promise to keep faith with him"?

Applying Technology Skills

30. Create a database of 5 to 10 primary sources on the regional civilizations in this chapter. Evaluate each source based on its language, correlation with other sources, and information about its author. Identify any bias the author reveals through his or her writing.

Making Decisions

31. Imagine that you are a Berber, used to living in the desert with your family. You have grown accustomed to the nomadic lifestyle. You are offered the opportunity to join another family in the city, go to school, and make new friends. What would you choose to do? Support your answer with logic and research from traditional and electronic sources.

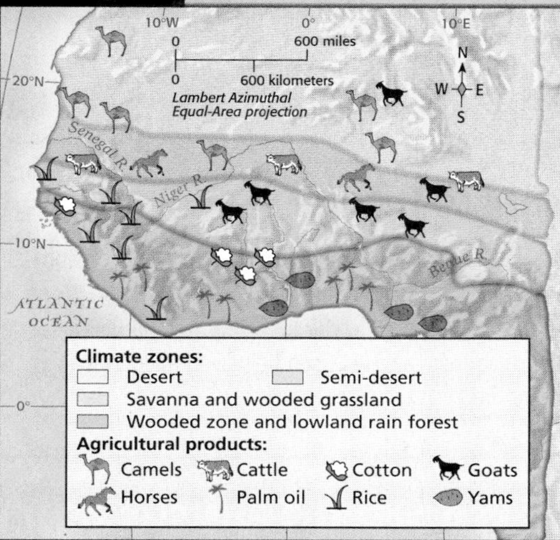

Analyzing Maps and Charts

Study the map above to answer the following questions.

32. Which zone produced the fewest number of different products? Where were most agricultural products grown?

33. In what zones were animals most plentiful? What geographical features allowed animals to thrive there?

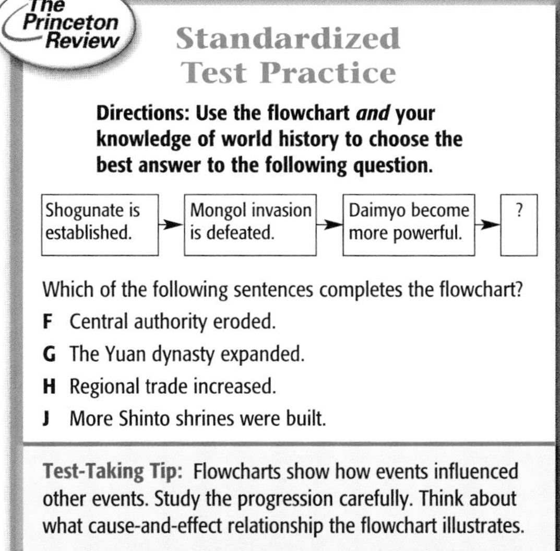

The Princeton Review — Standardized Test Practice

Directions: Use the flowchart *and* your knowledge of world history to choose the best answer to the following question.

Shogunate is established. → Mongol invasion is defeated. → Daimyo become more powerful. → ?

Which of the following sentences completes the flowchart?

F Central authority eroded.
G The Yuan dynasty expanded.
H Regional trade increased.
J More Shinto shrines were built.

Test-Taking Tip: Flowcharts show how events influenced other events. Study the progression carefully. Think about what cause-and-effect relationship the flowchart illustrates.

Have students visit the Web site at wh.mt.glencoe.com to review Chapter 3 and take the Self-Check Quiz.

Standardized Test Practice

Answer: F

Answer Explanation: Powerful aristocrats seized control of large territories, weakening central authority.

Bonus Question ?

Ask: **How can Europe in the Middle Ages be compared to Japan during the same time period?** *(Answers may include that in both places warfare, the culture of knighthood, and the political, economic, and social power of the knight dominated society.)*

Analyzing Primary Sources

28. It is a vow of loyalty that transcends other loyalties.

29. The lord had responsibilities to the vassal.

Applying Technology Skills

30. Students will develop a database and evaluate the validity of their sources.

Making Decisions

31. Some students may prefer the nomadic lifestyle; others may desire the advantages of a more cosmopolitan life.

Analyzing Maps and Charts

32. desert; wooded zone and lowland forest

33. savanna, wooded grassland, semi-desert; water, food supply

Chapter 4 Resources

Timesaving Tools

TeacherWorks™ All-In-One Planner and Resource Center

- **Interactive Teacher Edition** Access your Teacher Wraparound Edition and your classroom resources with a few easy clicks.
- **Interactive Lesson Planner** Planning has never been easier! Organize your week, month, semester, or year with all the lesson helps you need to make teaching creative, timely, and relevant.

Use Glencoe's **Presentation Plus!** multimedia teacher tool to easily present dynamic lessons that visually excite your students. Using Microsoft PowerPoint® you can customize the presentations to create your own personalized lessons.

Teaching Transparencies

Graphic Organizer Student Activity 4 Transparency

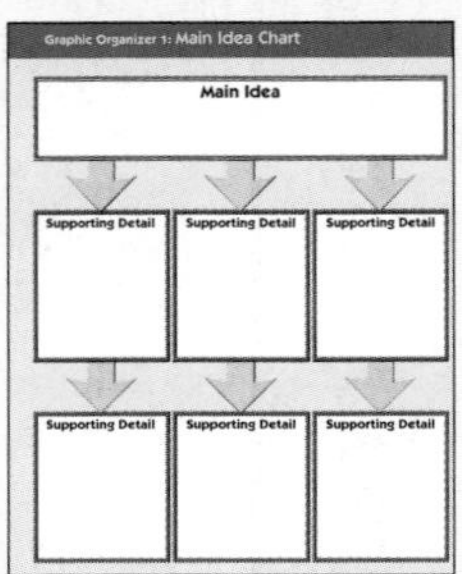

Chapter Transparency 4

Map Overlay Transparency 4

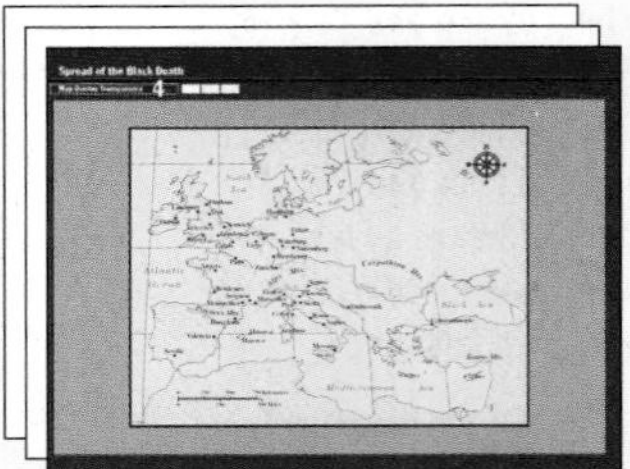

Application and Enrichment

Enrichment Activity 4

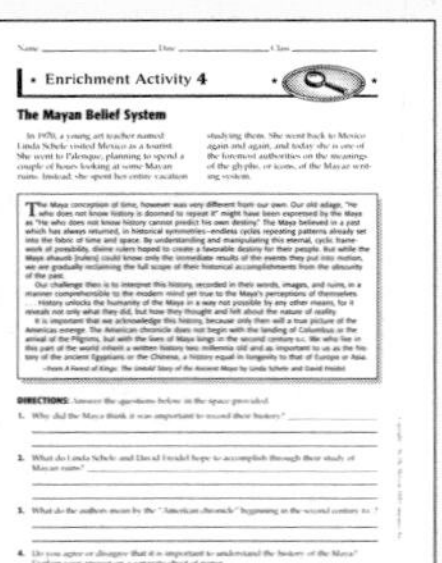

Primary Source Reading 4

History Simulation Activity 4

Historical Significance Activity 4

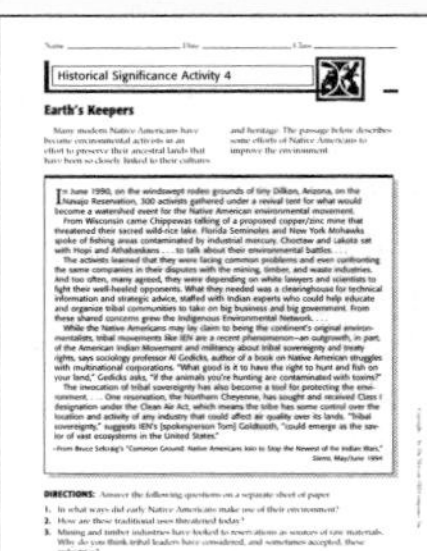

Cooperative Learning Activity 4

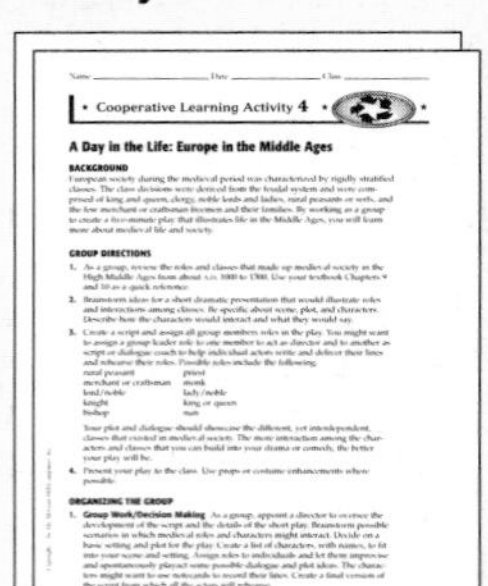

A&E HOME VIDEO

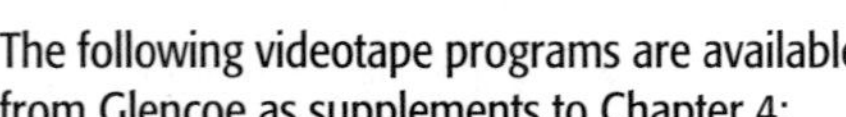

THE HISTORY CHANNEL.

The following videotape programs are available from Glencoe as supplements to Chapter 4:

- **Scourge of the Black Death** (ISBN 0–7670–0534–1)
- **The Mound Builders** (ISBN 0–7670–0822–7)
- **The Pueblo Cliff Dwellers** (ISBN 0–7670–0613–5)
- **Machu Picchu: City in the Sky** (ISBN 0–7670–0143–5)
- **The Maya** (ISBN 0–7670–0697–6)
- **Peru: Warriors and Treasure** (ISBN 0–7670–0861–3)

To order, call Glencoe at 1–800–334–7344. To find classroom resources to accompany many of these videos, check the following home pages:
A&E Television: www.aande.com
The History Channel: www.historychannel.com

Chapter 4 Resources

Review and Reinforcement

Linking Past and Present Activity 4

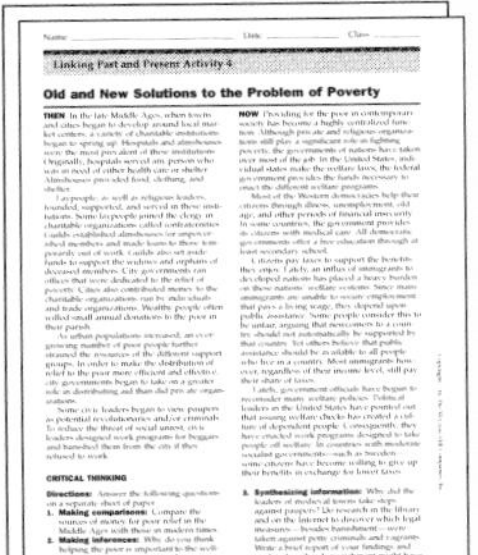

Time Line Activity 4

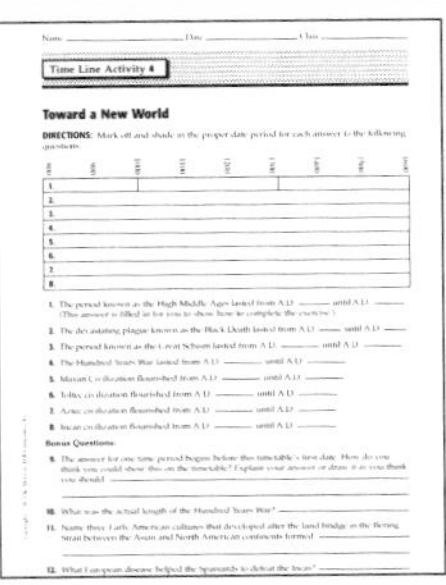

Reteaching Activity 4

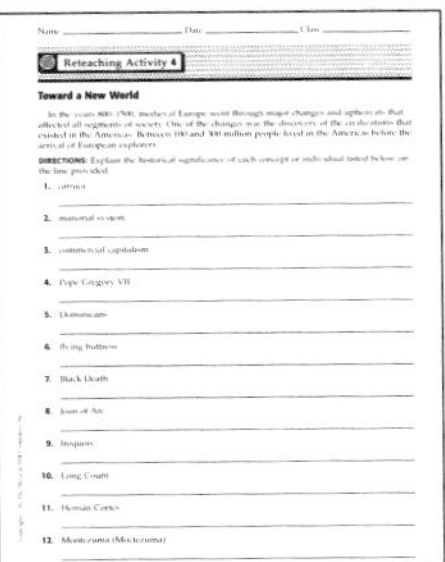

Vocabulary Activity 4

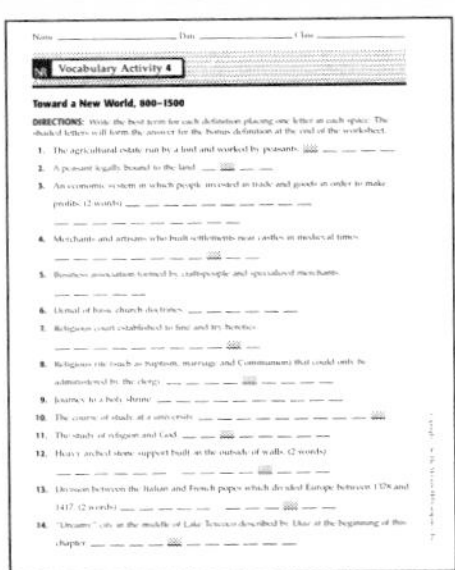

Critical Thinking Skills Activity 4

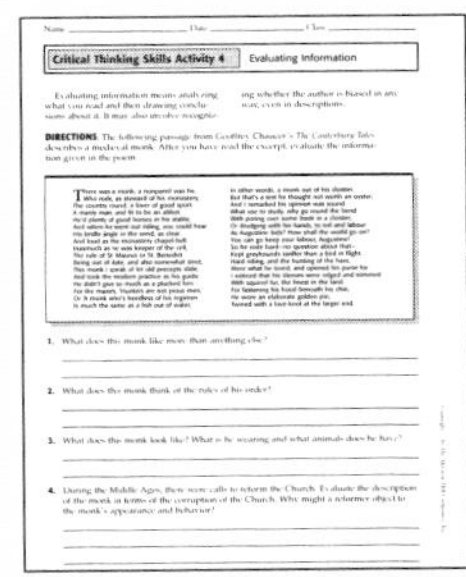

Assessment and Evaluation

Chapter 4 Test Form A

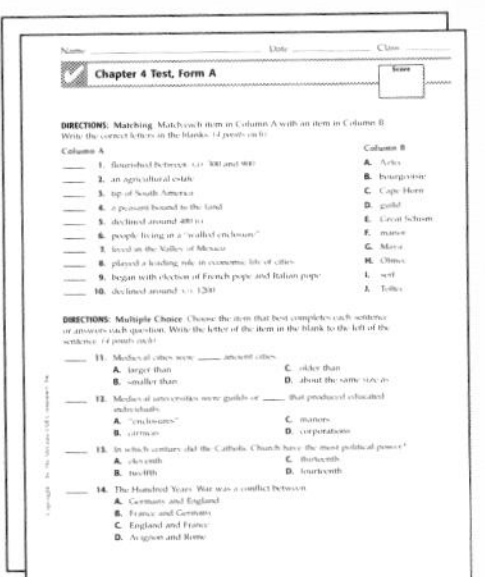

Chapter 4 Test Form B

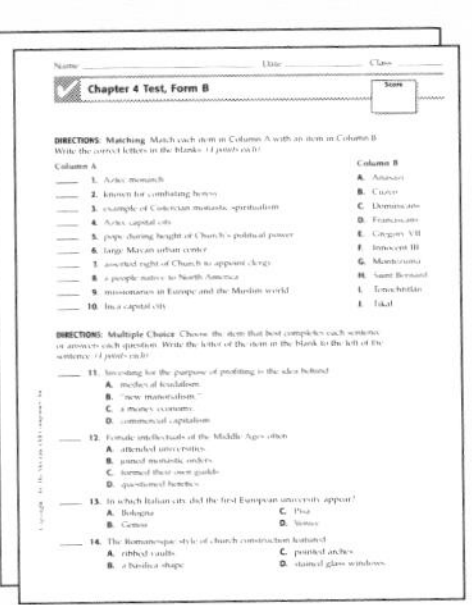

Performance Assessment Activity 4

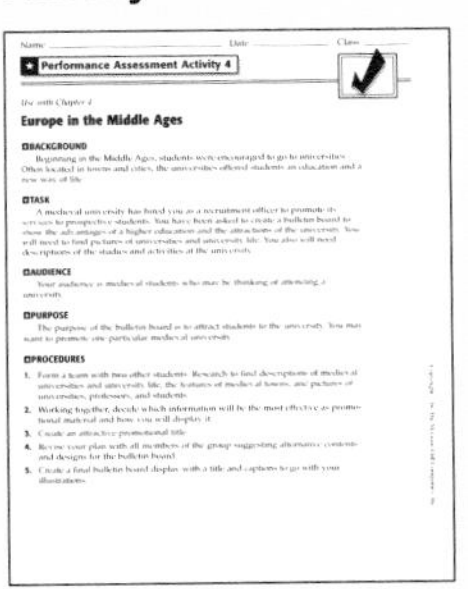

ExamView® Pro Testmaker CD-ROM

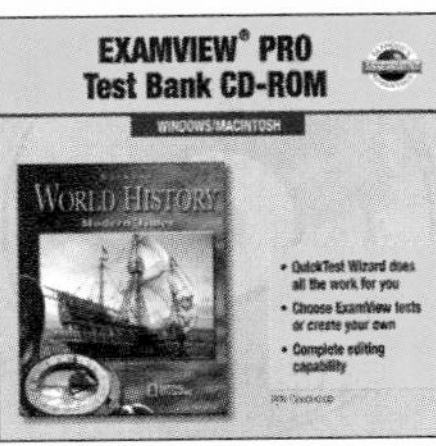

Standardized Test Skills Practice Workbook Activity 4

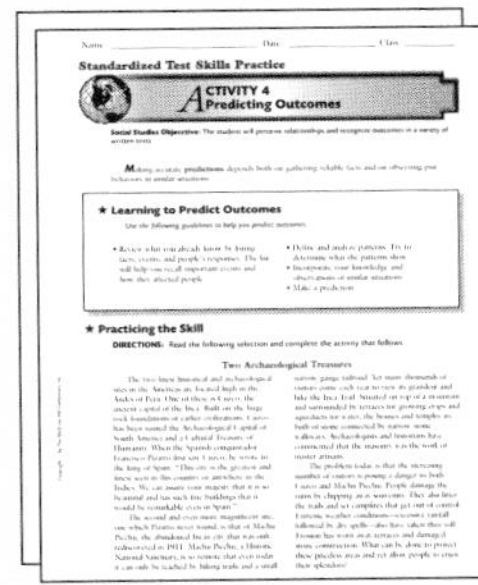

Interdisciplinary Activities

Mapping History Activity 4

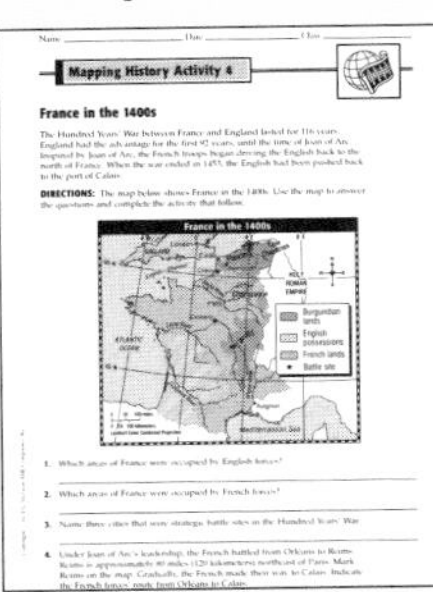

World Art and Music Activity 4

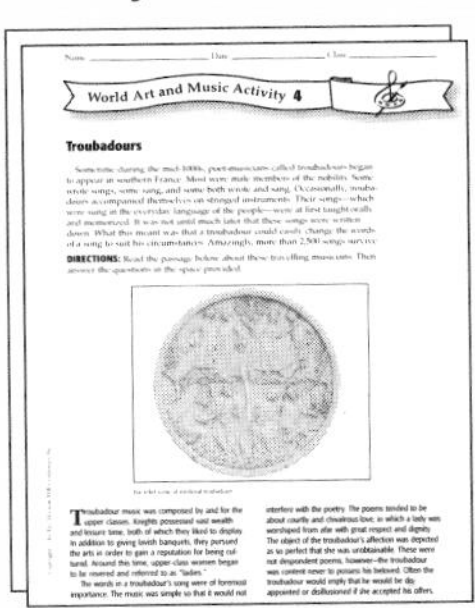

History and Geography Activity 4

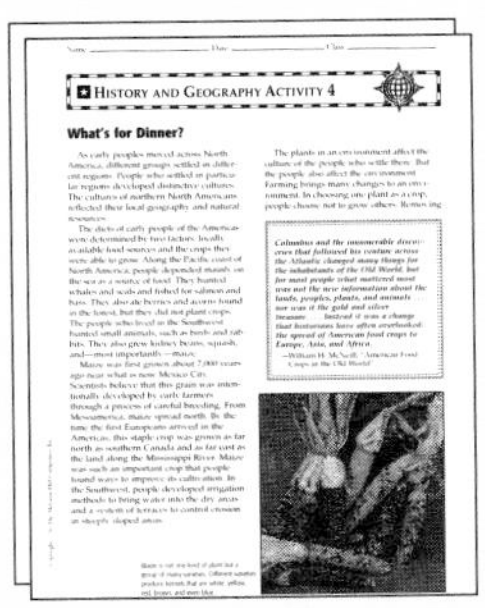

People in World History Activity 4

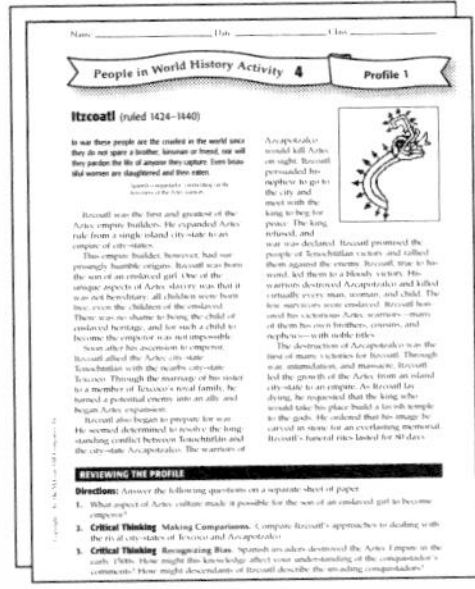

Multimedia

- Vocabulary PuzzleMaker CD-ROM
- Interactive Tutor Self-Assessment CD-ROM
- ExamView® Pro Testmaker CD-ROM
- Audio Program
- World History Primary Source Document Library CD-ROM
- MindJogger Videoquiz
- Presentation Plus! CD-ROM
- TeacherWorks CD-ROM
- Interactive Student Edition CD-ROM
- The World History—Modern Times Video Program

Spanish Resources

The following Spanish language materials are available in the Spanish Resources Binder:

- Spanish Guided Reading Activities
- Spanish Reteaching Activities
- Spanish Quizzes and Tests
- Spanish Vocabulary Activities
- Spanish Summaries

Chapter 4 Resources

SECTION RESOURCES

Daily Objectives	Reproducible Resources	Multimedia Resources
SECTION 1 **Europe in the Middle Ages** 1. Discuss the new farming practices, the growth of trade, and the rise of cities that created a flourishing European society. 2. Describe the various misfortunes that challenged Europe in the fourteenth century.	Reproducible Lesson Plan 4–1 Daily Lecture and Discussion Notes 4–1 Guided Reading Activity 4–1* Section Quiz 4–1* Reading Essentials and Study Guide 4–1	Daily Focus Skills Transparency 4–1 Interactive Tutor Self-Assessment CD-ROM ExamView® Pro Testmaker CD-ROM Presentation Plus! CD-ROM
SECTION 2 **The Americas** 1. Characterize early Mesoamerican civilizations that flourished with fully developed political, religious, and social structures. 2. Explain how the Aztec and the Inca succumbed to disease and to Spanish forces.	Reproducible Lesson Plan 4–2 Daily Lecture and Discussion Notes 4–2 Guided Reading Activity 4–2* Section Quiz 4–2* Reteaching Activity 4* Reading Essentials and Study Guide 4–2	Daily Focus Skills Transparency 4–2 Interactive Tutor Self-Assessment CD-ROM ExamView® Pro Testmaker CD-ROM Presentation Plus! CD-ROM

OUT OF TIME?
Assign the Chapter 4 **Reading Essentials and Study Guide.**

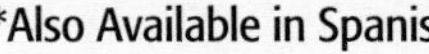

*Also Available in Spanish

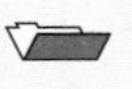 Blackline Master
 Transparency
 CD-ROM
 DVD
 Poster
 Music Program
 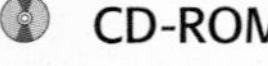 Audio Program
 Videocassette

Chapter 4 Resources

NATIONAL GEOGRAPHIC **Teacher's Corner**

INDEX TO NATIONAL GEOGRAPHIC MAGAZINE

The following articles relate to this chapter:

- "A Castle Under the Louvre," by Peter Miller, July 1989.
- "The Gothic Revolution," by James L. Stanfield and Victor R. Boswell, Jr., July 1989.
- "The Most Ancient Americans," by Rick Gore, October 1997.

NATIONAL GEOGRAPHIC SOCIETY PRODUCTS AVAILABLE FROM GLENCOE

To order the following products, call Glencoe at 1-800-334-7344:

- *PictureShow: The Middle Ages* (CD-ROM)
- *STV: Maya* (Videodisc)
- *PicturePack: Native Americans, 1 & 2* (Transparencies)

ADDITIONAL NATIONAL GEOGRAPHIC SOCIETY PRODUCTS

To order the following, call National Geographic at 1-800-368-2728:

- *The Soul of Spain* (Video)
- *The Builders: Marvels of Engineering* (Video)
- *Lost City of the Maya* (Video)
- *Lost Empire of the Tiwanaku* (Video)

NGS ONLINE

Access National Geographic's new dynamic MapMachine Web site and other geography resources at:
www.nationalgeographic.com
www.nationalgeographic.com/maps

KEY TO ABILITY LEVELS

Teaching strategies have been coded.

- **L1** BASIC activities for all students
- **L2** AVERAGE activities for average to above-average students
- **L3** CHALLENGING activities for above-average students
- **ELL** ENGLISH LANGUAGE LEARNER activities

Block Schedule

Activities that are suited to use within the block scheduling framework are identified by:

WORLD HISTORY Online

Use our Web site for additional resources. All essential content is covered in the Student Edition.

You and your students can visit www.wh.mt.glencoe.com, the Web site companion to *Glencoe World History—Modern Times.* This innovative integration of electronic and print media offers your students a wealth of opportunities. The student text directs students to the Web site for the following options:

- **Chapter Overviews**
- **Self-Check Quizzes**
- **Student Web Activities**
- **Textbook Updates**

Answers to the Student Web Activities are provided for you in the **Web Activity Lesson Plans.** Additional Web resources and Interactive Tutor Puzzles are also available.

From the Classroom of...

Hank Poehling
Central High School
La Crosse, Wisconsin

Compare and Contrast

The purpose of this project is to acquaint students with the historical impact of the Black Death on medieval European society. In comparing the Black Death to AIDS, students will understand the relevance of history as they also examine a contemporary problem. In addition, they receive beneficial AIDS education.

Have students produce a project comparing and contrasting the Black Death (bubonic plague) with AIDS, working either individually or in groups of up to four. The type of project can be left up to each individual or group—a display, a video newscast, a reenactment, or a news-style magazine. Tell students that the following areas must be addressed in the project:

- causes of both diseases
- symptoms of both diseases
- how both diseases are spread
- any known or possible cures for both diseases
- the effects of each disease on the individual
- the effects of each disease on society

Allow about two weeks for the projects. On the due date, have all groups and individuals make a formal presentation of their projects to the class.

Introducing CHAPTER 4

Performance Assessment

Refer to Activity 4 in the Performance Assessment Activities and Rubrics booklet.

The Impact Today

Have students explain the purpose and responsibilities of modern labor unions. Ask them to list products and services they use that are made or provided by union members. **L1**

GLENCOE TECHNOLOGY

The World History—Modern Times Video Program

To learn more about Europe in the Middle Ages, students can view the Chapter 4 video, "Chaucer's England," from **The World History—Modern Times Video Program.**

MindJogger Videoquiz

Use the **MindJogger Videoquiz** to preview Chapter 4 content.

 Available in VHS.

CHAPTER 4 Toward a New World

800–1500

Key Events

As you read, look for the key events in the history of medieval Europe and the Americas.

- *The revival of trade in Europe led to the growth of cities and towns.*
- *The Catholic Church was an important part of European people's lives during the Middle Ages.*
- *The Mayan, Aztec, and Incan civilizations developed and administered complex societies.*

The Impact Today

The events that occurred during this time period still impact our lives today.

- *The revival of trade brought with it a money economy and the emergence of capitalism, which is widespread in the world today.*
- *Modern universities had their origins in medieval Europe.*
- *The cultures of Central and South America reflect both Native American and Spanish influences.*

 ***World History—Modern Times Video*** *The Chapter 4 video,* "Chaucer's England," *chronicles the development of civilization in medieval Europe.*

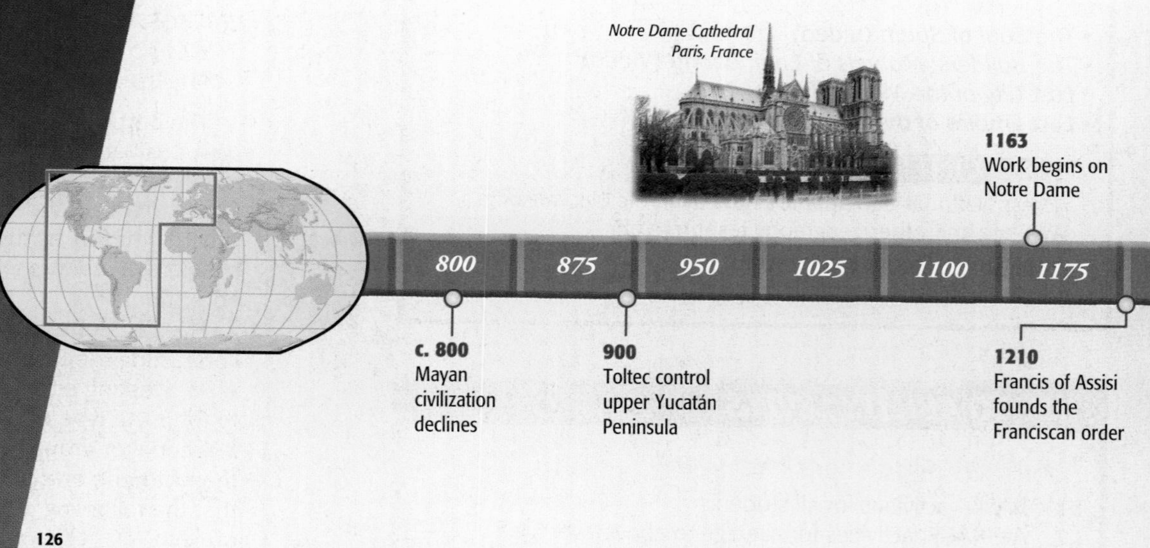

Notre Dame Cathedral
Paris, France
800
875
950
1025
1100
1175
c. 800 Mayan civilization declines
900 Toltec control upper Yucatán Peninsula
1163 Work begins on Notre Dame
1210 Francis of Assisi founds the Franciscan order

126

TWO-MINUTE LESSON LAUNCHER

Ask students to compile two lists: one, the responsibilities of citizens in a democratic society; and two, the responsibilities of the government toward its citizens. For the first list, encourage students to consider such factors as military service, taxes, loyalty, tolerance of diversity, voting, civic pride, and upkeep of property. For the second list, students can consider such factors as public works, social services, access to medical care, assistance for needy citizens, communication, infrastructure maintenance, education, and defense of freedoms. Post the class lists and refer to them as students discuss the roles of peasants and nobles during the medieval period. **L1**

Introducing
CHAPTER 4

The cathedral at Chartres, 50 miles (80 km) southwest of Paris, is but one of the many great Gothic cathedrals built in Europe during the Middle Ages.

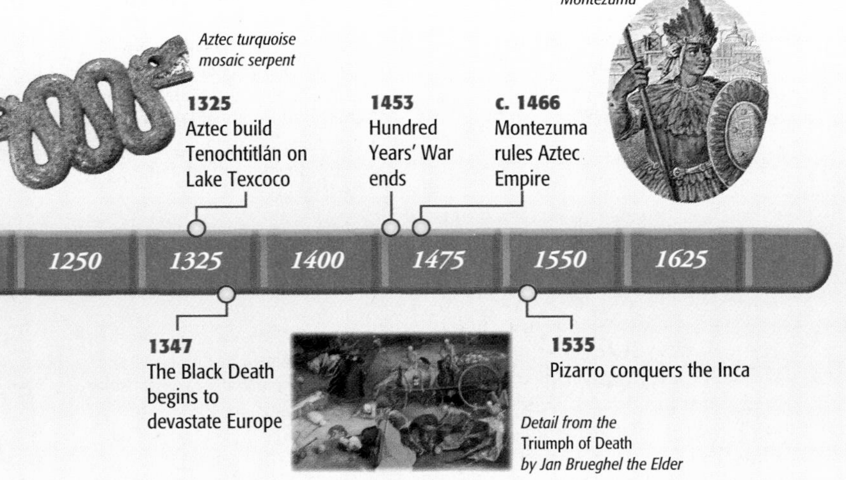

Aztec turquoise mosaic serpent
Montezuma
1325 Aztec build Tenochtitlán on Lake Texcoco
1453 Hundred Years' War ends
c. 1466 Montezuma rules Aztec Empire
1250
1325
1400
1475
1550
1625
1347 The Black Death begins to devastate Europe
1535 Pizarro conquers the Inca
Detail from the Triumph of Death by Jan Brueghel the Elder

HISTORY Online

Chapter Overview

Visit the *Glencoe World History—Modern Times* Web site at wh.mt.glencoe.com and click on **Chapter 4–Chapter Overview** to preview chapter information.

Chapter Objectives

After studying this chapter, students should be able to:

1. describe advances in farming and industry, the manorial system, and the rise of cities;
2. explain the dominant role played by the medieval Church;
3. list the cultural developments of the High Middle Ages;
4. name the various peoples who adapted to North American geography and formed societies;
5. describe the major cultures of Mesoamerica, particularly the Maya and the Aztec;
6. explain the rise and decline of the Incan Empire.

Chapter Overview

Introduce students to chapter content and key terms by having them access **Chapter Overview 4** at wh.mt.glencoe.com.

Time Line Activity

As students read the chapter, have them review the time line on these two pages. Ask students to list important events between the beginning of the plague in 1347 and the end of the Hundred Years' War in 1453, after which Europe began to recover. **L1**

MORE ABOUT THE ART

Chartres Cathedral The cathedral at Chartres was designed by an unknown architect and built between 1194 and 1220. It is one of the most famous cathedrals in France. Built of limestone, Chartres is 112 feet (34 m) high and 427 feet (130 m) long. Various architectural innovations at Chartres set the standard for thirteenth-century architecture. Chartres is particularly renowned for its beautiful stained glass windows—over 150 of them, covering nearly 3,000 square yards (2,508 sq m). Most are original, dating from about 1210 to about 1260. During both World Wars, they were taken down piece by piece for protection. More than 2,000 sculpted figures decorate the cathedral. Chartres reflects the medieval view that churches should inspire people and lead them to God.

CHAPTER PREVIEW

Introducing

A Story That Matters

Select from the following questions to reinforce the reading of *A Story That Matters.*

- Why were the Spanish surprised when they found cities and towns in Mexico? *(They expected to find only primitive people.)*
- What was the reaction of the Aztec to the Spanish army? *(They were terrified.)*
- What did the Spanish do to the cities they found? *(They destroyed them.)* **L1**

Critical Thinking

Ask the students to compare the passages written by Díaz and the unnamed Aztec. What inferences can they draw from these passages about the Spanish and the Aztec cultures? Have students develop descriptions of the two cultures based solely upon what they can determine from reading these passages. **L3**

About the Art

This mask of the Aztec god Xochipilli can be seen today in the National Museum of Anthropology in Mexico City, Mexico. The Aztec used many masks in their rites and ceremonies, which often involved human sacrifice. Masks made of human skulls were sometimes decorated with colorful mosaics. Many masks were designed to fit over the face of an important god or to be attached to the belt of a priest.

CHAPTER PREVIEW

A Story That Matters

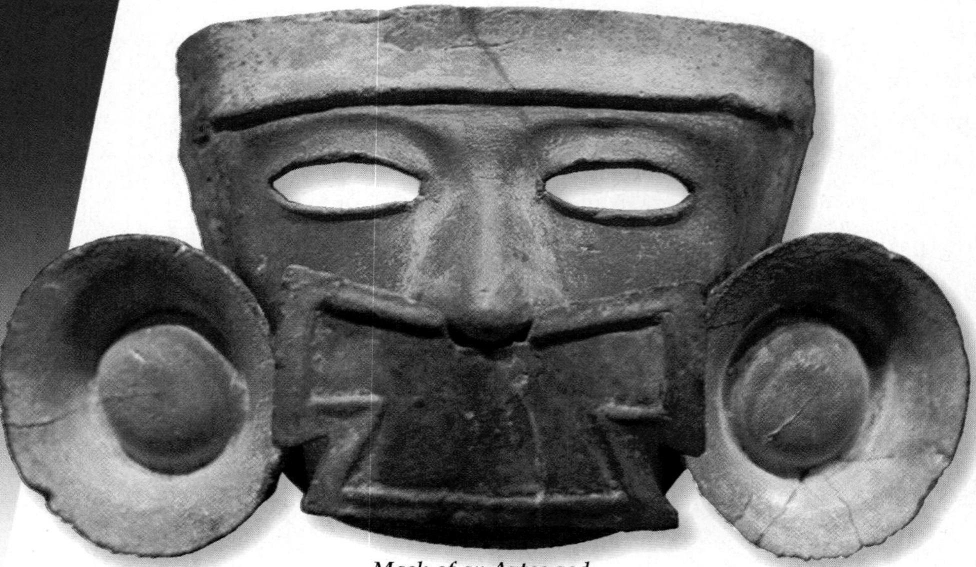

Mask of an Aztec god

Two Cultures Collide

Bernal Díaz, who accompanied Hernán Cortés on a Spanish expedition to Mexico in 1519, could not believe his eyes when he saw the Aztec city of Tenochtitlán in central Mexico:

> ❝When we beheld so many cities and towns on the water, and other large settlements built on firm ground, and that broad causeway running so straight and perfectly level to the city of Tenochtitlán, we were astonished because of the great stone towers and temples and buildings that rose up out of the water.❞

To some of the soldiers accompanying Cortés, "all these things seemed to be a dream."

The Aztec were equally astonished, but for quite different reasons. One wrote, "They [the Spanish] came in battle array, as conquerors, and the dust rose in whirlwinds on the roads, their spears glinted in the sun, and their flags fluttered like bats. Some of them were dressed in glistening iron from head to foot; they terrified everyone who saw them."

Within a short time, the Spanish had destroyed the Aztec Empire. Díaz remarked, "I thought that no land like it would ever be discovered in the whole world. But today all that I then saw is overthrown and destroyed; nothing is left standing."

Why It Matters

Organized societies had begun to take root in Central and South America by 1200 B.C. After A.D. 800, civilizations flourished on the plateau of central Mexico, the lowland regions along the Gulf of Mexico and extending into modern-day Guatemala, and the central Andes. The entry of Europeans into the Americas around A.D. 1500 led to the destruction of these civilizations.

History and You Using the Internet and traditional print sources, research the cities, innovations, and cultural contributions of the Aztec, Mayan, and Incan civilizations. Create a database that shows both the similarities and the differences among the three.

HISTORY AND YOU

Much of what we know about the early peoples of the Americas comes from the work of archaeologists. Archaeological digs have uncovered homes, burial mounds, pottery, baskets, stone tools, and the bones of people and animals. Ask students to investigate some of the important archaeological discoveries in the Americas. What has been learned? What are the most recent discoveries? What new methods of archaeological research are contributing to the advancement of knowledge about early American societies? When students present the results of their research, have them draw connections between what they discovered and what they learned about various early societies in this chapter. **L2**

SECTION 1

Europe in the Middle Ages

Guide to Reading

Main Ideas
- New farming practices and the growth of trade created a vigorous European society.
- The Catholic Church played a dominant role during the Middle Ages.

Key Terms
manor, serf, money economy, commercial capitalism, guild, heresy, Inquisition, sacrament, theology, new monarchies

People to Identify
Pope Gregory VII, Henry IV, Hildegard of Bingen, Saint Francis of Assisi

Places to Locate
Venice, Papal States, Rome, Avignon

Preview Questions
1. Why were church leaders often at odds with European rulers?
2. How did the Black Death impact European society?

Reading Strategy
Cause and Effect Use a chart like the one below to show the effects of the growth of towns on medieval European society.

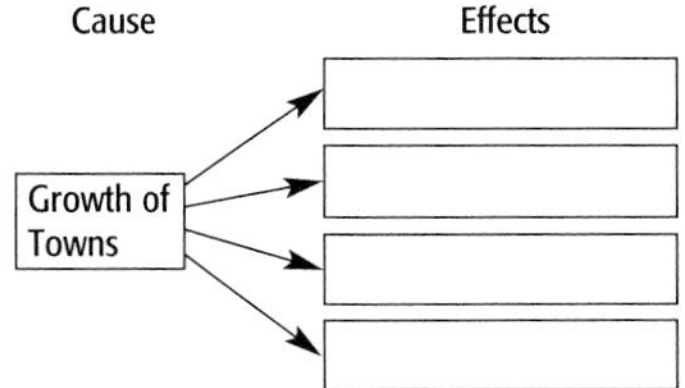

Preview of Events

1000	1100	1200	1300	1400	1500

- **1000s** Food production expands
- **1100s** Guilds are organized
- **1305** Pope moves to Avignon
- **1347** Black Death begins to devastate Europe
- **1417** Great Schism ends
- **1500** Europe has 80 universities

Voices from the Past

Pope Gregory VII, who served as pope from 1073 to 1085

In 1075, Pope Gregory VII issued the following decrees:

> ❝(1) That the Roman [Catholic] Church was founded by God alone. (2) That the pope alone can with right be called universal. (3) That he alone can depose or reinstate bishops. . . . (10) That [the pope's] name alone shall be spoken in the churches. (11) That his name is the only name in the world. (12) That it may be permitted to him to depose emperors. . . . (19) That he himself may be judged by no one. . . . (22) That the Roman Church has never erred; nor will it err to all eternity, the Scripture bearing witness.❞
>
> —***Select Historical Documents of the Middle Ages,*** **Ernest F. Henderson, ed., 1892**

The popes of the Catholic Church exerted their power, as is evident from these decrees. Christianity was a crucial element in medieval European society.

The New Agriculture

In the early Middle Ages, Europe had a relatively small population. In the High Middle Ages (1000–1300), however, population increased dramatically. The number of people almost doubled, from 38 million to 74 million. What caused this huge increase in population? For one thing, conditions in Europe were more settled and peaceful after the invasions of the early Middle Ages had stopped. This increased peace and stability also led to a dramatic expansion in food production after 1000.

SECTION RESOURCES

Reproducible Masters
- Reproducible Lesson Plan 4–1
- Daily Lecture and Discussion Notes 4–1
- Guided Reading Activity 4–1
- Section Quiz 4–1
- Reading Essentials and Study Guide 4–1

Transparencies
- Daily Focus Skills Transparency 4–1

Multimedia
- Interactive Tutor Self-Assessment CD-ROM
- ExamView® Pro Testmaker CD-ROM
- Presentation Plus! CD-ROM

1 FOCUS

Section Overview

This section traces the key events of the High Middle Ages in Europe, including technological advances that led to the growth of cities, the dominant role played by the Church, and the devastation caused by the Black Death.

BELLRINGER
Skillbuilder Activity

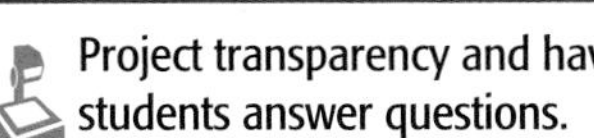

Project transparency and have students answer questions.

Available as a blackline master.

Daily Focus Skills Transparency 4–1

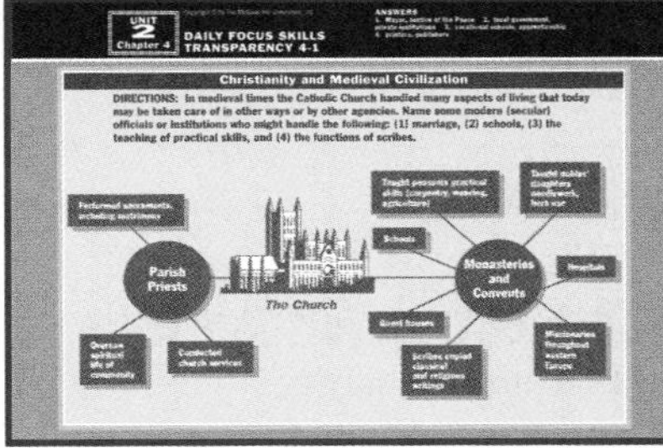

Guide to Reading

Answers to Graphic: merchants and artisans settled in cities; new cities and towns were founded; guilds were established; universities developed; Black Death spread

Preteaching Vocabulary: Be sure students understand what *heresy* meant to the medieval Church and why it was considered such a grave sin. **L1**

2 TEACH

SCIENCE, TECHNOLOGY & SOCIETY

Answer: Dams harness water for hydroelectric power, and windmills are used to produce electricity.

Daily Lecture and Discussion Notes 4–1

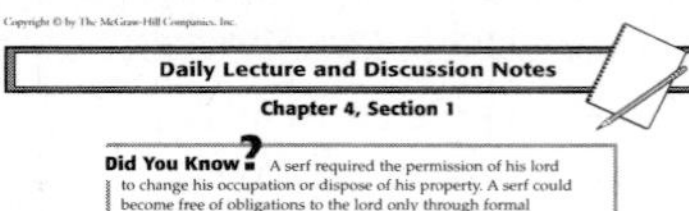

Connecting Across Time

Have students investigate the materials that are used to make tools today. How does their tensile strength compare to iron? Are modern tools more ergonomically designed than early farming tools? Which tools have changed? Which have not? **L2**

Critical Thinking

Ask students to give examples of major scientific discoveries and technological innovations that occurred during the Middle Ages and to describe the changes produced by these discoveries and innovations. **L1**

In part, food production increased because a change in climate during the High Middle Ages improved growing conditions. In addition, more land was cultivated as peasants of the eleventh and twelfth centuries cut down trees and drained swamps.

Changes in technology also aided the development of farming. The Middle Ages witnessed an explosion of labor-saving devices. For example, the people of the Middle Ages harnessed the power of water and wind to do jobs once done by humans or animals.

Many new devices were made from iron, which was mined in various areas of Europe. Iron was crucial in making the *carruca,* a heavy, wheeled plow with an iron plowshare. Unlike earlier plows, this plow could easily turn over heavy clay soils.

The shift from a two-field to a three-field system of crop rotation added to the increase in food production. In the early Middle Ages, peasants divided their land into two fields of equal size. One field was planted, while the other was allowed to lie fallow, or remain unplanted, to regain its fertility. Now, however, lands were divided into three parts. One field was planted in the fall with grains (such as rye and wheat) that were harvested in summer. The second field was planted in the spring with grains (oats and barley) and vegetables (peas and beans) that were harvested in the fall. The third field was allowed to lie fallow. The three-field system meant that only one-third, rather than one-half, of the land lay fallow at any time. The rotation of crops also kept the soil from becoming exhausted so quickly.

SCIENCE, TECHNOLOGY & SOCIETY

Harnessing the Power of Water and Wind

Watermill on Certovka River in Prague, Czech Republic

Watermills use the power of running water to do work. The watermill was invented as early as the second century B.C. It was not used much in the Roman Empire because the Romans had many slaves and had no need to mechanize. In the High Middle Ages, watermills became easier to build as the use of metals became more common. In 1086, the survey of English land known as the Domesday Book listed six thousand watermills in England.

Located along streams, mills powered by water were at first used to grind grains for flour. Gradually, mill operators were able to mechanize entire industries. Waterpower was used in mills for making cloth and in sawmills for cutting wood and stone, as well as in the working of metals.

Rivers, however, were not always available. Where this was the case, Europeans developed windmills to harness the power of the wind. Historians are unsure whether windmills were imported into Europe (they were invented in Persia) or designed independently by Europeans. Like the watermill, the windmill was first used for grinding grains. Later, however, windmills were used for pumping water and even cutting wood. However, they did not offer as great a range of possible uses as watermills.

The watermill and windmill were the most important devices for harnessing power before the invention of the steam engine in the eighteenth century. Their spread had revolutionary consequences, enabling Europeans to produce more food and to more easily manufacture a wide array of products.

Comparing ***How are water and wind power used today?***

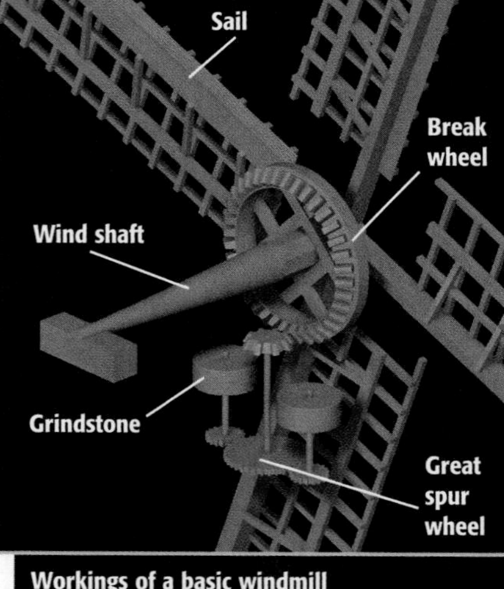

Workings of a basic windmill

MEETING INDIVIDUAL NEEDS

Visual Learners Draw a spider diagram (word web) with the word "farming" in the middle. Ask students to name factors that are necessary to farm successfully. Responses include availability of land and equipment, type of climate, workers, political stability. Then have students reread the section called "The New Agriculture" on pages 129 to 131 and draw another spider diagram with "New Agriculture" in the center. Ask students to supply factors that made the agricultural explosion of the Middle Ages possible. Discuss differences between agriculture then and now. Have students copy both diagrams for study purposes. **L1** ELL

Refer to the ***Inclusion for the High School Social Studies Classroom Strategies and Activities*** in the TCR.

The Manorial System Landholding nobles were a military elite whose ability to be warriors depended on their having the leisure time to pursue the arts of war. Landed estates, located on the fiefs given to a vassal by his lord, and worked by peasants, provided the economic support that made this way of life possible. *(See page 773 to read excerpts from Christine de Pizan's* A Woman May Need to Have the Heart of a Man *in the Primary Sources Library.)*

A manor was an agricultural estate run by a lord and worked by peasants. Although free peasants continued to exist, increasing numbers of free peasants became serfs, or peasants legally bound to the land. Serfs had to provide labor services, pay rents, and be subject to the lord's control. By 800, probably 60 percent of the people of western Europe were serfs.

Daily Life of the Peasants The life of peasants in Europe was simple. Their cottages had wood frames surrounded by sticks, with the spaces between sticks filled with straw and rubble and then plastered over with clay. Roofs were simply thatched.

The houses of poorer peasants consisted of a single room. Others, however, had at least two rooms—a main room for cooking, eating, and other activities and another room for sleeping. There was little privacy in a medieval peasant household.

The position of peasant women in manorial society was both important and difficult. They were expected to work in the fields and at the same time bear children. Their ability to manage the household might determine whether a peasant family would starve or survive in difficult times.

The seasons of the year largely determined peasant activities. Each season brought a new round of tasks. Harvest time in August and September was especially hectic. A good harvest of grains for making bread was crucial to survival in the winter months. In every season, of course, the serfs worked not only their own land but also the lords' lands.

A new cycle of labor began in October, when peasants worked the ground for the planting of winter crops. In November came the slaughter of excess livestock, because there was usually not enough food to keep the animals alive all winter. The meat would be salted to preserve it for winter use. In February and March, the land was plowed for the planting of spring crops—oats, barley, peas, and beans. Early summer was a fairly relaxed time, although there was still weeding and sheepshearing to be done.

Reading Check **Explaining** How did the seasons of the year affect peasant activities?

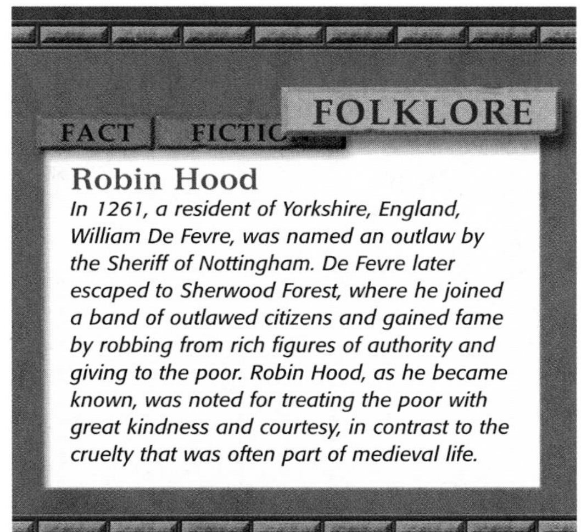

Robin Hood

In 1261, a resident of Yorkshire, England, William De Fevre, was named an outlaw by the Sheriff of Nottingham. De Fevre later escaped to Sherwood Forest, where he joined a band of outlawed citizens and gained fame by robbing from rich figures of authority and giving to the poor. Robin Hood, as he became known, was noted for treating the poor with great kindness and courtesy, in contrast to the cruelty that was often part of medieval life.

The Revival of Trade

Medieval Europe was an agricultural society in which most people lived in small villages. In the eleventh and twelfth centuries, however, a revival of trade and an associated growth of cities changed the economic foundation of European civilization.

Cities in Italy took the lead in the revival of trade. While **Venice** and other northern Italian cities were busy trading in the Mediterranean, the towns of Flanders (along the coast of present-day Belgium and northern France) were doing the same in northern Europe. By the twelfth century, a regular exchange of goods had developed between Flanders and Italy.

As trade increased, demand for gold and silver coins arose at fairs and trading markets of all kinds. Slowly, a money economy—an economic system based on money—began to emerge. New trading companies and banking firms were set up to manage the exchange and sale of goods. All of these new practices were part of the rise of commercial capitalism, an economic system in which people invested in trade and goods in order to make profits. Some historians have called this the beginnings of a **Commercial Revolution.**

Reading Check **Analyzing** How were increased trade and the development of a money economy related?

The Growth of Cities

The revival of trade led to a revival of cities. Towns had greatly declined in the early Middle Ages,

Reading Check

Answer: Because peasants were dependent on the land, the seasons of the year determined when and what they needed to plant in order to survive.

Connecting Across Time

Today's citizens do not pay their rents or taxes to a lord, but they do pay taxes to local and federal governments. Have students compare and contrast the services received for taxes with those received by peasants and serfs for their rents. **L1**

Reading Check

Answer: As trade increased, the demand for gold and silver coins arose. People began to trade goods for money, rather than goods for other goods.

Writing Activity

As students read this section, have them list as many features as possible pertaining to a serf's life. Then ask students to write a one-page paper, as if they were serfs, describing the activities of a typical day. Ask students to compare elements of their present-day lives that parallel a serf's day. **L1**

Charting Activity

Have students create a chart describing the major characteristics of the economic system of manorialism. Students should describe the economic obligations and benefits of serfs, peasants, and lords. Display charts in the classroom. **L2**

CRITICAL THINKING ACTIVITY

Making Decisions In the interdependent peasant communities, medieval women had a variety of duties and responsibilities. The nature of the community created an atmosphere where women were not isolated but had daily contact with traders, laborers, officers, and neighbors. They participated in the hard, heavy labor of planting and harvesting. Women were dairymaids, gardeners, bakers, brewers, and craftspeople. They were an integral part of the village network. Still, only men could be considered citizens. Ask students to discuss the justifications that might have been used to exclude women from citizenship. Do students think the societal attitudes reflected by women's lack of citizenship were held only by men? Why or why not? **L2**

CHAPTER 4
Section 1, 129–138

Guided Reading Activity 4–1

Name ________ Date ________ Class ________

Guided Reading Activity 4-1

Europe in the Middle Ages

DIRECTIONS: Fill in the blanks below as you read the section.

1. The population in the High Middle Ages (1000–1300) almost doubled from ________ million to ________ million people.
2. The shift from a ________-field to a ________-field system of crop rotation allowed for increased food production.
3. A ________ was an agricultural estate run by a lord and worked by peasants.
4. ________ was an economic system in which people invested their money in trade and goods in order to make a profit.
5. ________ was a fact of life in medieval cities as a result of the ever-present wood fires.
6. ________, king of Germany, and ________, elected as head of the Catholic church in 1073, struggled with each other over who had the right to appoint religious leaders—laity or clergy.
7. The ________ order was founded by a group of monks who were unhappy with the lack of discipline at their Benedictine monastery.
8. ________, founder of the Franciscan order, was born into a wealthy Italian merchant family.
9. Medieval Christians believed that a pilgrimage to a holy place, or ________, produced spiritual benefit.
10. The first ________ university appeared in Bologna, Italy.
11. Teaching at medieval universities was done by the ________ method in which instructors read to students from a basic text then added their own explanations.
12. Eleventh- and twelfth-century cathedrals were built in what is now known as ________ style.
13. The Black Death was the most devastating ________ disaster in European history.
14. Bubonic plague was spread by black ________ infested with ________ that carried the bacterium.
15. The ________ of the Church (1378–1417) divided Europe.
16. Since the thirteenth century, Russia had been dominated by the ________ until the reign of ________ when a new Russian state emerged.

118

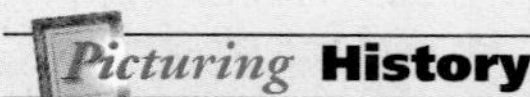

Picturing History

Answer: The picture shows raking and cutting tools. The season is summer.

Reading Check

Answer: Students should recognize that medieval cities were walled, had narrow, winding streets, and that the houses were crowded together. Cities were dirty, smelly, and had polluted air.

Writing Activity

Ask students to write two paragraphs describing what it might have been like to live in a medieval city. Have them mention both advantages *(jobs, safety, intellectual opportunity)* and disadvantages *(crowded conditions, lack of sanitation, disease)*. **L2**

Picturing History

This illustration is from the famous manuscript, *Très Riches Heures,* an example of a medieval Book of Hours. Books of Hours were personal prayer books that often contained calendars noting important dates of the year. What kinds of tools are the men and women in this illustration using to do their work? Which season is represented?

especially in Europe north of the Alps. Old Roman cities had continued to exist but had dwindled in size and population.

With the revival of trade, merchants began to settle in the old Roman cities. They were followed by craftspeople or artisans—people who had developed skills and saw a chance to make goods that could be sold by the merchants. In the course of the eleventh and twelfth centuries, the old Roman cities came alive with new populations and growth.

Many new cities or towns were also founded, especially in northern Europe. Usually, a group of merchants built a settlement near a castle because it was located along a trade route and because the lord of the castle would offer protection. If the settlement prospered and expanded, new walls were built to protect it. The merchants and artisans of these cities later came to be called *burghers* or bourgeoisie, from the German word *burg,* "a walled enclosure."

Medieval cities were small in comparison with either ancient or modern cities. A large trading city would number about five thousand inhabitants. Italian cities tended to be larger. Venice, Florence, Genoa, Milan, and Naples each had almost a hundred thousand inhabitants. Even the largest European city, however, seemed small alongside the Byzantine capital of Constantinople or the Arab city of Baghdad.

Life in the Medieval City Medieval towns were surrounded by stone walls. Because the walls were expensive to build, the space within was precious and tightly filled. Thus, medieval cities had narrow, winding streets. Houses were crowded against one another, and the second and third stories were built out over the streets.

The danger of fire was great. Dwellings were built mostly of wood before the fourteenth century, and candles and wood fires were used for light and heat. Medieval cities burned rapidly once a fire started.

The physical environment of medieval cities was not pleasant. The cities were often dirty and smelled from animal and human waste. Air pollution was also a fact of life from the ever present wood fires.

Industry and Guilds The revival of trade enabled cities and towns to become important centers for manufacturing a wide range of goods, such as cloth, metalwork, shoes, and leather goods. A host of craft activities were carried on in houses located in the narrow streets of the medieval cities.

From the twelfth century on, craftspeople began to organize themselves into guilds, or business associations. Guilds came to play a leading role in the economic life of the cities. By the thirteenth century, there were guilds for tanners, carpenters, bakers, and artisans of almost every other craft. There were also separate guilds for specialized groups of merchants, such as dealers in silk or money (banking).

Reading Check **Identifying** List three physical characteristics of medieval cities.

The Papal Monarchy

Since the fifth century, the popes of the Catholic Church had been supreme over the affairs of the Church. They had also gained control of territories in central Italy that came to be known as the **Papal States.** This control kept the popes involved in

EXTENDING THE CONTENT

Guilds The earliest form of workers' organizations or cooperatives were the medieval guilds. Guilds did not start out as the organizers and overseers of the production process for the craftspeople and merchants. Originally, guilds were organizations within communities that were developed to meet the common needs of the people. They functioned mainly as religious and social fraternities. The guilds provided needed assistance to widows, orphans, and elderly people. They also financed religious festivals and helped maintain and build local churches.

political matters, often at the expense of their spiritual duties.

During part of the 800s and 900s, the authority of the popes declined as the feudal lords became more powerful. Bishops and abbots, for example, began to obtain their offices as grants from nobles, not the pope. As vassals, these church officials carried out the usual feudal services, including military duties.

By the eleventh century, church leaders realized the need to be free from the interference of lords in the appointment of church officials. **Pope Gregory VII** decided to fight this interference. Elected pope in 1073, he was convinced that he had been chosen by God to reform the Church. To pursue this aim, Gregory claimed that the pope's authority extended over all the Christian world, including its rulers. He also asserted the right of the Church to appoint clergy and run its own affairs. If rulers did not accept this, the pope would remove them.

Gregory VII soon found himself in conflict with **Henry IV,** the king of Germany, over these claims. For many years, German kings had appointed high-ranking clerics, especially bishops, as their vassals in order to use them as administrators. Without them, the king could not hope to maintain his own power in the face of the powerful German nobles.

In 1075, Pope Gregory issued a decree forbidding high-ranking clerics from receiving their offices from lay (secular) leaders. Although Henry IV opposed the pope's actions, the new papal policy ultimately won out.

The popes of the twelfth century did not give up the reform ideals of Pope Gregory VII, and they were even more inclined to strengthen papal power and build a strong administrative system. During the papacy of Pope Innocent III in the thirteenth century, the Catholic Church reached the height of its political power. Innocent III's actions were those of a man who believed that he, the pope, was the supreme judge of European affairs. For example, he forced the king of France, Philip Augustus, to take back his wife and queen after Philip had tried to have his marriage annulled.

Reading Check **Summarizing** Briefly describe the conflict between Pope Gregory VII and King Henry IV.

New Religious Orders

In the second half of the eleventh century and the first half of the twelfth century, a wave of religious enthusiasm seized Europe. This movement led to a rise in the number of monasteries and the emergence of new monastic orders. Both men and women joined religious orders in increasing numbers.

A New Activism In the eleventh century, the most important new order to arise was the Cistercian (sis•TUHR•shuhn) order. It was founded in 1098 by a group of monks who were unhappy with the lack of discipline at their own Benedictine monastery. Cistercian monastacism spread rapidly from southern France into the rest of Europe.

The **Cistercians** played a major role in developing a new, activistic spiritual model for twelfth-century Europe. While Benedictine monks spent hours inside the monastery in personal prayer, the Cistercians took their religion to the people outside the monastery. More than any other person, Saint Bernard of Clairvaux embodied the new spiritual ideal of Cistercian monasticism: "Arise, soldier of Christ, arise! Get up off the ground and return to the battle from which you have fled! Fight more boldly after your flight, and triumph in glory!"

Women were also actively involved in the spiritual movements of the age. The number of women joining religious houses grew dramatically. In the High Middle Ages, most nuns were from the ranks of the landed aristocracy. Female intellectuals found convents a haven for their activities. Most of the learned women of the Middle Ages, especially in Germany, were nuns. This was true of **Hildegard of Bingen,**

People In History

Hildegard of Bingen
1098–1179—Medieval abbess

Hildegard entered a religious house for females at the age of eight, took her vows at fourteen, and twenty-four years later became abbess. After becoming abbess, she began to write an account of the mystical visions she had had for years. "A great flash of light from heaven pierced my brain and . . . in that instant my mind was imbued with the meaning of the sacred books," she wrote. Eventually she produced three books based on her visions. Hildegard gained fame as a mystic and prophetess. Popes, emperors, kings, dukes, bishops, abbots, and abbesses eagerly sought her advice. She wrote to them all as an equal and did not hesitate to be critical.

Reading Check

Answer: Pope Gregory VII issued a decree forbidding high-ranking clerics from receiving their offices from secular leaders. King Henry IV opposed this policy because he needed the power to appoint church leaders in order to maintain his own power in Germany.

Connecting Across Time

The pope today is still elected by a gathering of cardinals, called a "conclave." They meet no later than the twentieth day after the death of a pope and vote by secret ballot until they can achieve a two-thirds majority on a given candidate. Ask students to research the election of the current pope. L2

Who?What?Where?When?

Hildegard of Bingen For women like Hildegard of Bingen, entering a convent was the only means of acquiring an education and pursuing a life as a writer. Hildegard composed musical plays and wrote treatises on natural history and medicine. Her influence extended to advising bishops, popes, and kings. Students might wish to compare Hildegard's story with that of Sor Juana Inés de la Cruz, who joined a convent in Mexico when she was refused university admission in the seventeenth century. L3

Enrich

It is almost impossible for students today to understand the influence and authority of the Roman Catholic Church in the Middle Ages. As students read this section, have them take notes describing the major characteristics of the authority exerted by the Roman Catholic Church. Then have students develop an outline from their notes. L2

COOPERATIVE LEARNING ACTIVITY

Staging a Class Debate The struggle between Gregory VII and Henry IV was one of the great conflicts between Church and state in the High Middle Ages. Have students recreate the "debate" between pope and king. The debate can be formal if you have the time to teach debating skills, or it can be informal, more like a class discussion. Divide the class into two teams (one for Gregory VII and one for Henry IV) and have each team research the debate. Teams should designate roles for each member. When teams have had a chance to complete their research, schedule a class period for the debate/discussion. Afterwards, discuss the points each side made. What arguments can students make to support a contention that their team "won"? L2

CHAPTER 4
Section 1, 129–138

Reading Check

Answer: Franciscans, the religious order of monks founded by Saint Francis of Assisi, lived among the people, preached repentance, and aided the poor. Dominicans, the religious order of monks founded by Spanish priest Dominic de Guzmán, defended Church teachings from heresy. They were especially well known for their roles as examiners of people suspected of heresy.

Who?What?Where?When?

Giotto Florentine painter Giotto (c.1266–c.1337) painted a series of frescoes based on the life of Saint Francis of Assisi. The frescoes are in the cathedral at Assisi, Italy. In September 1997, a severe earthquake damaged the cathedral and some of the frescoes. The one on this page is called "Preaching to the Birds."

Writing Activity

Have students choose one of the religious leaders discussed in this section and research his or her life. Have students locate and use primary and secondary sources such as computer software (including CD-ROMS), databases, and biographies to research their subjects. Then, ask students to write a brief summary of the person's major accomplishments. Students should share their findings with the class. **L2**

who became abbess of a religious house for females in western Germany.

The Franciscans and Dominicans In the thirteenth century, two new religious orders emerged that had a strong impact on the lives of ordinary people. They were the Franciscans and the Dominicans.

The Franciscans were founded by **Saint Francis of Assisi.** Francis was born to a wealthy Italian merchant family in Assisi. After having been captured and imprisoned during a local war, he had a series of dramatic spiritual experiences. These experiences led him to abandon all worldly goods and material pursuits and to live and preach in poverty, working and begging for his food. His love for others soon attracted a band of followers.

The Franciscans became very popular. They lived among the people, preaching repentance and aiding the poor. They undertook missionary work, first throughout Italy and then in all parts of Europe and even in the Muslim world.

The Dominican order was founded by a Spanish priest, Dominic de Guzmán. Dominic wanted to defend Church teachings from **heresy**—the denial of basic Church doctrines. Heretical movements became especially widespread in southern France. Dominic believed that a new religious order of men who lived lives of poverty and were capable of preaching effectively would best be able to attack heresy.

Saint Francis of Assisi, founder of the Franciscan order, rejected wealth for a life of simplicity and poverty.

The Church's desire to have a method of discovering and dealing with heretics led to the creation of a court called the **Inquisition,** or Holy Office. The job of this court was to find and try heretics, and it developed a regular procedure to deal with them. The Dominicans became especially well known for their roles as examiners of people suspected of heresy.

Reading Check **Analyzing** What impact did the Franciscans and Dominicans have on the lives of people in the thirteenth century?

Popular Religion in the High Middle Ages

We have witnessed the actions of popes, bishops, monks, and friars. But what of ordinary people? What were their religious hopes and fears? What were their religious beliefs?

The **sacraments** (Christian rites) of the Catholic Church were central in importance to ordinary people. These rites, such as baptism, marriage, and the Eucharist (Communion), made the Church a crucial part of people's lives from birth to death. The sacraments were seen as means for receiving God's grace and were necessary for salvation. Only the clergy could administer the sacraments, so everyone who hoped to gain salvation depended on the clergy to help them achieve this goal.

Other church practices were also important to ordinary people. One practice involved veneration of saints. Saints were men and women who were considered especially holy and who had achieved a special position in Heaven. Saints were able to ask for favors before the throne of God for people who prayed to them. Their ability to help and protect people in this way made saints very popular with all Christians.

Jesus Christ's apostles, of course, were recognized throughout Europe as saints. There were also numerous local saints who were of special significance to a single area. The Italians, for example, had Saint Nicholas, the patron saint of children, who is known today as Santa Claus. New saints emerged rapidly, especially in the intensely religious atmosphere of the eleventh and twelfth centuries.

Medieval Christians also believed that a pilgrimage to a holy shrine produced a spiritual benefit. The greatest shrine, but the most difficult to reach, was the Holy City of Jerusalem. On the continent, two pilgrim centers were especially popular in the High Middle Ages: **Rome,** which contained the relics of Saints Peter and Paul, and the town of Santiago de Compostela, supposedly the site of the tomb of the apostle James.

EXTENDING THE CONTENT

Catholic Church Of the seven sacraments defined by the Catholic Church, five directly influenced the lives of Christians during medieval times. *Baptism* removed original sin and indicated membership in the Church. *Marriage* dignified the union of two people. In the *Eucharist,* bread and wine were thought to miraculously become the body and blood of Jesus. Through *penance,* Christians received forgiveness for their sins. *Extreme unction,* or the *last rites,* were administered to the dying. The other two sacraments included *holy orders,* which was reserved for the clergy, and *confirmation* of older children, which did not become a regular practice until the thirteenth century.

CONNECTIONS Past To Present

From Saint Nicholas to Santa Claus

Saint Nicholas was a bishop in Asia Minor (present-day Turkey) who died in 342. He was known as a generous man who was fond of children. During the Middle Ages in Europe, Saint Nicholas became known as the patron saint of children. He brought them simple gifts of fruit, nuts, and candies on his feast day, which was December 6. Saint Nicholas was portrayed as being dressed in a red-and-white bishop's robe and sporting a flowing white beard.

The Dutch brought the tradition of Saint Nicholas with them to their colonies in the Americas. In America, however, changes occurred in the practices associated with Saint Nicholas. For example, in Holland children placed wooden shoes next to the fireplace to be filled with gifts from Saint Nicholas. In America, stockings were hung by the chimney.

The Dutch words for Saint Nicholas were *Sint Nikolass.* In America, they became *Sinte Klaas.* After the English took control of the Dutch colonies, *Sinte Klaas* became *Santa Claus.* Later in the nineteenth century, the physical appearance of Santa Claus also changed. Saint Nicholas had been portrayed as a tall, thin man. By the 1880s, Santa Claus had become the jolly fat man that we still know today.

Saint Nicholas

Comparing Past and Present

Think about a special holiday or event that you celebrate every year. Has your celebration of that holiday changed over the years? If so, how? Can you predict any future changes that might take place?

Local attractions, such as shrines dedicated to the Blessed Virgin Mary, also became pilgrimage centers.

Reading Check **Examining** Why were saints important to Christians in the High Middle Ages?

The Rise of Universities

The university as we know it today, with faculty, students, and degrees, was a product of the High Middle Ages. The word *university* comes from the Latin word *universitas,* meaning "corporation" or "guild." Medieval universities were educational guilds, or corporations, that produced educated and trained individuals.

The First Universities The first European university appeared in Bologna (buh•LOH•nyuh), Italy. A great teacher named Irnerius, who taught Roman law, attracted students to Bologna from all over Europe. Most were men who were administrators for kings and princes. (Women did not attend universities.) These men were eager to learn more about the law in order to apply it in their own jobs.

The first university in northern Europe was the University of Paris. In the second half of the twelfth century, a number of students and masters (teachers) left Paris and started their own university at Oxford, England. Kings, popes, and princes thought it honorable to found new universities. By 1500, Europe had 80 universities.

University Curricula Students began their studies at a medieval university with the traditional liberal arts curriculum, or course of study. This curriculum consisted of grammar, rhetoric, logic, arithmetic, geometry, music, and astronomy.

Teaching at a medieval university was done by a lecture method. The word *lecture* is derived from Latin and means "to read." Before the development of the printing press in the fifteenth century, books were expensive. Few students could afford them, so teachers read from a basic text and then added their explanations.

No exams were given after a series of lectures. When a student applied for a degree, however, he was given an oral examination by a committee of

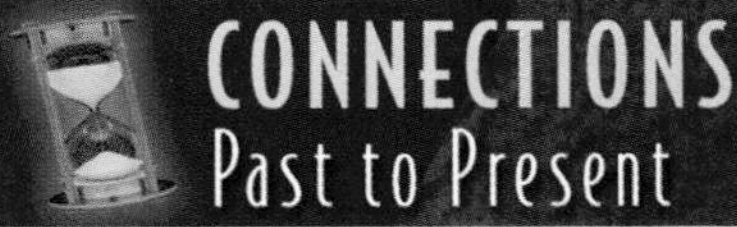

Answer: Answers will vary.

Reading Check

Answer: They had the ability to intercede between mortals and God, and, as such, they were believed to help and to protect the people.

Who?What?Where?When?

Universities Although modern universities had their origins in medieval Europe, Arabs founded universities nearly 200 years earlier. The Fatimids founded Cairo's al-Azhar University in 970. It remains the world's chief center of Islamic and Arabic learning.

Connecting Across Time

Compare and contrast schools of today with those of the High Middle Ages. Consider the roles of teachers and students, the curriculum, the role of the university, and its graduates. **L1**

3 ASSESS

Assign Section 1 Assessment as homework or as an in-class activity.

Have students use **Interactive Tutor Self-Assessment CD-ROM.**

MEETING INDIVIDUAL NEEDS

Visual/Spatial Have students who are visual learners or who have limited proficiency in English draw a series of illustrations depicting important events and people in this section. Ask the artists to work with other students to create text that explains their drawings. Display the completed drawings and accompanying text in the classroom. You might wish to ask each artist to work with another student to prepare an oral presentation to the class in which the students explain the significance of the events portrayed and why these events were chosen for illustration. **L1** ELL

Refer to the ***Inclusion for the High School Social Studies Classroom Strategies and Activities*** in the TCR.

Reading Check

Answer: Books were expensive and not readily available.

Section Quiz 4–1

Name ______ Date ______ Class ______

Chapter 4 Score

Section Quiz 4-1

DIRECTIONS: Matching Match each item in Column A with an item in Column B. Write the correct letters in the blanks. *(10 points each)*

Column A	Column B
____ 1. most highly regarded subject for university study	A. heresy
____ 2. struggled against papal supremacy	B. Hildegard of Bingen
____ 3. denial of basic Church doctrines	C. Henry IV
____ 4. abbess of a German religious house	D. Philip Augustus
____ 5. tried to have his marriage annulled	E. theology

DIRECTIONS: Multiple Choice In the blank, write the letter of the choice that best completes the statement or answers the question. *(10 points each)*

____ 6. Cities in ____ took the lead in the revival of trade.
A. Spain
B. France
C. England
D. Italy

____ 7. The Black Death devastated Europe in the
A. twelfth century.
B. thirteenth century.
C. fourteenth century.
D. fifteenth century.

____ 8. Most of the learned women of the Middle Ages were
A. nuns.
B. professors.
C. artisans.
D. merchants.

____ 9. One factor aiding the development of farming in medieval Europe was the
A. use of water and wind power.
B. formation of guilds.
C. growth of cities.
D. decline of Church power.

____ 10. What lasted from 1378 to 1417 and resulted in a decline of Church power?
A. the Hundred Years' War
B. the Black Death
C. the Great Schism
D. the Inquisition

Reading Check

Answer: Flying buttresses distributed the weight of the church's ceilings and roofs; therefore, the walls could be thinner and taller, and they could hold many large windows.

TURNING POINT

Not until the early 1900s were rats carrying bacteria-infected fleas identified as the carriers of bubonic plague. Today, knowledge of disease prevention and the development of vaccines have largely isolated plague outbreaks and reduced their devastating impact on societies.

teachers. These examinations were taken after a four- or six-year period of study. The first degree a student could earn was a bachelor of arts. Later, he might receive a master of arts.

After completing the liberal arts curriculum, a student could go on to study law, medicine, or theology. **Theology**—the study of religion and God—was the most highly regarded subject of the medieval university. A student who passed his final oral examinations in one of these areas was granted a doctor's degree.

Reading Check **Explaining** Why were most early university courses taught as lecture classes?

Architecture

The eleventh and twelfth centuries witnessed an explosion of building in medieval Europe, especially the building of churches. The cathedrals of the eleventh and twelfth centuries were built in the Romanesque style. Romanesque churches were normally built in the basilica shape used in the construction of churches in the late Roman Empire. (Basilicas were rectangular buildings with flat wooden roofs.)

Romanesque builders replaced the flat roofs with long, round, stone-arched structures called barrel vaults. Because stone roofs were heavy, Romanesque churches required massive pillars and walls to hold them up. This left little space for windows, so Romanesque churches were dark inside.

A new style, called Gothic, appeared in the twelfth century and was brought to perfection in the thirteenth. The Gothic cathedral remains one of the greatest artistic triumphs of the High Middle Ages. Two basic innovations of the twelfth century made Gothic cathedrals possible.

One innovation was the replacement of the round barrel vault of Romanesque churches with a combination of ribbed vaults and pointed arches. This change enabled builders to make Gothic churches higher than Romanesque churches, as if they were reaching to God.

Another technical innovation was the flying buttress—a heavy, arched support of stone, built onto the outside of the walls. Flying buttresses made it possible to distribute the weight of a church's vaulted ceilings outward and down. This eliminated the heavy walls that were needed in Romanesque churches. Gothic cathedrals were built, then, with relatively thin walls, which could be filled with magnificent stained glass windows.

Reading Check **Explaining** What were the benefits of flying buttresses?

The Late Middle Ages

TURNING POINT **In this section, you will learn how fourteenth-century Europe was devastated by the terrible plague known as the Black Death. This plague greatly decreased the population of Europe and brought about significant economic and social changes in the late Middle Ages.**

The Middle Ages in Europe had reached a high point in the thirteenth century. European society in the fourteenth and early fifteenth centuries (the Late Middle Ages), however, was challenged by an overwhelming number of disastrous forces. Especially catastrophic was the **Black Death.**

The Black Death The Black Death was the most devastating natural disaster in European history. One observer wrote that "father abandoned child, wife [abandoned] husband, one brother [abandoned] another, for the plague seemed to strike through breath and sight. And so they died." People were horrified by the plague, an evil force they could not understand.

A university classroom in fourteenth-century Germany

EXTENDING THE CONTENT

Stained Glass One of the most beautiful art forms to flourish during the Middle Ages was the craft of stained glass. Between the twelfth and sixteenth centuries, artisans created stained glass for some of the world's most magnificent cathedrals. Its original purpose was to illustrate Bible stories for illiterate peasants and serfs. The sun shining through the many pieces of colored glass, glittering like precious gems, was thought to convey the mystery of God. Artists created the colored glass by adding cobalt, silver, iron, or copper oxides to the glass. Details were painted on and then the glass was fired in a kiln. As shown on page 127, Chartres Cathedral, one of Europe's most majestic churches, has more than 150 stained glass windows.

History *through Architecture*

Answer: Students should recognize the ribbed vaults, pointed arches, and three-tiered elevations of Gothic church architecture.

Reading Essentials and Study Guide 4–1

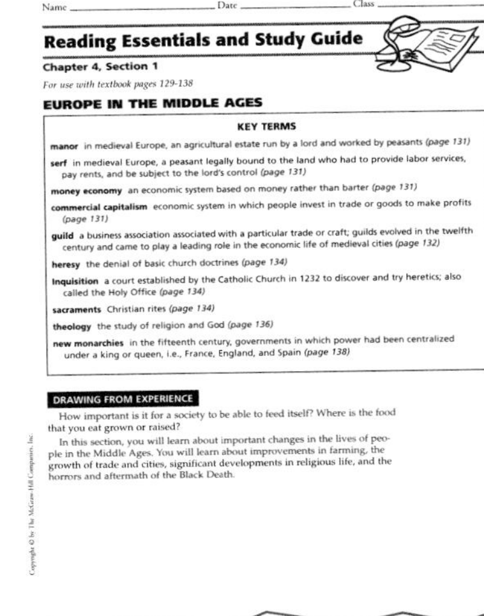

Name ______ Date ______ Class ______

Reading Essentials and Study Guide

Chapter 4, Section 1

For use with textbook pages 129-138

EUROPE IN THE MIDDLE AGES

KEY TERMS

manor in medieval Europe, an agricultural estate run by a lord and worked by peasants *(page 131)*

serf in medieval Europe, a peasant legally bound to the land who had to provide labor services, pay rents, and be subject to the lord's control *(page 131)*

money economy an economic system based on money rather than barter *(page 131)*

commercial capitalism economic system in which people invest in trade or goods to make profits *(page 131)*

guild a business association associated with a particular trade or craft; guilds evolved in the twelfth century and came to play a leading role in the economic life of medieval cities *(page 132)*

heresy the denial of basic church doctrines *(page 134)*

Inquisition a court established by the Catholic Church in 1232 to discover and try heretics; also called the Holy Office *(page 134)*

sacraments Christian rites *(page 134)*

theology the study of religion and God *(page 136)*

new monarchies in the fifteenth century, governments in which power had been centralized under a king or queen, i.e., France, England, and Spain *(page 138)*

DRAWING FROM EXPERIENCE

How important is it for a society to be able to feed itself? Where is the food that you eat grown or raised?

In this section, you will learn about important changes in the lives of people in the Middle Ages. You will learn about improvements in farming, the growth of trade and cities, significant developments in religious life, and the horrors and aftermath of the Black Death.

Connecting Across Time

Ask students to research the origins of the nursery rhyme "Ring Around the Rosies," which originally referred to the bubonic plague. Have student volunteers share the results of their research with the class. Have students research other nursery rhymes and traditional games to discover their connections to historical events. **L2**

History *through Architecture*

The evolution of architecture during the Middle Ages provided individuals with different ways to express their Christian faith. The use of flying buttresses, shown in the exterior above, allowed medieval architects to create a feeling of upward movement in Gothic cathedrals, as seen in the interior on the right. What other features associated with Gothic cathedrals can you identify from these photographs?

Bubonic plague was the most common form of the Black Death. It was spread by black rats infested with fleas carrying a deadly bacterium. Italian merchants brought the plague with them from Caffa, on the Black Sea, to the island of Sicily in October 1347. The plague had spread to southern Italy and southern France and Spain by the end of 1347.

Usually, the path of the Black Death followed trade routes. In 1348, the plague spread through France, the Low Countries (modern Belgium, Luxembourg, and the Netherlands), and Germany. It ravaged England in 1349 and expanded to northern Europe and Scandinavia. Eastern Europe and Russia were affected by 1351.

Out of a total European population of 75 million, possibly as many as 38 million people died of the plague between 1347 and 1351. Especially hard hit were Italy's crowded cities, where 50 to 60 percent of the people died. In England and Germany, entire villages disappeared.

The death of so many people in the fourteenth century had severe economic consequences. Trade declined, and a shortage of workers caused a dramatic rise in the price of labor. At the same time, the decline in the number of people lowered the demand for food, resulting in falling prices.

The Decline of Church Power The popes of the Roman Catholic Church reached the height of their power in the thirteenth century. Then, in the fourteenth century, a series of problems led to a decline in the Church's political and spiritual position.

The European kings had grown unwilling to accept papal claims of supremacy by the end of the thirteenth century. This is evident in the struggle between Pope Boniface VIII and King Philip IV of France. This struggle led a French pope in 1305 to take up residence in **Avignon** (a•veen•YOHN), in southern France.

From 1305 to 1377, the popes lived in Avignon. Sentiments against the papacy grew during this time. The pope was the bishop of Rome, and it seemed improper that he should reside in Avignon instead of Rome. When the pope did return in 1377, another disaster soon struck. After his death, a group of Italian cardinals elected an Italian pope, while a group of French cardinals elected a French pope.

The existence of two popes caused the **Great Schism,** which lasted from 1378 to 1417. It divided

COOPERATIVE LEARNING ACTIVITY

Creating a News Report Besides the massive social and economic consequences of the Black Death, it also had significant psychological effects on the people of the Middle Ages. Many, searching for answers, turned to mysticism and superstitious beliefs and practices. Some, seeking a scapegoat, persecuted their Jewish neighbors. AIDS is a modern-day plague, affecting millions around the world. Have students work together on a project comparing and contrasting the Black Death with AIDS. Ask them to address the causes, symptoms, and spread of each disease, any known or possible cures for each, and effects of each disease on individuals and society. They might present their information as a video or radio newscast, or as a newsmagazine article. **L2**

CHAPTER 4
Section 1, 129–138

Reading Check

Answer: New rulers began to reestablish the centralized power of monarchies.

Who?What?Where?When?

The Longbow In the Hundred Years' War, English soldiers were armed not only with pikes, or heavy spears, but also with longbows. This weapon was as tall as the man who carried it. He would draw it by stooping over with the bow parallel to the ground and then straighten up, using his leg and back muscles. The arrow was drawn to his ear. Bowmen could drive a 30-inch shaft tipped with a dagger through three inches of oak. In battle, the arrow storm was reported to darken the sky.

Reteaching Activity

Review the key terms from this section and ask students to explain the importance of each to the history of medieval Europe. **L1** ELL

4 CLOSE

Lead students in a discussion of the dominant role of the Church in the lives of medieval people. How dominant are the major religions today in people's lives? **L1**

The Battle of Crécy was the first major battle of the Hundred Years' War.

Europe. France and its allies supported the French pope, who had returned to Avignon. England and England's allies supported the pope in Rome.

The pope was widely believed to be the true leader of Christendom. When each line of popes denounced the other as the Antichrist (one who opposes Christ), people's faith in both the papacy and the Church were undermined. Although the schism was finally ended in 1417, the Church had lost much of its political and spiritual authority.

Political Crisis and Recovery War and political instability were also problems of the Late Middle Ages. The Hundred Years' War between England and France, which lasted from 1337 to 1453, was the most violent struggle during this period. It took the efforts of a simple peasant girl, Joan of Arc, to help the French armies and finally bring an end to the war.

In the fourteenth century, France, England, and other European states faced serious problems. In the fifteenth century, recovery set in as rulers attempted to reestablish the centralized power of monarchies. Some historians have spoken of these reestablished states as the **new monarchies**. This term applies especially to the monarchies of France, England, and Spain at the end of the fifteenth century.

Unlike France, England, and Spain, the Holy Roman Empire did not develop a strong monarchical authority. The failures of German emperors in the thirteenth century had made Germany a land of hundreds of independent states.

In eastern Europe, rulers also found it difficult to centralize their states. Religious differences troubled the area as Roman Catholics, Eastern Orthodox Christians, and other groups confronted one another. Since the thirteenth century, Russia had been under the domination of the Mongols. Gradually, the princes of Moscow rose to prominence. Under the great prince Ivan III, a new Russian state was born.

Reading Check **Explaining** How did European rulers begin to recover politically after the Hundred Years' War?

SECTION 1 ASSESSMENT

Checking for Understanding

1. **Define** manor, serf, money economy, commercial capitalism, guild, heresy, Inquisition, sacrament, theology, new monarchies.
2. **Identify** Commercial Revolution, Pope Gregory VII, Henry IV, Cistercians, Hildegard of Bingen, Saint Francis of Assisi, Black Death, Great Schism.
3. **Locate** Venice, Papal States, Rome, Avignon.
4. **Describe** the new religious orders created during the Middle Ages.
5. **List** the factors that led to increased food production.

Critical Thinking

6. **Explain** How did the ambitions of political rulers and the Catholic Church come into conflict during the Middle Ages?
7. **Compare and Contrast** Use a table like the one below to note the differences between the Romanesque and Gothic styles of church architecture.

Romanesque	Gothic

Analyzing Visuals

8. **Examine** the image of the medieval university classroom on page 136. In what ways was the educational process different in medieval universities than it is now? What elements of the traditional course of study in universities of the Middle Ages still exist in American high schools and colleges today?

Writing About History

9. **Persuasive Writing** Take the position of either Pope Gregory VII or King Henry IV of Germany. Argue whether popes or kings should have the authority to appoint clergy to high-ranking positions.

SECTION 1 ASSESSMENT

1. Key terms are in blue.
2. Commercial Revolution *(p. 131);* Pope Gregory VII *(p. 133);* Henry IV *(p. 133);* Cistercians *(p. 133);* Hildegard of Bingen *(p. 133);* Saint Francis of Assisi *(p. 134);* Black Death *(p. 136);* Great Schism *(p. 137)*
3. See chapter maps.
4. Cistercians took religion to people outside monastery. Franciscans lived among the people, preached repentance, aided poor. Dominicans defended Church against heresy.
5. peace, improved climate, more land, carruca, three-field system
6. Clergy had responsibilities to pope and kings. Pope Gregory VII claimed to have authority over rulers and clergy. Henry IV objected.
7. Romanesque: basilica shape, heavy walls, barrel vault roof, dark; Gothic: high roofs, ribbed vaults, pointed arches, thin walls, light
8. Teaching was by lecture since books were expensive. Oral exams were given at the end of a 4 to 6 year period of study. Theology was the most prestigious subject.
9. Essays will vary.

CRITICAL THINKING SKILLBUILDER

Analyzing Primary and Secondary Sources

Why Learn This Skill?

Suppose for a moment that a devastating tornado has struck a nearby town. On television that night, you watch an interview with an eyewitness. The eyewitness begins to cry as she describes the destruction of her own home and neighborhood. The next day, you read a newspaper account that describes the tornado's path. Is one of these accounts of the same event more accurate than the other?

Learning the Skill

To determine the accuracy of an account, you must analyze its source. There are two main types of sources—**primary** and **secondary.**

Primary sources are produced by eyewitnesses to events. Diaries, letters, autobiographies, interviews, artifacts, and paintings are primary sources. Because primary sources convey personal experiences, they often include the emotions and opinions of participants in an event.

Secondary sources use information gathered from others. Newspapers, textbooks, and biographies are secondary sources. Secondary sources, written later, help us to understand events in a larger context or time frame.

To determine reliability of a source, consider the type of source you are using. For a primary source, determine who the author is and when the material was written. An account written during or immediately after an event is often more reliable than one written years later. For a secondary source, look for good documentation. Researchers should cite their sources in footnotes and bibliographies.

For both types of sources you also need to evaluate the author. Is this author biased? What background and authority does he or she have? Finally, compare two accounts of the same event. If they disagree, you should question the reliability of the material and conduct further research to determine which can be corroborated with other reliable sources.

Practicing the Skill

Read the following excerpts and answer the questions:

> “Finally the two groups met. . . . When all was ready Montezuma placed his feet, shod in gold-soled, gem-studded sandals, on the carpeted pavement and . . . advanced to an encounter that would shape both his own destiny and that of his nation. . . . Montezuma had servants bring forward two necklaces of red shells hung with life-size shrimps made of gold. These he placed around Cortés's neck.”
>
> **—from *Cortés* by William Weber Johnson, 1975**

> “When we had arrived at a place not far from the town, the monarch raised himself in his sedan. . . . Montezuma himself was sumptuously attired, had on a species of half boot, richly set with jewels, and whose soles were made of solid gold. . . . Montezuma came up to Cortés, and hung about his neck a chaste necklace of gold, most curiously worked with figures all representing crabs.”
>
> **—from an account by Conquistador Bernal Díaz del Castillo, 1519**

1. What is the general topic of the two sources?
2. Identify the primary source.
3. Is one account more reliable than the other? If so, why? How do you know?

Applying the Skill

Find two accounts of a recent event or a historical event. Analyze the reliability of each. Be sure to document how you reached your conclusions about the reliability of the sources.

Glencoe's **Skillbuilder Interactive Workbook, Level 2,** provides instruction and practice in key social studies skills.

ANSWERS TO PRACTICING THE SKILL

1. the meeting between Cortés and Montezuma
2. the account by Bernal Díaz del Castillo
3. Answers may vary. Students should keep in mind that Bernal Díaz del Castillo's account may have been an eyewitness account; even if his account was *not* an eyewitness account, he accompanied Cortés, whereas the historian Johnson definitely was not there and must base his version on available documentation—which in this case is probably limited to Díaz's account.

Applying the Skill: Answers will vary. Be sure that students list full bibliographic citations.

TEACH

Analyzing Primary and Secondary Sources Have students analyze print advertisements. Point out the importance of analyzing information in ads, which are not usually objective. Emphasize the need to analyze the purpose and accuracy of all kinds of information.

Be sure students understand the difference between a primary and secondary source. **Ask:** How can you determine the reliability of a source? *(primary, determine author and date; secondary, check documentation; both, evaluate author)* **L1** ELL

Additional Practice

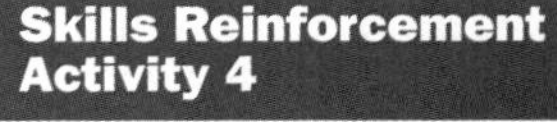

Skills Reinforcement Activity 4

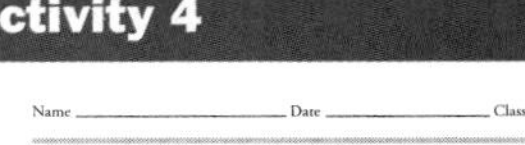

Name ______ Date ______ Class ______

Skills Reinforcement Activity 4

Analyzing Primary and Secondary Sources

Knowing the sources of information found in books and articles is critical to appraising their value as historical sources. Historians need a system to rate the accuracy of the information they collect.

DIRECTIONS: Read the following quotes, and determine which accurately represents the subject being discussed. The criteria to use in making your decisions should be: the type of source, who created it, when and where it was created, its topic, its purpose, and the source's reliability. Then answer the questions below in the space provided.

"The Spaniards had been allowed entry into the city so that they would learn to appreciate the extent of Moctezoma's [Montezuma's] greatness. Instead they seized him as hostage and puppet. As they clustered around him, gazing into his face, touching and prod-

"Cicuye is a village of nearly five hundred warriors, who are feared throughout that country. The pueblo is square, situated on a rock, with a large courtyard in the middle containing underground council chambers. The houses are all alike, four stories high. One

GLENCOE TECHNOLOGY

CD-ROM
Glencoe Skillbuilder Interactive Workbook CD-ROM, Level 2

This interactive CD-ROM reinforces student mastery of essential social studies skills.

1 FOCUS

Section Overview

This section describes early civilizations in the Americas, with an emphasis on Mesoamerica and South America.

BELLRINGER
Skillbuilder Activity

Project transparency and have students answer questions.

Available as a blackline master.

Daily Focus Skills Transparency 4–2

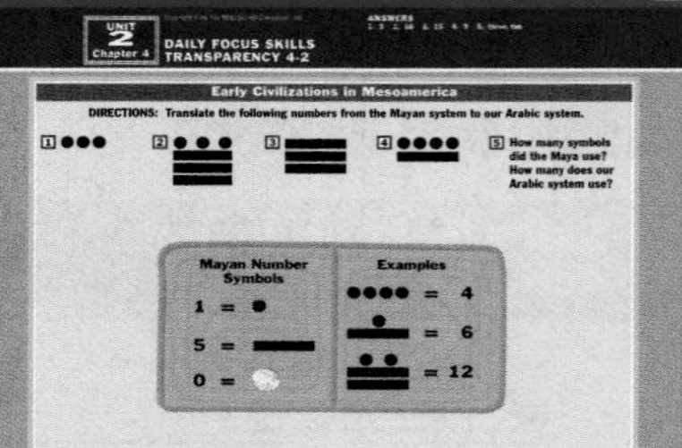

Guide to Reading

Answers to Graphic: Mayan: Yucatán Peninsula, Central America, southern Mexico; polytheistic; stone temples, pyramids, palaces; invasion, internal revolt, natural disaster, or lack of food. Aztec: Valley of Mexico; polytheistic; stone pyramids, temples, public buildings; c. 1520, Spanish forces. Inca: South America; polytheistic; road builders, stone buildings; c. 1535, Spanish forces.

Preteaching Vocabulary: Be sure students can define and locate on a map the region known as *Mesoamerica.* Ask them to describe the physical geography of the region. **L1**

SECTION 2 The Americas

Guide to Reading

Main Ideas
- Because of the variety of climate and geographic features, many different cultures emerged in the Americas.
- The Maya, Aztec, and Inca developed sophisticated civilizations in Mesoamerica and South America.

Key Terms
Mesoamerica, epidemic

People to Identify
Hernán Cortés, Montezuma, Pachacuti, Francisco Pizarro

Places to Locate
Gulf of Mexico, Yucatán Peninsula, Tikal, Chichén Itzá, Tenochtitlán

Preview Questions
1. Who were the first inhabitants of the Americas?
2. What forces ended the Aztec and Incan civilizations?

Reading Strategy
Summarizing Information Create a chart describing the characteristics of Mayan, Aztec, and Incan cultures.

People	
Location	
Religion	
Architecture	
Year/Reason Declined	

Preview of Events

1200 B.C. · A.D. 300 · A.D. 1100 · A.D. 1200 · A.D. 1300 · A.D. 1400 · A.D. 1500

- **c. 1200 B.C.** Olmec civilization emerges
- **A.D. 300** Mayan civilization begins
- **A.D. 1200** Toltec civilization declines
- **A.D. 1440s** Incan ruler Pachacuti builds empire
- **A.D. 1519** Cortés lands at Veracruz

Voices from the Past

One Sioux sacred woman said:

❝All of this creation is sacred, and so do not forget. Every dawn as it comes is a holy event, and every day is holy, for the light comes from your Father Wakan-Tanka, and also you must always remember that the two-leggeds and all the other peoples who stand upon this earth are sacred and should be treated as such." A Native American song says, "The whole Southwest was a House Made of Dawn. It was made of pollen and of rain. The land was old and everlasting. There were many colors on the hills and on the plain, and there was a dark wilderness on the mountains beyond. The land was tilled and strong and it was beautiful all around.❞

—*The Native Americans: An Illustrated History,* Betty and Ian Ballantine, eds., 1993

Sioux warrior shirt with beads and fringe

As these words illustrate, the first peoples who inhabited North America had great respect for the earth and its creatures.

Early Americans

The Americas make up an enormous land area, stretching about nine thousand miles (more than fourteen thousand km) from the Arctic Ocean in the north to Cape Horn at the tip of South America. Over this vast area are many different landscapes: ice-covered lands, dense forests, fertile river valleys ideal for hunting and farming, coastlines for fishing, lush tropical forests, and hot deserts.

Between 100,000 and 8,000 years ago, the last Ice Age produced low sea levels that in turn created a land bridge in the Bering Strait between the Asian and North American continents. Many scholars believe that small communities of people

SECTION RESOURCES

Reproducible Masters
- Reproducible Lesson Plan 4–2
- Daily Lecture and Discussion Notes 4–2
- Guided Reading Activity 4–2
- Section Quiz 4–2
- Reading Essentials and Study Guide 4–2

Transparencies
- Daily Focus Skills Transparency 4–2

Multimedia
- Interactive Tutor Self-Assessment CD-ROM
- ExamView® Pro Testmaker CD-ROM
- Presentation Plus! CD-ROM

from Asia crossed this land bridge. Most likely, they were hunters who were pursuing the herds of bison and caribou that moved in search of grazing land into North America as the glaciers receded. These people became the first Americans.

The peoples of North America created a remarkable number of different cultures. Inuits, Mound Builders, Anasazi, Plains Amerindians, and Iroquois all developed flourishing societies that responded in their own unique ways to the environmental conditions that they faced.

Reading Check **Summarizing** According to scholars, why did hunters cross the land bridge into North America?

The Maya and Toltec

Signs of civilization in Mesoamerica—a name we use for areas of Mexico and Central America that were civilized before the Spaniards arrived—appeared around 1200 B.C. with the Olmec. Located in the hot and swampy lowlands along the coast of the **Gulf of Mexico** south of Veracruz, the Olmec peoples farmed along the muddy riverbanks in the area. The Olmec had large cities that were centers for their religious rituals. Around 400 B.C., the Olmec civilization declined and eventually collapsed.

The Maya Later, on the **Yucatán Peninsula,** a major civilization arose—that of the **Maya,** which flourished between A.D. 300 and 900. It was one of the most sophisticated civilizations in the Americas. The Maya built splendid temples and pyramids and developed a complicated calendar. Mayan civilization came to include much of Central America and southern Mexico.

Mayan cities were built around a central pyramid topped by a shrine to the gods. Nearby were other temples, palaces, and a sacred ball court. Some scholars believe that urban centers such as **Tikal** (in present-day Guatemala) may have had a hundred thousand inhabitants.

Mayan civilization was composed of city-states, each governed by a hereditary ruling class. These Mayan city-states were often at war with each other. Ordinary soldiers who were captured in battle became slaves. Captured nobles and war leaders were used for human sacrifice.

Rulers of the Mayan city-states claimed to be descended from the gods. The Mayan rulers were helped by nobles and a class of scribes who may also have been priests. Mayan society also included townspeople who were skilled artisans, officials, and merchants. Most of the Mayan people were peasant farmers.

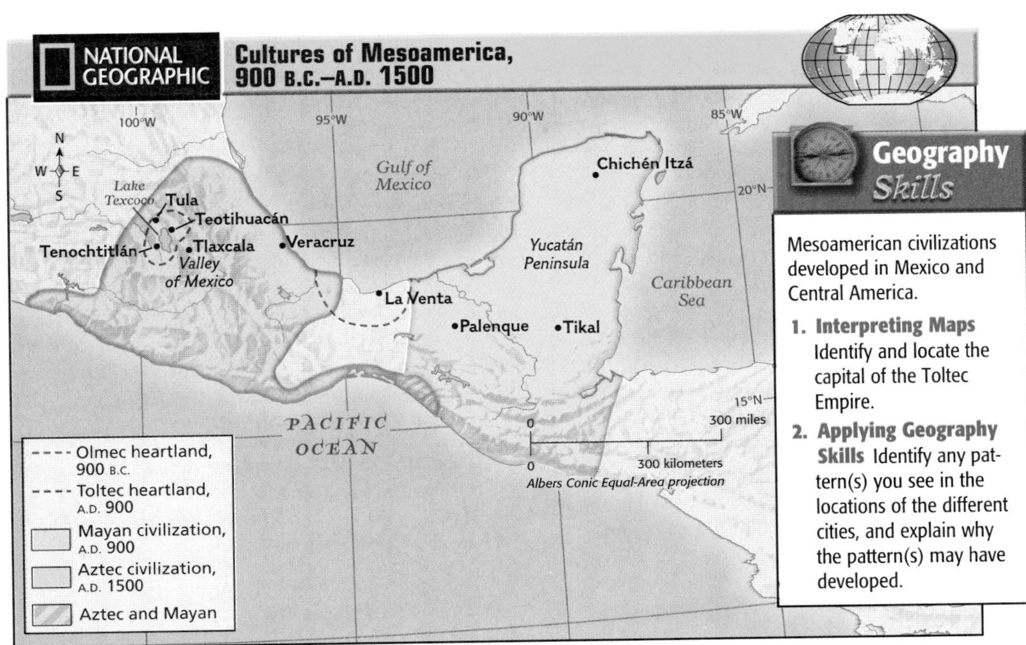

Geography Skills

Mesoamerican civilizations developed in Mexico and Central America.

1. **Interpreting Maps** Identify and locate the capital of the Toltec Empire.
2. **Applying Geography Skills** Identify any pattern(s) you see in the locations of the different cities, and explain why the pattern(s) may have developed.

2 TEACH

Reading Check

Answer: Hunters crossed into North America to pursue herds of bison and caribou.

Geography Skills

Answers:

1. Tula, northwest of modern-day Mexico City
2. cities clustered in Valley of Mexico suggests that the area was favorable to development; Lake Texcoco provided protection, as did the mountains surrounding the area; other cities located along the Gulf of Mexico, such as Veracruz, had the advantage of water for transportation

Daily Lecture and Discussion Notes 4–2

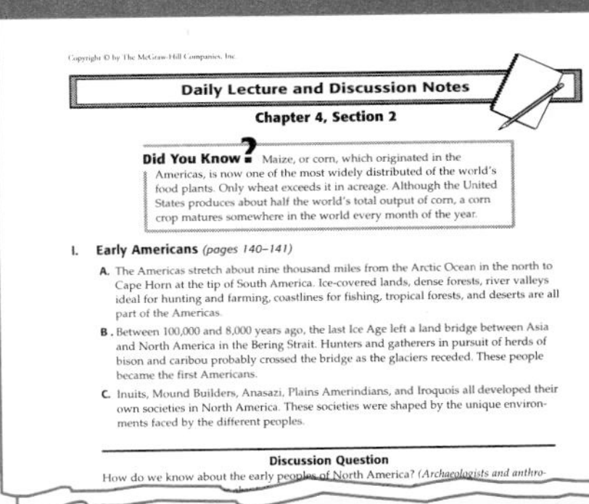

Daily Lecture and Discussion Notes

Chapter 4, Section 2

Did You Know? Maize, or corn, which originated in the Americas, is now one of the most widely distributed of the world's food plants. Only wheat exceeds it in acreage. Although the United States produces about half the world's total output of corn, a corn crop matures somewhere in the world every month of the year.

I. **Early Americans** *(pages 140–141)*

A. The Americas stretch about nine thousand miles from the Arctic Ocean in the north to Cape Horn at the tip of South America. Ice-covered lands, dense forests, river valleys ideal for hunting and farming, coastlines for fishing, tropical forests, and deserts are all part of the Americas.

B. Between 100,000 and 8,000 years ago, the last Ice Age left a land bridge between Asia and North America in the Bering Strait. Hunters and gatherers in pursuit of herds of bison and caribou probably crossed the bridge as the glaciers receded. These people became the first Americans.

C. Inuits, Mound Builders, Anasazi, Plains Amerindians, and Iroquois all developed their own societies in North America. These societies were shaped by the unique environments faced by the different peoples.

Discussion Question

How do we know about the early peoples of North America? *(Archaeologists and anthro-*

Writing Activity

Have students write a short report comparing Mayan hieroglyphics and pyramids with those of ancient Egypt. **L1**

COOPERATIVE LEARNING ACTIVITY

Creating a Bulletin Board Organize the class into five groups. Assign each group one of the following topics concerning the Maya: political and social structure, geography, economy, religion, writings and calendar, and collapse. Groups are to research their topics and use a poster board to display information not found in the text. Each group should select a coordinator who will assign specific tasks to each member. When the groups have finished, mount the displays so that they form a comprehensive chart presenting information on Mayan culture. Ask one member of each group to present its findings to the rest of the class. **L2**

For grading this activity, refer to the ***Performance Assessment Activities and Rubrics*** booklet.

CHAPTER 4
Section 2, 140–144

Reading Check

Answer: city-states governed by a hereditary ruling class; rulers helped by nobles and scribes

Enrich

Unlike early European and Asian cultures, the Mesoamericans did not put the wheel to practical use—remarkably, since small clay models with wheels suggest that the principle of the wheel was known to them. The Mayans built roads between their cities, but the wheel was never used for transport. Ask students whether they have any theories as to why the Mayans did not use wheels for transportation. **L1**

Who?What?Where?When?

Hieroglyphics The word "hieroglyphics" means *sacred writing.* Hieroglyphics use pictures rather than words to represent objects. The complex Mayan writing system contained more than 850 characters, including phonetic, ideographic, and hieroglyphic symbols. Do students think that if the Spanish had realized the significance of the Mayan hieroglyphic records, they would have treated Mayan books with more respect? **L1**

Guided Reading Activity 4–2

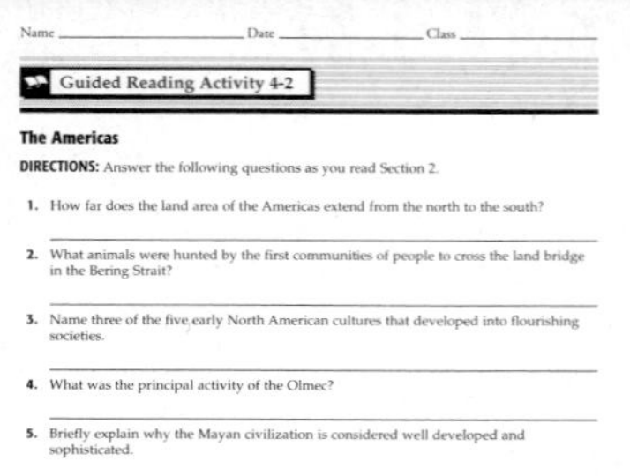

Name ______ Date ______ Class ______

Guided Reading Activity 4-2

The Americas

DIRECTIONS: Answer the following questions as you read Section 2.

1. How far does the land area of the Americas extend from the north to the south?
2. What animals were hunted by the first communities of people to cross the land bridge in the Bering Strait?
3. Name three of the five early North American cultures that developed into flourishing societies.
4. What was the principal activity of the Olmec?
5. Briefly explain why the Mayan civilization is considered well developed and sophisticated.

THE WAY IT WAS

SPORTS & CONTESTS

The Deadly Games of Central America

Mayan cities contained ball courts. Usually, a court consisted of a rectangular space surrounded by walls with highly decorated stone rings. The walls were covered with images of war and sacrificial victims. The contestants tried to drive a solid rubber ball through these rings. Ball players, usually two or three on a team, used their hips to propel the ball (they were not allowed to use hands or feet). Players donned helmets, gloves, and knee and hip protectors made of hide to protect themselves against the hard rubber balls.

Because the stone rings were placed 27 feet (more than 8 m) above the ground, it took considerable skill to score a goal. Some scholars believe that making a goal was so rare

This Mayan athlete is shown wearing protective padding.

The Maya created a sophisticated writing system based on hieroglyphs, or pictures. Mayan hieroglyphs remained a mystery to scholars for centuries. Then, modern investigators discovered that many passages contained symbols that recorded dates in the Mayan calendar known as the Long Count. This calendar was based on a belief in cycles of creation and destruction. According to the Maya, our present world was created in 3114 B.C. and is scheduled to complete its downward cycle on December 23, 2012.

HISTORY Online

Web Activity Visit the *Glencoe World History—Modern Times* Web site at wh.mt.glencoe.com and click on **Chapter 4–Student Web Activity** to learn more about early civilizations in the Americas.

The Mayan civilization in the central Yucatán Peninsula eventually began to decline. Explanations for the decline include invasion, internal revolt, or a natural disaster such as a volcanic eruption. A more recent theory is that overuse of the land led to reduced crop yields. Whatever the case, Mayan cities were abandoned and covered by dense jungle growth. They were not rediscovered until the nineteenth and twentieth centuries.

The Toltec The capital of the Toltec Empire was at Tula, built on a high ridge northwest of present-day Mexico City. The Toltec were a fierce and warlike people who extended their conquests into the Mayan lands of Guatemala and the northern Yucatán. The **Toltec** were also builders who constructed pyramids and palaces. They controlled the upper Yucatán Peninsula from the village of **Chichén Itzá** for several centuries, beginning around A.D. 900. In about 1200 their civilization, too, declined.

Reading Check **Describing** How was Mayan civilization organized and governed?

The Aztec

The origins of the **Aztec** are uncertain. Sometime during the twelfth century A.D., however, they began a long migration that brought them to the Valley of

INTERDISCIPLINARY CONNECTIONS ACTIVITY

Literature In the 1500s, Mayan myths were written down in an epic called the *Popul Voh.* The *Popul Voh* recounts the Mayan myth of creation. Here is the description of the universe before the creation of the earth: "There is not yet one person, one animal, bird, fish, crab, tree, rock, hollow, canyon, meadow, forest. Only the sky alone is there; the face of the earth is not clear. Only the sea alone is pooled under all the sky; there is nothing whatever gathered together. It is at rest; not a single thing stirs." Ask students to compare Mayan creation myths with those of other peoples, such as the Greeks, Romans, Norse, or Chinese. Have them prepare a class presentation, including illustrations or transparencies. **L3**

that players were rewarded with clothing and jewelry from the watching crowds.

The exact rules of the game are unknown, but we do know that it was more than a sport. The ball game had a religious meaning. The ball court was a symbol of the world, and the ball represented the sun and the moon. Apparently, it was believed that playing the game often would produce better harvests. The results of the game were deadly. The defeated players were sacrificed in ceremonies held after the end of the game. Similar courts have been found at sites throughout Central America, as well as present-day Arizona and New Mexico.

A present-day soccer match featuring Brazil and Canada

CONNECTING TO THE PAST

1. **Summarizing** Why was great skill required of the athletes who played the Mayan ball game?
2. **Describing** Explain the symbolism of the Mayan ball game.
3. **Writing about History** Research the gladiatorial contests of ancient Rome. How were those contests similar to the Mayan ball games?

Mexico. They eventually established their capital, beginning in 1325, at **Tenochtitlán** (tay•NAWCH•teet•LAHN), on an island in the middle of Lake Texcoco, now the location of Mexico City.

For the next hundred years, the Aztec built their city. They constructed temples, other public buildings, and houses. They built roadways of stone across Lake Texcoco to the north, south, and west, linking the many islands to the mainland. While they were building their capital city, the Aztec consolidated their rule over much of what is modern Mexico.

By 1500, as many as four million Aztec lived in the Valley of Mexico and the surrounding valleys of central Mexico. Power in the Aztec state was vested in the hands of the monarch, who claimed that he was descended from the gods.

At the center of the capital city of Tenochtitlán was a massive pyramid dedicated to Huitzilopochtli, god of the sun. A platform at the top held an altar for performing human sacrifices.

In 1519, a Spanish force under the command of **Hernán Cortés** landed at Veracruz, on the Gulf of Mexico. Cortés marched to Tenochtitlán at the head of a small body of troops (550 soldiers and 16 horses). The Aztec monarch **Montezuma** (also spelled Moctezuma) offered gifts of gold to the foreigners when they arrived.

Eventually, tensions arose between the Spaniards and the Aztec. Within a year, the forces of Cortés had had destroyed the Aztec pyramids, temples, and palaces. Tenochtitlán was no more.

Reading Check **Identifying** What was the capital of the Aztec civilization? What is the name of the modern-day city located there?

The Inca

In the fifteenth century, another remarkable civilization—that of the **Inca**—flourished in South America. In the 1440s, under the leadership of the powerful ruler **Pachacuti,** the Inca launched a campaign of conquest that eventually brought the entire region under their control.

Pachacuti and his immediate successors, Topa Inca and Huayna Inca (the word *Inca* means "ruler"), extended the boundaries of the Incan Empire as far as

EXTENDING THE CONTENT

Disease Much of the "conquest" of the Americas was accomplished without warfare. European infectious disease left its devastating mark on Native American cultures. Due to the relatively small, isolated population, basic hygiene practices, and temperate climates, many parts of the Americas were relatively disease-free. It was this good health that made the American peoples so vulnerable to European contact. Smallpox, contracted from European invaders and explorers, wiped out more people than all the wars combined. Lacking immunity, the population of the Americas was reduced by two-thirds. One estimate places the decline in population in Mesoamerica from 25 million to 3 million in 150 years.

THE WAY IT WAS

Answers:
1. players not allowed to use either their hands or feet; members of losing side were sacrificed after game
2. ball court symbolic of the world, and ball represented the sun and the moon
3. There was great honor in playing, but those who lost were put to death.

Reading Check

Answer: The Aztec capital was at Tenochtitlán on an island in the middle of Lake Texcoco. Mexico City is now located there.

Global Gourmet

Corn Corn and beans remain essential ingredients in the diet of the people of southern Mexico, Guatemala, and Belize. Corn is ground and pounded flat to make tortillas. This pancake-shaped bread is popular throughout the region and the world.

3 ASSESS

Assign Section 2 Assessment as homework or as an in-class activity.

Have students use **Interactive Tutor Self-Assessment CD-ROM.**

Section Quiz 4–2

Name ______ Date ______ Class ______

Chapter 4 Score

Section Quiz 4-2

DIRECTIONS: Matching Match each item in Column A with an item in Column B. Write the correct letters in the blanks. *(10 points each)*

Column A	Column B
____ 1. built cities around a central pyramid	A. Inca
____ 2. built a major road through the Andes	B. Aztec
____ 3. a people native to North America	C. Maya
____ 4. were destroyed by forces led by Cortés	D. Toltec
____ 5. had capital at Tula	E. Mound Builders

DIRECTIONS: Multiple Choice In the blank, write the letter of the choice that best completes the statement or answers the question. *(10 points each)*

____ 6. One feature of the Aztec is

CHAPTER 4
Section 2, 140–144

Reading Check

Answer: They expanded the Incan Empire to include parts of Ecuador, central Chile, and the edge of the Amazon basin. They ruled over about 12 million people.

Reading Essentials and Study Guide 4–2

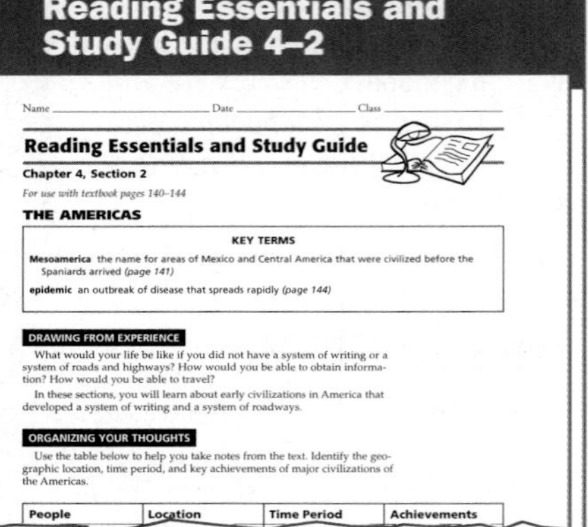

Name ______ Date ______ Class ______

Reading Essentials and Study Guide

Chapter 4, Section 2

For use with textbook pages 140–144

THE AMERICAS

KEY TERMS

Mesoamerica the name for areas of Mexico and Central America that were civilized before the Spaniards arrived *(page 141)*

epidemic an outbreak of disease that spreads rapidly *(page 144)*

DRAWING FROM EXPERIENCE

What would your life be like if you did not have a system of writing or a system of roads and highways? How would you be able to obtain information? How would you be able to travel?

In these sections, you will learn about early civilizations in America that developed a system of writing and a system of roadways.

ORGANIZING YOUR THOUGHTS

Use the table below to help you take notes from the text. Identify the geographic location, time period, and key achievements of major civilizations of the Americas.

People	Location	Time Period	Achievements

Writing Activity

Have students write a brief essay in which they summarize the major political, economic, and cultural developments of early American civilizations. **L1**

Reteaching Activity

Ask students to outline the section, focusing on the key features and events of each society discussed. **L1** ELL

4 CLOSE

Ask students to compare the rise, achievements, and decline of the Aztec and Incan Empires. **L1**

The 50-foot-tall stone walls of Cuzco were built without mortar by the Inca.

Ecuador, central Chile, and the edge of the Amazon basin. The empire included perhaps twelve million people. At the top of the system was the emperor, who was believed to be descended from Inti, the sun god.

The Incan state was built on war, so all young men were required to serve in the Incan army. With some two hundred thousand members, the army was the largest and best armed in the region.

The Inca also built roads. A system of some 24,800 miles (around 40,000 km) of roads extended from the border of modern-day Colombia to a point south of modern-day Santiago, Chile. Two major roadways extended in a north-south direction, one through the Andes and the other along the coast, with connecting routes between them.

The Incan Empire was still flourishing when the first Spanish expeditions arrived in the central Andes. In December 1530, **Francisco Pizarro** and a small band of about 180 men landed on the Pacific coast of South America. Pizarro brought steel weapons, gunpowder, and horses. The Inca had none of these.

The Incan Empire experienced an **epidemic** (an outbreak of disease that spreads rapidly) of smallpox. Like the Aztec, the Inca had no immunities to European diseases. All too soon, smallpox was devastating entire villages. Even the Incan emperor was a victim. Armed only with stones, arrows, and light spears, the Incan soldiers were little challenge to the Spaniard's charging horses, guns, and cannons.

Pizarro and his soldiers, aided by Incan allies, marched on Cuzco and captured the Incan capital. By 1535, Pizarro had established a new capital at Lima for a new colony of the Spanish Empire.

Reading Check **Describing** What were the accomplishments of Pachacuti and his immediate successors?

SECTION 2 ASSESSMENT

Checking for Understanding

1. **Define** Mesoamerica, epidemic.
2. **Identify** Maya, Toltec, Aztec, Hernán Cortés, Montezuma, Inca, Pachacuti, Francisco Pizarro.
3. **Locate** Gulf of Mexico,Yucatán Peninsula, Tikal, Chichén Itzá, Tenochtitlán.
4. **Explain** how Mayan hieroglyphics have helped us to understand Mayan culture.
5. **List** the accomplishments of the Aztec peoples.

Critical Thinking

6. **Analyze** Why would the Inca have found it important to build an extensive road system?
7. **Summarizing Information** Create a table like the one below listing the major civilizations and principle cities that developed in Mesoamerica.

Mesoamerica	
Civilizations	Cities

Analyzing Visuals

8. **Examine** the sculpture of a Mayan athlete on page 142. What inferences can you draw about the status of athletes in Mayan culture from examining this sculpture?

Writing About History

9. **Expository Writing** Using the Internet or library sources, research the political system of the Incan rulers. Write an essay in which you explain the advantages and disadvantages of the Incan political system.

SECTION 2 ASSESSMENT

1. Key terms are in blue.
2. Maya *(p. 141);* Toltec *(p. 142);* Aztec *(p. 142);* Hernán Cortés *(p. 143);* Montezuma *(p. 143);* Inca *(p. 143);* Pachacuti *(p. 143);* Francisco Pizarro *(p. 144)*
3. See chapter maps.
4. They provide a record of events in Mayan history, especially of the lives of Mayan rulers.
5. constructed temples and other public buildings; built stone roads; created a thriving civilization
6. The empire was geographically very large and held 12 million people; army needed roadways for travel.
7. Olmec: La Venta; Maya: Tikal, Palenque; Toltec: Tula, Chichén Itzá; Aztec: Tenochtitlán; Inca: Cuzco
8. Someone took the time, the resources, and great care to create this sculpture of a Mayan athlete, suggesting that athletes had great status in Mayan culture, just as athletes have in American culture.
9. Essays will vary. Students should document their resources and demonstrate knowledge of advantages and disadvantages.

EYEWITNESS TO HISTORY

The Quipu

THE INCA DID NOT POSSESS A WRITTEN language. To record events and other aspects of their lives that they wished to remember, they used a system of knotted strings, called the *quipu*. This is a sixteenth-century description of the process.

❝These men recorded on their knots all the tribute brought annually to the Inca, specifying everything by kind, species, and quality. They recorded the number of men who went to the wars, how many died in them, and how many were born and died every year, month by month. In short they may be said to have recorded on their knots everything that could be counted, even mentioning battles and fights, all the [ambassadors who] had come to visit the Inca, and all the speeches and arguments the king had uttered. But the purpose of the [diplomatic visits] or the contents of the speeches, or any other descriptive matter could not be recorded on the knots, consisting as it did of continuous spoken or written prose, which cannot be expressed by means of knots, since these can only give numbers and not words. To supply this want they used signs that indicated historical events or facts or the existence of any [diplomatic visit], speech, or discussion in time of peace or war. Such speeches were committed to memory and taught by tradition to their successors and descendants from father to son. . . . Another method too was used for keeping alive in the memory of the people their deeds and the [ambassadors] they sent to the Inca and the replies [the king] gave them. The philosophers and sages took the trouble to turn them into stories, no longer than fables, suitable for telling to children, young people, and the rustics of the countryside: they were thus passed from hand to hand and age to age, and preserved in the memories of all. . . . Similarly their poets composed short, compressed poems, embracing a history, or [a diplomatic visit], or the king's reply. In short, everything that could not be recorded on the knots was included in these poems, which were sung at their triumphs. Thus they remembered their history.❞

—Garcilaso de la Vega, *Royal Commentaries of the Incas: And General History of Peru*

The **quipu** *was made from woven strands of different-colored yarn.*

Analyzing Primary Sources

1. What did the *quipu* record? What was it unable to record?
2. In what other ways and from what other sources was the history of the Inca preserved?

145

TEACH

Analyzing Primary Sources Tell students that the *quipu* system of numbering is still used in parts of rural Peru today, although the meaning of the different lengths of cord has been lost. The system made use of single knots, double knots, and slipknots with loops to represent numbers. Different colored cords identified subjects such as tax and census information and other historical and financial records. Official messages were memorized and delivered by runners, or *chasquis*, who could cover as much as 150 miles (241 km) in a day. In this precursor to a postal system, pairs of *chasquis* were stationed in roadside huts placed every 1.8 miles (2.9 km) along the well-developed road network. As a runner approached one of the huts, he would shout out his message. The relief runner would memorize it, take the *quipu*, and leave for the next hut. Long, complex messages could be delivered very efficiently in this way.

Ask students why they think our society, unlike the Inca, relies less and less on oral traditions. *(We rely heavily on print and electronic media to store information. Oral traditions have lost their importance.)* **L1**

ANSWERS TO ANALYZING PRIMARY SOURCES

1. The *quipu* was used to record anything that could be numbered. It was not able to record events that could not be counted.
2. Incan history was recorded through memorization, then passed down from one generation to another orally, as stories or poems.

GLENCOE TECHNOLOGY

MindJogger Videoquiz

Use the **MindJogger Videoquiz** to review Chapter 4 content.

 Available in VHS.

Using Key Terms

1. Inquisition **2.** epidemic **3.** heresy **4.** manor **5.** Serfs **6.** money economy **7.** Mesoamerica **8.** commercial capitalism **9.** guilds **10.** sacraments **11.** theology

Reviewing Key Facts

12. had rustic homes, little privacy, a seasonal cycle of labor; were subject to lord

13. reestablished states with strong monarchical authority; France, England, Spain

14. crowded, smelly, polluted air

15. The Church ruled the Papal States so clergy had political interests. Church officials were granted their high positions as vassals of nobles, so they had feudal duties.

16. They were educated, and the intellectual and spiritual life available to nuns appealed to them.

17. veneration of saints, pilgrimages

18. In five years, 50 to 60 percent of the population died in some cities. Trade declined; a shortage of workers caused labor costs to rise; food prices fell.

19. Conflict between popes and kings and the Great Schism undermined people's faith in the papacy and the Church.

20. includes North, Central, and South America; has varied landscape including ice-covered lands, dense forests, fertile river valleys, coastlines, tropical forests, and hot deserts

21. pyramid

22. steel weapons, gunpowder, the riding of horses

CHAPTER 4 ASSESSMENT and ACTIVITIES

Using Key Terms

1. To discover and deal with heretics, the Church created a court called the _____.
2. The Incan Empire experienced an _____ of smallpox following the arrival of the Europeans.
3. The Dominicans attacked _____ through effective preaching.
4. A _____ was an agricultural estate owned by a lord and worked by peasants.
5. _____ were peasants, legally bound to the land.
6. In a _____ barter is replaced by coins, or money.
7. _____ is the name for the regions of Mexico and Central America that were settled before the arrival of the Spanish.
8. An economic system where people invest in goods and trade in order to make a profit is called _____.
9. Specialized business associations for crafts and banking were called _____.
10. The _____ were seen as necessary for salvation.
11. The study of religion and God, or _____, was the most highly regarded subject of medieval universities.

Reviewing Key Facts

12. **Culture** Describe the life of a peasant in the Middle Ages.
13. **Government** What were the "new monarchies"? In what countries were they established?
14. **Culture** Describe living conditions in a medieval city.
15. **History** How did the Church come to be involved in political matters and the feudal system?
16. **Culture** Why were most nuns from the ranks of landed aristocracy?
17. **Religion** What were some of the religious practices of ordinary people?
18. **Economics** What were the economic consequences of the Black Death?
19. **Culture** What factors led to the decline of Church power?
20. **Geography** Describe the region known as the Americas.
21. **Culture** What type of building was common to several of the Mesoamerican civilizations?
22. **Science and Technology** What technology did the Spanish bring to the Americas that contributed to the destruction of early civilizations?
23. **History** What are two of the reasons historians give for the decline of Mayan civilization?

Critical Thinking

24. **Drawing Conclusions** Tikal was a Mayan city that may have had up to a hundred thousand inhabitants. What type of organization, buildings, and services would be required for such a large city?
25. **Evaluating** Why was the Catholic Church such a powerful influence on the lives of people in the Middle Ages?
26. **Making Comparisons** Compare the design and function of Mesoamerican pyramids to Gothic cathedrals.

Chapter Summary

Cultural diffusion, innovation, and conflict marked the Middle Ages and the history of the Americas.

Movement	Growth	Innovation	Conflict
• Asian peoples cross a land bridge into North America. • An exchange of goods develops between Flanders and Italy. • Aztec peoples migrate to the Valley of Mexico in the 1100s. • Spanish forces sail to the Americas.	• Increase in trade leads to the growth of European cities. • The Catholic Church gains political power in Europe. • Four million Aztec live in or around the Valley of Mexico by 1500. • Incan ruler Pachacuti expands the Incan Empire.	• Universities are founded in Europe. • European churches are built in the Gothic style. • The Maya develop a hieroglyphic writing system. • An extensive road system is constructed in the Incan Empire.	• The Great Schism undermines Church authority. • England and France fight the Hundred Years' War. • Spanish forces destroy Aztec and Incan civilizations. • The Black Death and smallpox kill millions in Europe and South America.

146

23. invasion, internal revolt, natural disaster, food shortage

Critical Thinking

24. housing, roads, defense, administrators, communication, specialized jobs, food production and distribution

25. It was the only religious influence; people were dependent on the Church for salvation; marriage, birth, and death all involved the Church.

26. Both served religious functions. Both dominated the landscape and were central to the town. Pyramids used exterior space and were heavy; Gothic churches used interior space and were light and airy.

Writing About History

27. Students will write essays comparing medieval European and Mesoamerican farming techniques.

Analyzing Sources

28. He is concerned that his son is not studying and is wasting his time. The father uses shame and compares the son's behavior to the other students.

Self-Check Quiz
Visit the *Glencoe World History—Modern Times* Web site at wh.mt.glencoe.com and click on **Chapter 4–Self-Check Quiz** to prepare for the Chapter Test.

Writing About History

27. **Expository Writing** There are several explanations given in the chapter for the decline of the Maya. Write an essay comparing how overuse of the land may have led to the decline of the Maya with how the three-field system enhanced medieval food production.

Analyzing Sources

Read the following letter from a medieval father to his son away at a university.

> "I have recently discovered that you live dissolutely and slothfully, preferring license to restraint and play to work and strumming a guitar while the others are at their studies, whence it happens that you have read but one volume of law while your more industrious companions have read several. Wherefore I have decided to exhort you to repent utterly of your dissolute and careless ways, that you may no longer be called a waster and your shame may be turned to good repute."

28. What are the concerns of the father? What method does he use to motivate his son?
29. Write a reply from the son to his father.

Applying Technology Skills

30. **Using the Internet** Access the Internet to locate a Web site that has information about a Mesoamerican civilization. Use a search engine to focus your search using key words or phrases from this chapter. Create a bulletin board using the information gathered from the Web site. Be sure to incorporate photos, illustrations, and captions.

Analyzing Maps and Charts

31. Select an event or invention from each category on the chart at the top of the page. What was the effect of that event or invention?
32. Which factor leading to increased farm productivity was not the result of human intervention?
33. How did farming practices affect population?
34. How would peaceful conditions contribute to an increase in population?

Economic Changes in the Middle Ages

Better Farming
- Climatic change favorable to growing conditions
- Clearing of trees and draining of swamps by peasants
- Use of iron to make labor-saving devices, including scythes, axes, hoes, and wheeled plows
- Harnessing of wind and water power
- Shift from a two-field to a three-field system of crop rotation

Population Increase
- Peaceful conditions following the invasions of the early Middle Ages
- Dramatic expansion in food production

Growth of Cities
- Gradual revival of trade, including the initiation of trade fairs
- Slow emergence of an economy based on money (rather than barter)
- Movement of merchants and artisans to cities; organization of craftspeople into guilds
- Granting of basic liberties to townspeople by local lords
- Rise of city self-government

Standardized Test Practice

Directions: Choose the best answer to the following question.

What effect did the Black Death have on Europe?

F The plague resulted in an increase in the number of universities.
G The plague led to an acute labor shortage that resulted in higher wages.
H The plague inspired new ideas about faith that led to the formation of the Cistercian, Franciscan, and Dominican orders.
J The plague sparked the Hundred Years' War between France and England.

Test-Taking Tip: Although these questions mostly ask you about what you've learned in class, using common sense can help you arrive at the correct answers too. For example, to answer this question, think about what you know about the Black Death first and then read the answer choices.

Have students visit the Web site at wh.mt.glencoe.com to review Chapter 4 and take the Self-Check Quiz.

34. More time and energy could be devoted to finding ways to increase food production, which in turn would lead to an increase in population. Fewer casualties from battling invaders would also lead to population gains.

Standardized Test Practice

Answer: G
Answer Explanation: According to page 137, so many people died during the fourteenth century that the shortage of workers caused a dramatic rise in the price of labor.

Bonus Question ?

Ask: When did the first civilizations appear in Central America? What was happening in the Fertile Crescent at this time? *(American civilizations began around 1200 B.C., the time of Moses and the Exodus. Civilizations in the Fertile Crescent began a few thousand years earlier.)*

29. Students will write a reply. They may agree or disagree with the father's assessment.

Applying Technology Skills

30. Students will create a bulletin board with information from a Web site. You may wish to use this opportunity to remind students of the importance of finding and using reliable, authoritative Web sites.

Analyzing Maps and Charts

31. first category: led to population increase; second category: led to growth of cities; third category: led to decline of the feudal and manorial systems, rise of commercial capitalism
32. climatic change
33. Improved farming practices led to greater food supply, which led to population growth.

World Literature

Block Schedule

Team Teaching These poems of Li Bo may be presented in a team-teaching context, in conjunction with English or Language Arts.

Poetry of Li Bo

Historical Connection

Artistic, political, and economic advances often go together. The success of Li Bo was one indication of the prosperity of China during the Tang dynasty.

Background Information

Setting Li Bo often set his poems in natural surroundings. He traveled a great deal and, as a result, was sensitive to variations in landscape and climate.

Literary Elements Allusion is a reference, often indirect, to something that the writer assumes the reader knows about. For example, in "Hard Is the Journey," Li Bo's references to the Yellow River and T'ai-hang Mountains probably allude to his faraway home. Simile is the direct comparison of two things. In "Taking Leave of a Friend," Li Bo writes, "Sunset like the parting of old acquaintances." He is comparing the end of the day with the parting of friends.

World Literature

Five Poems

by Li Bo

Li Bo was born in A.D. 701 in western China. People began praising his beautiful poems even before he reached adulthood. Throughout his life he traveled extensively in China, amazing people with his ability to compose insightful, touching poems. He wrote about the world around him, the people he met, and the emotions he felt. By the time of his death in A.D. 762, he was regarded as one of China's greatest poets, a distinction he still holds today.

In the following poems, Li Bo interprets parting from a friend, life as a journey, and his experience with his homeland.

Read to Discover

As you read, note the ways in which Li Bo draws the reader into his descriptions. What emotions do his poems evoke in you?

Reader's Dictionary

brooklet: a small brook or creek

sparse: few and scattered

thrush: a type of small to medium sized bird that is an excellent singer

Taking Leave of a Friend

Blue mountains to the north of the walls,
White river winding about them;
Here we must make separation
And go out through a thousand miles
of dead grass.

Mind like a floating wide cloud,
Sunset like the parting of old acquaintances
Who bow over their clasped hands at a distance.
Our horses neigh to each other as we are departing.

▲ *This painting is titled* **Spring Dawn over Elixir Terrace.**

Clearing at Dawn

The fields are chill, the sparse
rain has stopped;
The colours of Spring teem
on every side.
With leaping fish the blue pond
is full;
With singing thrushes the green
boughs droop.
The flowers of the field have
dabbled their powdered cheeks;
The mountain grasses are bent
level at the waist.
By the bamboo stream the last
fragment of cloud
Blown by the wind slowly
scatters away.

148

ABOUT THE AUTHOR

Li Bo wrote more than 1,000 poems. Many were short, composed as thank-you notes and gifts to friends. Other poems, usually longer, were more like folk songs. Li Bo wrote these in a traditional ballad style to accompany music. As a follower of Daoism, he believed in intuition and loved nature. According to legend, he died when he jumped out of a boat to grab the reflection of the moon on the water. Li Bo lived in ancient China's greatest epoch for poetry. Three other revered poets, Wang Wei, Duo Fu, and Bo Juyi, also lived during the Tang dynasty.

Hard Is the Journey

Gold vessels of fine wines,
thousands a gallon,
Jade dishes of rare meats,
costing more thousands,
I lay my chopsticks down,
no more can banquet,
And draw my sword and stare
wildly about me:

Ice bars my way to cross
the Yellow River,
Snows from dark skies to climb
the T'ai-hang Mountains!

At peace I drop a hook
into a brooklet,
At once I'm in a boat
but sailing sunward . . .

(Hard is the Journey,
Hard is the Journey,
So many turnings,
And now where am I?)

So when a breeze breaks waves,
bringing fair weather,
I set a cloud for sails,
cross the blue oceans!

Landscape of the Four Seasons ***by Shen shih-Ch'ung*** ▲

In the Mountains on a Summer Day

Gently I stir a white feather fan,
With open shirt sitting in a green wood.
I take off my cap and hang it on a jutting stone;
A wind from the pine-tree trickles on my bare
head.

Listening to a Flute in Yellow Crane Pavilion

I came here a wanderer
thinking of home
remembering my far away Ch'ang-an.
And then, from deep in Yellow Crane Pavilion,
I heard a beautiful bamboo flute
play "Falling Plum Blossoms."
It was late spring in a city by the river.

Interpreting World Literature

1. What detail in *Taking Leave of a Friend* reveals a custom specific to Li Bo's times?
2. What happens between the beginning of the first stanza and the end of the second stanza of *Hard Is the Journey?*
3. What is the significance of the last line of *Listening to a Flute in Yellow Crane Pavilion?*
4. **CRITICAL THINKING** Li Bo describes beauty and peace and luxury in *Hard Is the Journey.* Why do you think he calls the journey "hard"?

Applications Activity

Write a poem describing your hometown. Make sure to include a description of something unique to that area.

WORLD LITERATURE

FOCUS

Before students read the first poem, describe Li Bo's life and his extensive travels. Ask students to predict what subjects would be emphasized by a poet who travels frequently.

TEACH

Evaluation

In "Taking Leave of a Friend," Li Bo uses hyperbole, or exaggeration. The "thousand miles of dead grass" is an exaggeration used for effect. Ask students if they think hyperbole works to convey the sense of bleakness one might feel if separated from a close friend. **L1**

Clarification

In "Hard Is the Journey," Li Bo refers to the Yellow River, also known as the Huang He. It flows through north and central China.

About the Art

Landscape painting became popular in China during the Tang dynasty, the period when Li Bo lived. Artists of this time painted scenes of craggy mountains, rocks, streams, and trees. Artists and poets used natural scenes to express their deepest feelings. "Outwardly, nature has been my teacher," said one Tang landscape painter, "but inwardly I follow the springs of my heart."

ANSWERS TO INTERPRETING WORLD LITERATURE

1. bowing to each other over clasped hands at a distance
2. There is a shift from a luxurious feast to a wintry nature scene.
3. Answers will vary, but many students will say that the beauty of the flute music heard in a city served as a substitute for the beauty of nature that could have been experienced at home.
4. Answers may include ideas such as the fact that life is full of difficult choices.

Application Activity

Answers will vary; students will write poems describing their hometowns.

Unit 2 Resources

Suggested Pacing Chart

	Unit 2 (1 day)	Chapter 5 (6 days)	Chapter 6 (5 days)	Chapter 7 (6 days)	Chapter 8 (4 days)	Chapter 9 (4 days)	Chapter 10 (6 days)	Chapter 11 (4 days)	Unit 2 (1 day)
Day 1	Introduction	Chapter 5 Intro, Section 1	Chapter 6 Intro, Section 1	Chapter 7 Intro, Section 1	Chapter 8 Intro, Section 1	Chapter 9 Intro, Section 1	Chapter 10 Intro, Section 1	Chapter 11 Intro, Section 1	Wrap-Up/ Projects/ Unit 2 Assessment
Day 2		Section 2	Section 2	Section 2	Section 2	Section 2	Section 2	Section 2	
Day 3		Section 3	Section 3	Section 3	Section 3	Section 3	Section 3	Section 3	
Day 4		Section 4	Chapter 6 Review	Section 4	Chapter 8 Review/ Assessment	Chapter 9 Review/ Assessment	Section 4	Chapter 11 Review/ Assessment	
Day 5		Chapter 5 Review	Chapter 6 Assessment	Chapter 7 Review			Chapter 10 Review		
Day 6		Chapter 5 Assessment		Chapter 7 Assessment			Chapter 10 Assessment		

Use the following tools to easily assess student learning in a variety of ways:

- Performance Assessment Activities and Rubrics
- Chapter Tests
- Section Quizzes
- Standardized Test Skills Practice Workbook
- SAT I/II Test Practice
- www.wh.mt.glencoe.com
- Interactive Tutor Self-Assessment CD-ROM
- MindJogger Videoquiz
- ExamView® Pro Testmaker CD-ROM

Teaching Transparencies

Unit Time Line Transparency 2

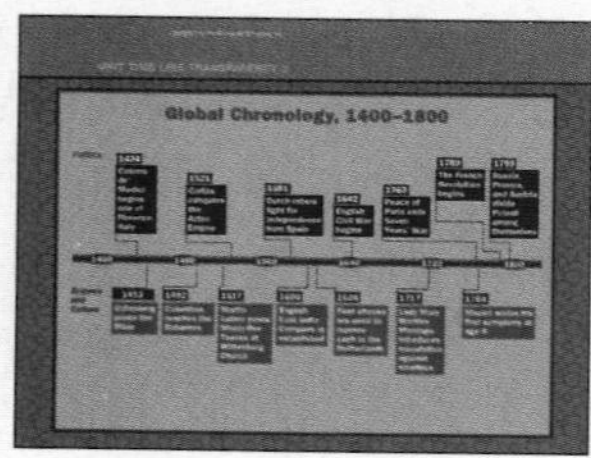

Cause-and-Effect Transparency 2

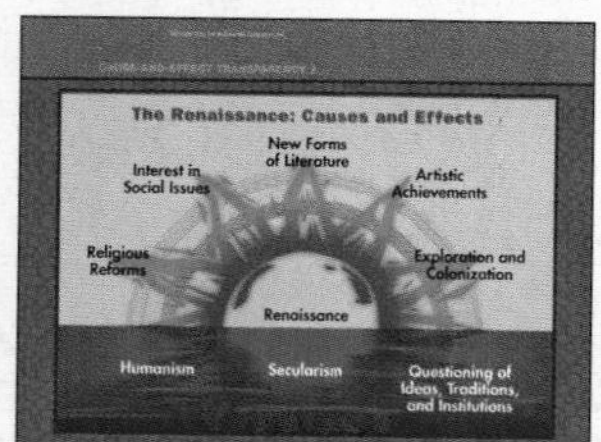

interNET RESOURCES

- www.wh.mt.glencoe.com

Glencoe World History—Modern Times
Visit the *Glencoe World History—Modern Times* Web site for history overviews, activities, assessments, and updated charts and graphs.

- www.socialstudies.glencoe.com

Glencoe Social Studies
Visit the Glencoe Web site for social studies activities, updates, and links to other sites.

- www.teachingtoday.glencoe.com

Glencoe Teaching Today
Visit the new Glencoe Web site for teacher development information, teaching tips, Web resources, and educational news.

- www.time.com

TIME Online
Visit the TIME Web site for up-to-date news and special reports.

Unit 2 Resources

ASSESSMENT

Unit 2 Tests Forms A and B

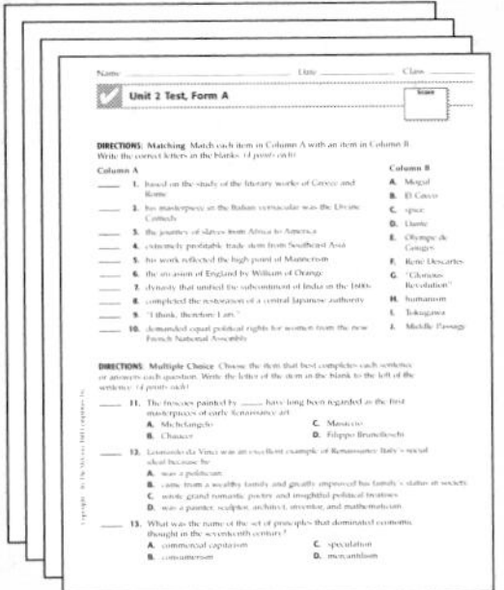

ExamView® Pro Testmaker CD-ROM

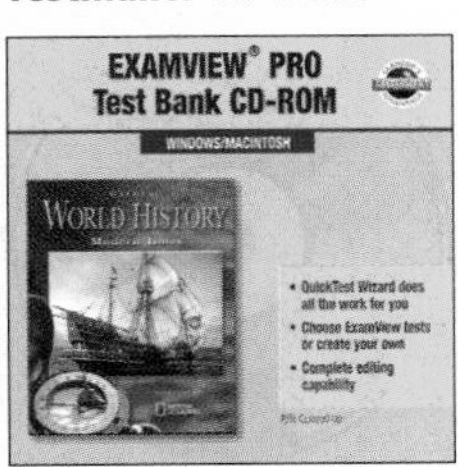

INTERDISCIPLINARY ACTIVITIES

World Literature Reading 2

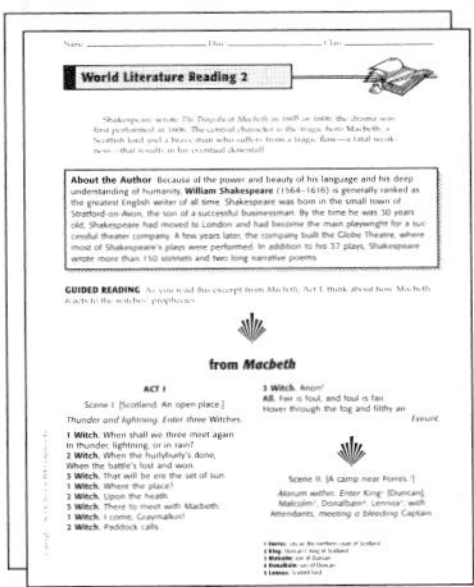

Economics and History Activity 2

APPLICATION AND ENRICHMENT

Charting and Graphing Activity 2

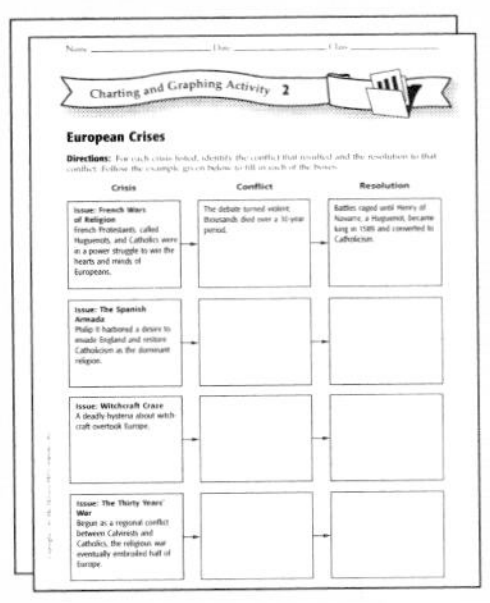

GEOGRAPHIC LITERACY

NGS Focus on Geographic Literacy

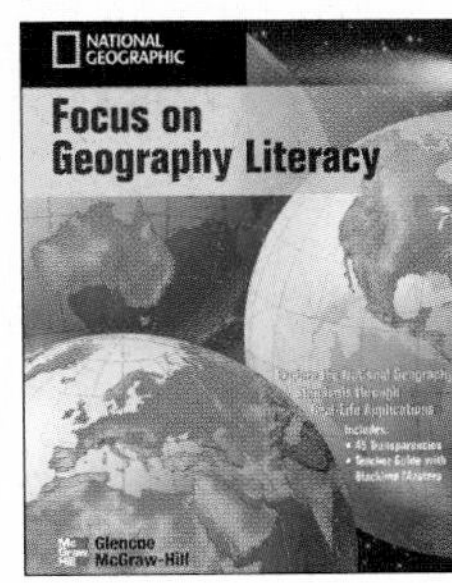

Building Geography Skills for Life

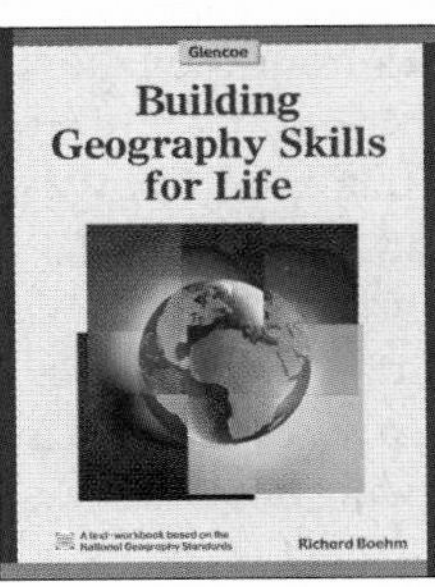

BIBLIOGRAPHY

Readings for the Student

Hudson, Jan. ***Sweetgrass.*** Paper Star, 1999. A teenage Blackfoot girl of the 1830s must prove herself as a capable woman.

Kahne, Heinz. ***Leonardo da Vinci: Dreams, Schemes, and Flying Machines.*** Prestel USA, 2000. Explore the inventions and art of da Vinci.

Johnson, Sylvia A. ***Tomatoes, Potatoes, Corn, and Beans: How the Foods of the Americas Changed Eating Around the World.*** Atheneum, 1997. Chronicles one aspect of how the world changed as a result of voyages of exploration.

Readings for the Teacher

Johnson, Paul. ***The Renaissance: A Short History.*** Modern Library, 2000. A concise history of events during the Renaissance.

Pagden, Anthony. ***Peoples and Empires: A Short History of European Migration, Exploration, and Conquest, from Greece to the Present.*** Modern Library, 2001. A history stretching from land-based to seagoing empires.

Hibbert, Christopher. ***The Days of the French Revolution.*** Quill, 1999. A historical narrative of the French Revolution.

Multimedia Resources

Video. ***Thomas Jefferson.*** PBS Video, 1–800–424–7963. Actors give voice to historical figures in the story of Jefferson.

Additional Glencoe Resources for this Unit:

- Glencoe Skillbuilder Interactive Workbook CD-ROM, Level 2
- Glencoe World History Primary Source Document Library
- World Art Prints
- World Biography: People in History
- Outline Map Resource Book
- World Desk Map
- World Art and Architecture Transparencies
- World Music: Cultural Traditions
- World Music: A Cultural Legacy
- Glencoe World Literature Library
- Reading in the Content Area
- Teaching Strategies for the World History Classroom (Including Block Scheduling Pacing Guides)
- Inclusion for the High School Social Studies Classroom Strategies and Activities

0:00 **Out of Time?**

If time does not permit teaching each chapter in this unit, you may use the **Reading Essentials and Study Guide** summaries.

Unit Objectives

After studying this unit, students should be able to:

1. explain the achievements of the Renaissance and the effects of the Protestant Reformation;
2. trace the growing power of monarchs and the rise of absolutism in Europe;
3. examine the Ottoman, Safavid, and Mogul Empires in Asia and India;
4. explain how the Scientific Revolution and Enlightenment changed the way people viewed their world;
5. compare the causes and evaluate effects of the English, French, and American Revolutions.

The Period in Perspective

In this unit students will learn about the emergence of powerful European nation-states and the creation of large empires in Asia. Discuss how both wealth and military power contribute to the rise of powerful nations.

Use these materials to enrich student understanding of the Renaissance and the Age of Exploration.

- **NGS PICTURE SHOW™ CD-ROMS**
  The Renaissance
  The Age of Exploration 1
- **NGS PICTURE PACK TRANSPARENCY SETS**
  The Renaissance
  The Age of Exploration
  The American Revolution

UNIT 2 The Early Modern World

1400–1800

The Period in Perspective

Beginning in the late fifteenth century, Europeans engaged in a vigorous period of state building. The result was the creation of independent monarchies in western and central Europe that formed the basis of a new European state system. These European states then began to expand into the rest of the world.

Also during this period, two great new Islamic empires, the Ottomans in Turkey and the Safavids in Persia, arose in Southwest Asia. A third Islamic empire—the Mogul Empire—unified the subcontinent of India. Least affected by the European expansion were the societies of East Asia: China and Japan.

Primary Sources Library

See pages 774–775 for primary source readings to accompany Unit 2.

Use The World History ***Primary Source Document Library CD-ROM*** *to find additional primary sources about The Early Modern World.*

▲ A model of the Copernican system

▶ A European navigator uses an astrolabe.

150

TEAM TEACHING ACTIVITY

Literature Life during the Renaissance, Reformation, and the Enlightenment gave rise to famous and influential pieces of literature, whose themes reflect the culture, values, and political concerns of their periods. These works also transcend their cultures and convey universal themes. Work with the English teacher to coordinate the study of a major piece of literature from this period. Works to consider include: *The Canterbury Tales*, to understand late medieval life in England; one of Shakespeare's plays to understand perceptions of English politics and monarchy; *A Tale of Two Cities* to understand the French Revolution; *Les Miserables* to understand social problems of eighteenth-century France; and *Frankenstein* to understand concerns about the Enlightenment. **L2**

"Dare to Know."
—Immanuel Kant

Introducing UNIT 2

GLENCOE
TECHNOLOGY

CD-ROM
World History Primary Source Document Library CD-ROM

Use the World History Primary Source Document Library CD-ROM to access primary source documents related to the early modern world.

More About the Art

Caravels had several features that originated in the Chinese and Muslim worlds. A caravel usually had three masts and a deep-sea rudder posted on the stern, first used by the Chinese. The triangular lateen sails that allowed the ship to sail into the wind originated in the Muslim world.

History *and the* Humanities

World Art and Architecture Transparencies
- 22 *May*
- 23 *Mona Lisa*
- 24 *The French Ambassadors*
- 25 *Herzogenburg Monastery*
- 27 *Ming Phoenix Crown*
- 28 *View of Toledo*
- 29 *Shah Jahan and One of His Sons Riding in Escort*
- 30 *Taj Mahal*
- 32 *The Letter*
- 34 *Blue Boy*
- 35 *Mission San Xavier del Bac*
- 36 *Napoleon Crossing the Alps*
- 38 *Persian Rugs*

World Music: Cultural Legacy, Lessons 8, 9

SERVICE-LEARNING PROJECT

Have students research revolutionary movements of the twentieth century by having them interview a member of their community who was directly involved in a revolutionary movement or whose family was affected by a revolution. How did it affect the person and that person's family? Did any international groups, such as Amnesty International or the Red Cross, assist the family? Have students identify and research one group dedicated to helping displaced people and then have students volunteer to help the agency meet its goals. Have students report back to the class on their activities and the agency's mission. **L2**

Refer to **Building Bridges: Connecting Classroom and Community through Service in Social Studies** from the National Council for the Social Studies for information about service-learning.

TEACH

Introduction

This feature focuses on the movements of revolutionary ideas between Europe and the Americas. The challenge of early scientists such as Galileo to established government and religious authority led to the questioning of long-held ideas about government, religion, and society, as well as science. In the United States, France, and Haiti, revolutionaries tried to put new ideas about government into practice.

Background Notes

Linking Past and Present

Revolutionary ideas of the 1700s continue to reverberate in this century. When Ho Chi Minh declared Vietnam's independence from France in 1945, his speech began: "All men are created equal. The Creator has given us certain inviolable Rights; the right to Life, the right to be Free, and the right to achieve Happiness." These immortal words are taken from the Declaration of Independence of the United States of America, which was written in 1776. Have students trace the historical development of the rule of law and rights and responsibilities, beginning in the ancient world and continuing to the beginning of the first modern constitutional republics.

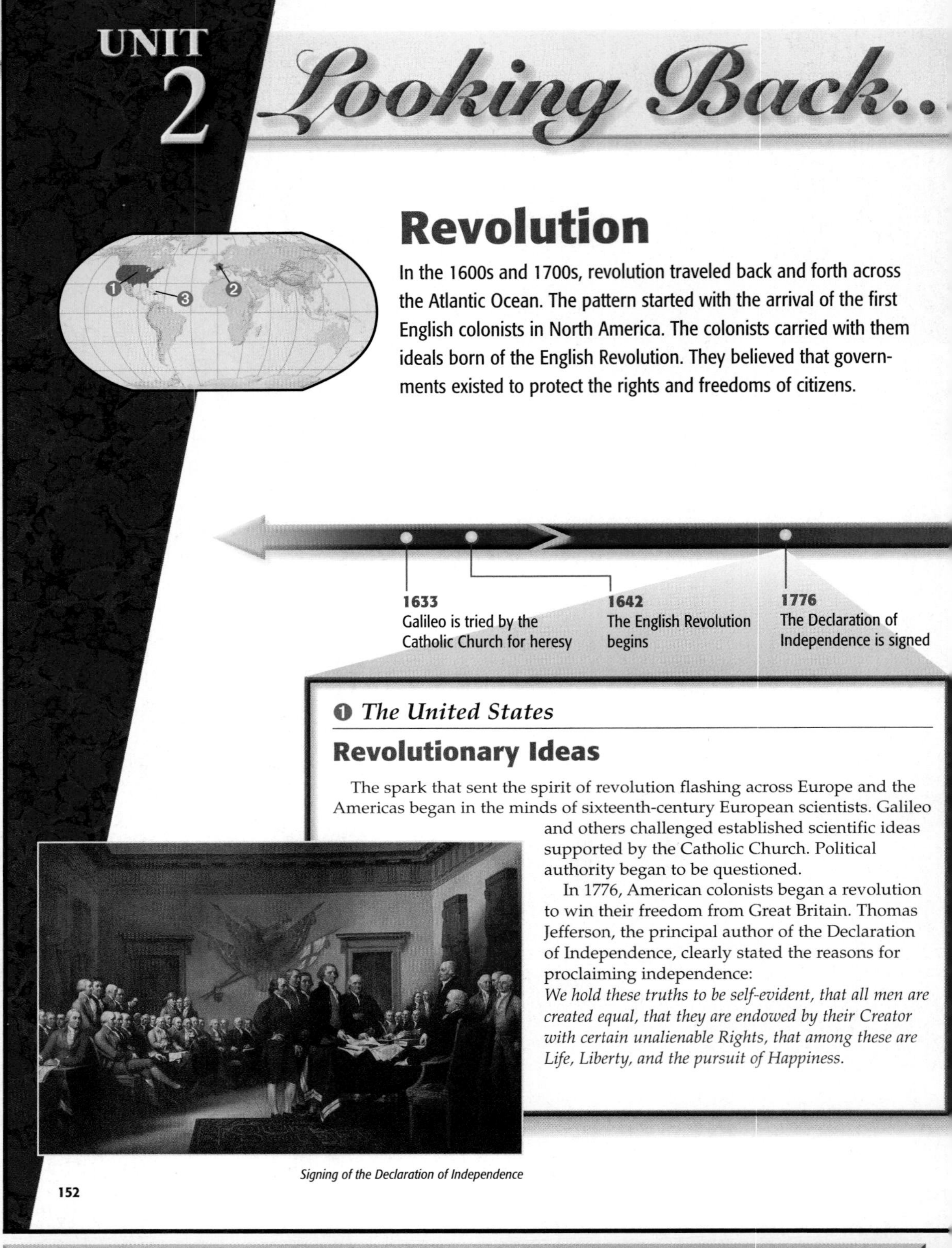

Revolution

In the 1600s and 1700s, revolution traveled back and forth across the Atlantic Ocean. The pattern started with the arrival of the first English colonists in North America. The colonists carried with them ideals born of the English Revolution. They believed that governments existed to protect the rights and freedoms of citizens.

1633 Galileo is tried by the Catholic Church for heresy

1642 The English Revolution begins

1776 The Declaration of Independence is signed

❶ *The United States*

Revolutionary Ideas

The spark that sent the spirit of revolution flashing across Europe and the Americas began in the minds of sixteenth-century European scientists. Galileo and others challenged established scientific ideas supported by the Catholic Church. Political authority began to be questioned.

In 1776, American colonists began a revolution to win their freedom from Great Britain. Thomas Jefferson, the principal author of the Declaration of Independence, clearly stated the reasons for proclaiming independence:

We hold these truths to be self-evident, that all men are created equal, that they are endowed by their Creator with certain unalienable Rights, that among these are Life, Liberty, and the pursuit of Happiness.

Signing of the Declaration of Independence

152

COOPERATIVE LEARNING ACTIVITY

Creating a Wall Map Have students work together to create a wall map and display that shows the origins of the ideas behind the American, French, and Haitian Revolutions. Organize the class into three groups, letting each group be responsible for one of the revolutions. Have members research the revolution, generating a list of philosophers, events, and other specific influences. For each item on the list, students should be sure to name the country of origin. When the lists have been completed, have students organize them by country in a format suitable for display. Have them mount the lists to the sides of a wall map, then use thumbtacks and colored yarn to show how various ideas traveled. **L2**

to See Ahead

French Revolution

❷ *France*

The Expanding Revolution

The revolutionary ideas contained within the Declaration of Independence traveled back across the Atlantic to influence the French Revolution. French rebels fought in defense of *Liberté, Egalité, and Fraternité.* In 1789, French revolutionaries drafted the Declaration of the Rights of Man and the Citizen. Echoing the principles of the Declaration of Independence, the French declaration proclaimed that, "Men are born and remain free and equal in rights."

1776 The American Revolution begins

1789 The French Revolution begins

1804 Saint Domingue achieves independence

❸ *Haiti*

Exporting Revolution

In 1791, the ideals of the American and French Revolutions traveled across the Atlantic and the Caribbean to the French-held colony of Saint Domingue on the island of Hispaniola. Inspired by talk of freedom, enslaved Africans took up arms. Led by a formerly enslaved man, Toussaint-Louverture, and other island leaders, the rebels fought for thirteen years against the French. On January 1, 1804, Saint Domingue, present-day Haiti, became the second nation in the Americas to achieve independence from colonial rule. "We have asserted our rights," declared the revolutionaries. "We swear never to yield them to any power on earth."

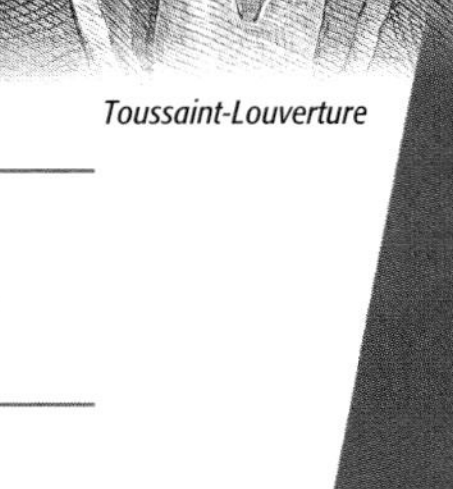
Toussaint-Louverture

Why It Matters

Political and intellectual revolutions changed the way people thought about established ideas and institutions. How did this change in perception eventually lead to the American view of government today?

153

Looking Back to See Ahead

Geography

Movement Americans living in France before the French Revolution promoted the principles of the new republic across the Atlantic. "Everyone here is trying their hands at forming declarations of rights," wrote Thomas Jefferson, whose advice was often sought by Lafayette and other moderate revolutionaries. Ask students to name other ways ideas of revolution may have traveled among the different locations of revolutions shown on the map on page 152. *(Answers may include trade, newspapers, scholars exchanging books.)*

CULTURAL DIFFUSION

Containing Antislavery The success of the Haitian Revolution terrified American slaveholders, who feared that the overthrow of slavery in Haiti would inspire their own enslaved people to rebel. In the southern United States, tighter restrictions were placed on both enslaved and free African Americans. In 1802, Jefferson's postmaster general advised a senator from Georgia against letting enslaved people deliver the mail: "After the scenes which St. Domingue has exhibited to the world, we cannot be too cautious in attempting to prevent similar evils. . . . Everything which tends to increase their knowledge of natural rights . . . or that affords them an opportunity . . . of establishing a chain and line of intelligence, must increase our hazard."

Why It Matters

ANSWER: Answers may include that the ideals of equality and liberty for all citizens are evident in the belief that all people should have a voice in choosing leaders and in making laws. Also, if all men and women are created equal, we do not believe in the "divine" right to rule. You might wish to guide students in a discussion of basic American rights often taken for granted, especially freedom of speech, press, and religion.

Chapter 5 Resources

Timesaving Tools

TeacherWorks™ All-In-One Planner and Resource Center

- **Interactive Teacher Edition** Access your Teacher Wraparound Edition and your classroom resources with a few easy clicks.
- **Interactive Lesson Planner** Planning has never been easier! Organize your week, month, semester, or year with all the lesson helps you need to make teaching creative, timely, and relevant.

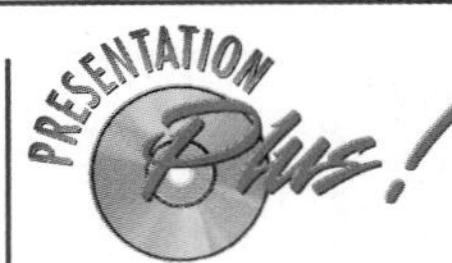

Use Glencoe's **Presentation Plus!** multimedia teacher tool to easily present dynamic lessons that visually excite your students. Using Microsoft PowerPoint® you can customize the presentations to create your own personalized lessons.

Teaching Transparencies

Graphic Organizer Student Activity 5 Transparency

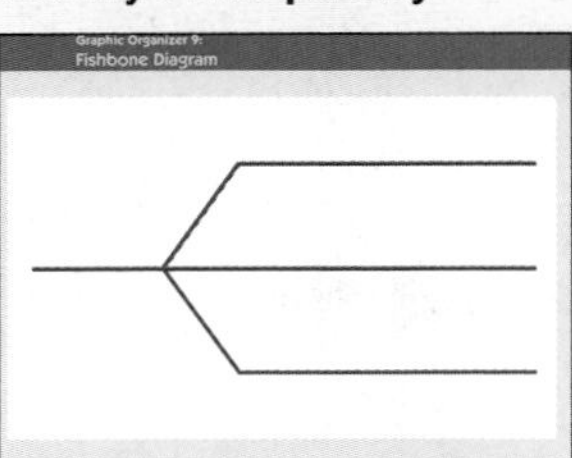

Chapter Transparency 5

Map Overlay Transparency 5

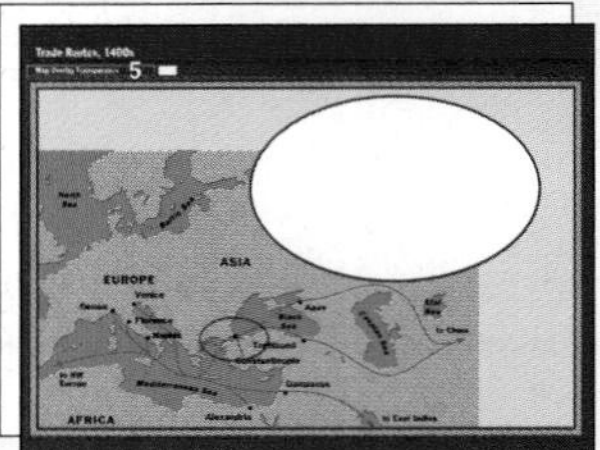

Application and Enrichment

Enrichment Activity 5

Primary Source Reading 5

History Simulation Activity 5

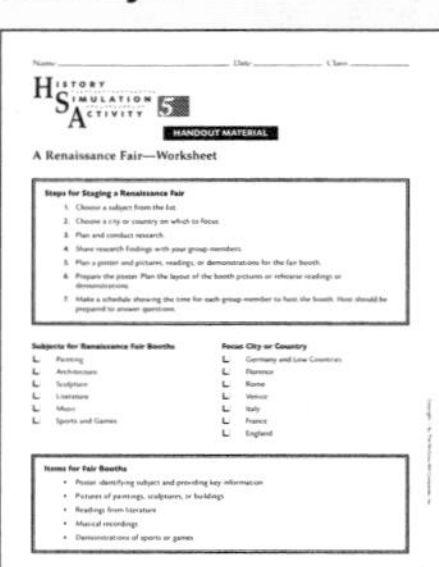

Historical Significance Activity 5

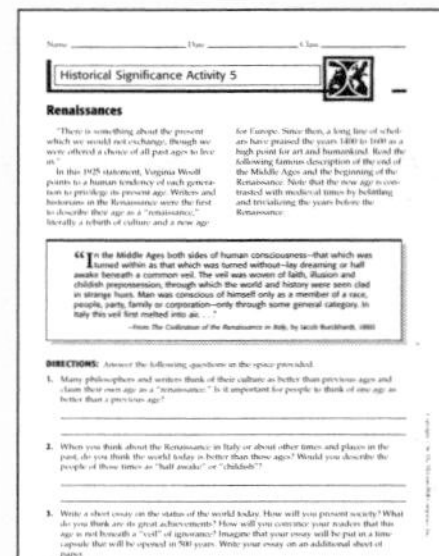

Cooperative Learning Activity 5

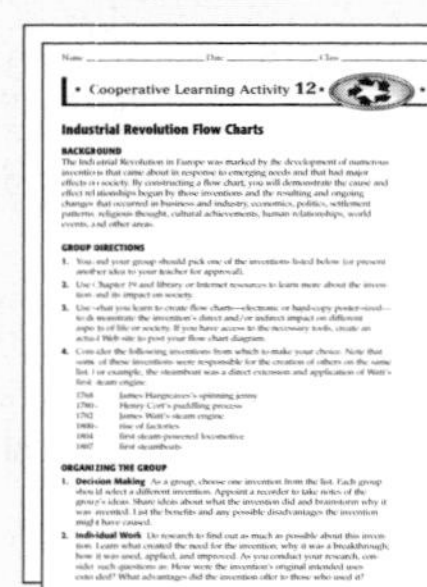

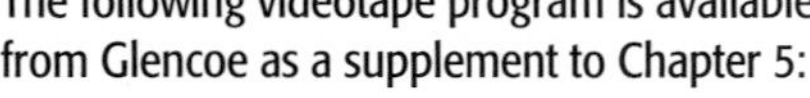

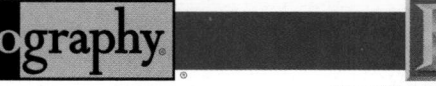

The following videotape program is available from Glencoe as a supplement to Chapter 5:

- **Michelangelo** (ISBN 1–56501–425–1)

To order, call Glencoe at 1–800–334–7344. To find classroom resources to accompany this video, check the following home pages:
A&E Television: www.aande.com
The History Channel: www.historychannel.com

Chapter 5 Resources

Review and Reinforcement

Linking Past and Present Activity 5

Time Line Activity 5

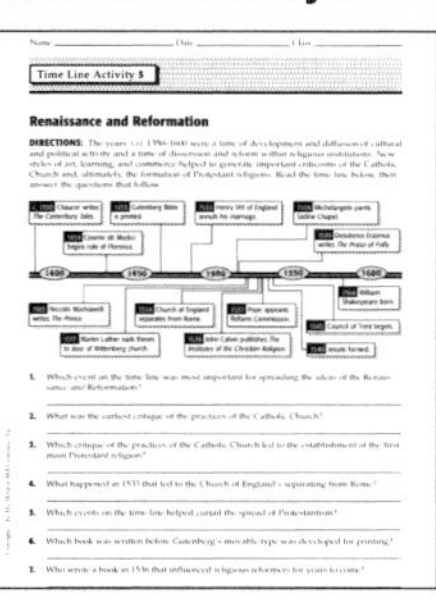

Reteaching Activity 5

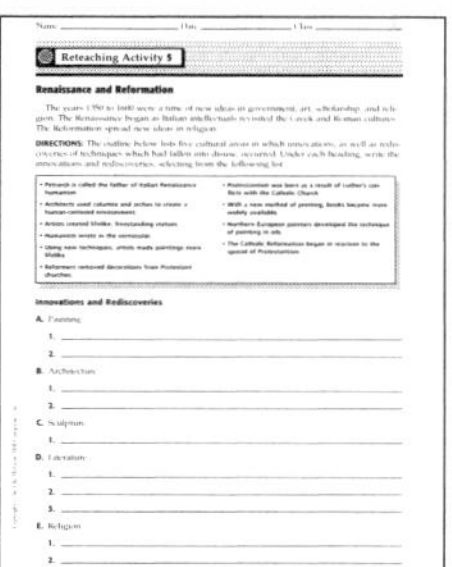

Vocabulary Activity 5

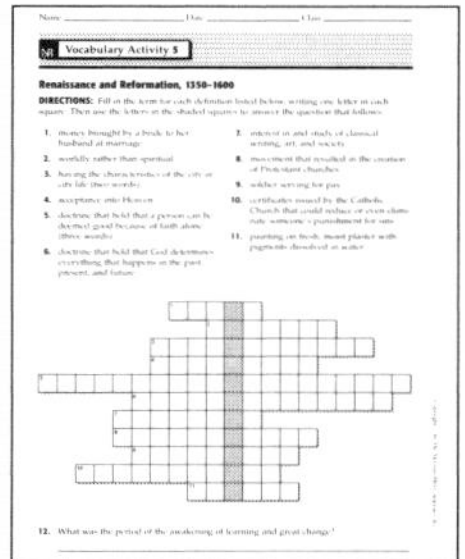

Critical Thinking Skills Activity 5

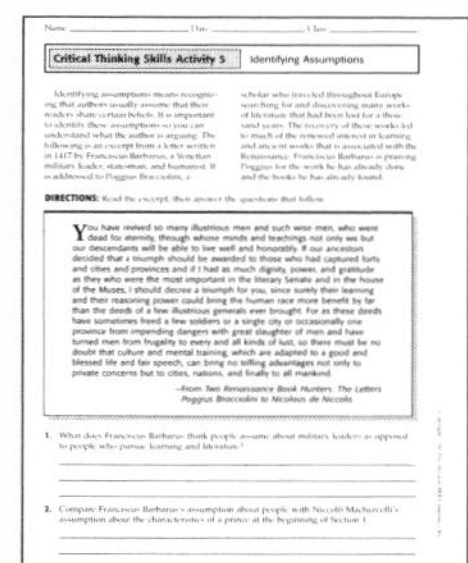

Assessment and Evaluation

Chapter 5 Test Form A

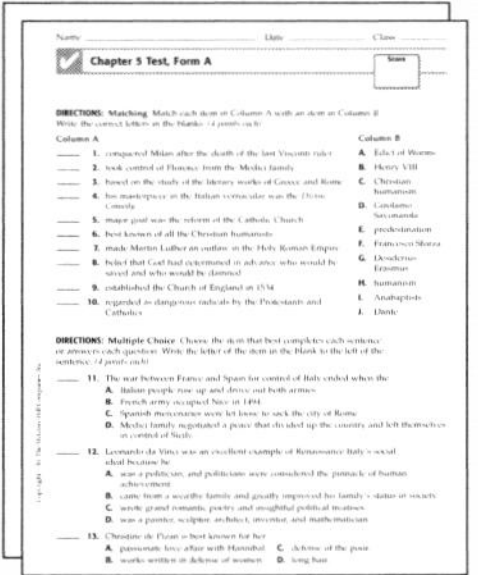

Chapter 5 Test Form B

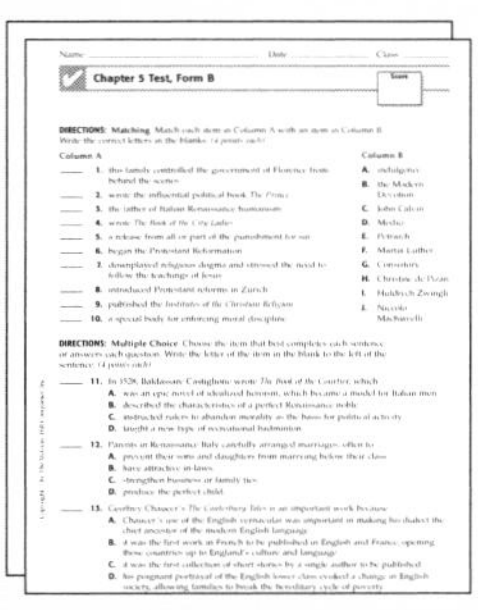

Performance Assessment Activity 5

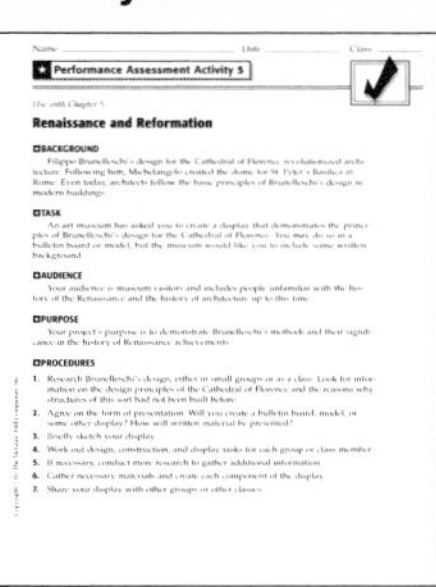

ExamView® Pro Testmaker CD-ROM

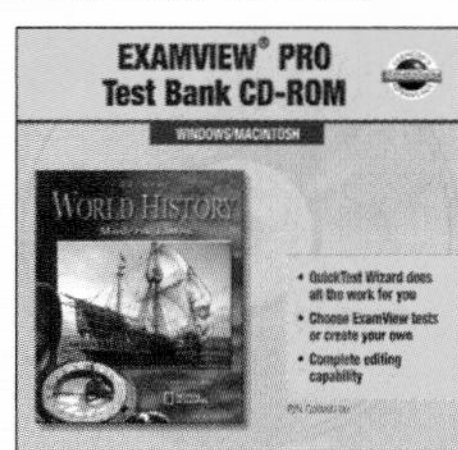

Standardized Test Skills Practice Workbook Activity 5

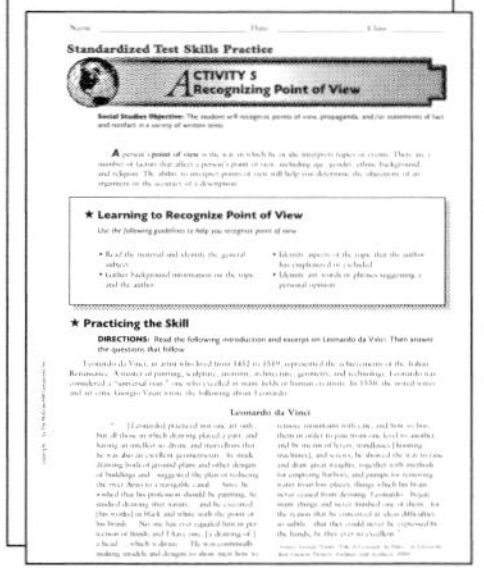

Interdisciplinary Activities

Mapping History Activity 5

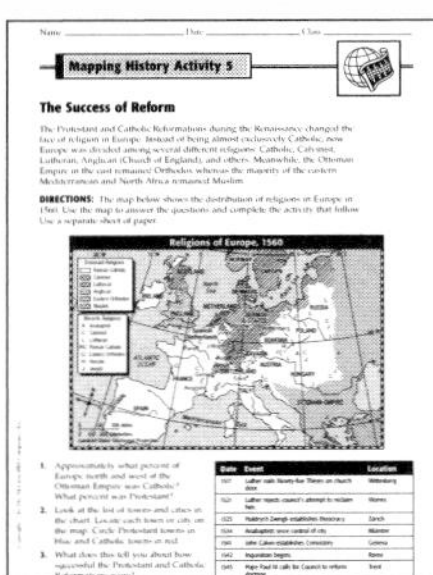

World Art and Music Activity 5

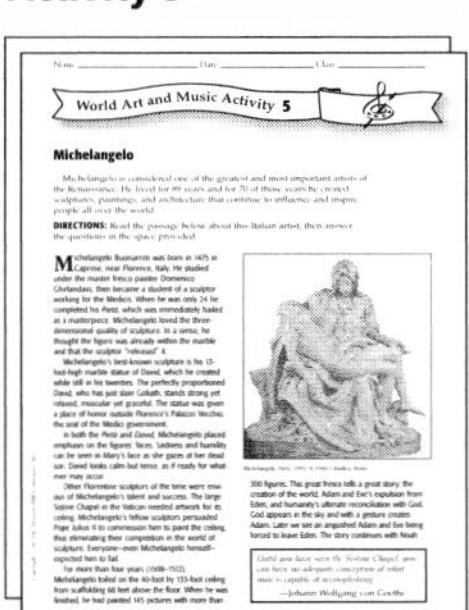

History and Geography Activity 5

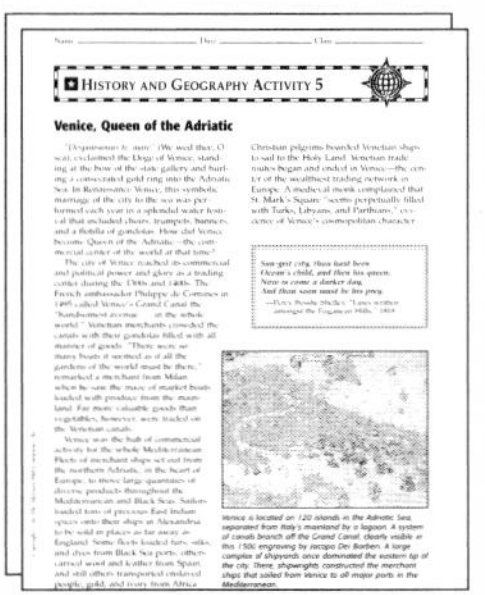

People in World History Activity 5

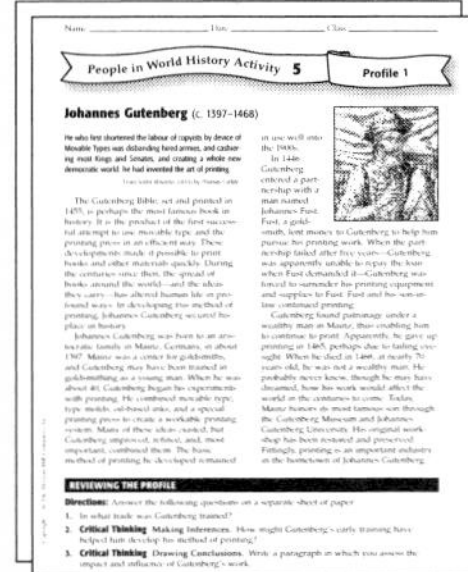

Multimedia

- Vocabulary PuzzleMaker CD-ROM
- Interactive Tutor Self-Assessment CD-ROM
- ExamView® Pro Testmaker CD-ROM
- Audio Program
- World History Primary Source Document Library CD-ROM
- MindJogger Videoquiz
- Presentation Plus! CD-ROM
- TeacherWorks CD-ROM
- Interactive Student Edition CD-ROM
- The World History—Modern Times Video Program

Spanish Resources

The following Spanish language materials are available in the Spanish Resources Binder:

- Spanish Guided Reading Activities
- Spanish Reteaching Activities
- Spanish Quizzes and Tests
- Spanish Vocabulary Activities
- Spanish Summaries

Chapter 5 Resources

SECTION RESOURCES

Daily Objectives	Reproducible Resources	Multimedia Resources
SECTION 1 **The Renaissance** 1. Explain why, between 1350 and 1550, Italian intellectuals believed they had entered a new age of human achievement. 2. Characterize city-states, which were centers of political, economic, and social life in Renaissance Italy.	Reproducible Lesson Plan 5–1 Daily Lecture and Discussion Notes 5–1 Guided Reading Activity 5–1* Section Quiz 5–1* Reading Essentials and Study Guide 5–1	Daily Focus Skills Transparency 5–1 Interactive Tutor Self-Assessment CD-ROM ExamView® Pro Testmaker CD-ROM Presentation Plus! CD-ROM
SECTION 2 **The Intellectual and Artistic Renaissance** 1. Discuss humanism—the most important intellectual movement associated with the Renaissance. 2. Identify the great artists and sculptors produced by the Renaissance, such as Michelangelo, Raphael, and Leonardo da Vinci.	Reproducible Lesson Plan 5–2 Daily Lecture and Discussion Notes 5–2 Guided Reading Activity 5–2* Section Quiz 5–2* Reading Essentials and Study Guide 5–2	Daily Focus Skills Transparency 5–2 Interactive Tutor Self-Assessment CD-ROM ExamView® Pro Testmaker CD-ROM Presentation Plus! CD-ROM
SECTION 3 **The Protestant Reformation** 1. Discuss the major goal of humanism in northern Europe, which was to reform Christendom. 2. Explain how Martin Luther's religious reforms led to the emergence of Protestantism.	Reproducible Lesson Plan 5–3 Daily Lecture and Discussion Notes 5–3 Guided Reading Activity 5–3* Section Quiz 5–3* Reading Essentials and Study Guide 5–3	Daily Focus Skills Transparency 5–3 Interactive Tutor Self-Assessment CD-ROM ExamView® Pro Testmaker CD-ROM Presentation Plus! CD-ROM
SECTION 4 **The Spread of Protestantism and the Catholic Response** 1. Summarize the different forms of Protestantism that emerged in Europe as the Reformation spread. 2. Summarize the religious rebirth of the Catholic Church.	Reproducible Lesson Plan 5–4 Daily Lecture and Discussion Notes 5–4 Guided Reading Activity 5–4* Section Quiz 5–4* Reteaching Activity 5* Reading Essentials and Study Guide 5–4	Daily Focus Skills Transparency 5–4 Interactive Tutor Self-Assessment CD-ROM ExamView® Pro Testmaker CD-ROM Presentation Plus! CD-ROM

0:00 **OUT OF TIME?**
Assign the Chapter 5 **Reading Essentials and Study Guide.**

*Also Available in Spanish

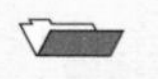 Blackline Master  Transparency  CD-ROM  DVD
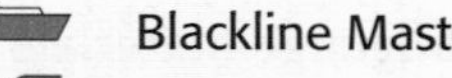 Poster 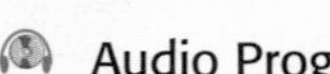 Music Program Audio Program 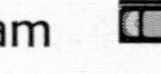 Videocassette

Chapter 5 Resources

Teacher's Corner

INDEX TO NATIONAL GEOGRAPHIC MAGAZINE

The following articles relate to this chapter:

- "Venice," by Erla Zwingle, February 1995.
- "Out of the Darkness: Michelangelo's Last Judgment," by Meg Nottingham Walsh, May 1994.
- "A Renaissance for Michelangelo," by David Jeffrey, December 1989.
- "Restoration Reveals the Last Supper," by Carlo Bertelli, November 1983.
- "Carrara Marble: Touchstone of Eternity," by Cathy Newman, July 1982.

NATIONAL GEOGRAPHIC SOCIETY PRODUCTS AVAILABLE FROM GLENCOE

To order the following products call Glencoe at 1-800-334-7344:

- *PictureShow: The Renaissance* (CD-ROM)
- *The Renaissance* (Transparencies, Poster Set)

NGS ONLINE

Access National Geographic's new dynamic MapMachine Web site and other geography resources at:
www.nationalgeographic.com
www.nationalgeographic.com/maps

KEY TO ABILITY LEVELS

Teaching strategies have been coded.

- **L1** BASIC activities for all students
- **L2** AVERAGE activities for average to above-average students
- **L3** CHALLENGING activities for above-average students
- **ELL** ENGLISH LANGUAGE LEARNER activities

Block Schedule

Activities that are suited to use within the block scheduling framework are identified by:

Use our Web site for additional resources. All essential content is covered in the Student Edition.

You and your students can visit www.wh.mt.glencoe.com, the Web site companion to *Glencoe World History—Modern Times.* This innovative integration of electronic and print media offers your students a wealth of opportunities. The student text directs students to the Web site for the following options:

- **Chapter Overviews**
- **Self-Check Quizzes**
- **Student Web Activities**
- **Textbook Updates**

Answers to the Student Web Activities are provided for you in the **Web Activity Lesson Plans.** Additional Web resources and Interactive Tutor Puzzles are also available.

From the Classroom of...

Kevin Witte
Kearney High School
Kearney, Nebraska

Ranking Renaissance Figures

Divide the class into groups of two to four students. Assign to each group a major figure of the Renaissance era such as Leonardo da Vinci, Joan of Arc, Niccolò Machiavelli, Lucretia Borgia, Petrarch, Desiderius Erasmus, the de' Medici family, Michelangelo, Thomas More, Martin Luther, and so on. Have the students of each group investigate their person's life, achievements, and influence, and prepare a fact sheet to be reproduced and distributed among the other students. Then ask one spokesperson from each group to make the case for that group's person being the most influential figure of the Renaissance era.

When all the presentations have been made, ask the students to rank the figures by the amount of influence each had on history starting with the most influential. Allow a limited amount of debate to occur before each vote.

Introducing Chapter 5

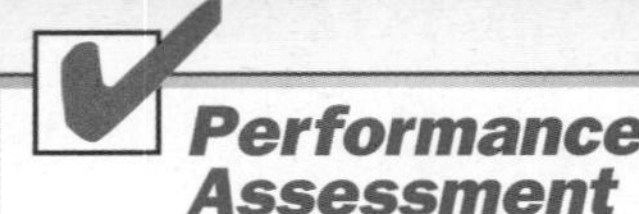

Performance Assessment

Refer to Activity 5 in the Performance Assessment Activities and Rubrics booklet.

The Impact Today

As they read the chapter, have students create a word web for either "Renaissance" or "Reformation." Have students record the information associated with their chosen term and summarize its importance today. **L1**

GLENCOE TECHNOLOGY

The World History—Modern Times Video Program

To learn more about the Renaissance and Reformation, students can view the Chapter 5 video, "Da Vinci: A Renaissance Man," from **The World History—Modern Times Video Program.**

MindJogger Videoquiz

Use the **MindJogger Videoquiz** to preview Chapter 5 content.

 Available in VHS.

CHAPTER 5 Renaissance and Reformation

1350–1600

Key Events

As you read, look for the key events in the history of the Renaissance and the Reformation in Europe.

- *Between 1350 and 1550, Italian intellectuals began to reexamine the culture of the Greeks and Romans. Historians later referred to this period of European history as the Renaissance.*
- *Martin Luther's break with the Catholic Church led to the emergence of the Protestant Reformation.*
- *During the period known as the Catholic Reformation, the Catholic Church enacted a series of reforms that were successful in strengthening the Church.*

The Impact Today

The events that occurred during this time period still impact our lives today.

- *Western art is founded on classical styles developed by the Greeks and Romans.*
- *Machiavelli's views on politics had a profound influence on later political leaders in the Western world and are still studied in universities today.*
- *The Jesuits have founded many Catholic colleges and universities in the United States.*

World History—Modern Times Video *The Chapter 5 video,* "Da Vinci: A Renaissance Man," *chronicles Leonardo da Vinci's numerous artistic and scientific innovations.*

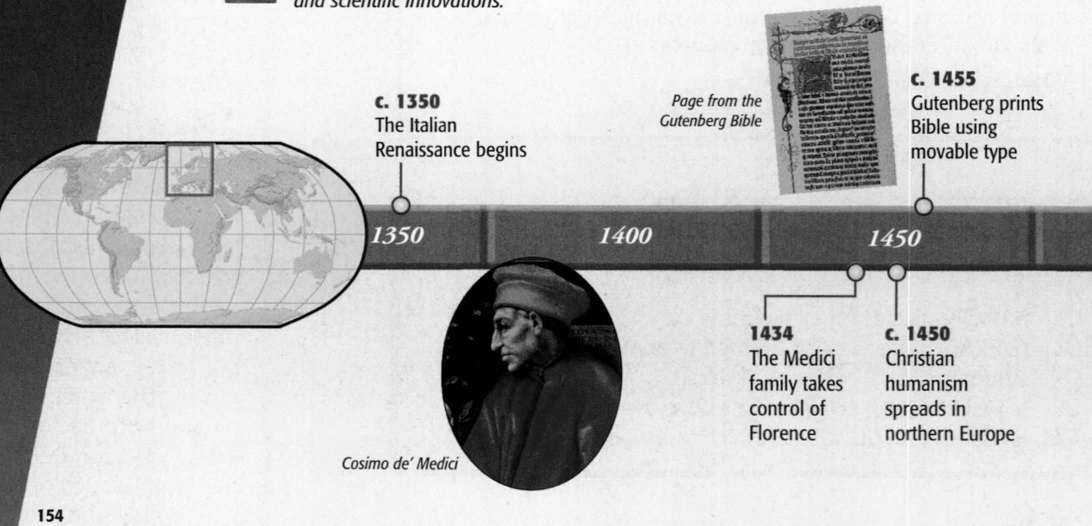
c. 1350
The Italian Renaissance begins
c. 1455
Gutenberg prints Bible using movable type
1350
1400
1450
1434
The Medici family takes control of Florence
c. 1450
Christian humanism spreads in northern Europe

Page from the Gutenberg Bible

Cosimo de' Medici

154

TWO-MINUTE LESSON LAUNCHER

Students may take for granted the varied subjects they study, failing to realize that our approach to education stems from the Renaissance's intellectual movement of humanism. Explain that humanists believed a liberal education was important for the full development of the individual. Ask students to name the subjects they study, and which they enjoy. Ask them to share their ideas about which subjects are valuable and why. Challenge them to think about why they must study subjects they may not personally enjoy or find valuable. Encourage them to discuss how their own education has helped them develop as individuals. **L1**

Renaissance art and architecture flourished in Florence. The Duomo, a Renaissance church, contains artwork by many important Renaissance artists.

1517 Martin Luther initiates the Protestant Reformation

1534 Henry VIII creates the Church of England

1500 — 1550 — 1600

1508 Michelangelo begins painting the Sistine Chapel

1519 Charles I of Spain is elected Holy Roman Emperor

1545 The Council of Trent is formed

langelo

HISTORY Online

Chapter Overview
Visit the *Glencoe World History—Modern Times* Web site at wh.mt.glencoe.com and click on **Chapter 5–Chapter Overview** to preview chapter information.

155

Introducing Chapter 5

Chapter Objectives

After studying this chapter, students should be able to:

1. list three characteristics of the Renaissance;
2. explain the three estates of Renaissance society;
3. explain Renaissance education;
4. describe artistic contributions of the Renaissance;
5. describe Christian humanism;
6. describe Luther's role in the Reformation;
7. describe religious changes in Switzerland, England and within the Catholic Church.

Chapter Overview
Introduce students to chapter content and key terms by having them access **Chapter Overview 5** at wh.mt.glencoe.com.

Time Line Activity

Have students examine the time line and note significant religious events. How many years passed between Gutenberg's printing of the Bible and the Council of Trent? How might Gutenberg's invention have led to the many changes in religion during this time? (*90 years; books, like the Bible and Luther's books were cheaper and more available, and ideas spread more quickly*) **L1**

MORE ABOUT THE ART

The Duomo of Florence is the result of six centuries of work. Although Arnolfo di Cambio designed the cathedral at the end of the thirteenth century, the façade was not completed until the nineteenth century. During the Renaissance, Filippo Brunelleschi created the enormous cupola, or dome. He worked on the cupola for sixteen years, completing it in 1436. Amazingly, the cupola was built without scaffolding. The interior of the dome features work by Renaissance artists, such as Vasari, Zuccari, Donatello, Uccello and Ghiberti. Behind the cathedral is the Duomo museum, which contains the work of many Renaissance artists, including sculptures by Michelangelo.

CHAPTER PREVIEW

Introducing

A Story That Matters

Depending upon the ability level of your students, select from the following questions to reinforce the reading of *A Story That Matters.*

- Who hired Michelangelo to paint the ceiling of the Sistine Chapel? *(Pope Julius II)*
- What was Michelangelo's attitude toward his art? *(very serious; he did not want to finish until he was satisfied)*
- How is the authority of the pope evident in this story? *(Michelangelo did not want to paint it, but the pope insisted; ceiling finished early to please the pope)* **L1 L2 L3**

About the Art

Michelangelo was a painter, sculptor, and architect. His figures on the ceiling of the Sistine Chapel reveal an ideal human being with perfect proportions. The beauty of this idealized human being is meant to be a reflection of divine beauty. The more beautiful the body, the more godlike the figure. In *The Creation of Adam*, God, from his place in heaven, provides Adam with the spark of life.

CHAPTER PREVIEW A Story That Matters

This detail from the Sistine Chapel is titled **The Creation of Adam.**

Painting the Sistine Chapel

Around 1500, Pope Julius II wanted the great Italian artist Michelangelo to paint the ceiling of the Sistine Chapel in Rome. "This is not my trade," Michelangelo protested; he was a sculptor, not a painter. He recommended other painters to the pope, but the pope persisted.

Michelangelo needed the money and undertook the project. He worked, on and off, for four years, from May 1508 to October 1512. For a long time he refused to allow anyone, including the pope, to see his work.

Julius grew anxious and pestered Michelangelo on a regular basis about when the ceiling would be finished. Tired of the pope's requests, Michelangelo once replied that the ceiling would be completed "when it satisfies me as an artist." The pope responded, "We want you to finish it soon." He then threatened that if Michelangelo did not "finish the ceiling quickly he would have him thrown down from the scaffolding."

Fearing the pope's anger, Michelangelo quickly completed his work. When he climbed down from the scaffold for the last time, he was tired and worn out. Because he had been on his back so long while painting the ceiling, it was said that he now found it easier to read by holding a book up rather than down. The Sistine Chapel ceiling, however, is one of the great masterpieces in the history of Western art.

Why It Matters

In the fifteenth century, intellectuals in Italy were convinced that they had made a decisive break with the Middle Ages and had entered a new age of human achievement. Today, we call this period of European history the Renaissance. Michelangelo was but one of the great figures of this time. Another was Martin Luther of Germany, whose break with the Roman Catholic Church at the beginning of the sixteenth century led to the Protestant Reformation and a new era in the history of Christianity.

History And You Identify two pieces of public art in your community. Research what commendations or criticism the city received following the unveiling of these pieces. Create a multimedia presentation with your findings.

HISTORY AND YOU

Renaissance art reflected the humanist emphasis on the individual or universal person. Bring in samples of the works of Michelangelo, Leonardo da Vinci, and Raphael for the class to see. Have students explain how the themes of the works emphasize the individual or universal person. Then ask students to list evidence of how the importance of the individual is still emphasized in our own times. Examples might be found in popular music, film, painting, and advertising. Ask students to identify how Renaissance art and the art of today demonstrate an artistic ideal or visual principle. **L2**

SECTION 1 The Renaissance

Guide to Reading

Main Ideas
- Between 1350 and 1550, Italian intellectuals believed they had entered a new age of human achievement.
- City-states were the centers of political, economic, and social life in Renaissance Italy.

Key Terms
urban society, secular, mercenary, dowry

People to Identify
Leonardo da Vinci, Francesco Sforza, Cosimo de' Medici, Lorenzo de' Medici, Niccolò Machiavelli

Places to Locate
Milan, Venice, Florence, Rome

Preview Questions
1. What was the Renaissance?
2. Describe the political world that existed in the Italian states.

Reading Strategy
Categorizing Information Use a web diagram like the one below to identify the major principles of Machiavelli's work, *The Prince.*

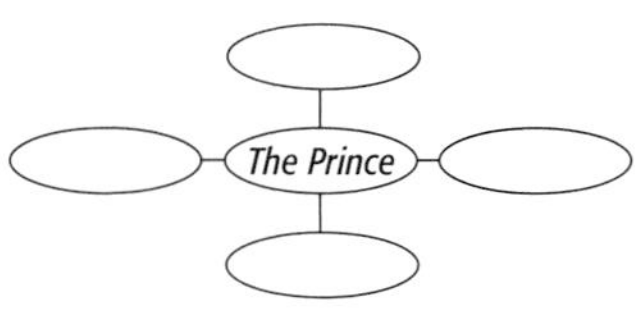

Preview of Events

1425 · 1450 · 1500 · 1525 · 1550

- **1447** Last Visconti ruler of Milan dies
- **1494** Charles VIII of France invades Naples
- **1513** Machiavelli writes *The Prince*
- **1527** Invading armies sack Rome
- **1528** Castiglione writes *The Book of the Courtier*

Voices from the Past

Cesare Borgia

Inspired by Cesare Borgia, who conquered central Italy and set up a state, Niccolò Machiavelli wrote *The Prince*, a short work on political power. He said:

> ❝Everyone realizes how praiseworthy it is for a prince to honor his word and to be straightforward rather than crafty in his dealings; nonetheless experience shows that princes who have achieved great things have been those who have given their word lightly, who have known how to trick men with their cunning, and who, in the end, have overcome those abiding by honest principles. . . . A prince, therefore, need not necessarily have all the good qualities I mentioned above, but he should certainly appear to have them. . . . He should not deviate from what is good, if that is possible, but he should know how to do evil, if that is necessary.❞
>
> —***The Prince*, George Bull, trans., 1981**

The Prince reflected the practice of politics in Renaissance Italy.

The Italian Renaissance

The word *renaissance* means rebirth. A number of people who lived in Italy between 1350 and 1550 believed that they had witnessed a rebirth of the ancient Greek and Roman worlds. To them, this rebirth marked a new age. Historians later called this period the Renaissance, or Italian Renaissance—a period of European history that began in Italy and spread to the rest of Europe. What, then, are the most important characteristics of the Italian Renaissance?

First, Renaissance Italy was largely an urban society. As the Middle Ages progressed, powerful city-states became the centers of Italian political, economic, and social life. Within this growing urban society, a secular, or worldly, viewpoint

1 FOCUS

Section Overview

This section describes the characteristics of the Renaissance, and the political and social structure of Renaissance society.

BELLRINGER
Skillbuilder Activity

Project transparency 5–1 and have students answer questions.

Available as a blackline master.

Daily Focus Skills Transparency 5–1

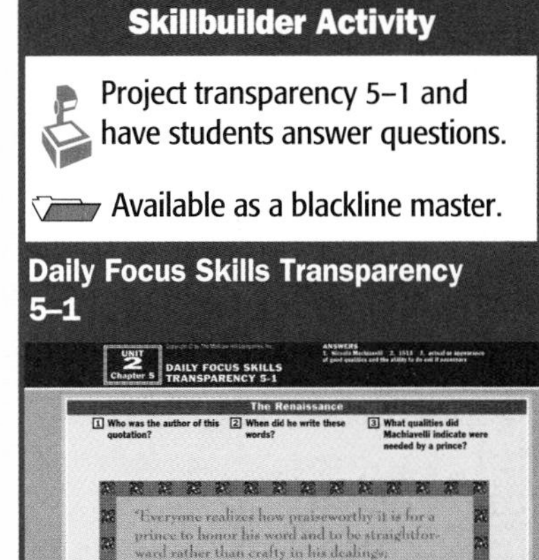

Guide to Reading

Answers to Graphic: *The Prince:* how to acquire and keep political power, attitude toward power based on understanding of human nature, political activity not restricted by moral principles, prince acts on behalf of the state

Preteaching Vocabulary: To understand the term *secular*, have students find as many synonyms and antonyms as possible for the word. *(synonyms: worldly, profane, temporal, non-religious, civil, lay, physical, non-clerical; antonyms: religious, spiritual)* **L1**

SECTION RESOURCES

Reproducible Masters
- Reproducible Lesson Plan 5–1
- Daily Lecture and Discussion Notes 5–1
- Guided Reading Activity 5–1
- Section Quiz 5–1
- Reading Essentials and Study Guide 5–1

Transparencies
- Daily Focus Skills Transparency 5–1

Multimedia
- Interactive Tutor Self-Assessment CD-ROM
- ExamView® Pro Testmaker CD-ROM
- Presentation Plus! CD-ROM

2 TEACH

Reading Check

Answer: A worldly viewpoint and increasing wealth brought renewed interest in ancient culture and a belief that a well-rounded individual should be capable of achievements in many areas.

Daily Lecture and Discussion Notes 5–1

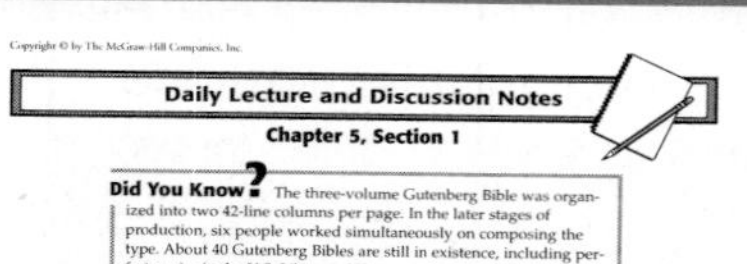

Daily Lecture and Discussion Notes

Chapter 5, Section 1

Did You Know? The three-volume Gutenberg Bible was organized into two 42-line columns per page. In the later stages of production, six people worked simultaneously on composing the type. About 40 Gutenberg Bibles are still in existence, including perfect copies in the U.S. Library of Congress, the French Bibliothèque Nationale, and the British Library.

I. **The Italian Renaissance** *(pages 157–158)*

A. The word *renaissance* means rebirth. The Italian Renaissance, which spread to the rest of Europe, occurred between 1350 and 1550. The rebirth was of the ancient Greek and Roman worlds.

B. Italy of the Renaissance was largely an **urban society.** The powerful city-states of the Middle Ages became political, economic, and social centers. A **secular,** or worldly, viewpoint developed in this urban society as increasing wealth created new opportunities for material enjoyment.

C. The Renaissance was also an age when the power of the Church declined, and society recovered from the plagues and instability of the Middle Ages. Part of this recovery was a rebirth of interest in the ancient Greek and Roman cultures.

D. A new view of human beings that emphasized individual ability and worth emerged in the Renaissance. The well-rounded, universal person was capable of achievements in many areas of life. For example, **Leonardo da Vinci** was a painter, sculptor, architect, inventor, and mathematician.

E. The upper classes were more affected by the Italian Renaissance than the lower classes, and they embraced its ideals more. Even so, many of the intellectual and artistic achievements were hard to ignore. Churches, wealthy homes, and public buildings displayed art that celebrated the human body, classical antiquity, and religious and secular themes.

Discussion Question

What term in English expresses the Renaissance ideal of a well-rounded, multi-talented person? *(The term is* Renaissance man.*)*

70

Enrich

Have students discuss the Greek concept of a sound mind in a sound body in relation to the quote "Men can do all things if they will." How do these two statements reflect the time periods in which they were uttered? *(both stress the value and strength of the individual, saw improving individual as a way to improve society)* **L2**

This painting by Luca Carlevaris, titled The Pier and the Ducal Palace, *shows the wealth associated with Venice.*

emerged as increasing wealth created new possibilities for the enjoyment of material things.

Second, the Renaissance was an age of recovery from the disasters of the fourteenth century such as the plague, political instability, and a decline of Church power. Recovery went hand in hand with a rebirth of interest in ancient culture. Italian thinkers became aware of their own Roman past—the remains of which were to be seen all around them. They also became intensely interested in the culture that had dominated the ancient Mediterranean world. This revival affected both politics and art.

Third, a new view of human beings emerged as people in the Italian Renaissance began to emphasize individual ability. As Leon Battista Alberti, a fifteenth-century Italian, said, "Men can do all things if they will." A high regard for human worth and a realization of what individuals could achieve created a new social ideal. The well-rounded, universal person was capable of achievements in many areas of life. **Leonardo da Vinci** (VIHN•chee), for example, was a painter, sculptor, architect, inventor, and mathematician.

Of course, not all parts of Italian society were directly affected by these three general characteristics of the Italian Renaissance. The wealthy upper classes, who made up a small percentage of the total population, more actively embraced the new ideas and activities. Indirectly, however, the Italian Renaissance did have some impact on ordinary people. Especially in the cities, many of the intellectual and artistic achievements of the period were highly visible and difficult to ignore. The churches, wealthy homes, and public buildings were decorated with art that celebrated religious and secular themes, the human body, and an appreciation of classical antiquity.

Reading Check **Summarizing** What were the characteristics of the Italian Renaissance?

The Italian States

During the Middle Ages, Italy had failed to develop a centralized monarchical state. The lack of a single strong ruler made it possible for a number of city-states in northern and central Italy to remain independent. Three of them—**Milan, Venice,** and

COOPERATIVE LEARNING ACTIVITY

Preparing a Summary Have students compare the Renaissance in Milan, Venice, and Florence. Organize students into three teams, each studying a city-state. Have each team split into subgroups to research a topic such as government, economy, patrons of the arts, women, painting, sculpture, or architecture. When research is complete, have subgroups report their findings to the whole team. Then have each team prepare an overall summary of its research. Ask each team to select a member to present the team's overall summary of its Renaissance city-state. **L2**

For grading this activity, refer to the ***Performance Assessment Activities*** booklet.

Florence—expanded and played crucial roles in Italian politics.

The Italian city-states prospered from a flourishing trade that had expanded in the Middle Ages. Italian cities traded with both the Byzantine and Islamic civilizations to the east. Italian trading ships had also moved into the western Mediterranean and then north along the Atlantic seaboard. These ships exchanged goods with merchants in both England and the Netherlands. Italian merchants had profited from the Crusades as well and were able to set up new trading centers in eastern ports. There, the Italian merchants obtained silks, sugar, and spices, which they carried back to Italy and the West.

Milan Milan, located in northern Italy at the crossroads of the main trade routes from Italian coastal cities to the Alpine passes, was one of the richest city-states in Italy. In the fourteenth century, members of the Visconti family established themselves as dukes of Milan and extended their power over all of Lombardy.

The last Visconti ruler of Milan died in 1447. **Francesco Sforza** then conquered the city and became its new duke. Sforza was the leader of a band of mercenaries—soldiers who sold their services to the highest bidder.

Francesco Sforza, Duke of Milan

Both the Visconti and Sforza rulers worked to build a strong centralized state. By creating an efficient tax system, they generated enormous revenues for the government.

Venice Another major northern Italian city-state was the republic of Venice. As a link between Asia and western Europe the city drew traders from all over the world. Officially Venice was a republic with an elected leader called a *Doge*. In reality a small group of merchant-aristocrats, who had become wealthy through their trading activities, ran the government of Venice on behalf of their own interests. Venice's trade empire was tremendously profitable and made Venice an international power.

Florence The republic of Florence dominated the region of Tuscany. In the course of the fourteenth century, a small but wealthy group of merchants established control of the Florentine government. They led the Florentines in a series of successful wars against their neighbors and established Florence as a major city-state in northern Italy.

In 1434, **Cosimo de' Medici** (MEH•duh•chee) took control of the city. The wealthy Medici family controlled the government from behind the scenes. Using their wealth and personal influence, Cosimo and later, **Lorenzo de' Medici,** his

Lorenzo de' Medici

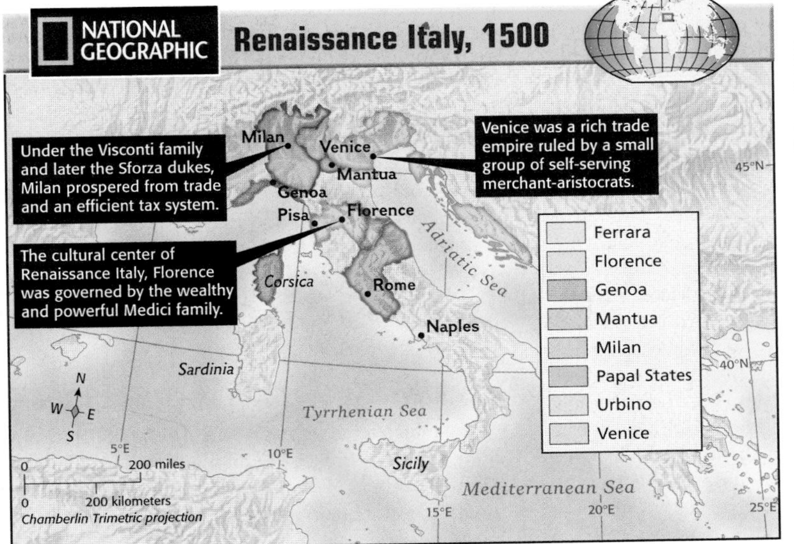

Geography Skills

Italian city-states prospered during the Renaissance.

1. **Interpreting Maps** Using your text, identify the three most powerful city-states. What geographic features did they have in common?
2. **Applying Geography Skills** Which city-state was in the best location to trade by land and sea with the Byzantine Empire to the east?

Geography Skills

Answers:

1. Milan, Venice, Florence; all in northern Italy
2. Venice **WH:** 11B

Guided Reading Activity 5–1

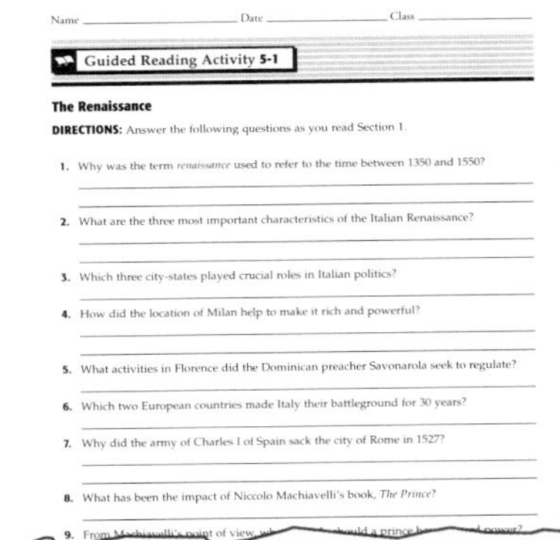

Name ______ Date ______ Class ______

Guided Reading Activity 5-1

The Renaissance

DIRECTIONS: Answer the following questions as you read Section 1.

1. Why was the term *renaissance* used to refer to the time between 1350 and 1550?
2. What are the three most important characteristics of the Italian Renaissance?
3. Which three city-states played crucial roles in Italian politics?
4. How did the location of Milan help to make it rich and powerful?
5. What activities in Florence did the Dominican preacher Savonarola seek to regulate?
6. Which two European countries made Italy their battleground for 30 years?
7. Why did the army of Charles I of Spain sack the city of Rome in 1527?
8. What has been the impact of Niccolo Machiavelli's book, *The Prince*?
9. From Machiavelli's point of view, ...

Who?What?Where?When?

Government The city-state of Florence had a republican form of government. Students should recognize the United States also has a republican form of government. Students should understand that in a republic, citizens vote for representatives who will make governmental decisions for them.

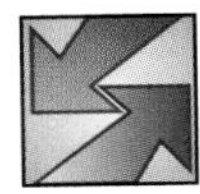

CURRICULUM CONNECTION

Cartography Have students work in pairs to create thematic maps showing the trade routes described in the text, including wool coming from England to be made into cloth in Italy, and spices and silks coming from the east. **L2**

CRITICAL THINKING ACTIVITY

Drawing Conclusions Have students research the impact of either the Medici family or Savonarola on Florence. Have students discuss the results of their findings. Ask students to decide whether they support or oppose the rule of the person they researched. Then have them write a letter to the editor of a Florence newspaper concerning either the Medicis or Savonarola. In their letters, they may choose to support or speak out against either the Medicis or Savonarola. Encourage students whose letters express opposite points of view to share them with the class. **L3**

History *through Art*

Answer: French and Spanish forces fought in Italy, so they would have seen the contributions of the Renaissance and taken new ideas back to their homelands.

Reading Check

Answer: worked to build a strong centralized state and created an efficient tax system that brought in enormous revenues for the government

Connecting Across Time

The Medici family was able to dominate Florentine politics for several generations. Ask students to suggest strategies that would have enabled one family to dominate city politics for such a long time. Can students identify American families who have dominated city or state governments for several generations? *(money, successful business, powerful ancestors, living in one place for generations; answers will vary)* **L1**

CURRICULUM CONNECTION

Study Skills Have students create a time line of the Italian Renaissance that includes ten to twenty important events, art works, or scientific achievements that were produced during this time. **L2**

History *through Art*

***Entry of Charles VIII into Naples* by Eloi Firmin Feron, 1837** Some scholars believe that the Italian wars helped spread Renaissance ideals and practices. How could the wars have had that effect?

grandson, dominated the city at a time when Florence was the cultural center of Italy.

During the late 1400s, Florence experienced an economic decline. Most of its economy was based on the manufacturing of cloth. Increased competition from English and Flemish cloth makers drove down profits.

During this time a Dominican preacher named Girolamo Savonarola began condemning the corruption and excesses of the Medici family. Citizens, tired of Medici rule, and frustrated by economic events, turned to Savonarola. So many people followed him that the Medici family turned Florence over to his followers.

Eventually people tired of Savonarola's strict regulations on gambling, horseracing, swearing, painting, music, and books. Savonarola also attacked the corruption of the Church, which angered the pope. In 1498, Savonarola was accused of heresy and sentenced to death. The Medici family returned to power.

The Italian Wars The growth of powerful monarchical states in the rest of Europe eventually led to trouble for the Italian states. Attracted by the riches of Italy, the French king Charles VIII led an army of thirty thousand men into Italy in 1494 and occupied the kingdom of Naples in southern Italy. Northern Italian states turned for help to the Spanish, who gladly agreed to send soldiers to Italy. For the next 30 years, the French and Spanish made Italy their battleground as they fought to dominate the country.

A decisive turning point in their war came in 1527. On May 5, thousands of troops belonging to the Spanish king Charles I arrived at the city of **Rome** along with mercenaries from different countries. They had not been paid for months. When they yelled, "Money! Money!" their leader responded, "If you have ever dreamed of pillaging a town and laying hold of its treasures, here now is one, the richest of them all, queen of the world." The next day the invading forces smashed down the gates and pushed their way into the city. The troops went berserk in a frenzy of bloodshed and looting. Church officials were sold as slaves, and churches and palaces were sacked while drunken soldiers fought over the spoils. The destruction did not end until the authorities were finally forced to establish some order. The terrible sack of Rome in 1527 by the armies of the Spanish king Charles I ended the Italian wars and left the Spanish a dominant force in Italy.

Reading Check **Describing** How did the Visconti and Sforza rulers become powerful in Milan?

Machiavelli and the New Statecraft

No one gave better expression to the Italians' love affair with political power than **Niccolò Machiavelli** (MA•kee•uh•VEH•lee). His book *The Prince* is one of the most influential works on political power in the Western world.

EXTENDING THE CONTENT

Diplomats The struggle for political and economic supremacy in northern Italy gave rise to a fundamental diplomatic procedure among the Italian city-states. This procedure spread to Europe and eventually the world. The Italians invented the machinery of modern diplomacy, such as placing resident ambassadors in capitals where political and commercial ties could be monitored. Diplomacy enabled rulers to win victories without the expense and risk of military operation. Diplomats from Milan and Florence negotiated the Peace of Lodi (1454). The role of the ambassador was four-fold: he or she won allies through negotiation, countered the designs of enemies, represented his government at official functions, and reported information relevant to aiding the preservation and expansion of his state.

Machiavelli, as portrayed by Santi di Tito

Machiavelli's central thesis in *The Prince* concerns how to acquire—and keep—political power. In the Middle Ages, many writers on political power had stressed the ethical side of a prince's activity—how a ruler ought to behave based on Christian principles. Machiavelli rejected this approach.

From Machiavelli's point of view, a prince's attitude toward power must be based on an understanding of human nature, which he believed was basically self-centered. He wrote, "One can make this generalization about men: they are ungrateful, fickle, liars, and deceivers, they shun danger and are greedy for profit." Political activity, therefore, should not be restricted by moral principles. A prince acts on behalf of the state. For the sake of the state, he must be willing to let his conscience sleep.

Machiavelli was among the first to abandon morality as the basis for analyzing political activity. His views on politics have had a profound influence on political leaders who followed.

Reading Check **Explaining** Why was *The Prince* an important work on political power?

Renaissance Society

In the Middle Ages, society was divided into three estates, or social classes. Although this social order continued into the Renaissance, some changes became evident. We examine the nobility and the peasants and townspeople here. The clergy are discussed later in the chapter.

The Nobility Throughout much of Europe, landholding nobles were faced with declining incomes during the greater part of the fourteenth and fifteenth centuries. Many members of the old nobility, however, retained their lands and titles; new blood also came into their ranks.

By 1500, nobles, old and new, again dominated society. Although they made up only about 2 to 3 percent of the population in most countries, the nobles held important political posts and served as advisers to the king.

By this time, the noble, or aristocrat, was expected to fulfill certain ideals. These ideals were clearly expressed in *The Book of the Courtier,* written by the Italian Baldassare Castiglione (KAHS•teel•YOH•NAY) in 1528.

In his work, Castiglione described the characteristics of a perfect Renaissance noble. First, a noble was born, not made. He was expected to have character, grace, and talent. Second, the perfect noble had to develop two basic skills. Because the chief aim of a noble was to be a warrior, he had to perform military and physical exercises. Unlike the medieval knight, however, who was primarily concerned with acquiring military skill, the Renaissance noble was also expected to gain a classical education and enrich his life with the arts. Third, the noble needed to follow a certain standard of conduct. Nobles were not supposed to hide their achievements but to show them with grace.

A portrait of Baldassare Castiglione by Raphael, c. 1516

Reading Check

Answer: Machiavelli rejected the ethical side of a prince's activity. He was among the first to abandon morality as the basis for the analysis of political activity.

Connecting Across Time

Have students compare the three characteristics of a noble as described by Castiglione to the American idea of a successful businessperson or community leader. How are the two similar and how are they different? You might also wish to have students compare the difference in views between Castiglione and Machiavelli. *(in America, we believe a "noble" can be made; it is not necessary to have military skill; students may or may not see classical education as important; may or may not see standard of conduct as important; Machiavelli believed moral conduct was not important, but Castiglione believed it was)* **L3**

CURRICULUM CONNECTION

Sociology Have students analyze the information presented in the text concerning the three estates and have them construct an accurate pyramid showing the percentage distribution of the first, second, and third estates. *(nobility—2–3%; clergy—7–12%; peasants—85–90%* **L1**

CRITICAL THINKING ACTIVITY

Analyzing Information Have students take the role of noble, merchant, artisan, or another citizen of Italy during the Renaissance. Pair students and have them write a series of letters to each other in which they give details of the events of the time and express their feelings and attitudes regarding developments and reforms. Students should indicate in their letters either how they are influencing the developments of the Renaissance or how they are influenced by the developments of the Renaissance. Each student should write at least five letters that are detailed, persuasive in tone and style, and that respond to the information contained in the letters written by their student partner. **L2**

Chapter 5
Section 1, 157-163

SCIENCE, TECHNOLOGY & SOCIETY

Answer: Printing made books much more common and less expensive. More people would see them and want to know what was in them.

3 ASSESS

Assign Performance Assessment Activity 1 as homework or as an in-class activity.

Have students use **Interactive Tutor Self-Assessment CD-ROM.**

Section Quiz 5–1

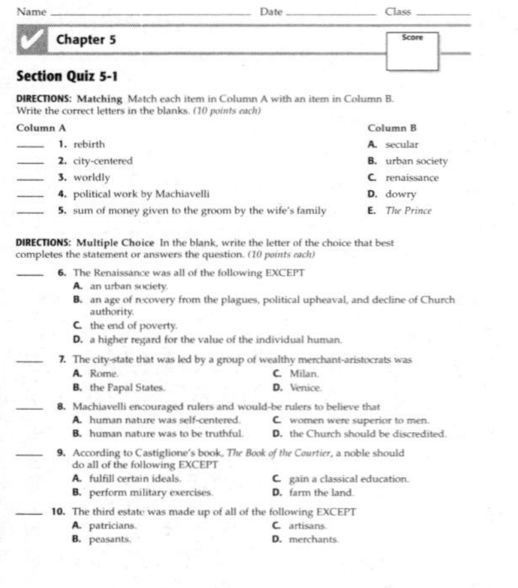
Name ______ Date ______ Class ______

Chapter 5 Score

Section Quiz 5-1

DIRECTIONS: Matching Match each item in Column A with an item in Column B. Write the correct letters in the blanks. *(10 points each)*

Column A	Column B
____ 1. rebirth	A. secular
____ 2. city-centered	B. urban society
____ 3. worldly	C. renaissance
____ 4. political work by Machiavelli	D. dowry
____ 5. sum of money given to the groom by the wife's family	E. *The Prince*

DIRECTIONS: Multiple Choice In the blank, write the letter of the choice that best completes the statement or answers the question. *(10 points each)*

____ 6. The Renaissance was all of the following EXCEPT
A. an urban society.
B. an age of recovery from the plagues, political upheaval, and decline of Church authority.
C. the end of poverty.
D. a higher regard for the value of the individual human.

____ 7. The city-state that was led by a group of wealthy merchant-aristocrats was
A. Rome. C. Milan.
B. the Papal States. D. Venice.

____ 8. Machiavelli encouraged rulers and would-be rulers to believe that
A. human nature was self-centered. C. women were superior to men.
B. human nature was to be truthful. D. the Church should be discredited.

____ 9. According to Castiglione's book, *The Book of the Courtier*, a noble should do all of the following EXCEPT
A. fulfill certain ideals. C. gain a classical education.
B. perform military exercises. D. farm the land.

____ 10. The third estate was made up of all of the following EXCEPT
A. patricians. C. artisans.
B. peasants. D. merchants.

Glencoe World History—Modern Times 33

SCIENCE, TECHNOLOGY & SOCIETY

The Impact of Printing

The Renaissance saw the development of printing in Europe. In the fifteenth century, Europeans gradually learned how to print with movable metal type. Johannes Gutenberg of Germany played a crucial role in the process. Gutenberg's Bible, printed about 1455, was the first European book produced from movable type.

By 1500, there were over a thousand printers in Europe. Almost forty thousand titles had been published. More than half of these were religious books, including Bibles in English, French, and German; prayer books; and sermons. Most others were Latin and Greek classics, legal and philosophical works, and romances.

The printing of books encouraged scholarly research and increased the public's desire to gain knowledge, which would eventually have an enormous impact on European society. The new religious ideas of the Reformation would not have spread as rapidly as they did in the sixteenth century without the printing press.

Printing allowed European civilization to compete for the first time with the civilization of China. The Chinese had invented printing much earlier, as well as printing with movable type.

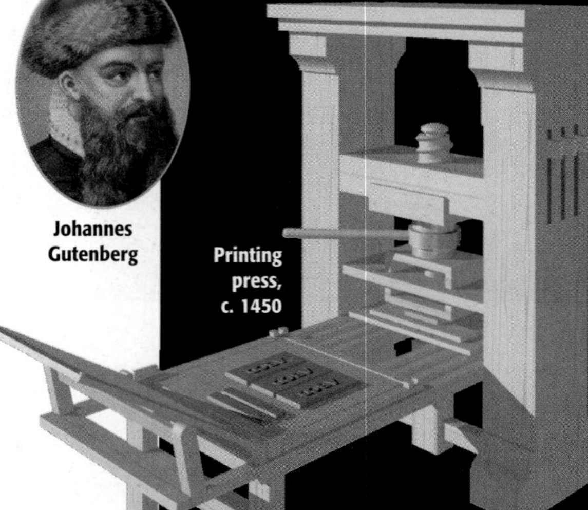
Johannes Gutenberg

Printing press, c. 1450

Fifteenth-century type design

H I K P

Analyzing ***Why do you think the printing of books encouraged people's desire to gain knowledge?***

What was the purpose of these standards?

> "I think that the aim of the perfect Courtier is so to win for himself the favor and mind of the prince whom he serves that he may be able to tell him, and always will tell him, the truth about everything he needs to know, without fear or risk of displeasing him; and that when he sees the mind of his prince inclined to a wrong action, he may dare to oppose him . . . so as to disuade him of every evil intent and bring him to the path of virtue."

The aim, then, of the perfect noble was to serve his prince in an effective and honest way. Nobles would adhere to Castiglione's principles for hundreds of years while they continued to dominate European life socially and politically.

Peasants and Townspeople In the Middle Ages, peasants had made up the overwhelming mass of the third estate. In the Renaissance, they still constituted 85 to 90 percent of the total European population, except in the highly urban areas of northern Italy and Flanders.

Serfdom continued to decrease with the decline of the manorial system. Increasingly, throughout the late Middle Ages, the labor owed by a peasant to a lord was converted into rent on land paid in money. By 1500, especially in western Europe, more and more peasants became legally free.

Townspeople made up the rest of the third estate. In the Middle Ages, townspeople were mostly merchants and artisans. The Renaissance town or city of the fifteenth century, however, was more diverse.

At the top of urban society were the patricians. Their wealth from trade, industry, and banking enabled them to dominate their communities economically, socially, and politically. Below them were the burghers—the shopkeepers, artisans, guild

MEETING INDIVIDUAL NEEDS

Visual/Auditory As a class, read the section entitled "Family and Marriage" on page 163. Have each student make a chart outlining what roles they feel fathers and mothers play in today's society. How are single parents able to perform all responsibilities necessary? How does this differ from Renaissance Italy? Various charts can be reproduced on the overhead or copied for the hearing-impaired. Students requiring assistance may list characteristics aloud while a partner constructs the chart. **L1**

Refer to ***Inclusion for the High School Social Studies Classroom Strategies and Activities*** in the TCR.

masters, and guild members who provided the goods and services for their fellow townspeople.

Below the patricians and the burghers were the workers, who earned pitiful wages, and the unemployed. Both groups lived miserable lives. These people made up perhaps 30 or 40 percent of the urban population.

During the late 1300s and the 1400s, urban poverty increased dramatically throughout Europe. One rich merchant of Florence, who had little sympathy for the poor, wrote:

> ❝Those that are lazy in a way that does harm to the city, and who can offer no just reason for their condition, should either be forced to work or expelled from the city. The city would thus rid itself of that most harmful part of the poorest class.❞

History *through Art*

***Celebration of a Marriage* by Ghirlandaio Domenico** During the Renaissance, a marriage was more of a business arrangement than a matter of love. How does this painting support or contradict that statement?

Family and Marriage The family bond was a source of great security in the dangerous urban world of Renaissance Italy. To maintain the family, parents carefully arranged marriages, often to strengthen business or family ties. Details were worked out well in advance, sometimes when children were only two or three years old. The most important aspect of the marriage contract was the size of the **dowry**, a sum of money given by the wife's family to the husband upon marriage.

The father-husband was the center of the Italian family. He gave it his name, managed all finances (his wife had no share in his wealth), and made the decisions that determined his children's lives. The mother's chief role was to supervise the household.

A father's authority over his children was absolute until he died or formally freed his children. In Renaissance Italy, children did not become adults on reaching a certain age. Instead, adulthood came to children when their fathers went before a judge and formally freed them. The age of adulthood varied from the early teens to the late twenties.

Reading Check **Contrasting** How was the Renaissance noble different from the medieval knight?

SECTION 1 ASSESSMENT

Checking for Understanding

1. **Define** urban society, secular, mercenary, dowry.
2. **Identify** Leonardo da Vinci, Francesco Sforza, Cosimo de' Medici, Lorenzo de' Medici, Niccolò Machiavelli.
3. **Locate** Milan, Venice, Florence, Rome.
4. **Explain** how the Spanish became involved in the Italian wars.
5. **Summarize** the characteristics of Castiglione's perfect noble.

Critical Thinking

6. **Explain** Why was a strong family bond so important in Renaissance Italy?
7. **Contrasting Information** Use a table like the one below to describe the differences between the social structure of the Middle Ages and the Renaissance.

	Middle Ages	Renaissance
Nobility		
Peasants		
Townspeople		

Analyzing Visuals

8. **Identify** details in the painting of Venice on page 158 that show it is a major city-state with a profitable trade empire. Find other images of Venice in your school library and compare them to this painting.

Writing About History

9. **Expository Writing** Read a few passages from *The Prince.* Write a brief essay explaining whether or not you agree with Machiavelli's theory of politics.

History *through Art*

Answer: Painting supports view that marriage was a business transaction. Lack of musicians and festive decorations, the man recording the ceremony, the sober expressions, are examples students could cite.

Reading Check

Answer: In addition to being a warrior, he must also gain a classical education and adorn his life with the arts.

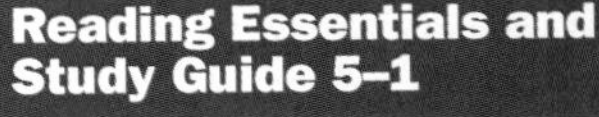

Reading Essentials and Study Guide 5–1

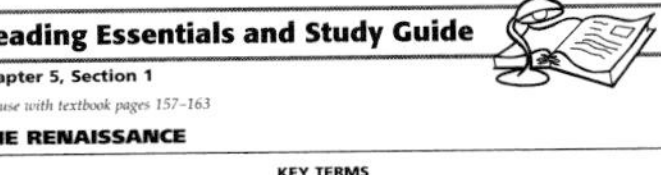

Name ______ Date ______ Class ______

Reading Essentials and Study Guide

Chapter 5, Section 1

For use with textbook pages 157–163

THE RENAISSANCE

KEY TERMS

urban society a society in which many of the people in cities *(page 157)*

secular worldly, rather than religious *(page 157)*

mercenary a soldier who sells his services to the highest bidder *(page 159)*

dowry in Renaissance Italy, a sum of money given by a wife's family to her husband upon marriage *(page 163)*

DRAWING FROM EXPERIENCE

What does being an individual mean to you? In what ways can a person foster his or her individuality?

In this section, you will learn about the beginnings of the Renaissance in Italy. During the Renaissance, a new view of human beings emerged that emphasized individual ability.

ORGANIZING YOUR THOUGHTS

Reteaching Activity

Have students make a three-column chart describing the Italian Renaissance with the headings: *Characteristics, Major City-States,* and *Three Estates.* **L1**

4 CLOSE

Review Greek and Roman civilization, their social roles, art, and architecture. Discuss specific ways in which the Renaissance was a rebirth of these ideals.

SECTION 1 ASSESSMENT

1. Key terms are in blue.
2. Leonardo da Vinci *(p. 158);* Francesco Sforza *(p. 159);* Cosimo de' Medici *(p. 159);* Lorenzo de' Medici *(p. 159);* Niccolò Machiavelli *(p. 160)*
3. See chapter maps.
4. When the French invaded, the northern Italian states turned to Spain for help.
5. born, not made; character, grace, talent; well rounded
6. financial security
7. Nobility—Middle Ages: primarily concerned with military skill; Renaissance: classical education, arts, warrior, standard of conduct
Peasants—Middle Ages: part of manorial system; Renaissance: more peasants were legally free
Townspeople—Middle Ages: merchants and artisans; Renaissance: patricians, shopkeepers, artisans, guild masters, workers.
8. impressive architecture, people at leisure, well-dressed
9. Answers should be supported by logic.

1 FOCUS

Section Opener

After reading this section, students should understand the intellectual movement of humanism and be able to identify the major artists and accomplishments of the artistic Renaissance.

BELLRINGER
Skillbuilder Activity

Project transparency 5–2 and have students answer questions.

Available as a blackline master.

Daily Focus Skills Transparency 5–2

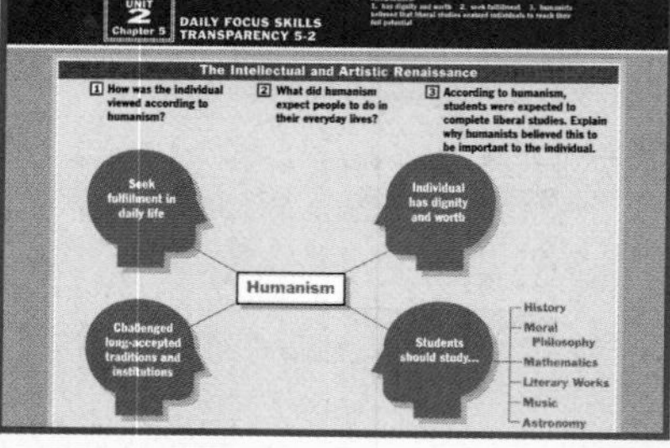

Guide to Reading

Answers to Graphic: *Divine Comedy:* soul's journey, written in Italian; *The Canterbury Tales:* stories of pilgrims journeying to Canterbury, portrays range of English society, written in English; *The Book of the City of Ladies:* argues that women were capable of learning, written in French

Preteaching Vocabulary: Have students explain how a *fresco* differs from an oil painting. *(frescoes done on wet plaster with water-based paints; oil paintings done on canvas with oil-based paints)*

SECTION 2 The Intellectual and Artistic Renaissance

Guide to Reading

Main Ideas
- The most important intellectual movement associated with the Renaissance was humanism.
- The Renaissance produced many great artists and sculptors such as Michelangelo, Raphael, and Leonardo da Vinci.

Key Terms
humanism, fresco

People to Identify
Petrarch, Dante, Michelangelo, Jan van Eyck, Albrecht Dürer

Places to Locate
Canterbury, Flanders

Preview Questions
1. What were the characteristics of Italian Renaissance humanism?
2. What were the chief achievements of European Renaissance painters?

Reading Strategy
Summarizing Information Use a table like the one below to describe the three pieces of literature written by Dante, Chaucer, and de Pizan. What was the primary importance of each of these works?

Divine Comedy	*The Canterbury Tales*	*The Book of the City of Ladies*

Preview of Events

1300 · 1350 · 1400 · 1450 · 1500

- **c. 1310** Dante writes the *Divine Comedy*
- **c. 1390** Chaucer writes *The Canterbury Tales*
- **c. 1415** Donatello creates his statue of St. George
- **c. 1434** Jan van Eyck paints the Arnolfini portrait
- **c. 1505** Leonardo da Vinci paints the Mona Lisa

Voices from the Past

Pico della Mirandola

Pico della Mirandola, a Renaissance philosopher, said in his *Oration on the Dignity of Man:*

❝You, constrained by no limits in accordance with your own free will, shall ordain for yourself the limits of your nature. We have set you at the world's center that you may from there more easily observe whatever is in the world. We have made you neither of heaven nor of earth, neither mortal nor immortal, so that with freedom of choice and with honor, as though the maker and molder of yourself, you may fashion yourself in whatever shape you shall prefer.❞

—***The Renaissance Philosophy of Man,*** **Ernest Cassirer, Paul Kristeller, and John Randall, Jr., eds., 1948**

There is no better expression of the Renaissance's exalted view of the importance of the individual.

Italian Renaissance Humanism

Secularism and an emphasis on the individual characterized the Renaissance. These characteristics are most noticeable in the intellectual and artistic accomplishments of the period. A key intellectual movement of the Renaissance was humanism.

SECTION RESOURCES

Reproducible Masters
- Reproducible Lesson Plan 5–2
- Daily Lecture and Discussion Notes 5–2
- Guided Reading Activity 5–2
- Section Quiz 5–2
- Reading Essentials and Study Guide 5–2

Transparencies
- Daily Focus Skills Transparency 5–2

Multimedia
- Interactive Tutor Self-Assessment CD-ROM
- ExamView® Pro Testmaker CD-ROM
- Presentation Plus! CD-ROM

Humanism was based on the study of the classics, the literary works of ancient Greece and Rome. Humanists studied such things as grammar, rhetoric, poetry, moral philosophy, and history—all of which was based on the works of ancient Greek and Roman authors. Today these subjects are called the humanities.

Petrarch (PEE•TRAHRK), who has often been called the father of Italian Renaissance humanism, did more than any other individual in the fourteenth century to foster the development of humanism. Petrarch looked for forgotten Latin manuscripts and set in motion a search for similar manuscripts in monastic libraries throughout Europe.

He also began the humanist emphasis on using pure classical Latin (Latin as used by the ancient Romans as opposed to medieval Latin). Humanists used the works of Cicero as a model for prose and those of Virgil for poetry.

In Florence, the humanist movement took a new direction at the beginning of the fifteenth century. Fourteenth-century humanists such as Petrarch had described the intellectual life as one of solitude. They rejected family and a life of action in the community. In contrast, humanists in the early 1400s took a new interest in civic life. They believed that it was the duty of an intellectual to live an active life for one's state, and that their study of the humanities should be put to the service of the state. It is no accident that they served as secretaries in the Italian city-states and to princes or popes.

✓Reading Check **Examining** Why is Petrarch called the father of Italian Renaissance humanism?

Vernacular Literature

The humanist emphasis on classical Latin led to its widespread use in the writings of scholars, lawyers, and theologians. However, some writers wrote in the vernacular (the language spoken in their own regions, such as Italian, French, or German). In the fourteenth century, the literary works of the Italian author **Dante** (DAHN•tay) and the English author Geoffrey Chaucer helped make vernacular literature more popular.

Dante

Dante's masterpiece in the Italian vernacular is the *Divine Comedy.* It is the story of the soul's journey to salvation. The lengthy poem is divided into three major sections: Hell, Purgatory, and Heaven, or Paradise. Dante is led on an imaginary journey through these three realms until he reaches Paradise, where he beholds God, or "the love that moves the sun and the other stars."

Chaucer used the English vernacular in his famous work *The Canterbury Tales.* His beauty of expression and clear, forceful language were important in making his dialect the chief ancestor of the modern English language.

The Canterbury Tales consists of a collection of stories told by a group of 29 pilgrims journeying to the tomb of Saint Thomas à Becket at **Canterbury,** England. This format gave Chaucer the chance to portray an entire range of English society, from the high to the low born.

Another writer who used the vernacular was Christine de Pizan, a Frenchwoman who is best known for her works written in defense of women. In *The Book of the City of Ladies,* written in 1404, she denounced the many male writers who had argued that women, by their very nature, are unable to learn and are easily swayed.

Christine de Pizan

Women, de Pizan argued, could learn as well as men if they could attend the same schools:

> “Should I also tell you whether a woman's nature is clever and quick enough to learn speculative sciences as well as to discover them, and likewise the manual arts. I assure you that women are equally well-suited and skilled to carry them out and to put them to sophisticated use once they have learned them.”

✓Reading Check **Explaining** What literary format does Chaucer use to portray English society?

Education in the Renaissance

The humanist movement had a profound effect on education. Renaissance humanists believed that education could dramatically change human beings.

2 TEACH

✓Reading Check

Answer: looked for forgotten Latin manuscripts; began the humanist emphasis on using pure classical Latin as opposed to medieval Latin

✓Reading Check

Answer: collection of stories told by a group of 29 pilgrims journeying to the tomb of Saint Thomas à Becket at Canterbury, England

Daily Lecture and Discussion Notes 5–2

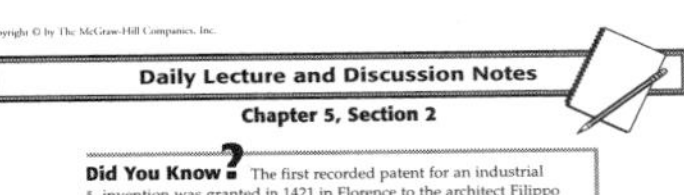

Daily Lecture and Discussion Notes

Chapter 5, Section 2

Did You Know? The first recorded patent for an industrial invention was granted in 1421 in Florence to the architect Filippo Brunelleschi. The patent gave him a three-year monopoly on the manufacture of a barge with hoisting gear used to transport marble.

I. **Italian Renaissance Humanism** *(pages 164–165)*

A. The secularism and individualism of the Renaissance was most apparent in its intellectual and artistic movements. One intellectual movement was **humanism.**

B. Humanism was based on the classics, the literary works of ancient Greece and Rome. Humanists studied the subjects that are now known as the humanities—for example, poetry, philosophy, and history.

C. **Petrarch** (fourteenth century) did the most to foster humanism's development. He generated a movement of finding forgotten Latin manuscripts, especially in monastic libraries. He emphasized using pure classical Latin (Roman Latin, not medieval Latin). Cicero was the model for prose and Virgil for poetry.

D. Fourteenth-century humanists had emphasized that the intellectual life was solitary, rejecting family and community engagement. Humanists of the early 1400s took an interest in civic life. They believed that the humanities and humanists should serve the state. Many humanists served as secretaries to popes and princes.

Discussion Question

CURRICULUM CONNECTION

Art and Literature Ask students to give examples from this section of innovations in literature and art that resulted from the influence of humanism. *(new forms of writing, such as sonnets and autobiography, literature in common language instead of Latin; more lifelike art; classical and religious themes in art)* **L3**

INTERDISCIPLINARY CONNECTIONS ACTIVITY

Sports The Renaissance revived the Greek concept that an ideal person participated in a variety of activities, including sports. Have students research and report to the class on one of the following popular Renaissance games or sports: javelin hurling, tennis, chess, archery, fencing, boxing, falconry, hunting, and gambling. Tell students to explain how these sports or games resemble or differ from the same activities today. Ask students to bring props for their reports and, if possible, if space and safety concerns are met, to give a brief demonstration of the skills needed for their game or sport. **L2**

History *through Art*

Answer: Painting is of a Biblical scene but uses Greek and Roman clothing, poses, and architectural elements. Renaissance elements include perspective and realistic portrayal of individuals.

Reading Check

Answer: enabled individuals to reach their full potential; liberal education produced individuals who followed a path of virtue and wisdom

Guided Reading Activity 5–2

Name ______ Date ______ Class ______

Guided Reading Activity 5-2

The Intellectual and Artistic Renaissance

DIRECTIONS: As you are reading the section, decide if a statement is true or false. Write **T** if the statement is true or **F** if the statement is false. For all false statements write a corrected statement.

____ 1. A key intellectual movement of the Renaissance was secularism.

____ 2. Humanists used the works of Cicero as a model for prose and those of Virgil for poetry.

____ 3. Dante's masterpiece, the *Divine Comedy*, is the story of two clowns in a medieval circus.

____ 4. *The Canterbury Tales* is a collection of stories told by a group of 29 pilgrims headed for the tomb of Saint Thomas à Becket.

____ 5. During the Renaissance, studies were called "liberal" because of their nonconservative approach.

____ 6. In Renaissance art, God was the focus of attention.

____ 7. By the end of the fifteenth century, Italian painters, sculptors, and architects had mastered the new techniques for symbolically portraying the world around them.

____ 8. The High Renaissance in Italy is associated with three artistic giants, Leonardo da Vinci, R[illegible] Michelangelo.

Critical Thinking

Guide students in a discussion of the humanist view of virtue. Why was this characteristic so central to the humanist education? You might wish to assign students to write a short essay explaining what they feel is the significance of virtue to the Renaissance education. *(to create a moral, elite ruling class; responsibility to better one's self in order to better society, etc.)* **L3**

History *through Art*

***The Tribute Money* by Masaccio, c. 1426**
In this church fresco, Masaccio creates a realistic relationship between the Biblical figures and the background. Identify the Renaissance artistic elements used by Masaccio in this work.

They wrote books on education and opened schools based on their ideas.

At the core of humanist schools were the liberal studies. Humanists believed that the liberal studies (what we call today the liberal arts) enabled individuals to reach their full potential. One humanist wrote, "We call those studies liberal by which we attain and practice virtue and wisdom; which calls forth and develops those highest gifts of body and mind which ennoble men."

What, then, were the liberal studies? According to the humanists, students should study history, moral philosophy, eloquence (or rhetoric), letters (grammar and logic), poetry, mathematics, astronomy, and music. In short, the purpose of a liberal education (and thus the reason for studying the liberal arts) was to produce individuals who follow a path of virtue and wisdom. These individuals should also possess rhetorical skills so they can persuade others to take this same path.

Following the Greek ideal of a sound mind in a sound body, humanist educators also stressed physical education. Pupils were taught the skills of javelin throwing, archery, and dancing, and they were encouraged to run, wrestle, hunt, and swim.

Humanist educators thought that a humanist education was a practical preparation for life. Its aim was not to create great scholars but complete citizens. Humanist schools provided the model for the basic education of the European ruling classes until the twentieth century.

Females were largely absent from these schools. The few female students who did attend humanist schools studied the classics and were encouraged to know some history as well as how to ride, dance, sing, play the lute (a stringed instrument), and appreciate poetry. They were told not to learn mathematics or rhetoric. It was thought that religion and morals should be foremost in the education of "Christian ladies" so that they could become good mothers and wives.

Reading Check **Explaining** How did a humanist education prepare a student for life?

The Artistic Renaissance in Italy

Renaissance artists sought to imitate nature in their works. They wanted onlookers to see the reality of the objects or events they were portraying. At the same time, these artists were developing a new world perspective. In this new view, human beings became the focus of attention—the "center and measure of all things," as one artist proclaimed.

New Techniques in Painting The frescoes painted by Masaccio (muh•ZAH•chee•oh) in Florence at the beginning of the fifteenth century have long been regarded as the first masterpieces of early Renaissance (1400–1490) art. A **fresco** is a painting done on fresh, wet plaster with water-based paints. Whereas human figures in medieval paintings look flat, Masaccio's have depth and come alive. By mastering the laws of perspective, which enabled him to create the illusion of three dimensions, Masaccio developed a new, realistic style of painting.

CRITICAL THINKING ACTIVITY

Analyzing Renaissance art represents themes reflective of the times. Select examples of Renaissance art based on the following Renaissance themes: individualism, worldliness, learning, antiquity, and reform. Study the pictures and write a sentence summary. Have students indicate in writing which of the themes are represented in each image. Suggested pictures include: *The School of Athens* by Raphael, *A Money Changer and His Wife* by Quentin Massy, *Proportional Study of a Man in the Manner of Vitrivius* by Leonardo da Vinci, *Erasmus* by Albrecht Dürer, *Charles V* by Titian, and *The Creation of Adam* by Michelangelo. **L3**

This new, or Renaissance, style was used and modified by other Florentine painters in the fifteenth century. Especially important were two major developments. One stressed the technical side of painting—understanding the laws of perspective and the organization of outdoor space and light through geometry. The second development was the investigation of movement and human anatomy. The realistic portrayal of the individual person, especially the human nude, became one of the chief aims of Italian Renaissance art.

Sculpture and Architecture The revolutionary achievements of Florentine painters in the fifteenth century were matched by equally stunning advances in sculpture and architecture. The sculptor Donatello spent time in Rome studying and copying the statues of the Greeks and Romans. Among his numerous works was a statue of Saint George, a realistic, freestanding figure.

The architect Filippo Brunelleschi (BROO•nuhl•EHS•kee) was inspired by the buildings of classical Rome to create a new architecture in Florence. The Medici, the wealthy ruling family of Florence, hired Brunelleschi to design the church of San Lorenzo. The classical columns and rounded arches that Brunelleschi used in the church's design create an environment that does not overwhelm the worshiper, as Gothic cathedrals might. Instead, the church provides comfort as a space created to fit human, and not divine, needs. Like painters and sculptors, Renaissance architects sought to reflect a human-centered world.

By the end of the fifteenth century, Italian painters, sculptors, and architects had created a new artistic world. Many artists had mastered the new techniques

David *by Michelangelo*

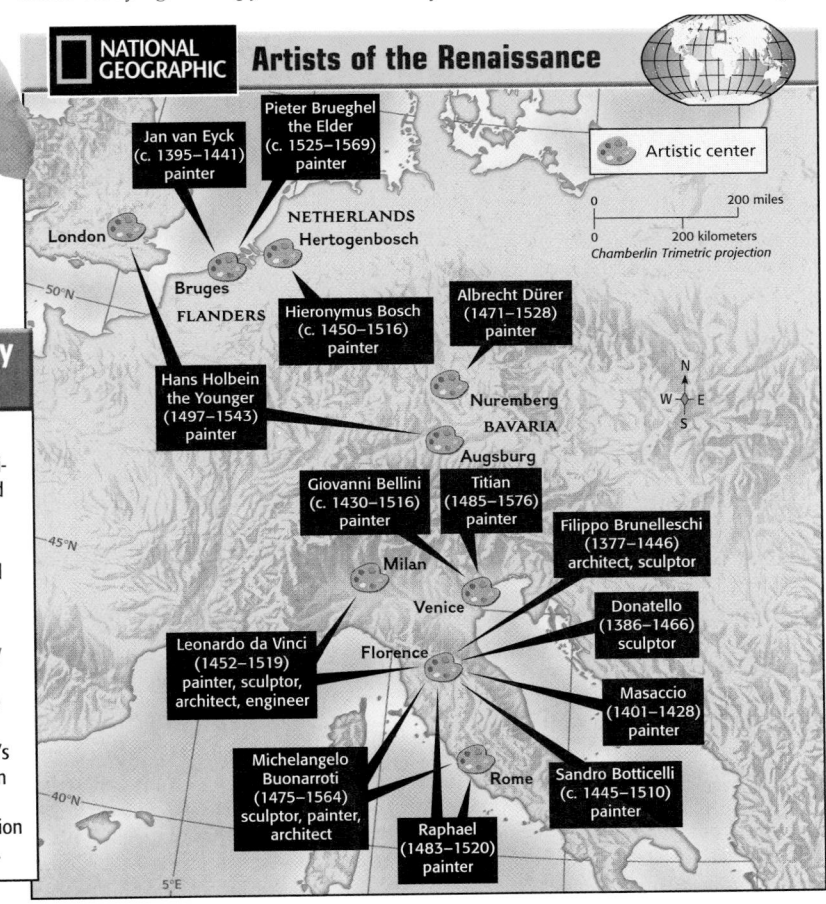

NATIONAL GEOGRAPHIC Artists of the Renaissance

Geography Skills

Renaissance art was influenced by the artistic principles of ancient Greece and Rome.

1. **Interpreting Maps** In which Italian city did the most Renaissance artists work?
2. **Applying Geography Skills** Create a chart listing the artists of the Renaissance. For each artist include the artist's date of birth, the city in which he worked, and the name and description of one of his creations.

Geography *Skills*

Answers:

1. Florence
2. Answers will vary. Students might include artists such as Raphael, Dürer, da Vinci, Titian, and Masaccio. **L1**

TURNING POINT

What changes did Renaissance artists bring to the arts of Europe? *(They broke with medieval symbolism and brought a new realism to the arts, experimenting with new techniques, such as perspective; much Renaissance art was devoted to religious topics, but Renaissance artists also turned to classical mythology.)* **L2**

Enrich

Students should gain a certain appreciation for the vast art riches of the Renaissance. You might wish to assign each student a research project based on the life and work of an artist and have students give their oral, illustrated presentations to the class. **L2**

Critical Thinking

Guide students in a discussion comparing the soaring, immense Gothic cathedrals built during the High Middle Ages with the Renaissance concept of smaller churches. How does the smaller size reflect the Renaissance emphasis on the universal person? *(church is not overwhelming; fits needs of person)* **L1**

EXTENDING THE CONTENT

Albrecht Dürer was perhaps the greatest artist of Renaissance Germany. This Nuremburg goldsmith-illustrator-painter was able to link Italian and Northern art. After spending time studying the Italian Renaissance artists he returned to Germany having grasped the possibilities of printing and engraving as artistic expression. In 1498, the publication of "The Apocalypse," was the first printed work designed entirely by an artist. It told the story of the biblical book of Revelation in a unique way—fourteen full-page wood cuttings on the right, and the corresponding text (in Latin or German editions) on the left. Because it could be enjoyed by the illiterate, and because of the uniqueness of woodcuts and prints together, "The Apocalypse" sold out rapidly and spread Dürer's fame far beyond Nuremburg.

History *through Art*

Answer: Answers will vary; the figures include Socrates, Plato (painted to look like Leonardo da Vinci), Aristotle, Zeno, Epicurus, Averroës, Pythagoras, Parmenides, Heraclitus (painted to look like Michelangelo), Diogenes, Euclid, Raphael, Ptolemy, Zoroaster, Xenophon, Alcibiades, and Alexander, among others.

Reading Check

Answer: Medieval paintings appeared flat and lifeless; in Renaissance paintings, perspective gave the illusion of depth and individual people were realistically portrayed.

Reading Check

Answer: Leonardo da Vinci, Raphael, Michelangelo

3 ASSESS

Assign Section 2 Assessment as homework or as an in-class activity.

Have students use **Interactive Tutor Self-Assessment CD-ROM.**

Section Quiz 5–2

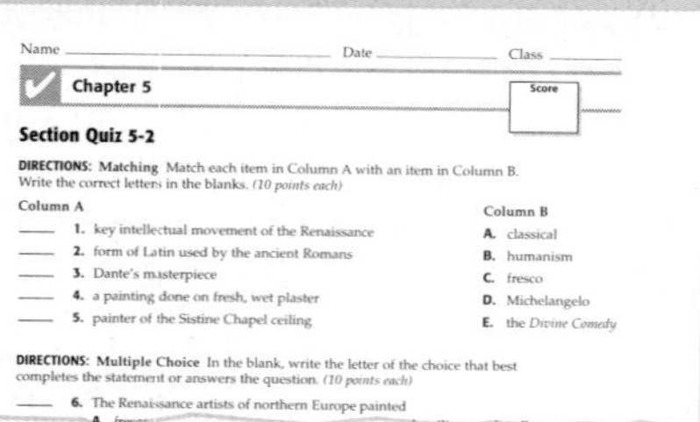

Name ________ Date ________ Class ________

Chapter 5 — Score

Section Quiz 5-2

DIRECTIONS: Matching Match each item in Column A with an item in Column B. Write the correct letters in the blanks. *(10 points each)*

Column A	Column B
____ 1. key intellectual movement of the Renaissance	A. classical
____ 2. form of Latin used by the ancient Romans	B. humanism
____ 3. Dante's masterpiece	C. fresco
____ 4. a painting done on fresh, wet plaster	D. Michelangelo
____ 5. painter of the Sistine Chapel ceiling	E. the *Divine Comedy*

DIRECTIONS: Multiple Choice In the blank, write the letter of the choice that best completes the statement or answers the question. *(10 points each)*

____ 6. The Renaissance artists of northern Europe painted

Raphael

History *through Art*

***School of Athens* by Raphael** Raphael created this painting for the pope to show the unity of Christian and classical works. Research the painting to discover the identities of the historical figures that Raphael depicted.

for realistically portraying the world around them and were now ready to move into new forms of creative expression.

Reading Check **Explaining** How did Renaissance paintings differ from medieval paintings?

Masters of the High Renaissance The final stage of Italian Renaissance painting, which flourished between 1490 and 1520, is called the High Renaissance. The High Renaissance in Italy is associated with three artistic giants, Leonardo da Vinci, Raphael, and Michelangelo.

Leonardo mastered the art of realistic painting and even dissected human bodies to better see how nature worked. However, he also stressed the need to advance beyond such realism. It was Leonardo's goal to create idealized forms that would capture the perfection of nature and the individual—perfection that could not be expressed fully by a realistic style.

At age 25, Raphael was already regarded as one of Italy's best painters. He was especially admired for his numerous madonnas (paintings of the Virgin Mary). In these, he tried to achieve an ideal of beauty far surpassing human standards.

Raphael is also well known for his frescoes in the Vatican Palace. His *School of Athens* reveals a world of balance, harmony, and order—the underlying principles of the art of the classical world of Greece and Rome.

Michelangelo, an accomplished painter, sculptor, and architect, was another artistic master of the High Renaissance. Fiercely driven by his desire to create, he worked with great passion and energy on a remarkable number of projects.

Michelangelo's figures on the ceiling of the Sistine Chapel in Rome reveal an ideal type of human being with perfect proportions. The beauty of this idealized human being is meant to be a reflection of divine beauty. The more beautiful the body, the more godlike the figure.

Reading Check **Identifying** Name the three Italian artists most closely associated with the High Renaissance.

The Northern Artistic Renaissance

Like the artists of Italy, the artists of northern Europe became interested in portraying their world realistically. However, their approach was different from the Italians'. This was particularly true of the artists of the Low Countries (present-day Belgium, Luxembourg, and the Netherlands).

COOPERATIVE LEARNING ACTIVITY

Analyzing Art Assign students to small groups to study the works of one of the following Northern Renaissance artists: Pieter Brueghel the Elder, Jan van Eyck, Albrecht Dürer, Lucas Cranach the Elder, or Hans Holbein the Younger. Tell students to use art history books to analyze their artist's works. Suggest that they record evidence of daily activities, occupations, social classes, entertainment, clothing, hairstyles, and housing shown in these works. Remind groups that each member should be responsible for a task, such as organizing research, recording the group's discussion, making photocopies, or presenting the group's analysis to the class. Tell students to include pictures of artworks in their reports to the class. **L2**

Circumstance played a role in the differences. The large wall spaces of Italian churches had given rise to the art of fresco painting. Italian artists used these spaces to master the technical skills that allowed them to portray humans in realistic settings. In the north, the Gothic cathedrals with their stained glass windows did not allow for frescoes. Thus, northern artists painted illustrations for books and wooden panels for altarpieces. Great care was needed to depict each object on a small scale.

Dürer

The most important northern school of art in the fifteenth century was found in **Flanders,** one of the Low Countries. The Flemish painter **Jan van Eyck** (EYEK) was among the first to use oil paint, which enabled the artist to use a wide variety of colors and create fine details as in his painting *Giovanni Arnolfini and His Bride*. Like other Northern Renaissance artists, however, van Eyck imitated nature not by using perspective, as the Italians did, but by simply observing reality and portraying details as best he could.

By 1500, artists from the north had begun to study in Italy and to be influenced by what artists were doing there. One German artist who was greatly affected by the Italians was **Albrecht Dürer.** He made two trips to Italy and absorbed most of what the Italians could teach on the laws of perspective.

As can be seen in his famous *Adoration of the Magi*, Dürer did not reject the use of minute details characteristic of northern artists. He did try, however, to fit those details more harmoniously into his works in accordance with Italian artistic theories. Like the Italian artists of the High Renaissance, Dürer tried to achieve a standard of ideal beauty that was based on a careful examination of the human form.

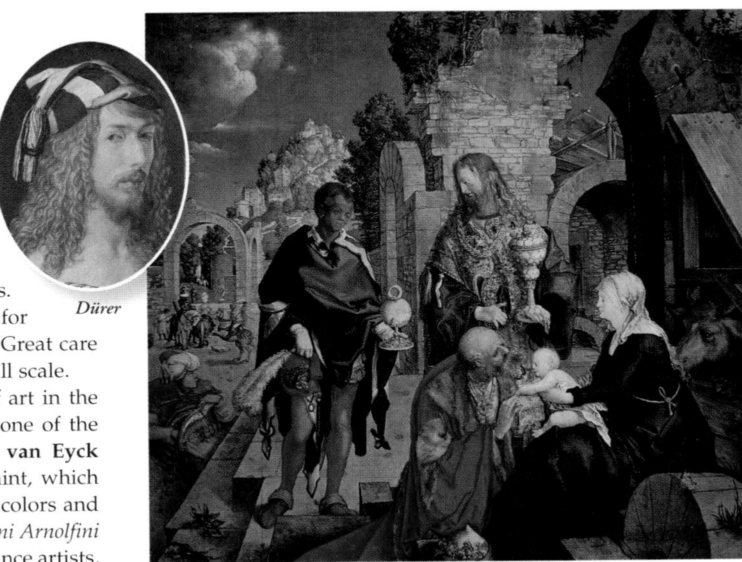

In the Adoration of the Magi, *Albrecht Dürer retains the minute details associated with northern European painting, but he also makes use of perspective and proportion.*

Reading Check **Examining** Why was Jan van Eyck's use of oil paint significant?

SECTION 2 ASSESSMENT

Checking for Understanding

1. **Define** humanism, fresco.
2. **Identify** Petrarch, Dante, Michelangelo, Jan van Eyck, Albrecht Dürer.
3. **Locate** Canterbury, Flanders.
4. **Summarize** Christine de Pizan's main argument in *The Book of the City of Ladies*. Why did her ideas receive so much attention?
5. **Compare** the underlying principles of both classical Greek and Roman art with Italian Renaissance art. How are the principles similar? How are they different?

Critical Thinking

6. **Compare and Contrast** How do the humanist goals and philosophy of education developed during the Renaissance compare with the goals of your high school education?
7. **Summarizing Information** Use a table like the one below to describe the greatest accomplishments of Leonardo da Vinci, Raphael, and Michelangelo.

Leonardo da Vinci	Raphael	Michelangelo

Analyzing Visuals

8. **Compare** the paintings of Raphael and Dürer, shown on page 168 and above. What themes does each artist explore? How does each painting reflect the history of the culture in which it was produced?

Writing About History

9. **Expository Writing** Assume the role of an art docent (a person who guides people through museums). Prepare a lecture to be given to a group of students on the works of Jan van Eyck and how they differ from Italian Renaissance paintings.

Reading Check

Answer: enabled him to use a wide variety of colors and create fine details

Reading Essentials and Study Guide 5–2

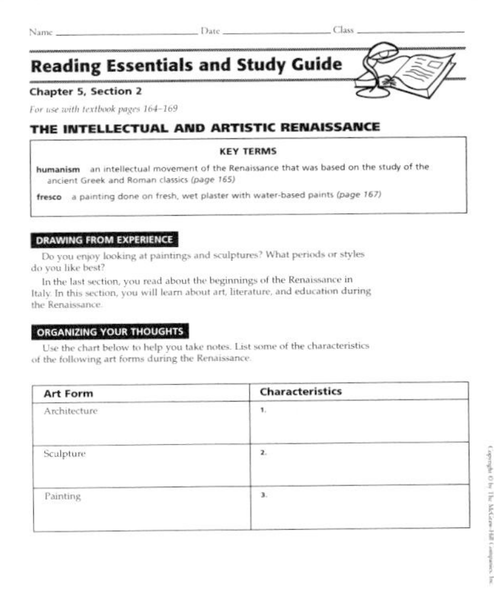

Name ______ Date ______ Class ______

Reading Essentials and Study Guide

Chapter 5, Section 2

For use with textbook pages 164–169

THE INTELLECTUAL AND ARTISTIC RENAISSANCE

KEY TERMS

humanism an intellectual movement of the Renaissance that was based on the study of the ancient Greek and Roman classics *(page 165)*

fresco a painting done on fresh, wet plaster with water-based paints *(page 167)*

DRAWING FROM EXPERIENCE

Do you enjoy looking at paintings and sculptures? What periods or styles do you like best?

In the last section, you read about the beginnings of the Renaissance in Italy. In this section, you will learn about art, literature, and education during the Renaissance.

ORGANIZING YOUR THOUGHTS

Use the chart below to help you take notes. List some of the characteristics of the following art forms during the Renaissance.

Art Form	Characteristics
Architecture	1.
Sculpture	2.
Painting	3.

Reteaching Activity

Ask students to list what they think were the most important innovations in literature, education, art, and architecture during the Renaissance. *(use of vernacular, humanist education, lifelike art, smaller churches)* **L2**

4 CLOSE

Students should recognize the impact of the art masterpieces that were created during this time and that it was wealthy Italian families and the Catholic Church who were the primary sponsors of Renaissance art.

SECTION 2 ASSESSMENT

1. Key terms are in blue.
2. Petrarch *(p. 165)*; Dante *(p. 165)*; Michelangelo *(p. 168)*; Jan van Eyck *(p. 169)*; Albrecht Dürer *(p. 169)*
3. See chapter maps.
4. Women could learn as well as men. Her ideas were revolutionary.
5. balance, harmony, order; subject matter differs
6. Students will compare Renaissance education to modern.
7. da Vinci: capture the perfection of nature and the individual; Raphael: achieve an ideal of beauty surpassing human standards; Michelangelo: ideal type of human being with perfect proportions
8. Raphael: philosophy, antiquity; It also reflects the Renaissance interest in antiquity. Dürer: religious
9. Answers may include that van Eyck painted in oils, used color, created fine details.

TEACH

Analyzing Primary Sources At a dinner party in 1546, Cardinal Farnese, a patron of the arts, asked Giorgio Vasari, an artist and architect, if he would assemble "a catalogue of artists and their works, listed in chronological order." Vasari complied and his famous "The Lives of the Most Excellent Painters, Sculptors, and Architects" was first published in 1550. The book has become an important source for historians despite some inaccuracies and bias. Using this source, ask students to explain and apply different methods that historians use to interpret the past, including the use of primary and secondary sources, points of view, frames of reference, and historical context.

Connecting Across Time

Encourage students to compare this painting with religious paintings of the Middle Ages and to note the differences in style and subject matter. **L2**

CURRICULUM CONNECTION

Arts Have students research specific achievements of Leonardo da Vinci and prepare an illustrated essay or chart detailing his contributions to fields other than art. **L2**

EYEWITNESS TO HISTORY

The Genius of Leonardo da Vinci

Leonardo da Vinci

DURING THE RENAISSANCE, artists came to be viewed as creative geniuses with almost divine qualities. The painter Giorgio Vasari helped create this image by writing a series of brief biographies of Italy's great artists, including Leonardo da Vinci.

❝In the normal course of events many men and women are born with various remarkable qualities and talents; but occasionally, in a way that transcends nature, a single person is marvelously endowed by heaven with beauty, grace, and talent in such abundance that he leaves other men far behind, all his actions seem inspired, and indeed everything he does clearly comes from God rather than from human art.

Everyone acknowledged that this was true of Leonardo da Vinci, an artist of outstanding physical beauty who displayed infinite grace in everything he did and who cultivated his genius so brilliantly that all problems he studied he solved with ease. He possessed great strength and dexterity; he was a man of regal spirit and tremendous breadth of mind; and his name became so famous that not only was he esteemed during his lifetime but his reputation endured and became even greater after his death. . . .

He was marvelously gifted, and he proved himself to be a first-class geometrician in his work as a sculptor and architect. In his youth, Leonardo made in clay several heads of women with smiling faces, of which plaster casts are still being made, as well as some children's heads executed as if by a mature artist. He also did many architectural drawings both of ground plans and of other elevations, and, while still young, he was the first to propose reducing the Arno River to a navigable canal between Pisa and Florence. He made designs for mills, . . . and engines that could be driven by water-power; and as he intended to be a painter by profession he carefully studied drawing from life. . . . Altogether, his genius was so wonderfully inspired by the grace of God, his powers of expression were so powerfully fed by a willing memory and intellect, and his writing conveyed his ideas so precisely, that his arguments and reasonings confounded the most formidable critics. In addition, he used to make models and plans showing how to excavate and tunnel through mountains without difficulty, so as to pass from one level to another; and he demonstrated how to lift and draw great weights by means of levers and hoists and ways of cleaning harbors and using pumps to suck up water from great depths.❞

—**Giorgio Vasari, *Lives of the Artists***

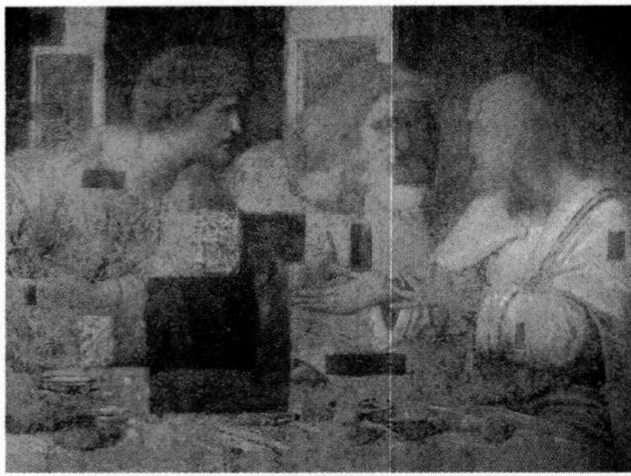

A detail from da Vinci's **Last Supper**, *shown as the painting was being restored in the late 1990s*

Analyzing Primary Sources

1. Name the qualities that Vasari admires in Leonardo da Vinci.
2. How does Vasari's description of da Vinci reflect the ideals of Italian Renaissance humanism?

ANSWERS TO ANALYZING PRIMARY SOURCES

1. physical beauty, infinite grace, genius, strength and dexterity, regal spirit, and tremendous breadth of mind
2. He was a well-rounded person who was very accomplished in a wide range of areas, including painting, sculpture, architecture, writing, geometry, and engineering.

SECTION 3

The Protestant Reformation

Guide to Reading

Main Ideas
- The major goal of humanism in northern Europe was to reform Christendom.
- Martin Luther's religious reforms led to the emergence of Protestantism.

Key Terms
Christian humanism, salvation, indulgence

People to Identify
Martin Luther, Desiderius Erasmus, Charles V

Places to Locate
Wittenberg, Bohemia, Hungary

Preview Questions
1. What were the beliefs of Christian humanists?
2. Explain what is meant by justification by grace through faith alone.

Reading Strategy
Cause and Effect Use a diagram like the one below to identify steps that led to the Reformation.

Steps Leading to the Reformation

Preview of Events

1500 · 1510 · 1520 · 1530 · 1540 · 1550

- **1509** Erasmus writes his satire *The Praise of Folly*
- **1517** Martin Luther posts the Ninety-five Theses in Wittenberg
- **1521** The Church excommunicates Luther
- **1555** The Peace of Augsburg divides Germany

Voices from the Past

On April 18, 1521, Martin Luther stood before the emperor and princes of Germany in the city of Worms and declared:

> ❝Since then Your Majesty and your lordships desire a simple reply, I will answer without horns and without teeth. Unless I am convicted by Scripture and plain reason—I do not accept the authority of popes and councils, for they have contradicted each other—my conscience is captive to the Word of God. I cannot and I will not recant anything, for to go against conscience is neither right nor safe. Here I stand, I cannot do otherwise. God help me. Amen.❞
>
> —***Here I Stand: A Life of Martin Luther,*** **Roland Bainton, 1950**

Martin Luther addressing the emperor in Worms

With these words Martin Luther refused to renounce his new religious ideas. Luther's words became the battle cry of the Protestant Reformation.

Erasmus and Christian Humanism

The Protestant Reformation is the name given to the religious reform movement that divided the western Church into Catholic and Protestant groups. Although **Martin Luther** began the Reformation in the early sixteenth century, several earlier developments had set the stage for religious change.

One such development grew from widespread changes in intellectual thought. During the second half of the fifteenth century, the new classical learning that was

1 FOCUS

Section Opener

After reading this section, students should understand the development of Protestantism.

BELLRINGER
Skillbuilder Activity

Project transparency 5–3 and have students answer questions.

Available as a blackline master.

Daily Focus Skills Transparency 5–3

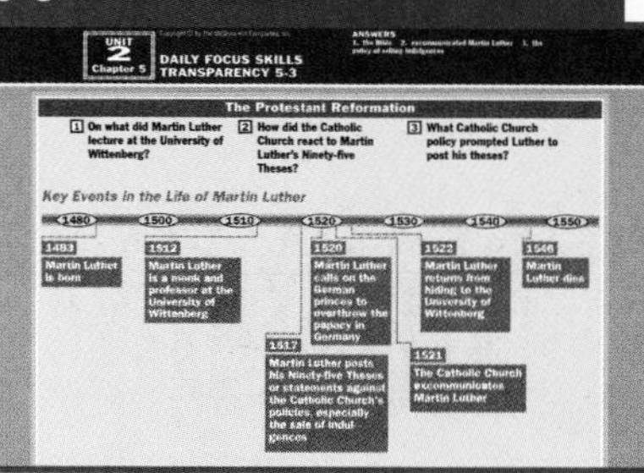

Guide to Reading

Answers to Graphic: Steps Leading to the Reformation: Christian humanism, corruption in the Catholic Church, people desired meaningful religious expression and assurance of their salvation, sale of indulgences, Modern Devotion

Preteaching Vocabulary: Ask students to explain the difference between *Christian humanism* and Renaissance humanism. *(Christian humanists believed that studying Christianity would lead to reform in the Church; Renaissance humanism believed that all studies made one a better individual.)*

SECTION RESOURCES

Reproducible Masters
- Reproducible Lesson Plan 5–3
- Daily Lecture and Discussion Notes 5–3
- Guided Reading Activity 5–3
- Section Quiz 5–3
- Reading Essentials and Study Guide 5–3

Transparencies
- Daily Focus Skills Transparency 5–3

Multimedia
- Interactive Tutor Self-Assessment CD-ROM
- ExamView® Pro Testmaker CD-ROM
- Presentation Plus! CD-ROM

2 TEACH

Reading Check

Answer: He criticized the abuses in the Church along with other aspects of his society and called for reform.

Daily Lecture and Discussion Notes 5–3

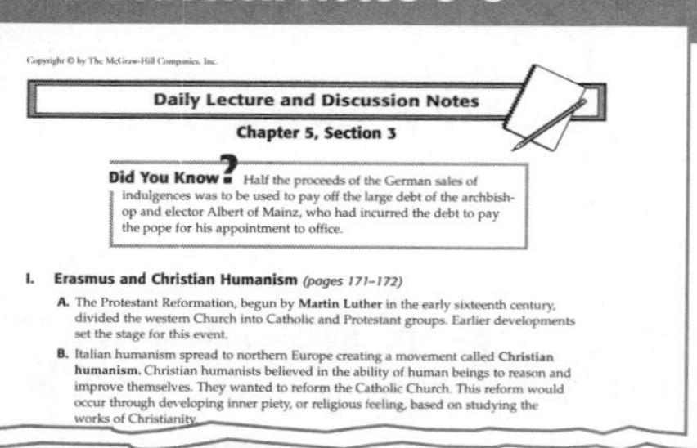

Daily Lecture and Discussion Notes

Chapter 5, Section 3

Did You Know? Half the proceeds of the German sales of indulgences was to be used to pay off the large debt of the archbishop and elector Albert of Mainz, who had incurred the debt to pay the pope for his appointment to office.

I. **Erasmus and Christian Humanism** *(pages 171–172)*

A. The Protestant Reformation, begun by **Martin Luther** in the early sixteenth century, divided the western Church into Catholic and Protestant groups. Earlier developments set the stage for this event.

B. Italian humanism spread to northern Europe creating a movement called **Christian humanism.** Christian humanists believed in the ability of human beings to reason and improve themselves. They wanted to reform the Catholic Church. This reform would occur through developing inner piety, or religious feeling, based on studying the works of Christianity.

ABCNEWS INTERACTIVE™

Turning Points in World History
The ABC News videotape includes a segment on the Reformation.

Connecting Across Time

On the eve of and during the Reformation, common people were concerned with salvation. They fasted, went on pilgrimages, attended mass, bought indulgences. The question of salvation was large in their lives. Ask students what people are concerned about today. What do those concerns reveal about our culture? *(Answers will vary, but list may reveal more secular concerns of success, solving world problems, etc.)* **L1**

part of Italian Renaissance humanism spread to northern Europe. From that came a movement called **Christian humanism,** or Northern Renaissance humanism. The major goal of this movement was the reform of the Catholic Church.

The Christian humanists believed in the ability of human beings to reason and improve themselves. They thought that if people read the classics, and especially the basic works of Christianity, they would become more pious. This inner piety, or inward religious feeling, would bring about a reform of the Church and society. Christian humanists believed that in order to change society, they must first change the human beings who make it up.

The best known of all the Christian humanists was **Desiderius Erasmus** (ih•RAZ•muhs). He called his view of religion "the philosophy of Christ." By this, he meant that Christianity should show people how to live good lives on a daily basis rather than provide a system of beliefs that people have to practice to be saved. Erasmus stressed the inwardness of religious feeling. To him, the external forms of medieval religion (such as pilgrimages, fasts, and relics) were not all that important.

To reform the Church, Erasmus wanted to spread the philosophy of Christ, provide education in the works of Christianity, and criticize the abuses in the Church. In his work *The Praise of Folly,* written in 1509, Erasmus humorously criticized aspects of his society that he believed were most in need of reform. He singled out the monks for special treatment. Monks, he said, "insist that everything be done in precise detail. . . . Just so many knots must be on each shoe and the shoelace must be of only one color."

Raphael's depiction of Pope Julius II

Erasmus sought reform within the Catholic Church. He did not wish to break away from the Church, as later reformers would. His ideas, however, did prepare the way for the Reformation. As people of his day said, "Erasmus laid the egg that Luther hatched."

Reading Check **Examining** How did Erasmus pave the way for the Reformation?

Religion on the Eve of the Reformation

Why were Erasmus and others calling for reform? Corruption in the Catholic Church was one reason. Between 1450 and 1520, a series of popes—known as the Renaissance popes—failed to meet the Church's spiritual needs. The popes were supposed to be the spiritual leaders of the Catholic Church. As leaders of the Papal States, however, they were all too often more concerned with Italian politics and worldly interests than with spiritual matters.

Julius II, the fiery "warrior-pope," personally led armies against his enemies. This disgusted Christians who viewed the pope as a spiritual, not a military, leader. One critic wrote, "How, O bishop standing in the room of the Apostles, dare you teach the people the things that pertain to war?"

Many church officials were also concerned with money and used their church offices to advance their careers and their wealth. At the same time, many ordinary parish priests seemed ignorant of their spiritual duties. People wanted to know how to save their souls, and many parish priests were unable to offer them advice or instruction.

While the leaders of the Church were failing to meet their responsibilities, ordinary people desired meaningful religious expression and assurance of their **salvation,** or acceptance into Heaven. As a result, for some, the process of obtaining salvation became almost mechanical. Collections of relics grew more popular as a means to salvation. According to church practice at that time, through veneration of a

EXTENDING THE CONTENT

Renaissance Popes Nicholas V (1447 to 1455) was the first pope of the Renaissance. He combined humanism with Christianity. He founded the Vatican Library and was a patron of the arts. Callistus III was a Spaniard who advanced his family, the Borgias. His nephew was the infamous Alexander VI. Alexander VI became pope in 1492 after bribing the cardinals. He worked shamelessly to further his own household. Julius II (1503 to 1513) worked to restore and extend papal territory. Leo X (1513 to 1521) made Rome a center of culture. He loved luxury and engaged in political intrigues. In 1517 there was a plot to poison him. Leo had the cardinal who led the plot tortured and executed. He created 31 new cardinals to ensure his control. He promoted the sale of indulgences in order to finance the building of St. Peter's Cathedral.

relic, a person could gain an **indulgence**—release from all or part of the punishment for sin. Frederick the Wise, Luther's prince, had amassed over five thousand relics. Indulgences attached to them could reduce time in purgatory by 1,443 years. The Church also sold indulgences, in the form of certificates.

Other people sought certainty of salvation in the popular mystical movement known as the Modern Devotion. The Modern Devotion downplayed religious dogma and stressed the need to follow the teachings of Jesus. This deepening of religious life was done within the Catholic Church. However, many people soon found that the worldly-wise clergy had little interest in the spiritual needs of their people. It is this environment that helps to explain the tremendous impact of Luther's ideas.

Reading Check **Explaining** What was the Modern Devotion?

Martin Luther

TURNING POINT **In this section, you will learn how, on October 31, 1517, Martin Luther nailed his Ninety-five Theses to the door of the Castle Church in Wittenberg, Germany. The publication of Luther's theses began the Protestant Reformation.**

Martin Luther was a monk and a professor at the University of Wittenberg, where he lectured on the Bible. Through his study of the Bible, Luther arrived at an answer to a problem—the certainty of salvation—that had bothered him since he had become a monk.

Catholic teaching had stressed that both faith and good works were needed to gain personal salvation. In Luther's eyes, human beings were powerless in the sight of an almighty God and could never do enough good works to earn salvation.

Through his study of the Bible, Luther came to believe that humans are not saved through their good works but through their faith in God. If an individual has faith in God, then God makes that person just, or worthy of salvation. God will grant salvation because God is merciful. God's grace cannot be earned by performing good works. This idea, called justification

Indulgence box

By posting his theses, Luther communicated his desire to debate the practice of selling indulgences. The advent of the printing press allowed his views to spread beyond Wittenberg.

(being made right before God) by faith, became the chief teaching of the Protestant Reformation. Because Luther had arrived at the doctrine of justification by faith by studying the Bible alone, the Bible became for Luther, as for all other Protestants, the primary source of religious truth.

The Ninety-five Theses Luther did not see himself as a rebel, but he was greatly upset by the widespread selling of indulgences. Especially offensive in his eyes was the monk Johann Tetzel, who sold indulgences with the slogan: "As soon as the coin in the coffer [money box] rings, the soul from purgatory springs." People, Luther believed, were simply harming their chances for salvation by buying these pieces of paper.

On October 31, 1517, Luther, who was greatly angered by the Church's practices, posted his Ninety-five Theses on the door of the Castle Church in **Wittenberg.** The theses were a stunning attack on abuses in the sale of indulgences. Thousands of copies of the Ninety-five Theses were printed and spread to all parts of Germany. Pope Leo X did not take the issue seriously, however. He said that Luther was simply "some drunken German who will amend his ways when he sobers up."

Reading Check

Answer: a mystical movement that rejected dogma and instead stressed the need to follow the teachings of Jesus

TURNING POINT

How did Luther's protest affect European religious life?
(His protest led to the rise of Protestantism. In challenging the pope's authority, Luther also contributed to ending the religious unity of western Europe.) **L1**

Guided Reading Activity 5–3

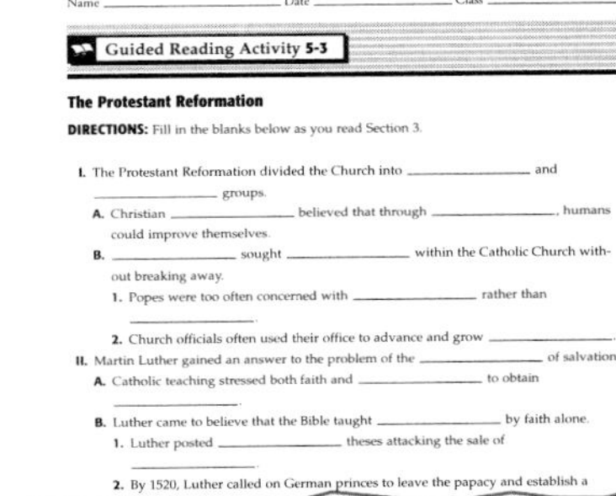

Name ________ Date ________ Class ________

Guided Reading Activity 5-3

The Protestant Reformation

DIRECTIONS: Fill in the blanks below as you read Section 3.

I. The Protestant Reformation divided the Church into ________ and ________ groups.
A. Christian ________ believed that through ________, humans could improve themselves.
B. ________ sought ________ within the Catholic Church without breaking away.
1. Popes were too often concerned with ________ rather than ________.
2. Church officials often used their office to advance and grow ________.
II. Martin Luther gained an answer to the problem of the ________ of salvation.
A. Catholic teaching stressed both faith and ________ to obtain ________.
B. Luther came to believe that the Bible taught ________ by faith alone.
1. Luther posted ________ theses attacking the sale of ________.
2. By 1520, Luther called on German princes to leave the papacy and establish a

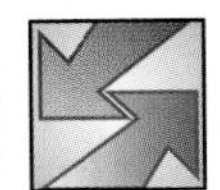

CURRICULUM CONNECTION

Vocabulary Some students may not understand the terms *indulgences, purgatory, remission,* and *dogma,* but these are critical to understanding the reform movement begun by Martin Luther. Allow time for students to look these terms up in the dictionary and discuss their meanings with the class. **L1**

EXTENDING THE CONTENT

Ninety-five Theses On October 31, 1517, Martin Luther nailed his Ninety-five Theses to the door of the Castle Church in Wittenberg launching the Reformation. Or did he? For hundreds of years people believed that Luther nailed his theses to the church door. In 1961, however, a researcher asserted that the famous image of Luther nailing the theses to the door belonged to the realm of legend. How did the researcher come to that conclusion? He noted that the first written account of the event comes from someone who could not have been an eyewitness. Also, the account appeared after Luther's death, and Luther himself had never mentioned the event. What is fact is that Luther wrote a letter to his superiors denouncing the sale of indulgences and included the theses, which were to be the basis for a discussion on the topic.

Geography Skills

Answers:

1. Worms
2. It was in Saxony. Luther benefited from Elector Frederick's protection. It was far from Rome and papal influence.

Enrich

Have students imagine that they are living in Germany in the 1500s. Ask them to assert a Catholic or Lutheran point of view in a letter to the editor about the implications of Luther's reforms on the Catholic Church in Germany. **L3**

3 ASSESS

Assign Section 3 Assessment as homework or as an in-class activity.

Have students use **Interactive Tutor Self-Assessment CD-ROM.**

Section Quiz 5–3

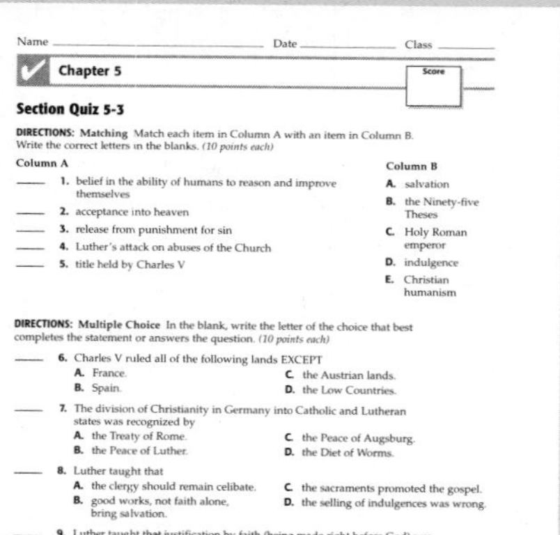

Name ______ Date ______ Class ______

Chapter 5 Score

Section Quiz 5-3

DIRECTIONS: Matching Match each item in Column A with an item in Column B. Write the correct letters in the blanks. *(10 points each)*

Column A

____ **1.** belief in the ability of humans to reason and improve themselves
____ **2.** acceptance into heaven
____ **3.** release from punishment for sin
____ **4.** Luther's attack on abuses of the Church
____ **5.** title held by Charles V

Column B

A. salvation
B. the Ninety-five Theses
C. Holy Roman emperor
D. indulgence
E. Christian humanism

DIRECTIONS: Multiple Choice In the blank, write the letter of the choice that best completes the statement or answers the question. *(10 points each)*

____ **6.** Charles V ruled all of the following lands EXCEPT
A. France. **B.** Spain. **C.** the Austrian lands. **D.** the Low Countries.

____ **7.** The division of Christianity in Germany into Catholic and Lutheran states was recognized by
A. the Treaty of Rome. **B.** the Peace of Luther. **C.** the Peace of Augsburg. **D.** the Diet of Worms.

____ **8.** Luther taught that
A. the clergy should remain celibate. **B.** good works, not faith alone, bring salvation. **C.** the sacraments promoted the gospel. **D.** the selling of indulgences was wrong.

____ **9.** Luther taught that justification by faith (being made right before God) was

A Break with the Church By 1520, Luther had begun to move toward a more definite break with the Catholic Church. He called on the German princes to overthrow the papacy in Germany and establish a reformed German church. Luther also attacked the Church's system of sacraments. In his view, they were the means by which the pope and the Church had destroyed the real meaning of the gospel for a thousand years. He kept only two sacraments—baptism and the Eucharist (also known as Communion). Luther also called for the clergy to marry. This went against the long-standing Catholic requirement that the clergy remain celibate, or unmarried.

Through all these calls for change, Luther continued to emphasize his new doctrine of salvation. It is faith alone, he said, and not good works, that justifies and brings salvation through Christ.

Unable to accept Luther's ideas, the Church excommunicated him in January 1521. He was also summoned to appear before the imperial diet—or legislative assembly—of the Holy Roman Empire, which was called into session at the city of Worms by the newly elected emperor Charles V. The emperor thought he could convince Luther to change his ideas, but Luther refused.

The young emperor was outraged. "A single friar who goes counter to all Christianity for a thousand years," he declared, "must be wrong!" By the **Edict of Worms,** Martin Luther was made an outlaw within the empire. His works were to be burned and Luther himself captured and delivered to the emperor. However, Luther's ruler, Elector Frederick of Saxony, was unwilling to see his famous professor killed. He sent Luther into hiding and then protected him when he returned to Wittenberg at the beginning of 1522.

The Rise of Lutheranism During the next few years, Luther's religious movement became a revolution. Luther was able to gain the support of many of the German rulers among the numerous states that made up the Holy Roman Empire. These rulers quickly took control of the Catholic churches in their territories, forming state churches whose affairs were supervised by the government.

As part of the development of these state-dominated churches, Luther also set up new religious services to replace the Catholic Mass. These featured a worship service consisting of Bible readings, preaching of the word of God, and song. The doctrine developed by Luther soon came to be known as Lutheranism, and the churches as Lutheran churches. Lutheranism was the first Protestant faith.

In June 1524, Luther faced a political crisis when German peasants revolted against their lords. The peasants looked to Luther to support their cause, but Luther instead supported the lords. To him, the state and its rulers were called by God to maintain the peace necessary for

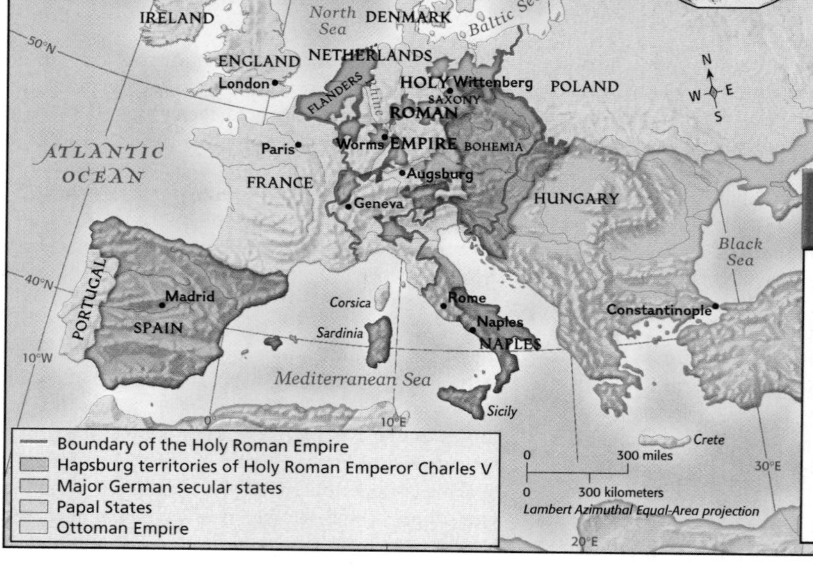

Geography Skills

Charles V wanted to keep his vast territories Catholic.

1. **Interpreting Maps** In which city was Luther declared an outlaw?
2. **Applying Geography Skills** How did the location of Wittenberg benefit the Protestant cause?

COOPERATIVE LEARNING ACTIVITY

Role-Playing Organize the class into five groups and have each group create a short television interview with Tetzel on the sale of indulgences, Luther on his Ninety-five Theses, Pope Leo X on excommunicating Luther, Elector Frederick of Saxony on hiding Luther, or Luther on the teachings of Lutheranism. Encourage students to conduct research at the library. Have each group select a member to act as an interviewer and another to be interviewed. All group members should prepare questions for the interview. After all interviews have been presented, have the class summarize the events that led to the Reformation. **L2**

For grading this activity, refer to the ***Performance Assessment Activities*** booklet.

the spread of the gospel. It was the duty of princes to stop revolt. By the following spring, the German princes had crushed the peasants. Luther found himself even more dependent on state authorities for the growth of his church.

✓Reading Check **Contrasting** How did Luther's theory of salvation differ from what the Catholic Church believed was necessary for salvation?

Politics in the German Reformation

From its very beginning, the fate of Luther's movement was closely tied to political affairs. **Charles V,** the Holy Roman emperor (who was also Charles I, the king of Spain), ruled an immense empire consisting of Spain and its colonies, the Austrian lands, **Bohemia, Hungary,** the Low Countries, the duchy of Milan in northern Italy, and the kingdom of Naples in southern Italy.

Politically, Charles wanted to keep this enormous empire under the control of his dynasty—the Hapsburgs. Religiously, he hoped to preserve the unity of his empire by keeping it Catholic. However, a number of problems kept him busy and cost him both his dream and his health. These same problems helped Lutheranism survive by giving Lutherans time to organize before having to face the Catholic forces.

The chief political concern of Charles V was his rivalry with the king of France, Francis I. Their conflict over disputed territories in a number of areas led to a series of wars that lasted more than 20 years. At the same time, Charles faced opposition from Pope Clement VII. Guided by political considerations, the pope had joined the side of the French king. The advance of the Ottoman Turks into the eastern part of Charles's empire forced the emperor to send forces there as well.

Finally, the internal political situation in the Holy Roman Empire was not in Charles's favor. Germany was a land of several hundred territorial states. Although all owed loyalty to the emperor, Germany's development in the Middle Ages had enabled these states to free themselves from the emperor's authority. Many individual rulers of the German states supported Luther as a way to assert their own local authority over the authority of the empire and Charles V.

By the time Charles V was able to bring military forces to Germany, the Lutheran princes were well organized. Unable to defeat them, Charles was forced to seek peace.

An end to religious warfare in Germany came in 1555 with the **Peace of Augsburg.** This agreement formally accepted the division of Christianity in Germany. The German states were now free to choose between Catholicism and Lutheranism. Lutheran states were to have the same legal rights as Catholic states. The peace settlement did not recognize the principle of religious toleration for individuals, however. The right of each German ruler to determine the religion of his subjects was accepted, but not the right of the subjects to choose their own religion.

✓Reading Check **Evaluating** How did the Peace of Augsburg influence the political and development of Germany?

SECTION 3 ASSESSMENT

Checking for Understanding

1. **Define** Christian humanism, salvation, indulgence.
2. **Identify** Martin Luther, Desiderius Erasmus, Edict of Worms, Charles V, The Peace of Augsburg.
3. **Locate** Wittenberg, Bohemia, Hungary.
4. **Explain** the impact of the Edict of Worms.
5. **List** the ways Erasmus wanted to reform the Catholic Church.

Critical Thinking

6. **Discuss** What were the consequences of Luther's Ninety-five Theses?
7. **Sequencing Information** Use a diagram like the one below to show Luther's actions leading to the emergence of Protestantism.

Luther's Actions

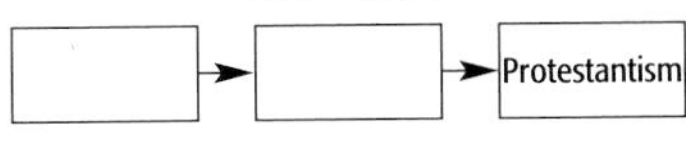

Analyzing Visuals

8. **Identify** the event illustrated in the painting on page 173. Why was this event significant? How has the painter portrayed Martin Luther?

Writing About History

9. **Persuasive Writing** Martin Luther's father wanted him to become a lawyer. Write a letter in which Martin Luther tries to convince his father that the path he chose was better than the law.

Chapter 5
Section 3, 171–175

✓Reading Check

Answer: Catholics believed that salvation came from both faith and good works; Luther believed that faith alone made a person worthy of salvation.

✓Reading Check

Answer: It formally ended religious warfare in Germany by allowing individual states to choose between Catholicism and Lutheranism.

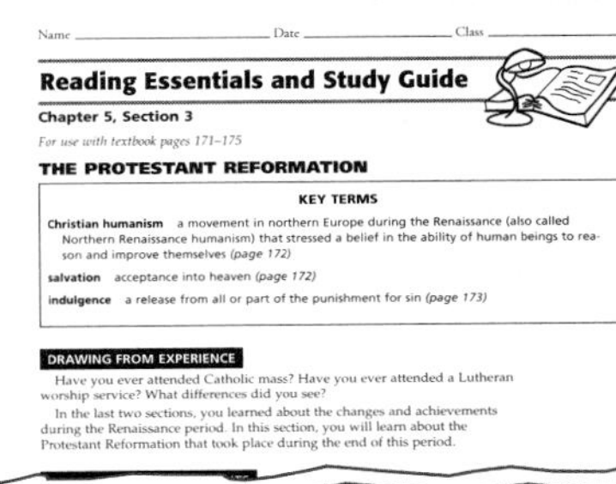
Reading Essentials and Study Guide 5–3

Name ____________ Date ____________ Class ____________

Reading Essentials and Study Guide

Chapter 5, Section 3

For use with textbook pages 171–175

THE PROTESTANT REFORMATION

KEY TERMS

Christian humanism a movement in northern Europe during the Renaissance (also called Northern Renaissance humanism) that stressed a belief in the ability of human beings to reason and improve themselves *(page 172)*

salvation acceptance into heaven *(page 172)*

indulgence a release from all or part of the punishment for sin *(page 173)*

DRAWING FROM EXPERIENCE

Have you ever attended Catholic mass? Have you ever attended a Lutheran worship service? What differences did you see?

In the last two sections, you learned about the changes and achievements during the Renaissance period. In this section, you will learn about the Protestant Reformation that took place during the end of this period.

Reteaching Activity

Have students list the main differences between Lutheranism and Catholicism. *(idea of salvation, sacraments, clergy could marry)* **L1**

4 CLOSE

Ask students to explain the relevance of justification by faith and the sale of indulgences to Luther's break from the Catholic Church. *(Luther did not believe actions brought salvation, but faith alone. The Church did not accept this.)* **L2**

SECTION 3 ASSESSMENT

1. Key terms are in blue.
2. Martin Luther *(p. 171);* Desiderius Erasmus *(p. 172);* Edict of Worms *(p. 174);* Charles V *(p. 175);* The Peace of Augsburg *(p. 175)*
3. See chapter maps.
4. outlawing Luther turned his religious movement into a revolution
5. spread the philosophy of Christ, provide education in works of Christianity, criticize abuses of the Church
6. gave rise to separate religious reform movements and to the breakdown of religious unity in Europe
7. Ninety-five Theses → called for German princes to establish a reformed German church → [additional reforms] → Protestantism
8. Luther posting his Ninety-five Theses on the church door. Answers will vary.
9. Students will compose a letter from Luther's point of view.

STUDY & WRITING SKILLBUILDER

TEACH

Summarizing Information

Before asking students to read the Skillbuilder, distribute copies of a newspaper editorial. Ask students which sentence best indicates the subject of the editorial. Ask them what this type of sentence is called *(topic sentence)*. Have them restate the point of the topic sentence in their own words. Now ask them to identify sentences that support the main point. Have students list, in as few words as possible, the supporting points. **L1**

Additional Practice

Skills Reinforcement Activity 5

Name ______ Date ______ Class ______

Skills Reinforcement Activity 5

Summarizing Information

The ability to summarize information is a part of note taking. Summarizing allows you to record and remember the most important ideas and facts from your reading. When you summarize, you record main ideas in your own words.

DIRECTIONS: Read the following excerpt from your text, pages 375–376. Then answer the questions below in the space provided.

The word *renaissance* means rebirth. A number of people who lived in Italy between 1350 and 1550 believed that they had witnessed a rebirth of the ancient Greek and Roman worlds. To them, this rebirth marked a new age. Historians later called this period the Renaissance, or Italian Renaissance—a period of European history that began in Italy and spread to the rest of Europe. What, then, are the most important characteristics of the Italian Renaissance?

First, Renaissance Italy was largely an

instability, and a decline of Church power. Recovery went hand in hand with a rebirth of interest in ancient culture. Italian thinkers became aware of their own Roman past—the remains of which were to be seen all around them. They also became intensely interested in the culture that had dominated the ancient Mediterranean world. This revival affected both politics and art.

Third, a new view of human beings emerged as people in the Italian Renaissance

GLENCOE TECHNOLOGY

CD-ROM
Glencoe Skillbuilder Interactive Workbook CD-ROM, Level 2

This interactive CD-ROM reinforces student mastery of essential social studies skills.

STUDY & WRITING SKILLBUILDER

Summarizing Information

Why Learn This Skill?

Imagine you have been assigned a chapter on the Renaissance for a midterm. After taking a short break, you discover that you cannot recall important information. What can you do to avoid this problem?

When you read a long selection, it is helpful to take notes. Summarizing information—reducing large amounts of information to a few key phrases—can help you remember the main ideas and important facts.

Learning the Skill

To summarize information, follow these guidelines when you read:

- Distinguish the main ideas from the supporting details. Use the main ideas in the summary.
- Use your own words to describe the main ideas. Do not copy the selection word for word.
- Summarize the author's opinion if you think it is important.
- If the summary is almost as long as the reading selection, you are including too much information. The summary should be very short.

Practicing the Skill

Read the selection below, and then answer the questions that follow.

For the next 30 years, the French and Spanish made Italy their battleground as they fought to dominate the country. A decisive turning point in their war came in 1527. On May 5, thousands of troops belonging to the Spanish king Charles I arrived at the city of Rome along with mercenaries from different countries. They had not been paid for months. When they yelled, "Money! Money!" their leader responded, "If you have ever dreamed of pillaging a town and laying hold of its treasures, here now is one, the richest of them all, queen of the world."

The next day the invading forces smashed down the gates and pushed their way into the city. The terrible sack of Rome in 1527 by the armies of the Spanish king Charles I ended the Italian wars and left the Spanish a dominant force in Italy.

1. What are the main ideas of this paragraph?
2. What are the supporting details of the main ideas?
3. Write a brief summary of two or three sentences that will help you remember what the paragraph is about.

St. Peter's Square, sixteenth-century Rome

Applying the Skill

Read and summarize two articles from the front page of a newspaper. Have a classmate ask you questions about them. How much were you able to remember after summarizing the information?

Glencoe's **Skillbuilder Interactive Workbook, Level 2,** provides instruction and practice in key social studies skills.

ANSWERS TO PRACTICING THE SKILL

1. The wars of the French and Spanish in Italy led to the sack of Rome.
2. dates, the name of the Spanish king, quotation
3. The French and Spanish fought in Italy for 30 years. When the Spanish king could not pay his troops, they sacked Rome. This ended the war, and Spain dominated Italy.

Applying the Skill: Students will work in pairs to summarize information.

SECTION 4

The Spread of Protestantism and the Catholic Response

Guide to Reading

Main Ideas
- Different forms of Protestantism emerged in Europe as the Reformation spread.
- The Catholic Church underwent a religious rebirth.

Key Terms
predestination, annul

People to Identify
Huldrych Zwingli, John Calvin, Henry VIII, Ignatius of Loyola

Places to Locate
Zürich, Geneva, Trent

Preview Questions
1. What different forms of Protestantism emerged in Europe?
2. What were the contributions of the Jesuits, the papacy, and the Council of Trent to the revival of Catholicism?

Reading Strategy
Cause and Effect Use a diagram like the one below to list some of the reforms proposed by the Council of Trent. Beside each, give the Protestant viewpoint to which it responded.

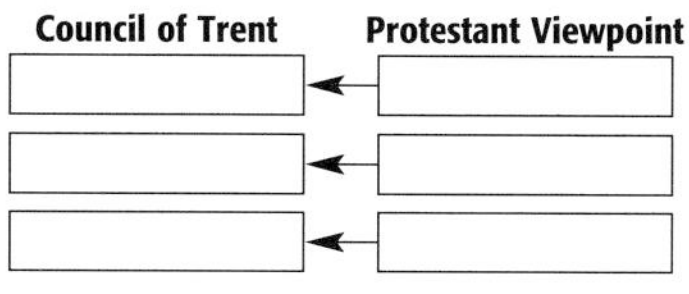

Council of Trent		Protestant Viewpoint
	←	
	←	
	←	

Preview of Events

1530 · 1535 · 1540 · 1545 · 1550 · 1555

- **1531** War between the Protestant and Catholic states in Switzerland
- **1534** The Act of Supremacy is passed in England
- **1540** The Society of Jesus becomes a religious order
- **1545** The Council of Trent is formed
- **1553** Mary Tudor, "Bloody Mary," becomes Queen of England

Ignatius Loyola

Voices from the Past

In order to fight Protestantism, the Catholic Ignatius Loyola founded a new religious order. He insisted on certain principles:

> "We must put aside all judgment of our own, and keep the mind ever ready and prompt to obey in all things the true Spouse of Jesus Christ, our holy Mother, the Roman Catholic Church. . . . If we wish to proceed securely in all things, we must hold fast to the following principle: What seems to me white, I will believe black if the Catholic Church so defines. For I must be convinced that in Christ our Lord, the bridegroom, and in His spouse the Catholic Church, only one Spirit holds sway, which governs and rules for the salvation of souls."
>
> —*Spiritual Exercises of Ignatius Loyola,* **Louis J. Puhl, trans., 1951**

Loyola's ideal of complete obedience to the church was the cornerstone of his fight against the spread of Protestant groups.

The Zwinglian Reformation

With the Peace of Augsburg, what had at first been merely feared was now certain: the ideal of Christian unity was forever lost. Even before the Peace of Augsburg, however, division had appeared in Protestantism. One of these new groups appeared in Switzerland.

1 FOCUS

Section Overview

This section discusses the different forms of Protestantism and reforms in the Catholic Church.

BELLRINGER
Skillbuilder Activity

Project transparency 5–4 and have students answer questions.

Available as a blackline master.

Daily Focus Skills Transparency 5–4

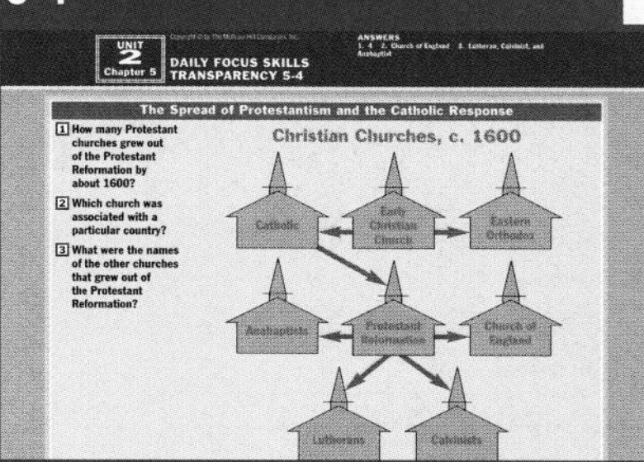

Guide to Reading

Answers to Graphic: Council of Trent: salvation through faith and works; Protestant viewpoint: salvation by faith alone
Council of Trent: seven sacraments; Protestant viewpoint: two sacraments
Council of Trent: clerical celibacy; Protestant viewpoint: called on clergy to marry

Preteaching Vocabulary: *Annul* and *divorce* are two terms we still use today. Ask students to think about how *annulment* differs from a divorce. *(annul pertains to religion; divorce is secular)* **L1**

SECTION RESOURCES

Reproducible Masters
- Reproducible Lesson Plan 5–4
- Daily Lecture and Discussion Notes 5–4
- Guided Reading Activity 5–4
- Section Quiz 5–4
- Reading Essentials and Study Guide 5–4

Transparencies
- Daily Focus Skills Transparency 5–4

Multimedia
- Interactive Tutor Self-Assessment CD-ROM
- ExamView® Pro Testmaker CD-ROM
- Presentation Plus! CD-ROM

2 TEACH

Reading Check

Answer: Relics and images were abolished. Painting and decorations were removed from the churches and replaced with whitewashed walls. Scripture reading, prayer, and sermons replaced the Catholic Mass.

Picturing History

Answer: Answers will vary. Calvin emphasized education, blending of clergy and laity in work of church, and the Consistory to oversee moral life and doctrinal purity. Artist conveys a favorable impression of Calvinism.

Daily Lecture and Discussion Notes 5–4

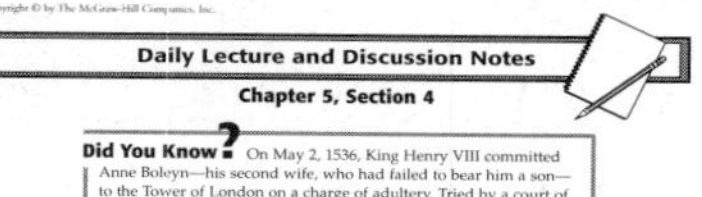

Daily Lecture and Discussion Notes

Chapter 5, Section 4

Did You Know? On May 2, 1536, King Henry VIII committed Anne Boleyn—his second wife, who had failed to bear him a son—to the Tower of London on a charge of adultery. Tried by a court of her peers and unanimously convicted, Boleyn was beheaded on May 19. On May 30, Henry married Jane Seymour.

I. **The Zwinglian Reformation and Calvin and Calvinism** *(pages 177–179)*

A. With the Peace of Augsburg, the ideal of Christian unity was lost forever. **Huldrych Zwingli,** a priest in **Zürich,** began a new Christian group in Switzerland. Relics and images were forbidden in the city, and a new service of scripture reading, prayer, and sermons replaced the Catholic Mass.

B. The Swiss and German reformers sought an alliance, but they could not agree on the meaning of the sacrament of Communion. In 1531 Zwingli was killed in a war between Protestant and Catholic states in Switzerland. John Calvin assumed the leadership of Protestantism in Switzerland.

C. **John Calvin** fled Catholic France for Switzerland after he converted to Protestantism. He placed a new emphasis on the all-powerful nature of God—what Calvin called the "power, grace, and glory of God." This led him to the important idea of **predestination,** which meant that God in an "eternal decree" had determined in advance who would be saved (the elect) and who would be damned (the reprobate).

Connecting Across Time

Guide students in a discussion concerning the decision of the city council of Zurich to follow Zwingli's religious reforms. Could such a thing happen in the city council chambers in the United States? Why or why not? *(no, because of separation of church and state)* **L1**

Huldrych Zwingli was a priest in **Zürich.** The city council of Zürich, strongly influenced by Zwingli, began to introduce religious reforms. Relics and images were abolished. All paintings and decorations were removed from the churches and replaced by whitewashed walls. A new church service consisting of scripture reading, prayer, and sermons replaced the Catholic Mass.

As his movement began to spread to other cities in Switzerland, Zwingli sought an alliance with Martin Luther and the German reformers. Both the German and Swiss reformers realized the need for unity to defend themselves against Catholic authorities, but they were unable to agree on the meaning of the sacrament of Communion. *(See page 774 to read excerpts from Martin Luther and Huldrych Zwingli's* A Reformation Debate *in the Primary Sources Library.)*

In October 1531, war broke out between the Protestant and Catholic states in Switzerland. Zürich's army was routed, and Zwingli was found wounded on the battlefield. His enemies killed him, cut up his body, and burned the pieces, scattering the ashes. The leadership of Protestantism in Switzerland now passed to John Calvin.

Reading Check **Describing** What religious reforms were introduced in Zürich?

Calvin and Calvinism

John Calvin was educated in his native France. After his conversion to Protestantism, however, he was forced to flee Catholic France for the safety of Switzerland. In 1536, he published the *Institutes of the Christian Religion,* a summary of Protestant thought. This work immediately gave Calvin a reputation as one of the new leaders of Protestantism.

On most important doctrines, Calvin stood very close to Luther. He, too, believed in the doctrine of justification by faith alone to explain how humans achieved salvation. However, Calvin also placed much emphasis on the all-powerful nature of God—what Calvin called the "power, grace, and glory of God."

Calvin's emphasis on the all-powerful nature of God led him to other ideas. One of these ideas was **predestination.** This "eternal decree," as Calvin called it, meant that God had determined in advance who would be saved (the elect) and who would be damned (the reprobate). According to Calvin, "He has once for all determined, both whom he would admit to salvation, and whom he would condemn to destruction."

The belief in predestination gave later Calvinists the firm conviction that they were doing God's work

Picturing History

John Calvin is shown speaking before leaders in Geneva. What attitudes about Calvin and the Protestant movement does the artist convey in this painting?

COOPERATIVE LEARNING ACTIVITY

Panel Discussion Organize the class into five groups to prepare and present a panel discussion of Reformation movements in one of the following countries: Switzerland, Scotland, the Netherlands, England, or Germany (Anabaptists). Using outside sources, each group member should focus on a specific topic, such as leadership, religious beliefs, relationship to government, or important political events. Have each group appoint a member to serve as moderator or timekeeper. After each group member presents his or her topic, have the moderator summarize the panel's main points. After all panels have made their presentations, encourage the class to compare and contrast these Reformation movements. **L2**

on Earth. This conviction, in turn, made them determined to spread their faith to other people. Calvinism became a dynamic and activist faith.

In 1536, Calvin began working to reform the city of **Geneva.** He created a church government that used both clergy and laity in the service of the church. The Consistory, a special body for enforcing moral discipline, was set up as a court to oversee the moral life and doctrinal purity of Genevans. The Consistory had the right to punish people who deviated from the church's teachings and moral principles. Citizens in Geneva were punished for such varied "crimes" as dancing, singing obscene songs, drunkenness, swearing, and playing cards.

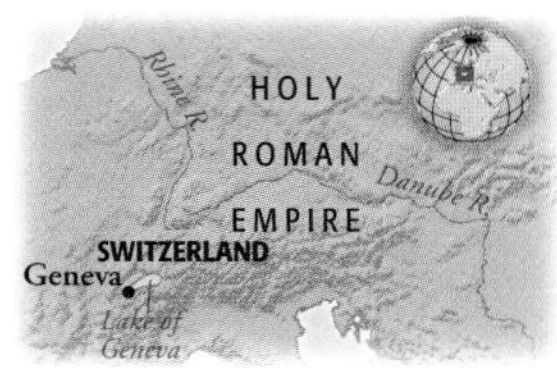

Calvin's success in Geneva made the city a powerful center of Protestantism. Following Calvin's lead, missionaries trained in Geneva were sent to all parts of Europe. Calvinism became established in France, the Netherlands, Scotland, and central and eastern Europe.

By the mid-sixteenth century, Calvinism had replaced Lutheranism as the most important and dynamic form of Protestantism. Calvin's Geneva stood as the fortress of the Protestant Reformation. John Knox, the Calvinist reformer of Scotland, called it "the most perfect school of Christ on earth."

Reading Check **Explaining** How did the Consistory enforce moral discipline in Geneva?

The Reformation in England

The English Reformation was rooted in politics, not religion. **King Henry VIII** wanted to divorce his first wife, Catherine of Aragon, with whom he had a daughter, Mary, but no son. Since he needed a male heir, Henry wanted to marry Anne Boleyn. Impatient with the pope's unwillingness to **annul** (declare invalid) his marriage to Catherine, Henry turned to England's own church courts.

As the archbishop of Canterbury, head of the highest church court in England, Thomas Cranmer ruled in May 1533 that the king's marriage to Catherine was "null and absolutely void." At the beginning of June, Anne was crowned queen. Three months later a child was born. Much to the king's disappointment, the baby was a girl. She would later become Queen Elizabeth I.

In 1534, at Henry's request, Parliament moved to finalize the break of the Catholic Church in England with the pope in Rome. The Act of Supremacy of 1534 declared that the king was "taken, accepted, and reputed the only supreme head on earth of the [new] Church of England." This position gave the king control over religious doctrine, clerical appointments, and discipline. Thomas More, a Christian humanist and devout Catholic, opposed the king's action and was beheaded.

Henry used his new powers to dissolve the monasteries and sell their land and possessions to wealthy landowners and merchants. The king received a great boost to his treasury and a group of supporters who now had a stake in the new order. In matters of doctrine, however, Henry remained close to Catholic teachings.

When Henry died in 1547, he was succeeded by Edward VI, a sickly nine-year-old, the son of his third wife. During Edward's reign, church officials who favored Protestant doctrines moved the Church of England, also called the Anglican Church, in a Protestant direction. New acts of Parliament gave the clergy the right to marry and created a new Protestant church service. These rapid changes aroused much opposition. When Mary, Henry's daughter by Catherine of Aragon, came to the throne in 1553, England was ready for a reaction.

Henry VIII disagreed with Luther's theology but found it politically convenient to break with the Catholic Church.

Reading Check

Answer: set up as a court, with the right to punish people who deviated from the church's teachings and moral principles; "crimes" included dancing, singing obscene songs, drunkenness, swearing, and playing cards

Guided Reading Activity 5–4

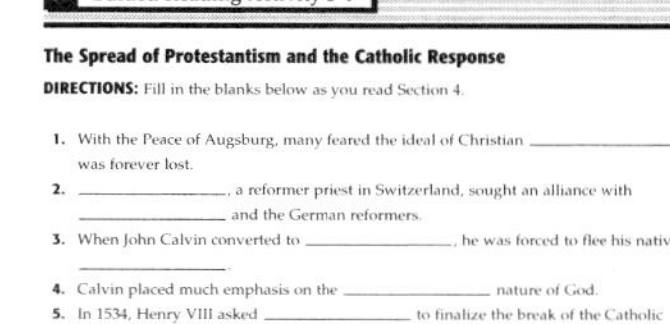

Name ______ Date ______ Class ______

Guided Reading Activity 5-4

The Spread of Protestantism and the Catholic Response

DIRECTIONS: Fill in the blanks below as you read Section 4.

1. With the Peace of Augsburg, many feared the ideal of Christian ______ was forever lost.
2. ______, a reformer priest in Switzerland, sought an alliance with ______ and the German reformers.
3. When John Calvin converted to ______, he was forced to flee his native ______.
4. Calvin placed much emphasis on the ______ nature of God.
5. In 1534, Henry VIII asked ______ to finalize the break of the Catholic Church in England with the pope in Rome.
6. During the reign of ______, church officials moved the Church of England, or Anglican Church, in a Protestant direction.
7. The ______ were a radical group that strongly disliked giving power to the state to control the affairs of the church.
8. Anabaptists considered all believers to be ______, chose their own ministers, and any member of the community was ______ to be a minister.
9. Protestantism eliminated the idea that special holiness was associated with

CURRICULUM CONNECTION

Politics Have students make a chart in which they show the country, leader, and basic beliefs and religious reforms of Zwinglism, Calvinism, the Anabaptists, and Anglicanism. *(Example: Zwinglism, Switzerland, Zwingli, salvation by faith alone, stripped church and changed church service)* **L1**

Who?What?Where?When?

Henry VIII was married a total of six times. Have students research his marriages and make a family tree showing his wives and his offspring.

EXTENDING THE CONTENT

Ireland The decisions made by King Henry VIII are still affecting Ireland's relations with England. Historically, their relations have not been good. The Irish, most of whom were Catholic, were angered by England's political and commercial domination. In the seventeenth century, Oliver Cromwell identified Catholicism with sedition and savagely crushed a rebellion. This, coupled with the nineteenth-century potato famine, led to the death of almost 1.5 million people, and another million immigrated to the U.S. and Great Britain. In the twentieth century, Britain granted Ireland autonomy, but retained Northern Ireland. In the 1990s, talks between the British government and the Irish Republican Army (IRA) resulted in some progress, but problems continue.

Reading Check

Answer: The pope would not annul his marriage to Catherine of Aragon so that he could remarry, so Henry broke with the Church.

CONNECTIONS Past to Present

Answer: Student answers should reflect understanding of religious basis for Amish way of life.

Enrich

Review with students Henry VIII's decision to create a different church in England. Discuss the reasons that his daughter, Mary, intended to restore the Catholic Church as the only church in England. Solicit input from the students on their reactions to Mary's motives.

Writing Activity

The European Renaissance and the Reformation were two very influential eras in world history. After they have read this chapter, ask students to write an essay in which they identify and describe the causes, characteristics, and effects of both the European Renaissance and the Reformation. **L1**

There was no doubt that Mary was a Catholic who wanted to restore England to Roman Catholicism. However, the way she went about it had the opposite effect. Among other actions, she had more than three hundred Protestants burned as heretics, earning her the nickname "Bloody Mary." As a result of her policies, England was even more Protestant by the end of Mary's reign than it had been at the beginning.

Reading Check **Examining** Why did Henry VIII form the Church of England?

The Anabaptists

Reformers such as Luther had allowed the state to play an important, if not dominant, role in church affairs. However, some people strongly disliked giving such power to the state. These were radicals known as the Anabaptists.

To Anabaptists, the true Christian church was a voluntary community of adult believers who had undergone spiritual rebirth and had then been baptized. This belief in adult baptism separated Anabaptists from Catholics and Protestants who baptized infants.

Anabaptists also believed in following the practices and the spirit of early Christianity. They considered all believers to be equal, a belief they based on the accounts of early Christian communities in the New Testament. Each Anabaptist church chose its own minister, or spiritual leader. Because all Christians were considered priests, any member of the community was eligible to be a minister (though women were often excluded).

Finally, most Anabaptists believed in the complete separation of church and state. Not only was government to be kept out of the realm of religion, it was not even supposed to have any political authority over real Christians. Anabaptists refused to hold political office or bear arms, because many took literally the biblical commandment "Thou shall not kill."

Their political beliefs, as much as their religious beliefs, caused the Anabaptists to be regarded as dangerous radicals who threatened the very fabric of sixteenth-century society. Indeed, the chief thing

CONNECTIONS Past To Present

The Descendants of the Anabaptists

Despite being persecuted for their belief in the complete separation of church and state, Anabaptists managed to survive.

Menno Simons was a popular leader of Anabaptism in the Netherlands. He dedicated his life to the spread of a peaceful Anabaptism that stressed separation from the world as the means for living a truly Christ-like life. Because of persecution, Menno Simons's followers, known as Mennonites, spread from the Netherlands into Germany and Russia. In the nineteenth century, many moved to Canada and the United States, where Mennonite communities continue to flourish.

In the 1690s, Jacob Ammann took the lead in encouraging a group of Swiss Mennonites to form their own church. They came to be known as the Amish (after the name Ammann). By the end of the seventeenth century, many of the Amish had come to North America in search of a land where they could practice their religion freely.

Today, Amish communities exist throughout Canada and the United States. One of the largest groups of Amish can be found in Pennsylvania, where they are known as the Pennsylvania Dutch. The Amish continue to maintain the Anabaptist way of life as it first developed in the sixteenth century. They live simple lives and refuse to use any modern devices, including cars and electricity.

▲ *The Amish are religious descendants of the Anabaptists.*

Comparing Past and Present

Today, many people living in the United States, such as the Amish, live without modern conveniences. Which appliances and conveniences would you be willing to give up? What cause or belief today might encourage people to give up a modern lifestyle?

180

MEETING INDIVIDUAL NEEDS

Visual Learners Create a stack of 3 x 5 cards with major events from 1400—1600 written on them. Events should include the Renaissance, humanism, Martin Luther's challenge, the rise of Calvinism, Catholicism, and various sub-events and details. Copy the cards so that you have one set for each group of four students in your class. Ask groups to arrange the cards in sequential order. Mix up the cards again. Have a race to see which group can place the cards in correct order. The cards can also be used for quizzing in pairs, or for fastening to the desktop for use by physically impaired students. The cards may be used by students who need repetition and for self-study. This activity is helpful for students who benefit from visual aids, practice in sequencing, or have difficulty with reading comprehension. **L1**

Geography Skills

Less than 100 years after Luther posted the Ninety-five Theses, the religious affiliations of Europeans were greatly altered.

1. **Interpreting Maps** What religions would not have been on this map prior to 1517?
2. **Applying Geography Skills** Summarize why Protestant religions spread as shown on the map.

other Protestants and Catholics could agree on was the need to persecute Anabaptists.

Reading Check **Describing** Why were the Anabaptists considered to be dangerous political radicals?

Effects on the Role of Women

The Protestants were important in developing a new view of the family. Protestantism had eliminated the idea that special holiness was associated with celibacy and had abolished both monasticism and the requirement of celibacy for the clergy. The family could now be placed at the center of human life. The "mutual love between man and wife" could be extolled.

Were idea and reality the same, however? More often, reality reflected the traditional roles of husband as the ruler and wife as the obedient servant whose chief duty was to please her husband. Luther stated it clearly:

> ❝The rule remains with the husband, and the wife is compelled to obey him by God's command. He rules the home and the state, wages war, defends his possessions, tills the soil, builds, plants, etc. The woman on the other hand is like a nail driven into the wall . . . so the wife should stay at home and look after the affairs of the household, as one who has been deprived of the ability of administering those

Geography Skills

Answers:

1. Anglican, Calvinism, Lutheran, Anabaptist
2. Lutheranism spread in northern German states because that is where it began, Anglicanism was the English form of Protestantism, Calvinism began in Switzerland and spread to Scotland via the Scots reformer John Knox, Anabaptists beliefs survived in areas where authorities did not persecute them. Protestantism was more widespread the farther it was geographically from Rome.

Reading Check

Answer: They believed in complete separation of church and state, and that the state had no authority over real Christians. They refused to hold political office or bear arms.

Connecting Across Time

During the Reformation, individuals, groups, and nations had to make difficult decisions as the Protestant religion spread throughout Europe. The choice between Catholicism and Protestantism was both a religious and a political choice, since a nation often determined the religion of its peoples. Have students evaluate the political choices and decisions that individuals, groups, and nations made during the Reformation era, taking into account historical context. Then ask students to apply this knowledge to the analysis of choices and decisions faced by contemporary societies. **L3**

CRITICAL THINKING ACTIVITY

Summarizing Have students research the more recent history of one of the Protestant groups mentioned in this section. Have them prepare brief reports that include the size of the sect today and where most members live, current beliefs and practices, and how the beliefs and practices have evolved since the group was founded. Students should include the role of women as part of their report. In a class discussion, encourage students to compare and contrast current practices and religious doctrines with their findings about other Protestant religions. **L1**

Answer: A greater emphasis was put on the family; the wife was compelled to obey her husband and to bear children.

History *through Art*

Answer: The painting conveys the power, unity, and authority of the Catholic Church.

Critical Thinking

Have students describe the impact of the Jesuits and the Council of Trent on the Catholic Church throughout the world. *(restored and spread Catholicism through education; reunited and strengthened the Church)* **L2**

3 ASSESS

Assign Section 4 Assessment as homework or as an in-class activity.

Have students use **Interactive Tutor Self-Assessment CD-ROM.**

Section Quiz 5–4

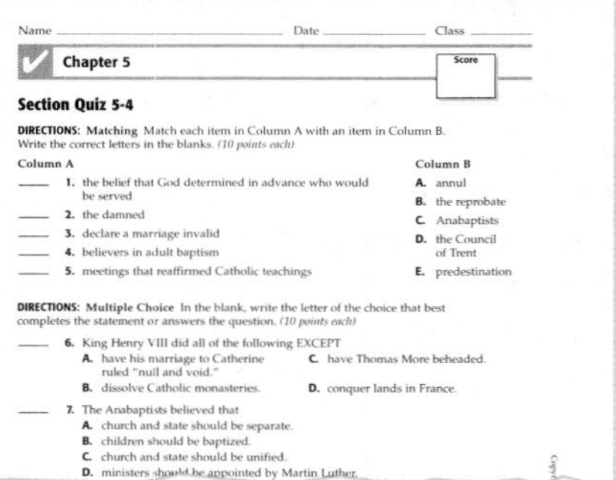

Name ______ Date ______ Class ______

Chapter 5 — Score

Section Quiz 5-4

DIRECTIONS: Matching Match each item in Column A with an item in Column B. Write the correct letters in the blanks. *(10 points each)*

Column A	Column B
____ 1. the belief that God determined in advance who would be served	A. annul
____ 2. the damned	B. the reprobate
____ 3. declare a marriage invalid	C. Anabaptists
____ 4. believers in adult baptism	D. the Council of Trent
____ 5. meetings that reaffirmed Catholic teachings	E. predestination

DIRECTIONS: Multiple Choice In the blank, write the letter of the choice that best completes the statement or answers the question. *(10 points each)*

____ 6. King Henry VIII did all of the following EXCEPT
- A. have his marriage to Catherine ruled "null and void."
- B. dissolve Catholic monasteries.
- C. have Thomas More beheaded.
- D. conquer lands in France.

____ 7. The Anabaptists believed that
- A. church and state should be separate.
- B. children should be baptized.
- C. church and state should be unified.
- D. ministers should be appointed by Martin Luther.

affairs that are outside and that concern the state. She does not go beyond her most personal duties.”

Obedience to her husband was not a woman's only role. Her other important duty was to bear children. To Calvin and Luther, this function of women was part of the divine plan. Family life was the only destiny for most Protestant women. Overall, then, the Protestant Reformation did not change women's subordinate place in society.

Reading Check **Evaluating** What impact did the Protestant Reformation have on women?

The Catholic Reformation

By the mid-sixteenth century, Lutheranism had become rooted in Germany and Scandinavia, and Calvinism had taken hold in Switzerland, France, the Netherlands, and eastern Europe. In England, the split from Rome had resulted in the creation of a national church. The situation in Europe did not look particularly good for the Catholic Church.

However, the Catholic Church also had a revitalization in the sixteenth century, giving it new strength and enabling it to regain much that it had lost. This Catholic Reformation was supported by three chief pillars: the Jesuits, reform of the papacy, and the Council of Trent.

HISTORY Online
Web Activity Visit the *Glencoe World History—Modern Times* Web site at wh.mt.glencoe.com and click on **Chapter 5–Student Web Activity** to learn more about the Reformation.

The Society of Jesus, known as the Jesuits, was founded by a Spanish nobleman, **Ignatius of Loyola.** Loyola gathered together a small group of followers, which was recognized as a religious order by the pope in 1540. All Jesuits took a special vow of absolute obedience to the pope, making them an important instrument for papal policy. Jesuits used education to spread their message. Jesuit missionaries were very successful in restoring Catholicism to parts of Germany and eastern Europe and in spreading it to other parts of the world.

History *through Art*

***Council of Trent* by Titian** The Council of Trent is thought to be the foundation of the Catholic Reformation. How does Titian's painting convey this idea?

COOPERATIVE LEARNING ACTIVITY

Visual Reports Organize the class into five groups. Using the map on page 181, have one group create a large map showing the distribution of religions in Europe after the Council of Trent. Have the second group research the *Index of Forbidden Books* and make a list of well-known authors and books that were on the list over the years. Have the third group research the Inquisition and make a drawing of the trials and punishments. Have the fourth group make an illustrated list of the main outcomes of the Council of Trent. Have the fifth group make a large world map showing areas of Jesuit missionary activities. Remind students to use library resources when needed. Have groups display their work on Catholic Reformation bulletin-board display.

Reform of the papacy was another important factor in the Catholic Reformation. The participation of Renaissance popes in dubious financial transactions and Italian political and military affairs had created many sources of corruption. It took the jolt of the Protestant Reformation to bring about serious reform.

Pope Paul III perceived the need for change and took the bold step of appointing a Reform Commission in 1537 to determine the Church's ills. The commission blamed the Church's problems on the corrupt policies of the popes. Paul III (who recognized the Jesuits as a new religious order) also began the Council of Trent, another pillar of the Catholic Reformation.

In March 1545, a group of cardinals, archbishops, bishops, abbots, and theologians met in the city of **Trent,** on the border between Germany and Italy. There, they began the Council of Trent, which met off and on for 18 years.

The final decrees of the Council of Trent reaffirmed traditional Catholic teachings in opposition to Protestant beliefs. Both faith and good works were declared necessary for salvation. The seven sacraments, the Catholic view of the Eucharist, and clerical celibacy were all upheld. Belief in purgatory and in the use of indulgences was strengthened, although the selling of indulgences was forbidden.

After the Council of Trent, the Roman Catholic Church possessed a clear body of doctrine and was unified under the supreme leadership of the pope.

Picturing History

Ignatius of Loyola, founder of the Jesuits, is shown kneeling before Pope Paul III. What role did the Jesuits play in the Catholic Reformation?

With a renewed spirit of confidence, the Catholic Church entered a new phase, as well prepared as the Calvinists to do battle for the Lord.

Reading Check **Describing** What was the relationship between the Jesuits and the pope?

SECTION 4 ASSESSMENT

Checking for Understanding

1. **Define** predestination, annul.
2. **Identify** Huldrych Zwingli, John Calvin, Henry VIII, Ignatius of Loyola.
3. **Locate** Zürich, Geneva, Trent.
4. **Describe** the results of "Bloody Mary's" religious policies. How might Mary's actions have indirectly affected the history of the United States?
5. **List** which countries had adopted Calvinism and which had adopted Lutheranism by the mid-sixteenth century.

Critical Thinking

6. **Analyze** How were the religious reforms in Zürich consistent with the aims of the Reformation?
7. **Contrasting Information** Use a diagram like the one below to describe how the Calvinists and the Anabaptists differed in their attitudes toward church members participating in government activities.

Calvinists		Anabaptists
	Church Participation in Government	

Analyzing Visuals

8. **Identify** the details shown in the portrait of Henry VIII on page 179 that illustrate his power and authority. How did the king use his position as "the only supreme head on earth of the Church of England"? Based on what you have read in your text, do you think that Henry was a religious man? Explain your answer.

Writing About History

9. **Expository Writing** Compose an unbiased account of the Council of Trent. Include who was involved, why it was convened, when it happened, and its final results.

Chapter 5
Section 4, 177–183

Picturing History

Answer: They helped turn back the Protestant tide by restoring Catholicism in parts of Germany and eastern Europe, as well as spreading it to other parts of the world.

Reading Check

Answer: Jesuits took a special vow of absolute obedience to the pope, making them an important instrument for papal policy.

Reading Essentials and Study Guide 5–4

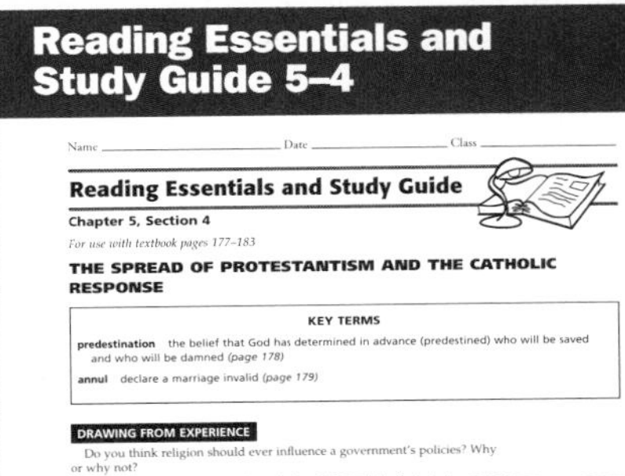
Name ______ Date ______ Class ______

Reading Essentials and Study Guide

Chapter 5, Section 4

For use with textbook pages 177–183

THE SPREAD OF PROTESTANTISM AND THE CATHOLIC RESPONSE

KEY TERMS

predestination the belief that God has determined in advance (predestined) who will be saved and who will be damned (page 178)

annul declare a marriage invalid (page 179)

DRAWING FROM EXPERIENCE

Do you think religion should ever influence a government's policies? Why or why not?

Reteaching Activity

On the chalkboard, draw a time line from 1500 to 1600. On the time line, have volunteers list important events from this section. **L1**

4 CLOSE

Ask students to summarize the major differences between the practices of Protestantism and Catholicism. *(justification by faith vs. good works; only two sacraments vs. all seven sacraments; unadorned church vs. decorated churches; emphasis on Bible vs. doctrine)* **L2**

SECTION 4 ASSESSMENT

1. Key terms are in blue.
2. Huldrych Zwingli *(p. 178);* John Calvin *(p. 178);* Henry VIII *(p. 179);* Ignatius of Loyola *(p. 182)*
3. See chapter maps.
4. English Protestants came to America.
5. Lutheranism in Germany and Scandinavia; Calvinism in Switzerland, France, the Netherlands, and eastern Europe
6. removed relics and images
7. Calvinists: church was government; Anabaptists: complete separation of church and state
8. marriage annulled; answers will vary
9. cardinals, archbishops, bishops, abbots, and theologians; called to reform the Catholic Church; convened in March 1545, and met off and on for the next 18 years; reaffirmed traditional Catholic teachings; established doctrine

GLENCOE TECHNOLOGY

MindJogger Videoquiz

Use the **MindJogger Videoquiz** to review Chapter 5 content.

 Available in VHS.

Using Key Terms

1. mercenaries **2.** humanism **3.** Christian humanism **4.** predestination **5.** secular **6.** urban society **7.** dowry **8.** indulgence **9.** fresco

Reviewing Key Facts

10. Medici

11. Geoffrey Chaucer

12. Greek and Roman

13. to show people how to live good lives on a daily basis rather than provide a system of beliefs that people have to practice to be saved

14. realistically

15. they were governed by wealthy families—the Visconti and Sforza families in Milan, the Medici family in Florence, and a group of merchant-aristocrats in the republic of Venice; nobility, townspeople (including wealthy patricians as well as burghers—shopkeepers, artisans, guild masters, and guild members), and peasants

16. by establishing the Society of Jesus, or Jesuits, a religious order that took a special vow of absolute obedience to the pope and used education to spread their message, restoring Catholicism to parts of Germany and eastern Europe and spreading it to other parts of the world

17. a worldly viewpoint and increasing wealth brought renewed interest in ancient culture; Italian thinkers became aware of their Roman past; emphasis on individual worth and ability began to emerge, leading to the ideal of the well-rounded individual

18. Niccolò Machiavelli, *The Prince*

19. when their fathers decided to give them their freedom

CHAPTER 5 ASSESSMENT and ACTIVITIES

Chapter Summary

The Renaissance was a period of great intellectual and artistic achievement. Religious rebirth followed in the 1500s.

1. Italy experiences an artistic, intellectual, and commercial awakening.

VENICE: The city becomes an international trading power.

FLORENCE: The Medici family improves city life and sponsors humanists and artists.

2. Ideas quickly spread from Italy to northern Europe.

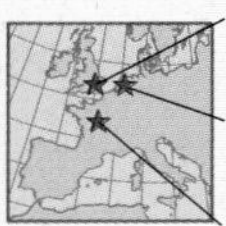

ENGLAND: King Henry VIII invites humanists to court.

FLANDERS: Artists use oil paints to depict fine detail in their paintings.

FRANCE: Architects create elegant castles that combine Gothic and classical styles.

3. Reformers begin to challenge both secular and religious rules and practices.

GERMANY: Martin Luther begins the Protestant Reformation. The Peace of Augsburg divides Germany into Catholic and Protestant states.

ENGLAND: King Henry VIII breaks with the pope to create the Church of England. Catholic Queen Mary executes Protestants.

SWITZERLAND: John Calvin promotes the concept of predestination.

4. The Catholic Church enacts reforms.

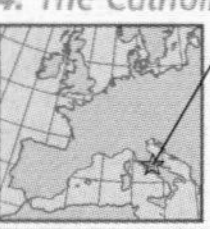

ITALY: The Council of Trent defines Catholic Church doctrine and tries to end Church abuses. The Jesuits, who take special vows of obedience to the pope, help spread Catholicism.

Using Key Terms

1. Soldiers who sell their services to the highest bidder are called ______.
2. The study of grammar, rhetoric, moral philosophy, and history was the basis of the intellectual movement called ______.
3. A movement whose major goal was the reform of Christendom was called ______.
4. John Calvin emphasized ______ , the belief that God chose who would be saved and who would be damned.
5. A ______ society places less emphasis on religion and more emphasis on a worldly spirit.
6. An ______ is one in which a great many people live in cities.
7. The money and goods given by the wife's family at the time of marriage is called a ______.
8. A remission, after death, from all or part of the punishment due to sin is called an ______.
9. An image painted on fresh, wet plaster is called a ______.

Reviewing Key Facts

10. **History** Which family dominated Florence during the Renaissance?
11. **Culture** Who wrote *The Canterbury Tales?*
12. **Culture** The Renaissance was a rebirth of the ideas of which ancient civilizations?
13. **History** According to Erasmus, what should be the chief concerns of the Christian church?
14. **Culture** How did Renaissance artists portray the human body?
15. **Government** How were the city-states of Renaissance Italy governed? What social classes were present in the typical city-state?
16. **History** How did Ignatius of Loyola help to reform Catholicism?
17. **History** Why did the Renaissance begin in Italy?
18. **Culture** Name the title and the author of one of the most influential works on political power.
19. **Culture** When were children considered adults in Renaissance Italy?

Critical Thinking

20. **Analyzing** Why did Martin Luther split with the Catholic Church? Identify the causes that led to the Protestant Reformation.
21. **Explaining** List one masterpiece of Renaissance literature or art and explain how it reflects Renaissance ideals.

Writing About History

22. **Expository Writing** Analyze how the Reformation shaped the political and religious life of Europe. Be sure to identify the historical effects of the Reformation.

Critical Thinking

20. Luther's study of the Bible led him to believe that humans are saved through their faith in God alone, and that grace could not be earned by performing good works. This was at odds with the Catholic doctrine that salvation depended on faith and good works. Luther also attacked abuses in the sale of indulgences in his Ninety-five Theses. He attacked the Church's view of the sacraments, keeping only baptism and the Eucharist. He was opposed to celibacy of the clergy. Eventually he called on the German princes to break with the Catholic Church and establish a reformed German church. Luther was excommunicated by the pope and made an outlaw within the Holy Roman Empire by Charles V. During the next few years, his movement became a revolution, and he gained the support of many of the German rulers who broke with the Catholic Church.

21. Answers will vary, depending on the work selected, but should reflect understanding of Renaissance ideals.

Self-Check Quiz

Visit the *Glencoe World History—Modern Times* Web site at wh.mt.glencoe.com and click on **Chapter 5–Self-Check Quiz** to prepare for the Chapter Test.

Analyzing Sources

Read the following description by Luther of a woman's role in marriage.

> ❝The rule remains with the husband, and the wife is compelled to obey him by God's command. He rules the home and the state, wages war, defends his possessions, tills the soil, builds, plants, etc. The woman on the other hand is like a nail driven into the wall . . . so the wife should stay at home and look after the affairs of the household, as one who has been deprived of the ability of administering those affairs that are outside and that concern the state. She does not go beyond her most personal duties.❞

23. What does this quote reveal about the woman's role in Protestant society?
24. What do you think Luther meant by the statement "The woman on the other hand is like a nail driven into the wall"?

Applying Technology Skills

25. **Using the Internet** Use the Internet to research a Renaissance artist. Find information about the person's life and achievements. Using your research, take on the role of that person and create an autobiography about your life and your contributions to the Renaissance.

Making Decisions

26. Select two of the following types of Renaissance people: a noble, merchant, shopkeeper, or peasant. Research what life was like for these individuals. How did their lives vary? Who had the more comfortable lifestyle? Take into account economic and social factors.

Analyzing Maps and Charts

27. Study the map at the top of the page. What are two of the bodies of water that border the Holy Roman Empire?
28. Using a contemporary atlas, name the modern countries that are within the boundaries of what was the Holy Roman Empire.
29. According to this map, was Rome a part of the Holy Roman Empire in 1400?

The Princeton Review

Standardized Test Practice

Directions: Use the passage below *and* your knowledge of world history to answer the following question.

from the Ninety-five Theses (1517)

Ignorant and wicked are the doings of those priests who, in the case of the dying, reserve canonical penances for purgatory.

Martin Luther's famous document attacked the Catholic Church for which practice?

F The Catholic Church had allowed humanism to spread through Europe.
G Luther disagreed with the doctrine of predestination.
H Many religious leaders sold indulgences.
J The Catholic popes were too concerned with worldly affairs.

Test-Taking Tip: If the question asks you to read a quote, look for clues that reveal its historical context. Such clues can be found in the title and date of the text as well as in the quote itself. Determining the historical context will help you to determine the quote's *historical significance* or the importance it has gained over time.

Chapter 5
Assessment and Activities

Have students visit the Web site at wh.mt.glencoe.com to review Chapter 5 and take the Self-Check Quiz.

Applying Technology Skills

25. Students will use the Internet to create a Renaissance autobiography.

Making Decisions

26. Answers will vary.

Analyzing Maps and Charts

27. North Sea, Mediterannean
28. Holland, Belgium, Luxembourg, Switzerland, Germany, Austria, parts of northern Italy
29. Rome was not a part of the Holy Roman Empire in 1400.

Standardized Test Practice

Answer: H
Test-Taking Tip: Read the title as well as the quote, then choose an answer.

Bonus Question ?

Ask: What factors lead to major changes in the structures of society, such as religion? *(education, technology, political strife)*

Writing About History

22. Answers will vary. Politically, the Reformation led to a power struggle between the Holy Roman Emperor and the German princes. It affected the religious life of Europe by introducing alternatives to Roman Catholicism, and by spurring a reformation within the Catholic Church to get rid of corruption.

Analyzing Sources

23. that her place was in the home, looking after household affairs
24. Answers will vary but should be supported by logic. It sounds as though Luther thought that women should remain at home.

Chapter 6 Resources

Timesaving Tools

TeacherWorks™ All-In-One Planner and Resource Center

- **Interactive Teacher Edition** Access your Teacher Wraparound Edition and your classroom resources with a few easy clicks.
- **Interactive Lesson Planner** Planning has never been easier! Organize your week, month, semester, or year with all the lesson helps you need to make teaching creative, timely, and relevant.

Use Glencoe's **Presentation Plus!** multimedia teacher tool to easily present dynamic lessons that visually excite your students. Using Microsoft PowerPoint® you can customize the presentations to create your own personalized lessons.

TEACHING TRANSPARENCIES

Graphic Organizer Student Activity 6 Transparency

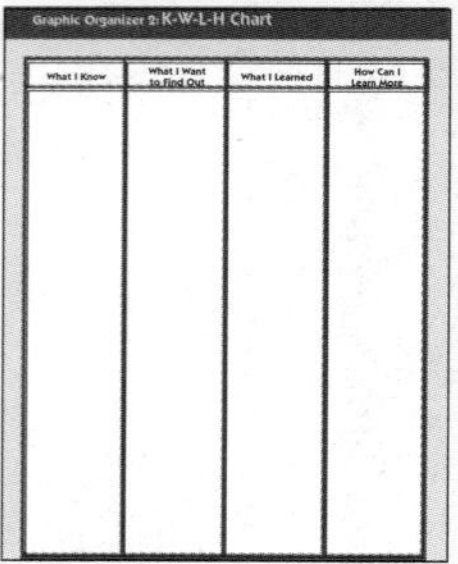

Chapter Transparency 6

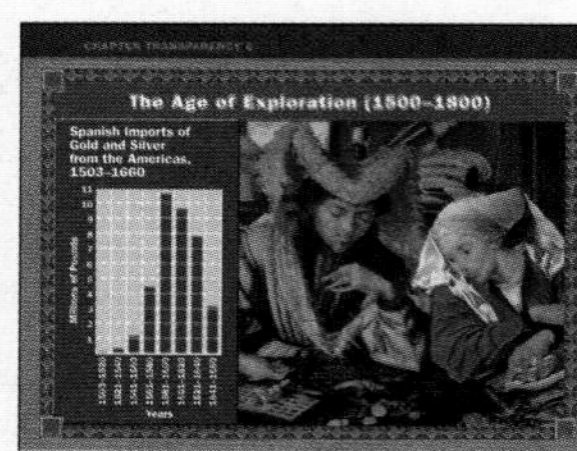

Map Overlay Transparency 6

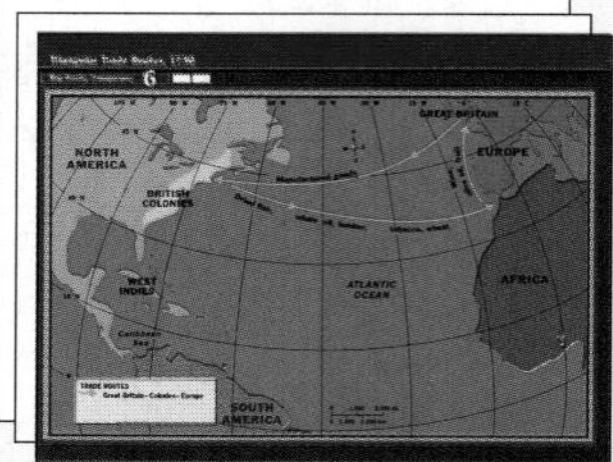

APPLICATION AND ENRICHMENT

Enrichment Activity 6

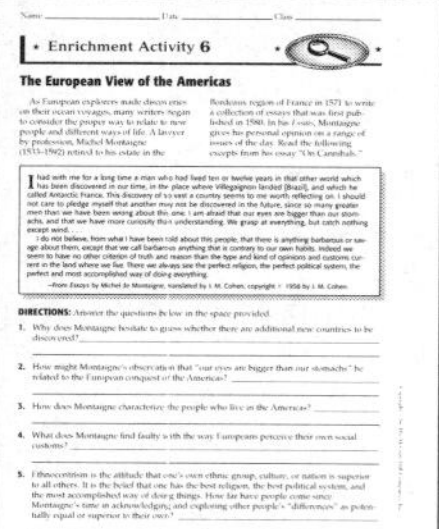

Primary Source Reading 6

History Simulation Activity 6

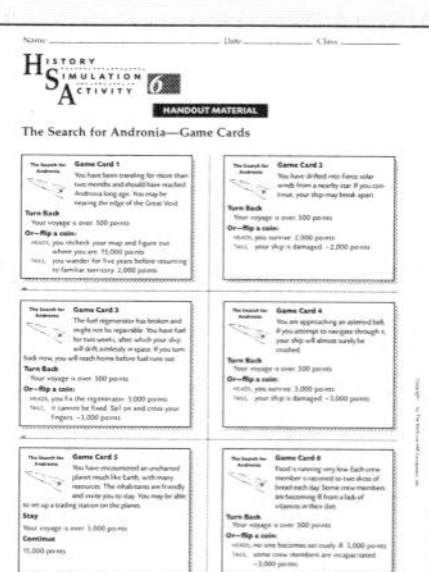

Historical Significance Activity 6

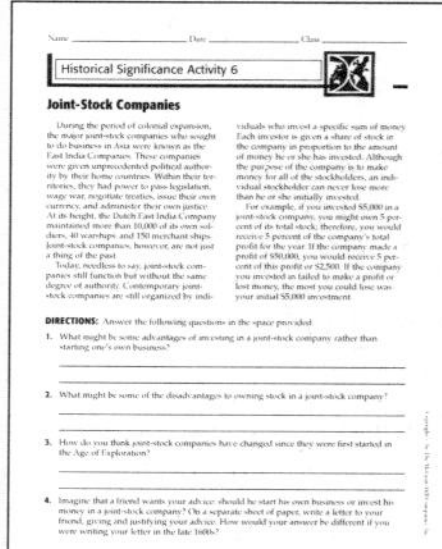

Cooperative Learning Activity 6

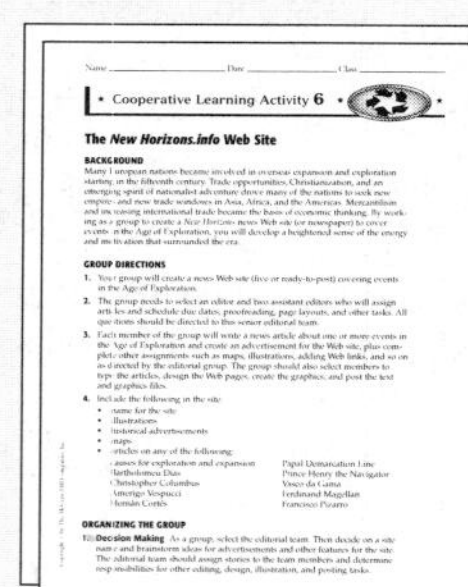

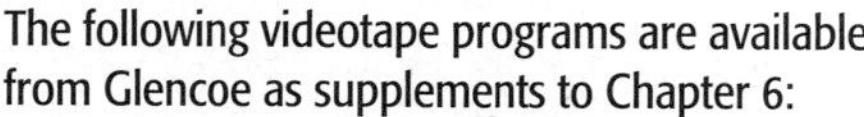

THE HISTORY CHANNEL.

The following videotape programs are available from Glencoe as supplements to Chapter 6:

- **Christopher Columbus: Explorer of the New World** (ISBN 1–56501–667–X)
- **Ponce de Leon: The First Conquistador** (ISBN 1–56501–669–6)

To order, call Glencoe at 1–800–334–7344. To find classroom resources to accompany many of these videos, check the following home pages:
A&E Television: www.aande.com
The History Channel: www.historychannel.com

Chapter 6 Resources

Review and Reinforcement

Linking Past and Present Activity 6

Time Line Activity 6

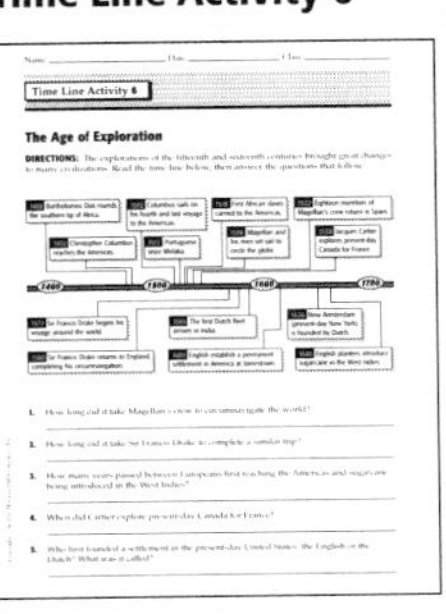

Reteaching Activity 6

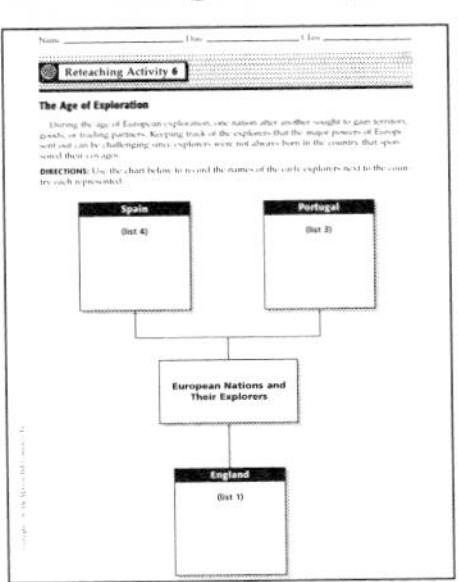

Vocabulary Activity 6

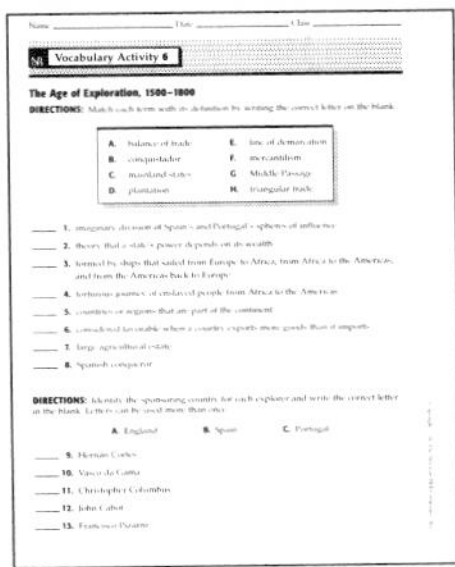

Critical Thinking Skills Activity 6

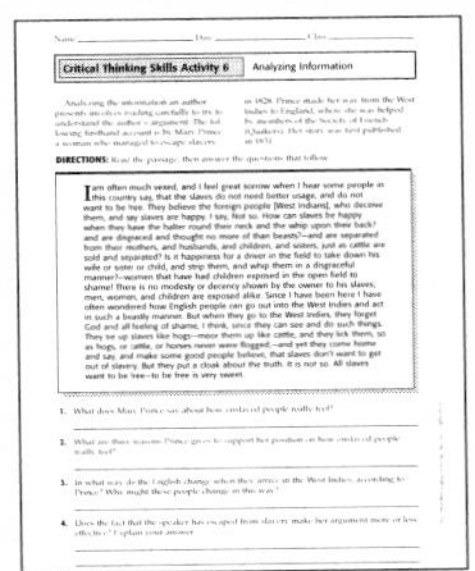

Assessment and Evaluation

Chapter 6 Test Form A

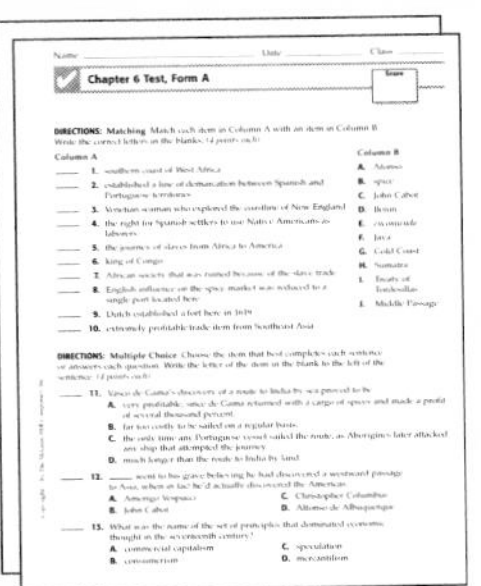

Chapter 6 Test Form B

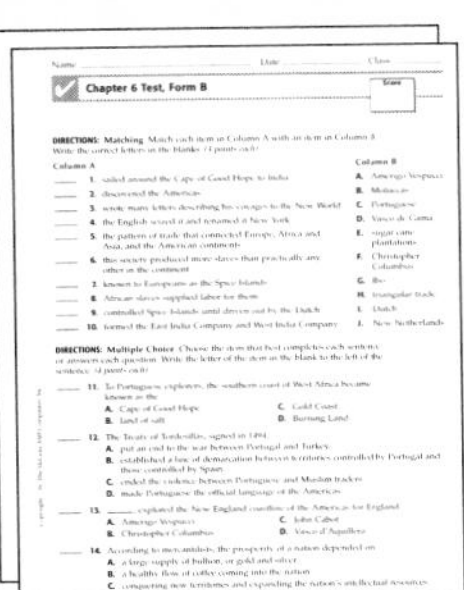

Performance Assessment Activity 6

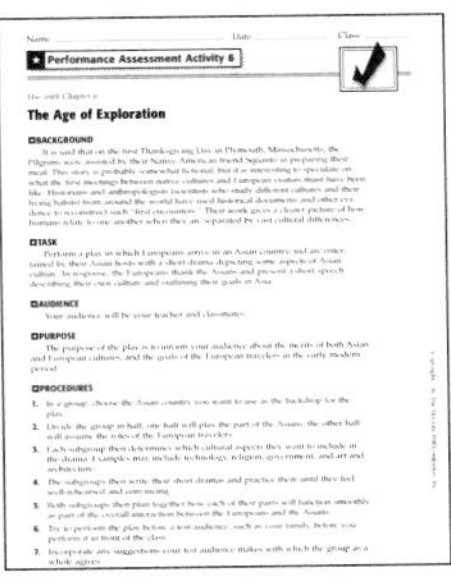

ExamView® Pro Testmaker CD-ROM

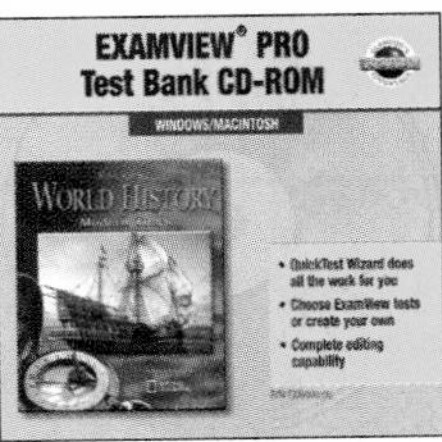

Standardized Test Skills Practice Workbook Activity 6

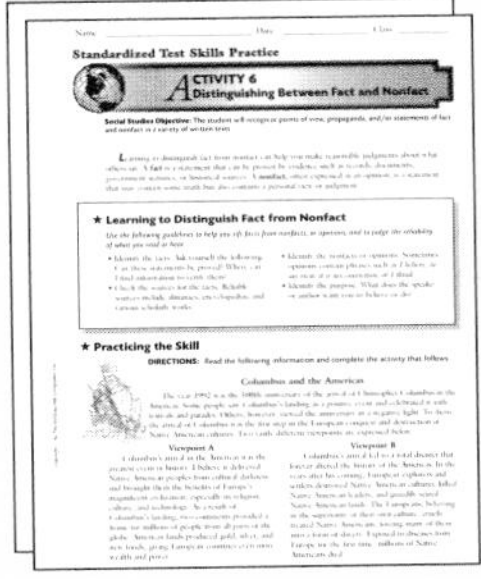

Interdisciplinary Activities

Mapping History Activity 6

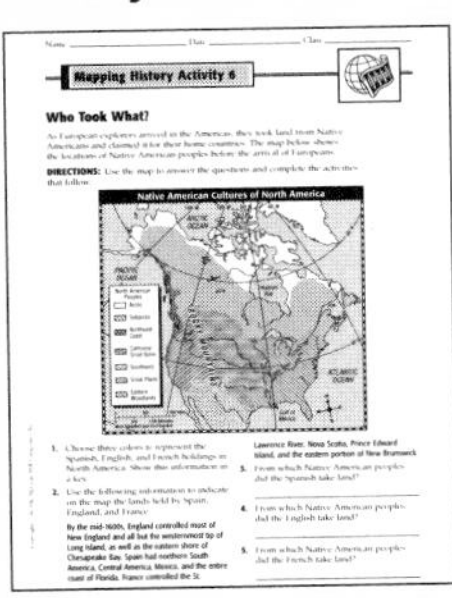

World Art and Music Activity 6

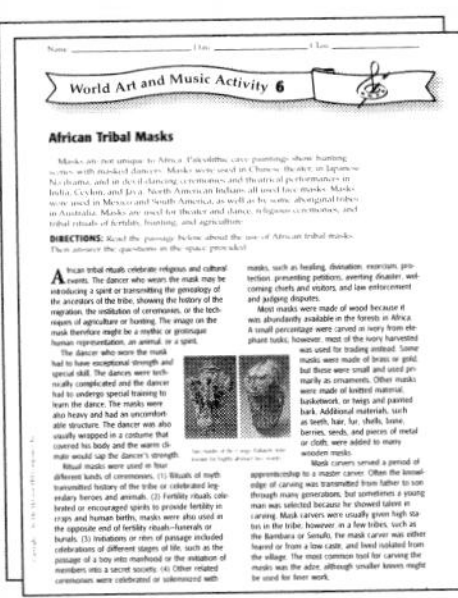

History and Geography Activity 6

People in World History Activity 6

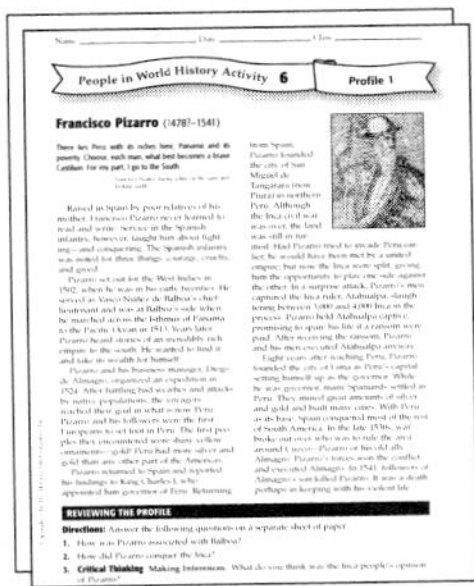

Multimedia

- Vocabulary PuzzleMaker CD-ROM
- Interactive Tutor Self-Assessment CD-ROM
- ExamView® Pro Testmaker CD-ROM
- Audio Program
- World History Primary Source Document Library CD-ROM
- MindJogger Videoquiz
- Presentation Plus! CD-ROM
- TeacherWorks CD-ROM
- Interactive Student Edition CD-ROM
- The World History—Modern Times Video Program

Spanish Resources

The following Spanish language materials are available in the Spanish Resources Binder:

- Spanish Guided Reading Activities
- Spanish Reteaching Activities
- Spanish Quizzes and Tests
- Spanish Vocabulary Activities
- Spanish Summaries

Chapter 6 Resources

SECTION RESOURCES

Daily Objectives	Reproducible Resources	Multimedia Resources
SECTION 1 **Exploration and Expansion** 1. Discuss how in the fifteenth century, Europeans began to explore the world. 2. Summarize how Portugal, Spain, the Dutch Republic, and England reached new economic heights through worldwide trade.	Reproducible Lesson Plan 6–1 Daily Lecture and Discussion Notes 6–1 Guided Reading Activity 6–1* Section Quiz 6–1* Reading Essentials and Study Guide 6–1	Daily Focus Skills Transparency 6–1 Interactive Tutor Self-Assessment CD-ROM ExamView® Pro Testmaker CD-ROM Presentation Plus! CD-ROM
SECTION 2 **Africa in an Age of Transition** 1. Explain how European expansion affected Africa with the dramatic increase of the slave trade. 2. Characterize the traditional political systems and cultures that continued to exist in most of Africa.	Reproducible Lesson Plan 6–2 Daily Lecture and Discussion Notes 6–2 Guided Reading Activity 6–2* Section Quiz 6–2* Reading Essentials and Study Guide 6–2	Daily Focus Skills Transparency 6–2 Interactive Tutor Self-Assessment CD-ROM ExamView® Pro Testmaker CD-ROM Presentation Plus! CD-ROM
SECTION 3 **Southeast Asia in the Era of the Spice Trade** 1. Summarize the Portuguese occupation of the Moluccas in search of spices and how the Dutch pushed the Portuguese out. 2. Relate how the arrival of the Europeans greatly affected the Malay.	Reproducible Lesson Plan 6–3 Daily Lecture and Discussion Notes 6–3 Guided Reading Activity 6–3* Section Quiz 6–3* Reteaching Activity 6* Reading Essentials and Study Guide 6–3	Daily Focus Skills Transparency 6–3 Interactive Tutor Self-Assessment CD-ROM ExamView® Pro Testmaker CD-ROM Presentation Plus! CD-ROM

0:00 **OUT OF TIME?**
Assign the Chapter 6 **Reading Essentials and Study Guide.**

*Also Available in Spanish

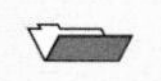 Blackline Master  Transparency 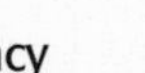 CD-ROM  DVD

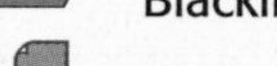 Poster 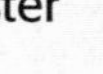 Music Program 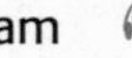 Audio Program  Videocassette

Chapter 6 Resources

Teacher's Corner

INDEX TO NATIONAL GEOGRAPHIC MAGAZINE

The following articles relate to this chapter:

- "La Salle's Last Voyage," by Lisa Moore LaRoe, May 1997.
- "San Diego: An Account of Adventure, Deceit, and Intrigue," by Frank Goddio, July 1994.
- "African Slave Trade: The Cruelest Commerce," by Colin Palmer, September 1992.
- "Portugal's Sea Road to the East," by Merle Severy, November 1982.
- "La Isabela: Europe's First Foothold in the New World," by Kathleen A. Deagan, January 1992.
- "Pizarro: Conqueror of the Inca," by John Hemming, February 1992.
- "Track of the Manila Galleons," by Eugene Lyon, September 1990.

NATIONAL GEOGRAPHIC SOCIETY PRODUCTS AVAILABLE FROM GLENCOE

To order the following products call Glencoe at 1-800-334-7344:

- *PictureShow: The Age of Exploration, 1 & 2* (CD-ROM)
- *Age of Exploration* (Transparencies)

NGS ONLINE

Access National Geographic's new dynamic MapMachine Web site and other geography resources at:
www.nationalgeographic.com
www.nationalgeographic.com/maps

KEY TO ABILITY LEVELS

Teaching strategies have been coded.

- **L1** BASIC activities for all students
- **L2** AVERAGE activities for average to above-average students
- **L3** CHALLENGING activities for above-average students
- **ELL** ENGLISH LANGUAGE LEARNER activities

Block Schedule

Activities that are suited to use within the block scheduling framework are identified by:

Use our Web site for additional resources. All essential content is covered in the Student Edition.

You and your students can visit www.wh.mt.glencoe.com, the Web site companion to *Glencoe World History—Modern Times.* This innovative integration of electronic and print media offers your students a wealth of opportunities. The student text directs students to the Web site for the following options:

- **Chapter Overviews**
- **Self-Check Quizzes**
- **Student Web Activities**
- **Textbook Updates**

Answers to the Student Web Activities are provided for you in the **Web Activity Lesson Plans.** Additional Web resources and Interactive Tutor Puzzles are also available.

From the Classroom of...

Scott Shephard
Watertown Senior High School
Watertown, South Dakota

Why We Explore

Encourage students to think about the general reasons humans explore. This activity also encourages students to compare the motives of explorers from the Age of Exploration with those of explorers from other eras of investigation.

On the board, write the following headings: *Motives, Risks,* and *Significant Gains.* Ask students what they know about Christopher Columbus and fill in the chart with facts about his explorations.

Next, give students a list of famous explorers such as Neil Armstrong, Lewis and Clark, Yury Gagarin, Marco Polo, and Edmund Hillary. Have students use classroom resources to find out about these people, then add facts about them to the chart on the board.

As a follow-up activity, ask students to draw some generalizations about the following: Why do we explore? Do the risks of exploration ever outweigh the gains? Was Columbus's voyage riskier than the *Apollo 11* moon mission? As a final evaluation, you might ask students to write an essay that compares and contrasts the motives, risks, and gains of Columbus with another explorer.

Introducing
CHAPTER 6

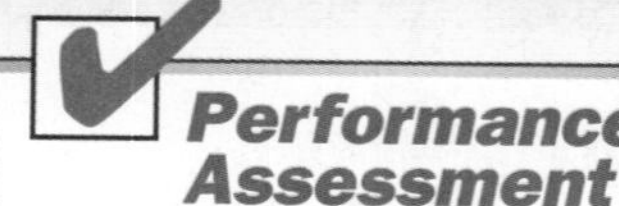

Performance Assessment

Refer to Activity 6 in the Performance Assessment Activities and Rubrics booklet.

The Impact Today

Today, people continue to explore the mysteries of Earth (oceans, jungles) and of space. Have students discuss how present-day exploration has benefited areas such as medicine and technology.

GLENCOE TECHNOLOGY

The World History—Modern Times Video Program

To learn more about the age of exploration students can view the Chapter 6 video, "Magellan's Voyage," from **The World History—Modern Times Video Program.**

MindJogger Videoquiz

Use the **MindJogger Videoquiz** to preview Chapter 6 content.

Available in VHS.

CHAPTER 6

The Age of Exploration

1500–1800

Key Events

As you read this chapter, look for the key events of the Age of Exploration.

- *Europeans risked dangerous ocean voyages to discover new sea routes.*
- *Early European explorers sought gold in Africa then began to trade slaves.*
- *Trade increased in Southeast Asia, and the Dutch built a trade empire based on spices in the Indonesian Archipelago.*

The Impact Today

The events that occurred during this time period still impact our lives today.

- *European trade was a factor in producing a new age of commercial capitalism that was one of the first steps toward today's world economy.*
- *The consequences of slavery continue to impact our lives today.*
- *The Age of Exploration led to a transfer of ideas and products, many of which are still important in our lives today.*

World History—Modern Times Video *The Chapter 6 video, "Magellan's Voyage," chronicles European exploration of the world.*

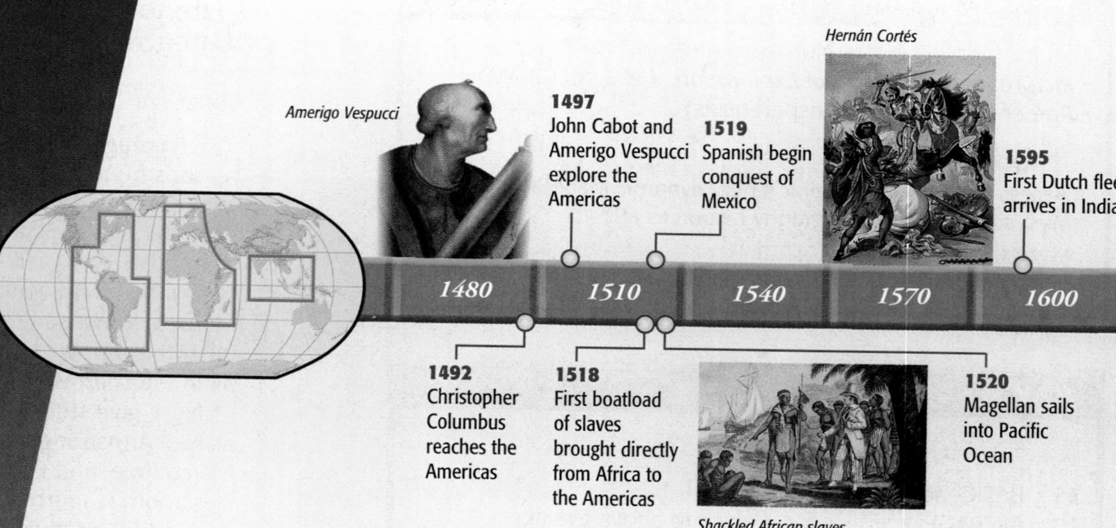

Hernán Cortés
Amerigo Vespucci
1497 John Cabot and Amerigo Vespucci explore the Americas
1519 Spanish begin conquest of Mexico
1595 First Dutch fleet arrives in India
1480
1510
1540
1570
1600
1492 Christopher Columbus reaches the Americas
1518 First boatload of slaves brought directly from Africa to the Americas
1520 Magellan sails into Pacific Ocean
Shackled African slaves

186

TWO-MINUTE LESSON LAUNCHER

To understand the appeal of exploration between 1500 and 1800, have students consider the reasons behind present-day space exploration. Ask students why people want to become astronauts and explore outer space? On the board write the headings *Motives, Risks,* and *Significant Gains.* Have the students share their ideas about the reasons why Europeans would have wanted to explore, the risks they faced, and the gains they made through exploration. **L1**

Ships of the Dutch East India Company

1630
English found Massachusetts Bay Colony

c. 1650
Dutch occupy Portuguese forts in Indian Ocean trading areas

c. 1700
English establish colonial empire in North America

1630 *1660* *1690* *1720* *1750*

1767
Burmese sack Thai capital

World map, 1630

HISTORY Online

Chapter Overview
Visit the *Glencoe World History—Modern Times* Web site at wh.mt.glencoe.com and click on **Chapter 6–Chapter Overview** to preview chapter information.

187

Introducing CHAPTER 6

Chapter Objectives

After studying this chapter, students should be able to:

1. explain the three main motives for exploration;
2. trace the development and decline of Portugal's trading empire and Spanish exploration;
3. describe the impact of Europeans on the peoples of Africa;
4. describe traditional African political systems;
5. discuss the shift in power from Portuguese to Dutch in the control of the spice trade;
6. contrast the impact of Europeans on mainland states of Southeast Asia with their impact on the Malay world;
7. describe the four main political systems in Southeast Asia.

HISTORY Online

Chapter Overview
Introduce students to chapter content and key terms by having them access **Chapter Overview 6** at wh.mt.glencoe.com.

Time Line Activity

As they read this chapter, have students examine the time line on these pages. Ask students to explain the significance of the date 1492. **L1**

MORE ABOUT THE ART

Dutch Shipping In 1602, the Dutch parliament granted a charter to the Dutch East India Company. As this company prospered, Dutch merchants increasingly replaced Portuguese traders in India and Southeast Asia. By the middle of the seventeenth century, the Netherlands was the primary commercial power in Europe. During this same period, the Dutch experienced a Golden Age in art. Wealthy Dutch merchants became patrons of the arts and encouraged artists to paint pictures that depicted the sea and shipping. This oil painting of the Dutch East India Company captures the commercial spirit that made the Netherlands such a powerful force in seventeenth-century trade.

CHAPTER PREVIEW

Introducing

A Story That Matters

Depending on the ability level of your students, select from the following questions to reinforce the reading of *A Story That Matters.*

- What was Magellan's goal when he set sail on August 10, 1519 *(passage to Asia by going west)*
- Given the details of the story, what words would students use to describe the voyage? *(dangerous, scary, miserable)*
- Why do students think sailors agreed to such voyages through unknown waters? *(fame, wealth, adventure)* **L1 L2**

About the Art

The picture shows Magellan's ships carefully navigating their way through the rocky islands that were scattered through the narrow passageway now called the Strait of Magellan. The Strait is narrow and experiences high winds, fog, and rain throughout the year. Until the opening of the Panama Canal in 1914, the Strait of Magellan remained an import route for sailing ships.

CHAPTER PREVIEW

A Story That Matters

Ferdinand Magellan

Discovery of Magellan Strait *by an unknown artist*

Magellan Sails Around the World

Convinced that he could find a sea passage to Asia through the Western Hemisphere, the Portuguese explorer Ferdinand Magellan persuaded the king of Spain to finance his voyage. On August 10, 1519, Magellan set sail on the Atlantic Ocean with five ships and a Spanish crew of 277 men.

After reaching South America, Magellan's fleet moved down the coast in search of a strait, or sea passage, that would take them through America. His Spanish ship captains thought he was crazy: "The fool is obsessed with his search for a strait," one remarked.

At last, in October 1520, Magellan passed through a narrow waterway (later named the Strait of Magellan) and emerged in the Pacific Ocean, which he called the Pacific Sea. Magellan reckoned that it would be a short distance from there to the Spice Islands of the East.

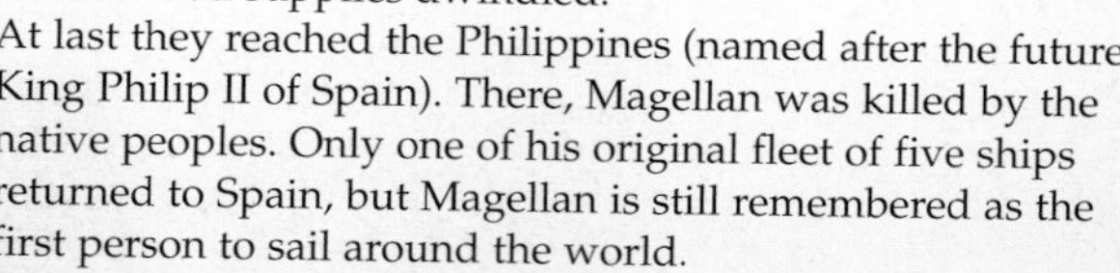

Week after week he and his crew sailed on across the Pacific as their food supplies dwindled. At last they reached the Philippines (named after the future King Philip II of Spain). There, Magellan was killed by the native peoples. Only one of his original fleet of five ships returned to Spain, but Magellan is still remembered as the first person to sail around the world.

Why It Matters

At the beginning of the sixteenth century, European adventurers launched their small fleets into the vast reaches of the Atlantic Ocean. They were hardly aware that they were beginning a new era, not only for Europe but also for the peoples of Asia, Africa, and the Americas. These European voyages marked the beginning of a process that led to radical changes in the political, economic, and cultural life of the entire non-Western world.

History and You Create a map to scale that shows Spain, South America, and the Philippines. Draw the route Magellan took from Spain to the Philippines. If the voyage took about 20 months, how many miles each day, on average, did Magellan travel? How long would a similar sea voyage take today?

HISTORY AND YOU

The discovery that one could sail around the southern tip of South America had a great impact on exploration and trade. Magellan himself did not actually complete this journey but died in the Philippines. Have students research the crew's journey from the Philippines to the Spice Islands and back to Spain. Who made it home safely? What happened to the other ships? What route did they take back to Spain? Students should also discuss how this voyage impacted commercial trade for the next several hundred years. Students should use primary and secondary sources and prepare a brief written report. **L2**

SECTION 1 Exploration and Expansion

Guide to Reading

Main Ideas
- In the fifteenth century, Europeans began to explore the world.
- Portugal, Spain, the Dutch Republic, and England reached new economic heights through worldwide trade.

Key Terms
conquistador, colony, mercantilism, balance of trade

People to Identify
Vasco da Gama, Christopher Columbus, John Cabot, Amerigo Vespucci, Francisco Pizarro, Ferdinand Magellan

Places to Locate
Portugal, Africa, Melaka, Cuba

Preview Questions
1. Why did Europeans travel to Asia?
2. What impact did European expansion have on the conquerors and the conquered?

Reading Strategy
Summarizing Information Use a chart like the one below to list reasons why Melaka, a port on the Malay Peninsula, was important to the Portuguese.

Importance of Melaka

Preview of Events

1450 · 1500 · 1550 · 1600 · 1650 · 1700

- **1488** Bartholomeu Dias rounds the Cape of Good Hope
- **1500** Pedro Cabral lands in South America
- **1550** Spanish gain control of northern Mexico
- **1630** English found Massachusetts Bay Colony

Voices from the Past

Christopher Columbus

In a letter to the treasurer of the king and queen of Spain, Christopher Columbus reported on his first journey:

> ❝Believing that you will rejoice at the glorious success that our Lord has granted me in my voyage, I write this to tell you how in thirty-three days I reached the Indies with the first fleet which the most illustrious King and Queen, our Sovereigns, gave me, where I discovered a great many thickly-populated islands. Without meeting resistance, I have taken possession of them all for their Highnesses. . . . When I reached [Cuba], I followed its coast to the westward, and found it so large that I thought it must be the mainland—the province of [China], but I found neither towns nor villages on the seacoast, save for a few hamlets.❞
>
> —***Letters from the First Voyage,*** **edited 1847**

To the end of his life, despite the evidence, Columbus believed he had found a new route to Asia.

Motives and Means

The dynamic energy of Western civilization between 1500 and 1800 was most apparent when Europeans began to expand into the rest of the world. First Portugal and Spain, then later the Dutch Republic, England, and France, all rose to new economic heights through their worldwide trading activity.

1 FOCUS

Section Overview

After reading this section, students should know the major European explorers and understand their accomplishments.

BELLRINGER
Skillbuilder Activity

Project transparency and have students answer questions.

Available as a blackline master.

Daily Focus Skills Transparency 6–1

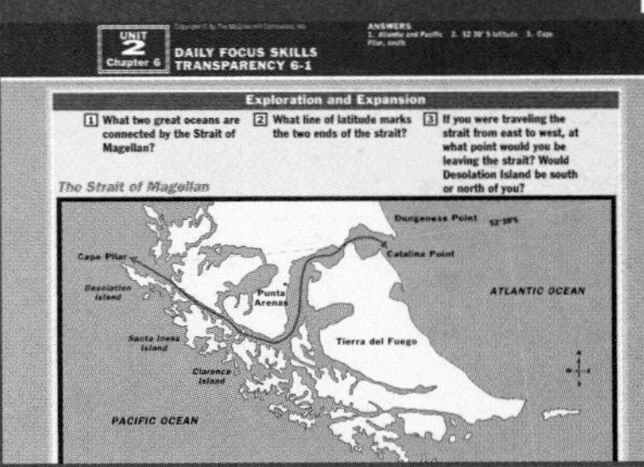

Guide to Reading

Answers to Graphic: strategically located, control could destroy Arab spice trade, gave Portuguese a way station en route to Spice Islands

Preteaching Vocabulary: Have students find the meaning of the Latin root of the word *mercantilism* and come up with two other words that come from the same root. *(mercari—to trade; merchant, merchandise)* **L1**

SECTION RESOURCES

Reproducible Masters
- Reproducible Lesson Plan 6–1
- Daily Lecture and Discussion Notes 6–1
- Guided Reading Activity 6–1
- Section Quiz 6–1
- Reading Essentials and Study Guide 6–1

Transparencies
- Daily Focus Skills Transparency 6–1

Multimedia
- Interactive Tutor Self-Assessment CD-ROM
- ExamView® Pro Testmaker CD-ROM
- Presentation Plus! CD-ROM

2 TEACH

Geography Skills

Answers:

1. Based on map, Australia and Antarctica
2. Tables will vary, should include explorer, date, sponsoring country, and area explored.

Daily Lecture and Discussion Notes 6–1

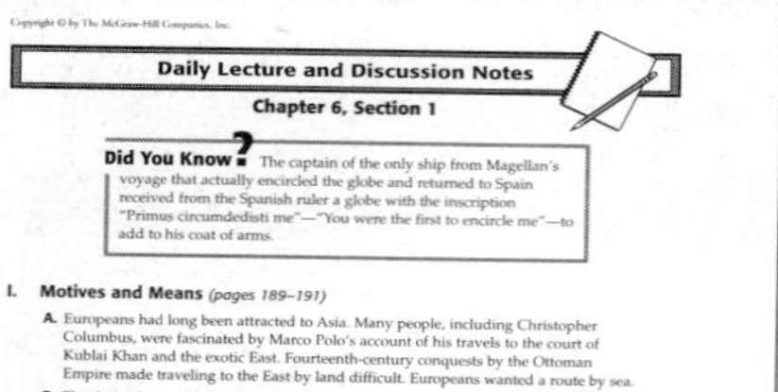

Copyright © by The McGraw-Hill Companies, Inc.

Daily Lecture and Discussion Notes

Chapter 6, Section 1

Did You Know? The captain of the only ship from Magellan's voyage that actually encircled the globe and returned to Spain received from the Spanish ruler a globe with the inscription "Primus circumdedisti me"—"You were the first to encircle me"—to add to his coat of arms.

I. **Motives and Means** *(pages 189–191)*

A. Europeans had long been attracted to Asia. Many people, including Christopher Columbus, were fascinated by Marco Polo's account of his travels to the court of Kublai Khan and the exotic East. Fourteenth-century conquests by the Ottoman Empire made traveling to the East by land difficult. Europeans wanted a route by sea.

B. The desire for wealth was a large part of European expansion. Merchants, adventurers, and government officials hoped to find precious metals in and expand trade with the

Enrich

Have students discuss why spices were especially prized by Europeans. *(needed to keep food from rotting; desired adding flavor)*

CURRICULUM CONNECTION

Science Have students research Europeans' understanding of wind currents, which helped them make long voyages. Ask them to draw or bring in diagrams explaining exactly how the compass and astrolabe work. **L2**

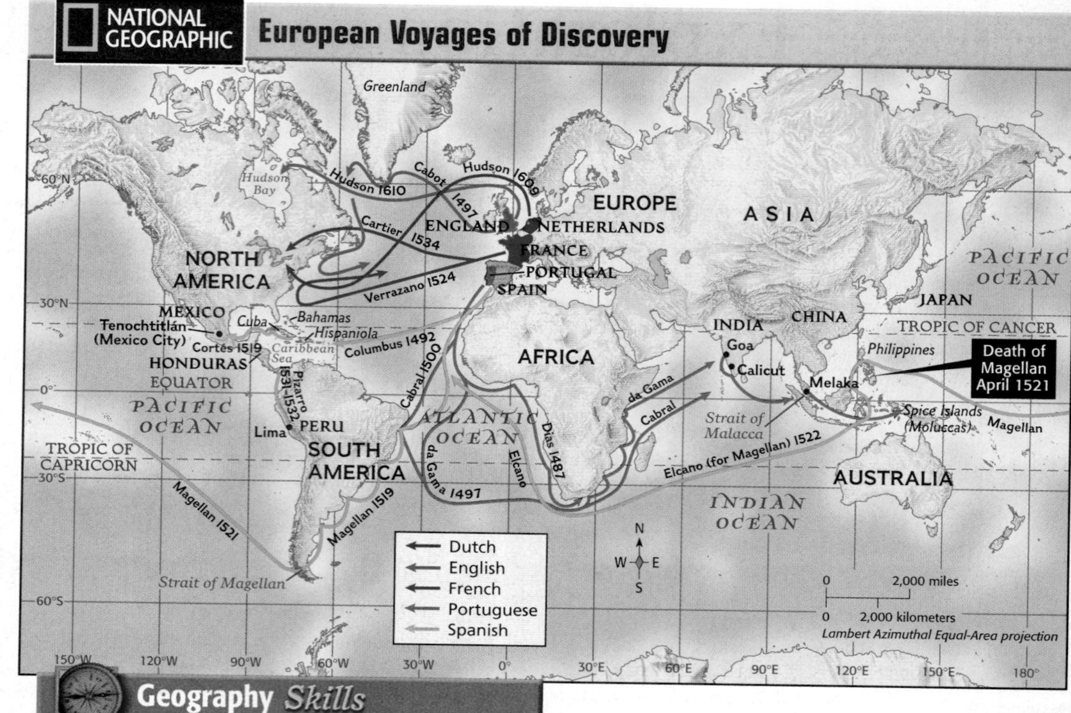

Geography Skills

For more than a hundred years European explorers sailed the globe searching for wealth and glory.

1. **Interpreting Maps** Which continents were left untouched by European explorers?
2. **Applying Geography Skills** Create a table that organizes the information on this map. Include the explorer, date, sponsoring country, and area explored.

For almost a thousand years, Europeans had mostly remained in one area of the world. At the end of the fifteenth century, however, they set out on a remarkable series of overseas journeys. What caused them to undertake such dangerous voyages to the ends of the earth?

Europeans had long been attracted to Asia. In the late thirteenth century, Marco Polo had traveled with his father and uncle to the Chinese court of the great Mongol ruler Kublai Khan. He had written an account of his experiences, known as *The Travels.* The book was read by many, including Columbus, who were fascinated by the exotic East. In the fourteenth century, conquests by the Ottoman Turks reduced the ability of westerners to travel by land to the East. People then spoke of gaining access to Asia by sea.

Economic motives loom large in European expansion. Merchants, adventurers, and state officials had high hopes of expanding trade, especially for the spices of the East. The spices, which were needed to preserve and flavor food, were very expensive after being shipped to Europe by Arab middlemen. Europeans also had hopes of finding precious metals. One Spanish adventurer wrote that he went to the Americas "to give light to those who were in darkness, and to grow rich, as all men desire to do."

This statement suggests another reason for the overseas voyages: religious zeal. Many people shared the belief of Hernán Cortés, the Spanish conqueror of Mexico, that they must ensure that the natives "are introduced into the holy Catholic faith."

There was a third motive as well. Spiritual and secular affairs were connected in the sixteenth century. Adventurers such as Cortés wanted to convert the natives to Christianity, but grandeur, glory, and a spirit of adventure also played a major role in European expansion.

"God, glory, and gold," then, were the chief motives for European expansion, but what made the voyages possible? By the second half of the fifteenth century, European monarchies had increased their

INTERDISCIPLINARY CONNECTIONS ACTIVITY

Geography Using a world map or globe, have students locate Portugal, Spain, the Netherlands, England, France, North and South America, the islands of the Caribbean, Africa, the East Indies (now Indonesia), India, and the Philippines. Into what three major oceans are the great waters of the world divided? Which ocean is the largest and which the smallest? *(Pacific, Atlantic, Indian; The Pacific is the largest and the Indian is the smallest.)* Have students note the distance from Europe to India, the islands of Indonesia, and the coast of the Americas. **L1** ELL

power and their resources. They could now turn their energies beyond their borders. Europeans had also reached a level of technology that enabled them to make a regular series of voyages beyond Europe. A new global age was about to begin.

Reading Check **Explaining** What does the phrase "God, glory, and gold" mean?

The Portuguese Trading Empire

Portugal took the lead in European exploration. Beginning in 1420, under the sponsorship of Prince Henry the Navigator, Portuguese fleets began probing southward along the western coast of **Africa.** There, they discovered a new source of gold. The southern coast of West Africa thus became known to Europeans as the Gold Coast.

Portuguese sea captains heard reports of a route to India around the southern tip of Africa. In 1488, Bartholomeu Dias rounded the tip, called the Cape of Good Hope. Later, **Vasco da Gama** went around the cape and cut across the Indian Ocean to the coast of India. In May of 1498, he arrived off the port of Calicut, where he took on a cargo of spices. He returned to Portugal and made a profit of several thousand percent. Is it surprising that da Gama's voyage was the first of many along this route?

Portuguese fleets returned to the area to destroy Muslim shipping and to gain control of the spice trade, which had been controlled by the Muslims. In

SCIENCE, TECHNOLOGY & SOCIETY

Sea Travel in an Age of Exploration

European voyagers acquired much of their knowledge about sailing from the Arabs. For example, sailors used charts that Arab navigators and mathematicians had drawn in the thirteenth and fourteenth centuries. Known as *portolani,* these charts recorded the shapes of coastlines and distances between ports. They were very valuable in European waters. Because the charts were drawn on a flat scale and took no account of the curvature of the earth, however, they were of little help on overseas voyages.

Only as sailors began to move beyond the coasts of Europe did they gain information about the actual shape of the earth. By 1500, cartography—the art and science of mapmaking—had reached the point where Europeans had fairly accurate maps of the areas they had explored.

Europeans also learned new navigational techniques from the Arabs. Previously, sailors had used the position of the North Star to determine their latitude. Below the Equator, though, this technique was useless. The compass and the astrolabe (also perfected by the Arabs) greatly aided exploration. The compass showed in what direction a ship was moving. The astrolabe used the sun or a star to ascertain a ship's latitude.

Finally, European shipmakers learned how to use lateen (triangular) sails, which were developed by the Arabs. New ships, called caravels, were more maneuverable and could carry heavy cannon and more goods.

Evaluating ***Which one advance was the most important for early explorers? Why?***

Caravel (small fifteenth- and sixteenth-century ship)

Cargo hold

Early compass

Map of the world, 1571

Reading Check

Answer: chief motives for European expansion: to convert the natives, for adventure, and for the riches that could be obtained

SCIENCE, TECHNOLOGY & SOCIETY

Answer: Answers will vary.

Guided Reading Activity 6–1

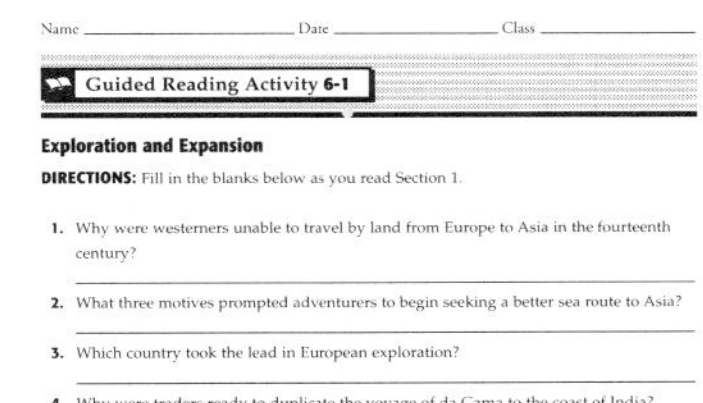

Name ______ Date ______ Class ______

Guided Reading Activity 6-1

Exploration and Expansion

DIRECTIONS: Fill in the blanks below as you read Section 1.

1. Why were westerners unable to travel by land from Europe to Asia in the fourteenth century?
2. What three motives prompted adventurers to begin seeking a better sea route to Asia?
3. Which country took the lead in European exploration?
4. Why were traders ready to duplicate the voyage of da Gama to the coast of India?

Critical Thinking

Although Europeans made voyages in part to "destroy Muslim shipping" and to convert "heathens," most of their sailing knowledge came from the Arabs. Ask students to research Arab technology. How did the Europeans acquire it? Did the Arabs make any effort to keep their knowledge secret? Did they themselves use what they discovered? **L2**

Writing Activity

Have students write a brief essay in which they identify the causes of European expansion beginning in the sixteenth century. **L1**

COOPERATIVE LEARNING ACTIVITY

Creating a Research Report Early Spanish and Portuguese explorers encountered many different cultures in the Americas (including Arawak, Carib, Maya, Aztec, Inca). Organize the class into small groups and have each group research and report on one of the indigenous American cultures. Each student should be assigned one of the following areas to research: geographic location and method of subsistence, arts and crafts, religious beliefs, customs, and the effect of European contact on the culture. Reports should be graded on how well students explain the political, economic, cultural and technological influence of European expansion on American cultures. One or more students may illustrate the report. **L2**

Reading Check

Answer: It would help destroy Arab control of the spice trade and provide the Portuguese a way station on the way to the Spice Islands.

ABCNEWS INTERACTIVE™

Turning Points in World History
The ABC News videotape includes a segment on the Age of Exploration.

CURRICULUM CONNECTION

Literature Have students read an excerpt from one of Columbus's journals. Discuss what the excerpt reveals about Columbus and his times. You might wish to ask other volunteers to read historical accounts of Columbus's journey that were written during differing time periods. Have students share what they learned and explore reasons for differences in these accounts with the class. **L2**

Critical Thinking

Have students identify and discuss the changes that resulted from the European age of exploration. Ask students to take notes as they read the chapter. From their notes have students describe the defining characteristics of this era. **L1**

1509, a Portuguese fleet of warships defeated a combined fleet of Turkish and Indian ships off the coast of India. A year later, Admiral Afonso de Albuquerque set up a port at Goa, on the western coast of India.

The Portuguese then began to range more widely in search of the source of the spice trade. Soon, Albuquerque sailed into **Melaka** on the Malay Peninsula. Melaka was a thriving port for the spice trade. For Albuquerque, control of Melaka would help to destroy Arab control of the spice trade and provide the Portuguese with a way station on the route to the Moluccas, then known as the Spice Islands.

From Melaka, the Portuguese launched expeditions to China and the Spice Islands. There, they signed a treaty with a local ruler for the purchase and export of cloves to the European market. This treaty established Portuguese control of the spice trade. The Portuguese trading empire was complete. However, it remained a limited empire of trading posts. The Portuguese had neither the power, the people, nor the desire to colonize the Asian regions.

Why were the Portuguese the first successful European explorers? Basically it was a matter of guns and seamanship. Later, however, the Portuguese would be no match for other European forces—the English, Dutch, and French.

Reading Check **Explaining** Why did Afonso de Albuquerque want control of Melaka?

Voyages to the Americas

The Portuguese sailed eastward through the Indian Ocean to reach the source of the spice trade. The Spanish sought to reach it by sailing westward across the Atlantic Ocean. With more people and greater resources, the Spanish established an overseas empire that was quite different from the Portuguese trading posts.

Opposing Viewpoints

What Was the Impact of Columbus on the Americas?

Historians have differed widely over the impact of Columbus on world history. Was he a hero who ushered in economic well being throughout the world? Or, was he a prime mover in the destruction of the people and cultures of the Americas?

"The whole history of the Americas stems from the Four Voyages of Columbus. . . . Today a core of independent nations unite in homage to Christopher, the stout-hearted son of Genoa, who carried Christian civilization across the Ocean Sea."

—Samuel Eliot Morison, 194
Admiral of the Ocean Se
A Life of Christopher Columbu

"Just twenty-one years after Columbus's first landing in the Caribbean, the vastly populous island that the explorer had re-named Hispaniola was effectively desolate; nearly 8,000,000 people. . . had been killed by violence, disease, and despair. [W]hat happened on Hispaniola was the equivalent of more than fifty Hiroshimas.* And Hispaniola was only the beginning."

—David E. Stannard, 199
American Holocaust: Columbu
and the Conquest of the New Worl

*The atom bomb dropped on Hiroshima, Japan, killed at leas 130,000 people.

MEETING INDIVIDUAL NEEDS

Visual/Spatial Have students work in pairs or small groups to summarize in pictures on poster board the achievements of Portugal and Spain described in this section. Try to pair competent illustrators with verbally proficient students. Tell students to discuss how the pictures should best convey the information. After the picture or pictures have been sketched and colored in, the groups should write labels summarizing the information the pictures convey. Display completed posters in the classroom. **L1** ELL

Refer to ***Inclusion for the High School Social Studies Classroom Strategies and Activities*** in the TCR.

The Voyages of Columbus An important figure in the history of Spanish exploration was an Italian, **Christopher Columbus.** Educated Europeans knew that the world was round, but had little understanding of its circumference or of the size of the continent of Asia. Convinced that the circumference of Earth was not as great as others thought, Columbus believed that he could reach Asia by sailing west instead of east around Africa.

Columbus persuaded Queen Isabella of Spain to finance an exploratory expedition. In October 1492, he reached the Americas, where he explored the coastline of **Cuba** and the island of Hispaniola.

Columbus believed he had reached Asia. Through three more voyages, he sought in vain to find a route through the outer islands to the Asian mainland. In his four voyages, Columbus reached all the major islands of the Caribbean and Honduras in Central America—all of which he called the Indies.

Columbus petitions Queen Isabella for financial support of his explorations.

"When the two races first met on the eastern coast of America, there was unlimited potential for harmony. The newcomers could have adapted to the hosts' customs and values. . . . But this did not happen . . . [Columbus] viewed the natives of America with arrogance and disdain . . . Columbus wrote of gold, . . . and of spices, . . . and 'slaves, as many as they shall order to be shipped. . .'"

—George P. Horse Capture, 1992
"An American Indian Perspective," *Seeds of Change*

You Decide

1. Using information from the text and outside sources, write an account of Columbus's voyages from his point of view. If Columbus were to undertake his voyages today, would he do anything differently? If not, why not?
2. Using the information in the text and your own research, evaluate the validity of these three excerpts. Which excerpt corroborates the information of the other? What might account for the difference in the viewpoints expressed here?

A Line of Demarcation By the 1490s, then, the voyages of the Portuguese and Spanish had already opened up new lands to exploration. Both Spain and Portugal feared that the other might claim some of its newly discovered territories. They resolved their concerns by agreeing on a line of demarcation, an imaginary line that divided their spheres of influence.

According to the Treaty of Tordesillas (TAWR•duh•SEE•yuhs), signed in 1494, the line would extend from north to south through the Atlantic Ocean and the easternmost part of the South American continent. Unexplored territories east of the line would be controlled by Portugal, and those west of the line by Spain. This treaty gave Portugal control over its route around Africa, and it gave Spain rights to almost all of the Americas.

Race to the Americas Other explorers soon realized that Columbus had discovered an entirely new frontier. Government-sponsored explorers from many countries joined the race to the Americas. A Venetian seaman, **John Cabot,** explored the New England coastline of the Americas for England. The Portuguese sea captain Pedro Cabral landed in South America in 1500. **Amerigo Vespucci** (veh•SPOO•chee), a Florentine, went along on several voyages and wrote letters describing the lands he saw. These letters led to the use of the name *America* (after Amerigo) for the new lands.

Opposing Viewpoints

Answers:
1. Answers will vary, but should be supported by logical arguments.
2. The Morison viewpoint is the traditional Eurocentric viewpoint that sees the arrival of the Europeans as a positive "civilizing" influence; the other two focus primarily on the negative effects of Columbus's discovery on the civilizations he found in the Americas.

Citrus Florida's citrus industry can be traced back to Columbus's second voyage to the Americas in 1493. The citrus seeds the navigator brought to the West Indies took root there and eventually made their way to Mexico and Florida.

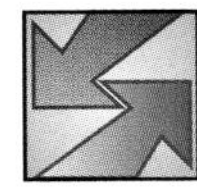

CURRICULUM CONNECTION

Science Ask interested students to research the impact of contagious diseases on Native American populations. How is immunity to such diseases built up? Were Europeans affected by American diseases? **L2**

Enrich

Have students use library resources to research the expeditions of one of the famous European explorers. Then have them prepare a script about the explorer's expedition. **L3**

EXTENDING THE CONTENT

Navigation In ancient times, sailors used the constellations and seasonal wind directions to navigate their ships. In the Middle Ages, sailors drew up charts that included sample calculations of wind directions for the different seasons. The invention of both the astrolabe and the compass had a combined impact on ancient civilization that somewhat mirrors the impact of radio on modern civilization. Sailors at last found an accurate way to measure the angle and movement of stars. Now, if a ship were blown off course by a storm, the astrolabe could show sailors how far they had drifted. The sextant, a device still used in modern-day navigation, was developed from the astrolabe.

CHAPTER 6
Section 1, 189–195

Reading Check

Answer: Each was afraid that the other might try to claim some of its newly discovered territories.

Reading Check

Answer: The majority of the natives quickly died off as a result of violence, forced labor, starvation, and disease.

TURNING POINT

How did governments respond to the new age of commercial capitalism? *(granted subsidies, improved transportation, higher taxes)* Ask students how international trade resulting from the Age of Exploration differed from earlier trade along the Silk Road. **L1**

3 ASSESS

Assign Section 1 Assessment as homework or as an in-class activity.

Have students use **Interactive Tutor Self-Assessment CD-ROM.**

Section Quiz 6–1

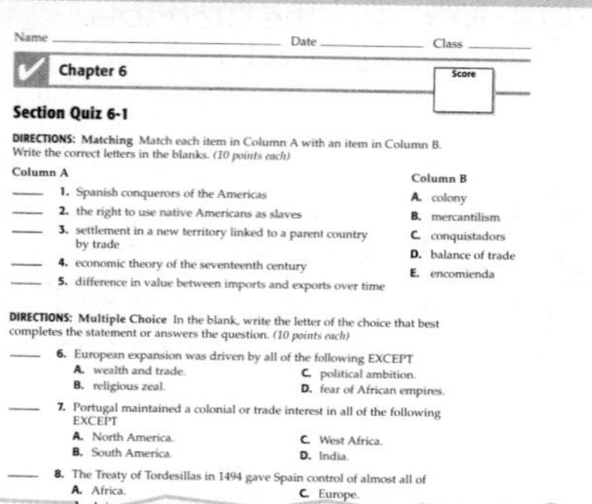
Name ______ Date ______ Class ______

Chapter 6 Score

Section Quiz 6-1

DIRECTIONS: Matching Match each item in Column A with an item in Column B. Write the correct letters in the blanks. *(10 points each)*

Column A

____ 1. Spanish conquerors of the Americas
____ 2. the right to use native Americans as slaves
____ 3. settlement in a new territory linked to a parent country by trade
____ 4. economic theory of the seventeenth century
____ 5. difference in value between imports and exports over time

Column B

A. colony
B. mercantilism
C. conquistadors
D. balance of trade
E. encomienda

DIRECTIONS: Multiple Choice In the blank, write the letter of the choice that best completes the statement or answers the question. *(10 points each)*

____ 6. European expansion was driven by all of the following EXCEPT
A. wealth and trade.
B. religious zeal.
C. political ambition.
D. fear of African empires.

____ 7. Portugal maintained a colonial or trade interest in all of the following EXCEPT
A. North America.
B. South America.
C. West Africa.
D. India.

____ 8. The Treaty of Tordesillas in 1494 gave Spain control of almost all of
A. Africa.
C. Europe.

Europeans called these territories the New World, but the lands were hardly new. They already had flourishing civilizations made up of millions of people when the Europeans arrived. The Americas were, of course, new to the Europeans, who quickly saw opportunities for conquest and exploitation.

Reading Check **Examining** Why did the Spanish and Portuguese divide the Americas in half by signing the Treaty of Tordesillas?

The Spanish Empire

The Spanish conquerors of the Americas—known as conquistadors—were individuals whose guns and determination brought them incredible success. The forces of Hernán Cortés took only three years to overthrow the mighty Aztec Empire in Central America. By 1550, the Spanish had gained control of northern Mexico. In South America, an expedition led by **Francisco Pizarro** took control of the Incan Empire high in the Peruvian Andes. Within 30 years, the western part of Latin America, as these lands in Mexico and Central and South America were called, had been brought under Spanish control. (The Portuguese took over Brazil, which fell on their side of the line of demarcation.)

By 1535, the Spanish had created a system of colonial administration in the Americas. Queen Isabella declared Native Americans (then called Indians, after the Spanish word *Indios,* "inhabitants of the Indies") to be her subjects. She granted the Spanish *encomienda,* or the right to use Native Americans as laborers.

The Spanish were supposed to protect Native Americans, but the settlers were far from Spain and largely ignored their rulers. Native Americans were put to work on sugar plantations and in gold and silver mines. Few Spanish settlers worried about protecting them.

Forced labor, starvation, and especially disease took a fearful toll on Native American lives. With little natural resistance to European diseases, the native peoples were ravaged by smallpox, measles, and typhus, and many of them died. Haiti, for example, had a population of 100,000 when Columbus arrived. By 1570, only 300 Native Americans had survived. In Mexico, the population dropped from 25 million in 1500 to 3 million in 1570.

Incan mask

In the early years of the conquest, Catholic missionaries converted and baptized hundreds of thousands of native peoples. With the arrival of the missionaries came parishes, schools, and hospitals—all the trappings of a European society. Native American social and political structures were torn apart and replaced by European systems of religion, language, culture, and government.

Reading Check **Evaluating** What was the impact of the Spanish settlement on the native populations in the Americas?

Economic Impact and Competition

TURNING POINT **As you will read, international trade was crucial in furthering a Commercial Revolution, a new age of commercial capitalism, one of the first steps in developing a world economy.**

Spanish conquests in the Americas affected not only the conquered but also the conquerors. This was especially true in the economic arena. Wherever they went, Europeans sought gold and silver. One Aztec commented that the Spanish conquerors "longed and lusted for gold. Their bodies swelled with greed; they hungered like pigs for that gold." Rich silver deposits were found and exploited in Mexico and southern Peru (modern Bolivia).

Gold and silver were only two of the products that were traded between Europe and the Americas. Sugar, dyes, cotton, vanilla, and hides from livestock raised in the South American pampas, or plains, flowed into Spain. Native agricultural products, such as potatoes, cocoa, corn, and tobacco, were also shipped to Europe. These new products changed European lifestyles.

In turn, Europeans brought horses and cattle to the Americas. Horses revolutionized the life of the Plains Indians in North America. Europeans also brought wheat and cane sugar, to be grown on large plantations by slave labor. This exchange of goods between Europe and the Americas was part of what historians call the Columbian Exchange, named after Christopher Columbus.

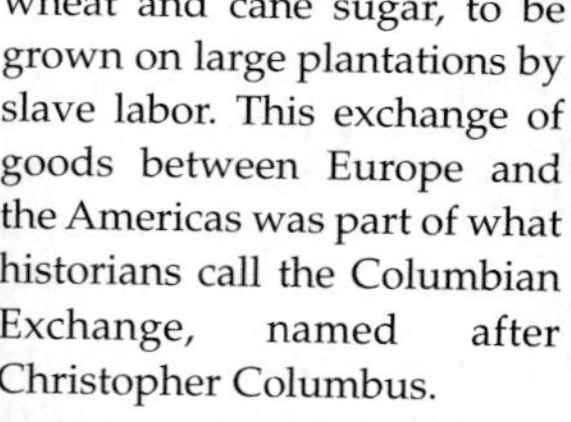

New Rivals Enter the Scene

By the end of the sixteenth century, several new European rivals had entered the scene for the eastern trade.

MEETING INDIVIDUAL NEEDS

Visual/Kinesthetic Have students refer to the world map in the Reference Atlas section of this text. Then ask students to study the historical map on page 191. Ask students to describe as many differences as they can between the two maps. Have students explain why the maps are different. *(tools and knowledge available to create the map, purpose of the map, cost of producing the map)* Have students interpret the maps to identify and explain the geographic factors that influenced the people and events of the Age of Exploration. To illustrate how difficult it was for explorers to create accurate maps, have your students create a map of the classroom. Encourage students to make scale and proportion as exact as possible **L1** ELL

The Spanish established themselves in the Philippine Islands, where **Ferdinand Magellan** had landed earlier. They turned the Philippines into a major Spanish base for trade across the Pacific. Spanish ships carried silver from Mexico to the Philippines and returned to Mexico with silk and other luxury goods.

At the beginning of the seventeenth century, an English fleet landed on the northwestern coast of India and established trade relations with the people there. Trade with Southeast Asia soon followed.

The first Dutch fleet arrived in India in 1595. Shortly after, the Dutch formed the East India Company and began competing with the English and the Portuguese.

The Dutch also formed the West India Company to compete with the Spanish and Portuguese in the Americas. The Dutch colony of New Netherlands stretched from the mouth of the Hudson River as far north as Albany, New York. Present-day names such as *Staten Island*, *Harlem*, and the *Catskill Mountains* are reminders of Dutch influence.

After 1650, however, rivalry with the English and the French brought the fall of the Dutch commercial empire in the Americas. The English seized the colony of New Netherlands and renamed it New York. Canada became a French colony.

The English, meanwhile, also moved into the Americas. The Massachusetts Bay Colony, founded in about 1630, had only four thousand settlers in its early years, but its numbers soon increased to forty thousand. By 1700, the English had established a colonial empire along the eastern seaboard of North America.

Trade, Colonies, and Mercantilism Led by Portugal and Spain, European nations in the 1500s and 1600s established many trading posts and colonies in the Americas and the East. A **colony** is a settlement of people living in a new territory, linked with the parent country by trade and direct government control.

With the development of colonies and trading posts, Europeans entered an age of increased international trade known as the Commercial Revolution. Colonies played a role in the theory of **mercantilism**, a set of principles that dominated economic thought in the 1600s: According to mercantilists, the prosperity of a nation depended on a large supply of bullion, or gold and silver. To bring in gold and silver payments, nations tried to have a favorable balance of trade. The **balance of trade** is the difference in value between what a nation imports and what it exports over time. When the balance is favorable, the goods exported are of greater value than those imported.

To encourage exports, governments stimulated export industries and trade. They granted subsidies, or payments, to new industries and improved transportation systems by building roads, bridges, and canals. By placing high tariffs, or taxes, on foreign goods, they tried to keep these goods out of their own countries. Colonies were considered important both as sources of raw materials and markets for finished goods.

Reading Check **Identifying** What products were sent from the Americas to Europe?

SECTION 1 ASSESSMENT

Checking for Understanding

1. **Define** conquistador, colony, mercantilism, balance of trade.
2. **Identify** Vasco da Gama, Christopher Columbus, John Cabot, Amerigo Vespucci, Francisco Pizarro, Ferdinand Magellan.
3. **Locate** Portugal, Africa, Melaka, Cuba.
4. **Explain** why the Spanish were so hungry for gold.
5. **List** the institutions of European society that were brought to the Americas by European missionaries.

Critical Thinking

6. **Describe** Identify and briefly describe the negative consequences of the Spanish *encomienda* system. Were there any positive consequences?
7. **Identifying Information** Use a web diagram like the one below to list motives for European exploration.

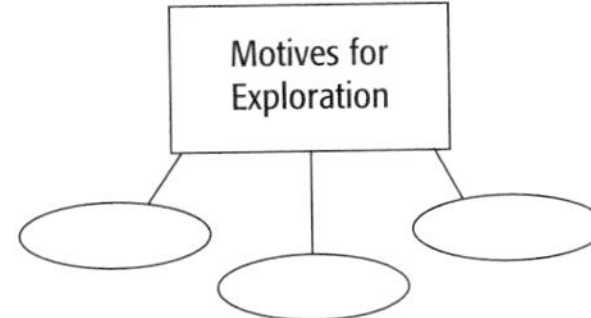

Analyzing Visuals

8. **Examine** the photograph of the Incan mask shown on page 194 of your text. How could artifacts such as this have increased the European desire to explore and conquer the Americas?

Writing About History

9. **Descriptive Writing** Research one of the expeditions discussed in this section. Write a journal entry describing your experiences as a sailor on the expedition. Provide details of your daily life on the ship and what you found when you first reached land.

CHAPTER 6
Section 1, 189–195

Reading Check

Answer: silver, dyes, gold, cotton, vanilla, hides, potatoes, cocoa, corn, tobacco

Reading Essentials and Study Guide 6–1

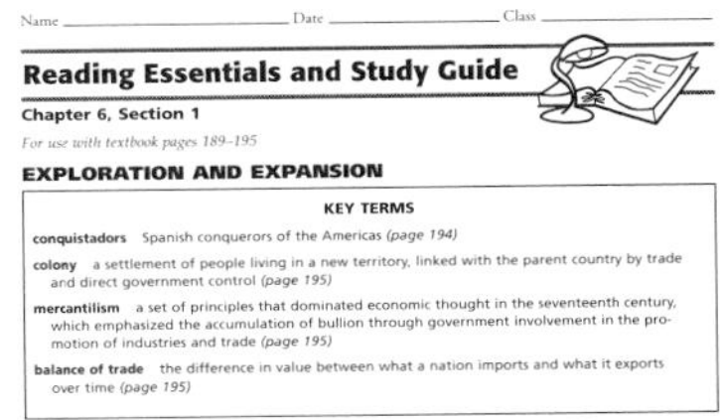
Name ____ Date ____ Class ____

Reading Essentials and Study Guide

Chapter 6, Section 1

For use with textbook pages 189–195

EXPLORATION AND EXPANSION

KEY TERMS

conquistadors Spanish conquerors of the Americas (page 194)

colony a settlement of people living in a new territory, linked with the parent country by trade and direct government control (page 195)

mercantilism a set of principles that dominated economic thought in the seventeenth century, which emphasized the accumulation of bullion through government involvement in the promotion of industries and trade (page 195)

balance of trade the difference in value between what a nation imports and what it exports over time (page 195)

Connecting Across Time

Ask students to research the Dutch East India Company and business strategies of multinational corporations. How has foreign trade changed since the seventeenth century? **L3**

Reteaching Activity

Have students work in pairs to outline this section. **L1**

4 CLOSE

Ask students how life in Europe was changed by exploration in Africa, Asia, and the Americas. What might the impact of expanded trade have been on Europeans' daily lives? Have students explain the political, economic, cultural, and technological influences of European expansion on Europeans. **L2**

SECTION 1 ASSESSMENT

1. Key terms are in blue.
2. Vasco da Gama *(p. 191)*; Christopher Columbus *(p. 193)*; John Cabot *(p. 193)*; Amerigo Vespucci *(p. 193)*; Francisco Pizarro *(p. 194)*; Ferdinand Magellan *(p. 194)*
3. See chapter maps.
4. mercantilism measured a nation's prosperity in bullion
5. parishes, schools, hospitals; also religion, language, culture, government
6. allowed the Spanish to use Native Americans as laborers, majority of the native population soon killed by forced labor, starvation, disease; positive: Spanish were supposed to protect the Native Americans
7. opportunities for riches, religious zeal, spirit of adventure
8. The mask is made of gold, which was highly desired by European explorers.
9. Students will create a journal entry.

TEACH

Analyzing Primary Sources
Based on this letter, how would students describe the attitude of the natives of Hispaniola toward Columbus and his men? *(Answers will vary.)* To whom was Columbus writing this letter? *(Spanish king and queen)* How do you know? *(Addresses "Your Highnesses")* How does the fact that he was writing to his sponsors explain why Columbus claims to have given the natives "good things," rather than worthless things? *(says he hoped natives would become Christian subjects of Spain, willing to give Spain what it wanted)* **L2**

Critical Thinking

Ask students to speculate why Columbus assumed the natives of Hispaniola were "very marvelously timid." **L2**

Connecting Across Time

During the Age of Exploration, most explorers were financed by their governments or by their monarchs. Guide students in a discussion of the ways contemporary explorers obtain financing for their work. **L2**

EYEWITNESS TO HISTORY

Columbus Lands in the Americas

ON RETURNING FROM HIS VOYAGE TO THE Americas, Christopher Columbus wrote a letter describing his experience. In this passage from the letter, he tells of his arrival on the island of Hispaniola.

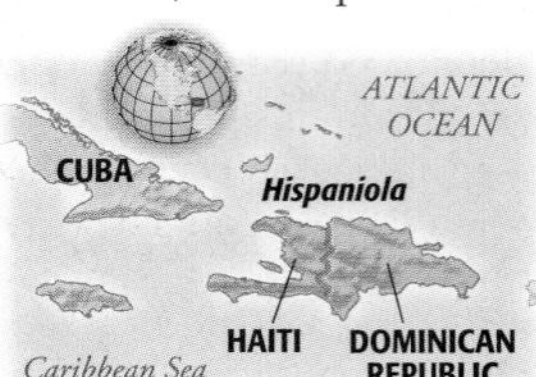

❝The people of this island and of all the other islands which I have found and of which I have information, all go naked, men and women, as their mothers bore them. They have no iron or steel or weapons, nor are they fitted to use them. This is not because they are not well built and of handsome stature, but because they are very marvelously timid. They have no other arms than spears made of canes, cut in seeding time, to the end of which they fix a small sharpened stick.

They refuse nothing that they possess, if it be asked of them; on the contrary, they invite any one to share it and display as much love as if they would give their hearts. They are content with whatever trifle of whatever kind they may be given to them, whether it be of value or valueless. I forbade that they should be given things so worthless as fragments of broken crockery, scraps of broken glass and lace tips, although when they were able to get them, they fancied that they possessed the best jewel in the world. So it was found that for a leather strap a soldier received gold to the weight of two and half castellanos, and others received much more for other things which were worthless. . . . I gave them a thousand handsome good things, which I had brought, in order that they might conceive affection for us and, more than that, might become Christians and be inclined to the love and service of Your Highnesses [king and queen of Spain], and strive to collect and give us of the things which they have in abundance and what are necessary to us.

Columbus landing in the Americas

They practice no kind of idolatry, but have a firm belief that all strength and power, and indeed all good things, are in heaven, and that I had descended from thence with these ships and sailors, and under this impression was I received after they had thrown aside their fears. Nor are they slow or stupid, but of very clear understanding; and those men who have crossed to the neighbouring islands give an abominable description of everything they observed; but they never saw any people clothed, nor any ships like ours.❞

—Christopher Columbus, *The Journal of Christopher Columbus*

Analyzing Primary Sources

1. Why did Columbus give the peoples of Hispaniola "a thousand handsome good things"?
2. How did the explorers take advantage of Native Americans?

196

ANSWERS TO ANALYZING PRIMARY SOURCES

1. Columbus wanted to win the affection of the people of Hispaniola, to encourage them to become Christians, to win their loyalty for the Spanish monarchs, and to encourage them to give things to him in return.
2. In trade transactions, Native Americans unwittingly exchanged disproportionate sums of gold for items of little worth that the explorers had brought with them.

SECTION 2 Africa in an Age of Transition

Guide to Reading

Main Ideas
- European expansion affected Africa with the dramatic increase of the slave trade.
- Traditional political systems and cultures continued to exist in most of Africa.

Key Terms
plantation, triangular trade, Middle Passage

People to Identify
King Afonso, Ibo

Places to Locate
Brazil, Benin, South Africa, Mozambique

Preview Questions
1. How did European expansion affect Africa's peoples and cultures?
2. How were the African states structured politically?

Reading Strategy
Cause and Effect Use a table like the one below to identify economic and political factors that caused the slave trade to be profitable. List the economic and political effects of the trade.

Economic/ Political Factors	Economic/ Political Effects

Preview of Events

1510 · 1525 · 1540 · 1555 · 1570 · 1585 · 1600

1518 A Spanish ship carries the first boatload of African slaves to the Americas

1590 Moroccan forces defeat the Songhai army

Voices from the Past

Captured Africans, yoked and shackled

Early European explorers sought gold in Africa but were soon involved in the slave trade. One Dutch trader noted:

> "As the slaves come down to Fida [a port on the west coast of Africa] from the inland country, they are put into a booth, or prison, built for that purpose, near the beach, all of them together; and when the Europeans are to receive them, they are brought out into a large plain, where the surgeons examine every part of them, men and women being all stark naked. Such as are found good and sound are set on one side. Each of those which have passed as good is marked . . . with a red-hot iron, imprinting the mark of the French, English, or Dutch companies, so that each nation may distinguish its own and prevent their being changed by the natives for worse."
>
> —***Documents Illustrative of the Slave Trade to America,*** **Elizabeth Dorman, ed.,1930**

The exchange of slaves became an important part of European trading patterns.

The Slave Trade

Traffic in slaves was not new, to be sure. As in other areas of the world, slavery had been practiced in Africa since ancient times. In the fifteenth century, it continued at a fairly steady level.

The primary market for African slaves was Southwest Asia, where most slaves were used as domestic servants. Slavery also existed in some European countries.

CHAPTER 6
Section 2, 197–200

1 FOCUS

Section Overview

This section explains the impact of European expansion on Africa and the cultures of Africa.

BELLRINGER
Skillbuilder Activity

Project transparency and have students answer questions.

Available as a blackline master.

Daily Focus Skills Transparency 6–2

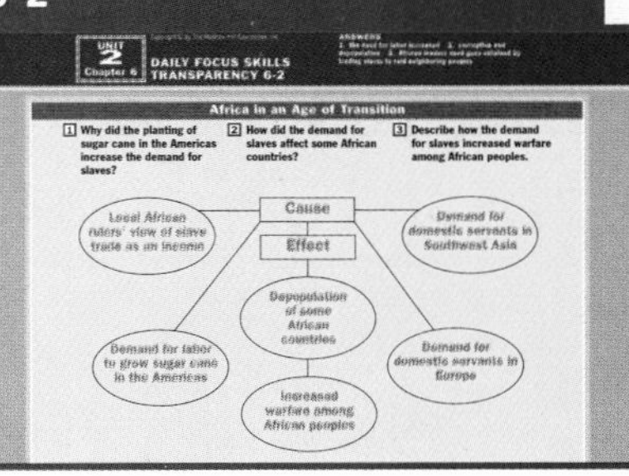

Guide to Reading

Answers to Graphic: Factors: market for African slaves in the Middle East, planting of sugarcane, demand for slaves increased; Effects: depopulation of some areas, increased warfare and violence

Preteaching Vocabulary: To understand *triangular trade,* have students draw a triangle and label the three points as Europe, Africa and Asia, and the Americas. Have them use arrows to indicate the shipping patterns of goods and slaves. **L1**

SECTION RESOURCES

Reproducible Masters
- Reproducible Lesson Plan 6–2
- Daily Lecture and Discussion Notes 6–2
- Guided Reading Activity 6–2
- Section Quiz 6–2
- Reading Essentials and Study Guide 6–2

Transparencies
- Daily Focus Skills Transparency 6–2

Multimedia
- Interactive Tutor Self-Assessment CD-ROM
- ExamView® Pro Testmaker CD-ROM
- Presentation Plus! CD-ROM

2 TEACH

Geography Skills

Answers:

1. the west coast, closest to ships from North and South America
2. They would have to wear more clothing, since both Europe and North America have cooler climates than the regions of Africa from which they came.

Daily Lecture and Discussion Notes 6–2

Daily Lecture and Discussion Notes

Chapter 6, Section 2

Did You Know? Historians define a slave as having the following characteristics: a slave is a form of property, either movable or immovable; a slave is the object of law, not its subject, and is not able to enter into contracts; a slave has fewer rights than his or her owner; few, if any, limits exist on how slaves may be abused; the product of the slave's labor belongs to someone else; a slave has few, if any, political rights.

I. **The Slave Trade** *(pages 197–199)*

A. In the fifteenth century the primary market for African slaves was Southwest Asia, where they were used principally as domestic servants. Some European countries also had slaves, used as servants for wealthy families.

B. The demand for slaves rose dramatically with the European voyages to the Americas and the planting of sugar cane there. **Plantations,** large agricultural estates, were set up on the eastern coast of **Brazil** and on islands in the Caribbean to grow sugar cane. Growing cane is labor intensive. The small native population, much of which had died from European diseases, could not provide the labor. African slaves were imported to meet the need.

Guided Reading Activity 6–2

Name ______________ Date ______________ Class ______________

Guided Reading Activity 6-2

Africa in an Age of Transition

DIRECTIONS: As you are reading the section, decide if a statement is true or false. Write **T** if the statement is true or **F** if the statement is false. For all false statements write a corrected statement.

____ 1. The primary market for African slaves was Southwest Asia, where most slaves were used as field hands.

____ 2. The demand for slaves changed dramatically with the discovery of the Americas and the planting of sugarcane there.

____ 3. In 1518, a Spanish ship carried the first boatload of African slaves directly from Africa to Spain.

Enrich

Guide students in a discussion of how the European discovery of the Americas and the planting of sugarcane in South America and the Caribbean changed African slavery. **L1**

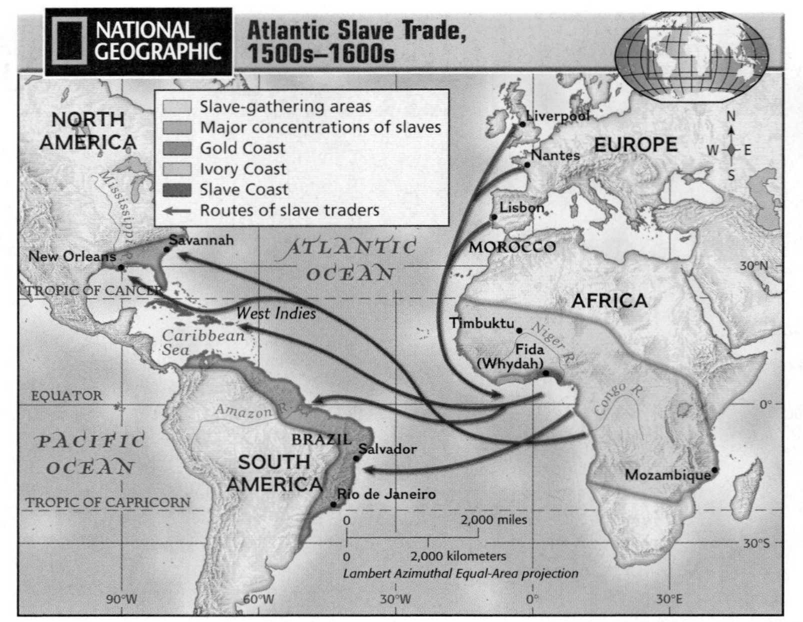

Geography Skills

More than a quarter of a million Africans were exported as slaves during the sixteenth century.

1. **Interpreting Maps** What part of Africa was the greatest source of slaves? Why?
2. **Applying Geography Skills** What, if any, adjustments to climate would African slaves have to make in North America and Europe?

During the last half of the fifteenth century, for example, about a thousand slaves were taken to Portugal each year. Most wound up serving as domestic servants. The demand for slaves changed dramatically, however, with the discovery of the Americas in the 1490s and the planting of sugarcane there.

Cane sugar was introduced to Europe from Southwest Asia during the Crusades. During the sixteenth century, **plantations,** large agricultural estates, were set up along the coast of **Brazil** and on islands in the Caribbean to grow sugarcane. Growing cane sugar demands much labor. The small Native American population, much of which had died of diseases imported from Europe, could not provide the labor needed. Thus, African slaves were shipped to Brazil and the Caribbean to work on the plantations.

Growth of the Slave Trade In 1518, a Spanish ship carried the first boatload of African slaves directly from Africa to the Americas. During the next two centuries, the trade in slaves grew dramatically and became part of the **triangular trade** that marked the emergence of a new world economy. The pattern of triangular trade connected Europe, Africa and Asia, and the American continents. European merchant ships carried European manufactured goods, such as guns and cloth, to Africa, where they were traded for a cargo of slaves. The slaves were then shipped to the Americas and sold. European merchants then bought tobacco, molasses, sugar, and raw cotton and shipped them back to Europe to be sold in European markets.

An estimated 275,000 African slaves were exported during the sixteenth century. Two thousand went every year to the Americas alone. In the seventeenth century, the total climbed to over a million and jumped to six million in the eighteenth century. By then the trade had spread from West Africa and Central Africa to East Africa. Altogether, as many as ten million African slaves were brought to the Americas between the early sixteenth and the late nineteenth centuries.

One reason for these astonishing numbers, of course, was the high death rate. The journey of slaves from Africa to the Americas became known as the **Middle Passage,** the middle portion of the triangular trade route. Many slaves died on the journey. Those who arrived often died from diseases to which they had little or no immunity.

Death rates were higher for newly arrived slaves than for those born and raised in the Americas. The new generation gradually developed at least a partial immunity to many diseases. Owners, however, rarely encouraged their slaves to have children. Many slave owners, especially on islands in the Caribbean, believed that buying a new slave was less expensive than raising a child from birth to working age.

Sources of Slaves Before the coming of Europeans in the fifteenth century, most slaves in Africa were prisoners of war. When Europeans first began to take part in the slave trade, they bought slaves from local African merchants at slave markets on the coasts in return for gold, guns, or other European goods.

CRITICAL THINKING ACTIVITY

Analyzing Slavery in Europe was well entrenched in the later Middle Ages. The bubonic plague, famine, and other epidemics created a severe labor shortage. This encouraged Italian bankers and merchants to buy slaves from Balkan Thrace, Southern Russia, and Central Anatolia. Profits were considerable and papal threats of excommunication failed to stop the slave trade. Genoese traders set up colonial stations in the Crimea and along the Black Sea for the needs of plantation agriculture in the Mediterranean area and the Americas. This form of slavery had nothing to do with race; almost all slaves were white. Have students discuss how black African slaves began to be traded in Europe. **L1**

At first, local slave traders obtained their supplies of slaves from the coastal regions nearby. As demand increased, however, they had to move farther inland to find their victims.

Local rulers became concerned about the impact of the slave trade on the well-being of their societies. In a letter to the king of Portugal in 1526, **King Afonso** of Congo (Bakongo) said, "so great is the corruption that our country is being completely depopulated."

Protests from Africans were generally ignored by Europeans, however, as well as by other Africans. As a rule, local rulers who traded slaves viewed the slave trade as a source of income. Many sent raiders into defenseless villages in search of victims.

Effects of the Slave Trade The effects of the slave trade varied from area to area. Of course, it always had tragic effects on the lives of individual victims and their families. The slave trade led to the depopulation of some areas, and it deprived many African communities of their youngest and strongest men and women.

The desire of local slave traders to provide a constant supply of slaves led to increased warfare in Africa. Coastal or near-coastal African leaders and their followers, armed with guns acquired from the trade in slaves, increased their raids and wars on neighboring peoples.

Slaves were kept in the ship's cargo deck, called the hold.

Only a few Europeans lamented what they were doing to traditional African societies. One Dutch slave trader remarked, "From us they have learned strife, quarrelling, drunkenness, trickery, theft, unbridled desire for what is not one's own, misdeeds unknown to them before, and the accursed lust for gold."

HISTORY Online

Web Activity Visit the *Glencoe World History—Modern Times* Web site at wh.mt.glencoe.com and click on **Chapter 6–Student Web Activity** to learn more about the Age of Exploration.

The slave trade had a devastating effect on some African states. The case of **Benin** in West Africa is a good example. A brilliant and creative society in the sixteenth century, Benin was pulled into the slave trade.

As the population declined and warfare increased, the people of Benin lost faith in their gods, their art deteriorated, and human sacrifice became more common. When the British arrived there at the end of the nineteenth century, they found a corrupt and brutal place. It took years to discover the brilliance of the earlier culture destroyed by slavery.

Reading Check **Describing** Describe the purpose and path of the triangular trade.

Political and Social Structures

The slave trade was one of the most noticeable effects of the European presence in Africa between 1500 and 1800. Generally, European influence did not extend beyond the coastal regions. Only in a few areas, such as **South Africa** and **Mozambique,** were there signs of a permanent European presence.

Traditional Political Systems In general, traditional African political systems continued to exist. By the sixteenth century, monarchy had become a common form of government throughout much of the continent. Some states, like the kingdom of Benin in West Africa, were highly centralized, with the king regarded as almost divine.

Other African states were more like collections of small principalities knit together by ties of kinship or other loyalties. The state of Ashanti on the Gold Coast was a good example. The kingdom consisted of a number of previously independent small states linked together by kinship ties and subordinated to the king. To provide visible evidence of this unity, each local ruler was given a ceremonial stool of office as a symbol of the kinship ties that linked the rulers

CHAPTER 6
Section 2, 197–200

Reading Check

Answer: it provided a market for manufactured goods from Europe (Africa), for slaves from Africa (the Americas), and for raw materials from the Americas (Europe)

Critical Thinking

Have students speculate on the effects of the slave trade on European traders and sailors. How might they justify their livelihoods? How might they rationalize the conditions on slave ships? How might Europeans develop a "comfort level" in thinking about African slavery? Remind students that views about the differences between races were very different three hundred years ago. **L2**

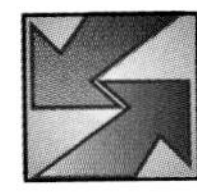

CURRICULUM CONNECTION

Music and Sociology The composer of the hymn "Amazing Grace" was a former slave trader. Ask students to research the composition of this song. Students might wish to watch Bill Moyers' program "Amazing Grace," produced for public television. Have students analyze how the hymn reflects the history of the culture in which it was produced. **L2**

3 ASSESS

Assign Section 2 Assessment as homework or as an in-class activity.

Have students use **Interactive Tutor Self-Assessment CD-ROM**.

COOPERATIVE LEARNING ACTIVITY

Creating a Newspaper By now, students have done a lot of thinking about and discussing the issue of slavery and its impact on the various people involved. Have students work in groups to prepare a one or two-page report for a Dutch newspaper of this era. Have the students write articles covering both sides of the slavery issue. Students might have an eyewitness account of a slaveship; a comparison of Dutch slaveships to those of Portugal or Spain; an interview with a slave (where he or she is from, what has happened, how he or she feels); or an interview with a ship's captain. Encourage students to be creative in both their writing and newspaper layout. Consider "publishing" the various newspapers for the entire class, or post them. **L3**

CHAPTER 6
Section 2, 197–200

Reading Check

Answer: monarchy; collections of small principalities, political units led by village leader

Section Quiz 6–2

Name ______ Date ______ Class ______

Chapter 6 Score

Section Quiz 6-2

DIRECTIONS: Matching Match each item in Column A with an item in Column B. Write the correct letters in the blanks. (10 points each)

Column A	Column B
___ 1. the pattern of trade connecting Europe, Africa, and the Americas	A. sugar cane
___ 2. the journey of slaves form Africa to America	B. Middle Passage
___ 3. large agricultural estates	C. triangular trade
___ 4. crop introduced to Europe from Southwest Asia	D. Ashanti
___ 5. Gold Coast state	E. plantations

DIRECTIONS: Multiple Choice In the blank, write the letter of the choice that best completes the statement or answers the question. (10 points each)

Reading Essentials and Study Guide 6–2

Name ______ Date ______ Class ______

Reading Essentials and Study Guide

Chapter 6, Section 2

For use with textbook pages 197–200

AFRICA IN AN AGE OF TRANSITION

KEY TERMS

plantations large agricultural estates that often depended on slavery to provide the labor they needed (page 198)

triangular trade a pattern of trade that connected Europe, Africa and Asia, and the American continents (page 198)

Middle Passage the journey of slaves from Africa to the Americas (the middle portion of the triangular trade route) (page 198)

DRAWING FROM EXPERIENCE

Have you ever visited a plantation? How did the plantation owners live?

Reteaching Activity

Have students create an outline of the information contained in this section. **L1**

4 CLOSE

Guide students in a discussion identifying the causes of European expansion in the sixteenth century. **L2**

People In History

King Afonso I
c.1456–c.1545—African king

Afonso I was the greatest king of Congo (present-day Angola and the Democratic Republic of the Congo). He was born Mvemba Nzinga, son of the king of Congo. After the Portuguese arrived in the kingdom, Mvemba converted to Catholicism and changed his name to Afonso. After he became king in 1506, Afonso sought friendly relations with the Portuguese. In return for trade privileges, the Portuguese sent manufactured goods, missionaries, and craftspeople to Congo. Afonso soon found, however, that the Portuguese could not be trusted. They made more and more raids for African slaves and even attempted to assassinate King Afonso when they thought that the king was hiding gold from them. Afonso remained a devout Christian, building churches and schools.

together. The king had an exquisite golden stool to symbolize the unity of the entire state.

Many Africans continued to live in small political units in which authority rested in a village leader. For example, the **Ibo** society of eastern Nigeria was based on independent villages. The Ibo were active traders, and the area produced more slaves than practically any other in the continent.

Foreign Influences Many African political systems, then, were affected little by the European presence. Nevertheless, the Europeans were causing changes, often indirectly. Europeans introduced new food products—sweet potatoes, maize (corn), and peanuts—to Africa in the sixteenth century. In the western Sahara, Europeans caused trade routes to shift toward the coast. This led to the decline of the Songhai trading empire.

Morocco had long hoped to expand its influence into the Sahara in order to seize control over the trade in gold and salt. In 1590, after a 20-week trek across the desert, Moroccan forces defeated the Songhai army and then occupied the great trading center of Timbuktu. Eventually, the Moroccans were forced to leave, but Songhai was beyond recovery. Its next two centuries were marked by civil disorder.

Foreigners also influenced African religious beliefs. Here, however, Europeans had less impact than the Islamic culture. In North Africa, Islam continued to expand. Muslim beliefs became dominant along the northern coast and began to spread southward.

Although their voyages centered on trade with the East, Europeans were also interested in spreading Christianity. The Portuguese engaged in some missionary activity, but the English, the Dutch, and the French made little effort to combine their trading activities with the message of the gospel. Except for a tiny European foothold in South Africa and the isolated kingdom of Ethiopia, Christianity did not stop the spread of Islam in Africa.

Reading Check **Describing** What was the most common form of government throughout Africa? What other political systems existed?

SECTION 2 ASSESSMENT

Checking for Understanding

1. **Define** plantation, triangular trade, Middle Passage.
2. **Identify** King Afonso, Ibo.
3. **Locate** Brazil, Benin, South Africa, Mozambique.
4. **Explain** how the Europeans obtained access to slaves. To what port cities in Europe and the Americas were the African slaves shipped?
5. **Identify** the effects of the slave trade on the culture of Benin.

Critical Thinking

6. **Analyze** Why did Africans engage in slave trade? Did they have a choice?
7. **Compare and Contrast** Use a table like the one below to compare and contrast the political systems of the Benin, the state of Ashanti, and the Ibo peoples.

Benin	Ashanti	Ibo

Analyzing Visuals

8. **Examine** the picture of the inside of a slave ship shown on page 199. From looking at this picture, what conclusions can you draw about the conditions that slaves endured during their voyage to the Americas?

Writing About History

9. **Persuasive Writing** Does the fact that Africans participated in enslaving other Africans make the European involvement in the slave trade any less reprehensible? Write an editorial supporting your position.

SECTION 2 ASSESSMENT

1. Key terms are in blue.
2. King Afonso *(p. 199)*; Ibo *(p. 200)*
3. See chapter maps.
4. bought them from African merchants; see cities noted on map
5. population declined, warfare increased, people lost faith in gods, art deteriorated, human sacrifice became more common
6. sale of enemies profitable, groups not engaged in slave trade likely to be victims; answers will vary
7. Benin: highly centralized, king almost divine; Ashanti: small states linked by kinship ties subordinated to king; Ibo: independent villages
8. slaves chained, had little room, tormented by slave handlers
9. Students will write an editorial. Encourage students to use other examples from history to support their position.

SECTION 3 Southeast Asia in the Era of the Spice Trade

Guide to Reading

Main Ideas
- The Portuguese occupied the Moluccas in search of spices but were pushed out by the Dutch.
- The arrival of the Europeans greatly impacted the Malay.

Key Terms
mainland states, bureaucracy

People to Identify
Khmer, Dutch

Places to Locate
Moluccas, Sumatra, Java, Philippines

Preview Questions
1. How did the power shift from the Portuguese to the Dutch in the control of the spice trade?
2. What religious beliefs were prevalent in Southeast Asia?

Reading Strategy
Summarizing Information Use a chart like the one below to list reasons why, unlike in Africa, the destructive effects of European contact in Southeast Asia were only gradually felt.

European Contact in Southeast Asia

Preview of Events

1510 · 1530 · 1550 · 1570 · 1590 · 1610 · 1630

- **1511** Portuguese seize Melaka
- **1600** Dutch begin to control spice trade
- **1619** Dutch establish a fort at Batavia (present-day Jakarta)

Voices from the Past

A parasol shades a European from the sun.

After establishing control of the island of Java, the Dutch encountered a problem in ruling it. One observer explained:

> "The greatest number of the Dutch settlers in Batavia [present-day Jakarta, Indonesia], such as were commonly seen at their doors, appeared pale and weak, and as if laboring with death. . . . Of the fatal effects of the climate upon both sexes, however, a strong proof was given by a lady there, who mentioned, that out of eleven persons of her family who had come to Batavia only ten months before, her father, brother-in-law, and six sisters had already died. The general reputation of the unhealthiness of Batavia for Europeans, deter most of those, who can reside at home with any comfort, from coming to it, notwithstanding the temptations of fortunes to be quickly amassed in it."
>
> —*Lives and Times: A World History Reader*, James P. Holoka and Jiu-Hwa L. Upsher, eds., 1995

Such difficult conditions kept Southeast Asia largely free of European domination.

Emerging Mainland States

In 1500, mainland Southeast Asia was a relatively stable region. Throughout mainland Southeast Asia, from Burma in the west to Vietnam in the east, kingdoms with their own ethnic, linguistic, and cultural characteristics were being formed.

SECTION RESOURCES

Reproducible Masters
- Reproducible Lesson Plan 6–3
- Daily Lecture and Discussion Notes 6–3
- Guided Reading Activity 6–3
- Section Quiz 6–3
- Reading Essentials and Study Guide 6–3

Transparencies
- Daily Focus Skills Transparency 6–3

Multimedia
- Interactive Tutor Self-Assessment CD-ROM
- ExamView® Pro Testmaker CD-ROM
- Presentation Plus! CD-ROM

1 FOCUS

Section Overview

This section discusses the impact of the European trade on Southeast Asia.

BELLRINGER
Skillbuilder Activity

Project transparency and have students answer questions.

Available as a blackline master.

Daily Focus Skills Transparency 6–3

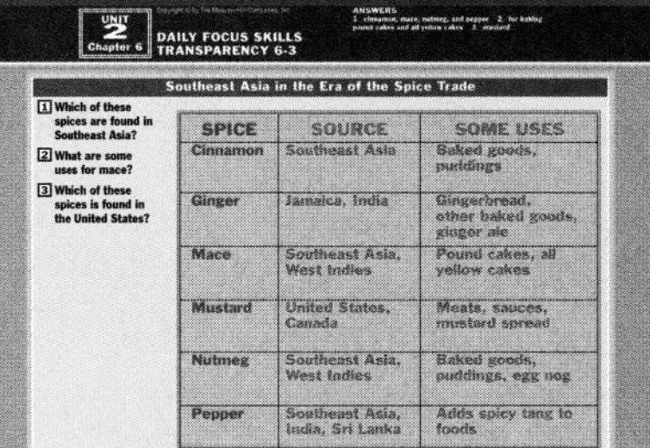
UNIT 2 Chapter 6
DAILY FOCUS SKILLS TRANSPARENCY 6-3

ANSWERS
1. cinnamon, mace, nutmeg, and pepper 2. for baking pound cakes and all yellow cakes 3. mustard

Southeast Asia in the Era of the Spice Trade

1. Which of these spices are found in Southeast Asia?
2. What are some uses for mace?
3. Which of these spices is found in the United States?

SPICE	SOURCE	SOME USES
Cinnamon	Southeast Asia	Baked goods, puddings
Ginger	Jamaica, India	Gingerbread, other baked goods, ginger ale
Mace	Southeast Asia, West Indies	Pound cakes, all yellow cakes
Mustard	United States, Canada	Meats, sauces, mustard spread
Nutmeg	Southeast Asia, West Indies	Baked goods, puddings, egg nog
Pepper	Southeast Asia, India, Sri Lanka	Adds spicy tang to foods

Guide to Reading

Answers to Graphic: cohesive character of the mainland states, Europeans did not colonize in Southeast Asia

Preteaching Vocabulary: Have students look up the word *bureaucracy* and explain its meaning. **L1**

2 TEACH

Reading Check

Answer: The growing spice trade resulted in the creation of an Islamic trade network; Islam was accepted first along the coast and gradually moved inland.

CONNECTIONS Around The World

Answer: Answers will vary, but should be backed by logical arguments. Encourage students to read *Guns, Germs, and Steel,* by Jared Diamond.

Daily Lecture and Discussion Notes 6–3

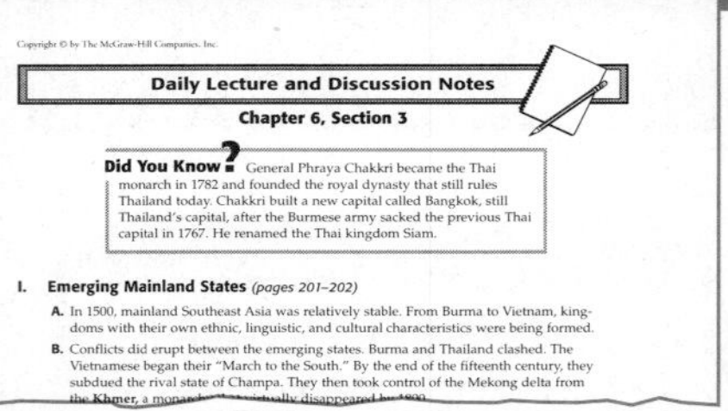

Daily Lecture and Discussion Notes

Chapter 6, Section 3

Did You Know? General Phraya Chakkri became the Thai monarch in 1782 and founded the royal dynasty that still rules Thailand today. Chakkri built a new capital called Bangkok, still Thailand's capital, after the Burmese army sacked the previous Thai capital in 1767. He renamed the Thai kingdom Siam.

I. **Emerging Mainland States** *(pages 201–202)*

A. In 1500, mainland Southeast Asia was relatively stable. From Burma to Vietnam, kingdoms with their own ethnic, linguistic, and cultural characteristics were being formed.

B. Conflicts did erupt between the emerging states. Burma and Thailand clashed. The Vietnamese began their "March to the South." By the end of the fifteenth century, they subdued the rival state of Champa. They then took control of the Mekong delta from the **Khmer,** a monar…

CURRICULUM CONNECTION

Geography Ask students to create a thematic map of exploration in Asia. Have students share their maps with the class. You might wish to create a bulletin board with the theme "Age of Exploration." L2

Conflicts did erupt among the emerging states on the Southeast Asian mainland. The Thai peoples had secured their control over the lower Chao Phraya River valley. Conflict between the Thai and the Burmese was bitter until a Burmese army sacked the Thai capital in 1767, forcing the Thai to create a new capital at Bangkok, farther to the south.

Across the mountains to the east, the Vietnamese had begun their "March to the South." By the end of the fifteenth century, they had subdued the rival state of Champa on the central coast. The Vietnamese then gradually took control of the Mekong delta from the **Khmer.** By 1800, the Khmer monarchy (the successor of the old Angkor kingdom—see Chapter 3) had virtually disappeared.

The situation was different in the Malay Peninsula and the Indonesian Archipelago. The area was gradually penetrated by Muslim merchants attracted to the growing spice trade. The creation of an Islamic trade network had political results as new states arose along the spice route. Islam was accepted first along the coast and then gradually moved inland.

The major impact of Islam, however, came in the fifteenth century, with the rise of the new sultanate at Melaka. Melaka owed its new power to its strategic location astride the strait of the same name, as well as to the rapid growth of the spice trade itself. Within a few years, Melaka had become the leading power in the region.

Reading Check **Examining** How did Muslim merchants affect the peoples of Southeast Asia?

The Arrival of Europeans

In 1511, the Portuguese seized Melaka and soon occupied the **Moluccas.** Known to Europeans as the Spice Islands, the Moluccas were the chief source of the spices that had originally attracted the Portuguese to the Indian Ocean.

The Portuguese, however, lacked the military and financial resources to impose their authority over broad areas. Instead, they set up small settlements along the coast, which they used as trading posts or as way stations en route to the Spice Islands.

A Shift in Power The situation changed with the arrival of the English and **Dutch** traders, who were better financed than were the Portuguese. The shift in

CONNECTIONS Around The World

Gunpowder and Gunpowder Empires

Gunpowder and guns were invented in China in the tenth century and spread to Europe and Southwest Asia in the fourteenth century. However, the full impact of gunpowder was not felt until after 1500.

Between 1500 and 1650, the world experienced a dramatic increase in the manufacture of weapons based on gunpowder. Large-scale production of cannons was especially evident in Europe, the Ottoman Empire, India, and China. By 1650, guns were also being made in Korea, Japan, Thailand, Iran, and, to a lesser extent, in Africa.

Firearms were a crucial element in the creation of new empires after 1500. Spaniards armed with firearms devastated the civilizations of the Aztec and Inca and carved out empires in Central and South America. The Ottoman Empire, the Mogul Empire in India, and the Safavid Empire in Persia also owed much of their success in creating and maintaining their large empires to the use of the new weapons. Historians have labeled these empires the "gunpowder empires."

The success of Europeans in creating new trade empires in the East owed much to the use of cannons as well. Portuguese ships, armed with heavy guns that could sink enemy ships at a distance of 100 yards (91 m) or more, easily defeated the lighter fleets of the Muslims in the Indian Ocean.

▲ *Spanish galleon with cannons*

◄ *Seventeenth-century pistol*

Comparing Cultures

Although gunpowder was invented in China, it was the Europeans who used it most effectively to establish new empires. Evaluate the reasons why this occurred. In your explanation, be sure to include the historical impact of European expansion throughout the world.

COOPERATIVE LEARNING ACTIVITY

Presenting an Oral Report Divide the class into four groups. Assign each group one of the four political systems discussed in this section—Buddhist, Javanese, Islamic, and Vietnamese. Have each group do outside research and prepare a report on their political system for oral presentation in class. Their report should include maps, charts, and illustrations of the era's dress, art, and so forth. Following the oral reports, you might want to ask the students to create a chart that compares the four political systems, or have a class discussion on the similarities and differences of the four systems. L2

European Trade in Southeast Asia, 1700

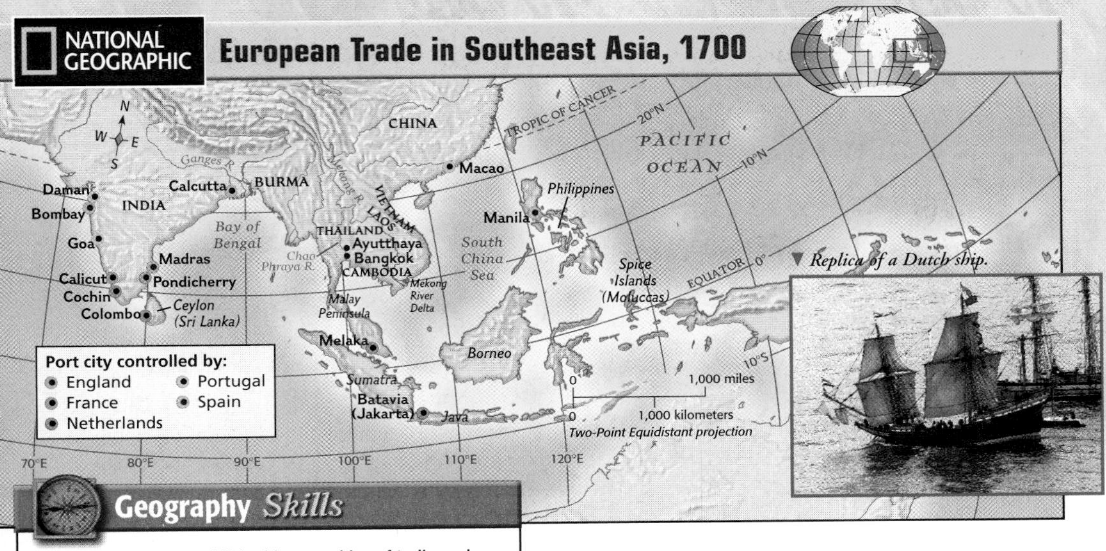

▼ Replica of a Dutch ship.

Geography Skills

Trading forts were established in port cities of India and Southeast Asia.

1. **Interpreting Maps** According to this map, which country controlled the most ports?
2. **Applying Geography Skills** Do outside research to create your own map of European trade. Show the trade routes each country used. What route do ships take today between Europe and Southeast Asia?

power began in the early 1600s when the Dutch seized a Portuguese fort in the Moluccas and then gradually pushed the Portuguese out of the spice trade.

During the next 50 years, the Dutch occupied most of the Portuguese coastal forts along the trade routes throughout the Indian Ocean, including the island of Ceylon (today's Sri Lanka) and Melaka. The aggressive Dutch traders drove the English traders out of the spice market, reducing the English influence to a single port on the southern coast of **Sumatra.**

The Dutch also began to consolidate their political and military control over the entire area. They tried to dominate the clove trade by limiting cultivation of the crop to one island and forcing others to stop growing and trading the spice. Then the Dutch turned their attention to the island of **Java,** where they established a fort at Batavia in 1619. The purpose of the fort was to protect Dutch possessions in the East. Gradually the Dutch brought the entire island under their control.

Impact on the Mainland Portuguese and then Dutch influence was mostly limited to the Malay Peninsula and the Indonesian Archipelago.

The arrival of the Europeans had less impact on mainland Southeast Asia. The Portuguese established limited trade relations with several **mainland states** (part of the continent, as distinguished from peninsulas or offshore islands), including Thailand, Burma, Vietnam, and the remnants of the old Angkor kingdom in Cambodia. By the early seventeenth century, other European nations had begun to compete actively for trade and missionary privileges. In general, however, the mainland states were able to unite and drive the Europeans out.

In Vietnam, a civil war temporarily divided the country into two separate states, one in the south and one in the north. After their arrival in the mid-seventeenth century, the European powers began to take sides in local politics. The Europeans also set up trading posts for their merchants.

By the end of the seventeenth century, however, it had become clear that economic opportunities were limited. Most of the posts were abandoned at that time. French missionaries tried to stay, but their efforts were blocked by the authorities, who viewed converts to Catholicism as a threat to the prestige of the Vietnamese emperor.

Why were the mainland states better able to resist the European challenge than the states in the Malay Peninsula and the Indonesian Archipelago? The mainland states of Burma, Thailand, and Vietnam had begun to define themselves as distinct political entities. They had strong monarchies that resisted foreign intrusion.

In the non-mainland states, there was less political unity. Moreover, these states were victims of their own

CHAPTER 6
Section 3, 201–204

Geography Skills

Answers:

1. Netherlands
2. Maps made by students will vary; Suez Canal

Guided Reading Activity 6–3

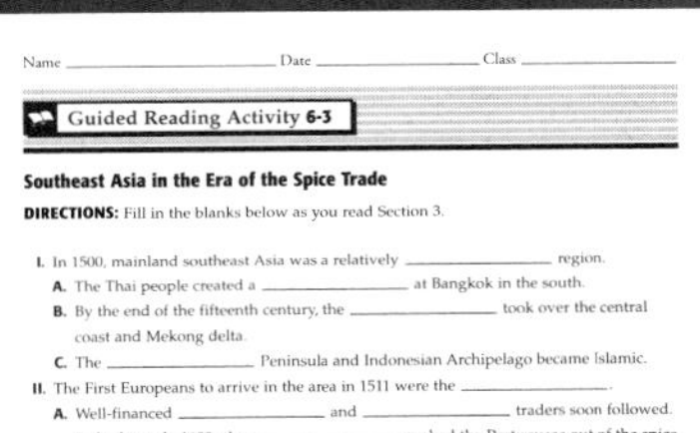

Name ________ Date ________ Class ________

Guided Reading Activity 6-3

Southeast Asia in the Era of the Spice Trade

DIRECTIONS: Fill in the blanks below as you read Section 3.

I. In 1500, mainland southeast Asia was a relatively ________ region.
  A. The Thai people created a ________ at Bangkok in the south.
  B. By the end of the fifteenth century, the ________ took over the central coast and Mekong delta.
  C. The ________ Peninsula and Indonesian Archipelago became Islamic.
II. The First Europeans to arrive in the area in 1511 were the ________.
  A. Well-financed ________ and ________ traders soon followed.
    1. In the early 1600s the ________ pushed the Portuguese out of the spice trade.

Writing Activity

After they have read the chapter, have students write an essay in which they explain the political, economic, cultural, and technological influences of European expansion on both Europeans and non-Europeans. **L2**

Enrich

Discuss with the students why Europeans had less impact on mainland Southeast Asia than they did on the islands along the spice route. *(strong monarchies, internal cohesion)*

3 ASSESS

Assign Section 3 Assessment as homework or as an in-class activity.

Have students use **Interactive Tutor Self-Assessment CD-ROM.**

INTERDISCIPLINARY CONNECTIONS ACTIVITY

Science and Technology Have students research and write a brief illustrated report on one of the following: developments in ship design and construction from antiquity through the age of exploration; the history of cartography from antiquity (beginning with Babylonian maps on clay tablets) through the age of exploration; the locations of various spices that Europeans sought. Ask the students to explain exactly what a spice is, why certain ones were especially prized, and why they were concentrated in certain parts of Asia. **L2**

For grading this activity, refer to the ***Performance Assessment Activities*** booklet.

Reading Check

Answer: the spice trade

Reading Check

Answer: Buddhist king considered superior; Javanese kings shared characteristics of the Buddhist system, both had a sacred quality.

Section Quiz 6–3

Name ______ Date ______ Class ______

Chapter 6 — Score

Section Quiz 6-3

DIRECTIONS: Matching Match each item in Column A with an item in Column B. Write the correct letters in the blanks. *(10 points each)*

Column A
____ 1. the Spice Islands
____ 2. Islamic sultanate in the Malay Peninsula
____ 3. portion of Southeast Asia comprised of Thailand, Burma, Vietnam, and Cambodia
____ 4. dominant new religion from Burma to Vietnam
____ 5. body of non-elective government officials

Column B
A. Melaka
B. mainland states
C. the Moluccas
D. bureaucracy
E. Buddhism

DIRECTIONS: Multiple Choice In the blank, write the letter of the choice that best completes the statement or answers the question. *(10 points each)*

Reading Essentials and Study Guide 6–3

Name ______ Date ______ Class ______

Reading Essentials and Study Guide

Chapter 6, Section 3

For use with textbook pages 201–204

SOUTHEAST ASIA IN THE ERA OF THE SPICE TRADE

KEY TERMS

mainland states states that are part of a continent, as distinguished from peninsulas or offshore islands *(page 203)*

bureaucracy a body of nonelective government officials *(page 204)*

DRAWING FROM EXPERIENCE

Have you ever thought what life would be like if you did not have spices for your food? What spices do you like best? How much would you be willing to pay for your favorite spices?

Reteaching Activity

Ask students to prepare a quiz, complete with answers, for this section. **L1** ELL

4 CLOSE

Ask students to discuss whether or not they believe that Southeast Asia became part of "the age of Western Dominance" during the years covered by this chapter. **L1**

resources. The spice trade there was enormously profitable. European merchants and rulers were determined to gain control of the sources of the spices.

Reading Check **Evaluating** Why were Europeans so interested in Southeast Asia?

Religious and Political Systems

Religious beliefs changed in Southeast Asia during the period from 1500 to 1800. Particularly in the nonmainland states and the **Philippines,** Islam and Christianity were beginning to attract converts. Buddhism was advancing on the mainland, where it became dominant from Burma to Vietnam. Traditional beliefs, however, survived and influenced the new religions.

The political systems in Southeast Asian states evolved into four styles of monarchy. Buddhist kings, Javanese kings, Islamic sultans, and Vietnamese emperors all adapted foreign models of government to local circumstances.

The Buddhist style of kingship became the chief form of government in the mainland states of Burma, Thailand, Laos, and Cambodia. In the Buddhist model, the king was considered superior to other human beings, and served as the link between human society and the universe.

The Javanese style of kingship was rooted in the political traditions of India and shared many of the characteristics of the Buddhist system. Like Buddhist rulers, Javanese kings were believed to have a sacred quality and they maintained the balance between the

Thai king

sacred and the material world. The royal palace was designed to represent the center of the universe. Rays spread outward to the corners of the realm.

Islamic sultans were found on the Malay Peninsula and in the small coastal states of the Indonesian Archipelago. In the Islamic pattern, the head of state was a sultan. He was viewed as a mortal, although he still possessed some special qualities. He was a defender of the faith and staffed his **bureaucracy** (a body of nonelective government officials) mainly with aristocrats.

In Vietnam, kingship followed the Chinese model. Like the Chinese emperor, the Vietnamese emperor ruled according to the teachings of Confucius. He was seen as a mortal appointed by Heaven to rule because of his talent and virtue. He also served as the intermediary between Heaven and Earth.

Reading Check **Comparing** How did the Javanese style of kingship compare to the Buddhist style of kingship?

SECTION 3 ASSESSMENT

Checking for Understanding

1. **Define** mainland states, bureaucracy.
2. **Identify** Khmer, Dutch.
3. **Locate** Moluccas, Sumatra, Java, Philippines.
4. **Explain** why the Portuguese decided to set up only small settlements in the Moluccas.
5. **List** the places where the Dutch established their forts. What were the major objectives of the Dutch? How did they go about accomplishing their objectives?

Critical Thinking

6. **Evaluate** Why did the Malay world fall to foreign traders, while the countries of mainland Southeast Asia retained their independence?
7. **Categorizing Information** Use a table like the one below to describe the four types of political systems that developed in Southeast Asia.

Region	Political System

Analyzing Visuals

8. **Examine** the picture of the Thai king shown above. How does this picture reflect the Buddhist model of kingship practiced in Southeast Asian states such as Thailand?

Writing About History

9. **Expository Writing** Pretend that you are a Portuguese merchant trying to establish trade relations with Southeast Asia. Write a letter to the authorities in Portugal explaining the particular difficulties you are encountering in Southeast Asia.

SECTION 3 ASSESSMENT

1. Key terms are in blue.
2. Khmer *(p. 202)*; Dutch *(p. 202)*
3. See chapter maps.
4. lacked military and financial resources
5. Moluccas, Ceylon, Melaka, Batavia; to control trade by limiting cultivation, establishing military and political control, driving out competition
6. less political unity
7. Burma, Thailand, Laos, Cambodia: Buddhist style of kingship; Java: kingship based on Indian political traditions; Malay Peninsula, Indonesian Archipelago: Islamic sultanates; Vietnam: emperor, rule according to teachings of Confucius
8. king elevated and isolated, reflecting his divine status and superiority over all other human beings
9. Students will compose a letter from the point of view of a Portuguese merchant.

CRITICAL THINKING SKILLBUILDER

Making Inferences and Drawing Conclusions

Why Learn This Skill?

While driving, you hear a news report about a fire downtown. As you approach downtown, traffic is very heavy. You cannot see any smoke, but you infer that the traffic is caused by the fire.

To **infer** *means to evaluate information and arrive at a conclusion. When you make inferences, you draw conclusions that are not stated directly.*

Bags of spices for sale

Learning the Skill

Follow the steps below to help make inferences and draw conclusions:

- Read carefully to determine the main facts and ideas.
- Write down the important facts.
- Consider any information you know that relates to this topic.
- Determine how your own knowledge adds to or changes the material.
- What inferences can you make about the material that are not specifically stated in the facts that you gathered from your reading?
- Use your knowledge and reason to develop conclusions about the facts.
- If possible, find specific information that proves or disproves your inference.

Practicing the Skill

Read the passage below, then answer the questions that follow.

In 1511, the Portuguese seized Melaka and soon occupied the Moluccas. Known to Europeans as the Spice Islands, the Moluccas were the chief source of the spices that had originally attracted the Portuguese to the Indian Ocean.

The Portuguese, however, lacked the military and financial resources to impose their authority over broad areas. Instead, they set up small settlements along the coast, which they used as trading posts or as way stations en route to the Spice Islands.

The situation changed with the arrival of the English and Dutch traders, who were better financed than were the Portuguese. The shift in power began in the early 1600s, when the Dutch seized a Portuguese fort in the Moluccas and drove out the Portuguese.

During the next fifty years, the Dutch occupied most of the Portuguese coastal forts along the trade routes throughout the Indian Ocean. The aggressive Dutch traders also drove the English traders out of the spice market, reducing the English influence to a single port on the southern coast of Sumatra.

1. What events does the writer describe?
2. What facts are presented?
3. What can you infer about the Dutch traders during this period?
4. What conclusion can you make about the spice market, other than those specifically stated by the author?

Applying the Skill

Scan the newspaper or a magazine for a political cartoon. Paste the cartoon on a piece of paper or poster board. Underneath, list three valid inferences based on the work.

Glencoe's **Skillbuilder Interactive Workbook, Level 2,** provides instruction and practice in key social studies skills.

TEACH

Making Inferences and Drawing Conclusions Bring to class a short news story from the local newspaper or, if appropriate, from the school newspaper. Duplicate and circulate the story, or read it aloud to the class. Have students summarize the facts as stated, review what they already know about the situation, and then form one or more conclusions about the topic. If time permits, have the class follow up later if additional information appears to support or refute the conclusions. **L1**

Additional Practice

Skills Reinforcement Activity 6

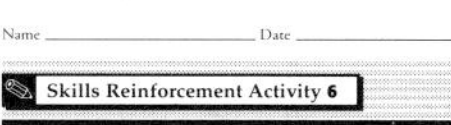

Making Inferences and Drawing Conclusions

GLENCOE TECHNOLOGY

CD-ROM
Glencoe Skillbuilder Interactive Workbook CD-ROM, Level 2

This interactive CD-ROM reinforces student mastery of essential social studies skills.

ANSWERS TO PRACTICING THE SKILL

1. The writer describes the European takeover of the spice market.
2. Among the facts presented are the date of the original European takeover, identities of the conquerors, territories conquered, date of beginning of the shift of power and the duration of the takeover.
3. Dutch traders wanted to control the spice market.
4. Among conclusions that students may draw is the fact that the spice market was very lucrative.

Applying the Skill: Answers will vary.

GLENCOE TECHNOLOGY

MindJogger Videoquiz

Use the **MindJogger Videoquiz** to review Chapter 6 content.

 Available in VHS.

Using Key Terms

1. mercantilism 2. Conquistadors 3. bureaucracy 4. plantations 5. mainland states 6. balance of trade 7. colony 8. Triangular trade 9. Middle Passage

Reviewing Key Facts

10. spices
11. Cortés; Pizarro
12. gold, silver, and agricultural products
13. Melaka
14. a cargo of spices; the profit was several thousand percent
15. prisoners of war; rewards of victors
16. Portugal
17. the compass and astrolabe aided in exploration, allowing them to determine what direction they were moving and to navigate; lateen sails made ships more maneuverable and allowed them to carry heavy cannon and more goods
18. He knew the world was round but underestimated the circumference.
19. They had little or no resistance to European diseases.

Critical Thinking

20. Answers will vary, but may include: may have killed newborns, discouraged or forbade marriage, kept the sexes apart.
21. Answers may include: the age of exploration brought the people of Europe, Asia, the Americas, and Africa into direct contact for the first time and led to a transfer of ideas and products. However, the European colonization took a great toll in human life and often had a negative impact on cultures that were conquered.

CHAPTER 6 ASSESSMENT and ACTIVITIES

Using Key Terms

1. A set of principles that dominated economic thought in the seventeenth century was called ______.
2. ______ were Spanish conquerors who were motivated by religious zeal and the desire for glory and riches.
3. A body of nonelective government officials is called a ______.
4. Many Africans were removed from their homes and shipped to large landed estates in the Americas called ______.
5. States that form part of a continent are called ______.
6. The ______ is the difference in value between what a nation imports and what it exports.
7. A settlement in a new territory, linked to the parent country, is called a ______.
8. ______ is the route between Europe, Africa, and America.
9. The journey of slaves from Africa to America on the worst portion of the triangular trade route was called the ______.

Reviewing Key Facts

10. **History** What did the Europeans want from the East?
11. **History** Who was the conquistador who overthrew the Aztec Empire? Who conquered the Inca?
12. **Economics** What did Europeans want from the Americas?
13. **Geography** What was the name of the city located on the Malay Peninsula that was the central point in the spice trade?
14. **Economics** When Vasco da Gama reached India, what cargo did he bring back? How profitable was his voyage?
15. **History** How did most Africans become slaves?
16. **History** What European country conquered Brazil?
17. **Science and Technology** How did the Portuguese make effective use of naval technology?
18. **Geography** What did Christopher Columbus believe about the size and shape of Earth?
19. **History** Why were European diseases devastating to the natives of America?

Chapter Summary

Listed below are the major European explorers of the fifteenth and sixteenth centuries. Marco Polo is the one explorer listed who predates the Age of Exploration.

Explorer	Date	Sponsoring Country	Discovery
Marco Polo	Late 13th cent.	Italy	Asia
Bartholomeu Dias	1487	Portugal	Cape of Good Hope
Christopher Columbus	1492	Spain	Bahamas, Cuba, Hispaniola
Vasco da Gama	1497	Portugal	India
John Cabot	1497	England	New England coastline
Amerigo Vespucci	1497	Portugal, Spain	South American coast
Pedro Cabral	1500	Portugal	Brazil
Afonso de Albuquerque	1509	Portugal	Melaka
Vasco de Balboa	1513	Spain	Pacific Ocean
Juan Ponce de León	1513	Spain	Florida
Hernán Cortés	1519	Spain	Mexico
Ferdinand Magellan	1520	Spain	Sailed around the world
Giovanni da Verrazano	1524	France	East coast of North America
Francisco Pizarro	1531	Spain	Peru
Jacques Cartier	1534	France	St. Lawrence River
Hernando de Soto	1539	Spain	North America's southeast
Francisco de Coronado	1540	Spain	North America's southwest
João Cabrilho	1542	Spain	California
Samuel de Champlain	1603	France	Great Lakes and Quebec
Henry Hudson	1609	Netherlands, England	Hudson River, Hudson Bay

206

Writing About History

22. Answers will vary but should be supported by logical arguments.

Analyzing Sources

23. Answers will vary but might include a discussion of morals and values.
24. Answers will vary, depending on how students interpret the words used.

Applying Technology Skills

25. Students will create a spreadsheet.

Making Decisions

26. Answers will vary.

CHAPTER 6
Assessment and Activities

Self-Check Quiz
Visit the *Glencoe World History—Modern Times* Web site at wh.mt.glencoe.com and click on **Chapter 6–Self-Check Quiz** to prepare for the Chapter Test.

Critical Thinking

20. Drawing Conclusions What might have resulted from the fact that many slave owners believed it was more economical to buy a new slave than to raise a child to working age?

21. Making Generalizations Describe the impact on history of the voyages of Christopher Columbus.

Writing About History

22. Informative Writing Write an essay in which you analyze the reasons why Native Americans in both North and South America might be offended by the term *New World.* What does the use of the term suggest about European attitudes toward the rest of the world? Refer to the Treaty of Tordesillas and use other specific examples.

Analyzing Sources

Read the following comment by an Aztec describing the Spanish conquerors:

> ❝[They] longed and lusted for gold. Their bodies swelled with greed, and their hunger was ravenous; they hungered like pigs for that gold.❞

23. Based on this quote, what might the Aztec have inferred about the Spaniards and their civilization?

24. What do you think is meant by "they hungered like pigs for that gold"?

Applying Technology Skills

25. Using the Internet Search the Internet for additional information about early European explorers and their achievements. Organize your information by creating a spreadsheet. Include headings such as name, regions of exploration, types of technology used, and contributions.

Making Decisions

26. Pretend that you are the leader of a country and must decide whether or not to explore outer space. What are the benefits and risks involved in undertaking space exploration? Compare and contrast modern space explorations with European voyages of exploration. Consider the technologies used, the ways explorations were funded, and the impact of these ventures on human knowledge.

Analyzing Maps and Charts

Study the chart on the opposite page to answer the following questions.

27. Approximately how many years separated the explorations of Marco Polo and those of Vasco da Gama?

28. Which countries sponsored the most explorations?

29. The voyages of discovery began in Europe. What continents did the explorers visit?

The Princeton Review — Standardized Test Practice

Directions: Use the map and your knowledge of world history to choose the best answer to the following question.

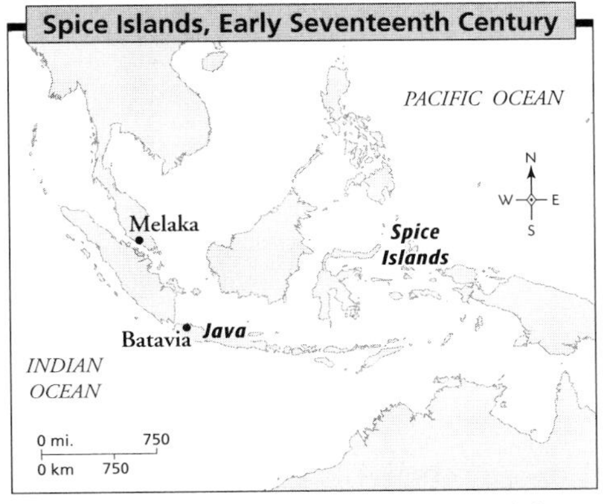

The Dutch established Batavia as a fort in 1619 to help them edge the Portuguese traders out of the area now called Indonesia. Today, which city is located where Batavia was established?

A New Delhi
B Jakarta
C Melaka
D Beijing

Test-Taking Tip: If a test question involves reading a map, make sure you read the title of the map and look at the map carefully for information before you try to answer the question.

HISTORY Online

Have students visit the Web site at wh.mt.glencoe.com to review Chapter 6 and take the Self-Check Quiz.

Standardized Test Practice

Answer: B
Answer Explanation: confirmed by modern map; students should start by eliminating the answers that are obviously incorrect based on their knowledge of world geography

Bonus Question ?

Ask: **How would the world be different if the age of exploration had never occurred?** *(only local, or regional economies; Native Americans would constitute entire population of North and South America; products and ideas would not have spread; geographical knowledge limited.)*

Analyzing Maps and Charts

27. 200 years
28. Spain, followed by Portugal
29. Asia, Africa, North America, South America

Chapter 7 Resources

Timesaving Tools

TeacherWorks™ All-In-One Planner and Resource Center

- **Interactive Teacher Edition** Access your Teacher Wraparound Edition and your classroom resources with a few easy clicks.
- **Interactive Lesson Planner** Planning has never been easier! Organize your week, month, semester, or year with all the lesson helps you need to make teaching creative, timely, and relevant.

Use Glencoe's **Presentation Plus!** multimedia teacher tool to easily present dynamic lessons that visually excite your students. Using Microsoft PowerPoint® you can customize the presentations to create your own personalized lessons.

Teaching Transparencies

Graphic Organizer Student Activity 7 Transparency

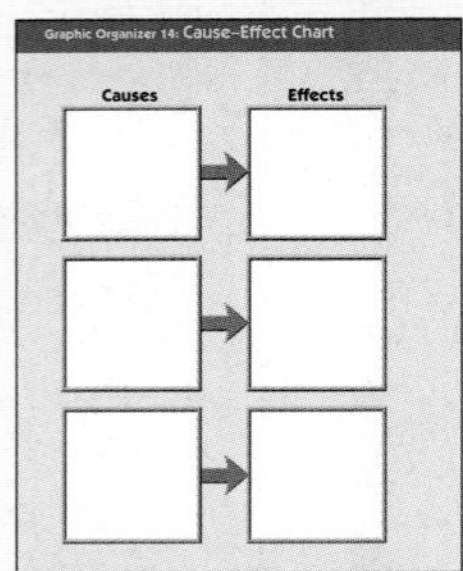

Chapter Transparency 7

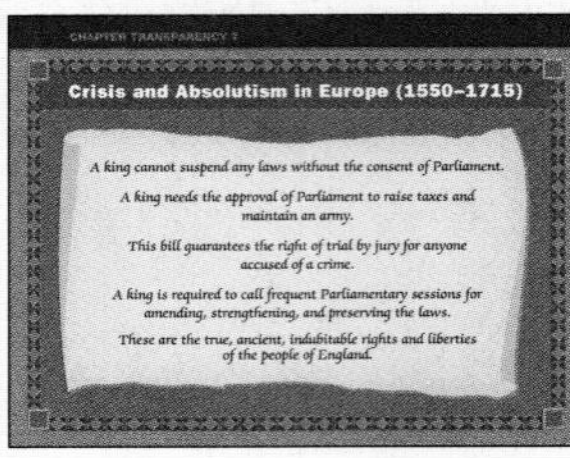

Map Overlay Transparency 7

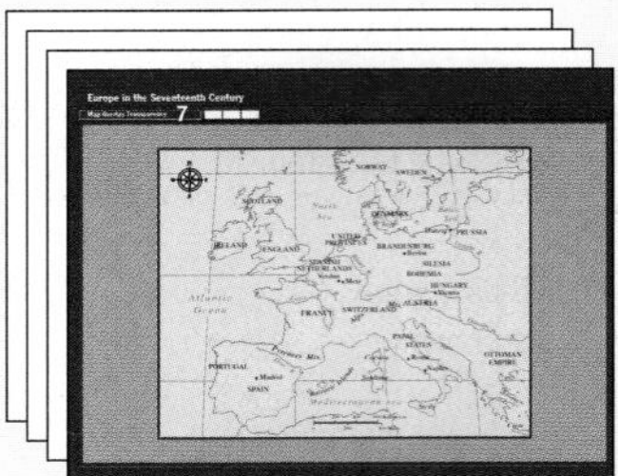

Application and Enrichment

Enrichment Activity 7

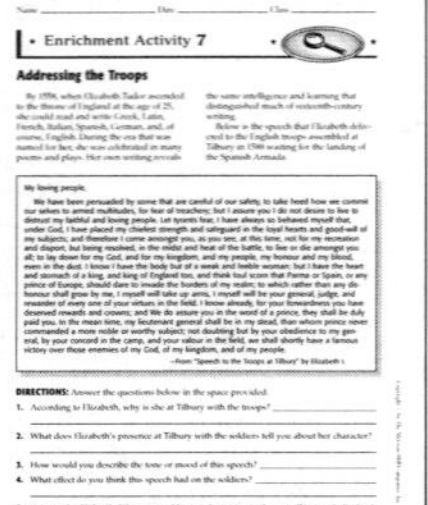

Primary Source Reading 7

History Simulation Activity 7

Historical Significance Activity 7

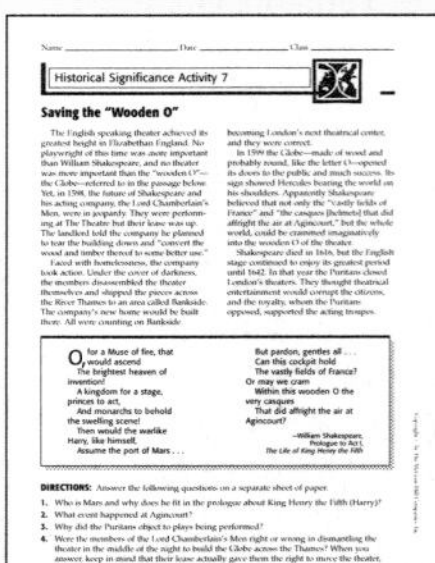

Cooperative Learning Activity 7

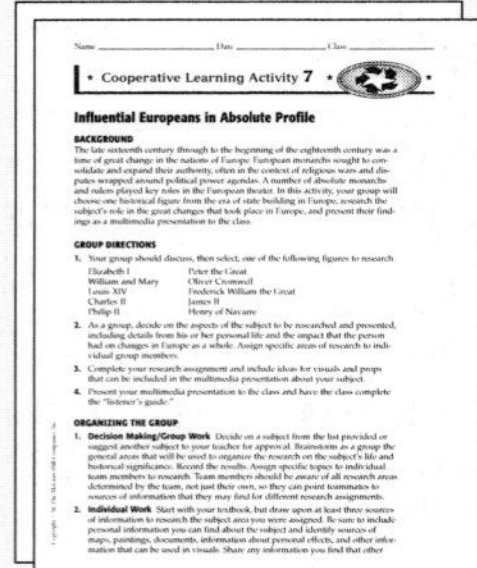

A&E HOME VIDEO. **Biography**® THE HISTORY CHANNEL®

The following videotape program is available from Glencoe as a supplement to Chapter 7:

- **Michelangelo** (ISBN 1–56501–425–1)

To order, call Glencoe at 1–800–334–7344. To find classroom resources to accompany this video, check the following home pages:
A&E Television: www.aande.com
The History Channel: www.historychannel.com

Chapter 7 Resources

Review and Reinforcement

Linking Past and Present Activity 7

Time Line Activity 7

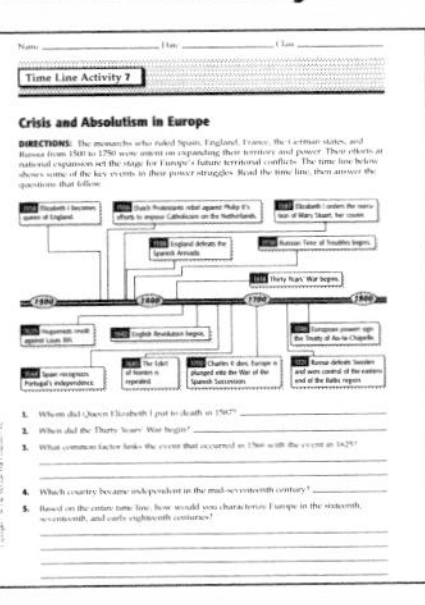

Reteaching Activity 7

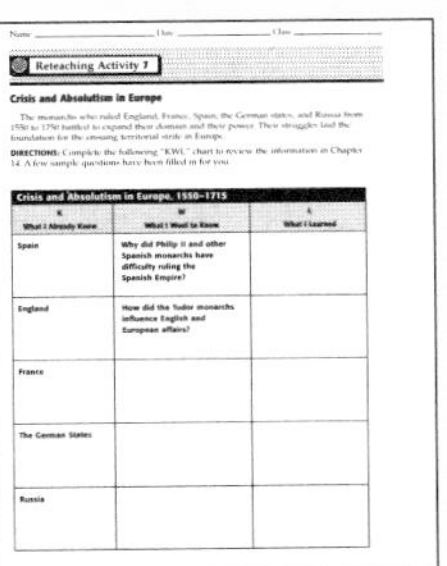

Vocabulary Activity 7

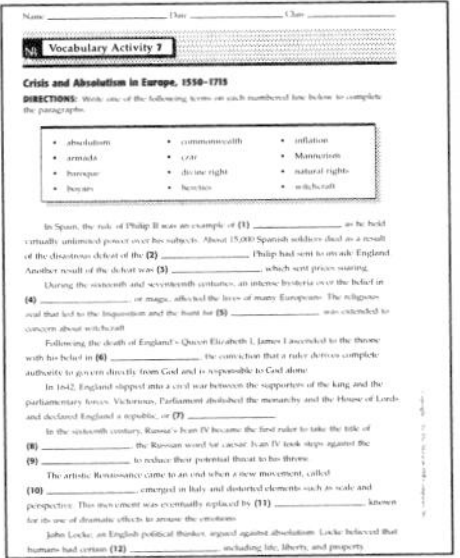

Critical Thinking Skills Activity 7

Assessment and Evaluation

Chapter 7 Test Form A

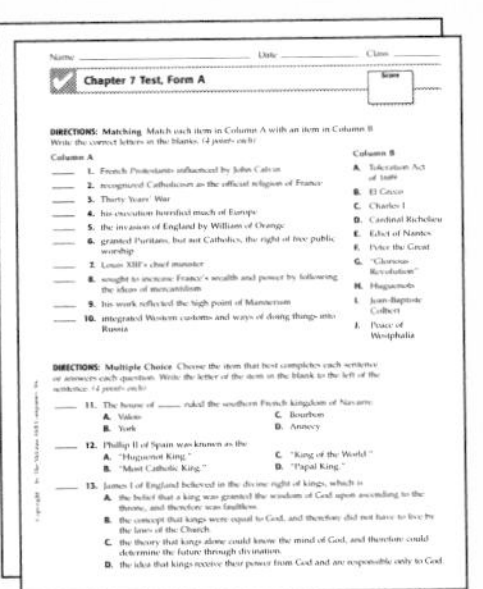

Chapter 7 Test Form B

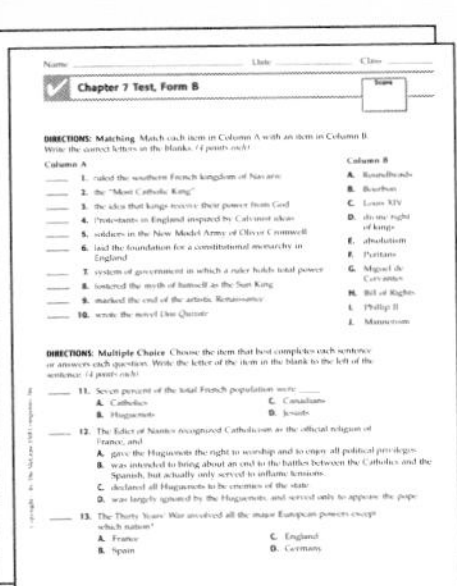

Performance Assessment Activity 7

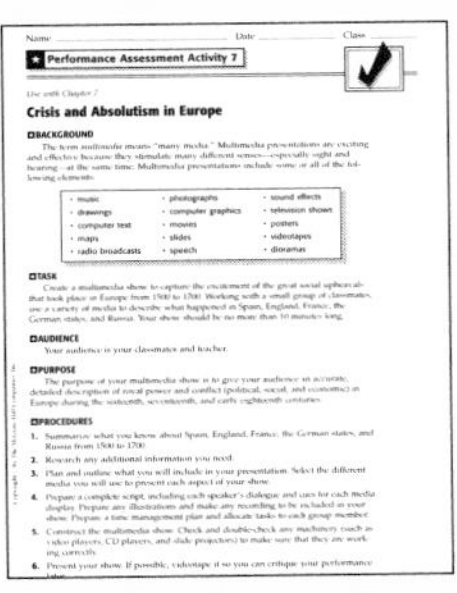

ExamView® Pro Testmaker CD-ROM

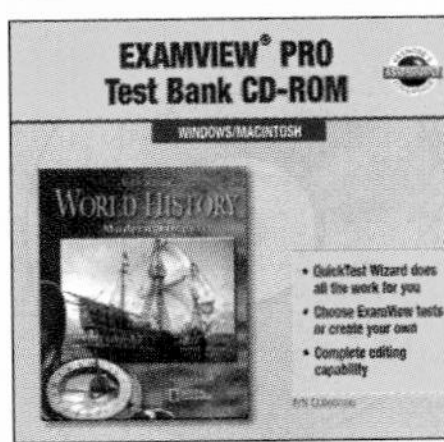

Standardized Test Skills Practice Workbook Activity 7

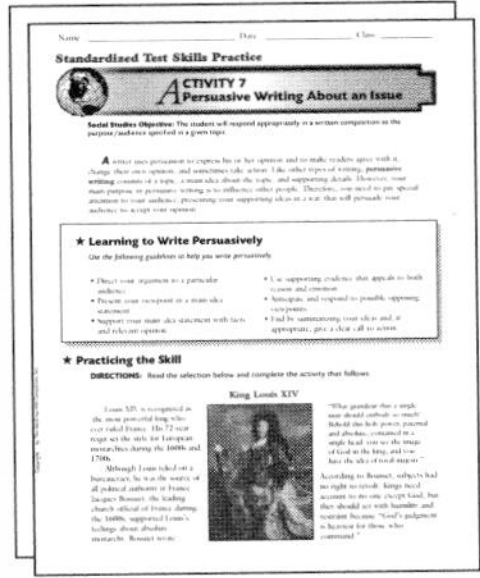

Interdisciplinary Activities

Mapping History Activity 7

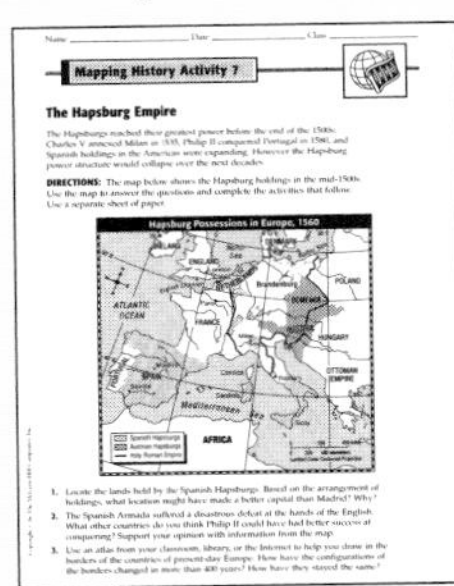

World Art and Music Activity 7

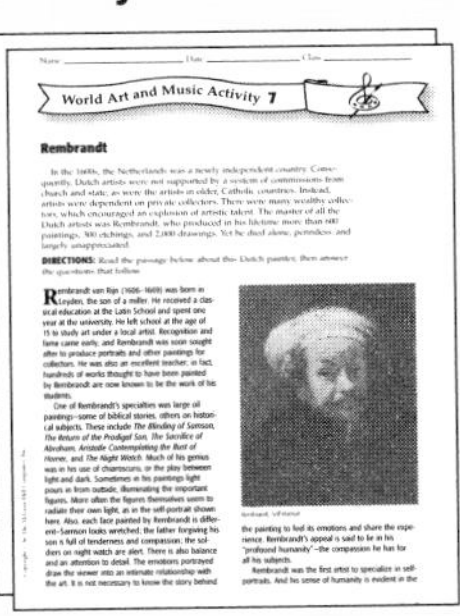

History and Geography Activity 7

People in World History Activity 7

Multimedia

- Vocabulary PuzzleMaker CD-ROM
- Interactive Tutor Self-Assessment CD-ROM
- ExamView® Pro Testmaker CD-ROM
- Audio Program
- World History Primary Source Document Library CD-ROM
- MindJogger Videoquiz
- Presentation Plus! CD-ROM
- TeacherWorks CD-ROM
- Interactive Student Edition CD-ROM
- The World History—Modern Times Video Program

Spanish Resources

The following Spanish language materials are available in the Spanish Resources Binder:

- Spanish Guided Reading Activities
- Spanish Reteaching Activities
- Spanish Quizzes and Tests
- Spanish Vocabulary Activities
- Spanish Summaries

Chapter 7 Resources

SECTION RESOURCES

Daily Objectives	Reproducible Resources	Multimedia Resources
SECTION 1 **Europe in Crisis: The Wars of Religion** 1. Discuss the situation in many European nations in which Protestants and Catholics fought for political and religious control. 2. Summarize how, during the sixteenth and seventeenth centuries, many European rulers extended their power and their borders.	Reproducible Lesson Plan 7–1 Daily Lecture and Discussion Notes 7–1 Guided Reading Activity 7–1* Section Quiz 7–1* Reading Essentials and Study Guide 7–1	Daily Focus Skills Transparency 7–1 Interactive Tutor Self-Assessment CD-ROM ExamView® Pro Testmaker CD-ROM Presentation Plus! CD-ROM
SECTION 2 **Social Crises, War, and Revolution** 1. Explain how the Thirty Years' War ended the unity of the Holy Roman Empire. 2. Relate how democratic ideals were strengthened as a result of the English and Glorious Revolutions.	Reproducible Lesson Plan 7–2 Daily Lecture and Discussion Notes 7–2 Guided Reading Activity 7–2* Section Quiz 7–2* Reading Essentials and Study Guide 7–2	Daily Focus Skills Transparency 7–2 Interactive Tutor Self-Assessment CD-ROM ExamView® Pro Testmaker CD-ROM Presentation Plus! CD-ROM
SECTION 3 **Response to Crisis: Absolutism** 1. Identify and describe Louis XIV, an absolute monarch whose extravagant lifestyle and military campaigns weakened France. 2. Discuss how Prussia, Austria, and Russia emerged as great European powers in the seventeenth and eighteenth centuries.	Reproducible Lesson Plan 7–3 Daily Lecture and Discussion Notes 7–3 Guided Reading Activity 7–3* Section Quiz 7–3* Reading Essentials and Study Guide 7–3	Daily Focus Skills Transparency 7–3 Interactive Tutor Self-Assessment CD-ROM ExamView® Pro Testmaker CD-ROM Presentation Plus! CD-ROM
SECTION 4 **The World of European Culture** 1. Describe the artistic movements of Mannerism and the baroque, which began in Italy and reflected the spiritual perceptions of the time. 2. Identify Shakespeare and Lope de Vega, prolific writers of dramas and comedies that reflected the human condition.	Reproducible Lesson Plan 7–4 Daily Lecture and Discussion Notes 7–4 Guided Reading Activity 7–4* Section Quiz 7–4* Reteaching Activity 7* Reading Essentials and Study Guide 7–4	Daily Focus Skills Transparency 7–4 Interactive Tutor Self-Assessment CD-ROM ExamView® Pro Testmaker CD-ROM Presentation Plus! CD-ROM

0:00 **OUT OF TIME?**
Assign the Chapter 7 **Reading Essentials and Study Guide.**

*Also Available in Spanish

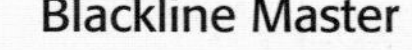

Blackline Master | Poster | Transparency | Music Program | CD-ROM | Audio Program | DVD | Videocassette

Chapter 7 Resources

NATIONAL GEOGRAPHIC Teacher's Corner

INDEX TO NATIONAL GEOGRAPHIC MAGAZINE

The following articles relate to this chapter:

- "The Tale of the San Diego," by Frank Goddio, July 1994.
- "The Living Tower of London," by William R. Newcott, October 1993.
- "St. Petersburg: Capital of the Tsars," by Steve Raymer, December 1993.
- "Inside the Kremlin," by Jon Thompson, January 1990.
- "Shakespeare Lives at the Folger," by Merle Severy, February 1987.
- "Legacy from the Deep: Henry VIII's Lost Warship," by Margaret Rule, May 1983.

NGS ONLINE

Access National Geographic's new dynamic MapMachine Web site and other geography resources at:
www.nationalgeographic.com
www.nationalgeographic.com/maps

KEY TO ABILITY LEVELS

Teaching strategies have been coded.

L1 BASIC activities for all students
L2 AVERAGE activities for average to above-average students
L3 CHALLENGING activities for above-average students
ELL ENGLISH LANGUAGE LEARNER activities

Block Schedule

Activities that are suited to use within the block scheduling framework are identified by:

Use our Web site for additional resources. All essential content is covered in the Student Edition.

You and your students can visit www.wh.mt.glencoe.com, the Web site companion to *Glencoe World History—Modern Times.* This innovative integration of electronic and print media offers your students a wealth of opportunities. The student text directs students to the Web site for the following options:

- **Chapter Overviews**
- **Self-Check Quizzes**
- **Student Web Activities**
- **Textbook Updates**

Answers to the Student Web Activities are provided for you in the **Web Activity Lesson Plans.** Additional Web resources and Interactive Tutor Puzzles are also available.

From the Classroom of...

Candice Frumson
Ladue Horton Watkins
High School
St. Louis, Missouri

What Kind of King am I?

Have students analyze and discuss primary source documents to gain an understanding of Louis XIV and absolutism. Choose from the writings of Louis or members of his court and distribute copies to students. Read the document aloud and provide time for students to take their own notes as to the main points and their interpretation. Then have students work in pairs to discuss the main points and take notes. Follow this activity with a class discussion. Ask if Louis's problems have a modern equivalent (use Hitler, the United States, the Soviet Union, and so on as examples). Ask students to write a "talk back" to Louis XIV telling him what they think of his ideas.

Performance Assessment

Refer to Activity 7 in the Performance Assessment Activities and Rubrics booklet.

The Impact Today

Have students explain the many ways in which their daily lives are affected by the U. S. Constitution. Remind students that European ideas and ideals influenced the Constitution's Framers as they prepared this living document that has profoundly shaped the way we live.

GLENCOE TECHNOLOGY

The World History—Modern Times Video Program

To learn more about early seventeenth-century France, students can view the Chapter 7 video, "Louis XIV: The Sun King," from **The World History—Modern Times Video Program.**

MindJogger Videoquiz

Use the **MindJogger Videoquiz** to preview Chapter 7 content.

Available in VHS.

CHAPTER 7 Crisis and Absolutism in Europe

1550–1715

Key Events

As you read this chapter, look for these key events in the history of Europe during the sixteenth, seventeenth, and early eighteenth centuries.

- *The French religious wars of the sixteenth century pitted Protestant Calvinists against Catholics.*
- *From 1560 to 1650, wars, including the devastating Thirty Years' War, and economic and social crises plagued Europe.*
- *European monarchs sought economic and political stability through absolutism and the divine right of kings.*
- *Concern with order and power was reflected in the writings of Thomas Hobbes and John Locke.*

The Impact Today

The events that occurred during this time period still impact our lives today.

- *The ideas of John Locke are imbedded in the Constitution of the United States.*
- *The works of William Shakespeare continue to be read and dramatized all over the world.*

World History—Modern Times Video *The Chapter 7 video,"Louis XIV: The Sun King," chronicles the practice of absolutism in France during the 1600s.*

Elizabeth I

c. 1520
Mannerism movement begins in Italy

1558
Elizabeth I becomes queen of England

1500

1550

1566
Violence erupts between Calvinists and Catholics in the Netherlands

St. Francis, as painted by Mannerist El Greco

208

TWO-MINUTE LESSON LAUNCHER

This chapter focuses on important monarchs throughout Europe during the sixteenth and seventeenth centuries. Help students understand how monarchs consolidated their power and how they ensured that their monarchies would survive into the next generation. Write the following words on the chalkboard or an overhead transparency: *prestige, privilege, organization, personality, diplomacy, opulence, conflict.* Have each student choose the quality he or she feels is most necessary for monarchs to maintain their power and then have students write a brief paragraph explaining why they chose that quality. **L1**

Introducing CHAPTER 14

Versailles was the center of court life during the reign of Louis XIV.

John Locke

1598 French Wars of Religion end

1618 Thirty Years' War begins in Germany

1648 Peace of Westphalia ends Thirty Years' War

1689 Toleration Act of 1689 is passed in English Parliament

1690 John Locke develops theory of government

1701 Frederick I becomes king of Prussia

1600 1650 1700

Gustavus Adolphus, the king of Sweden, on the battlefield

HISTORY Online

Chapter Overview
Visit the *Glencoe World History—Modern Times* Web site at wh.mt.glencoe.com and click on **Chapter 7–Chapter Overview** to preview chapter information.

209

Chapter Objectives

After studying this chapter, students should be able to:

1. describe the causes of the French Wars of Religion and explain how they were resolved;
2. explain the militant Catholicism of Philip II and its effects on Europe;
3. list the causes and results of the Thirty Years' War;
4. discuss the significance of the English Revolution and the Glorious Revolution;
5. explain absolutism in relation to Louis XIV, Ivan the Terrible, and Peter the Great;
6. distinguish between an absolute monarchy and a constitutional monarchy;
7. explain the significant movements in art, literature, and philosophy during the sixteenth and seventeenth centuries.

Chapter Overview
Introduce students to chapter content and key terms by having them access **Chapter Overview 7** at wh.mt.glencoe.com

Time Line Activity

Have students examine the events on the time line and list the events that relate to religious struggles. *(violence between Calvinists and Catholics in the Netherlands, French Wars of Religion, Toleration Act)* **L1**

MORE ABOUT THE ART

The Palace of Versailles is one of the most famous structures in Western architecture. It was originally built to reflect Louis XIV's power and grandeur. The palace was so expensive to build that Louis XIV destroyed some of the bills to avoid criticism from his ministers. On several occasions during his reign, the palace was the scene of elaborate and enormously expensive festivals that lasted for as long as a week. The armistice that ended World War I was signed in the palace, and the treaty named after it. Today, the palace is in great need of restoration. The Versailles Museum of France has been closed for nearly twenty years. Also closed to the public are the Hall of Battles and the magnificent Hall of the Crusades. Funds for restoring buildings and works of art are scarce.

CHAPTER PREVIEW

Introducing

A Story That Matters

Depending upon the ability level of your students, select from the following questions to reinforce the reading of *A Story That Matters.*

- What evidence is there in the story that suggests Louis XIV enjoyed being in control? *(He always appeared the same and did not lose control of himself.)*
- What was the one characteristic about himself that Louis XIV could not seem to control? *(his vanity)*
- Why do you think a monarch like Louis XIV, with limitless, unrestrained vanity, might make "mistakes of judgment"? *(He was too concerned with his own appearance and ego and did not always see the bigger picture.)* **L1 L2**

About the Art

Louis XIV was a great patron of the arts and increased the number of paintings in his galleries from 200 to 2,500. He demanded that artists meet classical standards that reflected elegance, self-restraint, and polish. French art became the expression of the nation and the king, but not of the people. French styles in both art and architecture spread to ruling classes all over Europe.

CHAPTER PREVIEW

A Story That Matters

Louis XIV with his army

Louis XIV holding court

The Majesty of Louis XIV

Louis XIV has been regarded by some as the perfect embodiment of an absolute monarch. Duc de Saint-Simon, who had firsthand experience of French court life, said in his memoirs that Louis was "the very figure of a hero, so imbued with a natural majesty that it appeared even in his most insignificant gestures and movements."

The king's natural grace gave him a special charm: "He was as dignified and majestic in his dressing gown as when dressed in robes of state, or on horseback at the head of his troops." He excelled at exercise and was never affected by the weather: "Drenched with rain or snow, pierced with cold, bathed in sweat or covered with dust, he was always the same."

He spoke well and learned quickly. He was naturally kind, and "he loved truth, justice, order, and reason." His life was orderly: "Nothing could be regulated with greater exactitude than were his days and hours." His self-control was evident: "He did not lose control of himself ten times in his whole life, and then only with inferior persons."

Even absolute monarchs had imperfections, however, and Saint-Simon had the courage to point them out: "Louis XIV's vanity was without limit or restraint." This trait led to his "distaste for all merit, intelligence, education, and most of all, for all independence of character and sentiment in others." It led as well as "to mistakes of judgment in matters of importance."

Why It Matters

The religious upheavals of the sixteenth century left Europeans sorely divided. Wars, revolutions, and economic and social crises haunted Europe, making the 90 years from 1560 to 1650 an age of crisis in European life. One response to these crises was a search for order. Many states satisfied this search by extending monarchical power. Other states, such as England, created systems where monarchs were limited by the power of a parliament.

History and You As you read through this chapter, you will learn about a number of monarchs. Create either a paper or electronic chart listing the following information: name of the ruler; country; religion; challenges; accomplishments. Using outside sources, add another category to your chart to reflect what you learn about the personal life and family of each king.

HISTORY AND YOU

Maintaining order and increasing political and economic stability has been the primary goal of most governments. What is the best way to do this—by extending governmental controls and powers or by guaranteeing individual rights and limiting government? Have students analyze this question by researching current examples of at least two governments that have taken different approaches to solving this issue. Students should familiarize themselves with John Locke and Thomas Hobbes who are discussed in Section 4 of this chapter before conducting their research. Have students write a brief report stating their opinion about this issue, as supported by the results of their research. **L2**

SECTION 1

Europe in Crisis: The Wars of Religion

Guide to Reading

Main Ideas
- In many European nations, Protestants and Catholics fought for political and religious control.
- During the sixteenth and seventeenth centuries, many European rulers extended their power and their borders.

Key Terms
militant, armada

People to Identify
Huguenots, Henry of Navarre, King Philip II, William the Silent, Elizabeth Tudor

Places to Locate
Netherlands, Scotland, Ireland

Preview Questions
1. What were the causes and results of France's wars of religion?
2. How do the policies of Elizabeth I of England and Philip II of Spain compare?

Reading Strategy
Compare and Contrast As you read this section, complete a chart like the one below comparing the listed characteristics of France, Spain, and England.

	France	Spain	England
Government			
Religion			
Conflicts			

Preview of Events

1560 · 1570 · 1580 · 1590 · 1600

- **1562** French Wars of Religion begin
- **1571** Spain defeats Turks in Battle of Lepanto
- **1588** England defeats the Spanish Armada
- **1598** Edict of Nantes recognizes rights of Huguenots in Catholic France

Saint Bartholomew's Day massacre

Voices from the Past

In August of 1572, during the French Wars of Religion, the Catholic party decided to kill Protestant leaders gathered in Paris. One Protestant described the scene:

❝In an instant, the whole city was filled with dead bodies of every sex and age, and indeed amid such confusion and disorder that everyone was allowed to kill whoever he pleased. . . . Nevertheless, the main fury fell on our people [the Protestants]. . . . The continuous shooting of pistols, the frightful cries of those they slaughtered, the bodies thrown from windows . . . the breaking down of doors and windows, the stones thrown against them, and the looting of more than 600 homes over a long period can only bring before the eyes of the reader an unforgettable picture of the calamity appalling in every way.❞

— ***The Huguenot Wars,*** Julian Coudy, 1969

Conflict between Catholics and Protestants was at the heart of the French Wars of Religion.

The French Wars of Religion

By 1560, Calvinism and Catholicism had become highly militant (combative) religions. They were aggressive in trying to win converts and in eliminating each other's authority. Their struggle for the minds and hearts of Europeans was the chief cause of the religious wars that plagued Europe in the sixteenth century.

SECTION RESOURCES

Reproducible Masters
- Reproducible Lesson Plan 7–1
- Daily Lecture and Discussion Notes 7–1
- Guided Reading Activity 7–1
- Section Quiz 7–1
- Reading Essentials and Study Guide 7–1

Transparencies
- Daily Focus Skills Transparency 7–1

Multimedia
- Interactive Tutor Self-Assessment CD-ROM
- ExamView® Pro Testmaker CD-ROM
- Presentation Plus! CD-ROM

1 FOCUS

Section Overview

This section explores the struggles between Catholics and Protestants during this period.

BELLRINGER
Skillbuilder Activity

Project transparency and have students answer questions.

Available as a blackline master.

Daily Focus Skills Transparency 7–1

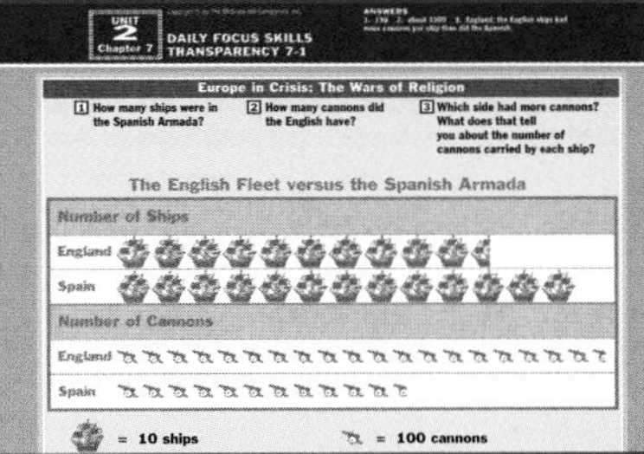

Guide to Reading

Answers to Graphic: France: Government: monarchy (Henry IV); Religion: Catholic; Conflicts: French Wars of Religion (1562–1598); Spain: Government: monarchy (Philip II); Religion: Catholic; Conflicts: Battle of Lepanto (1571), revolt in Netherlands (1566–1609), Armada attacked England (1588); England: Government: monarchy (Elizabeth I); Religion: Protestant; Conflicts: defeated Spanish Armada (1588)

Preteaching Vocabulary: Have students define *militant* and use the word in their own sentence, applying it to a contemporary situation. **L1**

CHAPTER 7
Section 1, 211–214

2 TEACH

Reading Check

Answer: Wars of Religion occurred; Henry of Navarre succeeded to throne; Henry converted to Catholicism and issued Edict of Nantes, making Catholicism the official religion of France.

Daily Lecture and Discussion Notes 7–1

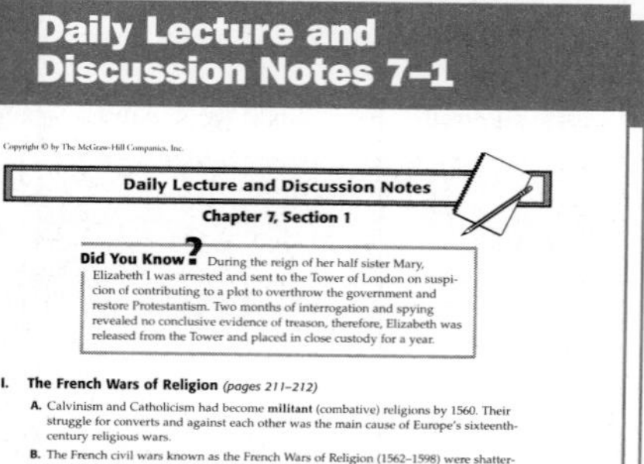

Daily Lecture and Discussion Notes

Chapter 7, Section 1

Did You Know? During the reign of her half sister Mary, Elizabeth I was arrested and sent to the Tower of London on suspicion of contributing to a plot to overthrow the government and restore Protestantism. Two months of interrogation and spying revealed no conclusive evidence of treason, therefore, Elizabeth was released from the Tower and placed in close custody for a year.

I. **The French Wars of Religion** *(pages 211–212)*

A. Calvinism and Catholicism had become **militant** (combative) religions by 1560. Their struggle for converts and against each other was the main cause of Europe's sixteenth-century religious wars.

B. The French civil wars known as the French Wars of Religion (1562–1598) were shattering. The **Huguenots** were French Protestants influenced by John Calvin. Only 7

Enrich

Under Philip II, Spain was intolerant of any diversity of belief, ready to undertake "holy war" against any who did not profess the Catholic faith. Philip II's reign was also the time when writers and artists such as Cervantes and El Greco lived and flourished. Ask students to speculate about how religious intolerance and artistic freedom might coexist. **L2**

Guided Reading Activity 7–1

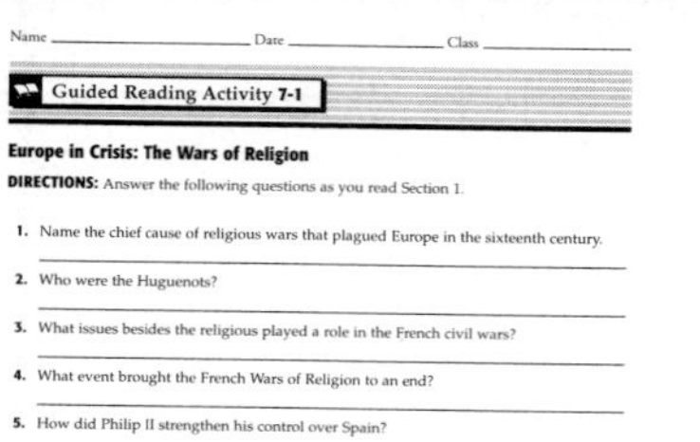

Name ____________ Date ____________ Class ____________

Guided Reading Activity 7-1

Europe in Crisis: The Wars of Religion

DIRECTIONS: Answer the following questions as you read Section 1.

1. Name the chief cause of religious wars that plagued Europe in the sixteenth century.
2. Who were the Huguenots?
3. What issues besides the religious played a role in the French civil wars?
4. What event brought the French Wars of Religion to an end?
5. How did Philip II strengthen his control over Spain?

However, economic, social, and political forces also played an important role in these conflicts.

Of the sixteenth-century religious wars, none was more shattering than the French civil wars known as the French Wars of Religion (1562–1598). Religion was at the center of these wars. The French kings persecuted Protestants, but the persecution did little to stop the spread of Protestantism.

Huguenots (HYOO•guh•NAWTS) were French Protestants influenced by John Calvin. They made up only about 7 percent of the total French population, but 40 to 50 percent of the nobility became Huguenots. Included in this group of nobles was the house of Bourbon, which ruled the southern French kingdom of Navarre and stood next to the Valois dynasty in the royal line of succession. The conversion of so many nobles made the Huguenots a powerful political threat to the Crown.

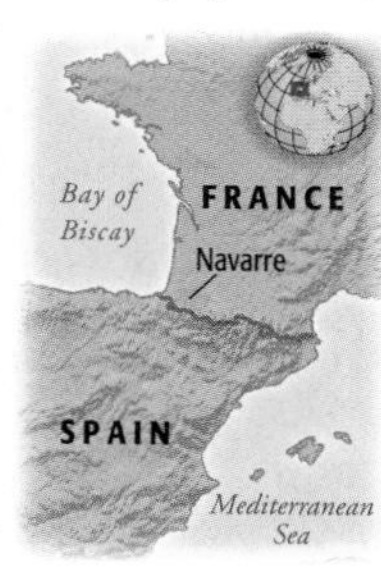

Still, the Catholic majority greatly outnumbered the Huguenot minority, and the Valois monarchy was strongly Catholic. In addition, an extreme Catholic party—known as the ultra-Catholics—strongly opposed the Huguenots. Possessing the loyalty of sections of northern and northwestern France, the ultra-Catholics could recruit and pay for large armies.

Although the religious issue was the most important issue, other factors played a role in the French civil wars. Towns and provinces, which had long resisted the growing power of the French monarchy, were willing to assist nobles in weakening the monarchy. The fact that so many nobles were Huguenots created an important base of opposition to the king.

For 30 years, battles raged in France between the Catholic and Huguenot sides. Finally, in 1589, **Henry of Navarre,** the political leader of the Huguenots and a member of the Bourbon dynasty, succeeded to the throne as Henry IV. He realized that as a Protestant he would never be accepted by Catholic France, so he converted to Catholicism. When he was crowned king in 1594, the fighting in France finally came to an end.

Henry of Navarre

To solve the religious problem, the king issued the **Edict of Nantes** in 1598. The edict recognized Catholicism as the official religion of France, but it also gave the Huguenots the right to worship and to enjoy all political privileges, such as holding public offices.

Reading Check **Identifying** List the sequence of events that led to the Edict of Nantes.

Philip II and Militant Catholicism

The greatest supporter of militant Catholicism in the second half of the sixteenth century was **King Philip II** of Spain, the son and heir of Charles V. The reign of King Philip II, which extended from 1556 to 1598, ushered in an age of Spanish greatness, both politically and culturally.

The first major goal of Philip II was to consolidate the lands he had inherited from his father. These included Spain, the **Netherlands,** and possessions in Italy and the Americas. To strengthen his control, Philip insisted on strict conformity to Catholicism and strong monarchical authority.

The Catholic faith was important to both Philip II and the Spanish people. During the late Middle Ages, Catholic kingdoms in Spain had reconquered Muslim areas within Spain and expelled the Spanish Jews. Driven by this crusading heritage, Spain saw itself as a nation of people chosen by God to save Catholic Christianity from the Protestant heretics.

Philip II, the "Most Catholic King," became a champion of Catholic causes, a role that led to spectacular victories and equally spectacular defeats. Spain's leadership of a Holy League against the Turks, for example, resulted in a stunning victory over the Turkish fleet in the Battle of Lepanto in 1571. Philip was not so fortunate in his conflicts with England (discussed in the following section) and the Netherlands.

The Spanish Netherlands, which consisted of 17 provinces (modern Netherlands and Belgium), was one of the richest parts of Philip's empire. Philip attempted to strengthen his control in this important region. The nobles of the Netherlands, who resented the loss of their privileges, strongly opposed Philip's efforts. To make matters worse, Philip tried to crush Calvinism in the Netherlands. Violence erupted in 1566 when Calvinists—especially nobles—began to destroy statues in Catholic churches. Philip sent ten thousand troops to crush the rebellion.

In the northern provinces, the Dutch, under the leadership of **William the Silent,** the prince of

COOPERATIVE LEARNING ACTIVITY

Creating a Report Organize the class into small groups. Assign a report on the life and actions of Henry of Navarre (Henry IV) of France. Each group should decide on a thesis for its report. Individual students could research Henry's personal and political life, Huguenot beliefs, the St. Bartholomew's Day Massacre, consequences of the Edict of Nantes, or other information that would support the group's thesis. Each member should submit research notes to the person who will write the draft of the report. After group approval and editing, a member should copy the report in final form. Students should use social studies terminology correctly in their reports as well as standard grammar, spelling, sentence structure, and punctuation. **L2**

Height of Spanish Power, c. 1560

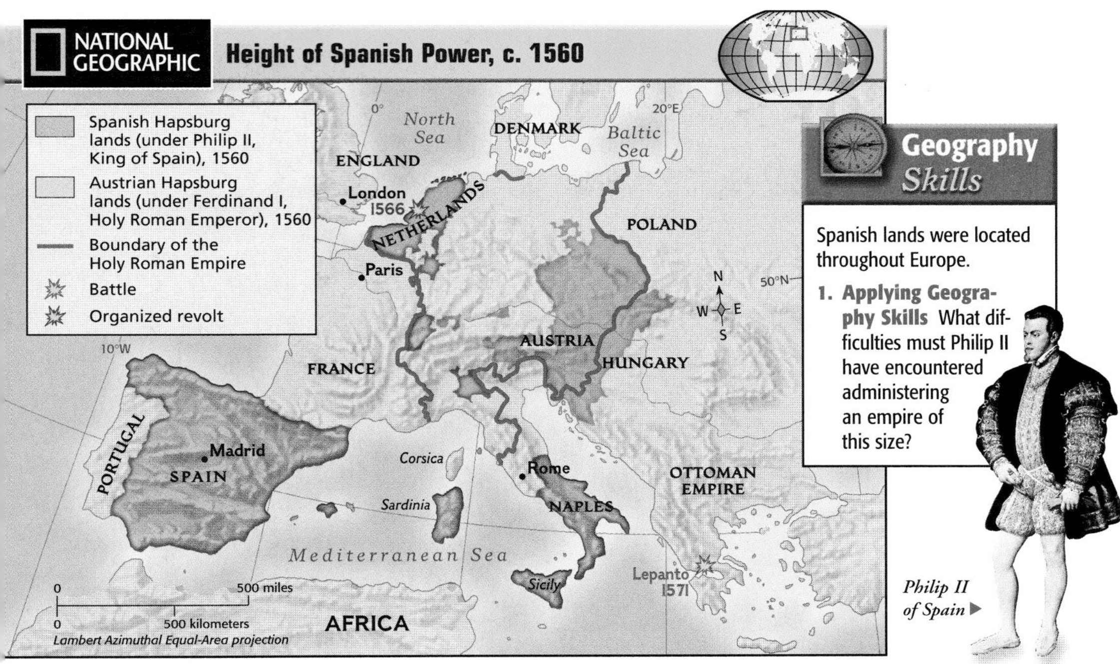

Philip II of Spain ▶

Geography Skills

Spanish lands were located throughout Europe.

1. **Applying Geography Skills** What difficulties must Philip II have encountered administering an empire of this size?

Orange, offered growing resistance. The struggle dragged on until 1609, when a 12-year truce ended the war. The northern provinces began to call themselves the United Provinces of the Netherlands and became the core of the modern Dutch state. In fact, the seventeenth century has often been called the golden age of the Dutch Republic because the United Provinces held center stage as one of Europe's great powers.

Philip's reign ended in 1598. At that time, Spain had the most populous empire in the world. Spain controlled almost all of South America and a number of settlements in Asia and Africa. To most Europeans, Spain still seemed to be the greatest power of the age.

In reality, however, Spain was not the great power that it appeared to be. Spain's treasury was empty. Philip II had gone bankrupt from spending too much on war, and his successor did the same by spending a fortune on his court. The armed forces were out-of-date, and the government was inefficient. Spain continued to play the role of a great power, but real power in Europe had shifted to England and France.

Reading Check **Describing** How important was Catholicism to Philip II and the Spanish people?

The England of Elizabeth

TURNING POINT **In this section, you will learn how the defeat of the Spanish Armada guaranteed that England would remain a Protestant country and signaled the beginning of Spain's decline as a sea power.**

When **Elizabeth Tudor** ascended the throne in 1558, England had fewer than four million people. During her reign, the small island kingdom became the leader of the Protestant nations of Europe and laid the foundations for a world empire.

Intelligent, careful, and self-confident, Elizabeth moved quickly to solve the difficult religious problem she inherited from her Catholic half-sister, Queen Mary Tudor. She repealed the laws favoring Catholics. A new Act of Supremacy named Elizabeth as "the only supreme governor" of both church and state. The Church of England under Elizabeth was basically Protestant, but it followed a moderate Protestantism that kept most people satisfied.

Elizabeth was also moderate in her foreign policy. The queen feared that war would be disastrous for England and for her own rule. She tried to keep Spain and France from becoming too powerful by supporting whichever was the weaker nation. Still, she allowed Francis Drake, an English navigator, to seize and plunder Spanish ships sailing the Caribbean.

Geography Skills

Answer: communication, travel, enforcing laws, collecting taxes

Reading Check

Answer: They saw themselves as chosen by God to save Catholicism from Protestant heretics.

TURNING POINT

Why was the defeat of the Spanish Armada significant for England? *(strengthened England and Protestantism)* **L1**

Critical Thinking

Have students discuss the ways Elizabeth I of England pursued policies based on moderation. *(religious policy, foreign policy, stayed out of allliances that might cause war)* **L1**

3 ASSESS

Assign Section 1 Assessment as homework or as an in-class activity.

Have students use **Interactive Tutor Self-Assessment CD-ROM.**

Section Quiz 7-1

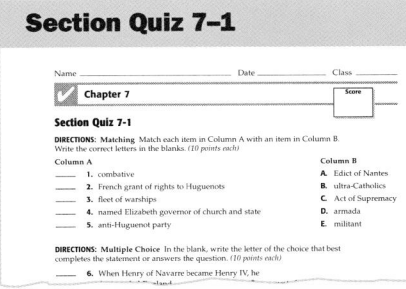

Name ______ Date ______ Class ______

Chapter 7 Score

Section Quiz 7-1

DIRECTIONS: Matching Match each item in Column A with an item in Column B. Write the correct letters in the blanks. *(10 points each)*

Column A	Column B
____ 1. combative	A. Edict of Nantes
____ 2. French grant of rights to Huguenots	B. ultra-Catholics
____ 3. fleet of warships	C. Act of Supremacy
____ 4. named Elizabeth governor of church and state	D. armada
____ 5. anti-Huguenot party	E. militant

DIRECTIONS: Multiple Choice In the blank, write the letter of the choice that best completes the statement or answers the question. *(10 points each)*

____ 6. When Henry of Navarre became Henry IV, he

MEETING INDIVIDUAL NEEDS

Visual/Spatial Divide the class into groups. Assign each group one of the three major religious wars of the period: French Wars of Religion, Philip II's battles in the Netherlands, and the Spanish Armada's battles with England. Allow ten minutes for each group to list the religious, social, and political issues involved in these wars. Then, as a class, combine the ideas into a chart or poster. You may want to assign a follow-up writing activity in which each student describes which war was the most important and explains why. **L1**

Refer to ***Inclusion for the High School Social Studies Classroom Strategies and Activities*** in the TCR.

Reading Check

Answer: He had been assured that the English would rise up against Elizabeth when the Spanish arrived.

Geography Skills

Answers:
1. length: 350 miles (560 km); width: west end: 112 miles (180 km); east end: 21 miles (34 km)
2. getting trapped in narrow east end of channel

Reading Essentials and Study Guide 7–1

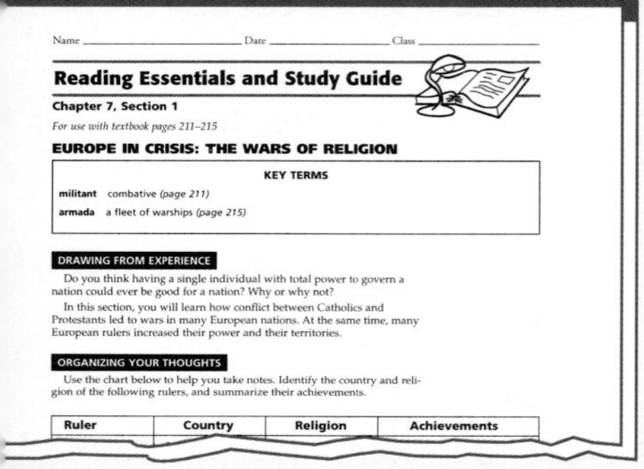

Name ______ Date ______ Class ______

Reading Essentials and Study Guide

Chapter 7, Section 1

For use with textbook pages 211–215

EUROPE IN CRISIS: THE WARS OF RELIGION

KEY TERMS

militant combative *(page 211)*

armada a fleet of warships *(page 215)*

DRAWING FROM EXPERIENCE

Do you think having a single individual with total power to govern a nation could ever be good for a nation? Why or why not?

In this section, you will learn how conflict between Catholics and Protestants led to wars in many European nations. At the same time, many European rulers increased their power and their territories.

ORGANIZING YOUR THOUGHTS

Use the chart below to help you take notes. Identify the country and religion of the following rulers, and summarize their achievements.

Ruler	Country	Religion	Achievements

Reteaching Activity

Ask students to give oral summaries of the French Wars of Religion, Philip II's reign, and the Spanish Armada's defeat. **L1**

4 CLOSE

Ask students to discuss which wars of religion they consider the most important and why. **L2**

Philip II of Spain had toyed for years with the idea of invading England. His advisers assured him that the people of England would rise against their queen when the Spaniards arrived. In any case, a successful invasion of England would mean the overthrow of Protestantism and a return to Catholicism.

In 1588, Philip ordered preparations for an armada—a fleet of warships—to invade England. The fleet that set sail had neither the ships nor the manpower that Philip had planned to send. An officer of the Spanish fleet reveals the basic flaw: "It is well known that we fight in God's cause. . . . But unless God helps us by a miracle, the English, who have faster and handier ships than ours, and many more long-range guns . . . will . . . stand aloof and knock us to pieces with their guns, without our being able to do them any serious hurt."

Defeat of the Spanish Armada

The hoped-for miracle never came. The Spanish fleet, battered by a number of encounters with the English, sailed back to Spain by a northward route around **Scotland** and **Ireland,** where it was pounded by storms. Many of the Spanish ships sank.

Reading Check **Explaining** Why was Philip II confident that the Spanish could successfully invade England?

NATIONAL GEOGRAPHIC **Defeat of the Spanish Armada, 1588**

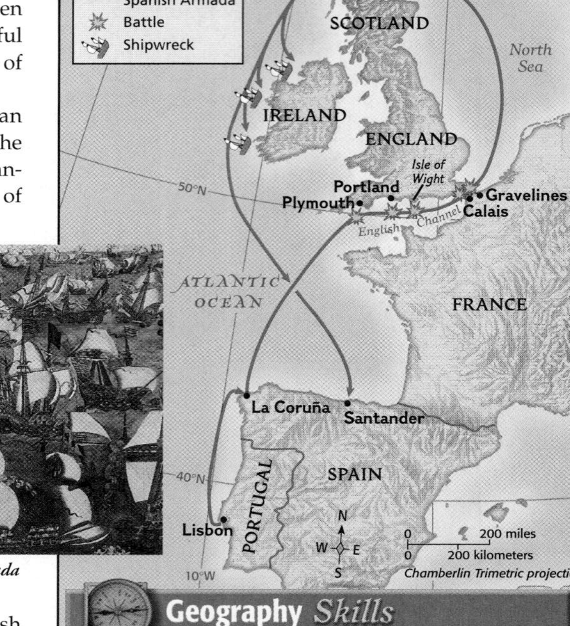

Geography Skills

England defeated the Spanish Armada in 1588.

1. **Interpreting Maps** Use the map's scale to estimate in miles the length and width of the English Channel.
2. **Applying Geography Skills** What were the Spanish hoping to avoid by taking the northern route back to Spain?

SECTION 1 ASSESSMENT

Checking for Understanding

1. **Define** militant, armada.
2. **Identify** Huguenots, Henry of Navarre, Edict of Nantes, King Philip II, William the Silent, Elizabeth Tudor.
3. **Locate** Netherlands, Scotland, Ireland.
4. **Describe** how the Edict of Nantes appeased both Catholics and Huguenots.
5. **List** the ways Elizabeth demonstrated moderation in her religious policy.

Critical Thinking

6. **Making Generalizations** Why did Philip II send out his fleet knowing he did not have enough ships or manpower?
7. **Compare and Contrast** Use a Venn diagram like the one below to compare and contrast the reigns of Henry of Navarre, Philip II, and Elizabeth Tudor.

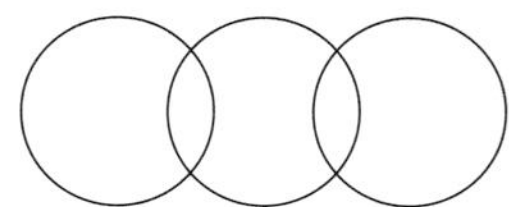

Analyzing Visuals

8. **Examine** the painting of the Saint Bartholomew's Day massacre shown on page 211 of your text. Is the work an objective depiction of the event, or can you find evidence of artistic bias in the painting?

Writing About History

9. **Persuasive Writing** Write a persuasive essay arguing whether or not it was a good idea for Philip II to sail against England. Identify the main reason the king of Spain decided to launch the invasion.

SECTION 1 ASSESSMENT

1. Key terms are in blue.
2. Huguenots (*p.212*); Henry of Navarre (*p.212*); Edict of Nantes (*p.212*); King Philip II (*p.212*); William the Silent (*p.212*); Elizabeth Tudor (*p.213*)
3. See chapter maps.
4. Catholicism: state religion; Huguenots: gained religious, political rights
5. repealed laws favoring Catholics, moderate Protestantism
6. believed in cause, had faith in a miracle
7. Henry: converted to Catholicism, moderate, kept Catholicism as state religion, gave Huguenots rights; Philip: Catholic, militant champion of Catholic causes; Elizabeth: Protestant, moderate in religion and politics, Henry/Elizabeth: moderate policies; Henry/Philip: Catholicism state religion
8. Answers should be supported by evidence.
9. Answers will vary. He had been assured that the English would revolt against their queen.

EYEWITNESS TO HISTORY

Queen Elizabeth's Golden Speech

IN 1601, NEAR THE END OF her life, Queen Elizabeth made a speech to Parliament, giving voice to the feeling that existed between the queen and her subjects.

Queen Elizabeth of England, Faced with the Spanish Armada 1588, Reviews Her Troops *by Ferdinand Piloty the Younger, 1861*

❝I do assure you there is no prince that loves his subjects better, or whose love can contradict our love. There is no jewel, be it of never so rich a price, which I set before this jewel; I mean your love. For I do esteem it more than any treasure or riches.

And, though God has raised me high, yet this I count the glory of my crown, that I have reigned with your love. This makes me that I do not so much rejoice that God has made me to be a Queen, as to be a Queen over so thankful a people.

Of myself I must say this: I never was any greedy, scraping grasper, nor a strait, fast-holding Prince, nor yet a waster. My heart was never set on any worldly goods, but only for my subjects' good. What you bestow on me, I will not hoard it up, but receive it to bestow on you again. Yea, mine own properties I account yours, to be expended for your good. . . .

I have ever used to set the Last-Judgement Day before mine eyes, and so to rule as I shall be judged to answer before a higher Judge, to whose judgement seat I do appeal, that never thought was cherished in my heart that tended not unto my people's good. . . .

There will never Queen sit in my seat with more zeal to my country, care for my subjects, and that will sooner with willingness venture her life for your good and safety, than myself. For it is my desire to live nor reign no longer than my life and reign should be for your good. And though you have had and may have many princes more mighty and wise sitting in this seat, you never had nor shall have any that will be more careful and loving.❞

—**Queen Elizabeth I, *The Golden Speech***

Analyzing Primary Sources

1. Identify phrases that convey Queen Elizabeth's feeling for her subjects.
2. To whom does Elizabeth feel accountable?
3. Which is more important: how subjects and rulers feel about each other or the policies and laws that rulers develop?

TEACH

Analyzing Primary Sources In this speech, Elizabeth characterizes her feelings toward her subjects. Have students, in a brief essay, compare and contrast her ideas about a ruler's attitude toward his or her subjects with Louis XIV's ideas, as reflected in his speech excerpted on page 225 of this chapter. How do their attitudes reflect the difference between a constitutional monarchy and an absolute monarchy? Ask students to incorporate specific quotations that support their conclusions. **L2**

Critical Thinking

In her speech, Elizabeth acknowledges the divine right of rulers when she says, "God has raised me high," and "God has made me to be a queen." However, her beliefs about divine right differ sharply from other rulers discussed in this chapter. Have students, in a brief essay, compare her views about divine right with the views of Jacques Bossuet, a seventeenth-century French bishop, excerpted on page 223 of this chapter. Ask students to incorporate specific quotations that support their conclusions. **L2 L3**

ANSWERS TO ANALYZING PRIMARY SOURCES

1. This passage is full of such phrases; for example: "I do esteem it [your love] more than any treasure or riches;" ". . . I have reigned with your love;" ". . . that never thought was cherished in my heart that tended not unto my people's good."
2. God ("a higher Judge")
3. Answers will vary, but students should support their point of view with logical arguments. You might wish to compare and contrast how modern-day citizens feel about their governments. You might also wish to discuss and compare how citizens living today can express their feelings toward government with the means that were available to citizens living during the time of absolute monarchs.

CHAPTER 7
Section 2, 216–221

1 FOCUS

Section Overview

This section describes the results of the Thirty Years' War and the English and Glorious Revolutions.

BELLRINGER
Skillbuilder Activity

Project transparency and have students answer questions.

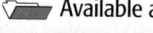

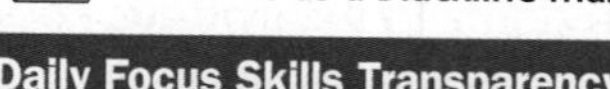
Available as a blackline master.

Daily Focus Skills Transparency 7–2

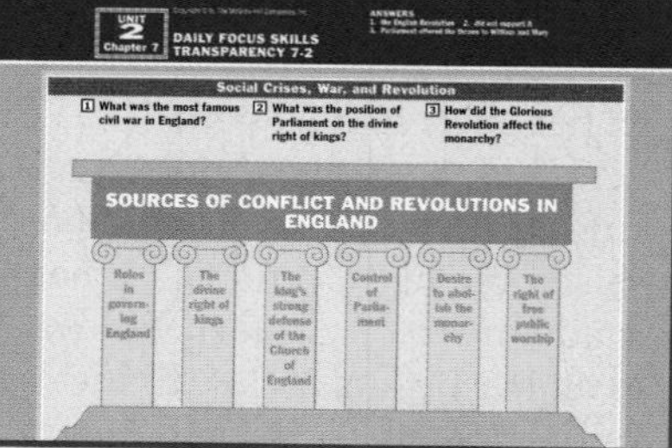

Guide to Reading

Answers to Graphic: Religious Conflicts: witchcraft craze, Thirty Years' War, English Civil War, Glorious Revolution

Preteaching Vocabulary: The text defines a *commonwealth* as a republic. Using a dictionary, have students research the archaic meaning of the term *commonwealth* and explain how it applies to the idea of a republic. **L1**

SECTION 2 Social Crises, War, and Revolution

Guide to Reading

Main Ideas
- The Thirty Years' War ended the unity of the Holy Roman Empire.
- Democratic ideals were strengthened as a result of the English and Glorious Revolutions.

Key Terms
inflation, witchcraft, divine right of kings, commonwealth

People to Identify
James I, Puritans, Charles I, Cavaliers, Roundheads, Oliver Cromwell, James II

Places to Locate
Holy Roman Empire, Bohemia

Preview Questions
1. What problems troubled Europe from 1560 to 1650?
2. How did the Glorious Revolution undermine the divine right of kings?

Reading Strategy
Summarizing Information As you read this section, use a chart like the one below to identify which conflicts were prompted by religious concerns.

Religious Conflicts

Preview of Events

1600 · 1620 · 1640 · 1660 · 1680 · 1700

- **1603** Elizabeth I dies
- **1642** Civil war in England begins
- **1649** Charles I is executed
- **1688** Glorious Revolution

Voices from the Past

Destruction of the city of Magdeburg

The Thirty Years' War (1618–1648) was a devastating religious war. A resident of Magdeburg, Germany, a city sacked ten times during the war, reported:

> ❝There was nothing but beating and burning, plundering, torture, and murder. Most especially was every one of the enemy bent on securing [riches]. . . . In this frenzied rage, the great and splendid city was now given over to the flames, and thousands of innocent men, women and children, in the midst of heartrending shrieks and cries, were tortured and put to death in so cruel and shameful a manner that no words would suffice to describe. Thus in a single day this noble and famous city, the pride of the whole country, went up in fire and smoke.❞
>
> —***Readings in European History,*** **James Harvey Robinson, 1934**

This destruction of Magdeburg was one of the disasters besetting Europe during this time.

Economic and Social Crises

From 1560 to 1650, Europe witnessed severe economic and social crises. One major economic problem was **inflation,** or rising prices. What caused this rise in prices? The great influx of gold and silver from the Americas was one factor. Then, too, a growing population in the sixteenth century increased the demand for land and food and drove up prices for both.

SECTION RESOURCES

Reproducible Masters
- Reproducible Lesson Plan 7–2
- Daily Lecture and Discussion Notes 7–2
- Guided Reading Activity 7–2
- Section Quiz 7–2
- Reading Essentials and Study Guide 7–2

Transparencies
- Daily Focus Skills Transparency 7–2

Multimedia
- Interactive Tutor Self-Assessment CD-ROM
- ExamView® Pro Testmaker CD-ROM
- Presentation Plus! CD-ROM

By 1600, an economic slowdown had begun in parts of Europe. Spain's economy, grown dependent on imported silver, was seriously failing by the 1640s. The mines were producing less silver, fleets were subject to pirate attacks, and the loss of Muslim and Jewish artisans and merchants hurt the economy. Italy, the financial center of Europe in the Renaissance, was also declining economically.

Population figures in the sixteenth and seventeenth centuries reveal Europe's worsening conditions. Population grew in the sixteenth century. The number of people probably increased from 60 million in 1500 to 85 million by 1600. By 1620, population had leveled off. It had begun to decline by 1650, especially in central and southern Europe. Warfare, plague, and famine all contributed to the population decline and to the creation of social tensions.

Reading Check **Explaining** Explain the causes for inflation in Europe in the 1600s.

The Witchcraft Trials

A belief in **witchcraft**, or magic, had been part of traditional village culture for centuries. The religious zeal that led to the Inquisition and the hunt for heretics was extended to concern about witchcraft. During the sixteenth and seventeenth centuries an intense hysteria affected the lives of many Europeans. Perhaps more than a hundred thousand people were charged with witchcraft. As more and more people were brought to trial, the fear of witches grew, as did the fear of being accused of witchcraft.

Common people—usually the poor and those without property—were the ones most often accused of witchcraft. More than 75 percent of those accused were women. Most of them were single or widowed and over 50 years old.

Under intense torture, accused witches usually confessed to a number of practices. Many said that they had sworn allegiance to the devil and attended sabbats, nightly gatherings where they feasted and danced. Others admitted using evil spells and special ointments to harm their neighbors.

By 1650, the witchcraft hysteria had begun to lessen. As governments grew stronger, fewer officials were willing to disrupt their societies with trials of witches. In addition, attitudes were changing. People found it unreasonable to believe in the old view of a world haunted by evil spirits.

Reading Check **Describing** What were the characteristics of the majority of those accused of witchcraft?

The Thirty Years' War

Religious disputes continued in Germany after the Peace of Augsburg in 1555. One reason for the disputes was that Calvinism had not been recognized by the peace settlement. By the 1600s, Calvinism had spread to many parts of Europe. Religion played an important role in the outbreak of the Thirty Years' War, called the "last of the religious wars," but political and territorial motives were evident as well. The war began in 1618 in the lands of the **Holy Roman Empire.** At first, it was a struggle between Catholic forces, led by the Hapsburg Holy Roman emperors, and Protestant (primarily Calvinist) nobles in **Bohemia** who rebelled against Hapsburg authority. Soon, however, the conflict became a political one. Cardinal Richelieu of France, Louis XIII's chief minister (see Section 3), helped cause this change. Richelieu had Catholic France join Protestant Sweden in fighting the Catholic Hapsburgs.

Geography Skills

The Thirty Years' War was fought primarily in the German states within the Holy Roman Empire.

1. **Interpreting Maps** List the towns that were sacked or plundered during the war.
2. **Applying Geography Skills** Research one of the battles on the map and describe its impact on the course of the war.

2 TEACH

Reading Check

Answer: influx of gold and silver from Americas; growing population increased demand for food and land

Reading Check

Answer: common people, usually poor, usually women, usually single or widowed and over 50 years old

Geography Skills

Answers:

1. Students should list the names of those towns that are printed in green.
2. Answers will vary depending on battle selected.

Daily Lecture and Discussion Notes 7–2

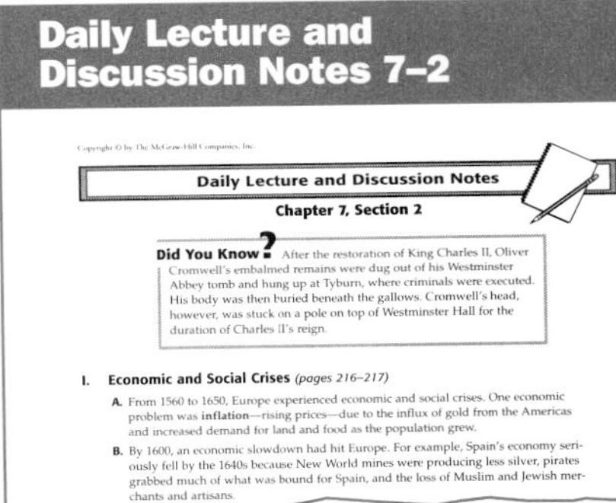

Enrich

Remind students that most people accused of witchcraft were poor, female, single or widowed, and over fifty. Ask students why those accused of being witches might fit this profile. *(people without power, no men to defend them, considered morally weak)* **L2**

EXTENDING THE CONTENT

The Thirty Years' War began in 1618 as a struggle between Roman Catholics and Protestants over the crown of Bohemia. Outside help for the Protestants came from King Adolphus of Sweden in 1630. The Catholic army sacked the city of Magdeburg, killing 20,000 citizens. Fearing that the Catholics would attack Leipzig, Protestants welcomed the help of King Adolphus and the Swedes. On the plains near Brentenfield, 70,000 Catholic and Swedish soldiers met. The Catholics lost 13,000 soldiers, while the Swedes lost fewer than 3,000. King Adolphus was applauded as the Protestant champion and laid the foundation for Sweden to become a leading European country for the next half a century. King Adolphus was killed at the battle of Lützen in 1632. France then entered the war, which lasted another 18 years.

Reading Check

Answer: all German states could determine their own religion; ended Holy Roman Empire by making all its states independent

SCIENCE, TECHNOLOGY & SOCIETY

Answer: Firearms came to be used widely, demanding armies that were better disciplined and trained. This led governments to fund regularly paid standing armies, so that wars were fought by professional soldiers.

Guided Reading Activity 7–2

Name ______ Date ______ Class ______

Guided Reading Activity 7-2

Social Crises, War, and Revolution

DIRECTIONS: Fill in the blanks below as you read Section 2.

The great influx of gold and silver from the **(1)** ______ and a growing population demanding land and food led to **(2)** ______ in Europe from 1560 to 1650. Spain's economy was seriously falling by the 1640s due to **(3)** ______ producing less silver, fleets subject to **(4)** ______ attacks, and the loss of Muslim and Jewish **(5)** ______ and **(6)** ______.

During the sixteenth and seventeenth centuries more than a hundred thousand people were charged with **(7)** ______. Under intense torture, accused witches usually **(8)** ______ to a number of practices. By 1650, people were finding it **(9)** ______ to believe in the old view of a world haunted by evil spirits.

(10) ______ played an important role in the outbreak of the Thirty Years' War, as well as **(11)** ______ and **(12)** ______ motives. The Peace of **(13)** ______ stated that all German states, including the Calvinist ones, could determine their own religion.

At the core of the English Revolution was the struggle between king and **(14)** ______ to determine what role each should play in governing England. James I of England believed kings receive their **(15)** ______ from God and are responsible only to him. Under the armies of **(16)** ______, Parliament finally proved victorious.

Dutch leader William of **(17)** ______ and his wife **(18)** ______ raised an army and invaded England in 1688 in an almost bloodless **(19)** ______. As William and Mary took the English throne,

Critical Thinking

Ask students to discuss the causes of the Thirty Years' War and results of the conflict. *(struggle between Catholicism and Calvinism, political motives; independence of German states.)* Have students create a thematic map illustrating this European war. **L1 L2**

The Thirty Years' War was the most destructive conflict that Europeans had yet experienced. Although most of the battles of the war were fought on German soil, all major European powers except England became involved. For 30 years Germany was plundered and destroyed. Rival armies destroyed the German countryside as well as entire towns. Local people had little protection from the armies. The Peace of Westphalia officially ended the war in Germany in 1648. The major contenders gained new territories, and one of them—France—emerged as the dominant nation in Europe.

The Peace of Westphalia stated that all German states, including the Calvinist ones, could determine their own religion. The more than three hundred states that had made up the Holy Roman Empire were virtually recognized as independent states, since each received the power to conduct its own foreign policy. This brought an end to the Holy Roman Empire as a political entity. Germany would not be united for another two hundred years.

Reading Check **Summarizing** How did the Peace of Westphalia impact the Holy Roman Empire?

SCIENCE, TECHNOLOGY & SOCIETY

The Changing Face of War

Gunpowder was first invented by the Chinese in the eleventh century and made its appearance in Europe by the fourteenth century. During the seventeenth century, firearms developed rapidly and increasingly changed the face of war.

By 1600, the flintlock musket had made firearms more deadly on the battlefield. Muskets were loaded from the front with powder and ball. In the flintlock musket, the powder that propelled the ball was ignited by a spark caused by a flint striking on metal. This mechanism made it easier to fire and more reliable than other muskets. Reloading techniques also improved, making it possible to make one to two shots per minute. The addition of the bayonet to the front of the musket made the musket even more deadly as a weapon. The bayonet was a steel blade used in hand-to-hand combat.

A military leader who made effective use of firearms during the Thirty Years' War was Gustavus Adolphus, the king of Sweden. The infantry brigades of Gustavus's army, six men deep, were composed of equal numbers of musketeers and pikemen. The musketeers employed the salvo, in which all rows of the infantry fired at once instead of row by row. These salvos of fire, which cut up the massed ranks of the opposing infantry squadrons, were followed by pike charges. Pikes were heavy spears 18 feet (about 5.5 m) long, held by pikemen massed together in square formations. Gustavus also used the cavalry in a more mobile fashion. After shooting a pistol volley, the cavalry charged the enemy with swords.

The increased use of firearms, combined with greater mobility on the battlefield, demanded armies that were better disciplined and trained. Governments began to fund regularly paid standing armies. By 1700, France had a standing army of four hundred thousand.

Analyzing ***How did the invention of gunpowder change the way wars were fought?***

Austrian flintlock pistol, c. 1680

Soldier firing

MEETING INDIVIDUAL NEEDS

Visual/Spatial Have visual learners make diagrams to better understand the Thirty Years' War. One diagram should list three motives for the war *(religious, political, territorial)* and three results of the Peace of Westphalia *(new territories, especially for France, German states could choose religion, states recognized as independent)*. Then have students make a second diagram that indicates which side the major European powers (Denmark, Sweden, France and Spain) took in the conflict between the Holy Roman Empire and the Protestants of Bohemia. *(All but Spain supported Protestants.)* **L1**

Refer to ***Inclusion for the High School Social Studies Classroom Strategies and Activities*** in the TCR.

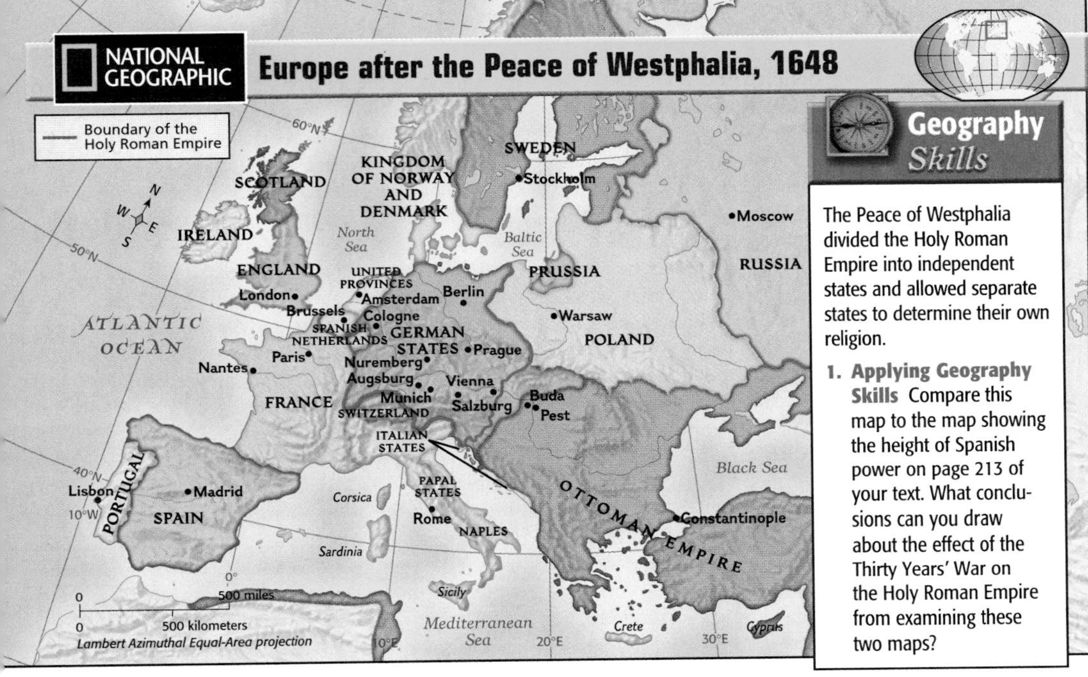

Geography Skills

The Peace of Westphalia divided the Holy Roman Empire into independent states and allowed separate states to determine their own religion.

1. **Applying Geography Skills** Compare this map to the map showing the height of Spanish power on page 213 of your text. What conclusions can you draw about the effect of the Thirty Years' War on the Holy Roman Empire from examining these two maps?

Revolutions in England

TURNING POINT **As you read this section, you will discover that Parliament held the real authority in the English system of constitutional monarchy.**

In addition to the Thirty Years' War, a series of rebellions and civil wars rocked Europe in the seventeenth century. By far the most famous struggle was the civil war in England known as the English Revolution. At its core was a struggle between king and Parliament to determine what role each should play in governing England. It would take another revolution later in the century to finally resolve this struggle.

The Stuarts and Divine Right With the death of Queen Elizabeth I in 1603, the Tudor dynasty came to an end. The Stuart line of rulers began with the accession to the throne of Elizabeth's cousin, the king of Scotland, who became **James I** of England.

James believed in the divine right of kings—that is, that kings receive their power from God and are responsible only to God. Parliament did not think much of the divine right of kings. It had come to assume that the king or queen and Parliament ruled England together.

Religion was an issue as well. The **Puritans** (Protestants in England inspired by Calvinist ideas) did not like the king's strong defense of the Church of England. The Puritans were members of the Church of England but wished to make the church more Protestant. Many of England's gentry, mostly well-to-do landowners, had become Puritans. The Puritan gentry formed an important part of the House of Commons, the lower house of Parliament. It was not wise to alienate them.

The conflict that began during the reign of James came to a head during the reign of his son, **Charles I.** Charles also believed in the divine right of kings. In 1628, Parliament passed a petition that prohibited the passing of any taxes without Parliament's consent. Although Charles I initially accepted this petition, he later changed his mind, realizing that it put limits on the king's power.

Charles also tried to impose more ritual on the Church of England. To the Puritans, this was a return to Catholic practices. When Charles tried to force the Puritans to accept his religious policies, thousands of them chose to go to America instead.

Civil War and the Commonwealth Complaints grew until England slipped into a civil war in 1642 between the supporters of the king (the **Cavaliers** or Royalists) and the parliamentary forces (called the **Roundheads** because of their short hair). Parliament proved victorious, due largely to the New Model Army of **Oliver Cromwell,** a military genius. The New Model Army was made up chiefly of more extreme Puritans, known as the Independents. These

Geography Skills

Answer:

1. The Holy Roman Empire contracted as a result of the Thirty Years' War. Students should note that the Holy Roman Empire lost parts of Switzerland and Italy.

TURNING POINT

What is the evidence that Parliament held the real authority in the English system of constitutional monarchy? *(Parliament's petition in 1628, Parliament overthrew and executed Charles I, passed laws after Restoration, the Glorious Revolution)* **L1**

Writing Activity

Ask students to use outside resources to further research the English Revolution. Then ask students to write an essay in which they identify and evaluate the causes and effects of the revolution and summarize the following ideas related to the revolution: separation of powers, "divine right of kings," liberty, equality, democracy, popular sovereignty, human rights, constitutionalism, and nationalism. Teachers may want to divide students into groups in which each student is assigned a particular topic or group of topics to research. **L2**

EXTENDING THE CONTENT

Charles I In 1628, the English Parliament forced Charles I to sign a Petition of Right in order to obtain money he needed to fund his wars. The Petition stated that the king could not collect taxes without Parliament's consent, imprison anyone without just cause, house troops in private homes without the owner's consent, or declare martial law (under which individual rights were limited) unless the country was at war. Nearly a year later, however, Charles dissolved Parliament and ruled for 11 years without its consent. During this time, Charles ignored the Petition and continued to collect taxes and imprison opponents at will. Religious freedoms also suffered as Puritans were denied the right to preach or publish. The king's actions and desire for absolute power eventually led to the English Revolution.

CONNECTIONS Around The World

Answers:

1. Answers may include: the cost of rebuilding can be very high and can affect the economy for years to come; whole families, neighborhoods, or cities can be wiped out.
2. Answers will vary, depending on the location.

CURRICULUM CONNECTION

Government Have students research and prepare a chart that compares rights in the English Bill of Rights with those in the United States Bill of Rights. Ask students to indicate on their charts the rights common to both countries' bills of rights. L2

3 ASSESS

Assign Section 2 Assessment as homework or as an in-class activity.

Have students use **Interactive Tutor Self Assessment CD-ROM.**

Section Quiz 7–2

Name ______ Date ______ Class ______

Chapter 7 — Score

Section Quiz 7-2

DIRECTIONS: Matching Match each item in Column A with an item in Column B. Write the correct letters in the blanks. *(10 points each)*

Column A	Column B
____ 1. rising prices	A. inflation
____ 2. magic in traditional European village culture	B. Roundheads
____ 3. William and Mary's 1688 "invasion" of England	C. Puritans
____ 4. parliamentary forces in the 1642 civil war	D. Glorious Revolution
____ 5. English Calvinist Protestant group	E. witchcraft

DIRECTIONS: Multiple Choice In the blank, write the letter of the choice that best completes the statement or answers the question. *(10 points each)*

____ 6. James I of England strongly believed in

men believed they were doing battle for God. As Cromwell wrote, "This is none other but the hand of God; and to Him alone belongs the glory." We might also give some credit to Cromwell; his soldiers were well disciplined and trained in the new military tactics of the seventeenth century.

The victorious New Model Army lost no time in taking control. Cromwell purged Parliament of any members who had not supported him. What was left—the so-called Rump Parliament—had Charles I executed on January 30, 1649. The execution of the king horrified much of Europe. Parliament next abolished the monarchy and the House of Lords and declared England a republic, or commonwealth.

Cromwell found it difficult to work with the Rump Parliament and finally dispersed it by force. As the members of Parliament departed, he shouted, "It is you that have forced me to do this, for I have sought the Lord night and day that He would slay me rather than put upon me the doing of this work." After destroying both king and Parliament, Cromwell set up a military dictatorship.

The Restoration Cromwell ruled until his death in 1658. After his death, Parliament restored the monarchy in the person of Charles II, the son of Charles I. With the return of monarchy in 1660, England's time of troubles seemed at an end.

However, problems soon arose. Charles II was sympathetic to Catholicism, and his brother James, heir to the throne, did not hide the fact that he was a Catholic. Parliament was suspicious about their Catholic leanings and introduced the Exclusion Bill, which would have barred James from the throne as a professed Catholic. Debate over the bill created two political groupings (later called political parties): the Whigs, who wanted to exclude James, and the Tories, who did not want to interfere with the principle of lawful succession to the throne.

To foil the Exclusion Bill, Charles dismissed Parlaiment in 1681. When Charles died in 1685, his brother became king. **James II** was an open and devout Catholic, making religion once more a cause of conflict between king and Parliament. James named Catholics to high positions in the government, army, navy, and universities.

Parliament objected to James's policies but stopped short of rebellion. Members knew that James was an old man, and his successors were his Protestant daughters Mary and Anne, born to his first wife.

CONNECTIONS Around The World

Natural Disasters in History

The religious wars in Europe, which led to many deaths, were manmade disasters that created economic, social, and political crises. Between 1500 and 1800, natural disasters around the world also took many lives and led to economic and social crises.

One of the worst disasters occurred in China in 1556. A powerful earthquake in northern China buried alive hundreds of thousands of peasants who had made their homes in cave dwellings carved out of soft clay hills.

In later years, earthquakes shattered other places around the world. On the last day of 1703, a massive earthquake struck the city of Tokyo. At the same time, enormous tidal waves caused by earthquakes flooded the Japanese coastline, sweeping entire villages out to sea. An earthquake that struck Persia in 1727 killed 75,000 people in the city of Tabriz.

Europe, too, had its share of natural disasters. A massive earthquake leveled the city of Lisbon, Portugal, in 1755, killing over 50,000 people and destroying more than 80 percent of the buildings in the city. The massive eruption of Mount Etna on the island of Sicily in 1669 devastated Catania, a nearby port city.

Earthquake at Lisbon in 1755

Comparing Cultures

1. How do natural disasters lead to economic and social crises?
2. What natural disasters can occur where you live?

220

MEETING INDIVIDUAL NEEDS

Verbal/Linguistic Have students imagine they have been selected by Parliament to write a letter either to Charles II asking him to return as king, or to William and Mary inviting them to be monarchs. Remind students to include reference to the current political problems and the conditions under which the monarchs will rule. Students may also choose to write a response letter or journal entry from the point of view of the potential monarch articulating reservations and concerns he or she may have about accepting the invitation. Suggest that students research styles for writing letters in the 1600s. Encourage students to share their completed letters with the class. L2

Picturing History

Here Cromwell is shown dismissing Parliament. After Cromwell's death, Parliament restored the monarchy. In 1689, Parliament offered the throne to William and Mary, shown above right. Why did English nobles want William and Mary to rule England, and not the heirs of James II?

However, in 1688, a son was born to James and his second wife, a Catholic. Now, the possibility of a Catholic monarchy loomed large.

A Glorious Revolution A group of English noblemen invited the Dutch leader, William of Orange, husband of James's daughter Mary, to invade England. William and Mary raised an army and in 1688 "invaded" England, while James, his wife, and his infant son fled to France. With almost no bloodshed, England had undergone a "Glorious Revolution." The issue was not if there would be a monarchy but who would be monarch.

In January 1689, Parliament offered the throne to William and Mary. They accepted it, along with a Bill of Rights. The Bill of Rights set forth Parliament's right to make laws and levy taxes. It also stated that standing armies could be raised only with Parliament's consent, thus making it impossible for kings to oppose or to do without Parliament. The rights of citizens to keep arms and have a jury trial were also confirmed. The Bill of Rights helped create a system of government based on the rule of law and a freely elected Parliament. This bill laid the foundation for a limited, or constitutional, monarchy.

Another important action of Parliament was the Toleration Act of 1689. This act granted Puritans, but not Catholics, the right of free public worship. Few English citizens, however, would ever again be persecuted for religion.

By deposing one king and establishing another, Parliament had destroyed the divine-right theory of kingship. William was, after all, king by the grace of Parliament, not the grace of God. Parliament had asserted its right to be part of the government.

Reading Check **Describing** Trace the sequence of events that led to the English Bill of Rights.

SECTION 2 ASSESSMENT

Checking for Understanding

1. **Define** inflation, witchcraft, divine right of kings, commonwealth.
2. **Identify** James I, Puritans, Charles I, Cavaliers, Roundheads, Oliver Cromwell, James II.
3. **Locate** Holy Roman Empire, Bohemia.
4. **Explain** why Oliver Cromwell first purged Parliament and then declared a military dictatorship.
5. **List** the countries involved in the Thirty Years' War.

Critical Thinking

6. **Drawing Conclusions** Which nation emerged stronger after the Thirty Years' War? Did thirty years of fighting accomplish any of the original motives for waging the war?
7. **Cause and Effect** Use a graphic organizer like the one below to illustrate the causes and effects of the Thirty Years' War.

Thirty Years' War	
Cause	Effect

Analyzing Visuals

8. **Examine** the cameo of William and Mary shown above. How does this painting compare to portraits of other rulers, such as the one of Louis XIV on page 226? How is the purpose of this painting different from the purpose of other royal portraits?

Writing About History

9. **Expository Writing** Write an essay analyzing the population figures in sixteenth- and seventeenth-century England. What accounts for the increases and decreases? Include a graph showing population.

SECTION 2 ASSESSMENT

1. Key terms are in blue.
2. James I (*p. 219*); Puritans (*p. 219*); Charles I (*p. 219*); Cavaliers (*p. 219*); Roundheads (*p. 219*); Oliver Cromwell (*p. 219*); James II (*p. 220*)
3. See chapter maps.
4. removed those who had not aided him; found Parliament difficult to work with
5. Bohemia, Holy Roman Empire, Denmark, Sweden, France, Spain
6. France. Protestants made some gains; Germany did not fare well.
7. Causes: Calvinism not recognized; Calvinist nobles rebelled against Hapsburgs; France, Spain, and Holy Roman Empire wanted European leadership; Effects: all German states could determine own religion; major contenders gained new lands; Holy Roman Empire ended
8. They look like an ordinary couple, not rulers by divine right.
9. Students should consult outside sources.

Picturing History

Answer: The nobles were concerned about the possibility of James II and his heirs instituting a Catholic monarchy in England.

Reading Check

Answers: Students should list the New Model Army of Cromwell, the Restoration, the Catholic king James II, and the invitation to William and Mary.

Reading Essentials and Study Guide 7–2

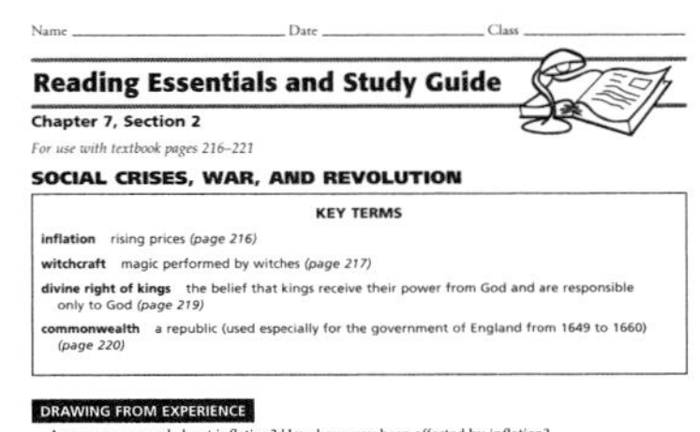

Name ______ Date ______ Class ______

Reading Essentials and Study Guide

Chapter 7, Section 2

For use with textbook pages 216–221

SOCIAL CRISES, WAR, AND REVOLUTION

KEY TERMS

inflation rising prices (page 216)

witchcraft magic performed by witches (page 217)

divine right of kings the belief that kings receive their power from God and are responsible only to God (page 219)

commonwealth a republic (used especially for the government of England from 1649 to 1660) (page 220)

DRAWING FROM EXPERIENCE

Are you concerned about inflation? How have you been affected by inflation?

Reteaching Activity

Have students list the causes of the English Revolution and Glorious Revolution. *(Charles I believed in divine right, added more ritual to Church of England; Charles II sympathized with Catholicism; James II was a Catholic, his wife and his son were Catholic.)* **L1**

4 CLOSE

Have students evaluate the political effects of both the Thirty Years' War on the German states and the English Revolution on England. **L1**

CRITICAL THINKING SKILLBUILDER

TEACH

Making Generalizations Write the following statement on the chalkboard: "Our school produces great football players (or debaters, or cheerleaders, etc.)." Ask students what information should be gathered in order to validate this generalization. *(number of awards; similar statistics for other schools in the area, etc.)* Then have students read the skill and complete the practice questions. **L1**

Additional Practice

Skills Reinforcement Activity 7

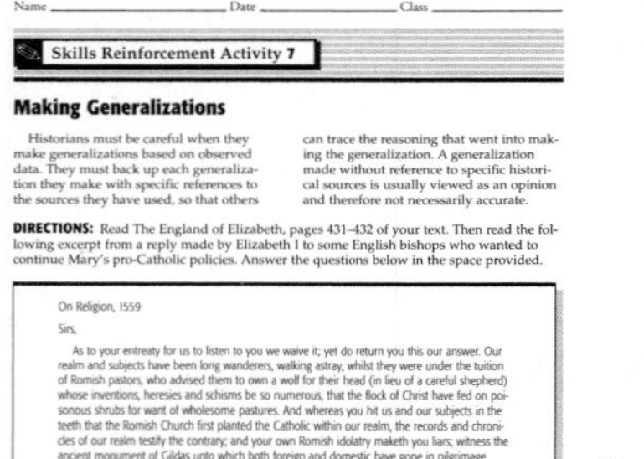
Name ______ Date ______ Class ______

Skills Reinforcement Activity 7

Making Generalizations

Historians must be careful when they make generalizations based on observed data. They must back up each generalization they make with specific references to the sources they have used, so that others can trace the reasoning that went into making the generalization. A generalization made without reference to specific historical sources is usually viewed as an opinion and therefore not necessarily accurate.

DIRECTIONS: Read The England of Elizabeth, pages 431–432 of your text. Then read the following excerpt from a reply made by Elizabeth I to some English bishops who wanted to continue Mary's pro-Catholic policies. Answer the questions below in the space provided.

On Religion, 1559

Sirs,

As to your entreaty for us to listen to you we waive it; yet do return you this our answer. Our realm and subjects have been long wanderers, walking astray, whilst they were under the tuition of Romish pastors, who advised them to own a wolf for their head (in lieu of a careful shepherd) whose inventions, heresies and schisms be so numerous, that the flock of Christ have fed on poisonous shrubs for want of wholesome pastures. And whereas you hit us and our subjects in the teeth that the Romish Church first planted the Catholic within our realm, the records and chronicles of our realm testify the contrary; and your own Romish idolatry maketh you liars; witness the ancient monument of Gildas unto which both foreign and domestic have gone in pilgrimage

GLENCOE TECHNOLOGY

CD-ROM
Glencoe Skillbuilder Interactive Workbook CD-ROM, Level 2

This interactive CD-ROM reinforces student mastery of essential social studies skills.

CRITICAL THINKING SKILLBUILDER

Making Generalizations

Why Learn This Skill?

Generalizations are broad statements or principles derived from specific facts. Here are some facts about Michigan and Florida:

Average monthly temperature (°F)

	January	April	July	October
Grand Rapids, Michigan	22	46.3	71.4	50.9
Vero Beach, Florida	61.9	71.7	81.1	75.2

One generalization that can be made from these facts is that Florida is warmer than Michigan. Generalizations are useful when you want to summarize large amounts of information and when detailed information is not required.

Learning the Skill

To make a valid generalization, follow these steps:

- **Identify the subject matter.** The example above compares Michigan to Florida.
- **Gather related facts and examples.** Each fact is about the climate of Michigan or Florida.
- **Identify similarities among these facts.** In each of the examples, the climate of Florida is more moderate than the climate of Michigan.
- **Use these similarities to form a general statement about the subject.** You can state either that Florida is warmer than Michigan or that Michigan is colder than Florida.

Practicing the Skill

Europe experienced economic crises and political upheaval from 1560 to 1650. Read the following excerpt from the text, then identify valid and invalid generalizations about what you have read.

Sixteenth-century gold coins

From 1560 to 1650, Europe witnessed severe economic and social crises, as well as political upheaval. The so-called price revolution was a dramatic rise in prices (inflation) that was a major economic problem in all of Europe in the sixteenth and early seventeenth centuries. What caused this price revolution? The great influx of gold and silver from the Americas was one factor. Perhaps even more important was an increase in population in the sixteenth century. A growing population increased the demand for land and food and drove up prices for both.

By the beginning of the seventeenth century, an economic slowdown had begun in some parts of Europe. Spain's economy, which had grown dependent on imported silver, was seriously failing by the decade of the 1640s. Italy, once the financial center of Europe in the age of the Renaissance, was also declining economically.

Identify each following generalization as valid or invalid based on the information presented:

1. Multiple factors can contribute to inflation.
2. If the government had taken measures to control an increase in population, inflation would have been prevented.
3. Nations should refrain from importing goods from other countries.
4. Less dependency on the importing of silver would have helped Spain's economy.

Applying the Skill

Over the next three weeks, read the editorials in your local newspaper. Write a list of generalizations about the newspaper's position on issues that have been discussed, either national or local.

Glencoe's **Skillbuilder Interactive Workbook, Level 2,** provides instruction and practice in key social studies skills.

ANSWERS TO PRACTICING THE SKILL

1. Valid; the text lists the influx of gold and silver into Europe and a growing population as two factors that contributed to inflation.
2. Invalid; controlling population growth would not have stopped the influx of gold and silver from the Americas.
3. Invalid; not importing goods does not account for other factors that can cause inflation such as population growth.
4. Valid; since the influx of silver helped cause inflation, less dependency on silver would have helped improve, but not necessarily solve, Spain's economic problems.

Applying the Skill: Answers will vary. Have students bring in their editorials or copies of editorials to share with the class. Ask students to analyze their editorials by examining the generalizations that they have already made.

SECTION 3

Response to Crisis: Absolutism

Guide to Reading

Main Ideas

- Louis XIV was an absolute monarch whose extravagant lifestyle and military campaigns weakened France.
- Prussia, Austria, and Russia emerged as great European powers in the seventeenth and eighteenth centuries.

Key Terms

absolutism, czar, boyar

People to Identify

Louis XIV, Cardinal Richelieu, Frederick William the Great Elector, Ivan IV, Michael Romanov, Peter the Great

Places to Locate

Prussia, Austria, St. Petersburg

Preview Questions

1. What is absolutism?
2. Besides France, what other European states practiced absolutism?

Reading Strategy

Summarizing Information As you read this section, complete a chart like the one below summarizing the accomplishments of Peter the Great.

Reforms	Government	Wars

Preview of Events

1600 · 1650 · 1700 · 1750

- **1613** Romanov dynasty begins in Russia
- **1643** Louis XIV comes to throne of France at age four
- **1715** Louis XIV dies
- **1725** Peter the Great dies

Voices from the Past

King Louis XIV

Jacques Bossuet, a seventeenth-century French bishop, explained a popular viewpoint:

> ❝It is God who establishes kings. They thus act as ministers of God and His lieutenants on earth. It is through them that he rules. This is why we have seen that the royal throne is not the throne of a man, but the throne of God himself. It appears from this that the person of kings is sacred, and to move against them is a crime. Since their power comes from on high, kings . . . should exercise it with fear and restraint as a thing which has come to them from God, and for which God will demand an account.❞
>
> — ***Western Civilization,*** Margaret L. King, 2000

Bossuet's ideas about kings became reality during the reign of King Louis XIV.

France under Louis XIV

One response to the crises of the seventeenth century was to seek more stability by increasing the power of the monarch. The result was what historians have called absolutism.

Absolutism is a system in which a ruler holds total power. In seventeenth-century Europe, absolutism was tied to the idea of the divine right of kings. It was thought that rulers received their power from God and were responsible to no one except God. Absolute monarchs had tremendous powers. They had the ability to

SECTION RESOURCES

Reproducible Masters

- Reproducible Lesson Plan 7–3
- Daily Lecture and Discussion Notes 7–3
- Guided Reading Activity 7–3
- Section Quiz 7–3
- Reading Essentials and Study Guide 7–3

Transparencies

- Daily Focus Skills Transparency 7–3

Multimedia

- Interactive Tutor Self-Assessment CD-ROM
- ExamView® Pro Testmaker CD-ROM
- Presentation Plus! CD-ROM

1 FOCUS

Section Overview

After studying this section, students should be able to define absolutism, describe the absolute monarchs, and explain the basis for their power.

BELLRINGER
Skillbuilder Activity

Project transparency and have students answer questions.

Available as a blackline master.

Daily Focus Skills Transparency 7–3

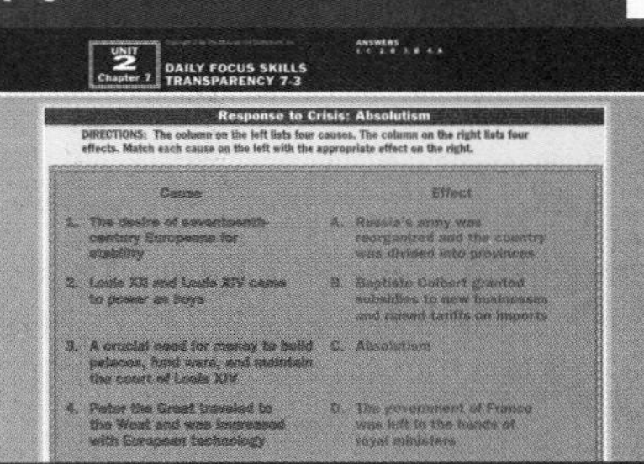

UNIT 2 Chapter 7
DAILY FOCUS SKILLS TRANSPARENCY 7-3

Response to Crisis: Absolutism

DIRECTIONS: The column on the left lists four causes. The column on the right lists four effects. Match each cause on the left with the appropriate effect on the right.

Cause	Effect
1. The desire of seventeenth-century Europeans for stability	A. Russia's army was reorganized and the country was divided into provinces
2. Louis XIII and Louis XIV came to power as boys	B. Baptiste Colbert granted subsidies to new businesses and raised tariffs on imports
3. A crucial need for money to build palaces, fund wars, and maintain the court of Louis XIV	C. Absolutism
4. Peter the Great traveled to the West and was impressed with European technology	D. The government of France was left to the hands of royal ministers

Guide to Reading

Answers to Graphic: Reforms: reorganized army; formed navy; introduced Western customs, practices, and manners; more freedom for upper-class women; Government: absolutist monarchy; divided Russia into provinces; tried to create "police" state; atmosphere of fear; built new capital at St. Petersburg; Wars: with Sweden to get a year-round Baltic port

Preteaching Vocabulary: Have students look up *absolutism* and brainstorm a list of synonyms. *(totalitarianism, fascism, dictatorship)* **L1**

CHAPTER 7
Section 3, 223–229

2 TEACH

Daily Lecture and Discussion Notes 7–3

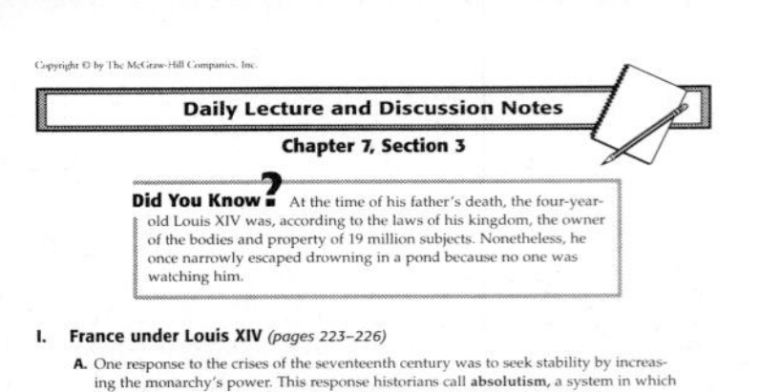

Daily Lecture and Discussion Notes

Chapter 7, Section 3

Did You Know? At the time of his father's death, the four-year-old Louis XIV was, according to the laws of his kingdom, the owner of the bodies and property of 19 million subjects. Nonetheless, he once narrowly escaped drowning in a pond because no one was watching him.

I. France under Louis XIV *(pages 223–226)*

A. One response to the crises of the seventeenth century was to seek stability by increasing the monarchy's power. This response historians call **absolutism,** a system in which the ruler has total power. It also includes the idea of the divine right of kings.

B. Absolute monarchs could make laws, levy taxes, administer justice, control the state's officials, and determine foreign policy.

C. The best example of seventeenth-century absolutism is the reign of **Louis XIV** of France. French power and culture spread throughout Europe. Other courts imitated the court of Louis XIV.

D. Louis XIII and Louis XIV were only boys when they came to power. A royal minister held power for each up to a certain age, **Cardinal Richelieu** for Louis XIII and Cardinal Marazin for Louis XIV. These ministers helped preserve the monarchy.

E. Richelieu took political and military rights from the Huguenots, a perceived threat to the throne, and thwarted a number of plots by nobles through a system of spies, executing the conspirators.

F. Louis XIV came to the throne in 1643 at age four. During Marazin's rule, nobles rebelled against the throne, but their efforts were crushed. Many French people concluded that the best chance for stability was with a monarch.

G. Louis XIV took power in 1661 at age 23. He wanted to be and was to be sole ruler of France. All were to report to him for orders or approval of orders. He fostered the myth of himself as the Sun King—the source of light for his people.

H. The royal court Louis established at **Versailles** served three purposes. It was the king's household, the location of the chief offices of the state, and a place where the powerful could find favors and offices for themselves. From Versailles, Louis controlled the central policy-making machinery of government.

I. Louis deposed nobles and princes from the royal council and invited them to Versailles where he hoped court life would distract them from politics. This tactic often worked. Louis' government ministers were to obey his every wish. He ruled with absolute authority in the three traditional areas of royal authority: foreign policy, the Church, and taxes.

turn

104

Guided Reading Activity 7–3

Name ____________ Date ____________ Class ____________

Guided Reading Activity 7-3

Response to Crisis: Absolutism

DIRECTIONS: Fill in the blanks below as you read Section 3.

I. ____________ is a system in which a ruler holds total ____________.

A. In seventeenth-century Europe, absolutism was tied to the divine ____________.

B. The reign of ____________ in France is the best example of absolutism.

1. Cardinal Richelieu strengthened the ____________ by limiting rights and spying on the nobles.
2. Louis XIV called himself the ____________.
3. Louis had complete authority over ____________, the ____________ and ____________.

II. ____________ and ____________ emerged as European powers after the Thirty Years' War.

A. Prussia was a small territory with no natural ____________ for defense.

1. Frederick William built the ____________ largest army in Europe.
2. In 1701, Frederick William's son ____________ officially became king.

B. The ____________ had long served as emperors in the Holy Roman Empire.

1. In the seventeenth century, they had lost the ____________ Empire.
2. After the defeat of the Turks in 1687, Austria took control of all of ____________, ____________, ____________, and ____________.

III. Ivan IV became the first Russian ruler to take the title of ____________, or caesar.

A. The most prominent member of the ____________ dynasty was Peter the Great.

Critical Thinking

Discuss with students the efforts of Cardinal Richelieu and Cardinal Mazarin to preserve the power of the monarchy. *(took away power of Huguenots, spied on plotting nobles, crushed revolts.)* **L1**

make laws, levy taxes, administer justice, control the state's officials, and determine foreign policy.

The reign of **Louis XIV** has long been regarded as the best example of the practice of absolutism in the seventeenth century. French culture, language, and manners reached into all levels of European society. French diplomacy and wars dominated the political affairs of western and central Europe. The court of Louis XIV was imitated throughout Europe.

Richelieu and Mazarin French history for the 50 years before Louis was a period of struggle as governments fought to avoid the breakdown of the state. The situation was made more difficult by the fact that both Louis XIII and Louis XIV were only boys when they came to the throne. The government was left in the hands of royal ministers. In France, two ministers played important roles in preserving the authority of the monarchy.

Cardinal Richelieu (RIH•shuh•LOO), Louis XIII's chief minister, strengthened the power of the monarchy. Because the Huguenots were seen as a threat to the king's power, Richelieu took away their political and military rights while preserving their religious rights. Richelieu also tamed the nobles by setting up a network of spies to uncover plots by nobles against the government. He then crushed the conspiracies and executed the conspirators.

Louis XIV came to the throne in 1643 at the age of four. Due to the king's young age, Cardinal Mazarin, the chief minister, took control of the government. During Mazarin's rule, a revolt led by nobles unhappy with the growing power of the monarchy broke out. This revolt was crushed. With its end, many French people concluded that the best hope for stability in France lay with a strong monarch.

Louis Comes to Power When Mazarin died in 1661, Louis XIV took over supreme power. The day after Cardinal Mazarin's death, the new king, at the age of 23, stated his desire to be a real king and the sole ruler of France:

THE WAY IT WAS

FOCUS ON EVERYDAY LIFE

At the Court of Versailles

In 1660, Louis XIV of France decided to build a palace at Versailles, near Paris. Untold sums of money were spent and tens of thousands of workers labored incessantly to complete the work. The enormous palace housed thousands of people.

Life at Versailles became a court ceremony, with Louis XIV at the center of it all. The king had little privacy. Only when he visited his wife, mother, or mistress or met with ministers was he free of the nobles who swarmed about the palace.

Most daily ceremonies were carefully staged, such as the king's rising from bed, dining, praying, attending mass, and going to bed. A mob of nobles competed to assist the king in carrying out these solemn activities. It was considered a great honor, for example, for a noble to be chosen to hand the king his shirt while dressing.

Why did the nobles take part in these ceremonies? Louis had made it clear that anyone who hoped to obtain an office, title, or pension from the king had to participate. This was Louis XIV's way of controlling their behavior.

Court etiquette became very complex. Nobles and royal princes were expected to follow certain rules. Who could sit where

View of the vast grounds and palace of Versailles

224

INTERDISCIPLINARY CONNECTIONS ACTIVITY

Art and Architecture Have students research and write a report on the building of Versailles, including when it was built, how it was built, the size of the grounds and the palace, and the style of architecture. Students should also discuss the art that is in the Versailles Museum. Students should analyze how the art and architecture reflect the power and grandeur associated with the reign of Louis XIV. They may also want to discuss the current status of Versailles. Students should design a visual aid to accompany their reports, using models, drawings, or photos to illustrate their research. The reports may be given orally and the visual aids displayed in the classroom to enhance the students' understanding of the architectural and artistic significance of the palace of Versailles. **L2**

❝Up to this moment I have been pleased to entrust the government of my affairs to the late Cardinal. It is now time that I govern them myself. You [secretaries and ministers of state] will assist me with your counsels when I ask for them. I request and order you to seal no orders except by my command. I order you not to sign anything, not even a passport without my command; to render account to me personally each day and to favor no one.❞

The king's mother, who was well aware of her son's love of fun and games and his affairs with the maids in the royal palace, laughed aloud at these words. Louis was serious, however. He established a strict routine from which he seldom deviated. He also fostered the myth of himself as the Sun King—the source of light for all of his people.

Government and Religion One of the keys to Louis's power was his control of the central policy-making machinery of government. The royal court that Louis established at Versailles (VUHR•SY) served three purposes. It was the personal household of the king. In addition, the chief offices of the state were located there, so Louis could watch over them. Finally, Versailles was the place where powerful subjects came to find favors and offices for themselves.

The greatest danger to Louis's rule came from very high nobles and royal princes. They believed they should play a role in the government of France. Louis got rid of this threat by removing them from the royal council. This council was the chief administrative body of the king, and it supervised the government. At the same time, Louis enticed the nobles and royal princes to come to his court, where he could keep them busy with court life and keep them out of politics.

Louis's government ministers were expected to obey his every wish. Said Louis, "I had no intention of sharing my authority with them." As a result, Louis had complete authority over the traditional areas of royal power: foreign policy, the Church, and taxes.

at meals with the king was carefully regulated. Once, at a dinner, the wife of a minister sat closer to the king than did a duchess. Louis XIV became so angry that he did not eat for the rest of the evening.

Daily life at Versailles included many forms of entertainment. Louis and his nobles hunted once a week. Walks through the Versailles gardens, boating trips, plays, ballets, and concerts were all sources of pleasure.

One form of entertainment—gambling—became an obsession at Versailles. Many nobles gambled regularly and lost enormous sums of money. One princess described the scene: "Here in France as soon as people get together they do nothing but play cards; they play for frightful sums, and the players seem bereft of their senses. One shouts at the top of his voice, another strikes the table with his fist. It is horrible to watch them." However, Louis did not think so. He was pleased by an activity that kept the Versailles nobles busy and out of politics.

The bedroom of Louis XIV at Versailles

Connecting to the Past

1. **Summarizing** How did Louis XIV attempt to control the behavior of his nobles?
2. **Explaining** Why did Louis like the gambling that went on at Versailles?
3. **Writing about History** In what way was the system of court etiquette another way in which Louis controlled his nobles?

The Way It Was

Answers:

1. by keeping them busy with court activities
2. it kept the nobles busy and out of politics; it also kept many nobles in debt and thus without resources to revolt against the king
3. nobles were expected to follow certain rules, such as where to sit at meals with the king

Critical Thinking

Discuss with students why, after the rule of Richelieu and Mazarin, many French citizens and noncitizens "concluded that the best hope for stability in France lay with a strong monarch." *(many plots against government, revolt of nobles)* **L1**

Enrich

Ask students to imagine what it was like to be a visitor to Louis XIV's court or to be Louis XIV himself: surrounded by nobles, servants, and hangers-on; determined to maintain absolute authority over foreign policy, the church, taxation, and the lives of his subjects. Have students write a diary entry from either the point of view of Louis, in which he confides his feelings about his court and reign, or from the point of view of a visitor describing life at Versailles and daily routines of the king. **L2**

CRITICAL THINKING ACTIVITY

Synthesizing Information Assign students to research the court of Louis XIV and to pay special attention to the development of the powerful cult surrounding Louis. What court ceremonies were involved in creating this cult of power? Have students explore the significance of both the ceremony of the *lever* and the *coucher.* Why were these types of ceremonies so important during his reign? How did they affect his style of governing? You might also want to have students compare Louis's court with cliques in their school or cults surrounding figures of pop culture. Do such cliques or cults exist? Why? How are they similar to the court of Louis XIV? Ask each student to write a report on his or her findings and observations. **L2**

Picturing History

Answer: Louis XIV developed a strong central government, improved internal transportation and communications, and created a merchant marine, all of which would have helped the state. However, his reckless spending and ambition left France in debt and surrounded by enemies, ultimately undermining the state.

Reading Check

Answer: kept the chief ministers at Versailles where he could watch over them; removed nobles and royal princes from the royal council and kept them busy with court life; expected his ministers to obey his wishes; attempted to stamp out Protestantism to maintain religious harmony

Etiquette By the time of Louis XIV, forks were in use, although the king used his fingers all of his life. People began to use napkins, and guests no longer had to use the tablecloth to wipe their fingers.

Economics Ask interested students to study mercantilism and to compare its principles with competing economic theories. L3

Picturing History

Louis XIV, shown here, had a clear vision of himself as a strong monarch. He had no intention of sharing his power with anyone. What effect did his views on monarchical government have on the development of the French state?

Although Louis had absolute power over France's nationwide policy making, his power was limited at the local level. The traditional groups of French society—the nobles, local officials, and town councils—had more influence than the king in the day-to-day operation of the local governments. As a result, the king bribed important people in the provinces to see that his policies were carried out.

Maintaining religious harmony had long been a part of monarchical power in France. The desire to keep this power led Louis to pursue an anti-Protestant policy aimed at converting the Huguenots to Catholicism. Early in his reign, Louis ordered the destruction of Huguenot churches and the closing of their schools. Perhaps as many as two hundred thousand Huguenots fled to England, the United Provinces, and the German states.

The Economy and War The cost of building palaces, maintaining his court, and pursuing his wars made finances a crucial issue for Louis XIV. He was most fortunate in having the services of Jean-Baptiste Colbert (kohl•BEHR) as controller-general of finances.

Colbert sought to increase the wealth and power of France by following the ideas of mercantilism. To decrease imports and increase exports, he granted subsidies to new industries. To improve communications and the transportation of goods within France, he built roads and canals. To decrease imports directly, Colbert raised tariffs on foreign goods and created a merchant marine to carry French goods.

The increase in royal power that Louis pursued led the king to develop a standing army numbering four hundred thousand in time of war. He wished to achieve the military glory befitting the Sun King. He also wished to ensure the domination of his Bourbon dynasty over European affairs.

To achieve his goals, Louis waged four wars between 1667 and 1713. His ambitions caused many nations to form coalitions to prevent him from dominating Europe. Through his wars, Louis added some territory to France's northeastern frontier and set up a member of his own dynasty on the throne of Spain.

Legacy of Louis XIV In 1715, the Sun King died. He left France with great debts and surrounded by enemies. On his deathbed, the 76-year-old monarch seemed remorseful when he told his successor (his great-grandson), "Soon you will be King of a great kingdom. . . . Try to remain at peace with your neighbors. I loved war too much. Do not follow me in that or in overspending. . . . Lighten your people's burden as soon as possible, and do what I have had the misfortune not to do myself."

Did Louis mean it? We do not know. In any event, the advice to his successor was probably not remembered; his great-grandson was only five years old.

Reading Check **Describing** What steps did Louis XIV take to maintain absolute power?

Absolutism in Central and Eastern Europe

After the Thirty Years' War, there was no German state, but over three hundred "Germanies." Of these states, two—**Prussia** and **Austria**—emerged in the seventeenth and eighteenth centuries as great European powers.

The Emergence of Prussia **Frederick William the Great Elector** laid the foundation for the Prussian state. Realizing that Prussia was a small, open territory with no natural frontiers for defense, Frederick William built a large and efficient standing army. He had a force of forty thousand men, which made the Prussian army the fourth-largest in Europe.

MEETING INDIVIDUAL NEEDS

Linguistic/Auditory To help students who learn better by discussing a topic and also to help those who are English language learners, have students work on this section in small groups of three. For homework, each student should select a part of the section to study, outline, and prepare to "teach." In class, students should clearly and logically present their section to the other members of the group, focusing on the significant people and events of their section. Each student should write a short quiz for the others to take at the end of the teaching session. L1 ELL

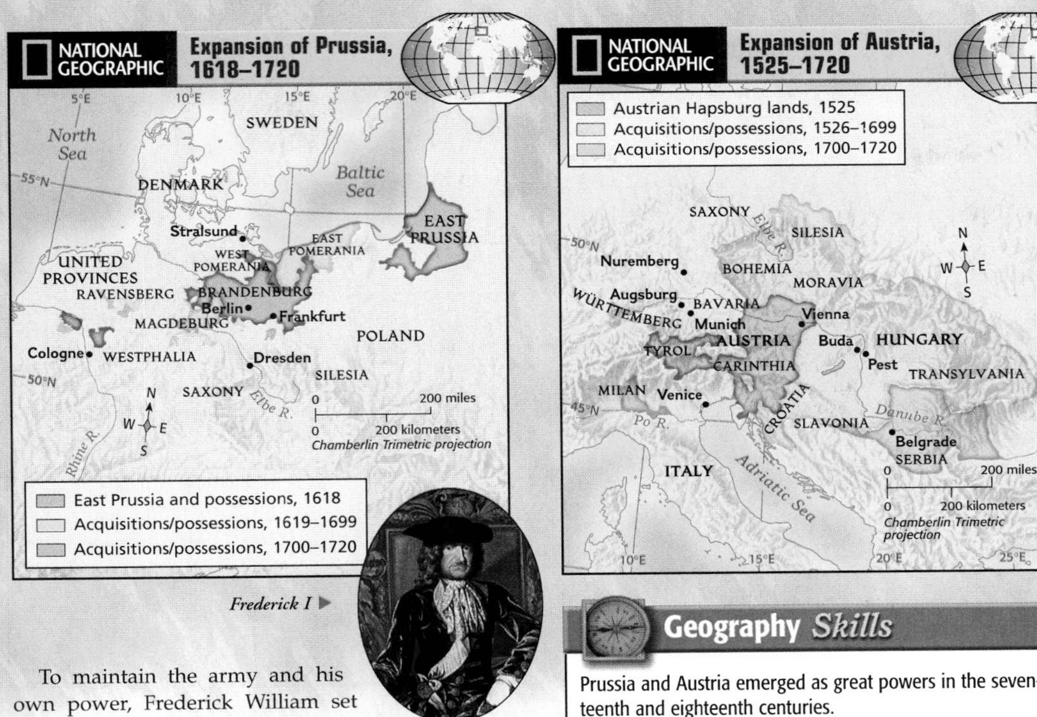

Frederick I ▶

To maintain the army and his own power, Frederick William set up the General War Commissariat to levy taxes for the army and oversee its growth. The Commissariat soon became an agency for civil government as well. The new bureaucratic machine became the elector's chief instrument to govern the state. Many of its officials were members of the Prussian landed aristocracy, known as the Junkers, who also served as officers in the army.

In 1701, Frederick William's son Frederick officially gained the title of king. Elector Frederick III became King Frederick I.

The New Austrian Empire The Austrian Hapsburgs had long played a significant role in European politics as Holy Roman emperors. By the end of the Thirty Years' War, their hopes of creating an empire in Germany had been dashed. The Hapsburgs made a difficult transition in the seventeenth century. They had lost the German Empire, but now they created a new empire in eastern and southeastern Europe.

The core of the new Austrian Empire was the traditional Austrian lands in present-day Austria, the Czech Republic, and Hungary. After the defeat of the Turks in 1687 (see Chapter 8), Austria took control of all of Hungary, Transylvania, Croatia, and Slavonia as well. By the beginning of the eighteenth century, the Austrian Hapsburgs had gained a new empire of considerable size.

Geography Skills

Prussia and Austria emerged as great powers in the seventeenth and eighteenth centuries.

1. **Interpreting Maps** What did Austria gain by expanding south?
2. **Applying Geography Skills** What destructive war happened during the time period covered by these maps?

The Austrian monarchy, however, never became a highly centralized, absolutist state, chiefly because it was made up of so many different national groups. The Austrian Empire remained a collection of territories held together by the Hapsburg emperor, who was archduke of Austria, king of Bohemia, and king of Hungary. Each of these areas had its own laws and political life. No common sentiment tied the regions together other than the ideal of service to the Hapsburgs, held by military officers and government officials.

Reading Check **Examining** Why was the Austrian monarchy unable to create a highly centralized, absolutist state?

Russia under Peter the Great

A new Russian state had emerged in the fifteenth century under the leadership of the principality of Muscovy and its grand dukes. In the sixteenth century, **Ivan IV** became the first ruler to take the title of czar, the Russian word for caesar.

Geography Skills

Answers:

1. Croatia, Slavonia, and Serbia
2. Thirty Years' War (1618–1648)

Reading Check

Answer: Empire was composed of so many different national groups that it remained a collection of territories.

Charting Activity

Ask students to create a chart that lists choices regarding local government, religion, finances, and war that led to the negative legacy of Louis XIV's reign. **L1**

Connecting Across Time

Ask students to describe the importance of military might to the practice of absolutism. *(military helps to enforce policies, ensure power)* **L1**

Critical Thinking

Have students discuss why the Austrian Empire, unlike Prussia, never became a centralized, absolutist state. *(composed of many different national groups, each had its own laws and political life.)* **L1**

Enrich

Both Ivan the Terrible and Peter the Great were complicated figures whose reigns included great successes and great failures. Invite interested students to research the life of one of these leaders, considering whether his reign was, on balance, good or bad for his people. **L2**

COOPERATIVE LEARNING ACTIVITY

Creating a Presentation Have students work in small groups to research and report on the daily life of women in Russia during the time of Peter the Great and Catherine the Great, as well as women in Russia today. Scholarly works on Russian feminism of the past and the present are available in local libraries. Have groups plan how to delegate the work—some students may research, and others may write the reports. Topics to consider might be family responsibilities, intellectual interests, types of work, and political concerns of the women. Groups should provide visuals with their reports to help the groups describe the life of women then and now. **L2**

For grading this activity, refer to the ***Performance Assessment Activities*** booklet.

CHAPTER 7
Section 3, 223–229

Geography *Skills*

Answers:

1. a "window to the west," an ice-free seaport with year-round access to Europe
2. The climate becomes unfavorable and very cold north of 60° N latitude.

Writing Activity

Have students write a brief essay in which they identify and evaluate the measures taken by Peter the Great to westernize Russia. What were the effects of these measures on his subjects? Ask students to discuss in their essays the ways in which Russian women benefited from Peter's reforms. *(removed veils, mixed more freely with men)* **L1**

3 ASSESS

Assign Section 3 Assessment as homework or as an in-class activity.

Have students use **Interactive Tutor Self-Assessment CD-ROM.**

Section Quiz 7–3

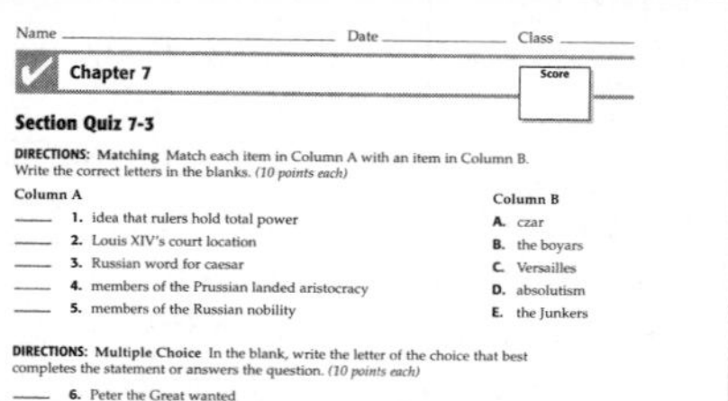

Name ______ Date ______ Class ______

Chapter 7 Score

Section Quiz 7-3

DIRECTIONS: Matching Match each item in Column A with an item in Column B. Write the correct letters in the blanks. *(10 points each)*

Column A	Column B
____ 1. idea that rulers hold total power	A. czar
____ 2. Louis XIV's court location	B. the boyars
____ 3. Russian word for caesar	C. Versailles
____ 4. members of the Prussian landed aristocracy	D. absolutism
____ 5. members of the Russian nobility	E. the Junkers

DIRECTIONS: Multiple Choice In the blank, write the letter of the choice that best completes the statement or answers the question. *(10 points each)*

____ 6. Peter the Great wanted

Geography *Skills*

Peter the Great organized Russia into provinces in an attempt to strengthen the power of the central government.

1. **Interpreting Maps** What did Russia gain by acquiring lands on the Baltic coast?
2. **Applying Geography Skills** Why are most cities in eastern Russia located near or south of 60°N latitude?

Ivan expanded the territories of Russia eastward. He also crushed the power of the Russian nobility, known as the **boyars.** He was known as Ivan the Terrible because of his ruthless deeds, among them stabbing his own son to death in a heated argument.

When Ivan's dynasty came to an end in 1584, a period of anarchy known as the Time of Troubles followed. This period did not end until the Zemsky Sobor, or national assembly, chose **Michael Romanov** as the new czar in 1613.

The Romanov dynasty lasted until 1917. One of its most prominent members was **Peter the Great.** Peter the Great became czar in 1689. Like the other Romanov czars who preceded him, Peter was an absolutist monarch who claimed the divine right to rule.

A few years after becoming czar, Peter made a trip to the West. When he returned to Russia, he was determined to westernize, or Europeanize, Russia. He was especially eager to borrow European technology. Only this kind of modernization could give him the army and navy he needed to make Russia a great power. Under Peter, Russia became a great military power. By his death in 1725, Russia was an important European state.

Military and Governmental Changes One of Peter's first goals was to reorganize the army. He employed both Russians and Europeans as officers. He drafted peasants for 25-year stints of service to build a standing army of 210,000 men. Peter has also been given credit for forming the first Russian navy, which was his overriding passion.

To impose the rule of the central government more effectively throughout the land, Peter divided Russia into provinces. He hoped to create a "police state," by which he meant a well-ordered community governed by law. However, few of his bureaucrats shared his concept of honest service and duty to the state. Peter hoped for a sense of civic duty, but his own personality created an atmosphere of fear that prevented it. He wrote to one administrator, "According to these orders act, act, act. I won't write more, but you will pay with your head if you interpret orders again." Peter wanted the impossible—that his administrators be slaves and free men at the same time.

EXTENDING THE CONTENT

St. Petersburg In 1703, Peter the Great obtained a pathway to Europe by gaining control of the Neva River from Sweden. On May 16, 1703, Russian workers laid the foundations for St. Petersburg at the mouth of the river. The city was built at an unprecedented speed; it became the capital of the Russian Empire only nine years after it was created. It was built by thousands of forced laborers, many of whom died from sickness, hunger, and accidents. St. Petersburg quickly became a major industrial center and, by 1726, it was the country's largest center of trade. The best artists in Europe and Russia created its masterpieces. Dozens of higher education establishments in St. Petersburg gave the country generations of prominent scientists and researchers. It is also the city of the great writers Pushkin, Gogol, Tolstoy, and Dostoevsky.

Cultural Changes After his first trip to the West, Peter began to introduce Western customs, practices, and manners into Russia. He ordered the preparation of the first Russian book of etiquette to teach Western manners. Among other things, the book pointed out that it was not polite to spit on the floor or to scratch oneself at dinner.

Because Westerners did not wear beards or the traditional long-skirted coat, Russian beards had to be shaved and coats shortened. At the royal court, Peter shaved off his nobles' beards and cut their coats at the knees with his own hands. Outside the court, barbers and tailors planted at town gates cut the beards and cloaks of those who entered.

One group of Russians—upper-class women—gained much from Peter's cultural reforms. Having watched women mixing freely with men in Western courts, Peter insisted that Russian upper-class women remove the veils that had traditionally covered their faces and move out into society. Peter also held gatherings in which both sexes could mix for conversation and dancing, a practice he had learned in the West.

St. Petersburg The object of Peter's domestic reforms was to make Russia into a great state and military power. An important part of this was to "open a window to the West," meaning a port with ready access to Europe. This could be achieved only on the Baltic Sea. At that time, however, the Baltic coast was controlled by Sweden, the most important power in northern Europe.

People In History

Peter the Great

1672–1725—Russian czar

Peter the Great, the man who made Russia a great power, was an unusual character. He was a towering, strong man 6 feet, 9 inches (2 m) tall. He was coarse in his tastes and rude in his behavior. He enjoyed a low kind of humor (belching contests and crude jokes) and vicious punishments (flogging, impaling, and roasting). Peter often assisted dentists and enjoyed pulling their patients' teeth.

During his first visit to the West, Peter immersed himself in the life of the people. He once dressed in the clothes of a Dutch sea captain and spent time with Dutch sailors. A German princess said of him: "He told us that he worked in building ships, showed us his hands, and made us touch the callous places that had been caused by work."

A long and hard-fought war with Sweden enabled Peter to acquire the lands he sought. On a marshland on the Baltic in 1703, Peter began the construction of a new city, **St. Petersburg,** his window on the West. St. Petersburg was finished during Peter's lifetime and remained the Russian capital until 1917.

Reading Check **Evaluating** Why was it so important that Peter the Great have a seaport on the Baltic?

SECTION 3 ASSESSMENT

Checking for Understanding

1. **Define** absolutism, czar, boyar.
2. **Identify** Louis XIV, Cardinal Richelieu, Frederick William the Great Elector, Ivan IV, Michael Romanov, Peter the Great.
3. **Locate** Prussia, Austria, St. Petersburg.
4. **Describe** the Western customs, practices, and manners that Peter the Great introduced to Russia.
5. **List** the purposes of the royal court at Versailles.

Critical Thinking

6. **Explain** What were Cardinal Richelieu's political goals? How did he reduce the power of the nobility and the Huguenots in France?
7. **Summarizing Information** Use a chart like the one below to summarize the reign of Louis XIV of France.

Government	Wars	Economics	Religion

Analyzing Visuals

8. **Examine** the photograph of the king's bedroom shown on page 225. How does this room reflect the nature of kingship under Louis XIV?

Writing About History

9. **Expository Writing** Historians have long considered the reign of Louis XIV to be the best example of the practice of absolute monarchy in the seventeenth century. Do you believe the statement is true? Why or why not? Write an essay supporting your opinion.

Reading Check

Answer: It was the only place where the Russians could have an ice-free port with year-round access to Europe.

Reading Essentials and Study Guide 7–3

Name ______ Date ______ Class ______

Reading Essentials and Study Guide

Chapter 7, Section 3

For use with textbook pages 223–229

RESPONSE TO CRISIS: ABSOLUTISM

KEY TERMS

absolutism a system of government in which a ruler holds total power *(page 223)*

czar the Russian word for caesar, which became the title of the Russian rulers beginning with Ivan IV *(page 227)*

boyars the Russian nobility *(page 228)*

DRAWING FROM EXPERIENCE

What do you think is the purpose of dress codes? Do you think dress codes should be enforced in public schools? Why or why not?

In the last section, you read about the wars, revolutions, and economic problems in Europe during the seventeenth century. In this section, you will learn how monarchs in certain countries gained absolute power during this time. One of these absolute monarchs, Peter the Great, even told people how they should dress.

ORGANIZING YOUR THOUGHTS

Use the chart below to help you take notes. Identify the countries of the following monarchs and summarize their achievements.

Monarch	Country	Achievements
Louis XIV	1.	2.
Frederick William the Great Elector	3.	4.
Peter the Great	5.	6.

Reteaching Activity

Have students analyze the information in this section by summarizing the achievements and the acts of oppression of each major ruler discussed. **L1**

4 CLOSE

Ask students to choose one of the monarchs from this period and discuss positive and negative effects of absolutism on their people and countries. **L1**

SECTION 3 ASSESSMENT

1. Key terms are in blue.
2. Louis XIV (*p. 224*); Cardinal Richelieu (*p. 224*); Frederick William the Great Elector (*p. 226*); Ivan IV (*p. 227*); Michael Romanov (*p. 228*); Peter the Great (*p. 228*)
3. See chapter maps.
4. etiquette, shave beards, women remove veils, mix freely in society
5. housed state offices, court life kept nobles out of politics
6. strengthen monarchy; revoked Huguenots' political and military rights, spied on nobles, executed conspirators
7. Government: absolute ruler; Wars: four wars, added lands in northeast, put relative on Spanish throne; Economics: mercantilism, subsidies to new industries, built roads and canals, created merchant marine, left France in debt; Religion: anti-Protestant, destroyed Huguenot churches, closed schools
8. extravagant; reflects public court life
9. Answers will vary.

1 FOCUS

Section Overview

This section discusses important artistic movements, writers, and philosophers of the sixteenth and seventeenth centuries.

BELLRINGER
Skillbuilder Activity

Project transparency and have students answer questions.

Available as a blackline master.

Daily Focus Skills Transparency 7–4

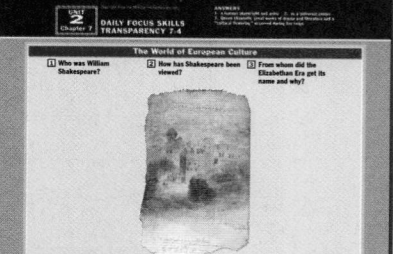

Guide to Reading

Answers to Graphic: Hobbes: humans struggled for self-preservation, agreed to be governed by absolute ruler, absolute power needed to preserve order; Locke: original state one of equality and freedom, have natural rights, established government to protect rights, if government breaks contract the people have right to form new one

Preteaching Vocabulary: Ask students to brainstorm a list of what they believe to be *natural rights*. L1

SECTION 4 The World of European Culture

Guide to Reading

Main Ideas
- The artistic movements of Mannerism and the baroque began in Italy and both reflected the spiritual perceptions of the time.
- Shakespeare and Lope de Vega were prolific writers of dramas and comedies that reflected the human condition.

Key Terms
Mannerism, baroque, natural rights

People to Identify
El Greco, Gian Lorenzo Bernini, William Shakespeare, Lope de Vega, Miguel de Cervantes, Thomas Hobbes, John Locke

Places to Locate
Madrid, Prague, Vienna, Brussels

Preview Questions
1. What two new art movements emerged in the 1500s?
2. Why are Shakespeare's works considered those of a "genius"?

Reading Strategy
Summarizing Information As you read this section, complete a chart like the one below summarizing the political thoughts of Thomas Hobbes and John Locke.

Thomas Hobbes	John Locke

Preview of Events

1575 · 1590 · 1605 · 1620 · 1635 · 1650 · 1665

- **1575** Baroque movement begins in Italy
- **1580** Golden Age of English theater begins
- **1599** Globe Theater built
- **1615** Cervantes completes *Don Quixote*
- **1651** *Leviathan* by Hobbes is published

William Shakespeare

Voices from the Past

In the play *Richard II,* William Shakespeare wrote the following lines about England:

> ❝This royal throne of kings, this sceptered isle,
> This earth of majesty, this seat of Mars,
> This other Eden, demi-Paradise,
> This fortress built by Nature for herself
> Against infection and the hand of war,
> This happy breed of men, this little world,
> This precious stone set in the silver sea,
> Which serves it in the office of a wall
> Or as a moat defensive to a house
> Against the envy of less happier lands—
> This blessed plot, this earth, this realm, this England.❞
>
> —***Richard II,*** **William Shakespeare**

In this play, one of the greatest playwrights of the English world expressed his patriotic enthusiasm.

Mannerism

The artistic Renaissance came to an end when a new movement, called Mannerism, emerged in Italy in the 1520s and 1530s. The Reformation's revival of religious values brought much political turmoil. Especially in Italy, the worldly

SECTION RESOURCES

Reproducible Masters
- Reproducible Lesson Plan 7–4
- Daily Lecture and Discussion Notes 7–4
- Guided Reading Activity 7–4
- Section Quiz 7–4
- Reading Essentials and Study Guide 7–4

Transparencies
- Daily Focus Skills Transparency 7–4

Multimedia
- Interactive Tutor Self-Assessment CD-ROM
- ExamView® Pro Testmaker CD-ROM
- Presentation Plus! CD-ROM

enthusiasm of the Renaissance declined as people grew anxious and uncertain and wished for spiritual experience.

Mannerism in art reflected this new environment by deliberately breaking down the High Renaissance principles of balance, harmony, and moderation. The rules of proportion were deliberately ignored as elongated figures were used to show suffering, heightened emotions, and religious ecstasy.

Mannerism spread from Italy to other parts of Europe and perhaps reached its high point in the work of **El Greco** ("the Greek"). El Greco was from the island of Crete. After studying in Venice and Rome, he moved to Spain.

In his paintings, El Greco used elongated and contorted figures, portraying them in unusual shades of yellow and green against an eerie background of stormy grays. The mood he depicts reflects well the tensions created by the religious upheavals of the Reformation.

Reading Check **Describing** What did the mood of El Greco's paintings reflect?

The Baroque Period

Mannerism was eventually replaced by a new movement—the **baroque**. This movement began in Italy in the last quarter of the sixteenth century and eventually spread to the rest of Europe and even Latin America. The Catholic reform movement most wholeheartedly adopted the baroque style. This can be seen in the buildings at Catholic courts, especially those of the Hapsburgs in **Madrid, Prague, Vienna,** and **Brussels.**

Baroque artists tried to bring together the classical ideals of Renaissance art with the spiritual feelings of the sixteenth-century religious revival. The baroque painting style was known for its use of dramatic effects to arouse the emotions. In large part, though, baroque art and architecture reflected the search for power that was such a part of the seventeenth century. Baroque churches and palaces were magnificent and richly detailed. Kings and princes wanted other kings and princes as well as their subjects to be in awe of their power.

Perhaps the greatest figure of the baroque period was the Italian architect and sculptor **Gian Lorenzo Bernini,** who completed Saint Peter's Basilica in Rome. Action, exuberance, and dramatic effects mark the work of Bernini in the interior of Saint Peter's.

Bernini's *Throne of Saint Peter* is a highly decorated cover for the pope's medieval wooden throne. The throne seems to hover in midair, held by the hands of the four great theologians of the early Catholic Church. Above the chair, rays of heavenly light drive a mass of clouds and angels toward the spectator.

History *through Art*

***Throne of Saint Peter* by Bernini, 1666**
It took Bernini eleven years to complete this monumental throne. How do you think Bernini wanted his work to impact the viewer?

Artemisia Gentileschi is less well-known than the male artists who dominated the seventeenth-century art world in Italy but prominent in her own right. Born in Rome, she studied painting with her father. In 1616, she moved to Florence and began a successful career as a painter. At the age of 23, she became the first woman to be elected to the Florentine Academy of Design. Although she was known internationally in her day as a portrait painter, her fame now rests on a series of pictures of heroines from the Old Testament. Most famous is her *Judith Beheading Holofernes*.

Reading Check **Identifying** How did baroque art and architecture reflect the seventeenth-century search for power?

A Golden Age of Literature

In both England and Spain, writing for the theater reached new heights between 1580 and 1640. Other forms of literature flourished as well.

2 TEACH

Reading Check

Answer: The tension created by the religious upheavals of the Reformation.

History *through Art*

Answer: Answers will vary, but might include to inspire awe or to impress the viewer with the power of the church.

Reading Check

Answer: through magnificence and rich details

Daily Lecture and Discussion Notes 7–4

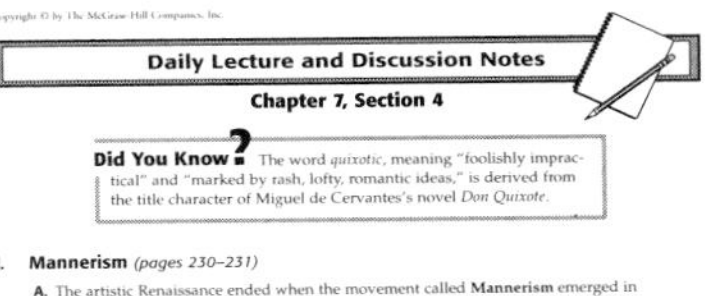

Daily Lecture and Discussion Notes

Chapter 7, Section 4

Did You Know? The word *quixotic*, meaning "foolishly impractical" and "marked by rash, lofty, romantic ideas," is derived from the title character of Miguel de Cervantes's novel *Don Quixote*.

I. **Mannerism** *(pages 230–231)*

A. The artistic Renaissance ended when the movement called **Mannerism** emerged in Italy in the 1520s and 1530s. The movement fit Europe's climate of the time, as people grew uncertain about worldly experience and wished for spiritual experience.

B. Mannerism broke down the High Renaissance values of balance, harmony, moderation, and proportion. Elongated figures showed suffering, heightened emotions, and religious ecstasy.

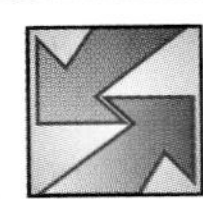

CURRICULUM CONNECTION

Literature Assign students to read all or part of a play by Shakespeare or Lope de Vega, or all or part of *Don Quixote*. Discuss with the class how the wider audiences for these works, "nobles, lawyers, merchants, and vagabonds," might have reacted to the themes and characters of these works. **L3**

INTERDISCIPLINARY CONNECTIONS ACTIVITY

Art Have students research and write a brief report on a major work of art by El Greco, Bernini, and Gentileschi. For each work they should describe the subject matter. They should also prepare a statement comparing and contrasting the subject matter of each of the works of art. Using what they have learned from the text, they should then identify the characteristics of each of the representative styles of Mannerism and Baroque as seen in the work of art and explain how each work of art achieves the goals of that particular style. Students should also identify symbols used by each artist. Finally, students should tell how they are affected by each of the works. **L3**

Reading Check

Answer: between 1580 and 1640; Lope de Vega

Guided Reading Activity 7–4

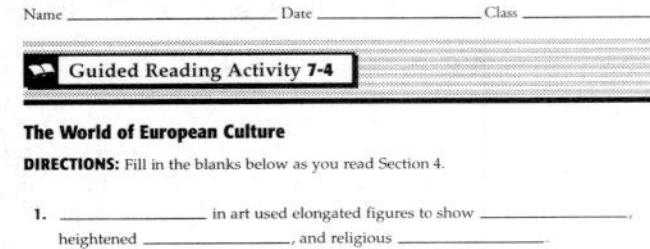

Name ______ Date ______ Class ______

Guided Reading Activity 7-4

The World of European Culture

DIRECTIONS: Fill in the blanks below as you read Section 4.

1. ______ in art used elongated figures to show ______, heightened ______, and religious ______.
2. The mood depicted by El Greco reflected well the tensions created by the religious upheavals of the ______.
3. The ______ painting style was known for its use of dramatic effects to arouse the emotions and reflect a search for power.
4. Perhaps the greatest figure of the baroque period was the Italian architect and sculptor ______, who completed St. Peter's ______ in Rome.
5. Of all the Elizabethan ______, none is more famous than ______.
6. The Globe theatre's admission charge of one or two pennies enabled even the ______ to attend.
7. Beginning in the 1580s, the standard for playwrights was set by ______ who wrote perhaps 1,500 plays in all.
8. Miguel de Cervantes' novel ______ has been hailed as one of the greatest literary works of all time.
9. Hobbes called the state "that great ______ to which we owe our peace and defense."
10. Locke believed ______ should protect the rights of the people, and the people would act ______ toward government.
11. John Locke's ideas were used to support demands for ______ government, the rule of law and the protection of rights.

CURRICULUM CONNECTION

Philosophy and Government Assign students to read the Declaration of Independence and to find those passages that reflect the political views of John Locke. **L2**

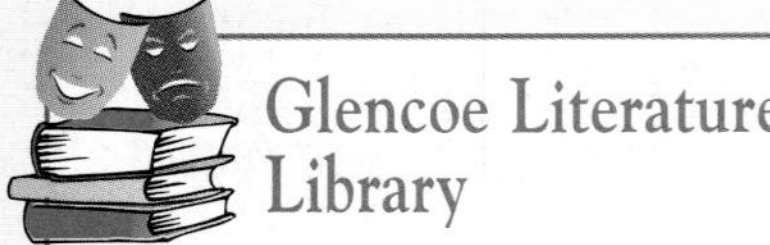

Glencoe Literature Library

The following literature from the **Glencoe Literature Library** may enrich the teaching of this chapter: *Hamlet* by William Shakespeare

HISTORY Online

Web Activity Visit the *Glencoe World History—Modern Times* Web site at wh.mt.glencoe.com and click on **Chapter 7–Student Web Activity** to learn more about William Shakespeare.

England's Shakespeare

A cultural flowering took place in England in the late sixteenth and early seventeenth centuries. The period is often called the Elizabethan Era, because so much of it fell within the reign of Queen Elizabeth. Of all the forms of Elizabethan literature, none expressed the energy of the era better than drama. Of all the dramatists, none is more famous than **William Shakespeare.**

When Shakespeare appeared in London in 1592, Elizabethans already enjoyed the stage. Elizabethan theater was a very successful business. London theaters ranged from the Globe, which was a circular, unroofed structure holding three thousand people, to the Blackfriars, a roofed structure that held only five hundred.

The Globe's admission charge of one or two pennies enabled even the lower classes to attend. The higher prices of the Blackfriars brought an audience of the well-to-do. Because Elizabethan audiences varied greatly, playwrights had to write works that pleased nobles, lawyers, merchants, and vagabonds alike.

William Shakespeare was a "complete man of the theater." Although best known for writing plays, he was also an actor and shareholder in the chief theater company of the time, the Lord Chamberlains' Company.

Shakespeare has long been viewed as a universal genius. He was a master of the English language and his language skills were matched by his insight into human psychology. Whether in his tragedies or his comedies, Shakespeare showed a remarkable understanding of the human condition.

Spanish Literature

The theater was one of the most creative forms of expression during Spain's golden century as well. The first professional theaters, created in Seville and Madrid, were run by actors' companies, as they were in England. Soon, every large town had a public playhouse, including Mexico City in the New World. Touring companies brought the latest Spanish plays to all parts of the Spanish Empire.

Beginning in the 1580s, the standard for playwrights was set by **Lope de Vega.** He wrote an extraordinary number of plays, perhaps 1,500 in all. Almost 500 of them survive. They have been characterized as witty, charming, action-packed, and realistic.

Lope de Vega made no apologies for the fact that he wrote his plays to please his audiences and satisfy public demand. He remarked once that if anyone thought he had written his plays for fame, "undeceive him and tell him that I wrote them for money."

One of the crowning achievements of the golden age of Spanish literature was the work of **Miguel de Cervantes** (suhr•VAN•TEEZ). His novel *Don Quixote* has been hailed as one of the greatest literary works of all time.

In the two main characters of this famous work, Cervantes presented the dual nature of the Spanish character. The knight, Don Quixote from La Mancha, is the visionary so involved in his lofty ideals that he does not see the hard realities around him. To him, for example, windmills appear to be four-armed giants. In contrast, the knight's fat and earthy squire, Sancho Panza, is a realist. Each of these characters finally comes to see the value of the other's perspective. We are left with the conviction that both visionary dreams and the hard work of reality are necessary to the human condition.

Reading Check **Describing** When was the "golden age" of Spanish literature? Who set the standard for playwrights?

Don Quixote and Sancho Panza

MEETING INDIVIDUAL NEEDS

Auditory Have students read together the section "A Golden Age of Literature" without pausing. Then have the students utilize note-taking skills and provide the following major topics:

I. Literature in England
- A Elizabethan Era
- B. Shakespeare

II. Literature in Spain
- A. Lope de Vega
- B. Miguel de Cervantes

Ask student to take notes on this handout as the class carefully rereads the selection. Use this outline as a basis for a quiz. This activity is useful for students with memory difficulties and attention deficit disorder. **L1**

Political Thought

The seventeenth-century concerns with order and power were reflected in the political thought of the time. The English revolutions of the seventeenth century prompted very different responses from two English political thinkers, Thomas Hobbes and John Locke.

Hobbes **Thomas Hobbes** was alarmed by the revolutionary upheavals in England. He wrote *Leviathan*, a work on political thought, to try to deal with the problem of disorder. *Leviathan* was published in 1651.

Hobbes claimed that before society was organized, human life was "solitary, poor, nasty, brutish, and short." Humans were guided not by reason and moral ideals but by a ruthless struggle for self-preservation.

To save themselves from destroying one another, people made a social contract and agreed to form a state. Hobbes called the state "that great Leviathan to which we owe our peace and defense." People in the state agreed to be governed by an absolute ruler who possessed unlimited power. Rebellion must be suppressed. To Hobbes, such absolute power was needed to preserve order in society.

Locke **John Locke,** who wrote a political work called *Two Treatises of Government*, 1690, viewed the exercise of political power quite differently. He argued against the absolute rule of one person.

Unlike Hobbes, Locke believed that before society was organized, humans lived in a state of equality and freedom rather than a state of war. In this state of nature, humans had certain natural rights—rights with which they were born. These included rights to life, liberty, and property.

Like Hobbes, however, Locke believed that problems existed in the state of nature. People found it difficult to protect their natural rights. For that reason, they agreed to establish a government to ensure the protection of their rights.

The contract between people and government involved mutual obligations. Government would protect the rights of the people, and the people would act reasonably toward government. However, if a government broke the contract—if a monarch, for example, failed to live up to the obligation to protect subjects' natural rights—the people might form a new government.

To Locke, people meant the landholding aristocracy, not landless masses. Locke was not an advocate of democracy, but his ideas proved important to both Americans and French in the eighteenth century. These ideas were used to support demands for constitutional government, the rule of law, and the protection of rights. Locke's ideas can be found in the American Declaration of Independence and the United States Constitution.

Reading Check **Explaining** According to Hobbes, why was absolute power needed?

SECTION 4 ASSESSMENT

Checking for Understanding

1. **Define** Mannerism, baroque, natural rights.
2. **Identify** El Greco, Gian Lorenzo Bernini, William Shakespeare, Lope de Vega, Miguel de Cervantes, Thomas Hobbes, John Locke.
3. **Locate** Madrid, Prague, Vienna, Brussels.
4. **Describe** what *Don Quixote* reveals about the nature of Spanish character.
5. **Summarize** the mutual obligations between people and government as understood by Locke.

Critical Thinking

6. **Describe** How did the Elizabethan theater experience provide a full reflection of English society?
7. **Compare and Contrast** Using a Venn diagram, compare and contrast Mannerism and baroque art.

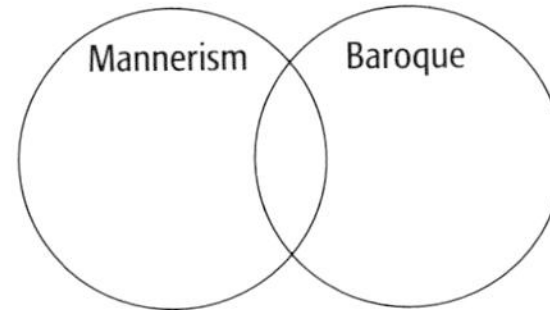

Analyzing Visuals

8. **Examine** the photograph of Bernini's *Throne of Saint Peter* shown on page 231 of your text. How does Bernini's artistic masterpiece reflect the political and social life of the period in which it was created?

Writing About History

9. **Persuasive Writing** In an essay, argue whether Shakespeare is stereotyping in this quote: "Frailty, thy name is woman." Support your position with quotes from other authors who either corroborate or disagree with Shakespeare.

SECTION 4 ASSESSMENT

1. Key terms are in blue.
2. El Greco (*p. 231*); Gian Lorenzo Bernini (*p. 231*); William Shakespeare (*p. 232*); Lope de Vega (*p. 232*); Miguel de Cervantes (*p. 232*); Thomas Hobbes (*p. 233*); John Locke (*p. 233*)
3. See chapter maps.
4. dual nature of visionary dreams and realism
5. government: protect people's rights; people: act reasonably toward government
6. The Globe: inexpensive; Blackfriars: served rich; playwrights had to please all classes
7. Mannerism: rejected Renaissance balance, harmony, moderation; ignored rules of proportion; Baroque: return to ideals of Renaissance art; action, exuberance, dramatic effects; detailed and ornate; Both: began in Italy; emotional, religious themes
8. highly ornate, rich details suggests awe at the power of pope
9. Answers should be supported by examples.

Reading Check

Answer: to preserve order in society

3 ASSESS

Assign Section 4 Assessment as homework or as an in-class activity.

Have students use **Interactive Tutor Self-Assessment CD-ROM.**

Section Quiz 7–4

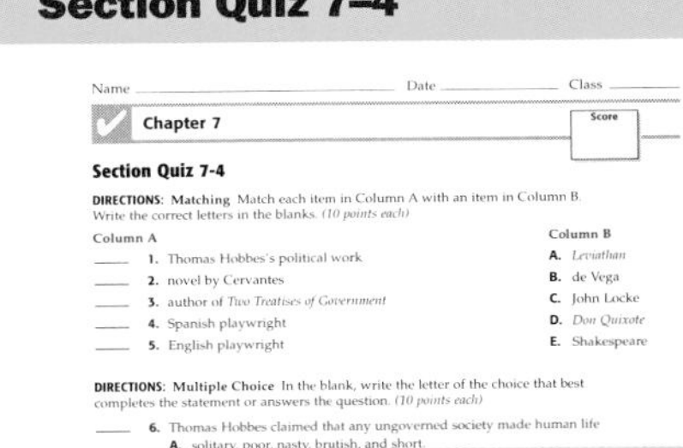

Reading Essentials and Study Guide 7–4

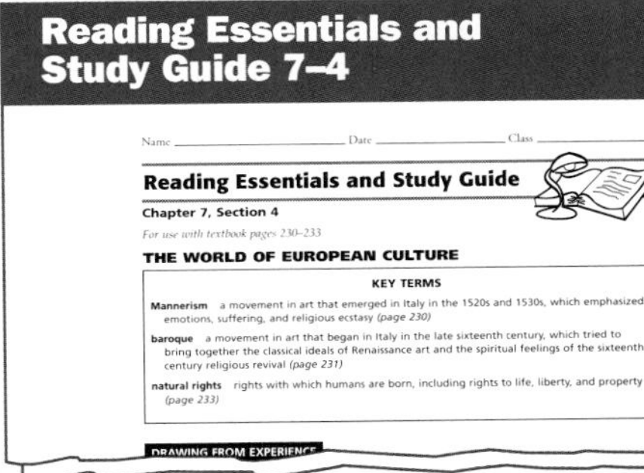

Reteaching Activity

Have students list the major artists and writers of this period and their major works. **L1**

4 CLOSE

Review with students how the art and literature of the period reflects the political conflicts discussed earlier in the chapter. **L2**

CHAPTER 7
Assessment and Activities

GLENCOE TECHNOLOGY

MindJogger Videoquiz

Use the **MindJogger Videoquiz** to review Chapter 7 content.

 Available in VHS.

Using Key Terms

1. armada **2.** commonwealth **3.** witchcraft **4.** divine right of kings **5.** Mannerism **6.** Absolutism **7.** Baroque **8.** czar **9.** boyars **10.** natural rights

Reviewing Key Facts

11. Huguenots

12. It gave Huguenots the right to worship and to enjoy political privileges in Catholic France.

13. Turks

14. Europe, North America, South America, Asia, Africa

15. 1618 to 1648, the Holy Roman Empire

16. France

17. to try to keep peace with his neighbors, not to love war too much, not to overspend, lighten his people's burden

18. for the money

19. One needs to balance visionary dreams with the reality of hard work in life.

20. to protect citizens' rights

Critical Thinking

21. Since Baroque art and architecture is ornate and detailed, the palace at Versailles is a perfect example. Its vastness alone projects power, as does its extravagance.

22. The more Philip cracked down on the Netherlands, the more rebellious the people became. The nobles resented the loss of their privileges and opposed his efforts. When he tried to crush Calvinism, the Calvinists—especially nobles—began to destroy statues in Catholic churches. He sent troops to crush the rebellion, resulting in growing resistance, war, and eventual independence for the Netherlands.

23. Locke believed that humans had certain natural rights to life, liberty, and property. This belief is reflected in our belief in the "inalienable rights" to "life, liberty, and the pursuit of happiness." He believed that the government had a duty to protect the rights of the people and, when it fails, that the people have a right to form a new government. This is similar to what happened when the American colonists declared independence from Britain. He would probably approve wholeheartedly of the American system of government.

Writing About History

24. Answers will vary. Students should support their positions with facts from the chapter.

Analyzing Sources

25. with fear and restraint, keeping in mind that they will be called on by God for an account

CHAPTER 7 ASSESSMENT and ACTIVITIES

Using Key Terms

1. Philip II sent a fleet of warships called an _____ to invade England in 1588.
2. Parliament abolished the monarchy and declared England a republic or _____.
3. The _____ hysteria began to end in 1650.
4. The belief that the monarch receives power directly from God is called _____.
5. In _____, elongated figures show suffering and heightened emotions.
6. _____ refers to the political system in which ultimate authority rests with the monarch.
7. _____ artists paired ideals of Renaissance art with sixteenth-century spiritual feelings.
8. The Russian monarch was called a _____.
9. The _____ were Russian nobility defeated by Ivan the Terrible.
10. John Locke believed people had certain _____—to life, liberty, and property.

Chapter Summary

The rulers of Europe during the sixteenth, seventeenth, and early eighteenth centuries battled to expand their borders, power, and religion. The chart below summarizes some of the events of this chapter.

Conflict

Spanish and English monarchs engage in a dynastic struggle.
- Philip II, a champion of Catholicism, resents English tolerance of Protestants.
- The defeat of the Spanish Armada in 1588 means that England will remain Protestant.

Change

Tudor monarchs bring stability and prosperity to England.
- The Act of Supremacy is passed.
- Foreign policy is moderate.
- Spain is defeated in 1588.

Uniformity

France's Louis XIV strengthens absolute monarchy in France and limits the rights of religious dissenters.
- He removes nobles and princes from royal council and keeps them busy with court life.
- He bribes people to make sure his policies are followed in the provinces.

Conflict

Dynastic and religious conflicts divide the German states.
- Two German states emerge as great powers in the seventeenth and eighteenth centuries: Prussia and Austria.
- Prussia has to build an army to protect its borders. Austria is diverse with no common culture or political rule.

Innovation

Peter the Great attempts to modernize Russian society.
- He introduces Western customs, practices, and manners.
- He prepares a Russian book of etiquette to teach Western manners.
- He mixes the sexes for conversation and dancing.

Reviewing Key Facts

11. **Religion** What is the name given to French Calvinists?
12. **Government** Why is the Edict of Nantes sometimes called the Edict of Tolerance?
13. **History** Whom did Spain defeat in the Battle of Lepanto in 1571?
14. **Geography** At the beginning of the seventeenth century, Spain controlled territory on which continents?
15. **History** When and where was the Thirty Years' War fought?
16. **History** After the Thirty Years' War, which country emerged as the most dominant in Europe?
17. **Government** On his deathbed, what advice did Louis XIV give to his great-grandson, the future king?
18. **Culture** What reason for writing did Lope de Vega give those who asked?
19. **Culture** What is the essential message of *Don Quixote* by Cervantes?
20. **Philosophy** According to John Locke, what was the purpose of government?

Critical Thinking

21. **Analyzing** Baroque art and architecture reflected a search for power. How can a particular style of art be more powerful than another? (Consider the palace at Versailles.)
22. **Explaining** "Repression breeds rebellion." Explain how this quote relates to the history of the Netherlands during the reign of Philip II.
23. **Compare and Contrast** Compare the political thought of John Locke to the American form of government. What would Locke support? What would he not support?

Self-Check Quiz

Visit the *Glencoe World History—Modern Times* Web site at wh.mt.glencoe.com and click on **Chapter 7 –Self-Check Quiz** to prepare for the Chapter Test.

Writing About History

24. Persuasive Writing Which of the monarchs described in this chapter do you most and least admire? Why? Write an essay supporting your answer with logic and reason.

Analyzing Sources

Read the following quote about absolutism by Jacques Bossuet, a seventeenth-century French bishop.

> ❝It is God who establishes kings. They thus act as ministers of God and His lieutenants on earth. It is through them that he rules. This is why we have seen that the royal throne is not the throne of man, but the throne of God himself. It appears from this that the person of kings is sacred, and to move against them is a crime. Since their power comes from on high, kings . . . should exercise it with fear and restraint as a thing which has come to them from God, and for which God will demand an account.❞

25. According to the quote, how should kings rule?

26. How do these words justify divine right of kings, and what does it mean that God will demand an account? What questions would you ask Bossuet about his ideas? How might he answer?

Applying Technology Skills

27. Using the Internet or library, research the current political status of France, Great Britain, Spain, and Germany. List the name of the current leader and the type of government (for example: Mexico, President Fox, constitutional democracy).

Making Decisions

28. Assume the role of King Louis XIV, or Queen Elizabeth I. Write a speech to your people about raising taxes and religion. Assess the needs of the state, the military, the court, and the people. Is it necessary to raise taxes? Which group is demanding the increase? How will this action affect each of these groups? Who will benefit the most, and who will suffer the most from the increase? After you have weighed options and considered the consequences, write a speech to your subjects announcing your decision. Persuade them that the increase is in the best interest of all.

NATIONAL GEOGRAPHIC **Growth of France under Louis XIV, 1643–1715**

Analyzing Maps and Charts

29. What natural borders help to define France during this period?

30. Study the map carefully. What means of transportation do you think most French people used for trade?

31. Using this map and your text, describe how Louis XIV expanded France. What was the legacy of Louis XIV's expansion for his successor?

32. How does the extent of France in 1715 compare to the extent of France today? Use an atlas to research your answer.

Standardized Test Practice

Directions: Choose the best answer to the following question.

All of the following resulted from the English "Glorious Revolution" EXCEPT

F the idea of the divine right of kings.

G the addition of a Bill of Rights to the English constitution.

H the restoration of a monarch in England.

J increased religious freedom for Protestants.

Test-Taking Tip: Key words such as *except* or *not* dramatically change the test question. Always read carefully so you do not miss key words.

Have students visit the Web site at wh.mt.glencoe.com to review Chapter 7 and take the Self-Check Quiz.

Standardized Test Practice

Answer: F

Answer Explanation: Remind students of the importance of reading the question carefully and then finding answers that fit and do not fit the question.

Bonus Question ?

Ask: If you could spend an evening with one of the rulers you have met in this chapter, who would it be and what would you do? Have students answer in the form of a brief essay. *(Students should support their answers with logic, reason, and historical evidence.)*

26. It says that the power to rule comes directly from God, and that God is the only one that the king has to answer to. Answers to last part of question will vary.

Applying Technology Skills

27. Answers will vary, depending on country chosen and its current political status.

Making Decisions

28. Answers will vary, but should be consistent with material presented in this chapter.

Analyzing Maps and Charts

29. Atlantic Ocean, Mediterranean Sea, Alps, Pyrenees

30. overland transportation and transportation by sea and fresh water (rivers)

31. By waging war, Louis added territory to France's northeastern frontier and along border with Spain. He left a legacy of debt and enemies.

32. France is larger today than in 1715.

Chapter 8 Resources

Timesaving Tools

TeacherWorks™ All-In-One Planner and Resource Center

- **Interactive Teacher Edition** Access your Teacher Wraparound Edition and your classroom resources with a few easy clicks.
- **Interactive Lesson Planner** Planning has never been easier! Organize your week, month, semester, or year with all the lesson helps you need to make teaching creative, timely, and relevant.

Use Glencoe's **Presentation Plus!** multimedia teacher tool to easily present dynamic lessons that visually excite your students. Using Microsoft PowerPoint® you can customize the presentations to create your own personalized lessons.

Teaching Transparencies

Graphic Organizer Student Activity 8 Transparency

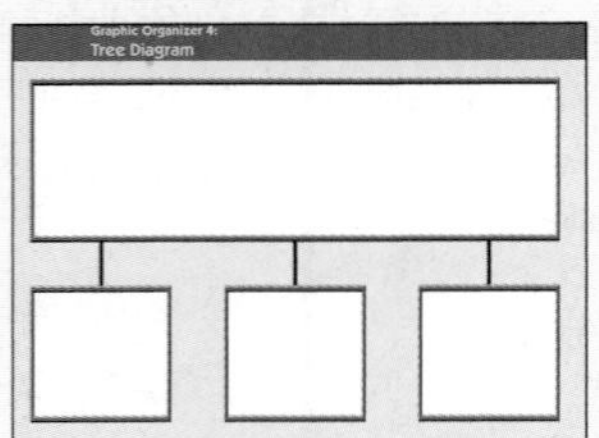

Chapter Transparency 8

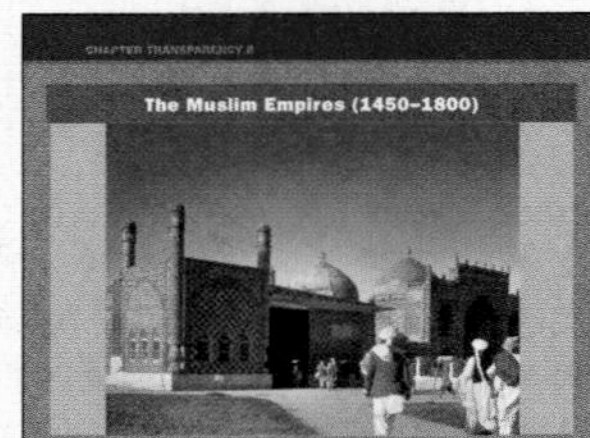

Map Overlay Transparency 8

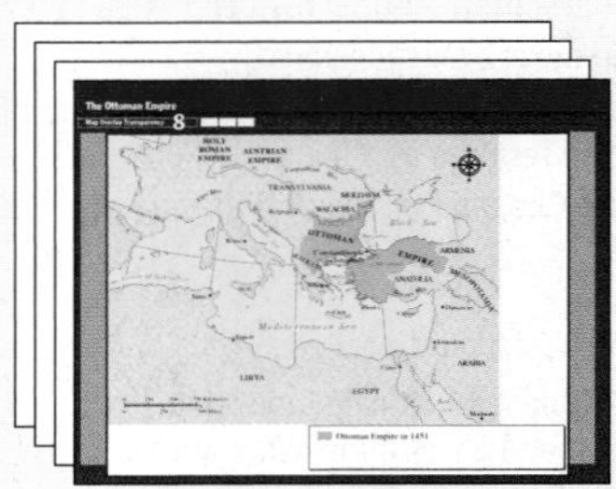

Application and Enrichment

Enrichment Activity 8

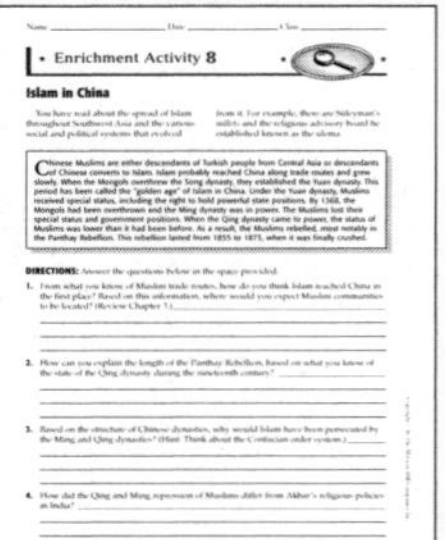
Enrichment Activity 8
Islam in China

Primary Source Reading 8

Primary Source Reading 8
Four Hundred Years of the East India Company

History Simulation Activity 8

History Simulation Activity 8
Handout Material
Lives in the Past—Planning Form

Historical Significance Activity 8

Historical Significance Activity 8
The Monument to Love

Cooperative Learning Activity 8

Cooperative Learning Activity 8
Muslim Empires Time Line

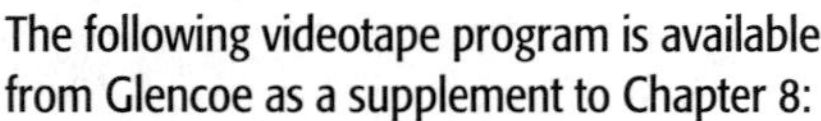

THE HISTORY CHANNEL.

The following videotape program is available from Glencoe as a supplement to Chapter 8:

- **Legends of the Arabian Knights** (ISBN 0–7670–0232–6)

To order, call Glencoe at 1–800–334–7344. To find classroom resources to accompany this video, check the following home pages:
A&E Television: www.aande.com
The History Channel: www.historychannel.com

Chapter 8 Resources

REVIEW AND REINFORCEMENT

Linking Past and Present Activity 8

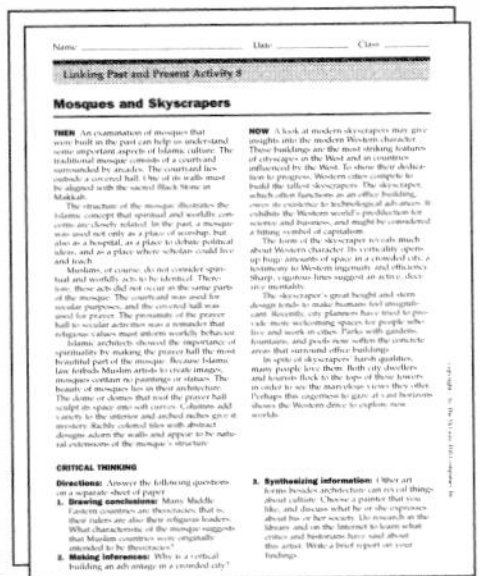

Time Line Activity 8

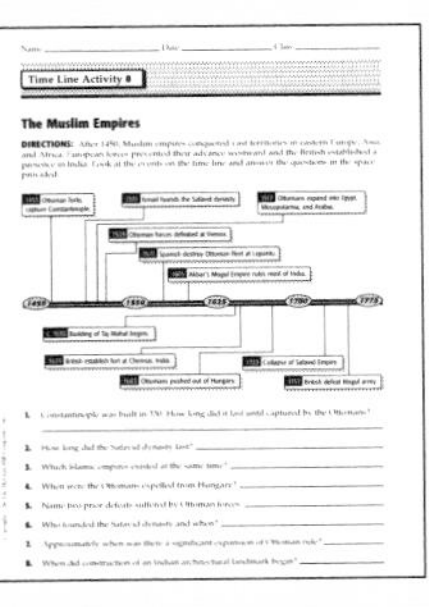

Reteaching Activity 8

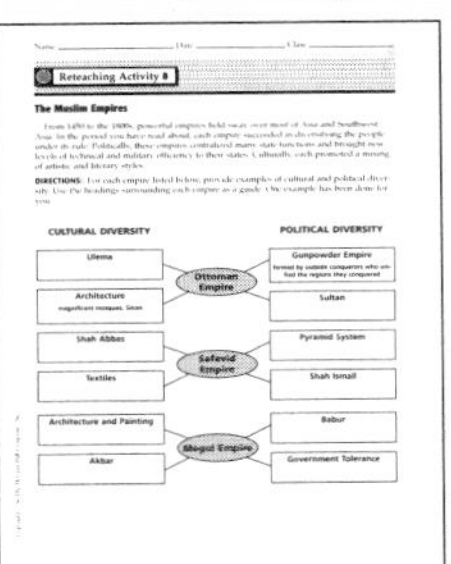

Vocabulary Activity 8

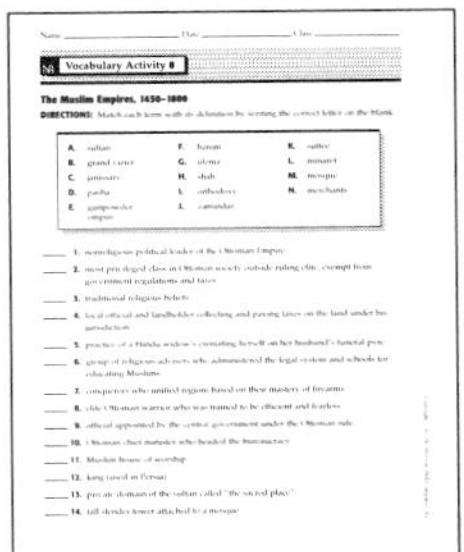

Critical Thinking Skills Activity 8

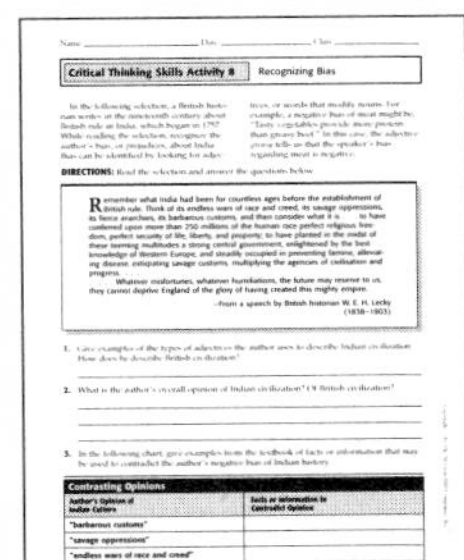

ASSESSMENT AND EVALUATION

Chapter 8 Test Form A

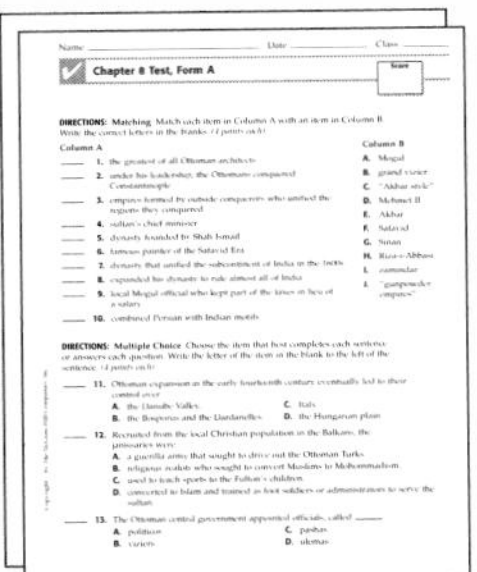

Chapter 8 Test Form B

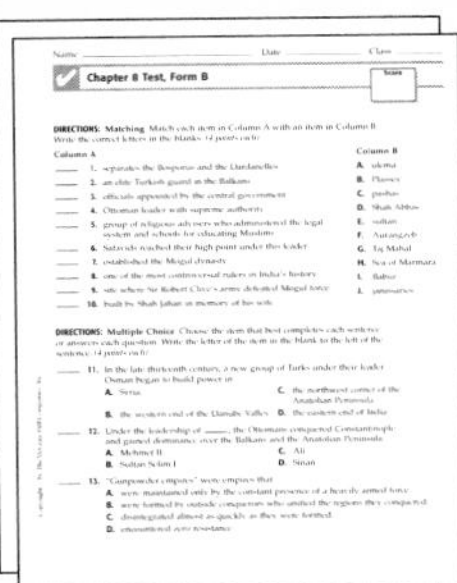

Performance Assessment Activity 8

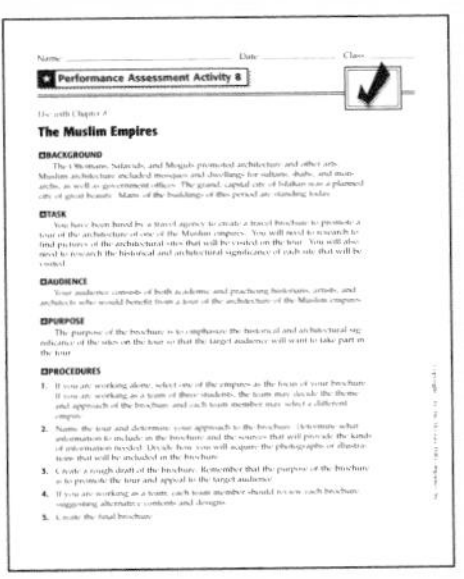

ExamView® Pro Testmaker CD-ROM

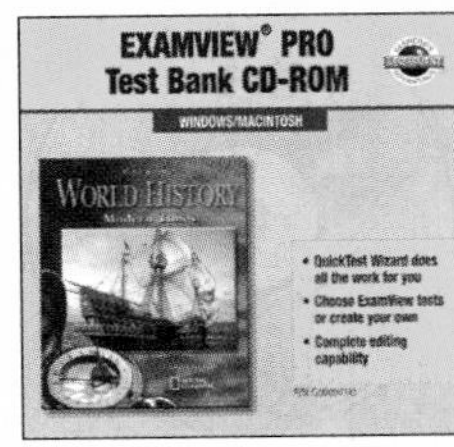

Standardized Test Skills Practice Workbook Activity 8

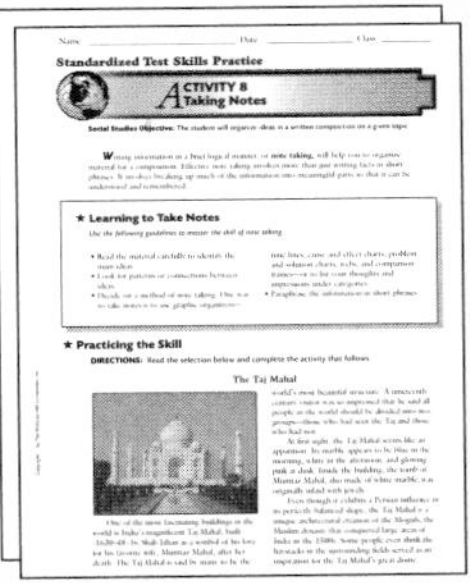

INTERDISCIPLINARY ACTIVITIES

Mapping History Activity 8

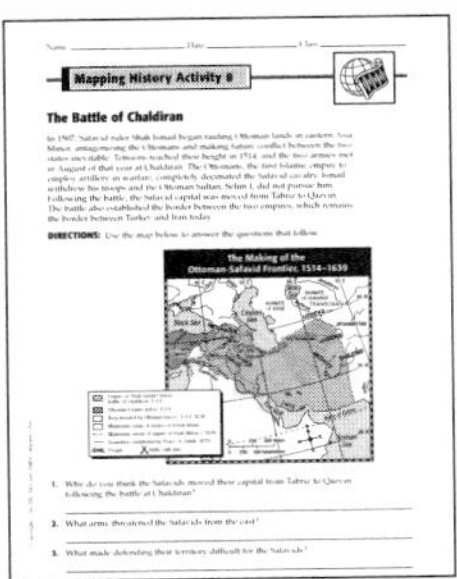

World Art and Music Activity 8

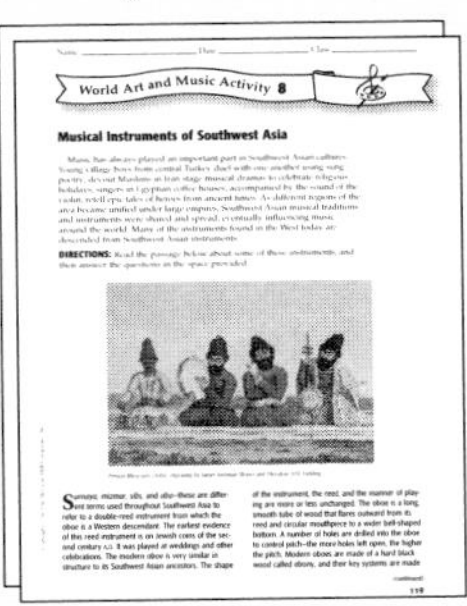

History and Geography Activity 8

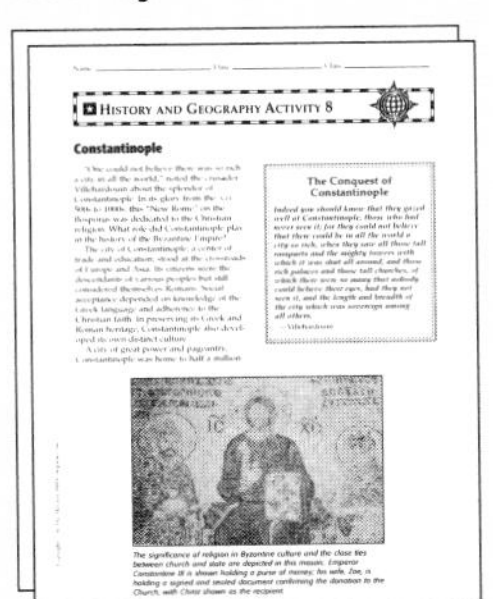

People in World History Activity 8

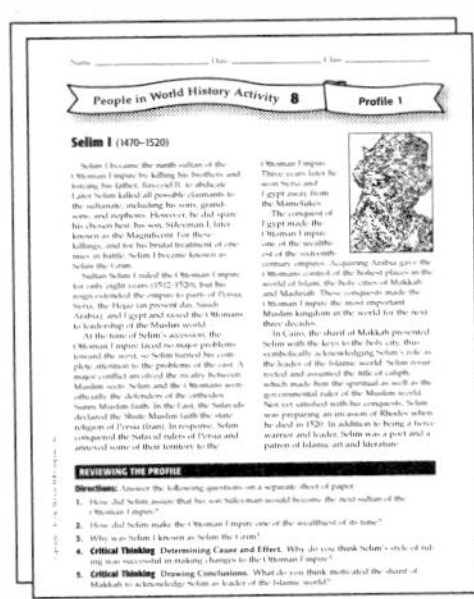

MULTIMEDIA

- Vocabulary PuzzleMaker CD-ROM
- Interactive Tutor Self-Assessment CD-ROM
- ExamView® Pro Testmaker CD-ROM
- Audio Program
- World History Primary Source Document Library CD-ROM
- MindJogger Videoquiz
- Presentation Plus! CD-ROM
- TeacherWorks CD-ROM
- Interactive Student Edition CD-ROM
- The World History—Modern Times Video Program

SPANISH RESOURCES

The following Spanish language materials are available in the Spanish Resources Binder:

- Spanish Guided Reading Activities
- Spanish Reteaching Activities
- Spanish Quizzes and Tests
- Spanish Vocabulary Activities
- Spanish Summaries

Chapter 8 Resources

SECTION RESOURCES

Daily Objectives	Reproducible Resources	Multimedia Resources
SECTION 1 **The Ottoman Empire** 1. Discuss how the Ottoman Turks used firearms to expand their lands and appointed local rulers to administer conquered regions. 2. Characterize the creation of a strong Ottoman Empire with religious tolerance and artistic achievements.	Reproducible Lesson Plan 8–1 Daily Lecture and Discussion Notes 8–1 Guided Reading Activity 8–1* Section Quiz 8–1* Reading Essentials and Study Guide 8–1	Daily Focus Skills Transparency 8–1 Interactive Tutor Self-Assessment CD-ROM ExamView® Pro Testmaker CD-ROM Presentation Plus! CD-ROM
SECTION 2 **The Rule of the Safavids** 1. Relate how the Safavids used their faith as a unifying force to bring Turks and Persians together. 2. Describe how the Safavid dynasty reached its height under Shah Abbas.	Reproducible Lesson Plan 8–2 Daily Lecture and Discussion Notes 8–2 Guided Reading Activity 8–2* Section Quiz 8–2* Reading Essentials and Study Guide 8–2	Daily Focus Skills Transparency 8–2 Interactive Tutor Self-Assessment CD-ROM ExamView® Pro Testmaker CD-ROM Presentation Plus! CD-ROM
SECTION 3 **The Grandeur of the Moguls** 1. Explain how the Moguls united India under a single government with a common culture. 2. Discuss how the introduction of foreigners seeking trade opportunities in India hastened the decline of the Mogul Empire.	Reproducible Lesson Plan 8–3 Daily Lecture and Discussion Notes 8–3 Guided Reading Activity 8–3* Section Quiz 8–3* Reteaching Activity 8* Reading Essentials and Study Guide 8–3	Daily Focus Skills Transparency 8–3 Interactive Tutor Self-Assessment CD-ROM ExamView® Pro Testmaker CD-ROM Presentation Plus! CD-ROM

0:00 **OUT OF TIME?**
Assign the Chapter 8 **Reading Essentials and Study Guide.**

*Also Available in Spanish

Blackline Master
 Transparency
 CD-ROM
 DVD
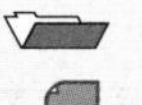 Poster
Music Program
Audio Program
Videocassette

Chapter 8 Resources

NATIONAL GEOGRAPHIC **Teacher's Corner**

INDEX TO NATIONAL GEOGRAPHIC MAGAZINE

The following articles relate to this chapter:

- "The World of Suleyman the Magnificent," by Merle Severy, November 1987.
- "When the Moguls Ruled India," by Mike Edwards, April 1985.

NGS ONLINE

Access National Geographic's new dynamic MapMachine Web site and other geography resources at:
www.nationalgeographic.com
www.nationalgeographic.com/maps

WORLD HISTORY Online

Use our Web site for additional resources. All essential content is covered in the Student Edition.

You and your students can visit www.wh.mt.glencoe.com, the Web site companion to *Glencoe World History—Modern Times.* This innovative integration of electronic and print media offers your students a wealth of opportunities. The student text directs students to the Web site for the following options:

- **Chapter Overviews**
- **Self-Check Quizzes**
- **Student Web Activities**
- **Textbook Updates**

Answers to the Student Web Activities are provided for you in the **Web Activity Lesson Plans.** Additional Web resources and Interactive Tutor Puzzles are also available.

KEY TO ABILITY LEVELS

Teaching strategies have been coded.

- **L1** BASIC activities for all students
- **L2** AVERAGE activities for average to above-average students
- **L3** CHALLENGING activities for above-average students
- **ELL** ENGLISH LANGUAGE LEARNER activities

Block Schedule

Activities that are suited to use within the block scheduling framework are identified by:

From the Classroom of...

Tom Cyrus
Kiana School
Kiana, Alaska

Commemorating the Reign of Süleyman

In the year 2020 we will observe the 500th anniversary of the beginning of Süleyman's reign. Encourage students to start preparing for the celebration now by designing commemorative coins, bills, postage stamps, costumes, a monument, and a convention center. Working in groups, students should research art and design during Süleyman's reign so that the commemorative materials will pay tribute to the period in which he lived.

Keep in mind that Süleyman was a student of poetry and a poet himself. Assign students the task of locating sixteenth-century Turkish poems to present and comment on to the class. Then consider extending this activity to include contemporary Turkish poems. Ask students to comment on how literature has changed. Ask if modern poets write about the same themes as the earlier poets.

Introducing CHAPTER 8

Performance Assessment

Refer to Activity 8 in the Performance Assessment Activities and Rubrics booklet.

The Impact Today

Before the fourteenth century, the cavalry, with its crossbows, usually had the advantage in war. Then the invention of gunpowder revolutionized warfare and changed the balance of power. Students should use primary and secondary sources to learn about other technological innovations that have affected the ways in which wars have been fought. **L2**

GLENCOE TECHNOLOGY

The World History—Modern Times Video Program

To learn more about the Muslim empires, students can view the Chapter 8 video, "Constantinople to Istanbul," from **The World History—Modern Times Video Program.**

MindJogger Videoquiz

Use the **MindJogger Videoquiz** to preview Chapter 8 content.

Available in VHS.

CHAPTER 8 The Muslim Empires

1450–1800

Key Events

As you read this chapter, look for the key events in the history of the Muslim empires.

- *Muslim conquerors captured vast territory in Europe and Asia using firearms.*
- *Religion played a major role in the establishment of the Ottoman, Safavid, and Mogul Empires.*
- *Trade and the arts flourished under the Muslim empires.*

The Impact Today

The events that occurred during this time period still impact our lives today.

- *Muslim art and architectural forms have endured, and examples can be found throughout the world.*
- *Since the territory once occupied by the Ottoman and Safavid dynasties produces one-third of the world's oil supply, these regions continue to prosper.*

World History—Modern Times Video *The Chapter 8 video, "Constantinople to Istanbul," chronicles the spread of Islam and Muslim cultural achievements.*

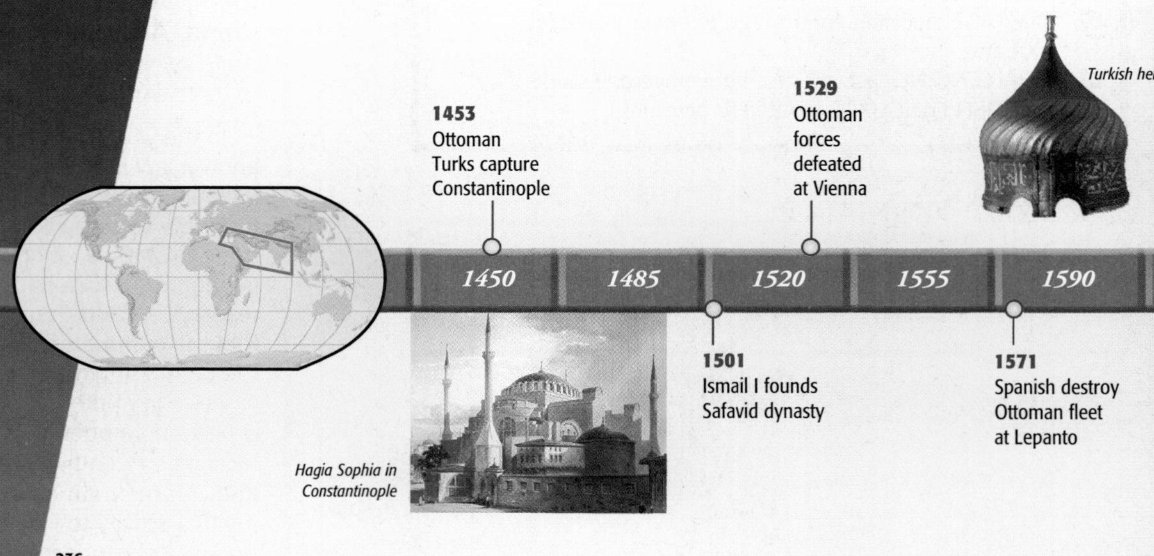

1453
Ottoman Turks capture Constantinople
1529
Ottoman forces defeated at Vienna
1450
1485
1520
1555
1590
1501
Ismail I founds Safavid dynasty
1571
Spanish destroy Ottoman fleet at Lepanto

Hagia Sophia in Constantinople

Turkish helr

236

TWO-MINUTE LESSON LAUNCHER

Ask students why Muslim peoples like the Ottomans, Safavids, and Moguls might have wanted to expand their territory. *(to gain control of trade routes; to spread their religion; to protect the lands they already governed)* Although these Muslim empires did not last, Islam remains one of the great religions of the world and its sphere of influence is expanding. Ask students to review the main tenets of Islam with emphasis on the Five Pillars. *(the confession of faith, prayer, almsgiving, fasting, and the pilgrimage to Makkah)* **L2**

This tilework features an inscription from the Quran, the sacred book of Islam.

Taj Mahal

c. 1632 Building of Taj Mahal begins

1757 British defeat Moguls at Battle of Plassey

1625 1660 1695 1730 1765

1600 Safavid dynasty peaks

1639 British establish fort at Chennai in India

1723 Safavid dynasty collapses

Persian painting

HISTORY Online

Chapter Overview
Visit the *Glencoe World History—Modern Times* Web site at wh.mt.glencoe.com and click on **Chapter 8–Chapter Overview** to preview chapter information.

237

Introducing CHAPTER 8

Chapter Objectives

After studying this chapter, students should be able to:

1. describe the gradual expansion of the Ottoman Empire;
2. discuss the achievements of Mehmet II and Süleyman the Magnificent;
3. discuss Ottoman rule, including the division of people by religion and occupation;
4. highlight Ottoman achievement in art and architecture;
5. describe the signs of decline of the Ottoman Empire.

Chapter Overview
Introduce students to chapter content and key terms by having them access **Chapter Overview 8** at wh.mt.glencoe.com

Time Line Activity

As students read the chapter, have them review the time line on pages 236 to 237. Have students select a world event on the time line, learn more about it, and write a brief description of the impact it had on the Muslim empires. **L1**

MORE ABOUT THE ART

Islamic Calligraphy Elegant calligraphy (artistic handwriting) transforms the words of the Quran into a work of art on this strikingly beautiful piece of Islamic tilework. Because the Hadith (a collection of sayings of Muhammad) warns against any attempt to imitate God by creating pictures of living beings, inscriptions from the Quran are often used to decorate Islamic art and architecture. Islamic calligraphers seek to convey both the power and the beauty of the Islamic religion through the stylized lettering of sacred words. This piece of tilework can be found today in a mosque in Turkey.

CHAPTER PREVIEW

Introducing

A Story That Matters

Depending on the ability levels of your students, select from the following questions to reinforce the reading of *A Story That Matters.*

- Describe Babur's "pitifully small" first army. *(on foot, wearing sandals and long frocks, armed with clubs)*
- What was different about Babur's second army, besides its greatly increased size? *(armed with artillery)*
- Describe the effects of Babur's words to his troops before the last battle. *(holy war; to fight until death)*
- What does it mean to be "flayed?" *(skinned)*
- Why do you think Babur ordered this dreadful death for the enemy leader? *(as an example to his enemies)* **L1**

About the Art

Gwalior is strategically situated atop a cliffed plateau that is nearly 2 miles (3.2 km) long and rises a sheer 300 feet (91 m) from the plain.

CHAPTER PREVIEW

A Story That Matters

The Fortress of Gwalior in India greatly impressed Babur.

The Conquests of Babur

At the beginning of the sixteenth century, to the north of India in present-day Afghanistan, lived a military adventurer named Babur, a descendant of the great Asian conqueror Timur Lenk (Tamerlane). Babur began with a pitifully small following: "The greater part of my followers (about 250 men) were on foot with sandals on their feet, clubs in their hands, and long frocks over their shoulders."

After seizing Kabul in 1504, Babur increased his forces, armed them with newly invented firearms, and extended his vision of conquest to the lands of India. With a force of eight thousand men armed with artillery, he destroyed the much larger army of the ruler of North India.

Nine months later, Babur's army faced yet another Indian prince with a considerably larger army. Babur rallied his forces with these words: "Let us, then, with one accord, swear on God's holy word, that none of us will even think of turning his face from this warfare, nor desert from the battle and slaughter that ensues, till his soul is separated from his body."

Babur's troops responded with enthusiasm. "Towards evening," he wrote later, "the confusion was complete, and the slaughter was dreadful. The fate of the battle was decided . . . I ordered the [enemy leader] to be flayed alive." Babur had won yet another decisive victory.

Why It Matters

During Europe's age of exploration, between 1500 and 1800, the world of Islam experienced new life with the rise of three great Muslim empires. With his victories, Babur created one of them—the Mogul Empire—in India. Along with the Ottomans and the Safavids, the Moguls dominated Southwest Asia and the South Asian subcontinent. For about two hundred years, these three powerful Muslim states brought stability to a region that had been in turmoil for centuries.

History and You The English language contains many words derived from Arabic. Research the subject of etymology (where words come from), using the Internet or a dictionary. Identify 25 English words derived from Arabic. List them in alphabetical order and then write a paragraph describing the influence of Arabic on English.

HISTORY AND YOU

Babur was not only a descendant of Timur Lenk, but also of Genghis Khan. He hoped to create an empire worthy of his ancestors. However, there is another side to Babur. He was a highly educated man who later in life wrote his memoirs. The *Baburnama,* as his work is known, was the first autobiography in Islamic literature. Historians have appreciated Babur's keen observations of the culture in which he lived. There are descriptions of political and military life, social events, family life, art and architecture. A primary source document, such as the *Baburnama,* is invaluable to historians.

SECTION 1 The Ottoman Empire

Guide to Reading

Main Ideas
- Ottoman Turks used firearms to expand their lands and appointed local rulers to administer conquered regions.
- The Ottomans created a strong empire with religious tolerance and artistic achievements.

Key Terms
janissary, pasha, gunpowder empire, sultan, harem, grand vizier, ulema

People to Identify
Mehmet II, Sultan Selim I, Sinan

Places to Locate
Anatolian Peninsula, Bosporus, Dardanelles, Sea of Marmara, Makkah

Preview Questions
1. What were the major events in the growth of the Ottoman Empire?
2. What role did religion play in the Ottoman Empire?

Reading Strategy
Organizing Information Create a chart to show the structure of Ottoman society. List groups in order of importance.

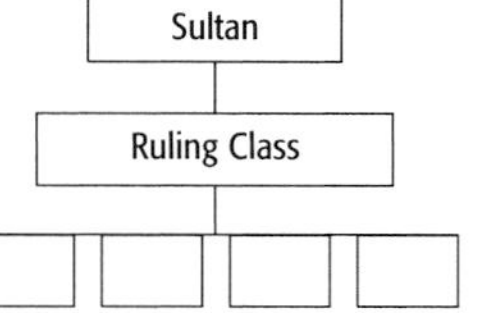

Preview of Events

1450 · 1475 · 1500 · 1525 · 1550 · 1575 · 1600

- **1453** Ottoman Turks capture Constantinople
- **1520** Süleyman I becomes Ottoman ruler
- **1526** Ottomans defeat Hungarians
- **1529** Austria defeats Ottomans at Vienna
- **1571** Spanish defeat Ottomans at Lepanto

Voices from the Past

In 1453, the Ottoman Turks conquered Constantinople, the Byzantine capital. One Greek described the scene:

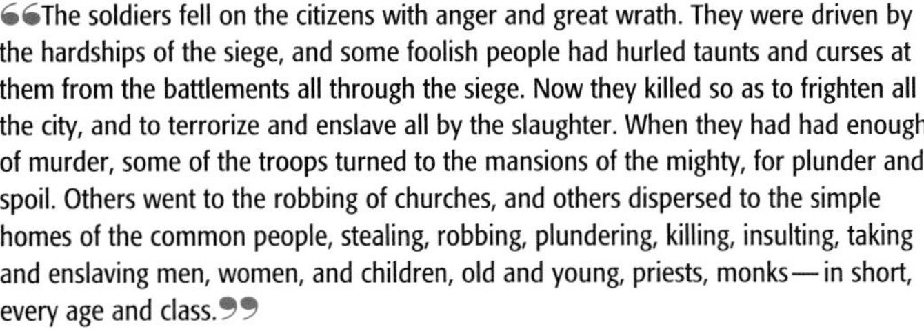

The siege of Constantinople

> ❝The soldiers fell on the citizens with anger and great wrath. They were driven by the hardships of the siege, and some foolish people had hurled taunts and curses at them from the battlements all through the siege. Now they killed so as to frighten all the city, and to terrorize and enslave all by the slaughter. When they had had enough of murder, some of the troops turned to the mansions of the mighty, for plunder and spoil. Others went to the robbing of churches, and others dispersed to the simple homes of the common people, stealing, robbing, plundering, killing, insulting, taking and enslaving men, women, and children, old and young, priests, monks—in short, every age and class.❞
>
> —***The Islamic World,*** **William H. McNeill and M.R. Waldham, 1973**

After this siege, Constantinople became the capital of the new Ottoman Empire.

Rise of the Ottoman Turks

In the late thirteenth century, a new group of Turks under their leader Osman began to build power in the northwest corner of the **Anatolian Peninsula.** That land had been given to them by the Seljuk Turk rulers as a reward for helping the rulers to defend their lands against the Mongols in the late thirteenth century.

At first, the Osman Turks were relatively peaceful and engaged in pastoral activities. However, as the Seljuk Empire began to decline in the early fourteenth century, the Osman Turks began to expand. This was the beginning of the Ottoman dynasty.

1 FOCUS

Section Overview

This section describes how the Ottoman Turks expanded and strengthened their empire.

BELLRINGER
Skillbuilder Activity

Project transparency and have students answer questions.

Available as a blackline master.

Daily Focus Skills Transparency 8–1

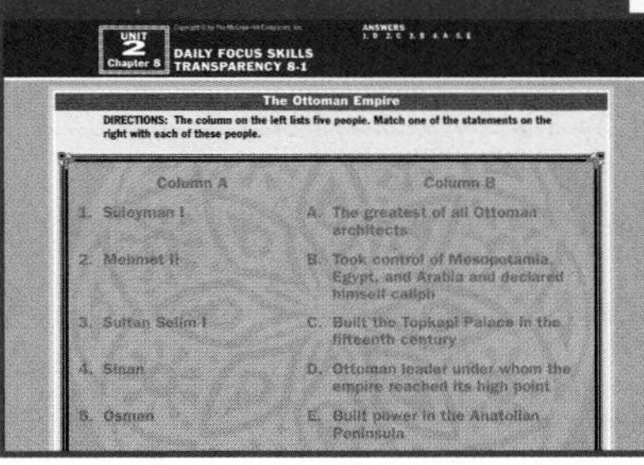

UNIT 2 Chapter 8
DAILY FOCUS SKILLS TRANSPARENCY 8-1
The Ottoman Empire
Column A
Column B
1. Süleyman I
2. Mehmet II
3. Sultan Selim I
4. Sinan
5. Osman
A. The greatest of all Ottoman architects
B. Took control of Mesopotamia, Egypt, and Arabia and declared himself caliph
C. Built the Topkapi Palace in the fifteenth century
D. Ottoman leader under whom the empire reached its high point
E. Built power in the Anatolian Peninsula

Guide to Reading

Answers to Graphic: Sultan; Ruling Class; Merchants, Artisans, Peasants, Pastoral Peoples

Preteaching Vocabulary: Have students define the term *gunpowder empire.* Ask students whether the term sounds positive or negative. Do students suppose contemporary Iranians, Indians, and Turks refer to these empires in this way? Why or why not? **L1**

SECTION RESOURCES

Reproducible Masters
- Reproducible Lesson Plan 8–1
- Daily Lecture and Discussion Notes 8–1
- Guided Reading Activity 8–1
- Section Quiz 8–1
- Reading Essentials and Study Guide 8–1

Transparencies
- Daily Focus Skills Transparency 8–1

Multimedia
- Interactive Tutor Self-Assessment CD-ROM
- ExamView® Pro Testmaker CD-ROM
- Presentation Plus! CD-ROM

CHAPTER 8
Section 1, 239–245

2 TEACH

Reading Check

Answer: the Bosporus, the Dardanelles, and the Sea of Marmara

Answer: Answers will vary, but should show an understanding of current events. You might wish to assign this activity to students as a research project and have them use current and historical sources to prepare a history of the Balkans.

Daily Lecture and Discussion Notes 8–1

Daily Lecture and Discussion Notes

Chapter 8, Section 1

Did You Know? The ottoman, a stuffed footstool also called a hassock, is named after the Ottoman Empire. Tales of this great empire excited the European imagination, and by the end of the eighteenth century a large market had formed for items of Eastern luxury—carpets, pillows, divans, and the like. Included was a small, backless couch the French called an *ottoman*, after the empire. The name was later applied in England to the smaller footstool.

I. **Rise of the Ottoman Turks** *(pages 239–240)*

A. The Ottoman dynasty began in the late thirteenth century when Turks under their leader Osman were given land in the northwest corner of the **Anatolian Peninsula** by the Seljuk Turks in return for help fighting against the Mongols.

B. The Ottomans expanded westward to control the strategic **Bosporus** and the **Dardanelles**. These two straits, separated by the **Sea of Marmara,** connect the Black Sea and the Aegean Sea. The Byzantine Empire had controlled the area.

C. The Ottomans expanded into the **Balkans** in the fourteenth century. Ottoman rulers claimed the name of sultan and built a strong military, first by developing an elite guard called **janissaries,** local Christians who converted to Islam and served as foot soldiers or admi…

Guided Reading Activity 8–1

Name ____________ Date ____________ Class ____________

Guided Reading Activity 8-1

The Ottoman Empire

DIRECTIONS: Answer the following questions as you read Section 1.

1. What change came over the Osman Turks as the Seljuk Empire began to decline?
2. What happened after the Ottomans recruited janissaries from the local Christian population of the Balkans?
3. What did Mehmet II say when he saw the ruin he had inflicted on the city of Constantinople?
4. What three things did Sultan Selim I declare himself to be after taking control of Mesopotamia?

From their location in the northwestern corner of the peninsula, the Ottomans expanded westward and eventually controlled the **Bosporus** and the **Dardanelles.** These two straits (narrow passageways), separated by the **Sea of Marmara,** connect the Black Sea and the Aegean Sea, which leads to the Mediterranean. The Byzantine Empire had controlled this area for centuries.

In the fourteenth century, the Ottoman Turks expanded into the **Balkans.** Ottoman rulers claimed the title of sultan and began to build a strong military by developing an elite guard called janissaries. Recruited from the local Christian population in the Balkans, the janissaries were converted to Islam and trained as foot soldiers or administrators to serve the sultan.

As knowledge of firearms spread in the late fourteenth century, the Ottomans began to master the new technology. The janissaries, trained as a well-armed infantry, began to spread Ottoman control in the Balkans. With their new forces, the Ottomans defeated the Serbs at the Battle of Kosovo in 1389. Around 1400, they advanced northward and annexed Bulgaria.

Reading Check **Identifying** What strategic lands and bodies of water did the Ottomans take from the Byzantine Empire?

Expansion of the Empire

Over the next three hundred years, Ottoman rule expanded to include large areas of Western Asia, as well as North Africa and additional lands in Europe.

The Fall of Constantinople Under the leadership of **Mehmet II,** the Ottomans moved to end the Byzantine Empire. With eighty thousand troops ranged against only seven thousand defenders, Mehmet laid siege to Constantinople. In their attack on the city, the Ottomans used massive cannons with 26-foot (8-m) barrels that could launch stone balls weighing up to 1,200 pounds (545 kg) each.

The attack began on April 6, 1453, with an Ottoman bombardment. The Byzantines took their final stand behind the walls along the western edge

CONNECTIONS Past To Present

Conflict in Yugoslavia

In 1919, Yugoslavia was formed as a new state in the Balkans. It consisted of six republics that had little interest in being part of a single nation. From 1945 to 1980, the dictator Marshal Tito held the country together.

In 1992, Yugoslavia began to disintegrate. The republics of Slovenia, Croatia, and Bosnia-Herzegovina declared their independence. When the republic of Serbia refused to accept the breakup of Yugoslavia, conflict erupted. The Serbians invaded Bosnia and pursued a policy of "ethnic cleansing," in which they killed Muslims or forcibly removed them from their homes.

Ethnic and religious struggles in Yugoslavia had deep roots in the past. In the Middle Ages, the Slavic peoples had accepted Christianity. While the Croatians and Slovenes became Roman Catholics, the Serbs remained Eastern Orthodox. In the fourteenth century, the Ottoman conquest of the Balkans brought the Muslims. Many Christians chose to convert to Islam. By 1500, the area that later became Yugoslavia was a land where Bosnian Muslims, Croatian Catholics, and Eastern Orthodox Serbs maintained an uneasy peace.

▼ *Ethnic Albanian refugees cross the Albanian border in 1999.*

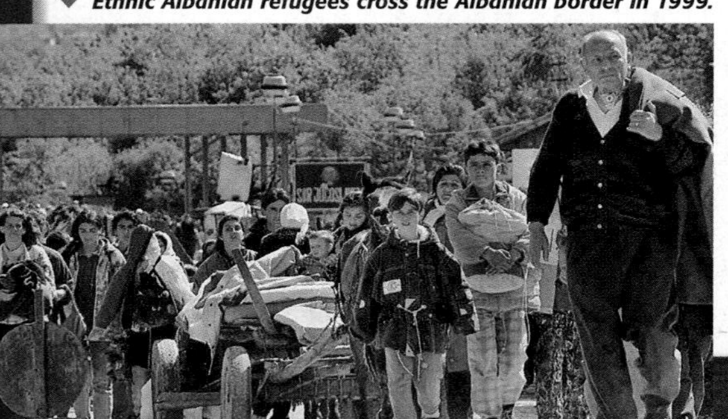

Comparing Past and Present

Using outside sources, research the current political situation in the Balkan states. How did the Balkan wars of the early 1990s end? How have those wars influenced the development of that region since 1992? What is the current political and economic situation in the Balkans?

EXTENDING THE CONTENT

The Janissaries The janissary corps were the elite soldiers and administrators of the sultan's army. As noted in the text, they were young Christian boys chosen because of their "good appearance and good physical build." This policy of recruiting janissaries lasted until 1634. After 1634, new recruits came from the sons of janissaries and the forces became less disciplined. To minimize the impact on the Ottoman treasury, the janissaries took jobs in the winter (when they were usually not fighting) as artisans. By 1826, the janissary force had grown so large—135,000 strong—and so powerful that the sultan was forced to massacre all its members. The demise of the janissaries corresponded with the decline of the Ottoman Empire.

Expansion of the Ottoman Empire, c. 1300–1699

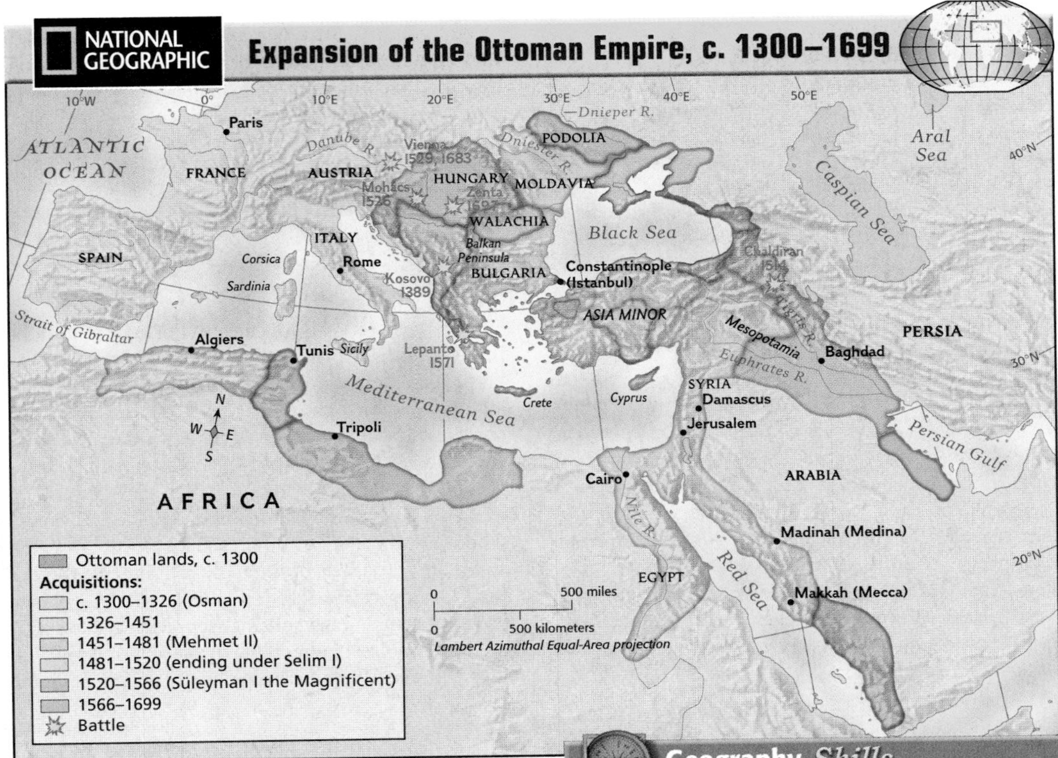

Geography Skills

For nearly four hundred years the Ottoman Empire continued to expand.

1. **Interpreting Maps** Name the places and dates for three battles that stopped Ottoman expansion into Europe.
2. **Applying Geography Skills** The Ottomans conquered Constantinople in 1453. How did that event impact their expansion?

of the city. They fought desperately for almost two months to save their city. Finally, on May 29, the walls were breached, and Ottoman soldiers poured into the city.

The Byzantine emperor died in the final battle, and a great three-day sack of the city began. When Mehmet II saw the ruin and destruction of the city, he was filled with regret and lamented, "What a city we have given over to plunder and destruction."

Western Asia and Africa With their new capital at Constantinople (later renamed **Istanbul**), the Ottoman Turks now dominated the Balkans and the Anatolian Peninsula. From approximately 1514 to 1517, **Sultan Selim I** took control of Mesopotamia, Egypt, and Arabia—the original heartland of Islam. Controlling several of the holy cities of Islam, including **Jerusalem, Makkah** (Mecca), and **Madinah,** Selim declared himself to be the new caliph, defender of the faith and successor to Muhammad.

After their victories in the east, Ottoman forces spent the next few years advancing westward along the African coast, eventually almost reaching the Strait of Gibraltar. The impact of Ottoman rule on the peoples of North Africa was relatively light, however.

Like their predecessors, the Ottomans were Muslims. Where possible, they preferred to administer their conquered regions through local rulers. The central government appointed officials, called pashas, who collected taxes, maintained law and order, and were directly responsible to the sultan's court in Constantinople.

Europe After their conquest of Constantinople in 1453, the Ottoman Turks tried to complete their conquest of the Balkans. They took the Romanian territory of Walachia, but the Hungarians stopped their advance up the Danube Valley.

Geography Skills

Answers:

1. The Ottomans were defeated in Vienna in 1529, by the Spanish at Lepanto in 1571, and again in Vienna in 1683.
2. The conquest of Constantinople marked the end of the Byzantine Empire; the Ottomans acquired a new capital and port, enabling them to expand further east.

Enrich

Ask students to identify which modern countries, wholly or in part, were ruled by the Ottoman Empire at its greatest extent. *(Turkey, Bulgaria, Romania, Greece, Hungary, Egypt, Libya, Tunisia, Algeria, Saudi Arabia, Yemen, Syria, Jordan, Israel, Iraq)* **L1**

CURRICULUM CONNECTION

Sociology Ask interested students to research the roles of women and families in the Ottoman Empire and compare them to those roles in Europe during the same time period. Ask the students to analyze the role that religion (Christianity and Islam) played in the attitudes toward women in these cultures and societies. **L2**

COOPERATIVE LEARNING ACTIVITY

Interpreting Maps Divide students into small groups. Ask them to examine the map on this page and locate Anatolia, where the Ottoman Empire began. Then ask them to find the Bosporus and the Dardanelles, and have them trace the passage between the Mediterranean and Black Seas. Then, have students find the Balkans, where the Ottoman Turks moved to pressure the Byzantine Empire. Ask students to determine how much territory the Ottoman Empire gained between 1451 and 1566. *(Students should realize that the Ottoman Empire more than tripled its size during this period.)* **L1**

For grading this activity, refer to the ***Performance Assessment Activities*** booklet.

Reading Check

Answer: Ottomans took control of Bosporus and Dardanelles, expanded into Balkans, seized Constantinople, controlled holy cities, advanced into Austria and Mediterranean

Who?What?Where?When?

Gunpowder Empires Before the fourteenth century, warriors like the Mongols with their cavalry and cross-bows had the advantage in battle. When gunpowder revolutionized war-fare, cannons became the decisive weapons. Because they required skilled technology and vast sums of money, they were only available to large, wealthy empires. Ask students how this impacted the development of other cultures that might have been emerging at this time in the areas controlled by the Ottomans. **L1**

Writing Activity

Have students write a brief essay in which they describe the political and economic impact of the Ottoman Empire on its conquered lands. **L1**

TURNING POINT

Ask students to discuss the following: "The Ottoman Empire reached its high point under Süleyman the Magnificent . . . but it was also Süleyman who probably started a period of decline." **L1**

The reign of Süleyman I, beginning in 1520, led to new Ottoman attacks on Europe. Advancing up the Danube, the Ottomans seized Belgrade. In 1526, at the Battle of Mohacs (MOH•hach) on the Danube, they won a major victory over the Hungarians.

Web Activity Visit the *Glencoe World History—Modern Times* Web site at wh.mt.glencoe.com and click on **Chapter 8–Student Web Activity** to learn more about the Ottoman Empire.

The Ottomans then conquered most of Hungary, moved into Austria, and advanced as far as Vienna, where they were finally defeated in 1529. At the same time, they extended their power into the western Mediterranean until a large Ottoman fleet was destroyed by the Spanish at Lepanto in 1571 (see Chapter 7).

During the first half of the seventeenth century, the Ottoman Empire in eastern Europe remained a "sleeping giant." Occupied with internal problems, the Ottomans were content with the status quo in eastern Europe. However, in the second half of the seventeenth century, they again went on the offensive.

By mid-1683, the Ottomans had marched through the Hungarian plain and laid siege to Vienna. Repulsed by an army of Europeans, the Ottomans retreated and were pushed out of Hungary. Although they retained the core of their empire, the Ottoman Turks would never again be a threat to central Europe.

Reading Check **Summarizing** List the sequence of events that led to the expansion of the Ottoman Empire.

The Nature of Ottoman Rule

Like the other Muslim empires in Persia and India, the Ottoman Empire is often labeled a **"gunpowder empire."** Gunpowder empires were formed by outside conquerors who unified the regions that they conquered. As the name suggests, such an empire's success was largely based on its mastery of the technology of firearms.

At the head of the Ottoman system was the **sultan**, who was the supreme authority in both a political and a military sense. The position of the sultan was hereditary. A son, although not necessarily the eldest, always succeeded the father. This practice led to struggles over succession upon the death of individual sultans. The losers in these struggles were often executed.

THE WAY IT WAS

YOUNG PEOPLE IN . . .

The Ottoman Empire

Every few years, as need arose, government commissioners went into the provinces of the Ottoman Empire to recruit a special class of slaves. Those chosen were usually Christian boys, because Muslims were not allowed to enslave other Muslims. This collecting of boys was known as the Devshirme—literally, the "boy levy." (The word *levy,* as used here, means the enlistment of people for military service.)

Most of the boys who were selected were from Christian peasant families in the Balkans. Recruits, usually between the ages of 10 and 20, were selected on the basis of good appearance and good physical build. These boys were brought to Constantinople, now the city of Istanbul, where most of them remained for training.

The boys were first converted to Islam. The brightest were then made pages (attendants) for the sultan and put into palace schools for a special education. Royal servants taught them languages (Turkish, Persian, and Arabic), literature, history, and of course, the Quran. The young boys also received physical and military training.

The boys were strictly disciplined. Sleep, study, and play were all done at very specific times. The boys were told to regard

CRITICAL THINKING ACTIVITY

Analyzing Ask students what *to recruit* commonly means. *(to fill up an army with new members; to secure the services of)* Do students think slaves can be "recruited?" Why or why not? Have students speculate on the reaction of Christian peasant families in the Balkans to the forcible recruitment of their sons. Ask the students how they would have reacted if they had been "recruited." Remind them that the chosen boys received an education and were treated as elite servants of the sultan. **L1**

As the empire expanded, the status and prestige of the sultan increased, and the position took on the trappings of imperial rule. A centralized administrative system was adopted, and the sultan became increasingly isolated in his palace.

The Topkapi ("iron gate") Palace in Istanbul, the new name for Constantinople, was the center of the sultan's power. The palace was built in the fifteenth century by Mehmet II. Like Versailles in France, it had an administrative purpose and served as the private residence of the ruler and his family.

The private domain of the sultan was called the **harem** ("sacred place"). Here, the sultan and his wives resided. Often a sultan chose four wives as his favorites.

When a son became a sultan, his mother became known as the queen mother and acted as a major adviser to the throne. This tradition often gave considerable power to the queen mother in the affairs of state.

The sultan controlled his bureaucracy through an imperial council that met four days a week. A chief minister, known as the **grand vizier,** led the meetings of the council. The sultan sat behind a screen and privately indicated his desires to the grand vizier.

The empire was divided into provinces and districts, each governed by officials. They were assisted by bureaucrats who had been trained in a palace school for officials in Istanbul. Senior officials were given land by the sultan. They were then responsible for collecting taxes and supplying armies for the empire from this landed area.

Reading Check **Describing** What was the relationship among the grand vizier, the sultan, and the imperial council?

Religion in the Ottoman World

Like most Turkic-speaking peoples in the Anatolian Peninsula and throughout Western Asia, the Ottomans were Sunni Muslims (see Chapter 3). Ottoman sultans had claimed the title of caliph since the early sixteenth century. In theory, they were responsible for guiding the flock and maintaining Islamic law.

In practice, the sultans gave their religious duties to a group of religious advisers known as the **ulema.** This group administered the legal system and schools for educating Muslims. Islamic law and customs were applied to all Muslims in the empire.

their families as dead and were kept isolated from the outside world. Punishments were severe. Any boy who broke the rules was beaten on the soles of his feet with a thin wooden rod.

At the age of 25, the young men were assigned different roles. Some who were well-trained in the use of firearms became janissaries. These foot soldiers also served as guards for the person of the sultan. Some became members of the regular cavalry, and others became government officials. Some of the latter even rose in importance to become chief ministers to the sultan.

The janissaries were an elite group who served the sultan.

Connecting to the Past

1. **Explaining** Why were Christian boys chosen to be the special class of slaves?
2. **Writing about History** Muslim boys could not be made into slaves, but Christian slaves could be converted to Muslims. What do you think about the logic of this system? Explain your answer.

Critical Thinking Activity

Decision Making Have the students write a letter from the perspective of a 15-year-old Balkan Christian boy who has been in the janissary corps for two years. Tell students that they must look at both the advantages (i.e., a chance to excel, better food, the excitement of court life) as well as the disadvantages (i.e., strict discipline, no contact with their families, being slaves to the sultan) of being in the corps. Then ask students to explain what they would do if they were placed in a similar situation. For example, what would students decide if they were offered an outstanding opportunity (a scholarship, a job in another country) that would force them to entirely give up their families and current way of life? **L1**

Reading Check

Answer: sultan controlled bureaucracy through imperial council; grand vizier led meetings of council while sultan sat behind a screen and indicated his desires to the grand vizier

The Way It Was

Answers:
1. Muslims were not allowed to enslave other Muslims.
2. Answers will vary.

Writing Activity

Have students write a one-page description of daily life in the Ottoman palace from the point of view of someone who lives there (the sultan, one of his wives, a son or daughter, a servant). **L2**

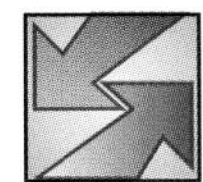

Curriculum Connection

Religion Ask students to speculate on and then research why mosques were part of a large complex with a library, school, hospital, and bazaar. Ask students what these complexes reveal about Islam as practiced by the Ottomans. **L3**

3 ASSESS

Assign Section 1 Assessment as homework or as an in-class activity.

Have students use **Interactive Tutor Self-Assessment CD-ROM.**

History *through Architecture*

Answer: because of the depictions of fruit on the walls

Reading Check

Answer: Theoretically, they were responsible for guiding the Muslim flock and maintaining Islamic law. In practice, they turned over religious duties to the ulema.

Reading Check

Answer: Women could own and inherit property, could not be forced into marriage, and could, under certain circumstances, obtain divorces.

Section Quiz 8–1

Name ______ Date ______ Class ______

Chapter 8 — Score

Section Quiz 8-1

DIRECTIONS: Matching Match each item in Column A with an item in Column B. Write the correct letters in the blanks. *(10 points each)*

Column A	Column B
____ 1. elite guard of the Ottoman Turks	A. harem
____ 2. empires united by outside conquerors	B. grand vizier
____ 3. residence of a sultan and his wives	C. the ulema
____ 4. chief official of a sultan	D. gunpowder empires
____ 5. Ottoman religious, legal, and educational advisers	E. janissaries

DIRECTIONS: Multiple Choice In the blank, write the letter of the choice that best completes the statement or answers the question. *(10 points each)*

CURRICULUM CONNECTION

Architecture Ask students to bring in pictures of official residences in various countries and throughout history. These could include the White House, Versailles, and the Forbidden City. Compare them to the Topkapi Palace. What do these structures convey about the cultures and systems of government that created them? **L1**

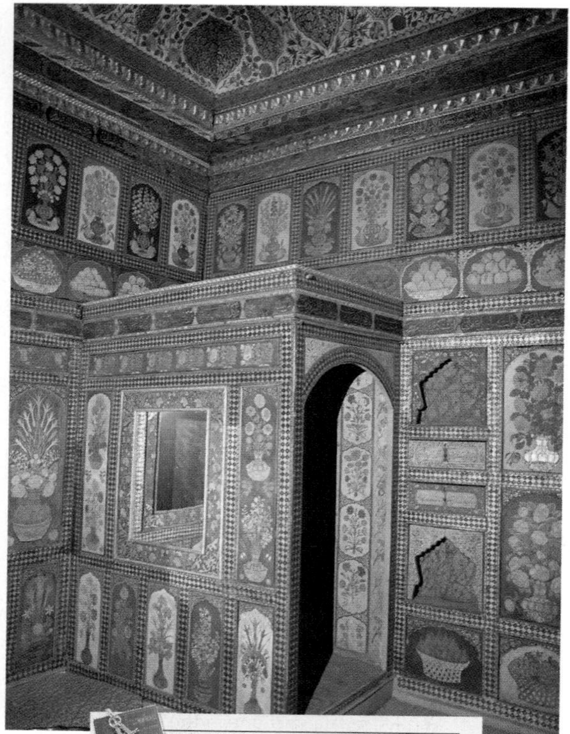

History *through Architecture*

Built by Mehmet II, the Topkapi Palace was the center of the sultan's power. This photo of the Fruit Room of Ahmet III in the palace is a beautiful reminder of the splendor of Islamic architecture and painting. How do you think this room acquired its name?

The Ottoman system was generally tolerant of non-Muslims, who made up a significant minority within the empire. Non-Muslims paid a tax, but they were allowed to practice their religion or to convert to Islam. Most people in the European areas of the empire remained Christian. In some areas, however, such as present-day Bosnia, large numbers converted to the Islamic faith.

Reading Check **Identifying** What religious responsibilities did the sultans have in their role as caliphs?

Ottoman Society

The subjects of the Ottoman Empire were divided by occupation. In addition to the ruling class, there were four main occupational groups: peasants, artisans, merchants, and pastoral peoples. Peasants farmed land that was leased to them by the state. Ultimate ownership of all land resided with the sultan. Artisans were organized according to craft guilds. Each guild provided financial services, social security, and training to its members. Outside the ruling elite, merchants were the most privileged class in Ottoman society. They were largely exempt from government regulations and taxes and were able, in many cases, to amass large fortunes. Pastoral peoples—nomadic herders—were placed in a separate group with their own regulations and laws.

Technically, women in the Ottoman Empire were subject to the same restrictions as women in other Muslim societies, but their position was somewhat better. As applied in the Ottoman Empire, Islamic law was more tolerant in defining the legal position of women. This relatively tolerant attitude was probably due to traditions among the Turkish peoples, which regarded women as almost equal to men.

Women were allowed to own and inherit property. They could not be forced into marriage and, in certain cases, were permitted to seek divorce. Women often gained considerable power within the palace. In a few instances, women even served as senior officials, such as governors of provinces.

Reading Check **Contrasting** How did the position of women in the Ottoman Empire contrast to that of women in other Muslim societies?

Problems in the Ottoman Empire

The Ottoman Empire reached its high point under Süleyman the Magnificent, who ruled from 1520 to 1566. It may also have been during Süleyman's rule that problems began to occur, however. Having executed his two most able sons on suspicion of treason, Süleyman was succeeded by his only surviving son, Selim II.

The problems of the Ottoman Empire did not become visible until 1699, when the empire began to lose some of its territory. However, signs of internal disintegration had already appeared at the beginning of the 1600s.

After the death of Süleyman, sultans became less involved in government and allowed their ministers to exercise more power. The training of officials declined, and senior positions were increasingly assigned to the sons or daughters of elites. Members of the elite soon formed a privileged group seeking wealth and power. The central bureaucracy lost its links with rural areas. As a result, local officials grew corrupt, and taxes rose. Constant wars

INTERDISCIPLINARY CONNECTIONS ACTIVITY

Literature Many of the kings and other members of the nobility in Shakespeare's plays exhibit both strengths and weaknesses. Students of Shakespeare's plays often analyze the "fatal flaw" in each of his protagonists to determine why they came to a tragic end. Ask students to research and describe what Süleyman's "fatal flaw" appears to have been. Which of Shakespeare's kings does he most resemble? Lear? Henry IV? Richard II? Macbeth? How did the deaths of his two most able sons contribute to the disintegration of the Ottoman Empire? **L3**

depleted the imperial treasury. Corruption and palace intrigue grew.

Another sign of change within the empire was the exchange of Western and Ottoman ideas and customs. Officials and merchants began to imitate the habits and lifestyles of Europeans. They wore European clothes and bought Western furniture and art objects. Europeans borrowed Ottoman military technology and decorated their homes with tiles, tulips, pottery, and rugs. During the sixteenth and seventeenth centuries, coffee was introduced to Ottoman society and spread to Europe.

Some sultans attempted to counter these trends. One sultan in the early seventeenth century issued a decree outlawing both coffee and tobacco. He even began to patrol the streets of Constantinople at night. If he caught any of his subjects in immoral or illegal acts, he had them immediately executed.

Reading Check **Summarizing** What changes ultimately led to the disintegration of the Ottoman Empire?

Ottoman Art

The Ottoman sultans were enthusiastic patrons of the arts. The period from Mehmet II to the early eighteenth century witnessed a flourishing production of pottery; rugs, silk, and other textiles; jewelry; and arms and armor. All of these adorned the palaces of the rulers. Artists came from all over the world to compete for the generous rewards of the sultans.

By far the greatest contribution of the Ottoman Empire to world art was in architecture, especially the magnificent mosques of the last half of the sixteenth century. The Ottoman Turks modeled their mosques on the open floor plan of Constantinople's Byzantine church of Hagia Sophia, creating a prayer hall with an open central area under one large dome.

In the mid-sixteenth century, the greatest of all Ottoman architects, **Sinan,** began building the first of his 81 mosques. One of Sinan's masterpieces was the Süleymaniye Mosque in Istanbul. Each of his mosques was topped by an imposing dome, and often the entire building was framed with four towers, or minarets.

The sixteenth century also witnessed the flourishing of textiles and rugs. The Byzantine emperor Justinian had introduced silk cultivation to the West in the sixth century. Under the Ottomans the silk industry resurfaced. Factories produced silks for wall hangings, sofa covers, and especially court costumes. Rugs were a peasant industry. The rugs, made of wool and cotton in villages from different regions, each boasted their own distinctive designs and color schemes.

Reading Check **Explaining** How were the arts tied to religion in Ottoman society?

SECTION 1 ASSESSMENT

Checking for Understanding

1. **Define** janissary, pasha, gunpowder empire, sultan, harem, grand vizier, ulema.
2. **Identify** Mehmet II, Sultan Selim I, Sinan.
3. **Locate** Anatolian Peninsula, Bosporus, Dardanelles, Sea of Marmara, Makkah.
4. **Evaluate** how the problems in the Ottoman Empire may have begun during the reign of Süleyman the Magnificent.
5. **Identify** the four main occupational groups in the Ottoman Empire.

Critical Thinking

6. **Drawing Inferences** Describe the organization of Ottoman government and explain why it was effective.
7. **Compare and Contrast** Create a chart like the one below to compare and contrast the contributions of Mehmet II, Selim I, and Süleyman I to the Ottoman Empire.

Ruler	Contributions	Effect on Empire
Mehmet II		
Selim I		
Süleyman I		

Analyzing Visuals

8. **Compare** the room shown on page 244 with the room from the palace of Versailles shown on page 225 of your text. How do the two rooms reflect the power of the rulers who had them built?

Writing About History

9. **Expository Writing** The Ottoman Empire was considered a "gunpowder empire." Research the history of gunpowder and write an essay explaining how the Ottomans acquired it. What impact did this acquisition have on the expansion of the Ottoman Empire? Use both primary and secondary sources for your research.

CHAPTER 8
Section 1, 239–245

Reading Check

Answer: training of officials declined, central bureacracy lost links to rural areas, corruption grew, taxes rose

Reading Check

Answer: The Ottomans' most dramatic artistic achievement was in architecture, especially their magnificent mosques.

Reading Essentials and Study Guide 8–1

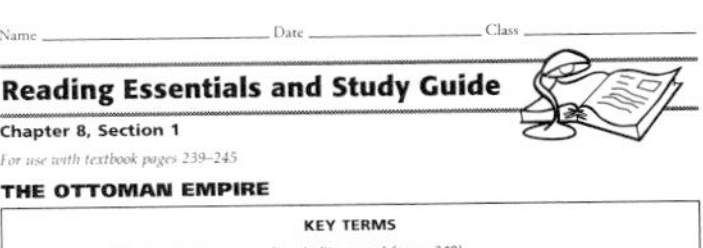

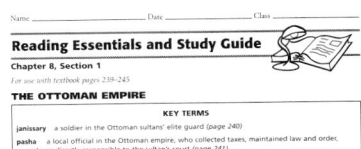

Name ______ Date ______ Class ______

Reading Essentials and Study Guide

Chapter 8, Section 1

For use with textbook pages 239–245

THE OTTOMAN EMPIRE

KEY TERMS

janissary a soldier in the Ottoman sultans' elite guard *(page 240)*

pasha a local official in the Ottoman empire, who collected taxes, maintained law and order, and was directly responsible to the sultan's court *(page 241)*

gunpowder empire an empire whose success was based largely on its mastery of the technology of firearms *(page 242)*

sultan the head of the Ottoman empire *(page 242)*

harem ("sacred place") the private domain of a sultan *(page 243)*

grand vizier a chief minister who led the meetings of the imperial council in the Ottoman Empire *(page 243)*

ulema a group of religious advisers in the Ottoman Empire who administered the legal system and the schools for educating Muslims *(page 243)*

DRAWING FROM EXPERIENCE

How is religious toleration guaranteed in the United States? Why do you think some people are not tolerant of religious beliefs that are different from their own?

In this section, you will learn about the empire of the Ottoman Turks. Although the Ottomans were Sunni Muslims, they were generally tolerant of other religions in their empire.

Reteaching Activity

Have students identify the historical figures mentioned in this section and explain the role each played in expanding the Ottoman Empire. **L1**

4 CLOSE

Ask students to discuss which achievement of the Ottoman Empire they consider the most important and why. **L1**

SECTION 1 ASSESSMENT

1. Key terms are in blue.
2. Mehmet II *(p. 240)*; Sultan Selim I *(p. 241)*; Sinan *(p. 245)*
3. See chapter maps.
4. He executed his two most able sons on suspicion of treason.
5. peasants, artisans, merchants, pastoral peoples
6. sultan controlled government through imperial council; grand vizier led the council; empire divided into provinces and districts governed by officials; bureaucracy helped administration of government
7. Mehmet II: captured Constantinople: gave empire dominance over Balkans and Anatolian Peninsula; Selim I: captured Mesopotamia, Egypt, Arabia, North Africa: gave empire control of holy cities; Süleyman I: led attacks on Europe: Europeans defeated Ottomans
8. Both rooms are lavishly decorated.
9. Answers will vary. Student work should reflect outside research.

SPECIAL REPORT SUMMARY

During the reign of Süleyman, the Ottoman Empire greatly expanded its size, from central Europe to Asia. Süleyman was also known as a builder and great patron of the arts.

■

Süleyman held absolute power, but was also known as the Lawgiver because he reformed the government and treated his subjects in a fair and just manner.

■

Süleyman was educated with Ibrahim, the son of a Greek fisherman. Ibrahim became a pasha and Süleyman later named him grand vizier and general supervisor of his administration.

■

The battle for successor to serve as emperor of the Ottoman Empire was long and bloody. Finally, five years after Süleyman's death, one of his sons, Selim, acceded to the throne. The reign of Selim II is usually viewed as the beginning of the decline of the Ottoman Empire.

TEACH

Points to Discuss

After students have read the selection, discuss the following: **What is the meaning of *jihad*?** *(It means a struggle against non-believers.)* **What event marked the Ottomans as a European power?** *(the capture of Constantinople)* **Who were the janissaries, and why were they important to Süleyman?** *(The janissaries were the sultan's elite army who gained their positions though their own skill. They were Christians recruited especially to serve in the sultan's elite army.)*

THE WORLD OF SÜLEYMAN

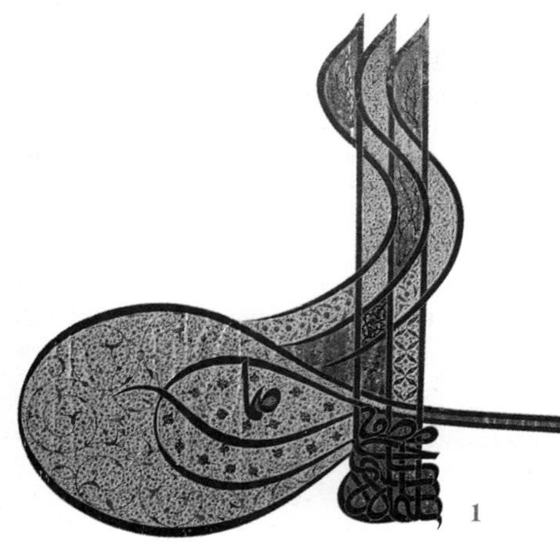

1

Called "the Magnificent" by Europeans who both feared and admired him, Süleyman I was a brilliant sixteenth-century military strategist who raised the Ottoman Empire to the height of its glory—more than doubling the landholdings he inherited from his father. During his 46-year reign (1520–1566), he personally led his armies on 13 campaigns, encouraged the growth of architecture and the fine arts, and played a key role in European politics of the day. Yet in spite of his power and his many achievements, Süleyman also endured great tragedy—driven to execute not only his dearest friend but also two of his own sons.

Arising from a nomadic Turkish-speaking tribe in western Anatolia (today's Turkey) in the late thirteenth century, the Ottomans were zealous Muslims who regarded the *jihad*, or holy war, against non-believers as their religious duty. Over the next century, they conquered Anatolia and ever larger portions of Byzantine territories in eastern Europe. In 1453, Süleyman's great-grandfather, Mehmet the Conqueror, delivered the final blow to the Byzantine Empire when he captured its capital, Constantinople. Renamed Istanbul, it became the rich Ottoman capital.

The fall of Constantinople sent a shock wave through Europe and confirmed the Ottomans as a European power. During Süleyman's reign, the empire would extend from Buda in central Europe to Basra in Asia. Süleyman would also greatly expand the practice begun by Mehmet the Conqueror of supporting the arts and architecture, building public baths, bridges, religious schools, and grand mosque complexes. One of the most famous still standing today is Istanbul's Süleymaniye Mosque.

Süleyman lived and ruled from the ornate palace of Topkapi. Also housed here were the empire's treasury, a school for training high officials, the sultan's advisers, and the harem. The women of the sultan's harem were drawn from non-Muslim enslaved women either captured or given as tribute by vassal states.

A small guard of janissaries, the sultan's elite army, also lived at the palace. Founded in the late fourteenth century—long before any standing army in Europe—the janissaries were recruited exclusively from Christian boys who were then brought up in the Islamic faith and trained in the use of arms. The sultan's high officials were also recruited as children from Christian families. After rigorous training, they gained their positions by their own skill. This system was so unusual for the times that one foreign ambassador who was granted an audience with Süleyman observed with astonishment that "there was not in all that great assembly a single man who

Teacher's Notes

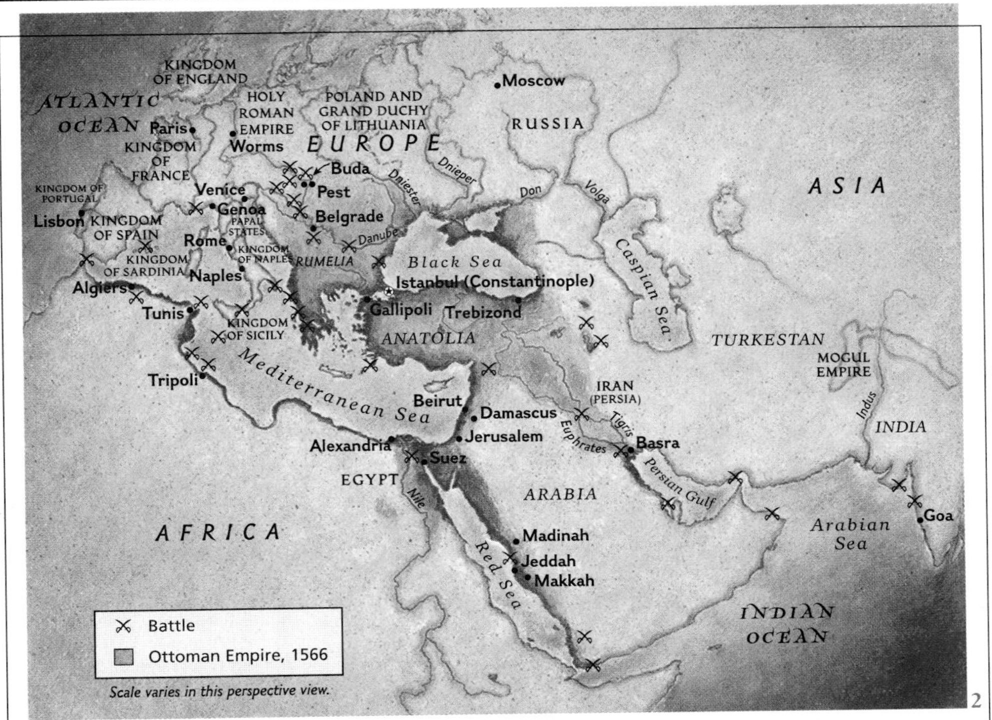

owed his position to aught save his valor and his merit."

Süleyman held absolute power and the right of life or death over his subjects. Yet one of his first official acts as sultan was to free 1,500 Egyptian and Iranian captives. He also paid merchants for any goods his father had confiscated, and ordered the execution of governors who were hated for their cruel abuses. This earned him a reputation as a just ruler who would protect the powerless among his people from illegal acts of corrupt officials.

His grateful subjects called Süleyman *Kanuni*, the Lawgiver. "I know of no State which is happier than this one," reported the Venetian ambassador. "It is furnished with all God's gifts. It controls war and peace with all; it is rich in gold, in people, in ships, and in obedience; no State can be compared with it." At the heart of this well-ordered system, however, lay the seeds of its eventual downfall.

■

"Whichever of my sons inherits the sultan's throne," declared Mehmet the Conqueror, "it behooves him to kill his brothers in the interest of the world order." Killing off all contenders early in a sultan's reign could protect the regime from the kind of civil wars that disrupted other monarchies during the sixteenth century. Because it was sacrilege to shed royal blood, the deed was carried out by strangling with a silken bowstring.

Mehmet himself began his rule by killing his infant brother. And according to one chronicler, Süleyman's father, Selim, claimed the throne by killing "his father and two brothers, and many nephews and sixty-two other relatives." Selim the Grim, as he was called, knew that failure to carry out the executions would have meant his own death—and that of Süleyman, his heir.

When his father became sultan, 18-year-old Prince Süleyman intensified his own training. Ottoman princes were assigned to serve as governors of provincial capitals, and to serve on military campaigns, ensuring

1 Süleyman's elaborate monogram endorsed many official documents issued during his 46-year reign.

2 Occupying a strategic position at the junction of three continents, the Ottoman Empire under Süleyman became a major world power. The broad sweep of the empire at the time of Süleyman's death in 1566 (shown in orange) included peoples of many religious and ethnic backgrounds.

How did Süleyman deal with cruel, oppressive governors? *(He had them executed.)* **Why did Mehmet believe it was prudent for potential heirs to the throne to kill their brothers?** *(It would protect the heir and the kingdom from palace intrigues and civil wars.)* **Why were Gulbahar and Roxelana enemies?** *(Both had sons who were potential heirs to the throne, and each wanted her own son to become sultan.)* **Why did Süleyman kill his oldest son, Mustafa?** *(He believed that Mustafa was plotting a rebellion, and that Mustafa was a danger to the state.)* **Who eventually took the throne, and what was his nickname?** *(Selim II; the Drunkard)* **How did the accession to the throne in European monarchies compare to the accession to sultan in the Ottoman Empire?** *(In some cases, they were somewhat similar. In European monarchies, it was not too uncommon for rivalries to occur and for siblings to be imprisoned. It was, however, accepted that the eldest male would inherit the throne.)*

FUN FACTS

- Charles V, the Holy Roman emperor, who ruled from 1519 to 1556, was a contemporary of Süleyman. Charles viewed the Ottomans as a major threat to his power, and considered Martin Luther only a minor annoyance, not nearly as significant as the Turkish threat to his empire.
- One European visitor had this to say about Süleyman: "His dignity of demeanor and his general physical appearance are worthy of the ruler of so vast an empire."
- Süleyman was responsible for building a bridge linking two parts of the Bosnian town of Mostar. The bridge lasted until November 9, 1993, when it was destroyed by Croatian artillery.

Who?What?Where?When?

Süleymaniye Mosque The Süleymaniye Mosque was built between 1550 and 1557, and many historians consider it to be the most beautiful example of Ottoman architecture in Istanbul. The mosque was designed by Sinan, one of the foremost architects of the Ottoman Empire and a close friend of Süleyman. The mosque sits atop a hill in old Istanbul. It is supported by four massive columns, one from Baalbek, one from Alexandria, and two from older Byzantine palaces. Inside the mosque the mihrab (a prayer niche indicating the direction of Makkah) and the *mimber* (pulpit from which the Friday sermon is preached) are carved from white marble. The four minarets, one at each corner of the courtyard, are said to represent Süleyman's position as the fourth Ottoman ruler of Istanbul. There are ten balconies on the minarets, and these are said to represent that Süleyman was the tenth sultan to reign since the founding of the Ottoman dynasty. Adjoining the mosque were theological schools, a medical school, a soup kitchen and a hospice for the poor, and a Turkish bath.

3

that whoever survived the battle for the throne would be well prepared to lead the empire. According to custom the prince of the house was supposed to be skilled in crafts as well as in gov ernment and war. Süleyman was trained as a goldsmith and was knowl edgeable about science and poetry.

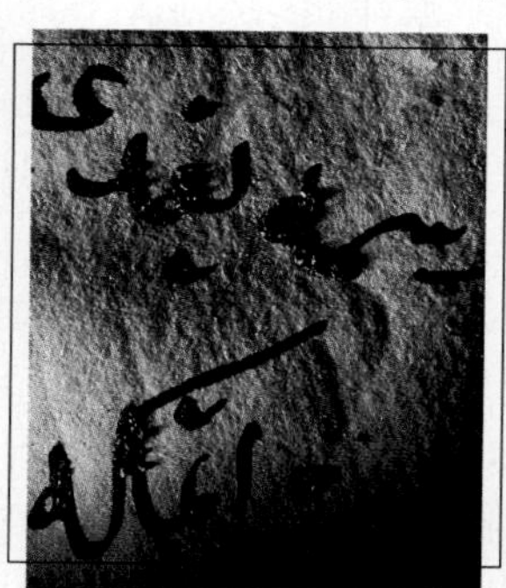

4

During his teens, he was educated with Ibrahim, a page at the prince's miniature court. A Greek fisherman's son who had been enslaved during a raid, Ibrahim was fluent in languages, charming, and intelligent. He and Süleyman were soon close friends. So high was Süleyman's opinion of his childhood friend that when he became sultan he made Ibrahim his grand vizier, the sultan's deputy and the general supervisor of the administration. He also put Ibrahim in charge of military campaigns when he himself did not ride into battle.

Süleyman set about producing several heirs to the throne. Three of his sons died in infancy, but the first to reach adulthood was Mustafa, whose mother was an enslaved girl named Gulbahar. Several sons by another concubine also reached adulthood. Their mother was a captive Russian bought for the sultan's harem at the slave market in Istanbul. Known in the West as Roxelana, she was nicknamed Hürrem—"Laughing One"—for her high spirits and lively storytelling. Much to Gulbahar's dis-

Teacher's Notes

may, Roxelana became one of Süleyman's favorites, appearing with him on some public occasions. His sons meant a lot to Süleyman at the beginning of his reign. He went hunting with them in many parts of his far-flung empire.

This abundance of male heirs set up a deadly rivalry between Gulbahar and Roxelana. Each mother knew that her sons would die if the other's ascended the throne. Roxelana seems to have taken every opportunity to strengthen her position with Süleyman and to undermine that of anyone she perceived as a rival. The rivals included not only Gulbahar but also the grand vizier, Ibrahim, who had openly opposed Süleyman's relationship with Roxelana. Süleyman's mother, who favored Ibrahim, was also a rival.

Then, in 1534, Süleyman's mother died. Two years later, convinced by Roxelana that Ibrahim was plotting against him, Süleyman ordered his lifelong friend executed. In addition, Roxelana managed to get her son-in-law, Rustem Pasha, appointed grand vizier.

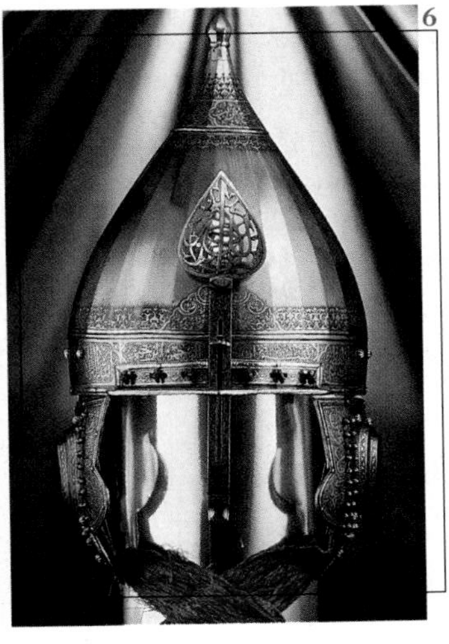

6

Meanwhile, all of Süleyman's sons were being trained just as he had been. Historians have speculated that he favored one or another of them at different times, but the record is hard to interpret. What is known is that Mustafa, Mehmet, Selim, and Bayezid each were assigned to governorships or military campaigns, and that Mehmet died of natural causes in 1543, only a year into his first governorship. Losing a son in adulthood was a great shock to Süleyman, who was, nonetheless, steadily conquering territory and using his influence to unsettle and destabilize Christian Europe.

5

Then in 1553, Rustem Pasha convinced Süleyman that Mustafa was plotting a rebellion. There may have been something to the rumor. Süleyman, at 59, was showing signs of his age and had recently been seriously ill. Mustafa, 39, had 20 years experience as a governor. He was respected by the soldiers he led and by the people, who considered him the best successor to his father.

Whatever the truth, Süleyman believed Mustafa to be a danger to the state. On campaign in Iran, he killed his oldest son. Very shortly thereafter, another son, Cihangir, died, leaving only Bayezid and Selim.

The battle for the throne turned into a decade-long civil war between Süleyman's two remaining sons and came to involve the empire's war with its longtime enemy, the Safavid dynasty of Iran. For the sultan, law and order in his empire was more important than any personal family ties. In 1561, Süleyman sided with Selim. He had Bayezid and all his sons—Süleyman's grandsons—killed.

Thus it happened that on Süleyman's death five years later, Selim II was the undisputed heir to the throne. Many date the slow decline of the empire to Selim's reign. Known as the Drunkard, he left the actual running of the state to his advisers. He also started the practice of choosing only one of his sons for training, thereby reducing the jockeying for power among sons, mothers, and palace officials.

In the seventeenth century, the sultans stopped killing their male relatives and began instead to imprison them. Thus, when a sultan was overthrown, or died without a male heir, the next person to sit on the throne would have spent years —and in some cases, their entire lives—in prison. Ill-equipped to lead, these sultans were easy prey for a corrupt bureaucracy.

3 **The soaring dome of Selimiye Mosque in Edirne is decorated with intricate patterns and phrases from the Quran. The vast mosque was built for Süleyman's son and successor, Selim II.**

4 **Transcribed by a court calligrapher, Süleyman's verses were often decorated with flecks of gold.**

5 **Solid gold and studded with rubies, emeralds, and other gems, this canteen was carried into battle for the sultan.**

6 **Ottoman armor, like this grand vizier's helmet, was frequently very ornate.**

INTERPRETING THE PAST

1. Why was Süleyman known as the Lawgiver? What kind of ruler was he?

2. What were Süleyman's main accomplishments?

3. What factors contributed to the decline of the Ottoman Empire after Süleyman's death?

CURRICULUM CONNECTION

Art Süleyman was known to be a great patron of the arts, and many projects were undertaken during his reign. You might wish to invite the art teacher to come to your class and discuss the contributions of the Ottoman Empire to our artistic heritage. Remind students that Islamic law prohibited using human or animal figures in artworks; however, it was believed that, if animals were drawn on a small scale or applied in everyday items, such as rugs and pottery, it would be harmless. As such, human and animal figures did survive in Islamic art, but they tended to become highly stylized, decorative motifs. Calligraphy also became highly decorative and stylized in the Ottoman Empire, and it remains a sophisticated and elegant Islamic art form.

Enrich

Guide students in a discussion of Süleyman's major accomplishments. What is the significance of Europeans calling him "Magnificent," but his people calling him "Lawgiver?" **L1**

INTERPRETING THE PAST

Answers:

1. Süleyman was known as the Lawgiver because he was considered to be a just and fair ruler, he reorganized the government so that corruption ended, regulated the laws of the empire, and saw that the laws were fairly enforced.
2. Süleyman's main accomplishments included governmental and legal reform; bringing prosperity to his people; greatly increasing the size of the Ottoman Empire.
3. Chief among the factors that contributed to the decline of the Ottoman Empire was the struggle for a successor. Süleyman left a number of male heirs, but did not appoint any one of them to serve as sultan. The heir who emerged alive, Selim, was known as the Drunkard, and he proved to be an incapable administrator.

1 FOCUS

Section Overview

This section describes the rise of the Safavid Empire and its cultural achievements.

BELLRINGER
Skillbuilder Activity

Project transparency and have students answer questions.

Available as a blackline master.

Daily Focus Skills Transparency 8–2

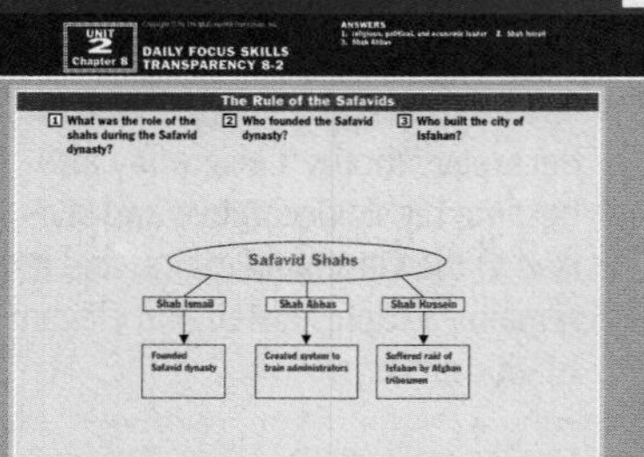

Guide to Reading

Answers to Graphics: Answers may include: Ottoman: ruled by sultan; Sunni Muslims; attempted to conquer central Europe; Safavid: ruled by shah; Shiite Muslims; allied with European states against Ottomans

Preteaching Vocabulary: Have students research the title *shah* which was used by the kings of Iran, or Persia. Was this title used in other places? (*The title* shah *was also used in Afghanistan until the overturn of the monarchy in 1973, and it has been used by rulers in other countries of central and southern Asia.*) **L1**

SECTION 2 The Rule of the Safavids

Guide to Reading

Main Ideas
- The Safavids used their faith as a unifying force to bring Turks and Persians together.
- The Safavid dynasty reached its height under Shah Abbas.

Key Terms
shah, orthodoxy, anarchy

People To Identify
Safavids, Shah Ismail, Shah Abbas, Riza-i-Abbasi

Places To Locate
Azerbaijan, Caspian Sea, Tabriz, Isfahan

Preview Questions
1. What events led to the creation and growth of the Safavid dynasty?
2. What cultural contributions were made by the Safavid dynasty?

Reading Strategy
Compare and Contrast Fill in the table below listing the key features of the Ottoman and Safavid Empires.

Ottoman Empire	Safavid Empire

Preview of Events

1500 · 1535 · 1570 · 1605 · 1640 · 1675 · 1710

- **1501** Ismail captures Iran and Iraq
- **1508** Safavid shah conquers Baghdad
- **1588** Shah Abbas becomes Safavid ruler
- **1612** Azerbaijan returned to Safavids
- **1723** Safavid Empire collapses

Voices from the Past

Aerial view of Isfahan, Iran

Under the Safavid dynasty of Persia, the capital city of Isfahan was known for its beauty. One English traveler reported:

> ❝The magnificently-arched bazaars, which form the Noble Square to the Palace, the several public inns, the stately rows of sycamore trees, which the world cannot parallel, the glorious summer-houses, the pleasant gardens, the stupendous bridges, sumptuous temples, the religious convents, the college for the professors of astronomy, are so many lasting monuments of Shah Abbas' fame. . . . Few cities in the world surpass Isfahan for wealth, and none come near it for those stately buildings, which for that reason are kept entire.❞
>
> —***A New Account of East India and Persia, Being Nine Years' Travels, 1672–1681,*** **John Fryer, edited 1911**

Isfahan was a planned city created by Shah Abbas the Great, ruler of the Safavids.

Rise of the Safavid Dynasty

After the collapse of the empire of Timur Lenk (Tamerlane) in the early fifteenth century, the area extending from Persia into central Asia fell into anarchy. At the beginning of the sixteenth century, however, a new dynasty known as the **Safavids** (sah•FAH•weedz) took control. Unlike many of their Islamic neighbors who were Sunni Muslims, the Safavids became ardent Shiites. (As discussed in

SECTION RESOURCES

Reproducible Masters
- Reproducible Lesson Plan 8–2
- Daily Lecture and Discussion Notes 8–2
- Guided Reading Activity 8–2
- Section Quiz 8–2
- Reading Essentials and Study Guide 8–2

Transparencies
- Daily Focus Skills Transparency 8–2

Multimedia
- Interactive Tutor Self-Assessment CD-ROM
- ExamView® Pro Testmaker CD-ROM
- Presentation Plus! CD-ROM

Chapter 3, the Sunnites and Shiites were the two major groups in the Islamic religion.)

The Safavid dynasty was founded by **Shah Ismail** (ihs•MAH•EEL), the descendant of Safi al-Din (thus the name *Safavid*). In the early fourteenth century, Safi al-Din had been the leader of a community of Turkish ethnic groups in **Azerbaijan,** near the **Caspian Sea.**

In 1501, Ismail used his forces to seize much of Iran and Iraq. He then called himself the shah, or king, of a new Persian state. Ismail sent Shiite preachers into Anatolia to convert members of Turkish tribes in the Ottoman Empire. The Ottoman sultan tried to halt this activity, but Ismail refused to stop. He also ordered the massacre of Sunni Muslims when he conquered Baghdad in 1508.

Alarmed by these activities, the Ottoman sultan, Selim I, advanced against the Safavids in Persia and won a major battle near **Tabriz.** However, Selim could not maintain control of the area. A few years later, Ismail regained Tabriz.

During the following decades, the Safavids tried to consolidate their rule throughout Persia and in areas to the west. Faced with the problem of integrating various Turkish peoples with the settled Persian-speaking population of the urban areas, the Safavids used the Shiite faith as a unifying force. Like the Ottoman sultan, the shah himself claimed to be the spiritual leader of all Islam.

In the 1580s, the Ottomans went on the attack. They placed Azerbaijan under Ottoman rule and controlled the Caspian Sea with their fleet. This forced the new Safavid shah, Abbas, to sign a peace treaty in which he lost much territory. The capital of the Safavids was moved from the northwestern city of Tabriz to the more centrally located city of **Isfahan.**

Reading Check **Identifying** What led to fighting between the Ottomans and the Safavids?

Glory and Decline

Under **Shah Abbas,** who ruled from 1588 to 1629, the Safavids reached the high point of their glory. A system similar to that of the janissaries in the Ottoman Empire was created to train administrators to run the kingdom. Shah Abbas also strengthened his army, which he armed with the latest weapons.

In the early seventeenth century, Shah Abbas moved against the Ottomans to regain lost territories. He was helped by European states, whose leaders viewed the Safavids as useful allies against their chief enemies, the Ottoman Turks. The Safavids had some initial success, but they could not hold all their territorial gains against the Ottoman armies. Nevertheless, in 1612, a peace treaty was signed that returned Azerbaijan to the Safavids.

After the death of Shah Abbas in 1629, the Safavid dynasty gradually lost its vigor. Most of his successors lacked his talent and political skills. The power of Shiite religious elements began to increase at court and in Safavid society at large.

While intellectual freedom had marked the height of the empire, the pressure to conform to traditional religious beliefs, called religious orthodoxy, increased. For example, Persian women who had considerable freedom during the early empire were now forced into seclusion and required to adopt the wearing of the veil.

In the early eighteenth century, during the reign of Shah Hussein, Afghan peoples invaded and seized the capital of Isfahan. The remnants of the Safavid ruling family were forced to retreat to Azerbaijan,

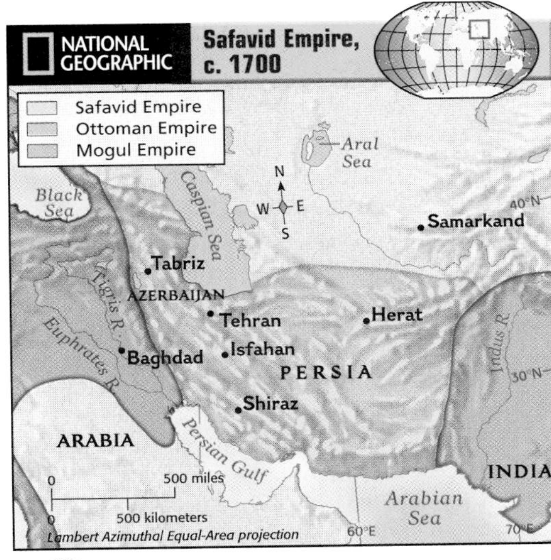

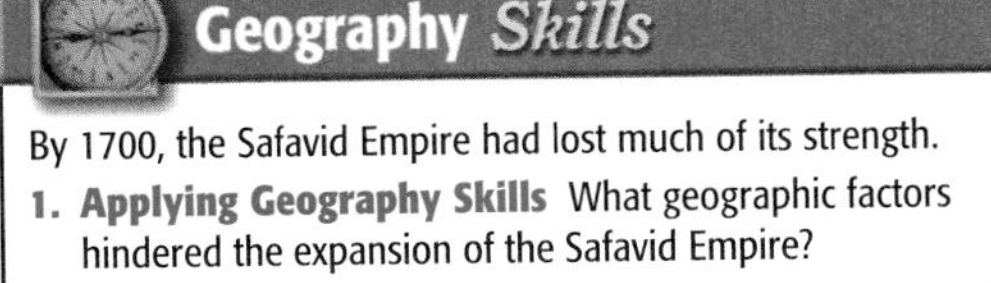

Geography Skills

By 1700, the Safavid Empire had lost much of its strength.

1. **Applying Geography Skills** What geographic factors hindered the expansion of the Safavid Empire?

CHAPTER 8
Section 2, 250–253

2 TEACH

Reading Check

Answer: religious differences (Ottomans were Sunni Muslims, Safavids were Shiite Muslims), competition for territory

Geography Skills

Answer:

1. surrounded by strong empires, sea power limited by Europeans, trade routes directed by Ottomans

Daily Lecture and Discussion Notes 8–2

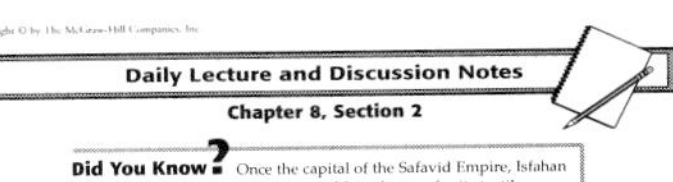

Daily Lecture and Discussion Notes

Chapter 8, Section 2

Did You Know? Once the capital of the Safavid Empire, Isfahan is today a major city in west-central Iran, known for its textiles, handicrafts, tiles, rugs, and cotton fabrics. Recovery of the city—which had declined greatly over the centuries since its peak of beauty during the reign of Shah Abbas—began in the second quarter of the twentieth century.

I. **Rise of the Safavid Dynasty** *(pages 250–251)*

A. In the sixteenth century a new dynasty know as the **Safavids** took control of the area extending from Persia into central Asia. The Safavids were Shiite Muslims.

B. **Shah Ismail** founded the Safavid dynasty. He was a descendant of Safi al-Din, who had been the leader of Turkish ethnic groups in **Azerbaijan,** near the **Caspian Sea,** in the early fourteenth century.

C. In 1501, Ismail seized much of Iran and Iraq. He called himself the **shah** (king) of a new Persian state. He sent Shiite preachers into **Anatolia** to convert Turks in the Ottoman Empire. Ismail also massacred Sunni Muslims when he conquered Baghdad in 1508.

D. Alarmed by the Safavids, the Ottoman ruler Selim I won a major battle against them near **Tabriz.** Within a few years, Ismail regained control of Tabriz.

E. Faced with integrating different peoples under their rule, the Safavids tried to use the Shiite faith as a unifying force. The shah claimed to be the spiritual leader of all Islam, as did the Ottoman sultan.

F. The Ottomans went on the attack in the 1580s, conquering Azerbaijan and controlling the Caspian Sea. Abbas, the Safavid shah, signed a peace treaty and lost much territory. The Safavid capital moved [illegible] Tabriz to **Isfahan.**

Guided Reading Activity 8–2

Name ____________ Date ____________ Class ____________

Guided Reading Activity 8-2

The Rule of the Safavids

DIRECTIONS: Fill in the blanks below as you read Section 2.

Unlike many of their Islamic neighbors who were **(1)** ____________ Muslims, the Safavids became ardent **(2)** ____________. Shah Ismail used his forces to seize much of **(3)** ____________ and **(4)** ____________ in 1501. He founded the Safavid dynasty. After the death of Shah **(5)** ____________ in 1629, the Safavid dynasty gradually lost its vigor. In the early eighteenth century, during the reign of Shah Hussein, **(6)** ____________ peoples invaded and seized the capital of Isfahan. Persia then sank into a long period of **(7)** ____________ and **(8)** ____________ anarchy.

The Safavid political system, like that in most empires, was organized in the

INTERDISCIPLINARY CONNECTIONS ACTIVITY

Religion Have students research and discuss the historical divisions between Sunni and Shiite Muslims and how they are relevant today. This religious division is still seen in Iran and Iraq. A shah survived as ruler of Iran until 1979 when the Ayatollah Khomeini, a Shiite Muslim imam, came to power. Today, Iran is the largest Shiite Muslim country in the world. Iraq is dominated by Sunni Muslims. In 1980, Iraq attacked Iran and the war between the two countries lasted until 1988. There were other reasons for this war (the desire to control oil revenue primary among them), but the religious tension between these two branches of Islam was a fundamental factor in this conflict that cost hundreds of thousands of lives. Ask students to provide contemporary examples of ongoing divisions between Sunni and Shiite Muslims. **L2**

Reading Check

Answer: He moved against the Ottomans to regain lost territories; his successors lacked his talent and political skills.

Graphic Organizer Skills

Answer: Ottoman; answers may include religious policies, ability to incorporate mixed ethnicities

Enrich

Have students locate Uzbekistan, Azerbaijan, Caspian Sea, Baghdad, Tabriz, and Isfahan on a contemporary map. Then have students compare the contemporary map to the one on page 251. Ask students what countries now comprise what was the Safavid Empire. *(parts of Saudi Arabia, Iran, Iraq)* The Ottoman Empire? *(Turkey, parts of Saudi Arabia, Iraq, Bulgaria, Greece, Yugoslavia, Romania)* **L1**

3 ASSESS

Assign Section 2 Assessment as homework or as an in-class activity.

Have students use **Interactive Tutor Self-Assessment CD-ROM.**

Section Quiz 8–2

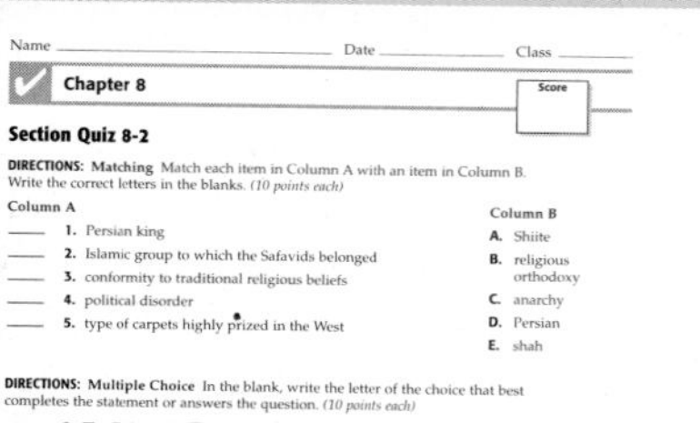
Name ______ Date ______ Class ______

Chapter 8 Score

Section Quiz 8-2

DIRECTIONS: Matching Match each item in Column A with an item in Column B. Write the correct letters in the blanks. *(10 points each)*

Column A	Column B
____ 1. Persian king	A. Shiite
____ 2. Islamic group to which the Safavids belonged	B. religious orthodoxy
____ 3. conformity to traditional religious beliefs	C. anarchy
____ 4. political disorder	D. Persian
____ 5. type of carpets highly prized in the West	E. shah

DIRECTIONS: Multiple Choice In the blank, write the letter of the choice that best completes the statement or answers the question. *(10 points each)*

Ottoman and Safavid Empires

Ottoman Empire	Both	Safavid Empire
Arose in early 14th century		Arose in early 16th century
Expanded from northwest Anatolian Peninsula to western Asia, eastern Europe, and North Africa	Conquered surrounding territory	Controlled area from Persia into central Asia; lost territory to Ottomans
Attempted to conquer central Europe	Strong military used latest weapons	Allied with European states against Ottomans
Sunni Muslims	Muslims	Shiite Muslims
Ruler: Sultan	Political and religious ruler inherited position and owned all land	Ruler: Shah
Was generally tolerant of non-Muslims in empire	Mixed ethnicities and religions in society	Used Shiite faith to unify peoples in empire
Began slow decline in 17th century	Encouraged trade and arts	Collapsed in 1723

Graphic Organizer Skills

Both the Ottomans and the Safavids created strong empires.

Compare and Contrast Which empire had a greater influence on Europe? What factors do you think most influenced the ability of both empires to expand?

their original homeland. The Turks took advantage of the situation to seize territories along the western border. Persia sank into a long period of political and social anarchy (lawlessness and disorder).

Reading Check **Evaluating** How did the Safavid Empire reach its pinnacle under Shah Abbas? Why did it decline after his death?

Political and Social Structures

Persia under the Safavids was a mixed society. The Safavids had come to power with the support of nomadic Turkish groups, but the majority of the people were Persian. Most of them were farmers or townspeople. The combination of Turkish and Persian elements affected virtually all aspects of Safavid society.

The Safavid political system, like that in most empires, was organized in the shape of a pyramid. The shah was at the top, the bureaucracy and landed classes were in the middle, and the common people were below.

The Role of the Shah The Safavid rulers were eagerly supported by Shiites who believed that the founder of the empire (Shah Ismail) was a direct successor of the prophet Muhammad. In return, the shahs declared Shiism to be the state religion.

Visitors reported that the shahs were more available to their subjects than were rulers elsewhere. "They show great familiarity to strangers," remarked one visitor, "and even to their own subjects, eating and drinking with them pretty freely." Indeed, the shahs even had their physical features engraved inside drinking cups so that people throughout their empire would know them.

Strong-minded shahs firmly controlled the power of the landed aristocracy. The shahs seized the large landed estates of the aristocrats and brought them under the control of the Crown. In addition, appointment to senior positions in the bureaucracy was based on merit rather than birth. To avoid competition between Turkish and non-Turkish elements, Shah Abbas, for example, hired a number of foreigners from neighboring countries for positions in his government.

Economy and Trade The Safavid shahs played an active part in trade and manufacturing activity. There

CRITICAL THINKING ACTIVITY

Compare and Contrast Ask students to refer to the diagram above and the time line on pages 236 to 237 at the beginning of this chapter. Ask students to note the political and cultural events involving the Safavid Empire. At what points do these intersect with similar events in the Ottoman Empire? Have students note what was happening in Europe during the years of Safavid prosperity. What similarities do they see? Ask students to analyze the Ottoman and Safavid Empires in terms of their governments, military might, and political, economic, and social structures. **L2**

was also a large and affluent urban middle class involved in trade.

Most goods in the empire traveled by horse or camel caravans. Although the road system was poor, the government provided resting places for weary travelers. In times of strong rulers, the roads were kept fairly clear of thieves and bandits.

At its height, Safavid Persia was a worthy successor to the great Persian empires of the past. However, it was probably not as prosperous as its neighbors to the east and west—the Moguls and the Ottomans. Hemmed in by the sea power of the Europeans to the south and the land power of the Ottomans to the west, the Safavids found trade with Europe difficult.

Reading Check **Describing** Describe the shah's power and its effect on society.

Safavid Culture

Knowledge of science, medicine, and mathematics under the Safavids was equal to that of other societies in the region. In addition, Persia witnessed an extraordinary flowering of the arts during the reign of Shah Abbas from 1588 to 1629.

The capital of Isfahan, built by Shah Abbas, was a grandiose planned city with wide spaces and a sense of order. Palaces, mosques, and bazaars were arranged around a massive polo ground. The immense mosques were richly decorated, and the palaces were delicate structures with slender wooden columns. To adorn the buildings, craftspeople created imaginative metalwork, elaborate tiles, and

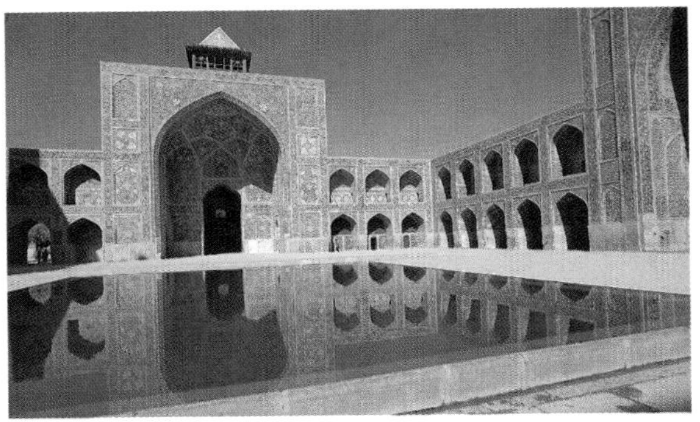

The Royal Academy of Isfahan

delicate glass vessels. Much of the original city still stands and is a gem of modern-day Iran.

Silk weaving based on new techniques flourished throughout the empire. The silks were a brilliant color, with silver and gold threads. The weavings portrayed birds, animals, and flowers.

Above all, carpet weaving flourished, stimulated by the great demand for Persian carpets in the West. Made primarily of wool, these carpets are still highly prized all over the world.

Persian painting enjoyed a long tradition, which continued in the Safavid Era. **Riza-i-Abbasi,** the most famous artist of this period, created exquisite works on simple subjects, such as oxen plowing, hunters, and lovers. Soft colors and flowing movement were the dominant features of the painting of this period.

Reading Check **Describing** What subjects were portrayed in many works of art from the Safavid Era?

SECTION 2 ASSESSMENT

Checking for Understanding

1. **Define** shah, orthodoxy, anarchy.
2. **Identify** Safavids, Shah Ismail, Shah Abbas, Riza-i-Abbasi.
3. **Locate** Azerbaijan, Caspian Sea, Anatolia, Tabriz, Isfahan.
4. **Describe** how the Safavids tried to bring the various Turkish and Persian peoples together.
5. **Summarize** how the increased pressures of religious orthodoxy influenced women's lives in the late Safavid dynasty.

Critical Thinking

6. **Explain** What was the shah's role in Safavid society and government?
7. **Organizing Information** Create a chart like the one below listing the Safavid shahs and significant developments that occurred during their administrations.

Shah	Significant Events

Analyzing Visuals

8. **Examine** the photograph of the Royal Academy of Isfahan shown on this page. Why would mosques have included schools like this academy?

Writing About History

9. **Expository Writing** Analyze the impact of the Safavid Empire's geographical location on its economy (what goods could be traded, trading partners, goods in high demand). Compare and contrast the Safavid economy with that of another economy.

CHAPTER 8
Section 2, 250–253

Reading Check

Answer: Shahs were available to their subjects and firmly controlled the power of the aristocracy; appointment to senior positions in the bureaucracy was based on merit.

Reading Check

Answer: simple subjects, such as oxen plowing, hunters, and flowers

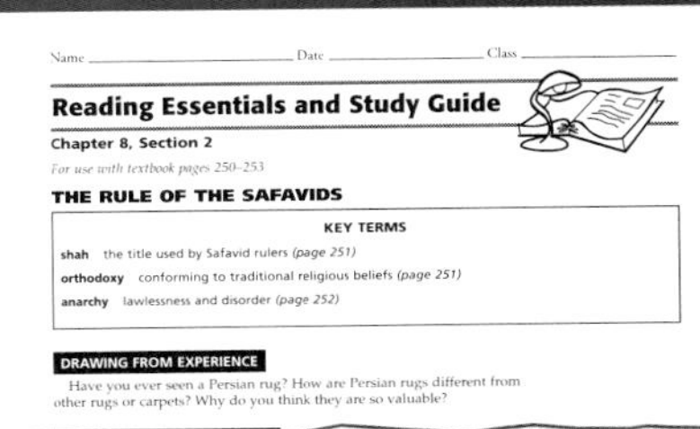
Name ____ Date ____ Class ____

Reading Essentials and Study Guide

Chapter 8, Section 2

For use with textbook pages 250–253

THE RULE OF THE SAFAVIDS

KEY TERMS

shah the title used by Safavid rulers *(page 251)*

orthodoxy conforming to traditional religious beliefs *(page 251)*

anarchy lawlessness and disorder *(page 252)*

DRAWING FROM EXPERIENCE

Have you ever seen a Persian rug? How are Persian rugs different from other rugs or carpets? Why do you think they are so valuable?

Reteaching Activity

Have students refer to the diagram on page 252. Have students note the political and cultural characteristics of the Safavid Empire. What characteristics did the Safavids share with the Ottomans? **L1**

4 CLOSE

Ask students to find examples and compare the artistic styles of the Safavid and Ottoman cultures. What characteristics do the styles share? How are they different? **L2**

SECTION 2 ASSESSMENT

1. Key terms are in blue.
2. Safavids *(p. 250)*; Shah Ismail *(p. 251)*; Shah Abbas *(p. 251)*; Riza-i-Abbasi *(p. 253)*
3. See chapter maps.
4. They used the Shiite faith as a unifying force.
5. They were forced into seclusion and required to adopt the wearing of the veil.
6. The shahs were actively involved in trade and the government; they controlled the power of the landed aristocracy and selected people for governmental positions.
7. Answers may include: Ismail: established Safavid dynasty; Abbas: trained administrators to run kingdom; Hussein: Isfahan seized by Afghan tribesmen
8. to provide education so that people could read the Quran
9. Answers will vary depending on the other economy selected.

STUDY & WRITING SKILLBUILDER

TEACH

Using Library Resources Make arrangements with the director of the school's resource center to have the class review various kinds of research sources: general and specialized encyclopedias, atlases, dictionaries, almanacs, periodical guides, the card catalog, and computerized databases such as Infotrak. Organize the class into several groups. Have each group familiarize itself with one of the above kinds of sources. Have each group describe to the class how to use the source and the kinds of information that can be found in that source.

Additional Practice

Skills Reinforcement Activity 8

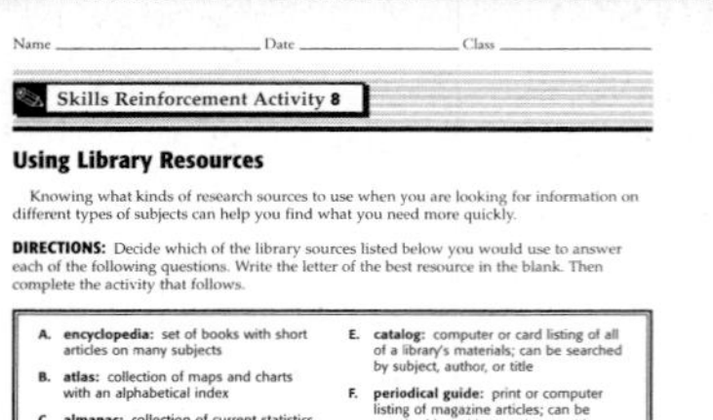
Name ______ Date ______ Class ______

Skills Reinforcement Activity 8

Using Library Resources

Knowing what kinds of research sources to use when you are looking for information on different types of subjects can help you find what you need more quickly.

DIRECTIONS: Decide which of the library sources listed below you would use to answer each of the following questions. Write the letter of the best resource in the blank. Then complete the activity that follows.

A. **encyclopedia:** set of books with short articles on many subjects
B. **atlas:** collection of maps and charts with an alphabetical index
C. **almanac:** collection of current statistics and facts that is updated annually
E. **catalog:** computer or card listing of all of a library's materials; can be searched by subject, author, or title
F. **periodical guide:** print or computer listing of magazine articles; can be searched by subject, author, or title

GLENCOE TECHNOLOGY

CD-ROM
Glencoe Skillbuilder Interactive Workbook CD-ROM, Level 2

This interactive CD-ROM reinforces student mastery of essential social studies skills.

STUDY & WRITING SKILLBUILDER

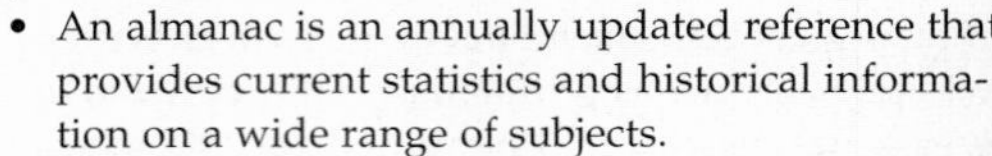

Using Library Resources

Why Learn This Skill?

You have been assigned a major research report. At the library, you wonder: Where do I start my research? Which reference works should I use?

Learning the Skill

Libraries contain many reference works. Here are brief descriptions of important reference sources:

Reference Books Reference books include encyclopedias, biographical dictionaries, atlases, and almanacs.

- An encyclopedia is a set of books containing short articles on many subjects arranged alphabetically.
- A biographical dictionary includes brief biographies listed alphabetically by last names.
- An atlas is a collection of maps and charts for locating geographic features and places. An atlas can be general or thematic.
- An almanac is an annually updated reference that provides current statistics and historical information on a wide range of subjects.

Card Catalogs Every library has a card catalog (on actual cards, computerized, or both), which lists every book in the library. Search for books by author, subject, or title. Computerized card catalogs can also advise you on the book's availability.

Periodical Guides A periodical guide lists topics covered in magazines and newspapers and tells you where the articles can be found.

Computer Databases Computer databases provide collections of information organized for rapid search and retrieval. For example, many libraries carry reference materials on CD-ROM.

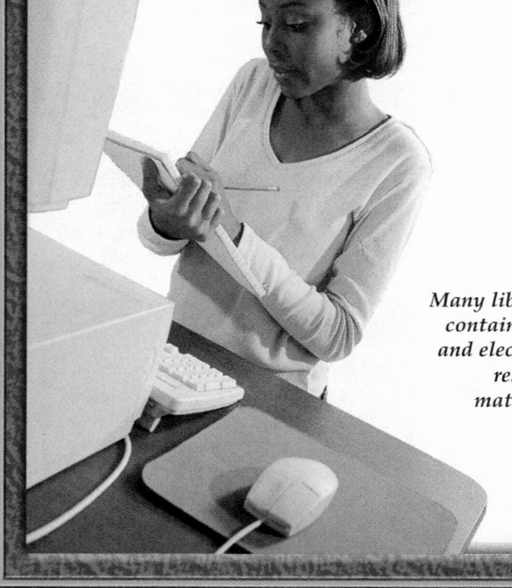

Many libraries contain print and electronic resource materials.

Practicing the Skill

Decide which source(s) described in this skill you would use to answer each of these questions for a report on the Safavid dynasty of Persia.

1. During what time period was the Safavid dynasty in control?
2. What present-day geographical area constitutes the territory occupied by the Safavids?
3. What type of leader was Shah Ismail?
4. What event was instrumental in moving the capital to Isfahan?

Application Activity

Using your school or local library, research the following and write a brief report to present your findings: Who established the East India Company and when? What was the work of the East India Company? Why was it important?

Glencoe's **Skillbuilder Interactive Workbook, Level 2,** provides instruction and practice in key social studies skills.

ANSWERS TO PRACTICING THE SKILL

1. An encyclopedia would have this information.
2. Both an atlas and an encyclopedia would have maps to show this.
3. A biographical dictionary or encyclopedia would be the best place to look for this information.
4. A historical account of this time period or an encyclopedia would contain this information.

Applying the Skill: Answers will vary. Students should list the reference(s) consulted.

SECTION 3

The Grandeur of the Moguls

Guide to Reading

Main Ideas
- The Moguls united India under a single government with a common culture.
- The introduction of foreigners seeking trade opportunities in India hastened the decline of the Mogul Empire.

Key Terms
zamindar, suttee

People to Identify
Babur, Akbar, Shah Jahan, Aurangzeb

Places to Locate
Khyber Pass, Delhi, Deccan Plateau, Calcutta, Chennai, Agra

Preview Questions
1. How did Mogul rulers develop the empire's culture?
2. What were the chief characteristics of Mogul society?

Reading Strategy
Summarizing Information As you read this section, create a chart listing the accomplishments and weaknesses of the Mogul rulers.

Ruler	Accomplishments	Weaknesses

Preview of Events

1500 · 1545 · 1590 · 1635 · 1680 · 1725 · 1770

- **1517** Babur crosses Khyber Pass into India
- **1556** Akbar becomes Mogul ruler
- **1605** Moguls rule most of India
- **1739** Persians sack Delhi
- **1763** Treaty of Paris gives British control in India

Voices from the Past

Persian cotton rug, c. 1630

The Mogul rulers of India lived in great splendor, as is evident in this report by an English traveler:

> "The first of September was the king's birthday. . . . Here attended the nobility all sitting on carpets until the king came; who at last appeared clothed, or rather laden with diamonds, rubies, pearls, and other vanities, so great, so glorious! His head, neck, breast, arms, above the elbows at the wrists, his fingers every one, with at least two or three rings; fettered with chains of diamonds; rubies as great as walnuts, and pearls, such as my eyes were amazed at. . . . He ascended his throne, and had basins of nuts, almonds, fruits, and spices made in thin silver, which he cast about."
>
> —*Eyewitness to History*, John Carey, ed.,1987

Mogul rulers united all of India under a single government with a common culture.

The Mogul Dynasty

In 1500, the Indian subcontinent was still divided into a number of Hindu and Muslim kingdoms. However, the Moguls established a new dynasty and brought a new era of unity to the region. The Moguls were not natives of India, but came from the mountainous region north of the Indus River valley.

The founder of the Mogul dynasty was **Babur.** His father was descended from the great Asian conqueror Timur Lenk, and his mother, from the Mongol

1 FOCUS

Section Overview

This section describes the Mogul dynasty, the decline of the Moguls, and the introduction of Western influence in India.

BELLRINGER
Skillbuilder Activity

 Project transparency and have students answer questions.

 Available as a blackline master.

Daily Focus Skills Transparency 8–3

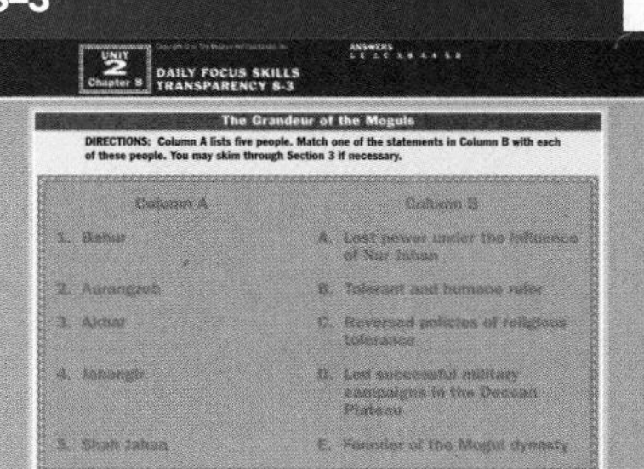
UNIT 2 Chapter 8 DAILY FOCUS SKILLS TRANSPARENCY 8-3

The Grandeur of the Moguls

DIRECTIONS: Column A lists five people. Match one of the statements in Column B with each of these people. You may skim through Section 3 if necessary.

Column A	Column B
1. Babur	A. Lost power under the influence of Nur Jahan
2. Aurangzeb	B. Tolerant and humane ruler
3. Akbar	C. Reversed policies of religious tolerance
4. Jahangir	D. Led successful military campaigns in the Deccan Plateau
5. Shah Jahan	E. Founder of the Mogul dynasty

Guide to Reading

Answers to Graphic: Answers may include: Babur: established Mogul dynasty: small forces; Akbar: extended Mogul rule throughout India: ruled young; Jahangir: strengthened central control of government: allowed wife to enrich her family; Shah Jahan: expanded empire's boundaries: strained empire's treasury; Aurangzeb: prohibited suttee, illegal taxes, drinking, gambling: created internal unrest

Preteaching Vocabulary: Have students explain the role that zamindars played in the Mogul government. **L1**

SECTION RESOURCES

Reproducible Masters
- Reproducible Lesson Plan 8–3
- Daily Lecture and Discussion Notes 8–3
- Guided Reading Activity 8–3
- Section Quiz 8–3
- Reading Essentials and Study Guide 8–3

Transparencies
- Daily Focus Skills Transparency 8–3

Multimedia
- Interactive Tutor Self-Assessment CD-ROM
- ExamView® Pro Testmaker CD-ROM
- Presentation Plus! CD-ROM

2 TEACH

Geography *Skills*

Answers:

1. European trading forts established in that area
2. greatest expansion under Akbar

Reading Check

Answer: His forces had advanced weapons, including artillery, which they used to capture Delhi and conquer much of North India.

Daily Lecture and Discussion Notes 8–3

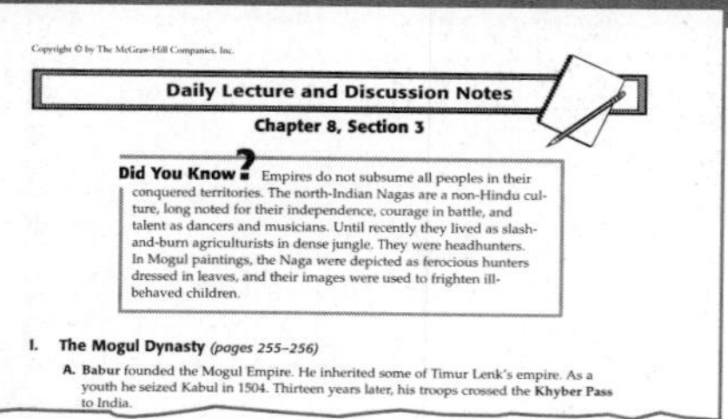

Daily Lecture and Discussion Notes

Chapter 8, Section 3

Did You Know? Empires do not subsume all peoples in their conquered territories. The north-Indian Nagas are a non-Hindu culture, long noted for their independence, courage in battle, and talent as dancers and musicians. Until recently they lived as slash-and-burn agriculturists in dense jungle. They were headhunters. In Mogul paintings, the Naga were depicted as ferocious hunters dressed in leaves, and their images were used to frighten ill-behaved children.

I. **The Mogul Dynasty** *(pages 255–256)*

A. **Babur** founded the Mogul Empire. He inherited some of Timur Lenk's empire. As a youth he seized Kabul in 1504. Thirteen years later, his troops crossed the **Khyber Pass** to India.

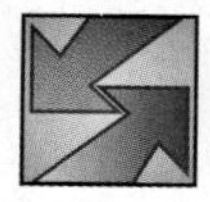

CURRICULUM CONNECTION

Economics Ask students to identify the ways that the economy of Akbar's India thrived during periods of political stability and peace. *(trade and manufacturing flourished)* How did Akbar's religious tolerance contribute to economic stability? *(answers will vary, but could include the idea that religious diversity strengthened Akbar's ability to understand and negotiate with other cultures)* **L2**

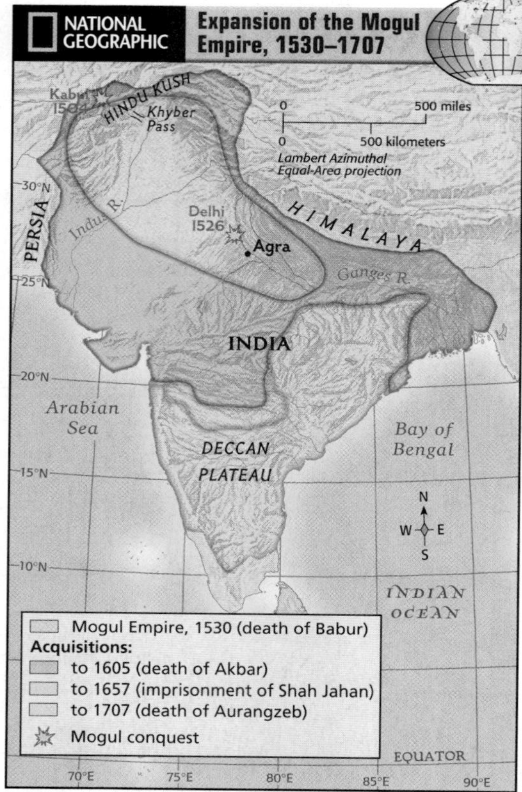

Geography *Skills*

Most of the people the Moguls encountered as they expanded into India were Hindu.

1. **Interpreting Maps** Why did the southern tip of India remain free from Mogul expansion?
2. **Applying Geography Skills** How does the map support the text's assertion that Akbar was the greatest of the conquering Mogul monarchs?

conqueror Genghis Khan. Babur had inherited a part of Timur Lenk's empire in an upland river valley of the Syr Darya. As a youth, he commanded a group of warriors who seized Kabul in 1504. Thirteen years later, his forces crossed the **Khyber Pass** to India.

Babur's forces were far smaller than those of his enemies, but they had advanced weapons, including artillery, and used them to great effect. With twelve thousand troops against an enemy force nearly ten times that size, Babur captured **Delhi** and established his power in the plains of North India. He continued his conquests in North India until his death in 1530 at the age of 47.

Reading Check **Summarizing** How did Babur begin the Mogul dynasty in India?

The Reign of Akbar

Babur's grandson **Akbar** was only 14 when he came to the throne. Highly intelligent and industrious, Akbar set out to extend his domain. By 1605, he had brought Mogul rule to most of India.

How was Akbar able to place almost all of India under his rule? By using heavy artillery, Akbar's armies were able to overpower the stone fortresses of their rivals. The Moguls were also successful negotiators.

Akbar's conquests created the greatest Indian empire since the Mauryan dynasty nearly two thousand years earlier. The empire appeared highly centralized but was actually a collection of semi-independent states held together by the power of the emperor.

Akbar was probably the greatest of the conquering Mogul monarchs, but he is best known for the humane character of his rule. Like all Mogul rulers, Akbar was born a Muslim, but he adopted a policy of religious tolerance. As emperor, he showed a keen interest in other religions and tolerated Hindu practices. He even welcomed the expression of Christian views by his Jesuit advisers at court. By taking a Hindu princess as one of his wives, Akbar put his policy of religious tolerance into practice.

Akbar was also tolerant in his administration of the government. The upper ranks of the government bureaucracy were filled with non-native Muslims, but many of the lower-ranking officials were Hindus.

It became common practice to give the lower-ranking officials plots of farmland for their temporary use. These local officials, known as **zamindars**, kept a portion of the taxes paid by the peasants in lieu of a salary. They were then expected to forward the rest of the taxes from the lands under their control to the central government. Zamindars came to exercise considerable power in their local districts.

Overall, the Akbar Era was a time of progress, at least by the standards of the day. All Indian peasants were required to pay about one-third of their annual harvest to the state but the system was applied justly. When bad weather struck in the 1590s, taxes were reduced, or suspended altogether. Thanks to a long period of peace and political stability, trade and manufacturing flourished.

EXTENDING THE CONTENT

Akbar There were three distinct stages to Akbar's life: an impetuous youth; a sober, empire-expanding maturity; and a religious mysticism later in his life. The foolishness of his youth is shown in a story from the *Akbarnama,* a picture history of his life that he commissioned because he could not read. One day he was told how Indian Rajputs would charge against a double-sided spear and impale themselves. He took this "challenge" and raced towards a sword fixed against a wall. Akbar was saved from senseless death only because someone kicked the sword away.

The era was an especially prosperous one in the area of foreign trade. Indian goods, notably textiles, tropical food products and spices, and precious stones, were exported in exchange for gold and silver. Much of the foreign trade was handled by Arab traders, because the Indians, like their Mogul rulers, did not care for travel by sea.

Reading Check **Explaining** How did Akbar's religious policy affect his government?

Decline of the Moguls

Akbar died in 1605 and was succeeded by his son Jahangir (juh•HAHN•GIHR). Jahangir was able and ambitious. During the early years of his reign, he continued to strengthen the central government's control over his vast empire.

Eventually, however, his grip began to weaken when he fell under the influence of one of his wives, Persian-born Nur Jahan. The empress used her position to enrich her own family. She arranged the marriage of her niece to her husband's third son and ultimate successor, **Shah Jahan.**

During his reign from 1628 to 1658, Shah Jahan maintained the political system established by earlier Mogul rulers. He also expanded the boundaries of the empire through successful campaigns in the **Deccan Plateau** and against the city of Samarkand, north of the Hindu Kush.

Shah Jahan's rule was marred by his failure to deal with growing domestic problems, however. He had inherited a nearly empty treasury. His military campaigns and expensive building projects put a heavy strain on the imperial finances and compelled him to raise taxes. Meanwhile, the majority of his subjects lived in poverty.

Shah Jahan's troubles worsened with his illness in the mid-1650s, which led to a struggle for power between two of his sons. One of Shah Jahan's sons, **Aurangzeb,** had his brother put to death and imprisoned his father. Aurangzeb then had himself crowned emperor in 1658.

Aurangzeb is one of the most controversial rulers in the history of India. A man of high principle, he attempted to eliminate many of what he considered to be India's social evils. He forbade both the Hindu custom of suttee (cremating a widow on her husband's funeral pyre) and the levying of illegal taxes. He tried to forbid gambling and drinking as well.

Aurangzeb was a devout Muslim and adopted a number of measures that reversed the Mogul policies of religious tolerance. The building of new Hindu temples was prohibited, and Hindus were forced to convert to Islam.

Aurangzeb's policies led to Hindu outcries and domestic unrest. In addition, a number of revolts against imperial authority broke out in provinces throughout the empire. Rebellious groups threatened the power of the emperor, leaving an increasingly divided India vulnerable to attack from abroad. In 1739, Delhi was sacked by the Persians, who left it in ashes.

Reading Check **Explaining** Why was Aurangzeb one of the most controversial rulers in the history of India?

The British in India

TURNING POINT **In this section, you will learn how a small British force defeated a Mogul army at the Battle of Plassey in 1757. A few years later, a similar victory over the French made the British a dominant presence in India until after World War II.**

The arrival of the British hastened the decline of the Mogul Empire. By 1650, British trading forts had been established at Surat, Fort William (now the city of **Calcutta**), and **Chennai** (Madras). From Chennai, British ships carried Indian-made cotton goods to the East Indies, where they were traded for spices.

British success in India attracted rivals, especially the French. The French established their own forts on the east coast at Pondicherry, south of Chennai, at Surat, and in the Bay of Bengal. For a brief period, the French went on the offensive, even capturing the British fort at Chennai.

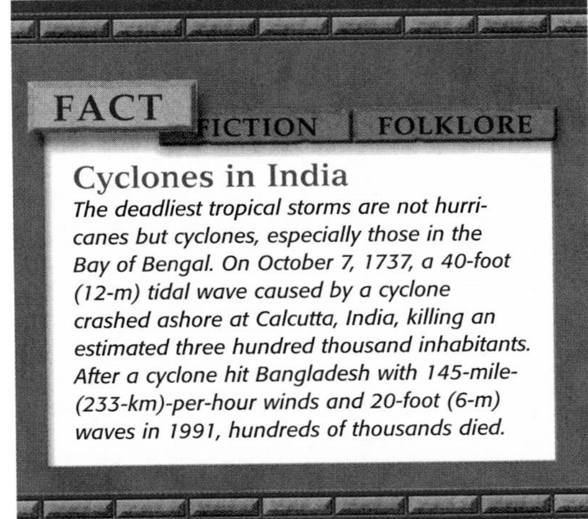

Cyclones in India

The deadliest tropical storms are not hurricanes but cyclones, especially those in the Bay of Bengal. On October 7, 1737, a 40-foot (12-m) tidal wave caused by a cyclone crashed ashore at Calcutta, India, killing an estimated three hundred thousand inhabitants. After a cyclone hit Bangladesh with 145-mile-(233-km)-per-hour winds and 20-foot (6-m) waves in 1991, hundreds of thousands died.

Reading Check

Answer: His religious tolerance allowed Hindus to become low-ranking government officials.

Reading Check

Answer: He was a man of high moral principles, but he was also ruthless and intolerant.

TURNING POINT

India became the crown jewel of the British Empire and was ruled by Britain until 1947. Ties between the two countries remain strong; today, many people from India and Pakistan live in Britain.

Guided Reading Activity 8–3

Name ______ Date ______ Class ______

Guided Reading Activity 8-3

The Grandeur of the Moguls

DIRECTIONS: Fill in the blanks below as you read Section 3.

I. In 1500 the Indian ______ was divided into a number of Hindu and Muslim kingdoms.
A. The founder of the ______ dynasty was Babur, descended from Timur Lenk.
B. Babur captured ______ and established his power in the plains of North India.
II. By 1605, ______ had brought Mogul rule to most of India.
A. Akbar was known for the ______ character of his rule.
1. A Muslim, he adopted a policy of religious ______

Enrich

Ask students to compare the treatment of subject peoples by the Ottomans, Safavids, and Moguls. *(Ottomans: Non-Muslims could practice their own religion and run their own communities; Safavids: forced everyone to adopt Shiite Islam; Moguls: Akbar encouraged religious tolerance, but later Moguls persecuted Hindus)*

COOPERATIVE LEARNING ACTIVITY

Conducting a Mock Trial Divide the class into two groups, prosecution and defense, and have the students conduct a mock trial of Aurangzeb, who is charged with contributing to the decline of the Mogul Empire. Prosecutors may argue that by forcing Hindus to convert to Islam and preventing them from building new temples, Aurangzeb turned Hindus against Muslims and weakened the country. The defense may point out that he strengthened India by attempting to abolish the practice of suttee, fighting against illegal taxes, and attempting to stop gambling and drinking **L1**

For grading this activity, refer to the ***Performance Assessment Activities*** booklet.

Geography Skills

Answers:

1. always along the coast, usually near a river or bay
2. Students should use atlases and other maps in the text.

Picturing History

Answer: Clive helped consolidate British control of India by exercising the power of the East India Company.

Reading Check

Answer: It was empowered by the British crown to act on its behalf; the company wanted to control markets in India and keep out foreign competition.

Connecting Across Time

Review with students the political situations in Britain, Portugal, and Holland at this time. Compare these nations' strengths and weaknesses with those of the Mogul Empire. In what ways were European powers expanding? How was the Mogul Empire at a point of weakness? Have students apply absolute and relative chronology to create a time line sequencing the significant individuals, events, and time periods in order to illustrate the comparison. **L2**

Critical Thinking

Guide students in a discussion of the following: How might history have been different had the British entered India during the reign of Akbar? How would Akbar have related to the British? Would he have been able to stand against them? **L2**

The British were saved by the military genius of Sir Robert Clive, an aggressive British empire builder. Clive eventually became the chief representative in India of the East India Company, a private company empowered by the British Crown to act on its behalf. As chief representative, it was Clive's job to fight any force, French or Indian, that threatened the East India Company's power in India. Owing to Clive's efforts, the French were ultimately restricted to the fort at Pondicherry and a handful of small territories on the southeastern coast.

While fighting the French, Clive was also consolidating British control in Bengal, the state in which Fort William was located. The Indian ruler of Bengal had attacked Fort William in 1756. He had imprisoned the British garrison overnight in what became known as the "Black Hole of Calcutta," an underground prison. The intense heat in the crowded space had led to disaster. Only 23 people (out of 146) had walked out alive.

In 1757, Clive led a small British force numbering about three thousand to victory over a Mogul-led army more than ten times its size in the Battle of Plassey in Bengal. As part of the spoils of victory, the failing Mogul court gave the British East India Company the power to collect taxes from lands in the area surrounding Calcutta.

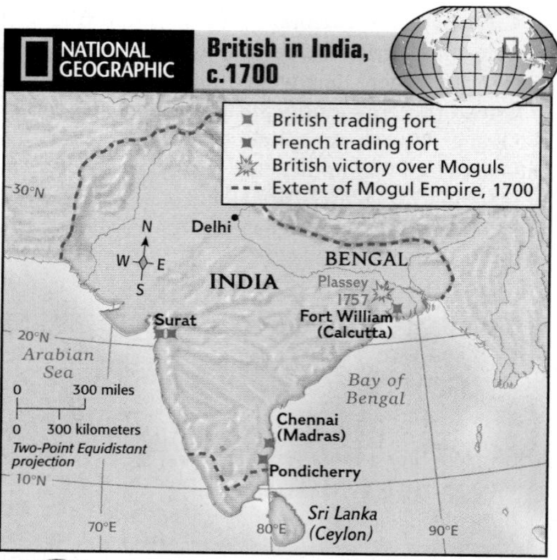

Geography Skills

The British East India Company gradually took over more and more land in India.

1. **Interpreting Maps** What do you notice about the placement of foreign trading forts in India?
2. **Applying Geography Skills** Create a map that shows the route British and French ships sailed to India.

Picturing History

Above is an engraved portrait of Lord Robert Clive. What was Clive's role in India?

Britain's rise to power in India, however, was not a story of constant success. Officials of the East India Company, from the governor-general on down, often combined arrogance with incompetence. They offended both their Indian allies and the local population, who were taxed heavily to meet the growing expenses of the East India Company. Intelligent Indian commanders avoided direct pitched battles with well-armed British troops. They preferred to harass and ambush them in the manner of modern-day guerrillas. Said one of India's commanders:

> "Shall I risk my cavalry which cost a thousand rupees each horse, against your cannon ball which cost two pice? No! I will march your troops until their legs swell to the size of their bodies. You shall not have a blade of grass, nor a drop of water. I will hear of you every time your drum beats, but you shall not know where I am once a month. I will give your army battle, but it must be when I please, and not when you choose."

In the late eighteenth century, the East India Company moved inland from the great coastal cities. British expansion brought great riches to individual British merchants, as well as to British officials who found they could obtain money from local rulers by selling trade privileges. The British were in India to stay.

Reading Check **Examining** How did the East India Company, a private company, become involved in the struggle over control of India?

CRITICAL THINKING ACTIVITY

Solving Problems After students have read the chapter, have them think about the problems that confronted the Ottoman, Safavid, or Mogul Empires. Direct students to use a problem-solving process to identify a problem and conduct research to provide a historical context for the problem they have identified. Each student should then list and consider options available to solve the problem, weigh the advantages and disadvantages of each option, choose and implement a solution, and then evaluate the effectiveness of the solution they implemented. **L2**

What If...

Britain's East India Company had been a financial disaster?

Chartered companies were the main instruments of imperial expansion for much of eighteenth-century Europe. They were private companies granted certain royal privileges—such as monopolies—that brought their rulers territorial and military dominance even as they sought their own commercial gains. However, some chartered companies did not prosper. The French East India companies, for example, did not survive.

Consider the Consequences Consider what would have happened to the political landscape of both India and Europe if Britain's East India Company had been a financial failure. What other country or company could have filled Britain's role in India?

Society and Daily Life in Mogul India

The Moguls were foreigners in India. In addition, they were Muslims ruling a largely Hindu population. The resulting blend of influences on the lives of ordinary Indians could be complicated. The treatment of women in Mogul India is a good example of this complexity.

Women had long played an active role in Mogul tribal society, and some actually fought on the battlefield alongside the men. Babur and his successors often relied on the women in their families for political advice.

To a degree, these Mogul attitudes toward women affected Indian society. Women from aristocratic families frequently received salaries and were allowed to own land and take part in business activities.

At the same time, the Moguls placed certain restrictions on women under Islamic law. These practices sometimes were compatible with existing tendencies in Indian society and were adopted by Hindus. The Islamic practice of isolating women, for example, was adopted by many upper-class Hindus.

In other ways, however, Hindu practices remained unchanged by Mogul rule. The custom of suttee continued despite efforts by the Moguls to abolish it. Child marriage also remained common.

The Mogul era saw the emergence of a wealthy landed nobility and a prosperous merchant class. During the late eighteenth century, this economic prosperity was shaken by the decline of the Mogul Empire and the coming of the British. However, many prominent Indians established trading ties with the foreigners, a relationship that temporarily worked to the Indians' benefit.

Most of what we know about the daily lives of ordinary Indians outside of the cities comes from the observations of foreign visitors. One such foreign visitor provided the following description of Indian life:

> ❝Their houses are built of mud with thatched roofs. Furniture there is little or none except some earthenware pots to hold water and for cooking and two beds, one for the man, the other for his wife; their bed cloths are scanty, merely a sheet or perhaps two, serving as under- and over-sheet. This is sufficient for the hot weather, but the bitter cold nights are miserable indeed, and they try to keep warm over little cow-dung fires.❞

Reading Check **Contrasting** How did women's lives under Islamic and Hindu religious laws differ from women's lives in Mogul society?

Mogul Culture

The Moguls brought together Persian and Indian influences in a new and beautiful architectural style. This style is best symbolized by the **Taj Mahal,** which was built in **Agra** by the emperor Shah Jahan in the mid-seventeenth century. The emperor built the Taj Mahal in memory of his wife, Mumtaz Mahal, who had died giving birth to her fourteenth child at the age of 39. The project employed twenty thousand workers and lasted more than twenty years. To finance it, the government raised land taxes, thus driving many Indian peasants into complete poverty.

The Taj Mahal is widely considered to be the most beautiful building in India, if not in the entire world. All the exterior and interior surfaces are decorated with cut-stone geometric patterns, delicate black stone tracery, or intricate inlays of colored precious stones in floral mosaics. The building seems to have monumental size, nearly blinding brilliance, and delicate lightness, all at the same time.

Another major artistic achievement of the Mogul period was in painting. Like architecture, painting in Mogul India resulted from the blending of two cultures: Persian and Indian. Akbar established a state

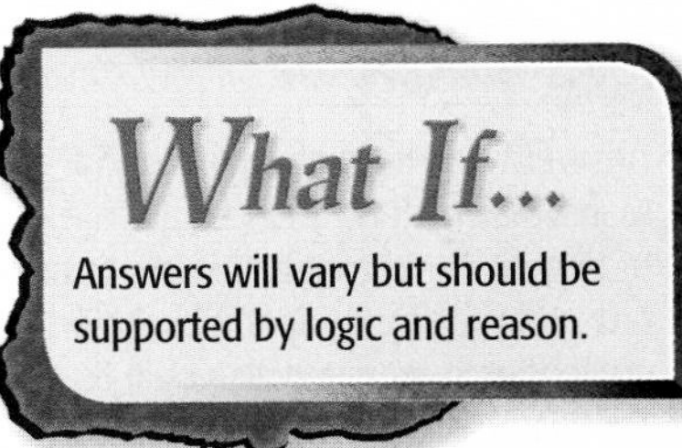

What If...
Answers will vary but should be supported by logic and reason.

Reading Check

Answer: Muslim law: women isolated, forced to wear veils; Hindu: women isolated, forced into child marriages, subjected to suttee; Mogul: women warriors, gave political advice, received salaries, owned land, took part in business and literary activities.

Charting Activity

Ask students to prepare a chart comparing the symptoms of decline for the Ottomans, Safavids, and the Moguls. **L2**

3 ASSESS

Assign Section 3 Assessment as homework or as an in-class activity.

Have students use **Interactive Tutor Self-Assessment CD-ROM.**

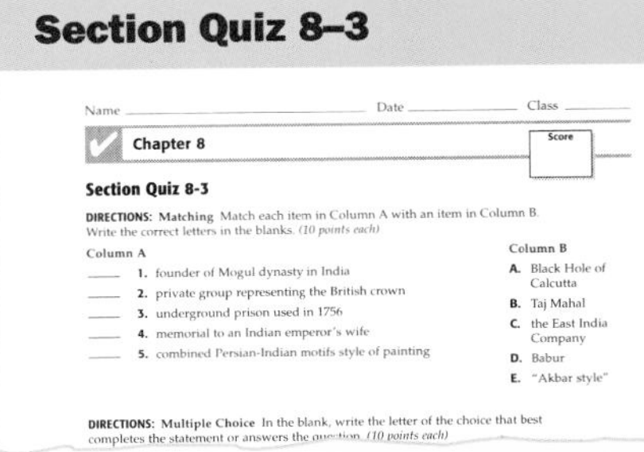
Section Quiz 8–3

Name ______ Date ______ Class ______

Chapter 8 Score

Section Quiz 8-3

DIRECTIONS: Matching Match each item in Column A with an item in Column B. Write the correct letters in the blanks. *(10 points each)*

Column A
____ 1. founder of Mogul dynasty in India
____ 2. private group representing the British crown
____ 3. underground prison used in 1756
____ 4. memorial to an Indian emperor's wife
____ 5. combined Persian-Indian motifs style of painting

Column B
A. Black Hole of Calcutta
B. Taj Mahal
C. the East India Company
D. Babur
E. "Akbar style"

DIRECTIONS: Multiple Choice In the blank, write the letter of the choice that best completes the statement or answers the question. *(10 points each)*

MEETING INDIVIDUAL NEEDS

Visual/Spatial By using the Internet and other reference sources, hearing-impaired or attention-deficit students can research the Taj Mahal. Have students find pictures and construct a time line depicting all work that has been done to the Taj Mahal. Have a few students make a list of all celebrity events that have occurred at the Taj Mahal. Share this list with the class orally, in writing, or as a visual presentation. For extension, ask if there is any comparable location in the United States or elsewhere. Compare and contrast orally the date of this building's original construction, size, and building materials. Does it really measure up to the Taj Mahal? **L1**

Refer to ***Inclusion for the High School Social Studies Classroom Strategies and Activities*** in the TCR.

History *through Architecture*

Answer: Legend claims that the Taj Mahal was built by Shah Jahan as a testament to his grief at the loss of his favorite wife. Contemporary scholars argue that Shah Jahan also built the Taj Mahal as a symbol of his power and wealth.

Reading Check

Answer: It combined Persian and Indian motifs, and included the portrayal of humans in action.

Reading Essentials and Study Guide 8–3

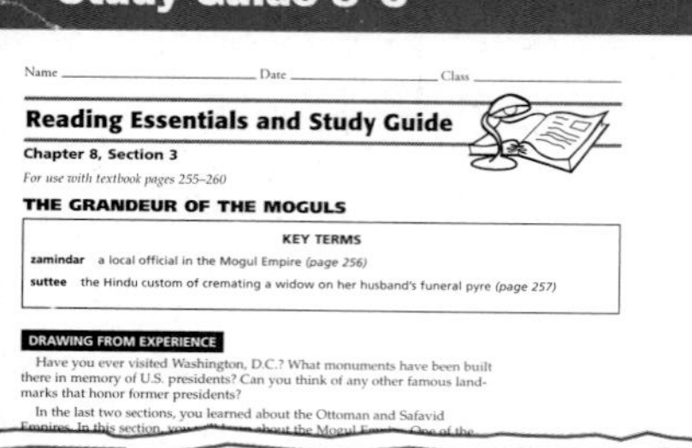

Name ______ Date ______ Class ______

Reading Essentials and Study Guide

Chapter 8, Section 3

For use with textbook pages 255–260

THE GRANDEUR OF THE MOGULS

KEY TERMS

zamindar a local official in the Mogul Empire (page 256)

suttee the Hindu custom of cremating a widow on her husband's funeral pyre (page 257)

DRAWING FROM EXPERIENCE

Have you ever visited Washington, D.C.? What monuments have been built there in memory of U.S. presidents? Can you think of any other famous landmarks that honor former presidents?

In the last two sections, you learned about the Ottoman and Safavid Empires. In this section, ...

Reteaching Activity

Review Akbar's religious policies with students. Then discuss those of Aurangzeb. You might ask students to compare and contrast the two men. Who was more devoted to his religion? What difference did that make in religious tolerance? **L2**

4 CLOSE

Ask students which ruler they would have preferred to live under: Süleyman, Shah Abbas, or Akbar. Have them explain why they would have preferred this ruler.

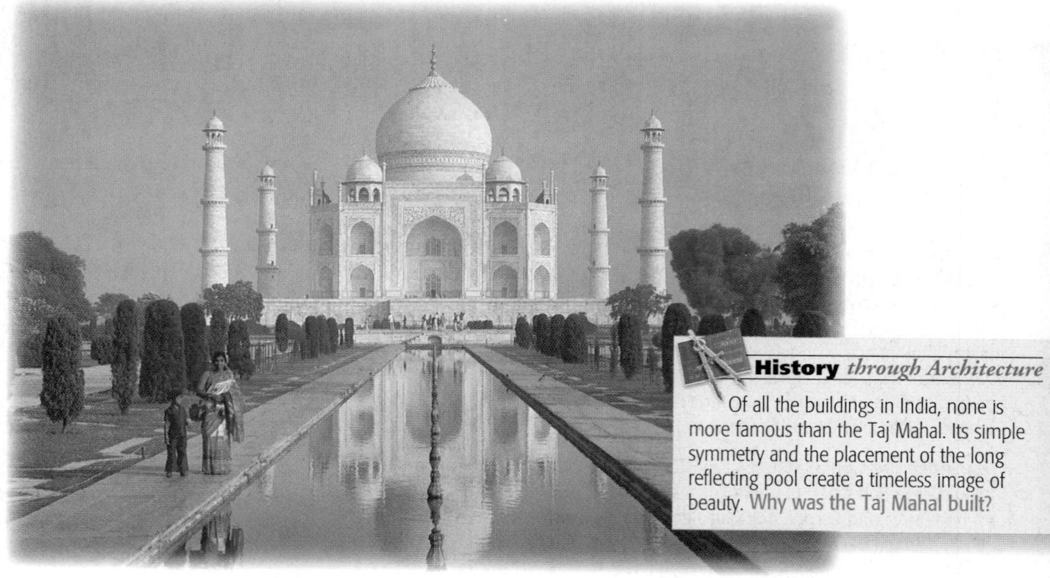

History *through Architecture*

Of all the buildings in India, none is more famous than the Taj Mahal. Its simple symmetry and the placement of the long reflecting pool create a timeless image of beauty. Why was the Taj Mahal built?

workshop for artists, mostly Hindus, who worked under the guidance of Persian masters to create the Mogul school of painting. The "Akbar style" combined Persian with Indian motifs. It included the portrayal of humans in action, for example—a characteristic not usually seen in Persian art. Akbar also encouraged his artists to imitate European art forms, including the use of perspective and lifelike portraits.

The Mogul emperors were dedicated patrons of the arts, and going to India was the goal of painters, poets, and artisans from as far away as the Mediterranean. Apparently, the generosity of the Moguls made it difficult to refuse a trip to India. It is said that the Moguls would reward a poet with his weight in gold.

Reading Check **Describing** What was the "Akbar style" of art?

SECTION 3 ASSESSMENT

Checking for Understanding

1. **Define** zamindar, suttee.
2. **Identify** Babur, Akbar, Shah Jahan, Aurangzeb.
3. **Locate** Khyber Pass, Delhi, Deccan Plateau, Calcutta, Chennai, Taj Mahal, Agra.
4. **Describe** the impact of the Moguls on the Hindu and Muslim peoples of the Indian subcontinent. How did the reign of Aurangzeb weaken Mogul rule in India?
5. **Summarize** the problems Shah Jahan faced during his rule. How did the rule of Shah Jahan come to an end?

Critical Thinking

6. **Evaluate** What role did the British play in the decline of the Mogul Empire in India?
7. **Cause and Effect** Create a chart like the one below listing the events that led to the decline of the Mogul Empire and tell how each contributed to the empire's decline.

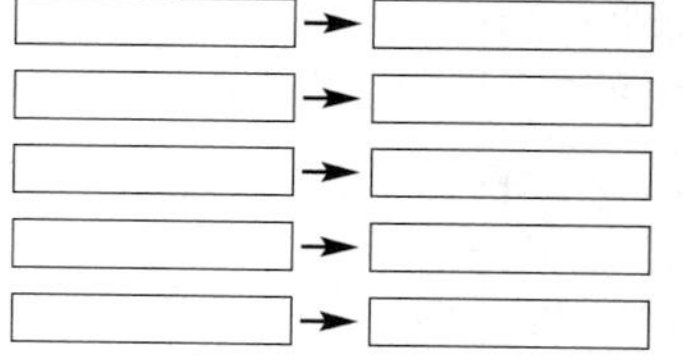

Analyzing Visuals

8. **Examine** the photograph above of the Taj Mahal, built as a tomb for the wife of Shah Jahan. How does the Taj Mahal compare to other buildings created to house the dead, such as the pyramids of Egypt? Which type of tomb is more impressive, in your opinion?

Writing About History

9. **Descriptive Writing** When the British established trading posts in India, their influence spread throughout the country. Present a speech describing how India would have developed if the British had not colonized the country.

SECTION 3 ASSESSMENT

1. Key terms are in blue.
2. Babur *(p. 255)*; Akbar *(p. 256)*; Shah Jahan *(p. 257)*; Aurangzeb *(p. 257)*
3. See chapter maps.
4. Mogul rulers tolerant of other religions; later attempts to force Hindus to convert led to domestic unrest.
5. had a nearly empty treasury; military campaigns and building projects forced him to raise taxes; imprisoned by his son
6. British defeated Mogul armies, gained ability to collect taxes
7. Jahangir influenced by wife → weakened succession to throne; Shah Jahan's expensive projects → government forced to raise taxes; Aurangzeb's strict social rules → domestic unrest; Aurangzeb's religious intolerance → Hindu revolt; arrival of British → weakened internal control
8. Answers will vary.
9. Answers will vary.

EYEWITNESS TO HISTORY

An Elephant Fight for the King's Entertainment

FRANÇOIS BERNIER WAS A WELL-TRAVELED Frenchman who visited India during the mid-seventeenth century. In this excerpt from his account of the visit, he describes a festival just outside the Red Fort at Delhi for the amusement of the emperor.

"The festivals generally conclude with an amusement unknown in Europe—a combat between two elephants; which takes place in the presence of all the people on the sandy space near the river: the King, the principal ladies of the court, and the nobles viewing the spectacle from different apartments in the fortress.

A wall of earth is raised three or four feet wide and five or six high. The two ponderous beasts meet one another face to face, on opposite sides of the wall, each having a couple of riders, that the place of the man who sits on the shoulders, for the purpose of guiding the elephant with a large iron hook, may immediately be supplied if he should be thrown down. The riders animate the elephants either by soothing words, or by chiding them as cowards, and urge them on with their heels, until the poor creatures approach the wall and are brought to the attack. The shock is tremendous, and it appears surprising that they ever survive the dreadful wounds and blows inflicted with their teeth, their heads, and their trunks. The stronger or more courageous elephant passes on and attacks his opponent, and, putting him to flight, pursues and fastens upon him with so much obstinacy, that the animals can be separated only by means of fireworks, which are made to explode between them; for they are naturally timid, and have a particular dread of fire, which is the reason why elephants have been used with so very little advantage in armies since the use of fire-arms.

This woodcut captures the fierceness of elephant fights.

The fight of these noble creatures is attended with much cruelty. It frequently happens that some of the riders are trodden underfoot; and killed on the spot. . . . So imminent is the danger considered, that on the day of combat the unhappy men take the same formal leave of their wives and children as if condemned to death. . . . The mischief with which this amusement is attended does not always end with the death of the rider: it happens that some spectators are knocked down and trampled upon by the elephants."

—**François Bernier, *Travels in the Mogul Empire***

Analyzing Primary Sources

1. What was the purpose of the elephant fights?
2. Did the elephant riders enjoy the sport? Explain your answer.
3. What other examples of animal fights can you think of? Why do you think people across cultures are entertained by watching such spectacles?

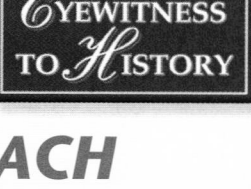

TEACH

Analyzing Primary Sources
Ask students to study the woodcut. How do the positions and postures of the onlookers contrast with the violence of what they are watching? How would students compare these elephant fights with bullfights? With other fights between animals that are engineered by humans for their "amusement"?

Who obviously has the French traveler's sympathy? *(the elephants)* How can you tell? *(use of "poor creatures," dreadful wounds and blows," "noble creatures")* Why does the Frenchman describe the riders as unhappy? How do the students think these riders were chosen? **L1**

ANSWERS TO ANALYZING PRIMARY SOURCES

1. to amuse the emperor
2. no; some of them were trodden underfoot and killed on the spot
3. Answers will vary. The ancient Romans enjoyed fights between animals and between animals and gladiators. Modern bullfighting carries on this tradition. Cockfighting was practiced extensively in ancient Persia, Greece, and Rome. It was popular in England for centuries before it was outlawed. It remains popular in parts of Latin America and Asia. Dogfighting was also popular and breeds such as boxers, bulldogs, and terriers were bred for that purpose. People enjoy these sports because of the thrill of real or implied danger and control over animals that the sports afford spectators. Today, many people consider these fights cruel to the animals.

CHAPTER 8 ASSESSMENT and ACTIVITIES

GLENCOE TECHNOLOGY

MindJogger Videoquiz

Use the **MindJogger Videoquiz** to review Chapter 8 content.

 Available in VHS.

Using Key Terms

1. zamindars **2.** grand vizier **3.** shah **4.** janissaries **5.** ulema **6.** harem **7.** Pashas **8.** sultan **9.** orthodoxy **10.** anarchy **11.** Gunpowder empires

Reviewing Key Facts

12. Ottomans dominated the Balkans and the Anatolian Peninsula.

13. major contribution was in architecture, especially the magnificent mosques, including the Süleymaniye Mosque in Istanbul, modeled partly on the Hagia Sophia; also silk wall hangings and wool and cotton rugs which boasted distinctive designs and color schemes

14. Turkish and Persian

15. He wanted people throughout the empire to know him.

16. carpets

17. He used advanced weapons, including artillery, and swift cavalry attacks.

18. custom of suttee, levying of illegal taxes, gambling, drinking

19. Mogul forces imprisoned their British captives in this underground prison. The intense heat and crowded space killed all but 23 of the 146 British captives.

20. it was believed that the company would increase British trade and expand British influence in India; France

21. Taj Mahal; new architectural and painting styles that combined Indian and Persian styles

Thinking Critically

22. Ottomans were Sunni Muslims who were tolerant of non-Muslims. Ottoman sultans led people, but the ulema acted as the supreme religious authority. Islamic law and customs were applied to all Muslims in the Ottoman Empire. Women were subject to some religious restrictions, but they could not be forced into marriages and they could seek divorce. The Safavids were Shiite Muslims led by the shah, who was supposed to be a direct descendant of Muhammad. The Shiites did not tolerate other religions, and they killed Sunni Muslims when they captured Baghdad and destroyed the city. The Shiites isolated women and forced them to wear veils.

23. Women gained considerable power within the palace in Ottoman society, and some served as senior officials or governors. In Mogul society women went to war and served as political advisors to the emperor. They took active roles in business and literary activities.

Writing About History

24. They were all "gunpowder empires" whose founders used advanced weaponry—firearms—to conquer them. Firearms allowed smaller forces to overcome

Using Key Terms

1. Mogul officials called _____ kept a portion of the taxes paid by peasants as their salaries.
2. The _____ led the meetings of the sultan's imperial council and served as his chief minister.
3. The _____ was the ruler of the Safavid Empire.
4. Boys from Christian families were recruited and trained as _____, the elite of the army.
5. The _____ administered the sultan's legal system and schools for educating Muslims.
6. The sultan's private living quarters was called the _____.
7. _____ collected taxes for the sultan.
8. The _____ was the political and military leader of the Ottoman Empire.
9. Adherence to traditional religious beliefs, called religious _____, increased as the Safavid dynasty started to decline.
10. A state of lawlessness or political disorder due to the absence of governmental authority is called _____.
11. _____ were formed by conquerors who had mastered the technology of firearms.

Reviewing Key Facts

12. **Geography** What effect did the capture of Constantinople have on Ottoman expansion?
13. **Culture** List and describe the Ottoman Empire's main contributions to world art.
14. **History** What two major ethnic groups were included in Safavid society?
15. **Government** Why did the shah have his physical features engraved in drinking cups?
16. **Economics** What Safavid goods were prized throughout the world?
17. **Science and Technology** How was Babur able to capture an enemy force nearly 10 times the size of his forces?
18. **Culture** What were the social evils Aurangzeb tried to eliminate?
19. **History** What happened at the Black Hole of Calcutta?
20. **Economics** Why was the British East India Company empowered to act on behalf of the British Crown? What other countries had financial interests in India?
21. **Culture** List the artistic contributions of Mogul society.

Chapter Summary

The following table shows the characteristics of the Ottoman, Safavid, and Mogul Empires.

	Ottomans	Safavids	Moguls
Warfare	• Train janissaries • Conquer Constantinople	• Battle Ottomans • Ally with European states	• Conquer India • Battle Persians and British
Arts	• Make magnificent mosques, pottery, rugs, and jewelry	• Blend Persian and Turkish influences • Excel at carpet making and painting	• Combine Persian and Indian motifs • Excel at architecture and painting
Government	• The sultan governs through local rulers called pashas.	• The shah trains administrators.	• The emperor controls semi-independent states.
Trade	• Merchants are the privileged class.	• Geography limits trade.	• Trade with Europeans
Religion	• Sunni Muslim • Religious tolerance	• Shiite Muslim • Religious orthodoxy	• Muslim, Hindu • Religious tolerance
Women	• Religious restrictions • Can own land, inherit property, seek divorce, and hold senior government posts	• Religious restrictions • Are kept secluded and made to wear veils	• Some religious restrictions • Serve as warriors, landowners, political advisors, and businesspeople

Self-Check Quiz
Visit the *Glencoe World History—Modern Times* Web site at wh.mt.glencoe.com and click on **Chapter 8–Self-Check Quiz** to prepare for the Chapter Test.

Critical Thinking

22. Compare and Contrast Compare the role of religion in Ottoman and Safavid societies.

23. Analyzing How did women play prominent roles in the Ottoman and Mogul cultures?

Writing About History

24. Expository Writing The acquisition of new technology can affect a country's development in many ways. Explain how the use of firearms affected the establishment of the three Muslim empires and tell how that same technology affects present-day society in the United States.

Analyzing Sources

Read a foreign visitor's description of Indian life:

> ❝Their houses are built of mud with thatched roofs. Furniture there is little or none except some earthenware pots to hold water and for cooking and two beds, one for the man, the other for his wife; their bed cloths are scanty, merely a sheet or perhaps two, serving as under- and over-sheet. This is sufficient for the hot weather, but the bitter cold nights are miserable indeed, and they try to keep warm over little cow-dung fires.❞

25. What type of furnishings did Indian families have?

26. From reading this passage, what can you conclude about the lives of Indian people during the Mogul Empire? Find two other sources describing Indian life during this time period. Do they corroborate this description? How is the information in the other passages similar to or different from this?

Making Decisions

27. The struggles to become the next sultan were often bitter and prolonged. Sometimes, those who lost were executed by the person who successfully gained the position and the power. Why do you think this occurred? Can you think of a better alternative, one that would have smoothly paved the way for the future sultan and guaranteed the security of the position without eliminating competitors? Explain your plan clearly and persuasively.

Expansion of the Ottoman Empire, 1451–1566

Sultan	Dates	Conquered Territory
Mehmet II	1451–1481	• Anatolian Peninsula • Balkans • Constantinople (Istanbul)
Selim I	1512–1520	• Arabia • Egypt • Mesopotamia
Süleyman I	1520–1566	• Austria • Hungary • Libya

Analyzing Maps and Charts

28. Which sultan ruled the longest?

29. Which sultan did *not* expand the empire in Europe?

30. Do you think the Ottoman army or navy made more conquests? Explain your reasoning.

Applying Technology Skills

31. Using the Internet Religion was one of the unifying forces in the creation of the Ottoman, Safavid, and Mogul Empires. Using the Internet, research the history of Iraq, a country established on a religious basis. Write an essay explaining the role religion plays in present-day Iraq.

Standardized Test Practice

Directions: Choose the best answer to the following question.

How were the Ottoman and the Mogul rulers similar?

A They controlled the Indian subcontinent.
B They were principally Shiite Muslims.
C Although Muslims, they tolerated other religions.
D They invaded and then controlled the Balkans for about a century.

Test-Taking Tip: Look at each answer choice carefully and ask yourself, "Is this statement true for *both* empires?" By eliminating answer choices you know are incorrect, you can improve your chances of identifying the correct answer.

Have students visit the Web site at wh.mt.glencoe.com to review Chapter 8 and take the Self-Check Quiz.

29. Selim I

30. Answers will vary but should be supported by logic. Students might say army, as chart suggests expansion followed land routes.

Applying Technology Skills

31. Answers will vary depending on material found and current events.

Standardized Test Practice

Answer: C
Answer Explanation: Students should read the question carefully so they realize that they are looking for a statement that is true for *both,* and not just *one,* of the empires noted.

Bonus Question ?

Ask students to explain the following sentence about the Mogul rulers: "They combined Muslim with Hindu and even Persian cultural values in a unique social and cultural synthesis."

larger ones, as when the Moguls conquered North India and the Ottomans laid siege to Constantinople. Answers will vary, but might include armed robbery, school shootings, or other uses and abuses of firearms.

Analyzing Sources

25. some earthenware pots for cooking and two beds, one for the man and one for his wife

26. Most Indian families lived simple lives and had few possessions. They were very poor and were at the mercy of the elements.

Making Decisions

27. Answers will vary but should be supported by logical arguments.

Analyzing Maps and Charts

28. Süleyman I

Chapter 9 Resources

Timesaving Tools

TeacherWorks™ All-In-One Planner and Resource Center

- **Interactive Teacher Edition** Access your Teacher Wraparound Edition and your classroom resources with a few easy clicks.
- **Interactive Lesson Planner** Planning has never been easier! Organize your week, month, semester, or year with all the lesson helps you need to make teaching creative, timely, and relevant.

Use Glencoe's **Presentation Plus!** multimedia teacher tool to easily present dynamic lessons that visually excite your students. Using Microsoft PowerPoint® you can customize the presentations to create your own personalized lessons.

TEACHING TRANSPARENCIES

Graphic Organizer Student Activity 9 Transparency

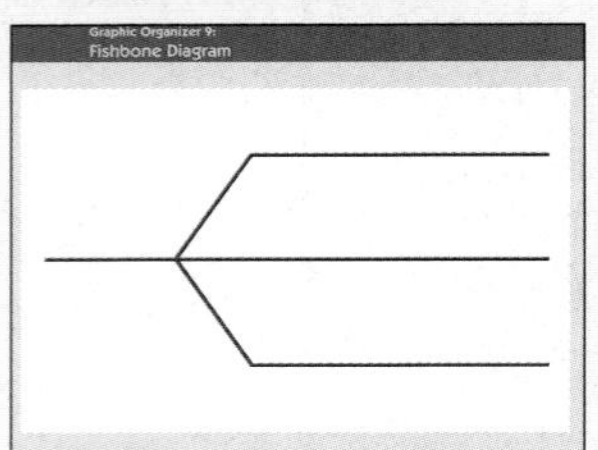

Chapter Transparency 9

Map Overlay Transparency 9

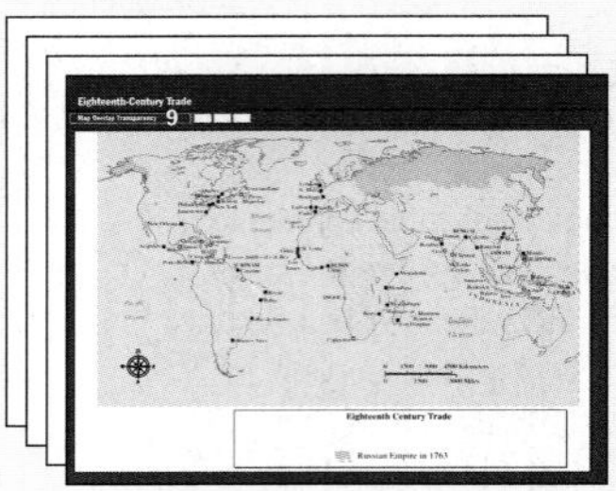

APPLICATION AND ENRICHMENT

Enrichment Activity 9

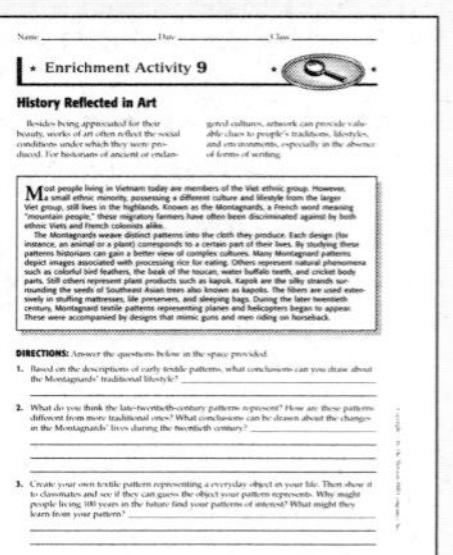

Primary Source Reading 9

History Simulation Activity 9

Historical Significance Activity 9

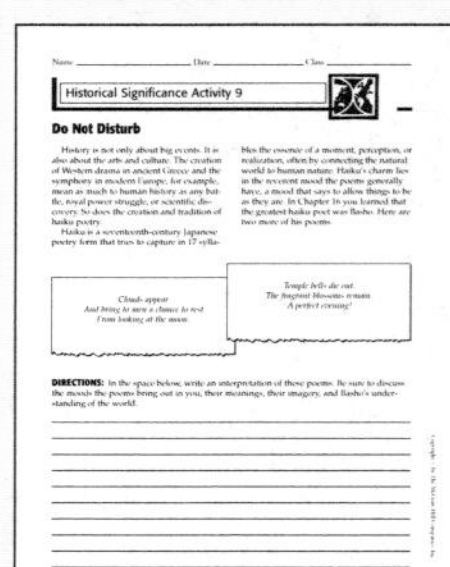

Cooperative Learning Activity 9

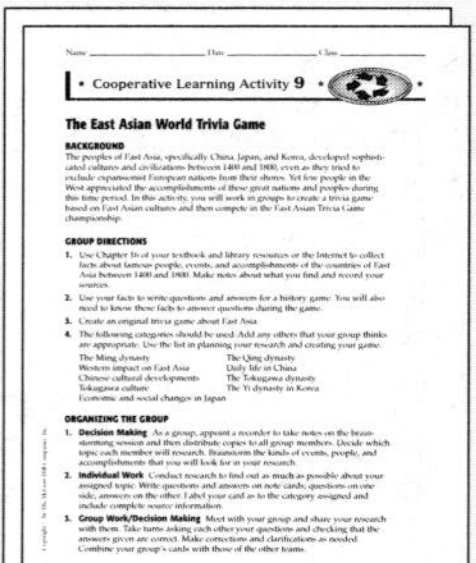

A&E HOME VIDEO. Biography® THE HISTORY CHANNEL®

The following videotape program is available from Glencoe as a supplement to Chapter 9:

- **China's Forbidden City** (ISBN 0–7670–0649–6)

To order, call Glencoe at 1–800–334–7344. To find classroom resources to accompany this video, check the following home pages:
A&E Television: www.aande.com
The History Channel: www.historychannel.com

Chapter 9 Resources

Review and Reinforcement

Linking Past and Present Activity 9

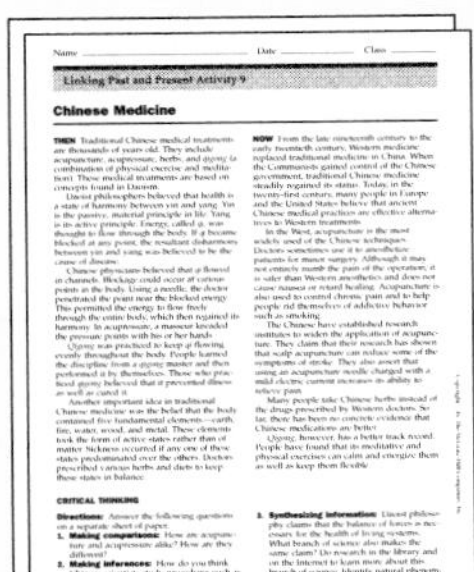

Time Line Activity 9

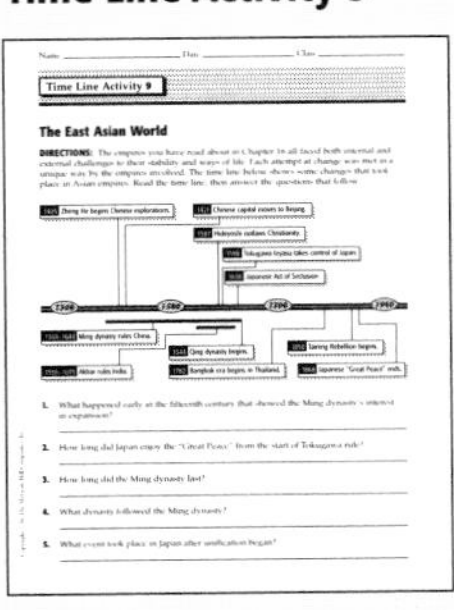

Reteaching Activity 9

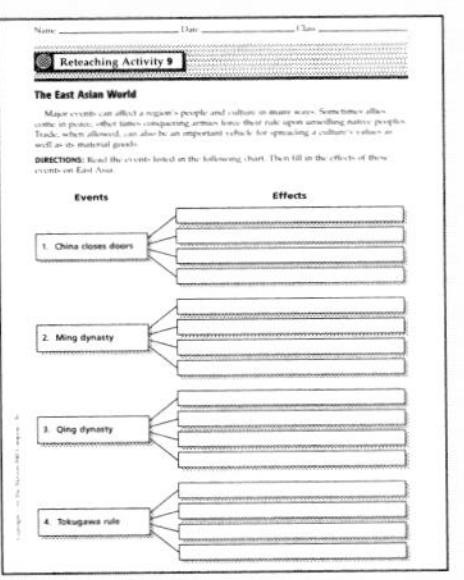

Vocabulary Activity 9

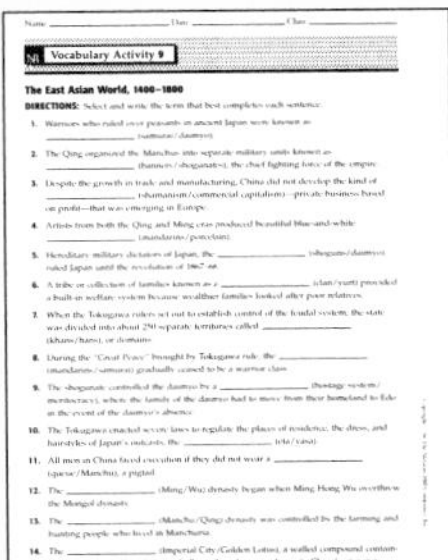

Critical Thinking Skills Activity 9

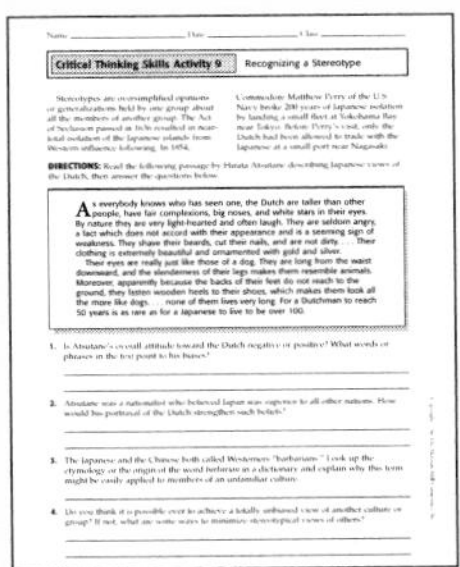

Assessment and Evaluation

Chapter 9 Test Form A

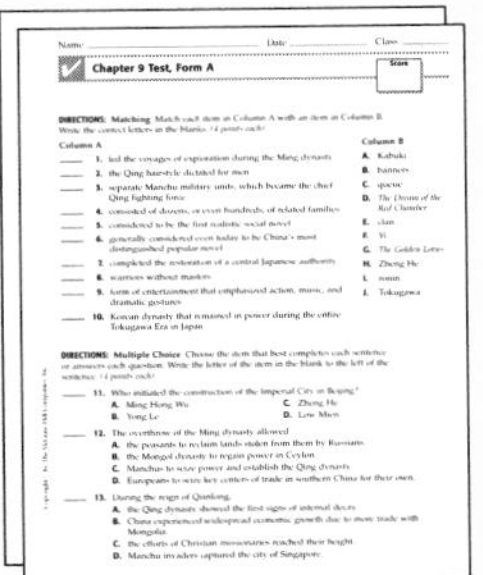

Chapter 9 Test Form B

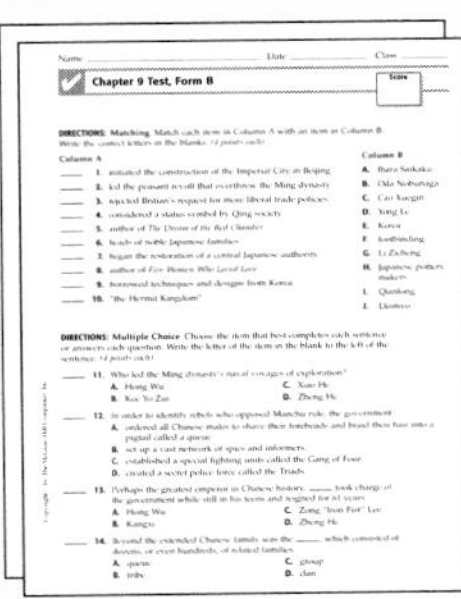

Performance Assessment Activity 9

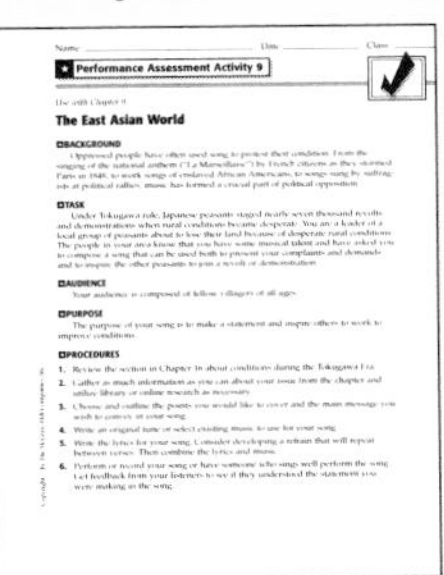

ExamView® Pro Testmaker CD-ROM

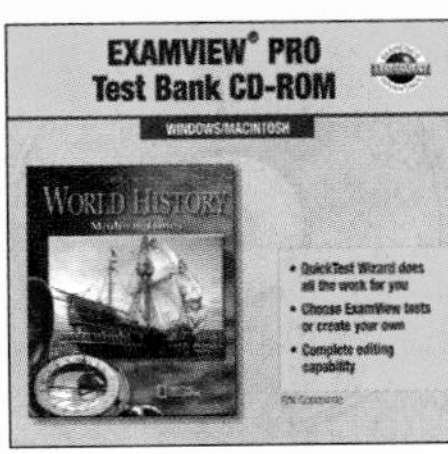

Standardized Test Skills Practice Workbook Activity 9

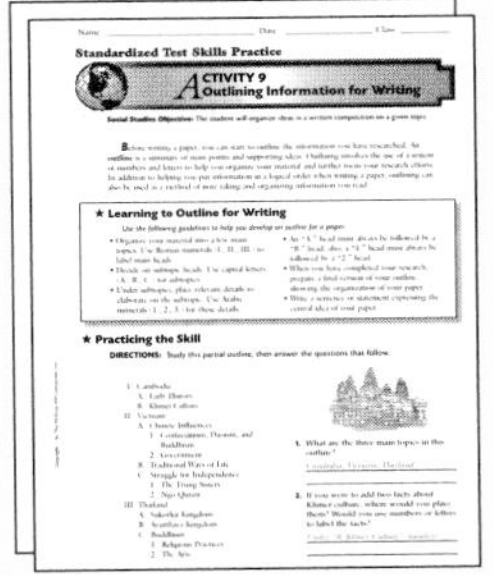

Interdisciplinary Activities

Mapping History Activity 9

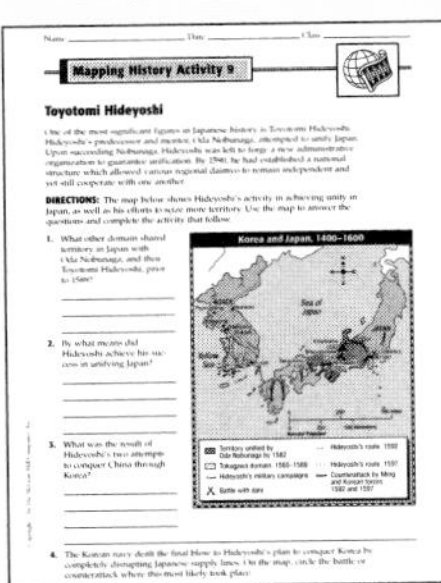

World Art and Music Activity 9

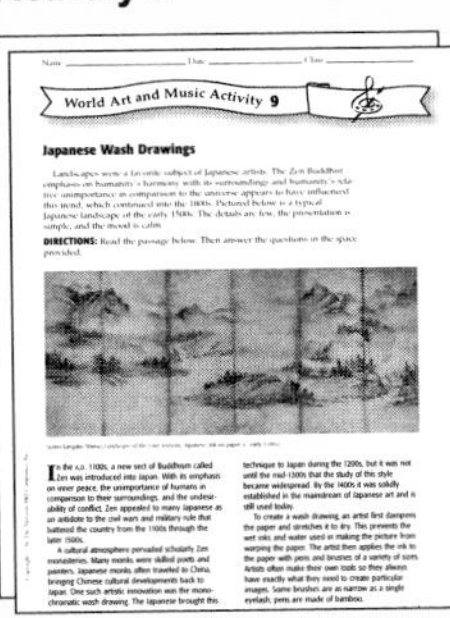

History and Geography Activity 9

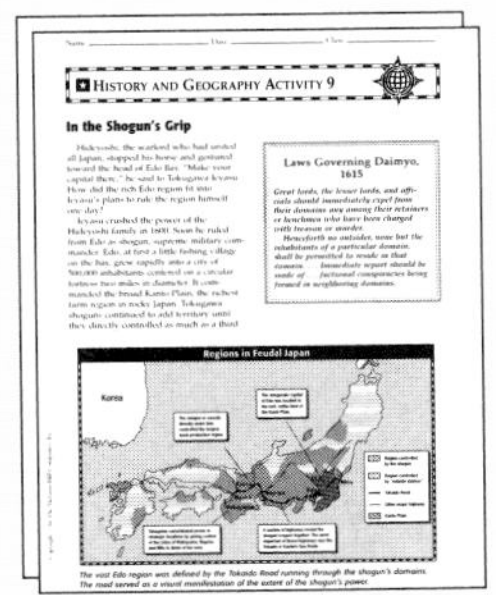

People in World History Activity 9

Multimedia

- Vocabulary PuzzleMaker CD-ROM
- Interactive Tutor Self-Assessment CD-ROM
- ExamView® Pro Testmaker CD-ROM
- Audio Program
- World History Primary Source Document Library CD-ROM
- MindJogger Videoquiz
- Presentation Plus! CD-ROM
- TeacherWorks CD-ROM
- Interactive Student Edition CD-ROM

- The World History—Modern Times Video Program

Spanish Resources

The following Spanish language materials are available in the Spanish Resources Binder:

- Spanish Guided Reading Activities
- Spanish Reteaching Activities
- Spanish Quizzes and Tests
- Spanish Vocabulary Activities
- Spanish Summaries

Chapter 9 Resources

SECTION RESOURCES

Daily Objectives	Reproducible Resources	Multimedia Resources
SECTION 1 **China at Its Height** 1. Summarize how China opened its doors to Europeans but closed those doors when it observed the effect of Western ideas on Chinese society. 2. Discuss how Chinese art and culture flourished between 1500 and 1800.	Reproducible Lesson Plan 9–1 Daily Lecture and Discussion Notes 9–1 Guided Reading Activity 9–1* Section Quiz 9–1* Reading Essentials and Study Guide 9–1	Daily Focus Skills Transparency 9–1 Interactive Tutor Self-Assessment CD-ROM ExamView® Pro Testmaker CD-ROM Presentation Plus! CD-ROM
SECTION 2 **Chinese Society and Culture** 1. Describe the rapid increase in population that led to rural land shortages. 2. Summarize Chinese society and its organization around the family. 3. Relate how architecture, decorative arts, and literature flourished during this period.	Reproducible Lesson Plan 9–2 Daily Lecture and Discussion Notes 9–2 Guided Reading Activity 9–2* Section Quiz 9–2* Reading Essentials and Study Guide 9–2	Daily Focus Skills Transparency 9–2 Interactive Tutor Self-Assessment CD-ROM ExamView® Pro Testmaker CD-ROM Presentation Plus! CD-ROM
SECTION 3 **Tokugawa Japan and Korea** 1. Identify the three powerful political figures who unified Japan. 2. Describe how between 1500 and 1800, Japan experienced many peasant uprisings. 3. Explain why Korea could not withstand invasions by the Japanese and Manchus.	Reproducible Lesson Plan 9–3 Daily Lecture and Discussion Notes 9–3 Guided Reading Activity 9–3* Section Quiz 9–3* Reteaching Activity 9* Reading Essentials and Study Guide 9–3	Daily Focus Skills Transparency 9–3 Interactive Tutor Self-Assessment CD-ROM ExamView® Pro Testmaker CD-ROM Presentation Plus! CD-ROM

0:00 **OUT OF TIME?**
Assign the Chapter 9 **Reading Essentials and Study Guide.**

*Also Available in Spanish

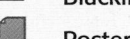

 Blackline Master  Transparency  CD-ROM DVD
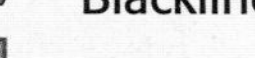 Poster Music Program Audio Program  Videocassette

Chapter 9 Resources

NATIONAL GEOGRAPHIC **Teacher's Corner**

INDEX TO NATIONAL GEOGRAPHIC MAGAZINE

The following articles relate to this chapter:

- "Sumo," by T.R. Reid, July 1997.
- "China's Gold Coast," by Mike Edwards, March 1997.

NGS ONLINE

Access National Geographic's new dynamic MapMachine Web site and other geography resources at:
www.nationalgeographic.com
www.nationalgeographic.com/maps

KEY TO ABILITY LEVELS

Teaching strategies have been coded.

- **L1** BASIC activities for all students
- **L2** AVERAGE activities for average to above-average students
- **L3** CHALLENGING activities for above-average students
- **ELL** ENGLISH LANGUAGE LEARNER activities

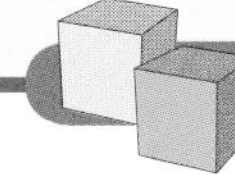

Block Schedule

Activities that are suited to use within the block scheduling framework are identified by:

WORLD HISTORY Online

Use our Web site for additional resources. All essential content is covered in the Student Edition.

You and your students can visit www.wh.mt.glencoe.com, the Web site companion to *Glencoe World History—Modern Times.* This innovative integration of electronic and print media offers your students a wealth of opportunities. The student text directs students to the Web site for the following options:

- **Chapter Overviews**
- **Self-Check Quizzes**
- **Student Web Activities**
- **Textbook Updates**

Answers to the Student Web Activities are provided for you in the **Web Activity Lesson Plans.** Additional Web resources and Interactive Tutor Puzzles are also available.

From the Classroom of...

N. Elijah Sivin
Poly Prep Country Day School
Brooklyn, New York

Celebrating Chinese Culture

As with other societies, the Chinese hold festivals to celebrate special occasions. People come together to acknowledge the event—a wedding or 60th birthday, perhaps—and to share food and one another's company. Have your students use the festival custom of sharing to celebrate Chinese culture itself.

Divide the class into pairs, then ask each pair to select a feature of Chinese culture. It might be opera, food preparation, martial arts, the Forbidden City, the yin/yang symbol, poetry, calligraphy, papermaking, the silk trade, Daoism, Confucianism, Buddhism, and so on.

Instead of food, the students will share knowledge they have gained. Each pair of students will prepare a visual and verbal display explaining their chosen subject. Individual students can write evaluations describing particular displays or features they particularly liked. A sampling of evaluations can be read aloud to the class.

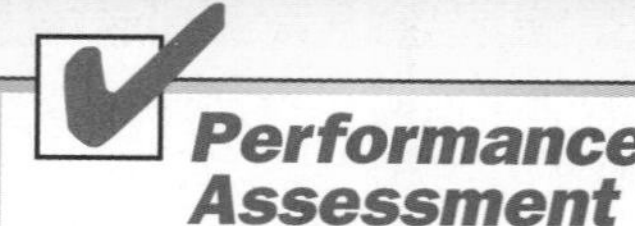

Performance Assessment

Refer to Activity 9 in the Performance Assessment Activities and Rubrics booklet.

The Impact Today

Relationships between Eastern and Western countries have often been marked by cultural misunderstandings. Have students explain why it is important for people in all cultures to understand and be familiar with cultural differences. **L1**

GLENCOE TECHNOLOGY

The World History—Modern Times Video Program

To learn more about the Japanese warrior class, students can view the Chapter 9 video, "The Samurai," from **The World History—Modern Times Video Program.**

MindJogger Videoquiz

Use the **MindJogger Videoquiz** to preview Chapter 9 content.

Available in VHS.

CHAPTER 9 The East Asian World

1400–1800

Key Events

As you read this chapter, look for the key events in the history of the East Asian world.

- *China closed its doors to the Europeans during the period of exploration between 1500 and 1800.*
- *The Ming and Qing dynasties produced blue-and-white porcelain and new literary forms.*
- *Emperor Yong Le began renovations on the Imperial City, which was expanded by succeeding emperors.*

The Impact Today

The events that occurred during this time still impact our lives today.

- *China today exports more goods than it imports.*
- *Chinese porcelain is collected and admired throughout the world.*
- *The Forbidden City in China is an architectural wonder that continues to attract people from around the world.*
- *Relations with China today still require diplomacy and skill.*

World History—Modern Times Video *The Chapter 9 video, "The Samurai," chronicles the role of the warrior class in Japanese history.*

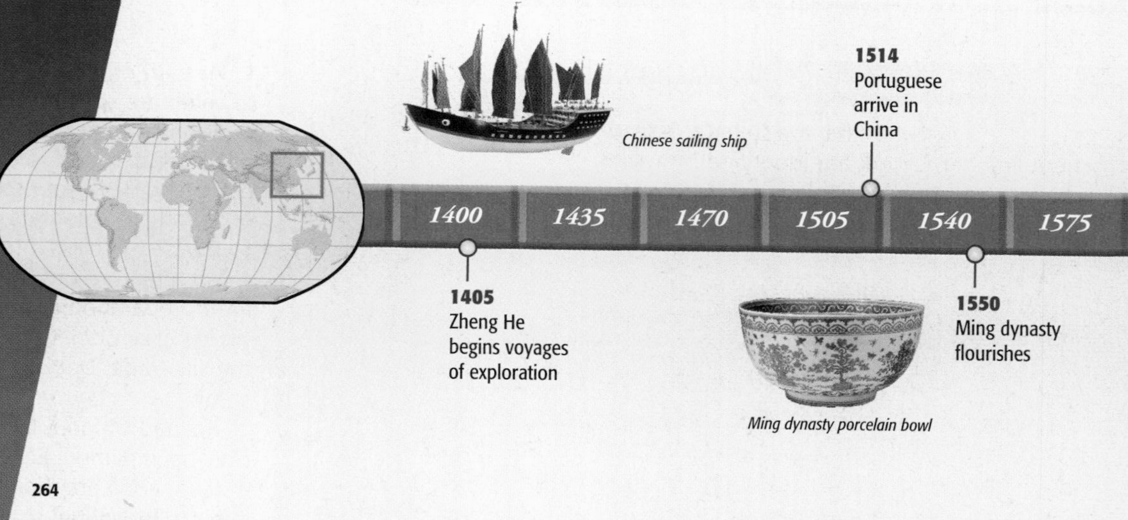
1514
Portuguese arrive in China
1400
1435
1470
1505
1540
1575
1405
Zheng He begins voyages of exploration
1550
Ming dynasty flourishes

Chinese sailing ship

Ming dynasty porcelain bowl

264

TWO-MINUTE LESSON LAUNCHER

Ask students to identify products they use every day (in the United States) that are made in Asia. Then ask students whether they can identify products made in the United States that are used in Asian countries. Ask students to analyze the products exported by the United States and by Asian countries. Do these products fall into categories? For example, does Japan export primarily electronics? What categories of products are exported by the United States? Do the United States or any Asian countries export culture or ideas? Ask students to examine their assumptions about American music, video, movies, or fashion. Do they assume that American products are superior? Why? **L3**

The Forbidden City in the heart of Beijing contains hundreds of buildings.

1598 Japanese unification begins

1603 Tokugawa rule begins "Great Peace"

1644 Last Ming emperor dies

1661 Emperor Kangxi begins 61-year reign

1750 Edo is one of the world's largest cities

1793 Britain's King George III sends trade mission to China

1796 White Lotus rebellion weakens Qing dynasty

1610 *1645* *1680* *1715* *1750* *1785*

Japanese samurai

HISTORY Online

Chapter Overview
Visit the *Glencoe World History—Modern Times* Web site at wh.mt.glencoe.com and click on **Chapter 9–Chapter Overview** to preview chapter information.

Introducing CHAPTER 9

Chapter Objectives

After studying this chapter, students should be able to:

1. trace the key events in the history of East Asia during the period from 1400 to 1800;
2. identify the major cultural and social elements in China and Japan.

Chapter Overview
Introduce students to chapter content and key terms by having them access **Chapter Overview 9** at wh.mt.glencoe.com.

Time Line Activity

As students read the chapter, they can review the time line on pages 264 to 265. Have students contrast the impact of exploration on the exploring countries with the isolation of the East Asian world. *(While other powerful countries were expanding trade and colonizing, the East Asian world was not. One result was that the European nations had a major impact on the development of territories such as North and South America, while the Chinese had little impact.)* **L2**

MORE ABOUT THE ART

The Forbidden City For five hundred years, the Forbidden City was the imperial palace of the Ming and Qing dynasties. The Forbidden City is the largest palace complex in the world and is surrounded by a moat and protective wall. Yellow, the symbol of the royal family, is the dominant color. There are dozens of halls and courtyards where the emperor, his family, and hundreds of retainers lived surrounded by treasures, artwork, and gardens. Commoners and even high-level officials were not allowed to enter the grounds. The last emperor was forced out of the Forbidden Palace in 1924. Today it is open to the public as a museum.

CHAPTER PREVIEW

Introducing

A Story That Matters

Depending on the ability levels of your students, select from the following questions to reinforce the reading of *A Story That Matters.*

- Why do many people assume that their ideas and products are better than those of foreign peoples? *(Answers will vary.)*
- Why are attempts to stop change almost certainly doomed to failure? *(Answers will vary. Students should support their ideas and opinions with specific examples.)*
- What obstacles did the participants in this meeting between the English and the Chinese have to overcome? *(Both parties spoke different languages and had different, conflicting protocols.)* **L1 L2**

About the Art

Before photography, important events were commemorated by artists in paintings and drawings. Sometimes an artist would flatter the patron, the individual paying for the artwork. To compress events that took place over several days into one painting, the artist might take some liberties with the actual order of events. Remind students that when looking at art, it is important to know the purpose of the artwork: the who, what, when, where, and why of its creation.

CHAPTER PREVIEW A Story That Matters

Emperor Qianlong

The meeting of Emperor Qianlong and Lord George Macartney

Mission to China

In 1793, a British official named Lord George Macartney led a mission on behalf of King George III to China. Macartney carried with him British products that he thought would impress the Chinese so much that they would be eager to open their country to trade with Great Britain. King George wrote in his letter to the Chinese emperor: "No doubt the exchange of goods between nations far apart tends to their mutual convenience, industry, and wealth."

Emperor Qianlong, however, was not impressed: "You, O King, are so inclined toward our civilization that you have sent a special envoy across the seas . . . to present your native products as an expression of your thoughtfulness. . . . As a matter of fact, the virtue and prestige of the Celestial Dynasty having spread far and wide, the kings of the myriad nations come by land and sea with all sorts of precious things. Consequently, there is nothing we lack, as your principal envoy and others have themselves observed. We have never set much store on strange or ingenious objects, nor do we need any more of your country's manufactures."

Macartney was shocked. He had believed that the Chinese would recognize, as he said, "that superiority which Englishmen, wherever they go, cannot conceal." An angered Macartney compared the Chinese Empire to "an old, crazy, first-rate man-of-war [naval warship]." It had once awed its neighbors "merely by [its] bulk and appearance" but was now destined, under poor leadership, to be "dashed to pieces on the shore."

Why It Matters

Between 1500 and 1800, China experienced one of its most glorious eras. The empire expanded, and Chinese culture flourished. In 1514, Portuguese ships arrived on the coast of China. At first, the new arrivals were welcomed. During the seventeenth century, however, most of the European merchants and missionaries were forced to leave. Chinese leaders adopted a "closed country" policy to keep out foreign ideas and protect their values and institutions. Until 1800, China was little affected by events taking place outside the region. Japan and Korea, too, remained isolated.

History and You Visit the Web site of a major art museum. Locate artifacts in their permanent collection from the dynasties discussed in this chapter, and explain how they typify the art of the time period.

HISTORY AND YOU

Today, there are several nations that practice a "closed country" policy. Ask students to do research to identify those nations. Point out to students that our culture has been enriched in many ways by other cultures. Ask students to brainstorm the ways in which our language, cuisine, music, and holiday customs have been influenced by other cultures. Social groups can also practice closed country policies. Have students discuss how social groups at their high school practice closed country policies through vocabulary, clothing, and activities associated with that social group. Do any of the groups practice a more "open door" policy? Have students identify the advantages and disadvantages of both types of policies. **L2**

SECTION 1 China at Its Height

Guide to Reading

Main Ideas
- China opened its doors to Europeans but closed those doors when it observed the effect of Western ideas on Chinese society.
- Between 1500 and 1800, Chinese art and culture flourished.

Key Terms
queue, banner

People to Identify
Ming, Zheng He, Manchu, Qing, Kangxi

Places to Locate
Guangzhou, Beijing, Manchuria, Taiwan

Preview Questions
1. What was remarkable about the naval voyages under Emperor Yong Le?
2. How did the Manchus gain the support of the Chinese?

Reading Strategy
Compare and Contrast As you read this section, complete a diagram like the one below to compare and contrast the achievements of the two dynasties.

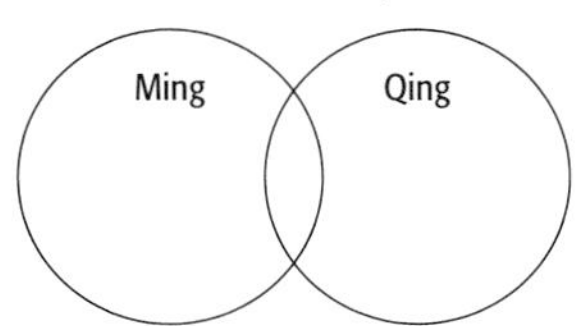

Preview of Events

1500 · 1540 · 1580 · 1620 · 1660 · 1700 · 1740

- **1514** China allows Portuguese to occupy Macao
- **1630** Major epidemic reduces the population in many areas
- **1736** Emperor Qianlong begins reign

Ferdinand Verbiest, a European missionary, reported on his experience with the Chinese emperor:

> ❝This emperor [Kangxi] [punishes] offenders of the highest as well as lowest class with marvelous impartiality, according to their misdeeds, depriving them of rank and dignity. . . . On this account men of all ranks and dignities whatsoever, even the nearest to him in blood, stand in his presence with the deepest awe, and recognize him as sole ruler. . . . The same goodwill he showed us on many other occasions, to wit, in frequently sending us dishes from his own table to ours. He even ordered us sometimes to be entertained in his own tent.❞
>
> —***Sources of World History,*** **Mark A. Kishlansky, ed.,1995**

Emperor Kangxi

Kangxi was one of the greatest of the many strong emperors who ruled China during the Ming and Qing dynasties.

The Ming Dynasty

As you read this section, you will discover how the decision to stop the voyages of exploration in the 1400s caused China to turn inward for four centuries, away from foreign trade and toward agriculture.

The Mongol dynasty in China was overthrown in 1368. The founder of the new dynasty took the title of Ming Hong Wu (the Ming Martial Emperor). This was the beginning of the **Ming** dynasty, which lasted until 1644.

Under Ming emperors, China extended its rule into Mongolia and central Asia and briefly reconquered Vietnam. Along the northern frontier, the Chinese

1 FOCUS

Section Overview

This section describes the Ming and Qing dynasties and the "closed country" policy of China.

BELLRINGER
Skillbuilder Activity

Project transparency and have students answer questions.

Available as a blackline master.

Daily Focus Skills Transparency 9–1

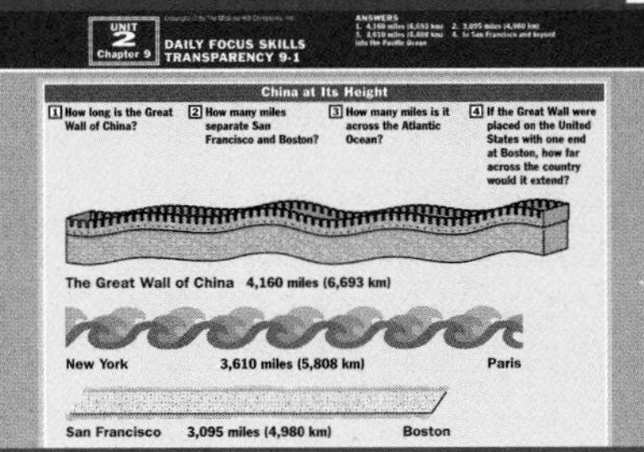

Guide to Reading

Answers to Graphic: Ming: Answers include extended rule into Mongolia, strengthened the Great Wall, increased manufacturing, conducted voyages of exploration; Qing: pacified country, restored peace and prosperity; Ming and Qing: centralized government, used civil service exam

Preteaching Vocabulary: Have students look up and discuss the different definitions of *queue.* **L1**

SECTION RESOURCES

Reproducible Masters
- Reproducible Lesson Plan 9–1
- Daily Lecture and Discussion Notes 9–1
- Guided Reading Activity 9–1
- Section Quiz 9–1
- Reading Essentials and Study Guide 9–1

Transparencies
- Daily Focus Skills Transparency 9–1

Multimedia
- Interactive Tutor Self-Assessment CD-ROM
- ExamView® Pro Testmaker CD-ROM
- Presentation Plus! CD-ROM

2 TEACH

Geography *Skills*

Answers:

1. Quanzhou, Bangkok, Melaka, Chittagong, Calicut, Hormuz, Aden, Jeddah, Mogadishu, Malindi, Mombasa; over 15,000 miles (24,135 km) **L2**
2. Answers will vary depending on the city chosen. **L3**

Daily Lecture and Discussion Notes 9–1

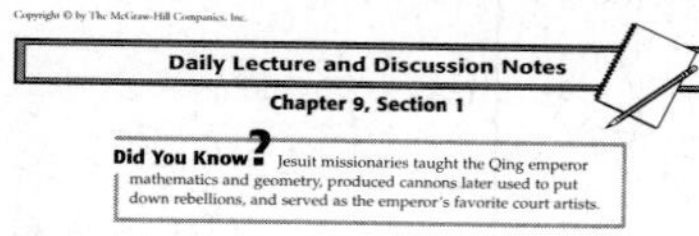

Daily Lecture and Discussion Notes

Chapter 9, Section 1

Did You Know? Jesuit missionaries taught the Qing emperor mathematics and geometry, produced cannons later used to put down rebellions, and served as the emperor's favorite court artists.

I. **The Ming Dynasty** *(pages 267–270)*

A. The **Ming** dynasty began with the overthrow of the Mongols in China in 1368. The Ming period lasted until 1644. China extended its rule into Mongolia and central Asia, and briefly reconquered Vietnam under the Ming emperors.

B. Ming rulers ran an effective government using a centralized bureaucracy staffed by officials who had taken the civil service examination. Ming emperors set up a nationwide school system. They completed the Grand Canal, on which grain was shipped south to north in China. The economy flourished. The Ming dynasty began a time of greatness in China.

C. Emperor Yong Le began construction of the Imperial City—known today as the Forbidden City—in Beijing in 1406. The Imperial City was the home to China's emperors for nearly 500 years.

D. Led by the court official **Zheng He,** China made seven voyages of exploration between 1405 and 1431. On the first, almost 28,000 men sailed on 62 ships. The fleet visited the western coast of India and city-states of East Africa. The voyages produced great profits, which alarmed Confucian traditionalist who thought trading was an unworthy activity. After the emperor Yong Le's death in 1424, the voyages halted.

E. In 1514 a Portuguese fleet arrived off the coast of China. The emperor was unimpressed with the Europeans, whom he considered at worst barbarians and at best "younger brothers" of the Chinese emperor, who was seen as the Son of Heaven. After outraging the Chinese with their behavior, the Portuguese were expelled from **Guangzhou** (Canton) but were allowed to occupy Macao.

F. Highly educated Jesuit missionaries made the trip to China and impressed Chinese officials with such devices as clocks and eyeglasses. The Jesuits were impressed with Chinese architecture and the printing of books. More importantly, both sides benefited from the exchange of ideas. The Jesuits were impressed with the teachings of Confucius, and they taught Christianity to the Chinese.

G. The Ming dynasty declined due to a series of weak rulers, government corruption, high taxes, low crop yields, peasant unrest, and a major epidemic in the 1630s. The suffering from the epidemic in part caused the peasant revolt led by Li Zicheng in 1644. He occupied **Beijing,** the capital, and the last Ming emperor committed suicide.

turn

123

Enrich

Have students research the voyages of Zheng He and then write a front-page newspaper article about the voyages. Include an interview with Zheng He. What did he accomplish? What did he see? **L2**

strengthened the Great Wall and made peace with the nomadic tribes that had troubled them for centuries.

At home, Ming rulers ran an effective government using a centralized bureaucracy staffed with officials chosen by the civil service examination system. They set up a nationwide school system. Manufactured goods were produced in workshops and factories in vastly higher numbers. New crops were introduced, which greatly increased food production. The Ming rulers also completed the Grand Canal, which made it possible to ship grain and other goods from southern to northern China. The Ming dynasty truly began a new era of greatness in Chinese history.

The Voyages of Zheng He Ming Hong Wu, founder of the dynasty, ruled from 1368 until 1398. After his death, his son Yong Le became emperor. This was after a four-year campaign to defeat the rightful heir. To establish the legitimacy of his rule, Yong Le built large monuments, strengthened the Great Wall, and restored Chinese rule over Vietnam.

In 1406, Yong Le began construction of the Imperial City in Beijing. In 1421 he moved the capital from Nanjing to Beijing, after construction was sufficiently far along. The Imperial City (known today as the Forbidden City) was created to convey power and prestige. For nearly 500 years the Imperial City was home to China's emperors. Yong Le died in 1424 and was buried with his wife and 16 concubines in a new cemetery for emperors outside of Beijing.

During his reign, Yong Le also sent a series of naval voyages into the Indian Ocean that sailed as far west as the eastern coast of Africa. Led by the court official **Zheng He** (JUNG HUH), seven voyages of exploration were made between 1405 and 1431. On the first voyage, nearly 28,000 men embarked on 62 ships. The largest ship was over 440 feet (134.1 m) long. (Columbus's Santa Maria was only 88 feet [26.8 m] long.) The fleet passed through Southeast Asia and visited the western coast of India and the city-states of East Africa. It returned with items unknown in China and information about the outside world. The emperor was especially fascinated by the giraffes from Africa, and he placed them in the imperial zoo.

The voyages led to enormous profits, which alarmed traditionalists within the bureaucracy. Some of them held the Confucian view that trading activities were unworthy. Shortly after Yong Le's death, the voyages were halted, never to be revived. One can only guess what difference it would have made if Zheng He's fleet had reached the Americas before Columbus did.

First Contacts with the West In 1514, a Portuguese fleet arrived off the coast of China. It was the first direct contact between the Chinese Empire and Europe since the journeys of Marco Polo.

At the time, the Ming government thought little of the arrival of the Portuguese. China was at the height of its power as the most magnificent civilization on

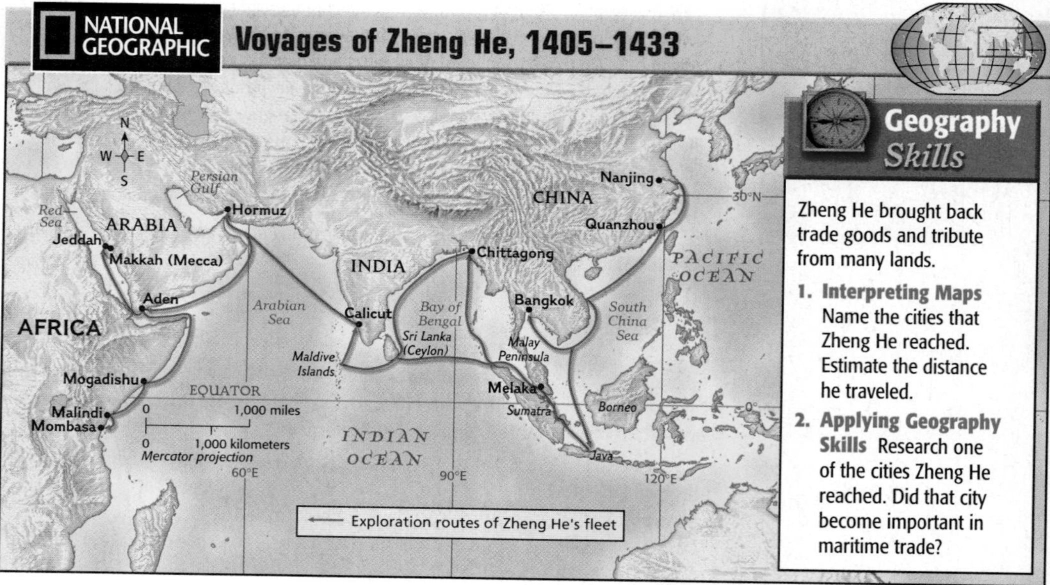

Geography Skills

Zheng He brought back trade goods and tribute from many lands.

1. **Interpreting Maps** Name the cities that Zheng He reached. Estimate the distance he traveled.
2. **Applying Geography Skills** Research one of the cities Zheng He reached. Did that city become important in maritime trade?

COOPERATIVE LEARNING ACTIVITY

Creating a Chart Organize students into two teams. Assign one team the Ming Dynasty, the other the Qing. Each team should make a chart that organizes the text's information about its assigned dynasty. Among the topics to be included are *Leaders, Religion, Trade Policies, Economics, European Contacts,* and *Cause of Decline.* Each team should determine responsibilities within the team for the six topics. The team members for each team should jointly decide on the format and organization of that team's chart. After they have been completed, the charts should be displayed for the entire class to see. **L1**

Earth. From the perspective of the emperor, the Europeans were only an unusual form of barbarian. To the Chinese ruler, the rulers of all other countries were simply "younger brothers" of the Chinese emperor, who was seen as the Son of Heaven.

The Portuguese soon outraged Chinese officials with their behavior. They were expelled from **Guangzhou** (Canton) but were allowed to occupy Macao.

At first, the Portuguese had little impact on Chinese society. Portuguese ships did carry goods between China and Japan but direct trade between Europe and China remained limited. Perhaps more important than trade, however, was the exchange of ideas.

Christian missionaries had also made the long voyage to China on European merchant ships. The Jesuits were among the most active. Many of them were highly educated men who brought along instruments, such as clocks, that impressed Chinese officials and made them more receptive to Western ideas.

Both sides benefited from this early cultural exchange. Chinese scholars marveled at their ability to read better with European eyeglasses. Christian missionaries were impressed with many aspects of Chinese civilization, such as the teachings of Confucius, the printing and availability of books, and Chinese architecture. Reports back home soon made Europeans even more curious about this great civilization on the other side of the world.

Fall of the Ming Dynasty After a period of prosperity and growth, the Ming dynasty gradually began to decline. During the late sixteenth century, a series of weak rulers led to a period of government corruption. High taxes, caused in part by this corruption, led to peasant unrest. Crop yields declined because of harsh weather.

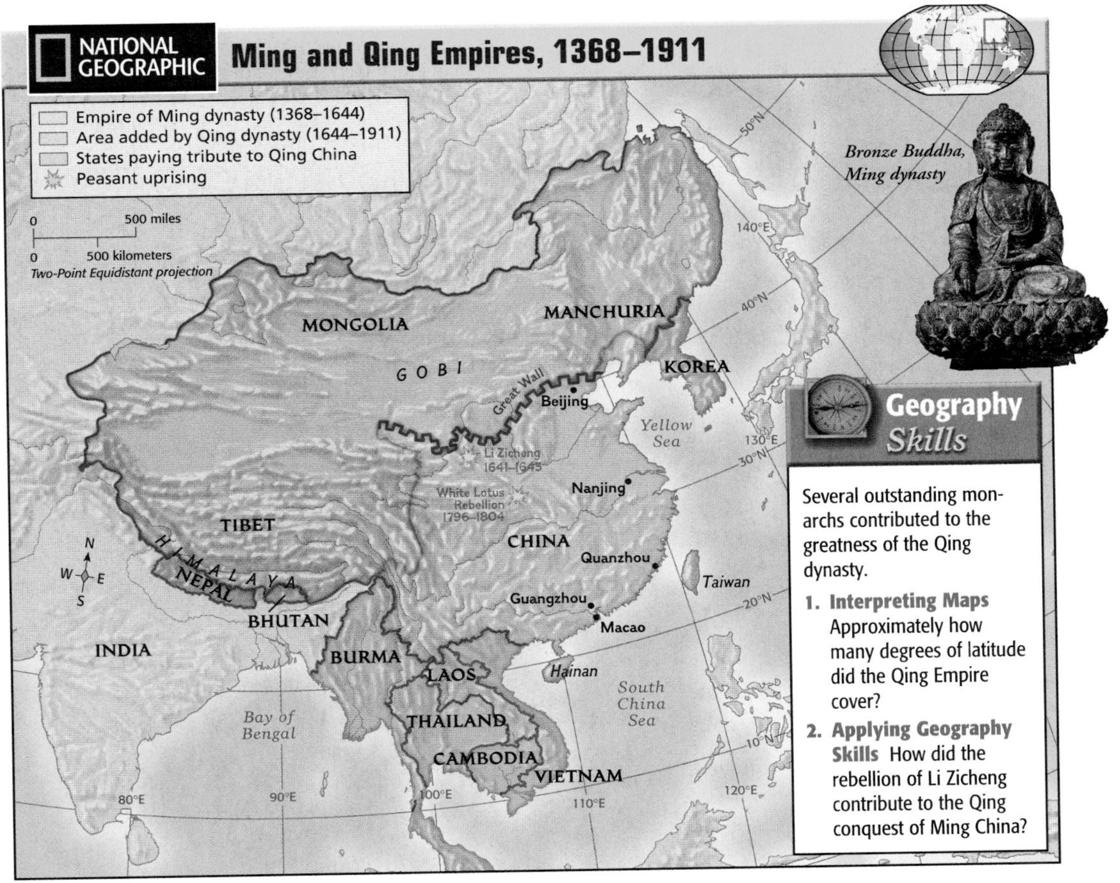

Geography Skills

Several outstanding monarchs contributed to the greatness of the Qing dynasty.

1. **Interpreting Maps** Approximately how many degrees of latitude did the Qing Empire cover?
2. **Applying Geography Skills** How did the rebellion of Li Zicheng contribute to the Qing conquest of Ming China?

COOPERATIVE LEARNING ACTIVITY

Staging A Debate The Chinese government prohibited its ships from sailing beyond the China Sea. This policy prevented Chinese owned ships from transporting goods to other lands. European captains transported Chinese goods wherever they could be sold. Divide the class into two groups. Have each group argue that this policy was or was not harmful to China's economy. Have students evaluate the arguments for sound reasoning, examples cited, and effectiveness of delivery. L3

For grading this activity, refer to the ***Performance Assessment Activity*** booklet.

Geography *Skills*

Answers:

1. approximately 70 degrees
2. When the rebels occupied the capital, the emperor committed suicide, which provided an opportunity for the Manchus to take over. L2

Guided Reading Activity 9–1

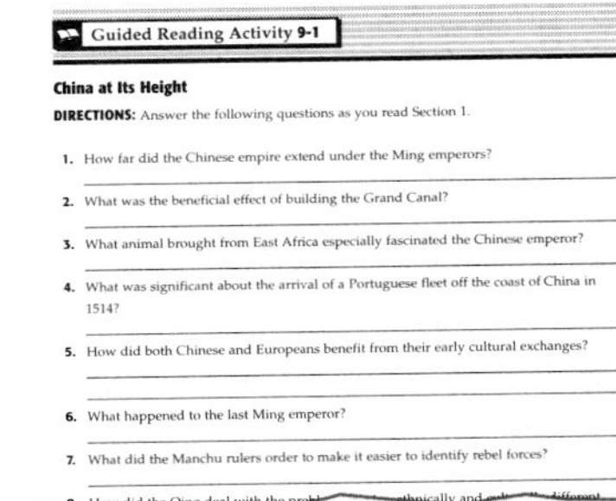

Name ______ Date ______ Class ______

Guided Reading Activity 9-1

China at Its Height

DIRECTIONS: Answer the following questions as you read Section 1.

1. How far did the Chinese empire extend under the Ming emperors?
2. What was the beneficial effect of building the Grand Canal?
3. What animal brought from East Africa especially fascinated the Chinese emperor?
4. What was significant about the arrival of a Portuguese fleet off the coast of China in 1514?
5. How did both Chinese and Europeans benefit from their early cultural exchanges?
6. What happened to the last Ming emperor?
7. What did the Manchu rulers order to make it easier to identify rebel forces?
8. How did the Qing deal with the prob...

Critical Thinking

Ask students to develop a hypothesis and supporting arguments about the Ming dynasty's policy of isolation. Was this policy an advantage or disadvantage to the Ming? L3

Who?What?Where?When?

Chinese New Year Although China today uses the Gregorian calendar, its traditional New Year is still celebrated in China and in Chinese communities outside China. The Chinese Dragon Dance, usually seen at the New Year celebration, dates back to the Sung dynasty. Other New Year traditions include housecleaning, paying debts, and giving to the poor.

CHAPTER 9
Section 1, 267–272

Reading Check

Answer: ran effective government using central bureaucracy with officials chosen by civil service examination system; extended rule into Mongolia and briefly reconquered Vietnam; strengthened Great Wall and made peace with nomadic tribes along northern border; set up nationwide school system; increased production of manufactured goods; introduced new crops; completed Grand Canal; began construction of new Imperial City in Beijing; conducted voyages of exploration

THE WAY IT WAS

Answers:

1. karate, judo, tae kwon do, kung fu, tai chi; empty-hand boxing, sparring, training in pairs, group exercises involving six or more athletes, weapons training
2. Answers will vary but may mention the influence of films and television. Student essays should include logical arguments and supporting examples.

CURRICULUM CONNECTION

Economics The Chinese government confined European traders to small trading areas. Paintings from the time depict British, Dutch and French flags flying over the same warehouse in China. Ask students to explain why it would have been unlikely to find this in any other part of the world in the eighteenth century. **L2**

In the 1630s, a major epidemic greatly reduced the population in many areas. One observer in a major city wrote, "There were few signs of human life in the streets and all that was heard was the buzzing of flies."

The suffering caused by the epidemic helped spark a peasant revolt led by Li Zicheng (LEE DZUH• CHUNG). The revolt began in central China and then spread to the rest of the country. In 1644, Li and his forces occupied the capital of **Beijing** (BAY• JING). The last Ming emperor committed suicide by hanging himself from a tree in the palace gardens.

The overthrow of the Ming dynasty created an opportunity for the **Manchus,** a farming and hunting people who lived northeast of the Great Wall in the area known today as **Manchuria.** The Manchus conquered Beijing, and Li Zicheng's army fell. The victorious Manchus then declared the creation of a new dynasty called the **Qing** (CHING), meaning "pure." This dynasty, created in 1644, remained in power until 1911.

Reading Check **Describing** What were the achievements of the Ming dynasty?

The Qing Dynasty

At first, the Chinese resisted the new rulers. At one point, rebels seized the island of **Taiwan** just off the coast of China. The new Manchu government evacuated the coastline across from the island in preparation for an attack on the rebels. To make it easier to identify the rebels, the government ordered all men to adopt Manchu dress and hairstyles. All Chinese males were to shave their foreheads and braid their hair into a pigtail called a **queue.** Those who refused were to be executed: "Lose your hair or lose your head."

The Manchus eventually adopted the Chinese political system and were gradually accepted as the legitimate rulers of the country. The Qing flourished under a series of strong early rulers. The emperors pacified the country, corrected serious social and economic ills, and restored peace and prosperity.

Qing Adaptations The Qing maintained the Ming political system but faced one major problem: the Manchus were ethnically and culturally different from their subject population. The Qing dealt with this reality in two ways.

THE WAY IT WAS

SPORTS & CONTESTS

The Martial Arts in China

The phrase *martial arts* refers to arts of combat and self-defense. Martial arts are a significant part of Asian history and culture. In recent years, they have become part of Western culture as well. Throughout the United States, for example, one can learn Japanese karate and judo, Korean tae kwon do, and Chinese kung fu and tai chi. Chinese martial arts are especially well known because of films featuring actors trained in the martial arts.

Chinese martial arts were already highly visible during the Han dynasty. Later, in 495, a Zen Buddhist monastery in Henan province developed methods of physical training that became Shaolin Quan. This style of boxing is known to the world today as kung fu.

Archery contest

270

COOPERATIVE LEARNING ACTIVITY

Preparing a Report Divide the class into two groups or teams. Assign one team to research life in a selected European country during this time period, and assign the other to research life in China. Suggest that the teams research the customs, clothing, music, housing, diet, and religion of their selected regions. Remind students that in both areas, clothing, housing, and diet, in particular, varied according to economic level. For the presentation of their research, have teams use maps, charts, models, music, clothing, and actual items from the culture. Encourage them to be creative. After the presentations, have the class compare and contrast the lifestyles of the two different areas at the same time in history. **L2**

First, the Qing tried to preserve their distinct identity within Chinese society. The Manchus, who made up only 2 percent of the population, were defined legally as distinct from everyone else in China. The Manchu nobility maintained large landholdings and received revenues from the state treasury. Other Manchus were organized into separate military units, called **banners.** The "bannermen" were the chief fighting force of the empire.

Second, the Qing dealt with the problem of ethnic and cultural differences by bringing Chinese into the top ranks of the imperial administration. All important government positions were shared equally by Chinese and Manchus. The Manchus' willingness to share power won the support of many Chinese.

Reign of Kangxi **Kangxi** (KONG•SEE), who ruled from 1661 to 1722, was perhaps the greatest emperor in Chinese history. A person with political skill and a strong character, Kangxi took charge of the government while still in his teens and reigned for 61 years.

Kangxi rose at dawn and worked until late at night. He wrote, "One act of negligence may cause sorrow all through the country, and one moment of negligence may result in trouble for thousands of generations." Kangxi calmed the unrest along the northern and western frontiers by force. As a patron of the arts and letters, he gained the support of scholars throughout the country.

During Kangxi's reign, the efforts of Christian missionaries reached their height. The emperor was quite tolerant of the Christians. Several hundred officials became Catholics, as did an estimated three hundred thousand ordinary Chinese. The Christian effort was undermined by squabbling among the Western religious orders who opposed the Jesuit policy of accommodating local beliefs and practices in order to facilitate conversion. Although Kangxi tried to resolve the problem, no solution was reached. After the death of Kangxi, however, his successor began to suppress Christian activities throughout China.

Westerners in China Qianlong, who ruled from 1736 to 1795, was another outstanding Qing ruler. During his reign, however, the first signs of internal decay began to appear in the Qing dynasty. As the emperor grew older, he fell under the influence of

Martial arts in China fell into five groups: empty-hand boxing, sparring, training in pairs, group exercises involving six or more athletes, and weapons training. Weapons included bows and arrows, swords, spears, and chains with a pointed tip.

The Tang dynasty began to select military officials through martial arts contests and established regular competitions. During the Ming dynasty, the martial arts became even more developed. The classic work on martial arts, *Treatise on Armament Technology,* was published, and martial arts techniques were organized into schools.

One method developed during the Ming era was tai chi. This method focused on providing for better health and longer life by unlocking the flow of energy (chi) in the body. Today, martial arts such as tai chi are used as methods of exercise.

After Communists came to power in China in 1949, the government again fostered the martial arts as a competitive sport. Martial arts teams

Tai chi practice outside the Forbidden City

have spread throughout the world. In 1990, an International Wushu (Martial Arts) Association was formed, consisting of representatives from 38 nations. One year later, the First World Martial Arts Championship took place in Beijing.

Connecting to the Past

1. **Summarizing Information** Identify at least five martial arts and the five groups of Chinese martial arts.
2. **Writing about History** Martial arts are very popular in the United States today. Why do you think this is so? Write a persuasive essay in which you present a case for offering martial arts classes as part of the physical educational program at your school.

EXTENDING THE CONTENT

The Question of Succession A common problem for monarchs is choosing a successor. The problem is particularly complicated for an emperor with many wives and children. Kangxi, who became emperor amidst controversy, wanted to prevent a similar problem for his heir. He chose his oldest son, Yinreng, as successor and educated him accordingly. Court officials were afraid to tell Kangxi that his son was violent and cruel. Eventually, the son had to be jailed for attempting a coup. As Kangxi lay dying, he was in the company of another son, Yongzheng, who told everyone after his father died that he was his father's choice for emperor. There were no witnesses, and Yongzheng ruled from 1723 to 1735. Yinreng and two other brothers died shortly after their father died.

3 ASSESS

Assign Section 1 Assessment as homework or as an in-class activity.

Have students use **Interactive Tutor Self-Assessment CD-ROM.**

Section Quiz 9–1

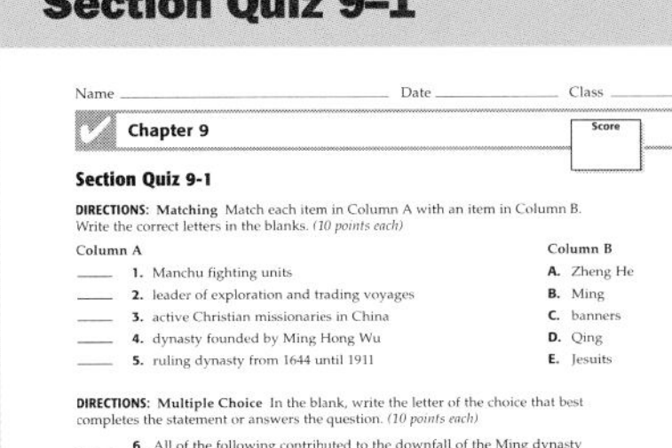

Name ______ Date ______ Class ______

Chapter 9 — Score

Section Quiz 9-1

DIRECTIONS: Matching Match each item in Column A with an item in Column B. Write the correct letters in the blanks. *(10 points each)*

Column A	Column B
____ 1. Manchu fighting units	A. Zheng He
____ 2. leader of exploration and trading voyages	B. Ming
____ 3. active Christian missionaries in China	C. banners
____ 4. dynasty founded by Ming Hong Wu	D. Qing
____ 5. ruling dynasty from 1644 until 1911	E. Jesuits

DIRECTIONS: Multiple Choice In the blank, write the letter of the choice that best completes the statement or answers the question. *(10 points each)*

____ 6. All of the following contributed to the downfall of the Ming dynasty

Reteaching Activity

Divide the class into two groups. Have each group prepare a section quiz for the other group to take. **L1**

Critical Thinking

Ask students to discuss the extent to which they would follow social expectations in other countries. For example, in some countries it is considered offensive to eat with your left hand or for students to look directly at a teacher. Would students follow these customs while living in these countries? Ask students why it is important to be aware of cultural differences. **L2**

Who? What? Where? When?

Matteo Ricci Known to the Chinese as Li Ma-tou, Matteo Ricci was the most famous Jesuit missionary to China. He and his fellow Jesuits impressed the Chinese with their knowledge of the Chinese language and their respect for Confucianism.

CHAPTER 9

Section 1, 267–272

Reading Check

Answer: Answers will vary.

Reading Essentials and Study Guide 9–1

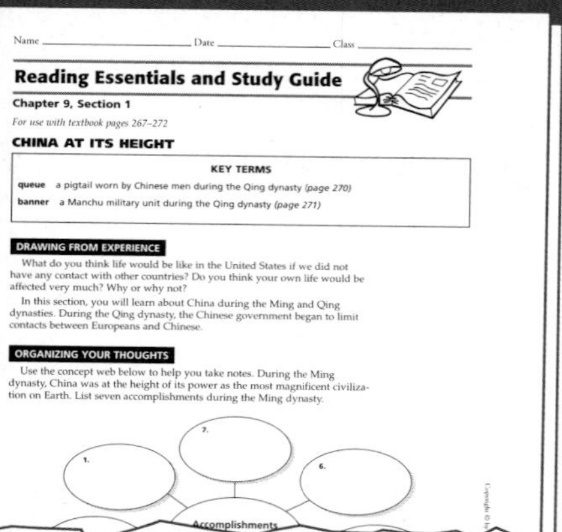
Name ______ Date ______ Class ______

Reading Essentials and Study Guide

Chapter 9, Section 1

For use with textbook pages 267–272

CHINA AT ITS HEIGHT

KEY TERMS

queue a pigtail worn by Chinese men during the Qing dynasty *(page 270)*

banner a Manchu military unit during the Qing dynasty *(page 271)*

DRAWING FROM EXPERIENCE

What do you think life would be like in the United States if we did not have any contact with other countries? Do you think your own life would be affected very much? Why or why not?

In this section, you will learn about China during the Ming and Qing dynasties. During the Qing dynasty, the Chinese government began to limit contacts between Europeans and Chinese.

ORGANIZING YOUR THOUGHTS

Use the concept web below to help you take notes. During the Ming dynasty, China was at the height of its power as the most magnificent civilization on Earth. List seven accomplishments during the Ming dynasty.

7.

1.

6.

Accomplishments

Critical Thinking

Tell students that it took eight years for the Qing dynasty to suppress the White Lotus Rebellion. What conclusions can students draw from that? Ask students to imagine a similar rebellion within the United States. What conclusions would they be able to draw about the government, rebels, and general population? Would students be able to predict the consequences of a sustained rebellion? **L3**

4 CLOSE

In a discussion, have students summarize the relationship between China and the rest of the world during the Ming and Qing dynasties. **L1**

Sixteenth-century farming in China

destructive elements at court. Corrupt officials and higher taxes led to unrest in rural areas. Growing pressure on the land because of population growth also led to economic hardship for many peasants. In central China, unhappy peasants launched a revolt known as the White Lotus Rebellion (1796–1804). The revolt was suppressed, but the enormous expenses of fighting the rebels weakened the Qing dynasty.

Unfortunately for China, the Qing dynasty was declining just as Europe was seeking more trade. At first, the Qing government sold trade privileges to the Europeans. However, to limit contacts between Europeans and Chinese, the Qing confined all European traders to a small island just outside Guangzhou. The traders could reside there only from October through March and could deal only with a limited number of Chinese firms licensed by the government.

For a while, the British accepted this system. By the end of the eighteenth century, however, some British traders had begun to demand access to additional cities along the Chinese coast. At the same time, the Chinese government was under pressure from its own merchants to open China to British manufactured goods.

In 1793, a British mission led by Lord George Macartney visited Beijing to seek more liberal trade policies. However, Emperor Qianlong wrote to King George III that China had no need of "your country's manufactures." The Chinese would later pay for their rejection of the British request.

Reading Check **Predict Consequences** Predict the consequences of the Chinese attitude toward trade with Europe.

SECTION 1 ASSESSMENT

Checking for Understanding

1. **Define** queue, banner.
2. **Identify** Ming, Zheng He, Manchu, Qing, Kangxi.
3. **Locate** Guangzhou, Beijing, Manchuria, Taiwan.
4. **Explain** how the pigtail became a political symbol under the Qing dynasty.
5. **List** the ways the Ming and Qing dynasties tried to limit contacts between Europeans and the Chinese people. Why did the British initially accept the restrictions?

Critical Thinking

6. **Make Generalizations** What was the general attitude of the Chinese regarding trade with the Western world? Give examples from the text to support your answer.
7. **Summarizing Information** Create a chart like the one below to show how both the Europeans and Chinese benefited from their early cultural exchange.

European Benefits	Chinese Benefits

Analyzing Visuals

8. **Examine** the picture of the Chinese peasants farming shown above. What conclusions can you draw about peasant life in China from looking at this picture? How do your conclusions compare and contrast with the depictions of peasant life found in other cultures you have already read about?

Writing About History

9. **Expository Writing** Using the Internet or print resources, research the voyages of Zheng He and Columbus. Write an essay comparing the technology, equipment, purpose, and results of the explorations of Zheng He and Columbus.

SECTION 1 ASSESSMENT

1. Key terms are in blue.
2. Ming *(p. 267)*; Zheng He *(p. 268)*; Manchu *(p. 270)*; Qing *(p. 270)*; Kangxi *(p. 271)*
3. See chapter maps.
4. The pigtails distinguished Manchu supporters from rebels.
5. Europeans were confined and restricted to certain places, times, and trading partners; the British had no other options.
6. The Chinese did not see any advantage to trade; examples will vary.
7. European Benefits include direct access to Chinese products and technology, income from trade; Chinese Benefits include access to European products and technology.
8. Answers will vary. Students may note that both men and women are in the field, which was true for many peasant societies.
9. Answers will vary. Students should document their findings.

SECTION 2 Chinese Society and Culture

Guide to Reading

Main Ideas
- A rapid increase in population led to rural land shortages.
- Chinese society was organized around the family.
- Architecture, decorative arts, and literature flourished during this period.

Key Terms
commercial capitalism, clan, porcelain

People to Identify
Cao Xuegin, Emperor Yong Le

Places to Locate
Imperial City, Beijing

Preview Questions
1. Why did the population increase between 1500 and 1800?
2. Why did commercial capitalism not develop in China during this period?

Reading Strategy
Organizing Information Use a concentric circle diagram like the one below to show the organization of the Chinese family.

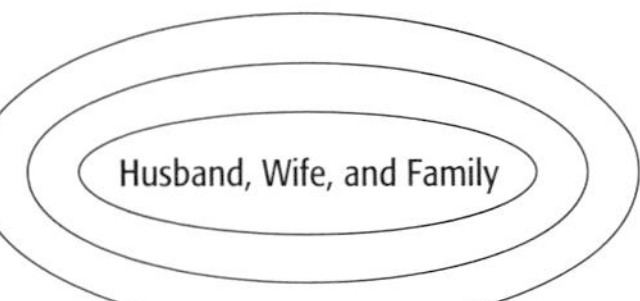

Preview of Events

1400 · 1475 · 1550 · 1625 · 1700 · 1775 · 1850

- **1368** Ming dynasty begins a new era of greatness in China
- **1406** Renovations are begun on the Imperial City
- **1791** Popular novel, *The Dream of the Red Chamber,* is published

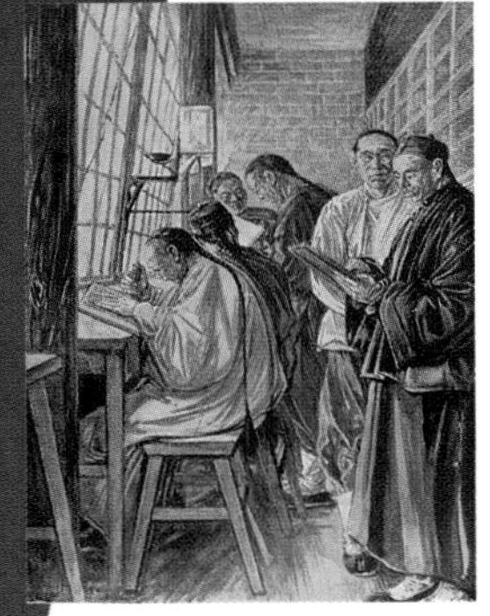
Chinese printers at work

Voices from the Past

In the sixteenth century, an Italian named Matteo Ricci expressed a great appreciation of Chinese printing:

“The Chinese method of printing has one decided advantage, namely, that once these tablets are made, they can be preserved and used for making changes in the text as often as one wishes. . . . The simplicity of Chinese printing is what accounts for the exceedingly large numbers of books in circulation here and the ridiculously low prices at which they are sold.”

—***China in the Sixteenth Century,*** **Louis J. Gallagher, trans., 1942**

Europeans who lived in China found much to admire in Chinese civilization.

Economic Changes

Between 1500 and 1800, China remained a mostly agricultural society. Nearly 85 percent of the people were small farmers. Nevertheless, the Chinese economy was changing.

The first change involved an increase in population, from less than 80 million in 1390 to more than 300 million at the end of the 1700s. The increase had several causes. A long period of peace and stability under the early Qing dynasty was one. Improvements in the food supply were another. A faster growing species of rice from Southeast Asia increased the food supply.

1 FOCUS

Section Overview

This section describes the population growth, family structure, daily life, and cultural elements of China.

BELLRINGER
Skillbuilder Activity

Project transparency and have students answer questions.

Available as a blackline master.

Daily Focus Skills Transparency 9–2

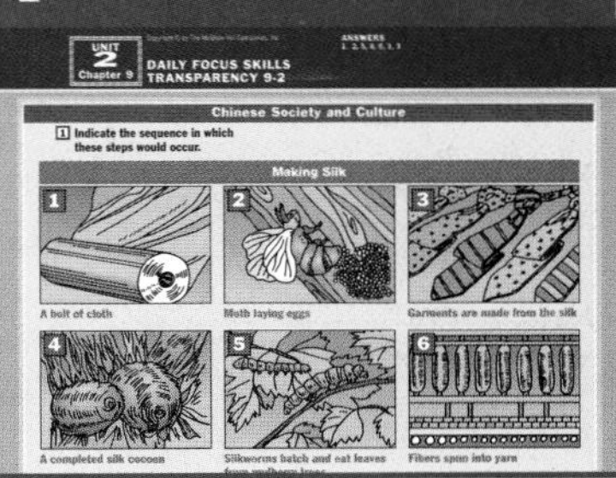

Guide to Reading

Answers to Graphic: Middle ring: Extended Family; Outer ring: Clan

Preteaching Vocabulary: Make sure students understand what is meant by *commercial capitalism* and how it differs from what was practiced in China. *(fewer government restrictions in commercial capitalism)* **L2**

SECTION RESOURCES

Reproducible Masters
- Reproducible Lesson Plan 9–2
- Daily Lecture and Discussion Notes 9–2
- Guided Reading Activity 9–2
- Section Quiz 9–2
- Reading Essentials and Study Guide 9–2

Transparencies
- Daily Focus Skills Transparency 9–2

Multimedia
- Interactive Tutor Self-Assessment CD-ROM
- ExamView® Pro Testmaker CD-ROM
- Presentation Plus! CD-ROM

2 TEACH

Reading Check

Answer: The Chinese government tended to discourage manufacturing and trade by levying heavy taxes, whereas European governments encouraged manufacturing and trade.

Answer: Answers will vary. Students should demonstrate ability to analyze sources for reliability.

Daily Lecture and Discussion Notes 9–2

Daily Lecture and Discussion Notes

Chapter 9, Section 2

Did You Know? Between 1500 and 1800 more than three-fourths of the Chinese people lived in rural areas and were small farmers. Farmers either worked as tenants and paid rent to a landlord or owned their land. Many Chinese believed that pursuing trade or manufacturing was inferior to farming.

I. **Economic Changes** *(pages 273–274)*

A. The population grew from 80 to 300 million between 1390 and the end of the 1700s. A long period of peace and stability was one reason. Another was that a faster-growing species of rice increased the food supply.

B. China's economy was changing from 1500 to 1800. There was less land for each family. By the 1700s almost all available farmland was under production. Shortages led to unrest.

C. Manufacturing and trade increased during this period. Nonetheless, China did not develop the **commercial capitalism**—private business based on profit—that Europe did. One reason is that merchants were not as independent in China. Government controlled trade and manufacturing and levied high taxes on it.

Discussion Question

Why might someone believe that farming was a more noble pursuit than trade or manufacturing? *(Answers will vary. Accept relevant, thoughtful answers. One common point of this position is that working the land leads to virtues such as honesty and thrift, while trade and manufacturing lead to the vice of greed.)*

Who?What?Where?When?

The Group In China, the group, whether it is family, business, or country, is more important than the individual. The way food is ordered illustrates this idea. In a typical American restaurant, everyone orders his or her own meal. In a Chinese restaurant, one order is placed for the group.

The population increase meant there was less land available for each family. The imperial court tried to make more land available by limiting the amount wealthy landowners could hold. By the eighteenth century, however, almost all the land that could be farmed was already being farmed. Shortages of land in rural areas led to unrest and revolts.

Another change in this period was a steady growth in manufacturing and increased trade between provinces. Taking advantage of the long era of peace and prosperity, merchants and manufacturers expanded their trade in silk, porcelain, cotton goods, and other products. *(See page 775 to read excerpts from Sung Ying-Hsing's* The Silk Industry in China *in the Primary Sources Library.)*

Despite the growth in trade and manufacturing, China did not develop the kind of commercial capitalism—private business based on profit—that was emerging in Europe. Some key differences between China and Europe explain this fact.

In the first place, middle-class merchants and manufacturers in China were not as independent as those in Europe. Trade and manufacturing remained under the firm control of the government. Many Chinese looked down on trade and manufacturing as inferior to farming. The state reflected this attitude by levying heavy taxes on manufacturing and trade and low taxes on farming.

Reading Check **Contrasting** What was the key difference in government policy toward trade and manufacturing in Europe and in China?

Daily Life

Daily life in China remained similar to what it had been in earlier periods. The emphasis on family relationships, based on Confucian ideals, contributed stability to Chinese society.

The Chinese Family Chinese society was organized around the family. The family was expected to provide for its members' needs, including the education of children, support of unmarried daughters, and care of the elderly. At the same time, all family members were expected to sacrifice their individual desires for the benefit of the family as a whole.

CONNECTIONS Around The World

A Population Explosion

Between 1700 and 1800, many areas in the world experienced a population explosion. In Europe, China, India, and the Muslim world, the number of people grew dramatically. Europe, for example, went from 120 million people in 1700 to almost 200 million by 1800; China, from less than 200 million to 300 million during the same period.

Four factors were important in causing this population explosion. First, better agricultural growing conditions affected wide areas of the world and enabled people to produce more food. Second, new foods provided additional sources of nutrition. Food crops were introduced in new areas: sweet potatoes in China, corn in Africa and Europe, and potatoes in northern Europe and Russia. Third, states controlled larger territories and were able to ensure a higher degree of order. Less violence led to fewer deaths.

Many cities experienced a growth in population.

Finally, by the eighteenth century, people had begun to develop immunities to epidemic diseases. The migration of people after 1500 had led to devastating epidemics. For example, the arrival of Europeans in Mexico led to millions of deaths from smallpox, measles, and chicken pox among a native population that had no immunities to European diseases. By 1750, however, the number and effects of plagues and epidemic diseases had decreased in Europe, India, China, and Southwest Asia.

Comparing Cultures

Many demographers believe that the world is currently experiencing another population boom. Research current population figures and predictions for the next 50 years. Check at least three sources. Is the information corroborated in three sources? If not, what reasons can explain the differences? How can you assess the reliability of the sources you used?

COOPERATIVE LEARNING ACTIVITY

Creating A Graph Ask students to create a graph showing the world population changes that occurred between 1700 and 1800. Students can use the information contained in the feature *A Population Explosion* as well as outside sources to research population changes in at least five different countries or regions during this period. Then ask students to interpret their information by posing and answering two questions about geographic distribution and patterns in world history shown on their graphs. Make sure that students use appropriate mathematical skills to interpret the information on their graphs. **L2**

For grading this activity, refer to the ***Performance Assessment Activity*** booklet.

Picturing History

Silk production began in China about 5,000 years ago. Describe the labor involved as shown in these paintings. Why was silk only worn by the wealthy?

The ideal family unit in Qing China was the extended family, in which as many as three or four generations lived under the same roof. When sons married, they brought their wives to live with them in the family home. Unmarried daughters also remained in the house, as did parents and grandparents. Chinese society held the elderly in high regard. Aging parents knew they would be cared for by their children.

Beyond the extended family was the clan, which consisted of dozens, or even hundreds, of related families. These families were linked by a clan council of elders and a variety of common social and religious activities. The clan system made it possible for wealthier families to help poorer relatives.

The Role of Women Women were considered inferior to men in Chinese society. Only males could have a formal education and pursue a career in government or scholarship. Within the family, capable women often played strong roles. Nevertheless, the wife was clearly subordinate to the husband. Legally, she could not divorce her husband or inherit property. The husband, in contrast, could divorce his wife if she did not produce sons. He could also take a second wife. Husbands were expected to provide support for their wives and children. In many cases, the head of the family would also be responsible for providing for more than just his own wife and children.

A feature of Chinese society that is often misunderstood by Westerners is the practice of footbinding. The origins of footbinding are not clear. Scholars believe it began among the wealthiest class of women and was later adopted by all classes. Bound feet were a status symbol. Women who had bound feet were more marriageable than those who did not, thus there was a status incentive as well as an economic incentive. An estimated one-half to two-thirds of the women in China bound their feet.

The process, begun in childhood, was very painful. Women who had their feet bound could not walk, they were carried. Not all clans looked favorably on footbinding. Women who worked in the fields or in occupations that required mobility did not bind their feet.

Reading Check **Describing** What was the legal status of women in China?

MEETING INDIVIDUAL NEEDS

Visual Learners Ask students to describe the role of women in traditional China. Then have students conduct research to learn about notable women throughout Chinese history. Have students look for women who were artists, writers, scientists, or government and business leaders. The task of students is to write the name, position, and a short biography of each selected woman on a card. On the other side of the card, have students attach a photo, if one is available. The cards can be used to help students recognize famous women and their accomplishments. L2

Refer to ***Inclusion for the High School Social Studies Classroom Strategies and Activities*** in the TCR.

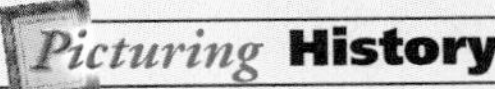

Picturing History

Answer: because it was expensive

Reading Check

Answer: Women were considered inferior to men. Only males could be educated. Within the family, women often played a strong role; however, wives were subordinate to husbands. They could not obtain a divorce or inherit property.

Guided Reading Activity 9–2

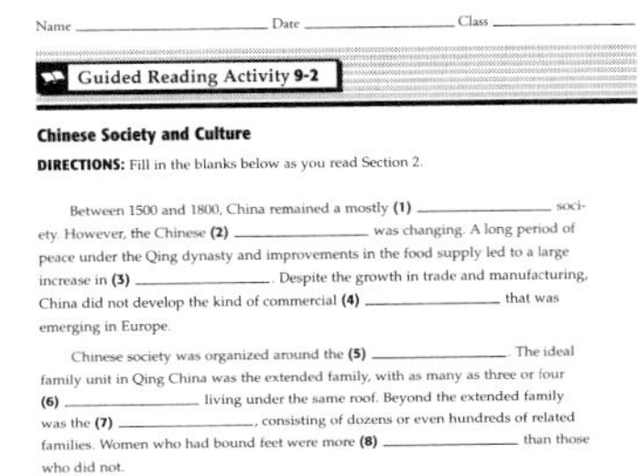

Name ______ Date ______ Class ______

Guided Reading Activity 9-2

Chinese Society and Culture

DIRECTIONS: Fill in the blanks below as you read Section 2.

Between 1500 and 1800, China remained a mostly **(1)** ______ society. However, the Chinese **(2)** ______ was changing. A long period of peace under the Qing dynasty and improvements in the food supply led to a large increase in **(3)** ______. Despite the growth in trade and manufacturing, China did not develop the kind of commercial **(4)** ______ that was emerging in Europe.

Chinese society was organized around the **(5)** ______. The ideal family unit in Qing China was the extended family, with as many as three or four **(6)** ______ living under the same roof. Beyond the extended family was the **(7)** ______, consisting of dozens or even hundreds of related families. Women who had bound feet were more **(8)** ______ than those who did not.

3 ASSESS

Assign Section 2 Assessment as homework or as an in-class activity.

Have students use **Interactive Tutor Self-Assessment CD-ROM.**

Section Quiz 9–2

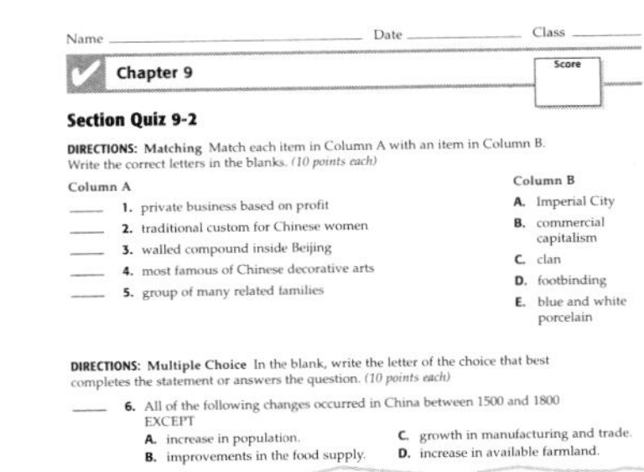

Name ______ Date ______ Class ______

Chapter 9 Score

Section Quiz 9-2

DIRECTIONS: Matching Match each item in Column A with an item in Column B. Write the correct letters in the blanks. *(10 points each)*

Column A

____ **1.** private business based on profit
____ **2.** traditional custom for Chinese women
____ **3.** walled compound inside Beijing
____ **4.** most famous of Chinese decorative arts
____ **5.** group of many related families

Column B

A. Imperial City
B. commercial capitalism
C. clan
D. footbinding
E. blue and white porcelain

DIRECTIONS: Multiple Choice In the blank, write the letter of the choice that best completes the statement or answers the question. *(10 points each)*

____ **6.** All of the following changes occurred in China between 1500 and 1800 EXCEPT
A. increase in population.
B. improvements in the food supply.
C. growth in manufacturing and trade.
D. increase in available farmland.

Reading Check

Answer: in architecture, the Imperial City in Beijing; decorative arts also flourished; blue-and-white porcelain of the Ming Dynasty

Reading Essentials and Study Guide 9–2

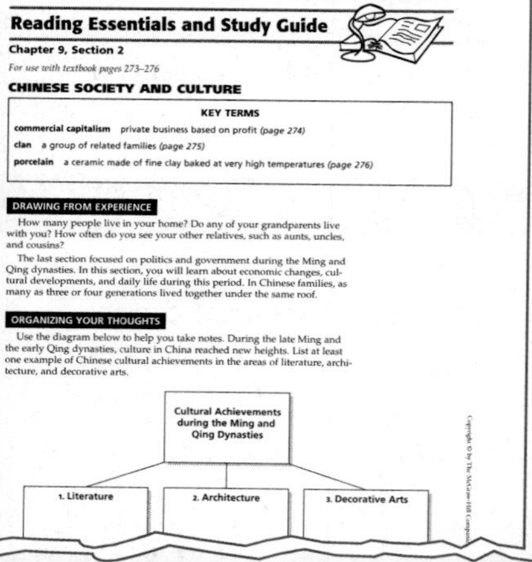
Name ______ Date ______ Class ______

Reading Essentials and Study Guide

Chapter 9, Section 2

For use with textbook pages 273–276

CHINESE SOCIETY AND CULTURE

KEY TERMS

commercial capitalism private business based on profit *(page 274)*

clan a group of related families *(page 275)*

porcelain a ceramic made of fine clay baked at very high temperatures *(page 276)*

DRAWING FROM EXPERIENCE

How many people live in your home? Do any of your grandparents live with you? How often do you see your other relatives, such as aunts, uncles, and cousins?

The last section focused on politics and government during the Ming and Qing dynasties. In this section, you will learn about economic changes, cultural developments, and daily life during this period. In Chinese families, as many as three or four generations lived together under the same roof.

ORGANIZING YOUR THOUGHTS

Use the diagram below to help you take notes. During the late Ming and the early Qing dynasties, culture in China reached new heights. List at least one example of Chinese cultural achievements in the areas of literature, architecture, and decorative arts.

Cultural Achievements during the Ming and Qing Dynasties

1. Literature
2. Architecture
3. Decorative Arts

Reteaching Activity

Ask students to summarize the major political, economic, and cultural developments that occurred in China during the period discussed in this section. **L1**

4 CLOSE

Ask students to identify the differences between their own culture and the culture described in this section. **L1**

Cultural Developments

During the late Ming and the early Qing dynasties, traditional culture in China reached new heights.

The Chinese Novel During the Ming dynasty, a new form of literature arose that eventually evolved into the modern Chinese novel. Works in this literary form were enormously popular, especially among well-to-do urban dwellers.

One Chinese novel, *The Golden Lotus,* is considered by many to be the first realistic social novel. *The Golden Lotus* depicts the corrupt life of a wealthy landlord in the late Ming period who cruelly manipulates those around him for sex, money, and power.

The Dream of the Red Chamber, by **Cao Xuegin,** is generally considered even today to be China's most distinguished popular novel. Published in 1791, it tells of the tragic love between two young people caught in the financial and moral disintegration of a powerful Chinese clan.

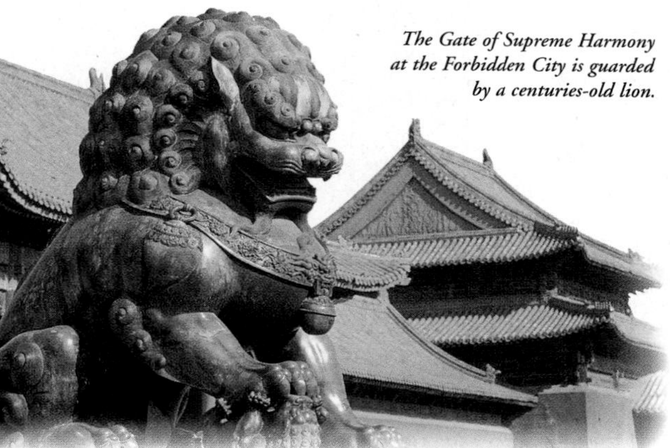
The Gate of Supreme Harmony at the Forbidden City is guarded by a centuries-old lion.

Ming and Qing Art During the Ming and the early Qing dynasties, China experienced an outpouring of artistic brilliance.

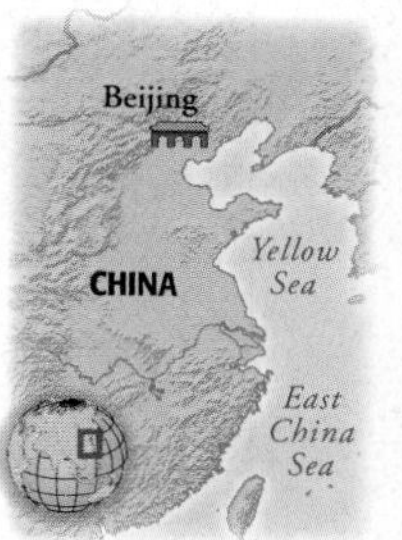

In architecture, the most outstanding example is the **Imperial City** in **Beijing. Emperor Yong Le** began renovations on the Imperial City—once the palace of the Mongol dynasty—in 1406. Succeeding emperors continued to add to the palace.

The Imperial City is an immense compound surrounded by six and one-half miles (10.5 km) of walls. It includes a maze of private apartments and offices, as well as stately halls for imperial audiences and banquets and spacious gardens. Because it was off-limits to commoners, the compound was known as the Forbidden City.

The decorative arts also flourished in this period. Perhaps the most famous of all the arts of the Ming Era was blue-and-white **porcelain.** Europeans admired the beauty of this porcelain and collected it in great quantities. Different styles of porcelain were produced during the reign of individual emperors.

Reading Check **Describing** What were the artistic accomplishments of the Ming and Qing dynasties?

SECTION 2 ASSESSMENT

Checking for Understanding

1. **Define** commercial capitalism, clan, porcelain.
2. **Identify** Cao Xuegin, Emperor Yong Le.
3. **Locate** Imperial City, Beijing.
4. **Explain** the significance of the Chinese extended family.
5. **Summarize** the plot of *The Dream of the Red Chamber.*

Critical Thinking

6. **Draw Conclusions** Although legally inferior to men, what important roles did women in the peasant class have?
7. **Identifying Information** Use a diagram to identify the economic changes in China from 1500 to 1800.

Analyzing Visuals

8. **Examine** the picture of women spinning silk shown on page 275 of your text. How does this picture reflect the role of women in Chinese society during the eighteenth century?

Writing About History

9. **Persuasive Writing** Pretend you are a Chinese mother talking to your daughter in 1700. Using research or your own ideas, convince her that footbinding is necessary and beneficial.

SECTION 2 ASSESSMENT

1. Key terms are in blue.
2. Cao Xuegin *(p. 276);* Emperor Yong Le *(p. 276)*
3. See chapter maps.
4. family was emphasized over individual; family members cared for each other.
5. It tells of the tragic love between two young people caught in the financial and moral disintegration of a powerful Chinese clan.
6. produce sons, work in fields
7. population increased; less land for each family; amount of land that could be held by wealthy landowners limited; steady growth in manufacturing and trade; heavy taxes levied on manufacturing and trade, low taxes on farming
8. participating in manufacturing, not just confined to home and family
9. Answers will vary. Students might refer to issues of status and female marriageability.

SOCIAL STUDIES SKILLBUILDER

Finding Exact Location on a Map

Why Learn This Skill?

A friend tells you that she lives at the northwest corner of Vine Street and Oak Avenue. By giving you the names of two streets that cross, she has pinpointed her exact location. We use a similar system to identify the exact location of any place on Earth.

Learning the Skill

Over many centuries, cartographers developed a grid system of imaginary lines—lines of latitude and lines of longitude. Lines of latitude run east and west around the earth. Because they always remain the same distance from each other, they are also called parallels. The parallel lines of latitude measure distance north and south of the Equator, which is located at 0 degrees latitude. Each line of latitude is one degree, or 69 miles (110 km), from the next. There are 90 latitude lines between the Equator and each pole. For example, New York City lies 41 degrees north of the Equator, or 41°N.

Lines of longitude, or meridians, run north and south from pole to pole. Unlike lines of latitude, lines of longitude are not always the same distance from each other. Lines of longitude are farthest apart at the Equator, and they intersect at the North and South Poles. The prime meridian marks 0 degrees longitude and runs through Greenwich, England, and western Africa. Longitude lines are measured by their distance east and west of the prime meridian up to 180 degrees. New York City, for example, lies 74 degrees west of the prime meridian, or 74°W.

With this system we can pinpoint the "grid address" of any place on Earth. For example, if we wanted to find a grid address for New York City, we would first find the line of latitude closest to it. Then, by following this line, we would locate the nearest line of longitude to cross it. The point where the lines intersect is the grid address. New York City's grid address would be 41°N, 74°W.

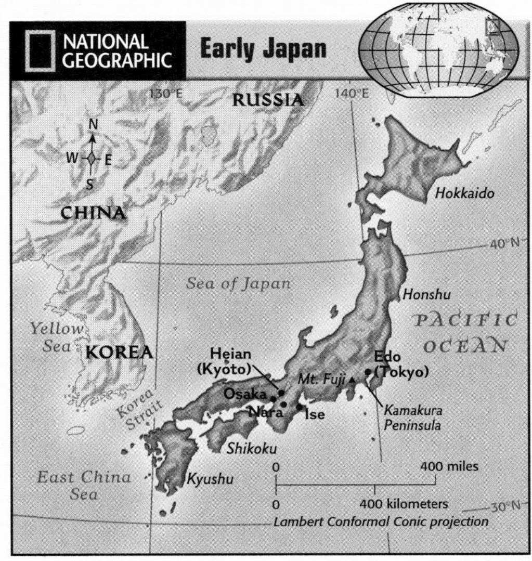

Practicing the Skill

Use the map above to answer the following questions.

1. What is Ise's approximate grid address?
2. What city sits at approximately 35°N, 140°E?
3. What is Osaka's approximate grid address?
4. What is Mt. Fuji's approximate grid address?

Applying the Skill

Create a travel itinerary for a tour of the ruins of ancient Egypt, Greece, or Southwest Asia. Choose at least 10 sites to visit. Draw a map of each region, including grid lines. On the map, identify each site's approximate grid location.

Glencoe's **Skillbuilder Interactive Workbook, Level 2,** provides instruction and practice in key social studies skills.

ANSWERS TO PRACTICING THE SKILL

1. The approximate grid address for Ise is 34° N, 136° E.
2. Edo (Tokyo) lies at 35° N, 140° E.
3. The approximate grid address for Osaka is 35° N, 135° E.
4. The approximate grid address for Mt. Fuji is 35° N, 139° E.

You might wish to remind students that because Japan is a small country, the grid addresses of its cities tend to be relatively close.

Applying the Skill: Student travel itineraries will vary greatly. You might call on volunteers to share their ideas and have the class create maps of the planned trips or trace the planned journeys on maps that are in the Reference Atlas section of the text.

SOCIAL STUDIES SKILLBUILDER

TEACH

Finding Exact Location on a Map Have one student draw a map of the area around your school on the chalkboard. Place the school in the center of the map, and label it "0." List north, south, east, and west on the board, with north at the top. Include four streets in each direction from the school and number them radiating from the school in each direction using the numerals 1–4. Insert street names. Now ask students to give grid locations for several street intersections. Then give them grid locations, and ask students to point to the intersections. **L1**

Additional Practice

Skills Reinforcement Activity 9

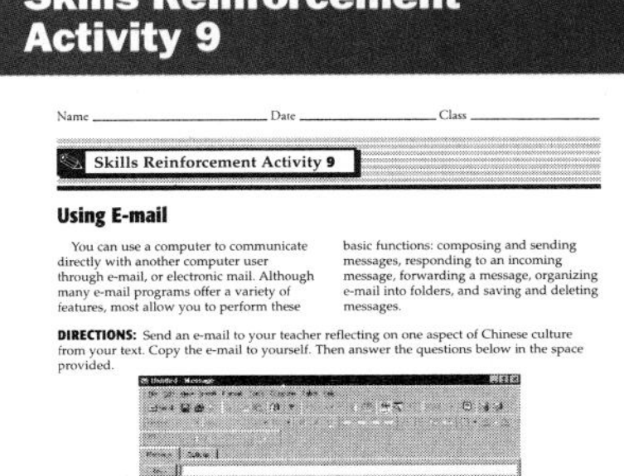

Name ______ Date ______ Class ______

Skills Reinforcement Activity 9

Using E-mail

You can use a computer to communicate directly with another computer user through e-mail, or electronic mail. Although many e-mail programs offer a variety of features, most allow you to perform these basic functions: composing and sending messages, responding to an incoming message, forwarding a message, organizing e-mail into folders, and saving and deleting messages.

DIRECTIONS: Send an e-mail to your teacher reflecting on one aspect of Chinese culture from your text. Copy the e-mail to yourself. Then answer the questions below in the space provided.

GLENCOE TECHNOLOGY

CD-ROM

Glencoe Skillbuilder Interactive Workbook CD-ROM, Level 2

This interactive CD-ROM reinforces student mastery of essential social studies skills.

1 FOCUS

Section Overview

This section describes the unification of Japan and economic and cultural changes up to 1750.

BELLRINGER
Skillbuilder Activity

Project transparency and have students answer questions.

Available as a blackline master.

Daily Focus Skills Transparency 9–3

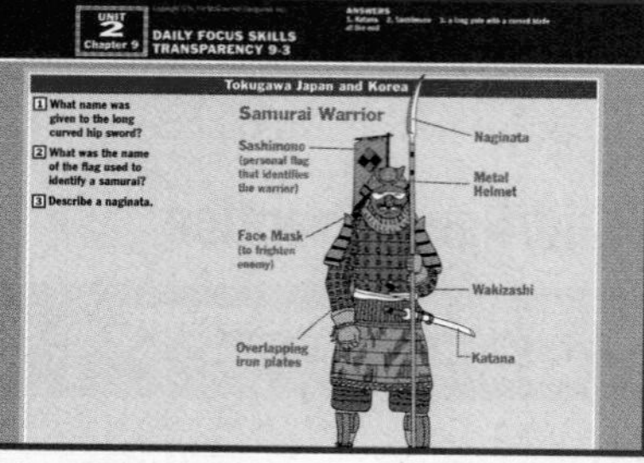

Guide to Reading

Answers to Graphic: Culture: Rise of popular fiction written by and for townspeople; Exquisite poetry remained a more serious form of literature; Rise of Kabuki dramas; Increase in building and furnishing mansions; Art enriched by other cultures, such as pottery techniques and designs from Korea; Japanese studied Western medicine, astronomy, languages, and even painting styles

Preteaching Vocabulary: Ask students to write a brief paragraph that explains how *daimyo* and *han* relate to each other. L2

SECTION 3 Tokugawa Japan and Korea

Guide to Reading

Main Ideas
- Japan was unified by three powerful political figures.
- Between 1500 and 1800, Japan experienced many peasant uprisings.
- Korea could not withstand invasions by the Japanese and Manchus.

Key Terms
daimyo, han, hostage system, eta

People to Identify
Oda Nobunaga, Toyotomi Hideyoshi, Tokugawa Ieyasu, Matsuo Basho

Places to Locate
Kyoto, Osaka, Edo, Korea

Preview Questions
1. What economic changes took place under the Tokugawa shoguns?
2. How did Japanese culture change during the Tokugawa Era?

Reading Strategy
Categorizing Information Using a diagram like the one below, categorize the different elements of Japanese culture.

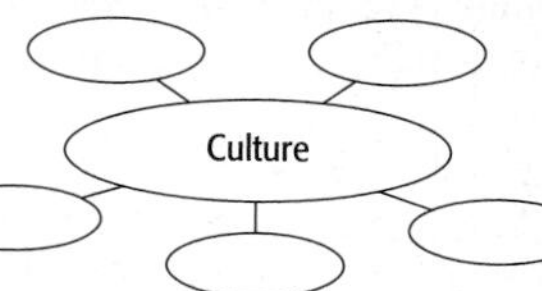

Preview of Events

c. 1450 · 1500 · 1550 · 1600 · 1650 · 1700 · 1750

- **1450** Power of shogun collapses
- **1550** Japan's unification begins
- **1750** Edo is one of the largest cities in the world

Voices from the Past

In 1649, the Japanese government issued an edict to be read in every village:

> ❝Peasants are people without sense or forethought. Therefore they must not give rice to their wives and children at harvest time, but must save food for the future. They should eat millet, vegetables, and other coarse food instead of rice. Even the fallen leaves of plants should be saved. The husband must work in the fields, the wife must work at the loom. However good-looking a wife may be, if she neglects her household duties by drinking tea or sightseeing or rambling on the hillsides, she must be divorced. Peasants must wear only cotton or hemp. They may not smoke tobacco. It is harmful to health, it takes up time and costs money.❞
>
> —*A History of World Societies*, J.P. McKay, B.D. Hill, and J. Buckler, eds., 1996

Japanese rice farmers

The life of the Japanese peasant was a difficult one, and there were many peasant revolts between 1500 and 1800.

The Three Great Unifiers

At the end of the fifteenth century, Japan was in chaos. The centralized power of the shogunate had collapsed. **Daimyo,** heads of noble families, controlled their own lands and warred with their neighbors. Soon, however, a dramatic reversal would unify Japan. The process of unification began in the mid-sixteenth century with three powerful political figures.

SECTION RESOURCES

Reproducible Masters
- Reproducible Lesson Plan 9–3
- Daily Lecture and Discussion Notes 9–3
- Guided Reading Activity 9–3
- Section Quiz 9–3
- Reading Essentials and Study Guide 9–3

Transparencies
- Daily Focus Skills Transparency 9–3

Multimedia
- Interactive Tutor Self-Assessment CD-ROM
- ExamView® Pro Testmaker CD-ROM
- Presentation Plus! CD-ROM

The first was **Oda Nobunaga** (oh•DAH noh•boo•NAH•gah). Nobunaga seized the imperial capital of **Kyoto** and placed the reigning shogun under his control. During the next few years, he tried to consolidate his rule throughout the central plains.

Nobunaga was succeeded by **Toyotomi Hideyoshi** (toh•yoh•TOH•mee HEE•day•YOH•shee), a farmer's son who had become a military commander. Hideyoshi located his capital at **Osaka.** By 1590, he had persuaded most of the daimyo on the Japanese islands to accept his authority.

After Hideyoshi's death in 1598, **Tokugawa Ieyasu** (toh•kuh•GAH•wah ee•YAH•soo), the powerful daimyo of **Edo** (modern-day Tokyo), took control of Japan. Ieyasu took the title of shogun in 1603. The Tokugawa rulers completed the restoration of central authority begun by Nobunaga and Hideyoshi. Tokugawa shoguns remained in power at their capital at Edo until 1868. Tokugawa rule brought a long period of peace known as the "Great Peace."

Reading Check **Identifying** Sequence the events that led to the unification of Japan.

Europeans in Japan

TURNING POINT **As you read this section, note how Japan's "closed country" policy removed European influence, allowing Japan to remain in isolation for centuries.**

As the three great commanders were unifying Japan, the first Europeans began to arrive. Portuguese traders landed on the islands in 1543. In a few years, Portuguese ships began stopping regularly at Japanese ports to take part in the regional trade between Japan, China, and Southeast Asia.

At first, the visitors were welcomed. The Japanese were fascinated by tobacco, clocks, eyeglasses, and other European goods. Daimyo were interested in buying all types of European weapons. Oda Nobunaga and Toyotomi Hideyoshi found the new firearms helpful in defeating their enemies and unifying the islands.

The first Jesuit missionary, Francis Xavier, arrived in 1549. The Jesuits converted a number of local daimyo. By the end of the sixteenth century, thousands of Japanese had become Christians. However, the Jesuit practice of destroying shrines caused a severe reaction. In 1587, Hideyoshi issued an edict prohibiting Christian activities within his lands.

Hideyoshi's edict was at first not strictly enforced. The Jesuits were allowed to continue their activities. Under Tokugawa Ieyasu, however, all missionaries were expelled, and Japanese Christians were persecuted.

European merchants were the next to go. Only a small Dutch community in Nagasaki was allowed to remain in Japan. Dutch ships were permitted to dock at Nagasaki harbor only once a year and could remain for only two or three months.

HISTORY Online

Web Activity Visit the *Glencoe World History—Modern Times* Web site at wh.mt.glencoe.com and click on **Chapter 9–Student Web Activity** to learn more about the role of the shogun in Japan.

Reading Check **Explaining** What was the effect of the Jesuit practice of destroying shrines?

Tokugawa Rule

The Tokugawa rulers set out to establish control of the feudal system that had governed Japan for over three hundred years. As before, the state was divided into about 250 separate territories called **hans,** or domains. Each was ruled by a daimyo. In theory, the

Jesuit priests in Japan

279

CHAPTER 9
Section 3, 278–282

2 TEACH

Reading Check

Answer: Oda Nobunaga seized the imperial capital and placed the reigning shogun under his control. He was succeeded by Toyotomi Hideyoshi, who established his capital at Osaka and by 1590 had persuaded most of the daimyo to accept his authority. After Hideyoshi's death, Tokugawa Ieyasu, the daimyo of Edo, took control of Japan and took the title of shogun. The Tokugawa rulers completed the restoration of central authority.

Reading Check

Answer: It backfired—Hideyoshi issued an edict prohibiting Christian activities within his lands.

Daily Lecture and Discussion Notes 9–3

Daily Lecture and Discussion Notes

Chapter 9, Section 3

Did You Know? The geisha (literally "art person") system was traditionally a form of indentured labor. Usually, her parents gave a young girl for a sum of money to a geisha house, which taught, fed, and clothed her. After a period of years, the geisha then began earning money to repay her parents' debt and her past keep.

I. **The Three Great Unifiers** *(pages 278–279)*

A. Japan was in chaos at the end of the fifteenth century. The shogunate had collapsed. **Daimyo,** the heads of noble families, controlled their own lands and warred with each other. Soon a reversal due to three powerful political figures would unify Japan.

B. **Oda Nobunaga** seized the capital of **Kyoto** and placed the shogun under his control. **Toyotomi Hideyoshi** succeeded him. He moved the capital to **Osaka.** By 1590 he had persuaded most of the daimyo to accept his authority.

C. **Tokugawa Ieyasu,** the powerful daimyo of **Edo,** succeeded him in 1598. He took the title of shogun in 1603 and completed the unification the earlier rulers had begun. Tokugawa shoguns remained in power at Edo, their capital, until 1868. Their rule brought a long period of peace known as the "Great Peace."

Discussion Question

What American political figures are comparable to the three unifiers in Japan? Why? *(Answers will vary. Major Founding Fathers and Abraham Lincoln are good answers.)*

TURNING POINT

The removal of European influence in Japan marked a movement away from the outside world. As Japanese culture grew inward-looking, a strong sense of nationalism developed.

COOPERATIVE LEARNING ACTIVITY

Creating an Oral Presentation Have students develop presentations on the samurai. Organize the class into small groups and have each group choose a particular topic to research. Possible topics include: the rise of samurai, famous samurai, clothing and armor, daily life, combat techniques, samurai as portrayed in film. Have each group decide on the format of its presentation, such as lecture, bulletin-board display, video, multimedia, role play, or drawings. Plan class time for the students to give their presentations. **L2**

For grading this activity, refer to the ***Performance Assessment Activities*** booklet.

CHAPTER 9
Section 3, 278–282

Reading Check

Answer: Each daimyo was required to maintain two residences, one in his own lands and one in Edo, where the shogun's court was located. When the daimyo was absent from his residence in Edo, his family was forced to stay there. The daimyo was under the shogun's control as his family members were hostages of the shogun.

Geography Skills

Answers:
1. Honshu **L1**
2. Students will create a diagram. Conclusion: access to trade increases population, which in turn increases trade. **L3**

Guided Reading Activity 9–3

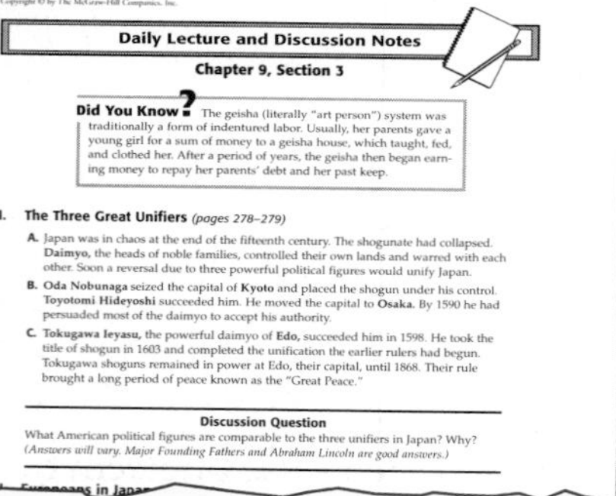

Daily Lecture and Discussion Notes

Chapter 9, Section 3

Did You Know? The geisha (literally "art person") system was traditionally a form of indentured labor. Usually, her parents gave a young girl for a sum of money to a geisha house, which taught, fed, and clothed her. After a period of years, the geisha then began earning money to repay her parents' debt and her past keep.

I. **The Three Great Unifiers** *(pages 278–279)*

A. Japan was in chaos at the end of the fifteenth century. The shogunate had collapsed. **Daimyo,** the heads of noble families, controlled their own lands and warred with each other. Soon a reversal due to three powerful political figures would unify Japan.

B. **Oda Nobunaga** seized the capital of **Kyoto** and placed the shogun under his control. **Toyotomi Hideyoshi** succeeded him. He moved the capital to **Osaka.** By 1590 he had persuaded most of the daimyo to accept his authority.

C. **Tokugawa Ieyasu,** the powerful daimyo of **Edo,** succeeded him in 1598. He took the title of shogun in 1603 and completed the unification the earlier rulers had begun. Tokugawa shoguns remained in power at Edo, their capital, until 1868. Their rule brought a long period of peace known as the "Great Peace."

Discussion Question

What American political figures are comparable to the three unifiers in Japan? Why? *(Answers will vary. Major Founding Fathers and Abraham Lincoln are good answers.)*

Critical Thinking

Ask students to compare the hostage system used by the shogunate to control the daimyo in Japan with the practice of French king Louis XIV requiring his nobles to live at Versailles. **L3**

daimyo were independent, because they were able to support themselves from taxes on their lands. In actuality, the shogunate controlled the daimyo by a **hostage system.**

In this system, the daimyo were required to maintain two residences—one in their own lands and one in Edo, where the court of the shogun was located. When the daimyo was absent from his residence in Edo, his family was forced to stay there.

During this long period of peace—known as the "Great Peace"—brought by Tokugawa rule, the samurai who had served the daimyo gradually ceased to be a warrior class. Many of them became managers on the lands of the daimyo.

Reading Check **Explaining** What was the hostage system? What was its effect on the daimyo?

Economic and Social Changes

A major economic change took place under the Tokugawa. Since the fourteenth century, many upper-class Japanese, influenced by Confucianism, had considered trade and industry beneath them. Under the Tokugawa, trade and industry began to flourish as never before, especially in the growing cities of Edo, Kyoto, and Osaka.

By 1750, Edo had a population of over a million and was one of the largest cities in the world. Banking flourished, and paper money became the normal medium of exchange in business transactions. A Japanese merchant class emerged and began to play a significant role in the life of the Japanese nation.

What effect did these economic changes have on Japanese peasants, who made up most of the population? Some farm families benefited by exploiting the growing demand for cash crops (crops grown for sale). Most peasants, however, experienced both declining profits and rising costs and taxes. Many were forced to become tenants or to work as hired help.

When rural conditions became desperate, some peasants revolted. Almost seven thousand peasant revolts and demonstrations against high taxes took place during the Tokugawa Era.

The Class System Social changes also marked the Tokugawa Era. These changes affected the class system and the role of women. During this era, Japan's class system became rigid. Rulers established strict

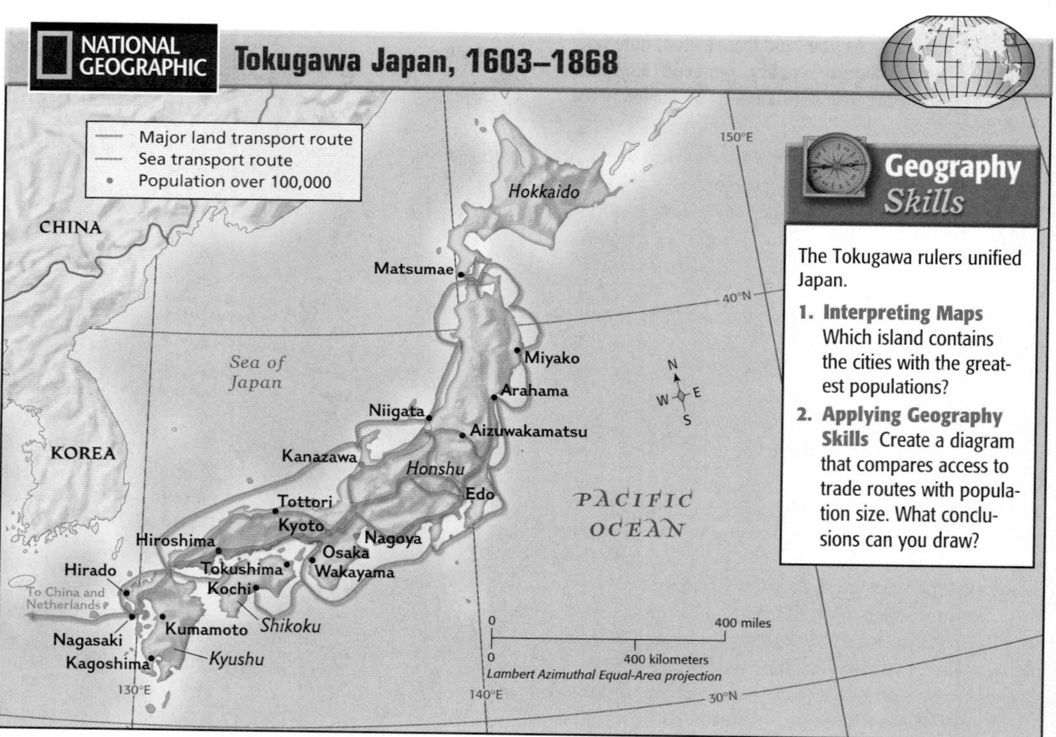

Geography Skills

The Tokugawa rulers unified Japan.

1. **Interpreting Maps** Which island contains the cities with the greatest populations?
2. **Applying Geography Skills** Create a diagram that compares access to trade routes with population size. What conclusions can you draw?

CRITICAL THINKING ACTIVITY

Evaluating The Tokugawa system of requiring the daimyo to live in Edo (Tokyo) or leave their families there helped keep the peace in Japan for over 250 years. No lord was willing to lose his family to attain political power. Pose the following to students for discussion: Governments of all countries with nuclear weapons must require that families of high officials live in hostile foreign lands. In which country might the family of the president of the United States live under this arrangement? What about families of government officials from China, India, or Israel? Divide the class into groups to discuss the effectiveness of such a system today. **L3**

legal distinctions among the four main classes: warriors, peasants, artisans, and merchants. Intermarriage between classes was forbidden.

The emperor and imperial court families were at the very top of the political and social structure. Next came the warrior class composed of the shogun, daimyo, samurai, and ronin. The shogun was supreme ruler below the emperor and distributor of the national rice crop. The local daimyo received land and rice from the shogun in exchange for military service. Samurai received rice from the daimyo in exchange for their services as advisors, castle guards, and government officials. Finally, the ronin were warriors without masters who traveled the countryside seeking employment.

Below the warriors were the farmers (peasants). Farmers produced rice and held a privileged position in society, but were often poor. The artisan class included craftspeople such as swordmakers and carpenters. Finally, the merchant class distributed food and essential goods. This class was at the bottom of the social hierarchy because they profited from the labor of others.

Below these classes were Japan's outcasts, the **eta**. The Tokugawa enacted severe laws to regulate the places of residence, the dress, and even the hairstyles of the eta.

The Role of Women The role of women in Tokugawa society became somewhat more restricted. Especially in the samurai class, where Confucian values were highly prized, the rights of females were restricted. Male heads of households had broad authority over property, marriage, and divorce.

Among the common people, women were also restricted. Parents arranged marriages, and a wife was expected to move in with her husband's family. A wife who did not meet the expectations of her husband or his family was likely to be divorced. Still, women were generally valued for their roles as childbearers and homemakers among the common people. Both sexes worked in the fields as well, although men did the heavier labor.

Reading Check **Explaining** In what ways were the rights of women of the common class restricted?

Tokugawa Culture

In the Tokugawa Era, a new set of cultural values began to appear, especially in the cities. It included the rise of popular literature written by and for the townspeople.

People In History

Matsuo Basho
1644–1694—Japanese poet

Basho was one of the chief literary figures in Tokugawa Japan. Although he lived most of his life in Kyoto and Edo, he also traveled to many other parts of the country. He was concerned with the search for the meaning of life and found answers to his quest in nature. His poems, called haiku, are grounded in natural images. This feature is evident in the following examples, which are among his most famous poems:

The ancient pond
A frog leaps in
The sound of the water.

On the withered branch
A crow has alighted—
The end of autumn.

Literature The best examples of the new urban fiction in the seventeenth century are the works of Ihara Saikaku, considered one of Japan's greatest writers. Saikaku's greatest novel, *Five Women Who Loved Love*, tells of a search for love by five women of the merchant class. The women are willing to die for love—and all but one eventually do.

Much of the popular literature of the Tokugawa Era was lighthearted and intended to please its audiences. Poetry remained a more serious form of literary expression. Exquisite poetry was written in the seventeenth century by the greatest of all Japanese poets, **Matsuo Basho.**

Theater and Art A new world of entertainment in the cities gave rise in the theater to Kabuki, which emphasized action, music, and dramatic gestures to entertain its viewers. Early Kabuki dramas dealt with the world of teahouses and dance halls in the cities.

Government officials feared that such activities could corrupt the nation's morals. Thus, the government forbade women to appear on stage. Officials therefore created a new professional class of male actors to impersonate female characters.

Art also reflected the changes in Japanese culture under the Tokugawa regime. The shogun's order that all daimyo and their families have residences in Edo sparked an increase in building. Nobles competed to erect the most magnificent mansions with lavish and beautiful furnishings. The abundant use of gold foil on

Reading Check

Answer: Parents arranged marriages. A wife was expected to move in with her husband's family. If a wife did not meet the expectations of her husband or his family, she was likely to be divorced.

Connecting Across Time

Today the works of Ihara Saikaku are considered literary classics because they are well-written and reveal a great deal about the culture for and about which they were written. Ask students to provide examples of popular culture today (books, movies, video) that will reveal a great deal about American culture to historians of the future. **L1**

Reteaching Activity

Ask students to list the Japanese social classes discussed in this section and write a descriptive phrase about each one. **L1**

3 ASSESS

Assign Section 3 Assessment as homework or as an in-class activity.

Have students use **Interactive Tutor Self-Assessment CD-ROM.**

Section Quiz 9–3

Name ______ Date ______ Class ______

Chapter 9 Score

Section Quiz 9-3

DIRECTIONS: Matching Match each item in Column A with an item in Column B. Write the correct letters in the blanks. *(10 points each)*

Column A
____ 1. heads of noble families
____ 2. territories or domains
____ 3. political control used by the shogunates
____ 4. crops grown for sale
____ 5. Japanese social outcasts

Column B
A. hostage system
B. hans
C. eta
D. daimyo
E. cash crops

DIRECTIONS: Multiple Choice In the blank, write the letter of the choice that best completes the statement or answers the question. *(10 points each)*

____ 6. Much of the prose literature of the Tokugawa Era was

EXTENDING THE CONTENT

The Eta As social outcasts in Tokugawa culture, the eta were forced to live in their own communities and were avoided by other groups. This was primarily due to their occupation, which was disposing of animal carcasses and tanning leather. Buddhism and Shintoism had regulations about taking a life and observed purification rituals when someone touched something dead. Today, many Japanese with eta ancestry are reluctant to reveal that information. They feel that discrimination still exists. Japanese parents may be reluctant to let their son or daughter marry someone of eta descent.

CHAPTER 9
Section 3, 278–282

Reading Check

Answer: They were afraid it would corrupt the nation's morals.

Reading Check

Answer: Korea's rulers tried to keep the country isolated from the outside world.

Reading Essentials and Study Guide 9–3

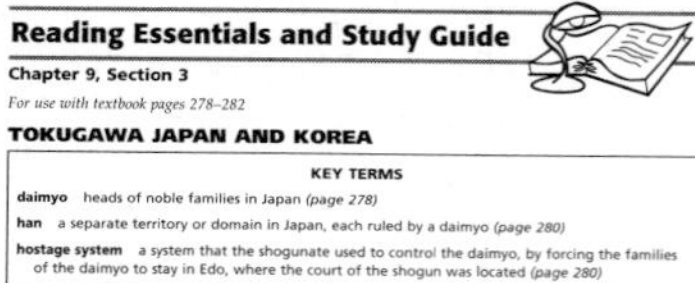

Name ______ Date ______ Class ______

Reading Essentials and Study Guide

Chapter 9, Section 3

For use with textbook pages 278–282

TOKUGAWA JAPAN AND KOREA

KEY TERMS

daimyo heads of noble families in Japan *(page 278)*

han a separate territory or domain in Japan, each ruled by a daimyo *(page 280)*

hostage system a system that the shogunate used to control the daimyo, by forcing the families of the daimyo to stay in Edo, where the court of the shogun was located *(page 280)*

eta outcasts in Japan during the Tokugawa Era *(page 281)*

DRAWING FROM EXPERIENCE

Are some occupations valued more highly than others in the United States? Which occupations do you think are the most highly valued? Which ones do you think are considered the least desirable?

In the last two sections, you learned about China during the Ming and Qing dynasties. In this section, you will learn about Japan and Korea during the Tokugawa Era, which lasted from 1598 to 1868. During this period, Japan developed a rigid class system, based largely on occupations.

Critical Thinking

Ask students to summarize the major political, economic, and cultural developments that occurred in Japan during the period discussed in this section. As part of their answer, have students explain the political, economic, cultural, and technological influences of European expansion on Tokugawa Japan. **L1**

4 CLOSE

Have students discuss similarities between the Ming, Qing, and Tokugawa dynasties. **L1**

walls and ceilings helped reflect the light in dark castle rooms, where windows were often small.

Japanese art was enriched by ideas from other cultures. Japanese pottery makers borrowed techniques and designs from Korea to create handsome ceramic pieces. The Japanese studied Western medicine, astronomy, languages, and even painting styles. In turn, Europeans wanted Japanese ceramics, which were prized as highly as the ceramics of the Chinese.

Reading Check **Summarizing** Why were government officials concerned about Kabuki theater?

Kabuki actor

Korea: The Hermit Kingdom

The Yi dynasty in **Korea,** founded at the end of the fourteenth century, remained in power during the entire Tokugawa Era in Japan. From their capital at Hanyang (modern-day Seoul), Yi rulers patterned their society after that of their powerful Chinese neighbors to the north.

Korean rulers tried to keep the country isolated from the outside world, earning it the name "the Hermit Kingdom." They were not always successful, however. A Japanese force under Toyotomi Hideyoshi invaded Korea in the late sixteenth century. Although the Japanese invaders were defeated, Korea was devastated, and the Yi dynasty was weakened. In the 1630s, a Manchu army invaded northern Korea and forced the Yi dynasty to become subject to China. Korea remained largely untouched by European merchants and Christian missionaries.

Reading Check **Summarizing** Why was Korea called "the Hermit Kingdom"?

SECTION 3 ASSESSMENT

Checking for Understanding

1. **Define** daimyo, han, hostage system, eta.
2. **Identify** Oda Nobunaga, Toyotomi Hideyoshi, Tokugawa Ieyasu, Matsuo Basho.
3. **Locate** Kyoto, Osaka, Edo, Korea.
4. **Sequence** the events that led to Japan's policy of isolation.
5. **List** the four main social classes that existed during the Tokugawa Era. Who was at the top of the social structure, and who was at the bottom?

Critical Thinking

6. **Draw Inferences** How were most peasants affected by the economic changes in Japan?
7. **Organizing Information** Using a chart like the one below, show how the new urban centers in Japan influenced the arts and entertainment.

urban centers	

Analyzing Visuals

8. **Examine** the photograph of a Kabuki actor shown above. What does this photograph tell you about Japanese Kabuki theater, and how does this theater compare to and contrast with the different forms of theater (opera, pantomime, realistic drama) that developed in the West?

Writing About History

9. **Descriptive Writing** Imagine that you are the literate wife of a samurai. Write a journal entry that describes your relationship to your husband, your children, and your mother-in-law.

SECTION 3 ASSESSMENT

1. Key terms are in blue.
2. Oda Nobunaga *(p. 279);* Toyotomi Hideyoshi *(p. 279);* Tokugawa Ieyasu *(p. 279);* Matsuo Basho *(p. 281)*
3. See chapter maps.
4. Jesuits burn shrines, Japan prohibits Christian activities, expels all missionaries, and turns away most European traders
5. warriors, farmers, artisans, merchants; top: warriors, bottom: merchants
6. experienced declining profits, rising costs, and taxes
7. urban centers: Rise of popular fiction written by and for townspeople; Rise of Kabuki theater dealing with world of teahouses, dance halls in cities; Increase in building (in Edo)
8. character is highly stylized: no indication of individual beneath costume; answers will vary
9. Answers will vary but should be consistent with material presented in this section.

Eyewitness to History

The Japanese Discover Firearms

THE PORTUGUESE BROUGHT handguns to Japan in the sixteenth century. In this selection, the daimyo of a small island off the southern tip of Japan provides an explanation of how to use the new weapons. Obviously, he is fascinated by the results.

This detail from a late sixteenth-century Japanese painting records the arrival of the first Portuguese traders at the port city of Nagasaki, Japan.

“There are two leaders among the traders. In their hands they carried something two or three feet [.6 or .9 m] long, straight on the outside with a passage inside, and made of a heavy substance. The inner passage runs through it although it is closed at the end. At its side, there is an opening which is the passageway for fire. Its shape defies comparison with anything I know. To use it, fill it with powder and small lead pellets. Set up a small target on a bank. Grip the object in your hand, compose your body, and closing one eye, apply fire to the opening. Then the pellet hits the target squarely. The explosion is like lightning and the report like thunder. Bystanders must cover their ears. This thing with one blow can smash a mountain of silver and a wall of iron. If one sought to do mischief in another man's domain and he was touched by it, he would lose his life instantly. . . . Lord Tokitaka saw it and thought it was the wonder of wonders. He did not know its name at first nor the details of its use. Then someone called it 'ironarms.'

Disregarding the high price of the arms, Tokitaka purchased from the aliens two pieces of the firearms for his family treasure. As for the art of grinding, sifting, and mixing of the powder, Tokitaka let his retainer learn it. Tokitaka occupied himself, morning and night, and without rest in handling the arms. As a result, he was able to convert the misses of his early experiments into hits—a hundred hits in a hundred attempts.”

—Lord Tokitaka, On the Use of Firearms

Analyzing Primary Sources

1. Who introduced firearms to Japan in the sixteenth century?
2. Considering the description of the firearm the Portuguese brought, what do you think we would call it today?
3. In the last paragraph, to whom does the term *aliens* refer?

TEACH

Analyzing Primary Sources
Ask students to write an essay in which they evaluate the reaction of the Japanese daimyo to firearms. Do students believe the daimyo was merely intrigued by these weapons or did he realize how important they would be to the future of Japan? How might Japan's history have been different if the Europeans had not sold Western military technology?

Enrich
Ask students to write a description of an object they use every day but tell them not to identify the object in their description. Have students read their descriptions out loud to the class to see if other students can identify the object. **L3**

ANSWERS TO ANALYZING PRIMARY SOURCES

1. The Portuguese were the first to bring firearms to Japan in the sixteenth century.
2. We would probably call it a shotgun or a rifle, although a very primitive one.
3. *Aliens* refers to the Portuguese. The term is used to describe people from other countries.

GLENCOE TECHNOLOGY

MindJogger Videoquiz

Use the **MindJogger Videoquiz** to review Chapter 9 content.

 Available in VHS.

Using Key Terms

1. banners **2.** commercial capitalism **3.** porcelain **4.** daimyo **5.** hostage system **6.** hans **7.** eta

Reviewing Key Facts

8. Europeans were considered a form of barbarian. Both sides benefited from the early cultural exchange. Eventually the Qing rulers attempted to limit contact with European traders.

9. It tried to preserve its distinct identity within Chinese society. It was defined legally as distinct. However, the Qing brought Chinese into the top ranks of the imperial administration, sharing important government positions equally with them.

10. because it was off-limits to commoners

11. With the long period of peace under the Tokugawa rule, a warrior class was no longer necessary. Many became managers on the land of the daimyo lords.

12. made it possible to ship grain and other goods from southern to northern China

13. originally, that anything the Europeans had to offer was superfluous because they lacked for nothing; later they came to be impressed by items such as clocks and eyeglasses

14. for destroying shrines

15. 1514

16. Tokyo; the Tokugawa rulers were the daimyo of Edo, so they made the city their capital, and by 1750 it had become one of the largest cities in the world.

17. Hanyang (modern-day Seoul)

CHAPTER 9 ASSESSMENT and ACTIVITIES

Using Key Terms

1. Military units called ____ were strategically placed throughout China as the chief fighting force of the Manchu Empire.
2. Trade and manufacturing in China did not develop into ____ as it did in Europe.
3. Chinese pottery makers were famous for their blue and white ____.
4. Heads of noble Japanese families, ____, controlled their own lands.
5. The shogunate controlled the daimyo by what has been called a ____, forcing the daimyo lords to leave their families in their Edo residence when the daimyo lords were away.
6. Japan was divided into 250 separate territories called ____, each ruled by a daimyo lord.
7. During the Tokugawa Era, Japan's class system became rigid with four classes and an underclass of outcasts, called the ____.

Reviewing Key Facts

8. **Culture** What was the Chinese view of Europeans, and how did interactions with Europeans impact Chinese society?
9. **Government** How did the Qing government solve the problem of being ethnically and culturally different from the people they governed?
10. **Culture** Why is the Imperial City in Beijing called the Forbidden City?
11. **Society** Explain how the samurai gradually ceased to be a warrior class.
12. **Government** How did the completion of the Grand Canal impact China?
13. **Economics** What was the Chinese attitude toward European products?
14. **Society** Why did Toyotomi Hideyoshi turn against the Jesuit missionaries?
15. **History** What year did the Portuguese make official contact with China?
16. **Geography** What is the current name of Edo, Japan? Why was Edo an important city to the Tokugawa rulers?
17. **Geography** Where was the ancient capital of Korea located?

Critical Thinking

18. **Making Generalizations** Do you believe that the plots of *The Golden Lotus* and *The Dream of the Red Chamber* would appeal to Western readers? Give your reasons.
19. **Analyzing** How might the surgeon general of the United States today respond to the portion of the Japanese government's edict in 1649 that said, "They [peasants] should eat millet and vegetables and other coarse food instead of rice. . . . They may not smoke tobacco. It is harmful to health. . . ."?

Chapter Summary

By the nineteenth century, Japanese and Chinese societies had changed as a result of the decisions and policies of their leaders.

Critical Thinking

18. Answers will vary. The plots of the novels are very similar to plots of popular modern Western novels.

19. The surgeon general would agree with it; grains, vegetables, and coarse foods are recognized as being beneficial to health, whereas tobacco products carry a warning from the surgeon general stating that they are harmful to health.

Writing About History

20. The Chinese isolationist period began as the Qing dynasty was declining. European traders were confined to a small island just outside Guanzhou, and they could reside there for only a few months each year and deal with only a few Chinese firms. In this way the Qing hoped to limit contact between Chinese and Europeans. Japan entered its isolationist phase as the country was in the process of unifying. The Jesuit

Self-Check Quiz
Visit the *Glencoe World History—Modern Times* Web site at wh.mt.glencoe.com and click on **Chapter 9–Self-Check Quiz** to prepare for the Chapter Test.

Writing About History

20. Expository Writing Compare the isolationist periods of China and Japan. Discuss each government's reasons for isolation, as well as the impact of isolation on their societies.

Analyzing Sources

Read the following excerpts from A Story That Matters, page 266.

> "... there is nothing we lack. We have never set much store on strange or ingenious objects, nor do we need any more of your country's manufactures."
>
> **—Emperor Qianlong**

> "... that superiority which Englishmen, wherever they go, cannot conceal."
>
> **—Lord George Macartney**

21. Compare the attitudes of Lord Macartney and Emperor Qianlong.
22. What have been some of the historical results of the political views of China and Britain?

Applying Technology Skills

23. Creating an Electronic Database Conduct outside research to learn more about the Tokugawa emperors in Japan. Then create an electronic database listing names of the emperors, dates each ruled, their significant accomplishments, and any problems that arose in Japan during their reigns. Share your database with your class.

Making Decisions

24. Imagine you are a Jesuit missionary in Japan. What would lead you to destroy Japanese religious shrines? When it becomes evident that the Japanese are outraged by your actions, what would you do and why?

Analyzing Maps and Charts

Study the map on this page to answer the following questions.

25. How many daimyo clans existed before the Tokugawa rulers?
26. How many miles separate Uesugi and Shimazu?
27. Which clans are located at the same latitudes?

NATIONAL GEOGRAPHIC **Japan, 1572**

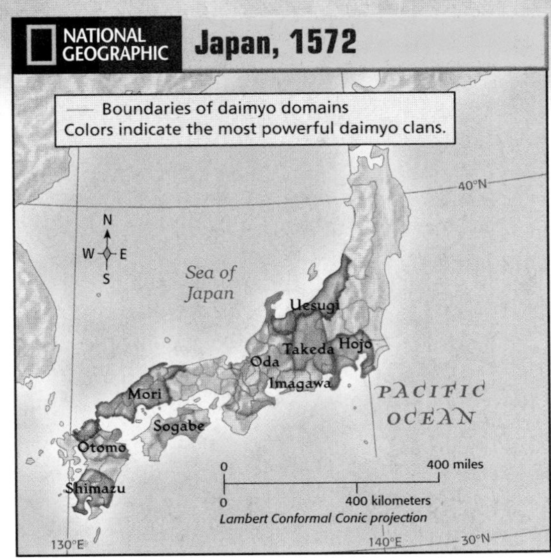

The Princeton Review

Standardized Test Practice

Directions: Use the passage *and* your knowledge of world history to answer the following question.

> "[I]t seems to be quite remarkable ... that in a kingdom of almost limitless expanse and innumerable population ... [that has] a well-equipped army and navy ... neither the King nor his people ever think of waging a war of aggression."
>
> **—Journals of Matteo Ricci**

The author suggests that people in the Ming dynasty

F lived in a militaristic society.
G adopted a "closed country" policy.
H were impoverished and starving.
J were prosperous but focused inward.

Test-Taking Tip: Do not rely on your memory of the passage to answer this question. Instead, look at each answer choice and check it against the quote.

Have students visit the Web site at wh.mt.glencoe.com to review Chapter 6 and take the Self-Check Quiz.

Making Decisions

24. Answers will vary. Answers may include that the Jesuit missionary destroys shrines to keep the Japanese from returning to their native religions. Consideration of the problem will weigh the importance of spreading Christianity against the risk of expulsion. Actual solutions should be creative.

Analyzing Maps and Charts

25. nine
26. approximately 600 miles (965.4 km)
27. Oda, Takeda, Hojo

Standardized Test Practice

Answer: J
Answer Explanation: Answers G and J may seem very similar. However, answer J matches the issues addressed in the quote more closely than G.

Bonus Question ?

Research the Yi dynasty of Korea and prepare a presentation for the class.

practice of destroying shrines led to the prohibition of Christian activities and the expulsions of all missionaries. Later, merchants were expelled, and only Dutch ships were permitted to dock at Nagasaki once a year, but only for two or three months.

Analyzing Sources

21. Both men were arrogant, conceited, and uninterested in the contributions of other civilizations.

22. Answers will vary. China's isolationism stymied its growth as a world power. The British attitude helped them dominate an empire on which the sun never set. As a result of less outside contact, Chinese society became more inward-looking. They considered everyone in the world but them to be backward and barbaric, as did the British.

Applying Technology

23. Answers will vary; students will create databases.

Introducing

World Languages

Language is an important source of self-identity, culture, and history. Language constantly changes, evolving to meet social and technological changes and adapting in order that we might understand and be understood by others.

TEACH

CURRICULUM CONNECTION

Linguistics The scientific study of language is called linguistics. Subfields include phonetics, which is concerned with the sounds of language; syntax, which deals with the structure of words and phrases; and semantics, which is the study of the meaning of words. Ask students to create a glossary of linguistic terms.

Critical Thinking

Ask students to study the map and chart on this page. Ask students to pose and answer two questions about geographic distributions and patterns shown on the map and chart. What conclusions can students draw about history from analyzing the chart and map? **L2**

World Languages

Language not only allows us to communicate, it affects the way we think and even how we may view ourselves. It creates an identity for a community of people and shapes their experiences.

Today about 6,500 languages are spoken around the world. Hundreds of these will disappear in this century because younger generations no longer speak them. Others will be overpowered by the influence of English, a language that has spread through technology, global commerce, telecommunications, and tourism.

World Languages

Language(s)	Native Speakers
Chinese languages	1,223,307,000
Spanish	332,000,000
English	322,000,000
Hindi/Urdu	240,000,000
Bengali	189,000,000
Arabic languages	174,950,000
Portuguese	170,000,000
Russian	170,000,000
Japanese	125,000,000
German	98,000,000
French	72,000,000

Source: SIL International, 1999.

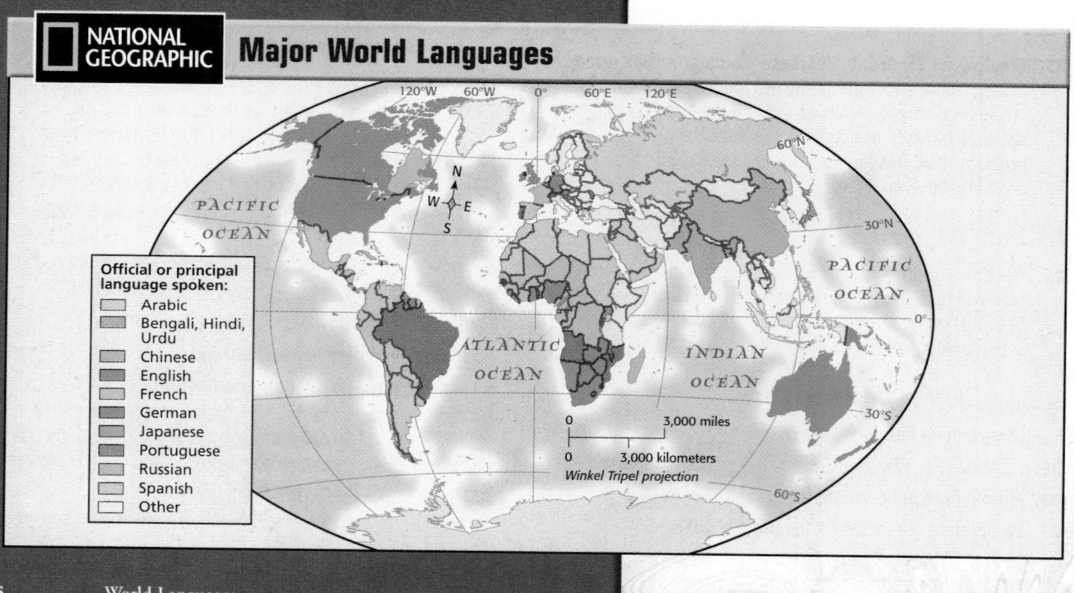

INTERDISCIPLINARY CONNECTIONS ACTIVITY

Language Skills Etymology is the history of a word, tracing its development since its earliest recorded occurrence in the language where it is found. Have students open a dictionary and select a page at random. Ask students to list the etymology of ten to fifteen words on the page. The etymology of a word is located in brackets before the definition. During a class discussion list on the board or overhead the different ways a word enters the English language. Student responses may include that a word has a French, German, or Latin history; the word is borrowed directly from another language (patio); the word is shortened (prom); the word is blended (motel); the word comes from a place name (calico); the word is a combination of initial letters (radar).

English Spoken Here

Old English (5th–11th Centuries)

If you were to travel back in time to visit Robin Hood, you would not be able to understand him. Even though you would both be speaking English, the language you speak has changed a great deal since the days of Robin and his merry men. Can you recognize any words from this old English conversation?

"Hast thu hafoc?"
Do you have a hawk?
"Ic habbe."
I have.
"Canst thu temian hig?"
Do you know how to tame them?
"Gea, ic cann. Hwat sceoldon hig me buton ic cuthe temian hig?"
Yes, I do. What use would they be to me if I could not tame them?
—From a tenth-century lesson

Middle English (11th–15th Centuries)

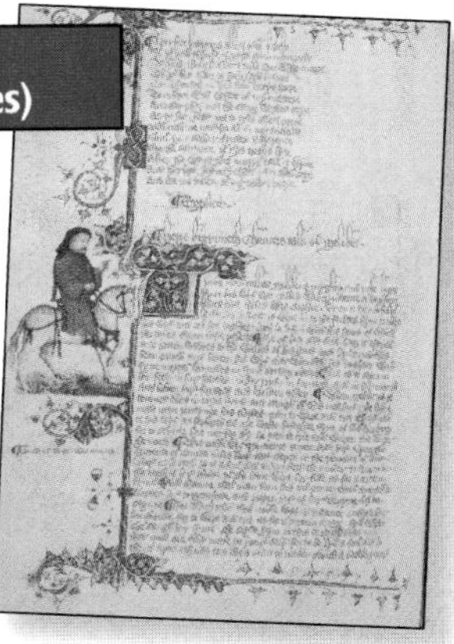

Middle English evolved when the Normans conquered England, bringing their language, French, with them. Many different dialects of English were spoken, but the dialect spoken in London became dominant. Geoffrey Chaucer's *Canterbury Tales* (1390) is an example.

In this viage shal telle tales tweye
To Caunterbury-ward I mene it so,
And homward he shal tellen othere two,
Of aventures that whilom han bifalle.

On this trip [you each] shall tell two tales
On the way to Canterbury,
And homeward [you] shall tell another two,
Of adventures that once had happened.
—From the Prologue of *Canterbury Tales*

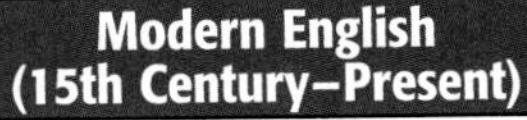

Modern English (15th Century–Present)

Although you might find Shakespeare difficult to understand, his English is essentially the language that evolved into the way we speak and read today.

JULIET: How camest thou
hither, tell me, and wherefore?
The orchard walls are high and hard
to climb,
And the place death, considering who
thou art,
If any of my kinsmen find thee here.

ROMEO: With love's light wings did I
o'er perch these walls,
For stony limits cannot hold love out,
And what love can do, that dares
love attempt,
Therefore thy kinsmen are no stop to me.
—From *Romeo and Juliet*

WORLD LANGUAGES

Connecting Across Time

The way we speak and the words we select when we speak are geared to occasion and audience. For example, students talking to each other on campus at lunch will use a different vocabulary and style than they would if they were interviewing for a job. Linguists call these differences registers. A register is the use of language defined by a social situation. Divide the class into two groups. Have one group rewrite Romeo and Juliet's dialogue on this page using very formal, modern English. Ask the second group to rewrite the dialogue in today's casual, informal style. Have students read their work aloud in class.

Who?What?When?Where?

American Sign Language Language is not necessarily oral or written. Sign language as practiced by hearing-impaired people is a visual-spatial language. Many people believe that American Sign Language (ASL) is a manual version of English. In fact, ASL is a completely separate language with its own syntax and grammatical structure. Hand gestures are just one component of ASL. Sign language makes use of the space surrounding the signer to describe places and people not present. Sign language is an important part of the communication process of the hearing impaired. You might wish to have a student or teacher sign several sentences or phrases to the class as a demonstration of another way to communicate.

EXTENDING THE CONTENT

J.R.R. Tolkien English fantasy fiction author John Ronald Reuel Tolkien, who lived from 1892 to1973, mastered Latin and Greek at an early age. Later he became proficient in a number of modern and ancient languages. He often made up his own languages for fun. When he wrote his trilogy, *The Lord of the Rings,* Tolkien created an entire system of languages for the marvelous inhabitants of Middle Earth. Fans of Tolkien appreciate how the author created an entirely believable world with its own history and languages. For Tolkien, "The invention of the languages is the foundation. The 'stories' were made rather to provide a world for the languages than the reverse."

Critical Thinking

Languages are classified by family. Languages that can be traced back to a common culture or civilization are related and belong in the same family. For example, English is an Indo-European language, related to other Indo-European languages such as German and Italian. Ask students to look at the languages listed on the chart to the right. Ask students to guess which languages are related to each other and belong in the same family. Students may be surprised to discover that Danish, Greek, Hindi, Spanish, and Persian are related to each other. Most linguists agree that Vietnamese, Tagalog, and Thai are related. Swahili is an African language but a great many of its words are derived from Arabic. Hebrew and Arabic have a common source. Most linguists believe that Chinese, Japanese, and Korean developed independently and are not part of the same language family. Have students choose a language, conduct outside research on its origin, and map its family tree.

CURRICULUM CONNECTION

Foreign Languages In many countries of the world people speak more than one language. Invite adults or fellow students who are proficient in more than one language to come to your classroom. Have them share how they came to learn several languages and how they feel they have benefited.

The ABCs of Language

How did writing begin? Early writing systems were derived from pictures. Every word would correspond to one or more symbols. For example, the word *house* might be written as a symbol that looked like a simplified house. Ancient Egyptian and Mayan hieroglyphics are examples.

The Phoenicians were among the first to develop an alphabet with characters that could be combined to make different sounds. The Greeks adapted it and passed it on to the Romans. The Roman alphabet is the alphabet most Western languages, such as English, use today.

How would you write "How are you?" to the people you meet around the world through the Internet?

"How Are You?"

Languages written from left to right →	
Danish	Hvordan gaar det?
Greek	Πως ειστε;
Hindi	आप कैसे है ?
Russian	Как пожйваете?
Spanish	¿Cómo está usted?
Swahili	Hujambo?
Tagalog (Philippines)	Kumusta po kayo?
Thai	สบายดีหรือ
Vietnamese	Anh (Chi) có khoe không?

Languages written from right to left ←	
Arabic	كيف حاكم ؟
Hebrew	סה שלוסר?
Persian	چطوريد؟

Languages written from top to bottom ↓	
Chinese	你好吗?
Japanese	お元気ですか
Korean	어떻개지내십니까?

Reading Chinese Characters

Chinese characters are combined in thousands of ways to make new words. In this example, when the character for tree is inserted into the character for box, you have a tree growing in a box, which is the character for "be in trouble."

Here are some other Chinese words divided into their elements. See if you can figure out what these characters mean.

EXAMPLE

木 + 口 = 困

tree + box = be in trouble

1. 火 + 山 = 火山
fire + mountain = ________

2. 木 + 木 + 木 = 森
tree + tree + tree = ________

Answers: 1. volcano 2. forest

COOPERATIVE LEARNING ACTIVITY

Creating a Presentation The map on page 286 highlights just ten of the world's 6,500 languages. Divide students into six groups. Assign a continent—North America, South America, Europe, Asia, Africa, or Australia—to each group. Have students research the language (or languages) spoken on their assigned continent. Students should discover who speaks which language and where the different language speakers are located. Have students discover which languages are growing and which are disappearing. Students should create a thematic illustration to show the results of their research, transferring statistical and written information into visual information. This illustration could be a thematic map, thematic graph, web graphic, or thematic time line. Have the groups share their visuals with the class.

WORLD LANGUAGES

Disappearing Languages

Before World War II, it is estimated that over 11 million people spoke Yiddish, a Jewish dialect. Many Yiddish speakers were killed in the Holocaust. Children of Holocaust survivors often forgot the language or chose not to use it in their new homelands. Today, the number of speakers is approximately 2 million, most of whom are elderly. When these people die, there will be few people left who speak the language, even though it's preserved in literature and oral records.

Many minority cultures around the world face the same problem. Often, these people live in areas that were once subjugated or conquered by other countries. The new rulers forced native peoples to adopt a new culture, often by prohibiting the use of the local language. In the United States, Native American children were frequently sent to boarding schools where they were forced to speak English and were punished if they spoke their own language. Not surprisingly, where there had once been hundreds of Native American languages, today there are only 175, and many of those will soon be extinct.

Fortunately, many struggling languages are making a comeback. In places like Ireland, northern Spain, and even Hawaii, schools are teaching traditional languages, and their usage is becoming widely accepted. Native Americans are also taking steps to revive their languages, as demonstrated by the Navajo newspaper at right. With language comes renewed interest in culture, and many ethnic groups who revive their language also find that they revive hope and self-worth within their people.

ADAHOONIŁIGII

THE NAVAHO LANGUAGE MONTHLY

VOL. 2 NO. 3

WINDOW ROCK, ARIZONA

'AHKEAH HONEESNA 'ÁKO BEESH BĄĄH DAH NAAZ NILIGII YÁ DAH NANIDAAHÍ SILĮĮ'!!

TSASK'EH BA HOOGHAN DIILTLA

English As an International Language

Mahesh is an Indian who lives in Trinidad. His wife is from Venezuela. To communicate they speak English. He works for an international oil company where he conducts business worldwide in English. On TV he watches CNN news, and he enjoys going to American movies.

English was first spread through colonization. Though usually unwelcome, English eventually became a way of communicating between ethnic groups who shared a country but not a common language. In the late twentieth century, English became even more dominant as American language and culture spread through global business (think Coca-Cola and McDonald's), media, and technology. The Israeli sign with English translations at left is an example of how English is being used worldwide.

Today, English is spoken in 115 countries as either the official language or as an important minority language. Although many people do not like it, the globalization of English has made communication and interaction between peoples easier. On the other hand, many smaller languages and cultures are being lost as the world becomes more homogeneous.

CURRICULUM CONNECTION

Foreign Languages Of the 6,500 languages spoken in the world today, close to 50 percent may be extinct within the next century. When a language is seen as culturally inferior, or when education and employment depend on proficiency in a national language, people conclude that their native language has lost its primary value. Loss of language, however, leads to loss of culture. In many parts of the world today, indigenous people are taking steps to preserve their languages. Have students research the various ways that languages are being preserved. Schedule class time so that students can make oral reports of their research results. Have students use the process of historical inquiry to research and to interpret the data they collect in their research.

Who?What?Where?When?

Translators In the nineteenth century, Christian missionaries working in foreign countries often insisted that local people learn to read and write in English. Today missionaries work hard to preserve local languages. If a culture has an unwritten language, missionaries work with locals to develop an alphabet so that through reading and writing, the language and history of a people and their culture will be preserved and continued.

Teacher's Notes

Chapter 10 Resources

Timesaving Tools

TeacherWorks™ All-In-One Planner and Resource Center

- **Interactive Teacher Edition** Access your Teacher Wraparound Edition and your classroom resources with a few easy clicks.
- **Interactive Lesson Planner** Planning has never been easier! Organize your week, month, semester, or year with all the lesson helps you need to make teaching creative, timely, and relevant.

Use Glencoe's **Presentation Plus!** multimedia teacher tool to easily present dynamic lessons that visually excite your students. Using Microsoft PowerPoint® you can customize the presentations to create your own personalized lessons.

TEACHING TRANSPARENCIES

Graphic Organizer Student Activity 10 Transparency

Chapter Transparency 10

Map Overlay Transparency 10

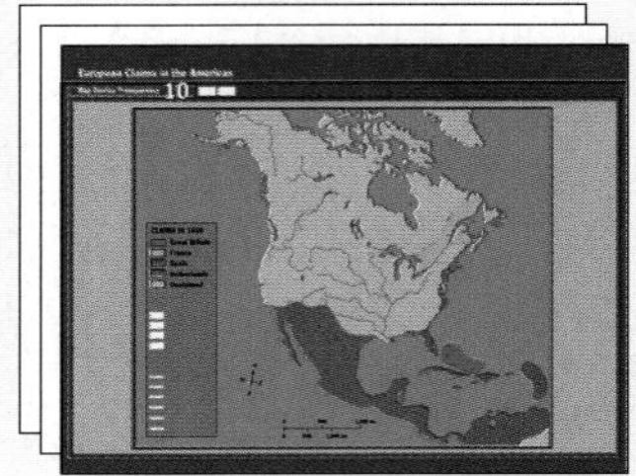

APPLICATION AND ENRICHMENT

Enrichment Activity 10

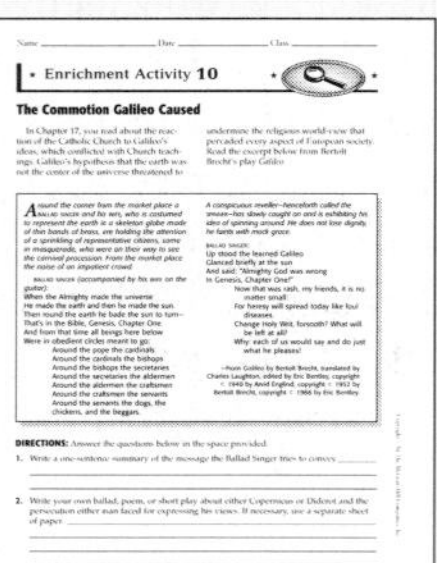

Enrichment Activity 10

The Commotion Galileo Caused

Primary Source Reading 10

Primary Source Reading 10

Of the *Encyclopedia*

History Simulation Activity 10

History Simulation Activity 10

HANDOUT MATERIAL

Science on Trial—Planning Form

Historical Significance Activity 10

Cooperative Learning Activity 10

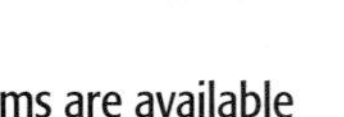

THE HISTORY CHANNEL.

The following videotape programs are available from Glencoe as supplements to Chapter 10:

- **Sir Isaac Newton: Gravity of Genius** (ISBN 1–56501–982–2)
- **Mozart** (ISBN 1–56501–590–8)
- **George Washington: Founding Father** (ISBN 1–56501–377–8)
- **The American Revolution** (ISBN 1–56501–436–7)

To order, call Glencoe at 1–800–334–7344. To find classroom resources to accompany many of these videos, check the following home pages:
A&E Television: www.aande.com
The History Channel: www.historychannel.com

Chapter 10 Resources

Review and Reinforcement

Linking Past and Present Activity 10

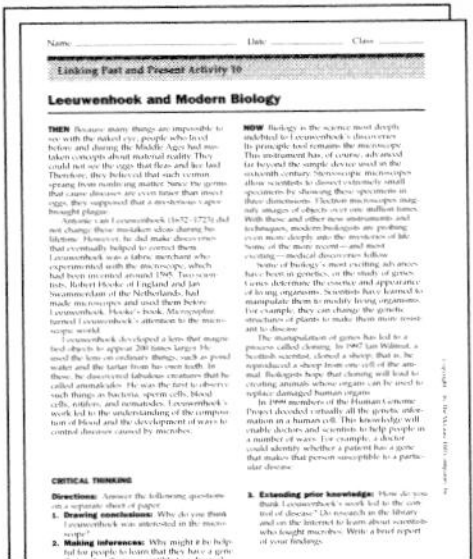

Time Line Activity 10

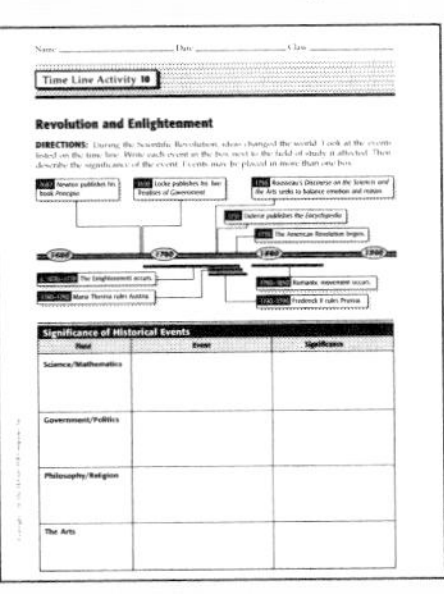

Reteaching Activity 10

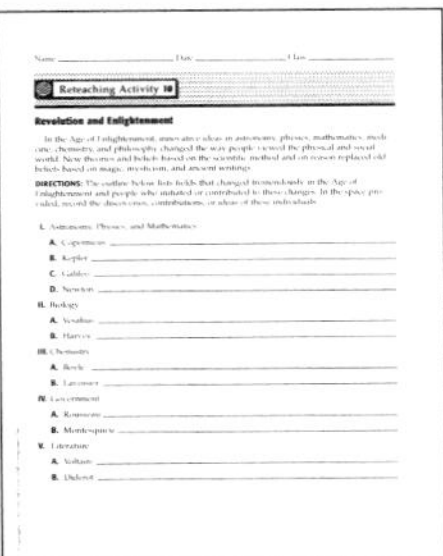

Vocabulary Activity 10

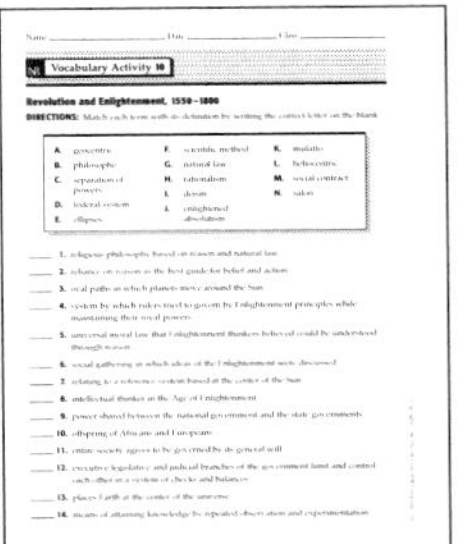

Critical Thinking Skills Activity 10

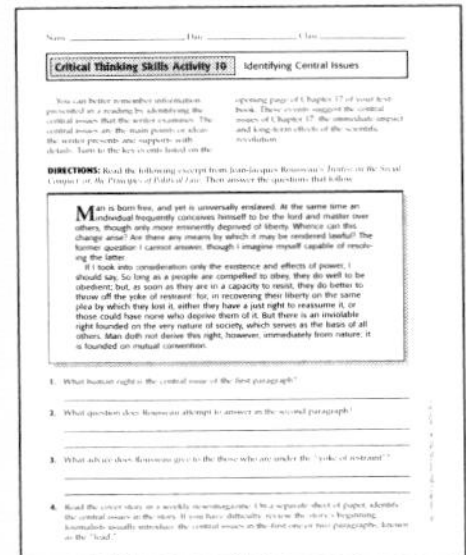

Assessment and Evaluation

Chapter 10 Test Form A

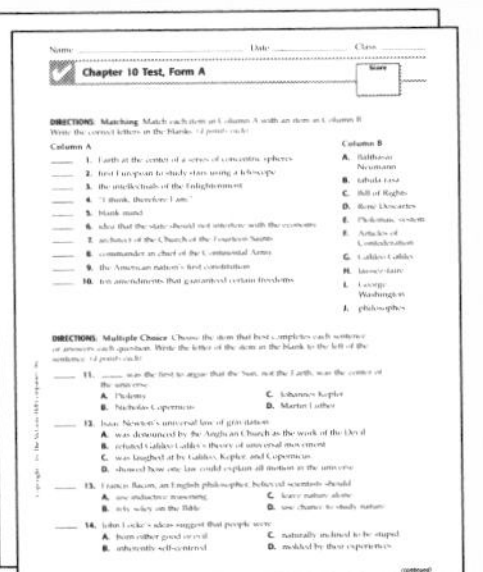

Chapter 10 Test Form B

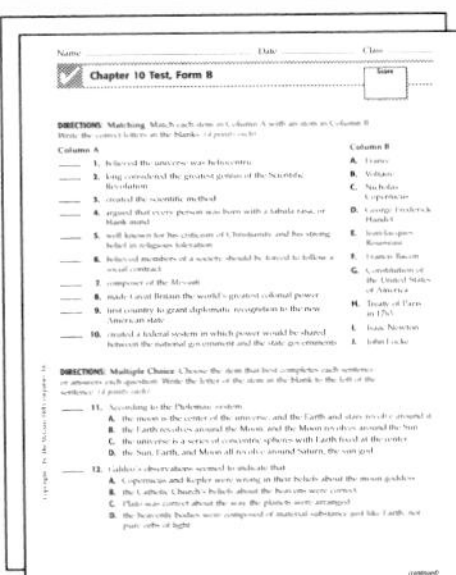

Performance Assessment Activity 10

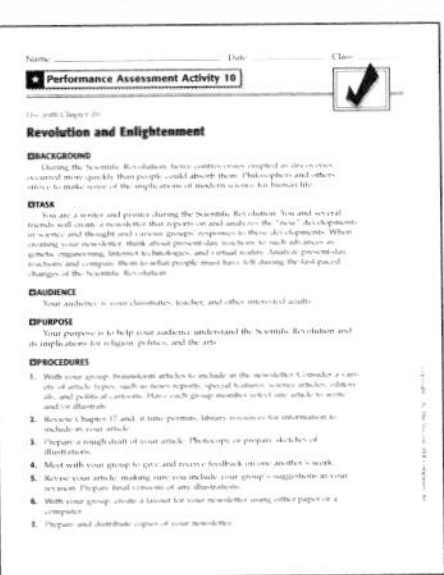

ExamView® Pro Testmaker CD-ROM

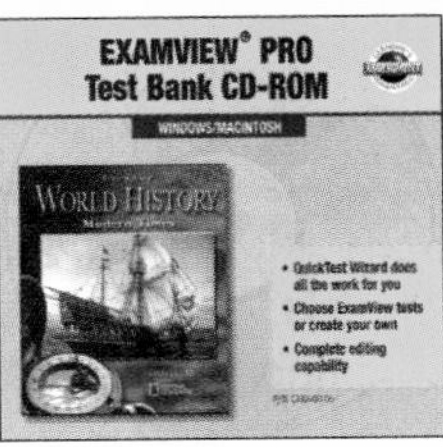

Standardized Test Skills Practice Workbook Activity 10

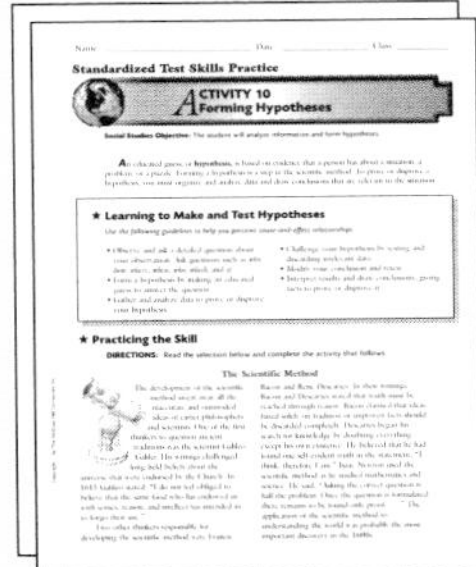

Interdisciplinary Activities

Mapping History Activity 10

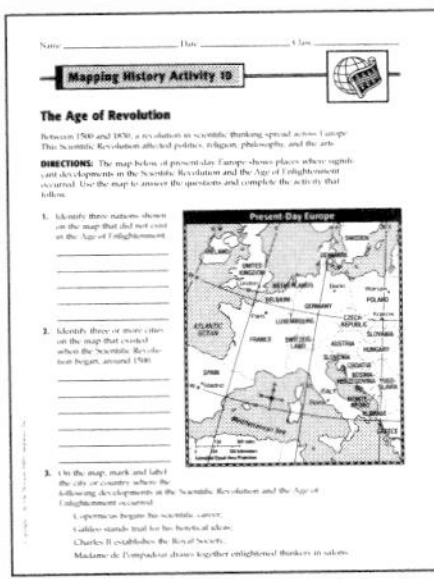

World Art and Music Activity 10

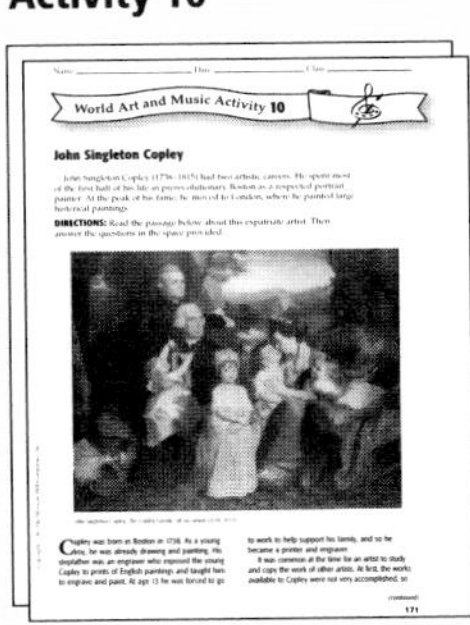

History and Geography Activity 10

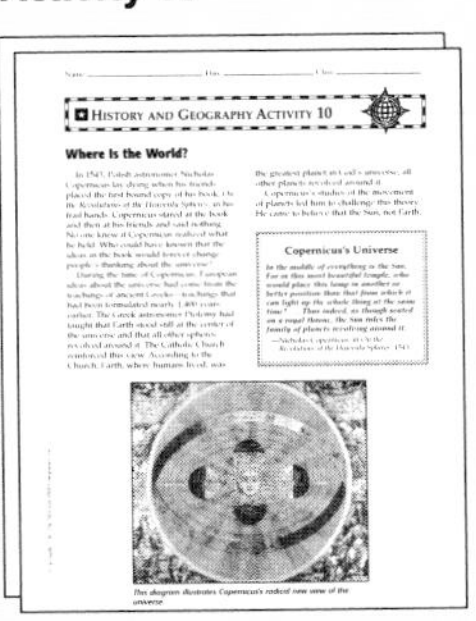

People in World History Activity 10

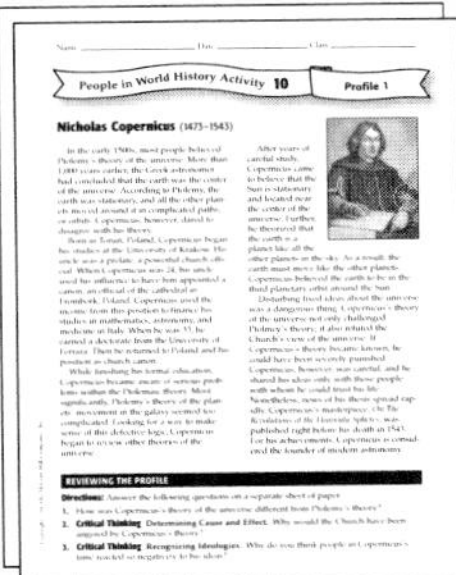

Multimedia

- Vocabulary PuzzleMaker CD-ROM
- Interactive Tutor Self-Assessment CD-ROM
- ExamView® Pro Testmaker CD-ROM
- Audio Program
- World History Primary Source Document Library CD-ROM
- MindJogger Videoquiz
- Presentation Plus! CD-ROM
- TeacherWorks CD-ROM
- Interactive Student Edition CD-ROM
- The World History—Modern Times Video Program

Spanish Resources

The following Spanish language materials are available in the Spanish Resources Binder:

- Spanish Guided Reading Activities
- Spanish Reteaching Activities
- Spanish Quizzes and Tests
- Spanish Vocabulary Activities
- Spanish Summaries

Chapter 10 Resources

SECTION RESOURCES

Daily Objectives	Reproducible Resources	Multimedia Resources
SECTION 1 **The Scientific Revolution** 1. Discuss how the Scientific Revolution gave Europeans a new way to view humankind's place in the universe.	Reproducible Lesson Plan 10–1 Daily Lecture and Discussion Notes 10–1 Guided Reading Activity 10–1* Section Quiz 10–1* Reading Essentials and Study Guide 10–1	Daily Focus Skills Transparency 10–1 Interactive Tutor Self-Assessment CD-ROM ExamView® Pro Testmaker CD-ROM Presentation Plus! CD-ROM
SECTION 2 **The Enlightenment** 1. Describe how eighteenth-century intellectuals used the ideas of the Scientific Revolution to reexamine all aspects of life. 2. Relate how people gathered in salons to discuss the ideas of the philosophes.	Reproducible Lesson Plan 10–2 Daily Lecture and Discussion Notes 10–2 Guided Reading Activity 10–2* Section Quiz 10–2* Reading Essentials and Study Guide 10–2	Daily Focus Skills Transparency 10–2 Interactive Tutor Self-Assessment CD-ROM ExamView® Pro Testmaker CD-ROM Presentation Plus! CD-ROM
SECTION 3 **The Impact of the Enlightenment** 1. Discuss how Enlightenment beliefs were reflected in the art, music, and literature of the time. 2. Summarize how Enlightenment thought influenced the politics of Europe in the eighteenth century.	Reproducible Lesson Plan 10–3 Daily Lecture and Discussion Notes 10–3 Guided Reading Activity 10–3* Section Quiz 10–3* Reading Essentials and Study Guide 10–3	Daily Focus Skills Transparency 10–3 Interactive Tutor Self-Assessment CD-ROM ExamView® Pro Testmaker CD-ROM Presentation Plus! CD-ROM
SECTION 4 **Colonial Empires and the American Revolution** 1. Explain how the colonies of Latin America and British North America were developing in ways that differed from their European mother countries. 2. Analyze why the American colonies revolted against Great Britain and formed a new nation.	Reproducible Lesson Plan 10–4 Daily Lecture and Discussion Notes 10–4 Guided Reading Activity 10–4* Section Quiz 10–4* Reteaching Activity 10* Reading Essentials and Study Guide 10–4	Daily Focus Skills Transparency 10–4 Interactive Tutor Self-Assessment CD-ROM ExamView® Pro Testmaker CD-ROM Presentation Plus! CD-ROM

0:00 **OUT OF TIME?**
Assign the Chapter 10 **Reading Essentials and Study Guide.**

*Also Available in Spanish

Blackline Master | Transparency | CD-ROM | DVD
Poster |   Music Program | 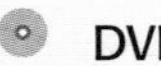 Audio Program | Videocassette

Chapter 10 Resources

NATIONAL GEOGRAPHIC Teacher's Corner

INDEX TO NATIONAL GEOGRAPHIC MAGAZINE

The following articles relate to this chapter:

- "The Hubble Telescope," by William R. Newcott, April 1997.
- "Sir Joseph Banks," by T.H. Watkins, November 1996.
- "Information Revolution," by Joel L. Swerdlow, October 1995.
- "Humboldt's Way," by Loren McIntyre, September 1985.
- "Two Revolutions," by Charles McCarry, July 1989.
- "Yorktown Shipwreck," by John D. Broadwater, June 1988.
- "James Madison, Architect of the Constitution," by Alice J. Hall, September 1987.

NATIONAL GEOGRAPHIC SOCIETY PRODUCTS AVAILABLE FROM GLENCOE

To order the following products call Glencoe at 1-800-334-7344:

- *The American People* (Videodiscs)
- *A Geographic Perspective on American History* (Videodiscs)

ADDITIONAL NATIONAL GEOGRAPHIC SOCIETY PRODUCTS

To order the following, call National Geographic at 1-800-368-2728:

- *PictureShow: Story of America's Library* (CD-ROM)

NGS ONLINE

Access National Geographic's new dynamic MapMachine Web site and other geography resources at:
www.nationalgeographic.com
www.nationalgeographic.com/maps

KEY TO ABILITY LEVELS

Teaching strategies have been coded.

L1 BASIC activities for all students
L2 AVERAGE activities for average to above-average students
L3 CHALLENGING activities for above-average students
ELL ENGLISH LANGUAGE LEARNER activities

Block Schedule

Activities that are suited to use within the block scheduling framework are identified by:

Use our Web site for additional resources. All essential content is covered in the Student Edition.

You and your students can visit www.wh.mt.glencoe.com, the Web site companion to *Glencoe World History—Modern Times.* This innovative integration of electronic and print media offers your students a wealth of opportunities. The student text directs students to the Web site for the following options:

- **Chapter Overviews**
- **Self-Check Quizzes**
- **Student Web Activities**
- **Textbook Updates**

Answers to the Student Web Activities are provided for you in the **Web Activity Lesson Plans.** Additional Web resources and Interactive Tutor Puzzles are also available.

From the Classroom of...

Susan Tufts
Rockville High School
Vernon, Connecticut

Parisian Salons

Discuss with students the role of salons during the Age of Enlightenment. Then explain that Madame de Geoffrin, a noted *salonnière* and patron, has invited a group of major philosophes, artists, writers, and musicians to her salon at the Hôtel de Rambouillet.

Have each student choose an Enlightenment figure to research and then portray at the salon. Although there were a number of well-known women in the Enlightenment era, such as Mary Wollstonecraft and Madame de Pompadour, girls may play the parts of men, if they wish. As teacher, you should also portray a character so that you can facilitate the conversation when necessary. Students should focus on the setting of the salon, group dynamics, and the ideas that would have been exchanged.

After the salon simulation, have students discuss what impact the free flow of ideas had on Europe and what effect those ideas have on the world today.

Introducing CHAPTER 10

Performance Assessment

Refer to Activity 10 in the Performance Assessment Activities and Rubrics booklet.

The Impact Today

Point out to students that scientists continually advance knowledge through experimentation in many areas. Many new findings and discoveries have far-ranging implications for science and for society. Ask students to generate lists of scientific breakthroughs that have occurred during the past five years. Also ask them to speculate on potential discoveries and innovations.

GLENCOE TECHNOLOGY

The World History—Modern Times Video Program

To learn more about the Scientific Revolution, students can view the Chapter 10 video, "New Scientific Thinking," from **The World History—Modern Times Video Program.**

MindJogger Videoquiz

Use the **MindJogger Videoquiz** to preview Chapter 10 content.

Available in VHS.

CHAPTER 10 Revolution and Enlightenment

1550–1800

Key Events

As you read this chapter, look for the key events in the history of the Scientific Revolution and the Enlightenment.

- *The ideas of the Scientific Revolution and the Enlightenment laid the foundation for a modern worldview based on rationalism and secularism.*
- *Enlightenment thought led some rulers to advocate such natural rights as equality before the law and freedom of religion.*
- *The American colonies formed a new nation and ratified the Constitution of the United States.*

The Impact Today

The events that occurred during this time period still impact our lives today.

- *Scientists use research techniques that are based on the scientific method.*
- *The intellectuals of the Enlightenment advocated the rights of the individual, paving the way for the rise of democracy.*
- *Montesquieu's idea of separation of powers strongly influenced the writing of the Constitution of the United States.*

World History—Modern Times Video The Chapter 10 video, "New Scientific Thinking," *chronicles the origins of the Scientific Revolution in Europe and its impact on scientific thinking worldwide.*

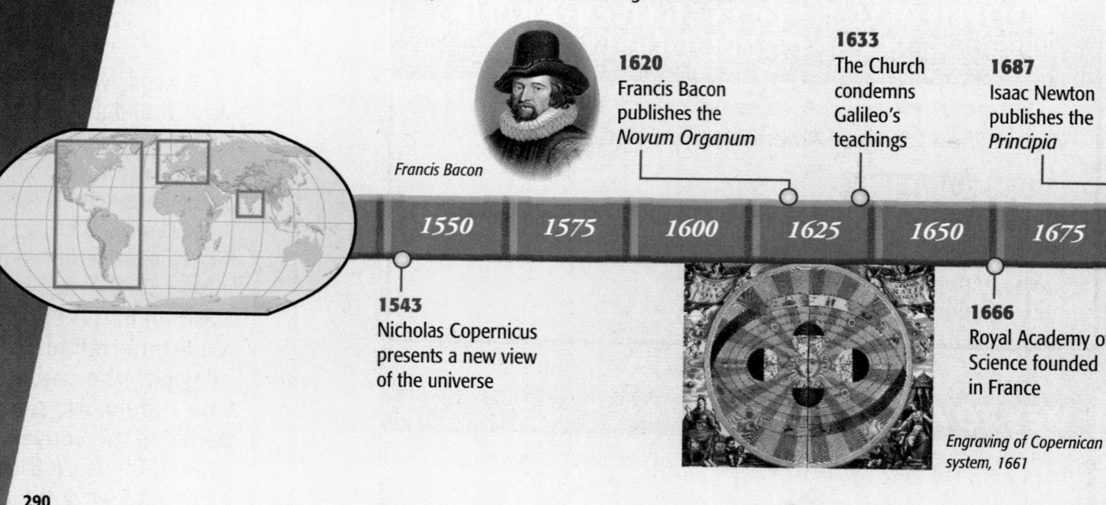
1550
1575
1600
1625
1650
1675
1543 Nicholas Copernicus presents a new view of the universe
1620 Francis Bacon publishes the *Novum Organum*
1633 The Church condemns Galileo's teachings
1666 Royal Academy of Science founded in France
1687 Isaac Newton publishes the *Principia*

Francis Bacon

Engraving of Copernican system, 1661

290

TWO-MINUTE LESSON LAUNCHER

On a table in front of the class, place three items that students would find desirable. Then divide the class into three groups. Each group should discuss which item it wants most and send a representative to the front of the class to take the item. Then track the outcomes. Each group could choose a different item, and everyone would be satisfied. If all three want the same item, ask the representatives to go back to their groups and discuss how they would obtain the item (using force or negotiation). Explain to students that this is similar to what happens when countries want to colonize or seize land belonging to other nations, as they will see in this chapter. **L1** ELL

Louis XIV at the French Royal Academy of Sciences

Denis Diderot

1751 Diderot becomes editor of the *Encyclopedia*

1763 The Seven Years' War ends

1788 The Constitution of the United States is ratified by nine states

1700 1725 1750 1775 1800 1825

1759 James Wolfe dies in battle outside Quebec, Canada

1776 American colonies declare independence from Britain

1792 Mary Wollstonecraft publishes *A Vindication of the Rights of Women*

British general, James Wolfe

HISTORY Online

Chapter Overview
Visit the *Glencoe World History—Modern Times* Web site at wh.mt.glencoe.com and click on **Chapter 10–Chapter Overview** to preview chapter information.

MORE ABOUT THE ART

The Academy of Science Louis XIV became king of France in 1643 at age four. He was an absolute monarch who called himself the Sun King because he believed he was a source of light to all his people. He supported building campaigns and the arts, including the founding of the Royal Academy of Science in 1666. The academy was built so that a group of French scientists who had been meeting informally for several years could hold regular meetings. Construction of the academy's observatory began in 1667. Today, the academy building in Paris is headquarters of the International Time Bureau, which sets standard time for the world's observatories.

Introducing CHAPTER 10

Chapter Objectives

After studying this chapter, students should be able to:

1. describe the scientific advances of the seventeenth and eighteenth centuries and their impact on society;
2. identify and describe conditions that led to the Enlightenment;
3. explain new philosophies and the social changes that arose during the Enlightenment;
4. describe the causes of the War of the Austrian Succession and the Seven Years' War;
5. explain the reasons for European exploration;
6. describe the impact of colonization;
7. explain the roots of revolution.

HISTORY Online

Chapter Overview
Introduce students to chapter content and key terms by having them access **Chapter Overview 10** at wh.mt.glencoe.com.

Time Line Activity

As students read the chapter, have them review the time line on pages 290 to 291. Ask them to explain the significance of 1633. *(The Catholic Church condemned Galileo's popularization of the Copernican theory because it challenged its belief that the universe was geocentric.)* **L1**

CHAPTER PREVIEW

Introducing

A Story That Matters

Depending on the ability levels of your students, select from the following questions to reinforce the reading of *A Story That Matters.*

- Have students debate the choice between self-respect and self-preservation that Galileo was forced to make by leaders of the Catholic Church. What do students believe they would have done in Galileo's situation? *(Answers will vary.)*
- Have students identify religious and ethical conflicts that scientific advancements have created in recent years. *(Answers will vary.)* **L2**

About the Art

Ask students to look at the image on this page. Have students locate Galileo in the painting. In a class discussion, have students describe how Galileo may have felt. Ask students to interpret what is happening in the foreground. Have students decide if the artist was recording the event or interpreting the event.

CHAPTER PREVIEW

A Story That Matters

Galileo sits before the Inquisition in Rome.

Galileo on Trial

The Italian scientist Galileo found himself in trouble with the authorities of the Catholic Church. Galileo believed in a new worldview. He explained to a friend, "I hold the Sun to be situated motionless in the center of the revolution of the celestial bodies, while . . . Earth rotates on its axis and revolves about the Sun." Moreover, "nothing physical that sense-experience puts before our eyes . . . ought to be called in question (much less condemned) upon the testimony of passages from the Bible."

The Catholic Church had a different view. In 1632, Galileo, 68 years old and in ill health, was called before the dreaded Inquisition in Rome. He was kept waiting for two months before he was tried and found guilty of heresy and disobedience. The report of the Inquisition said: "The view that the Sun stands motionless at the center of the universe is foolish, philosophically false, and utterly heretical, because contrary to Holy Scripture."

Completely shattered by the experience, Galileo recanted in 1633: "With a sincere heart I curse and detest the said errors contrary to the Holy Church, and I swear that I will nevermore in future say or assert anything that may give rise to a similar suspicion of me." Legend holds that when he left the trial room, Galileo muttered to himself, "And yet it [Earth] does move!"

Why It Matters

Galileo was one of the scientists of the seventeenth century who set the Western world on a new path. That path, known as the Scientific Revolution, developed a new way of viewing the universe.

In the eighteenth century, a group of intellectuals used the ideas of the Scientific Revolution to reexamine all aspects of life and began what came to be called the Age of Enlightenment. The ideas of the Enlightenment helped foster the American and French Revolutions.

History and You The philosopher Adam Smith used Enlightenment ideas to identify economic laws. Read the front page, business section, and classifieds of a newspaper. Create a poster with articles and advertisements reflecting Smith's economic principles.

HISTORY AND YOU

Galileo's theories caused people to question the nature of the universe and challenged the views of the Catholic Church. At the time he proposed his ideas, most people believed that Earth was at the center of the universe, and the moon and stars consisted of pure, unblemished, heavenly materials. It is popular to say that Galileo versus the Church is a case of science versus religion. In reality, the Church had paved the way for Galileo. Scholasticism and Thomas Aquinas insisted on the rationality of creation. Jesuit astronomers confirmed many of Galileo's discoveries. Some historians believe that Galileo angered the Church by insisting that the Church's interpretation of Scripture was wrong, not by insisting that his scientific theories were correct. By challenging accepted views, Galileo threatened the authority of the Church and laid the groundwork for rebellion. His beliefs formed the beginning of secular, rational thought—the hallmark of the Enlightenment.

SECTION 1 The Scientific Revolution

Guide to Reading

Main Idea
- The Scientific Revolution gave Europeans a new way to view humankind's place in the universe.

Key Terms
geocentric, Ptolemaic system, heliocentric, universal law of gravitation, rationalism, scientific method, inductive reasoning

People to Identify
Ptolemy, Nicholas Copernicus, Galileo Galilei, Isaac Newton, Robert Boyle, Margaret Cavendish, Maria Winkelmann, René Descartes, Francis Bacon

Places to Locate
Poland, Padua

Preview Questions
1. How did the Scientific Revolution begin?
2. What is the scientific method?

Reading Strategy
Summarizing Information Use a table like the one below to identify the contributions of Copernicus, Kepler, Galileo, and Newton to the development of a new concept of the universe.

Copernicus	
Kepler	
Galileo	
Newton	

Preview of Events

1545 · 1560 · 1575 · 1590 · 1605 · 1620 · 1635

- **1543** Vesalius publishes *On the Fabric of the Human Body*
- **1610** Galileo's discoveries are published
- **1628** Harvey publishes *On the Motion of the Heart and Blood*
- **1632** Galileo faces the Inquisition
- **1637** Descartes writes *Discourse on Method*

Galileo Galilei

Voices from the Past

In 1610, Galileo described what he had observed with his newly devised telescope:

> ❝Now let us review the observations made during the past two months. . . . Let us speak first of that surface of the Moon which faces us. For greater clarity I distinguish two parts of this surface, a lighter and a darker. . . . [T]he darker part makes the Moon appear covered with spots. . . . From observation of these spots . . . I have been led to the opinion and conviction that the surface of the Moon is not smooth, uniform, and precisely spherical as a great number of philosophers believe it and the other heavenly bodies to be, but is uneven, rough, and full of cavities, not unlike the face of . . . Earth, relieved by chains of mountains and deep valleys.❞
>
> —***Discoveries and Opinions of Galileo,* Stillman Drake, ed., 1957**

Galileo's observations helped to create a new view of the universe in the seventeenth century.

Background to the Revolution

In the Middle Ages, many educated Europeans took an intense interest in the world around them. However, these "natural philosophers," as medieval scientists were known, did not make observations of the natural world. These scientists relied on a few ancient authorities—especially Aristotle—for their scientific knowledge. A number of changes in the fifteenth and sixteenth centuries caused

1 FOCUS

Section Overview

This section explores how the Scientific Revolution changed humankind's view of the universe.

BELLRINGER
Skillbuilder Activity

Project transparency and have students answer questions.

Available as a blackline master.

Daily Focus Skills Transparency 10–1

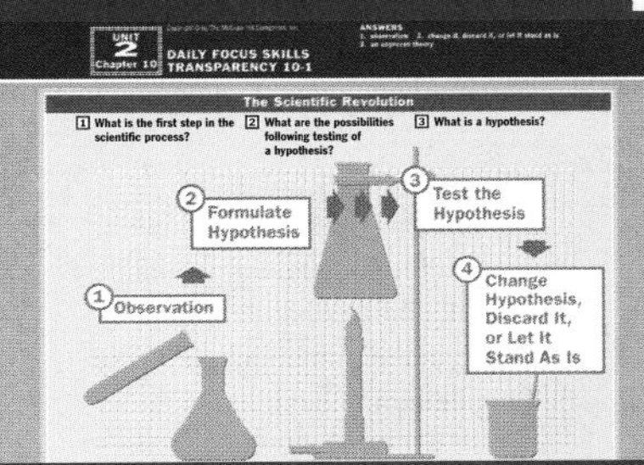

Guide to Reading

Answers to Graphic: Copernicus: Solar system is sun-centered; Kepler: Planets move around Sun in ellipses; Galileo: Heavenly bodies are composed of material substance, like Earth; Newton: Three laws of motion govern planetary bodies as well as objects on Earth.

Preteaching Vocabulary: Explain *rationalism. (Rationalism is a system of thought initiated by French philosopher René Descartes that claims reason is the chief source of knowledge.)* **L2**

SECTION RESOURCES

Reproducible Masters
- Reproducible Lesson Plan 10–1
- Daily Lecture and Discussion Notes 10–1
- Guided Reading Activity 10–1
- Section Quiz 10–1
- Reading Essentials and Study Guide 10–1

Transparencies
- Daily Focus Skills Transparency 10–1

Multimedia
- Interactive Tutor Self-Assessment CD-ROM
- ExamView® Pro Testmaker CD-ROM
- Presentation Plus! CD-ROM

2 TEACH

Reading Check

Answer: Humanists made available new works of Ptolemy, Archimedes, and Plato; invention of new instruments allowed accurate measurements; printing press spread ideas.

Picturing History

Answer: Both are dressed in rich clothing and hold models of the universe.

Daily Lecture and Discussion Notes 10–1

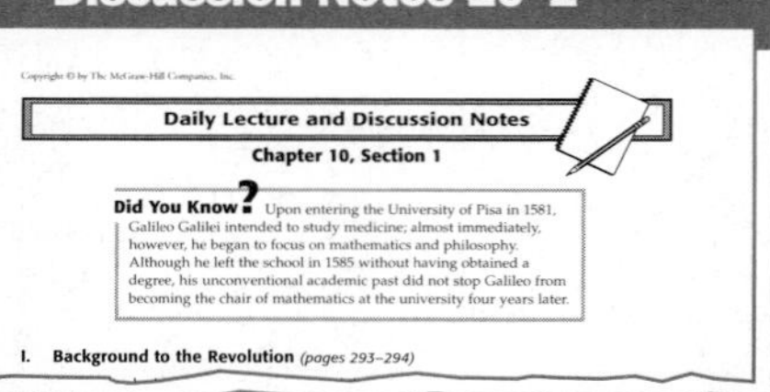

Daily Lecture and Discussion Notes

Chapter 10, Section 1

Did You Know? Upon entering the University of Pisa in 1581, Galileo Galilei intended to study medicine; almost immediately, however, he began to focus on mathematics and philosophy. Although he left the school in 1585 without having obtained a degree, his unconventional academic past did not stop Galileo from becoming the chair of mathematics at the university four years later.

I. **Background to the Revolution** *(pages 293–294)*

Who?What?Where?When?

Microscope and Telescope
Two new instruments, the microscope and the telescope, made many of the discoveries of the Scientific Revolution possible. Since the 1600s, many improvements have been made in both. Have students research and report to the class on new types of microscopes developed in the twentieth century, including the electron microscope and the scanning tunneling microscope. You could also have students report on twentieth-century telescopes, such as camera telescopes and radio telescopes. **L2**

the natural philosophers to abandon their old views and develop new ones.

Renaissance humanists had mastered Greek as well as Latin and thus had access to newly discovered works by **Ptolemy** (TAH•luh•mee), Archimedes, and Plato. These writings made it obvious that some ancient thinkers had disagreed with Aristotle and other accepted authorities of the Middle Ages.

Other developments also encouraged new ways of thinking. Technical problems that required careful observation and accurate measurements, such as calculating the amount of weight that ships could hold, served to stimulate scientific activity. Then, too, the invention of new instruments, such as the telescope and microscope, made fresh scientific discoveries possible. Above all, the printing press helped spread new ideas quickly and easily.

Mathematics played a very important role in the scientific achievements of the sixteenth and seventeenth centuries. The study of mathematics was promoted in the Renaissance by the rediscovery of the works of ancient mathematicians. Nicholas Copernicus, Johannes Kepler, Galileo Galilei, and Isaac Newton were all great mathematicians who believed that the secrets of nature were written in the language of mathematics. After studying and, sometimes, discarding the ideas of the ancient mathematicians, these intellectuals developed new theories that became the foundation of the Scientific Revolution.

Reading Check **Evaluating** What changes in the fifteenth and sixteenth centuries helped the natural philosophers develop new views?

A Revolution in Astronomy

Especially significant in the Scientific Revolution were discoveries in astronomy. These discoveries would overturn the conception of the universe held by Westerners in the Middle Ages.

The Ptolemaic System Ptolemy, who lived in the second century A.D., was the greatest astronomer of antiquity. Using his ideas, as well as those of Aristotle and of Christianity, the philosophers of the Middle

Ptolemaic Universe

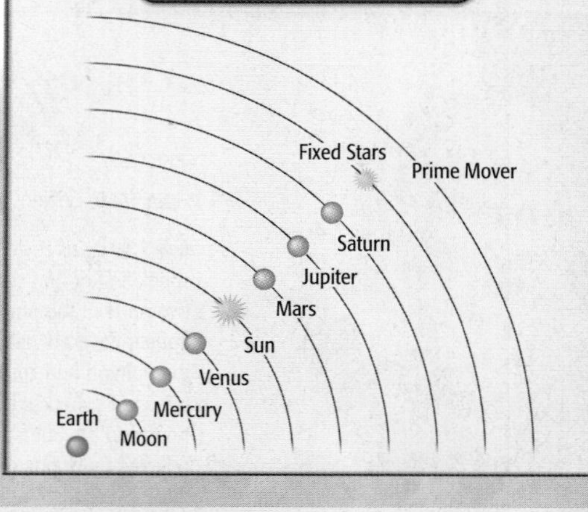

Picturing History

These astronomers, Ptolemy (left) and Copernicus (shown on page 295), were separated in time by approximately 1,400 years. Both men had a major impact on the way people viewed their place in the universe. What elements do you see in the two illustrations that help to convey to the viewer the importance of the two men and their scientific discoveries?

EXTENDING THE CONTENT

Copernicus The writings of Nicholas Copernicus are said to have triggered what is now known as the Copernican Revolution. However, there are several ironies associated with Copernicus. While he is credited with starting his eponymous revolution, he himself missed it. He died shortly before his theories were published, and his book was largely ignored until the next century. Furthermore, he thought that he would best be remembered for his theory of circularity, which is that the planets rotate in near-perfect circles. This theory was later proven incorrect. Nor was he the first person to suggest that Earth revolves around the Sun. That honor goes to Aristarchus, an ancient philosopher.

Ages had constructed a model of the universe known later as the Ptolemaic (TAH•luh•MAY•ik) system. This system is called geocentric because it places Earth at the center of the universe.

In the Ptolemaic system, the universe is a series of concentric spheres—spheres one inside the other. Earth is fixed, or motionless, at the center of these spheres. The spheres are made of a crystal-like, transparent substance, in which the heavenly bodies—pure orbs of light—are embedded. For example, the Moon is embedded in the first sphere, Mercury in the second, Venus in the third, and the Sun in the fourth. The rotation of the spheres makes these heavenly bodies rotate about the earth and move in relation to one another.

The tenth sphere in the Ptolemaic system was the "prime mover," which moved itself and gave motion to the other spheres. Beyond the tenth sphere was Heaven, where God and all the saved souls resided. God was at one end of the universe, then, and humans were at the center. Humans had been given power over the earth, but their real purpose was to achieve salvation.

Copernicus and Kepler In May 1543, **Nicholas Copernicus,** a native of **Poland,** published his famous book, *On the Revolutions of the Heavenly Spheres.* Copernicus, a mathematician, felt that the geocentric system was too complicated. He believed that his heliocentric, or sun-centered, conception of the universe offered a more accurate explanation than did the Ptolemaic system.

Copernicus argued that the Sun, not Earth, was at the center of the universe. The planets revolved around the Sun. The Moon, however, revolved around Earth. Moreover, according to Copernicus, the apparent movement of the Sun around Earth was really caused by the daily rotation of Earth on its axis and the journey of Earth around the Sun each year.

The next step in destroying the Ptolemaic system was taken by the German mathematician Johannes Kepler. Kepler used detailed astronomical data to arrive at his laws of planetary motion. His observations confirmed that the Sun was at the center of the universe and also added new information. In his first law, Kepler showed that the orbits of the planets around the Sun were not circular, as Copernicus

Copernican Universe

Fixed Stars
Saturn
Jupiter
Moon
Mars
Earth
Venus
Mercury
Sun

Chart Skills

Compare the illustrations of two different models of the universe on the previous page and this page, then answer the questions below.

1. **Compare and Contrast** Identify as many specific similarities and differences as you can find in the two models.
2. **Explaining** Explain the changes in the way people viewed the universe that resulted from the mathematical and scientific discoveries of Copernicus.

Chart Skills

Answers:

1. Ptolemaic model: Earth at the center, with Moon, planets, Sun, more planets, fixed stars, and "prime mover" rotating around it; Copernican model: Sun at center, with planets revolving around it and fixed stars beyond, Moon revolves around Earth, no "prime mover"
2. The Sun, not Earth, was now seen as the center of the universe. Many people, including popes, considered this heretical since it seemed to contradict the Bible. In the Ptolemaic universe, the "prime mover" (God) had a place; heaven was beyond the planets and stars. In the Copernican universe, there was seemingly no room for God or heaven. The Copernican model also introduced the notion that certain parts of the Bible might not be the literal truth.

Enrich

Have students evaluate this statement: "The Scientific Revolution largely resulted from the work of a handful of great intellectuals." Divide the class into groups and ask each group to evaluate the following alternative statement: "Changes in European civilization encouraged the development of new ideas that became the basis for the Scientific Revolution." The question is, did the people make the times or did the times make the people? **L3**

COOPERATIVE LEARNING ACTIVITY

Creating a Dramatic Presentation Organize the class into four groups. Have the members of three groups prepare five scenes each from Bertolt Brecht's *The Life of Galileo* to read dramatically to the class. Have the members of the fourth group make an intensive study of the facts of Galileo's life. After the three groups have completed their classroom reading of the entire play, have members of the fourth group participate in a panel discussion comparing Brecht's dramatic treatment of characters and events with their actual historical models. **L3**

For grading this activity, refer to the ***Performance Assessment Activities*** booklet.

Guided Reading Activity 10–1

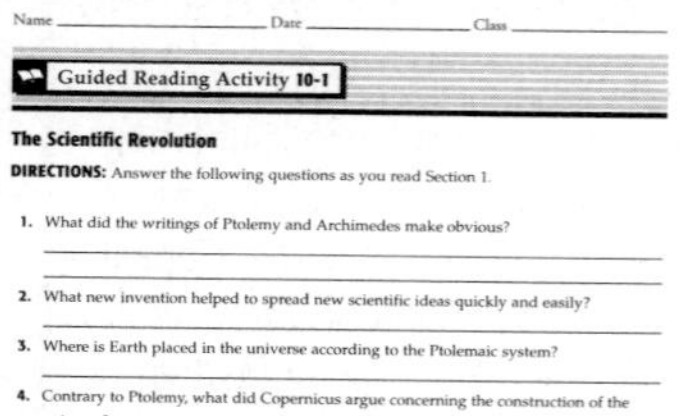
Name ______ Date ______ Class ______

Guided Reading Activity 10-1

The Scientific Revolution

DIRECTIONS: Answer the following questions as you read Section 1.

1. What did the writings of Ptolemy and Archimedes make obvious?
2. What new invention helped to spread new scientific ideas quickly and easily?
3. Where is Earth placed in the universe according to the Ptolemaic system?
4. Contrary to Ptolemy, what did Copernicus argue concerning the construction of the universe?

CURRICULUM CONNECTION

Science Ask students to relate the following factors to the Scientific Revolution in the sixteenth and seventeenth centuries during a class discussion: the telescope, Latin as a European intellectual language, the movable type printing press, and the rediscovery of mathematics. Which do students believe were most important? Which were least important? Are there other important factors they would include? **L2**

ABCNEWS INTERACTIVE™

Turning Points in World History
The ABC News videotape includes a segment on the Scientific Revolution.

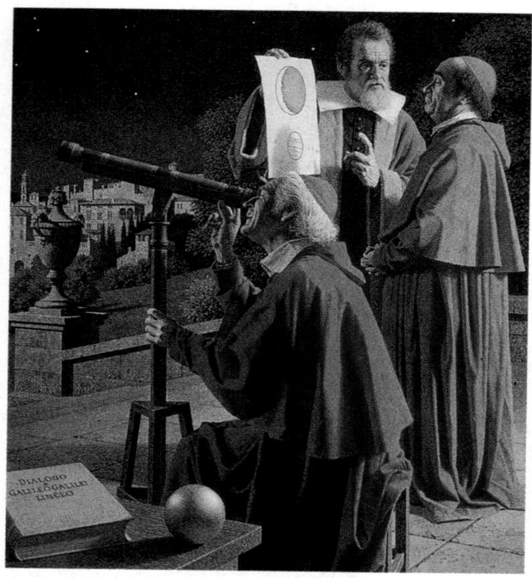
Galileo displays his drawings to the clergy.

had thought. Rather, the orbits were elliptical (egg-shaped), with the Sun toward the end of the ellipse instead of at the center. This finding, known as Kepler's law, contradicted the circular orbits and crystal-like spheres that were central to the Ptolemaic system.

Galileo Scientists could now think in terms of planets revolving around the Sun in elliptical orbits. Important questions remained unanswered, however. What are the planets made of? How does one explain motion in the universe? An Italian scientist answered the first question.

Galileo Galilei taught mathematics. He was the first European to make regular observations of the heavens using a telescope. With this tool, Galileo made a remarkable series of discoveries: mountains on the Moon, four moons revolving around Jupiter, and sunspots.

Galileo's observations seemed to destroy yet another aspect of the Ptolemaic conception. Heavenly bodies had been seen as pure orbs of light. Instead, it appeared that they were composed of material substance, just as Earth was.

Galileo's discoveries, published in *The Starry Messenger* in 1610, did more to make Europeans aware of the new view of the universe than did the works of Copernicus and Kepler. In the midst of his newfound fame, however, Galileo found himself under suspicion by the authorities of the Catholic Church.

The Church ordered Galileo to abandon the Copernican idea. The Copernican system threatened the Church's entire conception of the universe and seemed to contradict the Bible. In the Copernican view, the heavens were no longer a spiritual world but a world of matter. Humans were no longer at the center of the universe, and God was no longer in a specific place.

In spite of the Church's position, by the 1630s and 1640s, most astronomers had come to accept the heliocentric conception of the universe. However, the problem of explaining motion in the universe had not been solved, and the ideas of Copernicus, Kepler, and Galileo had yet to be tied together. This would be done by an Englishman who has long been considered the greatest genius of the Scientific Revolution.

Newton Born in 1642, **Isaac Newton** showed few signs of brilliance until he attended **Cambridge University.** Later, he became a professor of mathematics at the university and wrote his major work, *Mathematical Principles of Natural Philosophy.* This work is known simply as the *Principia,* by the first word of its Latin title.

In the first book of the *Principia,* Newton defined the three laws of motion that govern the planetary bodies, as well as objects on Earth. Crucial to his whole argument was the **universal law of gravitation.** This law explains why the planetary bodies do not go off in straight lines but instead continue in elliptical orbits about the Sun. The law states, in mathematical terms, that every object in the universe is attracted to every other object by a force called gravity.

Isaac Newton analyzing light rays

EXTENDING THE CONTENT

Galileo traveled to Rome in 1615 to ask Pope Paul V if he could teach the ideas of Copernicus. The pope said no. To circumvent the pope's ruling, Galileo wrote a book in which two laymen discussed the world views of Copernicus and Aristotle. Galileo took no position but spoke through his characters. The adherent of Aristotle was a fool, while the believer in Copernicus was a wise man. Galileo even took writings from the new pope, Urban VIII, and had them spoken by the fool. The new pope felt that Galileo had mocked him and broken his word. In 1992, Pope John Paul II admitted that the Catholic Church erred in persecuting Galileo.

Newton had shown that one universal law, mathematically proved, could explain all motion in the universe. At the same time, Newton's ideas created a new picture of the universe. It was now seen as one huge, regulated, uniform machine that worked according to natural laws. Newton's world-machine concept dominated the modern worldview until the twentieth century, when Albert Einstein's concept of relativity created a new picture of the universe.

Reading Check **Identifying** Name the four great mathematicians who had a profound impact on astronomy.

Breakthroughs in Medicine and Chemistry

A revolution in medicine also began in the sixteenth century. Medicine in the Late Middle Ages was dominated by the teachings of the Greek physician Galen, who had lived in the second century A.D. Galen had relied on animal, rather than human, dissection to arrive at a picture of human anatomy, and he was wrong in many instances.

The new anatomy of the sixteenth century was based on the work of Andreas Vesalius. In his 1543 book, *On the Fabric of the Human Body*, Vesalius discussed what he had found when dissecting human bodies while he was a professor of surgery at the University of **Padua.**

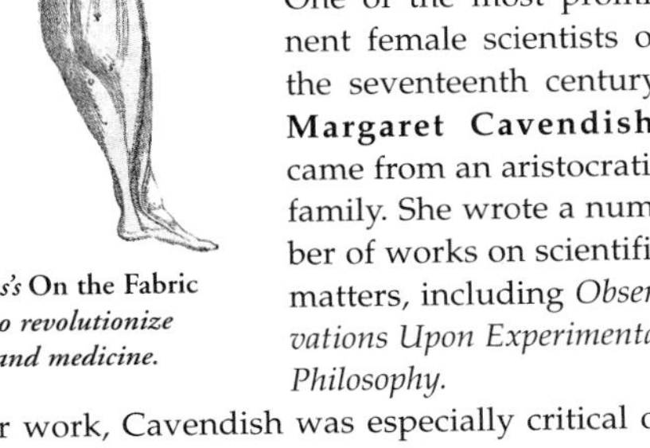

Drawings such as this from Vesalius's On the Fabric of the Human Body *did much to revolutionize knowledge of human anatomy and medicine.*

Vesalius presented a careful and accurate examination of the individual organs and general structure of the human body. His "hands-on" approach enabled him to overthrow some of Galen's theories. Nevertheless, Vesalius still clung to Galen's erroneous idea that two kinds of blood flowed in the veins and arteries.

William Harvey's reputation rests on his book *On the Motion of the Heart and Blood*, published in 1628. Harvey's work was based on close observations and experiments. Harvey showed that the heart—not the liver, as Galen had thought—was the beginning point for the circulation of blood in the body. He also proved that the same blood flows in both veins and arteries. Most important, he showed that the blood makes a complete circuit as it passes through the body.

A science of chemistry also arose in the seventeenth and eighteenth centuries. **Robert Boyle** was one of the first scientists to conduct controlled experiments. His pioneering work on the properties of gases led to Boyle's Law. This generalization states that the volume of a gas varies with the pressure exerted on it. In the eighteenth century, Antoine Lavoisier invented a system of naming the chemical elements, much of which is still used today. He is regarded by many as the founder of modern chemistry.

Reading Check **Describing** How did Vesalius and Harvey disprove many of Galen's theories?

Women and the Origins of Modern Science

Women as well as men were involved in the Scientific Revolution. One of the most prominent female scientists of the seventeenth century, **Margaret Cavendish,** came from an aristocratic family. She wrote a number of works on scientific matters, including *Observations Upon Experimental Philosophy*.

In her work, Cavendish was especially critical of the growing belief that humans, through science, were the masters of nature: "We have no power at all over natural causes and effects . . . for man is but a small part, his powers are but particular actions of Nature, and he cannot have a supreme and absolute power."

Margaret Cavendish

In Germany, many of the women who were involved in science were astronomers. These women had received the opportunity to become astronomers from working in family observatories, where they had been trained by their

Reading Check

Answer: Copernicus, Kepler, Galileo, Newton

Reading Check

Answer: By dissecting humans rather than animals, Vesalius was able to present a careful and accurate view of the individual organs and general structure of the human body, which enabled him to overthrow some of Galens's most glaring errors. Harvey showed that the heart, not the liver, was the beginning point for the circulation of blood in the body and proved that the same blood flows in veins and arteries and makes a complete circuit as it passes through the body.

Critical Thinking

Why was Newton's thinking important in the Scientific Revolution? *(Newton's work suggested that precise mathematical formulas could be used to describe an orderly universe. This idea greatly influenced the thinking of his time and all later scientific thought.)* **L2**

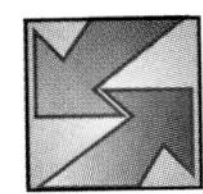

CURRICULUM CONNECTION

Science Assign students to prepare illustrated posters that include three types of information: key contributors to the Scientific Revolution, examples of their contributions at the time, and modern machines that may have resulted from their work. *(Example: Galileo, telescope, Hubble Space Telescope)* Display completed posters in the classroom. **L1** ELL

CRITICAL THINKING ACTIVITY

Drawing Conclusions In the seventeenth century, Peter Chamberlen invented a device to more easily remove a child from the womb during birth. His metal forceps clamped onto a baby's head and helped pull the child through the birth canal. He earned the title "man-midwife" (obstetrician) for this feat. Chamberlen's son formed a business to sell forceps, and it became impossible to obtain a medical license in Amsterdam without paying an enormous sum to purchase this device. Have students research other medical devices used in the seventeenth century, explain how they were distributed, choose one that they think is most important, and write a paragraph explaining why. **L3**

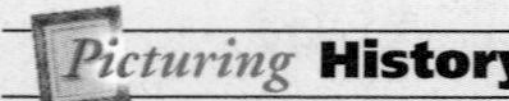

History

Answer: The concept of separation of mind and matter; reason is the chief source of knowledge.

Reading Check

Answer: Cavendish wrote *Observations Upon Experimental Philosophy*. She was critical of the belief that humans were the masters of nature; for her, humans were but a small part of the universe. Winkelmann discovered a comet.

3 ASSESS

Assign Section 1 Assessment as homework or as an in-class activity.

Have students use **Interactive Tutor Self-Assessment CD-ROM.**

Section Quiz 10–1

Name ________ Date ________ Class ________

Chapter 10 Score

Section Quiz 10-1

DIRECTIONS: Matching Match each item in Column A with an item in Column B. Write the correct letters in the blanks. *(10 points each)*

Column A	Column B
____ 1. Sun-centered model of the universe	A. Galileo
____ 2. egg-shaped	B. Kepler
____ 3. law of universal attraction	C. elliptical
____ 4. his observations suggested that planets had substance	D. gravity
____ 5. he developed laws of planetary motion	E. heliocentric

DIRECTIONS: Multiple Choice In the blank, write the letter of the choice that best completes the statement or answers the question. *(10 points each)*

____ 6. The scientific method was all of the following EXCEPT

Reading Essentials and Study Guide 10–1

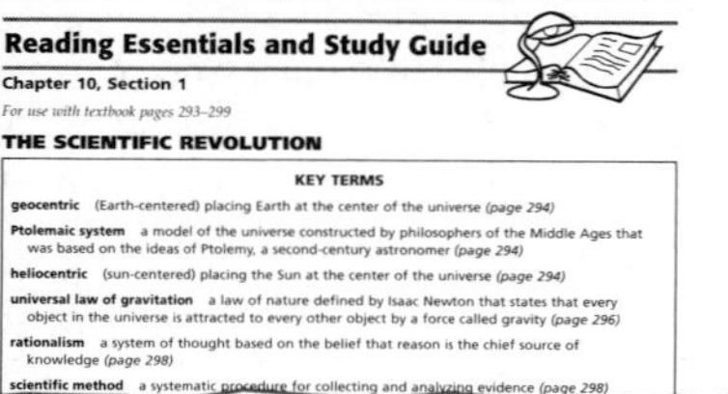

Name ________ Date ________ Class ________

Reading Essentials and Study Guide

Chapter 10, Section 1

For use with textbook pages 293–299

THE SCIENTIFIC REVOLUTION

KEY TERMS

geocentric (Earth-centered) placing Earth at the center of the universe *(page 294)*

Ptolemaic system a model of the universe constructed by philosophers of the Middle Ages that was based on the ideas of Ptolemy, a second-century astronomer *(page 294)*

heliocentric (sun-centered) placing the Sun at the center of the universe *(page 294)*

universal law of gravitation a law of nature defined by Isaac Newton that states that every object in the universe is attracted to every other object by a force called gravity *(page 296)*

rationalism a system of thought based on the belief that reason is the chief source of knowledge *(page 298)*

scientific method a systematic procedure for collecting and analyzing evidence *(page 298)*

fathers or husbands. Between 1650 and 1710, women made up 14 percent of all German astronomers.

The most famous of the female astronomers in Germany was **Maria Winkelmann.** She received training in astronomy from a self-taught astronomer. Her chance to be a practicing astronomer came when she married Gottfried Kirch, Prussia's foremost astronomer, and became his assistant.

Winkelmann made some original contributions to astronomy, including the discovery of a comet. Her husband described the discovery:

> “Early in the morning (about 2:00 A.M.) the sky was clear and starry. Some nights before, I had observed a variable star, and my wife (as I slept) wanted to find and see it for herself. In so doing, she found a comet in the sky. At which time she woke me, and I found that it was indeed a comet. . . . I was surprised that I had not seen it the night before.”

When her husband died, Winkelmann applied for a position as assistant astronomer at the Berlin Academy. She was highly qualified, but as a woman—with no university degree—she was denied the post. Members of the Berlin Academy feared that they would set a bad example by hiring a woman. “Mouths would gape,” they said.

Winkelmann's problems with the Berlin Academy reflect the obstacles women faced in being accepted as scientists. Such work was considered to be chiefly for males. In the view of most people in the seventeenth century, a life devoted to any kind of scholarship was at odds with the domestic duties women were expected to perform.

Reading Check **Summarizing** What did Margaret Cavendish and Maria Winkelmann contribute to the Scientific Revolution?

Picturing History

René Descartes is pictured here with Queen Christina of Sweden, who invited Descartes to her court. What philosophical principles did Descartes establish in his famous work *Discourse on Method?*

Descartes and Reason

The new conception of the universe brought about by the Scientific Revolution strongly influenced the Western view of humankind. Nowhere is this more evident than in the work of the seventeenth-century French philosopher **René Descartes** (day•KAHRT). Descartes began by thinking and writing about the doubt and uncertainty that seemed to be everywhere in the confusion of the seventeenth century. He ended with a philosophy that dominated Western thought until the twentieth century.

The starting point for Descartes's new system was doubt. In his most famous work, *Discourse on Method,* written in 1637, Descartes decided to set aside all that he had learned and to begin again. One fact seemed to him to be beyond doubt—his own existence:

> “But I immediately became aware that while I was thus disposed to think that all was false, it was absolutely necessary that I who thus thought should be something; and noting that this truth I think, therefore I am, was so steadfast and so assured . . . I concluded that I might without scruple accept it as being the first principle of the philosophy I was seeking.”

Descartes emphasized the importance of his own mind and asserted that he would accept only those things that his reason said were true.

From his first principle—“I think, therefore I am”—Descartes used his reason to arrive at a second principle. He argued that because “the mind cannot be doubted but the body and material world can, the two must be radically different.”

From this idea came the principle of the separation of mind and matter (and of mind and body).

MEETING INDIVIDUAL NEEDS

Visual/Auditory To help students organize and remember information about people discussed in this section, have them list the names of the people in the section. Then tell them that things are easier to remember if they are classified. Next to each name, students should write the scientific field in which the person was involved. Divide the class into pairs and have one student read a scientist's name and another state his or her scientific field. For example: “Who was Boyle?”, “Boyle was a chemist.” After students learn the names and classifications, add one more fact about each person, and then quiz again. For example: “Who was Boyle?”, “Boyle was a chemist who is often called the founder of modern chemistry.” **L1** ELL

298

Descartes's idea that mind and matter were completely separate allowed scientists to view matter as dead or inert—as something that was totally detached from themselves and that could be investigated independently by reason.

Descartes has rightly been called the father of modern rationalism. This system of thought is based on the belief that reason is the chief source of knowledge.

Reading Check **Explaining** What is the significance of Descartes's principle of the separation of mind and matter?

The Scientific Method

During the Scientific Revolution, people became concerned about how they could best understand the physical world. The result was the creation of a scientific method—a systematic procedure for collecting and analyzing evidence. The scientific method was crucial to the evolution of science in the modern world.

The person who developed the scientific method was actually not a scientist. **Francis Bacon,** an English philosopher with few scientific credentials, believed that instead of relying on the ideas of ancient authorities, scientists should use inductive reasoning to learn about nature. In other words, scientists should proceed from the particular to the general. Systematic observations and carefully organized experiments to test hypotheses (theories) would lead to correct general principles.

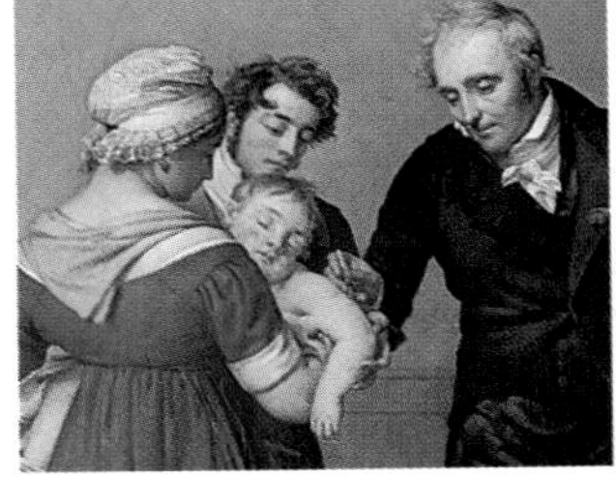

After years of study and experimentation, Edward Jenner developed the first vaccine for smallpox in 1796.

Bacon was clear about what he believed his scientific method could accomplish. He stated that "the true and lawful goal of the sciences is none other than this: that human life be endowed with new discoveries and power." He was much more concerned with practical matters than pure science.

Bacon wanted science to benefit industry, agriculture, and trade. He said, "I am laboring to lay the foundation, not of any sect or doctrine, but of human utility and power."

How would this "human power" be used? Bacon believed it could be used to "conquer nature in action." The control and domination of nature became an important concern of science and the technology that accompanied it.

Reading Check **Summarizing** What are the characteristics of the scientific method?

SECTION 1 ASSESSMENT

Checking for Understanding

1. **Define** geocentric, Ptolemaic system, heliocentric, universal law of gravitation, rationalism, scientific method, inductive reasoning.
2. **Identify** Ptolemy, Nicholas Copernicus, Galileo Galilei, Isaac Newton, Cambridge University, Robert Boyle, Margaret Cavendish, Maria Winkelmann, René Descartes, Francis Bacon.
3. **Locate** Poland, Padua.
4. **Contrast** the Ptolemaic, or geocentric, system of the universe to the heliocentric system developed by Copernicus.
5. **List** the pioneers of modern chemistry who lived during the seventeenth and eighteenth centuries.

Critical Thinking

6. **Analyze** Why did the Catholic Church condemn the work of Galileo during the seventeenth century?
7. **Identifying Information** Use a diagram to identify examples of new ideas in the form of mathematical discoveries, scientific discoveries, or technological innovations that appeared during the 1500s and 1600s. Then show in the diagram the changes produced by these discoveries or innovations.

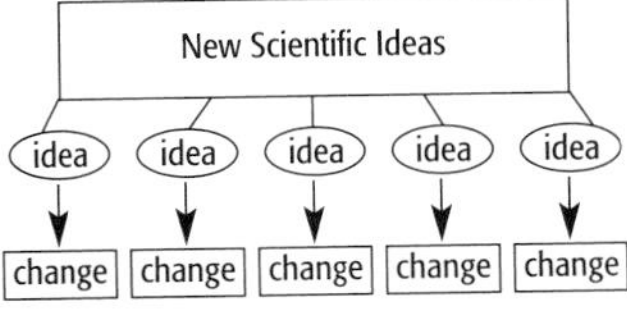

Analyzing Visuals

8. **Examine** the painting of Galileo on page 296. Why do you think that Galileo is showing his drawings to the clergyman standing beside him? Why might the other man be looking through Galileo's telescope? Based on what you have read in this section, do you think these men will support Galileo's views? Why or why not?

Writing About History

9. **Expository Writing** Do some research and then write an essay about either Copernicus, Galileo, or Newton. For the scientist you choose, discuss that person's individual contributions to the Scientific Revolution and how his ideas have influenced the development of modern society.

SECTION 1 ASSESSMENT

1. Key terms are in blue.
2. Ptolemy *(p. 294)*; Nicholas Copernicus *(p. 295)*; Galileo Galilei *(p. 296)*; Isaac Newton *(p. 296)*; Cambridge University *(p. 296)*; Robert Boyle *(p. 297)*; Margaret Cavendish *(p. 297)*; Maria Winkelmann *(p. 298)*; René Descartes *(p. 298)*; Francis Bacon *(p. 299)*
3. See chapter maps.
4. Ptolemaic system: Earth is the center of the universe; Copernican system: the Sun is the center of the universe.
5. Robert Boyle, Antoine Lavoisier
6. for violating church authority
7. heliocentric universe: threw doubt on literal interpretation of Bible; laws of motion, gravitation: concept of the universe as a machine; dissection of humans: better medical care; reason over faith: rationalism; scientific method: evolution of science
8. He may be presenting his theory. Answers will vary.
9. Students will write essays.

Reading Check

Answer: It allowed scientists to view matter as dead or inert, something totally detached from themselves that could be investigated independently by reason.

Reading Check

Answer: It is a systematic procedure for collecting and analyzing evidence. Scientists should proceed from the particular to the general. Systematic observations and carefully organized experiments to test hypotheses will lead to correct general principles.

Reteaching Activity

Ask students to identify the contributions of significant scientists introduced in this section such as Robert Boyle. **L1**

4 CLOSE

Write the words *Before* and *After* on the chalkboard. Have students take turns choosing a person mentioned in this section and describing an accepted theory before and after this person's work. For example, having chosen Copernicus, a student would describe astronomy before and after Copernicus's work. **L2**

1 FOCUS

Section Overview

This section explores how the ideas of the Scientific Revolution led to the Enlightenment and new philosophies that pervaded all aspects of life.

BELLRINGER
Skillbuilder Activity

Project transparency and have students answer questions.

Available as a blackline master.

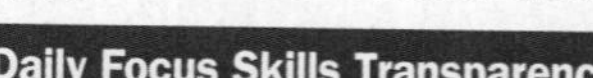
Daily Focus Skills Transparency 10–2

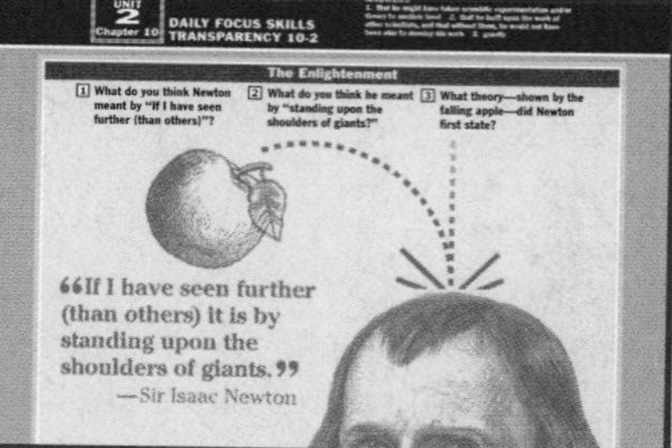

Guide to Reading

Answers to Graphic: Major Ideas of the Enlightenment: reason, deism, religious toleration, separation of powers, laissez-faire, natural law, social contract, progress

Preteaching Vocabulary: Explain the significance of *separation of powers. (The concept comes from the way England's government functioned with three separate branches that limited and controlled each other. It formed the model for the government of the United States.)* **L2**

SECTION 2 The Enlightenment

Guide to Reading

Main Ideas
- Eighteenth-century intellectuals used the ideas of the Scientific Revolution to reexamine all aspects of life.
- People gathered in salons to discuss the ideas of the philosophes.

Key Terms
philosophe, separation of powers, deism, laissez-faire, social contract, salon

People to Identify
John Locke, Montesquieu, Voltaire, Denis Diderot, Adam Smith, Jean-Jacques Rousseau, Mary Wollstonecraft, John Wesley

Places to Locate
Paris, London

Preview Questions
1. What was the Enlightenment?
2. What role did religion play during the Enlightenment?

Reading Strategy
Summarizing Information Use a diagram like the one below to list some of the main ideas introduced during the Enlightenment.

Preview of Events

1700 · 1715 · 1730 · 1745 · 1760 · 1775 · 1790

- **1702** The first daily newspaper is published in London
- **1748** Baron de Montesquieu publishes *The Spirit of the Laws*
- **1762** Rousseau publishes *The Social Contract*
- **1763** Voltaire writes his *Treatise on Toleration*
- **1776** Adam Smith publishes *The Wealth of Nations*

Voices from the Past

Voltaire

The French intellectual Voltaire attacked religious intolerance in *The Ignorant Philosopher:*

> "I say, there is scarce any city or borough in Europe, where blood has not been spilled for religious quarrels; I say, that the human species has been perceptibly diminished, because women and girls were massacred as well as men. I say that Europe would have a third larger population if there had been no theological disputes. In fine, I say, that so far from forgetting these abominable times, we should frequently take a view of them, to inspire an eternal horror for them. . . . It is for our age to make amends by toleration, for this long collection of crimes, which has taken place through the lack of toleration during sixteen barbarous centuries."
>
> **—From *Absolutism to Revolution* 1648–1848, Herbert H. Rowen, ed., 1963**

Religious toleration was one of the major themes of the Enlightenment.

Path to the Enlightenment

The Enlightenment was an eighteenth-century philosophical movement of intellectuals who were greatly impressed with the achievements of the Scientific Revolution. One of the favorite words of these intellectuals was *reason.* By this, they meant the application of the scientific method to an understanding of all life. They hoped that by using the scientific method, they could make progress toward a better society than the one they had inherited. *Reason, natural law, hope, progress*—these were common words to the thinkers of the Enlightenment.

The Enlightenment was especially influenced by the ideas of two seventeenth-century Englishmen, Isaac Newton and **John Locke.** To Newton, the physical

SECTION RESOURCES

Reproducible Masters
- Reproducible Lesson Plan 10–2
- Daily Lecture and Discussion Notes 10–2
- Guided Reading Activity 10–2
- Section Quiz 10–2
- Reading Essentials and Study Guide 10–2

Transparencies
- Daily Focus Skills Transparency 10–2

Multimedia
- Interactive Tutor Self-Assessment CD-ROM
- ExamView® Pro Testmaker CD-ROM
- Presentation Plus! CD-ROM

world and everything in it was like a giant machine (the Newtonian world-machine). If Newton could discover the natural laws that governed the physical world, then by using his methods, the intellectuals of the Enlightenment thought they could discover the natural laws that governed human society.

John Locke's theory of knowledge also greatly affected eighteenth-century intellectuals. In his *Essay Concerning Human Understanding,* Locke argued that every person was born with a tabula rasa, or blank mind:

> ❝Let us then suppose the mind to be, as we say, white paper, void of all characters, without any ideas. How comes it to be furnished? Whence has it all the materials of reason and knowledge? To this I answer, in one word, from experience. . . . Our observation, employed either about external sensible objects or about the internal operations of our minds perceived and reflected on by ourselves, is that which supplies our understanding with all the materials of thinking.❞

Locke's ideas suggested that people were molded by the experiences that came through their senses from the surrounding world. If environments were changed and people were exposed to the right influences, then people could be changed and a new society created.

How should the environment be changed? Using Newton's methods, people believed that they could discover the natural laws that all institutions should follow to produce the ideal society.

Reading Check **Explaining**

What was Newton's main contribution to Enlightenment thought?

Philosophes and Their Ideas

The intellectuals of the Enlightenment were known by the French name **philosophe** (FEE•luh•ZAWF), meaning "philosopher." Not all philosophes were French, however, and few were philosophers in the strict sense of the term. They were writers, professors, journalists, economists, and above all, social reformers. They came chiefly from the nobility and the middle class.

Most of the leaders of the Enlightenment were French, but even the French would have acknowledged that the English had provided the philosophical inspiration for the Enlightenment. It was definitely these French philosophes, however, who affected intellectuals elsewhere and created a movement that influenced the entire Western world. The Enlightenment was a truly international movement.

To the philosophes, the role of philosophy was to change the world. One writer said that the philosophe is one who "applies himself to the study of society with the purpose of making his kind better and happier." One conducts this study by using reason, or an appeal to facts. A spirit of rational criticism was to be applied to everything, including religion and politics.

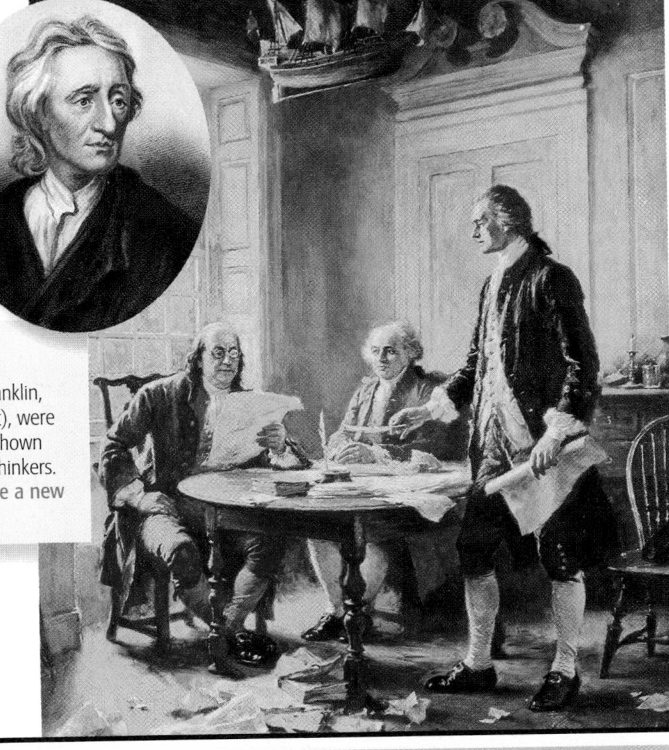

***Picturing* History**

Leaders of the American Revolution, such as Franklin, Adams, and Jefferson (pictured here left to right), were greatly influenced by the ideas of John Locke (shown above) and eighteenth-century Enlightenment thinkers. By what means or methods did Locke believe a new society could be created?

CHAPTER 10
Section 2, 300–307

2 TEACH

Reading Check

Answer: the idea that natural laws existed and that institutions could follow these laws to produce the ideal society

***Picturing* History**

Answer: By changing the environment and exposing people to the right influences, people and society could be changed.

Daily Lecture and Discussion Notes 10–2

Daily Lecture and Discussion Notes

Chapter 10, Section 2

Did You Know? The German Enlightenment philosopher Immanuel Kant maintained his regimen so reliably that people set their clocks according to his daily walk along the street in Königsberg now named for him, "The Philosopher's Walk." He is said to have missed this walk for only one short period: while reading Rousseau's *Emile*, he stayed at home for several days.

I. Path to the Enlightenment *(pages 300–301)*

A. The Enlightenment was an eighteenth-century philosophical movement built off the achievements of the Scientific Revolution. The Enlightenment philosophers hoped to make a better society by applying the scientific method and reason to social problems. They talked a lot about reason, natural law, hope, and progress.

B. Enlightenment philosophers thought that society was governed by natural laws just as the Newtonian physical universe was.

C. John Locke's theory of knowledge greatly influenced Enlightenment thinkers. He argued that people are born with a mind that is a tabula rasa, or blank slate, and that knowledge comes to it through the five senses. This meant that the right influences could create a new kind of society by creating a new way of understanding.

D. Enlightenment thinkers hoped to discover with the scientific method the laws that all institutions should follow to produce the ideal society.

Discussion Question

Are methods of understanding that work in the physical world applicable to the social world? *(Answers will vary. Accept relevant, thoughtful answers. The affirmative view emphasizes that humans are physical beings like the rest of nature. The negative view emphasizes that non-human nature is ordered by causality in a way that the social world is not. The social world emerges from freedom, reflection, and purpose.)*

II. Philosophes and Their Ideas *(pages 301–303)*

A. The Enlightenment intellectuals were called by the French name **philosophe** ("philosopher") Most were writers, professors, economists, journalists, and social reformers.

B. The ideas of the philosophes influenced the entire Western world. To them ideas were

Writing Activity

Ask students to evaluate Locke's theory that people are born with a blank mind. Do the students believe people are more a product of nature (genes) or nurture (environment)? Ask students to write a paragraph supporting their viewpoints. **L1**

CRITICAL THINKING ACTIVITY

Analyzing Information Although there is no single scientific method, you might suggest that students use the following procedure to conduct an investigation: 1) Identify a problem or ask a question; 2) develop a few hypotheses or educated guesses; 3) predict what will occur; 4) devise ways to test the accuracy of predictions based on the hypotheses; 5) check accuracy of tests; 6) repeat tests or devise new tests; 7) report results and conclusions objectively. Ask students if this method could be used to investigate nonscientific things. Then ask them to list things that they would test using this method. **L3**

History *through Art*

Answer: Answers will vary. Some members of the audience—other philosophes—would probably approve whole-heartedly, while the more conservative members—such as nobles—would probably be scandalized.

Critical Thinking

Have students describe some of the different ways specific people reacted to Enlightenment ideas. During a class discussion, ask them to consider the reactions of Locke, Diderot, Voltaire, Beccaria, and Rousseau. **L2**

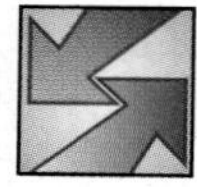

CURRICULUM CONNECTION

Philosophy Ask students to discuss why Descartes's conviction of his own existence should be regarded as an important philosophical realization. Ask students to explain what this statement had to do with the idea called *Cartesian dualism*. Do students believe this philosophical point of view was valid? Ask them to explain the reasons for their ideas. *(Answers will vary.)* **L3**

Writing Activity

Ask students to write a brief paper identifying changes that resulted from the Scientific Revolution.

History *through Art*

***Madame de Geoffrin's Salon* by Jean-Baptiste Lemoyner** shows the first reading of one of Voltaire's works. Describe the different reactions to Voltaire's ideas that you might hear from a typical Parisian eighteenth-century salon audience.

The philosophes often disagreed. The Enlightenment spanned almost a century, and it evolved over time. Each succeeding generation became more radical as it built on the contributions of the previous one. A few people, however, dominated the landscape. We begin our survey of the ideas of the philosophes by looking at the three French giants—Montesquieu (MAHN•tuhs•KYOO), Voltaire, and Diderot (dee•DROH).

Montesquieu Charles-Louis de Secondat, the Baron de **Montesquieu,** came from the French nobility. His most famous work, *The Spirit of the Laws,* was published in 1748. In this study of governments, Montesquieu tried to use the scientific method to find the natural laws that govern the social and political relationships of human beings.

Montesquieu identified three basic kinds of governments: (1) republics, suitable for small states; (2) despotism, appropriate for large states; and (3) monarchies, ideal for moderate-size states. He used England as an example of a monarchy.

Montesquieu believed that England's government had three branches: the executive (the monarch), the legislative (parliament), and the judicial (the courts of law). The government functioned through a **separation of powers.** In this separation, the executive, legislative, and judicial powers of the government limit and control each other in a system of checks and balances. By preventing any one person or group from gaining too much power, this system provides the greatest freedom and security for the state.

Montesquieu's analysis of the system of checks and balances through separation of powers was his most lasting contribution to political thought. The translation of Montesquieu's work into English made it available to American philosophes, who took his principles and worked them into the United States Constitution.

Voltaire The greatest figure of the Enlightenment was François-Marie Arouet, known simply as **Voltaire.** A Parisian, Voltaire came from a prosperous middle-class family. He wrote an almost endless stream of pamphlets, novels, plays, letters, essays, and histories, which brought him both fame and wealth.

Voltaire was especially well known for his criticism of Christianity and his strong belief in religious toleration. He fought against religious intolerance in France. In 1763, he penned his *Treatise on Toleration,* in which he reminded governments that "all men are brothers under God."

Throughout his life, Voltaire championed **deism,** an eighteenth-century religious philosophy based on reason and natural law. Deism built on the idea of the Newtonian world-machine. In the Deists' view, a

CRITICAL THINKING ACTIVITY

Drawing Conclusions The Enlightenment's ideals of reason, natural law, hope, and progress were the philosophical beliefs that led to the American Revolution and the creation of the United States. The Declaration of Independence and American Revolution were signals to Europeans that, for the first time, enlightened ideas were being put into action. Americans wanted the right to think freely and the right to express their opinions without fear of repression or censorship. Ask students if these ideals are still important to Americans. Have students explain why they think this is or is not so. You might also ask them to write a short essay expressing their opinions. **L2**

mechanic (God) had created the universe. To Voltaire and most other philosophes, the universe was like a clock. God, the clockmaker, had created it, set it in motion, and allowed it to run without his interference, according to its own natural laws.

Diderot **Denis Diderot** went to the University of **Paris** to fulfill his father's hopes that he would be a lawyer or pursue a career in the Church. He did neither. Instead, he became a freelance writer so that he could study and read in many subjects and languages. For the rest of his life, Diderot remained dedicated to new ideas.

Diderot's most famous contribution to the Enlightenment was the *Encyclopedia, or Classified Dictionary of the Sciences, Arts, and Trades*, a 28-volume collection of knowledge that he edited. First published in 1751, the purpose of the *Encyclopedia*, according to Diderot, was to "change the general way of thinking."

The *Encyclopedia* became a major weapon in the philosophes' crusade against the old French society. Many of its articles attacked religious superstition and supported religious toleration. Others called for social, legal, and political improvements that would lead to a society that was more tolerant and more humane. The *Encyclopedia* was sold to doctors, clergymen, teachers, and lawyers, thus spreading the ideas of the Enlightenment.

✓ Reading Check **Comparing** What were the major contributions of Montesquieu, Voltaire, and Diderot to the Enlightenment?

Toward a New Social Science

The philosophes, as we have seen, believed that Newton's methods could be used to discover the natural laws underlying all areas of human life. This led to what we would call the social sciences—areas such as economics and political science.

Economics The Physiocrats and Scottish philosopher Adam Smith have been viewed as the founders of the modern social science of economics. The Physiocrats, a French group, were interested in identifying the natural economic laws that governed human society. They maintained that if individuals were free to pursue their own economic self-interest, all society would ultimately benefit.

The state, then, should not interrupt the free play of natural economic forces by imposing government regulations on the economy. The state should leave the economy alone. This doctrine became known by its French name, **laissez-faire** (LEH•SAY FEHR), meaning "to let (people) do (what they want)."

The best statement of laissez-faire was made in 1776 by **Adam Smith** in his famous work *The Wealth of Nations*. Like the Physiocrats, Smith believed that the state should not interfere in economic matters. Indeed, Smith gave to government only three basic roles: protecting society from invasion (the army); defending citizens from injustice (the police); and keeping up certain public works, such as roads and canals, that private individuals could not afford.

History *through Art*

***Port of Marseille* by Claude-Joseph Vernet, 1754** Vernet was commissioned by the French king to paint the military and commercial seaports of France. What characteristic activities of a commercial port are included here? What information about the past could historians learn from this painting?

CHAPTER 10
Section 2, 300–307

✓ Reading Check

Answer: Montesquieu analyzed the idea of separation of powers to provide checks and balances; Voltaire advocated religious toleration and deism; Diderot edited the *Encyclopedia, or Classified Dictionary of the Sciences, Arts, and Trades.*

History *through Art*

Answer: Workers are unloading boats; merchants have come to inspect and buy goods. The wharf is a busy commercial center. Historians can determine how goods were shipped (in barrels), how trade was conducted, how goods were unloaded from the ships.

Guided Reading Activity 10–2

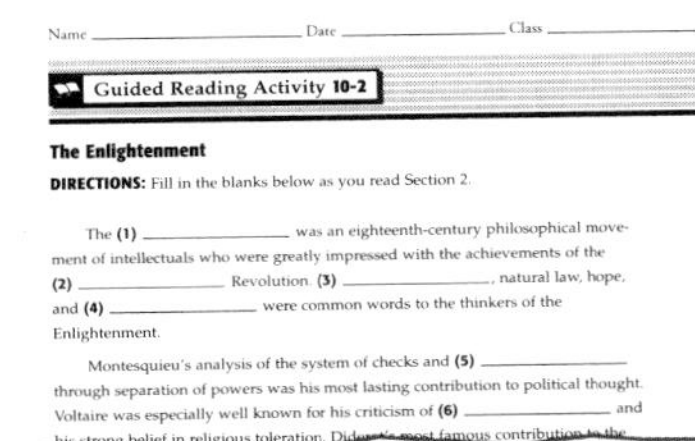

Name ________ Date ________ Class ________

Guided Reading Activity 10-2

The Enlightenment

DIRECTIONS: Fill in the blanks below as you read Section 2.

The **(1)** ________ was an eighteenth-century philosophical movement of intellectuals who were greatly impressed with the achievements of the **(2)** ________ Revolution. **(3)** ________, natural law, hope, and **(4)** ________ were common words to the thinkers of the Enlightenment.

Montesquieu's analysis of the system of checks and **(5)** ________ through separation of powers was his most lasting contribution to political thought. Voltaire was especially well known for his criticism of **(6)** ________ and his strong belief in religious toleration.

Critical Thinking

Ask students if they believe that a philosopher is one who "applies himself to the study of society with the purpose of making his kind better and happier." Were Voltaire's and Diderot's criticisms of Christianity intended to make people happier? (Answers will vary.) **L2**

INTERDISCIPLINARY CONNECTIONS ACTIVITY

Economics Adam Smith stated that government had three basic roles: protecting society from invasion, defending citizens from injustice, and engaging in public works that private industry could not afford. During a class discussion, ask students to support or oppose Smith's vision of government and state their reasons why. Then ask students to research the basic platforms of the major U.S. political parties: Democratic, Republican, Independent, Libertarian, Peace and Freedom, and Green. In which party would Smith have been most comfortable? Ask students to write paragraphs that answer this question and explain why this would have been a good fit. **L2**

Reading Check

Answer: The state should not interfere in economic matters.

Reading Check

Answer: *The Social Contract:* Society agreed to be governed by its general will and individuals must be forced to abide by the general will; *Emile:* Education should foster, not restrict, children's natural instincts.

Connecting Across Time

Ask students to evaluate the idea of Mary Wollstonecraft that women should have equal rights with men in education as well as in economic and political life. Why was she not taken seriously by many people during her life? How are the role and education of women during the Enlightenment reflected in today's society? **L1**

Enrich

To help students see the relationship between Enlightenment thought and today's political beliefs, have students list as many ideas as they can from the discussion of Enlightenment philosophy that are part of our current political, economic, and social systems. **L3**

Critical Thinking

Ask students to describe the origins of the Scientific Revolution in sixteenth-century Europe. Then have students explain the impact of the revolution on scientific thinking worldwide. **L2**

Beccaria and Justice By the eighteenth century, most European states had developed a system of courts to deal with the punishment of crime. Punishments were often cruel. The primary reason for extreme punishments was the need to deter crime in an age when a state's police force was too weak to ensure the capture of criminals.

One philosophe who proposed a new approach to justice was Cesare Beccaria. In his essay *On Crimes and Punishments,* written in 1764, Beccaria argued that punishments should not be exercises in brutality. He also opposed capital punishment. He did not believe that it stopped others from committing crimes. Moreover, it set an example of barbarism: "Is it not absurd, that the laws, which punish murder, should, in order to prevent murder, publicly commit murder themselves?"

Reading Check **Explaining** What is the concept of laissez-faire?

The Later Enlightenment

By the late 1760s, a new generation of philosophes had come to maturity. Most famous was **Jean-Jacques Rousseau** (ru•SOH). The young Rousseau wandered through France and Italy holding various jobs. Eventually he made his way to Paris, where he was introduced into the circle of the philosophes. He did not like city life, however, and often withdrew into long periods of solitude.

In his *Discourse on the Origins of the Inequality of Mankind,* Rousseau argued that people had adopted laws and government in order to preserve their private property. In the process, they had become enslaved by government. What, then, should people do to regain their freedom?

Jean-Jacques Rousseau

In his famous work *The Social Contract,* published in 1762, Rousseau presented his concept of the **social contract.** Through a social contract, an entire society agrees to be governed by its general will. Individuals who wish instead to follow their own self-interests must be forced to abide by the general will. "This means nothing less than that [they] will be forced to be free," said Rousseau. Thus, liberty is achieved by being forced to follow what is best for "the general will," because the general will represents what is best for the entire community.

Another important work by Rousseau is *Emile.* Written in the form of a novel, the work is a general discussion "on the education of the natural man." Rousseau argues that education should foster, and not restrict, children's natural instincts.

Unlike many Enlightenment thinkers, Rousseau believed that emotions, as well as reason, were important to human development. He sought a balance between heart and mind, between emotions and reason.

Rousseau did not necessarily practice what he preached. His own children were sent to orphanages, where many children died at a young age. Rousseau also viewed women as being "naturally" different from men: "To fulfill her functions, . . . [a woman] needs a soft life. . . . How much care and tenderness does she need to hold her family together." To Rousseau, women should be educated for their roles as wives and mothers by learning obedience and the nurturing skills that would enable them to provide loving care for their husbands and children. Not everyone in the eighteenth century agreed with Rousseau, however.

Reading Check **Summarizing** What were Rousseau's basic theories as presented in *The Social Contract* and *Emile?*

People In History

Mary Wollstonecraft
1759–1797—English writer

Mary Wollstonecraft is considered by many to be the founder of the European and American movements for women's rights. Wollstonecraft was largely self-educated. For a while, she earned a living as a governess but soon moved to a writing career and worked for a magazine publisher.

All along, Wollstonecraft continued to develop her ideas on education and women's rights. She wrote in 1792: "Make women rational creatures, and free citizens, and they will quickly become good wives; that is—if men do not neglect the duties of husbands and fathers!"

Mary Wollstonecraft married the philosopher William Godwin in 1797. She died shortly after the birth of their daughter—Mary Wollstonecraft Godwin Shelley—who wrote the famous novel *Frankenstein.*

COOPERATIVE LEARNING ACTIVITY

Role-Playing Organize the class into two groups to plan a gathering in a salon. Remind students that salons were places where writers, artists, and educated people could mingle with the nobility. Have each student in one group select a favorite individual from this chapter. Have students in the other group choose roles as members of the middle class or the nobility. Students should research the individuals, the lifestyles of the different social classes, and the salons. Then have them plan the setting and select a topic for the gathering. To stimulate conversation, you may wish to visit the salon in the guise of a noble person. **L1 L2**

For grading this activity, refer to the ***Performance Assessment Activities*** booklet.

CONNECTIONS Past To Present

Magazines, Then and Now

Bookstores and newsstands carry thousands of magazines that appeal to an enormous variety of interests. We can find magazines on fishing, car racing, fashion, politics, television, furniture making, tourism, wrestling, and a host of other subjects.

The first magazines in Europe were a product of a growing reading public in the seventeenth and eighteenth centuries, especially among the middle classes. The first magazine was published in Germany in 1633. It contained poems and articles on religion, the chief interest of its editor, Johann Rist.

Many early magazines had serious goals. Joseph Addison and Richard Steele's *Spectator,* begun in 1711, aimed to "bring Philosophy out of the closets and libraries, schools and colleges, to dwell in clubs and assemblies, at tea-tables and coffeehouses." It did not last long.

Some publishers began to broaden the appeal of their magazines. One goal was to attract women readers. *Ladies' Mercury,* published in Britain, provided advice on marriage and child rearing as well as sewing patterns and gossip. Its success brought forth a host of similar magazines.

Many early magazines failed because customers did not always pay for them on time. Isaiah Thomas, editor of the *Worcester Magazine,* became so desperate that he wrote: "The editor requests all those who are indebted to him for magazines, to make payment—butter will be received in small sums, if brought within a few days."

Argentine magazine stand

Comparing Past and Present

Pretend you are an eighteenth-century magazine editor assigned to write an article for the next edition. Choose a person or an event discussed in Chapter 10 to be the subject of your article (use outside resources if necessary). You could also select one Enlightenment idea and present it to your readers.

Rights of Women

For centuries, male intellectuals had argued that the nature of women made them inferior to men and made male domination of women necessary. By the eighteenth century, however, female thinkers began to express their ideas about improving the condition of women. The strongest statement for the rights of women was advanced by the English writer **Mary Wollstonecraft.** Many see her as the founder of the modern European and American movement for women's rights.

In *A Vindication of the Rights of Women,* Wollstonecraft identified two problems with the views of many Enlightenment thinkers. She noted that the same people who argued that women must obey men also said that government based on the arbitrary power of monarchs over their subjects was wrong. Wollstonecraft pointed out that the power of men over women was equally wrong.

Wollstonecraft further argued that the Enlightenment was based on an ideal of reason in all human beings. Because women have reason, then they are entitled to the same rights as men. Women, Wollstonecraft declared, should have equal rights in education, as well as in economic and political life.

Reading Check **Evaluating** How did Mary Wollstonecraft use the Enlightenment ideal of reason to advocate rights for women?

Social World of the Enlightenment

The Enlightenment was not a movement belonging exclusively to the nobles and aristocrats. For example, philosophes such as Diderot and Rousseau came from

COOPERATIVE LEARNING ACTIVITY

Creating a Database After they have read *Magazines, Then and Now,* ask students to list as many magazines as they can. Ask them to visit a newsstand or store and list twenty current magazines as homework. Then divide the class into three groups, and ask each group to compile a list of all its magazines. Have the groups compare lists in class, and create a master list with no duplicates. Then have students interpret the database they have created. Ask students: How many titles are on the list? What topics are covered? How do today's magazines compare to early magazines (topics, content, cost, number of pages, frequency of publication, type of paper, graphics, photographs, use of color)? **L2**

Answer: Answers will vary. Students should use visuals to accompany their presentations.

Reading Check

Answer: She argued that the Enlightenment was based on an ideal of reason in all human beings; if women have reason, then they are entitled to equal rights.

Connecting Across Time

Ask students whether they believe it is appropriate or desirable for governments to support the arts as was the practice during the Enlightenment. Students should debate the cost of artistic endeavors against the possibility that the government could control artistic expression through what it chose to support. Do students believe that our government should support artistic activity with public funds? What is their opinion of the National Endowment for the Arts? **L2**

Critical Thinking

Have students write an essay in which they analyze how ideas such as Judeo-Christian ethics and the rise of secularism and individualism in Western civilization, beginning with the Enlightenment, have influenced institutions and societies. **L2**

Geography Skills

Answers:

1. One key contains places of learning, the other denotes religions.
2. Students' work should be graded on depth and clarity of thought and quality of the charts.

3 ASSESS

Assign Section 2 Assessment as homework or as an in-class activity.

Have students use **Interactive Tutor Self-Assessment CD-ROM.**

Section Quiz 10–2

Name ______ Date ______ Class ______

Chapter 10 — Score

Section Quiz 10-2

DIRECTIONS: Matching Match each item in Column A with an item in Column B. Write the correct letters in the blanks. *(10 points each)*

Column A	Column B
____ 1. philosophers, writers, economists, social reformers	A. laissez-faire
____ 2. system of political limits and controls	B. philosophes
____ 3. to let (people) do (what they want)	C. deism
____ 4. idea that God lets the universe run by its own laws	D. natural economic laws
____ 5. interests of the Physiocrats and Adam Smith	E. separation of powers

DIRECTIONS: Multiple Choice In the blank, write the letter of the choice that best completes the statement or answers the question. *(10 points each)*

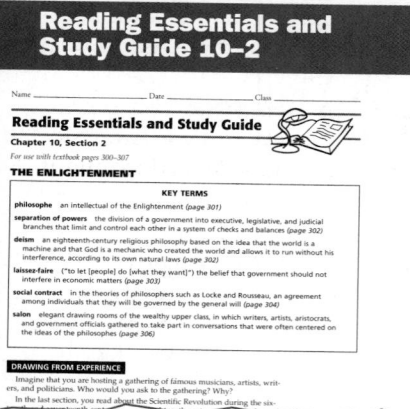

Reading Essentials and Study Guide 10–2

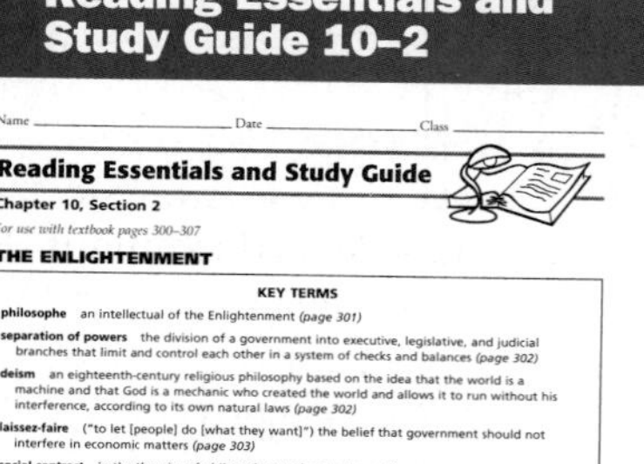

Name ______ Date ______ Class ______

Reading Essentials and Study Guide

Chapter 10, Section 2

For use with textbook pages 300–307

THE ENLIGHTENMENT

KEY TERMS

philosophe an intellectual of the Enlightenment *(page 301)*

separation of powers the division of a government into executive, legislative, and judicial branches that limit and control each other in a system of checks and balances *(page 302)*

deism an eighteenth-century religious philosophy based on the idea that the world is a machine and that God is a mechanic who created the world and allows it to run without his interference, according to its own natural laws *(page 302)*

laissez-faire ("to let [people] do [what they want]") the belief that government should not interfere in economic matters *(page 303)*

social contract in the theories of philosophers such as Locke and Rousseau, an agreement among individuals that they will be governed by the general will *(page 304)*

salon elegant drawing rooms of the wealthy upper class, in which writers, artists, aristocrats, and government officials gathered to take part in conversations that were often centered on the ideas of the philosophes *(page 306)*

DRAWING FROM EXPERIENCE

Imagine that you are hosting a gathering of famous musicians, artists, writers, and politicians. Who would you ask to the gathering? Why?

In the last section, you read about the Scientific Revolution during the six-

Geography Skills

The intellectuals of the Enlightenment created a movement that influenced the entire Western world.

1. **Interpreting Maps** Examine the keys of the two maps. What kind of information does each map contain?
2. **Applying Geography Skills** Pose and answer two questions about the geographic distributions shown on one of the maps on this page. Create a thematic chart that represents the same information.

the lower middle class. The movement did, however, have its greatest appeal with the aristocrats and upper classes in the larger cities. The common people, especially the peasants, were mostly unaware and little affected by the Enlightenment.

The Growth of Reading Of great importance to the Enlightenment was the spread of its ideas to the literate elite of European society. Especially noticeable in the eighteenth century was the growth of both publishing and the reading public. The number of titles issued each year by French publishers rose from 300 in 1750 to about 1,600 in the 1780s. Books had previously been aimed at small groups of the educated elite. Now, many books were directed at the new reading public of the middle classes, which included women and urban artisans.

An important aspect of the growth of publishing and reading in the eighteenth century was the development of magazines for the general public. In Great Britain, an important center for the new magazines, 25 periodicals were published in 1700, 103 in 1760, and 158 in 1780.

Along with magazines came daily newspapers. The first was printed in **London** in 1702. Newspapers were relatively cheap and were even provided free in many coffeehouses.

The Salon Enlightenment ideas were also spread through the salon. Salons were the elegant drawing rooms of the wealthy upper class's great urban houses. Invited guests gathered in these salons and took part in conversations that were often centered on the new ideas of the philosophes. The salons brought writers and artists together with aristocrats, government officials, and wealthy middle-class people.

The women who hosted the salons found themselves in a position to sway political opinion and influence literary and artistic taste. At her fashionable home in Paris, for example, Marie-Thérèse de

CRITICAL THINKING ACTIVITY

Drawing Inferences Ask students to do further research on the Parisian salons. Then ask students to analyze the information thay have found by drawing inferences. Who were the women who organized the salons? What were the political and social ties of these women? Why did they spend time and money organizing these evening affairs? Was this simply a passing social fad, or was it something more fundamental to the society and culture? Students might enjoy debating the extent to which these salon affairs provided political influence for a select group of women. **L2**

Geoffrin, wife of a wealthy merchant, held gatherings that became the talk of France and of all Europe. Distinguished foreigners, including a future king of Sweden and a future king of Poland, competed to receive invitations. These gatherings helped spread the ideas of the Enlightenment.

Reading Check **Examining** What was the importance of the salons?

Religion in the Enlightenment

Although many philosophes attacked the Christian churches, most Europeans in the eighteenth century were still Christians. Many people also sought a deeper personal devotion to God.

The Catholic parish church remained an important center of life for the entire community. How many people went to church regularly cannot be known. It has been established that 90 to 95 percent of Catholic populations did go to mass on Easter Sunday.

After the initial religious fervor that created Protestantism in the sixteenth century, Protestant churches settled into well-established patterns controlled by state authorities. Many Protestant churches were lacking in religious enthusiasm. The desire of ordinary Protestants for greater depths of religious experience led to new religious movements.

In England, the most famous new religious movement—Methodism—was the work of **John Wesley,** an Anglican minister. Wesley had a mystical experience in which "the gift of God's grace" assured him of salvation. This experience led him to become a missionary to the English people to bring them the "glad tidings" of salvation.

John Wesley

Wesley preached to the masses in open fields. He appealed especially to the lower classes. He tried, he said, "to lower religion to the level of the lowest people's capacities."

Wesley's powerful sermons often caused people to have conversion experiences. Many of these converts joined Methodist societies in which they helped each other do good works. In this way Wesley's Methodism gave the lower and middle classes in English society a sense of purpose and community. The Methodists stressed the importance of hard work and encouraged behaviors that led to spiritual contentment, which took the place of political equality.

After Wesley's death, Methodism became a separate Protestant group. Methodism proved that the need for spiritual experience had not been eliminated by the eighteenth-century search for reason.

Reading Check **Describing** What are some of the central ideas of Methodism?

SECTION 2 ASSESSMENT

Checking for Understanding

1. **Define** philosophe, separation of powers, deism, laissez-faire, social contract, salon.
2. **Identify** John Locke, Montesquieu, Voltaire, Denis Diderot, Adam Smith, Jean-Jacques Rousseau, Mary Wollstonecraft, John Wesley.
3. **Locate** Paris, London.
4. **Explain** the influence of Isaac Newton and John Locke on Enlightenment thinkers.
5. **List** the primary occupations of the philosophes.

Critical Thinking

6. **Discuss** What did Rousseau mean when he stated that if any individual wants to pursue his own self-interests at the expense of the common good, "He will be forced to be free"? Do you agree or disagree with Rousseau's ideas? Why?
7. **Summarizing Information** Use a diagram like the one below to identify factors that helped spread Enlightenment ideas throughout Europe.

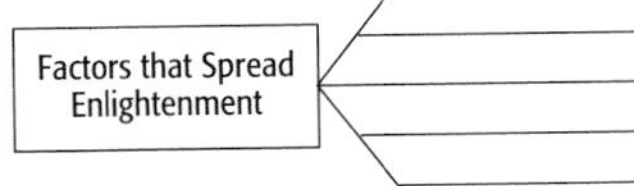

Analyzing Visuals

8. **Describe** the scene in the painting shown on page 303. What activities depicted in the painting are related to economics? What elements of the picture illustrate the economic principle of laissez-faire?

Writing About History

9. **Persuasive Writing** Mary Wollstonecraft argued that women are entitled to the same rights as men. Do you believe this premise to be true? Do you believe women are accorded equal rights today? Present your argument in an essay supported with evidence and logic.

Reading Check

Answer: The salons helped to spread the ideas of the Enlightenment. They brought writers and artists together with aristocrats. The women who hosted them found themselves in a position to sway political opinion and influence literary and artistic taste.

Reading Check

Answer: appealed to the lower classes; attempted to "lower religion to the level of the lowest people's capacities"; provided spiritual experience; good works; gave lower and middle classes a sense of purpose and community; stressed importance of hard work and encouraged behaviors that led to spiritual contentment, which took the place of political equality

Reteaching Activity

Have students list the names of all the people discussed in this section and state their contributions to their fields of endeavor. **L1**

4 CLOSE

Have students write their reactions to the Enlightenment. Ask them to imagine how they might have felt in the 1700s when faced with these new ideas. Collect the papers and read students' ideas aloud. Using the students' ideas as guidelines, review the ways people of the time reacted to the ideas of the Enlightenment. *(Answers will vary.)* **L2**

SECTION 2 ASSESSMENT

1. Key terms are in blue.
2. John Locke *(p. 300)*; Montesquieu *(p. 302)*; Voltaire *(p. 302)*; Denis Diderot *(p. 303)*; Adam Smith *(p. 303)*; Jean-Jacques Rousseau *(p. 304)*; Mary Wollstonecraft *(p. 305)*; John Wesley *(p. 307)*
3. See chapter maps.
4. Newton: Natural laws govern society; Locke: People are molded by experiences.
5. writers, professors, journalists, economists, social reformers
6. Answers should show understanding of Rousseau's ideas.
7. growth of publishing and reading; writings of philosophers and other Enlightenment thinkers; discussion in salons
8. busy commercial port; represents capitalist economy; goods are sold to those who need and want them
9. Answers should demonstrate understanding of women's rights.

CHAPTER 10
Section 3, 308–316

1 FOCUS

Section Overview

This section explores the impact of the Enlightenment on politics and the arts.

BELLRINGER
Skillbuilder Activity

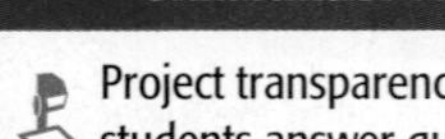

Project transparency and have students answer questions.

Available as a blackline master.

Daily Focus Skills Transparency 10–3

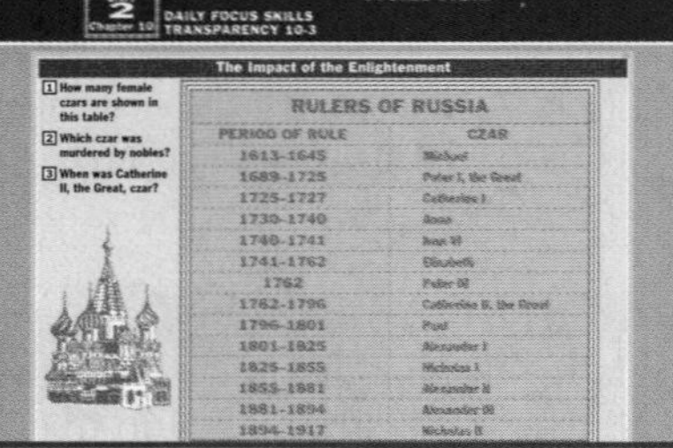

Guide to Reading

Answers to Graphic: Conflicts of the Seven Years' War: British and Prussians fought against the Austrians, Russians, and French; Britain and France fought in India; British and French fought over the waterways of the Gulf of St. Lawrence and the Ohio River Valley.

Preteaching Vocabulary: Explain how *enlightened absolutism* affected European governments. *(rulers tried to govern by Enlightenment principles, were reluctant to relinquish power, did not become "enlightened" leaders)* **L2**

SECTION 3 The Impact of the Enlightenment

Guide to Reading

Main Ideas
- Enlightenment beliefs were reflected in the art, music, and literature of the time.
- Enlightenment thought impacted the politics of Europe in the eighteenth century.

Key Terms
rococo, enlightened absolutism

People to Identify
Bach, Handel, Haydn, Mozart, Frederick the Great, Maria Theresa, Catherine the Great

Places to Locate
Prussia, Austria, Russia, Silesia

Preview Questions
1. What innovations in the arts occurred during the eighteenth century?
2. What were the causes and results of the Seven Years' War?

Reading Strategy
Describing Use a chart like the one below to list the conflicts of the Seven Years' War. Include the countries involved and where the conflicts were fought.

Conflicts of the Seven Years' War

Preview of Events

1735 · 1740 · 1745 · 1750 · 1755 · 1760 · 1765

- **1730s** Rococo style spreads through Europe
- **1740** War of the Austrian Succession begins
- **1748** The Treaty of Aix-la-Chapelle is signed
- **1756** The Seven Years' War erupts
- **1762** Catherine the Great becomes ruler of Russia
- **1763** The Treaty of Paris is signed

Prussian soldiers

Voices from the Past

The eighteenth-century Prussian king Frederick II once said:

> ❝[The services a monarch must provide for his people] consisted in the maintenance of the laws; a strict execution of justice; . . . and defending the state against its enemies. It is the duty of this magistrate to pay attention to agriculture; it should be his care that provisions for the nation should be in abundance, and that commerce and industry should be encouraged. He is a perpetual sentinel, who must watch the acts and the conduct of the enemies of the state. . . . If he be the first general, the first minister of the realm, it is not that he should remain the shadow of authority, but that he should fulfill the duties of such titles. He is only the first servant of the state.❞
>
> —***The Western Tradition,*** **Eugen Weber, 1972**

These comments reveal the impact of the ideas of the Enlightenment on the rulers of the period.

The Arts

The ideas of the Enlightenment also had an impact on the world of culture. Eighteenth-century Europe witnessed both traditional practices and important changes in art, music, and literature.

Architecture and Art The palace of Louis XIV at Versailles, in France, had made an enormous impact on Europe. The Austrian emperor, the Swedish king, and

SECTION RESOURCES

Reproducible Masters
- Reproducible Lesson Plan 10–3
- Daily Lecture and Discussion Notes 10–3
- Guided Reading Activity 10–3
- Section Quiz 10–3
- Reading Essentials and Study Guide 10–3

Transparencies
- Daily Focus Skills Transparency 10–3

Multimedia
- Interactive Tutor Self-Assessment CD-ROM
- ExamView® Pro Testmaker CD-ROM
- Presentation Plus! CD-ROM

other rulers also built grandiose residences. These palaces were modeled more on the Italian baroque style of the 1500s and 1600s than they were on the seventeenth-century French classical style of Versailles. Thus, a unique architectural style was created.

One of the greatest architects of the eighteenth century was Balthasar Neumann. Neumann's two masterpieces are the Church of the Fourteen Saints in southern Germany and the Residence, the palace of the prince-bishop of Würzburg. In these buildings, secular and spiritual become one as lavish and fanciful ornament, light, bright colors, and elaborate detail greet the visitor. Inside the church, a pilgrim in search of holiness is struck by the incredible richness of detail.

The baroque and neoclassical styles that had dominated seventeenth-century art continued into the eighteenth century. By the 1730s, however, a new artistic style, known as **rococo**, had spread all over Europe.

Unlike the baroque style, which stressed grandeur and power, rococo emphasized grace, charm, and gentle action. Rococo made use of delicate designs colored in gold with graceful curves. The rococo style was highly secular. Its lightness and charm spoke of the pursuit of pleasure, happiness, and love.

Rococo's appeal is evident in the work of Antoine Watteau. In his paintings, gentlemen and ladies in elegant dress reveal a world of upper-class pleasure and joy. Underneath that exterior, however, is an element of sadness as the artist suggests the fragility and passing nature of pleasure, love, and life.

Another aspect of rococo was a sense of enchantment and enthusiasm, especially evident in the work of Giovanni Battista Tiepolo. Many of Tiepolo's paintings came to adorn the walls and ceilings of churches and palaces. His masterpiece is the ceiling of the Bishop's Palace at Würzburg, a massive scene representing the four continents.

Music The eighteenth century was one of the greatest periods in the history of European music. In the first half of the century, two composers—Johann Sebastian Bach and George Frederick Handel—stand out as musical geniuses.

Bach, a renowned org-anist as well as a composer, spent his entire life in Germany. While he was music director at the Church of Saint Thomas in Leipzig, he composed his *Mass in B Minor* and other works that gave him the reputation of being one of the greatest composers of all time.

Handel was a German who spent much of his career in England. He is probably best known for his religious music. Handel's *Messiah* has been called a rare work that appeals immediately to everyone and yet is a masterpiece of the highest order.

HISTORY Online

Web Activity Visit the *Glencoe World History—Modern Times* Web site at **wh.mt.glencoe.com** and click on **Chapter 10–Student Web Activity** to learn more about the rococo style.

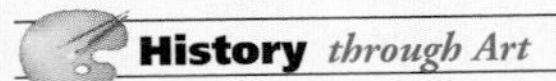
History *through Art*

***Danse dans un Pavillon* by Antoine Watteau**
Watteau began his career as an interior decorator and rose to become the court painter to King Louis XV. What details in this painting by Watteau are examples of the rococo style of painting?

2 TEACH

History *through Art*

Answer: The painting's theme is happy and light. It is a fanciful work; the dance emphasizes the grace of the woman.

Daily Lecture and Discussion Notes 10–3

Daily Lecture and Discussion Notes

Chapter 10, Section 3

Did You Know? Some Enlightenment thinkers believed that human reason was so powerful that one day human beings would be able to predict the condition of the entire universe in the next moment.

I. **The Arts** *(pages 308–310)*

A. The Enlightenment had a large impact on culture.

B. European monarchs tried to emulate Versailles, but in the Italian baroque style, not the French classical. They created a new kind of architecture. By the 1730s a new artistic style—**rococo**—had emerged. While the baroque style stressed grandeur and power, the rococo style emphasized grace, charm, and gentle action. It was highly secular, valuing the pursuit of pleasure, happiness, and love. The greatest rococo painter was Antoine Watteau.

C. Enchantment and enthusiasm are also part of rococo, as is evident in the painting of Giovanni Battista Tiepolo. Much of his work is in churches and palaces. His masterpiece is the ceiling of the Bishop's Palace at Würzburg, a huge scene representing the four continents.

D. The eighteenth century was one of the greatest in history for European music. Johann Sebastian Bach and George Frederick Handel, both German, were the two baroque standouts at the beginning of the century. Bach was a great organist and composer. *Mass in B Minor* is one of his famous works. Handel is best known for his *Messiah*.

E. Franz Joseph **Haydn** and Wolfgang Amadeus **Mozart** were the two standouts of the classical style in the second half of the eighteenth century. Hayden's *The Creation* is one of his greatest works. Mozart was a child prodigy, known for symphonies, concerti, and operas. His perpetual poverty made his life miserable. Haydn once said to Mozart's father, "Your son is the greatest composer known to me."

F. The novel developed in Europe in the eighteenth century. Henry Fielding wrote novels about people with no morals surviving by their wits, such as *The History of Tom Jones, a Foundling*. His characters reflect real types in eighteenth-century England.

Discussion Question

Who are some important twentieth-century composers of classical music? *(Sergei Prokofiev, Anton Bruckner, Benjamin Britten, and Aaron Copland are some.)*

turn

142

Guided Reading Activity 10–3

Name ____________ Date ____________ Class ____________

Guided Reading Activity 10-3

The Impact of the Enlightenment

DIRECTIONS: Fill in the blanks below as you read Section 3.

I. The Enlightenment brought important changes in art, ____________, and literature.

A. By the 1730s, a new artistic style known as ____________ had spread over Europe.

B. The eighteenth century was one of the greatest periods in the history of ____________ music.

1. Johann Sebastian ____________ was one of the greatest composers of all time.

2. Wolfgang Amadeus ____________ was a true child prodigy of the age.

C. The eighteenth century was important in the development of the European ____________.

II. Enlightenment thought had an effect on ____________ life in European states.

A. Frederick II of ____________ was well-versed in the ideas of the Enlightenment

B. Joseph II of Austria said, "Philosophy is the ____________ of my empire."

C. Catherine II of Russia said Diderot's ____________ theories "would have turned everything in my kingdom upside down."

III. The philosophes ____________ war as a foolish waste of life and resources.

A. In 1740, a major war broke out in connection with the succession to the ____________ throne.

B. The ____________ Years' War had three major areas of conflict: Europe, India, and North America.

C. The struggle between Britain and France in the rest of the world, known as the ____________, was fought in India and North America.

MEETING INDIVIDUAL NEEDS

Auditory Listening to authentic musical pieces will help students with a sensitivity to harmony, melody, rhythm, and tone better understand the different musical styles of the Age of Enlightenment. Play some works from the baroque period (1600–1750) by Bach or Handel and then some from the classical period (1750–1820) by Haydn or Mozart. Ask students to describe some of the ways the two styles differ. *(Answers may include the following: the use of repetition in baroque music, and the balance and contrast among movements of classical works.)* **L2**

Refer to ***Inclusion for the High School Social Studies Classroom Strategies and Activities*** in the TCR.

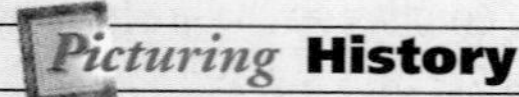

Answer: emphasized grace, charm, and gentle action; made use of delicate designs colored in gold with graceful curves; highly secular; sense of enchantment and enthusiasm

Picturing History

Answer: A child prodigy is a person who displays extraordinary talent at an early age. Answers to second question will vary.

Connecting Across Time

During the War of the Austrian Succession and the Seven Years' War, countries shifted their alliances in order to achieve political goals. This practice has continued to the present. During a class discussion, ask students if these decisions to shift alliances were made by wise monarchs or were simply signs of disloyalty and ingratitude. Have students support their viewpoints with concrete examples from the past and the present. **L2**

CURRICULUM CONNECTION

Music Play a brief selection of medieval religious music and of Mozart's *The Magic Flute* for your class. (See question 9, page 316.) Have students describe their reactions to and feelings for each selection. How does Mozart's music reflect the values of the Age of Enlightenment? **L2**

Bach and Handel perfected the baroque musical style. Two geniuses of the second half of the eighteenth century—Franz Joseph Haydn and Wolfgang Amadeus Mozart—were innovators who wrote music called classical rather than baroque.

Haydn spent most of his adult life as musical director for wealthy Hungarian princes. Visits to England introduced him to a world where musicians wrote for public concerts rather than princely patrons. This "liberty," as he called it, led him to write two great works, *The Creation* and *The Seasons.*

Mozart was truly a child prodigy. His failure to get a regular patron to support him financially made his life miserable. Nevertheless, he wrote music passionately. His *The Marriage of Figaro, The Magic Flute,* and *Don Giovanni* are three of the world's greatest operas. Haydn remarked to Mozart's father, "Your son is the greatest composer known to me."

Literature The eighteenth century was also important in the development of the European novel. The novel was especially attractive to a growing number of middle-class readers.

The Englishman Henry Fielding wrote novels about people without morals who survive by their wits. Fielding's best-known work is *The History of Tom Jones, a Foundling,* which describes the adventures of a young scoundrel. In a number of hilarious episodes, Fielding presents scenes of English life from the slums of London to the country houses of the English aristocracy. His characters reflect real types in eighteenth-century English society.

Reading Check **Identifying** What are the characteristics of the rococo style?

Enlightenment and Enlightened Absolutism

Enlightenment thought had an effect on the political life of European states in the eighteenth century. The philosophes believed in natural rights for all people. These rights included equality before the law; freedom of religious worship; freedom of speech; freedom of the press; and the right to assemble, hold property, and pursue happiness. As the American Declaration of Independence expressed, "We hold these truths to be self-evident, that all men are created equal; that they are endowed by their creator with certain unalienable rights; that among these are life, liberty and the pursuit of happiness."

How were these natural rights to be established and preserved? Most philosophes believed that people needed to be governed by enlightened rulers. What are enlightened rulers? They allow religious toleration, freedom of speech and of the press, and the rights of private property. They nurture the arts, sciences, and education. Above all, enlightened

Picturing History

In this painting, c. 1763, a seven-year-old Mozart is shown with his father and sister. Above is the original manuscript of Mozart's first attempt at writing choral music. What is a child prodigy? Do you know anyone who could be described as a child prodigy?

INTERDISCIPLINARY CONNECTIONS ACTIVITY

Art Many artistic styles flourished during the Enlightenment, including baroque, classical, and rococo. Assign students to write individual reports on an artist, writer, or musician of the seventeenth or eighteenth century whose work exemplifies one of these styles. Ask students to include examples and illustrations of their subject's work and to explain his or her contribution to the period. Their subjects might include artists Gian Lorenzo Bernini, Peter Paul Rubens, Caravaggio; musicians Handel, Haydn, Liszt, Mozart, J.S. Bach; writers Voltaire, Diderot, Fielding. Have students present their reports to the class orally. **L2 L3**

rulers obey the laws and enforce them fairly for all subjects. Only strong, enlightened monarchs could reform society.

Many historians once assumed that a new type of monarchy emerged in the later eighteenth century, which they called **enlightened absolutism.** In the system of enlightened absolutism, rulers tried to govern by Enlightenment principles while maintaining their royal powers.

Did Europe's rulers, however, actually follow the advice of the philosophes and become enlightened? To answer this question, we can examine three states—**Prussia, Austria,** and **Russia**.

Prussia: Army and Bureaucracy Two able Prussian kings, Frederick William I and Frederick II, made Prussia a major European power in the eighteenth century. Frederick William I strove to maintain a highly efficient bureaucracy of civil service workers. The supreme values of the bureaucracy were obedience, honor, and, above all, service to the king. As Frederick William asserted: "One must serve the king with life and limb, and surrender all except salvation. The latter is reserved for God. But everything else must be mine."

Frederick William's other major concern was the army. By the end of his reign in 1740, he had doubled the army's size. Although Prussia was tenth in physical size and thirteenth in population in Europe, it had the fourth largest army after France, Russia, and Austria. The Prussian army, because of its size and its reputation as one of the best armies in Europe, was the most important institution in the state.

Members of the nobility, who owned large estates with many serfs, were the officers in the Prussian army. These officers, too, had a strong sense of service to the king or state. As Prussian nobles, they believed in duty, obedience, and sacrifice.

Frederick II, or **Frederick the Great,** was one of the best educated and most cultured monarchs in the eighteenth century. He was well versed in the ideas of the Enlightenment and even invited Voltaire to live at his court for several years. Frederick was a dedicated ruler. He, too, enlarged the Prussian army, and he kept a strict watch over the bureaucracy.

For a time, Frederick seemed quite willing to make enlightened reforms. He abolished the use of torture except in treason and murder cases. He also granted limited freedom of speech and press, as well as complete religious toleration. However, he kept Prussia's serfdom and rigid social structure intact and avoided any additional reforms.

People In History

Frederick II (Frederick the Great)

1712–1786 — Prussian king

Frederick II, known as Frederick the Great, is credited with making Prussia a great European power. As a young man, Frederick was quite different from his strict father, Frederick William I. Frederick, who had a high regard for French culture, poetry, and flute playing, resisted his father's wishes that he immerse himself in government and military affairs. His father's frustration expressed itself in anger: "As I entered the room he seized me by the hair and threw me to the ground."

Frederick once tried to escape his father by fleeing to England with his friend Lieutenant Hans von Katte. Frederick William had both arrested and made his son watch the beheading of his good friend. One year later, Frederick asked for forgiveness and began to do what his father wanted.

The Austrian Empire The Austrian Empire had become one of the great European states by the beginning of the eighteenth century. It was difficult to rule, however, because it was a sprawling empire composed of many different nationalities, languages, religions, and cultures. Empress **Maria Theresa,** who inherited the throne in 1740, worked to centralize the Austrian Empire and strengthen the power of the state. She was not open to the philosophes' calls for reform, but her successor was.

Joseph II was determined to make changes. He believed in the need to sweep away anything standing in the path of reason. As he said, "I have made Philosophy the lawmaker of my empire, her logical applications are going to transform Austria."

Joseph's reform program was far reaching. He abolished serfdom, eliminated the death penalty, established the principle of equality of all before the law, and enacted religious reforms, including religious toleration. In his effort to change Austria, Joseph II issued thousands of decrees and laws.

Joseph's reform program, however, largely failed. He alienated the nobles by freeing the serfs. He alienated the Catholic Church with his religious reforms. Even the serfs were unhappy, because they were unable to make sense of the drastic changes in Joseph's policies. Joseph realized his failure when he

Who?What?Where?When?

***Sans Souci* Palace** Frederick II planned and had built a one-story summer palace, *Sans Souci.* The name is French and means "without cares." *Sans Souci* was the king's favorite retreat. It was famous for its midnight suppers, at which Frederick surrounded himself with educated men.

Many world leaders have retreats. Can you name and locate the retreat used by American presidents? *(Camp David in Maryland)* **L1**

Critical Thinking

Ask students to discuss why the Austrian monarchy, unlike that of Prussia, never became a centralized, absolutist state. *(state composed of many different national groups, each with its own laws and political life)* **L1**

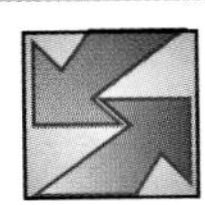

CURRICULUM CONNECTION

Literature English poet Alexander Pope (1688–1744) reflected the tenets of the Scientific Revolution in his *An Essay on Man*. In it he described nature as "A mighty maze! But not without plan."

CRITICAL THINKING ACTIVITY

Creating a Chart Ask each student to create a five-column chart listing the rulers studied in this chapter. The column headings should be labeled from left to right as follows: *Ruler, Country, Religion, Challenges,* and *Accomplishments.* Students should fill in the columns as they read the chapter, listing names and significant information to help them organize and recall key facts. The charts will be helpful for class discussions and to review material studied. After students have completed their charts, assign them to small groups to study specific rulers in depth. Each group should study a different ruler and report its research in an oral presentation. **L1** ELL

Picturing History

Answer: The carriage symbolizes the regal aspects and the riches of their monarchy. Joseph sought radical reform based on Enlightenment ideals but his reforms were overturned. Catherine seemed to favor financial reform but actually did little.

Critical Thinking

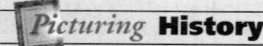

Both Catherine the Great and Maria Theresa were complicated figures whose reigns included great successes and great failures. Invite interested students to research the life of one of these leaders, considering whether her reign was, on balance, good or bad for her people. **L3**

Who?What?Where?When?

St. Petersburg Czar Peter the Great gained control of the Neva River and Russian access to the Baltic coast in 1703. This date marks the birth of St. Petersburg, the grand capital built on a group of islands in the Neva. Peter the Great erected magnificent buildings that included churches, establishments of higher education, government offices, and museums. The city spawned many scientists, writers, and government officials.

Today, St. Petersburg is a major Russian center of industry and tourism.

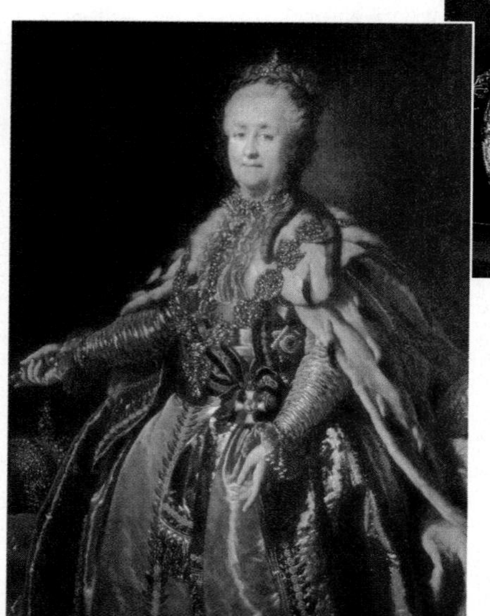

Picturing History

Pictured from left to right are Catherine the Great, a carriage used by Catherine, and Joseph II. How might the carriage symbolize the differences between Catherine's and Joseph's attempts at reform?

wrote his own epitaph for his gravestone: "Here lies Joseph II who was unfortunate in everything that he undertook." His successors undid almost all of Joseph II's reforms.

Russia under Catherine the Great In Russia, Peter the Great was followed by six weak successors who were put in power and deposed by the palace guard. After the last of these six successors, Peter III, was murdered by a group of nobles, his German wife emerged as ruler of all the Russians.

Catherine II, or **Catherine the Great,** ruled Russia from 1762 to 1796. She was an intelligent woman who was familiar with the works of the philosophes and seemed to favor enlightened reforms. She invited the French philosophe Denis Diderot to Russia and, when he arrived, urged him to speak frankly, "as man to man." He did so, outlining an ambitious program of political and financial reform.

Catherine, however, was skeptical about what she heard. Diderot's impractical theories, she said, "would have turned everything in my kingdom upside down." She did consider the idea of a new law code that would recognize the principle of the equality of all people in the eyes of the law. In the end, however, she did nothing, because she knew that her success depended on the support of the Russian nobility.

Catherine's policy of favoring the landed nobility led to worse conditions for the Russian peasants and eventually to rebellion. Led by an illiterate Cossack (a Russian warrior), Emelyan Pugachev, the rebellion spread across southern Russia, but soon collapsed. Catherine took stronger measures against the peasants. All rural reform was halted, and serfdom was expanded into newer parts of the empire.

Catherine proved to be a worthy successor to Peter the Great in her policies of territorial expansion. Russia spread southward to the Black Sea by defeating the Turks under Catherine's rule. To the west, Russia gained about 50 percent of Poland's territory.

Enlightened Absolutism? Of the rulers we have discussed, only Joseph II sought truly radical changes based on Enlightenment ideas. Both Frederick II and Catherine II liked to talk about enlightened reforms. They even attempted some, but they never took reform seriously. To Frederick II and Catherine II, maintaining the existing system took priority.

In fact, all three rulers were chiefly guided by a concern for the power and well-being of their states. In the final analysis, heightened state power in Prussia, Austria, and Russia was not used to undertake enlightened reforms. Rather, it was used to collect more taxes and thus to create armies, to wage wars, and to gain more power.

EXTENDING THE CONTENT

Seeds of Change The sixteenth century began with European explorers traveling the globe and initiating a process that led to radical changes in the world; the sixteenth century fostered creativity and change, resulting in new inventions; it experienced the growth of material wealth; it inspired new interest in learning; and it led to the formation of strong national states. These states would battle for the next few centuries over political freedom, absolutism, constitutionalism, and nationalism, and make western Europe a world leader. The forces that began in the sixteenth century have spread to every continent and influenced development all over the world. Emphasize the importance of this era in world history. Have students create their own charts that identify changes in world history that resulted from the European age of exploration and colonization.

The philosophes condemned war as a foolish waste of life and resources. Despite their words, the rivalry among states that led to costly struggles remained unchanged in eighteenth-century Europe. Europe's self-governing, individual states were chiefly guided by the self-interest of the rulers.

The eighteenth-century monarchs were concerned with the balance of power, the idea that states should have equal power in order to prevent any one from dominating the others. This desire for a balance of power, however, did not imply a desire for peace. Large armies created to defend a state's security were often used to conquer new lands as well. As Frederick the Great of Prussia remarked, "The fundamental rule of governments is the principle of extending their territories."

Reading Check **Evaluating** What effect did enlightened reforms have in Prussia, Austria, and Russia?

War of the Austrian Succession

In 1740, a major war broke out in connection with the succession to the Austrian throne. When the Austrian emperor Charles VI died, he was succeeded by his daughter, Maria Theresa. King Frederick II of Prussia took advantage of the succession of a woman to the throne of Austria by invading Austrian **Silesia.** France then entered the war against Austria, its traditional enemy. In turn, Maria Theresa made an alliance with Great Britain.

The War of the Austrian Succession (1740 to 1748) was fought in three areas of the world. In Europe, Prussia seized Silesia while France occupied the Austrian Netherlands. In the Far East, France took Madras (today called Chennai) in India from the British. In North America, the British captured the French fortress of Louisbourg at the entrance to the St. Lawrence River.

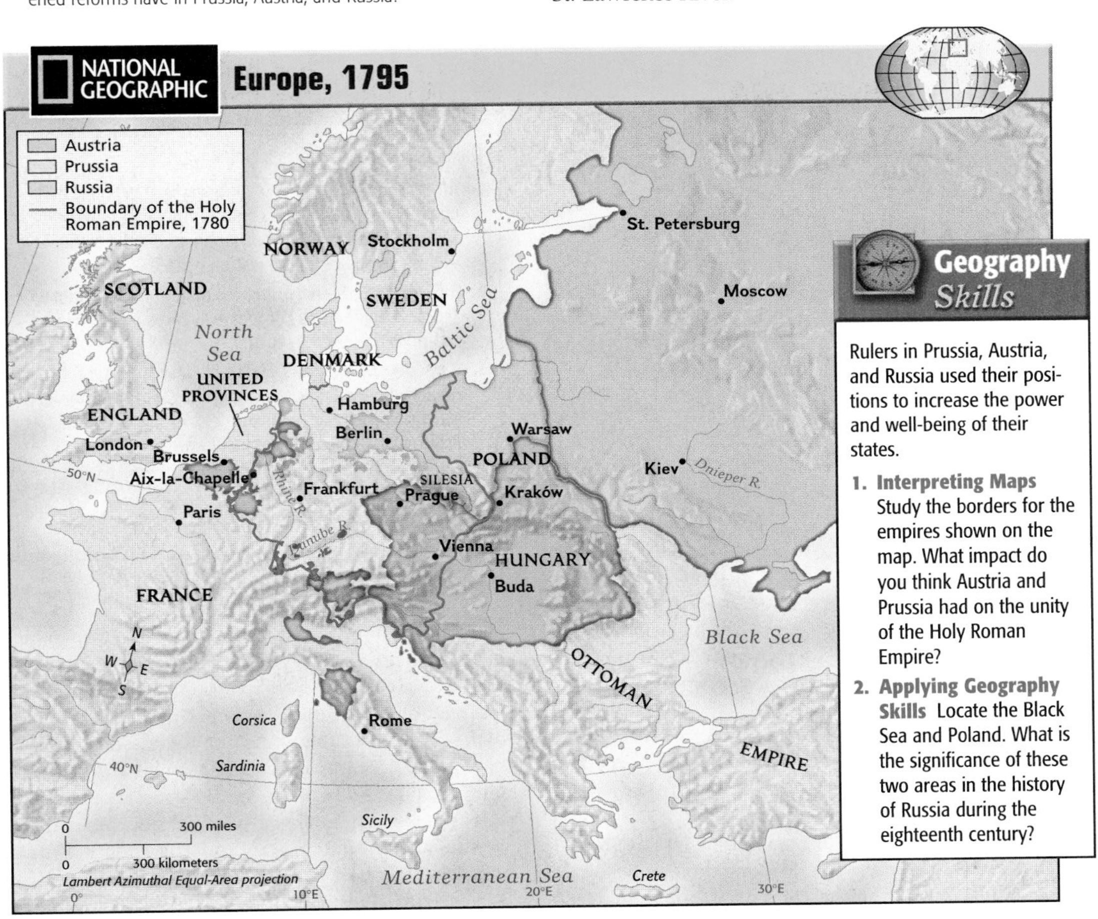

Geography Skills

Rulers in Prussia, Austria, and Russia used their positions to increase the power and well-being of their states.

1. **Interpreting Maps** Study the borders for the empires shown on the map. What impact do you think Austria and Prussia had on the unity of the Holy Roman Empire?
2. **Applying Geography Skills** Locate the Black Sea and Poland. What is the significance of these two areas in the history of Russia during the eighteenth century?

Reading Check

Answer: They had little effect. In Prussia, reforms were very limited and had no affect on the rigid social structure. In Austria, the far-reaching reforms of Joseph II largely failed. In Russia, Catherine appeared receptive to enlightened reforms but in the end did nothing.

Geography Skills

Answers:

1. Austria and Prussia diminished the size of the Holy Roman Empire.
2. Russia acquired parts of Poland and gained access to an ice-free port on the Black Sea.

Connecting Across Time

The sprawling Austrian Empire was difficult to rule because it was composed of many separate states with different nationalities, languages, religions, and cultures. Ask students to identify and describe other states they have studied that were difficult to rule. Then ask them to name present-day nations that face the same problems. **L2**

Writing Activity

Ask students to write a hypothetical newspaper article that might have appeared at the end of the War of the Austrian Succession. Tell them to describe the causes of the war and to evaluate the war's results. **L2**

EXTENDING THE CONTENT

Austrian Royal Family The Hapsburg family was one of the oldest and most distinguished royal dynasties in Europe, connected to virtually every royal house in Europe. Through marriages and inheritance, the family came to dominate much of Europe. The male line died out in 1740 with Emperor Charles VI, but his daughter Maria Theresa married Francis of Lorraine and began the Hapsburg-Lorraine line. The War of the Austrian Succession and the Napoleonic Wars diminished the Hapsburg fortune. By 1918, the Austrian Empire had been completely broken up into independent republics, although the claim to hereditary titles has been maintained by descendants of the once great family.

CHAPTER 10
Section 3, 308–316

Geography *Skills*

Answers:

1. Europe, North America, India; North America
2. British and Prussians allied against Austrians, Russians, and French
3. the waterways of the Gulf of St. Lawrence and the Ohio River Valley; British colonies heavily populated, British invested in navy and focused on war in North America, blocked French reinforcements

Answer: Austria and Great Britain; Prussia and France

Charting Activity

Assign students to construct a chart that shows which countries were allied with each other before and after the War of the Austrian Succession. Ask them to explain how these new alliances contributed to the causes of the Seven Years' War. **L1**

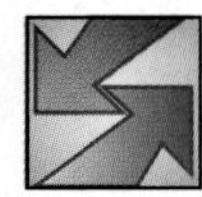

CURRICULUM CONNECTION

Economics Ask students to form and defend a hypothesis based on economic reasons Britain was willing to spend the money necessary to fight the French in North America during the Seven Years' War. **L2**

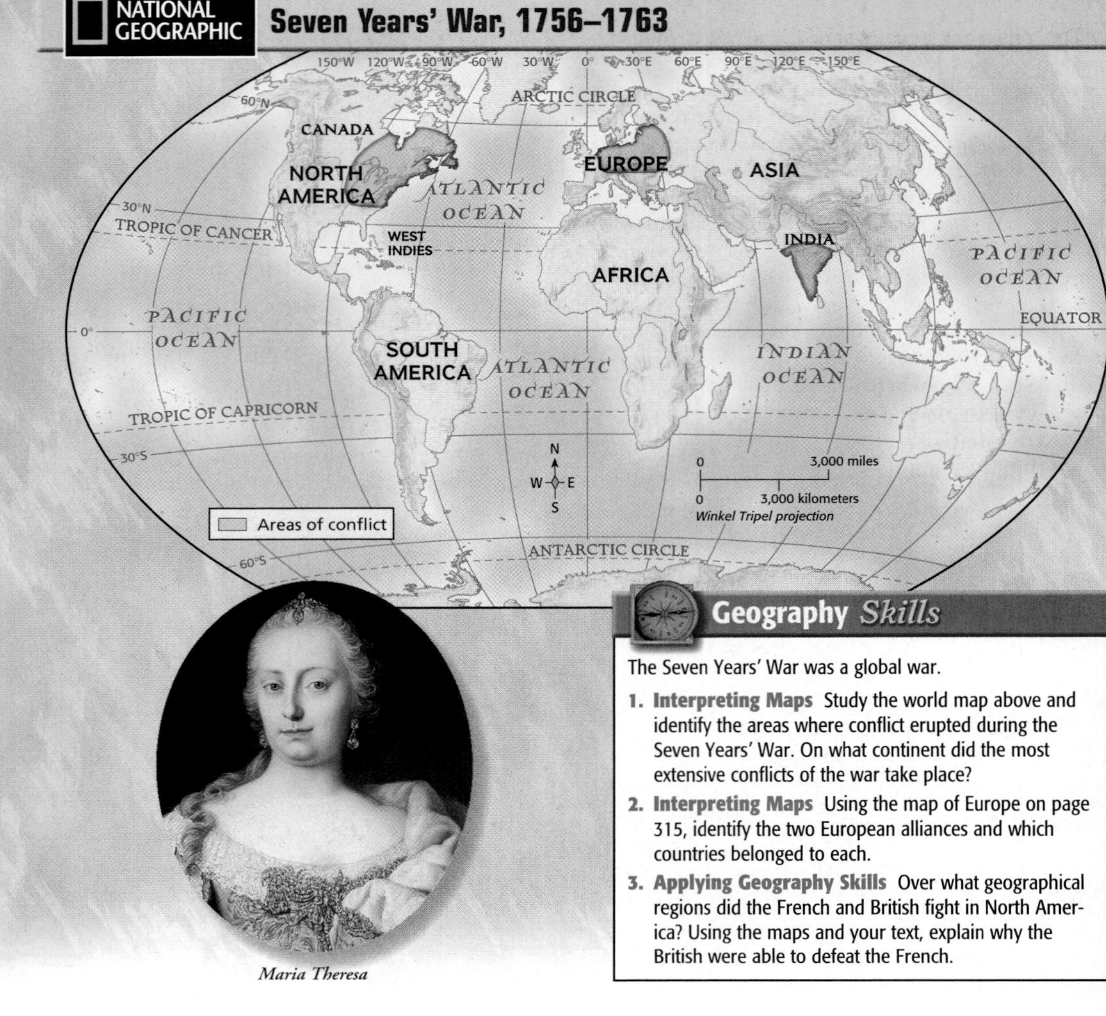

Maria Theresa

Geography *Skills*

The Seven Years' War was a global war.

1. **Interpreting Maps** Study the world map above and identify the areas where conflict erupted during the Seven Years' War. On what continent did the most extensive conflicts of the war take place?
2. **Interpreting Maps** Using the map of Europe on page 315, identify the two European alliances and which countries belonged to each.
3. **Applying Geography Skills** Over what geographical regions did the French and British fight in North America? Using the maps and your text, explain why the British were able to defeat the French.

After seven years of warfare, all parties were exhausted and agreed to the Treaty of Aix-la-Chapelle in 1748. This treaty guaranteed the return of all occupied territories except Silesia to their original owners. Prussia's refusal to return Silesia meant yet another war between Prussia and Austria.

Reading Check **Describing** Name the countries that fought together on each side of the War of the Austrian Succession.

The Seven Years' War

Maria Theresa refused to accept the loss of Silesia. She rebuilt her army while working diplomatically to separate Prussia from its chief ally, France. In 1756, Austria achieved what was soon labeled a diplomatic revolution.

New Allies French-Austrian rivalry had been a fact of European diplomacy since the late sixteenth century. However, two new rivalries now replaced the old one: the rivalry of Britain and France over colonial empires and the rivalry of Austria and Prussia over Silesia. France abandoned Prussia and allied with Austria. Russia, which saw Prussia as a major threat to Russian goals in central Europe, joined the new alliance with France and Austria. In turn, Britain allied with Prussia. This diplomatic revolution of 1756 led to another worldwide war. The war had

COOPERATIVE LEARNING ACTIVITY

Staging a Debate Have students hold a mock debate centering on Maria Theresa's right to rule the Hapsburg Empire after her father's death. Although women were not allowed to rule Austria, Holy Roman Emperor Charles VI convinced the monarchs of Europe to accept a *pragmatic sanction*. This royal decree asked Europe's rulers to promise not to divide the Hapsburg lands and to accept female succession to the Austrian throne. The debate topic is: "Should the pragmatic sanction have been honored by Austria's neighbors? Why or why not?" Students should research the life and times of Maria Theresa, her father Charles VI, and the status of women at that time. **L2**

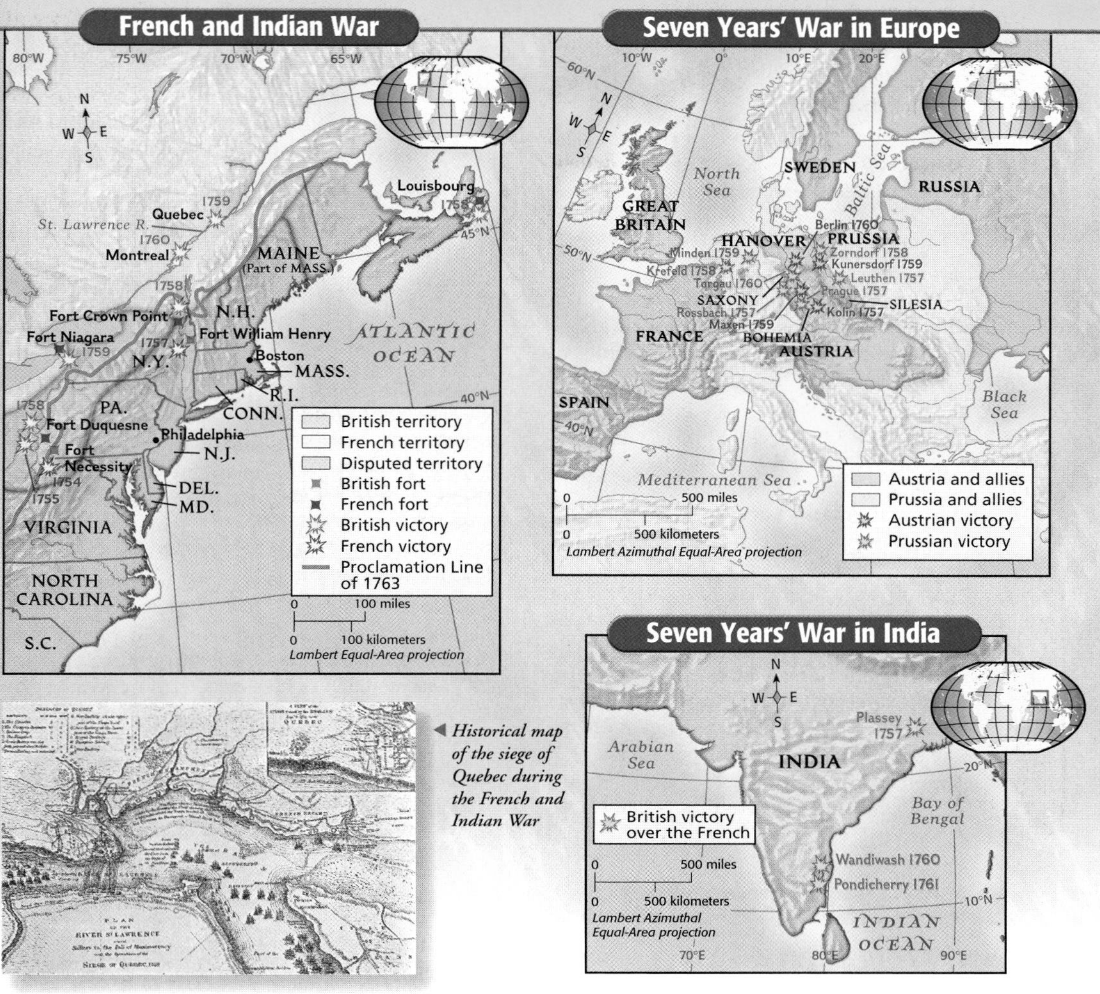

◀ *Historical map of the siege of Quebec during the French and Indian War*

three major areas of conflict: Europe, India, and North America.

The War in Europe Europe witnessed the clash of the two major alliances: the British and Prussians against the Austrians, Russians, and French. With his superb army and military skill, Frederick the Great of Prussia was able for some time to defeat the Austrian, French, and Russian armies. His forces were under attack from three different directions, however, and were gradually worn down.

Frederick faced disaster until Peter III, a new Russian czar who greatly admired Frederick, withdrew Russian troops from the conflict and from the Prussian lands that the Russians had occupied. This withdrawal created a stalemate and led to the desire for peace. The European war ended in 1763. All occupied territories were returned to their original owners, while Austria officially recognized Prussia's permanent control of Silesia.

The War in India The struggle between Britain and France in the rest of the world had more decisive results. Known as the Great War for Empire, it was fought in India and North America. The French had returned Madras to Britain after the War of the Austrian Succession, but the struggle in India continued. The British ultimately won out, not because they

Writing Activity

In this chapter, students have read about the impact of Enlightenment thought on political systems. Enlightenment thought emphasized ideals of equality and reason that can also be found in political philosophies from earlier civilizations. Ask students to summarize in an essay the worldwide influence of ideas concerning rights and responsibilities that originated from Greco-Roman and Judeo-Christian ideals such as equality before the law. **L2**

3 ASSESS

Assign Section 3 Assessment as homework or as an in-class activity.

Have students use **Interactive Tutor Self-Assessment CD-ROM.**

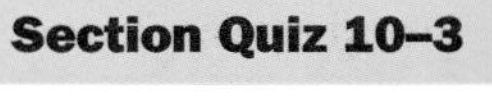

Section Quiz 10–3

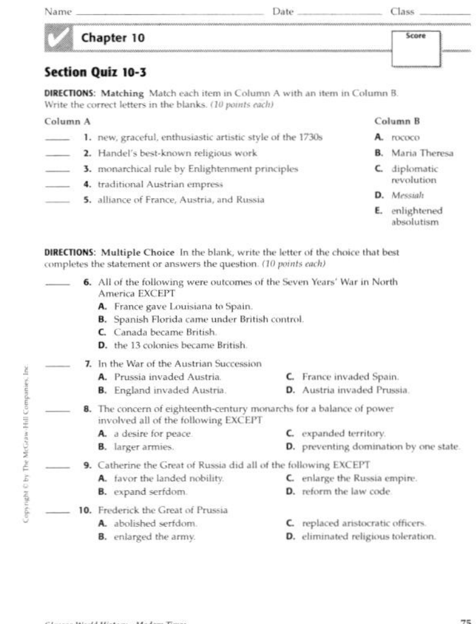

Name ________ Date ________ Class ________

Chapter 10 Score

Section Quiz 10-3

DIRECTIONS: Matching Match each item in Column A with an item in Column B. Write the correct letters in the blanks. *(10 points each)*

Column A	Column B
____ **1.** new, graceful, enthusiastic artistic style of the 1730s	**A.** rococo
____ **2.** Handel's best-known religious work	**B.** Maria Theresa
____ **3.** monarchical rule by Enlightenment principles	**C.** diplomatic revolution
____ **4.** traditional Austrian empress	**D.** *Messiah*
____ **5.** alliance of France, Austria, and Russia	**E.** enlightened absolutism

DIRECTIONS: Multiple Choice In the blank, write the letter of the choice that best completes the statement or answers the question. *(10 points each)*

____ **6.** All of the following were outcomes of the Seven Years' War in North America EXCEPT
A. France gave Louisiana to Spain.
B. Spanish Florida came under British control.
C. Canada became British.
D. the 13 colonies became British.

____ **7.** In the War of the Austrian Succession
A. Prussia invaded Austria. **C.** France invaded Spain.
B. England invaded Austria. **D.** Austria invaded Prussia.

____ **8.** The concern of eighteenth-century monarchs for a balance of power involved all of the following EXCEPT
A. a desire for peace. **C.** expanded territory.
B. larger armies. **D.** preventing domination by one state.

____ **9.** Catherine the Great of Russia did all of the following EXCEPT
A. favor the landed nobility. **C.** enlarge the Russia empire.
B. expand serfdom. **D.** reform the law code.

____ **10.** Frederick the Great of Prussia
A. abolished serfdom. **C.** replaced aristocratic officers.
B. enlarged the army. **D.** eliminated religious toleration.

Glencoe World History—Modern Times 75

CRITICAL THINKING ACTIVITY

Evaluating Have students assume the role of a political cartoonist or a columnist during the War of the Austrian Succession or the Seven Years' War. Ask students to depict or write about a major event in a cartoon for a fictitious newspaper, *The Prussian Press*. Subjects might include the balance of power in Europe, the fight over Silesia, or alliances formed by different countries. Ask students to consider whether Prussia would have invaded Austrian Silesia if it had known England would ally itself with Austria and enter the war against Prussia. Have students share their work with the class. **L2**

CHAPTER 10
Section 3, 308–316

Reading Check

Answer: by defeating the French in India and in North America; India was left to the British, and French North American possessions in Canada and east of the Mississippi were transferred to Britain

Reading Essentials and Study Guide 10–3

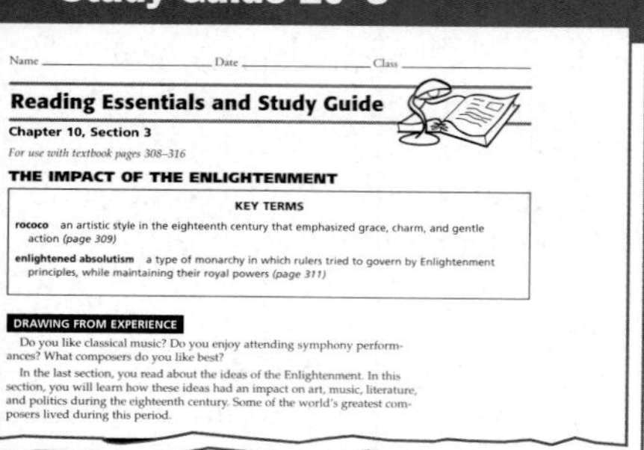
Name ______ Date ______ Class ______

Reading Essentials and Study Guide

Chapter 10, Section 3

For use with textbook pages 308–316

THE IMPACT OF THE ENLIGHTENMENT

KEY TERMS

rococo an artistic style in the eighteenth century that emphasized grace, charm, and gentle action *(page 309)*

enlightened absolutism a type of monarchy in which rulers tried to govern by Enlightenment principles, while maintaining their royal powers *(page 311)*

DRAWING FROM EXPERIENCE

Do you like classical music? Do you enjoy attending symphony performances? What composers do you like best?

In the last section, you read about the ideas of the Enlightenment. In this section, you will learn how these ideas had an impact on art, music, literature, and politics during the eighteenth century. Some of the world's greatest composers lived during this period.

Reteaching Activity

Ask students to explain the causes and effects of the War of the Austrian Succession and tell how the Seven Years' War grew out of a realignment of power in Europe. **L1** ELL

4 CLOSE

Both absolute and limited monarchies were attempts by European nations to restore order and increase stability in their societies. Which countries and rulers do students think best succeeded in reaching this goal? **L2**

had better forces but because they were more persistent. With the Treaty of Paris in 1763, the French withdrew and left India to the British.

The War in North America The greatest conflicts of the Seven Years' War took place in North America. On the North American continent, the French and British colonies were set up differently. French North America (Canada and Louisiana) was run by the French government as a vast trading area. It was valuable for its fur, leather, fish, and timber. The French state was unable to get people to move to North America, so its colonies were thinly populated.

British North America consisted of 13 prosperous colonies on the eastern coast of the present United States. Unlike the French colonies, the British colonies were more populated, containing about 1.5 million people by 1750.

The British and French fought over two primary areas in North America. One consisted of the waterways of the Gulf of St. Lawrence, which were protected by the fortress of Louisbourg and by forts that guarded French Quebec. The other area that was fought over was the unsettled Ohio River valley. The French began to move down from Canada and up from Louisiana to establish forts in the Ohio River valley. This French activity threatened to cut off the British settlers in the 13 colonies from expanding into this vast area. The French were able to gain the support of the Indians. As traders and not settlers, the French were viewed by the Indians with less hostility than the British.

The French scored a number of victories, at first. British fortunes were revived, however, by the efforts of William Pitt the Elder, Britain's prime minister. Pitt was convinced that the French colonial empire would have to be destroyed for Britain to create its own colonial empire. Pitt's policy focused on doing little in the European theater of war while putting resources into the colonial war, especially through the use of the British navy. The French had more troops in North America but not enough naval support. The defeat of French fleets in major naval battles gave the British an advantage, because the French could no longer easily reinforce their garrisons.

A series of British victories soon followed. In 1759, British forces under General Wolfe defeated the French under General Montcalm on the Plains of Abraham, outside Quebec. Both generals died in the battle. The British went on to seize Montreal, the Great Lakes area, and the Ohio River Valley. The French were forced to make peace. By the Treaty of Paris, they transferred Canada and the lands east of the Mississippi to England. Their ally Spain transferred Spanish Florida to British control. In return, the French gave their Louisiana territory to the Spanish. By 1763, Great Britain had become the world's greatest colonial power.

Reading Check **Explaining** How did Great Britain become the world's greatest colonial power?

SECTION 3 ASSESSMENT

Checking for Understanding

1. **Define** rococo, enlightened absolutism.
2. **Identify** Bach, Handel, Haydn, Mozart, Frederick the Great, Maria Theresa, Catherine the Great.
3. **Locate** Prussia, Austria, Russia, Silesia.
4. **Describe** the characteristics of an ideal enlightened ruler. Do any of the eighteenth-century rulers discussed in this section have the characteristics of an ideal ruler?
5. **List** all the countries in the world that fought in the Seven Years' War. Which country gained the most territory?

Critical Thinking

6. **Analyze** Why were Enlightenment ideals never fully practiced by eighteenth-century rulers?
7. **Compare and Contrast** Use a table like the one below to compare and contrast the reforms of Joseph II of Austria with those of Frederick II of Prussia and Catherine II of Russia.

Joseph II	Frederick II	Catherine II

Analyzing Visuals

8. **Identify** the theme of the Watteau painting on page 309. Find another example of rococo painting in an art history book in your school's library (such as a work by Giovanni Battista Tiepolo). Compare this painting to Watteau's. How are they similar?

Writing About History

9. **Expository Writing** Listen to a selection of medieval religious music and of Mozart's *The Magic Flute*. Write an essay describing how the two pieces are similar and different. What kind of emotion does each piece convey?

SECTION 3 ASSESSMENT

1. Key terms are in blue.
2. Bach *(p. 309)*; Handel *(p. 309)*; Haydn *(p. 310)*; Mozart *(p. 310)*; Frederick the Great *(p. 311)*; Maria Theresa *(p. 311)*; Catherine the Great *(p. 312)*
3. See chapter maps.
4. allows religious toleration and freedom of speech, nurtures arts, sciences, and education, obeys the laws and enforces them fairly for all subjects; Answers will vary.
5. Britain and Prussia against Austria, Russia, and France; Britain
6. They did not want to lose power.
7. Joseph II: abolished serfdom and death penalty, supported religious reform; Frederick II: abolished torture, granted limited freedom of speech and press; Catherine II: favored the nobility and expanded serfdom
8. Answers will vary.
9. Answers will vary.

STUDY & WRITING

SKILLBUILDER

Outlining

Why Learn This Skill?

Outlining is a useful skill for both taking notes and writing papers. When you are studying written material, use outlining to organize information. This not only helps you absorb the material, but later you will have useful notes to review for class or tests. When you are writing a paper, outlining is a good starting point for putting information in a logical order. Then use the material in the outline to write your paragraphs and arrange your essay.

Learning the Skill

There are two kinds of outlines—formal and informal. An informal outline is similar to taking notes and is useful for reviewing for a test.

- Write only words and phrases needed to remember ideas.
- Note related but less important details under the main ideas.

A formal outline has a standard format. In a formal outline:

- Label main heads with Roman numerals, subheads with capital letters, and details with Arabic numerals.
- Have at least two entries for each level.
- Indent each level from the level above.
- Use the same grammatical form for all entries. If one entry is a complete sentence, all other entries at that level must be complete sentences.

Practicing the Skill

Study the following outline and then answer these questions.

I. Changes in Astronomy
  A. Galileo Galilei
    1. Used the telescope to observe the heavens
    2. Condemned by the Catholic Church
  B. Isaac Newton
    1. Tied together the work of Copernicus, Kepler, and Galileo
    2. Published the *Principia*
      a. Defined the three laws of motion
      b. Proved the universal law of gravitation
II. Changes in Medicine
  A. Andreas Vesalius
    1. Dissected human bodies for the first accurate descriptions of human anatomy
    2. Published *On the Fabric of the Human Body*
  B. William Harvey
    1. Wrote the theory of blood circulation
    2. Published *Motion of the Heart and Blood*

1. Is this a formal or an informal outline?
2. What are the two main headings?
3. How does each subhead under "Isaac Newton" support the topic of the level above it?
4. Give two examples of grammatical consistency.

Nicholas Copernicus observing an eclipse of the moon

Applying the Skill

Using the guidelines above, create a formal outline for Section 3 of this chapter.

Glencoe's **Skillbuilder Interactive Workbook, Level 2,** provides instruction and practice in key social studies skills.

ANSWERS TO PRACTICING THE SKILL

1. This is a formal outline.
2. I. Changes in Astronomy; and II. Changes in Medicine
3. They both relate to Newton, telling us more about him.
4. All entries at the third level (Arabic numerals) begin with a verb, which is followed by a phrase that serves as the object of that verb.

Applying the Skill: Students will create an outline of Section 3 of this chapter. After they are finished, have students review their outlines to make sure that they are grammatically consistent.

STUDY & WRITING SKILLBUILDER

TEACH

Outlining On the chalkboard, write the following main headings for an informal outline about activities of a typical school day: *Morning, Afternoon, Evening.* Have students add indented subheads and further indented supporting details under each main head. For example: *At home* and *At school* could be subheads under *Morning. Get up, Get dressed,* and *Eat breakfast* could be details under *At home.* Be sure students have at least two subheads under each head and at least two details under each subhead. Convert students' outlines to formal outlines by placing Roman numerals, capital letters, and Arabic numerals in the appropriate places. Then have students read the skill and complete the practice questions. **L1**

Additional Practice

Skills Reinforcement Activity 10

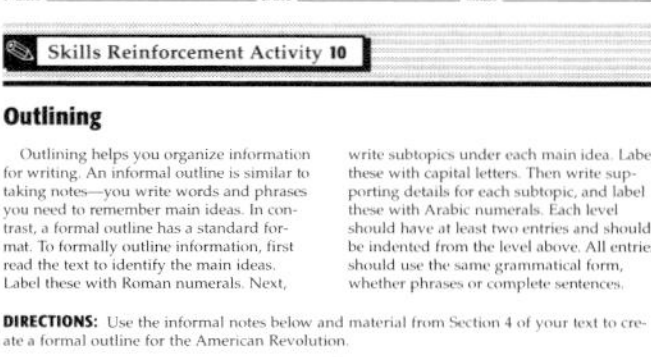

Name ______ Date ______ Class ______

Skills Reinforcement Activity 10

Outlining

Outlining helps you organize information for writing. An informal outline is similar to taking notes—you write words and phrases you need to remember main ideas. In contrast, a formal outline has a standard format. To formally outline information, first read the text to identify the main ideas. Label these with Roman numerals. Next, write subtopics under each main idea. Label these with capital letters. Then write supporting details for each subtopic, and label these with Arabic numerals. Each level should have at least two entries and should be indented from the level above. All entries should use the same grammatical form, whether phrases or complete sentences.

DIRECTIONS: Use the informal notes below and material from Section 4 of your text to create a formal outline for the American Revolution.

Seven Years' War results in need for

GLENCOE TECHNOLOGY

CD-ROM

Glencoe Skillbuilder Interactive Workbook CD-ROM, Level 2

This interactive CD-ROM reinforces student mastery of essential social studies skills.

CHAPTER 10
Section 4, 318–322

1 FOCUS

Section Overview

This section explores European colonization in North America and South America and how it led to revolution.

BELLRINGER
Skillbuilder Activity

 Project transparency and have students answer questions.

 Available as a blackline master.

Daily Focus Skills Transparency 10–4

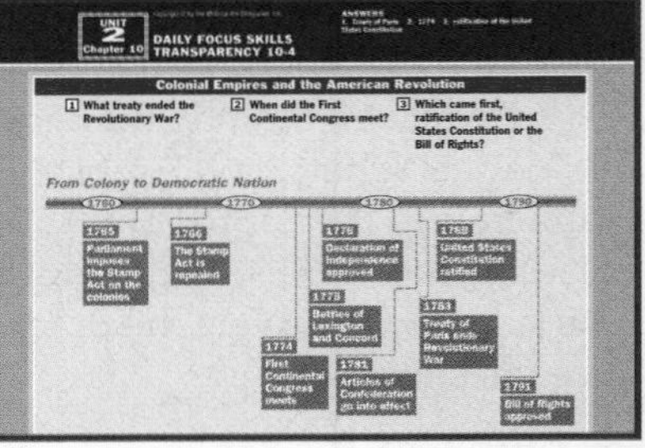

Guide to Reading

Answers to Graphic: New American Government: central federal government superior to governments of the individual states; divided into three branches (executive, legislative, judicial); Constitution the supreme law of the land; Bill of Rights guarantees specific rights

Preteaching Vocabulary: Explain the *federal system* of government. *(The federal system shares power between the state governments and the national government. It is the model upon which the United States Constitution is based.)* **L2**

SECTION 4 Colonial Empires and the American Revolution

Guide to Reading

Main Ideas
- The colonies of Latin America and British North America were developing in ways that differed from their European mother countries.
- The American colonies revolted against Great Britain and formed a new nation.

Key Terms
mestizo, mulatto, federal system

People to Identify
Sor Juana Inés de la Cruz, Hanoverians, Robert Walpole

Places to Locate
Brazil, Yorktown

Preview Questions
1. What were the chief characteristics of Latin American society?
2. What caused the American Revolution, and what did it accomplish?

Reading Strategy
Summarizing Information Use a chart like the one below to identify key aspects of the government created by the American colonists.

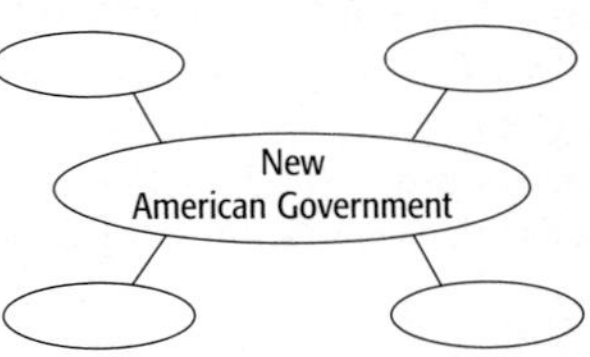

Preview of Events

1715	1730	1745	1760	1775	1790

- **1714** The Hanoverian dynasty is established
- **1721** Robert Walpole becomes prime minister of Britain
- **1757** William Pitt the Elder becomes prime minister
- **1776** American Revolution begins
- **1783** Treaty of Paris recognizes American independence

Voices from the Past

Thomas Jefferson

On July 2, 1776, the Second Continental Congress adopted a resolution declaring the independence of the American colonies. It read:

> ❝We hold these truths to be self-evident, that all men are created equal, that they are endowed by their Creator with certain unalienable Rights, that among these are Life, Liberty, and the pursuit of Happiness. That to secure these rights, Governments are instituted among Men, deriving their just powers from the consent of the governed. That whenever any Form of Government becomes destructive of these ends, it is the Right of the People to alter or to abolish it and to institute new Government.❞
>
> —***The Federal and State Constitutions,*** **S.N. Thorpe, ed., 1909**

The ideas of the Enlightenment had clearly made an impact on the colonies in North America. Despite their close ties to their European mother countries, the colonies of Latin America and British North America were developing in ways that sometimes differed significantly from those of Europe.

Colonial Empires in Latin America

In the sixteenth century, Portugal came to dominate **Brazil.** At the same time, Spain established an enormous colonial empire in the Western Hemisphere that included parts of North America, Central America, and most of South America. Within the lands of Central America and South America, a new civilization arose, which we call Latin America.

SECTION RESOURCES

Reproducible Masters
- Reproducible Lesson Plan 10–4
- Daily Lecture and Discussion Notes 10–4
- Guided Reading Activity 10–4
- Section Quiz 10–4
- Reading Essentials and Study Guide 10–4

Transparencies
- Daily Focus Skills Transparency 10–4

Multimedia
- Interactive Tutor Self-Assessment CD-ROM
- ExamView® Pro Testmaker CD-ROM
- Presentation Plus! CD-ROM

Latin America was a multiracial society. Already by 1501, Spanish rulers permitted intermarriage between Europeans and Native Americans, whose offspring became known as **mestizos** (meh•STEE•zohz). In addition, over a period of three centuries, possibly as many as 8 million African slaves were brought to Spanish and Portuguese America to work the plantations. **Mulattoes**—the offspring of Africans and Europeans—joined mestizos and other descendants of Europeans, Africans, and Native Americans to produce a unique society in Latin America.

Economic Foundations Both the Portuguese and the Spanish sought ways to profit from their colonies in Latin America. One source of wealth came from abundant supplies of gold and silver, which were sent to Europe. Farming, however, proved to be a more long-lasting and rewarding source of prosperity for Latin America.

A noticeable feature of Latin American agriculture was the dominant role of the large landowner. Both Spanish and Portuguese landowners created immense estates. Native Americans either worked on the estates or worked as poor farmers on marginal lands. This system of large landowners and dependent peasants has remained a lasting feature of Latin American society.

Trade provided another avenue for profit. In addition to gold and silver, a number of other natural products were shipped to Europe, including sugar, tobacco, diamonds, and animal hides. In turn, the mother countries supplied their colonists with manufactured goods.

Both Spain and Portugal closely regulated the trade of their American colonies to keep others out. By the beginning of the eighteenth century, however, both the British and the French had become too powerful to be kept out of the lucrative Latin American markets.

State and Church Portuguese Brazil and Spanish Latin America were colonial empires that lasted over three hundred years. The difficulties of

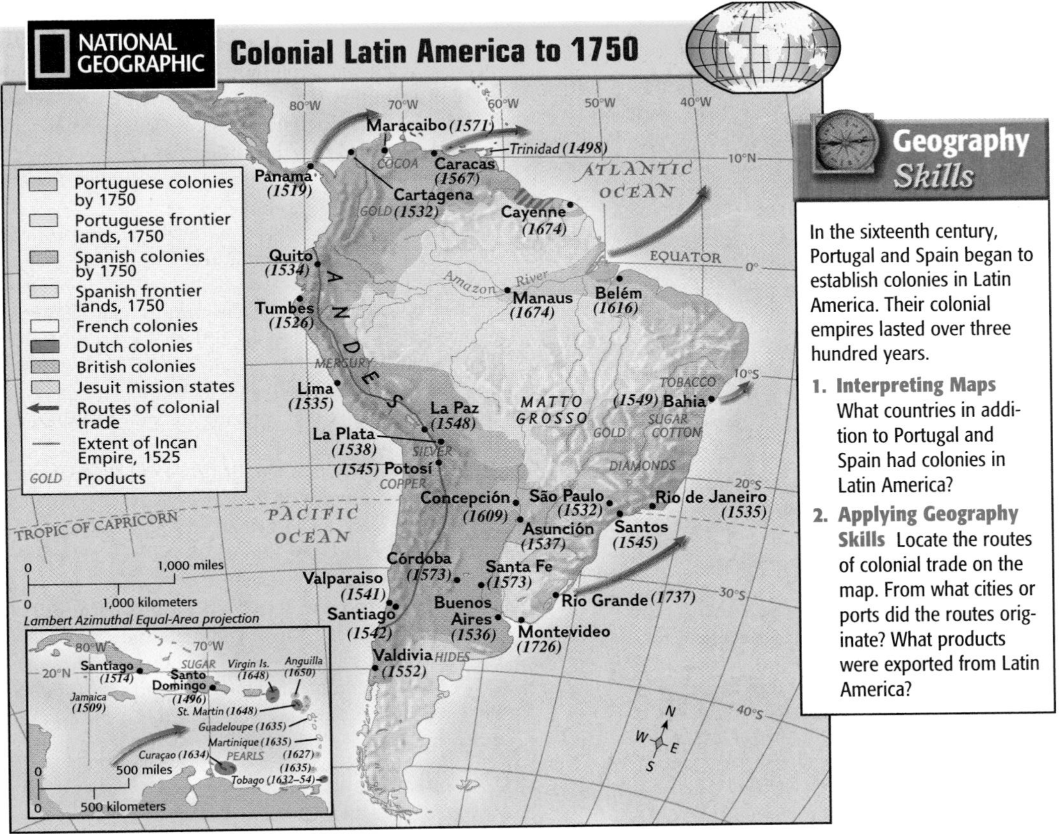

Geography Skills

In the sixteenth century, Portugal and Spain began to establish colonies in Latin America. Their colonial empires lasted over three hundred years.

1. **Interpreting Maps** What countries in addition to Portugal and Spain had colonies in Latin America?
2. **Applying Geography Skills** Locate the routes of colonial trade on the map. From what cities or ports did the routes originate? What products were exported from Latin America?

2 TEACH

Geography Skills

Answers:

1. French, Dutch, and British
2. Rio Grande, Bahia, Belém, Caracas, Panama; products included tobacco, sugar, cotton, diamonds, hides, copper, silver, mercury, cocoa, and gold

Daily Lecture and Discussion Notes 10–4

Daily Lecture and Discussion Notes
Chapter 10, Section 4

Did You Know? Some believe that Crispus Attucks, a former slave, was the first American to fall during the Boston Massacre on March 5, 1770. He is generally considered the first man to have lost his life in the fight for American independence. His body lay in state for three days in Boston's Faneuil Hall. In 1888 a monument honoring Attucks was unveiled in the Boston Commons.

I. Colonial Empires in Latin America (pages 318–320)
A. After the Spanish and Portuguese colonized the Americas, a new civilization arose that we call Latin America. Colonies often developed differently from the parent country.
B. Latin America was a multiracial society. Europeans and Native Americans intermarried; their offspring were known as mestizos. Close to 8 million African slaves were brought to these countries. Mulattoes—offspring of Europeans and Africans—were also part of the unique society of Latin America.
C. The Portuguese and Spanish sought ways to profit from their colonies. One source of wealth was gold and silver, but farming was more lucrative in the long run. An important feature of Latin American agriculture was the dominant role of the large landowner. The system of large landowners and dependent peasants has remained a lasting part of Latin America.
D. Trade between the parent country and colony also was profitable. Spain and Portugal both regulated their colonies to keep others out. By the beginning of the eighteenth

Guided Reading Activity 10–4

Name ______ Date ______ Class ______

Guided Reading Activity 10-4

Colonial Empires and the American Revolution

DIRECTIONS: Fill in the blanks below as you read Section 4.

1. In the sixteenth century, Portugal came to dominate ______. Spain's empire included parts of ______, ______, and ______ America.
2. By 1501, Spanish rulers permitted ______ between Europeans and Native Americans, whose offspring became known as ______.
3. A noticeable feature of Latin American ______ was the dominant role of the large landowner.
4. Portuguese Brazil and Spanish Latin America were colonial ______ that lasted over three hundred years.

Critical Thinking

After they have read this section, ask students to identify the causes and evaluate the effects of the American Revolution. **L1**

COOPERATIVE LEARNING ACTIVITY

Staging a Debate As European powers colonized the Americas, they carried on the agricultural tradition of landowners creating immense estates. The native inhabitants of the colonized areas could either work on the estates or subsist as poor farmers on the margins of these estates. Organize a class debate in which the two sides discuss whether this seems to be a fair system. One factor students should consider is whether this system leads to social unrest, considering that it emerged at the same time capitalism and industrialization were establishing themselves in Europe and the colonies. Students should also research if this system is still used, and if so, where. **L1**

CHAPTER 10
Section 4, 318–322

Reading Check

Answer: gold and silver that were sent to Europe; farming; trade

Reading Check

Answer: England and Scotland; both the English and the Scots

CURRICULUM CONNECTION

Economics Ask students to identify other conflicts that they have studied that were based on heavy taxation. Do students believe that the American Revolution would have been avoided if the British had allowed colonists to have a voice in the passage of tax laws? **L2**

Writing Activity

Ask students to research acts of Parliament that caused conflicts in the colonies. *(Stamp Act, Declaratory Act, Intolerable Acts, Quebec Act, tax on tea)* Have students write essays discussing why the colonists disliked these acts. *(They had no representation in Parliament.)* **L1 L2**

Enrich

The United States Declaration of Independence is one of the world's most significant historical documents. Have students locate a copy of this document and read it together in class. Guide students in a discussion in which they identify the impact of the political and legal ideas contained in the Declaration. **L2**

communication and travel between the Americas and Europe made the attempts of the Spanish and Portuguese monarchs to provide close regulation of their empires virtually impossible. As a result, colonial officials in Latin America had much freedom in carrying out imperial policies.

From the beginning of their conquest of the New World, Spanish and Portuguese rulers were determined to Christianize the native peoples. This policy gave the Catholic Church an important role to play in the Americas—a role that added considerably to the Church's power.

Catholic missionaries—especially the Dominicans, Franciscans, and Jesuits—fanned out to different parts of the Spanish Empire. To make their efforts easier, the missionaries brought Native Americans together into villages, or missions, where the native peoples could be converted, taught trades, and encouraged to grow crops. Missions enabled missionaries to control the lives of the Native Americans and keep them as docile members of the empire.

The Catholic Church built cathedrals, hospitals, orphanages, and schools in the colonies. The schools taught Native American students the basics of reading, writing, and arithmetic. The Catholic Church also provided an outlet other than marriage for women. They could enter convents and become nuns.

As in Europe, women in colonial religious orders—many of them of aristocratic background—often lived well. Many nuns worked outside their convents by running schools and hospitals. Indeed, one of these nuns, **Sor Juana Inés de la Cruz,** urged that women be educated.

Reading Check **Explaining** How did the Portuguese and the Spanish profit from their colonies in Latin America?

People In History

Sor Juana Inés de la Cruz
1651–1695—Mexican poet

Juana Inés de la Cruz was one of seventeenth-century Latin America's best-known literary figures. She was an avid learner but was denied admission to the University of Mexico because she was a woman. As a result of this rejection, she chose to enter a convent, where she could write poetry and plays. She said, "Who has forbidden women to engage in private and individual studies? Have they not a rational soul as men do?"

By her late thirties, she had become famous as a great poet. Denounced by her bishop for writing secular literature, she agreed to stop writing and devote herself to purely religious activities. She died at the age of 43 while nursing the sick during an epidemic in Mexico City.

Britain and British North America

The United Kingdom of Great Britain came into existence in 1707, when the governments of England and Scotland were united. The term *British* came to refer to both the English and the Scots.

In eighteenth-century Britain, the monarch and the Parliament shared power, with Parliament gradually gaining the upper hand. The monarch chose ministers who were responsible to the Crown and who set policy and guided Parliament. Parliament had the power to make laws, levy taxes, pass the budget, and indirectly influence the ministers of the monarch.

In 1714, a new dynasty—the **Hanoverians**—was established when the last Stuart ruler, Queen Anne, died without an heir. The crown was offered to her nearest relatives, Protestant rulers of the German state of Hanover. The first Hanoverian king, George I, did not speak English, and neither the first nor the second George knew the British system very well. Therefore, their chief ministers were allowed to handle Parliament.

Robert Walpole served as prime minister from 1721 to 1742 and pursued a peaceful foreign policy. However, growing trade and industry led to an ever-increasing middle class. The middle class favored expansion of trade and of Britain's world empire. They found a spokesman in William Pitt the Elder, who became prime minister in 1757. He expanded the British Empire by acquiring Canada and India in the Seven Years' War.

In North America, then, Britain controlled Canada as well as 13 colonies on the eastern coast of the present United States. The British colonies were thickly populated, containing about 1.5 million people by 1750. They were also prosperous.

The colonies were supposedly run by the British Board of Trade, the Royal Council, and Parliament, but the colonies actually had legislatures that tended to act independently. Merchants in port cities such as Boston, Philadelphia, New York, and Charleston did not want the British government to run their affairs.

Reading Check **Explaining** What countries made up Great Britain in the 1700s? To whom does the term *British* refer?

EXTENDING THE CONTENT

Margaret Brent If students are interested in the story of Sor Juana Inés de la Cruz, they might also be interested in learning about another woman who wanted her share of civil and political rights. Margaret Brent, who was born a Roman Catholic, emigrated to Maryland in 1683 and was the first single woman to own land in her own name. She acted as an attorney for Lord Baltimore and won fame as being "as brave as a man." Feeling she had proved her abilities, she asked for the right to vote. The colonial assembly refused her request, so she simply took her assets to Virginia where, still without a vote, she lived for the remainder of her life.

The American Revolution

After the Seven Years' War, British leaders wanted to get new revenues from the colonies. These revenues would be used to cover war costs, as well as to pay for the expenses of maintaining an army to defend the colonies.

In 1765, the Parliament imposed the Stamp Act on the colonies. The act required that certain printed materials, such as legal documents and newspapers, carry a stamp showing that a tax had been paid to Britain. Opposition was widespread and often violent, and the act was repealed in 1766. The crisis was over, but the cause of the dispute was not resolved.

Lord Cornwallis surrendering to George Washington (left of the American flag)

The War Begins Crisis followed crisis in the 1770s. To counteract British actions, the colonies organized the First Continental Congress, which met in Philadelphia in September 1774. Outspoken members urged colonists to "take up arms and organize militias."

Fighting finally erupted between colonists and the British army in April 1775 in Lexington and Concord, Massachusetts. The Second Continental Congress met soon afterward and formed an army, called the Continental Army, with George Washington as commander in chief. Still, the colonists did not rush headlong into war. After the fighting in Lexington and Concord, more than a year passed before the decision was made to declare independence from the British Empire.

On July 4, 1776, the Second Continental Congress approved a declaration of independence written by Thomas Jefferson. Based on the ideas of John Locke (see page 233), the Declaration of Independence declared the colonies to be "free and independent states absolved from all allegiance to the British Crown." The American Revolution had formally begun.

The war against Great Britain was a great gamble. Britain was a strong military power with enormous financial resources. The Continental Army of the Americans was made up of undisciplined amateurs who agreed to serve for only a short time.

Foreign Support and British Defeat Of great importance to the colonies' cause was support from foreign countries. These nations were eager to gain revenge for earlier defeats at the hands of the British.

The French supplied arms and money to the rebels from the beginning of the war. French officers and soldiers also served in Washington's army. In October 1777, following a British defeat, the French granted diplomatic recognition to the American state.

Spain and the Dutch Republic also entered the war against Great Britain. Now, the British were faced with war against much of Europe, as well as against the Americans.

When the army of General Cornwallis was forced to surrender to combined American and French forces under Washington at **Yorktown** in 1781, the British decided to end the war. The Treaty of Paris, signed in 1783, recognized the independence of the American colonies and granted the Americans control of the western territory from the Appalachians to the Mississippi River.

Reading Check **Explaining** Why did foreign countries support the American cause?

The Birth of a New Nation

TURNING POINT **Americans created a new social contract in 1788. The creation of the Constitution made Enlightenment concepts of liberty and representative government a reality for the first time.**

The 13 American colonies had gained their independence. The former colonies were now states. The states feared concentrated power, however, and each one was primarily concerned for its own interests. For these reasons, they had little enthusiasm for creating a united nation with a strong central government.

Reading Check

Answer: Some foreign countries were eager to gain revenge for earlier defeats at the hands of the British.

TURNING POINT

Discuss with students the historical and global impact of the U.S. Constitution and the U.S. representative government. **L1** **ELL**

Charting Activity

Have students create a chart that summarizes the ideas from the American Revolution concerning separation of powers, liberty, equality, democracy, popular sovereignty, human rights, constitutionalism, and nationalism. **L3**

3 ASSESS

Assign Section 4 Assessment as homework or as an in-class activity.

Have students use **Interactive Tutor Self-Assessment CD-ROM.**

Section Quiz 10–4

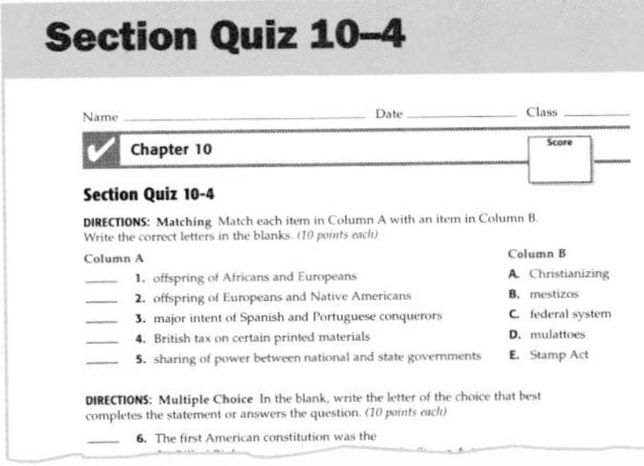

Name ________ Date ________ Class ________

Chapter 10 Score

Section Quiz 10-4

DIRECTIONS: Matching Match each item in Column A with an item in Column B. Write the correct letters in the blanks. *(10 points each)*

Column A	Column B
____ **1.** offspring of Africans and Europeans	**A.** Christianizing
____ **2.** offspring of Europeans and Native Americans	**B.** mestizos
____ **3.** major intent of Spanish and Portuguese conquerors	**C.** federal system
____ **4.** British tax on certain printed materials	**D.** mulattoes
____ **5.** sharing of power between national and state governments	**E.** Stamp Act

DIRECTIONS: Multiple Choice In the blank, write the letter of the choice that best completes the statement or answers the question. *(10 points each)*

____ **6.** The first American constitution was the

CRITICAL THINKING ACTIVITY

Drawing Inferences In spite of the many hardships of life in North America, colonists, in general, had longer lives, produced more children, and had a higher standard of living than their European counterparts. Food was more plentiful and famine was rare. Many colonists wrote to family members back in England that they ate food every day that English peasants would only eat on holidays. Because the population was more scattered and younger (16 was the average age in the colonies in 1790), Americans were less susceptible to disease and epidemics. Ask students to infer why life for colonists generally improved as soon as they settled in North America. **L2 L3**

CHAPTER 10
Section 4, 318–322

Reading Check

Answer: The Constitution created a stronger central government.

Reading Essentials and Study Guide 10–4

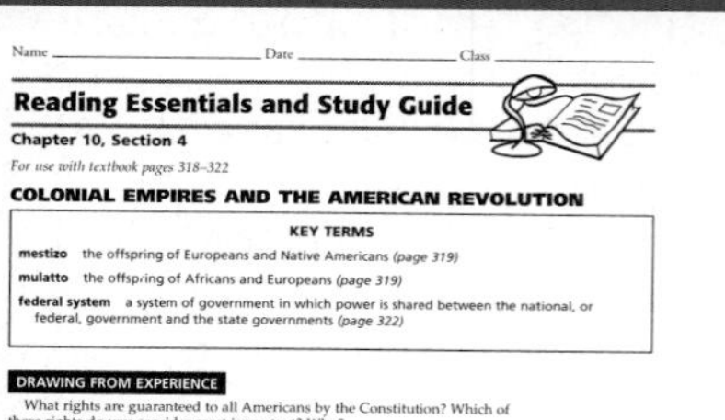
Name ______ Date ______ Class ______

Reading Essentials and Study Guide

Chapter 10, Section 4

For use with textbook pages 318–322

COLONIAL EMPIRES AND THE AMERICAN REVOLUTION

KEY TERMS

mestizo the offspring of Europeans and Native Americans *(page 319)*

mulatto the offspring of Africans and Europeans *(page 319)*

federal system a system of government in which power is shared between the national, or federal, government and the state governments *(page 322)*

DRAWING FROM EXPERIENCE

What rights are guaranteed to all Americans by the Constitution? Which of these rights do you consider most important? Why?

In the last two sections, you read about the impact of Enlightenment ideas on European life during the eighteenth century. The ideas of the Enlightenment also made a strong impact on the colonies in North America, which eventually led to the

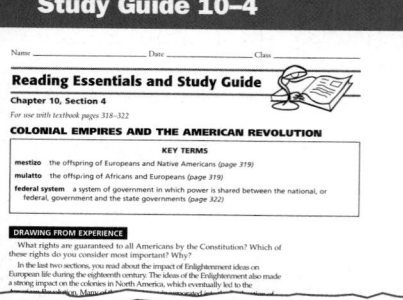

Reteaching Activity

Ask students to make charts that list the events that led to the American Revolution. Help them fill in information under the following headings: *Event, Date, What Occurred, Outcome.* **L1** ELL

4 CLOSE

Review the social and economic conditions in Latin America during the eighteenth century. Then ask students to describe how the British ruled their American colonies. Ask students to identify what aspects of British rule led to the American Revolution. **L2**

The Articles of Confederation, the American nation's first constitution, thus did little to provide for a strong central government. It soon became clear that the government under the Articles lacked the power to deal with the new nation's problems. A movement for a different form of national government arose.

The Articles of Confederation had been approved in 1781. In the summer of 1787, 55 delegates met in Philadelphia to revise the Articles. That meeting became the Constitutional Convention. The convention's delegates decided to write a plan for an entirely new national government.

The Constitution The proposed Constitution created a **federal system** in which power would be shared between the national government and the state governments. The national, or federal, government was given the power to levy taxes, raise an army, regulate trade, and create a national currency.

The federal government was divided into three branches, each with some power to check the workings of the others. The first branch was the executive branch. A president served as the chief executive. The president had the power to execute laws, veto the legislature's acts, supervise foreign affairs, and direct military forces.

The second branch of government was the legislative branch. It consisted of two house—the Senate, with memebers elected by the state legislatures, and the House of Representatives. Representatives were elected directly by the people.

The Supreme Court and other courts "as deemed necessary" by Congress provided the third branch of government, the judicial branch. The courts would enforce the Constitution as the "supreme law of the land."

According to the Constitutional Convention, the Constitution would have to be ratified, or approved, by a majority of the states before it could take effect. The Constitution was eventually approved, but by a slim margin.

The Bill of Rights Important to the eventual adoption of the Constitution was a promise to add a bill of rights. In 1789, the new Congress proposed 12 amendments, and the 10 that were approved by the states became known as the Bill of Rights.

These 10 amendments guaranteed freedom of religion, speech, press, petition, and assembly. They gave Americans the right to bear arms and to be protected against unreasonable searches and arrests. They guaranteed trial by jury, due process of law, and the protection of property rights.

Many of the rights in the Bill of Rights were derived from the natural rights proposed by the eighteenth-century philosophes. Many European intellectuals saw the American Revolution as the embodiments of the Enlightenment's political dreams. The premises of the Enlightenment seemed confirmed. A new age and a better world could be achieved.

Reading Check **Contrasting** What was the main difference between the Articles of Confederation and the Constitution?

SECTION 4 ASSESSMENT

Checking for Understanding

1. **Define** mestizo, mulatto, federal system.
2. **Identify** Sor Juana Inés de la Cruz, Hanoverians, Robert Walpole.
3. **Locate** Brazil, Yorktown.
4. **Explain** the role of the Catholic Church and its missionaries in colonial Latin America.
5. **List** the freedoms guaranteed under the American Bill of Rights.

Critical Thinking

6. **Summarize** Why did the American colonies declare their independence from the British Empire?
7. **Summarizing Information** Use a chart like the one below to identify the significant events and conflicts between the British and the colonists leading to the American Revolution.

Conflicts between British and Colonists

Analyzing Visuals

8. **Examine** the depiction of the signing of the Declaration of Independence on page 152. What principles of government and citizenship are illustrated in the painting?

Writing About History

9. **Expository Writing** Do further research on how the French supported the colonies during the American Revolution. Based on your research, write an essay analyzing the importance of the French assistance to the American colonists.

SECTION 4 ASSESSMENT

1. Key terms are in blue.
2. Sor Juana Inés de la Cruz *(p. 320)*; Hanoverians *(p. 320)*; Robert Walpole *(p. 320)*
3. See chapter maps.
4. established missions to convert natives; taught trades and encouraged agriculture; built cathedrals, hospitals, orphanages, and schools where natives could be taught basics of reading, writing, and arithmetic
5. freedom of religion, speech, press, petition, and assembly
6. The British Parliament imposed unpopular taxes on the colonists, which led to widespread opposition and eventually to fighting between the colonists and the British army.
7. See p. 321.
8. The painting shows a collaborative, representative government.
9. Answers will vary but should be supported by logic.

Eyewitness to History

The Mission

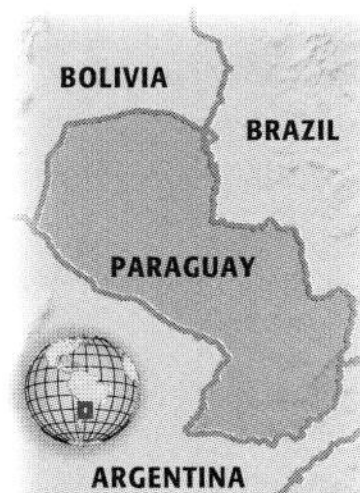

IN 1609, TWO JESUIT PRIESTS set out as missionaries to the Guarani Indians in eastern Paraguay. Eventually, the Jesuits established more than 30 missions in the region. This description of a Jesuit mission in Paraguay was written by Félix de Azara, a Spanish soldier and scientist.

Seventeenth-century mission in Paraguay

❝Having spoken of the towns founded by the Jesuit fathers, and of the manner in which they were founded, I shall discuss the government which they established in them. . . . In each town resided two priests, a curate and a sub-curate, who had certain assigned tasks.

The curate allowed no one to work for personal gain; he compelled everyone, without distinction of age or sex, to work for the community, and he himself saw to it that all were equally fed and dressed. For this purpose the curates placed in storehouses all the fruits of agriculture and the products of industry, selling in the Spanish towns their surplus of cotton, cloth, tobacco, vegetables, skins, and wood, transporting them in their own boats down the nearest rivers, and returning with whatever was required.

From the foregoing one may infer that the curates disposed of the surplus funds of the Indian towns, and that no Indian could aspire to own private property. This deprived them of any incentive to use reason or talent, since the most industrious, able, and worthy person had the same food, clothing, and pleasures as the most wicked, dull, and indolent. It also follows that although this form of government was well designed to enrich the communities it also caused the Indian to work at a languid pace, since the wealth of his community was of no concern to him.

It must be said that although the Jesuit fathers were supreme in all respects, they employed their authority with a mildness and restraint that command admiration. They supplied everyone with abundant food and clothing. They compelled the men to work only half a day, and did not drive them to produce more. Even their labor was given a festive air, for they went in procession to the fields, to the sound of music. . . . They gave them many holidays, dances, and tournaments, dressing the actors and the members of the municipal councils in gold or silver tissue and the most costly European garments, but they permitted the women to act only as spectators.❞

—**Félix de Azara, *Description and History of Paraguay and Rio de la Plata***

Analyzing Primary Sources

1. How is the mission town's government and economic system structured?
2. According to Azara, what are some of the problems with the town's system?
3. How might a Native American's description of the mission differ from Azara's European perspective?

323

TEACH

Analyzing Primary Sources

Explain to the class that Spain and Portugal were predominantly Roman Catholic countries. The Jesuits were extremely dedicated to proselytizing their faith, especially among native people in Latin America.

Discuss with students how the Jesuits changed the social structure of Indian towns, and ask them to describe life within the mission.

Ask students to explain how the Jesuits ruled the Indian converts. *(with kindness, fairly)* To what do they attribute this exercise of authority? *(their religion)* **L2**

Enrich

Ask interested students to research the Jesuit missions in South America. Where did the Jesuits establish missions? Were all of their interactions with Native Americans similar to what is described in *The Mission?* What happened to the Jesuit missions in South America? Do they still exist? Have students report their findings to the class. **L2**

ANSWERS TO ANALYZING PRIMARY SOURCES

1. The town is governed by two priests, a curate and a sub-curate. Everything in the mission (food, clothing) is owned by the entire community, and the surplus is taken to Spanish towns where it is traded for needed goods.
2. Azara thinks that it deprives people of any incentive to work hard, or to use their reason or talent.
3. Answers will vary. Students should support their answers with specific references to Azara's description. Students should realize that the lives of the Guarani were tightly controlled, and labor was forced, not voluntary.

CHAPTER 10
Assessment and Activities

GLENCOE TECHNOLOGY

MindJogger Videoquiz

Use the **MindJogger Videoquiz** to review Chapter 10 content.

 Available in VHS.

Using Key Terms

1. scientific method **2.** Ptolemaic, geocentric **3.** mestizos **4.** enlightened absolutism **5.** federal system **6.** inductive principles **7.** heliocentric **8.** philosophes **9.** rationalism **10.** laissez-faire

Reviewing Key Facts

11. a movement of intellectuals who were greatly impressed with achievements of the Scientific Revolution

12. British Board of Trade, the Royal Council, and Parliament (students will name only two of these)

13. to protect society from invasion, defend its citizens, and maintain certain public works such as roads (it should *not* interfere in economic matters)

14. Bach and Handel

15. Britain

16. people without morals who survived by their wits; *The History of Tom Jones, a Foundling*

17. in mathematical terms, that every object in the universe is attracted to every other object by a force called gravity

18. She made a strong argument for the rights of women in her book *A Vindication of the Rights of Women.*

19. Every person is born with a tabula rasa; all knowledge comes from our environment and reason.

20. On July 4, 1776, it approved the Declaration of Independence, triggering the American War of Independence.

CHAPTER 10 ASSESSMENT and ACTIVITIES

Using Key Terms

1. The _____ is a systematic procedure for collecting and analyzing evidence.
2. The idea that Earth is at the center of the universe is called a _____ or _____ system.
3. In the Americas, the offspring of European and American native peoples were called _____.
4. A new type of monarchy called _____ was influenced by reform-minded philosophes.
5. In the _____, power is shared between the national government and the state government.
6. When scientists proceed from the particular to the general they are using _____.
7. The belief that the Sun is at the center of the universe is called a _____ theory.
8. The intellects, or thinkers, of the Enlightenment, were generally called _____.
9. Descartes is known as the father of _____.
10. The doctrine that maintains that the state should not intervene in economics is called _____.

Reviewing Key Facts

11. **History** What was the Enlightenment?
12. **Government** Name two of the three groups that officially ran the 13 British colonies in North America.
13. **Government** According to Adam Smith, what is the proper role of government in society?
14. **Culture** Name two early eighteenth-century composers who have stood out as musical geniuses of the baroque style.
15. **History** What country challenged Spanish power in the Americas?
16. **Culture** What did Henry Fielding write about in his novels? What was his most popular work?
17. **Science and Technology** How did Newton explain the universal law of gravitation?
18. **Culture** Why is Mary Wollstonecraft often considered the founder of the modern women's movement?
19. **Culture** In his *Essay Concerning Human Understanding,* what ideas did John Locke propose?
20. **History** What was the major accomplishment of the Second Continental Congress?

Critical Thinking

21. **Making Generalizations** Describe inductive reasoning and give an example of finding scientific truth by using inductive principles.
22. **Summarizing** Explain how separation of powers works in the American government today and give specific examples.

Chapter Summary

As the Scientific Revolution and the ideas of the Enlightenment spread across Europe, innovations based on science and reason came into conflict with traditional beliefs, as shown in the chart below.

Innovation	Conflict or Reaction
Copernicus theorizes that Earth revolves around the Sun.	The Church teaches that Earth is the center of the universe.
Vesalius makes discoveries in anatomy.	French lawmakers consider dissecting human bodies illegal.
Boyle discovers that air is not a basic element.	Alchemists believe that all matter is made from four elements: earth, water, fire, and air.
Philosophes believe that the universe is structured, orderly, and governed by systematic laws.	Rousseau criticizes the emphasis on reason and promotes acting upon instinct.
Deism, a new religious concept based on reason and natural law, emerges.	Traditional views of established, organized religions are widespread.
Diderot publishes new scientific theories in the *Encyclopedia.*	The Catholic Church bans the *Encyclopedia,* and its editor is sent to prison.
Enlightened rulers implement political and humanitarian reforms.	Powerful nobles and church leaders fear losing power and reject most political reforms.

324

Critical Thinking

21. Inductive reasoning proceeds from the particular to the general. Systematic observations and carefully organized experiments to test hypotheses lead to correct general principles. Examples will vary but should illustrate these principles.

22. The president serves as head of the executive branch, Congress makes up the legislative branch, and the Supreme Court and other courts make up the judicial branch. Specific examples will vary but may include the president's vetoing legislation, the Supreme Court's overturning laws, etc.

Writing About History

23. John Locke believed that people are molded by experience, and if they were exposed to the right influences they could be changed and a new society created. Montesquieu probably had the most influence on the writers of the Constitution, with his proposal for a system of checks and balances that would be provided by a sepa-

Self-Check Quiz

Visit the *Glencoe World History—Modern Times* Web site at wh.mt.glencoe.com and click on **Chapter 10–Self-Check Quiz** to prepare for the Chapter Test.

Writing About History

23. Expository Writing Analyze how the ideas of John Locke, Montesquieu, Rousseau, and Voltaire influenced the development of the United States Constitution. Which thinker(s) had the most impact on the writers of the Constitution? Why has the Constitution remained so strong while so many reform efforts of the eighteenth century failed?

Analyzing Sources

Read the following quote from John Locke's *Essay Concerning Human Understanding:*

> ❝Let us then suppose the mind to be, as we say, white paper, void of all characters, without any ideas. How comes it to be furnished? Whence has it all the materials of reason and knowledge? To this I answer, in one word, from experience. . . . Our observation, employed either about external sensible objects or about the internal operations of our minds perceived and reflected on by ourselves, is that which supplies our understanding with all the materials of thinking.❞

24. According to Locke, how did the blank mind become knowledgeable?

25. How did one gain the experience necessary to nurture the mind?

Applying Technology Skills

26. Creating a Database Search the Internet for information about the great thinkers of the Enlightenment. Use a word processor to organize your research into a chart. Include headings such as name of philosopher, country, and ideas. Write a paragraph explaining which philosopher you believe had the greatest impact on modern civilization. Support your selection with facts and examples.

Making Decisions

27. As the reigns of Joseph II and Catherine the Great illustrate, it was very difficult to put the ideas of the Enlightenment into practice. Imagine that you are an enlightened monarch who wants to reform your country. What reforms will you initiate? Which thinker will most influence your reform plans? What problems might you encounter?

NATIONAL GEOGRAPHIC **Seven Years' War in the West Indies**

British possession
French possession
British/French battle
Havana 1762
Cuba
Hispaniola
Saint Domingue
Jamaica
Puerto Rico
ATLANTIC OCEAN
Caribbean Sea
Guadeloupe 1759
Dominica
Martinique 1762
St. Lucia
Barbados
0 300 miles
0 300 kilometers
Lambert Azimuthal Equal-Area projection
20°N
10°N
80°W
70°W
60°W

Analyzing Maps and Charts

28. What are the two largest islands in the Caribbean?

29. Name the battles fought in the West Indies during the Seven Years' War.

30. What is the approximate distance from Havana to Martinique?

The Princeton Review

Standardized Test Practice

Directions: Use the time line *and* your knowledge of world history to answer the following question.

Selected Milestones in Political Thought

1762 *The Social Contract* describes Rousseau's belief that governments are created from the people's general will

1760 | 1765 | 1770 | 1775 | 1780 | 1785 | 1790 | 1795

1776 The Declaration of Independence asserts the right to overthrow an unjust king

1792 Mary Wollstonecraft argues for equal rights for women

Which one of the following statements is supported by the information on the time line?

A Most Europeans supported their monarchs completely.

B Many people questioned the nature of their governments.

C There were few political problems in the 1750s.

D Only men thought and wrote about politics.

Test-Taking Tip: With a time line question, you may need to make an inference. Look for clues in the test question and time line. In this case, think about what the events on the time line have in common. These clues can help you make an inference that is supported by the time line.

CHAPTER 10
Assessment and Activities

Have students visit the Web site at wh.mt.glencoe.com to review Chapter 10 and take the Self-Check Quiz.

ration of the powers of government. Rousseau believed in a social contract, whereby an entire society agrees to be governed by its general will, and that people gain freedom by being forced to follow what is best for the general will. The Constitution is, in essence, a social contract, and our democratic government "forces" citizens to abide by the general will in the form of laws passed by our elected representatives. Voltaire believed that all men are brothers and that governments should be tolerant of all religions, which may have influenced the guarantee of freedom of religion provided by the Bill of Rights. Last part of question calls for opinion. Students' answers should be backed by logical arguments.

Analyzing Sources

24. through experience

25. by observation of external sensible objects

Applying Technology Skills

26. Answers will vary. Students will create charts.

Making Decisions

27. Answers will vary but should be consistent with the material presented in this chapter.

Analyzing Maps and Charts

28. Cuba and Hispaniola

29. Havana, Guadeloupe, Martinique

30. 1,400 miles (2,253 km)

Standardized Test Practice

Answer: B

Answer Explanation: Students should use their knowledge of world history to determine the validity of each statement.

Bonus Question ?

In 1611, English poet John Donne wrote that "new philosophy calls all in doubt." Similarly, in our times, many people are troubled by the destabilizing effects of new scientific methods. **Ask:** **What are three areas of scientific research today that some people find unsettling?** *(Answers may include manipulation of human reproduction, tinkering with genetic information, stem cell research, human and animal cloning.)* **L2**

Chapter 11 Resources

Timesaving Tools

TeacherWorks™ All-In-One Planner and Resource Center

- **Interactive Teacher Edition** Access your Teacher Wraparound Edition and your classroom resources with a few easy clicks.
- **Interactive Lesson Planner** Planning has never been easier! Organize your week, month, semester, or year with all the lesson helps you need to make teaching creative, timely, and relevant.

Use Glencoe's **Presentation Plus!** multimedia teacher tool to easily present dynamic lessons that visually excite your students. Using Microsoft PowerPoint® you can customize the presentations to create your own personalized lessons.

TEACHING TRANSPARENCIES

Graphic Organizer Student Activity 11 Transparency

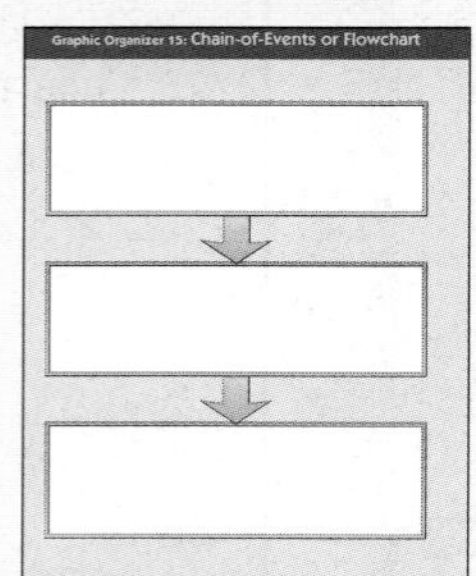

Chapter Transparency 11

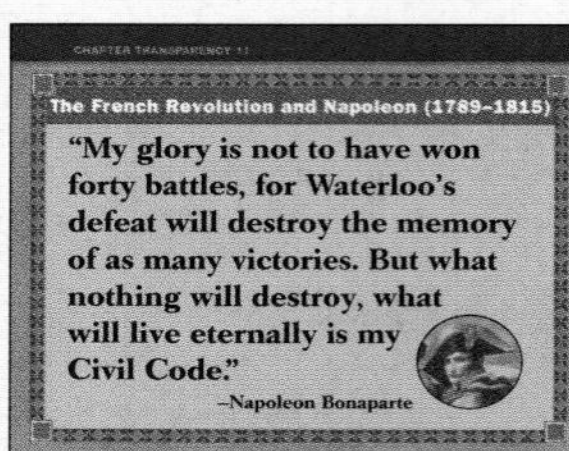

Map Overlay Transparency 11

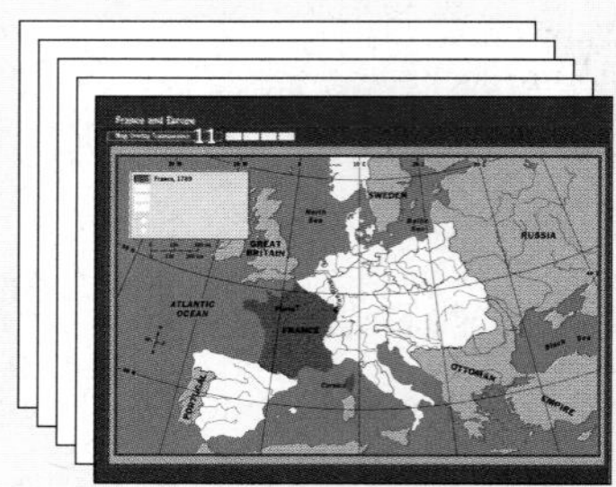

APPLICATION AND ENRICHMENT

Enrichment Activity 11

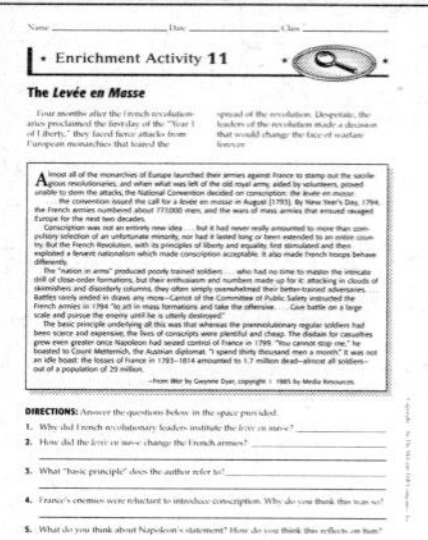

Primary Source Reading 11

History Simulation Activity 11

Historical Significance Activity 11

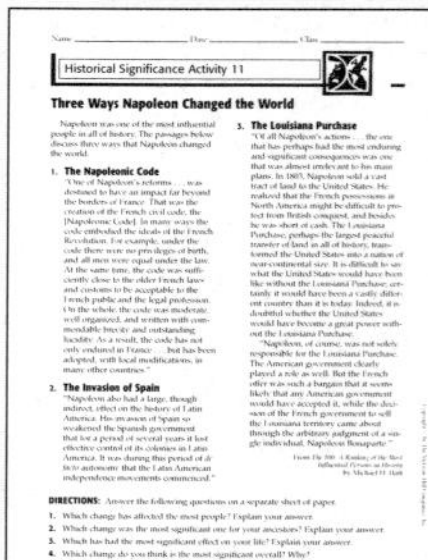

Cooperative Learning Activity 11

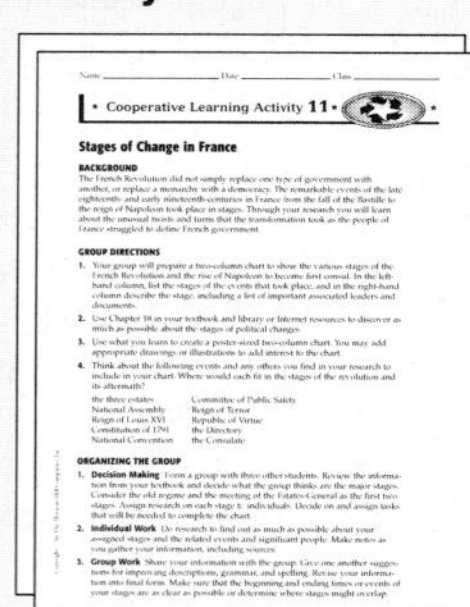

The following videotape program is available from Glencoe as a supplement to Chapter 11:

- **Napoleon Bonaparte: The Glory of France** (ISBN 0–7670–1211–9)

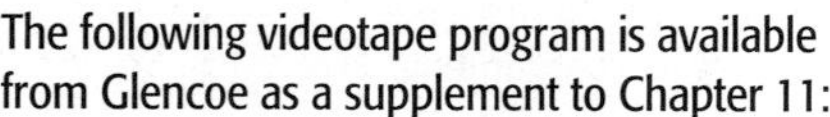

To order, call Glencoe at 1–800–334–7344. To find classroom resources to accompany this video, check the following home pages:
A&E Television: www.aande.com
The History Channel: www.historychannel.com

Chapter 11 Resources

Review and Reinforcement

Linking Past and Present Activity 11

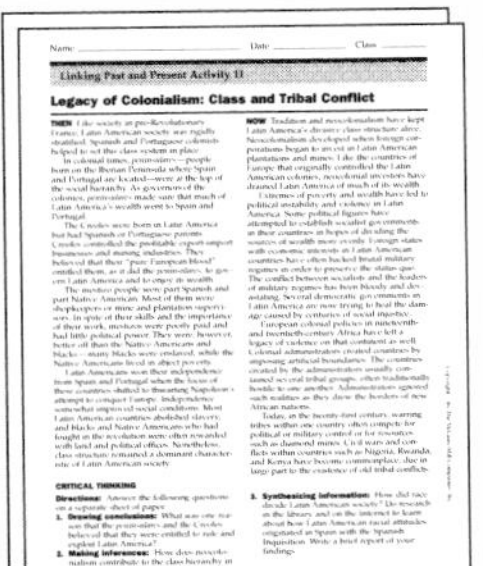

Time Line Activity 11

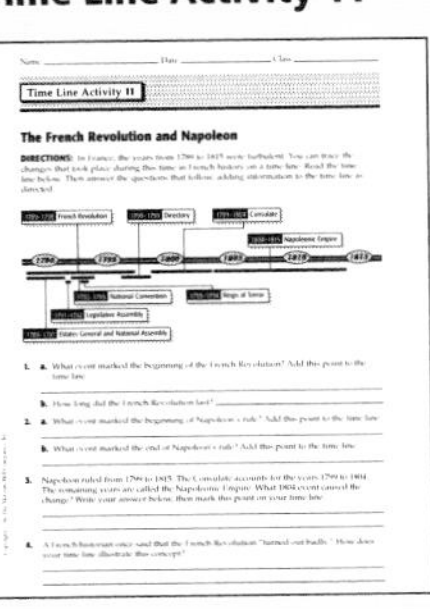

Reteaching Activity 11

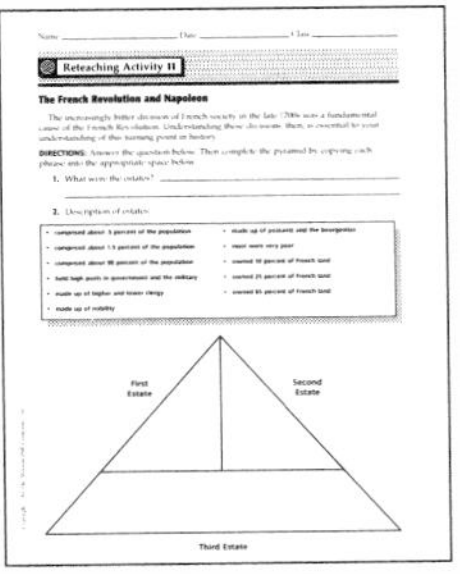

Vocabulary Activity 11

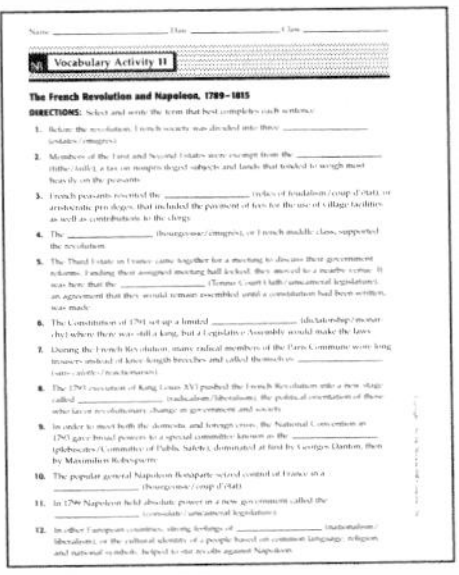

Critical Thinking Skills Activity 11

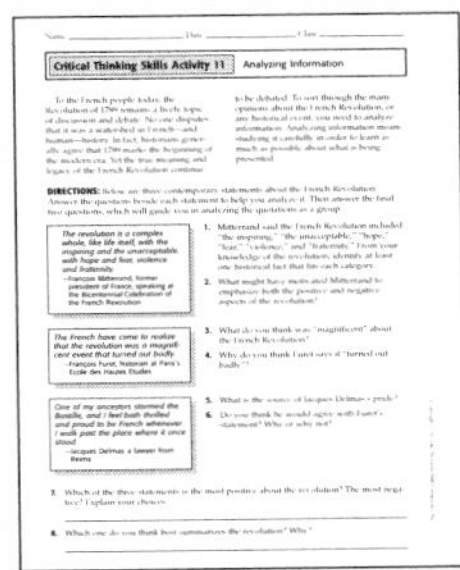

Assessment and Evaluation

Chapter 11 Test Form A

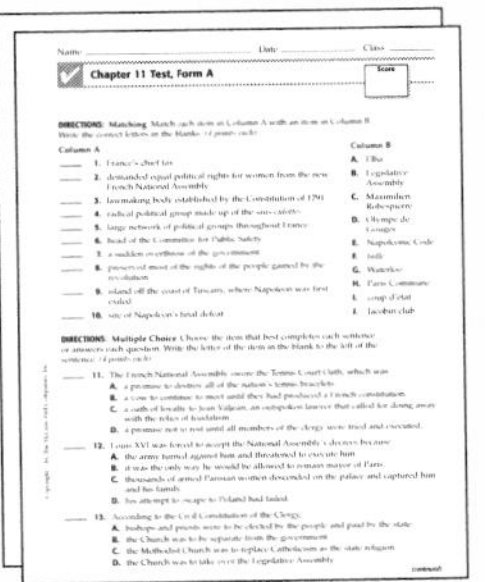

Chapter 11 Test Form B

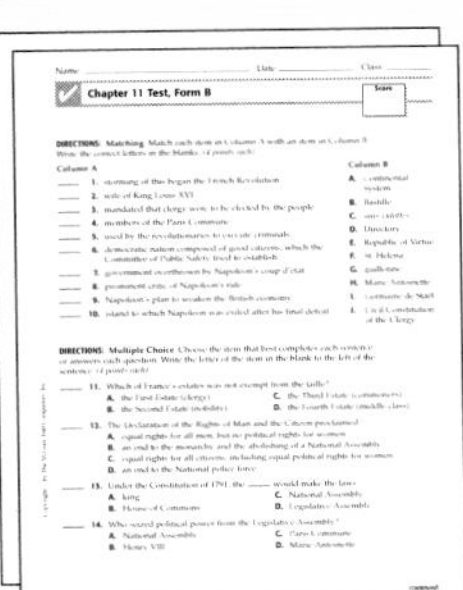

Performance Assessment Activity 11

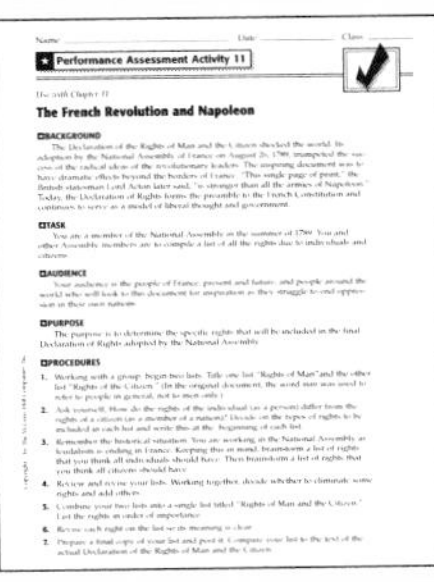

ExamView® Pro Testmaker CD-ROM

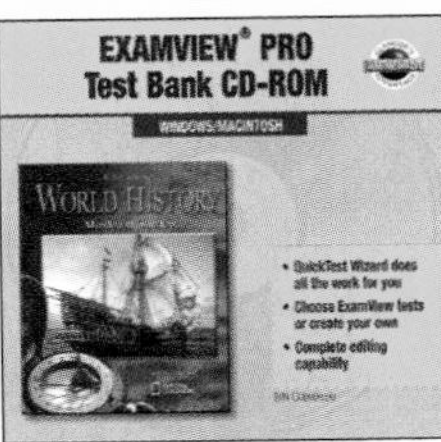

Standardized Test Skills Practice Workbook Activity 11

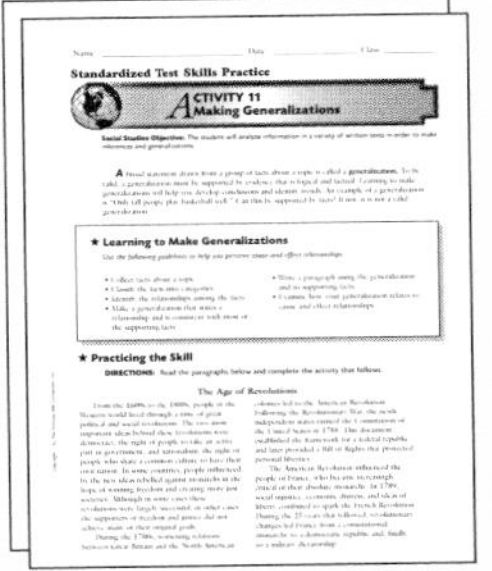

Interdisciplinary Activities

Mapping History Activity 11

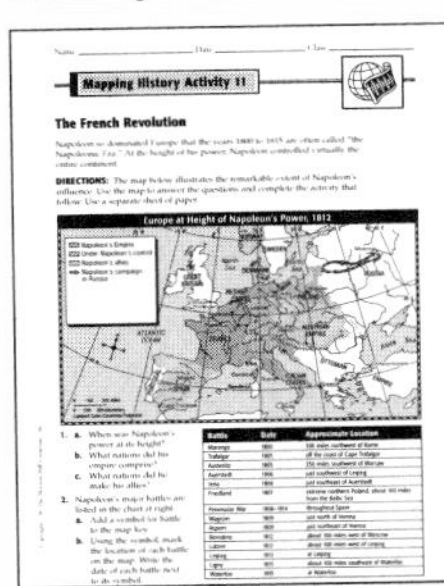

World Art and Music Activity 11

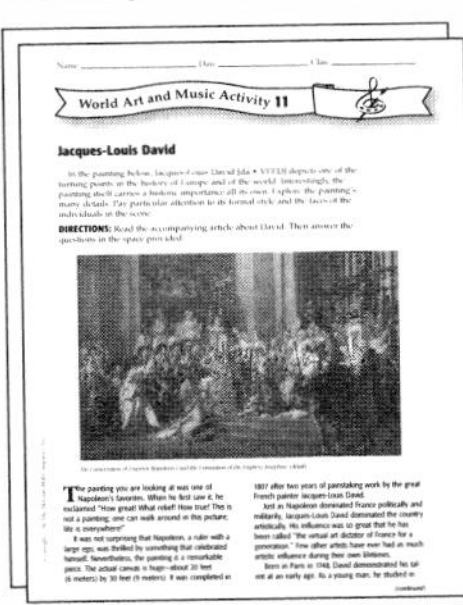

History and Geography Activity 11

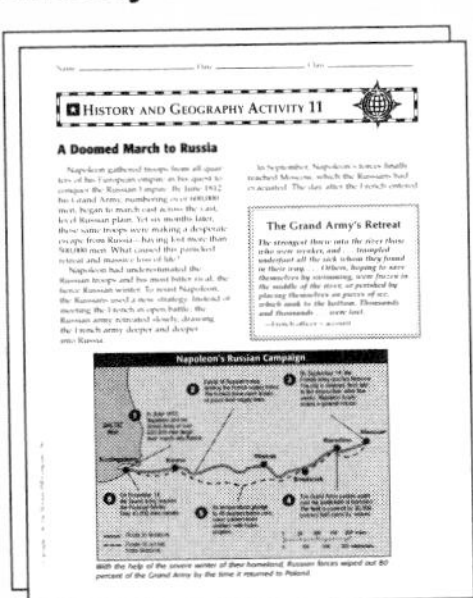

People in World History Activity 11

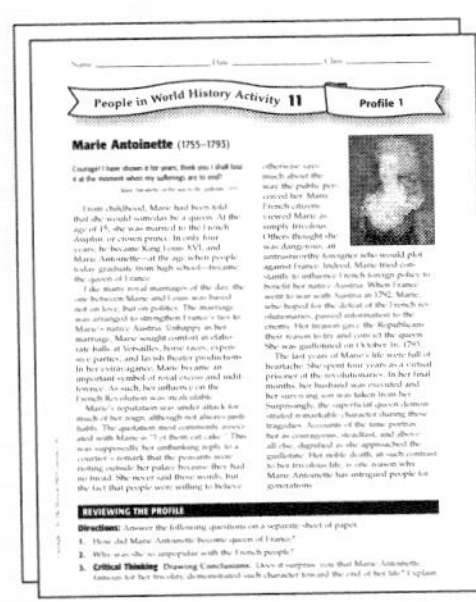

Multimedia

- Vocabulary PuzzleMaker CD-ROM
- Interactive Tutor Self-Assessment CD-ROM
- ExamView® Pro Testmaker CD-ROM
- Audio Program
- World History Primary Source Document Library CD-ROM
- MindJogger Videoquiz
- Presentation Plus! CD-ROM
- TeacherWorks CD-ROM
- Interactive Student Edition CD-ROM
- The World History—Modern Times Video Program

Spanish Resources

The following Spanish language materials are available in the Spanish Resources Binder:

- Spanish Guided Reading Activities
- Spanish Reteaching Activities
- Spanish Quizzes and Tests
- Spanish Vocabulary Activities
- Spanish Summaries

Chapter 11 Resources

SECTION RESOURCES

Daily Objectives	Reproducible Resources	Multimedia Resources
SECTION 1 **The French Revolution Begins** 1. Specify why social inequality and economic problems contributed to the French Revolution. 2. Explain why radicals, Catholic priests, nobles, and the lower classes opposed the new order.	Reproducible Lesson Plan 11–1 Daily Lecture and Discussion Notes 11–1 Guided Reading Activity 11–1* Section Quiz 11–1* Reading Essentials and Study Guide 11–1	Daily Focus Skills Transparency 11–1 Interactive Tutor Self-Assessment CD-ROM ExamView® Pro Testmaker CD-ROM Presentation Plus! CD-ROM
SECTION 2 **Radical Revolution and Reaction** 1. Report how radical groups and leaders controlled the Revolution. 2. Discuss why the new French Republic faced enemies at home and abroad.	Reproducible Lesson Plan 11–2 Daily Lecture and Discussion Notes 11–2 Guided Reading Activity 11–2* Section Quiz 11–2* Reading Essentials and Study Guide 11–2	Daily Focus Skills Transparency 11–2 Interactive Tutor Self-Assessment CD-ROM ExamView® Pro Testmaker CD-ROM Presentation Plus! CD-ROM
SECTION 3 **The Age of Napoleon** 1. Summarize how Napoleon built and lost an empire. 2. Discuss how nationalism spread as a result of the French Revolution. 3. Describe how Napoleon was exiled first to Elba, and then to St. Helena, where he died.	Reproducible Lesson Plan 11–3 Daily Lecture and Discussion Notes 11–3 Guided Reading Activity 11–3* Section Quiz 11–3* Reteaching Activity 11* Reading Essentials and Study Guide 11–3	Daily Focus Skills Transparency 11–3 Interactive Tutor Self-Assessment CD-ROM ExamView® Pro Testmaker CD-ROM Presentation Plus! CD-ROM

0:00 **OUT OF TIME?**
Assign the Chapter 11 **Reading Essentials and Study Guide.**

*Also Available in Spanish

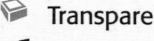

 Blackline Master
 Transparency
 CD-ROM
 DVD
 Poster
 Music Program
 Audio Program
 Videocassette
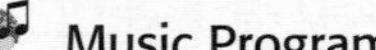

Chapter 11 Resources

NATIONAL GEOGRAPHIC **Teacher's Corner**

INDEX TO NATIONAL GEOGRAPHIC MAGAZINE

The following articles relate to this chapter:

- France: Bicentennial of the Great Revolution, Special Issue, July 1989.
- "Two Revolutions," by Charles McCarry, July 1989.
- "Napoleon," by John J. Putnam, February 1982.

ADDITIONAL NATIONAL GEOGRAPHIC SOCIETY PRODUCTS

To order the following, call National Geographic at 1-800-368-2728:

- *Democratic Government Series, "France"* (Video)

NGS ONLINE

Access National Geographic's new dynamic MapMachine Web site and other geography resources at:

www.nationalgeographic.com
www.nationalgeographic.com/maps

KEY TO ABILITY LEVELS

Teaching strategies have been coded.

L1 BASIC activities for all students
L2 AVERAGE activities for average to above-average students
L3 CHALLENGING activities for above-average students
ELL ENGLISH LANGUAGE LEARNER activities

Block Schedule

Activities that are suited to use within the block scheduling framework are identified by:

WORLD HISTORY Online

Use our Web site for additional resources. All essential content is covered in the Student Edition.

You and your students can visit www.wh.mt.glencoe.com, the Web site companion to *Glencoe World History—Modern Times.* This innovative integration of electronic and print media offers your students a wealth of opportunities. The student text directs students to the Web site for the following options:

- **Chapter Overviews**
- **Self-Check Quizzes**
- **Student Web Activities**
- **Textbook Updates**

Answers to the Student Web Activities are provided for you in the **Web Activity Lesson Plans.** Additional Web resources and Interactive Tutor Puzzles are also available.

From the Classroom of...

Susan E. Szachowicz
Brockton High School
Brockton, Massachusetts

The Congress of Vienna Convenes

Organize the class into five groups, representing Austria, Great Britain, Russia, Prussia, and France, and direct each group to select one spokesperson to be Metternich, Castlereagh, Alexander I, Frederick William III, and Talleyrand. Provide each group with an overview of the Congress and its purpose; information specific to their country, which includes their delegate's role at the Congress and their country's goals, vital interests, and demands; and an outline map of Europe at the height of Napoleon's power.

Each group should develop its lists of demands and redraw the map of Europe as it would like to see it. Then convene the Congress by having the representative from each group offer his or her proposals and maps to the entire class. Questioning and negotiating should proceed until a plan acceptable to all is developed. Finally, the class plan should be compared to the actual decision made at the Congress of Vienna with similarities and differences noted.

Introducing
CHAPTER 11

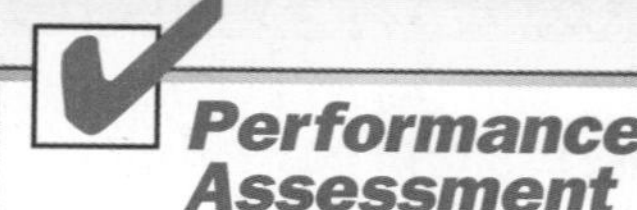

Performance Assessment

Refer to Activity 11 in the Performance Assessment Activities and Rubrics booklet.

The Impact Today

Ask students to consider the importance of revolutions and reasons people decide to revolt against their governments. Discuss how life in the United States might be different today if the American Revolution had never happened. Would the United States still be a possession or colony of Britain? Of Spain or France?

GLENCOE TECHNOLOGY

The World History—Modern Times Video Program

To learn more about the French Revolution and Napoleon, students can view the Chapter 11 video, "Napoleon," from **The World History—Modern Times Video Program.**

MindJogger Videoquiz

Use the **MindJogger Videoquiz** to preview Chapter 11 content.

Available in VHS.

CHAPTER 11 The French Revolution and Napoleon

1789–1815

Key Events

As you read this chapter, look for the key events of the French Revolution and French Empire.

- *The fall of the Bastille marked the beginning of the French Revolution.*
- *The Committee of Public Safety began the Reign of Terror.*
- *Napoleon Bonaparte created the French Empire.*
- *Allied forces defeated Napoleon at Waterloo.*

The Impact Today

The events that occurred during this time period still impact our lives today.

- *The French Revolution became the model for revolution in the modern world.*
- *The power of nationalism was first experienced during the French Revolution, and it is still powerful in existing nations and emerging nations today.*
- *The French Revolution spread the principles of liberty and equality, which are held dear by many nations and individuals today.*

World History—Modern Times Video *The Chapter 11 video, "Napoleon," chronicles the rise and fall of Napoleon Bonaparte.*

1789 French Revolution begins

1789 Olympe de Gouges writes declaration of rights for women

1792 National Convention establishes French Republic

1793 King Louis XVI is executed

1795 The Directory is formed

1799 Napoleon participates in coup d'état that topples French government

1790 1792 1794 1796 1798 1800

Louis XVI

Olympe de Gouges

326

TWO-MINUTE LESSON LAUNCHER

Have students brainstorm definitions of the term *revolution* and write their definitions on the chalkboard. Then guide students in a discussion of whether or not people are justified in choosing revolution as a solution to political and social problems. Ask students to think about the social and economic conditions in the United States today and whether or not those conditions could potentially lead to a revolution. Do students believe that a revolution in the United States would be likely? Why or why not? What alternatives to revolution do we have that other forms of government do not? How does the structure of our government prevent the need for revolution? **L2**

Napoleon Crossing the Great St. Bernard by Jacques-Louis David David was the leading artist of the French Revolution.

oleon
1801
Napoleon reaches agreement with the pope
1802
Napoleon made consul for life
1802
1804
Napoleon is crowned Emperor
1804
1805
British defeat French and Spanish at Trafalgar
1806
1808
1810
1812
Napoleon invades Russia
1812
1815
Duke of Wellington and his army defeat Napoleon at Waterloo
Duke of Wellington

HISTORY Online

Chapter Overview
Visit the *Glencoe World History—Modern Times* Web site at wh.mt.glencoe.com and click on **Chapter 11–Chapter Overview** to preview chapter information.

327

Introducing CHAPTER 11

Chapter Objectives

After studying this chapter, students should be able to:

1. identify and explain the causes of the French Revolution;
2. explain how the French Revolution brought about the destruction of the old regime;
3. identify and explain the causes of the Reign of Terror;
4. identify and explain the Age of Napoleon;
5. identify and describe the rise and fall of Napoleon's empire.

Chapter Overview
Introduce students to chapter content and key terms by having them access **Chapter Overview 11** at wh.mt.glencoe.com.

Time Line Activity

Have students examine the time line on these pages to understand the phases of the French Revolution. How many years passed between the beginning of the French Revolution and the execution of Louis XVI? *(4 years)* How many years passed between the execution of Louis XVI and the coup d'état that toppled French government (this period is also known as the Reign of Terror)? *(6 years)* How many years did Napoleon's reign last? *(16 years)* **L1**

MORE ABOUT THE ART

Jacques-Louis David Napoleon spread his image throughout Europe with copies of this portrait, commissioned in 1800, and others painted by the artist Jacques-Louis David. David had developed a neoclassical style early in his career that reflected the influence of Roman sculpture and emphasized the civic virtues of self-sacrifice and devotion to duty. After 1789, David began to paint more realistic scenes that depicted the people and events of the French Revolution. From 1799 to 1815, David was Napoleon's official painter. During this period, he adopted a more romantic style that promoted a heroic image of France's new leader. After Napoleon's defeat, David was exiled to Brussels, where he died in 1825.

CHAPTER PREVIEW

Introducing

A Story That Matters

Depending on the ability levels of your students, select from the following questions to reinforce the reading of *A Story That Matters.*

- Do you believe the Bastille was stormed to set prisoners free, because it was a symbol of oppression, or as the first step to overthrow the French monarchy? *(Answers may vary.)*
- What is the difference between a revolt and revolution? *(revolt: renouncing allegiance; armed uprising; vigorous dissent; revolution: a sudden radical, complete change; an overthrow of one government in favor of another)* **L1 L2**

About the Art

Encourage students to study the painting of the storming of the Bastille. Divide students into two groups. Ask one group to write descriptions of the storming of the Bastille from the point of view of a common soldier defending the prison. The other group should write descriptions from the point of view of a member of the mob. **L2**

CHAPTER PREVIEW

A Story That Matters

The storming of the Bastille

Fall of the Bastille

On the morning of July 14, 1789, a Parisian mob of some eight thousand men and women in search of weapons streamed toward the Bastille, a royal armory filled with arms and ammunition. The Bastille was also a state prison. Although it contained only seven prisoners at the time, in the eyes of those angry Parisians it was a glaring symbol of the government's harsh policies. The armory was defended by the Marquis de Launay and a small garrison of 114 men.

The assault began at one o'clock in the afternoon when a group of attackers managed to lower two drawbridges over the moat surrounding the fortress. The mob was joined by members of the French Guard, who began to bombard the fortress with cannon balls. After four hours of fighting, 98 attackers lay dead or dying. Only one defender had been killed.

As more attackers arrived, de Launay realized that he and his troops could not hold out much longer and surrendered. Angered by the loss of its members, the victorious mob beat de Launay to death, cut off his head, and carried it aloft in triumph through the streets of Paris.

When King Louis XVI returned to his palace at Versailles after a day of hunting, he was told about the fall of the Bastille by the duc de La Rochefoucauld-Liancourt. Louis exclaimed, "Why, this is a revolt." "No, Sire," replied the duke, "It is a revolution."

Why It Matters

The French Revolution began a new age in European political life. The old political order in France was destroyed. The new order was based on individual rights, representative institutions, and loyalty to the nation rather than the monarch. The revolutionary upheaval of the era, especially in France, created new political ideals, summarized in the French slogan, "Liberty, Equality, and Fraternity." These ideals transformed France, then spread to other European countries and the rest of the world.

History and You Using print or Internet sources, familiarize yourself with the lyrics to *The Marseillaise, God Save the Queen,* and *The Star Spangled Banner.* How do they vary in subject matter, tone, theme, and style, and how are they similar? Create a chart listing your findings.

HISTORY AND YOU

The revolutionaries believed in the political ideals of "Liberty, Equality, and Fraternity." The Bastille was attacked, in part, because it was a symbol of the very opposite of these ideals—royal oppression and unfair treatment under the law. Have students discuss the symbolic significance of structures, buildings, works of art, or monuments in our own country that represent our political ideals, such as the Statue of Liberty, the White House, the Washington Monument, Mt. Rushmore, and any other monuments with which students are familiar. What do these works represent? Why are they important to our society? **L2**

SECTION 1

The French Revolution Begins

Guide to Reading

Main Ideas

- Social inequality and economic problems contributed to the French Revolution.
- Radicals, Catholic priests, nobles, and the lower classes opposed the new order.

Key Terms

estate, relics of feudalism, bourgeoisie, *sans-culottes*

People to Identify

Louis XVI, Olympe de Gouges

Places to Locate

Versailles, Paris, Austria, Prussia

Preview Questions

1. How was the population of France divided into three estates?
2. How did the fall of the Bastille save the National Assembly?

Reading Strategy

Cause and Effect As you read this section, use a web diagram like the one below to list the factors that contributed to the French Revolution.

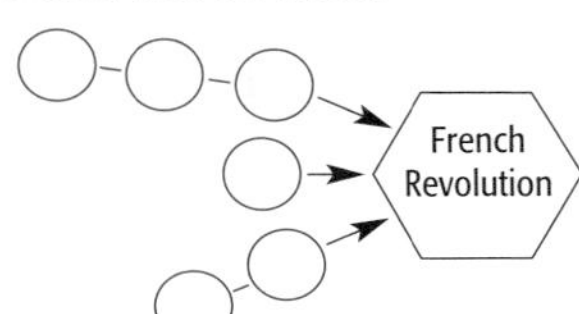

Preview of Events

1780 — 1790 — 1800

- **1787** Bad harvests lead to food shortages
- **1789** National Assembly adopts Declaration of the Rights of Man
- **1791** National Assembly completes new constitution

Voices from the Past

A correspondent with the London *Times* sent this report to his newspaper editor on July 20, 1789:

❝The number of armed men in Paris is supposed to amount to 300,000 men, and they called themselves the Militia. The way by which so many people have procured arms is, that all the public storehouses where weapons were lodged, have been broken open, as well as several private houses plundered, which they thought contained them. The Archbishop of Paris is among the number of those who have been sacrificed to the people's rage. He was assassinated at Versailles on Tuesday night. The city of Paris is entirely surrounded with a guard, and not a soul suffered to go out who has an appearance of wealth.❞

—***History in the First Person*, Louis L. Snyder and Richard B. Morris, eds., 1951**

The correspondent may not have realized the full significance of the events he reported, but the French Revolution had begun.

Conquerors of the Bastille

Background to the Revolution

The year 1789 witnessed two far-reaching events: the beginning of a new United States of America and the beginning of the French Revolution. Compared with the American Revolution, the French Revolution was more complex, more violent, and far more radical. It tried to create both a new political order and a new

1 FOCUS

Section Overview

This section describes the problems and conditions in France that led to the revolution in 1789 and the establishment of a limited monarchy in 1791.

BELLRINGER
Skillbuilder Activity

Project transparency and have students answer questions.

Available as a blackline master.

Daily Focus Skills Transparency 11-1

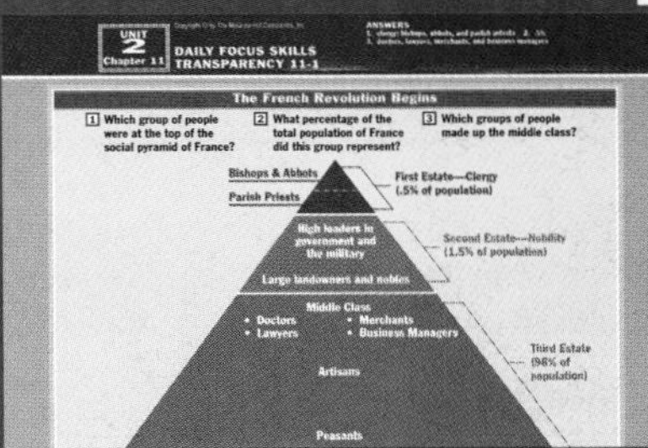

Guide to Reading

Answers to Graphic: Third Estate demands one vote per deputy → denied by king → National Assembly; relics of feudalism → popular uprising; other causes include food shortages, unemployment

Preteaching Vocabulary: Ask students to list synonyms for *relic*. If necessary, they may use a dictionary or thesaurus. Then, have students brainstorm some examples of what is meant by *relics of feudalism*. **L1 L2**

SECTION RESOURCES

Reproducible Masters

- Reproducible Lesson Plan 11–1
- Daily Lecture and Discussion Notes 11–1
- Guided Reading Activity 11–1
- Section Quiz 11–1
- Reading Essentials and Study Guide 11–1

Transparencies

- Daily Focus Skills Transparency 11–1

Multimedia

- Interactive Tutor Self-Assessment CD-ROM
- ExamView® Pro Testmaker CD-ROM
- Presentation Plus! CD-ROM

2 TEACH

Graph Skills

Answer:

1. Two percent of the population owned 35 percent of the land. The peasants constituted about 75 percent of the population and were heavily taxed to support the nobility and the clergy. The common people made up 98 percent of the population, owned 65 percent of land, and paid 100 percent of the taxes. Each estate had one vote. Even though the Third Estate made up 98 percent of the population, it would always be outvoted by the First Estate and the Second Estate, which would always vote to keep their tax exemptions.

Daily Lecture and Discussion Notes 11–1

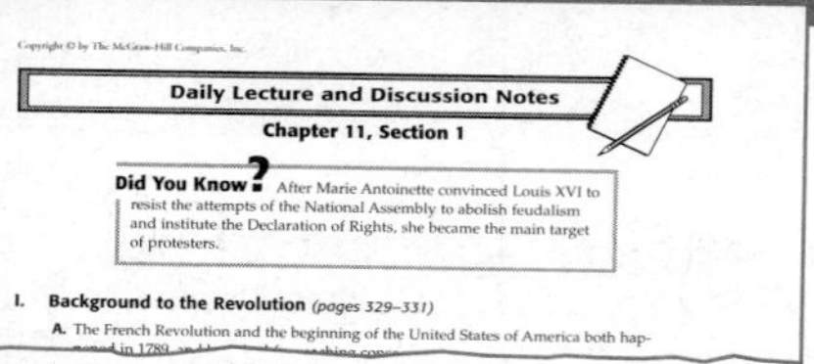

Daily Lecture and Discussion Notes
Chapter 11, Section 1
Did You Know? After Marie Antoinette convinced Louis XVI to resist the attempts of the National Assembly to abolish feudalism and institute the Declaration of Rights, she became the main target of protesters.
I. Background to the Revolution (pages 329–331)
A. The French Revolution and the beginning of the United States of America both hap-

CURRICULUM CONNECTION

Economics Remind students that the immediate causes of the French Revolution were financial. Ask students to explain why people often become more upset over issues of economic conditions than over a lack of political freedom. **Ask:** What economic events precipitated the American Revolution? *(British taxation on colonists)* **L2**

social order. Indeed, it has often been seen as a major turning point in European political and social history.

The causes of the French Revolution include both long-range problems and immediate forces. The long-range causes are to be found in the condition of French society. Before the revolution, French society was based on inequality. France's population of 27 million was divided, as it had been since the Middle Ages, into three orders, or **estates.**

The Three Estates The First Estate consisted of the clergy and numbered about 130,000 people. These people owned approximately 10 percent of the land. They were exempt from the *taille* (TAH•yuh), France's chief tax. The clergy were radically divided. The higher clergy, members of aristocratic families, shared the interests of the nobility. The parish priests were often poor and from the class of commoners.

The Second Estate, the nobility, included about 350,000 people. Nobles owned about 25 to 30 percent of the land. They played an important, and even a crucial, role in French society in the eighteenth century. They held many of the leading positions in the government, the military, the law courts, and the higher church offices. Moreover, they possessed many privileges, including tax exemptions. Like the clergy, they were exempt from the *taille.*

The nobles sought to expand their power at the expense of the monarchy. Many nobles said they were defending liberty by resisting the arbitrary actions of the monarchy. They also sought to keep their control over positions in the military, the Church, and the government.

The Third Estate, or the commoners of society, made up the overwhelming majority of the French population. Unlike the First and Second Estates, the Third Estate was divided by vast differences in occupation, level of education, and wealth.

The peasants, who constituted 75 to 80 percent of the total population, were by far the largest segment of the Third Estate. As a group, they owned about 35 to 40 percent of the land. However, landholdings varied from area to area, and over half of the peasants had little or no land on which to survive.

Serfdom no longer existed on any large scale in France, but French peasants still had obligations to their local landlords that they deeply resented. These **relics of feudalism,** or aristocratic privileges, were obligations that survived from an earlier age. They included the payment of fees for the use of village facilities such as the flour mill, community oven, and winepress, as well as contributions to the clergy.

Another part of the Third Estate consisted of skilled craftspeople, shopkeepers, and other wage earners in the cities. In the eighteenth century, a rise in consumer prices that was greater than the increase in wages left these urban groups with a decline in buying power. The struggle for survival led many of these people to play an important role in the revolution, especially in Paris.

The **bourgeoisie** (BURZH•WAH•ZEE), or middle class, was another part of the Third Estate. This group included about 8 percent of the population, or 2.3 million people. They owned about 20 to 25 percent of the land. This group included merchants, bankers, and industrialists, as well as professional people—lawyers, holders of public offices, doctors, and writers.

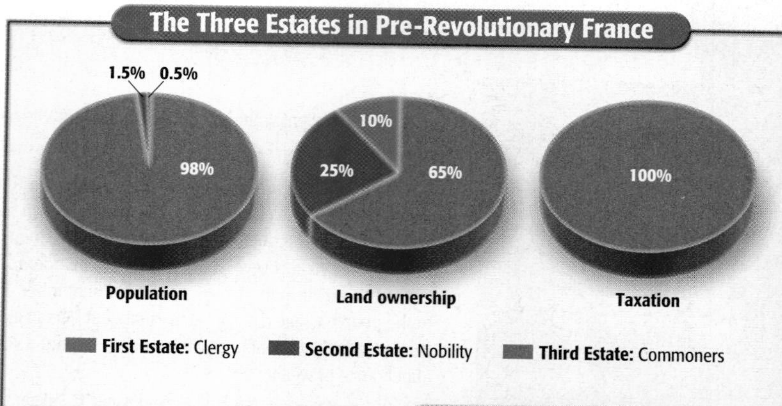

Graph Skills

The Third Estate included peasants, craftspeople, and the bourgeoisie. In the Third Estate, peasants owned about 40 percent of the land in France, and the bourgeoisie owned about 25 percent.

1. **Drawing Inferences** From looking at these circle graphs, what inferences can you draw about why a revolution occurred in France?

INTERDISCIPLINARY CONNECTIONS ACTIVITY

Literature/English Language Arts As a way of using literature as a key to understanding history, have your students read Charles Dickens's *A Tale of Two Cities*. Provide students with study guides to help them with the nineteenth-century language and style of writing. Students, in cooperation with an English teacher, might wish to develop the study guides. Then divide the class into groups and assign each group responsibility for reading different parts of the novel. Each group will create a presentation for its part of the book. The presentations can be given as a series. **L2**

Members of the middle class were unhappy with the privileges held by nobles. At the same time, they shared a great deal with the nobility. Indeed, by obtaining public offices, wealthy middle-class individuals could enter the ranks of the nobility. During the eighteenth century, 6,500 new noble families were created.

In addition, both aristocrats and members of the bourgeoisie were drawn to the new political ideas of the Enlightenment. Both groups were increasingly upset with a monarchical system resting on privileges and on an old and rigid social order. The opposition of these elites to the old order ultimately led them to drastic action against the monarchy.

Picturing **History**

Les Halles, the market area of Paris, is pictured with the Grand Chatelet in the background. Would this market have been quieter or busier twenty years before the revolution? Why?

Financial Crisis Social conditions, then, formed a long-range background to the French Revolution. The immediate cause of the revolution was the near collapse of government finances.

The French economy, although it had been expanding for 50 years, suffered periodic crises. Bad harvests in 1787 and 1788 and a slowdown in manufacturing led to food shortages, rising prices for food, and unemployment. The number of poor, estimated by some at almost one-third of the population, reached crisis proportions on the eve of the revolution.

An English traveler noted the misery of the poor in the countryside: "All the country girls and women are without shoes or stockings; and the plowmen at their work have neither shoes nor stockings to their feet. This is a poverty that strikes at the root of national prosperity."

In spite of these economic problems, the French government continued to spend enormous sums on costly wars and court luxuries. The queen, Marie Antoinette, was especially known for her extravagance. The government had also spent large amounts to help the American colonists against Britain.

On the verge of a complete financial collapse, the government of **Louis XVI** was finally forced to call a meeting of the Estates-General to raise new taxes. This was the French parliament, and it had not met since 1614.

Reading Check **Identifying** What groups were part of the Third Estate?

From Estates-General to National Assembly

The Estates-General was composed of representatives from the three orders of French society. The First and Second Estates had about three hundred delegates each. The Third Estate had almost six hundred delegates, most of whom were lawyers from French towns. To fix France's financial problems, most members of the Third Estate wanted to set up a constitutional government that would abolish the tax exemptions of the clergy and nobility.

The meeting of the Estates-General opened at **Versailles** on May 5, 1789. It was troubled from the start with a problem about voting. Traditionally, each estate had one vote. That meant that the First and Second Estates together could outvote the Third Estate two to one.

The Third Estate demanded that each deputy have one vote. With the help of a few nobles and clerics, that would give the Third Estate a majority. The king, however, declared he was in favor of the current system, in which each estate had one vote.

The Third Estate reacted quickly. On June 17, 1789, it called itself a National Assembly and decided to draft a constitution. Three days later, on June 20, the deputies of the Third Estate arrived at their meeting place, only to find the doors locked.

The deputies then moved to a nearby indoor tennis court and swore that they would continue to meet

CHAPTER 11
Section 1, 329–335

Reading Check

Answer: peasants; craftspeople, shopkeepers, and wage earners; and the bourgeoisie, or middle class, which included merchants, bankers, industrialists, and professionals such as lawyers, holders of public offices, doctors, and writers

Picturing **History**

Answer: It would probably have been busier, since the French economy was in a slowdown at the time of the revolution and there were food shortages and rising food prices. **L1**

Guided Reading Activity 11–1

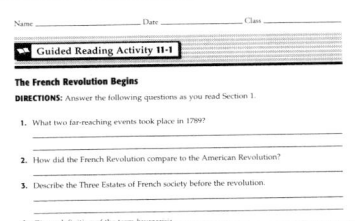

Name ____ Date ____ Class ____

Guided Reading Activity 11-1

The French Revolution Begins

DIRECTIONS: Answer the following questions as you read Section 1.

1. What two far-reaching events took place in 1789?
2. How did the French Revolution compare to the American Revolution?
3. Describe the Three Estates of French society before the revolution.
4. Give a definition of the term *bourgeoisie*.

Connecting Across Time

Discuss with students the concept of "one person, one vote." Why did the First and Second Estates in France oppose this concept? Discuss with students the election of 2000 in the United States and the controversy surrounding electoral votes versus popular vote in our own country. **L2**

COOPERATIVE LEARNING ACTIVITY

Taking a Vote Explain that the French government faced heavy debt in 1789. To pay the debt, the king wanted to increase taxes. The clergy and nobility (the First and Second Estates) had been exempt from taxation. Would they accept some of the burden now? Organize students into three groups, representing the First, Second, and Third Estates. Each group should prepare a statement and choose a person to present its position on taxation. Allow time for discussion, then have the class vote on each proposal for tax apportionment. Each estate, not each class member, receives one vote. Members of each estate must arrive at a consensus before casting its vote. **L3**

CHAPTER 11
Section 1, 329–335

Reading Check

Answer: because the First and Second Estates together could outvote the Third Estate two to one

History *through Art*

Answer: the fact that the doors of their meeting place were locked L1

Critical Thinking

Guide students in a discussion of whether they believe the French Revolution was caused more by economic issues or political grievances people had against the leadership of France. L2

CURRICULUM CONNECTION

Politics Ask students to explain why economic difficulties coupled with a lack of political cooperation often leads to a rise of political extremist groups. What other examples of this phenomenon can students identify? L3

ABCNEWS INTERACTIVE™

Turning Points in World History The ABC News videotape includes a segment on the French Revolution.

History *through Art*

***The Tennis Court Oath* by Jacques-Louis David** Members of the National Assembly swore that they would produce a French constitution. What caused members to fear that the National Assembly would be dissolved by force?

until they had produced a French constitution. The oath they swore is known as the **Tennis Court Oath.**

Louis XVI prepared to use force against the Third Estate. The common people, however, saved the Third Estate from the king's forces. On July 14, a mob of Parisians stormed the Bastille (ba•STEEL), an armory and prison in **Paris,** and dismantled it, brick by brick. Paris was abandoned to the rebels.

Louis XVI was soon informed that he could no longer trust the royal troops. Royal authority had collapsed. Louis XVI could enforce his will no more. The fall of the Bastille had saved the National Assembly.

At the same time, popular revolutions broke out throughout France, both in the cities and in the countryside. A growing hatred of the entire landholding system, with its fees and obligations, led to the popular uprisings.

Peasant rebellions took place throughout France and became part of the Great Fear, a vast panic that spread quickly through France in the summer of 1789. Citizens, fearing invasion by foreign troops that would support the French monarchy, formed militias.

Reading Check **Examining** Why did the Third Estate object to each estate's having one vote in the Estates-General?

The Destruction of the Old Regime

The peasant revolts and fear of foreign troops had a strong effect on the National Assembly, which was meeting in Versailles. One of the assembly's first acts was to destroy the relics of feudalism, or aristocratic privileges. On the night of August 4, 1789, the National Assembly voted to abolish the rights of landlords, as well as the financial privileges of nobles and clergy.

Declaration of the Rights of Man On August 26, the National Assembly adopted the **Declaration of the Rights of Man and the Citizen.** Inspired by the American Declaration of Independence and Constitution, and the English Bill of Rights, this charter of basic liberties began with a ringing affirmation of "the natural and imprescriptible rights of man" to "liberty, property, security, and resistance to oppression."

Reflecting Enlightenment thought, the declaration went on to proclaim freedom and equal rights for all men, access to public office based on talent, and an end to exemptions from taxation. All citizens were to have the right to take part in the making of laws. Freedom of speech and the press were affirmed.

MEETING INDIVIDUAL NEEDS

Reading Comprehension Have students carefully read this section. Then, have students develop and present a newscast on the beginning of the French Revolution. The students should play roles, such as reporters, representatives of each estate, and peasants. The newscast should include: 1) a reporter describing some of France's long-range problems, as well as some of the immediate issues that led to the revolution; 2) interviews with different representatives of the estates; 3) a reporter interviewing women on the role that they believe they should be playing in the revolution and subsequent governments; and 4) highlights of events that took place on June 20, July 14, and August 26, 1789. This type of active involvement is useful for students who need review and understanding of main ideas. L2

The declaration also raised an important issue. Did its ideal of equal rights for all men also include women? Many deputies insisted that it did, provided that, as one said, "women do not hope to exercise political rights and functions."

Olympe de Gouges, a woman who wrote plays and pamphlets, refused to accept this exclusion of women from political rights. Echoing the words of the official declaration, she penned a Declaration of the Rights of Woman and the Female Citizen. In it, she insisted that women should have all the same rights as men.

She wrote:

> ❝Believing that ignorance, omission, or scorn for the rights of woman are the only causes of public misfortunes and of the corruption of governments, the women have resolved to set forth in a solemn declaration the natural, inalienable, and sacred rights of woman in order that this declaration, constantly exposed before all the members of the society, will ceaselessly remind them of their rights and duties.❞

The National Assembly ignored her demands. *(See page 775 to read excerpts from Olympe de Gouges's* Declaration of the Rights of Woman and the Female Citizen *in the Primary Sources Library.)*

The King Concedes In the meantime, Louis XVI had remained at Versailles. He refused to accept the National Assembly's decrees on the abolition of feudalism and the Declaration of Rights. On October 5, however, thousands of Parisian women—described by one eyewitness as "detachments of women coming up from every direction, armed with broomsticks, lances, pitchforks, swords, pistols and muskets"—marched to Versailles. A delegation of the women met with Louis XVI and described how their children were starving from a lack of bread. They forced the king to accept the new decrees.

The crowd now insisted that the royal family return to Paris to show the king's support of the National Assembly. On October 6, the family journeyed to Paris. As a goodwill gesture, Louis XVI brought along wagonloads of flour from the palace

CONNECTIONS Around The World

A National Holiday

The French Revolution gave rise to the concept of the modern nation-state. With the development of the modern state came the celebration of one day a year as a national holiday—usually called Independence Day. The national holiday is a day that has special significance in the history of the nation-state.

In France, the fall of the Bastille on July 14, 1789, has been celebrated ever since as the beginning of the French nation-state. Independence Day in the United States is celebrated on July 4. On July 4, 1776, the Second Continental Congress approved the Declaration of Independence.

In Norway, people celebrate Constitution Day as a national holiday on May 17. On that day in 1814, Norway received a constitution, although it did not gain its independence from Sweden until 1905.

Most Latin American countries became independent of Spain or Portugal in the early nineteenth century. Mexico, for example, celebrates its Independence Day on September 16 with a colorful festival. On September 16, 1810, a crowd of local people attacked Spanish authorities in a small village near Mexico City. They were crushed, but their action eventually led to Mexico's independence from Spanish control in 1821.

Most nations in Africa and Asia gained their independence from Western colonial powers after World War II. India celebrates Independence Day on August 15. On that day in 1947, India won its independence from the British Empire.

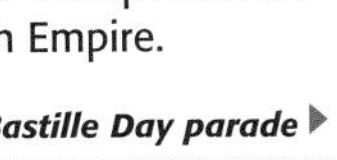

Bastille Day parade ▶

Comparing Cultures

Every nation celebrates its Independence Day with different kinds of festivities. For example, in the United States, many people have barbecues and watch firework displays. Choose two other nations and research how each nation and its people celebrate their Independence Day. Create an illustrated poster or chart showing your results.

EXTENDING THE CONTENT

Revolution and Immigration The French Revolution was one of the first revolts begun by common citizens that came to influence much of world history for the next two centuries. The Russian, Chinese, and Cuban Revolutions, and countless other revolutions and revolutionary groups were influenced and inspired by the French Revolution. Have students research one of the impacts of revolution—immigration. Have students study U.S. immigration patterns and develop explanations of the links between U.S. immigration and revolution in other countries. You might wish to have students chart their data or prepare visuals to support the evidence they find. L2

Answer: Answers will vary depending on the countries chosen.

Enrich

Ask students to explain the significance of the date 1789. Then have students create a time line of the important events of 1789 discussed in this section. *(1789: May 5, Meeting of Estates-General; June 17, National Assembly; June 20, Tennis Court Oath; August 4, National Assembly abolishes landlords and financial privileges; August 26, Declaration of the Rights of Man and the Citizen; October 6, Louis returns to Paris)* L1

Writing Activity

Have students prepare speeches that might have been made by women organizing the march to Versailles in 1789. Speeches should include reasons for the march. L2

Connecting Across Time

The French Revolution gave rise to the idea of a national holiday. In the United States, we have many national holidays. Ask students: "If you could add a national holiday commemorating an important person or national event, what would it be? How would it be celebrated?" L1

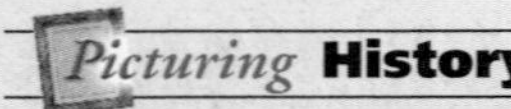

Picturing History

Answer: They were returned to Paris and eventually executed.

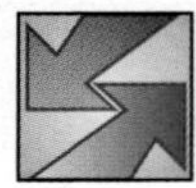

CURRICULUM CONNECTION

Government Ask students to define the phrase *separation of church and state. (Religions have no say in government; government has no control over religions)* Discuss the relationship between Church and state in France during the 1790s and how the changing relationship affected both common citizens and the government. *(Government controlled religion; made enemies of Catholics)* **L2**

3 ASSESS

Assign Section 1 Assessment as homework or as an in-class activity.

Have students use **Interactive Tutor Self-Assessment CD-ROM.**

Section Quiz 11–1

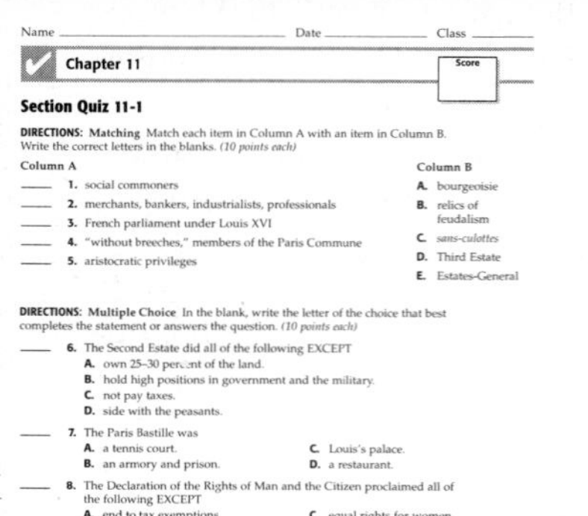

Name ______ Date ______ Class ______

Chapter 11 Score

Section Quiz 11-1

DIRECTIONS: Matching Match each item in Column A with an item in Column B. Write the correct letters in the blanks. *(10 points each)*

Column A	Column B
____ 1. social commoners	A. bourgeoisie
____ 2. merchants, bankers, industrialists, professionals	B. relics of feudalism
____ 3. French parliament under Louis XVI	C. *sans-culottes*
____ 4. "without breeches," members of the Paris Commune	D. Third Estate
____ 5. aristocratic privileges	E. Estates-General

DIRECTIONS: Multiple Choice In the blank, write the letter of the choice that best completes the statement or answers the question. *(10 points each)*

____ 6. The Second Estate did all of the following EXCEPT
A. own 25–30 percent of the land.
B. hold high positions in government and the military.
C. not pay taxes.
D. side with the peasants.

____ 7. The Paris Bastille was
A. a tennis court. C. Louis's palace.
B. an armory and prison. D. a restaurant.

____ 8. The Declaration of the Rights of Man and the Citizen proclaimed all of the following EXCEPT
A. end to tax exemptions. C. equal rights for women.

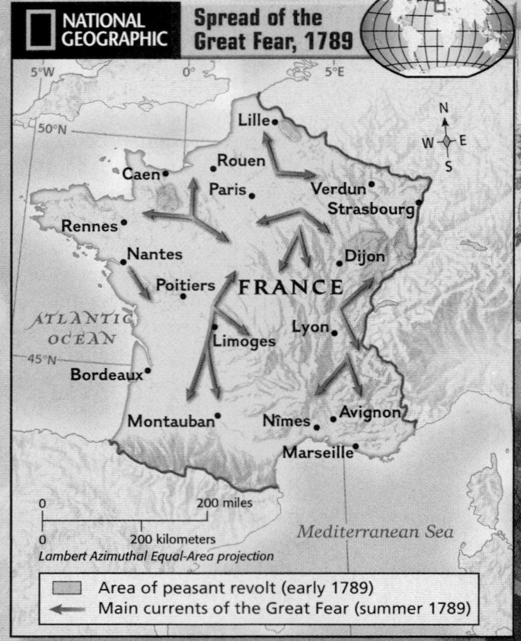

▲ *Parisian women march on Versailles.*

▲ *Louis XVI is arrested at Varennes.*

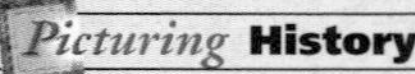

Picturing History

Louis XVI remained at Versailles during the great panic that swept through France in the summer of 1789. On October 5, 1789, thousands of women marched to Versailles and persuaded Louis to return to Paris with his family. Louis later tried to escape from France in 1791 but was captured at Varennes and returned to Paris. What happened to the royal family after their capture?

stores. The royal family and the supplies were escorted by women armed with pikes. The women sang, "We are bringing back the baker, the baker's wife, and the baker's boy" (the king; Marie Antoinette, the queen; and their son). The king and his family became virtual prisoners in Paris.

Church Reforms Because the Catholic Church was seen as an important pillar of the old order, it, too, was reformed. Because of the need for money, the National Assembly seized and sold the lands of the Church.

The Church was also secularized. A new Civil Constitution of the Clergy was put into effect. Both bishops and priests were to be elected by the people and paid by the state. The French government now controlled the Church. Many Catholics became enemies of the revolution.

A New Constitution and New Fears The National Assembly completed a new constitution, the Constitution of 1791, which set up a limited monarchy. According to the constitution, there would still be a king, but a Legislative Assembly would make the laws.

The Assembly was to consist of 745 representatives. The way they were to be chosen ensured that only the more affluent members of society would be elected. Though all male citizens had the same rights, only men over 25 who paid a specified amount in taxes could vote.

MEETING INDIVIDUAL NEEDS

Visual/Spatial Encourage students who are strong visual learners to draw pictures of some of the early events of the French Revolution. Topics for drawings might include the poverty of France, Marie Antoinette and her luxuries, the meeting of the Estates-General, the Third Estate locked out of its meeting place, the Tennis Court Oath, the storming of the Bastille, the women protesting the lack of bread, the return of Louis XVI to Paris, and the war with Austria. Then have a group of students arrange the drawings in chronological order along a time line on a bulletin board. **L1**

Refer to ***Inclusion for the High School Social Studies Classroom Strategies and Activities*** in the TCR.

By 1791, the old order had been destroyed. However, many people—including Catholic priests, nobles, lower classes hurt by a rise in the cost of living, and radicals who wanted more drastic solutions—opposed the new order. Louis XVI also made things difficult for the new government. He attempted to flee France in June 1791. He almost succeeded but was recognized, captured, and brought back to Paris.

In this unsettled situation, with a seemingly disloyal monarch, the new Legislative Assembly held its first session in October 1791. France's relations with the rest of Europe would soon lead to the downfall of Louis XVI.

War with Austria Over time, some European leaders began to fear that revolution would spread to their countries. The rulers of **Austria** and **Prussia** even threatened to use force to restore Louis XVI to full power. Insulted by this threat, the Legislative Assembly declared war on Austria in the spring of 1792.

The French fared badly in the initial fighting. A frantic search for scapegoats began. One observer noted, "Everywhere you hear the cry that the king is betraying us, the generals are betraying us, that nobody is to be trusted; . . . that Paris will be taken in six weeks by the Austrians . . . we are on a volcano ready to spout flames."

Rise of the Paris Commune Defeats in war, coupled with economic shortages at home in the spring of 1792, led to new political demonstrations, especially against Louis XVI. In August, radical political groups in Paris, declaring themselves a commune, organized a mob attack on the royal palace and Legislative Assembly.

Members of the new Paris Commune took the king captive. They forced the Legislative Assembly to suspend the monarchy and call for a National Convention, chosen on the basis of universal male suffrage, to decide on the nation's future form of government. (Under a system of universal male suffrage, all adult males had the right to vote.)

The French Revolution was about to enter a more radical and violent stage. Power now passed from the Assembly to the Paris Commune. Many of its members proudly called themselves the *sans-culottes,* ordinary patriots without fine clothes. (They wore long trousers instead of knee-length breeches; *sans-culottes* means "without breeches.") It has become customary to equate the more radical *sans-culottes* with working people or the poor. However, many were merchants and better-off artisans who were the elite of their neighborhoods.

Parisian sans-culottes

Reading Check **Evaluating** What was the significance of the Constitution of 1791?

SECTION 1 ASSESSMENT

Checking for Understanding

1. **Define** estate, relics of feudalism, bourgeoisie, *sans-culottes.*
2. **Identify** Louis XVI, Tennis Court Oath, Declaration of the Rights of Man and the Citizen, Olympe de Gouges.
3. **Locate** Versailles, Paris, Austria, Prussia.
4. **Explain** why the Catholic Church was targeted for reform.
5. **List** the reasons for the near collapse of government finances in France.

Critical Thinking

6. **Summarize** What were the main affirmations of the Declaration of the Rights of Man and the Citizen?
7. **Organizing Information** Equality was one of the slogans of the French Revolution. In a web diagram, identify five occasions when different groups expressed concern for equality during the revolution.

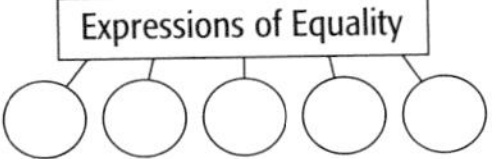

Analyzing Visuals

8. **Examine** the painting of the Tennis Court Oath shown on page 332. How does David's painting reflect the ideals of the French Revolution?

Writing About History

9. **Persuasive Writing** Olympe de Gouges wrote, "ignorance, omission, or scorn for the rights of woman are the only causes of public misfortune and corruption of governments." Do you agree or disagree? Write a paragraph supporting your point of view.

SECTION 1 ASSESSMENT

1. Key terms are in blue.
2. Louis XVI *(p. 331);* Tennis Court Oath *(p. 332);* Declaration of the Rights of Man and the Citizen *(p. 332);* Olympe de Gouges *(p. 333)*
3. See chapter maps.
4. It was part of the old order that was being torn down.
5. The government was spending enormous sums on costly wars and court luxuries.
6. right to liberty, property, security; freedom from oppression; equal rights for all men; equal access to public office; equal, fair taxation
7. Third Estate's call for one vote per deputy; Declaration of the Rights of Man; Declaration of the Rights of Woman; end of aristocratic privileges; peasant uprising during Great Fear
8. It appears that everyone is participating equally in the process of making policy.
9. Answers will vary. Students' opinions should be supported by logical arguments.

Reading Check

Answer: It set up a limited monarchy. There would still be a king, but a Legislative Assembly would make the laws.

Reading Essentials and Study Guide 11–1

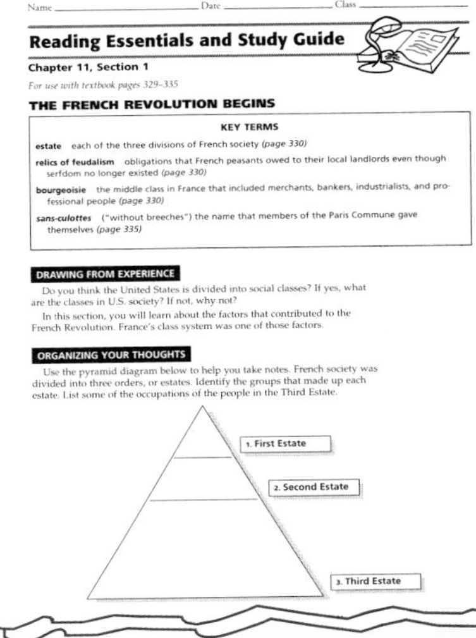

Name ______ Date ______ Class ______

Reading Essentials and Study Guide

Chapter 11, Section 1

For use with textbook pages 329–335

THE FRENCH REVOLUTION BEGINS

KEY TERMS

estate each of the three divisions of French society *(page 330)*

relics of feudalism obligations that French peasants owed to their local landlords even though serfdom no longer existed *(page 330)*

bourgeoisie the middle class in France that included merchants, bankers, industrialists, and professional people *(page 330)*

sans-culottes ("without breeches") the name that members of the Paris Commune gave themselves *(page 335)*

DRAWING FROM EXPERIENCE

Do you think the United States is divided into social classes? If yes, what are the classes in U.S. society? If not, why not?

In this section, you will learn about the factors that contributed to the French Revolution. France's class system was one of those factors.

ORGANIZING YOUR THOUGHTS

Use the pyramid diagram below to help you take notes. French society was divided into three orders, or estates. Identify the groups that made up each estate. List some of the occupations of the people in the Third Estate.

1. First Estate
2. Second Estate
3. Third Estate

Reteaching Activity

Have students write a letter to King Louis XVI identifying the causes of the French Revolution. **L2**

4 CLOSE

Have students review the groups that made up each estate and explain the role each group played in the revolution. **L1**

TEACH

Analyzing Primary Sources
Ask students to rewrite each of the rights listed in simplified, more contemporary language. You may wish to have students work in pairs for this activity. **L1** ELL

Charting Activity

Provide students with a copy of the U.S. Bill of Rights. Ask students to create a chart that identifies and explains similarities between this document and the French Declaration of Rights of Man and the Citizen. To what extent do students believe the authors of these documents were influenced by each other? **L2**

Critical Thinking

Have students read the excerpt from the Declaration of the Rights of Woman and the Female Citizen (pages 333 and 775). Ask students why they think de Gouges felt the need to create a separate declaration for the rights of women. **L2**

Critical Thinking

Legal and political concepts, such as ideas about rights, republicanism, responsibilities, the rule of law, constitutionalism, and democracy developed over time. Have students trace the historical development of these concepts from the ancient world to the beginning of the first modern constitutional republics. **L3**

EYEWITNESS TO HISTORY

Declaration of the Rights of Man and the Citizen

ONE OF THE MOST IMPORTANT DOCUMENTS of the French Revolution, the Declaration of the Rights of Man and the Citizen, was adopted in August 1789 by the National Assembly.

Painting of the declaration

❝The representatives of the French people, organized as a national assembly, considering that ignorance, neglect, and scorn of the rights of man are the sole causes of public misfortunes and of corruption of governments, have resolved to display in a solemn declaration the natural, inalienable, and sacred rights of man, so that this declaration, constantly in the presence of all members of society, will continually remind them of their rights and their duties . . . Consequently, the National Assembly recognizes and declares, in the presence and under the auspices of the Supreme Being, the following rights of man and citizen:

1. Men are born and remain free and equal in rights; social distinctions can be established only for the common benefit.
2. The aim of every political association is the conservation of the natural . . . rights of man; these rights are liberty, property, security, and resistance to oppression. . . .
4. Liberty consists in being able to do anything that does not harm another person. . . .
6. The law is the expression of the general will; all citizens have the right to concur personally or through their representatives in its formation; it must be the same for all, whether it protects or punishes.
7. No man can be accused, arrested, or detained except in cases determined by the law, and according to the forms which it has prescribed. . . .
10. No one may be disturbed because of his opinions, even religious, provided that their public demonstration does not disturb the public order established by law.
11. The free communication of thoughts and opinions is one of the most precious rights of man: every citizen can therefore freely speak, write, and print . . .
16. Any society in which guarantees of rights are not assured nor the separation of powers determined has no constitution.❞

—Declaration of the Rights of Man and the Citizen

Analyzing Primary Sources

1. According to this document, what are the natural, inalienable rights of man?
2. According to this document, can a person be arrested or otherwise "disturbed" because of his religious beliefs?
3. How do the rights listed in number 2 of the document compare to the rights listed in the U.S. Bill of Rights?

ANSWERS TO ANALYZING PRIMARY SOURCES

1. The natural, inalienable rights of man include liberty, property, security, and resistance to oppression.
2. No. A person should not be arrested for religious beliefs as long as any public demonstration involving that religion does not disturb the public order.
3. The rights guaranteed in item number 2 of the Declaration of the Rights of Man and the Citizen are not as inclusive as the rights guaranteed by the U.S. Bill of Rights. The U.S. Bill of Rights is a document consisting of 10 amendments to the Constitution; this is just one item in a long document guaranteeing many rights. Other rights, such as the right to religious freedom, are guaranteed elsewhere. (Numbers 7, 10, and 11 guarantee other rights included in the U.S. Bill of Rights.)

SECTION 2 Radical Revolution and Reaction

Guide to Reading

Main Ideas
- Radical groups and leaders controlled the Revolution.
- The new French Republic faced enemies at home and abroad.

Key Terms
faction, elector, coup d'état

People to Identify
Georges Danton, Jean-Paul Marat, Jacobins, Maximilien Robespierre

Places to Locate
Lyon, Nantes, Austrian Netherlands

Preview Questions
1. Why did a coalition of European countries take up arms against France?
2. Why did the Reign of Terror occur?

Reading Strategy
Summarizing Information As you read the section, list in a table like the one shown below the actions taken by the National Convention.

Actions taken by the National Convention
1.
2.
3.
4.

Preview of Events

♦1792 ♦1793 ♦1794 ♦1795

- **1792** National Convention splits into factions
- **1793** King Louis XVI is executed
- **1794** Reign of Terror ends
- **1795** New constitution is created

Voices from the Past

King Louis XVI

Henry de Firmont reported on the major event of January 21, 1793:

❝The path leading to the scaffold was extremely rough and difficult to pass; the King was obliged to lean on my arm, and from the slowness with which he proceeded, I feared for a moment that his courage might fail; but what was my astonishment, when arrived at the last step, he suddenly let go of my arm, and I saw him cross with a firm foot the breadth of the whole scaffold; and in a loud voice, I heard him pronounce distinctly these words: 'I die innocent of all the crimes laid to my charge; I pardon those who had occasioned my death; and I pray to God that the blood you are going to shed may never be visited on France.'❞

—***Eyewitness to History***, **John Carey, ed., 1987**

The execution of King Louis XVI in 1793 pushed the French Revolution into a new radical stage.

The Move to Radicalism

The Paris Commune had forced the Legislative Assembly to call a National Convention. Before the Convention met, the Paris Commune dominated the political scene. Led by the newly appointed minister of justice, **Georges Danton,** the *sans-culottes* sought revenge on those who had aided the king and resisted the popular will. Thousands of people were arrested and then massacred. New

1 FOCUS

Section Overview

This section discusses the events that occurred during the Reign of Terror and explains how Napoleon Bonaparte was able to seize power during a coup d'état in 1799.

BELLRINGER
Skillbuilder Activity

Project transparency and have students answer questions.

Available as a blackline master.

Daily Focus Skills Transparency 11–2

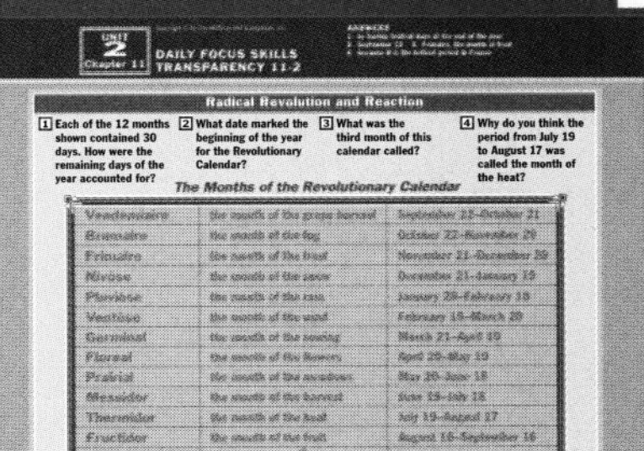
UNIT 2 Chapter 11 DAILY FOCUS SKILLS TRANSPARENCY 11-2

Radical Revolution and Reaction

1. Each of the 12 months shown contained 30 days. How were the remaining days of the year accounted for?
2. What date marked the beginning of the year for the Revolutionary Calendar?
3. What was the third month of this calendar called?
4. Why do you think the period from July 19 to August 17 was called the month of the heat?

The Months of the Revolutionary Calendar

Guide to Reading

Answers to Graphic:
1. abolished the monarchy
2. established the French Republic
3. passed a decree condemning the king to death
4. gave broad powers to the Committee of Public Safety

Preteaching Vocabulary: Have students look up the meaning of *faction* and use it in a sentence about a contemporary situation or personal experience. **L1** ELL

SECTION RESOURCES

Reproducible Masters
- Reproducible Lesson Plan 11–2
- Daily Lecture and Discussion Notes 11–2
- Guided Reading Activity 11–2
- Section Quiz 11–2
- Reading Essentials and Study Guide 11–2

Transparencies
- Daily Focus Skills Transparency 11–2

Multimedia
- Interactive Tutor Self-Assessment CD-ROM
- ExamView® Pro Testmaker CD-ROM
- Presentation Plus! CD-ROM

2 TEACH

Daily Lecture and Discussion Notes 11–2

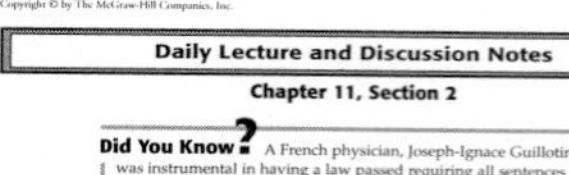

Daily Lecture and Discussion Notes

Chapter 11, Section 2

Did You Know? A French physician, Joseph-Ignace Guillotin, was instrumental in having a law passed requiring all sentences of death to be carried out by "means of a machine" to be humane. Use of the guillotine, named for Guillotin, continued in France through the 1970s. In 1981 France outlawed capital punishment.

I. **The Move to Radicalism** *(pages 337–339)*

A. Led by the minister of justice, **Georges Danton,** the *sans-culottes* sought revenge on those who had aided the king and resisted the popular will. Thousands of people were arrested and massacred.

B. One of the more important radical leaders was **Jean-Paul Marat,** who published the radical journal *Friend of the People*. He argued that the poor had a right to take from the rich whatever they needed, even by violence.

C. The National Convention met in 1792, acting not only as a constitutional convention but also as a sovereign ruling body. Its first act was to end the monarchy and establish the French Republic. The members disagreed over the king's fate. Two **factions**—the urban Mountain and the rural Girondins—of the **Jacobin** political club divided over the issue. The Girondins wanted to keep the king alive. The Mountain won and the king was beheaded, using the guillotine because they thought it was humane. The split got Marat, a Mountain, killed; Charlotte Corday, a Girondin, stabbed him to death in his bathtub.

D. France had other domestic problems besides a split in the National Convention. The Paris Commune pressured the Convention to enact more and more radical measures, and parts of France refused to accept the rule of the Convention.

E. A foreign crisis also loomed because the execution of the king outraged European monarchies. Spain, Portugal, Britain, and other monarchies formed a loose coalition to invade France. The revolution would be destroyed. To respond, the National Convention formed the 12-member **Committee of Public Safety,** led first by Danton and then by **Maximilien Robespierre.**

F. Robespierre was a la[illegible] activist, so known for his honesty that he was called

CURRICULUM CONNECTION

Literature Write the following quote from the opening of Charles Dickens's *A Tale of Two Cities* on the chalkboard: "It was the best of times, it was the worst of times. . . ." Discuss how this quote applies to the French Revolution. **L2**

Global Gourmet

Bread was the mainstay in the diet of the average Parisian in 1789. A typical French worker ate a four-pound loaf a day. Supplying bread for the city's more than 600,000 inhabitants was a major production. It is not surprising that it was often a problem as well. Bread shortages played a significant role in the onset of the French Revolution.

leaders of the people emerged, including **Jean-Paul Marat,** who published a radical journal called *Friend of the People.*

The Fate of the King In September 1792, the newly elected National Convention began its sessions. Although it had been called to draft a new constitution, it also acted as the sovereign ruling body of France.

The Convention was dominated by lawyers, professionals, and property owners. Two-thirds of its deputies were under the age of 45. Almost all had had political experience as a result of the revolution. Almost all distrusted the king. It was therefore no surprise that the National Convention's first major step on September 21 was to abolish the monarchy and establish a republic, the French Republic.

That, however, was as far as members of the convention could agree. They soon split into **factions** (dissenting groups) over the fate of the king. The two most important factions were the Girondins (juh•RAHN•duhns) and the Mountain. Both factions were members of the **Jacobin** (JA•kuh•buhn) club, a large network of political groups throughout France. The Girondins represented the provinces, areas outside the cities. Girondins feared the radical mobs in Paris and leaned toward keeping the king alive. The Mountain represented the interests of radicals in the city of Paris.

The Mountain won at the beginning of 1793 when it convinced the National Convention to pass a decree condemning Louis XVI to death. On January 21, 1793, the king was beheaded on the guillotine. Revolutionaries had adopted this machine because it killed quickly and, they believed, humanely. The execution of the king created new enemies for the revolution, both at home and abroad. A new crisis was at hand.

Crises and Response Disputes between Girondins and the Mountain were only one aspect of France's domestic crisis in 1792 and 1793. Within Paris, the local government—the Commune—favored radical change and put constant pressure on the National Convention to adopt ever more radical positions. Moreover, the National Convention itself still did not rule all of France. Peasants in western France as well as inhabitants of France's major provincial cities refused to accept the authority of the National Convention.

People In History

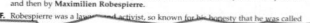

Jean-Paul Marat
1743–1793
French revolutionary

Jean-Paul Marat was a popular revolutionary leader in Paris at the beginning of the radical stage of the French Revolution. Born in Switzerland, he practiced medicine in London before returning to France in 1777. Marat was an intense man, always in a hurry: "I allot only two of the twenty-four hours to sleep. I have not had fifteen minutes play in over three years." He often worked in the bathtub because the water soothed the pain of a severe skin disorder.

In his newspaper, *Friend of the People,* Marat expressed his ideas, which were radical for his time. He called for mob violence and the right of the poor to take by force whatever they needed from the rich. He helped make the Jacobins more radical, especially by condemning the Girondins. This also led to his death: Charlotte Corday, a Girondin, stabbed him to death in his bathtub.

Maximilien Robespierre
1758–1794
French revolutionary

Robespierre was one of the most important French revolutionary leaders. He received a law degree and later became a member of the National Convention, where he preached democracy and advocated suffrage (the right to vote) for all adult males. He lived simply and was known to be extremely honest. In fact, in 1791, he received the title, "The Incorruptible." A believer in Rousseau's social contract idea, Robespierre thought that anyone opposed to being governed by the general will, as he interpreted it, should be executed.

One observer said of Robespierre, "That man will go far; he believes all that he says." Robespierre himself said, "How can one reproach a man who has truth on his side?" His eagerness and passion in pursuing the Reign of Terror frightened many people. Eventually, he was arrested and guillotined.

COOPERATIVE LEARNING ACTIVITY

Creating a Speech Help students understand why people willing to inflict harm on others have gained power during times of crisis. Ask students to create a list of problems faced by leaders of the French Revolution in 1792. Ask students to work in small groups to write a speech that might have been given by a member of the Committee of Public Safety to justify the committee's radical actions. Encourage students to think about why so many French people were willing to tolerate the actions of this committee. What problems might the committee member cite? How might a committee member explain the committee's actions as solutions to these problems? What promises for the future might the committee have made? **L2**

Reign of Terror execution list ▼

Model of a guillotine ▼

▲ *Marie Antoinette goes to her execution.*

Picturing History

During the Reign of Terror, thousands of people, including aristocrats and the queen of France, were killed by the guillotine. Why did the revolutionaries decide to use the guillotine to execute people?

A foreign crisis also loomed large. The execution of Louis XVI had outraged the royalty of most of Europe. An informal coalition of Austria, Prussia, Spain, Portugal, Britain, the Dutch Republic, and Russia took up arms against France. The French armies began to fall back.

By late spring of 1793, the coalition was poised for an invasion of France. If successful, both the revolution and the revolutionaries would be destroyed, and the old regime would be reestablished. The revolution had reached a decisive moment.

To meet these crises, the National Convention gave broad powers to a special committee of 12 known as the **Committee of Public Safety**. It was dominated at first by Georges Danton, then by **Maximilien Robespierre.**

Reading Check **Examining** What were the differences between the Girondins and the Mountain?

The Reign of Terror

For a 12-month period, from 1793 to 1794, the Committee of Public Safety took control. The Committee acted to defend France from foreign and domestic threats.

To meet the crisis at home, the National Convention and the Committee of Public Safety set in motion an effort that came to be known as the **Reign of Terror.** Revolutionary courts were set up to prosecute internal enemies of the revolutionary republic. During the course of the Reign of Terror, close to 40,000 people were killed. Of those, 16,000 people, including Marie Antoinette and Olympe de Gouges, died under the blade of the guillotine. Peasants and persons who had opposed the *sans-culottes* were among the victims. Most executions were held in places that had openly rebelled against the authority of the National Convention.

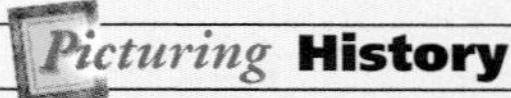

Picturing History

Answer: The guillotine was believed to kill quickly and humanely.

Reading Check

Answer: The Girondins represented the provinces. They feared the radical mobs in Paris and leaned toward keeping the king alive. The Mountain represented the interests of the radicals in Paris.

Guided Reading Activity 11–2

Name ________ Date ________ Class ________

Guided Reading Activity 11-2

Radical Revolution and Reaction

DIRECTIONS: As you are reading the section, decide if a statement is true or false. Write **T** if the statement is true or **F** if the statement is false. For all false statements write a corrected statement.

____ 1. The National Convention's first major step on September 21, 1792, was to reestablish the authority of King Louis XVI.

____ 2. The political faction known as the Mountain convinced the National Convention to pass a decree condemning Louis XVI to death.

____ 3. During the Reign of Terror, revolutionary courts were established to settle property disputes between the church and state.

____ 4. In the new French Republic, the titles "citizen" and "citizeness" replaced "mister" and "madame."

____ 5. In the dechristianization of France, the National Convention held a public ceremony dedicated to the worship of the monarchy.

Connecting Across Time

Ask students to compare the executions and destruction during the Reign of Terror in France with the destruction of cities and killing of native peoples by Spanish and Portuguese forces in Latin America. What might these events have had to do with the respect, or lack of respect, that people felt for human life? How could the oppressors justify their actions? **L3**

EXTENDING THE CONTENT

Jacobins The word *Jacobin* was originally used to refer to priests of the Dominican order whose first religious house in Paris was on the Rue St. Jacques. When the radical group made up of Robespierre, Marat, and others met in a former Dominican religious house, the French radicals became known as Jacobins. Today the word is used to refer to people with radical views. The Jacobins wore a *bonnet rouge* or red liberty cap to their meetings. The cap was modeled after the headdress worn by slaves in the Roman Empire who had gained their freedom. The cap became a symbol of loyalty to the French Revolution and became the obligatory headgear of all French patriots.

Critical Thinking

Ask students to name some of the tactics of the Reign of Terror. *(executions, military force, change in language [citizen, citizeness], new schools, dechristianization)* Then ask students if they can think of any other historical periods when such tactics were used. *(Answers may include Hitler's Germany and Salem, Massachusetts, during the witch trials.)* **L3**

Enrich

Have students create a time line of significant events that occurred between 1792 and 1799. Ask students to write a paragraph describing each event and its impact. **L1**

Writing Activity

In 1792, the National Convention abolished the monarchy and established the French Republic. Have students write an essay in which they trace the process by which democratic-republican government evolved. Students should identify the beginnings of this form of government in classical Greece and Rome and then trace its evolution through developments in England and the Enlightenment. **L2**

Crushing Rebellion Revolutionary armies were set up to bring rebellious cities back under the control of the National Convention. The Committee of Public Safety decided to make an example of **Lyon.** Some 1,880 citizens of that city were executed. When guillotining proved too slow, grapeshot (a cluster of small iron balls) was used to shoot the condemned into open graves. A German observer noted the terror of the scene:

> “Whole ranges of houses, always the most handsome, burnt. The churches, convents, and all the dwellings of the former patricians were in ruins. When I came to the guillotine, the blood of those who had been executed a few hours beforehand was still running in the street . . . I said to a group of *sans-culottes* that it would be decent to clear away all this human blood. Why should it be cleared? one of them said to me. It's the blood of aristocrats and rebels. The dogs should lick it up.”

In western France, too, revolutionary armies were brutal in defeating rebel armies. The commander of the revolutionary army ordered that no mercy be given: "The road is strewn with corpses. Women, priests, monks, children, all have been put to death. I have spared nobody." Perhaps the most notorious act of violence occurred in **Nantes,** where victims were executed by being sunk in barges in the Loire River.

People from all classes were killed during the Terror. Clergy and nobles made up about 15 percent of the victims, while the rest were from the bourgeoisie and peasant classes. The Committee of Public Safety held that all this bloodletting was only temporary. Once the war and domestic crisis were over, the true "Republic of Virtue" would follow, and the Declaration of the Rights of Man and the Citizen would be fully realized.

The Republic of Virtue Along with the terror, the Committee of Public Safety took other steps both to control France and to create a new order, called by

THE WAY IT WAS

YOUNG PEOPLE IN . . .

Revolutionary France

In 1794, deputies in the National Convention proposed a new military school that would train several thousand young males aged 16 and 17 in the arts of war and the love of country. A few months later, the *École de Mars*, or School of Mars (the Roman god of war), opened on the outskirts of Paris.

Much was expected of the 3,400 young recruits. They were expected to maintain high moral standards and become enthusiastic patriots. Students, however, ignored discipline and expressed the desire to return home. After the death of Robespierre, authorities shut the school down. The plan to train young people in a few weeks to be dedicated patriots had failed.

At the same time, many of these youths now became part of the reaction against the Reign of Terror. They formed what were called "golden youth," gangs of young men who attacked Jacobins and destroyed public statues of revolutionary figures, such as Jean-Paul Marat.

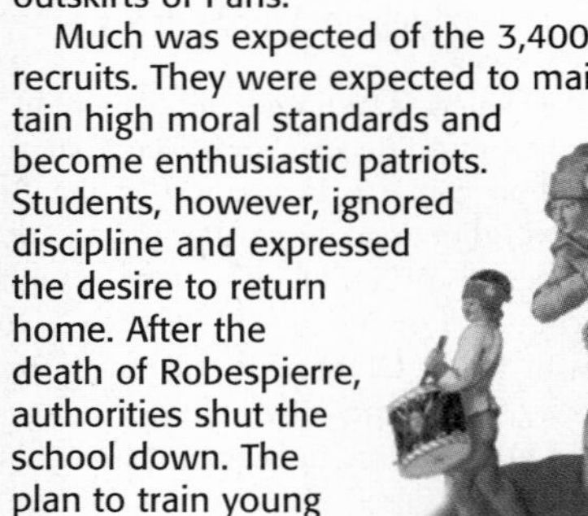

Young Men Off to Practice Using the Cannon, *c. 1789*

340

INTERDISCIPLINARY CONNECTIONS ACTIVITY

Philosophy The ideas of John Locke and Jean-Jacques Rousseau had a strong influence on leaders of the French Revolution. Ask students to research and write reports on Locke's *Two Treatises on Government* and Rousseau's *The Social Contract.* Students should summarize the philosophy of each work and discuss specific evidence that each influenced the French Revolution. Is one philosophy more evident than the other in the actions of French leaders? In what ways did the French fail to implement each philosophy correctly? Did leaders abuse the philosophy or take it too far? Did they lose sight of the philosophy altogether? Have students identify the impact of the political and legal ideas contained in Locke's *Two Treatises.* **L3**

Robespierre the Republic of Virtue—a democratic republic composed of good citizens. In the new French Republic, the titles "citizen" and "citizeness" had replaced "mister" and "madame." Women wore long dresses inspired by the clothing worn in the great republic of ancient Rome.

By spring 1793, the Committee was sending "representatives on mission" as agents of the central government to all parts of France to implement laws dealing with the wartime emergency. The Committee opened new schools to help educate individuals and produce good citizens. Slavery was abolished in France's colonies.

The committee also attempted to provide some economic controls by establishing price limits on goods considered necessities, ranging from food and drink to fuel and clothing. The controls failed to work very well, since the government lacked the machinery to enforce them.

In 1789, it had been a group of women who convinced Louis XVI to return to Paris from Versailles. Women remained actively involved in the revolution, even during its more radical stage. Women observed sessions of the National Convention and made their demands known to those in charge. In 1793, two women founded the Society for Revolutionary Republican Women. This Parisian group, which was mainly composed of working-class women, stood ready to defend the new French Republic. Many men, however, continued to believe that women should not participate in political or military affairs.

In its attempts to create a new order that reflected its belief in reason, the National Convention pursued a policy of dechristianization. The word *saint* was removed from street names, churches were pillaged and closed by revolutionary armies, and priests were encouraged to marry. In Paris, the cathedral of Notre Dame was designated a "temple of reason." In

For many young people who had shared in the revolutionary enthusiasm, however, the reaction against the Reign of Terror was a disaster. One good example is Marc-Antoine Jullien. At 18, he had been an assistant to Robespierre. After the execution of Robespierre, he was hunted down and put in prison for two years.

While in prison, Jullien wrote a diary expressing the hardships of a young revolutionary who had grown old before his time. He wrote: "I was born in a volcano, I lived in the midst of its eruption. I will be buried in its lava." He expressed his pain: "My life is a dark and terrible story, but one that is touching and educational for inexperienced youth."

When Jullien was released from prison, he wrote, "I am leaving, I never wish to see Paris again, I want cows and milk. I am twenty-one years old, may the dawn of my life no longer be clouded by dark images."

Disillusioned by his troubles, Jullien came to long for a savior who would restore the freedom of the republic. When

Closing of the Salle des Jacobins in Paris, symbolizing the end of the Reign of Terror

Connecting to the Past

1. **Examine** Why did the National Convention choose to open a school dedicated to training patriots? Are there comparable schools in the United States today?
2. **Writing about History** Marc-Antoine Jullien lived during troubled times. In the world today, many young people are undergoing similar experiences. Research an area of political unrest. Write a one-page paper describing the effect of that unrest on a person your age.

The Way It Was

Answers:

1. to turn out military leaders who had high moral standards and were enthusiastic patriots; yes, West Point is an example
2. Answers will vary.

Curriculum Connection

Art Ask students to create a recruiting poster that might have been used to encourage young men to join and fight for the French revolutionary army. **L1** ELL

Writing Activity

Women played a significant role in the revolution. Have students research and prepare a report about the role of French women during this time and how women impacted the revolution. **L2**

Who? What? Where? When?

Revolutionary Titles Just as the French revolutionaries addressed every person as *Citizen* rather than by titles such as *Sir* or *Madame*, the Communists during the Russian Revolution addressed one another as *Tovarishch* (meaning "Comrade"). In both cases, the attempt was to show equality of people within a cause. *Comrade* later came to mean a member of the Communist party, not just a citizen of the country.

Critical Thinking Activity

Solving Problems The French Revolution and the subsequent Reign of Terror led to many problems of government, economics, culture, and society. Assign students to work in small groups to use a problem-solving process to identify a problem that arose during this time period and conduct research to provide a historical context for the problem they have identified. Students should then list and consider options available to solve the problem, weigh the advantages and disadvantages of each option, work collaboratively to choose and implement a solution, and then evaluate the effectiveness of the solution they implemented. **L1**

Reading Check

Answer: Anyone who opposed the National Convention was considered an enemy.

TURNING POINT

Ask students how the army created by the French Republic changed the nature of modern warfare. Also have students identify other changes that resulted from the French Revolution. **L1**

Reading Check

Answer: It was the creation of a people's government, not a professional army established by a ruling dynasty. Its wars were people's wars, not dynastic wars.

3 ASSESS

Assign Section 2 Assessment as homework or as an in-class activity.

Have students use **Interactive Tutor Self-Assessment CD-ROM.**

Section Quiz 11–2

Name ______ Date ______ Class ______

Chapter 11 Score

Section Quiz 11-2

DIRECTIONS: Matching Match each item in Column A with an item in Column B. Write the correct letters in the blanks. *(10 points each)*

Column A	Column B
___ 1. Minister of Justice for the Paris Commune	A. coup d'état
___ 2. individuals qualified to vote	B. Georges Danton
___ 3. sudden overthrow of a government	C. Council of Elders
___ 4. dissenting groups	D. factions
___ 5. upper legislative house under the Constitution of 1795	E. electors

DIRECTIONS: Multiple Choice In the blank, write the letter of the choice that best completes the statement or answers the question. *(10 points each)*

___ 6. The Reign of Terror set up revolutionary courts to prosecute
A. Austrian prisoners. C. enemies of the republic.
B. the *sans-culottes*. D. Robespierre's followers.

___ 7. The two dissenting groups within the National Convention were the
A. Girondins and the Mountain. C. Commune and the Paris mob.
B. Jacobins and the Marats. D. Dantons and the Robespierres.

___ 8. During its rule, the government of the Directory was opposed by
A. Robespierre. C. the Jacobins.
B. royalists and radicals. D. moderates.

___ 9. The Directory was eventually toppled by
A. Robespierre. C. the Jacobins.
B. Louis XVI.

November 1793, a public ceremony dedicated to the worship of reason was held in the former cathedral. Patriotic maidens in white dresses paraded before a temple of reason where the high altar had once stood.

Another example of dechristianization was the adoption of a new calendar. Years would no longer be numbered from the birth of Christ but from September 22, 1792—the first day of the French Republic. The calendar contained 12 months. Each month consisted of three 10-day weeks, with the tenth day of each week a day of rest. This eliminated Sundays and Sunday worship services, as well as church holidays.

The anti-Christian purpose of the calendar was reinforced in the naming of the months of the year. The months were given names that were supposed to invoke the seasons, the temperature, or the state of the vegetation (for example, the month of *Vendémiaire,* or "seed time"). As Robespierre came to realize, however, dechristianization failed to work because France was still overwhelmingly Catholic.

Reading Check **Identifying** Whom did the Committee of Public Safety consider to be enemies of the state?

A Nation in Arms

TURNING POINT **As you will learn, the French Republic created a new kind of army that would ultimately change the nature of modern warfare.**

As you read earlier, France was threatened by external forces during this time. To save the republic from its foreign enemies, the Committee of Public Safety decreed a universal mobilization of the nation on August 23, 1793:

> "Young men will fight, young men are called to conquer. Married men will forge arms, transport military baggage and guns and will prepare food supplies. Women, who at long last are to take their rightful place in the revolution and follow their true destiny, will forget their futile tasks: their delicate hands will work at making clothes for soldiers; they will make tents and they will extend their tender care to shelters where the defenders of the Patrie [homeland] will receive the help that their wounds require. Children will make lint of old cloth. It is for them that we are fighting: children, those beings destined to gather all the fruits of the revolution, will raise their pure hands toward the skies. And old men, performing their missions again, as of yore, will be guided to the public squares of the cities where they will kindle the courage of young warriors and preach the doctrines of hate for kings and the unity of the Republic."

In less than a year, the French revolutionary government had raised an army of 650,000. By September 1794, the army numbered 1,169,000. The republic's army was the largest ever seen in European history. It pushed the allies invading France back across the Rhine and even conquered the **Austrian Netherlands.**

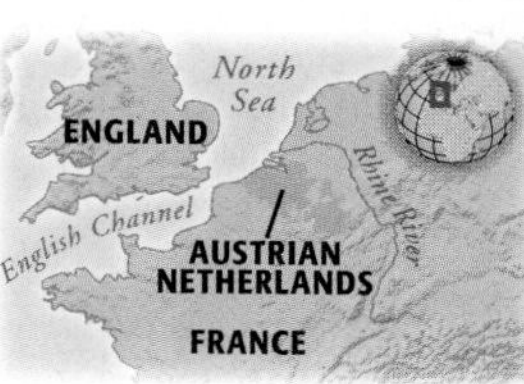

The French revolutionary army was an important step in the creation of modern nationalism. Previously, wars had been fought between governments or ruling dynasties by relatively small armies of professional soldiers. The new French army was the creation of a people's government. Its wars were people's wars. When dynastic wars became people's wars, however, warfare became more destructive.

End of the Terror By the summer of 1794, the French had largely defeated their foreign foes. There was less need for the Reign of Terror, but it continued nonetheless. Robespierre, who had become very powerful, was obsessed with ridding France of all its corrupt elements. Only then could the Republic of Virtue follow.

Many deputies in the National Convention who feared Robespierre decided to act. They gathered enough votes to condemn him, and Robespierre was guillotined on July 28, 1794.

After the death of Robespierre, revolutionary fervor began to cool. The Jacobins lost power and more moderate middle-class leaders took control. Much to the relief of many in France, the Reign of Terror came to a halt.

Reading Check **Evaluating** How did the French revolutionary army help to create modern nationalism?

The Directory

With the terror over, the National Convention reduced the power of the Committee of Public Safety. Churches were allowed to reopen for public worship. In addition, a new constitution was created in August 1795 that reflected the desire for more stability.

In an effort to keep any one governmental group from gaining control, the Constitution of 1795 established a national legislative assembly consisting of two chambers: a lower house, known as the Council of 500, which initiated legislation; and an upper house, the Council of Elders, which accepted or rejected the

CRITICAL THINKING ACTIVITY

Evaluating Have students evaluate how the American Revolution differed from the French Revolution. What was the long-term impact of each revolution on political developments around the world? Why do students think the French Revolution was so much more violent than the American Revolution? It is sometimes said that the American Revolution was a political revolution, but the French Revolution was social, economic, as well as political. Have the students assess the validity of this comparison and state their views to the class. You might also wish to have students prepare charts showing the number of deaths that resulted from each of the revolutions, estimates of property damages, and other costs. **L2**

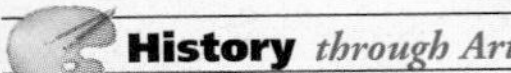
History *through Art*

***The Eighteenth of Brumaire* by Francois Bouchot**
This painting depicts Napoleon's coup d'état, November 10, 1799. What factors helped Napoleon (shown center) overthrow the Directory?

proposed laws. The 750 members of the two legislative bodies were chosen by electors (individuals qualified to vote in an election). The electors had to be owners or renters of property worth a certain amount, a requirement that limited their number to 30,000.

From a list presented by the Council of 500, the Council of Elders elected five directors to act as the executive committee, or Directory. The Directory, together with the legislature, ruled. The period of the revolution under the government of the Directory (1795–1799) was an era of corruption and graft. People reacted against the sufferings and sacrifices that had been demanded in the Reign of Terror. Some of them made fortunes in property by taking advantage of the government's severe money problems.

At the same time, the government of the Directory was faced with political enemies. Royalists who desired the restoration of the monarchy, as well as radicals unhappy with the turn toward moderation, plotted against the government. The Directory was unable to find a solution to the country's continuing economic problems. In addition, it was still carrying on wars left from the Committee of Public Safety.

Increasingly, the Directory relied on the military to maintain its power. In 1799, a coup d'état (KOO day•TAH), a sudden overthrow of the government, led by the successful and popular general Napoleon Bonaparte, toppled the Directory. Napoleon seized power.

Reading Check **Describing** Describe the government that replaced the National Convention.

SECTION 2 ASSESSMENT

Checking for Understanding

1. **Define** faction, elector, coup d'état.
2. **Identify** Georges Danton, Jean-Paul Marat, Jacobins, Committee of Public Safety, Maximilien Robespierre, Reign of Terror.
3. **Locate** Lyon, Nantes, Austrian Netherlands.
4. **Explain** both the similarities and the differences between the Girondins and the Mountain.
5. **List** the members of the informal coalition that took up arms against France. What was the result of this conflict?

Critical Thinking

6. **Drawing Conclusions** Did the French Republic live up to the revolution's ideals of Liberty, Equality, and Fraternity? Write a paragraph in support of your opinion.
7. **Contrasting Information** Using a table like the one below, contrast the changes in French governmental policy during and after Robespierre's possession of power.

During	After

Analyzing Visuals

8. **Examine** the painting shown on page 339. Explain whether or not you think this is a realistic depiction of Marie Antoinette before her execution, or whether the artist is promoting a particular version of her death.

Writing About History

9. **Expository Writing** Propaganda is the spreading of information for the purpose of helping or injuring a cause. How does the decree of universal mobilization quoted on page 342 fit the definition of propaganda? Use examples from the decree to support your argument in an essay.

SECTION 2 ASSESSMENT

1. Key terms are in blue.
2. Georges Danton *(p. 337);* Jean-Paul Marat *(p. 338);* Jacobins *(p. 338);* Committee of Public Safety *(p. 339);* Maximilien Robespierre *(p. 339);* Reign of Terror *(p. 339)*
3. See chapter maps.
4. Girondins: represented provinces, feared radical mobs, moderate toward king; Mountain: represented city, more radical group, wanted to execute king
5. Austria, Prussia, Spain, Portugal, Britain, Dutch Republic, Russia; new French army repelled invasion
6. Answers will vary.
7. Answers may include: During: Reign of Terror; dechristianization; After: more moderate leaders; churches reopen
8. Answers will vary.
9. It is designed to make people want to join the struggle, which is depicted as being pure and selfless. Examples will vary.

History *through Art*

Answer: The Directory's era was one of corruption and graft. It was faced with political enemies, was unable to find a solution to the country's economic problems, was still carrying on wars left from the Committee of Public Safety, and it relied increasingly on the military to maintain its power. Napoleon was a successful and popular general.

Reading Check

Answer: The new government had a legislative assembly with two chambers and an executive committee called the Directory.

Reading Essentials and Study Guide 11–2

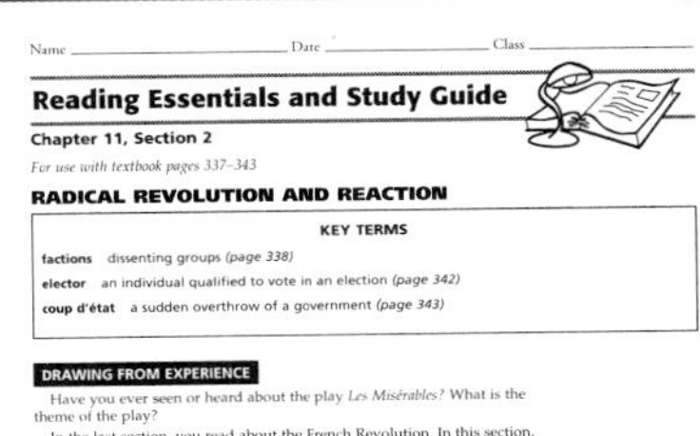
Name ______ Date ______ Class ______

Reading Essentials and Study Guide

Chapter 11, Section 2

For use with textbook pages 337–343

RADICAL REVOLUTION AND REACTION

KEY TERMS

factions dissenting groups *(page 338)*

elector an individual qualified to vote in an election *(page 342)*

coup d'état a sudden overthrow of a government *(page 343)*

DRAWING FROM EXPERIENCE

Have you ever seen or heard about the play *Les Misérables?* What is the theme of the play?

In the last section, you read about the French Revolution. In this section, you will learn how radical groups and leaders began to control the revolution and how other countries reacted to the revolution.

Reteaching Activity

Ask students to discuss the significance of the National Convention, the death of Louis XVI, Jacobins, Robespierre, Reign of Terror, and Directory. **L1**

4 CLOSE

Ask students to list and evaluate the effects of the French Revolution. **L2**

Social Studies Skillbuilder

TEACH

Interpreting Graphs Count the number of students who usually travel to school on foot, by bicycle, on a school bus, by public transportation, or by car. Note the results on the chalkboard and call on volunteers to convert these numbers into percentages. Next, draw a circle on the chalkboard and explain that the circle represents the whole class, or 100 percent. Divide the circle into sections to represent the percentages of the subgroups. Have students note how the circle illustrates the relationship of the parts to the whole. **L1**

Additional Practice

Skills Reinforcement Activity 11

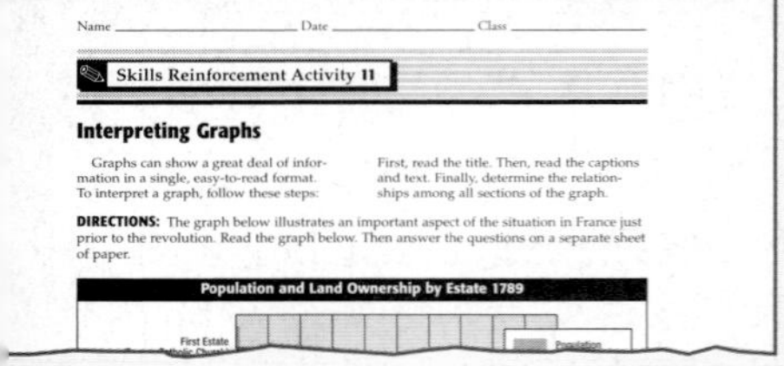

Name ______ Date ______ Class ______

Skills Reinforcement Activity 11

Interpreting Graphs

Graphs can show a great deal of information in a single, easy-to-read format. To interpret a graph, follow these steps: First, read the title. Then, read the captions and text. Finally, determine the relationships among all sections of the graph.

DIRECTIONS: The graph below illustrates an important aspect of the situation in France just prior to the revolution. Read the graph below. Then answer the questions on a separate sheet of paper.

Population and Land Ownership by Estate 1789

First Estate

GLENCOE TECHNOLOGY

CD-ROM
Glencoe Skillbuilder Interactive Workbook CD-ROM, Level 2

This interactive CD-ROM reinforces student mastery of essential social studies skills.

Social Studies Skillbuilder

Interpreting Graphs

Why Learn This Skill?

Graphs are one method of illustrating dates, facts, and figures. With a graph, you can compare change or differences easily. For example, your parents say you are spending too much money on clothes. You disagree, but they show you a bar graph of your weekly expenses. The bar for each week shows how the money you have spent on clothes is higher than the week before. With a quick glance, you immediately see that they are right. You decide to make a graph of your own to show them how your allowance is not keeping up with inflation.

Learning the Skill

There are basically three types of graphs:

- **Circle graphs** They look like a pizza that has been divided into different size slices. They are useful for showing comparisons and percentages.
- **Bar graphs** Individual bars are drawn for each item being graphed. The length of the bars easily illustrates differences or changes over time.
- **Line graph** Each item is indicated by a point on the graph. The points are then connected by a line. You can tell how values have changed by whether the line is going up or down.

Most graphs also use words to identify or label information. The steps below will help you interpret graphs.

- **Read the title** If the graph is called "Randy's Weekly Clothing Expenses," then it will be plotting Randy's expenses every week.
- **Read the captions and text** In Randy's graph, each bar would be captioned with a weekly date, and the amounts that each bar represents would be clearly marked.
- **Determine the relationships among all sections of the graph** By looking at each bar, you can see the amount spent for that week. By comparing the bars with each other, you can see how Randy's expenses have changed from week to week.

Periods of Revolution and Empire in France, 1789–1815

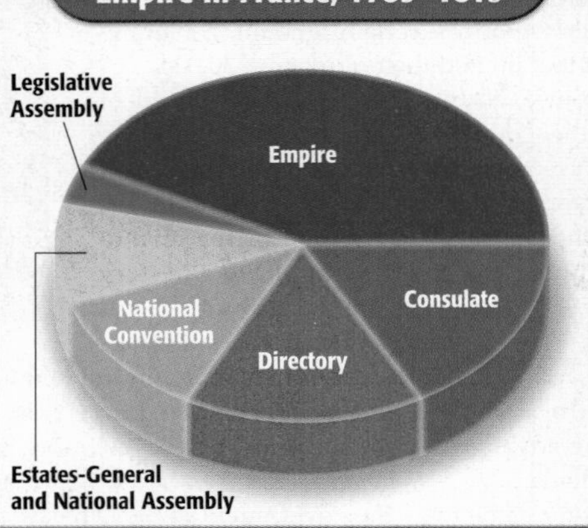

Practicing the Skill

The circle graph above visually compares the length of time for different periods discussed in this chapter. Study the graph and answer the following:

1. What was the longest of the six periods of the French Revolution?
2. What was the shortest of the six periods?
3. About what percentage of the total time did Napoleon rule France (he ruled during the Consulate and Empire)?
4. About what percentage of the time did the Directory rule?

Applying the Skill

Pick a recent day and make a list of all of your activities in a 24-hour period. Now create a circle graph that shows the division of the day.

Glencoe's **Skillbuilder Interactive Workbook, Level 2,** provides instruction and practice in key social studies skills.

344

ANSWERS TO PRACTICING THE SKILL

1. The Empire was the longest of the six periods.
2. The Legislative Assembly was the shortest period.
3. Napoleon ruled approximately 55 to 60 percent of the time during the Consulate and Empire.
4. The Directory ruled for approximately 17 percent (one-sixth) of this time.

Applying the Skill: Students will make circle graphs. Ask students to share their graphs with the class, either in small groups or with the entire class, depending upon time constraints.

SECTION 3 The Age of Napoleon

Guide to Reading

Main Ideas
- Napoleon built and lost an empire.
- Nationalism spread as a result of the French Revolution.
- Napoleon was exiled first to Elba, and then to St. Helena, where he died.

Key Terms
consulate, nationalism

People to Identify
Napoleon Bonaparte, Anne-Louise-Germaine de Staël, Duke of Wellington

Places to Locate
Corsica, Moscow, Elba, Waterloo

Preview Questions
1. Why did Napoleon want to stop British goods from reaching Europe?
2. What were two reasons for the collapse of Napoleon's empire?

Reading Strategy
Summarizing Information In a table like the one below, list the achievements of Napoleon's rule.

Achievements of Napoleon's Rule

Preview of Events

1790 · 1800 · 1810 · 1820

- **1799** Napoleon takes part in coup d'état
- **1804** Napoleon is crowned emperor
- **1805** French are defeated at Trafalgar
- **1815** Napoleon is defeated at Waterloo

Voices from the Past

Napoleon Bonaparte

Napoleon once wrote:

❝But let that impatiently awaited savior give a sudden sign of his existence, and the people's instinct will divine him and call upon him. The obstacles are smoothed before his steps, and a whole great nation, flying to see him pass, will seem to be saying: 'Here is the man.' . . . A consecutive series of great actions never is the result of chance and luck; it always is the product of planning and genius. Great men are rarely known to fail in their most perilous enterprises. . . . Is it because they are lucky that they become great? No, but being great, they have been able to master luck.❞

—*The Mind of Napoleon*, J. Christopher Herold, 1955

Napoleon possessed an overwhelming sense of his own importance. He was convinced that he was the man of destiny who would save the French people.

The Rise of Napoleon

Napoleon Bonaparte dominated French and European history from 1799 to 1815. In a sense, he brought the French Revolution to an end in 1799, but he was also a child of the revolution. The French Revolution made possible his rise first in the military and then to supreme power in France. Indeed, Napoleon once said, "I am the revolution." He never ceased to remind the French that they owed to him the preservation of all that was beneficial in the revolutionary program.

Early Life Napoleon was born in 1769 in **Corsica,** an island in the Mediterranean Sea, only a few months after France had annexed the island. He was the son of a lawyer whose family came from the Florentine nobility. The young Napoleon

1 FOCUS

Section Overview

This section chronicles Napoleon's rise to power, his victories, and his ultimate defeat.

BELLRINGER
Skillbuilder Activity

 Project transparency and have students answer questions.

 Available as a blackline master.

Daily Focus Skills Transparency 11–3

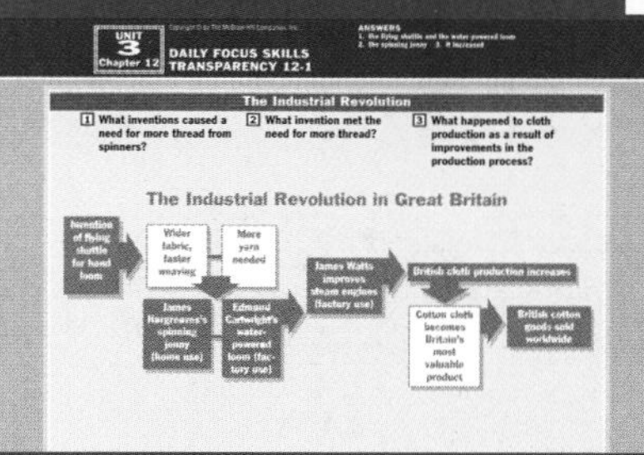

Guide to Reading

Answers to Graphic: peace with the Catholic Church; codification of laws; development of capable bureaucracy; principles of the French Revolution spread throughout Europe

Preteaching Vocabulary: Discuss the meaning of *nationalism* and have students come up with a list of examples that illustrate the spirit of nationalism in the United States today. **L1**

SECTION RESOURCES

Reproducible Masters
- Reproducible Lesson Plan 11–3
- Daily Lecture and Discussion Notes 11–3
- Guided Reading Activity 11–3
- Section Quiz 11–3
- Reading Essentials and Study Guide 11–3

Transparencies
- Daily Focus Skills Transparency 11–3

Multimedia
- Interactive Tutor Self-Assessment CD-ROM
- ExamView® Pro Testmaker CD-ROM
- Presentation Plus! CD-ROM

2 TEACH

Reading Check

Answer: energy, charm, ability to make quick decisions, keen intelligence, ease with words, and supreme confidence in himself

Picturing **History**

Answer: Napoleon had made an agreement with the pope recognizing Catholicism as the religion of the majority of the French people.

Daily Lecture and Discussion Notes 11–3

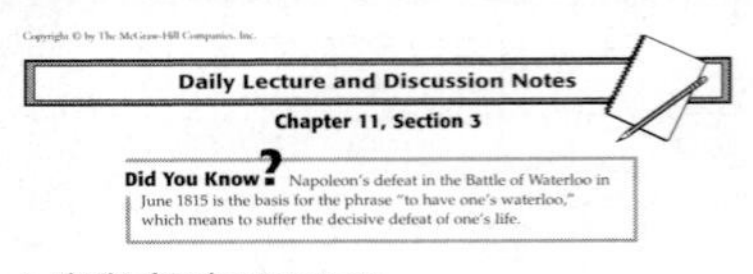

Daily Lecture and Discussion Notes

Chapter 11, Section 3

Did You Know? Napoleon's defeat in the Battle of Waterloo in June 1815 is the basis for the phrase "to have one's waterloo," which means to suffer the decisive defeat of one's life.

I. **The Rise of Napoleon** *(pages 345–346)*

A. **Napoleon Bonaparte** dominated European history from 1799 to 1815. He never stopped reminding the French that he preserved what was beneficial in the revolutionary program.

B. Napoleon was born in 1769 on the Mediterranean island of **Corsica.** He went to a military school in France on a royal scholarship. In 1785 he was commissioned as a lieutenant in the French army.

C. For the next seven years Napoleon educated himself in philosophy and the world's great military campaigns. The French Revolution and the European wars that followed it gave him the chance to use his knowledge.

D. By the age of only 25, Napoleon was made a brigadier general by the Committee of Public Safety. He won a series of victories as the French commander against armies in Italy.

E. Napoleon's combination of intelligence, charm, wit, and decisiveness allowed him to win the support of his troops and other people. He returned to France in 1797 as a conquering hero. Napoleon's attempt to strike at Britain by taking Egypt and threatening India failed. In 1799 he returned to Paris.

F. Napoleon took part in the coup d'état that overthrew the Directory. Even though in theory France was a republic, Napoleon held absolute power as the first consul of a new government called the **consulate.** He appointed members of the bureaucracy, controlled the army, conducted foreign affairs, and influenced the legislature.

G. In 1802 Napoleon made himself consul for life, and in 1804 he had himself crowned Emperor Napoleon I.

Discussion Question

Besides harming Britain at the behest of the French government, what might have attracted Napoleon to invade Egypt? *(He wanted to make it a part of the empire he planned to build. Napoleon saw himself as a new Roman caesar.)*

Critical Thinking

Ask students to discuss the apparent contradiction between Napoleon having himself crowned emperor and his creation of the Napoleonic Code, which recognized the principle of equality of all citizens. **L2**

received a royal scholarship to study at a military school in France.

Napoleon's education in French military schools led to his commission in 1785 as a lieutenant in the French army. He was not well liked by his fellow officers because he was short, spoke with an Italian accent, and had little money.

For the next seven years, Napoleon read the works of the philosophes and educated himself in military matters by studying the campaigns of great military leaders from the past. The revolution and the European war that followed gave him new opportunities to use his knowledge.

Military Successes Napoleon rose quickly through the ranks of the French army. In 1792, he became a captain. Two years later, at the age of only 25, he was made a brigadier general by the Committee of Public Safety. In 1796, he was made commander of the French armies in Italy, where he used speed, deception, and surprise to win a series of victories.

Throughout his Italian campaigns, Napoleon won the confidence of his men with his energy, charm, and ability to make quick decisions. These qualities, combined with his keen intelligence, ease with words, and supreme confidence in himself, enabled him to influence people and win their firm support.

In 1797, Napoleon returned to France as a conquering hero. He was given command of an army in training to invade Britain. Knowing that the French were not ready for such an invasion, Napoleon proposed instead to strike indirectly at Britain by taking Egypt and threatening India, a major source of British wealth.

The British, however, controlled the seas. By 1799, they had cut off Napoleon's army in Egypt. Seeing certain defeat, Napoleon abandoned his army and returned to Paris.

Consul and Emperor In Paris, Napoleon took part in the coup d'état that overthrew the government of the Directory. He was only 30 years old at the time. With the coup d'état of 1799, a new government—called the **consulate**—was proclaimed. Although theoretically it was a republic, in fact Napoleon held absolute power.

As first consul, Napoleon controlled the entire government. He appointed members of the bureaucracy, controlled the army, conducted foreign affairs, and influenced the legislature.

In 1802, Napoleon was made consul for life. Two years later, he crowned himself Emperor Napoleon I.

Reading Check **Describing** What personal qualities did Napoleon possess that gained him popular support?

Picturing **History**

In this painting, Napoleon is shown crowning his wife Josephine empress. During his own coronation, Napoleon seized the crown from Pope Pius VII and placed it on his own head. How had Napoleon earlier made peace with the Catholic Church?

CRITICAL THINKING ACTIVITY

Analyzing Napoleon is the archetype for the "great man on a horse," the autocratic, popular leader who will take charge if the people give him absolute authority. Mussolini, Franco, Hitler, Pinochet, and countless other leaders have followed in Napoleon's footsteps. Ask students to analyze how Napoleon's influence on subsequent leaders may have impacted students personally. For example, were any of their ancestors involved in World War II? Ask students to evaluate how the style of leadership in the United States compares to the model of the autocratic leader. **L1**

Napoleon's Domestic Policies

Napoleon once claimed that he had preserved the gains of the revolution for the French people. The ideal of republican liberty had, of course, been destroyed by Napoleon's takeover of power. However, were the ideals of the French Revolution maintained in other ways? An examination of his domestic policies will enable us to judge the truth or falsehood of Napoleon's claim.

Peace with the Church One of Napoleon's first moves at home was to establish peace with the oldest enemy of the revolution, the Catholic Church. Napoleon himself had no personal religious faith. He was an eighteenth-century believer in reason who regarded religion at most as a convenience. In Egypt, he called himself a Muslim; in France, a Catholic. However, he saw the need to restore stability to France, and most of the French were Catholic.

In 1801, Napoleon made an agreement with the pope. The agreement recognized Catholicism as the religion of a majority of the French people. In return, the pope agreed not to ask for the return of the church lands seized in the revolution.

With this agreement, the Catholic Church was no longer an enemy of the French government. At the same time, those who had bought church lands during the revolution became avid supporters of the Napoleonic regime.

Codification of the Laws Napoleon's most famous domestic achievement was his codification of the laws. Before the revolution, France did not have a single set of laws but rather had almost 300 different legal systems. During the revolution, efforts were made to prepare a single law code for the entire nation. However, it remained for Napoleon to bring the work to completion in seven codes of law.

The most important of the codes was the **Civil Code,** or Napoleonic Code. This code preserved most of the gains of the revolution by recognizing the principle of the equality of all citizens before the law, the right of the individual to choose a profession, religious toleration, and the abolition of serfdom and feudalism. Property rights continued to be carefully protected, and the interests of employers were safeguarded by outlawing trade unions and strikes.

The rights of some people were strictly curtailed by the Civil Code, however. During the radical phase of the French Revolution, new laws had made divorce an easy process for both husbands and wives and had allowed all children (including daughters) to inherit property equally. Napoleon's Civil Code undid these laws.

French marriage ceremony, nineteenth century

Divorce was still allowed, but the Civil Code made it more difficult for women to obtain divorces. Women were now "less equal than men" in other ways as well. When they married, their property was brought under the control of their husbands. In lawsuits, they were treated as minors, and their testimony was regarded as less reliable than that of men.

A New Bureaucracy Napoleon also developed a powerful, centralized administrative machine. He worked hard to develop a bureaucracy of capable officials. Early on, the regime showed that it cared little whether the expertise of officials had been gained in royal or revolutionary bureaucracies. Promotion, whether in civil or military offices, was to be based not on rank or birth but on ability only. Opening government careers to individuals based on their ability was one change the middle class had wanted before the revolution.

Napoleon also created a new aristocracy based on merit in the state service. Napoleon created 3,263 nobles between 1808 and 1814. Nearly 60 percent were military officers, while the remainder came from the upper ranks of the civil service and other state and local officials. Socially, only 22 percent of Napoleon's aristocracy came from the nobility of the old regime. Almost 60 percent were middle class in origin.

Guided Reading Activity 11–3

Name ________ Date ________ Class ________

Guided Reading Activity 11-3

The Age of Napoleon

DIRECTIONS: Fill in the blanks below as you read Section 3.

Napoleon Bonaparte dominated **(1)** ________ and **(2)** ________ history from 1799 to 1815. Napoleon once said, **(3)** "________." He was born in 1769 on the island of **(4)** ________ in the Mediterranean Sea. His education in French military schools led to his commission in 1785 as a **(5)** ________ in the French army. At the age of only 25, Napoleon was made a brigadier general by the **(6)** ________. In 1796, he was made commander of the French armies in **(7)** ________ where he won a series of victories.

Although theoretically the new government of 1799 was a republic, Napoleon held **(8)** ________ power. In 1802, Napoleon was made **(9)** ________ for life and two years later he had himself crowned **(10)** ________ Napoleon I.

Napoleon was a believer in reason who regarded religion to be at most a **(11)** ________. But in Egypt he called himself a **(12)** ________; in France, a **(13)** ________. In an agreement made with the Pope, **(14)** ________ was recognized as the religion of a majority of the French people. Napoleon's most famous domestic achievement was his **(15)** ________ of the laws. The most important of the codes was the **(16)** ________, or Napoleonic Code. This code preserved most of the **(17)** ________ of the revolution. However, Napoleon also destroyed some revolutionary ideals through **(18)** ________. He shut down 60 of 73 French **(19)** ________.

Two major reasons help to explain the rapid decline of Napoleon's Grand Empire: the **(20)** ________ of Great Britain and the force of **(21)** ________. The beginning of Napoleon's downfall came in 1812 with his disastrous invasion of **(22)** ________.

204

Writing Activity

Ask students to research and write an essay on one of the following two topics. They can either: 1) assess the ways in which Napoleon fulfilled the ideals of the French Revolution; or 2) assess the ways in which Napoleon betrayed the ideals of the revolution. Have students alternate the reading of their essays between the two topics. You might also wish to stage a class debate on this topic. **L3**

Enrich

Ask students to list and discuss possible reasons for the Catholic Church's decision to give up its claim to lands in France in 1801. **Ask: How did Napoleon benefit from this agreement?** *(helped bring stability, put Catholic Church on his side, new landholders supported him)* **L1**

COOPERATIVE LEARNING ACTIVITY

Creating an Oral Report Organize the class into groups to research the changes Napoleon brought to France and whether these changes are still in effect. Assign each group one of the following topics: restructuring of government, educational system, financial system, legal system (Napoleonic Code), and Concordat of 1801, the agreement Napoleon made with the pope. Have each group present an oral report of its findings to the class. Encourage groups to use charts, graphs, and pictures to illustrate their reports. Some students may wish to make a multimedia presentation using software programs suitable to the project. After groups have given their reports, encourage a class discussion about Napoleon's impact on France. **L2 L3**

CHAPTER 11
Section 3, 345–351

Reading Check

Answer: It was the most important of the seven codes of law that replaced almost 300 different legal systems in France.

Charting Activity

Have students create a chart that lists the lands of Napoleon's Grand Empire. Columns should have the following headings: "French Empire" *(France, half of Italy)*; "Dependent states" *(Spain, Holland, Italy, Swiss Republic, the Grand Duchy of Warsaw, and Confederation of the Rhine)*; and "Allied states" *(Prussia, Austria, Russia, and Sweden)*. **L1**

Critical Thinking

Napoleon tried to spread the principles of the French Revolution throughout his empire, including the principles of equality, religious toleration, and economic freedom. Ask students to identify which principle Napoleon is emphasizing in his advice to his brother Jerome. Have students refer specifically to his words to support their answers. *(equality; says commoners should have the same rights as nobles, hierarchy should be abolished)* **L2**

Writing Activity

Have students write a brief essay in which they analyze the French Empire by describing its political and economic impact on other European states. **L1**

Preserver of the Revolution? In his domestic policies, then, Napoleon did preserve aspects of the revolution. The Civil Code preserved the equality of all citizens before the law. The concept of opening government careers to more people was another gain of the revolution that he retained.

On the other hand, Napoleon destroyed some revolutionary ideals. Liberty was replaced by a despotism that grew increasingly arbitrary, in spite of protests by such citizens as the prominent writer **Anne-Louise-Germaine de Staël.** Napoleon shut down 60 of France's 73 newspapers. He insisted that all manuscripts be subjected to government scrutiny before they were published. Even the mail was opened by government police.

Reading Check **Evaluating** What was the significance of Napoleon's Civil Code?

Napoleon's Empire

Napoleon is, of course, known less for his domestic policies than for his military leadership. His conquests began soon after he rose to power.

Building the Empire When Napoleon became consul in 1799, France was at war with a European coalition of Russia, Great Britain, and Austria. Napoleon realized the need for a pause in the war. He remarked that "the French Revolution is not finished so long as the scourge of war lasts. . . . I want peace, as much to settle the present French government, as to save the world from chaos."

Napoleon achieved a peace treaty in 1802, but it did not last long. War was renewed in 1803 with Britain. Soon, Britain was joined by Austria, Russia, and Prussia. In a series of battles at Ulm, Austerlitz, Jena, and Eylau from 1805 to 1807, Napoleon's Grand Army defeated the Austrian, Prussian, and Russian armies. Napoleon now had the opportunity to create a new European order.

From 1807 to 1812, Napoleon was the master of Europe. His Grand Empire was composed of three major parts: the French Empire, dependent states, and allied states.

The French Empire was the inner core of the Grand Empire. It consisted of an enlarged France extending to the Rhine in the east and including the western half of Italy north of Rome.

Dependent states were kingdoms under the rule of Napoleon's relatives. These came to include Spain, Holland, the kingdom of Italy, the Swiss Republic, the Grand Duchy of Warsaw, and the Confederation of the Rhine (a union of all German states except Austria and Prussia).

Allied states were those defeated by Napoleon and forced to join his struggle against Britain. The allied states included Prussia, Austria, Russia, and Sweden.

Spreading the Principles of the Revolution Within his empire, Napoleon sought to spread some of the principles of the French Revolution, including legal equality, religious toleration, and economic freedom. He explained to his brother Jerome after he had made Jerome king of Westphalia:

> "What the peoples of Germany desire most impatiently is that talented commoners should have the same right to your esteem and to public employments as the nobles, that any trace of serfdom and of an intermediate hierarchy between the sovereign and the lowest class of the people should be completely abolished. The benefits of the Code Napoleon, the publicity of judicial procedure, the creation of juries must be so many distinguishing marks of your monarchy. . . . The peoples of Germany, the peoples of France, of Italy, of Spain all desire equality and liberal ideas. . . . the buzzing of the privileged classes is contrary to the general opinion. Be a constitutional king."

People In History

Anne-Louise-Germaine de Staël
1766–1817—French writer

Anne-Louise-Germaine de Staël was a prominent writer of the revolutionary and Napoleonic eras in France. She established a salon for the powerful that lasted from 1790 until 1804. It was said of her that she was "so spoiled by admiration for her wit that it [would] be hard to make her realize her shortcomings." During the Reign of Terror, she helped friends escape France. She also left France but returned in 1795.

Although she at first supported Napoleon, she clashed repeatedly with him. She once asked him, "Who was the greatest woman of history?" Napoleon responded, "The one who had the most children." Eventually, she denounced Napoleon's rule as tyrannical. Napoleon banned her books in France and exiled her to the German states, where she continued to write.

MEETING INDIVIDUAL NEEDS

Auditory/Musical Tell students that the composer Beethoven had initially greatly admired Napoleon, seeing the general as the embodiment of the spirit of the French Revolution. Beethoven originally dedicated his Third Symphony to Napoleon. He retracted the dedication when Napoleon proclaimed himself emperor, renaming the work "Heroic Symphony to celebrate the memory of a great man." It has become known as the *Eroica*. Have students who are strong auditory/musical learners listen to the Third Symphony. Have them select segments that they feel especially express the spirit of Napoleonic or revolutionary France and play these for the rest of the class. **L1** ELL

From 1807 to 1812, Napoleon controlled a vast empire in Europe.

1. **Interpreting Maps** Compare the map of Napoleon's Grand Empire to the map of the Roman Empire shown on page 69 of your text. How were these two empires similar, and how were they different? What geographic factors could help to account for these similarities and differences?
2. **Applying Geography Skills** Examine the locations of the states that were allied against Napoleon in 1812. What geographic factors would have helped these states to remain independent from Napoleon's control?

In the inner core and dependent states of his Grand Empire, Napoleon tried to destroy the old order. The nobility and clergy everywhere in these states lost their special privileges. Napoleon decreed equality of opportunity with offices open to talents, equality before the law, and religious toleration. The spread of French revolutionary principles was an important factor in the development of liberal traditions in these countries.

Reading Check **Identifying** What were the three parts of Napoleon's Grand Empire?

The European Response

Like Hitler 130 years later, Napoleon hoped that his Grand Empire would last for centuries. Like Hitler's empire, it collapsed almost as rapidly as it had been formed. Two major reasons help to explain this: the survival of Great Britain and the force of nationalism.

Britain's Survival Britain's survival was due primarily to its sea power. As long as Britain ruled the waves, it was almost invulnerable to military attack.

Reading Check

Answer: the French Empire, dependent states, and allied states

Geography Skills

Answers:

1. Roman Empire extended further to the east, water not a primary barrier to expansion; Napoleon limited by British navy; Both: Germany, Russia limited expansion-due to factors including climate
2. Great Britain: sea; Sweden, Russia, Portugal: distance, water

Who?What?Where?When?

Napoleonic Code France exported the Napoleonic Code to its empire in Europe and its colonies in North America. Today, Louisiana, once part of France's lands in America, is the only state with laws still based on the Napoleonic Code.

Critical Thinking

Have students label two columns "Positive" and "Negative" on a sheet of paper. Ask students to list Napoleon's actions as both a government leader and a general, placing the specific actions under the appropriate heading. Some actions may be viewed as both positive and negative. *(Example: Positive: replaced turmoil of revolution with orderly government; Negative: put himself as head of a dictatorship.)* **L3**

COOPERATIVE LEARNING ACTIVITY

Creating a Newspaper Have the class work together to plan the front page of the *Napoleonic Times,* a newspaper chronicling the events of Napoleon's rule, beginning in 1799. After students have read Section 3, organize them into groups and have each group list the stories and visuals they would put on the front page. Students may get ideas for visuals from illustrations in Chapter 11. Groups can decide which event gets the top headline and where the other lead articles and visuals should go. Then, as a class, have groups decide on final placement of stories and visuals. **L2**

For grading this activity, refer to the ***Performance Assessment Activities*** booklet.

Reading Check

Answer: Since Britain is an island, it was only possible to invade by sea, and its strong navy provided defense against invasion.

Writing Activity

Have students write a diary entry and draw an illustration from the viewpoint of a French soldier involved in the march toward Moscow or in the retreat from Russia. **L2** ELL

3 ASSESS

Assign Section 3 Assessment as homework or as an in-class activity.

Have students use **Interactive Tutor Self-Assessment CD-ROM.**

Section Quiz 11–3

Name ______ Date ______ Class ______

Chapter 11 Score

Section Quiz 11-3

DIRECTIONS: Matching Match each item in Column A with an item in Column B. Write the correct letters in the blanks. *(10 points each)*

Column A	Column B
____ 1. Napoleon's government after 1799	A. allied states
____ 2. Napoleon's unified law system	B. the consulate
____ 3. Napoleon's birthplace	C. nationalism
____ 4. Napoleon's allies against Britain	D. Corsica
____ 5. unique cultural identity of a people	E. Civil Code

DIRECTIONS: Multiple Choice In the blank, write the letter of the choice that best completes the statement or answers the question. *(10 points each)*

____ 6. Napoleon's Continental System was designed to

Reading Essentials and Study Guide 11–3

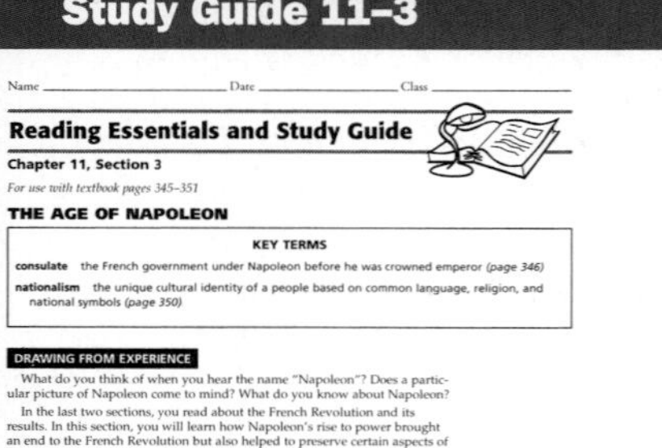

Name ______ Date ______ Class ______

Reading Essentials and Study Guide

Chapter 11, Section 3

For use with textbook pages 345–351

THE AGE OF NAPOLEON

KEY TERMS

consulate the French government under Napoleon before he was crowned emperor *(page 346)*

nationalism the unique cultural identity of a people based on common language, religion, and national symbols *(page 350)*

DRAWING FROM EXPERIENCE

What do you think of when you hear the name "Napoleon"? Does a particular picture of Napoleon come to mind? What do you know about Napoleon?

In the last two sections, you read about the French Revolution and its results. In this section, you will learn how Napoleon's rise to power brought an end to the French Revolution but also helped to preserve certain aspects of the revolution.

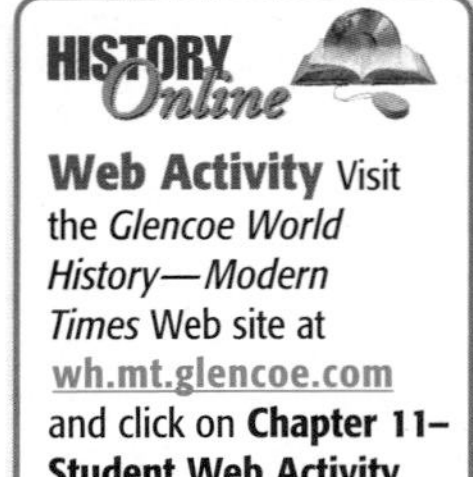

Web Activity Visit the *Glencoe World History—Modern Times* Web site at wh.mt.glencoe.com and click on **Chapter 11–Student Web Activity** to learn more about Napoleon Bonaparte.

Napoleon hoped to invade Britain and even collected ships for the invasion. The British navy's decisive defeat of a combined French-Spanish fleet at Trafalgar in 1805 destroyed any thought of an invasion, however.

Napoleon then turned to his Continental System to defeat Britain. The aim of the Continental System was to stop British goods from reaching the European continent to be sold there. By weakening Britain economically, Napoleon would destroy its ability to wage war.

The Continental System, too, failed. Allied states resented being told by Napoleon that they could not trade with the British. Some began to cheat. Others resisted. Furthermore, new markets in the Middle East and in Latin America gave Britain new outlets for its goods. Indeed, by 1809–1810, British overseas exports were at near-record highs.

Nationalism A second important factor in the defeat of Napoleon was nationalism. **Nationalism** is the unique cultural identity of a people based on common language, religion, and national symbols. The spirit of French nationalism had made possible the mass armies of the revolutionary and Napoleonic eras. However, Napoleon's spread of the principles of the French Revolution beyond France indirectly brought a spread of nationalism as well.

The French aroused nationalism in two ways. First, they were hated as oppressors. This hatred stirred the patriotism of others in opposition to the French. Second, the French showed the people of Europe what nationalism was and what a nation in arms could do. It was a lesson not lost on other peoples and rulers.

Reading Check **Explaining** Why did being a sea power help Britain to survive an attack by the French?

The Fall of Napoleon

The beginning of Napoleon's downfall came in 1812 with his invasion of Russia. Within only a few years, the fall was complete.

Disaster in Russia The Russians had refused to remain in the Continental System, leaving Napoleon with little choice but to invade. He knew the risks in invading such a large country. However, he also knew that if the Russians were allowed to challenge the Continental System unopposed, others would soon follow suit.

In June 1812, a Grand Army of over six hundred thousand men entered Russia. Napoleon's hopes for victory depended on a quick defeat of the Russian armies. The Russian forces, however, refused to give battle. They retreated for hundreds of miles. As they retreated, they burned their own villages and countryside to keep Napoleon's army from finding food. When the Russians did stop to fight at Borodino, Napoleon's forces won an indecisive and costly victory.

When the remaining Grand Army arrived in **Moscow,** they found the city ablaze. Lacking food

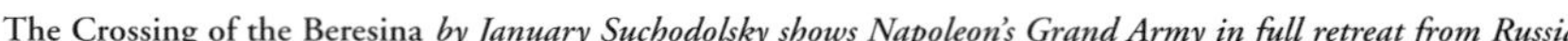

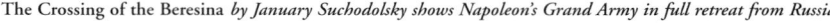

The Crossing of the Beresina *by January Suchodolsky shows Napoleon's Grand Army in full retreat from Russia.*

INTERDISCIPLINARY CONNECTIONS ACTIVITY

Family and Consumer Sciences During the years of the French Empire, clothing and furniture were made in what became known as the Empire style. Have students prepare an oral report about this style, using reference material (from the school or local library) on the history of fashion and furniture. Encourage students to find out how this style became popular, if it spread to other countries, if it influenced other styles, and if it remained popular in later years. Ask students to make sketches or use pictures showing the Empire style in their reports. **L1** ELL

What If...

Napoleon had won at Waterloo?

Napoleon dominated much of the world stage until his loss at Waterloo. Waterloo was a close battle against the Duke of Wellington and the allied forces. Military strategists speculate that had Napoleon's commanders been better, Napoleon might have won the battle.

Consider the Consequences Consider Napoleon's impact on history had he defeated Wellington. Explain why this victory might have marshaled enough support for Napoleon to have resumed his rule as emperor.

and supplies, Napoleon abandoned Moscow late in October and began the "Great Retreat" across Russia. The retreat proceeded in terrible winter conditions. Only forty thousand out of the original army managed to arrive back in Poland in January 1813.

This military disaster led other European states to rise up and attack the crippled French army. Paris was captured in March 1814. Napoleon was soon sent into exile on the island of **Elba,** off the coast of Tuscany. The Bourbon monarchy was restored to France in the person of Louis XVIII, brother of the executed king, Louis XVI.

The Final Defeat The new king had little support, and Napoleon, bored on the island of Elba, slipped back into France. Troops were sent to capture him. Napoleon opened his coat and addressed them: "Soldiers of the 5th regiment, I am your Emperor. . . . If there is a man among you [who] would kill his Emperor, here I am!"

No one fired a shot. Shouting "Vive l'Empereur! Vive l'Empereur!" ("Long Live the Emperor! Long Live the Emperor!") the troops went over to his side. Napoleon made his entry into Paris in triumph on March 20, 1815.

The powers that had defeated Napoleon pledged once more to fight this person they called the "Enemy and Disturber of the Tranquility of the World." Napoleon raised yet another army and moved to attack the nearest allied forces stationed in Belgium.

At **Waterloo** in Belgium on June 18, 1815, Napoleon met a combined British and Prussian army under the **Duke of Wellington** and suffered a bloody defeat. This time, the victorious allies exiled him to St. Helena, a small island in the south Atlantic. Only Napoleon's memory would continue to haunt French political life.

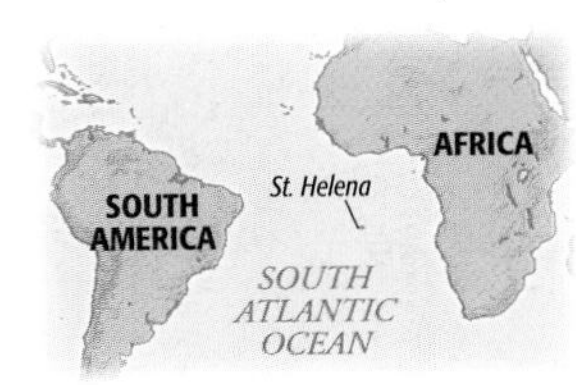

Reading Check **Examining** Why did Napoleon invade Russia?

SECTION 3 ASSESSMENT

Checking for Understanding

1. **Define** consulate, nationalism.
2. **Identify** Napoleon Bonaparte, Civil Code, Anne-Louise-Germaine de Staël, Duke of Wellington.
3. **Locate** Corsica, Moscow, Elba, Waterloo.
4. **Explain** how nationalism contributed to Napoleon's defeat. Be sure to discuss how French nationalism produced nationalism outside of France.
5. **List** the powers Napoleon exercised as first consul.

Critical Thinking

6. **Describe** How did the principles of the French Revolution spread throughout Europe?
7. **Sequencing Information** Using a diagram like the one below, identify the reasons for the rise and fall of Napoleon's Grand Empire.

Napoleon's Rise and Fall

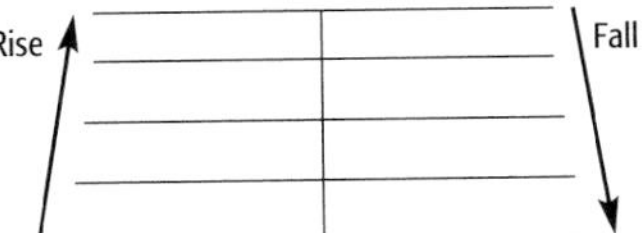

Analyzing Visuals

8. **Examine** the portrait shown on page 327 of your text. Napoleon commissioned this painting in 1800. How does David portray Napoleon, and why do you think Napoleon wanted artists to produce portraits like the one created by David?

Writing About History

9. **Persuasive Writing** In your opinion, was Napoleon an enlightened ruler or a tyrant? Write a position paper supporting your view. Be sure to include pertinent information about Napoleon's Civil Code.

What If...

Answers will vary. The French still had great loyalty to the man who brought their nation to such dominance. This victory might have been enough to quash the allied forces, and would have given Napoleon the time and the influence to collect more support.

Reading Check

Answer: Russia refused to remain in the Continental System. Napoleon feared that others would follow if Russia was not punished.

Reteaching Activity

Have students summarize Napoleon's greatest accomplishments and greatest defeats. *(accomplishments: legal and educational reforms; defeats: Trafalgar, retreat from Russia, Waterloo)* **L1** ELL

4 CLOSE

Lead students in a discussion of the important changes in Europe that were, or may have been, caused by Napoleon's rule in France. **L1**

SECTION 3 ASSESSMENT

1. Key terms are in blue.
2. Napoleon Bonaparte *(p. 345);* Civil Code *(p. 347);* Anne-Louise-Germaine de Staël *(p. 348);* Duke of Wellington *(p. 351)*
3. See chapter maps.
4. Conquered people were brought together in their hatred for their French oppressors.
5. appointed bureaucrats, controlled army, conducted foreign affairs, influenced legislature
6. Within his empire, Napoleon ended special privileges of nobility, clergy; appointed people based on talent; and decreed legal equality and religious toleration.
7. Rise: military genius, peace with Catholics, Civil Code, turned conquered into allies; Fall: nationalism, survival of Britain, failure of Continental System, invasion of Russia
8. as a romantic hero; answers will vary
9. Answers should be supported by logical arguments and facts from this chapter.

GLENCOE TECHNOLOGY

MindJogger Videoquiz

Use the **MindJogger Videoquiz** to review Chapter 11 content.

 Available in VHS.

Using Key Terms

1. relics of feudalism **2.** estates
3. bourgeoisie **4.** *sans-culottes*
5. factions **6.** coup d'état **7.** consulate
8. Nationalism

Reviewing Key Facts

9. document adopted in August 1789 by the National Assembly that proclaims freedom and equal rights for all

10. the fall of the Bastille

11. abolished the privileges of the aristocracy and clergy, adopted the Declaration of the Rights of Man, created a new constitution limiting the monarchy, seized control of Church property

12. Answers may include a radical element controlled the National Convention and condemned the king.

13. They murdered their opponents. Others feared Robespierre's power and had him executed.

14. He emerged as first consul, then consul for life, and finally emperor.

15. Other nations feared that the rebellions and uprisings would spread to their countries.

16. to weaken Britain economically so it could no longer wage war; Britain opened new trade markets and allies of France circumvented the system

17. Russian tactic of retreating and destroying areas caused French to starve; harsh winter further hurt French army.

Critical Thinking

18. National Assembly: limited monarchy; National Convention: more radical, executed the king; Robespierre: Committee of Public Safety; Directory: government by property owners. National Assembly was most democratic. Answers will vary but should be supported logically.

19. social contract, inalienable human rights, equality, religious toleration, separation of powers

Writing About History

20. Answers may include all three revolutions were reactions to oppressive regimes; American: overseas colonial power; French and Russian: despotic monarchy. The American and French revolutions were influenced by Enlightenment ideals, both issued Declarations, and citizens were willing to fight to gain freedom. The Russian Revolution promised to redistribute the nation's wealth to the people, but really replaced one repressive regime with an even more repressive one. The transitional period between the time of the revolution to the establishment of a stable government was peaceful in America, but marked by violence in both France and Russia.

CHAPTER 11 ASSESSMENT and ACTIVITIES

Chapter Summary

The French Revolution was one of the great turning points in history. The years from 1789 to 1815 in France were chaotic, and change came in unexpected ways. The chart below will help you understand and remember some of the major events of this time and the changes they caused.

The French Revolution

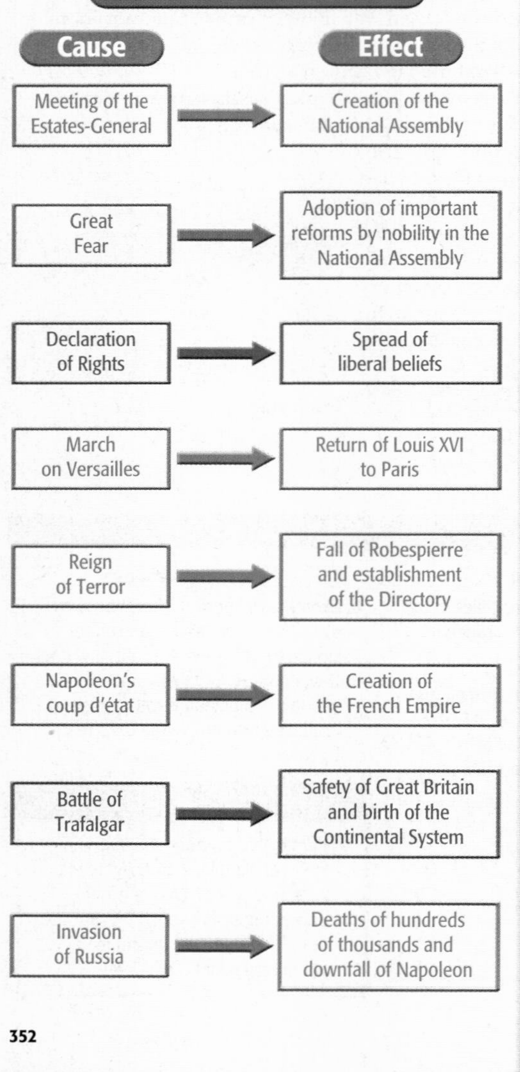

Cause
Effect
Meeting of the Estates-General
Creation of the National Assembly
Great Fear
Adoption of important reforms by nobility in the National Assembly
Declaration of Rights
Spread of liberal beliefs
March on Versailles
Return of Louis XVI to Paris
Reign of Terror
Fall of Robespierre and establishment of the Directory
Napoleon's coup d'état
Creation of the French Empire
Battle of Trafalgar
Safety of Great Britain and birth of the Continental System
Invasion of Russia
Deaths of hundreds of thousands and downfall of Napoleon

Using Key Terms

1. Aristocratic privileges, or ______, were obligations of the French peasants to local landlords.
2. From the period of the Middle Ages until the creation of the French Republic, France's population was divided into three orders or ______.
3. Members of the French middle class, the ______, were part of the Third Estate.
4. Members of the Paris Commune were called ______ because of their clothing.
5. During the National Convention of 1792, dissenting groups or ______ disagreed over the fate of Louis XVI.
6. Napoleon seized power during an overthrow of the French government, which is called a ______.
7. In 1799, Napoleon controlled the ______, a new government in which Napoleon had absolute power.
8. ______ is the cultural identity of a people based on common language, religion, and national symbols.

Reviewing Key Facts

9. **Government** What was the Declaration of the Rights of Man and the Citizen?
10. **History** What event started the French Revolution?
11. **Government** What reforms did the National Assembly make between 1789 and 1791?
12. **History** Why was Louis XVI executed?
13. **Government** How did Robespierre and the Committee of Public Safety deal with opponents of the government? What was the effect of their policies?
14. **Government** How did Napoleon assume power in France and become emperor?
15. **Geography** How did the French Revolution lead to war with other European nations?
16. **Economics** What was the purpose of the Continental System? Did it succeed? Explain.
17. **History** Why was the French invasion of Russia a failure?

Critical Thinking

18. **Making Comparisons** Examine the different systems of government in France from 1789 to 1812. Which was the most democratic? Which form of government was the most effective and why?
19. **Evaluating** Evaluate which Enlightenment ideals affected the French Revolution.

Self-Check Quiz

Visit the *Glencoe World History—Modern Times* Web site at wh.mt.glencoe.com and click on **Chapter 11–Self-Check Quiz** to prepare for the Chapter Test.

Writing About History

20. **Expository Writing** Look ahead to Section 3 in Chapter 16. Compare and contrast the American, French, and Russian Revolutions. Consider their causes and effects and summarize the principles of each revolution regarding ideas such as democracy, liberty, separation of powers, equality, popular sovereignty, human rights, constitutionalism, and nationalism.

Analyzing Sources

Read the following quotation by Napoleon, then answer the questions below.

> "What the peoples of Germany desire most impatiently is that talented commoners should have the same right to your esteem and to public employments as the nobles, that any trace of serfdom and of an intermediate hierarchy between the sovereign and the lowest class of the people should be completely abolished. The benefits of the Code Napoleon, the publicity of judicial procedure, the creation of juries must be so many distinguishing marks of your monarchy."

21. What does Napoleon say that the people of Germany want and do not want?
22. What were Napoleon's views about how civil and military workers should be hired and promoted? Where in this quote does Napoleon refer to these views?

Applying Technology Skills

23. **Using the Internet** Use the Internet to do a keyword search for "Declaration of the Rights of Man." Identify the places where the ideals of liberty, equality, and fraternity are still being debated today. Are there places where these ideals are not being discussed and should be?

Making Decisions

24. Think about the execution of Robespierre. Why did the National Convention decide to execute Robespierre? Can you think of another solution that would have addressed their concerns?

NATIONAL GEOGRAPHIC **Reign of Terror, 1793–1794**

Analyzing Maps and Charts

Study the map above to answer the following questions.

25. What cities served as centers of execution?
26. Approximately how far from Paris were centers of execution established?
27. Research one of the towns on the map and write a brief essay that describes the impact of the Reign of Terror on the people who lived there.

The Princeton Review **Standardized Test Practice**

Directions: Choose the best answer to the following question.

The "Republic of Virtue" signaled that the French Revolution

F was controlled by royalists who supported King Louis XVI.

G established a long-lasting constitutional monarchy.

H became a centralized military force under Napoleon.

J grew more violent as extremists took control.

Test-Taking Tip: If you do not know the answer to a question, eliminate any answer choices that you know are incorrect. Then choose the best answer from the remaining choices.

HISTORY Online

Have students visit the Web site at wh.mt.glencoe.com to review Chapter 11 and take the Self-Check Quiz.

26. Toulon and Marseille are approximately 400 miles (644 km) from Paris; Bordeaux is approximately 300 miles (483 km); Angers and Arras are approximately 100 miles (161 km).
27. Essays should be concise and provide a bibliography of sources used in the research.

Standardized Test Practice

Answer: J

Answer Explanation: Review each answer with the students and have them list reasons why J is the best answer to this question.

Bonus Question ?

Ask: Why was the time ripe for revolution in France in 1789? *(widespread knowledge of Enlightenment ideas; example of the successful American Revolution; high national debt plus several poor harvests; indifference of ruling classes for plight of peasants and workers)*

Analyzing Sources

21. They want equality of all classes. They do not want serfdom or an intermediate hierarchy between the sovereign and the lowest classes.
22. Promotion was to be based not on birth but on ability; "talented commoners should have the same right to your esteem and to public employments as the nobles."

Applying Technology Skills

23. Answers will vary.

Making Decisions

24. Because he was getting too powerful and they feared his fanaticism; answers will vary.

Analyzing Maps and Charts

25. Arras, Paris, Angers, Nantes, Bordeaux, Lyon, Orange, Marseille, Toulon

World Literature

Block Schedule

Team Teaching This excerpt from *Candide* can be presented in a team-teaching context, in conjunction with English or Language Arts.

Candide

Historical Connection

Voltaire's first-hand observations of the Prussian Army served as the basis for this portion of *Candide.*

Background Information

Setting This excerpt satirizes the reign of Frederick the Great of Prussia, who increased the Prussian army to 200,000 men.

Characters Candide is the innocent wanderer who seems to fall from one catastrophe into another. Dr. Pangloss is his mentor and instructor, and Cunégonde is a beautiful princess who did not wish to marry him.

Plot Students need to be reminded that *Candide* is a satire in which Voltaire criticizes both nobility and inhumane cruelty. Some consider this piece a landmark for the ideals of the Enlightenment. Voltaire argues for freedom of thought, social justice, and religious tolerance throughout the work.

Literary Element *Candide* is a novel. Students may need assistance recognizing the excerpt's irony. A careful reading will put the piece in its proper historical perspective.

World Literature

from Candide

by Voltaire

Voltaire was born François-Marie Arouet on November 21, 1694. He assumed the pen name "Voltaire" in 1718. Voltaire was a critical and satiric writer who used his wit to attack both church and state. *Candide* is one of Voltaire's most brilliant and most well-known works.

Read to Discover

Candide has been taught that "everything is for the best." However, his adventures usually prove the opposite. Here, he has just been cast out of a castle. The "men in blue" he meets are army recruiters for Frederick the Great, king of Prussia, who was at war with the French when Voltaire wrote *Candide.* How can you tell that Voltaire is making fun of the Prussian king and his army?

Reader's Dictionary

bulwark: strong support or protection

summarily: done without delay or formality

Candide . . . dragged himself into the neighboring village, which was called Waldberghofftrarbkdikdorff; he was penniless, famished, and exhausted. At the door of a tavern he paused forlornly. Two men dressed in blue [Prussian soldiers] took note of him:

—Look, chum, said one of them, there's a likely young fellow of just about the right size.

They approached Candide and invited him very politely to dine with them.

—Gentlemen, Candide replied with charming modesty, I'm honored by your invitation, but I really don't have enough money to pay my share.

—My dear sir, said one of the blues, people of your appearance and your merit don't have to pay; aren't you five feet five inches tall?

—Yes, gentlemen, that is indeed my stature, said he, making a bow.

—Then, sire, you must be seated at once; not only will we pay your bill this time, we will never allow a man like you to be short of money; for men were made only to render one another mutual aid.

—You are quite right, said Candide; it is just as Dr. Pangloss always told me, and I see clearly that everything is for the best.

They beg him to accept a couple of crowns, he takes them, and offers an I.O.U.; they won't hear of it, and all sit down at table together.

—Don't you love dearly . . . ?

—I do indeed, says he, I dearly love Miss Cunégonde.

▲ *Prussian soldiers*

354

ABOUT THE AUTHOR

François-Marie Arouet was born in Paris and educated at a Jesuit school. Even at an early age, Voltaire was known for his wit, intelligence, and sense of justice. In 1717, the young Arouet was arrested and imprisoned for writing satirical verses criticizing the French government. Not long after his release from prison, Voltaire was exiled to England, where he studied the ideas of John Locke and Isaac Newton. Upon his return to France, he wrote a book praising the ideals represented by these two men, and again angered the government. From 1745 to 1750, however, he served as historiographer to Louis XV and, in 1746, was elected to the French Academy. After having lived in Berlin and Switzerland, Voltaire returned to France in 1778, where he remained until his death.

—No, no, says one of the gentlemen, we are asking if you don't love dearly the King of the Bulgars [Frederick the Great].

—Not in the least, says he, I never laid eyes on him

—What's that you say? He's the most charming of kings, and we must drink his health.

—Oh, gladly, gentlemen; and he drinks.

—That will do, they tell him; you are now the bulwark, the support, the defender, the hero of the Bulgars; your fortune is made and your future assured.

Promptly they slip irons on his legs and lead him to the regiment. There they cause him to right face, left face, present arms, order arms, aim, fire, doubletime, and they give him thirty strokes of the rod. Next day he does the drill a little less awkwardly and gets only twenty strokes; the third day, they give him only ten, and he is regarded by his comrades as a prodigy.

Candide, quite thunderstruck, did not yet understand very clearly how he was a hero. One fine spring morning he took it into his head to go for a walk, stepping straight out as if it were a privilege of the human race, as of animals in general, to use his legs as he chose. He had scarcely covered two leagues when four other heroes [Prussian soldiers], each six feet tall, overtook him, bound him, and threw him into a dungeon. At the court-martial they asked which he preferred, to be flogged thirty-six times by the entire regiment or to receive summarily a dozen bullets in the brain. In vain did he argue that the human will is free and insist that he preferred neither alternative; he had to choose; by virtue of the divine gift called "liberty" he decided to run the gauntlet thirty-six times, and actually endured two floggings. The regiment was composed of two thousand men. That made four thousand strokes. As they were preparing for the third beating, Candide, who could endure no more, begged as a special favor that they would have the goodness to smash his head. His plea was granted; they bandaged his eyes and made him kneel down. The King of the Bulgars [Frederick the Great], passing by at this moment, was told of the culprit's crime; and as this king had a rare genius, he understood, from everything they told him of Candide, that this was a young metaphysician, extremely ignorant of the ways of the world, so he granted his royal pardon, with a generosity which will be praised in every newspaper in every age. A worthy surgeon cured Candide in three weeks with the ointments described by Dioscorides. He already had a bit of skin back and was able to walk when the King of the Bulgars went to war with the King of the Abares.

▲ *Frederick the Great, king of Prussia*

Nothing could have been so fine, so brisk, so brilliant, so well-drilled as the two armies. The trumpets, the fifes, the oboes, the drums, and the cannon produced such a harmony as was never heard in hell. First the cannons battered down about six thousand men on each side; then volleys of musket fire removed from the best of worlds about nine or ten thousand rascals who were cluttering up its surface.

Interpreting World Literature

1. Why do the men choose Candide to kidnap into the army?
2. Explain the irony of the soldiers' statement, "your fortune is made and your future assured."
3. Why is Candide punished? How does this relate to the philosophy of the Enlightenment?
4. **CRITICAL THINKING** What is Voltaire's attitude toward the "King of the Bulgars"?

Applications Activity

Write a satirical piece criticizing something about a television show or movie. Remember that a satire does not directly attack but criticizes by showing how ridiculous something is.

World Literature

FOCUS

Ask students to propose ways in which government can and should recruit soldiers for their armies. Is there a fair and equitable way to recruit military personnel, especially during times of war?

TEACH

Reading Comprehension

After the class has read this excerpt, assign them to work in small groups and have each group rewrite a particular part of the piece in modern English. When groups have finished their work, have one member of each group read the selection written by the group. How does the modern version compare to Voltaire's original writing?

Critical Thinking

Read aloud to the class the sentence on page 355, "One fine spring morning he took it into his head to go for a walk, stepping straight out as if it were a privilege of the human race, . . . to use his legs as he chose." Ask students how this passage relates to the following quote by Voltaire, "Liberty of thought is the life of the soul." How does the passage relate to the ideals of the Enlightenment?

ANSWERS TO INTERPRETING WORLD LITERATURE

1. Candide is chosen because he is the right size.
2. Soldiers were poorly paid, and their future was most likely death in battle.
3. Candide is punished for running away, thinking he has free will. (The concept of free will is a central ideal of the Enlightenment).
4. The king is modeled on Frederick the Great, at whose court Voltaire lived for some time. The fact that he recognizes Candide's action as a mistake only a metaphysician (philosopher) would make is a dig at Frederick, who was not as enlightened as he liked to think himself; for example, he did not free the serfs because to do so would have angered the nobility, on whom he relied to lead his army.

Applications Activity: Answers will vary.

Unit 3 Resources

Suggested Pacing Chart

Unit 3 (1 day)	Chapter 12 (6 days)	Chapter 13 (6 days)	Chapter 14 (6 days)	Chapter 15 (4 days)	Unit 3 (1 day)
Day 1 Introduction	**Day 1** Chapter 12 Intro, Section 1 **Day 2** Section 2 **Day 3** Section 3 **Day 4** Section 4 **Day 5** Chapter 12 Review **Day 6** Chapter 12 Assessment	**Day 1** Chapter 13 Intro, Section 1 **Day 2** Section 2 **Day 3** Section 3 **Day 4** Section 4 **Day 5** Chapter 13 Review **Day 6** Chapter 13 Assessment	**Day 1** Chapter 14 Intro, Section 1 **Day 2** Section 2 **Day 3** Section 3 **Day 4** Section 4 **Day 5** Chapter 14 Review **Day 6** Chapter 14 Assessment	**Day 1** Chapter 15 Intro, Section 1 **Day 2** Section 2 **Day 3** Section 3 **Day 4** Chapter 15 Review/Assessment	**Day 1** Wrap-Up/ Projects/Unit 3 Assessment

Use the following tools to easily assess student learning in a variety of ways:

- Performance Assessment Activities and Rubrics
- Chapter Tests
- Section Quizzes
- Standardized Test Skills Practice Workbook
- SAT I/II Test Practice
- www.wh.mt.glencoe.com
- Interactive Tutor Self-Assessment CD-ROM
- MindJogger Videoquiz
- ExamView® Pro Testmaker CD-ROM

Teaching Transparencies

Unit Time Line Transparency 3

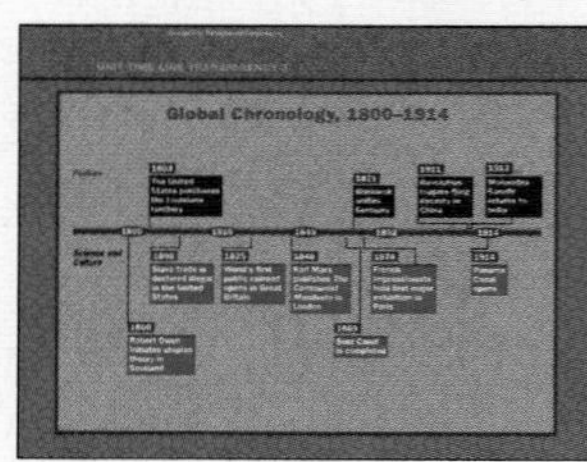

Cause-and-Effect Transparency 3

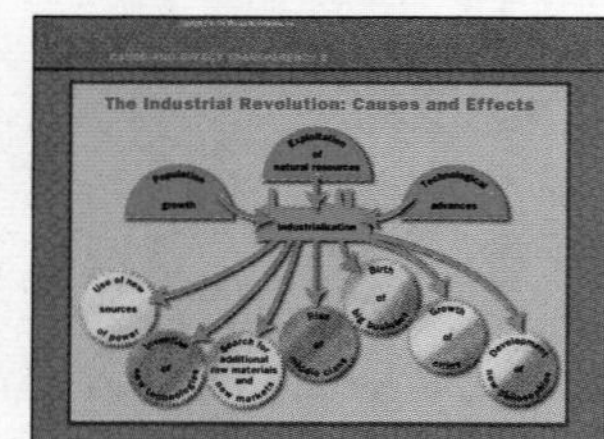

interNET RESOURCES

- www.wh.mt.glencoe.com

Glencoe World History—Modern Times
Visit the *Glencoe World History—Modern Times* Web site for history overviews, activities, assessments, and updated charts and graphs.

- www.socialstudies.glencoe.com

Glencoe Social Studies
Visit the Glencoe Web site for social studies activities, updates, and links to other sites.

- www.teachingtoday.glencoe.com

Glencoe Teaching Today
Visit the new Glencoe Web site for teacher development information, teaching tips, Web resources, and educational news.

- www.time.com

TIME Online
Visit the TIME Web site for up-to-date news and special reports.

Unit 3 Resources

Assessment

Unit 3 Tests Forms A and B

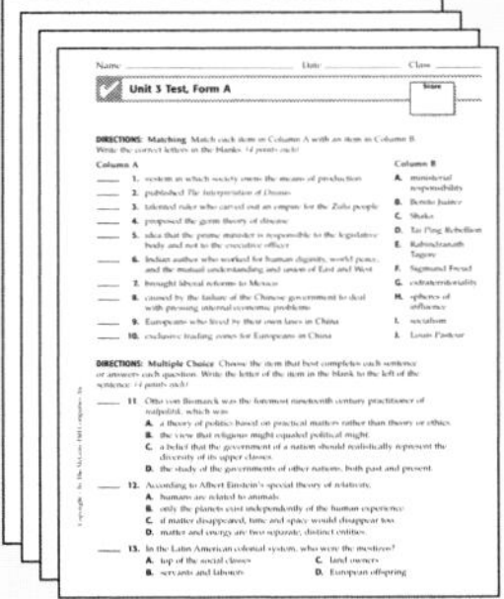

ExamView® Pro Testmaker CD-ROM

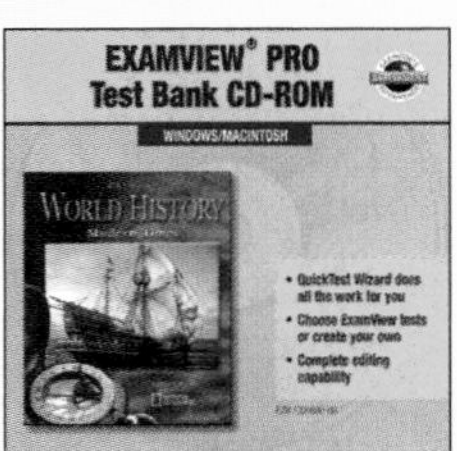

Interdisciplinary Activities

World Literature Reading 3

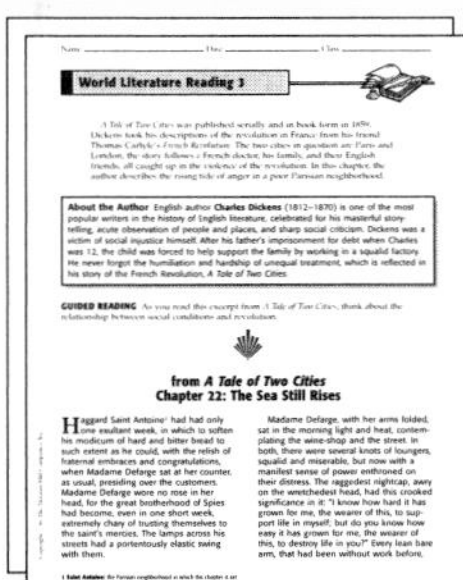

Economics and History Activity 3

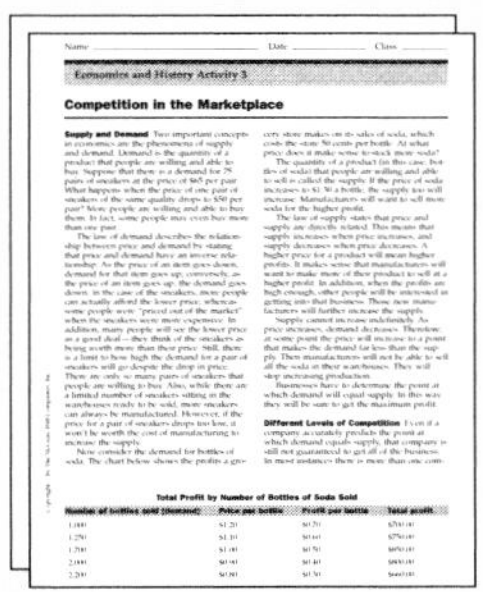

Application and Enrichment

Charting and Graphing Activity 3

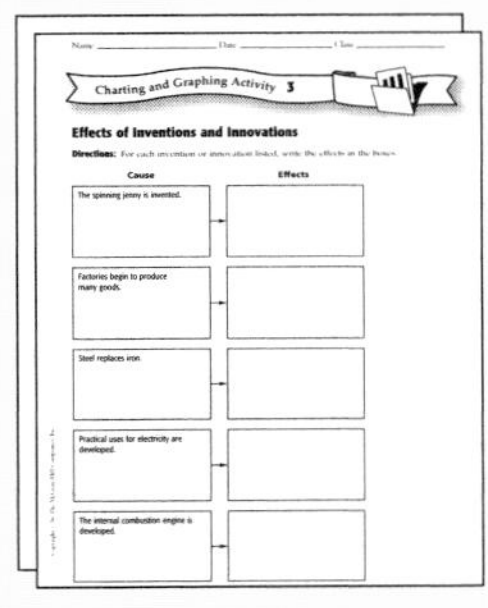

Geographic Literacy

NGS Focus on Geographic Literacy

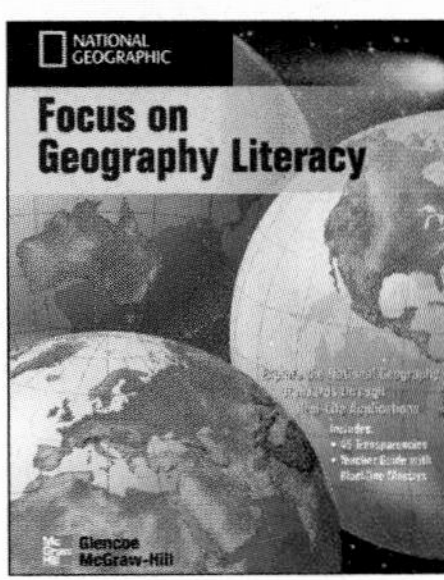

Building Geography Skills for Life

Bibliography

Readings for the Student

Martin, Valerie. ***Mary Reilly.*** Vintage Books, 2001. Fiction — account of Dr. Jekyll that takes place in Victorian England.

Marrin, Albert. ***Terror of the Spanish Main: Sir Henry Morgan and His Buccaneers.*** Dutton Books, 1998. Account of Henry Morgan, the Spanish Empire, and its colonies.

Readings for the Teacher

Forster, Edward Morgan. ***A Passage to India.*** Harvest Books, 1984. A look at the relationship between an Indian man and a British man in 1924.

Young, Helen Praeger. ***Choosing Revolution: Chinese Women Soldiers on the Long March.*** University of Illinois Press, 2001. Interviews with veterans of the Red Army in Communist China.

Jansen, Marius B. ***The Making of Modern Japan.*** Belknap Press, 2000. A study of continuing strands in Japanese history.

Multimedia Resources

DVD/VHS. ***Gandhi.*** Directed by Richard Attenborough, 1982. Follows the life of Mahatma Gandhi as he leads the movement for Indian independence from Great Britain.

Additional Glencoe Resources for this Unit:

- Glencoe Skillbuilder Interactive Workbook CD-ROM, Level 2
- Glencoe World History Primary Source Document Library
- World Art Prints
- World Biography: People in History
- Outline Map Resource Book
- World Desk Map
- World Art and Architecture Transparencies
- World Music: Cultural Traditions
- World Music: A Cultural Legacy
- Glencoe World Literature Library
- Reading in the Content Area
- Teaching Strategies for the World History Classroom (Including Block Scheduling Pacing Guides)
- Inclusion for the High School Social Studies Classroom Strategies and Activities

0:00 Out of Time?

If time does not permit teaching each chapter in this unit, you may use the **Reading Essentials and Study Guide** summaries.

Unit Objectives

After studying this unit, students should be able to:

1. describe the impact of the Industrial Revolution;
2. describe the revolutionary and reform movements that reshaped politics of Europe and the Americas in the 1800s;
3. explain how nationalists unified Italy and Germany and challenged autocracy in Russia and Austria-Hungary;
4. discuss the effects of imperialism in Asia, Africa, and Latin America.

The Period in Perspective

Direct students' attention to the title of this unit. Explain that unit and chapter titles in this text reflect major eras in world history. Have students turn to the Table of Contents that begins on page iv and identify what they think are the major eras of world history. Then have students describe at least two defining characteristics of each era. Discuss these descriptions in class, and use this discussion to help students understand that such distinctions are arbitrary, that historians frequently differ in their opinions about what periods constitute the major eras of world history.

Use these materials to enrich student understanding of European imperialism.

- **NGS PICTURE SHOW™ CD-ROMs**
  The Age of Exploration 2
- **NGS PICTURE PACK TRANSPARENCY SETS**
  The Age of Exploration

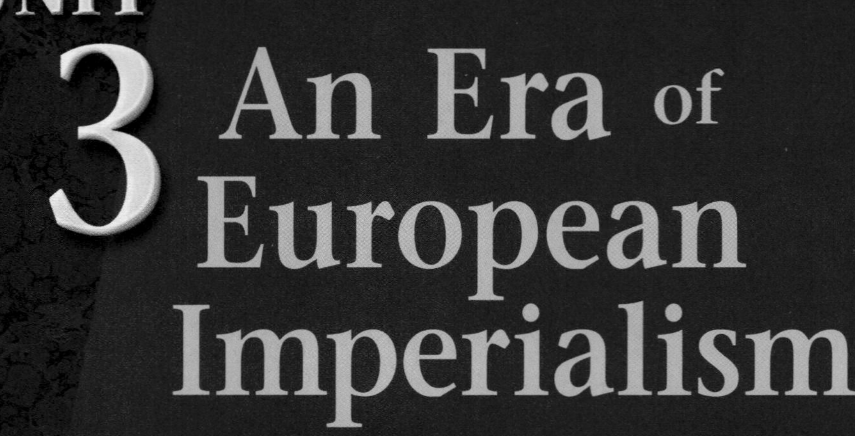

UNIT 3 An Era of European Imperialism

1800–1914

The Period in Perspective

The period of world history from 1800 to 1914 was characterized by two major developments: the growth of industrialization and Western domination of the world. The Industrial Revolution became one of the major forces for change, leading Western civilization into the industrial era that has characterized the modern world. At the same time, the Industrial Revolution created the technological means, including new weapons, by which the West achieved domination over much of the rest of the world.

Primary Sources Library

See pages 776–777 for primary source readings to accompany Unit 3.

*Use The World History **Primary Source Document Library CD-ROM** to find additional primary sources about An Era of European Imperialism.*

▲ Zulu lodging

► Zulu king Cetewayo meeting with British ambassadors

356

TEAM TEACHING ACTIVITY

Literature This unit discusses Western imperialism and its impact on the colonized peoples and lands. Nowhere were the excesses of colonialism more evident than in Africa. King Leopold of Belgium, in spite of his claims of bringing civilization to Africa, exemplifies the worst treatment of African natives. In conjunction with the English teacher, assign students to read Joseph Conrad's *Heart of Darkness*. Students should research the geography of the Congo, the historical background of the period, especially King Leopold's statements about the sacred mission of civilization, and the life of the author. From a literary standpoint, students should focus on Conrad's use of irony and symbolism to convey the atrocities of imperialism in the Congo. L3

"The world's surface is limited, therefore the great object should be to take as much of it as possible."

—Cecil John Rhodes

GLENCOE TECHNOLOGY

CD-ROM
World History Primary Source Document Library CD-ROM

Use the World History Primary Source Document Library CD-ROM to access primary source documents related to European imperialism.

More About the Art

In 1879, the Zulu king Cetewayo met with British ambassadors who were representing Lord Chelmsford. Cetewayo was the last king of independent Zululand. Cetewayo tried to ally himself with the British against the Afrikaners, but the British invaded Zululand and eventually defeated the Zulu forces.

History *and the* Humanities

World Art and Architecture Transparencies

- 37 *Ono Waterfall*
- 39 *Le Moulin de la Galette*
- 40 *Sunday Afternoon on the Island of La Grande Jatte*
- 41 *Starry Night*
- 42 *In the Garden*
- 43 *The Banjo Lesson*

SERVICE-LEARNING PROJECT

As students work their way through the school year, they are often asked to consider ways to improve the general morale at the school or to improve the academic curriculum. Assign each student the task of using a problem-solving process to identify one problem that exists at the school that the student believes can be corrected. Then have students gather information about the problem they have identified. Have students list and consider critically the options that are available to solve the problem. Have students consider the advantages and disadvantages of each of their proposed solutions. Have students choose and implement the solution they have identified as being the most effective for the identified problem. Finally, have students evaluate the effectiveness of the solution they have implemented. **L1** ELL

Looking Back to See Ahead

TEACH

Introduction

This feature focuses on the spread of the Industrial Revolution from its beginnings in Great Britain to the United States and Japan.

Background Notes

Linking Past and Present

Spread of Technology Today, industrial technology moves quickly from one country to another. For example, computer software, microelectronics, and industrial chemicals, once produced almost entirely in Europe, Japan, and the United States, are now exported from Brazil, India, Korea, and Taiwan. The reduction in trade barriers under GATT (General Agreement on Tariffs and Trade) has made the movement of technology even easier. To expand on the themes of trade regulation and the global economy, have students use outside sources to research current economic conditions in a number of countries. Then have students compare the relationships between and among contemporary countries with differing economic systems.

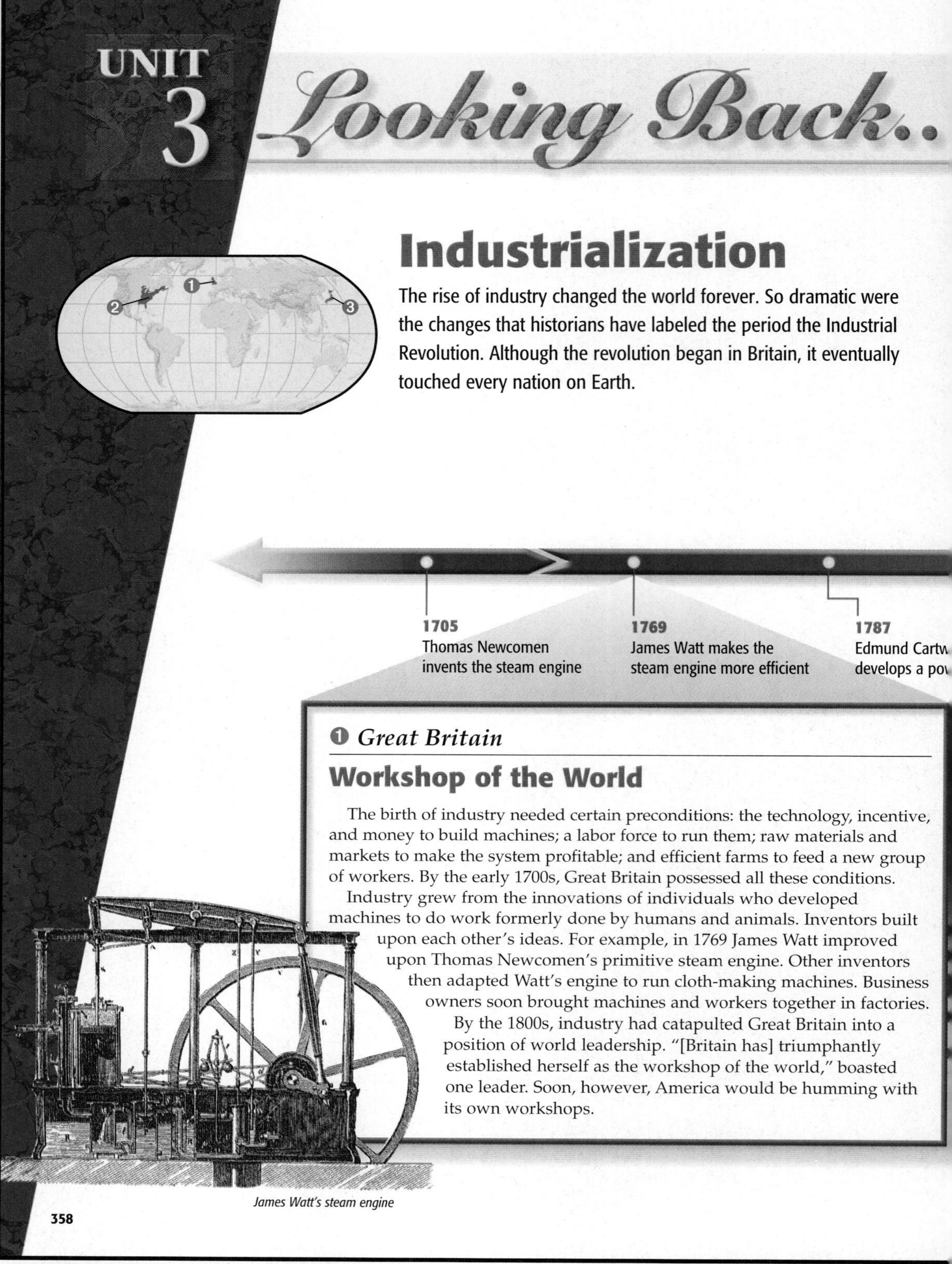

UNIT 3
Looking Back...

Industrialization

The rise of industry changed the world forever. So dramatic were the changes that historians have labeled the period the Industrial Revolution. Although the revolution began in Britain, it eventually touched every nation on Earth.

1705
Thomas Newcomen invents the steam engine
1769
James Watt makes the steam engine more efficient
1787
Edmund Cartw
develops a pow

❶ *Great Britain*

Workshop of the World

The birth of industry needed certain preconditions: the technology, incentive, and money to build machines; a labor force to run them; raw materials and markets to make the system profitable; and efficient farms to feed a new group of workers. By the early 1700s, Great Britain possessed all these conditions.

Industry grew from the innovations of individuals who developed machines to do work formerly done by humans and animals. Inventors built upon each other's ideas. For example, in 1769 James Watt improved upon Thomas Newcomen's primitive steam engine. Other inventors then adapted Watt's engine to run cloth-making machines. Business owners soon brought machines and workers together in factories.

By the 1800s, industry had catapulted Great Britain into a position of world leadership. "[Britain has] triumphantly established herself as the workshop of the world," boasted one leader. Soon, however, America would be humming with its own workshops.

James Watt's steam engine

358

COOPERATIVE LEARNING ACTIVITY

Technology Today Have students brainstorm a list of important technologies today (prompt them if necessary to consider semiconductors, satellites, fiber optics, biotechnology, software, and high-definition television). Then organize the class into groups and have each group research and prepare an oral report on one technology. Reports should indicate, if possible, where the technology was first developed and where it is produced today. Then have students from each group present their report to the class. Encourage students to include visuals in their reports. L2

to See Ahead

Samuel Slater's mill

❷ *The United States*

The Revolution Spreads

Great Britain prohibited the export of machines and machine operators. In 1789, however, a factory supervisor named Samuel Slater escaped by disguising himself as a farmhand and boarding a ship to New York. Working from memory, Slater built a cotton mill in Rhode Island in 1793.

Soon after, the United States began churning out its own industrial inventors. Standardized parts and the assembly line led to mass production—a concept that would revolutionize people's lives around the globe.

1793 Samuel Slater opens the first machine-run cotton mill in the U.S.

1855 Henry Bessemer develops an inexpensive method of producing steel

1913 Henry Ford uses assembly lines to mass produce cars

1914 Japan expands foreign trade

❸ *Japan*

The Search for Markets

In 1853, the Industrial Revolution traveled to Japan in the form of a fleet of United States steamships sent to open the islands to trade. "What we had taken as a fire at sea," recalled one Japanese observer, "was really smoke coming out of the smokestacks."

The military power produced by United States industry shook the Japanese. They temporarily gave in to American trade demands, but they also vowed that they too would possess industry. By 1914, Japan's merchant fleet was the sixth largest in the world, and its trade had increased one hundred-fold in value in 50 years.

Matthew Perry's steamship in Tokyo Bay

Why It Matters

The increase in industry made it necessary to find new sources of raw materials and new markets for manufactured goods. How could competition for resources and markets lead to the wars of the twentieth century?

Why It Matters

ANSWER: In an effort to acquire more resources, powerful countries that need the resources, such as oil, minerals, and trade routes, may threaten the sovereignty of countries that have the resources. Also, countries may raise taxes on imports from wealthier countries with the resources and markets, causing tensions to build between nations.

Geography

Movement The Industrial Revolution caused unprecedented movement among peoples as farmers in many lands left their farms to work in factories, often in far-off places. Skilled European workers came to the United States in the early 1800s to work in cotton mills like the one Slater built in Pawtucket. In the 1820s one observer noted that a mix of workers from different parts of Britain made problems for one mill owner: "I cannot conceive a more uncomfortable situation than . . . to be surrounded by a mixture of Irish, Yorkshire, and West of England workmen. Whatever advice they might receive from the one party would be condemned by the other. . . ." Ask students if there are any contemporary parallels to the situation above.

CULTURAL DIFFUSION

Military-Industrial Complex The Japanese understood that a nation could not have a strong military without industrializing. After Britain defeated China in the Opium War of the 1830s, one Japanese individual commented: "Why did an upright and righteous great country like China lose to an insolent, unjust, and contemptible country like England? It is because [the rulers of China] prided themselves on their superiority, regarded the outside world with contempt, and paid no heed to the progress of machinery in foreign countries."

Chapter 12 Resources

Timesaving Tools

TeacherWorks™ All-In-One Planner and Resource Center

- **Interactive Teacher Edition** Access your Teacher Wraparound Edition and your classroom resources with a few easy clicks.
- **Interactive Lesson Planner** Planning has never been easier! Organize your week, month, semester, or year with all the lesson helps you need to make teaching creative, timely, and relevant.

Use Glencoe's **Presentation Plus!** multimedia teacher tool to easily present dynamic lessons that visually excite your students. Using Microsoft PowerPoint® you can customize the presentations to create your own personalized lessons.

Teaching Transparencies

Graphic Organizer Student Activity 12 Transparency

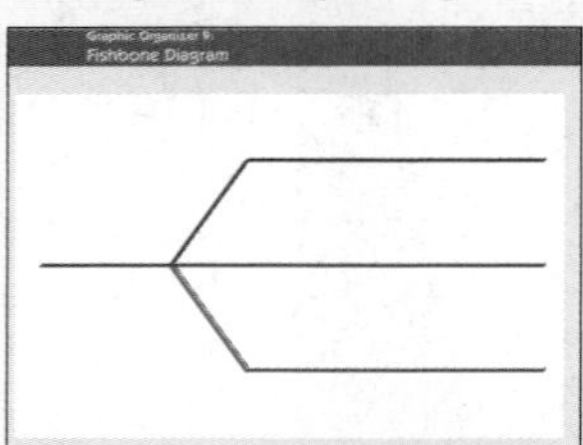

Chapter Transparency 12

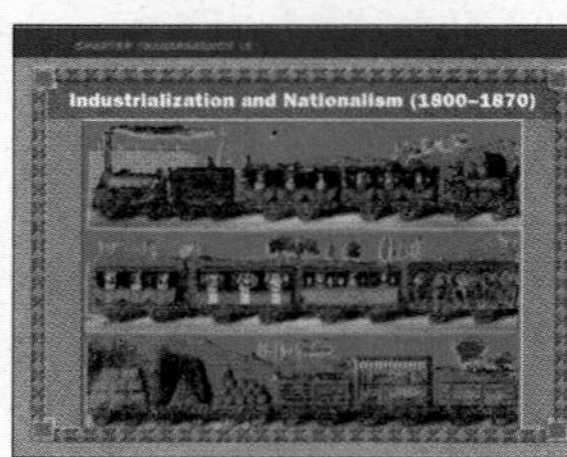

Map Overlay Transparency 12

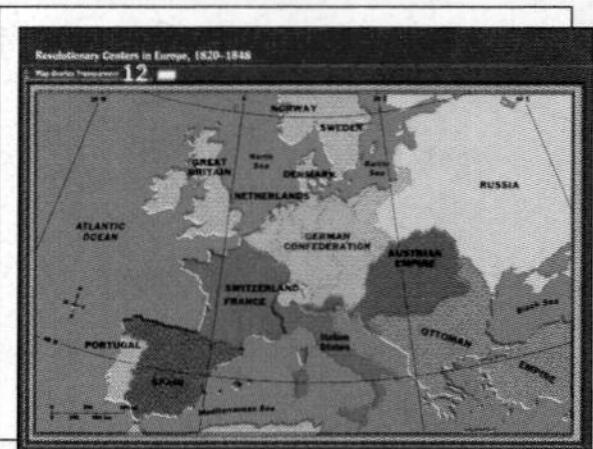

Application and Enrichment

Enrichment Activity 12

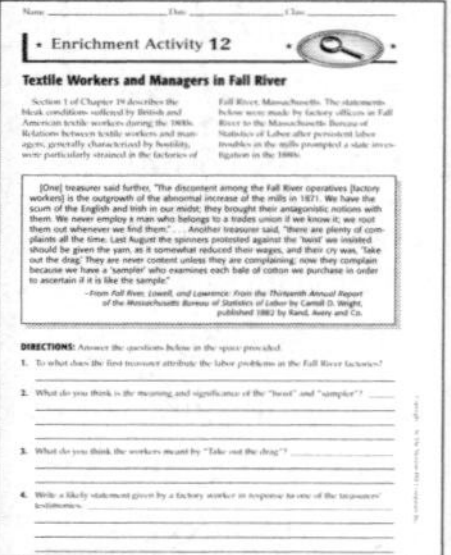

Primary Source Reading 12

History Simulation Activity 12

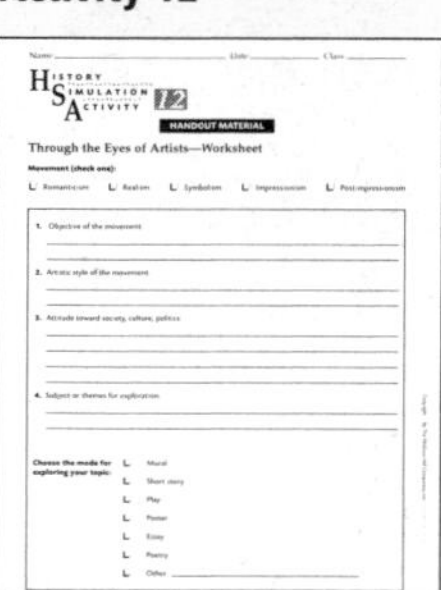

Historical Significance Activity 12

Cooperative Learning Activity 12

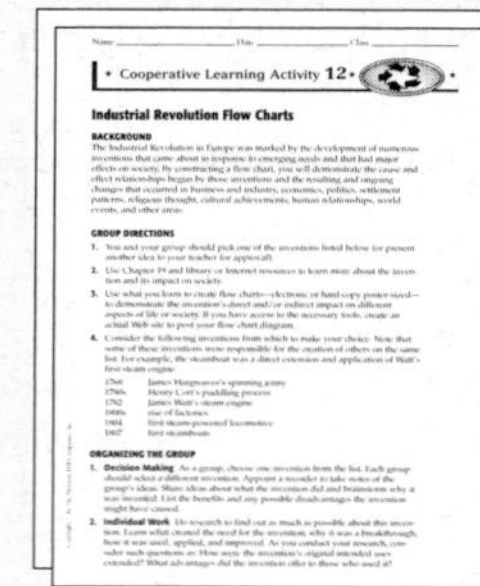

A&E HOME VIDEO. Biography® THE HISTORY CHANNEL.

The following videotape programs are available from Glencoe as supplements to Chapter 12:

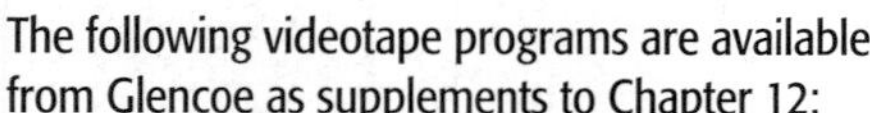

- **Railroads That Tamed the West** (ISBN 0–7670–0033–1)
- **Textiles: Birth of an American Industry** (ISBN 0–7670–0624–0)

To order, call Glencoe at 1–800–334–7344. To find classroom resources to accompany many of these videos, check the following home pages:
A&E Television: www.aande.com
The History Channel: www.historychannel.com

Chapter 12 Resources

REVIEW AND REINFORCEMENT

Linking Past and Present Activity 12

Time Line Activity 12

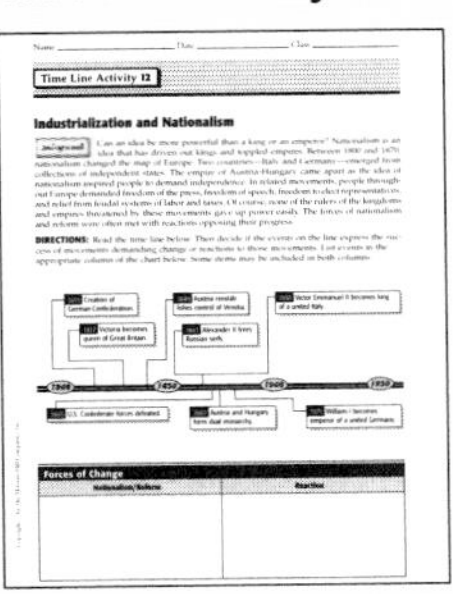

Reteaching Activity 12

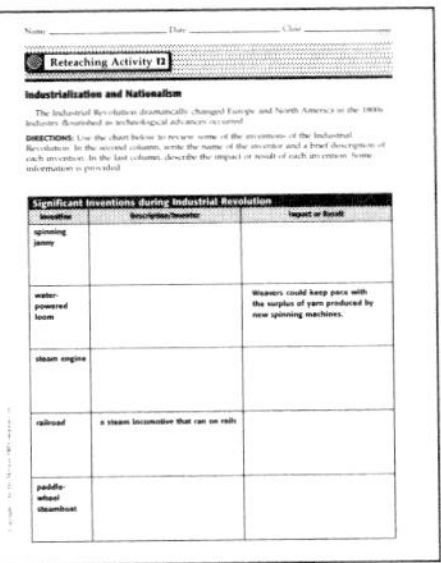

Vocabulary Activity 12

Critical Thinking Skills Activity 12

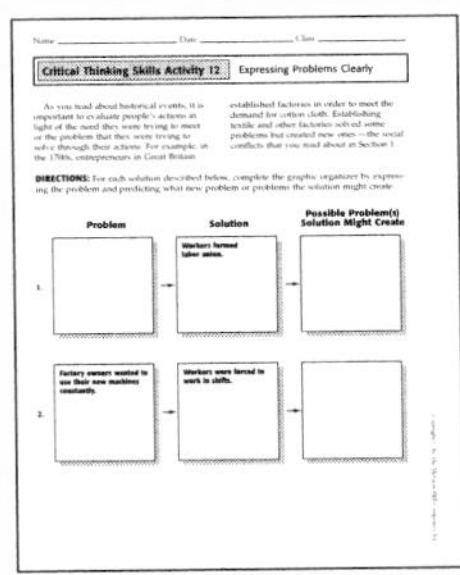

ASSESSMENT AND EVALUATION

Chapter 12 Test Form A

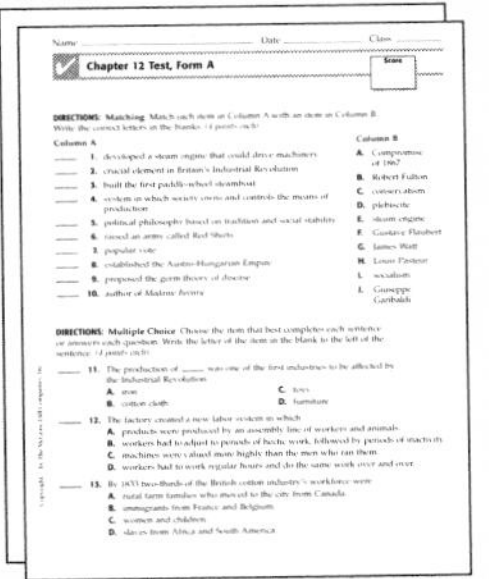

Chapter 12 Test Form B

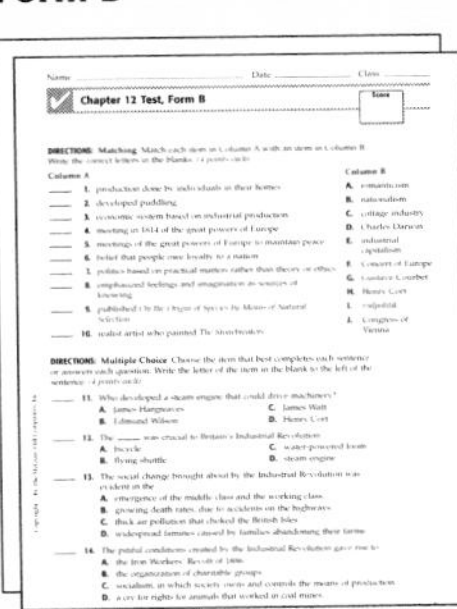

Performance Assessment Activity 12

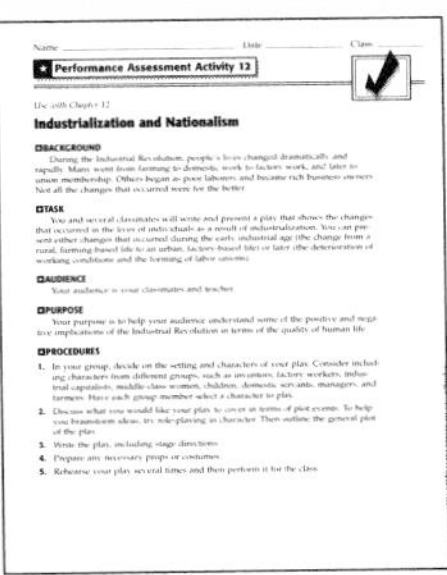

ExamView® Pro Testmaker CD-ROM

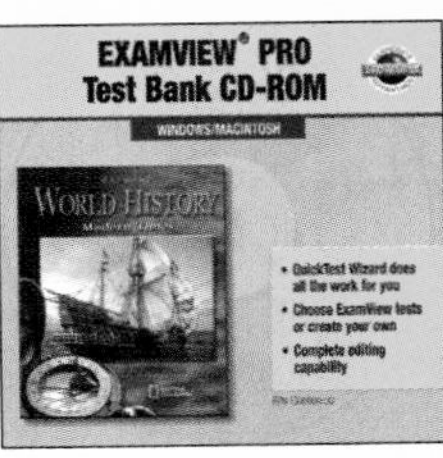

Standardized Test Skills Practice Workbook Activity 12

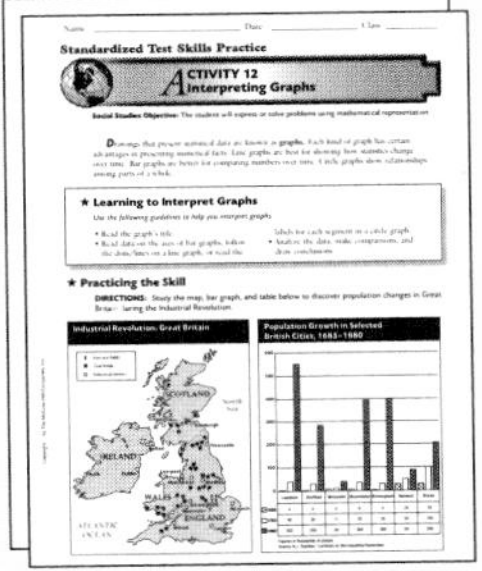

INTERDISCIPLINARY ACTIVITIES

Mapping History Activity 12

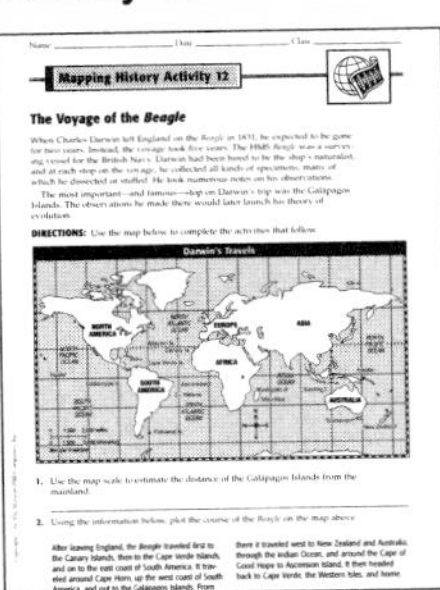

World Art and Music Activity 12

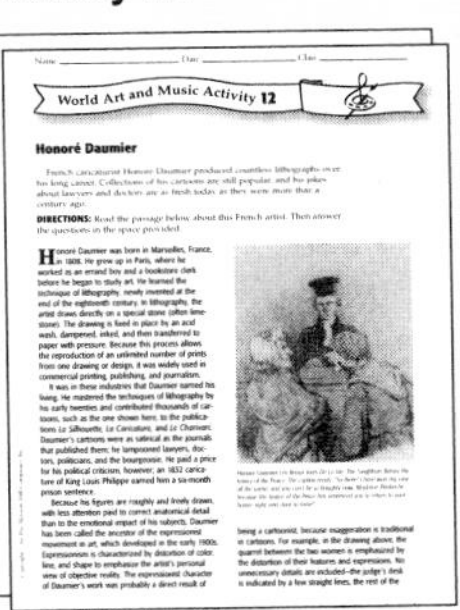

History and Geography Activity 12

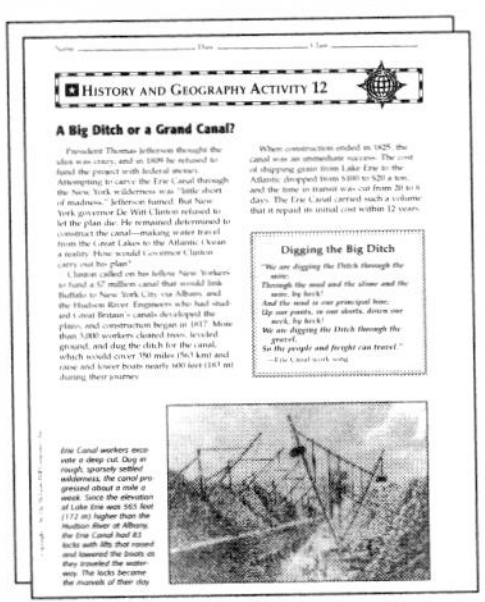

People in World History Activity 12

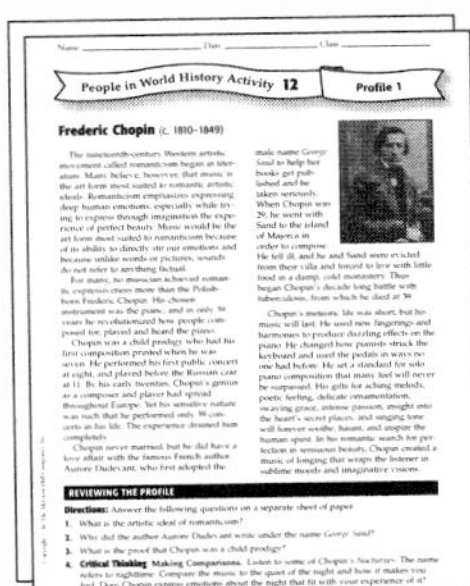

MULTIMEDIA

- Vocabulary PuzzleMaker CD-ROM
- Interactive Tutor Self-Assessment CD-ROM
- ExamView® Pro Testmaker CD-ROM
- Audio Program
- World History Primary Source Document Library CD-ROM
- MindJogger Videoquiz
- Presentation Plus! CD-ROM
- TeacherWorks CD-ROM
- Interactive Student Edition CD-ROM
- The World History—Modern Times Video Program

SPANISH RESOURCES

The following Spanish language materials are available in the Spanish Resources Binder:

- Spanish Guided Reading Activities
- Spanish Reteaching Activities
- Spanish Quizzes and Tests
- Spanish Vocabulary Activities
- Spanish Summaries

Chapter 12 Resources

SECTION RESOURCES

Daily Objectives	Reproducible Resources	Multimedia Resources
SECTION 1 **The Industrial Revolution** 1. Explain why coal and steam replaced wind and water as new sources of energy and power. 2. Describe the growth of cities as people moved from the country to work in factories.	Reproducible Lesson Plan 12–1 Daily Lecture and Discussion Notes 12–1 Guided Reading Activity 12–1* Section Quiz 12–1* Reading Essentials and Study Guide 12–1	Daily Focus Skills Transparency 12–1 Interactive Tutor Self-Assessment CD-ROM ExamView® Pro Testmaker CD-ROM Presentation Plus! CD-ROM
SECTION 2 **Reaction and Revolution** 1. Summarize how the great powers worked to maintain a conservative order throughout Europe. 2. Characterize the forces of liberalism and nationalism and their continued growth, which led to the revolutions of 1848.	Reproducible Lesson Plan 12–2 Daily Lecture and Discussion Notes 12–2 Guided Reading Activity 12–2* Section Quiz 12–2* Reading Essentials and Study Guide 12–2	Daily Focus Skills Transparency 12–2 Interactive Tutor Self-Assessment CD-ROM ExamView® Pro Testmaker CD-ROM Presentation Plus! CD-ROM
SECTION 3 **National Unification and the National State** 1. Report how the rise of nationalism contributed to the unification of Italy and Germany. 2. Explain that while nationalism had great appeal, not all peoples achieved the goal of establishing their own national states.	Reproducible Lesson Plan 12–3 Daily Lecture and Discussion Notes 12–3 Guided Reading Activity 12–3* Section Quiz 12–3* Reading Essentials and Study Guide 12–3	Daily Focus Skills Transparency 12–3 Interactive Tutor Self-Assessment CD-ROM ExamView® Pro Testmaker CD-ROM Presentation Plus! CD-ROM
SECTION 4 **Culture: Romanticism and Realism** 1. Describe how romanticism emerged as a reaction to the ideas of the Enlightenment at the end of the eighteenth century. 2. Characterize the Industrial Revolution, which created a new interest in science and helped produce the realist movement.	Reproducible Lesson Plan 12–4 Daily Lecture and Discussion Notes 12–4 Guided Reading Activity 12–4* Section Quiz 12–4* Reteaching Activity 12* Reading Essentials and Study Guide 12–4	Daily Focus Skills Transparency 12–4 Interactive Tutor Self-Assessment CD-ROM ExamView® Pro Testmaker CD-ROM Presentation Plus! CD-ROM

0:00 **OUT OF TIME?**
Assign the Chapter 12 **Reading Essentials and Study Guide.**

*Also Available in Spanish

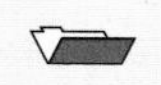 Blackline Master  Transparency  CD-ROM  DVD

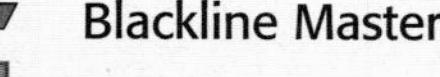 Poster  Music Program 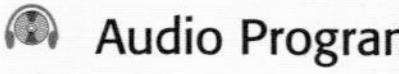 Audio Program  Videocassette

Chapter 12 Resources

NATIONAL GEOGRAPHIC **Teacher's Corner**

INDEX TO NATIONAL GEOGRAPHIC MAGAZINE

The following articles relate to this chapter:

- "Robot Revolution," by Curt Suplee, July 1997.
- "Information Revolution," by Joel L. Swerdlow, October 1995.
- "George Washington's Patowmack Canal," by Wilbur E. Garrett, June 1987.
- "Reinventing Berlin," by Peter Ross Range, December 1996.

ADDITIONAL NATIONAL GEOGRAPHIC SOCIETY PRODUCTS

To order the following, call National Geographic at 1-800-368-2728:

- *Inventors and Inventions* (Video)
- *Wired World* (Video)
- *Technology's Price* (Video)

NGS ONLINE

Access National Geographic's new dynamic MapMachine Web site and other geography resources at:
www.nationalgeographic.com
www.nationalgeographic.com/maps

KEY TO ABILITY LEVELS

Teaching strategies have been coded.

- **L1** BASIC activities for all students
- **L2** AVERAGE activities for average to above-average students
- **L3** CHALLENGING activities for above-average students
- **ELL** ENGLISH LANGUAGE LEARNER activities

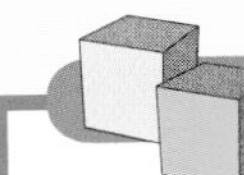

Block Schedule

Activities that are suited to use within the block scheduling framework are identified by:

WORLD HISTORY Online

Use our Web site for additional resources. All essential content is covered in the Student Edition.

You and your students can visit www.wh.mt.glencoe.com, the Web site companion to *Glencoe World History—Modern Times.* This innovative integration of electronic and print media offers your students a wealth of opportunities. The student text directs students to the Web site for the following options:

- **Chapter Overviews**
- **Self-Check Quizzes**
- **Student Web Activities**
- **Textbook Updates**

Answers to the Student Web Activities are provided for you in the **Web Activity Lesson Plans.** Additional Web resources and Interactive Tutor Puzzles are also available.

From the Classroom of...

Edward Thomas
Elmont Memorial High School
Elmont, New York

Analyzing Effects of Industrialization

Ask students what products or inventions have been important during the 1990s and early 2000s. Have students discuss the ways each product or invention has affected their lives and society as a whole, both positively and negatively. Then have students list products and inventions from the Industrial Revolution, along with their effects in both rural and urban regions. Use these lists as a springboard for a general discussion of the changes in lifestyle brought about by industrialization. Be sure students mention the movement of many people from rural to urban areas. Ask students if any of the problems brought about by industrialization are still present in society.

Introducing CHAPTER 12

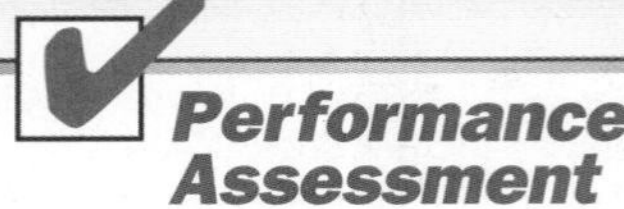

Performance Assessment

Refer to Activity 12 in the Performance Assessment Activities and Rubrics booklet.

The Impact Today

Ask students to consider the positive and negative effects of industrialization in the past, and of the current technological revolution. Overall, is the impact of technology a positive or negative one on society today?

GLENCOE TECHNOLOGY

The World History—Modern Times Video Program

To learn more about the cultural and social changes of the nineteenth century, students can view the Chapter 12 video, "The Romantic Era," from **The World History—Modern Times Video Program.**

MindJogger Videoquiz

Use the **MindJogger Videoquiz** to preview Chapter 12 content.

 Available in VHS.

CHAPTER 12 Industrialization and Nationalism

1800–1870

Key Events

As you read this chapter, look for the key events in the development of industrialization and nationalism.

- *The Industrial Revolution saw a shift from an economy based on farming and handicrafts to an economy based on manufacturing by machines and industrial factories.*
- *Three important ideologies—conservatism, nationalism, and liberalism—emerged to play an important role in world history.*
- *Romanticism and realism reflected changes in society in Europe and North America.*

The Impact Today

The events that occurred during this time period still impact our lives today.

- *The early conflicts between workers and employers produced positive effects for workers in modern society.*
- *The Industrial Revolution replaced many handcrafted items with mass-produced items, many of which we still use today.*
- *Nationalism has had a profound effect on world developments in the twentieth century.*

World History—Modern Times Video *The Chapter 12 video,* "The Romantic Era," *chronicles cultural and social changes in nineteenth-century Europe.*

The Clermont, *built by Robert Fulton*

1807 Robert Fulton builds the first paddle-wheel steamboat

1800 | 1810 | 1820 | 1830

1814 Congress of Vienna meets

1830 First public railway line opens in Britain

360

TWO-MINUTE LESSON LAUNCHER

Have students brainstorm ideas associated with liberalism and conservatism in modern-day American politics. Ask them to consider what each believes about the responsibility of the government, personal freedoms, economic problems, social problems, and reforms in the society. Based on their feedback, write a definition of both terms as they apply today. You may also want to ask students which group would more likely be viewed as "nationalist" in its outlook. Encourage students, as they read the chapter, to compare the struggle between liberalism and conservatism of the nineteenth century with today. In what way is the struggle the same? How has it changed? Is the struggle as significant today as it was then?

Introducing
CHAPTER 12

Chapter Objectives

After studying this section, students should be able to:

1. describe the impact of the Industrial Revolution;
2. explain changes in the popularity of conservative, liberal, and nationalist movements;
3. identify and explain reasons for revolutionary outbursts and reforms in Europe;
4. describe the events that led to the unification of Italy and of Germany;
5. describe developments in the United States and Canada;
6. identify and explain characteristics of romanticism and realism;
7. describe events in the new age of science.

Coalbrookedale by Night by Philippe Jacques de Loutherbourg Artists painted the dramatic changes brought on by the Industrial Revolution.

Francis I, Austrian emperor

1837 Victoria becomes queen of Great Britain

1848 Revolutions erupt in Europe

1853 Crimean War begins

1855 Czar Alexander II frees the Russian serfs

1865 U.S. Confederate troops surrender

1871 German unification achieved

1840 | 1850 | 1860 | 1870

Queen Victoria

Czar Alexander II of Russia

HISTORY Online

Chapter Overview
Visit the *Glencoe World History—Modern Times* Web site at wh.mt.glencoe.com and click on **Chapter 12–Chapter Overview** to preview chapter information.

361

Chapter Overview
Introduce students to chapter content and key terms by having them access **Chapter Overview 12** at wh.mt.glencoe.com.

Time Line Activity

According to the time line, what period of the nineteenth century had the most wars? *(1848 to 1870; 22 years)* Why do you think there were so many revolutions in one period? *(ideas spread; similar problems in western countries)* **L2**

MORE ABOUT THE ART

Coalbrookedale Ask students to study the art on this page. Ask students to identify visual clues that tell the observer how this artist feels about the Industrial Revolution. *(Use of color, night setting, and smoke portrays Industrial Revolution as menacing and chaotic.)* Many artists and poets did not view the changes brought to the landscape by the Industrial Revolution favorably. Wordsworth penned these lines: "I have lived to mark/A new and unforeseen creation rise/From out of the labors of a peaceful Land/Wielding her potent energy to frame/And to produce, with appetite keen/As that of war, which rests not night or day/Industrious to destroy."

CHAPTER PREVIEW

Introducing

A Story That Matters

Depending on the ability levels of your students, select from the following questions to reinforce the reading of *A Story That Matters.*

- Why would leaders of the Old Order choose to celebrate the defeat of Napoleon with such a display of wealth and pageantry? *(to show their power)*
- Why might this have been a sign of the need for change in Europe? *(shows the decadence and arrogance of ruling class, unconcerned with lower classes)*
- Why do some historians believe the Industrial Revolution was as much a cause for the fall of the Old Order as were the revolutions of the early nineteenth century? *(new middle class gained power)* **L1 L2 L3**

About the Art

This painting records a meeting of the Congress of Vienna. In this elegant setting aristocratic negotiators from around Europe gathered to work out the treaties that ensured peace in Europe for almost one hundred years. Ask students to describe specific aspects of the painting that convey the aristocratic nature of the scene. *(Answers will vary.)*

CHAPTER PREVIEW

A Story That Matters

Austrian emperor Francis I (left) hosted the Congress of Vienna.

The Congress of Vienna

In the fall of 1814, hundreds of foreigners began to converge on Vienna, the capital city of the Austrian Empire. Many of these foreigners were members of European royalty—kings, archdukes, princes, and their wives—accompanied by their political advisers and scores of servants.

Their congenial host was the Austrian emperor Francis I, who was quite willing to spend a fortune to entertain the visitors. A Festivals Committee arranged entertainment on a daily basis for nine months. Francis I never tired of providing Vienna's guests with glittering balls, hunting parties, picnics, hot-air balloon displays, and sumptuous feasts.

A banquet for forty tables of guests was held every night in the Hofburg Palace. Then, too, there were the concerts. Actors, actresses, singers, and composers were engaged to entertain, and Beethoven even composed a new piece of music for the event. One participant remembered, "Eating, fireworks, public illuminations. For eight or ten days, I haven't been able to work at all. What a life!"

Of course, not every waking hour was spent in pleasure during this gathering of notables, known to history as the Congress of Vienna. These people were representatives of all the states that had fought Napoleon. Their real business was to arrange a final peace settlement after almost 10 years of war.

Why It Matters

The Congress of Vienna tried to find a way to undo the changes brought about by the French Revolution and Napoleon. However, the new forces of change had become too powerful to be contained. They called forth political revolutions that would shake Europe for years to come. At the beginning of the nineteenth century, another kind of revolution began to transform the economic and social structure of Europe. The Industrial Revolution led to the industrialization that shaped the modern world.

History and You List several inventions developed during your lifetime. What are their purposes? Do they save time or make manual work easier? Have they impacted society as a whole? Have there been any negative consequences to any of these inventions? Write a paper summarizing your thoughts.

HISTORY AND YOU

Have students imagine that they are either a member of European royalty or a servant visiting or working at the king's palace at the Congress of Vienna. Ask them to write a diary entry about their perceptions of the celebrations and meetings following the Napoleonic era. How would they feel about all the festivities? What would they think the king was trying to accomplish with all of the celebrating? How would they feel about the end of the Napoleonic era? What would they hope the outcome of the Congress would be? Why? How would their social position or the country they were from influence their feelings? **L2**

SECTION 1 The Industrial Revolution

Guide to Reading

Main Ideas
- Coal and steam replaced wind and water as new sources of energy and power.
- Cities grew as people moved from the country to work in factories.

Key Terms
capital, entrepreneur, cottage industry, puddling, industrial capitalism, socialism

People to Identify
James Watt, Robert Fulton

Places to Locate
Liverpool, Manchester

Preview Questions
1. What technological changes led to the development of industrialization?
2. What was the social impact of the Industrial Revolution in Europe, especially on women and children?

Reading Strategy
Categorizing Information Use a table like the one below to name important inventors mentioned in this section and their inventions.

Inventors	Inventions

Preview of Events

1750 · 1770 · 1790 · 1810 · 1830 · 1850

- **1768** James Hargreaves invents spinning jenny
- **1782** James Watt builds steam engine that can drive machinery
- **1807** Steamboats make transportation easier
- **1833** Factory Act reduces child labor in Britain
- **1840** Steamships begin to cross the Atlantic

Factory workers

Voices from the Past

In 1844, a factory in Berlin posted the following rules for its workers:

❝The normal working day begins at all seasons at 6 A.M. precisely and ends, after the usual break of half an hour for breakfast, an hour for dinner and half an hour for tea, at 7 P.M. . . . Workers arriving 2 minutes late shall lose half an hour's wages; whoever is more than 2 minutes late may not start work until after the next break, or at least shall lose his wages until then. . . . No worker may leave his place of work otherwise than for reasons connected with his work. . . . All conversation with fellow-workers is prohibited . . .❞

—***Documents of European Economic History,*** **Sidney Pollard and Colin Holmes, 1968**

The new factories of the Industrial Revolution demanded a rigorous discipline to force employees to become accustomed to a new kind of work life.

The Industrial Revolution in Great Britain

TURNING POINT **As you will learn, during the Industrial Revolution, Europe saw a shift from an economy based on farming and handicrafts to an economy based on manufacturing by machines in factories.**

The Industrial Revolution began in Great Britain in the 1780s and took several decades to spread to other Western nations. Several factors contributed to make Great Britain the starting place.

CHAPTER 12
Section 1, 363–370

1 FOCUS

Section Overview

This section discusses industrialization and its effects on Western countries.

BELLRINGER
Skillbuilder Activity

Project transparency and have students answer questions.

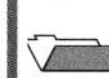
Available as a blackline master.

Daily Focus Skills Transparency 12–1

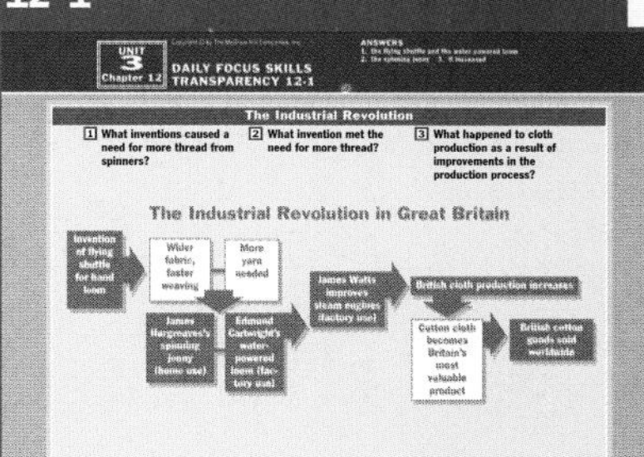

DAILY FOCUS SKILLS TRANSPARENCY 12-1
The Industrial Revolution
1 What inventions caused a need for more thread from spinners?
2 What invention met the need for more thread?
3 What happened to cloth production as a result of improvements in the production process?
The Industrial Revolution in Great Britain

Guide to Reading

Answers to Graphic: James Hargreaves: spinning jenny; Edmund Cartwright: water-powered loom; James Watt: steam engine; Henry Cort: puddling; Robert Fulton: paddle-wheel steamboat

Preteaching Vocabulary: Have students define the terms *capitalism, socialism, capital, entrepreneur.* Then have them write a sentence explaining the difference between capitalism and socialism, and a sentence explaining the relationship between capital and entrepreneur. **L1**

SECTION RESOURCES

Reproducible Masters
- Reproducible Lesson Plan 12–1
- Daily Lecture and Discussion Notes 12–1
- Guided Reading Activity 12–1
- Section Quiz 12–1
- Reading Essentials and Study Guide 12–1

Transparencies
- Daily Focus Skills Transparency 12–1

Multimedia
- Interactive Tutor Self-Assessment CD-ROM
- ExamView® Pro Testmaker CD-ROM
- Presentation Plus! CD-ROM

2 TEACH

Daily Lecture and Discussion Notes 12–1

Daily Lecture and Discussion Notes

Chapter 12, Section 1

Did You Know? Within four years of his arrival, Samuel Slater constructed the first successful water-powered cotton mill in the United States, on the Blackstone River in Pawtucket, Rhode Island. The construction of this mill, now a national historic site, is popularly recognized as the beginning of the Industrial Revolution in America.

I. The Industrial Revolution in Great Britain *(pages 363–365)*

A. The Industrial Revolution began in Great Britain in the 1780s for several reasons.

B. Improved farming methods increased the food supply, which drove food prices down and gave families more money for manufactured goods. The increased food supply also supported a growing population.

C. Britain had a ready supply of **capital**—money to invest—for industrial machines and factories. Wealthy **entrepreneurs** were looking for ways to invest and make profits. Finally, Britain had abundant natural resources and a supply of markets, in part because of its colonial empire.

D. In the eighteenth century Great Britain had surged ahead in the production of cotton goods. The two-step process of spinning and weaving had been done by individuals in their homes, a production method called **cottage industry.**

E. A series of inventions—the flying shuttle, the spinning jenny, and the water-powered loom invented by Edmund Cartwright in 1787—made both weaving and spinning faster. It was now efficient to bring workers to the new machines in factories. Cottage industry no longer was efficient.

F. The cotton industry became even more productive after the Scottish engineer, **James Watt,** improved the steam engine in 1782 so it could drive machinery. Steam power was used to spin and weave cotton. Steam-powered cotton mills proliferated throughout Britain. The steam engines used coal. Mills no longer had to be located near water.

G. By 1840 cotton cloth was Britain's most valuable product. Its cotton goods were sold all over the world.

H. The steam engine drove Britain's Industrial Revolution, and it ran on coal. This led to the coal industry expanding. The coal supply seemed unlimited. Coal also transformed the iron industry. Iron had been made in England since the Middle Ages. Using the process developed by Henry Cort called **puddling,** industry produced a better quality of iron. The British iron industry boomed. In 1740 Britain produced 17,000 tons of iron. Cort's process quadrupled production, and by 1852 Britain was producing almost 3 million tons of iron annually.

turn

163

TURNING POINT

How did population growth and abundant natural resources contribute to the shift of Britain's economy to one based on manufacturing? *(More people meant more laborers; natural resources provided power necessary for manufacturing.)*

Who? What? Where? When?

James Hargreaves (who may have named the spinning jenny after his wife) tried to keep his invention secret. But other spinners became suspicious because his family produced so much yarn. They burst into his house, destroyed his machine, and forced the family to move away.

Young woman at work in a textile mill

Contributing Factors First, agricultural practices in the eighteenth century had changed. Expansion of farmland, good weather, improved transportation, and new crops, such as the potato, led to a dramatic increase in the food supply. More people could be fed at lower prices with less labor.

Second, with more abundant food supplies, the population grew. In the 1700s, Parliament passed laws that allowed large landowners to fence off common lands. As a result of this **enclosure movement,** many peasants were forced to move to towns to work in the new factories.

Third, Britain had a ready supply of money, or **capital,** to invest in the new industrial machines and the factories needed to house them. Many British people were very wealthy. Some, called **entrepreneurs,** were interested in finding new business opportunities and new ways to make profits.

Fourth, natural resources were plentiful in Britain. The country's many rivers provided water power and a means for transporting raw materials and finished products from one place to another. Britain also had abundant supplies of coal and iron ore, essential in manufacturing processes.

Finally, a supply of markets gave British manufacturers a ready outlet for their goods. Britain had a vast colonial empire, and British ships could transport goods anywhere in the world. In addition, because of population growth and cheaper food at home, domestic markets were increasing. A growing demand for cotton cloth led British manufacturers to begin to look for ways to increase production.

Changes in Cotton Production In the eighteenth century, Great Britain had surged ahead in the production of inexpensive cotton goods. The manufacture of cotton cloth was a two-step process. First, spinners made cotton thread from raw cotton. Then, weavers wove the thread into cloth on looms. In the eighteenth century, these tasks were done by individuals in their rural homes—a production method known as **cottage industry.**

A series of technological advances in the eighteenth century made cottage industry inefficient. First, the invention of the "flying shuttle" made weaving faster. Now, weavers needed more thread from spinners because they could produce cloth at a faster rate.

By 1768, James Hargreaves had invented a spinning machine called the spinning jenny, which met this need. Other inventors made similar contributions. The spinning process became much faster. In fact, thread was being produced faster than weavers could use it.

Another invention made it possible for the weaving of cloth to catch up with the spinning of thread. This was a water-powered loom invented by Edmund Cartwright by 1787. It now became more efficient to bring workers to the new machines and have them work in factories near streams and rivers, which were used to power many of the early machines.

The cotton industry became even more productive when the steam engine was improved in the 1760s by a Scottish engineer, **James Watt.** In 1782, Watt made changes that enabled the engine to drive machinery. Steam power could now be used to spin and weave cotton. Before long, cotton mills using steam engines were found all over Britain. Because steam engines were fired by coal, they did not need to be located near rivers.

British cotton cloth production increased dramatically. In 1760, Britain had imported 2.5 million pounds (1.14 million kg) of raw cotton, which was used to produce cloth in cottage industries. In 1787, the British imported 22 million pounds (10 million kg) of cotton, most of it spun on machines. By 1840, 366 million pounds (166 million kg) of cotton were imported each year. By this time, cotton cloth was Britain's most valuable product. British cotton goods were sold everywhere in the world and were produced mainly in factories.

MEETING INDIVIDUAL NEEDS

Kinesthetic To help students grasp the timesaving qualities of mass production, select ten students to work together to complete a particular task. It can be as simple as a drawing or involve a more complicated assembly. Five students will perform the entire task as individuals; the others will divide the work. For example—with a drawing of a person, have five students complete the entire task, while the other five choose a particular part (arm, legs, face, torso) and pass it on to the next person. Both can be timed and judged for quality. Discuss the results as a class. In which way was the task finished more quickly? Who had greater satisfaction? The better product? **L2**

Refer to ***Inclusion for the High School Social Studies Classroom Strategies and Activities*** in the TCR.

The Coal and Iron Industries The steam engine was crucial to Britain's Industrial Revolution. For fuel, the engine depended on coal, a substance that seemed then to be unlimited in quantity. The success of the steam engine increased the need for coal and led to an expansion in coal production. New processes using coal aided the transformation of another industry—the iron industry.

Britain's natural resources included large supplies of iron ore. At the beginning of the eighteenth century, the basic process of producing iron had changed little since the Middle Ages. It became possible to produce a better quality of iron in the 1780s, when Henry Cort developed a process called **puddling.**

In this process, coke, which was derived from coal, was used to burn away impurities in crude iron, called pig iron, and produce an iron of high quality. The British iron industry boomed. In 1740, Britain had produced 17,000 tons (15,419 t) of iron. After Cort's process came into use in the 1780s, production jumped to nearly 70,000 tons (63,490 t). In 1852, Britain produced almost 3 million tons (2.7 million t)—more iron than was produced by the rest of the world combined. The high-quality iron was used to build new machines, especially new means of transportation.

Railroads In the eighteenth century, more efficient means of moving resources and goods developed. All-weather roads improved year-round transport, but it was the railroads that were particularly important.

In 1804, the first steam-powered locomotive ran on an industrial rail-line in Britain. It pulled 10 tons (9 t) of ore and 70 people at 5 miles (8.05 km) per hour. Better locomotives followed. One called the *Rocket* was used on the first public railway line, which opened in 1830 and extended 32 miles (51.5 km) from **Liverpool** to **Manchester,** England. The *Rocket* sped along at 16 miles (25.7 km) per hour while pulling a 40-ton (36-t) train. Within 20 years, locomotives were able to reach 50 miles (80.5 km) per hour, an incredible speed to passengers. In 1840, Britain had almost 2,000 miles (3,218 km) of railroads. By 1850, 6,000 miles (9,654 km) of railroad track crisscrossed much of that country.

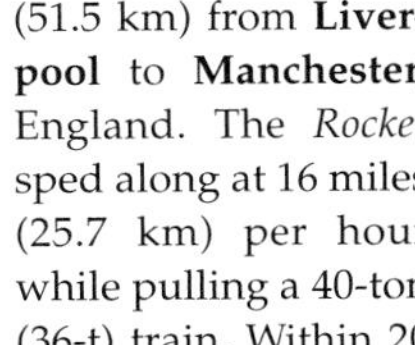

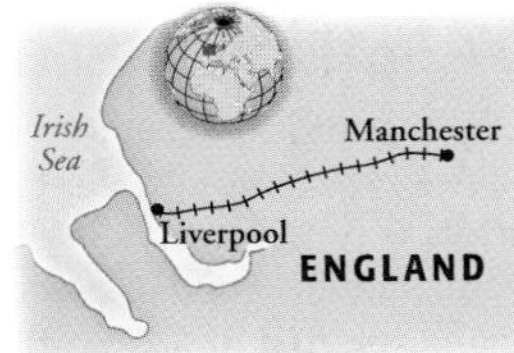

Building railroads created new jobs for farm laborers and peasants. Less expensive transportation led to lower-priced goods, thus creating larger markets. More sales meant more factories and more machinery. Business owners could reinvest their profits in new equipment, adding to the growth of the economy. This type of regular, ongoing economic growth became a basic feature of the new industrial economy.

The New Factories The factory was another important element in the Industrial Revolution. From its beginning, the factory created a new labor system. Factory owners wanted to use their new machines constantly. So, workers were forced to work in shifts to keep the machines producing at a steady rate.

Early factory workers came from rural areas, where they were used to periods of hectic work, followed by periods of inactivity. Early factory owners therefore had to create a system of work discipline in which employees became used to working regular hours and doing the same work over and over. For example, adult workers were fined for being late and were dismissed for serious misconduct, especially for being drunk. Child workers were often beaten. One early industrialist said that his aim was "to make the men into machines that cannot err."

Reading Check **Describing** How were adult and child factory workers disciplined?

Picturing History

In the *Rocket* (left), it took just two hours to travel 32 miles (51.5 km). How does this picture capture people's sense of wonder about train travel?

CHAPTER 12
Section 1, 363–370

Reading Check

Answer: Adults were fined for being late or dismissed for more serious misconduct; children were often beaten.

Picturing History

Answer: They seem to be trying to figure out how it moves. It is obviously an object of great interest.

Guided Reading Activity 12–1

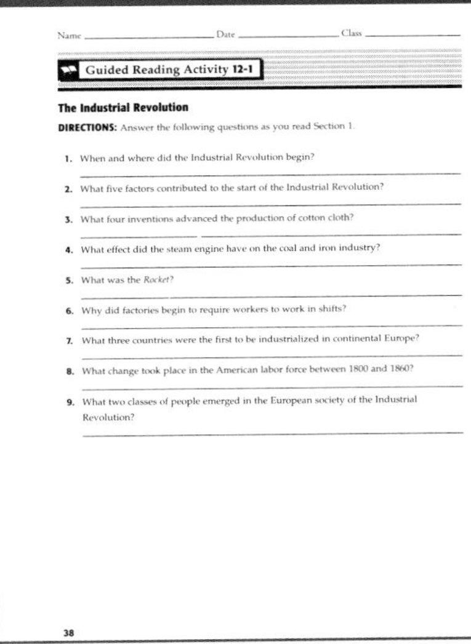

Name ________ Date ________ Class ________

Guided Reading Activity 12-1

The Industrial Revolution

DIRECTIONS: Answer the following questions as you read Section 1.

1. When and where did the Industrial Revolution begin?
2. What five factors contributed to the start of the Industrial Revolution?
3. What four inventions advanced the production of cotton cloth?
4. What effect did the steam engine have on the coal and iron industry?
5. What was the *Rocket*?
6. Why did factories begin to require workers to work in shifts?
7. What three countries were the first to be industrialized in continental Europe?
8. What change took place in the American labor force between 1800 and 1860?
9. What two classes of people emerged in the European society of the Industrial Revolution?

38

TURNING POINT

The Industrial Revolution dramatically changed the way that people lived in the nineteenth century, and it continues to impact our lives today. Ask students to identify changes that resulted from the Industrial Revolution. **L1**

COOPERATIVE LEARNING ACTIVITY

Researching Organize the class into groups. Have each group research innovations in one of these areas: farming, textiles, power sources, transportation. Each team member should be assigned a specific topic; for example, a student in the group examining power sources could research the use of wood or coal. After completing their research, the groups should meet to share their findings. Each team member should summarize his or her research for the group. Then each team should create a general summary to be delivered orally to the class. **L2**

For grading this activity, refer to the ***Performance Assessment Activities*** booklet.

CHAPTER 12
Section 1, 363–370

Reading Check

Answer: The railroad turned the United States into a single, massive market for the manufactured goods of the Northeast.

Graph Skills

Answers:
1. Britain's population did not increase as much as the population of the United States. The United States expanded the quantity of railroad tracks far more than Britain.
2. Britain; Britain

CURRICULUM CONNECTION

Environmental Science Railroads and other industries relied on burning coal for energy. This created sulfuric clouds over British cities. Ask students how this would have affected the lives of all British citizens. Why might wealthy people have chosen to spend more time at their country estates? *(buildings became sooty, more illness, city became less beautiful; the country was cleaner and more beautiful)* **L1**

Critical Thinking

In general, working conditions in American industry were better than in Europe until after the 1840s. Ask students to discuss why. What might it have had to do with the supply of workers? *(more work and fewer workers in the United States made them less expendable)* **L3**

The Spread of Industrialization

By the mid-nineteenth century, Great Britain had become the world's first and richest industrial nation. It produced one-half of the world's coal and manufactured goods. Its cotton industry alone in 1850 was equal in size to the industries of all other European countries combined.

Europe The Industrial Revolution spread to the rest of Europe at different times and speeds. First to be industrialized in continental Europe were Belgium, France, and the German states.

In these places, governments were very active in encouraging the development of industrialization. For example, governments provided funds to build roads, canals, and railroads. By 1850, a network of iron rails had spread across Europe.

North America An Industrial Revolution also occurred in the new nation of the United States. In 1800, six out of every seven American workers were farmers, and there were no cities with more than 100,000 people. Between 1800 and 1860, the population in the United States grew from 5 million to 30 million people. Cities grew, too. Nine cities had populations over 100,000. Only 50 percent of American workers were farmers.

The United States was a large country in the 1800s. A transportation system to move goods across the nation was vital. Thousands of miles of roads and canals were built to link east and west. **Robert Fulton** built the first paddle-wheel steamboat, the *Clermont*, in 1807. By 1860, a thousand steamboats plied the Mississippi River and made transportation easier on the Great Lakes and along the Atlantic coast.

Most important in the development of an American transportation system was the railroad. It began with fewer than 100 miles (160.9 km) of track in 1830. By 1860, about 30,000 miles (48,270 km) of railroad track covered the United States. The railroad turned the United States into a single massive market for the manufactured goods of the Northeast.

Labor for the growing number of factories in the Northeast came chiefly from the farm population. Many of the workers in the new factories of New England were women. Indeed, women made up more than 80 percent of the workers in large textile (cotton and wool) factories.

Factory owners sometimes sought entire families, including children, to work in their factories. One advertisement in a newspaper in the town of Utica, New York read: "Wanted: A few sober and industrious families of at least five children each, over the age of eight years, are wanted at the cotton factory in Whitestown. Widows with large families would do well to attend this notice."

Reading Check **Evaluating** Why was the railroad important to the American Industrial Revolution?

Comparing Britain and the United States*

*As you study these comparisons, keep in mind the vast difference in area encompassed by Britain and the United States. Britain (England, Scotland, and Wales) totals 67,390 square miles (174,540 sq km); the continental United States totals 3,017,630 square miles (7,815,661 sq km).

Graph Skills

Britain was the leading industrial nation in the early and mid-nineteenth century, but countries such as the United States eventually surpassed Britain in industrial production.

1. **Comparing** How did Britain's population growth, from 1830 to 1870 and 1870 to 1900, compare to the United States's growth? How did Britain's expansion in railroad tracks compare to that of the United States during the same period?
2. **Problem Solving** Which country had the highest percentage of railroad track miles in comparison to total square miles in 1870? In 1900?

COOPERATIVE LEARNING ACTIVITY

Visual Presentations Organize the class into groups. Have each group study innovations in transportation during the Industrial Revolution: railroads, steamships, and automobiles. Assign each team member a specific topic, such as method of operation, economic impact, and most common uses. After completing their research, team members should share information. Each team should then combine individual reports into a summary, and design a visual aid, such as a drawing or graph, to enhance their report. One member of each team should present the group's summary and visual aid to the rest of the class. **L2**

NATIONAL GEOGRAPHIC

Industrialization of Europe by 1870

— German Confederation

0 400 miles
0 400 kilometers
Chamberlin Trimetric projection

Geography Skills

The Industrial Revolution spread throughout nineteenth-century Europe.

1. **Interpreting Maps** What was the predominate industry in the United Kingdom?
2. **Applying Geography Skills** What patterns do you see in the distribution of the major industries? What geographical factors could account for these patterns?

Social Impact in Europe

The Industrial Revolution drastically changed the social life of Europe and the world. This change was evident in the first half of the nineteenth century in the growth of cities and the emergence of two new social classes: the industrial middle class and the industrial working class.

Growth of Population and Cities In 1750, European population stood at an estimated 140 million. By 1850, the population had almost doubled to 266 million. The key to this growth was a decline in death rates, wars, and diseases, such as smallpox and plague. Because of an increase in the food supply, more people were better fed and resistant to disease. Famine largely disappeared from western Europe.

Cities and towns in Europe grew dramatically in the first half of the nineteenth century. The growth was directly related to industrialization. By 1850,

Geography Skills

Answers:

1. coal mining
2. Most of the industries are located in northern Europe, especially around the border between France, Netherlands, and Germany. This was an area very rich in natural resources, which is probably why industries clustered there. Presence of mountains in southern Europe could also account for reduced industry since difficult to transport goods in that region.

Connecting Across Time

Ask students to interview a parent or grandparent about significant technological changes that have occurred during their lifetimes. How have the changes affected their lives? **L1**

Critical Thinking

Ask students to list some of the activities that were part of the Industrial Revolution but which could not be accomplished at home. Discuss why these activities contributed to the growth of towns near factories. *(mining, iron production, building railways, weaving cloth and spinning yarn on machines, use of steam engine to power machinery)* **L2**

INTERDISCIPLINARY CONNECTIONS ACTIVITY

Journalism Divide the class into groups and provide each group with a selection from such Charles Dickens works as *Oliver Twist, Hard Times,* or *The Old Curiosity Shop.* Let each group use its selection to write an exposé-style newspaper article on working class conditions in Britain during the Industrial Revolution. Students should write interviews with the characters or report on an event from the story. Compile the articles into a newsletter/newspaper for the class. You might want to have students add political cartoons, want ads, etc. **L2**

For grading this activity, refer to the ***Performance Assessment Activities*** booklet.

CHAPTER 12
Section 1, 363–370

Critical Thinking
In a class discussion ask students to explain why the growth of the bourgeoisie shifted political as well as economic power in Europe. Why did the masses of factory workers not have any effective political power? *(factory owners made a lot of money, stimulated the economy, paid more taxes and contributed to the growth of cities. Workers had little say in politics because they had little money and little time)* **L2**

Connecting Across Time
Ask students to describe what would happen to a present-day firm that used the methods described on page 369 to maintain control over its workers. What does this indicate about the need for government protection of workers? *(They might face fines, prosecution, or be shut down. Government needs to regulate labor policies.)* **L1**

ABCNEWS INTERACTIVE™

Turning Points in World History
The ABC News videotape includes a segment on the Industrial Revolution.

especially in Great Britain and Belgium, cities were rapidly becoming home to many industries. With the steam engine, factory owners did not need water power and could locate their plants in cities. People moved from the country to the cities to find work, traveling on the new railroads.

In 1800, Great Britain had one major city, London, with a population of 1 million, and six cities with populations between 50,000 and 100,000. Fifty years later, London's population had swelled to 2,363,000. Nine cities had populations over 100,000, and 18 cities had populations between 50,000 and 100,000. Over 50 percent of the British population lived in towns and cities by 1850. Urban populations also grew in other European countries, but less dramatically.

The rapid growth of cities in the first half of the nineteenth century led to pitiful living conditions for many of the inhabitants. Eventually, these conditions prompted urban reformers to call on local governments to clean up their cities. The calls for reform would be answered in the second half of the nineteenth century.

The Industrial Middle Class The Middle Ages had seen the rise of commercial capitalism, an economic system based on trade. With the Industrial Revolution came the rise of **industrial capitalism,** an economic system based on industrial production. Industrial capitalism produced a new middle-class group—the industrial middle class.

In the Middle Ages, the bourgeois, or middle-class person, was the burgher or town dweller, who may have been active as a merchant, official, artisan, lawyer, or intellectual. Later, the term *bourgeois* came to include people involved in industry and banking, as well as professionals, such as lawyers, teachers, doctors, and government officials.

The new industrial middle class was made up of the people who built the factories, bought the machines, and figured out where the markets were.

THE WAY IT WAS

YOUNG PEOPLE IN . . .

The Industrial Revolution

Children had been an important part of the family economy in preindustrial times. They worked in the fields or at home in cottage industries. In the Industrial Revolution, however, child labor was exploited.

Children represented a cheap supply of labor. In 1821, 49 percent of the British people were under 20 years of age. Hence, children made up a large pool of workers. Children were paid only about one-sixth to one-third of what a man was paid.

The owners of cotton factories in England found child labor especially useful.

Young laborers

Children had a delicate touch as spinners of cotton. Their smaller size made it easier for them to move under machines to gather loose cotton. Furthermore, they were more easily trained to factory work than adults.

In the cotton factories in 1838, children under the age of 18 made up 29 percent of the total workforce. In cotton mills, children as young as age seven worked 12 to 15 hours per day, six days a week.

Discipline was often harsh. A report from a British parliamentary inquiry into the condition of child factory workers in 1838 stated:

368

MEETING INDIVIDUAL NEEDS

Auditory/Visual Have the students read pages 368–370 and "Young People in the Industrial Revolution" on pages 368–369. Divide the class into two groups and designate one group as "The Industrial Middle Class" and the other as "The Industrial Working Class." Have each group identify the following: 1) Who makes up their group? *(Middle Class: merchants, officials, lawyers, bankers, teachers, doctors, factory builders, marketers; Working Class: factory workers, cotton mill workers, coal miners, many women and children)* 2) How do they feel about the employment of children? *(Middle Class: helpful, delicate touch as cotton spinners, more easily trained, cheap labor; Working class: exploited, abused, dangerous, unhealthy, brings in needed money)* Have each group prepare a chart listing the above information and share it with the class.

Their qualities included initiative, vision, ambition, and often, greed. One manufacturer said, "Getting of money . . . is the main business of the life of men."

The Industrial Working Class The Industrial Revolution also created an industrial working class. Industrial workers faced wretched working conditions. Work hours ranged from 12 to 16 hours a day, six days a week, with a half-hour for lunch and dinner. There was no security of employment and no minimum wage.

The worst conditions were in the cotton mills, where temperatures were especially harmful. One report noted that "in the cotton-spinning work, these creatures are kept, 14 hours in each day, locked up, summer and winter, in a heat of from 80 to 84 degrees." Mills were also dirty, dusty, dangerous, and unhealthy.

Conditions in the coal mines were also harsh. Although steam-powered engines were used to lift coal from the mines to the top, inside the mines men still bore the burden of digging the coal out. Horses, mules, women, and children hauled coal carts on rails to the lift. Dangerous conditions, including cave-ins, explosions, and gas fumes (called "bad air"), were a way of life. The cramped conditions in mines—tunnels were often only three or four feet high—and their constant dampness led to deformed bodies and ruined lungs.

In Britain, women and children made up two-thirds of the cotton industry's workforce by 1830. However, the number of children declined under the Factory Act of 1833, which set 9 as the minimum age for employment. Children between 9 and 13 could work only 8 hours a day; those between 13 and 18 could work 12 hours.

As the number of children employed declined, their places were taken by women. Women made up 50 percent of the labor force in British textile factories before 1870. They were mostly unskilled labor and

"It is a very frequent thing at Mr. Marshall's . . . for Mr. Horseman to start the mill earlier in the morning than he formerly did; and provided a child should be drowsy, the overlooker walks round the room with a stick in his hand, and he touches that child on the shoulder, and says, 'Come here.' In a corner of the room there is an iron cistern; it is filled with water; he takes this boy, and takes him up by the legs, and dips him over head in the cistern, and sends him to work for the remainder of the day. . . . What means were taken to keep the children to their work?—Sometimes they would tap them over the head, or nip them over the nose, or give them a pinch of snuff, or throw water in their faces, or pull them off where they were, and job them about to keep them awake."

The same inquiry also reported that, in some factories, children were often beaten with a rod or whip to keep them at work.

Supervisors made sure children worked continuously.

Connecting to the Past

1. **Identifying** What kind of working conditions did children face in the factories during the early Industrial Revolution?
2. **Analyzing** Why did factory owners permit such conditions and such treatment of children?
3. **Writing about History** What are conditions like today for factory workers? Write an essay contrasting current conditions with those of 100 years ago.

Critical Thinking Activity

Supporting a Point of View Assign students to one of two groups: factory owner and factory workers. The owners can research the basic ideas behind Social Darwinism and the capitalist system, while the workers can draw on the ideas of Robert Owen and utopian socialists. As a class, prepare a debate outlining the major differences between the two and the philosophies in which they believed. You may want to encourage the class to work together to compile the major points of each side in a chart on the chalkboard or poster. Finish the lesson by assigning the students to write essays in which they must support the beliefs and views of either the factory owners or the factory workers. **L2**

The Way It Was

Answers:

1. they worked long hours, harshly disciplined, and poorly paid
2. They had a delicate touch as spinners of cotton, their smaller size made it easier to move under machines; also, they were easier to train than adults.
3. much better—children no longer work in factories, hours are shorter, and working conditions are much better; corporal punishment is no longer condoned

3 ASSESS

Assign Section 1 Assessment as homework or as an in-class activity.

Have students use **Interactive Tutor Self-Assessment CD-ROM.**

Section Quiz 12–1

Name ______ Date ______ Class ______

Chapter 12 Score

Section Quiz 12-1

DIRECTIONS: Matching Match each item in Column A with an item in Column B. Write the correct letters in the blanks. *(10 points each)*

Column A	Column B
____ 1. seekers of new business opportunities	A. capital
____ 2. money supply	B. cottage industry
____ 3. production method using rural, at-home workers	C. socialism
____ 4. governmental ownership and control of production	D. spinning jenny
____ 5. invention that improved thread production	E. entrepreneurs

DIRECTIONS: Multiple Choice In the blank, write the letter of the choice that best completes the statement or answers the question. *(10 points each)*

____ 6. Which of the following did NOT contribute to Britain's Industrial

Picturing History

Answer: Cities and towns grew dramatically as industries moved to them from the country. People crowded in to find work, and the rapid growth led to pitiful living conditions such as the ones shown here.

✓ Reading Check

Answer: long hours; no job security; no minimum wage; harmful conditions

Reading Essentials and Study Guide 12–1

Name ____________ Date ____________ Class ____________

Reading Essentials and Study Guide

Chapter 12, Section 1

For use with textbook pages 363–370

THE INDUSTRIAL REVOLUTION

KEY TERMS

capital money available for investment *(page 364)*

entrepreneur a person who invests in a new business or businesses in order to make profits *(page 365)*

cottage industry a production method in which individuals did the work in their rural homes *(page 364)*

puddling a process developed by Henry Cort in the 1780s that produced high quality iron by using coke to burn away impurities in crude iron *(page 365)*

industrial capitalism an economic system based on industrial production *(page 368)*

socialism a system in which society, usually in the form of the government, owns and controls

Reteaching Activity

Write the following headings on the board: *agriculture, population, machinery, transportation.* Ask students to discuss how changes in each area contributed to the Industrial Revolution. **L2**

4 CLOSE

Ask students to discuss whether they agree with the following statement: "In the long run, the Industrial Revolution was good for all classes of British society because it created so much new wealth in that nation."

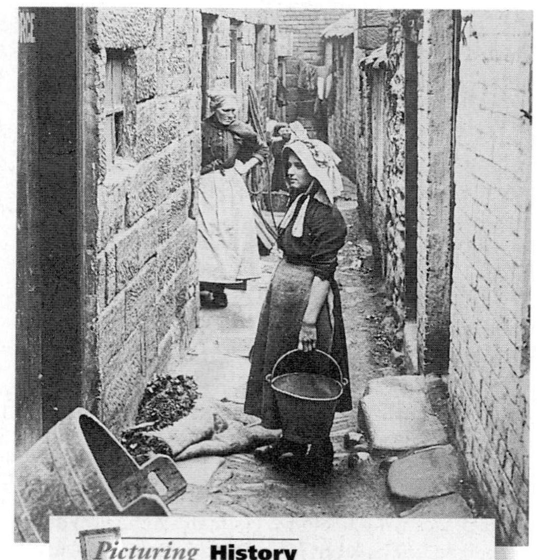

Picturing **History**

A late nineteenth-century photo shows housing conditions in England. How did the Industrial Revolution contribute to such scenes?

were paid half or less than half of what men received. Excessive working hours for women were outlawed in 1844.

The employment of children and women was in large part carried over from an earlier pattern. Husband, wife, and children had always worked together in cottage industry. The laws that limited the work hours of children and women thus gradually led to a new pattern of work.

Men were now expected to earn most of the family income by working outside the home. Women, in contrast, took over daily care of the family and performed low-paying jobs, such as laundry work, that could be done in the home. Working at home for pay made it possible for women to continue to help with the family's financial survival.

Early Socialism In the first half of the nineteenth century, the pitiful conditions created by the Industrial Revolution gave rise to a movement known as **socialism**. Socialism is a system in which society, usually in the form of the government, owns and controls the means of production—natural resources, factories, and so forth.

Early socialism was largely the idea of intellectuals who believed in the equality of all people and who wanted to replace competition with cooperation in industry. To later socialists, especially the followers of Karl Marx, such ideas were merely impractical dreams. The later socialists contemptuously labeled the earlier theorists utopian socialists. The term has lasted to this day.

Robert Owen, a British cotton manufacturer, was one utopian socialist. He believed that humans would show their natural goodness if they lived in a cooperative environment. At New Lanark in Scotland, Owen transformed a squalid factory town into a flourishing community. He created a similar community at New Harmony, Indiana, in the United States in the 1820s, which failed.

✓ Reading Check **Describing** What type of working conditions did the industrial workers face?

SECTION 1 ASSESSMENT

Checking for Understanding

1. **Define** capital, entrepreneur, cottage industry, puddling, industrial capitalism, socialism.
2. **Identify** enclosure movement, James Watt, Robert Fulton.
3. **Locate** Liverpool, Manchester.
4. **Describe** the importance of the railroads in the growth of cities in Europe and North America.
5. **List** the members of the new industrial middle class.

Critical Thinking

6. **Cause and Effect** Analyze how the Industrial Revolution changed the way families lived and worked.
7. **Cause and Effect** Use a diagram like the one below to list the causes and effects of the Industrial Revolution.

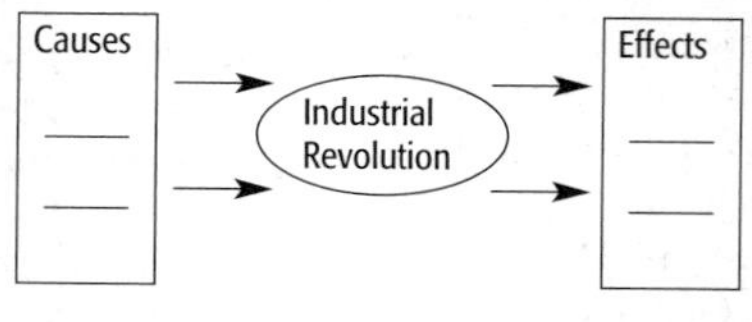

Analyzing Visuals

8. **Examine** the picture of a female textile worker shown on page 364 of your text. How does this picture reflect the role that women played in the Industrial Revolution?

Writing About History

9. **Informative Writing** You are a nineteenth-century journalist. Write a brief article depicting the working conditions in cotton mills and an explanation of how owners defend such conditions.

SECTION 1 ASSESSMENT

1. Key terms are in blue.
2. enclosure movement *(p. 364)*; James Watt *(p. 364)*; Robert Fulton *(p. 366)*
3. See chapter maps.
4. less expensive transportation, led to lower-priced goods, larger markets
5. the people who built the factories, bought the machines
6. people from land into cities; subjecting them to poverty, overcrowding, illness
7. Causes: more food for more people, factory system based on steam power; Effects: more and cheaper goods, new social classes; growth of cities, short-term suffering for workers, long-term improvement in standards of living
8. Women entered workforce, worked in factories, or took low-paying jobs that could be done at home.
9. Answers should be consistent with material presented in this section.

SECTION 2 Reaction and Revolution

Guide to Reading

Main Ideas
- The great powers worked to maintain a conservative order throughout Europe.
- The forces of liberalism and nationalism continued to grow and led to the revolutions of 1848.

Key Terms
conservatism, principle of intervention, liberalism, universal male suffrage

People to Identify
Klemens von Metternich, Louis-Napoleon

Places to Locate
Vienna, Prague

Preview Questions
1. What did the Congress of Vienna try to accomplish?
2. Why did revolutions occur in 1848?

Reading Strategy
Cause and Effect Use a chart like the one below to identify the causes of the revolutions in France in 1830 and 1848.

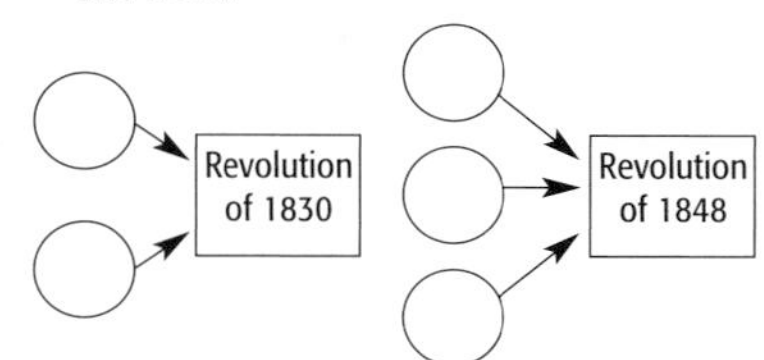

Preview of Events

1810	1820	1830	1840	1850	1860

- **1814** Congress of Vienna meets to create balance of power
- **1830** Liberals overthrow Charles X and establish a constitutional monarchy in France
- **1848** Revolutions sweep through Europe
- **1849** Austria reestablishes control over Lombardy

Klemens von Metternich confers with Napoleon.

Voices from the Past

Prince Klemens von Metternich, the foreign minister of the Austrian Empire, wrote:

> ❝The first principle to be followed by the monarchs, united as they are by the coincidence of their desires and opinions, should be that of maintaining the stability of political institutions against the disorganized excitement which has taken possession of men's minds. . . . The first and greatest concern for the immense majority of every nation is the stability of the laws, and their uninterrupted action—never their change. Therefore, let the governments govern, let them maintain the groundwork of their institutions, both ancient and modern; for it is at all times dangerous to touch them.❞
>
> —***Memoirs,*** **Alexander Napler, trans., 1881**

Metternich worked tirelessly for 30 years to repress the "revolutionary seed," as he called it, that had been spread by Napoleon Bonaparte.

The Congress of Vienna

After the defeat of Napoleon, European rulers moved to restore the old order. This was the goal of the great powers—Great Britain, Austria, Prussia, and Russia—when they met at the **Congress of Vienna** in September 1814 to arrange a final peace settlement. The leader of the congress was the Austrian foreign minister, Prince **Klemens von Metternich** (MEH•tuhr•NIHK).

Metternich claimed that he was guided at **Vienna** by the principle of legitimacy. This meant that lawful monarchs from the royal families that had ruled before Napoleon would be restored to their positions of power in order to keep peace and stability in Europe. This had already been done in France with the

1 FOCUS

Section Overview

This section discusses the political forces that led to revolutions across Europe.

BELLRINGER
Skillbuilder Activity

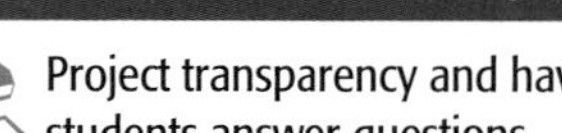
Project transparency and have students answer questions.

Available as a blackline master.

Daily Focus Skills Transparency 12–2

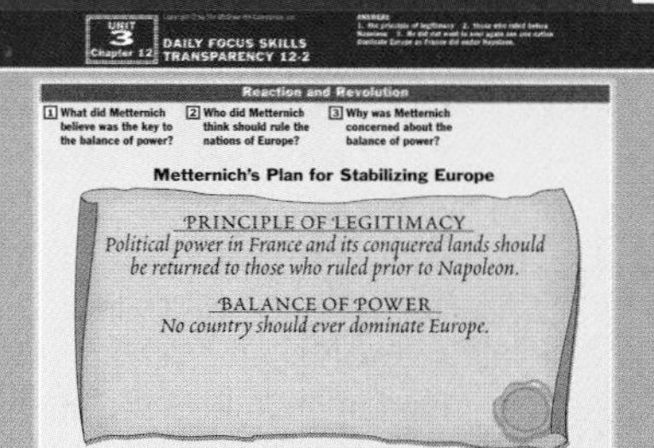

Guide to Reading

Answers to Graphic: Revolution of 1830: dissolution of legislature; suspension of freedom of press Revolution of 1848: economic problems; worker revolt; voting rights

Preteaching Vocabulary: Ask students to define *conservatism* and *liberalism*, and write a sentence that applies each word to a contemporary political situation. **L1**

SECTION RESOURCES

Reproducible Masters
- Reproducible Lesson Plan 12–2
- Daily Lecture and Discussion Notes 12–2
- Guided Reading Activity 12–2
- Section Quiz 12–2
- Reading Essentials and Study Guide 12–2

Transparencies
- Daily Focus Skills Transparency 12–2

Multimedia
- Interactive Tutor Self-Assessment CD-ROM
- ExamView® Pro Testmaker CD-ROM
- Presentation Plus! CD-ROM

CHAPTER 12
Section 2, 371–376

2 TEACH

Reading Check

Answer: Lawful monarchs from the royal families that had ruled before Napoleon would be restored to their positions of power in order to keep peace and stability in Europe. This was done in France but largely ignored elsewhere.

Geography *Skills*

Answers:

1. Within the German Confederation; Austria
2. France lost areas in northern and central Italy, the Illyrian Provinces, Netherlands and areas of Prussia and the German States. Russia gained the Grand Duchy of Warsaw. Remind students that when comparing areas on maps, it is important to look at the map scales. Point out that the map on page 349 and the one on this page have different scales, and that areas may appear larger or smaller because of this difference in scale.

Daily Lecture and Discussion Notes 12–2

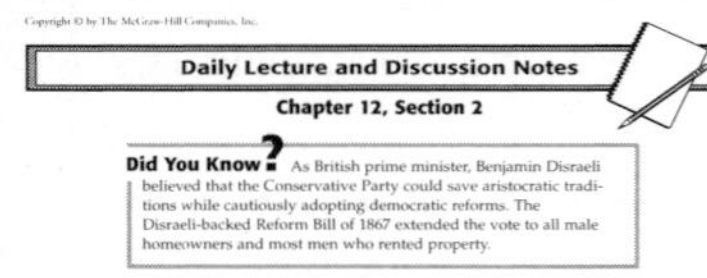

Daily Lecture and Discussion Notes

Chapter 12, Section 2

Did You Know? As British prime minister, Benjamin Disraeli believed that the Conservative Party could save aristocratic traditions while cautiously adopting democratic reforms. The Disraeli-backed Reform Bill of 1867 extended the vote to all male homeowners and most men who rented property.

I. **The Congress of Vienna** *(pages 371–372)*

A. When the great powers of Austria, Prussia, Russia, and Great Britain met at the **Congress of Vienna** in 1814, they wanted to restore the old order after Napoleon's defeat.

B. Prince **Klemens von Metternich** was the Austrian foreign minister who led the Congress. He said he was guided at **Vienna** by the principle of legitimacy: legitimate monarchs deposed by Napoleon would be restored in the interest of peace and stability.

C. Some countries accepted the principle of legitimacy and some did not.

D. The participants in the Congress of Vienna also rearranged European territories to form a new balance of military and political power to keep one country from dominating Europe. To balance Russian territorial gains, Prussia and Austria were given new territories, for example.

Geography *Skills*

The Congress of Vienna tried to create a new balance of power in Europe.

1. **Interpreting Maps** Within what political boundries is Vienna located? Of what nation is Vienna the capital today?
2. **Applying Geography Skills** Compare this map to the map of Napoleonic Europe shown on page 349 of your text. What territories that belonged to the French Empire in 1812 were *not* part of France after the Congress of Vienna? What land did Russia gain?

restoration of the Bourbon monarchy. However, the principle of legitimacy was largely ignored elsewhere.

Practical considerations of power were addressed at the Congress of Vienna. The great powers rearranged territories in Europe, believing that this would form a new balance of power. The powers at Vienna wanted to keep any one country from dominating Europe. This meant balancing political and military forces that guaranteed the independence of the great powers. To balance Russian territorial gains, for example, new territories were given to Prussia and Austria.

Reading Check **Explaining** What was the "principle of legitimacy"?

The Conservative Order

The arrangements worked out at the Congress of Vienna were a victory for rulers who wanted to contain the forces of change unleashed by the French Revolution. These rulers, like Metternich, believed in the political philosophy known as **conservatism**.

Conservatism is based on tradition and social stability. Most conservatives at that time favored obedience to political authority and believed that organized religion was crucial to order in society. Conservatives hated revolutions and were unwilling to accept demands from people who wanted either individual rights or representative governments.

To maintain the new balance of power, Great Britain, Russia, Prussia, and Austria (and later France) agreed to meet at times in conferences to take steps that would maintain the peace in Europe. These meetings came to be called the Concert of Europe.

MEETING INDIVIDUAL NEEDS

Study Strategy To help students learn the information in this section, suggest that they outline it. They should list each major heading and any subheads, saving space under these heads to write the key figures, dates, and events as they read about them. They should focus on writing information in their own words, rather than copying information directly from the book. They should look up words they do not understand and write the definitions to reinforce their understanding of the new terms. It may be helpful for auditory learners to work in pairs and read the section aloud to each other. **L1**

Refer to ***Inclusion for the High School Social Studies Classroom Strategies and Activities*** in the TCR.

Eventually, the great powers adopted a **principle of intervention.** According to this principle, the great powers had the right to send armies into countries where there were revolutions in order to restore legitimate monarchs to their thrones. Britain refused to accept the principle, arguing that the great powers should not interfere in the internal affairs of other states. Austria, Prussia, Russia, and France, however, used military forces to crush revolutions in Spain and Italy, as well as to restore monarchs to their thrones.

✓Reading Check **Summarizing** What were the views of the conservative movement?

Forces of Change

Between 1815 and 1830, conservative governments throughout Europe worked to maintain the old order. However, powerful forces for change—known as liberalism and nationalism—were also at work.

Liberalism **Liberalism,** a political philosophy based largely on Enlightenment principles, held that people should be as free as possible from government restraint.

Liberals had a common set of political beliefs. Chief among them was the protection of civil liberties, or the basic rights of all people. These civil liberties included equality before the law and freedom of assembly, speech, and press. Liberals believed that all these freedoms should be guaranteed by a written document, such as the American **Bill of Rights.**

Most liberals wanted religious toleration for all, as well as separation of church and state. Liberals also demanded the right of peaceful opposition to the government. They believed that laws should be made by a representative assembly (legislature) elected by qualified voters.

Many liberals, then, favored government ruled by a constitution such as in a constitutional monarchy, in which a king is regulated by a constitution. They believed that written constitutions would guarantee the rights they sought to preserve.

Liberals did not, however, believe in a democracy in which everyone had a right to vote. They thought that the right to vote and hold office should be open only to men of property. Liberalism, then, was tied to middle-class men, especially industrial middle-class men, who wanted voting rights for themselves so that they could share power with the landowning classes. The liberals feared mob rule and had little desire to let the lower classes share that power.

Nationalism Nationalism was an even more powerful force for change in the nineteenth century than was liberalism. Nationalism arose out of people's awareness of being part of a community with common institutions, traditions, language, and customs. This community is called a nation. For nationalists, people owe their chief political loyalty to the nation rather than to a dynasty, city-state, or other political unit.

Nationalism did not become a popular force for change until the French Revolution. From then on, nationalists came to believe that each nationality should have its own government. Thus, the Germans, who were separated into many principalities, wanted national unity in a German nation-state with one central government. Subject peoples, such as the Hungarians, wanted the right to establish their own governments rather than be subject to the Austrian emperor.

Nationalism, then, was a threat to the existing political order. A united Germany, for example, would upset the balance of power set up at the Congress of Vienna in 1815. At the same time, an independent Hungarian state would mean the breakup of the Austrian Empire. Conservatives feared such change and thus tried hard to repress nationalism.

In the first half of the nineteenth century, nationalism found a strong ally in liberalism. Most liberals

People In History

Klemens von Metternich
1773–1859—Austrian statesman

There was no greater symbol of conservatism in the first half of the nineteenth century than Prince Klemens von Metternich. Born in the Rhineland of Germany, he fled to Austria in 1794 and joined the Austrian diplomatic service. He was made Austrian foreign minister in 1809.

An experienced diplomat, Metternich was conceited and self-assured. He described himself in his memoirs in 1819: "There is a wide sweep about my mind. I am always above and beyond the preoccupation of most public men; I cover a ground much vaster than they can see. I cannot keep myself from saying about twenty times a day: 'How right I am, and how wrong they are.'" When revolution erupted in 1848, Metternich fled to England.

✓Reading Check

Answer: based on tradition and social stability; favors obedience to political authority; organized religion considered crucial to order in society; unwilling to accept liberal demands for individual rights or representative governments

Guided Reading Activity 12–2

Name ____________ Date ____________ Class ____________

Guided Reading Activity 12-2

Reaction and Revolution

DIRECTIONS: Fill in the blanks below as you read Section 2.

After the defeat of **(1)** ____________, European rulers moved to restore the old order with **(2)** ____________, **(3)** ____________, **(4)** ____________, and **(5)** ____________ in power. This goal was addressed at the Congress of **(6)** ____________ in September 1814.

The arrangements made at this Congress were a victory for rulers who wanted to contain the forces of **(7)** ____________ unleashed by the French Revolution. Their political philosophy, based on tradition and social stability, is known as **(8)** ____________. The great powers assumed the right of intervention whereby they could send armies into countries where there were revolutions in order to restore legitimate **(9)** ____________ to their thrones.

Liberals believed in the protection of **(10)** ____________ liberties, or the basic rights of all people. Many favored government ruled by a **(11)** ____________ which regulates the monarchy. They thought that the right to vote and hold office should be open only to men of **(12)** ____________. Liberals had no desire for the **(13)** ____________ classes to share in power.

(14) ____________ in the nineteenth century arose out of people's awareness of being part of a community with common institutions. After the French Revolution, nationalists came to believe that each **(15)** ____________ should have its own government. **(16)** ____________ feared the implications of such thinking and tried to repress nationalism.

Nationalistic/liberal thinking led to **(17)** ____________ in the countries of Europe. The **(18)** ____________ of France was finally overthrown in 1848. Cries for change led many German rulers to promise **(19)** ____________, a free press, and jury trials. In Vienna, Austria, revolutionary forces took control of the **(20)** ____________ and demanded a liberal constitution.

39

Critical Thinking

Have students think through and debate the views of conservatives and liberals. You might have them evaluate the success of the Congress of Vienna based on the two views. **L3**

Critical Thinking

In the first half of the nineteenth century, nationalism found a strong ally in liberalism. Ask students if they believe that these two concepts are allies today. Why or why not? What is the difference between the two concepts? **L3**

CRITICAL THINKING ACTIVITY

Categorizing Information Nationalism has been an impetus to conflict and change throughout world history. In some countries, nationalist conflict has been resolved peacefully. In other cases, attempts at resolution have created more conflict and tension. There are also places where no attempts have been made to resolve nationalist issues. Ask students to research nationalism and identify countries and regions where nationalism has been an issue. Ask students to create a thematic graph with their research results. Students may choose to use nationalism as the theme or narrow the theme based on their research. **L2**

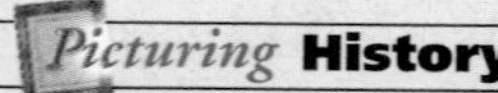

Picturing History

Answer: The upper middle class supported him as the new constitutional monarch.

Reading Check

Answer: In France, liberals overthrew Charles X and established a constitutional monarchy. Nationalism was the force in three revolutions in 1830. Belgium created an independent state, but revolts in Poland and Italy failed to free these lands of foreign domination.

Critical Thinking

Based on their knowledge of the French Revolution, students should discuss how the events described in this section can be called a continuation of the French Revolution. *(French revolted against new monarchy; still demanding many of the same rights)* **L1**

Enrich

Ask students to explain why people in Europe would be likely to feel a greater sense of nationalism after the wars in the Napoleonic era. *(they had seen overthrow of monarchs; had ended foreign domination by Napoleon)* **L2**

Connecting Across Time

Help students define *nationalism.* Discuss how nationalism can unify people in a country or can lead to war and to discrimination against minority groups. Conclude by asking students to give examples of nationalism at work in the world today. **L1**

Picturing History

In 1830, Charles X of France dissolved the French legislature and suspended freedom of the press. Revolution followed. The rebels (left) demanded a republic. How was Louis-Philippe involved in these events?

Louis-Philippe

believed that freedom could only be possible in people who ruled themselves. Each group of people should have its own state: no state should attempt to dominate another state. The association with liberalism meant that nationalism had a wider scope.

Revolutionary Outbursts Beginning in 1830, the forces of change—liberalism and nationalism—began to break through the conservative domination of Europe. In France, liberals overthrew the Bourbon monarch Charles X in 1830 and established a constitutional monarchy. Political support for the new monarch, Louis-Philippe, a cousin of Charles X, came from the upper middle class.

Nationalism was the chief force in three other revolutions the same year. Belgium, which had been annexed to the Dutch Republic in 1815, rebelled and created an independent state. Revolutions in Poland and Italy were much less successful. Russian forces crushed the attempt of Poles to free themselves from foreign domination. Austrian troops marched into Italy and put down revolts in a number of Italian states.

Reading Check **Evaluating** How did liberalism and nationalism begin to break through the conservative domination of Europe?

The Revolutions of 1848

Despite liberal and nationalist successes in France and Belgium, the conservative order still dominated much of Europe as the midpoint of the nineteenth century approached. However, the forces of liberalism and nationalism continued to grow. These forces of change erupted once more in the revolutions of 1848.

Another French Revolution Revolution in France was again the spark for revolution in other countries. Severe economic problems beginning in 1846 brought untold hardship in France to the lower middle class, workers, and peasants. At the same time, members of the middle class clamored for the right to vote. The government of Louis-Philippe refused to make changes, and opposition grew.

The monarchy was finally overthrown in 1848. A group of moderate and radical republicans set up a provisional, or temporary, government. The republicans were people who wished France to be a republic—a government in which leaders are elected.

The provisional government called for the election of representatives to a Constituent Assembly that would draw up a new constitution. Election was to be by **universal male suffrage**—that is, all adult men could vote.

The provisional government also set up national workshops to provide work for the unemployed. From March to June, the number of unemployed enrolled in the national workshops rose from 6,100 to almost 120,000. This emptied the treasury and frightened the moderates, who reacted by closing the workshops on June 21.

The workers refused to accept this decision and poured into the streets. In four days of bitter and

COOPERATIVE LEARNING ACTIVITY

Creating a News Broadcast Organize students into groups and assign each group one of the revolutions described in this chapter. Each team should prepare a news broadcast by dividing up responsibility to research and prepare stories that provide a rounded picture of events in one of the revolutions. Each team should have a news anchor, on-the-scene reporter, and a subject for the interview. Have teams report on events, reactions of conservative and nationalistic leaders and persons-in-the-street. Remind students to base their reports on actual events and actual people when possible. Have them write scripts and present their broadcasts to the class. You may want to videotape the presentations. **L2**

bloody fighting, government forces crushed the working-class revolt. Thousands were killed, and thousands more were sent to the French prison colony of Algeria in northern Africa.

The new constitution, ratified on November 4, 1848, set up a republic, called the Second Republic. The Second Republic had a single legislature elected by universal male suffrage. A president, also chosen by universal male suffrage, served for four years. In the elections for the presidency held in December 1848, Charles Louis Napoleon Bonaparte (called **Louis-Napoleon**), the nephew of the famous French ruler, won a resounding victory.

Trouble in the German States News of the 1848 revolution in France led to upheaval in other parts of Europe. The Congress of Vienna in 1815 had recognized the existence of 38 independent German states (called the **Germanic Confederation**). Of these, Austria and Prussia were the two great powers. The other states varied in size.

In 1848, cries for change led many German rulers to promise constitutions, a free press, and jury trials. Indeed, an all-German parliament, called the Frankfurt Assembly, was held to fulfill a liberal and nationalist dream—the preparation of a constitution for a new united Germany. Deputies to the parliament were elected by universal male suffrage.

Ultimately, however, the Frankfurt Assembly failed to achieve its goal. The members drafted a constitution but had no real means of forcing the German rulers to accept it. German unification was not achieved.

Revolutions in Central Europe The Austrian Empire also had its problems. The empire was a **multinational state**—a collection of different peoples, including Germans, Czechs, Magyars (Hungarians), Slovaks, Romanians, Slovenes, Poles, Croats, Serbians, and Italians. Only the Hapsburg emperor provided a common bond. The Germans, though only a quarter of the population, played a leading role in governing the Austrian Empire.

In March 1848, demonstrations in the major cities led to the dismissal of Metternich, the Austrian foreign minister. In Vienna, revolutionary forces took control of the capital and demanded a liberal constitution. To appease the revolutionaries, the government gave Hungary its own legislature. In Bohemia, the Czechs clamored for their own government.

Austrian officials had made concessions to appease the revolutionaries but were determined to reestablish their control over the empire. In June 1848, Austrian

CONNECTIONS Past To Present

Russian Troops in Hungary

On November 1, 1956, Imry Nagy, leader of Hungary, declared Hungary a free nation and promised new elections. Hungary was at that time under the control of the Soviet Union. Fearing that these elections would mean the end of Communist rule in Hungary, Nikita Khrushchev, leader of the Soviet Union, reacted dramatically.

On November 4, two hundred thousand Soviet (mostly Russian) troops and four thousand Soviet tanks invaded Budapest, Hungary's capital city. An estimated fifty thousand Hungarians died on that day. Nagy fled but was later arrested and executed. The Hungarian Revolution of 1956 had failed.

To Hungarians who knew their country's history, the use of Russian troops to crush their independence had an all-too-familiar ring. In 1848, Louis Kossuth had led a revolt that forced Hungary's Austrian rulers to grant Hungary its own legislature and a separate national army. In April 1849, the Hungarian legislature declared Hungary a republic. Kossuth was made the new president.

Meanwhile, the Austrians were unwilling to give up their control of Hungary. Unable to subdue the Hungarians, the Austrian government asked the Russians for help. Czar Nicholas I of Russia, who feared revolution anywhere, gladly agreed. A Russian army of 140,000 men crushed the Hungarian forces, and Kossuth fled abroad. The Hungarian Revolution of 1848–1849 had failed.

▲ *Soviet tanks in Hungary*

Comparing Past and Present

There have been other, more recent revolts against repressive governments that have been met with force, violence, and loss of life. Review recent newsmagazines to locate one such event. Write a historical account of the event, using both primary and secondary sources.

MEETING INDIVIDUAL NEEDS

Visual/Spatial Have students create a chart with the following headings across the top: *conservatives* and *liberals/nationalists.* Down the left side, have students list *France, Germany, Austria,* and *Italy.* For each country, have students list the demands and actions of the conservative and liberal sides in that country's revolution. This exercise is useful in helping students to understand the basic differences between conservatism and liberalism/nationalism by applying it to the history of each country. This exercise is also helpful for students who learn material more easily when it is presented in a graphic or chart. **L1**

Refer to ***Inclusion for the High School Social Studies Classroom Strategies and Activities*** in the TCR.

CHAPTER 12
Section 2, 371–376

Answer: Answers will vary. Verify that students use multiple sources.

Writing Activity

Ask students to write a statement about the possible unification of nineteenth-century Germany from the viewpoint of a ruler of a small German state. **L3 WH:** 8A

Critical Thinking

In the last few chapters, students have studied several revolutions that radically impacted the development of world politics. After they have read this chapter, ask students to identify changes that resulted from the political revolutions of the eighteenth and nineteenth centuries. **L1**

3 ASSESS

Assign Section 2 Assessment as homework or as an in-class activity.

Have students use **Interactive Tutor Self-Assessment CD-ROM.**

Section Quiz 12–2

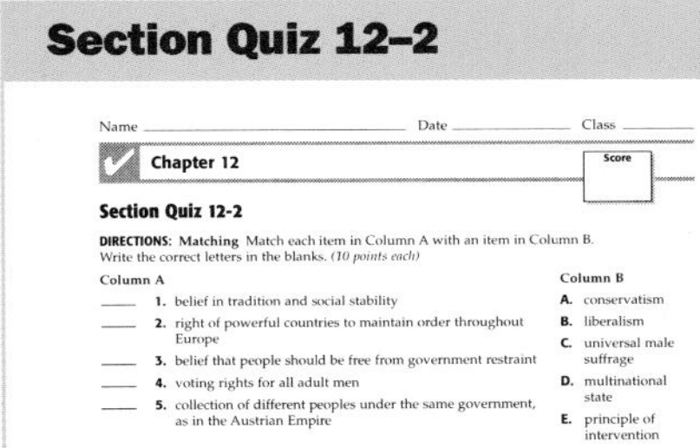

Name ________ Date ________ Class ________

Chapter 12 | Score

Section Quiz 12-2

DIRECTIONS: Matching Match each item in Column A with an item in Column B. Write the correct letters in the blanks. *(10 points each)*

Column A	Column B
____ **1.** belief in tradition and social stability	**A.** conservatism
____ **2.** right of powerful countries to maintain order throughout Europe	**B.** liberalism
____ **3.** belief that people should be free from government restraint	**C.** universal male suffrage
____ **4.** voting rights for all adult men	**D.** multinational state
____ **5.** collection of different peoples under the same government, as in the Austrian Empire	**E.** principle of intervention

Reading Check

Answer: began in France; other countries: German states, Austrian Empire, Italian states

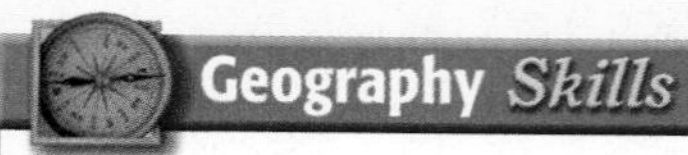

Geography Skills

Answers:

1. to Palermo in Sicily
2. Answers will vary.

Reading Essentials and Study Guide 12–2

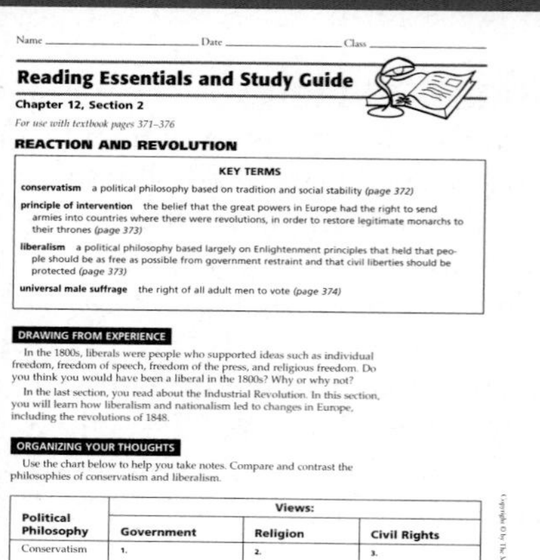

Name ______ Date ______ Class ______

Reading Essentials and Study Guide

Chapter 12, Section 2

For use with textbook pages 371–376

REACTION AND REVOLUTION

KEY TERMS

conservatism a political philosophy based on tradition and social stability *(page 372)*

principle of intervention the belief that the great powers in Europe had the right to send armies into countries where there were revolutions, in order to restore legitimate monarchs to their thrones *(page 373)*

liberalism a political philosophy based largely on Enlightenment principles that held that people should be as free as possible from government restraint and that civil liberties should be protected *(page 373)*

universal male suffrage the right of all adult men to vote *(page 374)*

DRAWING FROM EXPERIENCE

In the 1800s, liberals were people who supported ideas such as individual freedom, freedom of speech, freedom of the press, and religious freedom. Do you think you would have been a liberal in the 1800s? Why or why not?

In the last section, you read about the Industrial Revolution. In this section, you will learn how liberalism and nationalism led to changes in Europe, including the revolutions of 1848.

ORGANIZING YOUR THOUGHTS

Use the chart below to help you take notes. Compare and contrast the philosophies of conservatism and liberalism.

Political Philosophy	Views:		
	Government	Religion	Civil Rights
Conservatism	1.	2.	3.

Reteaching Activity

Ask students to write six new Reading Checks covering the material in this section. **L1**

4 CLOSE

Ask students to support or oppose the following statement: "Acts of civil disobedience, violence, and terrorism have made guaranteeing personal freedoms less desirable for society." **L2**

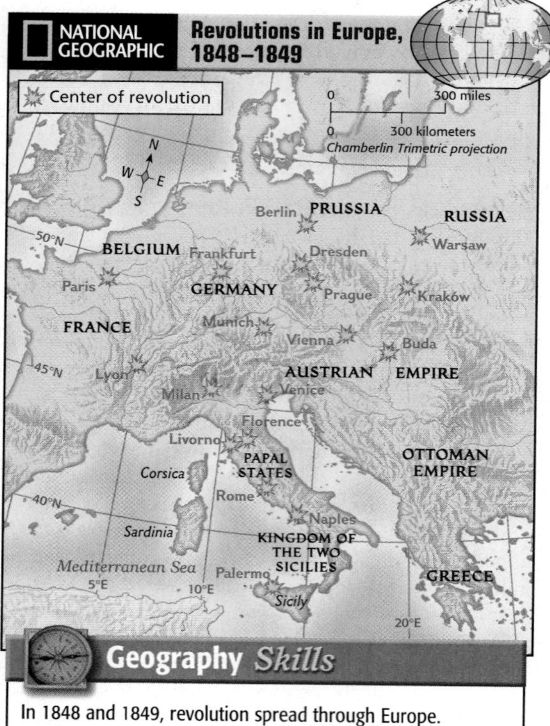

Geography Skills

In 1848 and 1849, revolution spread through Europe.

1. **Interpreting Maps** How far south did the revolutions of 1848 to 1849 extend?
2. **Applying Geography Skills** Pose and answer one question about the pattern in world history shown on this map.

military forces crushed the Czech rebels in **Prague.** By the end of October, the rebels in Vienna had been defeated as well. With the help of a Russian army of 140,000 men, the Hungarian revolutionaries were finally subdued in 1849. The revolutions in the Austrian Empire had failed.

Revolts in the Italian States The Congress of Vienna had set up nine states in Italy, including the Kingdom of Piedmont in the north; the Kingdom of the Two Sicilies (Naples and Sicily); the Papal States; a handful of small states; and the northern provinces of Lombardy and Venetia, which were now part of the Austrian Empire.

In 1848, a revolt broke out against the Austrians in Lombardy and Venetia. Revolutionaries in other Italian states also took up arms and sought to create liberal constitutions and a unified Italy. By 1849, however, the Austrians had reestablished complete control over Lombardy and Venetia. The old order also prevailed in the rest of Italy.

Throughout Europe in 1848, popular revolts started upheavals that had led to liberal constitutions and liberal governments. However, moderate liberals and more radical revolutionaries were soon divided over their goals, and so conservative rule was reestablished. Even with the reestablishment of conservative governments, however, the forces of nationalism and liberalism continued to influence political events.

Reading Check **Identifying** What countries experienced revolutions in 1848?

SECTION 2 ASSESSMENT

Checking for Understanding

1. **Define** conservatism, principle of intervention, liberalism, universal male suffrage.
2. **Identify** Congress of Vienna, Klemens von Metternich, Bill of Rights, Louis-Napoleon, Germanic Confederation, multinational state.
3. **Locate** Vienna, Prague.
4. **Explain** the effect of conservatism in 1848.
5. **List** the different peoples living in the Austrian Empire.

Critical Thinking

6. **Analyze** How did the social and economic changes from the Industrial Revolution contribute to the spread of liberalism?
7. **Compare and Contrast** Use a table like the one below to compare and contrast the ideologies of conservatism, liberalism, and nationalism.

Conservatism	Liberalism	Nationalism

Analyzing Visuals

8. **Examine** the portrait of Louis-Philippe shown on page 374. How does this portrait reflect Louis-Philippe's position in France? How is this portrait different from that of earlier French rulers like Louis XIV or Napoleon?

Writing About History

9. **Expository Writing** Select one of the following ideologies: conservatism, liberalism, or nationalism. Write an essay in which you identify contemporary ideas that are influenced by that ideology.

SECTION 2 ASSESSMENT

1. Key terms are in blue.
2. Congress of Vienna *(p. 371)*; Klemens von Metternich *(p. 371)*; Bill of Rights *(p. 373)*; Louis-Napoleon *(p. 375)*; Germanic Confederation *(p. 375)*; multinational state *(p. 375)*
3. See chapter maps.
4. Conservative governments led to liberal calls for reforms.
5. Germans, Czechs, Magyars (Hungarians), Slovaks, Romanians, Slovenes, Poles, Croats, Serbs, and Italians
6. Industrial Revolution led to growth of industrial middle class. Liberalism was tied to middle-class men.
7. Conservatism: tradition, social stability, obedience to political authority; Liberalism: civil liberties, religious tolerance, constitution; Nationalism: common institutions, traditions, language, customs
8. less emphasis on majesty
9. Essays will identify influence on contemporary ideology.

EYEWITNESS TO HISTORY

Revolutionary Excitement

THE EXCITEMENT WITH WHICH GERMAN liberals and nationalists received the news of the revolution in France are captured well in the *Reminiscences* of Carl Schurz. After the failure of the German revolution of 1848, Schurz went to the United States, where he fought in the Civil War and became secretary of the interior.

Carl Schurz and the Frankfurt Assembly

❝One morning, toward the end of February, 1848, I sat quietly in my attic-chamber, working hard at my tragedy of "Ulrich von Hutten" [a sixteenth-century German knight], when suddenly a friend rushed breathlessly into the room, exclaiming: "What, you sitting here! Do you not know what has happened?"

"No; what?"

"The French have driven away Louis Philippe and proclaimed the republic."

I threw down my pen—and that was the end of "Ulrich von Hutten." I never touched the manuscript again. We tore down the stairs, into the street, to the market-square, the accustomed meeting-place for all the student societies after their midday dinner. Although it was still forenoon, the market was already crowded with young men talking excitedly. . . . We were dominated by a vague feeling as if a great outbreak of elemental forces had begun, as if an earthquake was impending of which we had felt the first shock, and we instinctively crowded together. . . .

The next morning there were the usual lectures to be attended. But how profitless! The voice of the professor sounded like a monotonous drone coming from far away. What he had to say did not seem to concern us. At last we closed with a sigh the notebook and went away, pushed by a feeling that now we had something more important to do—to devote ourselves to the affairs of the fatherland. . . . Now had arrived in Germany the day for the establishment of "German Unity," and the founding of a great, powerful national German Empire. In the first line the meeting of a national parliament. Then the demands for civil rights and liberties, free speech, free press, the right of free assembly, equality before the law, a freely elected representation of the people with legislative power . . . the word *democracy* was soon on all tongues. . . . Of course the regeneration of the fatherland must, if possible, be accomplished by peaceable means. Like many of my friends, I was dominated by the feeling that at last the great opportunity had arrived for giving to the German people the liberty which was their birthright and to the German fatherland its unity and greatness, and that it was now the first duty of every German to do and to sacrifice everything for this sacred object.❞

—**Carl Schurz, *Reminiscences***

Analyzing Primary Sources

1. Why were Schurz and other Germans so excited about the revolution in France?
2. Would you be willing to sacrifice everything for your freedom and liberty? Why or why not?

TEACH

Analyzing Primary Sources
Have students study the reminiscences of Carl Schurz, then ask students to consider how an old guard conservative would reply to him. Have students write a dialogue between Carl Schurz and a conservative. You might wish to organize a class debate regarding what might have transpired between Carl Schurz and a conservative government official. As an interesting historical footnote, ask students to predict if Carl Schurz fought for the North or South during the Civil War. Ask students to conduct further research to discover the answer. **L2**

Critical Thinking

Ask students to discuss their opinions of the following statement: "It is impossible for an oppressive government to give its people just a little freedom." Do students believe the statement is true or false? **L1**

ANSWERS TO ANALYZING PRIMARY SOURCES

1. They felt that the French Revolution had unleashed elemental forces that would sweep into Germany and result in the establishment of a liberal German nation with a parliament, civil rights, and other trappings of a democracy.
2. Answers will vary but should be supported by logical arguments.

1 FOCUS

Section Overview

This section describes the unification of Italy and Germany and the impact of nationalism in other parts of Europe and in North America.

BELLRINGER
Skillbuilder Activity

Project transparency and have students answer questions.

Available as a blackline master.

Daily Focus Skills Transparency 12–3

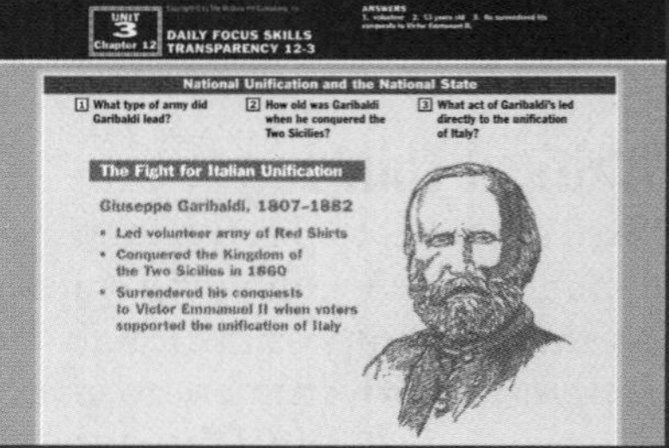

Guide to Reading

Answers to Graphic: Great Britain: vote extended to males of industrial middle class, Parliament made social, political reforms; France: economic expansion, Paris rebuilt, France went to war with Prussia, Second Empire fell; Austrian Empire: dual monarchy of Austria-Hungary; Russia: Russia defeated in Crimean War, Alexander II freed serfs, Alexander II assassinated

Preteaching Vocabulary: Have students use a dictionary to research the Latin root of *plebiscite.* *(plebiscite—Latin, plebs—the people; scitum—decree, vote for)* **L1**

SECTION 3 National Unification and the National State

Guide to Reading

Main Ideas
- The rise of nationalism contributed to the unification of Italy and Germany.
- While nationalism had great appeal, not all peoples achieved the goal of establishing their own national states.

Key Terms
militarism, kaiser, plebiscite, emancipation, abolitionism, secede

People to Identify
Giuseppe Garibaldi, Otto von Bismarck, Queen Victoria, Czar Alexander II

Places to Locate
Piedmont, Alsace, Lorraine, Budapest

Preview Questions
1. What were the roles of Camillo di Cavour and Otto von Bismarck in the unification of their countries?
2. What caused the American Civil War?

Reading Strategy
Summarizing Information Use a table like the one below to list the changes that took place in the indicated countries during the nineteenth century.

Great Britain	France	Austrian Empire	Russia

Preview of Events

1850 · 1855 · 1860 · 1865 · 1870 · 1875

- **1852** Second Empire begins in France
- **1861** Kingdom of Italy proclaimed
- **1867** The British North American Act is passed
- **1870** Franco-Prussian War begins
- **1871** William I becomes kaiser of a united Germany

Giuseppe Garibaldi

Voices from the Past

On June 13, 1860, the *Times* of London made the following report:

❝In the afternoon, Garibaldi made a tour of inspection round [Palermo]. The popular idol [Garibaldi], in his red flannel shirt, with a loose colored handkerchief around his neck, was walking on foot among those cheering, laughing, crying, mad thousands; and all his few followers could do was to prevent him from being bodily carried off the ground. The people threw themselves forward to kiss his hands, or at least, to touch the hem of his garment. Children were brought up, and mothers asked on their knees for his blessing.❞

—**The *Times* of London, June 13, 1860**

Garibaldi, hailed by the Italians as a great hero, was one of the most colorful figures involved in the unification of Italy.

Breakdown of the Concert of Europe

The revolutions of 1848 had failed. By 1871, however, both Germany and Italy would be unified. The changes that made this possible began with the Crimean War.

The Crimean War was the result of a long-standing struggle between Russia and the Ottoman Empire. The Ottoman Empire had long controlled much of the territory in the Balkans in southeastern Europe. By the beginning of the

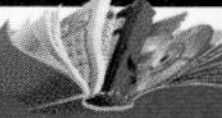

SECTION RESOURCES

Reproducible Masters
- Reproducible Lesson Plan 12–3
- Daily Lecture and Discussion Notes 12–3
- Guided Reading Activity 12–3
- Section Quiz 12–3
- Reading Essentials and Study Guide 12–3

Transparencies
- Daily Focus Skills Transparency 12–3

Multimedia
- Interactive Tutor Self-Assessment CD-ROM
- ExamView® Pro Testmaker CD-ROM
- Presentation Plus! CD-ROM

nineteenth century, however, the Ottoman Empire was in decline, and its authority over its territories in the Balkans began to weaken.

Russia was especially interested in expanding its power into Ottoman lands in the Balkans. This expansion would give Russia access to the Dardanelles and thus the Mediterranean Sea. Russia would become the major power in eastern Europe and could challenge British naval control of the eastern Mediterranean. Other European powers feared Russian ambitions and had their own interest in the decline of the Ottoman Empire.

In 1853, the Russians invaded the Turkish Balkan provinces of Moldavia and Walachia. In response, the Ottoman Turks declared war on Russia. Great Britain and France, fearful of Russian gains, declared war on Russia the following year. This conflict came to be called the Crimean War.

The Crimean War was poorly planned and poorly fought. Eventually, heavy losses caused the Russians to seek peace. By the Treaty of Paris, signed in March 1856, Russia agreed to allow Moldavia and Walachia to be placed under the protection of all the great powers.

The effect of the Crimean War was to destroy the Concert of Europe. Austria and Russia had been the two chief powers maintaining the status quo in the first half of the nineteenth century. They were now enemies because Austria, which had its own interests in the Balkans, had refused to support Russia in the Crimean War. A defeated and humiliated Russia withdrew from European affairs for the next 20 years. Austria was now without friends among the great powers. This new international situation opened the door for the unification of both Italy and Germany.

✓Reading Check **Explaining** How did the Crimean War destroy the Concert of Europe?

Italian Unification

In 1850, Austria was still the dominant power on the Italian Peninsula. After the failure of the revolution of 1848, people began to look to the northern Italian state of **Piedmont** for leadership in achieving the unification of Italy. The royal house of Savoy ruled the Kingdom of Piedmont, which included Piedmont, the island of Sardinia, Nice, and Savoy. The ruler of the kingdom, beginning in 1849, was King Victor Emmanuel II.

The king named Camillo di Cavour his prime minister in 1852. Cavour was a dedicated political leader. As prime minister, he pursued a policy of economic expansion that increased government revenues and enabled the kingdom to equip a large army. Cavour, however, knew that Piedmont's army was not strong enough to defeat the Austrians. He would need help, so he made an alliance with the French emperor Louis-Napoleon. He then provoked the Austrians into invading Piedmont in 1859.

The final result of the conflict that followed was a peace settlement that gave the French Nice and Savoy. Cavour had promised Nice and Savoy to the French for making the alliance. Lombardy, which had been under Austrian control, was given to Piedmont, while Austria retained control of Venetia. Cavour's success caused nationalists in some other northern Italian states (Parma, Modena, and Tuscany) to overthrow their governments and join their states to Piedmont.

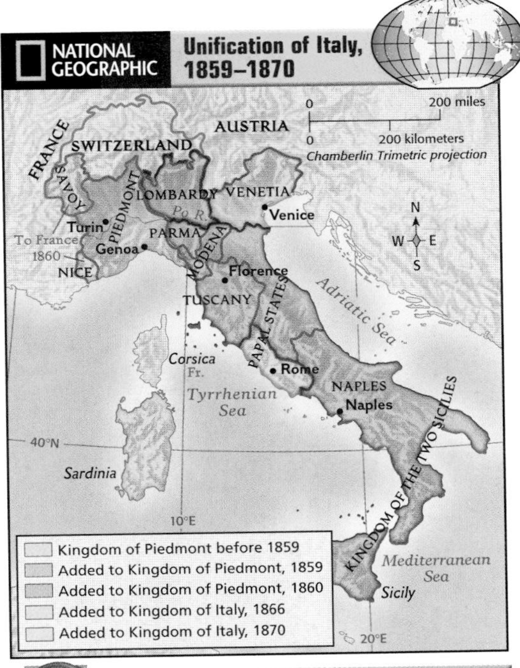

Geography Skills

From 1859 to 1870, Italy struggled to become a unified country.

1. **Interpreting Maps** Looking at the map, explain the sequence of events in Italian unification.
2. **Applying Geography Skills** What geographic factors help to explain why the state of Piedmont became the leader in the struggle to unify Italy?

CHAPTER 12
Section 3, 378–385

2 TEACH

✓Reading Check

Answer: Austria and Russia had been the two chief powers maintaining the status quo in Europe, but now they were enemies because Austria had refused to support Russia in the war.

Geography Skills

Answers:

1. Lombardy, Parma, Modena, and Tuscany were added to Piedmont; after the Kingdom of the Two Sicilies was added to Piedmont, it became the kingdom of Italy in 1861. Next, Venetia came under Italian control. Rome was the last state annexed, in 1870, and became the capital.
2. Piedmont was between France and Austrian-controlled territories. Cavour allied with France, provoking Austrians into attacking Piedmont. Lombardy became part of Piedmont, and several northern Italian states to its south overthrew their governments and joined Piedmont as well, putting it well on the way to unifying Italy.

Daily Lecture and Discussion Notes 12–3

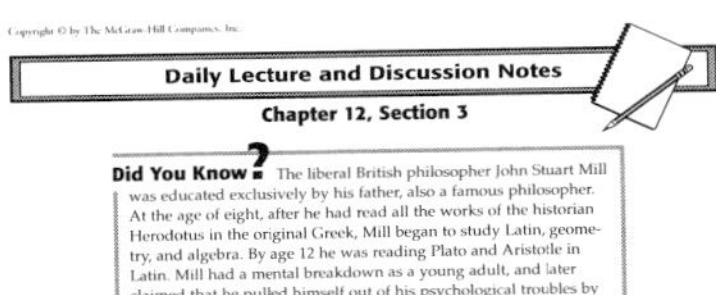

Daily Lecture and Discussion Notes

Chapter 12, Section 3

Did You Know? The liberal British philosopher John Stuart Mill was educated exclusively by his father, also a famous philosopher. At the age of eight, after he had read all the works of the historian Herodotus in the original Greek, Mill began to study Latin, geometry, and algebra. By age 12 he was reading Plato and Aristotle in Latin. Mill had a mental breakdown as a young adult, and later claimed that he pulled himself out of his psychological troubles by reading Romantic poetry.

I. **Breakdown of the Concert of Europe** *(pages 378–379)*

A. The nationalist goals of the 1848 revolutionaries would be achieved later. By 1871 both Germany and Italy were unified, a change caused by the Crimean War.

B. The Crimean War was rooted in a conflict between Russia and the Ottoman Empire, which controlled much of the Balkans in southeastern Europe. The power of the Ottoman Empire declined in the nineteenth century.

COOPERATIVE LEARNING ACTIVITY

Making a Time Line Organize students into three groups to construct a chronology showing the unification of Italy. Have one group gather information on key people, writing short descriptions of their roles. Have the second group prepare short written descriptions about key events and their dates. Have the third group design and draw the time line, incorporating information from the other two groups. Have this group post the time line on a classroom bulletin board or wall. Encourage the class to use the time line as a reference. **L1**

Reading Check

Answer: After he conquered the Kingdom of the Two Sicilies, he turned them over to Piedmont, resulting in a new kingdom of Italy.

Geography *Skills*

Answers:

1. Unification occurred from north to south.
2. Italy's peninsular shape and northern mountains may have aided in unification, Germany may have been influenced by surrounding strong countries.

Guided Reading Activity 12-3

Name ________ Date ________ Class ________

Guided Reading Activity 12-3

National Unification and the National State

DIRECTIONS: Fill in the blanks below as you read Section 3.

I. The Crimean War was the result of a struggle between ________ and the ________.
   A. Russia was interested in expanding its power into the ________.
   B. Fearful of Russian power, ________ and ________ declared war on Russia.
   C. The Crimean War destroyed the ________ of Europe.
II. On March 17, 1861, King Victor ________ II proclaimed a new kingdom of Italy.
III. Under Bismarck, Prussia organized the Northern German states into a ________.
   A. In 1870, ________ armies defeated an entire French army and the French ruler.
   B. The southern German states agreed to enter the ________ German Confederation.
IV. By giving the ________ class a voice in rule, Britain avoided revolution in 1848.
V. The French were defeated in the ________ and the Second Napoleonic Empire fell.
VI. The ________ of 1867 created dual monarchies in Austria and Hungary.
VII. The ________ of Alexander II in 1881 returned Russia to the old methods of repression.

Charting Activity

Have students create a chart with the following column headings: Count Cavour, Victor Emmanuel II, Garibaldi. Include the following topics for rows: *Goals and Ideals, Events and Dates, Impact on Unification.* Suggest students use outside sources to complete the chart. **L2** ELL

Meanwhile, in southern Italy, a new leader of Italian unification had arisen. **Giuseppe Garibaldi,** a dedicated Italian patriot, raised an army of a thousand volunteers—called Red Shirts because of the color of their uniforms.

The Kingdom of the Two Sicilies (Sicily and Naples) was ruled by France, and a revolt had broken out in Sicily against the Bourbon king. Garibaldi's forces landed in Sicily and, by the end of July 1860, controlled most of the island. In August, Garibaldi and his forces crossed over to the mainland and began a victorious march up the Italian Peninsula. Naples, and with it the entire Kingdom of the Two Sicilies, fell in early September.

Garibaldi chose to turn over his conquests to Piedmont. On March 17, 1861, a new kingdom of Italy was proclaimed under King Victor Emmanuel II. The task of unification was not yet complete, however. Venetia in the north was still held by Austria, and Rome was under the control of the pope, supported by French troops.

The Italians gained control of Venetia as a result of a war between Austria and Prussia. In the Austro-Prussian War of 1866, the new Italian state became an ally of Prussia. Prussia won the war, and the Italians were given Venetia.

In 1870, during the Franco-Prussian War, French troops withdrew from Rome. Their withdrawal enabled the Italian army to annex Rome on September 20, 1870. Rome became the capital of the united Italian state.

Reading Check **Explaining** How did Giuseppe Garibaldi contribute to Italian unification?

Geography *Skills*

On January 18, 1871, the united German states formed the Second German Empire.

1. **Interpreting Maps** Looking at the map, explain the sequence of German unification.
2. **Applying Geography Skills** Compare this map with the map of Italian unification shown on page 379. What geographic factors influenced the process of unification for both Germany and Italy?

German Unification

After the failure of the Frankfurt Assembly to achieve German unification in 1848 and 1849, Germans looked to Prussia for leadership in the cause of German unification. In the course of the nineteenth century, Prussia had become a strong and prosperous state. Its government was authoritarian. The Prussian king had firm control over both the government and the army. Prussia was also known for its **militarism,** or reliance on military strength.

In the 1860s, King William I tried to enlarge the Prussian army. When the Prussian legislature refused to levy new taxes for the proposed military changes, William I appointed a new prime minister, Count **Otto von Bismarck.**

Bismarck has often been seen as the foremost nineteenth-century practitioner of *realpolitik*—the "politics of reality," or politics based on practical matters rather than on theory or ethics. Bismarck was open about his strong dislike of anyone who opposed him.

COOPERATIVE LEARNING ACTIVITY

Dramatizing Organize the class into six groups to role-play the diplomatic stands taken by Germany and its rivals in its war with Denmark, the war with Austria (Seven Weeks' War), and the Franco-Prussian War. Have three groups research Germany's position in each war and the other three groups each research Denmark's, Austria's, and France's positions. Suggest that students gather data about their assigned country's goals and relations with their opposing country. Then ask each pair of rival groups to present their dramatizations in the order in which they occurred: the war with Denmark, the war with Austria, and the Franco-Prussian War. **L2**

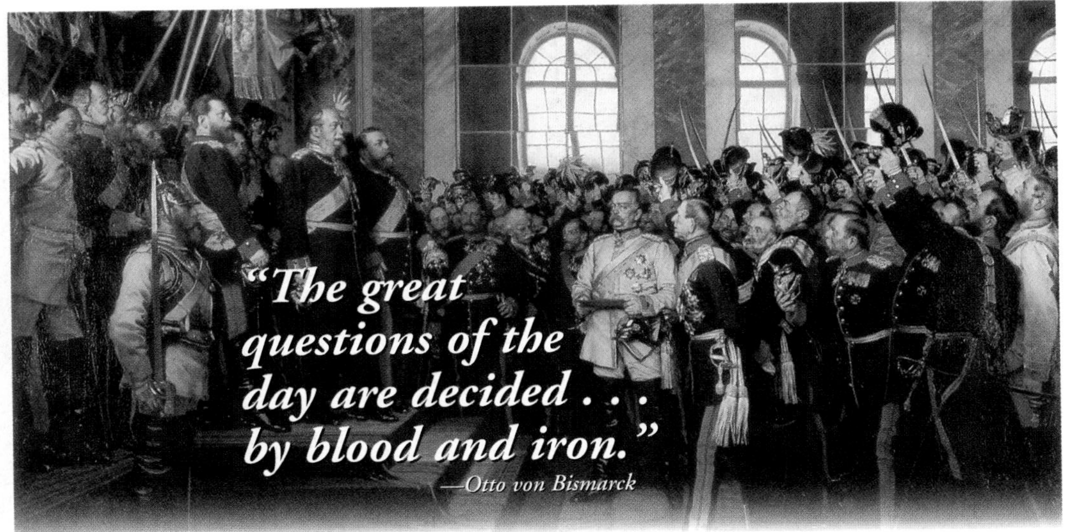

"The great questions of the day are decided . . . by blood and iron."
—Otto von Bismarck

Bismarck stands at the center as William I is named Emperor William I of the Second German Empire.

After his appointment, Bismarck ignored the legislative opposition to the military reforms. He argued instead that "Germany does not look to Prussia's liberalism but to her power."

Bismarck proceeded to collect taxes and strengthen the army. From 1862 to 1866, Bismarck governed Prussia without approval of the parliament. In the meantime, he followed an active foreign policy, which soon led to war.

After defeating Denmark with Austrian help in 1864 and gaining control of the duchies of Schleswig and Holstein, Bismarck created friction with the Austrians and forced them into a war on June 14, 1866. The Austrians, no match for the well-disciplined Prussian army, were decisively defeated on July 3.

Prussia now organized the German states north of the Main River into a North German Confederation. The southern German states, which were largely Catholic, feared Protestant Prussia. However, they also feared France, their western neighbor. As a result, they agreed to sign military alliances with Prussia for protection against France.

Prussia now dominated all of northern Germany, but problems with France soon arose. Bismarck realized that France would never be content with a strong German state to its east because of the potential threat to French security.

In 1870, Prussia and France became embroiled in a dispute over the candidacy of a relative of the Prussian king for the throne of Spain. Bismarck took advantage of the misunderstandings between the French and Prussians to goad the French into declaring war on Prussia on July 15, 1870. This conflict was called the Franco-Prussian War.

The French proved to be no match for the better led and better organized Prussian forces. The southern German states honored their military alliances with Prussia and joined the war effort against the French. Prussian armies advanced into France. At Sedan, on September 2, 1870, an entire French army and the French ruler, Napoleon III, were captured.

Paris finally surrendered on January 28, 1871, and an official peace treaty was signed in May. France had to pay 5 billion francs (about $1 billion) and give up the provinces of **Alsace** and **Lorraine** to the new German state. The loss of these territories left the French burning for revenge.

Even before the war had ended, the southern German states had agreed to enter the North German Confederation. On January 18, 1871, Bismarck and six hundred German princes, nobles, and generals filled the Hall of Mirrors in the palace of Versailles, 12 miles outside Paris. William I of Prussia was proclaimed kaiser, or emperor, of the Second German Empire (the first was the medieval Holy Roman Empire).

German unity had been achieved by the Prussian monarchy and the Prussian army. The authoritarian and militaristic values of Prussia were triumphant in the new German state. With its industrial resources and military might, the new state had become the strongest power on the European continent.

Reading Check **Summarizing** What events led to German unification?

Reading Check

Answer: Bismarck's active foreign policy; war with Austrians in 1866 led to the organization of a North German Confederation; Franco-Prussian War led southern German states to agree to enter the North German Confederation; in 1871 William I of Prussia was proclaimed kaiser of the Second German Empire

Critical Thinking

Ask students to describe what might have happened to the German states if their leader had been less assertive and self-confident than Bismarck. *(Germany would not have become the strongest power in Europe, the unification of Germany would not have happened.)* **L1**

Who?What?Where?When?

German Unification Bismarck used three wars to unify Germany, but another German-caused war—World War II—left Germany divided for 45 years. In 1990, West Germany and East Germany were reunited as one country.

Enrich

Ask students to discuss the idea that a country should only fight a war that it is sure it can win. What did Prussia gain by fighting France (beyond a victory over the French army)? *(provinces of Alsace and Lorraine, 5 billion francs)* **L1**

EXTENDING THE CONTENT

German Unification World Wars I and II were essentially the same fight—for German hegemony in Europe. Even today, the German people enjoy one of the world's highest standards of living, despite Germany's devastation during World War II and its subsequent division for over forty years. Germany's role on the world's stage will become increasingly important as a new generation, a united generation, emerges. As Western Europe's richest and most populous nation, Germany remains a key member of the continent's economic, political, and defense organizations.

History *through Art*

Answer: At first it worked, but by the 1860s opposition to his policies arose and he was forced to liberalize his regime.

Writing Activity

Ask students to discuss and evaluate the following statement: "Economic prosperity in Great Britain was a good substitute for political reform." Have students write a brief paper arguing for or against the validity of that statement. **L2**

Who?What?Where?When?

Victor Hugo lived and wrote during the time of Napoleon III. The novels of Hugo combine historical detail and concern for social issues with beautiful prose and moving plots. Hugo was a fervent supporter of the republican form of government. When Napoleon III came to power, Hugo went into exile. It was at this time he wrote *Les Miserables.* In this book, Hugo hoped to counter the prevailing perception of the poor as criminals, and to describe their life under an authoritarian government.

Charting Activity

Ask students to make a chart listing the positive and negative aspects of Napoleon III's regime. *(positive—expanded economy, rebuilt Paris, had support of people; negative—authoritarian, limited civil liberties, took all power, including legislative)* **L1**

Nationalism and Reform in Europe

While Italy and Germany were being unified, other states in Europe were also experiencing changes.

Great Britain Great Britain managed to avoid the revolutionary upheavals of the first half of the nineteenth century. In 1815, Great Britain was governed by aristocratic landowning classes, which dominated both houses of Parliament. In 1832, Parliament passed a bill that increased the number of male voters. The new voters were chiefly members of the industrial middle class. By giving the industrial middle class an interest in ruling Britain, Britain avoided revolution in 1848. In the 1850s and 1860s, Parliament continued to make both social and political reforms that helped the country to remain stable.

Another reason for Britain's stability was its continuing economic growth. By 1850, the British middle class was already prosperous as a result of the Industrial Revolution. After 1850, the working classes at last began to share some of this prosperity. Real wages for laborers increased more than 25 percent between 1850 and 1870.

The British feeling of national pride was well reflected in **Queen Victoria,** whose reign from 1837 to 1901 was the longest in English history. Her sense of duty and moral respectability reflected the attitudes of her age, which has ever since been known as the Victorian Age.

France In France, events after the revolution of 1848 moved toward the restoration of the monarchy. Four years after his election as president in 1848, Louis-Napoleon returned to the people to ask for the restoration of the empire. In this plebiscite, or popular vote, 97 percent responded with a yes vote. On December 2, 1852, Louis-Napoleon assumed the title of Napoleon III, Emperor of France. (The first Napoleon had named his son as his successor and had given him the title of Napoleon II. Napoleon II never ruled France, however.) The Second Empire had begun.

HISTORY Online

Web Activity Visit the *Glencoe World History—Modern Times* Web site at wh.mt.glencoe.com and click on **Chapter 12–Student Web Activity** to learn more about Queen Victoria.

The government of Napoleon III was clearly authoritarian. As chief of state, Napoleon III controlled the armed forces, police, and civil service. Only he could introduce legislation and declare war. The Legislative Corps gave an appearance of representative government, because the members of the group were elected by universal male suffrage for six-year terms. However, they could neither initiate legislation nor affect the budget.

Napoleon III completely controlled the government and limited civil liberties. Nevertheless, the

Napoleon III

History *through Art*

***La Place Clichy* by Eugene Galien-Laloue**
To distract citizens from their loss of civil liberties, Napoleon III beautified the city of Paris. How successful was this policy?

MEETING INDIVIDUAL NEEDS

Auditory/Visual/Tactile This activity will enhance understanding of the concept of "nation" and "nationalism." Have students review the map of Italy on page 379 and the map of Germany on page 380. Also, share with the class a map of the United States. Ask students to describe how they feel about the United States being their country. For students from other countries, have them share their feelings about being from their respective countries. Relate their descriptions to the concept of nationalism. Bring to class objects associated with Italian and German traditions (for example, foods, traditional songs, pictures of traditional dress, etc.). Have the students express how having these traditions in common enhances the feeling of nationalism. **L1**

first five years of his reign were a spectacular success. To distract the public from their loss of political freedom, he focused on expanding the economy. Government subsidies helped foster the rapid construction of railroads, harbors, roads, and canals. Iron production tripled.

In the midst of this economic expansion, Napoleon III also carried out a vast rebuilding of the city of Paris. The old Paris of narrow streets and walls was replaced by a modern Paris of broad boulevards, spacious buildings, public squares, an underground sewage system, a new public water supply system, and gaslights. The new Paris served a military purpose as well. Broad streets made it more difficult for would-be rebels to throw up barricades and easier for troops to move rapidly through the city in the event of revolts.

Peasants had to pay for the poor-quality land they received from the Russian government.

In the 1860s, opposition to some of Napoleon's economic and governmental policies arose. In response, Napoleon III began to liberalize his regime. For example, he gave the legislature more power. In a plebiscite held in 1870, the French people gave Napoleon another victory. This triumph was short-lived, however. After the French were defeated in the Franco-Prussian War in 1870, the Second Empire fell.

The Austrian Empire As we have seen, nationalism was a major force in nineteenth-century Europe. However, one of Europe's most powerful states—the Austrian Empire—was a multinational empire that had been able to frustrate the desire of its ethnic groups for independence.

After the Hapsburg rulers crushed the revolutions of 1848 and 1849, they restored centralized, autocratic government to the empire. Austria's defeat at the hands of the Prussians in 1866, however, forced the Austrians to make concessions to the fiercely nationalistic Hungarians.

The result was the Compromise of 1867. This compromise created the dual monarchy of Austria-Hungary. Each of these two components of the empire now had its own constitution, its own legislature, its own government bureaucracy, and its own capital (Vienna for Austria and **Budapest** for Hungary). Holding the two states together were a single monarch (Francis Joseph was both emperor of Austria and king of Hungary) and a common army, foreign policy, and system of finances.

In domestic affairs, then, the Hungarians had become an independent nation. The compromise, of course, did not satisfy the other nationalities that made up the multinational Austro-Hungarian Empire.

Russia At the beginning of the nineteenth century, Russia was overwhelmingly rural, agricultural, and autocratic. The Russian czar was still regarded as a divine-right monarch with unlimited power. The Russian government, based on soldiers, secret police, repression, and censorship, withstood the revolutionary fervor of the first half of the nineteenth century.

In 1856, however, as described earlier, the Russians suffered a humiliating defeat in the Crimean War. Even staunch conservatives now realized that Russia was falling hopelessly behind the western European powers. **Czar Alexander II** decided to make serious reforms.

Serfdom was the largest problem in czarist Russia. On March 3, 1861, Alexander issued an **emancipation** edict, which freed the serfs. Peasants could now own property and marry as they chose. The government provided land for the peasants by buying it from the

CURRICULUM CONNECTION

Literature *Les Miserables* is popular today as a movie and musical. Ask students to watch the video. In a class discussion have students identify ways that *Les Miserables* transcends the culture in which it was created and conveys universal themes.

Enrich

As a class discussion, compare the life of a Russian serf following emancipation with the life of an English factory worker. How were their lives similar and how did they differ? In which situation would your students have preferred to live? Have the students define freedom from the perspective of the factory worker and the emancipated serf. **L1**

Critical Thinking

Ask students to explain why emancipation of serfs or slaves is not the same as creating equality for these people. What other conditions would be needed for true equality? *(economic opportunity, education, social opportunity)* **L2**

3 ASSESS

Assign Section 3 Assessment as homework or as an in-class activity.

Have students use **Interactive Tutor Self-Assessment CD-ROM.**

INTERDISCIPLINARY CONNECTIONS ACTIVITY

Literature Have students research and present an oral report on one of the following Russian writers: Alexander Pushkin, Mikhail Lermontov, Nikolay Gogol, Ivan Turgenev, Fyodor Dostoyevsky, or Leo Tolstoy. Ask students to include the following information in their reports: the writer's education; social, economic, and political background; titles of major works; how the writer portrayed Russian history and society in the works; and the writer's lasting impact on Russian culture. **L3**

For grading this activity, refer to the ***Performance Assessment Activities*** booklet.

CHAPTER 12
Section 3, 378–385

Reading Check

Answer: Parliament increased the number of male voters, giving the industrial middle class an interest in ruling Britain. The country and its people were fairly prosperous.

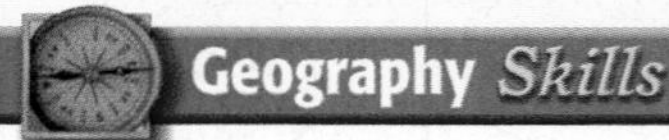

Geography Skills

Answer: Southern states needed large amounts of human labor because they were not industrialized.

Section Quiz 12–3

Name ______ Date ______ Class ______

Chapter 12 Score

Section Quiz 12-3

DIRECTIONS: Matching Match each item in Column A with an item in Column B. Write the correct letters in the blanks. *(10 points each)*

Column A	Column B
____ 1. emperor	A. militarism
____ 2. Bismarck's theory of practical, as opposed to idealistic, governance	B. secede
____ 3. reliance on military strength	C. kaiser
____ 4. law that freed Russian serfs	D. emancipation edict
____ 5. withdraw from or choose not to be part of	E. realpolitik

DIRECTIONS: Multiple Choice In the blank, write the letter of the choice that best completes the statement or answers the question. *(10 points each)*

____ 6. The Compromise of 1867 did all of the following EXCEPT
A. create the dual monarchy of Austria-Hungary.
B. create a single monarch to govern both Austria and Hungary.
C. establish a common Austria-Hungary army.
D. allow Huns within the empire to vote.

____ 7. Napoleon III became Emperor of France and, at first,
A. limited civil liberties.
B. expanded freedoms.
C. restored the monarchy.
D. formed a shared empire with Hungary.

____ 8. A major threat to American national unity during the nineteenth century was
A. the Revolutionary War.
B. the War of 1812.
C. slavery.
D. liberalism.

____ 9. Bismarck faced challenges to his authority from all of the following EXCEPT
A. German Catholics.
B. France.
C. the legislature.
D. the Prussian army.

____ 10. Britain avoided any form of revolution in 1848 by
A. giving the industrial middle class the vote.
B. giving women the vote.
C. building up the British army.
D. expanding railroads.

Writing Activity

In this chapter, students have read about different political philosophies and systems that shaped Western states in the nineteenth century. Ask students to write an essay in which they explain the impact of parliamentary and constitutional systems of government on significant world political developments. **L2**

landlords. (*See page 776 to read excerpts from Czar Alexander II's* Imperial Decree to Free the Serfs *in the Primary Sources Library.*)

The new land system, however, was not that helpful to the peasants. The landowners often kept the best lands for themselves. The Russian peasants soon found that they did not have enough good land to support themselves. Emancipation of the serfs, then, led not to a free, landowning peasantry, but to an unhappy, land-starved peasantry that largely followed old ways of farming.

Alexander II attempted other reforms as well, but he soon found that he could please no one. Reformers wanted more changes and a faster pace for change. Conservatives thought that the czar was trying to destroy the basic institutions of Russian society. When a group of radicals assassinated Alexander II in 1881, his son and successor, Alexander III, turned against reform and returned to the old methods of repression.

Reading Check **Examining** How was Great Britain able to avoid a revolution in 1848?

Nationalism in the United States

The government under the U.S. Constitution had committed the United States to two of the major forces of the first half of the nineteenth century: liberalism and nationalism. National unity had not come easily, however.

Two factions had fought bitterly about the division of power in the new government. The Federalists had favored a strong central government. The Republicans, fearing central power, had wanted the federal government to be subordinate to the state governments. These early divisions had ended with the War of 1812 against the British. A surge of national feeling had served to cover over the nation's divisions.

Slavery challenged national unity in the United States.

The election of Andrew Jackson as president in 1828 had opened a new era in American politics. Property qualifications for voting had been dropped. The right to vote was eventually extended to almost all adult white males.

By the mid-nineteenth century, slavery had become a threat to American national unity. There were four million African American slaves in the South by 1860, compared with one million in 1800.

The South's economy was based on growing cotton on plantations, chiefly by slave labor. The invention of the cotton gin by Eli Whitney in 1793 had made it easier to clean cotton of its seeds, thus increasing cotton production. The South was determined to maintain both its cotton economy and plantation-based slavery. At the same time, **abolitionism**, a movement to end slavery, arose in the North and challenged the southern way of life.

As opinions over slavery grew more divided, compromise became less possible. Abraham Lincoln said in a speech in Illinois in 1858 that "this government cannot endure permanently half slave and half free."

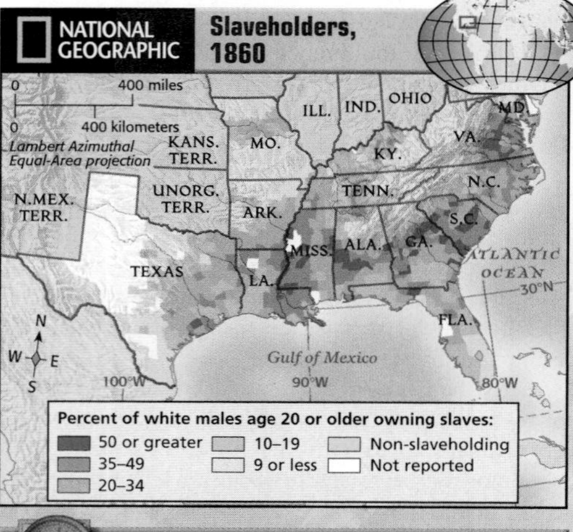

Geography Skills

By 1860, there were four million African American slaves in the South.

1. **Applying Geography Skills** What conclusions can you draw about economic conditions in the southern United States in 1860 from looking at this map?

COOPERATIVE LEARNING ACTIVITY

Facilitating a Discussion Organize the class into groups to discuss the ways American life might be different if the Civil War had not been fought and the country had remained divided into two separate nations. Have each group focus on a different topic, such as economy, international relations, labor, government, or culture. Also, encourage students to consider how their own personal lives might be different. One person from each group should take notes on the discussion and report the group's ideas to the class. Encourage students from the other groups to ask questions after each presentation. **L1**

When Lincoln was elected president in November 1860, the die was cast.

On December 20, 1860, a South Carolina convention voted to **secede**, or withdraw, from the United States. In February 1861, six more southern states did the same, and a rival nation—the Confederate States of America—was formed. In April, fighting erupted between North and South—the Union and the Confederacy.

The American Civil War (1861 to 1865) was an extraordinarily bloody struggle. Over 600,000 soldiers died, either in battle or from deadly diseases spawned by filthy camp conditions. The Union, with more men and resources, gradually wore down the Confederacy. On January 1, 1863, Lincoln's Emancipation Proclamation declared most of the nation's slaves "forever free." The surrender of Confederate forces on April 9, 1865, meant that the United States would be "one nation, indivisible." National unity had prevailed in the United States.

Reading Check **Explaining** How did the election of Andrew Jackson influence American politics?

The Emergence of a Canadian Nation

By the Treaty of Paris in 1763, signed at the end of the Seven Years' War, Canada passed from the French to the British. By 1800, most of the Canadian people favored more freedom from British rule. However, there were also serious differences among the colonists. Upper Canada (now Ontario) was mostly English speaking, whereas Lower Canada (now Quebec) was mostly French speaking.

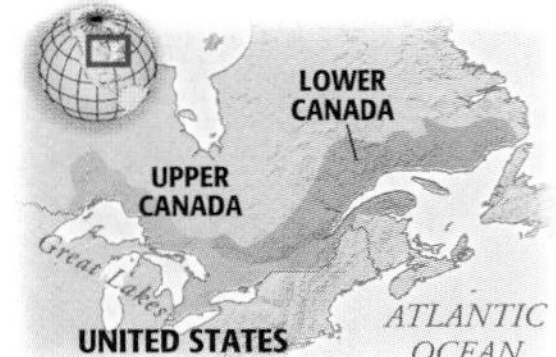

After two short rebellions against the government broke out in Upper and Lower Canada in 1837 and 1838, the British moved toward change. In 1840, the British Parliament formally joined Upper and Lower Canada into the United Provinces of Canada. The United Provinces was not self-governed.

The head of Upper Canada's Conservative Party, John Macdonald, became a strong voice for self-government. The British, fearful of American designs on Canada, finally gave in. In 1867, Parliament passed the **British North American Act,** which established a Canadian nation—the Dominion of Canada—with its own constitution. John Macdonald became the first prime minister of the Dominion. Canada now possessed a parliamentary system and ruled itself, although foreign affairs remained in the hands of the British government.

Reading Check **Describing** How did the British North American Act change the government of Canada?

SECTION 3 ASSESSMENT

Checking for Understanding

1. **Define** militarism, kaiser, plebiscite, emancipation, abolitionism, secede.
2. **Identify** Giuseppe Garibaldi, Otto von Bismarck, Queen Victoria, Czar Alexander II, British North American Act.
3. **Locate** Piedmont, Alsace, Lorraine, Budapest.
4. **Explain** why you think Alexander III turned against the reforms of his father.
5. **List** the Prussian values and assets that caused the Second German Empire to become the strongest European state.

Critical Thinking

6. **Drawing Inferences** Explain how the forces of liberalism and nationalism affected events in the United States during the nineteenth century.
7. **Compare and Contrast** Use a Venn diagram to compare and contrast Bismarck's and Cavour's methods for achieving unification in Germany and Italy.

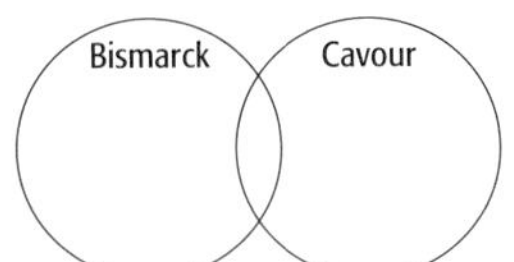

Analyzing Visuals

8. **Examine** the photographs of a peasant and a slave family shown on pages 383 and 384. Based on the visual evidence of the two photographs, how do you think the living conditions of Russian peasants compared to living conditions of slaves in the United States?

Writing About History

9. **Expository Writing** Write an essay comparing the events and outcomes of the rules of Bismarck and Napoleon III. What personal characteristics did each man have that contributed to his accomplishments?

SECTION 3 ASSESSMENT

1. Key terms are in blue.
2. Giuseppe Garibaldi *(p. 380)*; Otto von Bismarck *(p. 380)*; Queen Victoria *(p. 382)*; Czar Alexander II *(p. 383)*; British North American Act *(p. 385)*
3. See chapter maps.
4. He may have felt they led to father's assassination, restore stability
5. values: authoritarianism, militarism; assets: industrial, military
6. divided nation, led to Civil War
7. Bismarck: relied on military, ignored legislative opposition; Cavour: relied on others (France, Garibaldi, Prussia) for help, policy of economic expansion; Bismarck and Cavour: planned the unification of his country, used military means to accomplish unification, provoked Austria into war to reach objectives
8. They appear to be similar, very poor.
9. Students will write essays.

CHAPTER 12
Section 3, 378–385

Reading Check

Answer: He was the first president to be elected after the dropping of property qualifications for voting, and the right to vote was eventually extended to virtually all adult white males.

Reading Check

Answer: The act established a self-governing Canadian nation with its own constitution, although foreign affairs were still handled by the British.

Reading Essentials and Study Guide 12–3

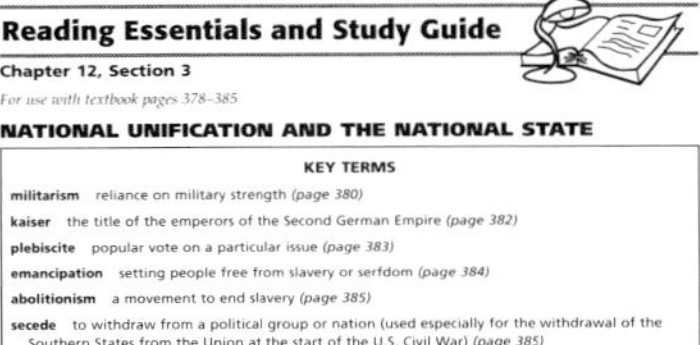
Name ______ Date ______ Class ______

Reading Essentials and Study Guide

Chapter 12, Section 3

For use with textbook pages 378–385

NATIONAL UNIFICATION AND THE NATIONAL STATE

KEY TERMS

militarism reliance on military strength *(page 380)*

kaiser the title of the emperors of the Second German Empire *(page 382)*

plebiscite popular vote on a particular issue *(page 383)*

emancipation setting people free from slavery or serfdom *(page 384)*

abolitionism a movement to end slavery *(page 385)*

secede to withdraw from a political group or nation (used especially for the withdrawal of the Southern States from the Union at the start of the U.S. Civil War) *(page 385)*

Reteaching Activity

Write a time line on the chalkboard with the dates 1850 to 1875. Assign groups of students one of the following: *Italy, Germany, Britain, France, Austria, Russia, America,* and *Canada.* Students should add important events for their country to the time line. **L1**

4 CLOSE

Discuss with students how nationalism led to revolution in some cases, and, in others, resulted in political, social, and economic reforms.

Critical Thinking

Skillbuilder

TEACH

Identifying an Argument In preparation for this lesson, find two newspaper editorials or opinion pieces that make opposing arguments on the same issue. Before having students read the skill, distribute copies of the articles. After students have read the editorials, ask them to identify the argument and supporting reasons in each piece. Now have students read the skill and complete the practice questions. **L1**

Additional Practice

Skills Reinforcement Activity 12

Name ____________ Date ____________ Class ____________

Skills Reinforcement Activity 12

Identifying an Argument

An argument is the presentation of an opinion. The main idea, or thesis, of an argument is the writer's or speaker's basic position or viewpoint. To evaluate an argument, consider its strengths and weaknesses. Does the writer or speaker support the thesis with facts and examples?

DIRECTIONS: Read the statement below from Robert Owen, a utopian socialist. Then answer the questions below in the space provided.

"By my own experience and reflection I had ascertained that human nature is radically good, and is capable of being trained, educated and placed from birth in such manner, that all ultimately (that is as soon as the gross errors and corruptions of the present false and wicked system are overcome and destroyed) must become united, good, wise, wealthy and happy. And I felt that to attain this glorious result, the sacrifices of the character, fortune and life of an individual was not deserving a moment's consideration. And my decision was made to overcome all

GLENCOE TECHNOLOGY

CD-ROM
Glencoe Skillbuilder Interactive Workbook CD-ROM, Level 2

This interactive CD-ROM reinforces student mastery of essential social studies skills.

Critical Thinking

Skillbuilder

Identifying an Argument

Why Learn This Skill?

In everyday conversation, the word **argument** *refers to a conflict involving two or more opinions. However, in writing and in formal debate, an argument is the full presentation of a single opinion. An argument uses facts to support a particular opinion. After hearing these facts, it is then up to you to determine whether the argument is valid or not.*

Learning the Skill

There are three basic elements to consider in an argument.

- **What is the thesis?** The main idea of an argument is its thesis, or the writer's basic position or viewpoint on the subject. In some arguments the thesis is stated explicitly. In others, you must read carefully to determine the writer's position.
- **What are the supporting reasons, examples, and facts?** The writer supports the thesis with reasons and supports the reasons with examples or facts.
- **What are its strengths and weaknesses?** Before accepting or rejecting an argument, evaluate its strengths and weaknesses. How well is each reason supported by facts and examples? Does the author's bias invalidate the argument?

Practicing the Skill

Read the following quotation published in 1842 in *L'Atelier (The Workshop),* a Parisian newspaper. Then answer the following questions.

> ❝Who has not heard of the women silkworkers . . . working fourteen to sixteen hours (except for one hour for both meals); always standing, without a single minute for repose [rest], putting forth an enormous amount of effort. And many of them have to walk a league or more, morning and evening, to get home, which is often a cause for moral disorder. Nor should we neglect to mention the danger that exists merely from working in these large factories, surrounded by wheels, gears, enormous leather belts that always threaten to seize you and pound you to pieces. There is not a factory in which some kind of accident has not happened—some woman worker caught by the hair or her clothing, and thereby pulverized; some mutilation of the fingers or the hands.❞

Men, women, and children working in a factory

1. What is the writer's thesis?
2. What reasons does the writer give to support this thesis?
3. What facts support the statement that danger exists for the workers in the workplace?
4. What is your reaction to the author's argument?

Applying the Skill

Find a recent article that states an argument about a political or historical issue. Identify the thesis of the argument and the major reasons and evidence supporting it. Decide whether you accept or reject this argument and explain why.

GO TO Glencoe's **Skillbuilder Interactive Workbook, Level 2,** provides instruction and practice in key social studies skills.

ANSWERS TO PRACTICING THE SKILL

1. Women factory workers face deplorable working conditions.
2. long hours, no rest, danger of walking to and from work, dangers from the factory equipment
3. The author does not present any specific facts (dates, names, etc.) to support his argument, just examples of the sorts of things that happen based on factual conditions in factories.
4. Answers will vary.

Applying the Skill: Students will identify the thesis and major reasons of an article.

SECTION 4 Culture: Romanticism and Realism

Guide to Reading

Main Ideas
- At the end of the eighteenth century, romanticism emerged as a reaction to the ideas of the Enlightenment.
- The Industrial Revolution created a new interest in science and helped produce the realist movement.

Key Terms
romanticism, secularization, organic evolution, natural selection, realism

People to Identify
Ludwig van Beethoven, Louis Pasteur, Charles Darwin, Charles Dickens

Places to Locate
London, France

Preview Questions
1. What were the major features of romanticism and realism?
2. How did the Scientific Revolution lead to secularization?

Reading Strategy
Summarizing Information Use a table like the one below to list popular literature from the romantic and realist movements.

Romanticism	Realism

Preview of Events

1820 · 1830 · 1840 · 1850 · 1860 · 1870 · 1880

- **1820** Walter Scott writes *Ivanhoe*
- **1849** Courbet paints *The Stonebreakers*
- **1859** Charles Darwin publishes *On the Origin of Species by Means of Natural Selection*
- **1869** Mendeleyev presents classification of material elements

Charles Dickens

Voices from the Past

In *The Old Curiosity Shop,* Charles Dickens described the English mill town of Birmingham:

> ❝A long suburb of red brick houses—some with patches of garden ground, where coal-dust and factory smoke darkened the shrinking leaves, and coarse rank flowers; and where the struggling vegetation sickened and sank under the hot breath of kiln and furnace . . . —a long, flat, straggling suburb passed, they came by slow degrees upon a cheerless region, where not a blade of grass was seen to grow; where not a bud put forth its promise in the spring; where nothing green could live but on the surface of the stagnant pools, which here and there lay idly sweltering by the black roadside.❞
>
> —Charles Dickens, *The Old Curiosity Shop,* 1840–1841

Dickens, a highly successful English novelist, realistically portrayed the material surroundings of his time, but an element of romanticism still pervaded his novels.

Romanticism

At the end of the eighteenth century, a new intellectual movement, known as romanticism, emerged as a reaction to the ideas of the Enlightenment. The Enlightenment had stressed reason as the chief means for discovering truth. The romantics emphasized feelings, emotion, and imagination as sources of knowing.

1 FOCUS

Section Overview

This section discusses romanticism, science, and the realist movement of the nineteenth century.

BELLRINGER
Skillbuilder Activity

Project transparency and have students answer questions.

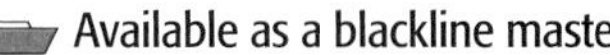
Available as a blackline master.

Daily Focus Skills Transparency 12–4

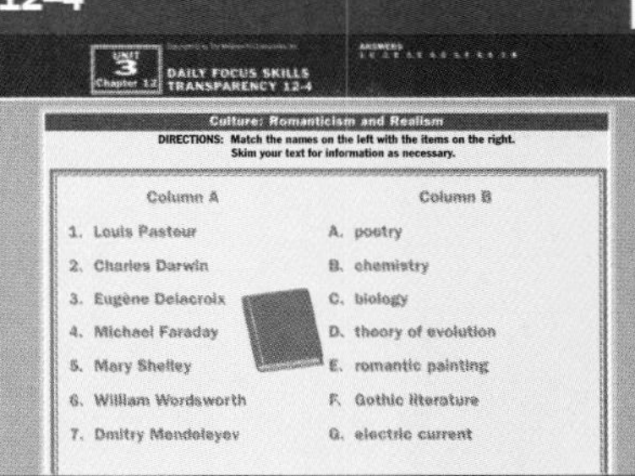
DAILY FOCUS SKILLS TRANSPARENCY 12-4

Culture: Romanticism and Realism

DIRECTIONS: Match the names on the left with the items on the right. Skim your text for information as necessary.

Column A	Column B
1. Louis Pasteur	A. poetry
2. Charles Darwin	B. chemistry
3. Eugène Delacroix	C. biology
4. Michael Faraday	D. theory of evolution
5. Mary Shelley	E. romantic painting
6. William Wordsworth	F. Gothic literature
7. Dmitry Mendeleyev	G. electric current

Guide to Reading

Answers to Graphic: Romanticism: Scott's *Ivanhoe*, Shelley's *Frankenstein*, Poe's short stories, Wordsworth's poetry; Realism: Flaubert's *Madame Bovary*, Dickens's *Oliver Twist* and *David Copperfield*

Preteaching Vocabulary: Have students define *secularization* and discuss its role today. To what extent is *secularization* still tied to science and technology and to what extent does it transcend these fields? Have students describe the effects of secularization on society today. **L1**

SECTION RESOURCES

Reproducible Masters
- Reproducible Lesson Plan 12–4
- Daily Lecture and Discussion Notes 12–4
- Guided Reading Activity 12–4
- Section Quiz 12–4
- Reading Essentials and Study Guide 12–4

Transparencies
- Daily Focus Skills Transparency 12–4

Multimedia
- Interactive Tutor Self-Assessment CD-ROM
- ExamView® Pro Testmaker CD-ROM
- Presentation Plus! CD-ROM

CHAPTER 12
Section 4, 387–391

2 TEACH

History *through Architecture*

Answer: pointed arches and tall spires

Daily Lecture and Discussion Notes 12–4

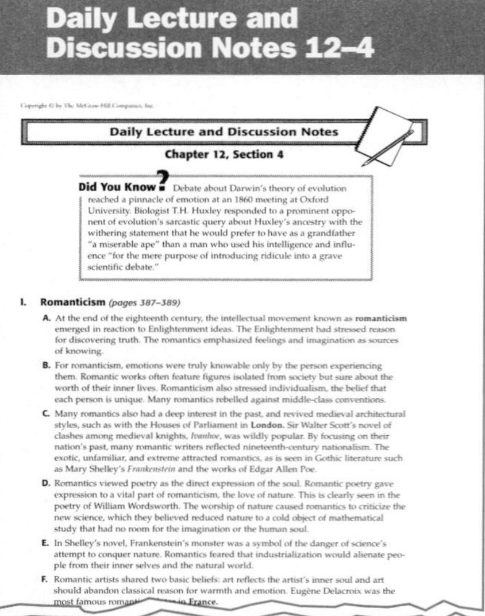

Daily Lecture and Discussion Notes

Chapter 12, Section 4

Did You Know? Debate about Darwin's theory of evolution reached a pinnacle of emotion at an 1860 meeting at Oxford University. Biologist T.H. Huxley responded to a prominent opponent of evolution's sarcastic query about Huxley's ancestry with the withering statement that he would prefer to have as a grandfather "a miserable ape" than a man who used his intelligence and influence "for the mere purpose of introducing ridicule into a grave scientific debate."

I. **Romanticism** *(pages 387–389)*

A. At the end of the eighteenth century, the intellectual movement known as **romanticism** emerged in reaction to Enlightenment ideas. The Enlightenment had stressed reason for discovering truth. The romantics emphasized feelings and imagination as sources of knowing.

B. For romanticism, emotions were truly knowable only by the person experiencing them. Romantic works often feature figures isolated from society but sure about the worth of their inner lives. Romanticism also stressed individualism, the belief that each person is unique. Many romantics rebelled against middle-class conventions.

C. Many romantics also had a deep interest in the past, and revived medieval architectural styles, such as with the Houses of Parliament in **London.** Sir Walter Scott's novel of clashes among medieval knights, *Ivanhoe*, was wildly popular. By focusing on their nation's past, many romantic writers reflected nineteenth-century nationalism. The exotic, unfamiliar, and extreme attracted romantics, as is seen in Gothic literature such as Mary Shelley's *Frankenstein* and the works of Edgar Allen Poe.

D. Romantics viewed poetry as the direct expression of the soul. Romantic poetry gave expression to a vital part of romanticism, the love of nature. This is clearly seen in the poetry of William Wordsworth. The worship of nature caused romantics to criticize the new science, which they believed reduced nature to a cold object of mathematical study that had no room for the imagination or the human soul.

E. In Shelley's novel, Frankenstein's monster was a symbol of the danger of science's attempt to conquer nature. Romantics feared that industrialization would alienate people from their inner selves and the natural world.

F. Romantic artists shared two basic beliefs: art reflects the artist's inner soul and art should abandon classical reason for warmth and emotion. Eugène Delacroix was the most famous roman[illegible] in France.

Connecting Across Time

Ask students to identify similarities and differences between the romantic vision that abandoned classical ideas of the past and some examples of modern art and music. **L2**

Writing Activity

Have students research the life of one of the artists of the period and write a brief biography. Tell students to include information on education, training, major works, and public acceptance. **L1**

The romantics believed that emotion and sentiment were only understandable to the person experiencing them. In their novels, romantic writers created figures who were often misunderstood and rejected by society but who continued to believe in their own worth through their inner feelings.

Romantics also valued individualism, the belief in the uniqueness of each person. Many romantics rebelled against middle-class conventions. Male romantics grew long hair and beards and both men and women wore outrageous clothes to express their individuality.

Many romantics had a passionate interest in the past. They revived medieval architecture and built castles, cathedrals, city halls, parliamentary buildings (such as the Houses of Parliament in **London**), and even railway stations in a style called neo-Gothic. Literature, too, reflected this interest in the past. The novels of Walter Scott became best-sellers in the first half of the nineteenth century. *Ivanhoe,* in which Scott tried to evoke clashes between knights in medieval England, became his most popular novel. By focusing on their nations' past, many romantic writers created literature that reflected the nineteenth century's fascination with nationalism.

The exotic and unfamiliar also attracted many romantics. This attraction gave rise to Gothic literature. Chilling examples are Mary Shelley's *Frankenstein* in Britain and Edgar Allen Poe's short stories of horror in the United States. Some romantics even sought the unusual in their own lives by exploring their dreams and nightmares and seeking altered states of consciousness.

The romantics viewed poetry as the direct expression of the soul. Romantic poetry gave expression to one of the most important characteristics of romanticism—its love of nature. Romantics believed that nature served as a mirror into which humans could look to learn about themselves. This is especially evident in the poetry of William Wordsworth, the foremost English romantic poet of nature. His experience of nature was almost mystical:

> ❝One impulse from a vernal wood
> May teach you more of man,
> Of moral evil and of good,
> Than all the sages can.❞

The worship of nature also caused Wordsworth and other romantic poets to be critical of eighteenth-century science, which, they believed, had reduced nature to a cold object of study. To Wordsworth, the scientists' dry, mathematical approach left no room for the imagination or for the human soul. The poet who left to the world "one single moral precept," or principle, said Wordsworth, did more for the world than did scientists, who were soon forgotten. The monster created by Frankenstein in Mary Shelley's novel was a symbol of the danger of science's attempt to conquer nature. Many romantics were convinced that the emerging industrialization would cause people to become alienated from their inner selves and the natural world around them.

Like the literary arts, the visual arts were deeply affected by romanticism. Romantic artists shared at least two features. First, to them, all art was a reflection of

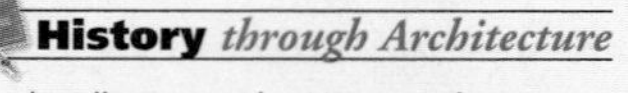

History *through Architecture*

Lights illuminate the Houses of Parliament and Big Ben in London. What are the Gothic architectural elements of these buildings?

COOPERATIVE LEARNING ACTIVITY

Producing an Art Magazine Familiarize students with romanticism and realism by bringing in samples of writing by authors such as Wordsworth and Dickens, and paintings by Delacroix and Courbet. It may be helpful to coordinate this lesson with the English and/or art teachers. Have students work together to produce a magazine displaying their own literary and artistic accomplishments. Contributions must be in the style of either romantic or realist art. Contributions may include paintings, drawings, poetry, songs, and so on. Some students should be responsible for assembling and organizing the materials. Others may do interviews of the contributors or write articles evaluating the works as they relate to the principles of romanticism or realism. **L2** ELL

Like his contemporary William Wordsworth, English artist John Constable sought to capture nature's dramatic beauty in his works. Constable's watercolor of Stonehenge from 1835 reflects the romantic emphasis on emotion over reason.

the artist's inner feelings. A painting should mirror the artist's vision of the world and be the instrument of the artist's own imagination. Second, romantic artists abandoned classical reason for warmth and emotion.

Eugène Delacroix (DEH•luh•KWAH) was one of the most famous romantic painters from **France.** His paintings showed two chief characteristics: a fascination with the exotic and a passion for color. His works reflect his belief that "a painting should be a feast to the eye."

To many romantics, music was the most romantic of the arts, because it enabled the composer to probe deeply into human emotions. Music historians have called the nineteenth century the age of romanticism. One of the greatest composers of all time, **Ludwig van Beethoven,** was the bridge between the classical and romantic periods in music.

Beethoven was one of the few composers who was able singlehandedly to transform the art of music. For Beethoven, music had to reflect his deepest inner feelings: "I must write, for what weighs on my heart, I must express." Beethoven's early work fell largely within the classical framework of the eighteenth century. However, his Third Symphony embodied the elements of romanticism with its use of powerful melodies to create dramatic intensity.

Reading Check **Examining** How did the popularity of *Ivanhoe* reflect the interests of the nineteenth century?

A New Age of Science

The Scientific Revolution had created a modern, rational approach to the study of the natural world. For a long time, only the educated elite understood its importance. By the 1830s, however, new discoveries in science had led to many practical benefits that affected all Europeans. In 1796, for example, Edward Jenner had discovered a vaccine for smallpox, a widespread disease that killed mostly infants and young children.

In biology, the Frenchman **Louis Pasteur** proposed the germ theory of disease, which was crucial to the development of modern scientific medical practices. In chemistry, the Russian Dmitry Mendeleyev in the 1860s classified all the material elements then known on the basis of their atomic weights. In Great Britain, Michael Faraday put together a primitive generator that laid the foundation for the use of electric current.

The dramatic material benefits often provided by science and technology led Europeans to have a growing faith in science. This faith, in turn, undermined the religious faith of many people. It is no accident that the nineteenth century was an age of increasing **secularization** (indifference or rejection of religion or religious consideration). For many people, truth was now to be found in science and the concrete material existence of humans. No one did more to create a picture of humans as material beings that

Reading Check

Answer: It deals with medieval England, reflecting the romantic interest in the past and fascination with nationalism.

Guided Reading Activity 12–4

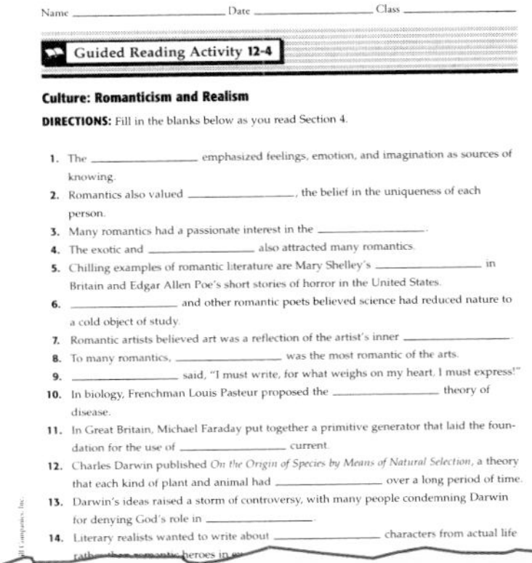

Name ______ Date ______ Class ______

Guided Reading Activity 12-4

Culture: Romanticism and Realism

DIRECTIONS: Fill in the blanks below as you read Section 4.

1. The ______ emphasized feelings, emotion, and imagination as sources of knowing.
2. Romantics also valued ______, the belief in the uniqueness of each person.
3. Many romantics had a passionate interest in the ______.
4. The exotic and ______ also attracted many romantics.
5. Chilling examples of romantic literature are Mary Shelley's ______ in Britain and Edgar Allen Poe's short stories of horror in the United States.
6. ______ and other romantic poets believed science had reduced nature to a cold object of study.
7. Romantic artists believed art was a reflection of the artist's inner ______.
8. To many romantics, ______ was the most romantic of the arts.
9. ______ said, "I must write, for what weighs on my heart, I must express!"
10. In biology, Frenchman Louis Pasteur proposed the ______ theory of disease.
11. In Great Britain, Michael Faraday put together a primitive generator that laid the foundation for the use of ______ current.
12. Charles Darwin published *On the Origin of Species by Means of Natural Selection*, a theory that each kind of plant and animal had ______ over a long period of time.
13. Darwin's ideas raised a storm of controversy, with many people condemning Darwin for denying God's role in ______.
14. Literary realists wanted to write about ______ characters from actual life

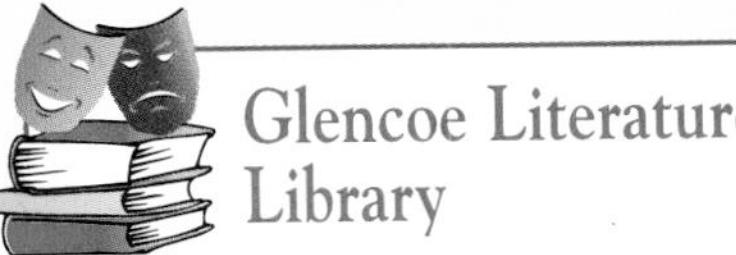

Glencoe Literature Library

The following literature from the **Glencoe Literature Library** may enrich the teaching of this chapter:

A Tale of Two Cities by C. Dickens
Great Expectations by C. Dickens
Cyrano de Bergerac by E. Rostand
Frankenstein by M. Shelley

CURRICULUM CONNECTION

Geography Have students research Darwin's voyage. Have them locate on a world map the stops Darwin made and report his conclusions. **L2**

INTERDISCIPLINARY CONNECTIONS ACTIVITY

Science Have students make a chart in which they identify the contributions of significant scientists and inventors discussed in this chapter such as Louis Pasteur, Robert Fulton, and James Watt. After they have examined eighteenth- and nineteenth-century achievements in science and technology, have students form groups to research the scientific breakthroughs of the twentieth century. Groups should choose specific areas of science to research; for example, space exploration, medical research, environmental research. Group members should discuss the breakthroughs in their field and develop a poster written and designed by students. The posters should answer such questions as: What was the breakthrough? Who was responsible for it? Why is it important? What effect does it have on our lives today? **L2**

Reading Check

Answer: It created a picture of human beings as part of the natural world, not higher beings that were above it. This upset many people, who objected that it turned life into a mere struggle for survival where moral values had no place, or that Darwin had denied God's role in creation. (It also led to the search for our earliest ancestors that is discussed in Chapter 1.)

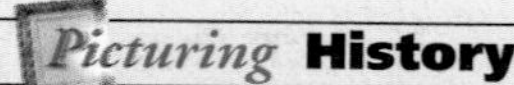

Picturing **History**

Answer: Students will research medical advances in the 1800s.

3 ASSESS

Assign Section 4 Assessment as homework or as an in-class activity.

Have students use **Interactive Tutor Self-Assessment CD-ROM.**

Section Quiz 12–4

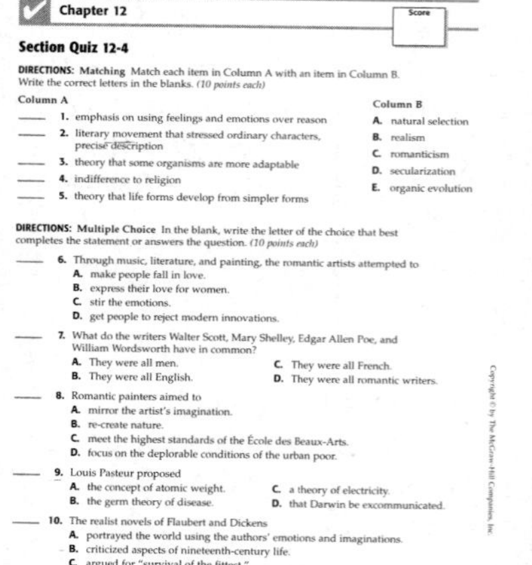

Name ______ Date ______ Class ______

Chapter 12 — Score

Section Quiz 12-4

DIRECTIONS: Matching Match each item in Column A with an item in Column B. Write the correct letters in the blanks. *(10 points each)*

Column A	Column B
___ 1. emphasis on using feelings and emotions over reason	A. natural selection
___ 2. literary movement that stressed ordinary characters, precise description	B. realism
___ 3. theory that some organisms are more adaptable	C. romanticism
___ 4. indifference to religion	D. secularization
___ 5. theory that life forms develop from simpler forms	E. organic evolution

DIRECTIONS: Multiple Choice In the blank, write the letter of the choice that best completes the statement or answers the question. *(10 points each)*

___ 6. Through music, literature, and painting, the romantic artists attempted to
A. make people fall in love.
B. express their love for women.
C. stir the emotions.
D. get people to reject modern innovations.

___ 7. What do the writers Walter Scott, Mary Shelley, Edgar Allen Poe, and William Wordsworth have in common?
A. They were all men.
B. They were all English.
C. They were all French.
D. They were all romantic writers.

___ 8. Romantic painters aimed to
A. mirror the artist's imagination.
B. re-create nature.
C. meet the highest standards of the École des Beaux-Arts.
D. focus on the deplorable conditions of the urban poor.

___ 9. Louis Pasteur proposed
A. the concept of atomic weight.
B. the germ theory of disease.
C. a theory of electricity.
D. that Darwin be excommunicated.

___ 10. The realist novels of Flaubert and Dickens
A. portrayed the world using the authors' emotions and imaginations.
B. criticized aspects of nineteenth-century life.
C. argued for "survival of the fittest."
D. condem[illegible]

were simply part of the natural world than Charles Darwin.

In 1859, **Charles Darwin** published *On the Origin of Species by Means of Natural Selection.* The basic idea of this book was that each kind of plant and animal had evolved over a long period of time from earlier and simpler forms of life. Darwin called this principle **organic evolution.**

How did this natural process work? According to Darwin, in every species, "many more individuals of each species are born than can possibly survive." This results in a "struggle for existence." Darwin believed that some organisms are more adaptable to the environment than others, a process that Darwin called **natural selection.**

Those that are naturally selected for survival ("survival of the fittest") reproduce and thrive. The unfit do not survive. The fit who survive pass on the variations that enabled them to survive until, according to Darwin, a new, separate species emerges. In *The Descent of Man,* published in 1871, Darwin argued that human beings had animal origins and were not an exception to the rule governing other species.

Darwin's ideas raised a storm of controversy. Some people objected that Darwin's theory made human beings ordinary products of nature rather than unique beings. Others were bothered by his idea of life as a mere struggle for survival. "Is there a place in the Darwinian world for moral values?" they asked. Many people also condemned Darwin for denying God's role in creation. Gradually, however, many scientists and other intellectuals came to accept Darwin's theory.

Reading Check **Describing** How did Darwin's theory of natural selection influence the way in which people viewed the world?

Realism

The belief that the world should be viewed realistically, a view frequently expressed after 1850, was closely related to the scientific outlook. In politics, Bismarck had practiced the "politics of reality." **Realism** became a movement in the literary and visual arts as well.

The literary realists of the mid-nineteenth century rejected romanticism. They wanted to write about ordinary characters from actual life rather than romantic heroes in exotic settings. They also tried to avoid emotional language by using precise description. They preferred novels to poems.

Many literary realists combined their interest in everyday life with an examination of social issues. These artists expressed their social views through their characters. Although this type of realistic writing occurred worldwide, the French led the way.

The realist novel was perfected by the French author Gustave Flaubert, who was a leading novelist of the 1850s and 1860s. His work *Madame Bovary* presents a critical description of small-town life in France. The British novelist **Charles Dickens** became very successful with his realistic novels focusing on the lower and middle classes in Britain's early Industrial Age. In such novels as *Oliver Twist* and *David Copperfield,* Dickens described the urban poor and the brutal life they led with vivid realism.

Picturing **History**

Louis Pasteur developed a vaccine against rabies. In 1993, the Louis Pasteur Institute researchers were the first to isolate the AIDS virus. Research other medical advances that were made during the 1800s.

EXTENDING THE CONTENT

Charles Darwin As a young man, Charles Darwin became increasingly bored with his studies of medicine. He then went to Cambridge with the idea of becoming a minister. However, he became preoccupied with natural history. After graduation he got the job of naturalist aboard *H.M.S. Beagle.* Darwin was most impressed by the flora and fauna in the Galápagos Islands. He found it curious that God had created a unique type of finch for each of the Galápagos Islands. Darwin also realized that the populations of animals would constantly exceed their food supply. The most likely to survive were those most skilled in finding food for themselves and their offspring. The most controversial part of his theory pertained to this idea of survival of the fittest.

History *through Art*

***The Stonebreakers* by Gustave Courbet, 1849** As an artist of the realist school, Courbet broke with the mystical and imaginative romantic period. Which style do you prefer?

In art, too, realism became dominant after 1850. Realist artists sought to show the everyday life of ordinary people and the world of nature with photographic realism. The French became leaders in realist painting, as they had become leaders in realistic writing.

Gustave Courbet was the most famous artist of the realist school. He loved to portray scenes from everyday life. His subjects were factory workers, peasants, and the wives of saloon keepers. "I have never seen either angels or goddesses, so I am not interested in painting them," Courbet said.

One of his famous works, *The Stonebreakers*, shows two roadworkers engaged in the deadening work of breaking stones to build a road. There were those who objected to Courbet's "cult of ugliness" and who found such scenes of human misery scandalous. To Courbet, however, no subject was too ordinary, too harsh, or too ugly.

Reading Check **Evaluating** What factors helped to produce the movement known as realism?

SECTION 4 ASSESSMENT

Checking for Understanding

1. **Define** romanticism, secularization, organic evolution, natural selection, realism.
2. **Identify** Ludwig van Beethoven, Louis Pasteur, Charles Darwin, Charles Dickens.
3. **Locate** London, France.
4. **Explain** how scientific developments affected the cultural movements of the nineteenth century.
5. **List** the values of the romantics.

Critical Thinking

6. **Compare and Contrast** How did romanticism compare to the ideas of the Enlightenment?
7. **Organizing Information** Use a table to list scientists and their discoveries in the mid-nineteenth century.

Scientist	Discovery
Pasteur	
Mendeleyev	
Faraday	
Darwin	

Analyzing Visuals

8. **Examine** the painting by John Constable shown on page 389 of your text. How does this painting reflect the characteristics of the romantic movement?

Writing About History

9. **Expository Writing** Read poetry by two different poets of romanticism. Write a paper describing the elements of romanticism found in the poems. Be sure to include quotations.

SECTION 4 ASSESSMENT

1. Key terms are in blue.
2. Ludwig van Beethoven (*p. 389*); Louis Pasteur (*p. 389*); Charles Darwin (*p. 390*); Charles Dickens (*p. 390*)
3. See chapter maps.
4. linked with realism, the belief that the world should be viewed scientifically, replaced emotional language of romanticism
5. emphasis on feelings, imagination, individualism, rebellion against convention, interest in past, exotic
6. Romanticism: emphasized feelings and imagination; Enlightenment: used reason and logic
7. Pasteur: germ theory of disease; Mendeleyev: classified material elements on the basis of their atomic weights; Faraday: primitive generator laid foundation for use of electricity; Darwin: organic evolution and natural selection
8. Answer should mention emotion, feeling.
9. Answers will vary.

History *through Art*

Answer: Answers will vary but should be logically supported.

Reading Check

Answer: scientific outlook, rejection of romanticism, the desire to write about ordinary characters from actual life; belief that no subject was too ordinary

Reading Essentials and Study Guide 12–4

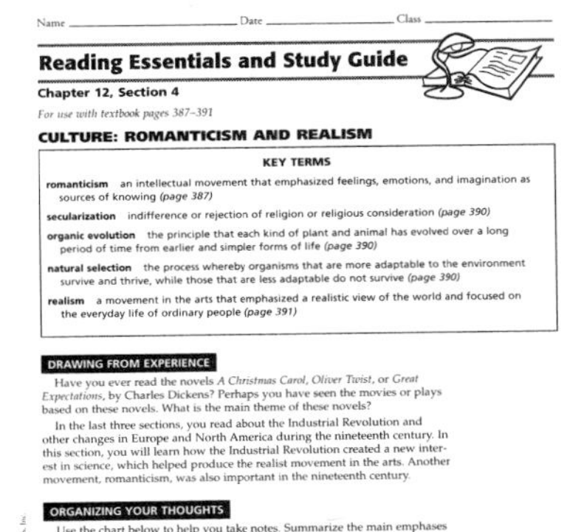

Name ______ Date ______ Class ______

Reading Essentials and Study Guide

Chapter 12, Section 4

For use with textbook pages 387–391

CULTURE: ROMANTICISM AND REALISM

KEY TERMS

romanticism an intellectual movement that emphasized feelings, emotions, and imagination as sources of knowing *(page 387)*

secularization indifference or rejection of religion or religious consideration *(page 390)*

organic evolution the principle that each kind of plant and animal has evolved over a long period of time from earlier and simpler forms of life *(page 390)*

natural selection the process whereby organisms that are more adaptable to the environment survive and thrive, while those that are less adaptable do not survive *(page 390)*

realism a movement in the arts that emphasized a realistic view of the world and focused on the everyday life of ordinary people *(page 391)*

DRAWING FROM EXPERIENCE

Have you ever read the novels *A Christmas Carol*, *Oliver Twist*, or *Great Expectations*, by Charles Dickens? Perhaps you have seen the movies or plays based on these novels. What is the main theme of these novels?

In the last three sections, you read about the Industrial Revolution and other changes in Europe and North America during the nineteenth century. In this section, you will learn how the Industrial Revolution created a new interest in science, which helped produce the realist movement in the arts. Another movement, romanticism, was also important in the nineteenth century.

ORGANIZING YOUR THOUGHTS

Use the chart below to help you take notes. Summarize the main emphases and themes of romanticism and realism, and list some of the important writers and artists in these two movements.

Movement	Emphases/Themes	Important Writers	Important Artists
Romanticism	1.	2.	3.

Reteaching Activity

Have students work in groups of three to summarize each of the three headings in this section. **L1**

4 CLOSE

Lead students in a discussion about how political, economic, and social systems are reflected in artistic works of both romanticism and realism.

GLENCOE TECHNOLOGY

MindJogger Videoquiz

Use the **MindJogger Videoquiz** to review Chapter 12 content.

 Available in VHS.

Using Key Terms

1. Abolitionism **2.** principle of legitimacy **3.** Universal male suffrage **4.** puddling **5.** organic evolution **6.** conservatism **7.** cottage industry **8.** plebiscite **9.** socialism **10.** Romanticism

Reviewing Key Facts

11. Crimean

12. Austria, Prussia, Russia, and France

13. hereditary monarchies without constitutions, such as Austria, Prussia, Russia, and France

14. a reflection of the artist's inner feelings; warmth and emotion

15. It involved Russia versus the Ottoman Empire, Great Britain, and France. The war broke out over Russian aspirations in the Balkans and desire to take advantage of Turkish weakness.

16. cities grew dramatically, the population shifted from mostly rural to mostly urban as former farm workers moved to cities, a large industrial middle class arose, squalid working conditions and slums prevailed, but eventually members of the working class began to share in the prosperity, eventually universal male suffrage, development of socialism

17. It provided a source of power that enabled factories to be built in more locations, not just near sources of water power.

18. increased the number of male voters

19. Landlords kept the best lands for themselves, so peasants found themselves without enough land to support themselves; conservatives thought that the czar was trying to destroy the basic institutions of Russian society.

CHAPTER 12 ASSESSMENT and ACTIVITIES

Using Key Terms

1. _____ was the movement to end slavery in the United States.
2. At the Congress of Vienna in 1814, the _____ became the guiding political principle for the great powers.
3. _____ means that all adult men have the right to vote.
4. The process invented by Henry Cort to produce high quality iron is called _____.
5. The basic idea of Charles Darwin's book, *On the Origin of Species,* was the principle of _____.
6. Obedience to political authority, emphasis on organized religion to maintain the social order, and resistance to the ideas of individual rights and representative government are characteristics of _____.
7. Before the Industrial Revolution, goods were often produced by individuals working in their own homes, a method known as _____.
8. Louis-Napoleon became president when 97 percent of the _____ responded with a yes vote.
9. A system in which society and not individuals owns the means of production is called _____.
10. _____ emphasized feeling, emotion, and imagination as sources of knowing.

Reviewing Key Facts

11. **History** The Concert of Europe was destroyed by which war?
12. **History** What four nations were prepared to use military forces to crush revolts in other nations?
13. **Government** Which governments supported the ideology of conservatism?
14. **Culture** What features can be found in paintings of the romantic style?
15. **History** What countries were involved in the Crimean War? What were the causes of the war?
16. **Economics** How did the Industrial Revolution affect Great Britain's social structure?
17. **Science and Technology** Explain the role of the steam engine in the development of the factory system.
18. **Government** What were the provisions of the British voting bill in 1832?
19. **Government** Why did the reforms of Czar Alexander II satisfy few Russians?
20. **History** Between 1815 and 1830, what forces for change threatened the conservative governments throughout Europe?
21. **Culture** Name the social classes that tended to support conservatism.
22. **Science and Technology** How did new discoveries in science in the 1800s provide practical benefits to Europeans?
23. **Government** Identify and describe the Compromise of 1867. To what was the compromise a response, and how successful was it?
24. **Government** Describe how Otto von Bismarck contributed to German unification.
25. **Economics** What was the economic impact of railroads on the Industrial Revolution?

Chapter Summary

In this chapter, you have studied developments from industry to art, faith to science, and liberalism to conservatism. The chart below summarizes some of these developments.

Advances	Conflict	Change	Reaction	Diversity
• Steam and coal are new sources of power. • Higher-quality iron leads to better railroads.	• Nationalism and liberalism become forces for change. • Conservatives attempt to suppress nationalism.	• People move to cities for factory work. • Italy unifies. • Germany emerges as a strong European power.	• Russian czars oppose the forces of liberalism and nationalism. • Science has a greater impact on people, undermining religious faith.	• Austria-Hungary contains many different ethnic groups seeking self-rule. • Romanticism and realism are opposite artistic styles.

20. liberalism and nationalism

21. rulers, nobles, and the wealthy elites who wanted to retain the status quo

22. modern medical practices, foundation for use of electric current, growing faith in science

23. It divided the Austrian Empire into a dual monarchy, Austria-Hungary. It sought to appease nationalist Hungarians by giving Hungary its own capital, constitution, and legislature, as well as control over domestic affairs. It did not satisfy the many other nationalities in the Austro-Hungarian Empire.

24. His authoritarian rule, and a well-organized, well-trained army, helped Prussia to organize the German states into the North German Confederation, and then the Second German Empire, with the Prussian king as kaiser.

25. Railroads were less expensive transportation, which led to lower-priced goods and larger markets.

Self-Check Quiz

Visit the *Glencoe World History—Modern Times* Web site at wh.mt.glencoe.com and click on **Chapter 12–Self-Check Quiz** to prepare for the Chapter Test.

Critical Thinking

26. **Making Comparisons** Compare the motives for Czar Alexander II's emancipation of the serfs with Abraham Lincoln's motives for issuing the Emancipation Proclamation in 1862.
27. **Cause and Effect** Describe how the Crimean War indirectly contributed to the unification of the Italian and German states.

Writing About History

28. **Expository Writing** How did the political, economic, and social injustices that existed during the nineteenth century contribute to romanticism and realism?

Analyzing Sources

Read the following excerpt from the poetry of William Wordsworth:

> “One impulse from a vernal wood
> May teach you more of man,
> Of moral evil and of good,
> Than all the sages can.”

29. What characteristic of romantic poetry is evident in Wordsworth's poem?
30. What message is Wordsworth trying to convey? Do you agree?

Applying Technology Skills

31. **Using the Internet** Search the Internet to find information about Charles Dickens. Use a search engine to help focus your search by using words such as *Charles Dickens, Industrial Revolution, London,* and *Oliver Twist.* Prepare a report on the life of Charles Dickens, including his views on the working conditions in Britain and how he portrayed the lower and middle classes in his novels.

Making Decisions

32. Pretend that you are a monarch in Europe in 1847. You can tell that agitation is spreading in your country and you fear revolution. Using what you know about the causes of revolution and how other countries (i.e., Britain) have been able to avoid it, what reforms might you choose to enact? What steps or policies would you avoid?
33. Evaluate the political choices and decisions that European rulers made at the Congress of Vienna in 1814. What were the consequences of the decisions these leaders made?

Analyzing Maps and Charts

Study the map, Industrialization of Europe by 1870, on page 367 to answer the following questions.

34. In which part of the United Kingdom is industrialization concentrated?
35. What relationship exists between railways and industrial centers?

Standardized Test Practice

Directions: Choose the best answer to the following question.

Use the information in the box *and* your knowledge of world history to answer the following question.

British Economic Conditions During the Early 1800s
- Canal miles tripled between 1760 and 1830.
- Britain had built more than 6,000 miles (9,654 km) of railroad tracks by 1850.
- Britain produced nearly 3 million tons (2.7 million t) of iron ore by 1852.
- London's population grew by 236 percent between 1800 and 1850.

Which of the following statements is based on the information in this box?

A The Industrial Revolution led to massive urbanization.
B London neighborhoods in the 1800s were sharply divided between rich and poor.
C A boom in railroad and canal construction made transportation more difficult.
D Parliament disagreed with the king over taxes and spending.

Test-Taking Tip: This question asks for an answer that is supported by the facts provided in the box. Find the answer choice that is *proven true* by the information listed in the box.

Critical Thinking

26. Alexander II was concerned with modernization; Lincoln felt that the issue of slavery was dividing the United States, and the solution was to abolish it.
27. It led to the breakdown of the Concert of Europe and left Austria without friends among the great powers. Both Piedmont and Prussia were able to take advantage of Austria's weakened position to unify Italy and Germany.

Writing About History

28. Romanticism offered an escape, emphasizing feelings, emotion, imagination; novelists like Scott fostered nationalism while offering escape into their countries' past. Realist artists portrayed the grim realities of lower-class life.

Analyzing Sources

29. the love of nature
30. that nature serves as a mirror into which humans can look to learn more about themselves

HISTORY Online

Have students visit the Web site at wh.mt.glencoe.com to review Chapter 12 and take the Self-Check Quiz.

Applying Technology Skills

31. Students should include a list of references.

Making Decisions

32. Answers will include specific reforms.
33. rearranging territories to form new balance of power, guarantee independence of the great powers, attempt to maintain peace in Europe, lead to Concert of Europe.

Analyzing Maps and Charts

34. in central England
35. Rail lines developed near industrial cities.

Standardized Test Practice

Answer: A
Test-Taking Tip: Only one statement is based on information in the box.

Bonus Question ?

Ask: What political, social, economic, or other conditions make it easiest for a country to achieve democratic government with civil rights for all citizens? What conditions make it most difficult? *(Answers may include that some history of self-government or of limitations on monarchical power make it easiest; traditions of absolute rule and a rigid social class structure make it most difficult.)*

Chapter 13 Resources

Timesaving Tools

TeacherWorks™ All-In-One Planner and Resource Center

- **Interactive Teacher Edition** Access your Teacher Wraparound Edition and your classroom resources with a few easy clicks.
- **Interactive Lesson Planner** Planning has never been easier! Organize your week, month, semester, or year with all the lesson helps you need to make teaching creative, timely, and relevant.

Use Glencoe's **Presentation Plus!** multimedia teacher tool to easily present dynamic lessons that visually excite your students. Using Microsoft PowerPoint® you can customize the presentations to create your own personalized lessons.

TEACHING TRANSPARENCIES

Graphic Organizer Student Activity 13 Transparency

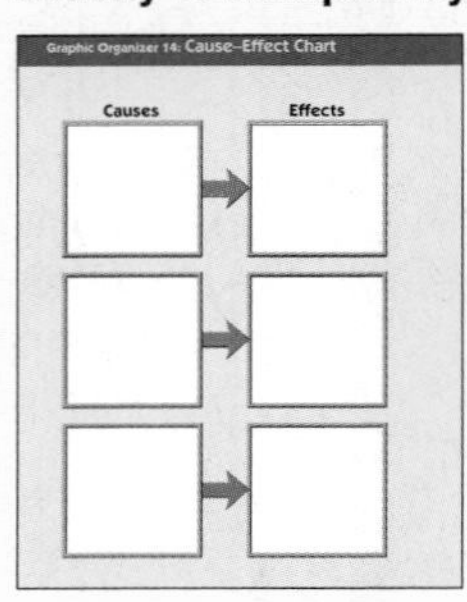

Chapter Transparency 13

Map Overlay Transparency 13

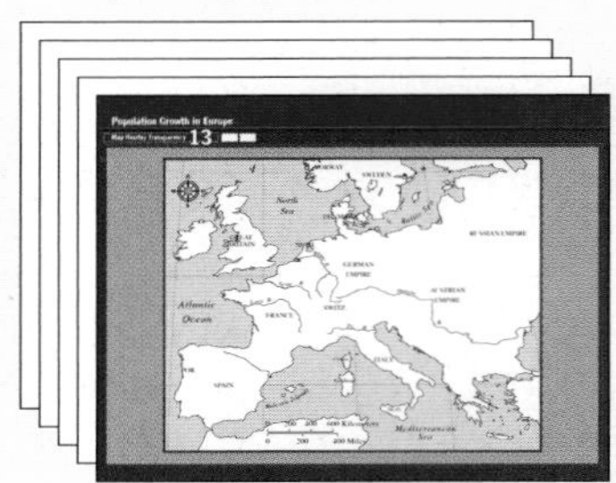

APPLICATION AND ENRICHMENT

Enrichment Activity 13

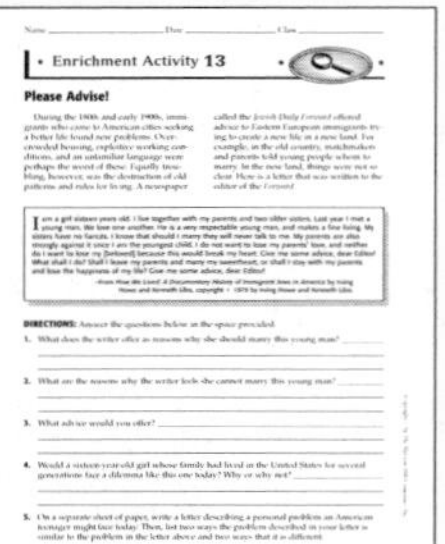

Primary Source Reading 13

History Simulation Activity 13

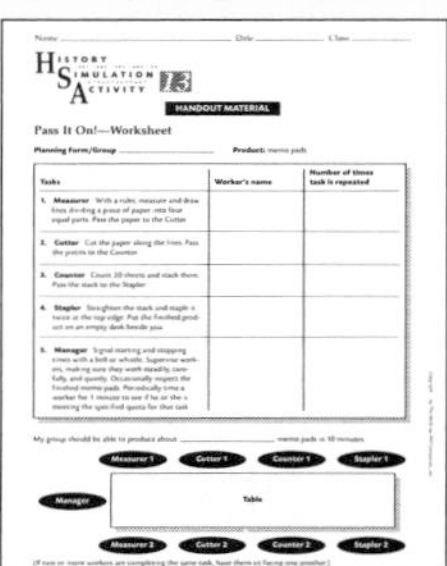

Historical Significance Activity 13

Cooperative Learning Activity 13

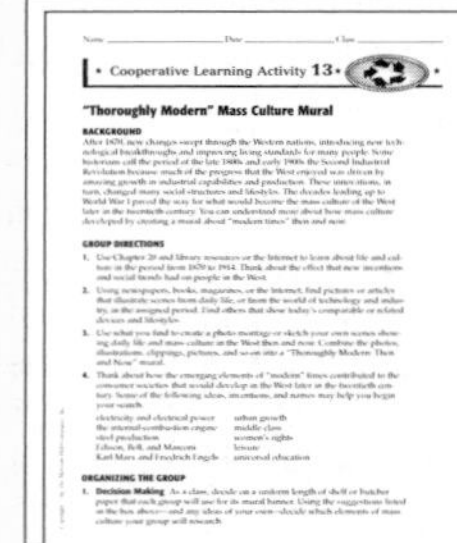

THE HISTORY CHANNEL.

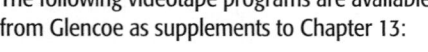

The following videotape programs are available from Glencoe as supplements to Chapter 13:

- **Alexander Graham Bell: Voice of Invention** (ISBN 1–56501–946-6)
- **Marconi: Whisper in the Air** (ISBN 1–56501–551–7)
- **Henry Ford: Tin Lizzy Tycoon** (ISBN 1–56501–380–8)
- **American Civil War** (ISBN 0–7670–0102–8)
- **The Homes of Frank Lloyd Wright** (ISBN 0–7670–0009–9)

To order, call Glencoe at 1–800–334–7344. To find classroom resources to accompany many of these videos, check the following home pages:
A&E Television: www.aande.com
The History Channel: www.historychannel.com

Chapter 13 Resources

Review and Reinforcement

Linking Past and Present Activity 13

Time Line Activity 13

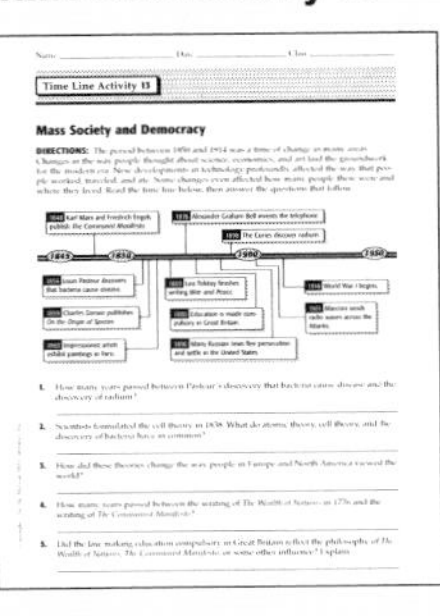

Reteaching Activity 13

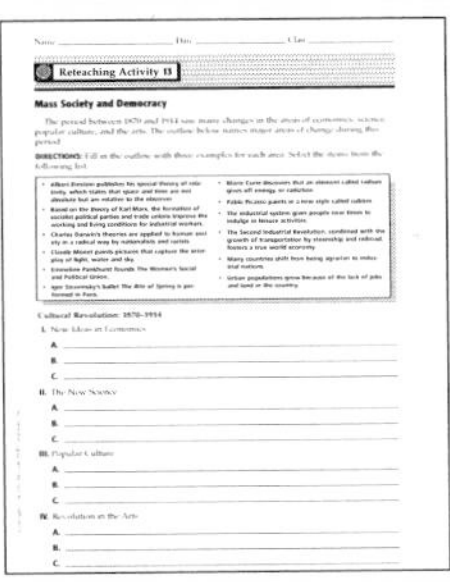

Vocabulary Activity 13

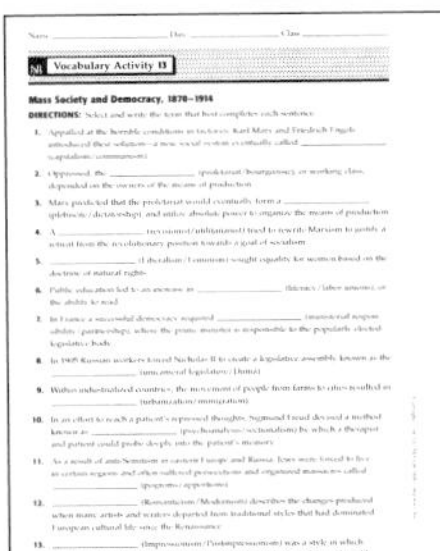

Critical Thinking Skills Activity 13

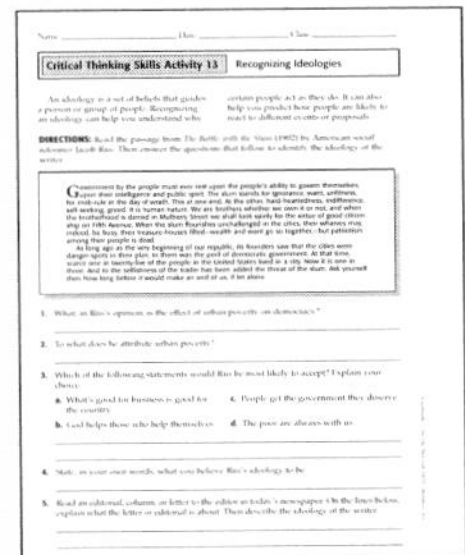

Assessment and Evaluation

Glencoe's Assessment Advantage

Chapter 13 Test Form A

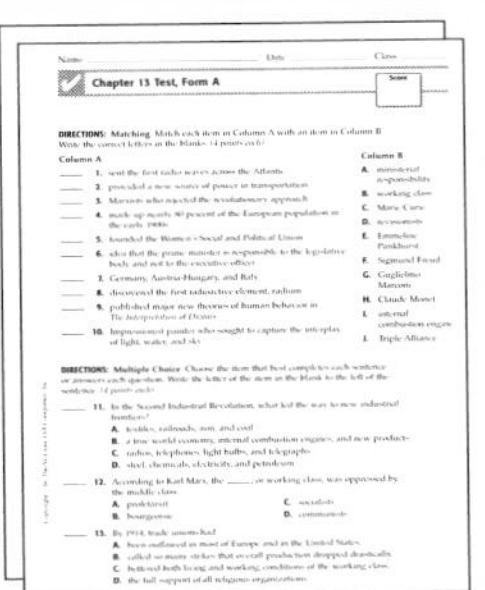

Chapter 13 Test Form B

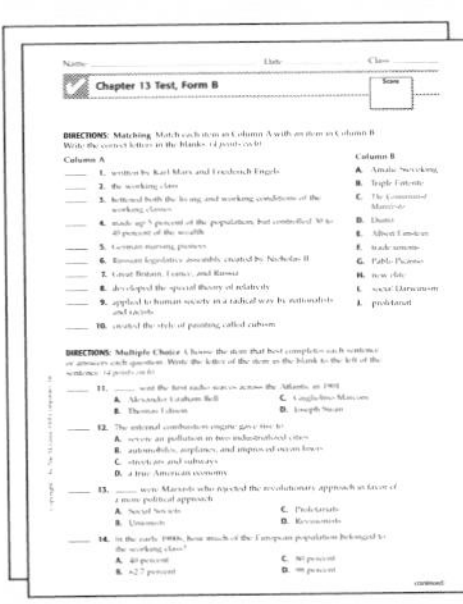

Performance Assessment Activity 13

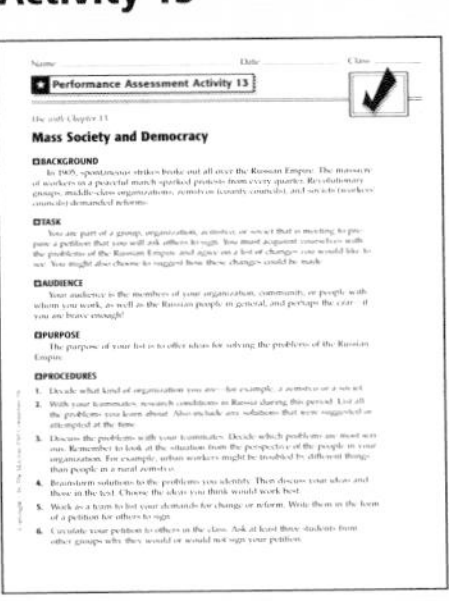

ExamView® Pro Testmaker CD-ROM

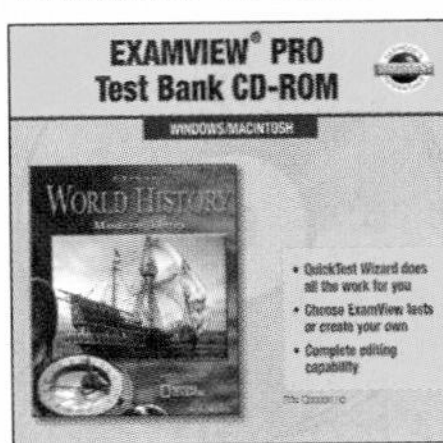

Standardized Test Skills Practice Workbook Activity 13

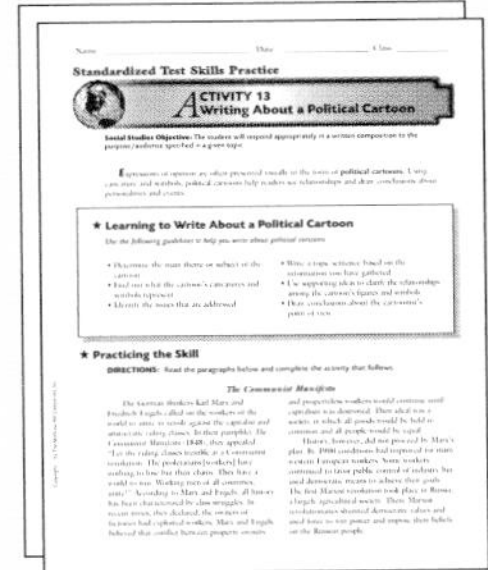

Interdisciplinary Activities

Mapping History Activity 13

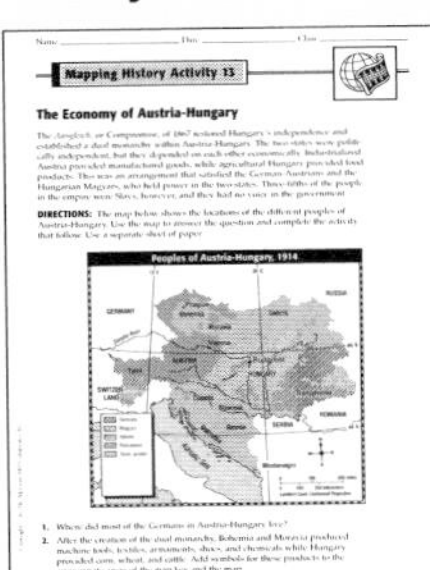

World Art and Music Activity 13

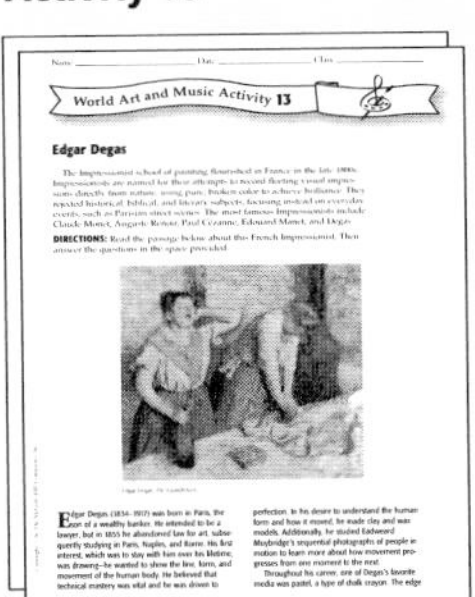

History and Geography Activity 13

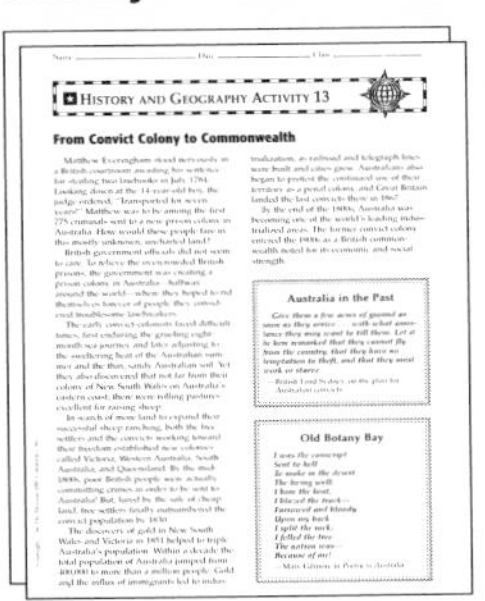

People in World History Activity 13

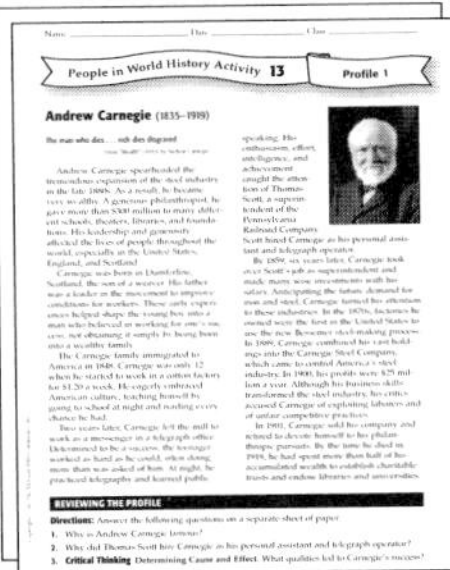

Multimedia

- Vocabulary PuzzleMaker CD-ROM
- Interactive Tutor Self-Assessment CD-ROM
- ExamView® Pro Testmaker CD-ROM
- Audio Program
- World History Primary Source Document Library CD-ROM
- MindJogger Videoquiz
- Presentation Plus! CD-ROM
- TeacherWorks CD-ROM
- Interactive Student Edition CD-ROM
- The World History—Modern Times Video Program

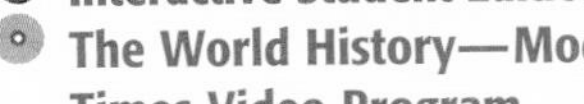

Spanish Resources

The following Spanish language materials are available in the Spanish Resources Binder:

- Spanish Guided Reading Activities
- Spanish Reteaching Activities
- Spanish Quizzes and Tests
- Spanish Vocabulary Activities
- Spanish Summaries

Chapter 13 Resources

SECTION RESOURCES

Daily Objectives	Reproducible Resources	Multimedia Resources
SECTION 1 **The Growth of Industrial Prosperity** 1. Describe how new sources of energy and consumer products transformed the standard of living for all social classes in many European countries. 2. Summarize how working-class leaders used Marx's ideas to form socialist parties.	Reproducible Lesson Plan 13–1 Daily Lecture and Discussion Notes 13–1 Guided Reading Activity 13–1* Section Quiz 13–1* Reading Essentials and Study Guide 13–1	Daily Focus Skills Transparency 13–1 Interactive Tutor Self-Assessment CD-ROM ExamView® Pro Testmaker CD-ROM Presentation Plus! CD-ROM
SECTION 2 **The Emergence of Mass Society** 1. Characterize the varied middle class in Victorian Britain and their belief in the principles of hard work and good conduct. 2. Discuss how the new opportunities for women and the working class improved their lives.	Reproducible Lesson Plan 13–2 Daily Lecture and Discussion Notes 13–2 Guided Reading Activity 13–2* Section Quiz 13–2* Reading Essentials and Study Guide 13–2	Daily Focus Skills Transparency 13–2 Interactive Tutor Self-Assessment CD-ROM ExamView® Pro Testmaker CD-ROM Presentation Plus! CD-ROM
SECTION 3 **The National State and Democracy** 1. Discuss how new political parties and labor unions challenged the governments of western Europe. 2. Explain how international rivalries led to conflicts in the Balkans and World War I.	Reproducible Lesson Plan 13–3 Daily Lecture and Discussion Notes 13–3 Guided Reading Activity 13–3* Section Quiz 13–3* Reading Essentials and Study Guide 13–3	Daily Focus Skills Transparency 13–3 Interactive Tutor Self-Assessment CD-ROM ExamView® Pro Testmaker CD-ROM Presentation Plus! CD-ROM
SECTION 4 **Toward the Modern Consciousness** 1. Describe how innovative artistic movements during the late 1800s and early 1900s rejected traditional styles. 2. Explain how extreme nationalism and racism led to an increase in anti-Semitism. 3. Summarize how developments in science changed how people saw themselves and their world.	Reproducible Lesson Plan 13–4 Daily Lecture and Discussion Notes 13–4 Guided Reading Activity 13–4* Section Quiz 13–4* Reteaching Activity 13* Reading Essentials and Study Guide 13–4	Daily Focus Skills Transparency 13–4 Interactive Tutor Self-Assessment CD-ROM ExamView® Pro Testmaker CD-ROM Presentation Plus! CD-ROM

0:00 **OUT OF TIME?**
Assign the Chapter 13 **Reading Essentials and Study Guide.**

*Also Available in Spanish

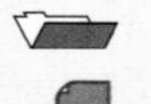 Blackline Master
 Transparency
 CD-ROM
 DVD
 Videocassette

Poster · Music Program · Audio Program

Chapter 13 Resources

NATIONAL GEOGRAPHIC **Teacher's Corner**

INDEX TO NATIONAL GEOGRAPHIC MAGAZINE

The following articles relate to this chapter:

- "Vincent van Gogh," by Joel L. Swerdlow, October 1997.
- "The World of Tolstoy," by Peter T. White, June 1986.
- "Paris: La Belle Epoque," by Eugen Weber, July 1989.

ADDITIONAL NATIONAL GEOGRAPHIC SOCIETY PRODUCTS

To order the following, call National Geographic at 1-800-368-2728:

- *Capitalism, Socialism, Communism Series, "Communism," "Socialism," "Capitalism"* (Videos)

NGS ONLINE

Access National Geographic's new dynamic MapMachine Web site and other geography resources at:
www.nationalgeographic.com
www.nationalgeographic.com/maps

KEY TO ABILITY LEVELS

Teaching strategies have been coded.

- **L1** BASIC activities for all students
- **L2** AVERAGE activities for average to above-average students
- **L3** CHALLENGING activities for above-average students
- **ELL** ENGLISH LANGUAGE LEARNER activities

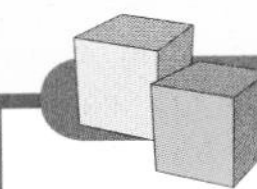

Block Schedule

Activities that are suited to use within the block scheduling framework are identified by:

WORLD HISTORY Online

Use our Web site for additional resources. All essential content is covered in the Student Edition.

You and your students can visit www.wh.mt.glencoe.com, the Web site companion to *Glencoe World History—Modern Times.* This innovative integration of electronic and print media offers your students a wealth of opportunities. The student text directs students to the Web site for the following options:

- **Chapter Overviews**
- **Self-Check Quizzes**
- **Student Web Activities**
- **Textbook Updates**

Answers to the Student Web Activities are provided for you in the **Web Activity Lesson Plans.** Additional Web resources and Interactive Tutor Puzzles are also available.

From the Classroom of...

Daniel W. Blackmon
Coral Gables Senior High School
Miami, Florida

Agents for Social Change

Direct the students to the following Web site: Spartacus Educational — www.spartacus.schoolnet.co.uk/

This is a history Web site based in the United Kingdom. From among the topics available, have the students frame, and then answer, a question relating to social change in the period from 1870 to 1914. Examples of questions include: "What was the role of the National Union of Women's Suffrage Societies in obtaining the right to vote for women in Great Britain?" "What was the significance of the London Dockers' Strike of 1889?" Completed questions and answers can be exchanged among students for peer review and criticism.

Introducing
CHAPTER 13

Performance Assessment

Refer to Activity 13 in the Performance Assessment Activities and Rubrics booklet.

The Impact Today

Ask students to review how production grew during the Industrial Revolution. What impact did increased production have on prosperity in the Western world? Ask students why the Industrial Revolution would have encouraged development of organizations to protect the rights of workers. In addition, ask students to describe changes in the daily life of women resulting from the Industrial Revolution. **L1**

GLENCOE TECHNOLOGY

The World History—Modern Times Video Program

To learn more about mass society and democracy, students can view the Chapter 13 video, "The Industrial Movement," from **The World History—Modern Times Video Program.**

MindJogger Videoquiz

Use the **MindJogger Videoquiz** to preview Chapter 13 content.

 Available in VHS.

CHAPTER 13 Mass Society and Democracy

1870–1914

Key Events

As you read this chapter, look for the key events in the development of mass society.

- *The Second Industrial Revolution resulted in changes in political, economic, and social systems.*
- *After 1870, higher wages and improved conditions in cities raised the standard of living for urban workers.*
- *The late 1800s and early 1900s were a time of political conflict that led to the Balkan crises and, eventually, World War I.*
- *New discoveries radically changed scientific thought, art, architecture, and social consciousness between 1870 and 1914.*

The Impact Today

The events that occurred during this time period still impact our lives today.

- *Because of poor working conditions, labor unions were organized to fight for improvements. Millions of workers are members of various unions today.*
- *Many of the inventions produced during this time, such as telephones and automobiles, are still used today.*

World History—Modern Times Video The Chapter 13 video, "The Industrial Movement," *chronicles the impact of the development and advancements of the Second Industrial Revolution.*

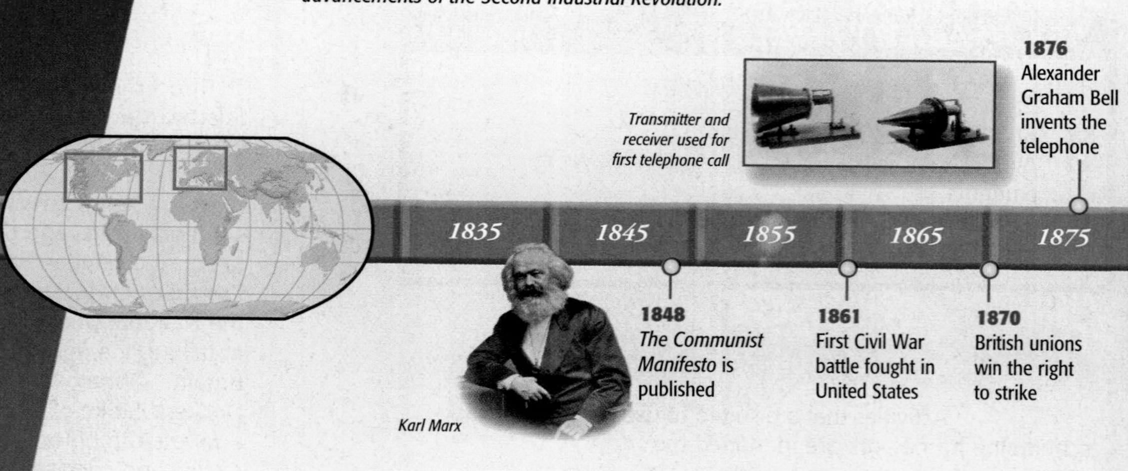

Transmitter and receiver used for first telephone call

1876 Alexander Graham Bell invents the telephone

1848 *The Communist Manifesto* is published

1861 First Civil War battle fought in United States

1870 British unions win the right to strike

Karl Marx

394

TWO-MINUTE LESSON LAUNCHER

The period from 1870 through 1914 was an age of inventive geniuses, including Guglielmo Marconi, Alexander Graham Bell, and many others. Have students brainstorm to create a list of other creative geniuses from science, economics, and the arts who worked during this period. Then have students create a list of contemporary innovators, writers, and artists who are transforming our society.

The Gare Saint-Lazare: Arrival of a Train by Claude Monet, 1877 This painting illustrates Monet's fascination with light as it is reflected and absorbed by the sky, clouds, windows, and trains.

World War I recruitment poster

1888 Eastman creates the Kodak camera

1889 Daimler and Maybach build gasoline-powered car

1901 Marconi sends radio waves across the Atlantic

1905 A revolution in Russia produces limited reforms

1914 World War I begins

1885 | 1895 | 1905 | 1915 | 1925

an automobile, ...hlradwagen, 1889

HISTORY Online

Chapter Overview
Visit the *Glencoe World History—Modern Times* Web site at wh.mt.glencoe.com and click on **Chapter 13–Chapter Overview** to preview chapter information.

395

Introducing CHAPTER 13

Chapter Objectives

After studying this chapter, students should be able to:

1. describe the Second Industrial Revolution;
2. discuss the roles played by inventive individual geniuses such as Guglielmo Marconi, Alexander Graham Bell, and Michael Faraday;
3. understand how the development of new ideas such as socialism, modern physics, and psychology affected people's lives;
4. discuss important cultural developments between 1870 and 1914.

Chapter Overview
Introduce students to chapter content and key terms by having them access **Chapter Overview 13** at wh.mt.glencoe.com.

Time Line Activity

As students read the chapter, have them review the time line on pages 394 to 395. Have students select an event on the time line, learn more about it, and write a brief description of the impact it had.

MORE ABOUT THE ART

Impressionism French painter Claude Monet was the initiator, leader, and dedicated advocate of the Impressionist style. Monet often painted works in series, each depicting the same subject in different light and weather conditions. This painting of the train station (the Gare Saint-Lazare) in Paris, is usually considered the first of his series painting. Executed during the winter of 1876–77, the work represents a total break with the usual Impressionist subjects. Here, the steam engines belch smoke and steam in the train station, prefiguring the mechanical subjects painted by Italian Futurists after 1909.

CHAPTER PREVIEW

Introducing

A Story That Matters

Depending on the ability levels of your students, select from the following questions to reinforce the reading of *A Story That Matters.*

- How have leisure time activities changed over the years?
- What kinds of leisure activities do people engage in now? Fifty years ago? One hundred years ago?
- How much time do students spend on leisure activities? How much time did people spend on leisure activities in the early 1900s?
- How available is transportation today for those who do not have their own automobiles, compared to 100 years ago? **L1** ELL

About the Art

The Steeplechase swimming pool was the largest heated outdoor swimming pool in the world at that time. The pool was part of a larger amusement complex built by George Tilyou. The complex featured rides, a scenic railroad, a rose garden, and a pier. Postcards such as this were used as souvenirs of the Steeplechase Funny Place.

CHAPTER PREVIEW A Story That Matters

Steeplechase swimming pool at Coney Island, New York, c. 1919

The New Leisure

By the second half of the nineteenth century, new work patterns had established the concept of the weekend as a distinct time of recreation and fun. New forms of transportation—railroads and streetcars—enabled workers to make brief trips to amusement parks. Coney Island was only eight miles from central New York City; Blackpool, in England, was a short train ride from nearby industrial towns.

With their Ferris wheels and other daring rides that threw young men and women together, amusement parks offered a whole new world of entertainment. Before leaving, people purchased picture postcards to remember the day's fun.

Thanks to the railroad, seaside resorts—once visited only by the wealthy—became accessible to more people for weekend visits. One upper-class seaside resort regular expressed his disgust with the new "day-trippers":

"They swarm upon the beach, wandering about with apparently no other aim than to get a mouthful of fresh air. You may see them in groups of three or four—the husband, a pale man, dressed in black coat, carries the baby; the wife, equally pale and thin, decked out in her best, labors after with a basket of food. And then there is generally another child . . . wandering behind."

Businessmen in resorts like Blackpool, however, welcomed the crowds of new visitors and built for them boardwalks laden with food, drink, and entertainment.

Why It Matters

A new leisure was one part of the mass society that emerged in the late nineteenth century. The development of this new mass society helped improve the lives of the lower classes, who benefited from extended voting rights, a better standard of living, and public education. In addition, the European nation-states now fostered national loyalty and created mass armies. Political democracy grew as the right to vote was extended to all adult males.

History and You In 1850, a person could expect to live 41 years. By 1910, life expectancy had increased to 54 years. Using a recent almanac, compare the life expectancy rates of people in the United States, United Kingdom, and Russia today with the rates in 1910. Create a bar graph with the data you find.

HISTORY AND YOU

Both the Ferris wheel and another dazzling new marvel—electricity—were first presented to the American people in 1893 at the World's Columbian Exposition held in Chicago, Illinois. To inaugurate the exhibition, President Grover Cleveland dramatically turned on the electric power by pushing a button in the White House. The engine, dynamo, and alternating-current generator that turned on in Chicago were displayed for the first time by George Westinghouse and would later became the basic tools of the electric power industry. Ask students if they have had to endure lengthy periods without electricity. How would they describe this experience? How do they think their lives would be different on a day-to-day basis without electricity?

SECTION 1

The Growth of Industrial Prosperity

Guide to Reading

Main Ideas
- New sources of energy and consumer products transformed the standard of living for all social classes in many European countries.
- Working-class leaders used Marx's ideas to form socialist parties and unions.

Key Terms
bourgeoisie, proletariat, dictatorship, revisionist

People to Identify
Thomas Edison, Alexander Graham Bell, Guglielmo Marconi, Karl Marx

Places to Locate
Netherlands, Austria-Hungary, Spain, Portugal, Russia

Preview Questions
1. What was the Second Industrial Revolution?
2. What were the chief ideas of Karl Marx?

Reading Strategy
Cause and Effect As you read this section, complete a diagram like the one below showing the cause and effect relationship between the resources and the products produced.

Cause	Effect
Electricity →	
Steel →	
Internal-combustion engine →	

Preview of Events

1845 · 1855 · 1865 · 1875 · 1885 · 1895 · 1905

- **1848** Marx and Engels publish *The Communist Manifesto*
- **1875** Creation of German Social Democratic Party
- **1879** Thomas Edison invents the light bulb
- **1889** The Second International socialist association forms
- **1903** Wright brothers make first flight

Voices from the Past

On December 12, 1901, Guglielmo Marconi reported a remarkable discovery:

> ❝Shortly before mid-day I placed the single earphone to my ear and started listening. . . . I was at last on the point of putting . . . my beliefs to test. The answer came at 12:30 when I heard, faintly but distinctly, *pip-pip-pip*. I handed the phone to Kemp: 'Can you hear anything?' I asked. 'Yes,' he said, 'the letter S'—he could hear it. . . . The electric waves sent out into space from Britain had traversed the Atlantic—the distance, enormous as it seemed then, of 1,700 miles [2,735 km] —It was an epoch in history. I now felt for the first time absolutely certain the day would come when mankind would be able to send messages without wires . . . between the farthermost ends of the earth.❞
>
> —***Eyewitness to History***, **John Carey, ed., 1987**

Guglielmo Marconi and his wireless apparatus, 1896

Marconi's discovery of radio waves was one of the many advances of the Second Industrial Revolution.

The Second Industrial Revolution

Westerners in the late 1800s worshiped progress. At the heart of this belief in progress was the stunning material growth produced by what is called the Second Industrial Revolution. The first Industrial Revolution had given rise to textiles, railroads, iron, and coal. In the Second Industrial Revolution, steel, chemicals, electricity, and petroleum led the way to new industrial frontiers.

1 FOCUS

Section Overview

This section describes new products and patterns of production, the birth of a world economic system, and efforts to organize the working class.

BELLRINGER
Skillbuilder Activity

Project transparency and have students answer questions.

Available as a blackline master.

Daily Focus Skills Transparency 13–1

Guide to Reading

Answers to Graphic: Electricity → electric lights; streetcars and subways; conveyor belts, cranes, and machines in factories. Steel → railroads; ships; weapons; lighter, smaller, and faster machines and engines. Internal combustion engines → ocean liners; airplanes; automobiles

Preteaching Vocabulary: Discuss the words *proletariat* and *bourgeoisie*. Ask students to draw pictures representing typical members of each group. Have students explain their drawings.

SECTION RESOURCES

Reproducible Masters
- Reproducible Lesson Plan 13–1
- Daily Lecture and Discussion Notes 13–1
- Guided Reading Activity 13–1
- Section Quiz 13–1
- Reading Essentials and Study Guide 13–1

Transparencies
Daily Focus Skills Transparency 13–1

Multimedia
- Interactive Tutor Self-Assessment CD-ROM
- ExamView® Pro Testmaker CD-ROM
- Presentation Plus! CD-ROM

CHAPTER 13
Section 1, 397–401

2 TEACH

SCIENCE, TECHNOLOGY & SOCIETY

Answer: because they were handmade

Daily Lecture and Discussion Notes 13–1

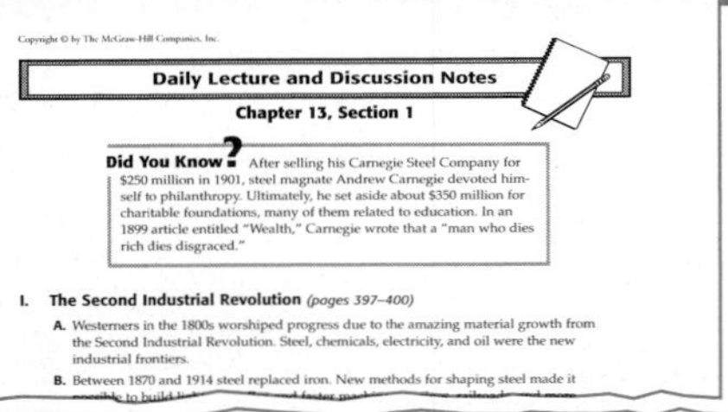

Daily Lecture and Discussion Notes

Chapter 13, Section 1

Did You Know? After selling his Carnegie Steel Company for $250 million in 1901, steel magnate Andrew Carnegie devoted himself to philanthropy. Ultimately, he set aside about $350 million for charitable foundations, many of them related to education. In an 1899 article entitled "Wealth," Carnegie wrote that a "man who dies rich dies disgraced."

I. **The Second Industrial Revolution** *(pages 397–400)*

A. Westerners in the 1800s worshiped progress due to the amazing material growth from the Second Industrial Revolution. Steel, chemicals, electricity, and oil were the new industrial frontiers.

B. Between 1870 and 1914 steel replaced iron. New methods for shaping steel made it

Guided Reading Activity 13–1

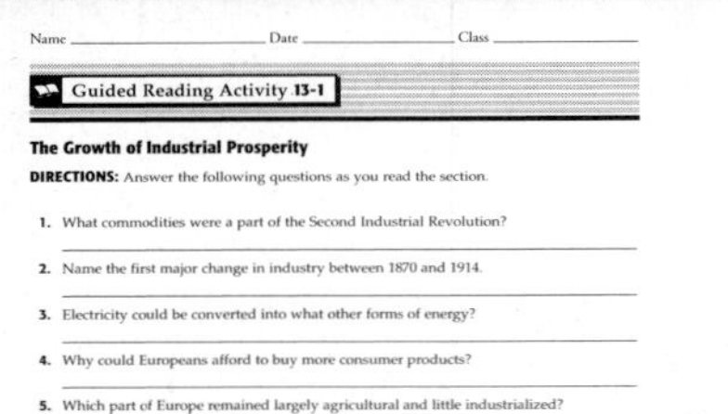
Name ______ Date ______ Class ______

Guided Reading Activity 13-1

The Growth of Industrial Prosperity

DIRECTIONS: Answer the following questions as you read the section.

1. What commodities were a part of the Second Industrial Revolution?
2. Name the first major change in industry between 1870 and 1914.
3. Electricity could be converted into what other forms of energy?
4. Why could Europeans afford to buy more consumer products?
5. Which part of Europe remained largely agricultural and little industrialized?

CURRICULUM CONNECTION

Economics Remind students that the invention of the automobile not only created new industries, it destroyed old ones. Ask students to identify and describe businesses that were harmed by the automobile. **L2**

New Products The first major change in industry between 1870 and 1914 was the substitution of steel for iron. New methods for shaping steel made it useful in the building of lighter, smaller, and faster machines and engines, as well as railways, ships, and weapons. In 1860, Great Britain, France, Germany, and Belgium produced 125,000 tons (112,500 t) of steel. By 1913, the total was an astounding 32 million tons (29 million t).

Electricity was a major new form of energy that proved to be of great value. It could be easily converted into other forms of energy, such as heat, light, and motion, and moved easily through space by means of wires. In the 1870s, the first practical generators of electrical current were developed. By 1910, hydroelectric power stations and coal-fired steam-generating plants enabled homes and factories to be tied to a single, common source of power.

Electricity gave birth to a series of inventions. The creation of the light bulb by **Thomas Edison** in the United States and Joseph Swan in Great Britain opened homes and cities to electric lights. A revolution in communications began when **Alexander Graham Bell** invented the telephone in 1876 and **Guglielmo Marconi** sent the first radio waves across the Atlantic in 1901.

By the 1880s, streetcars and subways powered by electricity had appeared in major European cities. Electricity transformed the factory as well. Conveyor belts, cranes, and machines could all be powered by electricity. With electric lights, factories could remain open 24 hours a day.

The development of the internal-combustion engine, fired by oil and gasoline, provided a new source of power in transportation. This engine gave rise to ocean liners with oil-fired engines, as well

SCIENCE, TECHNOLOGY & SOCIETY

The Automobile

Many new forms of transportation were created in the Industrial Revolution, but none affected more people on a daily basis than the automobile. It was the invention of the internal-combustion engine that made the automobile possible.

A German engineer, Gottlieb Daimler, invented a light, portable internal-combustion engine in 1885. In 1889, Daimler and Wilhelm Maybach produced an automobile powered by a gasoline engine that reached a speed of 10 miles [16 km] per hour. In 1926, Daimler and Karl Benz, another German, merged to form Daimler-Benz, an automotive company that would later manufacture the Mercedes-Benz.

Early cars were handmade and expensive. Only several hundred were sold between 1893 and 1901. Their slow speed, 14 miles [22.5 km] per hour, was a problem, too. Early models were not able to climb steep hills.

An American, Henry Ford, revolutionized the car industry in 1908 by using an assembly line to mass-produce his Model T. Before, it had taken a group of workers 12 hours to build a single car. Now, the same number of workers could build a car in an hour and a half. By cutting production costs, Ford lowered the price of the automobile. A Model T cost $850 in 1908 but only $360 by 1916. By 1916, Ford's factories were producing 735,000 cars a year. By 1925, Ford's Model T cars would make up half of the automobiles in the world.

Analyzing ***Why were early cars expensive?***

Distributor
Cylinder
Piston
Internal-combustion engine

1914 Ford Model T

2001 Ford Explorer

MEETING INDIVIDUAL NEEDS

Visual After students have read this chapter, have them prepare a chart in which they identify the contributions of significant scientists and inventors of the late nineteenth and early twentieth centuries, such as Marie Curie, Albert Einstein, and Thomas Edison. The chart should contain three columns: 1) name 2) country, and 3) contribution. The chart should include Thomas Edison/U.S./lightbulb; Alexander Graham Bell/U.S./telephone; Guglielmo Marconi/Italy/radio waves; Wright Brothers/U.S./airplane; plus others. Have students prepare a collage or poster of the inventions that emerged in this period: conveyor belts, cranes, sewing machines, etc. Students may use the library, Internet, or magazines to accomplish this. **L1**

Industrialization of Europe by 1914

Geography Skills

Steel, electricity, and chemicals were some of the products of the Second Industrial Revolution.

1. **Interpreting Maps** Locate the areas shown on the map that have the heaviest concentrations of industry. What geographic factors could have helped these areas become heavily industrialized?
2. **Applying Geography Skills** Use the information provided in this map to create a chart that shows the type of industry in each European country.

as to the airplane and the automobile. In 1903, Orville and Wilbur Wright made the first flight in a fixed-wing plane at Kitty Hawk, North Carolina. In 1919, the first regular passenger air service was established.

New Patterns Industrial production grew at a rapid pace because of greatly increased sales of manufactured goods. Europeans could afford to buy more consumer products for several reasons. Wages for workers increased after 1870. In addition, prices for manufactured goods were lower because of reduced transportation costs.

In the cities, the first department stores began to sell a new range of consumer goods made possible by the development of the steel and electrical industries. Clocks, bicycles, electric lights, and typewriters were sold in great quantities.

Not all nations benefited from the Second Industrial Revolution. By 1900, Europe was divided into two economic zones. Great Britain, Belgium, France, the **Netherlands,** Germany, the western part of the Austro-Hungarian Empire, and northern Italy made up an advanced industrialized core. These nations had a high standard of living and decent systems of transportation.

Another part of Europe was still largely agricultural. This was the little-industrialized area to the south and east, consisting of southern Italy, most of **Austria-Hungary, Spain, Portugal,** the Balkan kingdoms, and **Russia.** These countries provided food and raw materials for the industrial countries.

CHAPTER 13
Section 1, 397–401

Geography Skills

Answers:

1. Netherlands, Belgium, Germany, France, northern Italy, United Kingdom, western Austria-Hungary; located near navigable rivers, ports, near other nations, abundant natural resources
2. Answers will vary but should be consistent with information in map.

TURNING POINT

Discovery of the passage around Africa in the fifteenth century allowed a great increase in trade between Europe and the Far East. Ask students to explain why the internal combustion engine had the same impact on trade in the nineteenth century. **L2**

CURRICULUM CONNECTION

Science and Society Ask students to write an essay in which they explain the causes of industrialization and evaluate both the short-term and the long-term impact of industrialization on societies in the eighteenth, nineteenth, and twentieth centuries. Students may wish to review Chapter 12 and to consider the impact of industrialization on their own lives when writing this essay. **L2**

COOPERATIVE LEARNING ACTIVITY

Making Maps Have students break into small groups and do additional research on the Second Industrial Revolution, especially world trading patterns. Have them draw a world map that shows the products that were traded, especially foodstuffs, raw materials, and manufactured products. What does the map reveal about industrially developed and industrially undeveloped nations? Ask students to discuss the differences between the standards of living in the advanced, industrial countries and the "backward," little-industrialized areas that were still largely agricultural. How is this information relevant to today? **L1**

For grading this activity, refer to the ***Performance Assessment Activities*** booklet.

CHAPTER 13
Section 1, 397–401

Reading Check

Answer: because of its capital, industries, and military might

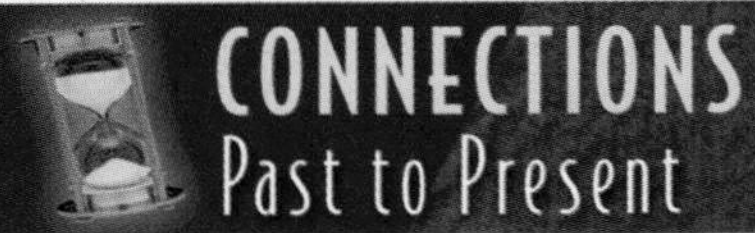

Answer: Answers will vary but should be supported by references.

CURRICULUM CONNECTION

Writing Assign students to write a capitalist manifesto that might have been created by owners of industry. It should emphasize the good they are doing workers, society, and their nations in general. It should also condemn people who would limit their economic and political powers. **L2**

3 ASSESS

Assign Section 1 Assessment as homework or as an in-class activity.

Have students use **Interactive Tutor Self-Assessment CD-ROM.**

Section Quiz 13–1

Name ______ Date ______ Class ______

Chapter 13 Score

Section Quiz 13-1

DIRECTIONS: Matching Match each item in Column A with an item in Column B. Write the correct letters in the blanks. *(10 points each)*

Column A	Column B
____ 1. the working class	A. strikes
____ 2. Marxists who rejected violent revolution	B. dictatorship
____ 3. organized work stoppages called by unions	C. revisionists
____ 4. absolute governmental power by an individual or group	D. internal-combustion
____ 5. engine type fired by oil or gasoline	E. proletariat

DIRECTIONS: Multiple Choice In the blank, write the letter of the choice that best completes the statement or answers the question. *(10 points each)*

Toward a World Economy The Second Industrial Revolution, combined with the growth of transportation by steamship and railroad, fostered a true world economy. By 1900, Europeans were receiving beef and wool from Argentina and Australia, coffee from Brazil, iron ore from Algeria, and sugar from Java.

European capital was also invested abroad to develop railways, mines, electrical power plants, and banks. Of course, foreign countries also provided markets for the manufactured goods of Europe. With its capital, industries, and military might, Europe dominated the world economy by the beginning of the twentieth century.

Reading Check **Explaining** Why did Europe dominate the world economy by the beginning of the twentieth century?

Organizing the Working Classes

The desire to improve their working and living conditions led many industrial workers to form socialist political parties and socialist trade unions. These organizations emerged after 1870, but the theory on which they were based had been developed earlier by Karl Marx.

Marx's Theory In 1848, *The Communist Manifesto* was published. It was written by two Germans, **Karl Marx** and Friedrich Engels, who were appalled at the horrible conditions in factories. They blamed the system of industrial capitalism for these conditions. Their solution was a new social system. One form of Marxist socialism was eventually called communism (see Chapter 16).

Marx believed that all of world history was a "history of class struggles." According to Marx, oppressor and oppressed have "stood in constant opposition to one another" throughout history.

One group of people—the oppressors—owned the means of production (land, raw materials, money, and so forth) and thus had the power to control government and society. Indeed, government itself was an instrument of this ruling class. The other group, which depended on the owners of the means of production, were the oppressed.

In the industrialized societies of Marx's day, the class struggle continued. According to Marx, "society as a

CONNECTIONS Past To Present

May Day

On May 1, 1997, parades and demonstrations took place around the world. Mexican workers poured into the streets of Mexico City to denounce the North American Free Trade Agreement (NAFTA). Workers believed it had caused a decline in their wages. In Seoul, Korean workers hurled rocks at police to protest government corruption in South Korea. In Berlin and Leipzig, union workers marched to protest high unemployment in Germany. In Beijing, people filled Tiananmen Square to praise workers at the beginning of a three-day vacation. In Japan, two million workers attended rallies across the country. Fifteen thousand workers marched in the streets of San Salvador to demand that the government pass laws to benefit the workers of El Salvador.

Why did these marches and demonstrations occur around the world on May 1? In the nineteenth century, the rise of socialist parties in Europe led to a movement to form an international organization. The purpose of this organization was to strengthen the position of socialist parties against international capitalism.

In 1889, leaders of various socialist parties formed the Second International, a loose association of national groups. Its first action was to declare May 1 as May Day, an international labor day to be marked by strikes and mass labor demonstrations. Although the Second International no longer exists, workers around the world still observe May Day.

May Day rally near St. Basil's cathedral in Moscow, May 1, 1997

Comparing Past and Prese

Using outside sources, research what occurred last May 1. Were May Day celebrations held, and if so, where? Is May 1 still an international labor day or has the meaning of the date changed?

CRITICAL THINKING ACTIVITY

Researching Many people thought that by implementing Marx's ideas about socialism they could eliminate oppression and create a society in which all people were equal. Have students use methods historians use to show why this goal was unattainable. Have them explain and then apply different methods that historians use to interpret the past, including using primary and secondary sources, points of view, frames of reference, and historical context to refute this claim. Have students use the process of historical inquiry to research, interpret, and use multiple sources of evidence in this project. Ask students to prepare a final report, which should include databases, a research outline, a bibliography, visuals, charts, time lines, and maps as appropriate. **L2 L3**

whole is more and more splitting up into two great hostile camps, into two great classes directly facing each other: Bourgeoisie and Proletariat." The **bourgeoisie**—the middle class—were the oppressors. The **proletariat**—the working class—were the oppressed.

Marx predicted that the struggle between the two groups would finally lead to an open revolution where the proletariat would violently overthrow the bourgeoisie. After their victory, the proletariat would form a **dictatorship** (government in which a person or group has absolute power) to organize the means of production. However, since the proletariat victory would essentially abolish the economic differences that create separate social classes, Marx believed that the final revolution would ultimately produce a classless society. The state—which had been an instrument of the bourgeois interests—would wither away.

Socialist Parties In time, working-class leaders formed socialist parties based on Marx's ideas. Most important was the German Social Democratic Party (SPD), which emerged in 1875. Under the direction of its Marxist leaders, the SPD advocated revolution while organizing itself into a mass political party that competed in elections for the German parliament. Once in the parliament, SPD delegates worked to pass laws that would improve conditions for the working class.

Despite government efforts to destroy it, the German Social Democratic Party grew. When it received four million votes in the 1912 elections, it became the largest single party in Germany.

Socialist parties also emerged in other European states. In 1889, leaders of the various socialist parties joined together and formed the Second International, an association of national socialist groups that would fight against capitalism worldwide. (The First International had failed in 1872.)

Marxist parties were divided over their goals. Pure Marxists thought that capitalism would be overthrown in a violent revolution. Other Marxists, called **revisionists**, rejected the revolutionary approach and argued that workers must continue to organize in mass political parties and even work with other parties to gain reforms. As workers received the right to vote, they could push for laws to benefit the lives of workers, including women and children.

Trade Unions Another force for workers' rights was the trade, or labor, union. In Great Britain, unions won the right to strike in the 1870s. (A strike is a work stoppage called by members of a union to pressure an employer into meeting their demands.) Labor unions used strikes to raise wages, better working conditions, and gain the right of collective bargaining (negotiation between union workers and employers).

By 1914, there were almost four million workers in British trade unions. Trade unions in the rest of Europe had varying degrees of success in improving both the living and the working conditions of the working classes.

Reading Check **Summarizing** How would you summarize Marx's theory as expressed in *The Communist Manifesto?*

SECTION 1 ASSESSMENT

Checking for Understanding

1. **Define** bourgeoisie, proletariat, dictatorship, revisionist.
2. **Identify** Thomas Edison, Alexander Graham Bell, Guglielmo Marconi, Karl Marx.
3. **Locate** Netherlands, Austria-Hungary, Spain, Portugal, Russia.
4. **Explain** how Marx's ideas came to directly impact society.
5. **List** the European nations that were still largely agricultural in 1900.

Critical Thinking

6. **Drawing Inferences** Do you think there is a relationship between the large number of technical innovations made during this period and the growing need for labor reforms and unions?
7. **Compare and Contrast** Use a Venn diagram like the one below to compare and contrast the first and second Industrial Revolutions.

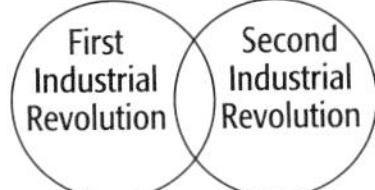

Analyzing Visuals

8. **Compare** the photos of the two Ford vehicles on page 398. Identify the differences and similarities.

Writing About History

9. **Expository Writing** After Marconi's first transmission across radio waves, he said, "I now felt for the first time absolutely certain the day would come when mankind would be able to send messages without wires. . . ." Write a paragraph about how this was a prophecy of technology to come.

SECTION 1 ASSESSMENT

1. Key terms are in blue.
2. Thomas Edison *(p. 398);* Alexander Graham Bell *(p. 398);* Guglielmo Marconi *(p. 398);* Karl Marx *(p. 400)*
3. See chapter maps.
4. socialist parties formed based on his ideas; worked to pass laws to improve conditions for working class; some socialist parties became very powerful
5. southern Italy, most of Austria-Hungary, Spain, Portugal, Balkan kingdoms, Russia
6. Answers will vary but should be supported by logical arguments.
7. First: textiles, railroads, iron, coal; Second: steel, chemicals, electricity, petroleum; Both: new technologies, products, forms of transportation
8. Similarities: four wheels, internal combustion engines; Differences: Explorer larger, enclosed interior
9. Answers will vary; wireless transmission led to radio, television, mobile telephones, and wireless computer networks.

Reading Check

Answer: All of world history was a "history of class struggles"—the oppressor versus the oppressed. This struggle would end in open revolution and the overthrow of the bourgeoisie by the proletariat. A classless society would emerge, and the state would wither away.

Reading Essentials and Study Guide 13–1

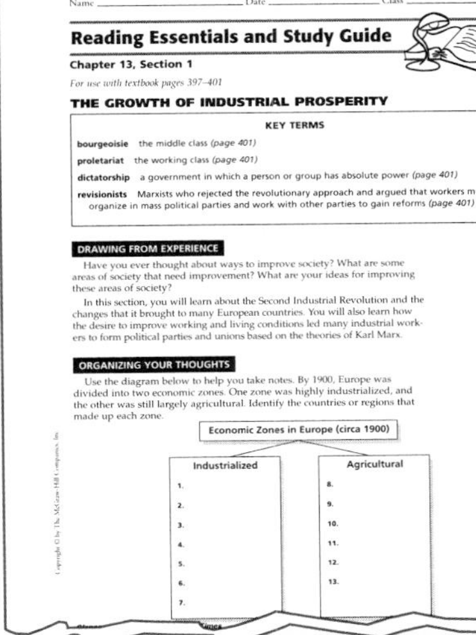

Reteaching Activity

Have students identify the reasons why nineteenth-century workers might have been dissatisfied with capitalism and therefore turned to socialism. **L1**

4 CLOSE

Discuss the relationship between progress in the Second Industrial Revolution and the need workers felt to organize to protect their rights.

TEACH

Analyzing Primary Sources

Discuss with students the fact that Marxist thought had a substantial effect on the world scene for most of the twentieth century. Point out that the perceived threat of communism, the antithesis of capitalism, formed the basis for U.S. foreign policy during the Cold War. Communism contributed an ideological edge to the existing military threat of the Soviet Union after World War II. Twice after the Russian Revolution of 1917, the United States experienced "Red Scares," when constitutional freedoms were revoked to protect the country from the "evils" of communism. Tell students that most Americans understood the fear, but they had little understanding of what communism actually was.

EYEWITNESS TO HISTORY

Marx and Engels Proclaim the Classless Society

IN *THE COMMUNIST MANIFESTO,* Karl Marx and Friedrich Engels expressed their view that a classless society would be the end product of the struggle between the bourgeoisie and the proletariat.

German poster proclaiming "Proletarians of the World, Unite!"

❝We have seen above, that the first step in the revolution by the working class, is to raise the proletariat to the position of ruling class. . . . The proletariat will use its political supremacy to wrest, by degrees, all capital from the bourgeoisie, to centralize all instruments of production in the hands of the State, i.e., of the proletariat organized as the ruling class; and to increase the total of productive forces as rapidly as possible. . . .

When, in the course of development, class distinctions have disappeared, and all production has been concentrated in the whole nation, the public power will lose its political character. Political power, properly so called, is merely the organized power of one class for oppressing another. If the proletariat during its contest with the bourgeoisie is compelled, by the force of circumstances, to organize itself as a class, if, by means of a revolution, it makes itself the ruling class, and, as such, sweeps away by force the old conditions of production, then it will, along with these conditions, have swept away the conditions for the existence of class antagonisms and of classes generally, and will thereby have abolished its own supremacy as a class.

In place of the old bourgeois society, with its classes and class antagonisms, we shall have an association, in which the free development of each is the condition for the free development of all. . . .

The Communists disdain to conceal their views and aims. They openly declare that their ends can be attained only by the forcible overthrow of all existing social conditions. Let the ruling classes tremble at a Communist revolution. The proletarians have nothing to lose but their chains. They have a world to win. Workingmen of all countries, unite!❞

—Karl Marx and Friedrich Engels, *The Communist Manifesto*

Analyzing Primary Sources

1. Do you agree with Marx's definition of political power? Why or why not?
2. Do you think Marx's idea of a classless society is realistic? Why or why not?

402

ANSWERS TO ANALYZING PRIMARY SOURCES

1. Answers will vary but should be supported by logical arguments. Students should recognize that, according to Marx and Engels, political power is the oppression of one class by another. In the classless society, such oppression could not occur. Hence, political power would be shared equally.
2. Answers will vary but should be supported by logical arguments. Students should recognize that all totalitarian regimes contain a ruling class.

SECTION 2 The Emergence of Mass Society

Guide to Reading

Main Ideas
- A varied middle class in Victorian Britain believed in the principles of hard work and good conduct.
- New opportunities for women and the working class improved their lives.

Key Terms
feminism, literacy

People to Identify
Amalie Sieveking, Florence Nightingale, Clara Barton, Emmeline Pankhurst

Places to Locate
London, Frankfurt

Preview Questions
1. What were the chief characteristics of the middle class in the nineteenth century?
2. How did the position of women change between 1870 and 1914?

Reading Strategy
Summarizing Information As you read this section, complete a graphic organizer like the one below summarizing the divisions among the social classes.

Social Classes		
Working	Middle	Wealthy

Preview of Events

1870 · 1875 · 1880 · 1885 · 1890 · 1895 · 1900

- **1870** Women win right to own property in Great Britain
- **1881** First publication of London's *Evening News*
- **1885** 10,000 people watch British Soccer Cup finals
- **1903** Women's Social and Political Union established

Voices from the Past

Sylvia Pankhurst, feminist and daughter of Emmeline Pankhurst

In *History of the Suffrage Movement,* Sylvia Pankhurst described the efforts of women to enter the House of Commons to petition for the right to vote:

❝Those of us who took refuge in doorways were dragged roughly down the steps and hurled back in front of the horses. When even this failed to banish us, the foot constables rushed at us and, catching us fiercely by the shoulders, turned us round again and then seizing us by the back of the neck and thumping us cruelly between the shoulders forced us at a running pace along the streets until we were far from the House of Commons. They had been told to drive us away and to make as few arrests as possible. Still we returned, until at last sixty-five women, all of them bruised, had been taken to the police station.❞

—***Sources of the West,*** **Mark A. Kishlansky, ed., 1998**

The movement for women's rights was one aspect of the new mass society.

The New Urban Environment

By the end of the nineteenth century, the new industrial world had led to the emergence of a mass society in which the concerns of the majority of the population—the lower classes—were central. More and more people lived in cities. In 1800, urban dwellers made up 40 percent of the population in Britain, 25 percent in France and Germany, and 10 percent in eastern Europe. By 1914, urban

SECTION RESOURCES

Reproducible Masters
- Reproducible Lesson Plan 13–2
- Daily Lecture and Discussion Notes 13–2
- Guided Reading Activity 13–2
- Section Quiz 13–2
- Reading Essentials and Study Guide 13–2

Transparencies
- Daily Focus Skills Transparency 13–2

Multimedia
- Interactive Tutor Self-Assessment CD-ROM
- ExamView® Pro Testmaker CD-ROM
- Presentation Plus! CD-ROM

1 FOCUS

Section Overview

This section describes the development of a new urban environment and new social structures, the growth of opportunities for women, and changes in education and leisure.

BELLRINGER
Skillbuilder Activity

Project transparency and have students answer questions.

Available as a blackline master.

Daily Focus Skills Transparency 13–2

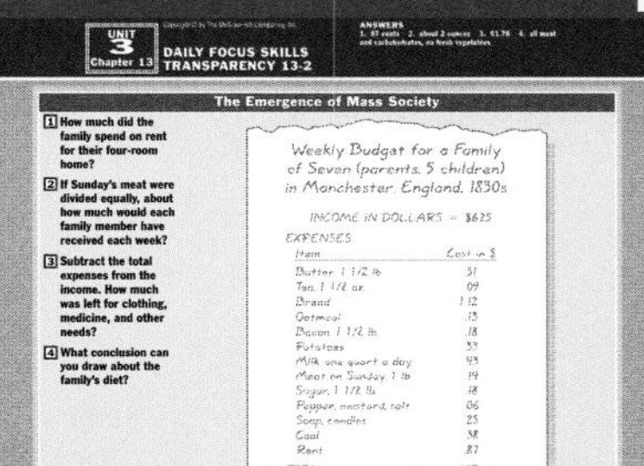

UNIT 3 Chapter 13 DAILY FOCUS SKILLS TRANSPARENCY 13-2

The Emergence of Mass Society

1. How much did the family spend on rent for their four-room home?
2. If Sunday's meat were divided equally, about how much would each family member have received each week?
3. Subtract the total expenses from the income. How much was left for clothing, medicine, and other needs?
4. What conclusion can you draw about the family's diet?

Weekly Budget for a Family of Seven (parents, 5 children) in Manchester, England, 1830s

INCOME IN DOLLARS = $625

EXPENSES

Item	Cost in $
Butter, 1 1/2 lb	.51
Tea, 1 1/2 oz	.09
Bread	1.12
Oatmeal	.13
Bacon, 1 1/2 lb	.18
Potatoes	.33
Milk, one quart a day	.43
Meat on Sunday, 1 lb	.14
Sugar, 1 1/2 lb	.18
Pepper, mustard, salt	.06
Soap, candles	.25
Coal	.38
Rent	.87

Guide to Reading

Answers to Graphic: Working: Rural (landholding peasants, farm laborers, sharecroppers), Urban (artisans, laborers, domestic servants); Middle: Upper (industrialists, bankers, merchants); Middle (lawyers, doctors, civil servants); Lower (shopkeepers, traders, prosperous peasants); Wealthy: aristocrats, business tycoons

Preteaching Vocabulary: Discuss the impact of *literacy* on *feminism.* **L1**

2 TEACH

Geography *Skills*

Answers:

1. Students should refer to key.
2. Databases will vary but should be based on information on the map.

Reading Check

Answer: because of migration from rural areas; in second half of century, they grew faster because living conditions improved so much that more people could survive there longer

Daily Lecture and Discussion Notes 13–2

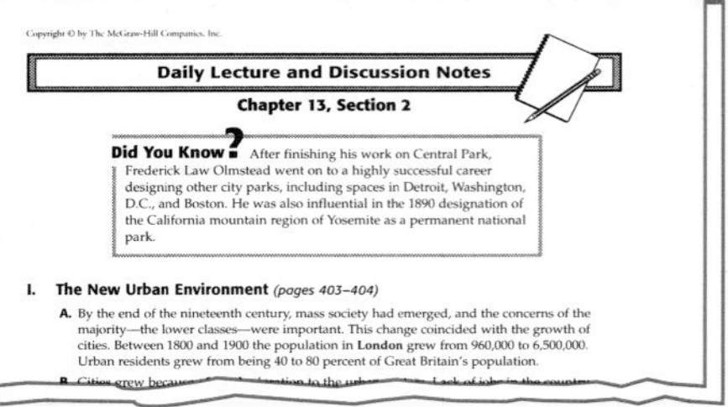

Daily Lecture and Discussion Notes

Chapter 13, Section 2

Did You Know? After finishing his work on Central Park, Frederick Law Olmstead went on to a highly successful career designing other city parks, including spaces in Detroit, Washington, D.C., and Boston. He was also influential in the 1890 designation of the California mountain region of Yosemite as a permanent national park.

I. **The New Urban Environment** *(pages 403–404)*

A. By the end of the nineteenth century, mass society had emerged, and the concerns of the majority—the lower classes—were important. This change coincided with the growth of cities. Between 1800 and 1900 the population in **London** grew from 960,000 to 6,500,000. Urban residents grew from being 40 to 80 percent of Great Britain's population.

Guided Reading Activity 13–2

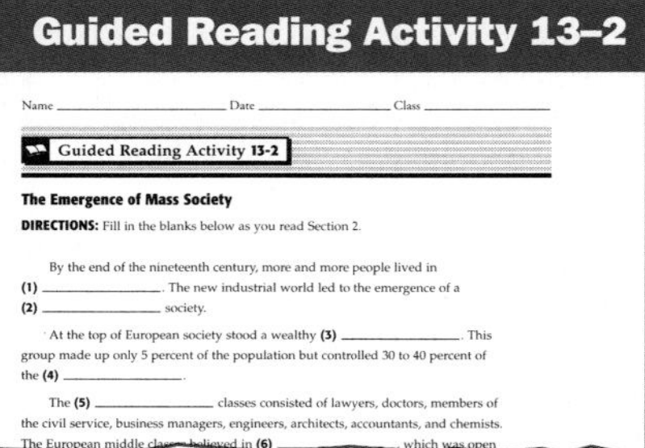

Name ____________ Date ____________ Class ____________

Guided Reading Activity 13-2

The Emergence of Mass Society

DIRECTIONS: Fill in the blanks below as you read Section 2.

By the end of the nineteenth century, more and more people lived in **(1)** ____________. The new industrial world led to the emergence of a **(2)** ____________ society.

At the top of European society stood a wealthy **(3)** ____________. This group made up only 5 percent of the population but controlled 30 to 40 percent of the **(4)** ____________.

The **(5)** ____________ classes consisted of lawyers, doctors, members of the civil service, business managers, engineers, architects, accountants, and chemists.

residents had increased to 80 percent of the population in Britain, 45 percent in France, 60 percent in Germany, and 30 percent in eastern Europe. The size of cities also grew, especially in industrialized countries. Between 1800 and 1900, the population in **London** grew from 960,000 to 6,500,000.

Urban populations grew quickly because of the vast migration to cities from rural areas. Lack of jobs and lack of land drove people from the countryside to the city. There, they found jobs in factories and, later, in service trades and professions.

Cities also grew faster in the second half of the nineteenth century because living conditions improved so much that more people could survive there longer. In the 1840s, a number of urban reformers had pointed to filthy living conditions as the chief cause of deadly epidemic diseases in the cities. Cholera, for example, had ravaged Europe in the early 1830s and 1840s, especially in the overcrowded cities.

Following the advice of reformers, city governments created boards of health to improve the quality of housing. City medical officers and building inspectors now inspected dwellings for public health hazards. New building regulations required running water and internal drainage systems for all new buildings.

Essential to the public health of the modern European city was the ability to bring in clean water and to expel sewage. The need for fresh water was met by a system of dams and reservoirs that stored the water and by aqueducts and tunnels that carried it from the countryside to the city and into individual dwellings. Gas heaters in the 1860s, and later electric heaters, made regular hot baths available to many people.

The treatment of sewage was improved by building mammoth underground pipes that carried raw sewage far from the city for disposal. The city of **Frankfurt,** Germany began its program for sewers with a lengthy public campaign featuring the slogan "from the toilet to the river in half an hour."

Reading Check **Explaining** Why did cities grow so quickly in the nineteenth century?

Social Structure of Mass Society

After 1871, most people enjoyed an improved standard of living. Even so, great poverty remained a part of Western society. Between the few who were rich and the many who were very poor existed several middle-class groups.

NATIONAL GEOGRAPHIC **European Population Growth and Relocation, 1820–1900**

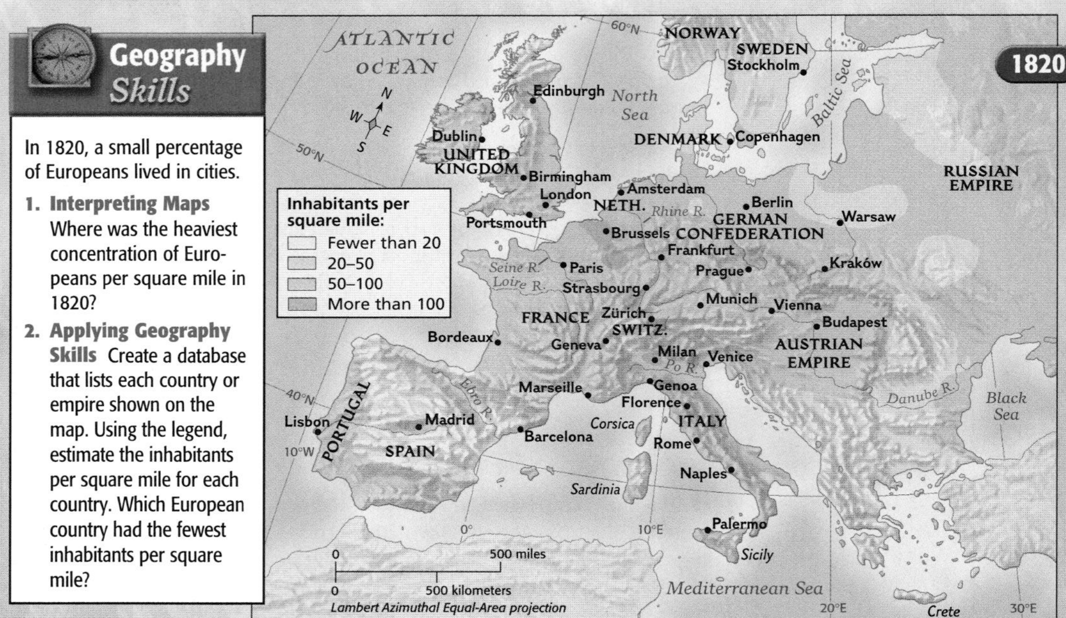

Geography *Skills*

In 1820, a small percentage of Europeans lived in cities.

1. **Interpreting Maps** Where was the heaviest concentration of Europeans per square mile in 1820?
2. **Applying Geography Skills** Create a database that lists each country or empire shown on the map. Using the legend, estimate the inhabitants per square mile for each country. Which European country had the fewest inhabitants per square mile?

404

MEETING INDIVIDUAL NEEDS

Visual Have students work in small groups to research the industrialization of a major European city. Aspects to consider include the following: Which geographical advantages and technological innovations helped this city become an industrial center? What were the most important industries in this city? What positive and negative effects did industrialization bring to this city and its population? How does this city today compare and contrast with itself at the time of industrialization? Students should create thematic maps, pictorial collages, or other visual displays and then share their knowledge with the class. **L2**

Refer to ***Inclusion for the High School Social Studies Classroom Strategies and Activities*** in the TCR.

The New Elite At the top of European society stood a wealthy elite. This group made up only 5 percent of the population but controlled between 30 and 40 percent of the wealth. During the nineteenth century, landed aristocrats had joined with the most successful industrialists, bankers, and merchants—the wealthy upper middle class—to form this new elite. Members of the elite, whether aristocratic or upper middle class in background, became leaders in the government and military.

Marriage also served to unite the two groups. Daughters of business tycoons gained aristocratic titles and aristocratic heirs gained new sources of cash. For example, when wealthy American Consuelo Vanderbilt married the British duke of Marlborough, the new duchess brought approximately $10 million to her husband.

The Middle Classes The middle classes consisted of a variety of groups. Below the upper middle class, which formed part of the new elite, was a middle group that included lawyers, doctors, members of the civil service, business managers, engineers, architects, accountants, and chemists. Beneath this solid and comfortable middle group was a lower middle class of small shopkeepers, traders, and prosperous peasants. The members of this group provided goods and services for the classes above them.

The Second Industrial Revolution produced a new group of white-collar workers between the lower middle class and the lower classes. This group included traveling salespeople, bookkeepers, telephone operators, department store salespeople, and secretaries. Although not highly paid, these white-collar workers were often committed to middle-class ideals.

The middle classes shared a certain lifestyle with values that tended to dominate much of nineteenth-century society. The members of the middle class liked to preach their worldview both to their children and to the upper and lower classes of their society. This was especially evident in Victorian Britain, often considered a model of middle-class society.

The European middle classes believed in hard work, which was open to everyone and guaranteed to have positive results. They were also regular churchgoers who believed in the good conduct associated with Christian morality. The middle class was concerned with the right way of doing things, which gave rise to such best-selling manners and etiquette books as *The Habits of Good Society*.

1900

Inhabitants per square mile:
- Fewer than 20
- 20–50
- 50–100
- More than 100

ATLANTIC OCEAN, North Sea, Baltic Sea, Black Sea, Mediterranean Sea, NORWAY, SWEDEN, Stockholm, DENMARK, Copenhagen, UNITED KINGDOM, Edinburgh, Dublin, Birmingham, London, Portsmouth, NETH., Amsterdam, BELG., Brussels, GERMAN EMPIRE, Berlin, Frankfurt, RUSSIAN EMPIRE, Warsaw, Kraków, Prague, Munich, Vienna, Budapest, AUSTRIAN EMPIRE, FRANCE, Paris, Strasbourg, Bordeaux, Marseille, SWITZ., Zürich, Geneva, ITALY, Milan, Venice, Genoa, Florence, Rome, Naples, Palermo, Sicily, Sardinia, Corsica, SPAIN, Madrid, Barcelona, PORTUGAL, Lisbon, Crete, Seine R., Loire R., Rhine R., Po R., Ebro R., Danube R.

0 500 miles / 0 500 kilometers
Lambert Azimuthal Equal-Area projection

Geography Skills

Two population changes occurred in Europe from 1820 to 1900: the overall population increased, and it shifted from rural to urban areas.

1. **Interpreting Maps** Which areas had *no* change in population density between 1820 and 1900?
2. **Applying Geography Skills** Analyze the relationship between the increased urban populations shown here and the areas of industrial concentration shown on the map on page 399.

405

EXTENDING THE CONTENT

Social Forces In the late nineteenth century, Thorstein Veblen's ideas about social forces helped to create a new discipline called sociology. Sociology, the study of people living together in society, teaches that institutions mold and shape our thoughts. Institutions form an accepted pattern for the entire group, and are formed by a combination of customs, beliefs, and traditions. Images of success, as shown through advertising and the media, seduce people into buying "status" items. People in the upper and middle classes tend to buy goods that are expensive, useless, or wasteful to impress others with their wealth. Veblen called this type of buying "conspicuous consumption."

Geography Skills

Answers:
1. Students should refer to key.
2. Students should recognize the correlation between industrial centers and high population density.

Charting Activity

Ask students to make a list of activities in which Americans can participate only if they live in cities. Ask them to explain what the Industrial Revolution had to do with the growth of cities. Finally, ask them to write an essay that describes the relationship between the Industrial Revolution and the growth of urban mass society. **L1**

3 ASSESS

Assign Section 2 Assessment as homework or as an in-class activity.

Have students use **Interactive Tutor Self-Assessment CD-ROM.**

Section Quiz 13–2

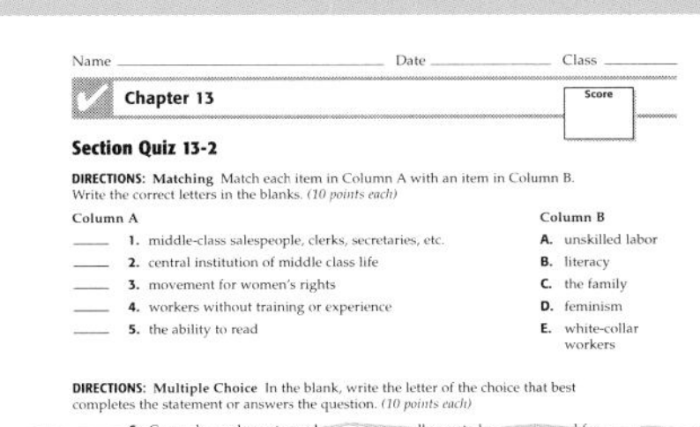
Name ____ Date ____ Class ____

Chapter 13 Score

Section Quiz 13-2

DIRECTIONS: Matching Match each item in Column A with an item in Column B. Write the correct letters in the blanks. (10 points each)

Column A	Column B
____ 1. middle-class salespeople, clerks, secretaries, etc.	A. unskilled labor
____ 2. central institution of middle class life	B. literacy
____ 3. movement for women's rights	C. the family
____ 4. workers without training or experience	D. feminism
____ 5. the ability to read	E. white-collar workers

DIRECTIONS: Multiple Choice In the blank, write the letter of the choice that best completes the statement or answers the question. (10 points each)

Reading Check

Answer: The major groups in the social structure included a wealthy elite, middle classes (high, middle, and low), and working classes.

Reading Essentials and Study Guide 13–2

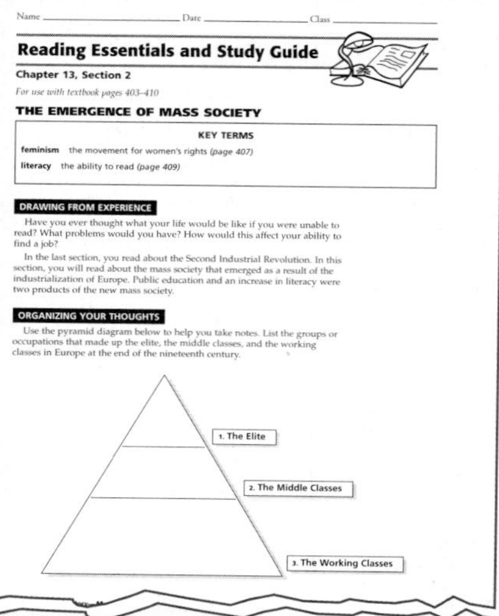
Name ____________ Date ____________ Class ____________

Reading Essentials and Study Guide

Chapter 13, Section 2

For use with textbook pages 403–410

THE EMERGENCE OF MASS SOCIETY

KEY TERMS

feminism the movement for women's rights *(page 407)*

literacy the ability to read *(page 409)*

DRAWING FROM EXPERIENCE

Have you ever thought what your life would be like if you were unable to read? What problems would you have? How would this affect your ability to find a job?

In the last section, you read about the Second Industrial Revolution. In this section, you will read about the mass society that emerged as a result of the industrialization of Europe. Public education and an increase in literacy were two products of the new mass society.

ORGANIZING YOUR THOUGHTS

Use the pyramid diagram below to help you take notes. List the groups or occupations that made up the elite, the middle classes, and the working classes in Europe at the end of the nineteenth century.

1. The Elite
2. The Middle Classes
3. The Working Classes

Connecting Across Time

Assign students to find a photograph or copy of an illustration that shows a typical location where women might work today. Ask students to identify and explain differences between their picture and the picture on this page. What changes in technology and social values have benefited women in the past century? Ask students to analyze the ways in which the economic influence of working women has been enhanced. Also ask students to analyze the ways in which the economic influence has remained the same. **L1**

The Working Classes Below the middle classes on the social scale were the working classes, which made up almost 80 percent of the European population. Many of the members of these classes were landholding peasants, farm laborers, and sharecroppers, especially in eastern Europe.

Women worked as operators and secretaries at the Paris telephone exchange in 1904.

The urban working class consisted of many different groups, including skilled artisans and semiskilled laborers. At the bottom of the urban working class were the unskilled laborers. They were the largest group of workers and included day laborers and large numbers of domestic servants. One out of every seven employed persons in Great Britain in 1900 was a domestic servant. Most domestic servants were women.

Urban workers experienced an improvement in the material conditions of their lives after 1870. Reforms created better living conditions in cities. In addition, a rise in wages, along with a decline in many consumer costs, made it possible for workers to buy more than just food and housing. Workers now had money for more clothes and even leisure activities. At the same time, strikes were leading to 10-hour workdays and Saturday afternoons off.

Reading Check **Identifying** Name the major groups in the social structure of the late nineteenth century.

The Experiences of Women

In 1800, women were mainly defined by family and household roles. They remained legally inferior and economically dependent upon men. In the course of the nineteenth century, women struggled to change their status.

New Job Opportunities During much of the nineteenth century, working-class groups maintained the belief that women should remain at home to bear and nurture children and should not be allowed in the industrial workforce. Working-class men argued that keeping women out of industrial work would ensure the moral and physical well-being of families.

The Second Industrial Revolution, however, opened the door to new jobs for women. A high demand for relatively low paid white-collar workers, coupled with a shortage of male workers, led many employers to hire women. Both industrial plants and retail shops needed clerks, typists, secretaries, file clerks, and salesclerks.

The expansion of government services created opportunities for women to be secretaries and telephone operators, and to take jobs in the fields of education, health, and social services. While some middle-class women held these jobs, they were mainly filled by the working class who aspired to a better quality of life.

Marriage and the Family Many people in the nineteenth century believed in the ideal expressed in Lord Tennyson's *The Princess*, published in 1847:

> “Man for the field and woman for the hearth:
> Man for the sword and for the needle she:
> Man with the head and woman with the heart:
> Man to command and woman to obey. . . .”

This view of the sexes was strengthened during the Industrial Revolution. As the chief family wage earners, men worked outside the home. Women were left with the care of the family.

Throughout the 1800s, marriage remained the only honorable and available career for most women. There was also one important change. The number of children born to the average woman began to decline—the most significant development in the modern family. This decline in the birthrate was tied to improved economic conditions, as well as increased use of birth control. In 1882, Europe's first birth control clinic was founded in Amsterdam.

COOPERATIVE LEARNING ACTIVITY

Role-Playing Assign students to work in pairs to investigate a social issue discussed in this section. Students should take the roles of an interviewer and an interviewee, write a script for an interview, and perform it for the class. Possible interview “pairs” include a journalist and a factory worker, a public official and an urban newcomer discussing the difficulty of adjusting to crowded living and working conditions, or a woman working as a telephone operator and a woman who did not work outside the home discussing their domestic lives. **L1**

For grading this activity, refer to the ***Performance Assessment Activities*** booklet.

The family was the central institution of middle-class life. With fewer children in the family, mothers could devote more time to child care and domestic leisure.

The middle-class family fostered an ideal of togetherness. The Victorians created the family Christmas with its Yule log, tree, songs, and exchange of gifts. By the 1850s, Fourth of July celebrations in the United States had changed from wild celebrations to family picnics.

The lives of working-class women were different from those of their middle-class counterparts. While they may have aspired to middle-class ideals, most working-class women had to earn money to help support their families. Daughters in working-class families were expected to work until they married. After marriage, they often did small jobs at home to support the family. For the children of the working classes, childhood was over by the age of nine or ten, when children became apprentices or were employed in odd jobs. *(See page 777 to read excerpts from L'Atelier's* The Unfortunate Situation of Working Women *in the Primary Sources Library.)*

Between 1890 and 1914, however, family patterns among the working class began to change. Higher-paying jobs in heavy industry and improvements in the standard of living made it possible for working-class families to depend on the income of husbands alone.

By the early twentieth century, some working-class mothers could afford to stay at home, following the pattern of middle-class women. At the same time, working-class families aspired to buy new consumer products, such as sewing machines and cast-iron stoves.

The Movement for Women's Rights Modern **feminism**, or the movement for women's rights, had its beginnings during the Enlightenment, when some women advocated equality for women based on the doctrine of natural rights. In the 1830s, a number of women in the United States and Europe argued for the right of women to divorce and own property. (By law, a husband had almost complete control over his wife's property.) These early efforts were not very successful, and women in Britain did not win the right to own property until 1870.

The fight for property rights was only the beginning of the women's movement. Some middle- and upper-middle-class women fought for and gained access to universities, and others sought entry into occupations dominated by men.

Though training to become doctors was largely closed to women, some entered the medical field by becoming nurses. In Germany, **Amalie Sieveking** was a nursing pioneer who founded the Female Association for the Care of the Poor and Sick in Hamburg. More famous is the British nurse **Florence Nightingale.** Her efforts during the Crimean War (1854–1856), combined with those of **Clara Barton** in the U.S. Civil War (1861–1865), transformed nursing into a profession of trained, middle-class "women in white."

By the 1840s and 1850s, the movement for women's rights expanded as women called for equal political rights. Many feminists believed that the right to vote was the key to improving the overall position of women.

The British women's movement was the most active in Europe. The Women's Social and Political Union, founded in 1903 by **Emmeline Pankhurst** and her daughters, used unusual publicity stunts to call attention to its demands. Its members pelted

Picturing History

Shown below are Emmeline Pankhurst, her daughters, and a fellow suffragist. Why do you think women such as these had to fight so hard and long to obtain the right to vote?

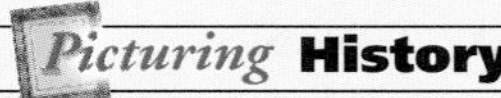

Picturing History

Answer: Answers will vary but should be supported by logical arguments.

Who?What?Where?When?

Women's Rights Middle-class married women during the industrial age benefited from domestic help, but they had few legal rights. In England, for example, a woman forfeited to her husband not only her property, but also her right to control it. A man could will his wife's property to someone without her consent.

Enrich

Have students research and report on men's and women's clothing during some period of the Industrial Revolution. Their reports should answer such questions as: Did social classes dress differently from one another, and if so, how? Ask students what conclusions they can draw about the period by studying its clothing. **L1**

Who?What?Where?When?

Nurses Nursing was one of the few careers open to women of the industrial age. Let students work together in groups to develop biographies on Amalie Sieveking, Florence Nightingale, Clara Barton, and other women who made names for themselves in occupations dominated by men. Assign one woman to be researched by each group. Encourage groups to develop creative ways to present their findings to the rest of class. **L1**

EXTENDING THE CONTENT

British Suffragists The Pankhursts were determined activists in the struggle for women's suffrage and were often arrested for damaging property or disturbing the peace. Once in jail, the Pankhursts, like other suffragists, went on hunger strikes, a potentially dangerous action since the government allowed prison authorities to force-feed hunger strikers by pouring liquids into their stomachs "through a rubber tube clamped to the nose or mouth." But neither jail nor abusive treatment could stop the Pankhursts. Through their efforts and those of other suffragists, by 1918 British women over age 30 eventually received the right to vote. Males could vote at age 21.

Reading Check

Answer: the right of women to full citizenship in the nation-state

Connecting Across Time

Ask students to describe changes in the social role of the nuclear family from the beginning of the twentieth century to the present. Have students work in small groups to analyze the specific roles of women, children, and families in different historical cultures. Students might wish to review the chapters on Greece, Rome, the Islamic and Byzantine Empires, the Middle Ages, and the Renaissance to help with this analysis. Have groups share their information in a class discussion. **L1**

CURRICULUM CONNECTION

Economics Wages are defined as the payments made to labor for its contribution to the production of wealth. In the United States, wages make up three-quarters of all payments to the factors of production. "Real wages" refer to the purchasing power of money wages— how much real wealth money can buy at current prices. When money wages increase and inflation increases at the same rate, real wages remain constant.

THE WAY IT WAS

SPORTS & CONTESTS

The New Team Sports

Sports were by no means a new activity in the late nineteenth century. Soccer games had been played by peasants and workers, and these games had often been bloody and even deadly. However, in the late nineteenth century, sports became strictly organized. The English Football Association (founded in 1863) and the American Bowling Congress (founded in 1895), for example, provided strict rules and officials to enforce them.

The new sports were not just for leisure or fun. Like other forms of middle-class recreation, they were intended to provide excellent training, especially for youth. The participants could not only develop individual skills but also acquire a sense of teamwork useful for military service.

These characteristics were already evident in British schools in the 1850s and 1860s. Such schools as Harrow and Loretto placed organized sports at the center of education. At Loretto, for example, education was supposed to instill "First—Character. Second—Physique. Third—Intelligence. Fourth—Manners. Fifth—Information."

The new team sports rapidly became professionalized as well. The English Football Association, mentioned above, regulated professional soccer. In the United States, the first national association to recognize professional baseball players was

Woodcut of scene from 1886 baseball game between New York and Boston

government officials with eggs, chained themselves to lampposts, burned railroad cars, and smashed the windows of department stores on fashionable shopping streets. These suffragists (people who advocate the extension of political rights, such as voting rights) had one basic aim: the right of women to full citizenship in the nation-state.

Before World War I, demands for women's rights were being heard throughout Europe and the United States. However, only in Norway and some states in the United States did women actually receive the right to vote before 1914. It would take the dramatic upheaval of World War I to make male-dominated governments give in on this basic issue of the rights of women.

Reading Check **Identifying** What was the basic aim of the suffragists?

Universal Education

Universal education was a product of the mass society of the late nineteenth and early twentieth centuries. Education in the early nineteenth century was primarily for the elite and the wealthier middle class. However, between 1870 and 1914, most Western governments began to set up state-financed primary schools. Both boys and girls between the ages of 6 and 12 were required to attend these schools. States also took responsibility for training teachers by setting up teacher-training schools.

Why did Western nations make this commitment to public education? One reason was industrialization. In the first Industrial Revolution, unskilled labor (workers without training or experience) was able to meet factory needs. The new firms of the Second Industrial Revolution, however, needed trained,

EXTENDING THE CONTENT

Public Education In 1900, only 10 percent of American adolescents aged 14 to 17 were enrolled in high schools and most of those students were from affluent families. High school attendance grew after the introduction of strict child labor laws and more students regarded education as the key to success. Schools also played a key role in "Americanizing" immigrants to fit into mainstream society. From 1900 to 1996, the percentage of teenagers who graduated from high school increased from about 6 percent to about 85 percent.

formed in 1863. By 1900, the National League and the American League had complete control over professional baseball.

Mass spectator sports became a big business. In 1872, two thousand people watched the British Soccer Cup finals. By 1885, the crowd had increased to ten thousand and by 1901, to a hundred thousand. Spectator sports even reflected class differences. Upper-class soccer teams in Britain viewed working-class teams as vicious and inclined to "money-grubbing, tricks, sensational displays, and utter rottenness."

Sports in the late nineteenth century were mostly for men, who believed that females were not well suited for "vigorous physical activity." Nevertheless, middle-class women could play "easy" sports—croquet and lawn tennis. Eventually, some sports began to appear at women's colleges and girls' public schools in England.

Late nineteenth-century game of croquet

CONNECTING TO THE PAST

1. **Describing** What did sports offer middle-class men of the late nineteenth century?
2. **Evaluating** Why do you think spectator sports became such a big business?
3. **Writing about History** Write a brief essay comparing the educational goals at your school with those at Loretto. What are the differences and similarities?

THE WAY IT WAS

Answers:

1. They were intended to provide excellent training, especially for youth. Participants developed individual skills and gained a sense of teamwork useful for military service.
2. Answers will vary but should be supported by logical arguments.
3. Answers will vary but should be supported by examples.

skilled labor. Both boys and girls with an elementary education now had new job possibilities beyond their villages or small towns. These included white-collar jobs in railways, post offices, and the teaching and nursing fields.

The chief motive for public education, however, was political. Giving more people the right to vote created a need for better-educated voters. Even more important was the fact that primary schools instilled patriotism. As people lost their ties to local regions and even to religion, nationalism gave them a new faith.

Compulsory elementary education created a demand for teachers, and most of them were women. Many men saw teaching as a part of women's "natural role" as nurturers of children. Females were also paid lower salaries, which in itself was a strong incentive for states to set up teacher-training schools for women. The first female colleges were really teacher-training schools.

The most immediate result of public education was an increase in **literacy**, or the ability to read. In western and central Europe, most adults could read by 1900. Where there was less schooling, the story was very different. Nearly 79 percent of adults in Serbia and Russia still could not read by 1900.

With the increase in literacy after 1870 came the rise of mass newspapers, such as the *Evening News* (1881) and the *Daily Mail* (1896) in London. Millions of copies were sold each day. These newspapers were all written in an easily understood style. They were also sensationalistic—that is, they provided gossip and gruesome details of crimes.

Reading Check **Explaining** Why did states make a commitment to provide public education?

Reading Check

Answer: partly to provide trained, skilled labor, but primarily because the extension of voting rights created a need for better-educated voters (and to instill patriotism)

Writing Activity

Review the goals of Western nations in making a commitment to mass education. Have students write an essay comparing and contrasting those goals with the goals of modern society. Student answers should include comments on the need for a skilled labor force and better-educated voters. **L2**

TURNING POINT

Assign students to ask their parents or other adults about the need young people had for an education thirty years ago. Was it possible to obtain a good job without a diploma? What has happened to make an education almost essential for financial success in today's world? **L1**

EXTENDING THE CONTENT

Middle-Class Children The Boy Scouts were created in 1908 in Victorian Great Britain to promote recreational activities centered around military concerns and character-building. Many viewed these activities as a way of counteracting the possible dangers that female domination of the home posed for boys. There was little organized recreational activity of this kind for girls. When a girls' division of the Boy Scouts was formed, its founder stated that "you do not want to make tomboys of refined girls. The main object is to give them all the ability to be better mothers and guides to the next generation."

CHAPTER 13
Section 2, 403–410

Reading Check

Answer: Subways and streetcars meant that even the working classes could make their way to athletic games, amusement parks, and dance halls.

Enrich

During the early twentieth century, technological developments dramatically changed the way that many people lived, worked, and played. Have students write an essay in which they describe the connection between scientific discoveries and technological innovations and new patterns of social and cultural life in the twentieth century. Students should consider, for example, how developments in transportation and communication affected social mobility. Students may also want to consider the impact of technology on their own lives. **L2**

Reteaching Activity

Have students construct a chart of the social pyramid in Europe at the turn of the century. Students should include the percentage at each level, and the groups that belonged at each level. **L1**

4 CLOSE

Ask students to identify and discuss ways in which compulsory education created career opportunities for many women. **L1**

This English train (c. 1845) was an early form of the mass transportation that enabled more people to participate in leisure activities.

New Forms of Leisure

The Second Industrial Revolution allowed people to pursue new forms of leisure. The new forms of popular mass leisure both entertained large crowds and distracted them from the realities of their work lives. Leisure came to be viewed as what people do for fun after work. The industrial system gave people new times—evening hours, weekends, and a week or two in the summer—to indulge in leisure activities.

Amusement parks introduced people to exciting new experiences and technology. By the late nineteenth century, team sports had developed into yet another form of leisure. Subways and streetcars meant that even the working classes could make their way to athletic games, amusement parks, and dance halls.

The new mass leisure was quite different from earlier forms of popular culture. The earlier festivals and fairs had been based on community participation. The new forms of leisure were standardized for largely passive audiences. Amusement parks and professional sports teams were essentially big businesses organized to make profits.

Reading Check **Explaining** How did innovations in transportation change leisure activities during the Second Industrial Revolution?

SECTION 2 ASSESSMENT

Checking for Understanding

1. **Define** feminism, literacy.
2. **Identify** Amalie Sieveking, Florence Nightingale, Clara Barton, Emmeline Pankhurst.
3. **Locate** London, Frankfurt.
4. **Explain** what is meant by the term *universal education.* How did industrialization help propel the movement for universal education?
5. **List** the explanations given in this section for the decline in birthrate during the 1800s.

Critical Thinking

6. **Explain** Why have certain occupations such as elementary teaching and nursing historically been dominated by women?
7. **Summarizing Information** Use a graphic organizer like the one below to summarize the results of urban reforms.

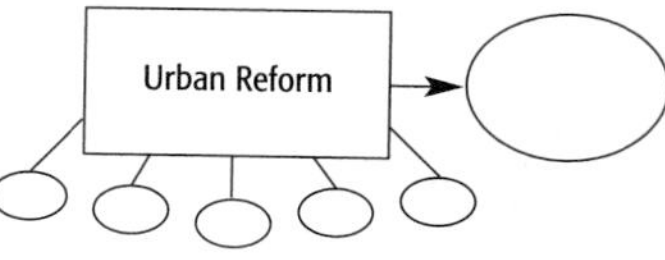

Analyzing Visuals

8. **Examine** the clothing worn by the women in the photos on pages 406, 407, and 409. How have women's fashions changed since the late nineteenth century? How have women's political rights changed? In what ways might these changes be related?

Writing About History

9. **Persuasive Writing** The feminist movement changed the role of women. In an essay, argue whether these changes had a positive or negative impact on society.

SECTION 2 ASSESSMENT

1. Key terms are in blue.
2. Amalie Sieveking *(p. 407);* Florence Nightingale *(p. 407);* Clara Barton *(p. 407);* Emmeline Pankhurst *(p. 407)*
3. See chapter maps.
4. mandatory attendance at state-financed schools; needed trained, skilled labor and better-educated voters
5. better economic conditions, increased use of birth control
6. women seen as nurturers, cared for children and sick, would work for less pay
7. Reform: boards of health; building inspectors and regulations; fresh water; treatment of sewage; hot water; Results: better living conditions, healthier people
8. long, restrictive dresses then, now better suited to active lifestyles; Western women have gained full political rights; in past, women restricted in dress and in rights
9. Answers will vary but should be supported by logical arguments.

SECTION 3 The National State and Democracy

Guide to Reading

Main Ideas
- The governments of western Europe were challenged by the development of new political parties and labor unions.
- International rivalries led to conflicts in the Balkans and to World War I.

Key Terms
ministerial responsibility, Duma

People to Identify
Otto von Bismarck, William II, Francis Joseph, Nicholas II, Queen Liliuokalani

Places to Locate
St. Petersburg, Montenegro

Preview Questions
1. What domestic problems did the United States and Canada face?
2. What issues sparked the crises in the Balkans?

Reading Strategy
Summarizing Information As you read this section, complete a diagram like the one below listing the countries in each alliance.

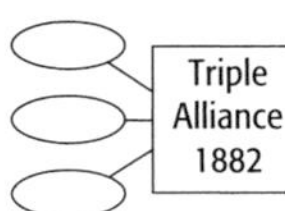

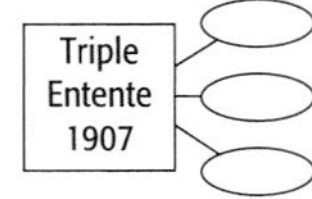

Preview of Events

1860 · 1870 · 1880 · 1890 · 1900 · 1910

- **1867** Dual monarchy of Austria-Hungary created
- **1875** France establishes the Third Republic
- **1882** Triple Alliance created
- **1900** Labour Party emerges in Great Britain
- **1907** Triple Entente formed

Voices from the Past

Czar Nicholas II

On January 22, 1905, a group of peaceful demonstrators tried to present a petition of grievances to Czar Nicholas II. One described the result:

> ❝We were not more than thirty yards from the soldiers, being separated from them only by the bridge over the Tarakanovskii Canal, when suddenly, without any warning and without a moment's delay, was heard the dry crack of many rifle-shots. . . . A little boy of ten years, who was carrying a church lantern, fell pierced by a bullet. Both the [black]smiths who guarded me were killed, as well as all those who were carrying the icons and banners; and all these emblems now lay scattered on the snow. The soldiers were actually shooting into the courtyards of the adjoining houses, where the crowd tried to find refuge.❞
>
> —***Eyewitness to History,*** **John Carey, ed., 1987**

As a result of the massacre of peaceful demonstrators, the czar faced a revolution. In Russia and other parts of central and eastern Europe, many groups struggled for independence. Throughout much of the Western world, however, the national state had become the focus of people's loyalties.

Western Europe and Political Democracy

By the late nineteenth century, progress had been made toward establishing constitutions, parliaments, and individual liberties in the major European states.

1 FOCUS

Section Overview

This section describes developments in the United States and Canada, the growth of democracy in Western Europe, the reasons for the continued existence of the old order in Eastern Europe, and the results of international rivalry and war in the Balkans.

BELLRINGER Skillbuilder Activity

Project transparency and have students answer questions.

Available as a blackline master.

Daily Focus Skills Transparency 13–3

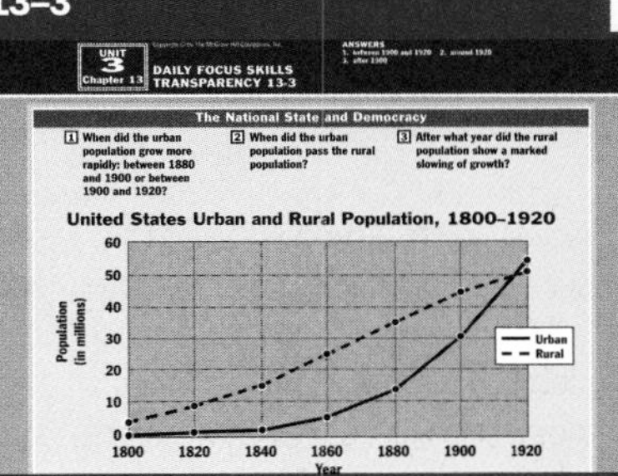

Guide to Reading

Answers to Graphic: Triple Alliance 1882: Germany, Austria-Hungary, Italy; Triple Entente 1907: Great Britain, France, Russia

Preteaching Vocabulary: Discuss with students the concept of *ministerial responsibility*. Why is this concept crucial for democracy?

SECTION RESOURCES

Reproducible Masters
- Reproducible Lesson Plan 13–3
- Daily Lecture and Discussion Notes 13–3
- Guided Reading Activity 13–3
- Section Quiz 13–3
- Reading Essentials and Study Guide 13–3

Transparencies
- Daily Focus Skills Transparency 13–3

Multimedia
- Interactive Tutor Self-Assessment CD-ROM
- ExamView® Pro Testmaker CD-ROM
- Presentation Plus! CD-ROM

CHAPTER 13
Section 3, 411–416

2 TEACH

Geography Skills

Answers:

1. French Empire, Ottoman Empire, and Russian Empire
2. Answers will vary but should be supported by logic.

Daily Lecture and Discussion Notes 13–3

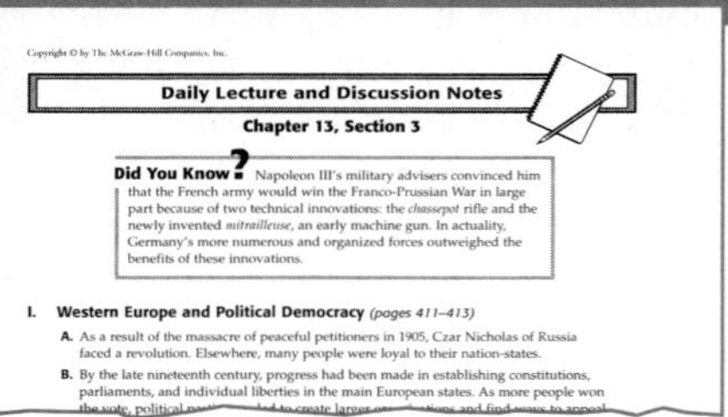

Daily Lecture and Discussion Notes

Chapter 13, Section 3

Did You Know? Napoleon III's military advisers convinced him that the French army would win the Franco-Prussian War in large part because of two technical innovations: the *chassepot* rifle and the newly invented *mitrailleuse*, an early machine gun. In actuality, Germany's more numerous and organized forces outweighed the benefits of these innovations.

I. **Western Europe and Political Democracy** *(pages 411–413)*

A. As a result of the massacre of peaceful petitioners in 1905, Czar Nicholas of Russia faced a revolution. Elsewhere, many people were loyal to their nation-states.

B. By the late nineteenth century, progress had been made in establishing constitutions, parliaments, and individual liberties in the main European states. As more people won the vote, political parties needed to create larger organizations and find ways to appeal

TURNING POINT

Help students understand that a more equal distribution of income and wealth often leads to a more equal distribution of political power. Ask students to write an essay explaining why poor people are less able to participate in the political process than people who are in the middle and upper economic classes. **L1**

Critical Thinking

Ask students who could vote in Great Britain by 1918. *(all males over age 21, females over age 30)* Have students generate a list of possible reasons for these different age requirements for voting.

Geography Skills

Various empires dominated the European political scene in the late nineteenth century.

1. **Interpreting Maps** Which three empires extend beyond the boundaries shown on this map?
2. **Applying Geography Skills** Pose and answer your own question about how the geographic relationships shown on this map might result in major conflicts, such as the impending world war.

Political democracy, characterized by universal male suffrage and ministerial responsibility, expanded. As more and more men (and later, women) were able to vote, political parties needed to create larger organizations and to find ways to appeal to the masses of people who were now part of the political process.

Great Britain By 1871, Great Britain had a working two-party parliamentary system. For the next 50 years, these two parties—the Liberal Party and the Conservative Party—alternated in power at regular intervals. Both parties were led by a ruling class composed of aristocratic landowners and upper-middle-class businesspeople.

The Liberals and Conservatives competed with each other in passing laws that expanded the right to vote. Reform acts in 1867 and 1884 increased the number of adult males who could vote. By the end of World War I (1918), all males over age 21 and women over age 30 could vote.

At the end of the nineteenth century, then, political democracy was becoming well established in Britain. Social reforms for the working class soon followed. The working class in Great Britain supported the Liberal Party. Two developments made Liberals fear that they would lose this support. First, trade unions grew, and they began to favor a more radical change of the economic system. Second, in 1900, a new party—the Labour Party, which dedicated itself to the interests of workers—emerged.

The Liberals held the government from 1906 to 1914. To retain the support of the workers, they voted for a series of social reforms. The National Insurance Act of 1911 provided benefits for workers in case of sickness and unemployment. Additional laws provided a small pension for those over 70 and compensation for those injured in accidents while at work.

France In France, the collapse of Louis-Napoleon's Second Empire left the country in confusion. In 1875,

INTERDISCIPLINARY CONNECTIONS ACTIVITY

Economics While Marx and Engels advocated state intervention on behalf of the downtrodden workers, a "right wing" argued that the free market was the most efficient and prosperous system. One voice, Henry George, differed from the common left and right wing views and became one of the most influential reformers of the late nineteenth century. George held that it was society's institutions that were responsible for poverty, and that the institution of land ownership was at the very heart of the problem. Land is owned by the few, while the many are forced to pay the few to make use of it. Taxing land values with a "Single Tax" would loosen the economic shackles imposed by land owners. Lead students in a discussion of private versus public land ownership.

a new constitution turned the nation into a republic—the Third Republic. The new French government had a president and a legislature made up of two houses. Members of the upper house, called the Senate, were elected indirectly. In the lower house, called the Chamber of Deputies, members were elected by universal male suffrage.

The powers of the president were not well defined in the constitution. A premier (or prime minister) actually led the government. The premier and his ministers were responsible to the Chamber of Deputies, not to the president. This principle of **ministerial responsibility**—the idea that the prime minister is responsible to the popularly elected legislative body and not to the executive officer—is crucial for democracy.

France failed to develop a strong parliamentary system. The existence of a dozen political parties forced the premier to depend on a coalition of parties to stay in power. Frequent changes of government leadership plagued the republic. Nevertheless, by 1914, the Third Republic commanded the loyalty of most French people.

Italy Italy had emerged by 1870 as a united national state. The nation had little sense of unity, however, because a great gulf separated the poverty-stricken south from the industrialized north. Constant turmoil between labor and industry weakened the social fabric of the nation. Widespread corruption among government officials prevented the government from dealing with these problems. Universal male suffrage was granted in 1912 but did little to stop corruption and weakness in the government.

Reading Check **Summarizing** What is the principle of ministerial responsibility?

Analyzing *Political Cartoons*

In 1890, Emperor William II fired Otto von Bismarck and took control of Germany's relations with other countries. In this scene, the emperor is shown relaxing on a throne made of cannonballs and artillery, while Bismarck bids him good-bye. The woman watching represents Germany. What do you think the cartoonist is trying to say?

Central and Eastern Europe: The Old Order

Germany, Austria-Hungary (or the Austro-Hungarian Empire), and Russia pursued policies that were quite different from those of some western European nations.

Germany The constitution of the new imperial Germany begun by **Otto von Bismarck** in 1871 provided for a two-house legislature. The lower house of the German parliament, the Reichstag, was elected on the basis of universal male suffrage.

Ministers of government, however, were responsible not to the parliament, but to the emperor. The emperor also controlled the armed forces, foreign policy, and the government bureaucracy. As chancellor (prime minister), Bismarck worked to keep Germany from becoming a democracy.

By the reign of **William II,** emperor from 1888 to 1918, Germany had become the strongest military and industrial power in Europe. With the expansion of industry and cities came demands for democracy.

Conservative forces—especially the landowning nobility and big industrialists, two powerful ruling groups in imperial Germany—tried to block the movement for democracy by supporting a strong

Reading Check

Answer: A premier (or prime minister) actually leads the government. The premier is directly responsible to the legislative body, not to the executive officer.

Analyzing *Political Cartoons*

Answer: Answers will vary. The cartoon indicates that Germany fears the emperor will not rule wisely and that he is foolish and dangerous.

Guided Reading Activity 13–3

Name ________ Date ________ Class ________

Guided Reading Activity 13-3

The National State and Democracy

DIRECTIONS: Fill in the blanks below as you read Section 3.

I. By the late nineteenth century, major European states were establishing ________, ________, and individual ________.

A. In Great Britain, the ________ and ________ Parties alternated in power.

B. In 1875, a new ________ turned France into a republic

C. Constant turmoil between ________ and ________ weakened the social fabric of Italy.

II. The ________ and ________ European nations pursued much different policies from their western counterparts.

Critical Thinking

Outwardly, the governments of Great Britain and Germany appeared similar. What traits did they share? *(two houses, prime minister, lower house elected by the people)* What were key differences? *(In Germany, ministers of the government were responsible to the emperor, not the people.)*

MEETING INDIVIDUAL NEEDS

Researching/Writing Ask students to select a country (Great Britain, France, Italy, Germany, the United States, Canada, Russia), then research and write a short essay that explains the social, political, and economic situation in that country at the turn of the century. Students should state whether or not the Industrial Revolution resulted in a political revolution in that country and explain why or why not. Ask the students to imagine what life might have been like for an average worker in that country, and have them write a journal entry detailing the events of one day. **L2**

Refer to ***Inclusion for the High School Social Studies Classroom Strategies and Activities*** in the TCR.

Reading Check

Answer: The Duma was created as a legislative assembly in the wake of "Bloody Sunday," but the czar quickly curtailed its power.

TURNING POINT

Ask students to compare the revolutions in western Europe between 1815 and 1848 with the events in Russia on "Bloody Sunday." Why were all of these events a sign of the decline and eventual fall of the old order? Why did this type of event take place in Russia almost a century after a similar event happened in western Europe? **L2**

Connecting Across Time

Assign students to find a political cartoon that is critical of a national leader. Ask students to compare the manner in which the cartoon on page 413 depicts William II with the way the modern leader is depicted. What similarities and differences can they find? Why do people often react more strongly to cartoons than to written descriptions of their leaders?

foreign policy. They believed that expansion abroad would not only increase their profits, but would also divert people from pursuing democratic reforms.

Austria-Hungary After the creation of the dual monarchy of Austria-Hungary in 1867, Austria enacted a constitution that, in theory, set up a parliamentary system with ministerial responsibility. In reality, the emperor, **Francis Joseph,** largely ignored this system. He appointed and dismissed his own ministers and issued decrees, or laws, when the parliament was not in session.

Austria remained troubled by conflicts between the various nationalities in the state. The German minority that governed Austria felt increasingly threatened by Czechs, Poles, and other Slavic groups within the empire. Representatives of these groups in the parliament agitated for their freedom, which further encouraged the emperor to ignore the parliament and govern by imperial decrees.

Unlike Austria, Hungary had a parliament that worked. It was controlled by Magyar landowners who dominated the peasants and ethnic groups.

Russia In Russia, **Nicholas II** began his rule in 1894 believing that the absolute power of the czars should be preserved: "I shall maintain the principle of autocracy just as firmly and unflinchingly as did my unforgettable father." Conditions were changing, however.

Industrialization in Russia progressed rapidly after 1890. By 1900, Russia had become the fourth largest producer of steel behind the United States, Germany, and Great Britain. With industrialization came factories, an industrial working class, and pitiful working and living conditions. Socialist parties developed, including the Marxist Social Democratic Party and the Social Revolutionaries, but government repression forced both parties to go underground. After the defeat of Russia by Japan, growing discontent and opposition to the czarist regime exploded into the Revolution of 1905.

On January 22, 1905, a massive procession of workers went to the Winter Palace in **St. Petersburg** to present a petition of grievances to the czar. Troops foolishly opened fire on the peaceful demonstration, killing hundreds. This "Bloody Sunday" caused workers throughout Russia to call strikes.

Nicholas II was eventually forced to grant civil liberties and create a legislative assembly, called the **Duma.** These reforms, however, proved short-lived. By 1907, the czar had already curtailed the power of the Duma, and again used the army and bureaucracy to rule Russia.

Reading Check **Identifying** What was the role of the Duma in the Russian government?

Scene at the Narva Gate in St. Petersburg, January 22, 1905, the day known as "Bloody Sunday"

EXTENDING THE CONTENT

"Bloody Sunday" The workers attending the mass demonstration peacefully carried religious icons, pictures of Nicholas, and petitions citing their grievances and desired reforms to the square before the Winter Palace. Nicholas was not in the city. The chief of the security police—Nicholas's uncle, Grand Duke Vladimir—tried to stop the march, then ordered his police to fire upon the demonstrators. More than 100 marchers were killed and several hundred more were wounded. The massacre was followed by a series of strikes, uprisings and mutinies in other cities, and became known as the Revolution of 1905.

The United States and Canada

Between 1870 and 1914, the United States became an industrial power with a foreign empire. Canada faced problems of national unity during this period.

Aftermath of the Civil War Four years of bloody civil war had preserved American national unity, but the old South had been destroyed. One-fifth of the adult white male population in the South had been killed, and four million African American slaves had been freed.

In 1865, the Thirteenth Amendment to the Constitution was passed, abolishing slavery. Later, the Fourteenth and Fifteenth Amendments gave citizenship to African Americans and the right to vote to African American males. However, new state laws in southern states soon stripped African Americans of their right to vote. By 1880, supporters of white supremacy were in power everywhere in the South.

Economy Between 1860 and 1914, the United States made the shift from an agrarian to an industrial nation. American heavy industry (steel and iron production, for example) was the best in the world in 1900. In that year, the Carnegie Steel Company alone produced more steel than did Great Britain's entire steel industry. As in Europe, industrialization in the United States led to urbanization. Whereas 20 percent of Americans lived in cities in 1860, over 40 percent did in 1900.

By 1900, the United States had become the world's richest nation. Yet serious problems remained. In 1890, the richest 9 percent of Americans owned an incredible 71 percent of the wealth. Labor unrest over unsafe working conditions and regular cycles of devastating unemployment led workers to organize unions. By the turn of the century, the American Federation of Labor had emerged as labor's chief voice, but it lacked real power. In 1900, only 8.4 percent of American workers were members.

Expansion Abroad At the end of the nineteenth century, the United States began to expand abroad. The Samoan Islands in the Pacific became the first important United States colony. By 1887, American settlers had gained control of the sugar industry on the Hawaiian Islands.

As more Americans settled in Hawaii, they sought to gain political power. When **Queen Liliuokalani** (lee•lee•oo•oh•kah•LAH•nee) tried to strengthen the power of the monarchy to keep the islands under her peoples' control, the United States government sent military forces to the islands. The queen was deposed, and Hawaii was annexed by the United States in 1898.

In 1898, the United States also defeated Spain in the Spanish-American War. As a result, the United States acquired the formerly Spanish possessions of Puerto Rico, Guam, and the Philippines.

The Filipino people hoped for independence, but the United States refused to grant it. It took the United States three years to pacify the Philippines and establish control. By the beginning of the twentieth century, the United States, the world's richest nation, had an empire.

Canada At the beginning of 1870, the Dominion of Canada had four provinces: Quebec, Ontario, Nova Scotia, and New Brunswick. With the addition in 1871 of two more provinces—Manitoba and British Columbia—the Dominion of Canada extended from the Atlantic to the Pacific.

Real unity was difficult to achieve, however, because of distrust between the English-speaking and French-speaking peoples of Canada. Wilfred Laurier, who became the first French-Canadian prime minister in 1896, was able to reconcile these two major groups. During his administration, industrialization boomed, and immigrants from Europe helped populate Canada's vast territories.

Reading Check **Identifying** Name the territories acquired by the United States in 1898.

International Rivalries

Otto von Bismarck realized that Germany's emergence in 1871 as the most powerful state in continental Europe had upset the balance of power established at Vienna in 1815. Fearing that France intended to create an anti-German alliance, Bismarck made a defensive alliance with Austria-Hungary in 1879. In 1882, Italy joined this alliance.

The Triple Alliance of 1882 united the powers of Germany, Austria-Hungary, and Italy in a defensive alliance against France. At the same time, Bismarck maintained a separate treaty with Russia and tried to remain on good terms with Great Britain.

In 1890, Emperor William II fired Bismarck and took control of Germany's foreign policy. The emperor embarked on an activist policy dedicated to enhancing German power. He wanted, as he put it, to find Germany's rightful "place in the sun."

One of the changes he made in Bismarck's foreign policy was to drop the treaty with Russia. The ending

CHAPTER 13
Section 3, 411–416

Reading Check

Answer: Puerto Rico, Guam, and the Philippines

3 ASSESS

Assign Section 3 Assessment as homework or as an in-class activity.

Have students use **Interactive Tutor Self-Assessment CD-ROM.**

Section Quiz 13–3

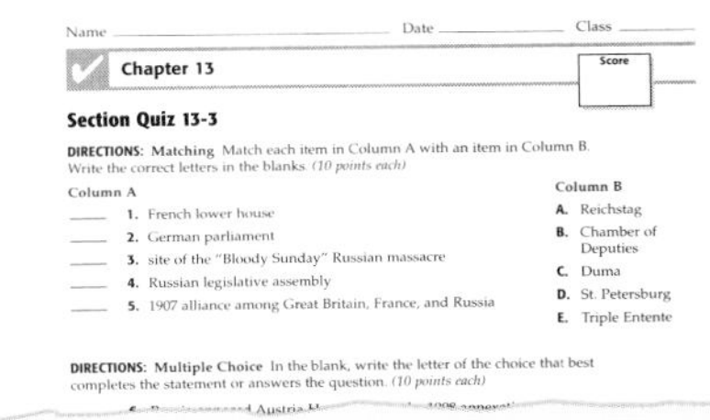
Name ______ Date ______ Class ______

Chapter 13 Score

Section Quiz 13-3

DIRECTIONS: Matching Match each item in Column A with an item in Column B. Write the correct letters in the blanks. (10 points each)

Column A	Column B
___ 1. French lower house	A. Reichstag
___ 2. German parliament	B. Chamber of Deputies
___ 3. site of the "Bloody Sunday" Russian massacre	C. Duma
___ 4. Russian legislative assembly	D. St. Petersburg
___ 5. 1907 alliance among Great Britain, France, and Russia	E. Triple Entente

DIRECTIONS: Multiple Choice In the blank, write the letter of the choice that best completes the statement or answers the question. (10 points each)

Mathematics To help students understand the concept of distribution of wealth, pick up a few dozen miniature candy bars. Distribute them to the class as follows: ten percent of the class receives 70 percent of the candy bars, the next ten percent receives 15 percent and the remaining eighty percent receives the last 15 percent of the treats. Refer to the distribution of wealth in the United States at the beginning of the twentieth century (page 415). Then break out some extra candy before your students revolt!

EXTENDING THE CONTENT

Kaiser William Fires Bismarck When 29-year-old William II ascended to the imperial throne of Germany, a power struggle quickly developed with Prince Otto von Bismarck, national hero and unifier of Germany. Kaiser William wanted to rescind an order requiring Bismarck's permission before ministers conferred with the kaiser. Rather than discussing this issue with the kaiser, Bismarck changed the topic to the kaiser's proposed visit with the Russian czar. Bismarck produced reports but refused to let the kaiser read them. William grabbed one and found in it insulting comments about himself. Shortly afterwards, he asked Bismarck to resign.

Reading Check

Answer: Triple Alliance: Germany, Austria-Hungary, Italy; Triple Entente: Great Britain, France, Russia

Reading Check

Answer: They had hoped to create a large Serbian kingdom that would include most of the southern Slavs, including Bosnia and Herzegovina.

Reading Essentials and Study Guide 13–3

Name ______ Date ______ Class ______

Reading Essentials and Study Guide

Chapter 13, Section 3

For use with textbook pages 411–416

THE NATIONAL STATE AND DEMOCRACY

KEY TERMS

ministerial responsibility the idea that the prime minister is responsible to the popularly elected legislative body not to the executive *(page 413)*

Duma a legislative assembly in Russia during the time of Nicholas II *(page 414)*

DRAWING FROM EXPERIENCE

Have you ever thought what your life would be like if you had been born in a different country? What do you think would affect you more—the differ-

Reteaching Activity

Have students identify the various alliances in the Balkans described on this page. *(Russian protection of Slavs, Serbia's hopes for a large Serbian kingdom, Austria-Hungary's protection of Bosnia and Herzegovina)* Discuss how these overlapping territorial goals produced instability in the Balkans. **L2**

4 CLOSE

Ask students to discuss why the location of the Balkans made it unlikely that they would be left alone in peace by the more powerful states. Why were they important from both military and economic points of view? **L1**

of that alliance brought France and Russia together. In 1894, these two powers formed a military alliance.

Over the next 10 years, German policies abroad caused the British to draw closer to France. By 1907, an alliance of Great Britain, France, and Russia—known as the Triple Entente—stood opposed to the Triple Alliance of Germany, Austria-Hungary, and Italy.

Europe was now dangerously divided into two opposing camps that became more and more unwilling to compromise. A series of crises in the Balkans between 1908 and 1913 set the stage for World War I.

Reading Check **Summarizing** What countries formed the Triple Alliance and the Triple Entente?

Crises in the Balkans

Over the course of the nineteenth century, the Balkan provinces of the Ottoman Empire had gradually gained their freedom, although regional rivalries between Austria-Hungary and Russia had complicated the process. By 1878, Greece, Serbia, Romania, and **Montenegro** had become independent states. Bulgaria did not become totally independent, but was allowed to operate under Russian protection. The Balkan territories of Bosnia and Herzegovina were placed under the protection of Austria-Hungary.

In 1908, Austria-Hungary took the drastic step of annexing Bosnia and Herzegovina. Serbia was outraged. The annexation of these two Slavic-speaking territories dashed the Serbians' hopes of creating a large Serbian kingdom that would include most of the southern Slavs.

The Russians, as protectors of their fellow Slavs, supported the Serbs and opposed the annexation. Backed by the Russians, the Serbs prepared for war against Austria-Hungary. At this point, Emperor William II of Germany demanded that the Russians accept Austria-Hungary's annexation of Bosnia and Herzegovina or face war with Germany.

Weakened from their defeat in the Russo-Japanese War in 1905, the Russians backed down but vowed revenge. Two wars between Balkan states in 1912 and 1913 further embittered the inhabitants and created more tensions among the great powers.

The Serbians blamed Austria-Hungary for their failure to create a large Serbian kingdom. Austria-Hungary was convinced that Serbia was a mortal threat to its empire and must at some point be crushed. As Serbia's chief supporters, the Russians were angry and determined not to back down again in the event of another confrontation with Austria-Hungary or Germany in the Balkans. The allies of Austria-Hungary and Russia were determined to support their respective allies more strongly in another crisis. By the beginning of 1914, these countries viewed each other with suspicion.

Reading Check **Explaining** Why were the Serbs outraged when Austria-Hungary annexed Bosnia and Herzegovina?

SECTION 3 ASSESSMENT

Checking for Understanding

1. **Define** ministerial responsibility, Duma.
2. **Identify** Otto von Bismarck, William II, Francis Joseph, Nicholas II, Queen Liliuokalani.
3. **Locate** St. Petersburg, Montenegro.
4. **Explain** how the United States became an industrial power. What problems did industrialization cause in the United States and how did people attempt to solve some of these problems?
5. **List** the series of events leading to unrest in Russia at the turn of the century. What were the consequences of "Bloody Sunday"?

Critical Thinking

6. **Analyze** Which country do you think had a stronger democracy at the end of the nineteenth century, France or England? Why?
7. **Compare and Contrast** Use this chapter and Chapter 10 to create a Venn diagram like the one below comparing and contrasting the systems of government in France and the United States.

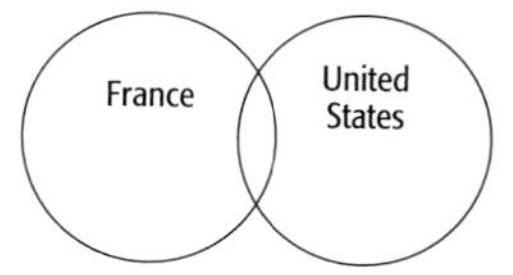

Analyzing Visuals

8. **Examine** the illustration of "Bloody Sunday" on page 414. What does the artist seem to be saying about the events that occurred on January 22, 1905? Does the picture reflect a particular point of view? Where might an illustration such as this have been exhibited and why?

Writing About History

9. **Expository Writing** Do some research about recent conflicts in the Balkans. Write one or two paragraphs comparing the causes of the recent conflicts with the causes of the conflicts between Balkan countries in the early twentieth century.

SECTION 3 ASSESSMENT

1. Key terms are in blue.
2. Otto von Bismarck *(p. 413);* William II *(p. 413);* Francis Joseph *(p. 414);* Nicholas II *(p. 414);* Queen Liliuokalani *(p. 415)*
3. See chapter maps.
4. invested in heavy industry; problems: distribution of wealth, labor unrest, unemployment; formed unions
5. poor working, living conditions, underground socialist parties oppose czar, workers demonstrate, troops open fire, workers strike, czar grants civil liberties, reforms short-lived
6. Answers should be supported by logical arguments.
7. France: premier leads government, many political parties, coalition governments; United States: president chief executive, two major political parties, federal system; Both: representative democracies with popularly elected legislatures
8. Answers should be supported by logical arguments.
9. Answers should be supported by logical arguments.

CRITICAL THINKING SKILLBUILDER

Detecting Bias

Why Learn This Skill?

Suppose you see an ad showing two happy customers shaking hands with a used-car salesman. The ad says, "Visit Honest Harry for the best deal on wheels." That evening you see a television program that investigates used-car sales businesses. The report says that many of these businesses cheat their customers.

Each message expresses a bias—an inclination or prejudice that inhibits impartiality. Harry wants to sell cars; the television program wants to attract viewers. Most people have preconceived feelings, opinions, and attitudes that affect their judgment on many topics. Ideas stated as facts may be opinions. Detecting bias enables us to evaluate the accuracy of information.

Learning the Skill

In detecting bias:

- Identify the writer's or speaker's purpose.
- Watch for emotionally charged language such as *exploit, terrorize,* and *cheat.*
- Look for visual images that provoke a strong emotional response.
- Look for overgeneralizations such as *unique, honest,* and *everybody.*
- Notice italics, underlining, and punctuation that highlight particular ideas.
- Examine the material to determine whether it presents equal coverage of differing views.

Practicing the Skill

Industrialization produced widespread changes in society and widespread disagreement on its effects. Karl Marx and Friedrich Engels presented their viewpoint on industrialization in *The Communist Manifesto* in 1848. Read the following excerpt and then answer these questions.

> "The bourgeoisie . . . has put an end to all feudal, patriarchal, idyllic relations. It has pitilessly torn asunder the motley feudal ties that bound man to his 'natural superiors,' and has left remaining no other nexus [link] between man and man than naked self-interest, than callous 'cash payment.' It has drowned the most heavenly of ecstasies of religious fervor, of chivalrous enthusiasm . . . in the icy water of egotistical calculation. . . . In one word, for exploitation, veiled by religious and political illusions, it has substituted naked, shameless, direct, brutal exploitation."

1. What is the purpose of this quote?
2. What are three examples of emotionally charged language?
3. According to Marx and Engels, which is more inhumane—the exploitation by feudal lords or by the bourgeoisie? Why?
4. What bias about the bourgeoisie is expressed in this excerpt?

Applying the Skill

Find written material about a topic of interest in your community. Possible sources include editorials, letters to the editor, and pamphlets from political candidates and interest groups. Write a short report analyzing the material for evidence of bias.

Glencoe's **Skillbuilder Interactive Workbook, Level 2,** provides instruction and practice in key social studies skills.

CRITICAL THINKING SKILLBUILDER

TEACH

Detecting Bias Point out that everyone is biased. Without using reason, people rely on gut emotional reactions, favoring some things—a sports team, a political party—and disapproving of others—a nationality, a breed of dog. Have students list, anonymously, two biases of theirs, either positive or negative. After collecting these, read some of them aloud for class discussion. Which are positive and which negative? How might they be helpful or harmful? **L1**

Additional Practice

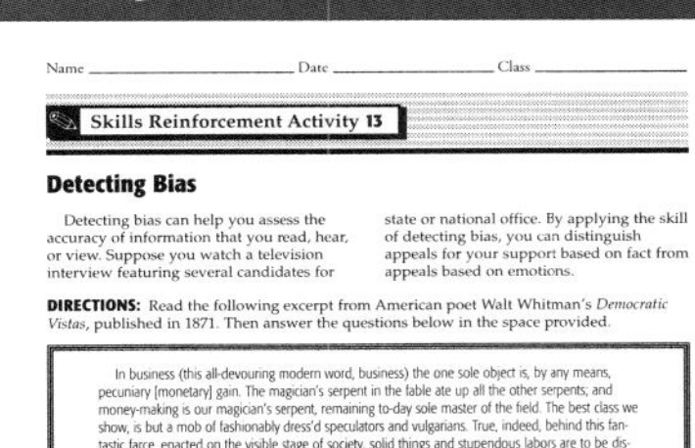

Name ______ Date ______ Class ______

Skills Reinforcement Activity 13

Detecting Bias

Detecting bias can help you assess the accuracy of information that you read, hear, or view. Suppose you watch a television interview featuring several candidates for state or national office. By applying the skill of detecting bias, you can distinguish appeals for your support based on fact from appeals based on emotions.

DIRECTIONS: Read the following excerpt from American poet Walt Whitman's *Democratic Vistas,* published in 1871. Then answer the questions below in the space provided.

In business (this all-devouring modern word, business) the one sole object is, by any means, pecuniary [monetary] gain. The magician's serpent in the fable ate up all the other serpents; and money-making is our magician's serpent, remaining to-day sole master of the field. The best class we show, is but a mob of fashionably dress'd speculators and vulgarians. True, indeed, behind this fantastic farce, enacted on the visible stage of society, solid things and stupendous labors are to be discover'd, existing crudely and going on in the background, to advance and tell themselves in time. Yet

GLENCOE TECHNOLOGY

CD-ROM

Glencoe Skillbuilder Interactive Workbook CD-ROM, Level 2

This interactive CD-ROM reinforces student mastery of essential social studies skills.

ANSWERS TO PRACTICING THE SKILL

1. The purpose of the quote is to inflame the reader against the bourgeoisie.
2. Answers will vary but might include: "pitilessly torn asunder," "callous 'cash payment,'" "icy water of egotistical calculation."
3. According to Marx and Engels, the bourgeoisie is more inhumane because it is "naked, shameless, direct, brutal."
4. Marx and Engels are extremely biased *against* the bourgeoisie.

Applying the Skill: Answers will vary but should be supported by logical arguments.

CHAPTER 13
Section 4, 418–423

1 FOCUS

Section Overview

This section describes the developments in physics and psychology, the relationship between the concept of social Darwinism and racism, anti-Semitism in Europe, and the growth of modernism in literature and the arts.

BELLRINGER
Skillbuilder Activity

Project transparency and have students answer questions.

Available as a blackline master.

Daily Focus Skills Transparency 13–4

Guide to Reading

Answers to Graphic: Impressionism: Monet, paint nature directly; Postimpressionism: van Gogh, stress color; Cubism: Picasso, geometric designs; Abstract Expressionism: Kandinsky, avoid visual reality

Preteaching Vocabulary: Discuss how *psychoanalysis* relates to *modernism.*

SECTION 4 Toward the Modern Consciousness

Guide to Reading

Main Ideas
- Innovative artistic movements during the late 1800s and early 1900s rejected traditional styles.
- Extreme nationalism and racism led to an increase in anti-Semitism.
- Developments in science changed how people saw themselves and their world.

Key Terms
psychoanalysis, pogrom, modernism

People to Identify
Marie Curie, Albert Einstein, Sigmund Freud, Claude Monet, Pablo Picasso

Places to Locate
Vienna, France

Preview Questions
1. How did Einstein and Freud challenge people's views of the world?
2. How did modernism revolutionize architecture?

Reading Strategy
Identifying Information As you read this section, complete a chart like the one below that lists an artist and a characteristic of the art movement indicated.

Impressionism		
Post-Impressionism		
Cubism		
Abstract Expressionism		

Preview of Events

1890 · 1895 · 1900 · 1905 · 1910 · 1915 · 1920

- **1896** Herzl publishes *The Jewish State*
- **1900** Freud publishes *The Interpretation of Dreams*
- **1905** Einstein publishes his special theory of relativity
- **1913** Stravinsky's *The Rite of Spring* performed in Paris

Voices from the Past

Self-Portrait
by Camille Pissarro

Camille Pissarro, a French artist, expressed his philosophy of painting in this way:

"Do not define too closely the outlines of things; it is the brush stroke of the right value and color which should produce the drawing. . . . The eye should not be fixed on one point, but should take in everything, while observing the reflections which the colors produce on their surroundings. Work at the same time upon sky, water, branches, ground, keeping everything going on an equal basis. . . . Don't proceed according to rules and principles, but paint what you observe and feel. Paint generously unhesitatingly, for it is best not to lose the first impression."

—*History of Impressionism,* John Rewald, 1961

Pissarro was part of a revolution in the arts. Between 1870 and 1914, radical ideas in the arts and sciences opened the way to a modern consciousness.

A New Physics

TURNING POINT **As you will learn, Albert Einstein challenged the Newtonian idea of a mechanical universe, thus introducing an element of uncertainty into humankind's perception of space and time.**

Before 1914, many people in the Western world continued to believe in the values and ideals that had been put forth by the Scientific Revolution and the Enlightenment. *Reason, science,* and *progress* were still important words to Europeans.

SECTION RESOURCES

Reproducible Masters
- Reproducible Lesson Plan 13–4
- Daily Lecture and Discussion Notes 13–4
- Guided Reading Activity 13–4
- Section Quiz 13–4
- Reading Essentials and Study Guide 13–4

Transparencies
- Daily Focus Skills Transparency 13–4

Multimedia
- Interactive Tutor Self-Assessment CD-ROM
- ExamView® Pro Testmaker CD-ROM
- Presentation Plus! CD-ROM

Science was one of the chief pillars supporting the optimistic view of the world that many Westerners shared in the nineteenth century. Science, which was supposedly based on hard facts and cold reason, offered a certainty of belief in the orderliness of nature. Many believed that by applying already known scientific laws, humans could arrive at a complete understanding of the physical world and an accurate picture of reality.

Throughout much of the nineteenth century, Westerners believed in a mechanical conception of the universe that was based on the ideas of Isaac Newton. In this perspective, the universe was viewed as a giant machine. Time, space, and matter were objective realities that existed independently of those observing them. Matter was thought to be composed of solid material bodies called atoms.

Marie Curie, c. 1910

These views were seriously questioned at the end of the nineteenth century. The French scientist **Marie Curie** discovered that an element called radium gave off energy, or radiation, that apparently came from within the atom itself. Atoms were not simply hard material bodies but small, active worlds.

At the beginning of the twentieth century, **Albert Einstein,** a German-born scientist working in Switzerland, provided a new view of the universe. In 1905, Einstein published his special theory of relativity, which stated that space and time are not absolute but are relative to the observer.

According to this theory, neither space nor time has an existence independent of human experience. As Einstein later explained to a journalist, "It was formerly believed that if all material things disappeared out of the universe, time and space would be left. According to the relativity theory, however, time and space disappear together with the things."

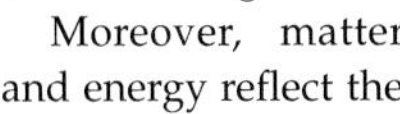

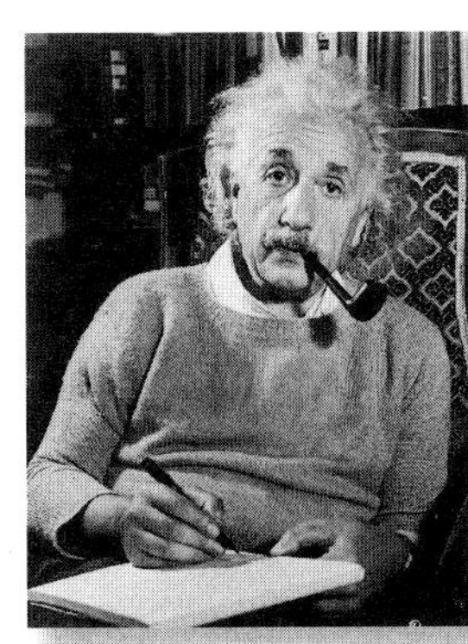
Albert Einstein, 1940

Moreover, matter and energy reflect the relativity of time and space. Einstein concluded that matter is nothing but another form of energy. This idea led to an understanding of the vast energies contained within the atom and to the Atomic Age. To some, however, a relative universe—unlike Newton's universe—was a universe without certainty.

Reading Check **Explaining** How did Marie Curie's discovery change people's ideas about the atom?

Freud and Psychoanalysis

At the turn of the century, **Sigmund Freud** (FROYD), a doctor from **Vienna,** proposed a series of theories that raised questions about the nature of the human mind. Freud's ideas, like the new physics, added to the uncertainties of the age. His major theories were published in 1900 in *The Interpretation of Dreams.*

Sigmund Freud, c. 1938

According to Freud, human behavior was strongly determined by past experiences and internal forces of which people were largely unaware. Freud argued that painful and unsettling experiences were repressed, or hidden from a person's conscious awareness. Freud believed that these hidden feelings continued to influence behavior, however, because they were part of the unconscious.

According to Freud, repression of such experiences began in childhood, so he devised a method—known as psychoanalysis—by which a therapist and patient could probe deeply into the patient's memory. In this way, they could retrace the chain of repressed thoughts all the way back to their childhood origins. If the patient's conscious mind could be made aware of the unconscious and its repressed contents, the patient could be healed.

The full importance of Sigmund Freud's thought was not felt until after World War I. In the 1920s, his ideas gained worldwide acceptance. Freudian terms, such as *unconscious* and *repression,* became standard vocabulary words. Psychoanalysis, pioneered by Freud, developed into a major profession.

Reading Check **Summarizing** What is Freud's theory of the human unconscious?

2 TEACH

Reading Check

Answer: It showed that atoms were not simply hard material bodies but small, active worlds.

Reading Check

Answer: that past experiences are repressed but continue to influence behavior because they are part of the unconscious

Daily Lecture and Discussion Notes 13–4

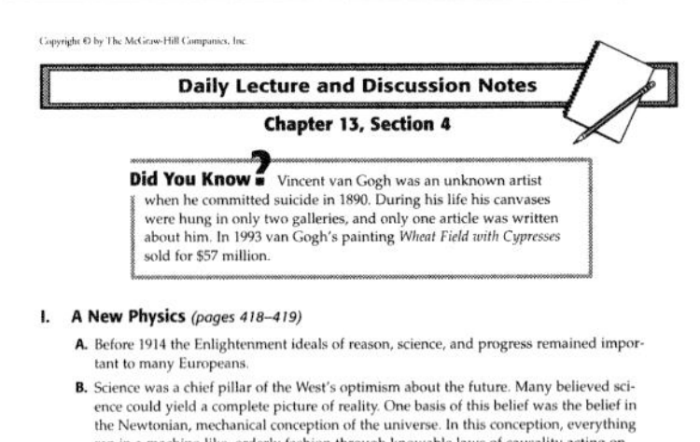
Daily Lecture and Discussion Notes

Chapter 13, Section 4

Did You Know? Vincent van Gogh was an unknown artist when he committed suicide in 1890. During his life his canvases were hung in only two galleries, and only one article was written about him. In 1993 van Gogh's painting *Wheat Field with Cypresses* sold for $57 million.

I. A New Physics (pages 418–419)

A. Before 1914 the Enlightenment ideals of reason, science, and progress remained important to many Europeans.

B. Science was a chief pillar of the West's optimism about the future. Many believed science could yield a complete picture of reality. One basis of this belief was the belief in the Newtonian, mechanical conception of the universe. In this conception, everything ran in a machine-like, orderly fashion through knowable laws of causality acting on

CURRICULUM CONNECTION

Psychology Ask students to write their opinion of the value of psychoanalysis on an unsigned piece of paper. Survey their opinions. Discuss why some people have a high regard for this process while others do not. What does this show about our different social values? L2

MEETING INDIVIDUAL NEEDS

Auditory/Visual Divide the class into five groups. Each group will be responsible for presenting to the class major figures in each of the following areas: 1) Physics (Albert Einstein); 2) Psychoanalysis (Freud); 3) Social Darwinism (Herbert Spencer, Bernhardi, Chamberlain); 4) Literature (Ibsen, Zola); and 5) Art (Pissarro, Monet, van Gogh). Have each group pick an interviewer and interviewee. After discussion and preparation, have the "interviewers" for each group introduce the respective "main characters" to the class. Particularly for the group dealing with art, the students may bring pictures exemplifying Impressionism, for example. L1

Refer to ***Inclusion for the High School Social Studies Classroom Strategies and Activities*** in the TCR.

Chart *Skills*

1. Answers will vary but might include the following: Ornamentalism: Gian Lorenzo Bernini; Naturalism: Émile Zola; Romanticism: Ludwig van Beethoven; Realism: Gustave Courbet; Physics: Isaac Newton; Psychology: René Descartes
2. Answers will vary but should be supported by examples.

Reading Check

Answer: Social progress comes from "the struggle for survival" as the "fit," or strong, advanced while the weak declined.

Guided Reading Activity 13–4

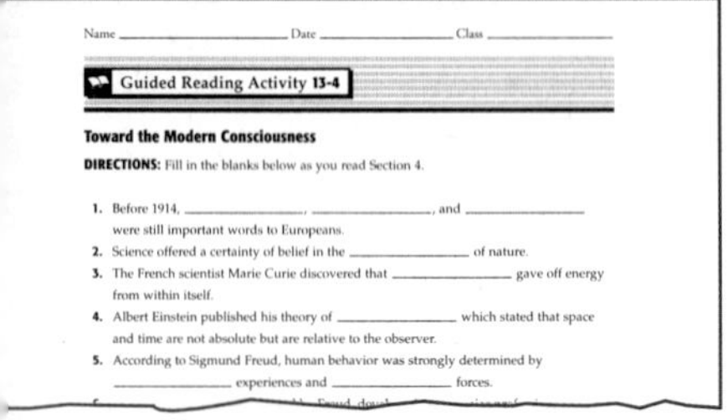

Name ______ Date ______ Class ______

Guided Reading Activity 13-4

Toward the Modern Consciousness

DIRECTIONS: Fill in the blanks below as you read Section 4.

1. Before 1914, ______, ______, and ______ were still important words to Europeans.
2. Science offered a certainty of belief in the ______ of nature.
3. The French scientist Marie Curie discovered that ______ gave off energy from within itself.
4. Albert Einstein published his theory of ______ which stated that space and time are not absolute but are relative to the observer.
5. According to Sigmund Freud, human behavior was strongly determined by ______ experiences and ______ forces.

TURNING POINT

Adolf Hitler (1889–1945) is often viewed as a single, irrational creature who used political power to enforce his personal prejudice and hatred. Discuss how social Darwinism was applied in Hitler's childhood and youth. Discuss whether Hitler may have become powerful partly because of widespread, or at least influential, agreement with his views.

Revolution in the Arts and Sciences

	Old View	New View
Architecture	Ornamentalism	Functionalism
Literature	Naturalism	Symbolism
Music	Romanticism	• Impressionism • Chromaticism • Expressionism
Painting	Realism	• Impressionism • Postimpressionism • Cubism • Abstract expressionism
Physics	Newton's mechanical universe	Einstein's relative universe
Psychology	Conscious awareness	Freud's unconscious mind

Chart *Skills*

In the late nineteenth century, major changes occurred in the arts and sciences.

1. **Identifying** Review earlier chapters of your text and identify artists and scientists whose work exemplified the "Old Views," as listed above.
2. **Evaluating** After reading about the changes that took place in each of the areas listed above, write a paragraph or two explaining which area of change you think had the biggest impact on societies and cultures of the early twentieth century.

Social Darwinism and Racism

In the late nineteenth and early twentieth centuries, scientific theories were sometimes applied inappropriately to achieve desired results. For example, Charles Darwin's theories were applied to human society in a radical way by nationalists and racists. Their ideas are known as social Darwinism.

The most popular exponent of social Darwinism was the British philosopher Herbert Spencer. He argued that social progress came from "the struggle for survival" as the "fit"—the strong—advanced while the weak declined. Some prominent businessmen used social Darwinism to explain their success. To them, the strong and fit—the able and energetic—had risen to the top; the stupid and lazy had fallen by the wayside.

In their pursuit of national greatness, extreme nationalists often insisted that nations, too, were engaged in a "struggle for existence" in which only the fittest (the strongest) survived. The German general Friedrich von Bernhardi argued in 1907, "War is a biological necessity of the first importance, . . . since without it an unhealthy development will follow, which excludes every advancement of the race, and therefore all real civilization. War is the father of all things."

Perhaps nowhere was the combination of extreme nationalism and racism more evident than in Germany. One of the chief exponents of German racism was Houston Stewart Chamberlain, a Briton who became a German citizen. He believed that modern-day Germans were the only pure successors of the Aryans, who were portrayed as the original creators of Western culture. Chamberlain singled out Jews as the racial enemy who wanted to destroy the Aryan race.

Reading Check **Explaining** What does the theory of social Darwinism state?

Anti-Semitism and Zionism

Anti-Semitism—hostility toward and discrimination against Jews—was not new to European civilization. Since the Middle Ages, the Jews had been portrayed as the murderers of Christ and subjected to mob violence. Their rights had been restricted, and they had been physically separated from Christians by being required to live in areas of cities known as ghettos.

In the nineteenth century, Jews were increasingly granted legal equality in many European countries. Many Jews now left the ghettos and became assimilated into the cultures around them. Many became successful as bankers, lawyers, scientists, scholars, and journalists.

CRITICAL THINKING ACTIVITY

Solving Problems Simulate a congressional hearing in which the class is divided into five groups. Have each group choose from the following list of organizations or others of their own choosing. Each group will prepare an argument and represent that organization before a congressional hearing convened to discuss the following: What are the causes and possible solutions to the problems of racism and discrimination? Organizations: Anti-Defamation League, the National Association for the Advancement of Colored People, Gay and Lesbian Alliance Against Defamation, National Organization for Women, Aryan Nations, United Farm Workers, etc. L1

These achievements were only one side of the picture, however, as is evident from the Dreyfus affair in France. Alfred Dreyfus, a Jew, was a captain in the French general staff. Early in 1895, a secret military court found him guilty of selling army secrets and condemned him to life imprisonment. During his trial, angry right-wing mobs yelled anti-Semitic sayings such as, "Death to the Jews."

Soon after the trial, however, evidence emerged that pointed to Dreyfus's innocence. Another officer, a Catholic aristocrat, was more obviously the traitor. The army refused a new trial. A wave of public outrage finally forced the government to hold a new trial and pardon Dreyfus in 1899.

In Germany and Austria-Hungary during the 1880s and 1890s, new parties arose that used anti-Semitism to win the votes of people who felt threatened by the changing economic forces of the times. However, the worst treatment of Jews at the turn of the century occurred in eastern Europe, where 72 percent of the world Jewish population lived. Russian Jews were forced to live in certain regions of the country. Persecutions and **pogroms** (organized massacres) were widespread.

Hundreds of thousands of Jews decided to emigrate to escape the persecution. Many went to the United States. Some (probably about 25,000) moved to Palestine, which became home for a Jewish nationalist movement called Zionism.

For many Jews, Palestine, the land of ancient Israel, had long been the land of their dreams. A key figure in the growth of political Zionism was Theodor Herzl, who stated in his book *The Jewish State* (1896), "The Jews who wish it will have their state."

Settlement in Palestine was difficult, however, because it was then part of the Ottoman Empire, which was opposed to Jewish immigration. Although three thousand Jews went annually to Palestine between 1904 and 1914, the Zionist desire for a homeland in Palestine remained only a dream on the eve of World War I.

Reading Check **Explaining** Why did Jews begin to move to Palestine?

The Culture of Modernity

Between 1870 and 1914, many writers and artists rebelled against the traditional literary and artistic styles that had dominated European cultural life since the Renaissance. The changes that they produced have since been called **modernism.**

People In History

Berthe Morisot
1841–1895—French painter

Berthe Morisot was the first woman painter to join the Impressionists. She came from a wealthy French family that had settled in Paris when she was seven. Her dedication to the new style of painting won her the disfavor of more traditional French artists.

Morisot believed that women had a special vision, which was, as she said, "more delicate than that of men." She developed her own unique style, using lighter colors and flowing brushstrokes. Near the end of her life, she lamented the refusal of men to take her work seriously: "I don't think there has ever been a man who treated a woman as an equal, and that's all I would have asked, for I know I'm worth as much as they."

Literature Throughout much of the late nineteenth century, literature was dominated by naturalism. Naturalists felt that literature should be realistic and address social problems. These writers, such as Henrik Ibsen and Émile Zola, explored issues such as the role of women in society, alcoholism, and the problems of urban slums.

At the beginning of the twentieth century, a group of writers known as the **symbolists** caused a literary revolution. Primarily interested in writing poetry and strongly influenced by the ideas of Freud, the symbolists believed that objective knowledge of the world was impossible. The external world was only a collection of symbols that reflected the true reality—the individual human mind. Art, the symbolists believed, should function for its own sake instead of serving, criticizing, or seeking to understand society.

Painting The period from 1870 to 1914 was one of the most productive in the history of art. Since the Renaissance, the task of artists had been to represent reality as accurately as possible. By the late nineteenth century, artists were seeking new forms of expression to reflect their changing views of the world.

HISTORY Online

Web Activity Visit the *Glencoe World History—Modern Times* Web site at wh.mt.glencoe.com and click on **Chapter 13–Student Web Activity** to learn more about Impressionism.

CHAPTER 13
Section 4, 418–423

Reading Check

Answer: to escape persecution

CURRICULUM CONNECTION

Politics Many artists of the time took sides in the Dreyfus affair. Monet and Pissarro were among the artists believing that the charge of treason against Captain Dreyfus, the only Jew on the General Staff of the French army, was unfounded. Cézanne, Rodin, Renoir, and Degas believed in Dreyfus's guilt.

Critical Thinking

Ask students to explain why Zionism may have grown in Europe as a response to prejudice against Jewish people. Why have some Europeans who are prejudiced against Jewish people supported this movement?

3 ASSESS

Assign Section 4 Assessment as homework or as an in-class activity.

Have students use **Interactive Tutor Self-Assessment CD-ROM.**

Section Quiz 13–4

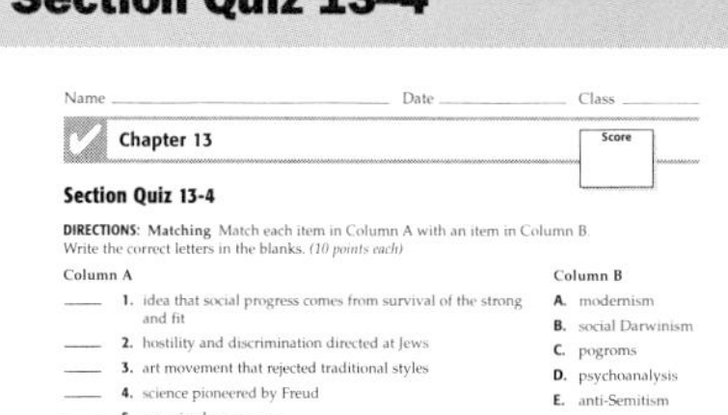
Name ______ Date ______ Class ______

Chapter 13 Score

Section Quiz 13-4

DIRECTIONS: Matching Match each item in Column A with an item in Column B. Write the correct letters in the blanks. *(10 points each)*

Column A	Column B
____ 1. idea that social progress comes from survival of the strong and fit	A. modernism
____ 2. hostility and discrimination directed at Jews	B. social Darwinism
____ 3. art movement that rejected traditional styles	C. pogroms
____ 4. science pioneered by Freud	D. psychoanalysis
____ 5. organized massacres	E. anti-Semitism

DIRECTIONS: Multiple Choice In the blank, write the letter of the choice that best completes the statement or answers the question. *(10 points each)*

INTERDISCIPLINARY CONNECTIONS ACTIVITY

Literature Select and distribute several poems written by the French symbolist poets Stephane Mallarmé, Paul Verlaine, or Arthur Rimbaud. Engage students in a discussion about Mallarmé's belief that "to name an object is to destroy three-quarters of the enjoyment of a poem, which is made up of the pleasure of guessing little by little." Ask students how Mallarmé and his followers gave impressions by suggestion rather than direct statement. Explain that symbolism spread to the other arts and to other countries and, while intellectuals applauded this effort, the average person found symbolism difficult to understand. L3

History *through Art*

Answer: Answers will vary depending on students' individual responses to the painting.

Reading Essentials and Study Guide 13–4

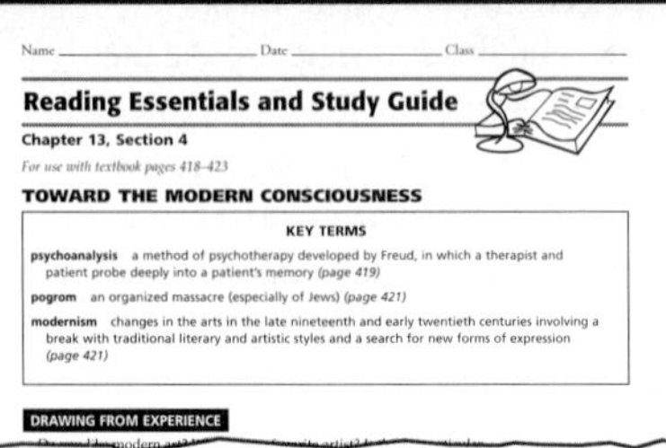

Name ______ Date ______ Class ______

Reading Essentials and Study Guide

Chapter 13, Section 4

For use with textbook pages 418–423

TOWARD THE MODERN CONSCIOUSNESS

KEY TERMS

psychoanalysis a method of psychotherapy developed by Freud, in which a therapist and patient probe deeply into a patient's memory *(page 419)*

pogrom an organized massacre (especially of Jews) *(page 421)*

modernism changes in the arts in the late nineteenth and early twentieth centuries involving a break with traditional literary and artistic styles and a search for new forms of expression *(page 421)*

DRAWING FROM EXPERIENCE

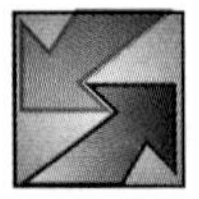

CURRICULUM CONNECTION

Art Have students assemble copies of paintings from the period covered in this section, identify the movement each work represents, and point out characteristics of the movement. **L1**

Enrich

Ask students to examine the painting on this page. Why do some art critics believe that van Gogh was more interested in color than in form? *(Van Gogh's work is less representational and invokes the viewer's imagination with startling and vibrant colors.)*

History *through Art*

Starry Night **by Vincent van Gogh, 1889**
During the last two years of his life, van Gogh painted many night scenes such as this one. What adjectives would you use to describe the feelings van Gogh conveyed in this painting?

Impressionism was a movement that began in **France** in the 1870s, when a group of artists rejected the studios where artists had traditionally worked and went out into the countryside to paint nature directly. One important Impressionist is **Claude Monet** (moh•NAY), who painted pictures in which he sought to capture the interplay of light, water, and sky. Other Impressionist painters include Pierre-Auguste Renoir (REHN• WAHR) and Berthe Morisot.

In the 1880s, a new movement, known as Postimpressionism, arose in France and soon spread to other European countries. A famous Postimpressionist is Vincent van Gogh (GOH). For van Gogh, art was a spiritual experience. He was especially interested in color and believed that it could act as its own form of language. Van Gogh maintained that artists should paint what they feel.

By the beginning of the twentieth century, the belief that the goal of art was to represent reality had lost much of its meaning. This was especially true in the visual arts. Perhaps the most important factor in the decline of realism in painting was the spread of photography to the mass markets. Photography had been invented in the 1830s and became widespread after George Eastman created the first Kodak camera in 1888. Now, anyone could take a photograph that looked exactly like the subject.

Artists came to realize that their strength was not in mirroring reality, which the camera could do, but in creating reality. The visual artists, like the symbolist writers of the time, sought meaning in individual consciousness. Between 1905 and 1914, this search for individual expression created modern art. One of the most outstanding features of modern art is the attempt of the artist to avoid "visual reality."

By 1905, one of the most important figures in modern art was beginning his career. **Pablo Picasso** was from Spain but settled in Paris in 1904. He painted in a remarkable variety of styles. He created a new style, called cubism, that used geometric designs to recreate reality in the viewer's mind. In his paintings, Picasso attempted to view human form from many sides. In this aspect he seems to have been influenced by the increasingly popular theory of relativity.

COOPERATIVE LEARNING ACTIVITY

Creating an Art Magazine Have students work together to produce a magazine displaying their literary and artistic accomplishments. Contributions must be in the style of one of the artistic movements of the period described in this section and may include drawings, poetry, songs, and so on. Some students should be responsible for assembling and organizing the materials by movement. Others may do interviews of the contributors or write articles evaluating the works. **L1**

For grading this activity, refer to the ***Performance Assessment Activities*** booklet.

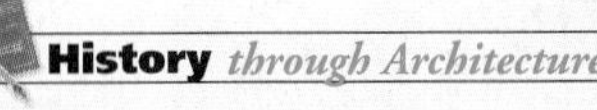

History *through Architecture*

***Fallingwater* by Frank Lloyd Wright, 1936** Why do you think this Pennsylvania house is a good example of modern architecture?

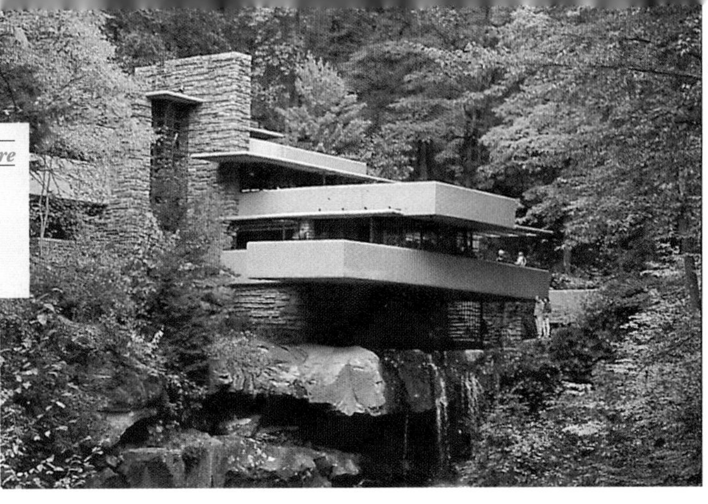

In 1910, abstract painting began. Wassily Kandinsky, a Russian who worked in Germany, was one of the founders of abstract expressionism. Kandinsky sought to avoid visual reality altogether. He believed that art should speak directly to the soul. To do so, it must use only line and color.

Architecture Modernism in the arts revolutionized architecture and gave rise to a new principle known as functionalism. Functionalism was the idea that buildings, like the products of machines, should be functional, or useful. They should fulfill the purpose for which they were built. All unnecessary ornamentation should be stripped away.

The United States was a leader in the new architecture. The country's rapid urban growth and lack of any architectural tradition allowed for new building methods. The Chicago School of the 1890s, led by Louis H. Sullivan, used reinforced concrete, steel frames, and electric elevators to build skyscrapers virtually free of external ornamentation.

One of Sullivan's most successful pupils was Frank Lloyd Wright. Wright's private houses, built chiefly for wealthy patrons, were geometric structures with long lines and overhanging roofs. Wright pioneered the modern American house.

Music At the beginning of the twentieth century, developments in music paralleled those in painting. The music of the Russian composer Igor Stravinsky was the first to reflect expressionist theories.

Stravinsky's ballet *The Rite of Spring* revolutionized music. When it was performed in Paris in 1913, the sounds and rhythms of the music and dance caused a near riot by an outraged audience.

Reading Check **Explaining** How did the Impressionists radically change the art of painting in the 1870s?

SECTION 4 ASSESSMENT

Checking for Understanding

1. **Define** psychoanalysis, pogrom, modernism.
2. **Identify** Marie Curie, Albert Einstein, Sigmund Freud, symbolists, Claude Monet, Pablo Picasso.
3. **Locate** Vienna, France.
4. **Explain** why photography caused some artists to reject realism.
5. **List** some of the modernist movements in art, music, and architecture and an individual associated with each of the movements.

Critical Thinking

6. **Analyze** Why are times of political and economic change often associated with times of artistic change?
7. **Organizing Information** Use a web diagram to summarize the problems the Jews faced during the time period discussed in this section.

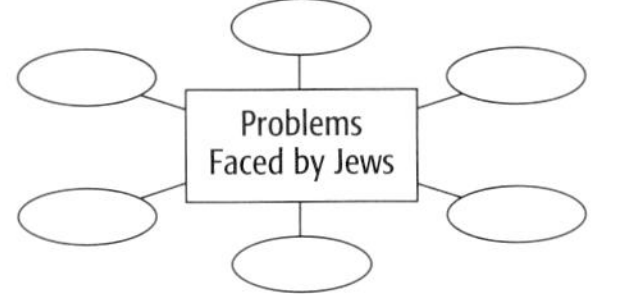

Analyzing Visuals

8. **Compare** the painting by van Gogh on page 422 to other paintings of night scenes in art history books. Pick one such painting and tell why you enjoy that painting either more or less than the van Gogh painting.

Writing About History

9. **Expository Writing** Research the symbolist writers. Who were they and what did they write about? Write a short biography about one of the symbolists who interests you. Include the titles of this symbolist's best-known works.

CHAPTER 13
Section 4, 418–423

History *through Architecture*

Answer: Answers will vary but might include that it is virtually free of external ornamentation or that it is a geometric structure with long lines and overhanging roofs.

Reading Check

Answer: They rejected the studios where artists had traditionally worked and went out into the countryside to paint nature directly.

Glencoe Literature Library

The following literature from the **Glencoe Literature Library** may enrich the teaching of this chapter: *The Metamorphosis* by F. Kafka

Reteaching Activity

Have students research the life of one of the artists of the period and write a brief biography, including information on education, training, major works, and public acceptance. **L1**

4 CLOSE

Have students write a brief paragraph explaining which artistic movement described in this section they find most visually pleasing and which they like least.

SECTION 4 ASSESSMENT

1. Key terms are in blue.
2. Marie Curie *(p. 419);* Albert Einstein *(p. 419);* Sigmund Freud *(p. 419);* symbolists *(p. 421);* Claude Monet *(p. 422);* Pablo Picasso *(p. 422)*
3. See chapter maps.
4. Artists had tried to represent reality as accurately as possible, but the camera could achieve this much more efficiently. Instead of mirroring reality, many artists turned to creating a reality of their own.
5. See pages 421–423.
6. Artists express their reactions to these changes in their art.
7. Problems Faced by Jews: ghettos, restriction of rights, persecution, pogroms, anti-Semitism
8. Answers will vary but should be supported by logical arguments.
9. Answers will vary depending on the symbolist chosen. Answers should demonstrate an understanding of symbolist themes.

GLENCOE TECHNOLOGY

MindJogger Videoquiz
Use the **MindJogger Videoquiz** to review Chapter 13 content.

 Available in VHS.

Using Key Terms
1. revisionists 2. bourgeoisie; proletariat 3. Feminism 4. ministerial responsibility 5. Duma 6. Psychoanalysis 7. modernism 8. Pogroms 9. dictatorship 10. literacy

Reviewing Key Facts
11. radio, light bulb, telephone
12. Karl Marx and Friedrich Engels
13. helped nurse soldiers during Crimean and Civil Wars, helped transform nursing into a profession of trained middle-class women
14. educated voters and instilled patriotism; gave people skills necessary to gain employment in the Second Industrial Revolution; created a demand for teachers, providing work for women; increased literacy; led to rise of mass newspapers
15. the Third Republic
16. workers called for strikes, forced Nicholas II to grant civil rights and create the Duma
17. because of labor unrest over unsafe working conditions and regular cycles of devastating unemployment
18. use of reinforced concrete, steel frames, electric elevators, skyscrapers
19. William II
20. Postimpressionist artist; believed art was a spiritual experience and artists should paint what they feel, interested in color and believed it could act as its own form of language
21. the right to vote
22. steel

CHAPTER 13 ASSESSMENT and ACTIVITIES

Using Key Terms
1. The _____ were Marxists who rejected the revolutionary approach of pure Marxists.
2. According to Marx, the middle-class oppressors were the _____, and the working-class oppressed were the _____.
3. _____ is the movement for gaining women's rights.
4. The principle by which a prime minister is directly answerable to a popularly elected representative body is _____.
5. The _____ is the Russian legislative assembly.
6. _____ is a method by which a therapist and a patient probe for repressed experiences.
7. A literary and artistic style that rejected traditional styles was called _____.
8. _____ were organized massacres of helpless people, such as the acts against the Jews.
9. A _____ is a government in which a person or group has absolute power.
10. The introduction of universal education in the late nineteenth century led to an increase in _____.

Reviewing Key Facts
11. **Science and Technology** List one invention each of Guglielmo Marconi, Thomas Edison, and Alexander Graham Bell.
12. **Government** Who wrote *The Communist Manifesto?*
13. **Culture** How did Florence Nightingale and Clara Barton transform nursing?
14. **Culture** What purposes were served by compulsory education?
15. **Government** What was the name given to France's government after the adoption of a new constitution in 1875?
16. **Government** What was the result of "Bloody Sunday" in St. Petersburg in 1905?
17. **Economics** Why did American workers organize unions?
18. **Culture** What did Louis H. Sullivan contribute to the field of architecture?
19. **Government** Who was the emperor of Germany at the end of the nineteenth century?
20. **Culture** Who was Vincent van Gogh and why was he important?
21. **Government** What basic right were women denied until World War I?
22. **Economics** By 1900, Russia had become the fourth largest producer of what product?

Critical Thinking
23. **Evaluating** Why was revisionist socialism more powerful in western Europe than in eastern Europe?
24. **Drawing Conclusions** Was the Revolution of 1905 in Russia a success or a failure? Why?
25. **Summarizing** Identify changes that resulted from the Second Industrial Revolution.

Chapter Summary
Innovations in technology and production methods created great economic, political, social, and cultural changes between 1870 and 1914, as shown in the chart below. The development of a mass society led to labor reforms and the extension of voting rights. New scientific theories radically changed people's vision of the world. Change also brought conflict as tensions increased in Europe and new alliances were formed.

Economics	Politics	Society	Culture	Conflict
• Industrial growth and the development of new energy resources lead to increased production of consumer goods.	• Growth of mass politics leads to the development of new political parties. • Labor leaders use ideas of socialism and Marxism to form unions.	• Women fight for equal rights. • Society adopts middle-class values. • Unions fight for labor reforms. • Mass leisure develops.	• Many artists reject traditional styles and develop new art movements. • New scientific ideas radically change people's perception of the world.	• Nationalism and imperialism create conflict in the Balkans and eventually lead to World War I. • Growth of nationalism leads to increased anti-Semitism.

Critical Thinking
23. Revisionists believed that workers could achieve their aims by working within democratic systems, and western European countries tended to have democratic systems while eastern European countries tended to have autocratic systems.
24. Answers will vary. It was a success in that it led to reforms and the creation of the Duma. Ultimately, it was a failure; the reforms were short-lived and the czar soon curtailed the power of the Duma.
25. Answers will vary. Changes are summarized at the bottom of this page.

Writing about History
26. Answers will vary. Newton believed the universe was like a machine in which time, space, and matter existed independently, while Einstein believed time and space are relative to the observer and not independent. Newton's universe was one of certainty, in which natural laws could explain anything, while

Have students visit the Web site at wh.mt.glencoe.com to review Chapter 13 and take the Self-Check Quiz.

Analyzing Maps and Charts

32. Autocratic government has no public involvement in political decision-making while democratic government has public involvement in political decision-making.

33. Both have some amount of public involvement in government, but a republic has more public involvement than a constitutional monarchy.

34. Switzerland; the city-states of classical Greece and the Roman Republic

Standardized Test Practice

Answer: F
Question Type: cause and effect
Answer Explanation: The shift in power as the Ottoman Empire waned is the only one of the options given that would facilitate the emergence of different factions in the Balkan Peninsula.

Bonus Question ?

Ask: How have biological arguments been used to defend racism? *(Many people who have held racist views justified them in terms of creating what they believed would be a racially superior society.)*

HISTORY Online

Self-Check Quiz
Visit the *Glencoe World History—Modern Times* Web site at wh.mt.glencoe.com and click on **Chapter 13–Self-Check Quiz** to prepare for the Chapter Test.

Forms of Government, 1900

Dictatorship or Absolute Monarchy	**Authoritarian State***	Constitutional Monarchy	Republic	**Direct Democracy**
Ottoman Empire, Russia	Austria-Hungary, Germany	Italy, Great Britain	United States, France	Switzerland

Autocracy — Rule by one — *auto* (self) + *kratos* (might) — *No public involvement in political decision making*

Democracy — Rule by the people — *demos* (people) + *kratos* (might) — *Direct public involvement in political decision making*

*Austria-Hungary and Germany had parliaments chosen by the people.

Writing About History

26. Expository Writing Compare and contrast Einstein's and Newton's understandings of the universe. Explain how they differ and how they are related.

Analyzing Sources

Read the following quote from a regular visitor to an upper-class seaside resort.

> "They swarm upon the beach, wandering about with apparently no other aim than to get a mouthful of fresh air. You may see them in groups of three or four—the husband, a pale man, dressed in black coat, carries the baby; the wife, equally pale and thin, decked out in her best, labors after with a basket of food. And then there is generally another child . . . wandering behind."

27. What can you infer about the husband and the wife from the way in which they are described?

28. In what way do the ideas expressed in this quote reflect the class-consciousness of this time period?

Applying Technology Skills

29. Using the Internet Use the Internet to find examples of paintings by Monet and Picasso. Carefully examine the paintings, then describe their main differences and similarities. Some features to look for include each artist's subject matter, use of color, and method of painting.

Making Decisions

30. Assume the role of a working-class laborer at a newly unionized factory. What demands would you present to management? Do these demands cover everything that is wrong with the factory? If not, how did you decide what to present?

31. Reread the information in your text and do further research on similarities and differences among the British Conservative, Liberal, and Labour parties of 1914. Decide which of these three parties you would belong to if you lived in England at that time. Explain your choice of parties.

Analyzing Maps and Charts

Use the chart above to answer the following questions.

32. According to the chart, what is the major difference between an autocratic and a democratic form of government?

33. How are a constitutional monarchy and a republic similar? How do they differ?

34. Where was direct democracy practiced in 1900? Which earlier civilizations also practiced direct democracy?

Standardized Test Practice

Directions: Choose the best answer to the following question.

The emergence of different factions in the Balkan Peninsula at the end of the nineteenth century was a result of

F shifting power as the Ottoman Empire waned.
G Serbia's dominance of the region.
H America's victory in the Spanish-American War.
J Nicholas II of Russia's repressive regime.

Test-Taking Tip: This question asks you for a *cause*. Because causes always happen before effects, think about which answer choices happened *before* the disintegration of the Balkan Peninsula.

Einstein's universe was one without certainty. Both Newton and Einstein put forth theories of the universe that were revolutionary, completely changing the way people viewed the world around them.

Analyzing Sources

27. that they are a working-class couple from a city

28. It is apparent that the writer feels disdain for the people he is writing about, that he feels that they are very much beneath him socially.

Applying Technology Skills

29. Answers will vary. Students should list the paintings they used for their comparisons.

Making Decisions

30. Answers will vary but should be consistent with material presented in this chapter.

31. Answers will vary but should be supported by logical arguments.

Chapter 14 Resources

Timesaving Tools

TeacherWorks™ All-In-One Planner and Resource Center

- **Interactive Teacher Edition** Access your Teacher Wraparound Edition and your classroom resources with a few easy clicks.
- **Interactive Lesson Planner** Planning has never been easier! Organize your week, month, semester, or year with all the lesson helps you need to make teaching creative, timely, and relevant.

Use Glencoe's **Presentation Plus!** multimedia teacher tool to easily present dynamic lessons that visually excite your students. Using Microsoft PowerPoint® you can customize the presentations to create your own personalized lessons.

Teaching Transparencies

Graphic Organizer Student Activity 14 Transparency

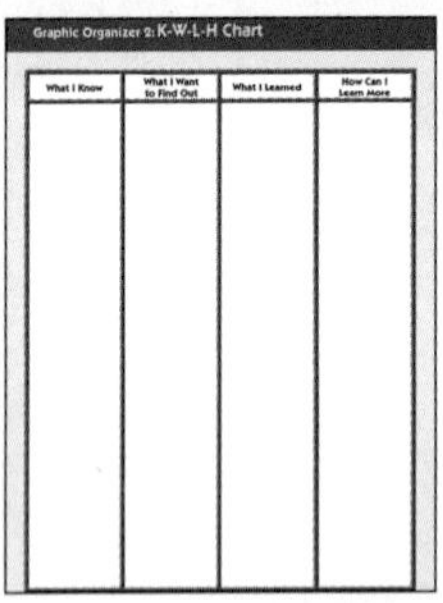

Chapter Transparency 14

Map Overlay Transparency 14

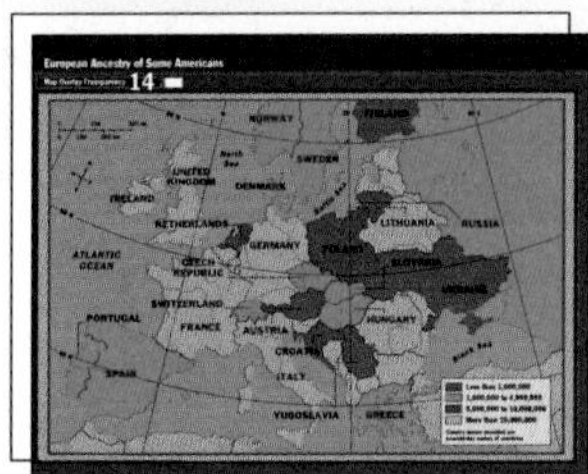

Application and Enrichment

Enrichment Activity 14

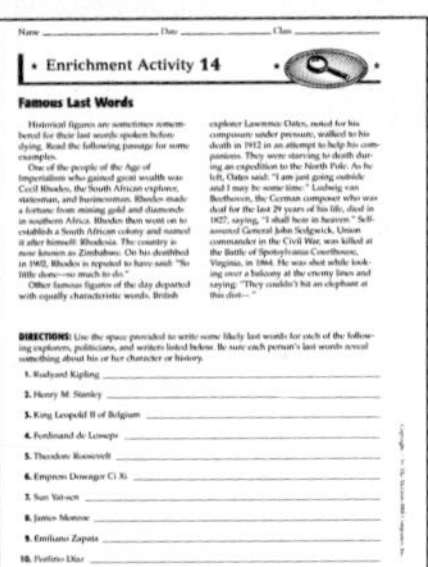

Primary Source Reading 14

History Simulation Activity 14

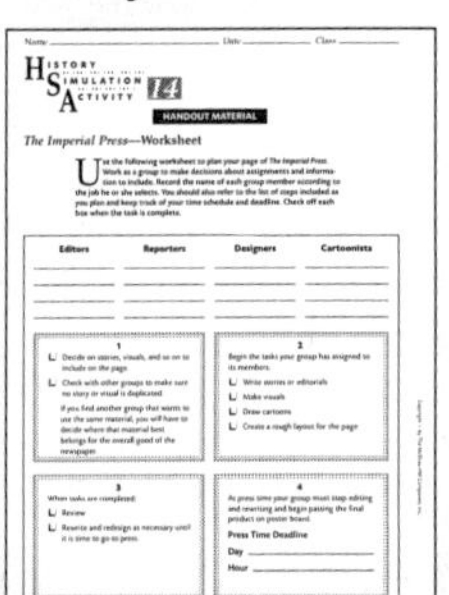

Historical Significance Activity 14

Cooperative Learning Activity 14

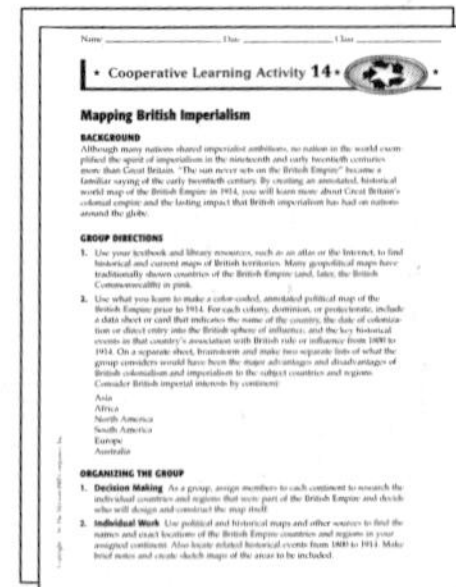

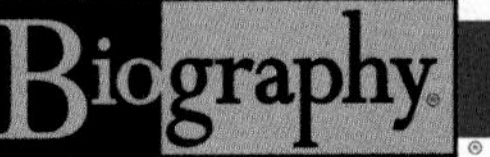

THE HISTORY CHANNEL.

The following videotape program is available from Glencoe as a supplement to Chapter 14:

- **Mahatma Gandhi: Pilgrim of Peace** (ISBN 0–7670–0668–2)

To order, call Glencoe at 1–800–334–7344. To find classroom resources to accompany this video, check the following home pages:
A&E Television: www.aande.com
The History Channel: www.historychannel.com

Chapter 14 Resources

Review and Reinforcement

Linking Past and Present Activity 14

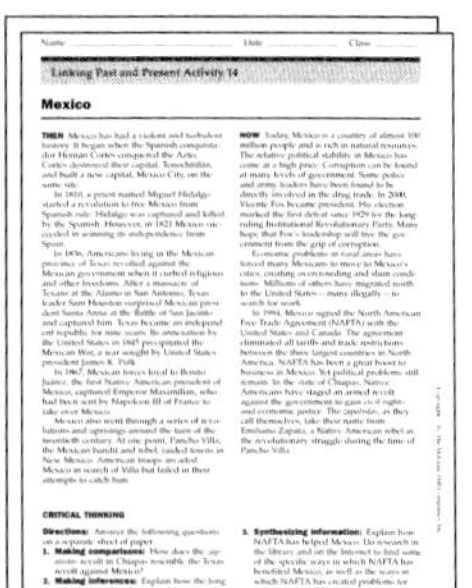

Time Line Activity 14

Reteaching Activity 14

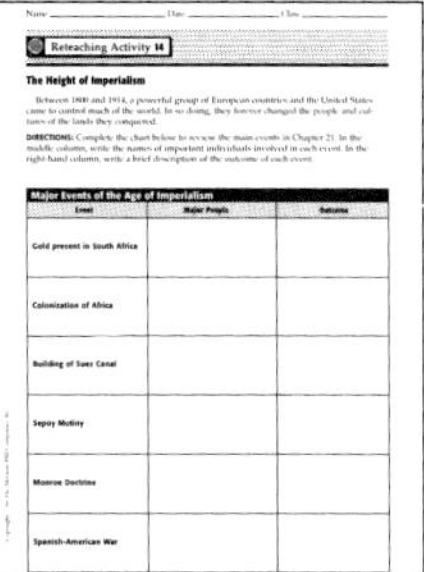

Vocabulary Activity 14

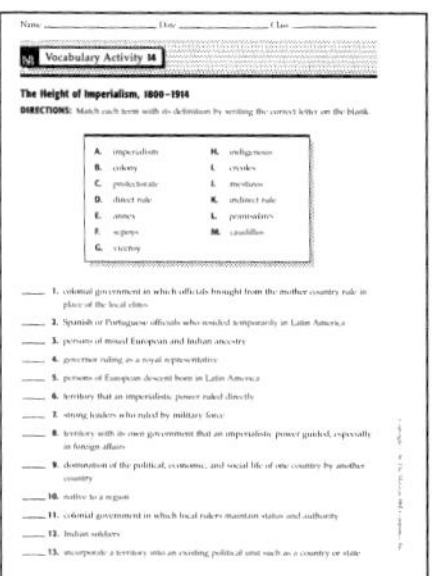

Critical Thinking Skills Activity 14

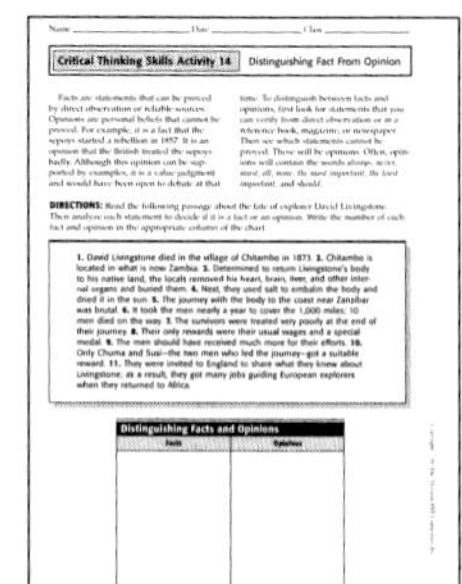

Assessment and Evaluation

Chapter 14 Test Form A

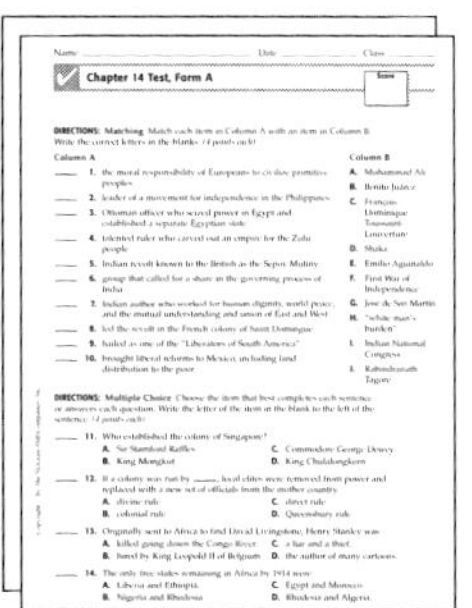

Chapter 14 Test Form B

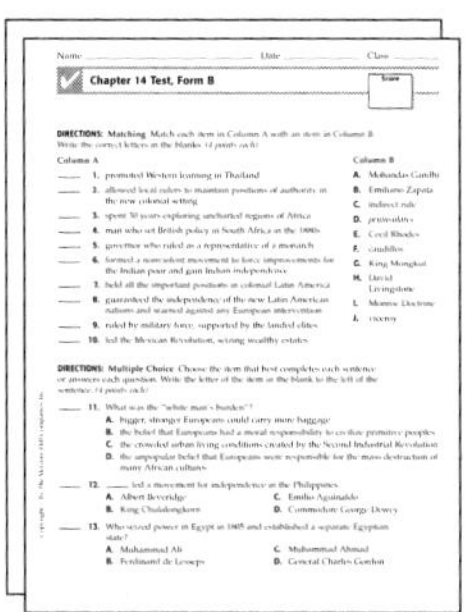

Performance Assessment Activity 14

ExamView® Pro Testmaker CD-ROM

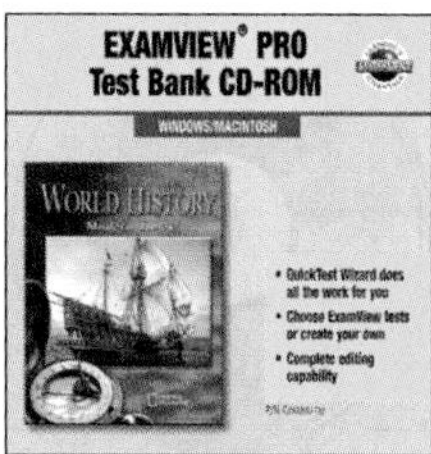

Standardized Test Skills Practice Workbook Activity 14

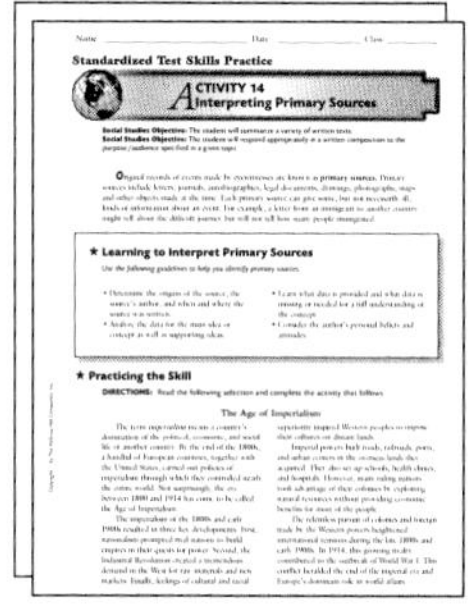

Interdisciplinary Activities

Mapping History Activity 14

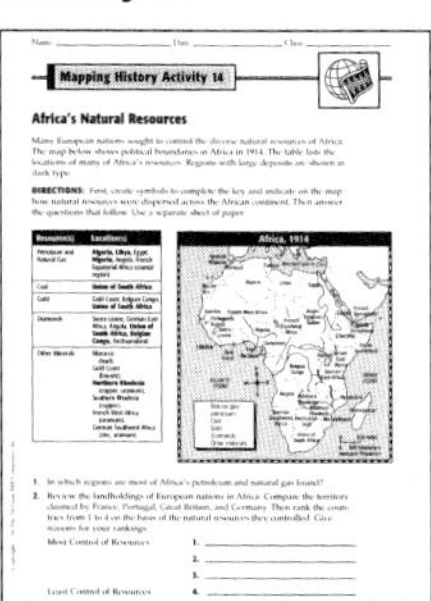

World Art and Music Activity 14

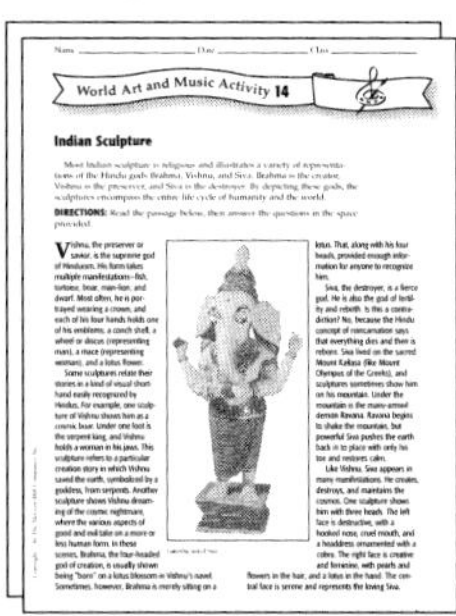

History and Geography Activity 14

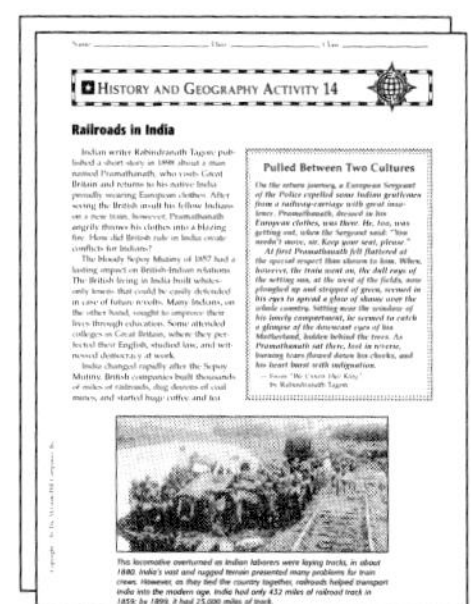

People in World History Activity 14

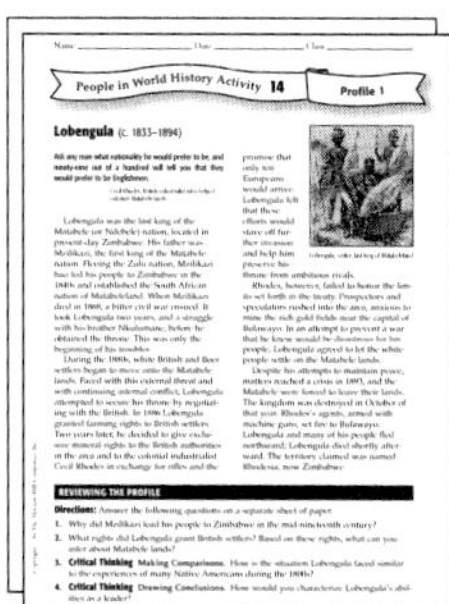

Multimedia

- Vocabulary PuzzleMaker CD-ROM
- Interactive Tutor Self-Assessment CD-ROM
- ExamView® Pro Testmaker CD-ROM
- Audio Program
- World History Primary Source Document Library CD-ROM
- MindJogger Videoquiz
- Presentation Plus! CD-ROM
- TeacherWorks CD-ROM
- Interactive Student Edition CD-ROM
- The World History—Modern Times Video Program

Spanish Resources

The following Spanish language materials are available in the Spanish Resources Binder:

- Spanish Guided Reading Activities
- Spanish Reteaching Activities
- Spanish Quizzes and Tests
- Spanish Vocabulary Activities
- Spanish Summaries

Chapter 14 Resources

SECTION RESOURCES

Daily Objectives	Reproducible Resources	Multimedia Resources
SECTION 1 **Colonial Rule in Southeast Asia** 1. Explain how, through the "new imperialism," Westerners sought to control vast territories. 2. Describe how colonial export policies exploited native populations and opened up markets for European manufactured goods.	Reproducible Lesson Plan 14–1 Daily Lecture and Discussion Notes 14–1 Guided Reading Activity 14–1* Section Quiz 14–1* Reading Essentials and Study Guide 14–1	Daily Focus Skills Transparency 14–1 Interactive Tutor Self-Assessment CD-ROM ExamView® Pro Testmaker CD-ROM Presentation Plus! CD-ROM
SECTION 2 **Empire Building in Africa** 1. Discuss how Great Britain, France, Germany, Belgium, and Portugal placed virtually all of Africa under European rule. 2. Report how native peoples sought an end to colonial rule.	Reproducible Lesson Plan 14–2 Daily Lecture and Discussion Notes 14–2 Guided Reading Activity 14–2* Section Quiz 14–2* Reading Essentials and Study Guide 14–2	Daily Focus Skills Transparency 14–2 Interactive Tutor Self-Assessment CD-ROM ExamView® Pro Testmaker CD-ROM Presentation Plus! CD-ROM
SECTION 3 **British Rule in India** 1. Discuss how British rule brought stability to India but destroyed native industries and degraded Indians. 2. Identify Mohandas Gandhi, who advocated nonviolent resistance to gain Indian independence from Great Britain.	Reproducible Lesson Plan 14–3 Daily Lecture and Discussion Notes 14–3 Guided Reading Activity 14–3* Section Quiz 14–3* Reading Essentials and Study Guide 14–3	Daily Focus Skills Transparency 14–3 Interactive Tutor Self-Assessment CD-ROM ExamView® Pro Testmaker CD-ROM Presentation Plus! CD-ROM
SECTION 4 **Nation Building in Latin America** 1. Explain how Latin American countries served as a source of raw materials for Europe and the United States. 2. Explain that because land remained the basis of wealth and power, landed elites dominated Latin American countries.	Reproducible Lesson Plan 14–4 Daily Lecture and Discussion Notes 14–4 Guided Reading Activity 14–4* Section Quiz 14–4* Reteaching Activity 14* Reading Essentials and Study Guide 14–4	Daily Focus Skills Transparency 14–4 Interactive Tutor Self-Assessment CD-ROM ExamView® Pro Testmaker CD-ROM Presentation Plus! CD-ROM

0:00 **OUT OF TIME?**
Assign the Chapter 14 **Reading Essentials and Study Guide.**

*Also Available in Spanish

 Blackline Master  Transparency  CD-ROM DVD
  Poster 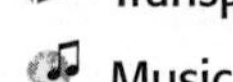  Music Program  Audio Program  Videocassette

NATIONAL GEOGRAPHIC Teacher's Corner

INDEX TO NATIONAL GEOGRAPHIC MAGAZINE

The following articles relate to this chapter:

- "El Libertador: Simon Bolivar," by Bryan Hodgson, March 1994.
- "Malaysia," by T.R. Reid, August 1997.
- "India," by Geoffrey C. Ward, May 1997.
- "Burma, the Richest of Poor Countries," by Joel L. Swerdlow, July 1995.

NGS ONLINE

Access National Geographic's new dynamic MapMachine Web site and other geography resources at:

www.nationalgeographic.com
www.nationalgeographic.com/maps

KEY TO ABILITY LEVELS

Teaching strategies have been coded.

L1 BASIC activities for all students
L2 AVERAGE activities for average to above-average students
L3 CHALLENGING activities for above-average students
ELL ENGLISH LANGUAGE LEARNER activities

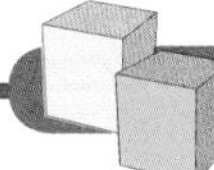

Block Schedule

Activities that are suited to use within the block scheduling framework are identified by:

WORLD HISTORY Online

Use our Web site for additional resources. All essential content is covered in the Student Edition.

You and your students can visit www.wh.mt.glencoe.com, the Web site companion to *Glencoe World History—Modern Times.* This innovative integration of electronic and print media offers your students a wealth of opportunities. The student text directs students to the Web site for the following options:

- **Chapter Overviews**
- **Self-Check Quizzes**
- **Student Web Activities**
- **Textbook Updates**

Answers to the Student Web Activities are provided for you in the **Web Activity Lesson Plans.** Additional Web resources and Interactive Tutor Puzzles are also available.

From the Classroom of...

Anna Mae Grimm
Homestead High School
Mequon, Wisconsin

Experiencing Apartheid

One of the legacies of European settlement in Africa was the separation of races, called apartheid, enacted in South Africa in 1948. For one class period, designate about half the students to be part of an "underclass" that will not be allowed to participate in activities with the rest of the class. Have the "underclass" sit at the back of the room. Provide an interesting activity for the rest of the class, and assign the separated students routine worksheets. Hold an election during the class period (for example, elect a discussion leader) and exclude the separated students from voting.

During the next class period, discuss how students felt during the simulation—both those in the "underclass" and those in the mainstream. Use this as a springboard for discussing apartheid in South Africa.

Introducing CHAPTER 14

Performance Assessment

Refer to Activity 14 in the Performance Assessment Activities and Rubrics booklet.

The Impact Today

Few nations retain colonies, but problems that arose from colonialism are still visible, especially in Africa and Latin America. Discuss these problems, and possible solutions, with students. Help students to locate remnants of imperialism that exist around the world today.

GLENCOE TECHNOLOGY

The World History—Modern Times Video Program

To learn more about nineteenth-century imperialism, students can view the Chapter 14 video, "Imperialism," from **The World History—Modern Times Video Program.**

MindJogger Videoquiz

Use the **MindJogger Videoquiz** to preview Chapter 14 content.

Available in VHS.

CHAPTER 14 The Height of Imperialism

1800–1914

Key Events

As you read this chapter, look for the key events in the history of imperialism.

- *Competition among European nations led to the partition of Africa.*
- *Colonial rule created a new social class of westernized intellectuals.*
- *British rule brought order and stability to India, but with its own set of costs.*
- *As a colonial power, the United States practiced many of the same imperialist policies as European nations.*

The Impact Today

The events that occurred during this time period still impact our lives today.

- *Rhodesia became the nation of Zimbabwe.*
- *India adopted a parliamentary form of government like that of Great Britain.*
- *The United States gave up rights to the Panama Canal Zone on December 31, 1999.*

World History—Modern Times Video *The Chapter 14 video, "Imperialism," chronicles imperialism on three continents.*

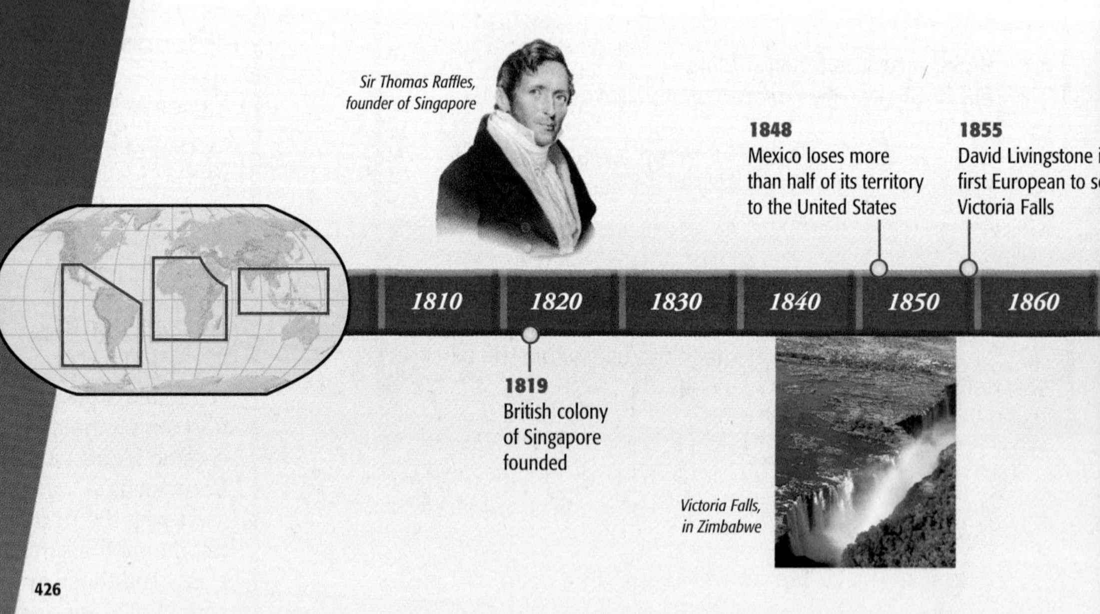

Sir Thomas Raffles, founder of Singapore
1848
Mexico loses more than half of its territory to the United States
1855
David Livingstone is first European to see Victoria Falls
1810
1820
1830
1840
1850
1860
1819
British colony of Singapore founded
Victoria Falls, in Zimbabwe

426

TWO-MINUTE LESSON LAUNCHER

Ask students to speculate about how the spread of empires might have affected peoples in Asia, Africa, and Latin America. **Ask:** **How did colonial peoples respond to Western rule?** *(Colonized people were introduced to Western traditions and technologies–sometimes against their will. Often, they were also led to reject native customs and beliefs. Imperialists exploited laborers and sometimes split up families and villages. Western rule inspired nationalist movements that led to independence.)* **L1**

British family celebrating Christmas in India, c. 1900

Zulus meet the British.

	1879 Zulu king meets with British ambassadors		**1896** Britain and France agree to maintain Thailand as a buffer state	**1900** Virtually all of Southeast Asia is under European rule	
1870	*1880*	*1890*	*1900*	*1910*	*1920*
1880 "New imperialism" begins	**1884** France makes the Vietnam Empire a protectorate		**1898** The United States defeats Spain for control over the Philippines	**1910** Emiliano Zapata leads peasant movement in Mexico	

Emiliano Zapata

HISTORY Online

Chapter Overview

Visit the *Glencoe World History—Modern Times* Web site at wh.mt.glencoe.com and click on **Chapter 14–Chapter Overview** to preview chapter information.

427

Introducing CHAPTER 14

Chapter Objectives

After studying this chapter, students should be able to:

1. describe how colonial powers took over and ruled other territories;
2. discuss how Western nations imposed their values and institutions;
3. describe how nationalism gave subjects means for seeking their freedom;
4. describe how colonies provided raw materials and new markets for industrialized nations;
5. describe the social divisions in the colonies between the colonizers and those who were colonized.

Chapter Overview

Introduce students to chapter content and key terms by having them access **Chapter Overview 14** at wh.mt.glencoe.com.

Time Line Activity

Have students select a region noted on the time line and write a brief description of the impact of imperialism on native peoples in that region. **L1**

MORE ABOUT THE ART

Colonial Families The view above of an English family enjoying an afternoon together portrays just a few of the large number of servants assigned to British families during colonial times. Prosperous families had at least 25 servants, and even a single man had a minimum of a dozen. In this illustration, a very small child is seen in the care of an Indian nurse. It was the custom to send European children who were over the ages of eight or ten to boarding schools in England where they could start to prepare for a successful career. Because older children were often at school and husbands were frequently away on official business, family times such as the one depicted were infrequent in British colonies.

CHAPTER PREVIEW

Introducing

A Story That Matters

Depending on the ability levels of your students, select from the following questions to reinforce the reading of *A Story That Matters.*

- How did David Livingstone's description of Africa differ from people's perception of the region? *(People thought Africa was barren, hot, dry, windy, and full of dangerous creatures. Livingstone found a bountiful region of fruit trees and rivers.)*
- How did David Livingstone say Great Britain could bring "civilization" to Africa? *(through Christianity and commerce)* **L1**

About the Art

The large illustration shows the Livingstone expedition in Africa. Ask students if they feel this is a highly romantic view or a realistic view of expeditions in Africa during this time. Why might illustrations such as this have been produced, and who would have been their intended audience? Students will learn more about Livingstone in the *National Geographic* feature that begins on page 444.

CHAPTER PREVIEW

A Story That Matters

David Livingstone

Livingstone expedition in Africa, c. 1855

Livingstone in Africa

In 1841, the Scottish doctor and missionary David Livingstone began a series of journeys that took him through much of central and southern Africa. Livingstone was a gentle man whose goal was to find locations for Christian missions on behalf of the London Missionary Society. He took great delight in working with the African people.

Livingstone's travels were not easy. Much of his journey was done by foot, canoe, or mule. He suffered at times from rheumatic fever, dysentery, and malaria. He survived an attack by armed warriors and a mutiny by his own servants.

Back in Great Britain, his exploits made Livingstone a national hero. His book *Missionary Travels and Researches in South Africa* was a best-seller. People jammed into lecture halls to hear him speak of the beauty of Africa. As the *London Journal* reported, "Europe had always heard that the central regions of southern Africa were bleak and barren, heated by poisonous winds, infested by snakes . . . [but Livingstone spoke of] a high country, full of fruit trees, abounding in shade, watered by a perfect network of rivers."

Livingstone tried to persuade his listeners that Britain needed to send both missionaries and merchants to Africa. Combining Christianity and commerce, he said, would achieve civilization for Africa.

Why It Matters

During the nineteenth and early twentieth centuries, Western colonialism spread throughout the non-Western world. Great Britain, Spain, Holland, France, Germany, Russia, and the United States competed for markets and raw materials for their expanding economies. By the end of the nineteenth century, virtually all of the peoples of Asia and Africa were under colonial rule. Although Latin America successfully resisted European control, it remained economically dependent on Europe and the United States.

History and You Territorial and trade dominance are among the primary goals of imperialist nations. Create a map of either Asia or Africa to help you understand how the various imperialists viewed those regions. Code the territories according to exports or European dominance.

HISTORY AND YOU

Emphasize with students that the "new imperialism" of the nineteenth century was based on the idea of the right and duty of Western nations to impose their values and institutions on subject peoples. Imperialism tended to create severe social divisions in the colonies between imperial rulers and subjects, who were often treated as social inferiors. Even the education of native peoples often meant the education of native elites in the languages and ideas of the colonial power in the hope that they would share the outlook of the colonial rulers. After colonies gained their independence, Western and native institutions continued to influence each other as states sought to reestablish their own identities and traditions. Ask students to speculate on their possible reponses to becoming subjects of an imperialistic regime.

SECTION 1 Colonial Rule in Southeast Asia

Guide to Reading

Main Ideas
- Through the "new imperialism," Westerners sought to control vast territories.
- Colonial export policies exploited native populations and opened up markets for European manufactured goods.

Key Terms
imperialism, protectorate, indirect rule, direct rule

People to Identify
King Mongkut, King Chulalongkorn, Commodore George Dewey, Emilio Aguinaldo

Places to Locate
Singapore, Burma, Thailand, Philippines

Preview Questions
1. Why were Westerners so determined to colonize Southeast Asia?
2. What was the chief goal of the Western nations?

Reading Strategy
Identifying Information Make a chart showing which countries controlled what parts of Southeast Asia.

Spain (until 1898)	
Holland	
United States (after 1898)	
France	
Great Britain	

Preview of Events

1850 · 1870 · 1890 · 1910 · 1930 · 1950

- **1896** France and Great Britain agree to maintain Thailand as a buffer state
- **1900** France calls new possessions Union of Indochina
- **1930** Saya San leads Burma uprising

Voices from the Past

Dutch plantation in Java, mid-1800s

In 1860, E. Douwes Dekker wrote a book on the Dutch colonial system on the island of Java. He said:

> "The [Dutch government] compels [the Javanese farmer] to cultivate certain products on his land; it punishes him if he sells what he has produced to any purchaser but itself; and it fixes the price actually paid. The expenses of transport to Europe through a privileged trading company are high; the money paid to the chiefs for encouragement increases the prime cost; and because the entire trade must produce profit, that profit cannot be got in any other way than by paying the Javanese just enough to keep him from starving, which would lessen the producing power of the nation."
>
> —***The World of Southeast Asia: Selected Historical Readings*, Harry J. Benda and John A. Larkin, eds., 1967**

Dekker, a Dutch colonial official, was critical of the havoc the Dutch had wreaked on the native peoples of Java.

The New Imperialism

In the nineteenth century, a new phase of Western expansion into Asia and Africa began. European nations began to view Asian and African societies as a source of industrial raw materials and a market for Western manufactured goods. No longer were Western gold and silver traded for cloves, pepper, tea,

1 FOCUS

Section Overview

This section describes the "new imperialism," the three colonial powers that established control of Southeast Asia, the differences between direct and indirect rule, the impact of colonialism on local economies and cultures, and the rise of nationalist movements in Southeast Asia.

BELLRINGER
Skillbuilder Activity

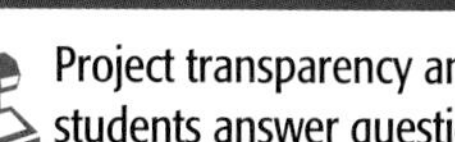

Project transparency and have students answer questions.

Available as a blackline master.

Daily Focus Skills Transparency 14–1

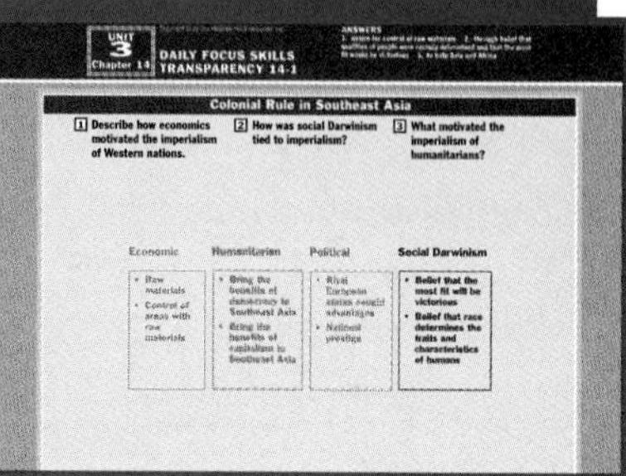

Guide to Reading

Answers to Graphic: Spain: Philippines; Holland: Dutch East Indies; United States: Philippines; France: Union of French Indochina; Great Britain: Singapore, Burma

Preteaching Vocabulary: Discuss how the word *imperialism* means the policy of extending central authority outside a nation's natural boundaries. **L1** ELL

SECTION RESOURCES

Reproducible Masters
- Reproducible Lesson Plan 14–1
- Daily Lecture and Discussion Notes 14–1
- Guided Reading Activity 14–1
- Section Quiz 14–1
- Reading Essentials and Study Guide 14–1

Transparencies
- Daily Focus Skills Transparency 14–1

Multimedia
- Interactive Tutor Self-Assessment CD-ROM
- ExamView® Pro Testmaker CD-ROM
- Presentation Plus! CD-ROM

CHAPTER 14
Section 1, 429–434

2 TEACH

Reading Check

Answer: (1) economic, (2) desire for political power, (3) sense of racial superiority (social Darwinism), (4) moral responsibility to civilize primitive people ("the white man's burden")

Chart *Skills*

Answers:

1. Sweden, Finland, Denmark, Switzerland, Austria-Hungary, Greece, Russia
2. Britain; because they had territories in every part of the world, so that it was always daylight somewhere in the British Empire

Daily Lecture and Discussion Notes 14–1

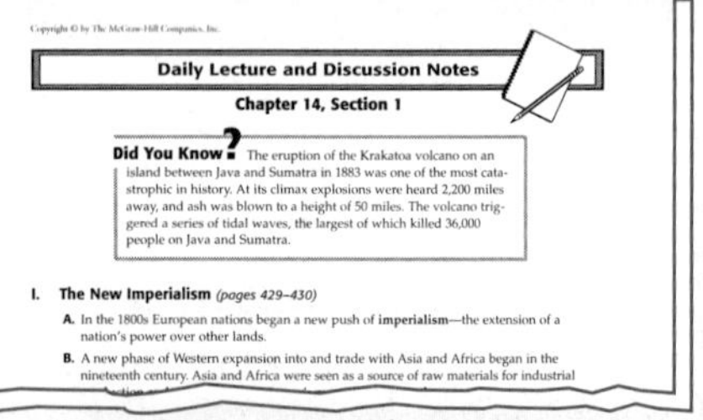

Daily Lecture and Discussion Notes

Chapter 14, Section 1

Did You Know? The eruption of the Krakatoa volcano on an island between Java and Sumatra in 1883 was one of the most catastrophic in history. At its climax explosions were heard 2,200 miles away, and ash was blown to a height of 50 miles. The volcano triggered a series of tidal waves, the largest of which killed 36,000 people on Java and Sumatra.

I. **The New Imperialism** *(pages 429–430)*

A. In the 1800s European nations began a new push of **imperialism**—the extension of a nation's power over other lands.

B. A new phase of Western expansion into and trade with Asia and Africa began in the nineteenth century. Asia and Africa were seen as a source of raw materials for industrial

Guided Reading Activity 14–1

Name ______ Date ______ Class ______

Guided Reading Activity 14-1

Colonial Rule in Southeast Asia

DIRECTIONS: Fill in the blanks below as you read Section 1.

1. Beginning in the 1880s, European states began an intense scramble for ______ territory.
2. ______ is the extension of a nation's power over other lands.
3. Through "new imperialism," European states sought nothing less than ______ over vast territories.
4. As European affairs grew tense, states sought to acquire colonies abroad to gain an ______ over rivals.
5. Some Europeans argued that they had a ______ responsibility to civilize primitive people.

and silk. Now the products of European factories were sent to Africa and Asia in return for oil, tin, rubber, and the other resources needed to fuel European industries.

Beginning in the 1880s, European states began an intense scramble for overseas territory. **Imperialism,** the extension of a nation's power over other lands, was not new. Europeans had set up colonies in North and South America and trading posts around Africa and the Indian Ocean by the sixteenth century.

However, the imperialism of the late nineteenth century, called the "new imperialism" by some, was different. Earlier, European states had been content, especially in Africa and Asia, to set up a few trading posts where they could carry on trade and perhaps some missionary activity. Now they sought nothing less than direct control over vast territories.

Why did Westerners begin to increase their search for colonies after 1880? There was a strong economic motive. Capitalist states in the West were looking for both markets and raw materials, such as rubber, oil, and tin, for their industries. Europeans also wanted more direct control of the areas with the raw materials and markets.

The issue was not simply an economic one, however. European nation-states were involved in heated rivalries. As European affairs grew tense, states sought to acquire colonies abroad in order to gain an advantage over their rivals.

Colonies were also a source of national prestige. To some people, in fact, a nation could not be great without colonies. One German historian wrote that "all great nations in the fullness of their strength have the desire to set their mark upon barbarian lands and those who fail to participate in this great rivalry will play a pitiable role in time to come."

In addition, imperialism was tied to social Darwinism and racism. Social Darwinists believed that in the struggle between nations, the fit are victorious. Racism is the belief that race determines traits and capabilities. Racists erroneously believe that particular races are superior or inferior. Racist beliefs have led to the use of military force against other nations. One British professor argued in 1900, "The path of progress is strewn with the wrecks of nations; traces are everywhere to be seen of the [slaughtered remains] of inferior races. Yet these dead people are, in very truth, the stepping stones on which mankind has arisen to the higher intellectual and deeper emotional life of today."

Some Europeans took a more religious and humanitarian approach to imperialism. They argued that Europeans had a moral responsibility to civilize primitive people. They called this responsibility the "white man's burden."

These people believed that the nations of the West should help the nations of Asia and Africa. To some, this meant bringing the Christian message to the "heathen masses." To others, it meant bringing the benefits of Western democracy and capitalism to these societies.

Reading Check **Describing** What were four primary motivations for the "new imperialism"?

Height of European Imperialism

	Southeast Asia	Africa	India
Britain	flag	flag	flag
Belgium		flag	
France	flag	flag	
Germany	flag	flag	
Italy		flag	
Netherlands	flag	flag	
Portugal	flag	flag	
Spain		flag	

Chart *Skills*

In the late 1800s a "new imperialism" flourished, with most of the major European countries attempting to take control of territories in Asia and Africa.

1. **Identifying** Look at a political map of Europe in Chapter 13. Which European countries did *not* try to colonize parts of Asia or Africa?
2. **Analyzing** It has been said about one of the countries identified in the chart that "the sun never sets" on this particular empire. To which country does this phrase refer? What do you think the phrase means?

CRITICAL THINKING ACTIVITY

Evaluating Social Darwinists seized on the theory of evolution, particularly the idea of the survival of the fittest, to justify racist attitudes toward non-Western people. According to this theory, it was the duty of the "superior" European nations to spread Western civilization to the "backward" countries. These theorists argued that the loss of culture and tradition was a natural consequence of social evolution. Ask students how social Darwinism would have been used by the African slave traders or the Spanish explorers. Does this theory justify their actions? Was it a justification for imperialism in the nineteenth century? Is it a valid argument for cultural prejudice today?

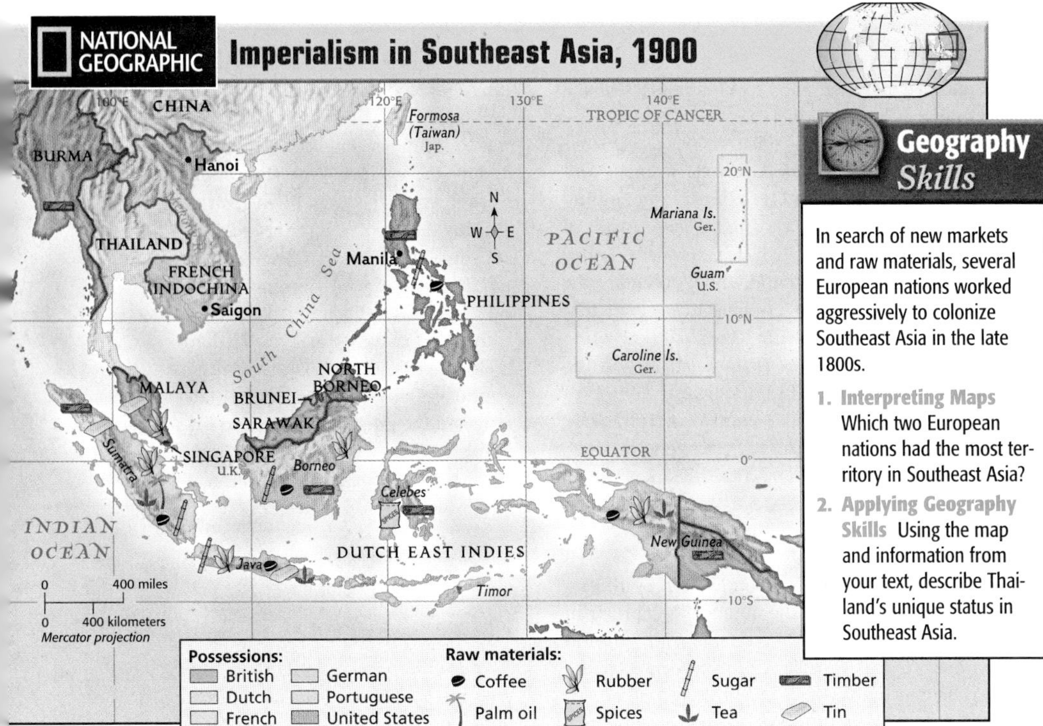

Geography Skills

In search of new markets and raw materials, several European nations worked aggressively to colonize Southeast Asia in the late 1800s.

1. **Interpreting Maps** Which two European nations had the most territory in Southeast Asia?
2. **Applying Geography Skills** Using the map and information from your text, describe Thailand's unique status in Southeast Asia.

Colonial Takeover in Southeast Asia

The new imperialism of the late nineteenth century was evident in Southeast Asia. In 1800, only two societies in this area were ruled by Europeans: the Spanish Philippines and the Dutch East Indies. By 1900, virtually the entire area was under Western rule.

Great Britain The process began with Great Britain. In 1819, Great Britain, under Sir Thomas Stamford Raffles, founded a new colony on a small island at the tip of the Malay Peninsula called **Singapore** ("city of the lion"). In the new age of steamships, Singapore soon became a major stopping point for traffic going to or from China. Raffles was proud of his new city and wrote to a friend in England, "Here all is life and activity; and it would be difficult to name a place on the face of the globe with brighter prospects."

During the next few decades, the British advance into Southeast Asia continued. Next to fall was the kingdom of **Burma** (modern Myanmar). Britain wanted control of Burma in order to protect its possessions in India. It also sought a land route through Burma into South China. Although the difficult terrain along the frontier between Burma and China caused this effort to fail, British activities in Burma led to the collapse of the Burmese monarchy. Britain soon established control over the entire country.

France The British advance into Burma was watched nervously by France, which had some missionaries operating in Vietnam. The French missionaries were persecuted by the local authorities, who viewed Christianity as a threat to Confucian doctrine. However, Vietnam failed to stop the Christian missionaries. Vietnamese internal rivalries divided the country into two separate governments, in the north and the south.

France was especially alarmed by British attempts to monopolize trade. To stop any British move into Vietnam, the French government decided in 1857 to force the Vietnamese to accept French protection.

The French eventually succeeded in making the Vietnamese ruler give up territories in the Mekong River delta. The French occupied the city of Saigon and, during the next 30 years, extended their control over the rest of the country. In 1884, France seized the city of Hanoi and made the Vietnamese Empire a French **protectorate**—a political unit that depends on another government for its protection.

Geography Skills

Answers:

1. The Netherlands (Dutch) and Great Britain
2. Thailand's independence was supported by both Britain and France to provide a buffer between French Indochina and British Burma.

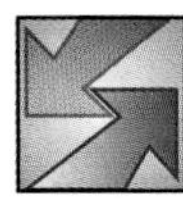

CURRICULUM CONNECTION

Sociology Ask students to research how the culture of a city or a country is modified when colonial powers dominate a region. For example, Singapore acquired many British traits, and the official language of Vietnam became French. L2

Enrich

In order to administer and control their new colonies, European governments encouraged citizens to move to the colonies with their families to run the economy and the government. Have students design an advertisement intended to induce people to relocate to the new territories. Remind them that many people were attracted to the economic opportunities and lavish lifestyle available in the new territories. L1 ELL

INTERDISCIPLINARY CONNECTIONS ACTIVITY

Geography Ask students to name the countries on the above map and to identify the colonizer and date of claim or control of each country. Ask students what they notice about the dates of colonization. *(Except for Malaya [1786], all countries were colonized before the early 1600s or after 1800.)* Ask students what feature of Vietnam might explain its having been divided several times in its history *(very long and narrow country with north and south connected by a narrow strip).* How long (north to south) is Vietnam? *(about 1,200 miles [1,931 km])* How wide (east to west) is it at its narrowest point? *(less than 50 miles [80 km])*

CHAPTER 14
Section 1, 429–434

Reading Check

Answer: Both were important in providing access to China. However, Britain's primary interest in Burma was to protect its possessions in India.

CURRICULUM CONNECTION

Speech Have one of your students read Senator Beveridge's speech as a politician might. What are the two reasons given in the speech for the United States to retain control over the Philippines? *(to provide access to markets in China and to spread civilization)* How would the senator feel about the "white man's burden"? *(He would accept it as valid.)* **L1**

Writing Activity

Have students write an essay identifying the causes and effects of imperialism. The essays should include an introduction; a paragraph each for political, economic, and social causes and effects; and a conclusion. **L1**

Critical Thinking

Ask students to describe the connection between the Industrial Revolution in Europe and the rise of imperialism in the nineteenth century. Then ask students to evaluate the impact of the Industrial Revolution on colonial societies. **L2**

In the 1880s, France extended protection over neighboring Cambodia, Annam, Tonkin, and Laos. By 1900, France included all of its new possessions in a new Union of French Indochina.

Thailand—The Exception After the French conquest of Indochina, **Thailand** was the only remaining free state in Southeast Asia. During the last quarter of the nineteenth century, British and French rivalry threatened to place Thailand, too, under colonial rule.

Two remarkable rulers were able to prevent that from happening. One was **King Mongkut** (known to theatergoers as the king in *The King and I*), and the other was his son **King Chulalongkorn.** Both promoted Western learning and maintained friendly relations with the major European powers. In 1896, Britain and France agreed to maintain Thailand as an independent buffer state between their possessions in Southeast Asia.

The United States One final conquest in Southeast Asia occurred at the end of the nineteenth century. In 1898, during the Spanish-American War, United States naval forces under **Commodore George Dewey** defeated the Spanish fleet in Manila Bay.

Believing it was his moral obligation to "civilize" other parts of the world, President William McKinley decided to turn the **Philippines,** which had been under Spanish control, into an American colony. This action would also prevent the area from falling into the hands of the Japanese. In fact, the islands gave the United States a convenient jumping-off point for trade with China.

This mixture of moral idealism and desire for profit was reflected in a speech given in the Senate in January 1900 by Senator Albert Beveridge of Indiana:

> "Mr. President, the times call for candor. The Philippines are ours forever. And just beyond the Philippines are China's unlimited markets. We will not retreat from either. We will not abandon an opportunity in [Asia]. We will not renounce our part in the mission of our race, trustee, under God, of the civilization of the world."

Scene from decisive Manila Bay battle

The Filipinos did not agree with the American senator. **Emilio Aguinaldo** (ah•gee•NAHL•doh) was the leader of a movement for independence in the Philippines. He began his revolt against the Spanish. When the United States acquired the Philippines, Aguinaldo continued the revolt and set himself up as the president of the Republic of the Philippines. Led by Aguinaldo, the guerrilla forces fought bitterly against the United States troops to establish their independence. However, the United States defeated the guerrilla forces, and President McKinley had his steppingstone to the rich markets of China.

Emilio Aguinaldo

Reading Check **Identifying** What spurred Britain to control Singapore and Burma?

Colonial Regimes in Southeast Asia

Western powers governed their new colonial empires by either indirect or direct rule. Their chief goals were to exploit the natural resources of these lands and open up markets for their own manufactured goods. To justify their actions, they often spoke of bringing the blessings of Western civilizations to their colonial subjects.

EXTENDING THE CONTENT

Filipinos As a result of anti-Chinese immigration laws in the United States in the early twentieth century, many sugar, pineapple, and other agricultural planters in Hawaii and California began to recruit cheap Filipino labor. Because the overwhelming proportion of Filipino immigrants were male, and because of racial prejudice, many states prohibited marriage or any other contact between Asian males and Caucasian females. In fact, Filipinos were not even eligible for U.S. citizenship until the late 1940s. Today more immigrants to the United States come from the Philippines than from any other Asian nation.

Indirect and Direct Rule Sometimes, a colonial power could realize its goals most easily through cooperation with local political elites. In these cases, **indirect rule** was used. Local rulers were allowed to maintain their positions of authority and status in a new colonial setting.

In Southeast Asia, colonial powers, wherever possible, tried to work with local elites. This made it easier to gain access to the region's natural resources. Indirect rule also lowered the cost of government, because fewer officials had to be trained. Moreover, indirect rule had less effect on local culture.

One example of indirect rule was in the Dutch East Indies. Officials of the Dutch East India Company allowed local landed aristocrats in the Dutch East Indies to control local government. These local elites maintained law and order and collected taxes in return for a payment from the Dutch East India Company.

Local peasants, shown here in Ceylon in the late 1800s, worked at poverty-level wages for foreign plantation owners during the colonial period.

Indirect rule, then, was convenient and cost less. Indirect rule was not always possible, however, especially when local elites resisted the foreign conquest. In such cases, the local elites were removed from power and replaced with a new set of officials brought from the mother country. This system is called **direct rule.**

In Burma, for example, the monarchy staunchly opposed colonial rule. As a result, Great Britain abolished the monarchy and administered the country directly through its colonial government in India.

In Indochina, France used both direct and indirect rule. It imposed direct rule on the southern provinces in the Mekong delta, which had been ceded to France as a colony after the first war in 1858 to 1860. The northern parts of Vietnam, seized in the 1880s, were governed as a protectorate. The emperor still ruled from his palace in Hue, but he had little power.

To justify their conquests, Western powers had spoken of bringing the blessings of advanced Western civilization to their colonial subjects. Many colonial powers, for example, spoke of introducing representative institutions and educating the native peoples in the democratic process. However, many Westerners came to fear the idea of native peoples (especially educated ones) being allowed political rights.

Colonial Economies The colonial powers did not want their colonists to develop their own industries. Thus, colonial policy stressed the export of raw materials—teak wood from Burma; rubber and tin from Malaya; spices, tea, coffee, and palm oil from the East Indies; and sugar from the Philippines. In many cases, this policy led to some form of plantation agriculture, in which peasants worked as wage laborers on plantations owned by foreign investors.

Plantation owners kept the wages of their workers at poverty levels in order to increase the owners' profits. Conditions on plantations were often so unhealthy that thousands died. In addition, high taxes levied by colonial governments to pay for their administrative costs were a heavy burden for peasants.

Nevertheless, colonial rule did bring some benefits to Southeast Asia. It led to the beginnings of a modern economic system. Colonial governments built railroads, highways, and other structures that could benefit native peoples as well as colonials. The development of an export market helped to create an entrepreneurial class in rural areas. In the Dutch East Indies, for example, small growers of rubber, palm oil, coffee, tea, and spices began to share in the profits of the colonial enterprise. Most of the profits, however, were taken back to the colonial mother country.

Reading Check **Explaining** Why did colonial powers prefer that colonists not develop their own industries?

Resistance to Colonial Rule

Many subject peoples in Southeast Asia were quite unhappy with being governed by Western powers. At first, resistance came from the existing ruling class. In Burma, for example, the monarch himself fought Western domination. By contrast, in Vietnam, after

INTERDISCIPLINARY CONNECTIONS ACTIVITY

Literature "The White Man's Burden" is the title of the Rudyard Kipling poem written in 1899. Ask student volunteers to find the poem and read it to the class. Arrange with a literature teacher to discuss other literature from this period that deals with imperialism or life in colonized countries. Possibilities include E.M. Forster's *A Passage to India,* a novel about life in India under British rule, or *Heart of Darkness* by Joseph Conrad, a story about one man's journey up the Congo River. Ask students to read excerpts from these novels and to prepare oral reports that summarize the works' themes and views on imperialism. L2

For grading this activity, refer to the ***Performance Assessment Activities*** booklet.

Reading Check

Answer: They wanted the colonies to provide a market for their own manufactured goods and to provide raw materials for those goods.

Writing Activity

Have students imagine the circumstances of a European colonist living in a new territory. Ask students to write a one-page letter home describing their new environment, lifestyle, and interactions with the indigenous peoples. L1

3 ASSESS

Assign Section 1 Assessment as homework or as an in-class activity.

Have students use **Interactive Tutor Self-Assessment CD-ROM.**

Section Quiz 14–1

Name ______ Date ______ Class ______

Chapter 14 Score

Section Quiz 14-1

DIRECTIONS: Matching Match each item in Column A with an item in Column B. Write the correct letters in the blanks. *(10 points each)*

Column A	Column B
____ 1. extension of a nation's power over other lands	A. direct rule
____ 2. governing by working with existing political elites	B. Singapore
____ 3. replacement of local rulers with officials from the mother country	C. imperialism
____ 4. political unit dependent on another for protection	D. protectorate
____ 5. "city of the lion"	E. indirect rule

DIRECTIONS: Multiple Choice In the blank, write the letter of the choice that best completes the statement or answers the question. *(10 points each)*

____ 6. The Spanish-American War resulted in
A. humiliating defeat for the U.S.
B. an important peace conference.
C. war with Thailand.
D. new territories for the U.S.

____ 7. All of the following came under French control EXCEPT for one. Which one?
A. Vietnam
B. Cambodia
C. Thailand
D. Laos

Critical Thinking

Have students look at the photo on page 434 and identify the means of restraint used on the prisoners *(stocks).* Why would the French have believed it acceptable to hold prisoners in such harsh, inhuman conditions? L1 ELL

Reading Check

Answer: (1) resistance from the ruling class to Western takeover; (2) peasant revolts, often as a result of being driven off their land to make way for plantation agriculture; (3) Westernized urban middle class began to demand independence

Reading Essentials and Study Guide 14–1

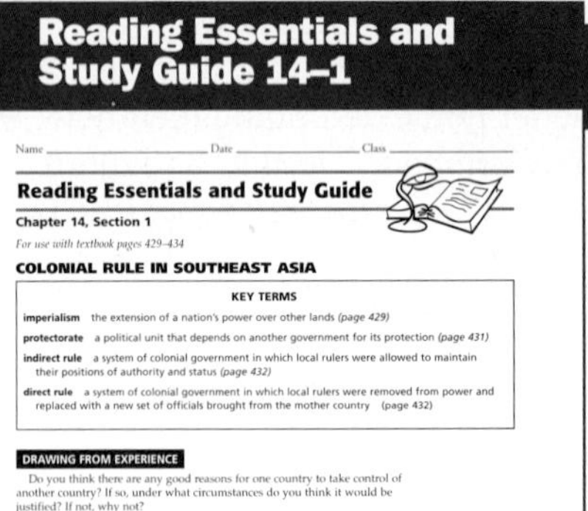

Name ______ Date ______ Class ______

Reading Essentials and Study Guide

Chapter 14, Section 1

For use with textbook pages 429–434

COLONIAL RULE IN SOUTHEAST ASIA

KEY TERMS

imperialism the extension of a nation's power over other lands *(page 429)*

protectorate a political unit that depends on another government for its protection *(page 431)*

indirect rule a system of colonial government in which local rulers were allowed to maintain their positions of authority and status *(page 432)*

direct rule a system of colonial government in which local rulers were removed from power and replaced with a new set of officials brought from the mother country (page 432)

DRAWING FROM EXPERIENCE

Do you think there are any good reasons for one country to take control of another country? If so, under what circumstances do you think it would be justified? If not, why not?

In this section, you will learn about the "new imperialism" of the late nine-

Reteaching Activity

Have students identify the historical figures mentioned in this section and explain the role each played in the conquest of Southeast Asia. **L1**

4 CLOSE

The economy for colonies was based on *unequal exchange.* Low-value raw materials were exported to Europe and high-cost manufactured goods were imported. Ask students to list the benefits and negative effects that resulted from this policy. *(Benefits: jobs, infrastructure development. Negative effects: low-paying jobs, destroying local crafts and industries, preventing growth of local economy, establishing a class system, creating dependence on Europe)* **L1**

In 1907, Vietnamese prisoners await trial for plotting against the French.

the emperor had agreed to French control of his country, a number of government officials set up an organization called Can Vuoug ("Save the King"). They fought against the French without the emperor's help.

Sometimes, resistance to Western control took the form of peasant revolts. Under colonial rule, peasants were often driven off the land to make way for plantation agriculture. Angry peasants then vented their anger at the foreign invaders. For example, in Burma, in 1930, the Buddhist monk Saya San led a peasant uprising against the British colonial regime many years after the regime had completed its takeover.

Early resistance movements failed, overcome by Western powers. At the beginning of the twentieth century, a new kind of resistance began to emerge that was based on the force of nationalism. The leaders were often a new class that had been created by colonial rule: westernized intellectuals in the cities.

In many cases, this new urban middle class—composed of merchants, clerks, students, and professionals—had been educated in Western-style schools. They were the first generation of Asians to understand the institutions and values of the West. Many spoke Western languages and worked in jobs connected with the colonial regimes.

At first, many of the leaders of these movements did not focus clearly on the idea of nationhood but simply tried to defend the economic interests or religious beliefs of the natives. In Burma, for example, the first expression of modern nationalism came from students at the University of Rangoon. They formed an organization to protest against official persecution of the Buddhist religion and British lack of respect for local religious traditions. They protested against British arrogance and failure to observe local customs in Buddhist temples. Not until the 1930s, however, did these resistance movements begin to demand national independence.

Reading Check **Summarizing** Explain three forms of resistance to Western domination.

SECTION 1 ASSESSMENT

Checking for Understanding

1. **Define** imperialism, protectorate, indirect rule, direct rule.
2. **Identify** King Mongkut, King Chulalongkorn, Commodore George Dewey, Emilio Aguinaldo.
3. **Locate** Singapore, Burma, Thailand, Philippines.
4. **Explain** how the "new imperialism" differed from old imperialism. Also explain how imperialism came to be associated with social Darwinism.
5. **List** some of the benefits colonial rule brought to Southeast Asia. Do you think these benefits outweighed the disadvantages? Why or why not?

Critical Thinking

6. **Making Inferences** Why were resistance movements often led by natives who had lived and been educated in the West? Initially, what were the goals of these resistance leaders? How did their goals change over time?
7. **Cause and Effect** In a diagram like the one below, identify the effects of colonial rule on the colonies.

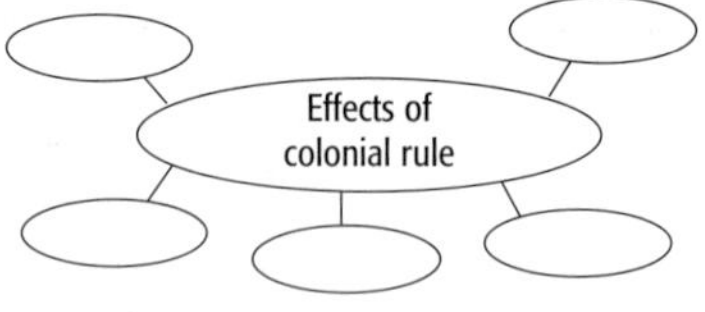

Analyzing Visuals

8. **Describe** the situation being endured by the Vietnamese prisoners in the photo above. Be specific in your description of their confinement. Based on your reading of the living conditions in Southeast Asian colonies at this time, do you think you would have risked this type of punishment if you had been in their position? Explain.

Writing About History

9. **Expository Writing** Use varied media to determine what the United States's relationship is today with the Philippines and how Filipino political groups view this relationship. Write an essay based on your findings.

SECTION 1 ASSESSMENT

1. Key terms are in blue.
2. King Mongut *(p. 432);* King Chulalongkorn *(p. 432);* Commodore George Dewey *(p. 432);* Emilio Aguinaldo *(p. 432)*
3. See chapter maps.
4. old: European states set up a few trading posts; new: European states wanted direct control of colonial raw materials and markets; in the struggle between nations, the fit—Western imperialists—are victorious
5. built railroads, highways, and other structures, created an entrepreneurial class; answers will vary
6. understood Western institutions; defend peoples; independence
7. introduced representative institutions; developed plantation agriculture; high taxes; began modern economic system; built railroads, highways; developed export market; resistance movements
8. Answers will vary.
9. Students will write an essay.

Eyewitness to History

A Call to Arms

IN 1862, THE VIETNAMESE emperor granted three provinces in southern Vietnam to the French. In outrage, many patriotic Vietnamese military officers and government officials appealed to their fellow Vietnamese to rise up and resist the foreigners. The following lines were written in 1864.

French troops battle Vietnamese resistance fighters.

❝This is a general proclamation addressed to the scholars and the people. . . .
Our people are now suffering through a period of anarchy and disorder. . . .
Let us now consider our situation with the French today.
We are separated from them by thousands of mountains and seas.
By hundreds of differences in our daily customs.
Although they were very confident in their copper battleships surmounted by chimneys,
Although they had a large quantity of steel rifles and lead bullets,
These things did not prevent the loss of some of their best generals in these last years, when they attacked our frontier in hundreds of battles. . . .
You, officials of the country,
Do not let your resistance to the enemy be blunted by the peaceful stand of the court,
Do not take the lead from the three subjected provinces and leave hatred unavenged.
So many years of labor, of energy, of suffering–shall we now abandon all?
Rather, we should go to the far ends of jungles or to the high peaks of mountains in search of heroes.
Rather, we should go to the shores of the sea in search of talented men.
Do not envy the scholars who now become provincial or district magistrates [in the French administration]. They are decay, garbage, filth, swine.
Do not imitate some who hire themselves out to the enemy. They are idiots, fools, lackeys, scoundrels.❞

—An Appeal to Vietnamese Citizens to Resist the French

Analyzing Primary Sources

1. What do the writers of the quoted lines want their fellow Vietnamese to do?
2. What are the writer's feelings toward those who worked with the French administration? How can you tell?

TEACH

Analyzing Primary Sources

Although students may not recognize it as such, this selection may be classified as propaganda—information that is presented with the purpose of persuading people to accept or believe a particular point of view. Ask students to identify some particularly emotional passage from the writing. Then ask students to create a list of questions that might be used as a guide to determine whether a piece of writing is propaganda. Ask students to bring in an article, speech, or pamphlet that they consider to be propaganda and to explain why. **L2**

Critical Thinking

This image depicts a battle scene from the French invasion of Southeast Asia. Ask students to decide whether they perceive a bias toward one side or the other in the representation. *(Students may note that the Vietnamese forces appear to be in disarray and in retreat while the French are fighting in a well-organized formation.)* **L1**

ANSWERS TO ANALYZING PRIMARY SOURCES

1. The writers want their fellow Vietnamese to resist the French.
2. The writer despises those who collaborated with the French. His language reveals his feelings toward the collaborators. In his proclamation, the author says that the collaborators are "decay, garbage, filth, swine" and "idiots, fools, lackeys, scoundrels."

1 FOCUS

Section Overview

This section describes the effects imperialism had on the continent of Africa.

BELLRINGER
Skillbuilder Activity

 Project transparency and have students answer questions.

 Available as a blackline master.

Daily Focus Skills Transparency 14–2

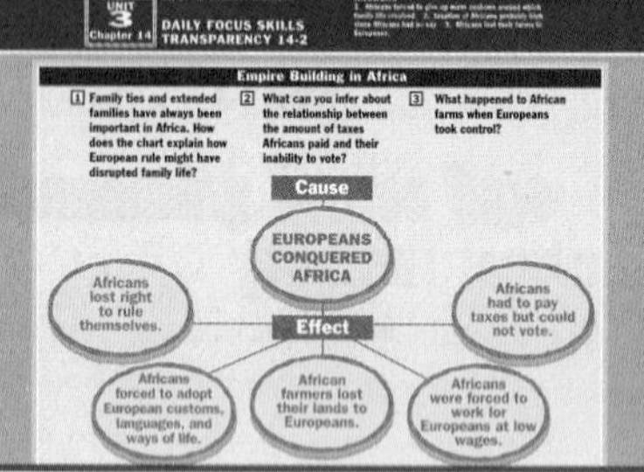

Guide to Reading

Answers to Graphic: West Africa: Great Britain, France; North Africa (including Egypt): France, Great Britain, Italy; Central Africa: Belgium, France; East Africa: Great Britain, Portugal, Germany, Belgium; South Africa: Great Britain

Preteaching Vocabulary: Have students research the word *indigenous.* *(originating in a specified place or country; native)* L1 ELL

SECTION 2 Empire Building in Africa

Guide to Reading

Main Ideas
- Great Britain, France, Germany, Belgium, and Portugal placed virtually all of Africa under European rule.
- Native peoples sought an end to colonial rule.

Key Terms
annex, indigenous

People to Identify
Muhammad Ali, David Livingstone, Henry Stanley, Zulu

Places to Locate
Suez Canal, Rhodesia, Union of South Africa

Preview Questions
1. What new class of Africans developed in many African nations?
2. What was the relationship between the Boers and the Zulu?

Reading Strategy
Categorizing Information Make a chart like the one below showing what countries controlled what parts of Africa.

Controlling Country	Part of Africa
	West Africa
	North Africa (including Egypt)
	Central Africa
	East Africa
	South Africa

Preview of Events

1860 · 1870 · 1880 · 1890 · 1900 · 1910 · 1920

- **1869** Suez Canal completed
- **1884** Berlin Conference divides Africa among Europeans
- **1896** Ethiopia defeats Italian forces
- **1915** Egypt becomes British protectorate

Voices from the Past

King Lo Bengula, seated, c. 1880

A southern African king, Lo Bengula, wrote a letter to Queen Victoria about how he had been cheated:

❝Some time ago a party of men came to my country, the principal one appearing to be a man called Rudd. They asked me for a place to dig for gold, and said they would give me certain things for the right to do so. I told them to bring what they could give and I would show them what I would give. A document was written and presented to me for signature. I asked what it contained, and was told that in it were my words and the words of those men. I put my hand to it. About three months afterwards I heard from other sources that I had given by the document the right to all the minerals of my country.❞

—***The Imperialism Reader,*** **Louis L. Snyder, ed., 1962**

Europeans did not hesitate to deceive native Africans in order to get African lands.

West Africa

Before 1880, Europeans controlled little of the African continent directly. They were content to let African rulers and merchants represent European interests. Between 1880 and 1900, however, fed by intense rivalries among themselves, Great Britain, France, Germany, Belgium, and Portugal placed virtually all of Africa under European rule.

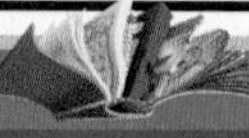

SECTION RESOURCES

Reproducible Masters
- Reproducible Lesson Plan 14–2
- Daily Lecture and Discussion Notes 14–2
- Guided Reading Activity 14–2
- Section Quiz 14–2
- Reading Essentials and Study Guide 14–2

Transparencies
- Daily Focus Skills Transparency 14–2

Multimedia
- Interactive Tutor Self-Assessment CD-ROM
- ExamView® Pro Testmaker CD-ROM
- Presentation Plus! CD-ROM

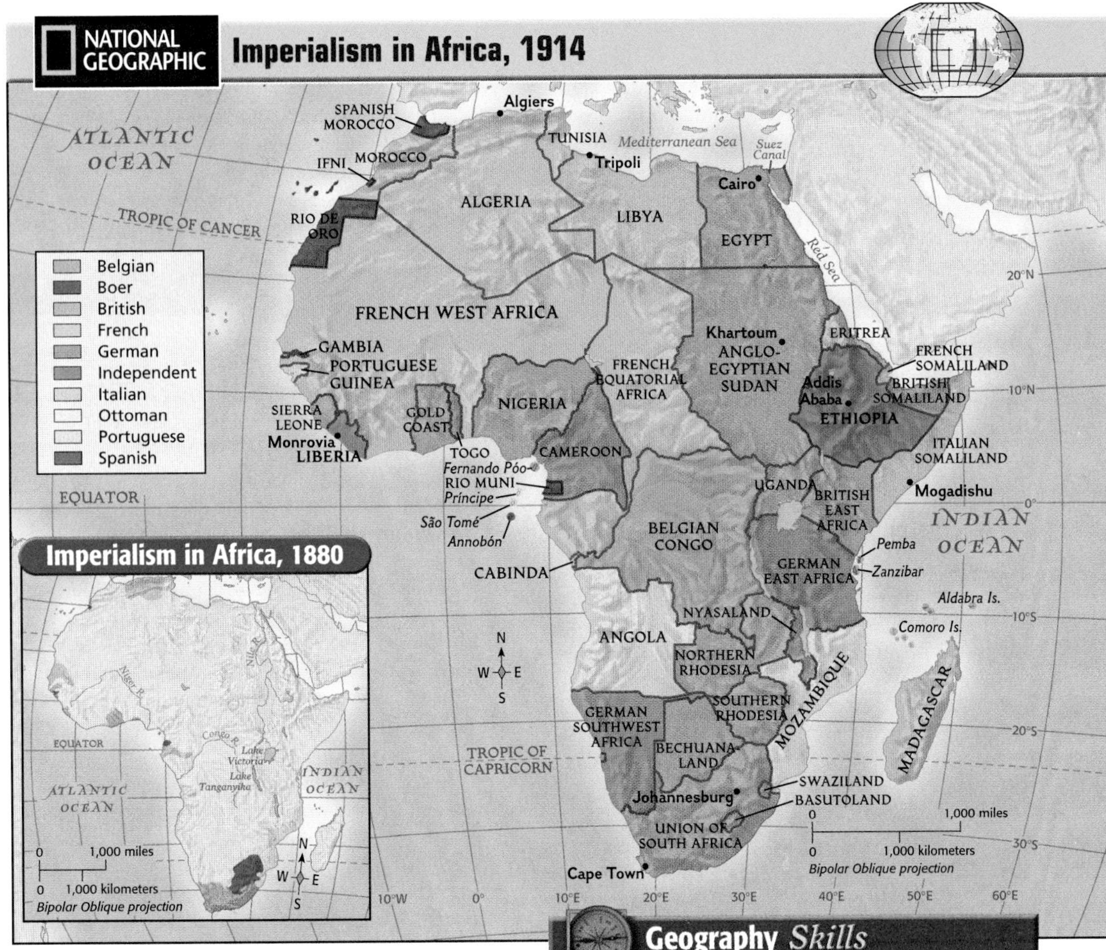

West Africa had been particularly affected by the slave trade, but that had begun to decline by 1800. By 1808, both Great Britain and the United States had declared the slave trade illegal. Other European countries eventually followed suit. Slavery was abolished in the United States in 1865 and in Cuba and Brazil within the next 25 years. By the 1890s, slavery had been abolished in all major countries of the world.

As slavery declined, Europe's interest in other forms of trade increased. Europeans sold textiles and other manufactured goods in exchange for such West African natural resources as peanuts, timber, hides, and palm oil. Encouraged by this growing trade, European governments began to push for a more permanent presence along the coast. Early in the nineteenth century, the British set up settlements along the Gold Coast and in Sierra Leone.

Geography Skills

More so in Africa than in Asia, European countries competed against each other in their attempts to colonize new territories.

1. **Interpreting Maps** Identify the two independent countries in Africa in 1914.
2. **Applying Geography Skills** Describe the changes that occurred in Africa from 1880 to 1914 for the Ottoman Empire, France, Britain, and the Boers.

The growing European presence in West Africa led to increasing tensions with African governments in the area. For a long time, most African states were able to maintain their independence. However, in 1874, Great Britain stepped in and annexed (incorporated a country within a state) the west coastal states as the first British colony of Gold Coast. At about the same time, Britain established a protectorate over

2 TEACH

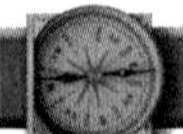

Geography Skills

Answers:

1. Liberia, Ethiopia
2. Ottomans lost territory to Britain and Italy; Britain also expanded into southern Africa; France expanded into northwest and central Africa; Boer territory was incorporated into British-held Union of South Africa; most of Africa was under European control.

Daily Lecture and Discussion Notes 14–2

Daily Lecture and Discussion Notes

Chapter 14, Section 2

Did You Know? The imperialist Cecil Rhodes established in his will a scheme to award scholarships at Oxford to men throughout the English-speaking world. Although Rhodes himself used the words "white" and "civilized" interchangeably, his will forbade disqualification on the grounds of race, so many nonwhite students have benefited from the Rhodes Scholarship. In 1976 the program was expanded to include women.

I. **West Africa** *(pages 436–438)*

A. Europeans did not hesitate to deceive Africans in order to get their land and natural resources.

B. Driven by of rivalries among themselves, Great Britain, France, Germany, Belgium, and Portugal placed almost all of Africa under European rule between 1880 and 1890.

C. West Africa was particularly affected by the slave trade, but trafficking in slaves had declined after it was declared illegal by both Great Britain and the United States by 1808. By the 1890s slavery was abolished in all the major countries of the world.

D. As slavery declined, Europe's interest in other forms of trade increased—for example, trading manufactured goods for peanuts, timber, hides, and palm oil. In the early nineteenth century, the British established settlements along the Gold Coast and in Sierra Leone. The growing European presence in West Africa caused increasing tensions with local African governments, who feared for their independence.

Guided Reading Activity 14–2

Name ______________ Date ______________ Class ______________

Guided Reading Activity 14-2

Empire Building in Africa

DIRECTIONS: Answer the following questions as you read Section 2.

1. Which five European countries placed virtually all of Africa under European control between 1880 and 1900?
2. What reforms did Muhammad Ali introduce during a 30-year reign in Egypt?
3. What did Great Britain believe concerning the Suez Canal?
4. In 1879, France established control over which North African country?
5. What humiliation did Italy suffer in North Africa in 1896?
6. State the famous words of Henry Stanley upon discovering David Livingstone in Central Africa.
7. By what means did King Leopold II of Belgium, colonize Central Africa?
8. What part did African delegates pl[...] Berlin Conference as their continent was

CRITICAL THINKING ACTIVITY

Drawing Conclusions The resistance to colonial rule points out the inherent contradictions in colonial policy. In a class discussion, ask students to consider the expected and unintended effects of colonial policies. Under education, for example, an expected result was suppression of traditional culture and values. An unintended result was pride in tradition and resentment of colonial disrespect. Conclude the discussion by pointing out to students that the Europeans' attempts to ensure their own dominance, power, and control, as well as their lavish lifestyle, sowed the seeds for their own downfall. L2

Refer to ***Inclusion for the High School Social Studies Classroom Strategies and Activities*** in the TCR.

CHAPTER 14
Section 2, 436–442

Reading Check

Answer: Slavery was gradually abolished in all major countries.

Reading Check

Answer: Because the Suez Canal linked the Red Sea and the Mediterranean, Britain considered it the "lifeline to India."

Critical Thinking

Ask students to conduct outside research and report on French colonies in North Africa. What problems did the French encounter in maintaining control over these colonies during the mid twentieth century? L1

Charting Activity

Divide the class into groups and ask each group to create a chart listing reasons why Africa was important to the European countries. Have groups share their charts with the class. *(to exploit the continent's resources for their own purposes, to control trade to their own advantage, to enhance national prestige by increasing overseas possessions, and to establish Christian missions)* L1 ELL

Writing Activity

Have students research and write a brief essay describing how advances in medicine, travel, and communications increased the pace of nineteenth-century imperialism. L2

warring groups in Nigeria. By 1900, France had added the huge area of French West Africa to its colonial empire. This left France in control of the largest part of West Africa. In addition, Germany controlled Togo, Cameroon, and German Southwest Africa (now Namibia) along the west coast.

Reading Check **Explaining** Why did the slave trade decline in the 1800s?

North Africa

Egypt had been part of the Ottoman Empire, but as Ottoman rule declined, the Egyptians sought their independence. In 1805, an officer of the Ottoman army named **Muhammad Ali** seized power and established a separate Egyptian state.

During the next 30 years, Muhammad Ali introduced a series of reforms to bring Egypt into the modern world. He modernized the army, set up a public school system, and helped create small industries in refined sugar, textiles, munitions, and ships.

The growing economic importance of the Nile Valley in Egypt, along with the development of steamships, gave Europeans the desire to build a canal east of Cairo to connect the Mediterranean and Red Seas. In 1854, a French entrepreneur, Ferdinand de Lesseps, signed a contract to begin building the **Suez Canal.** The canal was completed in 1869.

Ferdinand de Lesseps

The British took an active interest in Egypt after the Suez Canal was opened. Believing that the canal was its "lifeline to India," Great Britain sought as much control as possible over the canal area. In 1875, Britain bought Egypt's share in the Suez Canal. When an Egyptian army revolt against foreign influence broke out in 1881, Britain suppressed the revolt. Egypt became a British protectorate in 1915.

The British believed that they should also control the Sudan, south of Egypt, to protect their interests in Egypt and the Suez Canal. In 1881, Muslim cleric Muhammad Ahmad, known as the Mahdi ("the rightly guided one," in Arabic), launched a revolt that brought much of the Sudan under his control.

General Gordon's Last Stand *by George William Joy*

Britain sent a military force under General Charles Gordon to restore Egyptian authority over the Sudan. However, Gordon's army was wiped out at Khartoum in 1885 by Muhammad Ahmad's troops. Gordon himself died in the battle. Not until 1898 were British troops able to seize the Sudan.

The French also had colonies in North Africa. In 1879, after 150,000 French people had settled in the region of Algeria, the French government established control there. Two years later, France imposed a protectorate on neighboring Tunisia. In 1912, France established a protectorate over much of Morocco.

Italy joined in the competition for colonies in North Africa by attempting to take over Ethiopia, but Italian forces were defeated by Ethiopia in 1896. Italy now was the only European state defeated by an African state. This humiliating loss led Italy to try again in 1911. Italy invaded and seized Turkish Tripoli, which it renamed Libya.

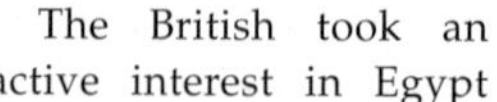

Reading Check **Explaining** Great Britain was determined to have complete control of the Suez Canal. Why?

Central Africa

Territories in Central Africa were also added to the list of European colonies. Explorers aroused

COOPERATIVE LEARNING ACTIVITY

Staging a Debate Divide the class into small groups and have some groups research the development, history, and ownership of the Suez Canal. Groups should prepare a map of the Eastern Hemisphere, using the Suez Canal as the central focus of the map. Students should provide statistical information to support their analysis of the effects of physical and human geographic factors on the effects of the opening of the Suez Canal on world trade patterns. Other groups should prepare similar reports on the Panama Canal. When the groups have finished their work, organize a class debate over the question of which canal is more important in terms of worldwide economy and strategic location. L2

popular interest in the dense tropical jungles of Central Africa. **David Livingstone,** as we have seen, was one such explorer. He arrived in Africa in 1841. For 30 years he trekked through unchartered regions. He spent much of his time exploring the interior of the continent.

When Livingstone disappeared for a while, the *New York Herald* hired a young journalist, **Henry Stanley,** to find him. Stanley did, on the eastern shore of Lake Tanganyika, and greeted the explorer with the now famous words, "Dr. Livingstone, I presume."

After Livingstone's death in 1873, Stanley remained in Africa to carry on the great explorer's work. Unlike Livingstone, however, Stanley had a strong dislike of Africa. He once said, "I detest the land most heartily."

In the 1870s, Stanley explored the Congo River in Central Africa and sailed down it to the Atlantic Ocean. Soon, he was encouraging the British to send settlers to the Congo River basin. When Britain refused, he turned to King Leopold II of Belgium.

King Leopold II was the real driving force behind the colonization of Central Africa. He rushed enthusiastically into the pursuit of an empire in Africa. "To open to civilization," he said, "the only part of our globe where it has not yet penetrated, to pierce the darkness which envelops whole populations, is a crusade, if I may say so, a crusade worthy of this century of progress." Profit, however, was equally important to Leopold. In 1876, he hired Henry Stanley to set up Belgian settlements in the Congo.

Leopold's claim to the vast territories of the Congo aroused widespread concern among other European states. France, in particular, rushed to plant its flag in the heart of Africa. Leopold ended up with the territories south of the Congo River. France occupied the areas to the north.

Reading Check **Examining** What effect did King Leopold II of Belgium have on European colonization of the Congo River basin?

East Africa

By 1875, Britain and Germany had become the chief rivals in East Africa. Germany came late to the ranks of the imperialist powers. At first, the German chancellor Otto von Bismarck had downplayed the importance of colonies. As more and more Germans called for a German empire, however, Bismarck became a convert to colonialism. As he expressed it, "All this colonial business is a sham, but we need it for the elections."

CONNECTIONS Around The World

The Role of Quinine

Before 1850, the fear of disease was a major factor in keeping Europeans from moving into Africa. Especially frightening was malaria, an often fatal disease spread by parasites. Malaria is especially devastating in tropical and subtropical regions, which offer good conditions for breeding the mosquitoes that carry and spread the malaria parasites.

By 1850, European doctors had learned how to treat malaria with quinine, a drug that greatly reduced the death rate from the disease. Quinine is a bitter drug obtained from the bark of the cinchona tree, which is native to the slopes of the Andes in South America. The Indians of Peru were the first people to use the bark of the cinchona tree to treat malaria.

The Dutch took the cinchona tree and began to grow it in the East Indies. The East Indies eventually became the chief source of quinine. With the use of quinine and other medicines, Europeans felt more secure about moving into Africa.

By the beginning of the twentieth century, more than 90 percent of African lands were under the control of the European powers. A drug found in the bark of Latin American trees, which were then grown in Asia, had been used by Europeans to make possible their conquest of Africa.

The bark from cinchona trees dries in the sun.

Comparing Cultures

Fear of disease kept Europeans from moving into Africa. Once quinine was discovered, Europeans felt safer about Africa.

1. What fears do we have today that prevent or inhibit exploration or research?
2. What technological advances would be required to overcome those fears?

INTERDISCIPLINARY CONNECTIONS ACTIVITY

Government and Economics Nowhere were the excesses of colonialism more evident than in Africa. Leopold, in spite of his claims of bringing civilization, exemplifies the worst treatment of the African natives. He enslaved the Congolese people to work on his plantations, had forests cut down to build rubber plantations, and had elephant herds slaughtered for ivory. In twenty years of brutal rule, Leopold "The Civilizer" stripped the Congo of its culture, its people, and its resources. Ask students to research the situation in the Democratic Republic of the Congo (formerly Zaire) today. What problems does this country face today? Are these current problems an outgrowth of Leopold's colonial legacy? Why or why not? L2

Reading Check

Answer: By putting Belgian settlements in the Congo, he aroused widespread concern among other European states, and France rushed in to stake its claims in central Africa.

Answers:

1. Students will identify fears that inhibit exploration and research.
2. Answers will vary depending on the answers to the previous question.

Who? What? Where? When?

Malaria People who have contracted malaria sometimes suffer relapses after their first infection. Malaria is still a common disease in Africa, Central America, and Southeast Asia.

Who? What? Where? When?

David Livingstone Although remembered primarily for his explorations and humanitarian work, David Livingstone worked to bring Africa into the world community of nations. His body is buried in Westminster Abbey, but he gave instructions that his heart was to remain in Africa. It is buried in Blantyre, Malawi, a city named after his birthplace in Scotland.

Reading Check

Answer: Conflicting claims over East Africa were settled without African delegates present.

CURRICULUM CONNECTION

Geography Have students use maps in this chapter or in the Reference Atlas to measure the distance involved in Cecil Rhodes's "Cape to Cairo" railroad. What terrain would this railroad have to go through? L2

Who?What?Where?When?

The Zulu The Zulu army that defeated the British at the Battle of Isandhlwana in 1870 included a regiment of men in their sixties. Zulu regiments were divided by age, and each regiment lived in a separate village in peacetime.

Enrich

The imperialists, with their desire to colonize and control Africa, often clashed with the diverse indigenous groups. Have students research some of the original inhabitants of Africa and their relations with the imperialists and report to the class on their findings. This exercise may be done in small groups. L2

In addition to its West African holdings, Germany tried to develop colonies in East Africa. Most of East Africa had not yet been claimed by any other power. However, the British were also interested in the area because control of East Africa would connect the British Empire in Africa from South Africa to Egypt. Portugal and Belgium also claimed parts of East Africa.

To settle these conflicting claims, the Berlin Conference was held in 1884. The conference gave official recognition to both British and German claims for territory in East Africa. Portugal received a clear claim on Mozambique. No African delegates were present at this conference, which carved up their continent.

Reading Check **Evaluating** What was significant about the Berlin Conference in 1884?

South Africa

Nowhere in Africa did the European presence grow more rapidly than in the south. By 1865, the total white population of the area had risen to nearly two hundred thousand people.

The Boers, or Afrikaners—as the descendants of the original Dutch settlers were called—had occupied Cape Town and surrounding areas in South Africa since the seventeenth century. During the Napoleonic Wars, however, the British seized these lands from the Dutch. Afterward, the British encouraged settlers to come to what they called Cape Colony.

In the 1830s, disgusted with British rule, the Boers fled northward on the Great Trek to the region between the Orange and Vaal (VAHL) Rivers and to the region north of the Vaal River. In these areas, the Boers formed two independent republics—the Orange Free State and the Transvaal (later called the South African Republic). The Boers, who believed white superiority was ordained by God, put many of the **indigenous** (native to a region) peoples in these areas on reservations.

The Boers had frequently battled the indigenous **Zulu** people. In the early nineteenth century, the

Opposing Viewpoints

Who Benefited from the New Imperialism?

Europeans justified colonization of Africa and Asia in many ways. Native peoples viewed the takeover of their lands differently. Rudyard Kipling and Edward Morel were British journalists who held opposing viewpoints about imperialism.

"Take up the White Man's burden—
Send forth the best ye breed—
Go bind your sons to exile
To serve your captives' needs;
To wait in heavy harness,
On fluttered folk and wild—
Your new-caught sullen peoples,
Half-devil and half-child. . . .
Take up the White Man's burden—
And reap his old reward:
The blame of those ye better,
The hate of those ye guard—
The cry of hosts ye humour
(Ah, slowly;) toward the light: —
'Why brought he us from bondage,
Our loved Egyptian night?'"

—**Rudyard Kipling, 1899**
The White Man's Burden

"It is [the Africans] who carry the 'Black man's burden. . . . ' In hewing out for himself a fixed abode in Africa, the white man has massacred the African in heaps. . . .

EXTENDING THE CONTENT

African Civilization It is important that students realize that there was already an established civilization in southern Africa before the arrival of the Europeans. Great city-states, such as Great Zimbabwe, existed and had established trade routes, built elaborate cities with administrative centers, mined precious minerals, and had distinctive cultures and traditions. For many years, white explorers and historians refused to accept evidence of these civilizations and made up fantastic stories of lost white civilizations to explain away the advanced artifacts. Edgar Rice Burroughs's "Tarzan" stories grew out of this tradition.

Zulu, under a talented ruler named Shaka, had carved out their own empire. After Shaka's death, the Zulu remained powerful. Finally, in the late 1800s, the British became involved in conflicts with the Zulu, and the Zulu were defeated.

In the 1880s, British policy in South Africa was largely set by Cecil Rhodes. Rhodes had founded diamond and gold companies that had made him a fortune. He gained control of a territory north of the Transvaal, which he named **Rhodesia** after himself.

Rhodes was a great champion of British expansion. He said once, "I think what [God] would like me to do is to paint as much of Africa British red as possible." One of Rhodes's goals was to create a series of British colonies "from the Cape to Cairo"—all linked by a railroad.

Rhodes's ambitions eventually led to his downfall in 1896. The British government forced him to resign as prime minister of Cape Colony after discovering that he planned to overthrow the Boer government of the South African Republic without his government's approval. The British action was too late to avoid a war between the British and the Boers, however.

This war, called the Boer War, dragged on from 1899 to 1902. Fierce guerrilla resistance by the Boers angered the British. They responded by burning crops and herding more than 150,000 Boer women and children into detention camps, where lack of food caused 26,000 deaths. Eventually, the vastly larger British army won.

In 1910, the British created an independent **Union of South Africa,** which combined the old Cape Colony and the Boer republics. The Union of South Africa would be a self-governing nation within the British Empire. To appease the Boers, the British agreed that only whites would vote.

Reading Check **Describing** What happened to the Boers at the end of the Boer War?

Colonial Rule in Africa

By 1914, Great Britain, France, Germany, Belgium, and Portugal had divided up Africa. Only Liberia, which had been created as a homeland for freed United States slaves, and Ethiopia remained free states. Native peoples who dared to resist were simply devastated by the superior military force of the Europeans.

As was true in Southeast Asia, most European governments ruled their new territories in Africa with the least effort and expense possible. Indirect rule meant relying on existing political elites and institutions. The British especially followed this approach. At first, in some areas, the British simply asked a local ruler to accept British authority and to fly the British flag over official buildings.

The concept of indirect rule was introduced in the Islamic state of Sokoto, in northern Nigeria, in 1900. This system of indirect rule in Sokoto had one good feature: it did not disrupt local customs and institutions. However, it did have some unfortunate consequences.

The system was basically a fraud because British administrators made all major decisions. The native authorities served chiefly to enforce those decisions. Another problem was that indirect rule kept the old African elite in power. Such a policy provided few opportunities for ambitious and talented young Africans from outside the old elite. In this way British indirect rule sowed the seeds for class and tribal tensions, which erupted after independence came in the twentieth century.

What the partial occupation of his soil by the white man has failed do; . . . what the [machine gun] and the rifle, the slave gang, labour in the bowels of the earth and the lash, have failed to do; what imported measles, smallpox and syphilis have failed to do; whatever the overseas slave trade failed to do; the power of modern capitalistic exploitation, assisted by modern engines of destruction, may yet succeed in accomplishing. . . .

Thus the African is really helpless against the material gods of the white man, as embodied in the trinity of imperialism, capitalistic exploitation, and militarism.”

—**Edward Morel, 1903**
The Black Man's Burden

You Decide

1. What was the impact of imperialism on the colonized territories in Africa, according to Morel?
2. Quote lines in Rudyard Kipling's poem that reflect his view of colonized peoples. What values did Kipling assume his readers shared with him?

Opposing Viewpoints

Answers:

1. The impact was negative: Africans died from guns and disease and were forced into slave labor.
2. Answers will vary. He assumed readers believed in the superiority of European culture.

Reading Check

Answer: Their lands were combined with Cape Colony to form the Union of South Africa, a self-governing nation within the British Empire. To appease the Boers, the British agreed that only whites could vote.

3 ASSESS

Assign Section 2 Assessment as homework or as an in-class activity.

Have students use **Interactive Tutor Self-Assessment CD-ROM.**

Section Quiz 14–2

Name ______ Date ______ Class ______

Chapter 14 Score

Section Quiz 14-2

DIRECTIONS: Matching Match each item in Column A with an item in Column B. Write the correct letters in the blanks. *(10 points each)*

Column A	Column B
____ 1. shortcut between Europe and Asia	A. Muhammad Ali
____ 2. Scottish explorer, missionary, and doctor	B. David Livingstone
____ 3. nineteenth-century Egyptian ruler	C. Afrikaners
____ 4. Dutch settlers in South Africa	D. annex
____ 5. incorporate a country within another state	E. Suez Canal

DIRECTIONS: Multiple Choice In the blank, write the letter of the choice that best completes the statement or answers the question. *(10 points each)*

INTERDISCIPLINARY CONNECTIONS ACTIVITY

Technology Shaka Zulu, called "The Napoleon of Africa," rose from being an obscure tribal chief to building one of the greatest empires ever seen in southern Africa. He accomplished this primarily by exerting great discipline over his army and with two technical innovations. Shaka Zulu gave his soldiers large shields which fitted together to protect soldiers from flying spears. Soldiers carried just one stabbing spear (*assagai*) instead of a number of long-handled throwing spears so they could run fast and tackle the enemy in hand-to-hand combat. Shaka Zulu's disciplined army surprised the British with its fierce resistance to "superior" British military resources. Ask students to research the Zulu's military technology. How does their technology compare to that used by other great armies discussed in previous chapters? How did the British finally defeat the Zulu?

CHAPTER 14
Section 2, 436–442

Reading Check

Answer: The French wanted to assimilate their African subjects into the French culture. The British used indirect rule, ruling through existing political elites and institutions.

Reading Check

Answer: Westerners exalted democracy, equality, and political freedom, but they did not apply these values in the colonies.

Reading Essentials and Study Guide 14–2

Name ________ Date ________ Class ________

Reading Essentials and Study Guide

Chapter 14, Section 2

For use with textbook pages 436–442

EMPIRE BUILDING IN AFRICA

KEY TERMS

annex to incorporate a country within a state (page 437)

indigenous native to a region (page 440)

DRAWING FROM EXPERIENCE

Has anyone ever told you that your traditions and customs were wrong? How would this make you feel?

In the last section, you read about imperialism in Southeast Asia. In this section, you will learn about imperialism in Africa. Most colonial powers did

Reteaching Activity

Ask students to identify the role each of the following played in the imperialist expansion in Africa: Stanley and Livingstone, Suez Canal, Leopold II, Afrikaners, palm oil, Liberia. **L2**

4 CLOSE

Have students summarize the effects of imperialism on Africa. What benefits and hardships did colonization bring to the continent? Have students explain the political, economic, cultural, and technological influences of expansion on both Europeans and non-Europeans. **L1**

Most other European nations governed their African possessions through a form of direct rule. This was true in the French colonies. At the top was a French official, usually known as a governor-general. He was appointed from Paris and governed with the aid of a bureaucracy in the capital city of the colony.

The French ideal was to assimilate African subjects into French culture rather than preserve native traditions. Africans were eligible to run for office and even serve in the French National Assembly in Paris. A few were appointed to high positions in the colonial administration.

Reading Check **Comparing** How did the French system of colonial rule differ from that of Great Britain?

Rise of African Nationalism

As in Southeast Asia, a new class of leaders emerged in Africa by the beginning of the twentieth century. Educated in colonial schools or in Western nations, they were the first generation of Africans to know a great deal about the West.

On the one hand, the members of this new class admired Western culture and sometimes disliked the ways of their own countries. They were eager to introduce Western ideas and institutions into their own societies.

On the other hand, many came to resent the foreigners and their arrogant contempt for African peoples. These intellectuals recognized the gap between theory and practice in colonial policy. Westerners had exalted democracy, equality, and political freedom but did not apply these values in the colonies.

There were few democratic institutions. Native peoples could have only low-paying jobs in the colonial bureaucracy. To many Africans, colonialism had meant the loss of their farmlands or employment on plantations or in factories run by foreigners.

Middle-class Africans did not suffer as much as poor African peasant plantation workers. However, members of the middle class also had complaints. They usually qualified only for menial jobs in the government or business. Even then, their salaries were lower than those of Europeans in similar jobs.

Europeans expressed their superiority over Africans in other ways. Segregated clubs, schools, and churches were set up as more European officials brought their wives and began to raise families. Europeans also had a habit of addressing Africans by their first names or calling an adult male "boy."

Such conditions led many members of the new urban educated class to feel great confusion toward their colonial masters and the civilization the colonists represented. The educated Africans were willing to admit the superiority of many aspects of Western culture. However, these intellectuals fiercely hated colonial rule and were determined to assert their own nationality and cultural destiny. Out of this mixture of hopes and resentments emerged the first stirrings of modern nationalism in Africa.

During the first quarter of the twentieth century, resentment turned to action. Across Africa, native peoples began to organize political parties and movements seeking the end of foreign rule.

Reading Check **Evaluating** Why were many African intellectuals frustrated by colonial policy?

SECTION 2 ASSESSMENT

Checking for Understanding

1. **Define** annex, indigenous.
2. **Identify** Muhammad Ali, David Livingstone, Henry Stanley, Zulu.
3. **Locate** Suez Canal, Rhodesia, Union of South Africa.
4. **Explain** why the British were interested in East Africa. What other countries claimed parts of East Africa?
5. **List** the ways in which the French system of direct rule included Africans.

Critical Thinking

6. **Drawing Conclusions** What can you conclude from the fact that African delegates were not included in the Berlin Conference of 1884?
7. **Organizing Information** Using a chart like the one below, identify key figures of African resistance to colonial rule.

Leader	Country opposed	Dates of resistance

Analyzing Visuals

8. **Examine** the painting on page 438. What was the painter trying to say about the hostilities between the British and the people of the Sudan? If forced to choose, whom would you support in this confrontation?

Writing About History

9. **Expository Writing** Research the importance of the Suez Canal today. Write a paper comparing the present-day significance of the canal to its historical significance.

SECTION 2 ASSESSMENT

1. Key terms are in blue.
2. Muhammad Ali *(p. 438);* David Livingstone *(p. 439);* Henry Stanley *(p. 439);* Zulu *(p. 440)*
3. See chapter maps.
4. Acquiring East Africa would connect the British Empire in Africa from South Africa to Egypt; Germany
5. Africans could run for public office and even serve in the National Assembly in Paris.
6. Answers may include that no one wanted to hear what they thought of European plans for their continent.
7. Muhammad Ahmad (Sudan): Britain:1881–1898; Shaka (Zulu): Boers: early nineteenth century
8. The British were not intimidated, even when they appear to be outnumbered and unarmed, compared to the Sudanese.
9. Students will compare past and present significance of the Suez Canal.

TECHNOLOGY

SKILLBUILDER

Evaluating a Web Site

Why Learn This Skill?

Your little sister has developed a strange rash on her back, so you decide to check the Internet to see whether or not it might be chicken pox and how the rash should be treated. When you look for a Web site, however, you find dozens, and they are all giving different advice. How do you determine which site is giving the most accurate and up-to-date information?

The Internet has become a valuable research tool. It is convenient to use and contains plentiful information. Unfortunately, some Web site information is not necessarily correct or reliable. When using the Internet as a research tool, the user must distinguish between quality information and inaccurate or incomplete information.

Learning the Skill

To evaluate a Web site, ask yourself the following questions:

- Where does the site originate? If it is a university, a well-known organization or agency, or a respected publication, then the information is likely to be trustworthy.
- Are the facts on the site documented? Where did this information originally come from? Is the author clearly identified?
- Are the links to other parts of the site appropriate? Do they take you to information that helps you learn more about the subject?
- Is more than one source used for background information within the site? If so, does the site contain a bibliography?
- When was the last time the site was updated?
- Does the site explore the topic in-depth?
- Does the site contain links to other useful and up-to-date resources? Although many legitimate sites have products to sell, some sites are more interested in sales than in providing accurate information.
- Is the information easy to access? Is it properly labeled?
- Is the design appealing?

Practicing the Skill

Visit the Web site about Mohandas Gandhi at *http://www.mkgandhi.org* featured on this page. Then, answer the following questions.

1. Who is the author or sponsor of the Web site?
2. What information does the home page link you to? Are the links appropriate to the topic?
3. What sources were used for the information contained on the site? When was it last updated?
4. Does the site explore the topic in-depth? Why or why not?
5. Are there links to other useful sources and are they up-to-date?
6. Is the design of the site appealing? Why or why not? When was Gandhi born? How easy or difficult was it to locate this information?

Applying the Skill

Comparing Web Sites Locate two other Web sites that provide information about Mohandas Gandhi. Evaluate each one for accuracy and usefulness, and then compare them to the site featured above (http://www.mkgandhi.org).

TECHNOLOGY SKILLBUILDER

TEACH

Evaluating a Web Site It is as important to evaluate Web sites as it is to evaluate print sources. Students should corroborate the information found on a Web site with the information found on at least one other site. As with print sources, students should identify the author or sponsor of a Web site to help evaluate the purpose and accuracy of the information posted. Remind students to check whether university Web sites are authored by a professor or by students since this could affect the accuracy of the information posted.

Additional Practice

Skills Reinforcement Activity 14

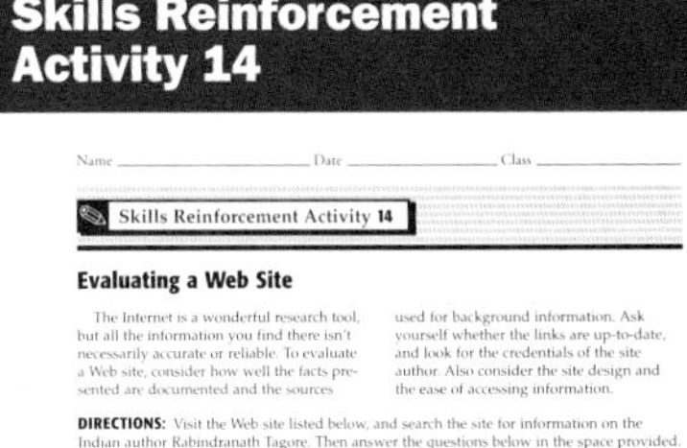

Name ________ Date ________ Class ________

Skills Reinforcement Activity 14

Evaluating a Web Site

The Internet is a wonderful research tool, but all the information you find there isn't necessarily accurate or reliable. To evaluate a Web site, consider how well the facts presented are documented and the sources used for background information. Ask yourself whether the links are up-to-date, and look for the credentials of the site author. Also consider the site design and the ease of accessing information.

DIRECTIONS: Visit the Web site listed below, and search the site for information on the Indian author Rabindranath Tagore. Then answer the questions below in the space provided.

http://www.nobel.se/

1. Who is the author or sponsor of this site? What does this tell you about the reliability of the site?

GLENCOE TECHNOLOGY

CD-ROM
Glencoe Skillbuilder Interactive Workbook CD-ROM, Level 2

This interactive CD-ROM reinforces student mastery of essential social studies skills.

ANSWERS TO PRACTICING THE SKILL

1. The sponsors of the Web site are the supporters of Mohandas Gandhi.
2. The home page links to works by and about Gandhi, a time line of his life, images of Gandhi, and links to other useful sources.
3. The "About Us" feature explains the sources and contains the date of the last update.
4. The site has extensive written and multimedia material both by and about Gandhi.
5. By clicking on "On Gandhi" you get to "Other Links." These have summaries that describe the resource.
6. It is very visual, with pictures of Gandhi, as well as audio and video clips and an interactive time line.

Applying the Skill: Answers will vary depending on the Web sites students locate.

NATIONAL GEOGRAPHIC

SPECIAL REPORT SUMMARY

David Livingstone was both an explorer and a missionary who was the first European to explore extensive regions of Africa. His detailed notes and reports were used to revise maps of the African continent.

■

Livingstone's primary goal was to find a navigable river that would open the center of Africa to European commerce.

■

Livingstone was the first European to travel to the mouth of the Zambezi River and named Victoria Falls after the British queen.

■

Henry Stanley was sent by a newspaper to find Livingstone in Africa, and when Stanley finally found him near Lake Tanganyika, Livingstone was near death. Stanley traveled with Livingstone for five months, exploring Lake Tanganyika.

TEACH

Points to Discuss

After students have read this selection, discuss the following: **What two very different concepts motivated Livingstone to travel to Africa?** *(He wanted to find a navigable river that would open the center of Africa to European commerce, and he wanted to end the slave trade.)* **What medical problems did Livingstone encounter during his first years in Africa?** *(He suffered from malaria and lost the use of his left arm from a lion attack.)* **How did Livingstone differ from other European explorers to Africa?**

STANLEY AND LIVINGSTONE IN AFRICA

1

More than three years had passed with no word from Dr. David Livingstone. The renowned Scottish missionary and explorer had left Britain in August 1865, bound for East Africa, where the Royal Geographical Society had asked him, among other things, to try to determine the source of the Nile River. The explorer Richard Burton favored Lake Tanganyika while the late John Hanning Speke had been certain the Nile arose in Lake Victoria. The 52-year-old Livingstone had arrived at the island of Zanzibar in January 1866. He and his party of about 60 men were taken to the mainland some six weeks later and were known to have headed into the interior. Months later, the first rumors of his death reached the coast.

In October 1869, James Gordon Bennett, son of the publisher of the *New York Herald*, met with reporter Henry M. Stanley in the Grand Hotel in Paris. "Go and find him wherever you may hear that he is and get what news you can of him," Bennett told Stanley. "And perhaps the old man may be in want; take enough with you to help him should he require it. Of course, you will act according to your own plans, and do what you think best—but find Livingstone!"

The man Stanley was supposed to find was known and admired both for his achievements as an explorer and for his dedicated efforts to end the slave trade. Since going out to Africa in 1840 as a 27-year-old medical missionary, David Livingstone had covered thousands of miles of territory previously unexplored by Europeans. Sometimes he traveled by canoe or on the back of an ox, but mostly he went on foot. In the early years he traveled with his wife, Mary, and their young children.

Though he suffered from malaria and had lost the use of his left arm after being attacked by a wounded lion, Livingstone remained determined. He made detailed notes and reports, which he sent to London whenever he could. The information he sent was used to revise the maps of Africa.

All the exploration that Livingstone did in the mid-1850s had one goal: to find a navigable river that would open the center of Africa to legitimate European commerce and to Christianity. In so doing, Livingstone hoped to drive out the slave trade, an evil that he called "this open sore of the world."

In the spring of 1852, Livingstone sent his family back to England. Then, starting from Cape Town, South Africa, he trekked north to the Upper Zambezi and then west to Luanda on the Atlantic coast (in present-day Angola). After a brief rest, he headed to Quelimane on the east coast (now in Mozambique). The trip of some 4,300 miles (6,919 km) finally ended in May 1856. Livingstone traveled with a small party of 25 or so

Teacher's Notes

3

Africans. In contrast to other European expedition leaders, the missionary regarded the men not as his servants but as his friends. His loyalty to them was returned manyfold.

The expedition traveled light, although Livingstone always carried his navigational instruments, a Bible, a nautical almanac, and his journal. He also carried a magic lantern (an early slide projector) and slides, so he could tell Bible stories to any who would listen. On the second half of the journey, from the interior to the mouth of the Zambezi River, Livingstone became the first European to see the spectacular waterfall the Africans called "Mosi-oa-tunya" (the smoke that thunders). Livingstone named it Victoria Falls, after the British queen.

2

■

When the missionary got back to Britain in late 1856, he found that word of his explorations and discoveries had preceded him. He was now famous. The following year Livingstone turned his journals into a book—*Missionary Travels and Researches in South Africa*—which quickly became a best-seller. In his book and at every public opportunity he could find, he raised the issue of the slave trade. He condemned those who tolerated it and profited by it.

When he sailed back to Africa in the spring of 1858, Dr. Livingstone was the newly appointed British Con-

1 Tipping his pith helmet, Henry Morton Stanley greets the explorer with his restrained inquiry: "Dr. Livingstone, I presume?"

2 The scarcity of paper did not prevent Livingstone from recording his observations in meticulous detail, as seen in this fragment from his journals. He would also record topographical measurements taken with the sextant.

3 "It had never been seen before by European eyes," Livingstone wrote of his first view of Victoria Falls, "but scenes so lovely must have been gazed upon by angels in their flight." His drawing of the falls and the meandering Zambezi River below it (inset) hardly does the scene justice.

(Students should note that Livingstone sent back notes and diaries to London so that maps of Africa could be revised; in addition, he regarded the native Africans with whom he traveled as friends, not as servants. He was loyal to them, and they were loyal to Livingstone.) **Why did Livingstone carry a projector and slides with him?** *(He told Bible stories to any who would listen and illustrated the stories with his slides.)* **How did the waterfall known as "Mosi-oa-tunya" become Victoria Falls?** *(Livingstone named the falls after the British queen, Victoria.)* **What were some of the problems Livingstone encountered during his trip that began in 1858?** *(Although Livingstone had backing from the British government, he encountered numerous problems. His wife fell ill; his six European assistants quarreled among themselves; the boat was not appropriate for Africa; and he was greatly hampered by the Quebrasa Falls; later, in 1862, Mary Livingstone died while on expedition with her husband.)* **What is the source of the Nile?** *(Lake Victoria)*

FUN FACTS

- Henry Stanley was born in Wales, came to the United States and fought in the Civil War as a Confederate and then as a Union soldier.
- Henry Stanley was as famous for being an author as he was for being an explorer. He was a contemporary of Mark Twain and Joseph Conrad.
- After Livingstone was attacked by a lion he was asked what profound thoughts he was thinking. Livingstone answered, "I was wondering what part of me he would eat first."
- Charles Dickens had a low opinion of missionaries. However, after he read Livingstone's work *Missionary Travels and Researches in South Africa,* Dickens said they were written by "as honest and as courageous a man as ever lived."

CURRICULUM CONNECTION

Geography Have students use the map of Africa in the Reference Atlas in their textbooks to locate the areas in Africa explored by Livingstone. Have students create their own maps that trace Livingstone's path from Britain to Victoria Falls and Lake Tanganyika. You might also wish to assign students to research place names in Africa to see which have or have had European names. (For example, Zimbabwe was formerly known as Rhodesia, named for Cecil Rhodes.)

Writing Activity

Have students imagine that they are either David Livingstone or Henry Stanley. Ask them to write either a diary account of the meeting between the two men or the newspaper account that Stanley might have written following his meeting with Livingstone. Have students illustrate their writings and share results with other class members.

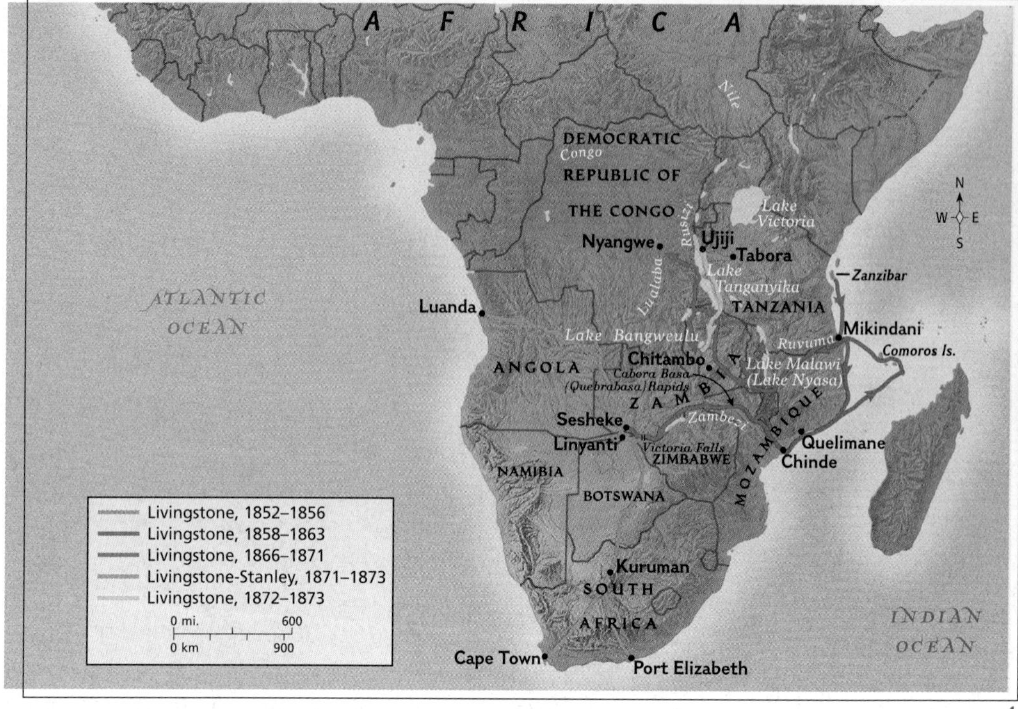

4

sul for the East Coast of Africa. With substantial government backing and far more equipment and personnel than he had previously enjoyed, he continued to explore the Zambezi and its tributaries. His wife sailed with him but then fell ill and went to rest in Cape Town.

Despite its advantages, this expedition was plagued with problems. There was quarreling among Livingstone's six European assistants, and the fuel-eating boat he had been given was more trouble than it was worth.

Worst of all was the discovery that on his previous trip down the Zambezi he had bypassed a bend in the river that held big problems. When the party headed upriver from the east coast of Africa, they came around that bend only to be stopped by the Quebrabasa Rapids. Try as he might—and Livingstone insisted on trying, until everyone in his expedition was exhausted— this was an obstacle no boat could get past.

Even though his efforts were adding daily to European knowledge of the African interior and would be of benefit to all who came after him, Livingstone was frustrated at not finding the navigable river that would surely bring an end to the slave trade.

Then, tragedy struck. In early 1862, Mary Livingstone was well enough to join her husband, but a few months later she fell ill again. In April, she died. Grief stricken, Livingstone threw himself into his work, but his increased efforts did not pay off. In July 1863, the expedition was ordered to return home.

Livingstone stayed in Britain only long enough to write a second book, *The Zambezi and Its Tributaries*, and to drum up support for his next expedition. On his third and final trip to Africa, the great explorer disappeared.

Henry Stanley left to carry out his employer's orders soon after the Paris meeting. He took a roundabout route to Africa to cover other stories for the *Herald*, including the opening of the Suez Canal in Egypt. James Bennett hoped that by delaying Stanley's arrival in Africa, the reporter would come back with definite news of Livingstone—that he was dead or alive and not just missing. ("If he is dead," Bennett had said, "bring back every possible proof of his death.")

By the time Stanley finally reached Africa in late January 1871, Livingstone had been struggling with near-starvation, chronic dysentery, sore-covered feet, and hostile groups. Of the 60 men he had started with, only a small handful remained, including Chuma, a freed slave, and

Teacher's Notes

Susi, a Yao servant. Both of them had been with him for years. Desperately sick and without medicine, Livingstone had been repeatedly nursed back to relatively good health by Arab slave traders. The passionate anti-slavery activist owed his life to the very people he wished to banish from Africa.

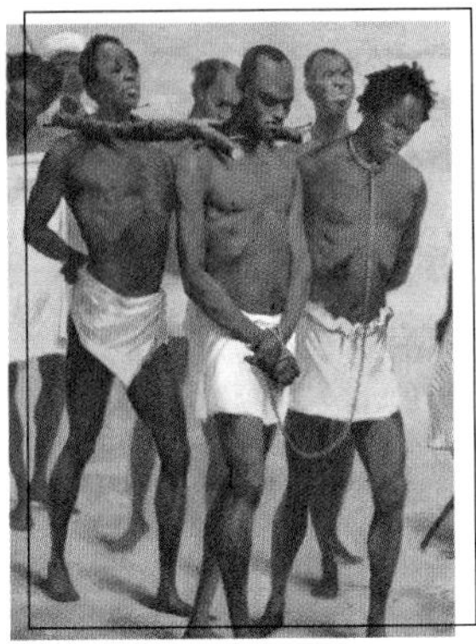

5

In July 1871, ill and discouraged, Livingstone headed to Ujiji, on the east bank of Lake Tanganyika. He expected to find several months' worth of supplies, medicine, and mail waiting for him there. In late October, "reduced to a skeleton," as he put it, he hobbled into the village—only to learn that all his supplies and precious medicines had been plundered by the headman of the place. Extremely depressed, he felt he couldn't do anything but wait for a miracle.

Several weeks later, the miracle arrived under a waving Stars and Stripes. Henry Stanley could hardly contain his emotion as he approached the pale white man."I would have run to him, only I was a coward in the presence of such a mob," Stanley later wrote, "[I] would have embraced him, only he being an Englishman, I did not know how he would receive me; so I did what cowardice and false pride suggested was the best thing—walked deliberately to him, took off my hat, and said: 'Dr. Livingstone, I presume?' 'Yes,' said he, with a kind smile, lifting his cap slightly."

Stanley remained with Livingstone for five months and explored Lake Tanganyika with him. That trip proved that Burton was wrong about the Ruzizi, the river he thought led from the lake to become the Nile. Livingstone was now determined to prove his own theory, which was that the Nile originated with the headwaters of a river called the Lualaba. (As it turns out, the Lualaba is actually part of the Congo River system. Speke was right all along: The Nile's source is Lake Victoria.)

Unable to persuade the older man to return to Britain, Stanley left in March 1872. Reaching the coast in May, his news of finding Livingstone reached Europe and America in August. At about that time, Livingstone received the fresh supplies and men that Stanley had promised to send back to him. He promptly set off toward Lakes Tanganyika and Bangweulu.

The old explorer's will was great, but his long-suffering body was no longer up to the demands of the trip. By April 22, 1873, he was being carried in a litter. On the night of April 30, in the village of Chitambo, Susi helped him to bed, last speaking with him at midnight. The next morning, his companions found Livingstone kneeling by the bed, his head in his hands in prayer—dead.

6

Resolving that Livingstone should be returned to Britain, they buried his heart under a large tree near the hut where he died. Then they filled the body with salt, smeared it with brandy, and left it to dry for two weeks before beginning the long journey to the coast. Eight months and a thousand miles (1,609 km) later, they delivered Livingstone's body to the British Consul in Zanzibar. April 18, 1874, was declared a national day of mourning and all of London came to a halt as Dr. Livingstone was buried in Westminster Abbey.

4 **Livingstone made two significant crossings of the African continent—from the interior west to Luanda in 1853–1854, and then east to Quelimane in 1855–1856. On his expedition in 1866 to find the source of the Nile, illness and other difficulties hampered his progress. Henry Stanley found him at Ujiji on November 10, 1871.**

5 **The all-too familiar sight of captives in chains drove Livingstone to denounce the collaboration of European authorities in the widespread traffic in slaves.**

6 **Henry Morton Stanley developed a great interest in exploring Africa after he found Livingstone.**

INTERPRETING THE PAST

1. What were two of Dr. Livingstone's reasons for exploring Africa?

2. What waterfall did Livingstone encounter on his trip from the interior to the mouth of the Zambezi River ?

3. What were the main obstacles that Livingstone faced?

Who?What?Where?When?

Lake Tanganyika Bordered by four countries, Burundi, Congo DR, Tanzania, and Zambia, Lake Tanganyika is the longest fresh water lake in the world. It is the second deepest, after Lake Baikal in Russia. It lies in the Great Rift Valley, which accounts for its great depth, just under 0.9 miles (1,433 m). Lake Tanganyika has about 1,181 miles (1,900 km) of shoreline; north to south it is 420 miles (677 km) long and 31 miles (50 km) wide. Over 350 different species of fish live in the lake. The bottom half-mile (805 m) of the lake is either too low in oxygen or too high in hydrogen sulphide to support life, and some scientists believe that this "fossil water" may be as much as 20 million years old.

Who?What?Where?When?

Sir Richard Francis Burton (1814–1890) Richard Burton was a British explorer. He and his companion John Speke were the first Europeans to visit Somalia. Burton then received a commission from the British Royal Geographical Society to identify the sources of the Nile, and in 1857, he led an expedition that began in Zanzibar. He and Speke were the first Europeans to view Lake Tanganyika, but it was Speke who would discover that the actual source of the Nile is Lake Victoria. Burton was also a linguist and a prolific writer who authored and translated many books during his lifetime.

INTERPRETING THE PAST

Answers:

1. Livingstone's two main objectives were to find the source of the Nile and to find a navigable river that would open Africa to trade and Christianity, thus eliminating slave trade.
2. He encountered Victoria Falls.
3. The main obstacles he faced included the sheer size of Africa, disease, the need for supplies, hostile groups, and long separations from his family.

1 FOCUS

Section Overview

This section describes the expansion of British control over India; the effects of British rule on the economy, politics, and culture of India; the causes of Indian nationalism; and the establishment of a modern Indian identity.

BELLRINGER
Skillbuilder Activity

 Project transparency and have students answer questions.

 Available as a blackline master.

Daily Focus Skills Transparency 14–3

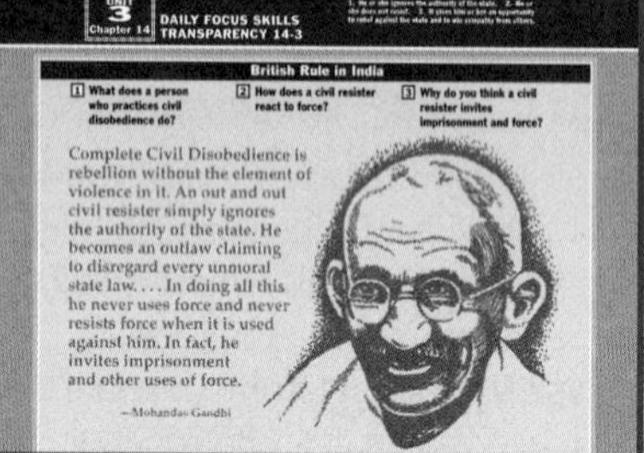

Guide to Reading

Answers to Graphic: textiles: local industry severely damaged; cotton: food supplies unable to keep up with growing population; school: trained children to serve in government, army; railroad: improved transportation, communications

Preteaching Vocabulary: Ask students to use dictionaries to define the two key terms in this section. Review definitions with the class. L2

SECTION 3 British Rule in India

Guide to Reading

Main Ideas
- British rule brought stability to India but destroyed native industries and degraded Indians.
- Mohandas Gandhi advocated nonviolent resistance to gain Indian independence from Great Britain.

Key Terms
sepoy, viceroy

People to Identify
Queen Victoria, Mohandas Gandhi

Places to Locate
Kanpur, Mumbai

Preview Questions
1. What was the goal of the Indian National Congress?
2. Why was India called the "Jewel in the Crown" of Queen Victoria, the Empress of India?

Reading Strategy
Cause and Effect Using a chart like the one below, identify some causes and effects of British influence on India.

Cause	Effect
1. British textiles	
2. cotton crops	
3. school system	
4. railroad, telegraph, telephone services	

Preview of Events

1840 · 1850 · 1860 · 1870 · 1880 · 1890 · 1900

- **1857** Sepoy Mutiny fails
- **1876** Queen Victoria is named "Empress of India"
- **1885** Indian National Congress forms

Voices from the Past

Thomas Macaulay

Thomas Macaulay, who was charged with the task of introducing an educational system into India, decided that it would use the English language:

> "What, then shall the language of education be? [Some] maintain that it should be the English. The other half strongly recommend the Arabic and Sanskrit. The whole question seems to me to be, which language is the best worth knowing? . . . It is, I believe, no exaggeration to say that all the historical information which has been collected from all the books written in the Sanskrit language is less valuable than what may be found in short textbooks used at preparatory schools in England."
>
> —*A New History of India*, Stanley Wolpert, 1977

Macaulay's attitude reflects the sense of superiority that the British brought with them to India.

The Sepoy Mutiny

Over the course of the eighteenth century, British power in India had increased while the power of the Mogul rulers had declined (see Chapter 8). A trading company, the British East India Company, was given power by the British government to become actively involved in India's political and military affairs.

To rule India, the British East India Company had its own soldiers and forts. It also hired Indian soldiers, known as sepoys, to protect the company's interests in the region.

In 1857, a growing Indian distrust of the British led to a revolt. The revolt was known to the British as the Great Rebellion or the Sepoy Mutiny. Indians call it the First War of Independence.

SECTION RESOURCES

Reproducible Masters
- Reproducible Lesson Plan 14–3
- Daily Lecture and Discussion Notes 14–3
- Guided Reading Activity 14–3
- Section Quiz 14–3
- Reading Essentials and Study Guide 14–3

Transparencies
- Daily Focus Skills Transparency 14–3

Multimedia
- Interactive Tutor Self-Assessment CD-ROM
- ExamView® Pro Testmaker CD-ROM
- Presentation Plus! CD-ROM

Picturing History

After the 1857 revolt, officials of the British government ruled India. The sepoys were unsuccessful and paid dearly, as is shown by the British execution of Indian soldiers above. Why did the Indian revolt fail?

The major immediate cause of the revolt was the spread of a rumor that the British were issuing their Indian troops new bullets that were greased with cow and pig fat. The cow was sacred to Hindus; the pig was taboo to Muslims. A group of sepoys at an army post near Delhi refused to load their rifles with the new bullets. When the British arrested them, the sepoys went on a rampage and killed 50 European men, women, and children.

From this beginning, the revolt quickly spread. Within a year, however, Indian troops loyal to the British, along with fresh British troops, had crushed the rebellion. Although Indian troops fought bravely and outnumbered the British by 240,000 to 40,000, they were not well organized. Rivalries between Hindus and Muslims kept Indians from working together.

Atrocities were terrible on both sides. At **Kanpur** (Cawnpore), Indians armed with swords and knives massacred two hundred defenseless women and children in a building known as the House of the Ladies. When the British recaptured Kanpur, they took their revenge before executing the Indians.

As a result of the uprising, the British Parliament transferred the powers of the East India Company directly to the British government. In 1876, the title of Empress of India was bestowed on **Queen Victoria.** The people of India were now her colonial subjects, and India became her "Jewel in the Crown."

Reading Check **Describing** What were two effects of the Great Rebellion?

Colonial Rule

The British government ruled India directly through a British official known as a viceroy (a governor who ruled as a representative of a monarch), who was assisted by a British civil service staff. This staff of about 3,500 officials ruled almost 300 million people, the largest colonial population in the world. British rule involved both benefits and costs for Indians.

2 TEACH

Picturing History

Answer: Rivalries between Hindus and Muslims kept them from working together.

Reading Check

Answer: The East India Company became an agent of the British government. Queen Victoria was made Empress of India.

Daily Lecture and Discussion Notes 14–3

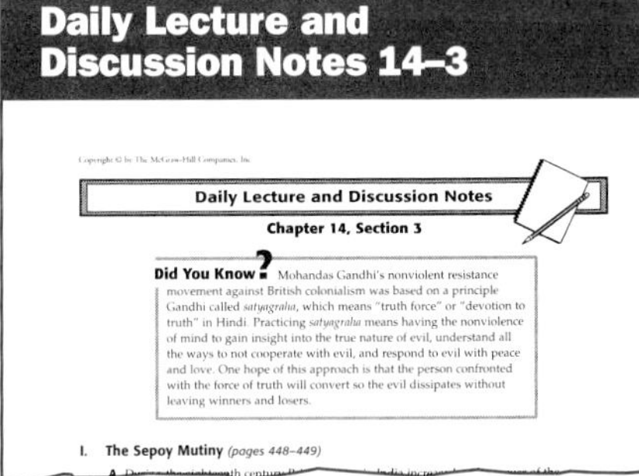

Daily Lecture and Discussion Notes

Chapter 14, Section 3

Did You Know? Mohandas Gandhi's nonviolent resistance movement against British colonialism was based on a principle Gandhi called *satyagraha*, which means "truth force" or "devotion to truth" in Hindi. Practicing *satyagraha* means having the nonviolence of mind to gain insight into the true nature of evil, understand all the ways to not cooperate with evil, and respond to evil with peace and love. One hope of this approach is that the person confronted with the force of truth will convert so the evil dissipates without leaving winners and losers.

I. **The Sepoy Mutiny** *(pages 448–449)*

Guided Reading Activity 14–3

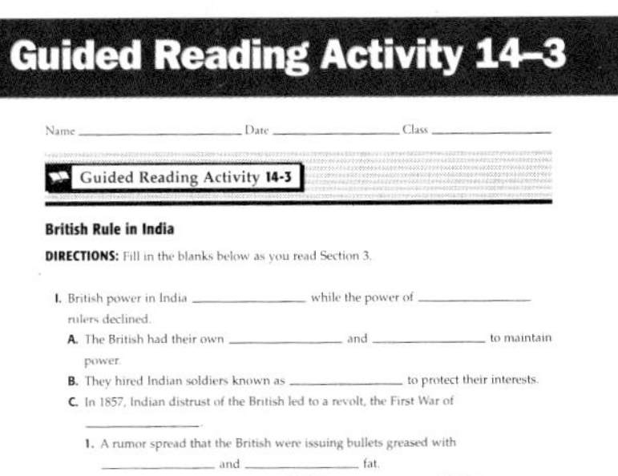

Name ________ Date ________ Class ________

Guided Reading Activity 14-3

British Rule in India

DIRECTIONS: Fill in the blanks below as you read Section 3.

I. British power in India ________ while the power of ________ rulers declined.
  A. The British had their own ________ and ________ to maintain power.
  B. They hired Indian soldiers known as ________ to protect their interests.
  C. In 1857, Indian distrust of the British led to a revolt, the First War of ________.
    1. A rumor spread that the British were issuing bullets greased with ________ and ________ fat.

Enrich

Guide students in a discussion of British insensitivity to Indian culture. Is a lack of sensitivity or understanding common to all European colonization attempts? L1

CRITICAL THINKING ACTIVITY

Compare and Contrast Have students write two different histories of the events surrounding the 1857 revolt in India. One should be a British account of the Sepoy Mutiny, the other the Indian account of the First War of Independence (different names for the same event). These could be written as newspaper articles explaining the events to a specific audience (the British community in India, the Hindu community, or Muslim readers). Ask the students to discuss how opinions and points of view will affect a historian's perception of historical facts. L2

CURRICULUM CONNECTION

Economics After the Sepoy rebellion, the British spent immense sums of money on economic development in India. Ask students what the British motives might have been for this investment. *(to support the needs of the British Empire while repressing any rebellion or conflict with the Indians)* What seems to have been of little concern to the British? *(the beliefs and culture of the Indians or their economic security)* L2

Charting Activity

Have students research and list the various languages spoken in India. *(Fourteen languages are recognized in the Indian constitution including Hindi, English, Telugu, Bengali, Tamil, and Urdu.)* What conclusions can students draw about Indian society from examining the number of languages spoken in the country? L2

Glencoe Literature Library

The following literature from the **Glencoe Literature Library** may enrich the teaching of this chapter:

Nectar in a Sieve by K. Markandaya

A House for Mr. Biswas by V.S. Naipaul

Benefits of British Rule British rule in India had several benefits for subjects. It brought order and stability to a society that had been badly divided by civil war. It also led to a fairly honest and efficient government.

Through the efforts of the British administrator and historian Lord Thomas Macaulay, a new school system was set up. Its goal was to train Indian children to serve in the government and army. The new system served only elite, upper-class Indians, however. Ninety percent of the population remained illiterate.

Railroads, the telegraph, and a postal service were introduced to India shortly after they appeared in Great Britain. The first rail network, from Calcutta to Delhi, was begun in 1839 and opened in 1853. By 1900, 25,000 miles (40,225 km) of railroads crisscrossed India. *(See page 777 to read excerpts from Dadabhai Naroji's* The Impact of British Rule in India *in the Primary Sources Library.)*

Costs of British Rule The Indian people, however, paid a high price for the peace and stability brought by British rule. Perhaps the greatest cost was economic. British entrepreneurs and a small number of Indians reaped financial benefits from British rule, but it brought hardship to millions of others in both the cities and the countryside. British manufactured goods destroyed local industries. The introduction of British textiles put thousands of women out of work and severely damaged the Indian textile industry.

In rural areas, the British sent the zamindars to collect taxes. The British believed that using these local officials would make it easier to collect taxes from the peasants. However, the zamindars in India took advantage of their new authority. They increased taxes and forced the less fortunate peasants to become tenants or lose their land entirely. Peasant unrest grew.

The British also encouraged many farmers to switch from growing food to growing cotton. As a result, food supplies could not keep up with the growing population. Between 1800 and 1900, thirty million Indians died of starvation.

Finally, British rule was degrading, even for the newly educated upper classes, who benefited the

THE WAY IT WAS

FOCUS ON EVERYDAY LIFE

British Official's Home in India

During the time that India was a British colony, many British government officials spent a considerable amount of time there fulfilling their administrative duties. Their families usually came with them during their tours of duty, bringing their Victorian lifestyle and many of the furnishings that went with it.

British officials in India built comfortable bungalows, as they were called. Bungalows (The name comes from the Indian word *bungla,* which means *Bengali.*) were elegant and spacious country houses. Many had large porches that were open to breezes while protecting the inhabitants from the sun. Surrounding the bungalows were cottages where dozens of Indian servants lived with their families.

The official was the sahib—the master. The official's wife was the memsahib, or madam-sahib. The memsahib was expected to oversee the running of the household on a daily basis, especially since the sahib was often away on official business. At the beginning of each day, she assigned duties to all the servants. For example, she fixed the menu for the day with the cook and directed the gardeners about how to plant the gardens with seeds from home. In the evening, she was expected to entertain. Supper parties with other British families were the usual form of entertainment.

450

INTERDISCIPLINARY CONNECTIONS ACTIVITY

Economics There were positive and negative effects of British rule in India. The British instituted improvements in the health, education, infrastructure, and customs of India, but they did so primarily to serve their own interests. Ask students to discuss how these changes benefited Britain economically. *(The British were attempting to create stable conditions to produce materials for British industry and markets for British goods. Most of the changes were necessary to provide workers, land, and social conditions for British industry, administration, and colonial lifestyle.)* L1

most from it. The best jobs and the best housing were reserved for Britons. Although many British colonial officials sincerely tried to improve the lot of the people in India, British arrogance cut deeply into the pride of many Indians.

Despite their education, the Indians were never considered equals of the British. Lord Kitchener, one of Britain's military commanders in India, said, "It is this consciousness of the inherent superiority of the European which has won for us India. However well educated and clever a native may be, and however brave he may prove himself, I believe that no rank we can bestow on him would cause him to be considered an equal of the British officer."

The British also showed disrespect for India's cultural heritage. The Taj Mahal, for example, a tomb for the beloved wife of an Indian ruler, became a favorite site for English weddings and parties. Many partygoers even brought hammers to chip off pieces as souvenirs. British racial attitudes led to the rise of an Indian nationalist movement.

Reading Check **Examining** How was British rule degrading to Indians?

An Indian Nationalist Movement

The first Indian nationalists were upper class and English-educated. Many of them were from urban areas, such as **Mumbai** (then called Bombay), Chennai (Madras), and Calcutta. Some were trained in British law and were members of the civil service.

At first, many preferred reform to revolution, but the slow pace of reform convinced many Indian nationalists that relying on British goodwill was futile. In 1885, a small group of Indians met in Mumbai to form the **Indian National Congress** (INC). The INC did not demand immediate independence but did call for a share in the governing process.

The INC had difficulties because of religious differences. The goal of the INC was to seek independence for all Indians, regardless of class or religious background. However, many of its leaders were Hindu and reflected Hindu concerns. Eventually, Muslims began to call for the creation of a separate Muslim League to represent the interests of the millions of Muslims in Indian society.

In 1915, the return of a young Hindu from South Africa brought new life to India's struggle for

A British officer receives a pedicure from an Indian servant.

The wife of a British officer is attended by Indian servants. A British merchant waits to speak to her.

Many British officials had a high standard of living and were expected to have a large number of servants. One woman wrote in 1882: "It is one of the social duties of Indian life that you must keep three servants to do the work of one." A well-to-do family had at least 25 servants. Even bachelors had at least a dozen. Indians served as cooks, maids, butlers, gardeners, tailors, and nursemaids for the children. All household servants wore uniforms—usually white with bands on their turbans—and went barefoot in the house.

CONNECTING TO THE PAST

1. **Identifying** What were the responsibilities of the wife of a British officer in India?
2. **Writing about History** What do you learn about British-Indian social relations from this reading?

EXTENDING THE CONTENT

British Rule of India Over time, the British rulers of India became increasingly isolated from India and Indians. The British viceroy of India spent half the year at his mountain retreat and the other half in Calcutta where most of his dealings were with English gentlemen, merchants, and civil service workers. The establishment of an overland telegraph in 1865, the opening of the Suez Canal in 1869, and the installation of a submarine cable in 1870 meant that British officials would often have closer contact with London than with the people of India. As a result, they had little understanding of the effects of their policies on the people in the land that they ruled.

Reading Check

Answer: The British were arrogant about their "inherent superiority," the best housing and jobs were reserved for Britons, and the British showed disrespect for India's cultural heritage.

THE WAY IT WAS

Answers:

1. oversee running of the household, entertain in the evening
2. that the most common relationship between British and Indian was probably as master and servant

Connecting Across Time

Ask students to research and discuss the ways in which the teaching of Mohandas Gandhi directly affected Martin Luther King, Jr., and the American civil rights movement. **L2**

3 ASSESS

Assign Section 3 Assessment as homework or as an in-class activity.

Have students use **Interactive Tutor Self-Assessment CD-ROM.**

Section Quiz 14–3

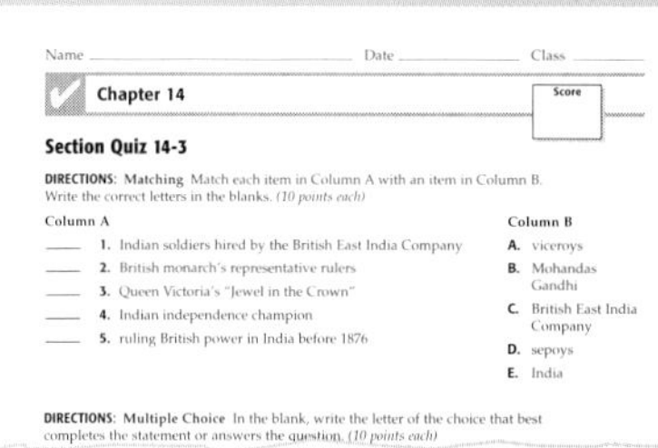

Name ______ Date ______ Class ______

Chapter 14 Score

Section Quiz 14-3

DIRECTIONS: Matching Match each item in Column A with an item in Column B. Write the correct letters in the blanks. *(10 points each)*

Column A	Column B
____ 1. Indian soldiers hired by the British East India Company	A. viceroys
____ 2. British monarch's representative rulers	B. Mohandas Gandhi
____ 3. Queen Victoria's "Jewel in the Crown"	C. British East India Company
____ 4. Indian independence champion	D. sepoys
____ 5. ruling British power in India before 1876	E. India

DIRECTIONS: Multiple Choice In the blank, write the letter of the choice that best completes the statement or answers the question. *(10 points each)*

CHAPTER 14
Section 3, 448–452

Reading Check

Answer: to force the British to help the poor, and to grant independence to India

Reading Check

Answer: Indian novelists and poets began writing historical romances and epics, both of which typically foster nationalism.

Reading Essentials and Study Guide 14–3

Name ______ Date ______ Class ______

Reading Essentials and Study Guide

Chapter 14, Section 3

For use with textbook pages 448–452

BRITISH RULE IN INDIA

KEY TERMS

sepoy an Indian soldier serving in the British army (page 448)

viceroy a governor who ruled as a representative of a monarch (page 449)

DRAWING FROM EXPERIENCE

Have you ever read any stories or poems by the British writer Rudyard Kipling? What insights do his stories and poems give us into life in India during the Age of Imperialism?

In the last two sections, you learned about imperialism in Southeast Asia

Enrich

The Age of Exploration (covered in Chapter 6) led to expansion and colonization and ultimately to "new imperialism" covered in this chapter. Ask students to identify the changes that resulted from the European age of colonization. **L2**

Reteaching Activity

Create a group outline of the section on the board. Have students contribute oral summaries of each part for class discussion. **L1**

4 CLOSE

To show their understanding of the political and economic impact of imperialism, ask students to analyze the British Empire. **L1**

independence. **Mohandas Gandhi** was born in 1869 in Gujarat, in western India. He studied in London and became a lawyer. In 1893, he went to South Africa to work in a law firm serving Indian workers there. He soon became aware of the racial exploitation of Indians living in South Africa.

On his return home to India, Gandhi became active in the independence movement. Using his experience in South Africa, he set up a movement based on nonviolent resistance. Its aim was to force the British to improve the lot of the poor and grant independence to India. Ultimately, Gandhi's movement would lead to Indian independence.

Reading Check **Summarizing** What were the two goals of Mohandas Gandhi?

Colonial Indian Culture

The love-hate tension in India that arose from British domination led to a cultural, as well as a political, awakening. The cultural revival began in the early nineteenth century with the creation of a British college in Calcutta. A local publishing house was opened. It issued textbooks on a variety of subjects, including the sciences, Sanskrit, and Western literature. The publisher also printed grammars and dictionaries in the various Indian languages.

This revival soon spread to other regions of India, leading to a search for modern literary expression and a new national identity. Indian novelists and poets began writing historical romances and epics. Some wrote in English, but most were uncomfortable with a borrowed colonial language. They preferred to use their own regional tongues.

The most illustrious Indian author was Rabindranath Tagore. A great writer and poet, Tagore was also a social reformer, spiritual leader, educator, philosopher, singer, painter, and international spokesperson for the moral concerns of his age. He liked to invite the great thinkers of the time to his country estate. There he set up a school that became an international university.

Tagore's life mission was to promote pride in a national Indian consciousness in the face of British domination. He wrote a widely read novel in which he portrayed the love-hate relationship of India toward its colonial mentor. The novel depicted a country that admired and imitated the British model while also agonizing over how it could establish a modern identity separate from that of Great Britain.

Tagore, however, was more than an Indian nationalist. His life's work was one long prayer for human dignity, world peace, and the mutual understanding and union of East and West. As he once said, "It is my conviction that my countrymen will truly gain their India by fighting against the education that teaches them that a country is greater than the ideals of humanity."

Reading Check **Comparing** How did the nationalist movement parallel cultural developments in India?

SECTION 3 ASSESSMENT

Checking for Understanding

1. **Define** sepoy, viceroy.
2. **Identify** Queen Victoria, Indian National Congress, Mohandas Gandhi.
3. **Locate** Kanpur, Mumbai.
4. **Explain** why the Muslim League was created. What were the advantages of its formation? What were the disadvantages?
5. **List** the economic costs to the Indian people that resulted from India being ruled by the British. What benefits to the Indian population, if any, resulted from British rule?

Critical Thinking

6. **Predict Consequences** Many British lived in India for decades. Do you think living in India would have changed British attitudes toward Indians? Explain.
7. **Organizing Information** Draw a graph like the example below to show the percentage of India's population that died of starvation in the 1800s.

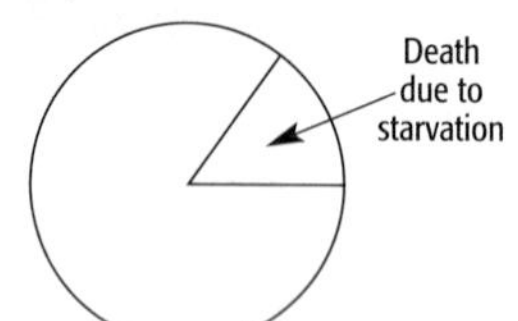

Analyzing Visuals

8. **Interpret** the messages conveyed by the two images on page 451. Describe your reactions to the paintings. Why might your reactions be the same as or different from reactions of English teenagers viewing these paintings in the late 1800s?

Writing About History

9. **Descriptive Writing** Imagine you are a member of India's upper-class. You have just attended a reception at the home of a British official. Describe in writing your impressions of the home, making a comparison to your own residence.

SECTION 3 ASSESSMENT

1. Key terms are in blue.
2. Queen Victoria *(p. 449)*; Indian National Congress *(p. 451)*; Mohandas Gandhi *(p. 452)*
3. See chapter maps.
4. Hindus dominated National Congress; represented Muslim interests; split nationalist movement
5. British textiles destroyed local industry, peasants overtaxed by zamindars, cotton growing led to mass starvation; new school system, improved transportation and communications
6. Answers will vary.
7. Ten percent died.
8. Answers should be supported by logical arguments. Remind students that servants were common even in middle-class British homes during this time.
9. Answers will vary.

SECTION 4

Nation Building in Latin America

Guide to Reading

Main Ideas

- Latin American countries served as a source of raw materials for Europe and the United States.
- Because land remained the basis of wealth and power, landed elites dominated Latin American countries.

Key Terms

creole, *peninsulare*, mestizo, Monroe Doctrine, caudillo

People to Identify

José de San Martín, Simón Bolívar, Antonio López de Santa Anna, Benito Juárez

Places to Locate

Puerto Rico, Panama Canal, Haiti, Nicaragua

Preview Question

1. How did the American Revolution inspire political changes in Latin America?

Reading Strategy

Compare and Contrast Create a Venn diagram comparing and contrasting colonial rule in Africa and in Latin America.

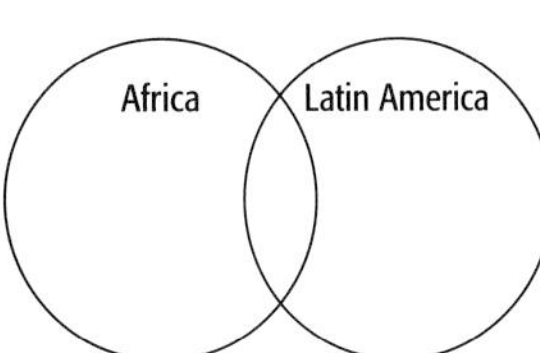

Preview of Events

♦1800	♦1805	♦1810	♦1815	♦1820	♦1825	♦1830

- **1810** Mexico experiences its first revolt
- **1821** Mexico declares independence
- **1825** Most of Latin America becomes independent

Portrait of Simón Bolívar

On August 15, 1818, Simón Bolívar issued a proclamation to the people of New Granada (present-day Colombia):

“Granadans! America's day is come; no human power can stay the course of nature guided by the hand of Providence. Join your efforts to those of your brothers: Venezuela marches with me to free you, as in past years you marched with me to free Venezuela. Already our advance guard fills whole provinces of your territory with the luster of its arms; and the same advance guard, powerfully aided, will hurl the destroyed of New Granada into the seas. The sun will not have completed the course of its present round through the heavens without beholding in all your territory the proud altars of liberty.”

—***World Civilizations*, Philip J. Adler, 1996**

Bolívar was one of the leaders in liberating South America from Spanish and Portuguese control.

Nationalist Revolts

By the end of the eighteenth century, the new political ideals stemming from the successful revolution in North America were beginning to influence Latin America. European control would soon be in peril.

1 FOCUS

Section Overview

This section describes the import and export of materials and goods in Latin American nations, how the domination of the landed elite caused political instability in Latin America, and the causes of the Mexican Revolution.

BELLRINGER
Skillbuilder Activity

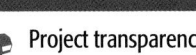

 Project transparency and have students answer questions.

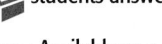

 Available as a blackline master.

Daily Focus Skills Transparency 14–4

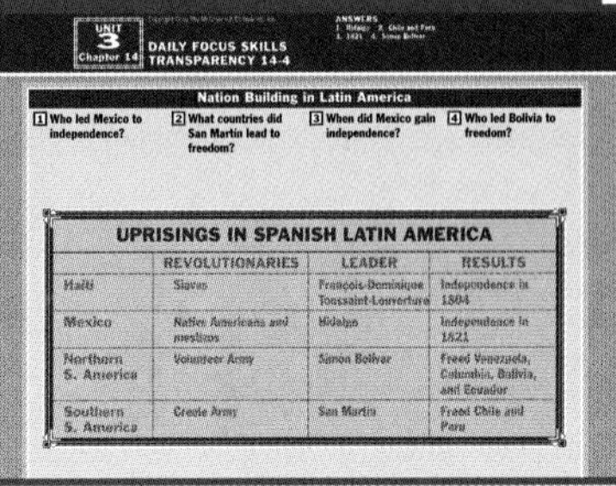

Guide to Reading

Answers to Graphic: Africa: direct or indirect rule, some democratic institutions; Latin America: direct rule, no democratic institutions; Both: trade dominated by colonizers, Europeans felt superior to native peoples

Preteaching Vocabulary: Ask students to describe the significance of the *Monroe Doctrine.* L1

SECTION RESOURCES

Reproducible Masters

- Reproducible Lesson Plan 14–4
- Daily Lecture and Discussion Notes 14–4
- Guided Reading Activity 14–4
- Section Quiz 14–4
- Reading Essentials and Study Guide 14–4

Transparencies

- Daily Focus Skills Transparency 14–4

Multimedia

- Interactive Tutor Self-Assessment CD-ROM
- ExamView® Pro Testmaker CD-ROM
- Presentation Plus! CD-ROM

CHAPTER 14
Section 4, 453–459

2 TEACH

Reading Check

Answer: When Napoleon overthrew the monarchies of Spain and Portugal, it weakened their authority over their empires, giving the creole elites the opportunity to overthrow colonial rule.

Daily Lecture and Discussion Notes 14–4

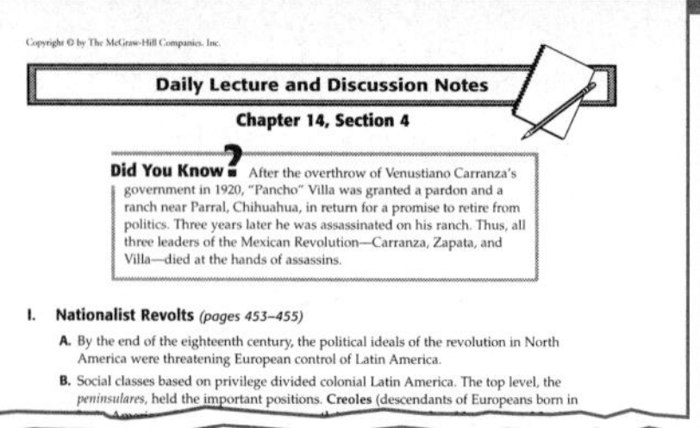

Guided Reading Activity 14–4

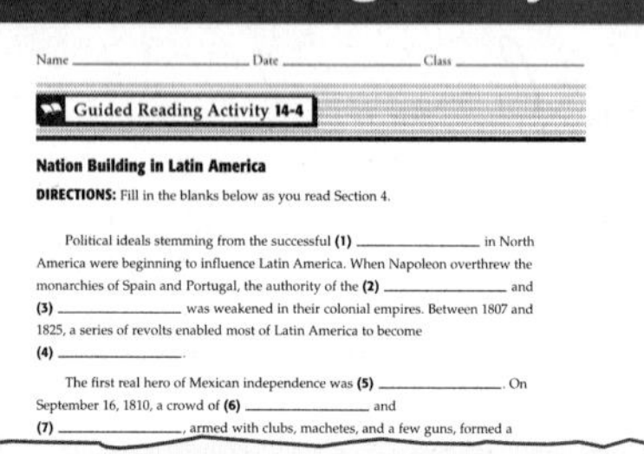

CURRICULUM CONNECTION

Government Ask students to choose a country mentioned in this section, research the current political situation using Internet resources, write a brief summary about that country, and present it to the class. **L1**

Father Hidalgo leads Mexicans in revolt against the Spaniards.

Social classes based on privilege divided colonial Latin America. *Peninsulares*, at the top, held all important positions. Creoles controlled land and business but were regarded as second-class citizens by *peninsulares.* Mestizos were the largest group but worked as servants or laborers.

Prelude to Revolution The creole elites were especially influenced by revolutionary ideals. Creoles were descendants of Europeans born in Latin America and lived there permanently. They found the principles of the equality of all people in the eyes of the law, free trade, and a free press very attractive. In addition, they, along with a growing class of merchants, disliked the domination of their trade by Spain and Portugal.

Creoles deeply resented the *peninsulares,* Spanish and Portuguese officials who resided temporarily in Latin America for political and economic gain and then returned to their mother countries. These Europeans dominated Latin America and drained the Americas of their wealth.

The creole elites soon began to denounce the rule of the Spanish and Portuguese. At the beginning of the nineteenth century, Napoleon's wars provided them with an opportunity for change. When Napoleon overthrew the monarchies of Spain and Portugal, the authority of the Spaniards and Portuguese in their colonial empires was severely weakened. Between 1807 and 1825, a series of revolts enabled most of Latin America to become independent.

Before the main independence movements began, an unusual revolution took place in the French colony of Saint Domingue, on the island of Hispaniola. Led by François-Dominique Toussaint-Louverture (TOO•SAN LOO•vuhr•TYUR), more than a hundred thousand slaves rose in revolt and seized control of all of Hispaniola. On January 1, 1804, the western part of Hispaniola, now called Haiti, announced its freedom and became the first independent state in Latin America.

Reading Check **Describing** How did Napoleon's wars affect Latin America?

Revolt in Mexico Beginning in 1810, Mexico, too, experienced a revolt. The first real hero of Mexican independence was Miguel Hidalgo, a parish priest in a small village about a hundred miles (160 km) from Mexico City.

Hidalgo, who had studied the French Revolution, roused the local Native Americans and mestizos (people of European and Native American descent) to free themselves from the Spanish: "My children, this day comes to us as a new dispensation. Are you ready to receive it? Will you be free? Will you make the effort to recover from the hated Spaniards the lands stolen from your forefathers 300 years ago?"

On September 16, 1810, a crowd of Native Americans and mestizos, armed with clubs, machetes, and a few guns, formed a mob army to attack the Spaniards. Hidalgo was an inexperienced military leader, however, and his forces were soon crushed. A military court sentenced Hidalgo to death, but his memory lived on. In fact, September 16, the first day of the uprising, is Mexico's Independence Day.

The participation of Native Americans and mestizos in Mexico's revolt against Spanish control frightened both creoles and *peninsulares* there. Afraid of the masses, they cooperated in defeating the popular revolutionary forces. Conservative elites—both creoles and *peninsulares*—then decided to overthrow Spanish rule as a way of

HISTORY Online

Web Activity Visit the *Glencoe World History—Modern Times* Web site at wh.mt.glencoe.com and click on **Chapter 14–Student Web Activity** to learn more about independence movements in Latin America.

EXTENDING THE CONTENT

Toussaint-Louverture François-Dominique Toussaint-Louverture, the grandson of an African king, was born a slave in Saint Domingue in 1746. Inspired by news of the French Revolution, black slaves in Saint Domingue revolted in 1791 under Toussaint-Louverture's leadership. By 1801, Toussaint-Louverture controlled Saint Domingue and freed all slaves. Napoleon Bonaparte refused to accept Toussaint-Louverture's control of France's richest colony. In 1802, Toussaint-Louverture was tricked into surrendering, arrested, and taken to France where he died a year later. Haiti, however, became free when Toussaint-Louverture's lieutenant drove out the French forces in 1804.

preserving their own power. They selected a creole military leader, Agustín de Iturbide (EE•TUR•BEE•thay), as their leader.

In 1821, Mexico declared its independence from Spain. Iturbide named himself emperor in 1822 but was deposed in 1823. Mexico then became a republic.

Painting of early twentieth-century coffee plantation by Candido Portinari

Revolts in South America **José de San Martín** of Argentina and **Simón Bolívar** of Venezuela, both members of the creole elite, were hailed as the "Liberators of South America." These men led revolutions throughout the continent. San Martín believed that the Spaniards must be removed from all of South America if any South American nation was to be free.

By 1810, the forces of San Martín had liberated Argentina from Spanish authority. Bolívar began the struggle for independence in Venezuela in 1810 and then went on to lead revolts in New Granada (Colombia) and Ecuador.

In January 1817, San Martín led his forces over the Andes to attack the Spanish in Chile. The journey was an amazing feat. Two-thirds of the pack mules and horses died during the trip. Soldiers suffered from lack of oxygen and severe cold while crossing mountain passes that were more than two miles (3.218 km) above sea level.

The arrival of San Martín's forces in Chile completely surprised the Spaniards. Spanish forces were badly defeated at the Battle of Chacabuco on February 12, 1817. In 1821, San Martín moved on to Lima, Peru, the center of Spanish authority.

Convinced that he could not complete the liberation of Peru alone, San Martín welcomed the arrival of Bolívar and his forces. The "Liberator of Venezuela" took on the task of crushing the last significant Spanish army at Ayacucho on December 9, 1824.

By the end of 1824, Peru, Uruguay, Paraguay, Colombia, Venezuela, Argentina, Bolivia, and Chile had all become free states. Earlier, in 1822, the prince regent of Brazil had declared Brazil's independence from Portugal. The Central American states had become independent in 1823. In 1838 and 1839, they divided into five republics: Guatemala, El Salvador, Honduras, Costa Rica, and Nicaragua.

In the early 1820s, only one major threat remained to the newly won independence of the Latin American states. Members of the Concert of Europe favored the use of troops to restore Spanish control in Latin America. The British, who wished to trade with Latin America, disagreed. They proposed joint action with the United States against any European moves in Latin America.

Distrustful of British motives, United States president James Monroe acted alone in 1823. In the Monroe Doctrine, he guaranteed the independence of the new Latin American nations and warned against any European intervention in the Americas.

More important to Latin American independence than American words, however, was Britain's navy. Other European powers feared British naval power, which stood between Latin America and any European invasion force.

Reading Check **Evaluating** How did the French Revolution affect Mexico?

Difficulties of Nation Building

The new Latin American nations faced a number of serious problems between 1830 and 1870. The wars for independence had resulted in a staggering loss of people, property, and livestock. Unsure of their precise boundaries, the new nations went to war with one another to settle border disputes. Poor roads, a lack of railroads, thick jungles, and mountains made communication, transportation, and national unity difficult. During the course of the nineteenth century, the new Latin American nations would become economically dependent on Western nations once again.

Reading Check

Answer: Miguel Hidalgo, who had studied the French Revolution, led the local Indians and mestizos in a revolt against the Spanish that failed. The Mexican elites then revolted and declared Mexico independent.

Enrich

The text explains how San Martín surprised the Spanish in Chile by an unexpected attack through the Andes Mountains. Ask students to name two other examples of victories won by soldiers who appeared from an unexpected direction. *(Students might suggest Hannibal descending into northern Italy by crossing the Alps; or George Washington crossing the Delaware and surprising the British at Trenton.)* L2

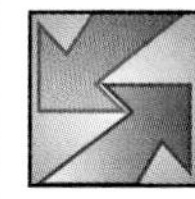

CURRICULUM CONNECTION

Journalism Ask students to draw a political cartoon depicting a major event from this section and present it to the class. L1

Charting Activity

Have students create a chart that identifies and explains the political, economic, cultural, and technological influences of European expansion on both Europeans and non-Europeans. L3

CRITICAL THINKING ACTIVITY

Evaluating Ask students to research the Monroe Doctrine and compile their findings into an essay. The Monroe Doctrine laid the foundations of U.S. policy in Latin America. It was developed because the United States and Britain were concerned about possible European colonial expansion. By separating Europe from America, Monroe emphasized the existence of distinctly American, and specifically U.S., interests. Ask students to evaluate the effectiveness of the Monroe Doctrine. How did the doctrine change to reflect world events? What countries benefited the most and the least from the Monroe Doctrine? How did the doctrine influence the development of Latin American states, and what is its legacy today? L1

Geography *Skills*

Answers:

1. Atlantic and Pacific
2. 7,700 miles (12,389 km)
3. because that was where the isthmus was the narrowest; also, Nicaragua was an independent nation and Panama needed support that the United States could provide in exchange for control of the isthmus

Critical Thinking

Organize a class debate on the following topic: "Resolved: Imperialism was a necessary, if sometimes painful, stage in the evolution and modernization of non-European societies." You will need to choose (1) an affirmative team, (2) a negative team, (3) a moderator, and (4) judges. The order of the debate should be (1) affirmative case, (2) negative case, (3) affirmative rebuttal, (4) negative rebuttal, (5) questions from judges directed to the affirmative team, (6) questions from judges directed to the negative team, (7) negative summary, and (8) affirmative summary. L2

NATIONAL GEOGRAPHIC **Panama Canal**

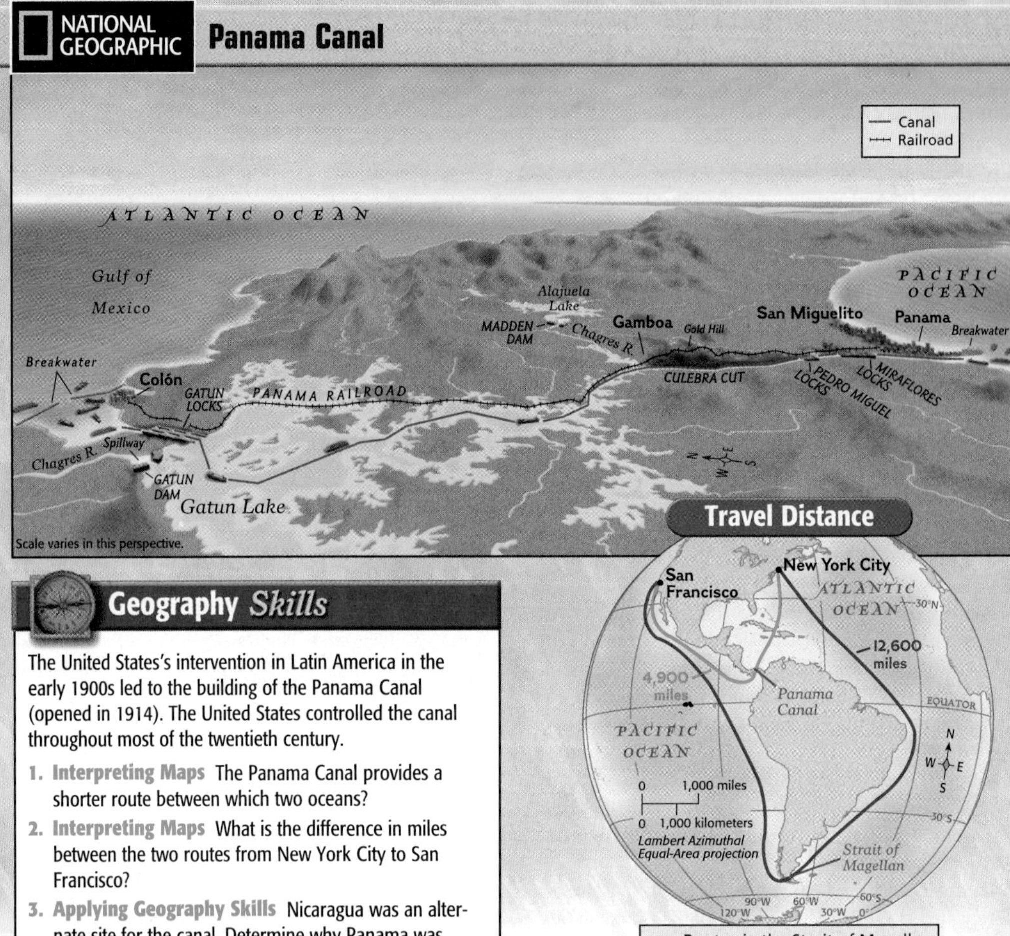

Geography *Skills*

The United States's intervention in Latin America in the early 1900s led to the building of the Panama Canal (opened in 1914). The United States controlled the canal throughout most of the twentieth century.

1. **Interpreting Maps** The Panama Canal provides a shorter route between which two oceans?
2. **Interpreting Maps** What is the difference in miles between the two routes from New York City to San Francisco?
3. **Applying Geography Skills** Nicaragua was an alternate site for the canal. Determine why Panama was selected.

Rule of the Caudillos Most of the new nations of Latin America began with republican governments, but they had had no experience in ruling themselves. Soon after independence, strong leaders known as caudillos came into power.

Caudillos ruled chiefly by military force and were usually supported by the landed elites. Many kept the new national states together. Some were also modernizers who built roads and canals, ports, and schools. Others were destructive.

Antonio López de Santa Anna, for example, ruled Mexico from 1829 to 1855. He misused state funds, halted reforms, and created chaos. In 1835, American settlers in the Mexican state of Texas revolted against Santa Anna's rule.

Texas gained its independence in 1836 and United States statehood in 1845. War between Mexico and the United States soon followed (1846–1848). Mexico was defeated and lost almost one-half of its territory to the United States in the Mexican War.

Fortunately for Mexico, Santa Anna's disastrous rule was followed by a period of reform from 1855 to 1876. This era was dominated by **Benito Juárez,** a Mexican national hero. The son of Native American peasants, President Juárez brought liberal reforms to Mexico, including separation of church and state, land distribution to the poor, and an educational system for all of Mexico.

Other caudillos, such as Juan Manual de Rosas in Argentina, were supported by the masses, became extremely popular, and brought about radical change. Unfortunately, the caudillo's authority depended on his personal power. When he died or lost power, civil wars for control of the country often erupted.

MEETING INDIVIDUAL NEEDS

Visual/Kinesthetic Divide the class into four groups: 1) Southeast Asia, 2) Africa, 3) India, and 4) Latin America. Have each group re-read their respective section. Each group should then prepare a bulletin board display that will show how imperialism affected their part of the world. The bulletin boards may include items such as maps, examples of art, religious symbols, products associated with the regions, etc. For example, Southeast Asia: Christianity, production of rubber, palm oil, coffee, tea; Africa: sugar, textiles, ivory; India: Hinduism, spices; Latin America: sugar, Christianity, beef, coffee, bananas, silver. L1

Refer to ***Inclusion for the High School Social Studies Classroom Strategies and Activities*** in the TCR.

Panama Canal Locks

1. A ship arrives from the Atlantic Ocean or the Pacific Ocean.
2. The ship enters the first lock and steel gates close behind it. Water flows into the lock from an artificial lake. When the water reaches the level of the next higher lock, gates open and the ship moves forward.
3. Electric towing locomotives called mules pull the ship by cables through the locks.
4. In a descending lock, water is drained to the level of the next lower lock and the ship advances.

Workers building the Panama Canal

Panama Canal Facts

- In 1534, Holy Roman Emperor Charles V ordered the first survey of a proposed canal route across the Isthmus of Panama. The survey came back "impossible."
- The canal was constructed in two stages: between 1881 and 1888 by a French company and between 1904 and 1914 by the United States.
- The canal is 51 miles (82 km) long. The average time a ship spends in transit is 8 to 10 hours.
- There are 6 pairs of locks, or a total of 12 locks. Each lock is 1,000 feet (305 m) long and 110 feet (34 m) wide. The lock system lifts ships 85 feet (26 m) above sea level.
- About 140 million tons (127 million t) of commercial cargo pass through the canal each year.

A New Imperialism Political independence brought economic independence, but old patterns were quickly reestablished. Instead of Spain and Portugal, Great Britain now dominated the Latin American economy. British merchants moved into Latin America in large numbers, and British investors poured in funds. Old trade patterns soon reemerged.

Latin America continued to serve as a source of raw materials and foodstuffs for the industrial nations of Europe and the United States. Exports included wheat, tobacco, wool, sugar, coffee, and hides. At the same time, finished consumer goods, especially textiles, were imported.

The emphasis on exporting raw materials and importing finished products ensured the ongoing domination of the Latin American economy by foreigners. Latin American countries remained economic colonies of Western nations, even though they were no longer political colonies.

Persistent Inequality A fundamental, underlying problem for all of the new Latin American nations was the domination of society by the landed elites. Large estates remained a way of life in Latin America. By 1848, for example, the Sánchez Navarro family in Mexico possessed 17 estates made up of 16 million acres (6,480,000 ha). Estates were often so large that they could not be farmed efficiently.

Land remained the basis of wealth, social prestige, and political power throughout the nineteenth century. Landed elites ran governments, controlled courts, and kept a system of inexpensive labor. These landowners made enormous profits by growing single, specialized crops, such as coffee, for export. The

CHAPTER 14
Section 4, 453–459

Connecting Across Time

Have students research and write short reports on public reaction to a more recent attempt by the United States to shape political events in Latin America by supporting the Nicaraguan contras. Ask students to consider how attitudes toward American intervention in the Western Hemisphere may have changed over the century. **L2**

3 ASSESS

Assign Section 4 Assessment as homework or as an in-class activity.

Have students use **Interactive Tutor Self-Assessment CD-ROM.**

Section Quiz 14–4

Chapter 14

Section Quiz 14-4

Reading Essentials and Study Guide 14–4

Reading Essentials and Study Guide

Chapter 14, Section 4

NATION BUILDING IN LATIN AMERICA

INTERDISCIPLINARY CONNECTIONS ACTIVITY

Economics The theory of "economic dependency" means that developing countries can never catch up with developed countries. Technological products have more value than raw materials. Since developing countries cannot afford to buy technology, and have only low-valued goods to exchange, they are forever dependent on the developed countries for technological products. Have students choose one of the countries discussed in this section and research that country's current economic condition. Ask students to prepare an oral report that summarizes the country's major imports and exports, industry, and economic relations with other countries.

For grading this activity, refer to the ***Performance Assessment Activities*** booklet.

Reading Check

Answer: fighting over boundaries; poor roads, lack of railroads, thick jungles, and mountains made communication, transportation, and national unity difficult

TURNING POINT

The construction of the Panama Canal greatly increased the military and economic capabilities of the United States by drastically reducing the time it took to sail between the country's two coasts.

Picturing History

Answer: Puerto Rico, the Philippines, and Guam

Reading Check

Answer: American military forces were sent to many Latin American countries to protect American investments; in some cases, military occupation lasted for many years.

Critical Thinking

Ask students to summarize the main barriers to national unity in Latin America. *(the failure of nationalists to address the unequal class system; the continued economic dependence on Europe created by the colonial system; the rebel elite continued to profit from the sale of raw materials; Latin America exchanged political colonialism for economic colonialism)*

masses, with no land to grow basic food crops, experienced dire poverty.

Reading Check **Describing** What were some of the difficulties faced by the new Latin American republics?

Political Change in Latin America

TURNING POINT **One hundred years of direct United States involvement in the Panama Canal ended on December 31, 1999, when the canal reverted to Panamanian control.**

After 1870, Latin American governments, led by large landowners, wrote constitutions similar to those of the United States and European democracies. The ruling elites were careful to keep their power by limiting voting rights, however.

The United States in Latin America By 1900, the United States, which had emerged as a world power, had begun to interfere in the affairs of its southern neighbors. As a result of the Spanish-American War (1898), Cuba became a United States protectorate, and **Puerto Rico** was annexed to the United States.

In 1903, the United States supported a rebellion that enabled Panama to separate itself from Colombia and establish a new nation. In return, the United States was granted control of a strip of land 10 miles (16.09 km) wide running from coast to coast in Panama. There, the United States built the **Panama Canal,** which was opened in 1914.

American investments in Latin America soon followed, as did American resolve to protect those investments. Beginning in 1898, American military forces were sent to Cuba, Mexico, Guatemala, Honduras, Nicaragua, Panama, Colombia, Haiti, and the Dominican Republic to protect American interests.

Some expeditions remained for many years. United States Marines were in **Haiti** from 1915 to 1934, and **Nicaragua** was occupied from 1909 to 1933. Increasing numbers of Latin Americans began to resent this interference from the "big bully" to the north.

Revolution in Mexico In some countries, large landowners supported dictators who looked out for the interests of the ruling elite. Porfirio Díaz, who ruled Mexico between 1877 and 1911, created a conservative, centralized government with the support of the army, foreign capitalists, large landowners, and the Catholic Church. All these groups benefited from their alliance. However, forces for change in Mexico led to a revolution.

During Díaz's dictatorial reign, the wages of workers had declined. Ninety-five percent of the rural population owned no land, whereas about a thousand families owned almost all of Mexico. When a liberal landowner, Francisco Madero, forced Díaz from power in 1911, he opened the door to a wider revolution.

Madero's ineffectiveness created a demand for agrarian reform. This new call for reform was led by Emiliano Zapata. Zapata aroused the masses of landless peasants and began to seize the estates of wealthy landholders.

Between 1910 and 1920, the Mexican Revolution caused great damage to the Mexican economy. Finally, a new constitution enacted in 1917 set up a government led by a president, created land-reform policies, established limits on foreign investors, and set an agenda to help the workers. The revolution also led to an outpouring of patriotism. Intellectuals and artists sought to capture what was unique about Mexico, with special emphasis on its past.

Reading Check **Describing** What was the United States's role as a colonial power?

Picturing History

United States marines hoist the American flag following a United States victory in the Spanish-American War. What territories in addition to Cuba came under American control as a result of the Spanish-American War?

EXTENDING THE CONTENT

The Panama Canal President Theodore Roosevelt wanted to boost American power and to compete more effectively with the imperial powers of Europe and Japan. The Panama Canal helped accomplish this goal by strengthening the military posture of the United States. The canal eliminated 7,700 miles (12,389 km) from the sea voyage between New York City and San Francisco. It cost $380 million and tens of thousands of lives, and took ten years to complete. It was a testament to the skill of American engineers. Without the significant advances made in technology during the 1800s, the canal could not have been built.

Economic Change in Latin America

After 1870, Latin America began an age of prosperity based to a large extent on the export of a few basic items. These included wheat and beef from Argentina, coffee from Brazil, coffee and bananas from Central America, and sugar and silver from Peru. These foodstuffs and raw materials were largely exchanged for finished goods—textiles, machines, and luxury items—from Europe and the United States. After 1900, Latin Americans also increased their own industrialization, especially by building textile, food-processing, and construction material factories.

One result of the prosperity that came from increased exports was growth in the middle sectors (divisions) of Latin American society—lawyers, merchants, shopkeepers, businesspeople, schoolteachers, professors, bureaucrats, and military officers. These middle sectors accounted for only 5 to 10 percent of the population, hardly enough in numbers to make up a true middle class. Nevertheless, after 1900, the middle sectors of society continued to expand.

Regardless of the country in which they lived, middle-class Latin Americans shared some common characteristics. They lived in the cities; sought education and decent incomes; and saw the United States as a model, especially in regard to industrialization.

The middle sectors in Latin America sought liberal reform, not revolution. Once they had the right to vote, they generally sided with the landholding elites.

Picturing History

This photo shows Montevideo, Uruguay, in the early twentieth century. What signs of increasing prosperity do you see in this photo?

Reading Check **Evaluating** What caused the growth of a middle class in Latin America?

SECTION 4 ASSESSMENT

Checking for Understanding

1. **Define** creole, *peninsulare*, mestizo, Monroe Doctrine, caudillo.
2. **Identify** José de San Martín, Simón Bolívar, Antonio López de Santa Anna, Benito Juárez.
3. **Locate** Puerto Rico, Panama Canal, Haiti, Nicaragua.
4. **Describe** British motives for protecting Latin American states.
5. **List** the powers and privileges of the landed elites.

Critical Thinking

6. **Examine** Why did eliminating European domination from Latin America not bring about significant economic and social change?
7. **Organizing Information** Fill in the chart below to identify which country exported each product listed.

Product	Country
coffee	
bananas and coffee	
beef and wheat	
sugar and silver	

Analyzing Visuals

8. **Describe** the painting on page 454. What action is taking place? How would you describe the emotions of the people in the scene? How has the painter tried to convey the importance of the event?

Writing About History

9. **Expository Writing** Why did Latin American countries remain economic colonies of Western nations when they were no longer political colonies? Write a brief essay explaining why this happened.

Picturing History

Answer: The buildings are well maintained, people are well dressed; there seems to be an abundance of automobiles.

Reading Check

Answer: prosperity from increased exports

Enrich

Using information from this text, have students describe the defining characteristics of this era of imperialism. L2

Reteaching Activity

Ask students which country in Latin America was the first to obtain independence. *(Haiti, 1804)* Which country was the last to obtain independence? *(Dominican Republic, 1844)* What is ironic about the answers to the above questions? *(Both countries share the same island.)* L1

4 CLOSE

Ask students to discuss the causes of instability that led to revolution in Latin America. Students can focus on either internal problems like land distribution, churches, etc., or external events like the American Revolution or the Napoleonic wars in Europe. Allow each student the opportunity to participate. L2

SECTION 4 ASSESSMENT

1. Key terms are in blue.
2. José de San Martín *(p. 455);* Simón Bolívar *(p. 455);* Antonio López de Santa Anna *(p. 456);* Benito Juárez *(p. 456)*
3. See chapter maps.
4. The British wanted to trade with Latin America.
5. They ran governments, controlled courts, and kept a system of inexpensive labor.
6. Landed elites excluded the vast majority of the population from any role in governing.
7. coffee: Brazil; bananas and coffee: Central America; beef and wheat: Argentina; sugar and silver: Peru
8. An angry mob is taking up arms. Prominent swords, flames, and banners convey energy and motion. Answers will vary.
9. New nations relied on exporting a few basic raw materials and importing manufactured goods until they could develop their own industries.

GLENCOE
TECHNOLOGY

MindJogger Videoquiz

Use the **MindJogger Videoquiz** to review Chapter 14 content.

 Available in VHS.

Using Key Terms

1. imperialism **2.** protectorate **3.** indirect rule **4.** direct rule **5.** annexed **6.** indigenous **7.** sepoys **8.** viceroy **9.** Monroe Doctrine **10.** creole

Reviewing Key Facts

11. as a source of raw materials and markets for their manufactured goods; source of national prestige; belief in their inherent superiority over indigenous peoples

12. Liberia

13. Great Britain, France, Germany, Belgium, Portugal

14. destroyed local textile industry; tax collectors overtaxed peasants; farmers encouraged to grow cotton instead of food, leading to mass starvation; new school system to train Indian children; establishment of railroads, telegraph, and postal service improved transportation and communications

15. Zamindars were local officials used by the British to collect taxes. Many took advantage of their authority to increase taxes, forcing the less fortunate peasants to become tenants or lose their land entirely.

16. to force the British to help the poor and grant independence to India

17. More than 100,000 slaves revolted, overthrowing French rule.

18. It would support Panama's rebellion against Colombia in exchange for control of a 10-mile-wide (16.09 km) strip of land running from coast to coast.

19. Thailand; to serve as a buffer state between British and French possessions in Southeast Asia

CHAPTER 14 ASSESSMENT and ACTIVITIES

Chapter Summary

The Age Of Imperialism

The imperialist powers of the nineteenth century conquered weaker countries and carved up the lands they seized. Their actions had a lasting effect on the world, especially the conquered peoples of Asia and Africa. The chart below organizes selected events that occurred during the age of imperialism according to four themes.

Movement

- Imperialistic nations set up colonies and protectorates.
- Christian missionaries preach in Africa and Asia.
- Cecil Rhodes makes a fortune in South Africa.

Change

- Ferdinand de Lesseps completes the Suez Canal in 1869.
- King Leopold II of Belgium colonizes the Congo Basin.
- The United States gains new territory after the Spanish-American War.
- The Panama Canal opens in 1914.

Reaction

- The British East India Company controls India.
- Afrikaners set up independent republics.

Nationalism

- The United States creates the Monroe Doctrine in 1823.
- In May 1857, the Sepoys rebel against British commanders.
- Afrikaners fight the British in the Boer War from 1899 to 1902.

Using Key Terms

1. The extension of a nation's power over other lands is called _____.
2. A _____ is a political unit that depends on another state for its protection, such as Cambodia in its relationship with France in the 1880s.
3. The method of colonial government in which local rulers maintain their authority is called _____.
4. When foreigners govern the colony instead of locals it is called _____.
5. Puerto Rico was _____ by the United States.
6. People who are native to a country are known as _____.
7. Indian soldiers in the service of the British East India Company were called _____.
8. The _____ of India was assisted by a large British civil service staff.
9. To prevent foreign interference in Latin America, the president of the United States issued the _____.
10. The _____ elite led the fight for independence in South America.

Reviewing Key Facts

11. **Economics** Why did European states wish to establish colonies?
12. **Geography** What African state was founded as refuge for former slaves?
13. **History** By 1914, what European countries had divided up Africa?
14. **Culture** What were the effects of British rule in India?
15. **Government** Describe the zamindar system, which was used by the British in India.
16. **History** What were the goals of Mohandas Gandhi?
17. **History** Why was the Haitian revolution unique?
18. **History** What arrangement did the United States make with Panama?
19. **Geography** What country in Southeast Asia remained independent? Why?

Critical Thinking

20. **Analyzing** Explain the circumstances surrounding the building of the Panama Canal. How did the United States benefit?
21. **Making Comparisons** Discuss the various concerns of people under colonial rule. Did social class affect how they viewed colonial power? How were the concerns of different social classes similar? How were they different?

Critical Thinking

20. In 1903, the United States supported Panama's revolt against Colombia in exchange for control of a 10-mile-wide (16.09 km) strip of land running from coast to coast. The canal built there shortened the traveling distance between the U.S. coasts, making shipping faster and cheaper.

21. Most people under colonial rule resented it. In many cases, the elite classes resented foreign rule the most because they understood the institutions and values of the West. Peasant unrest often came about as a result of displacement from lands that were seized by colonists; peasants were often forced into virtual slavery on new plantations. The colonists' superior attitude resulted in a growing resentment and native pride.

Writing About History

22. Answers should be consistent with material presented in this chapter.

Self-Check Quiz

Visit the *Glencoe World History—Modern Times* Web site at wh.mt.glencoe.com and click on **Chapter 14–Self-Check Quiz** to prepare for the Chapter Test.

Writing About History

22. **Persuasive Writing** Pretend you are a British colonist who has been living abroad for a year. Decide whether you are for or against colonialism and write a letter to your family convincing them of your views. Use examples from the text or your own research.

Analyzing Sources

Read the following quote by Miguel Hidalgo:

> "My children, this day comes to us as a new dispensation. Are you ready to receive it? Will you be free? Will you make the effort to recover from the hated Spanish the lands stolen from your forefathers 300 years ago?"

23. Describe the tone of this quote. What emotions is Hidalgo trying to arouse? Is Hidalgo correct when he claims that the Spanish stole the land?
24. Do you think Native Americans in North America are justified in feeling that their lands were stolen? Why or why not?

Applying Technology Skills

25. **Using the Internet** Use the Internet to research Emilio Aguinaldo and the Philippine quest for independence. Create a map showing the various battle sites.

Making Decisions

26. You are a local ruler in your country. You deeply resent the colonial power that has asked you to rule in its interest. Do you continue to rule or do you resign? What are the consequences of your decision?
27. Originally the Panama Canal was a French project. When the French ran into difficulties, they attempted to sell their project to the United States. As a United States senator, decide whether or not the United States should take over the project. Give reasons for your decision.
28. Simón Bolívar is considered to be the George Washington of South America. Do further research on Bolívar in your school library. If necessary, review information you have previously learned about George Washington. Decide whether or not you think the comparison between Bolívar and Washington is fair. Explain your decision.

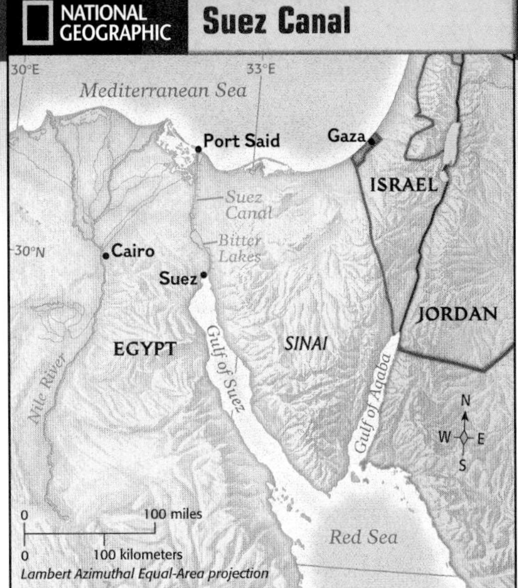

Analyzing Maps and Charts

Use your text and the map above to answer the following questions.

29. Approximately how long is the Suez Canal?
30. Why is control of the Suez Canal so important?
31. What alternative transportation exists across the land masses surrounding the Suez Canal?
32. What route was used for trade and transportation in this area prior to the building of the Suez Canal?

Standardized Test Practice

Directions: Choose the best answer to the following question.

Which of the following was a consequence of British colonial rule in India?

A the defeat of the Mogul dynasty
B the popularity of the joint-stock company
C the exploitation of resources
D the Berlin Conference of 1884

Test-Taking Tip: If you do not immediately know the right answer to a question, look at each answer choice carefully. Try to recall the context in which these events were discussed in class. Remembering this context may help you eliminate incorrect answer choices.

CHAPTER 14
Assessment and Activities

Have students visit the Web site at wh.mt.glencoe.com to review Chapter 14 and take the Self-Check Quiz.

28. Answers will vary but should be supported by references and logical arguments.

Analyzing Maps and Charts

29. about 100 miles (160 km)
30. It links the Mediterranean Sea to the Red Sea and provides a shorter route from Europe to Asia.
31. railroad runs parallel to canal
32. Without the canal, ships in the Mediterranean Sea had to travel around Africa to reach Asia.

Standardized Test Practice

Answer: C
Answer Explanation: Students can automatically eliminate answers not related to India, such as D.

Bonus Question ?

Have students write a definition of *nationalism.* **Ask:** What do nationalist movements hope to gain or preserve? *(cultural and political independence)*

Analyzing Sources

23. He is trying to inflame their anger against the "hated Spanish," as well as a feeling of righteous indignation. Answers will vary.
24. Answers will vary but should be supported by logical arguments and information about recent legal cases.

Applying Technology Skills

25. Answers will vary. Students will create maps.

Making Decisions

26. Answers will vary but should be consistent with the material presented in this chapter.
27. Answers will vary but should be supported by logical arguments.

Chapter 15 Resources

Timesaving Tools

TeacherWorks™ All-In-One Planner and Resource Center

- **Interactive Teacher Edition** Access your Teacher Wraparound Edition and your classroom resources with a few easy clicks.
- **Interactive Lesson Planner** Planning has never been easier! Organize your week, month, semester, or year with all the lesson helps you need to make teaching creative, timely, and relevant.

Use Glencoe's **Presentation Plus!** multimedia teacher tool to easily present dynamic lessons that visually excite your students. Using Microsoft PowerPoint® you can customize the presentations to create your own personalized lessons.

TEACHING TRANSPARENCIES

Graphic Organizer Student Activity 15 Transparency

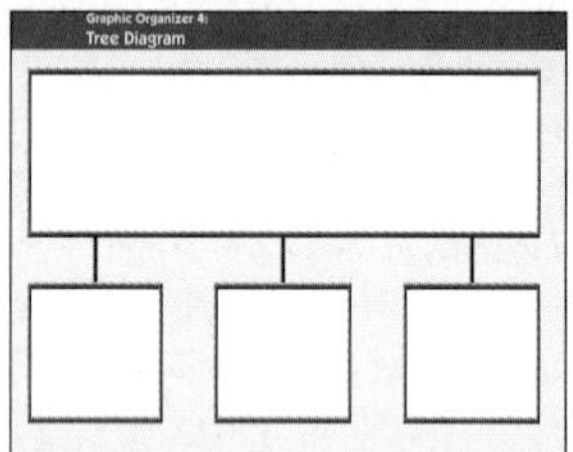

Chapter Transparency 15

Map Overlay Transparency 15

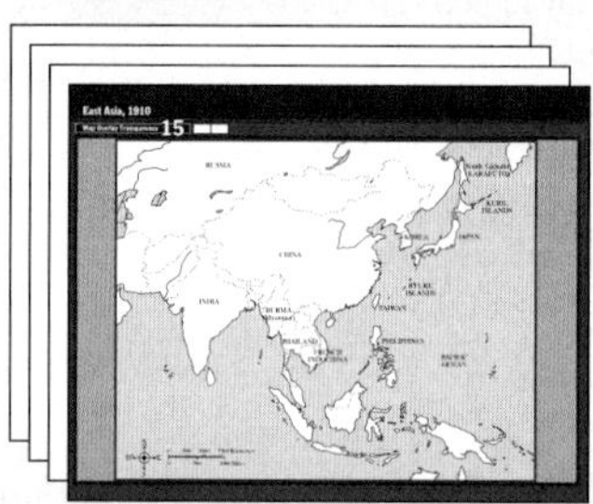

APPLICATION AND ENRICHMENT

Enrichment Activity 15

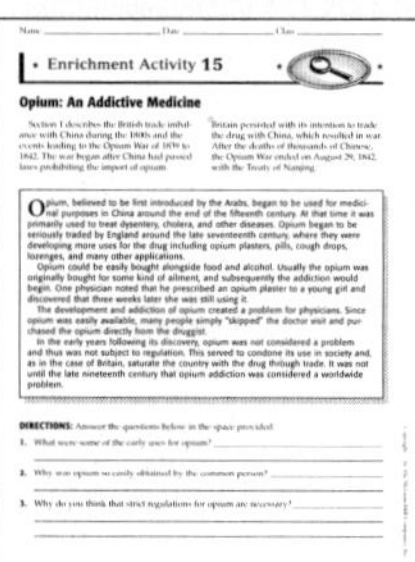

Primary Source Reading 15

History Simulation Activity 15

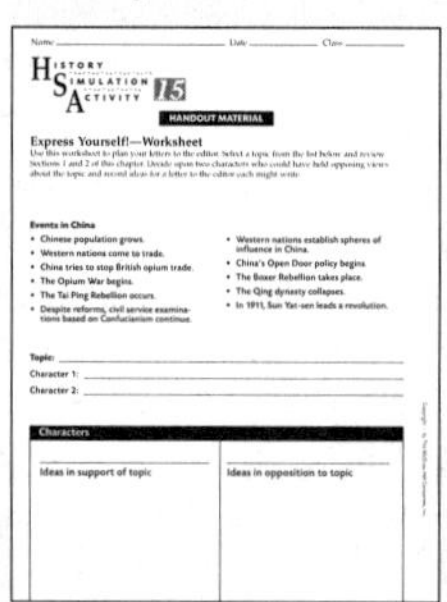

Historical Significance Activity 15

Cooperative Learning Activity 15

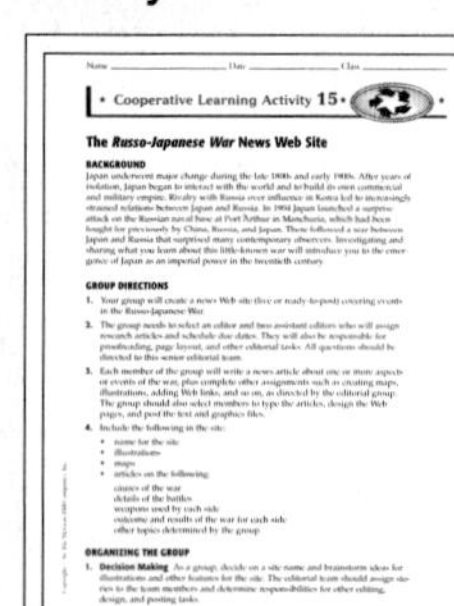

A&E HOME VIDEO. Biography® THE HISTORY CHANNEL®

The following videotape program is available from Glencoe as a supplement to Chapter 15:

- **China's Boxer Rebellion** (ISBN 0-7670-0617-8)

To order, call Glencoe at 1-800-334-7344. To find classroom resources to accompany this video, check the following home pages:

A&E Television: www.aande.com

The History Channel: www.historychannel.com

Chapter 15 Resources

Review and Reinforcement

Linking Past and Present Activity 15

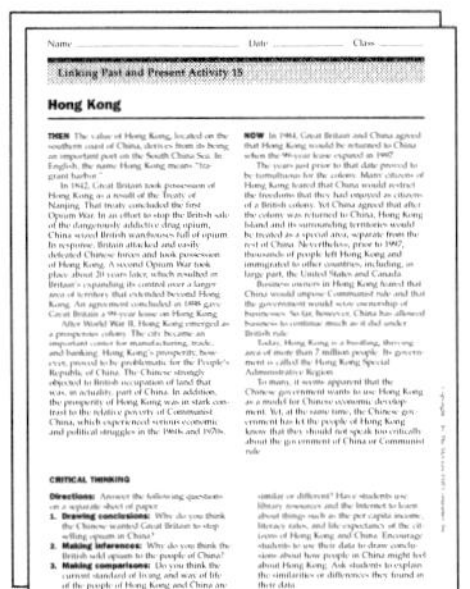

Time Line Activity 15

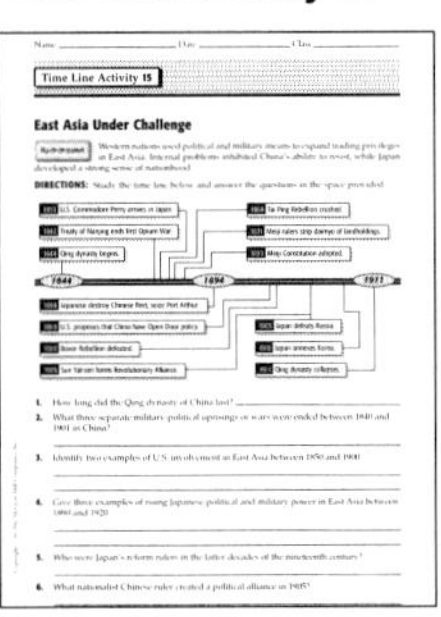

Reteaching Activity 15

Vocabulary Activity 15

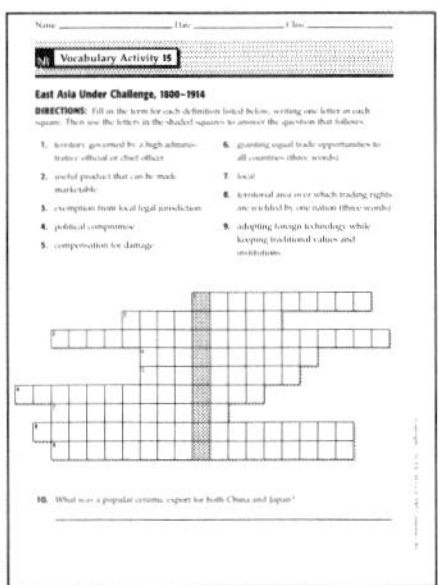

Critical Thinking Skills Activity 15

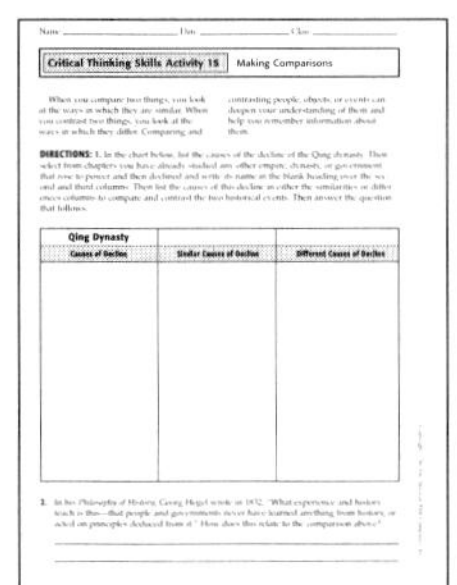

Assessment and Evaluation

Chapter 15 Test Form A

Chapter 15 Test Form B

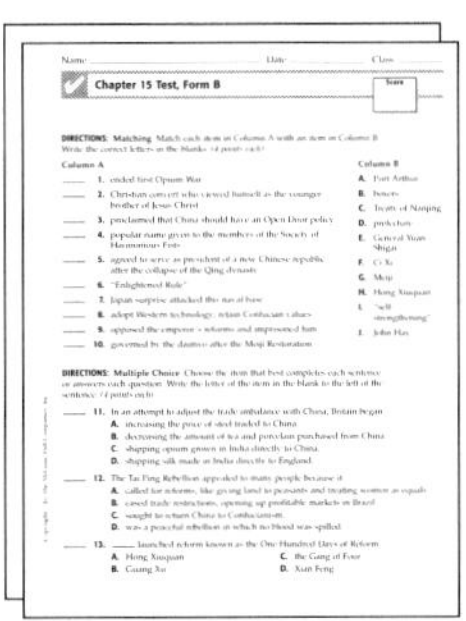

Performance Assessment Activity 15

ExamView® Pro Testmaker CD-ROM

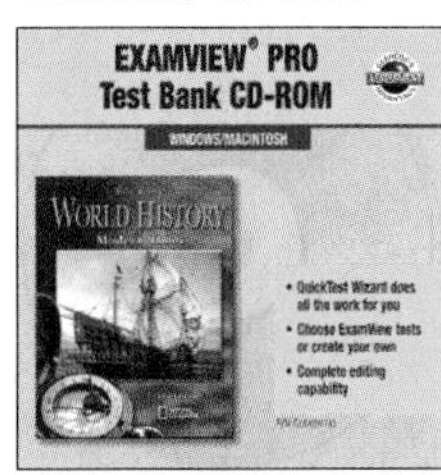

Standardized Test Skills Practice Workbook Activity 15

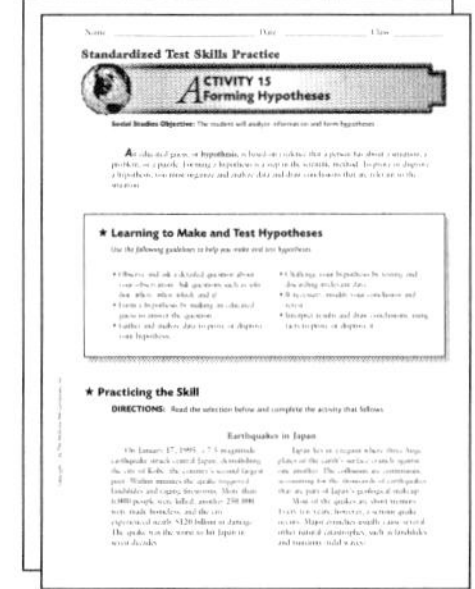

Interdisciplinary Activities

Mapping History Activity 15

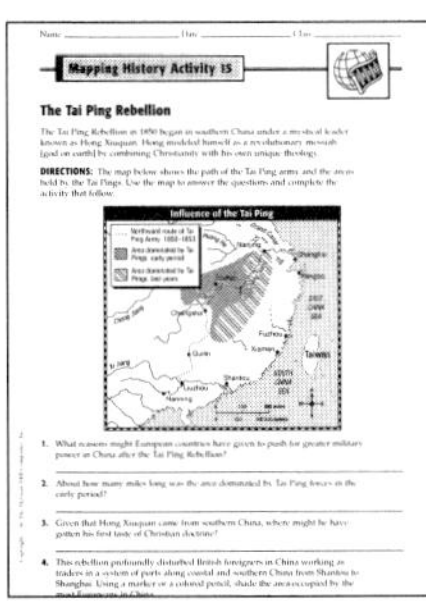

World Art and Music Activity 15

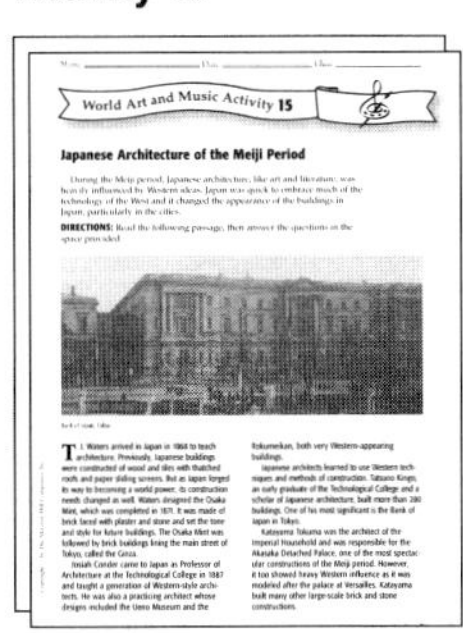

History and Geography Activity 15

People in World History Activity 15

Multimedia

- Vocabulary PuzzleMaker CD-ROM
- Interactive Tutor Self-Assessment CD-ROM
- ExamView® Pro Testmaker CD-ROM
- Audio Program
- World History Primary Source Document Library CD-ROM
- MindJogger Videoquiz
- Presentation Plus! CD-ROM
- TeacherWorks CD-ROM
- Interactive Student Edition CD-ROM
- The World History—Modern Times Video Program

Spanish Resources

The following Spanish language materials are available in the Spanish Resources Binder:

- Spanish Guided Reading Activities
- Spanish Reteaching Activities
- Spanish Quizzes and Tests
- Spanish Vocabulary Activities
- Spanish Summaries

Chapter 15 Resources

SECTION RESOURCES		
Daily Objectives	**Reproducible Resources**	**Multimedia Resources**
SECTION 1 **The Decline of the Qing Dynasty** 1. Explain that the Qing dynasty declined because of internal and external pressures. 2. Summarize how Western nations increased their economic involvement with China.	Reproducible Lesson Plan 15–1 Daily Lecture and Discussion Notes 15–1 Guided Reading Activity 15–1* Section Quiz 15–1* Reading Essentials and Study Guide 15–1	Daily Focus Skills Transparency 15–1 Interactive Tutor Self-Assessment CD-ROM ExamView® Pro Testmaker CD-ROM Presentation Plus! CD-ROM
SECTION 2 **Revolution in China** 1. Identify Sun Yat-sen and his reforms, which led to a revolution in China. 2. Discuss how the arrival of Westerners brought changes to the Chinese economy and culture.	Reproducible Lesson Plan 15–2 Daily Lecture and Discussion Notes 15–2 Guided Reading Activity 15–2* Section Quiz 15–2* Reading Essentials and Study Guide 15–2	Daily Focus Skills Transparency 15–2 Interactive Tutor Self-Assessment CD-ROM ExamView® Pro Testmaker CD-ROM Presentation Plus! CD-ROM
SECTION 3 **Rise of Modern Japan** 1. Describe how Western intervention opened Japan, an island that had been isolated for 200 years, to trade. 2. Discuss the interaction between Japan and Western nations that gave birth to a modern industrial society.	Reproducible Lesson Plan 15–3 Daily Lecture and Discussion Notes 15–3 Guided Reading Activity 15–3* Section Quiz 15–3* Reteaching Activity 15* Reading Essentials and Study Guide 15–3	Daily Focus Skills Transparency 15–3 Interactive Tutor Self-Assessment CD-ROM ExamView® Pro Testmaker CD-ROM Presentation Plus! CD-ROM

0:00 **OUT OF TIME?**
Assign the Chapter 15 **Reading Essentials and Study Guide.**

*Also Available in Spanish

 Blackline Master  Transparency CD-ROM DVD
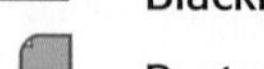 Poster Music Program  Audio Program  Videocassette

Chapter 15 Resources

Teacher's Corner

INDEX TO NATIONAL GEOGRAPHIC MAGAZINE

The following articles relate to this chapter:

- "Hong Kong," by Mike Edwards, March 1997.
- "Hagi: Where Japan's Revolution Began," N. Taylor Gregg, June 1984.

NGS ONLINE

Access National Geographic's new dynamic MapMachine Web site and other geography resources at:

www.nationalgeographic.com
www.nationalgeographic.com/maps

KEY TO ABILITY LEVELS

Teaching strategies have been coded.

- L1 BASIC activities for all students
- L2 AVERAGE activities for average to above-average students
- L3 CHALLENGING activities for above-average students
- ELL ENGLISH LANGUAGE LEARNER activities

Block Schedule

Activities that are suited to use within the block scheduling framework are identified by:

WORLD HISTORY Online

Use our Web site for additional resources. All essential content is covered in the Student Edition.

You and your students can visit www.wh.mt.glencoe.com, the Web site companion to *Glencoe World History—Modern Times.* This innovative integration of electronic and print media offers your students a wealth of opportunities. The student text directs students to the Web site for the following options:

- **Chapter Overviews**
- **Self-Check Quizzes**
- **Student Web Activities**
- **Textbook Updates**

Answers to the Student Web Activities are provided for you in the **Web Activity Lesson Plans.** Additional Web resources and Interactive Tutor Puzzles are also available.

From the Classroom of...

Anna Mae Grimm
Homestead High School
Mequon, Wisconsin

Leading a Developing Republic

Students will play the roles of the newly elected president and cabinet of a fictitious developing country to gain a perspective on the complexities involved in national development. Students should take the roles of president; military leader; ministers of health, industry, finance, trade, agriculture, public works; leaders of two religious groups; farmers; businesspeople; feminists; and the unemployed—all of them with competing interests.

Have students participate in a roundtable discussion to try to create a national structure that keeps everyone happy. Students should keep in mind that their country is poor, with health and literacy problems. It does, however, have abundant natural resources. Remind students that their contributions to the discussion should reflect the interests of their chosen role. Ask students to discuss whether their discussion gave them insight into the complexities involved in industrializing a developing country.

Performance Assessment

Refer to Activity 15 in the Performance Assessment Activities and Rubrics booklet.

The Impact Today

Today, China and Japan are two of the United States's largest trading partners. In 2000, the trade deficit with Japan was approximately $81 billion, and the trade deficit with China was almost $84 billion. Ask students to examine labels and stickers on products in their homes to get an idea of how much and what kinds of products the United States imports from these countries.

GLENCOE TECHNOLOGY

The World History—Modern Times Video Program

To learn more about Japan during the nineteenth century, students can view the Chapter 15 video, "The Russo-Japanese War," from **The World History—Modern Times Video Program.**

MindJogger Videoquiz

Use the **MindJogger Videoquiz** to preview Chapter 15 content.

 Available in VHS.

CHAPTER 15 East Asia Under Challenge

1800–1914

Key Events

As you read this chapter, look for the key events in the development of East Asia.

- *Western nations used political persuasion and military strength to gain trading privileges with China and Japan.*
- *China's internal problems made it easier for Western nations to penetrate the country and strengthen their influence.*
- *Japan's ability to adopt Western ways and to maintain its own traditions enabled it to develop into a modern, powerful nation.*

The Impact Today

The events that occurred during this time period still impact our lives today.

- *The issues raised by the Opium War continue to be addressed, since drug addiction is still a major international problem.*
- *Japan has one of the world's largest industrialized, free-market economies.*
- *China's large market continues to attract Western business and trade.*

World History—Modern Times Video *The Chapter 15 video, "The Russo-Japanese War," chronicles the conflict between Russia and Japan.*

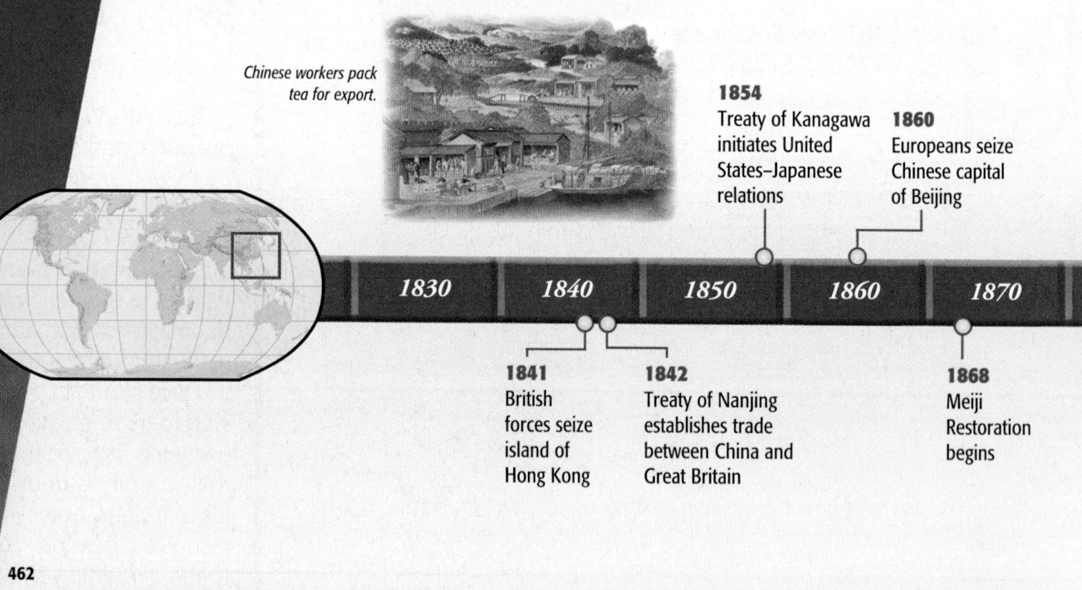
1830
1840
1850
1860
1870
1841 British forces seize island of Hong Kong
1842 Treaty of Nanjing establishes trade between China and Great Britain
1854 Treaty of Kanagawa initiates United States–Japanese relations
1860 Europeans seize Chinese capital of Beijing
1868 Meiji Restoration begins

Chinese workers pack tea for export.

462

TWO-MINUTE LESSON LAUNCHER

This chapter deals with the challenges faced by Asian countries during the nineteenth century. This exercise reinforces geographic and population problems in Japan. Let one student represent 8 million people. Put five chairs at the front of the room and have four students sit in the chairs, leaving one empty. Tell students that these four represent the total population of California (32 million people). The empty chair represents unpopulated land in the state. Now call 12 additional students to the front of the room so that the population of Japan (126 million) is represented. Explain that the land areas of California and Japan are very close. Tell the 16 students that they must arrange to sit on only 2 of the chairs since sixty percent of Japan's land is mountainous and uninhabitable. Harmony, cooperation, and tolerance are essential characteristics of this populous society. L1

A British steamship attacks Chinese naval forces off the coast of China during the Opium War.

Sun Yat-sen

1905
Sun Yat-sen forms Revolutionary Alliance in China

1911
Chinese revolution starts

1880	1890	1900	1910	1920

c. 1900
Japan's industrial sector begins to grow

1910
Japan annexes Korea

Meiji-era train depot

HISTORY Online

Chapter Overview
Visit the *Glencoe World History—Modern Times* Web site at wh.mt.glencoe.com and click on **Chapter 15–Chapter Overview** to preview chapter information.

MORE ABOUT THE ART

Naval Forces Great Britain demonstrated its naval power in countries that were *not* part of the British Empire. In 1839, when the Opium War began, the Chinese military forces were no match for their well-armed British opponents. This painting shows Chinese junks under attack from British steamships during the Opium War. What do students observe about the Chinese navy's boats? Ask students to discuss why the Chinese, who invented gunpowder, had not modernized their military weapons.

Introducing CHAPTER 15

Chapter Objectives

After studying this chapter, students should be able to:

1. describe changes that led to the decline of the Qing dynasty, including the Opium War, the Tai Ping Rebellion, and the Boxer Rebellion;
2. describe the "self-strengthening reforms" of the Qing dynasty;
3. list the three stages of Sun Yat-sen's proposal to reform China's government;
4. list three effects Western trade had on the Chinese economy;
5. describe the new political system of Japan;
6. explain the influence of Western culture on Japanese social structure and culture.

Chapter Overview
Introduce students to chapter content and key terms by having them access **Chapter Overview 15** at wh.mt.glencoe.com.

Time Line Activity

Ask students to propose significant Western events from Chapter 12 that they would add to the time line on these pages to get a sense of world politics during this period. L2

CHAPTER PREVIEW

Introducing

A Story That Matters

Depending upon the ability levels of your students, select from the following questions to reinforce the reading of *A Story That Matters.*

- Which groups were trying to carry out activities in China and Japan? *(European merchants and missionaries)*
- How did China respond to the challenge of Western influences? *(resistant, but eventually gave in)*
- What role did the military play in the opening of China and Japan to European merchants and missionaries? *(a threat of force)* **L1 L2**

About the Art

The Summer Palace at Beijing was built in 1750, destroyed by the British and French in the war of 1860, and restored in 1895. The palace is an outstanding example of Chinese landscape design. It integrates the natural landscape with manmade pavilions, halls, palaces, temples, and bridges, forming a harmonious whole.

CHAPTER PREVIEW

A Story That Matters

The Summer Palace in Beijing today

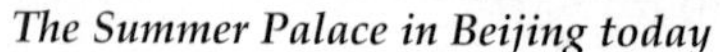

Palace interior

Looting of the Summer Palace

Like the countries of South Asia, Southeast Asia, and Africa, the nations of East Asia faced a growing challenge from the power of the West in the nineteenth century. In China, Westerners used their military superiority to pursue their goals.

In 1860, for example, Great Britain and France decided to retaliate against the Chinese, who had tried to restrict British and French activities. In July, combined British and French forces arrived on the outskirts of Beijing. There, they came upon the Old Summer Palace of the Chinese emperors. The soldiers were astounded by the riches they beheld and could not resist the desire to steal them.

Beginning on October 6, British and French troops moved through the palace. They took anything that looked valuable and smashed what they could not cart away. One British observer wrote, "You would see several officers and men of all ranks with their heads and hands brushing and knocking together in the same box." In another room, he said, "a scramble was going on over a collection of handsome state robes . . . others would be amusing themselves by taking shots at chandeliers."

Lord Elgin, leader of the British forces in China, soon restored order. After the Chinese took hostage and then murdered 20 British and French soldiers, however, Lord Elgin ordered the Old Summer Palace to be burned. Intimidated, the Chinese government agreed to Western demands.

Why It Matters

The events of 1860 were part of a regular pattern in East Asia in the nineteenth century. Backed by European guns, European merchants and missionaries pressed for the right to carry out their activities in China and Japan. The Chinese and Japanese resisted but were eventually forced to open their doors to the foreigners. Unlike other Asian societies, however, both Japan and China were able to maintain their national independence.

History and You International contact continues to shrink differences among nations. Using the information in this chapter and outside research, create a chart comparing the development of the United States and Japan during the twentieth century. Include data on material goods as well as economic, political, or social trends.

HISTORY AND YOU

The opening of China and Japan to Western trade and influence changed the face of world trade forever. Have students research the current trade situation between the United States and either Japan or China. What products are traded and how cordial are trade relations between the two countries? Have students focus their reports on a specific current issue. They might examine the interdependence of Japanese and American economies or examine the controversy granting "Most Favored Nation" trading status to China in the late 1990s. **L2**

SECTION 1 The Decline of the Qing Dynasty

Guide to Reading

Main Ideas
- The Qing dynasty declined because of internal and external pressures.
- Western nations increased their economic involvement with China.

Key Terms
extraterritoriality, self-strengthening, spheres of influence, indemnity

People to Identify
Hong Xiuquan, Guang Xu, Empress Dowager Ci Xi, John Hay

Places to Locate
Guangzhou, Chang Jiang, Hong Kong

Preview Questions
1. What internal problems led to the decline of the Qing dynasty?
2. What role did Western nations play in the Qing dynasty's decline?

Reading Strategy
Compare and Contrast Create a chart comparing and contrasting the Tai Ping and Boxer Rebellions.

	Tai Ping	Boxer
Reforms Demanded		
Methods Used to Obtain Reforms		
Outcomes		

Preview of Events

1840 · 1850 · 1860 · 1870 · 1880 · 1890 · 1900

- **1839** Opium War begins
- **1850** Tai Ping Rebellion begins
- **1898** Ci Xi opposes reforms
- **1900** Boxer Rebellion defeated

Nobleman, Qing dynasty

Voices from the Past

In the second half of the nineteenth century, calls for political reform were heard in China. However, a leading court official, Zhang Zhidong, argued:

> "The doctrine of people's rights will bring us not a single benefit but a hundred evils. Are we going to establish a parliament? Among the Chinese scholars and people there are still many today who are content to be vulgar and rustic. They are ignorant of the general situation in the world, they do not understand the basic system of the state. They have not the most elementary idea about foreign countries. . . . Even supposing the confused and clamorous people are assembled in one house, for every one of them who is clear-sighted, there will be a hundred others whose vision is clouded; they will converse at random and talk as if in a dream—what use will it be?"
>
> —***China's Response to the West: A Documentary Survey, 1839–1923,*** **Ssu-yu Teng and John K. Fairbank, eds., 1970**

Zhang's view prevailed, and no reforms were enacted.

Causes of Decline

In 1800, after a long period of peace and prosperity, the Qing dynasty of the Manchus was at the height of its power. A little over a century later, however, humiliated and harassed by the Western powers, the Qing dynasty collapsed.

1 FOCUS

Section Overview

This section discusses the decline of the Qing dynasty and the increase of Western involvement with China.

BELLRINGER
Skillbuilder Activity

 Project transparency and have students answer questions.

 Available as a blackline master.

Daily Focus Skills Transparency 15–1

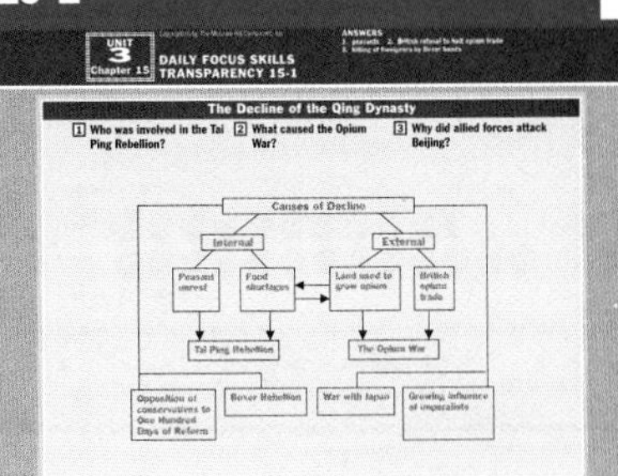

Guide to Reading

Answers to Graphic: Tai Ping: See pages 467 to 469. Boxer: See page 471.

Preteaching Vocabulary: A *sphere of influence* is an area where foreign governments have exclusive trading rights and use of ports but do not have administrative control. By the end of the nineteenth century, large parts of China were claimed as spheres of influence by European countries, Russia, and Japan. Notably, the United States did not claim a sphere of influence in China.

SECTION RESOURCES

Reproducible Masters
- Reproducible Lesson Plan 15–1
- Daily Lecture and Discussion Notes 15–1
- Guided Reading Activity 15–1
- Section Quiz 15–1
- Reading Essentials and Study Guide 15–1

Transparencies
- Daily Focus Skills Transparency 15–1

Multimedia
- Interactive Tutor Self-Assessment CD-ROM
- ExamView® Pro Testmaker CD-ROM
- Presentation Plus! CD-ROM

2 TEACH

Reading Check

Answer: Internal factors included corruption, peasant unrest, incompetent leadership, rapid population growth, and a serious food shortage. External pressure was applied by the modern West.

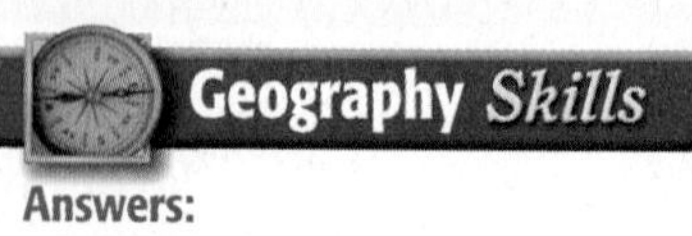

Geography Skills

Answers:

1. mountains
2. China was a dominant force in East Asia.

Daily Lecture and Discussion Notes 15–1

Daily Lecture and Discussion Notes

Chapter 15, Section 1

Did You Know? Under the pseudonym of Sax Rohmer, the British mystery novelist Arthur Sarsfield Ward (1886–1959) wrote books featuring a character named Fu Manchu. The long, drooping Fu Manchu moustache is named after this character.

I. **Causes of Decline** *(pages 465–466)*

A. In 1800 the Qing dynasty of the Manchus was at the height of its power. After more than a century of Western humiliation and harassment, the Qing dynasty collapsed in the early 1900s.

B. Internal changes also played a role in the downfall of the Qing dynasty. It began to suffer from corruption, peasant unrest, and incompetence. Rapid population growth—400 million by 1900—along with food shortages and regular famine made these matters worse.

C. The ships, guns, and ideas of foreigners probably hastened the end of the Qing Era.

Enrich

Have students conduct additional research on the fall of the Qing dynasty using print and Internet sources. Ask students to interpret the bibliographies used in the research, and then create their own bibliographies of at least five sources that could be used for writing a report on the Qing dynasty. Students may require some assistance in interpreting bibliographies. L2

One important reason for the abrupt decline and fall of the Qing dynasty was the intense external pressure applied to Chinese society by the modern West. However, internal changes also played a role in the dynasty's collapse.

After an extended period of growth, the Qing dynasty began to suffer from corruption, peasant unrest, and incompetence. These weaknesses were made worse by rapid growth in the country's population. By 1900, there were 400 million people in China. Population growth created a serious food shortage. In the 1850s, one observer wrote, "Not a year passes in which a terrific number of persons do not perish of famine in some part or other of China."

The ships, guns, and ideas of foreigners highlighted the growing weakness of the Qing dynasty and probably hastened its end.

Reading Check **Examining** What factors led to the decline of the Qing dynasty?

The Opium War

By 1800, Europeans had been in contact with China for more than two hundred years. European merchants, however, were restricted to a small trading outlet at **Guangzhou** (GWONG•JO), or Canton. The British did not like this arrangement.

The British also had an unfavorable trade balance in China. That is, they imported more goods from China than they exported to China. For years, Britain had imported tea, silk, and porcelain from the Chinese and sent Indian cotton to China to pay for these imports. The cotton, however, did not cover the entire debt, and the British were forced to pay for their imports with silver. The British sent increasing quantities of silver to China, especially in exchange for tea, which was in great demand by the British.

At first, the British tried to negotiate with the Chinese to improve the trade imbalance. When negotiations failed, the British turned to trading opium.

Opium was grown in northern India under the sponsorship of the British East India Company and then shipped directly to Chinese markets. Demand for opium—a highly addictive drug—in South China jumped dramatically. Soon, silver was flowing out of China and into the pockets of the officials of the British East India Company.

The Chinese reacted strongly. The British were not the first to import opium into China. The Chinese government had already seen opium's dangerous qualities, and had made its trade illegal. They appealed to the British government on moral grounds to stop the traffic in opium. A government official wrote to Queen Victoria: "Suppose there were

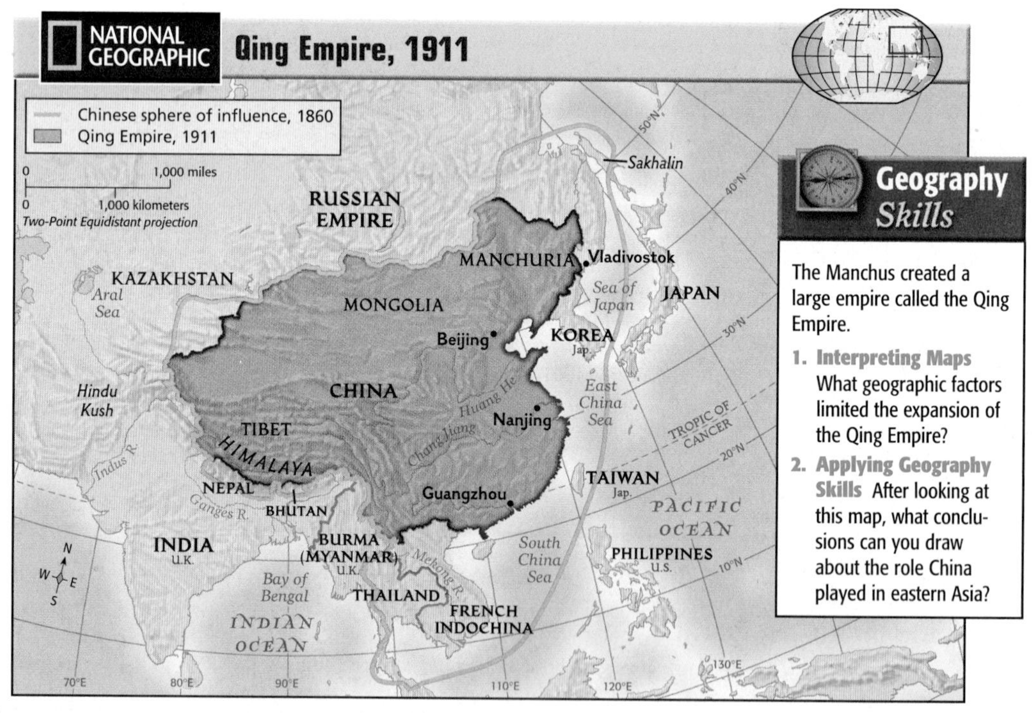

Geography Skills

The Manchus created a large empire called the Qing Empire.

1. **Interpreting Maps** What geographic factors limited the expansion of the Qing Empire?
2. **Applying Geography Skills** After looking at this map, what conclusions can you draw about the role China played in eastern Asia?

COOPERATIVE LEARNING ACTIVITY

Making Generalizations and Drawing Conclusions The rapid decline of the Qing dynasty was due to a combination of internal and external causes. Have students work in pairs to list internal and external factors that force change and how a government may respond. Have students come together to compare their lists. Students should reach the conclusion that the resources the government requires to respond to internal factors are limited by the demands of external forces *(military or police intervention, applying funds to alleviate worst symptoms, increasing representation, etc.)*, and the resources needed to respond to external forces are restricted by internal factors *(unified government response, dedicated military, citizen resistance, etc.)*. L2

people from another country who carried opium for sale to England and seduced your people into buying and smoking it; certainly your honorable ruler would deeply hate it and be bitterly aroused."

The British refused to halt their activity, however. As a result, the Chinese government blockaded the foreign area in Guangzhou in order to force traders to surrender their chests of opium. The British responded with force, starting the Opium War (1839–1842).

The Chinese were no match for the British. British warships destroyed Chinese coastal and river forts. When a British fleet sailed almost unopposed up the **Chang Jiang** (Yangtze River) to Nanjing, the Qing dynasty made peace.

In the Treaty of Nanjing in 1842, the Chinese agreed to open five coastal ports to British trade, limit taxes on imported British goods, and pay for the costs of the war. China also agreed to give the British the island of **Hong Kong.** Nothing was said in the treaty about the opium trade. Moreover, in the five ports, Europeans lived in their own sections and were subject not to Chinese laws but to their own laws—a practice known as extraterritoriality.

The Opium War marked the beginning of the establishment of Western influence in China. For the time being, the Chinese tried to deal with the problem by pitting foreign countries against one another. Concessions granted to the British were offered to other Western nations, including the United States. Soon, thriving foreign areas were operating in the five treaty ports along the southern Chinese coast.

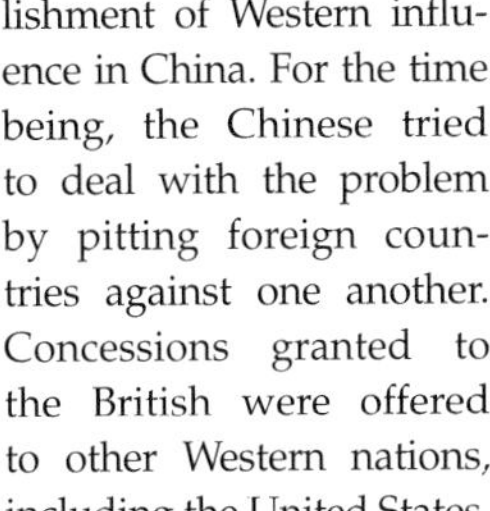

Web Activity Visit the *Glencoe World History—Modern Times* Web site at wh.mt.glencoe.com and click on **Chapter 15–Student Web Activity** to learn more about Western influence in China.

Reading Check **Summarizing** What did the British do to adjust their trade imbalance with China?

The Tai Ping Rebellion

In the meantime, the failure of the Chinese government to deal with pressing internal economic problems led to a peasant revolt, known as the Tai Ping (TIE PING) Rebellion (1850–1864). It was led by

CONNECTIONS Past To Present

The Return of Hong Kong to China

In 1984, Great Britain and China signed a joint declaration in which Britain agreed to return its colony of Hong Kong to China on July 1, 1997. China promised that Hong Kong would keep its free market, its capitalist economy, and its way of life. The formula was "one country, two systems."

In 1841, Hong Kong was a small island with a few fishing villages on the southeastern coast of China. A British naval force seized the island and used it as a port for shipping opium into China. A year later, after a humiliating defeat in the Opium War, China agreed to give the island of Hong Kong to Britain.

Later, the British took advantage of the declining power of China's Qing dynasty to gain additional lands next to Hong Kong. In 1861, the Chinese government granted the Kowloon Peninsula to Britain. In 1898, the Chinese granted the British a 99-year lease on the nearby New Territories, an area that provided much of the food for the colony of Hong Kong.

In the 1950s and 1960s, Hong Kong was filled with refugees from the new Communist regime in mainland China. The population of Hong Kong swelled to six million. The economy of Hong Kong boomed. Today, Hong Kong is the eighth largest trading nation in the world.

Troops take down the British flag in Hong Kong in 1997.

Comparing Past and Present

Using outside sources, research the current political and cultural situation in Hong Kong. Explain what the formula "one country, two systems" means. Evaluate whether or not the formula has been successful since Hong Kong was returned to China.

Reading Check

Answer: They started to trade opium instead of paying for imports with silver.

Answer: "One country, two systems" refers to the fact that Hong Kong is now part of China, which is Communist, but that Hong Kong maintains its capitalist economic system. Answers should be supported by facts and logic.

Guided Reading Activity 15-1

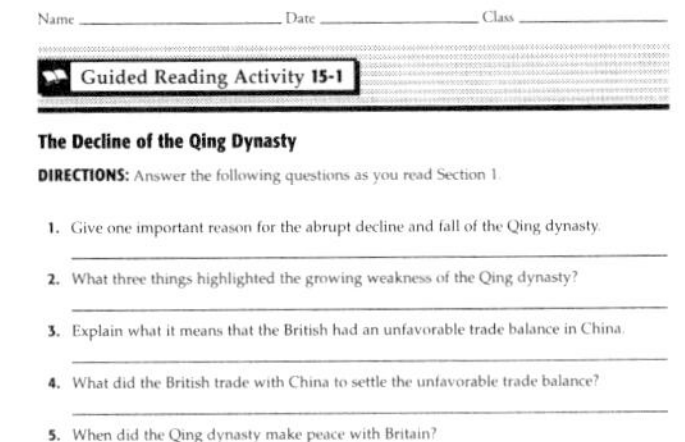
Name ______ Date ______ Class ______

Guided Reading Activity 15-1

The Decline of the Qing Dynasty

DIRECTIONS: Answer the following questions as you read Section 1.

1. Give one important reason for the abrupt decline and fall of the Qing dynasty.
2. What three things highlighted the growing weakness of the Qing dynasty?
3. Explain what it means that the British had an unfavorable trade balance in China.
4. What did the British trade with China to settle the unfavorable trade balance?
5. When did the Qing dynasty make peace with Britain?

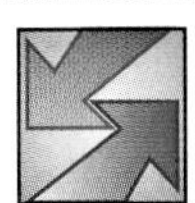

CURRICULUM CONNECTION

Economics Conduct a debate on the issue of foreign trade. Have students assume the roles of Chinese officials and European merchants. The debate topic should be: What should the Chinese trade policy be? Should the Chinese keep foreign merchants out of China? L3

EXTENDING THE CONTENT

The Tai Ping Rebellion An American mercenary from Salem, Massachusetts, named Frederick Townsend Ward went to China in 1859 and, at the age of 28, he raised an army of Chinese soldiers commanded by Western officers to fight the Tai Ping rebels. Using Western weapons and tactics, Ward defeated armies much larger than his own *Chang-sheng-chun* ("Ever Victorious Army"). Such was his reputation that the followers of Hong Xiuquan called his men the "devil soldiers." When Ward was killed three years after coming to China, the Manchu government built a temple and shrine to honor his memory.

Then and Now

Answer: Without the British, Hong Kong probably would have remained an island of fishing villages, of little importance in the world. Under the British, Hong Kong developed into a huge city with a thriving economy.

Reading Check

Answer: give land to all peasants, treat men and women equally, abolish private property, outlaw alcohol and tobacco, eliminate binding of women's feet

Charting Activity

Have students create a chart to help them understand the results of the Opium War. Columns should be labeled *The Treaty of Nanjing* and *The Treaty of Tianjin.* Rows should be labeled *year of treaty, with whom,* and *the agreement. (Nanjing: 1842; with the British; opened five ports to trade, limited taxes on British imports, paid for war, gave Britain Hong Kong. Tianjin: 1860; with the British and French; legalized opium, opened new ports, gave Kowloon to Great Britain.)* **L3**

Writing Activity

Have students write a brief essay in which they explain the political, economic, cultural, and technological influences of European expansion on China in the nineteenth century. **L1**

Hong Xiuquan, a Christian convert who viewed himself as a younger brother of Jesus Christ.

Hong was convinced that God had given him the mission of destroying the Qing dynasty. Joined by great crowds of peasants, Hong captured the town of Yongan and proclaimed a new dynasty, the Heavenly Kingdom of Great Peace (*Tai Ping Tianguo* in Chinese—hence the name *Tai Ping Rebellion*).

The Tai Ping Rebellion appealed to many people because it called for social reforms. These reforms included giving land to all peasants and treating women as equals of men. Women even served in their own units in the Tai Ping army.

Hong's rebellion also called for people to give up private possessions. Peasants were to hold lands and farms in common, and money, food, and clothing were to be shared equally by all. Hong outlawed alcohol and tobacco and eliminated the practice of binding women's feet. The Chinese Communist Revolution of the twentieth century (see Chapter 24) would have similar social goals.

In March 1853, the rebels seized Nanjing, the second largest city of the empire, and massacred 25,000 men, women, and children. The revolt continued for 10 more years but gradually began to fall apart. Europeans came to the aid of the Qing dynasty when they realized the destructive nature of the Tai Ping forces. As one British observer noted, there was no hope "of any good ever coming of the rebel movement. They do nothing but burn, murder, and destroy."

Then and Now

Victoria served as the capital of Britain's Hong Kong colony. How did the presence of the British impact the island of Hong Kong?

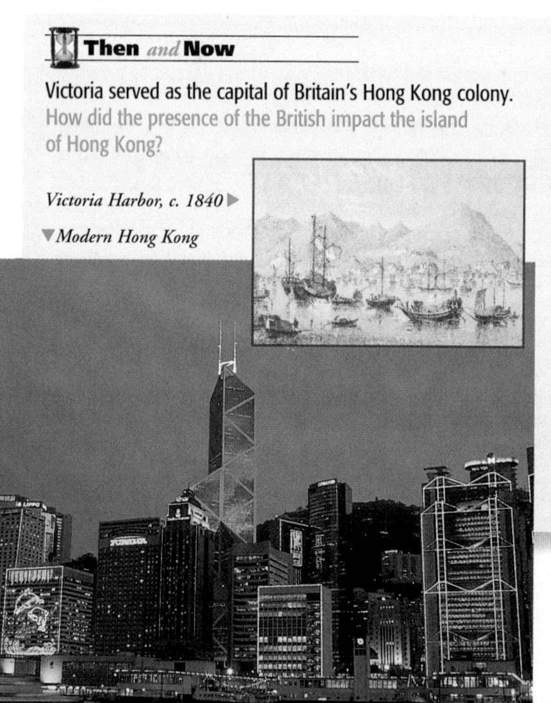

Victoria Harbor, c. 1840 ▶

▼*Modern Hong Kong*

European troops battle Tai Ping soldiers in Guangzhou during the Tai Ping Rebellion.

In 1864, Chinese forces, with European aid, recaptured Nanjing and destroyed the remaining rebel force. The Tai Ping Rebellion proved to be one of the most devastating civil wars in history. As many as twenty million people died in the course of the 14-year struggle.

One reason for the Qing dynasty's failure to deal effectively with the internal unrest was its ongoing struggle with the Western powers. In 1856, Great Britain and France launched another series of attacks against China. They seized the capital, Beijing, in 1860. In the ensuing Treaty of Tianjin, the Chinese government agreed to legalize the opium trade, open new ports to foreign trade, and surrender the peninsula of Kowloon (opposite the island of Hong Kong) to Great Britain.

Reading Check **Summarizing** What social reforms did the Tai Ping Rebellion demand?

Efforts at Reform

By the late 1870s, the Qing dynasty was in decline. Unable to restore order themselves, government troops had relied on forces recruited by regional warlords to help fight the Tai Ping Rebellion. To finance their private armies, warlords had collected taxes from local people. After crushing the revolt, many of these warlords refused to dismiss their units. With the support of the local gentry, they continued to collect local taxes for their own use.

In its weakened state, the Qing court finally began to listen to the appeals of reform-minded officials. The reformers called for a new policy they called **"self-strengthening."** By this, they meant that China

MEETING INDIVIDUAL NEEDS

Visual/Auditory As students read this chapter, have them find as many of the following words as possible: China, porcelain, Guangzhou, tea, silk, Hong Kong, Nanjing, Beijing, Zhang Zhidong, Russia, Siberia, Tibet, weapons, Great Britain, Japan, Korea, Guang Xu, Empress Dowager Ci Xi, John Hay, Sun Yat-sen. Use an overhead transparency divided into 3 columns—Places, People, and Products—and ask students to tell under which column each word belongs. Then have the students share the significance of the item according to what they read in the chapter. **L1**

Refer to ***Inclusion for the High School Social Studies Classroom Strategies and Activities*** in the TCR.

should adopt Western technology while keeping its Confucian values and institutions. Under this policy, factories were built to produce modern weapons and ships, increasing China's military strength. However, the traditional Chinese imperial bureaucracy was also retained, and civil service examinations based on Confucian writers were still used to select government staff members. This new policy guided Chinese foreign and domestic policy for the next 25 years.

Some reformers wanted to change China's traditional political institutions by introducing democracy. However, such ideas were too radical for most reformers. During the last quarter of the nineteenth century, the Chinese government tried to modernize China's military forces and build up industry without touching the basic elements of Chinese civilization. Railroads, weapons factories, and shipyards were built, but the Chinese value system remained unchanged.

✓Reading Check **Explaining** What was China's policy of "self-strengthening"?

The Advance of Imperialism

In the end, however, the changes did not help the Qing stay in power. The European advance into China continued during the last two decades of the nineteenth century, while internal conditions continued to deteriorate.

Mounting Pressures In the north and northeast, Russia took advantage of the Qing dynasty's weakness to force China to give up territories north of the Amur River in Siberia. In Tibet, a struggle between Russia and Great Britain kept both powers from seizing the territory outright. This allowed Tibet to become free from Chinese influence.

Even more ominous changes were taking place in the Chinese heartland. European states began to create **spheres of influence**, areas where the imperial powers had exclusive trading rights. After the Tai Ping Rebellion, warlords in the provinces began to negotiate directly with foreign nations. In return for money,

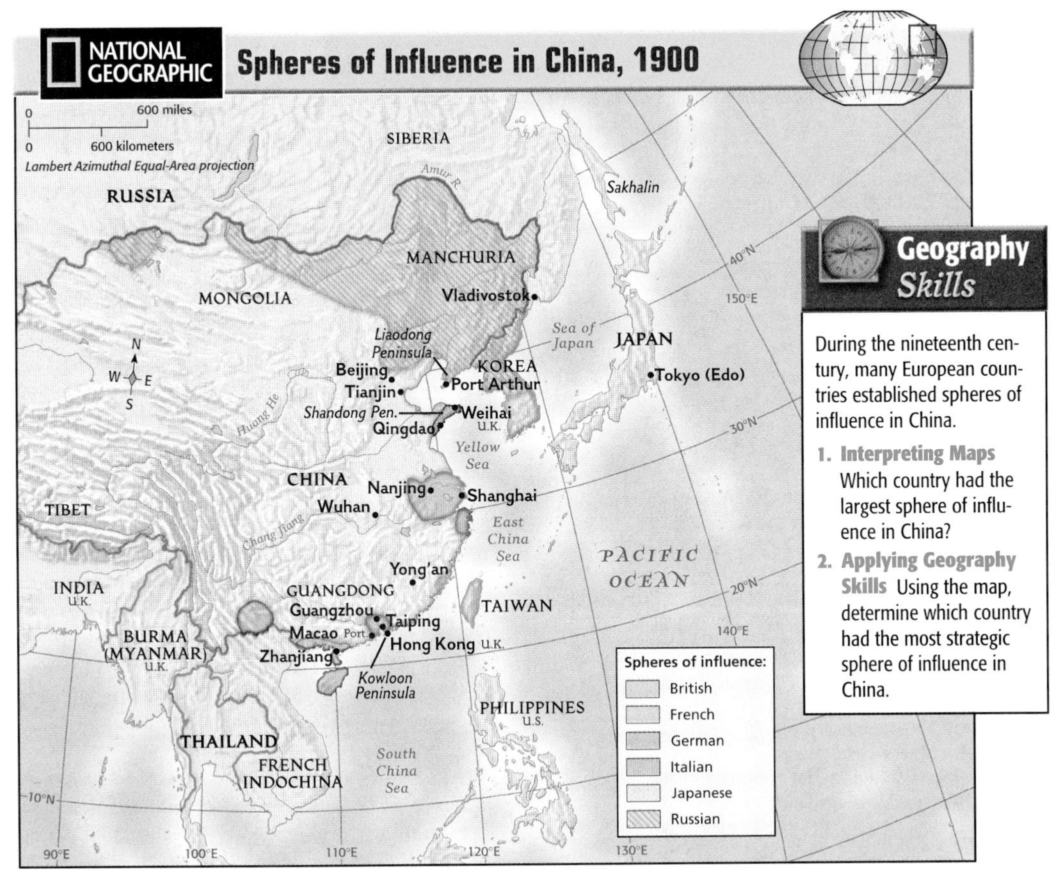

Geography Skills

During the nineteenth century, many European countries established spheres of influence in China.

1. **Interpreting Maps** Which country had the largest sphere of influence in China?
2. **Applying Geography Skills** Using the map, determine which country had the most strategic sphere of influence in China.

CHAPTER 15
Section 1, 465–471

✓Reading Check

Answer: Self-strengthening meant adopting Western technology while retaining Confucian values and institutions. (The government built up China's military and its industry without changing its value system.)

Geography Skills

Answers:
1. Russia, then Britain
2. Britain because of its access to the East China Sea

Critical Thinking

Ask students what effect the Open Door policy had on imperialist countries in China. *(All countries were granted access to China. Tariffs were lowered to allow equal access.)* Why would the United States want to allow open access to China? *(United States did not have a sphere of influence there. Open access would allow United States to compete with other countries.)* Only twenty-five years after the United States proposed the Open Door policy, the Monroe Doctrine was imposed in Latin America. Ask students to compare the two policies. Are they consistent? *(The Open Door policy allowed all countries access to China. The Monroe Doctrine warned against European intervention in Latin America.)* **L2**

EXTENDING THE CONTENT

The Confucian Code China maintained its cultural and territorial integrity for over 2000 years due, in part, to the teachings of Confucius. Confucian principles were state policy from 210 B.C. until A.D. 1912. The three concepts of Confucian teachings are 1) the emperor is superior to all others on Earth and is considered accountable for all events that influence the welfare of his people; 2) administrators in the government are selected on the basis of merit and competence; 3) the Chinese people are taught to value order and social cohesion above personal gain. This meant submission to authority, respect for tradition, and moderation in all things. The self-strengthening policy attempted to reconcile these values with Western technology.

CHAPTER 15
Section 1, 465–471

Reading Check

Answer: Britain, France, Germany, Russia, Japan

Enrich

Have students compare and contrast the Tai Ping Rebellion with the Boxer Rebellion. Be sure they include the motivation, tactics, and outcomes of each. **L2**

3 ASSESS

Assign Section 1 Assessment as homework or as an in-class activity.

Have students use **Interactive Tutor Self-Assessment CD-ROM.**

Reteaching Activity

Create a group outline of this section on the board. Have students give oral summaries of each part for a class discussion. **L1**

Section Quiz 15–1

Name ________ Date ________ Class ________

Chapter 15 Score

Section Quiz 15-1

DIRECTIONS: Matching Match each item in Column A with an item in Column B. Write the correct letters in the blanks. *(10 points each)*

Column A	Column B
____ **1.** division of exclusive trading rights with China	**A.** spheres of influence
____ **2.** Hay's proposal to ensure equal access to Chinese markets	**B.** extraterritoriality
____ **3.** members of a Chinese nationalist secret organization	**C.** indemnity
____ **4.** payment to the injured for damages	**D.** Boxers
____ **5.** European freedom from Chinese laws	**E.** Open Door Policy

DIRECTIONS: Multiple Choice In the blank, write the letter of the choice that best completes the statement or answers the question. *(10 points each)*

____ **6.** To improve their balance of trade with China, the British sold the Chinese
A. porcelain. **C.** tea.
B. opium. **D.** silk.

____ **7.** As a result of China losing the first Opium War to Britain, all of the following happened EXCEPT
A. Britain received Hong Kong.
B. five ports were opened to British trade.
C. the British in China accepted Chinese laws.
D. China paid for the cost of the war.

____ **8.** In the Treaty of Tianjin after the second Opium War, China agreed to
A. legalize trade in opium. **C.** recognize Hong as leader.
B. close several ports to trade. **D.** take back Kowloon.

____ **9.** The Qing dynasty's "self strengthening" reforms included
A. ending trade. **C.** moving toward democracy.
B. adopting Western technology. **D.** eliminating Confucian ideals.

____ **10.** The Qing dynasty was weakened by all of the following EXCEPT
A. war with Japan. **C.** warlord independence.
B. disputes with Russia. **D.** a changing value system.

the warlords granted these nations exclusive trading rights or railroad-building and mining privileges. In this way, Britain, France, Germany, Russia, and Japan all established spheres of influence in China.

In 1894, another blow further disintegrated the Qing dynasty. The Chinese went to war with Japan over Japanese inroads into Korea, a land that the Chinese had controlled for a long time. The Chinese were soundly defeated. As a reward, Japan demanded and received the island of Taiwan (known to Europeans at the time as Formosa), and the Liaodong (LYOW•DOONG) Peninsula. Fearing Japan's growing power, however, the European powers forced Japan to give the Liaodong Peninsula back to China.

New pressures for Chinese territory soon arose. In 1897, two German missionaries were murdered by Chinese rioters. Germany used this pretext to demand territories in the Shandong (SHON•DOONG) Peninsula. When the Chinese government approved the demand, other European nations made new claims on Chinese territory.

Internal Crisis This latest scramble for territory took place at a time of internal crisis in China. In the spring of 1898, the young emperor **Guang Xu** (GWANG SHYOO) launched a massive reform program based on changes in Japan (see the discussion later in this chapter). During the following weeks, known as the One Hundred Days of Reform, the emperor issued edicts calling for major political, administrative, and educational reforms. With these reforms, the emperor intended to modernize government bureaucracy by following Western models; to adopt a new educational system that would replace the traditional civil service examinations; to adopt Western-style schools, banks and a free press; and to train the military to use modern weapons and Western fighting techniques.

Many conservatives at court, however, opposed these reforms. They saw little advantage in copying the West. As one said, "An examination of the causes of success and failure in government reveals that . . . the adoption of foreignism leads to disorder." According to this conservative, traditional Chinese rules needed to be reformed and not rejected in favor of Western changes.

Most important, the new reform program was opposed by the emperor's aunt, **Empress Dowager Ci Xi** (TSUH•SEE). She became a dominant force at court and opposed the emperor's reforms. With the aid of the imperial army, she eventually imprisoned the emperor and ended his reform efforts.

Reading Check **Identifying** What countries claimed Chinese lands between 1880 and 1900?

People In History

Ci Xi
1835–1908—Chinese empress

Empress Dowager Ci Xi, through her unwillingness to make significant reforms, helped bring about the overthrow of the Qing dynasty. Ci Xi was at first a low-ranking concubine to Emperor Xian Feng. Her position became influential in 1856, when she gave birth to the emperor's first and only son.

When the emperor died, Ci Xi ruled China on behalf of her son. Later, she ruled on behalf of her nephew Guang Xu. With the aid of conservatives at court and the imperial army, she had Guang Xu jailed in the palace.

Empress Dowager Ci Xi ruled China for almost 50 years, during a crucial period in the nation's history. She was well aware of her own power. "I have often thought that I am the cleverest woman who ever lived . . . I have 400 million people all dependent on my judgement."

Opening the Door to China

As foreign pressure on the Qing dynasty grew stronger, both Great Britain and the United States feared that other nations would overrun the country should the Chinese government collapse. In 1899, U.S. secretary of state **John Hay** presented a proposal that ensured equal access to the Chinese market for all nations and preserved the unity of the Chinese Empire. When none of the other imperialist governments opposed the idea, Hay proclaimed that all major states with economic interests in China had agreed that the country should have an **Open Door policy.**

In part, the Open Door policy reflected American concern for the survival of China. However, it also reflected the interests of some trading companies in the United States. These companies wanted to operate in open markets and disliked the existing division of China into separate spheres of influence dominated by individual states.

The Open Door policy did not end the system of spheres of influence. However, it did reduce restrictions on foreign imports imposed by the dominating power within each sphere.

EXTENDING THE CONTENT

The Boxer Rebellion The Empress Dowager Ci Xi also had a hand in the Boxer Rebellion. Initially the Boxers' objectives were to overthrow the government and to rid China of foreigners, then to drop their opposition to the government and to join with it to destroy the foreigners. The Empress Dowager and officials in the government supported the Boxers and encouraged their anti-foreigner and anti-Christian campaigns. When the Empress Dowager ordered that all foreigners in Beijing be killed, foreign ministry staff and hundreds of Chinese Christians took refuge in the Roman Catholic cathedral in Beijing for more than two months. It is because of Ci Xi's participation that the allies were able to claim that the Chinese government should pay heavy reparations.

The Open Door policy also helped to reduce imperialist hysteria over access to the China market. The policy lessened fears in Britain, France, Germany, and Russia that other powers would take advantage of China's weakness and attempt to dominate the China market for themselves.

Reading Check **Analyzing** Why did the United States want an Open Door policy in China?

The Boxer Rebellion

The Open Door policy came too late to stop the Boxer Rebellion. *Boxer* was the popular name given to members of a secret organization called the Society of Harmonious Fists. Members practiced a system of exercise—a form of shadowboxing, or boxing with an imaginary opponent—that they thought would protect them from bullets.

The Boxers were upset by the foreign takeover of Chinese lands. Their slogan was "destroy the foreigner." They especially disliked Christian missionaries and Chinese converts to Christianity who seemed to threaten Chinese traditions. At the beginning of 1900, Boxer bands roamed the countryside and slaughtered foreign missionaries and Chinese Christians. Their victims also included foreign businessmen and even the German envoy to Beijing.

Response to the killings was immediate and overwhelming. An allied army consisting of twenty thousand British, French, German, Russian, American, and Japanese troops attacked Beijing in August 1900. The army restored order and demanded more concessions from the Chinese government. The Chinese government was forced to pay a heavy indemnity—a payment for damages—to the powers that had crushed the uprising. The imperial government was now weaker than ever.

Boxers are rounded up after the failed rebellion.

Reading Check **Explaining** How did the Boxers get their name?

SECTION 1 ASSESSMENT

Checking for Understanding

1. **Define** extraterritoriality, self-strengthening, spheres of influence, indemnity.
2. **Identify** Hong Xiuquan, Guang Xu, Empress Dowager Ci Xi, John Hay, Open Door policy.
3. **Locate** Guangzhou, Chang Jiang, Hong Kong.
4. **Analyze** how the Tai Ping Rebellion helped to weaken the Qing dynasty.
5. **List** the countries that supplied troops for the allied army, which was formed to fight the Boxers in 1900.

Critical Thinking

6. **Drawing Inferences** Why did European nations agree to follow the Open Door policy proposed by the United States?
7. **Organizing Information** Create a diagram listing the factors that led to the decline of the Qing dynasty.

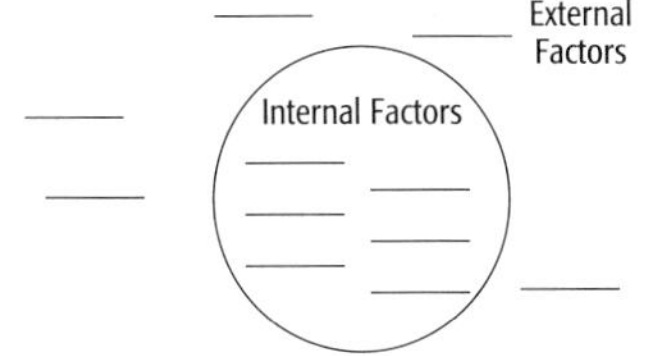

Analyzing Visuals

8. **Examine** the illustration of the Tai Ping Rebellion shown on page 468 of your text. What visual evidence in this picture shows that both the British and the Chinese were determined to win the battle?

Writing About History

9. **Expository Writing** Using outside sources, research, write, and present a report explaining the effects of population on modern China. Remember to include government laws enacted to curtail population growth and explain the consequences of disobeying these laws.

Reading Check

Answer: United States trading companies wanted to operate in open markets and disliked the division of China into spheres of influence dominated by individual states.

Reading Check

Answer: *Boxer* was the name given to members of the Society of Harmonious Fists, who practiced shadowboxing.

Reading Essentials and Study Guide 15–1

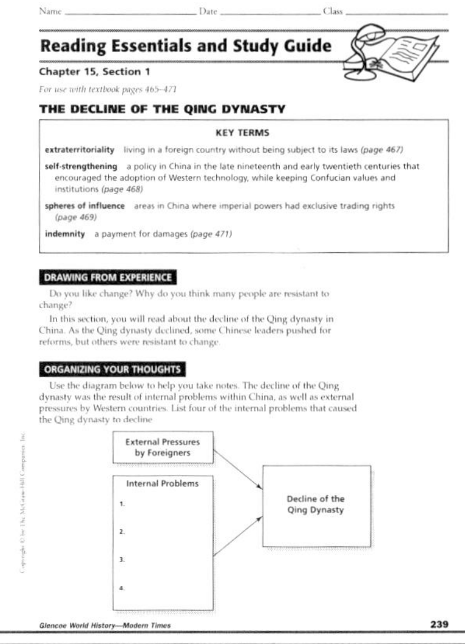

Name ______ Date ______ Class ______

Reading Essentials and Study Guide

Chapter 15, Section 1

For use with textbook pages 465–471

THE DECLINE OF THE QING DYNASTY

KEY TERMS

extraterritoriality living in a foreign country without being subject to its laws *(page 467)*

self-strengthening a policy in China in the late nineteenth and early twentieth centuries that encouraged the adoption of Western technology, while keeping Confucian values and institutions *(page 468)*

spheres of influence areas in China where imperial powers had exclusive trading rights *(page 469)*

indemnity a payment for damages *(page 471)*

DRAWING FROM EXPERIENCE

Do you like change? Why do you think many people are resistant to change?

In this section, you will read about the decline of the Qing dynasty in China. As the Qing dynasty declined, some Chinese leaders pushed for reforms, but others were resistant to change.

ORGANIZING YOUR THOUGHTS

Use the diagram below to help you take notes. The decline of the Qing dynasty was the result of internal problems within China, as well as external pressures by Western countries. List four of the internal problems that caused the Qing dynasty to decline

External Pressures by Foreigners

Internal Problems
1.
2.
3.
4.

Decline of the Qing Dynasty

Glencoe World History—Modern Times 239

4 CLOSE

Have students compare the activities of European countries in China to European activities in Southeast Asia and India. Ask why European countries did not attempt to exert direct control over China as they did in other countries. L2

SECTION 1 ASSESSMENT

1. Key terms are in blue.
2. Hong Xiuquan *(p. 468)*; Guang Xu *(p. 470)*; Empress Dowager Ci Xi *(p. 470)*; John Hay *(p. 470)*; Open Door policy *(p. 470)*
3. See chapter maps.
4. a devastating civil war; lasted 14 years; almost 20 million people died; the Qing dynasty was forced to rely on European aid
5. Britain, France, Germany, Russia, United States, Japan
6. helped reduce imperialist hysteria over access to the China market, and lessened attempt of any one country to dominate the market
7. Internal: corruption, peasant unrest, rapid population growth, serious food shortage, Tai Ping Rebellion, Boxer Rebellion; External: Opium War, trade concessions, extraterritoriality, spheres of influence, imperialist advances, Open Door policy, indemnities
8. Both are fierce and committed.
9. Answers will vary.

STUDY & WRITING SKILLBUILDER

TEACH

Writing a Report Have students review the process of choosing a topic. Practice this process with them by suggesting a number of general topics about nineteenth-century China that students must narrow down. General topics might include Chinese foreign policy, domestic problems in China, and attempts at reforms in China. These could be narrowed down to the internal problems of the Tai Ping Rebellion and the Boxer Rebellion, the Opium War's effects on foreign policy, and the policy of self-strengthening. L2

Additional Practice

Skills Reinforcement Activity 15

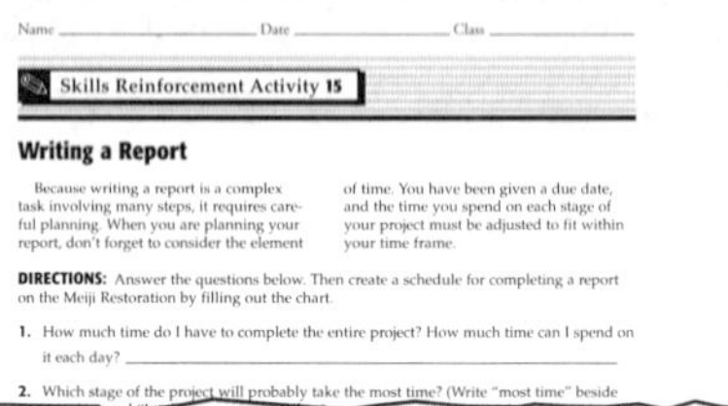

Name ______ Date ______ Class ______

Skills Reinforcement Activity 15

Writing a Report

Because writing a report is a complex task involving many steps, it requires careful planning. When you are planning your report, don't forget to consider the element of time. You have been given a due date, and the time you spend on each stage of your project must be adjusted to fit within your time frame.

DIRECTIONS: Answer the questions below. Then create a schedule for completing a report on the Meiji Restoration by filling out the chart.

1. How much time do I have to complete the entire project? How much time can I spend on it each day? ______
2. Which stage of the project will probably take the most time? (Write "most time" beside

GLENCOE TECHNOLOGY

CD-ROM
Glencoe Skillbuilder Interactive Workbook CD-ROM, Level 2

This interactive CD-ROM reinforces student mastery of essential social studies skills.

STUDY & WRITING SKILLBUILDER

Writing a Report

Why Learn This Skill?

You have learned about taking notes, making outlines, and finding sources for researching a paper. Now how do you put all those skills together to actually write a report?

Learning the Skill

Use the following guidelines to help you in writing a report:

- **Select an interesting topic.** As you identify possible topics, focus on resources that are available. Do preliminary research to determine whether your topic is too broad or too narrow. For example, writing about Japan in the nineteenth century is very broad. There is too much information to research and write about. Narrowing it down to one event in the nineteenth century, such as the Treaty of Kanagawa, is much more practical. If, however, you cannot find enough information about your topic, it is probably too narrow.
- **Write a thesis statement.** The thesis defines what you want to prove, discover, or illustrate in your report.

- **Prepare and do research on your topic.** Make a list of main idea questions, and then do research to answer those questions. Prepare note cards on each main idea question, listing the source information.
- **Organize your information.** Use an outline or another kind of organizer. Then follow your outline or organizer in writing a rough draft of your report.
- **Include an introduction, main body, and conclusion.** The introduction briefly presents the topic and gives your topic statement. The main body should follow your outline to develop the important ideas in your argument. The conclusion summarizes and restates your findings.
- **Revise the first draft.** Before writing the final draft of your report, wait one day and then reread and revise your first draft.

Practicing the Skill

Suppose you are writing a report on the decline of the Qing dynasty. Answer the following questions about the writing process.

1. What is a possible thesis statement?
2. What are three main idea questions?
3. What are three possible sources of information?
4. What are the next two steps in the process of writing a report?

Applying the Skill

Review the thesis, questions, and resources you came up with for the report on the Qing dynasty. Using this information, continue your research on this topic, organize your information, and write a short report.

Glencoe's **Skillbuilder Interactive Workbook, Level 2,** provides instruction and practice in key social studies skills.

ANSWERS TO PRACTICING THE SKILL

1. Answers will vary. Thesis statements define what you want to prove, discover, or illustrate in your report.
2. Answers will vary but might include the following: What were the internal causes? What were the external causes? What could the Qing rulers have done differently to stop or reverse the decline?
3. Answers might include the Internet, encyclopedias, and books on the Qing dynasty.
4. Create an outline; write a rough draft.

Applying the Skill: Student reports should be logically organized and list references. You might wish to have individual students review the process they used to develop a thesis, conduct research, organize their ideas, and then draft and edit their reports.

SECTION 2 Revolution in China

Guide to Reading

Main Ideas
- Sun Yat-sen introduced reforms that led to a revolution in China.
- The arrival of Westerners brought changes to the Chinese economy and culture.

Key Terms
provincial, commodity

People to Identify
Sun Yat-sen, Henry Pu Yi, General Yuan Shigai

Places to Locate
Shanghai, Wuhan

Preview Questions
1. What was Sun Yat-sen's role in the collapse of the Qing dynasty?
2. How did Western influence affect the Chinese economy and culture?

Reading Strategy
Compare and Contrast Create a chart like the one below listing the reforms requested by Sun Yat-sen and those implemented by Empress Dowager Ci Xi.

Sun Yat-sen's Proposals	Empress Dowager Ci Xi's Reforms

Preview of Events

1902 · 1905 · 1908 · 1911 · 1914 · 1917 · 1920

- **1905** Sun Yat-sen issues reform program
- **1908** Emperor Guang Xu and Empress Dowager Ci Xi die
- **1911** Qing dynasty collapses
- **1916** General Yuan Shigai dies

Voices from the Past

Sun Yat-sen presides over the parliament.

In 1905, a reformer named Sun Yat-sen presented a program that called for the following changes:

> "Establish the Republic: Now our revolution is based on equality, in order to establish a republican government. All our people are equal and all enjoy political rights. The president will be publicly chosen by the people of the country. The parliament will be made up of members publicly chosen by the people of the country. Equalize land ownership: The good fortune of civilization is to be shared equally by all the people of the nation. We should assess the value of all the land in the country. Its present price shall be received by the owner, but all increases in value resulting from reform and social improvements after the revolution shall belong to the state, to be shared by all the people."
>
> —***Sources of Chinese Tradition,*** **William Theodore de Bary et al., eds., 1960**

These ideas helped start a revolution in China in 1911.

The Fall of the Qing

After the Boxer Rebellion, the Qing dynasty in China tried desperately to reform itself. Empress Dowager Ci Xi, who had long resisted her advisers' suggestions for change, now embraced a number of reforms in education, administration, and the legal system.

The civil service examination system was replaced by a new educational system based on the Western model. After 1905, legislative assemblies were formed at the **provincial,** or local, level. Elections for a national assembly were even held in 1910.

1 FOCUS

Section Overview

This section discusses revolution in China and the effect of Western influence on China.

BELLRINGER Skillbuilder Activity

Project transparency and have students answer questions.

Available as a blackline master.

Daily Focus Skills Transparency 15–2

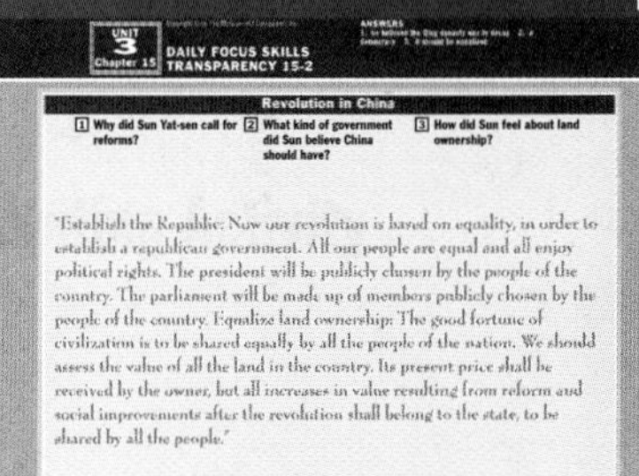

UNIT 3 Chapter 15 DAILY FOCUS SKILLS TRANSPARENCY 15-2

Revolution in China

1. Why did Sun Yat-sen call for reforms?
2. What kind of government did Sun believe China should have?
3. How did Sun feel about land ownership?

"Establish the Republic: Now our revolution is based on equality, in order to establish a republican government. All our people are equal and all enjoy political rights. The president will be publicly chosen by the people of the country. The parliament will be made up of members publicly chosen by the people of the country. Equalize land ownership: The good fortune of civilization is to be shared equally by all the people of the nation. We should assess the value of all the land in the country. Its present price shall be received by the owner, but all increases in value resulting from reform and social improvements after the revolution shall belong to the state, to be shared by all the people."

Guide to Reading

Answers to Graphic: Proposals: military takeover, prepare for democratic rule, establish constitutional democracy; Reforms: replaced civil service exam with educational system, established legislative assemblies, elections for a national assembly

Preteaching Vocabulary: Ask students to use a thesaurus to find synonyms and antonyms for the term *provincial. (synonyms: rural, rustic, local; antonyms: cosmopolitan, universal, sophisticated)* **L1**

SECTION RESOURCES

Reproducible Masters
- Reproducible Lesson Plan 15–2
- Daily Lecture and Discussion Notes 15–2
- Guided Reading Activity 15–2
- Section Quiz 15–2
- Reading Essentials and Study Guide 15–2

Transparencies
- Daily Focus Skills Transparency 15–2

Multimedia
- Interactive Tutor Self-Assessment CD-ROM
- ExamView® Pro Testmaker CD-ROM
- Presentation Plus! CD-ROM

2 TEACH

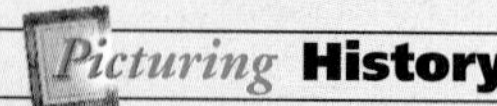

Picturing History

Answer: definitely the first phase, military takeover of the government; probably also the second phase, to keep order while his party prepared the people for democratic rule

Daily Lecture and Discussion Notes 15–2

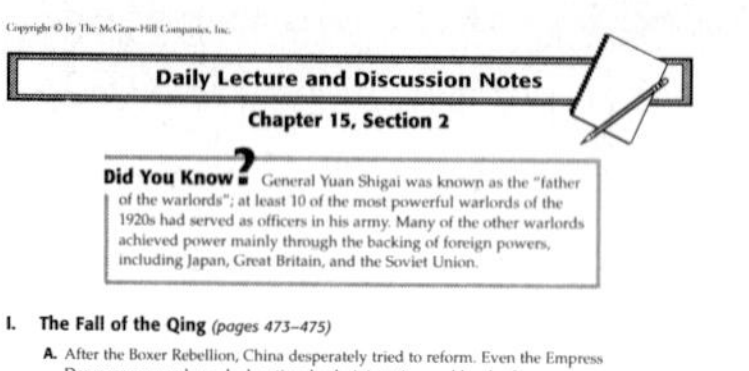

Daily Lecture and Discussion Notes

Chapter 15, Section 2

Did You Know? General Yuan Shigai was known as the "father of the warlords"; at least 10 of the most powerful warlords of the 1920s had served as officers in his army. Many of the other warlords achieved power mainly through the backing of foreign powers, including Japan, Great Britain, and the Soviet Union.

I. **The Fall of the Qing** *(pages 473–475)*

A. After the Boxer Rebellion, China desperately tried to reform. Even the Empress Dowager now embraced educational, administrative, and legal reforms.

B. A Western educational system replaced the traditional civil service examination educational system. After 1905, legislative assemblies were formed at the **provincial** (local) level. Elections for a national assembly were held in 1910.

Enrich

Have students prepare for and stage a class debate by assuming the roles of advisers to the Qing emperor. One set of advisers favors making reforms to modernize China. The other set of advisers favors maintaining the traditional Confucian system. What arguments would each side use to support its position? **L3**

Critical Thinking

Ask students to discuss why Sun Yat-sen gave up power to General Yuan Shigai. What was Sun Yat-sen's motivation? *(Sun Yat-sen realized he did not have the support or power he needed to unite China.)* **L1**

The emerging new elite, composed of merchants, professionals, and reform-minded gentry, soon became impatient with the slow pace of political change. They were angry when they discovered that the new assemblies were not allowed to pass laws but could only give advice to the ruler.

Moreover, the recent reforms had done nothing for the peasants, artisans, and miners, whose living conditions were getting worse as taxes increased. Unrest grew in the countryside as the dynasty continued to ignore deep-seated resentments.

The Rise of Sun Yat-sen The first signs of revolution appeared during the last decade of the nineteenth century, when the young radical **Sun Yat-sen** formed the Revive China Society. Sun Yat-sen believed that the Qing dynasty was in a state of decay and could no longer govern the country. Unless the Chinese were united under a strong government, they would remain at the mercy of other countries.

Although Sun believed that China should follow the pattern of Western countries, he also knew that the Chinese people were hardly ready for democracy. He instead developed a three-stage reform process that included: (1) a military takeover, (2) a transitional phase in which Sun's own revolutionary party would prepare the people for democratic rule, and (3) the final stage of a constitutional democracy.

In 1905, at a convention in Tokyo, Sun united radical groups from across China and formed the Revolutionary Alliance, which eventually became the Nationalist Party. The new organization advocated Sun's Three People's Principles, which promoted nationalism, democracy, and the right for people to pursue their own livelihoods. Although the new organization was small, it benefited from the rising discontent generated by the Qing dynasty's failure to improve conditions in China.

People In History

Sun Yat-sen
1866–1925
Chinese revolutionary

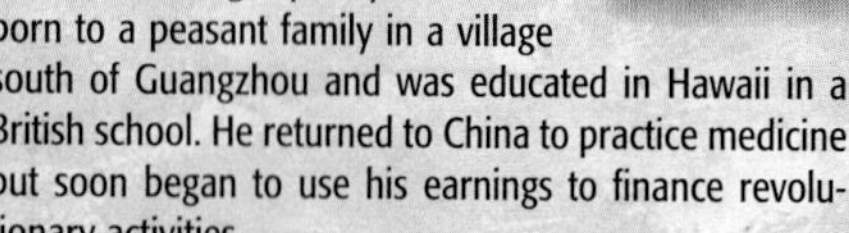

Sun Yat-sen was the leader of the revolutionary movement that overthrew the Qing dynasty. Sun was born to a peasant family in a village south of Guangzhou and was educated in Hawaii in a British school. He returned to China to practice medicine but soon began to use his earnings to finance revolutionary activities.

A failed rebellion forced Sun to flee to Japan and later to the United States and London. There, he raised money and recruited Chinese exiles to help carry out his revolutionary plans. After the Qing government collapsed in 1911, he returned to China.

Sun was never able to fully realize his dream of leading a new Chinese republic. Nevertheless, the governments of both the Republic of China on Taiwan and the Communist People's Republic of China honor him as the founder of modern China.

Picturing History

Sun Yat-sen's Nationalist soldiers arrive at a village in search of bandits. Sun Yat-sen's revolutionary forces rose against the Qing dynasty in 1911. What stage(s) in his reform process was Sun attempting to undertake with his army?

CRITICAL THINKING ACTIVITY

Synthesizing Information Revolutions frequently fail to bring about the anticipated changes. This was the case in China. Sun Yat-sen led a successful revolution to end the rule of the Qing dynasty, but he was unable to establish rule over the new government. Ask students to discuss reasons why most revolutions do not bring about intended changes. Organize students into groups and ask them to list the reasons for a revolution, the characteristics of a revolution, the characteristics of a revolution that is successful in overthrowing a government, and what conditions might be like following a revolution. Use group ideas to generate a class discussion on the nature of revolutions generally, as well as apply the ideas to Sun Yat-sen's revolution. **L2**

The Revolution of 1911 The Qing dynasty was near its end. In 1908, Empress Dowager Ci Xi died. Her nephew Guang Xu, a prisoner in the palace, died one day before his aunt. The throne was now occupied by China's "last emperor," the infant **Henry Pu Yi.**

In October 1911, followers of Sun Yat-sen launched an uprising in central China. At the time, Sun was traveling in the United States. Thus, the revolt had no leader, but the government was too weak to react. The Qing dynasty collapsed, opening the way for new political forces.

Sun's party had neither the military nor the political strength to form a new government. The party was forced to turn to a member of the old order, **General Yuan Shigai** (YOO•AHN SHUR•GIE), who controlled the army.

Yuan was a prominent figure in military circles, and he had been placed in charge of the imperial army sent to suppress the rebellion. Instead, he abandoned the government and negotiated with members of Sun Yat-sen's party. General Yuan agreed to serve as president of a new Chinese republic and to allow the election of a legislature. Sun himself arrived in China in January 1912, after reading about the revolution in a Denver, Colorado, newspaper.

In the eyes of Sun Yat-sen's party, the events of 1911 were a glorious revolution that ended two thousand years of imperial rule. However, the 1911 uprising was hardly a revolution. It produced no new political or social order. Sun Yat-sen and his followers still had much to accomplish.

The Revolutionary Alliance was supported mainly by an emerging urban middle class, and its program was based largely on Western liberal democratic principles. However, the urban middle class in China was too small to support a new political order. Most of the Chinese people still lived on the land, and few peasants supported Sun Yat-sen's party. In effect, then, the events of 1911 were less a revolution than a collapse of the old order.

Reading Check **Evaluating** What changes did the Revolution of 1911 actually produce in China?

An Era of Civil War

After the collapse of the Qing dynasty, the military took over. Sun Yat-sen and his colleagues had accepted General Yuan Shigai as president of the new Chinese republic in 1911 because they lacked the military force to compete with his control over the army. Many feared that if the revolt lapsed into chaos, the Western powers would intervene. If that happened, the last shreds of Chinese independence would be lost. However, even the general's new allies distrusted his motives.

"As Heaven has unified [the earth] under one sky, it will harmonize the various teachings of the world and bring them back to the same source."

—Wang Tao on the need for reform in China, 1800s

Picturing History

Sun Yat-sen and his wife, third and second from the left, stand with other members of the Revolutionary Alliance in Hangzhou, China. How does the clothing of the people in the photograph reflect Sun Yat-sen's beliefs about the future of China and Wang Tao's thoughts on the process of reform in the country?

Answer: the collapse of the Qing dynasty; General Yuan Shigai agreed to serve as president of a new Chinese republic and to allow the election of a legislature

Picturing History

Answer: The illustration shows a blending of East and West. While these people are wearing Western clothing and hairstyles, they are neither extravagant nor fashionable.

Guided Reading Activity 15–2

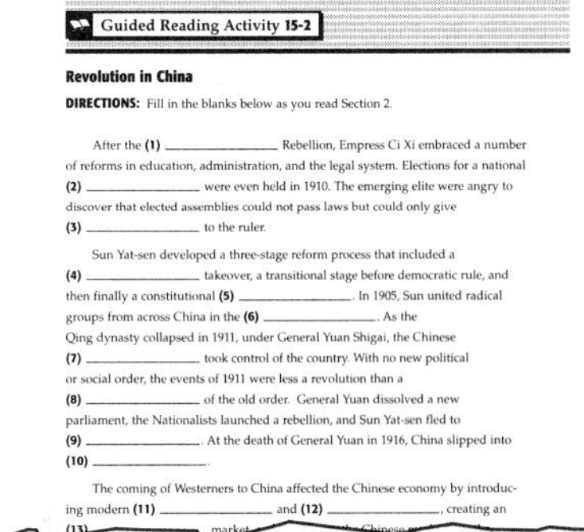

Name ____________ Date ____________ Class ____________

Guided Reading Activity 15-2

Revolution in China

DIRECTIONS: Fill in the blanks below as you read Section 2.

After the **(1)** ____________ Rebellion, Empress Ci Xi embraced a number of reforms in education, administration, and the legal system. Elections for a national **(2)** ____________ were even held in 1910. The emerging elite were angry to discover that elected assemblies could not pass laws but could only give **(3)** ____________ to the ruler.

Sun Yat-sen developed a three-stage reform process that included a **(4)** ____________ takeover, a transitional stage before democratic rule, and then finally a constitutional **(5)** ____________. In 1905, Sun united radical groups from across China in the **(6)** ____________. As the Qing dynasty collapsed in 1911, under General Yuan Shigai, the Chinese **(7)** ____________ took control of the country. With no new political or social order, the events of 1911 were less a revolution than a **(8)** ____________ of the old order. General Yuan dissolved a new parliament, the Nationalists launched a rebellion, and Sun Yat-sen fled to **(9)** ____________. At the death of General Yuan in 1916, China slipped into **(10)** ____________.

The coming of Westerners to China affected the Chinese economy by introducing modern **(11)** ____________ and **(12)** ____________, creating an

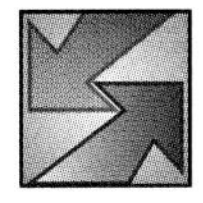

CURRICULUM CONNECTION

Language Arts Have students watch the 1987 film *The Last Emperor*. Have them write reports analyzing the way the film uses the story of Pu Yi as a mirror reflecting China's passage from feudalism through revolution toward a modern society. **L3**

EXTENDING THE CONTENT

Ba Jin Inform students that Ba Jin, the author discussed on page 478, wrote under the pseudonym Li Fei-Kan. His writing was exalted by the Communist regime after 1949, although he lost favor during the time of the Cultural Revolution (1966–1969). The title Ba Jin gave to his trilogy *Family, Spring,* and *Autumn* was *Torrent*. Ask students what torrent means and what the choice of this term must have meant to the author. *(The dictionary defines torrent as a rushing, violent, or abundant and unceasing stream of anything. This imagery might refer to the force of destruction exerted by the family on an individual, or perhaps to the revolutionary forces in China.)*

Reading Check

Answer: Yuan tried to destroy new democratic institutions; when he dissolved the parliament, the Nationalists rebelled.

Connecting Across Time

Have students identify characteristics of the collapse of previously studied empires or civilizations (Roman Empire, Aztec Empire, Mayan Empire, etc.). Then have students compare these characteristics with those impacting the decline of China's old order. Have students analyze information by identifying cause-and-effect relationships. There are also many parallels with countries today that are trying to modernize their economies while maintaining their cultures and traditions. Ask students to identify and describe some contemporary examples. *(There are a number of examples from Latin America, Africa, and the Middle East.)* **L3**

3 ASSESS

Assign Section 2 Assessment as homework or as an in-class activity.

Have students use **Interactive Tutor Self-Assessment CD-ROM**

Section Quiz 15–2

Name ______ Date ______ Class ______

Chapter 15 Score

Section Quiz 15-2

DIRECTIONS: Matching Match each item in Column A with an item in Column B. Write the correct letters in the blanks. *(10 points each)*

Column A	Column B
____ **1.** local, as opposed to national	**A.** Sun Yat-sen
____ **2.** formed the Revive China Society	**B.** provincial
____ **3.** dynasty that ended in 1911	**C.** Guomindang
____ **4.** reform party that accepted General Yuan as president	**D.** Qing
____ **5.** new name for the Nationalist Party	**E.** Revolutionary Alliance

Yuan understood little of the new ideas sweeping into China from the West. He ruled in a traditional manner and even tried to set up a new imperial dynasty. Yuan was hated by reformers for using murder and terror to destroy the new democratic institutions. He was hated by traditionalists (those who supported the Qing) for being disloyal to the dynasty he had served.

Yuan's dictatorial efforts rapidly led to clashes with Sun's party, now renamed the *Guomindang,* or Nationalist Party. When Yuan dissolved the new parliament, the Nationalists launched a rebellion. The rebellion failed, and Sun Yat-sen fled to Japan.

Yuan was strong enough to brush off the challenge from the revolutionary forces, but he could not turn back history. He died in 1916 and was succeeded by one of his officers. For the next several years, China slipped into civil war as the power of the central government disintegrated and military warlords seized power in the provinces. Their soldiers caused massive destruction throughout China.

Reading Check **Explaining** Why were there rebellions in China after General Yuan Shigai became president?

Chinese Society in Transition

When European traders began to move into China in greater numbers in the mid-1800s, Chinese society was already in a state of transition. The growth of industry and trade was especially noticeable in the cities, where a national market for such **commodities**—marketable products—as oil, copper, salt, tea, and porcelain had appeared. Faster and more reliable transportation and a better system of money and banking had begun to create the foundation for a money economy. New crops brought in from abroad increased food production and encouraged population growth. The Chinese economy had never been more productive.

The coming of Westerners to China affected the Chinese economy in three ways. Westerners: (1) introduced modern means of transportation and communications; (2) created an export market; and (3) integrated the Chinese market into the nineteenth-century world economy.

To some, these changes were beneficial. Shaking China out of its old ways quickened a process of change that had already begun in Chinese society. Western influences forced the Chinese to adopt new ways of thinking and acting.

THE WAY IT WAS

YOUNG PEOPLE IN . . .

China

In traditional China, children were thought of not as individuals but as members of a family. Indeed, children were valued because they—especially the sons—would help with the work in the fields, carry on the family name, and care for their parents in old age. By the beginning of the twentieth century, however, these attitudes had changed in some parts of Chinese society.

Some of the changes resulted from the new educational system. After the government abolished the civil service examinations in 1905, a Confucian education was no longer the key to a successful career. New schools based on the Western model were set up. Especially in the cities, both public and private schools educated a new generation of Chinese, who began to have less respect for the past.

By 1915, educated youth had launched an intense attack on the old system and old values. The main focus of the attack was the Confucian concept of the family. Young people rejected the old family ideas of respect for elders, supremacy of men over women, and sacrifice of individual needs to the demands of the family.

Chinese youth in Western-style clothing

476

COOPERATIVE LEARNING ACTIVITY

Staging a Debate Ask students to break into groups to prepare for and then to debate the following proposition: *Resolved: Individuals in the United States today have too many rights. Society as a whole is jeopardized by its inability to control individuals.* Ask the groups to appoint a spokesperson and allow each group five minutes to present its response to the proposition. Then ask the class to vote on the proposition as a whole. **L2**

For grading this activity, refer to the ***Performance Assessment Activities*** booklet.

At the same time, however, China paid a heavy price for the new ways. Its local industry was largely destroyed. Also, many of the profits in the new economy went to foreign countries rather than back into the Chinese economy.

During the first quarter of the twentieth century, the pace of change in China quickened even more. After World War I, which temporarily drew foreign investment out of the country, Chinese businesspeople began to develop new ventures. **Shanghai, Wuhan,** Tianjin, and Guangzhou became major industrial and commercial centers with a growing middle class and an industrial working class.

✓Reading Check **Evaluating** How did the arrival of Westerners affect China?

China's Changing Culture

In 1800, daily life for most Chinese was the same as it had been for centuries. Most were farmers, living in millions of villages in rice fields and on hillsides throughout the countryside. A farmer's life was governed by the harvest cycle, village custom, and family ritual. Most males were educated in the Confucian classics. Females remained in the home or in the fields. All children were expected to obey their parents, and wives were expected to submit to their husbands.

A visitor to China 125 years later would have seen a different society, although it would still have been recognizably Chinese. The changes were most striking in the cities. Here the educated and wealthy had been visibly affected by the growing Western cultural presence. Confucian social ideals were declining rapidly in influence and those of Europe and North America were on the rise.

Nowhere in China was the struggle between old and new more visible than in the field of culture. Radical reformers wanted to eliminate traditional culture, condemning it as an instrument of oppression. They were interested in creating a new China that would be respected by the modern world.

The first changes in traditional culture came in the late nineteenth century. Intellectuals began to introduce Western books, paintings, music, and ideas to China. By the first quarter of the twentieth century, China was flooded by Western culture as intellectuals called for a new culture based on that of the modern West.

Western literature and art became popular in China, especially among the urban middle class.

A spirit of individualism emerged out of the revolt of the youth. Young people now saw themselves as important in and for themselves. Sons no longer believed they had to sacrifice their wishes for the concerns of the larger family. Young people demanded the right to choose their own mates and their own careers.

Young Chinese also demanded that women have rights and opportunities equal to those enjoyed by men. They felt that women no longer should be subject to men.

The effect of the young people's revolt could be seen mainly in the cities. There, the tyranny of the old family system began to decline. Women sought education and jobs alongside men. Free choice in marriage became commonplace among affluent families in the cities. The teenage children of Westernized elites copied the clothing and even the music of young people in Europe and America.

These changes generally did not reach the villages, where traditional attitudes and customs persisted. Marriages arranged by parents continued to be the rule rather than the exception. According to a survey taken in the 1930s, well over two-thirds of marriages were still arranged, even among urban couples. In one rural area, only 3 villagers out of 170 had even heard of the idea of "modern marriage," or a marriage in which people freely choose their marriage partners.

Connecting to the Past

1. **Contrasting** Contrast the traditional way of life with life after 1915 for young people in China.
2. **Writing about History** How do the teenagers in China during the early twentieth century compare to the young people in the United States today? What common problems might both experience? Write a one-page essay explaining your ideas. Give specific examples to support your point of view.

477

✓Reading Check

Answer: Westerners transformed China by increasing industry and trade, improving transportation and communications, establishing a new money economy, creating export markets, integrating China into the nineteenth-century world economy, and introducing new crops that increased food production and encouraged population growth.

The Way It Was

Answers:

1. Traditionally, children were valued not as individuals but as part of the family. After 1915, young people developed a spirit of individualism and rejected ideas such as respect for elders, supremacy of men over women, and sacrifice of individual needs to the demands of the family.
2. Answers should be supported by examples and logical arguments.

Reteaching Activity

Have students analyze information by creating a time line that sequences the important events that occurred in China from 1900 to 1920. Have them share their time lines with the class. L1

MEETING INDIVIDUAL NEEDS

Visual/Spatial Students have been provided with considerable information in this chapter on political events and culture in China during the early twentieth century. Those students who are visual learners or have artistic talent should create a wall mural that depicts an event or scene described in this section. The mural should show progress in chronological order. Encourage students to add as many details and to be as culturally and historically accurate as possible. Display the mural in the classroom and ask other students to identify the people and events depicted in the mural. L2

Refer to ***Inclusion for the High School Social Studies Classroom Strategies and Activities*** in the TCR.

CHAPTER 15
Section 2, 473–478

 **History**

Answer: The family appears to be very traditional, with the eldest seated. All are wearing traditional clothing.

Reading Check

Answer: Western books, paintings, music, and ideas became popular with China's urban middle class. Intellectuals called for a new culture based on that of the modern West. More conservative elements of the population, especially in rural areas, clung to traditional Chinese culture.

Reading Essentials and Study Guide 15–2

Name ________ Date ________ Class ________

Reading Essentials and Study Guide

Chapter 15, Section 2

For use with textbook pages 473–478

REVOLUTION IN CHINA

KEY TERMS

provincial local, as opposed to national (page 473)

commodity a marketable product (page 476)

DRAWING FROM EXPERIENCE

Have you ever read any books about China? What are some customs or traditions in China? How are they the same or different from your family's customs or traditions?

In the last section, you read about the decline of the Qing dynasty. In this section, you will learn about the fall of the Qing dynasty in the early twentieth century, and the changes in Chinese society and culture during this time.

ORGANIZING YOUR THOUGHTS

Use the diagram below to help you take notes. The coming of Westerners dramatically affected China. List three ways that the Chinese economy was affected by Westerners. Also list three ways that the West influenced Chinese culture.

4 CLOSE

The conflict between tradition and change is never resolved and seems to be repeated, usually with less intensity than in China, every generation. Ask students to describe how they have experienced or witnessed the conflicts between culture and change. L2

Picturing History

Ba Jin (far right) is pictured with his four brothers and his stepmother. In his novel *Family*, Ba Jin shows readers how traditional patterns of family life prevailed in China's villages. From the photo, what inferences can be made about Ba Jin's family?

Traditional culture, however, remained popular with the more conservative elements of the population, especially in rural areas. Most creative artists followed foreign trends, while traditionalists held on to Chinese culture.

Literature in particular was influenced by foreign ideas. Western novels and short stories began to attract a larger audience. Although most Chinese novels written after World War I dealt with Chinese subjects, they reflected the Western tendency toward a realistic portrayal of society. Often, they dealt with the new Westernized middle class. Mae Dun's *Midnight*, for example, described the changing customs of Shanghai's urban elites. Most of China's modern authors showed a clear contempt for the past.

Ba Jin, the author of numerous novels and short stories, was one of China's foremost writers at the turn of the century. Born in 1904, Ba Jin was well attuned to the rigors and expected obedience of Chinese family life. In his trilogy, *Family, Spring,* and *Autumn,* he describes the distintegration of traditional Confucian ways as the younger members of a large family attempt to break away from their elders.

Reading Check **Describing** What effects did Western culture have on China?

SECTION 2 ASSESSMENT

Checking for Understanding

1. **Define** provincial, commodity.
2. **Identify** Sun Yat-sen, Henry Pu Yi, General Yuan Shigai.
3. **Locate** Shanghai, Wuhan.
4. **Describe** the attitudes toward Western culture held by Chinese in rural and urban areas. Which of these two groups do you think benefited more from Western involvement in the Chinese economy and society?
5. **List** the stages in Sun Yat-sen's three-stage process for reform. What principles did he hope to promote in China?

Critical Thinking

6. **Analyze** Why did the reforms introduced by Empress Dowager Ci Xi and General Yuan Shigai fail to improve the way China was governed?
7. **Cause and Effect** Create a diagram like the one below showing the changes resulting from European traders' contact with China in the mid-nineteenth century.

Contact		Effects
	→	
	→	
	→	

Analyzing Visuals

8. **Examine** the photograph of Sun Yat-sen's soldiers shown on page 474. What inferences can you draw about his army from looking at the photo? How important was this army in overthrowing the Qing dynasty?

Writing About History

9. **Expository Writing** Research and compare the reasons why both the United States and China experienced civil war. Write an essay offering alternatives to war that might have solved the internal problems of one of the two nations.

SECTION 2 ASSESSMENT

1. Key terms are in blue.
2. Sun Yat-sen *(p. 474)*; Henry Pu Yi *(p. 475)*; General Yuan Shigai *(p. 475)*
3. See chapter maps.
4. Urban areas embraced Western culture, rural areas retained traditional ideas; urban.
5. (1) military takeover, (2) transitional phase, (3) constitutional democracy; nationalism, democracy, pursuit of livelihood
6. reforms too slow and limited; conditions did not improve for many
7. Answers may include: trade → creation of export market; banking → money-based economy; industry → growth of industrial centers
8. well equipped but more relaxed and less regimented than expected; army not significant to the overthrow of the government
9. Answers should be supported by logical arguments.

SECTION 3 Rise of Modern Japan

Guide to Reading

Main Ideas

- Western intervention opened Japan, an island that had been isolated for 200 years, to trade.
- The interaction between Japan and Western nations gave birth to a modern industrial society.

Key Terms

concession, prefecture

People to Identify

Matthew Perry, Millard Fillmore, Mutsuhito, Ito Hirobumi

Places to Locate

Edo Bay, Kyoto, Edo, Port Arthur

Preview Questions

1. What effect did the Meiji Restoration have on Japan?
2. What steps did Japan take to become an imperialist nation?

Reading Strategy

Categorizing Information Create a table like the one below listing the promises contained in the Charter Oath of 1868 and the provisions of the Meiji constitution of 1890.

Charter Oath	Constitution

Preview of Events

1850 · 1860 · 1870 · 1880 · 1890 · 1900 · 1910

- **1853** Commodore Perry arrives in Japan
- **1871** Government seizes daimyo's lands to strengthen executive power
- **1874** Japan pursues imperialist policy
- **1890** Adoption of Meiji constitution
- **1905** Japan defeats Russia

Voices from the Past

Hand-colored photograph of Japanese children, c. 1890

In 1890, Japanese leaders issued a decree to be read to every schoolchild:

> "You, our subjects, be filial to your parents, affectionate to your brothers and sisters, as husbands and wives be harmonious, as friends true; bear yourselves in modesty and moderation; extend your goodness to all; pursue learning and cultivate arts, and thereby develop intellectual faculties and perfect moral powers; furthermore, advance public good and promote common interests; always respect the Constitution and observe the laws; should emergency arise, offer yourselves to the State; and thus guard and maintain the prosperity of our imperial throne."
>
> —***Sources of Japanese Tradition,*** **Ryusaku Tsunoda et al., eds., 1958**

Obedience and the community were valued in Japan.

An End to Isolation

TURNING POINT **In this section, you will learn how the Treaty of Kanagawa brought Japan out of isolation and started its development into an imperialist nation.**

By 1800, the Tokugawa shogunate had ruled the Japanese islands for two hundred years. It had driven out foreign traders and missionaries and isolated the country from virtually all contact with the outside world. The Tokugawa maintained formal relations only with Korea. Informal trading links with Dutch and Chinese merchants continued at Nagasaki. Foreign ships, which were beginning to prowl along the Japanese coast in increasing numbers, were driven away.

To the Western powers, the continued isolation of Japanese society was a challenge. Western nations were convinced that the expansion of trade on a global

1 FOCUS

Section Overview

This section discusses the events and transformations that opened Japan to trade and industrialization.

BELLRINGER
Skillbuilder Activity

 Project transparency and have students answer questions.

 Available as a blackline master.

Daily Focus Skills Transparency 15–3

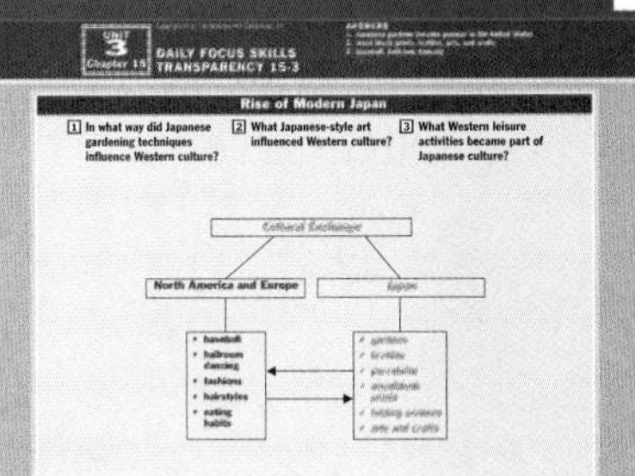

Guide to Reading

Answers to Graphic: Oath: emperor rules, legislative assembly assists emperor, country divided into prefectures; Constitution: emperor a figurehead, prime minister exercises executive authority, lower house of parliament elected

Preteaching Vocabulary: Have students research the meaning of the root *cede*. Ask them to give examples of other words that come from the root *cede*. *(yield; cease, concede, accede, access, exceed, intercede, precede, proceed, secede, succeed)* **L1**

SECTION RESOURCES

Reproducible Masters

- Reproducible Lesson Plan 15–3
- Daily Lecture and Discussion Notes 15–3
- Guided Reading Activity 15–3
- Section Quiz 15–3
- Reading Essentials and Study Guide 15–3

Transparencies

- Daily Focus Skills Transparency 15–3

Multimedia

- Interactive Tutor Self-Assessment CD-ROM
- ExamView® Pro Testmaker CD-ROM
- Presentation Plus! CD-ROM

2 TEACH

TURNING POINT

What were the conditions of the Treaty of Kanagawa that helped make Japan an imperialist nation? *(opening of ports to Western traders, establishing a United States consulate in Japan)* Have students analyze the information in this section by contrasting Japan before and after the Treaty of Kanagawa. **L2**

Reading Check

Answer: return of shipwrecked American sailors, opening of two ports to Western traders, establishment of a United States consulate in Japan

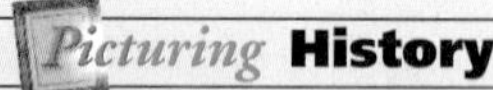

Picturing **History**

Answer: Trade with West began; resistance led to end of shogunate system.

Reading Check

Answer: Sat-Cho alliance forces shogun to promise to end relations with West; Western ships destroy Choshu fortifications; alliance forces shogun to resign and restore emperor to power, ending the shogunate system

Daily Lecture and Discussion Notes 15–3

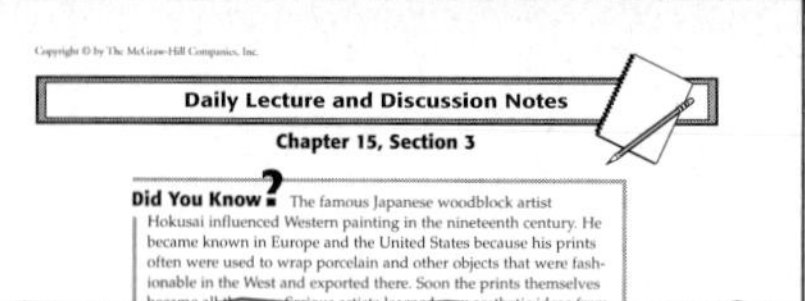
Daily Lecture and Discussion Notes
Chapter 15, Section 3
Did You Know? The famous Japanese woodblock artist Hokusai influenced Western painting in the nineteenth century. He became known in Europe and the United States because his prints often were used to wrap porcelain and other objects that were fashionable in the West and exported there. Soon the prints themselves

basis would benefit all nations. They now began to approach Japan in the hope of opening it up to foreign economic interests.

The first foreign power to succeed with Japan was the United States. In the summer of 1853, an American fleet of four warships under Commodore **Matthew Perry** arrived in **Edo Bay** (now Tokyo Bay). They sought, as Perry said, "to bring a singular and isolated people into the family of civilized nations."

Perry brought with him a letter from President **Millard Fillmore.** The U.S. president asked for better treatment of sailors shipwrecked on the Japanese islands. (Foreign sailors shipwrecked in Japan were treated as criminals and exhibited in public cages.) He also requested the opening of foreign relations between the United States and Japan.

Picturing **History**

This Japanese painting records Commodore Perry's arrival in Edo Bay in July 1853. What was the economic and political impact of Perry's visits on Japan?

A few months later, Perry, accompanied by an even larger fleet, returned to Japan for an answer. Shogunate officials had been discussing the issue. Some argued that contacts with the West would hurt Japan. Others pointed to the military superiority of the United States and recommended concessions, or political compromises. The question was ultimately decided by the guns of Commodore Perry's ships.

Under military pressure, Japan agreed to the Treaty of Kanagawa. This treaty between Japan and the United States provided for the return of shipwrecked American sailors, the opening of two ports to Western traders, and the establishment of a U.S. consulate in Japan.

In 1858, U.S. consul Townsend Harris signed a more detailed treaty. It called for the opening of several new ports to U.S. trade and residence, as well as an exchange of ministers. Similar treaties were soon signed by Japan and several European nations.

Reading Check **Identifying** What benefits did the Treaty of Kanagawa grant the United States?

Resistance to the New Order

The decision to open relations with the Western powers was highly unpopular in parts of Japan. Resistance was especially strong among the samurai warriors in two territories in the south, Satsuma and Choshu. Both had strong military traditions, and neither had been exposed to heavy Western military pressure. In 1863, the Sat-Cho alliance (from Satsuma-Choshu) forced the shogun to promise to end relations with the West.

The rebellious groups soon showed their own weakness, however. When Choshu troops fired on Western ships in the Strait of Shimonoseki, which leads into the Sea of Japan, the Westerners fired back and destroyed the Choshu fortifications.

The incident convinced the rebellious forces of the need to strengthen their military. They also became more determined not to give in to the West. As a result, Sat-Cho leaders urged the shogun to take a stronger position against the foreigners.

The Sat-Cho leaders demanded that the shogun resign and restore the power of the emperor. In January 1868, their armies attacked the shogun's palace in **Kyoto** and proclaimed that the authority of the emperor had been restored. After a few weeks, the shogun's forces collapsed, ending the shogunate system.

Reading Check **Identifying** What events led to the collapse of the shogunate system in Japan?

The Meiji Restoration

The Sat-Cho leaders had genuinely mistrusted the West, but they soon realized that Japan must change to survive. The new leaders embarked on a policy of reform that transformed Japan into a modern industrial nation.

EXTENDING THE CONTENT

Western Influence in Japan As part of the reforms of the Meiji era, the Japanese sent fifty men and women to study Western culture. The Iwakura Mission, as it was known, brought back to Japan ideas about government, industry, and culture. One European idea that had a powerful effect on the Japanese was Herbert Spencer's philosophy of social Darwinism. This idea, that people and nations are in constant struggle for the "survival of the fittest," mirrored the Japanese nationalist ideology of *fukoku-hyohei* (wealth and strength). Many of the negative results of the Meiji Restoration (the dehumanization of labor, growth of the military, Japan's expansionist policies) came about as a result of the merger of these similar Western and Japanese philosophies.

Emperor Mutsuhito

The symbol of the new era was the young emperor **Mutsuhito.** He called his reign the Meiji (MAY•jee), or "Enlightened Rule." This period has thus become known as the Meiji Restoration.

Of course, the Meiji ruler was controlled by the Sat-Cho leaders, just as earlier emperors had been controlled by the shogunate. In recognition of the real source of political power, the capital was moved from Kyoto to **Edo** (now named Tokyo), the location of the new leaders. The imperial court was moved to the shogun's palace in the center of the city.

Transformation of Japanese Politics Once in power, the new leaders moved first to abolish the old order and to strengthen power in their hands. To undercut the power of the daimyo—the local nobles—the new leaders stripped these great lords of the titles to their lands in 1871. As compensation, the lords were given government bonds and were named governors of the territories formerly under their control. The territories were now called prefectures.

The Meiji reformers set out to create a modern political system based on the Western model. In 1868, the new leaders signed a Charter Oath, in which they promised to create a new legislative assembly within the framework of continued imperial rule. Although senior positions in the new government were given to the daimyo, the key posts were held by modernizing leaders from the Sat-Cho group. The country was divided into 75 prefectures. (The number was reduced to 45 in 1889 and remains at that number today.)

During the next 20 years, the Meiji government undertook a careful study of Western political systems. A commission under **Ito Hirobumi** traveled to Great Britain, France, Germany, and the United States to study their governments.

As the process evolved, two main factions appeared, the Liberals and the Progressives. The Liberals wanted political reform based on the Western liberal democratic model, with supreme authority vested in the parliament as the representative of the people. The Progressives wanted power to be shared between the legislative and executive branches, with the executive branch having more control.

During the 1870s and 1880s, these factions fought for control. In the end, the Progressives won. The Meiji constitution, adopted in 1890, was modeled after that of Imperial Germany. Most authority was given to the executive branch.

In theory, the emperor exercised all executive authority, but in practice he was a figurehead. Real executive authority rested in the hands of a prime minister and his cabinet of ministers. These ministers were handpicked by the Meiji leaders.

Under the new constitution, members of the upper house of the parliament were to be appointed, while members of the lower house were to be elected. The two houses were to have equal legislative powers.

The final result was a political system that was democratic in form but authoritarian in practice. Although modern in external appearance, it was still traditional, because power remained in the hands of a ruling oligarchy (the Sat-Cho leaders). Although a new set of institutions and values had emerged, the system allowed the traditional ruling class to keep its influence and economic power.

Meiji Economics The Meiji leaders also set up a new system of land ownership. A land reform program made the traditional lands of the daimyo into the private property of the peasants. The daimyo, as mentioned, were compensated with government bonds.

The Meiji leaders levied a new land tax, which was set at an annual rate of 3 percent of the estimated value of the land. The new tax was an excellent source of revenue for the government. However, it was quite burdensome for the farmers.

Under the old system, farmers had paid a fixed percentage of their harvest to the landowners. In bad

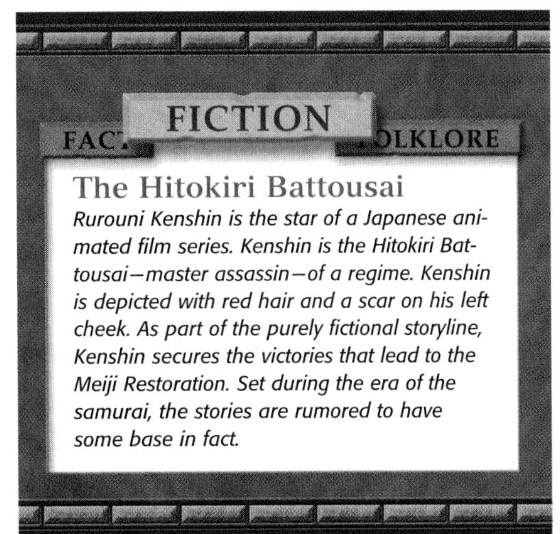

The Hitokiri Battousai

Rurouni Kenshin is the star of a Japanese animated film series. Kenshin is the Hitokiri Battousai—master assassin—of a regime. Kenshin is depicted with red hair and a scar on his left cheek. As part of the purely fictional storyline, Kenshin secures the victories that lead to the Meiji Restoration. Set during the era of the samurai, the stories are rumored to have some base in fact.

CHAPTER 15
Section 3, 479–486

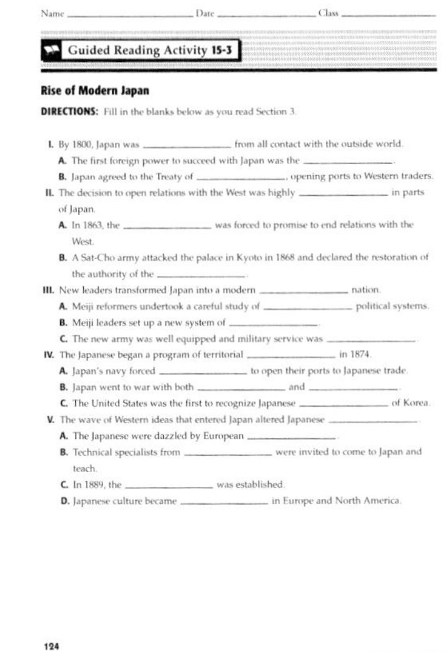

Guided Reading Activity 15–3

Name ______ Date ______ Class ______

Guided Reading Activity 15-3

Rise of Modern Japan

DIRECTIONS: Fill in the blanks below as you read Section 3.

I. By 1800, Japan was ______ from all contact with the outside world.
A. The first foreign power to succeed with Japan was the ______.
B. Japan agreed to the Treaty of ______, opening ports to Western traders.
II. The decision to open relations with the West was highly ______ in parts of Japan.
A. In 1863, the ______ was forced to promise to end relations with the West.
B. A Sat-Cho army attacked the palace in Kyoto in 1868 and declared the restoration of the authority of the ______.
III. New leaders transformed Japan into a modern ______ nation.
A. Meiji reformers undertook a careful study of ______ political systems.
B. Meiji leaders set up a new system of ______.
C. The new army was well equipped and military service was ______.
IV. The Japanese began a program of territorial ______ in 1874.
A. Japan's navy forced ______ to open their ports to Japanese trade.
B. Japan went to war with both ______ and ______.
C. The United States was the first to recognize Japanese ______ of Korea.
V. The wave of Western ideas that entered Japan altered Japanese ______.
A. The Japanese were dazzled by European ______.
B. Technical specialists from ______ were invited to come to Japan and teach.
C. In 1889, the ______ was established.
D. Japanese culture became ______ in Europe and North America.

124

Who?What?Where?When?

Matthew Perry On his first visit to Japan, Commodore Perry was careful to bring examples of modern technology to leave with the Japanese, in order to impress the Japanese with the power and scientific advances of the West. Perry even set up a miniature railroad along the coast that whirled Japanese officials around its tracks. A telegraph link was set up between Perry's ship and the royal palace. The technological and military significance of these gifts was not lost on the Japanese. Ask students why Perry would try to impress the Japanese with Western technology. *(Perry was hoping to intimidate the Japanese government with the ineffectiveness of resistance and also to interest them in obtaining these "marvels" for themselves.)* **L2**

CRITICAL THINKING ACTIVITY

Evaluating Inform students that the members of the Sat-Cho alliance were from the samurai class and held traditional values that helped them in the drive to industrialize Japan. One samurai founder of a large corporation created the following "corporate guidelines." Ask students to "translate" them into modern-day terms. Do they believe that these values operate today in the American corporate climate? 1) Do not be preoccupied with small matters but aim at the management of large enterprises. 2) Once you start an enterprise, be sure to succeed. 3) Do not engage in speculative enterprises. 4) Operate enterprises with the national interest in mind. 5) Never forget the pure spirit of public service, sincerity, and fidelity. **L2**

Chart *Skills*

Answers:

1. Industrialization encouraged; universal system of education developed; Western practices adopted
2. Reestablishment of imperial rule led to the other political changes. To create a stronger central government, the daimyo were stripped of their land. Land given to peasants was taxed to fund changes such as the new army, educational system, and industrialization, which led many farmers into tenancy.

Writing Activity

Have students research Matthew Perry's dealing with the Japanese and prepare a television "Special News Report" for U.S. citizens eager to know the outcome. Ask students to write interview questions and answers for Perry and the shoguns who signed treaties with him. Some students can take the role of reporters and others can represent Perry, members of his crew, and the Japanese.

CURRICULUM CONNECTION

Music Puccini's popular opera *Madama Butterfly*, which was first performed in 1904, dramatizes some of the consequences of Japan's relationship with the West. Ask students to research the opera and summarize its central themes. L1

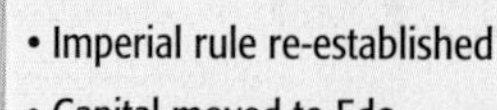

Meiji Restoration: Birth of Modern Japan

	Changes and Events
Politics	• Imperial rule re-established • Capital moved to Edo • Most power in executive branch (emperor, prime minister, cabinet)
Economics	• Daimyo's lands given to peasants • Many farmers, unable to pay new land tax, forced into tenancy • Industrialization encouraged
Social Structure	• New imperial army created • Universal system of education developed • Western practices adopted

Chart *Skills*

The Meiji government began reforms that transformed Japan's political, economic, and social structures.

1. **Cause and Effect** What changes noted on the chart most reflect the influence of Western ideas upon Japan?
2. **Making Generalizations** How are the changes in the three areas of politics, economics, and social structure interrelated?

harvest years, they had owed little or nothing. Under the new system, the farmers had to pay the land tax every year, regardless of the quality of the harvest.

As a result, in bad years, many peasants were unable to pay their taxes. This forced them to sell their lands to wealthy neighbors and become tenant farmers who paid rent to the new owners. By the end of the nineteenth century, about 40 percent of all farmers were tenants.

With its budget needs met by the land tax, the government turned to the promotion of industry. The chief goal of the reformers was to create a "rich country and a strong state" to guarantee Japan's survival against the challenge of Western nations.

The Meiji government gave subsidies to needy industries, provided training and foreign advisors, improved transportation and communications, and started a new educational system that stressed applied science. In contrast to China, Japan was able to achieve results with little reliance on foreign money. By 1900, Japan's industrial sector was beginning to grow. Besides tea and silk, other key industries were weapons, shipbuilding, and sake (SAH•kee), or Japanese rice wine.

From the start, a unique feature of the Meiji model of industrial development was the close relationship between government and private business. The government encouraged the development of new industries by providing businesspeople with money and privileges. Once an individual enterprise or industry was on its feet, it was turned over entirely to private ownership. Even then, however, the government continued to play some role in the industry's activities.

Building a Modern Social Structure The Meiji reformers also transformed other institutions. A key focus of their attention was the military. The reformers were well aware that Japan would need a modern military force to compete with the Western powers. Their motto was "Strengthen the Army."

A new imperial army based on compulsory military service was formed in 1871. All Japanese men now served for three years. The new army was well equipped with modern weapons.

Education also changed. The Meiji leaders realized the need for universal education, including instruction in modern technology. A new ministry of education, established in 1871, guided the changes.

After a few years of experimentation, the education ministry adopted the American model of elementary schools, secondary schools, and universities. It brought foreign specialists to Japan to teach in the new schools. In the meantime, it sent bright students to study abroad.

CRITICAL THINKING ACTIVITY

Drawing Inferences Have students identify the primary and secondary causes of the Meiji Restoration. Using the historical skills of analyzing information and drawing inferences, students should predict how Chinese history might have been different if China had undergone a similar restoration. Also, explain to students that Japan's modernization movement thrust it into the modern era and eventually resulted in Japan's dominant economic position in the twenty-first century. Ask students to list as many ways as possible in which Japan's economic capabilities have affected the students' lives either directly or indirectly. L2

Much of the content of the new educational system was Western in inspiration. However, a great deal of emphasis was still placed on the virtues of loyalty to the family and community. Loyalty to the emperor was especially valued. Both teachers and students were required to bow before a portrait of the emperor each day.

Daily Life and Women's Rights Japanese society in the late Tokugawa Era, before the Meiji reforms, could be described by two words: *community* and *hierarchy.* The lives of all Japanese people were determined by their membership in a family, village, and social class. At the same time, Japanese society was highly hierarchical. Belonging to a particular social class determined a person's occupation and social relationships with others. Women were especially limited by the "three obediences": child to father, wife to husband, and widow to son. Whereas husbands could easily obtain a divorce, wives could not. Marriages were arranged, and the average marital age of females was sixteen years. Females did not share inheritance rights with males. Few received any education outside the family.

The Meiji Restoration had a marked effect on the traditional social system in Japan. Special privileges for the aristocracy were abolished. For the first time, women were allowed to seek an education. As the economy shifted from an agricultural to an industrial base, thousands of Japanese began to get new jobs and establish new social relationships.

Western fashions became the rage in elite circles. The ministers of the first Meiji government were known as the "dancing cabinet" because of their love for Western-style ballroom dancing. The game of baseball was imported from the United States.

Young people were increasingly influenced by Western culture and values. A new generation of modern boys and girls began to imitate the clothing styles, eating habits, hairstyles, and social practices of European and American young people.

The social changes brought about by the Meiji Restoration also had a less attractive side. Many commoners were ruthlessly exploited in the coal mines and textile mills. Workers labored up to 20 hours a day, often under conditions of incredible hardship. Coal miners employed on a small island in the harbor of Nagasaki worked in temperatures up to 130 degrees Fahrenheit (54 degrees C). When they tried to escape, they were shot.

Resistance to such conditions was not unknown. In many areas, villagers sought new political rights. In some cases, they demanded increased attention to human rights. Women took part in this process and formed the Freedom and People's Rights Movement. This movement was demanding voting rights for women as early as 1876.

Picturing History

For a recital at a music school in 1889, Japanese musicians played Western music and wore Western clothing. In what other ways did Japanese culture change under the Meiji government?

Picturing History

Answer: Other changes included the abolition of special privileges for the aristocracy, education for women, introduction of baseball, exploitation of workers, and the growth of a movement for women's rights.

Connecting Across Time

Life for factory workers in Japan was just as bad as it was in Europe during the early stages of the Industrial Revolution. Twelve-hour shifts in factories were common. Low wages for workers produced high profits for factory owners. Crowded slums sprang up near factory districts. However, most citizens accepted the belief that personal sacrifice was necessary to make Japan a powerful industrial nation.

Critical Thinking

The text discusses the Japanese concept of the three obediences: child to father, wife to husband, and widow to son. Ask students to write their own concepts of three obediences. For instance, a student might write child to parent, friend to friend, citizen to government, or employee to employer. Afterwards, ask volunteers to share their obediences with the class. This activity should lead to some lively discussion of cultural values. Some artistic students may even wish to illustrate the older Japanese obediences and some of the class's examples. L2

INTERDISCIPLINARY CONNECTIONS ACTIVITY

Sports Have students research the introduction of baseball in Tokyo in 1871 by Horace Wilson and the first organized baseball team, the Shimbashi Athletic Club Athletics, in 1878. They should also note the differences between Meiji baseball and contemporary American baseball, as well as the role of baseball in Japan today. Ask students to consider the following questions: Why did baseball become popular in Japan? Does baseball have the same status in Japan as it does in America, or do the two countries value the game for different reasons? What imported sporting events, if any, have become popular in the United States? L2

For grading this activity, refer to the ***Performance Assessment Activities*** booklet.

CHAPTER 15
Section 3, 479–486

Reading Check

Answer: Emperor theoretically had executive authority but was actually a figurehead; prime minister and his cabinet had real executive authority; upper house of parliament was appointed; lower house of parliament was elected; both houses of parliament had equal legislative powers.

Geography *Skills*

Answers:

1. Japan acquired South Sakhalin Island, Korea, and Taiwan.
2. distance from Japan, accessibility to water, Japan's strong navy

CURRICULUM CONNECTION

Sociology Remind students that the Japanese in America had already suffered discrimination before World War II. In reaction to a wave of Japanese immigration in the late 1890s and early 1900s, Californians organized a Japanese and Korean Exclusion League with the aim of combating the "Japanese menace." In 1906, a San Francisco school board assigned all Asian students to one segregated school. The Japanese government officially protested this intended slur to the government. Theodore Roosevelt fashioned an agreement whereby San Francisco retracted the segregation order in exchange for a promise from Japan to limit immigration of farmers and workers to the United States and to Hawaii.

The transformation of Japan into a "modern society" did not detach the country entirely from its old values, however. Traditional values based on loyalty to the family and community were still taught in the new schools. Traditional values were also given a firm legal basis in the 1890 constitution, which limited the right to vote to men. The Civil Code of 1898 played down individual rights and placed women within the context of their family role.

Reading Check **Explaining** How was Japan's government structured under the Meiji constitution?

Joining the Imperialist Nations

We have seen that the Japanese modeled some of their domestic policies on Western practices. They also copied the imperialist Western approach to foreign affairs. Japan, after all, is small, lacking in resources, and densely populated. There is no natural room for expansion. To some Japanese, the lessons of history were clear. Western nations had amassed wealth and power not only because of their democratic, economic, and educational systems, but also because of their colonies. Colonies had provided the Western powers with sources of raw materials, inexpensive labor, and markets for their manufactured products. To compete, Japan would also have to expand.

Beginnings of Expansion The Japanese began their program of territorial expansion close to home. In 1874, Japan claimed control of the Ryukyu (ree•YOO•KYOO) Islands, which had long been subject to the Chinese Empire. Two years later, Japan's navy forced the Koreans to open their ports to Japanese trade.

The Chinese had long controlled Korea and were concerned by Japan's growing influence there. During the 1880s, Chinese-Japanese rivalry over Korea intensified. In 1894, the two nations went to war. Japanese ships destroyed the Chinese fleet and seized the Manchurian city of **Port Arthur.**

In the treaty that ended the war, the Manchu rulers of China recognized the independence of Korea. They also ceded (transferred) Taiwan and the Liaodong Peninsula, with its strategic naval base at Port Arthur, to Japan.

Shortly thereafter, the Japanese gave the Liaodong Peninsula back to China. In the early twentieth century, however, the Japanese returned to the offensive.

Rivalry with Russia over influence in Korea had led to increasingly strained relations between Japan and Russia. The Russians thought little of the Japanese and even welcomed the possibility of war. One adviser to Nicholas II said, "We will only have to throw our caps at them and they will run away."

War with Russia In 1904, Japan launched a surprise attack on the Russian naval base at Port Arthur, which Russia had taken from China in 1898. When Japanese forces moved into Manchuria and the Liaodong Peninsula, Russian troops proved to be no match for them. The Russian commander in chief said, "It is impossible not to admire the bravery and

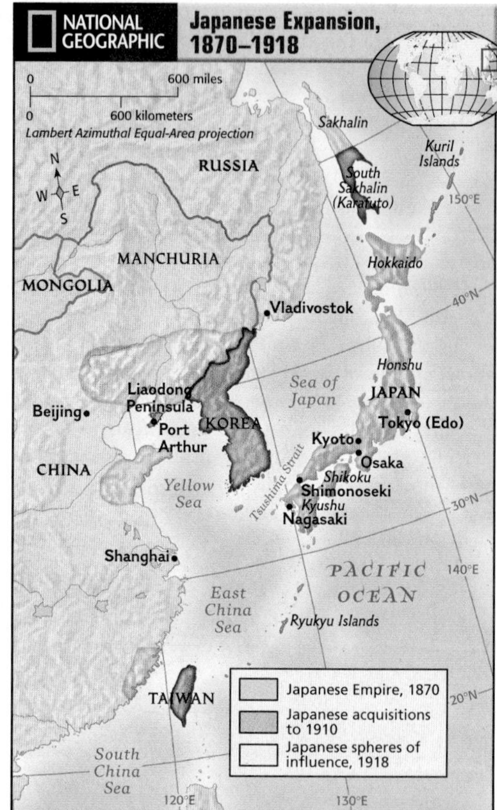

Geography *Skills*

In the late nineteenth century, Japan transformed itself into an imperialist nation.

1. **Interpreting Maps** Between 1870 and 1910, approximately how much land did Japan acquire through expansion?
2. **Applying Geography Skills** What geographic factors might have influenced Japan's expansion?

EXTENDING THE CONTENT

The Russo-Japanese War Students should realize that the United States played a diplomatic role very early in the war. Theodore Roosevelt helped negotiate peace at Port Arthur, ending the Russo-Japanese War and earning the Nobel Peace Prize. President Roosevelt became the first American to win this prestigious award. Neither Russia nor Japan was grateful for Roosevelt's efforts. Both countries felt they had received the worse end of the deal and bore a grudge against the United States because of the settlement.

Picturing History

The Japanese surprise attack on Port Arthur in 1904 reflected the growing power of Japan and its navy. What impact did the Japanese victory have on Russia? How did it affect relations between Japan and the United States?

activity of the Japanese. The attack of the Japanese is a continuous succession of waves, and they never relax their efforts by day or by night."

In the meantime, Russia had sent its Baltic fleet halfway around the world to East Asia, only to be defeated by the new Japanese navy off the coast of Japan. After their defeat, the Russians agreed to a humiliating peace in 1905. They gave the Liaodong Peninsula back to Japan, as well as the southern part of Sakhalin (SA•kuh•LEEN), an island north of Japan. The Japanese victory stunned the world. Japan had become one of the great powers.

U.S. Relations During the next few years, Japan consolidated its position in northeastern Asia. The Japanese government annexed Korea in 1910. The United States was the first nation to recognize this annexation. In return, the United States asked for Japan's support for American authority in the Philippines.

Mutual suspicion between the two countries was growing, however. The Japanese resented U.S. efforts to restrict immigration. Moreover, some Americans began to fear the rise of Japanese power in East Asia. In 1907, President Theodore Roosevelt made a "gentlemen's agreement" with Japan that essentially stopped Japanese immigration to the United States.

Reading Check **Explaining** Why did Japan turn itself into an imperialist power?

Culture in an Era of Transition

The wave of Western technology and ideas that entered Japan in the last half of the nineteenth century greatly altered the shape of traditional Japanese culture. Literature was especially affected. Dazzled by European literature, Japanese authors began translating and imitating the imported models.

The novel showed the greatest degree of change. People began to write novels that were patterned after the French tradition of realism. Naturalist Japanese authors tried to present existing social conditions and the realities of war as objectively as possible.

Other aspects of Japanese culture were also changed. The Japanese invited technicians, engineers, architects, and artists from Europe and the United States to teach their "modern" skills to eager Japanese students. The Japanese copied Western artistic techniques and styles. Huge buildings of steel and reinforced concrete, adorned with Greek columns, appeared in many Japanese cities.

A national reaction had begun by the end of the nineteenth century, however. Many Japanese artists

Reading Check

Answer: Japan was a small nation, lacking in resources, and densely populated; there was no room for expansion. It imitated the Western nations in creating a colonial empire, providing raw materials, inexpensive labor, and markets for manufactured goods.

Picturing History

Answer: Russia was humiliated by its defeat; the United States grew suspicious as Japan became a world power.

3 ASSESS

Assign Section 3 Assessment as homework or as an in-class activity.

Have students use **Interactive Tutor Self-Assessment CD-ROM.**

Reteaching Activity

Have students create a table showing the major changes described in this section. The table will have five columns, labeled *Territorial, Political, Economic, Diplomatic,* and *Cultural.* The left side of the table should be a time line from 1875 to 1925. Students should list events in each column according to the dates they occurred. L1

MEETING INDIVIDUAL NEEDS

Visual/Auditory Have students prepare a visual display depicting one of the Asian countries studied in this chapter during the period from 1800 to 1914. The display may include typical dress, maps, lists of the Japanese colonies, pictures of the Qing dynasty, Chinese and Japanese products, pictures of daily life, farmers, villages, rice fields, etc. Have the students present their displays to the class. Encourage them to look through their homes and find products made in Japan or China. Have them share some of these items with the class. You might wish to play Japanese music during the presentation. L2

Refer to ***Inclusion for the High School Social Studies Classroom Strategies and Activities*** in the TCR.

CHAPTER 15
Section 3, 479–486

History *through Art*

Answer: The print's subject is from a Japanese novel written during the Heian period (c. 1010).

Reading Check

Answer: Western nations developed tastes for Japanese arts and crafts; Japanese gardens became popular.

Section Quiz 15–3

Name ______ Date ______ Class ______

Chapter 15 — Score

Section Quiz 15-3

DIRECTIONS: Matching Match each item in Column A with an item in Column B. Write the correct letters in the blanks. *(10 points each)*

Column A	Column B
____ 1. U.S. presidential emissary to Japan	A. daimyo
____ 2. political compromises	B. Port Arthur
____ 3. traditional local Japanese nobles	C. Commodore Perry
____ 4. territories of the new governors	D. prefectures
____ 5. Manchurian city seized by Japan	E. concessions

DIRECTIONS: Multiple Choice In the blank, write the letter of the choice that best completes the statement or answers the question. *(10 points each)*

Reading Essentials and Study Guide 15–3

Name ______ Date ______ Class ______

Reading Essentials and Study Guide

Chapter 15, Section 3

For use with textbook pages 479–486

RISE OF MODERN JAPAN

KEY TERMS

concession a political compromise *(page 480)*

prefecture a territory in Japan during the Meiji government *(page 481)*

DRAWING FROM EXPERIENCE

What is the first thing that comes to mind when you hear the word "Japanese"? Do you think first of Japanese products, such as cars? Or do you

4 CLOSE

Reform efforts in Japan produced dramatic changes but did not provide security or stability. Discuss changes and developments in Japan that contributed to social and economic instability. **L1**

History *through Art*

***The Lady Fujitsubo Watching Prince Genji Departing in the Moonlight* by A. Hiroshige and U. Toyokuni, 1853**

How does this print reflect the artist's interest in Japan's cultural past?

began to return to older techniques. In 1889, the Tokyo School of Fine Arts was established to promote traditional Japanese art. Japanese artists searched for a new but truly Japanese means of expression. Some artists tried to bring together native and foreign techniques. Others returned to past artistic traditions for inspiration.

Cultural exchange also went the other way. Japanese arts and crafts, porcelains, textiles, fans, folding screens, and woodblock prints became fashionable in Europe and North America. Japanese art influenced Western painters. Japanese gardens, with their close attention to the positioning of rocks and falling water, became especially popular in the United States.

Reading Check **Describing** What effect did Japanese culture have on other nations?

SECTION 3 ASSESSMENT

Checking for Understanding

1. **Define** concession, prefecture.
2. **Identify** Matthew Perry, Millard Fillmore, Mutsuhito, Ito Hirobumi.
3. **Locate** Edo Bay, Kyoto, Edo, Port Arthur.
4. **Explain** how the Japanese educational system promoted traditional values even as it adopted Western educational models.
5. **List** the professionals that the Japanese invited from abroad to teach "modern" skills.

Critical Thinking

6. **Explain** How did the Japanese land reform program create internal problems?
7. **Cause and Effect** Create a diagram listing the results of Western influence on Japanese culture.

Analyzing Visuals

8. **Examine** the photograph on page 482. What characteristics of modern Japan does it illustrate?

Writing About History

9. **Persuasive Writing** Pretend that you wish to study abroad in China or Japan. Write a letter of application stating which country you would like to visit and why. State what you hope to learn while abroad, and how you would overcome or minimize the drawbacks of being a foreign student.

SECTION 3 ASSESSMENT

1. Key terms are in blue.
2. Matthew Perry *(p. 480)*; Millard Fillmore *(p. 480)*; Mutsuhito *(p. 481)*; Ito Hirobumi *(p. 481)*
3. See chapter maps.
4. retained emphasis on loyalty to family, community, emperor
5. technicians, engineers, architects, artists
6. New tax did not vary by size of harvest; many farmers were forced to sell their land.
7. Meiji constitution modeled after imperial Germany; industry grew; established colonial empire; compulsory military service; women's rights movement; universal education; adopted Western technology; baseball introduced
8. highly mechanized; worker wears Western clothing
9. Answers will vary.

EYEWITNESS TO HISTORY

A Letter to the Emperor

WHEN U.S. COMMODORE MATTHEW C. Perry arrived in Tokyo Bay on his first visit to Japan in July 1853, he carried a letter from Millard Fillmore, the president of the United States. This excerpt is from Fillmore's letter.

Millard Fillmore

Japanese officials greet Commodore Perry.

❝Millard Fillmore, President of the United States of America, To His Imperial Majesty, The Emperor of Japan. Great and Good Friend! . . .

I have directed Commodore Perry to assure your Imperial Majesty that I entertain the kindest feelings towards your Majesty's person and government; and that I have no other object in sending him to Japan, but to propose to your Imperial Majesty that the United States and Japan should live in friendship, and have [trade] with each other. . . . I have particularly charged Commodore Perry to abstain from any act, which could possibly disturb the peace of your Imperial Majesty's lands.

The United States of America reaches from ocean to ocean, and our territory of Oregon and state of California lie directly opposite to the dominions of your Imperial Majesty. Our steam-ships can go from California to Japan in eighteen days. Our great state of California produces about sixty millions of dollars in gold, every year, besides silver, quicksilver, precious stones, and many other valuable articles.

Japan is also a rich and fertile country, and produces many very valuable articles. . . . I am desirous that our two countries should trade with each other, for the benefit both of Japan and the United States.

We know that the ancient laws of your Imperial Majesty's government do not allow of foreign trade except with the Dutch. But as the state of the world changes, and new governments are formed, it seems to be wise from time to time to make new laws. . . . If your Imperial Majesty were so far to change the ancient laws, as to allow a free trade between the two countries, it would be extremely beneficial to both.

Many of our ships pass every year from California to China; and great numbers of our people pursue the whale fishery near the shores of Japan. It sometimes happens in stormy weather that one of our ships is wrecked on your Imperial Majesty's shores. In all such cases we ask and expect that our unfortunate people should be treated with kindness, and that their property should be protected, till we can send a vessel and bring them away.

Your Good Friend,
Millard Fillmore❞

—Letter from President Fillmore to the Emperor of Japan

Analyzing Primary Sources

1. What did President Fillmore want from the Japanese?
2. Why can his letter be seen as a masterful combination of salesmanship, diplomacy, and firmness?
3. From the perspective of President Fillmore and others in the United States, the emperor's decision may have looked like an easy one. Explain why this would not have been a simple decision for the emperor.

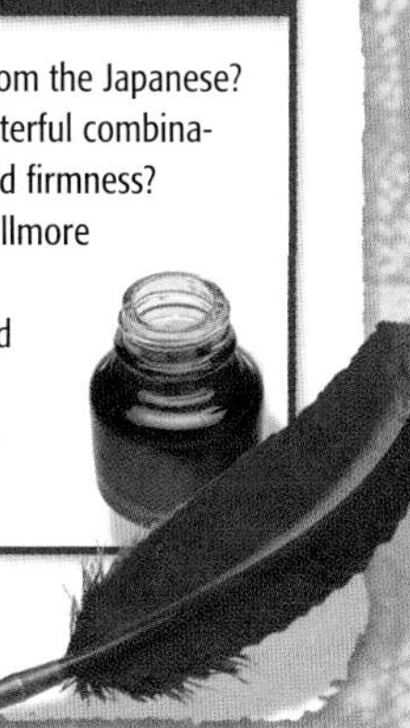

TEACH

Analyzing Primary Sources In his letter to the emperor, President Fillmore states, "I am desirous that the two countries should trade with each other, for the benefit of both Japan and the United States." Today, Japan is one of the leading trade nations, and the United States has a trade deficit with Japan.

From a purely geographical standpoint, Japan has relatively few economic advantages. Ask students to identify geographical features that would work against Japan's becoming a world power. *(Japan is small, made of small mountainous islands scattered over 1,500 miles [2,414 km]. Japan lacks natural resources, especially land and oil. Only 15 percent of Japan's land is arable. Japan is situated on the Ring of Fire—subject to volcanoes, tsunamis, and earthquakes.)*

Ask students to identify ways Japan has overcome these geographic obstacles. *(Cities are compact, lifestyles are simple. The diet does not include large amounts of meat or milk products because cattle require lots of space. Cultural values have developed that reward cooperation, hard work, and the submission of individualism to the needs of the state. The Japanese value of loyalty to authority carries the country through difficult times. International trade is the mainstay of its economy.)* **L2**

ANSWERS TO ANALYZING PRIMARY SOURCES

1. He wanted to be permitted to trade with them and to have shipwrecked American sailors treated justly and protected until they could be picked up.
2. President Fillmore was very complimentary and conciliatory but also direct and persuasive.
3. Answers will vary. Students may argue that, while trade with the United States might be advantageous, the emperor probably knew that if he made concessions to the Americans, he would be forced to make concessions to the British, the French, the Germans, and the Russians. The Japanese would be inundated with foreign ideas, which would threaten the Japanese way of life. The emperor probably also realized that, if he refused, the United States would use force. He was in a no-win situation and forced to make the best of it.

GLENCOE TECHNOLOGY

MindJogger Videoquiz

Use the **MindJogger Videoquiz** to review Chapter 15 content.

 Available in VHS.

Using Key Terms

1. prefectures **2.** extraterritoriality **3.** spheres of influence **4.** Open Door policy **5.** self-strengthening **6.** indemnities **7.** provincial **8.** commodities

Reviewing Key Facts

9. tea, silk, porcelain; payment: Indian cotton, silver, opium

10. Chinese agreed to open five coastal ports to British trade, limit taxes on imported British goods, pay for the Opium War, and give the island of Hong Kong to the British.

11. Emperor Guang Xu issued edicts calling for major political, administrative, and educational reforms based on changes in Japan. Conservatives and Empress Dowager Ci Xi opposed the reforms. Ci Xi imprisoned Guang Xu and ended his reform efforts.

12. Sun Yat-sen called for a three-stage process to introduce democracy to China: military takeover, a transitional phase, and constitutional democracy. No, the Revolution of 1911 marked the collapse of the old order, not the creation of a new system.

13. It united radical groups from across China. It advocated Sun Yat-sen's Three People's Principles, which promoted nationalism, democracy, and the right for people to pursue their own livelihoods.

14. traditionalists against radical reformers

15. United States

16. It provided for the return of shipwrecked American sailors, the opening of two ports to the United States, the establishment of a U.S. consulate in Japan.

17. the samurai warriors of the Satsuma and Choshu territories in the south

18. the transformation of Japan into a modern industrial nation under Emperor Mutsuhito, who called his reign Meiji, or "Enlightened Rule"

19. introduced modern transportation, communications; created export market; integrated Chinese market into nineteenth-century world economy

20. To improve an unfavorable balance of trade, the British began to ship opium to China. The Chinese protested, but the British refused to halt their activity. The Chinese government then blockaded the foreign area in Guangzhou to force the traders to surrender their chests of opium. The British responded with force, starting the Opium War.

21. 1874: Ryukyu Islands; 1876: forced Koreans to open ports; 1894: Port Arthur; 1904: reclaimed port; 1910: annexed Korea

CHAPTER 15 ASSESSMENT and ACTIVITIES

Using Key Terms

1. The daimyo governed _____ after the Meiji Restoration seized their lands.
2. Europeans who lived by their own laws while on Chinese soil practiced _____.
3. European traders established _____ in which they negotiated directly with Chinese warlords.
4. Secretary of State John Hay proposed the _____ to further U.S. trade interests in China.
5. The policy of _____ called for the Chinese people to adopt Western technology while retaining their Confucian values and institutions.
6. The Chinese government was forced to pay heavy _____ to the powers that crushed the Boxer Rebellion.
7. After 1905, Chinese legislative assemblies were formed at the _____ level.
8. When Westerners visited China in the mid-1800s, a market for _____ such as oil, copper, salt, tea, and porcelain already existed.

Reviewing Key Facts

9. **Economics** What items did the British import from China, and how did they pay for them?
10. **Government** List the terms of the Treaty of Nanjing.
11. **Culture** Explain the One Hundred Days of Reform and their outcome.
12. **Citizenship** Summarize the terms of Sun Yat-sen's reform program and tell whether or not they were implemented.
13. **Government** What was the role of the Revolutionary Alliance?
14. **Government** What opposing forces formed in China after the civil war?
15. **History** Who was the first foreign power to penetrate Japan?
16. **Economics** What were the terms of the Treaty of Kanagawa?
17. **Citizenship** Which Japanese groups opposed Japanese relations with Western powers?
18. **Government** What was the Meiji Restoration?
19. **Economics** In what three ways did Westerners affect the Chinese economy during the mid-1800s?
20. **Economics** Identify the sequence of events that led to the Opium War of 1839 to 1842.
21. **History** In chronological order, list the territories and countries Japan took control of in its program of expansion.

Critical Thinking

22. **Summarizing** Summarize the effects of imperialism on nineteenth-century China.
23. **Analyzing** How effective was Japan's territorial expansion program?
24. **Identifying Options** Instead of importing opium to China, what else might the British have done to restore the balance of trade?

Chapter Summary

Imperialist powers advanced into China and Japan in the nineteenth century. China's government fell, but Japan's modernized and endured.

Movement	Change	Reaction	Nationalism
• British secure trade outlets at five coastal ports in China. • Commodore Perry sails into Edo Bay. • Japan invades Port Arthur, Manchuria.	• Japan's Tokugawa shogunate and China's Qing dynasty collapse. • Meiji reformers institute compulsory military service in Japan. • United States initiates Open Door policy in China.	• Tai Ping Rebellion breaks out in China. • Sat-Cho leaders demand the resignation of Japan's shogun. • Boxer Rebellion occurs in China.	• Meiji government reforms Japan. • Japan adopts the Meiji constitution. • Sun Yat-sen establishes the Republic of China.

Self-Check Quiz

Visit the *Glencoe World History—Modern Times* Web site at wh.mt.glencoe.com and click on **Chapter 15–Self-Check Quiz** to prepare for the Chapter Test.

Writing About History

25. **Persuasive Writing** Imagine you are a court official living in China during the reign of Emperor Guang Xu. The emperor is planning his reform program and needs advice concerning how to help strengthen China. Write a letter to the emperor telling him how you think China should either change or stay the same. Choose two or three specific issues such as the educational system, the development of the military, or the structure of the government to discuss in your letter.

Analyzing Sources

Zhang Zhidong, a leading Chinese court official, argued:

> "The doctrine of people's rights will bring us not a single benefit but a hundred evils. Are we going to establish a parliament? Among the Chinese scholars and people there are still many today who are content to be vulgar and rustic. They are ignorant of the general situation in the world, they do not understand the basic system of the state."

26. Does Zhang Zhidong think that the Chinese people are well informed?
27. How does Zhang Zhidong's quote apply to China today?

Applying Technology Skills

28. **Using the Internet** Use the Internet to research the causes of revolution in the world. Research specific examples, such as the American, French, and Russian Revolutions, to determine why they occurred. Compare the causes of these revolutions to those of the 1911 revolution in China.

Making Decisions

29. To build a "rich country and a strong state," the Japanese government subsidized (provided funds for) its industries. Evaluate the reasons for Japan's decision. The potential need for subsidy is not unique to Japan. Imagine that you are the president of a newly colonized island. Write a brief essay explaining how you would promote the growth of industry on your island.

Analyzing Maps and Charts

Examine the chart of the Meiji Restoration shown on page 482 of your text. Then answer the following questions.

30. What impact did the Meiji Restoration have on the social structure of Japan?
31. How do you think the daimyo felt about the Meiji Restoration?
32. What effect did the Meiji Restoration have on industry?

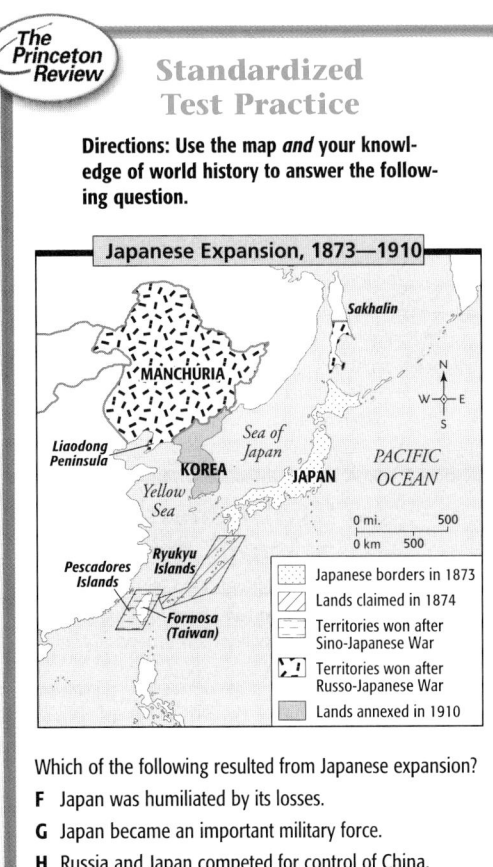

The Princeton Review

Standardized Test Practice

Directions: Use the map *and* your knowledge of world history to answer the following question.

Japanese Expansion, 1873—1910

Which of the following resulted from Japanese expansion?

F Japan was humiliated by its losses.
G Japan became an important military force.
H Russia and Japan competed for control of China.
J China's government was strengthened and reformed.

Test-Taking Tip: Any time you get a map, pay careful attention to the title and to the map legend. The legend gives information crucial to understanding the map. The information in the legend may also help you eliminate answer choices that are incorrect.

HISTORY Online

Have students visit the Web site at wh.mt.glencoe.com to review Chapter 15 and take the Self-Check Quiz.

Applying Technology Skills

28. Students will conduct research on the Internet.

Making Decisions

29. Answers will vary. The Japanese practice of subsidizing new industries helped to encourage the development of new industries, leading to a stronger economy.

Analyzing Maps and Charts

30. Japanese adopt many Western practices; see chart on page 482.
31. Answers will vary. Students might say that the daimyo were angry to lose their land. The text states that they were compensated with government bonds and by being made governors of their prefectures. In the long run, they probably appreciated the political stability and economic progress that resulted.
32. The Restoration encouraged it.

Standardized Test Practice

Answer: B
Answer Explanation: The amount of land gained indicates that answer F is obviously incorrect.

Critical Thinking

22. Western demands undermined authority of Qing dynasty, strengthened provincial warlords, opened China up to more contact with the West; benefits include development of modern transportation and communications, creation of an export market, and the integration of the Chinese market into the nineteenth-century world economy.
23. Students might argue that Japan's territorial expansion program was very successful.
24. Answers will vary but should be supported by logical arguments

Writing About History

25. Answers will vary.

Analyzing Sources

26. no
27. Education is now compulsory, and the Chinese have a high rate of literacy. However, contact with the outside world is carefully controlled by the government.

Bonus Question ?

Ask: How does cultural diffusion today differ from what it was in the period covered by this chapter? *(Answers will vary but should make the point that today it is affected by sophisticated systems of communication and transportation and thus happens much more quickly.)*

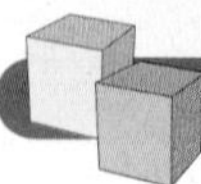

World Literature

Block Schedule

Team Teaching This excerpt from *Shooting an Elephant* may be presented in a team teaching context, in conjunction with English or Language Arts.

Shooting an Elephant

Historical Connection

Burma was part of the British Empire from the 1820s until 1948. Orwell's essay gives a personal account of the corrupting effects of imperialism, both on the colonizers and on the colonized.

Background Information

Setting The essay is set in Burma (present-day Myanmar) during the 1920s.

Characters The narrator is a British Imperial police officer.

Plot The narrator is informed that an elephant has been found wandering loose in the town, and he, as the British official, must do something about it.

Literary Element Recognizing the tone is key to student understanding of this excerpt. Tone is a writer's attitude toward his or her subject, audience, or a character. It is conveyed through details and word choice.

World Literature

from Shooting an Elephant

George Orwell

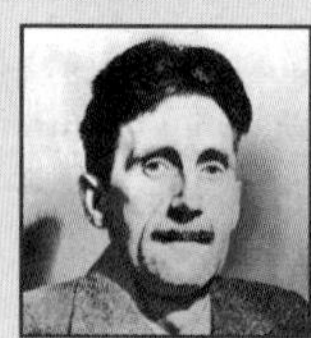

George Orwell was the pen name of English author Eric Arthur Blair, who was born in Motihari, India, on June 25, 1903. He lived for 46 years, and during that time, he wrote many influential essays, novels, and newspaper articles. His two most famous works are *1984* and *Animal Farm,* both of which are commentaries against totalitarianism. He served for several years as an assistant superintendent in the Indian Imperial Police but resigned due to his distaste of imperialism. In *Shooting an Elephant,* Orwell describes an incident that happened to him, and he satirizes the problems of colonial rule.

Read to Discover

Examine the ways in which George Orwell describes the relationship between the British colonial officer and the "natives." Can you think of a modern parallel to this situation?

Reader's Dictionary

mahout: a keeper and driver of an elephant

dominion: rule, control

sahib: title meaning "sir" or "master"

I had halted on the road. As soon as I saw the elephant I knew with perfect certainty that I ought not to shoot him. It is a serious matter to shoot a working elephant—it is comparable to destroying a huge and costly piece of machinery—and obviously one ought not to do it if it can possibly be avoided. And at that distance, peacefully eating, the elephant looked no more dangerous than a cow. I thought then and I think now that his attack of "must" was already passing off; in which case he would merely wander harmlessly about until the mahout came back and caught him. Moreover, I did not in the least want to shoot him. I decided that I would watch him for a little while to make sure that he did not turn savage again, and then go home.

But at that moment I glanced round at the crowd that had followed me. It was an immense crowd, two thousand at the least and growing every minute. It blocked the road for a long distance on either side. I looked at the sea of yellow faces above the garish clothes—faces all happy and excited over this bit of fun, all certain that the elephant was going to be shot. They were watching me as they would watch a conjurer about to perform a trick. They did not like me, but with the magical rifle in my hands I was momentarily worth watching. And suddenly I realized that I should have to shoot the elephant after all. The people expected it

◀ *Colonial hunter*

ABOUT THE AUTHOR

George Orwell was born in India but educated in England. At the age of 19, he joined the Imperial Police in Burma instead of continuing on to a university. After five years in Burma (1922–1927), he became disgusted and outraged at the colonial system. Orwell then left Burma and became a writer. He spent time living among beggars in both London and Paris, and he worked as a dishwasher, a miner, and a field hand. Orwell wrote about these experiences in *Down and Out in Paris and London.* He became a socialist and fought on the side of the Republicans in the Spanish Civil War. During World War II, he worked as a journalist. He believed passionately in political freedom and his two most famous books, *Animal Farm* and *1984,* fiercely attack totalitarian governments. He died at the age of forty-six of tuberculosis.

World Literature

▲ *Working elephants, 1890s*

of me and I had got to do it; I could feel their two thousand wills pressing me forward irresistibly. And it was at this moment, as I stood there with the rifle in my hands, that I first grasped the hollowness, the futility of the white man's dominion in the East. Here was I, the white man with his gun, standing in front of the unarmed native crowd—seemingly the leading actor of the piece; but in reality I was only an absurd puppet pushed to and fro by the will of those yellow faces behind. I perceived in this moment that when the white man turns tyrant it is his own freedom that he destroys. He becomes a sort of hollow, posing dummy, the conventionalized figure of a sahib. For it is the condition of his rule that he shall spend his life in trying to impress the "natives," and so in every crisis he has got to do what the "natives" expect of him. He wears a mask, and his face grows to fit it. I had got to shoot the elephant. I had committed myself to doing it when I sent for the rifle. A sahib has got to act like a sahib; he has got to appear resolute, to know his own mind and do definite things. To come all that way, rifle in hand, with two thousand people marching at my heels, and then to trail feebly away, having done nothing—no, that was impossible. The crowd would laugh at me. And my whole life, every white man's life in the East, was one long struggle not to be laughed at.

. . . But I did not want to shoot the elephant. . . . The sole thought in my mind was that if anything went wrong those two thousand Burmese would see me . . . trampled on, and reduced to a grinning corpse. And if that happened it was quite probable that some of them would laugh. That would never do.

Interpreting World Literature

1. What is the context of this story? Why is the narrator following an elephant?
2. Why does the narrator ultimately decide that he must shoot the elephant?
3. What does this story reveal about Orwell's attitudes about imperialism? How can you tell?
4. **CRITICAL THINKING** According to Orwell in this piece, who held the power in colonial India?

Applications Activity
Write a narrative account of an incident when you felt people were pushing you to act in opposition to your original intentions.

FOCUS

Ask students to recall a time when they were treated as outsiders, perhaps at a new school or at a party where they didn't know the other guests. How did it feel to be viewed as a person who didn't belong to the group? Have the students ever made others feel like outsiders? **L1**

TEACH

Interpretation

The tone of a literary piece might be sad, angry, joyful, or sarcastic. Have students work in small groups or as a class to brainstorm as many words as possible that could describe tone. Orwell's tone toward colonialism is made clear through his word choice and characterization of events. Ask students to describe in their own words Orwell's tone toward the Burmese and the British. Have them support their interpretations with specific examples from the excerpt. Is Orwell's tone negative or positive toward each group? Why do students think that an individual in the narrator's position might feel this way? What impression does this excerpt give about the effects of imperialism on humanity? **L1 L2**

ANSWERS TO INTERPRETING WORLD LITERATURE

1. An elephant had escaped from its owner, and the narrator is supposed to kill him.
2. The narrator does not want to be laughed at by the local people for walking away from the elephant.
3. Imperialism has many negative consequences for both the oppressor as well as the oppressed. Orwell states this in the narration: ". . . when the white man turns tyrant it is his own freedom that he destroys."
4. Although the British were officially in power, they were actually subject to the expectations of the people they ruled.

Applications Activity
Answers will vary.

Unit 4 Resources

Suggested Pacing Chart

Unit 4 (1 day)	Chapter 16 (6 days)	Chapter 17 (6 days)	Chapter 18 (6 days)	Chapter 19 (6 days)	Unit 4 (1 day)
Day 1 Introduction	**Day 1** Chapter 16 Intro, Section 1 **Day 2** Section 2 **Day 3** Section 3 **Day 4** Section 4 **Day 5** Chapter 16 Review **Day 6** Chapter 16 Assessment	**Day 1** Chapter 17 Intro, Section 1 **Day 2** Section 2 **Day 3** Section 3 **Day 4** Section 4 **Day 5** Chapter 17 Review **Day 6** Chapter 17 Assessment	**Day 1** Chapter 18 Intro, Section 1 **Day 2** Section 2 **Day 3** Section 3 **Day 4** Section 4 **Day 5** Chapter 18 Review **Day 6** Chapter 18 Assessment	**Day 1** Chapter 19 Intro, Section 1 **Day 2** Section 2 **Day 3** Section 3 **Day 4** Section 4 **Day 5** Chapter 19 Review **Day 6** Chapter 19 Assessment	**Day 1** Wrap-Up/Projects/ Unit 4 Assessment

Use the following tools to easily assess student learning in a variety of ways:

- Performance Assessment Activities and Rubrics
- Chapter Tests
- Section Quizzes
- Standardized Test Skills Practice Workbook
- SAT I/II Test Practice
- www.wh.mt.glencoe.com
- Interactive Tutor Self-Assessment CD-ROM
- MindJogger Videoquiz
- ExamView® Pro Testmaker CD-ROM

Teaching Transparencies

Unit Time Line Transparency 4

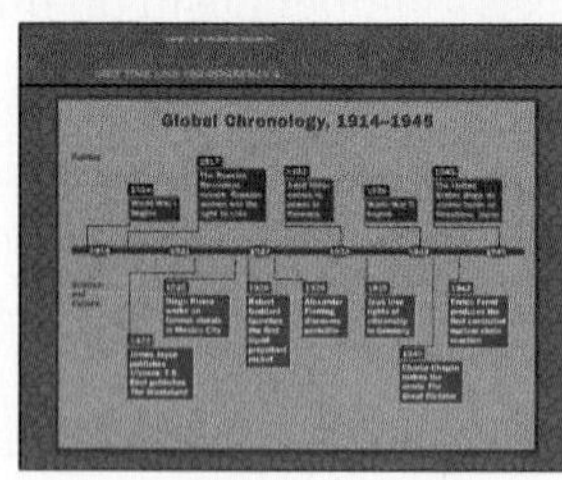

Cause-and-Effect Transparency 4

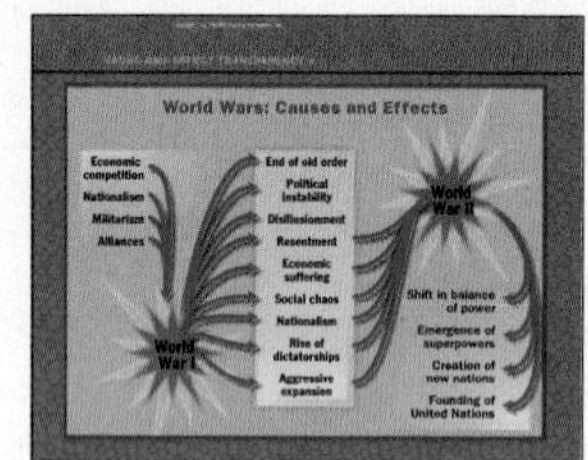

interNET RESOURCES

- www.wh.mt.glencoe.com

Glencoe World History—Modern Times
Visit the *Glencoe World History—Modern Times* Web site for history overviews, activities, assessments, and updated charts and graphs.

- www.socialstudies.glencoe.com

Glencoe Social Studies
Visit the Glencoe Web site for social studies activities, updates, and links to other sites.

- www.teachingtoday.glencoe.com

Glencoe Teaching Today
Visit the new Glencoe Web site for teacher development information, teaching tips, Web resources, and educational news.

- www.time.com

TIME Online
Visit the TIME Web site for up-to-date news and special reports.

Unit 4 Resources

Assessment

Unit 4 Tests Forms A and B

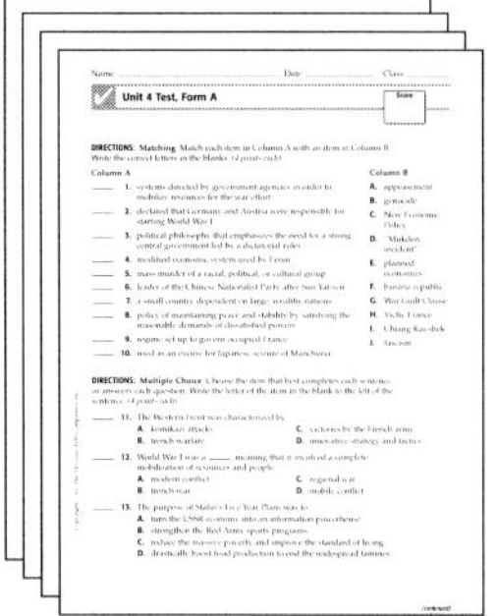

ExamView® Pro Testmaker CD-ROM

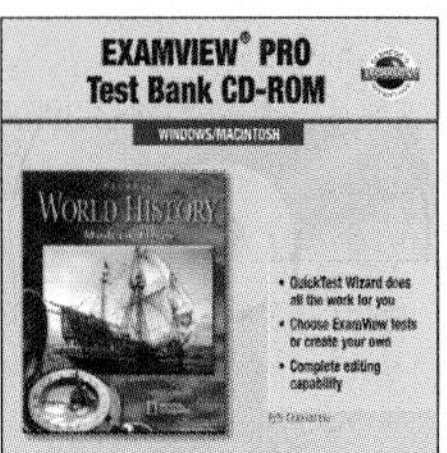

Interdisciplinary Activities

World Literature Reading 4

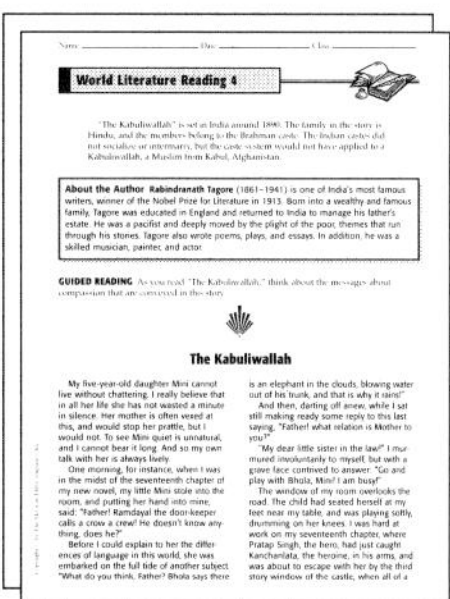

Economics and History Activity 4

Application and Enrichment

Charting and Graphing Activity 4

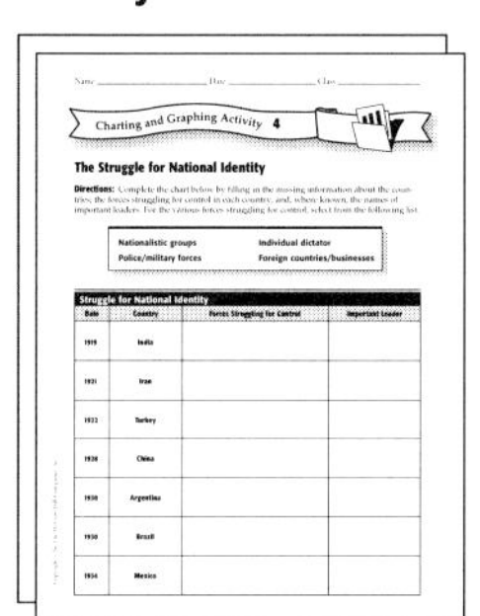

Geographic Literacy

NGS Focus on Geographic Literacy

Building Geography Skills for Life

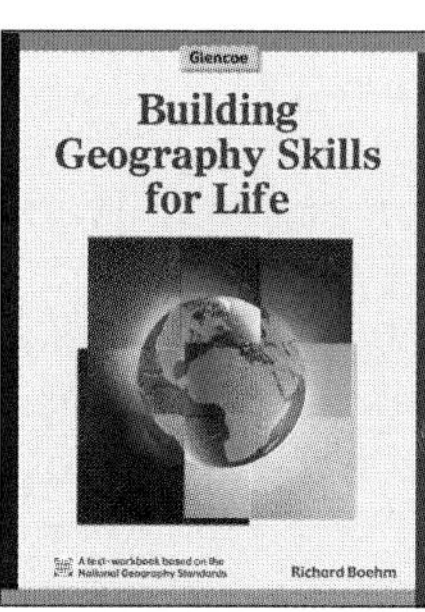

BIBLIOGRAPHY

Readings for the Student

Choi, Sook Nyul. ***Year of Impossible Goodbyes.*** Yearling Books, 1993. A fictional account of a North Korean family who survives the Japanese occupation of World War II, only to flee Russian Communists.

Sevitin, Sonia. ***Silver Days.*** Aladdin Paperbacks, 1992. After escaping from Nazi Germany, the Platt family struggles to make a home in America (fiction).

Opdyke, Irene Gut. ***In My Hands: Memories of a Holocaust Rescuer.*** Anchor Books, 2001. The (nonfiction) personal story of a Polish nursing student during the German occupation of World War II.

Readings for the Teacher

Vinen, Richard. ***A History in Fragments: Europe in the Twentieth Century.*** Da Capo Press, 2001. A history of Europe's evolution from imperialism to democracy to the present-day.

Multimedia Resources

VHS. ***American Civil Liberties: A History.*** (57 minutes) Films for the Humanities & Sciences. P.O. Box 2053, Princeton, NJ 08543, 1–800–257–5126. Traces the rise of this organization from its beginnings after World War I.

VHS. ***After the Cloud Lifted: Hiroshima's Stories of Recovery.*** (35 minutes) RMS Communications, 1996. Survivors talk about their lives before and after the dropping of the atomic bomb.

Additional Glencoe Resources for this Unit:

- Glencoe Skillbuilder Interactive Workbook CD-ROM, Level 2
- Glencoe World History Primary Source Document Library
- World Art Prints
- World Biography: People in History
- Outline Map Resource Book
- World Desk Map
- World Art and Architecture Transparencies
- World Music: Cultural Traditions
- World Music: A Cultural Legacy
- Glencoe World Literature Library
- Reading in the Content Area
- Teaching Strategies for the World History Classroom (Including Block Scheduling Pacing Guides)
- Inclusion for the High School Social Studies Classroom Strategies and Activities

0:00 Out of Time?

If time does not permit teaching each chapter in this unit, you may use the **Reading Essentials and Study Guide** summaries.

Unit Objectives

After studying this unit, students should be able to:

1. describe the causes and impact of World War I;
2. trace the growth of Fascist and Communist dictatorships in Italy, Germany, and the Soviet Union;
3. explain the upsurge of nationalism in Asia, Africa, and Latin America;
4. trace the events that led to World War II;
5. describe major events and turning points of World War II;
6. describe events that took place during the Holocaust;
7. describe the impact of World War II on civilian populations.

The Period in Perspective

To build student interest in this unit prior to assigning the first reading, discuss the general causes of war, particularly more recent wars like the Vietnam War, the Persian Gulf War, and the war on terrorism.

NATIONAL GEOGRAPHIC

Use these materials to enrich student understanding of World War I and World War II.

- **NGS PICTURE SHOW™ CD-ROMs**
  World War I Era
  World War II Era
- **NGS PICTURE PACK TRANSPARENCY SETS**
  World War I Era
  World War II Era

UNIT 4 The Twentieth-Century Crisis

1914–1945

The Period in Perspective

The period between 1914 and 1945 was one of the most destructive in the history of humankind. As many as 60 million people died as a result of World Wars I and II, the global conflicts that began and ended this era. As World War I was followed by revolutions, the Great Depression, totalitarian regimes, and the horrors of World War II, it appeared to many that European civilization had become a nightmare. By 1945, the era of European domination over world affairs had been severely shaken. With the decline of Western power, a new era of world history was about to begin.

Primary Sources Library

See pages 778–779 for primary source readings to accompany Unit 4.

Use The World History ***Primary Source Document Library CD-ROM*** *to find additional primary sources about The Twentieth-Century Crisis.*

▲ Gate, Dachau Memorial

▶ Former Russian prisoners of war honor the American troops who freed them.

492

TEAM TEACHING ACTIVITY

Art With the art teacher, coordinate a study of the major modern art movements of the 1920s and 1930s. Students should examine the philosophy and works of the Dada movement, surrealism, cubism, and the functionalist movement of the Bauhaus school. After students are familiar with each of these movements and its philosophy, discuss the possible influence that World War I had on the art of this period. You may want to have students write reports analyzing an artist's work and the historical influences on that artist, or you may want students, with the help of the art teacher, to create their own artistic creations that reflect the philosophies of one of the movements. L2

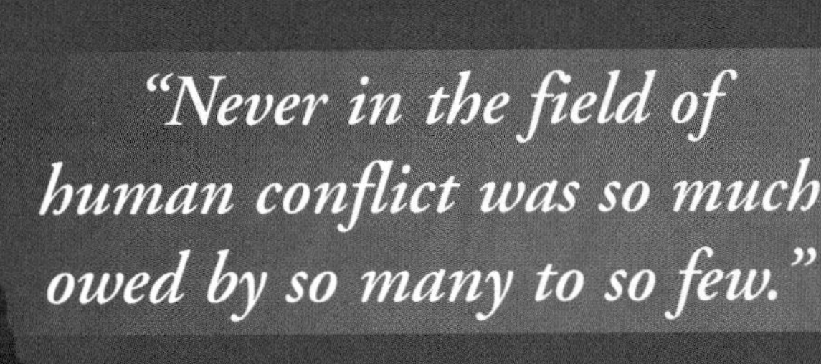

"Never in the field of human conflict was so much owed by so many to so few."

—*Winston Churchill*

Introducing UNIT 4

GLENCOE TECHNOLOGY

CD-ROM
World History Primary Source Document Library CD-ROM

Use the World History Primary Source Document Library CD-ROM to access primary source documents related to the twentieth-century crisis.

More About the Photo

The inscription above the gate at Dachau reads "Work will make you free" ("Arbeit Macht Frei"). Dachau was Germany's first concentration camp, opened in 1933. Almost 30,000 prisoners were living there upon liberation in 1945. In 1965 the camp was made into a memorial.

History *and the* Humanities

World Art and Architecture Transparencies

- 45 *I Want You for the U.S. Army*
- 46 *Three Musicians*
- 48 *Empire State Building*
- 49 *Zapatistas*
- 50 *The Persistence of Memory*
- 51 *Migrant Mother*
- 52 *Bird in Space*
- 53 *The Red Stairway*

SERVICE-LEARNING PROJECT

Some of the best primary sources for information about World War II live in our own communities. Have students work in pairs to interview a World War II survivor. Students may choose to contact the local Veterans Affairs office or local senior centers to identify a veteran. Have students interview the person and write a report about that person's experiences. Also have students reflect on how learning about the war from someone directly involved in it has expanded their understanding of the war. L2

Refer to **Building Bridges: Connecting Classroom and Community through Service in Social Studies** from the National Council for the Social Studies for information about service-learning.

Looking Back to See Ahead

TEACH

Introduction

This feature focuses on efforts by the international community to achieve collective security, first through the League of Nations, established after World War I, and later through the United Nations, set up in the aftermath of World War II.

Background Notes

Linking Past and Present

United Nations As students will read in this unit, American president Woodrow Wilson strongly supported the concept of collective security and was one of the strongest proponents of the League of Nations; the failure of the United States Senate to approve American participation was a blow to Wilson and to the League. In contrast, today, the United States is a leading member of the United Nations. Even with the strong leadership role of the United States in the United Nations, however, there is often heated debate in Congress about American participation in UN peacekeeping missions. The United Nations has been far more than an agent for collective security. Remind students that the UN, in addition to the Security Council has an Economic and Social Council and an International Court of Justice.

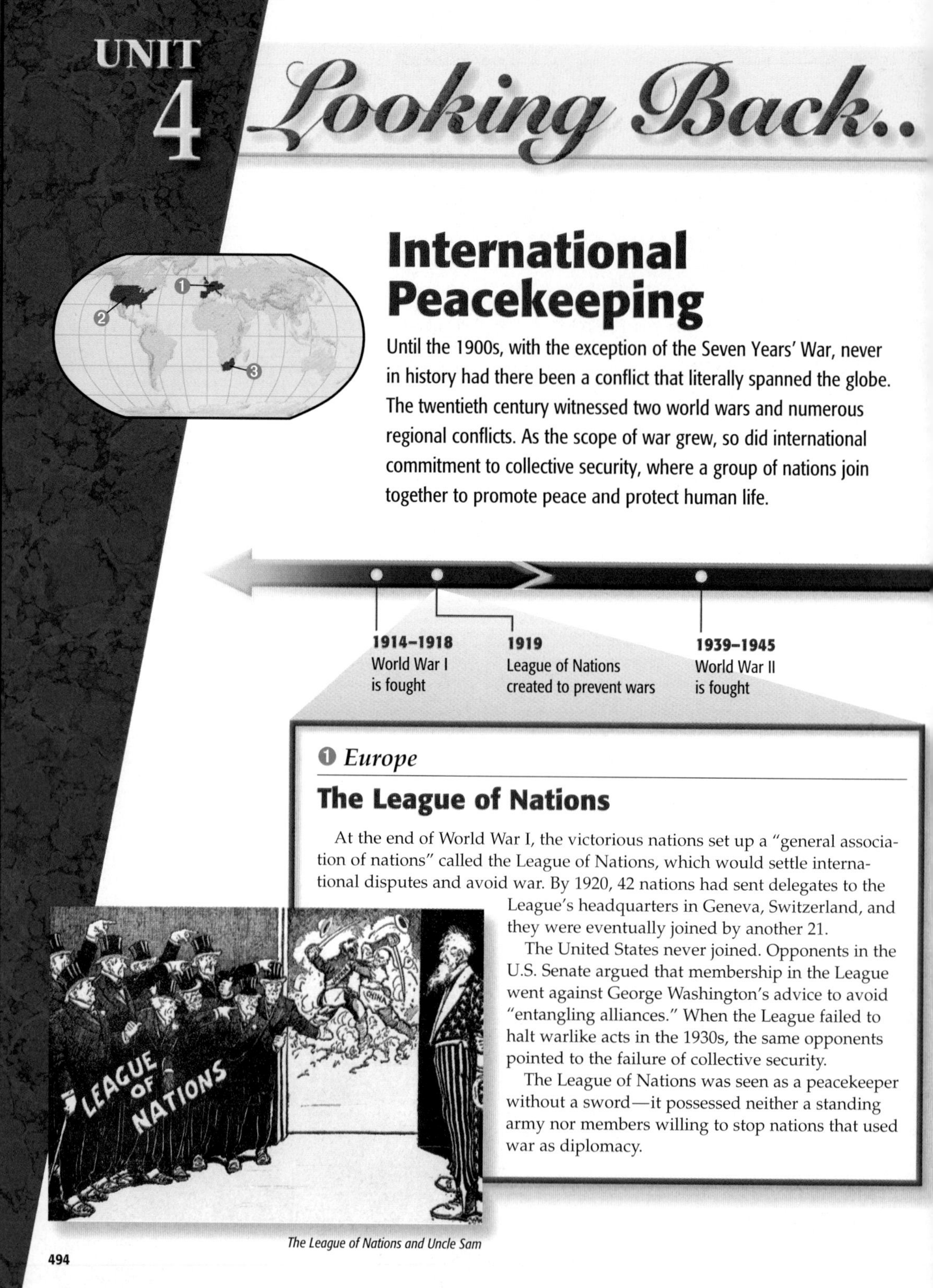

UNIT 4 *Looking Back..*

International Peacekeeping

Until the 1900s, with the exception of the Seven Years' War, never in history had there been a conflict that literally spanned the globe. The twentieth century witnessed two world wars and numerous regional conflicts. As the scope of war grew, so did international commitment to collective security, where a group of nations join together to promote peace and protect human life.

1914–1918 World War I is fought

1919 League of Nations created to prevent wars

1939–1945 World War II is fought

❶ *Europe*

The League of Nations

At the end of World War I, the victorious nations set up a "general association of nations" called the League of Nations, which would settle international disputes and avoid war. By 1920, 42 nations had sent delegates to the League's headquarters in Geneva, Switzerland, and they were eventually joined by another 21.

The United States never joined. Opponents in the U.S. Senate argued that membership in the League went against George Washington's advice to avoid "entangling alliances." When the League failed to halt warlike acts in the 1930s, the same opponents pointed to the failure of collective security.

The League of Nations was seen as a peacekeeper without a sword—it possessed neither a standing army nor members willing to stop nations that used war as diplomacy.

The League of Nations and Uncle Sam

494

COOPERATIVE LEARNING ACTIVITY

Model United Nations Have students compile a list of international conflicts that are currently raging around the world. Then organize students into small groups. Assign each group a conflict from the list. Have them role-play an attempt by the United Nations to resolve the situation. In each group, have some students represent the two parties in the conflict and others represent UN mediators. Have students discuss the sources of the conflict and then negotiate a peace treaty. Each group can describe its dilemma to the class, and explain why they could or could not resolve the conflict. L2

For grading this activity, refer to the ***Performance Assessment Activities*** booklet.

to See Ahead

UN membership flags

❷ *The United States*

The United Nations

After World War II, the United States hosted a meeting to create a new peacekeeping organization. Delegates from 50 nations hammered out the Charter of the United Nations. To eliminate the root causes of war, the UN created agencies that promoted global education and the well-being of children. In 1948, United States delegate Eleanor Roosevelt convinced the UN to adopt the Universal Declaration of Human Rights, which committed the UN to eliminate oppression. The headquarters for the UN are located in New York City.

1945
United Nations replaces the League of Nations

1948
UN adopts the Universal Declaration of Human Rights

1950–1953
UN troops participate in the Korean War

1994
UN actions lead to the end of apartheid in South Africa

❸ *South Africa*

The Power of World Opinion

By 1995, the UN had taken part in 35 peacekeeping missions—some successful, some not. It also had provided protection for over 30 million refugees.

The UN used world opinion to promote justice. In 1977, it urged nations to enforce economic sanctions and an arms embargo against South Africa until apartheid was lifted. In 1994, South Africa held its first all-race elections. Many believed this was a major triumph for collective international action.

Casting a vote in South Africa

Why It Matters

The UN hopes to use collective international actions to promote peace around the world. Often this involves preventing injustice and improving living conditions. What are some recent UN actions that support these principles?

Why It Matters

Student answers will vary depending on current events. Students may identify the efforts in Somalia, Sudan, and Sarajevo to provide food and supplies; the campaign to create international policy for the elimination of land mines; food drops into Afghanistan during the war on terrorism; relief to refugees and victims of civil and tribal warfare in Rwanda and other African nations.

Geography

Movement Since 1989, troops from around the world have participated in UN observer and peacekeeping missions in Latin America, Africa, and Europe. Among the most important have been the observer groups sent to monitor elections in Nicaragua, Haiti, and South Africa and the peacekeeping missions in Bosnia, the Republic of Georgia, and Somalia. Ask students what problems the growing numbers of UN missions in recent years may have created. *(The UN has been burdened with ballooning costs and funding shortages.)*

Cultural Diffusion

International Cooperation and Popular Music Since the 1970s the spirit of international cooperation has influenced the world of rock music. In the early 1970s, a number of rock musicians, including George Harrison and Bob Dylan, held a concert to raise money for famine victims in the newly created nation of Bangladesh (formerly part of Pakistan). In the 1980s, Bob Geldof of the Boomtown Rats organized Band Aid, featuring many recording artists such as Sting and Phil Collins, to raise money for famine relief in Ethiopia.

Chapter 16 Resources

Timesaving Tools

TeacherWorks™ All-In-One Planner and Resource Center

- **Interactive Teacher Edition** Access your Teacher Wraparound Edition and your classroom resources with a few easy clicks.
- **Interactive Lesson Planner** Planning has never been easier! Organize your week, month, semester, or year with all the lesson helps you need to make teaching creative, timely, and relevant.

Use Glencoe's **Presentation Plus!** multimedia teacher tool to easily present dynamic lessons that visually excite your students. Using Microsoft PowerPoint® you can customize the presentations to create your own personalized lessons.

TEACHING TRANSPARENCIES

Graphic Organizer Student Activity 16 Transparency

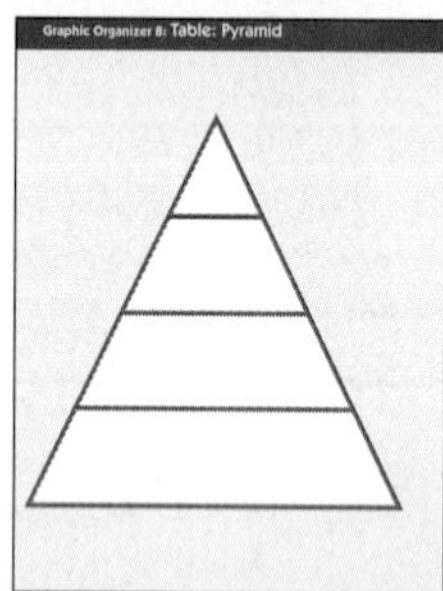

Chapter Transparency 16

Map Overlay Transparency 16

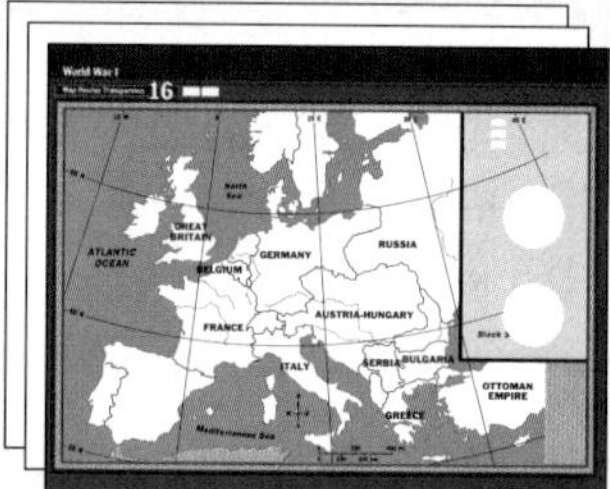

APPLICATION AND ENRICHMENT

Enrichment Activity 16

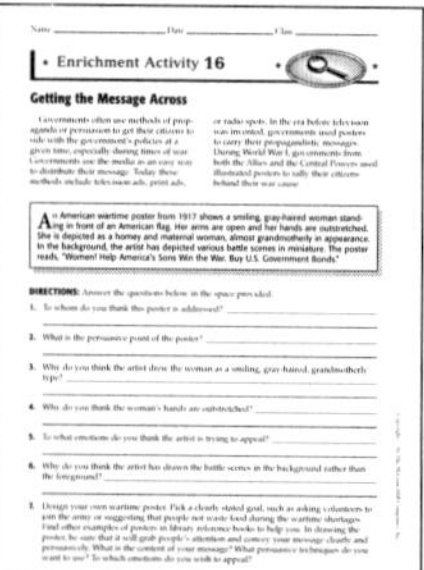

Primary Source Reading 16

History Simulation Activity 16

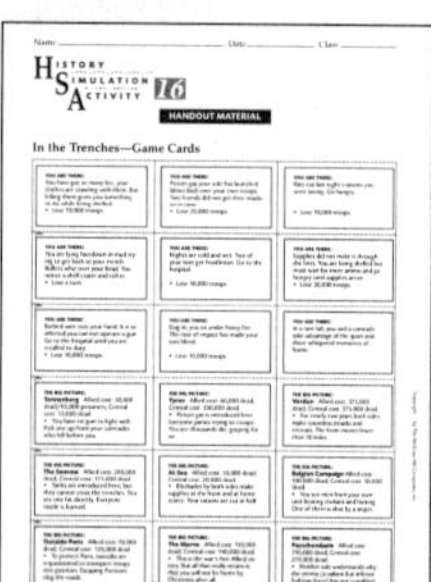

Historical Significance Activity 16

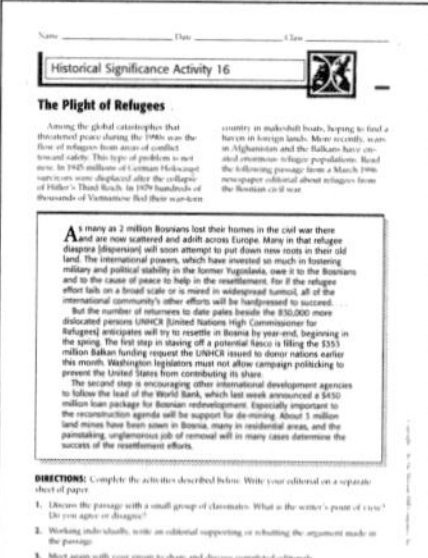

Cooperative Learning Activity 16

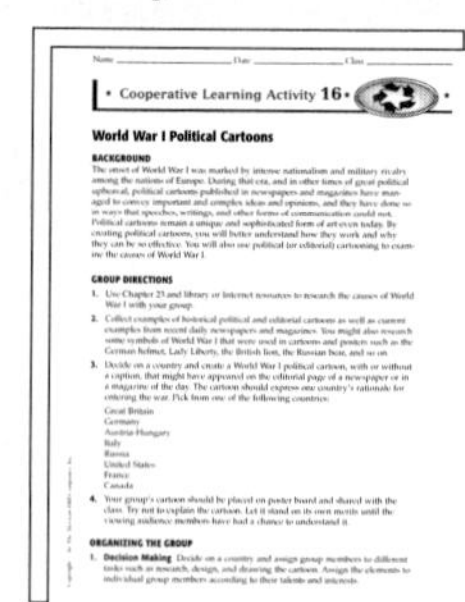

Biography®

THE HISTORY CHANNEL®

The following videotape programs are available from Glencoe as supplements to Chapter 16:

- **Woodrow Wilson: Reluctant Warrior** (ISBN 0–7670–0101–X)
- **Nicholas and Alexandra** (ISBN 1–56501–514–2)
- **Rasputin: The Mad Monk** (ISBN 0–7670–0189–3)

To order, call Glencoe at 1–800–334–7344. To find classroom resources to accompany many of these videos, check the following home pages:
A&E Television: www.aande.com
The History Channel: www.historychannel.com

Chapter 16 Resources

Review and Reinforcement

Linking Past and Present Activity 16

Time Line Activity 16

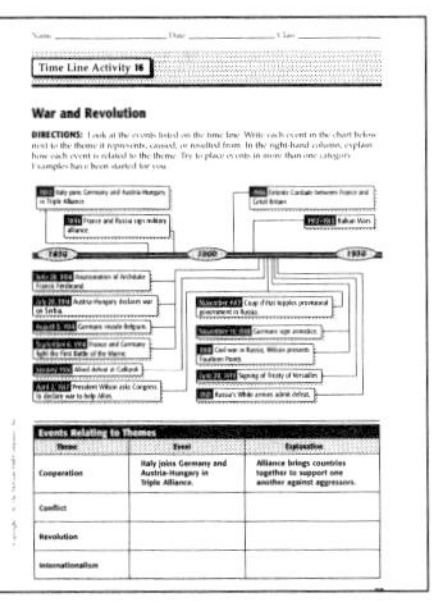

Reteaching Activity 16

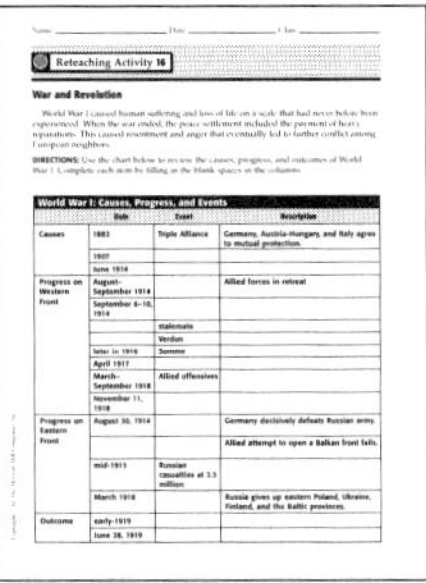

Vocabulary Activity 16

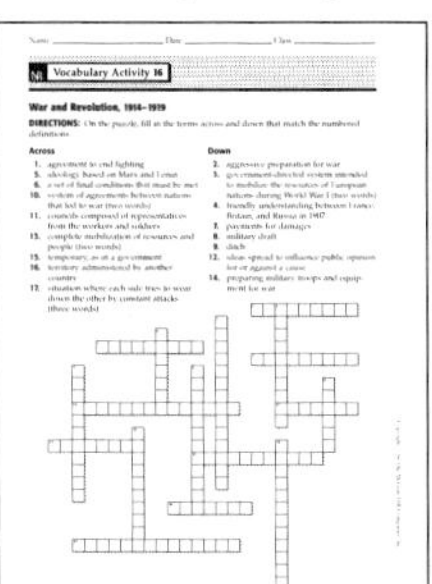

Critical Thinking Skills Activity 16

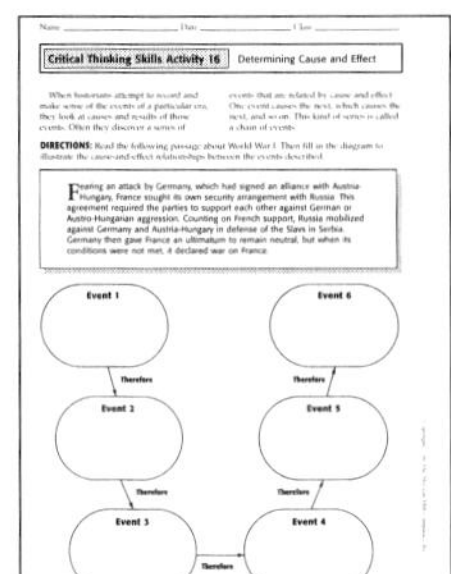

Assessment and Evaluation

Chapter 16 Test Form A

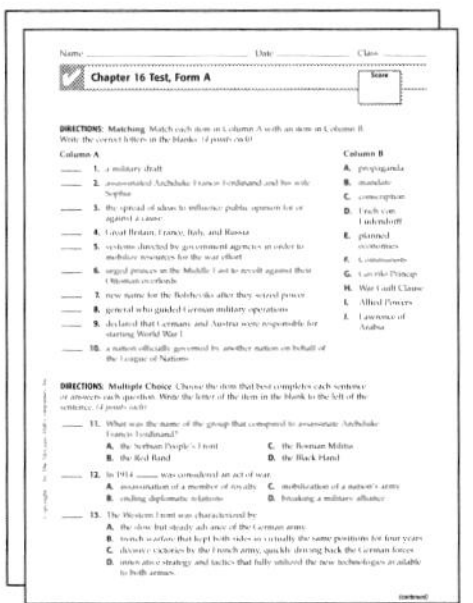

Chapter 16 Test Form B

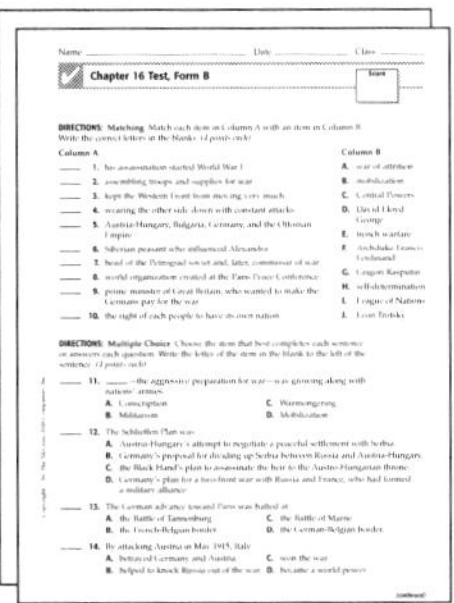

Performance Assessment Activity 16

ExamView® Pro Testmaker CD-ROM

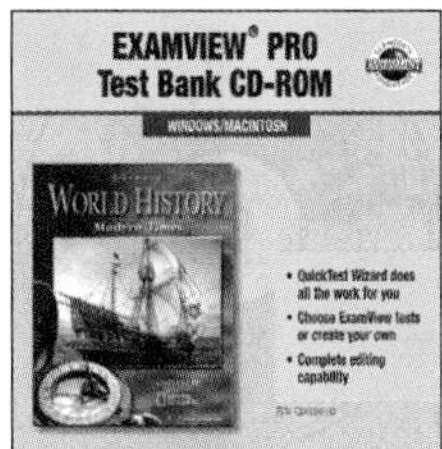

Standardized Test Skills Practice Workbook Activity 16

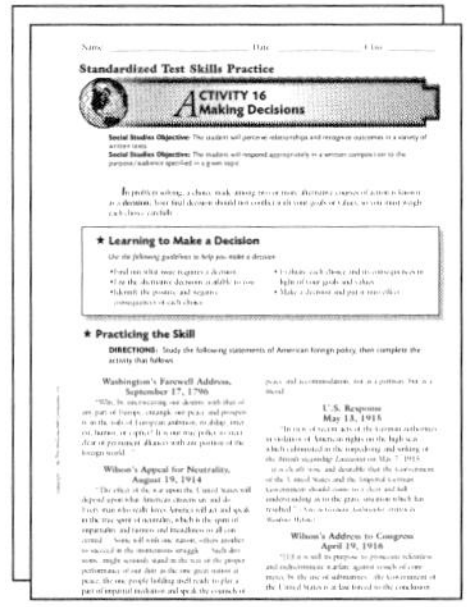

Interdisciplinary Activities

Mapping History Activity 16

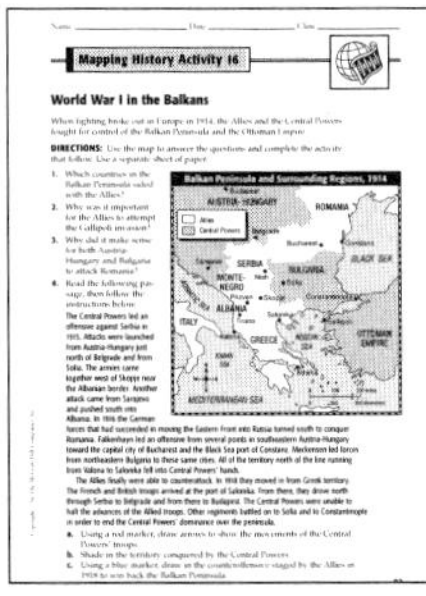

World Art and Music Activity 16

History and Geography Activity 16

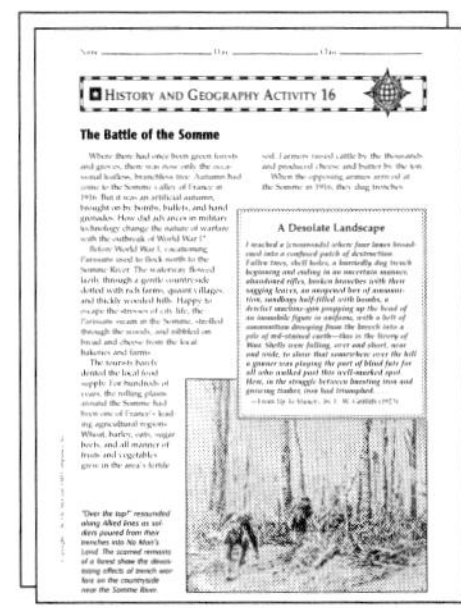

People in World History Activity 16

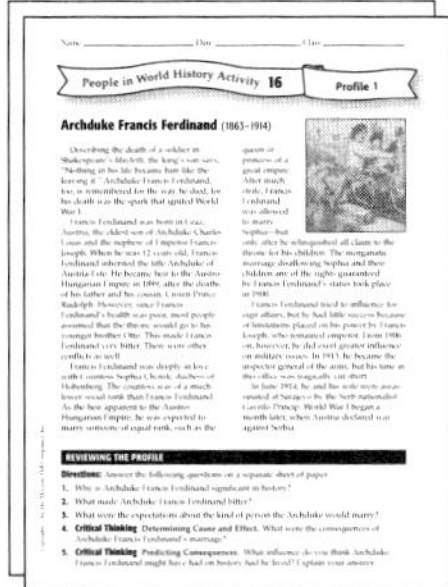

Multimedia

- Vocabulary PuzzleMaker CD-ROM
- Interactive Tutor Self-Assessment CD-ROM
- ExamView® Pro Testmaker CD-ROM
- Audio Program
- World History Primary Source Document Library CD-ROM
- MindJogger Videoquiz
- Presentation Plus! CD-ROM
- TeacherWorks CD-ROM
- Interactive Student Edition CD-ROM
- The World History—Modern Times Video Program

Spanish Resources

The following Spanish language materials are available in the Spanish Resources Binder:

- Spanish Guided Reading Activities
- Spanish Reteaching Activities
- Spanish Quizzes and Tests
- Spanish Vocabulary Activities
- Spanish Summaries

Chapter 16 Resources

SECTION RESOURCES

Daily Objectives	Reproducible Resources	Multimedia Resources
SECTION 1 **The Road to World War I** 1. Discuss how militarism, nationalism, and a crisis in the Balkans led to World War I. 2. Explain why Serbia's determination to become a large, independent state angered Austria-Hungary and initiated hostilities.	Reproducible Lesson Plan 16–1 Daily Lecture and Discussion Notes 16–1 Guided Reading Activity 16–1* Section Quiz 16–1* Reading Essentials and Study Guide 16–1	Daily Focus Skills Transparency 16–1 Interactive Tutor Self-Assessment CD-ROM ExamView® Pro Testmaker CD-ROM Presentation Plus! CD-ROM
SECTION 2 **The War** 1. Report how the stalemate at the Western Front led to new alliances, a widening of the war, and new weapons. 2. Summarize how governments expanded their powers, increased opportunities for women, and made use of propaganda.	Reproducible Lesson Plan 16–2 Daily Lecture and Discussion Notes 16–2 Guided Reading Activity 16–2* Section Quiz 16–2* Reading Essentials and Study Guide 16–2	Daily Focus Skills Transparency 16–2 Interactive Tutor Self-Assessment CD-ROM ExamView® Pro Testmaker CD-ROM Presentation Plus! CD-ROM
SECTION 3 **The Russian Revolution** 1. Explain how poor leadership led to the fall of the czarist regime in Russia. 2. Relate how the Bolsheviks came to power under Lenin. 3. Describe how Communist forces triumphed over anti-Communist forces.	Reproducible Lesson Plan 16–3 Daily Lecture and Discussion Notes 16–3 Guided Reading Activity 16–3* Section Quiz 16–3* Reading Essentials and Study Guide 16–3	Daily Focus Skills Transparency 16–3 Interactive Tutor Self-Assessment CD-ROM ExamView® Pro Testmaker CD-ROM Presentation Plus! CD-ROM
SECTION 4 **End of the War** 1. Report how combined Allied forces stopped the German offensive. 2. Explain how peace settlements brought political and territorial changes to Europe and created bitterness and resentment in several nations.	Reproducible Lesson Plan 16–4 Daily Lecture and Discussion Notes 16–4 Guided Reading Activity 16–4* Section Quiz 16–4* Reteaching Activity 16* Reading Essentials and Study Guide 16–4	Daily Focus Skills Transparency 16–4 Interactive Tutor Self-Assessment CD-ROM ExamView® Pro Testmaker CD-ROM Presentation Plus! CD-ROM

0:00 **OUT OF TIME?**
Assign the Chapter 16 **Reading Essentials and Study Guide.**

*Also Available in Spanish

 Blackline Master  Transparency   DVD
 Poster  Music Program  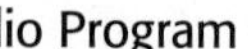 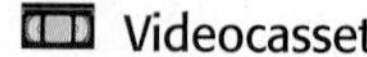

CD-ROM · Audio Program · Videocassette

Chapter 16 Resources

NATIONAL GEOGRAPHIC Teacher's Corner

INDEX TO NATIONAL GEOGRAPHIC MAGAZINE

The following articles relate to this chapter:

- "Riddle of the *Lusitania,*" by Robert D. Ballard, April 1994.
- "The Bolshevik Revolution: Experiment That Failed," by Dusko Doder, October 1992.

ADDITIONAL NATIONAL GEOGRAPHIC SOCIETY PRODUCTS

To order the following, call National Geographic at 1-800-368-2728:

- *1914–1918: World War I* (Video)
- *1917: Revolution in Russia* (Video)
- *The Rise and Fall of the Soviet Union* (Video)
- *Last Voyage of the* Lusitania (Video)
- *Russia's Last Tsar* (Video)
- *Voices of Leningrad* (Video)

NGS ONLINE

Access National Geographic's new dynamic MapMachine Web site and other geography resources at:
www.nationalgeographic.com
www.nationalgeographic.com/maps

KEY TO ABILITY LEVELS

Teaching strategies have been coded.

- L1 BASIC activities for all students
- L2 AVERAGE activities for average to above-average students
- L3 CHALLENGING activities for above-average students
- ELL ENGLISH LANGUAGE LEARNER activities

Block Schedule

Activities that are suited to use within the block scheduling framework are identified by:

WORLD HISTORY Online

Use our Web site for additional resources. All essential content is covered in the Student Edition.

You and your students can visit www.wh.mt.glencoe.com, the Web site companion to *Glencoe World History—Modern Times.* This innovative integration of electronic and print media offers your students a wealth of opportunities. The student text directs students to the Web site for the following options:

- **Chapter Overviews**
- **Self-Check Quizzes**
- **Student Web Activities**
- **Textbook Updates**

Answers to the Student Web Activities are provided for you in the **Web Activity Lesson Plans.** Additional Web resources and Interactive Tutor Puzzles are also available.

From the Classroom of...

Daniel W. Blackmon
Coral Gables Senior High School
Miami, Florida

Terrorism Then and Now

Direct students to the "World War I Primary Document Archive" site maintained by Brigham Young University Library: www.lib.byu.edu/~rdh/wwi/. Have them do a word search for the Serbian nationalist society, Narodna Odbrana. It was within this society that another secret band was formed called The Black Hand, whose members were responsible for the assassination of Archduke Francis Ferdinand, an act that ultimately resulted in the start of World War I.

Of the 30 or so documents found, ask students to read "World War I, the Narodna Odbrana," "The Black Hand," "World War I, the Assassination of Archduke Ferdinand" plus three documents of their choosing. At a later date, when the students have completed the assigned reading, lead a class discussion comparing and contrasting the Narodna Odbrana with known terrorist groups of today.

Introducing
CHAPTER 16

Performance Assessment

Refer to Activity 16 in the Performance Assessment Activities and Rubrics booklet.

The Impact Today

Explain to students that World War I was larger in scope and scale than any prior war and that it left lasting resentments, some of which still exist today. Ask students to find evidence of World War I's repercussions in current world events or in their own family history.

GLENCOE TECHNOLOGY

The World History—Modern Times Video Program

To learn more about World War I, students can view the Chapter 16 video, "Modern Warfare," from **The World History—Modern Times Video Program.**

MindJogger Videoquiz

Use the **MindJogger Videoquiz** to preview Chapter 16 content.

Available in VHS.

CHAPTER 16 War and Revolution

1914–1919

Key Events

As you read this chapter, look for the key events of World War I, the Russian Revolution, and the Paris Peace Conference.

- *Archduke Francis Ferdinand was assassinated by a Serbian nationalist.*
- *Militarism, nationalism, and alliances drew nations into war.*
- *The United States's entry into the war helped the Allies.*
- *The impact of the war at home led to an increase in the federal government's powers and changed the status of women.*
- *The Russian Revolution ended with the Communists in power.*
- *Peace settlements caused lingering resentment.*
- *The League of Nations was formed.*

The Impact Today

The events that occurred during this period still impact our lives today.

- *World War I led to the disintegration of empires and the creation of new states. This process continues today.*
- *Communism became a factor in global conflict as other nations turned to its ideology.*
- *The Balkans continue to be an area of political unrest.*

World History—Modern Times Video *The Chapter 16 video, "Modern Warfare," chronicles innovations in warfare during the twentieth century.*

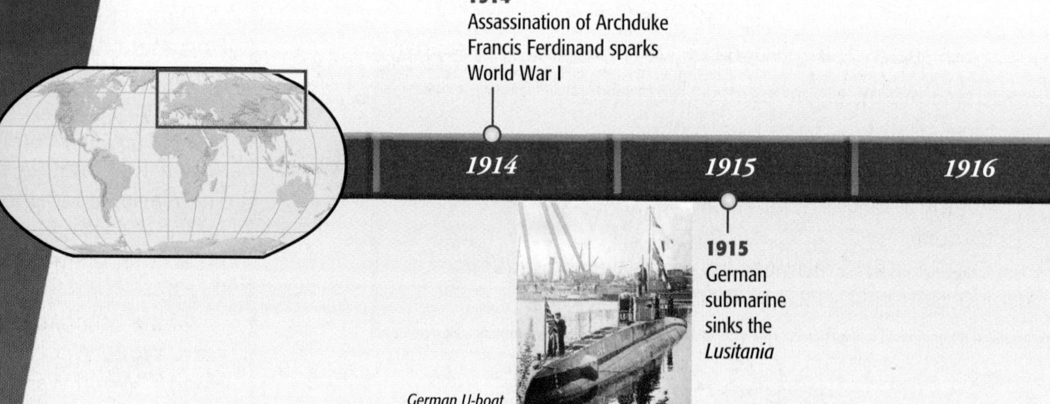
1914
Assassination of Archduke Francis Ferdinand sparks World War I
1914
1915
1916
1915
German submarine sinks the *Lusitania*

German U-boat

TWO-MINUTE LESSON LAUNCHER

An important theme of this chapter is how technology changed the way the world waged war. Students will learn how changes in technology created a new concept: that of "total war." List the following warfare innovations on the chalkboard: *trench warfare, poison gas, tanks, machine guns,* and *airplanes*. Ask students to speculate on the effects of these innovations on the war effort. They should consider how these innovations might have affected the number of casualties, amount of land involved, length of the conflict, the economic impact on the nations involved, and the psychological impact on the individuals fighting. Ask students to identify elements of current military strategy and technology that parallel what students are studying in this chapter. L2

Introducing CHAPTER 16

Chapter Objectives

After studying this chapter, students should be able to:

1. name the members of the Triple Alliance and the Triple Entente/Central Powers;
2. summarize the causes of World War I;
3. describe the stalemate on the Western Front and events on the Eastern Front;
4. explain innovations in warfare;
5. explain what is meant by "total war" and its effects on society;
6. trace the fall of czarist Russia and the rise of the Communists;
7. explain the Allies' victory;
8. list the major provisions of the Treaty of Versailles.

HISTORY *Online*

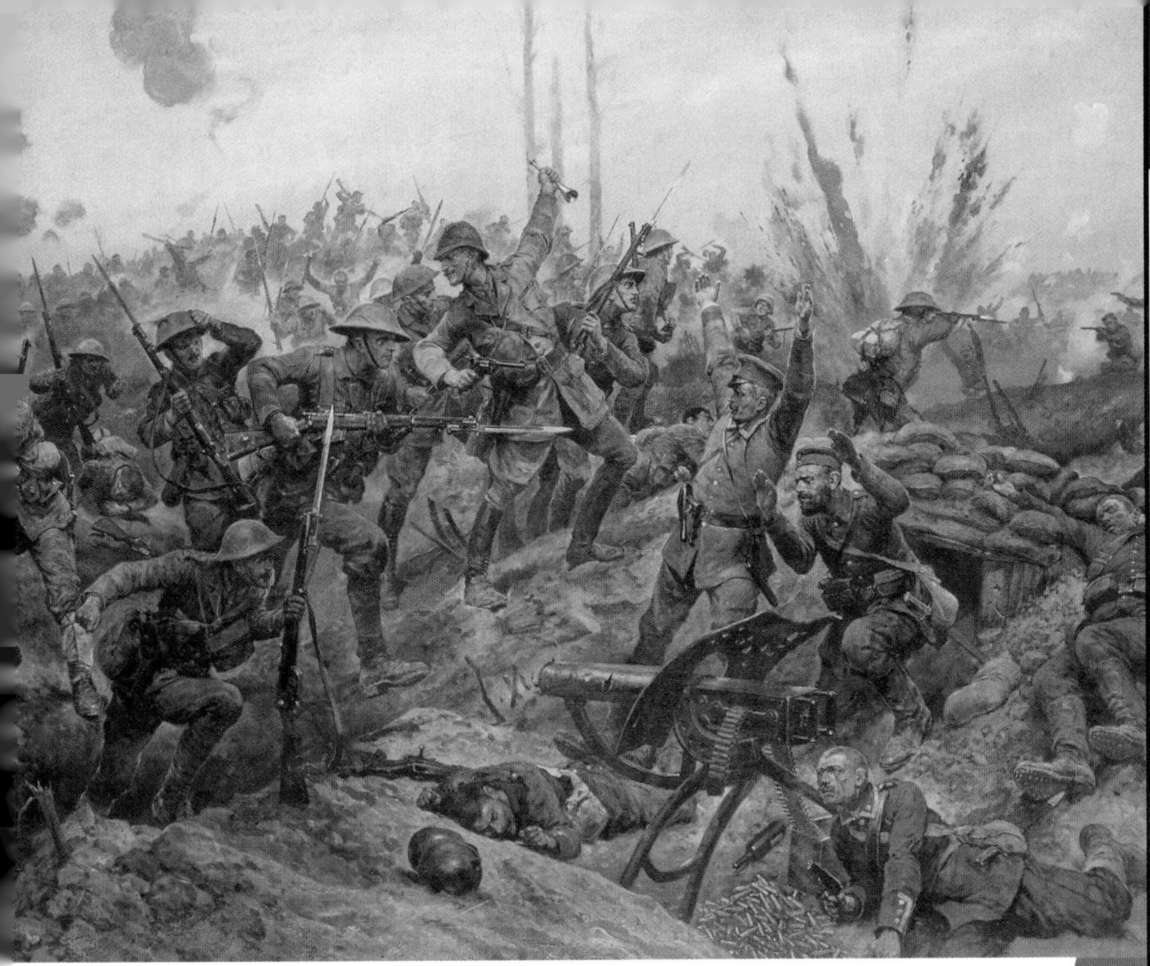

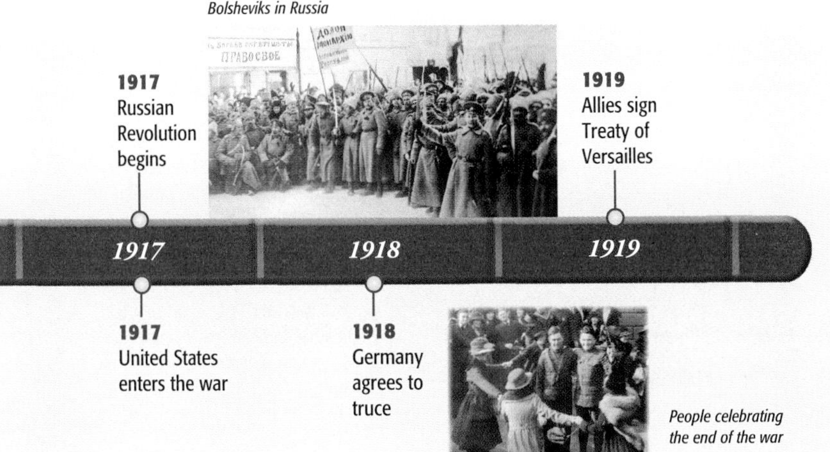

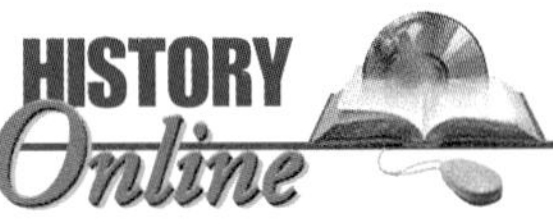

Chapter Overview

Introduce students to chapter content and key terms by having them access **Chapter Overview 16** at wh.mt.glencoe.com.

Time Line Activity

Have students examine the time line. Ask them to explain the significance of the dates 1914 through 1918. How many years after the start of World War I did the United States become involved in the war? *(3 years)* How long after the United States's involvement did Germany agree to a truce? *(1 year)* What does this suggest about the importance of U.S. involvement? *(The United States played a major role in defeating Germany.)* **L1**

Battle of the Somme by Richard Woodville The Battle of the Somme was one of the bloodiest battles of World War I.

Bolsheviks in Russia

1917 Russian Revolution begins

1919 Allies sign Treaty of Versailles

1917	1918	1919

1917 United States enters the war

1918 Germany agrees to truce

People celebrating the end of the war

HISTORY *Online*

Chapter Overview

Visit the *Glencoe World History—Modern Times* Web site at wh.mt.glencoe.com and click on **Chapter 16–Chapter Overview** to preview chapter information.

497

MORE ABOUT THE ART

Battle of the Somme The Battle of the Somme began on July 1, 1916, along a 25-mile (40.2 km) front near the Somme River in France. It was a devastating campaign for both Allied and German forces. As students will read in *A Story That Matters* on the next page, on the first day of fighting the British lost almost 21,000 men. Six months later, the Allied forces had advanced just five miles (8 km). Allied and German casualties totaled approximately one million. The battle was one of the costliest in history. In Britain, the enormous costs of this battle contributed to the first signs of war weariness. An interesting exercise for students would be to compare the depiction of the battle on this page with firsthand accounts.

CHAPTER PREVIEW

Introducing
A Story That Matters

Depending upon the ability levels of your students, select from the following questions to reinforce the reading of *A Story That Matters*.

1. When and where did this battle begin? *(July 1, 1916)* Who were the opposing forces? *(British and French against the Germans)*
2. What was "No-Man's-Land"? *(unoccupied area between opposing armies)*
3. What details in the story suggest that this was, in fact, a Great War? *(the great number of lives lost, the large amount of equipment, the violence and destruction described)* **L1 L2**

About the Art

At the Battle of the Somme, the British introduced a new weapon—an armored vehicle called the tank. However, it made little difference to the outcome of the struggle. Tanks were still too clumsy, too slow, and too prone to mechanical failure to be an effective weapon. The generals on both sides did not yet understand how best to use them.

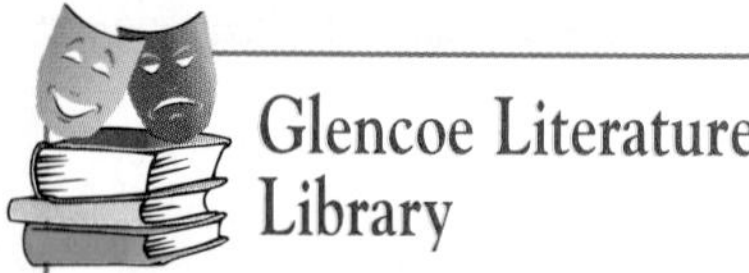

Glencoe Literature Library

The following literature from the **Glencoe Literature Library** may enrich the teaching of this chapter: *All Quiet on the Western Front* by E. M. Remarque

CHAPTER PREVIEW A Story That Matters

Advancing troops in the Battle of the Somme

British artillery firing on the Germans at the Battle of the Somme

The Battle of the Somme

On July 1, 1916, British and French infantry forces attacked German defensive lines along a front about 25 miles (40 km) long near the Somme River in France. Each soldier carried almost 70 (32 kg) pounds of equipment, including a rifle, ammunition, grenades, a shovel, a mess kit, and a full water bottle. This burden made it "impossible to move much quicker than a slow walk."

German machine guns soon opened fire. "We were able to see our comrades move forward in an attempt to cross No-Man's-Land, only to be mown down like meadow grass," recalled one British soldier. Another wrote later, "I felt sick at the sight of this carnage and remember weeping."

Philip Gibbs, an English journalist with the troops, reported on what he found in the German trenches that the British forces overran: "Victory! . . . Groups of dead lay in ditches which had once been trenches, flung into chaos by that bombardment I had seen. . . . Some of the German dead were young boys, too young to be killed for old men's crimes, and others might have been old or young. One could not tell because they had no faces, and were just masses of raw flesh in rags of uniforms. Legs and arms lay separate without any bodies thereabouts."

In the first day of the Battle of the Somme, more than 21,000 British soldiers died. After six months of fighting, the British had advanced five miles (eight km). One million British, French, and German soldiers had died.

Why It Matters

World War I (1914–1918) devastated the economic, social, and political order of Europe. People at the time, overwhelmed by the size of the war's battles and the number of casualties, simply called it the Great War. The war was all the more disturbing to Europeans because it came after a period that many believed to have been an age of progress. World War I and the revolutions it spawned can properly be seen as the first stage in the crisis of the twentieth century.

History and You Look online or in the library for a speech delivered by Woodrow Wilson or another leader, explaining the reasons for entering the war. Analyze the arguments. How might someone opposed to the war counter those arguments?

498

HISTORY AND YOU

After reading the story, ask students to imagine that they are a soldier on the Western Front fighting for either side. Have them write a letter to their country's leader about life at war. How would they feel about life on the Western Front? How would they characterize their purpose for being there? How would they feel about the enemy? What requests would they make of their leader? What would their hopes be for the future? Encourage students to be creative in their approach and writing style and to share their letters with the class. **L1**

SECTION 1 The Road to World War I

Guide to Reading

Main Ideas
- Militarism, nationalism, and a crisis in the Balkans led to World War I.
- Serbia's determination to become a large, independent state angered Austria-Hungary and initiated hostilities.

Key Terms
conscription, mobilization

People to Identify
Archduke Francis Ferdinand, Gavrilo Princip, Emperor William II, Czar Nicholas II, General Alfred von Schlieffen

Places to Locate
Serbia, Bosnia

Preview Questions
1. How did the assassination of Archduke Francis Ferdinand lead to World War I?
2. How did the system of alliances help cause the war?

Reading Strategy
Cause and Effect Use a diagram like the one below to identify the factors that led to World War I.

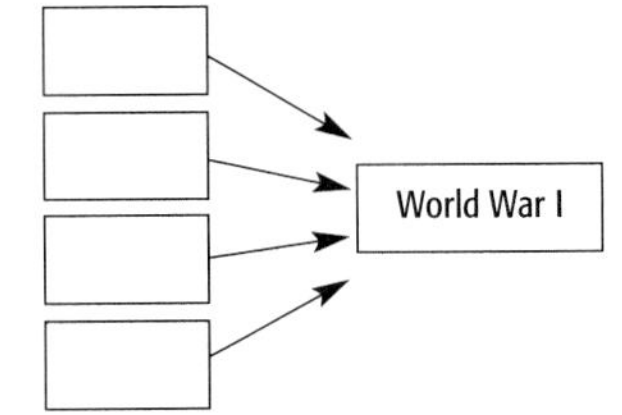

Preview of Events

♦1860 ♦1870 ♦1880 ♦1890 ♦1900 ♦1910 ♦1920

- **1882** Triple Alliance forms
- **1907** Triple Entente forms
- **1914** World War I begins

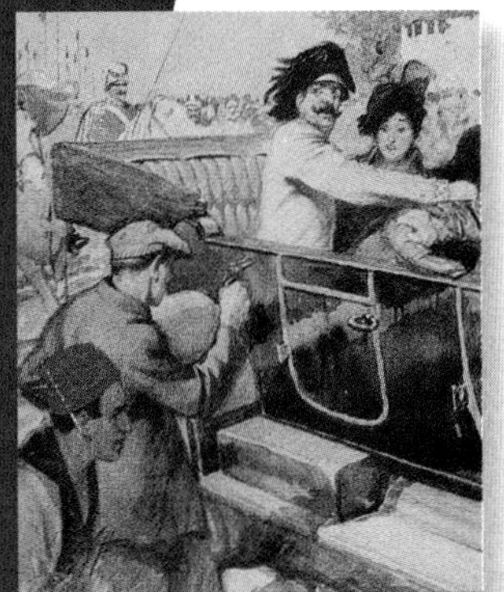
Assassination at Sarajevo

Voices from the Past

On June 28, 1914, the heir to the Austro-Hungarian throne, Archduke Francis Ferdinand, was assassinated in the Bosnian city of Sarajevo. One of the conspirators described the scene:

❝As the car came abreast, [the assassin] stepped forward from the curb, drew his automatic pistol from his coat and fired two shots. The first struck the wife of the Archduke, the Archduchess Sophia, in the abdomen. She was an expectant mother. She died instantly. The second bullet struck the Archduke close to the heart. He uttered only one word: 'Sophia'—a call to his stricken wife. Then his head fell back and he collapsed. He died almost instantly.❞

—***Eyewitness to History*, John Carey, ed., 1987**

This event was the immediate cause of World War I, but underlying forces had been moving Europeans toward war for some time.

Nationalism and the System of Alliances

In the first half of the nineteenth century, liberals believed that if European states were organized along national lines, these states would work together and create a peaceful Europe. They were wrong.

The system of nation-states that emerged in Europe in the last half of the nineteenth century led not to cooperation but to competition. Rivalries over colonies

1 FOCUS

Section Overview

This section discusses the causes of World War I.

BELLRINGER
Skillbuilder Activity

 Project transparency and have students answer questions.

 Available as a blackline master.

Daily Focus Skills Transparency 16–1

Guide to Reading

Answers to Graphic: World War I: system of alliances, growth of nationalism, internal dissent, militarism

Preteaching Vocabulary: Discuss the meaning of *conscription* and *mobilization* with the students. Ask them to consider why both of these actions might be seen as a threat to opposing nations. *(expands the size of the army; prepares the army to go to war)*

SECTION RESOURCES

Reproducible Masters
- Reproducible Lesson Plan 16–1
- Daily Lecture and Discussion Notes 16–1
- Guided Reading Activity 16–1
- Section Quiz 16–1
- Reading Essentials and Study Guide 16–1

Transparencies
- Daily Focus Skills Transparency 16–1

Multimedia
- Interactive Tutor Self-Assessment CD-ROM
- ExamView® Pro Testmaker CD-ROM
- Presentation Plus! CD-ROM

CHAPTER 16
Section 1, 499–502

2 TEACH

Geography *Skills*

Answers:

1. Britain was separated from the rest of Europe by water, making it harder to invade.
2. Triple Alliance: Austria-Hungary, Germany, Italy; Triple Entente: Britain, France, Russia; Other: Portugal, Spain, Switzerland, Belgium, Netherlands, Denmark, Norway, Sweden, Romania, Serbia, Bulgaria, Greece, Albania

Reading Check

Answer: increased competition

Reading Check

Answer: Conservative leaders feared that their countries were on the verge of revolution; the desire to suppress internal disorder may have encouraged them to plunge into war.

Daily Lecture and Discussion Notes 16–1

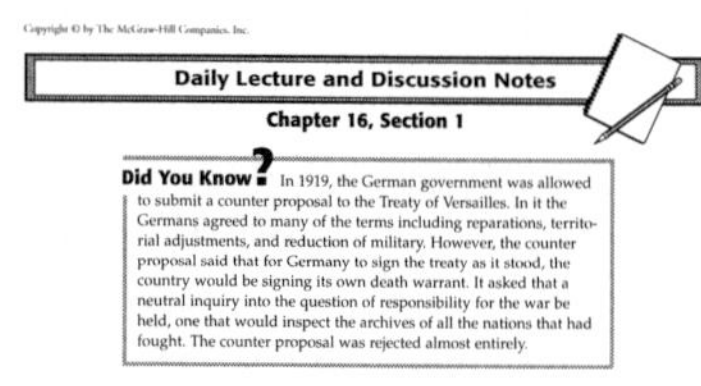

Daily Lecture and Discussion Notes

Chapter 16, Section 1

Did You Know? In 1919, the German government was allowed to submit a counter proposal to the Treaty of Versailles. In it the Germans agreed to many of the terms including reparations, territorial adjustments, and reduction of military. However, the counter proposal said that for Germany to sign the treaty as it stood, the country would be signing its own death warrant. It asked that a neutral inquiry into the question of responsibility for the war be held, one that would inspect the archives of all the nations that had fought. The counter proposal was rejected almost entirely.

I. **Nationalism and the System of Alliances** *(pages 499–500)*

A. Liberals during the first half of the 1800s hoped that the formation of European nation-states would lead to peace. However, the imperialist states that emerged during the second half of the 1800s became highly competitive over trade and colonies.

B. Two main alliances divided Europe: The **Triple Alliance** (1882) was made up of Germany, Austria-Hungary, and Italy; and the **Triple Entente** (1907) was made up of France, Great Britain, and Russia.

C. During the early 1900s, several crises erupted, particularly in the Balkans, which created a great deal of anger and tension between the nations of the two alliances. Each nation was willing to go to war to preserve its power.

D. European ethnic groups, such as Slavs in the Balkans and the Irish in the British Empire, dreamed of creating their own national states, which also increased tensions in Europe.

Geography *Skills*

The alliance system was one of the major causes of World War I.

1. **Interpreting Maps** What geographic factor made it unlikely that World War I battles would be fought in Great Britain?
2. **Applying Geography Skills** Create a three-column chart with the headings Triple Entente, Triple Alliance, and Other. Place all the countries labeled on the map in the proper column.

and trade grew during an age of frenzied nationalism and imperialist expansion.

At the same time, Europe's great powers had been divided into two loose alliances. Germany, Austria-Hungary, and Italy formed the **Triple Alliance** in 1882. France, Great Britain, and Russia created the **Triple Entente** in 1907.

In the early years of the twentieth century, a series of crises tested these alliances. Especially troublesome were the crises in the Balkans between 1908 and 1913. These events left European states angry at each other and eager for revenge. Each state was guided by its own self-interest and success. They were willing to use war as a way to preserve the power of their national states.

The growth of nationalism in the nineteenth century had yet another serious result. Not all ethnic groups had become nations. Slavic minorities in the Balkans and the Hapsburg Empire, for example, still dreamed of creating their own national states. The Irish in the British Empire and the Poles in the Russian Empire had similar dreams.

Reading Check **Identifying** Did the growth of nationalism in the first half of the nineteenth century lead to increased competition or increased cooperation among European nations?

Internal Dissent

National desires were not the only source of internal strife at the beginning of the twentieth century. Socialist labor movements also had grown more powerful. The Socialists were increasingly inclined to use strikes, even violent ones, to achieve their goals.

Some conservative leaders, alarmed at the increase in labor strife and class division, feared that European nations were on the verge of revolution. In the view of some historians, the desire to suppress internal disorder may have encouraged various leaders to take the plunge into war in 1914.

Reading Check **Explaining** According to some historians, how might internal disorder have been one of the causes of World War I?

Militarism

The growth of mass armies after 1900 heightened the existing tensions in Europe. The large size of these armies also made it obvious that if war did come, it would be highly destructive.

Conscription, a military draft, had been established as a regular practice in most Western countries before 1914. (The United States and Britain were

CRITICAL THINKING ACTIVITY

Synthesizing Information Have students do additional research on the origins of World War I and then conduct a class debate on this topic. Have students assume the roles of the leaders of Austria-Hungary, Germany, Serbia, Russia, France, and Britain. Debate which country was most responsible for starting World War I and which country bore little or no responsibility for starting the war. Or, have students use a map of 1914 Europe to explain the role geography played in the development of the Schlieffen plan. Ask students how geography affected the war plans of the other World War I participants. L2

exceptions.) European armies doubled in size between 1890 and 1914.

With its 1.3 million men, the Russian army had grown to be the largest. The French and German armies were not far behind, with 900,000 each. The British, Italian, and Austro-Hungarian armies numbered between 250,000 and 500,000 soldiers each.

Militarism—aggressive preparation for war— was growing. As armies grew, so too did the influence of military leaders. They drew up vast and complex plans for quickly mobilizing millions of men and enormous quantities of supplies in the event of war.

Military leaders feared that any changes in these plans would cause chaos in the armed forces. Thus, they insisted that their plans could not be altered. In the 1914 crises, this left European political leaders with little leeway. They were forced to make decisions for military instead of political reasons.

Reading Check **Examining** What was the effect of conscription on events leading up to World War I?

The Outbreak of War: Summer 1914

Militarism, nationalism, and the desire to stifle internal dissent may all have played a role in the starting of World War I. However, it was the decisions made by European leaders in response to another crisis in the Balkans in the summer of 1914 that led directly to the conflict.

The Serbian Problem As we have seen, states in southeastern Europe had struggled for many years to free themselves of Ottoman rule. Furthermore, the rivalry between Austria-Hungary and Russia for domination of these new states created serious tensions in the region.

By 1914, **Serbia,** supported by Russia, was determined to create a large, independent Slavic state in the Balkans. Austria-Hungary, which had its own Slavic minorities to contend with, was equally determined to prevent that from happening.

Many Europeans saw the potential danger in this explosive situation. The British ambassador to Vienna anticipated war in 1913:

> “Serbia will some day set Europe by the ears, and bring about a universal war on the Continent. . . . I cannot tell you how exasperated people are getting here at the continual worry which that little country causes to Austria under encouragement from Russia. . . . It will be lucky if Europe succeeds in avoiding war as a result of the present crisis.”

It was against this backdrop of mutual distrust and hatred that the events of the summer of 1914 were played out.

Assassination in Sarajevo On June 28, 1914, **Archduke Francis Ferdinand,** the heir to the throne of Austria-Hungary, and his wife Sophia, visited the Bosnian city of Sarajevo (SAR•uh•YAY•VOH). A group of conspirators waited there in the streets. The conspirators were members of the Black Hand, a Serbian terrorist organization that wanted **Bosnia** to be free of Austria-Hungary and to become part of a large Serbian kingdom.

The conspirators planned to kill the archduke, along with his wife. That morning, one of the conspirators threw a bomb at the archduke's car, but it glanced off and exploded against the car behind him. Later in the day, however, **Gavrilo Princip,** a 19-year-old Bosnian Serb, succeeded in shooting both the archduke and his wife.

Austria-Hungary Responds The Austro-Hungarian government did not know whether or not the Serbian government had been directly involved in the archduke's assassination, but it did not care. It saw an opportunity to "render Serbia innocuous [harmless] once and for all by a display of force," as the Austrian foreign minister put it.

Austrian leaders wanted to attack Serbia but feared Russian intervention on Serbia's behalf, so they sought the backing of their German allies. **Emperor William II** of Germany and his chancellor responded with a "blank check," saying that Austria-

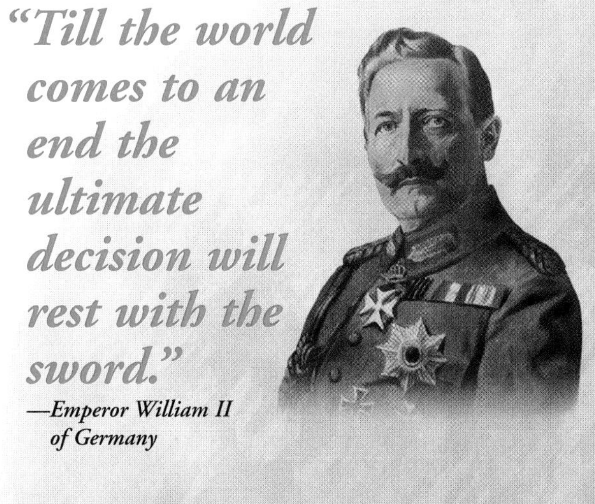

"Till the world comes to an end the ultimate decision will rest with the sword."
—Emperor William II of Germany

CHAPTER 16
Section 1, 499–502

Reading Check

Answer: European armies doubled in size between 1890 and 1914.

Guided Reading Activity 16–1

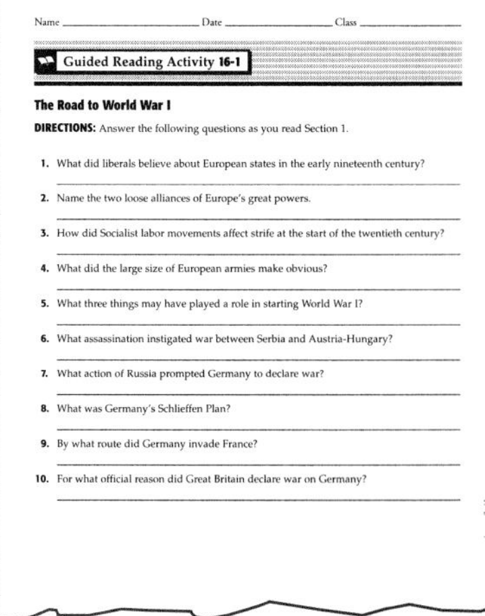
Guided Reading Activity 16–1

Name ____________ Date ____________ Class ____________

Guided Reading Activity 16-1

The Road to World War I

DIRECTIONS: Answer the following questions as you read Section 1.

1. What did liberals believe about European states in the early nineteenth century?
2. Name the two loose alliances of Europe's great powers.
3. How did Socialist labor movements affect strife at the start of the twentieth century?
4. What did the large size of European armies make obvious?
5. What three things may have played a role in starting World War I?
6. What assassination instigated war between Serbia and Austria-Hungary?
7. What action of Russia prompted Germany to declare war?
8. What was Germany's Schlieffen Plan?
9. By what route did Germany invade France?
10. For what official reason did Great Britain declare war on Germany?

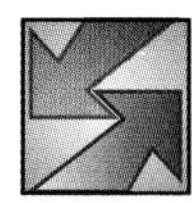

CURRICULUM CONNECTION

Government Ask students to research the concept of neutrality as defined by international law and practiced in the twentieth century. Suggest they consider the U.S. Neutrality Acts of 1935, 1936, and 1937. **L2**

3 ASSESS

Assign Section 1 Assessment as homework or as an in-class activity.

Have students use **Interactive Tutor Self-Assessment CD-ROM.**

COOPERATIVE LEARNING ACTIVITY

Preparing a News Report Organize students into small groups and have them stage a series of radio or television newscasts devoted to the outbreak of World War I. Each group should select a crucial date from June 28 to August 4, 1914. Students should incorporate researched information with the text material and design visual aids, such as maps and charts, when appropriate. Groups should assign members tasks, such as researching and compiling information, writing, designing, visual aids, and performing. Have groups include participants' comments and citizens' responses. **L2**

For grading this activity, refer to the ***Performance Assessment Activities*** booklet.

Hungary could rely on Germany's "full support," even if "matters went to the length of a war between Austria-Hungary and Russia."

Strengthened by German support, Austrian leaders sent an ultimatum to Serbia on July 23. In it, they made such extreme demands that Serbia had little choice but to reject some of them in order to preserve its sovereignty. On July 28, Austria-Hungary declared war on Serbia.

Russia Mobilizes Russia was determined to support Serbia's cause. On July 28, **Czar Nicholas II** ordered partial mobilization of the Russian army against Austria-Hungary. Mobilization is the process of assembling troops and supplies and making them ready for war. In 1914, mobilization was considered an act of war.

Leaders of the Russian army informed the czar that they could not partially mobilize. Their mobilization plans were based on a war against both Germany and Austria-Hungary. Mobilizing against only Austria-Hungary, they claimed, would create chaos in the army. Based on this claim, the czar ordered full mobilization of the Russian army on July 29, knowing that Germany would consider this order an act of war.

The Conflict Broadens Indeed, Germany reacted quickly. The German government warned Russia that it must halt its mobilization within 12 hours. When Russia ignored this warning, Germany declared war on Russia on August 1.

Like the Russians, the Germans had a military plan. It had been drawn up under the guidance of **General Alfred von Schlieffen** (SHLEE•fuhn), so was known as the Schlieffen Plan. The plan called for a two-front war with France and Russia, who had formed a military alliance in 1894.

According to the Schlieffen Plan, Germany would conduct a small holding action against Russia while most of the German army would carry out a rapid invasion of France. This meant invading France by moving quickly along the level coastal area through Belgium. After France was defeated, the German invaders would move to the east against Russia.

Under the Schlieffen Plan, Germany could not mobilize its troops solely against Russia. Therefore, it declared war on France on August 3. About the same time, it issued an ultimatum to Belgium demanding the right of German troops to pass through Belgian territory. Belgium, however, was a neutral nation.

On August 4, Great Britain declared war on Germany, officially for violating Belgian neutrality. In fact, Britain, which was allied with the countries of France and Russia, was concerned about maintaining its own world power. As one British diplomat put it, if Germany and Austria-Hungary won the war, "what would be the position of a friendless England?" By August 4, all the great powers of Europe were at war.

Reading Check **Evaluating** What was the Schlieffen Plan and how did it complicate the events leading to World War I?

SECTION 1 ASSESSMENT

Checking for Understanding

1. **Define** conscription, mobilization.
2. **Identify** Triple Alliance, Triple Entente, Archduke Francis Ferdinand, Gavrilo Princip, Emperor William II, Czar Nicholas II, General Alfred von Schlieffen.
3. **Locate** Serbia, Bosnia.
4. **Explain** why Great Britain became involved in the war.
5. **List** the ethnic groups that were left without nations after the nationalist movements of the nineteenth century.

Critical Thinking

6. **Analyze** How did the creation of military plans help draw the nations of Europe into World War I? In your opinion, what should today's national and military leaders have learned from the military plans that helped initiate World War I? Explain your answer.
7. **Sequencing Information** Using a diagram like the one below, identify the series of decisions made by European leaders in 1914 that led directly to the outbreak of war.

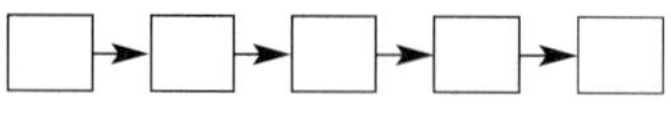

Analyzing Visuals

8. **Examine** the painting of Emperor William II of Germany shown on page 501 of your text. How does this portrait of the emperor reflect the nature of leadership before World War I?

Writing About History

9. **Expository Writing** Some historians believe that the desire to suppress internal disorder may have encouraged leaders to take the plunge into war. As an adviser, write a memo to your country's leader explaining how a war might be advantageous with regard to domestic policy.

Reading Check

Answer: It called for a two-front war with France and Russia. By declaring war on France, Germany brought Great Britain into the war.

Section Quiz 16–1

Name ______ Date ______ Class ______

Chapter 16 Score

Section Quiz 16-1

DIRECTIONS: Matching Match each item in Column A with an item in Column B. Write the correct letters in the blanks. *(10 points each)*

Column A	Column B
____ 1. military draft	A. mobilization
____ 2. aggressive preparation for war	B. militarism
____ 3. readying troops and supplies for war	C. Germany
____ 4. ally of Austria-Hungry	D. Russia
____ 5. protector of Serbia	E. conscription

DIRECTIONS: Multiple Choice In the blank, write the letter of the choice that best completes the statement or answers the question. *(10 points each)*

____ 6. The Triple Alliance was a loose agreement of cooperation among

Reading Essentials and Study Guide 16–1

Name ______ Date ______ Class ______

Reading Essentials and Study Guide

Chapter 16, Section 1

For use with textbook pages 499–502

THE ROAD TO WORLD WAR I

KEY TERMS

conscription a military draft *(page 500)*

mobilization the process of assembling troops and supplies and making them ready for war *(page 502)*

DRAWING FROM EXPERIENCE

Have you ever been given an ultimatum? How did you react to the ultimatum?

In this section, you will learn about the events that led to the start of World War I. Ultimatums played an important role in starting World War I.

ORGANIZING YOUR THOUGHTS

Use the time line below to help you take notes. Identify seven key events during the summer of 1914 that led to World War I.

1. → 2. → 3. →

Reteaching Activity

Ask students to identify the specific events that led to World War I. **L1**

4 CLOSE

Ask students to give examples that explain the following sentence: "It was against this backdrop of mutual distrust and hatred that the events of the summer of 1914 were played out." **L1**

SECTION 1 ASSESSMENT

1. Key terms are in blue.
2. Triple Alliance *(p. 500)*, Triple Entente *(p. 500)*, Archduke Francis Ferdinand *(p. 501)*, Gavrilo Princip *(p. 501)*, Emperor William II *(p. 501)*, Czar Nicholas II *(p. 502)*, General Alfred von Schlieffen *(p. 502)*
3. See chapter maps.
4. official cause: Germany violated Belgian neutrality; actual cause: Britain concerned about own power
5. Slavic minorities in Balkans and Hapsburg Empire; Irish in British Empire; Poles in Russian Empire
6. Countries could not partially mobilize or limit war fronts.
7. Austria-Hungary punishes Serbia → Germany helps Austria-Hungary → Russia against Austria-Hungary, Germany → German war against Russia and France → Britain declares war on Germany
8. rise of militarism
9. Answers should be consistent with material presented in this section.

SECTION 2 The War

Guide to Reading

Main Ideas
- The stalemate at the Western Front led to new alliances, a widening of the war, and new weapons.
- Governments expanded their powers, increased opportunities for women, and made use of propaganda.

Key Terms
propaganda, trench warfare, war of attrition, total war, planned economies

People to Identify
Lawrence of Arabia, Admiral Holtzendorff, Woodrow Wilson

Places to Locate
Marne, Tannenberg, Masurian Lakes, Verdun, Gallipoli

Preview Questions
1. How did trench warfare lead to a stalemate?
2. Why did the United States enter the war?

Reading Strategy
Organizing Information Identify which countries belonged to the Allies and the Central Powers. What country changed allegiance? What country withdrew from the war?

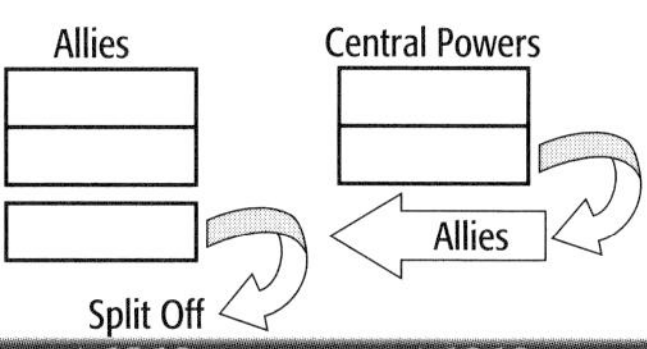

Preview of Events

1914 · 1915 · 1916 · 1917 · 1918 · 1919

- **1915** *Lusitania* sunk by German forces
- **1916** Battle of Verdun
- **1917** United States enters the war

Voices from the Past

Troops going to war

Stefan Zweig, an Austrian writer, described the excitement Austrians felt going to war in 1914:

> ❝What did the people know of war in 1914, after nearly half a century of peace? They did not know war; they had hardly given it a thought. They still saw it in the perspective of their school readers and of paintings in museums; brilliant cavalry attacks in glittering uniforms, the fatal shot always straight through the heart, the entire campaign a resounding march of victory—'We'll be home at Christmas,' the recruits shouted laughingly to their mothers in August of 1914. . . . The young people were honestly afraid that they might miss this most wonderful and exciting experience of their lives; . . . that is why they shouted and sang in the trains that carried them to the slaughter.❞
>
> —***The World of Yesterday,*** **Helmut Ripperger and B. W. Buebsch, trans., 1943**

Europeans went to war in 1914 with remarkable enthusiasm.

1914 to 1915: Illusions and Stalemate

Before 1914, many political leaders had thought that war involved so many political and economic risks that it would not be worth fighting. Others had believed that diplomats could easily control any situation and prevent war. At the beginning of August 1914, both ideas were shattered. However, the new illusions that replaced them soon proved to be equally foolish.

Government **propaganda**—ideas spread to influence public opinion for or against a cause—had worked in stirring up national hatreds before the war. Now, in August 1914, the urgent pleas of European governments for defense against

CHAPTER 16
Section 2, 503–509

1 FOCUS

Section Overview

This section discusses the widening of World War I and the expansion of government powers to accommodate the war.

BELLRINGER
Skillbuilder Activity

 Project transparency and have students answer questions.

 Available as a blackline master.

Daily Focus Skills Transparency 16–2

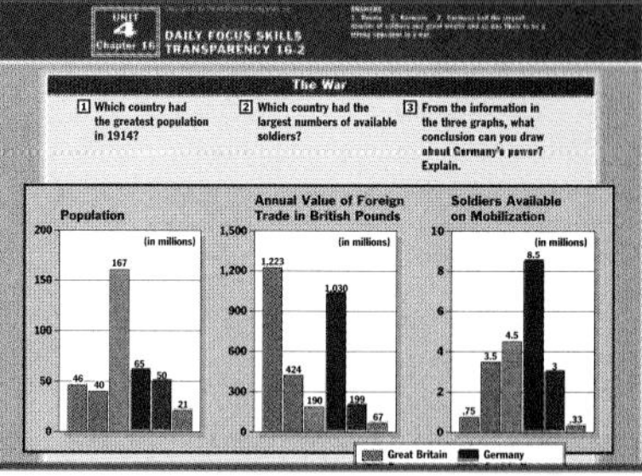

Guide to Reading

Answers to Graphic: Allies: Great Britain, France, United States, Italy, Russia;
Central Powers: Germany, Austria-Hungary, Bulgaria, Ottoman Empire; Italy changed from Central Powers to Allies; Russia withdrew from the war

Preteaching Vocabulary: Have students define *war of attrition, propaganda,* and *total war,* and discuss why a war of attrition might require more propaganda and lead to a total war. **L2**

SECTION RESOURCES

Reproducible Masters
- Reproducible Lesson Plan 16–2
- Daily Lecture and Discussion Notes 16–2
- Guided Reading Activity 16–2
- Section Quiz 16–2
- Reading Essentials and Study Guide 16–2

Transparencies
- Daily Focus Skills Transparency 16–2

Multimedia
- Interactive Tutor Self-Assessment CD-ROM
- ExamView® Pro Testmaker CD-ROM
- Presentation Plus! CD-ROM

2 TEACH

Daily Lecture and Discussion Notes 16–2

Daily Lecture and Discussion Notes

Chapter 16, Section 2

Did You Know? When President Woodrow Wilson declared war in 1917, he called it the "war to end all wars" and said that the United States would fight to "make the world safe for democracy." The government asked for volunteers, saying it needed a million men. However, public support was not as strong as the government would have liked. In the first six weeks after war was declared, about 70,000 men volunteered, which led Congress to start the draft.

I. **1914 to 1915: Illusions and Stalemate** *(pages 503–505)*

A. The events of August 1914 shattered two previously held ideas: that war was not worth fighting and that diplomats could prevent war.

B. Government **propaganda**—ideas spread to influence public opinion—had stirred up national hatreds before the war. When the war began, propaganda was used to urge people to defend their own country. The majority of people thought their country's cause was just.

C. All European wars since 1815 had only lasted a few weeks. In August, 1914, most people thought the war would be over by Christmas.

D. On the Western Front, Germany swept through Belgium into northern France and was stopped a short distance from Paris at the First Battle of the **Marne.** The Western Front turned into a stalemate, with neither side able to push the other out of the system of **trench warfare** they had begun. The trenches stretched from the English Channel nearly to the Swiss border. For four years both sides remained in almost the same positions.

E. On the Eastern Front, the war was far more mobile. The Russian army moved into eastern Germany but was defeated at the Battle of **Tannenberg** and the Battle of **Masurian Lakes,** making them no longer a threat to invade Germany. The Russians defeated Austria-Hungary and dislodged them from Serbia. The Italians, who had been allied with Germany and Austria-Hungary, broke their alliance in 1915 and attacked Austria-Hungary. The Germans came to the aid of the Austrians and together they defeated the Russians in several battles and drove them back. 2.5 million Russians had been killed, captured, or wounded. The Russians were almost out of the war. After defeating Serbia, Germany turned its attention back to the Western Front.

turn

CURRICULUM CONNECTION

Art Ask interested students to bring in copies of visual arts used as propaganda before and during World War I, including posters, cartoons, or paintings. Who were the artists? How effective was their work? **L2**

Critical Thinking

Have students explain the significance of the First Battle of the Marne. *(It ended the Schlieffen Plan, began trench warfare, and showed that the war would last a long time.)*

aggressors fell on receptive ears in every nation at war. Most people seemed genuinely convinced that their nation's cause was just.

A new set of illusions also fed the enthusiasm for war. In August 1914, almost everyone believed that the war would be over in a few weeks. People were reminded that almost all European wars since 1815 had, in fact, ended in a matter of weeks. Both the soldiers who boarded the trains for the war front in August 1914, and the jubilant citizens who showered them with flowers as they left, believed that the warriors would be home by Christmas.

The Western Front German hopes for a quick end to the war rested on a military gamble. The Schlieffen Plan had called for the German army to make a vast encircling movement through Belgium into northern France. According to the plan, the German forces would sweep around Paris. This would enable them to surround most of the French army.

The German advance was halted a short distance from Paris at the First Battle of the **Marne** (September 6–10). To stop the Germans, French military leaders loaded two thousand Parisian taxicabs with fresh troops and sent them to the front line.

The war quickly turned into a stalemate, as neither the Germans nor the French could dislodge each other from the trenches they had dug for shelter. These trenches were ditches protected by barbed wire. Two lines of trenches soon reached from the English Channel to the frontiers of Switzerland. The Western Front had become bogged down in **trench warfare** that kept both sides in virtually the same positions for four years.

The Eastern Front In contrast to the Western Front, the war on the Eastern Front was marked by mobility. The cost in lives, however, was equally enormous.

At the beginning of the war, the Russian army moved into eastern Germany but was decisively defeated at the Battle of **Tannenberg** on August 30 and the Battle of **Masurian Lakes** on September 15. As a result of these defeats, the Russians were no longer a threat to German territory.

THE WAY IT WAS

FOCUS ON EVERYDAY LIFE

Trench Warfare

Warfare in the trenches of the Western Front produced unimaginable horrors. Battlefields were hellish landscapes of barbed wire, shell holes, mud, and injured and dying men. The introduction of poison gas in 1915 produced new forms of injuries. One British writer described them: "I wish those people who write so glibly about this being a holy war could see a case of mustard gas . . . could see the poor things burnt and blistered all over with great mustard-coloured suppurating [pus-forming] blisters with blind eyes all sticky . . . and stuck together, and always fighting for breath, with voices a mere whisper, saying that their throats are closing and they know they will choke."

Soldiers in the trenches also lived with the persistent presence of death. Because combat went on for months, soldiers had to carry on in the midst of countless bodies of dead men or the remains of men blown apart by artillery barrages. Many soldiers remembered the stench of decomposing bodies and the swarms of rats that grew fat in the trenches.

Daily life in the trenches was predictable. Thirty minutes before sunrise, troops had to "stand to," or be combat-ready to repel any attack. If no attack came that day,

British gas mask and pack

EXTENDING THE CONTENT

Trench Warfare Trench warfare caused new types of illness and injury. Soldiers developed trench foot from standing in water-filled trenches for days or weeks. Some came down with trench fever, an illness carried by lice, trench nephritis, and trench foot. The use of shrapnel shells caused infection from the thousands of metal splinters embedded in wounds. Poison gas deployed in the trenches resulted in thousands of deaths, and millions of soldiers suffered with inflamed lungs and severe burns. Trench warfare also resulted in many facial injuries that eventually led to advances in plastic surgery techniques.

Austria-Hungary, Germany's ally, fared less well at first. The Austrians had been defeated by the Russians in Galicia and thrown out of Serbia as well. To make matters worse, the Italians betrayed their German and Austrian allies in the Triple Alliance by attacking Austria in May 1915. Italy thus joined France, Great Britain, and Russia, who had formed the Triple Entente, but now were called the Allied Powers, or Allies.

By this time, the Germans had come to the aid of the Austrians. A German-Austrian army defeated the Russian army in Galicia and pushed the Russians far back into their own territory. Russian casualties stood at 2.5 million killed, captured, or wounded. The Russians had almost been knocked out of the war.

Buoyed by their success, Germany and Austria-Hungary, joined by Bulgaria in September 1915, attacked and eliminated Serbia from the war. Their successes in the east would enable the Germans to move back to the offensive in the west.

Reading Check **Contrasting** How did the war on the Eastern Front differ from the war on the Western Front?

1916 to 1917: The Great Slaughter

On the Western Front, the trenches dug in 1914 had by 1916 become elaborate systems of defense. The lines of trenches for both sides were protected by barbed wire entanglements up to 5 feet (about 1.5 m) high and 30 yards (about 27 m) wide, concrete machine-gun nests, and other gun batteries, supported further back by heavy artillery. Troops lived in holes in the ground, separated from each other by a strip of territory known as no-man's-land.

Tactics of Trench Warfare The unexpected development of trench warfare baffled military leaders. They had been trained to fight wars of movement and maneuver. The only plan generals could devise was to attempt a breakthrough by throwing masses of men against enemy lines that had first been battered by artillery. Once the decisive breakthrough had been achieved, they thought, they could return to the war of movement that they knew best.

At times, the high command on either side would order an offensive that would begin with an artillery

the day's routine consisted of breakfast followed by inspection, sentry duty, work on the trenches, care of personal items, and attempts to pass the time. Soldiers often recalled the boredom of life in the dreary, lice-ridden, and muddy or dusty trenches.

At many places along the opposing lines of trenches, a "live and let live" system evolved. It was based on the realization that neither side was going to drive out the other. The "live and let live" system resulted in such arrangements as not shelling the latrines and not attacking during breakfast.

On both sides, troops produced their own humor magazines to help pass the time and fulfill the need to laugh in the midst of their daily madness. The British trench magazine, the *B. E. F. Times*, devoted one of its issues to defining military terms, including "DUDS—These are of two kinds. A shell on impact failing to explode is called a dud. They are unhappily not as plentiful as the other kind, which often draws a big salary and explodes for no reason."

British soldiers in the trenches

Connecting to the Past

1. **Explain** What was the rationale behind the "live and let live" system?
2. **Writing about History** Write several journal entries as if you were a soldier in the trenches.

CHAPTER 16
Section 2, 503–509

Reading Check

Answer: The Western Front reached a stalemate due to trench warfare; the Eastern Front was a more typical war of movement and maneuver.

The Way It Was

Answers:

1. Each side realized that it was not going to drive out the other, so they could refrain from shelling latrines or attacking during breakfast.
2. Answers should be consistent with material presented in this section.

Guided Reading Activity 16–2

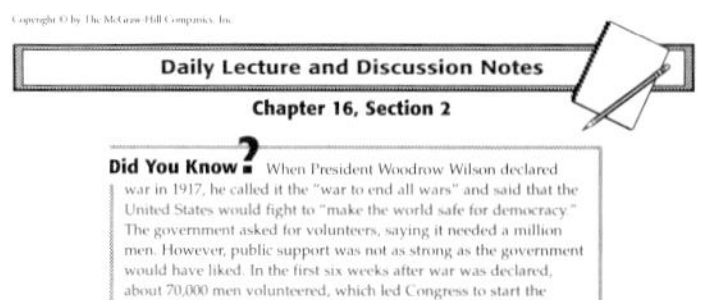

Daily Lecture and Discussion Notes

Chapter 16, Section 2

Did You Know? When President Woodrow Wilson declared war in 1917, he called it the "war to end all wars" and said that the United States would fight to "make the world safe for democracy." The government asked for volunteers, saying it needed a million men. However, public support was not as strong as the government would have liked. In the first six weeks after war was declared, about 70,000 men volunteered, which led Congress to start the draft.

I. **1914 to 1915: Illusions and Stalemate** *(pages 503–505)*

A. The events of August 1914 shattered two previously held ideas: that war was not worth fighting and that diplomats could prevent war.

B. Government **propaganda**—ideas spread to influence public opinion—had stirred up national hatreds before the war. When the war began, propaganda was used to urge

CURRICULUM CONNECTION

Literature Have students read all or parts of *All Quiet on the Western Front* and then write a letter in which they try to explain to their friends and family back home exactly what they are experiencing in the trenches on the Western Front. What difficulties do they face in trying to describe what they are experiencing? L2

MEETING INDIVIDUAL NEEDS

Visual Learners Have students identify the Triple Alliance and Triple Entente countries on the map on page 500, and ask them to list each country in its correct category. Then have students find photographs depicting scenes from each of the countries in the early 1900s. Have the students share their lists and pictures with the class. To aid in memorization and learning, pass out 3×5 cards upon which students list all countries in the Triple Alliance and Triple Entente. Ask students to sort the cards into these two categories. L1

Refer to ***Inclusion for the High School Studies Classroom Strategies and Activities*** in the TCR.

Answer: Traditional military methods did not work in trenches.

Reading Check

Answer: Both sides had to search for new allies who might provide a winning advantage, bringing more countries into the war.

Then *and* Now

Answer: In addition to airplanes, they used zeppelins.

CURRICULUM CONNECTION

Science and Technology Ask students to prepare a display showing the development of aviation during World War I. L2

Critical Thinking

Ask students to identify the important American figures arguing for and against U. S. neutrality. Ask students to speculate on the outcome of the war had the United States chosen to remain neutral. L3

Critical Thinking

When students finish reading this section, have them explain why World War I is considered a major era in world history. Have students describe the defining characteristics of this era. L1

barrage to flatten the enemy's barbed wire and leave the enemy in a state of shock. After "softening up" the enemy in this fashion, a mass of soldiers would climb out of their trenches with fixed bayonets and hope to work their way toward the enemy trenches.

The attacks rarely worked because men advancing unprotected across open fields could be fired at by the enemy's machine guns. In 1916 and 1917, millions of young men died in the search for the elusive breakthrough. In 10 months at **Verdun,** France, in 1916, seven hundred thousand men lost their lives over a few miles of land. World War I had turned into a war of attrition, a war based on wearing the other side down by constant attacks and heavy losses.

(See page 778 to read an excerpt from Arthur Guy Empey's Over the Top *in the Primary Sources Library.)*

War in the Air By the end of 1915, airplanes had appeared on the battlefront for the first time in history. At first, planes were used to spot the enemy's position. However, planes soon began to attack ground targets, especially enemy communications.

Fights for control of the air occurred and increased over time. At first, pilots fired at each other with handheld pistols. Later, machine guns were mounted on the noses of planes, which made the skies considerably more dangerous.

The Germans also used their giant airships—the zeppelins—to bomb London and eastern England. This caused little damage but frightened many people. Germany's enemies, however, soon found that zeppelins, which were filled with hydrogen gas, quickly became raging infernos when hit by antiaircraft guns.

Reading Check **Explaining** Why were military leaders baffled by trench warfare?

Widening of the War

Because of the stalemate on the Western Front, both sides sought to gain new allies who might provide a winning advantage. The Ottoman Empire had already come into the war on Germany's side in August 1914. Russia, Great Britain, and France—the Allies—declared war on the Ottoman Empire in November.

The Allies tried to open a Balkan front by landing forces at **Gallipoli** (guh•LIH•puh•lee), southwest of Constantinople, in April 1915. However, Bulgaria entered the war on the side of the Central Powers, as Germany, Austria-Hungary, and the Ottoman Empire were called. A disastrous campaign at Gallipoli forced the Allies to withdraw.

In return for Italy entering the war on the Allied side, France and Great Britain promised to let Italy have some Austrian territory. Italy on the side of the Allies opened up a front against Austria-Hungary.

By 1917, the war that had started in Europe had truly become a world conflict. In the Middle East, a British officer known as **Lawrence of Arabia,** in 1917, urged Arab princes to revolt against their Ottoman overlords. In 1918, British forces from Egypt destroyed the Ottoman Empire in the Middle East. For their Middle East campaigns, the British mobilized forces from India, Australia, and New Zealand.

The Allies also took advantage of Germany's preoccupations in Europe and lack of naval strength to seize German colonies in the rest of the world. Japan, a British ally beginning in 1902, seized a number of German-held islands in the Pacific. Australia seized German New Guinea.

Reading Check **Describing** What caused the widening of the war?

Then *and* Now

The introduction of airplanes greatly changed the nature of warfare during the twentieth century. What kind of aircraft did the Germans use during World War I?

British fighter plane, c. 1917 ▶

U.S. jet fighter, 2001 ▼

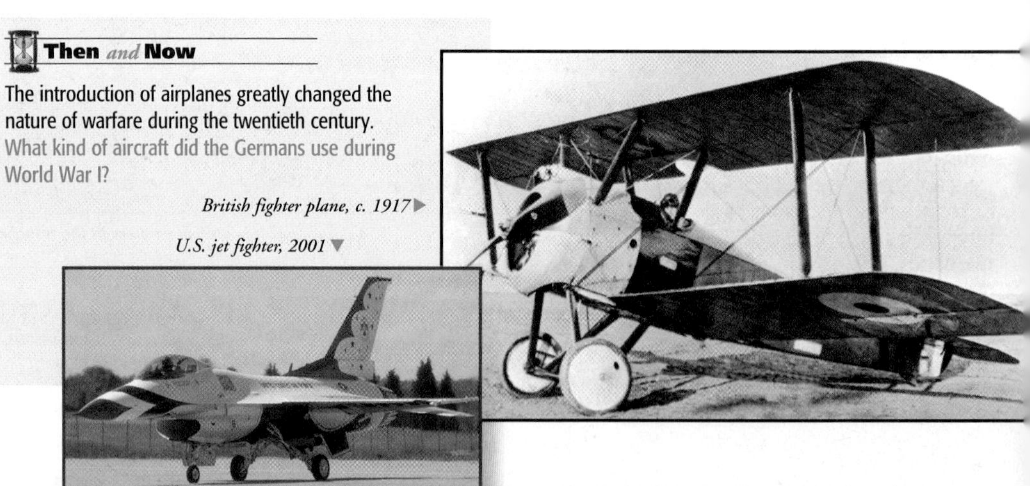

506

CRITICAL THINKING ACTIVITY

Decision Making New machines and devices were first used on a large scale during World War I. These included submarines, airplanes, tanks, motor trucks, machine guns, rapid-fire artillery, barbed wire, and poison gas. Break students into groups and ask them to complete a project (visual display, oral report, multimedia presentation) that answers the following question: What mistake did military leaders continue to make even though new technology was available? Remind students to define tasks thoroughly and to assign roles and responsibilities. After the project is complete, the group should evaluate everyone's contribution, highlighting aspects of the work that went well and suggesting ways the team might have functioned better. L2 L3

Entry of the United States

At first, the United States tried to remain neutral. As World War I dragged on, however, it became more difficult to do so. The immediate cause of United States involvement grew out of the naval war between Germany and Great Britain.

Britain had used its superior naval power to set up a naval blockade of Germany. The blockade kept war materials and other goods from reaching Germany by sea. Germany had retaliated by setting up its own blockade of Britain. Germany enforced its blockade with the use of unrestricted submarine warfare, which included the sinking of passenger liners.

On May 7, 1915, the British ship *Lusitania* was sunk by German forces. There were 1,100 civilian casualties, including over 100 Americans. After strong United States protests, the German government suspended unrestricted submarine warfare in September 1915 to avoid antagonizing the United States further. Only once did the German and British naval forces actually engage in direct battle—at the Battle of Jutland on May 31, 1916, when neither side won a conclusive victory.

Geography *Skills*

Trench warfare produced a stalemate on the Western Front.

1. **Applying Geography Skills** Create a bar graph with dates as one axis and miles as the other. Using Berlin as the starting point, plot the Central Powers advances from the earliest to the latest dates shown on the map.

By January 1917, however, the Germans were eager to break the deadlock in the war. German naval officers convinced Emperor William II that resuming the use of unrestricted submarine warfare could starve the British into submission within five months.

When the emperor expressed concern about the United States, he was told not to worry. The British would starve before the Americans could act. Even if the Americans did intervene, **Admiral Holtzendorff** assured the emperor, "I give your Majesty my word as an officer that not one American will land on the continent."

The German naval officers were quite wrong. The British were not forced to surrender, and the return to unrestricted submarine warfare brought the United States into the war in April 1917. United States troops

Geography *Skills*

Answer:

1. Students will create a graph based on the map.

CURRICULUM CONNECTION

Cartography Have students draw their own thematic maps to show the widening of the war into the Balkans, the Middle East, Africa, and Asia. Students should include an appropriate legend for their maps. Discuss reasons why military leaders sought to expand the conflict into these areas. *(Because of the stalemate in the west, both sides sought to gain strength in new allies.)*

Critical Thinking

Ask students to discuss the following sentence: "The immediate cause of U.S. involvement grew out of the naval war between Germany and Great Britain."

Critical Thinking

Ask students why the psychological impact of the United States's entry into World War I might have been greater than the actual military impact. *(The entry would have given a desperately needed morale boost to the Allies and discouraged Germany and Austria-Hungary. The opposition would have been more willing to seek a settlement.)* **L2**

MEETING INDIVIDUAL NEEDS

Auditory/Visual Encourage students needing extra reinforcement to summarize the material under each subhead in this section in a manner of their own choosing. Some students may elect to prepare oral summaries. Visual learners might draw a series of cartoons depicting such subjects as the battle, the weapons used, or trench warfare. Gifted students may use outside resources to enhance their summaries. You may wish to have students work in small groups to complete this activity. **L1** ELL

CHAPTER 16
Section 2, 503–509

Reading Check

Answer: The Germans wanted to starve Britain into submission. They believed they could accomplish that before the United States would enter the war.

3 ASSESS

Assign Section 2 Assessment as homework or as an in-class activity.

Have students use **Interactive Tutor Self-Assessment CD-ROM.**

Section Quiz 16–2

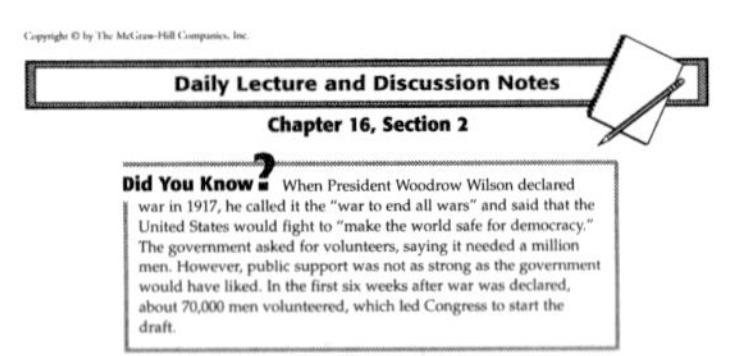

Daily Lecture and Discussion Notes

Chapter 16, Section 2

Did You Know? When President Woodrow Wilson declared war in 1917, he called it the "war to end all wars" and said that the United States would fight to "make the world safe for democracy." The government asked for volunteers, saying it needed a million men. However, public support was not as strong as the government would have liked. In the first six weeks after war was declared, about 70,000 men volunteered, which led Congress to start the draft.

I. **1914 to 1915: Illusions and Stalemate** *(pages 503–505)*

A. The events of August 1914 shattered two previously held ideas: that war was not worth fighting and that diplomats could prevent war.

B. Government **propaganda**—ideas spread to influence public opinion—had stirred up national hatreds before the war. When the war began, propaganda was used to urge people to defend their own country. The majority of people thought their country's cause was just.

C. All European wars since 1815 had only lasted a few weeks. In August, 1914, most people thought the war would be over by Christmas.

D. On the Western Front, Germany swept through Belgium into northern France and was stopped a short distance from Paris at the First Battle of the **Marne.** The Western Front turned into a stalemate, with neither side able to push the other out of the system of **trench warfare** they had begun. The trenches stretched from the English Channel nearly to the Swiss border. For four years both sides remained in almost the same positions.

E. On the Eastern Front, the war was far more mobile. The Russian army moved into eastern Germany but was defeated at the Battle of **Tannenberg** and the Battle of **Masurian Lakes,** making them no longer a threat to invade Germany. The Russians defeated Austria-Hungary and dislodged them from Serbia. The Italians, who had been allied with Germany and Austria-Hungary, broke their alliance in 1915 and attacked Austria-Hungary. The Germans came to the aid of the Austrians and together they defeated the Russians in several battles and drove them back. 2.5 million Russians had been killed, captured, or wounded. The Russians were almost out of the war. After defeating Serbia, Germany turned its attention back to the Western Front.

turn

231

Who?What?Where?When?

African American Soldiers More than 350,000 African Americans served in segregated units in World War I. Several units saw action alongside French soldiers fighting against the Germans. The French Legion of Honor was awarded to 171 African Americans.

American troops leave for war.

did not arrive in large numbers in Europe until 1918. However, the entry of the United States into the war not only gave the Allied Powers a psychological boost, but also brought them a major new source of money and war goods.

Reading Check **Evaluating** Why did the Germans resort to unrestricted submarine use?

The Home Front: The Impact of Total War

As World War I dragged on, it became a **total war,** involving a complete mobilization of resources and people. It affected the lives of all citizens in the warring countries, however remote they might be from the battlefields.

Masses of men had to be organized and supplies had to be manufactured and purchased for years of combat. (Germany alone had 5.5 million men in uniform in 1916.) This led to an increase in government powers and the manipulation of public opinion to keep the war effort going. The home front was rapidly becoming a cause for as much effort as the war front.

Increased Government Powers Most people had expected the war to be short, so little thought had been given to long-term wartime needs. Governments had to respond quickly, however, when the war machines failed to achieve their goals. Many more men and supplies were needed to continue the war. To meet these needs, governments expanded their powers. Countries drafted tens of millions of young men for that elusive breakthrough to victory.

Throughout Europe, wartime governments also expanded their power over their economies. Free-market capitalistic systems were temporarily put aside. Governments set up price, wage, and rent controls; rationed food supplies and materials; regulated imports and exports; and took over transportation systems and industries. In effect, in order to mobilize all the resources of their nations for the war effort, European nations set up **planned economies**—systems directed by government agencies.

Under conditions of total war mobilization, the differences between soldiers at war and civilians at home were narrowed. In the view of political leaders, all citizens were part of a national army dedicated to victory. As United States president **Woodrow Wilson** said, the men and women "who remain to till the soil and man the factories are no less a part of the army than the men beneath the battle flags."

Manipulation of Public Opinion As the war continued and casualties grew worse, the patriotic enthusiasm that had marked the early stages of World War I waned. By 1916, there were signs that civilian morale was beginning to crack under the pressure of total war. War governments, however, fought back against the growing opposition to the war.

Authoritarian regimes, such as those of Germany, Russia, and Austria-Hungary, relied on force to subdue their populations. Under the pressures of the war, however, even democratic states expanded their police powers to stop internal dissent. The British Parliament, for example, passed the Defence of the Realm Act (DORA). It allowed the government to arrest protestors as traitors. Newspapers were censored, and sometimes their publication was even suspended.

Wartime governments made active use of propaganda to arouse enthusiasm for the war. At the beginning, public officials needed to do little to achieve this goal. The British and French, for example, exaggerated German atrocities in Belgium and found that their citizens were only too willing to believe these accounts.

As the war progressed and morale sagged, governments were forced to devise new techniques for motivating the people. In one British recruiting poster, for example, a small daughter asked her father, "Daddy, what did YOU do in the Great War?" while her younger brother played with toy soldiers.

Total War and Women World War I created new roles for women. Because so many men left to fight at the front, women were asked to take over jobs that had not been available to them before. Women were employed in jobs that had once been considered

INTERDISCIPLINARY CONNECTIONS ACTIVITY

Sociology and Economics Have students research and report on the effects of the war on civilians. Among the subjects students might investigate are rationing, restrictions on transportation, popular entertainment, and the changing role of women. Ask students to describe the specific roles of women, children, and families during this time. Ask students to examine the economic and cultural influence of women during the time, as well. Finally, ask students to research and report on how the war was financed, with special attention to the sale of war bonds. L2

beyond their capacity. These included such occupations as chimney sweeps, truck drivers, farm laborers, and factory workers in heavy industry. For example, 38 percent of the workers in the Krupp Armaments works in Germany in 1918 were women.

The place of women in the workforce was far from secure, however. Both men and women seemed to expect that many of the new jobs for women were only temporary. This was evident in the British poem "War Girls," written in 1916:

> ❝There's the girl who clips your ticket for the train,
> And the girl who speeds the lift [elevator] from floor
> to floor,
> There's the girl who does a milk-round [milk delivery]
> in the rain,
> And the girl who calls for orders at your door.
> Strong, sensible, and fit,
> They're out to show their grit,
> And tackle jobs with energy and knack.
> No longer caged and penned up,
> They're going to keep their end up
> Till the khaki soldier boys come marching back.❞

At the end of the war, governments would quickly remove women from the jobs they had encouraged them to take earlier. The work benefits for women from World War I were short-lived as men returned to the job market. By 1919, there would be 650,000 unemployed women in Great Britain. Wages for the women who were still employed would be lowered.

Nevertheless, in some countries the role played by women in wartime economies had a positive impact on the women's movement for social and political emancipation. The most obvious gain was the right to vote, which was given to women in Germany, Austria, and the United States immediately after the war. In Britain, women had obtained this right in January 1918.

Many upper- and middle-class women had also gained new freedoms. In ever-larger numbers, young women from these groups took jobs; had their own apartments; and showed their new independence.

Reading Check **Summarizing** What was the effect of total war on ordinary citizens?

People In History

Edith Cavell
1865–1915—British nurse

Edith Cavell was born in Norfolk, England. She trained as a nurse and moved to Brussels in 1907 to head the Berkendael Medical Institute. After the outbreak of war, the institute became a Red Cross hospital. Cavell worked to shelter French and British soldiers and help them reach safety in the Netherlands.

Outraged, German military authorities in Brussels put her on trial for aiding the enemy and ordered her to be shot. Before her execution, Cavell said, "I am glad to die for my country." To arouse anti-German sentiment, both the French and British used her as an example of German barbarism. The Germans insisted they had the right to execute a traitor—whether man or woman.

SECTION 2 ASSESSMENT

Checking for Understanding

1. **Define** propaganda, trench warfare, war of attrition, total war, planned economies.
2. **Identify** Lawrence of Arabia, Admiral Holtzendorff, Woodrow Wilson.
3. **Locate** Marne, Tannenberg, Masurian Lakes, Verdun, Gallipoli.
4. **Explain** why World War I required total warfare.
5. **List** some of the occupations opened to women by the war.

Critical Thinking

6. **Identify** What methods did governments use to counter the loss of enthusiasm and opposition to the war at home?
7. **Organizing Information** Use a diagram like the one below to identify ways in which government powers increased during the war.

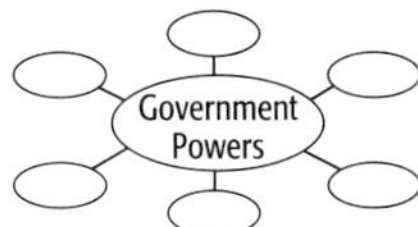

Analyzing Visuals

8. **Examine** the photograph of British soldiers shown on page 505. How does this photograph illustrate the type of warfare that emerged during World War I? What aspects of trench warfare are *not* shown in the photo?

Writing About History

9. **Expository Writing** What lasting results occurred in women's rights due to World War I? What were the temporary results? Write an essay discussing the effect of the war on women's rights.

Reading Check

Answer: Citizens were subject to rationing, propaganda, the draft, and loss of free speech. Women took jobs formerly considered beyond their capacity.

Enrich

Have students discuss the impact of World War I on the status of women. How did their acceptance, even if temporary, into occupations previously considered beyond their ability empower women to demand equal rights with men? **L2**

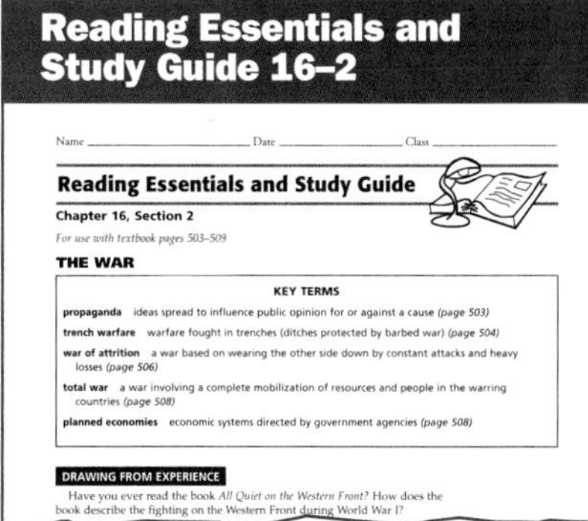
Reading Essentials and Study Guide 16–2

Name ____ Date ____ Class ____

Reading Essentials and Study Guide
Chapter 16, Section 2
For use with textbook pages 503–509

THE WAR

KEY TERMS
propaganda ideas spread to influence public opinion for or against a cause *(page 503)*
trench warfare warfare fought in trenches (ditches protected by barbed war) *(page 504)*
war of attrition a war based on wearing the other side down by constant attacks and heavy losses *(page 506)*
total war a war involving a complete mobilization of resources and people in the warring countries *(page 508)*
planned economies economic systems directed by government agencies *(page 508)*

DRAWING FROM EXPERIENCE
Have you ever read the book *All Quiet on the Western Front?* How does the book describe the fighting on the Western Front during World War I?

Reteaching Activity

Discuss the war's major events on both fronts and at sea; the effects of technological advances; the entrance of the United States into the war. **L1**

4 CLOSE

Have students summarize the situations of the Allies and the Central Powers in the spring of 1917. *(The prospect of victory was slim for both sides at this point.)*

SECTION 2 ASSESSMENT

1. Key terms are in blue.
2. Lawrence of Arabia *(p. 506)*; Admiral Holtzendorff *(p. 507)*; Woodrow Wilson *(p.508)*
3. See chapter maps.
4. Masses of men had to be organized and supplies had to be manufactured and purchased for years of combat, which led to measures that affected the lives of all citizens in the warring countries.
5. chimney sweeps, truck drivers, farm laborers, factory workers in heavy industry
6. propaganda, expanded police powers, protesters arrested, censorship
7. draft; rationing; price, wage, and rent controls; takeover of transportation; import and export regulation
8. trench warfare, waiting for next assault; the disease, death, uncomfortable conditions
9. Essays should reflect students' grasp of material.

NATIONAL GEOGRAPHIC

SPECIAL REPORT SUMMARY

In 1915, a German submarine sank the British luxury liner *Lusitania,* killing more than 1,000 people and helping draw the United States into World War I.

■

To clear up questions about the sinking, scientists used a robot vehicle to examine the wreck on the ocean floor.

■

Although the ship was carrying arms, the team found that the weapons had not exploded when a torpedo struck the *Lusitania.* This disproved a once-popular theory of why the ship sank so fast.

■

The team hypothesized that the powerful secondary explosion that caused the ship to sink in only 18 minutes was probably caused by the ignition of coal dust in a storage compartment.

TEACH

Points to Discuss

After students have read the feature, ask the following: **Why did the Germans see the *Lusitania* as a threat?** *(They believed the ship was carrying ammunition and other war materials to England.)* **Why did so many people lose their lives when the *Lusitania* sank?** *(The boat sank quickly, and the lifeboats were almost impossible to reach and board.)* **Why did the sinking of the *Lusitania* anger many Americans?** *(because sinking the unarmed passenger vessel*

THE LUSITANIA

1

Passengers boarding the British liner *R.M.S. Lusitania* in New York on May 1, 1915, for the voyage to Liverpool, England, knew of Germany's threat to sink ships bound for the British Isles. Britain and Germany had been fighting for nine months. Still, few passengers imagined that a civilized nation would attack an unarmed passenger steamer without warning.

Built eight years earlier, the *Lusitania* was described as a "floating palace." German authorities, however, saw her as a threat. They accused the British government of using the *Lusitania* to carry ammunition and other war supplies across the Atlantic.

With her four towering funnels, the liner looked invincible as she left New York on her last voyage. Six days later, at 2:10 P.M. on May 7, 1915, Walther Schwieger, the 30-year-old commander of the German submarine U 20, fired a single torpedo at the *Lusitania* from a range of about 750 yards (686 m).

Captain William Turner of the *Lusitania* saw the torpedo's wake from the navigation bridge just before impact. It sounded like a "million-ton hammer hitting a steam boiler a hundred feet high," one passenger said. A second, more powerful explosion followed, sending a geyser of water, coal, and debris high above the deck.

Listing to starboard, the liner began to sink rapidly at the bow, sending passengers tumbling down her slanted decks. Lifeboats on the port side were hanging too far inboard to be readily launched, those on the starboard side too far out to be easily boarded. Several overfilled lifeboats spilled occupants into the sea. The great liner disappeared under the waves in only 18 minutes, leaving behind a jumble of swimmers, corpses, deck chairs, and wreckage. Looking back upon the scene from his submarine, even the German commander Schwieger was shocked. He later called it the most horrible sight he had ever seen.

2

2

Teacher's Notes

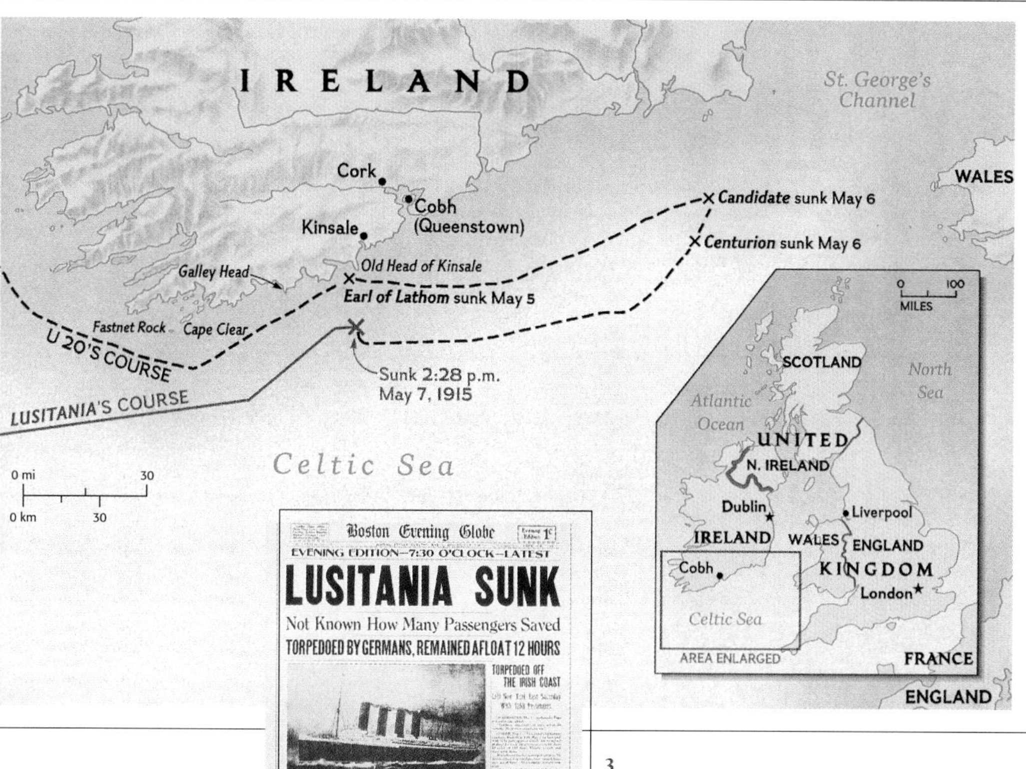

Boston Evening Globe

EVENING EDITION—7:30 O'CLOCK—LATEST

LUSITANIA SUNK

Not Known How Many Passengers Saved

TORPEDOED BY GERMANS, REMAINED AFLOAT 12 HOURS

TORPEDOED OFF THE IRISH COAST

3

News of the disaster raced across the Atlantic. Of 1,959 people aboard, only 764 were saved. The dead included 94 children and infants.

Questions were immediately raised. Did the British Admiralty give the *Lusitania* adequate warning? How could one torpedo have sunk her? Why did she go down so fast? Was there any truth to the German claim that the *Lusitania* had been armed?

From the moment the *Lusitania* sank, she was surrounded by controversy. Americans were outraged by the attack, which claimed the lives of 123 U.S. citizens. Newspapers called the attack "deliberate murder" and a "foul deed," and former President Theodore Roosevelt demanded revenge against Germany. The attack on the *Lusitania* is often credited with drawing the United States into World War I. However, President Woodrow Wilson—though he had vowed to hold Germany responsible for its submarine attacks—knew that the American people were not ready to go to war. It was almost two years before the United States joined the conflict in Europe.

A British judge laid full blame on the German submarine commander, while the German government claimed that the British had deliberately made her a military target. Tragically, inquiries following the sinking of the *Lusitania* revealed that Captain Turner had received warnings by wireless from the British Admiralty,

1 **The *Lusitania* arrives in New York on her maiden voyage in 1907 (opposite page).**

2 **Captain William Turner of the *Lusitania*, (opposite page, center); Walther Schwieger, commander of the German submarine U 20 (opposite page, right).**

3 **Headlines in Boston and New York (above) report the terrible news of the sinking of the *Lusitania* on May 7, 1915. In the two days prior to the attack on the *Lusitania*, the German submarine U 20 had sunk three ships off Ireland's southern coast. Yet the captain of the *Lusitania*, who had received warnings by wireless from the British Admiralty, took only limited precautions as he approached the area.**

killed more than 1,000 civilians, including 128 Americans) **What questions were raised about the sinking?** *(Was the ship warned about German submarines? Why did one torpedo sink it so fast? Was it armed, as Germany claimed? What caused a second explosion?)* **How do British and German accounts of responsibility for the sinking of the ship differ?** *(A British judge claimed Germany was completely responsible. The German government claimed that the British had purposely made the ship a target.)*

Enrich

Ask students to evaluate the political choices and decisions made by Britain, Germany, and the United States in regard to the *Lusitania.* Be sure students take into account the historical context. Then ask students to apply this knowledge to the analysis of choices and decisions faced by societies today. Students should use current news media for the second part of this activity. **L3**

FUN FACTS

- Woodrow Wilson's secretary of state, William Jennings Bryan, resigned rather than sign a strongly worded protest Wilson sent to Germany after the *Lusitania's* sinking.
- The name of the ship came from the ancient Roman province of Lusitania, which made up the region that is now Portugal and western Spain.
- The cargo of arms and ammunition that the *Lusitania* was carrying weighed about 173 tons.
- The British admiralty had recommended that the *Lusitania* follow a zigzag course, changing direction every few minutes, to avoid torpedo attacks.

CURRICULUM CONNECTION

Science and Technology The first submarine to be used in combat was built by an American, David Bushnell, in 1776 and was used during the Revolutionary War. It was made of wood and moved by means of a hand-turned propeller. (The craft was used in an unsuccessful attempt to blow up a British warship in New York harbor.) By the late 1800s, an American engineer named Simon Lake had made considerable advances in submarine technology, including the use of horizontal rudders for diving and water ballast for submergence. The U.S. Navy was slow to see the merits of Lake's work. In the early 1900s, however, Lake was hired by the United States.

Connecting to the Past

In recent years a number of wrecked ships have been raised from the ocean bottom by scientists and entrepreneurs. The salvage operations have generated controversy about the ownership of the materials recovered, which can be worth millions of dollars.

Among the better-known cases are the Padre Island wrecks in Texas and the case of *Nuestra Señora de la Atocha* in Florida.

but took only limited precautions as he approached the area where the U 20 was waiting.

Rumors of diamonds, gold, and valuables locked away in *Lusitania's* safes have prompted salvage attempts over the years. To date, no treasure has ever been reported.

Perhaps the biggest puzzle has been the hardest to solve: Why did the liner sink so fast? Newspapers speculated that the torpedo had struck munitions in a cargo hold, causing the strong secondary explosion. Divers later reported a huge hole in the port side of the bow, opposite where munitions would have been stored.

■

Hoping to settle the issue, a team from the Woods Hole Oceanographic Institution, sponsored by the National Geographic Society, sent their robot vehicle Jason down to photograph the damage. Fitted with cameras and powerful lights, the robot sent video images of the wreck by fiber-optic cable to a control room on the surface ship, *Northern Horizon*. A pilot maneuvered Jason with a joystick, while an engineer relayed instructions to the robot's computers. Other team members watched for recognizable objects on the monitors. In addition to using Jason to make a visual survey of the *Lusitania*, the team of researchers and scientists also used sonar to create a computerized, three-dimensional diagram of how the wreck looks today.

From this data, it was discovered that the *Lusitania's* hull had been flattened—in part by the force of gravity—to half its original width. But when Jason's cameras swept across the hold, looking for the hole reported by divers shortly after the sinking, there was none to be found. Indeed, no evidence was found that would indicate that the torpedo had detonated an explosion in a cargo hold, undermi[ning] one theory of why the liner san[k].

Questions about her cargo have haunted the *Lusitania* since the day she went down. Was she carrying il[le]gal munitions as the Germans have always claimed? In fact, she was. Th[e] manifest for her last voyage include[d] wartime essentials such as motorcyc[le] parts, metals, cotton goods, and foo[d] as well as 4,200 cases of rifle ammu[ni]tion, 1,250 cases of shrapnel (not explosive), and 18 boxes of percussi[on] fuses. However, the investigation co[n]ducted by the Woods Hole team an[d] Jason suggested that these munition[s] did not cause the secondary blast th[at] sent the *Lusitania* to the bottom. So what did?

One likely possibility was a coal-dust explosion. The German torpe[do] struck the liner's starboard side abou[t] 10 feet (3 m) below the waterline, rupturing one of the long coal

4

CRITICAL THINKING ACTIVITY

Ask students to review the maps in this feature and throughout this chapter. Then have students create a thematic database from the information contained on the maps. Students should interpret the database by posing and answering questions about geographic distributions and patterns in world history as revealed by information contained in the database. Make sure that students use appropriate mathematical skills to interpret the information on the maps. L2

5

6

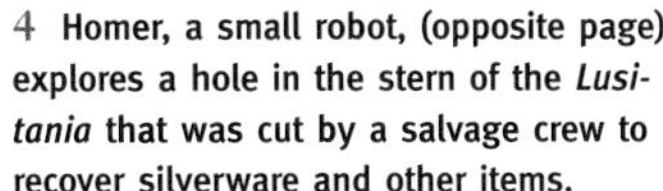

4 Homer, a small robot, (opposite page) explores a hole in the stern of the *Lusitania* that was cut by a salvage crew to recover silverware and other items.

5 A provocative poster (left) depicted drowning innocents and urged Americans to enlist in the armed forces.

6 Alice Drury (above left) was a young nanny for an American couple on the *Lusitania*. She and another nanny were caring for the couple's children: Audrey (above right), Stuart, Amy, and Susan. Alice was about to give Audrey a bottle when the torpedo hit. Alice wrapped Audrey in a shawl, grabbed Stuart, and headed for the lifeboats. A crewman loaded Stuart, but when Alice tried to board, the sailor told her it was full. Without a life jacket and with Audrey around her neck, Alice jumped into the water. A woman in the lifeboat grabbed her hair and pulled her aboard. Audrey's parents were rescued too, but Amy, Susan, and the other nanny were lost. Alice and Audrey Lawson Johnston have remained close ever since.

bunkers [storage bins] that stretched along both sides. If that bunker, mostly empty by the end of the voyage, contained explosive coal dust, the torpedo might have ignited it. Such an occurrence would explain all the coal that was found scattered on the seafloor near the wreck.

The *Lusitania's* giant funnels have long since turned to rust, an eerie marine growth covers her hull, and her superstructure is ghostly wreckage. Yet the horror and fascination surrounding the sinking of the great liner live on. With today's high-technology tools, researchers and scientists at Woods Hole and the National Geographic Society have provided another look—and some new answers—to explain the chain of events that ended with the *Lusitania* at the bottom of the sea.

INTERPRETING THE PAST

1. How did the *Lusitania* contribute to drawing the United States into World War I?

2. Describe the *Lusitania's* route. Where was it when it sank?

3. What mysteries were researchers able to solve by using underwater robot technology?

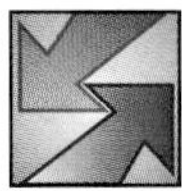

CURRICULUM CONNECTION

Geography Have students study the map on page 511. How far was the *Lusitania* from the Irish coast when it was sunk? *(about 10 miles [16 km])* How far apart were the two ships sunk by the U 20 on May 6, 1915? *(about 10 miles [16 km])* What was the approximate distance between Ireland and Wales? *(about 50 miles [81 km])*

Who?What?Where?When?

German U-Boat Attacks After the sinking of the *Lusitania*, German submarines continued to torpedo merchant vessels without warning. In March 1916, fearing the United States would enter the war, Germany stopped the attacks. With the war stalemated, however, Germany resumed unrestricted submarine attacks in February 1917, sinking four American ships in just two months. Wilson cited German violations of "freedom of the seas" as a reason for entering the war in April 1917.

INTERPRETING THE PAST

Answers:

1. Americans were outraged by this action by the Germans against a civilian target.
2. The *Lusitania* was traveling from New York City, across the Atlantic Ocean, and then along the southern coast of Ireland en route to Liverpool (on the western coast), England. The *Lusitania* was sunk off the southern coast of Ireland.
3. Researchers were able to determine that weapons carried by the *Lusitania* had not exploded, and they hypothesized that the second explosion was caused by the ignition of coal dust.

1 FOCUS

Section Overview

This section discusses the fall of Czar Nicholas II in Russia and the ensuing Russian Revolution, which put the Communists in power.

BELLRINGER
Skillbuilder Activity

Project transparency and have students answer questions.

Available as a blackline master.

Daily Focus Skills Transparency 16–3

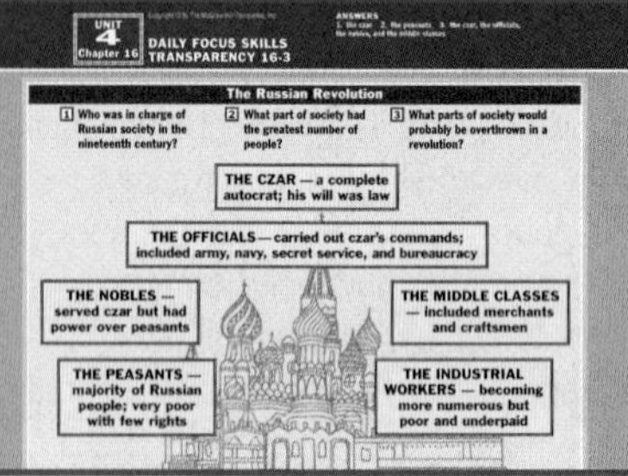
UNIT 4 Chapter 16
DAILY FOCUS SKILLS TRANSPARENCY 16-3

The Russian Revolution

1 Who was in charge of Russian society in the nineteenth century?
2 What part of society had the greatest number of people?
3 What parts of society would probably be overthrown in a revolution?

THE CZAR — a complete autocrat; his will was law
THE OFFICIALS — carried out czar's commands; included army, navy, secret service, and bureaucracy
THE NOBLES — served czar but had power over peasants
THE MIDDLE CLASSES — included merchants and craftsmen
THE PEASANTS — majority of Russian people; very poor with few rights
THE INDUSTRIAL WORKERS — becoming more numerous but poor and underpaid

Guide to Reading

Answers to Graphic: strikes by working class women, workers, and soldiers → provisional government established → czarist regime falls Germans ship Lenin back to Russia → Bolsheviks use soviets to overthrow Provisional Government

Preteaching Vocabulary: Ask students to define *soviet* and discuss it with the class. L2

SECTION 3 The Russian Revolution

Guide to Reading

Main Ideas
- The czarist regime in Russia fell as a result of poor leadership.
- The Bolsheviks under Lenin came to power.
- Communist forces triumphed over anti-Communist forces.

Key Terms
soviets, war communism

People to Identify
Alexandra, Grigori Rasputin, Alexander Kerensky, V. I. Lenin, Leon Trotsky

Places to Locate
Petrograd, Ukraine, Siberia, Urals

Preview Questions
1. After Lenin's arrival in Russia, what promises did the Bolsheviks make to the Russian people?
2. Why did civil war break out in Russia after the Russian Revolution?

Reading Strategy
Categorizing Information Using a chart like the one below, identify the factors and events that led to Lenin coming to power in 1917.

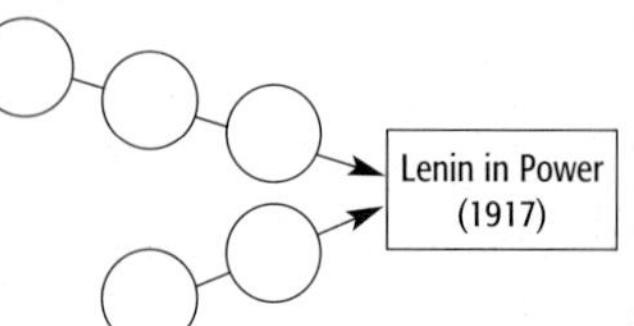

Preview of Events

1916 · 1917 · 1918 · 1919 · 1920 · 1921

- **1916** Rasputin assassinated
- **1917** Czar Nicholas II steps down
- **1918** Lenin signs Treaty of Brest-Litovsk
- **1921** Communists control Russia

Voices from the Past

John Reed

John Reed, an American journalist, described an important event that took place in St. Petersburg, Russia, on the night of November 6, 1917:

“After a few minutes huddling there, some hundreds of men began again to flow forward. By this time, in the light that streamed out of the Winter Palace windows, I could see that the first two or three hundred men were Red Guards [revolutionaries], with only a few scattered soldiers. Over the barricade of firewood we clambered, and leaping down inside gave a triumphant shout as we stumbled on a heap of rifles thrown down by the guards who had stood there. On both sides of the main gateway the doors stood wide open, and from the huge pile came not the slightest sound.”

—***Eyewitness to History,*** **John Carey, ed., 1987**

Reed was describing the Bolshevik seizure of the Winter Palace, seat of the Russian Government, by Bolshevik revolutionaries. This act led to a successful revolution in Russia.

Background to Revolution

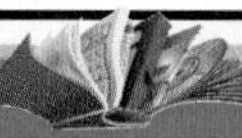

As you will learn, out of Russia's collapse in 1917 came the Russian Revolution. Its impact would be felt all over the world.

After its defeat by Japan in 1905 and the Revolution of 1905, Russia was unprepared both militarily and technologically for the total war of World War I. Russia

SECTION RESOURCES

Reproducible Masters
- Reproducible Lesson Plan 16–3
- Daily Lecture and Discussion Notes 16–3
- Guided Reading Activity 16–3
- Section Quiz 16–3
- Reading Essentials and Study Guide 16–3

Transparencies
- Daily Focus Skills Transparency 16–3

Multimedia
- Interactive Tutor Self-Assessment CD-ROM
- ExamView® Pro Testmaker CD-ROM
- Presentation Plus! CD-ROM

Picturing History

Rasputin (shown upper right corner) had great influence over Czar Nicholas II and his family, shown here in a 1913 photograph. Why was Rasputin able to influence Russian political affairs?

had no competent military leaders. Czar Nicholas II insisted on taking charge of the armed forces despite his lack of training.

In addition, Russian industry was unable to produce the weapons needed for the army. Many soldiers trained using broomsticks. Others were sent to the front without rifles and told to pick one up from a dead comrade.

Given these conditions, it is not surprising that the Russian army suffered incredible losses. Between 1914 and 1916, two million soldiers were killed, and another four to six million wounded or captured. By 1917, the Russian will to fight had vanished.

Beginnings of Upheaval Czar Nicholas II was an autocratic ruler who relied on the army and bureaucracy to hold up his regime. Furthermore, he was increasingly cut off from events by his German-born wife, **Alexandra.** She was a willful and stubborn woman who had fallen under the influence of **Grigori Rasputin** (ra•SPYOO•tuhn), an uneducated Siberian peasant who claimed to be a holy man. Alexandra believed that Rasputin was holy, for he alone seemed able to stop the bleeding of her son Alexis. Alexis, the heir to the throne, had hemophilia (a deficiency in the ability of the blood to clot).

With the czar at the battlefront, Alexandra made all of the important decisions. She insisted on first consulting Rasputin, the man she called "her beloved, never-to-be-forgotten teacher, savior, and mentor." Rasputin's influence made him an important power behind the throne. He did not hesitate to interfere in government affairs.

As the leadership at the top stumbled its way through a series of military and economic disasters, the Russian people grew more and more upset with the czarist regime. Even conservative aristocrats who supported the monarchy felt the need to do something to save the situation.

For a start, they assassinated Rasputin in December 1916. It was not easy to kill this man of incredible physical strength. They shot him three times and then tied him up and threw him into the Neva River. He drowned, but not before he had managed to untie the knots underwater. The killing of Rasputin occurred too late, however, to save the monarchy.

The March Revolution At the beginning of March 1917, a series of strikes led by working-class women broke out in the capital city of **Petrograd** (formerly St. Petersburg). A few weeks earlier, the government had started bread rationing in Petrograd after the price of bread had skyrocketed.

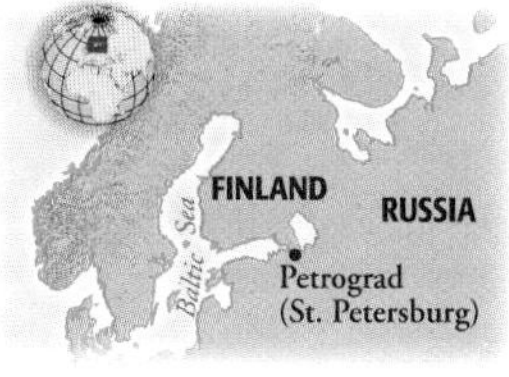

Many of the women who stood in the lines waiting for bread were also factory workers who worked 12-hour days. A police report warned the government:

> "Mothers of families, exhausted by endless standing in line at stores, distraught over their half-starving and sick children, are today perhaps closer to revolution than [the liberal opposition leaders] and of course they are a great deal more dangerous because they are the combustible material for which only a single spark is needed to burst into flame."

CHAPTER 16
Section 3, 514–519

2 TEACH

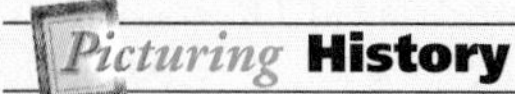

Picturing History

Answer: Alexandra believed that Rasputin was a holy man who could stop her son's bleeding, and this belief gave Rasputin influence at court.

Daily Lecture and Discussion Notes 16–3

Daily Lecture and Discussion Notes

Chapter 16, Section 3

Did You Know? Vladimir Ilyich Ulianov (V.I. Lenin) was born in 1870 to a middle class family. He was educated and became a lawyer. In 1887, his older brother was executed by the czarist police for planning to assassinate the czar. This event turned Lenin into a revolutionary, and he dedicated his life to overthrowing the czar.

I. **Background to Revolution** *(pages 514–516)*

A. Due to a lack of experienced military leaders and technology, Russia was unprepared for World War I. The Russian army was poorly trained and equipped and suffered terrible losses.

B. By 1917, the Russian will to continue fighting in the war had disappeared.

C. Czar Nicholas II relied on his army and government to keep him in power. His wife **Alexandra** cut him off from events. She was strongly influenced by **Grigori Rasputin,** who claimed to be a holy man. Though he had no military experience, Czar Nicholas II insisted on commanding the army in the field and was away from the capital. In his absence, Alexandra made important decisions with the help of Rasputin.

D. The Russian people became increasingly upset with the czar and his wife due to military and economic disasters. Conservatives wanted to save the deteriorating situation and assassinated Rasputin late in 1916. However, this did not save the monarchy.

E. In March 1917, working-class women led a series of strikes in the capital city of **Petrograd.** They were upset about bread shortages and rationing. They called a general strike that shut down all the factories.

F. Alexandra reported the situation to Nicholas, describing the demonstrators as hooligans. Nicholas responded by ordering troops to break up the crowds with force. However, many soldiers refused to shoot and joined the demonstrators. On March 12, the Duma, or legislature, met and established a provisional government. The government then urged the czar to step down, which he did.

G. The provisional government was headed by **Alexander Kerensky** and decided to continue fighting the war. This was a grave mistake, as it upset workers and peasants who wanted to end the years of fighting.

H. The government was also challenged by the **soviets**—councils representing workers and soldiers—who came to play an important role in Russian politics. Soviets sprang up around the country, and were mostly made up of socialists.

235

Critical Thinking

Ask students to research and analyze further how Rasputin's interference in Russia's political affairs contributed to the undermining of the czarist government. L2

COOPERATIVE LEARNING ACTIVITY

Creating a Presentation Divide students into four groups and assign each group a major figure in the Russian Revolution: Czar Nicholas II, Rasputin, Lenin, and Trotsky. Have each group research its assigned individual. Students should include his background, education, beliefs, and role in the revolution. Students should divide up the research appropriately and combine their findings to prepare a written or oral report to present to the class. If possible, the report should be accompanied by illustrations. Following the presentations, students should analyze the influence of each of these individuals on political events of the twentieth century. L2

Reading Check

Answer: The Russian army suffered incredible losses in the war. Nicholas II's wife made decisions under the influence of Rasputin; then came a series of military and economic disasters. At the beginning of March 1917, strikes led by working-class women broke out in Petrograd, which developed into a general strike. Large numbers of the soldiers joined the demonstrators. The Duma met and established a provisional government. Nicholas II stepped down on March 15.

Answer: One reason may have been to obtain the Romanov wealth.

Guided Reading Activity 16–3

Name ________ Date ________ Class ________

Guided Reading Activity 16-3

The Russian Revolution

DIRECTIONS: Fill in the blanks below as you read Section 3.

I. Russia was ________ for the total war of World War I.
A. ________ was increasingly cut off from events by his wife.
B. In March 1917, a series of strikes led by ________ started in Petrograd.
C. Nicholas ordered troops to break up crowds by ________ if necessary.
D. A socialist group, the ________ represented the radical interests of lower classes.
II. The Bolsheviks were a ________ party called the Russian Social Democrats.
A. The Bolsheviks came under the leadership of V.I. ________
1. They became a party dedicated to ________ revolution.

CURRICULUM CONNECTION

Literature Have students research and report on one of the following: Maksim Gorky, a champion of the revolutionary movement in Russia; Alexander Blok, who wrote "The Twelve," a poem about the revolution; or Vladimir Mayakovski, a poet who popularized the revolution. L3

On March 8, about 10,000 women marched through the city of Petrograd demanding "Peace and Bread" and "Down with Autocracy." Soon the women were joined by other workers. Together they called for a general strike. The strike shut down all the factories in the city on March 10.

Web Activity Visit the *Glencoe World History—Modern Times* Web site at wh.mt.glencoe.com and click on **Chapter 16–Student Web Activity** to learn more about the Russian royal family.

Alexandra wrote her husband Nicholas II at the battlefront, "This is a hooligan movement. If the weather were very cold they would all probably stay at home." Nicholas ordered troops to break up the crowds by shooting them if necessary. Soon, however, large numbers of the soldiers joined the demonstrators and refused to fire on the crowds.

The Duma, or legislative body, which the czar had tried to dissolve, met anyway. On March 12, it established the provisional government, which mainly consisted of middle-class Duma representatives. This government urged the czar to step down. Because he no longer had the support of the army or even the aristocrats, Nicholas II did step down, on March 15, ending the 300-year-old Romanov dynasty.

The provisional government, headed by **Alexander Kerensky** (keh•REHN•skee), now decided to carry on the war to preserve Russia's honor. This decision to remain in World War I was a major blunder. It satisfied neither the workers nor the peasants, who, tired and angry from years of suffering, wanted above all an end to the war.

The government was also faced with a challenge to its authority—the **soviets.** The soviets were councils composed of representatives from the workers and soldiers. The soviet of Petrograd had been formed in March 1917. At the same time, soviets sprang up in army units, factory towns, and rural areas. The soviets, largely made up of socialists, represented the more radical interests of the lower classes. One group—the Bolsheviks—came to play a crucial role.

Reading Check **Identifying** Develop a sequence of events leading to the March Revolution.

CONNECTIONS Past To Present

The Mystery of Anastasia

Czar Nicholas II, his wife Alexandra, and their five children were murdered on the night of July 16, 1918. Soon after, rumors began to circulate that some members of the family had survived.

In 1921, a young woman in Dalldorf, Germany, claimed to be the Grand Duchess Anastasia, youngest daughter of Nicholas II. Some surviving members of the Romanov family became convinced that she was Anastasia. Grand Duke Andrew, Nicholas II's first cousin, said after meeting with her, "For me there is definitely no doubt; it is Anastasia."

Later, the woman claiming to be Anastasia came to the United States. While in New York, she registered at a Long Island hotel as Anna Anderson and soon became known by that name. In 1932, she returned to Germany. During the next 30 years, she pursued a claim in German courts for part of the estate left to Empress Alexandra's German relatives. In the 1960s in the United States, she became even better known as a result of a popular play and film, *Anastasia.*

In 1968, Anna Anderson returned to the United States, where she died in 1984. In 1994, DNA testing of tissues from Anna Anderson revealed that she was not the Grand Duchess Anastasia. In all probability, Anna Anderson was Franziska Schanzkowska, a Polish farmer's daughter who had always dreamed of being an actress.

▲ *Grand Duchess Anastasia*

◀ *Anna Anderson*

Comparing Past and Present

The woman claiming to be Anastasia convinced many people of the authenticity of her claim. What do you think might have motivated her to act out the part of Anastasia for so many years?

EXTENDING THE CONTENT

Health As if the world war, revolution, and civil war were not devastating enough to the Russian people, an even greater danger appeared in the form of lice. Lice carry *Rickettsia* bacteria, which causes typhus. During the war years, between 1914 and 1916, the typhus outbreak on the Eastern Front was serious (there were no similar outbreaks on the Western Front due to the use of fumigants). After the revolution of 1917, Russia experienced the worst typhus epidemic in history. Between 1917 and 1921, over 25 million Russians came down with typhus and more than 2.5 million died. Ask students to compare this typhus epidemic with the fourteenth-century plague and identify any contemporary situations that parallel these historical situations.

Russian Revolution and Civil War, 1917–1922

Geography *Skills*

The Russian Revolution and civil war resulted in significant changes to Russia's boundaries.

1. **Interpreting Maps** Compare the area of Russia under Bolshevik control in 1919 with the area *not* under Bolshevik control. Which is larger? Which contained Russia's main cities?
2. **Applying Geography Skills** Pose two questions for your classmates to determine whether or not they can describe the changes in Russia's boundaries resulting from the Russian Revolution and World War I.

The Rise of Lenin

The **Bolsheviks** began as a small faction of a Marxist party called the Russian Social Democrats. The Bolsheviks came under the leadership of Vladimir Ilyich Ulianov (ool•YAH•nuhf), known to the world as **V. I. Lenin.**

Under Lenin's direction, the Bolsheviks became a party dedicated to violent revolution. Lenin believed that only violent revolution could destroy the capitalist system. A "vanguard" (forefront) of activists, he said, must form a small party of well-disciplined professional revolutionaries to accomplish the task.

Between 1900 and 1917, Lenin spent most of his time in Switzerland. When the provisional government was formed in March 1917, he saw an opportunity for the Bolsheviks to seize power. In April 1917, German military leaders, hoping to create disorder in Russia, shipped Lenin to Russia. Lenin and his associates were in a sealed train to prevent their ideas from infecting Germany.

Lenin's arrival in Russia opened a new stage of the Russian Revolution. Lenin maintained that the soviets of soldiers, workers, and peasants were ready-made instruments of power. He believed that the Bolsheviks should work toward gaining control of these groups and then use them to overthrow the provisional government.

At the same time, the Bolsheviks reflected the discontent of the people. They promised an end to the war, the redistribution of all land to the peasants, the transfer of factories and industries from capitalists to committees of workers, and the transfer of government power from the provisional government to the soviets. Three simple slogans summed up the Bolshevik program: "Peace, Land, Bread," "Worker Control of Production," and "All Power to the Soviets."

Reading Check **Examining** What was Lenin's plan when he arrived in Russia?

Geography *Skills*

Answers:

1. area not under Bolshevik control is larger, but area under Bolshevik control contained main cities
2. Questions and answers will vary.

Reading Check

Answer: to gain control of the soviets of soldiers, workers, and peasants and use them to overthrow the provisional government

Critical Thinking

Have students research and analyze the three Bolshevik slogans: "Peace, Land, Bread," "Worker Control of Production," and "All Power to the Soviets." Which did Lenin attempt to address? Which were strictly propaganda? What is the appeal of these slogans? L2

Turning Points in World History
The ABC News videotape includes a segment on the Russian Revolution.

Writing Activity

Have students write an essay in which they identify and explain the causes and effects of the rise of communism on the Soviet Union. L3

INTERDISCIPLINARY CONNECTIONS ACTIVITY

Art Have students use the Internet or library to research Communist propaganda posters from this period. Ask them to write a brief report analyzing at least one of the posters. Students should consider the following questions: What can be learned by examining the poster? What message is the poster trying to convey? Does the poster elicit an emotional response? How do the images in the poster portray Communist ideology and values? Students' reports should include a copy of the poster, and reports can be presented orally to the class. L2

The Bolsheviks Seize Power

By the end of October, Bolsheviks made up a slight majority in the Petrograd and Moscow soviets. The number of party members had grown from 50,000 to 240,000. With Leon Trotsky, a dedicated revolutionary, as head of the Petrograd soviet, the Bolsheviks were in a position to claim power in the name of the soviets. During the night of November 6, Bolshevik forces seized the Winter Palace, the seat of the provisional government. The government quickly collapsed with little bloodshed.

V. I. Lenin

This overthrow of the provisional government coincided with a meeting in Petrograd of the all-Russian Congress of Soviets, which represented local soviets from all over the country. Outwardly, Lenin turned over the power of the provisional government to the Congress of Soviets. The real power, however, passed to a Council of People's Commissars, headed by Lenin.

The Bolsheviks, who soon renamed themselves the Communists, still had a long way to go. Lenin had promised peace, and that, he realized, would not be an easy task. It would mean the humiliating loss of much Russian territory. There was no real choice, however.

On March 3, 1918, Lenin signed the Treaty of Brest-Litovsk with Germany and gave up eastern Poland, **Ukraine,** Finland, and the Baltic provinces. To his critics, Lenin argued that it made no difference. The spread of the socialist revolution throughout Europe would make the treaty largely irrelevant. In any case, he had promised peace to the Russian people. Real peace did not come, however, because the country soon sank into civil war.

Reading Check **Describing** What was the impact of the Treaty of Brest-Litovsk on Russia?

Civil War in Russia

Many people were opposed to the new Bolshevik, or Communist, regime. These people included not only groups loyal to the czar but also liberals and anti-Leninist socialists. These groups were joined by the Allies, who were extremely concerned about the Communist takeover. The Allies sent thousands of troops to various parts of Russia in the hope of bringing Russia back into the war. The Allied forces rarely fought on Russian soil, but they did give material aid to anti-Communist forces.

Between 1918 and 1921, the Communist (Red) Army was forced to fight on many fronts against these opponents. The first serious threat to the Communists came from **Siberia.** Here an anti-Communist (White) force attacked westward and advanced almost to the Volga River before being stopped.

Attacks also came from the Ukrainians in the southeast and from the Baltic regions. In mid-1919, White forces swept through Ukraine and advanced almost to Moscow before being pushed back.

By 1920, however, the major White forces had been defeated and Ukraine retaken. The next year, the Communist regime regained control over the independent nationalist governments in Georgia, Russian Armenia, and Azerbaijan (A•zuhr•BY•JAHN).

The royal family was another victim of the civil war. After the czar abdicated, he, his wife, and their five children had been taken into captivity. In April 1918, they were moved to Ekaterinburg, a mining town in the **Urals.** On the night of July 16, members of the local soviet murdered the czar and his family and burned their bodies in a nearby mine shaft.

Reading Check **Identifying** Who opposed the new Bolshevik regime?

Triumph of the Communists

How had Lenin and the Communists triumphed in the civil war over what seemed to be overwhelming forces? One reason was that the Red Army was a well-disciplined fighting force. This was largely due to the organizational genius of **Leon Trotsky.** As commissar of war, Trotsky reinstated the draft and insisted on rigid discipline. Soldiers who deserted or refused to obey orders were executed on the spot.

Furthermore, the disunity of the anti-Communist forces weakened their efforts. Political differences created distrust among the Whites and prevented them from cooperating effectively with one another. Some Whites insisted on restoring the czarist regime. Others believed that only a more liberal and democratic program had any chance of success.

Reading Check

Answer: Russia gained peace but lost eastern Poland, Ukraine, Finland, and the Baltic provinces.

Reading Check

Answer: groups loyal to the czar, liberals, anti-Leninist socialists, Communist White Russians, Allied forces, and Ukrainians

Writing Activity

Ask students to write an essay in which they identify the historic origins of the economic systems of capitalism and socialism. Then have students identify the historical origins of the economic and political system of communism. Finally, ask students to state the reasons for the Communist victory in the Russian civil war. L3

3 ASSESS

Assign Section 3 Assessment as homework or as an in-class activity.

Have students use **Interactive Tutor Self-Assessment CD-ROM.**

Section Quiz 16–3

Name ______ Date ______ Class ______

Chapter 16 Score

Section Quiz 16-3

DIRECTIONS: Matching Match each item in Column A with an item in Column B. Write the correct letters in the blanks. *(10 points each)*

Column A	Column B
____ 1. Russian legislative body in 1917	A. Trotsky
____ 2. representative councils of workers and soldiers	B. Duma
____ 3. small faction of the Russian Social Democrat Party	C. soviets
____ 4. Red Army's commissar	D. war communism
____ 5. temporary suspension of communist practices	E. Bolsheviks

DIRECTIONS: Multiple Choice In the blank, write the letter of the choice that best completes the statement or answers the question. *(10 points each)*

____ 6. Russia was unprepared for war in all of the following ways EXCEPT one. Which one?

COOPERATIVE LEARNING ACTIVITY

Creating a Chart Organize the class into three groups. Have one group create a chart identifying the causes and evaluating the effects of the English, American, French, and Russian Revolutions. The second group will create a chart summarizing the ideas from the same revolutions concerning separation of powers, liberty, equality, democracy, popular sovereignty, human rights, constitutionalism, nationalism, capitalism, socialism, and communism. The third group will identify and explain the causes and effects of World War I. Have groups share their information, and have all students write a summary of this information. L2

For grading this activity, refer to the ***Performance Assessment Activities*** booklet.

Picturing **History**

The Red Army is shown here marching through Moscow. Between 1918 and 1921, the Communist (Red) Army faced resistance from both the Allies and the anti-Communist (White) forces. Who was the Communist commissar of war during this period?

The Whites, then, had no common goal. The Communists, in contrast, had a single-minded sense of purpose. Inspired by their vision of a new socialist order, the Communists had the determination that comes from revolutionary zeal and convictions.

The Communists were also able to translate their revolutionary faith into practical instruments of power. A policy of **war communism**, for example, was used to ensure regular supplies for the Red Army. War communism meant government control of banks and most industries, the seizing of grain from peasants, and the centralization of state administration under Communist control.

Another Communist instrument was revolutionary terror. A new Red secret police—known as the Cheka—began a Red Terror aimed at the destruction of all those who opposed the new regime (much like the Reign of Terror in the French Revolution). The Red Terror added an element of fear to the Communist regime.

Finally, the presence of foreign armies on Russian soil enabled the Communists to appeal to the powerful force of Russian patriotism. At one point, over a hundred thousand foreign troops—mostly Japanese, British, American, and French—were stationed in Russia in support of anti-Communist forces. Their presence made it easy for the Communist government to call on patriotic Russians to fight foreign attempts to control the country.

By 1921, the Communists were in total command of Russia. In the course of the civil war, the Communist regime had transformed Russia into a centralized state dominated by a single party. The state was also largely hostile to the Allied powers, because the Allies had tried to help the Communists' enemies in the civil war.

Reading Check **Contrasting** Why did the Red Army prevail over the White Army?

SECTION 3 ASSESSMENT

Checking for Understanding

1. **Define** soviets, war communism.
2. **Identify** Alexandra, Grigori Rasputin, Alexander Kerensky, Bolsheviks, V.I. Lenin, Leon Trotsky.
3. **Locate** Petrograd, Ukraine, Siberia, Urals.
4. **Explain** why Lenin accepted the loss of so much Russian territory in the Treaty of Brest-Litovsk.
5. **List** some of the different opinions that split the White forces.

Critical Thinking

6. **Explain** How did the presence of Allied troops in Russia ultimately help the Communists?
7. **Organizing Information** Using a chart like the one below, sequence the steps the Communists took to turn Russia into a centralized state dominated by a single party.

Steps to Communist control
1.
2.

Analyzing Visuals

8. **Examine** the photograph of Czar Nicholas II and his family shown on page 515 of your text. Is this photograph an idealized view of royalty? Do you think the people of Russia would have agreed with this view of the royal family as portrayed in this photograph, especially during World War I?

Writing About History

9. **Expository Writing** Write an essay comparing the economic, political, and social causes of the American, French, and Russian Revolutions.

SECTION 3 ASSESSMENT

1. Key terms are in blue.
2. Alexandra *(p. 515)*; Grigori Rasputin *(p. 515)*; Alexander Kerensky *(p. 516)*; Bolsheviks *(p. 517)*; V. I. Lenin *(p. 517)*; Leon Trotsky *(p. 518)*
3. See chapter maps.
4. Lenin promised the people peace, thinking the socialist revolution would make the treaty irrelevant.
5. a restoration of the czarist regime, a liberal democracy
6. The presence of foreign forces stirred Russian patriotism, to which the Communists appealed.
7. well-disciplined, zealous Red Army; political differences among anti-Communists; war communism; Cheka
8. appear prosperous, country was poor
9. Essays should be supported from material in the text.

Picturing **History**

Answer: Leon Trotsky

Reading Check

Answer: The Red Army had the organizational genius of Leon Trotsky and a common goal; there were conflicting goals among the anti-Communist White forces.

Enrich

Have students write a brief essay explaining why the police believed that Russian women were "a great deal more dangerous" than political leaders, as stated in the report on page 515. **L2**

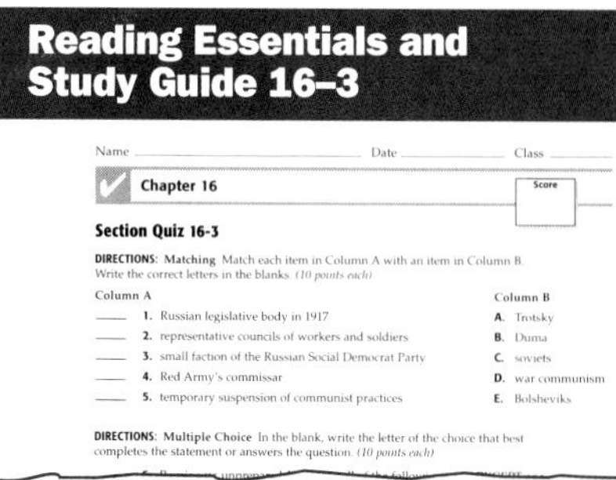

Reading Essentials and Study Guide 16–3

Name ______ Date ______ Class ______

Chapter 16 Score

Section Quiz 16-3

DIRECTIONS: Matching Match each item in Column A with an item in Column B. Write the correct letters in the blanks. *(10 points each)*

Column A	Column B
____ 1. Russian legislative body in 1917	A. Trotsky
____ 2. representative councils of workers and soldiers	B. Duma
____ 3. small faction of the Russian Social Democrat Party	C. soviets
____ 4. Red Army's commissar	D. war communism
____ 5. temporary suspension of communist practices	E. Bolsheviks

DIRECTIONS: Multiple Choice In the blank, write the letter of the choice that best completes the statement or answers the question. *(10 points each)*

Reteaching Activity

Have students construct a chart using dates from 1916 to 1922 along the side and these headings at the top: *Government Leader(s); Political/Social Events.* Have students fill in their charts. **L1**

4 CLOSE

Have students summarize the effects of World War I on the Russian Revolution.

TEACH

Analyzing Primary Sources
This selection captures the fervor and excitement of the early days of communism. What aspects of the Communist program would have seemed most attractive to people exhausted by war? What would have been the fascination for people like John Reed, who had become disenchanted with capitalism and angry about continuing social inequalities? Why did the Bolsheviks have such revolutionary fervor? How do Lenin's use of language and his mannerisms affect the crowd? Compare Reed's enthusiasm and the Bolsheviks' fervor to the new revolutionary fervor that overthrew communism in the revolutions of 1989. **L3**

Glencoe Literature Library

The following literature from the **Glencoe Literature Library** may enrich the teaching of this chapter:
Animal Farm by G. Orwell

EYEWITNESS TO HISTORY

Ten Days That Shook the World

Lenin speaks to the troops in Moscow.

JOHN REED WAS AN AMERICAN JOURNALIST who helped found the American Communist Labor party. Accused of treason, he fled the United States and went to Russia. In *Ten Days That Shook the World,* Reed left an eyewitness account of the Russian Revolution. He considered V. I. Lenin the great hero of the Bolshevik success.

❝It was just 8:40 when a thundering wave of cheers announced the entrance of the presidium [executive committee], with Lenin—great Lenin—among them. A short, stocky figure, with a big head set down in his shoulders, bald and bulging. Little eyes, a snubbish nose, wide, generous mouth, and heavy chin. Dressed in shabby clothes, his trousers much too long for him. Unimpressive, to be the idol of a mob, loved and revered as perhaps few leaders in history have been. . . .

Now Lenin, gripping the edge of the reading stand, letting his little winking eyes travel over the crowd as he stood there waiting, apparently oblivious to the long-rolling ovation, which lasted several minutes. When it finished, he said simply, 'We shall now proceed to construct the socialist order!' Again that overwhelming human roar.

'The first thing is the adoption of practical measures to realize peace. . . . We shall offer peace to the peoples of all the warring countries upon the basis of the Soviet terms—no annexations, no indemnities, and the right of self-determination of peoples. . . . This proposal of peace will meet with resistance on the part of the imperialist governments—we don't fool ourselves on that score. But we hope that revolution will soon break out in all the warring countries; that is why we address ourselves especially to the workers of France, England and Germany. . . .'

'The revolution of November 6th and 7th,' he ended, 'has opened the era of the Social Revolution. . . . The labour movement, in the name of peace and socialism, shall win, and fulfill its destiny. . . .'

There was something quiet and powerful in all this, which stirred the souls of men. It was understandable why people believed when Lenin spoke.❞

—**John Reed, *Ten Days That Shook the World***

Analyzing Primary Sources

1. Did John Reed agree or disagree with Lenin?
2. How do you know that Reed's account of Lenin is biased?

ANSWERS TO ANALYZING PRIMARY SOURCES

1. John Reed agreed with Lenin and considered Lenin a hero.
2. Answers will vary, but students should support their answers with examples from the excerpt. Students should know that phrases such as "great Lenin" and "the idol of the mob, loved and revered as perhaps few leaders in history have been" show bias.

SECTION 4 End of the War

Guide to Reading

Main Ideas
- Combined Allied forces stopped the German offensive.
- Peace settlements brought political and territorial changes to Europe and created bitterness and resentment in several nations.

Key Terms
armistice, reparation, mandate

People to Identify
Erich von Ludendorff, Friedrich Ebert, David Lloyd George, Georges Clemenceau

Places to Locate
Kiel, Alsace, Lorraine, Poland

Preview Questions
1. What were the key events in bringing about an end to the war?
2. What was the intended purpose of the League of Nations?

Reading Strategy
Organizing Information At the Paris Peace Conference, the leaders of France, Britain, and the United States were motivated by different concerns. Using a chart, identify the national interests of each country as it approached the peace deliberations.

France	Britain	United States

Preview of Events
1917 · 1918 · 1919 · 1920

1918 Germany agrees to an armistice

1919 Treaty of Versailles signed at the Paris Peace Conference

Voices from the Past

On September 15, 1916, on the Western Front, a new weapon appeared:

> "We heard strange throbbing noises, and lumbering slowly towards us came three huge mechanical monsters such as we had never seen before. My first impression was that they looked ready to topple on their noses, but their tails and the two little wheels at the back held them down and kept them level. . . . Instead of going on to the German lines the three tanks assigned to us straddled our front line, stopped and then opened up a murderous machine-gun fire. . . . They finally realized they were on the wrong trench and moved on, frightening the Germans out of their wits and making them scuttle like frightened rabbits."
>
> —*Eyewitness to History,* John Carey, ed., 1987

British tank

The tank played a role in bringing an end to World War I and foreshadowed a new kind of warfare.

The Last Year of the War

The year 1917 had not been a good one for the Allies. Allied offensives on the Western Front had been badly defeated. The Russian Revolution, which began in November 1917, led to Russia's withdrawal from the war a few months later. The cause of the Central Powers looked favorable, although war weariness was beginning to take its toll.

On the positive side, the entry of the United States into the war in 1917 gave the Allies a much-needed psychological boost, along with fresh men and material. In 1918, American troops would prove crucial.

1 FOCUS

Section Overview
This section discusses the end of the Great War and the peace settlements that followed.

BELLRINGER
Skillbuilder Activity

 Project transparency and have students answer questions.

 Available as a blackline master.

Daily Focus Skills Transparency 16–4

Guide to Reading

Answers to Graphic: France: strip Germany of weapons; reparations; separate Rhineland;
Britain: make Germany pay for war
United States: reduce armaments; ensure self-determination; League of Nations

Preteaching Vocabulary: Ask students to define *armistice, reparation,* and *mandate* and use each word in sentences of their own. L1

SECTION RESOURCES

Reproducible Masters
- Reproducible Lesson Plan 16–4
- Daily Lecture and Discussion Notes 16–4
- Guided Reading Activity 16–4
- Section Quiz 16–4
- Reading Essentials and Study Guide 16–4

Transparencies
- Daily Focus Skills Transparency 16–4

Multimedia
- Interactive Tutor Self-Assessment CD-ROM
- ExamView® Pro Testmaker CD-ROM
- Presentation Plus! CD-ROM

2 TEACH

Daily Lecture and Discussion Notes 16–4

Daily Lecture and Discussion Notes

Chapter 16, Section 4

Did You Know? The 1919 Treaty of Versailles demanded that Germany pay $5 billion in reparations for damages caused by the war. In 1921, Germany had paid nearly half the amount. However, the reparations committee met and decided that Germany should pay a total of $32.5 billion by 1963, an amount that many experts agreed could cause the German people to starve.

I. **The Last Year of the War** *(pages 521–523)*

A. During 1917, the Allies had been defeated in their offensives on the Western Front, and the Russians had withdrawn from the war. The Central Powers appeared to have the advantage.

B. The German military official **Erich von Ludendorff** decided to take a military gamble. In March 1918, the Germans launched a large offensive on the Western Front and came to within 50 miles of Paris. The Germans were stopped at the Second Battle of the Marne by French, Moroccan, and American troops and hundreds of tanks.

C. In 1918, the addition of more than 2 million American troops helped the Allies begin to advance toward Germany. By the end of September, General Ludendorff told German leaders that the war was lost.

D. The Allies were not willing to negotiate with the German government under Emperor William II. The German people were angry and exhausted by the war. In spite of attempted government reforms, German workers and soldiers in towns such as **Kiel** revolted and set up their own councils. On November 9, William II left the country.

E. The German Social Democratic party, led by **Friedrich Ebert,** declared that Germany would become a democratic republic. On November 11, the new German government signed an **armistice** with the Allies that ended the war.

F. In December 1918, a group of radical socialists formed the German Communist Party and then tried to seize power. They were defeated by the new government, which was backed by the army. The revolutionary leaders were killed.

G. The attempt by the Communists to take over the government left many middle-class Germans deeply afraid of communism.

H. At the end of the war, ethnic groups in Austria-Hungary sought independence. The Austro-Hungarian Empire disintegrated into the independent republics of Austria, Hungary, and Czechoslovakia and the monarchial state of Yugoslavia. National rivalries in the region would weaken eastern Europe for years to come.

Enrich

Ask students to define an idealist. *(One guided by ideals—lofty, high principles—rather than by practical considerations.)* Have them discuss the ways in which Woodrow Wilson was an idealist. Since ideals are usually considered positive and admirable, why didn't European leaders embrace Wilson's proposals? L2

Writing Activity

Have students write an essay analyzing the influence of Woodrow Wilson on political events of the twentieth century. L3

A New German Offensive For Germany, the withdrawal of the Russians offered new hope for a successful end to the war. Germany was now free to concentrate entirely on the Western Front. **Erich von Ludendorff,** who guided German military operations, decided to make one final military gamble—a grand offensive in the west to break the military stalemate.

The German attack was launched in March 1918. By April, German troops were within about 50 miles (80 km) of Paris. However, the German advance was stopped at the Second Battle of the Marne on July 18. French, Moroccan, and American troops (140,000 fresh American troops had just arrived), supported by hundreds of tanks, threw the Germans back over the Marne. Ludendorff's gamble had failed.

With the arrival of two million more American troops, Allied forces began making a steady advance toward Germany. On September 29, 1918, General Ludendorff informed German leaders that the war was lost. He demanded that the government ask for peace at once.

Collapse and Armistice German officials soon discovered that the Allies were unwilling to make peace with the autocratic imperial government of Germany. Reforms were begun to create a liberal government, but these efforts came too late for the exhausted and angry German people.

On November 3, sailors in the town of **Kiel,** in northern Germany, mutinied. Within days, councils of workers and soldiers were forming throughout northern Germany and taking over civilian and military offices. William II gave in to public pressure and left the country on November 9.

After William II's departure, the Social Democrats under **Friedrich Ebert** announced the creation of a democratic republic. Two days later, on November 11, 1918, the new German government signed an **armistice** (a truce, an agreement to end the fighting).

Opposing Viewpoints

Who Caused World War I?

Immediately after World War I, historians began to assess which nation was most responsible for beginning the war. As these four selections show, opinions have varied considerably.

"The Allied and Associated Governments affirm and Germany accepts the responsibility of Germany and her allies for causing all the loss and damage to which the Allied and Associated Governments have been subjected as a consequence of the war imposed upon them by the aggression of Germany and her allies."

Treaty of Versailles, Article 231, 1919

"None of the powers wanted a European War. . . . But the verdict of the Versailles Treaty that Germany and her allies were responsible for the War, in view of the evidence now available, is historically unsound. It should therefore be revised."

—**Sidney Bradshaw Fay**
Origins of the World War, 1930

COOPERATIVE LEARNING ACTIVITY

Preparing a Presentation Organize the class into four groups to research and report on World War I in the Middle East. One group should research the life of T.E. Lawrence. The second group should research Britain's role in the Middle Eastern front, including its broken promise of Arab independence. The third group should research the goals and participation of the Arab people involved. The fourth group should research the immediate results and long-term effects that the peace agreement has had on the people living in the Middle East. All four groups should then meet to share their data in presentations to the rest of the class. L3

Revolutionary Forces The war was over, but the revolutionary forces it had set in motion in Germany were not yet exhausted. A group of radical socialists, unhappy with the moderate policies of the Social Democrats, formed the German Communist Party in December 1918. A month later, the Communists tried to seize power in Berlin.

The new Social Democratic government, backed by regular army troops, crushed the rebels and murdered Rosa Luxemburg and Karl Liebknecht (LEEP• KNEHKT), leaders of the German Communists. A similar attempt at Communist revolution in the city of Munich, in southern Germany, was also crushed.

The new German republic had been saved from radical revolution. The attempt at revolution, however, left the German middle class with a deep fear of communism.

Austria-Hungary, too, experienced disintegration and revolution. As war weariness took hold of the empire, ethnic groups increasingly sought to achieve their independence. By the time the war ended, the Austro-Hungarian Empire was no more.

The empire had been replaced by the independent republics of Austria, Hungary, and Czechoslovakia, along with the large monarchical state called Yugoslavia. Rivalries among the nations that succeeded Austria-Hungary would weaken eastern Europe for the next 80 years.

Reading Check **Describing** What happened within Germany after the armistice?

The Peace Settlements

In January 1919, representatives of 27 victorious Allied nations met in Paris to make a final settlement of the Great War. Over a period of years, the reasons for fighting World War I had changed dramatically. When European nations had gone to war in 1914 they sought territorial gains. By the beginning of 1918, more idealistic reasons were also being expressed.

Wilson's Proposals No one expressed these idealistic reasons better than the U.S. president, Woodrow Wilson. Even before the end of the war, Wilson outlined "Fourteen Points" to the United States Congress—his basis for a peace settlement that he believed justified the enormous military struggle being waged.

Wilson's proposals for a truly just and lasting peace included reaching the peace agreements openly rather than through secret diplomacy; reducing armaments (military forces or weapons) to a "point consistent with domestic safety"; and ensuring self-determination (the right of each people to have its own nation).

Wilson portrayed World War I as a people's war against "absolutism and militarism." These two enemies of liberty, he argued, could be eliminated only by creating democratic governments and a "general association of nations." This association would guarantee "political independence and territorial integrity to great and small states alike."

Wilson became the spokesperson for a new world order based on democracy and international cooperation. When he arrived in Europe for the peace conference, he was enthusiastically cheered by many Europeans. Wilson soon found, however, that more practical motives guided other states.

The Paris Peace Conference Delegates met in Paris in early 1919 to determine the peace settlement. At the Paris Peace Conference, complications became obvious. For one thing, secret treaties and agreements that had been made before the war had raised

"In estimating the order of guilt of the various countries we may safely say that the only direct and immediate responsibility for the World War falls upon Serbia, France and Russia, with the guilt about equally divided."

—Harry Elmer Barnes
The Genesis of the World War, 1927

"As Germany willed and coveted the Austro-Serbian war and, in her confidence in her military superiority, deliberately faced the risk of a conflict with Russia and France, her leaders must bear a substantial share of the historical responsibility for the outbreak of general war in 1914."

—Fritz Fischer
Germany's Aims in the First World War, 1961

You Decide

1. Write a quote of your own that reflects your views on which nation caused World War I. Support your quote with passages from the text.

CHAPTER 16
Section 4, 521–526

Reading Check

Answer: William II left country; Social Democrats formed republic; Communists tried to seize power, leaving German middle class with deep fear of communism

Opposing Viewpoints

Answer: Have students share their quotes with the class.

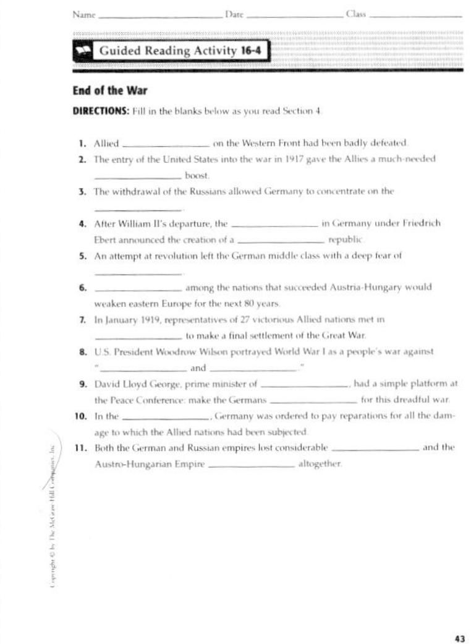
Guided Reading Activity 16–4

Name ____ Date ____ Class ____

Guided Reading Activity 16-4

End of the War

DIRECTIONS: Fill in the blanks below as you read Section 4.

1. Allied ____ on the Western Front had been badly defeated.
2. The entry of the United States into the war in 1917 gave the Allies a much-needed ____ boost.
3. The withdrawal of the Russians allowed Germany to concentrate on the ____.
4. After William II's departure, the ____ in Germany under Friedrich Ebert announced the creation of a ____ republic.
5. An attempt at revolution left the German middle class with a deep fear of ____.
6. ____ among the nations that succeeded Austria-Hungary would weaken eastern Europe for the next 80 years.
7. In January 1919, representatives of 27 victorious Allied nations met in ____ to make a final settlement of the Great War.
8. U.S. President Woodrow Wilson portrayed World War I as a people's war against "____ and ____."
9. David Lloyd George, prime minister of ____, had a simple platform at the Peace Conference: make the Germans ____ for this dreadful war.
10. In the ____, Germany was ordered to pay reparations for all the damage to which the Allied nations had been subjected.
11. Both the German and Russian empires lost considerable ____ and the Austro-Hungarian Empire ____ altogether.

43

TURNING POINT

World War I and the Russian Revolution were important turning points in world history. Ask students to identify changes that resulted from these two events. L2

EXTENDING THE CONTENT

Treaty of Versailles The mishandling of the peace accords of World War I directly led to World War II and the eventual dominant role of the United States in the world. Ask students to identify the two key nations that were not at the Paris Peace Conference. *(Germany and Russia)* Guide students in a discussion concerning how national interests, desire for revenge, and hopes for territorial gains figured in the peace talks. Have students list as many ways as they can in which the Paris Peace Conference and the Treaty of Versailles led to future problems. How did the absence of Germany and Russia impact future prospects for peace? Then have students debate the relative importance and possible results of each item on the list. L2

Critical Thinking

Many different political systems are represented by the nations mentioned in this chapter. Ask students to define and give examples of different political systems of the past and present. L2

CURRICULUM CONNECTION

Political Science Ask students to research and compare the League of Nations and the United Nations. Or, students may choose to research the Treaty of Versailles to discover what, specifically, were its provisions. L2

Who?What?Where?When?

The Windsor family Anti-German feeling reached near-hysteria in many of the Allied countries during World War I. In the United States, German-language instruction was dropped from schools. In Britain, King George V changed his family name from the German Saxe-Coburg-Gotha to the English name Windsor.

CURRICULUM CONNECTION

Government Ask students to discuss the failure of Wilson's approach to the peace. Since the United States entered the war so late and since no battles were fought on United States soil, was it fair for Wilson to expect the European nations to share his views? L2

the hopes of European nations for territorial gains. These hopes could not be totally ignored, even if they did conflict with the principle of self-determination put forth by Wilson.

National interests also complicated the deliberations of the Paris Peace Conference. **David Lloyd George,** prime minister of Great Britain, had won a decisive victory in elections in December of 1918. His platform was simple: make the Germans pay for this dreadful war.

France's approach to peace was chiefly guided by its desire for national security. To **Georges Clemenceau** (KLEH•muhn•SOH), the premier of France, the French people had suffered the most from German aggression. The French desired revenge and security against future German aggression. Clemenceau wanted Germany stripped of all weapons, vast German payments—**reparations**—to cover the costs of the war, and a separate Rhineland as a buffer state between France and Germany.

The most important decisions at the Paris Peace Conference were made by Wilson, Clemenceau, and Lloyd George. Italy, as one of the Allies, was considered one of the so-called Big Four powers. However, it played a smaller role than the other key powers—the United States, France, and Great Britain, called the Big Three. Germany was not invited to attend, and Russia could not be present because of its civil war.

People In History

Georges Clemenceau
1841–1929—French statesman

Georges Clemenceau was one of France's wartime leaders. He had a long political career before serving as French premier (prime minister) from 1906 to 1909 and from 1917 to 1920.

When Clemenceau became premier in 1917, he suspended basic civil liberties for the rest of the war. He had the editor of an antiwar newspaper executed on a charge of helping the enemy. Clemenceau also punished journalists who wrote negative war reports by having them drafted.

Clemenceau strongly disliked and distrusted the Germans and blamed them for World War I. "For the catastrophe of 1914 the Germans are responsible," he said. "Only a professional liar would deny this."

In view of the many conflicting demands at the peace conference, it was no surprise that the Big Three quarreled. Wilson wanted to create a world organization, the League of Nations, to prevent future wars. Clemenceau and Lloyd George wanted to punish Germany. In the end, only compromise made it possible to achieve a peace settlement.

Wilson's wish that the creation of an international peacekeeping organization be the first order of business was granted. On January 25, 1919, the conference accepted the idea of a League of Nations. In return, Wilson agreed to make compromises on territorial arrangements. He did so because he believed that the League could later fix any unfair settlements.

Clemenceau also compromised to obtain some guarantees for French security. He gave up France's wish for a separate Rhineland and instead accepted a defensive alliance with Great Britain and the United States. Both Great Britain and the United States pledged to help France if it was attacked by Germany.

The Treaty of Versailles The final peace settlement of Paris consisted of five separate treaties with the defeated nations—Germany, Austria, Hungary, Bulgaria, and Turkey. The Treaty of Versailles with Germany, signed at Versailles near Paris, on June 28, 1919, was by far the most important.

The Germans considered it a harsh peace. They were especially unhappy with Article 231, the so-called War Guilt Clause, which declared that Germany (and Austria) were responsible for starting the war. The treaty ordered Germany to pay reparations for all the damage to which the Allied governments and their people had been subjected as a result of the war "imposed upon them by the aggression of Germany and her allies."

The military and territorial provisions of the Treaty of Versailles also angered the Germans. Germany had to reduce its army to a hundred thousand men, cut back its navy, and eliminate its air force. **Alsace** and **Lorraine,** taken by the Germans from France in 1871, were now returned. Sections of eastern Germany were awarded to a new Polish state.

German land along both sides of the Rhine was made a demilitarized zone and stripped of all weapons and fortifications. This, it was hoped, would serve as a barrier to any future German military moves westward against France. Outraged by the "dictated peace," the new German government complained but, unwilling to risk a renewal of the war, they accepted the treaty.

MEETING INDIVIDUAL NEEDS

Auditory Have the class read carefully pages 521 to 526. Assist the students with the reading or have them read it aloud. Divide the class into three groups representing France, Britain, and the United States. Have the students work in their groups to prepare their country's opinions about how to deal with Germany and make a final settlement of World War I. Once each group is ready, they may come together and discuss their respective concerns in a role-playing activity where each student plays the role of a delegate from the country they represent. Some of the expected responses should be: 1) from the United States: reduction of military forces and weapons; self-determination of people (liberty); 2) Britain: revenge; 3) France: national security, strip Germany of all weapons, make Germany pay reparations. L2

Geography Skills

World War I dramatically changed political boundaries.

1. **Interpreting Maps** Rank the countries and empires listed in the map legend according to the amount of lost territory, from largest loss to smallest loss.
2. **Applying Geography Skills** Look back at the map on page 500, then examine the map above. Now, knowing the outcome of the war, predict which countries would lose the most territory. Why does the actual loss of territory, as shown above, differ from (or match) your predictions?

A New Map of Europe As a result of the war, the Treaty of Versailles, and the separate peace treaties made with the other Central Powers—Austria, Hungary, Bulgaria, and Turkey—the map of eastern Europe was largely redrawn. Both the German and Russian empires lost much territory in eastern Europe. The Austro-Hungarian Empire disappeared.

New nation-states emerged from the lands of these three empires: Finland, Latvia, Estonia, Lithuania, Poland, Czechoslovakia, Austria, and Hungary. New territorial arrangements were also made in the Balkans. Romania acquired additional lands from Russia, Hungary, and Bulgaria. Serbia formed the nucleus of a new state, called Yugoslavia, which combined Serbs, Croats, and Slovenes.

The Paris Peace Conference was supposedly guided by the principle of self-determination. However, the mixtures of peoples in eastern Europe made it impossible to draw boundaries along neat ethnic lines. Compromises had to be made, sometimes to satisfy the national interests of the victors. France, for example, had lost Russia as its major ally on Germany's eastern border. Thus, France wanted to strengthen and expand Poland, Czechoslovakia, Yugoslavia, and Romania as much as possible. Those states could then serve as barriers against Germany and Communist Russia.

As a result of compromises, almost every eastern European state was left with ethnic minorities: Germans in Poland; Hungarians, Poles, and Germans in Czechoslovakia; Hungarians in Romania, and the

CHAPTER 16
Section 4, 521–526

Geography Skills

Answers:

1. Russia, Austria-Hungary, Ottoman Empire, Germany
2. Many students might have predicted that Germany would lose the most territory, but answers will vary.

Connecting Across Time

Ask students to look at a contemporary map of Europe and the Middle East and compare it with the map on page 525. Have students list the ways in which Europe and the Middle East have changed since the end of World War I. What do these changes suggest about the effectiveness of the peace treaties to satisfy the nations in Europe? L2

3 ASSESS

Assign Section 4 Assessment as homework or as an in-class activity.

Have students use **Interactive Tutor Self-Assessment CD-ROM.**

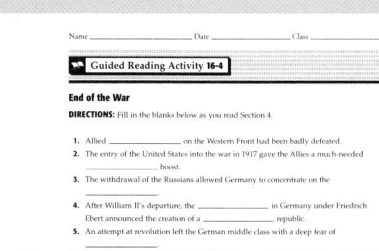

Section Quiz 16–4

Name ______ Date ______ Class ______

Guided Reading Activity 16-4

End of the War

DIRECTIONS: Fill in the blanks below as you read Section 4.

1. Allied ______ on the Western Front had been badly defeated.
2. The entry of the United States into the war in 1917 gave the Allies a much-needed ______ boost.
3. The withdrawal of the Russians allowed Germany to concentrate on the ______.
4. After William II's departure, the ______ in Germany under Friedrich Ebert announced the creation of a ______ republic.
5. An attempt at revolution left the German middle class with a deep fear of ______.

INTERDISCIPLINARY CONNECTIONS ACTIVITY

Literature For writers who were involved in the military during World War I, the war was an especially unforgettable experience. Have students research and write brief biographies of authors who created fiction or memoirs about their experiences. Possible subjects include Robert Graves, Siegfried Sassoon, e.e. cummings, John Dos Passos, and Ernest Hemingway. Students should focus on how the war affected the individual and his (or her) writing. Encourage students to read an actual work by their subject and discuss with the class how the literary work reflects the writer's attitude and feelings about the experience of World War I. Students may want to include a passage or excerpt that supports their view. L2

Answer: Woodrow Wilson (United States), David Lloyd George (Great Britain), Georges Clemenceau (France)

Reading Check

Answer: Article 231, the War Guilt Clause, which declared that Germany (and Austria) were responsible for starting the war

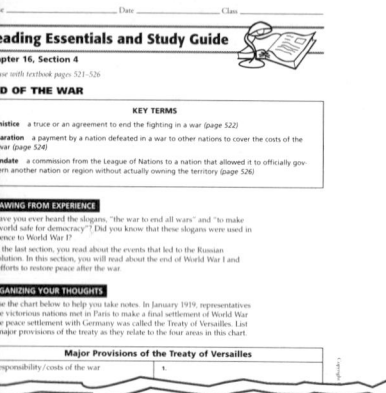

Reading Essentials and Study Guide 16–4

Reading Essentials and Study Guide
Chapter 16, Section 4
END OF THE WAR

Reteaching Activity

Have students list the major participants at the Paris Peace Conference and summarize the aims of each. **L1**

4 CLOSE

Review with students the major consequences of World War I on European society. In what sense did the conflict undermine "the whole idea of progress"?

History through Art

***Signing of the Treaty of Versailles* by John Christen Johansen, 1919** A peace settlement with Germany was signed at Versailles on June 28, 1919. What were the names of the representatives of the Big Three powers at the Paris Peace Conference?

combination of Serbs, Croats, Slovenes, Macedonians, and Albanians in Yugoslavia. The problem of ethnic minorities within nations would lead to later conflicts.

Yet another centuries-old empire—the Ottoman Empire—was broken up by the peace settlement. To gain Arab support against the Ottoman Turks during the war, the Western Allies had promised to recognize the independence of Arab states in the Ottoman Empire. Once the war was over, however, the Western nations changed their minds. France took control of Lebanon and Syria, Britain received Iraq and Palestine.

These acquisitions were officially called **mandates.** Woodrow Wilson had opposed the outright annexation of colonial territories by the Allies. As a result, the peace settlement created the mandate system. According to this system, a nation officially governed another nation as a mandate on behalf of the League of Nations but did not own the territory.

The War's Legacy World War I shattered the liberal, rational society that had existed in late-nineteenth- and early twentieth-century Europe. The death of almost 10 million people, as well as the incredible destruction caused by the war, undermined the whole idea of progress. Entire populations had participated in a devastating slaughter.

World War I was a total war—one that involved a complete mobilization of resources and people. As a result, the power of governments over the lives of their citizens increased. Freedom of the press and speech were limited in the name of national security. World War I made the practice of strong central authority a way of life.

The turmoil created by the war also seemed to open the door to even greater insecurity. Revolutions broke up old empires and created new states, which led to new problems. The hope that Europe and the rest of the world would return to normalcy was, however, soon dashed.

Reading Check **Identifying** What clause in the Treaty of Versailles particularly angered the Germans?

SECTION 4 ASSESSMENT

Checking for Understanding

1. **Define** armistice, reparation, mandate.
2. **Identify** Erich von Ludendorff, Friedrich Ebert, David Lloyd George, Georges Clemenceau.
3. **Locate** Kiel, Alsace, Lorraine, Poland.
4. **Explain** why the mandate system was created. Which countries became mandates? Who governed them?
5. **List** some of President Wilson's proposals for creating a truly just and lasting peace. Why did he feel the need to develop these proposals?

Critical Thinking

6. **Making Generalizations** Although Woodrow Wilson came to the Paris Peace Conference with high ideals, the other leaders had more practical concerns. Why do you think that was so?
7. **Compare and Contrast** Using a Venn diagram like the one below, compare and contrast Wilson's Fourteen Points to the Treaty of Versailles.

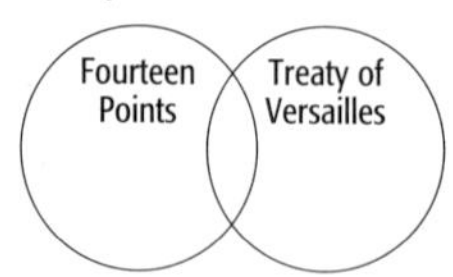

Analyzing Visuals

8. **Compare** the photograph of troops going to war on page 503 with the painting on page 497. How do you think the soldiers' expectations compared to their actual experiences?

Writing About History

9. **Informative Writing** You are a reporter for a large newspaper, sent to the Paris Peace Conference to interview one of the leaders of the Big Three. Prepare a written set of questions you would like to ask the leader you have selected.

SECTION 4 ASSESSMENT

1. Key terms are in blue.
2. Erich von Ludendorff *(p. 522)*; Friedrich Ebert *(p. 522)*; David Lloyd George *(p. 524)*; Georges Clemenceau *(p. 524)*
3. See chapter maps.
4. as an alternative to territorial annexation; France oversaw Lebanon, Syria; Britain oversaw Iraq, Palestine
5. open peace agreements reducing armaments; self-determination; creating a "general association of nations"
6. national interests
7. Fourteen Points: open diplomacy; self-determination of people; Treaty of Versailles: assignment of war guilt; reparations; demilitarized zone in Germany; map of Europe redrawn: Fourteen Points *and* Treaty of Versailles: reduction of arms; establishment of League of Nations
8. long war, not short adventure
9. Questions will vary.

Interpreting Military Movements on Maps

Why Learn This Skill?

Although wars begin over many different issues, they end as fights to control territory. Because wars are basically fought over land, maps are particularly useful tools for seeing the "big picture" of a war.

Learning the Skill

The map key is essential in interpreting military maps. The key explains what the map's colors and symbols represent. Use the following steps to study the key:

- Determine the meanings of the colors on the map. Usually, colors represent different sides in the conflict.
- Identify all symbols. These may include symbols for battle sites, victories, and types of military units and equipment.
- Study the arrows, which show the direction of military movements. Because these movements occur over time, some maps give dates showing when and where troops advanced and retreated.

Once you have studied the key and the map, follow the progress of the campaign that is shown. Notice where each side began, in which direction it moved, where the two sides fought, and which side claimed victory.

Practicing the Skill

The map on this page shows the Middle East front during World War I. Study the map and then answer the following questions.

1. On which side did Arabia and Egypt fight?
2. Who won the battle at the Dardanelles?
3. Describe the movement of the Central Powers offensives.
4. When did the Allies win the most battles in the Middle East?

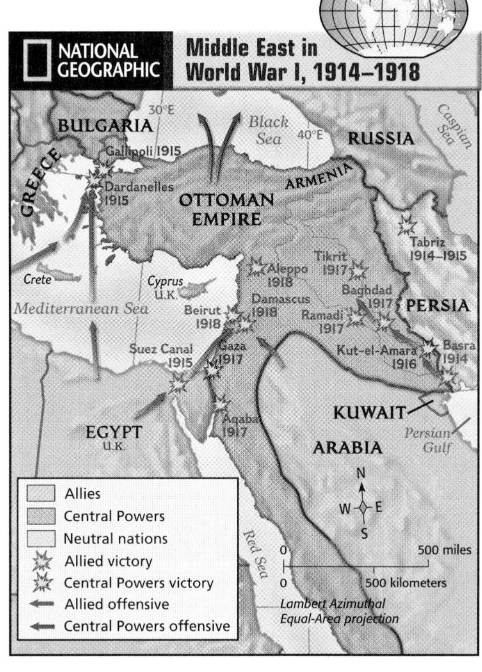

Applying the Skill

Choose a military map from this text or select one from another source. Study the map selection carefully. Write a paragraph about the war or conflict as it is depicted in the map. You should respond to issues such as where most of the fighting occurred; the year in which the most significant advance was made, and by whom; and whether or not there was a decisive victory by either side. Attach a copy of the map to your report.

Glencoe's **Skillbuilder Interactive Workbook, Level 2,** provides instruction and practice in key social studies skills.

527

TEACH

Interpreting Military Movements on Maps Ask students to make their own military maps of an engagement in an imaginary war. They should use two different colors to represent the opposing sides. Have students use different symbols or colors for the victories of each side and arrows to show the direction of troop movements. The students should label land and water areas and a few important towns or cities. The map should also include a legend explaining what the various colors and symbols represent. **L1**

Additional Practice

Skills Reinforcement Activity 16

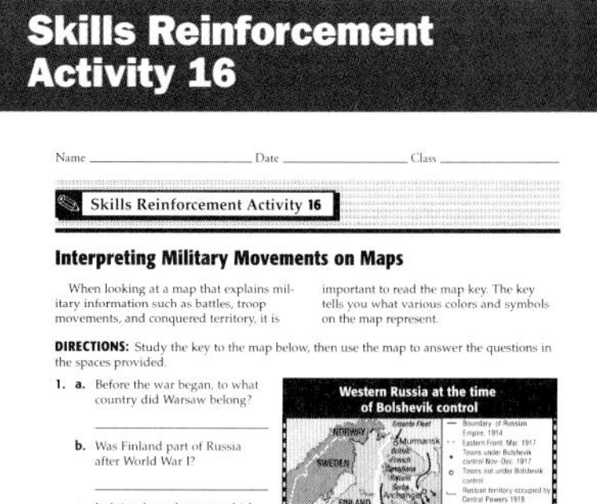

Name ____ Date ____ Class ____

Skills Reinforcement Activity 16

Interpreting Military Movements on Maps

When looking at a map that explains military information such as battles, troop movements, and conquered territory, it is important to read the map key. The key tells you what various colors and symbols on the map represent.

DIRECTIONS: Study the key to the map below, then use the map to answer the questions in the spaces provided.

1. a. Before the war began, to what country did Warsaw belong?

b. Was Finland part of Russia after World War I?

c. Judging from the map, which

GLENCOE TECHNOLOGY

CD-ROM
Glencoe Skillbuilder Interactive Workbook CD-ROM, Level 2

This interactive CD-ROM reinforces student mastery of essential social studies skills.

ANSWERS TO PRACTICING THE SKILL

1. Arabia and Egypt fought with the Allied forces.
2. The Central Powers won the battle at the Dardanelles.
3. The Central Powers moved north from the Ottoman Empire across the Black Sea into Russia.
4. The Allies won the most battles in the Middle East in 1917 and 1918.

Applying the Skill: Essays should be supported by information on maps that students will attach. Students should use social studies teminology correctly. They should also use standard grammar, spelling, sentence structure, and punctuation in their essays.

CHAPTER 16
Assessment and Activities

GLENCOE TECHNOLOGY

MindJogger Videoquiz
Use the **MindJogger Videoquiz** to review Chapter 16 content.

 Available in VHS.

Using Key Terms
1. conscription **2.** mobilization
3. trench warfare **4.** war of attrition
5. total war **6.** planned economies
7. soviets **8.** War communism
9. reparations

Reviewing Key Facts
10. by passing the Defence of the Realm Act, which allowed the government to arrest protesters as traitors and to censor or shut down newspapers

11. They promised an end to the war, redistribution of land to peasants, transfer of factories and industries from capitalists to committees of workers, and transfer of government power to soviets.

12. 1914: start of World War I; 1917: beginning of the Russian Revolution, and U.S. enters the war; 1918: end of World War I

13. During the war, women assumed many of the jobs men had vacated. After the war, women were encouraged to relinquish those jobs. They retained some social freedom and in some countries received the right to vote.

14. Czar Nicholas II was away leading the Russian army, leaving Alexandra to make decisions; she had come under Rasputin's influence.

15. Because nations were allies, they were bound to respond.

CHAPTER 16 ASSESSMENT and ACTIVITIES

Using Key Terms

1. The practice of requiring young people to join the military, which was followed by many nations before World War I, was called ______.
2. Before World War I, many European nations completed the ______ of their military by assembling troops and supplies for war.
3. The development of ______ baffled military leaders who had been trained to fight wars of movement.
4. World War I became a ______, or war based on wearing the other side down by constant attacks and heavy losses.
5. World War I involved a complete mobilization of resources and people that affected the lives of all citizens in the warring countries—a situation called ______.
6. European nations set up ______, or systems directed by government agencies to mobilize the entire resources of their nations.
7. Councils of workers and soldiers called ______ challenged the provisional government established after Nicholas II stepped down.
8. ______ is the term used to describe the Communists' centralization of control over its economy.
9. Germany was required by the Treaty of Versailles to make payments called ______ to the nations that won the war.

Reviewing Key Facts

10. **Government** How did the British government try to eliminate opposition from the people who were opposed to World War I?
11. **Culture** Explain the social changes promised by the Bolshevik slogans.
12. **History** State the significance of the following dates: 1914, 1917, and 1918.
13. **Culture** Describe the role and contribution of women during World War I. What was their status after the war?
14. **History** Why were Alexandra and Rasputin able to control the czar's government during much of World War I?
15. **Government** How did international alliances help to draw nations into World War I?
16. **History** Why was a "breakthrough" such an important military goal during the war?
17. **Government** What did the creation of a League of Nations have to do with Woodrow Wilson's willingness to sign the Treaty of Versailles?
18. **History** Why did Russia withdraw from the war? How did that affect Germany?
19. **Science and Technology** What innovations in military warfare occurred during World War I?

Chapter Summary

The outline below shows four themes of the chapter.

Cooperation: Alliance System	Conflict: World War I	Revolution: Russian Revolution	Internationalism: Peace of Paris
• Two loose alliances form in Europe: the Triple Alliance (Germany, Austria-Hungary, and Italy) and the Triple Entente (France, Great Britain, and Russia). • Alliances draw France and Great Britain into a conflict in which they have no direct interest.	• Combat takes the forms of trench warfare on the Western Front, a war of movement on the Eastern Front, and German submarine warfare in the waters surrounding Great Britain. • For the first time in history, airplanes are used for reconnaissance, combat, and bombing.	• Military and economic crises lead to a spontaneous revolution that ends the reign of the czars. • The Bolsheviks overthrow the provisional government and establish a Communist regime.	• The peace is a compromise between international and national interests. • Germany's reparation payments, military reductions, and territorial losses create a lasting bitterness that helps spark World War II.

16. Trench warfare caused a stalemate; a "breakthrough" would allow a return to the war of movement that the generals knew best.

17. He agreed to make compromises on territorial arrangements in the Treaty of Versailles, believing that the League of Nations could later fix any unfair settlements.

18. Russia withdrew due to the Russian Revolution—the Bolsheviks had promised peace in return for the support of the people. It meant that Germany only had to fight a war on the Western Front, giving them hope of winning.

19. fighter planes, tanks, submarines, bioweapons

Critical Thinking
20. Lenin stressed revolution and dictatorial government. Wilson affirmed democratic values, self-determination, and free institutions. Answers to final part of question will vary but should be supported by logical arguments.

Self-Check Quiz

Visit the *Glencoe World History—Modern Times* Web site at wh.mt.glencoe.com and click on **Chapter 16–Self-Check Quiz** to prepare for the Chapter Test.

Critical Thinking

20. **Decision Making** Compare Lenin's beliefs and goals with those of Woodrow Wilson. Which leader has had the greater impact on world history? Why?
21. **Analyzing** Why do some people feel that it is unlikely that a lasting peace could have been created at the end of World War I?

Writing About History

22. **Persuasive Writing** Both Britain and the United States passed laws during the war to silence opposition and censor the press. Are the ideals of a democratic government consistent with such laws? Provide arguments for and against.

Analyzing Sources

Reread the quote below by the British Ambassador to Vienna (see page 501), then answer the questions below.

> "I cannot tell you how exasperated people are getting here at the continual worry which that little country [Serbia] causes to Austria under encouragement from Russia. . . . It will be lucky if Europe succeeds in avoiding war as a result of the present crisis."

23. Where is Vienna located? Is the ambassador neutral in his comments or does he favor one country over another?
24. Compare the ways in which the actual events that started World War I mirror this ambassador's concerns.

Applying Technology Skills

25. **Interpreting the Past** Use the Internet to research the total costs of World War I. Determine how many people, both military and civilian, were killed or wounded on both sides. Also find the monetary costs of the war for both sides. Create a table that clearly shows your findings.

Making Decisions

26. Some historians argue that the heavy psychological and economic penalties placed on Germany by the Treaty of Versailles created the conditions for World War II. How might the treaty have been written to alleviate worldwide concern over German militarism without exacting such a heavy toll?

Paris Peace Conference: The Big Three

Country	United States	Great Britain	France
Leader	Wilson	Lloyd George	Clemenceau
Goal	Lasting peace	Germany pays	French security

Treaty of Versailles

International Relations	• League of Nations is formed.
Responsibility	• Germany accepts responsibility for starting the war and agrees to make reparations to the Allies.
Territory	• New nations are formed. • Germany returns Alsace and Lorraine to France. • France and Great Britain acquire mandates in the Middle East.
Military Strength	• Germany will reduce its army and navy and eliminate its air force. • German land along the Rhine River is demilitarized.

Analyzing Maps and Charts

Using the chart above, answer the following questions:

27. Which of the three nations involved in the Treaty of Versailles wanted to punish Germany for World War I?
28. What was the effect of the Treaty of Versailles on Germany's military?
29. Why did France demand the return of the regions of Alsace and Lorraine from Germany?

Standardized Test Practice

Directions: Choose the best answer to the following statement.

Which of these statements is **NOT** true about World War I?

A Most Europeans believed the conflict would be short-lived.
B Brutal hardships in Russia caused it to withdraw from the war in 1918.
C A system of alliances meant that many countries became mired in the dispute.
D Propaganda played a minor role in the war effort.

Test-Taking Tip: If a question includes the key word "not" or "except," read the question carefully. Make sure you understand the question completely before you pick your answer choice.

Have students visit the Web site at wh.mt.glencoe.com to review Chapter 16 and take the Self-Check Quiz.

Making Decisions

26. Answers will vary.

Analyzing Maps and Charts

27. Britain
28. reduce Germany's army and navy, eliminate its air force; German land along the Rhine River demilitarized
29. areas rich in iron ore and coal; provided a buffer between France and Germany

Answer: D

Answer Explanation:
Remind students that the Triple Alliance, the Triple Entente relied heavily on propaganda to promote the war effort. You might refer students to the *Lusitania* feature to reinforce this point.

Bonus Question ?

Was it just to place all the blame for causing World War I on Germany? *(Yes: war might have been avoided if Germany had not given Austria-Hungary permission to do with Serbia as it pleased. No: The intransigence of Austria-Hungary was also to blame and without the terrorism of Serbian nationalists, the war might not have broken out at all.)*

21. too many compromises; many unresolved issues; resentments among nations; no agreement satisfactory to all

Writing about History

22. Answers should be supported by logical arguments.

Analyzing Sources

23. Vienna is in Austria; answers will vary.
24. A Serbian nationalist shot the heir to the Austrian throne; Russia backed Serbia when Austria-Hungary declared war, while Germany backed Austria and declared war on France.

Applying Technology Skills

25. Answers will vary depending on sources. Only cost estimates are available because many were unaccounted for.

Chapter 17 Resources

Timesaving Tools

TeacherWorks™ All-In-One Planner and Resource Center

- **Interactive Teacher Edition** Access your Teacher Wraparound Edition and your classroom resources with a few easy clicks.
- **Interactive Lesson Planner** Planning has never been easier! Organize your week, month, semester, or year with all the lesson helps you need to make teaching creative, timely, and relevant.

Use Glencoe's **Presentation Plus!** multimedia teacher tool to easily present dynamic lessons that visually excite your students. Using Microsoft PowerPoint® you can customize the presentations to create your own personalized lessons.

Teaching Transparencies

Graphic Organizer Student Activity 17 Transparency

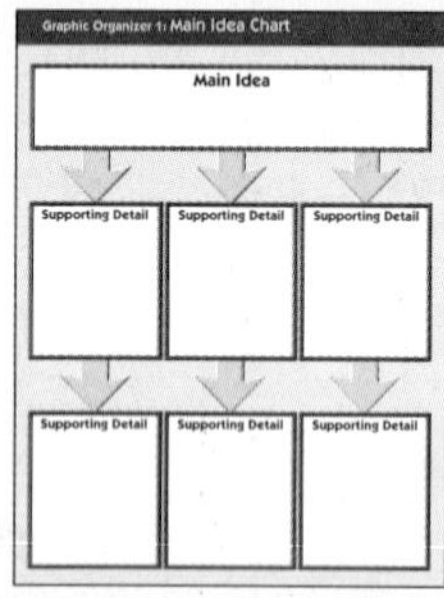

Chapter Transparency 17

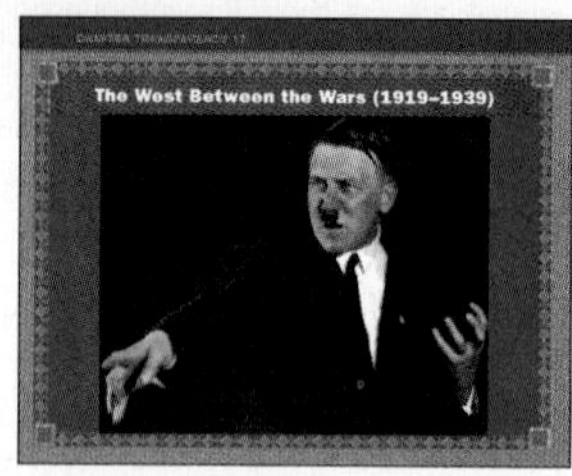

Map Overlay Transparency 17

Application and Enrichment

Enrichment Activity 17

Primary Source Reading 17

History Simulation Activity 17

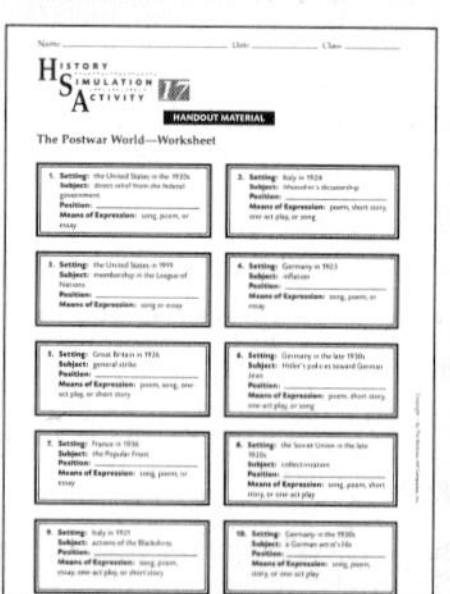

Historical Significance Activity 17

Historical Significance Activity 17 — Stock Market Crashes: Then and Now

Cooperative Learning Activity 17

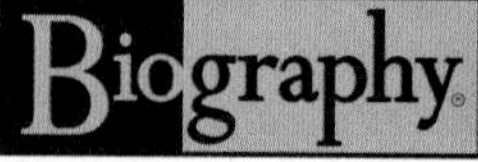

A&E HOME VIDEO.

THE HISTORY CHANNEL.

The following videotape programs are available from Glencoe as supplements to Chapter 17:

- **The Great Depression** (ISBN 0–7670–0859–6)
- **Mussolini: Italy's Nightmare** (ISBN 1–56501–818–4)
- **Joseph Stalin** (ISBN 1–56501–820–6)

To order, call Glencoe at 1–800–334–7344. To find classroom resources to accompany many of these videos, check the following home pages:
A&E Television: www.aande.com
The History Channel: www.historychannel.com

Chapter 17 Resources

Review and Reinforcement

Linking Past and Present Activity 17

Time Line Activity 17

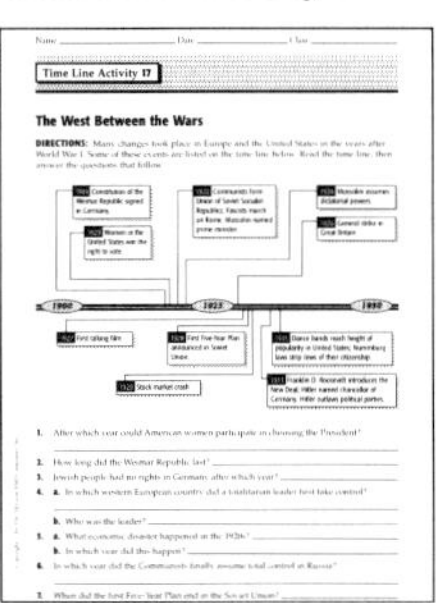

Reteaching Activity 17

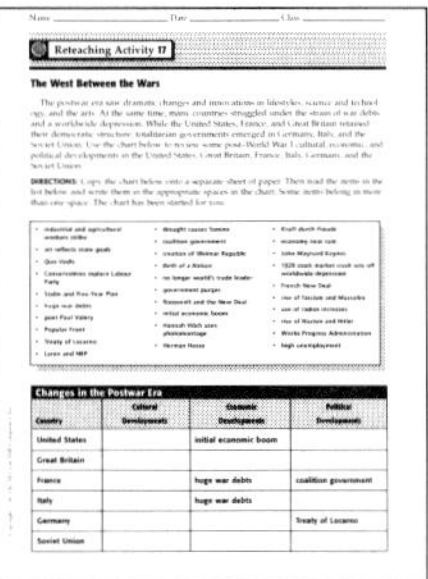

Vocabulary Activity 17

Critical Thinking Skills Activity 17

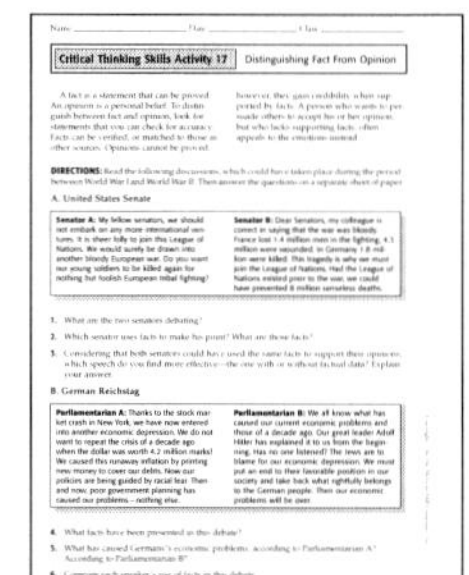

Assessment and Evaluation

Chapter 17 Test Form A

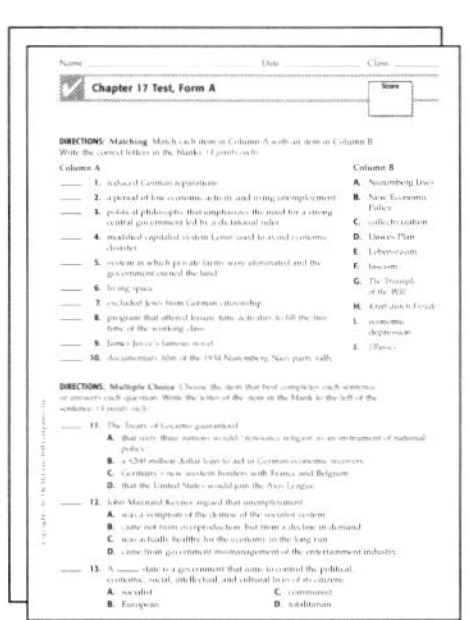

Chapter 17 Test Form B

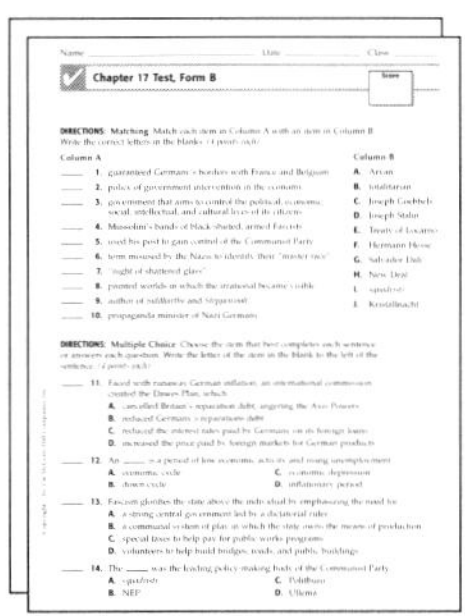

Performance Assessment Activity 17

ExamView® Pro Testmaker CD-ROM

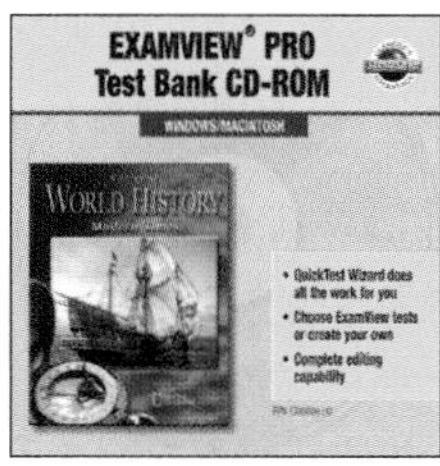

Standardized Test Skills Practice Workbook Activity 17

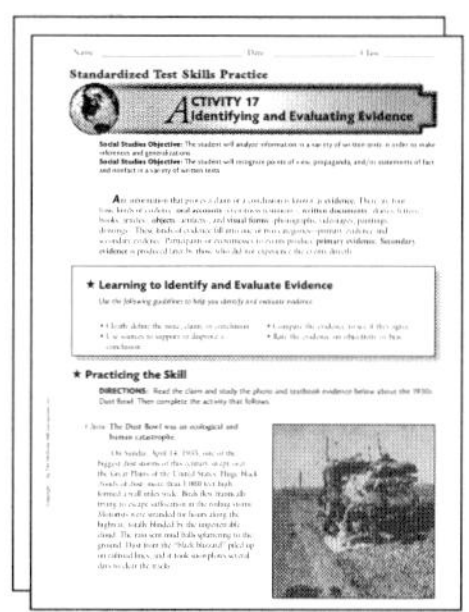

Interdisciplinary Activities

Mapping History Activity 17

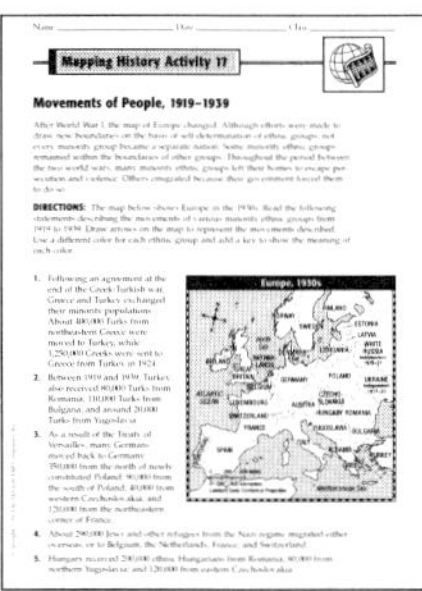

World Art and Music Activity 17

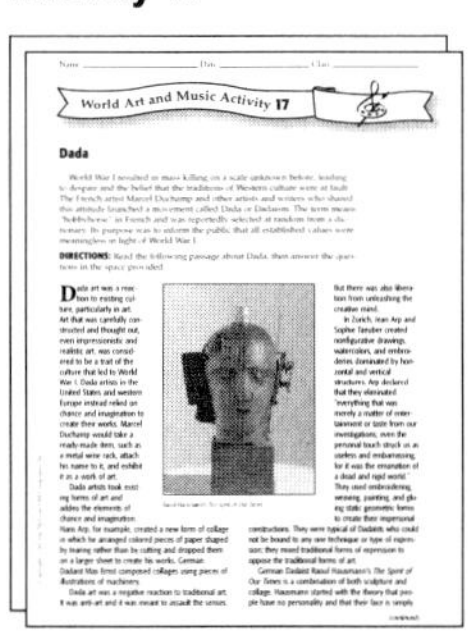

History and Geography Activity 17

People in World History Activity 17

Multimedia

- Vocabulary PuzzleMaker CD-ROM
- Interactive Tutor Self-Assessment CD-ROM
- ExamView® Pro Testmaker CD-ROM
- Audio Program
- World History Primary Source Document Library CD-ROM
- MindJogger Videoquiz
- Presentation Plus! CD-ROM
- TeacherWorks CD-ROM
- Interactive Student Edition CD-ROM
- The World History—Modern Times Video Program

Spanish Resources

The following Spanish language materials are available in the Spanish Resources Binder:

- Spanish Guided Reading Activities
- Spanish Reteaching Activities
- Spanish Quizzes and Tests
- Spanish Vocabulary Activities
- Spanish Summaries

Chapter 17 Resources

SECTION RESOURCES

Daily Objectives	Reproducible Resources	Multimedia Resources
SECTION 1 **The Futile Search for Stability** 1. Explain why peace and prosperity were short-lived after World War I. 2. Describe how a global economic depression weakened the Western democracies after 1929.	Reproducible Lesson Plan 17–1 Daily Lecture and Discussion Notes 17–1 Guided Reading Activity 17–1* Section Quiz 17–1* Reading Essentials and Study Guide 17–1	Daily Focus Skills Transparency 17–1 Interactive Tutor Self-Assessment CD-ROM ExamView® Pro Testmaker CD-ROM Presentation Plus! CD-ROM
SECTION 2 **The Rise of Dictatorial Regimes** 1. Characterize the modern totalitarian state established by Mussolini. 2. Report how Stalin, the leader of the Soviet Union, eliminated people who threatened his power.	Reproducible Lesson Plan 17–2 Daily Lecture and Discussion Notes 17–2 Guided Reading Activity 17–2* Section Quiz 17–2* Reading Essentials and Study Guide 17–2	Daily Focus Skills Transparency 17–2 Interactive Tutor Self-Assessment CD-ROM ExamView® Pro Testmaker CD-ROM Presentation Plus! CD-ROM
SECTION 3 **Hitler and Nazi Germany** 1. Characterize the totalitarian state in Germany established by Hitler and the Nazi Party. 2. Explain why many Germans accepted the Nazi dictatorship while other Germans suffered greatly under Hitler's rule.	Reproducible Lesson Plan 17–3 Daily Lecture and Discussion Notes 17–3 Guided Reading Activity 17–3* Section Quiz 17–3* Reading Essentials and Study Guide 17–3	Daily Focus Skills Transparency 17–3 Interactive Tutor Self-Assessment CD-ROM ExamView® Pro Testmaker CD-ROM Presentation Plus! CD-ROM
SECTION 4 **Cultural and Intellectual Trends** 1. Relate how radios and movies were popular forms of entertainment that were used to spread political messages. 2. Summarize the new artistic and intellectual trends that reflected the despair created by World War I and the Great Depression.	Reproducible Lesson Plan 17–4 Daily Lecture and Discussion Notes 17–4 Guided Reading Activity 17–4* Section Quiz 17–4* Reteaching Activity 17* Reading Essentials and Study Guide 17–4	Daily Focus Skills Transparency 17–4 Interactive Tutor Self-Assessment CD-ROM ExamView® Pro Testmaker CD-ROM Presentation Plus! CD-ROM

0:00 **OUT OF TIME?**
Assign the Chapter 17 **Reading Essentials and Study Guide.**

*Also Available in Spanish

 Blackline Master  Transparency 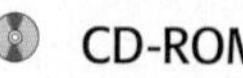 CD-ROM  DVD
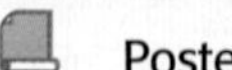 Poster Music Program Audio Program Videocassette

Chapter 17 Resources

NATIONAL GEOGRAPHIC **Teacher's Corner**

INDEX TO NATIONAL GEOGRAPHIC MAGAZINE

The following articles relate to this chapter:

- "Our Man in China," by Mike Edwards, January 1997.
- "U.S.S. *Macon:* Lost and Found," by J. Gordon Vaeth, January 1992.

NATIONAL GEOGRAPHIC SOCIETY PRODUCTS AVAILABLE FROM GLENCOE

To order the following products call Glencoe at 1-800-334-7344:

- *GTV: The American People* (Videodiscs)
- *GTV: A Geographic Perspective on American History* (Videodiscs)

ADDITIONAL NATIONAL GEOGRAPHIC SOCIETY PRODUCTS

To order the following, call National Geographic at 1-800-368-2728:

- *1929–1941: The Great Depression* (Video)
- *The Superliners: Twilight of an Era* (Video)
- *Secrets of the Titantic* (Video)

NGS ONLINE

Access National Geographic's new dynamic MapMachine Web site and other geography resources at:
www.nationalgeographic.com
www.nationalgeographic.com/maps

KEY TO ABILITY LEVELS

Teaching strategies have been coded.

- L1 BASIC activities for all students
- L2 AVERAGE activities for average to above-average students
- L3 CHALLENGING activities for above-average students
- ELL ENGLISH LANGUAGE LEARNER activities

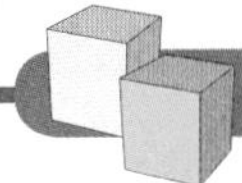

Block Schedule

Activities that are suited to use within the block scheduling framework are identified by:

WORLD HISTORY Online

Use our Web site for additional resources. All essential content is covered in the Student Edition.

You and your students can visit www.wh.mt.glencoe.com, the Web site companion to *Glencoe World History—Modern Times.* This innovative integration of electronic and print media offers your students a wealth of opportunities. The student text directs students to the Web site for the following options:

- **Chapter Overviews**
- **Self-Check Quizzes**
- **Student Web Activities**
- **Textbook Updates**

Answers to the Student Web Activities are provided for you in the **Web Activity Lesson Plans.** Additional Web resources and Interactive Tutor Puzzles are also available.

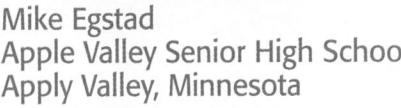

From the Classroom of...

Mike Egstad
Apple Valley Senior High School
Apply Valley, Minnesota

Fascism

Use the fasces from ancient Rome to demonstrate the essential meaning of fascism. The fasces was a battle ax (the state), a bundle of sticks (the citizens), and a strong cord (the law), which bound the sticks around the ax. It represented authority in Roman times and came to symbolize the relationship between the citizen and the state.

Bring to class a long, fairly thin dowel to represent the ax. Have each student contribute a pencil and use string or rubber bands to bind them into a bundle around the dowel. Then have students try to break the bundle with their bare hands. Remove the pencil that you have contributed and snap it in half with your fingers. Then demonstrate to students how easily the dowel with all pencils gone will break.

Point out to students that the primary goal and duty of individual citizens in a fascist state was to serve and protect the state. Remind them of Hitler's remark after the disaster at Stalingrad. "What is life? Life is the nation. The individual must die anyway. Beyond the life of the individual is the nation." Lead a class discussion evaluating this comment in relation to the demonstration of the fasces.

Introducing CHAPTER 17

Performance Assessment

Refer to Activity 17 in the Performance Assessment Activities and Rubrics booklet.

The Impact Today

Guide students in a discussion of both the negative and positive impact of automobiles, radio, and television on their lives and on the lives of their families. How would their lives differ without these technological developments? What leisure activities would they pursue?

GLENCOE TECHNOLOGY

The World History—Modern Times Video Program

To learn more about individuals who came to power following World War I, students can view the Chapter 17 video, "The Rise of Dictators," from **The World History—Modern Times Video Program.**

MindJogger Videoquiz

Use the **MindJogger Videoquiz** to preview Chapter 17 content.

 Available in VHS.

CHAPTER 17 The West Between the Wars

1919–1939

Key Events

As you read this chapter, look for the key events in the history of the Western countries between the wars.

- *Europe faced severe economic problems after World War I, including inflation and the Great Depression.*
- *Dictatorial regimes began to spread into Italy, Germany, and across eastern Europe.*
- *The uncertainties and disillusionment of the times were reflected in the art and literature of the 1920s and 1930s.*

The Impact Today

The events that occurred during this time period still impact our lives today.

- *The current debate over the federal government's role in local affairs and social problems developed in part from Franklin D. Roosevelt's solution to the Great Depression.*
- *Automobiles, motion pictures, and radios transformed the ways in which people lived during the 1920s and 1930s and still impact how we live our lives today.*

World History—Modern Times Video *The Chapter 17 video, "The Rise of Dictators," chronicles the growth of dictatorial regimes in Europe after 1918.*

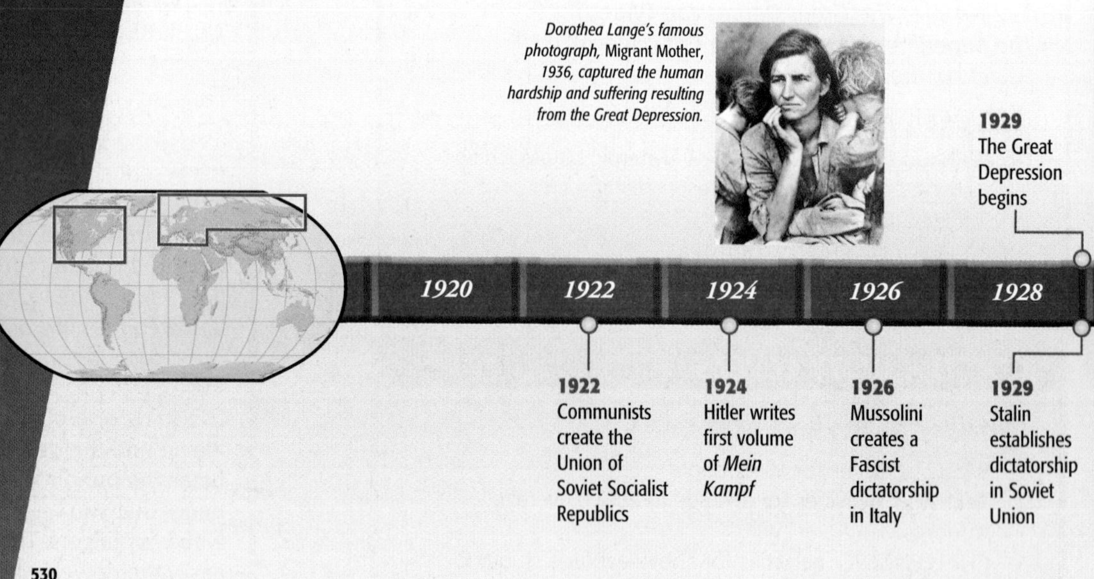
1929
The Great Depression begins
1920
1922
1924
1926
1928
1922
Communists create the Union of Soviet Socialist Republics
1924
Hitler writes first volume of *Mein Kampf*
1926
Mussolini creates a Fascist dictatorship in Italy
1929
Stalin establishes dictatorship in Soviet Union

Dorothea Lange's famous photograph, Migrant Mother, *1936, captured the human hardship and suffering resulting from the Great Depression.*

530

TWO-MINUTE LESSON LAUNCHER

Choose three students to come to the front of the class and ask them to pretend that they are farmers. Farmer Brown has a large farm and works hard seven days a week. Farmer Green has a medium-sized farm and works six days a week. Farmer White has a small farm and works five days a week. Farmer Brown earns 30 tokens for his work. Farmer Green earns 20 for his work, and Farmer White earns 10 for his. The government decides that it will take over the farms, and each farmer must continue to work his own land. Each will be paid 15 tokens for a week's work. Ask the farmers what they think of this government move. Explain that this is an example of socialism. L1 ELL

Hitler and the Nazi Party used rallies, such as this one at Nuremberg in 1937, to create support for their policies.

Franklin D. Roosevelt

1932
Franklin Delano Roosevelt is elected president of the United States

1933
Hitler becomes chancellor of Germany

Flags of the Hitler Youth organization

1936
John Maynard Keynes publishes *General Theory of Employment, Interest, and Money*

1936
Spanish Civil War begins

1930 — 1932 — 1934 — 1936 — 1938

HISTORY Online

Chapter Overview
Visit the *Glencoe World History—Modern Times* Web site at wh.mt.glencoe.com and click on **Chapter 17–Chapter Overview** to preview chapter information.

Introducing CHAPTER 17

Chapter Objectives

After studying this chapter, students should be able to:

1. explain the weaknesses of the League of Nations;
2. list the factors leading to the Great Depression;
3. discuss the response to economic hardships by Great Britain, France, Germany, and the United States;
4. distinguish between dictatorship and totalitarianism;
5. discuss how Mussolini, Stalin, Franco, and Hitler came to power;
6. describe Hitler's anti-Semitic policies and activities;
7. summarize the developments in the areas of art, music, literature, and science.

Chapter Overview
Introduce students to chapter content and key terms by having them access **Chapter Overview 17** at wh.mt.glencoe.com.

Time Line Activity

As students read the chapter, have them review the time line on this page. Ask them to explain the significance of 1933. *(Hitler became chancellor of Germany and began to establish the Nazi state.)* **L1**

MORE ABOUT THE ART

Nuremberg Rally On September 5, 1937, Adolf Hitler arrived in Nuremberg for the opening of the National Socialist Congress. The event was the largest display of Nazi power in Germany's history. Church bells rang and storm troopers lined the streets of Nuremberg to greet the führer. The size of the Congress was staggering, as Hitler reviewed a parade of 600,000 men. Hundreds of trains transported army and paramilitary units to the gathering, and tent cities were erected to house the participants. Days later Hitler met with foreign diplomats, including representatives from the United States and Italian leader Benito Mussolini.

CHAPTER PREVIEW

Introducing
A Story That Matters

Depending upon the ability levels of your students, select from the following questions to reinforce the reading of *A Story That Matters*.

- What were people's hopes during the 1920s? *(international peace, economic growth, political democracy)*
- Of all the severe economic problems, which was the most devastating? *(The Great Depression)* Why? *(widespread hunger, homelessness, despair)*
- Why do you think social unrest sometimes leads people to follow extremists and demagogues? *(Answers will vary.)*
- Do you think that a second Great Depression could occur today? Answers should be supported by examples and logical arguments. *(Answers will vary.)* **L1 L2**

CHAPTER PREVIEW

A Story That Matters

During the Great Depression, many people had to resort to desperate measures to find food.

The Great Depression

After World War I, Europe was faced with severe economic problems. Most devastating of all was the Great Depression that began at the end of 1929. The Great Depression brought misery to millions of people. Begging for food on the streets became widespread, especially when soup kitchens were unable to keep up with the demand.

More and more people were homeless and moved around looking for work and shelter. One observer in Germany reported, "An almost unbroken chain of homeless men extends the whole length of the great Hamburg-Berlin highway . . . [w]hole families had piled all their goods into baby carriages and wheelbarrows that they were pushing along as they plodded forward in dumb despair." In the United States, the homeless set up shantytowns they named "Hoovervilles" after President Herbert Hoover.

In their misery, some people saw suicide as the only solution. One unemployed person said, "Today, when I am experiencing this for the first time, I think that I should prefer to do away with myself, to take gas, to jump into the river, or leap from some high place. . . . Would I really come to such a decision? I do not know."

Social unrest spread rapidly. Some of the unemployed staged hunger marches to get attention. In democratic countries, people began to listen to, and vote for, radical voices calling for extreme measures.

Why It Matters

In the 1920s, many people assumed that Europe and the world were about to enter a new era of international peace, economic growth, and political democracy. These hopes were not realized, however. Most people wanted peace but were unsure how to maintain it. Plans for economic revival gave way to inflation and then to the Great Depression. Making matters worse, economic hard times gave rise to dictatorial regimes across much of Europe. The world was filled with uncertainty.

History and You Make a diagram listing the problems faced by the United States, Germany, and France during the Great Depression. Indicate how the problems were interrelated. Using what you learn from your diagram, explain how recovery would also have a chain effect.

HISTORY AND YOU

During the Great Depression, unemployment led to widespread hunger, homelessness, and despair on the part of many Americans. Yet the American spirit endured. Multiple families shared homes, strangers sheltered and fed those less fortunate, and people pulled together for the common good. That spirit was reawakened on the morning of September 11, 2001, when terrorists attacked the United States, wreaking death, destruction, and despair. Americans showed their strength of spirit once more. They pulled together to help people directly affected by the attacks and vowed to defeat terrorism. Hard times often promote unity, patriotism, and inner resolve. L2

SECTION 1

The Futile Search for Stability

Guide to Reading

Main Ideas
- Peace and prosperity were short-lived after World War I.
- After 1929, a global economic depression weakened the Western democracies.

Key Terms
depression, collective bargaining, deficit spending

People to Identify
John Maynard Keynes, Franklin Delano Roosevelt

Places to Locate
Ruhr Valley, Switzerland

Preview Questions
1. What was the significance of the Dawes Plan and the Treaty of Locarno?
2. How was Germany affected by the Great Depression?

Reading Strategy
Compare and Contrast Use a table like the one below to compare France's Popular Front with the New Deal in the United States.

Popular Front	New Deal

Preview of Events

1920 · 1925 · 1930 · 1935 · 1940

- **1921** German debt determined
- **1924** German debt restructured
- **1925** Treaty of Locarno
- **1929** U.S. stock market crashes
- **1935** WPA is established
- **1936** Popular Front is formed in France

Voices from the Past

Hunger marchers in London, 1932

On October 27, 1932, a group of workers marched in London to protest government policies. One observer reported:

❝By mid-day approximately 100,000 London workers were moving towards Hyde Park from all parts of London, to give the greatest welcome to the hunger marchers that had ever been seen in Hyde Park. . . . As the last contingent of marchers entered the park gates, trouble broke out with the police. It started with the special constables [police officers]; not being used to their task, they lost their heads, and, as the crowds swept forward on to the space where the meetings were to be held, the specials drew their truncheons [billy clubs] in an effort to control the sea of surging humanity. This incensed the workers, who turned on the constables and put them to flight.❞

—***Eyewitness to History,*** **John Carey, ed., 1987**

Worker unrest was but one of the social problems in Europe in the 1920s and 1930s.

Uneasy Peace, Uncertain Security

The peace settlement at the end of World War I had tried to fulfill nineteenth-century dreams of nationalism by creating new boundaries and new states. From the beginning, however, the settlement left nations unhappy. Border disputes poisoned relations in eastern Europe for years. Many Germans vowed to revise the terms of the Treaty of Versailles.

1 FOCUS

Section Overview
This section explores the Great Depression and its effect on governments after World War I.

BELLRINGER
Skillbuilder Activity

 Project transparency and have students answer questions.

 Available as a blackline master.

Daily Focus Skills Transparency 17–1

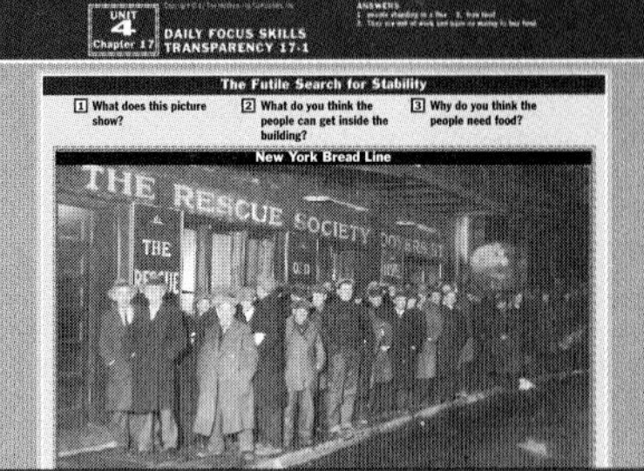

Guide to Reading

Answers to Graphic: Popular Front: right to collective bargaining, forty-hour work week, two-week paid vacation, minimum wage; New Deal: active government intervention in the economy, increased public works programs, new social legislation that began the U.S. welfare system

Preteaching Vocabulary: Explain the economic use of the word *depression. (A depression is a period of low economic activity and rising unemployment.)* L2

SECTION RESOURCES

Reproducible Masters
- Reproducible Lesson Plan 17–1
- Daily Lecture and Discussion Notes 17–1
- Guided Reading Activity 17–1
- Section Quiz 17–1
- Reading Essentials and Study Guide 17–1

Transparencies
- Daily Focus Skills Transparency 17–1

Multimedia
- Interactive Tutor Self-Assessment CD-ROM
- ExamView® Pro Testmaker CD-ROM
- Presentation Plus! CD-ROM

CHAPTER 17
Section 1, 533–538

2 TEACH

Answer: Answers will vary but should be supported by documentation and logical arguments.

Daily Lecture and Discussion Notes 17–1

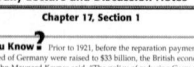

Daily Lecture and Discussion Notes

Chapter 17, Section 1

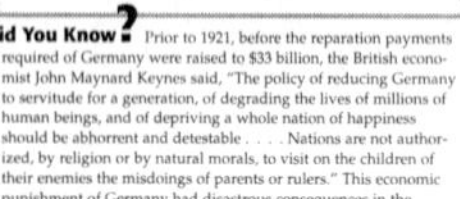

Did You Know? Prior to 1921, before the reparation payments required of Germany were raised to $33 billion, the British economist John Maynard Keynes said, "The policy of reducing Germany to servitude for a generation, of degrading the lives of millions of human beings, and of depriving a whole nation of happiness should be abhorrent and detestable . . . . Nations are not authorized, by religion or by natural morals, to visit on the children of their enemies the misdoings of parents or rulers." This economic punishment of Germany had disastrous consequences in the decades to come.

I. **Uneasy Peace, Uncertain Security** *(pages 533–536)*

A. The peace settlement at the end of World War I created repeated border disputes among new nations and left many Germans determined to change the terms of the Treaty of Versailles.

B. Though President Wilson and others hoped that the League of Nations could solve many of the new conflicts, the League was not able to maintain peace. One reason for this was that the United States never ratified the Treaty of Versailles and could not become a member of the League of Nations. Americans did not want to be involved in European affairs. Also, the League could not use military force and had to rely only on economic sanctions to stop aggression.

C. The French demanded that the Treaty of Versailles be strictly enforced. The Germans said that due to economic problems they could no longer continue to pay back the $33 billion that was required. The French army occupied the **Ruhr Valley,** an industrial and mining center. The French planned to take the reparations by operating German industries themselves.

D. In response, German workers went on strike. The government paid them by printing more money. This devalued the German currency and increased the inflation that had begun before the end of the war. The German mark became completely worthless. By the end of 1923, it took more than 4 trillion marks to equal one U.S. dollar.

E. The huge inflation meant that people suffered terribly. The economic problems led to political unrest in Germany. Other countries stepped in to help. **The Dawes Plan** began by reducing reparation payments and coordinating Germany's payments with what the nation could afford. The plan also loaned Germany $200 million and led to other American investments, which lasted between 1924 and 1929.

242

Guided Reading Activity 17–1

Name ________ Date ________ Class ________

Guided Reading Activity 17-1

The Futile Search for Stability

DIRECTIONS: Answer the following questions as you read Section 1.

1. What did the settlement at the end of World War I try to accomplish?
2. What wishes of Woodrow Wilson did the U.S. Senate refuse to fulfill?
3. How did France intend to collect unpaid war reparations from Germany?
4. Name two things the Dawes plan accomplished.
5. What did the League of Nations Covenant suggest that nations do with their military?
6. List two factors that played a major role in the start of the Great Depression.
7. How bad was the Great Depression in Great Britain in 1932?
8. List three problems faced by the Weimar Republic.
9. What was the old theory of how economic depressions should be solved?
10. How did Franklin Roosevelt propose to reform capitalism in order to save it?

A Weak League of Nations President Woodrow Wilson had realized that the peace settlement included unwise provisions that could serve as new causes for conflict. He had placed many of his hopes for the future in the League of Nations. This organization, however, was not very effective in maintaining the peace.

One problem was the failure of the United States to join the league. Most Americans did not wish to be involved in European affairs. The U.S. Senate, despite Wilson's wishes, refused to ratify, or approve, the Treaty of Versailles. That meant the United States could not be a member of the League of Nations, which automatically weakened the organization's effectiveness. Furthermore, the league could use only economic sanctions, and not military force, to stop aggression.

French Demands Between 1919 and 1924, desire for security led the French government to demand strict enforcement of the Treaty of Versailles. This tough policy toward Germany began with the issue of reparations, which were the payments that the Germans were supposed to make for the damage they had done in the war.

In April 1921, the Allied Reparations Commission determined that Germany owed 132 billion German marks (33 billion U.S. dollars) for reparations, payable in annual installments of 2.5 billion marks. The new German republic made its first payment in 1921.

By the following year, however, the German government, faced with financial problems, announced that it was unable to pay any more. France was outraged and sent troops to occupy the **Ruhr Valley,** Germany's chief industrial and mining center. France planned to collect reparations by operating and using the Ruhr mines and factories.

Inflation in Germany The German government adopted a policy of passive resistance to French occupation. German workers went on strike, and the government mainly paid their salaries by printing more paper money. This only added to the inflation (rise in prices) that had already begun in Germany by the end of the war.

CONNECTIONS Around The World

The Great Flu Epidemic

A flu epidemic at the end of World War I proved disastrous to people all over the world. Some observers believe that it began among American soldiers in Kansas. When they were sent abroad to fight, they carried the virus to Europe. By the end of 1918, many soldiers in European armies had been stricken with the flu.

The disease spread quickly throughout Europe. The three chief statesmen at the peace conference—the American president Woodrow Wilson, the British prime minister David Lloyd George, and the French premier Georges Clemenceau—all were sick with the flu during the negotiations that led to the Treaty of Versailles.

◀ *Flu victim*

The Spanish flu, as this strain of influenza was called, was known for its swift and deadly action. Many people died within a day of being infected. Complications also arose from bacterial infections in the lungs, which caused a deadly form of pneumonia.

In 1918 and 1919, the Spanish flu spread around the world with devastating results. Death tolls were enormous: in Russia, 450,000; in India, 5,000,000; in the United States, 550,000. It has been estimated that 22 million people, or more than twice the number of people killed in World War I, died from the great flu epidemic between 1918 and 1919.

Comparing Cultures

Using outside sources, research the medical advancements made since 1919 in treating and preventing influenza viruses. Could another flu epidemic occur today? Has the flu danger been replaced by other medical concerns?

COOPERATIVE LEARNING ACTIVITY

Conducting an Interview Organize the class into small groups, and ask each group to interview people who lived through the Great Depression of the 1930s. (If some students have no such contacts, direct them to local retirement or nursing homes.) Within each group, students should choose a topic, such as memories of Hoover and Roosevelt, New Deal programs, family experiences, and base their interview questions on these topics. Groups should assign each member a job, such as planning the interview questions, selecting people to interview, conducting interviews, and summarizing results. Ask each group to share their research by presenting an oral report to the class. **L2**

The German mark soon became worthless. In 1914, 4.2 marks equaled 1 U.S. dollar. By November 1, 1923, it took 130 billion marks to equal 1 dollar. By the end of November, the ratio had increased to an incredible 4.2 trillion marks to 1 dollar.

Evidence of runaway inflation was everywhere. Workers used wheelbarrows to carry home their weekly pay. One woman left a basket of money outside while she went into a store. When she came out, the money was there, but the basket had been stolen.

Economic adversity led to political upheavals, and both France and Germany began to seek a way out of the disaster. In August 1924, an international commission produced a new plan for reparations. **The Dawes Plan,** named after the American banker who chaired the commission, first reduced reparations. It then coordinated Germany's annual payments with its ability to pay.

The Dawes Plan also granted an initial $200 million loan for German recovery. This loan soon opened the door to heavy American investment in Europe. A brief period of European prosperity followed, but it only lasted from 1924 to 1929.

NATIONAL GEOGRAPHIC **Europe, 1923**

Territories administered by the League of Nations

Territory administered by the League of Nations

Lambert Azimuthal Equal-Area projection

Geography *Skills*

The new nationalism, as reflected by the European political map of the 1920s, did not solve Europe's problems after the war.

1. **Interpreting Maps** Compare the map above to the map of Europe before World War I on page 500. List all the countries shown on this map that are *not* shown on the earlier map. What does your list tell you about the political results of World War I?
2. **Applying Geography Skills** Again, compare the map above to the one on page 500. Create a two-column table. Label one column Changed Boundaries, and the other Unchanged Boundaries. List countries under the appropriate column.

The Treaty of Locarno With prosperity came a new European diplomacy. A spirit of cooperation was fostered by the foreign ministers of Germany and France, Gustav Stresemann and Aristide Briand. In 1925, they signed the **Treaty of Locarno,** which guaranteed Germany's new western borders with France and Belgium.

The Locarno pact was viewed by many as the beginning of a new era of European peace. On the day after the pact was concluded, the headlines in *The New York Times* read "France and Germany Ban War Forever." The London *Times* declared "Peace at Last."

The new spirit of cooperation grew even stronger when Germany joined the League of Nations in March 1926. Two years later, the Kellogg-Briand pact brought even more hope. Sixty-three nations signed this accord written by U.S. secretary of state Frank B. Kellogg and French foreign minister Aristide Briand. These nations pledged "to renounce war as an instrument of national policy." Nothing was said, however, about what would be done if anyone violated the pact.

Unfortunately, the spirit of Locarno was based on little real substance. Promises not to go to war were worthless without a way to enforce these promises. Furthermore, not even the spirit of Locarno could convince nations to cut back on their weapons. The League of Nations Covenant had suggested that

Geography *Skills*

Answers:

1. Turkey, Yugoslavia, Czechoslovakia, Hungary, Poland, Latvia, Estonia, Lithuania, Finland (East Prussia was a province of Germany); old empires dissolved, new states created
2. Changed: Germany, Austria-Hungary, Serbia, Albania (Yugoslavia); Unchanged: United Kingdom, France, Spain, Switzerland, Italy, Norway, Sweden

Critical Thinking

Ask students to speculate why Europe's economic and political upturn was short-lived despite the Dawes Plan, the Treaty of Locarno, the League of Nations, and the Kellogg-Briand pact. L2

Enrich

Guide students in a discussion and comparison of Great Britain and France's responses to postwar economic adversity. L2

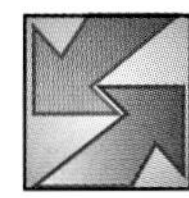

CURRICULUM CONNECTION

Economics Assign interested students sections of Keynes's *General Theory of Employment, Interest, and Money*. Ask them to prepare a lesson for the class on the basics of Keynesian economics. L3

CRITICAL THINKING ACTIVITY

Drawing Conclusions Economic events affected the world's governments after World War I. During the 1920s and 1930s, economic conditions resulted in unemployment, hunger, homelessness, and despair. In Europe and Latin America, these conditions allowed dictators and military governments to assume power, as people became more willing to surrender personal liberties in exchange for food, jobs, shelter, and security. In the United States, the federal government abandoned its *laissez-faire* policy and created public works and social programs to aid the ailing economy. Ask students to define the word *depression* and write a paragraph concluding why another depression could or could not occur today. L2

Reading Check

Answer: could use only economic sanctions to stop aggression

TURNING POINT

The Great Depression was one of the most extensive and significant economic downturns that the world had ever seen.

Reading Check

Answer: increased government activity in the economy; renewed interest in Marxist doctrines; led people to follow dictatorial leaders

Connecting Across Time

Guide students in a discussion of the factors leading to the Great Depression and how it differed from other economic downturns. Ask students to research how the Great Depression affected colonial economies. Who suffered more, the colonial powers or those living in the colonies? **L2**

Who?What?Where?When?

Dorothea Lange Ask students to bring in copies of photographs taken by Dorothea Lange during the depression. Discuss what makes these photographs so powerful. **L1**

Enrich

Have students create their own time lines of important economic events of the 1920s and 1930s. **L1** ELL

nations reduce their military forces to make war less probable. Germany, of course, had been forced to reduce its military forces. At the time, it was thought that other states would later do the same. However, states were simply unwilling to trust their security to anyone but their own military forces.

Reading Check **Explaining** Why was the League of Nations unable to maintain peace?

The Great Depression

TURNING POINT **In this section, you will learn how Western nations suffered a major economic collapse in the 1930s. This collapse, called the Great Depression, devastated morale, led to extremist political parties, and created the conditions for World War II.**

The brief period of prosperity that began in Europe in 1924 ended in an economic collapse that came to be known as the Great Depression. A **depression** is a period of low economic activity and rising unemployment.

Causes of the Depression Two factors played a major role in the start of the Great Depression. One important factor was a series of downturns in the economies of individual nations in the second half of the 1920s. By the mid-1920s, for example, prices for farm products, especially wheat, were falling rapidly because of overproduction.

The second factor in the coming of the Great Depression was an international financial crisis involving the U.S. stock market. We have seen that much of the European prosperity between 1924 and 1929 was built on U.S. bank loans to Germany. Germany needed the U.S. loans to pay reparations to France and Great Britain.

During the 1920s, the U.S. stock market was booming. By 1928, American investors had begun to pull money out of Germany to invest it in the stock market. Then, in October 1929, the U.S. stock market crashed, and the prices of stocks plunged.

In a panic, U.S. investors withdrew even more funds from Germany and other European markets. This withdrawal weakened the banks of Germany and other European states. The Credit-Anstalt, Vienna's most famous bank, collapsed in May 1931. Other banks soon followed, industrial production declined, and unemployment rose.

Economic downturns led to labor unrest in many countries.

Responses to the Depression Economic depression was by no means new to Europe. However, the extent of the economic downturn after 1929 truly made this the Great Depression. During 1932, the worst year of the depression, one British worker in every four was unemployed. Six million Germans, or 40 percent of the German labor force, were out of work at the same time. The unemployed and homeless filled the streets.

Governments did not know how to deal with the crisis. They tried a traditional solution of cutting costs by lowering wages and raising protective tariffs to exclude foreign goods from home markets. These measures made the economic crisis worse, however, and had serious political effects.

One effect of the economic crisis was increased government activity in the economy. This occurred even in countries that, like the United States, had a strong laissez-faire tradition—a belief that the government should not interfere in the economy.

Another effect was a renewed interest in Marxist doctrines. Marx's prediction that capitalism would destroy itself through overproduction seemed to be coming true. Communism thus became more popular, especially among workers and intellectuals.

Finally, the Great Depression led masses of people to follow political leaders who offered simple solutions in return for dictatorial power. Everywhere, democracy seemed on the defensive in the 1930s.

Reading Check **Summarizing** What were the results of the Great Depression?

EXTENDING THE CONTENT

Folk Music Woody Guthrie was an American balladeer who rode the railroads during the Great Depression, writing and singing songs about poverty and social justice. Although his folk music was written during the Great Depression, it was not at all depressing. Guthrie celebrated the indomitable human spirit in more than a thousand ballads. His most popular song is probably "This Land Is Your Land," still sung by countless school children. It is a song of democracy and equality, written at a time when such values were being challenged throughout the world.

Democratic States after the War

President Woodrow Wilson had claimed that the war had been fought to make the world safe for democracy. In 1919, his claim seemed justified. Most major European states and many minor ones had democratic governments.

In a number of states, women could now vote. Male political leaders had rewarded women for their contributions to the war effort by granting them voting rights. (Exceptions were Italy, **Switzerland,** France, and Spain, where women had to wait until the end of World War II for the right to vote.)

In the 1920s, Europe seemed to be returning to the political trends of the prewar era—parliamentary regimes and the growth of individual liberties. This was not, however, an easy process. Four years of total war and four years of postwar turmoil made a "return to normalcy" difficult.

Germany The Imperial Germany of William II had come to an end in 1918 with Germany's defeat in the war. A German democratic state known as the **Weimar** (VY•MAHR) **Republic** was then created. The Weimar Republic was plagued by problems.

For one thing, the republic had no truly outstanding political leaders. In 1925, Paul von Hindenburg, a World War I military hero, was elected president at the age of 77. Hindenburg was a traditional military man who did not fully endorse the republic he had been elected to serve.

The Weimar Republic also faced serious economic problems. As we have seen, Germany experienced runaway inflation in 1922 and 1923. With it came serious social problems. Widows, teachers, civil servants, and others who lived on fixed incomes all watched their monthly incomes become worthless, or their life savings disappear. These losses increasingly pushed the middle class toward political parties that were hostile to the republic.

To make matters worse, after a period of relative prosperity from 1924 to 1929, Germany was struck by the Great Depression. In 1930, unemployment had grown to 3 million people by March and to 4.38 million by December. The depression paved the way for fear and the rise of extremist parties.

France After the defeat of Germany, France became the strongest power on the European continent. Its greatest need was to rebuild the areas that had been devastated in the war. However, France, too, suffered financial problems after the war.

This German woman is using her worthless money to start a fire in her kitchen stove.

Because it had a more balanced economy than other nations, France did not begin to feel the full effects of the Great Depression until 1932. The economic instability it then suffered soon had political effects. During a nineteen-month period in 1932 and 1933, six different cabinets were formed as France faced political chaos. Finally, in June 1936, a coalition of leftist parties—Communists, Socialists, and Radicals—formed the Popular Front government.

The Popular Front started a program for workers that some have called the French New Deal. This program was named after the New Deal in the United States (discussed later in this section). The French New Deal gave workers the right to collective bargaining (the right of unions to negotiate with employers over wages and hours), a 40-hour workweek, a two-week paid vacation, and a minimum wage.

The Popular Front's policies, however, failed to solve the problems of the depression. By 1938, the French had little confidence in their political system.

Great Britain During the war, Britain had lost many of the markets for its industrial products to the United

3 ASSESS

Assign Section 1 Assessment as homework or as an in-class activity.

Have students use **Interactive Tutor Self-Assessment CD-ROM.**

Section Quiz 17–1

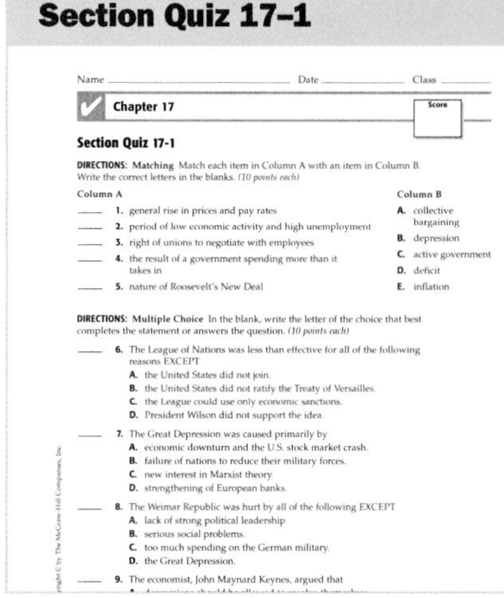

Name ______ Date ______ Class ______

Chapter 17 Score

Section Quiz 17-1

DIRECTIONS: Matching Match each item in Column A with an item in Column B. Write the correct letters in the blanks. *(10 points each)*

Column A	Column B
____ 1. general rise in prices and pay rates	A. collective bargaining
____ 2. period of low economic activity and high unemployment	B. depression
____ 3. right of unions to negotiate with employees	C. active government
____ 4. the result of a government spending more than it takes in	D. deficit
____ 5. nature of Roosevelt's New Deal	E. inflation

DIRECTIONS: Multiple Choice In the blank, write the letter of the choice that best completes the statement or answers the question. *(10 points each)*

____ 6. The League of Nations was less than effective for all of the following reasons EXCEPT
A. the United States did not join.
B. the United States did not ratify the Treaty of Versailles.
C. the League could use only economic sanctions.
D. President Wilson did not support the idea.

____ 7. The Great Depression was caused primarily by
A. economic downturn and the U.S. stock market crash.
B. failure of nations to reduce their military forces.
C. new interest in Marxist theory.
D. strengthening of European banks.

____ 8. The Weimar Republic was hurt by all of the following EXCEPT
A. lack of strong political leadership.
B. serious social problems.
C. too much spending on the German military.
D. the Great Depression.

____ 9. The economist, John Maynard Keynes, argued that

Reading Essentials and Study Guide 17–1

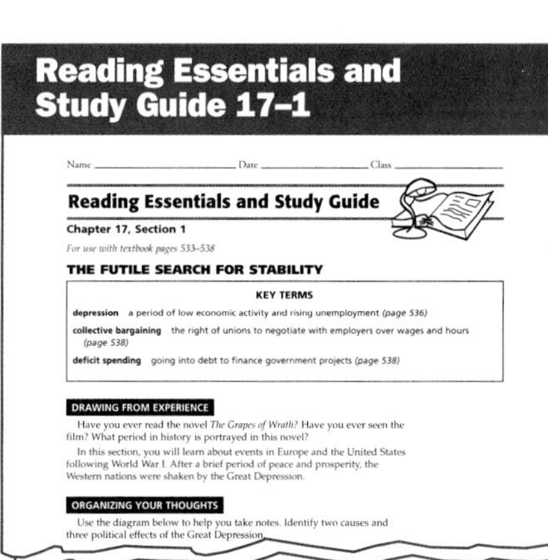

Name ______ Date ______ Class ______

Reading Essentials and Study Guide

Chapter 17, Section 1

For use with textbook pages 533–538

THE FUTILE SEARCH FOR STABILITY

KEY TERMS

depression a period of low economic activity and rising unemployment *(page 536)*

collective bargaining the right of unions to negotiate with employers over wages and hours *(page 538)*

deficit spending going into debt to finance government projects *(page 538)*

DRAWING FROM EXPERIENCE

Have you ever read the novel *The Grapes of Wrath?* Have you ever seen the film? What period in history is portrayed in this novel?

In this section, you will learn about events in Europe and the United States following World War I. After a brief period of peace and prosperity, the Western nations were shaken by the Great Depression.

ORGANIZING YOUR THOUGHTS

Use the diagram below to help you take notes. Identify two causes and three political effects of the Great Depression.

Critical Thinking

Economic downturns often occur in free-market economies. Have students identify elements from a recent recession that parallel conditions of the Great Depression. L2

MEETING INDIVIDUAL NEEDS

Multiple Intelligences Divide the class into eight small groups. Assign each group a topic from this section, as follows: the League of Nations, France, Germany, Great Britain, the United States, the Dawes Plan, the Treaty of Locarno, and the Great Depression. Ask each group to discuss and write down the important points of this topic presented in this section. Then have each group discuss what it has written and explain why it is important. Select one representative from each group to present the group's findings to the class. L1 ELL

Refer to ***Inclusion for the High School Social Studies Classroom Strategies and Activities*** in the TCR.

Reading Check

Answer: Governments should put people back to work building highways and public buildings, financing public works projects even if they have to engage in deficit spending.

Connecting Across Time

During the 1920s and 1930s, economic downturns led to labor unrest in many Western democracies. British workers often carried out strikes for better wages. A general strike is labor's strongest weapon, and when it occurs society can be thrown into upheaval. During a class discussion, ask students to give examples of present-day strikes and their effects on society. L2

Reteaching Activity

Ask students to review the section and list ways in which the bitterness of national rivalries were fed by the World War I settlements and post-war events. Have students speculate about the results of these new rivalries. L1

4 CLOSE

Guide students in a discussion about why democracy survived in the United States, Great Britain, and France after World War I despite serious economic and political problems. Then ask students to suggest examples that illustrate the following sentence: "Everywhere, democracy seemed on the defensive in the 1930s." L2

States and Japan. Such industries as coal, steel, and textiles declined after the war, leading to a rise in unemployment. In 1921, 2 million Britons were out of work. Britain soon rebounded, however, and experienced limited prosperity from 1925 to 1929.

By 1929, Britain faced the growing effects of the Great Depression. The Labour Party, which had become the largest party in Britain, failed to solve the nation's economic problems and fell from power in 1931. A new government, led by the Conservatives, claimed credit for bringing Britain out of the worst stages of the depression. It did so by using the traditional policies of balanced budgets and protective tariffs.

John Maynard Keynes

Political leaders in Britain largely ignored the new ideas of a British economist, **John Maynard Keynes,** who published his *General Theory of Employment, Interest, and Money* in 1936. He condemned the old theory that, in a free economy, depressions should be left to resolve themselves without governmental interference.

Keynes argued that unemployment came not from overproduction, but from a decline in demand. Demand, in turn, could be increased by putting people back to work building highways and public buildings. The government should finance such projects even if it had to engage in deficit spending, or had to go into debt.

The United States After Germany, no Western nation was more affected by the Great Depression than the United States. By 1932, U.S. industrial production had fallen 50 percent from its 1929 level. By 1933, there were 15 million unemployed.

Under these circumstances, the Democrat **Franklin Delano Roosevelt** was able to win a landslide victory in the 1932 presidential election. A believer in free enterprise, Roosevelt realized that capitalism had to be reformed if it was to be "saved." He pursued a policy of active government intervention in the economy that came to be known as the **New Deal.**

The New Deal included an increased program of public works, including the Works Progress Administration (WPA). The WPA, established in 1935, was a government organization that employed between 2 and 3 million people. They worked at building bridges, roads, post offices, and airports.

The Roosevelt administration was also responsible for new social legislation that began the U.S. welfare system. In 1935, the Social Security Act created a system of old-age pensions and unemployment insurance.

The New Deal provided reforms that perhaps prevented a social revolution in the United States. However, it did not solve the unemployment problems of the Great Depression. In 1938, American unemployment still stood at 11 million. Only World War II and the growth of weapons industries brought U.S. workers back to full employment.

Reading Check **Explaining** What did John Maynard Keynes think would resolve the Great Depression?

SECTION 1 ASSESSMENT

Checking for Understanding

1. **Define** depression, collective bargaining, deficit spending.
2. **Identify** Dawes Plan, Treaty of Locarno, John Maynard Keynes, Weimar Republic, Franklin Delano Roosevelt, New Deal.
3. **Locate** Ruhr Valley, Switzerland.
4. **Summarize** the intent of the Roosevelt administration's New Deal.
5. **List** the provisions of the Dawes Plan.

Critical Thinking

6. **Evaluate** Determine the validity of the following quotation: "Promises not to go to war were worthless without a way to enforce these promises."
7. **Cause and Effect** Use a diagram like the one below to list the causes of the Great Depression.

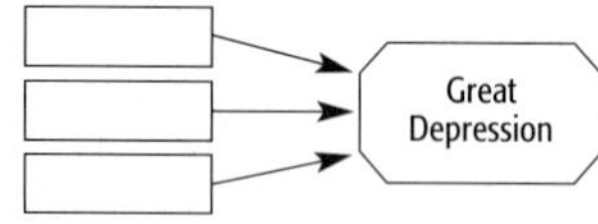

Analyzing Visuals

8. **Examine** the photograph on page 537. How would you survive if currency became worthless? Who would be at an advantage?

Writing About History

9. **Informative Writing** Research and write an essay that explains how the Great Depression caused extremist political parties to emerge throughout the world. Identify which parties are still active in the United States.

SECTION 1 ASSESSMENT

1. Key terms are in blue.
2. Dawes Plan *(p. 535)*; Treaty of Locarno *(p. 535)*; John Maynard Keynes *(p. 538)*; Weimar Republic *(p. 537)*; Franklin Delano Roosevelt *(p. 538)*; New Deal *(p. 538)*
3. See chapter maps.
4. New Deal: a policy of active government intervention in the economy; featured increased public works and new social legislation that began the U.S. welfare system
5. reduced reparations, coordinated Germany's annual payments with its ability to pay, and granted an initial $200 million loan for German recovery
6. Answers will vary.
7. series of downturns in the economies of individual nations; international financial crisis; crash of the U.S. stock market
8. Answers will vary.
9. Answers will vary. Communist and Socialist parties are still active.

CRITICAL THINKING SKILLBUILDER

Analyzing Political Cartoons

Why Learn This Skill?

What is your favorite comic strip? Why do you read it? Many people enjoy comics because they use interesting or amusing visuals to convey a story or idea.

Cartoons do not only appear in the newspaper's funny pages. They are also in the editorial section, where they give opinions on political issues. Political cartoons have been around for centuries and are good historical sources because they reflect the popular views on current affairs.

Learning the Skill

Using caricature and symbols, political cartoonists help readers see relationships and draw conclusions about events. A caricature exaggerates a detail such as a subject's features. Cartoonists use caricature to create a positive or negative impression. For example, if a cartoon shows one figure three times larger than another, it implies that one figure is more powerful than the other.

A symbol is an image or object that represents something else. For example, a cartoonist may use a crown to represent monarchy. Symbols often represent nations or political parties. Uncle Sam is a common symbol for the United States.

To analyze a political cartoon:

- Examine the cartoon thoroughly.
- Identify the topic and principal characters.
- Read labels and messages.
- Note relationships between the figures and symbols.
- Determine what point the cartoon is making.

Practicing the Skill

In the next section of this chapter, you will be reading about several dictators who rose to power in Europe in the years following World War I. The political cartoon on this page, published in 1938, makes a statement about these dictators and the reaction of the Western democracies toward them. Study the cartoon and then answer these questions.

1. What do the figures represent?
2. Why is the standing figure so large?
3. What is the standing figure holding and what is it attached to?
4. What is the sitting figure doing?
5. What is the message of the cartoon?

WOULD YOU OBLIGE ME WITH A MATCH PLEASE?

David Low, *London Evening Standard*

Applying the Skill

Choose a current issue on which you hold a strong opinion. Draw a political cartoon expressing your opinion on this issue. Show it to a friend to find out if the message is clear. If not, revise the cartoon to clarify its point.

Glencoe's **Skillbuilder Interactive Workbook, Level 2,** provides instruction and practice in key social studies skills.

TEACH

Analyzing Political Cartoons
Bring some political cartoons to class, such as the ones that appear on the editorial pages of many newspapers. Before the class reads the skill, distribute copies of the cartoons. Ask: What is the message of each cartoon and how did you figure it out? After a short class discussion, ask students to read the skill and complete the practice questions.

Ask students to look for political cartoons in newspapers and magazines and bring copies of them to class. Have students apply what they learned about analyzing political cartoons to explain the cartoons to the class. You might wish to prepare a class bulletin board with the cartoons. **L2**

Enrich

Have interested students create a political cartoon about one of the events or issues discussed in this chapter. Students should consider the audience for their cartoon, and what message they wish to convey to this particular audience. Have students share their work with the class, and add their cartoons to a class bulletin board. **L2**

ANSWERS TO PRACTICING THE SKILL

1. The seated figure represents the Western democracies; the standing figure represents dictatorships.
2. Dictatorships were very powerful and very active.
3. He is holding a rope, probably a fuse, which is attached to a bomb.
4. The seated figure is studying a photograph and smoking.
5. The dictators are setting the stage for another war; Western democracies seem oblivious to the danger. The caption implies that Western democracies might help dictatorships to create destruction if they are not aware and careful.

Applying the Skill: Have students share their final cartoons with the class.

1 FOCUS

Section Overview

This section explores the emergence of dictatorial regimes in Italy, Russia, and Spain.

BELLRINGER
Skillbuilder Activity

 Project transparency and have students answer questions.

 Available as a blackline master.

Daily Focus Skills Transparency 17–2

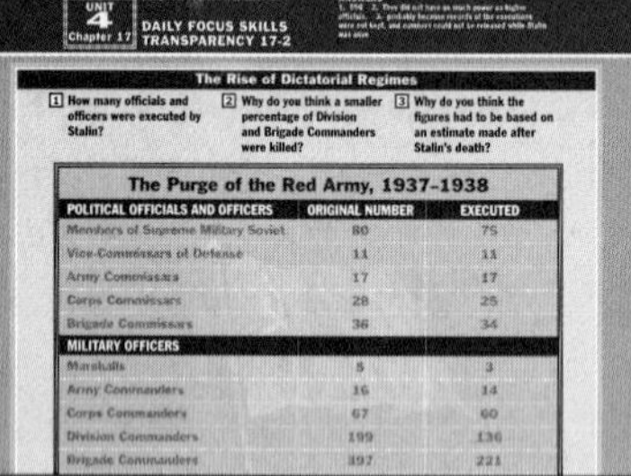
UNIT 4 Chapter 17 DAILY FOCUS SKILLS TRANSPARENCY 17-2

The Rise of Dictatorial Regimes

1. How many officials and officers were executed by Stalin?
2. Why do you think a smaller percentage of Division and Brigade Commanders were killed?
3. Why do you think the figures had to be based on an estimate made after Stalin's death?

The Purge of the Red Army, 1937–1938

POLITICAL OFFICIALS AND OFFICERS	ORIGINAL NUMBER	EXECUTED
Members of Supreme Military Soviet	80	75
Vice-Commissars of Defense	11	11
Army Commissars	17	17
Corps Commissars	28	25
Brigade Commissars	36	34
MILITARY OFFICERS		
Marshalls	5	3
Army Commanders	16	14
Corps Commanders	67	60
Division Commanders	199	136
Brigade Commanders	397	221

Guide to Reading

Answers to Graphic: Methods used by Mussolini: laws made by decree; police had unrestricted authority; outlawed other political parties; established secret police; exercised control over mass media; used organizations such as Fascist youth groups; made deal with Catholic Church to get its support

Preteaching Vocabulary: Explain the significance of *a totalitarian state. (a government that aims to control the political, economic, social, intellectual, and cultural lives of its citizens)* **L2**

SECTION 2 The Rise of Dictatorial Regimes

Guide to Reading

Main Ideas
- Mussolini established a modern totalitarian state in Italy.
- As leader of the Soviet Union, Stalin eliminated people who threatened his power.

Key Terms
totalitarian state, fascism, New Economic Policy, Politburo, collectivization

People to Identify
Benito Mussolini, Joseph Stalin, Francisco Franco

Places to Locate
Russia, Madrid

Preview Questions
1. To what extent was Fascist Italy a totalitarian state?
2. How did Joseph Stalin establish a totalitarian regime in the Soviet Union?

Reading Strategy
Categorizing Information Use a web diagram like the one below to list methods used by Mussolini to create a Fascist dictatorship.

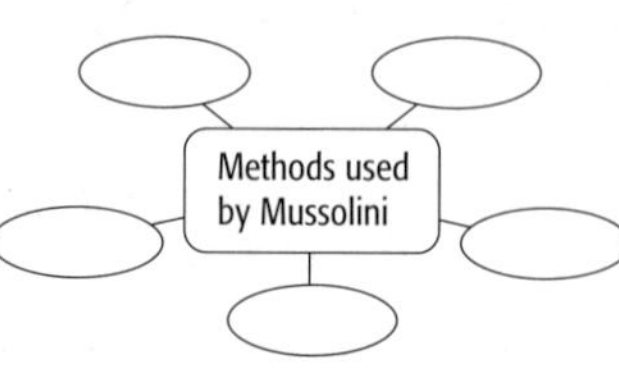

Preview of Events

1920 · 1925 · 1930 · 1935 · 1940

- **1919** Mussolini creates the *Fascio di Combattimento*
- **1924** Lenin dies
- **1928** Stalin launches his First Five-Year Plan
- **1929** Mussolini recognizes independence of Vatican City
- **1939** The Spanish Civil War ends

Voices from the Past

Benito Mussolini

In 1932, Benito Mussolini, the dictator of Italy, published a statement of his movement's principles:

> ❝Anti-individualistic, the Fascist conception of life stresses the importance of the State and accepts the individual only in so far as his interests coincide with those of the State. . . . The Fascist conception of the State is all-embracing; outside of it no human or spiritual values can exist. Thus understood, fascism is totalitarian, and the Fascist State . . . interprets, develops, and potentiates [makes effective] the whole life of a people . . . fascism does not, generally speaking, believe in the possibility or utility of perpetual peace. . . . War alone keys up all human energies to their maximum tension and sets the seal of nobility on those people who have the courage to face it.❞
>
> —**Benito Mussolini, "The Doctrine of Fascism,"** ***Italian Fascisms,*** **Adrian Lyttleton, ed., 1973**

These were the principles of the movement Mussolini called fascism.

The Rise of Dictators

The apparent triumph of democracy in Europe in 1919 was extremely short-lived. By 1939, only two major European states—France and Great Britain—remained democratic. Italy, the Soviet Union, Germany, and many other European states adopted dictatorial regimes. These regimes took both old and new forms.

SECTION RESOURCES

Reproducible Masters
- Reproducible Lesson Plan 17–2
- Daily Lecture and Discussion Notes 17–2
- Guided Reading Activity 17–2
- Section Quiz 17–2
- Reading Essentials and Study Guide 17–2

Transparencies
- Daily Focus Skills Transparency 17–2

Multimedia
- Interactive Tutor Self-Assessment CD-ROM
- ExamView® Pro Testmaker CD-ROM
- Presentation Plus! CD-ROM

A new form of dictatorship was the modern totalitarian state. A **totalitarian state** is a government that aims to control the political, economic, social, intellectual, and cultural lives of its citizens. New totalitarian regimes pushed the power of the central state far beyond what it had been in the past.

These totalitarian states wanted more than passive obedience. They wanted to conquer the minds and hearts of their subjects. They achieved this goal through mass propaganda techniques and high-speed modern communication. Modern technology also provided totalitarian states with an unprecedented ability to impose their wishes on their subjects.

The totalitarian states that emerged were led by a single leader and a single party. They rejected the ideal of limited government power and the guarantee of individual freedoms. Instead, individual freedom was subordinated to the collective will of the masses. This collective will of the masses, however, was organized and determined by the leader. The totalitarian state expected the active involvement of the masses in the achievement of its goals, whether those goals included war, a socialist state, or a thousand-year empire like the one Adolf Hitler wanted to establish.

Reading Check **Summarizing** What is the goal of a totalitarian state?

Fascism in Italy

In the early 1920s, **Benito Mussolini** (MOO•suh•LEE•nee) established the first European Fascist movement in Italy. Mussolini began his political career as a Socialist. In 1919, he created a new political group, the *Fascio di Combattimento,* or League of Combat. The term *Fascist* is derived from that name.

As a political philosophy, **fascism** (FA•SHIH•zuhm) glorifies the state above the individual by emphasizing the need for a strong central government led by a dictatorial ruler. In a Fascist state, people are controlled by the government, and any opposition is suppressed.

Rise of Fascism Like other European countries, Italy experienced severe economic problems after World War I. Inflation grew, and both industrial and agricultural workers staged strikes. Socialists spoke of revolution. The middle class began to fear a Communist takeover like the one that had recently occurred in **Russia.** Industrial and agricultural strikes created more division. Mussolini emerged from this background of widespread unrest.

Geography Skills

Many European countries adopted dictatorial regimes to solve their problems in the 1920s and 1930s.

1. **Interpreting Maps** Which countries shown on the map above are Fascist? Which are authoritarian? Which are democratic states?
2. **Applying Geography Skills** Pose and answer a question that creates a comparison between a country's political status as shown on this map and the side that country fought on in World War I.

In 1920 and 1921, Mussolini formed bands of black-shirted, armed Fascists called *squadristi* or Blackshirts. These bands attacked socialist offices and newspapers. They also used violence to break up strikes. Both middle-class industrialists who feared working-class strikes and large landowners who objected to agricultural strikes began to support Mussolini's Fascist movement.

By 1922, Mussolini's movement was growing quickly. The middle-class fear of socialism, communism, and disorder made the Fascists increasingly attractive to many people. In addition, Mussolini realized that the Italian people were angry over Italy's failure to receive more land in the peace settlement that followed the war. He understood that nationalism was a powerful force. Thus, he demanded more land for Italy and won thousands of converts to fascism with his patriotic and nationalistic appeals.

2 TEACH

Reading Check

Answer: to control the political, economic, social, intellectual, and cultural lives of its citizens

Geography Skills

Answers:

1. Germany, Austria, Italy; Estonia, Latvia, Lithuania, Poland, Hungary, Romania, Yugoslavia, Bulgaria, Albania, Greece, Portugal, Spain; Ireland, United Kingdom, Norway, Sweden, Finland, Netherlands, Belgium, Luxembourg, France, Switzerland, Czechoslovakia
2. Answers will vary.

Daily Lecture and Discussion Notes 17–2

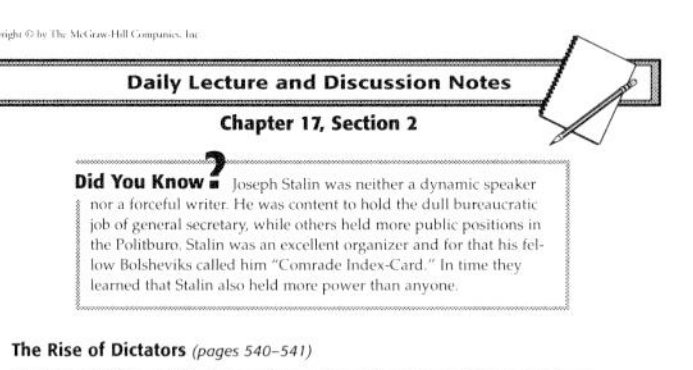

Daily Lecture and Discussion Notes

Chapter 17, Section 2

Did You Know? Joseph Stalin was neither a dynamic speaker nor a forceful writer. He was content to hold the dull bureaucratic job of general secretary, while others held more public positions in the Politburo. Stalin was an excellent organizer and for that his fellow Bolsheviks called him "Comrade Index-Card." In time they learned that Stalin also held more power than anyone.

I. **The Rise of Dictators** *(pages 540–541)*

A. Between 1919 and 1939, all the major countries of Europe except France and Great Britain had adopted some form of dictatorial government.

B. A new form of dictatorship was the modern **totalitarian state.** Totalitarian governments aimed to control all aspects of their citizens' lives. Totalitarian governments

Guided Reading Activity 17–2

Name ______ Date ______ Class ______

Guided Reading Activity 17-2

The Rise of Dictatorial Regimes

DIRECTIONS: Fill in the blanks below as you read Section 2.

By 1939, only France and Great Britain remained (1) ______. Other states fell to (2) ______ forms of government. A (3) ______ state is a government that aims to control the political, economic, social, intellectual, and cultural lives of its citizens. Totalitarian states wanted to (4) ______ the hearts and the minds of their subjects. The (5) ______ will of the masses was organized and determined by the leader.

(6) ______ glorifies the state above the individual by emphasizing the need for a strong central government led by a dictator. (7) ______

CRITICAL THINKING ACTIVITY

Analyzing Information Depression refers to a severe economic downturn in production and consumption that continues over a significant period of time. A depression can only occur in a free-market economy. Students have become familiar with the effects of the Great Depression in the United States. Ask students to research Latin American countries affected by the Great Depression and select one for further research. In their reports, have students identify how individual lives were changed, how people made ends meet, what economic measures taken by the state, and how political developments were affected. Ask students to analyze if, and how, the impact of the Great Depression differed from country to country.

Who?What?Where?When?

Benito Mussolini Italian dictator Benito Mussolini dreamed of making Italy a great nation and reviving the Roman Empire. To become Italy's leader, he promised "something to everyone," then used street violence and political pressure to destroy his opponents and become prime minister. He did not conduct purges, but he used terror to intimidate people.

Connecting Across Time

Ask students to list some of the freedoms that we take for granted that would be suppressed under Fascist rule. Have a student read the United States Bill of Rights to stimulate a follow-up discussion. L3

Critical Thinking

In 1936, a civil war began in Spain between the forces of General Francisco Franco and the country's republican government. Franco wanted to establish a dictatorship in Spain similar to the one established by Mussolini in Italy. Going to Spain and fighting for the republican cause captured the imaginations of many British and American young people. Ask students to speculate why this bloody conflict became important to freedom-loving people around the world. L2

People In History

Benito Mussolini
1883–1945—Italian dictator

Benito Mussolini was the founder of the first Fascist movement. He was an unruly and rebellious child who was expelled from school once for stabbing a fellow pupil. Ultimately, he received a diploma and worked for a short time as an elementary school teacher.

Mussolini became a Socialist and gradually became well known in Italian Socialist circles. In 1912, he obtained the important position of editor of *Avanti (Forward)*, the official Socialist daily newspaper.

After being expelled from the Socialist Party, he formed his own political movement, the Fascist movement. When the Fascists did poorly in the Italian election of November 1919, Mussolini said that fascism had "come to a dead end." He then toyed with the idea of emigrating to the United States to become a journalist.

In 1922, Mussolini and the Fascists threatened to march on Rome if they were not given power. Mussolini exclaimed, "Either we are allowed to govern, or we will seize power." Victor Emmanuel III, the king of Italy, gave in and made Mussolini prime minister.

Mussolini used his position as prime minister to create a Fascist dictatorship. New laws gave the government the right to suspend any publications that criticized the Catholic Church, the monarchy, or the state. The prime minister was made head of the government with the power to make laws by decree. The police were given unrestricted authority to arrest and jail anyone for either nonpolitical or political crimes.

In 1926, the Fascists outlawed all other political parties in Italy, and established a secret police, known as the OVRA. By the end of the year, Mussolini ruled Italy as *Il Duce* (eel DOO•chay), "The Leader."

The Fascist State Since Mussolini believed that the Fascist state should be totalitarian, he used various means to establish complete control over the Italian people. As we have seen, Mussolini created a secret police force, the OVRA, whose purpose was to watch citizens' political activities and enforce government policies. Police actions in Italy, however, were never as repressive or savage as those in Nazi Germany (discussed later in this chapter).

The Italian Fascists also tried to exercise control over all forms of mass media, including newspapers, radio, and film. The media was used to spread propaganda. Propaganda was intended to mold Italians into a single-minded Fascist community. Most Italian Fascist propaganda, however, was fairly unsophisticated, and mainly consisted of simple slogans like "Mussolini Is Always Right."

The Fascists also used organizations to promote the ideals of fascism and to control the population. For example, by 1939, Fascist youth groups included about 66 percent of the population between the ages of 8 and 18. These youth groups particularly focused on military activities and values.

With these organizations, the Fascists hoped to create a nation of new Italians who were fit, disciplined, and war-loving. In practice, however, the Fascists largely maintained traditional social attitudes. This is especially evident in their policies regarding women. The Fascists portrayed the family as the pillar of the state and women as the foundation of the family. Women were to be homemakers and mothers, which was "their natural and fundamental mission in life," according to Mussolini.

Despite his attempts, Mussolini never achieved the degree of totalitarian control seen in Hitler's Germany or Stalin's Soviet Union (discussed later in this chapter). The Italian Fascist Party did not completely destroy the country's old power structure. Some institutions, including the armed forces, were not absorbed into the Fascist state but managed to keep most of their independence. Victor Emmanuel was also retained as king.

Mussolini's compromise with the traditional institutions of Italy was especially evident in his relationship with the Catholic Church. In the Lateran Accords of February 1929, Mussolini's regime recognized the sovereign independence of a small area within Rome known as Vatican City. This territory had belonged to the Catholic Church since 1870. In return for this land, the pope recognized the Italian state.

Mussolini's regime also gave the Church a large grant of money and recognized Catholicism as the "sole religion of the state." In return, the Catholic Church urged Italians to support the Fascist regime.

In all areas of Italian life under Mussolini and the Fascists, there was a large gap between Fascist ideals and practices. The Italian Fascists promised

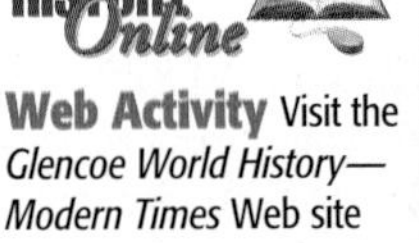

Web Activity Visit the *Glencoe World History—Modern Times* Web site at wh.mt.glencoe.com and click on **Chapter 17–Student Web Activity** to learn more about the rise of fascism.

COOPERATIVE LEARNING ACTIVITY

Staging a Debate Divide the class into two groups to debate this statement: Mussolini's rule was good for Italy. Have the members of each group agree on assignments within the group as they prepare for the debate. Inform students that they will need to conduct research to support their positions. Remind students that to hold a good debate, statements must be based on fact, not opinion. Be sure to allow both sides time to make rebuttal arguments. Explain to students the basis on which you determine the winning team (thoroughness of research, clarity and force of arguments, presentation, and so forth). L3

For grading this activity, refer to the ***Performance Assessment Activities*** booklet.

much but delivered considerably less. They would soon be overshadowed by a much more powerful Fascist movement to the north—that of Adolf Hitler, a student and admirer of Mussolini.

Reading Check **Examining** How did Mussolini gain power in Italy?

A New Era in the Soviet Union

As we have seen, Lenin followed a policy of war communism during the civil war in Russia. The government controlled most industries and seized grain from peasants to ensure supplies for the army.

Once the war was over, peasants began to sabotage the communist program by hoarding food. The situation became even worse when drought caused a great famine between 1920 and 1922. As many as 5 million lives were lost. With agricultural disaster came industrial collapse. By 1921, industrial output was only 20 percent of its 1913 level.

Russia was exhausted. A peasant banner proclaimed, "Down with Lenin and horseflesh. Bring back the czar and pork." As Leon Trotsky said, "The country, and the government with it, were at the very edge of the abyss."

Lenin's New Economic Policy In March 1921, Lenin pulled Russia back from the abyss. He abandoned war communism in favor of his New Economic Policy (NEP). The NEP was a modified version of the old capitalist system. Peasants were allowed to sell their produce openly. Retail stores, as well as small industries that employed fewer than 20 workers, could be privately owned and operated. Heavy industry, banking, and mines, however, remained in the hands of the government.

In 1922, Lenin and the Communists formally created a new state called the Union of Soviet Socialist Republics, which is also known as the USSR (by its initials), or as the Soviet Union (by its shortened form). By that time, a revived market and a good harvest had brought an end to famine. Soviet agricultural production climbed to 75 percent of its prewar level.

Overall, the NEP saved the Soviet Union from complete economic disaster. Lenin and other leading Communists, however, only intended the NEP to be a temporary retreat from the goals of communism.

The Rise of Stalin Lenin died in 1924. A struggle for power began at once among the seven members of the Politburo (PAH•luht•BYOOR•OH)—a committee that had become the leading policy-making body of the Communist Party. The Politburo was severely divided over the future direction of the Soviet Union.

One group, led by Leon Trotsky, wanted to end the NEP and launch Russia on a path of rapid industrialization, chiefly at the expense of the peasants. This group also wanted to spread communism abroad and believed that the revolution in Russia would not survive without other communist states.

Another group in the Politburo rejected the idea of worldwide communist revolution. Instead, it wanted to focus on building a socialist state in Russia and to continue Lenin's NEP. This group believed that rapid industrialization would harm the living standards of the Soviet peasants.

These divisions were underscored by an intense personal rivalry between Leon Trotsky and another Politburo member, **Joseph Stalin.** In 1924, Trotsky held the post of commissar of war. Stalin held the bureaucratic job of party general secretary. Because the general secretary appointed regional, district, city, and town party officials, this bureaucratic job actually became the most important position in the party.

Stalin used his post as general secretary to gain complete control of the Communist Party. The thousands of officials Stalin appointed provided him with support in his bid for power. By 1929, Stalin had eliminated from the Politburo the Bolsheviks of the revolutionary era and had established a powerful

People In History

Joseph Stalin
1879–1953—Soviet dictator

Joseph Stalin established a strong personal dictatorship over the Soviet Union. He joined the Bolsheviks in 1903 and came to Lenin's attention after staging a daring bank robbery to get funds for the Bolshevik cause. His real last name was Dzhugashvili, but he adopted the name Stalin, which means "man of steel."

Stalin was neither a dynamic speaker nor a forceful writer. He was a good organizer, however. His fellow Bolsheviks called him "Comrade Index-Card."

Like Hitler, Stalin was one of the greatest mass murderers in human history. It is estimated that his policies and his deliberate executions led to the death of as many as 25 million people. At the time of his death in 1953, he was planning yet another purge of party members.

Reading Check

Answer: He exploited the middle-class fear of socialism by having his *squadristi* attack Socialist offices and newspapers and break up strikes. He appealed to nationalism: realizing that the Italian people were angry over the failure of Italy to receive more land after World War I, he demanded more land for Italy and won thousands of converts. He and the Fascists threatened to march on Rome, forcing the king to make him prime minister, then set about to create a Fascist dictatorship.

CURRICULUM CONNECTION

Government Guide students in a discussion of Stalin's programs of rapid industrialization coupled with the collectivization of agriculture. What were three major results of these programs on the lives and fortunes of the Russian people? L2

Connecting Across Time

It has been said that communism is dictatorship of the lower class, fascism is dictatorship of the middle class, and monarchy is a dictatorship of the upper class. Have students find examples from history they have studied thus far to support this statement. If they disagree, ask them to be prepared to discuss why. L3

COOPERATIVE LEARNING ACTIVITY

Creating an Advertisement Organize the class into three groups and have each group create an advertising plan. One group's plan should promote the Bolshevik policy of communism, or government control over all major industries; another group should promote Lenin's New Economic Policy (NEP) that allowed some private businesses to operate but maintained government control over steel, railroad, and large-scale manufacturing; the last group should create an advertisement to support Stalin's Five-Year Plan, which set Soviet economic goals for that period and brought industrial and agricultural production under government control. Each group should research its topic, create an ad, and present it to the class. L2

Geography *Skills*

Answers:

1. Southwest
2. the area near Odessa and the Black Sea; strong concentration of iron and steel production

Connecting Across Time

As Stalin's crimes against humanity became known, people sympathetic to communism had to decide where they stood. Have students research, for example, "destalinization" in the Soviet Union after Stalin's death and the changing opinions of Stalin held by American Communists. **L2**

Writing Activity

Ask students to research and write an essay about Socialist realism, or the literary and artistic styles that became obligatory under Stalin's rule. Ask students to explain what the aim of art was under Socialist realism. How does this art reflect the history of the culture in which it was produced? What was the role of artistic expression in the production of art under Stalin's rule? **L3**

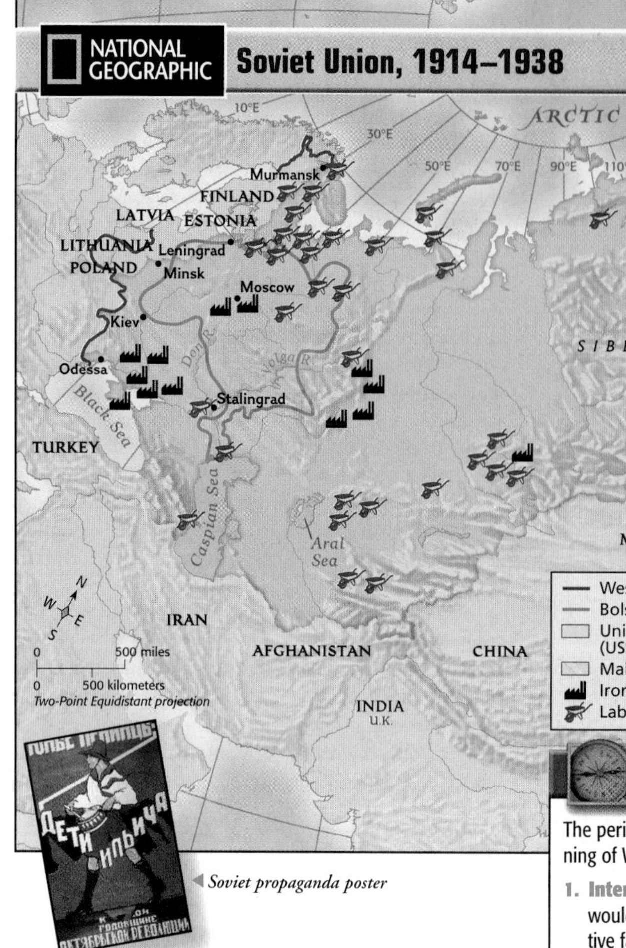

Soviet propaganda poster

Geography *Skills*

The period from the beginning of World War I to the beginning of World War II was one of dramatic change in Russia.

1. **Interpreting Maps** From Moscow, in which direction would you go to find the Soviet Union's most productive farming area: northeast, southwest, northwest, or southeast?
2. **Applying Geography Skills** Identify a particular area of the Soviet Union as shown on the map and explain why that area would have been of particular interest to Stalin during his First Five-Year Plan.

dictatorship. Trotsky, expelled from the party in 1927, eventually made his way to Mexico, where he was murdered in 1940, probably on Stalin's orders.

Five-Year Plans The Stalinist Era marked the beginning of an economic, social, and political revolution that was more sweeping in its results than were the revolutions of 1917. Stalin made a significant shift in economic policy in 1928 when he ended the NEP and launched his First Five-Year Plan. The **Five-Year Plans** set economic goals for five-year periods. Their purpose was to transform Russia virtually overnight from an agricultural into an industrial country.

The First Five-Year Plan emphasized maximum production of capital goods (goods devoted to the production of other goods, such as heavy machines) and armaments. The plan quadrupled the production of heavy machinery and doubled oil production. Between 1928 and 1937, during the first two Five-Year Plans, steel production in Russia increased from 4 million to 18 million tons (3.628 to 16.326 million t) per year.

The social and political costs of industrialization were enormous. Little provision was made for caring for the expanded labor force in the cities. The number of workers increased by millions between 1932 and 1940, but total investment in housing actually declined after 1929. The result was that millions of workers and their families lived in pitiful conditions. Real wages in industry also declined by 43 percent between 1928 and 1940. Strict laws even limited where workers could move. To keep workers content, government propaganda stressed the need for sacrifice to create the new socialist state.

MEETING INDIVIDUAL NEEDS

Visual Learners Assign students to work in groups of two. Create a two-column chart on the chalkboard that summarizes the changes brought about by Lenin and Stalin in the Soviet Union. Label the columns *Lenin* and *Stalin*. Label the individual rows in the chart as follows: *Major Industries, Small Businesses, Agriculture, Non-Russian Nationalities, Communist Party,* and *The Arts*. Ask each group to copy your chart and work together to fill it in. When groups have completed their charts, have them present their answers. Insert students' answers in the blank chart on the chalkboard. **L1** **ELL**

Refer to ***Inclusion for the High School Social Studies Classroom Strategies and Activities*** in the TCR.

With rapid industrialization came an equally rapid collectivization of agriculture. **Collectivization** was a system in which private farms were eliminated. Instead, the government owned all of the land while the peasants worked it.

Strong resistance to Stalin's plans came from peasants, who responded by hoarding crops and killing livestock. However, these actions only led Stalin to step up the program. By 1930, 10 million peasant households had been collectivized. By 1934, 26 million family farms had been collectivized into 250,000 units.

Costs of Stalin's Programs Collectivization was done at tremendous cost. The hoarding of food and the slaughter of livestock produced widespread famine. Stalin himself is supposed to have said that 10 million peasants died in the famines of 1932 and 1933. The only concession Stalin made to the peasants was that each collective farm worker was allowed to have one tiny, privately owned garden plot.

Stalin's programs had other costs as well. To achieve his goals, Stalin strengthened his control over the party bureaucracy. Those who resisted were sent into forced labor camps in Siberia.

Stalin's desire to make all decisions by himself also led to the Great Purge of the 1930s. First to be removed were the Old Bolsheviks—those who had been involved in the early days of the movement. Between 1936 and 1938, the most prominent Old Bolsheviks were put on trial and condemned to death.

During this same time, Stalin purged army officers, diplomats, union officials, party members, intellectuals, and numerous ordinary citizens. An estimated eight million Russians were arrested. Millions were sent to forced labor camps in Siberia, from which they never returned. Others were executed.

The Stalin Era also overturned much of the permissive social legislation that was enacted in the early 1920s. To promote equal rights for women, the Communists had made the divorce process easier and they had also encouraged women to work outside the home. After Stalin came to power, the family was praised as a small collective in which parents were responsible for teaching the values of hard work, duty, and discipline to their children. Divorced fathers who did not support their children were heavily fined.

Reading Check **Summarizing** What was Lenin's New Economic Policy?

Authoritarian States in the West

A number of governments in the Western world were not totalitarian but were authoritarian. These states adopted some of the features of totalitarian states, in particular, their use of police powers. However, the main concern of these authoritarian governments was not to create a new kind of mass society, but to preserve the existing social order.

Eastern Europe Some of these governments were found among the new states of eastern Europe. At first, it seemed that political democracy would become well established in eastern Europe after the war. Austria, Poland, Czechoslovakia, Yugoslavia (known as the kingdom of the Serbs, Croats, and Slovenes until 1929), Romania, Bulgaria, and Hungary all adopted parliamentary systems. However, most of these systems were soon replaced by authoritarian regimes.

Parliamentary systems failed in most eastern European states for several reasons. These states had little tradition of political democracy. In addition, they were mostly rural and agrarian. Many of the peasants were illiterate, and much of the land was still dominated by large landowners who feared the peasants. Ethnic conflicts also threatened these countries.

Powerful landowners, the churches, and even some members of the small middle class feared land

What If...

Trotsky had succeeded Lenin?

Lenin's death in 1924 caused a bitter political struggle to determine his successor. Although he had no influence over the final outcome, Lenin's testament, written in December 1922, predicted a split between Trotsky and Stalin. In his testament, read to delegates at the Thirteenth Congress, Lenin advised removing Stalin from his post as general secretary to prevent a power struggle.

Consider the Consequences Consider what would have happened if Stalin had not maintained his position of influence and had lost to Trotsky. Research Trotsky's beliefs, then write a short essay describing the direction the Soviet Union would have taken under his leadership.

EXTENDING THE CONTENT

Joseph Stalin was born in 1879. He was forced to learn Russian in school, although neither of his parents spoke it at home. As the best student in his church school, Stalin earned a full scholarship to a theological seminary. While there, he read the works of Karl Marx and converted to Russian Marxism; he then left the seminary to become a full-time revolutionary. He joined the Social-Democratic Party and spent years being arrested and imprisoned on various charges. He proved his abilities with the Social-Democratic Party as a writer and organizer and became its leader after Lenin's death.

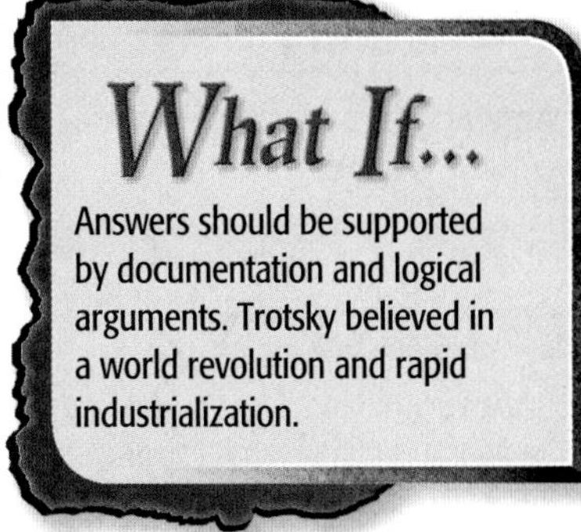

What If...
Answers should be supported by documentation and logical arguments. Trotsky believed in a world revolution and rapid industrialization.

Reading Check

Answer: a modified version of the old capitalist system intended to save Russian communism

3 ASSESS

Assign Section 2 Assessment as homework or as an in-class activity.

Have students use **Interactive Tutor Self-Assessment CD-ROM.**

Section Quiz 17–2

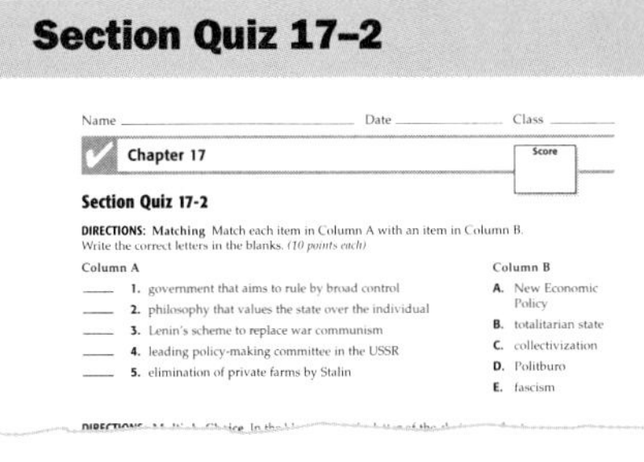
Name ______ Date ______ Class ______

Chapter 17 Score

Section Quiz 17-2

DIRECTIONS: Matching Match each item in Column A with an item in Column B. Write the correct letters in the blanks. *(10 points each)*

Column A	Column B
____ 1. government that aims to rule by broad control	A. New Economic Policy
____ 2. philosophy that values the state over the individual	B. totalitarian state
____ 3. Lenin's scheme to replace war communism	C. collectivization
____ 4. leading policy-making committee in the USSR	D. Politburo
____ 5. elimination of private farms by Stalin	E. fascism

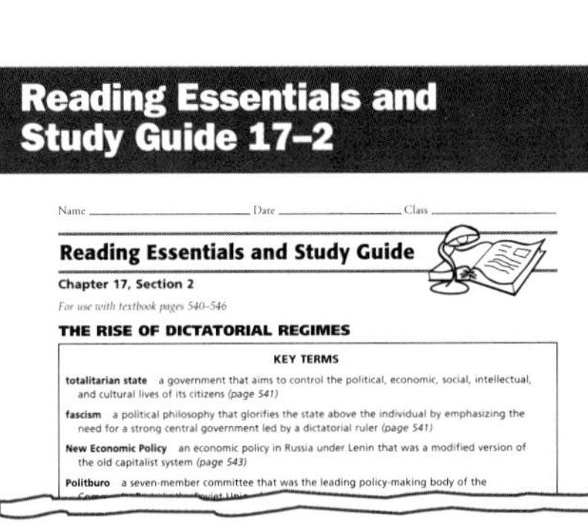
Reading Essentials and Study Guide 17–2

Name ______ Date ______ Class ______

Reading Essentials and Study Guide

Chapter 17, Section 2

For use with textbook pages 540–546

THE RISE OF DICTATORIAL REGIMES

KEY TERMS

totalitarian state a government that aims to control the political, economic, social, intellectual, and cultural lives of its citizens *(page 541)*

fascism a political philosophy that glorifies the state above the individual by emphasizing the need for a strong central government led by a dictatorial ruler *(page 541)*

New Economic Policy an economic policy in Russia under Lenin that was a modified version of the old capitalist system *(page 543)*

Politburo a seven-member committee that was the leading policy-making body of the

History *through Art*

Answer: War is brutal, and no living creature is spared.

Reading Check

Answer: It had a large middle class, a liberal tradition, and a strong industrial base.

Critical Thinking

Ask students to analyze the nature of the totalitarian regime in the Soviet Union. Students should be asked to include, identify, and describe examples of politically motivated mass murders, as well as examples of political, economic, and social oppression and violations of human rights in the Soviet Union. L1

Reteaching Activity

Ask students to list the major features of Mussolini's and Stalin's dictatorships. Ask them to explain how Franco seized power in Spain. L1

4 CLOSE

Ask students to discuss the personal qualities of Mussolini and Stalin that helped bring them to power. Have them describe how each leader represented his nation and his culture. L2

History *through Art*

***Guernica* by Pablo Picasso, 1937**
This famous painting is a strong antiwar statement. What do the images say about the realities of war?

reform, communist upheaval, and ethnic conflict. For this reason these groups looked to authoritarian governments to maintain the old system. Only Czechoslovakia, which had a large middle class, a liberal tradition, and a strong industrial base, maintained its political democracy.

Spain In Spain, too, political democracy failed to survive. Led by General **Francisco Franco,** Spanish military forces revolted against the democratic government in 1936. A brutal and bloody civil war began.

Foreign intervention complicated the Spanish Civil War. The fascist regimes of Italy and Germany aided Franco's forces with arms, money, and men. Hitler used the Spanish Civil War as an opportunity to test the new weapons of his revived air force. The horrible destruction of Guernica by German bombers in April 1937 was immortalized in a painting by the Spanish artist Pablo Picasso.

The Spanish republican government was aided by forty thousand foreign volunteers and by trucks, planes, tanks, and military advisers from the Soviet Union.

The Spanish Civil War came to an end when Franco's forces captured **Madrid** in 1939. Franco established a dictatorship that favored large landowners, businesspeople, and the Catholic clergy. Because it favored traditional groups and did not try to control every aspect of people's lives, Franco's dictatorship is an example of a regime that was authoritarian rather than totalitarian.

Reading Check **Explaining** How did Czechoslovakia maintain its political democracy?

SECTION 2 ASSESSMENT

Checking for Understanding

1. **Define** totalitarian state, fascism, New Economic Policy, Politburo, collectivization.
2. **Identify** Benito Mussolini, New Economic Policy, Politburo, Joseph Stalin, Five-Year Plan, Francisco Franco.
3. **Locate** Russia, Madrid.
4. **Explain** how Stalin gained control of the Communist Party after Lenin died.
5. **List** the countries that participated in the Spanish Civil War.

Critical Thinking

6. **Evaluate** What was the major purpose of the Five-Year Plans during the 1920s and 1930s in the Soviet Union?
7. **Organizing Information** Use a diagram like the one below to identify ways in which Stalin changed the Soviet Union. Include the economic, social, and political results of his programs.

How Stalin Changed the Soviet Union

Analyzing Visuals

8. **Contrast** the above painting with the rally photo on page 531. Both images make political statements about war and militarism. How do they differ? How are they similar? Which makes the strongest statement?

Writing About History

9. **Persuasive Writing** What were the pros and cons of Mussolini's rule? In an essay, argue whether or not Mussolini was good for Italy. Conduct research to support your position and base your statements on fact.

SECTION 2 ASSESSMENT

1. Key terms are in blue.
2. Benito Mussolini *(p. 541)*; New Economic Policy *(p. 543)*; Politburo *(p. 543)*; Joseph Stalin *(p. 543)*; Five-Year Plan *(p. 544)*; Francisco Franco *(p. 546)*
3. See chapter maps.
4. As Politburo party general secretary, Stalin appointed all party officials. Then he eliminated the revolutionary era Bolsheviks from the Politburo.
5. Germany and Italy
6. intended to rapidly increase the Soviet Union's industrial capacity by setting economic goals for five-year periods
7. rapid industrialization; collectivization of agriculture; strengthened control over the party bureaucracy; purged Old Bolsheviks and the opposition; undid permissive social legislation of the early 1920s
8. *Guernica* shows the death and destruction resulting from war. The rally shows the strength and discipline of the military. Answers will vary.
9. Answers will vary.

EYEWITNESS TO HISTORY

The Formation of Collective Farms

THE COLLECTIVIZATION OF AGRICULTURE transformed Russia's 26 million family farms into 250,000 collective farms *(kolkhozes)*. In this first-hand account, we see how the process worked.

“General collectivization in our village was brought about in the following manner: Two representatives of the [Communist] Party arrived in the village. All the inhabitants were summoned by the ringing of the church bell to a meeting at which the policy of general collectivization was announced. . . . Although the meeting lasted two days, from the viewpoint of the Party representatives, nothing was accomplished.

After this setback, two more officials were sent to reinforce the first two. A meeting of our section of the village was held in a stable which had previously belonged to a kulak [wealthy peasant farmer]. The meeting dragged on until dark. Suddenly someone threw a brick at the lamp, and in the dark the peasants began to beat the Party representatives who jumped out the window and escaped from the village barely alive. The following day seven people were arrested. The militia was called in and stayed in the village until the peasants, realizing their helplessness, calmed down. . . .

By the end of 1930 there were two kolkhozes in our village. Though at first these collectives embraced at most only 70 percent of the peasant households, in the months that followed they gradually absorbed more and more of them.

In these kolkhozes the great bulk of the land was held and worked communally, but each peasant household owned a house of some sort, a small plot of ground and perhaps some livestock. All the members of the kolkhoz were required to work on the kolkhoz a certain number of days each month; the rest of the time they were allowed to work on their own holdings. They derived their income partly from what they grew on their garden strips and partly from their work in the kolkhoz.

When the harvest was over, and after the farm had met its obligations to the state and to various special funds and had sold on the market whatever undesignated produce was left, the remaining produce and the farm's monetary income were divided among the kolkhoz members according to the number of 'labor days' each one had contributed to the farm's work. . . . After they had received their earnings, one of them remarked, 'You will live, but you will be very, very thin. . . .' By late 1932 more than 80 percent of the peasant households had been collectivized.”

—**Max Belov, *The History of a Collective Farm***

Russian peasants using scythes to harvest grain

Analyzing Primary Sources

1. Why did the peasants resist the collective farms?
2. How would you characterize the writer's description of the collectivization process in his village? Was he fair and objective; or, do you think that he reveals a bias either for or against the process? Explain and support your answer using excerpts from his description.

TEACH

Analyzing Primary Sources
Guide students in a discussion about Belov's description of how collective farms were formed in the Soviet Union. Ask students what Belov's description of the violent end to the village meeting and the results of that rebellion suggests about the Soviet government's attitude toward collectivization. Although they held meetings with local people, how did Communist Party representatives actually get collective farms instituted? Who benefited from these "communal" farms? Also ask students what they can infer about the author and his possible biases from reading this passage.
(a peasant living in a village, probably hostile to collectivization) L2

CURRICULUM CONNECTION

Economics Ask students to write paragraphs describing why collective farms were a failure and why Stalin's agricultural policies contributed to famine in the Soviet Union. L2

ANSWERS TO ANALYZING PRIMARY SOURCES

1. The peasants made even less money on the collective farms than they had made on their own. They also had less time to devote to their own holdings.
2. Answers should be supported by examples and logical arguments. The author, Max Belov, seems to share the point of view of the villagers, that collectivization was not very successful, but he has used facts to back up his description. Students might cite the quote, "You will live, but you will be very, very thin."

CHAPTER 17
Section 3, 548–553

1 FOCUS

Section Overview

This section explores how Hitler and the Nazi Party seized control of Germany, and the tactics they employed to discriminate against a large portion of the German population.

BELLRINGER
Skillbuilder Activity

 Project transparency and have students answer questions.

 Available as a blackline master.

Daily Focus Skills Transparency 17–3

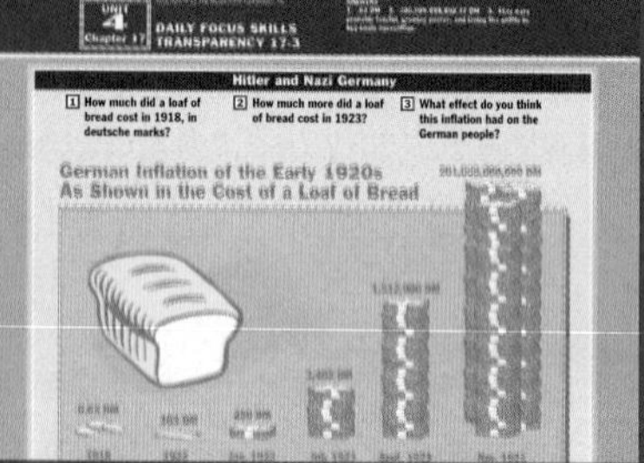

Guide to Reading

Answers to Graphic: Anti-Semitic Policies: Jews excluded from German citizenship, forbidden to marry citizens, required to wear Stars of David and carry identification cards, barred from public buildings and transportation, prohibited from owning, managing, or working in any retail stores; urged to emigrate, sent to concentration camps

Preteaching Vocabulary: Define *concentration camp. (a large prison camp where people who opposed Germany's Nazi regime were sent)* L2

SECTION 3 Hitler and Nazi Germany

Guide to Reading

Main Ideas
- Hitler and the Nazi Party established a totalitarian state in Germany.
- Many Germans accepted the Nazi dictatorship while other Germans suffered greatly under Hitler's rule.

Key Terms
Reichstag, concentration camp

People to Identify
Adolf Hitler, Heinrich Himmler

Places to Locate
Munich, Nuremberg

Preview Questions
1. How did Adolf Hitler rise to power?
2. What were the chief features of the Nazi total state?
3. How did the rise of Nazism affect Germany?

Reading Strategy
Categorizing Information Use a chart like the one below to list anti-Semitic policies enforced by the Nazi Party.

Anti-Semitic Policies

Preview of Events

1880 · 1890 · 1900 · 1910 · 1920 · 1930 · 1940

- **1889** Hitler is born
- **1921** Hitler takes control of the National Socialist German Workers' Party
- **1933** Reichstag passes Enabling Act
- **1935** Nazis enact Nuremberg laws
- **1938** The Kristallnacht occurs

Adolf Hitler

Voices from the Past

In September 1936, Adolf Hitler spoke to a mass rally in the city of Nuremberg:

"Do we not feel once again in this hour the miracle that brought us together? Once you heard the voice of a man, and it struck deep into your hearts; it awakened you, and you followed this voice. . . . When we meet each other here, the wonder of our coming together fills us all. Not everyone of you sees me, and I do not see everyone of you. But I feel you, and you feel me. It is the belief in our people that has made us small men great, that has made brave and courageous men out of us wavering, timid folk; this belief . . . joined us together into one whole! . . . You come, that you may, once in a while, gain the feeling that now we are together; we are with him and he with us, and we are now Germany!"

—***The Speeches of Adolf Hitler,*** **Norman Baynes, ed., 1942**

Hitler worked to create an emotional bond between himself and the German people.

Hitler and His Views

Adolf Hitler was born in Austria on April 20, 1889. A failure in secondary school, he eventually traveled to Vienna to become an artist but was rejected by the Vienna Academy of Fine Arts. He stayed in the city, supported at first by an inheritance. While in Vienna, however, Hitler developed his basic ideas, which he held for the rest of his life.

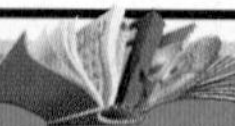

SECTION RESOURCES

Reproducible Masters
- Reproducible Lesson Plan 17–3
- Daily Lecture and Discussion Notes 17–3
- Guided Reading Activity 17–3
- Section Quiz 17–3
- Reading Essentials and Study Guide 17–3

Transparencies
- Daily Focus Skills Transparency 17–3

Multimedia
- Interactive Tutor Self-Assessment CD-ROM
- ExamView® Pro Testmaker CD-ROM
- Presentation Plus! CD-ROM

At the core of Hitler's ideas was racism, especially anti-Semitism. Hitler was also an extreme nationalist who understood how political parties could effectively use propaganda and terror. Finally, during his Viennese years, Hitler came to believe firmly in the need for struggle, which he saw as the "granite foundation of the world."

At the end of World War I, after four years of service on the Western Front, Hitler went to Germany and decided to enter politics. In 1919, he joined the little-known German Worker's Party, one of a number of right-wing extreme nationalist parties in **Munich.**

By the summer of 1921, Hitler had taken total control of the party, which he renamed the **National Socialist German Workers' Party** (NSDAP), or Nazi for short. Within two years, party membership had grown to 55,000 people, with 15,000 in the party militia. The militia was variously known as the SA, the Storm Troops, or the Brownshirts, after the color of their uniforms.

An overconfident Hitler staged an armed uprising against the government in Munich in November 1923. This uprising, called the Beer Hall Putsch, was quickly crushed, and Hitler was sentenced to prison. During his brief stay in jail, Hitler wrote ***Mein Kampf,*** or *My Struggle,* an account of his movement and its basic ideas.

In *Mein Kampf,* extreme German nationalism, strong anti-Semitism, and anticommunism are linked together by a social Darwinian theory of struggle. This theory emphasizes the right of superior nations to ***Lebensraum*** (LAY•buhnz•ROWM)—living space—through expansion. It also upholds the right of superior individuals to gain authoritarian leadership over the masses.

Reading Check **Summarizing** What main ideas does Hitler express in his book *Mein Kampf?*

Rise of Nazism

While he was in prison, Hitler realized that the Nazis would have to attain power by legal means, and not by a violent overthrow of the Weimar Republic. This meant that the Nazi Party would have to be a mass political party that could compete for votes with the other political parties.

After his release from prison, Hitler expanded the Nazi Party to all parts of Germany. By 1929, it had a national party organization. Three years later, it had 800,000 members and had become the largest party in the Reichstag—the German parliament.

No doubt, Germany's economic difficulties were a crucial factor in the Nazi rise to power. Unemployment had risen dramatically, growing from 4.35 million in 1931 to 6 million by the winter of 1932. The economic and psychological impact of the Great Depression made extremist parties more attractive.

Hitler promised to create a new Germany. His appeals to national pride, national honor, and traditional militarism struck an emotional chord in his listeners. After attending one of Hitler's rallies, a schoolteacher in Hamburg said, "When the speech was over, there was roaring enthusiasm and applause. . . . —How many look up to him with

Picturing History

In *Mein Kampf,* Hitler wrote that mass meetings were important because individuals who feel weak and uncertain become intoxicated with the power of the group. How do you think Hitler viewed the average person?

CHAPTER 17
Section 3, 548–553

2 TEACH

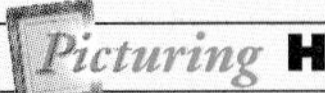

Picturing History

Hitler viewed the average person as one to be manipulated; who would respond to an appeal to national pride and honor.

Reading Check

Answer: extreme German nationalism, a strong anti-Semitism, and anticommunism linked together by a social Darwinian theory of struggle that emphasizes the right of superior nations to living space through expansion and the right of superior individuals to gain authoritarian leadership over the masses

Daily Lecture and Discussion Notes 17–3

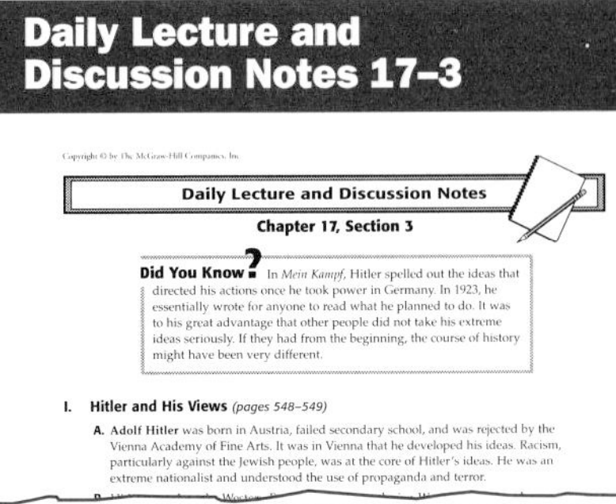

Daily Lecture and Discussion Notes

Chapter 17, Section 3

Did You Know? In *Mein Kampf,* Hitler spelled out the ideas that directed his actions once he took power in Germany. In 1923, he essentially wrote for anyone to read what he planned to do. It was to his great advantage that other people did not take his extreme ideas seriously. If they had from the beginning, the course of history might have been very different.

I. **Hitler and His Views** *(pages 548–549)*

A. **Adolf Hitler** was born in Austria, failed secondary school, and was rejected by the Vienna Academy of Fine Arts. It was in Vienna that he developed his ideas. Racism, particularly against the Jewish people, was at the core of Hitler's ideas. He was an extreme nationalist and understood the use of propaganda and terror.

Guided Reading Activity 17–3

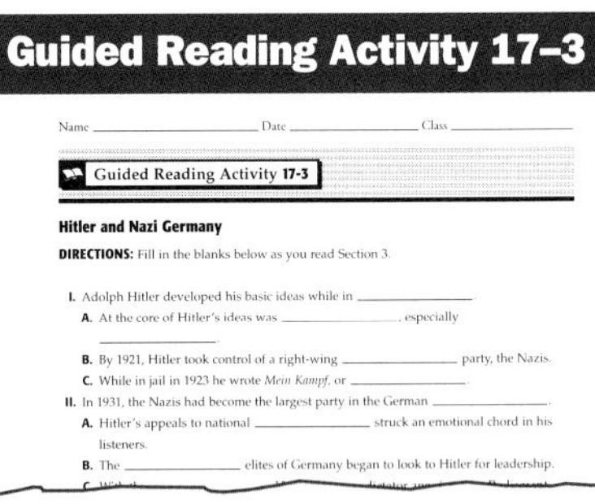

Name ________ Date ________ Class ________

Guided Reading Activity 17-3

Hitler and Nazi Germany

DIRECTIONS: Fill in the blanks below as you read Section 3.

I. Adolph Hitler developed his basic ideas while in ________.

A. At the core of Hitler's ideas was ________, especially ________.

B. By 1921, Hitler took control of a right-wing ________ party, the Nazis.

C. While in jail in 1923 he wrote *Mein Kampf,* or ________.

II. In 1931, the Nazis had become the largest party in the German ________.

A. Hitler's appeals to national ________ struck an emotional chord in his listeners.

B. The ________ elites of Germany began to look to Hitler for leadership.

MEETING INDIVIDUAL NEEDS

Visual/Kinesthetic Have students work in pairs to create charts comparing the characteristics of totalitarian states with those of a democracy. Have students make two columns and label them *Totalitarian* and *Democratic*. Then have them list the countries that were democracies and those that were totalitarian. Students should list characteristics of each form of government in the rows beneath the type of government. For example, democracies allow citizens to vote, have a congress or parliament, etc. Ask groups to share their charts. L2

Refer to ***Inclusion for the High School Social Studies Classroom Strategies and Activities*** in the TCR.

Reading Check

Answer: economic difficulties; Hitler appealed to national pride, national honor, and traditional militarism

Reading Check

Answer: It gave Hitler and his government the legal right to ignore the German constitution for four years; in essence, he was a dictator appointed by the parliament.

Charting Activity

Ask students to chart the four main ways the Nazis created their totalitarian state. *(mass demonstrations, control of economy, terror and repression, control of institutions)* **L1** **ELL**

Connecting Across Time

Guide students in a discussion of Hitler's main preoccupations and beliefs, as described in *Mein Kampf.* Ask them to compare and contrast Hitler's beliefs to those of present-day individuals and groups who operate outside of mainstream society. What threats do these contemporary fringe elements pose to civilized nations? **L3**

Critical Thinking

Have students identify and explain the causes and effects of the rise of Nazism in Germany and the rise of fascism in Italy. **L2**

touching faith as their helper, their saviour, their deliverer from unbearable distress."

Reading Check **Explaining** What factors helped the Nazi Party to gain power in Germany?

Victory of Nazism

After 1930, the German government ruled by decree with the support of President Hindenburg. The Reichstag had little power, and thus Hitler clearly saw that controlling the parliament was not very important.

More and more, the right-wing elites of Germany—the industrial leaders, landed aristocrats, military officers, and higher bureaucrats—looked to Hitler for leadership. He had the mass support to create a right-wing, authoritarian regime that would save Germany and people in privileged positions from a Communist takeover. In 1933, Hindenburg, under pressure, agreed to allow Hitler to become chancellor and create a new government.

Within two months, Hitler had laid the foundation for the Nazis' complete control over Germany. The crowning step of Hitler's "legal seizure" of power came on March 23, 1933, when a two-thirds vote of the Reichstag passed the **Enabling Act.** This law gave the government the power to ignore the constitution for four years while it issued laws to deal with the country's problems.

The Enabling Act gave Hitler's later actions a legal basis. He no longer needed the Reichstag or President Hindenburg. In effect, Hitler became a dictator appointed by the parliamentary body itself.

With their new source of power, the Nazis acted quickly to bring all institutions under Nazi control. The civil service was purged of Jews and democratic elements. Large prison camps called **concentration camps** were set up for people who opposed the new regime. Trade unions were dissolved. All political parties except the Nazis were abolished.

By the end of the summer of 1933, only seven months after being appointed chancellor, Hitler had established the basis for a totalitarian state. When Hindenburg died in 1934, the office of president was abolished. Hitler became sole ruler of Germany. Public officials and soldiers were all required to take a personal oath of loyalty to Hitler as their *Führer* (FYUR•uhr), or "Leader."

Reading Check **Examining** Why was the Enabling Act important to Hitler's success in controlling Germany?

THE WAY IT WAS

YOUNG PEOPLE IN . . .

Nazi Germany

In setting up a total state, the Nazis recognized the importance of winning young people over to their ideas. The Hitler Youth, an organization for young people between the ages of 10 and 18, was formed in 1926 for that purpose.

By 1939, all German young people were expected to join the Hitler Youth. Upon entering, each took an oath: "In the presence of this blood banner [Nazi flag], which represents our Führer, I swear to devote all my energies and my strength to the savior of our country, Adolf Hitler. I am willing and ready to give up my life for him, so help me God."

Young Germans waving flags

Members of the Hitler Youth had their own uniforms and took part in a number of activities. For males, these included camping and hiking trips, sports activities, and evenings together in special youth "homes." Almost all activities were competitive and meant to encourage fighting and heroic deeds.

Above all, the Hitler Youth organization worked to foster military values and virtues, such as duty, obedience, strength, and ruthlessness. Uniforms and drilling became

550

EXTENDING THE CONTENT

The Berlin Olympics in 1936 were so controversial that many nations planned on attending an alternate "People's Olympics" in Barcelona, Spain. However, when the Spanish Civil War broke out those games were canceled. The event that the world attended in Germany was a landmark in Olympic history for several reasons. It was the first Olympics to transmit results immediately throughout Europe, via a telex. The Germans also used zeppelins to quickly send newsreel footage to other countries. Furthermore, the 1936 games were the first televised Olympics. The Germans used a closed circuit to show the games in specially-equipped theaters in Berlin. Finally, the Berlin Games mark the beginning of the torch relay, a tradition that has since become synonymous with the Olympics.

The Nazi State, 1933–1939

Hitler wanted to develop the "total state." He had not simply sought power for power's sake. He had a larger goal—the development of an **Aryan** racial state that would dominate Europe and possibly the world for generations to come. (*Aryan* was a term linguists used to identify people speaking Indo-European languages. The Nazis misused the term and identified the Aryans with the ancient Greeks and Romans and twentieth-century Germans and Scandinavians.) Nazis thought the Germans were the true descendants and leaders of the Aryans and would create another empire like the one ruled by the ancient Romans. The Nazis believed that the world had already seen two German empires or Reichs: the Holy Roman Empire, and the German Empire of 1871 to 1918. It was Hitler's goal to create a Third Reich, the empire of Nazi Germany.

To achieve his goal, Hitler needed the active involvement of the German people. Hitler stated:

> "We must develop organizations in which an individual's entire life can take place. Then every activity and every need of every individual will be regulated by the collectivity represented by the party. There is no longer any arbitrary will, there are no longer any free realms in which the individual belongs to himself. . . . The time of personal happiness is over."

The Nazis pursued the creation of the totalitarian state in a variety of ways. Economic policies, mass spectacles, and organizations—both old and new—were employed to further Nazi goals. Terror was freely used. Policies toward women and, in particular, Jews reflected Nazi aims.

The State and Terror Nazi Germany was the scene of almost constant personal and institutional conflict. This resulted in administrative chaos. Struggle was a basic feature of relationships within the party, within the state, and between party and state. Hitler, of course, was the ultimate decision maker and absolute ruler.

For those who needed coercion, the Nazi total state used terror and repression. The *Schutzstaffeln* ("Guard Squadrons"), known simply as the SS, were an important force for maintaining order. The SS was originally created as Hitler's personal bodyguard. Under the direction of **Heinrich Himmler,** the SS came to control not only the secret police forces that Himmler had set up, but also the regular police forces.

a way of life. By 1938, training in the military arts was also part of the routine. Even boys 10 to 14 years old were given small-arms drill and practice with dummy hand grenades. Those who were 14 to 18 years old bore army packs and rifles while on camping trips in the countryside.

The Hitler Youth had a female division, known as the League of German Girls, for girls aged 10 to 18. They, too, had uniforms: white blouses, blue ankle-length skirts, and sturdy hiking shoes. Camping and hiking were also part of the girls' activities. More important, however, girls were taught domestic skills—how to cook, clean houses, and take care of children. In Nazi Germany, women were expected to be faithful wives and dutiful mothers.

Many German children were proud of being part of the Hitler Youth.

Connecting to the Past

1. **Explaining** What ideals and values did the Hitler Youth promote?
2. **Analyzing** How did the Hitler Youth help support the Nazi attempt to create a total state?
3. **Writing about History** Do organizations like the Hitler Youth exist today in the United States? How are they similar or different?

The Way It Was

Answers:

1. military values and virtues, such as duty, obedience, strength, and ruthlessness
2. by winning young people over to Nazi ideas
3. Students might mention Boy Scouts and Girl Scouts. Neither of those organizations is state-run, nor are all young people expected to join. Their goals, too, are very different.

Connecting Across Time

Some attribute the Nazi rise to power to their ability to use modern electioneering techniques. How would students compare Nazi use of conservative Germans' fear of communism to the McCarthy blacklist era of the 1950s in the United States? L3

Critical Thinking

Guide students in a discussion of the status of women under Nazism. Compare it to their status in Mussolini's Italy and Stalin's Soviet Union. L2

CURRICULUM CONNECTION

The Arts The musical stage play and film, *The Sound of Music*, by Rodgers and Hammerstein, depicts the Nazi takeover of Austria.

CRITICAL THINKING ACTIVITY

Analyzing Advise the students that Hitler and his followers were elected to power by a cultured and civilized people who experienced a drastic change in their way of life following World War I. The German people were searching for a leader and an identity to help them escape their economic woes. While Nazism at first glance seemed appealing, the Nazis began their reign of slaughter and extermination with incremental acts of prejudice and persecution, using innocent people as scapegoats. It is important to study the pattern in the rise of Nazism to ensure it never surfaces again in a similar form in our present world. Ask students to write an essay analyzing the totalitarian nature of Nazi Germany.

Chart *Skills*

Answers:

1. Methods for controlling the opposition were similar. All had one political leader who dominated the single political party.
2. Freedom of speech, opposition parties, and open and free elections are hallmarks of democracy. Opposition under dictators is either tightly controlled, prohibited, or eliminated.

3 ASSESS

Assign Section 3 Assessment as homework or as an in-class activity.

Have students use **Interactive Tutor Self-Assessment CD-ROM.**

Section Quiz 17–3

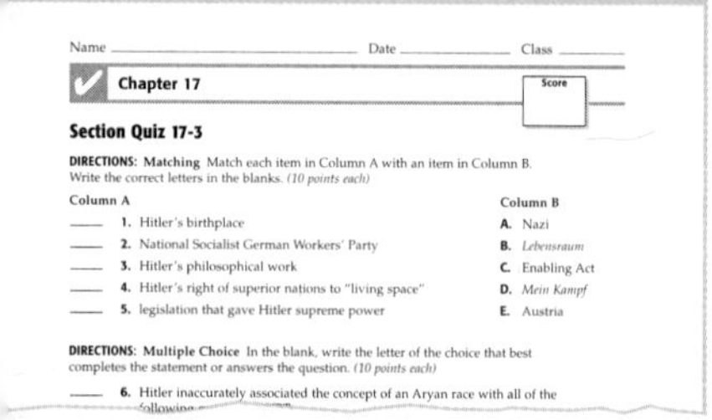

Name ______ Date ______ Class ______

Chapter 17 — Score

Section Quiz 17-3

DIRECTIONS: Matching Match each item in Column A with an item in Column B. Write the correct letters in the blanks. *(10 points each)*

Column A	Column B
____ 1. Hitler's birthplace	A. Nazi
____ 2. National Socialist German Workers' Party	B. *Lebensraum*
____ 3. Hitler's philosophical work	C. Enabling Act
____ 4. Hitler's right of superior nations to "living space"	D. *Mein Kampf*
____ 5. legislation that gave Hitler supreme power	E. Austria

DIRECTIONS: Multiple Choice In the blank, write the letter of the choice that best completes the statement or answers the question. *(10 points each)*

____ 6. Hitler inaccurately associated the concept of an Aryan race with all of the following

Reading Essentials and Study Guide 17–3

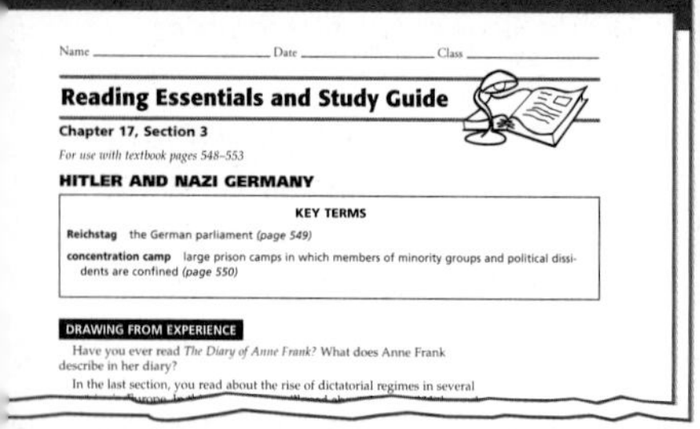

Name ______ Date ______ Class ______

Reading Essentials and Study Guide

Chapter 17, Section 3

For use with textbook pages 548–553

HITLER AND NAZI GERMANY

KEY TERMS

Reichstag the German parliament *(page 549)*

concentration camp large prison camps in which members of minority groups and political dissidents are confined *(page 550)*

DRAWING FROM EXPERIENCE

Have you ever read *The Diary of Anne Frank?* What does Anne Frank describe in her diary?

In the last section, you read about the rise of dictatorial regimes in several

Three Dictators: Mussolini, Stalin, and Hitler

	Benito Mussolini (1883–1945)	Joseph Stalin (1879–1953)	Adolf Hitler (1889–1945)
Country	Italy	USSR	Germany
Political Title	Prime Minister	General Secretary	Chancellor
Date in Power	1922	1929	1933
Political Party	Fascist Party	Communist Party	National Socialist German Workers' Party (NSDAP, or Nazi)
Type of Government	Fascist	Communist	Fascist
Source(s) of Support	Middle-class industrialists and large land owners	Party officials	Industrial leaders, landed aristocrats, military, and bureaucracy
Methods of Controlling Opposition	Secret police (OVRA), imprisonment, outlawing other parties, propaganda, censorship of the press	Purges, prison camps, secret police, state-run press, forced labor camps, executions	*Schutzstaffeln* (SS) police force, propaganda, state-run press, terror, repression, racial laws, concentration and death camps
Other Characteristics	Support for Catholic Church, nationalism, antisocialism, anticommunism	Five-Year Plans for rapid industrialization, collectivization of farms	Enabling Act, rearmament, public projects to put people to work, anti-Semitism, racism, social Darwinism, extreme nationalism

Chart *Skills*

Mussolini, Stalin, and Hitler all came to power after World War I.

1. **Making Comparisons** Compare the governments of Mussolini, Stalin, and Hitler. How were they similar?
2. **Identifying** What methods do people in a democracy use to express their opposition to government policies? Why would these methods not have worked under these dictators?

The SS was based on two principles: terror and ideology. Terror included the instruments of repression and murder—secret police, criminal police, concentration camps, and later, execution squads and death camps (concentration camps where prisoners are killed). For Himmler, the chief goal of the SS was to further the Aryan master race.

Economic Policies In the economic sphere, Hitler used public works projects and grants to private construction firms to put people back to work and end the depression. A massive rearmament program, however, was the key to solving the unemployment problem.

Unemployment, which had reached 6 million people in 1932, dropped to 2.6 million in 1934 and less than 500,000 in 1937. The regime claimed full credit for solving Germany's economic woes. The new regime's part in bringing an end to the depression was an important factor in leading many Germans to accept Hitler and the Nazis.

Spectacles and Organizations Mass demonstrations and spectacles were also used to make the German people an instrument of Hitler's policies. These meetings, especially the **Nuremberg** party rallies that were held every September, had great appeal. They usually evoked mass enthusiasm and excitement.

Institutions, such as the Catholic and Protestant churches, primary and secondary schools, and universities, were also brought under the control of the Nazi totalitarian state. Nazi professional organizations and leagues were formed for civil servants, teachers, women, farmers, doctors, and lawyers. In addition, youth organizations taught Nazi ideals.

Women and Nazism Women played a crucial role in the Aryan state as bearers of the children who, it

CRITICAL THINKING ACTIVITY

Synthesizing Information Ask each student to create a chart comparing and contrasting communism and fascism. The items to list in the chart include who holds authority in each system, how and why the authority is held, and what social and economic groups support the system. Ask students to list who owns the means of production, who makes decisions regarding production, and who owns the land and makes decisions on its use. Have students review their charts to determine in which ways the two systems are similar and in which ways they differ. Ask students to share their results during a class discussion. L2

was believed, would bring about the triumph of the Aryan race. The Nazis believed men were destined to be warriors and political leaders, while women were meant to be wives and mothers. By preserving this clear distinction, each could best serve to "maintain the whole community."

Nazi ideas determined employment opportunities for women. Jobs in heavy industry, it was thought, might hinder women from bearing healthy children. Certain professions, including university teaching, medicine, and law, were also considered unsuitable for women, especially married women. The Nazis instead encouraged women to pursue other occupations, such as social work and nursing. The Nazi regime pushed its campaign against working women with poster slogans such as "Get ahold of pots and pans and broom and you'll sooner find a groom!"

"The broad mass of a nation . . . will more easily fall victim to a big lie than to a small one."
—*Adolf Hitler*

Anti-Semitic Policies From its beginning, the Nazi Party reflected the strong anti-Semitic beliefs of Adolf Hitler. Once in power, the Nazis translated anti-Semitic ideas into anti-Semitic policies.

In September 1935, the Nazis announced new racial laws at the annual party rally in Nuremberg. These **"Nuremberg laws"** excluded Jews from German citizenship and forbade marriages between Jews and German citizens. Jews were also required to wear yellow Stars of David and to carry identification cards saying they were Jewish.

A more violent phase of anti-Jewish activity began on the night of November 9, 1938—the ***Kristallnacht,*** or "night of shattered glass." In a destructive rampage against the Jews, Nazis burned synagogues and destroyed some seven thousand Jewish businesses. At least a hundred Jews were killed. Thirty thousand Jewish males were rounded up and sent to concentration camps.

Kristallnacht led to further drastic steps. Jews were barred from all public transportation and all public buildings including schools and hospitals. They were prohibited from owning, managing, or working in any retail store. The Jews were forced to clean up all the debris and damage due to Kristallnacht. Finally, under the direction of the SS, Jews were encouraged to "emigrate from Germany."

Reading Check **Summarizing** What steps did Hitler take to establish a Nazi totalitarian state in Germany?

SECTION 3 ASSESSMENT

Checking for Understanding

1. **Define** Reichstag, concentration camp.
2. **Identify** Adolf Hitler, National Socialist German Workers' Party, *Mein Kampf, Lebensraum,* Enabling Act, Aryan, Heinrich Himmler, Nuremberg laws, *Kristallnacht.*
3. **Locate** Munich, Nuremberg.
4. **Summarize** the steps that Hitler took to become the sole ruler of Germany.
5. **List** the rights taken from the Jews by the Nazi government.

Critical Thinking

6. **Analyze** How did mass demonstrations and meetings contribute to the success of the Nazi Party?
7. **Organizing Information** Use a table to describe the policies and programs used by the Nazis to create a Third Reich. Identify the goals for each policy or program.

Policy/Program	Goals

Analyzing Visuals

8. **Examine** any two photos from this section. Compare and contrast the two photos. How do you think they relate to Hitler's vision of Nazi Germany?

Writing About History

9. **Expository Writing** Identify and read selected short segments of Hitler's *Mein Kampf.* Analyze a passage that seems especially meaningful to you. What is your evaluation of Hitler's argument? Give reasons for your assessment in an essay.

Reading Check

Answer: Hitler used mass demonstrations, control of economy, terror and repression, and control of institutions.

CURRICULUM CONNECTION

Literature Anne Frank was a Jewish girl who kept a diary during the two years she spent hiding with her family in an attic in Amsterdam. She was arrested in 1944 and sent to the Nazi death camp at Bergen-Belsen, where she died at the age of 15. Her account, *The Diary of a Young Girl,* was published in 1952. In 1987, more than thirty years later, Miep Gies, the woman who helped to hide the Frank family, wrote her own story, *Anne Frank Remembered,* about life under Nazi occupation and what she remembers of Anne Frank.

Reteaching Activity

Have students list the steps in Hitler's rise to power. They may begin with his forming the Brownshirts and conclude with his taking the title *Der Führer.* **L2**

4 CLOSE

Hold a class discussion to help students outline what led to the Nazis' rise to power in Germany. Have students create a flowchart on the chalkboard. Ask them to copy it and use it for reference. **L1 ELL**

SECTION 3 ASSESSMENT

1. Key terms are in blue.
2. Adolf Hitler *(p. 548)*; National Socialist German Workers' Party *(p. 549)*; *Mein Kampf (p. 549)*; *Lebensraum (p. 549)*; Enabling Act *(p. 550)*; Aryan *(p. 551)*; Heinrich Himmler *(p. 551)*; Nuremberg laws *(p. 553)*; *Kristallnacht (p. 553)*
3. See chapter maps.
4. increased size of Nazi Party in Reichstag; appointed chancellor; passed the Enabling Act
5. German citizenship; to marry German citizens; to use public transportation and buildings; to own, manage, or work in any retail store
6. They evoked mass enthusiasm and excitement.
7. Program: totalitarian state; Goal: control of citizens' lives; Program: Aryan racial state; Goals: elimination of Jews and domination of Germany and the world
8. Answers will vary.
9. Answers will vary depending on the passage selected.

CHAPTER 17
Section 4, 554–557

1 FOCUS

Section Overview

This section explores cultural and intellectual trends between World War I and World War II.

BELLRINGER
Skillbuilder Activity

 Project transparency and have students answer questions.

 Available as a blackline master.

Daily Focus Skills Transparency 17–4

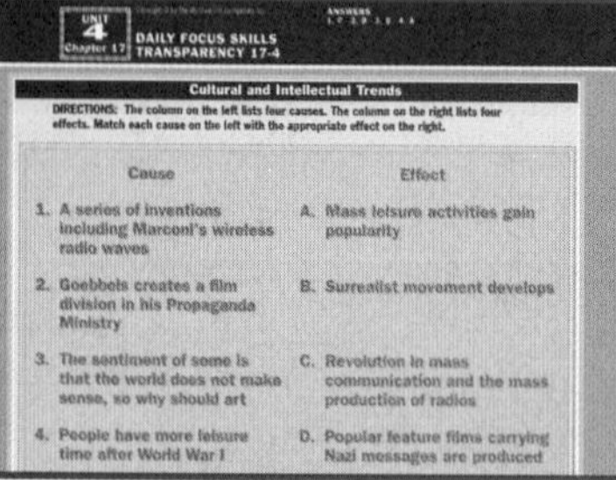

UNIT 4 Chapter 17
DAILY FOCUS SKILLS TRANSPARENCY 17-4

Cultural and Intellectual Trends

DIRECTIONS: The column on the left lists four causes. The column on the right lists four effects. Match each cause on the left with the appropriate effect on the right.

Cause	Effect
1. A series of inventions including Marconi's wireless radio waves	A. Mass leisure activities gain popularity
2. Goebbels creates a film division in his Propaganda Ministry	B. Surrealist movement develops
3. The sentiment of some is that the world does not make sense, so why should art	C. Revolution in mass communication and the mass production of radios
4. People have more leisure time after World War I	D. Popular feature films carrying Nazi messages are produced

Guide to Reading

Answers to Graphic: *Ulysses*; Joyce uses stream of consciousness to examine a day in the life of ordinary people. *Siddhartha* and *Steppenwolf*; Hesse uses Buddhist ideas to show the psychological confusion of modern existence.

Preteaching Vocabulary: Explain why *surrealism* arose during this period. *(Events in the material world were grim and made people want to escape. Surrealism sought a reality beyond the material world and found it in the world of the unconscious.)* L2

SECTION 4 Cultural and Intellectual Trends

Guide to Reading

Main Ideas

- Radios and movies were popular forms of entertainment that were used to spread political messages.
- New artistic and intellectual trends reflected the despair created by World War I and the Great Depression.

Key Terms

photomontage, surrealism, uncertainty principle

People to Identify

Salvador Dalí, James Joyce, Hermann Hesse

Places to Locate

Berlin, Dublin

Preview Questions

1. What trends dominated the arts and popular culture after 1918?
2. How did the new movements in arts and literature reflect the changes after World War I?

Reading Strategy

Categorizing Information Use a table like the one below to list literary works by Hesse and Joyce. Describe the techniques used in each work.

Literary Works	Techniques

Preview of Events

1915 · 1920 · 1925 · 1930

- **1920** First Dada show in Berlin
- **1922** James Joyce's *Ulysses* is published
- **1927** Werner Heisenberg explains the uncertainty principle

Voices from the Past

Tristan Tzara

In 1922, Tristan Tzara, a Romanian-French poet, gave a lecture on the new artistic movement called dadaism:

> "I know that you have come here today to hear explanations. Well, don't expect to hear any explanations about Dada. You explain to me why you exist. You haven't the faintest idea. . . . Dada is a state of mind. Dada applies itself to everything, and yet it is nothing, it is the point where the yes and the no and all the opposites meet, not solemnly in the castles of human philosophies, but very simply at street corners, like dogs and grasshoppers. Like everything in life, Dada is useless. Dada is without pretension, as life should be."
>
> —**Tristan Tzara, *The Dada Painters and Poets,* Robert Motherwell, ed., 1922**

Influenced by the insanity of World War I, dadaists attempted to give expression to what they saw as the absurdity of life.

Mass Culture: Radio and Movies

A series of inventions in the late nineteenth century had led the way for a revolution in mass communications. Especially important was Marconi's discovery of wireless radio waves. A musical concert transmitted in June of 1920 had a major impact on radio broadcasting. Broadcasting facilities were built in the United States, Europe, and Japan during 1921 and 1922. At the same time, the mass

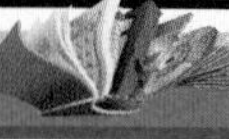

SECTION RESOURCES

Reproducible Masters

- Reproducible Lesson Plan 17–4
- Daily Lecture and Discussion Notes 17–4
- Guided Reading Activity 17–4
- Section Quiz 17–4
- Reading Essentials and Study Guide 17–4

Transparencies

- Daily Focus Skills Transparency 17–4

Multimedia

- Interactive Tutor Self-Assessment CD-ROM
- ExamView® Pro Testmaker CD-ROM
- Presentation Plus! CD-ROM

Picturing History

This 1920s movie camera (far right) and radio were part of a communications revolution. Millions of people could now hear or see the same entertainment, news, and advertisements. A more homogeneous, or uniform, culture resulted. What are the positive and negative results of a uniform culture?

production of radios began. In 1926, there were 2.2 million radios in Great Britain. By the end of the 1930s, there were 9 million.

Although motion pictures had first emerged in the 1890s, full-length features did not appear until shortly before World War I. The Italian film *Quo Vadis* and the American film *Birth of a Nation* made it apparent that cinema was an important new form of mass entertainment. By 1939, about 40 percent of adults in the more industrialized countries were attending a movie once a week. That figure had increased to 60 percent by the end of World War II.

Of course, radio and the movies could be used for political purposes. Hitler said, "Without motor-cars, sound films, and wireless, [there would be] no victory of Nazism." Radio offered great opportunities for reaching the masses. This became obvious when it was discovered that Adolf Hitler's fiery speeches made just as great an impact on people when heard over the radio as they did in person. The Nazi regime encouraged radio listening by urging manufacturers to produce inexpensive radios that could be bought on an installment plan.

Film, too, had propaganda potential, a fact not lost on Joseph Goebbels (GUH[R]•buhlz), the propaganda minister of Nazi Germany. Believing that film was one of the "most modern and scientific means of influencing the masses," Goebbels created a special film division in his Propaganda Ministry.

The Propaganda Ministry supported the making of both documentaries—nonfiction films—and popular feature films that carried the Nazi message. ***The Triumph of the Will***, for example, was a documentary of the 1934 Nuremberg party rally. This movie was filmed by Leni Riefenstahl, an actress turned director. It forcefully conveyed to viewers the power of National Socialism.

Reading Check **Explaining** Why was the radio an important propaganda tool for the Nazis?

Mass Leisure

After World War I, new work patterns provided people with more free time to take advantage of the leisure activities that had developed at the turn of the century. By 1920, the eight-hour day had become the norm for many office and factory workers in northern and western Europe.

Professional sporting events aimed at large audiences were an important aspect of mass leisure. Travel was another favorite activity. Trains, buses, and cars made trips to beaches or holiday resorts increasingly popular and affordable. Beaches, such as the one at Brighton in Great Britain, were mobbed by crowds of people from all social classes.

Mass leisure offered new ways for totalitarian states to control the people. The Nazi regime, for example, adopted a program called *Kraft durch Freude* ("Strength through Joy"). The program offered a variety of leisure activities to fill the free time of the working class. These activities included concerts, operas, films, guided tours, and sporting events. Especially popular were the program's inexpensive vacations, which were similar to modern package tours. A vacation could be a cruise to Scandinavia or the Mediterranean. More likely for workers, it was a shorter trip within Germany.

Reading Check **Examining** How did the "Strength through Joy" program help to support the Nazi regime?

2 TEACH

Picturing History

Answer: Positive results include helping members of a society bond; negative results include stifling creativity.

Reading Check

Answer: Radio offered great opportunities to reach the masses, and Hitler's fiery speeches were just as effective over the radio as in person.

Reading Check

Answer: It provided a new way to control the people—through leisure.

Daily Lecture and Discussion Notes 17–4

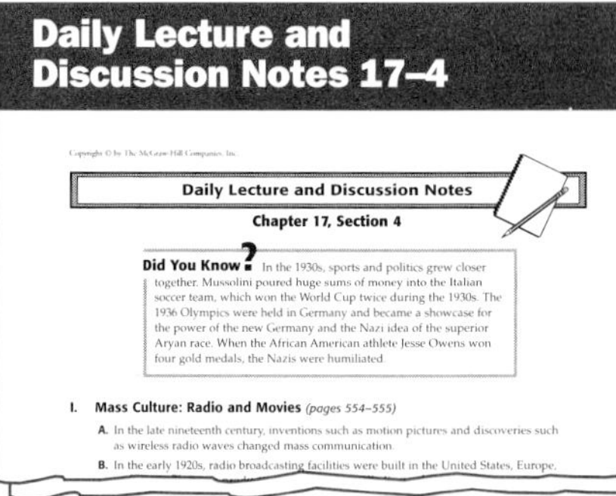

Daily Lecture and Discussion Notes

Chapter 17, Section 4

Did You Know? In the 1930s, sports and politics grew closer together. Mussolini poured huge sums of money into the Italian soccer team, which won the World Cup twice during the 1930s. The 1936 Olympics were held in Germany and became a showcase for the power of the new Germany and the Nazi idea of the superior Aryan race. When the African American athlete Jesse Owens won four gold medals, the Nazis were humiliated.

I. **Mass Culture: Radio and Movies** *(pages 554–555)*

A. In the late nineteenth century, inventions such as motion pictures and discoveries such as wireless radio waves changed mass communication.

B. In the early 1920s, radio broadcasting facilities were built in the United States, Europe,

Guided Reading Activity 17–4

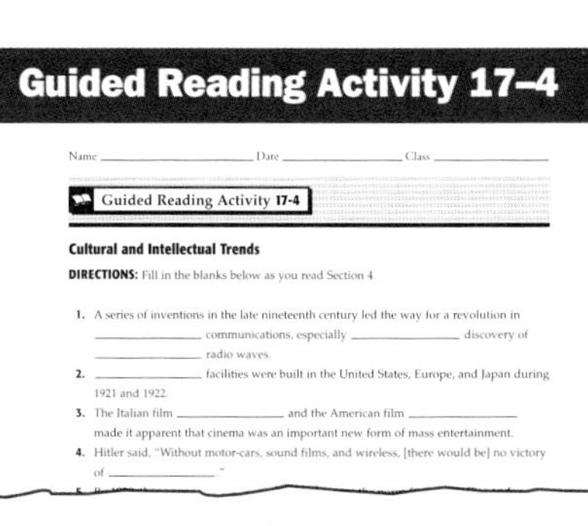
Name ______ Date ______ Class ______

Guided Reading Activity 17-4

Cultural and Intellectual Trends

DIRECTIONS: Fill in the blanks below as you read Section 4.

1. A series of inventions in the late nineteenth century led the way for a revolution in ______ communications, especially ______ discovery of ______ radio waves.
2. ______ facilities were built in the United States, Europe, and Japan during 1921 and 1922.
3. The Italian film ______ and the American film ______ made it apparent that cinema was an important new form of mass entertainment.
4. Hitler said, "Without motor-cars, sound films, and wireless, [there would be] no victory of ______."

INTERDISCIPLINARY CONNECTIONS ACTIVITY

Art and Language Arts Motion pictures became a major industry in the 1920s. One of the earliest silent film stars was British comedian Charlie Chaplin. Sound was added to films in the late 1920s. Have students research the movie industry and the technological advances it made during the postwar decade. Have students work in pairs to write a report on their findings and then design a poster advertising a movie of the era. Suggest that students bring a video of one of the old films to class, such as *Dracula*, starring Bela Lugosi; *Mata Hari* with Greta Garbo; *Rose Marie* with Jeanette MacDonald and Nelson Eddy; or *Top Hat* with Fred Astaire and Ginger Rogers. Ask students what values or ideals the films portray. L2

History *through Art*

Answer: After the nightmare landscapes of World War I battlefronts, the prewar fascination with the unconscious content of the mind seemed even more appropriate. Ask interested students to research and bring in examples of dadaist and surrealist art. **L1** ELL

3 ASSESS

Assign Section 4 Assessment as homework or as an in-class activity.

Have students use **Interactive Tutor Self-Assessment CD-ROM.**

Section Quiz 17–4

Name ______ Date ______ Class ______

Chapter 17 Score

Section Quiz 17-4

DIRECTIONS: Matching Match each item in Column A with an item in Column B. Write the correct letters in the blanks. *(10 points each)*

Column A	Column B
____ 1. non-fiction films	A. surrealism
____ 2. art movement that sought a reality in the unconscious	B. dadaism
____ 3. literary technique of portraying innermost thoughts	C. documentaries
____ 4. absurdist art form	D. stream of consciousness
____ 5. combination of individual photographs	E. photomontage

DIRECTIONS: Multiple Choice In the blank, write the letter of the choice that best completes the statement or answers the question. *(10 points each)*

Reading Essentials and Study Guide 17–4

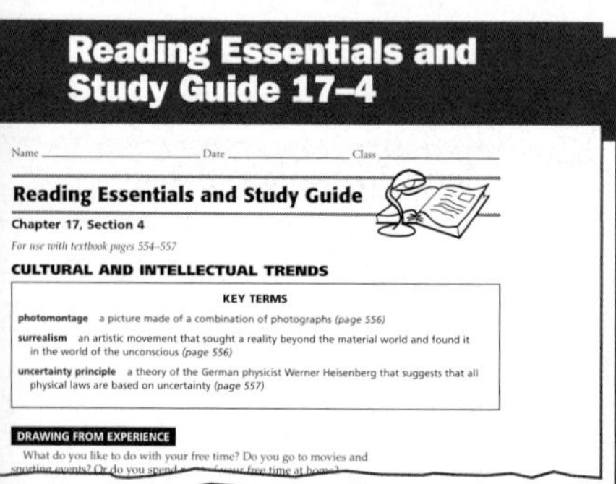

Name ______ Date ______ Class ______

Reading Essentials and Study Guide

Chapter 17, Section 4

For use with textbook pages 554–557

CULTURAL AND INTELLECTUAL TRENDS

KEY TERMS

photomontage a picture made of a combination of photographs *(page 556)*

surrealism an artistic movement that sought a reality beyond the material world and found it in the world of the unconscious *(page 556)*

uncertainty principle a theory of the German physicist Werner Heisenberg that suggests that all physical laws are based on uncertainty *(page 557)*

DRAWING FROM EXPERIENCE

What do you like to do with your free time? Do you go to movies and

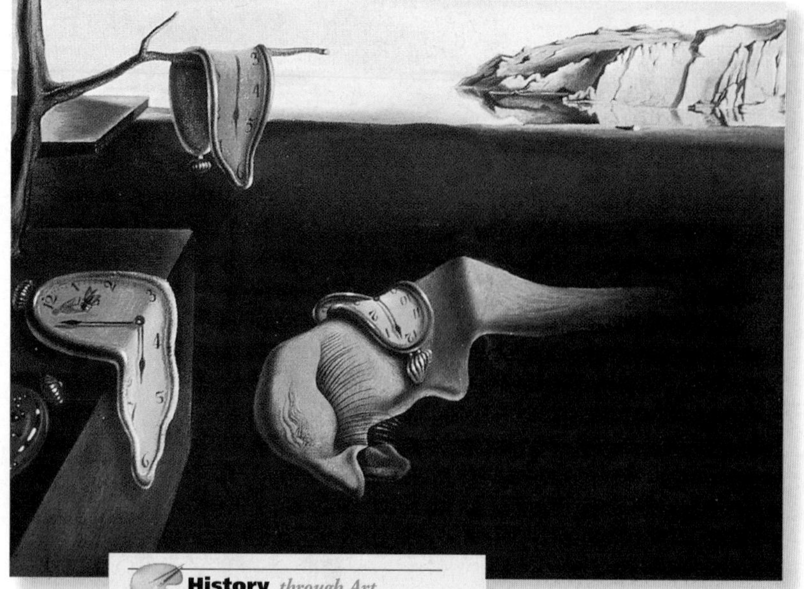

History *through Art*

***The Persistence of Memory* by Salvador Dalí, 1931** Surrealism gave everyday objects a dream-like quality. Dalí, like many surrealist artists, was influenced by Sigmund Freud's theory of the unconscious. Analyze why surrealism developed in the period between the wars.

Artistic and Literary Trends

Four years of devastating war had left many Europeans with a profound sense of despair. To many people, the horrors of World War I meant that something was dreadfully wrong with Western values, that human beings were violent animals who were incapable of creating a sane and rational world. The Great Depression and the growth of violent fascist movements only added to the despair created by the war.

With political, economic, and social uncertainties came intellectual uncertainties. These were evident in the artistic and intellectual achievements of the years following World War I.

Art: Nightmares and New Visions After 1918, artistic trends mainly reflected developments made before the war. Abstract expressionism, for example, became ever more popular. In addition, a prewar fascination with the absurd and the unconscious content of the mind seemed even more appropriate in light of the nightmare landscapes of the World War I battlefronts. "The world does not make sense, so why should art?" was a common remark. This sentiment gave rise to both the Dada movement and surrealism.

The dadaists were artists who were obsessed with the idea that life has no purpose. They were revolted by what they saw as the insanity of life and tried to express that feeling in their art. Dada artist Hannah Höch, for example, used **photomontage** (a picture made of a combination of photographs) to comment on women's roles in the new mass culture. Her work was part of the first Dada show in **Berlin** in 1920.

A more important artistic movement than dadaism was **surrealism.** This movement sought a reality beyond the material world and found it in the world of the unconscious. By portraying fantasies, dreams, and even nightmares, the surrealists sought to show the greater reality that exists beyond the world of physical appearances.

The Spaniard **Salvador Dalí** was the high priest of surrealism. Dalí painted everyday objects but separated them from their normal contexts. By placing recognizable objects in unrecognizable relationships, Dalí created a strange world in which the irrational became visible.

Not everybody accepted modern art forms. Many people denounced what they saw as decay in the arts. Nowhere was this more evident than in Nazi Germany. In the 1920s, Weimar Germany was one of the chief European centers for modern arts and sciences. Hitler and the Nazis, however, rejected modern art as "degenerate." In a speech in July 1937, Hitler proclaimed:

> "The people regarded this art [modern art] as the outcome of an impudent and shameless arrogance or of a simply shocking lack of skill; it felt that . . . these achievements which might have been produced by untalented children of from eight to ten years old—could never be valued as an expression of our own times or of the German future."

Hitler and the Nazis believed that they could create a new and genuine German art. It would glorify the strong, the healthy, and the heroic—the qualities

COOPERATIVE LEARNING ACTIVITY

Creating a Presentation Organize the class into small groups and assign a topic, such as science, literature, music, art, or technology to each group. Ask each group to compile a list of innovations in its assigned field between 1919 and 1939. Have each group describe the connection between discoveries and innovations in the assigned field and new patterns of social and cultural life in the twentieth century (for example, developments in transportation and communication that affected social mobility). Each group should create a pictorial display based on its list. Groups can find examples of innovations in books and magazines, or they may create their own illustrations. Have each group explain its display to the class, and post student products on the bulletin board. **L1** ELL

valued by the Aryan race. The new German art developed by the Nazis, however, was actually derived from nineteenth-century folk art, and emphasized realistic scenes of everyday life.

Literature: The Search for the Unconscious The interest in the unconscious that was evident in art was also found in new literary techniques. For example, "stream of consciousness" was a technique used by writers to report the innermost thoughts of each character. The most famous example of this approach is the novel *Ulysses,* published by the Irish writer **James Joyce** in 1922. *Ulysses* tells the story of one day in the life of ordinary people in **Dublin** by following the flow of their inner thoughts.

The German writer **Hermann Hesse** dealt with the unconscious in a quite different fashion. His novels reflect the influence of both Freud's psychology and Asian religions. The works focus on, among other things, the spiritual loneliness of modern human beings in a mechanized urban society. In both *Siddhartha* and *Steppenwolf,* Hesse uses Buddhist ideas to show the psychological confusion of modern existence. Hesse's novels had a great impact on German youth in the 1920s. He won the Nobel Prize for literature in 1946.

Reading Check **Examining** Why were artists and writers after World War I attracted to Freud's theory of the unconscious?

The Heroic Age of Physics

The prewar revolution in physics begun by Albert Einstein continued in the years between the wars. In fact, Ernest Rutherford, one of the physicists who showed that the atom could be split, called the 1920s the "heroic age of physics."

The new picture of the universe that was unfolding in physics undermined the old certainties of the classical physics of Newton. Newtonian physics had made people believe that all phenomena could be completely defined and predicted. In 1927, this belief was shaken when the German physicist Werner Heisenberg explained an observation he called the uncertainty principle.

Physicists knew that atoms were made up of smaller parts (subatomic particles). The fact that the behavior of these subatomic particles is unpredictable provides the foundation for the uncertainty principle. Heisenberg's theory essentially suggests that all physical laws are based on uncertainty. The theory's emphasis on randomness challenges Newtonian physics and thus, in a way, represents a new worldview. It is unlikely that many nonscientists understood the implications of Heisenberg's work. Nevertheless, the principle of uncertainty fit in well with the other uncertainties of the interwar years.

Reading Check **Explaining** How did Heisenberg's uncertainty principle challenge the Newtonian worldview?

SECTION 4 ASSESSMENT

Checking for Understanding

1. **Define** photomontage, surrealism, uncertainty principle.
2. **Identify** *The Triumph of the Will,* Salvador Dali, James Joyce, Hermann Hesse.
3. **Locate** Berlin, Dublin.
4. **Explain** how dadaism and surrealism reflected economic and political developments after World War I. Also explain how the painting on page 556, Dali's *The Persistence of Memory,* supports your explanation.
5. **List** the qualities that the Nazis wanted German art to glorify. Why do you think Hitler was concerned with issues such as the content and style of art?

Critical Thinking

6. **Evaluate** What impact did technological advances in transportation and communication have on Western culture between the wars?
7. **Compare and Contrast** Use a Venn diagram like the one below to compare the Dada movement and surrealism.

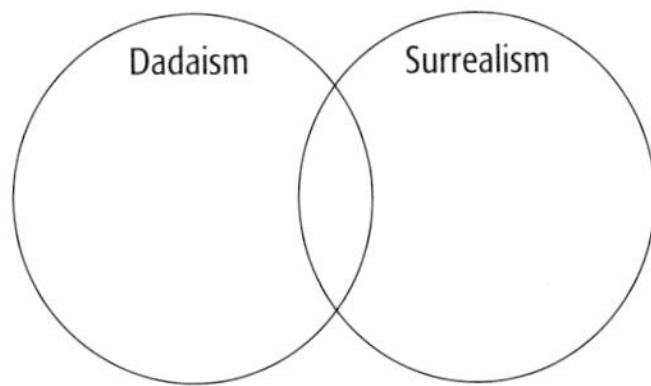

Analyzing Visuals

8. **Examine** the photographs on page 555. Describe how our culture has been influenced by radio and movies. What communication technology is most influential today?

Writing About History

9. **Informative Writing** Prepare a poster that shows the development of mass communication from the radio to modern technological advances in computers. Include photos and illustrations in your poster. Write a brief paragraph that summarizes twentieth-century innovations.

Reading Check

Answer: A fascination with Freud's theory of the unconscious content of the mind began before the war, but it seemed even more appropriate in light of the nightmare landscapes of the World War I battlefields.

Reading Check

Answer: Newton's physics had been based on certainty and natural laws, while Heisenberg's theory emphasizes randomness.

Critical Thinking

Ask students to discuss the following sentence: "More and more, mass culture and mass leisure had the effect of giving all the people in a nation similar ideas and similar experiences." L3

Reteaching Activity

Discuss with students how World War I changed the way people viewed the world. Review the artistic and scientific advances and cultural movements of the time. L1

4 CLOSE

Ask students to explain the significance of "mass entertainment," especially radio and movies. Discuss the growth of "mass leisure" and professional sports. Summarize developments in the areas of art, music, and literature. Identify the "heroic age of physics." L2

SECTION 4 ASSESSMENT

1. Key terms are in blue.
2. *The Triumph of the Will (p. 555)*; Salvador Dali *(p. 556)*; James Joyce *(p. 557)*; Hermann Hesse *(p. 557)*
3. See chapter maps.
4. Dadaists believed that life had no purpose, and surrealists sought a reality beyond the physical world. Their work reflected the nightmare mood caused by the Great Depression and totalitarian regimes. Answers will vary.
5. supposed to glorify the strong, the healthy, and the heroic; answers will vary
6. more free time, new leisure activities, rise in travel, mass entertainment
7. Dadaism: life has no purpose, tried to express the insanity of life in art; Surrealism: sought a reality beyond the material world; Both: reflect fascination with the absurd and the unconscious content of the mind
8. answers will vary; the Internet
9. Students will create posters.

GLENCOE TECHNOLOGY

MindJogger Videoquiz

Use the **MindJogger Videoquiz** to review Chapter 17 content.

 Available in VHS.

Using Key Terms

1. photomontage **2.** depression **3.** collectivization **4.** totalitarian state **5.** New Economic Policy **6.** deficit spending **7.** uncertainty principle **8.** Reichstag **9.** Politburo **10.** Collective bargaining

Reviewing Key Facts

11. the New Deal

12. Germany was faced with financial problems after the war.

13. It was an opportunity to test new weapons.

14. He felt that it was the outcome of arrogance or of a lack of skill that could never be valued as an expression of the German future. He wanted art to glorify the qualities of the Aryan race.

15. paid salaries by printing more money, which forced prices up

16. Because he was party general secretary, Stalin was in charge of appointing regional, district, city, and town party officials. The thousands of officials he appointed supported his bid for power. He then eliminated from the Politburo all the Bolsheviks of the revolutionary era.

17. Women were to be homemakers and mothers.

18. put heavy industry, banks, and mines under government control; permitted retail stores and small industries to be privately owned; allowed peasants to sell their produce openly

19. to exclude Jewish people from the rights of German citizenship

20. because they did not believe that the revolution in Russia could survive without other Communist states

CHAPTER 17 ASSESSMENT and ACTIVITIES

Using Key Terms

1. A ____ is a picture made of a combination of photographs.
2. A ____ is a period of low economic activity and rising unemployment.
3. The Soviet government followed a policy of ____ when it took private property after World War I without payments to the former owners.
4. A ____ exists when almost all power in a nation is held by the central government.
5. Lenin abandoned war communism in 1921 in favor of his ____, a modified version of the old capitalist system.
6. The government policy of going into debt to pay for public works projects, such as building highways, is called ____.
7. According to the ____, no one could determine the path of an electron, meaning all physical laws had elements of unpredictability.
8. The German parliament is known as the ____.
9. The ____ was the leading policy maker of the Communist Party.
10. ____ is the right of unions to negotiate with employers.

Reviewing Key Facts

11. **History** What did President Roosevelt call the program designed to fight the depression in the United States?
12. **Economics** Why were the Germans unable to pay all of the reparations assessed by the Treaty of Versailles?
13. **History** Why did Germany choose to become involved in the Spanish Civil War?
14. **Culture** Why did Hitler label modern art as degenerate?
15. **Economics** What did Germany do to cause high rates of inflation after World War I?
16. **Government** Describe how Stalin defeated Trotsky.
17. **Culture** What was the significance of the Italian Fascist slogan "Woman into the Home"?
18. **Economics** Describe Lenin's New Economic Policy.
19. **History** What was the basic purpose of the Nuremberg laws?
20. **Government** Why did Trotsky and his followers want to spread communism to other nations?

Critical Thinking

21. **Cause and Effect** Why did the depression help extremist leaders gain power in many nations during the 1930s?
22. **Compare and Contrast** How was Roosevelt's New Deal both similar to and different from Stalin's Five-Year Plan?

Writing About History

23. **Expository Writing** Write an essay in which you relate one of the following to the uncertainties and disillusionment of the interwar years: mass entertainment, mass leisure, professional sports, dadaism, surrealism, or the "stream of consciousness" technique in literature. Research your topic and provide references and a bibliography to accompany your essay.

Chapter Summary

Between 1919 and 1939, the West experienced great economic and political challenges.

Political and Economic Changes

- In Britain, the Conservative Party implements traditional economic policies.
- In the United States, President Roosevelt develops the New Deal, a policy of active government intervention in the economy.
- In France, the Popular Front establishes the French New Deal, which promotes workers' rights.

Rise of Totalitarianism

- In Italy, Mussolini leads the Fascists to power.
- Stalin becomes dictator of the Soviet Union and purges the Communist Party of Old Bolsheviks.
- In Germany, Hitler establishes a totalitarian Nazi regime and starts the large-scale persecution of Jews.

Innovations and Ideas

- The artistic movements of dadaism and surrealism reflect the uncertainty of life created by World War I.
- Radio and film transform communications.
- Literary techniques reflect an interest in the unconscious.
- Heisenberg's uncertainty principle suggests that physical laws are based on uncertainty.

Critical Thinking

21. During the Great Depression, many people who were in economic distress were willing to listen to any leader who promised improved economic conditions.

22. Both plans brought enormous changes in the two countries and increased the governments' involvement in social and economic affairs. Unlike the Five-Year Plans, the New Deal did not demand great sacrifices from the people.

Writing About History

23. Answers should be supported by logical arguments and include an accurate bibliography.

Analyzing Sources

24. Answers will vary but should be supported by examples and logical arguments. The use of the word *storm* indicates that there has been a period of great upheaval, such as a war or revolution, that has not been resolved.

Self-Check Quiz

Visit the *Glencoe World History—Modern Times* Web site at wh.mt.glencoe.com and click on **Chapter 17–Self-Check Quiz** to prepare for the Chapter Test.

Analyzing Sources

The crisis of confidence in Western civilization ran deep. It was well captured in the words of the French poet Paul Valéry in the early 1920s:

> ❝The storm has died away, and we are still restless, Uneasy, as if the storm were about to break. Almost all the affairs of men remain in a terrible uncertainty. We think of what has disappeared, and we are almost destroyed by what has been destroyed; we do not know what will be born, and we fear the future. . . . Doubt and disorder are in us and with us. There is no thinking man, however shrewd or learned he may be, who can hope to dominate this anxiety, to escape from this impression of darkness.❞

24. Pretend you do not know when Valéry wrote this poem. What might you be able to conclude about the time in which Valéry lived from this passage?

25. What do the first two lines of this poem convey?

Applying Technology Skills

26. **Creating a Multimedia Presentation** Search the Internet for sources on the Great Depression. Based on your research, create a multimedia presentation about the causes leading up to the depression and the effect the depression had on Europe and the United States. Use images from the Internet in your presentation. Include a plan describing the type of presentation you would like to develop and the steps you will take to ensure a successful presentation.

Making Decisions

27. Imagine that you are living in 1928. Pretend that you know everything that is going to occur because of the Great Depression and that you have the ability to move to any major country in the world. Where would you go and why? Would being part of a particular social class influence your decision?

28. Imagine that you are a young person living in Germany during 1935. Write a letter to your cousin who lives in the United States describing the influence of the increasingly powerful Nazi regime upon your life. Do you support Hitler's rise to power, or are you concerned about his policies?

NATIONAL GEOGRAPHIC **Spanish Civil War, 1936–1939**

Nationalist-controlled area, February 1939
Republican-controlled area, February 1939
Area of intense fighting

Analyzing Maps and Charts

Study the map above to answer the following questions.

29. What advantage would the Nationalists seem to have had over the Republicans in February 1939?

30. How would the geographic location of the Republicans in 1939 have affected their supply routes?

31. Where was the most intense fighting concentrated?

The Princeton Review

Standardized Test Practice

Directions: Choose the best answer to the following question.

The *General Theory of Employment, Interest, and Money* by John Maynard Keynes was published in 1936. The book argued for

A mercantilism.
B disarmament.
C deficit spending.
D isolationism.

Test-Taking Tip: If you do not know the right answer to this question, use common sense to eliminate answer choices that do not make sense. Recall the context in which Keynes has been discussed in class or in your textbook. Think about the title of his book. These clues may help you eliminate incorrect answer choices.

Have students visit the Web site at wh.mt.glencoe.com to review Chapter 17 and take the Self-Check Quiz.

31. Intense fighting occurred in central Spain near Toledo and Madrid and along the northern border near France.

Standardized Test Practice

Answer: C

Answer Explanation: Students should use the process of elimination to arrive at the best answer.

Bonus Question ?

Ask students: Given the state in which Germany, Italy, and Russia found themselves after World War I, could they have achieved economic health and national self-respect by any means other than totalitarianism? Ask students to explain their answer. L2

25. The war has ended, but there is great uncertainty as to what is yet to come.

Applying Technology Skills

26. Students will create multimedia presentations.

Making Decisions

27. Answers will vary but should be consistent with material presented in this chapter and supported by logical arguments.

28. Answers will vary but should be consistent with material presented in this chapter and supported by logical arguments.

Analyzing Maps and Charts

29. Nationalists controlled much more territory than the Republicans.

30. The Republicans controlled a number of major Mediterranean Sea ports but had no land routes to Europe and no water access to the Atlantic Ocean.

Chapter 18 Resources

Timesaving Tools

TeacherWorks™ All-In-One Planner and Resource Center

- **Interactive Teacher Edition** Access your Teacher Wraparound Edition and your classroom resources with a few easy clicks.
- **Interactive Lesson Planner** Planning has never been easier! Organize your week, month, semester, or year with all the lesson helps you need to make teaching creative, timely, and relevant.

Use Glencoe's **Presentation Plus!** multimedia teacher tool to easily present dynamic lessons that visually excite your students. Using Microsoft PowerPoint® you can customize the presentations to create your own personalized lessons.

Teaching Transparencies

Graphic Organizer Student Activity 18 Transparency

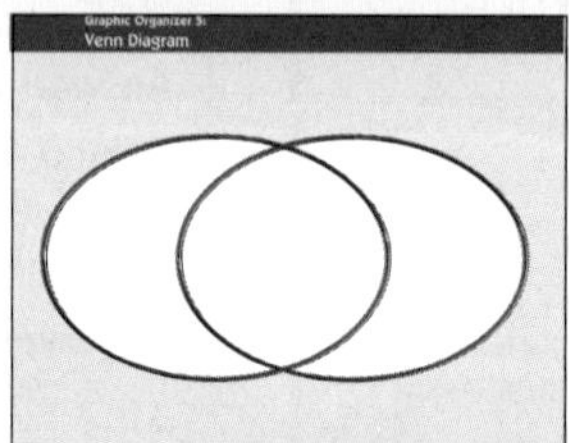

Chapter Transparency 18

Map Overlay Transparency 18

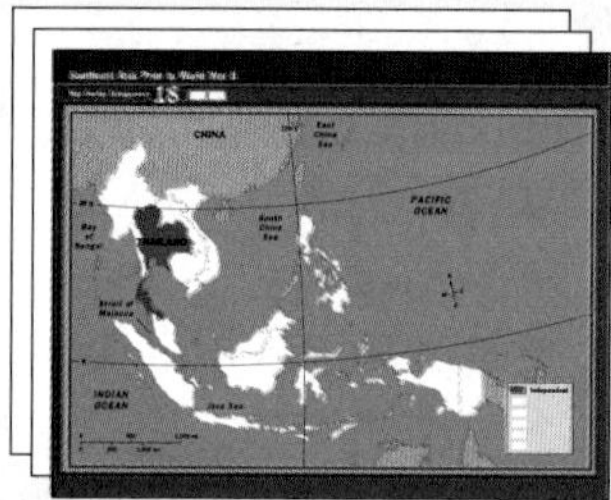

Application and Enrichment

Enrichment Activity 18

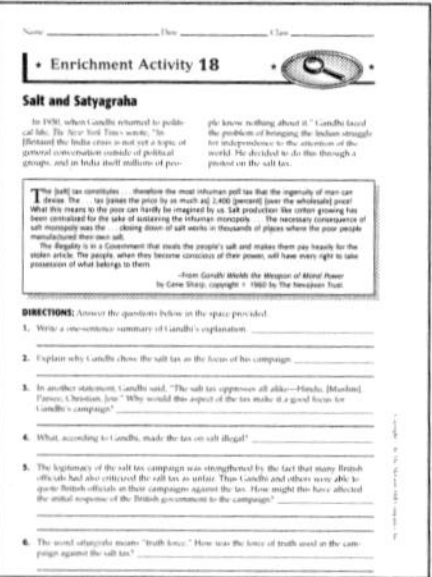

Primary Source Reading 18

History Simulation Activity 18

Historical Significance Activity 18

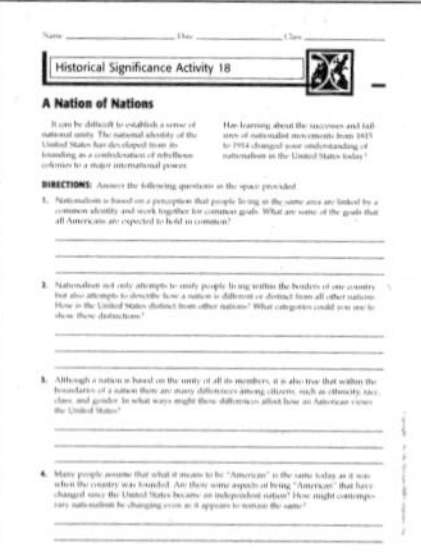

Cooperative Learning Activity 18

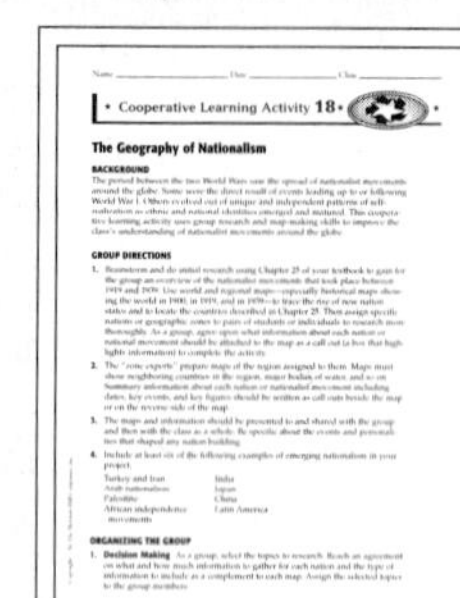

A&E HOME VIDEO

THE HISTORY CHANNEL.

The following videotape program is available from Glencoe as a supplement to Chapter 18:

- **Mahatma Gandhi: Pilgrim of Peace** (ISBN 0-7670-0668-2)

To order, call Glencoe at 1-800-334-7344. To find classroom resources to accompany this video, check the following home pages:
A&E Television: www.aande.com
The History Channel: www.historychannel.com

Chapter 18 Resources

Review and Reinforcement

Linking Past and Present Activity 18

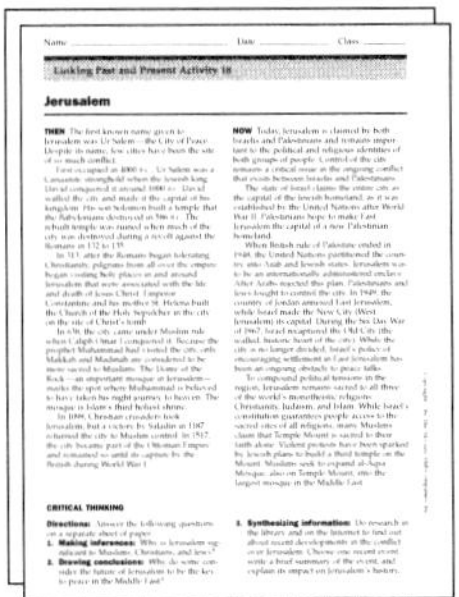

Time Line Activity 18

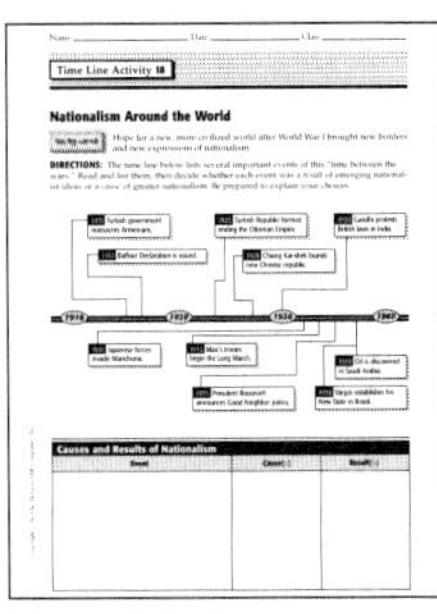

Reteaching Activity 18

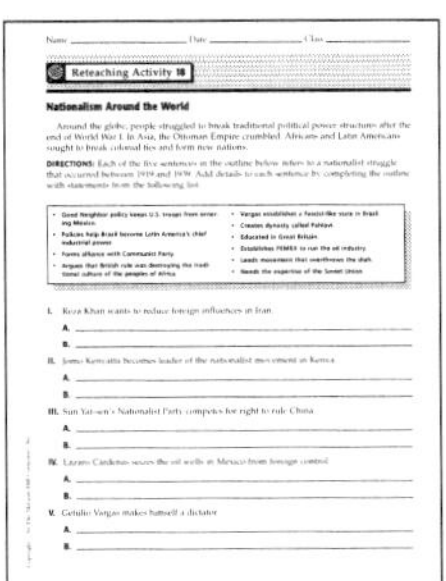

Vocabulary Activity 18

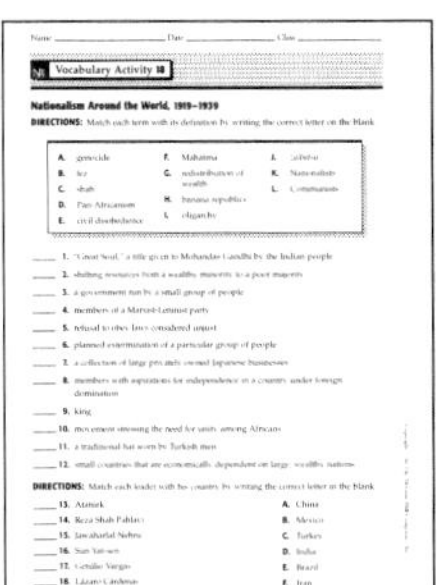

Critical Thinking Skills Activity 18

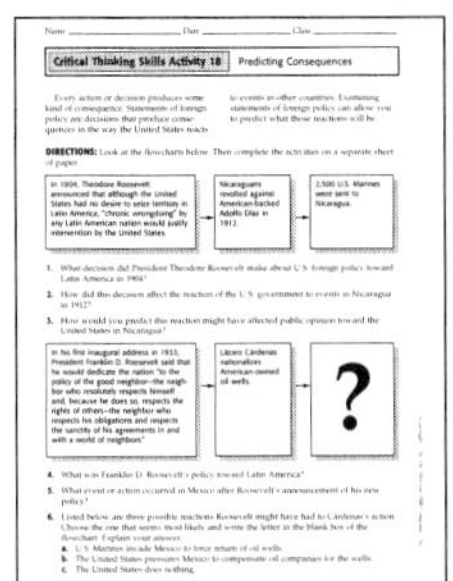

Assessment and Evaluation

Chapter 18 Test Form A

Chapter 18 Test Form B

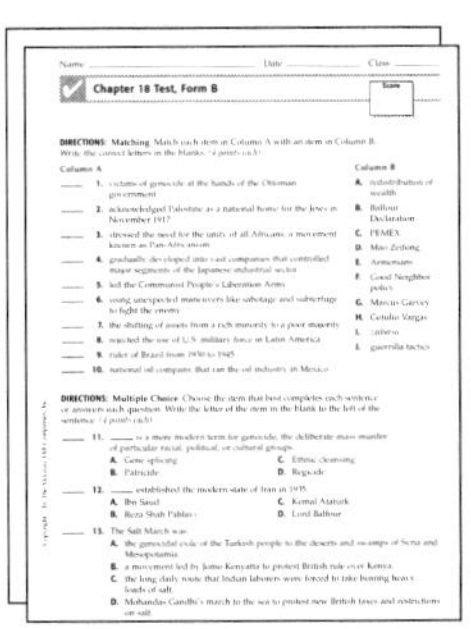

Performance Assessment Activity 18

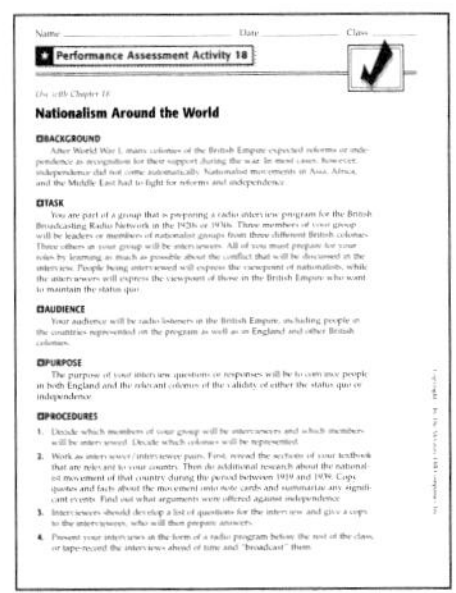

ExamView® Pro Testmaker CD-ROM

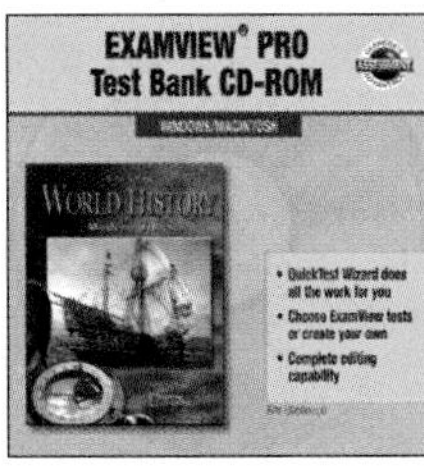

Standardized Test Skills Practice Workbook Activity 18

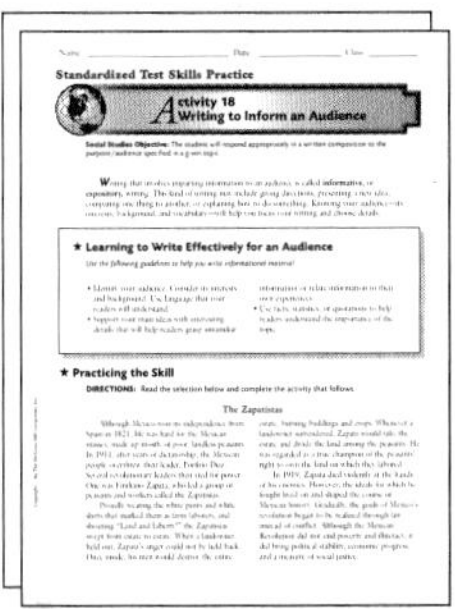

Interdisciplinary Activities

Mapping History Activity 18

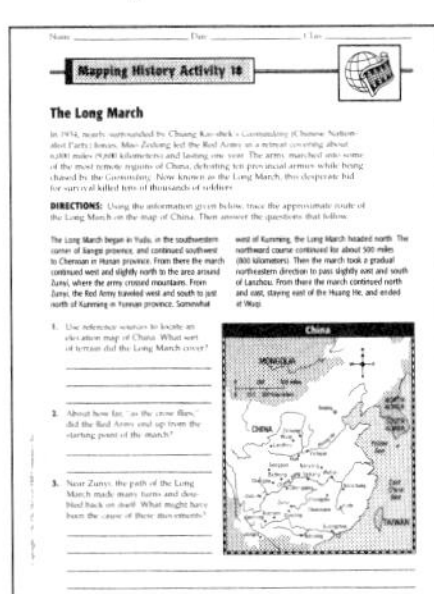

World Art and Music Activity 18

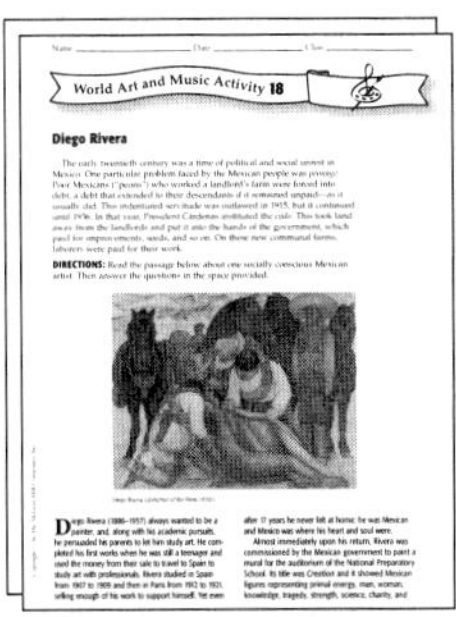

History and Geography Activity 18

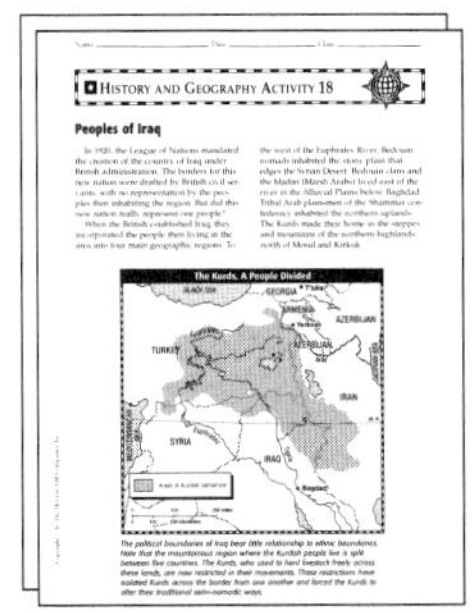

People in World History Activity 18

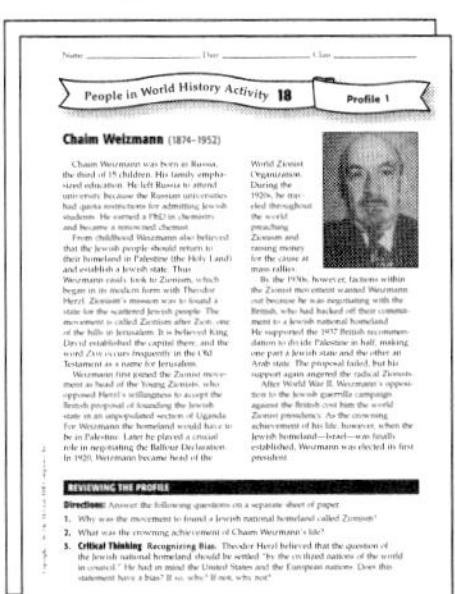

Multimedia

- Vocabulary PuzzleMaker CD-ROM
- Interactive Tutor Self-Assessment CD-ROM
- ExamView® Pro Testmaker CD-ROM
- Audio Program
- World History Primary Source Document Library CD-ROM
- MindJogger Videoquiz
- Presentation Plus! CD-ROM
- TeacherWorks CD-ROM
- Interactive Student Edition CD-ROM
- The World History—Modern Times Video Program

Spanish Resources

The following Spanish language materials are available in the Spanish Resources Binder:

- Spanish Guided Reading Activities
- Spanish Reteaching Activities
- Spanish Quizzes and Tests
- Spanish Vocabulary Activities
- Spanish Summaries

Chapter 18 Resources

SECTION RESOURCES

Daily Objectives	Reproducible Resources	Multimedia Resources
SECTION 1 **Nationalism in the Middle East** 1. Explain how nationalism led to the creation of the modern states of Turkey, Iran, and Saudi Arabia. 2. Specify how the Balfour Declaration made Palestine a national Jewish homeland.	Reproducible Lesson Plan 18–1 Daily Lecture and Discussion Notes 18–1 Guided Reading Activity 18–1* Section Quiz 18–1* Reading Essentials and Study Guide 18–1	Daily Focus Skills Transparency 18–1 Interactive Tutor Self-Assessment CD-ROM ExamView® Pro Testmaker CD-ROM Presentation Plus! CD-ROM
SECTION 2 **Nationalism in Africa and Asia** 1. Describe how peoples in Africa and Asia began to agitate for independence. 2. Relate how Japan became an aggressive military state. 3. Characterize how Soviet agents worked to spread communism around the world.	Reproducible Lesson Plan 18–2 Daily Lecture and Discussion Notes 18–2 Guided Reading Activity 18–2* Section Quiz 18–2* Reading Essentials and Study Guide 18–2	Daily Focus Skills Transparency 18–2 Interactive Tutor Self-Assessment CD-ROM ExamView® Pro Testmaker CD-ROM Presentation Plus! CD-ROM
SECTION 3 **Revolutionary Chaos in China** 1. Report how internal tensions led Chiang Kai-shek to violently end the Communist-Nationalist alliance. 2. Discuss Mao Zedong's belief that revolution in China would be led by peasants, not the urban working class.	Reproducible Lesson Plan 18–3 Daily Lecture and Discussion Notes 18–3 Guided Reading Activity 18–3* Section Quiz 18–3* Reading Essentials and Study Guide 18–3	Daily Focus Skills Transparency 18–3 Interactive Tutor Self-Assessment CD-ROM ExamView® Pro Testmaker CD-ROM Presentation Plus! CD-ROM
SECTION 4 **Nationalism in Latin America** 1. Describe how, before the Great Depression, the United States was the foremost investor in Latin America. 2. Report how the Great Depression created instability in Latin America, which led to military coups and the creation of military dictatorships.	Reproducible Lesson Plan 18–4 Daily Lecture and Discussion Notes 18–4 Guided Reading Activity 18–4* Section Quiz 18–4* Reteaching Activity 18* Reading Essentials and Study Guide 18–4	Daily Focus Skills Transparency 18–4 Interactive Tutor Self-Assessment CD-ROM ExamView® Pro Testmaker CD-ROM Presentation Plus! CD-ROM

0:00 **OUT OF TIME?**
Assign the Chapter 18 **Reading Essentials and Study Guide.**

*Also Available in Spanish

 Blackline Master  Transparency 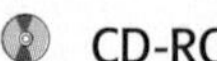 
CD-ROM DVD
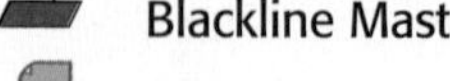  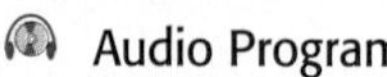 
Poster Music Program Audio Program Videocassette

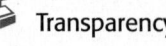

Chapter 18 Resources

NATIONAL GEOGRAPHIC **Teacher's Corner**

INDEX TO NATIONAL GEOGRAPHIC MAGAZINE

The following articles relate to this chapter:

- "The Promise of Pakistan," by John McCarry, October 1997.
- "India," by Geoffrey C. Ward, May 1997.
- "African Gold," by Carole Beckwith and Angela Fisher, October 1996.
- "Who are the Palestinians?" by Tad Szulc, June 1992.

NGS ONLINE

Access National Geographic's new dynamic MapMachine Web site and other geography resources at:
www.nationalgeographic.com
www.nationalgeographic.com/maps

KEY TO ABILITY LEVELS

Teaching strategies have been coded.

- L1 BASIC activities for all students
- L2 AVERAGE activities for average to above-average students
- L3 CHALLENGING activities for above-average students
- ELL ENGLISH LANGUAGE LEARNER activities

Block Schedule

Activities that are suited to use within the block scheduling framework are identified by:

WORLD HISTORY Online

Use our Web site for additional resources. All essential content is covered in the Student Edition.

You and your students can visit www.wh.mt.glencoe.com, the Web site companion to *Glencoe World History—Modern Times.* This innovative integration of electronic and print media offers your students a wealth of opportunities. The student text directs students to the Web site for the following options:

- **Chapter Overviews**
- **Self-Check Quizzes**
- **Student Web Activities**
- **Textbook Updates**

Answers to the Student Web Activities are provided for you in the **Web Activity Lesson Plans.** Additional Web resources and Interactive Tutor Puzzles are also available.

From the Classroom of...

Kimberly C. Felder
New Venture Academy
New York, New York

Nationalism Then and Now

Organize students into four groups: Mexico, Venezuela, Argentina, and Brazil. Have each group use the text to review the nationalistic struggle in its country, or provide groups with fact sheets. Then have each group write a letter to the editor of a newspaper in its country, arguing a nationalistic position.

Distribute magazine and newspaper articles about current nationalistic struggles. Try to include letters to the editor. Have the entire class compare the late twentieth-century struggles with nationalistic movements of Latin America.

Introducing
CHAPTER 18

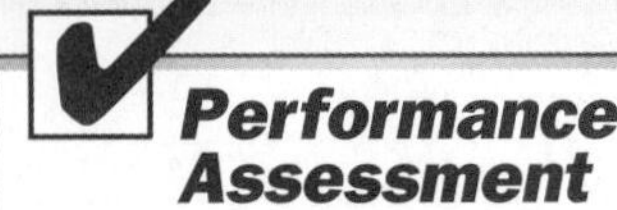

Refer to Activity 18 in the Performance Assessment Activities and Rubrics booklet.

The Impact Today

The struggle for national independence continues to be an important issue today. Point out to students as they begin to study this chapter that many ethnic and religious groups around the world are seeking national sovereignty. Ask students to bring to class newspaper and magazine accounts of situations involving nationalist movements.

GLENCOE TECHNOLOGY

The World History—Modern Times Video Program

To learn more about India's independence, students can view the Chapter 18 video, "Gandhi and Passive Resistance," from **The World History—Modern Times Video Program.**

MindJogger Videoquiz

Use the **MindJogger Videoquiz** to preview Chapter 18 content.

 Available in VHS.

CHAPTER 18 Nationalism Around the World

1919–1939

Key Events

As you read this chapter, look for the key events in the history of nationalism around the world.

- *The Balfour Declaration issued by the British foreign secretary in 1917 turned Palestine, a country with a 98 percent Muslim population, into a homeland for the Jews.*
- *Chiang Kai-shek positioned his Nationalist forces against Mao Zedong's Communists.*
- *Oil was discovered in the Persian Gulf area in 1938.*

The Impact Today

The events that occurred during this time period still impact our lives today.

- *The conflict over Palestine continues to bring violence and unrest to the region.*
- *Today China remains a communist state, and Mao Zedong is remembered as one of the country's most influential leaders.*
- *The Western world is very dependent upon oil from the Middle East.*

World History—Modern Times Video *The Chapter 18 video, "Gandhi and Passive Resistance," chronicles India's fight for independence between the two World Wars.*

1910
1915
1920
1925
1917 Britain issues Balfour Declaration
1923 Turkish Republic is formed, ending the Ottoman Empire
1928 Chiang Kai-shek founds a new Chinese republic

British enter Jerusalem, January 1918

Chiang Kai-shek

560

TWO-MINUTE LESSON LAUNCHER

This chapter concerns, among other things, people who rose to become national heroes. Ask students to brainstorm a list of adjectives and descriptive phrases that come to mind when they hear the word *hero.* Then divide the class into small groups. Give groups about ten minutes to discuss why nationalist feelings *(strong allegiance to one's own country, dislike of foreign presence, belief in the right to self-determination)* tend to inspire heroic leaders. Reunite the class and have them share the results of their discussions. L1

Introducing CHAPTER 18

The Destruction of the Old Order by José Clemente Orozco, c. 1922

1930
Gandhi's Salt March protests British laws in India

Aramco oil refinery in Ras Tanura, Saudi Arabia

1938
Oil is discovered in Saudi Arabia

1930 | 1935 | 1940 | 1945

1931
Japanese forces invade Manchuria

1935
Franklin D. Roosevelt announces the Good Neighbor policy

Franklin D. Roosevelt

HISTORY Online

Chapter Overview
Visit the *Glencoe World History—Modern Times* Web site at wh.mt.glencoe.com and click on **Chapter 18–Chapter Overview** to preview chapter information.

561

Chapter Objectives

After studying this chapter, students should be able to:

1. understand how the forces of nationalism affected events in the Middle East, Africa, Asia, and Latin America;
2. explain the role individual leaders played in the struggles for national independence;
3. describe how the creation of modern states included modernizing the economy;
4. explain how the lower classes led the way to social changes.

Chapter Overview
Introduce students to chapter content and key terms by having them access **Chapter Overview 18** at wh.mt.glencoe.com.

Time Line Activity

Have students select an event on the time line and learn more about it. From their research, have students write a brief report about the impact that event had on the emergence of nationalism. L2

MORE ABOUT THE ART

José Clemente Orozco is considered the most important contemporary muralist to work in fresco, the technique of applying watercolors to a moist plaster surface. While he did not fight in the Mexican Revolution, Orozco's political cartoons rallied support for General Venustiano Carranza. Orozco lived in the United States on several occasions. From 1932 to 1934 he painted a series of frescoes at Dartmouth College in Hanover, New Hampshire. The fresco pictured on this page was one of a series of murals painted on the walls of National Preparatory School, Mexico City, Mexico.

CHAPTER PREVIEW

Introducing
A Story That Matters

Depending on the ability levels of your students, select from the following questions and activities to reinforce the reading of *A Story That Matters.*

- What did Gandhi preach as he marched to Dandi? *(Civil disobedience is the inherent right of a citizen. He dare not give it up without ceasing to be a man.)*
- Why do you think Gandhi's nonviolent demonstrations were so successful against the British? *(The British could do little except imprison Gandhi; it is difficult to react against nonviolence.)*
- Do you agree or disagree with Gandhi's statement? Why or why not? *(Answers will vary.)* L1 L2

About the Art

Mohandas Gandhi's concern for and involvement with the poorer classes in India never ceased. Here he is joined by his followers on the Salt March in 1930.

Mohandas Gandhi was one of the most significant and influential persons of the twentieth century. His method of civil disobedience and nonviolence influenced Martin Luther King, Jr., and the civil rights movement in America. Gandhi also influenced Nelson Mandela and his efforts against apartheid in South Africa.

CHAPTER PREVIEW

A Story That Matters

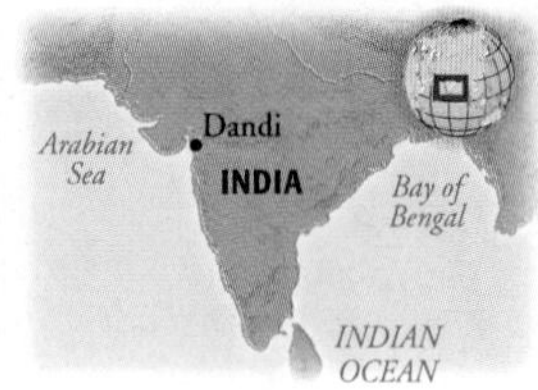

Gandhi leading the Salt March to Dandi to protest the British monopoly on salt production

Gandhi's March to the Sea

In 1930, Mohandas Gandhi, the 61-year-old leader of the Indian movement for independence from British rule, began a march to the sea with 78 followers. Their destination was Dandi, a little coastal town some 240 miles (386 km) away. The group covered about 12 miles (19 km) a day.

As they went, Gandhi preached his doctrine of nonviolent resistance to British rule in every village through which he passed: "Civil disobedience is the inherent right of a citizen. He dare not give it up without ceasing to be a man." By the time Gandhi reached Dandi, 24 days later, his small group had become a nonviolent army of thousands.

When Gandhi and his followers arrived at Dandi, Gandhi picked up a pinch of crystallized sea salt from the sand. Thousands of people all along the coast did likewise. In so doing, they were openly breaking British laws that prohibited Indians from making their own salt. The British had long profited from their monopoly on the making and selling of salt, an item much in demand in India. They used coastal saltflats to collect crystallized sea salt to sell.

By their simple acts of disobedience, Gandhi and the Indian people had taken yet another step on their long march to independence from the British. The Salt March was one of many nonviolent activities that Gandhi undertook to win India's national independence between World War I and World War II.

Why It Matters

With Europe in disorder after World War I, people living in colonies controlled by European countries began to think that the independence they desired might now be achieved. In Africa and Asia, movements for national independence began to take shape. In the Middle East, World War I ended the rule of the Ottoman Empire and created new states. For some Latin American countries, the fascist dictatorships of Italy and Germany provided models for change.

History and You You have read about many religious conflicts. In this chapter, you will learn about the conflict between the Muslims and the Hindus in India. Make a chart listing the differences between the groups. Explain how religious differences expand into other areas of conflict. How did this rivalry affect the development of India?

562

HISTORY AND YOU

Discuss the purpose of the Salt March led by Gandhi. Ask students to explain why the march might have been more effective at achieving change than a demonstration. Why were so many Indians attracted to Gandhi's message? How did the Salt March attack the underlying logic of imperialism? *(The empire was supposed to benefit England economically while preventing the Indians from reaping those same benefits.)* How did Gandhi's campaign affect India's relationship with Great Britain? *(His use of nonviolence weakened British authority and helped lead to India's independence.)* Ask students to analyze the influence of Gandhi on events of the twentieth century. Ask students to identify influential leaders today who are able to inspire followers as Gandhi did. L2

SECTION 1 Nationalism in the Middle East

Guide to Reading

Main Ideas
- Nationalism led to the creation of the modern states of Turkey, Iran, and Saudi Arabia.
- The Balfour Declaration made Palestine a national Jewish homeland.

Key Terms
genocide, ethnic cleansing

People to Identify
Abdulhamid II, T. E. Lawrence, Atatürk, Reza Shah Pahlavi, Ibn Saud

Places to Locate
Tehran, Iran, Saudi Arabia, Palestine

Preview Questions
1. What important force led to the fall of the Ottoman Empire?
2. What was the relationship between Arab nationalism and the mandate system?

Reading Strategy
Compare and Contrast Make a Venn diagram like the one below comparing and contrasting Atatürk's and Reza Shah Pahlavi's national policies.

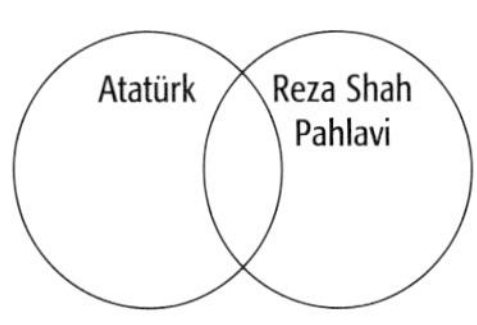

Preview of Events

1910 · 1915 · 1920 · 1925 · 1930 · 1935 · 1940

- **1915** Turkish government massacres Armenians
- **1916** The local governor of Makkah declares Arabia independent
- **1924** Caliphate formally abolished in Turkey
- **1932** Saudi Arabia is established

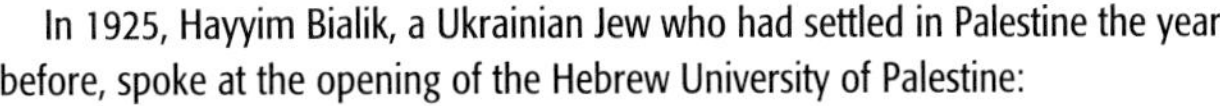

In 1925, Hayyim Bialik, a Ukrainian Jew who had settled in Palestine the year before, spoke at the opening of the Hebrew University of Palestine:

> ❝Through cruel and bitter trials and tribulations, through blasted hopes and despair of the soul, through innumerable humiliations, we have slowly arrived at the realization that without a tangible homeland, without private national premises that are entirely ours, we can have no sort of a life, either material or spiritual. . . . We have not come here to seek wealth, or dominion, or greatness. How much of these can this poor little country give us? We wish to find here only a domain of our own for our physical and intellectual labor.❞
>
> —***The Human Record: Sources of Global History,*** **Alfred J. Andrea and James H. Overfield, eds., 1998**

Committee discussing plans for a Jewish university in Palestine

Bialik was a believer in Zionism, a movement that supported the establishment of Palestine as a homeland for Jews.

Decline and Fall of the Ottoman Empire

The empire of the Ottoman Turks—which once had included parts of eastern Europe, the Middle East, and North Africa—had been growing steadily weaker since the end of the eighteenth century. Indeed, European nations called it "the sick man of Europe."

1 FOCUS

Section Overview

This section describes the Ottoman decline, the modernization of Turkey and Iran, and how Arab nationalism was affected by Jewish immigration to Palestine.

BELLRINGER
Skillbuilder Activity

Project transparency and have students answer questions.

Available as a blackline master.

Daily Focus Skills Transparency 18–1

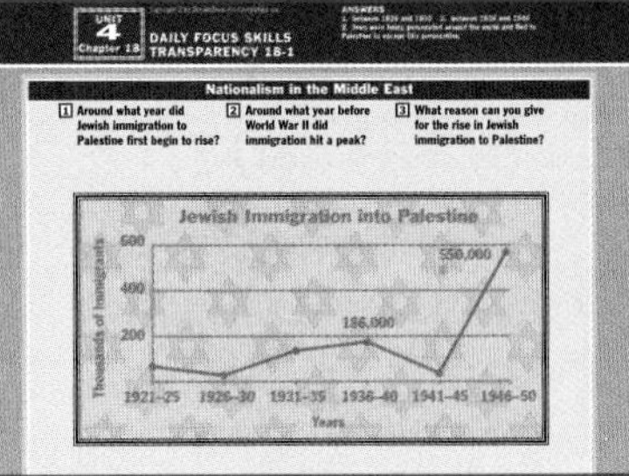

Guide to Reading

Answers to Graphic: Atatürk: democratic system, attempted to transform Turkey into a secular state; Pahlavi: no attempt to destroy Islamic beliefs; Atatürk *and* Pahlavi: modernized government, military, economic systems; encouraged education

Preteaching Vocabulary: Discuss the meaning of "genocide" *(a policy of killing people of a particular ethnic or religious group)* and "ethnic cleansing" *(attempt to purge an area of an ethnic group through deportation, intimidation, or genocide).* L2

SECTION RESOURCES

Reproducible Masters
- Reproducible Lesson Plan 18–1
- Daily Lecture and Discussion Notes 18–1
- Guided Reading Activity 18–1
- Section Quiz 18–1
- Reading Essentials and Study Guide 18–1

Transparencies
- Daily Focus Skills Transparency 18–1

Multimedia
- Interactive Tutor Self-Assessment CD-ROM
- ExamView® Pro Testmaker CD-ROM
- Presentation Plus! CD-ROM

2 TEACH

Daily Lecture and Discussion Notes 18–1

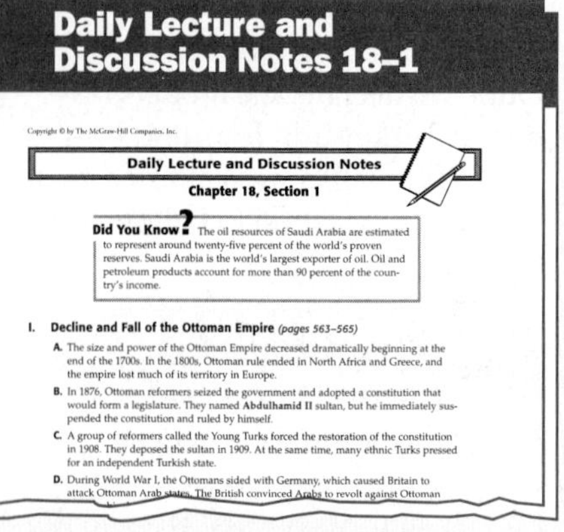

Copyright © by The McGraw-Hill Companies, Inc.

Daily Lecture and Discussion Notes

Chapter 18, Section 1

Did You Know? The oil resources of Saudi Arabia are estimated to represent around twenty-five percent of the world's proven reserves. Saudi Arabia is the world's largest exporter of oil. Oil and petroleum products account for more than 90 percent of the country's income.

I. **Decline and Fall of the Ottoman Empire** *(pages 563–565)*

A. The size and power of the Ottoman Empire decreased dramatically beginning at the end of the 1700s. In the 1800s, Ottoman rule ended in North Africa and Greece, and the empire lost much of its territory in Europe.

B. In 1876, Ottoman reformers seized the government and adopted a constitution that would form a legislature. They named **Abdulhamid II** sultan, but he immediately suspended the constitution and ruled by himself.

C. A group of reformers called the Young Turks forced the restoration of the constitution in 1908. They deposed the sultan in 1909. At the same time, many ethnic Turks pressed for an independent Turkish state.

D. During World War I, the Ottomans sided with Germany, which caused Britain to attack Ottoman Arab states. The British convinced Arabs to revolt against Ottoman

Guided Reading Activity 18–1

Name ____________ Date ____________ Class ____________

Guided Reading Activity **18-1**

Nationalism in the Middle East

DIRECTIONS: Answer the following questions as you read Section 1.

1. Which empire did the European nations call "the sick man of Europe"?
2. How did the British seek to undermine Ottoman rule in the Arabian Peninsula?
3. What is the deliberate mass murder of a particular racial, political, or cultural group called?
4. List three changes that came about in Turkey as a result of Ataturk's reforms.
5. In 1921, Reza Khan, an officer in the Persian army, led a military mutiny that seized control of what city in Iran?

Critical Thinking

Ask students to analyze why the final blow to the Ottoman Empire came from World War I. Why was it disastrous for the empire to ally itself with Germany and attempt to incite nationalist revolution against Britain, Russia, and France? **L2**

Enrich

Have students identify examples of political, economic, and social oppression, including human rights violations and genocide, which are discussed in this chapter. **L1**

The empire's size had decreased dramatically. Much of its European territory had been lost. In North Africa, Ottoman rule had ended in the nineteenth century when France seized Algeria and Tunisia and Great Britain took control of Egypt. Greece also declared its independence in the nineteenth century.

In 1876, Ottoman reformers seized control of the empire's government and adopted a constitution aimed at forming a legislative assembly. However, the sultan they placed on the throne, **Abdulhamid II,** suspended the new constitution and ruled by authoritarian means.

Abdulhamid paid a high price for his actions—he lived in constant fear of assassination. He kept a thousand loaded revolvers hidden throughout his guarded estate and insisted that his pets taste his food before he ate it.

The suspended constitution became a symbol of change to a group of reformers named the Young Turks. This group was able to force the restoration of the constitution in 1908 and to depose the sultan the following year. However, the Young Turks lacked strong support for their government. The stability of the empire was also challenged by many ethnic Turks who had begun to envision a Turkish state that would encompass all people of Turkish nationality.

Armenian children who have been orphaned wait to board a ship that will take them from Turkey to Greece. The Turks killed approximately 1 million Armenians and deported half a million.

Impact of World War I

The final blow to the old empire came from World War I. After the Ottoman government allied with Germany, the British sought to undermine Ottoman rule in the Arabian Peninsula by supporting Arab nationalist activities there. The nationalists were aided by the efforts of the dashing British adventurer **T. E. Lawrence,** popularly known as "Lawrence of Arabia."

T. E. Lawrence

In 1916, the local governor of Makkah, encouraged by Great Britain, declared Arabia independent from Ottoman rule. British troops, advancing from Egypt, seized Palestine. After suffering more than three hundred thousand deaths during the war, the Ottoman Empire made peace with the Allies in October 1918.

Massacre of the Armenians

During the war, the Ottoman Turks had alienated the Allies with their policies toward minority subjects, especially the Armenians. The Christian Armenian minority had been pressing the Ottoman government for its independence for years. In 1915, the government violently reacted to an Armenian uprising by killing Armenian men and expelling women and children from the empire.

Within seven months, six hundred thousand Armenians had been killed, and five hundred thousand had been deported (sent out of the country). Of those deported, four hundred thousand died while marching through the deserts and swamps of Syria and Mesopotamia.

By September 1915, an estimated 1 million Armenians were dead. They were victims of genocide, the deliberate mass murder of a particular racial, political, or cultural group. (A similar practice would be called ethnic cleansing in the Bosnian War of 1993 to 1996.) One eyewitness to the 1915 Armenian deportation wrote:

> "[She] saw vultures hovering over children who had fallen dead by the roadside. She saw beings crawling along, maimed, starving and begging for bread. From time to time she passed soldiers driving before them with whips and rifle-butts whole families, men, women and children, shrieking, pleading, wailing. These were the Armenian people setting out for exile into the desert from which there was no return."

EXTENDING THE CONTENT

The Turks and Armenians Angry at Armenian support for the Allies and fearful of Armenian nationalism, the Turkish government decided to use the war as an excuse to end the long history of animosity between Turks and Armenians. The Turkish army first removed all Armenian soldiers from its ranks and deported them to labor camps. They then rounded up Armenian civilians, roped them together, and drove them into the desert to starve. In other cases, the Turkish army destroyed whole Armenian villages and shot the inhabitants. The United States sent a formal note of protest to the Ottoman Empire on February 17, 1916.

NATIONAL GEOGRAPHIC **Middle East, 1919–1935**

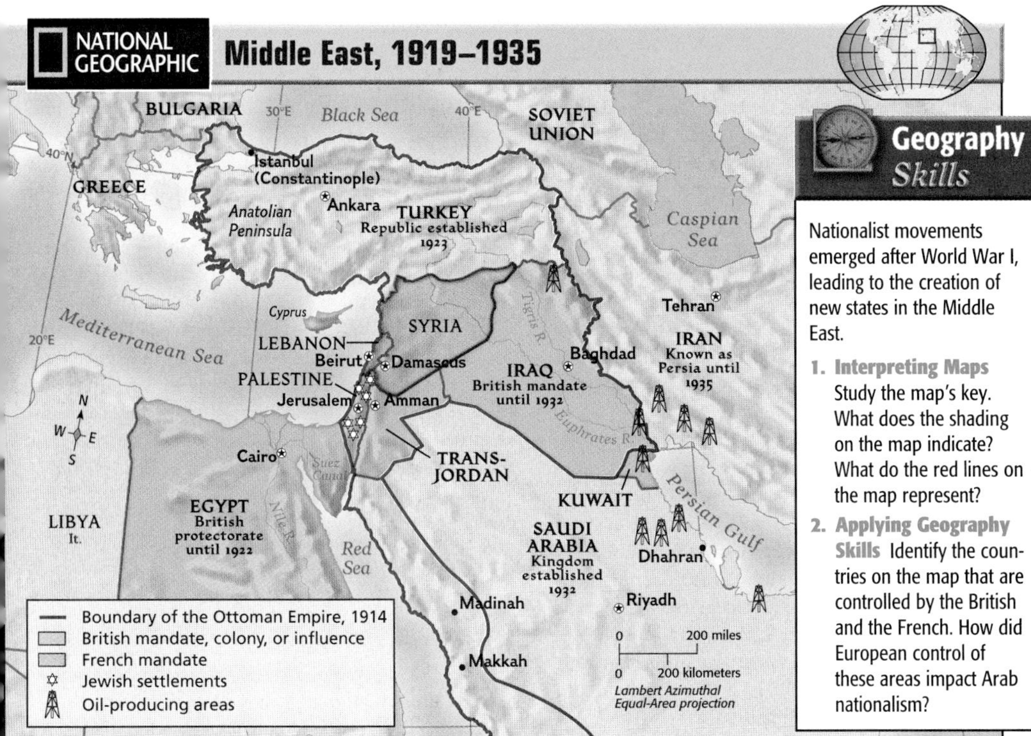

Geography Skills

Nationalist movements emerged after World War I, leading to the creation of new states in the Middle East.

1. **Interpreting Maps** Study the map's key. What does the shading on the map indicate? What do the red lines on the map represent?
2. **Applying Geography Skills** Identify the countries on the map that are controlled by the British and the French. How did European control of these areas impact Arab nationalism?

By 1918, another four hundred thousand Armenians had been massacred. Russia, France, and Britain denounced the Turkish killing of the Armenians as "against humanity and civilization." Because of the war, however, the killings went on.

Emergence of the Turkish Republic At the end of World War I, the tottering Ottoman Empire collapsed. Great Britain and France made plans to divide up Ottoman territories in the Middle East. Only the area of present-day Turkey remained under Ottoman control. Then, Greece invaded Turkey and seized the western parts of the Anatolian Peninsula.

The invasion alarmed key elements in Turkey, who were organized under the leadership of the war hero Colonel Mustafa Kemal. Kemal resigned from the army and summoned a national congress calling for the creation of an elected government and a new Republic of Turkey. His forces drove the Greeks from the Anatolian Peninsula. In 1923, the last of the Ottoman sultans fled the country, which was now declared to be the Turkish Republic. The Ottoman Empire had finally come to an end.

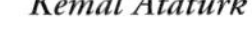
Kemal Atatürk

Reading Check **Evaluating** How did the Ottoman Empire finally end?

The Modernization of Turkey

President Kemal was now popularly known as **Atatürk** (AT•uh•TUHRK), or "father Turk." Over the next several years, he tried to transform Turkey into a modern state. A democratic system was put in place, but the president did not tolerate opposition and harshly suppressed his critics.

Atatürk's changes went beyond politics. Many Arabic elements were eliminated from the Turkish language, which was now written in the Roman alphabet. Popular education was introduced. All Turkish citizens were forced to adopt family (last) names, in the European style.

Atatürk also took steps to modernize Turkey's economy. Factories were established, and a five-year plan provided for state direction over the economy.

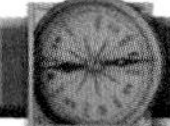

Geography Skills

Answers:

1. The shading indicates British, French, and Ottoman areas. The red lines indicate Ottoman boundaries.
2. Egypt, Palestine, Trans-Jordan, Lebanon, Iraq, Syria; Answers will vary but should include that mandates did not stifle, and sometimes increased, nationalist feeling.

Reading Check

Answer: After World War I, Britain and France divided up all the remaining Ottoman territories in the Middle East except present-day Turkey. Then, Greece invaded Turkey and seized the western parts of the Anatolian Peninsula. The invasion alarmed key elements in Turkey, who were under the leadership of Colonel Mustafa Kemal. Kemal resigned from the army and summoned a national congress that called for the creation of an elected government and a new Republic of Turkey. The last sultan fled in 1923.

CURRICULUM CONNECTION

Geography Locate Turkey on the map. What is important about its location? *(located in Europe and Asia, controls access to and from the Black Sea)* If 400,000 Armenians died in the deserts and swamps of Syria and Mesopotamia after expulsion from Turkey, from what part of Turkey do you think Armenians came? *(southeast)* **L2**

EXTENDING THE CONTENT

Modernization and Islam Since its beginnings in the seventh century, Islam has combined religious and political concerns. Muhammad was both a political/military leader and the religious leader of Islam. The four succeeding caliphs ("successors of the prophet") held both religious and political leadership. Similarly, Christian emperors of the Byzantine Empire held religious and political leadership. This is a contrast to many Western nations where the separation of church and state has been a controlling principle. Mustapha Kemal broke new ground as he secularized an Islamic society. Most of Islam, however, continues to blend religious belief and political principles.

Reading Check

Answer: His most radical step was his attempt to break the power of the Islamic religion and establish a secular state.

Reading Check

Answer: Reza Shah Pahlavi did not try to destroy the power of Islamic beliefs.

Enrich

In Iran, a revolutionary movement led by Muslim religious leader Ayatollah Ruhollah Khomeini overthrew Reza Shah's son, Mohammad Reza Pahlavi, and declared Iran an Islamic republic. Although Khomeini died in 1989, Iran continues to follow his commitment to Islamic revivalism. Ask students to do research to find out how Iran has changed in the years since Khomeini's death. L2

3 ASSESS

Assign Section 1 Assessment as homework or as an in-class activity.

Have students use **Interactive Tutor Self-Assessment CD-ROM.**

Section Quiz 18–1

Name ______ Date ______ Class ______

Chapter 18 Score

Section Quiz 18-1

DIRECTIONS: Matching Match each item in Column A with an item in Column B. Write the correct letters in the blanks. *(10 points each)*

Column A	Column B
____ 1. deliberate mass murder of a group	A. secular
____ 2. "father Turk," President Kemal	B. shah
____ 3. state that rejects religious influences	C. genocide
____ 4. king of Iran	D. Ibn Saud
____ 5. Arab nationalist leader	E. Atatürk

DIRECTIONS: Multiple Choice In the blank, write the letter of the choice that best completes the statement or answers the question. *(10 points each)*

____ 6. The Balfour Declaration of 1917 supported the idea of a

Atatürk also tried to modernize farming, although he had little effect on the nation's peasants.

Perhaps the most significant aspect of Atatürk's reform program was his attempt to break the power of the Islamic religion. He wanted to transform Turkey into a secular state—a state that rejects religious influence on its policies. Atatürk said, "Religion is like a heavy blanket that keeps the people of Turkey asleep."

The caliphate was formally abolished in 1924. Men were forbidden to wear the fez, the brimless cap worn by Turkish Muslims. When Atatürk began wearing a Western panama hat, one of his critics remarked, "You cannot make a Turk into a Westerner by giving him a hat."

Women were forbidden to wear the veil, a traditional Islamic custom. New laws gave women marriage and inheritance rights equal to men's. In 1934, women received the right to vote. All citizens were also given the right to convert to other religions.

The legacy of Kemal Atatürk was enormous. In practice, not all of his reforms were widely accepted, especially by devout Muslims. However, most of the changes that he introduced were kept after his death in 1938. By and large, the Turkish Republic was the product of Atatürk's determined efforts.

Reading Check **Identifying** What radical step did Atatürk take to modernize Turkey?

The Beginnings of Modern Iran

A similar process of modernization was underway in Persia. Under the Qajar dynasty (1794–1925), the country had not been very successful in resolving its domestic problems. Increasingly, the dynasty had turned to Russia and Great Britain to protect itself from its own people, which led to a growing foreign presence in Persia. The discovery of oil in the southern part of the country in 1908 attracted more foreign interest. Oil exports increased rapidly, and most of the profits went to British investors.

The growing foreign presence led to the rise of a native Persian nationalist movement. In 1921, Reza Khan, an officer in the Persian army, led a military mutiny that seized control of **Tehran,** the capital city. In 1925, Reza Khan established himself as shah, or king, and was called **Reza Shah Pahlavi.** The name of the new dynasty he created, Pahlavi, was the name of the ancient Persian language.

During the next few years, Reza Shah Pahlavi tried to follow the example of Kemal Atatürk in Turkey. He introduced a number of reforms to strengthen and modernize the government, the military, and the economic system. Persia became the modern state of **Iran** in 1935.

Unlike Kemal Atatürk, Reza Shah Pahlavi did not try to destroy the power of Islamic beliefs. However, he did encourage the creation of a Western-style educational system and forbade women to wear the veil in public.

Foreign powers continued to harass Iran. To free himself from Great Britain and the Soviet Union, Reza Shah Pahlavi drew closer to Nazi Germany. During World War II, the shah rejected the demands of Great Britain and the Soviet Union to expel a large number of Germans from Iran. In response, the Soviet Union and Great Britain sent troops into the country. Reza Shah Pahlavi resigned in protest and was replaced by his son, Mohammad Reza Pahlavi.

Reading Check **Comparing** How was Reza Shah Pahlavi's modernization of Persia different from Atatürk's transformation of Turkey?

Arab Nationalism

World War I offered the Arabs an opportunity to escape from Ottoman rule. However, there was a question as to what would replace that rule. The Arabs were not a nation, though they were united by their language and their Islamic cultural and religious heritage.

Because Britain had supported the efforts of Arab nationalists in 1916, the nationalists hoped this support would continue after the war ended. Instead, Britain made an agreement with France to create a number of mandates in the area. These mandates were former Ottoman territories that were now supervised by the new League of Nations. The league, in

Sultan Ibn Saud, who established the kingdom of Saudi Arabia

CRITICAL THINKING ACTIVITY

Solving Problems The land of the Kurds is a mountainous region that is divided among many nations. Seventeen million Kurds make up portions of Turkey, Iraq, Iran, Syria, Georgia, Azerbaijan, Armenia, and Lebanon. The Kurds have felt that they are being asked to give up their cultural identity because their language is often banned in schools. Ask students to research the history of the Kurds and to use a problem-solving process to identify a problem faced by the Kurds, gather information, list and consider options, consider advantages and disadvantages, choose and implement a solution, and evaluate the effectiveness of the solution. L2

turn, granted league members the right to govern particular mandates. Iraq and Jordan were assigned to Great Britain; Syria and Lebanon to France.

For the most part, Europeans created these Middle Eastern states. The Europeans determined the nations' borders and divided the peoples. In general, the people in these states had no strong identification with their designated country. However, a sense of Arab nationalism remained.

In the early 1920s, a reform leader, **Ibn Saud,** united Arabs in the northern part of the Arabian Peninsula. Devout and gifted, Ibn Saud (from whom came the name ***Saudi Arabia***) won broad support among Arab peoples. He established the kingdom of Saudi Arabia in 1932.

At first, the new kingdom, which consisted mostly of the vast desert of central Arabia, was desperately poor. Its main source of income came from the Muslim pilgrims who visited Makkah and Madinah.

During the 1930s, however, U.S. prospectors began to explore for oil. Standard Oil made a successful strike at Dhahran, on the Persian Gulf, in 1938. Soon, an Arabian-American oil company, popularly called Aramco, was created. The isolated kingdom was suddenly flooded with Western oil industries that brought the promise of wealth.

✓Reading Check **Examining** How were many Middle Eastern states created after World War I?

The Problem of Palestine

The situation in **Palestine** made matters even more complicated in the Middle East. While Palestine had been the home of the Jews in antiquity, few had lived there for almost two thousand years. While some Christians and Jews did live in Palestine, it was inhabited primarily by Muslim Palestinians. Britain, however, stated its intention to support a national home for the Jews in the 1917 Balfour Declaration: "His Majesty's Government views with favor the establishment in Palestine of a national home for the Jewish people."

The British promised that the Balfour Declaration would not undermine the rights of the non-Jewish peoples living in the area. Still, Arab nationalists were angered. They questioned how a national home for the Jewish people could be established in a territory that was 98 percent Muslim.

In the meantime, the promises of the Balfour Declaration drew Jewish settlers to Palestine. The Zionist movement (see Chapter 13) had advocated the return of Jews to Palestine since the late 1890s. During the 1930s, tensions increased between the new arrivals and the existing Muslim residents. At the same time, the rising persecution of Jews in Nazi Germany caused many European Jews to flee to Palestine. By 1939, there were about 450,000 Jews in Palestine.

The British, fearing aroused Arab nationalism, tried to restrict Jewish immigration into the territory. In 1939, the British declared that only 75,000 Jewish immigrants would be allowed into Palestine over the next five years. After that, no more Jews could enter the country. This decision would eventually produce severe conflicts in the region.

✓Reading Check **Explaining** Why did the Balfour Declaration produce problems in Palestine?

SECTION 1 ASSESSMENT

Checking for Understanding

1. **Define** genocide, ethnic cleansing.
2. **Identify** Abdulhamid II, T. E. Lawrence, Atatürk, Reza Shah Pahlavi, Ibn Saud.
3. **Locate** Tehran, Iran, Saudi Arabia, Palestine.
4. **Explain** why the British supported Arab nationalist activities in 1916.
5. **List** the mandates assigned to Great Britain and France.

Critical Thinking

6. **Evaluate** Why was it difficult for the Arab peoples to form one nation?
7. **Summarizing Information** Make a diagram like the one below showing eight aspects of the modernization of Turkey.

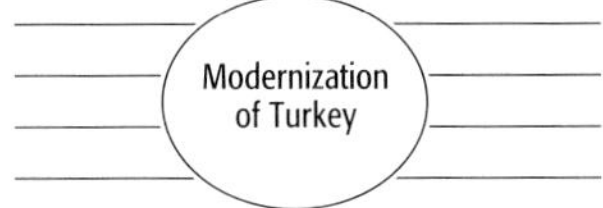

Analyzing Visuals

8. **Examine** the photo on page 564 showing Armenian children who lost their parents. Why were hundreds of thousands of Armenians killed or driven from their homes by the Turks?

Writing About History

9. **Expository Writing** Locate information regarding the current political policies of Iran. Write two paragraphs comparing this information with the policies of Reza Shah Pahlavi. Document your sources.

CHAPTER 18
Section 1, 563–567

✓Reading Check

Answer: Europeans determined the nations' borders and divided the peoples.

✓Reading Check

Answer: It stated Britain's intention to establish a Jewish homeland in Palestine, a territory in which most of the population was Muslim.

Reading Essentials and Study Guide 18–1

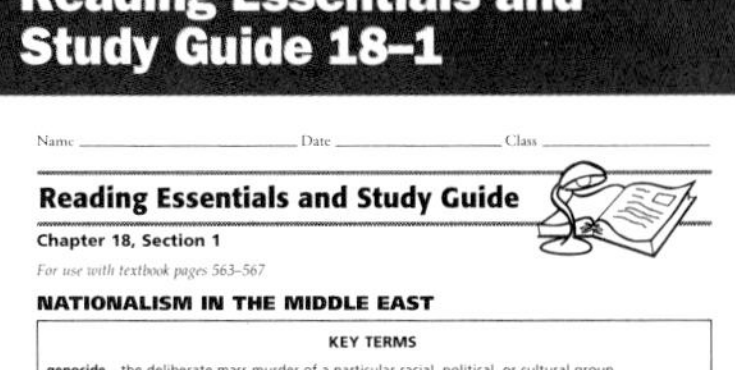
Reading Essentials and Study Guide
Chapter 18, Section 1
NATIONALISM IN THE MIDDLE EAST
KEY TERMS
genocide the deliberate mass murder of a particular racial, political, or cultural group (page 564)
ethnic cleansing another term for genocide, used during the Bosnian War of 1993 to 1996 (page 564)
DRAWING FROM EXPERIENCE

Reteaching Activity

Ask students to identify and explain the effects of World War I on the states and peoples discussed in this section. **L1**

4 CLOSE

Ask students to research and analyze the Balfour Declaration. Why was it issued? What were its effects? Why was Britain's commitment to it so short-lived? **L2**

SECTION 1 ASSESSMENT

1. Key terms are in blue.
2. Abdulhamid II *(p. 564)*; T. E. Lawrence *(p. 564)*; Atatürk *(p. 565)*; Reza Shah Pahlavi *(p. 566)*; Ibn Saud *(p. 567)*
3. See chapter maps.
4. to undermine Ottoman rule
5. Great Britain: Iraq, Jordan; France: Syria, Lebanon
6. They were a loose collection of peoples united by language and religion.
7. democratic system; modernized economy and farming; adopted Roman alphabet; popular education; family names; abolished caliphate; no fez or veil; new rights for women
8. The Christian Armenian minority wanted independence; the Turks reacted to revolt by killing Armenian men and forcing women, children out of the empire.
9. Answers should be supported by documentation. Many reforms in Iran have been reversed.

CHAPTER 18
Section 2, 568–573

1 FOCUS

Section Overview

This section describes the development of the African and Indian independence movements, religious conflict in India, the rise of militarism in Japan, and the spread of communism in Asia.

BELLRINGER
Skillbuilder Activity

 Project transparency and have students answer questions.

 Available as a blackline master.

Daily Focus Skills Transparency 18–2

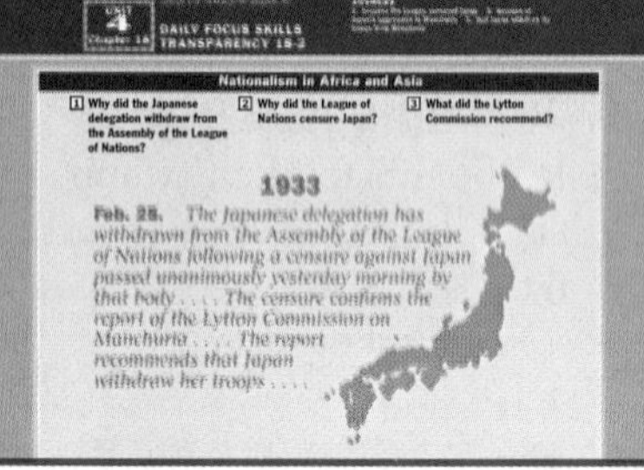

Guide to Reading

Answers to Graphic: Mahatma Gandhi: religious, Indian, traditional; Jawaharlal Nehru: secular, Western, modern

Preteaching Vocabulary: Discuss why Mohandas Gandhi was called "Great Soul" or Mahatma. L1

SECTION 2 Nationalism in Africa and Asia

Guide to Reading

Main Ideas
- Peoples in Africa and Asia began to agitate for independence.
- Japan became an aggressive military state.
- Soviet agents worked to spread communism around the world.

Key Terms
Pan-Africanism, Mahatma, civil disobedience, *zaibatsu*

People to Identify
W.E.B. Du Bois, Marcus Garvey, Mohandas Gandhi, Jawaharlal Nehru, Ho Chi Minh

Places to Locate
Kenya, Manchuria

Preview of Events
1. What different forms did protest against Western rule take?
2. How was communism received in Asia?

Reading Strategy
Contrasting Information Using a table like the one below, contrast the backgrounds and values of Gandhi and the younger Nehru.

Mahatma Gandhi	Jawaharlal Nehru

Preview of Events

1915 · 1920 · 1925 · 1930 · 1935 · 1940 · 1945

- **1920** Marcus Garvey issues *Declaration of the Rights of the Negro Peoples of the World*
- **1935** Government of India Act is passed
- **1938** Japan passes military draft law

Voices from the Past

Jomo Kenyatta

Jomo Kenyatta, an advocate of independence in Kenya, wrote:

> "By driving the African off his ancestral lands, the Europeans have reduced him to a state of serfdom incompatible with human happiness. The African is conditioned, by the cultural and social institutions of centuries, to a freedom of which Europe has little conception, and it is not in his nature to accept serfdom forever. He realizes that he must fight unceasingly for his own complete emancipation [freedom]; for without this he is doomed to remain the prey of rival imperialisms, which in every successive year will drive their fangs more deeply into his vitality and strength."
>
> —***Facing Mount Kenya,*** **Jomo Kenyatta, 1959**

Between 1919 and 1939, leaders emerged in Africa and Asia who sought to free their people from the power of the West. While none of these nationalist movements were successful before World War II, they did begin the journey toward independence.

Movements toward Independence in Africa

Black Africans had fought in World War I in British and French armies. Many Africans hoped they would be rewarded with independence after the war. As one newspaper in the Gold Coast argued, if African volunteers who fought on European battlefields were "good enough to fight and die in the Empire's cause, they were good enough to have a share in the government of their countries."

SECTION RESOURCES

Reproducible Masters
- Reproducible Lesson Plan 18–2
- Daily Lecture and Discussion Notes 18–2
- Guided Reading Activity 18–2
- Section Quiz 18–2
- Reading Essentials and Study Guide 18–2

Transparencies
- Daily Focus Skills Transparency 18–2

Multimedia
- Interactive Tutor Self-Assessment CD-ROM
- ExamView® Pro Testmaker CD-ROM
- Presentation Plus! CD-ROM

The peace settlement after World War I was a great disappointment. Germany was stripped of its African colonies, but these colonies were awarded to Great Britain and France to be administered as mandates for the League of Nations. Britain and France now governed a vast portion of Africa.

African Protests After World War I, Africans became more active politically. Africans who had fought in World War I had learned new ideas about freedom and nationalism in the West. In Africa itself, missionary schools taught their pupils about liberty and equality. As more Africans became aware of the enormous gulf between Western ideals and practices, they decided to seek reform.

Reform movements took different forms. In **Kenya** in 1921, the Young Kikuyu Association, organized by Harry Thuku, a telephone operator, protested the high taxes levied by the British rulers. His message was simple: "Hearken, every day you pay . . . tax to the Europeans of Government. Where is it sent? It is their task to steal the property of the Kikuyu people." Thuku was arrested. When an angry crowd stormed the jail and demanded his release, government authorities fired into the crowd and killed 50 people. Thuku was sent into exile.

A struggle against Italian rule in Libya also occurred in the 1920s. Forces led by Omar Mukhtar used guerrilla warfare against the Italians and defeated them a number of times. The Italians reacted ferociously. They established concentration camps and used all available modern weapons to crush the revolt. Mukhtar's death ended the movement.

Although colonial powers typically responded to such movements with force, they also began to make some reforms. They made these reforms in the hope of satisfying African peoples. Reforms, however, were too few and too late. By the 1930s, an increasing number of African leaders were calling for independence, not reform.

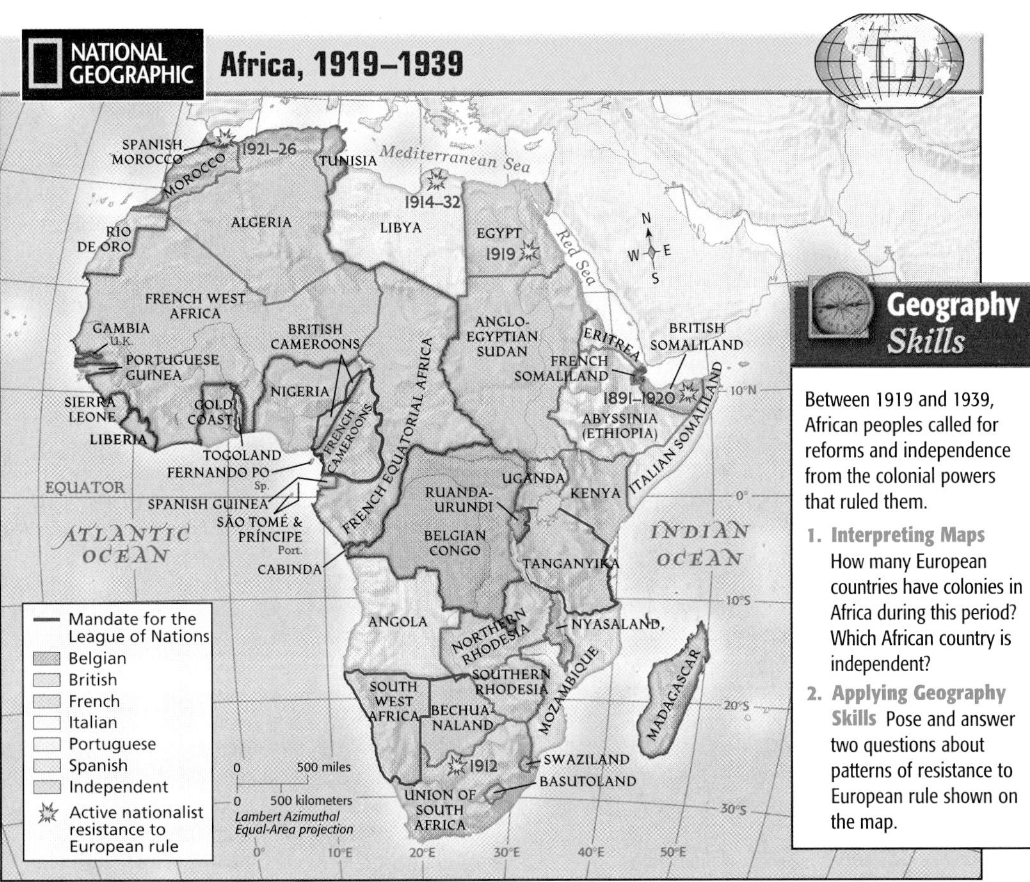

Geography Skills

Between 1919 and 1939, African peoples called for reforms and independence from the colonial powers that ruled them.

1. **Interpreting Maps** How many European countries have colonies in Africa during this period? Which African country is independent?
2. **Applying Geography Skills** Pose and answer two questions about patterns of resistance to European rule shown on the map.

2 TEACH

Geography *Skills*

Answers:

1. at least six; Liberia
2. Answers should demonstrate an understanding of the information shown on the map.

Daily Lecture and Discussion Notes 18–2

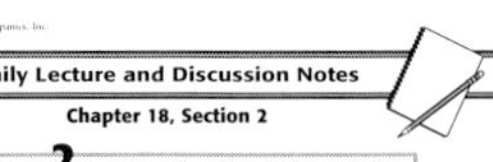

Daily Lecture and Discussion Notes

Chapter 18, Section 2

Did You Know? Ho Chi Minh was an experienced revolutionary obsessed by one goal: an independent Vietnam. In 1946, he told the French that they could kill ten of his men for every Frenchman killed and the Vietnamese would still win the war. The French ignored the warning and paid dearly for it.

I. **Movements toward Independence in Africa** *(pages 568–570)*

A. Even though black Africans had fought for the British and French in World War I, their hopes for independence after the war were not met. The Versailles peace settlements took away German colonies only to give them as mandates to France and Britain.

B. Many Africans became politically active after World War I. They sought reforms that would allow them the same ideals of liberty and equality espoused by Western democratic nations.

C. In **Kenya,** the Young Kikuyu Association protested in 1921 the high taxes imposed by Great Britain. Their leader Harry Thuku was jailed. When a crowd tried to free him, the British killed 50 of them and exiled Thuku.

D. In Libya, guerrilla fighters under Omar Mukhtar fought the Italian rulers and defeated them several times. The Italians put Libyans in concentration camps and eventually

CURRICULUM CONNECTION

Political Science Ask students to consider the following leaders of nationalist movements in Africa and Asia: Harry Thuku, Jomo Kenyatta, Mohandas Gandhi, Jawaharlal Nehru, and Ho Chi Minh. What qualities did these men share and how did they differ? Who would students say had the most far-reaching impact on the history of the twentieth century? L2

INTERDISCIPLINARY CONNECTIONS ACTIVITY

Literature and Political Science Ask students to read all or part of Jomo Kenyatta's book *Facing Mount Kenya* (1938). Ask students to summarize and discuss the book's main ideas in class. Kenyatta based the book on his graduate thesis in anthropology which he wrote while attending the London School of Economics. In *Facing Mount Kenya,* Kenyatta provides a powerful defense of African culture as he describes how the orderly and harmonious traditional Kikuyu society was disrupted and exploited by colonialism. After the book's publication, Kenyatta changed his name from Kamau Ngengi to Jomo ("Burning Spear") Kenyatta. He served as president of Kenya from 1964 until his death in 1978. L2

Reading Check

Answer: Educational opportunities and World War I ideals influenced some African leaders.

TURNING POINT

Ask students to identify the laws that Gandhi may have broken. Then have students discuss the right to assembly and freedom of speech granted to all Americans. Ask students to assess the degree to which human rights and democratic ideals and practices have been advanced throughout the world in the twentieth century. L2

Guided Reading Activity 18–2

Name ______ Date ______ Class ______

Guided Reading Activity 18-2

Nationalism in Africa and Asia

DIRECTIONS: Fill in the blanks below as you read Section 2.

Black Africans had fought in World War I in **(1)** ______ and French armies. Many Africans hoped they would be rewarded with **(2)** ______ after the war. The great **(3)** ______ was that colonies stripped from **(4)** ______ after World War I were awarded to Great Britain and France, who then controlled most of Africa.

As more Africans became aware of the enormous gulf between Western **(5)** ______ and **(6)** ______, they decided to seek reform. In **(7)** ______, Harry Thuku was arrested for protesting **(8)** ______ taxes. By the 1930s, an increasing number of African leaders were calling for independence, not **(9)** ______.

Young African leaders who had studied abroad were especially influenced by

CURRICULUM CONNECTION

Literature Assign one group of students to read *The Souls of Black Folk* by W.E.B. Du Bois. Ask another group to read Jomo Kenyatta's book *Facing Mount Kenya* (if you assigned the *Interdisciplinary Connections Activity* on page 569, choose other titles for this activity). Then ask each group to prepare a class presentation on the ideas presented in these influential books. L3

New Leaders Calls for independence came from a new generation of young African leaders. Many had been educated abroad, in Europe and the United States. Those who had studied in the United States were especially influenced by the ideas of **W.E.B. Du Bois** and **Marcus Garvey.**

> **HISTORY Online**
> **Web Activity** Visit the *Glencoe World History—Modern Times* Web site at wh.mt.glencoe.com and click on **Chapter 18–Student Web Activity** to learn more about nationalist movements.

Du Bois, an African American educated at Harvard University, was the leader of a movement that tried to make all Africans aware of their own cultural heritage. Garvey, a Jamaican who lived in Harlem in New York City, stressed the need for the unity of all Africans, a movement known as Pan-Africanism. His *Declaration of the Rights of the Negro Peoples of the World,* issued in 1920, had a strong impact on later African leaders.

Leaders and movements in individual African nations also appeared. Educated in Great Britain, Jomo Kenyatta of Kenya argued in his book *Facing Mount Kenya* that British rule was destroying the traditional culture of the peoples of Africa. Léopold Senghor, who had studied in France and written poetry about African culture, organized an independence movement in Senegal. Nnamdi Azikiwe, of Nigeria, began a newspaper, *The West African Pilot,* in 1937 and urged nonviolence as a method to gain independence. These are but three of the leaders who worked to end colonial rule in Africa. Success, however, would not come until after World War II.

Reading Check **Analyzing** Why did many Africans become more politically active after World War I?

The Movement for Indian Independence

TURNING POINT **As you read, you will learn how Mohandas Gandhi called on Indians to protest British laws by using the technique of civil disobedience. Gandhi was one leader in India's independence movement.**

Mohandas Gandhi had become active in the movement for Indian self-rule before World War I. By the time of World War I, the Indian people had already begun to refer to him as India's "Great Soul," or Mahatma. After the war, Gandhi remained an important figure, and new leaders also arose.

Protest and Reform After Gandhi's return to India from South Africa in 1913, he began to organize mass protests to achieve his aims. A believer in nonviolence, Gandhi protested British laws by using the methods of civil disobedience—refusal to obey laws considered to be unjust.

In 1919, the protests led to violence and a strong British reaction. British troops killed hundreds of unarmed protesters in the city of Amritsar, in northwestern India. Horrified at the violence, Gandhi briefly retreated from active politics. He was later arrested for his role in the protests and spent several years in prison.

In 1935, Great Britain passed the Government of India Act. This act expanded the role of Indians in the governing process. Before, the Legislative Council had only given advice to the British governor. Now, it became a two-house parliament. Two-thirds of its Indian members were to be elected. Similar bodies were created at the provincial level. Five million Indians (still only a small percentage of the total population) were given the right to vote.

A Push for Independence The Indian National Congress (INC) was founded in 1885 to seek reforms in Britain's government of India (see Chapter 14). Reforms, however, were no longer enough for many members of the INC. Under its new leader, Motilal Nehru, the INC wanted to push for full independence.

Gandhi, now released from prison, returned to his earlier policy of civil disobedience. He worked hard to inform ordinary Indians of his beliefs and methods. It was wrong, he said, to harm any living being. Hate could only be overcome by love, and love, rather than force, could win people over to one's position.

Nonviolence was central to Gandhi's campaign of noncooperation and civil disobedience. To protest unjust British laws, Gandhi told his people: "Don't pay your taxes or send your children to an English-supported school. . . . Make your own cotton cloth by spinning the thread at home, and don't buy English-made goods. Provide yourselves with home-made salt, and do not buy government-made salt."

Britain had introduced measures increasing the salt tax and prohibiting the Indian people from manufacturing or harvesting their own salt. In 1930, Gandhi protested these measures. Accompanied by supporters, he walked to the sea on what became known as the Salt March. On reaching the coast, Gandhi picked up a pinch of salt. Thousands of Indians followed his act of civil disobedience. Gandhi

EXTENDING THE CONTENT

Mohandas Gandhi Most students would not have recognized Gandhi as a young lawyer in South Africa at the beginning of the twentieth century. After immigrating to South Africa in search of professional opportunities, Gandhi set up a legal practice for the "colored" population of the country (i.e., those who were neither black African nor white European). He enjoyed modest success in an increasingly hostile South Africa. Eventually, he felt it was his duty to return to India to help the struggle for Indian independence from Britain. Leaving behind his law practice and his suits and ties, Gandhi became an influential Indian nationalist hero.

and many other members of the INC were arrested. (See page 779 to read excerpts from Gandhi Takes the Path of Civil Disobedience in the Primary Sources Library.)

New Leaders and New Problems In the 1930s, a new figure entered the movement. **Jawaharlal Nehru,** the son of Motilal Nehru, studied law in Great Britain. The younger Nehru was an example of a new kind of Indian politician. He was upper class and intellectual.

The independence movement split into two paths. The one identified with Gandhi was religious, Indian, and traditional. The other, identified with Nehru, was secular, Western, and modern. The existence of two approaches created uncertainty about India's future path.

In the meantime, another problem had arisen in the independence movement. Hostility between Hindus and Muslims had existed for centuries. Muslims were dissatisfied with the Hindu dominance of the INC and raised the cry "Islam is in danger."

In 1930, the Muslim League, under the leadership of Muhammad Ali Jinnah, called for the creation of a separate Muslim state of Pakistan (meaning "the land of the pure") in the northwest. Conflict between Muslims and Hindus grew.

Reading Check **Identifying** What three non-British conflicts affected the Indian independence movements in the 1930s?

The Rise of a Militarist Japan

During the first two decades of the twentieth century, Japanese society developed along a Western model. The economic and social reforms launched during the Meiji Era led to increasing prosperity and the development of a modern industrial and commercial sector.

A *Zaibatsu* Economy In the Japanese economy, various manufacturing processes were concentrated within a single enterprise called the *zaibatsu,* a large financial and industrial corporation. These firms gradually developed, often with government help, into vast companies that controlled major segments of the Japanese industrial sector. By 1937, the four largest *zaibatsu* (Mitsui, Mitsubishi, Sumitomo, and Yasuda) controlled 21 percent of the banking

CONNECTIONS Around The World

Paths to Modernization

After World War I, new states in the Middle East and Asia sought to modernize their countries. To many people, modernization meant westernization, the adoption of political and economic reforms based on Western models. These models included government based on democratic principles and a free-market, or capitalist, economic system based on industrialization.

After the success of the Communist revolution in Russia, however, a second model for modernization appeared. To some people, a Marxist system seemed to offer a better and quicker way to transform an agricultural state into a modern industrial state. The new system would be a socialist model in which an authoritarian state, not private industry, would own and control the economy.

Dubai, United Arab Emirates, a thriving, modern port city

Between World War I and World War II, some new republics combined features of both systems. In Turkey, Kemal Atatürk, creator of the new Turkish republic, set up a national assembly but ruled with an iron fist. His economic modernization combined private industries with state direction of the economy.

In China, the Nanjing Republic under Chiang Kai-shek supported the idea of democracy but maintained the need for dictatorial government as a first stage to prepare the Chinese people for democracy. Economic modernization in the new Chinese republic combined a modern industrial state with the traditional Chinese values of hard work and obedience.

Comparing Cultures

Using outside sources, research the current government of Turkey. How has the government developed since the rule of Kemal Atatürk? Does the current government reflect the influence of Western principles or has it evolved according to a Marxist model?

COOPERATIVE LEARNING ACTIVITY

Staging a Debate Organize the class into two groups to debate the following statement: "Gandhi's nonviolent philosophy made India's independence movement less effective than it would have been had force been used." Each group should research the issue and organize an argument before the debate takes place. Students might wish to divide the work into research, organization of information, and presentation of information and then assign these tasks to subgroups. You might have students conduct this debate in front of another class and let the members of that class vote on the most persuasive argument. L2

For grading this activity, refer to the ***Performance Assessment Activities*** booklet.

Reading Check

Answer: conflict between the path taken by Gandhi and the path taken by Nehru; conflict between Hindus and Muslims; calls by Muslims for a separate Muslim state

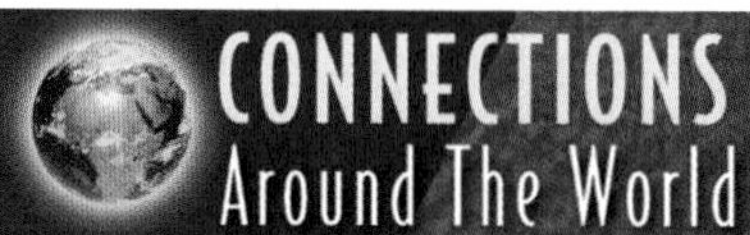

Answer: Students will prepare reports on Turkey. Despite brief interludes of military rule, Turkey's government reflects Western influence, having become a multiparty parliamentary democracy in 1950.

Enrich

Was Gandhi, in fact, the opposite of the "secular, Western, and modern" Nehru? Research Gandhi's background. Would you quarrel with any of these descriptors? If so, with which one(s)? L1

3 ASSESS

Assign Section 2 Assessment as homework or an in-class activity.

Have students use **Interactive Tutor Self-Assessment CD-ROM.**

Section Quiz 18–2

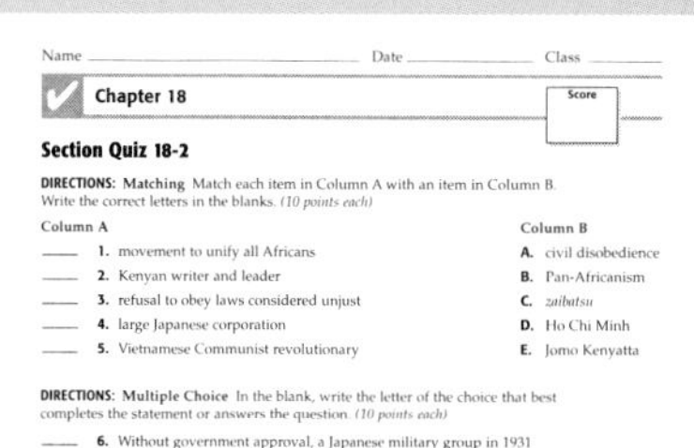
Name ______ Date ______ Class ______

Chapter 18 — Score

Section Quiz 18-2

DIRECTIONS: Matching Match each item in Column A with an item in Column B. Write the correct letters in the blanks. (10 points each)

Column A	Column B
___ 1. movement to unify all Africans	A. civil disobedience
___ 2. Kenyan writer and leader	B. Pan-Africanism
___ 3. refusal to obey laws considered unjust	C. *zaibatsu*
___ 4. large Japanese corporation	D. Ho Chi Minh
___ 5. Vietnamese Communist revolutionary	E. Jomo Kenyatta

DIRECTIONS: Multiple Choice In the blank, write the letter of the choice that best completes the statement or answers the question. (10 points each)

___ 6. Without government approval, a Japanese military group in 1931 invaded

Geography *Skills*

Answers:

1. Japan added Manchuria, more than doubling its size.
2. Japan is a mountainous island nation with no room to expand. A rapid increase in population led to food shortages. In addition, Japan needed raw materials and markets for its manufactured goods. Japan dealt with these problems by seizing territories overseas (Formosa, Korea, southern Manchuria) and making them part of the growing Japanese Empire.

CURRICULUM CONNECTION

Geography To increase their understanding of how population density affected Japanese expansionism, students should compare the size of Japan (145,856 square miles [377,767 sq km]) with that of their own state. By 1925, Japan's population was about 60 million. Have students find out the current population of their state. Ask students how Japan's growth led to its aggressive policies. **L1**

Critical Thinking

Ask students to analyze Japan as both an empire and a Fascist state. Ask students to identify and explain the causes and effects for the rise of fascism (militarism) in Japan. **L2**

industry, 26 percent of mining, 35 percent of shipbuilding, and over 60 percent of paper manufacturing and insurance.

The concentration of wealth led to growing economic inequalities. City workers were poorly paid and housed. Economic crises added to this problem shortly after World War I when inflation in food prices led to food riots. A rapid increase in population led to food shortages. (The population of the Japanese islands increased from 43 million in 1900 to 73 million in 1940.) Later, when the Great Depression struck, workers and farmers suffered the most.

With hardships came calls for a return to traditional Japanese values. Traditionalists especially objected to the growing influence of Western ideas and values on Japanese educational and political systems. At the same time, many citizens denounced Japan's attempt to find security through cooperation with the Western powers. Instead, they demanded that Japan use its own strength to dominate Asia and meet its needs.

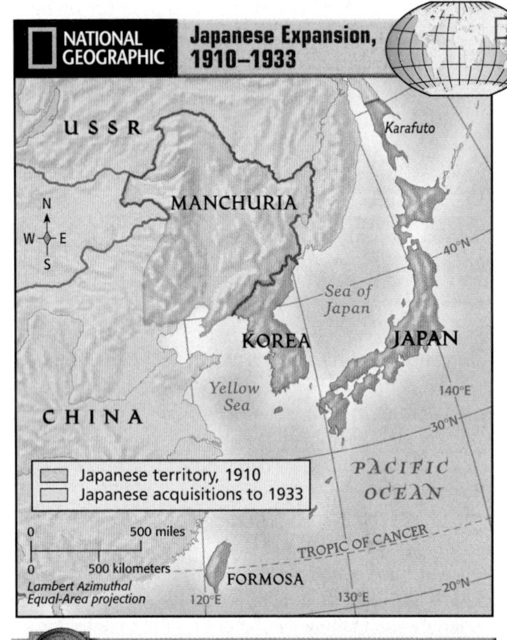

Geography *Skills*

The Japanese Empire expanded during the early twentieth century.

1. **Interpreting Maps** How did Japan's territory change between 1910 and 1933?
2. **Applying Geography Skills** Describe Japan's geographical features. How was geography a factor in Japanese expansion?

Japan and the West In the early twentieth century, Japanese leaders began to have difficulty finding sources of raw materials and foreign markets for the nation's manufactured goods. Until World War I, Japan had dealt with the problem by seizing territories—such as Formosa, Korea, and southern Manchuria—and making them part of the growing Japanese Empire. That policy succeeded but aroused the concern of the Western nations.

The United States was especially worried about Japanese expansion. The United States wanted to keep Asia open for U.S. trading activities. In 1922, the United States held a major conference of nations with interests in the Pacific. The major achievement of this conference was a nine-power treaty that recognized the territorial integrity of China and the maintenance of the Open Door policy. Japan accepted the provisions in return for recognition of its control of southern Manchuria.

During the remainder of the 1920s, the Japanese government tried to follow the rules established by the Washington Conference. This meant using diplomatic and economic means to realize Japanese interests in Asia. However, this approach did not prove popular.

Japanese industrialists began to expand into new areas, such as heavy industry, mining, chemicals, and the manufacturing of appliances and automobiles. These industries desperately needed resources not found in abundance in Japan. The Japanese government came under increasing pressure to find new sources for raw materials abroad.

The Rise of Militarism During the first two decades of the twentieth century, Japan moved toward a more democratic government. The parliament and political parties grew stronger. The influence of the old ruling oligarchy, however, remained strong. At the end of the 1920s, new problems led to the emergence of militant forces that encouraged Japan to become a militaristic state.

The rise of militant forces in Japan resulted when a group within the ruling party was able to gain control of the political system. Some of the militants were civilians convinced that the parliamentary system had been corrupted by Western ideas. Others were members of the military who were angered by the cuts in military spending and the government's pacifist policies during the early 1920s.

CRITICAL THINKING ACTIVITY

Solving Problems Have students make a list of the social and economic problems that Japan faced after World War I. The list should include rapid population growth, need for raw materials, scarce farmland, limited democracy, and political repression. Ask students to select one of the problems, gather information, list and consider options, consider advantages and disadvantages, choose and implement a solution, and evaluate the effectiveness of the solution. Have students write an essay describing the process and their solution. **L3**

During the early 1930s, civilians formed extremist patriotic organizations, such as the Black Dragon Society. Members of the army and navy created similar societies. One group of middle-level army officers invaded **Manchuria** without government approval in the autumn of 1931. Within a short time, all of Manchuria had been conquered.

The Japanese government opposed the conquest of Manchuria but the Japanese people supported it. Soon Hideki Tojo and other military leaders dominated the government and supported Japanese expansionism. Emperor Hirohito, fearing that the monarchy would be abolished, refused to oppose the action of the military leaders.

Japanese society was put on wartime status. A military draft law was passed in 1938. All political parties were merged into the Imperial Rule Assistance Association, which called for Japanese expansion abroad. Culture was purged of most Western ideas. Militant leaders insisted on the need for stressing traditional Japanese values instead.

Reading Check **Examining** How did the Japanese government change from the 1920s to the 1930s?

Nationalism and Revolution in Asia

Before World War I, the Marxist doctrine of social revolution had no appeal for Asian intellectuals. After all, most Asian societies were still agricultural and were hardly ready for revolution.

That situation began to change after the revolution in Russia in 1917. The rise to power of Lenin and the Bolsheviks showed that a revolutionary Marxist party could overturn an outdated system—even one that was not fully industrialized—and begin a new one.

The Spread of Communism In 1920, Lenin adopted a new revolutionary strategy aimed at societies outside the Western world. The chief means of spreading the word of Karl Marx was the Communist International, or Comintern for short. Formed in 1919, the Comintern was a worldwide organization of Communist parties dedicated to the advancement of world revolution.

At the Comintern's headquarters in Moscow, agents were trained and then returned to their own countries to form Marxist parties and promote the cause of social revolution. By the end of the 1920s, practically every colonial society in Asia had a Communist party.

Communist Parties in Asia How successful were these new parties? In some countries, the local Communists were briefly able to establish a cooperative relationship with existing nationalist parties in a common struggle against Western imperialism. This was true in French Indochina, where Vietnamese Communists were organized by the Moscow-trained revolutionary **Ho Chi Minh** in the 1920s. The strongest Communist-nationalist alliance was formed in China (see Section 3). In most colonial societies, though, Communist parties had little success in the 1930s. They failed to build a secure base of support among the mass of the population.

Reading Check **Evaluating** What was the relationship between communism and imperialism?

SECTION 2 ASSESSMENT

Checking for Understanding

1. **Define** Pan-Africanism, Mahatma, civil disobedience, *zaibatsu.*
2. **Identify** W.E.B. Du Bois, Marcus Garvey, Mohandas Gandhi, Jawaharlal Nehru, Ho Chi Minh.
3. **Locate** Kenya, Manchuria.
4. **Explain** the goals of the Comintern and how it pursued these goals.
5. **List** at least three leaders who worked to end colonial rule in Africa.

Critical Thinking

6. **Compare** What did young black leaders who wanted independence in Africa have in common?
7. **Sequencing Information** On a sequence chain like the one below, show five events that contributed to Japan's becoming a military state in the 1930s.

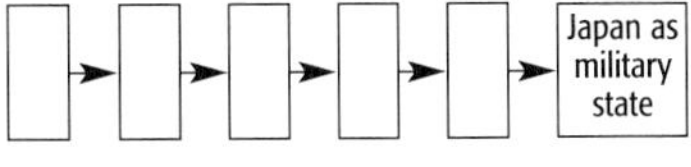

Analyzing Visuals

8. **Examine** the photo of Dubai in the feature on page 571. What do you see in the picture that tells you this is a modern port city?

Writing About History

9. **Expository Writing** Research contemporary Japanese conglomerates (*zaibatsu*) such as Mitsubishi and Sony. How are their operations different from those of American industries? Write two paragraphs and document your sources.

CHAPTER 18
Section 2, 568–573

Reading Check

Answer: During the early 1920s, the pacifist government cut military spending. At the end of the 1920s, militant forces were emerging that wanted Japan to become a militaristic state. The government was soon dominated by the military.

Reading Check

Answer: Communism was seen by some as a means to remove imperalistic rulers.

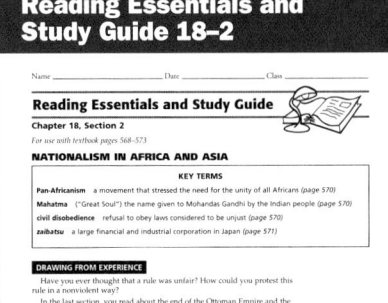

Reading Essentials and Study Guide 18–2

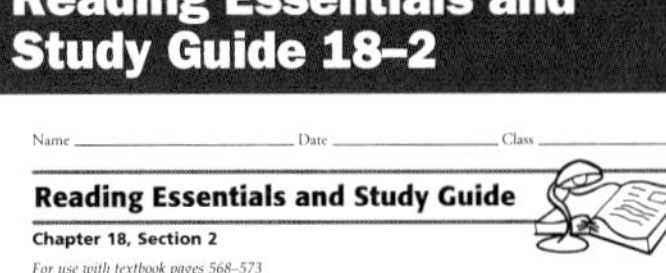
Name ______ Date ______ Class ______

Reading Essentials and Study Guide

Chapter 18, Section 2

For use with textbook pages 568–573

NATIONALISM IN AFRICA AND ASIA

KEY TERMS

Pan-Africanism a movement that stressed the need for the unity of all Africans *(page 570)*

Mahatma ("Great Soul") the name given to Mohandas Gandhi by the Indian people *(page 570)*

civil disobedience refusal to obey laws considered to be unjust *(page 570)*

zaibatsu a large financial and industrial corporation in Japan *(page 571)*

DRAWING FROM EXPERIENCE

Have you ever thought that a rule was unfair? How could you protest this rule in a nonviolent way?

In the last section, you read about the end of the Ottoman Empire and the rise of nationalism in the Middle East. In this section, you will read about nationalism in Africa and Asia. In India, the followers of Mahatma Gandhi used the methods of civil disobedience to [illegible]

Reteaching Activity

Ask students to summarize the effects of imperialism on the different societies discussed in this section. **L1**

4 CLOSE

Write the following on the chalkboard: *No matter how small or weak, every nation has the right to decide its own form of government and to manage its own affairs.* Ask students to discuss whether they agree or disagree with this statement. **L1**

SECTION 2 ASSESSMENT

1. Key terms are in blue.
2. W. E. B. Du Bois *(p. 570)*; Marcus Garvey *(p. 570)*; Mohandas Gandhi *(p. 570)*; Jawaharlal Nehru *(p. 571)*; Ho Chi Minh *(p. 573)*
3. See chapter maps.
4. The Comintern wanted to advance revolution. Agents were trained and returned to their countries to promote revolution.
5. Omar Mukhtar, Jomo Kenyatta, Léopold Senghor, Nnamdi Azikiwe
6. educated in West; wanted to make Africans aware of cultural heritage
7. Military draft law passed → Economic resources placed under government → Political parties merged → Labor unions disbanded → Education, culture purged of Western ideas; traditional values stressed
8. skyscrapers, several modes of transportation, evidence of economic activity
9. Answers should be well written and documented.

TEACH

Analyzing Primary Sources
Ask students to notice the words Ho Chi Minh uses to describe his reaction to Lenin's thesis: "emotion," "enthusiasm," "clear-sightedness," "confidence," "overjoyed to tears." Have students ever read anything that affected them this way? Ask the class to describe the personal and political conditions that might lead a person to experience such a "conversion" through the written word. **L1**

Critical Thinking

Ask students to supply evidence that supports or contradicts the following statement: "Harassed by colonial authorities, and saddled with direction from Moscow that often had little relevance to local conditions, Communist parties in most colonial societies had little success in the 1930s." **L2**

Critical Thinking

Have students analyze Lenin's strategy for spreading Marxist ideology. Was his decision to bring recruits to Moscow for training and then returning them to their own countries effective? What were the weaknesses of this strategy? How does Lenin's strategy relate to how Ho Chi Minh was converted to communism? **L2**

EYEWITNESS TO HISTORY

The Path to Liberation

THE VIETNAMESE REVOLUTIONARY Ho Chi Minh learned about the revolution in Bolshevik Russia in 1919 while living in France. He became a dedicated follower of Lenin and eventually became a leader of the Vietnamese Communist movement. In the following passage, Ho Chi Minh talks about his reasons for becoming a Communist.

▲ *Communist Party meeting in Hanoi, April 2001*

Ho Chi Minh, leader of the Vietnamese Communist movement ▶

❝After World War I, I made my living in Paris, now as a retoucher at a photographer's, now as a painter of 'Chinese antiquities' (made in France!). I would distribute leaflets denouncing the crimes committed by the French colonialists in Vietnam.

At that time, I supported the Russian Revolution only instinctively, not yet grasping all its historic importance. I loved and admired Lenin because he was a great patriot who liberated his compatriots; until then, I had read none of his books.

The reason for my joining the French Socialist Party was that these 'ladies and gentlemen'—as I called my comrades at that moment—had shown their sympathy toward me, toward the struggle of the oppressed peoples. But I understood neither what was a party, a trade-union, nor what was Socialism nor Communism. . . . A comrade gave me Lenin's 'Thesis on the National and Colonial Questions' to read.

There were political terms difficult to understand in this thesis. But by dint of reading it again and again, finally I could grasp the main part of it. What emotion, enthusiasm, clear-sightedness, and confidence it instilled in me! I was overjoyed to tears. Though sitting alone in my room, I shouted aloud as if addressing large crowds. 'Dear martyrs, compatriots! This is what we need, this is the path to our liberation!'

After that, I had entire confidence in Lenin.❞

—Ho Chi Minh, *The Path which Led Me to Leninism*

Analyzing Primary Sources

1. Why was Ho Chi Minh living in France?
2. What were Ho Chi Minh's feelings toward Lenin?
3. Why did Ho Chi Minh join the French Socialist Party?

ANSWERS TO ANALYZING PRIMARY SOURCES

1. He worked in Paris retouching photographs and painting "Chinese antiquities"; Ho Chi Minh was born in Vietnam and, at that time, Vietnam was a French colony, so there were ties between the two countries.
2. He loved and admired him and considered him a great patriot who had liberated his people. Ho Chi Minh wanted to use Lenin's ideas to liberate Vietnam from foreign rule.
3. He joined the French Socialist Party because it had shown sympathy toward him and toward the struggle of oppressed peoples.

SECTION 3 Revolutionary Chaos in China

Guide to Reading

Main Ideas
- Internal tensions led Chiang Kai-shek to violently end the Communist-Nationalist alliance.
- Mao Zedong believed revolution in China would be led by peasants, not the urban working class.

Key Terms
guerrilla tactics, redistribution of wealth

People to Identify
Sun Yat-sen, Chiang Kai-shek, Mao Zedong

Places to Locate
Shanghai, Chang Jiang, Nanjing

Preview Questions
1. Against whom were the Nationalist and Chinese Communist Parties aligned?
2. What obstacles did Chiang Kai-shek face in building a new China?

Reading Strategy
Summarizing Information Make a cluster diagram like the one below showing the Confucian values that Chiang Kai-shek used to bring modern Western ideas into a culturally conservative population.

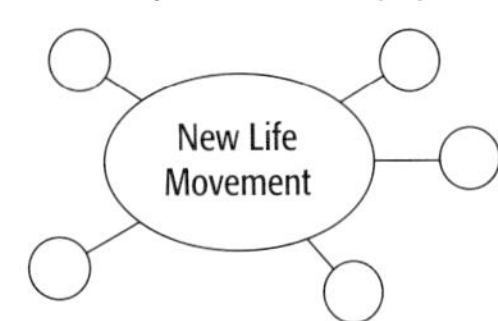

Preview of Events

1921 · 1923 · 1925 · 1927 · 1929 · 1931 · 1933

- **1921** Chinese Communist Party is formed in Shanghai
- **1923** Nationalists and Communists form an alliance
- **1933** Mao's troops begin Long March

Voices from the Past

In the fall of 1926, the young Communist Mao Zedong (Mao Tse-Tung) submitted a report to the Chinese Communist Party Central Committee calling for a massive peasant revolt against the ruling order:

> "In a very short time, in China's Central, Southern, and Northern provinces, several hundred million peasants will rise like a mighty storm, like a hurricane, a force so swift and violent that no power, however great, will be able to hold it back. They will smash all the restraints that bind them and rush forward along the road to liberation. They will sweep all the imperialists, warlords, corrupt officials, local tyrants, and evil gentry into their graves. . . . In force and momentum the attack is tempestuous; those who bow before it survive and those who resist perish."
>
> —***Selected Works of Mao Tse-Tung,* 1954**

Mao Zedong (at left)

The report shows Mao's confidence that peasants could play an active role in a Chinese revolution.

Nationalists and Communists

Revolutionary Marxism had its greatest impact in China. By 1920, central authority had almost ceased to exist in China. Two political forces began to emerge as competitors for the right to rule China: Sun Yat-sen's Nationalist Party, which had been driven from the political arena several years earlier, and the Chinese Communist Party.

1 FOCUS

Section Overview

This section discusses the Nationalist and Communist alliance to oppose the warlords and drive the imperialist powers out of China, the violent end of that alliance, Mao's "Long March," and Chiang Kai-shek's effort to create a "new China."

BELLRINGER
Skillbuilder Activity

Project transparency and have students answer questions.

Available as a blackline master.

Daily Focus Skills Transparency 18–3

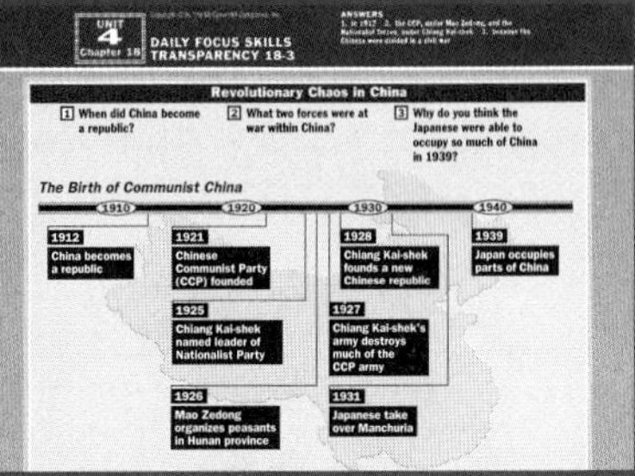

Guide to Reading

Answers to Graphic: hard work, obedience, integrity, propriety, righteousness

Preteaching Vocabulary: Have students describe the difference between guerrilla tactics and conventional military tactics.

SECTION RESOURCES

Reproducible Masters
- Reproducible Lesson Plan 18–3
- Daily Lecture and Discussion Notes 18–3
- Guided Reading Activity 18–3
- Section Quiz 18–3
- Reading Essentials and Study Guide 18–3

Transparencies
- Daily Focus Skills Transparency 18–3

Multimedia
- Interactive Tutor Self-Assessment CD-ROM
- ExamView® Pro Testmaker CD-ROM
- Presentation Plus! CD-ROM

2 TEACH

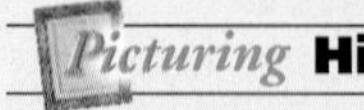

Picturing History

Answer: General Chiang Kai-shek believed that the Communists were a "disease of the heart."

Reading Check

Answer: Chiang Kai-skek destroyed the alliance. He only pretended that the Nationalist Party supported the Chinese Communist Party; shortly after succeeding Sun Yat-sen, he attacked the Communists and their supporters in Shanghai, killing thousands.

Daily Lecture and Discussion Notes 18–3

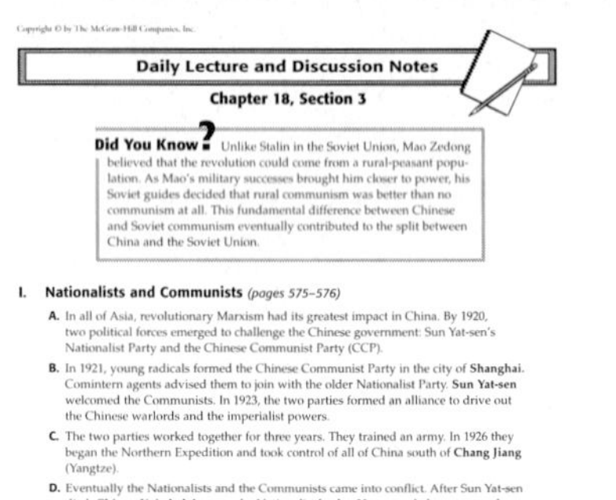

Daily Lecture and Discussion Notes

Chapter 18, Section 3

Did You Know? Unlike Stalin in the Soviet Union, Mao Zedong believed that the revolution could come from a rural-peasant population. As Mao's military successes brought him closer to power, his Soviet guides decided that rural communism was better than no communism at all. This fundamental difference between Chinese and Soviet communism eventually contributed to the split between China and the Soviet Union.

I. **Nationalists and Communists** *(pages 575–576)*

A. In all of Asia, revolutionary Marxism had its greatest impact in China. By 1920, two political forces emerged to challenge the Chinese government: Sun Yat-sen's Nationalist Party and the Chinese Communist Party (CCP).

B. In 1921, young radicals formed the Chinese Communist Party in the city of **Shanghai.** Comintern agents advised them to join with the older Nationalist Party. **Sun Yat-sen** welcomed the Communists. In 1923, the two parties formed an alliance to drive out the Chinese warlords and the imperialist powers.

C. The two parties worked together for three years. They trained an army. In 1926 they began the Northern Expedition and took control of all of China south of **Chang Jiang** (Yangtze).

D. Eventually the Nationalists and the Communists came into conflict. After Sun Yat-sen died, **Chiang Kai-shek** became the Nationalist leader. He pretended to support the Communists but did not. In 1927, he killed thousands of Communists in the **Shanghai Massacre.** The Communist-Nationalist alliance ended.

E. In 1928, Chiang Kai-

Critical Thinking

Have students identify and explain the difficulties faced by Sun Yat-sen in creating a new China. *(ousted shortly after taking office; failed in his attempt to overthrow Yuan with his Nationalist Party, failed to restore a strong central government)* **L2**

In 1921, a group of young radicals, including several faculty and staff members from Beijing University, founded the Chinese Communist Party (CCP) in the commercial and industrial city of **Shanghai.** Comintern agents soon advised the new party to join with the more experienced Nationalist Party.

Sun Yat-sen, leader of the Nationalists (see Chapter 15), welcomed the cooperation. He needed the expertise that the Soviet Union could provide. His anti-imperialist words had alienated many Western powers. One English-language newspaper in Shanghai wrote, "All his life, all his influence, are devoted to ideas that keep China in turmoil, and it is utterly undesirable that he should be allowed to prosecute those aims here." In 1923, the two parties—Nationalists and Communists—formed an alliance to oppose the warlords and drive the imperialist powers out of China.

For three years, the two parties overlooked their mutual suspicions and worked together. They mobilized and trained a revolutionary army to march north and seize control over China. This Northern Expedition began in the summer of 1926. By the following spring, revolutionary forces had taken control of all of China south of the **Chang Jiang** (Yangtze), including the major river ports of Wuhan and Shanghai.

Tensions between the two parties eventually rose to the surface. Sun Yat-sen died in 1925 and was succeeded as head of the Nationalist Party by the general **Chiang Kai-shek** (JEE•AHNG KY•SHEHK). Chiang pretended to support the alliance with the Communists. In April 1927, however, he struck against the Communists and their supporters in Shanghai, killing thousands in what is called the **Shanghai Massacre.** The Communist-Nationalist alliance ceased to exist.

In 1928, Chiang Kai-shek founded a new Chinese republic at **Nanjing.** During the next three years, he worked to reunify China. Although Chiang saw Japan as a serious threat to the Chinese nation, he believed that Japan was less dangerous than his other enemy, the Communists. He once remarked that "the Communists are a disease of the heart."

Reading Check **Explaining** How did Chiang Kai-shek change the Communist-Nationalist alliance?

The Communists in Hiding

After the Shanghai Massacre, most of the Communist leaders went into hiding in the city. There, they tried to revive the Communist movement among the working class. Shanghai was a rich recruiting ground for the party. People were discontented and looking for leadership.

Some party members fled to the mountainous Jiangxi (jee•AHNG•SHEE) Province south of the Chiang Jiang. They were led by the young Communist organizer **Mao Zedong** (MOW DZUH•DOONG). Unlike most other leading members of the Communist Party, Mao was convinced that a Chinese revolution would be driven by the poverty-stricken peasants in the countryside rather than by the urban working class.

Picturing History

Members of the Communist forces prepare to evacuate Shanghai during the Nationalists' takeover in 1927. Why did Chiang Kai-shek initiate this military action against the Communists?

COOPERATIVE LEARNING ACTIVITY

Creating a Report Organize the class into two groups to report on the influence of Chinese students on the politics of China. Each group should have a specific task, such as researching, organizing, or summarizing. Have one group examine the political role Chinese students played in the early part of this century. The other group can research the role Chinese students have played in politics in recent years, including the Tiananmen Square demonstrations of June 1989. Guide the class in a discussion comparing and contrasting the role of students during each period. **L2**

For grading this activity, refer to the ***Performance Assessment Activities*** booklet.

NATIONAL GEOGRAPHIC **China, 1926–1937**

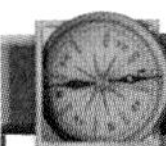

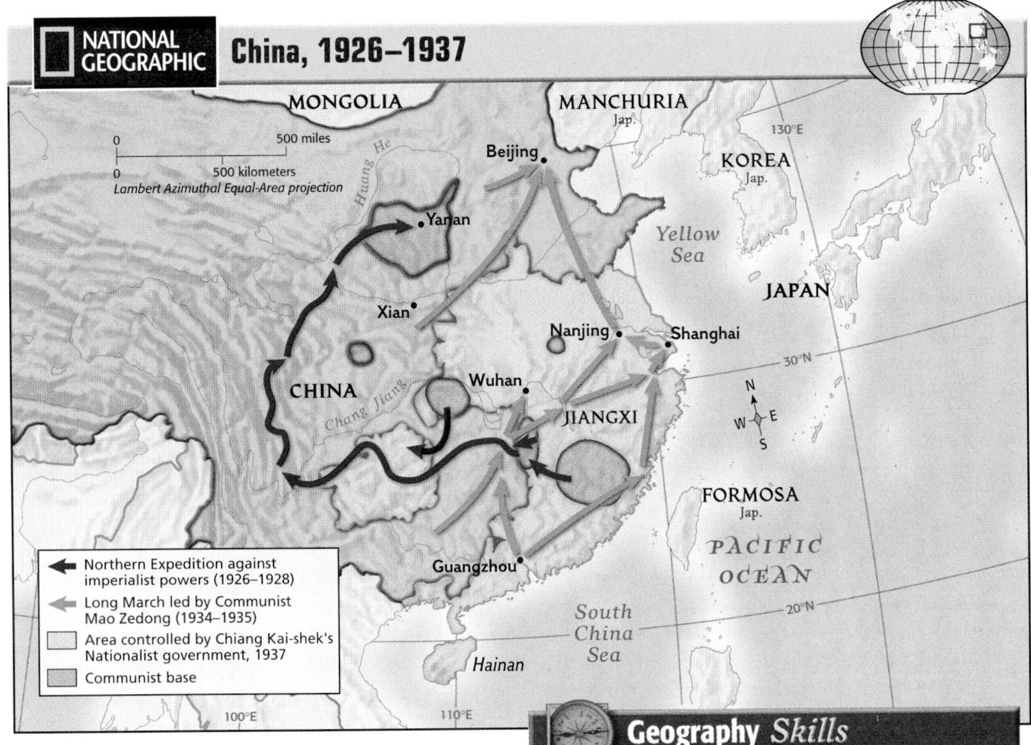

Chiang Kai-shek now tried to root the Communists out of their urban base in Shanghai and their rural base in Jiangxi Province. He succeeded in the first task in 1931. Most party leaders in Shanghai were forced to flee to Mao's base in South China.

Chiang Kai-shek then turned his forces against Mao's stronghold in Jiangxi Province. Chiang's forces far outnumbered Mao's, but Mao made effective use of guerrilla tactics, using unexpected maneuvers like sabotage and subterfuge to fight the enemy. Four slogans describe his methods: "When the enemy advances, we retreat! When the enemy halts and camps, we trouble them! When the enemy tries to avoid battle, we attack! When the enemy retreats, we pursue!"

Reading Check **Identifying** Which group did Mao believe would start the Communist revolution in China?

The Long March

In 1933, Chiang's troops, using their superior military strength, surrounded the Communist base in Jiangxi. However, Mao's army, the People's Liberation Army **(PLA)**, broke through the Nationalist lines and began its famous Long March.

Geography *Skills*

Communists and Nationalists fought imperialist powers and each other for control of China in the 1920s and 1930s.

1. **Interpreting Maps** Study the path of the arrows representing the Northern Expedition. Using the scale on the map, estimate the distance in miles and kilometers covered by the Northern Expedition.
2. **Applying Geography Skills** Use this map and others of China in this text to identify the mountains, rivers, and deserts Mao's army crossed during the Long March.

Moving on foot through mountains, marshes, and deserts, Mao's army traveled almost 6,000 miles (9,600 km) to reach the last surviving Communist base in the northwest of China. His troops had to fight all the way. Many froze or starved. One survivor remembered, "As the days went by, there was less and less to eat. After our grain was finished, we ate the horses, and then we lived on wild vegetables. When even the wild vegetables were finished, we ate our leather belts. After that we had to march on empty stomachs."

One year later, Mao's troops reached safety in the dusty hills of North China. Of the ninety thousand troops who had embarked on the journey, only nine

Reading Check

Answer: the poverty-stricken peasants rather than the working class

Geography *Skills*

Answers:

1. more than 3,000 miles (4,827 km)
2. Chang Jiang, Huang He, Himalaya, Mu Us Desert; students should consult the Reference Atlas.

Enrich

Ask students to explain how Mao's ideas differed from those of most other Chinese Communists. *(Mao believed a Chinese revolution must be based on the peasants in the countryside, not on the urban working class.)* Ask students to analyze the wisdom of this position. How does it help explain Mao's eventual triumph? What does it suggest about the workings of Mao's mind? **L2**

Guided Reading Activity 18–3

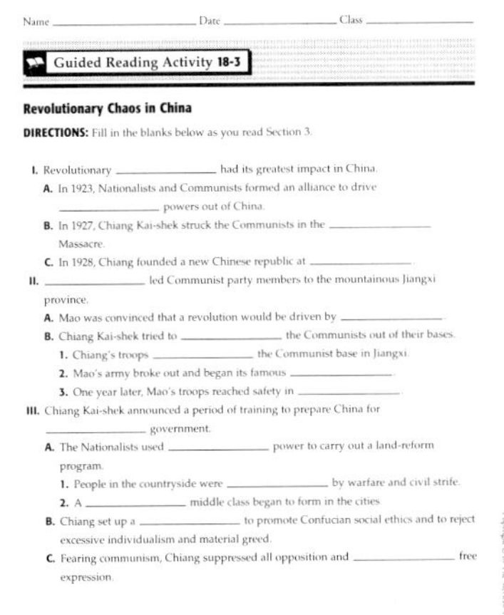

Name ____________ Date ____________ Class ____________

Guided Reading Activity **18-3**

Revolutionary Chaos in China

DIRECTIONS: Fill in the blanks below as you read Section 3.

I. Revolutionary ____________ had its greatest impact in China.
 A. In 1923, Nationalists and Communists formed an alliance to drive ____________ powers out of China.
 B. In 1927, Chiang Kai-shek struck the Communists in the ____________ Massacre.
 C. In 1928, Chiang founded a new Chinese republic at ____________.
II. ____________ led Communist party members to the mountainous Jiangxi province.
 A. Mao was convinced that a revolution would be driven by ____________.
 B. Chiang Kai-shek tried to ____________ the Communists out of their bases.
  1. Chiang's troops ____________ the Communist base in Jiangxi.
  2. Mao's army broke out and began its famous ____________.
  3. One year later, Mao's troops reached safety in ____________.
III. Chiang Kai-shek announced a period of training to prepare China for ____________ government.
 A. The Nationalists used ____________ power to carry out a land-reform program.
  1. People in the countryside were ____________ by warfare and civil strife.
  2. A ____________ middle class began to form in the cities.
 B. Chiang set up a ____________ to promote Confucian social ethics and to reject excessive individualism and material greed.
 C. Fearing communism, Chiang suppressed all opposition and ____________ free expression.

EXTENDING THE CONTENT

Mao's Communism When Marx and Engels envisioned a Communist society, they were exceedingly clear that a Communist society would develop only after capitalism had created an urban working class. This working class would rebel and create a new Socialist state, which would ultimately evolve into a Communist society. Mao Zedong believed that communism could be built on a rural-peasant foundation. Stalin distrusted the independent tendencies of the rural peasant. But as Mao's military achievements brought him closer to power, his Soviet guides decided that rural communism was better than no communism at all. Eventually, Chinese and Soviet communism split due to their fundamental differences.

CHAPTER 18
Section 3, 575–579

Reading Check

Answer: because 90 percent of Mao's troops had perished, and he was the only leader of the Chinese Communist Party

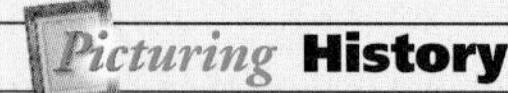

Picturing **History**

Answer: They had to travel almost 6,000 miles (9,600 km) on foot through mountains, marshes, and deserts, fighting all the way. Many froze or starved.

3 ASSESS

Assign Section 3 Assessment as homework or an in-class activity.

Have students use **Interactive Tutor Self-Assessment CD-ROM.**

Section Quiz 18–3

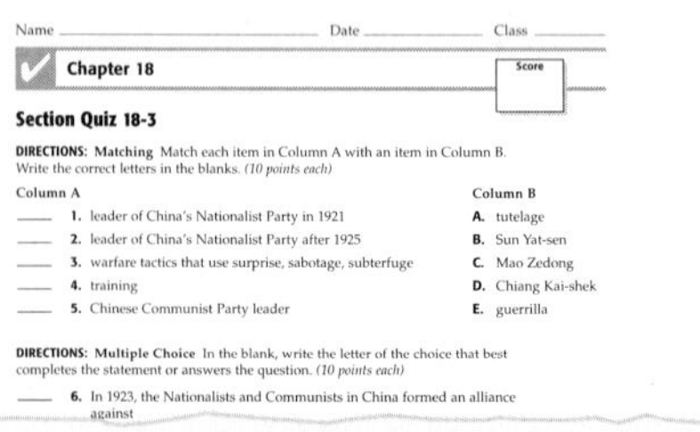

Name ____ Date ____ Class ____

Chapter 18 — Score

Section Quiz 18-3

DIRECTIONS: Matching Match each item in Column A with an item in Column B. Write the correct letters in the blanks. *(10 points each)*

Column A	Column B
____ **1.** leader of China's Nationalist Party in 1921	**A.** tutelage
____ **2.** leader of China's Nationalist Party after 1925	**B.** Sun Yat-sen
____ **3.** warfare tactics that use surprise, sabotage, subterfuge	**C.** Mao Zedong
____ **4.** training	**D.** Chiang Kai-shek
____ **5.** Chinese Communist Party leader	**E.** guerrilla

DIRECTIONS: Multiple Choice In the blank, write the letter of the choice that best completes the statement or answers the question. *(10 points each)*

____ **6.** In 1923, the Nationalists and Communists in China formed an alliance against

Reading Essentials and Study Guide 18–3

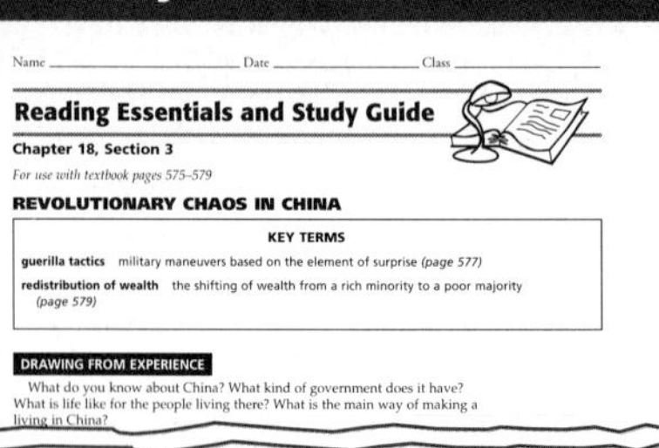

Name ____ Date ____ Class ____

Reading Essentials and Study Guide

Chapter 18, Section 3

For use with textbook pages 575–579

REVOLUTIONARY CHAOS IN CHINA

KEY TERMS

guerilla tactics military maneuvers based on the element of surprise *(page 577)*

redistribution of wealth the shifting of wealth from a rich minority to a poor majority *(page 579)*

DRAWING FROM EXPERIENCE

What do you know about China? What kind of government does it have? What is life like for the people living there? What is the main way of making a living in China?

Picturing **History**

Chinese Communists gather in North China following the year-long, 6,000-mile (9,600-km) Long March. Describe the difficulties Mao Zedong's forces had to overcome to reach safety in North China.

thousand remained. In the course of the Long March, Mao Zedong had become the sole leader of the Chinese Communist Party. To people who lived at the time, it must have seemed that the Communist threat to the Nanjing regime was over. To the Communists, however, there remained hope for the future.

Reading Check **Explaining** Why did it seem that communism was no longer a threat to China after the Long March?

The New China of Chiang Kai-shek

In the meantime, Chiang Kai-shek had been trying to build a new nation. Chiang had publicly declared his commitment to the plans of Sun Yat-sen, which called for a republican government. First, however, there would be a transitional period. In Sun's words:

> "China . . . needs a republican government just as a boy needs school. As a schoolboy must have good teachers and helpful friends, so the Chinese people, being for the first time under republican rule, must have a farsighted revolutionary government for their training. This calls for the period of political tutelage, which is a necessary transitional stage from monarchy to republicanism. Without this, disorder will be unavoidable."

In keeping with Sun's program, Chiang announced a period of political tutelage (training) to prepare the Chinese people for a final stage of constitutional government. In the meantime, the Nationalists would use their dictatorial power to carry out a land-reform program and to modernize industry.

It would take more than plans on paper to create a new China, however. Years of neglect and civil war had severely weakened the political, economic, and social fabric of the nation. Most of the people who lived in the countryside were drained by warfare and civil strife. The peasants there were still very poor and overwhelmingly illiterate, and they made up 80 percent of China's population.

A westernized middle class had begun to form in the cities. It was there that the new Nanjing government found much of its support. However, the new westernized elite pursued the middle-class values of individual advancement and material accumulation. They had few links with the peasants in the countryside.

Chiang Kai-shek was aware of the problem of introducing foreign ideas into a population that was still culturally conservative. Thus, while attempting to build a modern industrial state, he tried to bring together modern Western innovations with traditional Confucian values of hard work, obedience, and integrity. With his U.S.-educated wife Mei-ling Soong, Chiang set up a **"New Life Movement."** Its goal was to promote traditional Confucian social ethics, such as integrity, propriety, and righteousness.

INTERDISCIPLINARY CONNECTIONS ACTIVITY

Political Science Divide the students into two groups. Have one group of students imagine they are members of the Red Army trying to gain the support of peasants in the countryside. Have them write a short speech directed at Chinese peasants. The second group of students will imagine it supports Chiang Kai-shek's efforts to rule and reform China. Ask this group to prepare a short speech to convince Chinese peasants that their best hopes for the future are with Chiang and his "New Life Movement." End this activity with a discussion after students from the two groups read their speeches to the entire class. L3

People In History

Mao Zedong
1893–1976—Chinese leader

Mao Zedong was the creator of the People's Republic of China. The son of a prosperous peasant, he insisted that the Communist Party support peasant demands for land reform. In 1949, Communist forces under Mao drove out Chiang Kai-shek's Nationalists and assumed complete control of China. Mao's sayings were collected in *Quotations from Chairman Mao Zedong,* which came to be known simply as *The Little Red Book.*

Chiang Kai-shek
1887–1975—Chinese general

Chiang Kai-shek became the leader of the Chinese Nationalist Party in 1925 and established a Nationalist government over China three years later. After the defeat of Japan in 1945, Chiang became president of China, but his forces lost to the Communists in a civil war in 1949. Chiang fled with his forces to Taiwan, where he established a dictatorship, claiming all the while to be the only legitimate ruler of China.

At the same time, it rejected what was viewed as the excessive individualism and material greed of Western capitalist values.

Chiang Kai-shek faced a host of other problems as well. The Nanjing government had total control over only a handful of provinces in the Chang Jiang Valley. As we shall see in the next chapter, the Japanese threatened to gain control of northern China. The Great Depression was also having an ill effect on China's economy.

In spite of all of these problems, Chiang did have some success. He undertook a massive road-building project and repaired and extended much of the country's railroad system as well. He also established a national bank and improved the education system.

In other areas, Chiang was less successful and progress was limited. For example, a land-reform program was enacted in 1930, but it had little effect. Because Chiang's support came from the rural landed gentry, as well as the urban middle class, he did not press for programs that would lead to a **redistribution of wealth,** the shifting of wealth from a rich minority to a poor majority.

The government was also repressive. Fearing Communist influence, Chiang suppressed all opposition and censored free expression. In so doing, he alienated many intellectuals and political moderates.

Reading Check **Identifying** What was the intended final stage of Chiang Kai-shek's reform program?

SECTION 3 ASSESSMENT

Checking for Understanding

1. **Define** guerrilla tactics, redistribution of wealth.
2. **Identify** Sun Yat-sen, Chiang Kai-shek, Shanghai Massacre, Mao Zedong, PLA, New Life Movement.
3. **Locate** Shanghai, Chang Jiang, Nanjing.
4. **Explain** why the Communist Party aligned with the Nationalist Party.
5. **List** the external problems that threatened Chiang Kai-shek's regime.

Critical Thinking

6. **Analyze** What did Mao's Long March accomplish? Why was it successful?
7. **Summarizing Information** Use a diagram like the one below to show Chiang Kai-shek's successes during the 1930s.

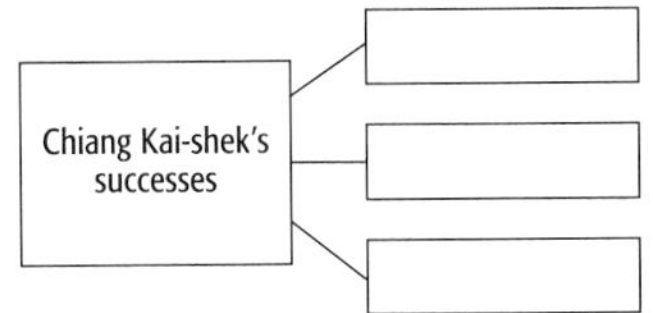

Analyzing Visuals

8. **Describe** the action taking place in the photo on page 576. What clues in the photo indicate the different kinds of warfare undertaken by soldiers during this time?

Writing About History

9. **Persuasive Writing** Conduct research to learn how the United States supported Chiang Kai-shek and why. Write an editorial for or against United States intervention in China.

Answer: a republican government

CURRICULUM CONNECTION

Historical Inquiry Have students research the propaganda techniques of Mao Zedong by using primary and secondary sources to find Chinese Communist Party political posters. What message did the party hope to convey and how did they convey it? Ask students to find a contemporary propaganda poster and analyze it for the class. L2

Reteaching Activity

Ask students to consider the following leaders of China's revolutionary movement: Sun Yat-sen, Chiang Kai-shek, and Mao Zedong. Why do students think it was Mao who emerged as the central figure in twentieth-century China? Ask students to analyze the influence of Mao Zedong on political events of the twentieth century. L2

4 CLOSE

Ask students to research and analyze Chiang Kai-shek's "New Life Movement." How did it attempt to merge traditional Confucian values with Western ideas? L2

SECTION 3 ASSESSMENT

1. Key terms are in blue.
2. Sun Yat-sen *(p. 576)*; Chiang Kai-shek *(p. 576)*; Shanghai Massacre *(p. 576)*; Mao Zedong *(p. 576)*; PLA *(p. 577)*; New Life Movement *(p. 578)*
3. See chapter maps.
4. because the Nationalists were more experienced
5. Nanjing only controlled a few provinces, the Japanese threatened northern China, economy depressed
6. The 10 percent who survived found safety, and Mao emerged as the leader; Communists had hope for the future.
7. transportation; a national bank; improved education
8. loading artillery onto a railroad car; hand-to-hand combat with swords, artillery fire
9. Answers should provide persuasive arguments.

TECHNOLOGY SKILLBUILDER

TEACH

Using an Electronic Spreadsheet This skill teaches students to work with a spreadsheet program on the computer. Review Learning the Skill with students. What types of information could be placed on spreadsheets? *(budgets, grades, schedules, population, temperatures, amount of precipitation, etc.)* Next, review Practicing the Skill with students. Then allow computer time to apply the directions. Students can find the information they need to complete Practicing the Skill in *The World Almanac, Statesmen's Yearbook*, and *The Population Data Sheet* from the Population Reference Bureau. L1

Additional Practice

Skills Reinforcement Activity 18

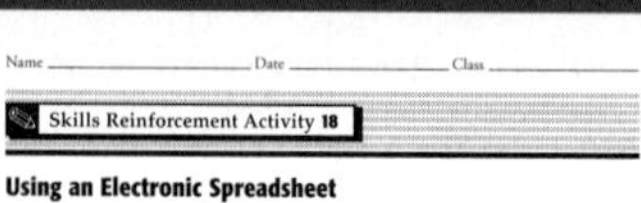

Name ________ Date ________ Class ________

Skills Reinforcement Activity **18**

Using an Electronic Spreadsheet

A spreadsheet is an electronic worksheet that can manage numbers quickly and easily. All spreadsheets follow a basic design of rows and columns. Each column is assigned a letter, and each row is assigned a number. Each point where a column and row intersect is called a cell. The cell's position on the spreadsheet is labeled according to its corresponding column and row, so A1 is column A, row 1. Spreadsheets use formulas to calculate numbers. To create a formula, highlight the cell you want the results in, and then build the formula, step by step.

DIRECTIONS: Use the information in the table below to create your own electronic spreadsheet and calculate the balance of trade for each of these Latin American countries. Then answer the questions on a separate sheet of paper. Your spreadsheet should have seven columns and six rows.

Value of Latin American Imports and Exports, 1989 and 1999

GLENCOE TECHNOLOGY

CD-ROM
Glencoe Skillbuilder Interactive Workbook CD-ROM, Level 2

This interactive CD-ROM reinforces student mastery of essential technology skills.

TECHNOLOGY SKILLBUILDER

Using an Electronic Spreadsheet

Why Learn This Skill?

Electronic spreadsheets can help people manage data quickly and easily. For example, if you want to know your grade average throughout the year, you could create a spreadsheet in which you enter your latest test and homework scores.

Learning the Skill

A spreadsheet is an electronic worksheet. All spreadsheets follow a basic design of columns and rows.

- Each *column* (vertical) is assigned a letter or number.
- Each *row* (horizontal) is assigned a number.
- A *cell* is where a column and row intersect.
- A cell's position on the spreadsheet is labeled according to its corresponding column and row—Column A, Row 1 (A1); Column B, Row 2 (B2); and so on (see diagram).

	A	B	C	D
1	A1	B1	C1	D1
2	A2	B2	C2	D2
3	A3	B3	C3	D3

Spreadsheets use standard formulas to calculate the numbers. You create a simple mathematical equation that uses these standard formulas and the computer does the calculations for you.

You can make changes in the spreadsheet by using the mouse or cursor to move to the appropriate cell. If you change any number in the cell, the computer will automatically recompute the totals. The computer will even copy a formula from one cell to another.

Practicing the Skill

Suppose you want to know the population densities (populations per square mile or square kilometer) of the countries in South Asia. Use these steps to create a spreadsheet.

1. In cell A1 type Country, in cell B1 type Population, in cell C1 type Land Area, and in cell D1 type Population Density.
2. In cells A2–A5 type India, Pakistan, Bangladesh, and Sri Lanka. In cell A6, type Total for South Asia.
3. In cells B2–B5, enter the population of each country shown in cells A2–A5.
4. In cells C2–C5, enter the land area (square miles or square kilometers) of each country.
5. In cell D2, use the mathematical formula (B2÷C2) to calculate the population density of each country. Copy this formula into cells D3–D5, changing the cell numbers in the formula as you enter each row.
6. In cell B6, create a formula to calculate the total population of South Asia (B2+B3+B4+B5).
7. In cell C6, create a formula to calculate the total land area of South Asia (C2+C3+C4+C5).
8. For cell D6, create a formula to calculate the total population density of South Asia (B6÷C6).

Applying the Skill

Use a spreadsheet to enter your test scores and your homework grades for each of your classes. Calculate your average grade in each class, and then calculate your average grade in all your classes.

ANSWERS TO PRACTICING THE SKILL

Questions 1–8: Students will set up a spreadsheet using the information in questions 1 to 8. Have students review their work at each step as they create their spreadsheets. Remind students to pay attention to details such as the spelling and capitalization of words used in their spreadsheets. Also remind students to be very careful when entering numbers into their spreadsheets. One incorrect number can invalidate a spreadsheet's calculation. Errors can be difficult to trace and correct.

Applying the Skill: Students will create spreadsheets with their test scores and homework grades.

SECTION 4 Nationalism in Latin America

Guide to Reading

Main Ideas
- Before the Great Depression, the United States was the foremost investor in Latin America.
- The Great Depression created instability in Latin America, which led to military coups and the creation of military dictatorships.

Key Terms
oligarchy

People to Identify
Juan Vicente Gómez, Hipólito Irigoyen, Getúlio Vargas, Lázaro Cárdenas

Places to Locate
Argentina, Chile, Brazil, Peru, Mexico

Preview Questions
1. What was the Good Neighbor policy?
2. How did the Great Depression affect the economies of Latin America?

Reading Strategy
Summarizing Information Make a chart like the one below listing the main exports of Latin America.

Country	Exports
Argentina	
Chile	
Brazil	
Peru	

Preview of Events

1915 — 1920 — 1925 — 1930 — 1935 — 1940

- **1920** United States becomes the main investor in Latin America
- **1930** Latin American exports decrease by 50 percent
- **1938** Getúlio Vargas establishes his New State in Brazil

Voices from the Past

In July 1938, Getúlio Vargas spoke to the Brazilian nation to explain his dictatorial regime, which he called the New State:

> ❝If you would ask me what is the program of the New State, I would tell you that its program is to crisscross the nation with railroads, highways, and airlines; to increase production; to provide for the workers and to encourage agriculture; to expand exports; to prepare the armed forces; to organize public opinion so that there is, body and soul, one Brazilian thought . . . finally [that] the preparation of internal and external defense by the rearmament of our brave armed forces and the simultaneous education of the new generations [is] inculcating [implanting] in them the spirit and love of the fatherland.❞
>
> —***A Documentary History of Brazil,*** **Bradford E. Burns, 1966**

Vargas's New State drew much of its inspiration from the Fascist regimes of Mussolini and Hitler.

Getúlio Vargas

The Latin American Economy

At the beginning of the twentieth century, the Latin American economy was based largely on the export of foodstuffs and raw materials. Some countries relied on only one or two products for sale abroad. **Argentina,** for example, sent beef and wheat; **Chile,** nitrates and copper; **Brazil** and Caribbean nations, sugar; and

1 FOCUS

Section Overview

This section describes U.S. investment in Latin America, the Good Neighbor policy, the impact of the Depression, and the move to authoritarianism in Latin America.

BELLRINGER
Skillbuilder Activity

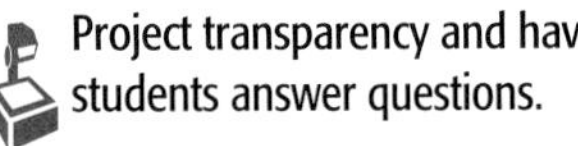

Project transparency and have students answer questions.

Available as a blackline master.

Daily Focus Skills Transparency 18–4

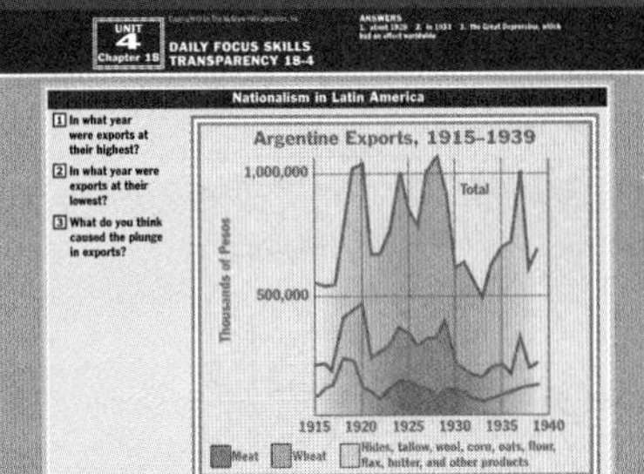

Guide to Reading

Answers to Graphic: Argentina: beef, wheat; Chile: nitrates, copper; Brazil: sugar; Peru: oil, copper

Preteaching Vocabulary: Have students create a chart showing the differences between an oligarchy, a democracy, and a monarchy.

SECTION RESOURCES

Reproducible Masters
- Reproducible Lesson Plan 18–4
- Daily Lecture and Discussion Notes 18–4
- Guided Reading Activity 18–4
- Section Quiz 18–4
- Reading Essentials and Study Guide 18–4

Transparencies
- Daily Focus Skills Transparency 18–4

Multimedia
- Interactive Tutor Self-Assessment CD-ROM
- ExamView® Pro Testmaker CD-ROM
- Presentation Plus! CD-ROM

2 TEACH

Geography Skills

Answers:

1. twenty-four
2. Some countries bear the name of the European countries (British Honduras, Dutch Guiana). Other countries have names in European languages (El Salvador, Colombia). The British, Dutch, and French all had colonies in northern South America. Students may infer the area had desirable resources, that European colonies were often located near the coast, or that there appears to be a direct sea route between Europe and northern South America.

Daily Lecture and Discussion Notes 18–4

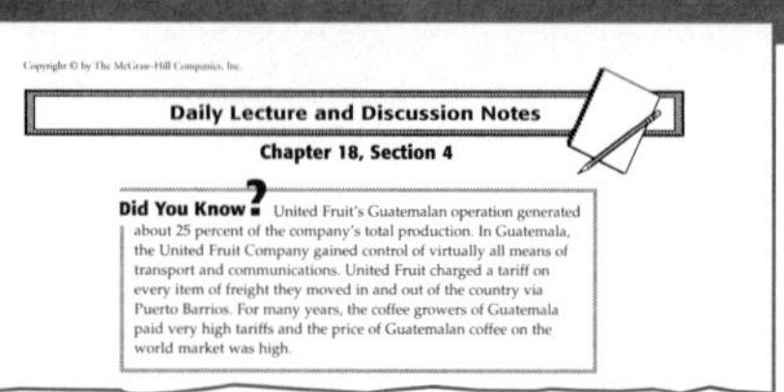

Daily Lecture and Discussion Notes

Chapter 18, Section 4

Did You Know? United Fruit's Guatemalan operation generated about 25 percent of the company's total production. In Guatemala, the United Fruit Company gained control of virtually all means of transport and communications. United Fruit charged a tariff on every item of freight they moved in and out of the country via Puerto Barrios. For many years, the coffee growers of Guatemala paid very high tariffs and the price of Guatemalan coffee on the world market was high.

CURRICULUM CONNECTION

Economics Ask interested students to study the process by which large segments of Latin America's export industries fell into U.S. hands. What was the strategy of U.S. companies? What was their attitude toward Latin America? What was the economic impact of U.S. ownership on Latin America? **L2**

Central America, bananas. A few reaped large profits from these exports. For the majority of the population, however, the returns were small.

Role of the United States Beginning in the 1920s, the United States began to replace Great Britain as the foremost investor in Latin America. British investors had put money into stocks and other forms of investment that did not give them direct control of Latin American companies. Unlike British investors, U.S. investors put their funds directly into production enterprises and ran companies themselves. In this way, large segments of Latin America's export industries fell into the hands of United States companies. A number of smaller Central American countries became independent republics, but their economies were often dependent on large, wealthy nations. The U.S.-owned United Fruit Company, for example, owned land, packing plants, and railroads in Central America. American firms also gained control of the copper-mining industry in Chile and **Peru,** as well as of the oil industry in **Mexico,** Peru, and Bolivia.

The fact that investors in the United States controlled many Latin American industries angered Latin Americans. A growing nationalist consciousness led many of them to view the United States as an imperialist power. It was not difficult for Latin American nationalists to show that profits from U.S. businesses were sometimes used to keep ruthless dictators in power. In Venezuela, for example, U.S. oil companies had a close relationship with the dictator **Juan Vicente Gómez.**

The United States had always cast a large shadow over Latin America. It had intervened militarily in Latin American affairs for years. This was especially true in Central America and the Caribbean. Many Americans considered both regions vital to the security of the United States.

The United States made some attempts to change its relationship with Latin America, however. In 1933, President Franklin D. Roosevelt announced the **Good Neighbor policy.** This policy rejected the use of U.S. military force in Latin America. Adhering to his word, the president withdrew the last United States Marines from Haiti in 1934. For the first time in 30 years, there were no U.S. troops in Latin American countries.

Impact of the Great Depression The Great Depression was a disaster for Latin America's economy. The weakening of the economies in the United States and Europe led to a decreased demand for Latin American foodstuffs and raw materials, especially coffee, sugar, metals, and meat. The total value of Latin American exports in 1930 was almost 50 percent below the figures for the years between 1925 and 1929. The countries that depended on the export of only one product, rather than multiple products, were especially damaged.

The Great Depression had one positive effect on the Latin American economy. With a decline in exports, Latin American countries no longer had the revenues to buy manufactured goods. Many Latin American governments encouraged the development of new industries that would produce goods that were formerly imported. This process of industrial development was supposed to achieve greater economic independence for Latin America.

NATIONAL GEOGRAPHIC **Latin America, 1939**

UNITED STATES
MEXICO
CUBA
HAITI
DOMINICAN REPUBLIC
TROPIC OF CANCER
BRITISH HONDURAS
HONDURAS
GUATEMALA
EL SALVADOR
NICARAGUA
COSTA RICA
PANAMA
VENEZUELA
BRITISH GUIANA
DUTCH GUIANA
FRENCH GUIANA
COLOMBIA
ECUADOR
EQUATOR
PERU
BRAZIL
BOLIVIA
TROPIC OF CAPRICORN
CHILE
PARAGUAY
PACIFIC OCEAN
ATLANTIC OCEAN
URUGUAY
ARGENTINA
0 1,000 miles
0 1,000 kilometers
Lambert Azimuthal Equal-Area projection
20°N 0° 20°S 40°S
120°W 100°W 80°W 60°W 40°W 20°W

Geography Skills

The economic and political stability of Latin America was strongly affected by World War I and the Great Depression.

1. **Interpreting Maps** How many countries made up Latin America in 1939?
2. **Applying Geography Skills** What evidence of the European occupation of Latin America can you find on this map? What inferences can you draw about this occupation by looking at northern South America?

COOPERATIVE LEARNING ACTIVITY

Geography Have students, working in groups, prepare a list of instances when the United States intervened in Latin America. The list should show the date, the reason the United States intervened, and the short-term outcome (i.e., how the United States "solved" the problem). What were the results of American intervention in Latin America over the long term? Has intervention cost the United States more than it gained? Ask the students to convert their lists to maps. Have students compare and analyze their maps. What patterns, if any, can be learned from their maps? **L2**

For grading this activity, refer to the ***Performance Assessment Activities*** booklet.

Often, however, the new industries were not started by individual capitalists. Because of a shortage of capital in the private sector, governments frequently invested in the new industries. This led to government-run steel industries in Chile and Brazil, along with government-run oil industries in Argentina and Mexico.

Reading Check **Comparing** How did the United States's method of investing in Latin America differ from that of Britain?

The Move to Authoritarianism

Most Latin American countries had republican forms of government. In reality, however, a relatively small group of church officials, military leaders, and large landowners dominated each country. This elite group controlled the masses of people, who were mostly poverty-stricken peasants. Military forces were crucial in keeping these special-interest groups in power. Indeed, military leaders often took control of the government.

This trend toward authoritarianism increased during the 1930s, largely because of the impact of the Great Depression. Domestic instability caused by economic crises led to the creation of many military dictatorships at the beginning of the 1930s. This trend was especially evident in Argentina, Brazil, and Mexico. Together, these nations possessed over half of the land and wealth of Latin America.

Argentina Argentina was controlled by an oligarchy, a government where a select group of people exercises control. This oligarchy of large landowners who had grown wealthy from the export of beef and wheat failed to realize the growing importance of industry and cities in their country. It also ignored the growing middle class, which reacted by forming the Radical Party in 1890.

In 1916, **Hipólito Irigoyen** (ee•PAW•lee•TOH IHR•ih•GOH•YEHN), leader of the Radical Party, was elected president of Argentina. The Radical Party, however, feared the industrial workers, who were using strikes to improve their conditions. The party thus drew closer to the large landowners and became more corrupt.

The military was also concerned with the rising power of the industrial workers. In 1930, the Argentine army overthrew President Irigoyen and reestablished the power of the large landowners. Through this action, the military hoped to continue the old export economy and thus stop the growth of working-class power that would come with more industrialization.

During World War II, restless military officers formed a new organization, known as the Group of United Officers (GOU). They were unhappy with the government and overthrew it in June 1943. Three years later, one GOU member, Juan Perón, seized sole power of the country (see Chapter 22).

Brazil In 1889, the army had overthrown the Brazilian monarchy and established a republic. The republic was controlled chiefly by the landed elites, who had become wealthy by growing coffee on large plantations.

By 1900, three-quarters of the world's coffee was grown in Brazil. As long as coffee prices remained high, the ruling oligarchy was able to maintain its power. The oligarchy largely ignored the growth of urban industry and the working class that came with it.

The Great Depression devastated the coffee industry. By the end of 1929, coffee prices had hit a record low. In 1930, a military coup made **Getúlio Vargas,** a wealthy rancher, president of Brazil. Vargas ruled Brazil from 1930 to 1945. Early in his rule, he appealed to workers by instituting an eight-hour day and a minimum wage.

Faced with strong opposition in 1937, Vargas made himself dictator. Beginning in 1938, he established his New State. It was basically an authoritarian state with some Fascist-like features. Political parties were outlawed and civil rights restricted. A secret police used torture to silence Vargas's opponents.

The price of coffee has had a major impact on almost every aspect of life in Brazil.

CHAPTER 18
Section 4, 581–585

Reading Check

Answer: British investors put money into stocks and other forms of investment that did not give them direct control of Latin American companies. American investors put funds directly into production enterprises and ran the companies themselves.

Guided Reading Activity 18–4

Name ______ Date ______ Class ______

Guided Reading Activity **18-4**

Nationalism in Latin America

DIRECTIONS: Fill in the blanks below as you read Section 4.

1. At the beginning of the twentieth century, the Latin American economy was based largely on the export of ______ and ______.
2. The fact that ______ in the United States controlled many Latin American industries ______ Latin Americans.
3. The United States had intervened ______ in Latin American for years.
4. In 1935, President Franklin Roosevelt announced the ______, a policy ______ the use of U.S. military force in Latin America.
5. The total value of Latin American ______ in 1930 was almost ______ below the figures for the years between 1925 and 1929.
6. Being low on ______ to buy manufactured goods, Latin American governments encouraged the development of new ______ to produce goods.
7. A trend toward ______ increased during the 1930s.
8. Argentina was controlled by an ______, a government where a select group of people exercises control.
9. A military coup made Getulio Vargas, a wealthy rancher, president of Brazil, and in 1937 Vargas made himself ______.
10. Lazaro Cardenas, president of Mexico from 1934 to 1940, distributed 44 million acres of land to landless Mexican ______, a move that made him enormously popular.

Enrich

Organize students into two groups. Have one group write a pamphlet in favor of the nationalization of foreign-owned oil wells in Mexico and have the other group write a pamphlet against nationalization. Tell students to support their arguments by forecasting the long-term effects of state ownership of the wells. **L2**

Writing Activity

After they have read this chapter, students should write brief essays in which they explain the impact of American political ideas on significant world political developments. **L2**

EXTENDING THE CONTENT

Coffee is an important export for nations in Latin America. For years, the traditional method of growing coffee in the shade of tall trees allowed a habitat beneficial to birds and insects to develop. As rainforests shrank, birds found a home on shade-grown coffee plantations. However, in recent years, a new high-yield sun-grown coffee has been developed. More and more land is devoted to sun-grown coffee. Since the introduction of sun-grown coffee, migratory bird watchers have noted a significant drop in the number of migratory birds. In addition, this type of coffee crop requires intensive use of pesticides, herbicides, and fertilizers.

CHAPTER 18
Section 4, 581–585

Chart *Skills*

Answers:

1. nationalism
2. Students' summaries should be consistent with material presented in this chapter.

3 ASSESS

Assign Section 4 Assessment as homework or an in-class activity.

Have students use **Interactive Tutor Self-Assessment CD-ROM.**

Section Quiz 18–4

Name ______ Date ______ Class ______

Chapter 18 Score

Section Quiz 18-4

DIRECTIONS: Matching Match each item in Column A with an item in Column B. Write the correct letters in the blanks. *(10 points each)*

Column A	Column B
____ 1. small countries dependent on larger, wealthier nations	A. oligarchies
____ 2. governments run by select groups of powerful people	B. Diego Rivera
____ 3. Mexican president who distributed land to peasants in the 1930's	C. banana republics
____ 4. Mexican fresco artist who studied in Europe	D. GetúlioVargas
____ 5. Brazilian reformer who turned dictator	E. Lázaro Cárdenas

DIRECTIONS: Multiple Choice In the blank, write the letter of the choice that best completes the statement or answers the question. *(10 points each)*

____ 6. Authoritarianism spread in Latin America during the 1930s largely

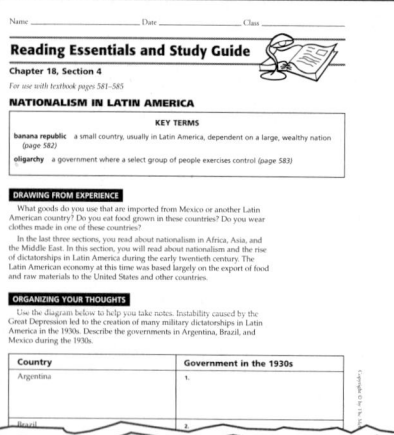

Reading Essentials and Study Guide 18–4

Name ______ Date ______ Class ______

Reading Essentials and Study Guide

Chapter 18, Section 4

For use with textbook pages 581–585

NATIONALISM IN LATIN AMERICA

KEY TERMS

banana republic a small country, usually in Latin America, dependent on a large, wealthy nation *(page 582)*

oligarchy a government where a select group of people exercises control *(page 583)*

DRAWING FROM EXPERIENCE

What goods do you use that are imported from Mexico or another Latin American country? Do you eat food grown in these countries? Do you wear clothes made in one of these countries?

In the last three sections, you read about nationalism in Africa, Asia, and the Middle East. In this section, you will read about nationalism and the rise of dictatorships in Latin America during the early twentieth century. The Latin American economy at this time was based largely on the export of food and raw materials to the United States and other countries.

ORGANIZING YOUR THOUGHTS

Use the diagram below to help you take notes. Instability caused by the Great Depression led to the creation of many military dictatorships in Latin America in the 1930s. Describe the governments in Argentina, Brazil, and Mexico during the 1930s.

Country	Government in the 1930s
Argentina	1.
Brazil	2.

Selected Nationalist Movements in the Early Twentieth Century

	Latin America			Africa and Asia			Middle East		
Country	Argentina	Brazil	Mexico	Kenya	Libya	India	Turkey	Persia	Northern Arabian Peninsula
Leader	Argentine army; Group of United Officers	Getúlio Vargas	Lázaro Cárdenas	Harry Thuku (Young Kikuyu Association); Jomo Kenyatta	Omar Mukhtar	Mohandas Gandhi	Mustafa Kemal (Atatürk)	Reza Khan (Reza Shah Pahlavi)	Ibn Saud
Driving Force	Fear of workers; dissatisfaction with government	Bad economy	Foreign control of oil industry	High taxes; British rule	Italian rule	British rule	Greek seizure of Anatolian Peninsula	British and Soviet presence	European creation of states
Outcome	New governments (1930, 1943)	Vargas's New State (1938)	Seizure of oil and property (1938); PEMEX	Exile of Thuku (1922)	Revolt crushed (1920s)	Government of India Act (1935)	Turkish Republic (1923)	Iran (1935)	Saudi Arabia (1932)

Chart *Skills*

Between World War I and World War II, many countries around the world struggled to achieve independence and national identity.

1. **Analyzing** What was the most frequent motivation for revolt in the countries identified above?
2. **Summarizing** How successful were those who sought to create a new nation or a new form of government? Using the information above and in this chapter, write a paragraph that summarizes the attempts at independence and nationalism made by the above countries.

Vargas also pursued a policy of stimulating new industries. The government established the Brazilian steel industry and set up a company to explore for oil. By the end of World War II, Brazil had become Latin America's chief industrial power. In 1945, the army, fearing that Vargas might prolong his power illegally after calling for new elections, forced him to resign.

Mexico Mexico was not an authoritarian state, but neither was it truly democratic. The Mexican Revolution of the early twentieth century had been the first significant effort in Latin America to overturn the system of large landed estates and raise the living standards of the masses (see Chapter 14). Out of the revolution had emerged a relatively stable political order.

The government was democratic in form. However, the official political party of the Mexican Revolution, known as the Institutional Revolutionary Party, or PRI, controlled the major groups within Mexican society. Every six years, party bosses of the PRI chose the party's presidential candidate. That candidate was then dutifully elected by the people.

A new wave of change began with **Lázaro Cárdenas** (KAHR•duhn•AHS), president of Mexico from 1934 to 1940. He moved to fulfill some of the original goals of the revolution. His major step was to distribute 44 million acres (17.8 million ha) of land to landless Mexican peasants, an action that made him enormously popular with the peasants.

Cárdenas also took a strong stand with the United States, especially over oil. By 1900, Mexico was known to have enormous oil reserves. Over the next 30 years, foreign oil companies from Britain and, in particular, the United States, made large investments in Mexico. After a dispute with the foreign-owned oil companies over workers' wages, the Cárdenas government seized control of the oil fields and the property of the oil companies.

MEETING INDIVIDUAL NEEDS

Visual/Tactile Have students work in groups with each group choosing a Latin American country. Suggested countries are: Argentina, Bolivia, Brazil, Chile, Cuba, Mexico, and Peru. Have each group prepare a bulletin board display that includes pictures, maps, and drawings of life and culture in the selected country. Foods, traditional dress, housing, arts, crafts, musical instruments, and other products associated with the country may also be displayed. Have each group make a presentation of its display to the class. In addition to the bulletin board, each group may enhance its presentation by bringing to class recordings of traditional music from the selected country. **L1**

Refer to ***Inclusion for the High School Studies Classroom Strategies and Activities*** in the TCR.

The U.S. oil companies were furious and asked President Franklin D. Roosevelt to intervene. He refused, reminding them of his promise in the Good Neighbor policy not to send U.S. troops into Latin America. Mexicans cheered Cárdenas as the president who had stood up to the United States.

Eventually, the Mexican government did pay the oil companies for their property. It then set up **PEMEX,** a national oil company, to run the oil industry.

Reading Check **Examining** How was the Mexican government democratic in form but not in practice?

Culture in Latin America

During the early twentieth century, European artistic and literary movements began to penetrate Latin America. In major cities, such as Buenos Aires in Argentina and São Paulo in Brazil, wealthy elites expressed great interest in the work of modern artists.

Latin American artists went abroad and brought back modern techniques, which they often adapted to their own native roots. Many artists and writers used their work to promote the emergence of a new national spirit. An example was the Mexican artist Diego Rivera.

Rivera had studied in Europe, where he was especially influenced by fresco painting in Italy. After his return to Mexico, he developed a monumental style that filled wall after wall with murals. Rivera's wall paintings can be found in such diverse places as the Ministry of Education, the Chapel of the Agriculture School at Chapingo, and the Social Security Hospital. His works were aimed at the masses of people, many of whom could not read.

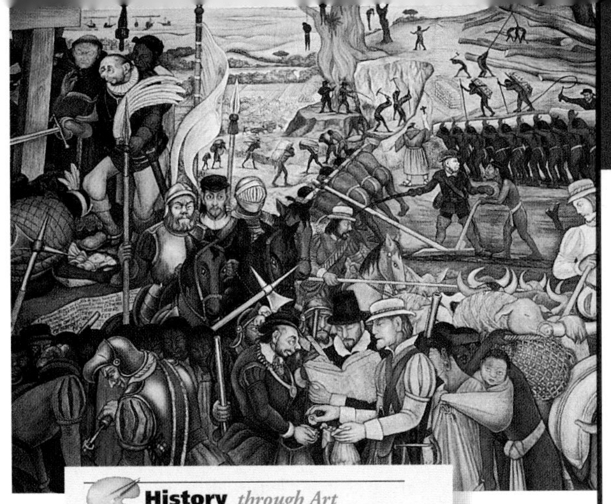

History *through Art*

***The Arrival of Cortez at Veracruz* (detail) by Diego Rivera, 1929–1935**
In this mural, what is Rivera saying about the impact of Europeans on Mexico's past?

Rivera sought to create a national art that would portray Mexico's past, especially its Aztec legends, as well as Mexican festivals and folk customs. His work also carried a political and social message. Rivera did not want people to forget the Mexican Revolution, which had overthrown the large landowners and the foreign interests that supported them.

Reading Check **Examining** How did Diego Rivera use his artistic talent as a political tool?

SECTION 4 ASSESSMENT

Checking for Understanding

1. **Define** oligarchy.
2. **Identify** Juan Vicente Gómez, Good Neighbor policy, Hipólito Irigoyen, Getúlio Vargas, Lázaro Cárdenas, PEMEX.
3. **Locate** Argentina, Chile, Brazil, Peru, Mexico.
4. **Explain** how Vargas's dictatorship ended.
5. **List** some of the industries the United States owned in Latin America.

Critical Thinking

6. **Examine** Why did the Great Depression cause many Latin American countries to improve their economic systems and gain more independence from foreign economic dominance?
7. **Compare and Contrast** Make a chart like the one below comparing and contrasting political struggles in Argentina and Brazil.

Argentina	Brazil

Analyzing Visuals

8. **Analyze** the photo on page 583. What does this photo reveal about what working conditions were like on Brazilian coffee plantations?

Writing About History

9. **Descriptive Writing** Using outside sources, find one or two examples of Diego Rivera's murals. In an essay, compare Rivera's paintings to the frescoes of medieval Italian painters like Giotto. How do Rivera's murals reflect the influence of Italian frescoes? How are they different?

CHAPTER 18
Section 4, 581–585

Answer: There was a single political party. The party selected presidential candidates who were then dutifully elected by the people.

History *through Art*

Answer: The mural shows Europeans dominating every aspect of Mexico and Mexican culture.

Reading Check

Answer: He sought to create a national art.

Reteaching Activity

Ask students to write a sentence for each boldfaced heading in this section.

4 CLOSE

Have students research Latin American artists and writers whose work dealt with nationalist issues. Then ask students to deliver brief oral reports describing how the artists' political beliefs shaped their work. Suggest that students bring in reproductions of artwork if possible. **L2**

SECTION 4 ASSESSMENT

1. Key terms are in blue.
2. Juan Vicente Gómez *(p. 582)*; Good Neighbor policy *(p. 582)*; Hipólito Irigoyen *(p. 583)*; Getúlio Vargas *(p. 583)*; Lázaro Cárdenas *(p. 584)*; PEMEX *(p. 585)*
3. See chapter maps.
4. The army forced him to resign.
5. copper-mining industry in Chile and Peru; oil industry in Mexico, Peru, and Bolivia
6. countries no longer could afford to import, resulted in the development of new industries
7. Argentina: oligarchy; army overthrew president, restored oligarchy; military officers overthrew government; Perón seized power; Brazil: oligarchy; military coup placed Vargas in power; Vargas forced to resign by army
8. required manual labor
9. Answers should be supported by examples.

GLENCOE TECHNOLOGY

MindJogger Videoquiz

Use the **MindJogger Videoquiz** to review Chapter 18 content.

 Available in VHS.

Using Key Terms

1. Mahatma **2.** ethnic cleansing **3.** genocide **4.** civil disobedience **5.** guerilla tactics **6.** oligarchy **7.** banana republics **8.** *zaibatsu* **9.** Pan-Africanism

Reviewing Key Facts

10. They questioned how a national home for the Jewish people could be established in a territory that was 98 percent Muslim.

11. *Comintern* is short for Communist International, a worldwide organization of Communist parties dedicated to the advancement of world revolution.

12. He introduced popular education, established factories, and modernized the economy. He took steps to break the power of the Islamic religion, abolishing the caliphate and forbidding women from wearing the veil. He gave women marriage and inheritance rights equal to men's and he gave women the right to vote.

13. The Communists were surrounded by Chiang Kai-shek's military strength; he had already been responsible for the Shanghai Massacre, and was determined to root out the Communists in their rural base.

14. The United States wanted to improve its relationship with Latin America.

15. to overthrow the warlords and to drive out imperialistic forces

16. One country exports raw materials to another and buys the other country's manufactured goods.

17. They passed the Government of India Act, which expanded the role of Indians in the governing process.

18. because there is only one party, which chooses all candidates for election

19. The largest *zaibatsu* controlled major portions of Japan's industrial sector, and the concentration of wealth led to economic inequalities. Inflation, a drastic population increase, and the Great Depression caused more hardships. Traditionalists blamed Western influence and promoted Japanese values. They opposed Japan's attempts to cooperate with Western powers and called for Japan to rely on its own strength to meet its needs and to dominate Asia.

20. Kenyatta said that foreign rule was destroying the traditional culture of native people in Africa.

Critical Thinking

21. It caused European Jews to flee to Palestine, where tensions increased between them and the original Muslim inhabitants.

CHAPTER 18 ASSESSMENT and ACTIVITIES

Using Key Terms

1. The name given by his followers to Mohandas Gandhi was _____, which means "great soul."
2. Serbian forces in the recent war in Bosnia followed a policy called _____ when they tried to eliminate Muslims from their land.
3. A policy of killing people of a particular ethnic or racial group is called _____.
4. An advocate of nonviolence, Gandhi urged _____ as a powerful method to achieve justice and bring an end to oppressive British rule in India.
5. When Mao Zedong's forces were outnumbered at their rural base in Jiangxi Province, they used _____ such as sabotage and subterfuge to fight Chiang Kai-shek's Nationalist troops.
6. Argentina, Brazil, and Mexico were controlled by _____, or governments where only a select group of people exercises control.
7. Chinese peasants did not support Chiang Kai-shek because he did not favor _____ .
8. The concentration of various manufacturing processes within a single Japanese industry is called a _____, or large financial and industrial corporation.
9. _____ was a movement stressing unity of all Africans.

Reviewing Key Facts

10. **Citizenship** Why were many Arabs opposed to the Balfour Declaration?
11. **Government** Identify the Comintern and explain why it was formed.
12. **Government** What reforms did Atatürk implement to transform the Turkish Republic into a modern and secular state?
13. **History** What happened to cause Chinese Communists to undertake the Long March in 1933?
14. **History** What did the United States hope to accomplish through its Good Neighbor policy toward Latin America?
15. **History** Why did the Nationalists and Communists in China form an alliance in 1928?
16. **Economics** Explain an import-export economy.
17. **Government** What did the British do to make Indian people less opposed to their colonial government in 1935?
18. **Citizenship** Why do people in some apparently democratic Latin American nations have little voice in their country's government?
19. **Economics** Explain how the entrenched system of *zaibatsu* contributed to increased nationalism and a move toward militarism in Japan.
20. **Citizenship** What message did Jomo Kenyatta use as the basic theme of his book *Facing Mount Kenya?*

Critical Thinking

21. **Cause and Effect** How did harsh treatment of Jewish people in Europe create problems for Arab people in the Middle East?
22. **Evaluating** How did Chiang Kai-shek's fear of communism cause him to alienate many intellectuals and political moderates?
23. **Making Generalizations** What was the cultural impact of World War I on Africans? How did the political status of Africa change after the war?

Chapter Summary

Between the two World Wars, a growing sense of nationalism inspired many countries to seek their independence from foreign rulers, as shown in the chart below.

Middle East	Africa and Asia	China	Latin America
The decline of the Ottoman Empire results in the emergence of many new Arab states.	Black Africans who fought in World War I become more politically active. They organize reform movements then call for independence.	In 1923, the Nationalists and the Communists form an alliance to oppose the warlords and drive the imperialist powers out of China.	After the Great Depression, Latin American countries work to become economically independent by creating new industries to produce goods that were formerly imported.

586

Self-Check Quiz

Visit the *Glencoe World History—Modern Times* Web site at wh.mt.glencoe.com and click on **Chapter 18–Self-Check Quiz** to prepare for the Chapter Test.

Writing About History

24. **Expository Writing** Nationalism first became a significant political force in the movement against Napoleon. Write an essay comparing the early nationalist movements to the later battles against imperialism discussed in this chapter.

Analyzing Sources

Chiang Kai-shek declared his commitment to Sun Yat-sen's plans for building a new nation. Chiang announced a period of political training, as described by Sun in the following quote.

> "China . . . needs a republican government just as a boy needs school. As a schoolboy must have good teachers and helpful friends, so the Chinese people, being for the first time under republican rule, must have a farsighted revolutionary government for their training. This calls for the period of political tutelage, which is a necessary transitional stage from monarchy to republicanism. Without this, disorder will be unavoidable."

25. What did Chiang Kai-shek mean when he compared China to a boy in school?
26. What does the quote seem to say, compared to what you think it really means? Is there a self-serving bias in Sun's statement? If so, explain.

Applying Technology Skills

27. **Using the Internet** Use the Internet to determine how the contemporary governments of Argentina and Brazil compare with the dictatorships that ruled these countries in the 1930s.
28. **Using the Internet** Use the Internet to learn more about Jomo Kenyatta, Léopold Senghor, Nnamdi Azikiwe, or other nationalist leaders who worked to end colonial rule in Africa. What methods did they use and how successful were they?

Making Decisions

29. Imagine that you are a female American foreign exchange student. Which Middle Eastern country would you choose to live in for a year? Discuss the reasons for your choice and also the concessions that would be required of you.

NATIONAL GEOGRAPHIC **Geography of China and Japan, c. 1920**

Analyzing Maps and Charts

Use the map above to answer the following questions.

30. Near what latitudes are the cities of Beijing and Tokyo located?
31. Name the bodies of water that separate Japan from North Korea and South Korea, and Japan from China.
32. List three geographical features of China.
33. Compare this map to the map shown on page 572. What major territory did Japan acquire between the date indicated on the above map and 1933?

Standardized Test Practice

Directions: Choose the best answer to the question below.

Which of the following is a true statement about the relationship between World War I and nationalism?

A World War I brought nationalist movements to a standstill.

B Most nationalist movements had reached their goals by the conclusion of World War I.

C The weakening of European countries fostered national independence movements.

D World War I helped the European economy, which fueled nationalist movements.

Test-Taking Tip: Read each answer choice carefully and eliminate any statements that you know are false. Getting rid of these wrong answer choices will help you find the correct answer.

22. He suppressed all opposition and censored free speech.
23. Africans in the war learned about ideas of freedom, nationalism, and equality from the West and they began to demand a voice in their own government. Culturally, the aftermath of the war led to the promotion of the unity of all Africans, African cultural heritage, and support for independence.

Writing about History

24. Answers should be supported by examples and logical arguments.

Analyzing Sources

25. Answers will vary. It sets the scene for the comparisons that follow. He saw China as a big, uneducated child that needed to grow up to be a responsible adult (republic).

HISTORY Online

Have students visit the Web site at wh.mt.glencoe.com to review Chapter 18 and take the Self-Check Quiz.

26. Sun Yat-sen believed the Chinese people were not ready for self-government and that he had to provide leadership. It justifies totalitarian rule.

Applying Technology Skills

27. Students should compare the contemporary governments of Argentina and Brazil and their counterparts during the 1930s.
28. Answers should be supported by references, examples, and logical arguments.

Making Decisions

29. Answers will vary but should be supported by logical arguments and based on facts.

Analyzing Maps and Charts

30. Beijing: 40°N; Tokyo: 35°N
31. Sea of Japan; East China Sea
32. desert, mountains, rivers, plains, coast
33. Manchuria

Standardized Test Practice

Answer: C

Answer Explanation: Throughout the chapter, nationalist movements began after World War I. Look for cause and effect statements.

Bonus Question ?

Ask students to identify the evidence that supports the following statement: "The United States has always cast a large shadow over Latin America." L2

Chapter 19 Resources

Timesaving Tools

TeacherWorks™ All-In-One Planner and Resource Center

- **Interactive Teacher Edition** Access your Teacher Wraparound Edition and your classroom resources with a few easy clicks.
- **Interactive Lesson Planner** Planning has never been easier! Organize your week, month, semester, or year with all the lesson helps you need to make teaching creative, timely, and relevant.

Use Glencoe's **Presentation Plus!** multimedia teacher tool to easily present dynamic lessons that visually excite your students. Using Microsoft PowerPoint® you can customize the presentations to create your own personalized lessons.

Teaching Transparencies

Graphic Organizer Student Activity 19 Transparency

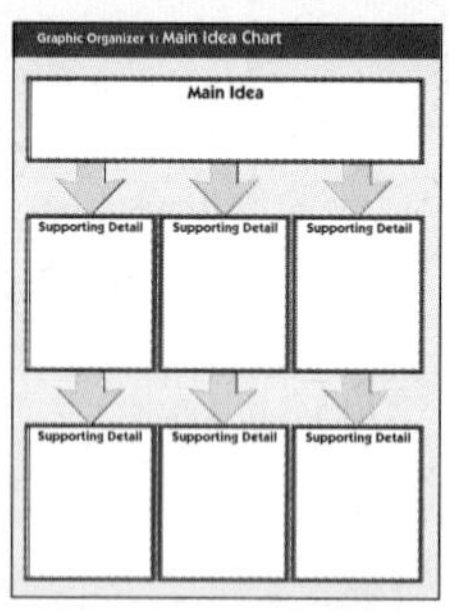

Chapter Transparency 19

Map Overlay Transparency 19

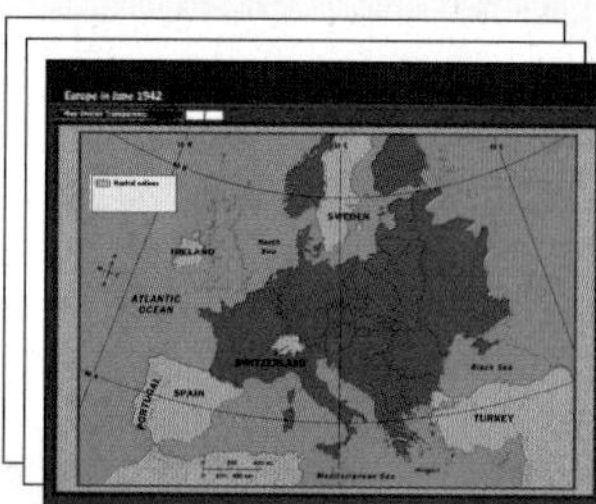

Application and Enrichment

Enrichment Activity 19

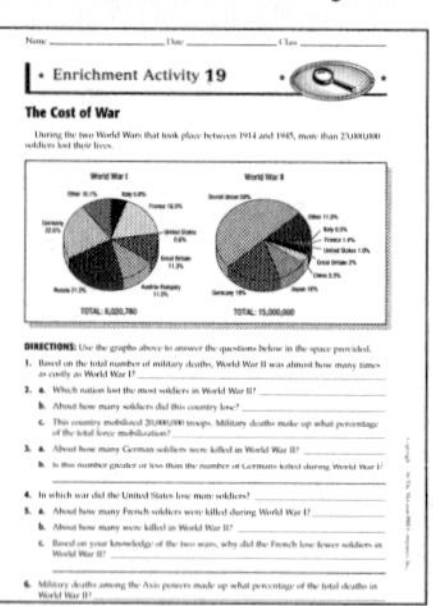

Primary Source Reading 19

History Simulation Activity 19

Historical Significance Activity 19

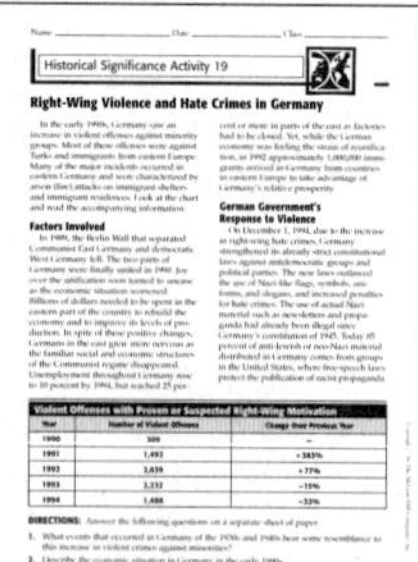

Cooperative Learning Activity 19

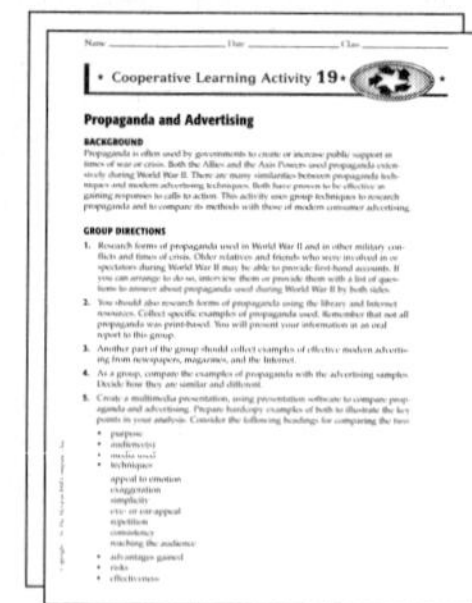

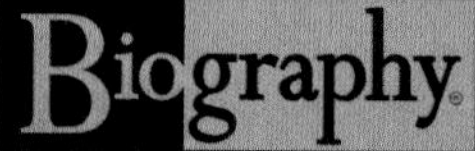

THE HISTORY CHANNEL.

The following videotape programs are available from Glencoe as supplements to Chapter 19:

- **World War II: The War Chronicles** (ISBN 1-56501-484-7)
- **The War in Europe** (ISBN 1-56501-993-8)
- **The War in the Pacific** (ISBN 1-56501-994-6)
- **Churchill and the War Cabinet Room** (ISBN 1-56501-813-3)
- **The Decision to Drop the Bomb** (ISBN 1-56501-600-9)
- **Anne Frank** (ISBN 0-7670-1409-X)

To order, call Glencoe at 1-800-334-7344. To find classroom resources to accompany many of these videos, check the following home pages:
A&E Television: www.aande.com
The History Channel: www.historychannel.com

Chapter 19 Resources

Review and Reinforcement

Linking Past and Present Activity 19

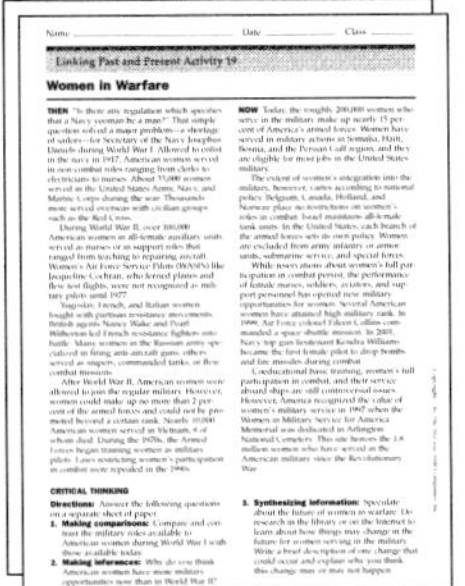

Time Line Activity 19

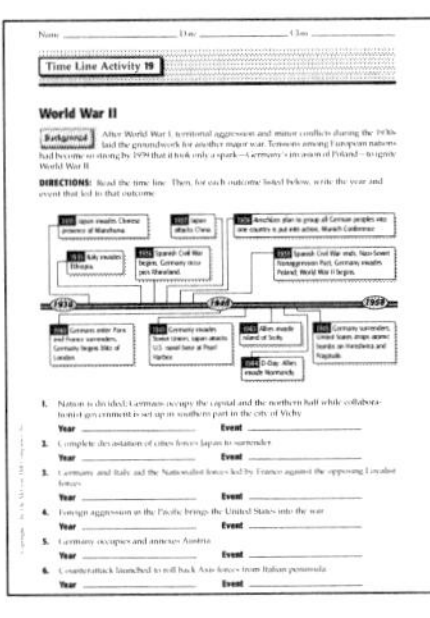

Reteaching Activity 19

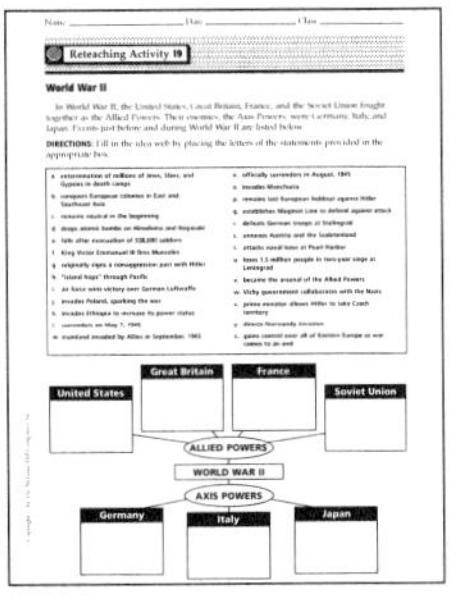

Vocabulary Activity 19

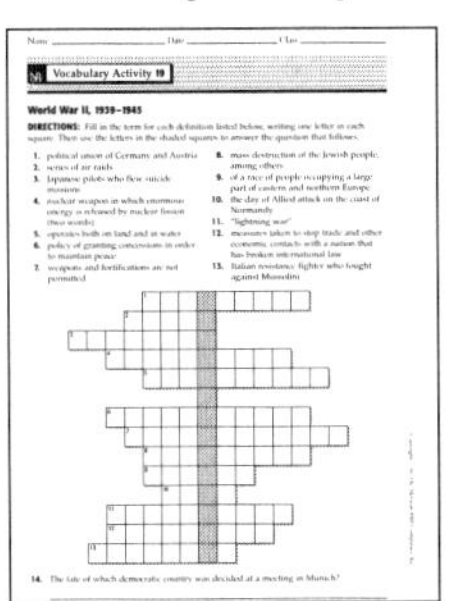

Critical Thinking Skills Activity 19

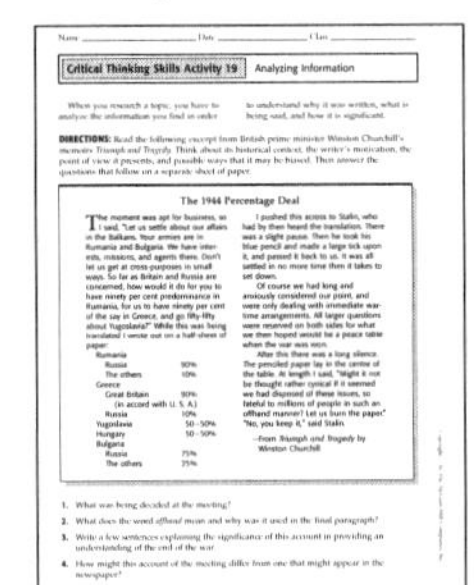

Assessment and Evaluation

Chapter 19 Test Form A

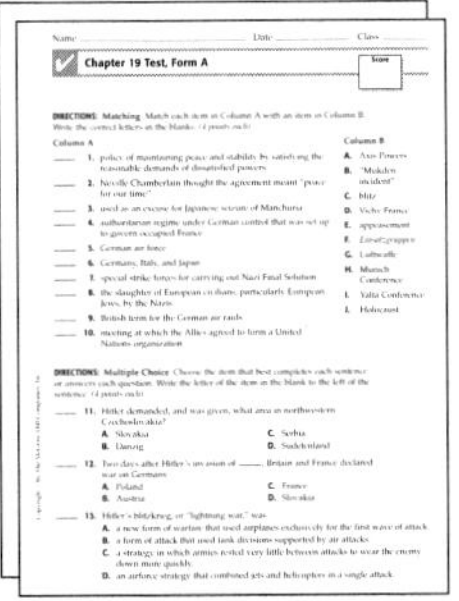

Chapter 19 Test Form B

Performance Assessment Activity 19

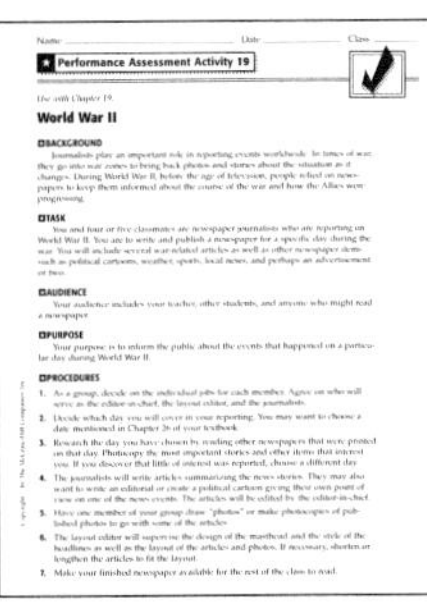

ExamView® Pro Testmaker CD-ROM

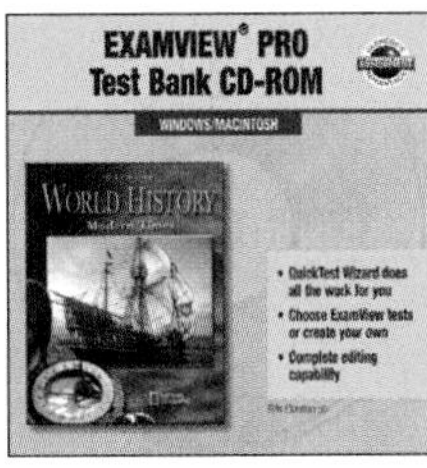

Standardized Test Skills Practice Workbook Activity 19

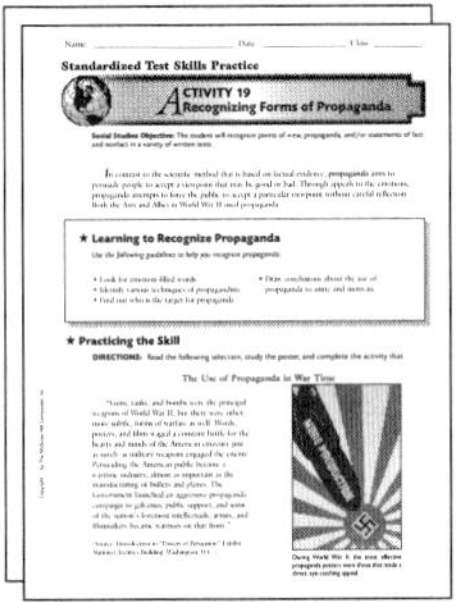

Interdisciplinary Activities

Mapping History Activity 19

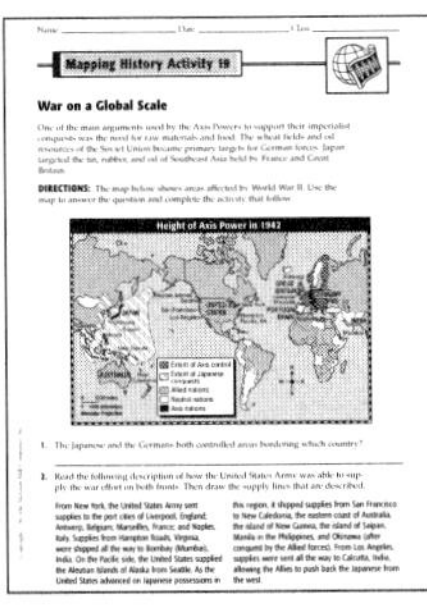

World Art and Music Activity 19

History and Geography Activity 19

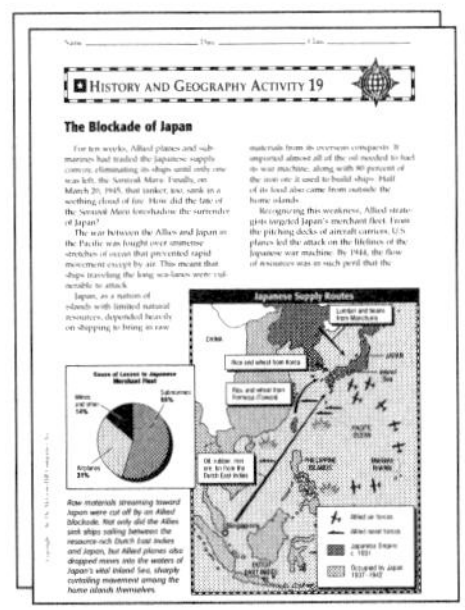

People in World History Activity 19

Multimedia

- Vocabulary PuzzleMaker CD-ROM
- Interactive Tutor Self-Assessment CD-ROM
- ExamView® Pro Testmaker CD-ROM
- Audio Program
- World History Primary Source Document Library CD-ROM
- MindJogger Videoquiz
- Presentation Plus! CD-ROM
- TeacherWorks CD-ROM
- Interactive Student Edition CD-ROM
- The World History—Modern Times Video Program

Spanish Resources

The following Spanish language materials are available in the Spanish Resources Binder:

- Spanish Guided Reading Activities
- Spanish Reteaching Activities
- Spanish Quizzes and Tests
- Spanish Vocabulary Activities
- Spanish Summaries

Chapter 19 Resources

SECTION RESOURCES

Daily Objectives	Reproducible Resources	Multimedia Resources
SECTION 1 **Paths to War** 1. Explain how Adolf Hitler's theory of Aryan racial domination laid the foundation for aggressive expansion outside of Germany. 2. Specify how the actions and ambitions of Japan and Germany paved the way of the outbreak of World War II.	Reproducible Lesson Plan 19–1 Daily Lecture and Discussion Notes 19–1 Guided Reading Activity 19–1* Section Quiz 19–1* Reading Essentials and Study Guide 19–1	Daily Focus Skills Transparency 19–1 Interactive Tutor Self-Assessment CD-ROM ExamView® Pro Testmaker CD-ROM Presentation Plus! CD-ROM
SECTION 2 **The Course of World War II** 1. Discuss how the bombing of Pearl Harbor created a global war between the Allied and the Axis forces. 2. Describe how Allied perseverance and effective military operations, as well as Axis miscalculations, brought an end to the war.	Reproducible Lesson Plan 19–2 Daily Lecture and Discussion Notes 19–2 Guided Reading Activity 19–2* Section Quiz 19–2* Reading Essentials and Study Guide 19–2	Daily Focus Skills Transparency 19–2 Interactive Tutor Self-Assessment CD-ROM ExamView® Pro Testmaker CD-ROM Presentation Plus! CD-ROM
SECTION 3 **The New Order and the Holocaust** 1. Report how Adolf Hitler's philosophy of Aryan superiority led to the Holocaust. 2. Analyze how the Japanese conquest of Southeast Asia forced millions of native peoples to labor for the Japanese war machine.	Reproducible Lesson Plan 19–3 Daily Lecture and Discussion Notes 19–3 Guided Reading Activity 19–3* Section Quiz 19–3* Reading Essentials and Study Guide 19–3	Daily Focus Skills Transparency 19–3 Interactive Tutor Self-Assessment CD-ROM ExamView® Pro Testmaker CD-ROM Presentation Plus! CD-ROM
SECTION 4 **The Home Front and the Aftermath of the War** 1. Discuss how World War II left a lasting impression on civilian populations. 2. Summarize how the end of the war created a new set of problems for the Allies as the West came into conflict with the Soviet Union.	Reproducible Lesson Plan 19–4 Daily Lecture and Discussion Notes 19–4 Guided Reading Activity 19–4* Section Quiz 19–4* Reteaching Activity 19* Reading Essentials and Study Guide 19–4	Daily Focus Skills Transparency 19–4 Interactive Tutor Self-Assessment CD-ROM ExamView® Pro Testmaker CD-ROM Presentation Plus! CD-ROM

0:00 **OUT OF TIME?**
Assign the Chapter 19 **Reading Essentials and Study Guide.**

*Also Available in Spanish

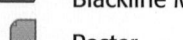

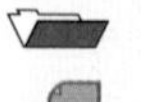 Blackline Master  Transparency  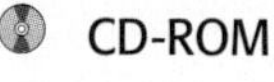 CD-ROM   DVD
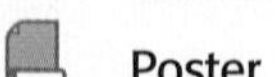  Poster 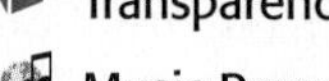 Music Program · Audio Program · Videocassette

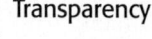

Chapter 19 Resources

NATIONAL GEOGRAPHIC Teacher's Corner

INDEX TO NATIONAL GEOGRAPHIC MAGAZINE

The following articles relate to this chapter:

- "Hiroshima," by Ted Gup, August 1995.
- "Blueprints for Victory," by John F. Shupe, May 1995.
- "The Wings of War," by Thomas B. Allen, March 1994.
- "Pearl Harbor: A Return to the Day of Infamy," by Thomas B. Allen, December 1991.
- "Remembering the Blitz," by Cameron Thomas, July 1999.
- "Ghosts of War in the South Pacific," by Peter Benchley, April 1988.

ADDITIONAL NATIONAL GEOGRAPHIC SOCIETY PRODUCTS

To order the following, call National Geographic at 1-800-368-2728:

- *Lost Fleet of Guadalcanal* (Video)
- *Search for Battleship Bismarck* (Video)

NGS ONLINE

Access National Geographic's new dynamic MapMachine Web site and other geography resources at:
www.nationalgeographic.com
www.nationalgeographic.com/maps

KEY TO ABILITY LEVELS

Teaching strategies have been coded.

- L1 BASIC activities for all students
- L2 AVERAGE activities for average to above-average students
- L3 CHALLENGING activities for above-average students
- ELL ENGLISH LANGUAGE LEARNER activities

Block Schedule

Activities that are suited to use within the block scheduling framework are identified by:

Use our Web site for additional resources. All essential content is covered in the Student Edition.

You and your students can visit www.wh.mt.glencoe.com, the Web site companion to *Glencoe World History—Modern Times.* This innovative integration of electronic and print media offers your students a wealth of opportunities. The student text directs students to the Web site for the following options:

- **Chapter Overviews**
- **Self-Check Quizzes**
- **Student Web Activities**
- **Textbook Updates**

Answers to the Student Web Activities are provided for you in the **Web Activity Lesson Plans.** Additional Web resources and Interactive Tutor Puzzles are also available.

From the Classroom of...

Loretta Smithson
Elsinore High School
Lake Elsinore, California

Experiencing the Holocaust

Organize the class into small groups to research the roots and results of anti-Semitism. Assign each group a different area to research: (1.) a history of the Hebrew people, including the Diaspora (A.D. 70); (2.) a history of Jewish expulsion from European countries (e.g., Spain, 1493); (3.) excerpts from books, writings, or speeches by famous people (e.g., Martin Luther); (4.) excerpts from books or stories of the Holocaust (e.g., *The Blue Tattoo*); (5.) reasons given by Nazis for their treatment of European Jews; and (6.) world reactions to Nazi treatment of Jews.

Provide students with the condensed materials they need for their categories, and encourage them to prepare their information in interesting ways for group presentations, such as charts, maps, diagrams, and slides.

After group presentations, let students share their analyses of the materials provided, then conduct a class discussion on the meaning of genocide and its implications for world events in recent years (in Kosovo, for example).

Introducing CHAPTER 19

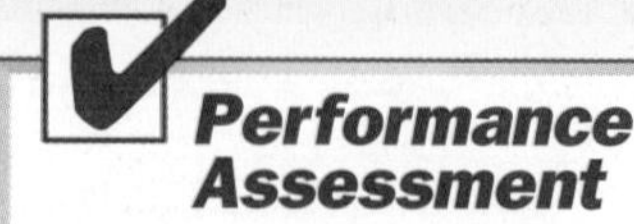

Performance Assessment

Refer to Activity 19 in the Performance Assessment Activities and Rubrics booklet.

The Impact Today

Remind students that World War II brought advances in medicine, transportation, and weapons. Today the World War II generation is honored as "The Greatest Generation" for the sacrifices they made. Have students identify and compile a list of the changes that resulted from the world wars of the twentieth century. Have students share their lists during a class discussion and ask them to refer to these lists as they study this chapter and those that follow. L1

GLENCOE TECHNOLOGY

The World History—Modern Times Video Program

To learn more about Jewish life under Hitler, students can view the Chapter 19 video, "The Holocaust," from **The World History—Modern Times Video Program.**

MindJogger Videoquiz

Use the **MindJogger Videoquiz** to preview Chapter 19 content.

 Available in VHS.

CHAPTER 19 World War II

1939–1945

Key Events

As you read this chapter, look for the key events in the history of World War II.

- *Adolf Hitler's philosophy of Aryan superiority led to World War II in Europe and was also the source of the Holocaust.*
- *Two separate and opposing alliances, the Allies and the Axis, waged a worldwide war.*
- *World War II left lasting impressions on civilian populations.*

The Impact Today

The events that occurred during this time period still impact our lives today.

- *By the end of World War II, the balance of power had shifted away from Europe.*
- *Germany and Japan's search for expanded "living space" is comparable to nations fighting over borders today.*
- *Atomic weapons pose a threat to all nations.*

World History—Modern Times Video *The Chapter 19 video,* "The Holocaust," *illustrates the horrors of Hitler's Final Solution.*

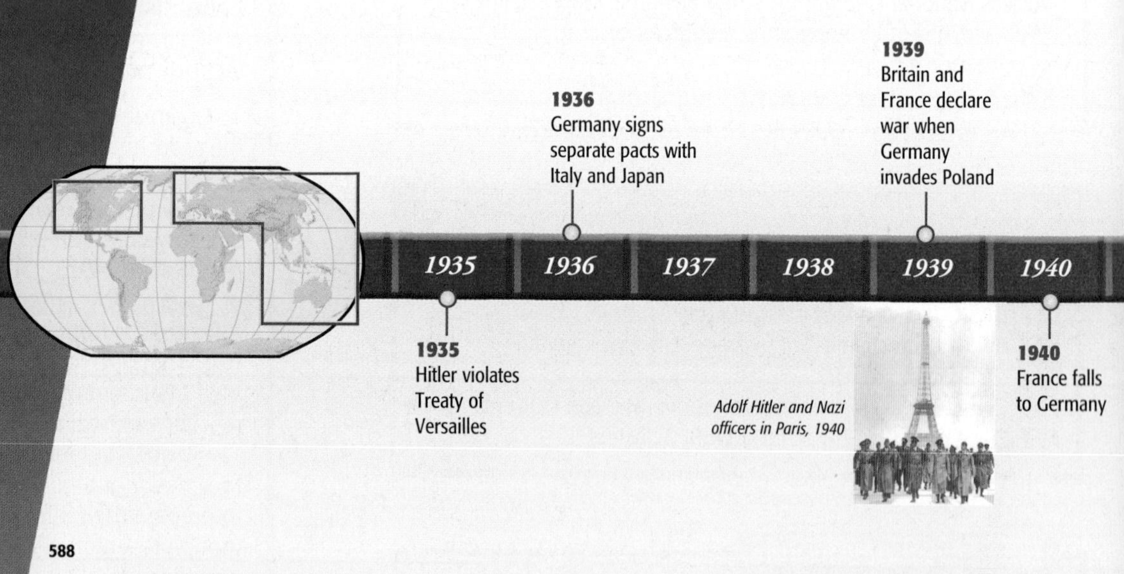
1935
1936
1937
1938
1939
1940
1936 Germany signs separate pacts with Italy and Japan
1939 Britain and France declare war when Germany invades Poland
1935 Hitler violates Treaty of Versailles
1940 France falls to Germany

Adolf Hitler and Nazi officers in Paris, 1940

588

TWO-MINUTE LESSON LAUNCHER

In just over 20 years after the end of World War I, "the war to end all wars," the world was engulfed in war again. Ask students to identify factors that contributed to both world wars. Then have students predict the likelihood of another world war. Ask students to identify real countries, issues, and leaders that they believe have the potential to trigger a third world war. Have the class discuss whether or not any of these scenarios is plausible. What steps (for example, treaties, UN involvement, humanitarian aid, economic loans) could be taken to avert potential crises? L2

Introducing
CHAPTER 19

Chapter Objectives

After studying this chapter, students should be able to:

1. identify the steps taken by Germany and Japan that led to the beginning of World War II;
2. describe the successes of Germany and Japan in the early years of the war;
3. list the major events of the last years of the war;
4. explain the causes and results of the Holocaust;
5. explain the conditions of the peace settlement and the ways in which the peace settlement led to the Cold War.

Chapter Overview

Introduce students to chapter content and key terms by having them access **Chapter Overview 19** at wh.mt.glencoe.com.

The Marine Corps War Memorial in Arlington County, Virginia, depicts marines raising the American flag on Iwo Jima in February 1945.

Self-Portrait with a Jewish Identity Card by Felix Nussbaum, 1943

Atomic bomb dropped on Hiroshima

1941 United States enters war after Japan attacks Pearl Harbor

1942 Nazi death camps in full operation

1943

1944

1945 Japanese surrender after United States drops atomic bombs on Japan

1945 Germany surrenders

Soldiers and civilians celebrate VE-Day, Paris

1946 Churchill proclaims existence of "iron curtain" in Europe

HISTORY Online

Chapter Overview

Visit the *Glencoe World History—Modern Times* Web site at wh.mt.glencoe.com and click on **Chapter 19–Chapter Overview** to preview chapter information.

Time Line Activity

As they read this chapter, have students interpret the time line on these pages by explaining the significance of the dates 1939 through 1945. L2

MORE ABOUT THE ART

Iwo Jima was a ferocious World War II battle in the Pacific that began in February 1945. Because the island of Iwo Jima is only 650 miles (1,046 km) from Tokyo, Japanese soldiers planned to defend it to the last man. After five days of intense fighting, the United States Marines were able to raise the flag. The moment was captured by a photographer. The photo caused a sensation in the United States. Within days, the public and government leaders were clamoring for a commemorative statue. Three of the original soldiers who raised the American flag survived the war and were used as models for the statue. The images of the other two soldiers were based on photographs. The inscription on the memorial reads, "Uncommon Valor was a Common Virtue."

CHAPTER PREVIEW

Introducing
A Story That Matters

Depending on the ability levels of your students, select from the following questions to reinforce the reading of *A Story That Matters.*

- Why would Hitler regard democracy as a "cancer"? *(He believed that certain races, certain people, were superior to others, and thus should be in control, whereas in a democracy all people are equal.)*
- What does Hitler mean by "ruthless Germanization?" *(fast, quick domination of lands and cultures by Germany to provide for the expansion of what Hitler believed was the superior race)*
- Ask students to study the maps on page 598, in the Reference Atlas, and in outside sources to identify the countries that took part in World War II, and those that did not. **L2**

About the Art

Before his entry into politics, Hitler was a struggling artist. As leader of Germany, Hitler mastered the art of propaganda. He used both auditory and visual means to appeal to the people of Germany. Simple slogans were developed and chanted at rallies. Visual elements, such as the "*Heil*-Hitler" salute, were used to create support for Hitler's Nazi Party policies. The poster combines a picture of Hitler with one of his slogans into an image that promotes the basic goals of fascism.

CHAPTER PREVIEW A Story That Matters

Poster, c. 1938, which proclaims "One People, one State, one Leader!"

After becoming dictator in 1933, Hitler often held large rallies to inspire the loyalty of Germans.

Hitler's Vision

On February 3, 1933, Adolf Hitler met secretly with Germany's leading generals. He had been appointed chancellor of Germany only four days before and was by no means assured that he would remain in office for long. Nevertheless, he spoke with confidence.

Hitler told the generals about his desire to remove the "cancer of democracy," create "the highest authoritarian state leadership," and forge a new domestic unity. All Germans would need to realize that "only a struggle can save us and that everything else must be subordinated to this idea." The youth especially would have to be trained and their wills strengthened "to fight with all means."

Hitler went on to say that Germany must rearm by instituting a military draft. Leaders must ensure that the men who were going to be drafted were not "poisoned by pacifism, Marxism, or Bolshevism." Once Germany had regained its military strength, how should this strength be used? Hitler had an answer. Because Germany's living space was too small for its people, it must prepare for "the conquest of new living space in the east and its ruthless Germanization."

Even before he had consolidated his power, Hitler had a clear vision of his goals. Reaching those goals meant another European war. Although World War I has been described as a total war, World War II was even more so. It was fought on a scale unprecedented in history and led to the most widespread human-made destruction that the world had ever seen.

Why It Matters

World War II in Europe was clearly Hitler's war. Other countries may have helped make the war possible by not resisting Germany earlier, before it grew strong, but it was Nazi Germany's actions that made the war inevitable. Globally, World War II was more than just Hitler's war. It consisted of two conflicts. One arose, as mentioned above, from the ambitions of Germany in Europe. The other arose from the ambitions of Japan in Asia. By 1941, with the involvement of the United States in both conflicts, these two conflicts merged into one global world war.

History and You The decision by the United States to use atomic bombs against Japan led to the end of World War II. Find two contrasting views on the potential of nuclear warfare today and analyze the perspectives.

HISTORY AND YOU

Had Hitler succeeded in destroying democracy and establishing German world domination, life today would be very different. Democratic nations, working together, ensured that democracy and democratic ideals would persevere by stopping German and Japanese aggression. At the end of World War II, nations joined together to form organizations such as NATO, CETO, and the United Nations to ensure mutual protection and to seek peaceful solutions to international conflicts. Ask students to speculate on how their lives might be different if Hitler had been victorious in Europe.

SECTION 1 Paths to War

Guide to Reading

Main Ideas
- Adolf Hitler's theory of Aryan racial domination laid the foundation for aggressive expansion outside of Germany.
- The actions and ambitions of Japan and Germany paved the way for the outbreak of World War II.

Key Terms
demilitarized, appeasement, sanction

People to Identify
Adolf Hitler, Benito Mussolini, Joseph Stalin, Chiang Kai-shek

Places to Locate
Rhineland, Sudetenland, Manchukuo

Preview Questions
1. What agreement was reached at the Munich Conference?
2. Why did Germany believe it needed more land?

Reading Strategy
Categorizing Information Create a chart listing examples of Japanese aggression and German aggression prior to the outbreak of World War II.

Japanese Aggression	German Aggression

Preview of Events

1931 · 1932 · 1933 · 1934 · 1935 · 1936 · 1937 · 1938 · 1939

- **1931** Japanese forces invade Manchuria
- **1936** Hitler and Mussolini create Rome-Berlin Axis
- **1937** Japanese seize Chinese capital
- **1938** Hitler annexes Austria
- **1939** World War II begins

Voices from the Past

Winston Churchill

After the leaders of France and Great Britain gave in to Hitler's demands on Czechoslovakia in 1938, Winston Churchill spoke to the British House of Commons:

> "I will begin by saying what everybody would like to ignore or forget but which must nevertheless be stated, namely, that we have sustained a total and unmitigated defeat. . . . And I will say this, that I believe the Czechs, left to themselves and told they were going to get no help from the Western Powers, would have been able to make better terms than they have got. . . . We are in the presence of a disaster of the first magnitude which has befallen Great Britain and France. . . . And do not suppose that this is the end. This is only the beginning of the reckoning."
>
> —***Parliamentary Debates,*** **London, 1938**

Churchill believed that Hitler's actions would lead to another war. He proved to be right.

The German Path to War

World War II in Europe had its beginnings in the ideas of **Adolf Hitler.** He believed that Aryans, particularly Germans, were superior to all other races and nationalities. Consequently, Hitler believed that Germany was capable of building a great civilization. To be a great power, however, Germany needed more land to support a larger population.

Already in the 1920s, Hitler had indicated that a Nazi regime would find this land to the east—in the Soviet Union. Germany therefore must prepare for war with the Soviet Union. Once the Soviet Union had been conquered, according to Hitler, its land would be resettled by German peasants. The Slavic peoples could

SECTION RESOURCES

Reproducible Masters
- Reproducible Lesson Plan 19–1
- Daily Lecture and Discussion Notes 19–1
- Guided Reading Activity 19–1
- Section Quiz 19–1
- Reading Essentials and Study Guide 19–1

Transparencies
- Daily Focus Skills Transparency 19–1

Multimedia
- Interactive Tutor Self-Assessment CD-ROM
- ExamView® Pro Testmaker CD-ROM
- Presentation Plus! CD-ROM

1 FOCUS

Section Overview

This section describes Hitler's racial theories and how the expansionist activities of Germany and Japan led to World War II.

BELLRINGER
Skillbuilder Activity

Project transparency and have students answer questions.

Available as a blackline master.

Daily Focus Skills Transparency 19–1

Guide to Reading

Answers to Graphic: Japanese: seized Manchuria; invaded China; cooperated with Nazi Germany; launched surprise attack on United States;
German: expanded armed forces; sent troops into Rhineland; annexed Austria; invaded Poland

Preteaching Vocabulary: Discuss the meaning of the word *appeasement.* In what ways did European nations follow a policy of appeasement and what was the result?

2 TEACH

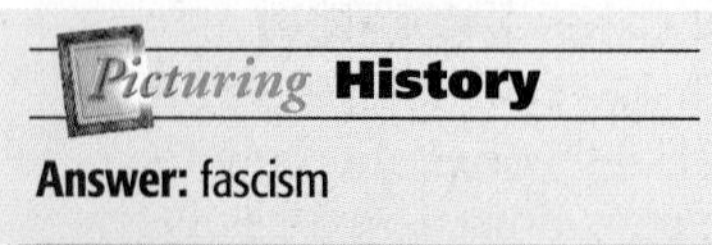

Picturing History

Answer: fascism

Daily Lecture and Discussion Notes 19–1

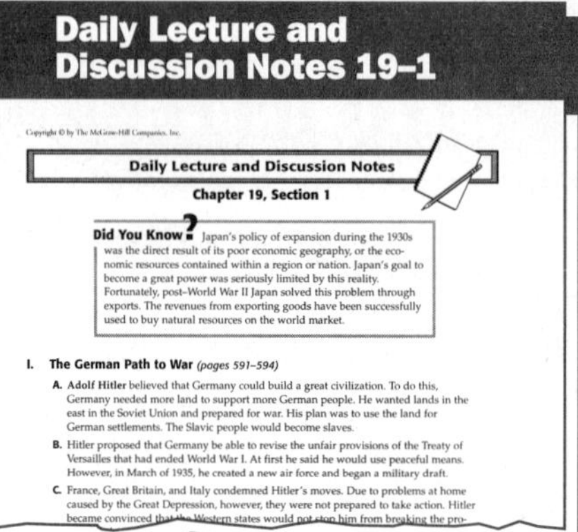

Daily Lecture and Discussion Notes

Chapter 19, Section 1

Did You Know? Japan's policy of expansion during the 1930s was the direct result of its poor economic geography, or the economic resources contained within a region or nation. Japan's goal to become a great power was seriously limited by this reality. Fortunately, post–World War II Japan solved this problem through exports. The revenues from exporting goods have been successfully used to buy natural resources on the world market.

I. **The German Path to War** *(pages 591–594)*

A. **Adolf Hitler** believed that Germany could build a great civilization. To do this, Germany needed more land to support more German people. He wanted lands in the east in the Soviet Union and prepared for war. His plan was to use the land for German settlements. The Slavic people would become slaves.

B. Hitler proposed that Germany be able to revise the unfair provisions of the Treaty of Versailles that had ended World War I. At first he said he would use peaceful means. However, in March of 1935, he created a new air force and began a military draft.

C. France, Great Britain, and Italy condemned Hitler's moves. Due to problems at home caused by the Great Depression, however, they were not prepared to take action. Hitler became convinced that the Western states would not stop him from breaking the pro-

CURRICULUM CONNECTION

Journalism Have students research and write a brief report on the work of one of the World War II correspondents or journalists such as Edward R. Murrow, Alan Moorehead, Robert Capa, Margaret Bourke-White, Max Alpert, or Henri Cartier-Bresson who gained fame due to their work during the war. L2

Enrich

Have students research the reasons for the downfall of Neville Chamberlain. Then guide the class in a discussion of the reasons for Great Britain's change of attitude toward Germany when Winston Churchill became prime minister. L2

be used as slave labor to build the Third Reich, an Aryan racial state that Hitler thought would dominate Europe for a thousand years.

The First Steps After World War I, the Treaty of Versailles had limited Germany's military power. As chancellor, Hitler, posing as a man of peace, stressed that Germany wished to revise the unfair provisions of the treaty by peaceful means. Germany, he said, only wanted its rightful place among the European states.

On March 9, 1935, however, Hitler announced the creation of a new air force. One week later, he began a military draft that would expand Germany's army from 100,000 to 550,000 troops. These steps were in direct violation of the Treaty of Versailles.

France, Great Britain, and Italy condemned Germany's actions and warned against future aggressive steps. In the midst of the Great Depression, however, these nations were distracted by their own internal problems and did nothing further.

Hitler was convinced that the Western states had no intention of using force to maintain the Treaty of Versailles. Hence, on March 7, 1936, he sent German troops into the **Rhineland.** The Rhineland was part of Germany, but, according to the Treaty of Versailles, it was a demilitarized area. That is, Germany was not permitted to have weapons or fortifications there. France had the right to use force against any violation of the demilitarized Rhineland but would not act without British support.

Great Britain did not support the use of force against Germany, however. The British government viewed the occupation of German territory by German troops as a reasonable action by a dissatisfied power. The London *Times* noted that the Germans were only "going into their own back garden." Great Britain thus began to practice a policy of appeasement. This policy was based on the belief that if European states satisfied the reasonable demands of dissatisfied powers, the dissatisfied powers would be content, and stability and peace would be achieved in Europe.

New Alliances Meanwhile, Hitler gained new allies. **Benito Mussolini** had long dreamed of creating a new Roman Empire in the Mediterranean, and, in October 1935, Fascist Italy invaded Ethiopia. Angered by French and British opposition to his invasion, Mussolini welcomed Hitler's support. He began to draw closer to the German dictator.

In 1936, both Germany and Italy sent troops to Spain to help General Francisco Franco in the Spanish Civil War. In October 1936, Mussolini and Hitler made an agreement recognizing their common political and economic interests. One month later, Mussolini spoke of the new alliance between Italy and Germany, called the Rome-Berlin Axis. Also in November, Germany and Japan signed the Anti-Comintern Pact, promising a common front against communism.

Union With Austria By 1937, Germany was once more a "world power," as Hitler proclaimed. He was convinced that neither France nor Great Britain would provide much opposition to his plans. In 1938, he decided to pursue one of his goals: *Anschluss* (ANSH•luhs), or union, with Austria, his native land.

By threatening Austria with invasion, Hitler forced the Austrian chancellor to put Austrian Nazis in charge of the government. The new government promptly invited German troops to enter Austria and "help" in maintaining law and order. One day later, on March 13, 1938, after his triumphal return to his native land, Hitler annexed Austria to Germany.

Picturing History

This 1937 Italian illustration depicts Hitler and Mussolini. What ideology brought Hitler and Mussolini together?

EXTENDING THE CONTENT

Benito Mussolini The *Fasci di Combattimento* were founded in March 1919 by Mussolini and other veterans of World War I. Taking their name from the fasces, an ancient symbol of Roman discipline, this nationalistic, antiliberal, and antisocialist movement attracted lower middle-class support in turbulent postwar Milan. Fascism grew rapidly after the mid-1920s, winning support in the countryside, where its black-shirt militia attacked peasant and socialist groups. By 1926, Mussolini had created an alliance with the army and the king, ultimately transforming the country into a single-party, totalitarian regime.

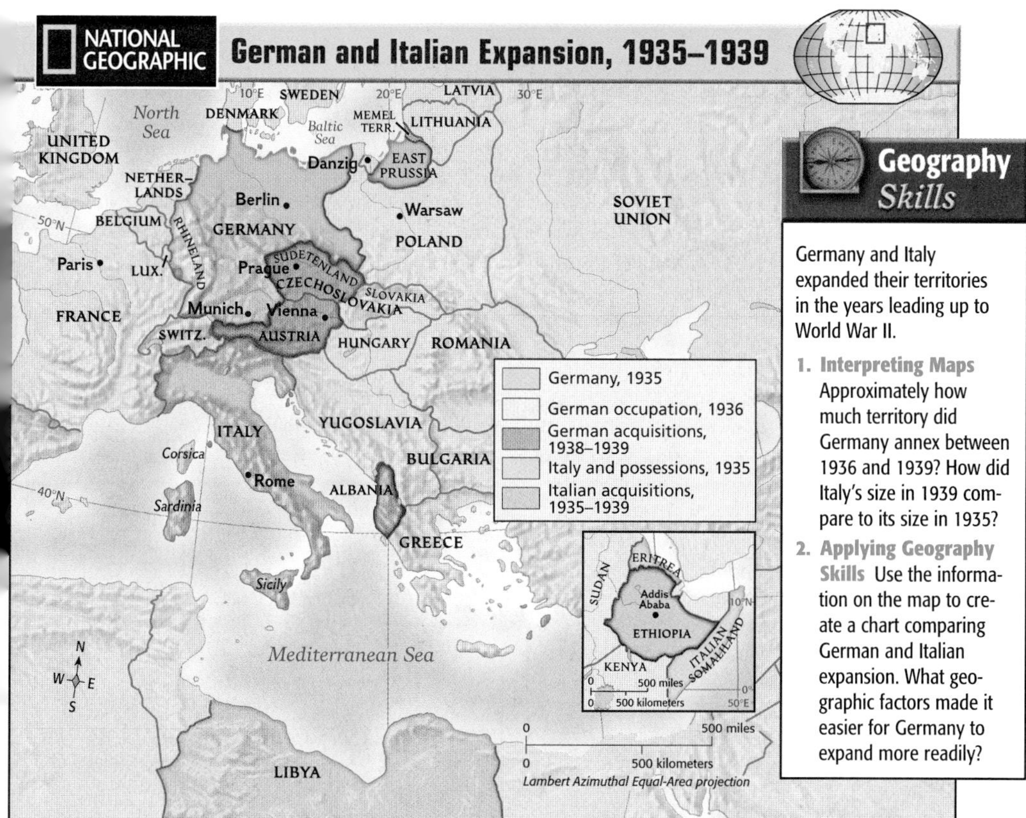

Geography Skills

Germany and Italy expanded their territories in the years leading up to World War II.

1. **Interpreting Maps** Approximately how much territory did Germany annex between 1936 and 1939? How did Italy's size in 1939 compare to its size in 1935?
2. **Applying Geography Skills** Use the information on the map to create a chart comparing German and Italian expansion. What geographic factors made it easier for Germany to expand more readily?

Demands and Appeasement Hitler's next objective was the destruction of Czechoslovakia. On September 15, 1938, he demanded that Germany be given the **Sudetenland,** an area in northwestern Czechoslovakia that was inhabited largely by Germans. He expressed his willingness to risk "world war" to achieve his objective.

At a hastily arranged conference in Munich, British, French, German, and Italian representatives did not object to Hitler's plans but instead reached an agreement that met virtually all of Hitler's demands. German troops were allowed to occupy the Sudetenland. The Czechs, abandoned by their Western allies, stood by helplessly.

The Munich Conference was the high point of Western appeasement of Hitler. When Neville Chamberlain, the British prime minister, returned to Britain from Munich, he boasted that the agreement meant "peace for our time." Hitler had promised Chamberlain that he would make no more demands. Like many others, Chamberlain believed Hitler's promises.

Great Britain and France React In fact, Hitler was more convinced than ever that the Western democracies were weak and would not fight. Increasingly, Hitler was sure that he could not make a mistake, and he had by no means been satisfied at Munich.

In March 1939, Hitler invaded and took control of Bohemia and Moravia in western Czechoslovakia. In the eastern part of the country, Slovakia became a puppet state controlled by Nazi Germany. On the evening of March 15, 1939, Hitler triumphantly declared in Prague that he would be known as the greatest German of them all.

At last, the Western states reacted to the Nazi threat. Hitler's aggression had made clear that his promises were worthless. When Hitler began to demand the Polish port of Danzig, Great Britain saw the danger and offered to protect Poland in the event of war. At the same time, both France and Britain realized that only the Soviet Union was powerful enough to help contain Nazi aggression. They began political and military negotiations with **Joseph Stalin,** the Soviet dictator.

Geography Skills

Answers:

1. Germany annexed approximately 50 percent more territory than it held. By 1939, the size of the country was about 50 percent larger.
2. Students will create charts. Answers may include that Germany wanted to repopulate the world with Aryan Germans, while Italy had no similar plans. Italy was also surrounded on three sides by water.

Critical Thinking

Ask students to examine the map on this page. Why would the transport of raw materials have been a problem for Germany during World War II? *(There were few ports that were accessible all year-round within Germany's territories.)* **L2**

Critical Thinking

Ask students why some people saluted Hitler and his entourage when he annexed the Sudetenland. *(The area had a German population of 3.5 million.)* **L2**

Connecting Across Time

The twentieth-century German and Japanese empires were transitory. Other empires and dynasties lasted for thousands of years. Have students analyze examples of major empires of the world. **L2**

COOPERATIVE LEARNING ACTIVITY

Creating an Oral Report Organize students into groups of four to six to research how the world reacted to the expansion of Japan into Nanjing, Italy into Ethiopia, and Germany into the Rhineland, Austria, and Czechoslovakia. Have each group choose one of these conquests and then find newspaper reports about it. Encourage students to apply different methods that historians have used to interpret the past, and to use the process of historical inquiry to research and to interpret the evidence. Also encourage students to use quotations that reveal the point of view of the reporter toward the conquest. Then have each group present its report to the class. **L2**

For grading this activity, refer to the ***Performance Assessment Activities*** booklet.

CHAPTER 19
Section 1, 591–595

Reading Check

Answer: in eastern Europe, including the Soviet Union

Geography Skills

Answer:
1. Student questions will vary but should be consistent with material presented in this section.

Guided Reading Activity 19-1

Name ______ Date ______ Class ______

Guided Reading Activity 19-1

Paths To War

DIRECTIONS: Answer the following questions as you read Section 1.

1. Where did Hitler plan to find the land he felt he needed to make Germany a great power?
2. What was the name given to the Aryan racial state that Hitler thought would dominate Europe for a thousand years?
3. When Hitler announced the creation of an air force, and expanded the German army, what agreement did he ...

Critical Thinking

Ask students to evaluate the following statement: "Building a powerful military leads a country to war because it is natural for military leaders to want to use and expand their power." Do students believe that this statement is true? To what extent might it explain why Japan's army invaded China? **L2**

3 ASSESS

Assign Section 1 Assessment as homework or as an in-class activity.

Have students use **Interactive Tutor Self-Assessment CD-ROM.**

Hitler and the Soviets Meanwhile, Hitler pressed on in the belief that the West would not fight over Poland. He now feared, however, that the West and the Soviet Union might make an alliance. Such an alliance could mean a two-front war for Germany. To prevent this possibility, Hitler made his own agreement with Joseph Stalin.

On August 23, 1939, Germany and the Soviet Union signed the Nazi-Soviet Nonaggression Pact. In it, the two nations promised not to attack each other. To get the nonaggression pact, Hitler offered Stalin control of eastern Poland and the Baltic states. Because he expected to fight the Soviet Union anyway, it did not matter to Hitler what he promised—he was accustomed to breaking promises.

Hitler shocked the world when he announced the nonaggression pact. The treaty gave Hitler the freedom to attack Poland. He told his generals, "Now Poland is in the position in which I wanted her. . . . I am only afraid that at the last moment some swine will submit to me a plan for mediation."

Hitler need not have worried. On September 1, German forces invaded Poland. Two days later, Britain and France declared war on Germany.

Reading Check **Identifying** Where did Hitler believe he could find more "living space" to expand Germany?

The Japanese Path to War

In September 1931, Japanese soldiers had seized Manchuria, which had natural resources Japan needed. Japan used as an excuse a Chinese attack on a Japanese railway near the city of Mukden. In fact, the "Mukden incident" had been carried out by Japanese soldiers disguised as Chinese.

Worldwide protests against the Japanese led the League of Nations to send investigators to Manchuria. When the investigators issued a report condemning the seizure, Japan withdrew from the league. Over the next several years, Japan strengthened its hold on Manchuria, which was renamed **Manchukuo.** Japan now began to expand into North China.

By the mid-1930s, militants connected to the government and the armed forces had gained control of Japanese politics. The United States refused to recognize the Japanese takeover of Manchuria but was unwilling to threaten force.

War With China **Chiang Kai-shek** tried to avoid a conflict with Japan so that he could deal with what he considered the greater threat from the Communists. When clashes between Chinese and Japanese troops broke out, he sought to appease Japan by allowing it to govern areas in North China.

As Japan moved steadily southward, protests against Japanese aggression grew stronger in Chinese cities. In December 1936, Chiang ended his military efforts against the Communists and formed a new united front against the Japanese. In July 1937, Chinese and Japanese forces clashed south of Beijing and hostilities spread.

Japan had not planned to declare war on China. However, the 1937 incident eventually turned into a major conflict. The Japanese seized the Chinese capital of Nanjing in December. Chiang Kai-shek refused to surrender and moved his government upriver, first to Hankou, then to Chongqing.

Geography Skills

Like Germany, Japan attempted to expand its territories prior to the beginning of the war.

1. **Applying Geography Skills** Pose and answer your own question about the territories Japan did *not* acquire but wanted to acquire.

CRITICAL THINKING ACTIVITY

Analyzing On page 595, the author suggests that the Japanese government might have rationalized its expansion into Asia in this fashion: "After all, who could better teach Asian societies how to modernize than the one Asian country that had already done it?" Ask students to identify what basic fallacy in logic Japan is making in this argument. *(Students might suggest that Japan assumes that the other countries want to modernize in the same way, and that because modernization worked in Japan, it would work anywhere.)* How does this compare to reasoning used by Western countries to justify their expansion? *(Western countries used similar thinking to justify their colonization of Africa and other regions of the world.)* Have students analyze the Japanese Empire and summarize the effect of its imperialism on other societies. **L2**

The New Asian Order Japanese military leaders had hoped to force Chiang to agree to join a New Order in East Asia, comprising Japan, Manchuria, and China. Japan would attempt to establish a new system of control in Asia with Japan guiding its Asian neighbors to prosperity. After all, who could better teach Asian societies how to modernize than the one Asian country that had already done it?

Part of Japan's plan was to seize Soviet Siberia, with its rich resources. During the late 1930s, Japan began to cooperate with Nazi Germany. Japan assumed that the two countries would ultimately launch a joint attack on the Soviet Union and divide Soviet resources between them.

When Germany signed the nonaggression pact with the Soviets in August 1939, Japanese leaders had to rethink their goals. Japan did not have the resources to defeat the Soviet Union without help. Thus, the Japanese became interested in the raw materials that could be found in Southeast Asia to fuel its military machine.

A move southward, however, would risk war with the European colonial powers and the United States. Japan's attack on China in the summer of 1937 had already aroused strong criticism, especially in the United States. Nevertheless, in the summer of 1940, Japan demanded the right to exploit economic resources in French Indochina.

The United States objected. It warned Japan that it would apply economic sanctions—restrictions intended to enforce international law—unless Japan withdrew from the area and returned to its borders of 1931. Japan badly needed the oil and scrap iron it was getting from the United States. Should these resources be cut off, Japan would have to find them elsewhere. Japan viewed the possibility of economic sanctions as a threat to its long-term objectives.

Japan was now caught in a dilemma. To guarantee access to the raw materials it wanted in Southeast Asia, Japan had to risk losing raw materials from the United States. Japan's military leaders, guided by Hideki Tojo, decided to launch a surprise attack on U.S. and European colonies in Southeast Asia.

Cabinet of Japanese prime minister Tojo (front center), 1941

Reading Check **Explaining** Why did Japan want to establish a New Order in East Asia?

SECTION 1 ASSESSMENT

Checking for Understanding

1. **Define** appeasement, demilitarized, sanction.
2. **Identify** Adolf Hitler, Benito Mussolini, Joseph Stalin, Chiang Kai-shek.
3. **Locate** Rhineland, Sudetenland, Manchukuo.
4. **Explain** why Japan felt the need to control other nations. Also explain the dilemma facing Japan as it sought to acquire access to needed resources.
5. **List** the reasons why Hitler's pact with Stalin was a key factor in forcing Britain and France to declare war on Germany.

Critical Thinking

6. **Explain** In what sense was World War II a product of World War I?
7. **Sequencing Information** Create a chart like the one below listing in chronological order the agreements that emboldened Hitler in his aggressive expansion policies.

Agreements Encouraging Hitler's Aggression Leading to World War II

Analyzing Visuals

8. **Analyze** the illustration on page 592 to determine what opinion the artist had about Italy's alliance with Germany. What aspects of the illustration indicate that its creator and its publisher either did or did not support Hitler's relationship with Mussolini and Italy?

Writing About History

9. **Persuasive Writing** Imagine you are the editor of a British newspaper in 1938. Write an editorial that captures the essence of your viewpoint. Use a headline that offers suggestions on how war can be avoided.

CHAPTER 19
Section 1, 591–595

Reading Check

Answer: Japan wanted to assert control and guide its neighbors to modernization and prosperity.

Section Quiz 19–1

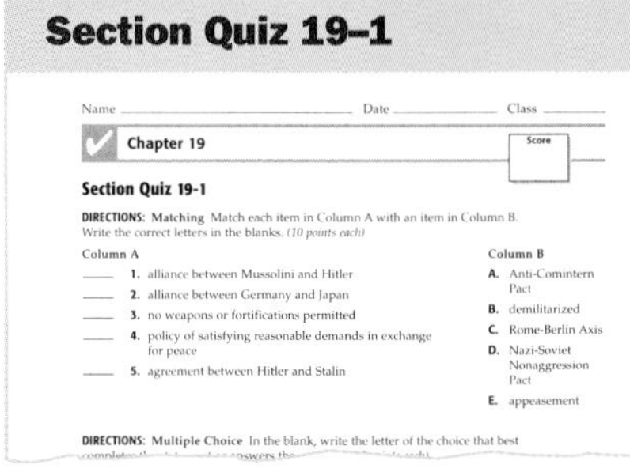

Name ______ Date ______ Class ______

Chapter 19 Score

Section Quiz 19-1

DIRECTIONS: Matching Match each item in Column A with an item in Column B. Write the correct letters in the blanks. *(10 points each)*

Column A	Column B
____ 1. alliance between Mussolini and Hitler	A. Anti-Comintern Pact
____ 2. alliance between Germany and Japan	B. demilitarized
____ 3. no weapons or fortifications permitted	C. Rome-Berlin Axis
____ 4. policy of satisfying reasonable demands in exchange for peace	D. Nazi-Soviet Nonaggression Pact
____ 5. agreement between Hitler and Stalin	E. appeasement

DIRECTIONS: Multiple Choice In the blank, write the letter of the choice that best

Reading Essentials and Study Guide 19–1

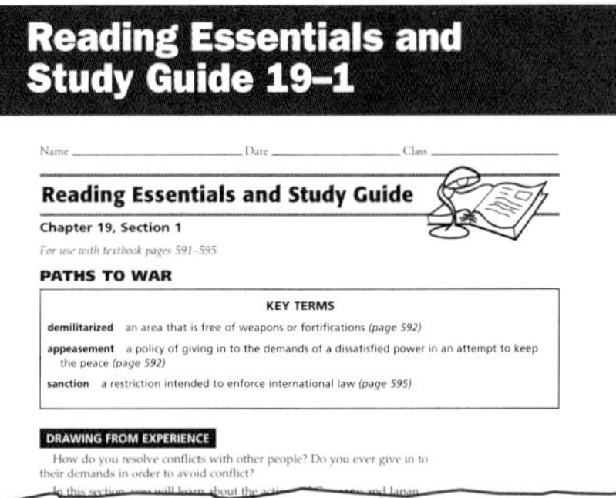

Name ______ Date ______ Class ______

Reading Essentials and Study Guide

Chapter 19, Section 1

For use with textbook pages 591–595

PATHS TO WAR

KEY TERMS

demilitarized an area that is free of weapons or fortifications *(page 592)*

appeasement a policy of giving in to the demands of a dissatisfied power in an attempt to keep the peace *(page 592)*

sanction a restriction intended to enforce international law *(page 595)*

DRAWING FROM EXPERIENCE

How do you resolve conflicts with other people? Do you ever give in to their demands in order to avoid conflict?

Reteaching Activity

Ask students to create a table that compares the political and economical conditions in Germany and Japan before World War II. **L1**

4 CLOSE

Ask students to find examples in Section 1 of countries forming alliances for their common good. Make a chart of the alliances made and the benefits received by the countries involved. **L1**

SECTION 1 ASSESSMENT

1. Key terms are in blue.
2. Adolf Hitler *(p. 591)*; Benito Mussolini *(p. 592)*; Joseph Stalin *(p. 593)*; Chiang Kai-shek *(p. 594)*
3. See chapter maps.
4. Japan depended on foreign sources for raw materials. Japan sought to expand on the Asian mainland, but risked losing raw materials from the United States if it did so.
5. Britain had offered to protect Poland in the event of war. The pact between Stalin and Hitler gave Hitler the freedom to invade Poland.
6. See *The First Steps* on page 592.
7. agreement with Mussolini, 1936; Anti-Comintern Pact with Japan, 1936; Munich Agreement, 1938; Hitler signs nonaggression pact with Soviet Union, 1939
8. The many Nazi flags in the background make it appear that the illustrator and publisher supported Hitler's relationship with Mussolini and Italy.
9. Answers will vary.

1 FOCUS

Section Overview

This section describes the expansion of World War II to a global conflict and the military and political operations that ultimately led to the Axis defeat by the Allies.

BELLRINGER
Skillbuilder Activity

 Project transparency and have students answer questions.

 Available as a blackline master.

Daily Focus Skills Transparency 19–2

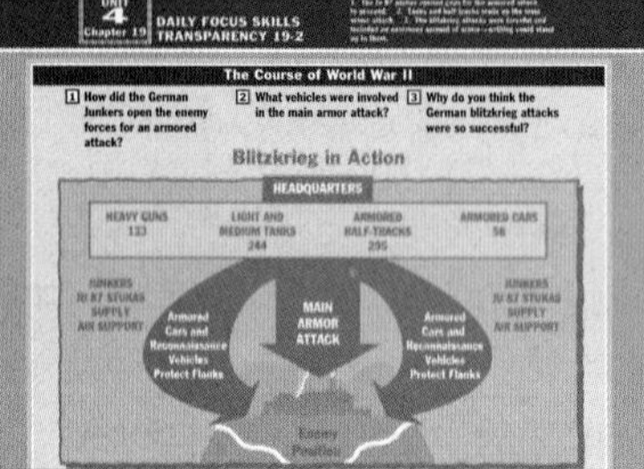

Guide to Reading

Answers to Graphic: Japan attacks Pearl Harbor: United States enters war; Battle of Midway: Japanese navy defeated; Invasion of Normandy: ends war in Europe; atomic bombs dropped on Japan: Japan surrenders

Preteaching Vocabulary: The British shortened the German word *blitzkrieg* to *blitz* to describe the intensive German bombardment of London. Ask students to identify how the word *blitz* is used today. L1

SECTION 2 The Course of World War II

Guide to Reading

Main Ideas
- The bombing of Pearl Harbor created a global war between the Allied and the Axis forces.
- Allied perseverance and effective military operations, as well as Axis miscalculations, brought an end to the war.

Key Terms
blitzkrieg, partisan

People to Identify
Franklin D. Roosevelt, Douglas MacArthur, Winston Churchill, Harry S Truman

Places to Locate
Stalingrad, Midway Island, Normandy, Hiroshima

Preview Questions
1. Why did the United States not enter the war until 1941?
2. What major events helped to end the war in Europe and Asia?

Reading Strategy
Cause and Effect Create a chart listing key events during World War II and their effect on the outcome of the war.

Event	Effect

Preview of Events

1939 · 1940 · 1941 · 1942 · 1943 · 1944 · 1945

- **1940** Germans bomb British cities
- **1942** Japanese defeated at the Battle of Midway Island
- **1943** Germans defeated at Stalingrad
- **1944** Allied forces invade France on D-Day

Hitler addresses the Reichstag on September 1, 1939.

Voices from the Past

On September 1, 1939, after beginning his attack on Poland, Hitler addressed the German Reichstag:

> "I do not want to be anything other than the first soldier of the German Reich. I have once more put on the uniform which was once most holy and precious to me. I shall only take it off after victory or I shall not live to see the end. . . . As a National Socialist and as a German soldier, I am going into this struggle strong in heart. My whole life has been nothing but a struggle for my people, for their revival, for Germany . . . Just as I myself am ready to risk my life any time for my people and for Germany, so I demand the same of everyone else. But anyone who thinks that he can oppose this national commandment, whether directly or indirectly, will die! Traitors can expect death."
>
> —*Nazism 1919–1945, A Documentary Reader,* J. Noakes and G. Pridham, 1995

Hitler had committed Germany to a life-or-death struggle.

Europe at War

Hitler stunned Europe with the speed and efficiency of the German attack on Poland. His **blitzkrieg**, or "lightning war," used armored columns, called panzer divisions, supported by airplanes. Each panzer division was a strike force of about three hundred tanks with accompanying forces and supplies.

SECTION RESOURCES

Reproducible Masters
- Reproducible Lesson Plan 19–2
- Daily Lecture and Discussion Notes 19–2
- Guided Reading Activity 19–2
- Section Quiz 19–2
- Reading Essentials and Study Guide 19–2

Transparencies
- Daily Focus Skills Transparency 19–2

Multimedia
- Interactive Tutor Self-Assessment CD-ROM
- ExamView® Pro Testmaker CD-ROM
- Presentation Plus! CD-ROM

The forces of the blitzkrieg broke quickly through Polish lines and encircled the bewildered Polish troops. Regular infantry units then moved in to hold the newly conquered territory. Within four weeks, Poland had surrendered. On September 28, 1939, Germany and the Soviet Union divided Poland.

Hitler's Early Victories After a winter of waiting (called the "phony war"), Hitler resumed the attack on April 9, 1940, with another blitzkrieg against Denmark and Norway. One month later, on May 10, Germany launched an attack on the Netherlands, Belgium, and France.

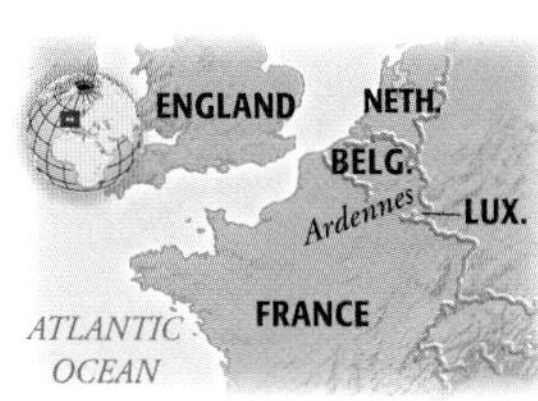

The main assault was through Luxembourg and the Ardennes (ahr•DEHN) Forest. German panzer divisions broke through weak French defensive positions there and raced across northern France. French and British forces were taken by surprise when the Germans went around, instead of across, the Maginot Line (a series of concrete and steel fortifications armed with heavy artillery along France's border with Germany). The Germans' action split the Allied armies, trapping French troops and the entire British army on the beaches of Dunkirk. Only by the heroic efforts of the Royal Navy and civilians in private boats did the British manage to evacuate 338,000 Allied (mostly British) troops.

The French signed an armistice on June 22. German armies now occupied about three-fifths of France. An authoritarian regime under German control was set up over the remainder of the country. It was known as Vichy France and was led by an aged French hero of World War I, Marshal Henri Pétain. Germany was now in control of western and central Europe, but Britain had still not been defeated. After Dunkirk, the British appealed to the United States for help.

President **Franklin D. Roosevelt** denounced the aggressors, but the United States followed a strict policy of isolationism. A series of neutrality acts, passed in the 1930s, prevented the United States from taking sides or becoming involved in any European wars. Many Americans felt that the United States had been drawn into World War I due to economic involvement in Europe and they wanted to prevent a recurrence. Roosevelt was convinced that the neutrality acts actually encouraged Axis aggression and wanted the acts repealed. They were gradually relaxed as the United States supplied food, ships, planes, and weapons to Britain.

The Battle of Britain Hitler realized that an amphibious (land-sea) invasion of Britain could succeed only if Germany gained control of the air. At the beginning of August 1940, the Luftwaffe (LOOFT•vah•fuh)—the German air force—launched a major offensive. German planes bombed British air and naval bases, harbors, communication centers, and war industries.

The British fought back with determination. They were supported by an effective radar system that gave them early warning of German attacks. Nevertheless, by the end of August, the British air force had suffered critical losses.

In September, in retaliation for a British attack on Berlin, Hitler ordered a shift in strategy. Instead of bombing military targets, the Luftwaffe began massive bombing of British cities. Hitler hoped in this way to break British morale. Instead, because military targets were not being hit, the British were able to rebuild their air strength quickly. Soon, the British air force was inflicting major losses on Luftwaffe bombers. At the end of September, Hitler postponed the invasion of Britain indefinitely.

London buildings collapse as a result of nightly German bombing.

CHAPTER 19
Section 2, 596–604

2 TEACH

Daily Lecture and Discussion Notes 19–2

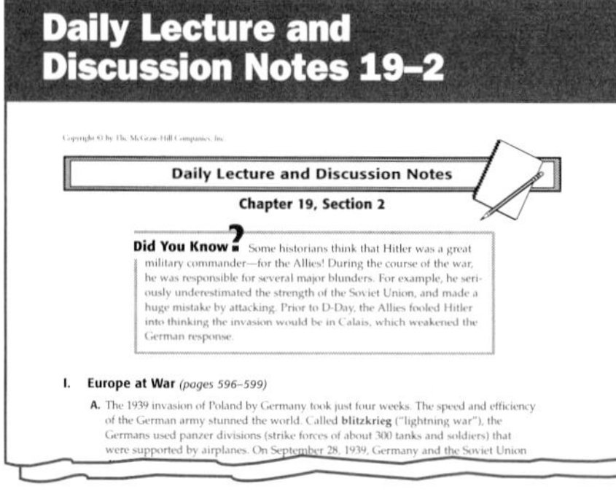

Daily Lecture and Discussion Notes

Chapter 19, Section 2

Did You Know? Some historians think that Hitler was a great military commander—for the Allies! During the course of the war, he was responsible for several major blunders. For example, he seriously underestimated the strength of the Soviet Union, and made a huge mistake by attacking. Prior to D-Day, the Allies fooled Hitler into thinking the invasion would be in Calais, which weakened the German response.

I. **Europe at War** *(pages 596–599)*

A. The 1939 invasion of Poland by Germany took just four weeks. The speed and efficiency of the German army stunned the world. Called **blitzkrieg** ("lightning war"), the Germans used panzer divisions (strike forces of about 300 tanks and soldiers) that were supported by airplanes. On September 28, 1939, Germany and the Soviet Union

Guided Reading Activity 19–2

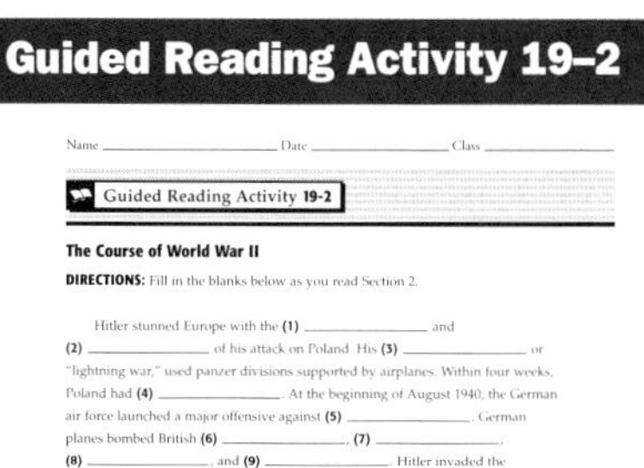

Name ________ Date ________ Class ________

Guided Reading Activity **19-2**

The Course of World War II

DIRECTIONS: Fill in the blanks below as you read Section 2.

Hitler stunned Europe with the **(1)** ________ and **(2)** ________ of his attack on Poland. His **(3)** ________ or "lightning war," used panzer divisions supported by airplanes. Within four weeks, Poland had **(4)** ________. At the beginning of August 1940, the German air force launched a major offensive against **(5)** ________. German planes bombed British **(6)** ________, **(7)** ________, **(8)** ________, and **(9)** ________. Hitler invaded the **(10)** ________ on June 22, 1941. An early **(11)** ________ and fierce Soviet **(12)** ________ halted the German advance.

Who?What?Where?When?

Radar In 1935, physicist Robert Watson-Watts developed radar, an early warning system used to detect incoming aircraft. This new invention (radio detecting and ranging) helped the British defeat the German Luftwaffe in the Battle of Britain.

Writing Activity

Ask students to write a hypothetical letter from a resident of London to an American relative describing how he or she feels after seeing the results of an air raid, such as the one pictured on this page. How might such destruction change this person's willingness to fight? **L1**

COOPERATIVE LEARNING ACTIVITY

Organizing a Group Discussion Break students into groups to discuss the answer to the following question: Why was it easier for a nation like Germany to take control of a vast area (such as it did in 1939) than it was to maintain control over the same area? *(It is easier to take over a territory through military power than to maintain control and administer an effective government. The German effort to occupy vast territories spread its power and people too thin.)* When students have finished their small group discussions, guide the class in a general discussion of this question and conclude with a list of other military leaders or empires that experienced the same problems Germany encountered. **L2**

CURRICULUM CONNECTION

Geography Ask students to study the map on this page. Which countries did Germany invade in 1941? *(Yugoslavia, Lithuania, Latvia, Estonia, the Soviet Union, Bulgaria, Greece, Finland)* **L1**

Connecting Across Time

Remind students that in Chapter 11 they read about how Napoleon Bonaparte suffered a stunning defeat just outside Moscow during the winter of 1812. In what ways did Napoleon and Hitler make the same mistakes? Have students refer to maps in the Reference Atlas and in these two chapters to identify and explain the answer to this question. *(These two leaders underestimated the effects of the Russian winter and the resistance of the Russian people.)* **L1**

Critical Thinking

By distorting history, Nazi ideology created the belief that "Aryans" were responsible for most advances in human history. As you discuss the validity, or lack of validity, of this view, ask students to be as specific as possible regarding the contributions of different cultures and civilizations. **L1**

Critical Thinking

Ask students to summarize the events that brought the Soviet Union and the United States into World War II. **L1**

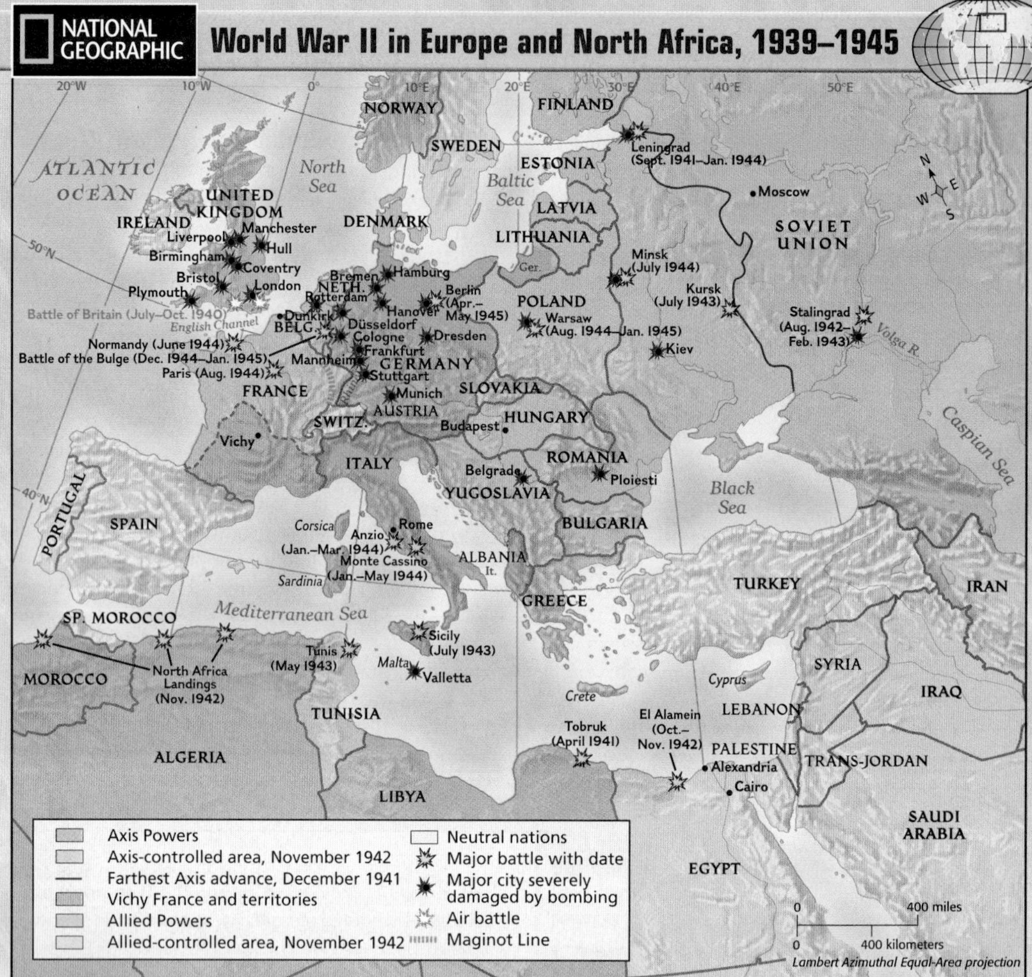

Attack on the Soviet Union Although he had no desire for a two-front war, Hitler became convinced that Britain was remaining in the war only because it expected Soviet support. If the Soviet Union was smashed, Britain's last hope would be eliminated. Moreover, Hitler had convinced himself that the Soviet Union had a pitiful army and could be defeated quickly.

Hitler's invasion of the Soviet Union was scheduled for the spring of 1941, but the attack was delayed because of problems in the Balkans. Hitler had already gained the political cooperation of Hungary, Bulgaria, and Romania. However, the failure of Mussolini's invasion of Greece in 1940 had exposed Hitler's southern flank to British air bases in Greece. To secure his Balkan flank, Hitler therefore seized both Greece and Yugoslavia in April.

Reassured, Hitler invaded the Soviet Union on June 22, 1941. He believed that the Russians could still be decisively defeated before the brutal winter weather set in.

The massive attack stretched out along a front some 1,800 miles (about 2,900 km) long. German troops advanced rapidly, capturing two million Russian soldiers. By November, one German army group had swept through Ukraine. A second army was besieging the city of Leningrad, while a third approached within 25 miles (about 40 km) of Moscow, the Soviet capital.

An early winter and fierce Soviet resistance, however, halted the German advance. Because of the planned spring date for the invasion, the Germans had no winter uniforms. For the first time in the war, German armies had been stopped. A counterattack in

EXTENDING THE CONTENT

The Blitz During World War II, German bombers rained destruction on London and strategic targets in an attempt to knock out Great Britain's defenses and force the British to surrender. Public shelters were set up throughout London in subway tunnels and other protected areas. At the height of the blitz, one out of every seven Londoners slept in a shelter. About two million children were evacuated to the countryside from London and other British cities. There, many of these city children played on grass and climbed trees for the first time. Parents and children reunited periodically when the government offered reduced train fares to the country.

Axis Offensives, 1939–1941

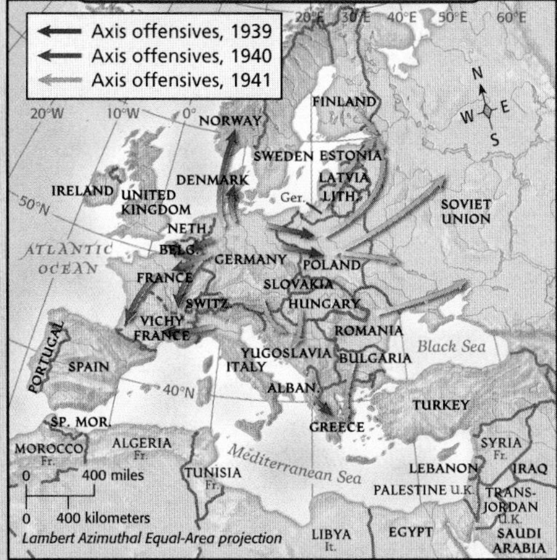

Allied Offensives, 1942–1945

Battle Deaths in World War II

Country	Battle Deaths
USSR	7,500,000
Germany	3,500,000
Yugoslavia	410,000
Poland	320,000
Romania	300,000
United States	292,000
United Kingdom	245,000
France	210,000
Hungary	140,000
Finland	82,000
Italy	77,000
Greece	74,000
Canada	37,000

Geography *Skills*

Heavy fighting took place in Europe and North Africa.

1. **Interpreting Maps** Name at least six major land battles of the war in Europe. Which side, the Allies or the Axis Powers, was more aggressive at the beginning of the war? Summarize the changes in direction of this side's offensives during the first three years of the war.
2. **Applying Geography Skills** Using information from all of the maps on pages 598 and 599, create an imaginary model of the war's outcome had Hitler chosen not to invade the Soviet Union. Your model could take the form of a map, a chart, or a database and include such items as battles, offensives, and casualties.

December 1941 by a Soviet army came as an ominous ending to the year for the Germans.

Reading Check **Evaluating** In the spring of 1941, what caused Hitler to delay his invasion of the Soviet Union? What halted the German advance once it had begun?

Japan at War

TURNING POINT **As you will learn, the Japanese attack on Pearl Harbor outraged Americans and led to the entry of the United States into the war.**

On December 7, 1941, Japanese aircraft attacked the U.S. naval base at Pearl Harbor in the Hawaiian Islands. The same day, other Japanese units launched additional assaults on the Philippines and began advancing toward the British colony of Malaya. Soon after, Japanese forces invaded the Dutch East Indies and occupied a number of islands in the Pacific Ocean. In some cases, as on the Bataan Peninsula and the island of Corregidor in the Philippines, resistance was fierce. By the spring of 1942, however, almost all of Southeast Asia and much of the western Pacific had fallen into Japanese hands.

A triumphant Japan now declared the creation of a community of nations. The name given to this new "community" was the Greater East-Asia Co-prosperity Sphere. The entire region would now be under Japanese direction. Japan also announced its intention to liberate the colonial areas of Southeast Asia from Western colonial rule. For the moment, however, Japan needed the resources of the region for its war machine, and it treated the countries under its rule as conquered lands.

Reading Check

Answer: Problems in the Balkans led Hitler to seize both Greece and Yugoslavia in April 1941. An early winter and fierce Soviet resistance halted the German advance.

TURNING POINT

How did Pearl Harbor change the course of World War II? *(The Japanese attack brought the United States, with its powerful military potential, into World War II.)*

Geography *Skills*

Answers:

1. Students should select sites marked with yellow icon; Axis; direction moved east in 1940, west in 1941, then east in 1942.
2. Students will create models.

Enrich

Have students research the raw materials Japan gained by invading French Indochina and the Dutch East Indies. Then ask students to write an essay in which they summarize and analyze the political and economic impact of Japanese imperialism on other societies. L2

MEETING INDIVIDUAL NEEDS

Creating Visual Aids Have students who are kinesthetic learners create a visual "war map" showing one of the following conflicts of the war: the Soviet offensive, the war in the desert, the invasion of Italy, or the war in the Pacific. Tell students to re-create the area of conflict and then illustrate how the Allied forces took the offensive and achieved victory. Suggest that they use markers, flags, or pictures to illustrate the actions in the conflict. Display completed maps in the classroom and encourage students to explain and interpret the visuals that they have created. L1

Refer to ***Inclusion for the High School Social Studies Classroom Strategies and Activities*** in the TCR.

CHAPTER 19
Section 2, 596–604

Reading Check

Answer: most of Southeast Asia and much of the western Pacific

Graphic Organizer → Skills

Answers:

1. 9 months; 5 years
2. Answers may include: the Russian Revolution took place during World War I, causing Russia to withdraw from the war. By the time of World War II, there was a strong totalitarian regime in power, and Russia was industrialized.

Who?What?Where?When?

Pearl Harbor By late 1941, there were more than 75 U.S. warships including battleships, destroyers, cruisers, and submarines stationed at Pearl Harbor. During the Japanese attack, the battleship U.S.S. *Arizona* was completely destroyed, the *Nevada* heavily damaged, and the *West Virginia* and the *California* were sunk. American losses were staggering, but Japan lost only 29 planes, 5 small submarines, and less than 100 soldiers. A national memorial has been built across the hull of the U.S.S. *Arizona* at Pearl Harbor, just outside Honolulu, Hawaii.

Critical Thinking

Ask students to analyze the information on pages 600 through 604 and suggest what they believe to be the two or three major reasons for the war turning in favor of the Allies.

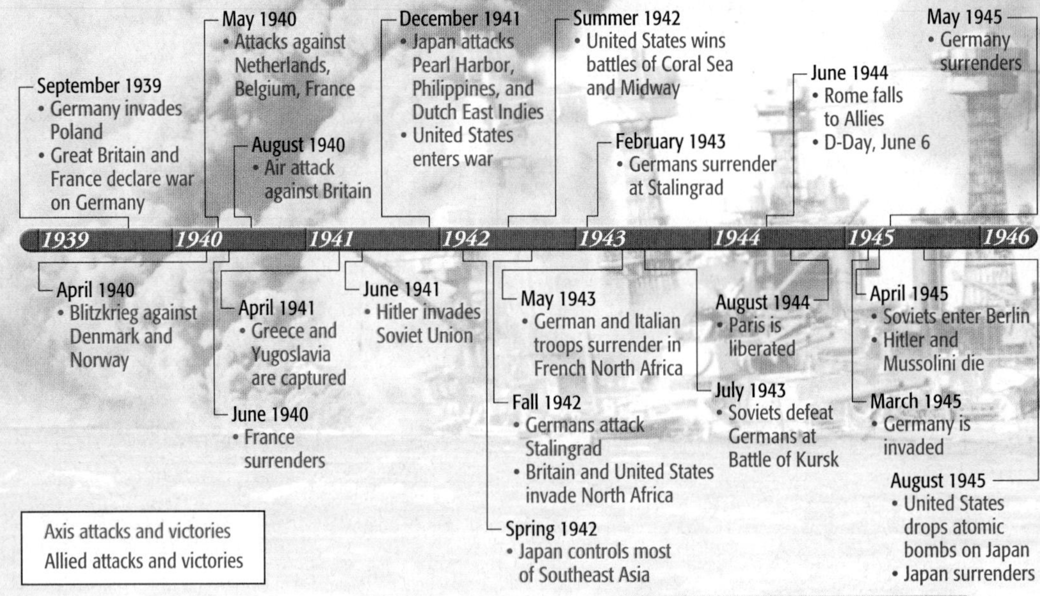

World War II: Attack and Counterattack
September 1939 • Germany invades Poland • Great Britain and France declare war on Germany
May 1940 • Attacks against Netherlands, Belgium, France
August 1940 • Air attack against Britain
December 1941 • Japan attacks Pearl Harbor, Philippines, and Dutch East Indies • United States enters war
Summer 1942 • United States wins battles of Coral Sea and Midway
February 1943 • Germans surrender at Stalingrad
June 1944 • Rome falls to Allies • D-Day, June 6
May 1945 • Germany surrenders
1939 1940 1941 1942 1943 1944 1945 1946
April 1940 • Blitzkrieg against Denmark and Norway
April 1941 • Greece and Yugoslavia are captured
June 1940 • France surrenders
June 1941 • Hitler invades Soviet Union
May 1943 • German and Italian troops surrender in French North Africa
Fall 1942 • Germans attack Stalingrad • Britain and United States invade North Africa
Spring 1942 • Japan controls most of Southeast Asia
August 1944 • Paris is liberated
July 1943 • Soviets defeat Germans at Battle of Kursk
April 1945 • Soviets enter Berlin • Hitler and Mussolini die
March 1945 • Germany is invaded
August 1945 • United States drops atomic bombs on Japan • Japan surrenders
Axis attacks and victories
Allied attacks and victories

Graphic Organizer → Skills

The time line above traces the major events of the war, from September 1939 to Japan's surrender in August 1945.

1. **Identifying** How much time elapsed from the beginning of the war until France's surrender? From France's surrender until Germany's surrender?
2. **Compare and Contrast** Use the time line and your knowledge of world history to compare the Soviet Union's involvement in World War II to Russia's involvement in World War I. How do you explain the successes and failures of the Soviet Union and Russia in these two wars?

Japanese leaders had hoped that their lightning strike at American bases would destroy the U.S. fleet in the Pacific. The Roosevelt administration, they thought, would now accept Japanese domination of the Pacific. The American people, in the eyes of Japanese leaders, had been made soft by material indulgence.

The Japanese miscalculated, however. The attack on Pearl Harbor unified American opinion about becoming involved in the war. The United States now joined with European nations and Nationalist China in a combined effort to defeat Japan. Believing the American involvement in the Pacific would make the United States ineffective in the European theater of war, Hitler declared war on the United States four days after Pearl Harbor. Another European conflict had turned into a global war.

Reading Check **Describing** By the spring of 1942, which territories did Japan control?

The Allies Advance

The entry of the United States into the war created a new coalition, the Grand Alliance. To overcome mutual suspicions, the three major Allies—Great Britain, the United States, and the Soviet Union—agreed to stress military operations and ignore political differences. At the beginning of 1943, the Allies agreed to fight until the Axis Powers—Germany, Italy, and Japan—surrendered unconditionally. The unconditional surrender principle, which required the Axis nations to surrender without any favorable condition, cemented the Grand Alliance by making it nearly impossible for Hitler to divide his foes.

The European Theater Defeat was far from Hitler's mind at the beginning of 1942. As Japanese forces advanced into Southeast Asia and the Pacific,

COOPERATIVE LEARNING ACTIVITY

Creating a Video Presentation Organize the class into three groups to create a 10- to 15-minute video documentary about Germany's early military offensives in World War II. Assign each group one of the following topics: the conquest of Poland, fall of France (include the Low Countries and Dunkirk), or the Battle of Britain. Suggest that students use pictures of events and people, sound effects, "interviews," speeches, and songs in their films. Each group should choose a narrator for its segment and one student to act as a coordinator with other groups. When the documentaries are completed, have students present their videos to other classes. L3

Hitler and his European allies continued fighting the war in Europe against the armies of Britain and the Soviet Union.

Until late 1942, it appeared that the Germans might still prevail on the battlefield. In North Africa, the Afrika Korps, German forces under General Erwin Rommel, broke through the British defenses in Egypt and advanced toward Alexandria. A renewed German offensive in the Soviet Union led to the capture of the entire Crimea in the spring of 1942. In August, Hitler boasted:

> "As the next step, we are going to advance south of the Caucasus and then help the rebels in Iran and Iraq against the English. Another thrust will be directed along the Caspian Sea toward Afghanistan and India. Then the English will run out of oil. In two years we'll be on the borders of India. Twenty to thirty elite German divisions will do. Then the British Empire will collapse."

This would be Hitler's last optimistic outburst. By the fall of 1942, the war had turned against the Germans.

In North Africa, British forces had stopped Rommel's troops at El Alamein (EL A•luh•MAYN) in the summer of 1942. The Germans then retreated back across the desert. In November 1942, British and American forces invaded French North Africa. They forced the German and Italian troops there to surrender in May 1943.

On the Eastern Front, after the capture of the Crimea, Hitler's generals wanted him to concentrate on the Caucasus and its oil fields. Hitler, however, decided that **Stalingrad,** a major industrial center on the Volga, should be taken first.

In perhaps the most terrible battle of the war, between November 1942 and February 2, 1943, the Soviets launched a counterattack. German troops were stopped, then encircled, and supply lines were cut off, all in frigid winter conditions. The Germans

CONNECTIONS Around The World

Women as Spies in World War II

For thousands of years, governments have relied on spies to gather information about their enemies. Until the twentieth century, most spies were men. During World War II, however, many women became active in the world of espionage.

Yoshiko Kawashima was born in China but raised in Japan. In 1932, she was sent to China by Japanese authorities to gather information for the invasion of China. Disguised as a young man, Kawashima was an active and effective spy until her arrest by the Chinese in 1945. The Chinese news agency announced that "a long-sought-for beauty in male costume was arrested today in Beijing." She was executed soon after her arrest.

Hekmath Fathmy was an Egyptian dancer. Her hatred of the British, who had occupied Egypt, caused her to become a spy for the Germans. Fathmy sang and danced for British troops in the Kit Kat Club, a nightclub in Cairo. After shows, she took British officers to her houseboat on the banks of the Nile. Any information she was able to obtain from her guests was passed on to John Eppler, a German spy in Cairo. Eventually, she was caught, but she served only a year in prison for her spying activities.

Violette Szabo of French/English background became a spy after her husband died fighting the Germans in North Africa. She joined Special Operations Executive, an arm of British Intelligence, and was sent to France several times. In August 1944, she parachuted into France to spy on the Germans. Caught by Gestapo forces at Salon La Tour, she was tortured and then shipped to Ravensbruck, a women's concentration camp near Berlin. She was executed there in April 1945.

▲ *Violette Szabo spied for the Allies to avenge her husband's death.*

Comparing Cultures

People have different motives for becoming spies. List several motives that might draw someone to espionage. Do you think the motives are different in peacetime? Investigate current espionage activities using the Internet or library. What various methods do governments use today to gather intelligence?

MEETING INDIVIDUAL NEEDS

Creating a Glossary To help students better understand terms used in Section 2, have them make a mini-dictionary for the following words: blitzkrieg, panzer, Luftwaffe, neutrality, coalition, unconditional surrender, isolationism, morale, and beachhead. Ask students to alphabetize the words, then find them in Section 2, and either determine their meaning from context or look them up in a dictionary or the Glossary of their textbook. Then have students write a definition for each word and use that word in a sentence. L1

Refer to ***Inclusion for the High School Social Studies Classroom Strategies and Activities*** in the TCR.

Answer: Answers should be supported by examples and logical arguments.

TURNING POINT

Why was Stalingrad a major turning point in World War II? *(The Battle of Stalingrad put the Germans on the defensive on the Eastern Front and marked the beginning of the turning of the tide in favor of the Allies.)*

Critical Thinking

Ask students to discuss why captured spies have often been treated more harshly than other enemy soldiers who were taken prisoner. What characteristics in enemy spies do we find particularly offensive? Why do we glorify the exploits of our own successful spies? L2

Writing Activity

Assign students to write the dialogue for an imaginary conversation between Winston Churchill and Hitler in 1941 before the United States entered the war. In this conversation, each man should explain to the other why his side is certain to win the war eventually. As part of this writing activity, ask students to analyze the influence of Churchill and Hitler on political events of the twentieth century. L2

Geography *Skills*

Answers:

1. nearly 4,000 miles (6,436 km)
2. Asia and the Pacific were sea-based, Europe was land-based.

CURRICULUM CONNECTION

Technology After D-Day, Pipe-Line Under The Ocean (PLUTO), a supply line under the English Channel, supplied 700 tons of gasoline a day for Allied trucks and tanks advancing across Europe. Ask students to research PLUTO and other technological innovations of the war. You might suggest radar, jet engines, special munitions, or Mulberry harbors.

Critical Thinking

Many difficult decisions were made during the course of World War II. Have students identify a situation that requires a similarly difficult decision. You might suggest that students assume roles of contemporary political or military leaders facing a decision about how to react to an event currently in the news. Then ask students to use a decision-making process to gather information, identify options, and predict consequences regarding their situation. Ask students to identify what actions would be needed to implement their decision. L2

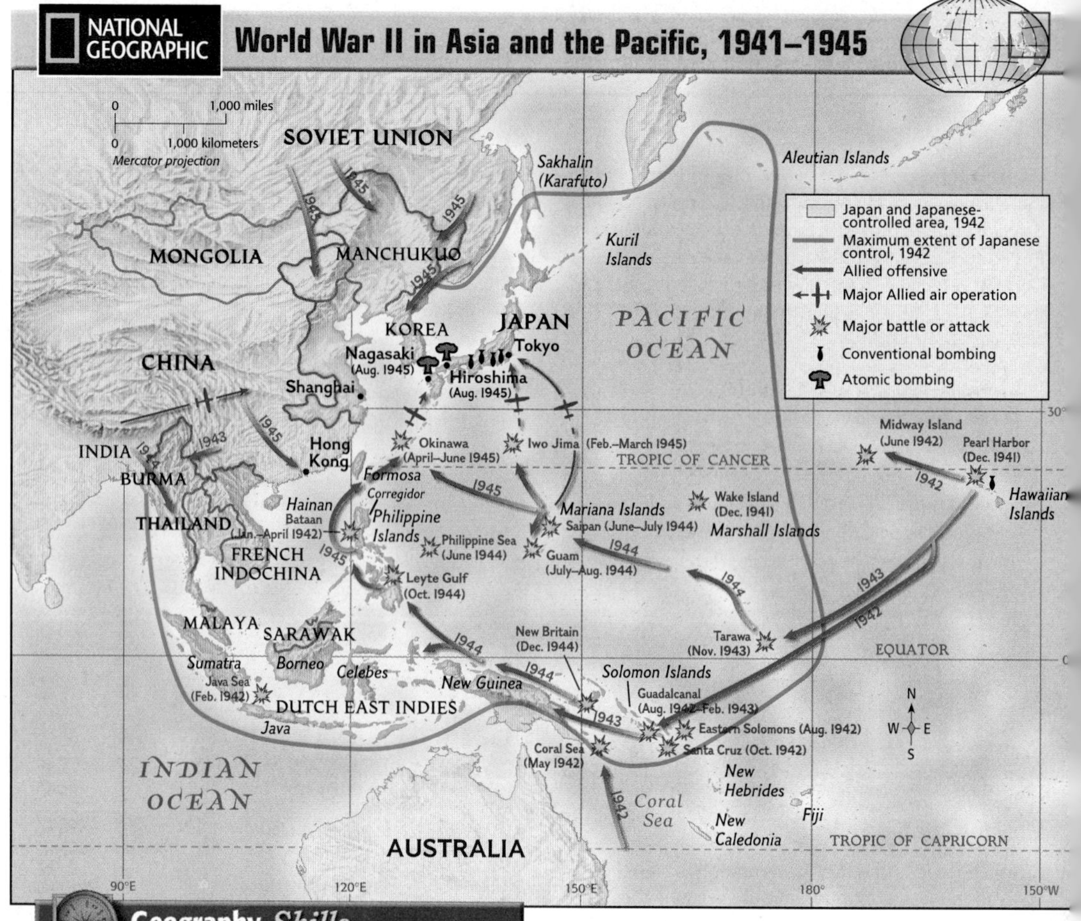

Geography *Skills*

"Island hopping," the Allied strategy in Asia and the Pacific, focused more on the islands in the Pacific than on the mainland of Asia.

1. **Interpreting Maps** What was the approximate distance from Japan, in miles and kilometers, to its farthest point of control?
2. **Applying Geography Skills** Compare this map to the earlier maps in the chapter dealing with the war in Europe. Then analyze the effects of geographic factors on the major events in the two different theatres of war.

were forced to surrender at Stalingrad. The entire German Sixth Army, considered the best of the German troops, was lost.

By February 1943, German forces in Russia were back to their positions of June 1942. By the spring of 1943, even Hitler knew that the Germans would not defeat the Soviet Union.

The Asian Theater In 1942, the tide of battle in the East also changed dramatically. In the Battle of the Coral Sea on May 7 and 8, 1942, American naval forces stopped the Japanese advance and saved Australia from the threat of invasion.

The turning point of the war in Asia came on June 4, at the Battle of **Midway Island.** U.S. planes destroyed four attacking Japanese aircraft carriers. The United States defeated the Japanese navy and established naval superiority in the Pacific.

By the fall of 1942, Allied forces in Asia were gathering for two chief operations. One, commanded by U.S. general **Douglas MacArthur,** would move into South China from Burma through the islands of Indonesia. The other would move across the Pacific with a combination of U.S. Army, Marine, and Navy attacks on Japanese-held islands. The policy was to capture some Japanese-held islands and bypass others, "island hopping" up to Japan. After a series of bitter engagements in the waters off the Solomon

INTERDISCIPLINARY CONNECTIONS ACTIVITY

Geography Geography is more than the study of a region's rivers, lakes, mountains, etc. For example, the economic geography of Japan (i.e., its economic resources) was a serious limitation to the Japanese aim to become a great power. Japan felt that it had to gain access to natural resources for a modern industrial economy. This meant expansion toward Korea, China, Russia, and adjoining Pacific areas. A weakness in economic geography directly led to aggression and imperialism. Today contemporary Japan peacefully meets its demands for natural resources. Through exports Japan can afford to buy natural resources in the world market. Ask students to create a chart that lists Japan's exports in one column and the natural resources it imports in a second column.

Islands from August to November 1942, Japanese fortunes were fading.

Reading Check **Summarizing** Why was the German assault on Stalingrad a crushing defeat for the Germans?

Last Years of the War

By the beginning of 1943, the tide of battle had turned against Germany, Italy, and Japan. Axis forces in Tunisia surrendered on May 13, 1943. The Allies then crossed the Mediterranean and carried the war to Italy, an area that **Winston Churchill** had called the "soft underbelly" of Europe. After taking Sicily, Allied troops began an invasion of mainland Italy in September.

The European Theater After the fall of Sicily, Mussolini was removed from office and placed under arrest by Victor Emmanuel III, king of Italy. A new Italian government offered to surrender to the Allied forces. However, Mussolini was liberated by the Germans in a daring raid and then set up as the head of a puppet German state in northern Italy. At the same time, German troops moved in and occupied much of Italy.

The Germans set up effective new defensive lines in the hills south of Rome. The Allied advance up the Italian Peninsula turned into a painstaking affair with very heavy casualties. Rome did not fall to the Allies until June 4, 1944. By that time, the Italian war had assumed a secondary role as the Allied forces opened their long-awaited "second front" in western Europe.

Since the autumn of 1943, the Allies had been planning an invasion of France from Great Britain, across the English Channel. Finally, on June 6, 1944 (D-Day), Allied forces under U.S. general Dwight D. Eisenhower landed on the **Normandy** beaches in history's greatest naval invasion. The Allies fought their way past underwater mines, barbed wire, and horrible machine gun fire. There was heavy German resistance even though the Germans thought the battle was a diversion and the real invasion would occur elsewhere. Their slow response enabled the Allied forces to set up a beachhead. Within three months, the Allies had landed two million men and a half-million vehicles. Allied forces then pushed inland and broke through German defensive lines.

After the breakout, Allied troops moved south and east. In Paris, resistance fighters rose up against the occupying Germans. The Allies liberated Paris by the end of August. In March 1945, they crossed the Rhine River and advanced into Germany. At the end of April 1945, Allied armies in northern Germany moved toward the Elbe River, where they linked up with the Soviets.

People In History

Winston Churchill
1874–1965
British prime minister

Winston Churchill was Great Britain's wartime leader. At the beginning of the war, Churchill had already had a long political career. He had advocated a hard-line policy toward Nazi Germany in the 1930s. On May 10, 1940, he became British prime minister.

Churchill was confident that he could guide Britain to ultimate victory. "I thought I knew a great deal about it all," he later wrote, "and I was sure I should not fail." Churchill proved to be an inspiring leader who rallied the British people with stirring speeches: "We shall fight on the beaches, we shall fight on the landing grounds, in the fields, in the streets, and in the hills. We shall never surrender." *Time* magazine designated Churchill the Man of the Year in 1940 and named him the Man of the Half Century in 1950.

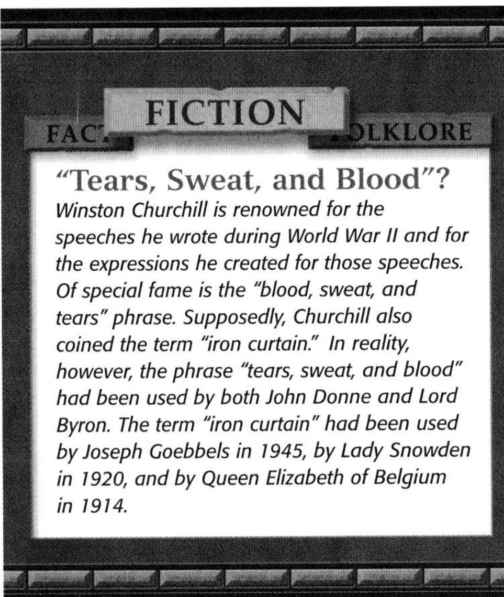
FACT FICTION FOLKLORE

"Tears, Sweat, and Blood"?

Winston Churchill is renowned for the speeches he wrote during World War II and for the expressions he created for those speeches. Of special fame is the "blood, sweat, and tears" phrase. Supposedly, Churchill also coined the term "iron curtain." In reality, however, the phrase "tears, sweat, and blood" had been used by both John Donne and Lord Byron. The term "iron curtain" had been used by Joseph Goebbels in 1945, by Lady Snowden in 1920, and by Queen Elizabeth of Belgium in 1914.

CHAPTER 19
Section 2, 596–604

Reading Check

Answer: The entire German Sixth Army, considered to be Hitler's best troops, was lost.

Who? What? Where? When?

Military Code In 1943, the United States Marine Corps recruited the Navajo to develop a military code that the Japanese could not break. Based on their oral language, the "Navajo Code Talkers" created the only unbreakable code in military history.

3 ASSESS

Assign Section 2 Assessment as homework or as an in-class activity.

Have students use **Interactive Tutor Self-Assessment CD-ROM.**

Section Quiz 19–2

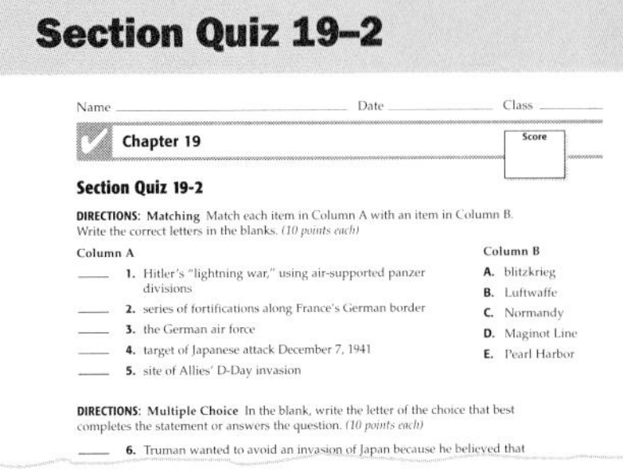
Name ______ Date ______ Class ______

Chapter 19 Score

Section Quiz 19-2

DIRECTIONS: Matching Match each item in Column A with an item in Column B. Write the correct letters in the blanks. (10 points each)

Column A	Column B
___ 1. Hitler's "lightning war," using air-supported panzer divisions	A. blitzkrieg
___ 2. series of fortifications along France's German border	B. Luftwaffe
___ 3. the German air force	C. Normandy
___ 4. target of Japanese attack December 7, 1941	D. Maginot Line
___ 5. site of Allies' D-Day invasion	E. Pearl Harbor

DIRECTIONS: Multiple Choice In the blank, write the letter of the choice that best completes the statement or answers the question. (10 points each)

___ 6. Truman wanted to avoid an invasion of Japan because he believed that

Reading Essentials and Study Guide 19–2

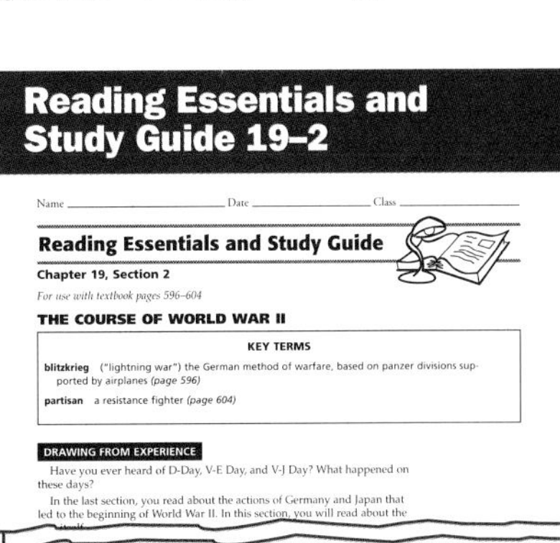
Name ______ Date ______ Class ______

Reading Essentials and Study Guide

Chapter 19, Section 2

For use with textbook pages 596–604

THE COURSE OF WORLD WAR II

KEY TERMS

blitzkrieg ("lightning war") the German method of warfare, based on panzer divisions supported by airplanes (page 596)

partisan a resistance fighter (page 604)

DRAWING FROM EXPERIENCE

Have you ever heard of D-Day, V-E Day, and V-J Day? What happened on these days?

In the last section, you read about the actions of Germany and Japan that led to the beginning of World War II. In this section, you will read about the

EXTENDING THE CONTENT

Hitler the General Contrary to the mythological picture of Hitler as a great military strategist, he actually committed many blunders that ultimately led to his defeat. Without subduing England, Hitler initiated an attack against the Soviet Union, creating a two-front war. He seriously underestimated the Soviet capability and paid a huge price for his mistake. Prior to D-Day, Hitler was fooled by the Allies into thinking that the invasion of Europe would take place at Calais. When the attack came on Normandy, he delayed the redeployment of his forces. By the time his troops became active, it was too late; the Normandy invasion had been a success.

CHAPTER 19
Section 2, 596–604

Reading Check

Answer: the one launched from Normandy after D-Day

ABCNEWS INTERACTIVE™

Turning Points in World History
The ABC News videotape includes a segment on the Holocaust and the dropping of the atomic bomb.

Critical Thinking

Ask students to debate Truman's decision to use the atomic bomb to end World War II. L2

Reteaching Activity

Using a large wall map, have students show Allied progress in the Atlantic, Soviet Union, North Africa, Italy, and the Pacific from 1942 to 1943.

4 CLOSE

Organize the class into two groups. Have each group make a list of ten key events from this section in chronological order. Combine the two lists into one top-ten list.

The Soviets had come a long way since the Battle of Stalingrad in 1943. In the summer of 1943, Hitler gambled on taking the offensive using newly developed heavy tanks. German forces were soundly defeated by the Soviets at the Battle of Kursk (July 5 to 12), the greatest tank battle of World War II.

Soviet forces now began a steady advance westward. They had reoccupied Ukraine by the end of 1943 and moved into the Baltic states by the beginning of 1944. Advancing along a northern front, Soviet troops occupied Warsaw in January 1945 and entered Berlin in April. Meanwhile, Soviet troops, along a southern front, swept through Hungary, Romania, and Bulgaria.

By January 1945, Adolf Hitler had moved into a bunker 55 feet (almost 17 m) under the city of Berlin to direct the final stages of the war. In his final political testament, Hitler, consistent to the end in his anti-Semitism, blamed the Jews for the war. He wrote, "Above all I charge the leaders of the nation and those under them to scrupulous observance of the laws of race and to merciless opposition to the universal poisoner of all peoples, international Jewry."

Hitler committed suicide on April 30, two days after Mussolini had been shot by Italian partisans, or resistance fighters. On May 7, 1945, German commanders surrendered. The war in Europe was finally over.

The Asian Theater The war in Asia continued. Beginning in 1943, U.S. forces had gone on the offensive and advanced, slowly at times, across the Pacific. As Allied military power drew closer to the main Japanese islands in the first months of 1945, **Harry S Truman,** who had become president on the death of Roosevelt in April, had a difficult decision to make. Should he use newly developed atomic weapons to bring the war to an end or find another way to defeat the Japanese forces?

Using atomic weapons would, Truman hoped, enable the United States to avoid an invasion of Japan. The Japanese had made extensive preparations to defend their homeland. Truman and his advisers had become convinced that American troops would suffer heavy casualties if they invaded Japan. At the time, however, only two bombs were available, and no one knew how effective they would be.

Truman decided to use the bombs. The first bomb was dropped on the Japanese city of **Hiroshima** on August 6. Three days later, a second bomb was dropped on Nagasaki. Both cities were leveled. Thousands of people died immediately, and thousands more died later from radiation. Emperor Hirohito now stepped in and forced the Japanese military leaders to surrender, which they did on August 14.

World War II was finally over. Seventeen million had died in battle. Perhaps twenty million civilians had perished as well. Some estimates place total losses at fifty million.

Reading Check **Identifying** What was the "second front" that the Allies opened in western Europe?

SECTION 2 ASSESSMENT

Checking for Understanding

1. **Define** blitzkrieg, partisan.
2. **Identify** Franklin D. Roosevelt, Douglas MacArthur, Winston Churchill, Harry S Truman.
3. **Locate** Stalingrad, Midway Island, Normandy, Hiroshima.
4. **Explain** Hitler's strategy of attacking the Soviet Union. Why did his delay in launching the attack ultimately contribute to the Soviet victory over the Germans?
5. **List** events leading to U.S. entry into the war.

Critical Thinking

6. **Evaluate** How might the Allied demand for unconditional surrender have helped Hitler to maintain his control over Germany?
7. **Sequencing Information** Using a chart like the one below, place the events of World War II in chronological order.

Year	Country	Event
1939		

Analyzing Visuals

8. **Examine** the photo on page 597 showing the destruction caused by the Luftwaffe's bombing raids on London. Explain how this strategy of Hitler's hurt, rather than helped, Germany's efforts.

Writing About History

9. **Descriptive Writing** Imagine you lived in California during World War II. Write an essay about your expectations of a Japanese invasion of California. You can choose to believe that an invasion was possible or impossible.

SECTION 2 ASSESSMENT

1. Key terms are in blue.
2. Franklin D. Roosevelt *(p. 597)*; General Douglas MacArthur *(p. 602)*; Winston Churchill *(p. 603)*; Harry S Truman *(p. 604)*
3. See chapter maps.
4. Hitler believed that the Soviets had a pitiful army and would be defeated quickly. Their defeat would cause Britain to fall. The delay left the German army in Russia in winter.
5. United States denounced Germany but remained neutral; United States supplied resources to Britain; Japan bombed Pearl Harbor
6. Answers will vary. It may have caused many Germans to continue to support Hitler because they saw him as the only alternative to national humiliation.
7. Students will create a time line of events.
8. By shifting from military targets to bombing British cities, Hitler gave the British an opportunity to rebuild their air strength.
9. Answers should be supported by logical arguments.

A German Soldier at Stalingrad

The Soviet victory at Stalingrad was a major turning point in World War II. These words come from the diary of a German soldier who fought and died there.

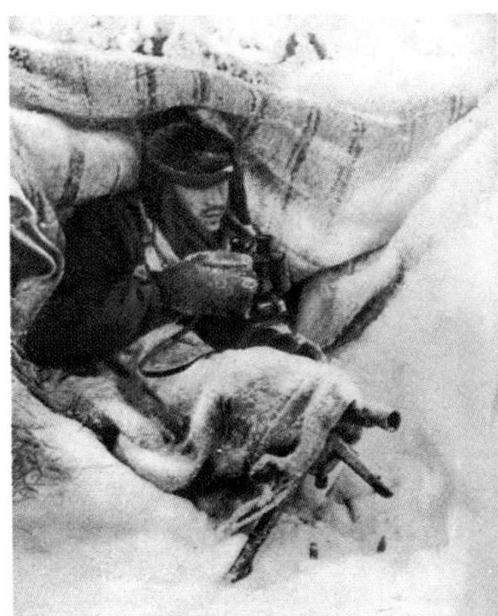

A German machine gunner endures the freezing Stalingrad winter in January 1943.

❝Today, after we'd had a bath, the company commander told us that if our future operations are as successful, we'll soon reach the Volga, take Stalingrad and then the war will inevitably soon be over. Perhaps we'll be home by Christmas.

July 29. The company commander says the Russian troops are completely broken, and cannot hold out any longer. To reach the Volga and take Stalingrad is not so difficult for us. The Führer knows where the Russians' [Soviets'] weak point is. Victory is not far away. . . .

September 4. We are being sent northward along the front towards Stalingrad. . . . It's a happy thought that the end of the war is getting nearer.

September 8. Two days of non-stop fighting. The Russians [Soviets] are defending themselves with insane stubbornness.

October 10. The Russians [Soviets] are so close to us that our planes cannot bomb them. We are preparing for a decisive attack. The Führer has ordered the whole of Stalingrad to be taken as rapidly as possible. . . .

October 22. Our regiment has failed to break into the factory. We have lost many men; every time you move you have to jump over bodies. . . .

November 10. A letter from Elsa today. Everyone expects us home for Christmas. In Germany everyone believes we already hold Stalingrad. How wrong they are. If they could only see what Stalingrad has done to our army. . . .

November 21. The Russians [Soviets] have gone over to the offensive along the whole front. Fierce fighting is going on. So, there it is—the Volga, victory and soon home to our families! We shall obviously be seeing them next in the other world.

November 29. We are encircled. It was announced this morning that the Führer has said: "The army can trust me to do everything necessary to rapidly break the encirclement."

December 3. We are on hunger rations and waiting for the rescue that the Führer promised. . . .

December 26. The horses have already been eaten. I would eat a cat; they say its meat is also tasty. The soldiers look like corpses or lunatics, looking for something to put in their mouths. They no longer take cover from Russian [Soviet] shells; they haven't the strength to walk, run away and hide. A curse on this war!❞

—A German Soldier, On the Battle of Stalingrad

Analyzing Primary Sources

1. What city was the German army trying to take?
2. How accurate was the information received by the German soldiers prior to the attack?
3. What evidence is there of both the effectiveness of Nazi propaganda, and of the soldiers' disenchantment?

TEACH

Analyzing Primary Sources

Hitler knew that capturing Stalingrad would be a tremendous victory for the German army. Initially the German army captured over half the city, but Soviet forces fought back causing a stalemate. With most of the German army engaged in fighting in the city, Stalin broke through the lines of the weaker Italian and Romanian armies, which were defending the flanks of the German army. Even though the German army was completely encircled and Hitler was advised that the situation was serious, he refused to allow his army to surrender. The temperature fell to minus 30° centigrade. The men had little to eat and began to succumb to cold, illness, and starvation.

Writing Activity

Assign students to create a similar diary that might have been written by a Soviet soldier who was defending Stalingrad. How many experiences would these two men share? Would either of them have spent much time or thought about which side in the battle was "right"? **L2**

ANSWERS TO ANALYZING PRIMARY SOURCES

1. The German army was trying to take Stalingrad.
2. The information received by German soldiers was not very accurate.
3. Apparently propaganda was very effective; everyone in Germany seems to have believed the siege of Stalingrad was going as Hitler had planned, when in fact it was not (see November 10 entry). Hitler failed to provide the support he had promised, leaving his soldiers to starve to death or be captured by the Soviets. In his November 21 entry, the soldier notes that he will next see his family "in the other world," which indicates his belief that the Germans were losing.

1 FOCUS

Section Overview

This section describes the development of the New Order in Europe, the Nazi Holocaust, Japan's expansion in Southeast Asia and its use of forced labor.

BELLRINGER
Skillbuilder Activity

Project transparency and have students answer questions.

Available as a blackline master.

Daily Focus Skills Transparency 19–3

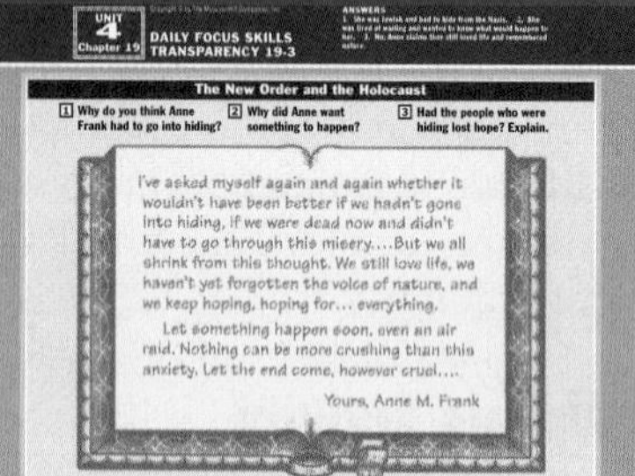
UNIT 4 Chapter 19 DAILY FOCUS SKILLS TRANSPARENCY 19-3

The New Order and the Holocaust

1. Why do you think Anne Frank had to go into hiding?
2. Why did Anne want something to happen?
3. Had the people who were hiding lost hope? Explain.

I've asked myself again and again whether it wouldn't have been better if we hadn't gone into hiding, if we were dead now and didn't have to go through this misery.... But we all shrink from this thought. We still love life, we haven't yet forgotten the voice of nature, and we keep hoping, hoping for... everything.

Let something happen soon, even an air raid. Nothing can be more crushing than this anxiety. Let the end come, however cruel....

Yours, Anne M. Frank

Guide to Reading

Answers to Graphic: Germany: directly annexed some occupied lands, Final Solution; Japan: Greater East-Asia Co-prosperity Sphere, retained power in colonies; Both: used slave labor from occupied lands

Preteaching Vocabulary: Ask students to review the meaning of *genocide*. Why is the word for "the deliberate mass murder of a group of people" not used to describe battlefield casualties in wartime? L2

SECTION 3 The New Order and the Holocaust

Guide to Reading

Main Ideas
- Adolf Hitler's philosophy of Aryan superiority led to the Holocaust.
- The Japanese conquest of Southeast Asia forced millions of native peoples to labor for the Japanese war machine.

Key Terms
genocide, collaborator

People to Identify
Heinrich Himmler, Reinhard Heydrich

Places to Locate
Poland, Auschwitz

Preview Questions
1. How did the Nazis carry out their Final Solution?
2. How did the Japanese create a dilemma for nationalists in the lands they occupied?

Reading Strategy
Compare and Contrast Using a Venn diagram like the one below, compare and contrast the New Order of Germany with the New Order of Japan.

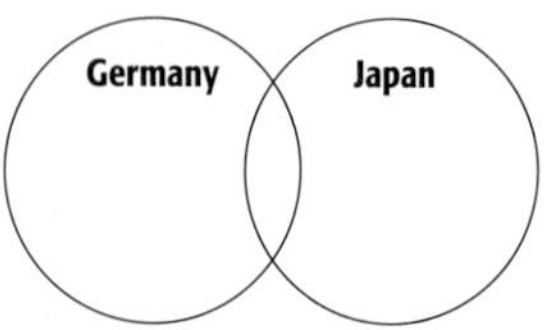

Preview of Events

1940 · 1941 · 1942 · 1943 · 1944 · 1945

- **1941** *Einsatzgruppen* created
- **1942** Two million ethnic Germans resettled in Poland
- **1943** Japan uses forced labor to build Burma-Thailand railroad
- **1944** Nazis continue Final Solution even as they start losing the war

Voices from the Past

Rudolf Höss

Rudolf Höss, commanding officer at the Auschwitz death camp, described the experience awaiting the Jews when they arrived there:

> "We had two SS doctors on duty at Auschwitz to examine the incoming transports of prisoners. The prisoners would be marched by one of the doctors who would make spot decisions as they walked by. Those who were fit for work were sent into the camp. Others were sent immediately to the extermination plants. Children of tender years were invariably exterminated since by reason of their youth they were unable to work. . . . At Auschwitz we fooled the victims into thinking that they were to go through a delousing process. Frequently they realized our true intentions and we sometimes had riots and difficulties due to that fact."
>
> —*Nazi Conspiracy and Aggression,* vol. 6, 1946

Millions of Jews died in the Nazi death camps.

The New Order in Europe

In 1942, the Nazi regime stretched across continental Europe from the English Channel in the west to the outskirts of Moscow in the east. Nazi-occupied Europe was largely organized in one of two ways. Some areas, such as western Poland, were directly annexed by Nazi Germany and made into German provinces. Most of occupied Europe, however, was run by German military or civilian officials with help from local people who were willing to collaborate with the Nazis.

SECTION RESOURCES

Reproducible Masters
- Reproducible Lesson Plan 19–3
- Daily Lecture and Discussion Notes 19–3
- Guided Reading Activity 19–3
- Section Quiz 19–3
- Reading Essentials and Study Guide 19–3

Transparencies
- Daily Focus Skills Transparency 19–3

Multimedia
- Interactive Tutor Self-Assessment CD-ROM
- ExamView® Pro Testmaker CD-ROM
- Presentation Plus! CD-ROM

Resettlement in the East Nazi administration in the conquered lands to the east was especially ruthless. These lands were seen as the living space for German expansion. They were populated, Nazis thought, by racially inferior Slavic peoples. Hitler's plans for an Aryan racial empire were so important to him that he and the Nazis began to put their racial program into effect soon after the conquest of **Poland.**

Heinrich Himmler, the leader of the SS, was put in charge of German resettlement plans in the east. Himmler's task was to move the Slavic peoples out and replace them with Germans. Slavic peoples included Czech, Polish, Serbo-Croatian, Slovene, and Ukrainian. This policy was first applied to the new German provinces created from the lands of western Poland.

One million Poles were uprooted and moved to southern Poland. Hundreds of thousands of ethnic Germans (descendants of Germans who had migrated years ago from Germany to different parts of southern and eastern Europe) were brought in to colonize the German provinces in Poland. By 1942, two million ethnic Germans had been settled in Poland.

The invasion of the Soviet Union made the Nazis even more excited about German colonization in the east. Hitler spoke to his intimate circle of a colossal project of social engineering after the war. Poles, Ukrainians, and Russians would be removed from their lands and become slave labor. German peasants would settle on the abandoned lands and "Germanize" them.

Himmler told a gathering of SS officers that 30 million Slavs might die in order to achieve German plans in the east. He continued, "Whether nations live in prosperity or starve to death interests me only insofar as we need them as slaves for our culture. Otherwise it is of no interest."

Slave Labor in Germany Labor shortages in Germany led to a policy of rounding up foreign workers for Germany. In 1942, a special office was set up to recruit labor for German farms and industries. By the summer of 1944, seven million European workers were laboring in Germany. They made up 20 percent of Germany's labor force. Another seven million workers were forced to labor for the Nazis in their own countries on farms, in industries, and even in military camps.

The use of forced labor often caused problems, however. Sending so many workers to Germany disrupted industrial production in the occupied countries that could have helped Germany. Then, too, the brutal way in which Germany recruited foreign workers led more and more people to resist the Nazi occupation forces.

People In History

Anne Frank
1929–1945
Dutch Holocaust victim

Anne Frank is one of the best-known victims of the Nazi Holocaust. When the Nazis began to round up Jews in the Netherlands, the Frank family, along with another family, moved into a secret annex above a warehouse owned by the family business. Employees of the Frank family provided food and a lifeline to the outside world.

Anne remained hopeful. She kept a diary to while away the time spent in hiding. On July 15, 1944, she wrote, "In spite of everything I still believe that people are really good at heart."

On August 4, 1944, after the Franks had spent two years in hiding, the Nazis found the secret annex. Anne and her sister were sent to Bergen-Belsen, a concentration camp in Germany. There they died of typhus. Anne's father, Otto Frank, who survived, later found Anne's diary. He had it published in 1947. *The Diary of Anne Frank* became an international best-seller.

Reading Check **Describing** What was Hitler's vision for the residents of eastern Europe?

The Holocaust

No aspect of the Nazi New Order was more terrifying than the deliberate attempt to exterminate the Jews. Racial struggle was a key element in Hitler's world of ideas. To him, racial struggle was a clearly defined conflict of opposites. On one side were the Aryans, creators of human cultural development. On the other side were the Jews, parasites, in Hitler's view, who were trying to destroy the Aryans.

Himmler and the SS closely shared Hitler's racial ideas. The SS was given responsibility for what the Nazis called their Final Solution to the Jewish problem. The Final Solution was **genocide** (physical extermination) of the Jewish people.

The *Einsatzgruppen* **Reinhard Heydrich,** head of the SS's Security Service, was given the task of administering the Final Solution. Heydrich created

2 TEACH

Reading Check

Answer: Hitler's goal was to remove Poles, Ukrainians, and Russians from their land, force them to become slave laborers, and replace them with Germans.

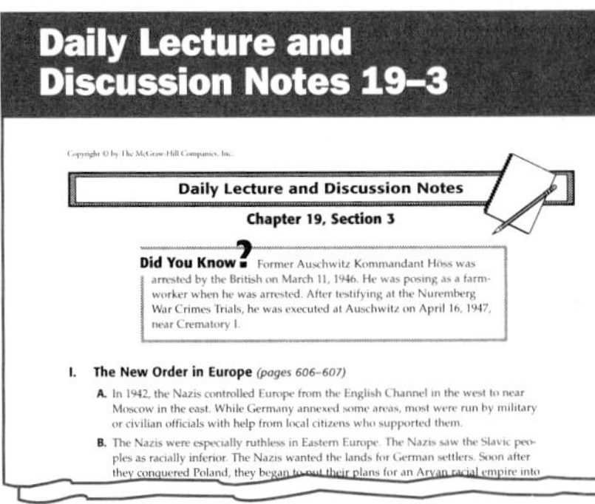
Daily Lecture and Discussion Notes 19–3

Daily Lecture and Discussion Notes

Chapter 19, Section 3

Did You Know? Former Auschwitz Kommandant Höss was arrested by the British on March 11, 1946. He was posing as a farmworker when he was arrested. After testifying at the Nuremberg War Crimes Trials, he was executed at Auschwitz on April 16, 1947, near Crematory I.

I. **The New Order in Europe** *(pages 606–607)*

A. In 1942, the Nazis controlled Europe from the English Channel in the west to near Moscow in the east. While Germany annexed some areas, most were run by military or civilian officials with help from local citizens who supported them.

B. The Nazis were especially ruthless in Eastern Europe. The Nazis saw the Slavic peoples as racially inferior. The Nazis wanted the lands for German settlers. Soon after they conquered Poland, they began to put their plans for an Aryan racial empire into

Critical Thinking

Ask students to refer to the quote on page 606 from Rudolph Höss. Discuss the description of the operation of death squads described in the quoted material. Point out to students that the writer is matter-of-fact and that he portrays little or no emotion. Ask students why they think this is. L2

Connecting Across Time

Unfortunately, war has often involved the killing of innocent civilians. Ask students to explain what made the killing of the Jewish people by the Nazis so different from civilian casualties in other wars. L2

CRITICAL THINKING ACTIVITY

Engaging in Historical Inquiry Remind students that in recent years there have been some efforts to prove that the Holocaust did not occur, or that the number of those who perished in German-run concentration camps has been greatly exaggerated. Have students explain and then apply different methods that historians use to interpret the past, including the use of primary and secondary sources, points of view, frames of reference, and historical context to refute this claim. Have students prepare a final report by first creating research outlines. Ask students to interpret each other's research outlines, looking for correct format and clarity of ideas. Then have students write a final report in which they include a bibliography, as well as databases, visuals, charts, time lines, and maps as appropriate. L2 L3

CHAPTER 19
Section 3, 606–611

Geography *Skills*

Answers:

1. six death camps, 25 concentration camps
2. located away from Germany, Poland had a large Jewish population

Guided Reading Activity 19–3

Name ______________ Date ______________ Class ______________

Guided Reading Activity 19-3

The New Order and the Holocaust

DIRECTIONS: Complete the outline below as you read Section 3.

I. In 1942, the Nazi regime stretched from the ______________ to ______________.
   A. ______________ moved Slavic people in the East and replaced them with ______________.
   B. By summer, 1944, seven million Europeans were ______________ to work for the Nazis.
II. The Final Solution in Hitler's Europe was ______________ of the Jewish people.
   A. ______________ formed death squads to kill Jews by mass murder.
   B. Six ______________ centers were built in Poland for mass executions of Jews.
   C. The Germans killed between five and six ______________ Jews.

Enrich

Assign small groups of students to research one of the following topics: *Kristallnacht;* the Warsaw Ghetto; German use of slave labor; artworks and gold stolen by Germany from occupied countries. Have each group present a panel discussion based on its research. After all panels have been presented, have the class discuss how Hitler's "New Order" was carried out through these various activities. **L2**

Critical Thinking

Ask students to explain why they believe any human being could be involved in the type of actions described in this section. Do students believe this could have happened without the unspoken support or tacit consent of most German people? **L2**

special strike forces, called *Einsatzgruppen,* to carry out Nazi plans. After the defeat of Poland, he ordered these forces to round up all Polish Jews and put them in ghettos set up in a number of Polish cities. Conditions in the ghettos were horrible. Families were crowded together in unsanitary housing. The Nazis attempted to starve residents by allowing only minimal amounts of food. Despite suffering, residents tried to carry on and some ghettos organized resistance against the Nazis.

In June 1941, the *Einsatzgruppen* were given the new job of acting as mobile killing units. These SS death squads followed the regular army's advance into the Soviet Union. Their job was to round up Jews in their villages, execute them, and bury them in mass graves. The graves were often giant pits dug by the victims themselves before they were shot.

The leader of one of these death squads described the mode of operation:

> "The unit selected for this task would enter a village or city and order the prominent Jewish citizens to call together all Jews for the purpose of resettlement. They were requested to hand over their valuables to the leaders of the unit, and shortly before the execution to surrender their outer clothing. The men, women, and children were led to a place of execution which in most cases was located next to a more deeply excavated anti-tank ditch. Then they were shot, kneeling or standing, and the corpses thrown into the ditch."

The Death Camps Probably one million Jews were killed by the *Einsatzgruppen.* As appalling as that sounds, it was too slow by Nazi standards. They

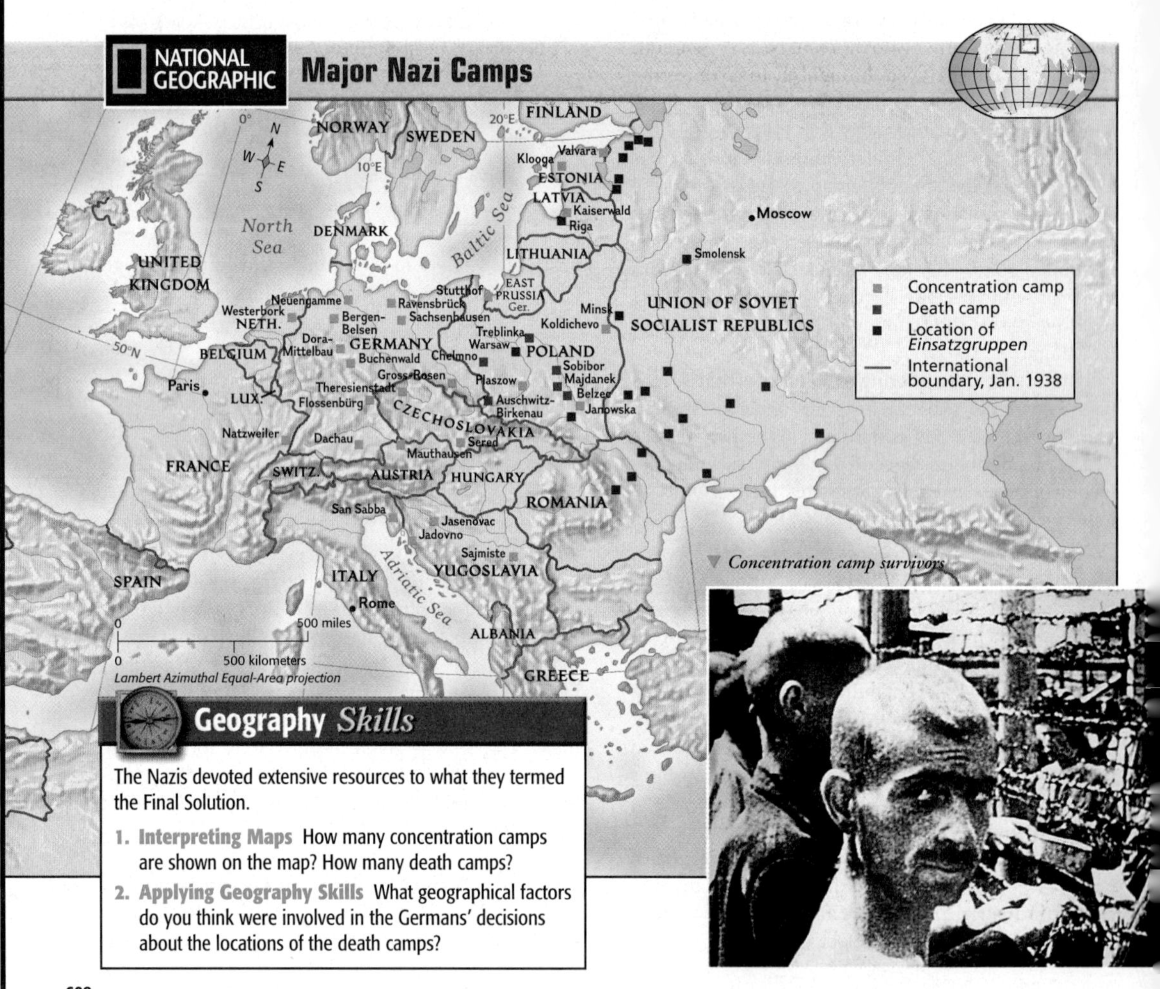

▼ *Concentration camp survivors*

Geography *Skills*

The Nazis devoted extensive resources to what they termed the Final Solution.

1. **Interpreting Maps** How many concentration camps are shown on the map? How many death camps?
2. **Applying Geography Skills** What geographical factors do you think were involved in the Germans' decisions about the locations of the death camps?

COOPERATIVE LEARNING ACTIVITY

Making a Presentation Organize the class into small groups to research the roots and results of anti-Semitism. Assign each group a different area to research: 1) a history of the Hebrew people, including the Diaspora (A.D. 70); 2) a history of the Jewish expulsion from European countries (e.g. Spain, 1492); 3) excerpts of writings or speeches by famous people (e.g. Theodor Herzl); 4) excerpts from books or stories of the Holocaust (e.g. *Night* by Elie Wiesel); 5) reasons given by Nazis for their treatment of European Jews; and 6) world reactions to Nazi treatment of the Jews. Provide students with the materials needed for their research and ask them to present their information to the class. **L2**

decided to kill the European Jewish population in specially built death camps.

Beginning in 1942, Jews from countries occupied by Germany (or sympathetic to Germany) were rounded up, packed like cattle into freight trains, and shipped to Poland. Six extermination centers were built in Poland for this purpose. The largest was **Auschwitz** (AUSH•VIHTS).

About 30 percent of the arrivals at Auschwitz were sent to a labor camp, where many were starved or worked to death. The remainder went to the gas chambers. Some inmates were subjected to cruel and painful "medical" experiments.

Jewish men, women, and children being taken by the Nazis

By the spring of 1942, the death camps were in full operation. First priority was given to the elimination of the ghettos in Poland. By the summer of 1942, however, Jews were also being shipped from France, Belgium, and Holland. Even as the Allies were winning the war in 1944, Jews were being shipped from Greece and Hungary. Despite desperate military needs, even late in the war when Germany faced utter defeat, the Final Solution had priority in using railroad cars to ship Jews to death camps.

The Death Toll The Germans killed between five and six million Jews, over three million of them in the death camps. Virtually 90 percent of the Jewish populations of Poland, the Baltic countries, and Germany were killed. Overall, the Holocaust was responsible for the death of nearly two out of every three European Jews.

The Nazis were also responsible for the deliberate death by shooting, starvation, or overwork of at least another nine to ten million non-Jewish people. The Nazis considered the Gypsies of Europe, like the Jews, to be a race containing alien blood. The Gypsies were rounded up for mass killing. About 40 percent of Europe's one million Gypsies were killed in the death camps.

The leading citizens of the Slavic peoples—the clergy, intellectuals, civil leaders, judges, and lawyers—were arrested and killed. Probably an additional four million Poles, Ukrainians, and Belorussians lost their lives as slave laborers for Nazi Germany. Finally, probably at least three million to four million Soviet prisoners of war were killed in captivity.

> **HISTORY Online**
> **Web Activity** Visit the *Glencoe World History—Modern Times* Web site at wh.mt.glencoe.com and click on **Chapter 19–Student Web Activity** to learn more about concentration camps.

This mass slaughter of European civilians, particularly European Jews, is known as the Holocaust. Jews in and out of the camps attempted to resist the Nazis. Some were aided by friends and even strangers, hidden in villages or smuggled into safe areas. Foreign diplomats would try to save Jews by issuing exit visas. The nation of Denmark saved almost its entire Jewish population.

Some people did not believe the accounts of death camps because, during World War I, allies had greatly exaggerated German atrocities to arouse enthusiasm for the war. Most often, people pretended not to notice what was happening. Even worse, collaborators (people who assisted the enemy) helped the Nazis hunt down Jews. The Allies were aware of the concentration camps and death camps but chose to concentrate on ending the war. Not until after the war did they learn the full extent of the horror and inhumanity of the Holocaust. *(See page 779 to read excerpts from* The Holocaust—The Camp Victims *in the Primary Sources Library.)*

The Other Victims Young people of all ages were also victims of World War II. Because they were unable to work, Jewish children, along with their mothers, were the first ones selected for gas chambers upon their arrival in the death camps of Poland. Young Jewish males soon learned to look as adult as possible in order to survive. Altogether, 1.2 million Jewish children died in the Holocaust.

> **Who? What? Where? When?**
> **Jewish Resistance** There were many acts of resistance to Nazi atrocities. For example, several hundred prisoners assigned to Crematorium IV at Auschwitz-Birkenau rebelled after learning that they were going to be killed. Jewish slave laborers in a nearby armaments factory smuggled explosives into the camp. On October 7, 1944, the prisoners killed three guards and blew up the crematorium and adjacent gas chamber. The Germans crushed the revolt and killed almost all of the prisoners involved in the rebellion. The Jewish women who had smuggled the explosives into the camp were publicly hanged.

Writing Activity

Ask students to research the Allied response to the Nazi persecution and killing of the Jews, Gypsies, and others. What actions did the Allies take to stop it? Have students write a report on the results of their research. L3

Connecting Across Time

The Holocaust is one of the most significant examples of human rights violations in the twentieth century. Ask students to identify other examples of political, economic, and social oppression and violations of human rights that have occurred throughout history. L2

CRITICAL THINKING ACTIVITY

Describing Ask students to describe the changes that must have taken place in communities surrounding Auschwitz-Birkenau in Poland. Citizens must have known or suspected what was happening nearby. What would they have thought? How could they have carried on normal day-to-day lives? Do students believe that any of them could really not have known what was being done? Ask students to research materials describing the reactions of people living in communities near Auschwitz and other extermination camps. Have the students imagine that they are members of one of those communities and write first-person narratives about their responses. L2

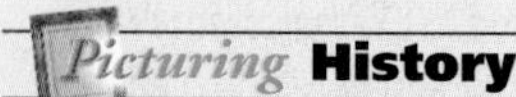

Answer: They were in charge of carrying out the Final Solution.

Picturing **History**

Answer: They were forced to be slave laborers in construction projects to help the Japanese war effort.

3 ASSESS

Assign Section 3 Assessment as homework or as an in-class activity.

Have students use **Interactive Tutor Self-Assessment CD-ROM.**

Section Quiz 19–3

Name ______ Date ______ Class ______

Chapter 19 — Score

Section Quiz 19-3

DIRECTIONS: Matching Match each item in Column A with an item in Column B. Write the correct letters in the blanks. *(10 points each)*

Column A	Column B
____ 1. Hitler's "Final Solution" for the Jews	A. Auschwitz
____ 2. crowded, designated containment or holding areas within cities for Jews	B. genocide
____ 3. Hitler's largest extermination center in Poland	C. Holocaust
____ 4. the mass slaughter of European civilians, especially Jews	D. ghettos
____ 5. French Indochinese Communist leader	E. Ho Chi Minh

DIRECTIONS: Multiple Choice In the blank, write the letter of the choice that best completes the statement or answers the question. *(10 points each)*

____ 6. After 1941, Germany ruled some areas like Poland through direct

Reading Essentials and Study Guide 19–3

Name ______ Date ______ Class ______

Reading Essentials and Study Guide

Chapter 19, Section 3

For use with textbook pages 606–611

THE NEW ORDER AND THE HOLOCAUST

KEY TERMS

genocide the physical extermination of a racial, political, or cultural group *(page 607)*

collaborator a person who assists the enemy *(page 609)*

DRAWING FROM EXPERIENCE

Have you ever heard about the Holocaust? Have you ever been to the Holocaust Museum in Washington, D.C.? What was the Holocaust? Why did it take place?

In the last two sections, you learned about events leading to World War II and the battles of the war. In this section, you will learn about the atrocities committed by the Nazis and the Japanese against the peoples they conquered.

ORGANIZING YOUR THOUGHTS

Use the chart below to help you take notes. Describe the following policies or programs of Hitler and the Nazis.

Nazi Policy	Description
resettlement	1.
forced labor	2.

Many children were evacuated from cities during the war in order to avoid the bombing. The Germans created about 9,000 camps for children in the countryside. In Japan, 15,000 children were evacuated from Hiroshima before its destruction. The British moved about 6 million children and their mothers in 1939.

Some British parents even sent their children to Canada and the United States. This, too, could be dangerous. When the ocean liner *Arandora Star* was hit by a German torpedo, it had 77 British children on board. They never made it to Canada.

Children evacuated to the countryside did not always see their parents again. Some of them, along with many other children, became orphaned when their parents were killed. In 1945, there were perhaps 13 million orphaned children in Europe.

In eastern Europe, children especially suffered under harsh German occupation policies. All secondary schools in German-occupied eastern Europe were closed. Their facilities and equipment were destroyed.

Heinrich Himmler, head of the SS, said of these Slavic children that their education should consist only "in teaching simple arithmetic up to 500, the writing of one's name, and that God has ordered obedience to the Germans, honesty, diligence, and politeness. I do not consider an ability to read as necessary."

At times, young people were expected to carry the burden of fighting the war. In the last year of the war, Hitler Youth members, often only 14 or 15 years old, could be found in the front lines. In the Soviet Union, children as young as 13 or 14 spied on German positions and worked with the resistance movement. Some were even given decorations for killing the enemy.

Reading Check **Summarizing** What was the job of the *Einsatzgruppen?*

The New Order in Asia

Japanese war policy in the areas in Asia occupied by Japan was basically defensive. Japan hoped to use its new possessions to meet its growing need for raw materials, such as tin, oil, and rubber. The new possessions also would be an outlet for Japanese manufactured goods. To organize these possessions, Japanese leaders included them in the Greater East Asia Co-prosperity Sphere. This was the economic community supposedly designed to provide mutual benefits to the occupied areas and the home country.

Japanese Policies The Japanese had conquered Southeast Asia under the slogan "Asia for the Asiatics." Japanese officials in occupied territories quickly made contact with anticolonialists. They promised the people that local governments would be established under Japanese control. Such governments were eventually set up in Burma, the Dutch East Indies, Vietnam, and the Philippines.

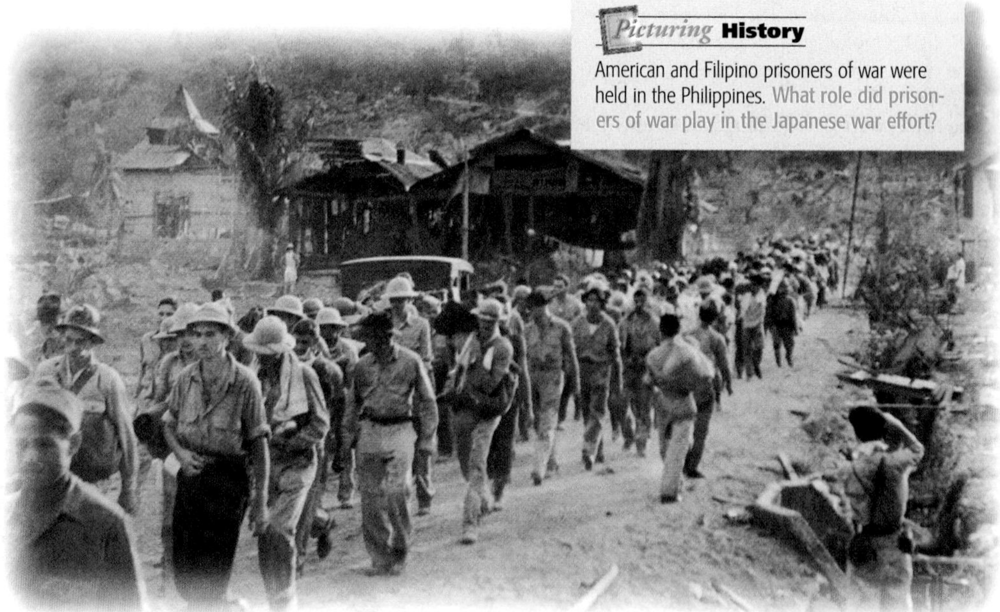

Picturing **History**

American and Filipino prisoners of war were held in the Philippines. What role did prisoners of war play in the Japanese war effort?

EXTENDING THE CONTENT

Nanjing Chinese citizens inside the walled city and in its vicinity showed fierce defiance toward the Japanese soldiers after the atrocities committed by the Imperial Army in 1937. Thousands of peasants organized a "Red Spear Society" that ambushed enemy soldiers. In other acts of resistance, anti-Japan leaflets were secretly printed and distributed in schools, movie theaters, and buses. Anti-Japan organizations inside and outside of the city received covert and overt aid from both the Nationalist Government and the Communist Party. In some instances, armed groups ambushed the Japanese occupying forces.

In fact, real power rested with Japanese military authorities in each territory. In turn, the local Japanese military command was directly subordinated to the Army General Staff in Tokyo. The economic resources of the colonies were used for the benefit of the Japanese war machine. The native peoples in occupied lands were recruited to serve in local military units or were forced to work on public works projects.

In some cases, these policies brought severe hardships to peoples living in the occupied areas. In Vietnam, for example, local Japanese authorities forcibly took rice and shipped it abroad. This led directly to a food shortage that caused over a million Vietnamese to starve to death in 1944 and 1945.

Japanese Behavior At first, many Southeast Asian nationalists took Japanese promises at face value and agreed to cooperate with their new masters. In Burma, for example, an independent government was set up in 1943 and declared war on the Allies. Eventually, the nature of Japanese occupation policies became clear, and sentiment turned against Japan.

Japanese officials provoked such attitudes by their arrogance and contempt for local customs. In the Dutch East Indies, for example, Indonesians were required to bow in the direction of Tokyo and to recognize the divinity of the Japanese emperor. In Burma, Buddhist pagodas were used as military latrines.

Like German soldiers in occupied Europe, Japanese military forces often had little respect for the lives of their subject peoples. After their conquest of Nanjing, China, in 1937, Japanese soldiers spent several days killing, raping, and looting. After the conquest of Korea, almost eight hundred thousand Korean people were sent to Japan, most of them as forced laborers.

In construction projects to help their war effort, the Japanese made extensive use of labor forces composed of both prisoners of war and local peoples. In building the Burma-Thailand railway in 1943, for example, the Japanese used 61,000 Australian, British, and Dutch prisoners of war and almost 300,000 workers from Burma, Malaya, Thailand, and the Dutch East Indies. An inadequate diet and appalling work conditions in an unhealthy climate led to the death of 12,000 Allied prisoners of war and 90,000 workers by the time the railway was completed.

Such Japanese behavior created a dilemma for many nationalists in the occupied lands. They had no desire to see the return of the colonial powers, but they did not like what the Japanese were doing. Some turned against the Japanese. Others simply did nothing.

Indonesian patriots tried to have it both ways. They pretended to support Japan while actually sabotaging the Japanese administration. In French Indochina, Ho Chi Minh's Communist Party made contact with U.S. military units in South China. The Communists agreed to provide information on Japanese troop movements and to rescue downed American fliers in the area. By the end of the war, little support remained in the region for the Japanese "liberators."

Reading Check **Examining** How did the Japanese treat the native peoples in occupied lands?

SECTION 3 ASSESSMENT

Checking for Understanding

1. **Define** genocide, collaborator.
2. **Identify** Heinrich Himmler, Reinhard Heydrich.
3. **Locate** Poland, Auschwitz.
4. **Explain** what the Nazis meant by the Final Solution. How did Hitler's commitment to the Final Solution hinder Germany's war effort?
5. **List** examples of objectionable Japanese occupation policies in Asia.

Critical Thinking

6. **Evaluate** What was the impact of the Holocaust on history? What lessons does the Holocaust have for us today?
7. **Cause and Effect** Create a chart giving examples of Hitler's actions to create a New World Order in Europe and the outcome of his efforts.

Hitler's Actions	Outcome

Analyzing Visuals

8. **Examine** the scene pictured on page 609. Describe, based on your reading, the series of events that will most likely follow.

Writing About History

9. **Persuasive Writing** Imagine you are a member of Hitler's inner circle in 1941 and are alarmed about Hitler's Final Solution. Compose a letter to Hitler, outlining the reasons why he should abandon plans to send Jews to the death camps.

Reading Check

Answer: Native peoples were recruited to serve in local military units or forced to work on public works projects.

Enrich

Have interested students do further research on the Nazi Holocaust by visiting the Web site of the U.S. Holocaust Memorial Museum. Ask these students to report back to the class any interesting facts or stories learned at the Web site. L1

Reteaching Activity

Have students compare the goals and methods of Hitler's "New Order" with Japan's plans to create an "Asia for Asiatics." L2

Glencoe Literature Library

The following literature from the **Glencoe Literature Library** may enrich the teaching of this chapter: *Night* by E. Wiesel

4 CLOSE

Ask students to analyze the information in this section by comparing the treatment of people in lands occupied by the Nazi forces of Germany and those of lands conquered by the Japanese. Did either of these powers have any apparent interest in the rights of the occupied people? L1

SECTION 3 ASSESSMENT

1. Key terms are in blue.
2. Heinrich Himmler *(p. 607)*; Reinhard Heydrich *(p. 607)*
3. See chapter maps.
4. The extermination of the Jewish people was meant to be the Final Solution to the "Jewish problem." Hitler diverted resources that could have been spent on the war.
5. forced Indonesians to recognize emperor's divinity; used Buddhist pagodas as military latrines; Japanese soldiers killed, raped, and looted Nanjing; used forced labor, many workers died
6. Answers should be supported by logical arguments.
7. Answers may include: Final Solution: millions of Jews killed; invaded Russia: German army defeated and weakened
8. herded up, packed into freight trains, shipped to death camps in Poland
9. Answers should be consistent with material presented in this section.

1 FOCUS

Section Overview

This section describes the impact of the war on civilians and how developments at the end of World War II led to the Cold War.

BELLRINGER
Skillbuilder Activity

 Project transparency and have students answer questions.

 Available as a blackline master.

Daily Focus Skills Transparency 19–4

Guide to Reading

Answers to Graphic: Soviet Union: shortages in food and housing; United States: widespread movement of people; Japanese Americans removed to camps; Japan: imported laborers from China and Korea; Germany: total mobilization of the economy near end of war closed schools, theaters, and cafes

Preteaching Vocabulary: Ask students to look up the meaning of the word *kamikaze*. Have students explain similarities between the *divine wind* that protected Japan in 1281 (Chapter 3), and the goal of pilots in 1945. L2

SECTION 4 The Home Front and the Aftermath of the War

Guide to Reading

Main Ideas
- World War II left a lasting impression on civilian populations.
- The end of the war created a new set of problems for the Allies as the West came into conflict with the Soviet Union.

Key Terms
mobilization, kamikaze, Cold War

People to Identify
Albert Speer, General Hideki Tojo

Places to Locate
London, Dresden, Hiroshima

Preview Questions
1. Why were the Japanese encouraged to serve as kamikaze pilots?
2. What was the outcome of the Yalta Conference in 1945?

Reading Strategy
Compare and Contrast Create a chart comparing and contrasting the impact of World War II on the lives of civilians.

Country	Impact on Lives of Civilians
Soviet Union	
United States	
Japan	
Germany	

Preview of Events

1942 · 1943 · 1944 · 1945 · 1946 · 1947

- **1943** Stalin, Roosevelt, and Churchill meet in Tehran to determine future course of war
- **1945** Allies bomb Dresden
- **1946** Churchill proclaims existence of "iron curtain" in Europe

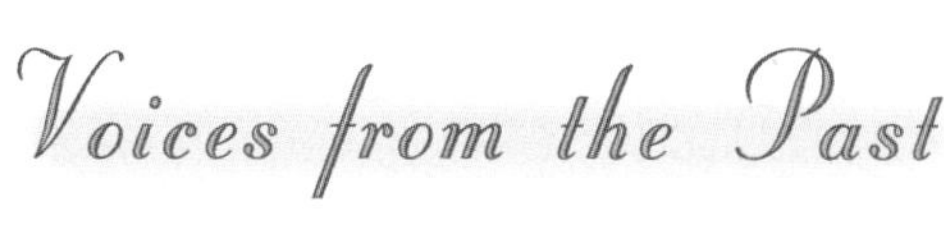

A B-26 drops bombs on Germany.

A German civilian described an Allied bombing raid on Hamburg in 1943:

❝As the many fires broke through the roofs of the burning buildings, a column of heated air rose more than two and a half miles high and one and a half miles in diameter. . . . This column was fed from its base by in-rushing cooler ground-surface air. One and one half miles from the fires this draft increased the wind velocity from eleven to thirty-three miles per hour. At the edge of the area the velocities must have been much greater, as trees three feet in diameter were uprooted. In a short time the temperature reached ignition point for all combustibles, and the entire area was ablaze. In such fires, complete burnout occurred, that is, no trace of combustible material remained.❞

—*The Bombing of Germany*, Hans Rumpf, 1963

The bombing of civilians in World War II made the home front dangerous.

The Mobilization of Peoples: Four Examples

Even more than World War I, World War II was a total war. Fighting was much more widespread and covered most of the world. Economic **mobilization** (the act of assembling and preparing for war) was more extensive; so, too, was the mobilization of women. The number of civilians killed—almost twenty million—was far higher. Many of these victims were children.

SECTION RESOURCES

Reproducible Masters
- Reproducible Lesson Plan 19–4
- Daily Lecture and Discussion Notes 19–4
- Guided Reading Activity 19–4
- Section Quiz 19–4
- Reading Essentials and Study Guide 19–4

Transparencies
- Daily Focus Skills Transparency 19–4

Multimedia
- Interactive Tutor Self-Assessment CD-ROM
- ExamView® Pro Testmaker CD-ROM
- Presentation Plus! CD-ROM

World War II had an enormous impact on civilian life in the Soviet Union, the United States, Germany, and Japan. We consider the home fronts of those four nations next.

The Soviet Union The initial defeats of the Soviet Union led to drastic emergency measures that affected the lives of the civilian population. Leningrad, for example, experienced nine hundred days of siege. Its inhabitants became so desperate for food that they ate dogs, cats, and mice. Probably 1.5 million people died in the city.

As the German army made its rapid advance into Soviet territory, Soviet workers dismantled and shipped the factories in the western part of the Soviet Union to the interior—to the Urals, western Siberia, and the Volga regions. Machines were placed on the bare ground. As laborers began their work, walls went up around them.

Stalin called the widespread military and industrial mobilization of the nation a "battle of machines." The Soviets won, producing 78,000 tanks and 98,000 artillery pieces. In 1943, 55 percent of the Soviet national income went for war materials, compared with 15 percent in 1940. As a result of the emphasis on military goods, Soviet citizens experienced severe shortages of both food and housing.

Soviet women played a major role in the war effort. Women and girls worked in industries, mines, and railroads. Overall, the number of women working in industry increased almost 60 percent. Soviet women were also expected to dig antitank ditches and work as air raid wardens. In addition, the Soviet Union was the only country in World War II to use women in battle. Soviet women served as snipers and also in aircrews of bomber squadrons.

The United States The home front in the United States was quite different from that of the other major powers. The United States was not fighting the war in its own territory. Eventually, the United States became the arsenal of the Allied Powers; it produced much of the military equipment the Allies needed. At the height of war production in November 1943, the country was building six ships a day and ninety-six thousand planes per year.

The mobilization of the American economy resulted in some social turmoil, however. The construction of new factories created boomtowns. Thousands came there to work but then faced a shortage of houses and schools. Widespread movements of people took place. Sixteen million men and women were enrolled in the military and moved frequently. Another sixteen million, mostly wives and girlfriends of servicemen or workers looking for jobs, also moved around the country.

Over a million African Americans moved from the rural South to the cities of the North and West, looking for jobs in industry. The presence of African Americans in areas where they had not lived before led to racial tensions and sometimes even racial riots. In Detroit in June 1943, for example, white mobs roamed the streets attacking African Americans.

One million African Americans enrolled in the military. There they were segregated in their own battle units. Angered by the way they were treated, some became militant and prepared to fight for their civil rights.

Picturing History

Many Japanese American families in southern California were transported to internment camps. Would you have supported the internment policy for Japanese Americans during the war? Explain.

CHAPTER 19
Section 4, 612–618

2 TEACH

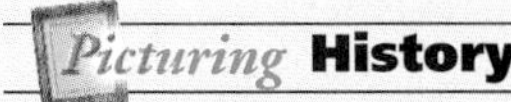

Picturing History

Answer: Answers should be supported by logical arguments.

Daily Lecture and Discussion Notes 19–4

Daily Lecture and Discussion Notes

Chapter 19, Section 4

Did You Know? President Truman said that he dropped the atomic bomb to avoid terrible American losses in the anticipated invasion of Japan. However, documents released under the Freedom of Information Act indicate that Truman may have overestimated these numbers. Many think that he had another purpose, which was to demonstrate American power to the possible new enemy, the Soviet Union.

I. The Mobilization of Peoples: Four Examples *(pages 612–614)*

A. Even more than World War I, World War II was a total war. Economic **mobilization** was more extensive. The war had an enormous impact on civilian life in many parts of the world.

B. In the Soviet Union initial defeats led to drastic emergency measures. For example, Leningrad was under siege for nine hundred days. Over a million people died there due to food shortages. People had to eat dogs, cats, and mice.

C. Soviet workers dismantled factories in the west and shipped them to the east, out of the way of the attacking German army. At times workers ran machines as new factory buildings were built up around them.

D. The military and industrial mobilization of the Soviet Union produced 78,000 tanks artillery pieces. In 1943, 55 percent of the national income went to war materials. As a result there were severe shortages of food and housing.

E. Soviet women were an important part of the war effort. Women working in industry increased 60 percent. They worked in industries, mines, and railroads. They dug antitank ditches and worked as air raid wardens. Some fought in battles and flew in bombers.

F. The war did not come to the home territory of the United States. The country became an arsenal for the Allies. The United States produced much of the military equipment needed to fight the Axis. In 1943, the United States was building six ships a day and ninety-six thousand planes per year.

G. The American mobilization created some social turmoil. There were widespread movements of people. For example, many women and men enrolled in the military moved frequently. Also, as millions of servicemen and workers looking for jobs moved around, their wives and children or girl friends often moved with them.

turn

283

Connecting Across Time

Although World War I was devastating for people who lived near the front, the homes, towns, and places of work of most Europeans were not damaged by the fighting. Ask students to compare this scenario with the physical destruction in Europe and Southeast Asia during World War II. **L1**

EXTENDING THE CONTENT

Women at War During the war there was a severe labor shortage, since men left their jobs to join the military and new jobs were created to meet wartime needs for munitions, food, and clothing. From 1942 to 1945, nearly six million American women joined the workforce and filled every conceivable kind of job. Most of those women lost their jobs when men returned home after the war. However, women had proven beyond a doubt that they were the equals of men. Since the 1960s, when women demanded equal access to economic opportunities, the legacy of their wartime counterparts facilitated their move into the economic mainstream.

CHAPTER 19
Section 4, 612–618

Reading Check

Answer: The movement of many African Americans from the South to cities in the North and West created racial tensions. Segregation in the military made some African Americans militant and prepared to fight for their civil rights.

Who?What?Where?When?

Japanese American Soldiers The 442nd Regimental Combat Team, a Japanese American unit, fought in eight major campaigns. Despite a climate of prejudice that interned thousands of Japanese Americans, the 442nd was an all-volunteer regiment that fought bravely for the United States. Altogether almost 26,000 Japanese Americans fought for the United States during World War II.

TURNING POINT

On February 19, 1942, President Roosevelt signed Executive Order 9066, which authorized the War Department to move 112,000 Japanese American men, women, and children from the West Coast to crude internment camps farther inland. These Americans lost their constitutional rights, property, businesses, and homes. Despite this policy, Japanese Americans remained loyal to the United States. None were ever brought to trial for espionage or sabotage. Ask students why they think Roosevelt signed this order.

Japanese Americans faced even more serious difficulties. On the West Coast, 110,000 Japanese Americans, 65 percent of whom had been born in the United States, were removed to camps surrounded by barbed wire and required to take loyalty oaths. Public officials claimed this policy was necessary for security reasons.

The racism in the treatment of Japanese Americans was evident when the California governor, Culbert Olson, said, "You know, when I look out at a group of Americans of German or Italian descent, I can tell whether they're loyal or not. I can tell how they think and even perhaps what they are thinking. But it is impossible for me to do this with inscrutable Orientals, and particularly the Japanese."

Germany In August 1914, Germans had enthusiastically cheered their soldiers marching off to war. In September 1939, the streets were quiet. Many Germans did not care. Even worse for the Nazi regime, many feared disaster.

Hitler was well aware of the importance of the home front. He believed that the collapse of the home front in World War I had caused Germany's defeat. In his determination to avoid a repetition of that experience, he adopted economic policies that may have cost Germany the war.

To maintain the morale of the home front during the first two years of the war, Hitler refused to cut consumer goods production or to increase the production of armaments. After German defeats on the Russian front and the American entry into the war, however, the economic situation in Germany changed.

Early in 1942, Hitler finally ordered a massive increase in armaments production and in the size of the army. Hitler's architect, **Albert Speer,** was made minister for armaments and munitions in 1942. Speer was able to triple the production of armaments between 1942 and 1943, despite Allied air raids.

A total mobilization of the economy was put into effect in July 1944. Schools, theaters, and cafes were closed. By that time, though, total war mobilization was too late to save Germany from defeat.

Nazi attitudes toward women changed over the course of the war. Before the war, the Nazis had worked to keep women out of the job market. As the war progressed and more and more men were called up for military service, this position no longer made sense. Nazi magazines now proclaimed, "We see the woman as the eternal mother of our people, but also as the working and fighting comrade of the man."

Kamikaze attacker being shot down in the Pacific, 1945

In spite of this change, the number of women working in industry, agriculture, commerce, and domestic service increased only slightly. The total number of employed women in September 1944 was 14.9 million, compared with 14.6 million in May 1939. Many women, especially those of the middle class, did not want jobs, particularly in factories.

Japan Wartime Japan was a highly mobilized society. To guarantee its control over all national resources, the government created a planning board to control prices, wages, labor, and resources. Traditional habits of obedience and hierarchy were used to encourage citizens to sacrifice their resources, and sometimes their lives, for the national cause.

The calls for sacrifice reached a high point in the final years of the war. Young Japanese were encouraged to volunteer to serve as pilots in suicide missions against U.S. fighting ships at sea. These pilots were known as **kamikaze**, or "divine wind."

Japan was extremely reluctant to mobilize women on behalf of Japan's war effort. **General Hideki Tojo,** prime minister from 1941 to 1944, opposed female employment. He argued that "the weakening of the family system would be the weakening of the nation . . . we are able to do our duties only because we have wives and mothers at home."

Female employment increased during the war, but only in such areas as the textile industry and farming, where women had traditionally worked. Instead of using women to meet labor shortages, the Japanese government brought in Korean and Chinese laborers.

Reading Check **Evaluating** How did World War II contribute to racial tensions in the United States?

COOPERATIVE LEARNING ACTIVITY

Creating an Oral Report Ask students to break into small groups and select one of the following countries: the United States, Great Britain, France, Germany, the Soviet Union, Japan, Korea, or China. Have students research and prepare an oral report on the daily activities of women in that country during the war. The report should include changes women experienced in home life, work opportunities, and military roles. Did the popular image of women change in that country during the war? If so, in what ways? If the popular image did not change, why not? After each group has made its report, discuss other unexpected social consequences of war regarding sex roles, race, and nationality. L2

Frontline Civilians: The Bombing of Cities

Bombing was used in World War II against a variety of targets, including military targets, enemy troops, and civilian populations. The bombing of civilians in World War II made the home front a dangerous place.

A few bombing raids had been conducted in the last year of World War I. The bombing of civilian populations had led to a public outcry. The bombings and the reaction to them had given rise to the argument that bombing civilian populations would be an effective way to force governments to make peace. As a result, European air forces began to develop long-range bombers in the 1930s.

Britain The first sustained use of civilian bombing began in early September 1940. Londoners took the first heavy blows. For months, the German air force bombed **London** nightly. Thousands of civilians were killed or injured, and enormous damage was done. Nevertheless, Londoners' morale remained high.

The blitz, as the British called the German air raids, soon became a national experience. The blitz was carried to many other British cities and towns. The ability of Londoners to maintain their morale set the standard for the rest of the British population. The theory that the bombing of civilian targets would force peace was proved wrong.

Germany The British failed to learn from their own experience, however. Churchill and his advisers believed that destroying German communities would break civilian morale and bring victory. Major bombing raids on German cities began in 1942. On May 31, 1942, Cologne became the first German city to be attacked by a thousand bombers.

Bombing raids added an element of terror to circumstances already made difficult by growing shortages of food, clothing, and fuel. Germans especially feared the incendiary bombs, which created firestorms that swept through cities. The ferocious bombing of **Dresden** from February 13 to 15, 1945, created a firestorm that may have killed as many as a hundred thousand inhabitants and refugees.

Germany suffered enormously from the Allied bombing raids. Millions of buildings were destroyed, and possibly half a million civilians died. Nevertheless, it is highly unlikely that Allied bombing sapped the morale of the German people. Instead, Germans, whether pro-Nazi or anti-Nazi, fought on stubbornly, often driven simply by a desire to live.

Nor did the bombing destroy Germany's industrial capacity. Production of war materials actually increased between 1942 and 1944, despite the bombing. Nevertheless, the widespread destruction of transportation systems and fuel supplies made it extremely difficult for the new materials to reach the German military.

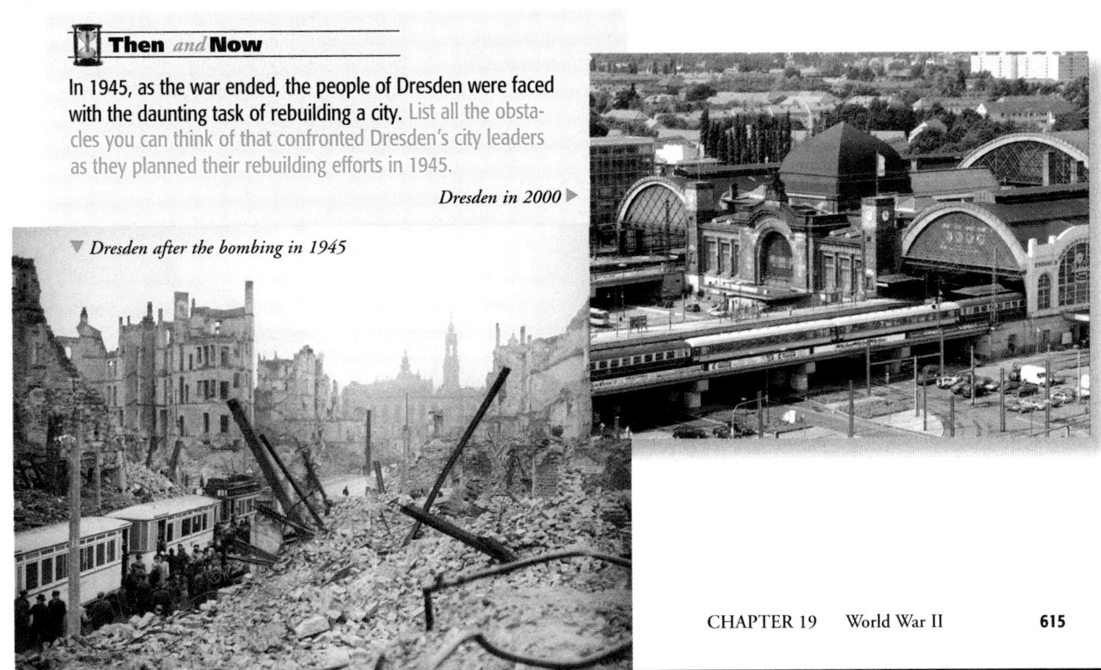

Then and Now

In 1945, as the war ended, the people of Dresden were faced with the daunting task of rebuilding a city. List all the obstacles you can think of that confronted Dresden's city leaders as they planned their rebuilding efforts in 1945.

Dresden in 2000 ▶

▼ *Dresden after the bombing in 1945*

Then and Now

Answer: Answers may include lack of finances, lack of able-bodied men, lack of raw materials.

Enrich

To help students understand how heavily German cities were bombed by the Allies, bring in photos of Dresden, Hamburg, Kiel, Hanover, or other cities that were almost totally demolished. Point out to students that the strategic bombing reduced German industrial capacity by less than eight percent, but it did necessitate a massive rebuilding effort after the war.

Guided Reading Activity 19–4

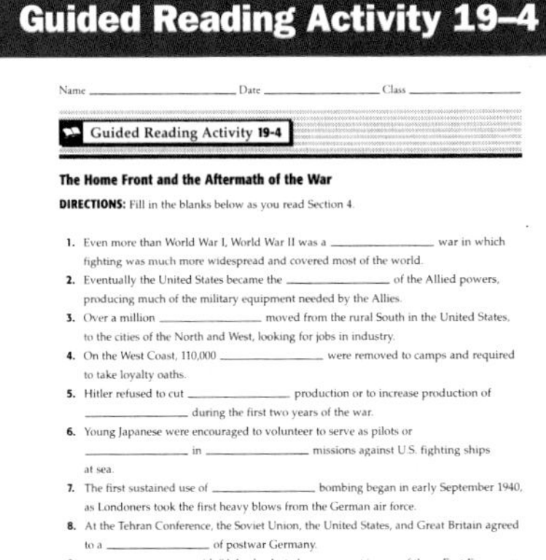

Name ____________ Date ____________ Class ____________

Guided Reading Activity 19-4

The Home Front and the Aftermath of the War

DIRECTIONS: Fill in the blanks below as you read Section 4.

1. Even more than World War I, World War II was a ____________ war in which fighting was much more widespread and covered most of the world.
2. Eventually the United States became the ____________ of the Allied powers, producing much of the military equipment needed by the Allies.
3. Over a million ____________ moved from the rural South in the United States, to the cities of the North and West, looking for jobs in industry.
4. On the West Coast, 110,000 ____________ were removed to camps and required to take loyalty oaths.
5. Hitler refused to cut ____________ production or to increase production of ____________ during the first two years of the war.
6. Young Japanese were encouraged to volunteer to serve as pilots or ____________ in ____________ missions against U.S. fighting ships at sea.
7. The first sustained use of ____________ bombing began in early September 1940, as Londoners took the first heavy blows from the German air force.
8. At the Tehran Conference, the Soviet Union, the United States, and Great Britain agreed to a ____________ of postwar Germany.
9. ____________ said, "A freely elected government in any of these East European countries would be anti-Soviet, and that we cannot allow."

Critical Thinking

Some people have compared Allied bombing of German cities and the American use of the atomic bomb against Hiroshima and Nagasaki with the Nazi death camps. Ask students to discuss this proposition. Do they believe it has merit? What reasons can they give to support their points of view? L2

MEETING INDIVIDUAL NEEDS

Developing Study Skills Set up a chart with four columns: *People, Places, Military Terms,* and *Other Terms* related to World War II. As you read the following words, have students identify the column in which each word should go. Ask the students to share what they have learned about each person, place, or term. The following words should be included: People: Hitler, Franco, Mussolini, Stalin, Roosevelt, Rommel, MacArthur, Churchill, Eisenhower, Aryans, Jews, Gypsies, Truman; Places: Czechoslovakia, Ethiopia, Austria, Munich, Poland, Manchuria, Beijing, Pearl Harbor, Midway, Auschwitz, London; Military Terms: blitzkrieg, panzer divisions, Luftwaffe, unconditional surrender, *Einsatzgruppen, blitz;* Other Terms: New Order, Final Solution, Cold War, Nazism, appeasement, Allies, führer, Holocaust, crematoriums. L1

SCIENCE, TECHNOLOGY & SOCIETY

Answer: Answers will vary but should be supported by logical arguments. Students might argue that it was quite different. It was a much more controversial decision, since a single atomic bomb caused such devastating damage and loss of life, as well as the lingering effects of radioactivity.

Reading Check

Answer: It was believed that bombing civilians would be an effective way to force governments to make peace.

3 ASSESS

Assign Section 4 Assessment as homework or as an in-class activity.

Have students use **Interactive Tutor Self-Assessment CD-ROM.**

Section Quiz 19–4

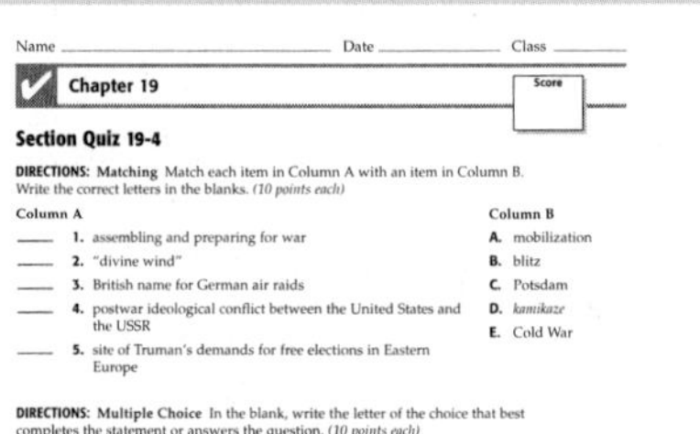

Name ________ Date ________ Class ________

Chapter 19 — Score

Section Quiz 19-4

DIRECTIONS: Matching Match each item in Column A with an item in Column B. Write the correct letters in the blanks. *(10 points each)*

Column A	Column B
____ 1. assembling and preparing for war	A. mobilization
____ 2. "divine wind"	B. blitz
____ 3. British name for German air raids	C. Potsdam
____ 4. postwar ideological conflict between the United States and the USSR	D. *kamikaze*
____ 5. site of Truman's demands for free elections in Eastern Europe	E. Cold War

DIRECTIONS: Multiple Choice In the blank, write the letter of the choice that best completes the statement or answers the question. *(10 points each)*

SCIENCE, TECHNOLOGY & SOCIETY

The Atomic Bomb

Scientists at the beginning of the twentieth century discovered that atoms contained an enormous amount of energy. The discovery gave rise to the idea that releasing this energy by splitting the atom might create a devastating weapon.

The idea was not taken seriously until World War II. Then, the fear that the Germans might make an atomic bomb convinced the U.S. government to try to develop one first. In 1942, the United States set in motion the Manhattan Project.

The Manhattan Project was a code name for the enormous industrial and technical enterprise that produced the first atomic bomb. It cost 2 billion dollars and employed the efforts of 600,000 people. U.S. Army Brigadier General Leslie Groves had overall supervision. The physicist J. Robert Oppenheimer was director of the Los Alamos, New Mexico, center where the bomb was actually built.

A successful test explosion on July 16, 1945, near Alamogordo, New Mexico, meant that the bomb was ready. The war in Europe had ended, but the bomb could be used against the Japanese. A committee had already chosen the city of Hiroshima as the first target.

The bomb was dropped on August 6, 1945, by a U.S. B-29 bomber nicknamed *Enola Gay.* The destruction was incredible. An area of about 5 square miles (13 sq km) was turned to ashes. Of the 76,000 buildings in Hiroshima, 70,000 were flattened. Of the city's 350,000 inhabitants, 140,000 had died by the end of 1945. By the end of 1950, another 50,000 had died from the effects of radiation. A second bomb was dropped on Nagasaki on August 9. The world had entered the Nuclear Age.

Evaluating ***Was the decision to use the atomic bomb in Japan any different from Allied decisions to bomb civilian population centers in Europe? Why or why not?***

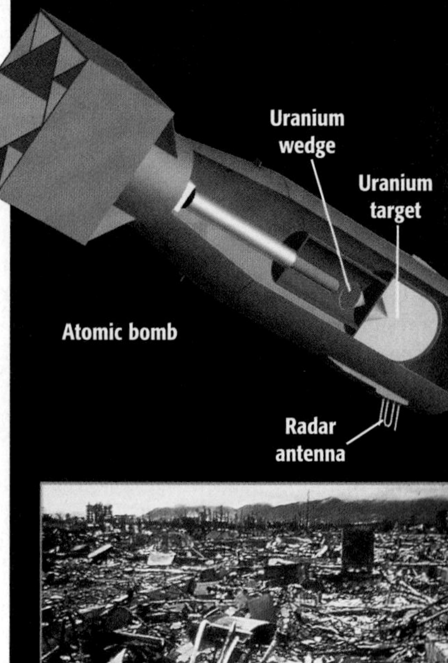

Hiroshima after atomic bomb dropped, August 1945

Japan In Japan, the bombing of civilians reached a new level with the use of the first atomic bomb. Japan was open to air raids toward the end of the war because its air force had almost been destroyed. Moreover, its crowded cities were built of flimsy materials that were especially vulnerable to fire.

Attacks on Japanese cities by the new U.S. B-29 Superfortresses, the biggest bombers of the war, had begun on November 24, 1944. By the summer of 1945, many of Japan's industries had been destroyed, along with one-fourth of its dwellings.

The Japanese government decreed the mobilization of all people between the ages of 13 and 60 into a People's Volunteer Corps. Fearing high U.S. casualties in a land invasion of Japan, President Truman and his advisers decided to drop the atomic bomb on Hiroshima and Nagasaki in August of 1945.

Reading Check **Explaining** Why were civilian populations targeted in bombing raids?

Peace and a New War

The total victory of the Allies in World War II was followed not by a real peace but by a period of political tensions, known as the Cold War. Primarily an ideological conflict between the United States and the Soviet Union, the Cold War was to dominate world affairs until the end of the 1980s.

INTERDISCIPLINARY CONNECTIONS ACTIVITY

Facilitating a Discussion To help students experience the complex decision-making process that led to the dropping of atomic bombs on Japan, assign students one of the following roles: member of U.S. Congress today, member of U.S. Congress in 1945, U.S. civilian in 1945, Japanese civilian in 1945, U.S. military officer in 1945, U.S. soldier in 1945, and a human rights activist today. Have students present their different views to the class as represented by the roles they are playing. Have the class discuss Truman's decision; then each student should vote for or against the use of atomic bombs. Students should use evidence and logical arguments to support their point of view on this social studies event. L2

Geography Skills

The political map of Europe changed dramatically as a result of World War II.

1. **Interpreting Maps** Compare the map on page 535 to this map and identify the political changes in Europe from the 1920s to 1945.
2. **Applying Geography Skills** Create a chart that shows how Europe was divided according to Soviet and Western influence.

The Tehran Conference Stalin, Roosevelt, and Churchill were the leaders of what was called the Big Three (the Soviet Union, the United States, and Great Britain) of the Grand Alliance. They met at Tehran in November 1943 to decide the future course of the war. Their major tactical decision had concerned the final assault on Germany. Stalin and Roosevelt had argued successfully for an American-British invasion through France. This was scheduled for the spring of 1944.

The acceptance of this plan had important consequences. It meant that Soviet and British-American forces would meet in defeated Germany along a north-south dividing line. Most likely, Eastern Europe would be liberated by Soviet forces. The Allies also agreed to a partition of postwar Germany.

The Yalta Conference The Big Three powers met again at Yalta in southern Russia in February 1945. By then, the defeat of Germany was obvious. The Western powers, which had once believed that the Soviets were in a weak position, were now faced with the reality of eleven million Soviet soldiers taking possession of Eastern and much of Central Europe.

Stalin was deeply suspicious of the Western powers. He wanted a buffer to protect the Soviet Union from possible future Western aggression. This would mean establishing pro-Soviet governments along the border of the Soviet Union.

Roosevelt, however, favored the idea of self-determination for Europe. This involved a pledge to help liberated Europe in the creation of "democratic institutions of their own choice." Liberated countries would hold free elections to determine their political systems.

At Yalta, Roosevelt sought Soviet military help against Japan. (At that time, the atomic bomb was not yet a certainty.) Roosevelt therefore agreed to Stalin's price for military aid against Japan: possession of Sakhalin and the Kuril Islands, which were ruled by Japan, as well as two warm-water ports and railroad rights in Manchuria.

The creation of the United Nations was a major American concern at Yalta. Roosevelt wanted the Big Three powers to pledge to be part of such an international organization before difficult issues divided them into hostile camps. Both Churchill and Stalin accepted Roosevelt's plans for the establishment of a United Nations organization and set the first meeting for San Francisco in April 1945.

The issues of Germany and Eastern Europe were treated less decisively. The Big Three reaffirmed that Germany must surrender unconditionally. It would be divided into four zones, which would be occupied and governed by the military forces of the United States, Great Britain, France, and the Soviet Union.

A compromise was also worked out on Poland. Stalin agreed to free elections in the future to determine a new government in that country. The issue of free elections in Eastern Europe, however, caused a split between the Soviets and Americans, as soon

Geography Skills

Answers:

1. Students will note changes in borders and influence.
2. Students will create a chart showing the division of Europe.

TURNING POINT

How did the American use of the atomic bomb affect future world events? *(For the first time, the atomic bomb was used in warfare, forcing Japan's surrender. It opened the atomic age, in which nuclear weapons would play a role in global rivalry.)*

Reading Essentials and Study Guide 19–4

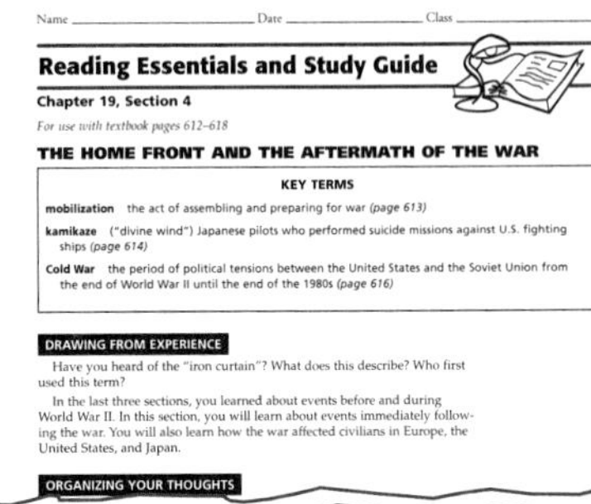
Name ______ Date ______ Class ______

Reading Essentials and Study Guide

Chapter 19, Section 4

For use with textbook pages 612–618

THE HOME FRONT AND THE AFTERMATH OF THE WAR

KEY TERMS

mobilization the act of assembling and preparing for war (page 613)

kamikaze ("divine wind") Japanese pilots who performed suicide missions against U.S. fighting ships (page 614)

Cold War the period of political tensions between the United States and the Soviet Union from the end of World War II until the end of the 1980s (page 616)

DRAWING FROM EXPERIENCE

Have you heard of the "iron curtain"? What does this describe? Who first used this term?

In the last three sections, you learned about events before and during World War II. In this section, you will learn about events immediately following the war. You will also learn how the war affected civilians in Europe, the United States, and Japan.

ORGANIZING YOUR THOUGHTS

Who? What? Where? When?

Veto Power At Yalta, Churchill, Roosevelt, and Stalin agreed that each of the five permanent members of the United Nations Security Council would have veto power over matters brought before the Council. During the early years of the United Nations, the Soviet Union often used its veto to prevent UN responses to Soviet actions in Eastern Europe.

CRITICAL THINKING ACTIVITY

Writing a Biography Ask students to prepare a biography of either Franklin Roosevelt or Winston Churchill, using both primary and secondary sources and the Internet. How did each man develop the qualities he needed to serve as a wartime leader? Students should examine factors such as education, military experience, personality traits, charisma, oratory skills, and ideals. Select volunteers to present their reports aloud to the class. Compile on the board a list of leadership qualities shared by Roosevelt and Churchill. **L1**

CHAPTER 19
Section 4, 612–618

Reading Check

Answer: He wanted absolute security, which could be gained only by the presence of Communist states in Eastern Europe.

Reteaching Activity

After they have read the chapter, ask students to identify and explain the causes and effects of World War II. **L1**

Critical Thinking

Ask students to discuss the likelihood of achieving the American objective of providing Europeans with "democratic institutions of their own choice" in light of the military and political situations at the end of World War II. **L3**

4 CLOSE

Ask students how the gains made by Stalin at Yalta were similar to those made by Hitler at the Munich conference. *(Both men got what they wanted in exchange for promises they did not keep: Hitler got the Sudetenland and then took over the rest of Czechoslovakia; Stalin got Poland, but instead of holding elections, made Poland a Communist state.)*

Churchill, Roosevelt, and Stalin at Yalta

became evident at the next conference of the Big Three powers at Potsdam, Germany.

The Potsdam Conference The Potsdam Conference of July 1945 began under a cloud of mistrust. Roosevelt had died on April 12 and had been succeeded as president by Harry Truman. At Potsdam, Truman demanded free elections throughout Eastern Europe. Stalin responded, "A freely elected government in any of these East European countries would be anti-Soviet, and that we cannot allow."

After a bitter and devastating war in which the Soviets had lost more people than any other country, Stalin sought absolute military security. To him, this security could be gained only by the presence of Communist states in Eastern Europe. Free elections might result in governments hostile to the Soviets.

War Crimes Trials By the summer of 1945, the Allies had agreed to hold a trial of war leaders for committing aggressive war and crimes against humanity. Nazi leaders were tried and condemned as war criminals at the Nuremberg war crimes trials in Germany in 1945 and 1946. War crimes trials were also held in Japan and Italy.

A New Struggle As the war slowly receded into the past, a new struggle was already beginning. Many in the West thought Soviet policy was part of a worldwide Communist conspiracy. The Soviets viewed Western, and especially American, policy as nothing less than global capitalist expansionism.

In March 1946, in a speech to an American audience, the former British prime minister Winston Churchill declared that "an iron curtain" had "descended across the continent," dividing Europe into two hostile camps. Stalin branded Churchill's speech a "call to war with the Soviet Union." Only months after the world's most devastating conflict had ended, the world seemed to be bitterly divided once again.

Reading Check **Identifying** Why did Stalin want to control Eastern Europe after World War II?

SECTION 4 ASSESSMENT

Checking for Understanding

1. **Define** mobilization, kamikaze.
2. **Identify** Albert Speer, General Hideki Tojo, Cold War.
3. **Locate** London, Dresden, Hiroshima.
4. **Explain** how Hitler's bombing of civilians in England backfired. What strategy do you think Hitler should have pursued instead?
5. **List** examples of Japan's vulnerability to Allied air attack in late 1944. What type of U.S. aircraft was used for the heaviest bombing of Japanese targets?

Critical Thinking

6. **Explain** Why did General Hideki Tojo oppose female employment in Japan?
7. **Organizing Information** Create a chart listing countries where bombing of heavily populated cities took place.

Country	City

Analyzing Visuals

8. **Analyze** the photo at the top of this page. How might the seating arrangement for the three leaders be significant? Which of the three leaders do you think came away from the meeting most pleased with the results?

Writing About History

9. **Persuasive Writing** President Truman concluded that dropping the atomic bomb on Japan was a justifiable way to end the war. Write an essay either condemning or agreeing with Truman's decision.

SECTION 4 ASSESSMENT

1. Key terms are in blue.
2. Albert Speer *(p. 614)*; General Hideki Tojo *(p. 614)*; Cold War *(p. 616)*
3. See chapter maps.
4. They failed to demoralize the British, allowed British to rebuild their air strength; bomb military targets.
5. air force almost destroyed; crowded cities built of flimsy materials that were vulnerable to fire; B29s
6. He felt women in the workforce would weaken the family unit, which in turn would weaken the nation.
7. England: London, many other cities and towns; Germany: Berlin, Dresden, Cologne, other cities; Japan: Hiroshima, Nagasaki, other cities
8. Answers should be supported by the text.
9. Student essays should be written logically with supporting proof.

CRITICAL THINKING SKILLBUILDER

Synthesizing Information

Why Learn This Skill?

Consider what it would be like to get funding for a new after-school club. In order to present your case, you would need to talk to other students and to school administrators, and to read reports and articles. Once you had gathered all the information you needed, you would synthesize—or put together—the most important points that could help you achieve your objective.

Synthesizing information involves combining information from two or more sources. The ability to synthesize information is important because information gained from one source often sheds new light upon other information. It is like putting the pieces of a puzzle together to form a complete picture. Being able to synthesize information will help you read and write more effectively.

Learning the Skill

To write a research report, you study several sources—encyclopedias, books, and articles. Once you have gathered information, you synthesize it into a report.

Before synthesizing information, analyze each source separately. Determine the value and reliability of each source. Then, look for connections and relationships among the different sources.

Practicing the Skill

Study the passage and the photo on this page.

> Bombing was used in World War II against a variety of targets, including military targets, enemy troops, and civilian populations. The bombing of civilians in World War II made the home front a dangerous place. A few bombing raids had been conducted in the last year of World War I. The bombings and the reaction to them had given rise to the argument that bombing civilian populations would be an effective way to force governments to make peace.
>
> Beginning in early September 1940, the German air force bombed London and many other British cities and towns nightly. The blitz, as the British called the German air raids, became a national experience. Londoners took the first heavy blows. Their ability to maintain their morale set the standard for the rest of the British population.

Scottish city bombed in 1941

1. What is the main idea of the passage?
2. What does the photo tell you about this topic?
3. By synthesizing the two sources, what information do you have about the bombing of Britain?

Applying the Skill

Find two sources of information about a current event and write a short report. For your report, try to use a primary and a secondary source, if possible. Answer these questions: What are the main ideas from these sources? How does each source add to your understanding of the topic? Do the sources support or contradict each other? If there are contradictions, how would you include the conflicting information in your report?

Glencoe's **Skillbuilder Interactive Workbook, Level 2,** provides instruction and practice in key social studies skills.

619

ANSWERS TO PRACTICING THE SKILL

1. Bombing of civilian populations made the home front a dangerous place but failed to destroy morale.
2. It appears to show a family making their way through the rubble with a few salvaged possessions.
3. Even though their cities were devastated, the British maintained their morale.

Applying the Skill: Students will write reports synthesizing information from two sources.

CRITICAL THINKING SKILLBUILDER

TEACH

Synthesizing Information Ask students to write detailed directions from your classroom to the principal's office or to the cafeteria. Have students exchange directions with a classmate. Then pass out copies of a school map. Have students compare the written directions with the map. How do the two differ? *(The written directions are more personal; the map gives options of other routes.)* Does the information from each source lead to the same location? *(yes)* Tell students that when they prepare material for reports, they must first synthesize, or combine, information from several sources.

Additional Practice

Skills Reinforcement Activity 19

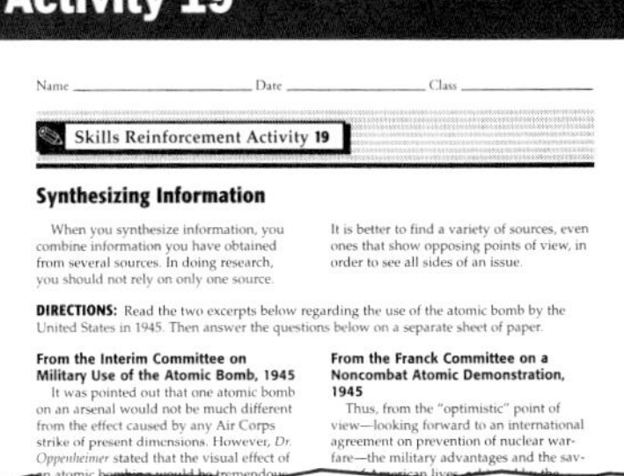

Name __________ Date __________ Class __________

Skills Reinforcement Activity 19

Synthesizing Information

When you synthesize information, you combine information you have obtained from several sources. In doing research, you should not rely on only one source. It is better to find a variety of sources, even ones that show opposing points of view, in order to see all sides of an issue.

DIRECTIONS: Read the two excerpts below regarding the use of the atomic bomb by the United States in 1945. Then answer the questions below on a separate sheet of paper.

From the Interim Committee on Military Use of the Atomic Bomb, 1945

It was pointed out that one atomic bomb on an arsenal would not be much different from the effect caused by any Air Corps strike of present dimensions. However, *Dr. Oppenheimer* stated that the visual effect of

From the Franck Committee on a Noncombat Atomic Demonstration, 1945

Thus, from the "optimistic" point of view—looking forward to an international agreement on prevention of nuclear warfare—the military advantages and the sav-

GLENCOE TECHNOLOGY

CD-ROM

Glencoe Skillbuilder Interactive Workbook CD-ROM, Level 2

This interactive CD-ROM reinforces student mastery of essential social studies skills.

GLENCOE TECHNOLOGY

MindJogger Videoquiz

Use the **MindJogger Videoquiz** to review Chapter 19 content.

 Available in VHS.

Using Key Terms

1. appeasement **2.** blitzkrieg **3.** demilitarized **4.** sanctions **5.** partisans **6.** genocide **7.** *kamikaze* **8.** collaborators

Reviewing Key Facts

9. northwestern Czechoslovakia; it was inhabited largely by Germans

10. an effective radar system that gave them early warning of German air attacks

11. U.S. planes destroyed four attacking Japanese aircraft carriers, defeating the Japanese navy and establishing American naval superiority in the Pacific.

12. The agreement made it impossible for Hitler to divide his foes.

13. Japanese Americans were rounded up and placed in camps for the duration of the war, while German Americans and Italian Americans were left alone.

14. 90 percent

15. Japan's attack on the U.S. naval base at Pearl Harbor in Hawaii

Critical Thinking

16. He wanted to avoid having to invade Japan, which he was convinced would cause heavy American casualties.

17. By the end of World War II, the balance of power had shifted away from Europe. The United States and the Soviet Union became world powers.

Writing About History

18. Answers will vary but should be supported by examples.

CHAPTER 19 ASSESSMENT and ACTIVITIES

Using Key Terms

1. The policy of giving in to Hitler's demands before World War II has been called ____.
2. The German style of attack that called for rapidly overrunning the positions of opposing forces was called a ____.
3. Because the Rhineland was ____, Germany was not permitted to have weapons or fortifications there.
4. The United States threatened economic ____ unless Japan returned to its borders of 1931.
5. Civilians in occupied countries who joined resistance movements were often called ____.
6. What the Nazis called the Final Solution was actually ____ of the Jewish people.
7. Japanese pilots who volunteered for suicide missions were known as ____.
8. People who assisted the Nazis in carrying out atrocities against Jewish people were known as ____.

Reviewing Key Facts

9. **Geography** Where was the Sudetenland located? Why was it important to Hitler?
10. **Science and Technology** What did the British develop to prepare for German air attack?
11. **History** What significant military action occurred at Midway Island in 1942?
12. **Government** Why did the Allied agreement to fight until the Axis Powers surrendered unconditionally possibly prolong the war?
13. **Citizenship** In what way were Japanese Americans treated differently than German Americans and Italian Americans?
14. **Citizenship** What percentage of the Jewish populations of Poland, the Baltic countries, and Germany were killed during the Holocaust?
15. **Government** What event triggered the entry of the United States into the war?

Chapter Summary

World War II was the most devastating total war in human history. Events engaged four continents, involved countless people and resources, and changed subsequent history. The chart below summarizes some of the themes and developments.

Country	Movement	Cooperation	Conflict
United States	• Retakes Japanese positions in Southeast Asia	• Relaxes neutrality acts • Meets with Allies at Tehran, Yalta, and Potsdam	• Leads war effort • Conducts island-hopping counterattacks • Drops atomic bombs on Japan
Great Britain	• Makes huge troop movements at Dunkirk and Normandy	• Meets with Allies at Tehran, Yalta, and Potsdam	• Stops Rommel at El Alamein • Withstands heavy German bombing
Soviet Union	• Demands Kuril and Sakhalin Islands • Takes control of much of eastern Europe	• Meets with Allies at Tehran, Yalta, and Potsdam	• Defeats Germany at Stalingrad • Forces Germany to fight war on two fronts
Germany	• Takes over Austria, Poland, and Sudetenland	• Forms Rome-Berlin Axis • Signs Anti-Comintern Pact	• Uses blitzkrieg tactics • Conducts genocide of Jews and others • Besieges Leningrad
Italy	• Invades Ethiopia	• Forms Rome-Berlin Axis	• Becomes German puppet state (northern Italy)
Japan	• Seizes Manchuria and renames it Manchukuo • Invades China	• Signs Anti-Comintern Pact	• Attacks Pearl Harbor • Conquers Southeast Asia from Indochina to Philippines

Analyzing Sources

19. As far as he was concerned, their only value was as slaves for the Germans.

20. Both the Germans and the Japanese were attempting to rid their lands of foreign elements. The Japanese used the slogan "Asia for the Asiatics" to get the support of anticolonialists in overthrowing Western colonial rule, but they turned out to be even worse colonialists than the Europeans they replaced. The Nazis wanted to get rid of the "contaminating" influences of the Jews, Gypsies, Slavs, and other groups by exterminating them. Both countries obtained slave labor from the lands they conquered and had little regard for the lives of the people they conquered.

Applying Technology Skills

21. Answers will vary but should be supported by examples and logical arguments.

CHAPTER 19
Assessment and Activities

Self-Check Quiz

Visit the *Glencoe World History—Modern Times* Web site at wh.mt.glencoe.com and click on **Chapter 19–Self-Check Quiz** to prepare for the Chapter Test.

Critical Thinking

16. **Cause and Effect** What factors caused President Truman to order the dropping of atomic bombs in Japan?
17. **Drawing Conclusions** How did World War II affect the world balance of power? What nations emerged from the conflict as world powers?

Writing About History

18. **Informative Writing** Write an essay that examines the different approaches to colonial governing in Asia taken by the Japanese during World War II and by Europeans before the war. Be sure to include information about key people, places, and events from each of the two periods in history.

Analyzing Sources

Heinrich Himmler, head of the German SS, argued:

> ❝Whether nations live in prosperity or starve to death interests me only insofar as we need them as slaves for our culture. Otherwise it is of no interest.❞

19. Describe Heinrich Himmler's opinion of the people that Germany conquered.
20. Compare the Nazi philosophy of creating a New Order with the Japanese philosophy of Asia for the Asiatics.

Applying Technology Skills

21. **Using the Internet** Use the Internet to research the daily life of a Japanese American citizen in a U.S. internment camp. Compare and contrast the treatment of Japanese Americans to that of German Americans and Italian Americans during this time.

Making Decisions

22. Some historians believe that President Truman dropped atomic weapons on Japan not to end the war in the Pacific, but to impress the Soviet Union with U.S. military power. Write a position paper evaluating this hypothesis in light of what you have learned about Stalin and the United States. What were Truman's other options? Do you think a leader today would make the same decision?

Analyzing Maps and Charts

Refer to the map on page 602 to answer the following questions.

23. Why did the Allies not retake every Japanese-held island?
24. How far is it from Pearl Harbor to Japan?

Standardized Test Practice

Directions: Use the map *and* your knowledge of world history to answer the following question.

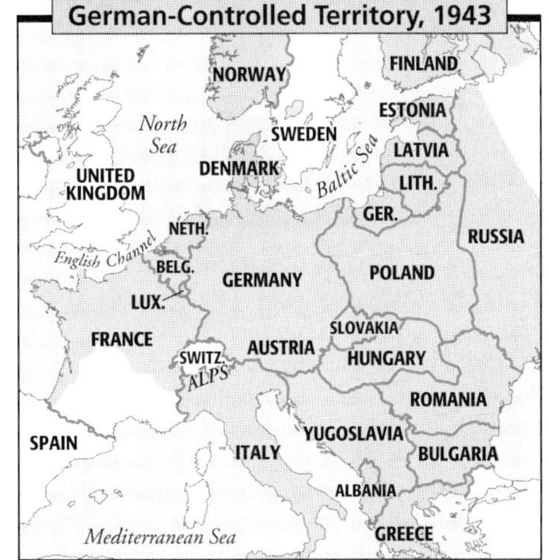

How did geographic factors influence German military advances?

F German troops had to cover long distances.
G German supply lines were vulnerable and easily breached.
H Colder climates created problems that the German military could not overcome.
J The blitzkrieg relied on tanks that were most effective on flatter terrain.

Test-Taking Tip: To answer this question about how geography affected history, look at the map carefully. Notice which areas the German military did not occupy. Use these clues to make an inference about how geography affected the German army.

Have students visit the Web site at wh.mt.glencoe.com to review Chapter 19 and take the Self-Check Quiz.

The Princeton Review

Standardized Test Practice

Answer: J
Answer Explanation: Note that the question asks about geographic features.

Bonus Question ?

Ask: Why did increased war production not do much to improve Germany's ability to fight the war? *(Germany lacked transportation to move supplies to the front.)*

Making Decisions

22. Answers will vary. Stalin had made clear his desire to surround the Soviet Union with other Communist countries to serve as a buffer. The fact that the United States had atomic weapons and the Soviet Union did not might have deterred him from making further demands. The Allies could have used conventional bombing raids or an actual invasion, but either might have taken months longer and cost many more lives. Today, many countries have nuclear capabilities, and it is hard to imagine any leader making a similar decision because of the fear of a full-scale nuclear war.

Analyzing Maps and Charts

23. They did not need to. By island hopping the Allies could cut off Japanese-held islands from supply lines.
24. more than 4,000 miles (6,640 km)

World Literature

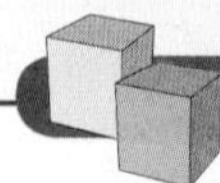

Block Schedule

Team Teaching
This excerpt from *A Room of One's Own* may be presented in a team-teaching context, in conjunction with English or Language Arts.

A Room of One's Own

Historical Connection

Virginia Woolf's writing reveals her concern over the limited opportunities available to women throughout much of Britain's history.

Background Information

Besides novels, Virginia Woolf also wrote many works of nonfiction, including two important essays exploring the roles of women in history and society: *A Room of One's Own* (1929) and *Three Guineas* (1938). Woolf was convinced that in order to produce creative work, an artist requires a private space in which to work ("A room of one's own") and enough money for basic survival ("three guineas"). She argues that the absence of one or both of these two basic requirements has made the development of women artists extraordinarily difficult, if not impossible (as it was for "Shakespeare's sister").

World Literature

from A Room of One's Own

by Virginia Woolf

Virginia Woolf, who was born in 1882 in London, is considered one of the most significant modernist writers of our time. Her work changed the ways the novel was perceived and written. She developed a technique known as stream of consciousness in which the writer portrays the inner lives and thoughts of multiple characters. Additionally, she is known for her feminist writings. One of the most famous of these is *A Room of One's Own.* The title of this work is based on her assertion that a woman "must have money and a room of her own" in order to write.

Read to Discover

How does Virginia Woolf express her belief that gender influences the development of talent? Do you think Woolf is being fair in her assessment? Does her analysis of the differences between treatment of men and women apply today?

Reader's Dictionary

agog: full of intense interest or excitement

moon: to dream

. . . Let me imagine, since facts are so hard to come by, what would have happened had Shakespeare had a wonderfully gifted sister, called Judith, let us say. Shakespeare himself went, very probably—his mother was an heiress—to the grammar school, where he may have learnt Latin—Ovid, Virgil and Horace—and the elements of grammar and logic. He was, it is well known, a wild boy who poached rabbits, perhaps shot a deer, and had, rather sooner than he should have done, to marry a woman in the neighbourhood, who bore him a child rather quicker than was right. That escapade sent him to seek his fortune in London. He had, it seemed, a taste for the theatre; he began by holding horses at the stage door. Very soon he got work in the theatre, became a successful actor, and lived at the hub of the universe, meeting everybody, knowing everybody, practising his art on the boards, exercising his wits in the street, and even getting access

◀ *Many of William Shakespeare's plays were performed at the Globe theater in London, shown left.*

ABOUT THE AUTHOR

Virginia Woolf, British novelist, essayist, and critic, was born Adeline Virginia Stephen in London. She was educated at home by her father and became a central figure in the creation of the modern novel. In 1917, Woolf, along with her husband, Leonard, founded Hogarth Press, which published the early works of authors such as E.M. Forster, Katherine Mansfield, and T. S. Eliot, and introduced the works of Sigmund Freud, founder of psychoanalysis, to English readers. Except for the first printing of Woolf's first novel, *The Voyage Out* (1915), Hogarth Press also published all of her works.

to the palace of the queen. Meanwhile his extraordinarily gifted sister, let us suppose, remained at home. She was as adventurous, as imaginative, as agog to see the world as he was. But she was not sent to school. She had no chance of learning grammar and logic, let alone of reading Horace and Virgil. She picked up a book now and then, one of her brother's perhaps, and read a few pages. But then her parents came in and told her to mend the stockings or mind the stew and not moon about with books and papers. They would have spoken sharply but kindly, for they were substantial people who knew the conditions of life for a woman and loved their daughter—indeed, more likely than not she was the apple of her father's eye. Perhaps she scribbled some pages up in an apple loft on the sly, but was careful to hide them or set fire to them. Soon, however, before she was out of her teens, she was to be betrothed to the son of a neighbouring wool-stapler. She cried out that marriage was hateful to her, and for that she was severely beaten by her father. Then he ceased to scold her. He begged her instead not to hurt him, not to shame him in this matter of her marriage. He would give her a chain of beads or a fine petticoat, he said; and there were tears in his eyes. How could she disobey him? How could she break his heart? The force of her own gift alone drove her to it. She made up a small parcel of her belongings, let herself down by a rope one summer's night and took the road to London. She was not seventeen. The birds that sang in the hedge were not more musical than she was. She had the quickest fancy, a gift like her brother's, for the tune of words. Like him, she had a taste for the theatre. She stood at the stage door; she wanted to act, she said. Men laughed in her face. The manager—a fat, loose-lipped man—guffawed. He bellowed something about poodles dancing and women acting—no woman, he said could possibly be an actress. He hinted—you can imagine what. She could get no training in her craft. Could she even seek her dinner in a tavern or roam the streets at midnight? Yet her genius was for fiction . . . At last—for she was very young, oddly like Shakespeare the poet in her face, with the same grey eyes and rounded brows—at last Nick Greene the actor-manager took pity on her; [but] she . . . killed herself one winter's night and lies buried at some cross-roads where the omnibuses now stop outside the Elephant and Castle. That, more or less, is how the story would run, I think, if a woman in Shakespeare's day had had Shakespeare's genius.

▲ *William Shakespeare*

Interpreting World Literature

1. What were "the conditions of life for a woman" that made Judith's parents scold her for attempting to read and write?
2. Why does Judith's father beat her?
3. What is Woolf's conclusion about the possibility of a woman becoming Shakespeare?
4. **CRITICAL THINKING** Why does Virginia Woolf have Shakespeare marry, but Shakespeare's sister run away from marriage?

Applications Activity

What does a person today need to succeed as a writer or artist? Write a descriptive account to illustrate your argument.

World Literature

FOCUS

Ask students to name other groups of people for whom social, political, and economic circumstances would have prevented the expression of individual genius. *(slaves in this country, women under the Taliban in Afghanistan, etc.)*

TEACH

Virginia Woolf was a fervent supporter of women's rights. In *A Room of One's Own* (1929), Woolf responds to those who would question the capabilities of women because there was no "female Shakespeare." By speculating about the fate of Shakespeare's brilliantly talented, imaginary sister, she is able to outline the difficulties of the woman artist in a world that denies her access to an education and the freedom to exercise her gift.

Interpretation

Ask students why "Shakespeare's sister" might have *"scribbled some pages up in an apple loft on the sly, but was careful to hide them or set fire to them."*

ANSWERS TO INTERPRETING WORLD LITERATURE

1. Women were supposed to marry and be good housewives and mothers. Reading and writing would not benefit them at all.
2. He believes that marriage is the only choice for a woman and that she must obey her father's wishes.
3. It could not have happened. Writing and acting were the province of men, and women were not allowed.
4. to prove that marriage was confining to a woman, but not to a man

Applications Activity: Answers should be supported by logical arguments.

Unit 5 Resources

Suggested Pacing Chart

Unit 5 (1 day)	Chapter 20 (4 days)	Chapter 21 (6 days)	Chapter 22 (4 days)	Chapter 23 (4 days)	Chapter 24 (4 days)	Chapter 25 (3 days)	Unit 5 (1 day)
Day 1 Introduction	**Day 1** Chapter 20 Intro, Section 1 **Day 2** Section 2 **Day 3** Section 3 **Day 4** Chapter 20 Review/ Assessment	**Day 1** Chapter 21 Intro, Section 1 **Day 2** Section 2 **Day 3** Section 3 **Day 4** Section 4 **Day 5** Chapter 21 Review **Day 6** Chapter 21 Assessment	**Day 1** Chapter 22 Intro, Section 1 **Day 2** Section 2 **Day 3** Section 3 **Day 4** Chapter 22 Review/ Assessment	**Day 1** Chapter 23 Intro, Section 1 **Day 2** Section 2 **Day 3** Chapter 23 Review **Day 4** Chapter 23 Assessment	**Day 1** Chapter 24 Intro, Section 1 **Day 2** Section 2 **Day 3** Section 3 **Day 4** Chapter 24 Review/ Assessment	**Day 1** Chapter 25 Intro, Section 1 **Day 2** Section 2 **Day 3** Chapter 25 Review/ Assessment	**Day 1** Wrap-Up/ Projects/ Unit 5 Assessment

Use the following tools to easily assess student learning in a variety of ways:

- Performance Assessment Activities and Rubrics
- Chapter Tests
- Section Quizzes
- Standardized Test Skills Practice Workbook
- SAT I/II Test Practice
- www.wh.mt.glencoe.com
- Interactive Tutor Self-Assessment CD-ROM
- MindJogger Videoquiz
- ExamView® Pro Testmaker CD-ROM

Teaching Transparencies

Unit Time Line Transparency 5

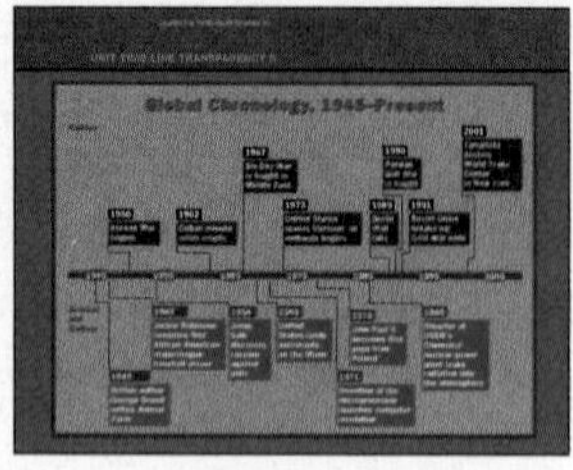

Cause-and-Effect Transparency 5

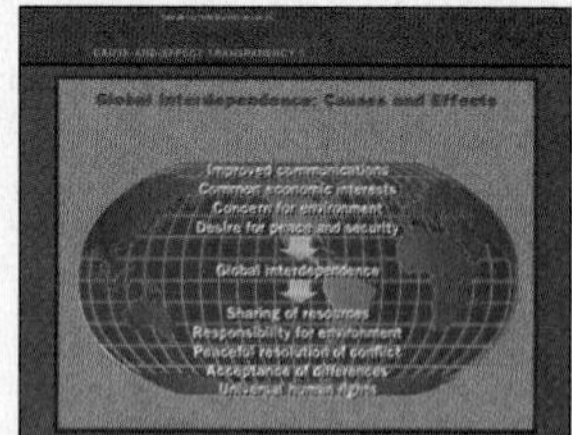

interNET RESOURCES

- www.wh.mt.glencoe.com

Glencoe World History—Modern Times
Visit the *Glencoe World History—Modern Times* Web site for history overviews, activities, assessments, and updated charts and graphs.

- www.socialstudies.glencoe.com

Glencoe Social Studies
Visit the Glencoe Web site for social studies activities, updates, and links to other sites.

- www.teachingtoday.glencoe.com

Glencoe Teaching Today
Visit the new Glencoe Web site for teacher development information, teaching tips, Web resources, and educational news.

- www.time.com

TIME Online
Visit the TIME Web site for up-to-date news and special reports.

Unit 5 Resources

ASSESSMENT

Unit 5 Tests Forms A and B

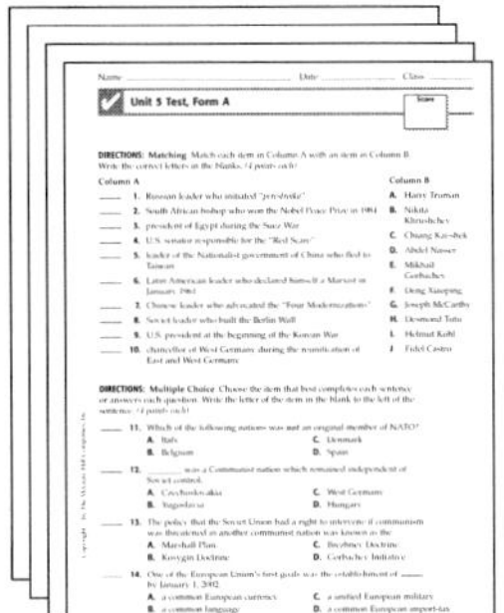
Unit 5 Test, Form A

ExamView® Pro Testmaker CD-ROM

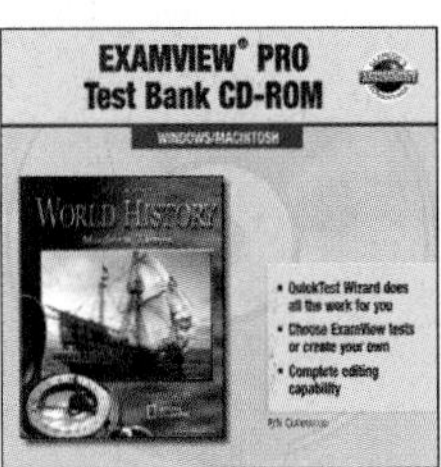

INTERDISCIPLINARY ACTIVITIES

World Literature Reading 5

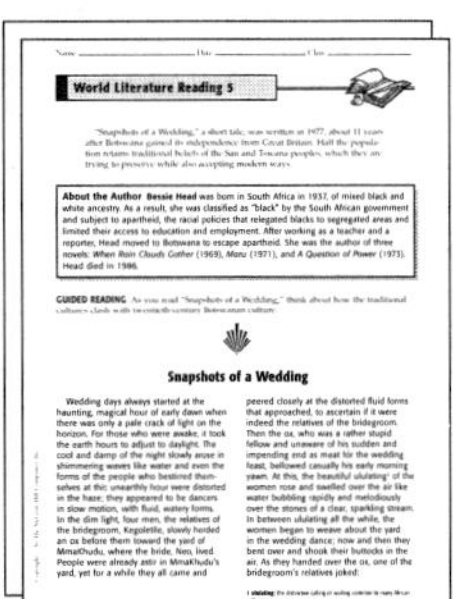
World Literature Reading 5

Snapshots of a Wedding

Economics and History Activity 5

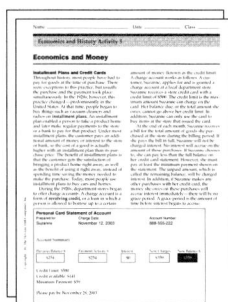

APPLICATION AND ENRICHMENT

Charting and Graphing Activity 5

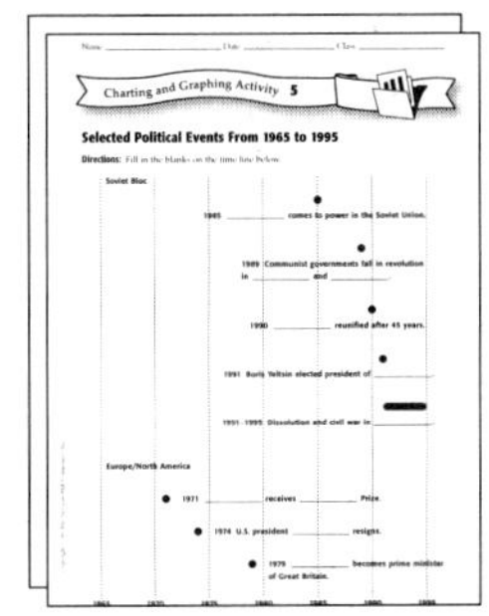
Charting and Graphing Activity 5

Selected Political Events From 1965 to 1995

GEOGRAPHIC LITERACY

NGS Focus on Geographic Literacy

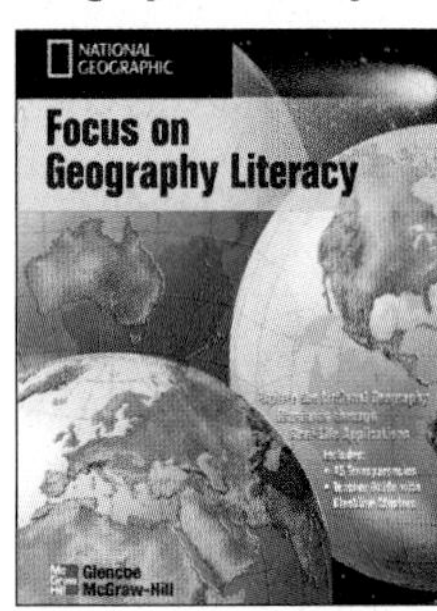

Building Geography Skills for Life

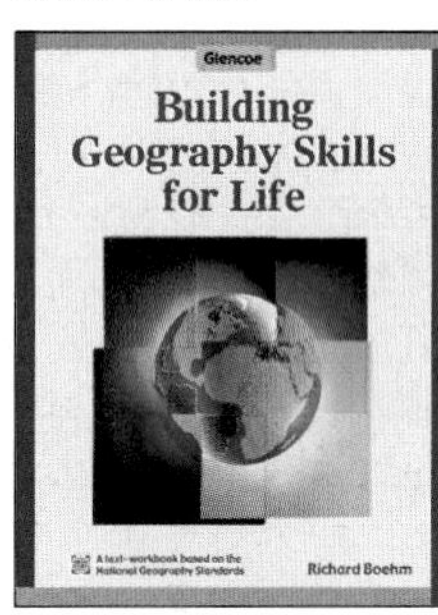

BIBLIOGRAPHY

Readings for the Student

Cart, Michael. ***Tomorrowland: Ten Stories About the Future.*** Scholastic, 2001. To celebrate the new millennium, writers contribute stories about the future.

Mazer, Anne. ***A Walk in My World: International Short Stories About Youth.*** Persea Books, 2000. Selected international stories.

Readings for the Teacher

Watkins, Michael, and Susan Rosegrant. ***Breakthrough International Negotiation: How Great Negotiators Transformed the World's Toughest Post-Cold War Conflicts.*** John Wiley & Sons, 2001. Examines conflict resolution in the Middle East, Korea, Africa, and Bosnia.

Skidmore, Thomas E., and Peter H. Smith. ***Modern Latin America.*** Oxford University Press, 2000. A lively history that includes coverage of trafficking, NAFTA, politics, and immigration.

Multimedia Resources

VHS. ***Jam Packed: The Challenge of Human Overpopulation.*** (1997, 30 minutes) Video Project, 200 Estates Drive, Ben Lomond, CA 95005, 1–800–475–2638.

Video. ***Sunrise over Tiananmen Square.*** First Run/Icarus, 1999. (29 minutes)

Additional Glencoe Resources for this Unit:

- Glencoe Skillbuilder Interactive Workbook CD-ROM, Level 2
- Glencoe World History Primary Source Document Library
- World Art Prints
- World Biography: People in History
- Outline Map Resource Book
- World Desk Map
- World Art and Architecture Transparencies
- World Music: Cultural Traditions
- World Music: A Cultural Legacy
- Glencoe World Literature Library
- Reading in the Content Area
- Teaching Strategies for the World History Classroom (Including Block Scheduling Pacing Guides)
- Inclusion for the High School Social Studies Classroom Strategies and Activities

Introducing UNIT 5

0:00 Out of Time?

If time does not permit teaching each chapter in this unit, you may use the **Reading Essentials and Study Guide** summaries.

Unit Objectives

After studying this unit, students should be able to:

1. summarize the causes and impact of the Cold War;
2. describe conflicts in Asia and the region's emergence as an economic powerhouse;
3. analyze the legacy of colonial rule in Africa and the challenges facing that continent;
4. examine the rival nationalistic movements in the Middle East and the region's search for peace;
5. identify political and economic trends in Latin America;
6. analyze factors that are leading toward globalization.

The Period in Perspective

Point out to students the nations that won their independence following World War II did so nearly 200 years after the United States became the first colony to become a sovereign nation. What challenges do newly independent nations face today?

Use these materials to enrich student understanding of events following World War II.

- **NGS PICTURE SHOW™ CD-ROMs**
  World War II Era
  Civil Rights
- **NGS PICTURE PACK TRANSPARENCY SETS**
  Civil Rights
  Physical Geography of the World
- **IMAGES OF THE WORLD POSTER SET**

UNIT 5 Toward a Global Civilization

1945–Present

The Period in Perspective

World War II can be seen as the end of an era of European domination of the world. After the war, Europe quickly divided into hostile camps as the Cold War rivalry between the United States and the Soviet Union forced nations to take sides. In the late 1980s, however, the Soviet Empire began to come apart, and the Cold War quickly ended.

World War II severely undermined the stability of the colonial order in Asia and Africa. By the end of the 1940s, most colonies in Asia had gained their independence. Later, African colonies, too, would become independent nations.

▲ Contemporary African art featuring Nelson Mandela

Primary Sources Library

See pages 780–781 for primary source readings to accompany Unit 5.

*Use The World History **Primary Source Document Library CD-ROM** to find additional primary sources about Global Civilization.*

▶ African National Congress campaign rally

624

TEAM TEACHING ACTIVITY

Science and Technology The text ends with a discussion of the challenges that face the world today. Many of these issues have developed as a result of, and may be solved by, advances in science and technology. Invite the science teacher to work with your class to compile a list of issues such as energy consumption and the greenhouse effect, consumption of material goods and pollution, terrorism and the resulting problems of land mines and biological warfare, and advances in medicine and the economics of pharmaceutical research. Assign students to research one issue addressed by the science teacher and then to prepare a multimedia report showing the relationship between the issue and world history.

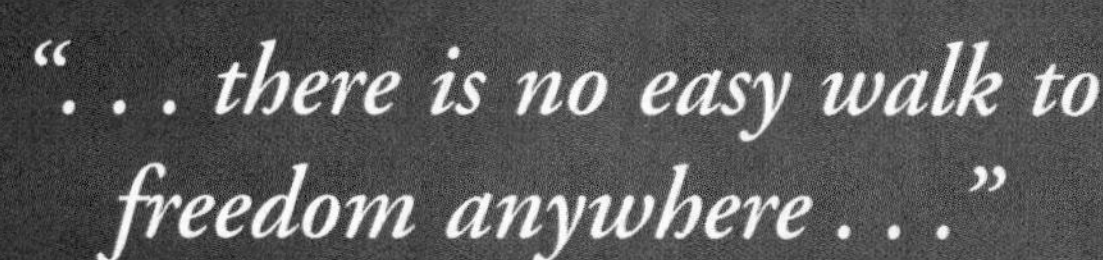

"... there is no easy walk to freedom anywhere ..."

—*Nelson Mandela*

Introducing UNIT 5

GLENCOE TECHNOLOGY

CD-ROM
World History Primary Source Document Library CD-ROM

Use the World History Primary Source Document Library CD-ROM to access primary source documents related to a global civilization.

More About the Art

The young Nelson Mandela was groomed to assume political office. Instead, he decided to become a lawyer and also dreamed of contributing to the freedom struggle of his people. Later, working with the then-banned African National Congress, Mandela became known as the "Black Pimpernel" because of his numerous disguises and successful evasion of the police. In 1994, he was elected president in the first election in South Africa open to all races.

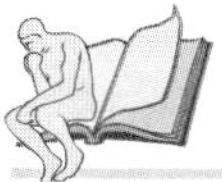

History *and the* Humanities

World Art and Architecture Transparencies
- 54 *Diego and I*
- 55 *Sydney Opera House*
- 56 *The Twelve Tribes of Israel*
- 57 *Figura*
- 58 *The Liberated African Woman*
- 59 *Vietnam Veterans Memorial*
- 60 *Petronas Towers*

World Music: Cultural Legacy, Lessons 2, 5, 6, 7, 8, 9

SERVICE-LEARNING PROJECT

Every community is faced with decisions that affect the citizens of that community. Assign students to read their local newspaper to identify situations in the community that require a decision. Assign students to use a decision-making process to identify a particular situation where a decision is required, to gather information about that situation, to identify options that are available in the community that will aid in the decision-making process, and to resolve the issue. Students should predict the consequences of the decision they would choose. Assign students to take action to implement the decision they have adopted. Finally, have students present reports of their actions or findings to the entire class. L2

Looking Back to See Ahead

TEACH

Introduction

This feature focuses on the political consequences of the development of modern international communications. Particular attention is given to the consequences of international satellite broadcasting and the benefits of the Internet.

Background Notes

Linking Past and Present

Space Race The early days of the space race between the U.S.S.R. and the United States were triggered by the Soviet launching of Sputnik I. The space race has also been the subject of numerous books and films, including Tom Wolfe's novel *The Right Stuff* and the popular film by the same title. Students interested in learning more about this period and the exploration of space may want to read Wolfe's novel or watch a video of the movie. Space exploration continues, although now often on an international, cooperative basis. You might wish to discuss the International Space Station and other joint space ventures with students.

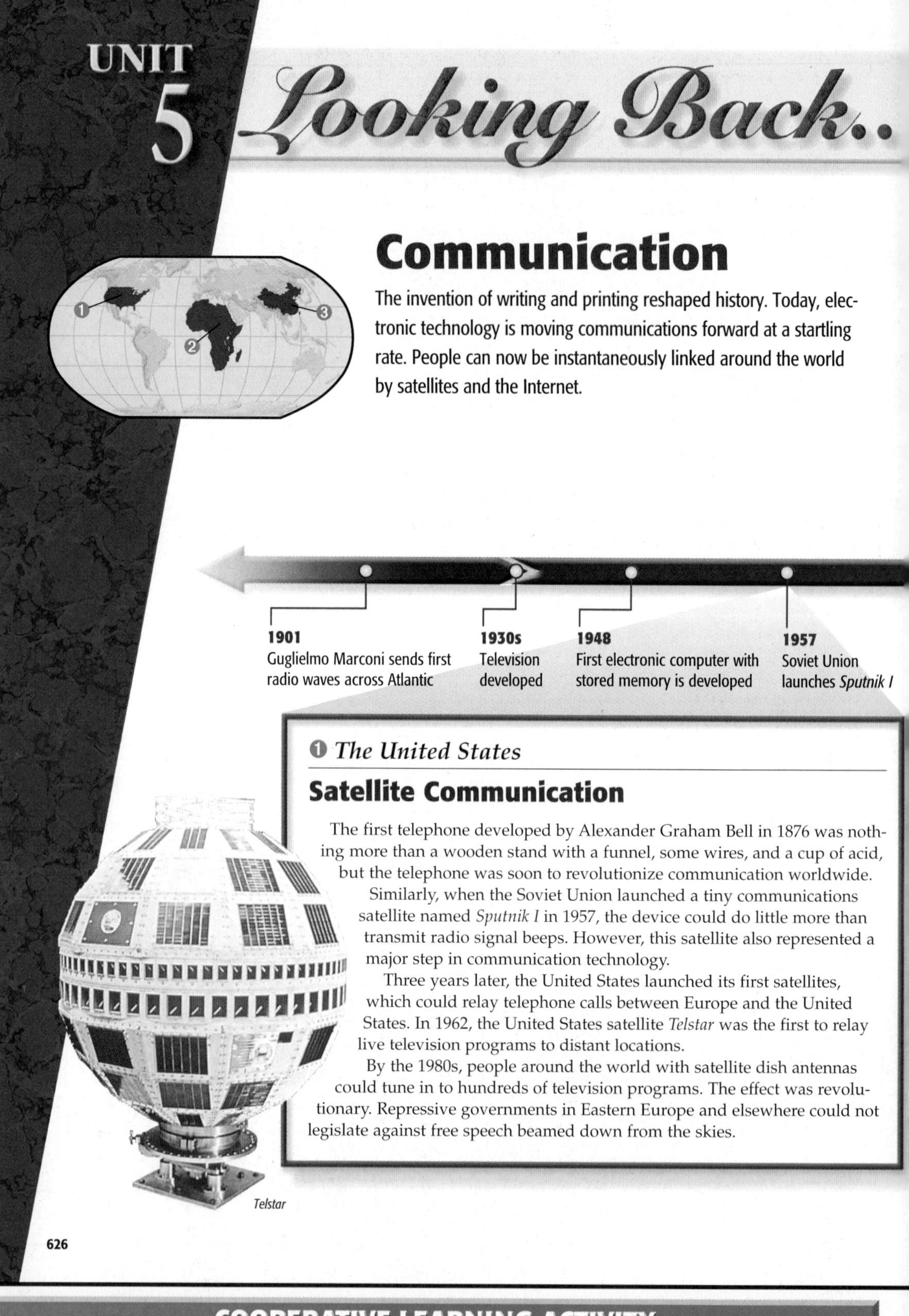

UNIT 5 *Looking Back...*

Communication

The invention of writing and printing reshaped history. Today, electronic technology is moving communications forward at a startling rate. People can now be instantaneously linked around the world by satellites and the Internet.

1901 Guglielmo Marconi sends first radio waves across Atlantic

1930s Television developed

1948 First electronic computer with stored memory is developed

1957 Soviet Union launches *Sputnik I*

❶ *The United States*

Satellite Communication

The first telephone developed by Alexander Graham Bell in 1876 was nothing more than a wooden stand with a funnel, some wires, and a cup of acid, but the telephone was soon to revolutionize communication worldwide.

Similarly, when the Soviet Union launched a tiny communications satellite named *Sputnik I* in 1957, the device could do little more than transmit radio signal beeps. However, this satellite also represented a major step in communication technology.

Three years later, the United States launched its first satellites, which could relay telephone calls between Europe and the United States. In 1962, the United States satellite *Telstar* was the first to relay live television programs to distant locations.

By the 1980s, people around the world with satellite dish antennas could tune in to hundreds of television programs. The effect was revolutionary. Repressive governments in Eastern Europe and elsewhere could not legislate against free speech beamed down from the skies.

Telstar

626

COOPERATIVE LEARNING ACTIVITY

Creating a Multimedia Presentation Organize students into small groups and have each group select one medium of communication, such as film, television, radio, newspaper, CD-ROM, or the Internet. Then ask each group to choose a current international news story and create a news feature on that topic for the medium they have chosen. Have each group present its report, explaining the features of the presentations that were specially adapted to the medium they chose, and estimating the size and nature of the audience they hoped to reach. L3

For grading this activity, refer to the ***Performance Assessment Activities*** booklet.

to See Ahead

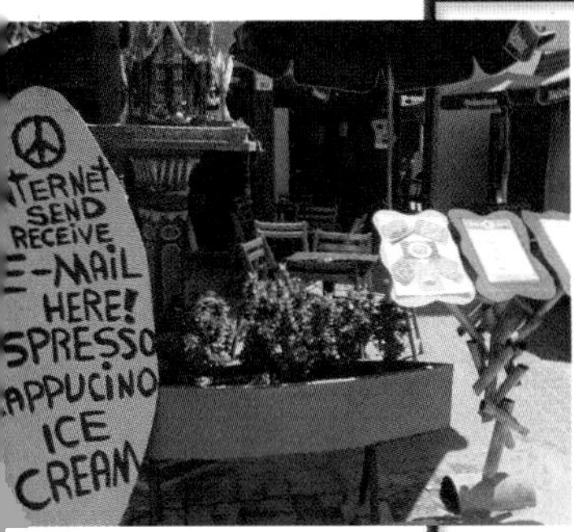

Cybercafe

❷ *Africa*

The Internet

In Africa, UNESCO is helping the Pan-African News Agency and others to link to the Internet. Project leaders see the Internet as one of the keys to unlocking Africa's economic potential. Currently, there is one Internet access site for every 200 Africans, compared to a world average of one site for every 30 people. Internet access will improve, and as it does, African communications, education, business, and government endeavors will be profoundly impacted.

1960 United States launches its first satellites

1971 Microprocessor is invented

1977 Apple II computer introduced

1990 African agencies link to the Internet

1993 Chinese government bans satellite dishes

❸ *China*

Satellite Dishes

Satellite dishes made it possible for people across the People's Republic of China to listen to Mandarin-speaking rappers out of Hong Kong, English broadcasts of CNN News, and movies from Japan. The uncensored broadcasts enraged government officials, who tried to ban satellite dishes in 1993. However, even as officials dismantled thousands of large dishes, kits for smaller dishes were being smuggled into the country.

Other countries with repressive policies, such as Iran and Myanmar, tried and failed to ban satellite reception. Even free governments, like India's, were concerned about the "cultural invasion," but satellite television was here to stay.

Satellite dish, Tibet

Why It Matters

While it used to take months to send a letter from the United States to Africa, today it can take only seconds. How has instantaneous communication made the world smaller? What are the good and bad results of this phenomenon?

Geography

Movement The United States is the leading source of television programs and films for the world market. Many countries have taken steps to limit the consumption of American cultural products for many reasons, including the desire to support their own film and television industries. Attempts by European nations to limit imports from the United States have led to conflicts under GATT (General Agreement on Tariffs and Trade), which seeks to open markets and reduce trade restrictions. GATT was first signed in 1947 and was amended several times. Then, in 1995, the World Trade Organization was formed to handle many of these international trade disputes.

Cultural Diffusion

Hollywood Abroad The internationalization of the film industry has changed the content of many American films. Many films produced in the United States now earn as much or more money in foreign distribution as they do inside the United States. Since these films are either dubbed or subtitled, those based on action and adventure rather than dialogue tend to be more successful. This phenomenon in part explains the trend toward producing blockbuster action thrillers.

Why It Matters

Students may list the following as possible benefits: instantaneous communication facilitates business interactions between distant nations; allows for more frequent contact between families and friends; allows more immediate and thorough access to important information about world events. Students may list the following as possible disadvantages: growing dependence on electronic communication; losing the art of writing; less travel and "real world" experiences; social relationships becoming dependent on technology; loss of emotional expression and interpersonal connections; inability to verify sources of information.

Chapter 20 Resources

Timesaving Tools

TeacherWorks™ All-In-One Planner and Resource Center

- **Interactive Teacher Edition** Access your Teacher Wraparound Edition and your classroom resources with a few easy clicks.
- **Interactive Lesson Planner** Planning has never been easier! Organize your week, month, semester, or year with all the lesson helps you need to make teaching creative, timely, and relevant.

Use Glencoe's **Presentation Plus!** multimedia teacher tool to easily present dynamic lessons that visually excite your students. Using Microsoft PowerPoint® you can customize the presentations to create your own personalized lessons.

Teaching Transparencies

Graphic Organizer Student Activity 20 Transparency

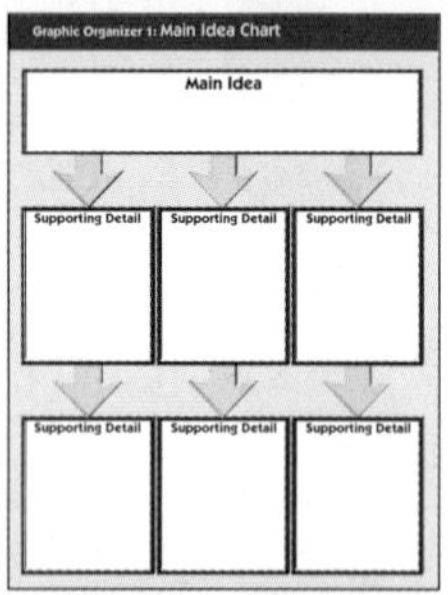

Chapter Transparency 20

Map Overlay Transparency 20

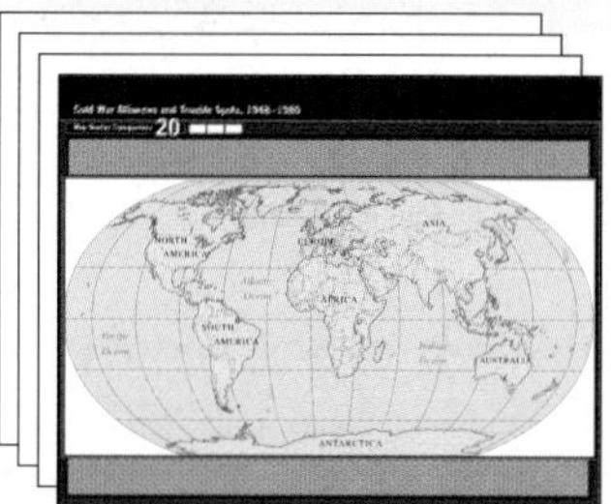

Application and Enrichment

Enrichment Activity 20

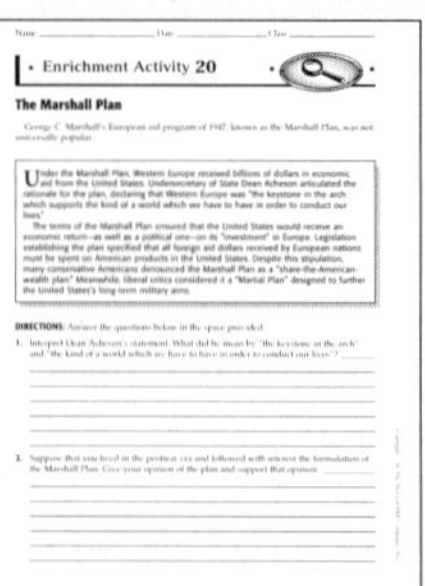

Primary Source Reading 20

History Simulation Activity 20

Historical Significance Activity 20

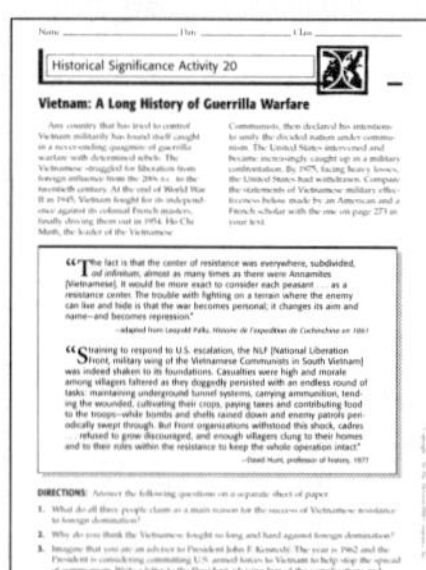

Cooperative Learning Activity 20

THE HISTORY CHANNEL.

The following videotape programs are available from Glencoe as supplements to Chapter 20:

- **Senator Joseph McCarthy: An American Inquisitor** (ISBN 1–56501–610–6)
- **Bay of Pigs/Cuban Missile Crisis** (ISBN 0–7670–1199–6)
- **The Fifties** (ISBN 0–7670–0413–2)
- **Martin Luther King, Jr.: The Man and the Dream** (ISBN 0–7670–1057–4)

To order, call Glencoe at 1–800–334–7344. To find classroom resources to accompany many of these videos, check the following home pages:

A&E Television: www.aande.com

The History Channel: www.historychannel.com

Chapter 20 Resources

REVIEW AND REINFORCEMENT

Linking Past and Present Activity 20

Time Line Activity 20

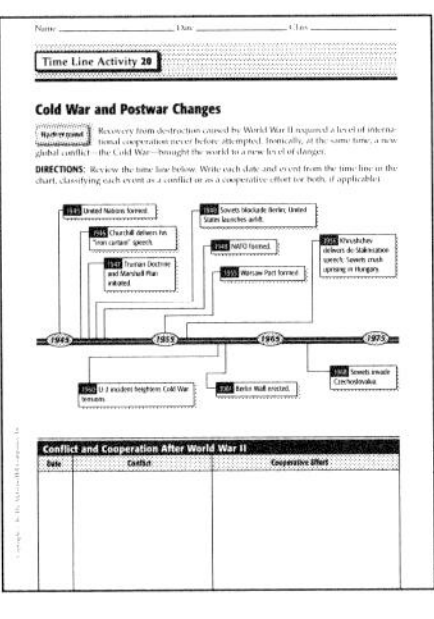

Reteaching Activity 20

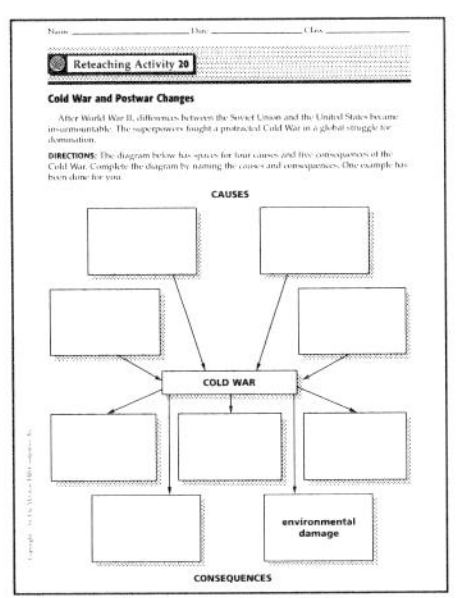

Vocabulary Activity 20

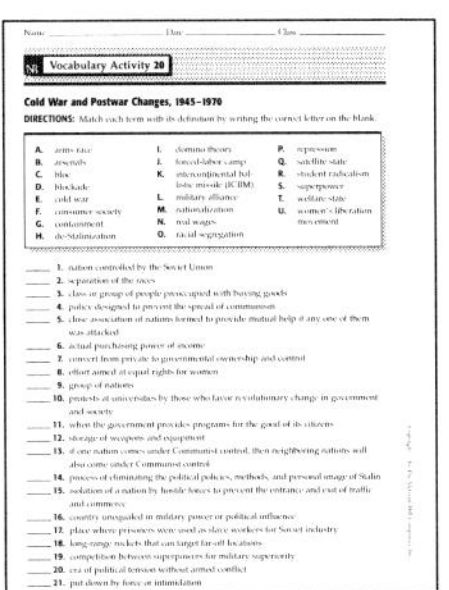

Critical Thinking Skills Activity 20

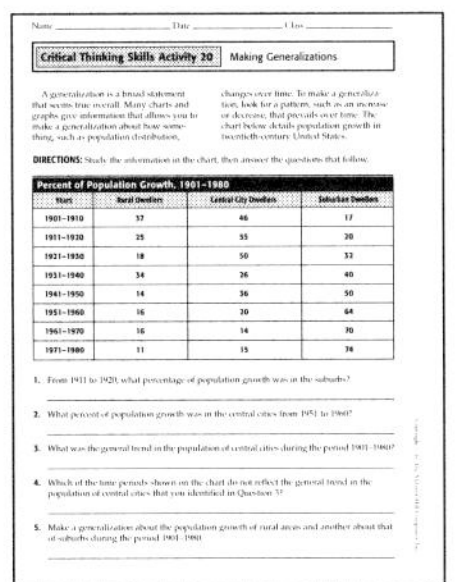

ASSESSMENT AND EVALUATION

Chapter 20 Test Form A

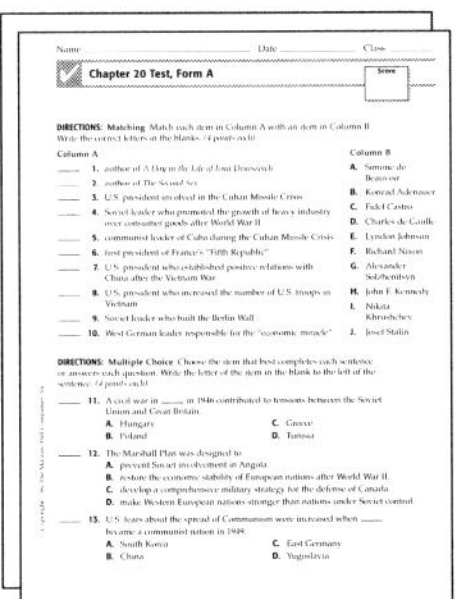

Chapter 20 Test Form B

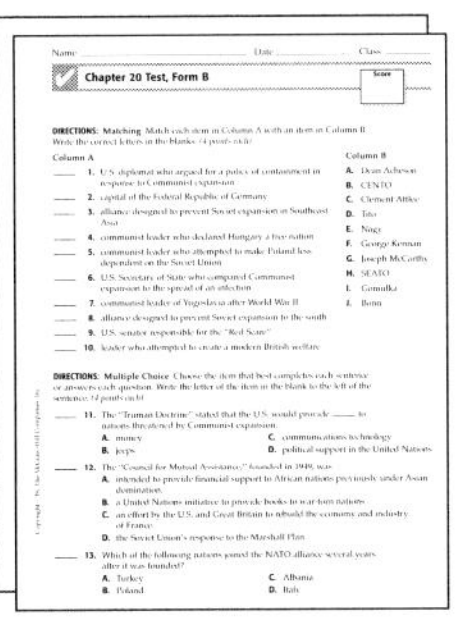

Performance Assessment Activity 20

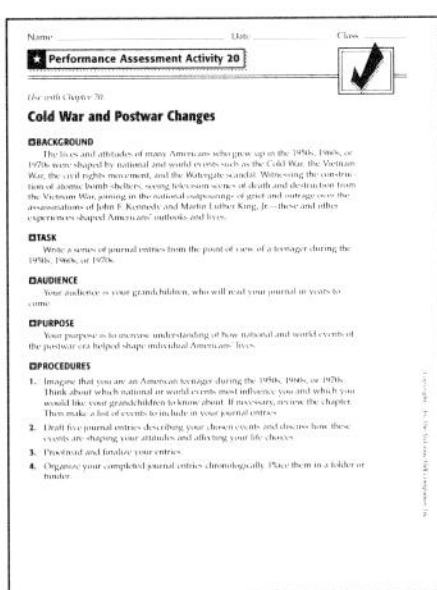

ExamView® Pro Testmaker CD-ROM

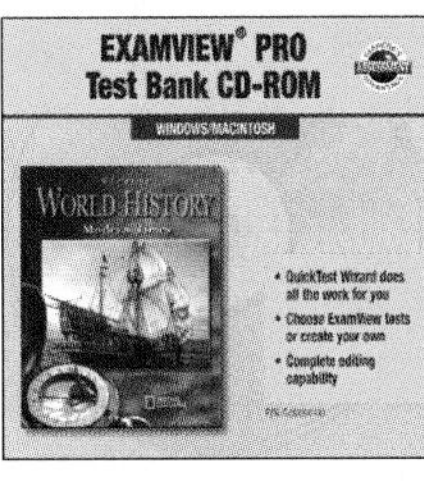

Standardized Test Skills Practice Workbook Activity 20

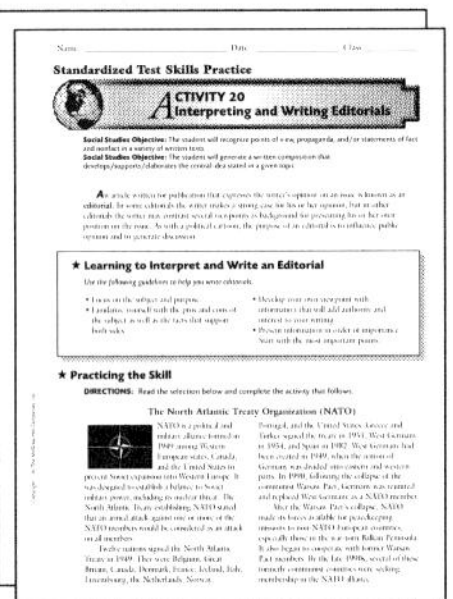

INTERDISCIPLINARY ACTIVITIES

Mapping History Activity 20

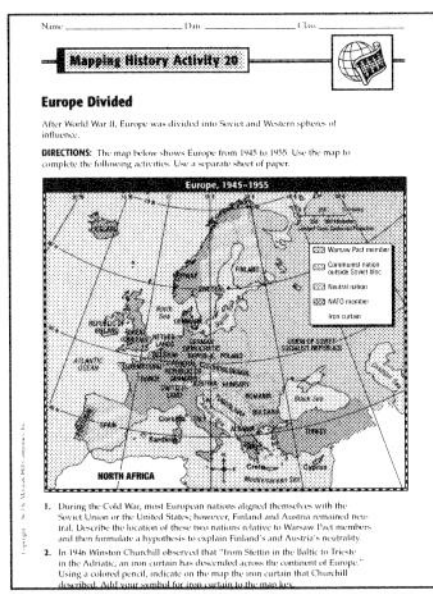

World Art and Music Activity 20

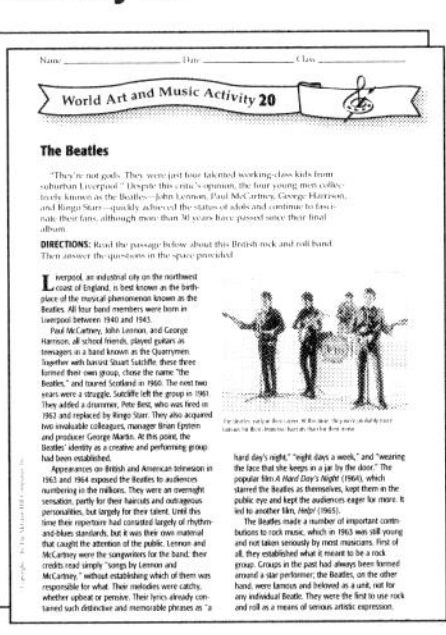

History and Geography Activity 20

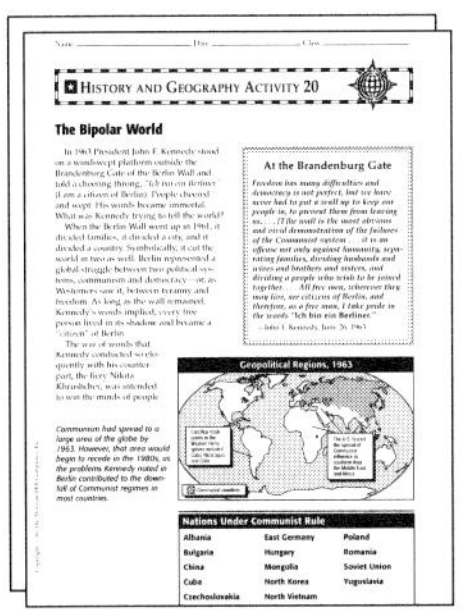

People in World History Activity 20

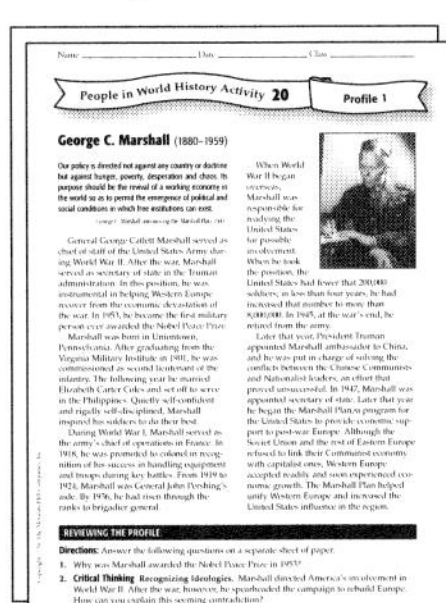

MULTIMEDIA

- Vocabulary PuzzleMaker CD-ROM
- Interactive Tutor Self-Assessment CD-ROM
- ExamView® Pro Testmaker CD-ROM
- Audio Program
- World History Primary Source Document Library CD-ROM
- MindJogger Videoquiz
- Presentation Plus! CD-ROM
- TeacherWorks CD-ROM
- Interactive Student Edition CD-ROM
- The World History—Modern Times Video Program

SPANISH RESOURCES

The following Spanish language materials are available in the Spanish Resources Binder:

- Spanish Guided Reading Activities
- Spanish Reteaching Activities
- Spanish Quizzes and Tests
- Spanish Vocabulary Activities
- Spanish Summaries

Chapter 20 Resources

SECTION RESOURCES

Daily Objectives	Reproducible Resources	Multimedia Resources
SECTION 1 **Development of the Cold War** 1. Identify and describe the period of conflict called the Cold War that developed between the United States and the Soviet Union after 1945. 2. Explain why, as the Cold War developed, European nations were forced to support one of the two major powers.	Reproducible Lesson Plan 20–1 Daily Lecture and Discussion Notes 20–1 Guided Reading Activity 20–1* Section Quiz 20–1* Reading Essentials and Study Guide 20–1	Daily Focus Skills Transparency 20–1 Interactive Tutor Self-Assessment CD-ROM ExamView® Pro Testmaker CD-ROM Presentation Plus! CD-ROM
SECTION 2 **The Soviet Union and Eastern Europe** 1. Describe the policies of de-Stalinization initiated by Soviet leader Khrushchev. 2. Discuss the revolts and protests faced by the Soviet Union in its attempt to gain and maintain control over Eastern Europe.	Reproducible Lesson Plan 20–2 Daily Lecture and Discussion Notes 20–2 Guided Reading Activity 20–2* Section Quiz 20–2* Reading Essentials and Study Guide 20–2	Daily Focus Skills Transparency 20–2 Interactive Tutor Self-Assessment CD-ROM ExamView® Pro Testmaker CD-ROM Presentation Plus! CD-ROM
SECTION 3 **Western Europe and North America** 1. Report how postwar Western societies rebuilt their economies and communities. 2. Explain how shifting social structures in the West led to upheaval and change.	Reproducible Lesson Plan 20–3 Daily Lecture and Discussion Notes 20–3 Guided Reading Activity 20–3* Section Quiz 20–3* Reteaching Activity 20* Reading Essentials and Study Guide 20–3	Daily Focus Skills Transparency 20–3 Interactive Tutor Self-Assessment CD-ROM ExamView® Pro Testmaker CD-ROM Presentation Plus! CD-ROM

0:00 **OUT OF TIME?**
Assign the Chapter 20 **Reading Essentials and Study Guide.**

*Also Available in Spanish

 Blackline Master  Transparency CD-ROM DVD

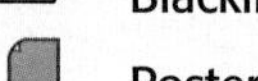 Poster  Music Program Audio Program  Videocassette

Chapter 20 Resources

NATIONAL GEOGRAPHIC Teacher's Corner

INDEX TO NATIONAL GEOGRAPHIC MAGAZINE

The following articles relate to this chapter:

- "Kaliningrad," by Priit J. Vesilind, March 1997.
- "The New Saigon," by Tracy Dahlby, April 1995.
- "East Europe's Dark Dawn," by Jon Thompson, June 1991.
- "Bikini: A Way of Life Lost," by William S. Ellis, June 1986.

ADDITIONAL NATIONAL GEOGRAPHIC SOCIETY PRODUCTS

To order the following, call National Geographic at 1-800-368-2728:

- *1945–1989: The Cold War* (Video)
- *Capitalism, Socialism, Communism Series, "Communism"* (Video)
- Europe: *The Road to Unity* (Video)

NGS ONLINE

Access National Geographic's new dynamic MapMachine Web site and other geography resources at:

www.nationalgeographic.com
www.nationalgeographic.com/maps

KEY TO ABILITY LEVELS

Teaching strategies have been coded.

- L1 BASIC activities for all students
- L2 AVERAGE activities for average to above-average students
- L3 CHALLENGING activities for above-average students
- ELL ENGLISH LANGUAGE LEARNER activities

Block Schedule

Activities that are suited to use within the block scheduling framework are identified by:

WORLD HISTORY Online

Use our Web site for additional resources. All essential content is covered in the Student Edition.

You and your students can visit www.wh.mt.glencoe.com, the Web site companion to *Glencoe World History—Modern Times.* This innovative integration of electronic and print media offers your students a wealth of opportunities. The student text directs students to the Web site for the following options:

- **Chapter Overviews**
- **Self-Check Quizzes**
- **Student Web Activities**
- **Textbook Updates**

Answers to the Student Web Activities are provided for you in the **Web Activity Lesson Plans.** Additional Web resources and Interactive Tutor Puzzles are also available.

From the Classroom of...

Jill M. Frimel
Solon High School
Solon, Ohio

Atomic Bombs

One of the most terrifying features of the Cold War was the building, by the United States and the Soviet Union, of intercontinental ballistic missiles (ICBMs) armed with nuclear devices. The launching of ICBMs would have resulted in the mutual assured destruction of both nations.

Ask students to review the development of nuclear weapons up to that point in history. Then have them discuss the practical and moral aspects of the "bomb" and its use in World War II. Assign individual students the following roles: member of a "ban-the-bomb" organization in 1960; "pro-bomb" member of the U.S. Congress in 1960; member of U.S. Congress in 1945; U.S. civilian in 1945; Japanese civilian in 1945; U.S. military officer in 1945; antinuclear scientist in 1945. Have these students present their views to the class, followed by a general discussion of Truman's decision to drop the bomb on Hiroshima and Nagasaki. Then have students vote for or against the deployment of nuclear weapons.

Introducing CHAPTER 20

Performance Assessment

Refer to Activity 20 in the Performance Assessment Activities and Rubrics booklet.

The Impact Today

Ask students to list the countries that they believe are known to or suspected of having nuclear weapons. *(U.S., Russia, India, Pakistan, Israel, France, England, etc.)* Discuss with students reasons for and against the United States maintaining a nuclear war capability in today's world. Also discuss what they think the United States's strategy should be for preventing and defending against nuclear attacks. L1

GLENCOE TECHNOLOGY

The World History—Modern Times Video Program

To learn more about the Soviet blockade of Berlin, students can view the Chapter 20 video, "The Berlin Airlift," from **The World History—Modern Times Video Program.**

MindJogger Videoquiz

Use the **MindJogger Videoquiz** to preview Chapter 20 content.

 Available in VHS.

CHAPTER 20 Cold War and Postwar Changes

1945–1970

Key Events

As you read this chapter, look for the key events of the Cold War.

- *At the end of World War II, the United States and the Soviet Union competed for political domination of the world.*
- *The United States fought in Korea and Vietnam to prevent the spread of communism.*
- *The Soviet Union used armies to maintain Soviet regimes in Eastern Europe.*
- *The creation of NATO and the European Economic Community helped Western Europe move toward political and economic unity during the Cold War.*

The Impact Today

The events that occurred during this time period still impact our lives today.

- *NATO continues to flourish. Representatives of its 19 member nations form the North Atlantic Council, which is headquartered in Brussels, Belgium.*
- *Nuclear weapons remain a threat to the peace and stability of the world.*
- *The civil rights struggle brought greater equality to African Americans and altered American attitudes toward race, discrimination, and poverty.*

World History—Modern Times Video *The Chapter 20 video, "The Berlin Airlift," shows how American and British planes circumvented the Soviet blockade.*

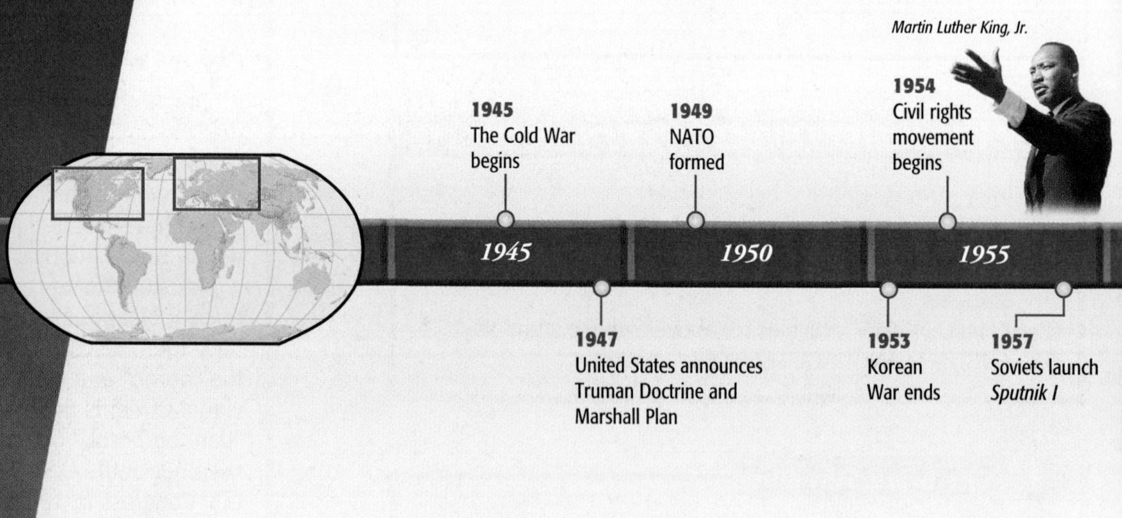
1945
The Cold War begins
1949
NATO formed
1954
Civil rights movement begins
1945
1950
1955
1947
United States announces Truman Doctrine and Marshall Plan
1953
Korean War ends
1957
Soviets launch *Sputnik I*

Martin Luther King, Jr.

628

TWO-MINUTE LESSON LAUNCHER

Ask students to list important differences between the Soviet Union and the United States that predated the end of World War II. *(totalitarian versus democratic political systems; planned Communist economy versus market capitalism; different wartime experiences)* Then ask students to brainstorm associations they have with the terms "cold war" and "iron curtain." Record and display their words and phrases, adding and subtracting as students study the chapter. You might mention that while Winston Churchill popularized the term "iron curtain," he did not originate it. As long ago as the early 1800s, it was used to refer to a fireproof curtain in theaters, installed to prevent the spread of flames between the stage area and the audience. L1

The Soviet government displays its military strength in Moscow's annual May Day parade.

1960 | 1965 | 1970

1961 Berlin Wall built

1962 Cuban missile crisis unfolds

1964 More U.S. troops sent to Vietnam

Fidel Castro

Berlin Wall

HISTORY Online

Chapter Overview
Visit the *Glencoe World History—Modern Times* Web site at wh.mt.glencoe.com and click on **Chapter 20–Chapter Overview** to preview chapter information.

629

MORE ABOUT THE ART

May Day May Day, a workers' holiday, has been the "Labor Day" for socialist and Communist countries since 1889. During the Soviet era, vast numbers of military vehicles and marchers paraded past Soviet leaders in Moscow's Red Square. People who studied the Kremlin used to analyze the lineup of leaders at these parades to see, by their positions (or nonappearance), who was in favor and who was not. Ask students to discuss the message conveyed by a parade like the one in this photograph. *(that the country is prepared militarily; it has the latest weapons; its people are united behind it)* **L1** ELL

Introducing CHAPTER 20

Chapter Objectives

After studying this chapter, students should be able to:

1. describe the development of the Cold War, the Cuban missile crisis, and the Vietnam War;
2. identify Stalin and Khrushchev and describe the spread of Soviet power;
3. explain developments in postwar Western societies.

Chapter Overview
Introduce students to chapter content and key terms by having them access **Chapter Overview 20** at wh.mt.glencoe.com.

Time Line Activity

As students read the chapter, have them review the time line on this page. Ask them which events were the direct result of the tension between the United States and the Soviet Union. Have them justify their responses. **L1**

Glencoe Literature Library

The following literature from the Glencoe Literature Library may enrich this chapter:

One Day in the Life of Ivan Denisovich by A. Solzhenitsyn

CHAPTER PREVIEW

Introducing

A Story That Matters

Depending on the ability levels of your students, select from the following questions to reinforce the reading of *A Story That Matters.*

- Why was the loss of 50 million people in World War II made even worse by the fact that many of them were young? *(Answers might include loss of work force, loss of people who might have started families.)*
- What would you say was the most pressing problem facing Europe after the war? Why do you think so? *(Answers will vary.)*
- How would you explain the title "A Sober Victory"? *(The war was over but Europe was devastated.)* L1

About the Art

The bombing of London by the Germans destroyed whole sections of the city. Buildings, roads, and railways, as well as light, power, and gas lines were heavily damaged. Using the photograph as a discussion starting point, ask students to imagine the physical and psychological hardships that would have confronted Europeans at the end of the war.

CHAPTER PREVIEW A Story That Matters

Cleaning up after the London Blitz

A Sober Victory

The end of World War II in Europe had been met with great joy. One visitor in Moscow reported, "I looked out of the window [at 2 A.M.], almost everywhere there were lights in the windows—people were staying awake. Everyone embraced everyone else, someone sobbed aloud."

After the victory parades and celebrations, however, Europeans awoke to a devastating realization: their civilization was in ruins. As many as fifty million people (both soldiers and civilians) had been killed over the last six years. Massive air raids had reduced many of the great cities of Europe to heaps of rubble.

An American general described Berlin: "Wherever we looked we saw desolation. It was like a city of the dead. Suffering and shock were visible in every face. Dead bodies still remained in canals and lakes and were being dug out from under bomb debris."

Millions of Europeans faced starvation. Grain harvests were only half of what they had been in 1939. Millions were also homeless. In the parts of the Soviet Union that had been occupied by the Germans, almost twenty-five million people were without homes. Fifteen million Germans and East Europeans were driven out of countries where they were no longer wanted. Millions of people had been uprooted by the war and became "displaced persons" who tried to find food and a way home.

Why It Matters

Despite the chaos, Europe was soon on the road to a remarkable recovery. However, World War II had destroyed European supremacy in world affairs, and from this, Europe did not recover. As the Cold War between the world's two superpowers—the United States and the Soviet Union—grew stronger, European nations were divided into two armed camps dependent on one of these two major powers. The United States and the Soviet Union, whose rivalry brought the world to the brink of nuclear war, seemed to hold the survival of Europe and the world in their hands.

History and You Create a world map. As you read the chapter, color the map as a United States policy maker might have during the Cold War. Indicate the Soviet and United States spheres of influence as well as areas under contention.

HISTORY AND YOU

The deadly products of the Cold War, nuclear weapons, remain a threat to the peace and stability of the world even though the United States and Russia are no longer enemies. National resources that were directed toward escalating arms production and military defenses, especially in the Soviet Union, slowed down progress in such areas as health and education. Based on what students know of Soviet and American history, have students explain why many Russians would be mistrustful of the West and why the Soviet Union would want to control Eastern Europe. Also have them explain the reasons for the United States's mistrust of the Soviet Union. Can they envision how the Cold War might have been avoided? L2

SECTION 1 Development of the Cold War

Guide to Reading

Main Ideas
- A period of conflict called the Cold War developed between the United States and the Soviet Union after 1945.
- As the Cold War developed, European nations were forced to support one of the two major powers.

Key Terms
satellite state, policy of containment, arms race, deterrence, domino theory

People to Identify
Dean Acheson, Nikita Khrushchev

Places to Locate
Berlin, Federal Republic of Germany, German Democratic Republic

Preview Questions
1. What were the major turning points in the development of the Cold War?
2. What was the Cuban missile crisis?

Reading Strategy
Summarizing Information Use a table like the one below to list the American presidents who held office during the Cold War and major events related to the Cold War that took place during their administrations.

President	Major Event

Preview of Events

1945 · 1950 · 1955 · 1960 · 1965

- **1948** Berlin Air Lift begins
- **1949** Chinese Communists take control of China
- **1950** Korean War begins
- **1961** Soviets and East Germans build the Berlin Wall
- **1964** Lyndon B. Johnson increases number of troops sent to Vietnam

Voices from the Past

Winston Churchill

On March 5, 1946, Winston Churchill said in a speech in Fulton, Missouri:

> "From Stettin in the Baltic to Trieste in the Adriatic, an iron curtain has descended across the continent. Behind that line lie all the capitals of the ancient states of central and eastern Europe, Warsaw, Berlin, Prague, Vienna, Budapest, Belgrade, Bucharest, and Sofia; all these famous cities and the populations around them lie in the Soviet sphere and all are subject, in one form or another, not only to Soviet influence but to a very high and increasing measure of control from Moscow."
>
> —*The Congressional Record,* 79th Congress, 1946

In 1946, Stalin replied: "In substance, Mr. Churchill now stands in the position of a firebrand of war." The division between Western Europe and Soviet-controlled Eastern Europe marked the beginning of the Cold War.

Confrontation of the Superpowers

Once the Axis powers were defeated, the differences between the United States and the Soviet Union became clear. Stalin still feared the capitalist West, and U.S. (and other Western) leaders continued to fear communism. Who, then, was responsible for beginning the Cold War between the United States and the Soviet Union? Both took steps that were unwise and might have been avoided. It should not surprise us that two such different systems would come into conflict.

1 FOCUS

Section Overview

This section describes the spread and effects of the Cold War.

BELLRINGER
Skillbuilder Activity

 Project transparency and have students answer questions.

 Available as a blackline master.

Daily Focus Skills Transparency 20–1

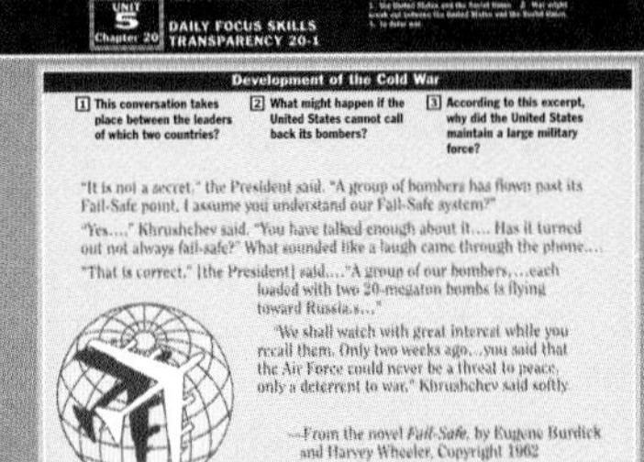
UNIT 5 Chapter 20 DAILY FOCUS SKILLS TRANSPARENCY 20-1

Development of the Cold War

1. This conversation takes place between the leaders of which two countries?
2. What might happen if the United States cannot call back its bombers?
3. According to this excerpt, why did the United States maintain a large military force?

"It is not a secret," the President said. "A group of bombers has flown past its Fail-Safe point. I assume you understand our Fail-Safe system?"

"Yes...." Khrushchev said. "You have talked enough about it.... Has it turned out not always fail-safe?" What sounded like a laugh came through the phone....

"That is correct," [the President] said...."A group of our bombers,...each loaded with two 20-megaton bombs is flying toward Russia...."

"We shall watch with great interest while you recall them. Only two weeks ago,...you said that the Air Force could never be a threat to peace, only a deterrent to war," Khrushchev said softly.

—From the novel *Fail-Safe,* by Eugene Burdick and Harvey Wheeler, Copyright 1962

Guide to Reading

Answers to Graphic: Truman: Truman Doctrine, Marshall Plan, Soviet blockade of Berlin; Communists take over in China; NATO; beginning of Korean War; Eisenhower: Warsaw Pact; development of intercontinental ballistic missiles; U.S.S.R. launches *Sputnik I;* Kennedy: Berlin Wall; Cuban missile crisis; Johnson: Vietnam War

Preteaching Vocabulary: Discuss the policy of containment and its relationship to the arms race. L1

SECTION RESOURCES

Reproducible Masters
- Reproducible Lesson Plan 20–1
- Daily Lecture and Discussion Notes 20–1
- Guided Reading Activity 20–1
- Section Quiz 20–1
- Reading Essentials and Study Guide 20–1

Transparencies
Daily Focus Skills Transparency 20–1

Multimedia
- Interactive Tutor Self-Assessment CD-ROM
- ExamView® Pro Testmaker CD-ROM
- Presentation Plus! CD-ROM

2 TEACH

Daily Lecture and Discussion Notes 20–1

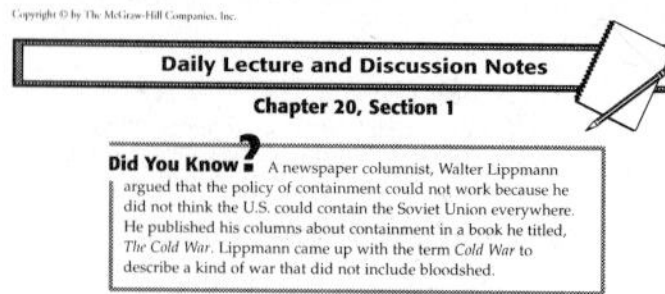

Daily Lecture and Discussion Notes

Chapter 20, Section 1

Did You Know? A newspaper columnist, Walter Lippmann argued that the policy of containment could not work because he did not think the U.S. could contain the Soviet Union everywhere. He published his columns about containment in a book he titled, *The Cold War*. Lippmann came up with the term *Cold War* to describe a kind of war that did not include bloodshed.

I. Confrontation of the Superpowers *(pages 631–633)*

A. The division between Western Europe and Soviet-controlled Eastern Europe was the beginning of the Cold War. The Soviet Union feared the capitalist West. The United States feared communism.

B. After World War II, the United States and Great Britain wanted the Eastern European nations to determine their own governments. Stalin feared that the Eastern European nations would be anti-Soviet if they were allowed free elections.

C. In early 1947 President Harry S. Truman issued the **Truman Doctrine,** which stated that the United States would give money to countries threatened by Communist expansion. As stated by **Dean Acheson,** the U.S. secretary of state, the United States was concerned that communism would spread throughout the free world if left unchecked.

D. In June 1947, the European Recovery Program, better known as the **Marshall Plan,** began. This program was set up to rebuild war-torn Europe.

E. The Soviet Union and its economically and politically dependent Eastern European **satellite states** refused to participate in the Marshall Plan.

F. In 1949, the Soviet Union set up the Council for Mutual Assistance (COMECON) as a response to the Marshall Plan. COMECON was established to help the economies of Eastern European states.

G. In 1947, the United States adopted the **policy of containment** to keep communism within its existing boundaries and prevent further Soviet aggressive moves.

H. By 1948, Great Britain, The United States, and France worked to unify the three western sections of Germany and **Berlin** and create a West German government. The Soviets opposed the creation of a West German state, so they tried to prevent it by setting up a blockade of West Berlin. The United States and Great Britain set up the Berlin Air Lift to fly in supplies to West Berlin. The Soviets ended the blockade of West Berlin in May 1949.

I. The **Federal Republic of Germany,** or West Germany, was formally created in September of 1949. A month later, the **German Democratic Republic** was set up by the Soviets. Berlin was divided into two parts.

288

Who? What? Where? When?

Truman Harry S Truman, a little-known senator from Missouri before he became Franklin Roosevelt's vice president, had relatively little experience in foreign affairs. When he succeeded to the presidency on Roosevelt's death, he had been vice president only 82 days and had met with the President just twice.

Critical Thinking

Assign students to review the text, and then to identify and compile a list of changes that resulted from the political revolutions of the eighteenth, nineteenth, and twentieth centuries. **L2**

Because of its need to feel secure on its western border, the Soviet government was not prepared to give up its control of Eastern Europe after Germany's defeat. American leaders were not willing to give up the power and prestige the United States had gained throughout the world. Suspicious of each other's motives, the United States and the Soviet Union soon became rivals. Between 1945 and 1949, a number of events led the two superpowers (a country whose military power is combined with political influence) to oppose each other.

Rivalry in Europe Eastern Europe was the first area of disagreement. The United States and Great Britain believed that the liberated nations of Eastern Europe should freely determine their own governments. Stalin, fearful that the Eastern European nations would be anti-Soviet if they were permitted free elections, opposed the West's plans. Having freed Eastern Europe from the Nazis, the Soviet army stayed in the conquered areas.

A civil war in Greece created another area of conflict between the superpowers. The Communist People's Liberation Army and anticommunist forces supported by Great Britain were fighting each other for control of Greece in 1946. However, Britain had its own economic problems, which caused it to withdraw its aid from Greece.

The Truman Doctrine President Harry S Truman of the United States, alarmed by the British withdrawal and the possibility of Soviet expansion into the eastern Mediterranean, responded in early 1947 with the **Truman Doctrine.** The Truman Doctrine stated that the United States would provide money to countries (in this case, Greece) threatened by Communist expansion. If the Soviets were not stopped in Greece, the Truman argument ran, then the United States would have to face the spread of communism throughout the free world.

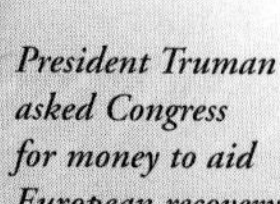

President Truman asked Congress for money to aid European recovery.

As **Dean Acheson,** the U.S. secretary of state, explained, "Like apples in a barrel infected by disease, the corruption of Greece would infect Iran and all the East . . . likewise Africa, Italy, France. . . . Not since Rome and Carthage had there been such a polarization of power on this earth."

The Marshall Plan The Truman Doctrine was followed in June 1947 by the European Recovery Program. Proposed by General George C. Marshall, U.S. secretary of state, it is better known as the **Marshall Plan.** Marshall, who had been the chief of staff for the U.S. Army during World War II, won the Nobel Peace Prize for his work on the European Recovery Program.

The Marshall Plan was designed to rebuild the prosperity and stability of war-torn Europe. It included $13 billion in aid for Europe's economic recovery. Underlying the Marshall Plan was the belief that Communist aggression was successful in countries where there were economic problems.

The Marshall Plan was not meant to shut out the Soviet Union or its economically and politically dependent Eastern European satellite states. They refused to participate, however. The Soviets saw the Marshall Plan as an attempt to buy the support of countries.

In 1949, the Soviet Union responded to the Marshall Plan by founding the Council for Mutual Assistance (COMECON) for the economic cooperation of the Eastern European states. COMECON largely failed, however, because of the inability of the Soviet Union to provide large amounts of financial aid.

By 1947, the split in Europe between the United States and the Soviet Union had become a fact of life. In July 1947, George Kennan, a well-known U.S. diplomat with much knowledge of Soviet affairs, argued for a policy of containment to keep communism within its existing boundaries and prevent further Soviet aggressive moves. Containment became U.S. policy.

The Division of Germany The fate of Germany also became a source of heated contention between the Soviets and the West. At the end of the war, the Allied Powers had divided Germany into four zones, each occupied by one of the Allies—the United States, the Soviet Union, Great Britain, and France. **Berlin,** located deep inside the Soviet zone, was also divided into four zones.

The foreign ministers of the four occupying powers met repeatedly in an attempt to arrive at a final peace treaty with Germany but had little success. By

632

EXTENDING THE CONTENT

Marshall Plan Explain to students that it was probably the Soviets themselves who were responsible for the Marshall Plan being approved by the United States Congress. Truman first asked Congress for the $13 billion (over a four-year period) for European recovery in September of 1947. Confident that they could defeat Truman in the upcoming election, the Republican-controlled Congress delayed action on the plan. The Soviets responded to news of the proposed Marshall Plan with their own military and financial aid package. Then, after the Soviet takeover of Czechoslovakia in February of 1948, Truman delivered a blistering speech to Congress demanding immediate passage of the Marshall Plan. Congress acted quickly to meet this request.

CHAPTER 20
Section 1, 631–636

February 1948, Great Britain, France, and the United States were making plans to unify the three Western sections of Germany (and Berlin) and create a West German government.

The Soviets opposed the creation of a separate West German state. They attempted to prevent it by mounting a blockade of West Berlin. Soviet forces allowed neither trucks, trains, nor barges to enter the city's three Western zones. Food and supplies could no longer get through to the 2.5 million people in these zones.

The Western powers faced a dilemma. No one wanted World War III, but how could the people in the Western zones of Berlin be kept alive, when the whole city was inside the Soviet zone? The solution was the Berlin Air Lift—supplies would be flown in by American and British airplanes. For more than 15 months, more than 200,000 flights carried 1.5 million tons (1.4 million t) of supplies. The Soviets, who wanted to avoid war as much as the Western powers, finally gave in and lifted the blockade in May 1949.

In September 1949, the **Federal Republic of Germany,** or West Germany, was formally created. Its capital was Bonn. A month later, a separate East German state, the **German Democratic Republic,** was set up by the Soviets. East Berlin became its capital. Berlin was now divided into two parts, a reminder of the division of West and East.

Reading Check **Describing** What was the intention of the Marshall Plan?

The Spread of the Cold War

TURNING POINT **As you will learn, the spread of the Cold War led to the creation of military alliances that influenced the development of the postwar world.**

In 1949, Chinese Communists took control of the government in China, strengthening U.S. fears about the spread of communism. The Soviet Union also exploded its first atomic bomb in 1949. All too soon, the United States and the Soviet Union were involved in a growing arms race, in which both countries built up their armies and weapons. Nuclear weapons became increasingly destructive.

Both sides came to believe that an arsenal of nuclear weapons would prevent war. They believed that if one nation attacked with nuclear weapons, the other nation would still be able to respond and devastate the attacker. According to this policy, neither side could risk using their massive supplies of weapons.

New Military Alliances The search for security during the Cold War led to the formation of new military alliances. The North Atlantic Treaty Organization **(NATO)** was formed in April 1949 when Belgium, Luxembourg, France, the Netherlands, Great Britain, Italy, Denmark, Norway, Portugal, and

Geography Skills

During the Berlin Air Lift, Western planes delivered food and supplies to the people of West Berlin.

1. **Interpreting Maps** Approximately how much German land was occupied by the Allies? How much was occupied by the Soviets?
2. **Applying Geography Skills** Why could the Allies not deliver food to West Berlin by land?

Reading Check

Answer: It provided financial aid to Europe to spur economic recovery and help strengthen countries so that they could resist Communist aggression.

TURNING POINT

How did the Cold War differ from past world conflicts? *(It was a long struggle between global superpowers that involved all means short of all-out war. The conditions of the Cold War were set by the superpowers' possession of nuclear weapons and their fear of mass destruction if these weapons were used.)* L1

Geography Skills

Answers:
1. approximately two-thirds, one-third
2. West Berlin was completely surrounded by Soviet-controlled East Germany, and the Soviet military prevented trucks, trains, and barges from entering West Berlin.

Connecting Across Time

Although the Warsaw Pact came to an end in 1991, NATO continues to flourish. In 1999, three Warsaw Pact countries — the Czech Republic, Hungary, and Poland — were admitted to NATO. Ask interested students to research the current membership and concerns of NATO, including its role in the war against terrorism. L2

COOPERATIVE LEARNING ACTIVITY

Organizing a Debate The Soviets, hardest hit by the war, took reparations from Germany in the form of industrial materials. By the summer of 1946, 200 chemical, paper, and textile factories in the Soviet East German zone had been taken apart and shipped to the Soviet Union. The United States, France, and Great Britain helped in the economic recovery of the three zones under their control. They sponsored free elections, agreed to combine their sectors of Berlin, and planned to form an independent West German state. Organize the class into groups for a debate, one side representing the Soviet Union and the other the Western powers. Each side should present its case for acting as it did. Encourage students to discuss why differing policies were adopted and what their long-term effects were. L3

CHAPTER 20
Section 1, 631–636

Geography *Skills*

Answers:

1. Warsaw Pact countries were closer to the Soviet Union, NATO countries were in Western Europe and North America.
2. Students will create a thematic chart. Spain, Yugoslavia, Ireland, Switzerland, Austria, Denmark

Guided Reading Activity 20–1

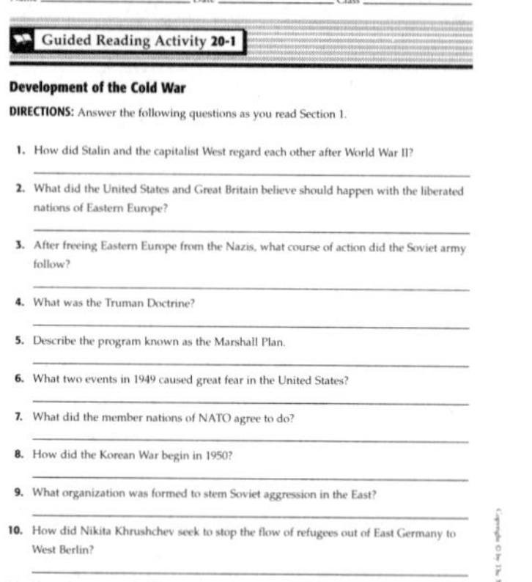

Name ________ Date ________ Class ________

Guided Reading Activity **20-1**

Development of the Cold War

DIRECTIONS: Answer the following questions as you read Section 1.

1. How did Stalin and the capitalist West regard each other after World War II?
2. What did the United States and Great Britain believe should happen with the liberated nations of Eastern Europe?
3. After freeing Eastern Europe from the Nazis, what course of action did the Soviet army follow?
4. What was the Truman Doctrine?
5. Describe the program known as the Marshall Plan.
6. What two events in 1949 caused great fear in the United States?
7. What did the member nations of NATO agree to do?
8. How did the Korean War begin in 1950?
9. What organization was formed to stem Soviet aggression in the East?
10. How did Nikita Khrushchev seek to stop the flow of refugees out of East Germany to West Berlin?
11. Name the event in 19[illegible] brought the world clo[illegible] nuclear war.

Enrich

After they have read this chapter, ask students to list the current members of NATO. **L1**

Connecting Across Time

Ask students to identify and discuss reasons why opposing alliances of Communist and non-Communist nations were successful in preventing another world war after 1945, while alliances formed in Europe at the beginning of the twentieth century were unsuccessful at preventing World War I. **L2**

Geography *Skills*

After World War II, the spread of the Cold War created new military alliances.

1. **Interpreting Maps** Are there any geographic factors that could have determined whether a country became a member of NATO or of the Warsaw Pact?
2. **Applying Geography Skills** Use the map to create a chart listing all of the countries in NATO and all the members of the Warsaw Pact. Which European countries did not join either alliance?

Iceland signed a treaty with the United States and Canada. All the powers agreed to provide mutual help if any one of them was attacked. A few years later, West Germany and Turkey joined NATO.

In 1955, the Soviet Union joined with Albania, Bulgaria, Czechoslovakia, East Germany, Hungary, Poland, and Romania in a formal military alliance known as the **Warsaw Pact.** Now, Europe was once again divided into hostile alliance systems, just as it had been before World War I.

New military alliances spread to the rest of the world after the United States became involved in the Korean War (discussed in Chapter 24). The war began in 1950 as an attempt by the Communist government of North Korea, which was allied with the Soviet Union, to take over South Korea. The Korean War confirmed American fears of Communist expansion. More determined than ever to contain Soviet power, the United States extended its military alliances around the world.

To stem Soviet aggression in the East, the United States, Great Britain, France, Pakistan, Thailand, the Philippines, Australia, and New Zealand formed the Southeast Asia Treaty Organization **(SEATO)**. The Central Treaty Organization **(CENTO),** which included Turkey, Iraq, Iran, Pakistan, Great Britain, and the United States, was meant to prevent the Soviet Union from expanding to the south. By the mid-1950s, the United States found itself allied militarily with 42 states around the world.

MEETING INDIVIDUAL NEEDS

Sequencing Events Events unfolded rapidly in the early years of the Cold War. To understand these events, their time frames, and the regions involved, students can construct a chart. Along the side, have them list the years 1945 to 1947, divided into three-month intervals. Along the top, students should enter the names of the countries most involved in the Cold War by region. At the appropriate places on the chart, students can indicate important events in the Cold War. Encourage them to add descriptions that explain the significance of each event. **L1** ELL

Refer to ***Inclusion for the High School Social Studies Classroom Strategies and Activities*** in the TCR.

The Arms Race The Soviet Union had set off its first atomic bomb in 1949. In 1952, both the Soviet Union and the United States developed hydrogen bombs, which were even more deadly. By the mid-1950s, both nations had intercontinental ballistic missiles (ICBMs) capable of sending bombs anywhere in the world.

The search for security soon took the form of deterrence. This policy held that huge arsenals of nuclear weapons on both sides prevented war. The belief was that neither side would launch a nuclear attack because the other side would be able to strike back with devastating power.

In 1957, the Soviets sent *Sputnik I*, the first manufactured space satellite, to orbit the earth. New fears seized the American public. Did the Soviet Union have a massive lead in building missiles? Was there a "missile gap" between the United States and the Soviet Union?

A Wall in Berlin **Nikita Khrushchev** (kroosh•CHAWF), who emerged as the new leader of the Soviet Union in 1955, tried to take advantage of the American concern over missiles to solve the problem of West Berlin. West Berlin remained a "Western island" of prosperity in the midst of the relatively poverty-stricken East Germany. Many East Germans, tired of Communist repression, managed to escape East Germany by fleeing through West Berlin.

Khrushchev realized the need to stop the flow of refugees from East Germany through West Berlin. In August 1961, the East German government began to build a wall separating West Berlin from East Berlin. Eventually it became a massive barrier guarded by barbed wire, floodlights, machine-gun towers, minefields, and vicious dog patrols. The Berlin Wall became a striking symbol of the division between the two superpowers.

Reading Check **Identifying** Name the military alliances formed during the Cold War.

The Cuban Missile Crisis

During the administration of John F. Kennedy, the Cold War confrontation between the United States and the Soviet Union reached frightening levels. In 1959, a left-wing revolutionary named Fidel Castro overthrew the Cuban dictator Fulgencio Batista and set up a Soviet-supported totalitarian regime in Cuba (see Chapter 22). President Kennedy approved a secret plan for Cuban exiles to invade Cuba in the hope of causing a revolt against Castro. The invasion was a disaster. Many of the exiles were killed or captured when they attempted a landing at the Bay of Pigs.

After the Bay of Pigs, the Soviet Union sent arms and military advisers to Cuba. Then, in 1962, Khrushchev began to place nuclear missiles in Cuba. The missiles were meant to counteract U.S. nuclear weapons placed in Turkey within easy range of the Soviet Union. Khrushchev was quick to point out, "Your rockets are in Turkey. You are worried by Cuba . . . because it is 90 miles from the American coast. But Turkey is next to us."

The United States was not willing to allow nuclear weapons within such close striking distance of its mainland. In October 1962, Kennedy found out that Soviet ships carrying missiles were heading to Cuba. He decided to blockade Cuba and prevent the fleet from reaching its destination. This approach gave each side time to find a peaceful solution. Khrushchev agreed to turn back the fleet and remove Soviet missiles from Cuba if Kennedy pledged not to invade Cuba. Kennedy quickly agreed.

The Cuban missile crisis seemed to bring the world frighteningly close to nuclear war. Indeed, in 1992 a high-ranking Soviet officer revealed that short-range rockets armed with nuclear devices would have been used against U.S. troops if the United States had invaded Cuba, an option that Kennedy fortunately had rejected. The realization that the world might have been destroyed in a few days had a profound influence on both sides. A hotline communications system between Moscow and Washington, D.C., was installed in 1963. The two superpowers could now communicate quickly in times of crisis.

Reading Check **Explaining** How was the Cuban missile crisis resolved?

Vietnam and the Domino Theory

By that time, the United States had been drawn into a new struggle that had an important impact on the Cold War—the Vietnam War (see Chapter 24). In 1964, under President Lyndon B. Johnson, increasing numbers of U.S. troops were sent to Vietnam. Their purpose was to keep the Communist regime of North Vietnam from gaining control of South Vietnam.

U.S. policy makers saw the conflict in terms of a domino theory. If the Communists succeeded

CHAPTER 20
Section 1, 631–636

Reading Check

Answer: North Atlantic Treaty Organization (NATO), Warsaw Pact, Southeast Asia Treaty Organization (SEATO), Central Treaty Organization (CENTO)

Reading Check

Answer: The Soviet Union agreed to turn back its fleet and remove its missiles from Cuba in exchange for a promise from the United States not to invade that country.

3 ASSESS

Assign Section 1 Assessment as homework or as an in-class activity.

Have students use **Interactive Tutor Self-Assessment CD-ROM.**

Section Quiz 20–1

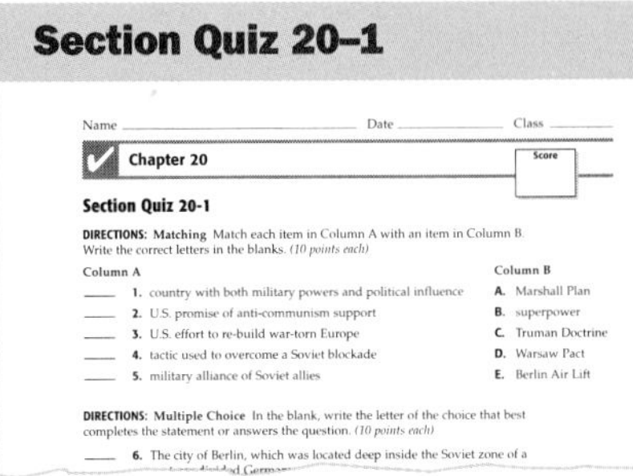
Name ______ Date ______ Class ______

Chapter 20 Score

Section Quiz 20-1

DIRECTIONS: Matching Match each item in Column A with an item in Column B. Write the correct letters in the blanks. *(10 points each)*

Column A	Column B
____ 1. country with both military powers and political influence	A. Marshall Plan
____ 2. U.S. promise of anti-communism support	B. superpower
____ 3. U.S. effort to re-build war-torn Europe	C. Truman Doctrine
____ 4. tactic used to overcome a Soviet blockade	D. Warsaw Pact
____ 5. military alliance of Soviet allies	E. Berlin Air Lift

DIRECTIONS: Multiple Choice In the blank, write the letter of the choice that best completes the statement or answers the question. *(10 points each)*

____ 6. The city of Berlin, which was located deep inside the Soviet zone of a

Reteaching Activity

Have students brainstorm a list of events that precipitated the Cold War on the board. Then arrange the events in chronological order. L1 ELL

CRITICAL THINKING ACTIVITY

Making Generalizations The members of NATO agreed to provide mutual help if any one of them were attacked. The Warsaw Pact was intended as much to strengthen the Soviet hold on Eastern Europe as to defend it. Ask students to discuss why it is reasonable to believe that European members of NATO would have worked harder to defend their governments than the Eastern European members of the Warsaw Pact. *(Answers will vary but should include that nations chose to join NATO while the nations of Eastern Europe were not given a choice about joining the Warsaw Pact.)* Ask students what significance this difference might have had to the eventual fall of the Soviet Union. L2

CHAPTER 20
Section 1, 631–636

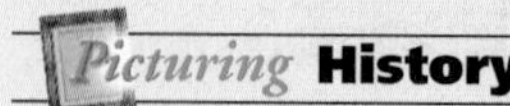

Answer: because of the growing number of American troops sent to Vietnam

Reading Check

Answer: It proved that the domino theory was unfounded.

Reading Essentials and Study Guide 20–1

Name ____________ Date ____________ Class ____________

Reading Essentials and Study Guide

Chapter 20, Section 1

For use with textbook pages 631–636

DEVELOPMENT OF THE COLD WAR

KEY TERMS

satellite state a state that is economically and politically dependent on a larger, more powerful state *(page 632)*

policy of containment the policy of the United States regarding the Soviet Union, with the goal of keeping communism within its existing boundaries and preventing further Soviet aggression *(page 632)*

arms race the build-up of huge arsenals of nuclear weapons and missiles by the United States and the Soviet Union *(page 635)*

domino theory the belief held by U.S. policymakers that if the Communists succeeded in South Vietnam, other countries in Asia would fall (like dominoes) to communism *(page 635)*

DRAWING FROM EXPERIENCE

Which countries of the world would you consider to be superpowers today? Why do you think so?

In this section, you will learn about the period of conflict called the Cold War that developed between the United States and the Soviet Union after the end of World War II.

ORGANIZING YOUR THOUGHTS

Use the chart below to help you take notes. During the Cold War period, new military alliances were created. Identify the members of the alliances in the chart below.

Alliance	Members
NATO	1.
Warsaw Pact	2.
SEATO	3.
CENTO	4.

4 CLOSE

Have students list the American presidents who held office during the Cold War. What major Cold War events took place during each administration? **L1**

Picturing History

Many young Americans were proud to serve their country in Vietnam, but increasingly the mood on college campuses was anti-war. Why?

in South Vietnam, the argument went, other countries in Asia would also fall (like dominoes) to communism.

Despite the massive superiority in equipment and firepower of the American forces, the United States failed to defeat the determined North Vietnamese. The growing number of American troops sent to Vietnam soon produced an antiwar movement in the United States, especially among college students of draft age. The mounting destruction of the conflict, brought into American homes every evening on television, also turned American public opinion against the war.

President Johnson, condemned for his handling of the costly and indecisive war, decided not to run for reelection. Former Vice President Richard M. Nixon won the election with his pledge to stop the war and bring the American people together. Ending the war was difficult, and Nixon's administration was besieged by anti-war forces.

Finally, in 1973, President Nixon reached an agreement with North Vietnam that allowed the United States to withdraw its forces. Within two years after the American withdrawal, Vietnam had been forcibly reunited by Communist armies from the North.

Despite the success of the North Vietnamese Communists, the domino theory proved unfounded. A split between Communist China and the Soviet Union, including border clashes and different implementations of communism, put an end to the Western idea that there was a single form of communism directed by Moscow. Under President Nixon, American relations with China were resumed. New nations in Southeast Asia managed to avoid Communist governments.

Above all, Vietnam helped show the limitations of American power. By the end of the Vietnam War, a new era in American-Soviet relations had begun to emerge.

Reading Check **Examining** What did the Vietnam War prove about the state of global communism?

SECTION 1 ASSESSMENT

Checking for Understanding

1. **Define** satellite state, policy of containment, arms race, deterrence, domino theory.
2. **Identify** Truman Doctrine, Dean Acheson, Marshall Plan, NATO, Warsaw Pact, SEATO, CENTO, Nikita Khrushchev.
3. **Locate** Berlin, Federal Republic of Germany, German Democratic Republic.
4. **Explain** why the Berlin Wall was built.
5. **List** the four powers that divided and occupied Germany.

Critical Thinking

6. **Evaluate** In your opinion, why did the United States assume global responsibility for containing communism?
7. **Organizing Information** Use a table like the one below to list the military alliances formed during the Cold War. In the next column list the countries belonging to the alliance.

Alliance	Countries

Analyzing Visuals

8. **Examine** the photo of a campus sit-in shown on this page. Students often used sit-ins to protest government policy in the 1960s and 1970s. What methods of protest do people use today?

Writing About History

9. **Informative Writing** Imagine that you are a resident of Berlin in 1948. Write a letter to a friend living in another part of Germany explaining what is happening in Berlin and your reaction to the actions of the foreign governments involved.

SECTION 1 ASSESSMENT

1. Key terms are in blue.
2. Truman Doctrine *(p. 632)*; Dean Acheson *(p. 632)*; Marshall Plan *(p. 632)*; NATO *(p. 633)*; Warsaw Pact *(p. 634)*; SEATO *(p. 634)*; CENTO *(p. 634)*; Nikita Khrushchev *(p. 635)*
3. See chapter maps.
4. to stop flow of refugees; a division between superpowers
5. U.S., Britain, France, USSR
6. Answers will vary.
7. NATO: Belgium, Luxembourg, France, Netherlands, Britain, Italy, Denmark, Norway, Portugal, Iceland, U.S., Canada, West Germany, Turkey; Warsaw Pact: USSR, Albania, Bulgaria, Czechoslovakia, East Germany, Hungary, Poland, Romania; SEATO: U.S., Britain, France, Pakistan, Thailand, Philippines, Australia, New Zealand; CENTO: Turkey, Iraq, Iran, Pakistan, Britain, U.S.
8. marches, advertising, coming before political bodies
9. Answers will vary.

SECTION 2 The Soviet Union and Eastern Europe

Guide to Reading

Main Ideas
- As Soviet leader, Khrushchev initiated policies of de-Stalinization.
- The Soviet Union faced revolts and protests in its attempt to gain and maintain control over Eastern Europe.

Key Terms
heavy industry, de-Stalinization

People to Identify
Alexander Solzhenitsyn, Tito, Imre Nagy, Alexander Dubček

Places to Locate
Soviet Union, Albania, Yugoslavia, Poland, Hungary, Czechoslovakia

Preview Questions
1. What were Khrushchev's policies of de-Stalinization?
2. How did the Soviet Union exert its power over Eastern Europe?

Reading Strategy
Categorizing Information Use a diagram like the one below to identify how the Soviet Union carried out Communist policies.

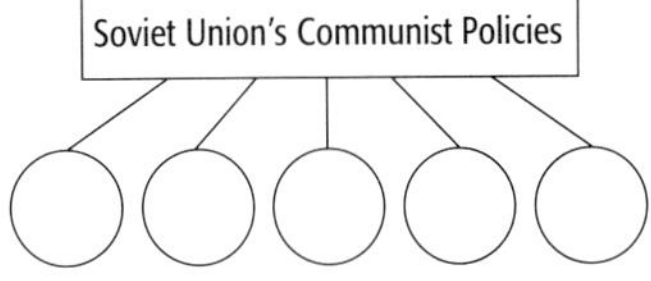

Preview of Events

1950 · 1955 · 1960 · 1965 · 1970

- **1953** Khrushchev named general secretary
- **1962** Solzhenitsyn's *One Day in the Life of Ivan Denisovich* is published
- **1964** Khrushchev is voted out of office
- **1968** The Soviet Army invades Czechoslovakia

Voices from the Past

Soviet tanks in Hungary

In 1956, Hungary revolted against Soviet control. The Soviet Union sent in troops and announced:

> "Forces of reaction and counterrevolution . . . are trying to take advantage of the discontent of part of the working people to undermine the foundations of the people's democratic order in Hungary and to restore the old landlord and capitalist order. The Soviet government and all the people deeply regret that the development of events in Hungary has led to bloodshed. On the request of the Hungarian People's Government the Soviet government consented to the entry into Budapest of the Soviet Army units to assist the Hungarian authorities to establish order in the town."
>
> —***Department of State Bulletin,*** **November 12, 1956**

After World War II, Stalin and the Soviet forces kept a tight hold on Eastern Europe—a hold that many countries struggled against.

The Reign of Stalin

World War II devastated the **Soviet Union.** To create a new industrial base, Stalin returned to the method that he had used in the 1930s. Soviet workers were expected to produce goods for export with little in return for themselves. The incoming capital from abroad could then be used to buy machinery and Western technology.

1 FOCUS

Section Overview

This section describes the spread of Soviet power in Eastern Europe.

BELLRINGER
Skillbuilder Activity

 Project transparency and have students answer questions.

 Available as a blackline master.

Daily Focus Skills Transparency 20–2

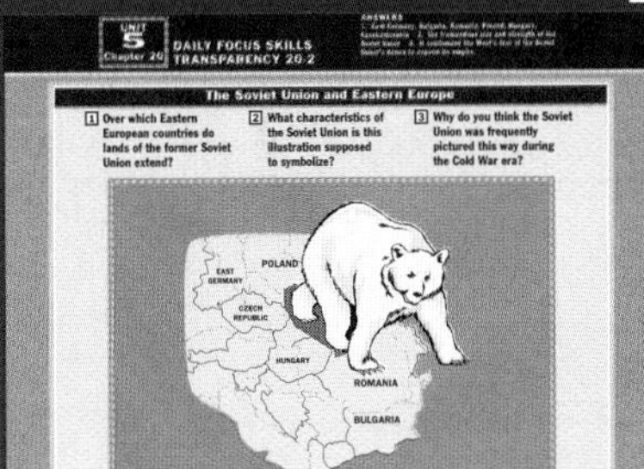

Guide to Reading

Answers to Graphic: Soviet Union's Communist Policies: emphasis on heavy industry rather than consumer goods, leaders exercised sole power, repression, stifled free expression, used political terror, military intervention

Preteaching Vocabulary: Be sure students understand the meaning and purpose of *de-Stalinization.* L1

SECTION RESOURCES

Reproducible Masters
- Reproducible Lesson Plan 20–2
- Daily Lecture and Discussion Notes 20–2
- Guided Reading Activity 20–2
- Section Quiz 20–2
- Reading Essentials and Study Guide 20–2

Transparencies
- Daily Focus Skills Transparency 20–2

Multimedia
- Interactive Tutor Self-Assessment CD-ROM
- ExamView® Pro Testmaker CD-ROM
- Presentation Plus! CD-ROM

2 TEACH

Reading Check

Answer: extreme hardship: shortage of consumer goods; average Russian family lived in a one-room apartment

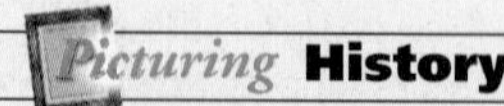

Picturing History

Answer: new spirit of cooperation now that the Cold War is over; enables nations to share the high costs as well as the research results

Daily Lecture and Discussion Notes 20–2

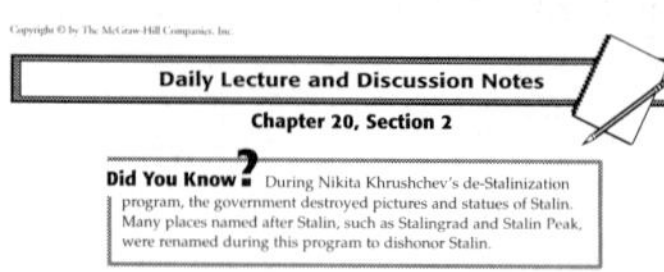

Daily Lecture and Discussion Notes

Chapter 20, Section 2

Did You Know? During Nikita Khrushchev's de-Stalinization program, the government destroyed pictures and statues of Stalin. Many places named after Stalin, such as Stalingrad and Stalin Peak, were renamed during this program to dishonor Stalin.

I. The Reign of Stalin *(pages 637–638)*

A. The economy of the **Soviet Union** was devastated by World War II. To create a new industrial base, goods were produced almost exclusively for export. The money from export goods was used to buy machinery and Western technology.

B. By 1950, the Soviet Union had built new power plants, canals, and giant factories. **Heavy industry**, the manufacture of machines and equipment for factories and mines, increased. The development of the hydrogen bomb in 1952 and the launch of the first space satellite, *Sputnik I*, in 1957 made the Soviet Union a world power.

C. In 1946, the Soviet government said that all literary and scientific work must conform to the political needs of the state.

D. Stalin died in 1953.

Discussion Question

What were the effects of the Soviet government's economic methods enacted after World War II? *(By 1950, Russian industrial production surpassed prewar levels by 40 percent. The Soviet people, however, had a shortage of consumer goods and a severe shortage of housing.)*

II. The Khrushchev Era *(pages 638–639)*

A. After Stalin's death, Nikita Khrushchev became the chief policy maker in the Soviet Union. Under his leadership, **de-Stalinization,** or the process of eliminating some of Stalin's ruthless policies, was put in place.

B. Khrushchev loosened government controls on literature. For example, he allowed the publication of a work by **Alexander Solzhenitsyn** that depicted life in a Siberian forced-labor camp. He tried to increase the production of consumer goods and agricultural output.

C. Khrushchev's attempts to increase agricultural output failed and the industrial growth rate also declined. In 1964, he was forced into retirement.

turn

Economic recovery in the Soviet Union was spectacular in some respects. By 1950, Russian industrial production had surpassed prewar levels by 40 percent. New power plants, canals, and giant factories were built. **Heavy industry** (the manufacture of machines and equipment for factories and mines) increased, chiefly for the benefit of the military. The development of hydrogen bombs in 1952 and the first space satellite, *Sputnik I,* in 1957 enhanced the Soviet state's reputation as a world power abroad.

The Soviet people, however, were shortchanged. The growth rate for heavy industry was three times that for consumer goods. Moreover, the housing shortage was severe. An average Russian family lived in a one-room apartment. A British official in Moscow reported that "every room is both a living room by day and a bedroom by night."

Stalin remained the undisputed master of the Soviet Union. He distrusted competitors, exercised sole power, and had little respect for other Communist Party leaders. He is reported to have said to members of his inner circle in 1952, "You are as blind as kittens. What would you do without me?"

Stalin's suspicions added to the increasing repression of the regime. In 1946, the government decreed that all literary and scientific work must conform to the political needs of the state. Along with this anti-intellectual campaign came political terror. A new series of purges seemed likely in 1953, but Stalin's death on March 5 prevented more blood-letting.

Reading Check **Summarizing** What costs did Stalin's economic policy impose on the Russian people?

The Khrushchev Era

A group of leaders succeeded Stalin, but the new general secretary of the Communist Party, Nikita Khrushchev, soon emerged as the chief Soviet policy maker. Once in power, Khrushchev took steps to undo some of the worst features of Stalin's regime.

At the Twentieth Congress of the Communist Party in 1956, Khrushchev condemned Stalin for his "administrative violence, mass repression, and terror." The process of eliminating the more ruthless policies of Stalin became known as **de-Stalinization.**

Khrushchev loosened government controls on literary works. In 1962, for example, he allowed the publication of *One Day in the Life of Ivan Denisovich,* a grim portrayal of life in a Siberian forced-labor camp written by **Alexander Solzhenitsyn** (SOHL•zhuh•NEET•suhn). Each day, as Solzhenitsyn related, prisoners were marched from the prison camp to a work project through subzero temperatures: "There were escort guards all over the place, . . . their machine guns sticking out and pointed right at your face. And there were guards with gray dogs." Many Soviets identified with Ivan as a symbol of the suffering they had endured under Stalin.

Khrushchev tried to place more emphasis on producing consumer goods. He also attempted to increase agricultural output by growing corn and cultivating vast lands east of the Ural Mountains. The attempt to increase agricultural output was not successful and damaged his reputation within the party. This failure, combined with increased military spending, hurt the Soviet economy. The industrial

Picturing History

A Soviet scientist is shown working on *Sputnik I.* The launch of *Sputnik I,* which orbited the earth for 57 days, stunned the United States and enhanced the prestige of the Soviet Union. Today, many space endeavors are international efforts. Why?

EXTENDING THE CONTENT

After World War II In 1992, a British expert on the Soviet military released a report indicating that the Soviet Union's losses during World War II were even more staggering than previously believed. With the declassification of many Soviet records after the fall of communism, John Erickson of Edinburgh University has estimated that Soviet deaths might have been as high as 49 million, or nearly 30 percent of its people. If this information proves to be accurate, it may hold a key to the beginning of the Cold War. Some historians speculate that Stalin, in an attempt to cover up the Soviet Union's post-war weakness, was deliberately hostile to the West, thereby contributing to worsening relations with the United States.

People In History

Nikita Khrushchev
1894–1971—Soviet leader

First secretary of the Communist Party after Stalin's death, Khrushchev eventually came to be the sole Soviet ruler. In 1956, he denounced the rule of Stalin, arguing that "Stalin showed in a whole series of cases his intolerance, his brutality and his abuse of power. . . . He was a very distrustful man, sickly suspicious. Everywhere and in everything he saw enemies, two-facers, and spies."

Khrushchev alienated other Soviet leaders by his policy in Cuba. He had other problems with the higher Soviet officials as well. They frowned on his tendency to crack jokes and play the clown. They also were displeased when he tried to curb their privileges.

growth rate, which had soared in the early 1950s, now declined dramatically from 13 percent in 1953 to 7.5 percent in 1964.

Foreign policy failures also damaged Khrushchev's reputation among his colleagues. His rash plan to place missiles in Cuba was the final straw. While he was away on vacation in 1964, a special meeting of the Soviet leaders voted him out of office (because of "deteriorating health") and forced him into retirement.

Reading Check **Explaining** Why did the Soviet leaders vote Khrushchev out of power?

Eastern Europe: Behind the Iron Curtain

At the end of World War II, Soviet military forces occupied all of Eastern Europe and the Balkans (except for Greece, Albania, and Yugoslavia). All of the occupied states came under Soviet control.

Communist Patterns of Control The timetable of the Soviet takeover varied from country to country. Between 1945 and 1947, Soviet-controlled Communist governments became firmly entrenched in East Germany, Bulgaria, Romania, Poland, and Hungary. In Czechoslovakia, where there was a strong tradition of democracy and a multi-party system, the Soviets did not seize control of the government until 1948. At that time they dissolved all but the Communist Party.

Albania and Yugoslavia were exceptions to this pattern of Soviet dominance. During the war, both countries had had strong Communist movements that resisted the Nazis. After the war, local Communist parties took control. Communists in **Albania** set up a Stalinist-type regime that grew more and more independent of the Soviet Union.

In **Yugoslavia,** Josip Broz, known as **Tito,** had been the leader of the Communist resistance movement. After the war, he moved toward the creation of an independent Communist state in Yugoslavia. Stalin hoped to take control of Yugoslavia, just as he had done in other Eastern European countries. Tito, however, refused to give in to Stalin's demands. He gained the support of the people by portraying the struggle as one of Yugoslav national freedom. Tito ruled Yugoslavia until his death in 1980. Although Yugoslavia had a Communist government, it was not a Soviet satellite state.

Between 1948 and Stalin's death in 1953, the Eastern European satellite states, directed by the Soviet Union, followed Stalin's example. They instituted Soviet-type five-year plans with emphasis on heavy industry rather than consumer goods. They began to collectivize agriculture. They eliminated all noncommunist parties and set up the institutions of repression—secret police and military forces.

Revolts Against Communism Communism did not develop deep roots among the peoples of Eastern Europe. Moreover, the Soviets exploited Eastern Europe economically for their own benefit and made living conditions harsh for most people.

After Stalin's death, many Eastern European states began to pursue a new course. In the late 1950s and 1960s, however, the Soviet Union made it clear—especially in **Poland, Hungary,** and **Czechoslovakia**—that it would not allow its Eastern European satellites to become independent of Soviet control.

In 1956, protests erupted in Poland. In response, the Polish Communist Party adopted a series of reforms in October 1956 and elected Wladyslaw Gomulka as first secretary. Gomulka declared that Poland had the right to follow its own socialist path. Fearful of Soviet armed response, however, the Poles compromised. Poland pledged to remain loyal to the Warsaw Pact.

CHAPTER 20
Section 2, 637–640

Reading Check

Answer: His failure to increase agricultural output, low production of consumer goods, and his plan to place missiles in Cuba weakened his political power.

Enrich

Ask students to write a short essay on the changes that took place in the Soviet Union under Khrushchev's leadership. Do students believe that Stalin would have been able to maintain his power had he lived longer? Was a period of de-Stalinization inevitable? **L2**

Guided Reading Activity 20–2

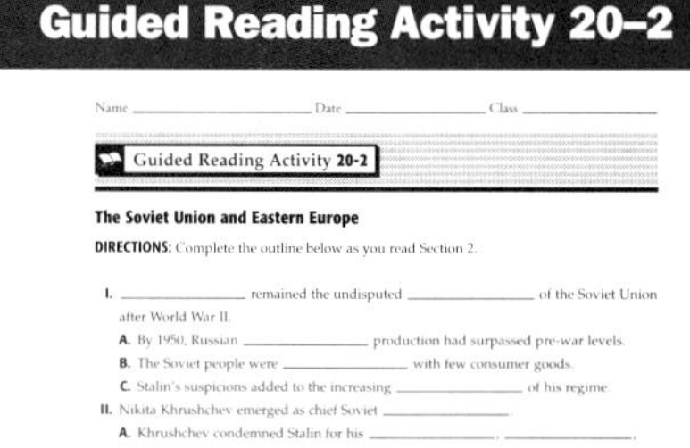

Name ________ Date ________ Class ________

Guided Reading Activity 20-2

The Soviet Union and Eastern Europe

DIRECTIONS: Complete the outline below as you read Section 2.

I. ________ remained the undisputed ________ of the Soviet Union after World War II.
- **A.** By 1950, Russian ________ production had surpassed pre-war levels.
- **B.** The Soviet people were ________ with few consumer goods.
- **C.** Stalin's suspicions added to the increasing ________ of his regime.

II. Nikita Khrushchev emerged as chief Soviet ________.
- **A.** Khrushchev condemned Stalin for his ________, ________, and ________.
- **B.** Government controls on ________ works were loosened.

3 ASSESS

Assign Section 2 Assessment as homework or as an in-class activity.

Have students use **Interactive Tutor Self-Assessment CD-ROM.**

Section Quiz 20–2

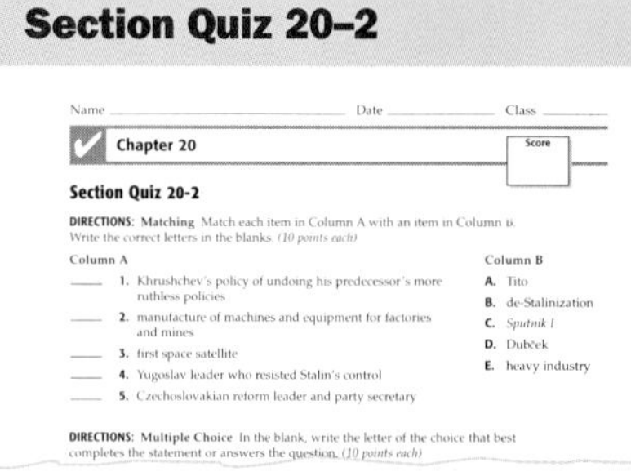

Name ________ Date ________ Class ________

Chapter 20 — Score

Section Quiz 20-2

DIRECTIONS: Matching Match each item in Column A with an item in Column B. Write the correct letters in the blanks. *(10 points each)*

Column A	Column B
____ **1.** Khrushchev's policy of undoing his predecessor's more ruthless policies	**A.** Tito
____ **2.** manufacture of machines and equipment for factories and mines	**B.** de-Stalinization
____ **3.** first space satellite	**C.** *Sputnik I*
____ **4.** Yugoslav leader who resisted Stalin's control	**D.** Dubček
____ **5.** Czechoslovakian reform leader and party secretary	**E.** heavy industry

DIRECTIONS: Multiple Choice In the blank, write the letter of the choice that best completes the statement or answers the question. *(10 points each)*

INTERDISCIPLINARY CONNECTIONS ACTIVITY

Music and Dance Artistic activity was closely regulated in the Soviet Union. For example, Russian ballet companies continued to tour the world during the Cold War, but dancers were closely supervised to prevent them from defecting. Several did manage to escape, including two of the greatest male dancers of modern times, Rudolf Nureyev and Mikhail Baryshnikov. Even composers were expected to glorify the Communist state. Have students research either the state of Russian dance during the Cold War and the defections of prominent dancers, or the effects of Communist repression on such composers as Sergey Prokofiev, Dmitry Shostakovich, or Aram Khachaturian. **L3**

CHAPTER 20
Section 2, 637–640

Reading Check

Answer: Communism's roots were not deep because it was imposed on Eastern Europe by a foreign power and went against national interests. Also, the Soviets exploited Eastern Europe economically for their own benefit and made living conditions harsh for most people.

Reteaching Activity

Ask students to outline the section, focusing on the key figures and events discussed. **L1** ELL

Reading Essentials and Study Guide 20–2

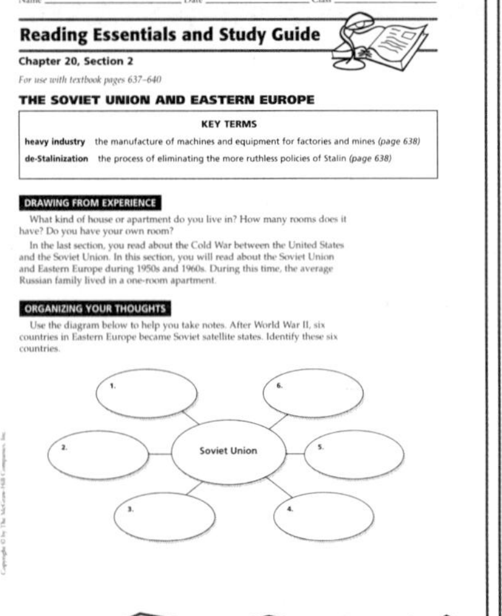
Name ______ Date ______ Class ______

Reading Essentials and Study Guide

Chapter 20, Section 2

For use with textbook pages 637–640

THE SOVIET UNION AND EASTERN EUROPE

KEY TERMS

heavy industry the manufacture of machines and equipment for factories and mines *(page 638)*

de-Stalinization the process of eliminating the more ruthless policies of Stalin *(page 638)*

DRAWING FROM EXPERIENCE

What kind of house or apartment do you live in? How many rooms does it have? Do you have your own room?

In the last section, you read about the Cold War between the United States and the Soviet Union. In this section, you will read about the Soviet Union and Eastern Europe during 1950s and 1960s. During this time, the average Russian family lived in a one-room apartment.

ORGANIZING YOUR THOUGHTS

Use the diagram below to help you take notes. After World War II, six countries in Eastern Europe became Soviet satellite states. Identify these six countries.

4 CLOSE

Guide students in a discussion of the doubtful nature of unity within the Soviet block. **L1**

The Soviet army invaded Czechoslovakia in 1968.

Developments in Poland in 1956 led Hungarian Communists to seek the same kinds of reforms. Unrest in Hungary, combined with economic difficulties, led to calls for revolt. To quell the rising rebellion, **Imre Nagy,** the Hungarian leader, declared Hungary a free nation on November 1, 1956, and promised free elections. It soon became clear that this could mean the end of Communist rule in Hungary.

Khrushchev was in no position at home to allow a member of the Communist group of nations to leave, however. Three days after Nagy's declaration, the Soviet Army attacked Budapest. The Soviets reestablished control over the country. Nagy was seized by the Soviet military and executed two years later.

The situation in Czechoslovakia in the 1950s was different. There, the "Little Stalin," Antonin Novotny, had been placed in power in 1952 by Stalin himself and remained firmly in control. By the late 1960s, however, Novotny had alienated many members of his own party. He was especially disliked by Czechoslovakia's writers. A writers' rebellion, which encouraged the people to take control of their own lives, led to Novotny's resignation, late in 1967.

Web Activity Visit the *Glencoe World History—Modern Times* Web site at wh.mt.glencoe.com and click on **Chapter 20–Student Web Activity** to learn more about the Cold War.

In January 1968, **Alexander Dubček** (DOOB•chehk) was elected first secretary of the Communist Party. He introduced a number of reforms, including freedom of speech and press and freedom to travel abroad. He relaxed censorship, began to pursue an independent foreign policy, and promised a gradual democratization of the Czechoslovakian political system. Dubček hoped to create "socialism with a human face." A period of euphoria broke out that came to be known as the "Prague Spring."

The euphoria proved to be short-lived, however. To forestall the spreading of this "spring fever," the Soviet Army invaded Czechoslovakia in August 1968 and crushed the reform movement. Gustav Husák replaced Dubček, did away with his reforms, and reestablished the old order.

Reading Check **Evaluating** What caused the battles between the Eastern European states and the Soviet Union?

SECTION 2 ASSESSMENT

Checking for Understanding

1. **Define** heavy industry, de-Stalinization.
2. **Identify** Alexander Solzhenitsyn, Tito, Imre Nagy, Alexander Dubček.
3. **Locate** Soviet Union, Albania, Yugoslavia, Poland, Hungary, Czechoslovakia.
4. **Explain** Khrushchev's relationship to Stalinism.
5. **List** two countries in Eastern Europe that resisted Soviet dominance.

Critical Thinking

6. **Explain** Why did Yugoslavia and Albania not come under the direct control of the Soviet Union?
7. **Organizing Information** Use a table like the one below to identify the policies of Stalin and the policies of Khrushchev.

Stalin	Khrushchev

Analyzing Visuals

8. **Compare** the photograph on page 638 with the one shown above. How does each photograph symbolize a different aspect of the Cold War?

Writing About History

9. **Informative Writing** You are a Western journalist in Hungary in 1956. Write an article for an American newspaper that describes the events leading to the Soviet attack on Budapest and what effect the attack will have on the Cold War.

SECTION 2 ASSESSMENT

1. Key terms are in blue.
2. Alexander Solzhenitsyn *(p. 638);* Tito *(p. 639);* Imre Nagy *(p. 640);* Alexander Dubček *(p. 640)*
3. See chapter maps.
4. set about eliminating Stalin's more ruthless policies
5. Albania, Yugoslavia
6. Because they had strong Communist governments already, they were able to resist Stalin's demands.
7. Stalin: economic recovery plan with emphasis on heavy industry, repression, political terror; Khrushchev: emphasis on producing consumer goods, attempted to increase agricultural output, eliminated most ruthless policies of Stalin, increased military spending
8. The photo on page 638 symbolizes the space race between the U.S. and U.S.S.R. The photo on page 640 symbolizes the repressive use of the military by the Soviet Union to keep the nations of Eastern Europe under its control.
9. Answers will vary.

SOCIAL STUDIES
SKILLBUILDER

Understanding World Time Zones

Why Learn This Skill?

Imagine that you work in Boston and call a client in London at 2:00 P.M. No one answers because, when it is 2:00 P.M. in Boston, it is already 7:00 P.M. in London.

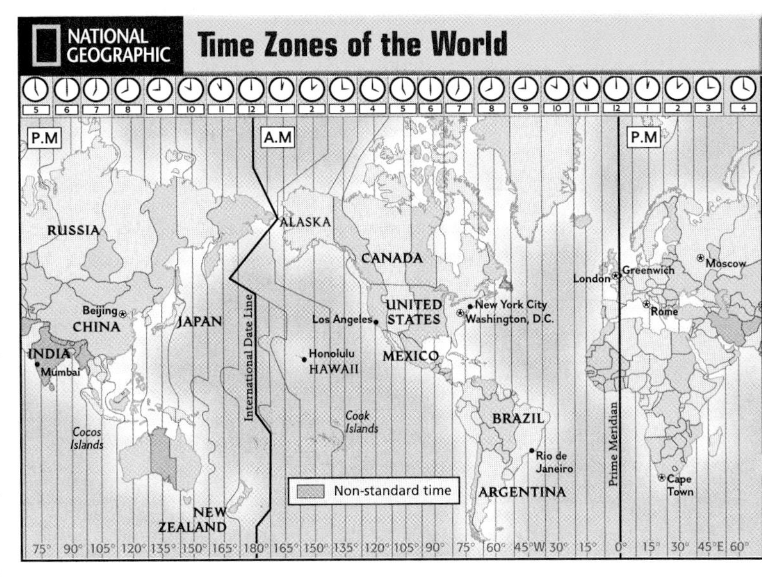

Learning the Skill

In 1884, an international conference divided the world into 24 time zones.

The Prime Meridian (0° longitude), which runs through Greenwich, England, became the reference point. Traveling east from Greenwich, the time is one hour later in each time zone. Traveling west from Greenwich, the time is one hour earlier per zone.

The International Date Line is at 180° longitude. When crossing this line from west to east, you lose one day; when crossing in the opposite direction, you gain a day.

Using the map on this page:

- Locate Los Angeles and note its time.
- Locate Mumbai, India.
- Determine whether Mumbai lies east or west of Los Angeles.
- Count the number of time zones between the two cities. Each time zone is an hour difference.
- Add or subtract the number of hours difference between Mumbai and Los Angeles.
- Is the International Date Line between the two points? If so, add or subtract a day.
- Check the time above Mumbai to see if you are correct.

Practicing the Skill

Use the map to calculate these times.

1. If it is 3:00 P.M. in Greenwich, what time is it in Moscow?
2. If it is 9:00 A.M. in Cape Town, what time is it in Washington, D.C.?
3. It is 5:00 P.M. on Tuesday in Beijing. What day and time is it in Honolulu?

Applying the Skill

Create four time zone problems. Be sure at least one problem involves the International Date Line. Exchange problems with a classmate and check the accuracy of each other's computation.

Glencoe's **Skillbuilder Interactive Workbook, Level 2,** provides instruction and practice in key social studies skills.

ANSWERS TO PRACTICING THE SKILL

1. In Moscow, Russia, the time would be 6:00 P.M.
2. In Washington, D.C., the time would be 3:00 A.M.
3. In Honolulu, Hawaii, the time would be 11:00 P.M. Monday.

Applying the Skill: Students will create time zone problems. Have students share their problems and answers with the class.

TEACH

Understanding World Time Zones Ask students why they think standard time was fixed in 1884. *(to prevent all the time differences that would result if each locality determined the mean solar time by different meridians, depending on its longitude)* What are the advantages of having a universal reference point? *(standardizes time for air and sea navigation and for scientific purposes, such as astronomy)* Have students use the hour your class begins and then figure out what the time would be in the following places: Washington, D.C.; Toronto, Ontario; Budapest, Hungary; and Cairo, Egypt. **L1** ELL

Additional Practice

Skills Reinforcement Activity 20

Name ______ Date ______ Class ______

Skills Reinforcement Activity 20

Understanding World Time Zones

Before 1800, people set their clocks by the sun. People lived by local time, and local times varied widely. Then, in 1884, an international conference established the Prime Meridian and the International Date Line in order to standardize time zones around the world.

DIRECTIONS: Read the scenario below about a fictitious journey to Berlin. Then use the map to answer the questions below in the space provided.

Imagine that you are going on a trip to Berlin. You will travel by airplane from your home in Denver, Colorado, to Berlin, Germany.

Time Zones of the World

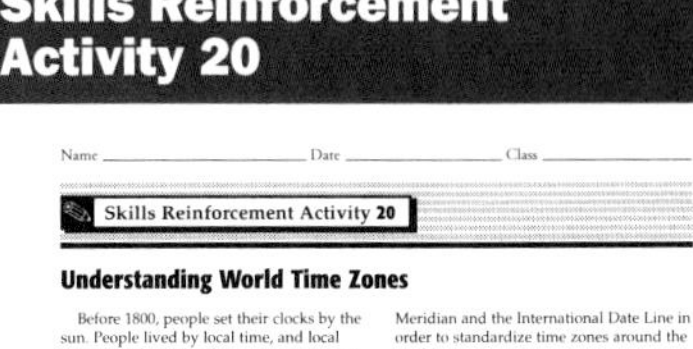

CD-ROM
Glencoe Skillbuilder Interactive Workbook CD-ROM, Level 2

This interactive CD-ROM reinforces student mastery of essential social studies skills.

CHAPTER 20
Section 3, 642–650

1 FOCUS

Section Overview

This section describes the major developments in postwar Western societies.

BELLRINGER
Skillbuilder Activity

 Project transparency and have students answer questions.

 Available as a blackline master.

Daily Focus Skills Transparency 20–3

Guide to Reading

Answers to Graphic: Great Britain: National Insurance Act, National Health Service Act; United States: Social Security, labor laws, health care for the elderly, various measures to combat poverty, federal assistance for education; Canada: Canada Pension Plan, national health insurance program

Preteaching Vocabulary: Be sure students understand what a *welfare state* is and how it differs from country to country. **L1**

SECTION 3 Western Europe and North America

Guide to Reading

Main Ideas
- Postwar Western societies rebuilt their economies and communities.
- Shifting social structures in the West led to upheaval and change.

Key Terms
welfare state, bloc, real wages

People to Identify
Charles de Gaulle, John F. Kennedy, Martin Luther King, Jr., Simone de Beauvoir

Places to Locate
France, West Germany

Preview Questions
1. How did the EEC benefit the member nations?
2. What were the major social changes in Western society after 1945?

Reading Strategy
Categorizing Information Use a table like the one below to list programs instituted by Great Britain, the United States, and Canada to promote social welfare.

Great Britain	United States	Canada

Preview of Events

1945 · 1950 · 1955 · 1960 · 1965 · 1970 · 1975

- **1949** Simone de Beauvoir publishes *The Second Sex*
- **1957** The Rome Treaty establishes the EEC
- **1964** The Civil Rights Act is passed
- **1968** Student revolts peak

Student protester in Paris

Voices from the Past

In 1968, student protestors scribbled the following on the walls of the University of Paris:

> "May 1968. World revolution is the order of the day.
> To be free in 1968 is to take part.
> Make love, not war.
> The mind travels farther than the heart but it doesn't go as far.
> Exam = servility, social promotion, hierarchic society.
> Love each other.
> Are you consumers or participants?
> Revolution, I love you."
>
> —***The Western Tradition from the Renaissance to the Present,*** **Eugen Weber, 1972**

Student revolts in the United States and Europe were a part of larger problems that faced Western society after 1945.

Western Europe: Recovery

With the economic aid of the Marshall Plan, the countries of Western Europe recovered relatively rapidly from the devastation of World War II. Between 1947 and 1950, European countries received $9.4 billion for new equipment and raw materials. By 1950, industrial output in Europe was 30 percent above prewar levels.

SECTION RESOURCES

Reproducible Masters
- Reproducible Lesson Plan 20–3
- Daily Lecture and Discussion Notes 20–3
- Guided Reading Activity 20–3
- Section Quiz 20–3
- Reading Essentials and Study Guide 20–3

Transparencies
- Daily Focus Skills Transparency 20–3

Multimedia
- Interactive Tutor Self-Assessment CD-ROM
- ExamView® Pro Testmaker CD-ROM
- Presentation Plus! CD-ROM

This economic recovery continued well into the 1950s and 1960s. The decades of the 1950s and 1960s were periods of dramatic economic growth and prosperity in Western Europe. Indeed, Western Europe had virtually full employment during these decades.

France and de Gaulle The history of **France** for nearly a quarter of a century after the war was dominated by one man—the war hero **Charles de Gaulle.** In 1946, de Gaulle helped establish a new government called the Fourth Republic. It featured a strong parliament and a weak presidency. No party was strong enough to dominate, and the government was largely ineffective.

Unhappy with the Fourth Republic, de Gaulle withdrew from politics. Then, in 1958, he returned. Leaders of the Fourth Republic, frightened by bitter divisions caused by a crisis in the French colony of Algeria (discussed in Chapter 23), asked de Gaulle to form a new government and revise the constitution.

In 1958, de Gaulle drafted a new constitution for the Fifth Republic that greatly enhanced the power of the president. The president would now have the right to choose the prime minister, dissolve parliament, and supervise both defense and foreign policy. The constitution was overwhelmingly approved by French voters, and de Gaulle became the first president of the Fifth Republic.

People In History

Charles de Gaulle

1890–1970—French president

Charles de Gaulle had an unshakable faith in his mission to restore the greatness of the French nation. De Gaulle followed a military career and, before World War II, he argued for a new type of mobile tank warfare. After France fell to the Nazis, he fled to Britain and became leader of the French Resistance.

As president of France, de Gaulle realized that France was wasting its economic strength by maintaining its colonial empire. By 1962, he had granted independence to France's black African colonies and to Algeria. At the same time, he believed that playing an important role in the Cold War would enhance France's stature. For that reason, he pulled France out of NATO, saying that France did not want to be an American "vassal state."

As the new president, de Gaulle sought to return France to a position of great power. To achieve the status of a world power, de Gaulle invested heavily in nuclear arms. France exploded its first nuclear bomb in 1960.

During de Gaulle's presidency, the French economy grew at an annual rate of 5.5 percent, faster than that of the United States. France became a major industrial producer and exporter, especially of automobiles and weapons.

Nevertheless, problems remained. Large government deficits and a rise in the cost of living led to unrest. In May 1968, a series of student protests was followed by a general labor strike. Tired and discouraged, de Gaulle resigned from office in April 1969 and died within a year.

The Economic Miracle of West Germany The three Western zones of Germany were unified as the Federal Republic of Germany in 1949. From 1949 to 1963, Konrad Adenauer (A•duhn•OWR), the leader of the **Christian Democratic Union** (CDU), served as chancellor (head of state). Adenauer sought respect for **West Germany.** He cooperated with the United States and other Western European nations and especially wanted to work with France—Germany's longtime enemy.

Konrad Adenauer

Under Adenauer, West Germany experienced an "economic miracle." This revival of the West German economy was largely guided by the minister of finance, Ludwig Erhard. Unemployment fell from 8 percent in 1950 to 0.4 percent in 1965. To maintain its economic expansion, West Germany even brought in hundreds of thousands of "guest" workers on visas from Italy, Spain, Greece, Turkey, and Yugoslavia.

Adenauer resigned in 1963, after 14 years of guiding West Germany through its postwar recovery. Ludwig Erhard succeeded Adenauer as chancellor and largely continued his policies.

An economic downturn in the mid-1960s opened the door to the Social Democratic Party, which became the leading party in 1969. The Social Democrats, a moderate socialist party, were led by Willy Brandt, mayor of West Berlin.

The Decline of Great Britain The end of World War II left Great Britain with massive economic

2 TEACH

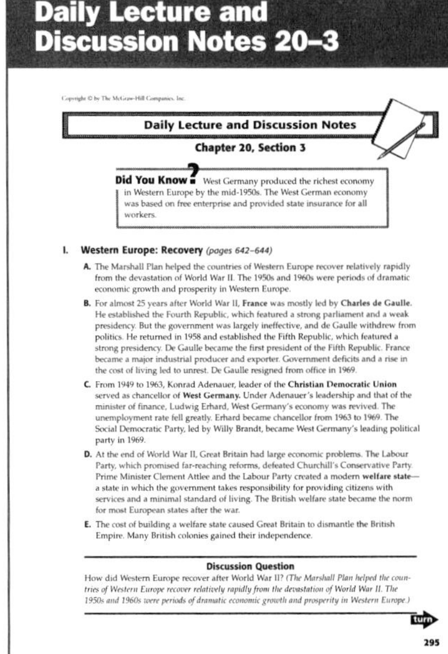

Daily Lecture and Discussion Notes 20–3

Daily Lecture and Discussion Notes

Chapter 20, Section 3

Did You Know? West Germany produced the richest economy in Western Europe by the mid-1950s. The West German economy was based on free enterprise and provided state insurance for all workers.

I. **Western Europe: Recovery** *(pages 642–644)*

A. The Marshall Plan helped the countries of Western Europe recover relatively rapidly from the devastation of World War II. The 1950s and 1960s were periods of dramatic economic growth and prosperity in Western Europe.

B. For almost 25 years after World War II, **France** was mostly led by **Charles de Gaulle.** He established the Fourth Republic, which featured a strong parliament and a weak presidency. But the government was largely ineffective, and de Gaulle withdrew from politics. He returned in 1958 and established the Fifth Republic, which featured a strong presidency. De Gaulle became the first president of the Fifth Republic. France became a major industrial producer and exporter. Government deficits and a rise in the cost of living led to unrest. De Gaulle resigned from office in 1969.

C. From 1949 to 1963, Konrad Adenauer, leader of the **Christian Democratic Union** served as chancellor of **West Germany.** Under Adenauer's leadership and that of the minister of finance, Ludwig Erhard, West Germany's economy was revived. The unemployment rate fell greatly. Erhard became chancellor from 1963 to 1969. The Social Democratic Party, led by Willy Brandt, became West Germany's leading political party in 1969.

D. At the end of World War II, Great Britain had large economic problems. The Labour Party, which promised far-reaching reforms, defeated Churchill's Conservative Party. Prime Minister Clement Attlee and the Labour Party created a modern **welfare state**—a state in which the government takes responsibility for providing citizens with services and a minimal standard of living. The British welfare state became the norm for most European states after the war.

E. The cost of building a welfare state caused Great Britain to dismantle the British Empire. Many British colonies gained their independence.

Discussion Question

How did Western Europe recover after World War II? *(The Marshall Plan helped the countries of Western Europe recover relatively rapidly from the devastation of World War II. The 1950s and 1960s were periods of dramatic economic growth and prosperity in Western Europe.)*

turn

295

Connecting Across Time

Ask students to identify and discuss similarities between the French decision to withdraw from NATO in 1968 and the independence of Communist Yugoslavia from the Soviet block. Why was it sometimes difficult for both the United States and the Soviet Union to maintain control over allied nations?

Writing Activity

Have students watch a video of the film *The Mouse That Roared* and then write a paper on the European attitude toward the United States that is reflected in the film. L2

INTERDISCIPLINARY CONNECTIONS ACTIVITY

Economics Have students identify reasons for the rapid economic recovery in West Germany after World War II. Also have students identify and discuss possible reasons for the economic decline of Great Britain after the war. Some believe Britain's decision to nationalize businesses was an important cause of the decline of the country's economy. Do students agree? Why or why not? Both West Germany and Great Britain created "welfare states"–a system in which the national government provides programs for the well-being of its citizens–yet Germany thrived while Britain struggled. Have students research conditions in both countries that suggest reasons for this disparity. Ask them to prepare a class exhibit of their findings. L2

For grading this activity, refer to the ***Performance Assessment Activities*** booklet.

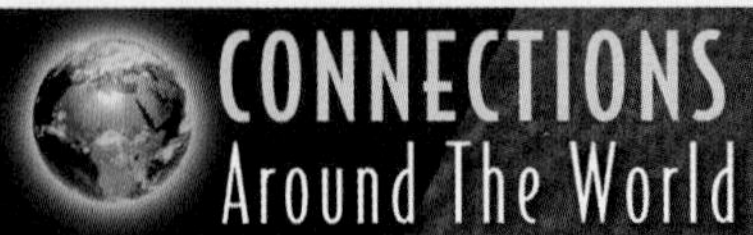

Answer: Answers will vary but should be supported by examples and logical arguments. Students might cite disruption in school, lack of housing, and crowded, congested streets and shops. Culturally, there might be a lack of entertainment activities or a lack of access to library materials.

Reading Check

Answer: Charles de Gaulle wanted to return France to a position of great power.

CURRICULUM CONNECTION

Economics Ask students to discuss ways in which the economic situation in Europe after World War II contributed to the political success of Socialist parties, particularly in Germany and Great Britain. Why would the United States have been so concerned about socialist successes? L3

Critical Thinking

The Soviet emphasis on production of heavy industrial goods resulted in a shortage of consumer goods throughout the Soviet sphere of influence. Do students believe the people of Eastern Europe would have been more tolerant of the Soviet presence in their countries if they had enjoyed a better standard of living? Ask students to compare the allocation of resources to heavy industry to the allocation of resources to infrastructure and consumer goods.

CONNECTIONS Around The World

Economic Miracles: Germany and Japan

Both Germany and Japan were devastated by World War II. Their economies were in shambles. Their cities lay in ruins. At the end of the twentieth century, though, Germany and Japan were two of the world's greatest economic powers. What explains their economic miracles?

Because of the destruction of the war, both countries were forced to build new industrial plants. For many years, neither country spent much on defense. Their governments focused instead on rebuilding the infrastructure (roads, bridges, canals, and b ildings) that had been destroyed during the war. Both German and Japanese workers had a long tradition of hard work and basic skills. In both countries, U.S. occupation policy was committed to economic recovery, a goal that was made easier by American foreign aid.

◀ German bridge

Today, Germany and Japan share many similarities in economic structure. Both rely on imports of raw materials for their industries. Both depend for their prosperity on exports of manufactured goods, including machinery, automobiles, steel, textiles, electrical and electronic equipment, and ships. Both nations must import food to feed their populations.

▲ Japanese railroad station

Comparing Cultures

The United States has never experienced the kind of destruction experienced by Germany and Japan during World War II. How might your life be different if the United States was in the process of rebuilding after a war? What cultural, political, and economic factors might influence the process of rebuilding in the United States?

problems. In elections held immediately after the war, the Labour Party overwhelmingly defeated Churchill's Conservative Party.

The Labour Party had promised far-reaching reforms, especially in the area of social welfare. Under Clement Attlee, the new prime minister, the Labour government set out to create a modern **welfare state**—a state in which the government takes responsibility for providing citizens with services and a minimal standard of living.

In 1946, the new government passed the National Insurance Act and the National Health Service Act. The insurance act provided government funds to help the unemployed, the sick, and the aged. The health act created a system of socialized medicine that ensured medical care for everyone. The British welfare state became the norm for most European states after the war.

The cost of building a welfare state at home forced Britain to reduce expenses abroad. This meant the dismantling of the British Empire. Economic necessity forced Britain to give in to the demands of its many colonies for national independence. Britain was no longer able to play the role of a world power.

Continuing economic problems brought the Conservatives back into power from 1951 to 1964. Although they favored private enterprise, the Conservatives accepted the welfare state and even extended it by financing an ambitious building program to improve British housing.

Reading Check **Explaining** Why did de Gaulle invest heavily in nuclear arms?

Western Europe: The Move toward Unity

As we have seen, the divisions created by the Cold War led the nations of Western Europe to form the North Atlantic Treaty Organization in 1949. The destructiveness of two world wars caused many thoughtful Europeans to consider the need for some additional form of European unity. National feeling was still too powerful, however, for European

EXTENDING THE CONTENT

British Government Clement Richard Attlee was born into the British middle class and worked as a social worker and lawyer until the outbreak of World War I. Attlee was an officer in the war. Entering the House of Commons in 1922, he became a minister in the minority Labour Party. During World War II, Attlee served in Churchill's coalition cabinet and in 1945 became prime minister. His government nationalized major public utilities and several industries, including coal mining; instituted free medical and hospital care; and established or improved numerous relief programs for underprivileged people. Attlee's government also granted independence to Burma (now Myanmar), India, Pakistan, Ceylon (now Sri Lanka), and Palestine (now Israel).

nations to give up their political sovereignty. As a result, the desire for unity focused chiefly on the economic arena, not the political one.

In 1957, France, West Germany, the Benelux countries (Belgium, the Netherlands, and Luxembourg), and Italy signed the Rome Treaty. This treaty created the **European Economic Community** (EEC), also known as the Common Market.

The EEC was a free-trade area made up of the six member nations. These six nations would impose no tariffs, or import charges, on each other's goods. However, as a group, they would be protected by a tariff imposed on goods from non-EEC nations. In this way, the EEC encouraged cooperation among the member nations' economies. All the member nations benefited economically.

By the 1960s, the EEC had become an important trading bloc (a group of nations with a common purpose). With a total population of 165 million, the EEC was the world's largest exporter and purchaser of raw materials.

Reading Check **Evaluating** Why did European unity come in the form of an economic alliance?

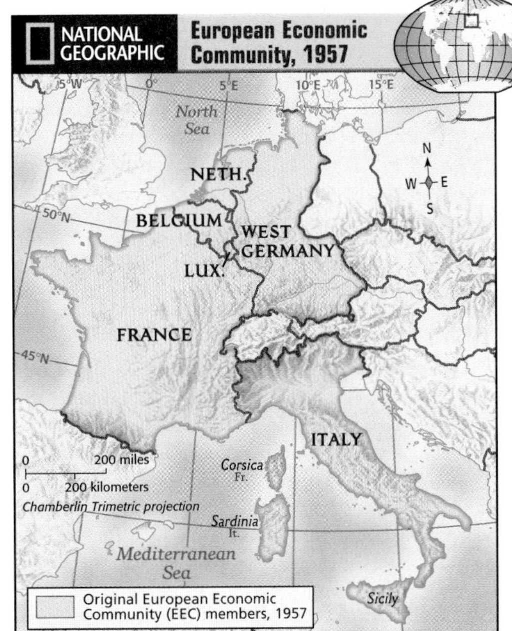

Geography Skills

The signing of the Rome Treaty in 1957 established the European Economic Community (EEC).

1. **Interpreting Maps** What countries were members of the EEC in 1957?
2. **Applying Geography Skills** What geographical factors could help to explain why some European countries joined the EEC in 1957 but others did not?

The United States in the 1950s

Between 1945 and 1970, the ideals of Franklin Delano Roosevelt's New Deal largely determined the patterns of American domestic politics. The New Deal had brought basic changes to American society. They included a dramatic increase in the role and power of the federal government, the rise of organized labor as a significant force in the economy and politics, the beginning of a welfare state, and a realization of the need to deal fairly with the concerns of minorities, especially African Americans.

The New Deal tradition in American politics was reinforced by the election of Democratic presidents—Harry S Truman in 1948, John F. Kennedy in 1960, and Lyndon B. Johnson in 1964. Even the election of a Republican president, Dwight D. Eisenhower, in 1952 and 1956 did not change the basic direction of the New Deal. Eisenhower said, "Should any political party attempt to abolish Social Security and eliminate labor laws, you would not hear of that party again in our political history."

An economic boom followed World War II. A shortage of consumer goods during the war had left Americans with both extra income and the desire to buy goods after the war. In addition, the growth of labor unions brought higher wages and gave more workers the ability to buy consumer goods. Between 1945 and 1973, real wages (the actual purchasing power of income) grew an average of 3 percent a year, the most prolonged advance in American history.

Prosperity was not the only characteristic of the early 1950s, however. Cold War struggles abroad led to the widespread fear that Communists had infiltrated the United States. President Truman's attorney general warned that Communists were "everywhere—in factories, offices, butcher stores, on street corners, in private businesses." For many Americans, proof of this threat became more evident when thousands of American soldiers were sent to Korea to fight and die in a war against Communist aggression.

This climate of fear produced a dangerous political agitator, Senator Joseph R. McCarthy of Wisconsin. His charges that hundreds of supposed communists were in high government positions helped create a massive "Red Scare"—fear of

Reading Check

Answer: National feeling was too powerful for European nations to give up their political sovereignty. Working together economically, however, these nations became a powerful bloc.

Geography Skills

Answers:

1. In 1957, France, West Germany, Belgium, the Netherlands, Luxembourg, and Italy were members of the EEC.
2. Nations that did not join were geographically isolated from the rest of the EEC—Great Britain by the English Channel and North Sea, Spain by the Pyrenees.

CURRICULUM CONNECTION

Economics Ask students to explain why the United States was in a better position to create a welfare state after World War II than most European nations. Why did the United States choose not to move as far along this path as some other nations? L2

Who? What? Where? When?

Eleanor Roosevelt Eleanor Roosevelt provided a voice of moderation during the postwar period. Roosevelt, who continued her public career after her husband died in 1945, was a member of the UN Commission on Human Rights. She tried to meet the Russians halfway. "All of us are going to die together or we are going to learn to live together," she said, "and if we are to live together we have to talk."

COOPERATIVE LEARNING ACTIVITY

Creating a Presentation Organize the class into eight small groups, one for each year from 1947 through 1954, the years of the post-World War II "Red Scare." Have each group research and report on relevant anticommunist activities that occurred in that year. Ask them to include proceedings of the House Un-American Activities Committee and the Senate Committee on Investigation, headed by Senator Joseph McCarthy of Wisconsin. Have each group develop its own definition of the term "McCarthyism." Once groups have completed their research, ask each group to work together to agree on a format to present their information. You might suggest that some groups adopt a radio or TV report format. L2

CHAPTER 20
Section 3, 642–650

Reading Check

Answer: Many Americans became convinced that there was a Communist plot to take over the world and that Communists had infiltrated the United States. For many Americans, the Korean War was proof of this threat.

Guided Reading Activity 20–3

Name ______ Date ______ Class ______

Guided Reading Activity 20-3

Western Europe and North America

DIRECTIONS: Fill in the blanks below as you read Section 3.

1. By 1950, ______ output in Europe was 30 percent above prewar levels.
2. Western Europe had virtually full ______ during the 1950s and 1960s.
3. One man—the war hero ______, dominated the history of France for nearly a quarter of a century after the war.
4. Under ______, West Germany experienced an "economic miracle."
5. An economic ______ in the mid-1960s opened the door to the Social Democratic Party.
6. Under Clement Attlee, the new Prime Minister, the British Labour government set out to create a modern ______.
7. In 1957, six Western European countries signed the Rome Treaty and created the ______.
8. The ideals of Franklin Roosevelt's ______ largely determined the patterns of American domestic politics.
9. Cold War struggles abroad led to the widespread fear that Communists had ______ the United States.
10. Thousands of American soldiers were sent to ______ to fight and die in a war against Communist aggression.
11. The civil rights movement had its beginnings in 1954, when the U.S. Supreme Court ruled that racial ______ in public schools was illegal.
12. With Richard Nixon's election in 1968, a shift to the political ______ in American politics began.

40

Enrich

Fear of Communist influence was very strong in American society during the Cold War years. Have students write about how and why this occurred. In their essays, have students discuss whether or not they think attitudes are different today, and if so, why. L2

communist subversion. Under McCarthy, several individuals including intellectuals and movie stars were questioned about Communist activities. When McCarthy attacked alleged "Communist conspirators" in the U.S. Army, he was condemned by Congress in 1954. Very quickly, his anticommunist crusade came to an end.

Reading Check **Describing** What effect did the Cold War have on many Americans?

The United States in the 1960s

The 1960s began on a youthful and optimistic note. At age 43, **John F. Kennedy** became the youngest elected president in the history of the United States. His administration was cut short when the president was killed by an assassin on November 22, 1963. Vice President Lyndon B. Johnson then became president. Johnson won a new term as president in a landslide victory in 1964.

Lyndon B. Johnson taking the oath of office

The Johnson Administration President Johnson used his stunning victory to pursue the growth of the welfare state, begun in the New Deal. Johnson's programs included health care for the elderly, various measures to combat poverty, and federal assistance for education.

Johnson's other domestic passion was the civil rights movement, or equal rights for African Americans. The civil rights movement had its beginnings in 1954, when the United States Supreme Court ruled that the practice of racial segregation (separation) in public schools was illegal. According to Chief Justice Earl Warren, "separate educational facilities

THE WAY IT WAS

FOCUS ON EVERYDAY LIFE

Youth Protest in the 1960s

The decade of the 1960s witnessed a dramatic change in traditional manners and morals. The new standards were evident in the breakdown of the traditional family as divorce rates increased dramatically. Movies, plays, and books broke new ground in the treatment of once-hidden subjects.

A new youth movement also emerged in the 1960s. New attitudes toward sex and the use of drugs were two of its features. Young people also questioned authority and rebelled against the older generation. Spurred on by the Vietnam War, the youth rebellion in the United States had become a youth protest movement by the second half of the 1960s. Active participants in the movement were often called "hippies."

In the 1960s, the lyrics of rock music reflected the rebellious mood of many young people. Bob Dylan, a well-known recording artist, expressed the feelings of the younger generation. His song "The Times They Are a-Changin'," released in 1964, has been called an "anthem for the protest movement." Some of its words, which follow, tell us why.

"The Times They Are a-Changin'"

Come gather round people
Wherever you roam
And admit that the waters

CRITICAL THINKING ACTIVITY

Drawing Conclusions Lyndon Johnson's dreams for a "Great Society" included health care for elderly people, a War on Poverty to be fought with food stamps and a Job Corps, a new Department of Housing and Urban Development to deal with the problems of the cities, federal assistance for education, and equal rights for African Americans. Despite all his accomplishments, including the Civil Rights Act of 1964 and the Voting Rights Act of 1965, Johnson's presidency and reputation ultimately foundered with U.S. involvement in the Vietnam War. Have students research the domestic achievements of Johnson's five years in office. Ask them to come to a conclusion they can defend about what Johnson's legacy should be: was he the architect of the Great Society or escalator of the Vietnam War? L2

are inherently unequal." African Americans also boycotted segregated buses and other public places.

In August 1963, The Reverend **Martin Luther King, Jr.,** leader of a growing movement for racial equality, led a march on Washington, D.C., to dramatize the African American desire for equality. King advocated the principle of passive disobedience practiced by Mohandas Gandhi. King's march and his impassioned plea for racial equality had an electrifying effect on the American people. By the end of 1963, a majority of the American people called civil rights the most significant national issue.

President Johnson took up the cause of civil rights. The Civil Rights Act in 1964 created the machinery to end segregation and discrimination in the workplace and all public places. The Voting Rights Act the following year made it easier for African Americans to vote in southern states.

Laws alone, however, could not guarantee the Great Society that Johnson talked about creating. He soon faced bitter social unrest.

Social Upheaval In the North and West, blacks had had voting rights for many years. However, local patterns of segregation led to higher unemployment rates for blacks than for whites. In the summer of 1965, race riots broke out in the Watts district of Los Angeles. Thirty-four people died, and over a thousand buildings were destroyed. In 1968, Martin Luther King, Jr., was assassinated. Riots hit over a hundred cities, including Washington, D.C. The riots led to a "white backlash" (whites became less sympathetic to the cause of racial equality) and continued the racial division of the United States.

Antiwar protests also divided the American people after President Johnson sent American troops to war in Vietnam (see Chapter 24). As the war progressed through the second half of the 1960s, the protests grew. Then, in 1970, four students at Kent State University were killed and nine others were wounded by the Ohio National Guard during a student demonstration. The tragedy startled the nation. By this time Americans were less willing to continue the war.

The combination of antiwar demonstrations and riots in the cities caused many people to call for "law and order." This was the appeal used by Richard Nixon, the Republican presidential candidate in 1968. With Nixon's election in 1968, a shift to the political right in American politics began.

Reading Check **Identifying** Name President Johnson's two most important domestic policy goals.

Around you have grown
And accept it that soon
You'll be drenched to the bone
If your time to you
Is worth savin'
Then you better start swimmin'
Or you'll sink like a stone
For the times they are a-changin' . . .

Come mothers and fathers
Throughout the land
And don't criticize
What you can't understand
Your sons and your daughters
Are beyond your command
Your old road
Is rapidly agin'
Please get out of the new one
If you can't lend your hand
For the times they are a-changin'

Young people expressed their rebellion through clothing, music, and government protests.

Connecting to the Past

1. **Identifying** What does Bob Dylan say is the consequence of not changing?
2. **Comparing** Are there songs or artists today who have the same cultural outlook as Bob Dylan?
3. **Writing about History** What social or political issues are being expressed in music, literature, television, or movies today? Write a brief essay highlighting one or two cultural examples, including lyrics or other relevant materials.

647

Reading Check

Answer: the growth of the welfare state and civil rights

The Way It Was

Answers:
1. If you don't "swim" (that is, change), you "sink like a stone."
2. Answers will vary but should be supported by examples.
3. Answers will vary but should be supported by examples.

Who? What? Where? When?

DEW line By the 1980s, the United States and the Soviet Union each had more than 12,000 ICBMs aimed at each other. The Distant Early Warning Line (DEW line) was a radar system built in 1957 to detect incoming missiles. The DEW line radars were placed in northern Canada because the most direct path of the missiles from the U.S.S.R. would be over the North Pole.

Critical Thinking

Citizens of the United States are guaranteed basic freedoms in the Bill of Rights. The First Amendment grants us the right to speech, assembly, and politics. Guide students in a discussion of these rights as they pertained to the civil rights movement of the 1960s and today. L1 ELL

EXTENDING THE CONTENT

Civil Rights Students and other young people played a key role in the civil rights struggle. In 1960, students in North Carolina organized the first sit-ins, occupying seats at a segregated lunch counter as a form of protest. The following year many students took part in freedom rides, demonstrating against segregated buses. In 1964, three young men — Michael Schwerner, Andrew Goodman, and James Chaney — were murdered while organizing voter registration in Mississippi. Ask students to research the role of young people in the fight for equal rights for African Americans. Have them consider whether they themselves might have been inspired to take part in this struggle. If so, what role might they have taken? L2

Picturing History

Answer: Answers will vary but should be supported by logical arguments.

Reading Check

Answer: Much of Canada's growth was financed by capital from the United States, which led to U.S. ownership of Canadian businesses.

CURRICULUM CONNECTION

Science A great scientific breakthrough of the Cold War period was the conquest of polio, a disease that had crippled and killed children and adults worldwide for centuries. (Franklin D. Roosevelt was one of its most prominent victims.) An inoculation, pioneered by Jonas Salk, was pronounced safe in 1955. An oral vaccine, developed by Albert Sabin, was approved in 1961. Today, polio has been almost eliminated throughout the world. Ask interested students to research and report on the work of Salk and Sabin. L2

Enrich

The text mentions that computers, televisions, and jet planes altered the pace of human life. Ask students to list specific ways in which this occurred. Also ask if other new inventions have had a similar effect. L2

Picturing History

Gunfire breaks up an anti-war protest at Kent State University, Ohio, in 1970. Today, a memorial inscribed "Inquire, Learn, Reflect" marks the site where four student protesters were killed by the National Guard. What message or lesson is conveyed to you by the events at Kent State?

The Development of Canada

For 25 years after World War II, a prosperous Canada set out on a new path of industrial development. Canada had always had a strong export economy based on its abundant natural resources. Now it developed electronic, aircraft, nuclear, and chemical engineering industries on a large scale. Much of the Canadian growth, however, was financed by capital from the United States, which led to U.S. ownership of Canadian businesses. Some Canadians feared American economic domination of Canada.

Canadians also worried about playing a secondary role politically and militarily to the United States. They sought to establish their own identity in world politics. Canada was a founding member of the United Nations in 1945 and joined the North Atlantic Treaty Organization in 1949.

The Liberal Party dominated Canadian politics throughout most of this period. Under Lester Pearson, the Liberal government created Canada's welfare state by enacting a national social security system (the Canada Pension Plan) and a national health insurance program.

Reading Check **Explaining** Why did some Canadians fear U.S. economic domination of Canada?

The Emergence of a New Society

After World War II, Western society witnessed rapid change. Such new inventions as computers, televisions, and jet planes altered the pace and nature of human life. The rapid changes in postwar society led many to view it as a new society.

A Changing Social Structure Postwar Western society was marked by a changing social structure.

Especially noticeable were changes in the middle class. Traditional middle-class groups were made up of businesspeople, lawyers, doctors, and teachers. A new group of managers and technicians, hired by large companies and government agencies, now joined the ranks of the middle class.

Changes also occurred among the lower classes. The shift of people from rural to urban areas continued. The number of people in farming declined drastically. By the 1950s, the number of farmers in most parts of

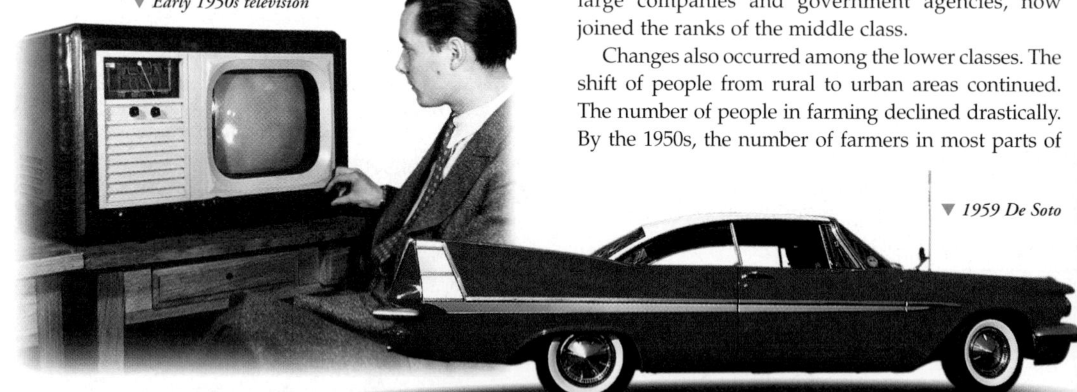

▼ *Early 1950s television*

▼ *1959 De Soto*

INTERDISCIPLINARY CONNECTIONS ACTIVITY

Language Arts Guide students in a discussion of any stories they have heard from family members or other adults about what it was like to be young in the 1960s and 1970s. Challenge students to create a "memory scrapbook" of their parents, relatives, and other community members' recollections, including details from those who observed or participated in the various student protests. Ask students to collect interesting stories, anecdotes, or poignant memories that they can write, edit, and illustrate as part of an oral history of their community. Suggest that they solicit photographs, letters, and preserved newspaper articles from the time. Create a class display. L2

Europe had dropped by 50 percent. The number of industrial workers also began to decline as the amount of white-collar workers increased.

At the same time, a noticeable increase in the real wages of workers made it possible for them to imitate the buying patterns of the middle class. This led to what some observers have called the **consumer society**—a society preoccupied with buying goods.

Buying on credit became widespread in the 1950s. Workers could now buy such products as televisions, washing machines, refrigerators, vacuum cleaners, and stereos. The automobile was the most visible symbol of the new consumerism. In 1948, there were 5 million cars in all of Europe. By the 1960s, there were almost 45 million.

Women in the Postwar World Women's participation in the world wars had resulted in several gains. They had achieved one of the major aims of the nineteenth-century feminist movement—the right to vote. After World War I, many governments had expressed thanks to women by granting them voting rights. Sweden, Great Britain, Germany, Poland, Hungary, Austria, and Czechoslovakia did so in 1918, followed by the United States in 1920. Women in France and Italy did not obtain the right to vote until 1945.

During World War II, women had entered the workforce in huge numbers. At the war's end, however, they were removed to provide jobs for soldiers returning home. For a time, women fell back into traditional roles. Birthrates rose, creating a "baby boom" in the late 1940s and the 1950s.

By the end of the 1950s, however, the birthrate had begun to fall, and with it, the size of families. The structure of the workplace changed once again as the number of married women in the workforce increased in both Europe and the United States.

These women, especially working-class women, faced an old problem. They still earned less than men for equal work. For example, in the 1960s, women earned 60 percent of men's wages in Britain, 50 percent in France, and 63 percent in West Germany.

In addition, women still tended to enter traditionally female jobs. Many faced the double burden of earning income on the one hand and raising a family on the other. Such inequalities led increasing numbers of women to rebel.

By the late 1960s, women had begun to assert their rights again. In the late 1960s came renewed interest in feminism, or the **women's liberation movement,** as it was now called.

Of great importance to the emergence of the postwar women's liberation movement was the work of **Simone de Beauvoir** (duh•boh•VWAHR). In 1949, she published her highly influential work, *The Second Sex.* As a result of male-dominated societies, she argued, women had been defined by their differences from men and consequently received second-class status. De Beauvoir's book influenced both the American and European women's movements.

Student Revolt As we have seen, students in U.S. universities in the mid- to late 1960s launched an antiwar protest movement. At the same time, European students were engaging in protests of their own.

Before World War II, it was mostly members of Europe's wealthier classes who went to universities. After the war, European states began to encourage more people to gain higher education by eliminating fees. As a result, universities saw an influx of students from the middle and lower classes. Enrollments grew dramatically. In France, 4.5 percent of young people went to university in 1950. By 1965, the figure had increased to 14.5 percent.

There were problems, however. Many European university classrooms were overcrowded, and many professors paid little attention to their students.

People In History

Simone de Beauvoir
1908–1986—French author

A prominent French intellectual, Simone de Beauvoir became a major voice in the European feminist movement. Born into a Catholic middle-class family and educated at the Sorbonne in Paris, she supported herself as a teacher and later as a novelist and writer.

De Beauvoir believed that she lived a "liberated" life for a twentieth-century European woman. Despite all her freedom, she still came to perceive that, as a woman, she faced limits that men did not: "What particularly signalizes the situation of woman is that she—a free autonomous being like all human creatures—nevertheless finds herself in a world where men compel her to assume the status of the Other."

Critical Thinking

Ask students to define and give examples of different political systems from the present. Then ask students to select a contemporary issue that is under debate. Students could select one of the issues mentioned in this chapter, such as how to avoid a nuclear war or the role of women in contemporary society. Once they have selected a topic, ask students to apply their knowledge of political systems to make decisions about the issue. How might different political systems hinder the resolution of the selected topic? Have students describe variables in their contemporary situation that could result in different outcomes. L2

3 ASSESS

Assign Section 3 Assessment as homework or as an in-class activity.

Have students use **Interactive Tutor Self-Assessment CD-ROM.**

Section Quiz 20–3

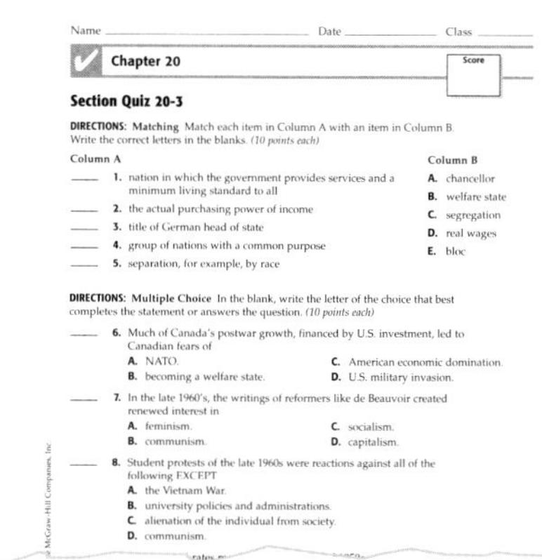

Name ______ Date ______ Class ______

Chapter 20 Score

Section Quiz 20-3

DIRECTIONS: Matching Match each item in Column A with an item in Column B. Write the correct letters in the blanks. *(10 points each)*

Column A	Column B
____ 1. nation in which the government provides services and a minimum living standard to all	A. chancellor
____ 2. the actual purchasing power of income	B. welfare state
____ 3. title of German head of state	C. segregation
____ 4. group of nations with a common purpose	D. real wages
____ 5. separation, for example, by race	E. bloc

DIRECTIONS: Multiple Choice In the blank, write the letter of the choice that best completes the statement or answers the question. *(10 points each)*

____ 6. Much of Canada's postwar growth, financed by U.S. investment, led to Canadian fears of
A. NATO.
B. becoming a welfare state.
C. American economic domination.
D. U.S. military invasion.

____ 7. In the late 1960's, the writings of reformers like de Beauvoir created renewed interest in
A. feminism.
B. communism.
C. socialism.
D. capitalism.

____ 8. Student protests of the late 1960s were reactions against all of the following EXCEPT
A. the Vietnam War.
B. university policies and administrations.
C. alienation of the individual from society.
D. communism.

EXTENDING THE CONTENT

Protest Songs Strictly speaking, folk music is music that "lives in oral tradition and is learned by ear, without the use of written music, primarily in rural cultures." Today, the concept of folk music has been greatly expanded and includes other forms of music, such as the protest song. These were songs written in the style of folk music but for political or social purposes. The most famous folk/protest composers in the United States are probably Bob Dylan, Woody Guthrie, and Pete Seeger. Dylan was perhaps the most influential voice of the early 1960s protest era and remains a leading composer and musician. He composed one of the signature songs of the sixties "Blowin' in the Wind," which became an anthem of the civil rights movement.

CHAPTER 20
Section 3, 642–650

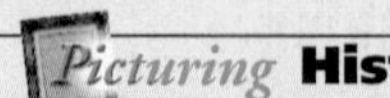

Answer: Answers will vary. They wanted to prevent cobblestones from being used as weapons in the future.

Reading Check

Answer: True equality — economic and social — with men.

Reading Essentials and Study Guide 20–3

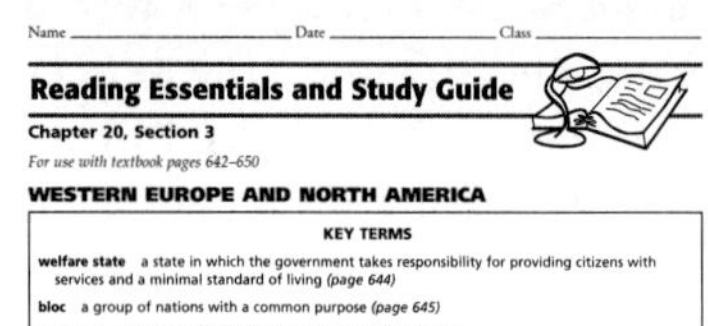
Name ____________ Date ____________ Class ____________

Reading Essentials and Study Guide

Chapter 20, Section 3

For use with textbook pages 642–650

WESTERN EUROPE AND NORTH AMERICA

KEY TERMS

welfare state a state in which the government takes responsibility for providing citizens with services and a minimal standard of living *(page 644)*

bloc a group of nations with a common purpose *(page 645)*

real wages the actual purchasing power of income *(page 645)*

DRAWING FROM EXPERIENCE

How do you feel about welfare? Do you think the government has a responsibility to provide citizens with basic needs, such as food and medical care?

In the last section, you read about developments in the Soviet Union and Eastern Europe following World War II. In this section, you will read about economic, political, and social changes in Western Europe, the United States, and Canada after the war. Some countries, such as Great Britain and the United States, developed welfare systems.

ORGANIZING YOUR THOUGHTS

Use the chart below to help you take notes. In the late 1950s, six countries in Western Europe created the European Economic Community, also known as the Common Market. Identify the six original members of the Common Market.

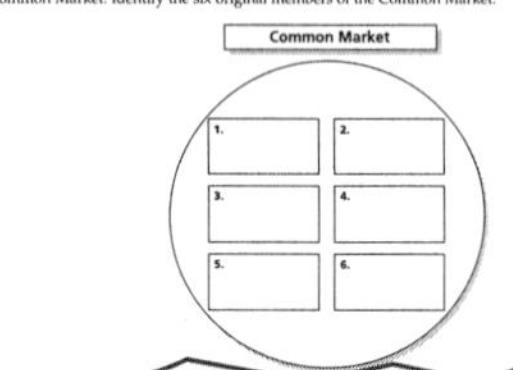

Reteaching Activity

Have students brainstorm a list of similarities and differences in the roles of women before and after World War II. **L1** **ELL**

4 CLOSE

Guide students in a discussion of the historical importance of student leadership in achieving social change. **L1**

Picturing History

Students threw cobblestones and the police retaliated with tear gas during the 1968 Paris demonstrations. Later, the streets were repaved with asphalt and concrete. After this incident, why do you think the authorities wanted paved streets rather than streets of cobblestone?

Growing discontent led to an outburst of student revolts in the late 1960s.

This student radicalism had several causes. Many of these protests were an extension of the revolts in U.S. universities, which were often sparked by student opposition to the Vietnam War. Some students, particularly in Europe, wished to reform the university system. They did not believe that universities responded to their needs or to the realities of the modern world. Others expressed concerns about becoming small cogs in the large and impersonal bureaucratic wheels of the modern world. Student protest movements in both Europe and the United States reached a high point in 1968. By the early 1970s, the movements had largely disappeared.

The student protests of the late 1960s caused many people to rethink some of their basic assumptions. Looking back, however, we can see that the student upheavals were not a turning point in the history of postwar Europe, as some people thought at the time. In the 1970s and 1980s, student rebels would become middle-class professionals. The vision of revolutionary politics would remain mostly a memory.

Reading Check **Identifying** What was the women's liberation movement trying to accomplish?

SECTION 3 ASSESSMENT

Checking for Understanding

1. **Define** welfare state, bloc, real wages.
2. **Identify** Charles de Gaulle, Christian Democratic Union, European Economic Community, John F. Kennedy, Martin Luther King, Jr., consumer society, women's liberation movement, Simone de Beauvoir.
3. **Locate** France, West Germany.
4. **Explain** why many British colonies gained their independence after World War II.
5. **List** the original members of the Common Market.

Critical Thinking

6. **Analyze** Do you think the student revolts of this period contributed positively or negatively to society? Why?
7. **Cause and Effect** Use a diagram like the one below to identify factors leading to the emergence of the postwar women's liberation movement.

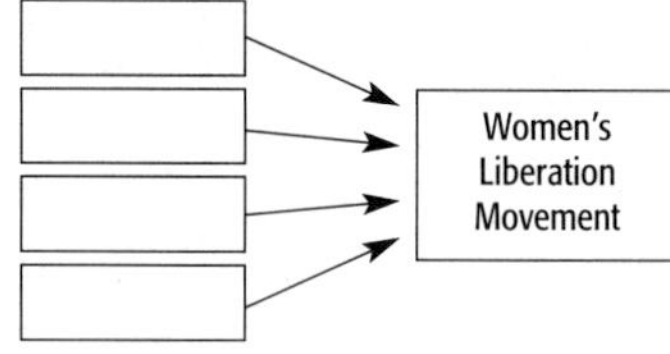

Analyzing Visuals

8. **Compare** the Kent State photo on page 648 with the photo above. What do these two scenes have in common? In your opinion, were the costs of these protests justified? What causes today could motivate this type of passion and sacrifice?

Writing About History

9. **Persuasive Writing** Demonstrations, marches, and riots were used in the 1960s and 1970s to communicate popular opinion. Write an essay that argues for or against the effectiveness of these methods for changing public opinion and policy.

SECTION 3 ASSESSMENT

1. Key terms are in blue.
2. Charles de Gaulle *(p. 643)*; Christian Democratic Union *(p. 643)*; European Economic Community *(p. 645)*; John F. Kennedy *(p. 646)*; Martin Luther King, Jr. *(p. 647)*; consumer society *(p. 649)*; women's liberation movement *(p. 649)*; Simone de Beauvoir *(p. 649)*
3. See chapter maps.
4. Britain was forced to reduce expenses abroad; demand for independence
5. France, West Germany, Belgium, Netherlands, Luxembourg, Italy
6. Answers will vary.
7. lower salaries than men; dual responsibilities of working outside the home and raising a family; status as second-class citizens in male-dominated society; publication of Simone de Beauvoir's *The Second Sex*
8. violent results of student revolt; answers to the last two questions will vary
9. Answers will vary.

Eyewitness to History

"I Have a Dream"

On August 28, 1963, Martin Luther King, Jr., led a civil rights march on Washington, D.C., and gave an inspired speech that energized the movement.

❝I am happy to join with you today in what will go down in history as the greatest demonstration for freedom in the history of our nation . . . .

I say to you today, my friends, so even though we face the difficulties of today and tomorrow, I still have a dream. It is a dream deeply rooted in the American dream. I have a dream that one day this nation will rise up and live out the true meaning of its creed, 'We hold these truths to be self-evident, that all men are created equal.' I have a dream that one day on the red hills of Georgia, sons of former slaves and the sons of former slave owners will be able to sit down together at the table of brotherhood. . . . I have a dream that my four little children will one day live in a nation where they will not be judged by the color of their skin, but by the content of their character . . . .

This is our hope. This is the faith that I go back to the South with. With this faith we will be able to hew out of the mountain of despair a stone of hope. With this faith we will be able to transform the jangling discords of our nation into a beautiful symphony of brotherhood. With this faith we will be able to work together, to pray together, to struggle together, to go to jail together, to stand up for freedom together, knowing that we will be free one day. And this will be the day. This will be the day when all of God's children will be able to sing with new meaning, 'My country 'tis of thee, sweet land of liberty, of thee I sing. Land where my father died, land of the pilgrims' pride, from every mountainside, let freedom ring.' And if America is to be a great nation, this must become true . . . .

And when this happens, and when we allow freedom to ring, when we let it ring from every village and every hamlet, from every state and every city, we will be able to speed up that day when all of God's children, black men and white men, Jews and Gentiles, Protestants and Catholics, will be able to join hands and sing in the words of the old Negro spiritual: 'Free at last, Free at last. Thank God Almighty, we are free at last.'❞

—Martin Luther King, Jr., Speech Delivered August 28, 1963, in Washington, D.C.

Martin Luther King, Jr., was an inspiring speaker.

Analyzing Primary Sources

1. Why do you think this speech has become so famous? Has King's dream been realized? Why or why not?
2. Describe King's dream in your own words.
3. Based on your earlier reading, how do you think Adolf Hitler would have reacted to King's speech? Explain.

TEACH

Analyzing Primary Sources
Martin Luther King, Jr., came to national prominence in 1955, when African Americans in Montgomery, Alabama, began a boycott against the local bus company, which practiced discrimination in seating and hiring. Montgomery had a municipal law that required African Americans to ride in the back of the city's buses. The boycott was successful, and in November 1956, the Supreme Court declared that segregation on public buses was unconstitutional.

In the spring of 1963, a bomb attack on a church in Birmingham, Alabama, killed four children and brought the nation's attention to the policies of racial segregation. A few months later, King delivered his famous speech.

Have students watch a videotape of Martin Luther King, Jr.'s, entire August 28, 1963 speech. Have students analyze its basic themes. Why do students think the speech was so effective?

Assign students to write their own "I Have a Dream" speech on a political or social issue of their choice. **L1** ELL

ANSWERS TO ANALYZING PRIMARY SOURCES

1. Answers will vary. It is powerful, poetic, and moving, full of vivid images and deeply felt emotion. Students should recognize that great care was devoted to language, especially repetition, in highly effective ways. Martin Luther King, Jr., was a highly skilled, gifted orator who clearly, and in simple words, spoke to the needs of our people.
2. Students should describe the themes that run through this speech, basic rights, equality, justice for all citizens of the United States.
3. Students should recall Hitler's idea of supreme race, and the horrors he inflicted upon non-Aryans. Answers will vary, but should be supported by examples and logical arguments.

GLENCOE TECHNOLOGY

MindJogger Videoquiz

Use the **MindJogger Videoquiz** to review Chapter 20 content.

 Available in VHS.

Using Key Terms

1. real wages **2.** domino theory **3.** de-Stalinization **4.** consumer society **5.** welfare states **6.** policy of containment **7.** women's liberation movement **8.** satellite state **9.** arms race

Reviewing Key Facts

10. It was the Soviet response to the Marshall Plan. It was supposed to provide for the economic cooperation of the Eastern European states, but failed because of the inability of the Soviet Union to provide large amounts of financial aid.

11. The British government created a welfare state.

12. Imre Nagy declared Hungary a free nation and promised free elections, which might have meant the end of Communist rule.

13. The Soviets responded by sending in their military to crush movements for reforms or independence.

14. It was Simone de Beauvoir's *The Second Sex*. The book argued that, in male-dominated societies, women had been defined by their differences from men, and consequently received second-class status.

15. computer, television, jet plane

16. The U.S. discovered that Soviet ships carrying missiles were headed to Cuba. The U. S. blockaded Cuba to prevent the Soviet fleet from reaching its destination. The Soviets agreed to turn back the fleet and to remove Soviet missiles from Cuba if the U.S. promised not to invade Cuba.

CHAPTER 20 ASSESSMENT and ACTIVITIES

Using Key Terms

1. The actual purchasing power of income is called ______.
2. The idea that allowing Communist aggressors to take over one country will encourage them to take over other nations has been called the______.
3. The process of removing Stalin's influence from the Soviet government, economy, and social system was called ______.
4. A nation that is preoccupied with the desire to provide its people with material goods may be said to be a ______.
5. Nations with governments that intervene in the economy to assure a minimal standard of living for all people are said to be ______.
6. The attempt of non-Communist world powers to prevent a further spread of communism to other states was called a ______.
7. The ______ is a force that is working for greater equality and rights for women.
8. A country that was economically and politically dependent on the Soviet Union was called a ______.
9. The United States and the Soviet Union were involved in a growing ______ in which both countries built up their armies and weapons.

Reviewing Key Facts

10. **Economics** What was COMECON and why was it formed?
11. **Economics** What changes were made in the British government's role in its economic system after World War II?
12. **History** What caused the Soviet Union to invade Hungary in 1956?
13. **History** Describe what happened when satellite states tried to become independent of the Soviet Union.
14. **Culture** What book influenced the women's movement in America and Europe? What was its significance to the movement?
15. **Science and Technology** Name some inventions that altered the pace and nature of life in postwar Western society.
16. **History** What happened during the Cuban missile crisis in 1962?
17. **Culture** Name the social movements that altered American society after World War II.
18. **Government** What prevented even greater repression and terror from taking place in the Soviet Union during the early 1950s?
19. **History** What were some of the political and economic "weapons" of the Cold War?

Chapter Summary

Following World War II, two new superpowers, the United States and the Soviet Union, engaged in a Cold War that was fought around the globe.

	Conflict/Crisis	Significant Event(s)	Result(s)
Greece (1944–1949)	Civil war erupts.	Great Britain aids government forces against communism.	United States creates Truman Doctrine.
Berlin (1949)	Soviets and Western powers divide Germany.	Western powers airlift supplies to Soviet-blockaded West Berlin.	Blockade is lifted.
Korea (1950–1952)	Civil war begins when North Korea invades South Korea.	United Nations forces fight to save South Korea from communism.	United States extends military alliances around the world.
Berlin (1961)	Refugees escape from East to West Berlin.	Soviets build Berlin Wall.	Berlin Wall becomes symbol of divided Germany.
Cuba (1962)	Soviets support Castro's totalitarian regime in Cuba.	United States invades Bay of Pigs; Soviets place nuclear missiles in Cuba; United States blockades Cuba.	Soviets withdraw missiles; hotline is established between Moscow and Washington, D.C.
Vietnam (1964–1973)	Civil war erupts between North and South Vietnam.	United States intervenes to prevent North Vietnam from taking over South Vietnam.	United States withdraws from Vietnam; Vietnam is reunited by Communists.

652

17. civil rights movement, women's liberation movement

18. Stalin's death in 1953; a new series of bloody purges seemed likely if he had lived

19. Political weapons: Truman Doctrine, new alliances (NATO, SEATO, CENTO, Warsaw Pact); Berlin Wall; active military intervention; Economic weapons: Marshall Plan, COMECON, EEC

Critical Thinking

20. Answers will vary but should be supported by logical arguments. De-Stalinization did help distance Khrushchev from his repressive predecessor.

21. No; the Cold War is over and the threat of Communist expansion appears to have ended.

Writing About History

22. Answers will vary but should be supported by logical arguments. The U.S. economy was not devastated by

Self-Check Quiz

Visit the *Glencoe World History—Modern Times* Web site at wh.mt.glencoe.com and click on **Chapter 20–Self-Check Quiz** to prepare for the Chapter Test.

Critical Thinking

20. **Analyzing** How did de-Stalinization help Khrushchev gain control of the Soviet government?
21. **Explaining** Is containment an important or pressing issue in American foreign policy today? Explain your reasoning.

Writing About History

22. **Expository Writing** In an essay, identify and explain possible reasons for the comparatively slow growth of social benefits provided to Americans, compared to the rapid growth of these programs in Europe, after World War II.

Analyzing Sources

Read the following excerpt from Solzhenitsyn's *One Day in the Life of Ivan Denisovich* in which prisoners march from the prison camp to a work project through temperatures of seventeen degrees below zero:

> "There were escort guards all over the place, . . . their machine guns sticking out and pointed right at your face. And there were guards with gray dogs."

23. Why might Soviets identify with this story?
24. Why did Khrushchev allow this book to be published?

Applying Technology Skills

25. **Using the Internet** Search the Internet for information about technological inventions since World War II that have greatly affected our lives. Use a search engine to focus your search. Create a time line including pictures and illustrations of the inventions you researched.

Making Decisions

26. The Cuban missile crisis developed out of a tense power struggle between two nuclear powers. What decisions created the crisis? What else might have been done?

Analyzing Maps and Charts

Using the map above, answer the following questions.

27. How many miles did the blockade zone of Cuba extend from west to east?

NATIONAL GEOGRAPHIC **Cuban Missile Crisis, 1962**

28. Why was the United States so concerned that the Soviets were placing missiles in Cuba? What other islands fall within the blockade zone?

The Princeton Review

Standardized Test Practice

Directions: Use the quote *and* your knowledge of world history to answer the following question.

> "And even today woman is heavily handicapped, though her situation is beginning to change. Almost nowhere is her legal status the same as man's, and frequently it is much to her disadvantage. Even when her rights are legally recognized in the abstract, long-standing custom prevents their full expression . . . ."
>
> **—*The Second Sex,* Simone de Beauvoir**

Simone de Beauvoir's book, *The Second Sex,* was published in 1949. Her book was influential because it

A helped women gain the right to vote.
B contributed to a women's movement in the 1950s and 1960s.
C greatly increased the number of married women in the labor force.
D influenced and shaped the student protest movement.

Test-Taking Tip: A date can be an important clue. When a question contains a date, think about major events that occurred during or around that time. Then eliminate answer choices that do not reflect that history.

Have students visit the Web site at wh.mt.glencoe.com to review Chapter 20 and take the Self-Check Quiz.

and Moscow. Answers for the second question will vary but should be supported by facts and logical arguments.

Analyzing Maps and Charts

27. The blockade zone extended approximately 300 miles (500 km).

28. Cuba is very close to the United States; Bahamas, Haiti, Dominican Republic, Puerto Rico, Jamaica

Standardized Test Practice

Answer: B
Answer Explanation: Choice B is discussing the same subject as the quote.

Bonus Question ?

Ask: Why did the successful Soviet invasion of Hungary in 1956 make it more difficult for the Soviet Union to influence nations in other parts of the world? *(The Soviet Union demonstrated that it would not tolerate any alternative forms of leadership and control in the nations it dominated.)*

World War II, while the economies of Europe were. Most Americans were not in need of help, while most Europeans were.

Analyzing Sources

23. It was a symbol of the suffering they had endured under Stalin.

24. It was part of his plan to undo some of the worst features of Stalin's regime.

Applying Technology Skills

25. Students will create a time line.

Making Decisions

26. President Kennedy's decision to support the Bay of Pigs invasion led to the Soviet Union's decision to place missiles in Cuba. Then Kennedy's decision to keep missiles out of Cuba nearly led to a confrontation between the U.S. and the U.S.S.R. Instead, the incident led to the creation of a hotline between Washington

Chapter 21 Resources

Timesaving Tools

TeacherWorks™ All-In-One Planner and Resource Center

- **Interactive Teacher Edition** Access your Teacher Wraparound Edition and your classroom resources with a few easy clicks.
- **Interactive Lesson Planner** Planning has never been easier! Organize your week, month, semester, or year with all the lesson helps you need to make teaching creative, timely, and relevant.

Use Glencoe's **Presentation Plus!** multimedia teacher tool to easily present dynamic lessons that visually excite your students. Using Microsoft PowerPoint® you can customize the presentations to create your own personalized lessons.

Teaching Transparencies

Graphic Organizer Student Activity 21 Transparency

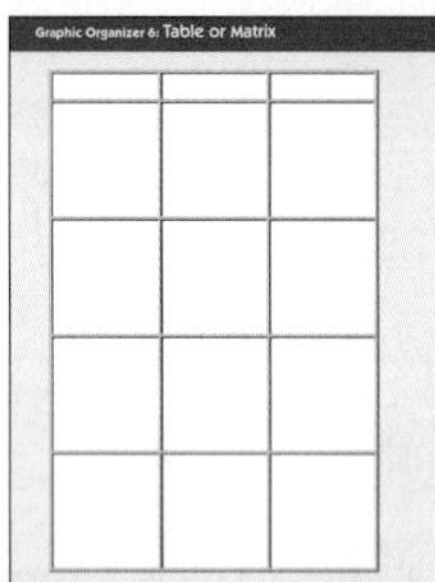

Chapter Transparency 21

Map Overlay Transparency 21

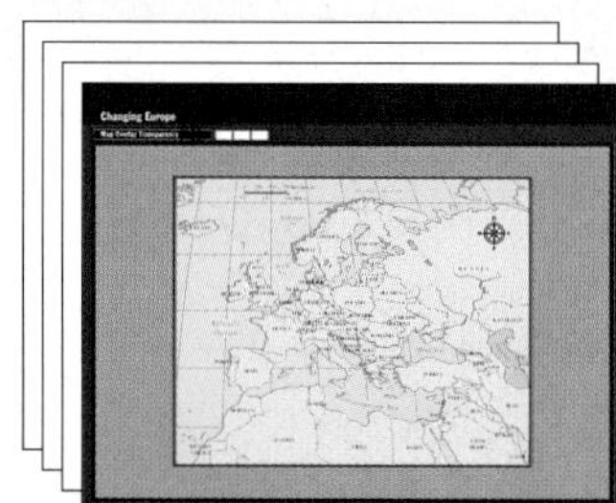

Application and Enrichment

Enrichment Activity 21

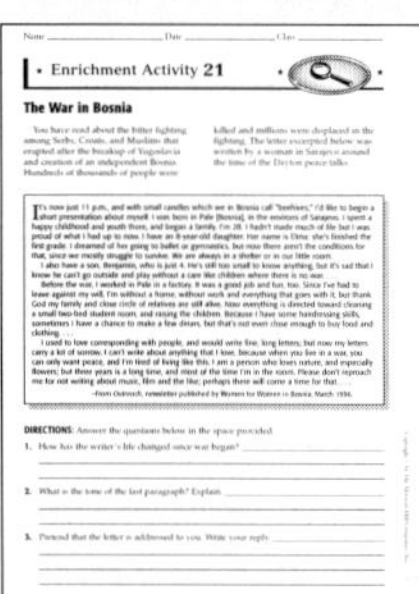

Primary Source Reading 21

History Simulation Activity 21

Historical Significance Activity 21

Cooperative Learning Activity 21

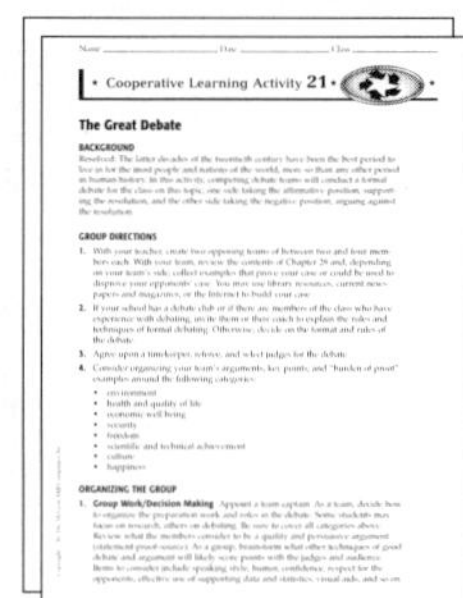

A&E HOME VIDEO.

Biography®

THE HISTORY CHANNEL.

The following videotape program is available from Glencoe as a supplement to Chapter 21:

- **Men in Space: From Goddard to Armstrong** (ISBN 1–56501–037–X)

To order, call Glencoe at 1–800–334–7344. To find classroom resources to accompany this video, check the following home pages:
A&E Television: www.aande.com
The History Channel: www.historychannel.com

Chapter 21 Resources

Review and Reinforcement

Linking Past and Present Activity 21

Time Line Activity 21

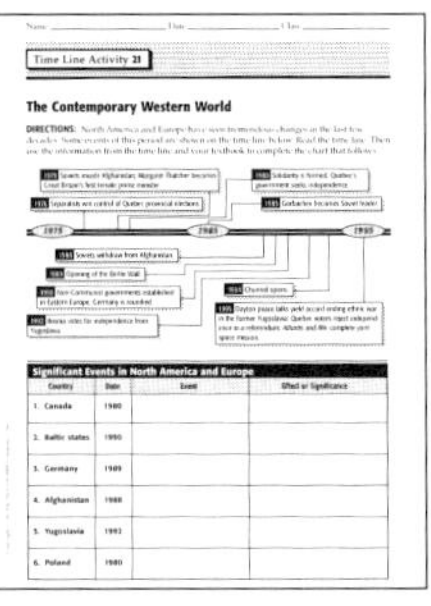

Reteaching Activity 21

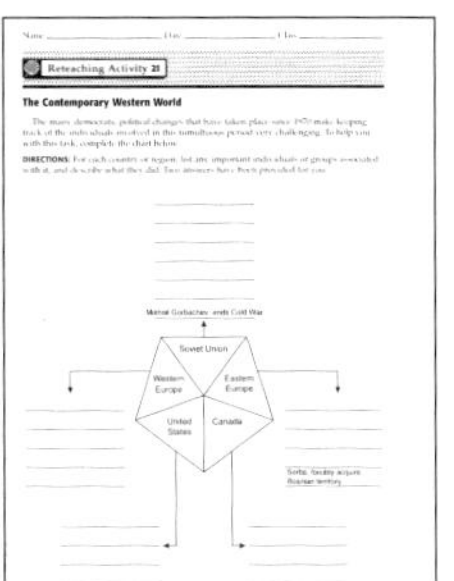

Vocabulary Activity 21

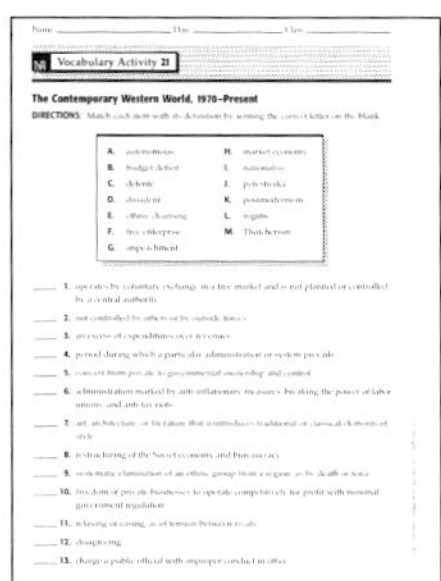

Critical Thinking Skills Activity 21

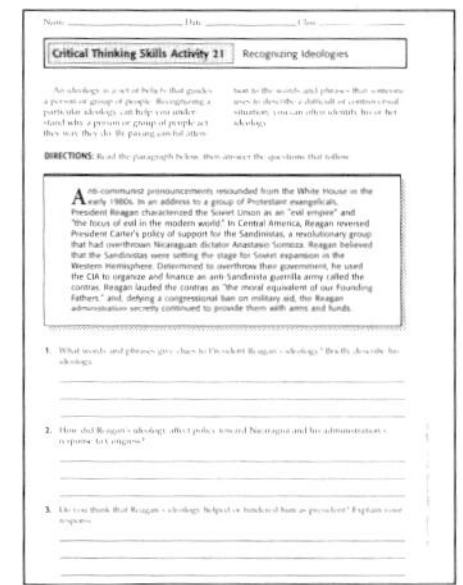

Assessment and Evaluation

Chapter 21 Test Form A

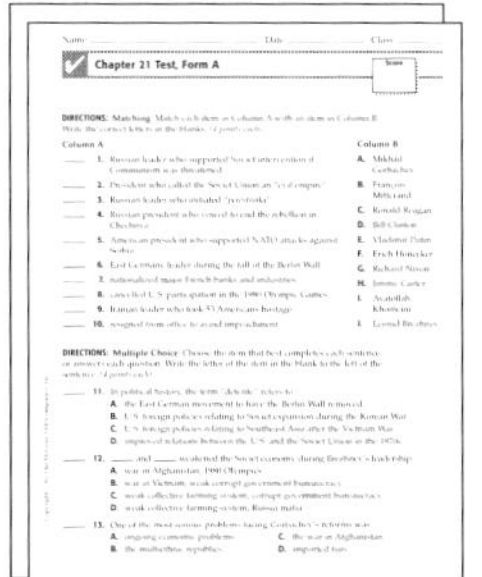

Chapter 21 Test Form B

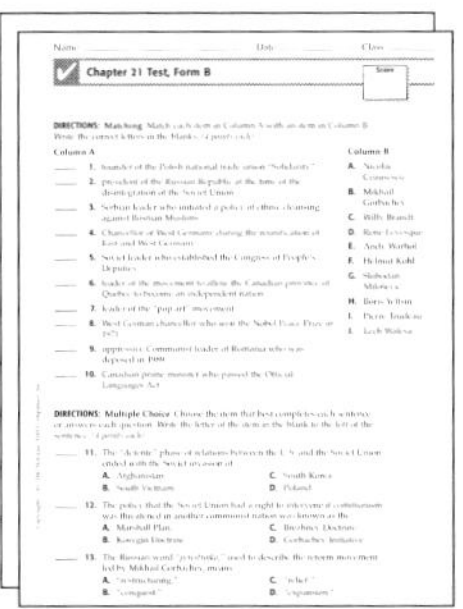

Performance Assessment Activity 21

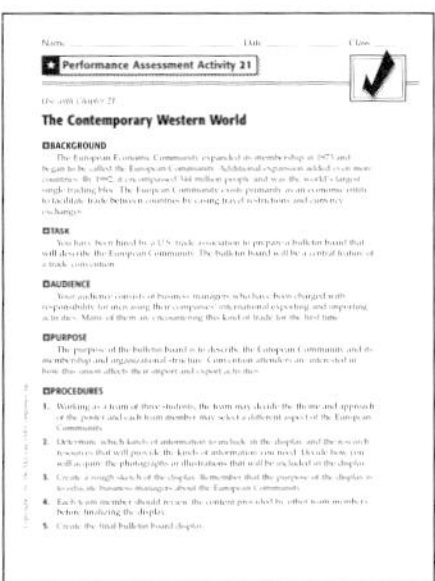

ExamView® Pro Testmaker CD-ROM

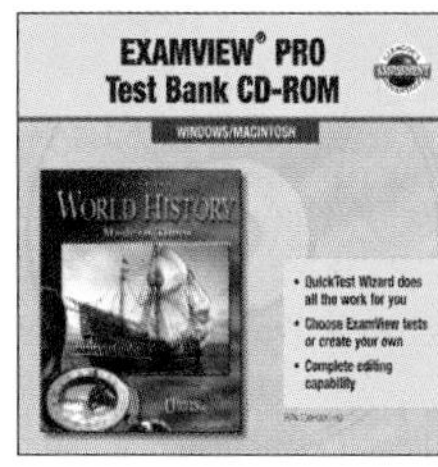

Standardized Test Skills Practice Workbook Activity 21

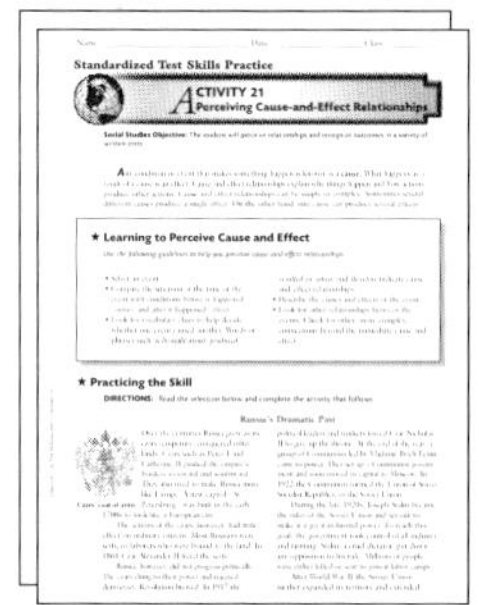

Interdisciplinary Activities

Mapping History Activity 21

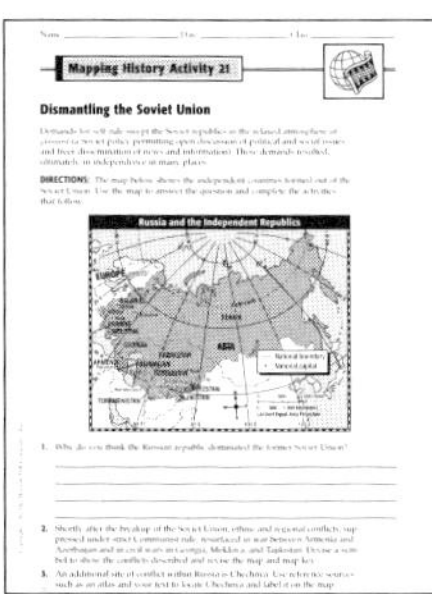

World Art and Music Activity 21

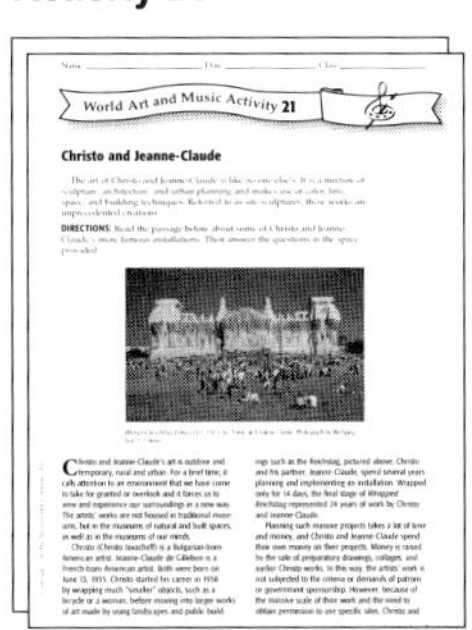

History and Geography Activity 21

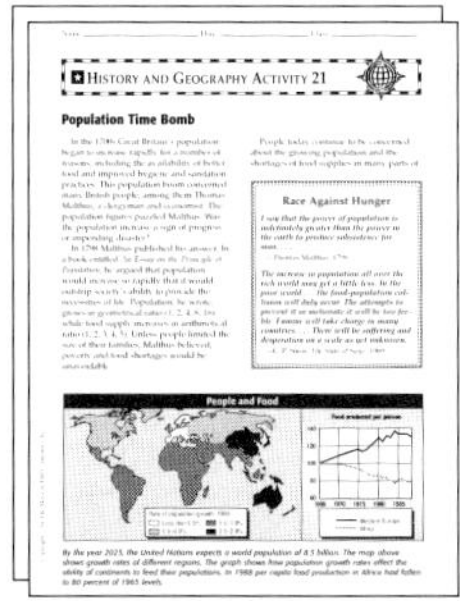

People in World History Activity 21

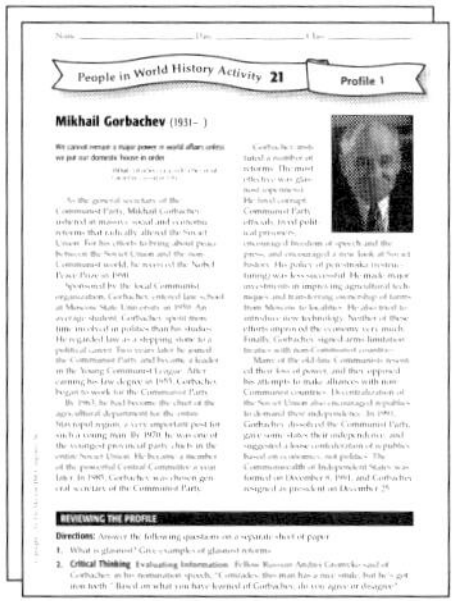

Multimedia

- Vocabulary PuzzleMaker CD-ROM
- Interactive Tutor Self-Assessment CD-ROM
- ExamView® Pro Testmaker CD-ROM
- Audio Program
- World History Primary Source Document Library CD-ROM
- MindJogger Videoquiz
- Presentation Plus! CD-ROM
- TeacherWorks CD-ROM
- Interactive Student Edition CD-ROM
- The World History—Modern Times Video Program

Spanish Resources

The following Spanish language materials are available in the Spanish Resources Binder:

- Spanish Guided Reading Activities
- Spanish Reteaching Activities
- Spanish Quizzes and Tests
- Spanish Vocabulary Activities
- Spanish Summaries

Chapter 21 Resources

SECTION RESOURCES

Daily Objectives	Reproducible Resources	Multimedia Resources
SECTION 1 **Decline of the Soviet Union** 1. Discuss how the Cold War ended after leadership changed in the Soviet Union. 2. Identify policies of Gorbachev that contributed to the disintegration of the Soviet Union. 3. Explain how conversion from a socialist to a free-market economy created many problems in the former Soviet states.	Reproducible Lesson Plan 21–1 Daily Lecture and Discussion Notes 21–1 Guided Reading Activity 21–1* Section Quiz 21–1* Reading Essentials and Study Guide 21–1	Daily Focus Skills Transparency 21–1 Interactive Tutor Self-Assessment CD-ROM ExamView® Pro Testmaker CD-ROM Presentation Plus! CD-ROM
SECTION 2 **Eastern Europe** 1. Describe Gorbachev's policy of not giving military support to Communist governments and how it created the opportunity for revolution. 2. Characterize the massive demonstrations that peacefully ended some Communist regimes and the violence that ended others.	Reproducible Lesson Plan 21–2 Daily Lecture and Discussion Notes 21–2 Guided Reading Activity 21–2* Section Quiz 21–2* Reading Essentials and Study Guide 21–2	Daily Focus Skills Transparency 21–2 Interactive Tutor Self-Assessment CD-ROM ExamView® Pro Testmaker CD-ROM Presentation Plus! CD-ROM
SECTION 3 **Europe and North America** 1. Discuss how Western European nations moved to unite their economies after 1970. 2. Identify the domestic problems that arose in the United States, Great Britain, France, Germany, and Canada.	Reproducible Lesson Plan 21–3 Daily Lecture and Discussion Notes 21–3 Guided Reading Activity 21–3* Section Quiz 21–3* Reading Essentials and Study Guide 21–3	Daily Focus Skills Transparency 21–3 Interactive Tutor Self-Assessment CD-ROM ExamView® Pro Testmaker CD-ROM Presentation Plus! CD-ROM
SECTION 4 **Western Society and Culture** 1. Relate how technological and scientific advances have created a global society. 2. Discuss artistic trends that reflect how the emerging global society led to a blending of cultural forms and ideas.	Reproducible Lesson Plan 21–4 Daily Lecture and Discussion Notes 21–4 Guided Reading Activity 21–4* Section Quiz 21–4* Reteaching Activity 21* Reading Essentials and Study Guide 21–4	Daily Focus Skills Transparency 21–4 Interactive Tutor Self-Assessment CD-ROM ExamView® Pro Testmaker CD-ROM Presentation Plus! CD-ROM

0:00 **OUT OF TIME?**
Assign the Chapter 21 **Reading Essentials and Study Guide.**

*Also Available in Spanish

 Blackline Master  Transparency  CD-ROM  DVD

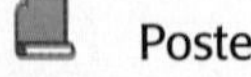 Poster  Music Program 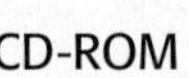 Audio Program  Videocassette

Chapter 21 Resources

NATIONAL GEOGRAPHIC Teacher's Corner

ADDITIONAL NATIONAL GEOGRAPHIC SOCIETY PRODUCTS

To order the following, call National Geographic at 1-800-368-2728:

- *Voices of Leningrad* (Video)
- *The Rise and Fall of the Soviet Union* (Video)

NGS ONLINE

Access National Geographic's new dynamic MapMachine Web site and other geography resources at:
www.nationalgeographic.com
www.nationalgeographic.com/maps

WORLD HISTORY Online

Use our Web site for additional resources. All essential content is covered in the Student Edition.

You and your students can visit www.wh.mt.glencoe.com, the Web site companion to *Glencoe World History—Modern Times.* This innovative integration of electronic and print media offers your students a wealth of opportunities. The student text directs students to the Web site for the following options:

- **Chapter Overviews**
- **Self-Check Quizzes**
- **Student Web Activities**
- **Textbook Updates**

Answers to the Student Web Activities are provided for you in the **Web Activity Lesson Plans.** Additional Web resources and Interactive Tutor Puzzles are also available.

KEY TO ABILITY LEVELS

Teaching strategies have been coded.

L1 BASIC activities for all students
L2 AVERAGE activities for average to above-average students
L3 CHALLENGING activities for above-average students
ELL ENGLISH LANGUAGE LEARNER activities

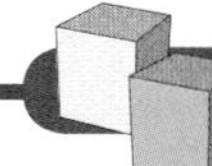

Block Schedule

Activities that are suited to use within the block scheduling framework are identified by: 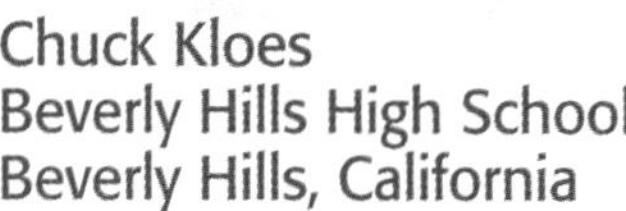

From the Classroom of...

Chuck Kloes
Beverly Hills High School
Beverly Hills, California

The Irish Question: A Solution Satisfactory to Whom?

Prepare "point of view" sheets for both sides of the Irish question—Sheet A listing four to five arguments in support of granting home rule to all of Ireland, and Sheet B listing four to five arguments in support of maintaining British control over Northern Ireland. Organize the class into A and B groups to debate the question and pass out the sheets.

Give the groups 15 minutes to study the sheets, collect data, and prepare their presentations. Have each group select two students to be spokespersons, and you can act as moderator. After the debate, hold a class discussion about what students learned from the exercise.

Performance Assessment

Refer to Activity 21 in the Performance Assessment Activities and Rubrics booklet.

The Impact Today

Explain to students that most of the topics in this chapter are still covered in current newspapers, magazines, and on television. Ask students to bring in current events that relate to the events and people discussed in this chapter.

GLENCOE TECHNOLOGY

The World History—Modern Times Video Program

To learn more about democracy in Poland, students can view the Chapter 21 video, "Solidarity," from **The World History—Modern Times Video Program.**

MindJogger Videoquiz

Use the **MindJogger Videoquiz** to preview Chapter 21 content.

Available in VHS.

CHAPTER 21

The Contemporary Western World

1970–Present

Key Events

As you read this chapter, look for the key events in the development of the contemporary Western world.

- *Political and social changes led to the end of the Cold War and the fall of communism in Eastern Europe and the Soviet Union.*
- *Economic challenges helped bring about and accompanied these sweeping political and social changes.*
- *Society and culture reflected these changes with the advent of the women's movement, the growth of technology, and a rise in terrorism.*

The Impact Today

The events that occurred during this time period still impact our lives today.

- *Energy prices continue to climb as world oil supplies diminish, causing economic challenges for oil-dependent nations.*
- *The computer and the Internet contribute to the creation of a global society.*
- *Film, television, music, and advertising spread the American way of life throughout the world.*

World History—Modern Times Video *The Chapter 21 video, "Solidarity," chronicles the history of the movement for democracy in Poland.*

1970 | 1974 | 1978 | 1982 | 1986

1970s
Equal Pay and Sex Discrimination Acts passed in United States

1980
Lech Walesa organizes trade union Solidarity in Poland

1987
Soviet Union and United States sign INF Treaty

Women's liberation march

654

TWO-MINUTE LESSON LAUNCHER

Explain to students that this chapter deals with contemporary issues that very much affect their lives today. Ask students to brainstorm a list of significant world events that occurred during their lifetime. What did they learn from a particular event? How did it affect their lives? Also, ask students to brainstorm a list of the challenges that face the world today. They might consider threats to the environment; the widening gap between rich and poor; terrorism; depletion of natural resources; civil rights abuses; the search for just political systems. What are the causes of these problems? How do they affect the students personally? What possible solutions do students see? Use their responses to introduce the contemporary issues discussed in this chapter.

Introducing
CHAPTER 21

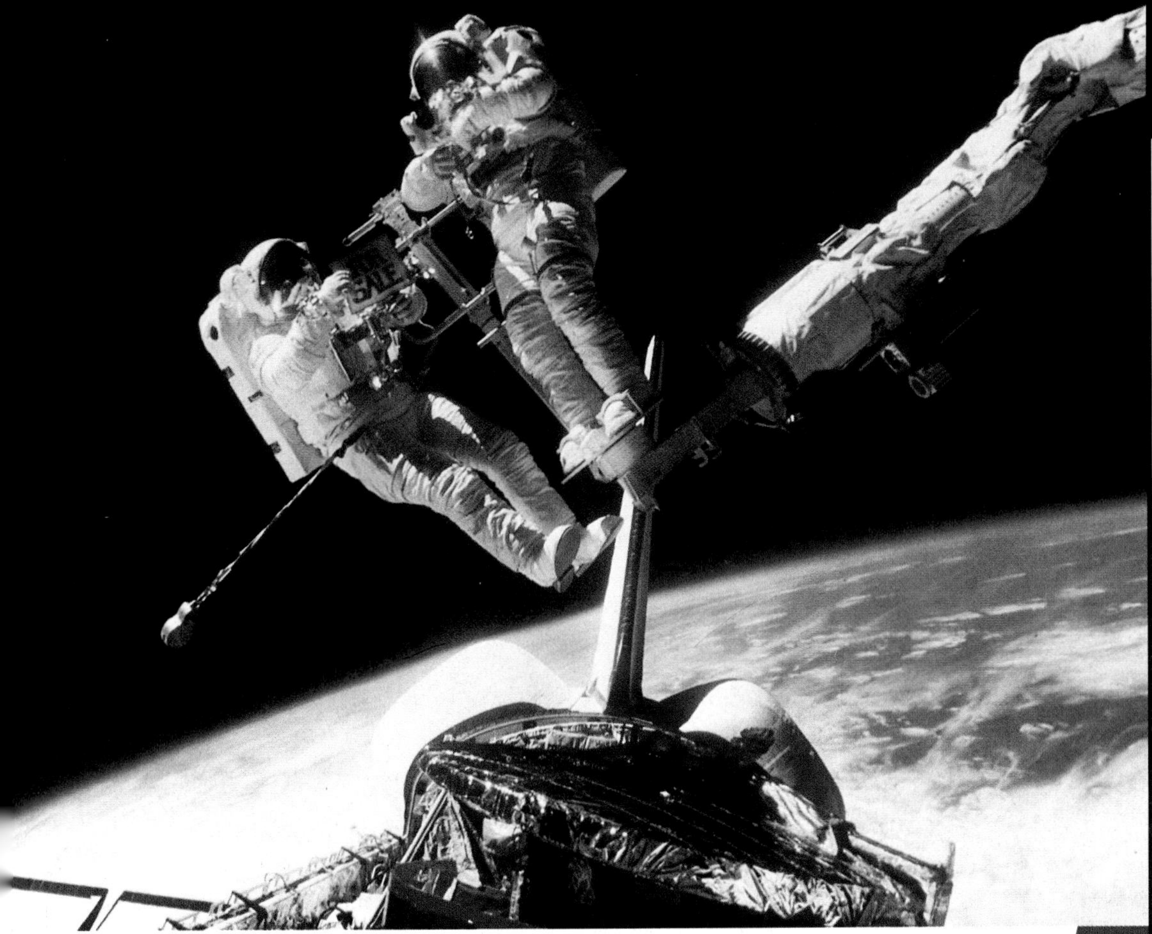

Advances in space exploration have been made possible by new technology.

The Berlin Wall comes down.

1989 Political upheaval and revolution occur in Eastern Europe; Berlin Wall falls

1990 Germany reunified

1991 Soviet Union is dissolved

2001 Terrorists attack World Trade Center and Pentagon in the United States

2002 Euro becomes common currency of several Western European nations

1990 *1994* *1998* *2002* *2006*

Euro coin

HISTORY Online

Chapter Overview
Visit the *Glencoe World History—Modern Times* Web site at wh.mt.glencoe.com and click on **Chapter 21 – Chapter Overview** to preview chapter information.

655

MORE ABOUT THE ART

Space Exploration and Earth New technology has helped advance space exploration. In turn, journeys into space have helped people to view the earth as a single unit with a shared environment. Space has become a laboratory in which scientists can assess what is happening to our planet. Spacecraft can orbit the earth and photograph areas of the planet to monitor changes. Using the unique perspective from space, scientists hope to be able to "watch the planet breathe" and to study global change with the aim of preventing more damage to the earth.

Chapter Objectives

After studying this chapter, students should be able to:

1. list and explain upheavals in the Soviet Union that led to its disintegration;
2. identify and explain events that led to the reunification of Germany;
3. identify and explain changes that took place in Eastern Europe after the fall of communism;
4. describe the unification of Western European economies;
5. identify and explain domestic events that affected Great Britain, the United States, and Canada;
6. describe the impact of terrorism on society;
7. identify and explain recent changes in women's roles, art, science and technology, and religion;
8. describe popular culture.

HISTORY Online

Chapter Overview
Introduce students to chapter content and key terms by having them access **Chapter Overview 21** at wh.mt.glencoe.com.

As students read the chapter, ask them to identify the four major events involving the Soviet Union and Eastern Europe that occurred within a span of five years. Why do they think these things happened in the order they did and with such rapid succession? L2

Introducing

A Story That Matters

Depending on the ability levels of your students, select from the following questions to reinforce the reading of *A Story That Matters.*

- Which superpower leader wanted the Berlin Wall to come down? *(Ronald Reagan)* Which leader thought it should remain? *(Mikhail Gorbachev)*
- Did the Berlin Wall prevent East Germans from escaping? *(No, tens of thousands fled.)*
- What did the wall symbolize? *(the Cold War)*
- What one person, event, or factor was most responsible for the wall coming down? *(Answers will vary. You may want to ask the question before assigning the chapter, telling students that you will want their answers after they complete the chapter.)*

About the Art

The Brandenburg Gate has always had symbolic significance for the people of Germany. It was built in 1791 as a "gate of peace," and it could only be used by Prussian royalty. When the Nazis took over and the avenue became a favorite parade route of Hitler, the gate became a symbol of fascism. In 1961, the gate was closed and became a symbol of division. With the tearing down of the Berlin Wall, the gate became a symbol of German reunification and the fall of communism.

CHAPTER PREVIEW

A Story That Matters

Near Berlin's Brandenburg Gate in 1990, crowds of people celebrate the reunification of Germany.

"Tear Down This Wall"

In 1988, the American president, Ronald Reagan, traveled to West Berlin. Facing the Berlin Wall, he challenged Mikhail Gorbachev, leader of the Soviet bloc, to "tear down this wall." During his own visit to West Germany a year later, Gorbachev responded, "The wall could disappear once the conditions that generated the need for it disappear. I do not see much of a problem here."

East Germany's Communist leaders, however, did see a problem, and they refused to remove the wall. In the summer of 1989, tens of thousands of East Germans fled their country while hundreds of thousands took to the streets to demand the resignation of the hard-line Communist leader, Erich Honecker.

Honecker finally relented. On November 9, 1989, a new East German government opened the wall and allowed its citizens to travel freely between West and East Berlin. The next day, government workers began to knock down the wall. They were soon joined by thousands of West and East Berliners who used sledgehammers and crowbars to rip apart the Cold War symbol.

Germans were overcome with joy. Many danced on the wall while orchestras played in the streets. Churches, theaters, and shops remained open day and night in West Germany as East Germans took advantage of their new freedom to travel. In 1990, West and East Germany became a single nation, and Berlin was once again the capital of Germany.

Why It Matters

In 1970, after more than two decades of the Cold War, the division of Europe between West and East seemed well established to most Europeans. A prosperous Western Europe that was allied to the United States stood opposed to a still-struggling Eastern Europe that remained largely subject to the Soviet Union. However, within 20 years, a revolutionary upheaval in the Soviet Union and Eastern Europe brought an end to the Cold War and the long-standing division of postwar Europe.

History and You Research contemporary Berlin. Use sources ranging from academic histories to travel guides. Make a list of the ways the East/West split still affects Berlin today. Which of these reminders of the past did you expect, and which surprised you? Why?

HISTORY AND YOU

It will be hard for some students to grasp the enormous impact of the collapse of the Soviet Union on world tensions and interrelations. Allow two weeks to complete the following activity that simulates how the Cold War contest between the superpowers divided the world into two camps. Arrange a method of dividing the class into two by a wall (to simulate the Berlin Wall). If possible, the wall should prevent students from seeing to the other side. In class, give privileges and rewards to only one side. At the end of the time, ask students how they felt about the people on the "other side." Remind them that the suspicion and doubt raised by this demonstration was nothing compared to the real distrust that grew between peoples of the West and the Soviet world.

SECTION 1 Decline of the Soviet Union

Guide to Reading

Main Ideas
- The Cold War ended after leadership changed in the Soviet Union.
- Gorbachev's policies contributed to the disintegration of the Soviet Union.
- Conversion from a socialist to a free-market economy has created many problems in the former Soviet states.

Key Terms
détente, dissident, perestroika

People to Identify
Ronald Reagan, Mikhail Gorbachev, Leonid Brezhnev, Boris Yeltsin, Vladimir Putin

Places to Locate
Afghanistan, Ukraine, Belarus

Preview Questions
1. How and why did the Cold War end?
2. What problems arose when the Soviet Union disintegrated?

Reading Strategy
Compare and Contrast Create a chart like the one below comparing the policies of Brezhnev and Gorbachev.

	Leonid Brezhnev	Mikhail Gorbachev
Foreign Policy		
Economic Policy		
Military Policy		
Personal Policy		

Preview of Events

1985 · 1988 · 1991 · 1994 · 1997 · 2000

- **1985** Mikhail Gorbachev assumes leadership of Soviet Union
- **1988** Communist Party conference initiates political reforms
- **1991** Boris Yeltsin becomes president of Russia
- **2000** Ex-KGB agent Vladimir Putin becomes president of Russia

Voices from the Past

Mikhail Gorbachev

In his book *Perestroika,* Soviet leader Mikhail Gorbachev wrote:

> ❝There is a great thirst for mutual understanding and mutual communication in the world. It is felt among politicians, it is gaining momentum among the intelligentsia, representatives of culture, and the public at large. And if the Russian word 'perestroika' has easily entered the international lexicon [vocabulary], this is due to more than just interest in what is going on in the Soviet Union. Now the whole world needs restructuring, i.e., progressive development, a fundamental change . . . I believe that more and more people will come to realize that through RESTRUCTURING in the broad sense of the word, the integrity of the world will be enhanced.❞
>
> —***Perestroika,* 1987**

After Mikhail Gorbachev came to power in 1985, the Soviet Union began to make changes in its foreign policy, and the Cold War rapidly came to an end.

From Cold War to Post-Cold War

By the 1970s, American-Soviet relations had entered a new phase, known as **détente,** which was marked by a relaxation of tensions and improved relations between the two superpowers. Grain and consumer goods were sold to the Soviet Union. Beginning in 1979, however, the apparent collapse of détente began a new period of East-West confrontation.

1 FOCUS

Section Overview

This section discusses the end of the Cold War and the Soviet Union.

BELLRINGER
Skillbuilder Activity

 Project transparency and have students answer questions.

 Available as a blackline master.

Daily Focus Skills Transparency 21–1

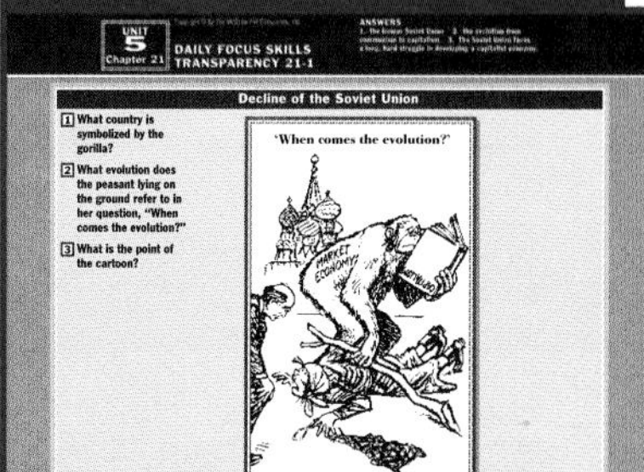

Guide to Reading

Answers To Graphic: Brezhnev: Foreign: intervention in Communist countries; Economic: heavy industry, collective farming; Military: invasion of Afghanistan; Political: dissidents punished; Gorbachev: Foreign: nonintervention; Economic: limited free enterprise; Military: nuclear arms treaty; Political: new Soviet parliament

Preteaching Vocabulary: Have students research the Latin origin of *dissident* and the French origin of *détente. (dissident: to sit apart; détente: to release hold)* **L1**

SECTION RESOURCES

Reproducible Masters
- Reproducible Lesson Plan 21–1
- Daily Lecture and Discussion Notes 21–1
- Guided Reading Activity 21–1
- Section Quiz 21–1
- Reading Essentials and Study Guide 21–1

Transparencies
- Daily Focus Skills Transparency 21–1

Multimedia
- Interactive Tutor Self-Assessment CD-ROM
- ExamView® Pro Testmaker CD-ROM
- Presentation Plus! CD-ROM

2 TEACH

Reading Check

Answer: Gorbachev became leader of the Soviet Union; he refused military support to Eastern European Communist countries.

TURNING POINT

How did Gorbachev's political restructuring in the Soviet Union lead to the movements for independence in Soviet Republics? *(He allowed non-Communist parties to form and eliminated the guarantee that the Communist Party would have a "leading role" in government.)* L1

Daily Lecture and Discussion Notes 21–1

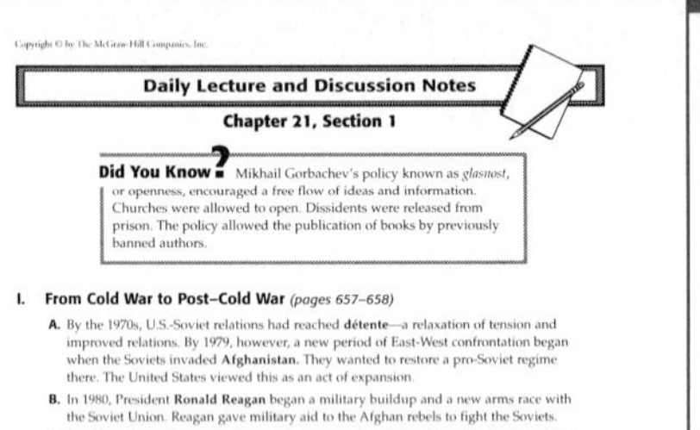

Daily Lecture and Discussion Notes

Chapter 21, Section 1

Did You Know? Mikhail Gorbachev's policy known as *glasnost*, or openness, encouraged a free flow of ideas and information. Churches were allowed to open. Dissidents were released from prison. The policy allowed the publication of books by previously banned authors.

I. **From Cold War to Post–Cold War** *(pages 657–658)*

A. By the 1970s, U.S.-Soviet relations had reached **détente**—a relaxation of tension and improved relations. By 1979, however, a new period of East-West confrontation began when the Soviets invaded **Afghanistan.** They wanted to restore a pro-Soviet regime there. The United States viewed this as an act of expansion.

B. In 1980, President **Ronald Reagan** began a military buildup and a new arms race with the Soviet Union. Reagan gave military aid to the Afghan rebels to fight the Soviets.

C. In 1985, **Mikhail Gorbachev** became the leader of the Soviet Union. His willingness to rethink Soviet foreign policy led to a dramatic end to the Cold War. In 1987 Gorbachev made an agreement with the United States—the Intermediate-range Nuclear Force (INF) Treaty—to eliminate intermediate-range nuclear missiles.

D. Gorbachev changed Soviet policy by stopping military support to Communist govern-

Enrich

In the nineteenth century, Alexis de Toqueville predicted that one day the United States and Russia would dominate the world as rivals. Have students analyze the present world situation and determine if they believe that the two countries are still rivals. L2

The Cold War Intensifies Détente received a major setback in 1979, when the Soviet Union invaded **Afghanistan.** The Soviet Union wanted to restore a pro-Soviet regime there, which the United States viewed as an act of expansion. President Jimmy Carter canceled American participation in the 1980 Olympic Games to be held in Moscow and placed an embargo on the shipment of American grain to the Soviets.

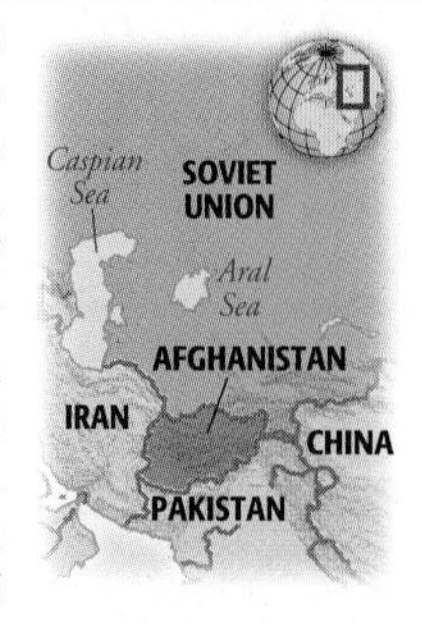

The Cold War further intensified when **Ronald Reagan** was elected president in 1980. Calling the Soviet Union an "evil empire," Reagan began a military buildup and a new arms race. Reagan also gave military aid to the Afghan rebels, in order to maintain a war in Afghanistan that the Soviet Union could not win.

End of the Cold War The accession of **Mikhail Gorbachev** (GAWR•buh•CHAWF) to power in the Soviet Union in 1985 eventually brought a dramatic end to the Cold War. Gorbachev's "New Thinking"—his willingness to rethink Soviet foreign policy—led to stunning changes.

Gorbachev made an agreement with the United States in 1987 (the Intermediate-range Nuclear Force [INF] Treaty) to eliminate intermediate-range nuclear weapons. Both sides had reasons to slow down the expensive arms race. Gorbachev hoped to make far-reaching economic and internal reforms. As its national debt tripled, the United States had moved from being a creditor nation (a country that exports more than it imports), to being the world's biggest debtor nation. By 1990, both countries knew that their large military budgets would make it difficult for them to solve their domestic problems.

In another policy change, Gorbachev stopped giving Soviet military support to Communist governments in Eastern Europe. This opened the door to the overthrow of Communist regimes in these countries. A mostly peaceful revolutionary movement swept through Eastern Europe in 1989. The reunification of Germany on October 3, 1990, was a powerful symbol of the end of the Cold War. In 1991, the Soviet Union was dissolved. Renewal of the rivalry between the two superpowers was now almost impossible.

Reading Check **Summarizing** What events immediately preceded the end of the Cold War?

Upheaval in the Soviet Union

TURNING POINT **You will learn how movements for independence caused the breakup of the Soviet Union.**

Between 1964 and 1982, drastic change in the Soviet Union had seemed highly unlikely. What happened to create such a dramatic turnaround in such a short time?

The Brezhnev Era When Nikita Khrushchev was removed from office in 1964, two men, Alexei Kosygin and **Leonid Brezhnev** (BREHZH•NEFF), replaced him. Brezhnev emerged as the dominant leader in the 1970s. He was determined to keep Eastern Europe in Communist hands and was uninterested in reform. Brezhnev insisted on the right of the Soviet Union to intervene if communism was threatened in another Communist state (known as the **Brezhnev Doctrine**).

At the same time, Brezhnev benefited from the more relaxed atmosphere associated with détente. The Soviet Union was roughly equal to the United States in nuclear arms. Its leaders thus felt secure and were willing to relax their authoritarian rule. Under Brezhnev, the regime allowed more access to Western styles of music, dress, and art. However, **dissidents**—those who spoke out against the regime—were still punished.

In his economic policies, Brezhnev continued to emphasize heavy industry. Two problems, however, weakened the Soviet economy. The government's central planning led to a huge, complex bureaucracy that discouraged efficiency and led to indifference. Moreover, collective farmers had no incentive to work hard. Many preferred working their own small private plots to laboring in the collective work brigades.

By the 1970s, the Communist ruling class in the Soviet Union had become complacent and corrupt. Party and state leaders—as well as leaders of the army and secret police (KGB)— enjoyed a high standard of living. Brezhnev was unwilling to tamper with the party leadership and state bureaucracy, regardless of the inefficiency and corruption that the system encouraged.

By 1980, the Soviet Union was seriously ailing, with a declining economy, a rise in infant mortality rates, a dramatic surge in alcoholism, and poor working conditions. Many felt the system was in trouble. Within the Communist Party, a small group of reformers emerged. One of these was Mikhail Gorbachev. A new era began in March 1985 when party leaders chose him to lead the Soviet Union.

MEETING INDIVIDUAL NEEDS

Visual/Auditory To help students understand the differences between Soviet leaders, use poster board and write the names Brezhnev, Gorbachev, and Yeltsin across the top. Then give groups of students index cards with characteristics of leadership during each leader's ruling period written on them. The following characteristics/events should be used: Brezhnev: emphasized industry, complex bureaucracy, bad harvests/farm problems, poor working conditions; Gorbachev: perestroika, market economy, glasnost, congress, began complete independence; Yeltsin: independent states, free market economy, organized crime. Have students glue or tack index cards under the name of the correct leader. L1

Breakup of the Soviet Union, 1991

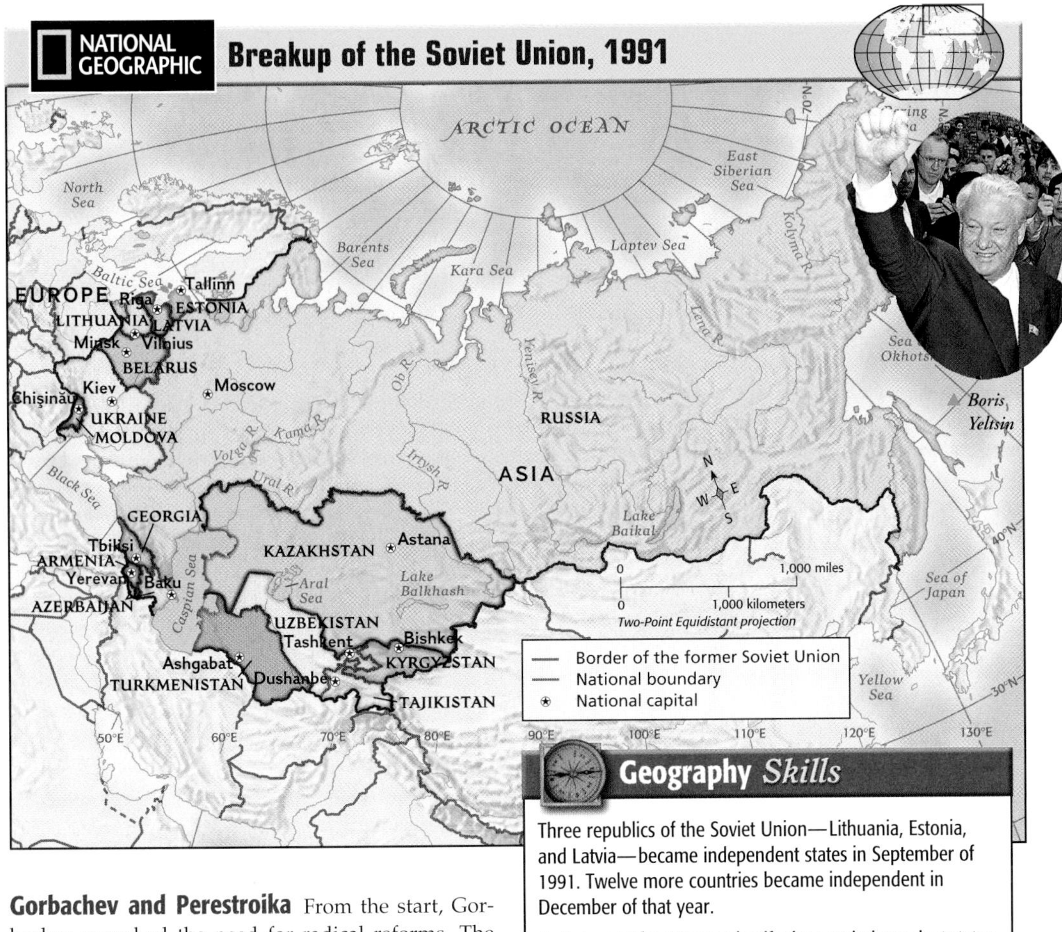

Geography *Skills*

Three republics of the Soviet Union—Lithuania, Estonia, and Latvia—became independent states in September of 1991. Twelve more countries became independent in December of that year.

1. **Interpreting Maps** Identify the new independent states.
2. **Applying Geography Skills** Why would trade become more difficult for Russia after the breakup?

Gorbachev and Perestroika From the start, Gorbachev preached the need for radical reforms. The basis of these reforms was perestroika (PEHR•uh•STROY•kuh) or restructuring. At first, this meant restructuring economic policy. Gorbachev wanted to start a market economy, where consumers influence what is produced. This economy would have limited free enterprise (based on private ownership of businesses) and some private property. Soon, however, Gorbachev realized that an attempt to reform the economy without political reform would be doomed to failure.

At the Communist Party conference in 1988, Gorbachev established a new Soviet parliament, the Congress of People's Deputies, whose members were to be elected. This parliament met in 1989—the first such meeting in Russia since 1918. Early in 1990, Gorbachev decreed that non-Communist political parties could organize. He also did away with a constitutional provision that guaranteed the Communist Party a "leading role" in government.

At the same time, Gorbachev strengthened his power by creating a new state presidency. The position of first secretary of the party (Gorbachev's position) had been the most important post in the Soviet Union. However, as the Communist Party became less closely tied to the state, the position of first secretary carried less power. In March 1990, Gorbachev became the Soviet Union's first (and last) president.

The End of the Soviet Union One of Gorbachev's most serious problems was the multiethnic nature of the Soviet Union. It included 92 nationalities and 112 different languages. The iron hand of the Communist Party, centered in Moscow, had kept centuries-old ethnic tensions contained.

Geography *Skills*

Answers:

1. Belarus, Ukraine, Moldova, Georgia, Turkmenistan, Armenia, Azerbaijan, Tajikistan, Kyrgyzstan, Uzbekistan, Kazakhstan, Russia
2. lost resources and access to water routes

Guided Reading Activity 21-1

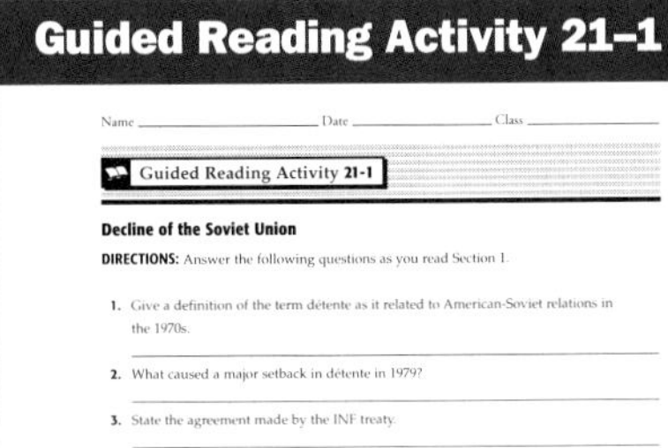
Name ______ Date ______ Class ______

Guided Reading Activity 21-1

Decline of the Soviet Union

DIRECTIONS: Answer the following questions as you read Section 1.

1. Give a definition of the term détente as it related to American-Soviet relations in the 1970s.
2. What caused a major setback in détente in 1979?
3. State the agreement made by the INF treaty.
4. What 1990 event was a powerful symbol of the end of the Cold War?

Writing Activity

After they have read this chapter, ask students to write a brief essay in which they summarize the significant events related to the spread and fall of communism. In their essays, have students summarize and describe the worldwide political and economic effects associated with the spread and fall of communism. L2

3 ASSESS

Assign Section 1 Assessment as homework or as an in-class activity.

Have students use **Interactive Tutor Self-Assessment CD-ROM.**

COOPERATIVE LEARNING ACTIVITY

Creating an Oral Report Organize the class into small groups. Assign each group one of the republics of the former Soviet Union to research in preparation for an oral report. Students should find information about the geographic features, the government, the people, the resources, major industries, the cities, and daily life of the republic. Suggest that each group divide the tasks and prepare information, including a map or copies of photographs, about one aspect of their republic. When their research is complete, ask each group to give a class presentation on its assigned republic. L2

For grading this activity, refer to the ***Performance Assessment Activities*** booklet.

CHAPTER 21
Section 1, 657–660

Reading Check

Answer: Reforms allowed centuries-old ethnic tensions in the Soviet Union to reemerge.

Section Quiz 21–1

Name ____ Date ____ Class ____

Chapter 21 Score

Section Quiz 21-1

DIRECTIONS: Matching Match each item in Column A with an item in Column B. Write the correct letters in the blanks. (10 points each)

Column A	Column B
___ 1. country that exports more than it imports	A. creditor nation
___ 2. agreement to eliminate mid-range nuclear weapons	B. détente
___ 3. Gorbachev's initial economic reforms	C. perestroika
___ 4. pre-1979 period of relaxed U.S.-Soviet tensions	D. INF Treaty
___ 5. economy influenced by consumer demand	E. market

DIRECTIONS: Multiple Choice In the blank, write the letter of the choice that best completes the statement or answers the question. (10 points each)

___ 6. By 1980, the Soviet Union was ailing from all of the following causes EXCEPT

Reading Essentials and Study Guide 21–1

Name ____ Date ____ Class ____

Reading Essentials and Study Guide

Chapter 21, Section 1

For use with textbook pages 657–660

DECLINE OF THE SOVIET UNION

KEY TERMS

détente a relaxation of tensions between nations, especially used for American-Soviet relations in the 1970s (page 657)

dissident a person who speaks out against a regime (page 658)

perestroika ("restructuring") the term used by Mikhail Gorbachev for economic reforms in the Soviet Union in the late 1980s (page 659)

DRAWING FROM EXPERIENCE

Have you heard of the "evil empire"? Who used this expression? What country was he talking about?

In this section, you will learn about changes in the Soviet Union in the 1980s and 1990s.

ORGANIZING YOUR THOUGHTS

Use the chart below to help you take notes. Identify the rulers of the Soviet

Reteaching Activity

Guide students in a discussion of the main points covered in this section. Ask volunteers to name key people and events and write them on the chalkboard. **L1**

4 CLOSE

Ask students to consider what problems they think the end of the Cold War solved and what problems it created. **L2**

As Gorbachev released this iron grip, these tensions again came to the forefront. Nationalist movements emerged throughout the republics of the Soviet Union. Between 1988 and 1990, there were calls for independence first in Soviet Georgia and then in Latvia, Estonia, Moldavia, Uzbekistan, Azerbaijan, and Lithuania.

During 1990 and 1991, Gorbachev struggled to deal with the problems unleashed by his reforms. By 1991, the conservative leaders of the traditional Soviet institutions—the army, government, KGB, and military industries—were worried. The possible breakup of the Soviet Union would mean an end to their privileges.

On August 19, 1991, a group of these conservative leaders arrested Gorbachev and tried to seize power. The attempt failed, however, when **Boris Yeltsin,** president of the Russian Republic, and thousands of Russians bravely resisted the rebel forces in Moscow.

The Soviet republics now moved for complete independence. Ukraine voted for independence on December 1, 1991. A week later, the leaders of Russia, **Ukraine,** and **Belarus** announced that the Soviet Union had "ceased to exist."

Gorbachev resigned on December 25, 1991, and turned over his responsibilities as commander in chief to Boris Yeltsin, the new president of Russia. By the end of 1991, one of the largest empires in world history had come to an end. A new era had begun in its now-independent states.

The New Russia Boris Yeltsin was committed to introducing a free market economy as quickly as possible, but the transition was not easy. Economic hardships and social disarray were made worse by a dramatic rise in the activities of organized crime. Yeltsin used brutal force to keep the province of Chechnya in Russia. He also opposed NATO's proposed expansion. After the end of the Cold War, Poland, Hungary, and the Czech Republic tried to join NATO. These countries were all former Soviet satellites.

At the end of 1999, Yeltsin resigned and was replaced by **Vladimir Putin,** who was elected president in 2000. Putin vowed to return the breakaway state of Chechnya to Russian authority and to adopt a more assertive role in international affairs. Fighting in Chechnya continued throughout 2000, nearly reducing the republic's capital city of Grozny to ruins.

In July 2001, Putin launched reforms aimed at boosting growth and budget revenues and keeping Russia on a strong economic track. The reforms included free sale and purchase of land, tax cuts, and efforts to join the international World Trade Organization. Since then, Russia has experienced a budget surplus and a growing economy.

Reading Check **Cause and Effect** How did Gorbachev's reforms cause the breakup of the Soviet Union?

SECTION 1 ASSESSMENT

Checking for Understanding

1. **Define** détente, dissident, perestroika.
2. **Identify** Ronald Reagan, Mikhail Gorbachev, Leonid Brezhnev, Brezhnev Doctrine, Boris Yeltsin, Vladimir Putin.
3. **Locate** Afghanistan, Ukraine, Belarus.
4. **Explain** why the conservative leaders of the traditional Soviet institutions opposed the breakup of the Soviet Union. Name the institutions these leaders represented.
5. **List** the problems that weakened the Soviet economy during the 1960s and 1970s.

Critical Thinking

6. **Drawing Inferences** Why did the former Soviet Union have problems adapting to a free-market society?
7. **Organizing Information** Create a diagram like the one below showing the problems the Soviet Union faced under communism and the problems the former Soviet republics face today.

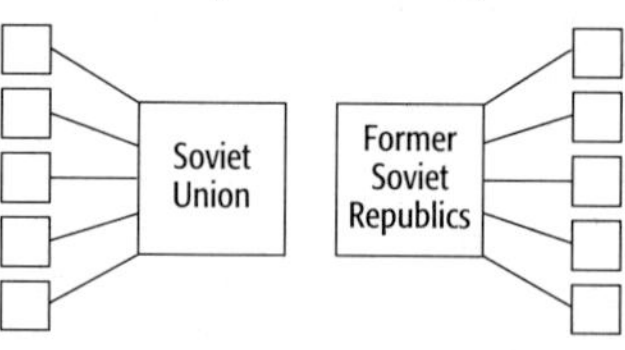

Analyzing Visuals

8. **Examine** the photographs of Mikhail Gorbachev and Boris Yeltsin on pages 657 and 659. What did each leader accomplish? What challenges did each man face? Which of these men had a greater impact on world history? Why?

Writing About History

9. **Expository Writing** Locate biographical information on Leonid Brezhnev, Mikhail Gorbachev, Boris Yeltsin, and Vladimir Putin. In an essay, analyze each leader's strengths and weaknesses. How did each man come to power?

SECTION 1 ASSESSMENT

1. Key terms are in blue.
2. Ronald Reagan *(p. 658)*; Mikhail Gorbachev *(p. 658)*; Leonid Brezhnev *(p. 658)*; Brezhnev Doctrine *(p. 658)*; Boris Yeltsin *(p. 660)*; Vladimir Putin *(p. 660)*
3. See chapter maps.
4. It would mean an end to their privileges. Army, government, KGB, military industries
5. Complex central bureaucracy discouraged efficiency and led to indifference.
6. because political reforms had not been made
7. Soviet Union: inefficiency; corruption; declining economy; alcoholism; high infant mortality; Former Soviet Republics: economic hardship; social disarray; organized crime; Chechnya; international relations
8. Gorbachev: radical economic and political reforms; problems unleashed by reforms; Yeltsin: committed to free market economy; hampered by economic hardships, social disarray, organized crime. Answers will vary.
9. Answers will vary.

SECTION 2 Eastern Europe

Guide to Reading

Main Ideas
- Gorbachev's policy of not giving military support to Communist governments created the opportunity for revolution.
- Massive demonstrations peacefully ended some Communist regimes, while violence ended others.

Key Terms
ethnic cleansing, autonomous

People to Identify
Lech Walesa, Václav Havel, Slobodan Milošević

Places to Locate
Bosnia-Herzegovina, Kosovo

Preview Questions
1. What caused the East German government to open its border in 1989?
2. What effect did the 1990 collapse of communism have on Yugoslavia?

Reading Strategy
Categorizing Information Create a chart listing one or two reasons for, and the results of, revolution.

Country	Reasons for Revolution	Results of Revolution
Poland		
Czechoslovakia		
Romania		
East Germany		
Yugoslavia		

Preview of Events

1987 · 1988 · 1989 · 1990 · 1991 · 1992

- **1988** Poland holds the first free elections in Eastern Europe in forty years
- **1989** Berlin Wall opens; communism falls in Czechoslovakia and Romania
- **1991** Slovenia and Croatia declare independence
- **1992** Serbs pursue policy of ethnic cleansing in Bosnia-Herzegovina

Voices from the Past

War-damaged Bosnia

Roy Gutman, a journalist for *Newsday,* wrote from Bosnia in July 1992:

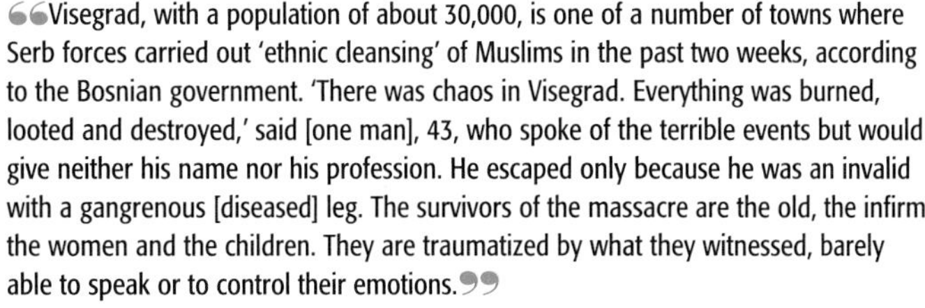

> "Visegrad, with a population of about 30,000, is one of a number of towns where Serb forces carried out 'ethnic cleansing' of Muslims in the past two weeks, according to the Bosnian government. 'There was chaos in Visegrad. Everything was burned, looted and destroyed,' said [one man], 43, who spoke of the terrible events but would give neither his name nor his profession. He escaped only because he was an invalid with a gangrenous [diseased] leg. The survivors of the massacre are the old, the infirm, the women and the children. They are traumatized by what they witnessed, barely able to speak or to control their emotions."
>
> —***The Mammoth Book of Eyewitness History,* Jon E. Lewis, 2000**

Ethnic cleansing was one aspect of an upheaval in Eastern Europe that began in 1989.

Revolutions in Eastern Europe

People in Eastern Europe had not always been happy with their Soviet-style Communist regimes. After Gorbachev made it clear that the Soviet Union would not intervene militarily in their states, revolutions broke out throughout Eastern Europe. By looking at four Eastern European states, we can see how the process worked.

Poland Workers' protests led to demands for change in Poland. In 1980, a worker named **Lech Walesa** (lehk vah•LEHN•suh) organized a national trade union known as Solidarity. Solidarity gained the support of the workers and of the

1 FOCUS

Section Overview

This section describes the changes and revolutions of Eastern Europe in the late twentieth century.

BELLRINGER
Skillbuilder Activity

Project transparency and have students answer questions.

Available as a blackline master.

Daily Focus Skills Transparency 21–2

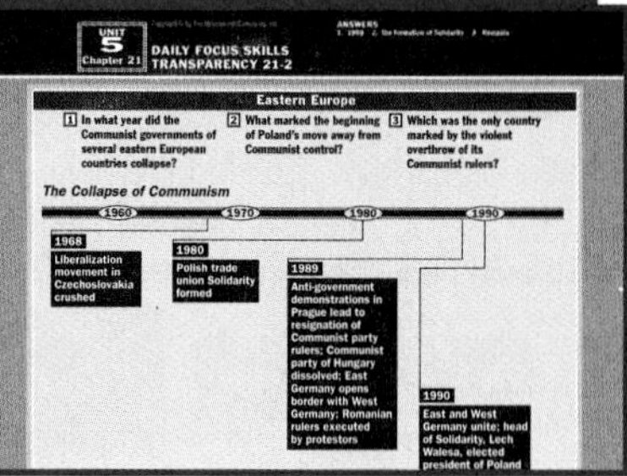

Guide to Reading

Answers to Graphic: Poland: worker protests: free elections; Czechoslovakia: repressive government: country divided; Romania: food shortages: dictator executed; East Germany: repressive government: reunification; Yugoslavia: collapse of Communist Party: republics declare independence

Preteaching Vocabulary: Introduce students to the term *ethnic cleansing.* Ask them to consider why a government might choose the term "ethnic cleansing" over "genocide." *("Cleansing" has a positive connotation, while "genocide" refers to murder.)* **L1**

SECTION RESOURCES

Reproducible Masters
- Reproducible Lesson Plan 21–2
- Daily Lecture and Discussion Notes 21–2
- Guided Reading Activity 21–2
- Section Quiz 21–2
- Reading Essentials and Study Guide 21–2

Transparencies
- Daily Focus Skills Transparency 21–2

Multimedia
- Interactive Tutor Self-Assessment CD-ROM
- ExamView® Pro Testmaker CD-ROM
- Presentation Plus! CD-ROM

2 TEACH

Daily Lecture and Discussion Notes 21–2

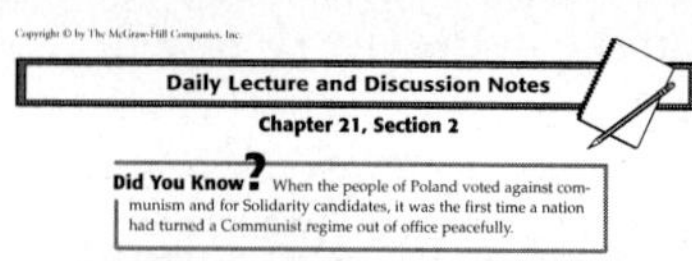

Daily Lecture and Discussion Notes

Chapter 21, Section 2

Did You Know? When the people of Poland voted against communism and for Solidarity candidates, it was the first time a nation had turned a Communist regime out of office peacefully.

I. **Revolutions in Eastern Europe** *(pages 661–663)*

A. Worker's protests led to demands for change in Poland. In 1980, **Lech Walesa** organized a national trade union in Poland known as Solidarity. In 1988, the Polish regime agreed to free parliamentary elections—the first free election in Eastern Europe in 40 years. In 1990, Walesa was elected president of Poland. Poland's rapid free-market reforms led to severe unemployment and discontent. Today Poland's free-market economy is becoming increasingly prosperous.

B. In 1968, Soviet troops crushed the reform movement in Czechoslovakia. In 1988 and 1989, mass demonstrations throughout Czechoslovakia led to the collapse of the Communist government. In December 1989, **Václav Havel,** a dissident against the Communist government, became president. In 1993 ethnic conflicts between Czechs and Slovaks led to the peaceful division of Czechoslovakia into the Czech Republic and Slovakia.

C. In 1965, Communist leader Nicolae Ceaușescu and his wife Elena led a dictatorial

CURRICULUM CONNECTION

Government Guide students in naming the different countries mentioned in this section whose Communist regimes ended. *(Poland, Czechoslovakia, Romania, East Germany, Yugoslavia)* Have students create a chart on the chalkboard that lists the names of the rulers involved in each country; have students tell whether the changes in each country were peaceful or violent. **L2** ELL

Turning Points in World History
The ABC News videotape includes a segment on the fall of the Berlin Wall.

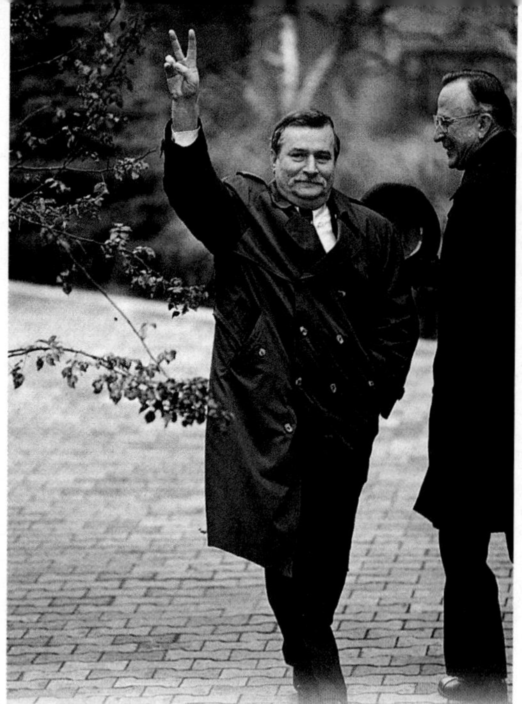

Solidarity organizer Lech Walesa became president of Poland in 1990.

Roman Catholic Church, which was under the leadership of Pope John Paul II, the first Polish pope. During a period of military rule in the 1980s, Walesa was arrested, but the movement continued.

Finally, after a new wave of demonstrations in 1988, the Polish regime agreed to free parliamentary elections—the first free elections in Eastern Europe in 40 years. A new government was elected, ending 45 years of Communist rule in Poland.

In December 1990, Walesa was chosen as president. Poland's new path, however, was not an easy one. Rapid free-market reforms led to severe unemployment and popular discontent.

At the end of 1995, Aleksander Kwasniewski, a former Communist, defeated Walesa and became the new president. He has continued Poland's move toward an increasingly prosperous free market economy.

Czechoslovakia After Soviet troops crushed the reform movement in Czechoslovakia in 1968, Communists used massive repression to maintain their power. Writers and other intellectuals continued to oppose the government, but they initially had little success.

Then, in 1988 and 1989, mass demonstrations took place throughout Czechoslovakia. By November 1989, crowds as large as five hundred thousand were forming in Prague. In December 1989, the Communist government collapsed.

At the end of December, **Václav Havel** (VAHT•SLAHF HAH•vel), a writer who had played an important role in bringing down the Communist government, became the new president. Havel became an eloquent spokesperson for Czech democracy and a new order in Europe.

Within Czechoslovakia, the new government soon faced old ethnic conflicts. The two national groups, Czechs and Slovaks, agreed to a peaceful division of the country. On January 1, 1993, Czechoslovakia split into the Czech Republic and Slovakia. Václav Havel was elected the first president of the new Czech Republic. Michal Kovác was elected president of Slovakia.

Romania In 1965, the Communist leader Nicolae Ceaușescu, (NEE•koh•lay chow•SHEHS•koo) and his wife, Elena, set up a rigid and dictatorial regime in Romania. Ceaușescu ruled Romania with an iron grip, using secret police to crush all dissent. Nonetheless, opposition to his regime grew.

Ceaușescu's economic policies led to a sharp drop in living standards, including food shortages and the rationing of bread, flour, and sugar. His plan for rapid urbanization, especially a program that called for the bulldozing of entire villages, further angered the Romanian people.

One incident ignited the flames of revolution. In December 1989, the secret police murdered thousands of men, women, and children who were peacefully demonstrating. Finally, the army refused to support any more repression. Ceaușescu and his wife were captured on December 22 and executed on Christmas Day. A new government was quickly formed.

German Reunification In 1971, Erich Honecker became head of the Communist Party in East Germany. He used the Stasi, the secret police, to rule for the next 18 years. In 1988, however, popular unrest, fueled by Honecker's harsh regime, led many East Germans to flee their country. Mass demonstrations against the regime broke out in the summer and fall of 1989.

On November 9, the Communist government

Web Activity Visit the *Glencoe World History—Modern Times* Web site at wh.mt.glencoe.com and click on **Chapter 21–Student Web Activity** to learn more about the fall of the Berlin Wall.

COOPERATIVE LEARNING ACTIVITY

Developing a Television Broadcast Organize the class into news teams and assign one team to cover West Germany, one to cover East Germany, and one to represent the team in the news studio in the United States. Each team will need to research the November 1989 reuniting of Berlin as the wall came down. Students are to conduct interviews to get firsthand reactions and accounts of reunited families and friends. (Teams should decide what parts each member will play.) The studio team should research details about the people in the West and the East and alert news teams about the questions they might ask when they air the show. If possible, have a video camera available to tape the broadcast. **L2**

surrendered to popular pressure by opening its entire border with the West. Hundreds of thousands of East Germans swarmed across the border. Families and friends who had not seen each other in decades were reunited. People on both sides of the wall began tearing it down. The government, helpless before this popular uprising, ordered the rest of the wall torn down. The Berlin Wall, long a symbol of the Cold War, was no more.

During East Germany's first free elections in March 1990, the Christian Democrats won almost 50 percent of the vote. The Christian Democrats supported political union with West Germany. The reunification of East and West took place on October 3, 1990. What had seemed almost impossible at the beginning of 1989 had become a reality by the end of 1990—the countries of West and East Germany had reunited to form one Germany.

Reading Check **Describing** How did the inhabitants of Eastern Europe respond to the repression of their totalitarian leaders?

The Disintegration of Yugoslavia

Although Yugoslavia had a Communist government, it had never been a Soviet satellite state. After World War II, its dictatorial leader, Josip Broz Tito, worked to keep the six republics and two provinces that made up Yugoslavia together. After Tito died in 1980, a collective federal government composed of representatives from the separate republics and provinces kept Yugoslavia under Communist rule. At the end of the 1980s, Yugoslavia was caught up in the reform movements sweeping Eastern Europe. By 1990, new parties had emerged, and the authority of the Communist Party had collapsed.

Calls for Independence The Yugoslav political scene was complex. In 1990, the Yugoslav republics of Slovenia, Croatia, **Bosnia-Herzegovina,** and Macedonia began to lobby for independence. **Slobodan Milošević** (SLOH•buh•DAHN muh•LOH•suh•VIHCH), who became leader of the Yugoslav republic of Serbia in 1987, rejected these efforts. The populations of these republics included Serb minorities. In Milošević's view, the republics could only be independent if their borders were re-drawn to include the Serb minorities in a new Greater Serbian state.

After negotiations failed, Slovenia and Croatia declared their independence in June 1991. In September 1991, the Yugoslavian army began a full assault against Croatia. Increasingly, the Yugoslavian army was dominated by Serbia, and it was aided by Serbian minorities in Croatia. Before a cease-fire was arranged, the Serbian forces had captured one-third of Croatia's territory in brutal fighting.

The War in Bosnia Early in 1992, the Serbs turned their guns on Bosnia-Herzegovina. By mid-1993, Serbian forces had acquired 70 percent of Bosnian territory.

Many Bosnians were Muslims. Toward them, the Serbs followed a policy they called ethnic cleansing—killing them or forcibly removing them from their lands. Ethnic cleansing revived memories of Nazi atrocities in World War II. By 1995, 250,000 Bosnians (mostly civilians) had been killed. Two million others were left homeless.

Geography Skills

The violence in Yugoslavia led to NATO involvement.

1. **Interpreting Maps** List the states that formed after the breakup of Yugoslavia and note their capitals.
2. **Applying Geography Skills** Explain why a peace boundary was created in Bosnia in 1995.

Reading Check

Answer: They held mass demonstrations that eventually brought about the collapse of the Communist governments.

Geography Skills

Answers:
1. See map.
2. to end the war in Bosnia

Guided Reading Activity 21-2

3 ASSESS

Assign Section 2 Assessment as homework or as an in-class activity.

Have students use **Interactive Tutor Self-Assessment CD-ROM.**

Section Quiz 21-2

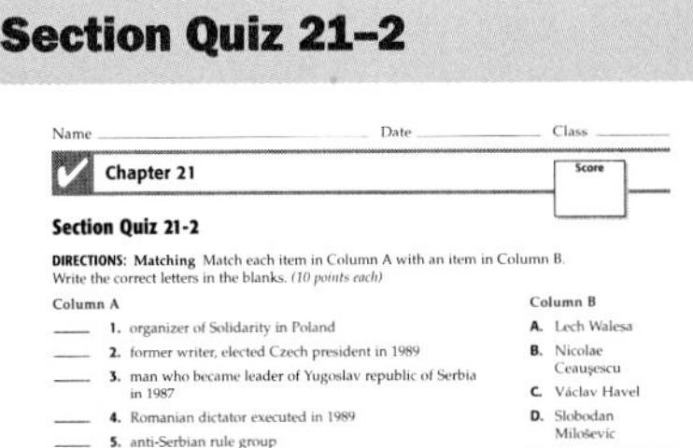

EXTENDING THE CONTENT

Berlin Wall Students may need to be reminded that the Berlin Wall was originally built in 1961 (at that time a barbed-wire barricade) in an attempt to control the movement of people from the eastern to the western sectors of Berlin. Before the more famous Berlin Wall was torn down, the government of Hungary began dismantling its own wall, which had been erected on its common border with Austria. Because of this, East Berliners were able to travel from East Berlin to Hungary, then on to Austria and back to West Berlin "by way of the West." At that point the Berlin Wall was merely a symbol of Communist oppression and served no practical purpose. The East Berlin government agreed to lift all immigration and traveling restrictions by November of 1989.

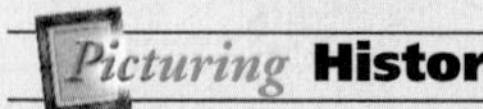

Picturing History

Answer: When Milošević stripped Kosovo of its autonomous status, ethnic Albanians began a campaign against Serbian rule. Serb forces began to massacre ethnic Albanians.

Reading Check

Answer: Wars broke out in Croatia, Bosnia, and Kosovo.

Reading Essentials and Study Guide 21–2

Name ________ Date ________ Class ________

Reading Essentials and Study Guide

Chapter 21, Section 2

For use with textbook pages 661–664

EASTERN EUROPE

KEY TERMS

ethnic cleansing the Serb policy of killing or forcibly removing Bosnians from their lands *(page 663)*

autonomous self-governing *(page 664)*

DRAWING FROM EXPERIENCE

Have you ever seen pictures of the Berlin Wall? What did it look like? Why was it built? Why did it fall?

In the last section, you read about the fall of communism in the Soviet Union. In this section, you will read about the fall of communism in other countries in Eastern Europe.

ORGANIZING YOUR THOUGHTS

Use the chart below to help you take notes. Describe how communism ended in the countries in this chart. Also indicate some results of the revolutions in these countries.

Country	How Communism Ended	Results of Revolution
Poland	1.	2.
Czechoslovakia	3.	4.
Romania	5.	6.
East Germany	7.	8.

Reteaching Activity

Have students prepare a detailed time line that shows the sequence of revolutionary events from 1989 to 1993 in Eastern Europe. **L1** **ELL**

4 CLOSE

Ask students to summarize recent changes in the Balkans and predict changes in Eastern Europe in the next decade. **L3**

In 1995, new offensives by Bosnian government army forces and by the Croatian army regained considerable territory that had been lost to Serbian forces. Air strikes by NATO bombers, strongly advocated by U.S. President Bill Clinton, were launched in retaliation for Serb attacks on civilians.

These attacks forced the Serbs to sign a formal peace treaty on December 14. The agreement split Bosnia into a loose union of a Serb republic and a Muslim-Croat federation. NATO sent a force of sixty thousand troops to monitor the frontier between the new political entities.

Picturing History

In 1999, Serbs forced hundreds of thousands of ethnic Albanians from their homes in Kosovo, creating a massive refugee crisis. What issues led to conflict in Kosovo?

The War in Kosovo Peace in Bosnia did not bring peace to the region. A new war erupted in 1998 over **Kosovo.** In 1974, Tito had made Kosovo an autonomous (self-governing) province within Yugoslavia. Kosovo's inhabitants were mainly ethnic Albanians who had kept their own language and customs.

In 1989, Slobodan Milošević stripped Kosovo of its autonomous status. Some groups of ethnic Albanians founded the Kosovo Liberation Army (KLA) in the mid-1990s and began a campaign against Serbian rule in Kosovo. In an effort to crush the KLA, Serb forces began to massacre ethnic Albanians. The United States and its NATO allies then sought to arrange a settlement.

After months of negotiations, the Kosovo Albanians agreed in 1999 to a peace plan that would give the ethnic Albanians in Kosovo broad autonomy for a three-year interim period. When Milošević refused to sign the agreement, the United States and its NATO allies began a bombing campaign that forced the Yugoslavian government to cooperate. In the fall elections of 2000, Milošević was ousted from power.

Reading Check **Identifying** What events resulted from the disintegration of Yugoslavia?

SECTION 2 ASSESSMENT

Checking for Understanding

1. **Define** ethnic cleansing, autonomous.
2. **Identify** Lech Walesa, Václav Havel, Slobodan Milošević.
3. **Locate** Bosnia-Herzegovina, Kosovo.
4. **Explain** why the Communist government ordered the Berlin Wall to be torn down.
5. **List** the four Eastern European states discussed in this section that had *not* been Soviet satellites. What events occurred in each state after the withdrawal of Soviet influence?

Critical Thinking

6. **Explain** Why did the inhabitants of Communist countries in Eastern Europe feel it was safe to rebel in 1989?
7. **Summarizing Information** Create a chart like the one below listing the Yugoslav republics that wanted independence after 1990, the inhabitants of these republics (if listed), and the reasons the republics fought each other.

Republics	Inhabitants	Causes of Fighting

Analyzing Visuals

8. **Study** the photo of ethnic Albanians shown on this page. What do they have in common with other victims of oppression throughout history? If you and your family were forced to leave your home, what would be your greatest concerns?

Writing About History

9. **Informative Writing** Research and write an essay about the Polish Solidarity movement begun by Lech Walesa in 1980. Why was it successful? Be sure to discuss Walesa's supporters, his adversaries, and the status of the movement today.

SECTION 2 ASSESSMENT

1. Key terms are in blue.
2. Lech Walesa *(p. 661)*; Václav Havel *(p. 662)*; Slobodan Milošević *(p. 663)*
3. See chapter maps.
4. After the East German government opened its border with the West, people on both sides of the Berlin Wall began tearing it down. The Communist government ordered the rest of the wall torn down.
5. Slovenia, Croatia, Bosnia-Herzegovina, Macedonia; they lobbied for their independence
6. The Soviet Union would no longer give military support to governments in Eastern Europe.
7. Slovenia: Serb minority; Croatia: Serb minority; Serbia wanted to retake area containing Serb population; Bosnia-Herzegovina: Bosnians (many of whom are Muslims), Serbs, Croats; ethnic differences, desire of Serbs to rid republic of Croats and Muslims; Macedonia: Serb minority
8. They are members of a minority; answers will vary.
9. Answers will vary.

Eyewitness to History

Václav Havel— The Call for a New Politics

IN THEIR ATTEMPTS TO DEAL WITH THE WORLD'S problems, some European leaders have pointed to the need for a new perspective. This excerpt is taken from a speech that Václav Havel delivered to the United States Congress on February 21, 1990, two months after he had become president of Czechoslovakia.

❝For this reason, the salvation of this human world lies nowhere else than in the human heart, in the human power to reflect, in human meekness and in human responsibility.

Without a global revolution in the sphere of human consciousness, nothing will change for the better in the sphere of our being as humans, and the catastrophe toward which this world is headed—be it ecological, social, demographic or a general breakdown of civilization—will be unavoidable. . . .

We are still a long way from that "family of man." In fact, we seem to be receding from the ideal rather than growing closer to it. Interests of all kinds—personal, selfish, state, nation, group, and if you like, company interests—still considerably outweigh genuinely common and global interests. We are still under the sway of the destructive and vain belief that man is the pinnacle of creation and not just a part of it and that therefore everything is permitted. . . .

In other words, we still don't know how to put morality ahead of politics, science and economics. We are still incapable of understanding that the only genuine backbone of all our actions, if they are to be moral, is responsibility.

Responsibility to something higher than my family, my country, my company, my success—responsibility to the order of being where all our actions are indelibly recorded and where and only where they will be properly judged.

After addressing the United States Congress, Václav Havel gives a victory sign.

The interpreter or mediator between us and this higher authority is what is traditionally referred to as human conscience.❞

—Václav Havel, Speech to the U.S. Congress

Analyzing Primary Sources

1. What is the difference between the way Václav Havel views politics and the way that most politicians have traditionally viewed politics?
2. Political ideas are of little value unless they can be implemented. What is your opinion—do you think that Havel's ideas could be turned into political reality? Why or why not?

665

TEACH

Analyzing Primary Sources
Have students analyze and evaluate Václav Havel's speech. Do they agree that people "don't know how to put morality ahead of politics, science and economics"? To what extent do students believe they are responsible for the values and actions of the society they belong to? **L2**

Who? What? Where? When?

Václav Havel was always opposed to the Communist regime in his native Czechoslovakia. Havel was born in 1936 into a well-to-do middle-class family. As he grew up, he struggled against the anti-intellectualism fostered by the Communist philosophy. He supported himself by working manual-labor jobs while he wrote plays depicting the "dehumanizing effects of mechanization on society and the individual spirit." Havel was a political, as well as a social, activist. He was imprisoned for nearly five years (1979 to 1983) for his efforts at founding a group dedicated to the relief of victims of political persecution. He was elected president of the Czechoslovak parliament in December of 1989, prior to the splitting of Czechoslovakia into the Czech Republic and Slovakia.

ANSWERS TO ANALYZING PRIMARY SOURCES

1. Havel believes responsibility should be the backbone of politics. Morality should be put ahead of politics, science, and economics. Most politicians have viewed responsibility and morality as being secondary to politics and economics. Politics tends to serve selfish interests, not necessarily what is best for the majority of the people.
2. Student answers will vary but should be supported by logical arguments. You might wish to use this question as the basis for a class debate or discussion.

CHAPTER 21
Section 3, 666–670

1 FOCUS

Section Overview

This section discusses the European Union and domestic affairs of Western nations in the late twentieth century.

BELLRINGER
Skillbuilder Activity

 Project transparency and have students answer questions.

 Available as a blackline master.

Daily Focus Skills Transparency 21–3

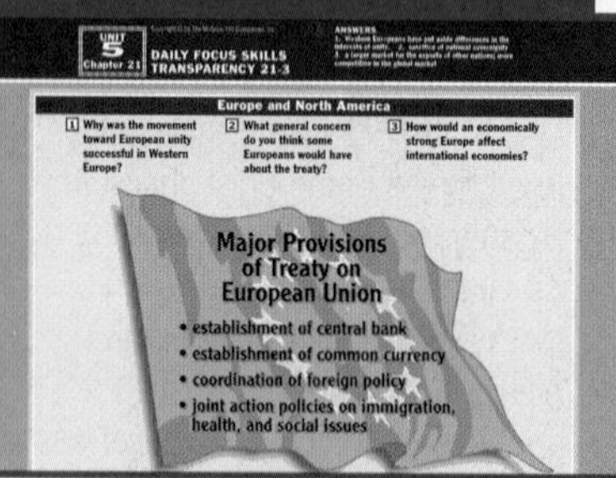

Guide to Reading

Answers to Graphic: Thatcherism: restricted union power, controlled inflation,tried to replace local property taxes with flat tax; Reagan: large military buildup, tripled government budget deficits, cut job programs; Both: limited social welfare

Preteaching Vocabulary: Ask students to find synonyms and antonyms for *deficit. (synonyms: shortage, lack, deficiency, scarcity; antonyms: surplus, abundance, excess, surfeit)* **L1**

SECTION 3 Europe and North America

Guide to Reading

Main Ideas
- Western European nations moved to unite their economies after 1970.
- Domestic problems arose in the United States, Great Britain, France, Germany, and Canada.

Key Terms
Thatcherism, budget deficit

People to Identify
Willy Brandt, Margaret Thatcher, Richard Nixon, Pierre Trudeau

Places to Locate
France, Northern Ireland

Preview Questions
1. What problems faced Western Europe after 1980?
2. What was the focus of U.S. domestic politics in the 1970s?

Reading Strategy
Compare and Contrast Draw a Venn diagram comparing and contrasting economic policies of Thatcherism with those of the Reagan Revolution.

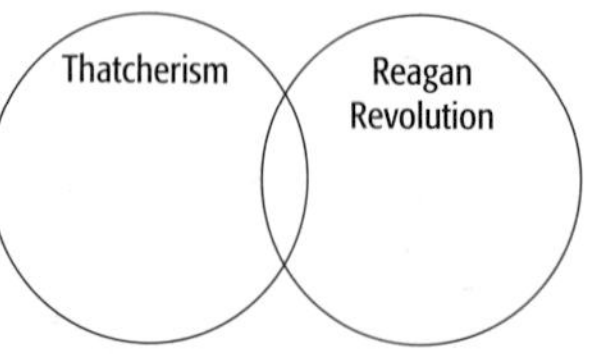

Preview of Events

1970 · 1975 · 1980 · 1985 · 1990 · 1995 · 2000

1971 West German chancellor Willy Brandt wins Nobel Peace Prize

1974 Richard Nixon resigns the presidency of the United States

1995 Canadian voters reject independence for Quebec

Voices from the Past

German neo-Nazis

A German reporter described violence against foreigners in Germany in 1991:

> ❝The municipality in northern Saxony has a population of just under 70,000, including 70 people from Mozambique and Vietnam who live in a hostel [inn] at the other end of town. The 'political situation' was triggered by an attack by a neo-Nazi gang on Vietnamese traders selling their goods on the market square on 17 September. After being dispersed by the police the Faschos [neo-Nazis] carried out their first attack on the hostel for foreigners. The attacks then turned into a regular evening hunt by a growing group of right-wing radicals, some of them minors, who presented their idea of a clean Germany by roaming the streets armed with truncheons, stones, steel balls, bottles and Molotov cocktails.❞
>
> —***The German Tribune,*** **October 6, 1991**

Attacks against foreigners by neo-Nazis became a problem in Germany during the 1990s.

Winds of Change in Western Europe

Between the early 1950s and late 1970s, Western Europe experienced virtually full employment. An economic downturn, however, occurred in the mid-1970s and early 1980s. Both inflation and unemployment rose dramatically. Undoubtedly, a dramatic increase in the price of oil following the Arab-Israeli conflict in 1973 (see Chapter 23) was a major cause for the downturn. Western European economies recovered in the course of the 1980s, but problems remained.

SECTION RESOURCES

Reproducible Masters
- Reproducible Lesson Plan 21–3
- Daily Lecture and Discussion Notes 21–3
- Guided Reading Activity 21–3
- Section Quiz 21–3
- Reading Essentials and Study Guide 21–3

Transparencies
- Daily Focus Skills Transparency 21–3

Multimedia
- Interactive Tutor Self-Assessment CD-ROM
- ExamView® Pro Testmaker CD-ROM
- Presentation Plus! CD-ROM

NATIONAL GEOGRAPHIC **Expansion of the European Union, 1957–1995**

Original members, 1957
Additional members:
by 1973
by 1986
by 1995

0 500 miles
0 500 kilometers
Lambert Azimuthal Equal-Area projection

Geography *Skills*

The European Union (EU) allows members to work together to increase trade and develop favorable economic policies.

1. **Interpreting Maps** How long have the original members been part of the EU?
2. **Applying Geography Skills** What does the EU's growth suggest about its value to European states?

The Western European nations moved toward a greater union of their economies after 1970. The European Economic Community (EEC) expanded in 1973 to include Great Britain, Ireland, and Denmark. By 1986, Spain, Portugal, and Greece had become members. Austria, Finland, and Sweden joined in 1995.

The EEC or European Community (EC) was chiefly an economic union. By 1992, it comprised 344 million people and made up the world's largest single trading bloc. The Treaty on European Union, which went into effect on January 1, 1994, turned the EC into the principal organization within the even more solidified European Union (EU). One of the EU's first goals was to establish a common European currency, the euro. Most of the EU nations planned to abandon their currency in favor of the euro by January 1, 2002.

Uncertainties in France France's deteriorating economic situation in the 1970s caused a shift to the left politically. By 1981, the Socialists had become the chief party in the National Assembly. The Socialist leader, François Mitterrand, was elected president.

Mitterrand initiated a number of measures to aid workers: an increased minimum wage, a 39-hour work week, and higher taxes for the rich. The Socialist government also nationalized, or took over, major banks, the steel industry, the space and electronics industries, and insurance firms.

Socialist policies, however, largely failed to work, and France's economic decline continued. In 1993, French unemployment stood at 10.6 percent. In the elections in March of that year, the Socialists won only 28 percent of the vote. A coalition of conservative parties gained 80 percent of the seats in the National Assembly. The move to the right in France was strengthened when the conservative mayor of Paris, Jacques Chirac, was elected president in May 1995.

From West Germany to Germany In 1969, the Social Democrats, a moderate Socialist party, replaced the Christian Democrats as the leading party in West Germany. The first Social Democratic chancellor of West Germany was **Willy Brandt.** In March 1971, Brandt worked out the details of a treaty with East Germany that led to greater cultural, personal, and economic contacts between West and East Germany. For this, he received the Nobel Peace Prize for 1971.

In 1982, the Christian Democratic Union of Helmut Kohl formed a new, more conservative government. Kohl was a smart politician who benefited greatly from an economic boom in the mid-1980s. Then events in East Germany led to the unexpected reunification of the two Germanies in 1990. With a population of 79 million people, the new Germany became the leading power in Europe.

The joy over reunification soon faded as new problems arose. It became clear that the rebuilding of eastern Germany would take far more money than had originally been thought.

Willy Brandt

2 TEACH

Geography *Skills*

Answers:

1. since 1957 (subtract that from current year)
2. it is valuable; work together for common economic policies, common currency

Daily Lecture and Discussion Notes 21–3

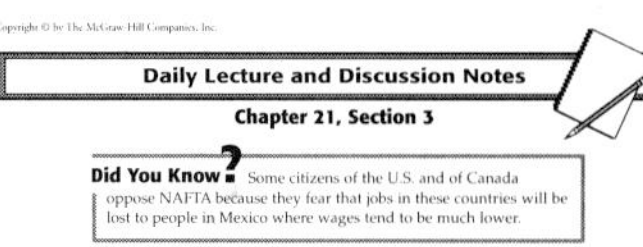

Daily Lecture and Discussion Notes

Chapter 21, Section 3

Did You Know? Some citizens of the U.S. and of Canada oppose NAFTA because they fear that jobs in these countries will be lost to people in Mexico where wages tend to be much lower.

I. **Winds of Change in Western Europe** *(pages 666–668)*

A. After 1970, Western European countries had greater economic unity. The European Economic Community (EEC) greatly expanded between 1973 and 1995. By 1992m the European Community (EC) made up the world's largest single trading bloc.

B. In 1994, the EC became the principle organization within the European Union (EU). Most EU nations planned to abandon their currency in favor of the common European currency, the euro, by January 2002.

C. **France's** economy declined in the 1970s. By 1981, the Socialists had become the main party in the National Assembly. Socialist president François Mitterand began measures to aid workers. He nationalized many businesses. Socialist policies failed, however, and France's economy continued to decline. In 1993, politics in France became conservative. In May 1995, conservative Jacques Chirac was elected president of France.

D. **Willy Brandt** was the first Social Democrat chancellor of West Germany. He received the Nobel Prize in 1971 for his work on a treaty with East Germany that led to greater contact and interaction between the two countries. In 1982, Helmut Kohl formed a new, more conservative government.

E. Reunification of the new Germany in 1989 made it the leading power in Europe. Reunification, however, led to economic problems. Eastern Germany needed to be rebuilt and the economy of eastern Germany collapsed. There was high unemployment and severe discontent. This led to attacks against foreigners by right-wing extremists.

F. Between 1964 and 1979, Great Britain's government faced the intense fighting between Catholics and Protestants in **Northern Ireland,** an ailing economy, and frequent labor

Critical Thinking

In many nations today, there is increasing fragmentation as ethnic groups break away to form their own countries *(Yugoslavia, Czech Republic, Slovakia)*. However, there is also a trend in other places toward unification and increased cooperation *(reunification of Germany, Western European unity, North American Free Trade Agreement, O.P.E.C.)*. Have your students hypothesize about which force is the stronger in the world today and why. L2

COOPERATIVE LEARNING ACTIVITY

Creating a Presentation Organize students into small groups. Have each group choose one of the countries studied in this section (France, Germany, Britain, Ireland, or Canada) to research contemporary life in that country. Have individual students in each group look at the people and culture, the music and literature, places of interest to visit, and the current political, economic, and social conditions. They should try to collect any visual materials they feel will help the presentation. Students should be asked to transfer information from one medium to another, including written to visual and statistical to written and visual, using computer software as appropriate. Have groups present these reports as panels of experts. L2

Chart Skills

Answers:

1. Answers will depend on countries chosen by students.
2. laissez-faire: right; command economy: left; capitalism: right; invisible hand: right; communism: left; socialism: left

Reading Check

Answer: to limit social welfare, restrict union power, and control inflation

Guided Reading Activity 21–3

Name ____________ Date ____________ Class ____________

Guided Reading Activity 21-3

Europe and North America

DIRECTIONS: Fill in the blanks below as you read Section 3.

1. By 1992, the EEC comprised 344 million people and made up the world's ____________ single trading bloc.
2. One of the European Union's first goals was to establish a common European currency, the ____________.
3. By 1981, the Socialists had become the chief party in the ____________ but ____________ policies largely failed to work.
4. A move to the right in France was strengthened when the ____________ mayor of Paris, Jacques Chirac, was elected president in May 1995.
5. West German chancellor Willy Brandt received the ____________ for 1971 when he initiated a cultural exchange treaty with East Germany.
6. When East and West Germany ____________ in 1989, the new Germany became the leading power in Europe.
7. Between 1964 and 1979, the ____________ and ____________ Parties alternated in power in Great Britain.
8. Margaret Thatcher pledged to limit ____________, restrict union power, and end ____________.
9. Much of President Bill Clinton's second term was overshadowed by charges of presidential ____________.
10. Pierre Trudeau became Prime Minister of Canada in 1968, and dedicated his administration to preserving a ____________ Canada.

66

Enrich

Have students research Margaret Thatcher. What was her background? What events in her early life made her want to pursue a career in politics? Was she a feminist? What was her overall strategy as prime minister? What did she hope to accomplish? In 1997, she became very critical of her successors. Why? **L2**

Kohl's government was soon forced to face the politically undesirable task of raising taxes. In addition, the virtual collapse of the economy in eastern Germany had led to extremely high levels of unemployment and severe discontent. One result was a return to power for the Social Democrats, who were victorious in the 1998 elections.

The collapse of the economy also led to increasing attacks on foreigners. For years, illegal immigrants and foreigners seeking refuge had found haven in Germany because of its very liberal immigration laws. In 1992, over 440,000 immigrants came to Germany seeking refuge; 123,000 came from former Yugoslavia alone. Increased unemployment and economic problems, however, caused tensions to grow between some Germans and immigrant groups. Attacks against foreigners by right-wing extremists—especially young neo-Nazis who believed in Hitler's idea of a pure Aryan race—became part of German life.

Economic Spectrum

Left	Right
• The economy is controlled by the state.	• The economy is based on free enterprise.
• Industries are owned by the national government.	• Industries are privately owned.
• The government determines allowable profit.	• Owners set prices and work for profit.
• Workers' rights are valued over owners' privileges.	• Workers and owners negotiate.
• The state supplies social services.	• Consumers pay for social services.

Chart Skills

The chart above represents a simplified view of two opposite economic models.

1. **Identifying** Select a minimum of five countries from this chapter. On which side of the economic spectrum would their economies belong?
2. **Describing** Look up the following words and phrases in a dictionary: *laissez-faire, command economy, capitalism, invisible hand, communism, socialism.* Decide if the definition describes a term on the left or the right of the economic spectrum.

Great Britain and Thatcherism Between 1964 and 1979, Great Britain's Conservative Party and Labour Party alternated being in power. One problem both parties had to face was the intense fighting between Catholics and Protestants in **Northern Ireland.** An ailing economy and frequent labor strikes were two other issues that the government struggled to solve.

In 1979, the Conservatives came to power under **Margaret Thatcher.** Thatcher pledged to limit social welfare, restrict union power, and end inflation. Although she did not eliminate the basic parts of the social welfare system, she did break the power of the labor unions and control inflation.

Thatcherism, as her economic policy was termed, improved the British economic situation, but at a price. The south of England, for example, prospered. Old industrial areas elsewhere, however, were beset by high unemployment, poverty, and even violence.

Thatcher dominated British politics in the 1980s. Only in 1990 did Labour's fortunes seem to revive. At that time, Thatcher's government tried to replace local property taxes with a flat-rate tax payable by every adult. In 1990, antitax riots broke out. Thatcher's popularity fell to an all-time low, and she resigned as prime minister.

The Conservative Party, now led by John Major, continued to hold a narrow majority. His government, however, failed to capture the imagination of most Britons. In new elections in 1997, the Labour Party won a landslide victory. Tony Blair, a moderate, became prime minister.

Reading Check **Explaining** What were the policies of Thatcherism?

The U.S. Domestic Scene

With the election of **Richard Nixon** as president in 1968, politics in the United States shifted to the right. Economic issues became the focus of domestic politics by the mid-1970s.

Nixon and Watergate In his campaign for the presidency, Nixon believed that "law and order" issues and a slowdown in racial desegregation would appeal to southern whites. The South, which had once been a stronghold for the Democrats, began to form a new allegiance to the Republican Party.

MEETING INDIVIDUAL NEEDS

English Language Learners Have students trace an outline map of Europe. Ask them to label the countries studied in this section and then color code each country. Have them make a color-code key for the map and in the key give specific information about each country, such as political leaders, important dates and events, and any other details they want to include. **L1** ELL

Refer to ***Inclusion for the High School Social Studies Classroom Strategies and Activities*** in the TCR.

Picturing History

Richard Nixon bids his staff goodbye after resigning his job as president of the United States. What events led Nixon to decide to leave office?

As president, Nixon began to use illegal methods to gain political information about his opponents. Nixon's zeal led to the Watergate scandal. A group of men working for Nixon's reelection campaign broke into the Democratic National Headquarters, located in the Watergate Hotel in Washington, D.C. They were caught there trying to install electronic listening devices.

Nixon repeatedly lied to the American public about his involvement in the affair. Secret tapes of his own conversations in the White House, however, revealed the truth. On August 9, 1974, Nixon resigned the presidency rather than face possible impeachment.

The Carter Administration Vice President Gerald Ford became president when Nixon resigned, only to lose in the 1976 election to the former governor of Georgia, Jimmy Carter. By 1980, the Carter administration was faced with two devastating problems. First, high rates of inflation and a noticeable decline in average weekly earnings were causing a drop in American living standards.

At the same time, a crisis abroad erupted when 52 Americans were held hostage by the Iranian government of the Ayatollah Ruhollah Khomeini (koh•MAY•nee) (see Chapter 23). Carter's inability to gain the release of the American hostages contributed to his overwhelming loss to Ronald Reagan in the election of 1980.

The Reagan Revolution The Reagan Revolution, as it has been called, sent U.S. policy in new directions. Reversing decades of policy, Reagan cut back on the welfare state by decreasing spending on food stamps, school lunch programs, and job programs. At the same time, his administration oversaw the largest peacetime military buildup in U.S. history.

Total federal spending rose from $631 billion in 1981 to over a trillion dollars by 1987. The spending policies of the Reagan administration produced record government budget deficits. A **budget deficit** exists when the government spends more than it collects in revenues. In the 1970s, the total deficit was $420 billion. Between 1981 and 1987, budget deficits were three times that amount.

The Clinton Years George Bush, Reagan's vice president, succeeded him as president. Bush's inability to deal with the deficit problem, as well as an economic downturn, enabled a Democrat, Bill Clinton, to be elected president in 1992.

The new president was a southern Democrat who claimed to be a new Democrat—one who favored a number of the Republican policies of the 1980s. This was a clear indication that the rightward drift in American politics was by no means ended by this Democratic victory.

President Clinton's political fortunes were aided considerably by a lengthy economic revival. Much of Clinton's second term, however, was overshadowed by charges of presidential misconduct. Clinton was threatened with removal from office when the House of Representatives voted two articles of impeachment—formal charges of misconduct—against him. He was tried in the Senate and acquitted after a bitter partisan struggle. Clinton's problems, however, helped the Republican candidate, George W. Bush, to win the presidential election in 2000.

Reading Check **Summarizing** What changes in U.S. policy were part of the Reagan Revolution?

Picturing History

Answer: He used illegal methods to get political information about his opponents and resigned to avoid impeachment.

Reading Check

Answer: cutbacks in welfare spending, increases in military spending

Enrich

As students begin their study of modern history, point out that events from the past impact our future. Ask students to evaluate how the American Revolution differed from the French and Russian Revolutions, and what its long-term impact on political developments around the world has been and will be.

3 ASSESS

Assign Section 3 Assessment as homework or as an in-class activity.

Have students use **Interactive Tutor Self-Assessment CD-ROM.**

Section Quiz 21–3

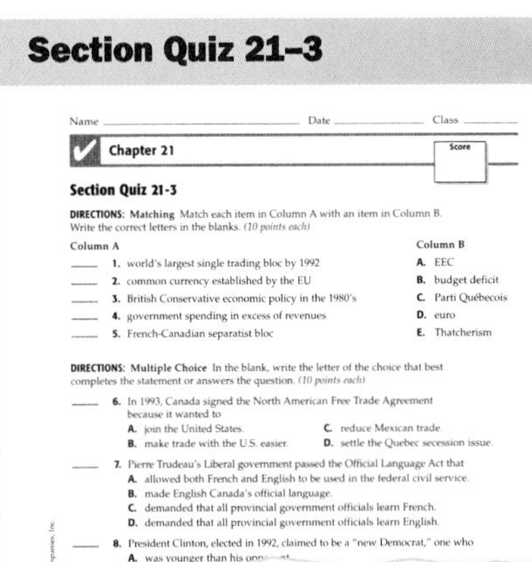

Name ______ Date ______ Class ______

Chapter 21 Score

Section Quiz 21-3

DIRECTIONS: Matching Match each item in Column A with an item in Column B. Write the correct letters in the blanks. *(10 points each)*

Column A	Column B
___ 1. world's largest single trading bloc by 1992	A. EEC
___ 2. common currency established by the EU	B. budget deficit
___ 3. British Conservative economic policy in the 1980's	C. Parti Québecois
___ 4. government spending in excess of revenues	D. euro
___ 5. French-Canadian separatist bloc	E. Thatcherism

DIRECTIONS: Multiple Choice In the blank, write the letter of the choice that best completes the statement or answers the question. *(10 points each)*

___ 6. In 1993, Canada signed the North American Free Trade Agreement because it wanted to
A. join the United States.
B. make trade with the U.S. easier.
C. reduce Mexican trade.
D. settle the Quebec secession issue.

___ 7. Pierre Trudeau's Liberal government passed the Official Language Act that
A. allowed both French and English to be used in the federal civil service.
B. made English Canada's official language.
C. demanded that all provincial government officials learn French.
D. demanded that all provincial government officials learn English.

___ 8. President Clinton, elected in 1992, claimed to be a "new Democrat," one who
A. was younger than his opp

COOPERATIVE LEARNING ACTIVITY

Creating a Presentation Organize students into small groups. Ask each group to research the administration of one of the following presidents: Nixon, Ford, Carter, Reagan, Bush, or Clinton. They should outline both foreign policy and domestic policy, and any major events of their presidency. They should also determine the positive and negative effects of the president's administration on the United States politically and economically. Encourage students to identify ways that the effects of the president's policies are still evident today. Groups should present their reports orally to the class and use visual aids, such as charts or time lines, to enhance their presentations.

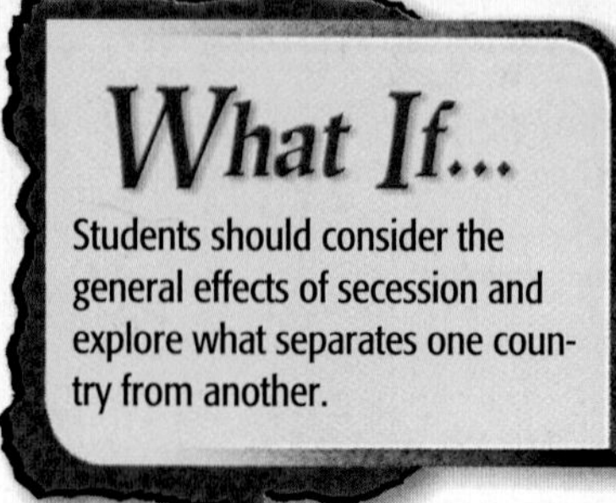

What If...

Students should consider the general effects of secession and explore what separates one country from another.

Reading Check

Answer: to preserve a united Canada, while acknowledging the rights of French-speaking Canadians

Reading Essentials and Study Guide 21–3

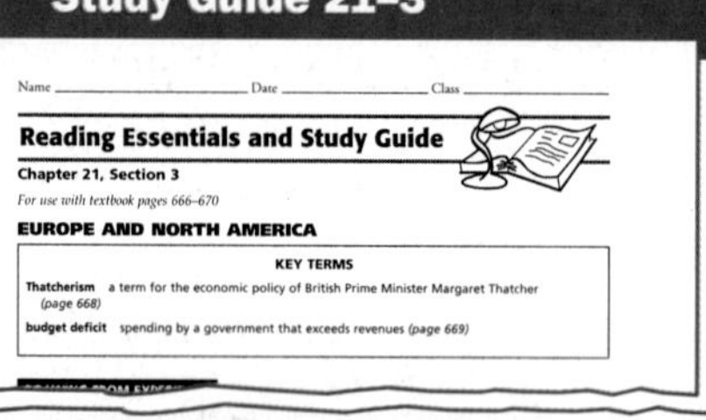

Name ______ Date ______ Class ______

Reading Essentials and Study Guide

Chapter 21, Section 3

For use with textbook pages 666–670

EUROPE AND NORTH AMERICA

KEY TERMS

Thatcherism a term for the economic policy of British Prime Minister Margaret Thatcher (page 668)

budget deficit spending by a government that exceeds revenues (page 669)

Reteaching Activity

Have students prepare a chart on the European Community showing the various nations that belong to it and the years they joined. What benefits does the European Community bring to its members? *(economic stability, military cooperation, immigration control, more trade)* **L2**

4 CLOSE

Discuss with students the problems that countries discussed in this section faced in the late twentieth century. **L2**

Canada

During a major economic recession in Canada in the early 1960s, the Liberals came into power. The most prominent Liberal government of the time was that of **Pierre Trudeau** (TROO•DOH), who became prime minister in 1968. Although he came from a French-Canadian background, Trudeau was dedicated to preserving a united Canada, while at the same time acknowledging the rights of French-speaking Canadians. His government passed the Official Languages Act, which allowed both English and French to be used in the federal civil service. Trudeau's government also supported a vigorous program of industrialization.

An economic recession in the early 1980s brought Brian Mulroney to power in 1984. Mulroney's government sought to return some of Canada's state-run corporations to private owners. In 1993, Canada approved the North American Free Trade Agreement (NAFTA) along with the United States and Mexico. The purpose of NAFTA was to make trade easier and more profitable by establishing guidelines for cooperation between the countries. The agreement, bitterly attacked by many Canadians as being too favorable to the United States, cost Mulroney much of his popularity. In 1993, the Liberal Party came to power with Jean Chrétien as prime minister. Chrétien was reelected in both 1997 and 2000.

Neither Trudeau's nor Mulroney's government was able to settle an ongoing crisis over the French-speaking province of Quebec. In the late 1960s, the Parti Québecois (KAY•buh•KWAH), headed by René Lévesque, had begun to advocate that Quebec secede from the Canadian union. In 1980, the party called for a vote that would grant Quebec's independence from the rest of Canada. In 1995, voters in Quebec narrowly rejected the plan. Debate over Quebec's status continues to divide Canada.

Reading Check **Summarizing** What was the purpose of the Official Languages Act?

What If...

Quebec had seceded from Canada?

Less than 50,000 votes kept Quebec a part of Canada in 1995. Although the separatists are still fighting to secede, the 1995 vote reflects how close they are to winning. Quebec's secession from Canada would make it an entirely independent country.

Consider the Consequences Consider what would be different if the separatists had won the 1995 referendum. Identify at least two changes that would have occurred if Quebec had become a separate country at that time.

SECTION 3 ASSESSMENT

Checking for Understanding

1. **Define** Thatcherism, budget deficit.
2. **Identify** Willy Brandt, Margaret Thatcher, Richard Nixon, Pierre Trudeau.
3. **Locate** France, Northern Ireland.
4. **Explain** the ongoing debate in Canada over the status of Quebec. Why do some people want Quebec to become independent?
5. **List** some of the changes initiated by François Mitterrand's government in France. How successful were Mitterrand's socialist policies?

Critical Thinking

6. **Cause and Effect** What factors led to the economic downturn of the 1970s? How did European nations respond?
7. **Organizing Information** Create a chart like the one below listing the problems faced by Germany when it was unified in 1990.

Problems Created by German Unification

Analyzing Visuals

8. **Compare** the photo on page 666 with the Hitler Youth photos on pages 531 and 550. What similarities and differences do you see among the photos?

Writing About History

9. **Expository Writing** When a country faces economic problems, its inhabitants often blame a person or a group. Look up the word *scapegoating.* Do you think that the way some Germans treated foreigners in the 1990s is an example of scapegoating? Write an essay about the use of scapegoating, including two or three examples from history.

SECTION 3 ASSESSMENT

1. Key terms are in blue.
2. Willy Brandt *(p. 667)*; Margaret Thatcher *(p. 668)*; Richard Nixon *(p. 668)*; Pierre Trudeau *(p. 670)*
3. See chapter maps.
4. Parties in Quebec have called for independence due to language and cultural differences.
5. increased minimum wage; 39-hour work week; higher taxes for the rich; nationalized major industries; economy declined
6. inflation, unemployment, and oil prices rose; nations of Western Europe moved toward greater union of their economies
7. lack of funds to rebuild eastern Germany; collapse of eastern Germany's economy; influx of refugees and illegal immigrants; attacks against foreigners
8. The photos on pages 749 and 768 show people using parades, flags, and propaganda to promote cause. Neo-Nazi parade is less unified than the Hitler Youth.
9. Answers should be supported by logical arguments and examples.

SECTION 4 Western Society and Culture

Guide to Reading

Main Ideas
- Technological and scientific advances have created a global society.
- Artistic trends reflect how the emerging global society has led to a blending of cultural forms and ideas.

Key Terms
pop art, postmodernism

People to Identify
Jackson Pollock, Andy Warhol, Elvis Presley, Beatles

Places to Locate
Northern Ireland, Afghanistan

Preview Questions
1. What have been the major social developments since 1970?
2. What have been the major cultural, scientific, and technological developments in the postwar world?

Reading Strategy
Categorizing Information Complete a cluster chart like the one below illustrating how women have been involved with causes related solely to women's issues and to broader, more universal causes.

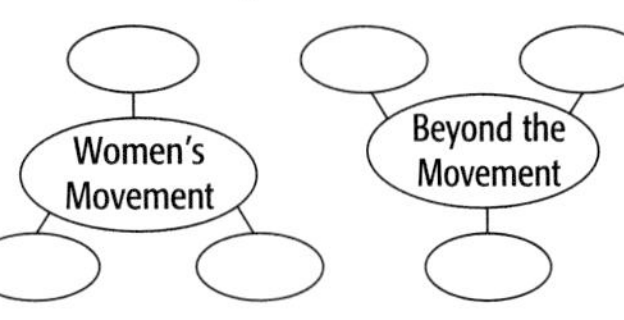

Preview of Events

1970 — 1975 — 1980 — 1985 — 1990 — 1995 — 2000

- **1972** Fighting escalates in Northern Ireland
- **1981** Women protest presence of American nuclear missiles in Britain
- **2001** Global opposition to terrorism forms

Voices from the Past

E. F. Schumacher

In his 1975 book *Small Is Beautiful,* the British economist E. F. Schumacher wrote:

> "We must begin to see the possibility of evolving a new lifestyle, with new methods of production and new patterns of consumption: a lifestyle designed for permanence. To give only two examples: in agriculture, we can interest ourselves in the perfection of production methods which are biologically sound and produce health, beauty and permanence. In industry, we can interest ourselves in small-scale technology, 'technology with a human face,' so that people have a chance to enjoy themselves while they are working, instead of working solely for their pay packet and hoping for enjoyment solely during their leisure time."
>
> —***Small Is Beautiful,*** **E. F. Schumacher, 1973**

Schumacher was a major critic of the sometimes destructive aspects of the new science and technology of the postwar world.

Changes in Women's Lives

Since 1970, the number of women in the work force has continued to rise. In Britain, for example, the number of women in the labor force went from 32 percent to 44 percent between 1970 and 1990. Greater access to universities enabled more women to pursue careers in such fields as law, medicine, and government. However, women continued to receive lower wages than men for the same work and to have fewer chances to advance to top positions.

1 FOCUS

Section Overview

This section discusses contemporary Western culture.

BELLRINGER
Skillbuilder Activity

Project transparency and have students answer questions.

Available as a blackline master.

Daily Focus Skills Transparency 21–4

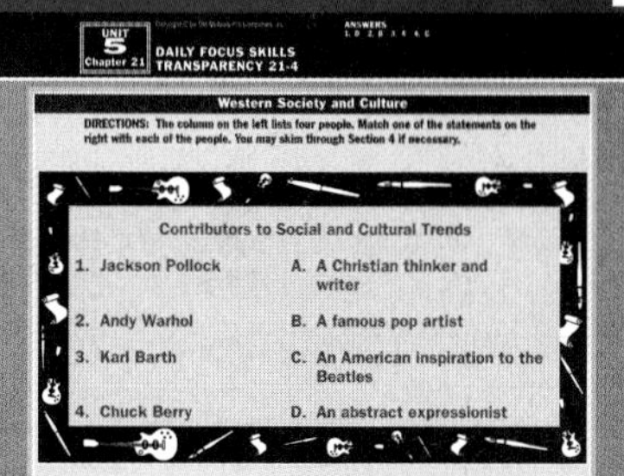

Guide to Reading

Answers to Graphic: Women's Movement: gender stereotyping, contraception, social and economic equality; Beyond the Movement: antinuclear movement, changing cultural attitudes, environmental causes

Preteaching Vocabulary: Discuss with students the meaning of *pop art.* Have them research the root of the word "popular." *(popularis, of the people).* How does this movement differ from past artistic movements they have studied? *(It is for everyone and sees the potential in everyday images to become "art.")* **L1**

SECTION RESOURCES

Reproducible Masters
- Reproducible Lesson Plan 21–4
- Daily Lecture and Discussion Notes 21–4
- Guided Reading Activity 21–4
- Section Quiz 21–4
- Reading Essentials and Study Guide 21–4

Transparencies
- Daily Focus Skills Transparency 21–4

Multimedia
- Interactive Tutor Self-Assessment CD-ROM
- ExamView® Pro Testmaker CD-ROM
- Presentation Plus! CD-ROM

2 TEACH

Reading Check

Answer: Women wanted to control the fundamental conditions of their lives. Some of the issues that became politicized were gender stereotyping, contraception, and social and economic equality.

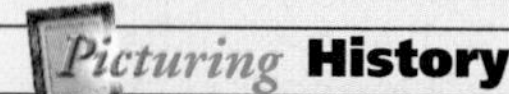

Picturing History

Answer: The United States vowed to wage a war on terrorism and began to create a coalition of nations around the world to cooperate in ridding the world of terrorist groups.

Daily Lecture and Discussion Notes 21–4

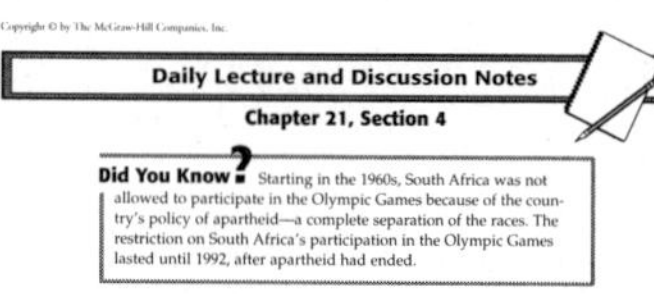

Daily Lecture and Discussion Notes

Chapter 21, Section 4

Did You Know? Starting in the 1960s, South Africa was not allowed to participate in the Olympic Games because of the country's policy of apartheid—a complete separation of the races. The restriction on South Africa's participation in the Olympic Games lasted until 1992, after apartheid had ended.

I. **Changes in Women's Lives** *(pages 671–672)*

A. Since 1970, the number of women in the workforce has continued to rise. Yet women continued to receive lower wages for the same work and fewer chances to advance.

B. During the 1960s and 1970s, women formed "consciousness-raising" groups to make people aware of women's issues, such as social and economic inequality.

C. During the 1980s and 1990s, women became involved in activities that affected the

Critical Thinking

Have students make a list of differences between the role of women in today's society compared to what it was thirty years ago. Ask them to make a second list of causes for these changes. Which causes do they believe have been most important? Which changes do they believe have been good for society? Which have been detrimental? **L1**

In the 1960s and 1970s, some women in the women's liberation movement came to believe that women themselves must transform the fundamental conditions of their lives. Women formed "consciousness-raising" groups to make people aware of women's issues. Gender stereotyping, contraception, and social and economic equality were a few of the issues that became politicized. During this time in the United States, for example, the Equal Pay and Sex Discrimination Acts were passed, giving legal support to equal rights for women.

As more women became activists in the 1980s and 1990s, they became involved in other issues. To affect the political environment, some women joined the antinuclear movement. In 1981, for example, a group of women protested American nuclear missiles in Britain by chaining themselves to the fence of an American military base. Other feminists focused on changing cultural attitudes through university programs in women's studies or worked for environmental causes.

In the 1990s, there was a backlash to the women's movement as some women advocated a return to traditional values and gender roles. Other women either rejected or attempted to redefine the term "feminism" as the struggle to balance career, family, and personal goals continued for both men and women.

Reading Check **Summarizing** What reforms did women want when they started the women's movement?

The Growth of Terrorism

Acts of terror have become a regular aspect of modern Western society. Bands of terrorists use the killing of civilians (especially by bombing), the taking of hostages, and the hijacking of airplanes to draw attention to their demands or to achieve their political goals.

Some terrorists are militant nationalists who wish to create separatist states. One such group is the Irish Republican Army (IRA), whose goal is to unite **Northern Ireland,** governed by Great Britain, with the Irish Republic. The IRA has resorted to attacks against government and civilian targets. Since the early 1970s, IRA terrorists have been responsible for the deaths of thousands of people.

State-sponsored terrorism has often been an important part of international terrorism. Some militant governments, such as those in Iraq, Syria, Cuba, and North Korea, have provided sanctuary and support to numerous terrorist organizations.

One of the most destructive acts of terrorism occurred on September 11, 2001, in the United States. Four groups of terrorists hijacked four commercial jet airplanes in Boston, Newark, and Washington, D.C. The hijackers flew two of the airplanes directly into the World Trade Center towers in New York City, destroying both buildings and causing a number of surrounding buildings to collapse. A third hijacked plane slammed into the Pentagon in Washington, D.C. The fourth plane crashed into an isolated area of Pennsylvania, diverted from its apparent objective in Washington, D.C. by heroic passengers. Thousands of people were killed, including all persons aboard the airliners.

The U.S. government accumulated evidence indicating that these acts had been carried out by al-Qaeda, the terrorist organization of Osama bin Laden. Bin Laden had used his inherited fortune to train

Picturing History

A New York firefighter surveys the remains of the twin towers of the World Trade Center. In addition to thousands of civilian casualties, many firefighters, police, and emergency workers were killed as they attempted rescue operations. What was the short-term impact of this act of terrorism on the United States and the world?

EXTENDING THE CONTENT

International Terrorism Osama bin Laden and his terrorist network are suspected of having coordinated several attacks intended to harm the United States and its international interests. On August 8, 1998, the U.S. embassies in Nairobi, Kenya, and in Dar es Salaam, Tanzania, were bombed in an attack that left 224 people dead. When the men accused of the attack went to trial, prosecutors of the case argued that bin Laden had used a satellite telephone to direct the bombings from Afghanistan. In 2000, the USS *Cole* was damaged by a bomb as the ship refueled in Aden, Yemen. Bin Laden was again suspected of having helped plan the terrorist attack that killed six U.S. sailors.

CONNECTIONS Around The World

Global Terrorism

Terrorist acts became more frequent in the second half of the twentieth century. A growing number of groups have used terrorism as a means to achieve their political goals. The U.S. State Department, for example, has designated close to 30 such groups around the world as Foreign Terrorist Organizations. These groups include urban guerrilla groups in Latin America; militants dedicated to the liberation of Palestine; Islamic militants fighting Western influence in the Middle East; and separatists seeking independent states, such as the Basques in Spain and the Tamils in Sri Lanka.

International terrorists have not limited their targets to their own countries. In 1972, three members of the neo-Marxist Japanese Red Army, who had been hired by the Popular Front for the Liberation of Palestine, opened fire at Tel Aviv's airport in Israel, killing 24 people, chiefly Christian pilgrims from Puerto Rico. The goal of the terrorists was to hurt Israel by discouraging people from visiting there.

Worldwide television newscasts have contributed to the expansion of global terrorism. International terrorists know that these news broadcasts create instant publicity for their causes. Televised images of American commercial jetliners flying into the twin towers of the World Trade Center in New York in 2001, for example, provided vivid evidence of the war that some militant groups have long threatened to wage against the United States.

Comparing Cultures

Using outside sources, locate recent acts of terrorism that occurred in two separate countries. Compare how these acts were similar and how they were different. Do you think the terrorists will achieve their goals by performing these acts?

terrorists in **Afghanistan,** which was controlled at the time by a militant Islamic group, the Taliban. Bin Laden was also suspected of directing earlier terrorist attacks against the United States, including the bombing of two U.S. embassies in Africa in 1998 and the attack on the USS *Cole* in 2000.

Following the World Trade Center and Pentagon attacks, United States president George W. Bush vowed to wage war on terrorism. The United States developed a global coalition of nations to rid the world of terrorist groups, a process that began with military action against Afghanistan in October 2001.

United States and NATO air strikes targeted Taliban-controlled command centers, airfields, and al-Qaeda hiding places. At the same time, food and supplies were dropped to aid the starving Afghan people. On the ground, opposition forces in Afghanistan pushed the Taliban out of the capital at Kabul and claimed control of more than half of the country by mid-November. Weeks later, representatives of rival Afghan factions met in Germany for UN-sponsored talks about Afghanistan's future.

At home, President Bush established the White House Office of Homeland Security for the purpose of protecting the United States from terrorism and responding to any future terrorist attacks. President Bush also signed an air security bill that made baggage screeners federal employees and required the inspection of all luggage checked on U.S. domestic flights. Across the nation, American flew flags, gave blood, and donated millions of dollars to charities to aid the families of victims of the September 11 attacks.

Reading Check **Explaining** What methods do terrorists use to achieve their goals?

Science and Technology

Scientific and technological achievements since World War II have revolutionized people's lives. During the war, many scientists were recruited by governments to develop new weapons and other instruments of war. Perhaps the most famous product of wartime scientific research was the atomic bomb, created by a team of American and European scientists. Most wartime devices, like the atomic

Answer: Answers will vary but should be supported by logical arguments.

Reading Check

Answer: killing of civilians, taking of hostages, hijacking of airplanes

Guided Reading Activity 21–4

Name ______ Date ______ Class ______

Guided Reading Activity 21-4

Western Society and Culture

DIRECTIONS: Fill in the blanks below as you read Section 4.

Since 1970, the number of women in the **(1)** ______ has continued to rise. In the 1960s and 1970s, some women came to believe that women themselves must **(2)** ______ the conditions of their lives. In the 1990s, there was a **(3)** ______ to the women's movement as some women advocated a return to traditional values and gender roles.

Bands of terrorists use the killing of **(4)** ______, the taking of hostages, and the **(5)** ______ of airplanes to draw attention to their demands or to achieve their political goals. One of the most destructive acts of ter-

Writing Activity

Have students research the 1969 Apollo II moon landing. Students should create a front-page newspaper headline and article discussing the moon landing as it would have been reported in 1969. **L2**

CURRICULUM CONNECTION

Economics Remind students that the space race did not just involve scientific research and accomplishment. It also required huge financial resources. Discuss with students why the Soviet successes were almost certain to be quickly surpassed by those of the United States.

EXTENDING THE CONTENT

Terrorism Terrorism is not a recent occurrence in history. It actually dates back to the first century A.D., if not earlier. During the first century, a Jewish religious sect called the Zealots fought to overthrow the occupation of the Romans in the present-day country of Israel. Terrorist acts were made against the political and religious leaders of Sunni Islam by the Assassins, a radical group of Shiite Muslims, in Iran during the twelfth century. Before the nineteenth century, terrorist attacks were fueled mainly by religious zeal. However, by the nineteenth century, terrorism began to have more political and revolutionary aims.

Reading Check

Answer: Complex projects during World War II required large teams of scientists, huge laboratories, and sophisticated equipment. Then, as now, only the government and large companies could provide such expensive facilities.

Reading Check

Answer: Some Christian thinkers have attempted to show how Christian teachings are still relevant for the modern world. Pope John XXIII liberalized a number of Catholic practices.

Connecting Across Time

Some people believe that the technological revolution is currently having as dramatic an effect on society as the industrial revolution had in the nineteenth century. Assign students to write an essay in which they evaluate this proposition. L3

Critical Thinking Activity

Have students look at examples of abstract expressionism and pop art and determine the basic characteristics of each one. What aspects of modern Western civilization do they reveal? L2

ABCNEWS INTERACTIVE™

Turning Points in World History
The ABC News videotape includes a segment on the moon landing.

bomb, were created for destructive purposes. Computers and jet airplanes, however, show how wartime technology can easily be adapted for peacetime uses.

By sponsoring projects, governments and the military created a new model for scientific research during World War II. Wartime projects were complex and required large teams of scientists, huge laboratories, and sophisticated equipment. Such facilities were so expensive that they could only be provided by governments and large corporations.

A stunning example of how the new scientific establishment operated is the space race. In 1961, four years after the Soviet Union sent *Sputnik I* into orbit, President Kennedy predicted that the United States would land astronauts on the Moon within a decade. Massive government funding enabled the United States to do so in 1969. *(See page 780 to read excerpts from John Glenn's* Progress Never Stops *in the Primary Sources Library.)*

The postwar alliance of science and technology led to a fast rate of change that became a fact of life in Western society. Underlying this alliance was the assumption that scientific knowledge gave human beings the ability and the right to manipulate the environment for their benefit.

Critics in the 1960s and 1970s noted that some technological advances had far-reaching side effects that were damaging to the environment. Chemical fertilizers, for example, were used for growing more abundant crops, but these fertilizers also destroyed the ecological balance of streams, rivers, and woodlands. In 2000, debates over organic farming and genetically enhanced food intensified as people continued to disagree over the role science should play in food production.

Reading Check **Summarizing** How did governmental projects help to create a new model for scientific research?

Religious Revival

Many people perceived a collapse in values during the twentieth century. The revival of religion was one response to that collapse. Ever since the Enlightenment of the eighteenth century, Christianity, as well as religion in general, had been on the defensive. A number of religious thinkers and leaders tried to bring new life to Christianity in the twentieth century. Despite the attempts of the Communist world to build an atheistic society and the attempts of the West to build a secular society, religion continued to play an important role in the lives of many people.

One expression of the religious revival was the attempt by Christian thinkers, such as the Protestant Karl Barth (BART), to breathe new life into traditional Christian teachings. In his numerous writings, Barth tried to show how the religious insights of the Reformation were still relevant for the modern world. To Barth the imperfect nature of human beings meant that humans could know religious truth not through reason but only through the grace of God.

In the Catholic Church, attempts at religious renewal came from two popes—John XXIII and John Paul II. Pope John XXIII reigned as pope for only a short time (1958 to 1963). Nevertheless, he sparked a dramatic revival of Catholicism when he summoned the twenty-first ecumenical council of the Catholic Church. Known as Vatican Council II, it liberalized a number of Catholic practices. For example, the mass could now be celebrated in the vernacular languages as well as Latin. New avenues of communication with other Christian faiths were also opened for the first time since the Reformation.

John Paul II, who had been the archbishop of Cracow in Poland before he became pope in 1978, was the first non-Italian pope since the sixteenth century. Pope John Paul's numerous travels around the world helped strengthen the Catholic Church throughout the non-Western world. Although he alienated a number of people by reasserting traditional Catholic teaching on such issues as birth control and a ban on women in the priesthood, John Paul II has been a powerful figure in reminding Catholics of the need to temper the pursuit of materialism with spiritual concerns.

Reading Check **Describing** What are two ways that the revival of religion was expressed in the twentieth century?

Trends in Art

For the most part, the United States has dominated the art world since the end of World War II. American art, often vibrantly colored and filled with activity, reflected the energy of the postwar United States. After 1945, New York City became the artistic center of the Western world.

Abstractionism, especially abstract expressionism, was the most popular form of modern art after World War II. Artists conveyed emotion and feeling and were less concerned about representing subject matter. The enormous canvases of the artist **Jackson Pollock** are filled with the vibrant energy of abstract expressionism.

The early 1960s saw the emergence of **pop art**, which took images of popular culture and transformed them into works of fine art. **Andy Warhol** was the most famous of the pop artists. Warhol took

CRITICAL THINKING ACTIVITY

Analyzing Guide students in a discussion of their perceptions of the role of religion in modern society. Do they believe that more people, or fewer people, make religion an important part of their lives today than in past generations? On what evidence do students base their opinions? Is there evidence in the media and popular culture that shows the increasing or decreasing significance of religion in people's lives? What factors or events in modern life affect the importance of religion in people's lives? How important is religion to them personally and to society as a whole? Ask students to make a chart listing reasons why they do or do not believe that society as a whole is affected by religion. L2

his subject matter from commercial art, such as Campbell soup cans, and photographs of celebrities such as Marilyn Monroe.

In the 1980s, styles emerged that some have referred to as postmodern. **Postmodernism** is marked by a revival of traditional elements and techniques, including not only traditional painting styles but also traditional crafts. Weavers, potters, glassmakers, metalsmiths, and furniture makers have all gained respect as postmodern artists.

During the 1980s and 1990s, many artists experimented with emerging technologies such as digital cameras and computer programs to create new art forms. These new art forms are often interactive, and they give the viewer the opportunity to influence the production of the art work itself—a process that blurs the line between the role of the artist and the role of the viewer.

Reading Check **Describing** What are the characteristics of pop art?

People In History

Jackson Pollock
1912–1956—American painter

Jackson Pollock became well known for his abstract expressionist paintings. Born in Wyoming, he was a child of the American West and was influenced by the sand paintings of Native Americans.

Pollock moved to New York in the early 1930s. Self-destructive and alcoholic, he saw painting as a way to deal with his problems. In such works as his *Lavender Mist* (1950), paint seems to explode, assaulting the viewer with emotion and movement.

In the 1940s, Pollock began to produce drip paintings. These he created by dropping paint with sticks and brushes on large canvases on the floor of his studio. He said: "On the floor I am more at ease. This way I can literally be in the painting. When I am in the painting I am not aware of what I am doing. There is pure harmony."

Popular Culture

The United States has been the most powerful force in shaping popular culture in the West and, to a lesser degree, in the world. Through movies, television, and music, the United States has spread its ideals and values of material prosperity—the American Dream—to millions around the world. Other countries object to the influence of American culture. It has often been called "cultural imperialism." Some nations, notably France, have taken active measures to resist the Americanization of their culture.

Already in 1923, the New York *Morning Post* noted that "the film is to America what the flag was once to Britain. By its means Uncle Sam may hope some day . . . to Americanize the world." That day has come. Movies were important vehicles for the spread of American popular culture in the years immediately after World War II. In the following decades, American movies have continued to dominate both European and American markets.

Television did not become readily available until the late 1940s. By 1954, there were 32 million television sets in the United States. Television became the centerpiece of middle-class life. In the 1960s, as television spread around the world, U.S. programs became popular in both European and non-Western nations.

The United States has also dominated popular music since the end of World War II. Jazz, blues, rhythm and blues, rock, and rap have been by far the most popular music forms in the Western world—and in much of the non-Western world—during this time. All of these genres began in the United States, and all are rooted in African American musical forms.

When American popular music spread to the rest of the world, it inspired local artists, who then transformed the music in their own way. For example, in the 1950s, American figures such as Chuck Berry and **Elvis Presley** inspired the **Beatles** and other British performers. The Beatles, in turn, led an "invasion" of the United States in the 1960s that inspired new American musicians.

The establishment of the video music channel MTV in the early 1980s changed the music scene by making image as important as sound to the selling of records. In the mid-1990s, teen and pre-teen consumers made performers such as 'N Sync and Britney Spears into multi-million dollar musical acts.

Between music videos and computer technology, consumer access to a variety of artists and musical genres has grown tremendously. An increasing number of performers are moving beyond regional boundaries to develop international audiences. For example, in the late 1990s, Latin American artists became popular in non-Latin markets. In this way, musical styles and markets continue to expand and diversify.

Reading Check **Identifying** Through what different media has American culture spread throughout the world?

Reading Check

Answer: It took images of popular culture, such as soup cans, and transformed them into works of art.

Reading Check

Answer: movies, television, music

Critical Thinking

Writer Susan Sontag said, "I think that there's been a decline in the capacity for seriousness—that society is dominated by entertainment values." Do students agree or disagree? Have students support their answers with specific observations about modern life. L2

3 ASSESS

Assign Section 4 Assessment as homework or as an in-class activity.

Have students use **Interactive Tutor Self-Assessment CD-ROM.**

Section Quiz 21–4

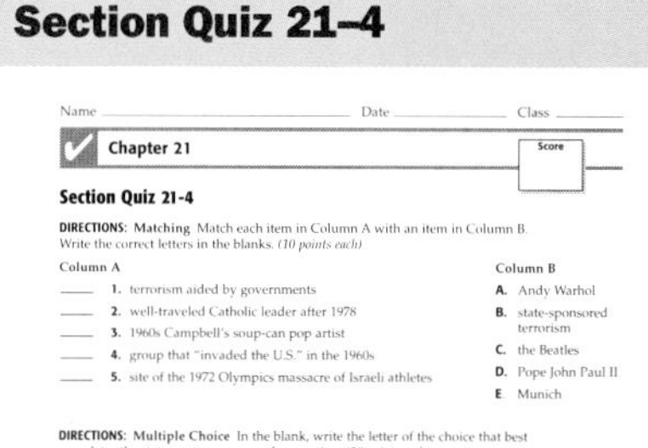

Name ______ Date ______ Class ______

Chapter 21 Score

Section Quiz 21-4

DIRECTIONS: Matching Match each item in Column A with an item in Column B. Write the correct letters in the blanks. *(10 points each)*

Column A	Column B
____ 1. terrorism aided by governments	A. Andy Warhol
____ 2. well-traveled Catholic leader after 1978	B. state-sponsored terrorism
____ 3. 1960s Campbell's soup-can pop artist	C. the Beatles
____ 4. group that "invaded the U.S." in the 1960s	D. Pope John Paul II
____ 5. site of the 1972 Olympics massacre of Israeli athletes	E. Munich

DIRECTIONS: Multiple Choice In the blank, write the letter of the choice that best completes the statement or answers the question. *(10 points each)*

MEETING INDIVIDUAL NEEDS

Visual/Auditory With your students, create an outline of the section "Popular Culture." Main headings should be 1) movies and television, 2) popular music, 3) sports. This can be done using the overhead projector or chalkboard. Discuss what trends students think will occur over the next several years in each category. Examples could include the Latin influence on music, and the emergence of soccer in the United States versus the increasing popularity of American football in Europe. How has the media helped to spread entertainment and culture across international borders? This is an excellent activity to foster critical thinking and synthesis skills for hard-to-motivate students. L1

Reading Check

Answer: Many countries have used the Olympic Games as a means to express political views. For example, the United States boycotted the 1980 Moscow Olympics, and, to retaliate, the Soviet Union boycotted the 1984 Los Angeles Games.

Reading Essentials and Study Guide 21–4

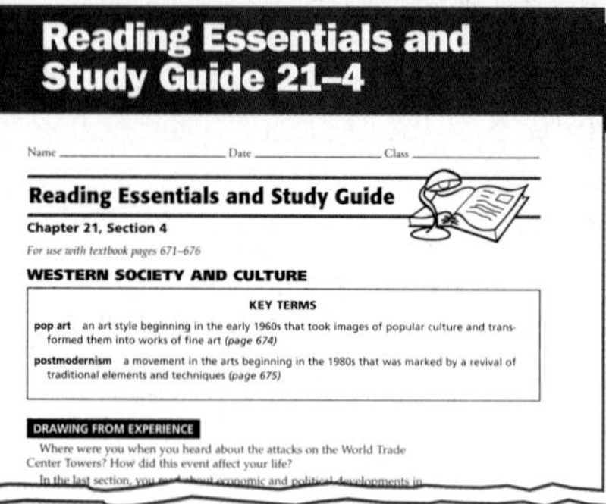
Name ________ Date ________ Class ________

Reading Essentials and Study Guide

Chapter 21, Section 4

For use with textbook pages 671–676

WESTERN SOCIETY AND CULTURE

KEY TERMS

pop art an art style beginning in the early 1960s that took images of popular culture and transformed them into works of fine art *(page 674)*

postmodernism a movement in the arts beginning in the 1980s that was marked by a revival of traditional elements and techniques *(page 675)*

DRAWING FROM EXPERIENCE

Where were you when you heard about the attacks on the World Trade Center Towers? How did this event affect your life?

Reteaching Activity

Ask students to create a chart showing the major changes in women's lives, the growth of terrorism, science and technology, religion, and art. **L1**

4 CLOSE

Guide students in a discussion about the positive and negative effects of the developments of the last decade, including the women's movement, technology, religion, and art. Ask students to analyze information in the section by making predictions for the future. **L2**

Television dominates popular culture around the world.

Sports, Television, Politics

In the postwar years, sports became a major product of both popular culture and the leisure industry. Through television, sports were transformed into a worldwide experience. The Olympic Games, for example, could now be broadcast across the globe from any location.

Televised sports were an inexpensive form of entertainment from consumers' point of view. Fans could now enjoy sporting events without buying tickets. In fact, some sports organizations at first resisted televising events because they feared that it would hurt ticket sales. Enormous revenues from television contracts helped change their minds.

Many sports organizations came to receive most of their yearly revenues from television contracts. The Olympics, for example, are now funded chiefly by American television. These funds come from advertising sponsors.

Sports have become big politics as well as big business. Indeed, politicization has been one of the most important recent trends in sports. Soccer, for example, is a vehicle for national feeling. Although the sport has been a positive outlet for national pride, all too often it has also been marked by violence.

The most telling example of the mix of politics and sport is the Olympic Games. When the Soviets entered Olympic competition in 1952, the Olympics became part of the Cold War. They were known as the "war without weapons." The Soviets used the Olympics to promote the Communist system as the best path for social progress.

The political nature of the games found expression in other ways as well. In 1972, at the Munich Games, a Palestinian terrorist group seized 11 Israeli athletes as hostages. Two hostages were killed immediately and the other 9 died in a shootout at the airport. The Soviets refused to participate in the Los Angeles Games in 1984 after the United States boycotted the 1980 Moscow Olympics.

Reading Check **Explaining** How have sports become big politics?

SECTION 4 ASSESSMENT

Checking for Understanding

1. **Define** pop art, postmodernism.
2. **Identify** Jackson Pollock, Andy Warhol, Elvis Presley, Beatles.
3. **Locate** Northern Ireland, Afghanistan.
4. **Explain** why some critics began to question the value of technological progress in postwar society. Give an example of a scientific or technological achievement that was criticized and explain why.
5. **List** the reasons why terrorists choose to pursue terrorism. What are some of the political goals of terrorists? In what ways are some terrorists associated with governments?

Critical Thinking

6. **Summarize** What are the components of the new scientific establishment? Explain the benefits and shortcomings of these components.
7. **Organizing Information** Create a chart like the one below listing the main goals of terrorists, the methods they use to achieve these goals, and how governments have responded.

Terrorism		
Goals	Methods	Government Responses

Analyzing Visuals

8. **Examine** the photograph of the destruction of the World Trade Center, shown on page 672. Describe the different roles citizens play during times of national or international crisis.

Writing About History

9. **Descriptive Writing** Abstractionism, abstract expressionism, and pop art became popular art forms after World War II. Research these art forms and make a list of two or three artists who followed each form. Find examples of these artists' works and describe in an essay how these works represent the innovations of the new art forms.

SECTION 4 ASSESSMENT

1. Key terms are in blue.
2. Jackson Pollock *(p. 674)*; Andy Warhol *(p. 674)*; Elvis Presley *(p. 675)*; Beatles *(p. 675)*
3. See chapter maps.
4. Some technological advances had far-reaching side effects that were damaging to the environment. Answers will vary.
5. draw attention to demands, achieve political goals; establishing states, draining a country's resources; some governments support or protect terrorists.
6. large teams of scientists, huge laboratories, sophisticated equipment, government or corporate funding; answers will vary.
7. Goals: draw attention to political demands; achieve political objectives; Methods: killing civilians; taking hostages; hijacking airplanes; Government Responses: coalition of nations to cooperate in ridding the world of terrorist groups
8. Answers should be supported by logical arguments.
9. Essays should demonstrate understanding of varying artistic expression.

Study & Writing SKILLBUILDER

Preparing A Bibliography

Why Learn This Skill?

In Chapter 15 you learned how to write a report. At the end of any report that you write, you need to list all the sources you used. A bibliography is a list of the books and articles used to research the material in your report.

Learning the Skill

A bibliography must follow a specific format:

- Entries should be arranged alphabetically by the author's last name. If there is no author, as in an encyclopedia reference, use the words in the title of the article to put it into alphabetical order.
- Different types of sources have different formats:

Books Author's last name, first name. *Full Title.* Place of publication: publisher, copyright date.
Reich, Charles. *The Greening of America.* New York: Random House, 1970.

Articles from magazines Author's last name, first name. "Title of Article." *Periodical* in which article appears, Volume number (issue date): page numbers.
Watson, Bruce. "The New Peace Corps in the New Kazakhstan." *Smithsonian,* Vol. 25 (August 1994): pp. 26–35.

Articles from newspapers Author's last name, first name (if given). "Title of Article." *Newspaper* in which article appears, date, section and page numbers. (If the newspaper has more than one edition, the edition should be cited rather than the page number, since the page number might be different in each edition.)
Finnonian, Albert. "The Iron Curtain Rises." *Wilberton Journal,* February 7, 1990, final edition.

Different types of sources require different formats in the bibliography.

Articles from encyclopedias "Title of article." *Encyclopedia's Name.* Edition (if not the first).
"Cold War." *Encyclopedia Britannica.* 11th Edition.

Web sites **Title of referenced source.** Web site's name (if given).
www.Internet address.com.
A Concrete Curtain: The Life and Death of the Berlin Wall.
www.wall-berlin.org.

Practicing the Skill

Review the sample bibliography, then answer the questions that follow.

Bibliography

Winkler, Allan M. *The Cold War: a history in documents.* Oxford, New York: Oxford University Press, 2000.
Hazen, Walter A. Post-Cold War Europe. Grand Rapids, Mich: Instructional Fair/TS Denison, 2000.
Havel, Václav. "The Call for New Politics." *The Washington Post.* February 22, 1990, p. A28.
The European Union: A Guide for Americans.
www.eurunion.org.

1. Are the bibliography entries in the correct order? Why or why not?
2. What is incorrect in the second book listing?
3. What is incorrect in the article listing?

Applying the Skill

Compile a bibliography for the research report you completed in Chapter 15. Include at least five sources.

Glencoe's **Skillbuilder Interactive Workbook, Level 2,** provides instruction and practice in key social studies skills.

ANSWERS TO PRACTICING THE SKILL

1. No; although the titles should be in alphabetical order, they are not.
2. The title is not italicized.
3. The name of the newspaper should be separated from the date by a comma, not a period.

Applying the Skill: Students will create bibliographies. Have students review their work carefully to check for small details such as periods versus commas. You may want to have students exchange papers so they can check each other's work.

Study & Writing SKILLBUILDER

TEACH

Preparing A Bibliography Write the following list on the chalkboard: *Author's name, Title, Place of publication, Publisher, Date of publication.* Ask students to find this information for their textbook. If necessary, guide students to the title and copyright pages. Have volunteers write the correct information from their text opposite the five categories on the chalkboard. Then tell students that this information is required for books in a bibliography. Direct students to read the skill and complete the practice questions to learn more about the purposes and formats of a bibliography. L1

Additional Practice

Skills Reinforcement Activity 21

Name ____________ Date ____________ Class ____________

Skills Reinforcement Activity 21

Preparing a Bibliography

A bibliography is a list of the resources used in writing a report. It establishes the reliability of your research and helps those who read your report to know where to find more information on your topic.

Bibliographies follow an established format. Entries are listed in alphabetical order and include the author, title, page numbers, publisher information, and publication date. Sample entries are shown below.

Books:
Hay, Peter. *Ordinary Heroes: The Life and Death of Chana Szenes, Israel's National Heroine.* New York: Paragon House, 1986.

Articles from magazines:
Watson, Bruce. "The New Peace Corps in the New Kazakhstan." *Smithsonian,* Vol. 25 (August 1994): pp. 26–35.

GLENCOE TECHNOLOGY

CD-ROM
Glencoe Skillbuilder Interactive Workbook CD-ROM, Level 2

This interactive CD-ROM reinforces student mastery of essential social studies skills.

GLENCOE TECHNOLOGY

MindJogger Videoquiz

Use the **MindJogger Videoquiz** to review Chapter 21 content.

 Available in VHS.

CHAPTER 21 ASSESSMENT and ACTIVITIES

Chapter Summary

The end of the Cold War brought dramatic economic, political, and social changes to Europe and North America. Many of these changes can be understood through the themes of conflict, change, regionalism, and cooperation. Below, some of the major events in postwar society are categorized according to these themes.

Conflict

- Serb forces carry out "ethnic cleansing" of Muslims.
- Terrorism becomes a regular aspect of modern society.
- Soviet troops crush a reform movement in Czechoslovakia.
- Nicolae Ceauşescu is arrested and executed.

Change

- The Soviet Union adopts a policy of perestroika under Gorbachev.
- Lech Walesa becomes the first elected president of an Eastern European nation in 40 years.
- The national debt triples in the United States during Ronald Reagan's presidency.
- Television, movies, and music spread American culture throughout the world.

Regionalism

- Ethnic Albanians declare Kosovo an independent province.
- Bosnian Serbs fight Bosnian Muslims and Croats.
- Bands of German youths attack illegal immigrants.
- Intense fighting breaks out between Protestants and Catholics in Northern Ireland.

Cooperation

- British women hold an antinuclear protest.
- American culture spreads through popular media.
- East Germany and West Germany are reunited into one nation.
- The Soviet Union and the United States sign the INF Treaty.

Using Key Terms

1. _____ was a phase in American/Soviet relations that was marked by decreased tension.
2. Serbian forces engaged in _____ to forcibly remove Bosnian Muslims from their lands.
3. The conservative British economic policy that limited social welfare, restricted union power, and ended inflation was known as _____.
4. _____ spoke out against the repressive Soviet regime.
5. Mikhail Gorbachev introduced _____ to restructure Soviet economic policy.

Reviewing Key Facts

6. **Government** What doctrine gave the Soviet Union the right to intervene if communism in another Communist state was threatened?
7. **Economics** What problems arose in Russia after the Soviet Union dissolved?
8. **Society** How did religion contribute to changes in Bosnia and Poland?
9. **Government** List the three Eastern European countries that made peaceful transitions from Communist to free-market societies.
10. **Government** Which countries' transitions to free-market societies were filled with violence and bloodshed?
11. **Economics** What caused the economic downturn in Western Europe from the mid-1970s to the early 1980s?
12. **Society** What problems surfaced in Germany as a result of reunification?
13. **Culture** Why was the Official Languages Act passed in Canada in 1968?
14. **Society** What goal did women in the United States and Europe work toward when the women's movement began?
15. **Society** List the methods terrorists use to draw attention to their causes or achieve their political goals.
16. **Science and Technology** Name the World War II invention that has become a fixture in homes, schools, and businesses in the United States and other developed countries.

Critical Thinking

17. **Evaluating** What were the results of the Reagan administration's military buildup?
18. **Analyzing** Explain why the United States, Great Britain, France, and Canada alternated between liberal and conservative government leaders from 1970 through 2000.

Using Key Terms

1. Détente **2.** ethnic cleansing **3.** Thatcherism **4.** Dissidents **5.** perestroika

Reviewing Key Facts

6. Brezhnev Doctrine
7. economic hardships, social disarray, a rise in organized crime, and the attempted secession of Chechnya
8. The Serbs wanted to kill many of the Bosnians because they were Muslims; they referred to this as "ethnic cleansing." The Catholic Church, under the leadership of the first Polish pope, supported the Solidarity movement in Poland.
9. Poland, Czechoslovakia, East Germany
10. Romania, Yugoslavia
11. The dramatic increase in the price of oil following the Arab-Israeli conflict in 1973 was a major cause of the economic downturn; both unemployment and inflation increased dramatically.
12. The cost of rebuilding eastern Germany was more than expected, forcing the government to raise taxes. The collapse of the economy in eastern Germany led to high levels of unemployment and severe discontent.
13. to preserve a united Canada by allowing both English and French to be used in the federal civil service
14. to transform the fundamental conditions of their lives; issues included gender stereotyping, contraception, and social and economic equality
15. They kill civilians, take hostages, and hijack airplanes.
16. the computer

Critical Thinking

17. Total federal spending rose from $631 billion in 1981 to over a trillion dollars in 1987, producing record government budget deficits. Budget deficits were triple those of the 1970s.
18. They were attempting to stabilize their economies.
19. It helps spread American ideals and values of material prosperity—the American Dream—to millions around the world, and may help foster democracy. On the negative side, it may lead to the erosion of the very features that define and distinguish other cultures. Latin American music has been popular even in non-Latin markets. (Other recent influences might include anime; *feng shui*; foreign foods; and reggae, *rai*, and Celtic music.)

Writing About History

20. Essays should be clearly written and supported by examples and logical arguments.

Self-Check Quiz

Visit the *Glencoe World History—Modern Times* Web site at wh.mt.glencoe.com and click on **Chapter 21–Self-Check Quiz** to prepare for the Chapter Test.

19. **Analyzing** The United States has been accused of "cultural imperialism." What positive and negative effects does the spread of American popular culture have? How has American popular culture been influenced in return?

Writing About History

20. **Persuasive Writing** In the latter part of the twentieth century, Communist governments ceased to exist in the Soviet Union and Eastern Europe. Countries instantly converted their economic systems from socialist to free-market societies. These conversions created many problems for the new societies. Write a paper listing the problems created by the fall of communism and describe solutions that would have made the transition easier.

Analyzing Sources

In his book *Perestroika,* Mikhail Gorbachev wrote:

❝There is a great thirst for mutual understanding and mutual communication in the world. It is felt among politicians, it is gaining momentum among the intelligentsia, representatives of culture, and the public at large. . . . Now the whole world needs restructuring, i.e., progressive development, a fundamental change . . . I believe that more and more people will come to realize that through restructuring in the broad sense of the word, the integrity of the world will be enhanced.❞

21. What does Gorbachev think is gaining momentum among the public at large?
22. How does Gorbachev's quote apply to today's world?

Making Decisions

23. Imagine that it is 1991 and you are in Ukraine, casting a vote for or against independence. What are the reasons you might choose to sever Ukraine from the Soviet Union? Why might you want to remain part of the Soviet Union? What factors do you consider most important? What is your final decision?
24. As the editor of a history textbook, you plan to include a feature on the popular culture of the 2000s. Who would you include as influential musicians, artists, and entertainers? What values do these individuals model? Who are the heroes and who are the superstars? Is there a difference?

NATIONAL GEOGRAPHIC **Caucasus Region, 1991**

Analyzing Maps and Charts

Study the map above to answer the following questions.

25. Which of these states is completely landlocked?
26. Which state's territory is separated by Armenia? What problems might that present?

Applying Technology Skills

27. **Using the Internet** Using the information in your text and outside sources, develop a PowerPoint presentation on the history of communism. Use specific examples.

Standardized Test Practice

Directions: Choose the best answer to the question below.

What happened in Czechoslovakia after the Communist Party collapsed?

F Rival ethnic states could not agree on national borders.
G East and West Germany were reunified.
H Conservative movements came to power in America and Great Britain.
J Mikhail Gorbachev invaded Czechoslovakia to regain control.

Test-Taking Tip: If you do not know the correct answer to this question, read the answer choices carefully. Eliminate any statement that is historically incorrect. This will help you focus on the remaining answer choices and increase your chances of choosing the correct answer.

Have students visit the Web site at wh.mt.glencoe.com to review Chapter 21 and take the Self-Check Quiz.

Analyzing Maps and Charts

25. Armenia
26. Azerbaijan; isolation, cultural and religious differences

Applying Technology Skills

27. Students will develop presentations based on chapter content and research.

Standardized Test Practice

Answer: F
Answer Explanation: The country of Czechoslovakia became two separate nations (p. 662)

Bonus Question ?

Ask: **What do you think will be the future of communism as an international political ideology?** *(Students should discuss the overthrowing of Communist regimes in the former Soviet Union and Eastern Europe and recent events in these countries, such as the election of former Communists in Hungary and Poland.)* **L2**

Analyzing Sources

21. the thirst for mutual understanding and mutual communication
22. People still seek mutual understanding and better communication. As long as people limit themselves to nationalistic goals, we will continue to have conflicts.

Making Decisions

23. Answers should be consistent with material presented in the chapter and supported by examples and logical arguments.
24. Answers should be consistent with material presented in the chapter and supported by examples and logical arguments.

Chapter 22 Resources

Timesaving Tools

TeacherWorks™ All-In-One Planner and Resource Center

- **Interactive Teacher Edition** Access your Teacher Wraparound Edition and your classroom resources with a few easy clicks.
- **Interactive Lesson Planner** Planning has never been easier! Organize your week, month, semester, or year with all the lesson helps you need to make teaching creative, timely, and relevant.

Use Glencoe's **Presentation Plus!** multimedia teacher tool to easily present dynamic lessons that visually excite your students. Using Microsoft PowerPoint® you can customize the presentations to create your own personalized lessons.

Teaching Transparencies

Graphic Organizer Student Activity 22 Transparency

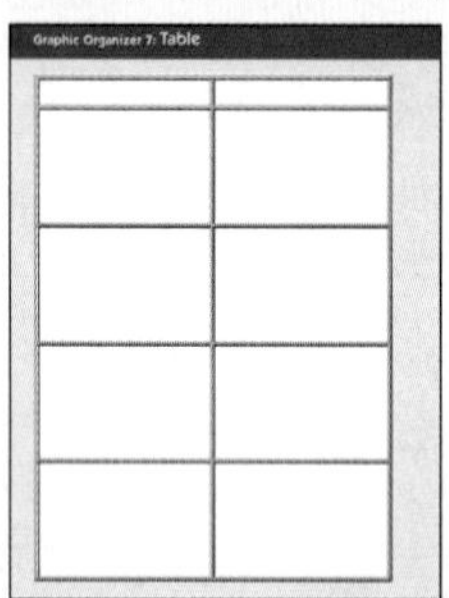

Chapter Transparency 22

Map Overlay Transparency 22

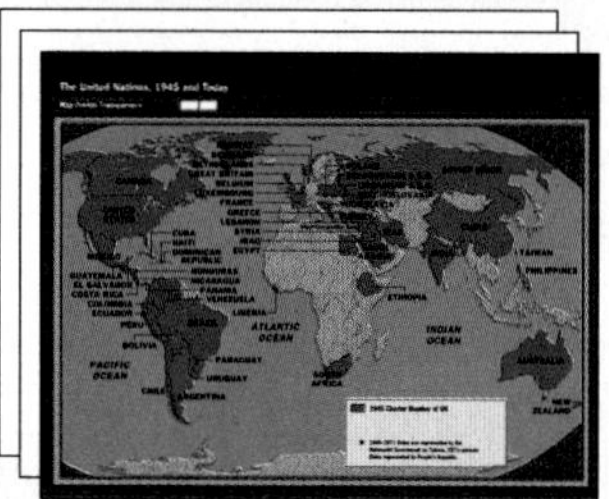

Application and Enrichment

Enrichment Activity 22

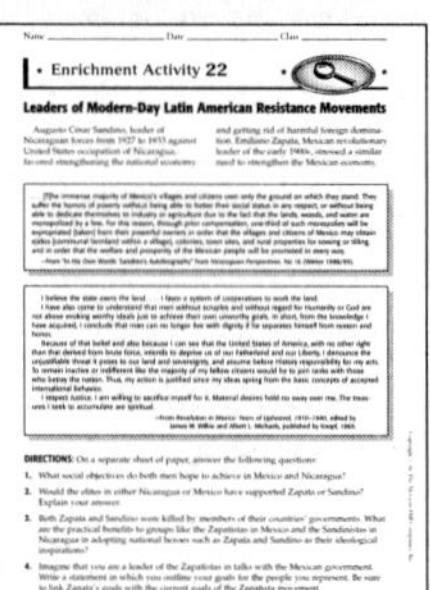

Primary Source Reading 22

History Simulation Activity 22

Historical Significance Activity 22

Cooperative Learning Activity 22

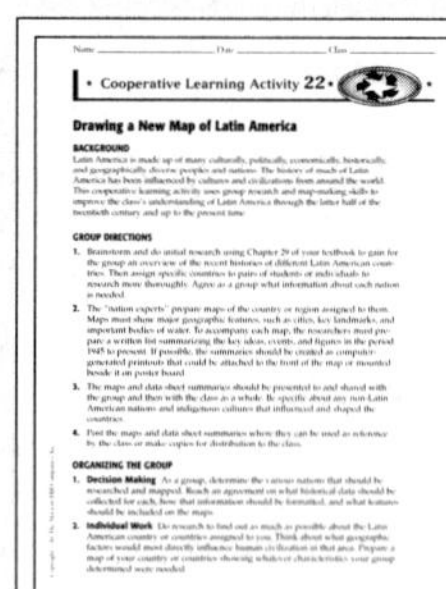

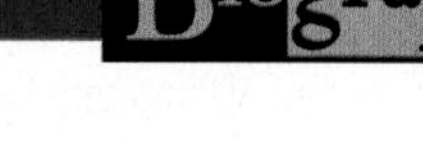

A&E HOME VIDEO

THE HISTORY CHANNEL.

The following videotape programs are available from Glencoe as supplements to Chapter 22:

- **Fidel Castro: El Commandante** (ISBN 0–7670–0237–7)
- **Cuba and Castro** (ISBN 0–7670–1426–X)
- **Evita: The Woman Behind the Myth** (ISBN 0–7670–0029–3)

To order, call Glencoe at 1–800–334–7344. To find classroom resources to accompany many of these videos, check the following home pages:
A&E Television: www.aande.com
The History Channel: www.historychannel.com

Chapter 22 Resources

Review and Reinforcement

Linking Past and Present Activity 22

Time Line Activity 22

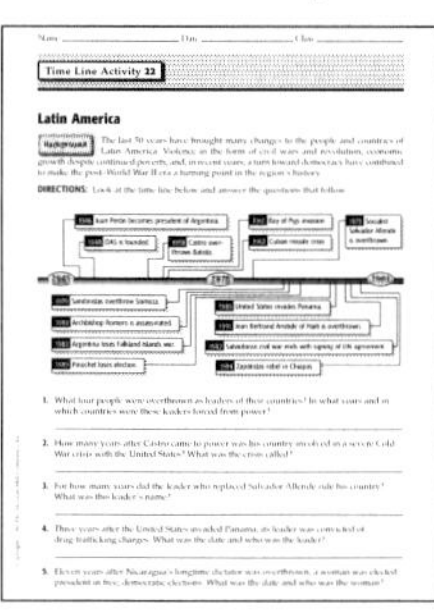

Reteaching Activity 22

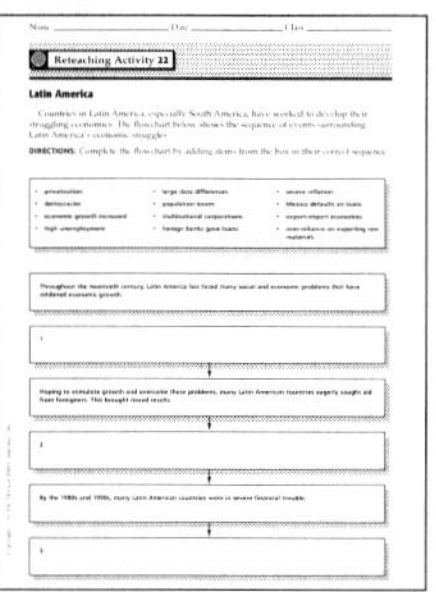

Vocabulary Activity 22

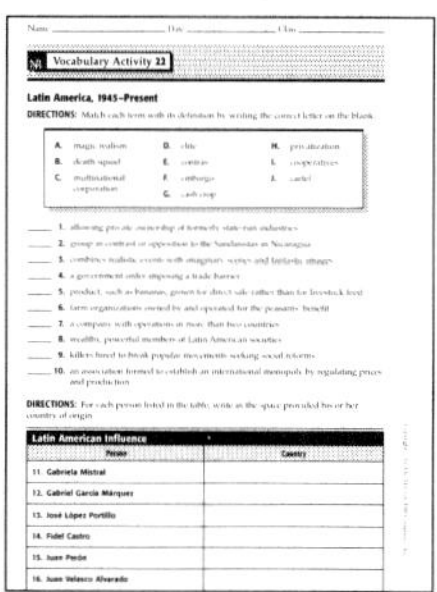

Critical Thinking Skills Activity 22

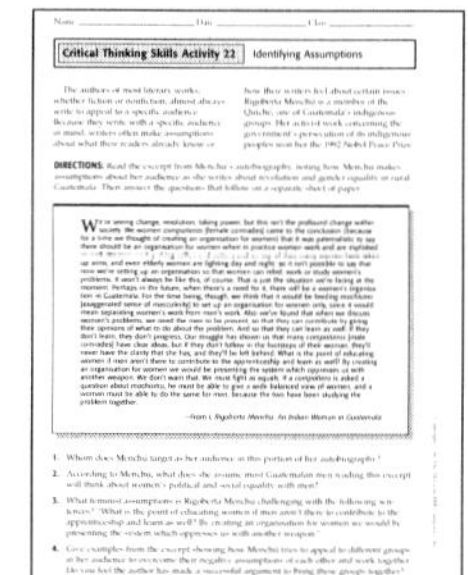

Assessment and Evaluation

Chapter 22 Test Form A

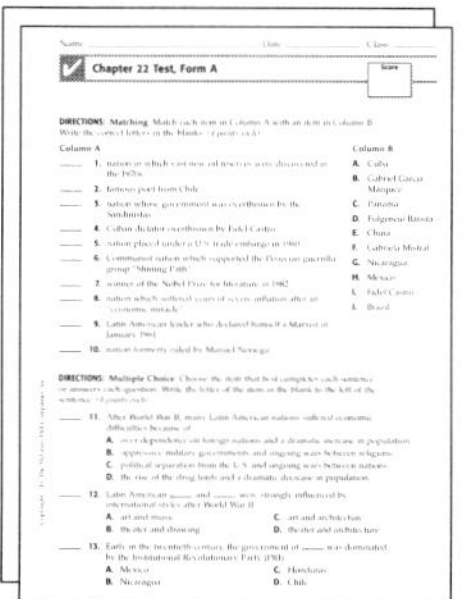

Chapter 22 Test Form B

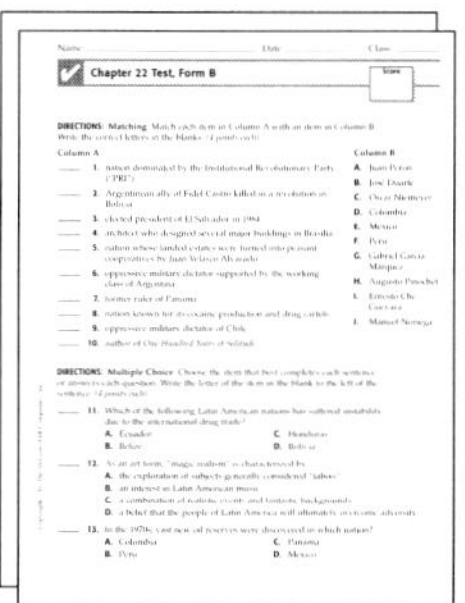

Performance Assessment Activity 22

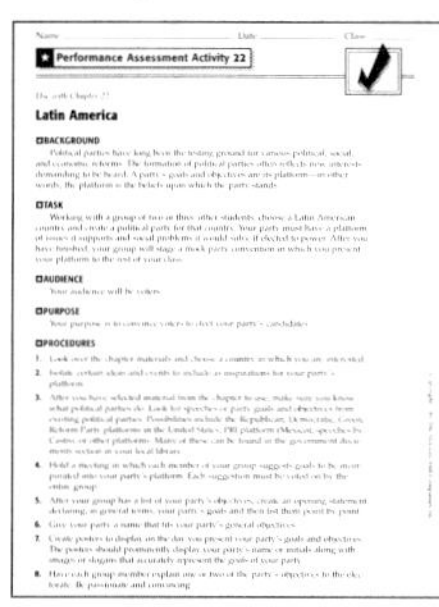

ExamView® Pro Testmaker CD-ROM

Standardized Test Skills Practice Workbook Activity 22

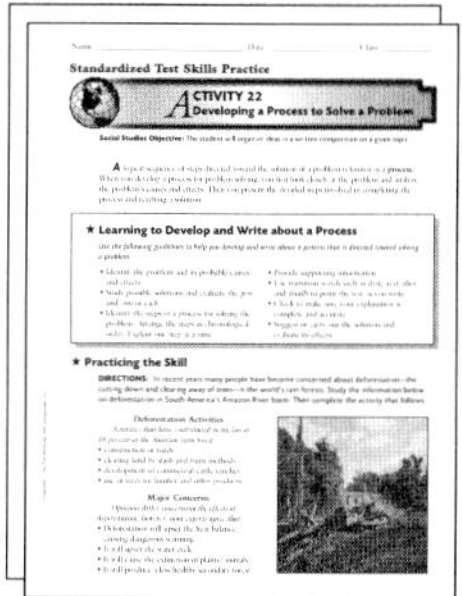

Interdisciplinary Activities

Mapping History Activity 22

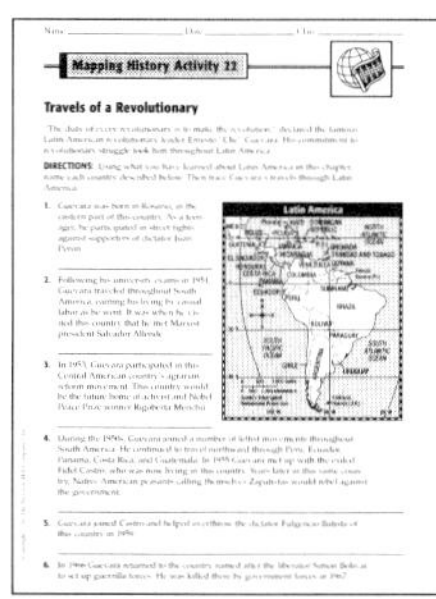

World Art and Music Activity 22

History and Geography Activity 22

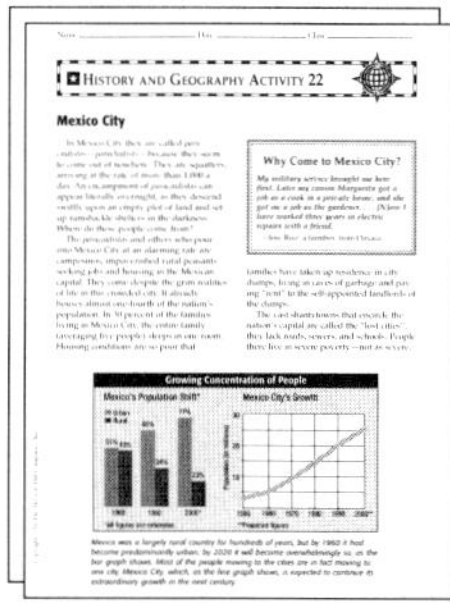

People in World History Activity 22

Multimedia

- Vocabulary PuzzleMaker CD-ROM
- Interactive Tutor Self-Assessment CD-ROM
- ExamView® Pro Testmaker CD-ROM
- Audio Program
- World History Primary Source Document Library CD-ROM
- MindJogger Videoquiz
- Presentation Plus! CD-ROM
- TeacherWorks CD-ROM
- Interactive Student Edition CD-ROM
- The World History—Modern Times Video Program

Spanish Resources

The following Spanish language materials are available in the Spanish Resources Binder:

- Spanish Guided Reading Activities
- Spanish Reteaching Activities
- Spanish Quizzes and Tests
- Spanish Vocabulary Activities
- Spanish Summaries

Chapter 22 Resources

SECTION RESOURCES

Daily Objectives	Reproducible Resources	Multimedia Resources
SECTION 1 **General Trends in Latin America** 1. Explain how exporting raw materials and importing manufactured goods has led to economic and political troubles for Latin American nations. 2. Characterize the democratic systems that many Latin American nations began to build in the late 1980s.	Reproducible Lesson Plan 22–1 Daily Lecture and Discussion Notes 22–1 Guided Reading Activity 22–1* Section Quiz 22–1* Reading Essentials and Study Guide 22–1	Daily Focus Skills Transparency 22–1 Interactive Tutor Self-Assessment CD-ROM ExamView® Pro Testmaker CD-ROM Presentation Plus! CD-ROM
SECTION 2 **Mexico, Cuba, and Central America** 1. Summarize the political and economic crises that Mexico and Central America faced after World War II. 2. Discuss the United States's fear of the spread of communism in Central American countries that led to active U.S. involvement in the region.	Reproducible Lesson Plan 22–2 Daily Lecture and Discussion Notes 22–2 Guided Reading Activity 22–2* Section Quiz 22–2* Reading Essentials and Study Guide 22–2	Daily Focus Skills Transparency 22–2 Interactive Tutor Self-Assessment CD-ROM ExamView® Pro Testmaker CD-ROM Presentation Plus! CD-ROM
SECTION 3 **The Nations of South America** 1. Discuss why South American nations have experienced economic, social, and political problems. 2. Explain why democracy has advanced in South America since the late 1980s.	Reproducible Lesson Plan 22–3 Daily Lecture and Discussion Notes 22–3 Guided Reading Activity 22–3* Section Quiz 22–3* Reteaching Activity 22* Reading Essentials and Study Guide 22–3	Daily Focus Skills Transparency 22–3 Interactive Tutor Self-Assessment CD-ROM ExamView® Pro Testmaker CD-ROM Presentation Plus! CD-ROM

0:00 **OUT OF TIME?**
Assign the Chapter 22 **Reading Essentials and Study Guide.**

*Also Available in Spanish

 Blackline Master  Transparency 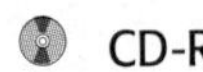 CD-ROM  DVD

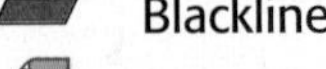 Poster 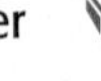 Music Program  Audio Program  Videocassette

Chapter 22 Resources

NATIONAL GEOGRAPHIC Teacher's Corner

INDEX TO NATIONAL GEOGRAPHIC MAGAZINE

The following articles relate to this chapter:

- "Peru Begins Again," by John McCarry, May 1996.
- "El Salvador," by Mike Edwards, September 1995.
- "Buenos Aires: Making Up for Lost Time," by John J. Putnam, December 1994.

ADDITIONAL NATIONAL GEOGRAPHIC SOCIETY PRODUCTS

To order the following, call National Geographic at 1-800-368-2728:

- *Capitalism, Socialism, Communism Series, "Communism"* (Video)
- *Nations of the World Series, "Mexico"* (Video)
- *Nations of the World Series, "Central America"* (Video)
- *Physical Geography of the Continents Series: South America* (Video)
- *The Mexicans: Through Their Eyes* (Video)

NGS ONLINE

Access National Geographic's new dynamic MapMachine Web site and other geography resources at:
www.nationalgeographic.com
www.nationalgeographic.com/maps

KEY TO ABILITY LEVELS

Teaching strategies have been coded.

- L1 BASIC activities for all students
- L2 AVERAGE activities for average to above-average students
- L3 CHALLENGING activities for above-average students
- ELL ENGLISH LANGUAGE LEARNER activities

Block Schedule

Activities that are suited to use within the block scheduling framework are identified by:

WORLD HISTORY Online

Use our Web site for additional resources. All essential content is covered in the Student Edition.

You and your students can visit www.wh.mt.glencoe.com, the Web site companion to *Glencoe World History—Modern Times.* This innovative integration of electronic and print media offers your students a wealth of opportunities. The student text directs students to the Web site for the following options:

- **Chapter Overviews**
- **Self-Check Quizzes**
- **Student Web Activities**
- **Textbook Updates**

Answers to the Student Web Activities are provided for you in the **Web Activity Lesson Plans.** Additional Web resources and Interactive Tutor Puzzles are also available.

From the Classroom of...

Mark Manning
Morristown High School
Morristown, New Jersey

Value of the Amazon Rain Forest

Provide students with fact sheets on the Amazon region. Then organize the class into two groups. Have one group research the economic potential of the rain forest, while the other investigates the region's unique ecology. Then have the class generate two lists comparing the economic and ecological worth of the Amazon region.

Have the full class discuss both sides of the issue of developing the Amazon rain forest. Given the struggling economies of the nations of the region, should economic development be a priority? Can economic development and ecological preservation be balanced?

Performance
Assessment

Refer to Activity 22 in the Performance Assessment Activities and Rubrics booklet.

The Impact Today

Emphasize with students the increasingly close relationships between the United States and Latin America due to trade agreements, cultural exchanges, and immigration policies. Before they begin reading this chapter, ask students to list ways in which the United States impacts the political, economic, and cultural life of Latin America, and how Latin America impacts life in the United States. Discuss how particular regions of the United States are affected in different ways or to varying degrees.

GLENCOE TECHNOLOGY

The World History—Modern Times Video Program

To learn more about events in Cuba, students can view the Chapter 22 video, "The Cuban Revolution," from **The World History—Modern Times Video Program.**

MindJogger Videoquiz

Use the **MindJogger Videoquiz** to preview Chapter 22 content.

 Available in VHS.

CHAPTER 22 Latin America

1945–Present

Key Events

As you read this chapter, look for the key events in the history of Latin American nations.

- *Many Latin American nations have experienced severe economic problems, and their governments have been led by military dictators.*
- *Successful Marxist revolutions in Cuba and Nicaragua fed fears in the United States about the spread of communism in the Americas.*

The Impact Today

The events that occurred during this time period still impact our lives today.

- *Latin American influence in the United States can be seen in art, music, literature, and foods.*
- *Rapid and unplanned industrial development in some Latin American countries has led to heightened concern about the environment.*

World History—Modern Times Video *The Chapter 22 video,* "The Cuban Revolution," *chronicles the causes and effects of Castro's revolution in Cuba.*

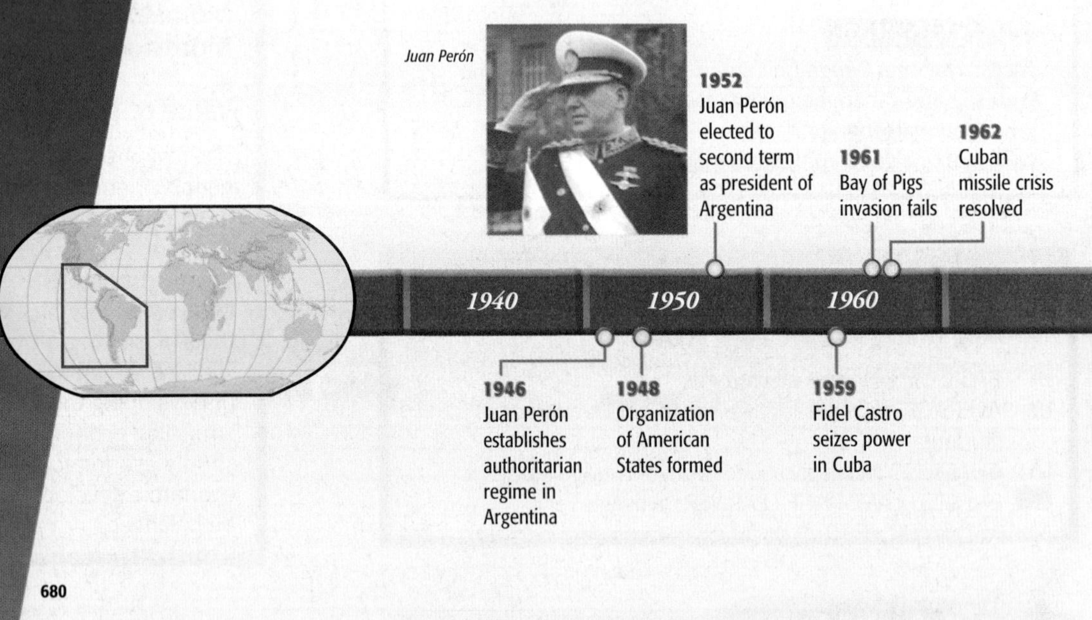
Juan Perón
1952
Juan Perón elected to second term as president of Argentina
1961
Bay of Pigs invasion fails
1962
Cuban missile crisis resolved
1940
1950
1960
1946
Juan Perón establishes authoritarian regime in Argentina
1948
Organization of American States formed
1959
Fidel Castro seizes power in Cuba

TWO-MINUTE LESSON LAUNCHER

Without letting them look at a map, ask students to name all the countries of North America. *(Canada, United States, and Mexico)* Ask them to identify the seven countries of Central America. *(Guatemala, Belize, Honduras, El Salvador, Nicaragua, Costa Rica, and Panama)* Find out if students are able to identify the countries of South America. *(Ecuador, Colombia, Venezuela, Guyana, Suriname, French Guiana, Brazil, Peru, Bolivia, Chile, Paraguay, Uruguay, Argentina)* Students may be surprised to discover that Mexico is a North American country. It is also listed as a Latin American country and as one of the countries of the Caribbean Basin. Using a map, help students to discover why Mexico is listed in three different categories. *(Geographically, Mexico is part of North America and the Caribbean Basin. Linguistically and culturally, it is part of Latin America.)* **L1**

Sugarloaf Mountain overlooks Rio de Janeiro, one of Brazil's most populous cities.

Ché Guevara

1967
Ché Guevara dies in Bolivia

1990
Violeta Barrios de Chamorro elected president of Nicaragua

1970 *1980* *1990* *2000*

Arrest of Panamanian leader Manuel Noriega

1989
United States invades Panama

2000
Vicente Fox becomes president of Mexico

HISTORY Online

Chapter Overview
Visit the *Glencoe World History—Modern Times* Web site at wh.mt.glencoe.com and click on **Chapter 22–Chapter Overview** to preview chapter information.

MORE ABOUT THE ART

Rio de Janeiro This photograph reveals a great deal about Rio de Janeiro. It is a vibrant city, popular among Brazilians and tourists. Five hundred years ago, Rio was founded by Portuguese explorers. Today, the city is a mix of Native American, African, European, and Asian descendants. Situated between the mountains and the ocean, eight million people live in a city designed for a third of that number. Million dollar condominiums are just blocks from overcrowded slums and the rainforest. Two of the most famous beaches in the world, Ipanema and Copacabana, are in Rio, contributing to a large tourist industry. Rio is a microcosm of Brazil, dealing with the same problems the nation faces: pollution, unequal distribution of income, and crime.

Introducing CHAPTER 22

Chapter Objectives

After studying this chapter, students should be able to:

1. list the economic and political changes that Latin America experienced after 1945;
2. describe the chief features and impact of the Cuban Revolution;
3. identify the major educational and cultural trends in Latin America since 1945;
4. understand that dictatorships were an oppressive consequence of political and economic instability;
5. summarize how Latin American countries have become more democratic.

Chapter Overview
Introduce students to chapter content and key terms by having them access **Chapter Overview 22** at wh.mt.glencoe.com .

Time Line Activity

As students read the chapter, have them review the time line on pages 680 to 681. Ask students to create a time line of their own which includes the events that they feel are significant in Latin American history.

CHAPTER PREVIEW

Introducing
A Story That Matters

Depending upon the ability levels of your students, select from the following questions to reinforce the reading of *A Story That Matters.*

- How successful was the attack on Moncada? *(Most troops were killed, wounded, or arrested.)*
- From today's vantage point, how would you evaluate Batista's decision to release the Castro brothers? *(resulted in Batista's overthrow)*
- What do you think will happen in Cuba when Castro is no longer the leader? *(Answers will vary.)* **L1 L2 L3**

About the Art

Fidel Castro has been the leader of Cuba for more than forty years. Castro's Cuba played an important role during the Cold War as a Soviet-financed Communist country ninety miles from the United States. Today some people feel that Castro is an anachronism, the last Communist dictator in Latin America, a leader who bet that the Soviet Union would triumph—a bet he lost. After years of economic instability, Cuba is suffering from poverty. An older, frailer Castro has considered limited capitalistic ventures to bring in revenue. The photos reinforce the fact that Fidel Castro is a military dictator. He has jailed political opponents and forced people who are looking for a better way of life to escape in boats and on rafts.

CHAPTER PREVIEW A Story That Matters

A victorious Fidel Castro rides through the streets of Havana in 1959.

The Castro Brothers

On July 26, 1953, two brothers, Fidel and Raúl Castro, led a band of 165 young people in an attack on the Moncada army camp at Santiago de Cuba. While a law student at the University of Havana, Fidel Castro had become a revolutionary. He was determined to overthrow the government of Fulgencio Batista, the dictator of Cuba.

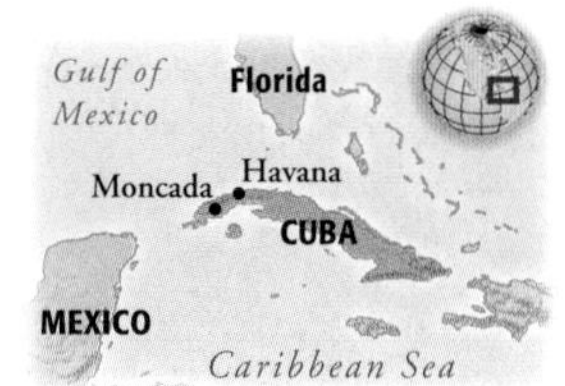

The attack on Moncada, however, was a disaster. Many of the troops led by the Castro brothers were killed, wounded, or arrested. Fidel and Raúl Castro escaped but were later captured and sentenced to prison for 15 years.

The Castro brothers could easily have died in prison, where political prisoners were routinely tortured. Instead, they were released after 11 months. By freeing political prisoners, Batista hoped to win the favor of the Cuban people.

He certainly did not gain the favor of the Castros. After his release, Fidel Castro fled to Mexico and built a new revolutionary army. Six years later, on January 1, 1959, Fidel Castro and his forces finally seized control of Cuba. Hundreds of thousands of Cubans swept into the streets, overcome with joy. One person remarked, "We were walking on a cloud." To the many Latin Americans who wanted major social and economic changes, Castro soon became a source of hope.

Why It Matters

Since 1945, the nations of Latin America have followed different paths of change. In some countries military dictators have maintained political stability and initiated economic changes. A few nations, like Cuba, have used Marxist revolutions to create a new political, economic, and social order. Many Latin American nations have struggled to build democratic systems, especially since the late 1980s. The Cold War has also had an impact on Latin America.

History and You As you read this chapter, document the struggle between democracy and dictatorship in the Latin American states. Make a chart or diagram comparing the different states, their leadership, and reasons why the regimes were able to gain power.

HISTORY AND YOU

Have students search newspapers or Internet news sources and ask students to bring in current articles that report on Latin American countries. Discuss the ways in which foreign countries are still involved in Latin American countries. *(aid, investment, military, judicial)* Are the problems that are mentioned in these news articles legacies of colonial history? Have students compare the charts they created (in the exercise above) to the news items they have collected. Challenge students to identify the relationship between what is happening in Latin America today and the history of Latin America that they are reading about in this chapter. **L3**

SECTION 1 General Trends in Latin America

Guide to Reading

Main Ideas
- Exporting raw materials and importing manufactured goods has led to economic and political troubles for Latin American nations.
- Many Latin American nations began to build democratic systems in the late 1980s.

Key Terms
multinational corporation, magic realism

People to Identify
Gabriel García Márquez, Oscar Niemeyer

Places to Locate
Chile, Brazil, Bolivia, Peru, Colombia

Preview Questions
1. What factors undermined the stability of Latin American countries?
2. How did the roles of women change in Latin America after 1945?

Reading Strategy
Categorizing Information Use a chart like the one below to identify social and political challenges in Latin America since 1945.

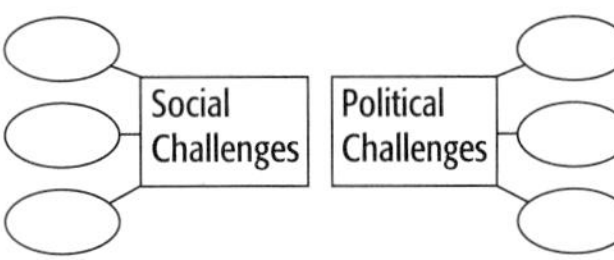

Preview of Events

1940 · 1950 · 1960 · 1970 · 1980 · 1990

- **1948** The Organization of American States is formed
- **1980** A movement toward democracy takes place in Latin America
- **1982** Gabriel García Márquez wins the Nobel Prize for literature
- **1990** Twenty-nine Latin American cities have over a million people

Voices from the Past

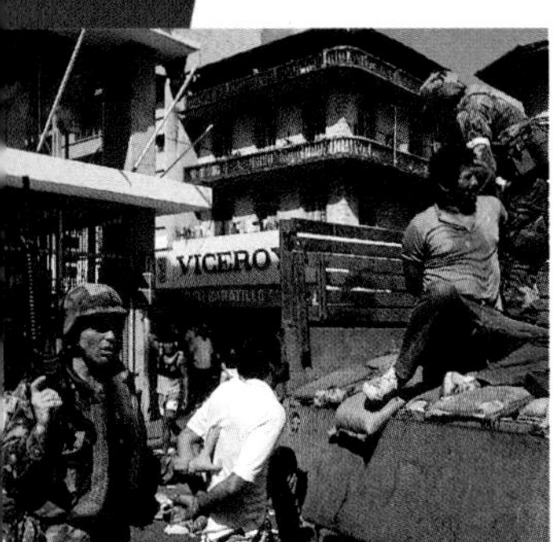

U.S. soldiers in Panama

One Latin American observer discussed the United States's invasion of Panama in 1989 in the following words:

> ❝The first official [U.S.] reason for the invasion of Panama was 'to protect American lives there.' This pretext was not credible, for the cry of 'wolf! wolf!' has been used before in Latin America. . . . The danger to American lives is a hundred times greater every day and night in Washington, D.C., 'the murder capital of the United States,' and in other American cities to which President Bush has hardly applied his policy of protecting North American lives and waging war against drugs (he prefers to wage that war on foreign battlefields).❞
>
> —***Latin American Civilization: History and Society, 1492 to the Present,*** **Benjamin Keen, 1996**

U.S. intervention in Latin American affairs has been a general trend in Latin American history since 1945.

Economic and Political Developments

Since the nineteenth century, Latin Americans had exported raw materials while buying manufactured goods from industrialized countries. As a result of the Great Depression, however, exports fell, and the revenues that had been used to buy manufactured goods declined. In response, many Latin American countries developed industries to produce goods that were formerly imported.

1 FOCUS

Section Overview

This section will give students a brief look at Latin American culture and political and economic trends.

BELLRINGER
Skillbuilder Activity

Project transparency and have students answer questions.

Available as a blackline master.

Daily Focus Skills Transparency 22-1

Guide to Reading

Answers to Graphic: Social Challenges: population growth; rapid rise in size of cities; enormous gap between the poor and the rich; international drug trade; Political Challenges: repressive military regimes; multinational corporations increased dependence on industrialized nations; movement toward democracy in 1980s in many countries

Preteaching Vocabulary: *Multinational corporation* is derived from three different Latin words. Ask students to look up those words and their meanings. **L1**

SECTION RESOURCES

Reproducible Masters
- Reproducible Lesson Plan 22–1
- Daily Lecture and Discussion Notes 22–1
- Guided Reading Activity 22–1
- Section Quiz 22–1
- Reading Essentials and Study Guide 22– 1

Transparencies
- Daily Focus Skills Transparency 22–1

Multimedia
- Interactive Tutor Self-Assessment CD-ROM
- ExamView® Pro Testmaker CD-ROM
- Presentation Plus! CD-ROM

2 TEACH

Daily Lecture and Discussion Notes 22–1

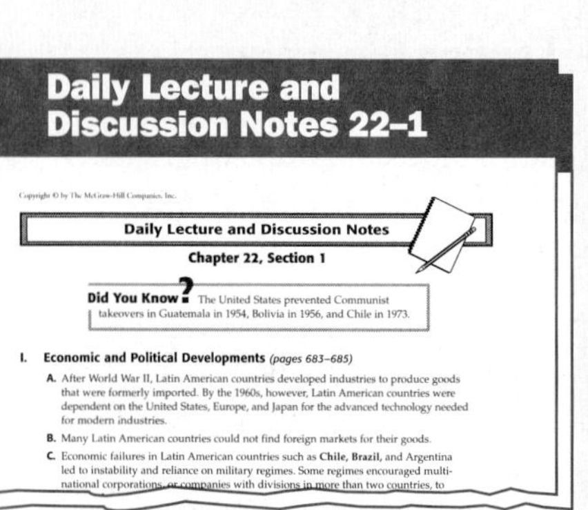

Daily Lecture and Discussion Notes

Chapter 22, Section 1

Did You Know? The United States prevented Communist takeovers in Guatemala in 1954, Bolivia in 1956, and Chile in 1973.

I. **Economic and Political Developments** *(pages 683–685)*

A. After World War II, Latin American countries developed industries to produce goods that were formerly imported. By the 1960s, however, Latin American countries were dependent on the United States, Europe, and Japan for the advanced technology needed for modern industries.

B. Many Latin American countries could not find foreign markets for their goods.

C. Economic failures in Latin American countries such as **Chile, Brazil,** and Argentina led to instability and reliance on military regimes. Some regimes encouraged multinational corporations, or companies with divisions in more than two countries, to

CURRICULUM CONNECTION

Economics Discuss why democracy is in a precarious position in any state that is experiencing economic instability. Point out that Bolivia had an annual inflation rate that exceeded 1,000 percent in the 1980s. What did that inflation rate do to the price of gas and utilities? Have students compute the price changes using the prices of items with which they are familiar. **L1**

Enrich

Latin American economies continue to evolve. Ask students to research and compare the relationships between and among contemporary Latin American countries with different economic systems. **L3**

Critical Thinking

Ask students to use the graph on page 685 to pose and answer questions about geographic distributions and patterns in world history as they relate to Latin America in the last half of the twentieth century. **L2**

NATIONAL GEOGRAPHIC
U.S. Involvement in Latin America since 1945
UNITED STATES
1 MEXICO
1994: U.S., Mexico, and Canada enter into North American Free Trade Agreement (NAFTA).
13 HONDURAS
1981–1990: U.S. supports contra rebels in Nicaragua from bases in Honduras.
12 CUBA
1959: Castro overthrows Batista.
1960: U.S. declares trade embargo upon Cuba.
1961: U.S. supports attempted overthrow of Castro's government (Bay of Pigs invasion).
1962: U.S. blockades Cuba during Cuban Missile Crisis.
1980: Thousands of Cuban refugees enter U.S.
TROPIC OF CANCER
HAITI
BELIZE
2 GUATEMALA
1954: U.S. supports overthrow of Socialist government.
11 DOMINICAN REPUBLIC
1965: U.S. military forces intervene to suppress possible communist influence.
3 EL SALVADOR
Late 1970s and 1980s: U.S. supports Salvadoran army against Marxist-led guerrillas in civil war.
1992: Peace settlement ends civil war.
COSTA RICA
GUYANA
FRENCH GUIANA Fr.
COLOMBIA
SURINAME
EQUATOR
10 GRENADA
1979: U.S. ends aid as Marxist government assumes power.
1983: Extremists overthrow government; U.S. invades to restore stable government.
4 NICARAGUA
1979: U.S. withdraws support for corrupt Somoza family; Somozas are overthrown by Sandinistas (Marxist guerrilla forces).
1981–1990: U.S. secretly aids contra rebel efforts to overthrow Sandinista government.
ECUADOR
9 PANAMA
1989: U.S. invades Panama and arrests and imprisons General Noriega on charges of drug trafficking.
1999: U.S relinquishes rights to Panama Canal Zone.
BRAZIL
5 PERU
1958: Riots against U.S.
BOLIVIA
8 VENEZUELA
1958: Riots against U.S.
PARAGUAY
TROPIC OF CAPRICORN
ATLANTIC OCEAN
6 CHILE
1970: U.S. tries and fails to prevent election of Socialist President Allende.
URUGUAY
PACIFIC OCEAN
N
W
E
S
7 ARGENTINA
1946: U.S. tries and fails to prevent election of President Perón.
0 1,000 miles
0 1,000 kilometers
Lambert Azimuthal Equal-Area projection
FALKLAND ISLANDS U.K.
30°N
10°N
20°S
30°S
40°S
130°W 120°W 110°W 100°W 90°W 80°W 70°W 60°W 50°W 40°W 30°W 20°W 10°W 0°

By the 1960s, however, Latin American countries were still experiencing economic problems. They were dependent on the United States, Europe, and Japan, especially for the advanced technology needed for modern industries. Also, many Latin American countries had failed to find markets abroad to sell their manufactured products.

These economic failures led to instability and reliance on military regimes. In the 1960s, repressive military regimes in **Chile, Brazil,** and Argentina abolished political parties and returned to export-import economies financed by foreigners. These regimes also encouraged multinational corporations (companies with divisions in more than two countries) to come to Latin America. This made these Latin American countries even more dependent on industrialized nations.

In the 1970s, Latin American nations grew more dependent as they attempted to maintain their weak economies by borrowing money. Between 1970 and 1982, debt to foreigners grew from $27 billion to $315.3 billion. By 1982, a number of Latin American economies had begun to crumble. Wages fell, and unemployment and inflation skyrocketed.

To get new loans, Latin American governments were now forced to make basic reforms. During this process, however, many people came to believe that

INTERDISCIPLINARY CONNECTIONS ACTIVITY

Economics Divide students into groups and have each group prepare a chart or map of Latin America that shows the population growth and change in economic productivity for each nation over the past fifty years,. Figures for each decade will be adequate. *The World Factbook,* published by the CIA, which is available on the Internet, and the reference section of the local library are good sources for information. When each group has prepared its map or chart, discuss the following questions: Which nations have experienced the greatest growth? the least? Which have the highest and lowest per capita GNP (GDP in recent years)? What conclusions can students draw from these facts? **L2**

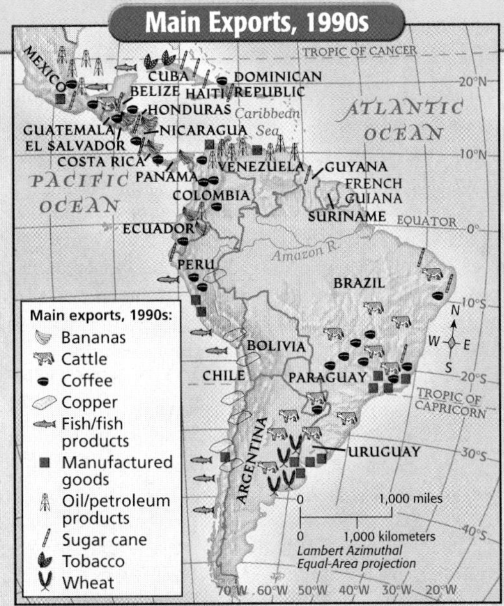

Geography Skills

Over the past 50 to 60 years, the United States has been actively involved in Latin American affairs.

1. **Interpreting Maps** What information can you find in the map on page 684 that supports the view that the people of Latin America would prefer that the United States *not* interfere in Latin American affairs?
2. **Applying Geography Skills** Create a thematic time line based on the data presented in the map on the left page. Then, pose and answer a question about the patterns in world history shown on your time line.
3. **Applying Geography Skills** Create a database for Latin America that includes elements from each of the maps and the graph on pages 684 and 685. Analyze your data, then write one paragraph stating which Latin American country you think will have the greatest population increase over the next 20 years.

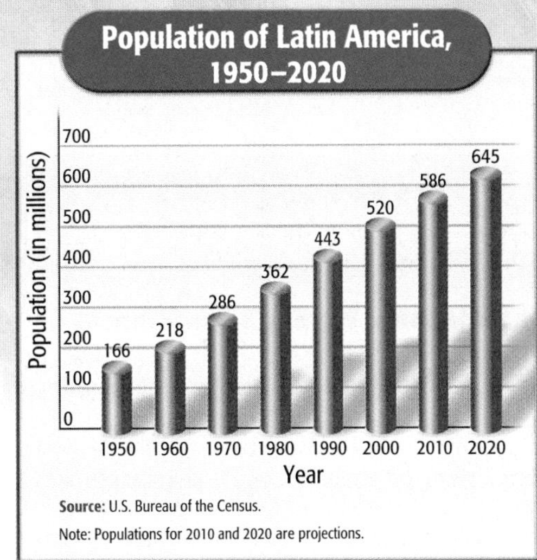

Source: U.S. Bureau of the Census.

Note: Populations for 2010 and 2020 are projections.

government had taken control of too many industries. Trying to industrialize too quickly had led to the decline of the economy in the countryside as well.

Many hoped that encouraging peasants to grow food for home consumption rather than export would stop the flow of people from the countryside to the cities. At the same time, they believed that more people would now be able to buy the products from Latin American industries.

With the debt crisis in the 1980s came a movement toward democracy. Some military leaders were unwilling to deal with the monstrous debt problems. At the same time, many people realized that military power without popular consent could not maintain a strong state. By the mid-1990s, several democratic regimes had been established.

The movement toward democracy was the most noticable trend of the 1980s and the early 1990s in Latin America. This revival of democracy was fragile. In 1992, President Alberto Fujimori returned Peru to an authoritarian system.

Reading Check **Explaining** Why did the debt crisis of the 1980s create a movement toward democracy?

CHAPTER 22
Section 1, 683–687

Geography Skills

Answers:

1. anti-United States riots, United States has acted secretly
2. Students will create time lines and pose questions about them.
3. Students will create databases; paragraphs will vary.

Reading Check

Answer: Some military leaders were unable to deal with the debt problems. At the same time, many people believed that their participation and a movement toward democracy would reverse the economic decline caused by the debt crisis.

Guided Reading Activity 22–1

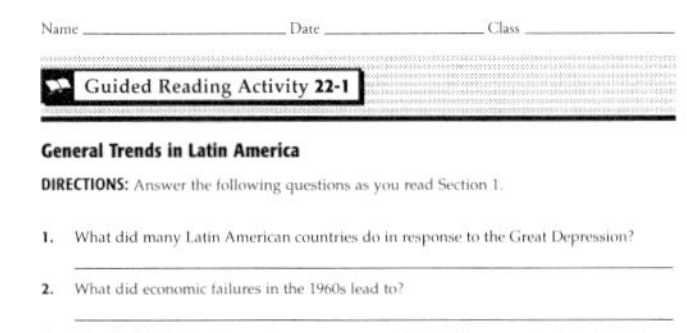
Name ______ Date ______ Class ______

Guided Reading Activity 22-1

General Trends in Latin America

DIRECTIONS: Answer the following questions as you read Section 1.

1. What did many Latin American countries do in response to the Great Depression?
2. What did economic failures in the 1960s lead to?

Who? What? Where? When?

Archbishop Oscar Romero In the 1970s and 1980s, El Salvador was torn by civil war. Oscar Romero was appointed archbishop because he was seen as a moderate figure. Shortly after his appointment, his friend Father Rutillo Grande was assassinated by a paramilitary death squad. This changed Romero from a moderate to an activist, speaking out openly against government-sponsored death squads. He was nominated for the Nobel Peace Prize for his courageous efforts. In 1980, as Romero was preparing Mass, a shot rang out from the back of the church. Romero was killed instantly.

INTERDISCIPLINARY CONNECTIONS ACTIVITY

Anthropology Before the European colonial conquests, Latin America was home to the most advanced Native American cultures and the largest population of Native Americans. Ask the students what has happened to the descendants of the Maya, Aztec, Inca, and other indigenous peoples. Have students research and report on Native Americans today and include information on geographical concentrations, living conditions, educational and career opportunities, languages spoken, involvement in government, and religious affiliation. Encourage students to identify current government leaders and other public figures who claim Native American ancestry. L1

CHAPTER 22
Section 1, 683–687

Reading Check

Answer: It made economic problems worse. Cities and slums grew rapidly, and the gap between rich and poor remained enormous.

Reading Check

Answer: The U.S. returned to a policy of taking action when it believed that Soviets were trying to establish Communist governments. It also provided massive military aid to anti-Communist regimes.

Answers:

1. concerns from industrialized nations: political, economic, cultural, and sexual rights; concerns from developing countries: bringing an end to violence, hunger, and disease
2. Answers should be supported by examples and logical arguments.

3 ASSESS

Assign Section 1 Assessment as homework or as an in-class activity.

Have students use **Interactive Tutor Self-Assessment CD-ROM.**

Section Quiz 22–1

Name ____ Date ____ Class ____

Chapter 22 | Score

Section Quiz 22-1

DIRECTIONS: Matching Match each item in Column A with an item in Column B. Write the correct letters in the blanks. (10 points each)

Column A	Column B
___ 1. companies with divisions in more than two countries	A. Oscar Niemeyer
___ 2. literary form developed in Latin America	B. magic realism
___ 3. received 1982 Nobel Prize for literature	C. multinational corporations
___ 4. Western Hemisphere political group	D. García Márquez
___ 5. famous architect who designed some of Brasília's buildings	E. Organization of American States

DIRECTIONS: Multiple Choice In the blank, write the letter of the choice that best completes the statement or answers the question. (10 points each)

Latin American Society

Latin America's economic problems were made worse by dramatic growth in population. By the mid-1980s, the population in Latin America had grown from about 165 million people in 1950 to 400 million.

With the increase in population came a rapid rise in the size of cities. By 1990, 29 Latin American cities had over a million people. Slums, or shantytowns, became part of many of these cities.

The gap between the poor and the rich remained enormous in Latin America. Landholding and urban elites owned huge estates and businesses, while peasants and the urban poor struggled just to survive.

The traditional role of homemaker continues for women, who have also moved into new jobs. In addition to farm labor, women have found jobs in industry, and as teachers, professors, doctors, and lawyers.

The international drug trade brought crime and corruption to some Latin American countries, undermining their stability. **Bolivia, Peru,** and **Colombia** were especially big producers of cocaine and marijuana.

Reading Check **Evaluating** Describe the effect(s) of Latin America's dramatic increase in population.

The United States and Latin America

The United States has always played a large role in Latin America. For years, the United States had sent troops into Latin American countries to protect U.S. interests and bolster friendly dictators.

In 1948, the states of the Western Hemisphere formed the **Organization of American States** (OAS), which called for an end to military action by one state in the affairs of any other state. The formation of the OAS, however, did not end U.S. involvement in Latin American affairs.

As the Cold War developed, so, too, did the anxiety of American policy makers about the possibility of Communist regimes in Latin America. As a result, the United States returned to a policy of taking action when it believed that Soviet agents were trying to establish Communist governments or governments hostile to United States interests. The United States also provided massive amounts of military aid to anti-Communist regimes.

Reading Check **Examining** How did the Cold War impact United States policy in Latin America?

CONNECTIONS Around The World

International Women's Conferences

As women around the world organized movements to change the conditions of their lives, an international women's movement emerged. Especially in the 1970s, much attention was paid to a series of international conferences on women's issues. Between 1975 and 1985, the United Nations celebrated the Decade for Women by holding conferences in such cities as Mexico City, Copenhagen, and Nairobi.

The conferences made clear how women in both industrialized and developing nations were organizing to make people aware of women's issues. They also made clear the differences between women from Western and non-Western countries.

Latin American mother with children

Women from Western countries spoke about political, economic, cultural, and sexual rights. In contrast, women from developing countries in Latin America, Africa, and Asia focused on bringing an end to the violence, hunger, and disease that haunt their lives.

At the International Women's Year Tribunal in Mexico in 1974, sponsored by the United Nations, Dimitila Barrios de Chungara, a miner's wife from Bolivia, expressed her lack of patience with professional women at the conference. She said, "So, I went up and spoke. I made them see that they don't live in our world. I made them see that in Bolivia human rights aren't respected. . . . Women like us, housewives, who get organized to better our people well, they [the Bolivian police] beat us up and persecute us."

Comparing Cultures

Women from industrialized and developing nations focus on very different issues.

1. Which concerns of women are most important?
2. Do you think women's conferences are needed? What purposes might conferences serve other than raising issues?

EXTENDING THE CONTENT

OAS The Organization of American States (OAS) began in 1948 with 21 member nations. These nations affirmed their commitment to common goals and respect for each other's sovereignty. Since then the OAS has expanded to include all 35 countries of North, South, and Central America, and the Caribbean. The goals of the OAS are to strengthen democracy, defend human rights, foster free trade, combat drugs, and promote sustainable development. In the practical arena they monitor elections, remove land mines, build homes, and fund programs to manage natural resources. After Hurricane Mitch in 1998, the OAS built 50 homes in Nicaragua. Residents provided the labor and patrolled the area at night. No one knew who was getting which home until each resident pulled a key from a box and opened the door of his or her new home.

Latin American Culture

Writers and artists have played important roles in Latin American society. They have been given a public status granted to very few writers and artists in other countries. In Latin America, writers and artists are seen as people who can express the hopes of the people. One celebrated Latin American writer is the Chilean poet Gabriela Mistral.

In literature, Latin Americans developed a unique form of expression called **magic realism.** Magic realism brings together realistic events with dreamlike or fantastic backgrounds.

Perhaps the foremost example of magic realism is *One Hundred Years of Solitude,* a novel by **Gabriel García Márquez.** In this story of the fictional town of Macondo, the point of view slips back and forth between fact and fantasy. Villagers are not surprised when a local priest rises into the air and floats. However, when these villagers are introduced to magnets, telescopes, and magnifying glasses, they are dumbfounded by what they see as magic. According to García Márquez, fantasy and fact depend on one's point of view.

García Márquez, a Colombian, was the most famous of the Latin American novelists. He was a former journalist who took up writing when he became angered by the negative reviews Latin American authors were receiving. He was awarded the Nobel Prize for literature in 1982.

People In History

Gabriela Mistral
1889–1957—Chilean poet

Gabriela Mistral, whose real name was Lucila Godoy Alcayaga, was a poet and educator. She was trained to be a teacher and became the director of a school for girls in Santiago, Chile. In 1922, she was invited by the Mexican government to introduce educational programs for the poor in that country. Later, she took up residence in the United States and taught at Middlebury and Barnard Colleges.

In 1945, she became the first Latin American author to win the Nobel Prize for literature. Her poems explored the many dimensions of love, tinged with an element of sadness.

Latin American art and architecture were strongly influenced by international styles after World War II. In painting, abstract styles were especially important. Perhaps the most notable example of modern architecture can be seen in Brasília, the capital city of Brazil, built in the 1950s and 1960s. Latin America's greatest modern architect, **Oscar Niemeyer,** designed some of the major buildings in Brasília.

Reading Check **Identifying** What novel is the foremost example of magic realism?

SECTION 1 ASSESSMENT

Checking for Understanding

1. **Define** multinational corporation, magic realism.
2. **Identify** Organization of American States (OAS), Gabriel García Márquez, Oscar Niemeyer.
3. **Locate** Chile, Brazil, Bolivia, Peru, Colombia.
4. **Explain** how the Great Depression hurt Latin American economies. Have these economies recovered from the problems caused by the Great Depression?
5. **List** two well-known Latin American writers. Why are writers and artists held in such high regard in Latin America?

Critical Thinking

6. **Analyze** Why did the rapid rate of population growth in many Latin American countries cause problems for their political and economic systems?
7. **Organizing Information** Draw a chart like the one below to list economic challenges in Latin America since 1945. On your chart, use dates and names of countries from the text to make each entry as specific as possible.

Analyzing Visuals

8. **Examine** the photograph of a Latin American mother with her children shown on page 686 of the text. How does this photograph reflect the concerns faced by many Latin American women?

Writing About History

9. **Descriptive Writing** A uniquely Latin American literary form is magic realism, which combines realistic events with elements of magic and fantasy. Research further the elements of magic realism and then write a short story about a real or imagined event, using that style.

CHAPTER 22
Section 1, 683–687

Reading Check

Answer: *One Hundred Years of Solitude* by García Márquez

Reading Essentials and Study Guide 22–1

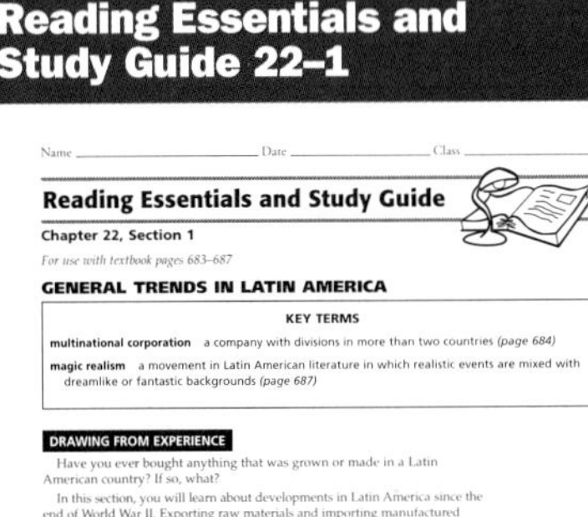
Name ______ Date ______ Class ______

Reading Essentials and Study Guide

Chapter 22, Section 1

For use with textbook pages 683–687

GENERAL TRENDS IN LATIN AMERICA

KEY TERMS

multinational corporation a company with divisions in more than two countries *(page 684)*

magic realism a movement in Latin American literature in which realistic events are mixed with dreamlike or fantastic backgrounds *(page 687)*

DRAWING FROM EXPERIENCE

Have you ever bought anything that was grown or made in a Latin American country? If so, what?

In this section, you will learn about developments in Latin America since the end of World War II. Exporting raw materials and importing manufactured goods led to economic and political problems for many Latin American nations.

ORGANIZING YOUR THOUGHTS

Use the chart below to help you take notes. For each topic in the chart, describe its effect on the countries of Latin America.

CURRICULUM CONNECTION

Population Within a few years, Hispanics will be the majority ethnic group in the United States. Ask students to determine the effect of immigration in their area. Perhaps they live in an area of Asian immigration. Help students to understand why people emigrate. **L1**

Reteaching Activity

Have students write one sentence about each of the major headings in this section. **L1**

4 CLOSE

Have students write a one-page study guide summarizing the main themes of this section.

SECTION 1 ASSESSMENT

1. Key terms are in blue.
2. OAS *(p. 686)*; Gabriel García Márquez *(p. 687)*; Oscar Niemeyer *(p. 687)*
3. See chapter maps.
4. Exports fell and revenues declined. Latin American countries developed industries to produce formerly imported goods.
5. Gabriela Mistral, Gabriel García Márquez; they express the hopes of the people
6. Cities and slums grew rapidly, creating a gap between rich and poor. Peasants and the urban poor struggled to survive. These conditions strain economies, lead to political instability, and repressive regimes.
7. dependent on U.S., Europe, and Japan; return to export-import economies financed by foreigners; presence of multinational corporations; growing foreign debt; wages fell, inflation skyrocketed; debt crisis
8. poverty, unemployment, lack of opportunity
9. Stories should use elements of magic realism.

1 FOCUS

Section Overview

This section describes the major events in Mexico, Cuba, and Central America following World War II.

BELLRINGER
Skillbuilder Activity

Project transparency and have students answer questions.

Available as a blackline master.

Daily Focus Skills Transparency 22–2

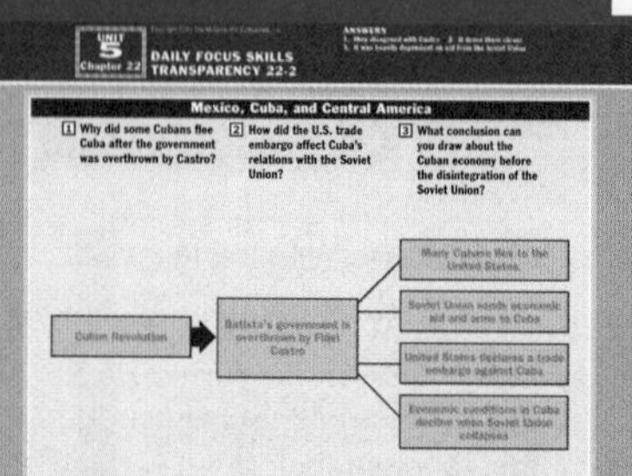

Guide to Reading

Answers to Graphic: El Salvador: government controlled by wealthy elite and military, U.S. supported Salvadoran military; Nicaragua: Somoza family ruled with U.S. support, U.S. supported contras in war; Panama: wealthy oligarchy ruled with U.S. support, National Guard takeover, Noriega took control, U.S. sent troops to arrest Noriega

Preteaching Vocabulary: Have students use dictionaries to look up the word *contra.* Have them write the definition that fits *contra* as used in this chapter. **L1**

SECTION 2 Mexico, Cuba, and Central America

Guide to Reading

Main Ideas
- Mexico and Central America faced political and economic crises after World War II.
- The United States feared the spread of communism in Central American countries, which led to active American involvement in the region.

Key Terms
privatization, trade embargo, contra

People to Identify
Vicente Fox, Fidel Castro, Manuel Noriega

Places to Locate
Havana, El Salvador, Nicaragua, Panama

Preview Questions
1. What problems did Mexico and the nations of Central America face after 1945?
2. What were the chief features and impact of the Cuban Revolution?

Reading Strategy
Categorizing Information Use a table like the one below to identify the political and economic challenges faced by El Salvador, Nicaragua, and Panama after 1945.

El Salvador	Nicaragua	Panama

Preview of Events

1950 · 1960 · 1970 · 1980 · 1990 · 2000

- **1959** Castro's revolutionaries seize Havana
- **1961** United States breaks diplomatic relations with Cuba
- **1979** The Sandinistas overthrow Somoza rule in Nicaragua
- **1983** Noriega takes control of Panama
- **2000** Vicente Fox defeats the PRI candidate for the presidency of Mexico

Voices from the Past

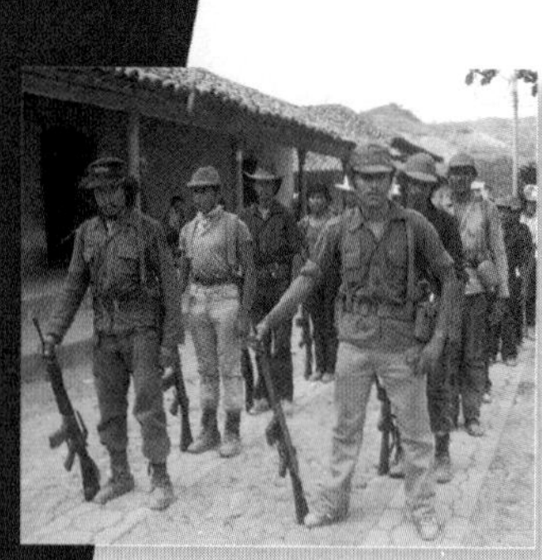

Contra soldiers

Nancy Donovan, a Catholic missionary in Nicaragua, described her encounter with the military forces known as the contras:

> ❝It is not easy to live in a war zone. The least of it was my being kidnapped by contras early this year. The hard part is seeing people die and consoling families. . . . In those eight hours I was held, as I walked in a column of 60 or so men and a few women—all in uniform—I could hear shooting and realized that people I knew were being killed. Earlier I had seen bodies brought back to town, some burned, some cut to pieces.❞
>
> —***Latin American Civilization: History and Society, 1492 to the Present,*** **Benjamin Keen, 1996**

Financed by the United States, the contras were trying to overthrow the Sandinista rulers of Nicaragua in one of several bloody wars fought in Central America.

The Mexican Way

The Mexican Revolution at the beginning of the twentieth century created a political order that remained stable for many years. The official political party of the Mexican Revolution—the Institutional Revolutionary Party, or PRI—came to dominate Mexico. Every six years, leaders of the PRI chose the party's presidential candidate, who was then elected by the people.

SECTION RESOURCES

Reproducible Masters
- Reproducible Lesson Plan 22–2
- Daily Lecture and Discussion Notes 22–2
- Guided Reading Activity 22–2
- Section Quiz 22–2
- Reading Essentials and Study Guide 22–2

Transparencies
- Daily Focus Skills Transparency 22–2

Multimedia
- Interactive Tutor Self-Assessment CD-ROM
- ExamView® Pro Testmaker CD-ROM
- Presentation Plus! CD-ROM

During the 1950s and 1960s, steady economic growth led to real gains in wages for more and more people in Mexico. At the end of the 1960s, however, students began to protest Mexico's one-party government system. On October 2, 1968, university students gathered in Mexico City to protest government policies. Police forces opened fire and killed hundreds. Leaders of the PRI grew concerned about the need for change in the system.

The next two presidents, Luís Echeverría and José López Portillo, made political reforms and opened the door to the emergence of new political parties. Greater freedom of debate in the press and universities was allowed. Economic problems, however, would soon reappear.

In the late 1970s, vast new reserves of oil were discovered in Mexico. The sale of oil abroad increased dramatically, and the government became more dependent on oil revenues. When world oil prices dropped in the mid-1980s, Mexico was no longer able to make payments on its foreign debt. The government was forced to adopt new economic policies. One of these policies was privatization, the sale of government-owned companies to private firms.

The debt crisis and rising unemployment increased dissatisfaction with the government. Support for the PRI dropped, and in 2000, **Vicente Fox** defeated the PRI candidate for the presidency.

Reading Check **Evaluating** How was Mexico's economy affected by its oil industry?

The Cuban Revolution

TURNING POINT **As you will learn, the Bay of Pigs invasion was an attempt by the United States to move forcefully against Fidel Castro and the threat of communism that he represented.**

In the 1950s, a strong opposition movement arose in Cuba. Led by **Fidel Castro,** the movement aimed to overthrow the government of the dictator Fulgencio Batista, who had controlled Cuba since 1934. Castro's army used guerrilla warfare against Batista's regime. As the rebels gained more support, the regime collapsed. Castro's revolutionaries seized **Havana** on January 1, 1959. Many Cubans who disagreed with Castro fled to the United States.

Relations between Cuba and the United States quickly deteriorated when the Castro regime began to receive aid from the Soviet Union. Arms from Eastern Europe also began to arrive in Cuba. In October 1960, the United States declared a trade embargo, prohibiting trade with Cuba, and just three months later, on January 3, 1961, broke all diplomatic relations with Cuba.

Web Activity Visit the *Glencoe World History—Modern Times* Web site at wh.mt.glencoe.com and click on **Chapter 22–Student Web Activity** to learn more about Fidel Castro.

Soon after that, in April 1961, the American president, John F. Kennedy, supported an attempt to overthrow Castro's government. When the invasion at the Bay of Pigs failed, the Soviets were encouraged to make an even greater commitment to Cuba. In December 1961, Castro declared himself a Marxist, drawing ever closer to the Soviet Union. The Soviets began placing nuclear missiles in Cuba in 1962, an act that led to a showdown with the United States (see Chapter 20).

The Cuban missile crisis caused Castro to realize that the Soviet Union had been unreliable. If the revolutionary movement in Cuba was to survive, the Cubans would have to start a social revolution in the rest of Latin America. They would do this by starting guerrilla wars and encouraging peasants to overthrow the old regimes. Ernesto Ché Guevara, an Argentinian and an ally of Castro, led such a war in

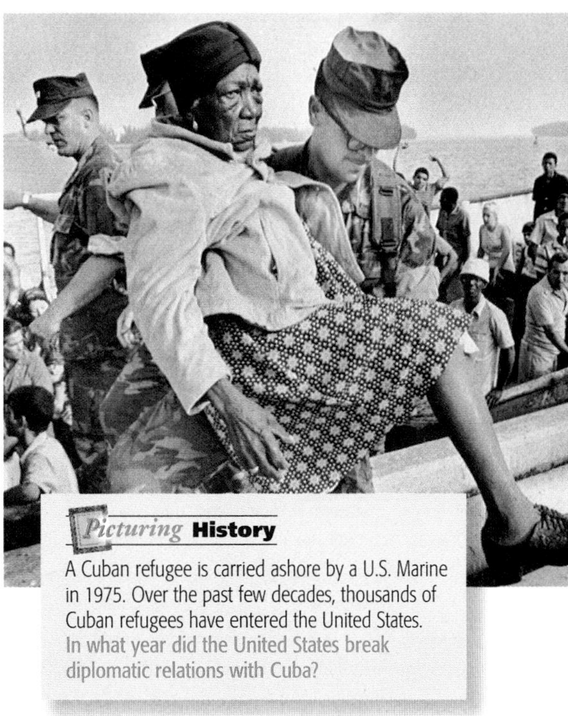

Picturing **History**

A Cuban refugee is carried ashore by a U.S. Marine in 1975. Over the past few decades, thousands of Cuban refugees have entered the United States. In what year did the United States break diplomatic relations with Cuba?

2 TEACH

Reading Check

Answer: Vast oil reserves were discovered in the late 1970s. Oil sales increased; the government became dependent on oil revenues. When oil prices dropped in the mid-1980s, Mexico was not able to make payments on its debt. The government adopted new economic policies, including privatization of government-owned companies.

TURNING POINT

Bay of Pigs About 1,500 anti-Castro exiles, trained by the United States, landed in Cuba at the Bay of Pigs. They wanted Cubans to revolt against Castro. The anti-Castro exiles were hoping for American military support, but President Kennedy barred open military support. The Cuban people did not join the anti-Castro invasion and most of the invaders were captured or killed. The invasion tarnished Kennedy's presidency and damaged the image of the United States.

Picturing **History**

Answer: 1961

Daily Lecture and Discussion Notes 22–2

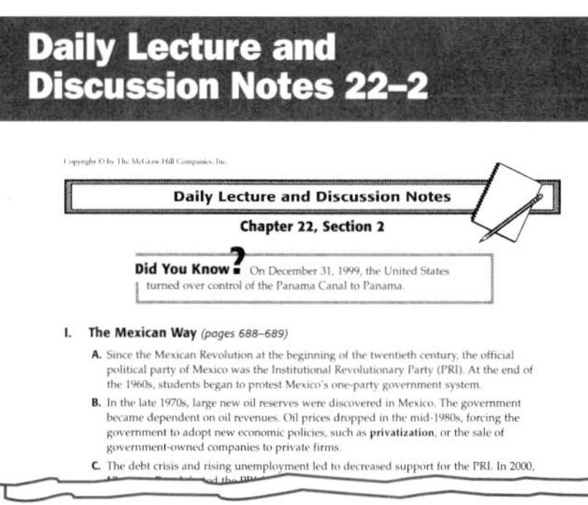

Daily Lecture and Discussion Notes

Chapter 22, Section 2

Did You Know? On December 31, 1999, the United States turned over control of the Panama Canal to Panama.

I. **The Mexican Way** *(pages 688–689)*

A. Since the Mexican Revolution at the beginning of the twentieth century, the official political party of Mexico was the Institutional Revolutionary Party (PRI). At the end of the 1960s, students began to protest Mexico's one-party government system.

B. In the late 1970s, large new oil reserves were discovered in Mexico. The government became dependent on oil revenues. Oil prices dropped in the mid-1980s, forcing the government to adopt new economic policies, such as **privatization**, or the sale of government-owned companies to private firms.

C. The debt crisis and rising unemployment led to decreased support for the PRI. In 2000,

COOPERATIVE LEARNING ACTIVITY

Staging a Debate Have students hold a debate about the Cuban missile crisis of 1962. Organize students into two groups, one group taking the position that the Soviet missiles had to be removed from Cuba at any cost, the other defending a negotiated settlement or even allowing the missiles to remain. Refer students to the following works: Samuel Dinerstein, *The Making of a Missile Crisis,* October 1962; Robert A. Divine, *The Cuban Missile Crisis;* and Robert F. Kennedy, *Thirteen Days: A Memoir of the Cuban Missile Crisis.* Students should present clear, well-supported arguments, and use effective verbal and non-verbal strategies. Students not involved in the oral presentations should evaluate and critique the debate participants. L3

CHAPTER 22
Section 2, 688–691

Chart *Skills*

Answer:

1. Students will use a problem-solving process.

Reading Check

Answer: Cuba lost the support of those countries, causing economic conditions to decline steadily.

Guided Reading Activity 22–2

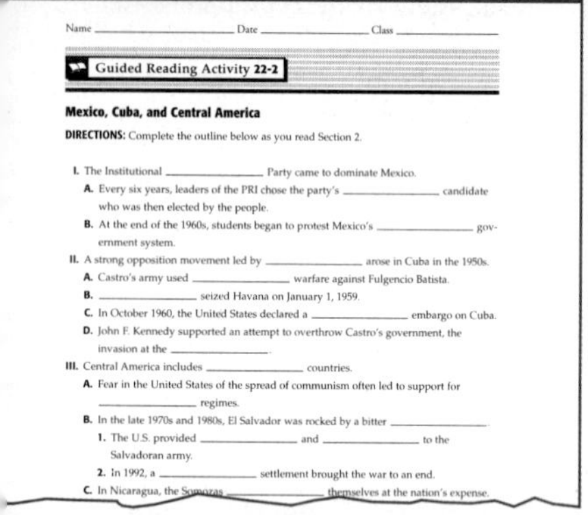

Name ______________ Date ______________ Class ______________

Guided Reading Activity 22-2

Mexico, Cuba, and Central America

DIRECTIONS: Complete the outline below as you read Section 2.

I. The Institutional ______________ Party came to dominate Mexico.
   A. Every six years, leaders of the PRI chose the party's ______________ candidate who was then elected by the people.
   B. At the end of the 1960s, students began to protest Mexico's ______________ government system.
II. A strong opposition movement led by ______________ arose in Cuba in the 1950s.
   A. Castro's army used ______________ warfare against Fulgencio Batista.
   B. ______________ seized Havana on January 1, 1959.
   C. In October 1960, the United States declared a ______________ embargo on Cuba.
   D. John F. Kennedy supported an attempt to overthrow Castro's government, the invasion at the ______________.
III. Central America includes ______________ countries.
   A. Fear in the United States of the spread of communism often led to support for ______________ regimes.
   B. In the late 1970s and 1980s, El Salvador was rocked by a bitter ______________.
      1. The U.S. provided ______________ and ______________ to the Salvadoran army.
      2. In 1992, a ______________ settlement brought the war to an end.
   C. In Nicaragua, the Somozas ______________ themselves at the nation's expense.

Critical Thinking

After they have read this section, have students assess the degree to which human rights and democratic ideals and practices have been advanced throughout the world during the twentieth century. **L1**

3 ASSESS

Assign Section 2 Assessment as homework or as an in-class activity.

Have students use **Interactive Tutor Self-Assessment CD-ROM.**

Government Reforms in Latin America

	Argentina	Brazil	Chile	El Salvador	Nicaragua	Panama	Peru
Military Regime	**1955:** Military overthrows Perón. **1973:** Perón is reelected. **1976:** Military takes over again.	**1964:** Military seizes control. **1982:** Severe recession undermines military control.	**1973:** Military, under Pinochet, overthrows Marxist Allende and establishes regime.	**1972:** Military prevents free elections. **1979:** Military takes over.	**1979:** Sandinistas (Marxist guerrilla forces) bring down dictatorship of Somoza family.	**1983:** National Guard, under Noriega, seizes control. **1989:** Noriega nullifies election results.	**1968:** Military, under Alvarado, takes over. **1975:** Military removes Alvarado.
Civilian Rule	**1983:** Civilian rule returns; Alfonsín is elected. **1994:** Constitution is reformed.	**1985:** Free elections held. **1989:** 80 million Brazilians vote. **1999:** Military put under civilian control.	**1989:** Pinochet is overthrown in free elections. **2000:** Socialist Ricardo Lagos Escobar elected president.	**1984:** Moderate Duarte is elected but civil war continues. **1992:** Peace settlement ends civil war.	**1990:** Sandinistas lose free elections but remain strongest party. **1996:** Elections result in peaceful transfer of power.	**1989:** U.S. troops arrest Noriega; democracy returns. **1999:** Female, Mireya Moscoso de Gruber, elected president.	**1980:** Civilian rule returns. **1990–2000:** Fujimori is dictatorial president. **2001:** Toledo wins free elections.

Chart *Skills*

Many Latin American countries have had problems maintaining stable governments.

1. **Problem Solving** Use a problem-solving process and the information in this chapter to list options and choose possible solutions to suggest how these countries might avoid takeovers by military regimes in the future.

Bolivia but was killed by the Bolivian army in the fall of 1967. The Cuban strategy failed.

Nevertheless, in Cuba, Castro's Marxist regime continued, but with mixed results. The Cuban people did secure some social gains. The regime provided free medical services for all citizens, and illiteracy was nearly eliminated.

The Cuban economy continued to rely on the production and sale of sugar. Economic problems forced the Castro regime to depend on Soviet aid and the purchase of Cuban sugar by Soviet bloc countries. After the collapse of these Communist regimes in 1989, Cuba lost their support. Economic conditions in Cuba have steadily declined. Nevertheless, Castro has managed to remain in power.

Reading Check **Describing** How was Castro's Cuba affected by the collapse of Communist governments in Eastern Europe?

Upheaval in Central America

Central America includes seven countries: Costa Rica, Nicaragua, Honduras, El Salvador, Panama, Belize, and Guatemala. Economically, Central America has depended on the export of bananas, coffee, and cotton. Prices for these products have varied over time, however, creating economic crises. In addition, an enormous gulf between a wealthy elite and poor peasants has created a climate of instability.

Fear in the United States of the spread of communism often led to American support for repressive regimes in the area. American involvement was especially evident in El Salvador, Nicaragua, and Panama.

El Salvador After World War II, the wealthy elite and the military controlled the government in **El Salvador.** The rise of an urban middle class led to some hopes for a more democratic government. The army, however, refused to allow free elections that were planned for 1972.

In the late 1970s and the 1980s, El Salvador was rocked by a bitter civil war. Marxist-led, leftist guerrillas and right-wing groups battled one another. During the presidency of Ronald Reagan, the United States provided weapons and training to the Salvadoran army to defeat the guerrillas.

In 1984, a moderate, José Duarte, was elected president. However, the elections failed to stop the savage killing. By the early 1990s, the civil war had led to the deaths of at least 75,000 people. Finally, in 1992, a peace settlement brought the war to an end.

Nicaragua In **Nicaragua,** the Somoza family seized control of the government in 1937 and kept control for the next 42 years. Over most of this period, the Somoza

CRITICAL THINKING ACTIVITY

Evaluating Organize students into three teams representing a Central American, South American, and a Caribbean basin country of their own choice. Have each team investigate U.S. and foreign news coverage about its country. Students should listen to radio news broadcasts; watch TV news; and read newspapers, news magazines, and Internet news. Students should summarize the information they gather and share it with the class. Have the class discuss how well and how fairly these countries are covered by the media. It might be interesting to have students discover what news sources immigrants from these countries use to keep informed. Are they the same sources the students used? Why or why not? **L2**

regime had the support of the United States. The Somozas enriched themselves at the nation's expense and used murder and torture to silence opposition.

By 1979, the United States, under President Jimmy Carter, had grown unwilling to support the corrupt regime. In that same year, Marxist guerrilla forces known as the Sandinista National Liberation Front won a number of military victories against government forces and gained virtual control of the country.

The Sandinistas inherited a poverty-stricken nation. Soon, a group opposed to the Sandinistas' policies, called the contras, began to try to overthrow the new government. The Reagan and Bush administrations in the United States, worried by the Sandinistas' alignment with the Soviet Union, supported the contras.

The war waged by the contras undermined support for the Sandinistas. In 1990, the Sandinistas agreed to free elections, and they lost to a coalition headed by Violeta Barrios de Chamorro. They lost again in 2001 but remained one of the strongest parties in Nicaragua.

Panama Panama became a nation in 1903, when it broke away from Colombia with help from the United States. In return for this aid, the United States gained control of the Panama Canal and extensive influence over the government and economy of Panama. A wealthy oligarchy ruled, with American support.

After 1968, power in Panama came into the hands of the military leaders of Panama's National Guard. One such leader was **Manuel Noriega,** who took control of Panama in 1983.

People In History

Rigoberta Menchú
1959– Guatemalan activist

Rigoberta Menchú is a reformer who worked to save her fellow Quiché Indians from the murder squads of the Guatemalan government. She grew up in a poor family. Her father helped organize a peasant movement, but he and other family members were killed by government troops.

Rigoberta Menchú then began to play an active role in her father's movement. Condemned by the Guatemalan government, she fled to Mexico. Her autobiography, *I . . . Rigoberta Menchú,* brought world attention to the fact that 150,000 Native Americans had been killed by the Guatemalan authorities. In 1992, she received the Nobel Peace Prize and used the money from the award to set up a foundation to help Native Americans.

At first, Noriega was supported by the United States. His brutality and involvement with the drug trade, however, turned American leaders against him. In 1989, President George Bush sent U.S. troops to Panama. Noriega was arrested and sent to prison in the United States on charges of drug trafficking.

Reading Check **Summarizing** What factors led to conflicts in Central America from the 1970s to the 1990s?

SECTION 2 ASSESSMENT

Checking for Understanding

1. **Define** privatization, trade embargo, contra.
2. **Identify** Vicente Fox, Fidel Castro, Manuel Noriega.
3. **Locate** Havana, Nicaragua, Panama, El Salvador.
4. **Explain** why the Cubans attempted to spur revolution in the rest of Latin America.
5. **List** the political reforms enacted by Mexican presidents Luís Echeverría and José López Portillo.

Critical Thinking

6. **Evaluate** Why did relations between the Soviet Union and Cuba become more difficult after 1962?
7. **Cause and Effect** Use a chart like the one below to show how Mexico has reacted to political and economic crises since World War II.

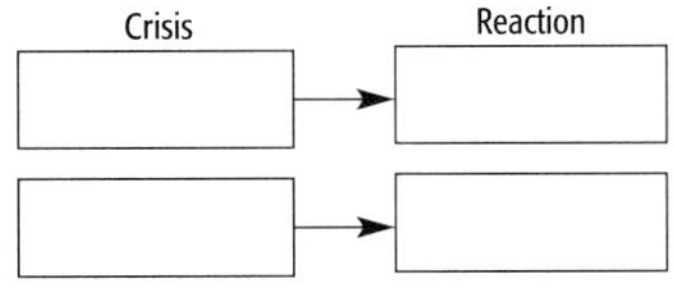

Analyzing Visuals

8. **Examine** the photo of Castro on page 682 and the photo of a Cuban refugee on page 689. What inferences can you draw about Castro's reign in Cuba from looking at these photos?

Writing About History

9. **Persuasive Writing** The United States has increasingly tried to negotiate conflicts using economic tools rather than military force. Research the trade embargo imposed upon Cuba. Write a persuasive argument for or against this embargo.

SECTION 2 ASSESSMENT

1. Key terms are in blue.
2. Vicente Fox *(p. 689)*; Fidel Castro *(p. 689)*; Manuel Noriega *(p. 690)*
3. See chapter maps.
4. to keep the revolutionary movement alive in Cuba
5. allowed greater freedom of debate in press and universities; opened door to new political parties
6. The Soviet Union had backed down in the 1962 Cuban missile crisis, leading Castro to realize that the Soviet Union was unreliable.
7. Crisis: students protested government policies and one-party system; Reaction: police forces opened fire and killed hundreds, PRI leaders grew concerned about need for change in system; Crisis: drop in oil prices; Reaction: Mexico unable to make payments on foreign debt
8. military based, poor nation, number of refugees implies that many disliked Castro's rule
9. Students should write a persuasive, fact-based argument.

Reading Check

Answer: Most of the countries had been dominated by wealthy elites and/or the military; the gulf between the elite and poor created a climate of instability; opposition usually came from Marxist rebels; fearing the spread of Communism, the United States often ended up supporting repressive regimes.

Section Quiz 22–2

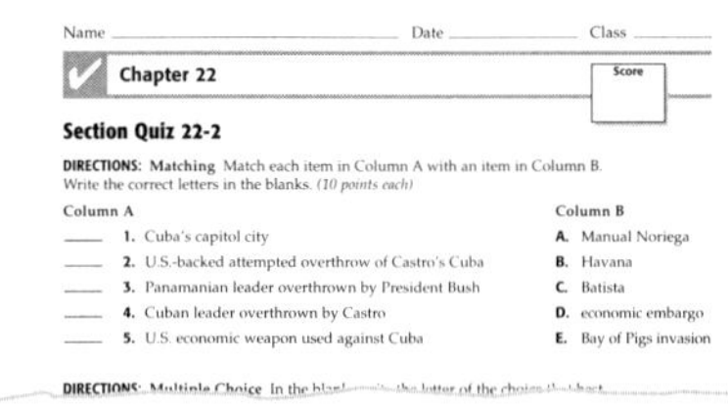
Name ______ Date ______ Class ______

Chapter 22 Score

Section Quiz 22-2

DIRECTIONS: Matching Match each item in Column A with an item in Column B. Write the correct letters in the blanks. *(10 points each)*

Column A	Column B
____ 1. Cuba's capitol city	A. Manual Noriega
____ 2. U.S.-backed attempted overthrow of Castro's Cuba	B. Havana
____ 3. Panamanian leader overthrown by President Bush	C. Batista
____ 4. Cuban leader overthrown by Castro	D. economic embargo
____ 5. U.S. economic weapon used against Cuba	E. Bay of Pigs invasion

Reading Essentials and Study Guide 22–2

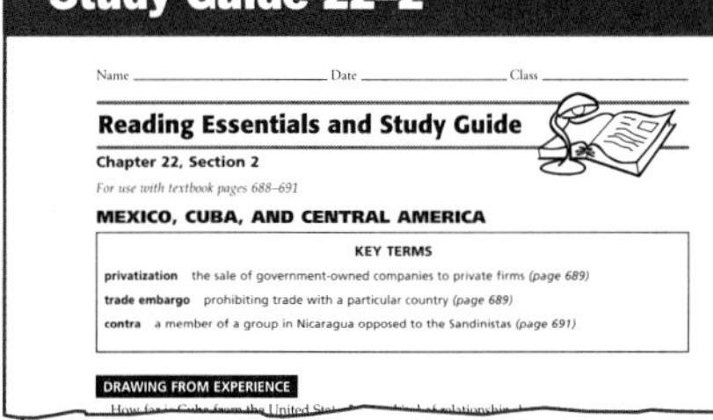
Name ______ Date ______ Class ______

Reading Essentials and Study Guide

Chapter 22, Section 2

For use with textbook pages 688–691

MEXICO, CUBA, AND CENTRAL AMERICA

KEY TERMS

privatization the sale of government-owned companies to private firms *(page 689)*

trade embargo prohibiting trade with a particular country *(page 689)*

contra a member of a group in Nicaragua opposed to the Sandinistas *(page 691)*

DRAWING FROM EXPERIENCE

Reteaching Activity

Have students develop an outline covering the information in Section 2. **L1**

4 CLOSE

Ask students to summarize the ways in which the United States has intervened in Central America and Cuba. Ask students to evaluate the consequences of U.S. involvement in these countries. **L1**

TEACH

Analyzing Primary Sources The 1968 Summer Olympics marked the first time the Olympic games had been held in a Latin American country. They were being held during a tumultuous time in world history: The Vietnam War was taking place, Martin Luther King, Jr., and Robert F. Kennedy had been assassinated, and the Soviet Union had invaded Czechoslovakia. Protesters in Mexico objected to the huge sums of money being spent to construct sporting venues.

The opening paragraph on this page states that there was a growing conflict between the government and university students. Ask students to recall information from previous chapters about conflicts in other countries between students and government. In 1968, many felt that the world was in revolt. Ask students to research events of 1968 and create a time line. How does the student revolt in Mexico fit into the time line? L1

Critical Thinking

Using the time line they created, students should select one of the countries and conflicts and research it further. Discuss the results in class. What are the common issues in each of the conflicts? Encourage students to read two primary sources, representing opposing views of the conflict. L3

EYEWITNESS TO HISTORY

Student Revolt in Mexico

A GROWING CONFLICT BETWEEN THE government and university students in Mexico came to a violent climax on October 2, 1968, just before the Olympic Games were to begin in Mexico City. The official government report said that Mexican authorities were fired upon, and they returned the gunfire. This excerpt is taken from an account of the events by the student National Strike Council.

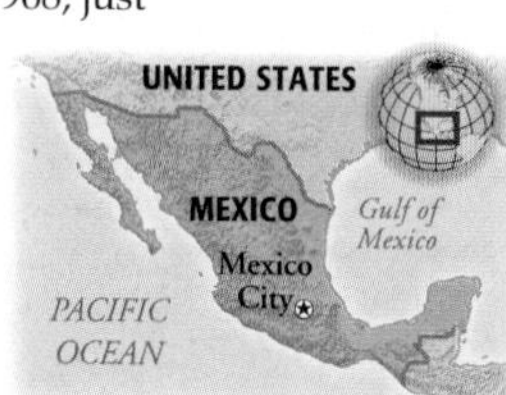

Student demonstrators in Mexico City

❝After an hour and a half of a peaceful meeting attended by 10,000 people and witnessed by scores of domestic and foreign reporters, a helicopter gave the army the signal to attack by dropping flares into the crowd. Simultaneously, the plaza was surrounded and attacked by members of the army and police forces.

The local papers have given the following information, confirmed by firsthand witnesses, about the attack:

1. Numerous secret policemen had infiltrated the meeting in order to attack it from within, with orders to kill. They were known to each other by the use of a white handkerchief tied around their right hands. . . .
2. High-caliber weapons and expansion bullets were used. Seven hours after the massacre began, tanks cleaned up the residential buildings of Nonoalco-Tlatelolco with short cannon blasts and machine-gun fire.
3. On the morning of October 3, the apartments of supposedly guilty individuals were still being searched, without a search warrant.
4. Doctors in the emergency wards of the city hospitals were under extreme pressure, being forced to forego attention to the victims until they had been interrogated and placed under guard. . . .
5. The results of this brutal military operation include hundreds of dead (including women and children), thousands of wounded, an unwarranted search of all the apartments in the area, and thousands of violent arrests. . . . It should be added that members of the National Strike Council who were captured were stripped and herded into a small archaeological excavation at Tlatelolco, converted for the moment into a dungeon. Some of them were put up against a wall and shot.

All this has occurred only ten days before the start of the Olympics. The repression is expected to become even greater after the Games. . . .

We are not against the Olympic Games. Welcome to Mexico.❞

—Account of the Clash Between the Government and Students in Mexico, October 2, 1968

Analyzing Primary Sources

1. What was the reason for the military attack on the students?
2. Why do you think the government reacted with such violence?
3. Do you think the government handled the situation well? Why or why not?

692

ANSWERS TO ANALYZING PRIMARY SOURCES

1. The official government report said that the Mexican authorities had been fired upon, and they returned the gunfire.
2. Answers should be supported by logical arguments. It was only days before the opening of the Mexico City Olympics, and the Mexican government wanted to avoid the possibility of any disturbances during the Olympic Games.
3. Answers should be supported by logical arguments.

SECTION 3 The Nations of South America

Guide to Reading

Main Ideas
- South American nations have experienced economic, social, and political problems.
- Democracy has advanced in South America since the late 1980s.

Key Terms
cooperative, Shining Path

People to Identify
Juan Perón, Salvador Allende, Augusto Pinochet, Juan Velasco Alvarado

Places to Locate
Argentina, Falkland Islands

Preview Questions
1. What obstacles does the new democratic government in Brazil face?
2. What factors have been the greatest causes of South American instability?

Reading Strategy
Categorizing Information Use a table like the one below to describe the factors leading to the change from military rule to civilian rule in Argentina, Brazil, and Chile.

Argentina	Brazil	Chile

Preview of Events

1945 · 1955 · 1965 · 1975 · 1985 · 1995 · 2005

- **1946** Juan Perón is elected president of Argentina
- **1973** Military forces overthrow Allende presidency in Chile
- **1982** Argentina sends troops to the Falkland Islands
- **2001** Alejandro Toledo is elected president of Peru

Voices from the Past

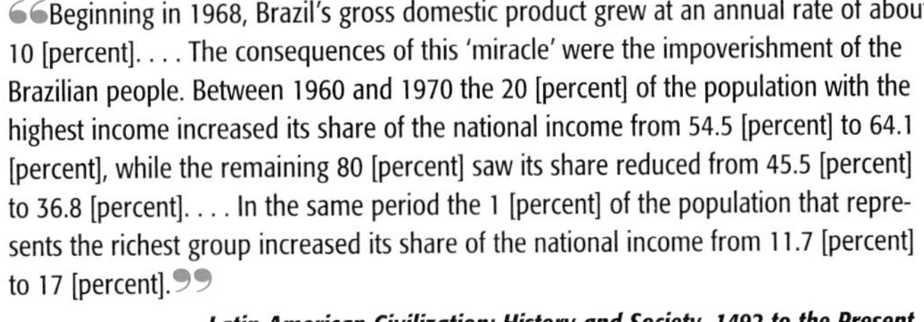

In 1974, a group of Brazilian Catholic priests talked about an economic miracle that had taken place in Brazil:

> "Beginning in 1968, Brazil's gross domestic product grew at an annual rate of about 10 [percent]. . . . The consequences of this 'miracle' were the impoverishment of the Brazilian people. Between 1960 and 1970 the 20 [percent] of the population with the highest income increased its share of the national income from 54.5 [percent] to 64.1 [percent], while the remaining 80 [percent] saw its share reduced from 45.5 [percent] to 36.8 [percent]. . . . In the same period the 1 [percent] of the population that represents the richest group increased its share of the national income from 11.7 [percent] to 17 [percent]."
>
> —***Latin American Civilization: History and Society, 1492 to the Present,* Benjamin Keen, 1996**

Brazilian city, 1971

The countries of South America shared in the economic, political, and social problems that plagued Latin America after 1945. Argentina, Brazil, Chile, Colombia, and Peru provide examples of these problems.

Argentina

Argentina is Latin America's second largest country. For years, it had been ruled by a powerful oligarchy whose wealth was based on growing wheat and

1 FOCUS

Section Overview

This section describes economic and political developments in five South American countries.

BELLRINGER
Skillbuilder Activity

Project transparency and have students answer questions.

Available as a blackline master.

Daily Focus Skills Transparency 22–3

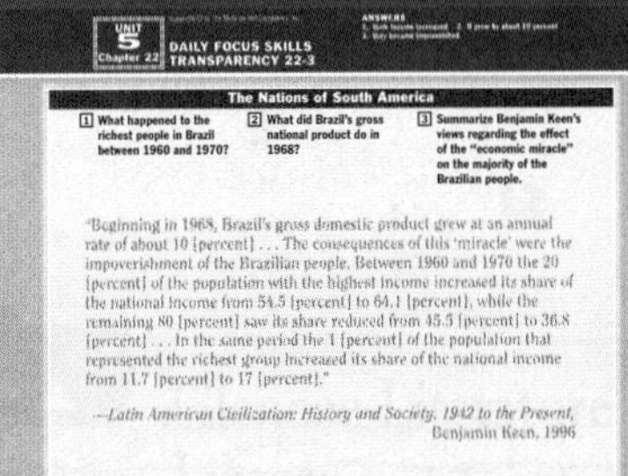

UNIT 5 Chapter 22 DAILY FOCUS SKILLS TRANSPARENCY 22-3

The Nations of South America

1. What happened to the richest people in Brazil between 1960 and 1970?
2. What did Brazil's gross national product do in 1968?
3. Summarize Benjamin Keen's views regarding the effect of the "economic miracle" on the majority of the Brazilian people.

"Beginning in 1968, Brazil's gross domestic product grew at an annual rate of about 10 [percent] . . . The consequences of this 'miracle' were the impoverishment of the Brazilian people. Between 1960 and 1970 the 20 [percent] of the population with the highest income increased its share of the national income from 54.5 [percent] to 64.1 [percent], while the remaining 80 [percent] saw its share reduced from 45.5 [percent] to 36.8 [percent] . . . In the same period the 1 [percent] of the population that represented the richest group increased its share of the national income from 11.7 [percent] to 17 [percent]."

—*Latin American Civilization: History and Society, 1942 to the Present,* Benjamin Keen, 1996

Guide to Reading

Answers to Graphic: Argentina: economic problems; Falklands defeat discredited the military
Brazil: "economic miracle" failed to benefit ordinary Brazilians; led to high inflation, military retreated, led to democratic society
Chile: horrible abuses of human rights led to growing unrest

Preteaching Vocabulary: Ask students to discover if any *cooperatives* (food co-op, child care co-op) are in their neighborhoods. **L1**

SECTION RESOURCES

Reproducible Masters
- Reproducible Lesson Plan 22–3
- Daily Lecture and Discussion Notes 22–3
- Guided Reading Activity 22–3
- Section Quiz 22–3
- Reading Essentials and Study Guide 22–3

Transparencies
- Daily Focus Skills Transparency 22–3

Multimedia
- Interactive Tutor Self-Assessment CD-ROM
- ExamView® Pro Testmaker CD-ROM
- Presentation Plus! CD-ROM

CHAPTER 22
Section 3, 693–696

2 TEACH

Reading Check

Answer: The government bought Argentina's railways and took over banking, insurance, shipping, and communications industries.

Daily Lecture and Discussion Notes 22–3

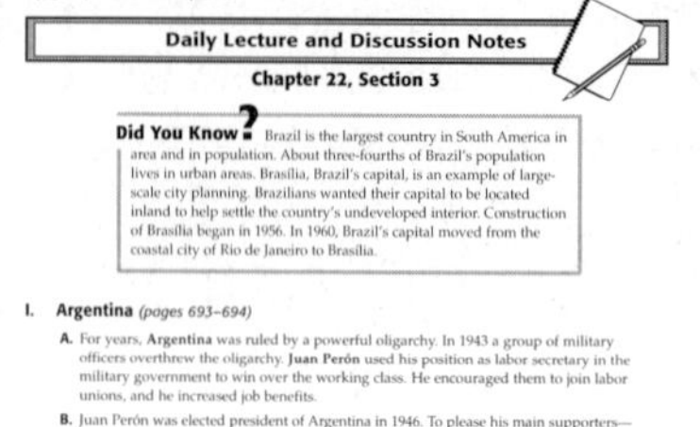

Daily Lecture and Discussion Notes

Chapter 22, Section 3

Did You Know? Brazil is the largest country in South America in area and in population. About three-fourths of Brazil's population lives in urban areas. Brasília, Brazil's capital, is an example of large-scale city planning. Brazilians wanted their capital to be located inland to help settle the country's undeveloped interior. Construction of Brasília began in 1956. In 1960, Brazil's capital moved from the coastal city of Rio de Janeiro to Brasília.

I. **Argentina** *(pages 693–694)*

A. For years, **Argentina** was ruled by a powerful oligarchy. In 1943 a group of military officers overthrew the oligarchy. **Juan Perón** used his position as labor secretary in the military government to win over the working class. He encouraged them to join labor unions, and he increased job benefits.

B. Juan Perón was elected president of Argentina in 1946. To please his main supporters—labor and the working middle class—Perón increased industrialization. He worked to rid Argentina of foreign investors. His regime was authoritarian.

C. Perón died in 1974. A new military regime took power in 1976. To divert people's attention from economic problems, the regime invaded the **Falkland Islands** but were defeated by Great Britain.

D. In 1983, Raúl Alfonsín was elected president of Argentina and worked to restore democratic practices. In 1989, Carlos Saúl Menem won the presidential election. The peaceful transfer of power gave rise to hope for democracy in Argentina.

Discussion Question

How did Juan Perón win over the working class of Argentina? *(He encouraged them to join labor unions, and he increased job benefits. He increased industrialization. He worked to rid Argentina of foreign inv*

Critical Thinking

Ask students to define and give examples of different political systems in contemporary Latin America. L2

Guided Reading Activity 22–3

Name ________ Date ________ Class ________

Guided Reading Activity 22-3

The Nations of South America

DIRECTIONS: Fill in the blanks below as you read Section 3.

1. Argentina is Latin America's ________ largest country.
2. Juan Peron became vice president of Argentina's ________ government in 1944.
3. When Peron was elected president in 1946, his chief support came from ________ and the ________ middle class.
4. Peron created ________ gangs modeled after Hitler's Brownshirts, who used violent means to terrify Peron's opponents.
5. The military stepped in and seized control of ________ in 1964.
6. Beginning in 1968, Brazil experienced an ________ as its economy grew spectacularly.
7. In the 1990s, a series of ________ elected presidents managed to restore some stability to Brazil's economy.
8. Salvador Allende tried to create a ________ society in Chile by constitutional means.
9. Wealthy landholders were angry when radical workers began to take control of their estates and the ________ did nothing to stop them.
10. A radical guerrilla group in Peru known as ________, killed mayors, missionaries, priests, and peasants.
11. Alberto Fujimori, the son of a ________ immigrant, was chosen as Peruvian president in 1990.
12. After World War II, Marxist guerrilla groups began to organize Colombian

raising cattle. Support from the army was crucial to the continuing power of the oligarchy.

In 1943, in the midst of World War II, a group of army officers overthrew the oligarchy. The new military regime was unsure of how to deal with the working classes until one of its members, **Juan Perón,** devised a new strategy.

Using his position as labor secretary in the military government, Perón sought to win over the workers, known as the descamisados (the shirtless ones). He encouraged them to join labor unions. He also increased job benefits, as well as the number of paid holidays and vacations.

In 1944, Perón became vice president of the military government and made sure that people knew he was responsible for the better conditions for workers. As Perón grew more popular, however, other army officers began to fear his power, and they arrested him. An uprising by workers forced the officers to back down.

Perón was elected president of Argentina in 1946. His chief support came from labor and the urban middle class, and to please them, he followed a policy of increased industrialization. At the same time, he sought to free Argentina from foreign investors. The government bought the railways and took over the banking, insurance, shipping, and communications industries.

People In History

Eva Perón
1919–1952—Argentine first lady

Eva Perón, known as Evita to her followers, was the first lady of Argentina from 1946 to 1952. Raised in poverty, Eva dreamed of being an actress. At 15, she moved to Buenos Aires, Argentina's largest city, where she eventually gained fame as a radio performer.

Eva met Juan Perón in 1944 and became his wife a year later. She was an important force in her husband's rise to power. Together, they courted the working-class poor with promises of higher wages and better working conditions. As first lady, Eva Perón formed a charitable organization that built hospitals, schools, and orphanages. She campaigned for women's rights. The masses adored her. To this day, monuments and street names in Argentina keep her memory alive. The American musical and movie *Evita* are based on her life.

Perón's regime was authoritarian. He created Fascist gangs modeled after Hitler's Brownshirts. The gangs used violent means to terrify Perón's opponents.

Fearing Perón's power, the military overthrew the Argentinian leader in September 1955. Perón went into exile in Spain. Overwhelmed by problems, however, military leaders later allowed Perón to return. He was reelected as president in 1973 but died a year later.

In 1976, the military once again took over power. The new regime tolerated no opposition. Perhaps 36,000 people were killed.

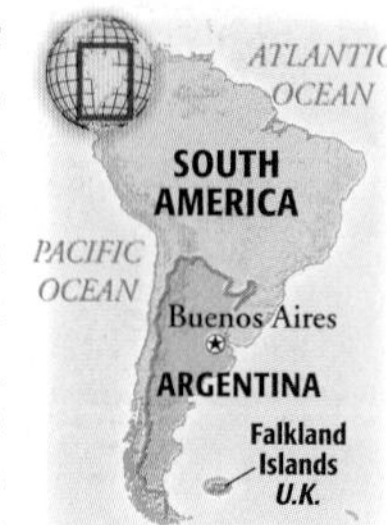

At the same time, economic problems plagued the nation. To divert people's attention, the military regime invaded the **Falkland Islands,** off the coast of Argentina, in April 1982. Great Britain, which had controlled the islands since the nineteenth century, sent ships and troops and took the islands back. The loss discredited the military and opened the door to civilian rule in Argentina.

In 1983, Raúl Alfonsín was elected president and worked to restore democratic practices. The Perónist Carlos Saúl Menem won the presidential elections of 1989. This peaceful transfer of power gave rise to the hope that Argentina was moving on a democratic path.

Reading Check **Explaining** How did Juan Perón free Argentina from foreign investors?

Brazil

Like other Latin American countries, Brazil experienced severe economic problems following World War II. When democratically elected governments proved unable to solve these problems, the military stepped in and seized control in 1964.

The armed forces remained in direct control of the country for the next 20 years. The military set a new economic direction, reducing government interference in the economy and stressing free market forces. Beginning in 1968, the new policies seemed to be working. Brazil experienced an "economic miracle" as its economy grew spectacularly.

Ordinary Brazilians benefited little from this economic growth, however. The gulf between rich and poor, which had always been wide, grew even wider.

EXTENDING THE CONTENT

Magic Realism The term *magic realism* applies predominantly to a Latin American literary movement. Realistic portrayals of everyday events and characters are combined with elements of fantasy and myth. Yet magic realism differs from works of fantasy. There are no wizards, or dragons, or the casting of spells. Magic realism is like a dream; in the morning you realize that what you dreamed does not make any sense, but while you were dreaming it seemed very normal. Latin American authors who employ the style include Gabriel García Márquez, Carlos Fuentes, and Julio Cortazar. American writer Toni Morrison uses elements of magic realism. Students who have seen the movies *The Truman Show* and *Pleasantville* have seen examples of magic realism.

Furthermore, rapid development led to an inflation rate of 100 percent a year. Overwhelmed, the generals retreated and opened the door for a return to democracy in 1985.

The new democratic government faced enormous obstacles—a massive foreign debt, increasingly severe inflation (it was 800 percent in 1987), and a lack of social unity. In the 1990s, however, a series of democratically elected presidents managed to restore some stability to Brazil's economy.

Reading Check **Evaluating** What factors led to the return to democracy in Brazil in 1985?

Chile

In elections held in 1970, **Salvador Allende** (ah•YEHN•day), a Marxist, became president of Chile. Allende tried to create a socialist society by constitutional means. He increased the wages of industrial workers and nationalized the largest domestic and foreign-owned corporations.

Allende's policies were not popular with everyone. Nationalization of the copper industry, Chile's major source of export income, angered the copper companies' American owners, as well as the American government. Wealthy landholders were angry when radical workers began to take control of their estates and the government did nothing to stop these takeovers.

In March 1973, new elections increased the number of Allende's supporters in the Chilean congress. Afraid of Allende's growing strength, the Chilean army, under the direction of General **Augusto Pinochet** (PEE•noh•CHEHT), moved to overthrow the government. In September 1973, military forces seized the presidential palace and shot Allende. The military then set up a dictatorship.

The Pinochet regime was one of the most brutal in Chile's history. Thousands of opponents were imprisoned. Thousands more were tortured and murdered. The regime also outlawed all political parties and did away with the congress. While some estates and industries were returned to their owners, the copper industries remained in government hands.

The regime's horrible abuses of human rights led to growing unrest in the mid-1980s. In 1989, free presidential elections led to the defeat of Pinochet, and Chile moved toward a more democratic system.

Reading Check **Explaining** Why did the armed forces of Chile overthrow the government of Salvador Allende in 1973?

What If...

Salvador Allende had lost the Chilean election?

In 1973, Salvador Allende beat Jorge Alessandri, former president of Chile, by 40,000 votes out of almost 3 million cast in the general election. Since Allende won by a plurality rather than a majority (over 50 percent of the vote), the election was referred to the Chilean National Congress for a final decision. The Congress chose Allende, bringing the Western world its first democratically elected Marxist president.

Consider the Consequences What if Alessandri had been reelected to continue his regime? Explain why the United States would not have had the same incentives to oppose Alessandri as it had to oppose Allende.

Peru

The history of Peru has been marked by instability. Peru's dependence on the sale abroad of its products has led to extreme ups and downs in the economy. With these ups and downs have come many government changes. A large, poor, and landless peasant population has created an additional source of unrest.

A military takeover in 1968 led to some change. General **Juan Velasco Alvarado** sought to help the peasants. His government seized almost 75 percent of the nation's large landed estates and put ownership of the land into the hands of peasant cooperatives (farm organizations owned by and operated for the peasants' benefit). The government also nationalized many foreign-owned companies and held food prices at low levels to help urban workers.

Economic problems continued, however, and Peruvian military leaders removed General Alvarado from power in 1975. Five years later, unable to cope with Peru's economic problems, the military returned Peru to civilian rule.

New problems made the task of the civilian government even more difficult. A radical guerrilla group with ties to Communist China, known as Shining Path, killed mayors, missionaries, priests, and peasants. The goal of Shining Path was to smash all authority and create a classless society.

Reading Check

Answer: rapid economic growth led to high inflation; the gap between rich and poor grew wider; the military regime retreated.

Reading Check

Answer: Allende was a Marxist who was trying to create a socialist society by constitutional means. When new elections increased the number of his supporters in the Chilean congress, the army, alarmed by the radical influence, overthrew the government.

What If...

The history of Chile would probably have been much less violent. There would have been no reason for the United States to support a military takeover, since there would have been no Marxist threat.

3 ASSESS

Assign Section 3 Assessment as homework or as an in-class activity.

Have students use **Interactive Tutor Self-Assessment CD-ROM.**

Section Quiz 22–3

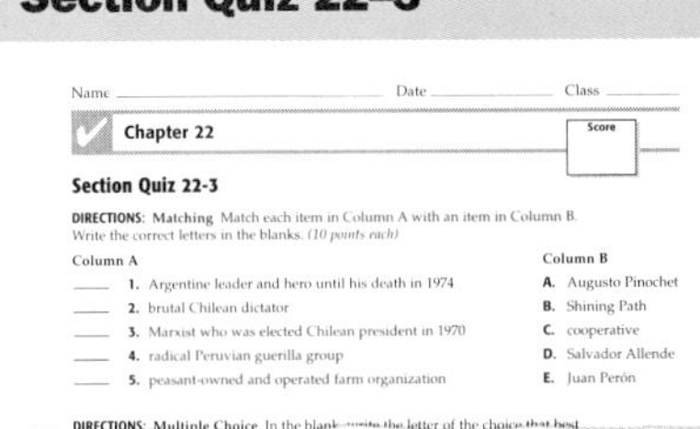
Name ______ Date ______ Class ______

Chapter 22 — Score

Section Quiz 22-3

DIRECTIONS: Matching Match each item in Column A with an item in Column B. Write the correct letters in the blanks. *(10 points each)*

Column A	Column B
____ 1. Argentine leader and hero until his death in 1974	A. Augusto Pinochet
____ 2. brutal Chilean dictator	B. Shining Path
____ 3. Marxist who was elected Chilean president in 1970	C. cooperative
____ 4. radical Peruvian guerilla group	D. Salvador Allende
____ 5. peasant-owned and operated farm organization	E. Juan Perón

DIRECTIONS: Multiple Choice In the blank write the letter of the choice that best

INTERDISCIPLINARY CONNECTIONS ACTIVITY

Environment The rain forests of Central and South America have been called "the lungs of the earth," producing much of the oxygen that we all breathe. The need for Latin Americans to find jobs and opportunities and to develop agriculture, while at the same time protecting and conserving the rain forest becomes a concern for the entire planet. Even protected areas are at risk. Scientists have discovered that deforestation in one area can result in harmful atmospheric conditions miles away. Replacing forests with farms and roads means less moisture evaporates from the soil, reducing clouds around forested peaks 65 miles (104.5 km) away. Ask students how nations can develop and become economically stable and still protect their natural resources. What obligations do developed nations have toward less developed nations? L3

CHAPTER 22
Section 3, 693–696

Reading Essentials and Study Guide 22–3

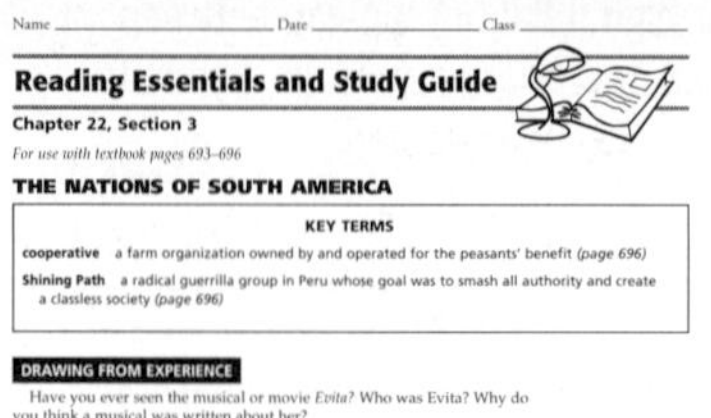
Name ______ Date ______ Class ______

Reading Essentials and Study Guide

Chapter 22, Section 3

For use with textbook pages 693–696

THE NATIONS OF SOUTH AMERICA

KEY TERMS

cooperative a farm organization owned by and operated for the peasants' benefit *(page 696)*

Shining Path a radical guerrilla group in Peru whose goal was to smash all authority and create a classless society *(page 696)*

DRAWING FROM EXPERIENCE

Have you ever seen the musical or movie *Evita?* Who was Evita? Why do you think a musical was written about her?

In the last section, you read about economic and political crises in Mexico, Cuba, and Central America following World War II. In this section, you will

Critical Thinking

Ask students to evaluate the long-term impact of the American Revolution on political developments around the world, focusing on its impact in Latin America. **L2**

Reading Check

Answer: He seized large landed estates and put the land into the hands of peasant cooperatives.

Reading Check

Answer: Coca is used to produce cocaine for sale in the illegal drug market; coca leaves gave impoverished peasants a new cash crop.

Reteaching Activity

Have students review the changes in government in Argentina, Chile, Brazil, Peru, and Colombia from 1980 to the present. **L1**

4 CLOSE

Have students list the challenges facing the countries of South America today. **L2**

In 1990, Peruvians chose Alberto Fujimori as president. Fujimori, the son of a Japanese immigrant, promised reforms. Two years later, he suspended the constitution and congress, became a dictator, and began a campaign against Shining Path guerrillas. Corruption led to his ouster from power in 2000. In June 2001, Alejandro Toledo became the first freely elected president of Native American descent.

Reading Check **Identifying** How did General Juan Velasco Alvarado earn the support of many Peruvian peasants?

Drug lords often use terrorism to threaten those people who try to stop the flow of illegal drugs.

Colombia

Colombia has long had a democratic political system, but a conservative elite led by the owners of coffee plantations has dominated the government.

After World War II, Marxist guerrilla groups began to organize Colombian peasants. The government responded violently. More than two hundred thousand peasants had been killed by the mid-1960s. Violence remained a constant feature of Colombian life in the 1980s and 1990s.

Peasants who lived in poverty turned to a new cash crop—coca leaves, used to make cocaine. The drug trade increased, and so, too, did the number of drug lords. Drug lords formed cartels (groups of drug businesses) that used bribes and violence to force government cooperation in the drug traffic and eliminate competitors. Attempts to stop the traffic in drugs had little success and drug traffickers thrived. Currently, Colombia supplies the majority of cocaine to the international drug market. The government has begun an aerial eradication program.

High unemployment (around 20 percent in 2000) continues to hamper Colombia's economic growth. Colombia's leading exports, coffee and oil, are subject to price fluctuations. However, President Andres Pastrana has a well respected economic team working to keep the economy on track.

Reading Check **Explaining** Why have some Colombian peasants turned to the production of coca leaves?

SECTION 3 ASSESSMENT

Checking for Understanding

1. **Define** cooperative, Shining Path.
2. **Identify** Juan Perón, Salvador Allende, Augusto Pinochet, Juan Velasco Alvarado.
3. **Locate** Argentina, Falkland Islands.
4. **Explain** why the Argentine military invaded the Falkland Islands. What was the impact of this invasion on the government of Argentina?
5. **List** the obstacles Brazil's new democratic government faced in 1985. How did economic conditions help this democratic government come to power?

Critical Thinking

6. **Analyze** Why is it often easier for the military to seize power in a nation than it is for the military to rule that nation effectively? Which countries discussed in this chapter seem to support this theory?
7. **Organizing Information** Use a chart like the one below to show how democracy has advanced in South America since the late 1980s.

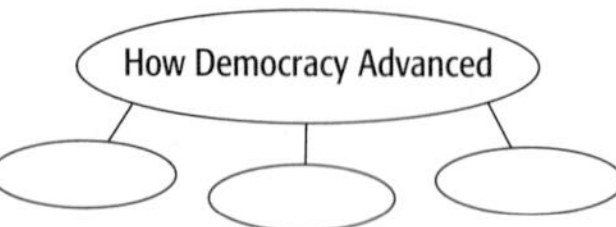

Analyzing Visuals

8. **Examine** the photograph of a Brazilian city shown on page 693 of your text. How does this photograph reflect the problems created by the Brazilian "economic miracle"?

Writing About History

9. **Informative Writing** Pretend you are an American journalist sent to Argentina to cover Perón's presidency. Write an article based on your interviews with the workers and government officials. Include the pros and cons of living under the Perón regime.

SECTION 3 ASSESSMENT

1. Key terms are in blue.
2. Juan Perón *(p. 694)*; Salvador Allende *(p. 695)*; Augusto Pinochet *(p. 695)*; Juan Velasco Alvarado *(p. 695)*
3. See chapter maps.
4. to divert attention from economic problems; the result was a defeat which discredited the military and opened the door to civilian rule
5. massive foreign debt, increasingly severe inflation, and a lack of social unity; economic problems overwhelmed the military regime
6. Military regimes are usually repressive, leading to popular unrest.
7. Argentina: military dictatorship discredited by the Falkland defeat, Alfonsín elected president in 1983; Brazil: inflation opened door to democratic society in 1985; Chile: human rights abuses under Pinochet's dictatorship led to his defeat
8. It increased the gulf between rich and poor.
9. Students will write an informative article.

TECHNOLOGY

SKILLBUILDER

Developing a Database

Why Learn This Skill?

Do you have an address book with your friends' names; addresses; and phone, fax, pager, and cell numbers? Do you have to cross out information when numbers change? When you have a party, do you address all the invitations by hand? If your address book were stored in a computer, you could find a name instantly. You could update your address book easily and use the computer to print out invitations and envelopes.

When you collect information in a computer file, the file is called an electronic database. The database can contain any kind of information: lists detailing your CD collection; notes for a research paper; your daily expenses. Using an electronic database can help you locate information quickly and organize and manage it, no matter how large the file.

Learning the Skill

An electronic database is a collection of facts that is stored in a file on the computer. Although you can build your own database, there is special software—called a database management system (DBMS)—that makes it easy to add, delete, change, or update information. Some popular commercial DBMS programs allow you to create address books, note cards, financial reports, family trees, and many other types of records.

A database can be organized and reorganized in any way that is useful to you.

- The DBMS software program will usually give clear instructions about entering and arranging your information.
- The information in a database is organized into different fields. For example, in an address book, one field might be your friends' names and another could be their addresses.
- When you retrieve information, the computer will search through the files and display the information on the screen. Often it can be organized and displayed in a variety of ways, depending on what you want.

Fidel Castro with farmers

Practicing the Skill

Fidel Castro is one of the Latin American leaders discussed in this chapter. Follow these steps to build a database of the political events that have taken place during his years as Cuba's leader.

1. Determine what facts you want to include in your database.
2. Follow the instructions in the DBMS that you are using to set up fields.
3. Determine how you want to organize the facts in the database—chronologically by the date of the event, or alphabetically by the name of the event.
4. Follow the instructions in your computer program to place the information in order of importance.

Applying the Skill

Research and build a database that organizes information about current political events in Latin American countries. Explain to a partner why the database is organized the way it is and how it might be used in this class.

ANSWERS TO PRACTICING THE SKILL

Using information from the textbook, students will create databases of political events that have taken place in Cuba while Castro was the leader. Information should be arranged logically.

Applying the Skill: Students will research and create databases. The database should organize information about current political events in Latin American countries. Information should be arranged logically.

TECHNOLOGY SKILLBUILDER

TEACH

Developing a Database Students who know how to use and construct a database will have a valuable skill that can save them time in locating specific facts and discovering relationships among facts.

Before students begin working on this exercise, have students review Chapter 22, noting the references to Cuba and Fidel Castro. Point out the fields that are used most often, as well as ideas that are original and practical. L2

Additional Practice

Skills Reinforcement Activity 22

Name ______ Date ______ Class ______

Skills Reinforcement Activity 22

Developing a Database

A large amount of information can be managed and organized with the help of a computerized database program. Once you enter data in a database table, you can quickly locate a record according to key information. If you have a newspaper delivery route, for example, you could have the program list all your customers that live on a particular street. You could also locate all customers who receive newspapers on weekends only.

DIRECTIONS: Research and use the information about events in Mexico from 1945 to the present. Use your text to complete the database table below by filling in the year, key event or events, and the president of Mexico at the time of the event.

Events in Mexico

Year	Event	President

GLENCOE TECHNOLOGY

CD-ROM
Glencoe Skillbuilder Interactive Workbook CD-ROM, Level 2

This interactive CD-ROM reinforces student mastery of essential social studies skills.

CHAPTER 22 ASSESSMENT and ACTIVITIES

GLENCOE TECHNOLOGY

MindJogger Videoquiz

Use the **MindJogger Videoquiz** to review Chapter 22 content.

 Available in VHS.

Using Key Terms

1. multinational corporations **2.** contras **3.** magic realism **4.** privatization **5.** trade embargo **6.** Shining Path **7.** cooperatives

Reviewing Key Facts

8. The OAS aims to end military action by one state in the affairs of another state in the Western Hemisphere.

9. Castro began to receive aid from the Soviet Union and arms from Eastern Europe.

10. Gabriel García Márquez

11. The United States provided weapons and training to the Salvadoran army to defeat the guerrillas.

12. The U.S. military invaded Panama and arrested him. He was sent to prison on charges of drug trafficking.

13. because of their corruption

14. The Shining Path's goal was to smash all authority and create a classless society.

15. It undermines stability.

16. Under Castro, the Cuban people have secured some social gains. The regime provides free medical services for all citizens, and illiteracy has nearly been eliminated.

Critical Thinking

17. Soviet control of Eastern European nations was much more comprehensive than the influence the United States has exerted on Latin American nations. The United States has generally avoided direct military intervention in Latin American nations. Instead, it has funded anti-Communist governments and guerrilla movements.

18. Answers will vary but should address the economic and strategic importance of the Panama Canal.

Using Key Terms

1. Corporations with headquarters in several countries are called ____.
2. The anti-Communist forces that fought the Sandinistas in Nicaragua were called ____.
3. A style of literature that combines elements of the real world with imaginary events is called ____.
4. Selling government-owned companies to individuals or to corporations is called ____.
5. The refusal to import or export goods to or from another country is a ________.
6. The Communist guerrilla movement in Peru is called the ____.
7. Farms owned and operated by groups of peasants are called ________.

Reviewing Key Facts

8. **History** What is the purpose of the Organization of American States?
9. **Economics** What did Fidel Castro do in 1960 that probably contributed to the decision of the United States to sponsor an invasion of Cuba at the Bay of Pigs in 1961?
10. **Culture** Who is considered the most famous of the Latin American novelists?
11. **History** How was the U.S. involved in El Salvador?
12. **History** What happened that ended Manuel Noriega's control of Panama in 1989?
13. **Government** Why was President Carter unwilling to continue support of the Somoza family?
14. **Government** What was the goal of the guerrilla group known as Shining Path?
15. **Economics** What effect does the wide gap between the rich and the poor have in Latin American countries?
16. **Government** Why was Castro able to maintain control of Cuba even after he lost his foreign support?

Critical Thinking

17. **Compare and Contrast** Compare the policies of the United States toward Latin American countries to those of the Soviet Union toward countries in Eastern Europe.
18. **Drawing Inferences** Analyze why the United States used its military power to arrest Manuel Noriega after ignoring many other dishonest and corrupt leaders in Latin America.

Writing About History

19. **Expository Writing** Analyze how Cuba's revolution affected the United States and the Soviet Union. Explain the background and context of the revolution. How were these events particular to the time period?

Chapter Summary

Several Latin American countries have moved from conflict to cooperation.

Country	Conflict	Revolution	Change	Cooperation
Cuba	Corruption and canceled elections create unrest.	Castro ousts Batista.	Castro improves social welfare system but suspends elections.	Castro allows limited foreign investment, improving relations with Canada and other countries.
Nicaragua	Repressive Somoza regime owns a quarter of the country's land.	Social movement led by Sandinistas overthrows Somoza in 1979.	Sandinistas initiate social reforms but are hampered by contras.	Sandinista regime agrees to hold free elections in 1990; Chamorro is elected president.
Mexico	PRI dominates.	University students protest government policies.	PRI allows new political parties and more freedoms.	Mexico elects non-PRI candidate as president.
Argentina	Economy is poor.	Argentine military overthrows Perón.	Economy recovers; many citizens lose lives to death squads.	Democracy is gradually restored after Falkland Islands disaster.
El Salvador	Elites control most wealth and land.	Leftist guerrillas and right-wing groups battle.	U.N.-sponsored peace agreement ends civil war in 1992.	Economy grows; ties with neighbors are renewed.

Writing About History

19. The Cuban Revolution brought the Cold War to Latin America. The United States worked to rid Cuba of Castro and to halt the spread of revolutionary ideas in Latin America. The Soviet Union gained a foothold in the Americas and used Cuba to further its foreign policy interests. With the disintegration of the Soviet Union, the Cold War ended, and Cuba was left without support.

Analyzing Sources

20. The contras were trying to overthrow the Marxist Sandinista government. The Reagan and Bush administrations were worried by the Sandinistas' alignment with the Soviet Union.

21. Answers will vary but should be supported by logical arguments.

Self-Check Quiz

Visit the *Glencoe World History—Modern Times* Web site at wh.mt.glencoe.com and click on **Chapter 22–Self-Check Quiz** to prepare for the Chapter Test.

Analyzing Sources

Read the following excerpt from Nancy Donovan, a Catholic missionary in Nicaragua:

> "It is not easy to live in a war zone. The least of it was my being kidnapped by contras early this year. The hardest part is seeing people die and consoling families. . . . In those eight hours I was held, as I walked in a column of 60 or so men and a few women—all in uniform—I could hear shooting and realized that people I knew were being killed. Earlier I had seen bodies brought back to town, some burned, some cut to pieces."

20. Why did the United States finance the contras?
21. What role do you think the United States should play in Central America? Should the United States have supported rebels capable of the type of warfare described in this passage?

Applying Technology Skills

22. **Create a Database** Research the major political events in South America since 1945. Include the following information in your database:
    - Year
    - Country
    - Event

Making Decisions

23. Identify one of the challenges faced by the countries of Latin America today. Create a poster that illustrates the issue you have selected. Include a clear statement of the issue, information you have gathered about the background of the challenge, and key individuals or countries involved with the issue. Identify options, predict consequences, and offer possible solutions.

Analyzing Maps and Charts

Using the map above, answer the following questions:

24. Which South American country has the largest geographic area? Which countries have the largest populations?

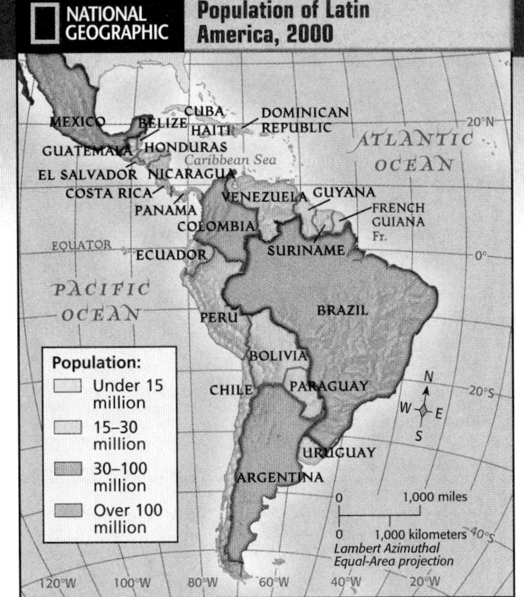

25. How do the populations of Central American countries compare to the populations of other Latin American countries?
26. Which South American countries are landlocked? Between what degrees of latitude and longitude are they located?

Standardized Test Practice

Directions: Choose the best answer to the following question.

Why are Latin American countries economically important to the United States?

A American banks need countries such as Brazil and Mexico to default on their loans.

B Latin American countries are popular destinations for American tourists.

C Latin American countries are colonies of European nations.

D America imports raw goods such as oil, coffee, and copper from Mexico, El Salvador, Colombia, and Chile.

Test-Taking Tip: Read test questions carefully because every word is important. This question asks why Latin America is *economically* important. Therefore, you can eliminate any answer choices that do not offer explanations about their economic importance.

Have students visit the Web site at wh.mt.glencoe.com to review Chapter 22 and take the Self-Check Quiz.

Standardized Test Practice

Answer: D

Answer Explanation: Answers A–C do not benefit the United States, so by process of elimination, D is the best answer.

Bonus Question ?

Ask: Which of the three regional groupings in this chapter—Mexico and the Caribbean, Central America, or South America—do you think has the best prospects for the future? *(When predicting, students should keep in mind the region's history, government, economic resources, and social structure.)* **L2**

Applying Technology Skills

22. Students will create databases. Information should be supported by multiple outside sources.

Making Decisions

23. Students will create posters; information should be consistent with material presented in this chapter.

Analyzing Maps and Charts

24. Brazil; Brazil, Mexico
25. less population due to smaller area
26. Bolivia, Paraguay; between 10° and 30° latitude, 70° and 55° longitude.

Chapter 23 Resources

Timesaving Tools

TeacherWorks™ All-In-One Planner and Resource Center

- **Interactive Teacher Edition** Access your Teacher Wraparound Edition and your classroom resources with a few easy clicks.
- **Interactive Lesson Planner** Planning has never been easier! Organize your week, month, semester, or year with all the lesson helps you need to make teaching creative, timely, and relevant.

Use Glencoe's **Presentation Plus!** multimedia teacher tool to easily present dynamic lessons that visually excite your students. Using Microsoft PowerPoint® you can customize the presentations to create your own personalized lessons.

TEACHING TRANSPARENCIES

Graphic Organizer Student Activity 23 Transparency

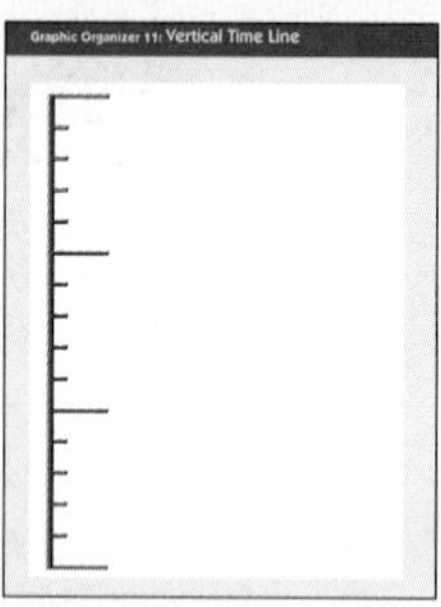

Chapter Transparency 23

Map Overlay Transparency 23

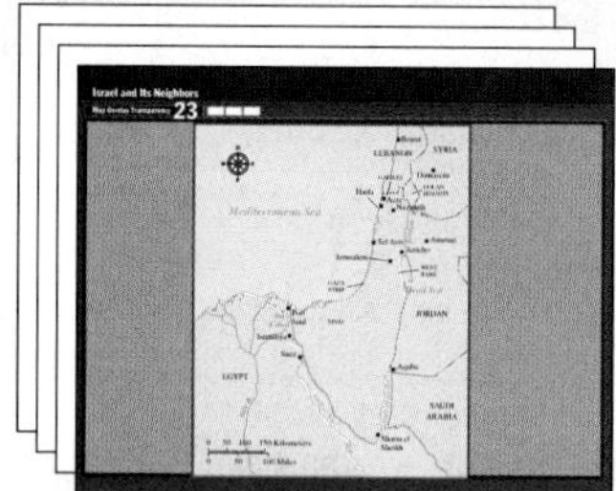

APPLICATION AND ENRICHMENT

Enrichment Activity 23

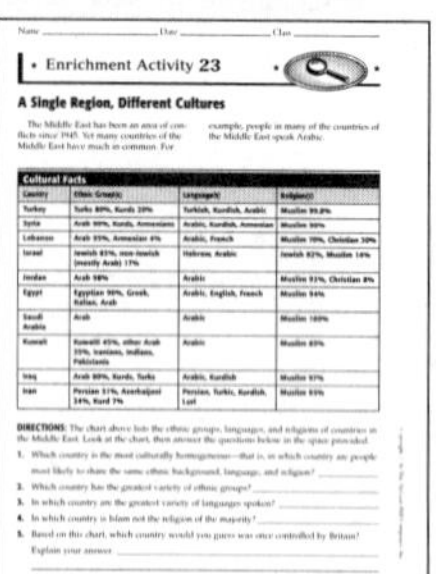

Primary Source Reading 23

History Simulation Activity 23

Historical Significance Activity 23

Cooperative Learning Activity 23

A&E HOME VIDEO. Biography®

THE HISTORY CHANNEL®

The following videotape program is available from Glencoe as a supplement to Chapter 23:

- **Nelson Mandela: Journey to Freedom** (ISBN 0–7670–0113–3)

To order, call Glencoe at 1–800 334–7344. To find classroom resources to accompany this video, check the following home pages:
A&E Television: www.aande.com
The History Channel: www.historychannel.com

Chapter 23 Resources

Review and Reinforcement

Linking Past and Present Activity 23

Time Line Activity 23

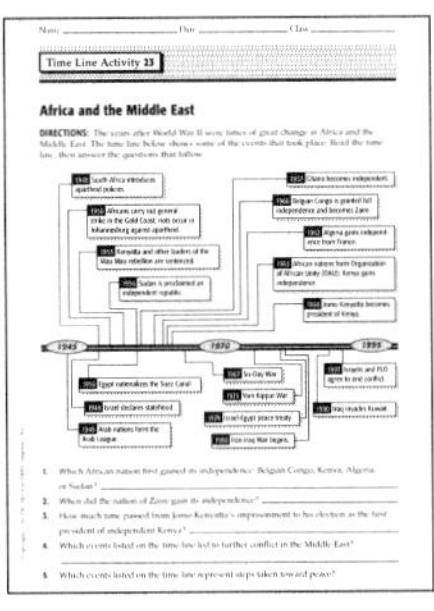

Reteaching Activity 23

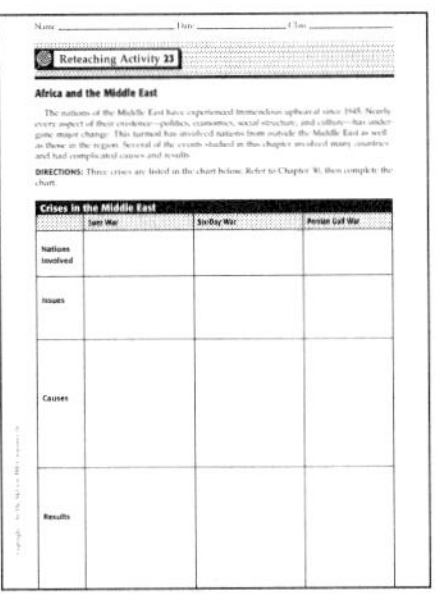

Vocabulary Activity 23

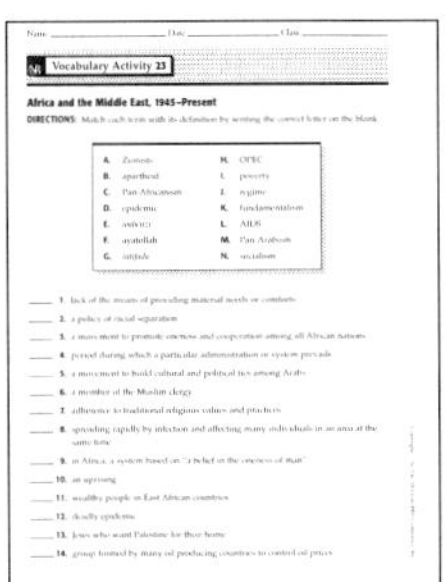

Critical Thinking Skills Activity 23

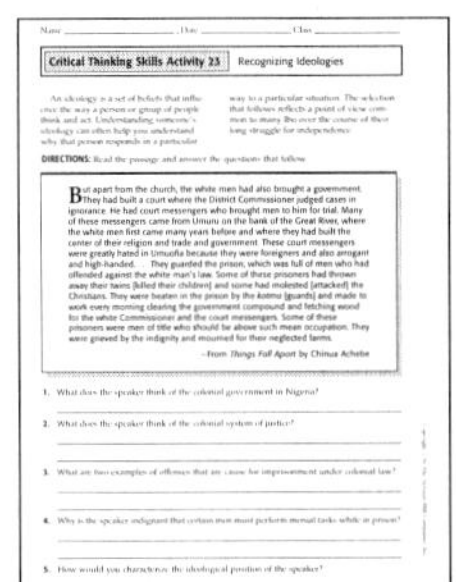

Assessment and Evaluation

Chapter 23 Test Form A

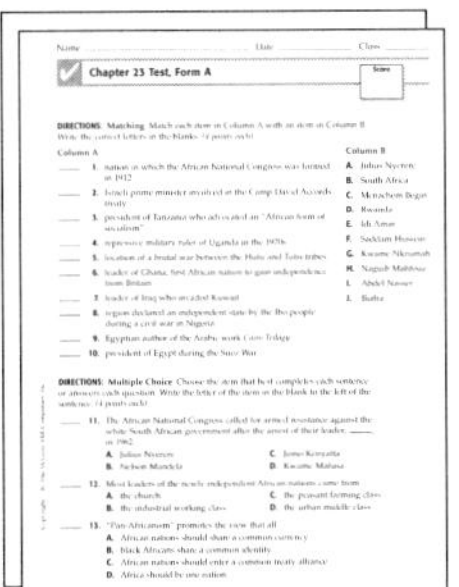

Chapter 23 Test Form B

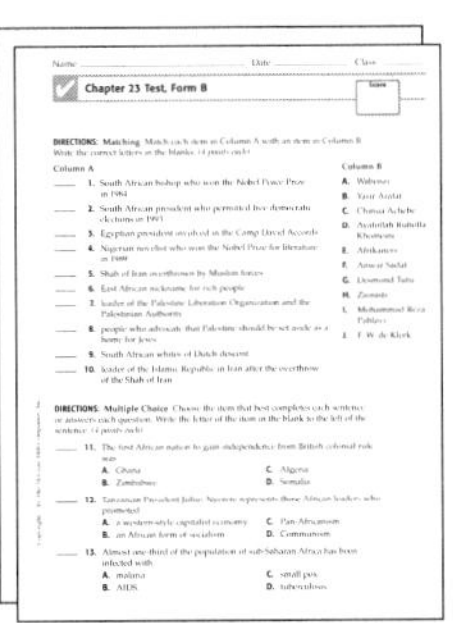

Performance Assessment Activity 23

ExamView® Pro Testmaker CD-ROM

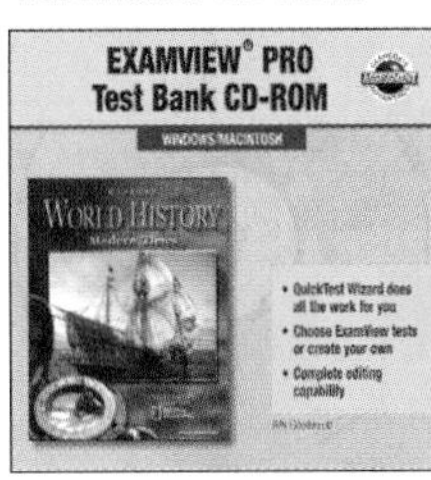

Standardized Test Skills Practice Workbook Activity 23

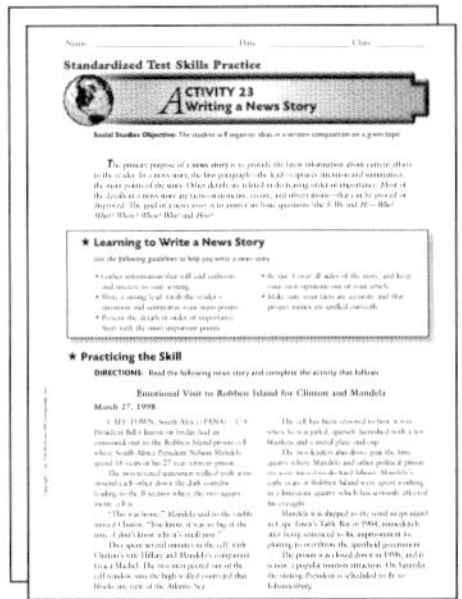

Interdisciplinary Activities

Mapping History Activity 23

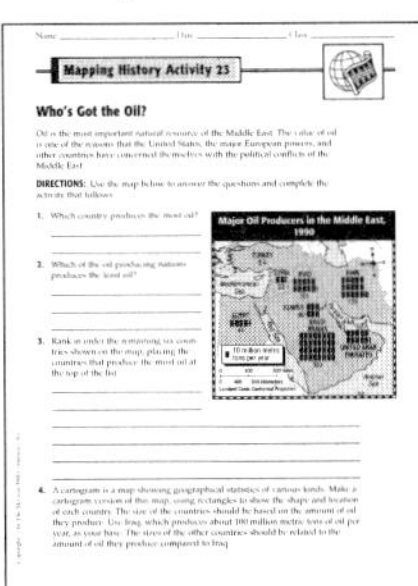

World Art and Music Activity 23

History and Geography Activity 23

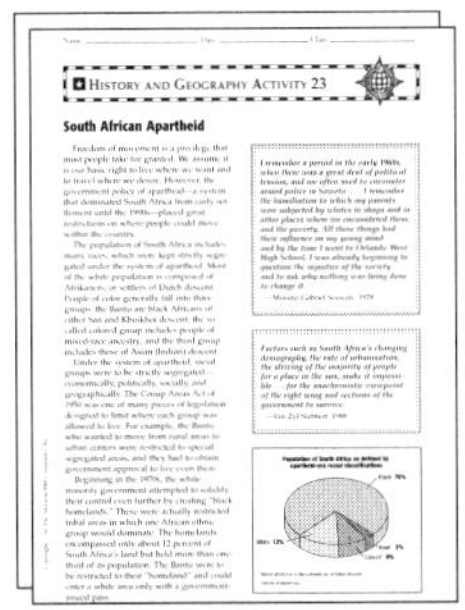

People in World History Activity 23

Multimedia

- Vocabulary PuzzleMaker CD-ROM
- Interactive Tutor Self-Assessment CD-ROM
- ExamView® Pro Testmaker CD-ROM
- Audio Program
- World History Primary Source Document Library CD-ROM
- MindJogger Videoquiz
- Presentation Plus! CD-ROM
- TeacherWorks CD-ROM
- Interactive Student Edition CD-ROM
- The World History—Modern Times Video Program

Spanish Resources

The following Spanish language materials are available in the Spanish Resources Binder:

- Spanish Guided Reading Activities
- Spanish Reteaching Activities
- Spanish Quizzes and Tests
- Spanish Vocabulary Activities
- Spanish Summaries

Chapter 23 Resources

SECTION RESOURCES

Daily Objectives	Reproducible Resources	Multimedia Resources
SECTION 1 **Independence in Africa** 1. Describe how people hoped that independence would bring democratic governments, but instead many African nations fell victim to military regimes and one-party states. 2. Discuss how African nations struggled to resolve the tension between modern and traditional cultures and economies.	Reproducible Lesson Plan 23–1 Daily Lecture and Discussion Notes 23–1 Guided Reading Activity 23–1* Section Quiz 23–1* Reading Essentials and Study Guide 23–1	Daily Focus Skills Transparency 23–1 Interactive Tutor Self-Assessment CD-ROM ExamView® Pro Testmaker CD-ROM Presentation Plus! CD-ROM
SECTION 2 **Conflict in the Middle East** 1. Explain how instability in various parts of the Middle East led to armed conflict and mediation attempts from countries outside the region. 2. Discuss the Islamic revival in many Middle Eastern countries, which influenced political and social life.	Reproducible Lesson Plan 23–2 Daily Lecture and Discussion Notes 23–2 Guided Reading Activity 23–2* Section Quiz 23–2* Reteaching Activity 23* Reading Essentials and Study Guide 23–2	Daily Focus Skills Transparency 23–2 Interactive Tutor Self-Assessment CD-ROM ExamView® Pro Testmaker CD-ROM Presentation Plus! CD-ROM

0:00 **OUT OF TIME?**
Assign the Chapter 23 **Reading Essentials and Study Guide.**

*Also Available in Spanish

 Blackline Master  Transparency  CD-ROM  DVD
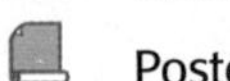 Poster Music Program Audio Program Videocassette

Chapter 23 Resources

Teacher's Corner

INDEX TO NATIONAL GEOGRAPHIC MAGAZINE

The following articles relate to this chapter:

- "Down the Zambezi," by Paul Theroux, October 1997.
- "African Gold," by Carol Beckwith and Angela Fisher, October 1996.
- "Ndoki—The Last Place on Earth," by Douglas Chadwick, July 1995.

NATIONAL GEOGRAPHIC SOCIETY PRODUCTS AVAILABLE FROM GLENCOE

To order the following products call Glencoe at 1-800-334-7344:

- *STV: World Geography, Vol. 2, Africa* (Videodisc)

ADDITIONAL NATIONAL GEOGRAPHIC SOCIETY PRODUCTS

To order the following, call National Geographic at 1-800-368-2728:

- *South Africa: After Apartheid* (Video)
- *Baka: People of the Forest* (Video)

NGS ONLINE

Access National Geographic's new dynamic MapMachine Web site and other geography resources at:
www.nationalgeographic.com
www.nationalgeographic.com/maps

KEY TO ABILITY LEVELS

Teaching strategies have been coded.

L1 BASIC activities for all students
L2 AVERAGE activities for average to above-average students
L3 CHALLENGING activities for above-average students
ELL ENGLISH LANGUAGE LEARNER activities

Block Schedule

Activities that are suited to use within the block scheduling framework are identified by:

WORLD HISTORY Online

Use our Web site for additional resources. All essential content is covered in the Student Edition.

You and your students can visit www.wh.mt.glencoe.com, the Web site companion to *Glencoe World History—Modern Times.* This innovative integration of electronic and print media offers your students a wealth of opportunities. The student text directs students to the Web site for the following options:

- **Chapter Overviews**
- **Self-Check Quizzes**
- **Student Web Activities**
- **Textbook Updates**

Answers to the Student Web Activities are provided for you in the **Web Activity Lesson Plans.** Additional Web resources and Interactive Tutor Puzzles are also available.

From the Classroom of...

Umbisa Kendeli-Gusa
Mifflin International School
Columbus, Ohio

Contemporary Lifestyle of African Teenagers

Have students make a direct link with a school in Africa and communicate one-on-one with an African teenager. This can be facilitated through e-mail or by calling an African embassy in Washington, D.C., which will provide the link between schools in Africa and the United States. It is recommended that students communicate with the English-speaking countries south of the Sahara.

Using their knowledge from Chapter 23, have students ask their African counterparts to focus on the way life is now compared to the way it was in the past. Students should investigate in detail the interaction between the church, parents, the government, and any other agencies that affect the lives of youth from early childhood through adolescence. Students may also wish to inquire about age sets.

Have students write to the local newspaper and share this experience and their new knowledge with the community at large.

Introducing
CHAPTER 23

Performance Assessment

Refer to Activity 23 in the Performance Assessment Activities and Rubrics booklet.

The Impact Today

Help students to understand that events in one part of the world increasingly have global impact. For example, tension in the Middle East impacts oil production, tourism, and political movements. Ask students to brainstorm ways in which events in places such as the Middle East have affected them personally. (*Answers will vary, but students should see that these events can affect such things as the prices of heating oil and gasoline, security measures at airports, and relatives and friends in the military being put in dangerous situations—all of which can affect their lives.*)

GLENCOE TECHNOLOGY

The World History—Modern Times Video Program

To learn more about South Africa, students can view the Chapter 23 video, "Apartheid," from **The World History—Modern Times Video Program.**

MindJogger Videoquiz

Use the **MindJogger Videoquiz** to preview Chapter 23 content.

Available in VHS.

CHAPTER 23 Africa and the Middle East

1945–Present

Key Events

As you read this chapter, look for the key events in the development of Africa and the Middle East.

- *From the 1950s to the 1970s, most African nations gained independence from colonial powers.*
- *Israel declared statehood on May 14, 1948, creating conflict and struggle between the new state and its neighbors.*

The Impact Today

The events that occurred during this time period still impact our lives today.

- *Many African nations struggle with political and economic stability.*
- *The United States continues to work with the Israelis and Palestinians to find a peaceful solution to their territorial disputes.*

World History—Modern Times Video *The Chapter 23 video, "Apartheid," chronicles segregation and its demise in South Africa.*

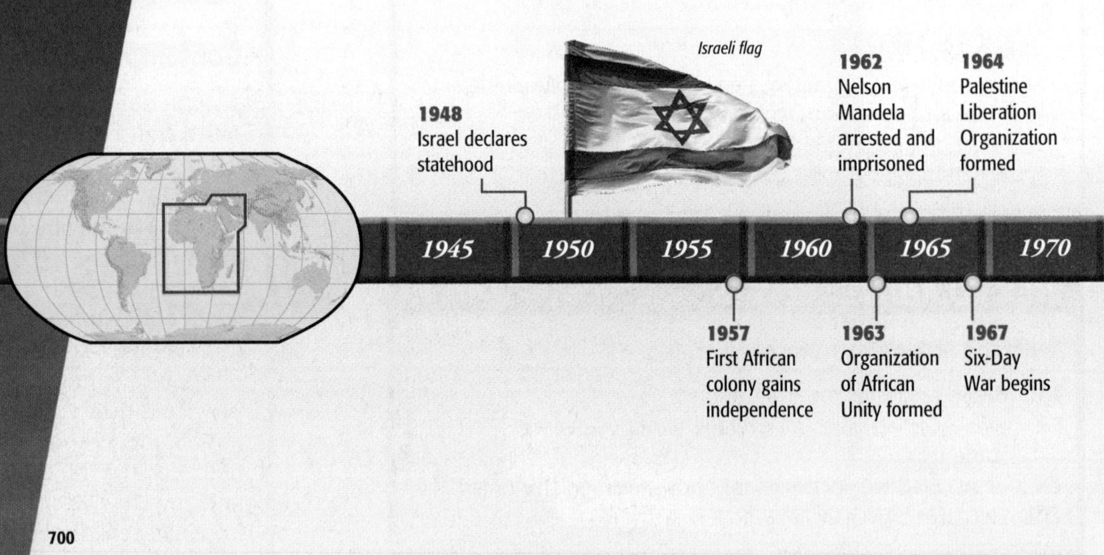
Israeli flag
1945
1950
1955
1960
1965
1970
1948 Israel declares statehood
1957 First African colony gains independence
1962 Nelson Mandela arrested and imprisoned
1963 Organization of African Unity formed
1964 Palestine Liberation Organization formed
1967 Six-Day War begins

700

TWO-MINUTE LESSON LAUNCHER

To arouse student curiosity, prepare a short quiz on African current events. Ask the students such questions as: Who is the president of South Africa? How many nations are in Africa? Where is Eritrea located? The war between the north and south in Sudan involves which groups? Which is the more pressing problem in Africa, desertification or lack of clean water? Which African nations have democratically elected governments? Depending upon the quiz results, you may want to assign students the task of doing research to answer these questions. You also may want to ask students to bring in newspaper articles about Africa to display in the room. L2

Kwame Nkrumah celebrates independence. Ghana gained its independence from Great Britain in 1957.

U.S. military planes during Gulf War

1990
Iraqi attack on Kuwait leads to Persian Gulf crisis

1975 | *1980* | *1985* | *1990* | *1995* | *2000*

1979
Israel and Egypt sign the Camp David Accords

1989
Chinua Achebe wins Nobel Prize in literature

1994
Nelson Mandela becomes South Africa's first black president

; of Camp David Accords

Inauguration of Nelson Mandela

HISTORY Online

Chapter Overview
Visit the *Glencoe World History—Modern Times* Web site at wh.mt.glencoe.com and click on **Chapter 23–Chapter Overview** to preview chapter information.

Introducing CHAPTER 23

Chapter Objectives

After studying this chapter, students should be able to:

1. describe the ways in which independent nations emerged in Africa;
2. list the ethnic, cultural, environmental, and economic challenges facing African nations;
3. describe how the Cold War and nationalism affected politics in the Middle East;
4. identify the steps and people involved in the Middle East peace process.

Chapter Overview
Introduce students to chapter content and key terms by having them access **Chapter Overview 23** at wh.mt.glencoe.com.

Time Line Activity

As students read the chapter, have them review the time line on pages 700–701. Ask them to explain the significance of the dates 1948, 1964, 1967, and 1980. Help students to understand the struggles associated with independence.

MORE ABOUT THE ART

Independence Kwame Nkrumah was a highly educated man who wanted to liberate Ghana from British rule. The motto of his political party was "Self-Government Now." Imprisoned several times by the British government, Nkrumah began a campaign of nonviolent protest that gained him public support in Africa and elsewhere. Nkrumah was a dynamic, emotional, and inspiring speaker. When the British government decided to grant independence, Nkrumah was elected prime minister of Ghana. He began building roads, schools, and clinics. When economic growth faltered, Nkrumah imposed socialism and undercut the power of traditional leaders. A coup ended his leadership, but he is remembered today for eradicating colonialism in his country.

CHAPTER PREVIEW

Introducing
A Story That Matters

Depending upon the ability levels of your students, select from the following questions to reinforce the reading of *A Story That Matters.*

- Who was the ruler of Iran in 1970? *(Mohammad Reza Pahlavi)*
- What can you infer from this story about the relationship between the shah of Iran and the United States? *(The United States supported the shah, he came to the United States for medical treatment.)* **L1 L2**

About the Art

The revolution in Iran is indicative of how Cold War struggles had unintended consequences. Iran bordered the Soviet Union. The West wanted to block Soviet influence in Iran. In 1951, the Iranian prime minister nationalized the British-owned oil industry. Great Britain called for a world boycott of Iranian oil. As Iranians began to suffer, their hatred of the West grew. A military coup in 1953 restored the shah to power, which increased his ties to the United States.

The photos show the deposed shah and an anti-American demonstration that happened eight months after Iran was declared an Islamic republic. Iran celebrated the 20th anniversary of the revolution in 1999.

CHAPTER PREVIEW

A Story That Matters

Mohammad Reza Pahlavi

Anti-American protesters in Iran

Revolution in Iran

In the 1970s, many Iranians began to grow dissatisfied with their ruler, Mohammad Reza Pahlavi, the shah of Iran. An opposition movement, led by the Muslim clergy under the guidance of the Ayatollah Ruhollah Khomeini, grew in strength. (An ayatollah is a major religious leader. The word means "the sign of God.")

One observer described a political rally in the capital city of Tehran in 1978: "On Sunday, December 11, hundreds of thousands of people held a procession in the center of Tehran. . . . Slogans against the shah rippled in the wind—'Death to the Shah!' 'Death to the Americans!' 'Khomeini is our leader,' and so on. People from all walks of life could be found in the crowd."

In January 1979, the shah left Iran, officially for a "period of rest and holiday." Three weeks later, the Ayatollah Khomeini returned to Iran from exile in Paris. On April 1, his forces seized control and proclaimed Iran to be an Islamic republic. Included in the new government's program was an attack on the United States, viewed by Khomeini as the "Great Satan."

On November 4, after the shah had gone to the United States for medical treatment, Iranian revolutionaries seized the United States Embassy in Tehran, taking 52 Americans hostage. Not until the inauguration of a new American president, Ronald Reagan, in January 1981 did the Iranians free their American captives.

Why It Matters

These revolutionary events in Iran are examples of the upheavals that changed both Africa and the Middle East after 1945. In both these areas of the world, Europeans were forced to give up their control and allow independent states to emerge. The change from colony to free nation was not easy. In Africa, the legacy of colonialism left arbitrary boundaries, political inexperience, and continued European economic domination. In the Middle East, ethnic and religious disputes persist.

History and You The Arab-Israeli war is not one war but a continual series of struggles. Using your textbook and outside resources, make a time line of the conflict. Choose three points on your time line to highlight, then describe the events that led to those specific episodes.

HISTORY AND YOU

For several decades the United States has worked for peace in the Middle East. The peace process involves meetings between Israeli and Palestinian leaders, as well as leaders of neighboring countries. Despite years of meetings, accords, and agreements, peace has been elusive since peace efforts have not always been supported by individuals within countries. President Anwar Sadat of Egypt was assassinated in 1981 by an Egyptian for recognizing Israel's right to exist. Prime Minister Yitzhak Rabin of Israel was shot by an Israeli student in 1995 for accepting self-rule in Palestine. In 2001, President George W. Bush said, "The idea of a Palestinian state has always been part of a vision, so long as the right of Israel to exist is respected." The peace process continues.

SECTION 1 Independence in Africa

Guide to Reading

Main Ideas
- People hoped that independence would bring democratic governments, but many African nations fell victim to military regimes and one-party states.
- Culturally and economically, African nations struggled to resolve the tension between the modern and the traditional.

Key Terms
apartheid, Pan-Africanism

People to Identify
Kwame Nkrumah, Nelson Mandela, Julius Nyerere, Desmond Tutu, Chinua Achebe

Places to Locate
South Africa, Kenya, Liberia, Nigeria

Preview Questions
1. What economic problems did independent African nations face?
2. How have social tensions impacted African culture?

Reading Strategy
Categorizing Information As you read this section, complete a chart like the one below identifying the problems in Africa during its first stages of independence.

	Africa
Economic	
Social	
Political	

Preview of Events

1960 · 1962 · 1964 · 1966 · 1968 · 1970 · 1972

- **1960** Blacks massacred in Sharpeville
- **1962** Arrest of ANC leader Nelson Mandela
- **1963** Organization of African Unity forms
- **1967** Civil war in Nigeria
- **1971** Idi Amin seizes control of Uganda

Voices from the Past

Demonstration against white rule

On March 21, 1960, Humphrey Taylor, a reporter, described a peaceful march by black South Africans against white rule:

> "We went into Sharpeville the back way, around lunch time last Monday, driving along behind a big grey police car and three armoured cars. As we went through the fringes of the township many people were shouting the Pan-Africanist slogan 'Our Land.' They were grinning and cheerful. . . . Then the shooting started. We heard the chatter of a machine gun, then another, then another. . . . One woman was hit about ten yards from our car. . . . Hundreds of kids were running, too. Some of the children, hardly as tall as the grass, were leaping like rabbits. Some of them were shot, too."
>
> —***The Mammoth Book of Eyewitness History 2000,*** **Jon E. Lewis, 2000**

The Sharpeville massacre was a stunning example of the white government's oppression of the black majority in South Africa.

The Transition to Independence

European rule had been imposed on nearly all of Africa by 1900. However, after World War II, Europeans realized that colonial rule in Africa would have to end. This belief was supported by the United Nations charter, which pledged that all colonial peoples should have the right to self-determination.

In 1957, the Gold Coast, renamed Ghana and under the guidance of **Kwame Nkrumah,** was the first former British colony to gain independence. Nigeria, the Belgian Congo (renamed Zaire, now the Democratic Republic of Congo), Kenya, and others soon followed. Seventeen new African nations emerged in 1960.

1 FOCUS

Section Overview

This section describes the challenges facing Africa after independence.

BELLRINGER
Skillbuilder Activity

Project transparency and have students answer questions.

Available as a blackline master.

Daily Focus Skills Transparency 23–1

Guide to Reading

Answers to Graphic: Economic: depended on export of single crop or resource; failed to invest in infrastructure; corruption; population growth; drought; AIDS; Social: poverty, massive slums; growth of cities overwhelmed sanitation, transportation systems; women in low-paying positions; Political: military regimes, one-party states; warring ethnic groups

Preteaching Vocabulary: Ask students to look up the two different pronunciations of the word *apartheid.* Which pronunciation is more familiar to students? L1

SECTION RESOURCES

Reproducible Masters
- Reproducible Lesson Plan 23–1
- Daily Lecture and Discussion Notes 23–1
- Guided Reading Activity 23–1
- Section Quiz 23–1
- Reading Essentials and Study Guide 23–1

Transparencies
- Daily Focus Skills Transparency 23–1

Multimedia
- Interactive Tutor Self-Assessment CD-ROM
- ExamView® Pro Testmaker CD-ROM
- Presentation Plus! CD-ROM

2 TEACH

Reading Check

Answer: Algerian nationalists organized the National Liberation Front and began guerrilla warfare in 1954 to liberate the country; granted independence in 1962

Geography Skills

Answers:

1. Morocco; Tunisia; Libya; Egypt; Sudan; Ethiopia; South Africa
2. Eritrea; Equatorial Guinea; São Tomé and Príncipe; Djibouti; Comoros; Angola; Namibia; Botswana; Zimbabwe; Swaziland; Mozambique; Malawi; Guinea-Bissau; Lesotho
3. States often seem to become independent in large blocks (i.e. most of the states in the western and central region of Africa became independent around 1960); suggests that independence movements reinforce each other and spread to neighboring areas

TURNING POINT

African soldiers fought with the Allies in World War II. They were inspired by the ideals for which they fought: self-rule and freedom from tyranny. Theo Ayoola, a Nigerian who fought with the British, said, "[We] overseas soldiers are coming back home with new ideas. We have been told what we fought for. That is freedom! We want freedom, nothing but freedom!" Ask students how postwar ideas contributed to African nationalism. **L1**

Another 11 nations followed between 1961 and 1965. After a series of brutal guerrilla wars, the Portuguese finally surrendered their colonies of Mozambique and Angola in the 1970s.

In North Africa, the French granted full independence to Morocco and Tunisia in 1956. Because Algeria was home to two million French settlers, France chose to keep control there. Meanwhile, however, Algerian nationalists had organized the National Liberation Front (FLN) and in 1954 initiated a guerrilla war to liberate their homeland. The French leader, Charles de Gaulle, granted Algeria its independence in 1962.

In **South Africa,** where the political system was dominated by European settlers, the process was more complicated. Political activity on the part of local blacks had begun with the formation of the African National Congress (ANC) in 1912. Its goal was economic and political reform. The ANC's efforts, however, met with little success.

At the same time, by the 1950s, South African whites (descendants of the Dutch, known as Afrikaners) had strengthened the laws separating whites and blacks. The result was a system of racial segregation known as apartheid ("apartness").

Blacks demonstrated against the apartheid laws, but the white government brutally repressed the demonstrators. In 1960, police opened fire on people who were leading a peaceful march in Sharpeville, killing 69, two-thirds of whom were shot in the back. After the arrest of ANC leader **Nelson Mandela** in 1962, members of the ANC called for armed resistance to the white government.

Reading Check **Describing** How did Algeria gain independence from France?

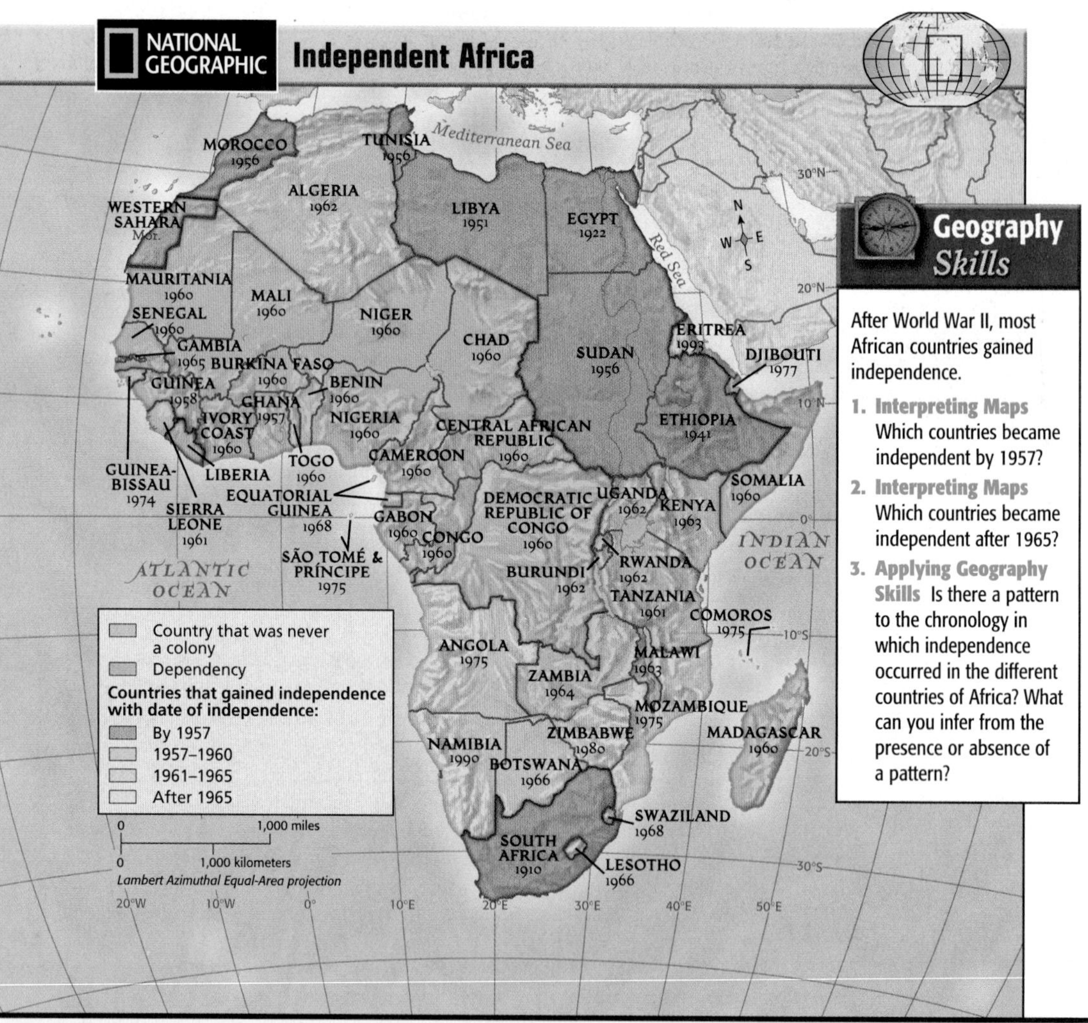

Geography Skills

After World War II, most African countries gained independence.

1. **Interpreting Maps** Which countries became independent by 1957?
2. **Interpreting Maps** Which countries became independent after 1965?
3. **Applying Geography Skills** Is there a pattern to the chronology in which independence occurred in the different countries of Africa? What can you infer from the presence or absence of a pattern?

COOPERATIVE LEARNING ACTIVITY

Creating a Map Have students separate the countries of Africa into five regions: north, west, central, east, and south. Organize the class into five teams, assigning one region to each team. Have the class create a relief map of the African continent, with each group researching its area and coordinating with other groups to produce the final map. Students should research the climate, landforms, elevation, and waterways of their region. Have team members supplement the map with three-dimensional models of animals and plants found in their region. Have students prepare a short oral presentation of their region. In their reports, have students identify ways in which geographers analyze limited evidence. **L2**

For grading this activity, refer to the ***Performance Assessment Activities*** booklet.

The New Nations

The African states that achieved independence in the 1950s, 1960s, and 1970s still faced many problems. The leaders of these states, as well as their citizens, dreamed of stable governments and economic prosperity. Many of these dreams have yet to be realized.

New African Leaders Most of the leaders of the newly independent African states came from the urban middle class and had studied in either Europe or the United States. They spoke and read European languages and believed in using the Western democratic model in Africa.

One of these leaders was Jomo Kenyatta. Educated in Great Britain, Kenyatta returned to Kenya in 1946 and founded the Kenya African National Union, which sought independence for Kenya. British authorities imprisoned him on a charge of supporting the Mau Mau movement, which used terrorism to gain freedom from the British. He led his country to independence in 1963 and served as its president from 1964 to his death in 1978.

The views of African leaders on economics were diverse. Some leaders, such as Jomo Kenyatta, believed in Western-style capitalism. Others, such as Kwame Nkrumah of Ghana, preferred an "African form of socialism." This meant a system in which ownership of the country's wealth would be put into the hands of the people.

Some African leaders believed in the dream of Pan-Africanism—the unity of all black Africans, regardless of national boundaries. In the view of Pan-Africanists, all black African peoples shared a common identity. Pan-Africanism was supported by several of the new African leaders, including Léopold Senghor of Senegal, Kwame Nkrumah, and Jomo Kenyatta.

Nkrumah in particular hoped that a Pan-African union would join all of the new countries of the continent in a broader community. Although his dream never became a reality, the Organization of African Unity (OAU), founded by the leaders of 32 African states in 1963, was a concrete result of the belief in Pan-Africanism. The OAU has contributed to African unity through such activities as settling border disputes.

Economic Problems Independence did not bring economic prosperity to the new African nations. Most still relied on the export of a single crop or natural resource. **Liberia,** for example, depended on the

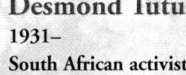

People In History

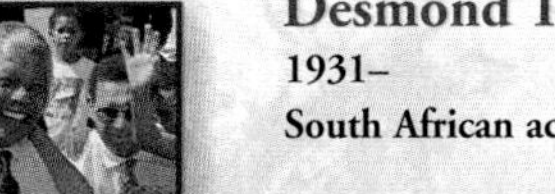

Nelson Mandela
1918–
South African leader

Nelson Mandela was the first black president of South Africa. Mandela was trained to be a leader of the Thembu people, and, later, he received a Western education.

In 1949, Mandela became one of the leaders of the African National Congress (ANC). The ANC at first advocated a policy of passive resistance to white rule in South Africa. Later, it supported more violent methods. The result was a sentence of life imprisonment for Mandela.

During his stay in prison, Mandela's reputation grew throughout Africa and the world. Finally, the South African government released Mandela and agreed to hold free elections. In 1994, he became president.

Desmond Tutu
1931–
South African activist

Head of the Anglican Church in South Africa, Archbishop Desmond Tutu became a leader of the nonviolent movement against apartheid. Raised in Johannesburg, he studied theology and was ordained an Anglican priest in 1961. He rose quickly through the ranks and became an archbishop and head of the Anglican Church in South Africa in 1986. As a passionate believer in nonviolence, he supported a policy of economic sanctions against his own country in order to break the system of apartheid peacefully. He wrote: "If we cannot consider all peaceful means then people are in effect saying that there are no peaceful means." For his efforts, he was awarded the Nobel Peace Prize in 1984.

Daily Lecture and Discussion Notes 23–1

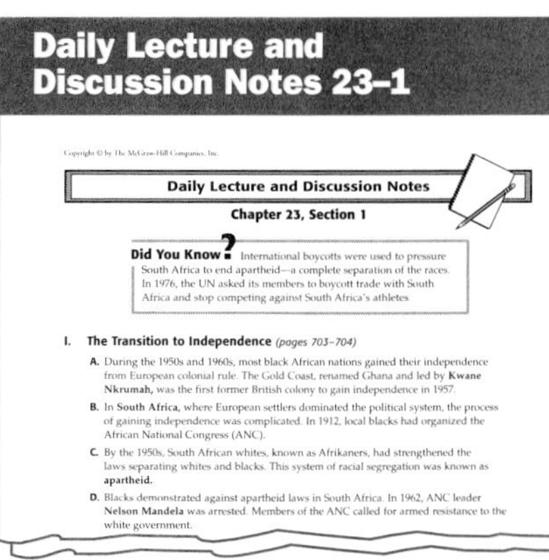

Daily Lecture and Discussion Notes

Chapter 23, Section 1

Did You Know? International boycotts were used to pressure South Africa to end apartheid—a complete separation of the races. In 1976, the UN asked its members to boycott trade with South Africa and stop competing against South Africa's athletes.

I. **The Transition to Independence** *(pages 703–704)*

A. During the 1950s and 1960s, most black African nations gained their independence from European colonial rule. The Gold Coast, renamed Ghana and led by **Kwane Nkrumah,** was the first former British colony to gain independence in 1957.

B. In **South Africa,** where European settlers dominated the political system, the process of gaining independence was complicated. In 1912, local blacks had organized the African National Congress (ANC).

C. By the 1950s, South African whites, known as Afrikaners, had strengthened the laws separating whites and blacks. This system of racial segregation was known as **apartheid.**

D. Blacks demonstrated against apartheid laws in South Africa. In 1962, ANC leader **Nelson Mandela** was arrested. Members of the ANC called for armed resistance to the white government.

Writing Activity

Have students research the policy of apartheid as practiced in South Africa from the 1940s until the 1990s. Ask them to write short reports explaining how the racial laws developed and how these laws affected the civil, human, and economic rights of black and mixed-race South Africans. L2

Enrich

Remind students that American colonists fought Britain and that Latin American countries fought Spain to become independent. Discuss why Europeans were so reluctant to grant independence to African nations. L2

Who?What?Where?When?

Independence After independence many African nations took names from African history. For example, the Gold Coast and the French Sudan were renamed Ghana and Mali after ancient African kingdoms (see Chapter 3). Southern Rhodesia, named for Cecil Rhodes, chose Zimbabwe, for the great Bantu cultural center.

MEETING INDIVIDUAL NEEDS

Visual/Spatial There are more than 50 nations in Africa, and each one has a unique history. Have students select a nation and create a print or Internet "home page" for that nation. Students should include language, customs, transition to independence, government, resources, geography, leaders, and celebrities. Encourage students to make the page visually interesting as well as informative. Have students pick one area that they are personally interested in to research in depth. It could be art, religion, music, tourism, or the environment. Display the "home pages" around the room. L2

Refer to ***Inclusion for the High School Social Studies Classroom Strategies and Activities*** in the TCR.

Guided Reading Activity 23-1

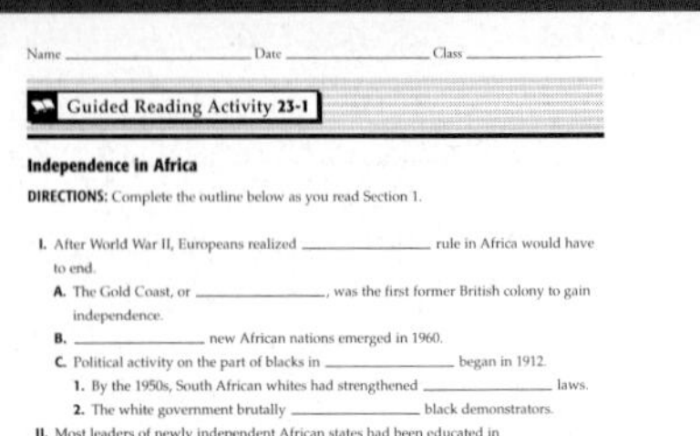

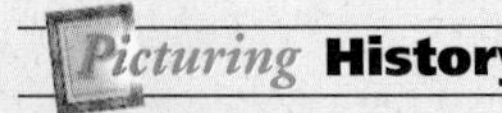

Picturing History

Answer: high population growth, droughts, spread of AIDS

Connecting Across Time

Ask students to explain why the former British colonies in North America had an easier time of creating a unified nation than states in Africa. Help students recognize the factors that can contribute to unity or divisiveness: language, religion, and ancestry to name a few. **L1**

Who?What?Where?When?

Ecology The centuries of white settlement in South Africa have affected the region's ecology and worsened its droughts. The native thorn trees and baobabs resist drought, as do traditional crops such as sorghum and tubers. The European settlers, however, planted crops that required more water and put in lawns and swimming pools. They also imported pine and eucalyptus trees that use great amounts of water.

export of rubber; **Nigeria,** on oil. When prices dropped, their economies suffered. To make matters worse, most African states had to import technology and manufactured goods from the West.

The new states also sometimes created their own problems. Scarce national resources were spent on military equipment or expensive consumer goods rather than on building the foundations for an industrial economy. In addition, corruption and bribery became common.

Population growth also crippled efforts to create modern economies. By the 1980s, population growth averaged nearly 3 percent throughout Africa, the highest rate of any continent.

Drought conditions led to widespread hunger and starvation, first in West African countries such as Niger and Mali and then in Ethiopia, Somalia, and the Sudan. Millions fled to neighboring countries in search of food.

In recent years, the spread of acquired immunodeficiency syndrome (AIDS) in Africa has reached epidemic proportions. According to one estimate, one-third of the entire population of sub-Saharan Africa is infected with the virus that causes AIDS.

As a result of all these problems, poverty is widespread in Africa, especially among the three-quarters of the population still living off the land. Cities have grown tremendously and are often surrounded by massive slums populated by rural people who came to the cities looking for employment. The growth of the cities has overwhelmed sanitation and transportation systems. Pollution and perpetual traffic jams are the result.

Millions live without water and electricity in their homes. In the meantime, the fortunate few enjoy lavish lifestyles. The rich in many East African countries are known as the *wabenzi,* or Mercedes-Benz people.

Political Challenges Many people had hoped that independence would lead to stable political order based on "one person, one vote." They were soon disappointed as democratic governments gave way to military regimes and one-party states. The Cold War also created problems for Africa as the superpowers competed for influence. For example, when the Soviet Union supported a Marxist government in Ethiopia, the United States established military bases in neighboring Somalia.

Within many African nations, the concept of nationhood was also undermined by warring ethnic groups. Since many of the boundaries of the African nations had been arbitrarily drawn by colonial powers, virtually all of these states included widely different ethnic, linguistic, and territorial groups.

During the late 1960s, civil war tore Nigeria apart. When northerners began to kill the Ibo people, thousands of Ibo fled to their home region in the eastern part of Nigeria. There, Lieutenant Colonel Odumegu Ojukwu organized the Ibo in a rebellion and declared the eastern region of Nigeria an independent state

Picturing History

This shantytown is in Cape Town, South Africa. Tremendous urban growth has led to the rise of slums outside many African cities. What factors contribute to the spread of poverty in Africa?

EXTENDING THE CONTENT

The Moving Sahara Deep in the Sahara, ancient rock paintings show grazing cattle and grasses where now there is only rock and sand. Before Africa was colonized, farming techniques allowed fields to lie uncultivated until the soil was replenished. During colonialism, Europeans pushed Africans to grow big cash crops for export. Farmers cut down trees and overfarmed the land. Drought caused plants to die, and without plants to anchor the topsoil it washed or blew away. The mixture of overfarming, overgrazing, cutting trees, and drought has pushed the Sahara south as fast as 90 miles (145 km) a year.

Picturing History

President F. W. de Klerk agreed to hold South Africa's first democratic national elections in 1993. Here you see people waiting to vote for the first time. Who was the first freely elected president of South Africa?

called Biafra. After three years of bloody civil war, Biafra finally surrendered and accepted the authority of the central government of Nigeria.

Conflicts also broke out among ethnic groups in Zimbabwe. In central Africa, fighting between the Hutu and Tutsi created unstable governments in both Burundi and Rwanda. In 1994, a Hutu rampage left some five hundred thousand Tutsi dead in Rwanda.

Reading Check **Explaining** Why was the Organization of African Unity formed?

New Hopes

TURNING POINT **As you will learn, worldwide pressure on the South African government led to the end of apartheid and the election of that country's first black president in 1994.**

Not all the news in Africa has been bad. In recent years, popular demonstrations have led to the collapse of one-party regimes and the emergence of democracies in several countries. One case was that of Idi Amin of Uganda. After ruling by terror and brutal repression throughout the 1970s, Amin was deposed in 1979. Dictatorships also came to an end in Ethiopia, Liberia, and Somalia. In these cases, however, the fall of the regime was later followed by bloody civil war.

One of the most remarkable events of recent African history was the election of Nelson Mandela to the presidency of the Republic of South Africa. Mandela had been sentenced to life imprisonment in 1962 for his activities with the African National Congress. He spent 27 years of his life in the maximum-security prison on Robben Island in South Africa. For all those years, Mandela never wavered from his determination to secure the liberation of his country. In January 1985, he was offered his freedom, given certain conditions, from then President Botha. At this point, Mandela had served over 21 years of a life sentence and had passed his 70th birthday. Yet, he refused to accept a conditional freedom: "Only free men can negotiate; prisoners cannot enter into contracts. Your freedom and mine cannot be separated." Over the years, Nobel Peace prize winner (1984) Bishop **Desmond Tutu** and others worked to free him and to end apartheid in South Africa. Worldwide pressure on the white South African government led to reforms and the gradual dismantling of apartheid laws. In 1990, Mandela was finally released from prison.

In 1993, the government of President F. W. de Klerk agreed to hold democratic national elections—the first in South Africa's history. In 1994, Nelson Mandela became South Africa's first black president. In his presidential inaugural address, he expressed his hopes for

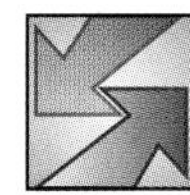

HISTORY Online

Web Activity Visit the *Glencoe World History—Modern Times* Web site at wh.mt.glencoe.com and click on **Chapter 23–Student Web Activity** to learn more about African independence.

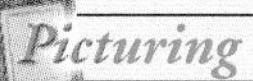

Picturing History

Answer: Nelson Mandela

Reading Check

Answer: to promote Pan-African unity

TURNING POINT

International public pressure was brought to bear on South Africa in the 1980s. Have students research the forms that pressure took. Include public condemnation of apartheid from individual nations and the United Nations, barring of South African athletes from the Olympics, a UN arms embargo, divestment policies, and limitations on trade and investment. Students should decide which forms of public pressure were the most effective and which, if any, were unfair. Have students present their conclusions in brief position papers. L3

CURRICULUM CONNECTION

Oratory Ask students to select one of the following names: Steven Biko, Desmond Tutu, Nelson Mandela, P. W. Botha, F. W. de Klerk. Have students research the life and influence of the person they select. Each student should prepare a speech, as if they were that person, summarizing that individual's contribution to or impact on South African history. L2

COOPERATIVE LEARNING ACTIVITY

Preparing a Presentation Assign pairs of students one African country to represent at a mock session of the United Nations General Assembly. Before holding the mock session, have students research how the United Nations General Assembly conducts debates and issues resolutions. Have students brainstorm issues they might discuss, including economic development, the environment, HIV education, foreign aid, free trade, crime, and urbanization. Ask students to research current events in their country so that they can represent its interests at the General Assembly session. L3

For grading this activity, refer to the ***Performance Assessment Activities*** booklet.

Reading Check

Answer: Uganda, Ethiopia, Liberia, Somalia

Picturing History

Answer: one-quarter

3 ASSESS

Assign Section 1 Assessment as homework or as an in-class activity.

Have students use **Interactive Tutor Self-Assessment CD-ROM.**

Section Quiz 23–1

Name ______ Date ______ Class ______

Chapter 23 Score

Section Quiz 23-1

DIRECTIONS: Matching Match each item in Column A with an item in Column B. Write the correct letters in the blanks. *(10 points each)*

Column A	Column B
____ 1. system of racial segregation used in South Africa	A. Desmond Tutu
____ 2. idea of the unity of all black Africans	B. apartheid
____ 3. South African bishop and Nobel Peace Prize winner	C. Pan-Africanism
____ 4. 1989 Nobel Prize-winning Nigerian novelist	D. AIDS
____ 5. widespread epidemic in sub-Saharan Africa	E. Chinua Achebe

DIRECTIONS: Multiple Choice In the blank, write the letter of the choice that best completes the statement or answers the question. *(10 points each)*

____ 6. The African form of socialism was based on

Enrich

Ask students to work in groups to apply knowledge of political systems to make a decision about a contemporary issue. Require students to describe variables in the contemporary situation that could result in different outcomes. The open-ended nature of this activity will allow students to take advantage of current news media. **L2**

unity: "We shall build a society in which all South Africans, both black and white, will be able to walk tall, without any fear in their hearts, assured of their inalienable right to human dignity—a rainbow nation at peace with itself and the world." *(See page 781 to read excerpts from Nelson Mandela's* An Ideal for Which I am Prepared to Die *in The Primary Sources Library.)*

Reading Check **Identifying** Which African countries overthrew dictatorships?

Society and Culture in Modern Africa

Africa is a study in contrasts. Old and new, native and foreign live side by side. One result is a constant tension between traditional ways and Western culture.

City and Countryside In general, the impact of the West has been greater in the cities than in the countryside. After all, the colonial presence was first and most firmly established in the cities. Many cities, including Dakar, Lagos, Cape Town, Brazzaville, and Nairobi, are direct products of colonial rule. Most African cities today look like cities elsewhere in the world. They have high-rise apartments, wide boulevards, neon lights, movie theaters, and, of course, traffic jams.

Outside the major cities, where about three-quarters of the inhabitants of Africa live, modern influence has had less of an impact. Millions of people throughout Africa live much as their ancestors did, in thatched dwellings without modern plumbing and electricity. They farm, hunt, or raise livestock by traditional methods, wear traditional clothing, and practice traditional beliefs. Conditions, such as drought or flooding, affect the ability of rural Africans to grow crops or tend herds. Migration to the cities for work is one solution. This can be very distruptive to families and villages. Many urban people view rural people as backward. Rural dwellers view the cities as corrupting and destructive to traditional African values and customs.

Women's Roles Independence from colonial powers had a significant impact on women's roles in African society. Almost without exception women were allowed to vote and run for political office. Few women hold political offices. Although women dominate some professions, such as teaching, child care, and clerical work, they do not have the range of career opportunities available to men. Most African women are employed in low-paid positions such as farm laborers, factory workers, and servants. Furthermore, in many rural areas, traditional attitudes toward women, including arranged marriages, still prevail.

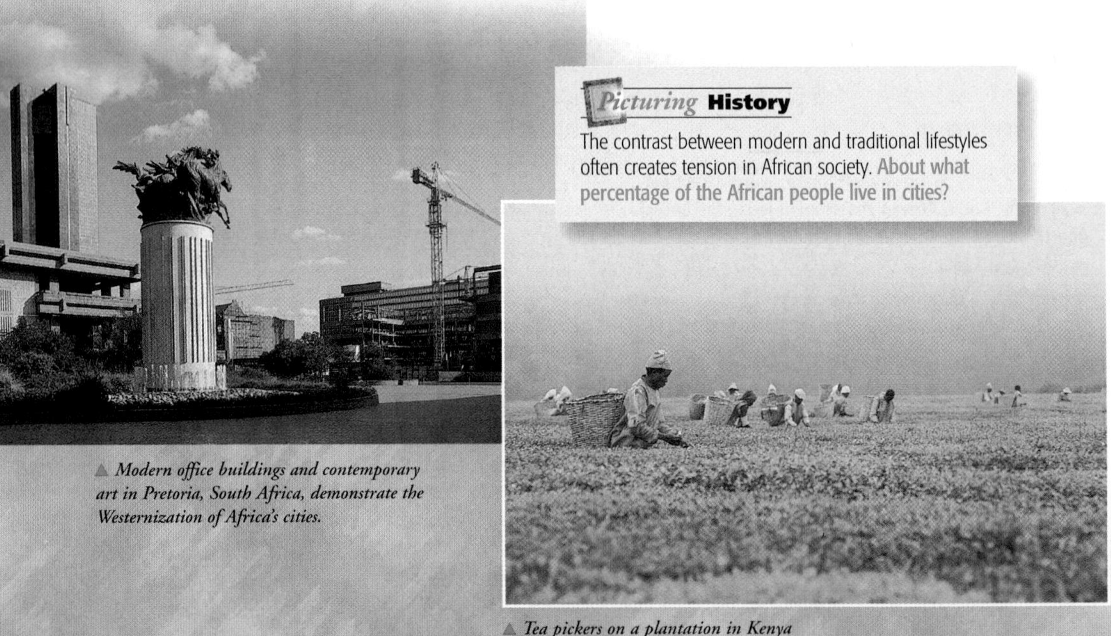

Picturing History

The contrast between modern and traditional lifestyles often creates tension in African society. About what percentage of the African people live in cities?

▲ *Modern office buildings and contemporary art in Pretoria, South Africa, demonstrate the Westernization of Africa's cities.*

▲ *Tea pickers on a plantation in Kenya*

COOPERATIVE LEARNING ACTIVITY

Creating a Display Have students form five teams, one for each region of Africa: north, west, central, east, and south. Individual team members should choose different types of African art to research within their region, such as painting, pottery, metal and wood sculpture, textiles, body ornamentation, and music. Have students find examples of each type of art and copy or record them to bring to class. Have the teams work together to create a classroom or hallway exhibit, complete with captions explaining the display. Organize the exhibit by region or by type of art. **L1** ELL

For grading this activity, refer to the ***Performance Assessment Activities*** booklet.

African Culture The tension between traditional and modern and between native and foreign also affects African culture. Africans have kept their native artistic traditions while adapting them to foreign influences. A dilemma for many contemporary African artists is the need to find a balance between Western techniques and training on the one hand, and the rich heritage of traditional African art forms on the other.

In some countries, governments make the artists' decisions for them. Artists are told to depict scenes of traditional African life. These works are designed to serve the tourist industry.

African writers have often addressed the tensions and dilemmas that modern Africans face. The conflicting demands of town versus country and native versus foreign were the themes of most of the best-known works of the 1960s and 1970s.

These themes certainly characterize the work of **Chinua Achebe,** a Nigerian novelist and winner of the Nobel Prize for literature in 1989. Achebe's four novels show the problems of Africans caught up in the conflict between traditional and Western values. Most famous of Achebe's four novels is *Things Fall Apart,* in which the author portrays the simple dignity of traditional African village life.

Reading Check **Summarizing** What themes are characterized in the work of Chinua Achebe?

Picturing **History**

A Nigerian craftsman is in the process of carving a wooden drum. How do you think tourism has affected traditional African art forms?

SECTION 1 ASSESSMENT

Checking for Understanding

1. **Define** apartheid, Pan-Africanism.
2. **Identify** Kwame Nkrumah, Nelson Mandela, Julius Nyerere, Desmond Tutu, Chinua Achebe.
3. **Locate** South Africa, Kenya, Liberia, Nigeria.
4. **Explain** how population growth has crippled the efforts of African nations to create stable, modern economies. Identify at least two other recent obstacles to an improved economy.
5. **Describe** the relationship between the Hutu and the Tutsi. Identify other nations in the news today with ethnic or religious conflict.

Critical Thinking

6. **Explain** Why was the idea of Pan-Africanism never realized?
7. **Organizing Information** Create a chart comparing the characteristics of the modern African city and rural areas.

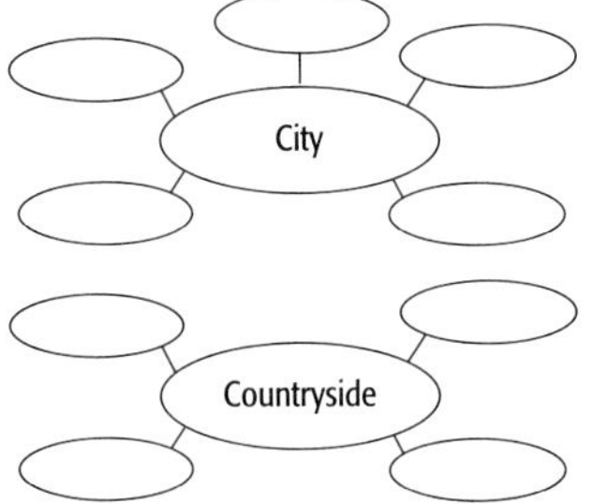

Analyzing Visuals

8. **Examine** the photograph of Kwame Nkrumah shown on page 701 of your text. How does this photograph reflect the pride that Kwame Nkrumah and his companions feel about Ghana's newly won independence? Use specific visual evidence from the photograph to support your answer.

Writing About History

9. **Persuasive Writing** Assume the role of an African leader of a newly independent nation. Write a speech to your citizens in which you explain Pan-Africanism and convince them that Pan-Africanism will benefit both the nation and the people.

CHAPTER 23
Section 1, 703–709

Reading Essentials and Study Guide 23–1

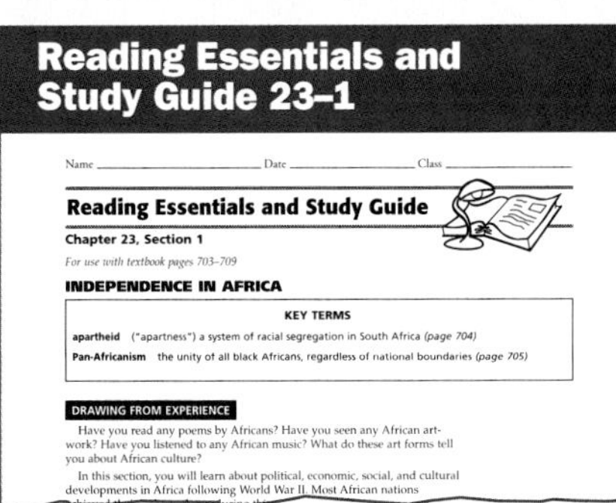
Name ______ Date ______ Class ______

Reading Essentials and Study Guide

Chapter 23, Section 1

For use with textbook pages 703–709

INDEPENDENCE IN AFRICA

KEY TERMS

apartheid ("apartness") a system of racial segregation in South Africa *(page 704)*

Pan-Africanism the unity of all black Africans, regardless of national boundaries *(page 705)*

DRAWING FROM EXPERIENCE

Have you read any poems by Africans? Have you seen any African artwork? Have you listened to any African music? What do these art forms tell you about African culture?

In this section, you will learn about political, economic, social, and cultural developments in Africa following World War II. Most African nations

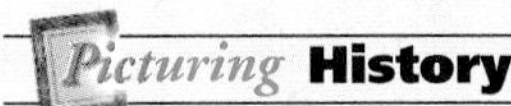

Answer: His novels show the problems of Africans caught up in the conflict between traditional and Western values.

Answer: In some countries artists have been told to depict scenes of traditional African life to serve the tourist industry.

Reteaching Activity

Have students review the section by taking notes for each page. **L1**

4 CLOSE

Have students write one paragraph in which they describe the main differences between pre-World War II Africa and Africa today.

SECTION 1 ASSESSMENT

1. Key terms are in blue.
2. Kwame Nkrumah *(p. 703)*; Nelson Mandela *(p. 704)*; Julius Nyerere *(p. 705)*; Desmond Tutu *(p. 707)*; Chinua Achebe *(p. 709)*
3. See chapter maps.
4. not enough food; drought, AIDS
5. tribal/ethnic conflicts that led to bloodshed; answers will vary, depending on current events
6. too much ethnic, cultural, political, and economic diversity
7. City: high-rise apartments; wide boulevards; neon lights; movie theaters; traffic jams; view rural people as backward; Countryside: thatched dwellings; no modern plumbing or electricity; farm, hunt, or raise livestock using traditional methods; traditional clothing and beliefs; view cities as destructive to traditional African values and customs
8. joyful expressions on men's faces; pride in wearing African clothing
9. Answers should be supported by logical arguments.

SOCIAL STUDIES SKILLBUILDER

TEACH

Interpreting Statistics Learning to interpret statistics is an important skill in this age of readily available information. Have students note the use of statistics in commercials and advertising. Have students bring in examples of the use of statistics in advertising. Discuss the examples in class. L2

Additional Practice

Skills Reinforcement Activity 23

Name ______________ Date ______________ Class ______________

Skills Reinforcement Activity 23

Interpreting Statistics

Statistics can help you support an opinion or make a point. Statistics are data collected and organized to help identify effects and make predictions. To interpret statistics, first read the title and any labels to get an overall idea of the information being shown. Analyze the numbers shown by looking for decreases, similarities, and differences. Look for sets of numbers or data that seem to be related or to have some correlation. Draw conclusions from the information based on the relationships and trends you find.

DIRECTIONS: Study the table below. Then answer the following questions in the space provided.

Selected Statistics for Selected African Countries

Country	Life Expectancy at Birth	Adult Literacy Rate	Percentage of Adult Population Living with HIV–1997	Percentage of Adult Population Living with HIV–1999
Botswana	37	70%	25.1	35.8
Kenya	48	78%	11.64	13.95
South Africa	48	82%	12.91	19.94
Zimbabwe	37	85%	25.84	25.06

Source: *The World Factbook, 2001.*

1. Which country experienced the greatest increase in HIV between 1997 and 1999?

2. Which country's population is most affected by HIV? Which country's population is least affected by HIV?

GLENCOE TECHNOLOGY

CD-ROM
Glencoe Skillbuilder Interactive Workbook CD-ROM, Level 2

This interactive CD-ROM reinforces student mastery of essential social studies skills.

SOCIAL STUDIES SKILLBUILDER

Interpreting Statistics

Why Learn This Skill?

A news report comes out that statistical evidence from a recent scientific study proves that chocolate can prevent cancer. The next day, a doctor is interviewed saying that the statistics are misleading. What are you to believe?

Statistics are used to support a claim or an opinion. They can be used to support opposing sides of an issue. To avoid being misled, it is important to understand how to interpret statistics.

Learning the Skill

Statistics are sets of tabulated information that may be gathered through surveys and other sources. When studying statistics, consider each of the following:

- **Biased sample** The sample may affect the results. A sample that does not represent the entire population is called a biased sample. An unbiased sample is called a representative sample.
- **Correlation** Two sets of data may be related or unrelated. If they are related, we say that there is a correlation between them. For example, there is a positive correlation between academic achievement and wages. There is a negative correlation, however, between smoking and life expectancy.
- **Statistical significance** Researchers determine whether the data support a generalization or whether the results are due to chance. If the probability that the results were due to chance is less than 5 percent, researchers say that the result is statistically significant.

Practicing the Skill

The table at the top of the next column rates countries according to economic freedom, that is the fewest restrictions on trade, property rights, and monetary policies. The scores are on a scale from 1 to 5, with 1 being the greatest economic freedom. Study the table. Then answer the questions that follow.

2001 Index of Economic Freedom

Nation (rank)	Trade	Gov't Intervention	Wages/ Prices	Overall Score
Hong Kong (1)	1.0	2.0	2.0	**1.30**
United States (5)	2.0	2.0	2.0	**1.75**
United Arab Emirates (14)	2.0	3.0	3.0	**2.05**
Israel (54)	2.0	3.5	2.0	**2.75**
Lebanon (59)	3.0	3.0	2.0	**2.85**
Botswana (68)	3.0	4.0	2.0	**2.95**
Cameroon (90)	4.0	2.0	3.0	**3.20**
Syria (141)	5.0	3.0	4.0	**4.00**
Zimbabwe (146)	5.0	2.5	4.0	**4.25**

Source: The Heritage Foundation.

1. Which category or categories show a positive correlation with economic freedom?
2. Which category or categories show a negative correlation with economic freedom?

Applying the Skill

Create a two-question survey that will generate answers that can be correlated. For example, ask: "How many hours of television do you watch per day?" and "How many hours of homework do you do per day?" Gather responses, then develop a correlation between the topics addressed by the two questions.

Glencoe's **Skillbuilder Interactive Workbook, Level 2,** provides instruction and practice in key social studies skills.

ANSWERS TO PRACTICING THE SKILL

1. Trade, Wages/Prices show a positive correlation with economic freedom.
2. Government intervention shows a negative correlation with economic freedom.

Applying the Skill: Students will gather samples, then tabulate and evaluate their statistics.

SECTION 2 Conflict in the Middle East

Guide to Reading

Main Ideas
- Instability in various parts of the Middle East has led to armed conflict and mediation attempts from countries outside the region.
- In many Middle Eastern countries, an Islamic revival has influenced political and social life.

Key Terms
Pan-Arabism, *intifada*

People to Identify
Gamal Abdel Nasser, Anwar el-Sadat, Yasir Arafat, Ayatollah Ruhollah Khomeini, Saddam Hussein, Naguib Mahfouz

Places to Locate
Israel, Egypt, Sinai Peninsula, West Bank, Iran, Iraq, Kuwait, Persian Gulf

Preview Questions
1. How was the state of Israel created?
2. How did the Islamic revival affect Middle Eastern Society?

Reading Strategy
Compare and Contrast As you read this section, complete a Venn diagram to compare and contrast the countries of Iran and Iraq.

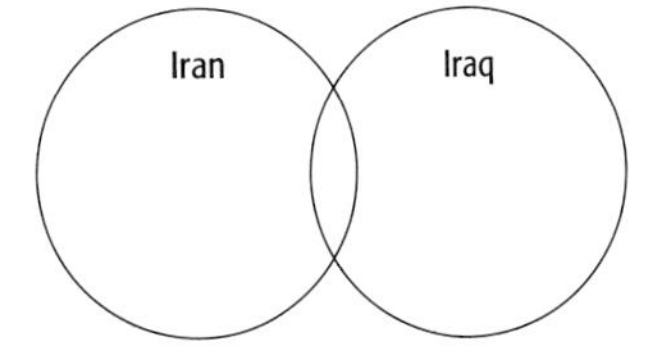

Preview of Events

1955 · 1960 · 1965 · 1970 · 1975 · 1980 · 1985

- **1956** Suez War begins
- **1964** Egypt forms the PLO with Yasir Arafat
- **1979** Khomeini seizes control of Iran
- **1981** Iran frees American hostages

Voices from the Past

David Ben-Gurion

On May 14, 1948, David Ben-Gurion stood in Museum Hall in Tel Aviv and announced to the people assembled there:

> “The land of Israel was the birthplace of the Jewish people. Here their spiritual, religious and national identity was formed. In their exile from the land of Israel the Jews remained faithful to it in all the countries of their dispersal, never ceasing to hope and pray for the restoration of their national freedom. Therefore by virtue of the natural and historic right of the Jewish people to be a nation as other nations, and of the Resolution of the General Assembly of the United Nations, we hereby proclaim the establishment of the Jewish nation in Palestine, to be called the State of Israel.”
>
> —Jon E. Lewis, ***The Mammoth Book of Eyewitness History,*** 2000

The creation of the state of Israel made Arab-Israeli conflict a certainty.

The Question of Palestine

TURNING POINT **As you will learn, in 1948, Palestine was divided into two states: an Arab state and a Jewish state.**

In the Middle East, as in other areas of Asia, World War II led to the emergence of new independent states. Syria and Lebanon gained their independence near the end of World War II. Jordan achieved complete self-rule soon after the war. These new states were predominantly Muslim.

1 FOCUS

Section Overview

This section describes political problems in the Middle East and efforts at intervention by countries outside the region.

BELLRINGER
Skillbuilder Activity

Project transparency and have students answer questions.

Available as a blackline master.

Daily Focus Skills Transparency 23–2

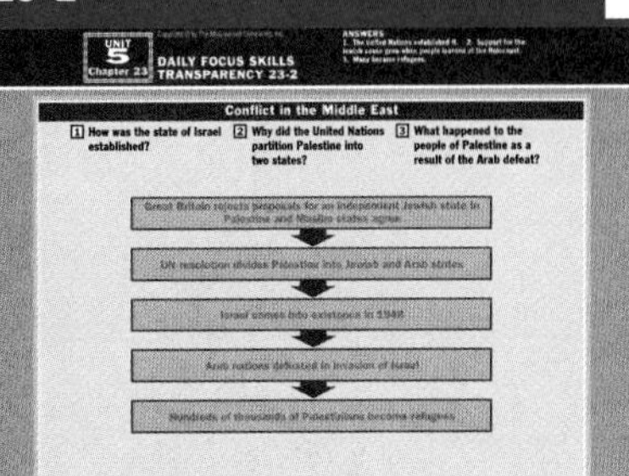

Guide to Reading

Answers to graphic: Iran: Shiite Muslim; traditional Muslim beliefs in clothing styles, social practices, legal system; Iraq: Sunni Muslim; militant and hostile; Both: Muslim countries; history of disputes, especially over Strait of Hormuz

Preteaching Vocabulary: The Arabic word *intifada* means uprising. It comes from a word that literally means to "shake off." The Palestinians in Israeli-controlled areas tried to "shake off" Israeli control and end the expansion of Jewish settlements.

SECTION RESOURCES

Reproducible Masters
- Reproducible Lesson Plan 23–2
- Daily Lecture and Discussion Notes 23–2
- Guided Reading Activity 23–2
- Section Quiz 23–2
- Reading Essentials and Study Guide 23–2

Transparencies
- Daily Focus Skills Transparency 23–2

Multimedia
- Interactive Tutor Self-Assessment CD-ROM
- ExamView® Pro Testmaker CD-ROM
- Presentation Plus! CD-ROM

2 TEACH

Reading Check

Answer: Many people had been shocked and outraged at the end of World War II when they learned about the Holocaust, which increased sympathy for the Jewish cause.

Answer: Answers will vary. Foreign workers may come to the United States for better wages and living conditions or to escape persecution under repressive governments.

Daily Lecture and Discussion Notes 23–2

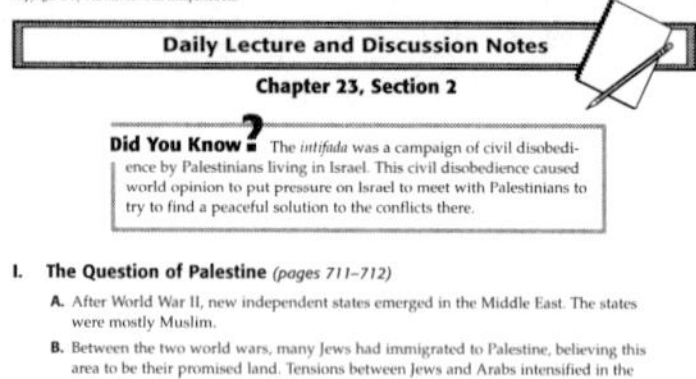

Daily Lecture and Discussion Notes

Chapter 23, Section 2

Did You Know? The *intifada* was a campaign of civil disobedience by Palestinians living in Israel. This civil disobedience caused world opinion to put pressure on Israel to meet with Palestinians to try to find a peaceful solution to the conflicts there.

I. **The Question of Palestine** *(pages 711–712)*

A. After World War II, new independent states emerged in the Middle East. The states were mostly Muslim.

B. Between the two world wars, many Jews had immigrated to Palestine, believing this area to be their promised land. Tensions between Jews and Arabs intensified in the 1930s. Great Britain, under a UN mandate to govern Palestine, rejected proposals for an independent Jewish state in Palestine.

C. The **Zionists** still wanted Palestine as a home for Jews. The Holocaust caused sympathy for the Jewish proposals for an independent Jewish state in Palestine. In 1948, the UN divided Palestine into two states—an Arab state and a Jewish state, **Israel.**

D. Several Arab countries invaded Israel, but the invasion failed. Arabs, however, refused to recognize Israel's right to exist.

E. The issue of a homeland and self-governance for the Palestinians remains a problem

Connecting Across Time

Assign students to write an essay that compares the decision of Nasser to nationalize the Suez Canal with the decision of Salvador Allende to nationalize foreign businesses in Chile (Chapter 22) in the 1970s. Ask students why nations were willing to go to war to protect the Suez Canal but not the copper mines of Chile. L2

In the years between the two world wars, many Jews had immigrated to Palestine, believing this area to be their promised land. Tensions between Jews and Arabs had intensified during the 1930s. Great Britain, which governed Palestine under a United Nations (UN) mandate, had limited Jewish immigration into the area and had rejected proposals for an independent Jewish state in Palestine. The Muslim states agreed with this position.

The **Zionists** who wanted Palestine as a home for Jews were not to be denied, however. Many people had been shocked at the end of World War II when they learned about the Holocaust, the deliberate killing of six million European Jews in Nazi death camps. As a result, sympathy for the Jewish cause grew. In 1948, a United Nations resolution divided Palestine into a Jewish state and an Arab state. The Jews in Palestine proclaimed the state of **Israel** on May 14, 1948.

Its Arab neighbors saw the new state as a betrayal of the Palestinian people, most of whom were Muslim. Outraged, several Arab countries invaded the new Jewish state. The invasion failed, but the Arab states still refused to recognize Israel's right to exist.

As a result of the division of Palestine, hundreds of thousands of Palestinians fled to neighboring Arab countries, where they lived in refugee camps. Other Palestinians came under Israeli rule. The issue of a homeland and self-governance for the Palestinians remains a problem today.

Reading Check **Identifying** Why was there international support for Palestine to serve as a home for Jews?

Nasser and Pan-Arabism

In **Egypt,** a new leader arose who would play an important role in the Arab world. Colonel **Gamal Abdel Nasser** took control of the Egyptian government in the early 1950s. On July 26, 1956, Nasser seized the Suez Canal Company, which had been under British and French administration.

Concerned over this threat to their route to the Indian Ocean, Great Britain and France decided to strike back. They were quickly joined by Israel. The forces of the three nations launched a joint attack on Egypt, starting the Suez War of 1956. The United States and the Soviet Union supported Nasser and forced Britain, France, and Israel to withdraw their troops

CONNECTIONS Around The World

Global Migrations

Since 1945, tens of millions of people have migrated from one part of the world to another. There are many reasons for these migrations. Persecution for political reasons caused many people from Pakistan, Bangladesh, Sri Lanka, Eastern Europe, and East Germany to seek refuge in Western European countries. Brutal civil wars in Asia, Africa, the Middle East, and Europe led millions of refugees to seek safety in neighboring countries. A devastating famine in Africa in 1984–1985 drove hundreds of thousands of Africans to relief camps throughout the continent to find food.

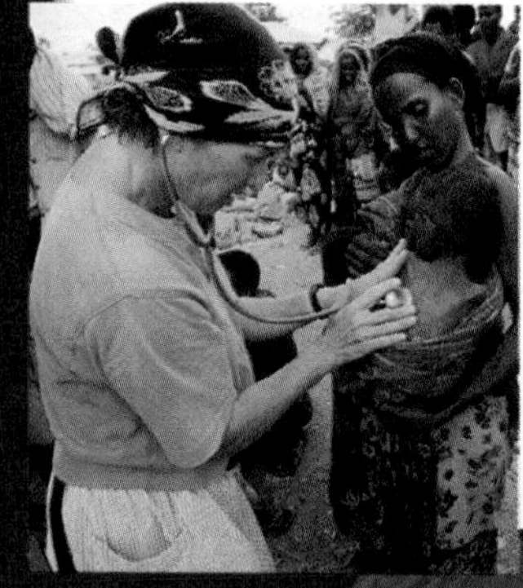

Mobile clinic in Somalia, Africa

Most people who have migrated, however, have done so to find jobs. Guest workers from Turkey, southern and Eastern Europe, North Africa, India, and Pakistan, for example, have flooded into the more prosperous Western European countries. Overall, some fifteen million guest workers worked and lived in Europe in the 1980s.

Many countries adopted policies that allowed guest workers to remain in the host countries for several years. In the 1980s and 1990s, however, foreign workers often became scapegoats when countries experienced economic problems. Political parties in France and Norway, for example, called for the removal of blacks and Arabs.

Comparing Cultures

Are there immigrant populations where you live? Describe some of the attitudes your friends and families have toward foreign workers. Think of several reasons why foreign populations have migrated to the United States.

INTERDISCIPLINARY CONNECTIONS ACTIVITY

Historical Inquiry Both Jews and Arabs have made strong claims for the land of Palestine. Have students use the process of historical inquiry to research, interpret, and consider multiple sources of evidence for those claims. Students should use primary and secondary sources, such as the Balfour Declaration and the British act that created the Transjordan. Students should identify bias and evaluate the validity of sources. Encourage students to organize their research by sequencing, identifying cause and effect, and summarizing. When students finish their inquiry, they should be able to come to a conclusion about who has the strongest historical claims to Palestine. Students should present their conclusion in a clearly written position paper. L3

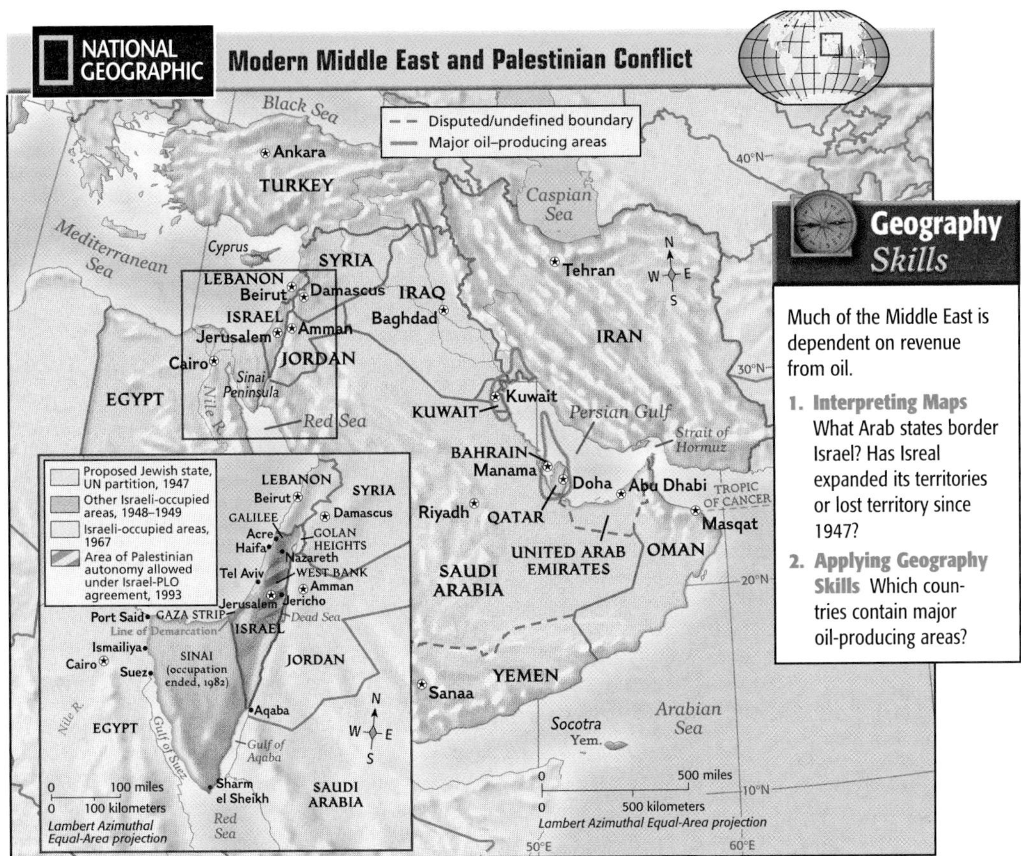

Geography Skills

Much of the Middle East is dependent on revenue from oil.

1. **Interpreting Maps** What Arab states border Israel? Has Isreal expanded its territories or lost territory since 1947?
2. **Applying Geography Skills** Which countries contain major oil-producing areas?

from Egypt. These Cold War enemies were opposed to French and British influence in the Middle East.

Nasser emerged from the conflict as a powerful leader. He now began to promote Pan-Arabism, or Arab unity. In March 1958, Egypt formally united with Syria in the United Arab Republic (UAR). Nasser was named the first president of the new state. Egypt and Syria hoped that the union would eventually include all the Arab states. Many other Arab leaders were suspicious of Pan-Arabism, however. Oil-rich Arab states were concerned they would have to share revenues with poorer states in the Middle East. Indeed, in Nasser's view, Arab unity meant that wealth derived from oil, which currently flowed into a few Arab states or to foreign interests, could be used to improve the standard of living throughout the Middle East.

In 1961, military leaders took over Syria and withdrew the country from its union with Egypt. Nasser continued to work on behalf of Arab interests.

Reading Check **Evaluating** Why were France and Great Britain threatened when Nasser seized the Suez Canal?

The Arab-Israeli Dispute

During the late 1950s and 1960s, the dispute between Israel and other states in the Middle East became more heated. In 1967, Nasser imposed a blockade against Israeli shipping through the Gulf of Aqaba. He declared: "Now we are ready to confront Israel. We are ready to deal with the entire Palestine question."

Fearing attack, on June 5, 1967, Israel launched air strikes against Egypt and several of its Arab neighbors. Israeli warplanes wiped out most of the Egyptian air force. Israeli armies broke the blockade and occupied the **Sinai Peninsula.** Israel seized territory on the **West Bank** of the Jordan River, occupied Jerusalem, and took control of the Golan Heights. During this Six-Day War, Israel tripled the size of its territory. Another million Palestinians now lived inside Israel's new borders, most of them on the West Bank.

Over the next few years, Arab states continued to demand the return of the occupied territories. Nasser died in 1970 and was succeeded in office by

CRITICAL THINKING ACTIVITY

Analyzing Put slips of paper of five different colors into a box. You will need to have enough slips so each student will be able to pull one from the box. Each color represents a different group: Palestinians who took part in the *intifada;* Israelis who took part in the Six-Day War; Egyptians under Nasser; Jordanians during the Gulf War; wealthy businessmen from Saudi Arabia during the Gulf War or the war on terrorism. Students should work alone or in groups to research the events that took place during the specified period or occurrence. Following the research, have students determine how their assigned group would view the current events in the Middle East. Have students write a position paper on the Middle East peace process and the violence in the Middle East that represents the point of view of their group. L2

Reading Check

Answer: It was their most direct route to the Indian Ocean.

Geography Skills

Answers:

1. Jordan, Syria, Lebanon; expanded
2. Iran; Iraq; Kuwait; Qatar; Saudi Arabia; United Arab Emirates

CURRICULUM CONNECTION

Journalism Have students write two editorials that might have appeared in newspapers in 1947. Have one editorial support the creation of a Jewish state in Palestine and the other one oppose the idea. Make sure students offer logical arguments based on fact. L2

Who?What?Where?When?

Jerusalem In 1950, Israel proclaimed Jerusalem as its capital. Jerusalem is considered a sacred site by Jews, Muslims, and Christians. The city was captured in about 1000 B.C. by King David. Many of the Christian monuments in Jerusalem date from the 4th century A.D. In the late 600s the Muslim caliph Abd al-Malik built the Dome of the Rock. Jerusalem has been occupied by Jews, Romans, Muslims, Crusaders, Turks, Ottomans, Egyptians, and the British.

CHAPTER 23
Section 2, 711–716

Reading Check

Answer: an agreement between Israel and Egypt to sign a peace treaty

Reading Check

Answer: The agreement called for Palestinian autonomy in certain areas of Israel; in return, the PLO recognized the Israeli state.

Guided Reading Activity 23–2

Name ______________ Date ______________ Class ______________

Guided Reading Activity 23-2

Conflict in the Middle East

DIRECTIONS: Fill in the blanks below as you read Section 2.

1. In 1948, a ______________ resolution divided Palestine into a Jewish state and an Arab state.
2. The Jews in Palestine proclaimed the state of ______________ on May 14, 1948.
3. Arab neighbors saw the new state as a ______________ of the Palestinian people.
4. The forces of Great Britain, France, and Israel launched a joint attack on Egypt, starting the ______________ of 1956.
5. In 1967, Abdel Nasser imposed a ______________ against Israeli shipping through the Gulf of Aqaba.
6. During the ______________, Israel tripled the size of its territory.

Critical Thinking

In 1978, the Nobel Peace Prize was awarded to Anwar el-Sadat and Menachem Begin for signing the Camp David Accords. Then in 1994, Yasir Arafat, Yitzhak Rabin, and Shimon Peres received the Nobel Peace Prize for initiating the peace process between Israel and the PLO. Ask students to identify other significant individuals, including social and religious leaders, from the twentieth century. Then have students analyze the influence of their selected individuals on the political, social, and religious events of the twentieth century. L2

Palestinians clash with Israeli soldiers.

Anwar el-Sadat. In 1973, Arab forces led by Sadat launched a new attack against Israel. This conflict was ended in 1974 by a cease-fire agreement negotiated by the UN.

Meanwhile, however, the war was having indirect results in Western nations. A number of Arab oil-producing states had formed the Organization of Petroleum Exporting Countries **(OPEC)** in 1960 to gain control over oil prices. During the 1973 war, some OPEC nations announced large increases in the price of oil to foreign countries. The price hikes, coupled with cuts in oil production, led to oil shortages and serious economic problems in the United States and Europe.

In 1977, U.S. president Jimmy Carter began to press for a compromise peace between Arabs and Israelis. In September 1978, Carter met with President Sadat of Egypt and Israeli Prime Minister Menachem Begin (BAY•gihn) at Camp David in the United States. The result was the Camp David Accords, an agreement to sign an Israeli-Egyptian peace treaty. The treaty, signed by Sadat and Begin in March 1979, ended the state of war between Egypt and Israel. Many Arab countries continued to refuse to recognize Israel, however.

Reading Check **Identifying** What are the Camp David Accords?

The PLO and the *Intifada*

In 1964, the Egyptians took the lead in forming the Palestine Liberation Organization (PLO) to represent the interests of the Palestinians. The PLO believed that only the Palestinian peoples had the right to create a state in Palestine. At the same time, a guerrilla movement called al-Fatah, headed by the PLO political leader **Yasir Arafat,** began to launch terrorist attacks on Israeli territory. Terrorist actions against Israel continued for decades.

Yasir Arafat

During the early 1980s, Palestinian Arabs, frustrated by their failure to achieve self-rule, became even more militant. This militancy led to a movement called the *intifada* ("uprising") among PLO supporters living inside Israel. The *intifada* was marked by protests throughout the nation. A second *intifada* began in September 2000 and continued for over a year.

As the 1990s began, U.S.-sponsored peace talks to address the Palestinian issue opened between Israel and a number of its Arab neighbors. Finally, in 1993, Israel and the PLO reached an agreement calling for Palestinian autonomy in certain areas of Israel. In return, the PLO recognized the Israeli state. Yasir Arafat became the head of the semi-independent area known as the Palestinian Authority. Progress in making this agreement work, however, has been slow.

Reading Check **Summarizing** What were the terms of the agreement reached in 1993?

Revolution in Iran

The leadership of Shah Mohammad Reza Pahlavi and revenue from oil helped **Iran** to become a rich country. Iran was also the chief ally of the United States in the Middle East in the 1950s and 1960s.

However, there was much opposition to the shah in Iran. Millions of devout Muslims looked with distaste at the new Iranian civilization. In their eyes, it was based on greed and materialism, which they identified with American influence.

Leading the opposition to the shah was the **Ayatollah Ruhollah Khomeini** (ko•MAY•nee), a member of the Muslim clergy. By the late 1970s, large numbers of Iranians had begun to respond to

Ayatollah Khomeini

INTERDISCIPLINARY CONNECTIONS ACTIVITY

Economics OPEC members are Algeria, Indonesia, Iran, Iraq, Kuwait, Libya, Nigeria, Qatar, Saudi Arabia, United Arab Emirates, and Venezuela. They hold more than 77 percent of the world's oil reserves. OPEC-engineered price controls in the 1970s and 1980s affected non-OPEC nations, causing non-OPEC nations to increase production, exploration, and refining abilities. Assign students to groups to research the differences in oil production between OPEC and non-OPEC nations. Each group should prepare a chart that illustrates one of the following: oil prices per barrel for the last six months, economic growth vs. oil demand, exports vs. imports, or a chart that reflects the economic conditions that result from oil usage and global demands for oil. Have students interpret charts by posing and answering questions about them. L2

Khomeini's words. In 1979, the shah's government collapsed and was replaced by an Islamic republic.

The new government, led by the Ayatollah Khomeini, moved to restore Islamic law. Supporters of the shah were executed or fled the country. Anti-American sentiments erupted when militants seized 52 Americans in the United States embassy in Tehran and held them hostage for over a year.

After the death of Khomeini in 1989, a new government, under President Hashemi Rafsanjani, began to loosen control over personal expression and social activities. Rising criticism of official corruption and a high rate of inflation, however, sparked a new wave of government repression in the mid-1990s.

Reading Check **Summarizing** List the reasons that the shah's government collapsed.

Iraq's Aggression

To the west of Iran was a militant and hostile **Iraq,** under the leadership of **Saddam Hussein** since 1979. Iraq and Iran have long had an uneasy relationship, fueled by religious differences. Both are Muslim nations. The Iranians, however, are largely Shiites, whereas most Iraqi leaders are Sunnis. Iran and Iraq have engaged for years in disputes over territory, especially the Strait of Hormuz, which connects the Persian Gulf and the Gulf of Oman.

In 1980, President Saddam Hussein launched an attack on Iran. The war was a brutal one. Poison gas was used against civilians, and children were used to clear dangerous minefields. A cease-fire was finally arranged in 1988.

In 1990, Iraqi troops moved across the border and occupied the country of **Kuwait,** at the head of the **Persian Gulf.** The invasion sparked an international outcry. The United States led an international force that freed Kuwait and destroyed a large part of Iraq's armed forces. The allies hoped that an internal revolt would overthrow Hussein, but he remained in power.

Reading Check **Describing** Describe why Iran and Iraq have been in conflict for many years.

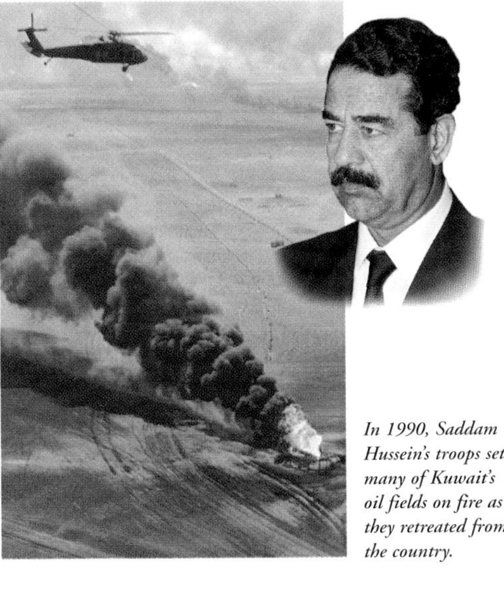

In 1990, Saddam Hussein's troops set many of Kuwait's oil fields on fire as they retreated from the country.

Afghanistan and the Taliban

After World War II, the king of Afghanistan, in search of economic assistance for his country, developed close ties with the Soviet Union. In 1973, the king was overthrown by his cousin, who himself was removed during a pro-Soviet coup in 1978. The new leaders, Noor Taraki and Babrak Karmal, attempted to create a Communist government but were opposed by groups wanting to create an Islamic state. Karmal called for aid from the Soviets, who launched a full-scale invasion of Afghanistan in 1979.

The Soviets occupied Afghanistan for 10 years but were forced to withdraw by anti-Communist forces supported by the United States and Pakistan. Though a pro-Soviet government was left in the capital at Kabul, various Islamic rebel groups began to fight for control. One of these, the Taliban, seized Kabul in 1996. By the fall of 1998, the Taliban controlled more than two-thirds of the country. Opposing factions controlled northern Afghanistan.

Condemned for its human rights abuses and imposition of harsh social policies, the Taliban was also suspected of sheltering Osama bin Laden and his al-Qaeda organization. In 1999 and 2000, the United Nations Security Council demanded the Taliban hand over bin Laden for trial, but it refused. In 2001, the Taliban was driven out of Kabul by rebel forces and American bombers.

Reading Check **Explaining** What was the political situation in Afghanistan in 1996?

Society and Culture

In recent years, conservative religious forces have tried to replace foreign culture and values with Islamic forms of belief and behavior. This movement is called Islamic revivalism or Islamic activism. For

CRITICAL THINKING ACTIVITY

Analyzing *Talib* means religious student. For many years, Afghan members of the Taliban studied in religious schools in Pakistan. In 1994, they were appointed by Islamabad to protect a convoy going from Pakistan to Central Asia. The Taliban proved to be effective fighters and, by 1996, had taken over most of Afghanistan. Weary of years of lawlessness, ordinary Afghans were happy to have the Taliban restore peace. Later, however, many came to resent the harsh rule of the Taliban. In 2001, opposition forces drove the Taliban out of power. Have students identify the many ethnic groups in Afghanistan including information about where each group lives and how much of the population the group represents. Ask students to discuss how ethnic divisions have complicated the political situation in Afghanistan. L2

Reading Check

Answer: devout Muslims disliked new Iranian culture; thought it was based on greed and materialism, blamed American influence

Reading Check

Answer: Most of the disputes concern territory, especially Strait of Hormuz.

Reading Check

Answer: A pro-Soviet government was in place, but in 1996, an Islamic rebel group, the Taliban, seized the capital city of Kabul.

3 ASSESS

Assign Section 2 Assessment as homework or as an in-class activity.

Have students use **Interactive Tutor Self-Assessment CD-ROM.**

Section Quiz 23–2

Name ______ Date ______ Class ______

Chapter 23 Score

Section Quiz 23-2

DIRECTIONS: Matching Match each item in Column A with an item in Column B. Write the correct letters in the blanks. *(10 points each)*

Column A	Column B
____ **1.** group that wanted Palestine to be a Jewish homeland	**A.** Zionists
____ **2.** concept of Arab unity	**B.** the United Arab Republic
____ **3.** short-lived union of Egypt and Syria starting in 1958	**C.** OPEC
____ **4.** bloc of Arab oil-producing states formed in 1960	**D.** Saddam Hussein
____ **5.** Iraqi military leader who invaded Kuwait in 1990	**E.** Pan-Arabism

DIRECTIONS: Multiple Choice In the blank, write the letter of the choice that best completes the statement or answers the question. *(10 points each)*

____ **6.** Which of the following was not a result of the UN resolution dividing

Connecting Across Time

Present-day Iran and Iraq are sites of ancient empires. Have students recall a conflict discussed in Chapter 1, then locate information on the Iran-Iraq war in 1980. Ask students to write a paragraph comparing the causes of these conflicts. L2

Answer: Naguib Mahfouz won the Nobel Prize for literature in 1988.

Reading Essentials and Study Guide 23–2

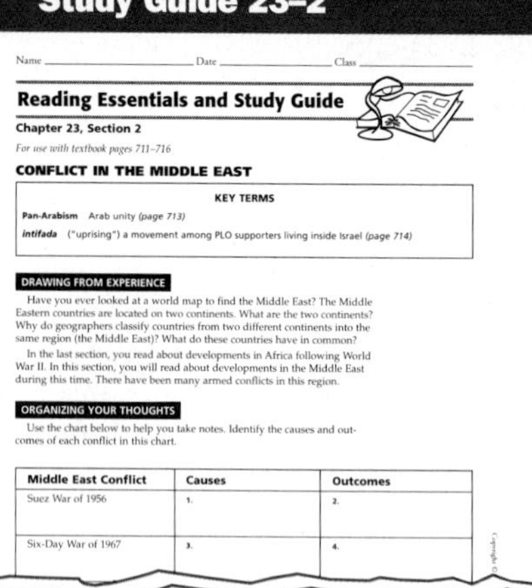

Name ______ Date ______ Class ______

Reading Essentials and Study Guide

Chapter 23, Section 2

For use with textbook pages 711–716

CONFLICT IN THE MIDDLE EAST

KEY TERMS

Pan-Arabism Arab unity *(page 713)*

intifada ("uprising") a movement among PLO supporters living inside Israel *(page 714)*

DRAWING FROM EXPERIENCE

Have you ever looked at a world map to find the Middle East? The Middle Eastern countries are located on two continents. What are the two continents? Why do geographers classify countries from two different continents into the same region (the Middle East)? What do these countries have in common?

In the last section, you read about developments in Africa following World War II. In this section, you will read about developments in the Middle East during this time. There have been many armed conflicts in this region.

ORGANIZING YOUR THOUGHTS

Use the chart below to help you take notes. Identify the causes and outcomes of each conflict in this chart.

Middle East Conflict	Causes	Outcomes
Suez War of 1956	1.	2.
Six-Day War of 1967	3.	4.

Critical Thinking

Have students use the map on page 713 to locate the Strait of Hormuz. Ask students to interpret the map to identify and explain how control of the Strait of Hormuz has influenced people and events in the past. **L2**

Reteaching Activity

Ask students to review this section and then write several Reading Check questions that focus on what students believe are the most important points in the section. **L1**

4 CLOSE

Review with students the issues and challenges faced by the Middle East.

most Muslims, the Islamic revival is a reassertion of cultural identity, formal religious observance, family values, and morality.

Islamic Militants Actions of militants have often been fueled by hostility to the culture of the West. In the eyes of some Islamic leaders, Western values and culture are based on materialism, greed, and immorality. The goal of extremists is to remove all Western influence in Muslim countries.

The movement to return to the pure ideals of Islam began in Iran under the Ayatollah Khomeini. In revolutionary Iran, traditional Muslim beliefs reached into clothing styles, social practices, and the legal system. These ideas and practices spread to other Muslim countries. In Egypt, for example, militant Muslims assassinated President Sadat in 1981. Unfortunately for Islam, the extreme and militant movements received much media exposure, giving many people an unfavorable impression of Islam.

Women's Roles At the beginning of the twentieth century, women's place in Middle Eastern society had changed little for hundreds of years. Early Muslim women had participated in the political life of society and had extensive legal, political, and social rights. Cultural practices in many countries had overshadowed those rights, however.

In the nineteenth and twentieth centuries, Muslim scholars debated issues surrounding women's roles in society. Many argued for the need to rethink outdated interpretations and cultural practices that prevented women from realizing their potential. This had an impact on a number of societies, including Turkey and Iran.

Until the 1970s, the general trend in urban areas was toward a greater role for women. Beginning in the 1970s, however, there was a shift toward more traditional roles for women. This trend was especially noticeable in Iran.

Middle Eastern Culture The literature of the Middle East since 1945 has reflected a rise in national awareness, which encouraged interest in historical traditions. Writers also began to deal more with secular themes. Literature is no longer the preserve of the elite but is increasingly written for broader audiences.

The most famous contemporary Egyptian writer is **Naguib Mahfouz.** He was the first writer in Arabic to win the Nobel Prize for literature (in 1988). His *Cairo Trilogy,* published in 1952, is considered the finest writing in Arabic since World War II. The story follows a merchant family in Egypt in the 1920s. The changes in the family parallel the changes in Egypt.

The artists of the Middle East at first tended to imitate Western models. Later, however, they began to experiment with national styles and returned to earlier forms for inspiration.

Reading Check **Identifying** Which Arabic writer won the Nobel Prize for literature?

SECTION 2 ASSESSMENT

Checking for Understanding

1. **Define** Pan-Arabism, *intifada.*
2. **Identify** Zionists, Gamal Abdel Nasser, Anwar el-Sadat, Yasir Arafat, Ayatollah Ruhollah Khomeini, OPEC, Saddam Hussein, Naguib Mahfouz.
3. **Locate** Israel, Egypt, Sinai Peninsula, West Bank, Iran, Iraq, Kuwait, Persian Gulf.
4. **Explain** the meaning and purpose of OPEC. What control does it have?
5. **Summarize** the events that led to the Six-Day War. What gains and losses resulted from the war?

Critical Thinking

6. **Explain** Why do some people believe it was a mistake for the UN and the United States not to occupy Iraq after the Persian Gulf crisis? What did the Allies hope would happen in Iraq after the Iraqi forces were defeated?
7. **Taking Notes** Organize the information presented in this section in outline form, following the model below.

   I. Palestine
      A. Great Britain limits Jewish immigration.
      B. Zionists want Jewish homeland.
   II. Nasser takes control of Egypt

Analyzing Visuals

8. **Examine** the photograph of Kuwait shown on page 715. Why do you think the Iraqi troops decided to set fire to the oil fields as they retreated from Kuwait? Do you think that they set the fires for military, political, or economic reasons, or for all three?

Writing About History

9. **Persuasive Writing** Choose the role of either an Arab Palestinian or a Jewish settler. Write a letter to the United Nations General Assembly arguing your position on the Palestine issue. What do you think should be done in Palestine and why?

SECTION 2 ASSESSMENT

1. Key terms are in blue.
2. Zionists *(p. 712)*; Gamal Abdel Nasser *(p. 712)*; Anwar el-Sadat *(p. 714)*; Yasir Arafat *(p. 714)*; Ayatollah Ruhollah Khomeini *(p. 714)*; Saddam Hussein *(p. 715)*; Naguib Mahfouz *(p. 716)*
3. See chapter maps.
4. Organization of Petroleum Exporting Countries; controls oil prices
5. Increased tensions between Israel and neighbors; Egypt blockaded Israeli shipping; Israel attacked Egypt, seized Sinai Peninsula, occupied West Bank, Golan Heights, tripling territory, gaining more Palestinians; Arab nations demanded return of occupied lands
6. might be only way to control Hussein, protect Persian Gulf; revolt to overthrow Hussein
7. Outlines should follow the format presented here.
8. military: fires created cover for retreating forces, hindered allied troops; economic/political: weakened Kuwait's economic, political power; threatened countries dependent on Kuwait's oil
9. Answers will vary.

EYEWITNESS TO HISTORY

The Suez Canal Belongs to Egypt

THE SUEZ CANAL WAS built between 1854 and 1869, using mainly French money and Egyptian labor. It was managed by a Paris-based corporation called the Suez Canal Company. In this excerpt from a speech, Egyptian president Gamal Abdel Nasser declared that it was time for the canal to be owned and managed by Egyptians.

Freighters in the Suez Canal

❝The Suez Canal is an Egyptian canal built as a result of great sacrifices. The Suez Canal Company is an Egyptian company that was expropriated [taken away] from Egypt by the British who, since the canal was dug, have been obtaining the profits of the Company. . . . And yet the Suez Canal Company is an Egyptian limited liability company. The annual Canal revenue is 35 million Egyptian pounds. From this sum Egypt–which lost 120,000 workers in digging the Canal–takes one million pounds from the Company.

It is a shame when the blood of people is sucked, and it is no shame that we should borrow for construction. We will not allow the past to be repeated again, but we will cancel the past by restoring our rights in the Suez Canal. . . .

The Suez Canal Company was a state within a state, depending on the conspiracies of imperialism and its supporters. The Canal was built for the sake of Egypt, but it was a source of exploitation. There is no shame in being poor, but it is a shame to suck blood. Today we restore these rights, and I declare in the name of the Egyptian people that we will protect these rights with our blood and soul. . . .

The people will stand united as one man to resist imperialist acts of treachery. We shall do whatever we like. When we restore all our rights, we shall become stronger and our production will increase. At this moment, some of your brethren, the sons of Egypt, are now taking over the Egyptian Suez Canal and directing it. We have taken this decision to restore part of the glories of the past and to safeguard our national dignity and pride. May God bless you and guide you in the path of righteousness.❞

—Nasser's Speech Nationalizing the Suez Canal Company

Analyzing Primary Sources

1. What problem was President Nasser addressing?
2. According to Nasser, why does the Suez Canal rightfully belong to Egypt?

TEACH

Analyzing Primary Sources The Suez crisis began when Nasser wanted to build a dam at Aswan in the Upper Nile River valley. The dam would end Nile flooding and generate electricity. Hoping to gain political influence in Egypt, the United States offered Egypt a $270 million loan to build the dam. Nasser also wanted weapons to modernize his army, but the West refused to sell arms to him. Nasser turned to the Soviets, who were willing to make an arms deal. This angered the United States, which cancelled the loan. Nasser retaliated by nationalizing the canal. He said he would use canal fees to finance the dam.

CURRICULUM CONNECTION

Art and Environment The Aswan High Dam was dedicated in 1971. It has helped control flooding and generates electricity, however, it is not without controversy. The huge artificial lake created by the dam covered archaeological sites that had not yet been investigated. Some ancient monuments were relocated, but not all. Ninety thousand people, most of whom lived in the Sudan, had to be relocated. Silt, that would have normally been carried down the Nile, builds up behind the dam. This has caused erosion to the Egyptian coastline. Ask students to select either the Art or Environment connection for further research. Then have students prepare a position paper answering the question: Was the Aswan Dam a good idea? L3

ANSWERS TO ANALYZING PRIMARY SOURCES

1. President Nasser addressed the fact that Egypt was being taken advantage of by the people who managed the Suez Canal. The Egyptian government was not getting a fair share of the profits.
2. Egypt was entitled to the Suez Canal, according to Nasser, because the canal was expropriated from Egypt by the British, who were keeping most of the profits and paying only a small share to Egypt. In addition, 120,000 Egyptians lost their lives building the canal; it was a matter of national dignity and pride to control the canal that was bought with the sacrifices of the Egyptian people.

GLENCOE TECHNOLOGY

MindJogger Videoquiz

Use the **MindJogger Videoquiz** to review Chapter 23 content.

 Available in VHS.

Using Key Terms

1. apartheid **2.** Pan-Arabism **3.** *intifada* **4.** Pan-Africanism

Reviewing Key Facts

5. because there were two million French settlers in Algeria

6. traditions of community: ownership of country's wealth in hands of the people

7. led armed resistance against white South African government

8. became first black president of South Africa

9. he is a leader of the nonviolent movement against apartheid

10. almost constant conflict with neighbors and Palestinians

11. millions of devout Muslims felt his regime was based on materialism and greed, reflecting American influence

12. rapid growth of cities, overwhelmed sanitation and transportation systems leading to poor living conditions

13. rise in national awareness has encouraged interest in historical traditions; more secular themes; no longer for elite but is increasingly written for a broader audience

14. The idea for Israel came out of a 1948 United Nations resolution dividing Palestine into a Jewish state and an Arab state. Factors: sympathy for Jews after Holocaust, fact that Palestine was ancient home of Jewish people, emergence of other independent states in Middle East

15. Israel tripled in size, increased Arab animosity, one million more Palestinians within new Israeli borders; Arab states demanded return of occupied lands; conflicts continued

CHAPTER 23 ASSESSMENT and ACTIVITIES

Using Key Terms

1. The former South African policy of separating the races was called ____.
2. The belief in Arab unity has been called ____.
3. The uprising to protest Israeli domination of Palestine was called the ____.
4. The Organization of African Unity was a result of the belief in ____.

Reviewing Key Facts

5. **Government** Why did France grant independence to Morocco and Tunisia in 1956, but not to Algeria?
6. **Government** What was the philosophy behind African socialism?
7. **History** Why was Nelson Mandela imprisoned by the white South African government?
8. **Citizenship** What did Nelson Mandela achieve in 1994?
9. **Government** Why is Desmond Tutu an important international leader?
10. **Economy** Why has Israel allocated a large part of its national production to maintaining highly trained and well-equipped military forces?
11. **Government** Why did Shah Mohammad Reza Pahlavi of Iran lose the support of his people despite rapid growth in Iran's economy and standard of living?
12. **Culture** What problems resulted from the migration of Africans from rural areas into cities?
13. **Culture** How has the literature of the Middle East dealt with traditional versus modern values?
14. **History** How was Israel created and which factors contributed to its founding?
15. **History** What effect did the Six-Day War have on the relationship between Arabs and Israelis?
16. **Government** Name some major accomplishments of Egyptian leader Gamal Abdel Nasser that elevated his status as a leader in the Arab world.
17. **History** How was the concept of nationhood undermined in many African countries?
18. **Economy** How did price increases and production cuts by OPEC nations in 1973 affect the United States and Europe?
19. **History** Give two reasons for the war that broke out in 1980 between Iran and Iraq.

Critical Thinking

20. **Evaluating** Why have English and French been used as official languages of government in many African nations?
21. **Analyzing** Could a lasting peace have been established between Iraq and its neighbors even if UN forces had captured Saddam Hussein? Explain your answer.
22. **Evaluating** Compare the legacy of European colonialism in Africa and the Middle East. Discuss the consequences of colonialism still being felt in these areas.
23. **Analyzing** Why do you think Israel was able to seize so much territory during the Six-Day War?

Writing About History

24. **Expository Writing** Compare and contrast the role of women and their positions and rights in the Middle East and Africa.

Chapter Summary

In the postwar period, Africa and the Middle East faced many challenges that threatened their stability.

	Government	Economy	Society
Africa	• Many new nations are undermined by civil war. • Democracy is threatened by military regimes. • Democratic national elections are held in South Africa.	• Most new nations rely on the export of a single crop or resource. • Population growth cripples efforts to create modern economies. • Poverty is widespread.	• Tension between traditional ways and Western culture continues.
Middle East	• Palestine is divided into two states. • Arab-Israeli dispute results in war and peace treaties. • Israel and PLO reach agreement about autonomy.	• Much of the Middle East is dependent on oil revenue. • OPEC is formed to gain control over oil prices.	• Islamic revival reasserts cultural identity and values over foreign, Western influences.

16. took control of Suez Canal for Egypt; won 1956 Suez war against Britain, France, and Israel; promoted Pan-Arabism; united with Syria to form United Arab Republic, and became its first president

17. boundaries were arbitrarily drawn by colonial powers and included widely different ethnic, linguistic, and territorial groups

18. oil shortages and serious economic problems

19. religious differences (Iraqis are Sunnis, Iranians are Shiites); dispute over territory

Critical Thinking

20. many were once French or British colonies; governments and economies developed using these languages; they unify different ethnic and linguistic groups within nations

21. Answers will vary.

Self-Check Quiz

Visit the *Glencoe World History—Modern Times* Web site at wh.mt.glencoe.com and click on **Chapter 23–Self-Check Quiz** to prepare for the Chapter Test.

Analyzing Sources

Read the following quote describing a political rally in Tehran in 1978.

> "On Sunday, December 11, hundreds of thousands of people held a procession in the center of Tehran . . . . Slogans against the shah rippled in the wind—'Death to the Shah!' 'Death to the Americans!' 'Khomeini is our leader,' and so on. People from all walks of life could be found in the crowd."

25. What is meant by the phrase "people from all walks of life?"
26. Why were the people protesting the shah? Why were anti-American slogans included in the protest? What resulted when the shah left Iran and the Ayatollah Khomeini became the leader? Who are the leaders of Iran today? Does the quote above reflect current sentiments?

Making Decisions

27. Create a new peace accord for Israel and the Palestinians. Why do the Israelis and the Palestinians need a peace accord? What do you need to consider in creating the terms of the agreement? What country would both parties agree to accept as an intermediary to help them settle their problems? What resistance to your accord might you face from either party? How do you get both Israelis and Palestinians to accept the accord? Once it is accepted, how would you enforce this agreement?
28. You have been elected South Africa's first president after the end of apartheid. What challenges will you face now that apartheid is over? How will you try to solve these problems? What are your hopes for South Africa?

Analyzing Maps and Charts

Refer to the map on page 713 of your textbook to answer the following questions.

29. What do you think Iraq hoped to gain by invading the country of Kuwait?
30. How far is Tehran from Baghdad?
31. How important is access to the Persian Gulf and the Strait of Hormuz for oil-producing countries?

Applying Technology Skills

32. **Using the Internet** Use the Internet to create a bibliography of resource materials about Nelson Mandela and Desmond Tutu. Design a Web page to organize the links.

The Princeton Review — Standardized Test Practice

Directions: Use the time line and your knowledge of world history to answer the following question.

Selected Events in Middle Eastern Politics

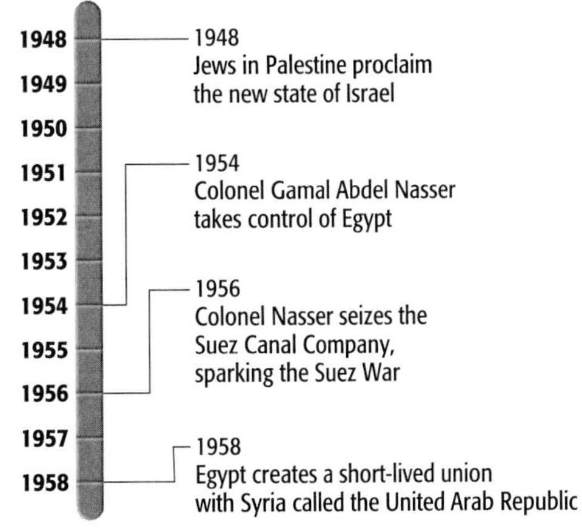
1948
1949
1950
1951
1952
1953
1954
1955
1956
1957
1958
1948
Jews in Palestine proclaim the new state of Israel
1954
Colonel Gamal Abdel Nasser takes control of Egypt
1956
Colonel Nasser seizes the Suez Canal Company, sparking the Suez War
1958
Egypt creates a short-lived union with Syria called the United Arab Republic

Which of the following events resulted from the events on this time line?

F Shock over the Holocaust helped Jews realize their goals for a homeland.
G Nasser imposed a blockade against Israeli shipping.
H Iraq launched an attack on its enemy, Iran.
J The Balfour Declaration gave support to Zionist Jews.

Test-Taking Tip: Time lines show chronology, or the order in which events happened. You can use your knowledge of chronology to get rid of incorrect answer choices. Think about what events happened *before* this time line begins. Those answer choices must be wrong.

22. national borders drawn by colonial powers remain roughly the same; led to weak national identities but strong regional identities, Arabs share language and religion; Africans divided by many ethnic, linguistic, and religious groups in nations created by Europeans. Many African cities founded by colonial powers, nationalist leaders educated in Europe and U.S. Colonialism left both regions without history of democratic government or industrial infrastructure, making it difficult to find economic success.

23. Answers will vary.

Writing About History

24. Women in most African countries could vote, run for political office; women dominate some professions; most in low-paying jobs; in rural areas, traditional attitudes prevail; in Middle East, trend toward a greater role for women until 1970s, then shift toward more traditional roles

HISTORY Online

Have students visit the Web site at wh.mt.glencoe.com to review Chapter 23 and take the Self-Check Quiz.

Analyzing Sources

25. people who work in all types of jobs, from all classes
26. felt regime was based on materialism and greed; blamed American influence; restored traditional Islamic law; answers will vary

Making Decisions

27. Answers will vary.
28. Answers will vary.

Analyzing Maps and Charts

29. improved access to the Persian Gulf
30. about 500 miles (804.5 km)
31. very important, they can access Suez Canal

Applying Technology Skills

32. Students will design a Web page.

Standardized Test Practice

Answer: G
Answer Explanation: Answer includes the same subject as the time line entries.

Bonus Question ?

Ask: What role did the end of the Cold War play in the formation of the coalition that opposed Iraq in the Persian Gulf War? *(If the Cold War had not ended, the Soviet Union might have backed Iraq against the United States, Saudi Arabia, and Kuwait.)* L3

Chapter 24 Resources

Timesaving Tools

TeacherWorks™ All-In-One Planner and Resource Center

- **Interactive Teacher Edition** Access your Teacher Wraparound Edition and your classroom resources with a few easy clicks.
- **Interactive Lesson Planner** Planning has never been easier! Organize your week, month, semester, or year with all the lesson helps you need to make teaching creative, timely, and relevant.

Use Glencoe's **Presentation Plus!** multimedia teacher tool to easily present dynamic lessons that visually excite your students. Using Microsoft PowerPoint® you can customize the presentations to create your own personalized lessons.

Teaching Transparencies

Graphic Organizer Student Activity 24 Transparency

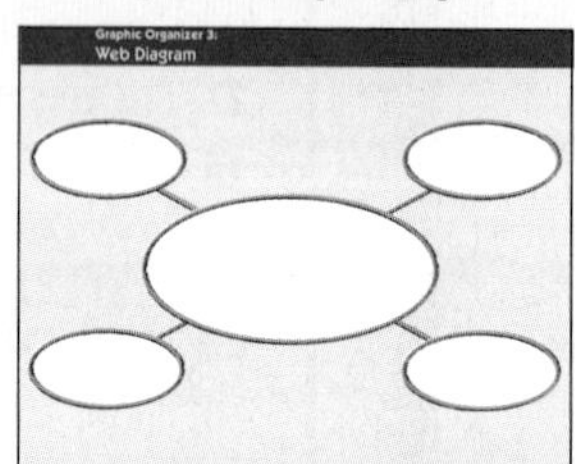

Chapter Transparency 24

Map Overlay Transparency 24

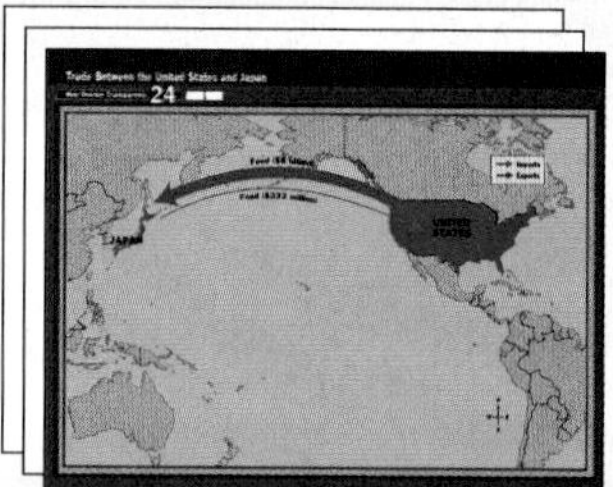

Application and Enrichment

Enrichment Activity 24

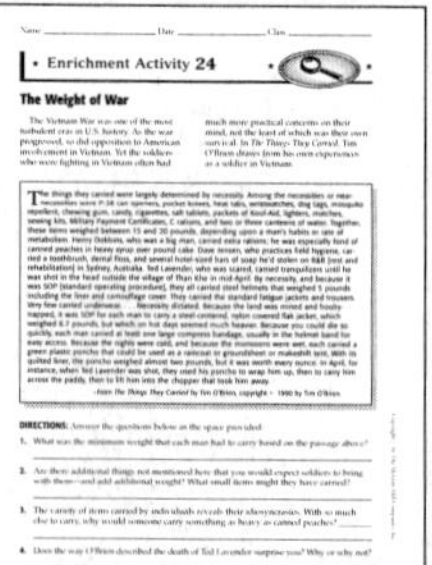

Primary Source Reading 24

History Simulation Activity 24

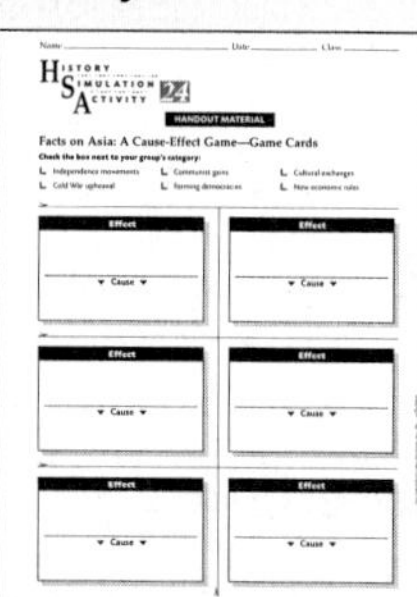

Historical Significance Activity 24

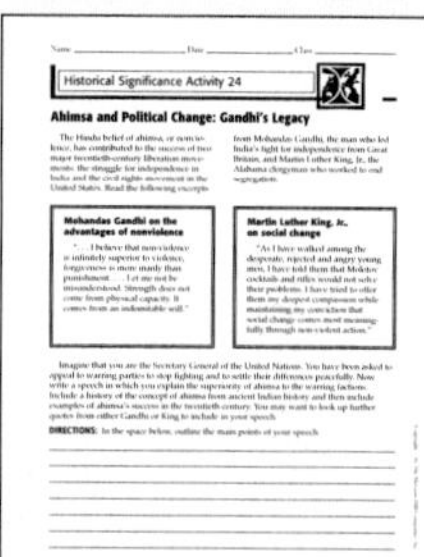

Cooperative Learning Activity 24

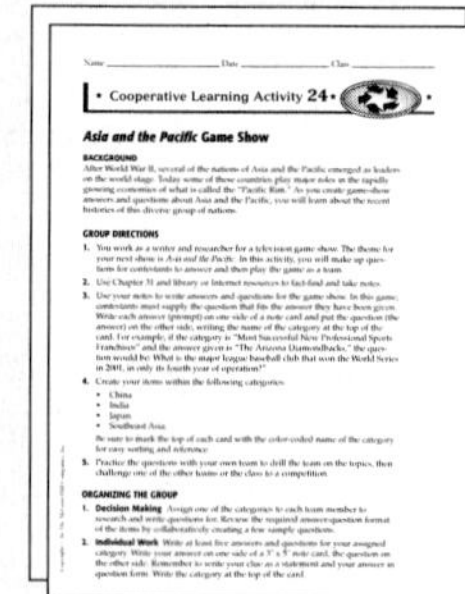

A&E HOME VIDEO

THE HISTORY CHANNEL.

The following videotape programs are available from Glencoe as supplements to Chapter 24:

- **Democracy Crushed: Tiananmen Square** (ISBN 0-7670-1459-6)
- **Korea: The Forgotten War** (ISBN 1-56501-540-1)
- **Vietnam: A Soldier's Diary** (ISBN 0-7670-0772-7)

To order, call Glencoe at 1-800-334-7344. To find classroom resources to accompany many of these videos, check the following home pages:
A&E Television: www.aande.com
The History Channel: www.historychannel.com

Chapter 24 Resources

Review and Reinforcement

Linking Past and Present Activity 24

Time Line Activity 24

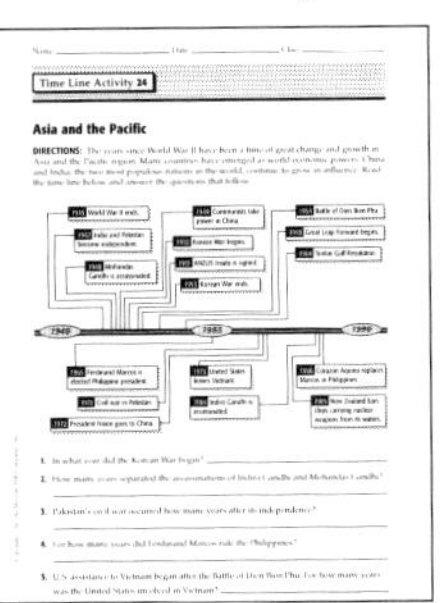

Reteaching Activity 24

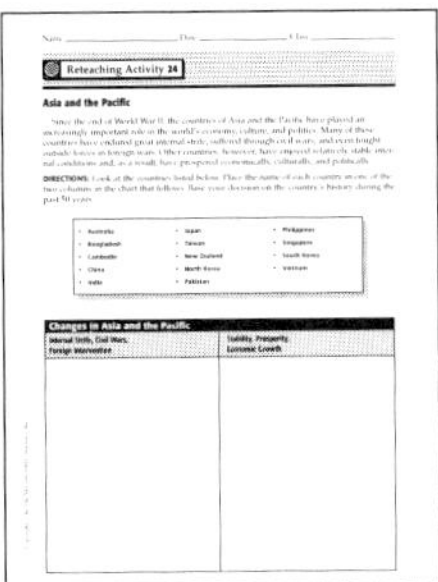

Vocabulary Activity 24

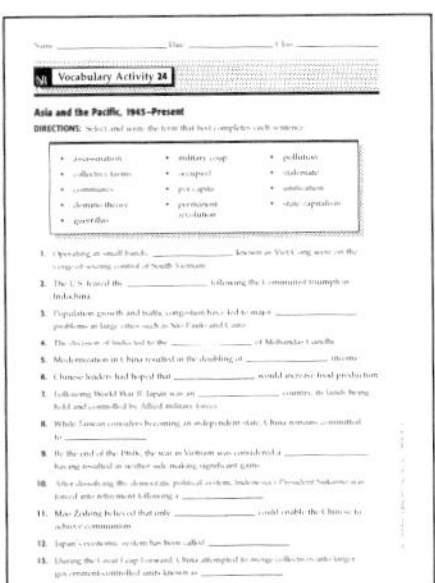

Critical Thinking Skills Activity 24

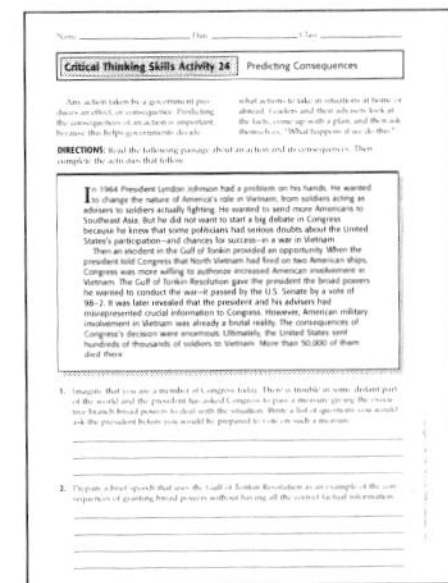

Assessment and Evaluation

Chapter 24 Test Form A

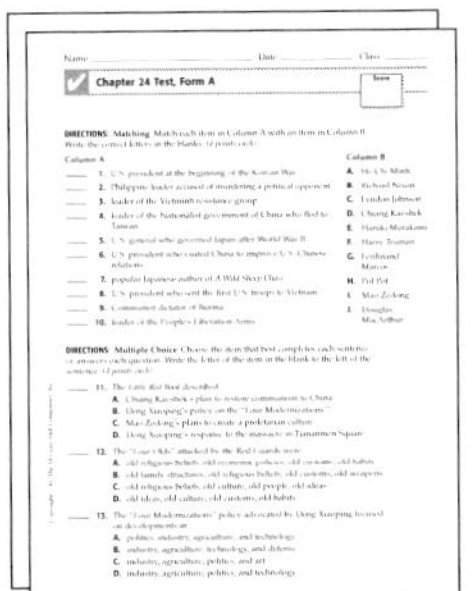

Chapter 24 Test Form B

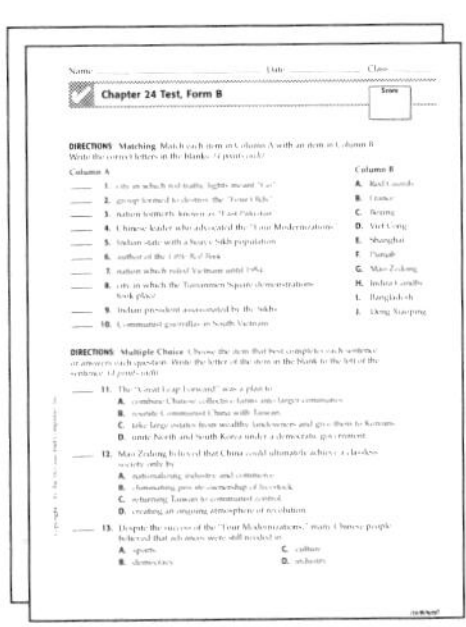

Performance Assessment Activity 24

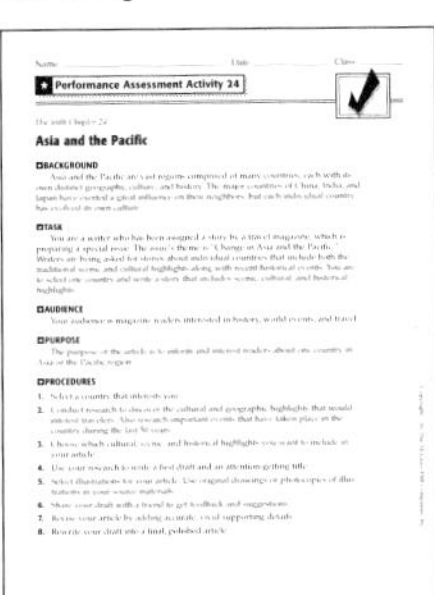

ExamView® Pro Testmaker CD-ROM

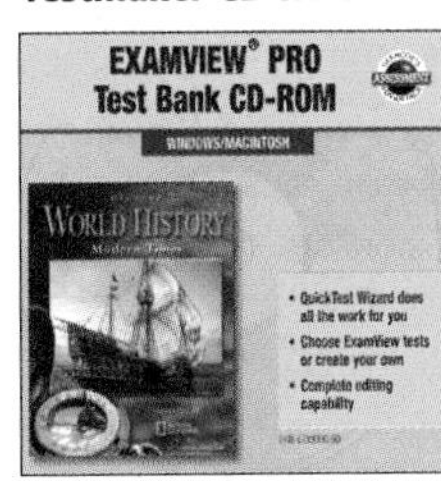

Standardized Test Skills Practice Workbook Activity 24

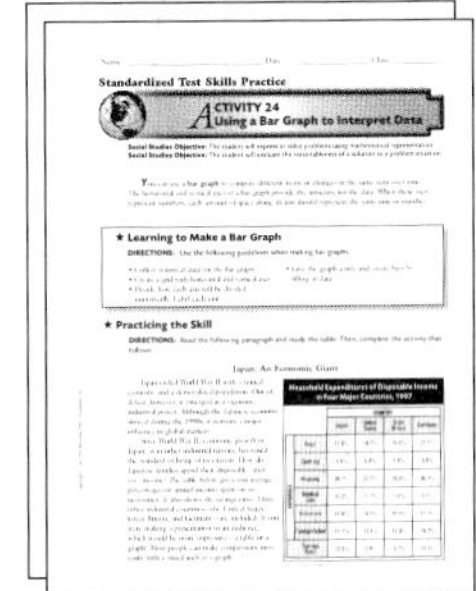

Interdisciplinary Activities

Mapping History Activity 24

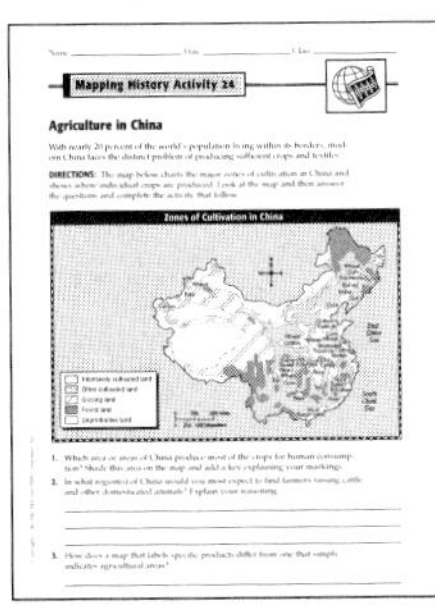

World Art and Music Activity 24

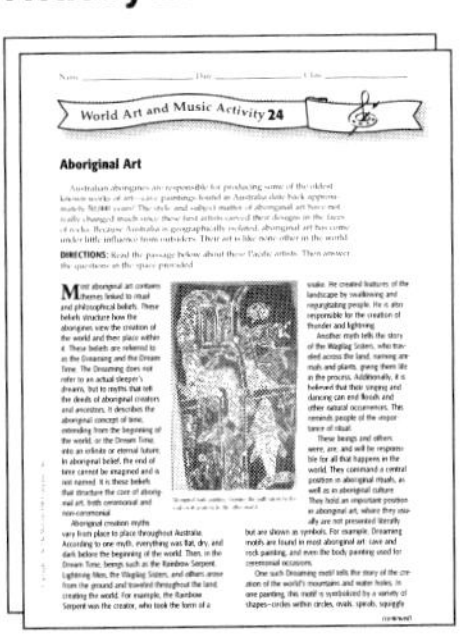

History and Geography Activity 24

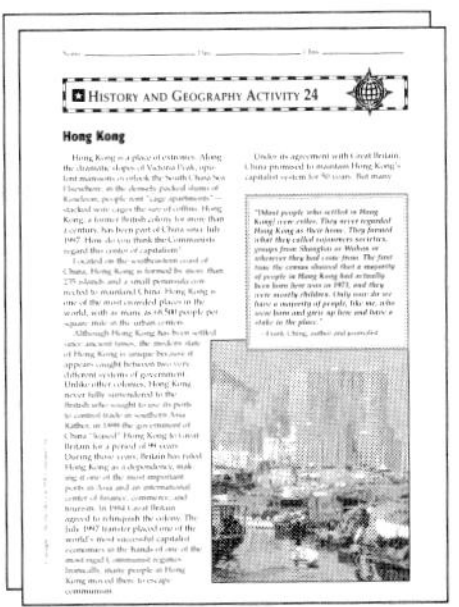

People in World History Activity 24

Multimedia

- Vocabulary PuzzleMaker CD-ROM
- Interactive Tutor Self-Assessment CD-ROM
- ExamView® Pro Testmaker CD-ROM
- Audio Program
- World History Primary Source Document Library CD-ROM
- MindJogger Videoquiz
- Presentation Plus! CD-ROM
- TeacherWorks CD-ROM
- Interactive Student Edition CD-ROM
- The World History—Modern Times Video Program

Spanish Resources

The following Spanish language materials are available in the Spanish Resources Binder:

- Spanish Guided Reading Activities
- Spanish Reteaching Activities
- Spanish Quizzes and Tests
- Spanish Vocabulary Activities
- Spanish Summaries

Chapter 24 Resources

SECTION RESOURCES		
Daily Objectives	**Reproducible Resources**	**Multimedia Resources**
SECTION 1 **Communist China** 1. Describe the socialist society in China established by Mao Zedong. 2. Discuss how after Mao's death, modified capitalist techniques were used to encourage growth in industry and farming.	Reproducible Lesson Plan 24–1 Daily Lecture and Discussion Notes 24–1 Guided Reading Activity 24–1* Section Quiz 24–1* Reading Essentials and Study Guide 24–1	Daily Focus Skills Transparency 24–1 Interactive Tutor Self-Assessment CD-ROM ExamView® Pro Testmaker CD-ROM Presentation Plus! CD-ROM
SECTION 2 **Independent States in South and Southeast Asia** 1. Explain how British India was divided into two states: India, mostly Hindu, and Pakistan, mostly Muslim. 2. Summarize how many of the newly independent states of Southeast Asia attempted to form democratic governments but often fell subject to military regimes.	Reproducible Lesson Plan 24–2 Daily Lecture and Discussion Notes 24–2 Guided Reading Activity 24–2* Section Quiz 24–2* Reading Essentials and Study Guide 24–2	Daily Focus Skills Transparency 24–2 Interactive Tutor Self-Assessment CD-ROM ExamView® Pro Testmaker CD-ROM Presentation Plus! CD-ROM
SECTION 3 **Japan and the Pacific** 1. Describe how Japan and the "Asian tigers" have created successful industrial societies. 2. Analyze why Australia and New Zealand have identified themselves culturally and politically with Europe, yet in recent years they have been drawing closer to their Asian neighbors.	Reproducible Lesson Plan 24–3 Daily Lecture and Discussion Notes 24–3 Guided Reading Activity 24–3* Section Quiz 24–3* Reteaching Activity 24* Reading Essentials and Study Guide 24–3	Daily Focus Skills Transparency 24–3 Interactive Tutor Self-Assessment CD-ROM ExamView® Pro Testmaker CD-ROM Presentation Plus! CD-ROM

0:00 **OUT OF TIME?**
Assign the Chapter 24 **Reading Essentials and Study Guide.**

*Also Available in Spanish

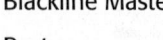

 Blackline Master  Transparency CD-ROM DVD
Poster Music Program Audio Program Videocassette

Chapter 24 Resources

Teacher's Corner

INDEX TO NATIONAL GEOGRAPHIC MAGAZINE

The following articles relate to this chapter:

- "The New Saigon," by Tracy Dahlby, April 1995.
- "Shanghai: Where China's Past and Future Meet," by William S. Ellis, March 1994.
- "Kyushu: Japan's Southern Gateway," by Tracy Dahlby, January 1994.
- "Taiwan: The Other China Changes Course," by Arthur Zich, November 1993.

ADDITIONAL NATIONAL GEOGRAPHIC SOCIETY PRODUCTS

To order the following, call National Geographic at 1-800-368-2728:

- *Capitalism, Socialism, Communism Series, "Communism"* (Video)
- *Nations of the World Series, "Japan"* (Video)
- *Democratic Governments Series "Japan"* (Video)
- *The Changing Faces of Communism Series, "Vietnam"* (Video)

NGS ONLINE

Access National Geographic's new dynamic MapMachine Web site and other geography resources at:
www.nationalgeographic.com
www.nationalgeographic.com/maps

KEY TO ABILITY LEVELS

Teaching strategies have been coded.

L1 BASIC activities for all students
L2 AVERAGE activities for average to above-average students
L3 CHALLENGING activities for above-average students
ELL ENGLISH LANGUAGE LEARNER activities

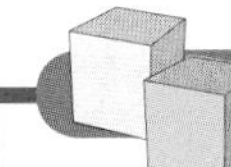

Block Schedule

Activities that are suited to use within the block scheduling framework are identified by: [icon]

Use our Web site for additional resources. All essential content is covered in the Student Edition.

You and your students can visit www.wh.mt.glencoe.com, the Web site companion to *Glencoe World History—Modern Times.* This innovative integration of electronic and print media offers your students a wealth of opportunities. The student text directs students to the Web site for the following options:

- **Chapter Overviews**
- **Self-Check Quizzes**
- **Student Web Activities**
- **Textbook Updates**

Answers to the Student Web Activities are provided for you in the **Web Activity Lesson Plans.** Additional Web resources and Interactive Tutor Puzzles are also available.

Clair Wiles
N. Eugene High School
Eugene, Oregon

Thinking About *Butsudans*

Explain to students that many Japanese homes have a Buddhist shrine or altar called a *butsudan*. The *butsudan* is usually a lacquered cabinet that contains many objects of symbolic and religious significance. One important purpose of the *butsudan* is to serve as a memorial for departed family members. As such, it may contain pictures and other memorabilia.

Share photos of *butsudans* that you have found on the Internet or in printed sources with students. Ask students to conduct further research themselves on *butsudans* and the sorts of objects they contain. Then have them design and draw their own *butsudans* and compile a list of contents to commemorate people, both living and dead, who have had a positive influence on their lives. They may be family members, friends, or even famous individuals.

Display the drawings and lists. After everyone has had a chance to view the drawings, hold a class discussion on how daily exposure to these objects could affect one's attitudes.

Performance Assessment

Refer to Activity 24 in the Performance Assessment Activities and Rubrics booklet.

The Impact Today

Emphasize that in a world increasingly linked by technology and the spread of ideas, students need to have a global view. Ask students to describe current events involving Asian countries, which students have read about or watched on television newscasts recently. In what specific ways is the interaction between the United States and Asia increasing? Why do students think this increased interaction is occurring?

GLENCOE TECHNOLOGY

The World History—Modern Times Video Program

To learn more about the changes and events in Vietnam since 1945, students can view the Chapter 24 video, "Vietnam," from **The World History—Modern Times Video Program.**

MindJogger Videoquiz

Use the **MindJogger Videoquiz** to preview Chapter 24 content.

Available in VHS.

CHAPTER 24 Asia and the Pacific

1945–Present

Key Events

As you read, look for the key events in the history of postwar Asia.

- *Communists in China introduced socialist measures and drastic reforms under the leadership of Mao Zedong.*
- *After World War II, India gained its independence from Britain and divided into two separate countries—India and Pakistan.*
- *Japan modernized its economy and society after 1945 and became one of the world's economic giants.*

The Impact Today

The events that occurred during this time period still impact our lives today.

- *Today China and Japan play significant roles in world affairs: China for political and military reasons, Japan for economic reasons.*
- *India and Pakistan remain rivals. In 1998, India carried out nuclear tests and Pakistan responded by testing its own nuclear weapons.*
- *Although the people of Taiwan favor independence, China remains committed to eventual unification.*

World History—Modern Times Video *The Chapter 24 video, "Vietnam," chronicles the history and impact of the Vietnam War.*

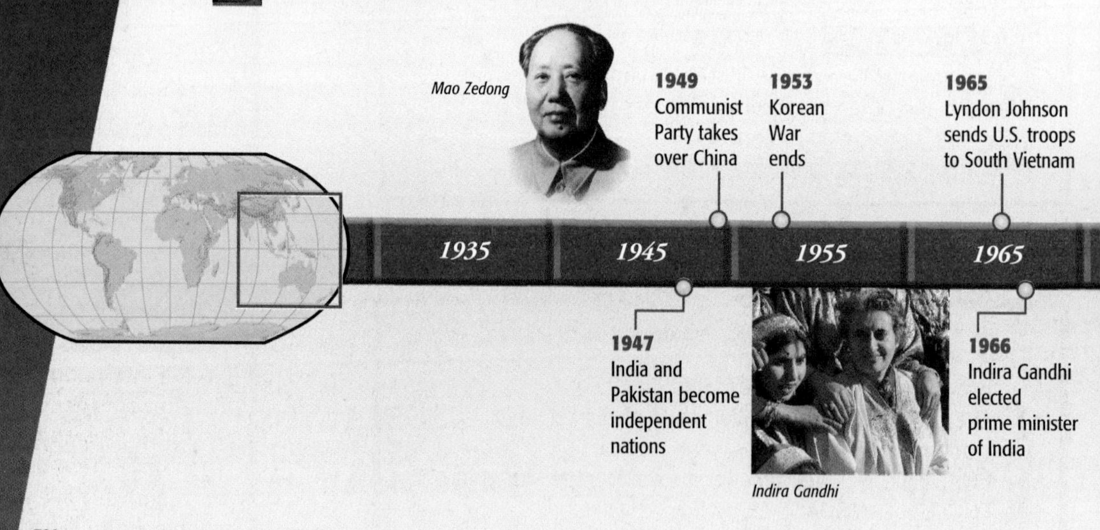

Mao Zedong
1949
Communist Party takes over China
1953
Korean War ends
1965
Lyndon Johnson sends U.S. troops to South Vietnam
1935
1945
1955
1965
1947
India and Pakistan become independent nations
1966
Indira Gandhi elected prime minister of India
Indira Gandhi

720

TWO-MINUTE LESSON LAUNCHER

Have students use globes to locate the countries discussed in this chapter: China, Taiwan, North Korea, South Korea, India, Pakistan, Bangladesh, Burma, Vietnam, Cambodia, Indonesia, the Philippines, Singapore, Australia, and New Zealand. Ask the following questions: Which countries are the largest geographically? *(China, India, Australia)* Do you think that size is a measure of a country's power or importance? *(No, India is relatively large, but much of its population is poor. Japan and Singapore are small but economically advanced.)* **L1**

Singapore's architecture is a mixture of modern and colonial buildings.

Nixon in China

1972
Richard Nixon establishes diplomatic relations with China

1989
Tiananmen Square massacre

1975 1985 1995 2005

1979
Mother Teresa receives the Nobel Peace Prize

1997
Return of Hong Kong to China

Fireworks celebrate the handover of Hong Kong to China.

HISTORY Online

Chapter Overview
Visit the *Glencoe World History—Modern Times* Web site at wh.mt.glencoe.com and click on **Chapter 24–Chapter Overview** to preview chapter information.

Introducing CHAPTER 24

Chapter Objectives

After studying this chapter, students should be able to:

1. describe economic and political changes in China;
2. describe Chinese culture;
3. describe China's role in the Cold War and the Korean War;
4. identify and describe India and Pakistan's formation and evolution;
5. explain religious, social, and cultural life in India;
6. identify and describe the independent states of Southeast Asia;
7. explain the allied occupation of Japan;
8. describe Japan's transformation since 1945.

Chapter Overview
Introduce students to chapter content and key terms by having them access **Chapter Overview 24** at wh.mt.glencoe.com.

Time Line Activity

As students read the chapter, have them review the time line on pages 720 and 721. Ask them to explain the significance of 1965. *(United States President Lyndon B. Johnson sent American troops to South Vietnam.)* **L1**

MORE ABOUT THE ART

Singapore is the capital city of a small island nation that bears the same name, located just 80 miles (128.7 km) north of the Equator. The city is home to many of the world's major banks, which are situated in Singapore's downtown skyscrapers. The city features a variety of architectural styles based upon its settlement pattern. Colonial buildings stand in the heart of the city, while other buildings mirror the ethnic and social groups that reside in Singapore. Among the more prominent areas of the city are Chinatown, Little India, the Arab District, and Orchard Road, where shops, hotels, restaurants, and nightclubs attract upscale clientele. Singapore boasts the world's busiest port, and the city has become a major tourist destination since independence in 1965.

CHAPTER PREVIEW

Introducing
A Story That Matters

Depending upon the ability level of your students, select from the following questions to reinforce the reading of *A Story That Matters.*

- Why would a government choose a military strategy to oppose unarmed civilians? *(The government wanted to end the pro-democracy movement and prevent further demonstrations.)*
- Forty years of Communist rule did not erase historical values and beliefs of the Chinese people. Why not? *(Governments shape societies and are often able to control actions, but belief and values are a matter of individual conscience and choice.)* L1

About the Art

Photography is a powerful communication tool. Without these photographs and others, Chinese authorities would have been able to deny the events of Tiananmen Square. Ask students to discuss other events in recent history that have been recorded by photographers. How has the photographic record increased our understanding of those events?

CHAPTER PREVIEW

A Story That Matters

The events in Tiananmen Square ended tragically for pro-democracy protesters.

A Movement for Democracy

In the spring of 1989, China began to experience a remarkable series of events. Crowds of students, joined by workers and journalists, filled Tiananmen Square in Beijing day after day to demonstrate in favor of a democratic government for China. Some students waged a hunger strike, and others carried posters calling for democracy.

To China's elderly rulers, calls for democracy were a threat to the dominant role that the Communist Party had played in China since 1949. Some leaders interested in reform advised restraint in handling the protesters. Most of the Communist leaders, however, wanted to repress the movement. When students erected a 30-foot (9-m)-high statue called "The Goddess of Democracy" that looked similar to the American Statue of Liberty, party leaders became especially incensed.

On June 3, 1989, the Chinese army moved into the square. Soldiers carrying automatic rifles fired into the unarmed crowds. Tanks and troops moved in and surrounded the remaining students. At 5:30 in the morning on June 4, the mayor of Beijing announced that Tiananmen Square had been "handed back to the people." Even then, the killing of unarmed citizens continued. In all, hundreds of civilians died in the streets of Beijing. The movement for democracy in China had ended.

Why It Matters

The movement for democracy in China in the 1980s was only one of many tumultuous events in Asia after World War II. In China, a civil war gave way to a new China under Communist control. Japan recovered from the devastation of World War II and went on to build an economic powerhouse. In South Asia and Southeast Asia, nations that had been dominated by Western colonial powers struggled to gain their freedom. Throughout Asia, nations worked to develop modern industrialized states.

History and You Find online or in the library a commentary on the Tiananmen Square incident written from the perspective of the Chinese government. Analyze the work to determine whether or not it displays bias. Support your opinion.

722

HISTORY AND YOU

The United States became a separate nation when the colonists rebelled against Great Britain and declared independence. From the time the United States Constitution and Bill of Rights were signed, Americans have, in most cases, been able to speak freely and demonstrate peacefully against the government without fear of government retaliation. During certain periods in United States history citizens have held mass demonstrations on behalf of civil rights or against government intervention in foreign lands, especially during the 1960s and early 1970s. The story of Tiananmen Square shows how totalitarian regimes exercise complete control over their citizens' public speech and actions. Ask students if they believe situations might occur in which the government would be justified in using force against *peaceful* public protest. L2

SECTION 1 Communist China

Guide to Reading

Main Ideas
- Mao Zedong established a socialist society in China.
- After Mao's death, modified capitalist techniques were used to encourage growth in industry and farming.

Key Terms
commune, permanent revolution, per capita

People to Identify
Deng Xiaoping, Richard Nixon

Places to Locate
Taiwan, South Korea, North Korea

Preview Questions
1. How did the Great Leap Forward and the Great Proletarian Cultural Revolution affect China?
2. What were the major economic, social, and political developments in China after the death of Mao Zedong?

Reading Strategy
Cause and Effect Use a chart like the one below to list communism's effects on China's international affairs.

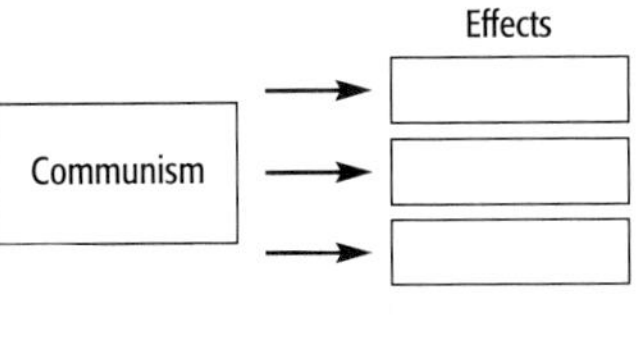

Preview of Events

1950	1958	1972	1979
A marriage law guarantees women equal rights with men in China	Mao Zedong institutes the Great Leap Forward	President Nixon visits China	China establishes diplomatic ties with the United States

Students in support of Mao Zedong

Voices from the Past

Nien Cheng, the widow of an official of Chiang Kai-shek's regime, described a visit by Red Guards to her home:

> ❝Mounting the stairs, I was astonished to see several Red Guards taking pieces of my porcelain collection out of their padded boxes. One young man . . . was stepping on them. . . . Impulsively I leapt forward and caught his leg just as he raised his foot to crush the next cup. He toppled. We fell in a heap together. . . . The young man whose revolutionary work of destruction I had interrupted said angrily, 'You shut up! These things belong to the old culture. . . . Our Great Leader Chairman Mao taught us, "If we do not destroy, we cannot establish." The old culture must be destroyed to make way for the new socialist culture.'❞
>
> —***Life and Death in Shanghai,*** **Nien Cheng, 1986**

The Red Guards were established to create a new order in China.

Civil War and the Great Leap Forward

By 1945, there were two Chinese governments. The Nationalist government of Chiang Kai-shek, based in southern and central China, was supported by the United States. The Communist government, under the leadership of Mao Zedong, had its base in North China.

In 1946, full-scale war between the Nationalists and the Communists broke out. In the countryside, millions of peasants were attracted to the Communists by promises of land. Many joined Mao's People's Liberation Army.

By the spring of 1949, the People's Liberation Army had defeated the Nationalists. Chiang and two million followers fled to the island of **Taiwan.**

1 FOCUS

Section Overview

This section explores the establishment of a socialist society in China.

BELLRINGER
Skillbuilder Activity

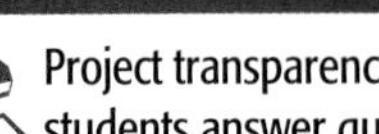

Project transparency and have students answer questions.

Available as a blackline master.

Daily Focus Skills Transparency 24–1

DAILY FOCUS SKILLS TRANSPARENCY 24-1

Communist China

1 According to this editorial, what was Chairman Mao Zedong's goal?
2 What obstacle stood in the way of achieving this goal?
3 Describe the editorial policy of the newspapers responsible for this editorial.

Chairman Mao points out: "Before a brand-new social system can be built on the site of the old, the site must be swept clean. Invariably, remnants of old ideas reflecting the old system remain in people's minds for a long time, and they do not easily give way." We must continue to criticize the old system and old ideas,....

Guide to Reading

Answers to Graphic: Effects: signed a pact of friendship and cooperation with the Soviet Union; sent troops to North Korea; isolated from major Western powers

Preteaching Vocabulary: Explain *permanent revolution. (Mao believed that a state of constant revolutionary fervor that focused on overcoming the past was the way to achieve true communism. This fervor is known as permanent revolution.)* L2

SECTION RESOURCES

Reproducible Masters
- Reproducible Lesson Plan 24–1
- Daily Lecture and Discussion Notes 24–1
- Guided Reading Activity 24–1
- Section Quiz 24–1
- Reading Essentials and Study Guide 24–1

Transparencies
- Daily Focus Skills Transparency 24–1

Multimedia
- Interactive Tutor Self-Assessment CD-ROM
- ExamView® Pro Testmaker CD-ROM
- Presentation Plus! CD-ROM

2 TEACH

Geography Skills

Answers:

1. Kunming, Shenzhen, Wuhan, Chongqing, Xian; Hefei, Nanjing, Shanghai, Beijing; sites from 20 years earlier include Beijing, Nanjing, Wuhan, Shenzhen (nearby), Chongqing
2. Distance is approximately 100 miles (161 km); answers will vary but may include Chicago, Illinois, and Milwaukee, Wisconsin.

Reading Check

Answer: Bad weather and the peasants' hatred of the new system reduced production and caused mass starvation.

Daily Lecture and Discussion Notes 24–1

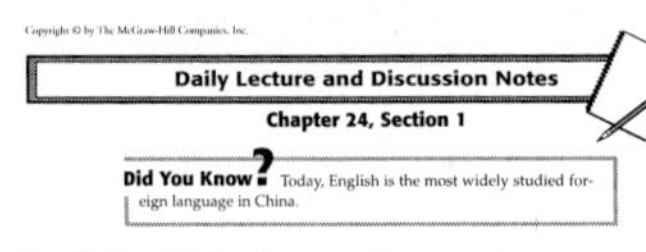

Daily Lecture and Discussion Notes

Chapter 24, Section 1

Did You Know? Today, English is the most widely studied foreign language in China.

I. **Civil War and the Great Leap Forward** *(pages 723–724)*

A. By 1945, China had two governments. The United States supported the Nationalist government of Chiang Kai-shek, based in southern and central China. The Communist government led by Mao Zedong was based in North China.

B. In 1946 war between the Nationalists and the Communists broke out. Millions of peasants joined Mao's People's Liberation Army because they were promised land. Mao's Communist army defeated the Nationalist army. Chiang and his followers fled to **Taiwan.** The Communist Party, led by Mao Zedong, ruled China.

C. In 1955, the Chinese government started a program to build a socialist society. Most

Guided Reading Activity 24–1

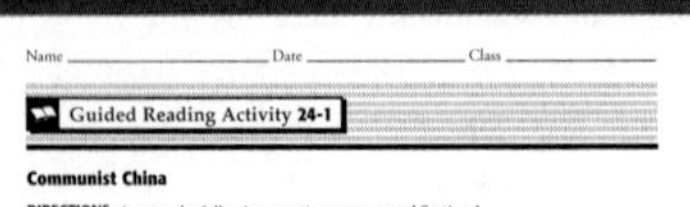

Name ____________ Date ____________ Class ____________

Guided Reading Activity 24-1

Communist China

DIRECTIONS: Answer the following questions as you read Section 1.

1. What happened between the Nationalists and Communists in China in 1946?
2. Where did Chiang Kai-shek and his followers flee when they were defeated?
3. Why did Mao begin the radical Great Leap Forward in 1958?
4. List the "Four Olds" targeted for elimination by the Red Guards.
5. State the Four Modernizations focused on by the policies of Deng Xiaoping.

NATIONAL GEOGRAPHIC China, 1949–1989

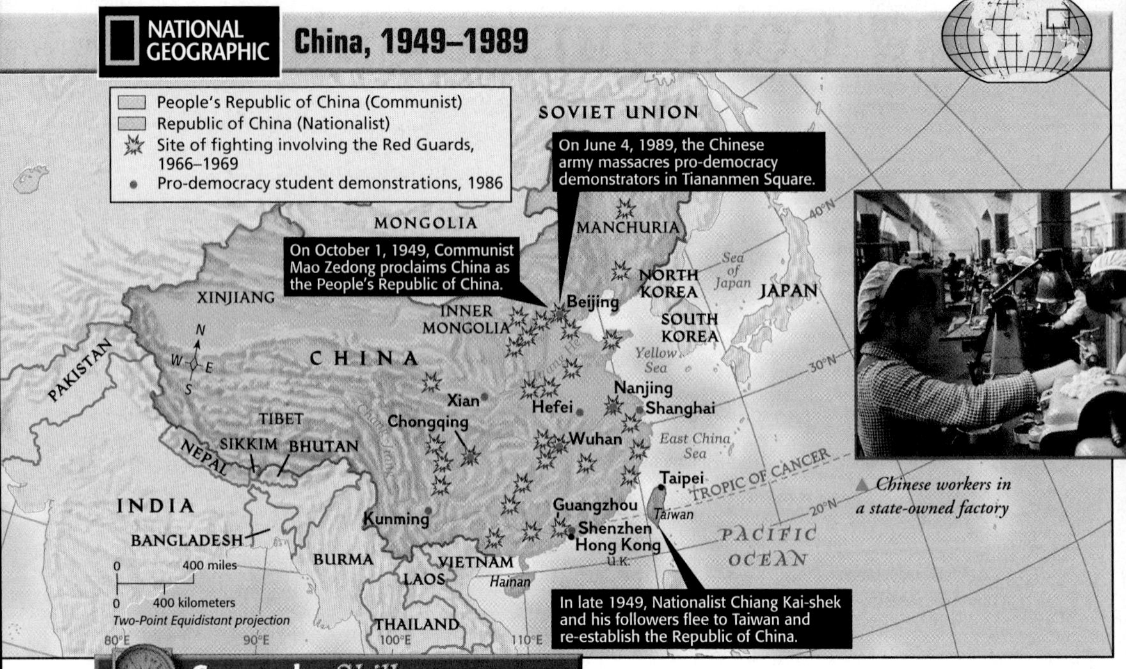

▲ *Chinese workers in a state-owned factory*

Geography Skills

The People's Republic of China originated in 1949.

1. **Interpreting Maps** Identify the places where pro-democracy student demonstrations took place in 1986. Which of these cities had also been sites of fighting involving the Red Guards 20 years earlier?
2. **Applying Geography Skills** Use the map's scale to determine the approximate distance from Taiwan to mainland China. Use an atlas to help you name two U.S. cities that are about this same distance apart.

The Communist Party, under the leadership of its chairman, Mao Zedong, now ruled China. In 1955, the Chinese government launched a program to build a socialist society. To win the support of the peasants, lands were taken from wealthy landlords and given to poor peasants. About two-thirds of the peasant households in China received land under the new program. Most private farmland was collectivized, and most industry and commerce was nationalized.

Chinese leaders hoped that collective farms would increase food production, allowing more people to work in industry. Food production, however, did not grow.

To speed up economic growth, Mao began a more radical program, known as the Great Leap Forward, in 1958. Existing collective farms, normally the size of a village, were combined into vast **communes.** Each commune contained more than thirty thousand people who lived and worked together. Mao hoped this program would enable China to reach the final stage of communism—the classless society—before the end of the twentieth century. The government official slogan promised the following: "Hard work for a few years, happiness for a thousand."

The Great Leap Forward was a disaster. Bad weather and the peasants' hatred of the new system drove food production down. As a result, almost fifteen million people died of starvation. In 1960, the government abandoned the communes and returned to collective farms.

Reading Check **Explaining** Why was the Great Leap Forward an economic disaster for China?

The Great Proletarian Cultural Revolution

Mao now faced opposition within the Communist Party. Despite this opposition and the commune failure, he still dreamed of a classless society. In Mao's eyes, only **permanent revolution,** an atmosphere of constant revolutionary fervor, could enable the

EXTENDING THE CONTENT

The Great Leap Forward The Great Leap Forward was similar to Stalin's collectivization and his first Five-Year Plan. Mao believed that by combining collectivization with industrial programs, he could avoid Stalin's disaster. Thousands of small agricultural collectives were merged into much larger communes. Thousands of people lived in paramilitary fashion with communal kitchens, mess halls, and nurseries. Each commune was expected to be self-supporting. The resulting dislocations appalled the Soviets, who withdrew their aid rather than see it wasted. Starvation was the result of the Great Leap Forward from 1959–1962. No one knows exactly how many people died of hunger, but the figure is thought to be in the millions.

Chinese to overcome the past and achieve the final stage of communism.

In 1966, Mao launched the **Great Proletarian Cultural Revolution.** The Chinese name literally meant "great revolution to create a proletarian (working class) culture." A collection of Mao's thoughts, called the ***Little Red Book,*** was hailed as the most important source of knowledge in all areas.

HISTORY Online

Web Activity Visit the *Glencoe World History—Modern Times* Web site at wh.mt.glencoe.com and click on **Chapter 24–Student Web Activity** to learn more about the Cultural Revolution.

To further the Cultural Revolution, the Red Guards were formed. These were revolutionary groups composed largely of young people. Red Guards set out across the nation to eliminate the "Four Olds"—old ideas, old culture, old customs, and old habits. The Red Guard destroyed temples, books written by foreigners, and foreign music. They tore down street signs and replaced them with ones carrying revolutionary names. The city of Shanghai even ordered that red (the revolutionary color) traffic lights would indicate that traffic could move, not stop.

Vicious attacks were made on individuals who had supposedly deviated from Mao's plan. Intellectuals and artists accused of being pro-Western were especially open to attack. Key groups, however, including Communist Party members, urban professionals, and many military officers, did not share Mao's desire for permanent revolution. People, disgusted by the actions of the Red Guards, began to turn against the movement.

Reading Check **Identifying** What were the "Four Olds" and how did the Red Guards try to eliminate them?

China After Mao

In September 1976, Mao Zedong died at the age of 83. A group of practical-minded reformers, led by **Deng Xiaoping** (DUNG SHOW•PIHNG), seized power and brought the Cultural Revolution to an end.

Policies of Deng Xiaoping Under Deng Xiaoping, the government followed a policy called the Four Modernizations, which focused on four areas—industry, agriculture, technology, and national defense. For over 20 years, China had been isolated from the technological advances taking place elsewhere in the world. To make up for lost time, the government invited foreign investors to China. Thousands of students were sent abroad to study science, technology, and modern business techniques.

A new agricultural policy was begun. Collective farms could now lease land to peasant families who paid rent to the collective. Anything produced on the land above the amount of that payment could be sold on the private market. Peasants were also allowed to make goods they could sell to others.

Overall, modernization worked. Industrial output skyrocketed. Per capita (per person) income, including farm income, doubled during the 1980s. The standard of living rose for most people. The average Chinese citizen in the early 1980s had barely earned enough to buy a bicycle, radio, or watch. By the 1990s, many were buying refrigerators and color television sets.

Movement for Democracy Despite these achievements, many people complained that Deng Xiaoping's program had failed to achieve a fifth modernization—democracy. The new leaders did not allow direct criticism of the Communist Party. Those who called for democracy were often sentenced to long terms in prison.

The problem began to intensify in the late 1980s. More Chinese began to study abroad. More information about Western society reached educated people

People In History

Deng Xiaoping
1904–1997—Chinese leader

Deng Xiaoping was one of China's major leaders after the death of Mao Zedong. Deng studied in France, where he joined the Chinese Communist Party. Back in China, he helped organize the Communist army. At the end of World War II, Deng became a member of the Central Committee of the Communist Party. An opponent of Mao's Cultural Revolution, he was labeled a "renegade, scab, and traitor" and sent to work in a tractor factory.

In 1978, after the failure of the Cultural Revolution, Deng became the leader of China's modernization and economic reform. Deng took a practical approach to change. He said, "I do not care whether a cat is black or white, the important thing is whether it catches mice." Between 1982 and 1989, Deng was the chief leader of China.

Reading Check

Answer: old ideas, old culture, old customs, and old habits; the Red Guards destroyed temples, books written by foreigners, jazz records, etc.; used violent methods, making vicious attacks on individuals who supposedly deviated from Mao's plan, especially intellectuals and artists who were accused of being pro-Western

TURNING POINT

How did Mao Zedong's rule affect China and its place in world affairs? *(Mao imposed a Communist system on China and tried to uproot traditional ways. Mao's China later became an independent Communist power, and it began to normalize relations with the West in the 1970s.)* L2

Critical Thinking

Have students analyze the nature of the totalitarian regime in China by categorizing information in this chapter. L2

COOPERATIVE LEARNING ACTIVITY

Creating a Multimedia Presentation Have students form five groups to research one of the following topics: the 1949 civil war, the Five-Year Plans of the 1950s, the Cultural Revolution of the 1960s, the pragmatists versus the Gang of Four in the 1970s, and the Tiananmen Square crackdown in 1989. Tell students to use their texts as well as outside research materials. After they have completed their research, have students prepare a multimedia presentation, including charts and other visuals to present their findings. Each group should then choose one student to present its research orally, using the multimedia presentation. L2

For grading this activity, refer to the ***Performance Assessment Activities*** booklet.

Reading Check

Answer: democracy; Chinese leaders did not allow direct criticism of the Communist Party, often sentencing those who called for democracy to long prison terms

Reading Check

Answer: women allowed to take part in politics, and increasing numbers became active in the Communist Party at the local level; marriage law guaranteed women equal rights with men; regime sought to destroy traditional family system because family loyalty considered to be against the basic principle of Marxism—dedication to society at large

What If...

Answers will vary but should be supported by logical arguments. The Communist movement might have died out in China, or at least have been reduced to a minor political faction, and the Nationalists might have maintained control of the mainland.

Enrich

Ask students to analyze the influence of Mao Zedong and Deng Xiaoping on the political events of the twentieth century. **L3**

inside the country. The economic improvements of the early 1980s led to pressure from students and other city residents for better living conditions and more freedom to choose jobs after graduation.

In the late 1980s, rising inflation led to growing discontent among salaried workers, especially in the cities. Corruption and special treatment for officials and party members led to increasing criticism as well. In May 1989, student protesters called for an end to the corruption and demanded the resignation of China's aging Communist Party leaders. These demands received widespread support from people in the cities and led to massive demonstrations in **Tiananmen Square** in Beijing.

Some Communist leaders were divided over how to respond. However, Deng Xiaoping saw the student desire for democracy as a demand for an end to the Communist Party. He ordered tanks and troops into Tiananmen Square to crush the demonstrators. Democracy remained a dream.

Throughout the 1990s, China's human rights violations and its determination to unify with Taiwan strained its relationship with the West. China's increasing military power has also created international concern. However, China still maintains diplomatic relations with the West.

Reading Check **Explaining** What was the fifth modernization, and why was it not achieved?

What If...

Mao Zedong had died on the Long March?

Chairman Mao was the dominant figure of Chinese communism. During his regime, he was close to a cult figure; schoolchildren would trade Mao cards, pins, and photographs like they were baseball cards or marbles. He rose to power during the Long March of 1934 to 1935 and quickly became the People's Republic of China's greatest leader.

Consider the Consequences The Communists lost over half of their forces during the 6,000-mile (9,660-km) trek of the Long March. Consider the consequences for Chinese communism if Mao had been one of the casualties. How might recent Chinese history have been altered if Mao had not survived this ordeal?

Chinese Society Under Communism

From the start, the Chinese Communist Party wanted to create a new kind of citizen. These new citizens would be expected to contribute their utmost for the good of all. In the words of Mao Zedong, the people "should be resolute, fear no sacrifice, and surmount every difficulty to win victory."

During the 1950s, the Communist government in China took steps to end the old system. One change involved the role of women. Women were now allowed to take part in politics. At the local level, an increasing number of women became active in the Communist Party. In 1950, a new marriage law guaranteed women equal rights with men.

The new regime also tried to destroy the influence of the traditional family system. To the Communists, loyalty to the family, an important element in the Confucian social order, undercut loyalty to the state. For Communist leaders, family loyalty was against the basic principle of Marxism—dedication to society at large.

During the Great Leap Forward, children were encouraged for the first time to report to the authorities any comments by their parents that criticized the system. These practices continued during the Cultural Revolution. Red Guards expected children to report on their parents, students on their teachers, and employees on their superiors.

At the time, many foreign observers feared that the Cultural Revolution would transform the Chinese people into robots spouting the slogans fed to them by their leaders. This did not happen, however. After the death of Mao Zedong there was a noticeable shift away from revolutionary fervor and a return to family traditions.

For most people, this shift meant better living conditions. Married couples who had been given patriotic names such as "Protect Mao Zedong" and "Build the Country" by their parents chose more elegant names for their own children.

The new attitudes were also reflected in people's clothing choices. For a generation after the civil war, clothing had been restricted to a baggy "Mao suit" in olive drab or dark blue. Today, young Chinese people wear jeans, sneakers, and sweat suits. *(See page 781 to read excerpts from Xiao-huang Yin's* China's Gilded Age *in the Primary Sources Library.)*

Reading Check **Evaluating** What was the impact of Communist rule on women, marriage, and family in China?

MEETING INDIVIDUAL NEEDS

Visual Learners In order to help students view the spectrum of change in China from World War II to the present, have students work together to create a time line showing the relative chronology of important events in China's history. Tell students to include political, economic, social, and cultural changes that occurred and to state why these changes were significant. Since repercussions of the events at Tiananmen Square are still being felt, ask students to research this 1989 incident in depth. You might ask students to predict what they envision for China's future. **L2**

Refer to ***Inclusion for the High School Social Studies Classroom Strategies and Activities*** in the TCR.

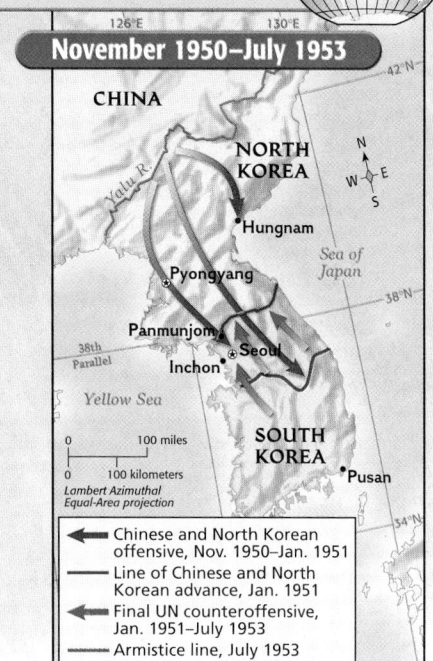

NATIONAL GEOGRAPHIC **Korean War, 1950–1953**

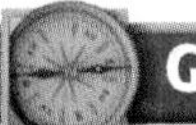

June–November 1950

CHINA
Yalu R.
NORTH KOREA
Sea of Japan
Pyongyang
38th Parallel
Inchon
Seoul
Yellow Sea
SOUTH KOREA
Pusan
126°E
130°E
42°N
38°N
34°N
0 100 miles
0 100 kilometers
Lambert Azimuthal Equal-Area projection

- North Korean offensive, June–Sept. 1950
- Farthest North Korean advance, Sept. 1950
- UN offensive, Sept.–Nov. 1950
- Farthest UN advance, Nov. 1950

November 1950–July 1953

CHINA
Yalu R.
NORTH KOREA
Hungnam
Sea of Japan
Pyongyang
Panmunjom
38th Parallel
Seoul
Inchon
Yellow Sea
SOUTH KOREA
Pusan
126°E
130°E
42°N
38°N
34°N
0 100 miles
0 100 kilometers
Lambert Azimuthal Equal-Area projection

- Chinese and North Korean offensive, Nov. 1950–Jan. 1951
- Line of Chinese and North Korean advance, Jan. 1951
- Final UN counteroffensive, Jan. 1951–July 1953
- Armistice line, July 1953

Geography *Skills*

Three years of fighting resulted in no change to the boundary between North and South Korea.

1. **Interpreting Maps** Identify the offensive shown in the map on the left that caused the Chinese to enter the war.
2. **Applying Geography Skills** How would you compare the UN offensives in the two maps? What reasons can you suggest for the differences?

China and the World: The Cold War in Asia

When Chinese Communists came to power, American fears about the spread of communism intensified. In 1950, China signed a pact of friendship and cooperation with the Soviet Union, and some Americans began to worry about a Communist desire for world domination. With the outbreak of war in Korea, the Cold War had clearly arrived in Asia.

The Korean War Korea was a part of the Japanese Empire from 1905 until 1945. In August 1945, the Soviet Union and the United States agreed to divide Korea into two zones at the 38th parallel. The plan was to hold elections after the war (World War II) to reunify Korea. As American-Soviet relations grew worse, however, two separate governments emerged in Korea—a Communist one in the north and an anti-Communist one in the south.

There was great tension between the two governments. With the approval of Joseph Stalin, North Korean troops invaded **South Korea** on June 25, 1950. President Harry Truman, with the support of the United Nations, sent U.S. troops to repel the invaders.

In September 1950, UN forces—mostly Americans—marched northward across the 38th parallel with the aim of unifying Korea. The Chinese, greatly alarmed, sent hundreds of thousands of Chinese troops into **North Korea** and pushed UN forces back across the 38th parallel.

Harry Truman

CHAPTER 24
Section 1, 723-728

Geography *Skills*

Answers:

1. Arrows indicating northward movement show the UN offensive of 1950.
2. UN offensive on left map crosses 38°N while offensive on right map stops at 38°N; reflects how Chinese forces kept UN forces from crossing 38°N after the 1950 offensive came too close to China

3 ASSESS

Assign Section 1 Assessment as homework or as an in-class activity.

Have students use **Interactive Tutor Self-Assessment CD-ROM.**

Section Quiz 24–1

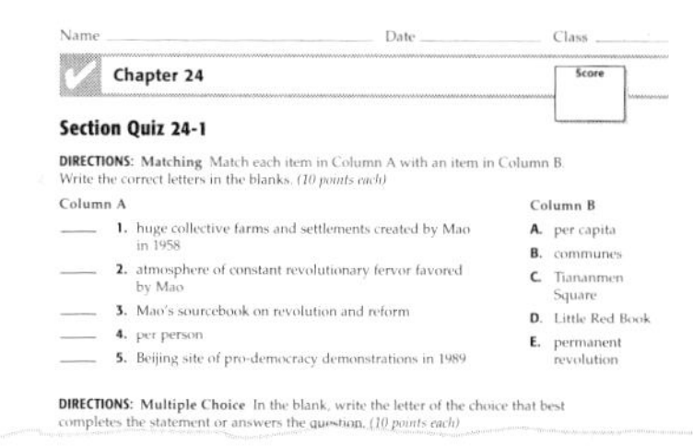

Name ______ Date ______ Class ______

Chapter 24 Score

Section Quiz 24-1

DIRECTIONS: Matching Match each item in Column A with an item in Column B. Write the correct letters in the blanks. *(10 points each)*

Column A	Column B
____ 1. huge collective farms and settlements created by Mao in 1958	A. per capita
____ 2. atmosphere of constant revolutionary fervor favored by Mao	B. communes
____ 3. Mao's sourcebook on revolution and reform	C. Tiananmen Square
____ 4. per person	D. Little Red Book
____ 5. Beijing site of pro-democracy demonstrations in 1989	E. permanent revolution

DIRECTIONS: Multiple Choice In the blank, write the letter of the choice that best completes the statement or answers the question. *(10 points each)*

Critical Thinking

Have students identify changes that resulted from the political revolutions of the twentieth century. L2

EXTENDING THE CONTENT

China and the United Nations China is one of five permanent members of the United Nations Security Council. The Council deals with peacekeeping operations, encourages nuclear non-proliferation treaties, and is concerned with international crime and human rights, just to name a few of its activities. The other members are France, Great Britain, the Russian Federation, and the United States. Each member has veto power. In the past, members have occasionally used their veto power to further their own interests. For example, China, which is interested in regaining Taiwan, has vetoed United Nations activities in countries that maintain diplomatic ties with Taiwan.

CHAPTER 24
Section 1, 723-728

Picturing History

Answer: Answers will vary depending on the results of students' research.

Reading Check

Answer: China was faced with a serious security threat from the Soviet Union, along with internal problems.

Reading Essentials and Study Guide 24–1

Name ______ Date ______ Class ______

Reading Essentials and Study Guide

Chapter 24, Section 1

For use with textbook pages 723–728

COMMUNIST CHINA

KEY TERMS

commune a vast collective farm in China that contained more than thirty thousand people who lived and worked together (page 724)

permanent revolution an atmosphere of constant revolutionary fervor (page 724)

per capita per person (page 725)

Reteaching Activity

Assign one student to be timekeeper and organize the rest of the class into two teams. Play a game in which you state names or terms from this section, and students must explain them within 10 seconds. Each correct answer is worth one point. **L1 ELL**

4 CLOSE

Have students review events in the Great Leap Forward and the Cultural Revolution. They should then describe changes that took place after Mao's death. End by having students summarize significant events related to the spread of communism, including worldwide political and economic effects. **L2**

Picturing History

The Korean War was the first war to utilize a United Nations coalition, the first to see integrated U.S. forces, and the first time that African American women enlisted in the Marines. Research other first time events of the Korean War.

Three more years of fighting produced no final victory. An armistice was finally signed in 1953. The 38th parallel remained, and remains today, the boundary line between North and South Korea.

The Shifting Power Balance in Asia Western fears led to China's isolation from the major Western powers. China was forced to rely almost entirely on the Soviet Union for both technological and economic aid. In the late 1950s, however, relations between China and the Soviet Union began to deteriorate. Matters grew worse in the 1960s, when military units on both sides of the frontier between the two countries often clashed.

Faced with a serious security threat from the Soviet Union, along with internal problems, Chinese leaders decided to improve relations with the United States. In 1972, President **Richard Nixon** made a state visit to China. He was the first U.S. president to visit the People's Republic of China since its inception in 1949. The two sides agreed to improve relations. In 1979, diplomatic ties were established with the United States. Chinese relations with the Soviet Union gradually improved throughout the 1980s. By the 1990s, China was playing an increasingly active role in Asian affairs.

Reading Check **Examining** Why did China decide to improve relations with the United States?

SECTION 1 ASSESSMENT

Checking for Understanding

1. **Define** commune, permanent revolution, per capita.
2. **Identify** Great Proletarian Cultural Revolution, *Little Red Book,* Deng Xiaoping,Tiananmen Square, Richard Nixon.
3. **Locate** Taiwan, South Korea, North Korea.
4. **Explain** the original plan developed by the United States and the Soviet Union for the future of Korea.
5. **List** the actions the Chinese government took to promote technological development.

Critical Thinking

6. **Compare and Contrast** Identify the changes the Communist takeover brought to China during the 1950s. Then, compare and contrast how policies have changed in China since the 1970s.
7. **Contrasting Information** Use a table like the one below to contrast the policies of the two Chinese leaders Mao Zedong and Deng Xiaoping.

Mao Zedong	Deng Xiaoping

Analyzing Visuals

8. **Compare** the photographs on pages 722 and 723. Imagine you are in each photo. What are you expressing? Is more than one point of view being expressed in each photo? What are some of the things that might happen to you after the event shown in each photo? How will you be remembered by historians?

Writing About History

9. **Descriptive Writing** Pretend that you are a visitor to China during the Cultural Revolution. Write a letter to a friend at home describing the purpose of the Red Guards.

SECTION 1 ASSESSMENT

1. Key terms are in blue.
2. Great Proletarian Cultural Revolution *(p. 725)*; *Little Red Book (p. 725)*; Deng Xiaoping *(p. 725)*; Tiananmen Square *(p. 726)*; Richard Nixon *(p. 728)*
3. See chapter maps.
4. to hold elections after World War II to reunify Korea
5. invited foreign investors, sent students abroad to study science, technology, business
6. 1950s: collectivized, nationalized industry, maintained ties to Soviet Union; since the 1970s: improved relations with United States, modernized industry
7. Mao Zedong: put China under the control of the Communist Party, set out to build a socialist society Deng: introduced economic reforms aimed at modernizing China
8. 722: expresses desire for democracy; 723: expresses support for Mao, communism
9. Answers should be consistent with material presented in this section.

CRITICAL THINKING SKILLBUILDER

Reading a Cartogram

Why Learn This Skill?

Most maps show countries in proportion to their amount of land area. For example, Japan is much smaller than China and is usually depicted that way on a map. Japan, however, has a greater gross national product than China. If we wanted to depict that on a map, how would it look?

Cartograms are maps that show countries according to a value other *than land area. They might portray features such as populations or economies. To visually compare these features, cartograms distort countries' sizes and shapes. This makes it possible to see at a glance how each country or region compares with another in a particular value. Therefore, on a cartogram showing gross national products, Japan looks larger than China.*

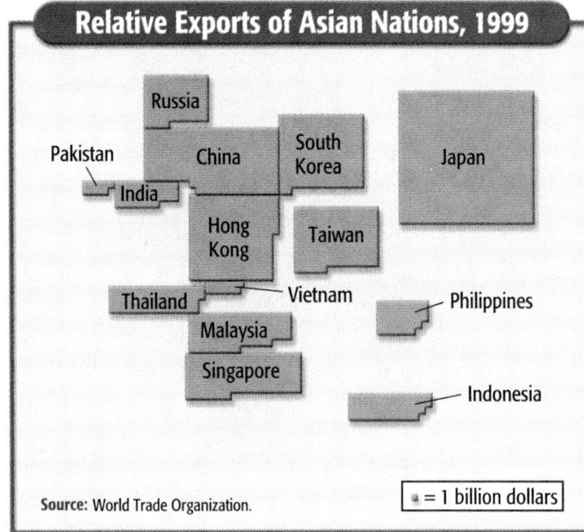

Learning the Skill

To use a cartogram:

- Read the title and key to identify what value the cartogram illustrates.
- Examine the cartogram to see which countries or regions appear.
- Find the largest and smallest countries.
- Compare the cartogram with a conventional land-area map to determine the degree of distortion of particular countries.
- Draw conclusions about the countries and the feature you are comparing.

Practicing the Skill

Study the cartogram on this page and answer these questions.

1. What is the subject of the cartogram?
2. What countries are represented?
3. Which country appears largest on the cartogram? Which appears smallest?
4. Compare the cartogram to the map of Asia found in the Atlas. Which countries are most distorted in size compared to a land-area map?
5. What accounts for these distortions?

Applying the Skill

At the library, find statistics that compare some value for different countries. For example, you might compare the amount of oil consumption of countries in North America.

Convert these statistics into a simple cartogram. Determine the relative size of each country according to the chosen value. If the United States consumes five times more oil than Mexico, then the United States should appear five times larger than Mexico on the cartogram.

Glencoe's **Skillbuilder Interactive Workbook, Level 2,** provides instruction and practice in key social studies skills.

729

ANSWER TO PRACTICING THE SKILL

1. The cartogram shows the relative value of exports of Asian nations in 1999.
2. Russia, Hong Kong, Taiwan, Japan, China, Malaysia, Indonesia, Pakistan, India, Singapore, Philippines, Thailand, Vietnam, South Korea
3. Japan appears as the largest; Pakistan appears as the smallest.
4. Hong Kong and Russia are the most distorted.
5. Hong Kong, which appears as very large, is a city with a tremendous economy and high industrial output; the Asian portion of Russia is sparsely settled and has relatively undeveloped industries compared to the European portion, thus Russia appears as smaller.

Applying the Skill: Students will create cartograms.

CRITICAL THINKING SKILLBUILDER

TEACH

Reading a Cartogram Suggest that students imagine they are members of a school board charged with the responsibility of planning where the city needs new schools. The standard city map shows the various residential areas and the borders of school districts. Ask students to consider how a cartogram would help them. Suggest that if it showed at a glance the relative numbers of school-age children in each district, this would help them to judge the capacity needs. Ask students to brainstorm other situations where a cartogram would be helpful. L2

Additional Practice

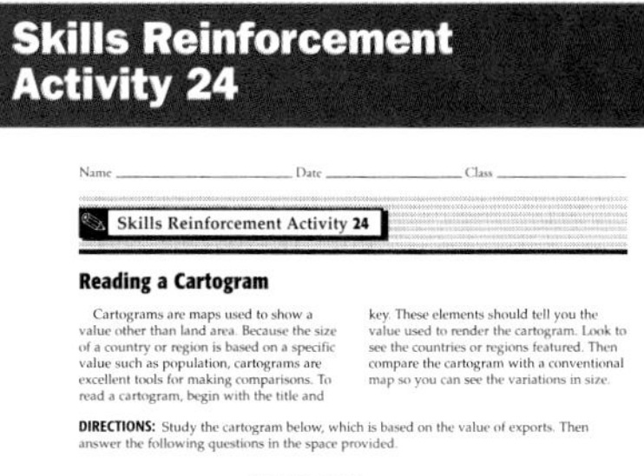
Skills Reinforcement Activity 24

Name ____ Date ____ Class ____

Skills Reinforcement Activity 24

Reading a Cartogram

Cartograms are maps used to show a value other than land area. Because the size of a country or region is based on a specific value such as population, cartograms are excellent tools for making comparisons. To read a cartogram, begin with the title and key. These elements should tell you the value used to render the cartogram. Look to see the countries or regions featured. Then compare the cartogram with a conventional map so you can see the variations in size.

DIRECTIONS: Study the cartogram below, which is based on the value of exports. Then answer the following questions in the space provided.

GLENCOE TECHNOLOGY

CD-ROM

Glencoe Skillbuilder Interactive Workbook CD-ROM, Level 2

This interactive CD-ROM reinforces student mastery of essential social studies skills.

SPECIAL REPORT SUMMARY

Established as a frontier outpost almost 3,000 years ago, old Beijing is being overtaken by hotels, office towers, and nightclubs.

■

Genghis Khan destroyed Beijing in 1215. His grandson rebuilt it 50 years later.

■

The city is laid out according to the principles of *feng shui* so that it will attract positive energy and good luck.

■

The Forbidden City, once open only to the emperor and his family, is now a museum.

■

Mao proclaimed the establishment of the People's Republic of China from the Gate of Heavenly Peace in 1949.

■

Today, entrepreneurs have been building to develop business. Residents wish to retain the character of the old city, and activists want more individual freedom.

TEACH

Points to Discuss

After students have read the selection, discuss the following: **How are Beijing and New York geographically similar?** *(both are near the 40th parallel, spring and autumn are the most comfortable seasons)* **How did the canal connecting Chang Jiang Valley to Beijing change the city?** *(gave Beijing a transportation link to the outside world)* **What evidence is**

TRANSFORMING BEIJING

1

In 1979, after decades of watching China's economy stagnate, Communist Party leade Deng Xiaoping took a gamble. He began relaxing the state's tight economic controls while trying to keep a firm grip on politica power. In the Chinese capital of Beijing, the result of Deng's "second revolution" has been a big construction boom, new foreign investment—and the kind of Western cultural influence that China has resisted for centuries.

Geographically, Beijing's location in Asia is roughly similar to New York's in North America. Both lie near the 40th parallel, and in both places the most comfortable seasons are autumn and spring. But the similarities end there. The city now known as Beijing began as a frontier outpost nearly 3,000 years ago. It was built to guard the North China Plain against marauding groups who attacked through mountain passes in the north.

Without access to the sea or a significant river to link it to the outside world, Beijing might have remained a dusty outpost. But in the seventh century A.D., a 1,000-mile (1,609-km) canal was dug to link the city with the fertile Chang Jiang Valley in the south. Three centuries later the city became the capital of the Liao dynasty. Then came the Mongols under Genghis Khan, who sacked and burned the capital in 1215.

About 50 years later, however, Genghis's grandson, Kublai Khan, rebuilt the city so gloriously that the Venetian traveler Marco Polo marveled at its streets "so straight and wide that you can see right along from end to end and from one gate to another." Kublai Khan's Dadu (meaning "Great Capital"), Marco Polo wrote, "is arranged like a chessboard."

Indeed, Beijing is laid out on a precise north-south axis, in harmony with the ancient practice of *feng shui* ("wind and water"). According to this tradition, buildings (and the furnishings inside them) must be properly aligned to take advantage of the natural energy (*qi*) that flows through all things. The proper placement of a house or temple will thus attract positive *qi* and good luck; the wrong placement invites disaster.

The north-south axis passes directly through Qian Men (Front Gate), proceeds through the red walls of Tian An Men (Gate of Heavenly Peace), and then on to Wu Men (Meridian Gate), beyond which lies the Forbidden City.

An area once barred to everyone except the emperor, his family, and his most favored concubines, guards, and

Teacher's Notes

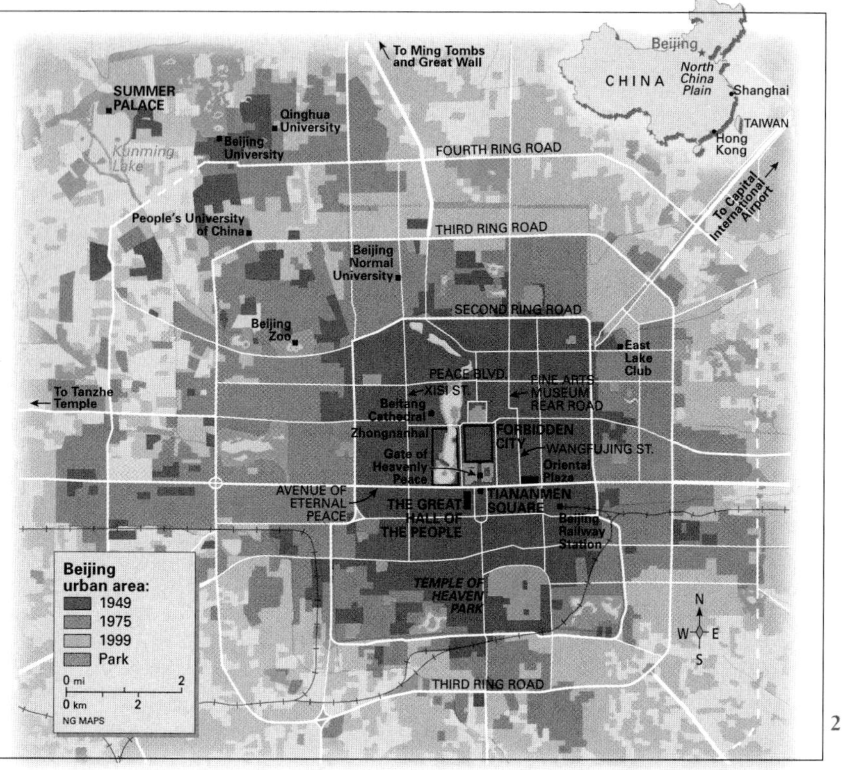

officials, the Forbidden City lay at the very center of a series of cities-within-cities, concentric rectangles defined by their high walls. Today the walls are largely gone and the Forbidden City is a museum overflowing with tourists.

The Gate of Heavenly Peace, on the north side of nearby Tiananmen Square, is the spiritual heart of all China. Centuries ago, orders from the emperor were sent down from the top of the gate to officials waiting below.

3

1 A migrant worker balances on his cart as he stacks bricks at the construction site of a large apartment complex.

2 The Forbidden City (above map) was once considered the stable core of the empire. In spite of its growth, urban Beijing accounts for only a fraction of the territory the city includes. By an administrative decision of 1959, Beijing's boundaries now cover a 6,600 square-mile (17,094 square-km) municipality that includes satellite towns and agricultural communes as well as such tourist attractions as the Ming Tombs and the Great Wall.

3 Mao Zedong's mausoleum and the Monument to the People's Heroes dominate Tiananmen Square.

there that Beijing was not rebuilt in a haphazard fashion? *(Marco Polo noted that the "streets were straight and wide" and "arranged like a chessboard." Principles of* feng shui *determined that the city would be laid out on a precise north-south axis.)* **Describe the layout of the Forbidden City?** *(It was a city within cities, set within concentric high-walled rectangles.)* **What is considered the spiritual heart of all China?** *(The Gate of Heavenly Peace)* **What monuments and displays around Tiananmen Square commemorate Mao and communism?** *(Mao's portrait, Monument to The People's Heroes, Great Hall of the People, mausoleum)* **What evidence is there of Deng Xiaoping's experiment in free enterprise?** *McDonald's, Kentucky Fried Chicken, night clubs, department stores, tourist centers, the Oriental Plaza)* **How many people will Tiananmen Square hold?** *(one million)* **What might be unusual to Westerners about the parking structure at the Oriental Plaza?** *(the fact that it only holds 2,000 cars, yet 10,000 bicycles)* **How has China benefited from the increase in free enterprise?** *(production has climbed steadily, per capita income has almost doubled, business opportunities have increased)* **Describe the 1989 events at Tiananmen Square.** *(Unarmed demonstrators protesting government corruption were attacked by the Chinese Army.)* **How many square miles are included within the boundaries of Beijing?** *(6,600 square miles [17,094 square km])*

FUN FACTS

- Color is symbolic in China. Red is a positive color. It stands for good fortune, prosperity, and fame. Brides wear red, and red envelopes of money are given at weddings. White can represent purity, but is also associated with sadness and death. It is considered bad luck to write words of congratulation on white paper. Yellow is the imperial color and represents China itself. The last emperor of China, Pu Yi, wrote that as a boy he believed everything was yellow, since he saw so much of it.
- The giant panda, found only in China, is an endangered species, with only 1,000 surviving in the wild.
- China extends across five time zones, however, all of China conforms to a single time zone. If you live in eastern or western China, the sun will not be directly overhead at noon.

NATIONAL GEOGRAPHIC

Connecting Across Time

Despite protests by human rights activists, the International Olympic Committee (IOC) voted to conduct the 2008 Summer Olympic games in Beijing, the first time such an event is to be held in China. China planned to spend more than $20 billion to construct an Olympic village for the athletes, build competition venues, improve transportation and communication systems, and cut down on industrial pollution. Thirty-two competition sites will be designated within the city of Beijing. The city was told by the IOC to develop an alternative to Tiananmen Square, which Beijing planned to use as a beach volleyball site.

Who? What? Where? When?

Imperial Gardens The gardens were constructed at the request of emperors of different generations. Because the Forbidden City was built to convey an atmosphere of royal authority, gardens were added to give the emperors and their families an area for recreation and relaxation. The Imperial Gardens are unlike Western gardens which are designed to showcase plants. The gardens of Beijing include long covered corridors, pavilions set over a lake, and free-standing decorative walls.

4

5

From that same high place, on the afternoon of October 1, 1949, Mao Zedong formally proclaimed the establishment of the People's Republic of China. His portrait now hangs on the wall of the gate, staring out at the square and providing a backdrop for tourist photographs.

In the late 1950s, during the Great Leap Forward, homes around Tiananmen Square were torn down to expand the square from 27 acres (10.9 ha) to 98 acres (39.7 ha)—large enough to hold a million people. In the center stands the 124-foot (37.8-m) high Monument to the People's Heroes. On the west side is the many-columned Great Hall of the People, where the government meets and visiting dignitaries are entertained. Across the square on the east side is the Historical Museum. To the south, opposite his portrait on Tian An Men, is the huge mausoleum where Mao Zedong's body is on display.

■

In the 20-some years since Deng Xiaoping's experiment in free enterprise began, the blocky Soviet-style monuments built by Mao have been overtaken by the bright lights of McDonald's, Kentucky Fried Chicken, and thousands of private restaurants and nightclubs catering to foreign visitors and investors.

The building boom has swept away much of what was once a major characteristic of the old city: the low, walled alleyways called *hutong*. Some of the family compounds were hundreds of years old and housed three generations. The government is moving more than 2 million of the city's 11 million residents out to the suburbs to make room for new tourism centers, department stores, and expensive apartment compounds.

As one long-time Beijing resident put it, "The old city is gone. Old things like the Forbidden City or a temple are scattered between skyscrapers like toys thrown here and there. Old Beijing is dismembered."

Along with all the tearing down

CRITICAL THINKING ACTIVITY

Analyzing Have students write an essay in which they identify examples of political, economic, and social oppression and violations of human rights throughout history. Make sure that students include examples of slavery, the Holocaust, and politically-motivated mass murders in Cambodia, China, and the Soviet Union. Ask students to assess the degree to which human rights and democratic ideals and practices have been advanced throughout the world during the twentieth century. If students need assistance identifying political, economic, and social oppression, have them consider examples and strategies of oppression such as forced assimilation, voting requirements, sanctions, and absence of labor laws for adults and children. **L2**

and building up that has occurred in the last two decades, China's production has climbed steadily. Per capita annual income for city dwellers has almost doubled since 1990 to more than $600. Foreign businesses hoping for a share of the vast Chinese market have rushed in.

Not all of these entrepreneurs have been welcomed by Beijing's residents, however. A mammoth complex called the Oriental Plaza, for example, has been the focus of controversy. Built by a Hong Kong business partnership, the complex contains eight office towers, two apartment towers, and a five-star international hotel. It also includes more than a million square feet (93,000 square m) of retail mall and a parking structure for 2,000 cars and 10,000 bicycles.

Even for a city of large monuments, the Oriental Plaza is beyond big. Residents complain that the project destroys the character of the old city, dwarfing as it does The Gate of Heavenly Peace.

As the site of countless demonstrations over the years, Tiananmen Square has become familiar to television viewers around the world. The most vivid scenes in recent memory are from early June 1989, when the Chinese Army attacked unarmed demonstrators who had been protesting government corruption. Perhaps as many as 2,000 people were killed. Although the government would prefer the event be forgotten, the anniversary of the June 4th attack has been marked repeatedly with some form of protest.

Yet even as the government clamps down on highly visible political demonstrations, activists have found a more subtle way to make their points—the Internet. More and more young Chinese are making their way online. Their access to an open market of ideas and uncensored information brings with it a new sense of individualism. Undoubtedly this will have a lasting impact on the future of their city and their nation.

4 **Demolition of the old makes way for the new as downtown Beijing undergoes a massive face-lift.**

5 **Residents of old family compounds haul out their belongings as they load a truck to move to housing projects in the suburbs.**

6 **Students protest in Tiananmen Square in 1989. The peaceful protests turned violent when the army attacked.**

INTERPRETING THE PAST

1. Why was Beijing established?
2. How is the capital city laid out ?
3. How has Beijing changed during the last twenty years?
4. Do you think the lives of the residents of Beijing have improved or deteriorated during the last two decades?

CURRICULUM CONNECTION

Architecture *Hutongs* are the lanes or alleyways formed by a series of compounds (houses set around a courtyard). Currently, one-third of Beijing's population lives in that style of housing. The Chinese government has provided modern housing but many residents prefer the traditional housing. The Chinese realize the architecture has great historical value as it reflects changes in the Yuan, Ming, and Qing dynasties. Today the *hutong* have become tourist destinations. The width of the lanes varies considerably. They can be 32 feet (10m) to slightly less than 16 inches (40 cm). Ask students to locate photographs of the *hutong.*

Enrich

Ask students to explain the following Chinese proverbs. Encourage students to see if there is an equivalent proverb in English.

1. Once on a tiger's back, it is hard to alight.
2. An ant may well destroy a whole dam.
3. A book holds a house of gold.
4. Great souls have wills; feeble ones have only wishes.

Critical Thinking

After students have read about the ancient city of Beijing, ask them to identify ways that archaeologists, anthropologists, historians, and geographers analyze limited evidence to find information about the past. **L2**

INTERPRETING THE PAST

Answers:

1. It was established as a frontier outpost, 3,000 years ago, to guard the North China Plain from marauding groups.
2. It is laid out in a north-south axis, with straight streets according to the principles of *feng shui.*
3. increasingly modern buildings, business opportunities, increased wages, and tearing down of old buildings
4. Students should consider carefully what is meant by better. Students should also recognize that people of different cultures might value things differently than they would.

1 FOCUS

Section Overview

This section explores the birth of India and Pakistan and the progress of newly independent states in Southeast Asia.

BELLRINGER
Skillbuilder Activity

 Project transparency and have students answer questions.

 Available as a blackline master.

Daily Focus Skills Transparency 24–2

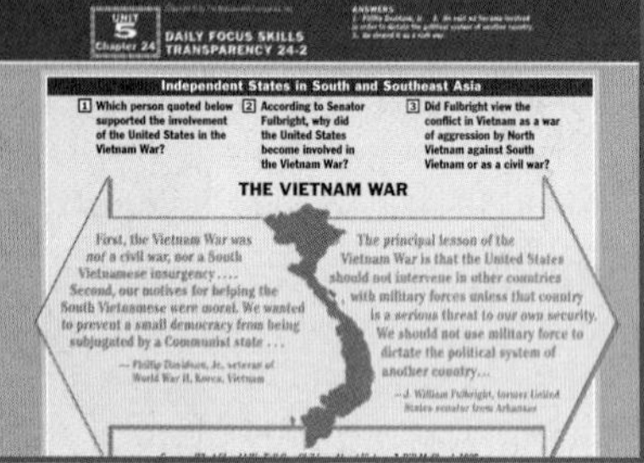

Guide to Reading

Answers to Graphic: Challenges in India: growing population, worsening poverty, ethnic strife, religious strife

Preteaching Vocabulary: Explain the significance of a *stalemate. (A stalemate is an impasse in which neither side in a conflict can make significant gains.)* L2

SECTION 2 Independent States in South and Southeast Asia

Guide to Reading

Main Ideas
- British India was divided into two states: India, mostly Hindu, and Pakistan, mostly Muslim.
- Many of the newly independent states of Southeast Asia attempted to form democratic governments but often fell subject to military regimes.

Key Terms
stalemate, discrimination

People to Identify
Pol Pot, Ferdinand Marcos

Places to Locate
Punjab, Bangladesh

Preview Questions
1. What policies did Jawaharlal Nehru put into effect in India?
2. What internal and external problems did the Southeast Asian nations face after 1945?

Reading Strategy
Categorizing Information Use a web diagram like the one below to identify challenges India faced after independence.

Preview of Events

1945 · 1950 · 1955 · 1960 · 1965 · 1970 · 1975

- **1948** A Hindu militant assassinates Mohandas Gandhi
- **1949** The independent Republic of Indonesia is established
- **1966** Indira Gandhi becomes prime minister of India
- **1971** East Pakistan becomes the independent nation of Bangladesh

Voices from the Past

An example of Western influence in India

In 1989, Maneka Gandhi, former minister of the environment for India, wrote an article entitled "Why India Doesn't Need Fast Food" in the *Hindustan Times:*

> ❝India's decision to allow Pepsi Foods Ltd. to open 60 restaurants in India—30 each of Pizza Hut and Kentucky Fried Chicken—marks the first entry of multinational, meat-based junk-food chains into India. . . . The implications of allowing junk-food chains into India are quite stark. As the name denotes, the foods served at Kentucky Fried Chicken are chicken-based and fried. This is the worst combination possible for the body and can create a host of health problems, including obesity, high cholesterol, heart ailments, and many kinds of cancer. . . . Can our health systems take care of the fallout from these chicken restaurants?❞
>
> —***World Press Review,*** **September 1995**

Many Indians continue to reject Western influence.

India Divided

At the end of World War II, British India's Muslims and Hindus were bitterly divided. The leaders in India realized that British India would have to be divided into two countries, one Hindu (India) and one Muslim (Pakistan). Pakistan consisted of two regions separated by India. One part, West Pakistan, was to the northwest of India. The other, East Pakistan, was to the northeast.

SECTION RESOURCES

Reproducible Masters
- Reproducible Lesson Plan 24–2
- Daily Lecture and Discussion Notes 24–2
- Guided Reading Activity 24–2
- Section Quiz 24–2
- Reading Essentials and Study Guide 24––2

Transparencies
- Daily Focus Skills Transparency 24–2

Multimedia
- Interactive Tutor Self-Assessment CD-ROM
- ExamView® Pro Testmaker CD-ROM
- Presentation Plus! CD-ROM

On August 15, 1947, India and Pakistan became independent. Millions of Hindus and Muslims fled across the new borders, Hindus toward India and Muslims toward Pakistan. As a result of these mass migrations, over a million people were killed including Mohandas Gandhi, who was assassinated by a Hindu militant on January 30, 1948.

In the same year, Ceylon, an island off the coast of India, also received its independence from Britain. Known as Sri Lanka since 1972, the new nation has been torn by ethnic conflict between the majority Sinhalese and the minority Tamils.

Reading Check **Summarizing** Why was British India divided into two new nations after World War II? What was the immediate result?

The New India

With independence, the Indian National Congress, renamed the Congress Party, began to rule India. Jawaharlal Nehru (jah•wah•HAR•lahl NAY•roo), the new prime minister, was a popular figure with strong ideas about the future of Indian society. He admired Great Britain's political institutions and the socialist ideals of the British Labour Party. Nehru's vision of the new India combined a parliamentary form of government led by a prime minister. In his view the new India would have a moderate socialist economic structure.

Accordingly, the state took over the ownership of major industries, utilities, and transportation. Private enterprise was permitted at the local level. Farmland remained in private hands. India developed a large industrial sector, and industrial production almost tripled between 1950 and 1965.

Nehru died in 1964. In 1966, the leaders of the Congress Party selected Nehru's daughter, Indira Gandhi (who was not related to Mohandas Gandhi), as the new prime minister. Except for a brief 22-month interval in the late 1970s, she retained that office until 1984.

India faced many problems during this period. Its growing population was one of the most serious. Even in 1948, the country had been unable to support its population. In the 1950s and 1960s, India's population grew at a rate of more than 2 percent per year. In spite of government efforts, India was unable to control this growth.

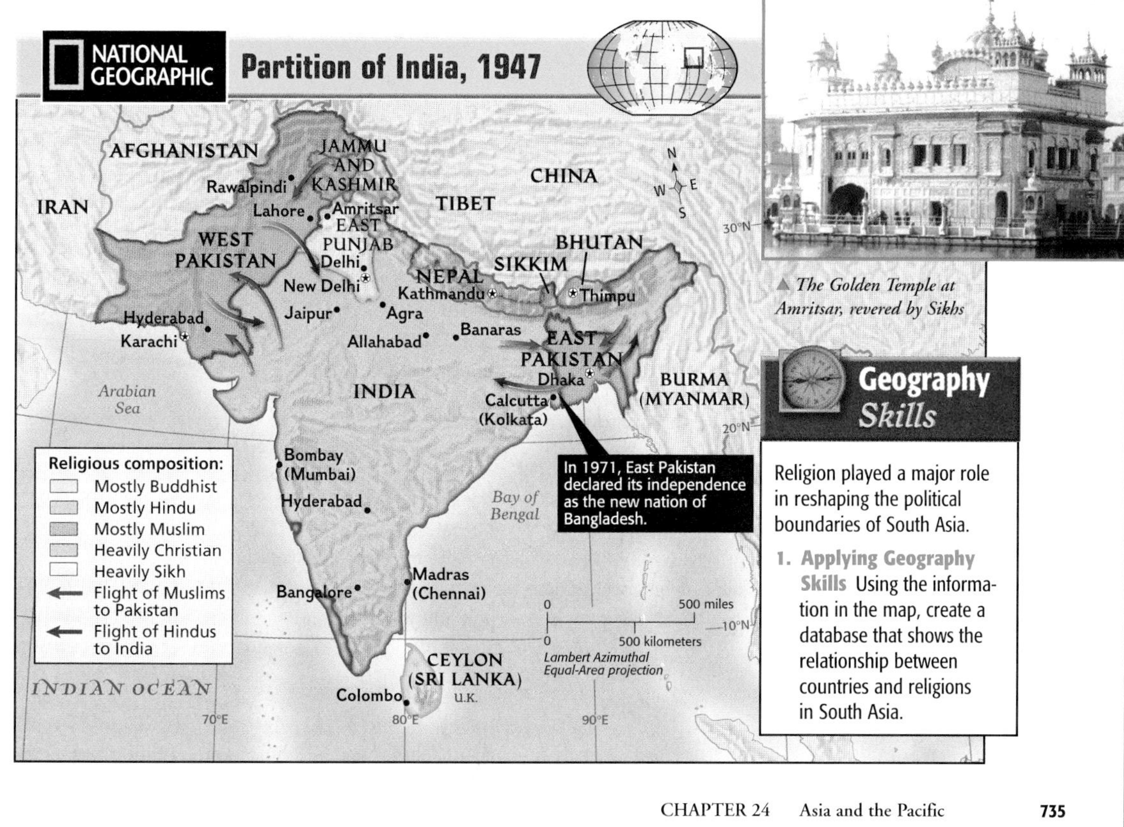

▲ *The Golden Temple at Amritsar, revered by Sikhs*

Geography Skills

Religion played a major role in reshaping the political boundaries of South Asia.

1. **Applying Geography Skills** Using the information in the map, create a database that shows the relationship between countries and religions in South Asia.

2 TEACH

Geography Skills

Answer:

1. Students will create a database.

Answer: because the Hindus and Muslims were bitterly divided; mass migrations and violence resulted; millions died

Daily Lecture and Discussion Notes 24–2

Guided Reading Activity 24–2

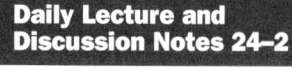

EXTENDING THE CONTENT

The Sikhs The Sikh religion is centered in the Indian state of Punjab, an important agricultural region. Sikhs represent a disproportionate number of the professional people in India. Sikh males are distinguished by their beards and the turbans that cover their hair (which they are forbidden to cut). They must carry a ceremonial dagger for religious reasons (which can lead to difficulties with U.S. authorities). Indira Gandhi used Sikhs as her bodyguards because they are renowned as warriors. An attack on the Sikh's holiest shrine, the Golden Temple at Amritsar, to clear out Sikh extremists, resulted in 1,200 deaths and led to Indira Gandhi's assassination by her own bodyguards.

Reading Check

Answer: religious and ethnic conflicts, poverty

Reading Check

Answer: internal conflicts, including growing division between East and West Pakistan that resulted in civil war and independence for East Pakistan as Bangladesh; both nations (Pakistan and Bangladesh) have had difficulty in establishing stable governments; both remain poor

TURNING POINT

How was independence finally achieved in Southeast Asia? *(World War II hastened the process of independence in Southeast Asia, just as it did in Africa.)* L1

Who?What?Where?When?

Independence Diversity contributed to the breakup of the Indian subcontinent. India and Pakistan separated because of religious differences, and Bangladesh later broke off from Pakistan because of language and cultural differences. Religious and ethnic diversity within India, Pakistan, and Sri Lanka continues to create unrest.

Critical Thinking

Ask students to write an essay in which they analyze the influence of Gandhi on events of the twentieth century. **WH:** 10B

People In History

Mother Teresa of Calcutta

1910–1997

Roman Catholic nun

Mother Teresa was born Agnes Gonxha Bojaxhiu to Albanian parents. At age 18, she went to Ireland to become a missionary nun. After training in both Ireland and Darjeeling, India, she took her religious vows in 1937 and adopted the name Teresa from Saint Theresa of Lisieux, the patron saint of foreign missionaries.

When she was sent to Calcutta, Teresa was amazed at the large numbers of suffering people she saw on the streets. She believed it was her destiny to help these people and, in 1948, the Vatican gave her permission to follow her calling. In 1950, she and her followers established the Missionaries of Charity to help the poor and the sick.

Over the years, Mother Teresa and her followers established numerous centers throughout the world to aid the hungry, the sick, and the poor. When she won the Nobel Peace Prize in 1979 for her humanitarian efforts, Mother Teresa asked that the money for the celebration banquet be donated to the poor. When Mother Teresa died in 1997, she left behind a legacy that continues to inspire people around the world.

One result was worsening poverty for many people. Millions lived in vast city slums. It was in the slums of Calcutta, India, that Mother Teresa helped the poor, sick, and dying Indian people.

Growing ethnic and religious strife presented another problem in India. This conflict involved the **Sikhs,** followers of a religion based on both Hindu and Muslim ideas. Many Sikhs lived in a northern province called the **Punjab.** Militant Sikhs demanded that this province be independent from India. Gandhi refused and, in 1984, she used military force against Sikh rebels taking refuge in the Golden Temple, one of the Sikhs' most important shrines. More than 450 Sikhs were killed. Seeking revenge for these killings, two Sikh members of Gandhi's personal bodyguard assassinated her later that year.

Indira Gandhi's son Rajiv replaced his mother as prime minister and began to move the government in new directions. Private enterprise was encouraged, as well as foreign investment. His successors have continued to transfer state-run industries into private hands and to rely on the free market. This has led to a noticeable growth in India's middle class.

Rajiv Gandhi was prime minister from 1984 to 1989. He was assassinated in 1991 while campaigning for reelection. In the following years, the Congress Party remained the leading political party, but its powerful hold over the Indian people was gone. New parties competed for control of the national and state governments. At the same time, tensions between Hindus and Muslims continued to disturb India's stability.

Reading Check **Examining** What are the underlying causes of political strife in India?

Pakistan

Unlike its neighbor India, Pakistan was a completely new nation when it attained independence in 1947. Its early years were marked by intense internal conflicts. Most dangerous was the growing division between East and West Pakistan. These two separate regions are very different in nature. West Pakistan, for example, is a dry and mountainous area, while East Pakistan has marshy land densely populated with rice farmers.

Many people in East Pakistan felt that the government, based in West Pakistan, ignored their needs. In 1971, East Pakistan declared its independence. After a brief civil war, it became the new nation of **Bangladesh.**

Both Bangladesh and Pakistan (as West Pakistan is now known) have had difficulty in establishing stable governments. In both nations, military officials have often seized control of the civilian government. Both nations also remain very poor.

Reading Check **Describing** What problems did Pakistan face after it achieved independence?

Southeast Asia

TURNING POINT **After World War II, most of the states of Southeast Asia received independence from their colonial rulers. France's refusal to let go of Indochina led to a long war in Vietnam that ultimately involved other Southeast Asian nations and the United States in a widening conflict.**

Colonies in Southeast Asia, like colonies elsewhere, gained their independence at the end of World War II. The process varied considerably across the region, however.

Independence In July 1946, the United States granted total independence to the Philippines. Great

MEETING INDIVIDUAL NEEDS

Visual Learners Have students work together in small groups to create two time lines. One time line should be based on important events in India's history between World War II and the present; the second one should be based on important events in Pakistan's history over the same period. Tell students to include political, economic, and cultural events. Before advising students on the appropriate scale to use (for example, three inches per year), determine how much wall space you have available to display all the time lines from this chapter. Ask each group to present its two time lines, and allow other groups to ask questions and add dates, if necessary. L2

Britain was also willing to end its colonial rule in Southeast Asia. In 1948, Burma became independent. Malaya's turn came in 1957.

The Netherlands and France were less willing to abandon their colonial empires in Southeast Asia. The Dutch tried to suppress a new Indonesian republic that had been set up by Achmed Sukarno. When the Indonesian Communist Party attempted to seize power, however, the United States pressured the Netherlands to grant independence to Sukarno and his non-Communist Nationalist Party. In 1949, the Netherlands recognized the new Republic of Indonesia.

The situation was very different in Vietnam. The leading force in the movement against colonial French rule there was the local Communist Party, led by Ho Chi Minh. In August 1945, the **Vietminh,** an alliance of forces under Communist leadership, seized power throughout most of Vietnam. Ho Chi Minh was elected president of a new provisional republic in Hanoi. France, however, refused to accept the new government and seized the southern part of the country.

The Vietnam War Over the following years, France fought Ho Chi Minh's Vietminh for control of Vietnam without success. In 1954, France finally agreed to a peace settlement. Vietnam was divided into two parts. In the north, the Communists were based in Hanoi, and in the south, the non-Communists were based in Saigon.

Both sides agreed to hold elections in two years to create a single government. Instead, however, the conflict continued. The United States, opposed to any

NATIONAL GEOGRAPHIC Vietnam War, 1968–1975

Major Viet Cong assault during the Tet Offensive, 1968
Ho Chi Minh Trail
U.S. and South Vietnamese offensives
Major U.S. base
Areas in neutral countries bombed by U.S.

U.S. conducts extensive bombing of Hanoi, Dec. 1972.
U.S. mines Haiphong Harbor, 1972.
Invasion of Laos, Feb.–Mar. 1971
Invasion of Cambodia, April–June 1970
Surrender of South Vietnam, U.S. withdrawal, April 1975

CHINA
Lao Cai
Pingxiang
Dien Bien Phu
Red R.
Hanoi
Haiphong
Red River Delta
MYANMAR (BURMA)
LAOS
NORTH VIETNAM
Gulf of Tonkin
Mekong R.
Vientiane
DMZ (Demilitarized Zone)
Quang Tri
17th Parallel
Hue
Da Nang
Duy Xuyen
Kham Duc
South China Sea
THAILAND
Khe Sanh
Dak To
Quang Ngai
Kontum
Pleiku
Qui Nhon
Bangkok
CAMBODIA
SOUTH VIETNAM
Tonle Sap
Ban Me Thuot
Nha Trang
Da Lat
Phnom Penh
Tay Ninh
Bien Hoa
Saigon
My Tho
Can Tho
Ben Tri
Mekong Delta
Gulf of Thailand
20°N
15°N
10°N
105°E
110°E
0 200 miles
0 200 kilometers
Mercator projection

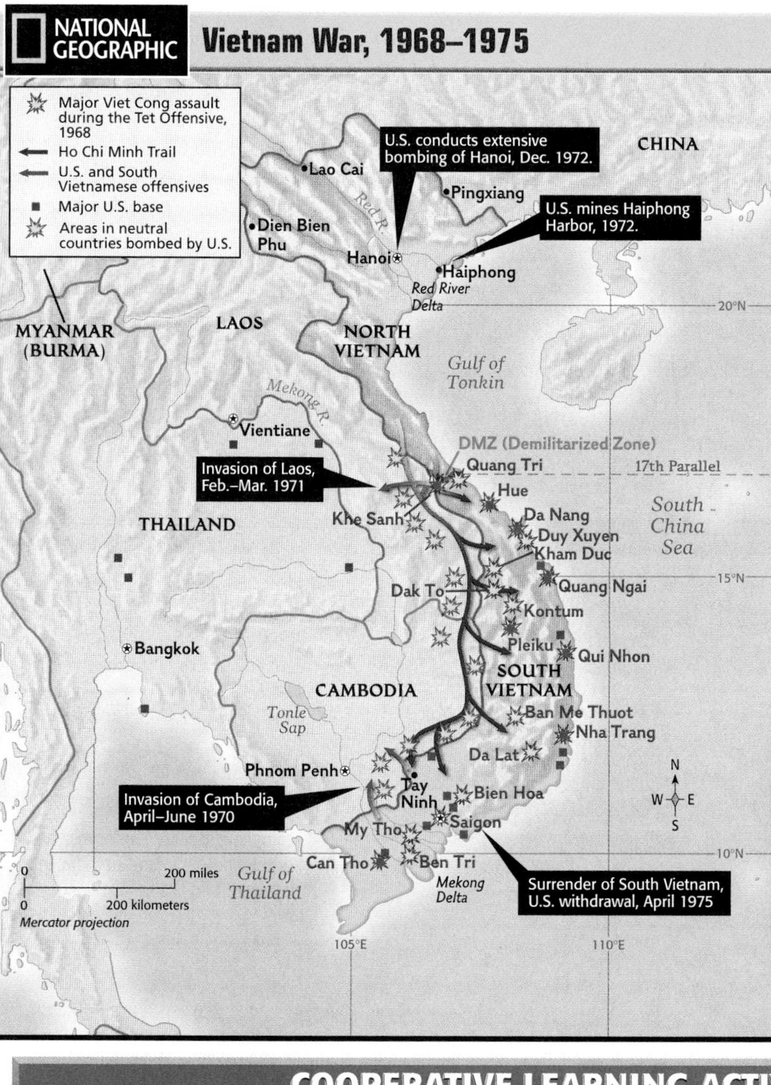

Geography Skills

Concern over the spread of communism led the United States to become involved in the Vietnam War.

1. **Interpreting Maps** Create a time line showing the key events in the Vietnam War as presented on this map.
2. **Applying Geography Skills** Do further research and write an essay explaining how geography impacted the war in Vietnam.

American soldiers in Vietnam

CHAPTER 24
Section 2, 734-738

Geography Skills

Answers:

1. Students should place dates from black boxes on map on a time line, creating an absolute time line of events.
2. Answers will vary depending on research; some topics students can investigate include the need for an air war in Vietnam and the relationship between Vietnam's geography and the use of guerrilla tactics in the war.

3 ASSESS

Assign Section 2 Assessment as homework or as an in-class activity.

Have students use **Interactive Tutor Self-Assessment CD-ROM.**

Section Quiz 24–2

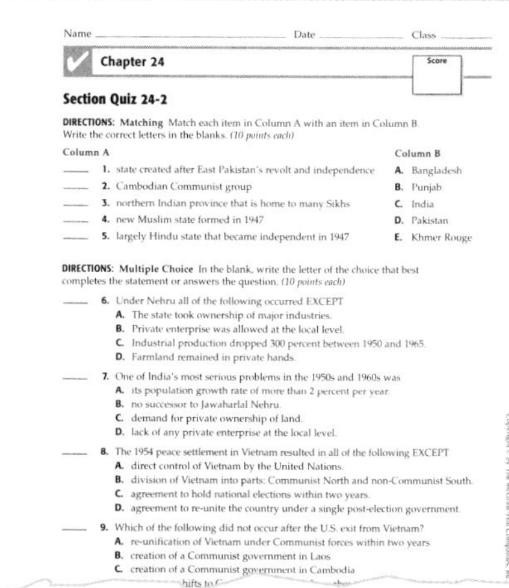

Name ______ Date ______ Class ______

Chapter 24 Score

Section Quiz 24-2

DIRECTIONS: Matching Match each item in Column A with an item in Column B. Write the correct letters in the blanks. *(10 points each)*

Column A	Column B
___ 1. state created after East Pakistan's revolt and independence	A. Bangladesh
___ 2. Cambodian Communist group	B. Punjab
___ 3. northern Indian province that is home to many Sikhs	C. India
___ 4. new Muslim state formed in 1947	D. Pakistan
___ 5. largely Hindu state that became independent in 1947	E. Khmer Rouge

DIRECTIONS: Multiple Choice In the blank, write the letter of the choice that best completes the statement or answers the question. *(10 points each)*

___ 6. Under Nehru all of the following occurred EXCEPT
A. The state took ownership of major industries.
B. Private enterprise was allowed at the local level.
C. Industrial production dropped 300 percent between 1950 and 1965.
D. Farmland remained in private hands.

___ 7. One of India's most serious problems in the 1950s and 1960s was
A. its population growth rate of more than 2 percent per year.
B. no successor to Jawaharlal Nehru.
C. demand for private ownership of land.
D. lack of any private enterprise at the local level.

___ 8. The 1954 peace settlement in Vietnam resulted in all of the following EXCEPT
A. direct control of Vietnam by the United Nations.
B. division of Vietnam into parts: Communist North and non-Communist South.
C. agreement to hold national elections within two years.
D. agreement to re-unite the country under a single post-election government.

___ 9. Which of the following did not occur after the U.S. exit from Vietnam?
A. re-unification of Vietnam under Communist forces within two years
B. creation of a Communist government in Laos
C. creation of a Communist government in Cambodia

COOPERATIVE LEARNING ACTIVITY

Creating a Poster Organize the class into seven teams, one for each country being studied: India, Pakistan, Bangladesh, Vietnam, Indonesia, Cambodia, and the Philippines. Each team should assign individual members to research one of the following topics: religion, economy, language, education, government (type, current leadership, and perceived strength and weaknesses). Instruct each team to create a chart in poster form that will summarize what they learn about their assigned country. Have students display the completed charts and compare and contrast the seven nations. L1

For grading this activity, refer to the ***Performance Assessment Activities*** booklet.

Reading Check

Answer: The U.S. was opposed to the further spread of communism and wanted to prevent a Communist victory in Vietnam. By 1973, American public opinion on the war was sharply divided, leading the U.S. to withdraw troops from Vietnam.

Reading Essentials and Study Guide 24–2

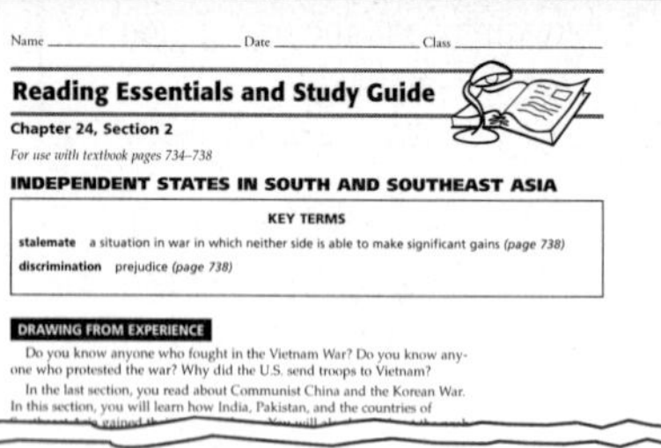

Name ______ Date ______ Class ______

Reading Essentials and Study Guide

Chapter 24, Section 2

For use with textbook pages 734–738

INDEPENDENT STATES IN SOUTH AND SOUTHEAST ASIA

KEY TERMS

stalemate a situation in war in which neither side is able to make significant gains *(page 738)*

discrimination prejudice *(page 738)*

DRAWING FROM EXPERIENCE

Do you know anyone who fought in the Vietnam War? Do you know anyone who protested the war? Why did the U.S. send troops to Vietnam?

In the last section, you read about Communist China and the Korean War. In this section, you will learn how India, Pakistan, and the countries of

Reteaching Activity

Have students locate India, Pakistan, Bangladesh, the Philippines, Burma, Indonesia, and Vietnam on a map. Ask them to identify the year each country achieved independence and to summarize the contemporary challenges each country faces. **L1**

4 CLOSE

Lead students in a discussion of the problems that ethnic, religious, economic, and social forces create when countries become independent. **L1**

further spread of communism, began to provide aid to South Vietnam. In spite of this aid, South Vietnamese Communist guerrillas known as Viet Cong, supported by military units from North Vietnam, were on the verge of seizing control of the entire country by early 1965.

In March 1965, President Lyndon Johnson decided to send U.S. troops to South Vietnam to prevent a total victory for the Communists. The Communist government in North Vietnam responded by sending more of its forces into the south.

By the end of the 1960s, the war had reached a stalemate—neither side was able to make significant gains. With American public opinion sharply divided, President Richard Nixon reached an agreement with North Vietnam in 1973 that allowed the United States to withdraw its forces. Within two years, Communist armies had forcibly reunited Vietnam.

The reunification of Vietnam under Communist rule had an immediate impact on the region. By the end of the year, both Laos and Cambodia had Communist governments. In Cambodia, a brutal revolutionary regime under the dictator **Pol Pot,** leader of the **Khmer Rouge** (kuh•MEHR ROOZH), massacred more than a million Cambodians. However, the Communist triumph in Indochina did not lead to the "falling dominoes" that many U.S. policy makers had feared (see Chapter 20).

Government in the Independent States In the beginning, many of the leaders of the newly independent states in Southeast Asia admired Western political and economic practices. They hoped to form democratic, capitalist states like those in the West.

By the end of the 1950s, however, hopes for rapid economic growth had failed. Internal disputes within the new countries weakened democratic governments, opening the door to both military and one-party autocratic regimes.

In more recent years, some Southeast Asian societies have shown signs of moving again toward more democratic governments. One example is the Philippines. There, President **Ferdinand Marcos** came to power in 1965. Fraud and corruption became widespread in the Marcos regime. In the early 1980s, Marcos was accused of involvement in the killing of Benigno Aquino, a leader of the political opposition. A massive public uprising forced Marcos to flee the country. In 1986, Corazon Aquino, wife of the murdered opposition leader, became president and worked for democratic reforms.

Women in South and Southeast Asia Across South and Southeast Asia, women's roles have changed considerably. After independence, India's leaders sought to extend women's rights. The constitution of 1950 forbade discrimination (prejudicial treatment) based on gender and called for equal pay for equal work. Child marriage was outlawed. Women were encouraged to attend school and to enter the labor market. In Southeast Asia, virtually all of the newly independent states granted women full legal and political rights. Women have become more active in politics and occasionally hold senior political or corporate positions.

Reading Check **Identifying** Give the reasons for the United States's entry into and withdrawal from the Vietnam War.

SECTION 2 ASSESSMENT

Checking for Understanding

1. **Define** stalemate, discrimination.
2. **Identify** Sikhs, Vietminh, Pol Pot, Khmer Rouge, Ferdinand Marcos.
3. **Locate** Punjab, Bangladesh.
4. **Explain** how the reunification of Vietnam under Communist rule affected the region.
5. **Summarize** Nehru's vision of the new India.

Critical Thinking

6. **Evaluate** Has the division of British India into two countries been beneficial? Explain your answer.
7. **Organizing Information** Use a table like the one below to list the political status or type of government of the Southeast Asian countries discussed in this section.

Country		
Government		

Analyzing Visuals

8. **Examine** the photograph on page 735, then locate Amritsar on the map. How does Amritsar's location support the statement that Sikhism has been influenced by both Hinduism and Islam?

Writing About History

9. **Expository Writing** Write an essay comparing political, economic, and cultural developments in India and Pakistan from World War II to the present.

SECTION 2 ASSESSMENT

1. Key terms are in blue.
2. Sikhs *(p. 736)*; Vietminh *(p. 737)*; Pol Pot *(p. 738)*; Khmer Rouge *(p. 738)*; Ferdinand Marcos *(p. 738)*
3. See chapter maps.
4. contributed to Communist rule in Laos, Cambodia
5. It combined a parliamentary form of government led by a prime minister with a moderate socialist economic structure.
6. The division allowed groups more autonomy but left a legacy of conflict.
7. Philippines: democracy; Vietnam: communism; Cambodia: communism; Laos: communism
8. The city is located in Hindu-dominated India but is near a traditionally Muslim region.
9. Students will write an essay comparing political, economic, and cultural developments in India and Pakistan.

SECTION 3 Japan and the Pacific

Guide to Reading

Main Ideas
- Japan and the "Asian tigers" have created successful industrial societies.
- Although Australia and New Zealand have identified themselves culturally and politically with Europe, in recent years they have been drawing closer to their Asian neighbors.

Key Terms
occupied, state capitalism

People to Identify
Douglas MacArthur, Kim Il Sung, Syngman Rhee

Places to Locate
Singapore, Hong Kong

Preview Questions
1. What important political, economic, and social changes have occurred in Japan since 1945?
2. What did the "Asian tigers" accomplish in Asia?

Reading Strategy
Categorizing Information Use a table like the one below to list the key areas of industrial development in South Korea, Taiwan, and Singapore.

South Korea	Taiwan	Singapore

Preview of Events

1940 · 1950 · 1960 · 1970 · 1980 · 1990 · 2000

- **1947** Japan adopts new constitution
- **1951** A peace treaty restores Japanese independence
- **1963** General Chung Hee Park is elected president of South Korea
- **1997** Great Britain returns control of Hong Kong to mainland China

Voices from the Past

Japanese woman at work in a Toyota factory

In an introduction to the book *Japanese Women,* published in 1995, Kumiko Fujimura-Fanselow wrote:

> ❝A quick glance at educational statistics reveals a higher percentage of female as compared to male high school graduates entering colleges and universities. The overwhelming majority of female college and university graduates, over 80 percent, are taking up employment and doing so in a wider range of fields than in the past. Better education and the availability of more job opportunites have increasingly made it possible for women to look upon marriage as an option rather than a prescribed lifestyle. . . . A dramatic development has been the advancement by married women, including those with children, into the labor force.❞
>
> **—*Japanese Women: New Feminist Perspectives on the Past, Present, and Future,* Kumiko Fujimura-Fanselow et al., eds., 1995**

After World War II, many Japanese women began to abandon their old roles to pursue new opportunities.

The Allied Occupation

From 1945 to 1952, Japan was an occupied country—its lands held and controlled by Allied military forces. An Allied administration under the command of United States general **Douglas MacArthur** governed Japan. As commander of the occupation administration, MacArthur was responsible for destroying the Japanese war machine, trying Japanese civilian and military officials charged with war crimes, and laying the foundations of postwar Japanese society.

CHAPTER 24
Section 3, 739-744

1 FOCUS

Section Overview
This section focuses on social and economic changes in postwar Japan and other Asian states.

BELLRINGER
Skillbuilder Activity

Project transparency and have students answer questions.

Available as a blackline master.

Daily Focus Skills Transparency 24–3

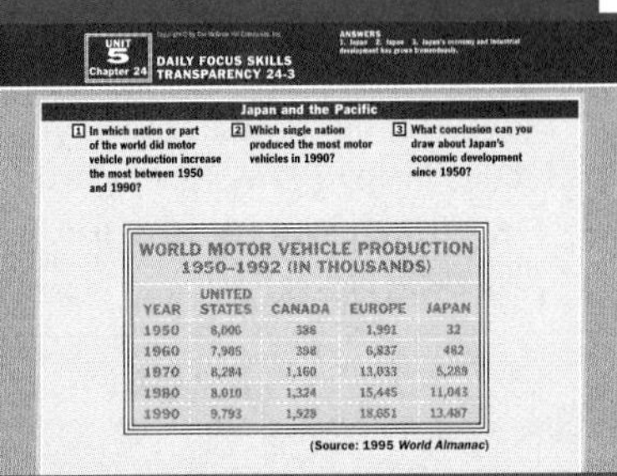

UNIT 5 Chapter 24 DAILY FOCUS SKILLS TRANSPARENCY 24-3

Japan and the Pacific

1. In which nation or part of the world did motor vehicle production increase the most between 1950 and 1990?
2. Which single nation produced the most motor vehicles in 1990?
3. What conclusion can you draw about Japan's economic development since 1950?

WORLD MOTOR VEHICLE PRODUCTION 1950–1992 (IN THOUSANDS)

YEAR	UNITED STATES	CANADA	EUROPE	JAPAN
1950	8,006	388	1,991	32
1960	7,905	398	6,837	482
1970	8,284	1,160	13,033	5,289
1980	8,010	1,324	15,445	11,043
1990	9,793	1,928	18,651	13,487

(Source: 1995 *World Almanac*)

Guide to Reading

Answers to Graphic: South Korea: chemicals, textiles, shipbuilding Taiwan: manufacturing, commerce Singapore: shipbuilding, oil refineries, electronics

Preteaching Vocabulary: Define *state capitalism. (State capitalism is Japan's way of dealing with its economy. The state establishes price and wage policies and subsidizes vital industries.)* L2

SECTION RESOURCES

Reproducible Masters
- Reproducible Lesson Plan 24–3
- Daily Lecture and Discussion Notes 24–3
- Guided Reading Activity 24–3
- Section Quiz 24–3
- Reading Essentials and Study Guide 24–3

Transparencies
- Daily Focus Skills Transparency 24–3

Multimedia
- Interactive Tutor Self-Assessment CD-ROM
- ExamView® Pro Testmaker CD-ROM
- Presentation Plus! CD-ROM

2 TEACH

Reading Check

Answer: new constitution, maintained armed forces only for self-defense, powers of emperor were reduced, guaranteed basic civil and political rights, women given right to vote

Geography *Skills*

Answers:

1. The upper part of Honshu has no industry.
2. Japan has limited natural resources to export, so it mainly relies on industry and manufacturing for income. Geographically, shipping is mandatory and fisheries are also crucial to the Japanese economy.

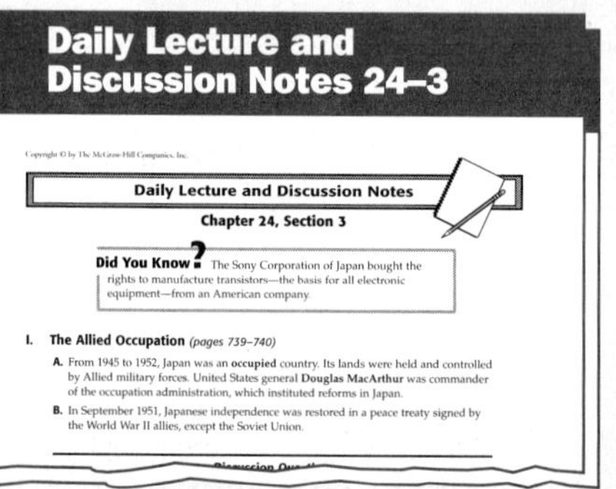

Daily Lecture and Discussion Notes 24–3

Daily Lecture and Discussion Notes

Chapter 24, Section 3

Did You Know? The Sony Corporation of Japan bought the rights to manufacture transistors—the basis for all electronic equipment—from an American company.

I. **The Allied Occupation** *(pages 739–740)*

A. From 1945 to 1952, Japan was an **occupied** country. Its lands were held and controlled by Allied military forces. United States general **Douglas MacArthur** was commander of the occupation administration, which instituted reforms in Japan.

B. In September 1951, Japanese independence was restored in a peace treaty signed by the World War II allies, except the Soviet Union.

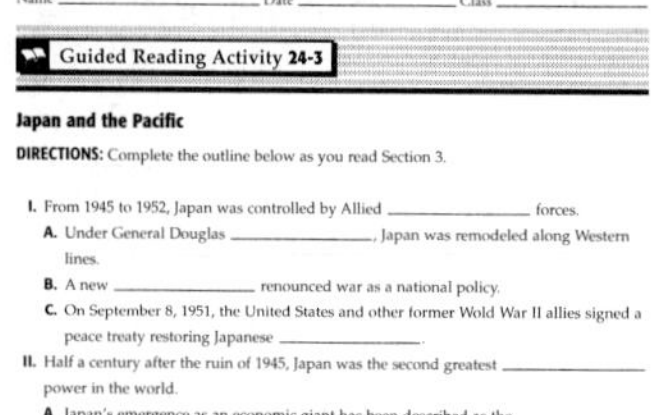

Guided Reading Activity 24–3

Name ______ Date ______ Class ______

Guided Reading Activity **24-3**

Japan and the Pacific

DIRECTIONS: Complete the outline below as you read Section 3.

I. From 1945 to 1952, Japan was controlled by Allied ______ forces.

A. Under General Douglas ______, Japan was remodeled along Western lines.

B. A new ______ renounced war as a national policy.

C. On September 8, 1951, the United States and other former Wold War II allies signed a peace treaty restoring Japanese ______.

II. Half a century after the ruin of 1945, Japan was the second greatest ______ power in the world.

A. Japan's emergence as an economic giant has been described as the

General Douglas MacArthur

Under MacArthur's firm direction, Japanese society was remodeled along Western lines. A new constitution renounced war as a national policy. Japan agreed to maintain armed forces at levels that were only sufficient for self-defense. The constitution also established a parliamentary system, reduced the power of the emperor (who was forced to announce that he was not a god), guaranteed basic civil and political rights, and gave women the right to vote.

On September 8, 1951, the United States and other former World War II allies (but not the Soviet Union) signed a peace treaty restoring Japanese independence. On the same day, Japan and the United States signed a defensive alliance in which the Japanese agreed that the United States could maintain military bases in Japan.

Reading Check **Identifying** What reforms were instituted in Japan under the command of U.S. general Douglas MacArthur?

The Japanese Miracle

In August 1945, Japan was in ruins and its land occupied by a foreign army. Half a century later, Japan was the second greatest industrial power in the world.

Japan's rapid emergence as an economic giant has often been described as the "Japanese miracle." Japan has made a dramatic recovery from the war. To understand this phenomenon fully, we must examine not just the economy but also the changes that have occurred in Japanese society.

Politics and Government Japan's new constitution embodied the principles of universal suffrage and a balance of power among the executive, legislative, and judicial branches of government. These principles have held firm. Japan today is a stable democratic society.

At the same time, the current Japanese political system retains some of Japan's nineteenth-century political system under the Meiji. An example involves the distribution of political power. Japan has a multiparty system with two major parties—the Liberal Democrats and the Socialists. In practice, however, the Liberal Democrats have dominated the government. At one point, they remained in office for 30 years. During this period decisions on key issues, such as who should become prime minister, were decided by a small group within the party. A dramatic change, however, did occur in 1993, when the Liberal Democrats were defeated on charges of government corruption. Mirohiro Hosokawa was elected prime minister and promised to clean up the political system.

Today, the central government plays an active role in the economy. It establishes price and wage policies and subsidizes vital industries. This government role in the economy is widely accepted in Japan. Indeed, it is often cited as a key reason for the efficiency of Japanese industry and the emergence of the country as an industrial giant. Japan's economic system has been described as "state capitalism."

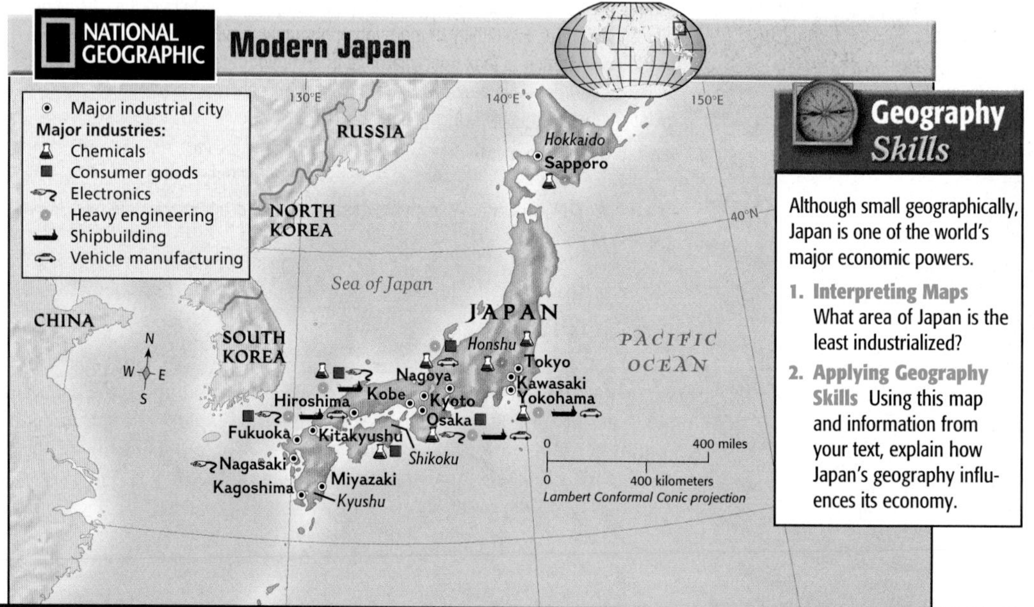

Geography *Skills*

Although small geographically, Japan is one of the world's major economic powers.

1. **Interpreting Maps** What area of Japan is the least industrialized?
2. **Applying Geography Skills** Using this map and information from your text, explain how Japan's geography influences its economy.

COOPERATIVE LEARNING ACTIVITY

Conducting an Interview Organize the class into two groups: one to prepare interview questions to ask General MacArthur, the other to prepare questions for Emperor Hirohito. Questions should be based on research of topics such as demilitarization, government, economic reform, and world affairs. Have students from both groups meet to combine their questions into a list. Then appoint students to act as MacArthur, Hirohito, and an interviewer, and have them practice role-playing a TV interview. When students are prepared, invite another class or students' families to attend the mock broadcast. L3

For grading this activity, refer to the ***Performance Assessment Activities*** booklet.

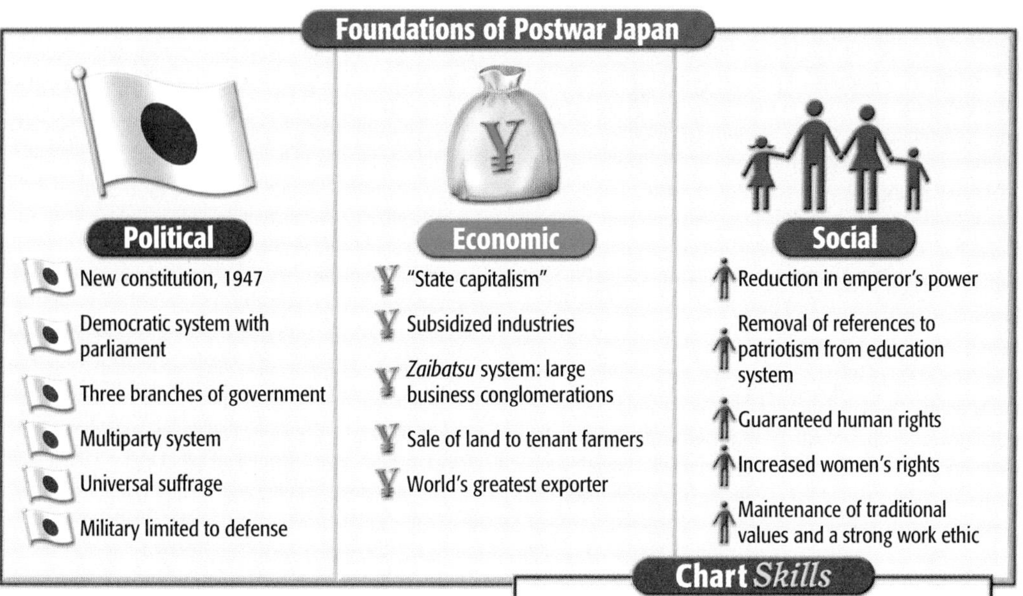

Foundations of Postwar Japan
Political
New constitution, 1947
Democratic system with parliament
Three branches of government
Multiparty system
Universal suffrage
Military limited to defense
Economic
"State capitalism"
Subsidized industries
Zaibatsu system: large business conglomerations
Sale of land to tenant farmers
World's greatest exporter
Social
Reduction in emperor's power
Removal of references to patriotism from education system
Guaranteed human rights
Increased women's rights
Maintenance of traditional values and a strong work ethic

Chart *Skills*

After 1945, Japan's society, government, and economy were modernized.

1. **Compare and Contrast** Pick another country discussed in this chapter and compare its economic characteristics to those of postwar Japan. What are the similarities and differences?

Some problems remain, however. Two recent prime ministers have been forced to resign over improper financial dealings with business associates. Critics at home and abroad have charged that, owing to government policies, the textbooks used in Japanese schools do not adequately discuss the crimes committed by the Japanese government and armed forces during World War II.

The Economy During their occupation of Japan, Allied officials had planned to dismantle the large business conglomerations known as the *zaibatsu*. With the rise of the Cold War, however, the policy was scaled back. Only the 19 largest companies were affected. In addition, the new policy did not keep Japanese companies from forming loose ties with each other, which basically gave rise to another *zaibatsu* system.

The occupation administration had more success with its land-reform program. Half of the population lived on farms, and half of all farmers were tenants of large landowners. Under the reform program, lands were sold on easy credit terms to the tenants. The reform program created a strong class of independent farmers.

At the end of the Allied occupation in 1952, the Japanese gross national product was one-third that of Great Britain or France. Today, it is larger than both put together and well over half that of the United States. Japan is the greatest exporting nation in the world. Its per capita income equals or surpasses that of most Western states.

What explains the Japanese success? Some analysts point to cultural factors. The Japanese are group oriented and find it easy to cooperate with one another. Hardworking and frugal, they are more inclined to save than to buy. This boosts the savings rate and labor productivity. The labor force is highly skilled. In addition, Japanese people share common values and respond in similar ways to the challenges of the modern world.

Other analysts have cited more practical reasons for the Japanese economic success. For example, because its industries were destroyed in World War II, Japan was forced to build entirely new, modern factories. Japanese workers spend a substantially longer period of time at their jobs than do workers in other advanced societies. Corporations reward innovation and maintain good management-labor relations. Finally, some experts contend that Japan uses unfair trade practices—that it dumps goods at prices below cost to break into a foreign market and restricts imports from other countries.

Chart *Skills*

Answer:

1. Students will compare the economy of Japan and another Asian country.

Enrich

How did Japan's economy change after World War II? *(American aid and Japanese know-how enabled Japan to rebuild its economy. Japan's government and business leaders invested heavily in electronics and automobiles for export. By the 1970s, Japan had become a leader in the world market.)* **L2**

Who?What?Where?When?

Emperor Hirohito Hirohito was the longest-reigning ruler in Japan's history, presiding over his nation from 1926 until his death in 1989. From the outset, the period of his rule was named Showa, or "Enlightened Peace." Even though World War II took place during Hirohito's reign, he wound up accepting the Allied terms of surrender. A new constitution stripped the imperial family of its political power, established a cabinet based on the British model, and barred Japan from all warfare except for defense. Hirohito also renounced the tradition of conferring divine status on Japan's emperors. His son, Akihito, succeeded him.

MEETING INDIVIDUAL NEEDS

Visual Learners Have students work in small groups to create both absolute and relative time lines of important events in Japan's history between World War II and the present. Before advising students on the appropriate scale to use (for example, three inches per year), determine how much wall space you have available to display all the time lines from this chapter. Tell students to include political, religious, economic, and cultural events, as well as natural disasters such as the 1995 Kobe earthquake. **L1 L2**

Refer to ***Inclusion for the High School Social Studies Classroom Strategies and Activities*** in the TCR.

Reading Check

Answer: Japan's government establishes price and wage policies and subsidizes vital industries.

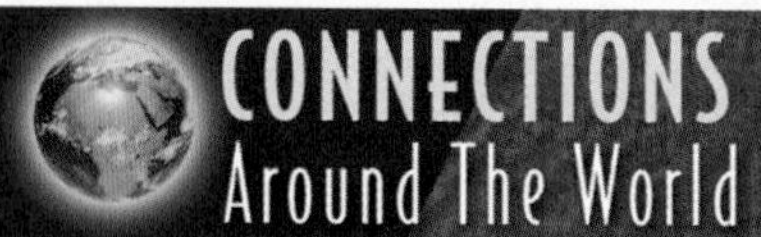

CONNECTIONS Around The World

Answer: Answers will vary but should be supported with factual information.

CURRICULUM CONNECTION

The Arts Arrange a classroom showing of the Japanese director Akira Kurosawa's *Rhapsody in August,* about the bombing of Nagasaki during World War II. After viewing the film have the class discuss it. L2

CURRICULUM CONNECTION

Economics Production of automobiles became the heart of Japan's industrial expansion in the 1960s. Between 1960 and 1980, Japan increased its share of world automobile production from three percent to 29 percent. By 1980, the Asian superpower had overtaken West Germany, France, Great Britain, and the United States to become the world's leading automotive producer. Today many Japanese auto companies have U.S. production facilities.

Social Changes During the occupation, Allied planners thought they could eliminate the aggressiveness that had characterized Japanese behavior before and during the war. A new educational system removed all references to patriotism and loyalty to the emperor. At the same time, it stressed individualism. Women were given the right to vote and were encouraged to enter politics.

Efforts to remake Japanese behavior through laws were only partly successful. Many of the distinctive characteristics of traditional Japanese society have persisted into the present day, although in altered form. Emphasis on the work ethic, for example, remains strong. The tradition of hard work is stressed in the educational system.

The subordinate role of women in Japanese society has not been entirely eliminated. Women are now legally protected against discrimination in employment, yet very few have reached senior levels in business, education, or politics. Japan has had no female prime ministers and few female cabinet ministers.

Women now make up nearly 50 percent of the workforce, but most are in retail or service occupations. Their average salary is only about half that of males.

Culture After the Japanese defeat in World War II, many of the writers who had been active before the war resurfaced. However, their writing was now more sober. This "lost generation" described its anguish and piercing despair. Several writers committed suicide. For them, defeat was made worse by fear of the Americanization of postwar Japan.

Since the 1970s, increasing wealth and a high literacy rate have led to a massive outpouring of books. In 1975, Japan already produced twice as much fiction as the United States. This trend continued into the 1990s. Much of this new literature deals with the common concerns of all the wealthy industrialized nations. Current Japanese authors were raised in the crowded cities of postwar Japan, where they soaked up movies, television, and rock music. These writers speak the universal language of today's world.

Haruki Murakami is one of Japan's most popular authors today. He was one of the first to discard the somber style of the earlier postwar period and to speak the contemporary language. *A Wild Sheep Chase,* published in 1982, is an excellent example of his gripping, yet humorous, writing.

Reading Check **Explaining** How is the Japanese government involved in Japan's economy?

CONNECTIONS Around The World

Cities and Cars

Since the beginning of the Industrial Revolution in the nineteenth century, the growth of industrialization has been accompanied by the growth of cities. In both industrialized and developing countries, congested and polluted cities have become a way of life. In recent years, as more people have been able to buy cars, traffic jams have also become a regular feature.

In São Paulo, Brazil, for example, traffic jams in which nobody moves last for hours. There are 4.5 million cars in São Paulo, twice the number in New York City, although the cities have about the same population (16 million people). Workers in auto factories in Brazil work around the clock to meet the demand for cars.

Traffic in Thailand

The same situation is evident in other cities around the world. In Cairo, a city of 14 million people, pollution from stalled traffic erodes the surface of the Sphinx outside the city. In Bangkok, the capital city of Thailand, it can take six hours to reach the airport.

A major cause of traffic congestion is lack of roads. As more and more poor people have fled the countryside for the city, many cities have tripled in population in just 20 years. At the same time, few new roads have been built.

Comparing Cultures

Using outside sources, research traffic problems in three cities in different parts of the world (for example, Los Angeles, Hong Kong, and Paris). How are the traffic problems in these cities similar, and how are they different? What solutions are people developing to solve traffic problems in these particular cities?

INTERDISCIPLINARY CONNECTIONS ACTIVITY

Science The Japanese have a deep reverence for nature and longevity. Both are reflected in the ancient Japanese art of bonsai, in which trees are carefully pruned to be no more than a few feet, or even inches, tall and may live for centuries. Bonsai trees are not just plants, but works of art. The goal of the bonsai gardener is to accurately portray nature in a miniature form. Have students research the techniques used in bonsai and do a demonstration for the class. You might wish to invite a local bonsai expert to bring plants to class to share with students. L3

The "Asian Tigers"

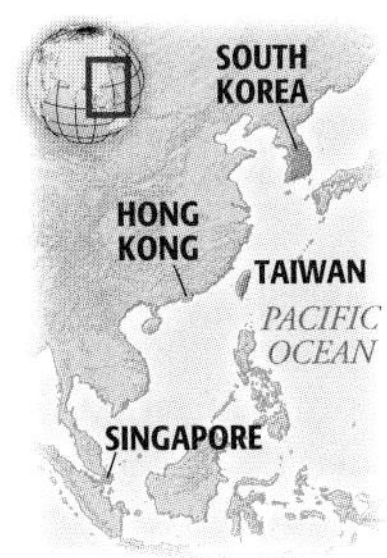

A number of Asian nations have imitated Japan in creating successful industrial societies. Sometimes called the "Asian tigers," they are South Korea, Taiwan, Singapore, and Hong Kong. Along with Japan, they have become economic powerhouses.

South Korea In 1953, the Korean Peninsula was exhausted from three years of bitter war. Two heavily armed countries now faced each other across the 38th parallel. North of this line was the People's Republic of Korea (North Korea) under the dictatorial rule of the Communist leader **Kim Il Sung.** To the south was the Republic of Korea (South Korea), under the dictatorial president **Syngman Rhee.**

After several years of harsh rule and government corruption in South Korea, demonstrations broke out in the capital city of Seoul in the spring of 1960. Rhee was forced to retire. A coup d'etat in 1961 put General Chung Hee Park in power. Two years later, Park was elected president and began to strengthen the South Korean economy with land reform and the promotion of free market policies.

South Korea gradually emerged as a major industrial power in East Asia. The key areas for industrial development were chemicals, textiles, and shipbuilding. By the 1980s, South Korea was moving into automobile production. The largest Korean corporations are Samsung, Daewoo, and Hyundai.

Like many other countries in the region, South Korea was slow to develop democratic principles. Park ruled by autocratic means and suppressed protest. However, opposition to military rule began to develop with the growth of a middle class. Students and city dwellers demonstrated against government policies. Finally, new elections in 1992 brought Kim Young Sam to the presidency. He promised that he would make South Korea "a freer democracy."

Taiwan: The Other China After they were defeated by the Communists and forced to retreat to Taiwan, Chiang Kai-shek and his followers established a capital at Taipei. The government continued to call itself the Republic of China.

Chiang Kai-shek's government maintained that it was the legitimate government of all the Chinese people and would eventually return in triumph to the mainland. At the same time, however, the Communist government on the mainland claimed to rule all of China, including Taiwan.

Protection by American military forces enabled the new regime to concentrate on economic growth without worrying about a Communist invasion. Making good use of foreign aid and the efforts of its own energetic people, the Republic of China built a modern industrialized society.

A land-reform program, which put farmland in the hands of peasants, doubled food production in Taiwan. With government help, local manufacturing and commerce expanded. During the 1960s and 1970s, industrial growth averaged well over 10 percent a year. By the mid-1980s, over three-quarters of the population lived in urban areas.

Prosperity, however, did not lead to democracy. Under Chiang Kai-shek, the government ruled by emergency decree and refused to allow the formation of new political parties. After the death of Chiang in 1975, the Republic of China slowly began to evolve toward a more representative form of government. By the end of the 1980s, democratic elections and opposition parties had come into being.

A major issue for Taiwan is whether it will become an independent state or will be united with mainland China. The United States supports self-determination for the people of Taiwan and believes that any final decision on Taiwan's future must be made by peaceful means. Meanwhile, the People's

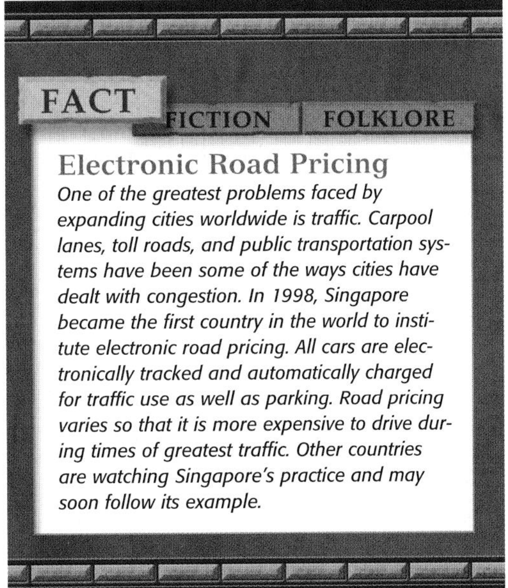

Electronic Road Pricing

One of the greatest problems faced by expanding cities worldwide is traffic. Carpool lanes, toll roads, and public transportation systems have been some of the ways cities have dealt with congestion. In 1998, Singapore became the first country in the world to institute electronic road pricing. All cars are electronically tracked and automatically charged for traffic use as well as parking. Road pricing varies so that it is more expensive to drive during times of greatest traffic. Other countries are watching Singapore's practice and may soon follow its example.

CRITICAL THINKING ACTIVITY

Analyzing Divide the class into five groups, and assign each group one of the following "Asian tigers" to research: Japan, South Korea, Taiwan, Singapore, and Hong Kong. Each group should determine the present economic situation in the nation they are researching and construct a chart that illustrates the various branches of the economy and the kinds of profits companies earn. Ask students to answer the following questions: Why have these states been so successful in their economic growth? Is their prosperity continuing? What economic setbacks has the nation faced recently? How have these been dealt with? What effects does the nation's economic situation have on the other four nations, and on the world?

CHAPTER 24
Section 3, 739-744

3 ASSESS

Assign Section 3 Assessment as homework or as an in-class activity.

Have students use **Interactive Tutor Self-Assessment CD-ROM.**

Section Quiz 24–3

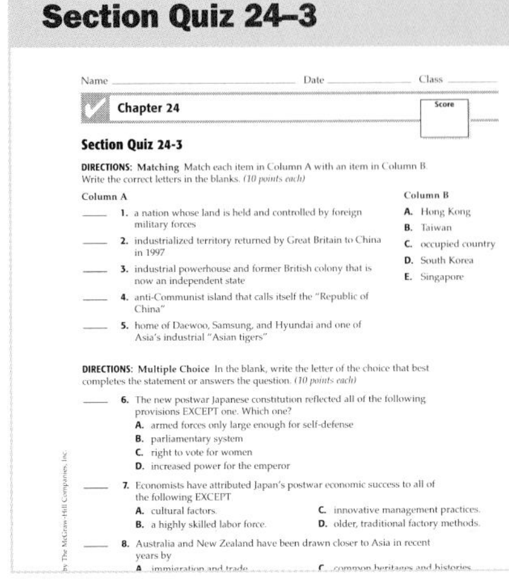

Name ______ Date ______ Class ______

Chapter 24 Score

Section Quiz 24-3

DIRECTIONS: Matching Match each item in Column A with an item in Column B. Write the correct letters in the blanks. *(10 points each)*

Column A

____ **1.** a nation whose land is held and controlled by foreign military forces

____ **2.** industrialized territory returned by Great Britain to China in 1997

____ **3.** industrial powerhouse and former British colony that is now an independent state

____ **4.** anti-Communist island that calls itself the "Republic of China"

____ **5.** home of Daewoo, Samsung, and Hyundai and one of Asia's industrial "Asian tigers"

Column B

A. Hong Kong
B. Taiwan
C. occupied country
D. South Korea
E. Singapore

DIRECTIONS: Multiple Choice In the blank, write the letter of the choice that best completes the statement or answers the question. *(10 points each)*

____ **6.** The new postwar Japanese constitution reflected all of the following provisions EXCEPT one. Which one?
A. armed forces only large enough for self-defense
B. parliamentary system
C. right to vote for women
D. increased power for the emperor

____ **7.** Economists have attributed Japan's postwar economic success to all of the following EXCEPT
A. cultural factors.
B. a highly skilled labor force.
C. innovative management practices.
D. older, traditional factory methods.

____ **8.** Australia and New Zealand have been drawn closer to Asia in recent years by
A. immigration and trade
C. common heritages and histories

Reading Essentials and Study Guide 24–3

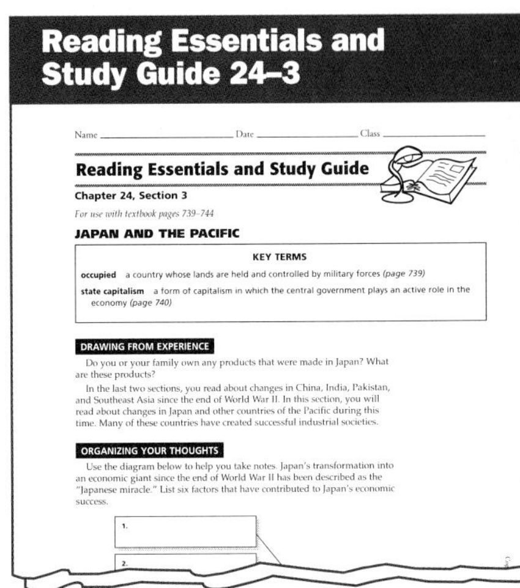

Name ______ Date ______ Class ______

Reading Essentials and Study Guide

Chapter 24, Section 3

For use with textbook pages 739–744

JAPAN AND THE PACIFIC

KEY TERMS

occupied a country whose lands are held and controlled by military forces *(page 739)*

state capitalism a form of capitalism in which the central government plays an active role in the economy *(page 740)*

DRAWING FROM EXPERIENCE

Do you or your family own any products that were made in Japan? What are these products?

In the last two sections, you read about changes in China, India, Pakistan, and Southeast Asia since the end of World War II. In this section, you will read about changes in Japan and other countries of the Pacific during this time. Many of these countries have created successful industrial societies.

ORGANIZING YOUR THOUGHTS

Use the diagram below to help you take notes. Japan's transformation into an economic giant since the end of World War II has been described as the "Japanese miracle." List six factors that have contributed to Japan's economic success.

1.

2.

Enrich

Ask students to explain the impact of parliamentary and constitutional systems of government on significant world political developments discussed in this chapter. L3

Reading Check

Answer: Since Chiang Kai-shek and his followers retreated to the island after their defeat by the Communists, Taiwan has continued to call itself the Republic of China. It is currently an independent state, although the People's Republic of China remains committed to eventual reunification.

Reading Check

Answer: Immigration has increased from East and Southeast Asia, and trade relations with Asia have been increasing. They have identified themselves culturally and politically with Europe rather than Asia, since the majority of their populations are of European origin. Their political institutions and values are derived from European models, and their economies resemble those of the industrial countries of the world. Both are members of the British Commonwealth.

Reteaching Activity

Ask students to explain the relevance of each of the following to the modern history of Japan: 1945–1952, 1947 constitution, and decentralization. **L1**

4 CLOSE

Discuss the Allied occupation of Japan and the country's transformation since 1945. Ask students to describe how women's roles have changed and how Japan has influenced other "Asian tigers."

Republic of China on the mainland remains committed to eventual unification.

Singapore and Hong Kong **Singapore,** once a British colony and briefly a part of the state of Malaysia, is now an independent state. Under the leadership of Prime Minister Lee Kuan Yew (kwahn yoo), Singapore developed an industrial economy based on shipbuilding, oil refineries, and electronics. Singapore has also become the banking center of the region.

In Singapore, an authoritarian political system has created a stable environment for economic growth. The prime minister once stated that the Western model of democracy was not appropriate for Singapore. Its citizens, however, are beginning to demand more political freedoms.

Like Singapore, **Hong Kong** became an industrial powerhouse with standards of living well above the levels of its neighbors. For over 150 years, Hong Kong was under British rule. In 1997, however, Great Britain returned control of Hong Kong to mainland China. China, in turn, promised that, for the next 50 years, the people of Hong Kong would live under a capitalist system and be self-governing. The shape of Hong Kong's future remains uncertain.

Reading Check **Evaluating** What is the relationship between Taiwan and China?

Australia and New Zealand

Both Australia and the country of New Zealand located to the south and east of Australia, have identified themselves culturally and politically with Europe rather than with their Asian neighbors. Their political institutions and values are derived from European models, and their economies resemble those of the industrialized countries of the world. Both are members of the British Commonwealth. Both are also part of the United States-led ANZUS defensive alliance (Australia, New Zealand, the United States).

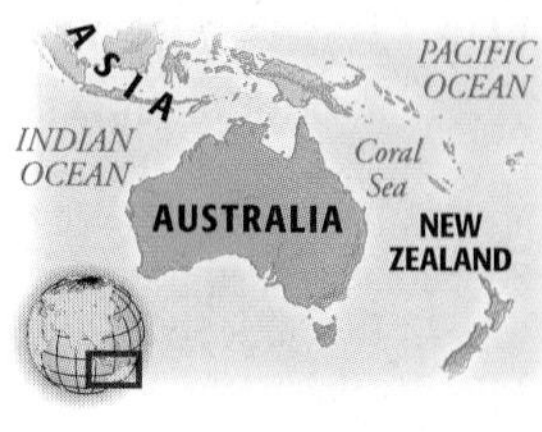

In recent years, however, trends have been drawing both states closer to Asia. First, immigration from East and Southeast Asia has increased rapidly. More than one-half of current immigrants into Australia come from East Asia.

Second, trade relations with Asia are increasing rapidly. About 60 percent of Australia's export markets today are in East Asia. Asian trade with New Zealand is also on the increase.

Whether Australia and New Zealand will ever become an integral part of the Asia-Pacific region is uncertain. Since the majority of the population in both Australia and New Zealand has European origins, cultural differences often hinder mutual understanding between the two countries and their Asian neighbors.

Reading Check **Examining** How have Australia and New Zealand been drawn closer to their Asian neighbors? How are they linked to Europe?

SECTION 3 ASSESSMENT

Checking for Understanding

1. **Define** occupied, state capitalism.
2. **Identify** Douglas MacArthur, Kim Il Sung, Syngman Rhee.
3. **Locate** Singapore, Hong Kong.
4. **Explain** the impact of Japan's land-reform program. What other programs or policies did the occupation administration implement in Japan?
5. **List** the ways in which Australia and New Zealand are similar to European nations.

Critical Thinking

6. **Predict Consequences** What further impact do you think the return of Hong Kong to China will have on either country?
7. **Organizing Information** Use a diagram like the one below to show factors contributing to Japan's economic success.

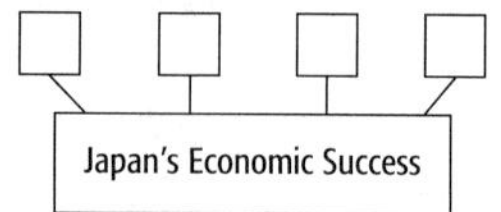

Analyzing Visuals

8. **Locate** the photo of Douglas MacArthur on page 740. What military rank did he hold? Why did the Allies choose a military leader instead of a politician or diplomat to command postwar Japan? What were some of MacArthur's responsibilities in Japan?

Writing About History

9. **Informative Writing** Do additional research on Japan and the "Asian tigers" and analyze their sources of growth. Explain in an essay why these states have been so successful.

SECTION 3 ASSESSMENT

1. Key terms are in blue.
2. Douglas MacArthur (*p. 739*); Kim Il Sung (*p. 743*); Syngman Rhee (*p. 743*)
3. See chapter maps.
4. It created a strong class of independent farmers; armed forces were for self-defense only; parliamentary system was instituted.
5. the majority of population is of European origin; political institutions, values, derived from European models
6. Hong Kong's economic power may open China to outside influences, or China may limit Hong Kong's liberties.
7. group oriented; more inclined to save than to buy; highly skilled labor force; people share common values
8. general; because Japan was an occupied country, tasks were militarily oriented i.e., dismantling war machine
9. Answers should be supported by examples and logical arguments.

Eyewitness to History

School Regulations, Japanese Style

JAPANESE CHILDREN ARE exposed to a school environment much more regimented than that of U.S. public school children. The following regulations are examples of rules adopted by middle school systems in various parts of Japan.

Japanese school children in their uniforms

"1. Boys' hair should not touch the eyebrows, the ears, or the top of the collar.
2. No one should have a permanent wave, or dye his or her hair. Girls should not wear ribbons or accessories in their hair. Hair dryers should not be used. . . .
3. Keep your uniform clean and pressed at all times. Girls' middy blouses should have two buttons on the back collar. Boys' pant cuffs should be of the prescribed width. No more than 12 eyelets should be on shoes.
4. Wear your school badge at all times. It should be positioned exactly.
5. Going to school in the morning, wear your book bag strap on the right shoulder; in the afternoon on the way home, wear it on the left shoulder.
6. When you raise your hand to be called on, your arm should extend forward and up at the angle prescribed in your handbook.
7. Your own route to and from school is marked in your student rule handbook; carefully observe which side of each street you are to use on the way to and from school.
8. After school you are to go directly home, unless your parent has written a note permitting you to go to another location. Permission will not be granted by the school unless this other location is a suitable one. You must not go to coffee shops.
9. Before and after school, no matter where you are, you represent our school, so you should behave in ways we can all be proud of."

—Japanese School Regulations

Analyzing Primary Sources

1. In your own words, describe the Japanese system of education for young people.
2. Compare the Japanese system of education to the American system with which you are familiar. How are they similar? How are they different?

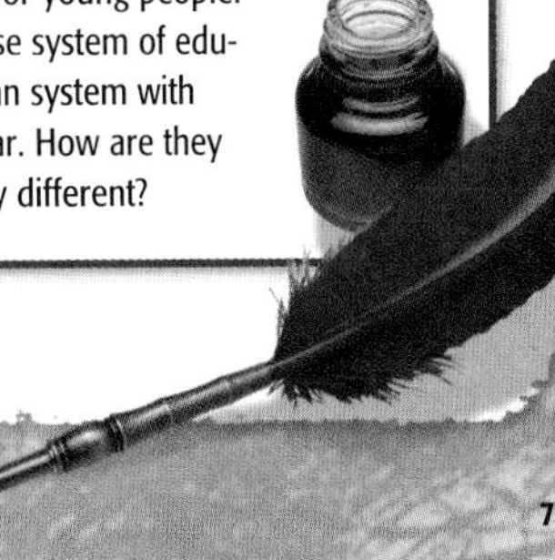

TEACH

Analyzing Primary Sources
Japanese students attend school 240 days a year and have an average of five hours of homework each day. Discipline is very strict and classes are very structured. Students are encouraged to conform and strict rules of behavior are enforced.

The Japanese system is more disciplined than the American system. American students are not encouraged to conform, rather they are encouraged to develop their individualism. Americans do not go to school as much as the Japanese, 180 days as compared to 240 days per year. The literacy rate in Japanese schools is higher than in American schools. American students have more freedom and less competition getting into colleges.

If you have students in your class who have attended school in other countries, ask them to share their experiences with the class.

ANSWERS TO ANALYZING PRIMARY SOURCES

1. Student answers will vary. Students should realize that school regulations in Japan are far more rigid and detailed than in U.S. public schools. Students should cite specific quotes from the document to support their answers.
2. Students will probably find more differences than similarities, based on the information presented in this excerpt.

GLENCOE TECHNOLOGY

MindJogger Videoquiz
Use the **MindJogger Videoquiz** to review Chapter 24 content.

 Available in VHS.

Using Key Terms
1. State capitalism **2.** permanent revolution **3.** occupied **4.** per capita **5.** stalemate **6.** communes **7.** discrimination

Reviewing Key Facts
8. South Korea, Taiwan, Singapore, Hong Kong; because thay have become economic powers

9. It could concentrate on economic growth without worrying about a Communist invasion.

10. violence between Hindus and Muslims and the division of British India into two countries, India and Pakistan

11. France

12. They massacred them.

13. invited foreign investors to China and sent thousands of students abroad to study science, technology, and modern business techniques

14. Great Britain returned control to China.

15. A demonstration for democratic reforms was crushed by the Chinese military.

16. daughter of Jawaharlal Nehru who succeeded him as prime minister of India; she was assassinated in 1984

Critical Thinking
17. Ethnic and religious strife contributed to the assassinations. Answers to second part of question will vary but should be supported by logical arguments.

18. Japan's creation of an economy geared for exports has made Japan one of the world's economic giants.

CHAPTER 24 ASSESSMENT and ACTIVITIES

Chapter Summary
Since 1945, Asia and the Pacific region have seen many changes, as shown below.

Change
Out of defeat comes a new political and economic system.
- After gaining independence, Japan becomes an economic powerhouse.
- Imitating Japan, other Asian nations also develop strong economies.

Revolution
Communists assume power and introduce socialist methods.
- In China, Mao Zedong initiates programs like the Great Leap Forward and the Great Proletarian Cultural Revolution. After Mao, Deng Xiaoping institutes the Four Modernizations.

Regionalism
Decades of rivalry and suspicion cause divisions.
- Tensions between Communist North Korea and non-Communist South Korea lead to war.
- China resists Taiwanese independence.

Conflict
Nationalism and Cold War competition lead to war.
- The United States enters the war in Vietnam.
- The Khmer Rouge devastates Cambodia.

Diversity
Religious and ethnic rivalries hinder unity and lead to violence.
- Religious and ethnic differences produce conflict between Hindus and Muslims in India and Pakistan.

Cultural Diffusion
Political and economic changes link Asian countries to the world.
- Democracy develops in the Philippines.
- Chinese students demand democratic reforms.
- Increased immigration and trade draw Australia and New Zealand closer to their Asian neighbors.

Using Key Terms
1. _____ is an economic system in which the central government plays an active role in the country's economy.
2. An idea supported by Mao, that a constant state of revolution could create perfect communism, was called _____.
3. A country is _____ when its lands are held and controlled by a foreign military force.
4. The amount of income earned by each person in a country is called _____ income.
5. A _____ is reached when neither side in a conflict is able to achieve significant gains.
6. Massive collective farms created in China's Great Leap Forward were called _____.
7. Many governments now have laws that forbid acts of prejudice or _____ from being committed against people in their countries.

Reviewing Key Facts
8. **Geography** What nations are called the "Asian tigers" and why?
9. **Economics** How did promises of military protection from the United States help Taiwan develop its economy?
10. **History** What were the consequences of Great Britain's withdrawal from India?
11. **History** What nation fought for control of Vietnam before the United States became involved?
12. **Government** What policy did the Khmer Rouge follow toward the people they regarded as enemies after they gained control of Cambodia?
13. **Economics** What help did China require to improve its economy after the Cultural Revolution?
14. **History** What happened to Hong Kong in 1997?
15. **History** What events took place in Tiananmen Square in 1989?
16. **Government** Who was Indira Gandhi?

Critical Thinking
17. **Making Predictions** Analyze what conditions in India contributed to the assassinations of political leaders. Do you believe it is possible for India to maintain a stable democratic government?
18. **Drawing Conclusions** Evaluate the impact Japan's recovery has had on global affairs since World War II.

Writing About History
19. They both have been under dictatorial rule. South Korea has prospered more than North Korea and has also moved toward democracy.

Analyzing Sources
20. It had changed drastically. During the war, women were discouraged from working outside the home and told that their primary role was to be wives and mothers. By 1955, more women than men were entering college, and the majority of college graduates were seeking employment in a wider range of fields than before.

Self-Check Quiz

Visit the *Glencoe World History—Modern Times* Web site at wh.mt.glencoe.com and click on **Chapter 24–Self-Check Quiz** to prepare for the Chapter Test.

Writing About History

19. **Expository Writing** Compare North and South Korea. In what ways are they similar? In what ways are they different? Do supplementary research online or at the library to learn about their cultures and histories.

Analyzing Sources

Read the following excerpt from the book *Japanese Women*, published in 1955:

> "A quick glance at educational statistics reveals a higher percentage of female as compared to male high school graduates entering colleges and universities. The overwhelming majority of female college and university graduates, over 80 percent, are taking up employment and doing so in a wider range of fields than in the past. Better education and the availability of more job opportunities have increasingly made it possible for women to look upon marriage as an option rather than a prescribed lifestyle. . . ."

20. What does this passage reveal about the role of women in Japan after World War II?
21. Do you think it was difficult for Japanese women to break from their old roles in society?

Applying Technology Skills

22. **Developing Multimedia Presentations** Locate sources about present-day Cambodia and Vietnam. Organize your findings by creating a fact sheet comparing the two countries. Use a word processor to create a chart. Headings to include are population, type of economy, type of government, currency, infant mortality rate, literacy rate, and official religion. Provide a map of each country that shows political boundaries, major cities, and natural resources.

Making Decisions

23. What is the conflict regarding Taiwan's independence? Research the reasons for the tension between China and Taiwan. How do you think this conflict would be best resolved? Create a compromise solution that would satisfy the demands of those who want a self-determined Taiwan, as well as those who want Taiwan reunified with China.

NATIONAL GEOGRAPHIC Indochina, 1946–1954

Analyzing Maps and Charts

24. Approximately how much of Vietnam was controlled by the Communists between 1946 and 1954?
25. Which countries separate North and South Vietnam from Thailand?
26. What river runs from China to the Gulf of Tonkin?

The Princeton Review Standardized Test Practice

Directions: Choose the best answer to the question below.

Between 1966 and 1976, the destruction of many temples, the seizure of many books, and the imprisonment of some artists and intellectuals were closely related to which movement?

A China's Cultural Revolution
B Conservatism
C Women's rights movement
D Humanism

Test-Taking Tip: Even if you know the correct answer immediately, read all of the answer choices and eliminate those you know are wrong. Doing so will help you confirm that the answer choice you think is correct is indeed correct.

Have students visit the Web site at wh.mt.glencoe.com to review Chapter 24 and take the Self-Check Quiz.

Standardized Test Practice

Answer: A
Answer Explanation: Students should review page 725 of their text.

Bonus Question ?

Ask: How convincing are arguments by developing nations that democracy should be sacrificed in the name of promoting economic growth and public safety? Support your answer with examples from specific countries studied in this chapter. *(Answers will vary, but may include the following: the end justifies the means, and countries such as Singapore are cleaner and safer than the United States, with a higher general standard of living, even if there is political repression; the end does not justify the means, and people are better served by democratic countries, even if some citizens do not have an economic safety net.)* L3

21. Answers will vary but should be supported by logical arguments.

Applying Technology Skills

22. Students will create fact sheets and maps.

Making Decisions

23. Students will use problem-solving skills to develop a solution to the conflict between Taiwan and China.

Analyzing Maps and Charts

24. approximately seventy-five percent
25. Cambodia and Laos
26. Mekong

Chapter 25 Resources

Timesaving Tools

TeacherWorks™ All-In-One Planner and Resource Center

- **Interactive Teacher Edition** Access your Teacher Wraparound Edition and your classroom resources with a few easy clicks.
- **Interactive Lesson Planner** Planning has never been easier! Organize your week, month, semester, or year with all the lesson helps you need to make teaching creative, timely, and relevant.

Use Glencoe's **Presentation Plus!** multimedia teacher tool to easily present dynamic lessons that visually excite your students. Using Microsoft PowerPoint® you can customize the presentations to create your own personalized lessons.

TEACHING TRANSPARENCIES

Graphic Organizer Student Activity 25 Transparency

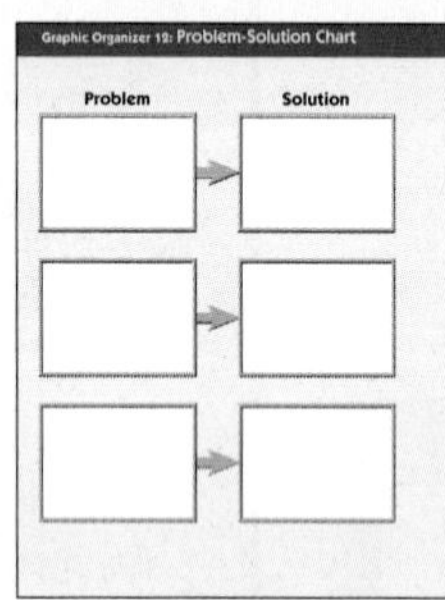

Chapter Transparency 25

Map Overlay Transparency 25

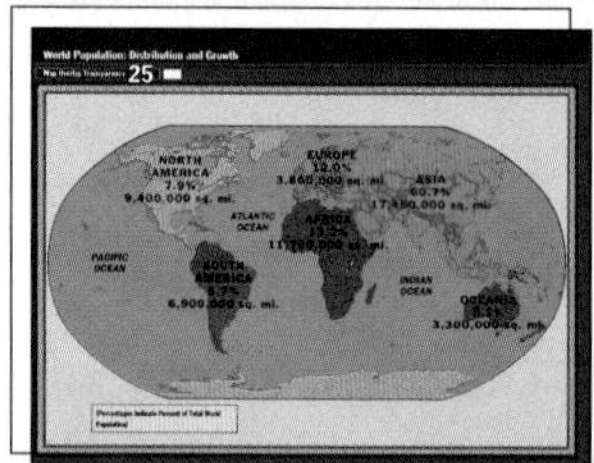

APPLICATION AND ENRICHMENT

Enrichment Activity 25

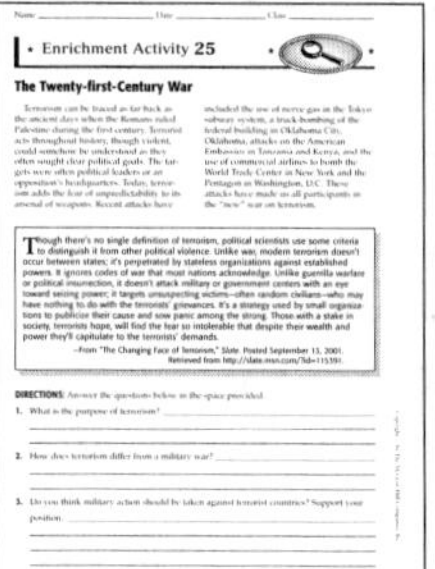

Primary Source Reading 25

History Simulation Activity 25

Historical Significance Activity 25

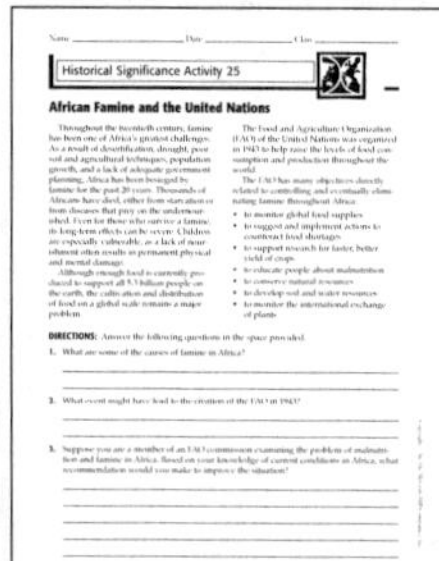

Cooperative Learning Activity 25

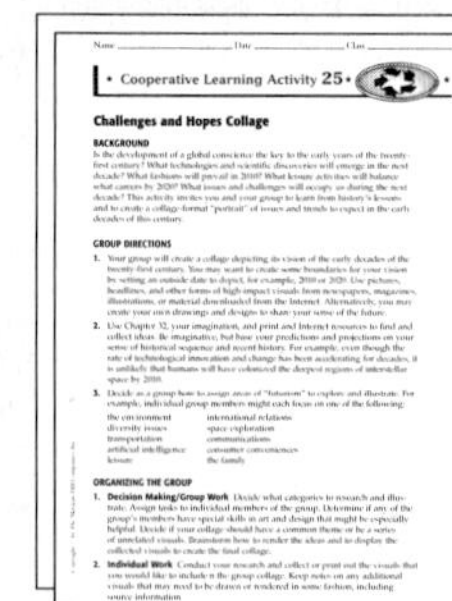

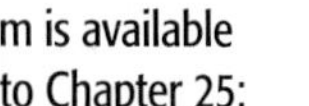

THE HISTORY CHANNEL®

The following videotape program is available from Glencoe as a supplement to Chapter 25:

- **Men in Space: From Goddard to Armstrong** (ISBN 1–56501–037–X)

To order, call Glencoe at 1–800–334–7344. To find classroom resources to accompany this video, check the following home pages:
A&E Television: www.aande.com
The History Channel: www.historychannel.com

Chapter 25 Resources

Review and Reinforcement

Linking Past and Present Activity 25

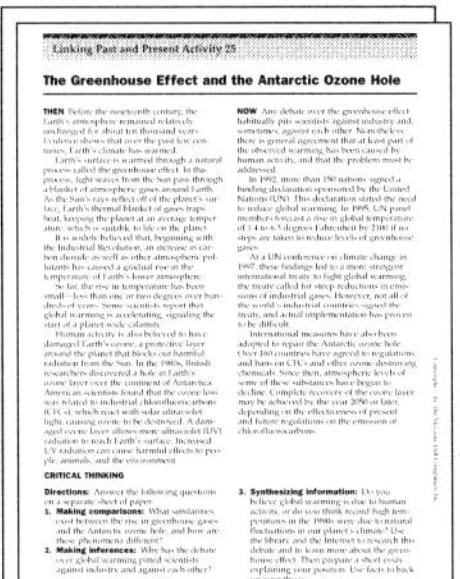

Time Line Activity 25

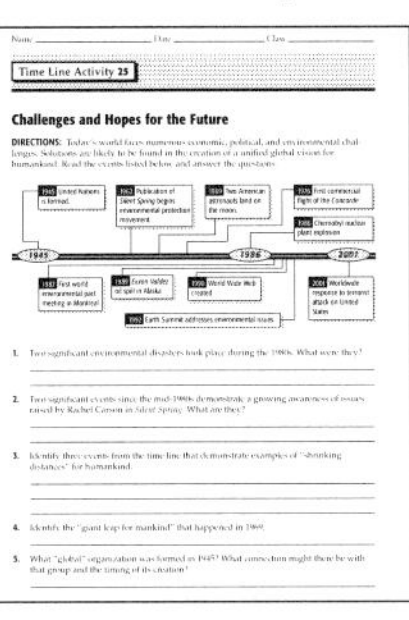

Reteaching Activity 25

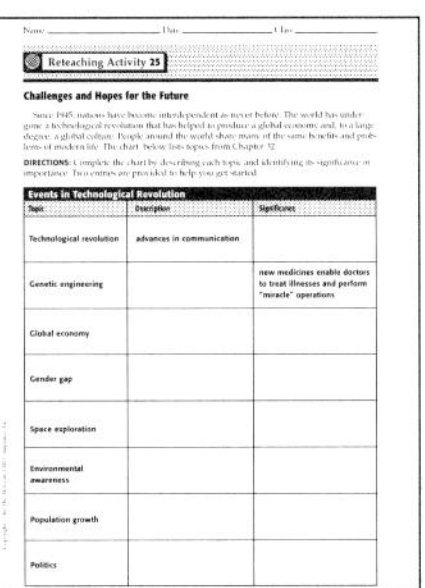

Vocabulary Activity 25

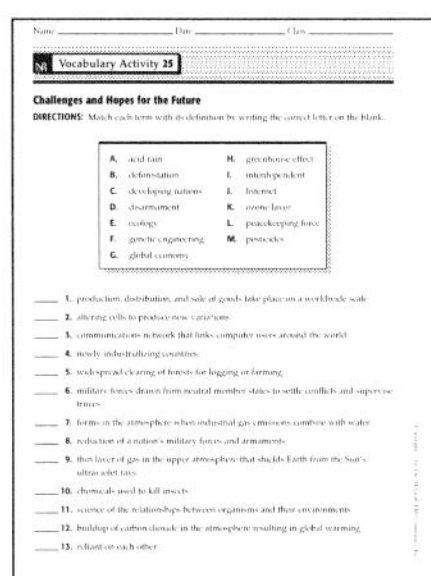

Critical Thinking Skills Activity 25

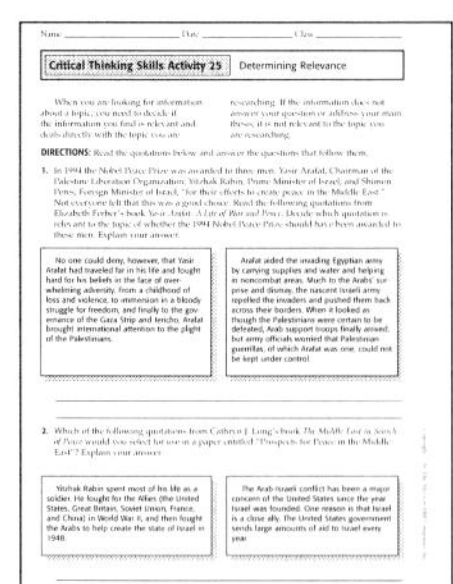

Assessment and Evaluation

Chapter 25 Test Form A

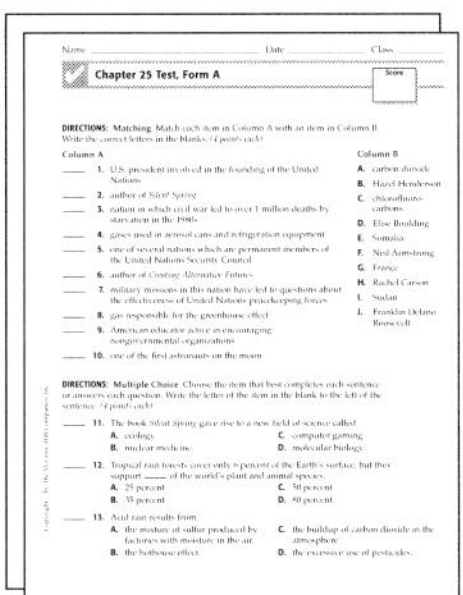

Chapter 25 Test Form B

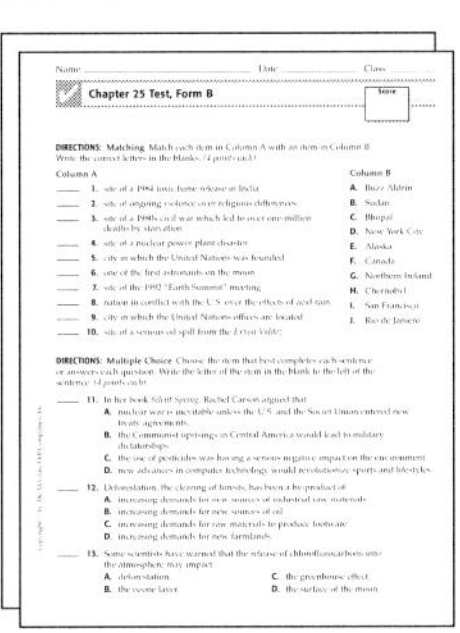

Performance Assessment Activity 25

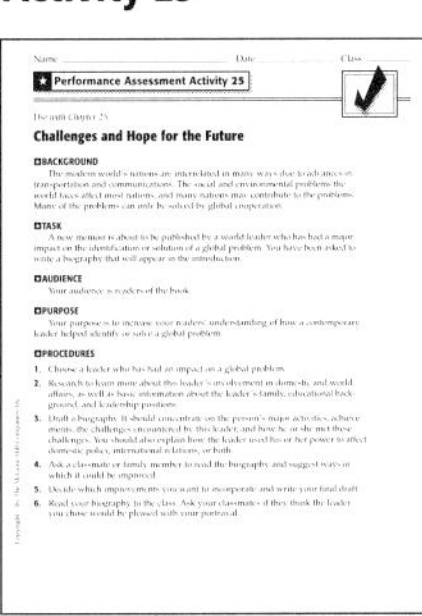

ExamView® Pro Testmaker CD-ROM

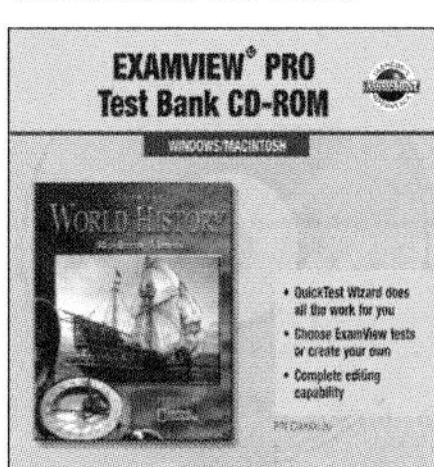

Standardized Test Skills Practice Workbook Activity 25

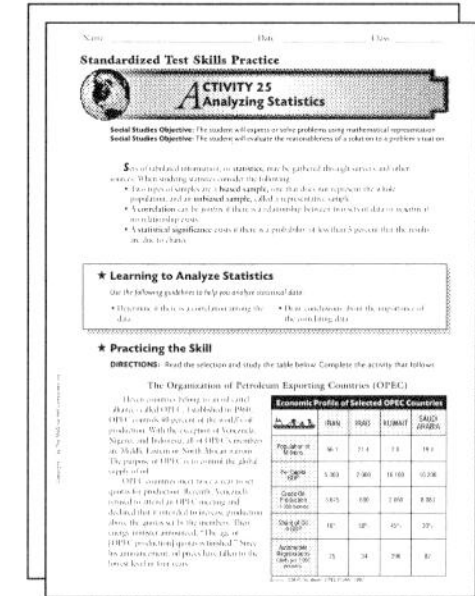

Interdisciplinary Activities

Mapping History Activity 25

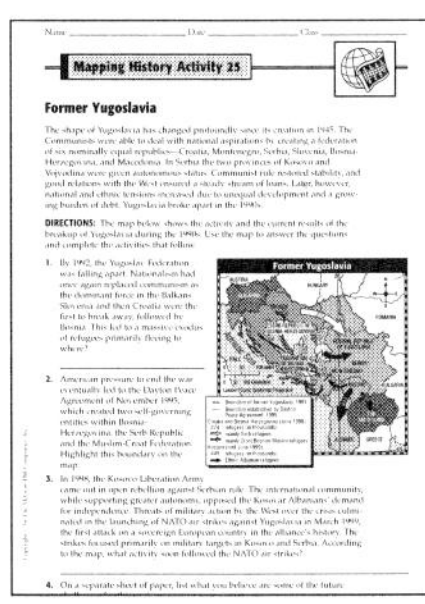

World Art and Music Activity 25

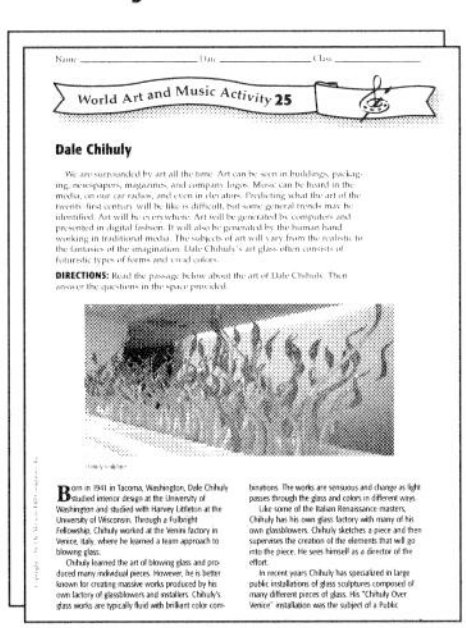

History and Geography Activity 25

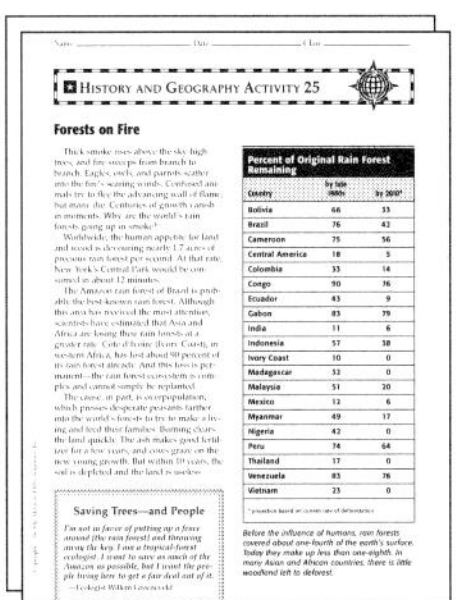

People in World History Activity 25

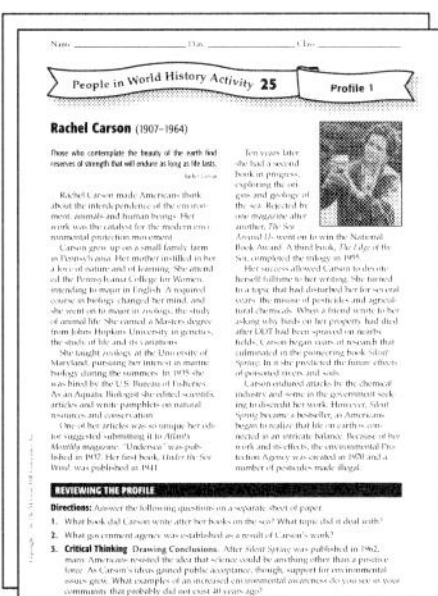

Multimedia

- Vocabulary PuzzleMaker CD-ROM
- Interactive Tutor Self-Assessment CD-ROM
- ExamView® Pro Testmaker CD-ROM
- Audio Program
- World History Primary Source Document Library CD-ROM
- MindJogger Videoquiz
- Presentation Plus! CD-ROM
- TeacherWorks CD-ROM
- Interactive Student Edition CD-ROM
- The World History—Modern Times Video Program

Spanish Resources

The following Spanish language materials are available in the Spanish Resources Binder:

- Spanish Guided Reading Activities
- Spanish Reteaching Activities
- Spanish Quizzes and Tests
- Spanish Vocabulary Activities
- Spanish Summaries

Chapter 25 Resources

SECTION RESOURCES

Daily Objectives	Reproducible Resources	Multimedia Resources
SECTION 1 **The Challenges of Our World** 1. Discuss the environmental, social, economic, and political challenges that the world faces. 2. Explain why the benefits of the technological revolution must be balanced against its costs.	Reproducible Lesson Plan 25–1 Daily Lecture and Discussion Notes 25–1 Guided Reading Activity 25–1* Section Quiz 25–1* Reading Essentials and Study Guide 25–1	Daily Focus Skills Transparency 25–1 Interactive Tutor Self-Assessment CD-ROM ExamView® Pro Testmaker CD-ROM Presentation Plus! CD-ROM
SECTION 2 **Global Visions** 1. Identify the organizations that have been established to respond to global challenges. 2. Characterize the citizens' groups and nongovernmental organizations that have also formed to address global concerns.	Reproducible Lesson Plan 25–2 Daily Lecture and Discussion Notes 25–2 Guided Reading Activity 25–2* Section Quiz 25–2* Reteaching Activity 25* Reading Essentials and Study Guide 25–2	Daily Focus Skills Transparency 25–2 Interactive Tutor Self-Assessment CD-ROM ExamView® Pro Testmaker CD-ROM Presentation Plus! CD-ROM
0:00 **OUT OF TIME?** Assign the Chapter 25 **Reading Essentials and Study Guide.**		

*Also Available in Spanish

 Blackline Master  Transparency  CD-ROM  DVD

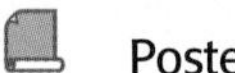 Poster  Music Program Audio Program 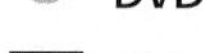 Videocassette

Chapter 25 Resources

NATIONAL GEOGRAPHIC Teacher's Corner

INDEX TO NATIONAL GEOGRAPHIC MAGAZINE

The following articles relate to this chapter:

- "A Dream Called Nunavut," by Michael Parfit, September 1997.
- "Sri Lanka," by Priit J. Vesilind, January 1997.
- "Information Revolution," by Joel L. Swerdlow, October 1995.

NATIONAL GEOGRAPHIC SOCIETY PRODUCTS AVAILABLE FROM GLENCOE

To order the following products call Glencoe at 1-800-334-7344:

- *GTV: The American People* (Videodisc)
- *GTV: A Geographic Perspective on American History* (Videodisc)
- *Picture Atlas of the World* (CD-ROM)

ADDITIONAL NATIONAL GEOGRAPHIC SOCIETY PRODUCTS

To order the following, call National Geographic at 1-800-368-2728:

- *Europe: The Road to Unity* (Video)
- *Technology's Price* (Video)
- *For All Mankind* (Video)

NGS ONLINE

Access National Geographic's new dynamic MapMachine Web site and other geography resources at:
www.nationalgeographic.com
www.nationalgeographic.com/maps

KEY TO ABILITY LEVELS

Teaching strategies have been coded.

L1 BASIC activities for all students
L2 AVERAGE activities for average to above-average students
L3 CHALLENGING activities for above-average students
ELL ENGLISH LANGUAGE LEARNER activities

Block Schedule

Activities that are suited to use within the block scheduling framework are identified by:

Use our Web site for additional resources. All essential content is covered in the Student Edition.

You and your students can visit www.wh.mt.glencoe.com, the Web site companion to Glencoe World History—Modern Times. This innovative integration of electronic and print media offers your students a wealth of opportunities. The student text directs students to the Web site for the following options:

- **Chapter Overviews**
- **Self-Check Quizzes**
- **Student Web Activities**
- **Textbook Updates**

Answers to the Student Web Activities are provided for you in the **Web Activity Lesson Plans.** Additional Web resources and Interactive Tutor Puzzles are also available.

From the Classroom of...

Peter Twomey
Brockton High School
Brockton, Massachusetts

Israel/Palestine—A Solution?

Assign each student a Middle Eastern or North African country to research. Then, using the text, library books, and current newspaper articles, each student should write a brief history of his or her country from the end of World War II to the present, including an economic profile.

Supply each student with a summary sheet of Arab-Israeli conflicts from 1948 to the present accompanied by maps of the Israeli-Palestinian area in 1948, 1967, and today. When students' research is completed, call a peacekeeping meeting. In round one, each country introduces itself and gives an oral summary of its recent history, including an economic profile. In round two, the countries give their views on the question at hand: What should be the nature of the Israeli and Palestinian states? Why?

To conclude, students should compare their views with those of current Israeli and Palestinian politicians.

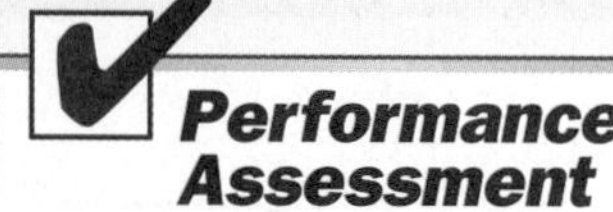

Performance Assessment

Refer to Activity 25 in the Performance Assessment Activities and Rubrics booklet.

The Impact Today

Guide students in a discussion of what they view as the most pressing challenges and the most promising hopes that face them and their families in the coming years.

GLENCOE TECHNOLOGY

The World History—Modern Times Video Program

To learn more about the world's future challenges and goals, students can view the Chapter 25 video, "In the Twenty-First Century," from **The World History—Modern Times Video Program.**

MindJogger Videoquiz

Use the **MindJogger Videoquiz** to preview Chapter 25 content.

Available in VHS.

CHAPTER 25 Challenges and Hopes for the Future

Key Events

As you read this chapter, look for key issues that challenge the contemporary world.

- *Today's world faces the challenges of protecting and preserving the environment, addressing economic and social changes, implementing new technologies, resolving political conflicts, and eliminating international terrorism.*
- *The world's inhabitants must adopt a cooperative global vision to address the problems that confront all humankind.*

The Impact Today

The events that occurred during this time period still impact our lives today.

- *The debate over nuclear weapons continues as European leaders question the United States government's desire to deploy a nuclear missile defense system in outer space.*
- *Peacekeeping forces remain in the Balkan Peninsula.*
- *Automakers, fuel companies, and other manufacturers are developing methods to reduce harmful emissions.*

World History—Modern Times Video *The Chapter 25 video, "In the Twenty-first Century," explores various issues that the world is facing today.*

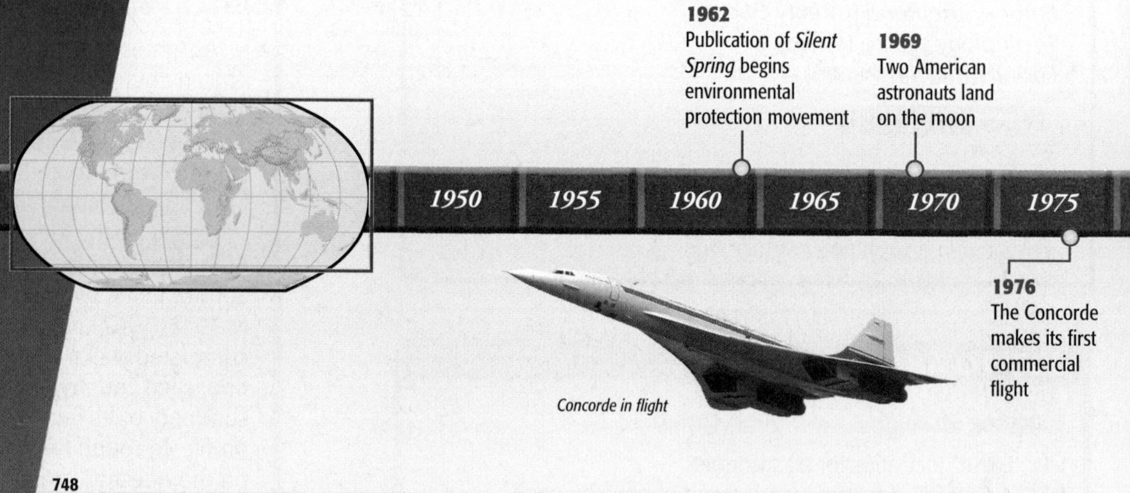
1962
Publication of *Silent Spring* begins environmental protection movement
1969
Two American astronauts land on the moon
1950
1955
1960
1965
1970
1975
1976
The Concorde makes its first commercial flight

Concorde in flight

748

TWO-MINUTE LESSON LAUNCHER

Ask students to list the problems that exist in their community and write their responses on the chalkboard. *(Answers may include traffic, no public transportation, lack of affordable housing, crime, gangs, lack of entertainment facilities for teens, lack of youth programs and athletic fields, need for more public schools, etc.).* Have students name some organizations formed to address these problems. *(Answers may include Boys and Girls Clubs, YMCA, citizens' advisory groups, Police Athletic League, Chamber of Commerce, etc.)* Ask students to determine if any of the problems occur elsewhere in the world. Have them think of ways to address these global problems. L1

Introducing
CHAPTER 25

The International Space Station, shown here in 2000, combines the scientific and technological resources of 16 nations.

Cleanup after oil spill in Alaska

1980 1985 1990 1995 2000 2005

1986 Explosion at nuclear plant in Chernobyl releases deadly radiation

1987 Montreal meeting creates first world environmental pact

1989 *Exxon Valdez* causes oil spill in Alaska

1990 World Wide Web created

1992 Earth Summit proposes solutions to environmental challenges

2001 World responds to terrorist attack on United States

HISTORY Online

Chapter Overview
Visit the *Glencoe World History—Modern Times* Web site at wh.mt.glencoe.com and click on **Chapter 25–Chapter Overview** to preview chapter information.

Chapter Objectives

After studying this chapter, students should be able to:

1. describe factors in the environmental crisis faced by all nations of the world;
2. identify and explain the costs and benefits of the technological revolution;
3. identify and describe the purpose and accomplishments of the United Nations;
4. identify and describe alternative global visions for the future.

Chapter Overview
Introduce students to chapter content and key terms by having them access **Chapter Overview 25** at wh.mt.glencoe.com.

Time Line Activity

As students read the chapter, have them review the time line on these pages. Ask them to explain the significance of the 2001 terrorist attack on the United States.
(On September 11, 2001, terrorists seized four U.S. commercial airliners and crashed three into major U.S. landmarks, killing thousands of individuals and prompting international cooperation to destroy terrorist cells throughout the world.) L1

MORE ABOUT THE ART

The International Space Station The International Space Station is the largest, most sophisticated, and most powerful spacecraft ever built. The 150-ton (136 t) complex has been the temporary home of astronauts from six countries since it opened its hatch on November 2, 2000. Equipment and experiments from the major space station partners – the United States, Russia, Canada, Japan, and the European Space Agency – have been launched to the complex to study space and to observe the earth with the aim of preventing more damage to the earth's environment. The International Space Station is the largest engineering project ever undertaken in space, and it is the first truly global space exploration effort.

CHAPTER PREVIEW

TEACH

Introducing

A Story That Matters

Depending on the ability levels of your students, select from the following questions to reinforce the reading of *A Story That Matters.*

- Discuss the meanings of the words *hero, courage, duty,* and *sacrifice. (Answers will vary.)*
- How did the individuals who responded to the terrorist attacks show these qualities? *(Answers will vary.)*
- What is the meaning of the sentence "Freedom and fear are at war"? (*Answers will vary. President George W. Bush may have meant that the terrorists who planned the attack were motivated by fear—a fear of freedom and democracy.*) **L1 L2 ELL**

About the Art

New York firefighters were among the first to arrive at the World Trade Center on the morning of September 11. Many lost their lives trying to rescue those who were trapped in the buildings. Many more took part in the search and rescue mission that followed. Ask students to describe other photos of this event and tell why those photos were memorable.

CHAPTER PREVIEW

A Story That Matters

Rescue workers search for survivors in the ruins of the World Trade Center.

A Time for Heroes

On September 11, 2001, international terrorists hijacked four commercial airplanes, two of which were used to destroy the twin towers of the World Trade Center in New York City. Thousands of people died in the attack when first one tower, and then the other, collapsed. Many of those who died were firefighters, police officers, and other rescue workers who rushed into the buildings to help people to safety.

In the days following the attack, countless tales of unimaginable bravery emerged. Two office workers carried a disabled woman down 68 floors to safety. Peter Ganci, a 33-year veteran of the New York City Fire Department, survived the collapse of the first tower but died trying to evacuate people from the second tower. Father Mychal Judge, the Fire Department chaplain, removed his helmet to give last rites to a dying firefighter but died himself when he was hit by debris. One firefighter, as he climbed toward the flames, stopped to give a fleeing woman a bottle of water. She escaped, but he did not.

George Howard, a Port Authority officer, raced to help people, even though it was his day off, and died in the effort. In an address to the American nation, President George W. Bush said that he would carry Howard's badge as a reminder of the horrors of terrorism, for "Freedom and fear are at war. The advance of human freedom, the great achievement of our time and the great hope of every time, now depends on us. . . . We will not falter and we will not fail."

Why It Matters

The destruction of the World Trade Center was not an attack on the United States alone. People from over 80 countries were killed in what the United Nations condemned as a "crime against humanity." More and more, people are coming to understand that destructive forces unleashed in one part of the world soon affect the entire world. As British prime minister Tony Blair said, "We are realizing how fragile are our frontiers in the face of the world's new challenges. Today, conflicts rarely stay within national boundaries." Terrorism, worldwide hunger, nuclear proliferation, global warming—these issues make us aware of the global nature of contemporary problems. Increasingly, the world's nations must unite to create lasting solutions.

History and You What contemporary global problem concerns you the most? Write an essay explaining what the world's nations should do, together, to solve this problem.

HISTORY AND YOU

The unprecedented attacks of September 11, 2001, marked a turning point in world history. In addition to causing a tremendous loss of life and the physical destruction of American landmarks, the terrorists inflicted psychological and economic damage. They did not, however, destroy the indomitable human spirit or the goodness of humankind. Instead of causing discord, the attacks promoted unity, cooperation, determination to continue, and the inspiration to rebuild shattered lives and centers of enterprise. It also united many of the world's countries in a global effort to destroy international terrorism.

SECTION 1

The Challenges of Our World

Guide to Reading

Main Ideas
- The world faces environmental, social, economic, and political challenges.
- The benefits of the technological revolution must be balanced against its costs.

Key Terms
ecology, deforestation, ozone layer, greenhouse effect, acid rain, bioethics, biowarfare, bioterrorism, global economy

People to Identify
Rachel Carson, Neil Armstrong, Buzz Aldrin

Places to Locate
Bhopal, Chernobyl, Sudan

Preview Questions
1. What challenges face the world in the twenty-first century?
2. What are the promises and perils of the technological revolution?

Reading Strategy
Cause and Effect Complete the table below as you read the chapter.

Concern	Cause	Effect
Deforestation		
Loss of ozone layer		
Greenhouse effect		
Acid rain		
Weapons		
Hunger		

Preview of Events

1984 · 1985 · 1986 · 1987 · 1988 · 1989 · 1990

1984 Toxic fumes kill 2,000 people in Bhopal, India

1989 Oil spill from tanker in Alaska devastates environment

Voices from the Past

Biologist and author, Rachel Carson

In 1962, Rachel Carson wrote:

> "It is not my contention that chemical pesticides must never be used. I do contend that we have put poisons and biologically potent chemicals into the hands of persons largely or wholly ignorant of their potentials for harm. We have subjected enormous numbers of people to contact with these poisons, without their consent and often without their knowledge. . . . I contend, furthermore, that we have allowed these chemicals to be used with little or no advance investigation of their effect on soil, water, wildlife, and man himself. Future generations are unlikely to condone our lack of prudent concern for the integrity of the natural world that supports all life."
>
> —*Silent Spring*, Rachel Carson, 1962

The modern movement to protect the environment began with Rachel Carson's *Silent Spring*.

The Environmental Crisis

In 1962, American scientist **Rachel Carson** argued that the use of pesticides—chemicals sprayed on crops to kill insects—was having deadly, unforeseen results. Besides insects, birds, fish, and other wild animals were being killed by the buildup of these pesticides in the environment. Also, the pesticide residue on food was harmful to human beings.

1 FOCUS

Section Overview

This section discusses the benefits of the technological revolution and explores the challenges the world faces.

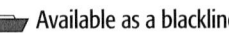

BELLRINGER
Skillbuilder Activity

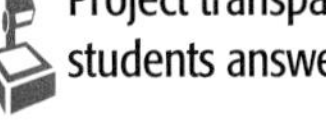
Project transparency and have students answer questions.

Available as a blackline master.

Daily Focus Skills Transparency 25–1

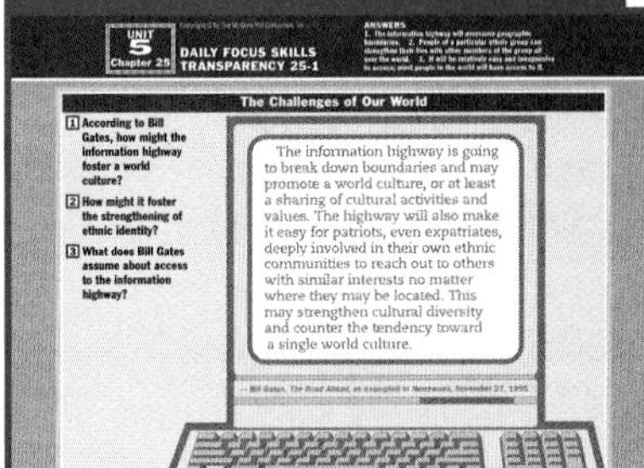

Guide to Reading

Answers to Graphic: Deforestation—Cause: population growth; Effect: destruction of natural habitat; Loss of ozone layer—Cause: chlorofluorocarbons; Effect: Earth loses ultraviolet protection; Greenhouse effect—Cause: carbon dioxide; Effect: global warming; Acid rain—Cause: sulfur; Effect: destroys forests; Weapons—Cause: technological and biological revolution; Effect: war; Hunger—Cause: population growth, natural catastrophes; Effect: starvation

Preteaching Vocabulary: Explain the *greenhouse effect. (buildup of carbon dioxide acts like the glass roof of a greenhouse, containing heat from the sun)* L2

SECTION RESOURCES

Reproducible Masters
- Reproducible Lesson Plan 25–1
- Daily Lecture and Discussion Notes 25–1
- Guided Reading Activity 25–1
- Section Quiz 25–1
- Reading Essentials and Study Guide 25–1

Transparencies
- Daily Focus Skills Transparency 25–1

Multimedia
- Interactive Tutor Self-Assessment CD-ROM
- ExamView® Pro Testmaker CD-ROM
- Presentation Plus! CD-ROM

CHAPTER 25
Section 1, 751-755

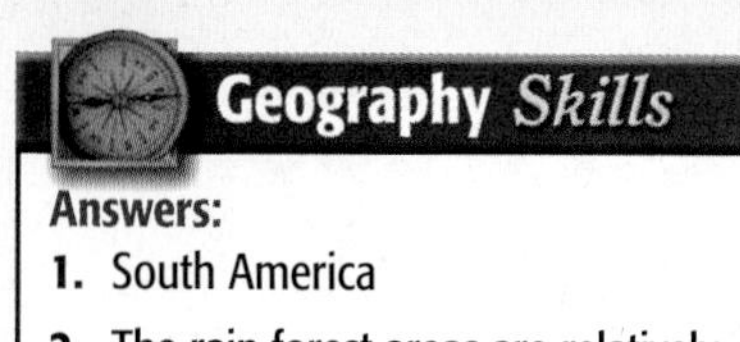

Geography Skills

Answers:
1. South America
2. The rain forest areas are relatively close to the Equator.

Daily Lecture and Discussion Notes 25–1

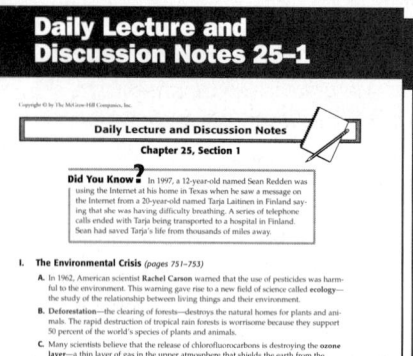

Daily Lecture and Discussion Notes
Chapter 25, Section 1

Did You Know? In 1997, a 12-year-old named Sean Redden was using the Internet at his home in Texas when he saw a message on the Internet from a 20-year-old named Tarja Laitinen in Finland saying that she was having difficulty breathing. A series of telephone calls ended with Tarja being transported to a hospital in Finland. Sean had saved Tarja's life from thousands of miles away.

I. **The Environmental Crisis** *(pages 751–753)*
   A. In 1962, American scientist **Rachel Carson** warned that the use of pesticides was harmful to the environment. This warning gave rise to a new field of science called **ecology**—the study of the relationship between living things and their environment.
   B. **Deforestation**—the clearing of forests—destroys the natural homes for plants and animals. The rapid destruction of tropical rain forests is worrisome because they support 50 percent of the world's species of plants and animals.
   C. Many scientists believe that the release of chlorofluorocarbons is destroying the **ozone layer**—a thin layer of gas in the upper atmosphere that shields the earth from the Sun's ultraviolet rays.

Guided Reading Activity 25–1

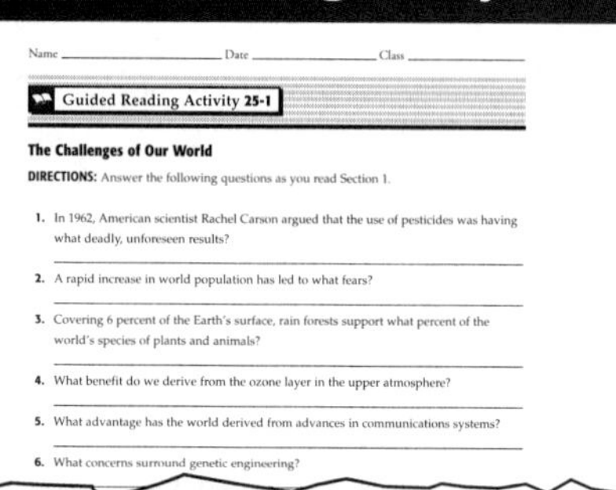

Name ______ Date ______ Class ______

Guided Reading Activity 25-1

The Challenges of Our World

DIRECTIONS: Answer the following questions as you read Section 1.

1. In 1962, American scientist Rachel Carson argued that the use of pesticides was having what deadly, unforeseen results?
2. A rapid increase in world population has led to what fears?
3. Covering 6 percent of the Earth's surface, rain forests support what percent of the world's species of plants and animals?
4. What benefit do we derive from the ozone layer in the upper atmosphere?
5. What advantage has the world derived from advances in communications systems?
6. What concerns surround genetic engineering?

Connecting Across Time

Have students list the social changes that took place as a result of the Industrial Revolution in the eighteenth and nineteenth centuries. Assign students to compare these changes with those that are taking place today in the United States as a result of the technological revolution. L2

NATIONAL GEOGRAPHIC **Global Deforestation**

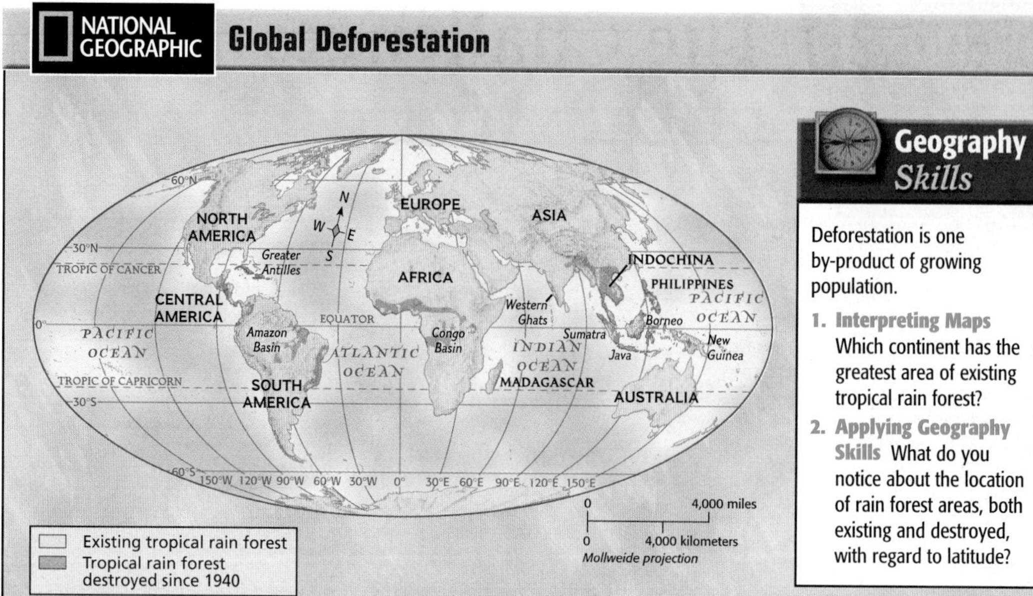

Geography Skills

Deforestation is one by-product of growing population.

1. **Interpreting Maps** Which continent has the greatest area of existing tropical rain forest?
2. **Applying Geography Skills** What do you notice about the location of rain forest areas, both existing and destroyed, with regard to latitude?

Carson's warnings alarmed many scientists and gave rise to a new field of science called ecology, the study of the relationship between living things and their environment. Many people became more aware of the dangers to the environment on which they depended for their survival.

Impact of Population Growth Dangers to the environment have many sources. A rapid increase in world population has led to fears that Earth's resources simply cannot support the growing number of human beings. Deforestation—the clearing of forests—is one by-product of the growing population. More and more forests and jungles have been cut down to provide farmland and firewood for the people on Earth. As forests are cut down, natural dwelling places for plants and animals are destroyed.

Especially worrisome is the rapid destruction of tropical rain forests near Earth's equator. Although the tropical rain forests cover only 6 percent of Earth's surface, they support 50 percent of the world's species of plants and animals. The tropical rain forests are also crucial to human survival. They remove carbon dioxide from the air and return oxygen to it.

Chemical Wastes and Disasters Another danger to the environment is chemical waste. One concern involves chlorofluorocarbons, which are gases used in aerosol cans, refrigerators, and automobile air conditioners. Many scientists warn that the release of chlorofluorocarbons is destroying the ozone layer, a thin layer of gas in the upper atmosphere that shields Earth from the Sun's ultraviolet rays.

Other scientists have proposed the existence of a greenhouse effect, global warming caused by the buildup of carbon dioxide in the atmosphere. Global warming could create various problems. Sea levels could rise because of melting polar ice, for example, and cause flooding of coastal areas.

Yet another problem is acid rain, the rainfall that results when sulfur produced by factories mixes with moisture in the air. Acid rain has been held responsible for killing forests in both North America and Europe.

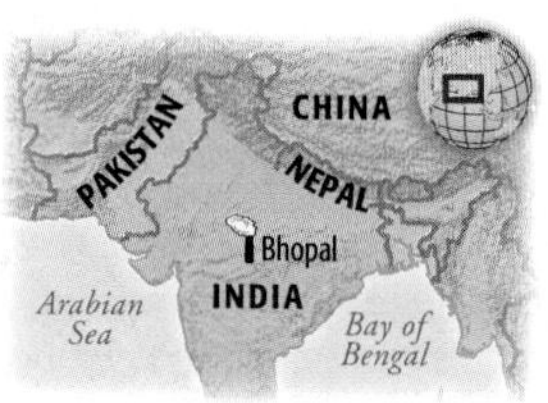

Major ecological disasters have also occurred during the last 20 years. In 1984, a chemical plant at **Bhopal,** India, released toxic fumes into the air, killing 2,000 people and injuring another 150,000. A nuclear explosion at **Chernobyl** in 1986 released radiation that killed hundreds. In 1989, the oil tanker *Exxon Valdez* ran aground in Alaska. Thousands of

COOPERATIVE LEARNING ACTIVITY

Creating a Newspaper Organize the class into four groups and assign each group a global-issue category: environmental, political, economic, and social. Each group should select a particular global issue in their category and study the issue by scanning newspapers, magazines, television and radio broadcasts, and the Internet. Group members will compile their information and transfer the information from one medium to another, including written to visual and statistical to written or visual, using computer software as appropriate. Groups will then create a newspaper devoted to the global issues in their category. As part of this assignment, students should be required to interpret databases they use in their research, and create new databases, research outlines, bibliographies, and visuals, including graphs, charts, time lines, and maps. L2

birds were killed, fishing grounds were polluted, and the local environment was devastated.

These ecological disasters made people more aware of the need to deal with environmental problems. In 1987, representatives of 46 nations meeting in Montreal agreed to protect Earth's ozone layer by reducing the use of chlorofluorocarbons. In 1992, an Earth Summit in Rio de Janeiro examined the challenges to the environment and proposed new solutions.

Individual nations have reacted to environmental problems by enacting recycling programs, curbing the dumping of toxic materials, and instituting water conservation measures. Whether these efforts will be sufficient to save the environment and keep Earth habitable will no doubt be one of the major questions of the early twenty-first century.

Reading Check **Summarizing** What global concerns have arisen since the 1960s?

The Technological Revolution

TURNING POINT **In this section, you will learn how two American astronauts landed on the moon in 1969. This landing opened the new frontier of space to world exploration.**

Since World War II, a stunning array of changes has created a technological revolution.

Transportation, Communications, and Space

Modern transportation and communication systems are transforming the world community. Since the 1970s, jumbo jet airliners have moved millions of people around the world each year. The Internet—the world's largest network of computers—provides quick access to enormous quantities of information. The development of the World Wide Web in the 1990s made the Internet even more accessible to people everywhere. Satellites, cable television, facsimile (fax) machines, and cellular telephones enable people to communicate almost instantaneously with others practically everywhere on Earth.

The exploration of space is another world-changing development. In 1969, the American astronauts **Neil Armstrong** and **Buzz Aldrin** landed on the moon. Since then, space probes have increased our understanding of distant planets, and several astronauts have orbited the earth in the space shuttle. Satellites provide information about weather on Earth, and transmit signals for radio, television, and telephone communications.

Health Care and Agriculture

In the field of health, new medicines enable doctors to treat both physical and mental illnesses. New technologies, including computer-aided imaging, have enabled doctors to perform "miracle" operations. Mechanical valves and pumps for the heart as well as organ transplants have allowed people to live longer and more productive lives.

Technological changes in the field of health have raised new concerns, however, and have led to a new field of study called bioethics, which deals with moral choices in medical research. For example, genetic engineering is a new scientific field that alters the genetic information of cells to produce new variations. Some scientists have questioned whether genetic engineering might accidentally create new strains of deadly bacteria that could not be controlled. The issues of stem-cell research and human cloning have also generated intense debate.

In agriculture, the Green Revolution has promised immense returns. The Green Revolution refers to the development of new strains of rice, corn, and other grains that have greater yields. It was promoted as the technological solution to feeding the world's ever-growing population. However, immense quantities of chemical fertilizers are needed to grow the new strains, and many farmers cannot afford them.

Astronaut Buzz Aldrin on the moon with the Apollo 11 *lunar module*

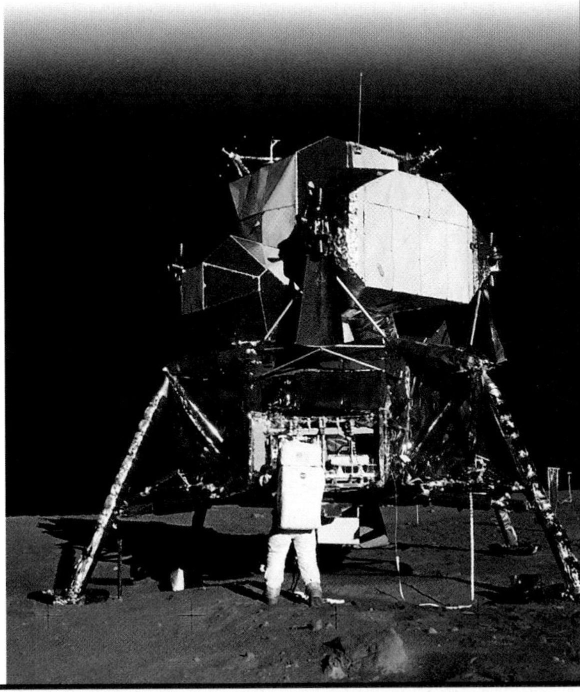

CHAPTER 25
Section 1, 751-755

Reading Check

Answer: Answers will include the environment, population growth, deforestation, disposal of chemical waste, and chemical and nuclear accidents.

TURNING POINT

In what ways has the technological revolution been a turning point? *(Computers and the Internet enable millions of people throughout the world to communicate with one another; new technologies have furthered space exploration, and new medical technologies have improved quality of life and research possibilities.)* L1

Critical Thinking

As students finish their study of world history, assign students to identify the major eras in world history and describe their defining characteristics. Students may wish to refer to unit and chapter titles as well as chapter time lines. Students should create a chart or table listing the major eras and their defining characteristics. Charts should be displayed in the room and will be a helpful study tool. Encourage students to study all the charts. L2

COOPERATIVE LEARNING ACTIVITY

Creating a Time Line Throughout this course, students have been made aware of changes that resulted from important turning points in world history. Have students review the turning points contained in each chapter. Break students into small groups and assign each group a time period or a unit from the text. Groups will research their time period or unit and then each group will create a time line illustrating the changes that resulted from important turning points. In creating their time lines, students should apply absolute and relative chronology through the sequencing of significant individuals, events, and time periods. Display the time lines around the room so that students can compare absolute and relative chronology. L2

Reading Check

Answer: transportation, communications, space exploration, health care, agriculture, weapons development

3 ASSESS

Assign Section 1 Assessment as homework or as an in-class activity.

Have students use **Interactive Tutor Self-Assessment CD-ROM.**

Section Quiz 25-1

Name ______ Date ______ Class ______

Chapter 25 Score

Section Quiz 25-1

DIRECTIONS: Matching Match each item in Column A with an item in Column B. Write the correct letters in the blanks. *(10 points each)*

Column A	Column B
____ 1. global warming caused by a build-up of carbon dioxide in the atmosphere	A. Rio de Janeiro
____ 2. site of Soviet Union nuclear disaster	B. greenhouse effect
____ 3. site of 1992 Earth Summit	C. Bhopal
____ 4. science of altering genetic information in cells to create new variations of cells	D. genetic engineering
____ 5. site of 1984 Indian chemical disaster	E. Chernobyl

DIRECTIONS: Multiple Choice In the blank, write the letter of the choice that best completes the statement or answers the question. *(10 points each)*

CURRICULUM CONNECTION

Political Systems Ask students to select a contemporary event that is under debate. Once they have chosen an event, ask students to apply their knowledge of political systems to make decisions about the event. Students may analyze information by drawing conclusions as part of their decision-making process. For example, students could consider how different political systems might influence the outcome or resolution of their chosen event. L2

In addition, the new crops have been subject to insects. The pesticides used to control the insects create environmental problems.

Weapons The technological revolution has also led to the development of more advanced methods of destruction. Most frightening are nuclear, biological, and chemical weapons.

The end of the Cold War in the late 1980s reduced the chances of a major nuclear war. However, nuclear weapons continue to spread, making a regional nuclear war possible. Another concern is whether nuclear materials—bombs or radioactive matter—will be obtained and used by terrorists.

After anthrax-filled letters were used to kill U.S. citizens in 2001, people around the world became more aware of the increased availability and the potential threat of biological and chemical weapons. **Biowarfare,** the use of disease and poison against civilians and soldiers in wartime, is not new, however. The first incident occurred in Europe in the 1300s when, during a siege, plague-infested corpses were launched over city walls to infect the populace. Biological weapons were used in World War I and in China and Manchuria in the 1930s and 1940s. Chemical weapons were used extensively in the Iran-Iraq war in the 1980s.

Governments have made agreements to limit the research, production, and use of biological and chemical weapons. The 1925 Geneva Protocol, for example, prohibits the use, though not the research or production, of biological and chemical weapons. In 1972, the United States and the Soviet Union agreed only to permit work on defensive biological weapons.

These measures have not prevented terrorists and terrorist-supporting governments from practicing **bioterrorism,** the use of biological and chemical weapons in terrorist attacks. For example, in 1995 members of a Japanese religious sect named Aum Shinrikyo released a chemical agent, sarin gas, in a Tokyo subway, killing 12 people and injuring thousands.

Reading Check **Identifying** List the industries that the technological revolution has affected since World War II.

Economic and Social Challenges

Since World War II, the nations of the world have developed a **global economy**—an economy in which the production, distribution, and sale of goods take place on a worldwide scale. In 1995, the **World Trade Organization** (WTO) was established. Trade agreements are negotiated, signed, and upheld by its member nations, which number over 140. The WTO has been criticized for placing commercial interests over environmental and health concerns and leaving out small and developing countries. Still, the WTO is the only global international organization dealing with rules of trade between nations.

Another symbol of the global economy is the multinational corporation. The growing number of these corporations (including banks, computer companies, airlines, and fast-food chains) do business around the world. In this way the multinational corporations help tie countries together in a global economy and create a more interdependent world.

The Gap Between Rich and Poor Nations One of the features of the global economy is the wide gap between rich and poor nations. The rich, industrialized nations are mainly in the Northern Hemisphere. They include countries such as the United States, Canada, and Japan, as well as countries in western Europe. These nations have well-organized industrial and agricultural systems, make use of advanced technologies, and have strong educational systems.

The poor nations, sometimes called developing countries, are located mainly in the Southern Hemisphere and include many nations in Africa, Asia, and Latin America. Developing countries are primarily farming nations with little technology.

A serious problem in developing countries is explosive population growth. The world's population today is 6.2 billion. The United Nations projects that by 2050, the world's population could reach 9 billion. Much of that rapid growth is taking place in developing countries, which can least afford it.

Rapidly growing populations have caused many people to move to cities to find jobs. In developing countries, the size of some cities has grown dramatically as a result of this shift. São Paulo, Brazil, for example, had 8.1 million people in 1970. Today, it has over 22 million. Millions of people in such cities live in terrible conditions in slums or shantytowns.

Hunger has also become a staggering problem. Every year, over 8 million people die of hunger, many of them children under five years of age. Besides rapid population growth, poor soil, natural catastrophes, and economic and political factors contribute to widespread hunger. In Afghanistan, for example, most of the population is hungry. Over the last two decades, the country has experienced a major earthquake, severe drought, and political and military upheaval.

CRITICAL THINKING ACTIVITY

Compare and Contrast Throughout this text, students have read about the historic origins and development of widely differing economic systems. Among them are: a centrally planned Communist economy, a free-market economy, a welfare state economy, and a Socialist economy. Ask students to write an essay in which they compare the relationships between and among contemporary countries with differing economic systems. What are the advantages and disadvantages of each system? In this era of globalization, are economic systems evolving? Are differing economic systems beginning to resemble each other or are they maintaining their distinctiveness? L2

Civil wars have been especially devastating in creating food shortages. In **Sudan,** civil war broke out in the 1980s. Both sides refused to allow food to be sent to their enemies. By the early 1990s, 1.3 million people had died in Sudan from starvation.

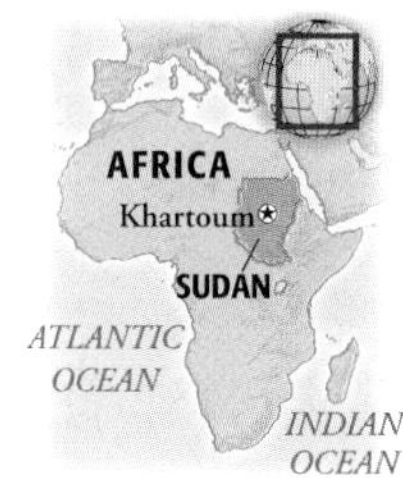

The Gender Gap The gap between rich and poor nations is also reflected in the status of women. In the Western world, the gap between men and women has been steadily narrowing. The number of women in the workforce continues to increase, along with the number of women university graduates. Many countries have passed laws that require equal pay for women and men who are doing the same work. A number of Western countries also have laws that prohibit discrimination based on gender.

Women in developing countries, by contrast, often remain bound to their homes and families and subordinate to their fathers and husbands. They continue to face difficulties in obtaining education, property rights, or decent jobs.

Reading Check **Comparing** What are the differences between developing and industrialized nations?

Political Challenges

After World War II, African and Asian leaders identified democracy as the defining theme of their new political cultures. Within a decade, however, democratic systems in many developing countries had been replaced by military dictatorships or one-party governments. Many leaders underestimated the difficulties of building democratic political institutions.

In recent years, there have been signs of renewed interest in democracy in various parts of the world, particularly in Asia, Africa, and Latin America. Examples are the free elections held in South Korea, Taiwan, and the Philippines. Similar developments have taken place in a number of African countries and throughout Latin America.

Unfortunately, regional, ethnic, and religious differences continue to create conflict around the world. In Europe, Yugoslavia has been torn apart by ethnic divisions. In the Middle East, the conflict between Israelis and Palestinians continues to produce acts of terror. Conflicts among hostile ethnic groups in Africa have led to massacres of hundreds of thousands. It remains to be seen how such conflicts can be resolved.

Reading Check **Explaining** Name the areas of the world where conflict exists. Describe the nature of the conflicts.

Reading Check

Answer: Developing nations are primarily farming nations with little technology. Developed nations have well-organized industrial and agricultural systems, make use of advanced technologies, and have strong educational systems.

Reading Check

Answer: Answers will depend on current events.

Reading Essentials and Study Guide 25–1

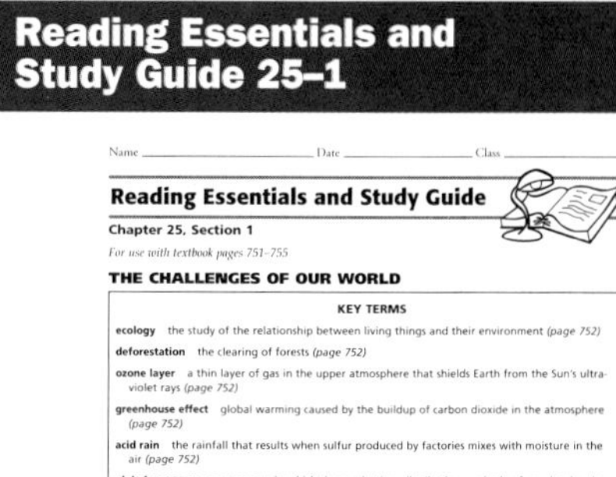

Name ______ Date ______ Class ______

Reading Essentials and Study Guide

Chapter 25, Section 1

For use with textbook pages 751–755

THE CHALLENGES OF OUR WORLD

KEY TERMS

ecology the study of the relationship between living things and their environment (page 752)

deforestation the clearing of forests (page 752)

ozone layer a thin layer of gas in the upper atmosphere that shields Earth from the Sun's ultraviolet rays (page 752)

greenhouse effect global warming caused by the buildup of carbon dioxide in the atmosphere (page 752)

acid rain the rainfall that results when sulfur produced by factories mixes with moisture in the air (page 752)

global economy an economy in which the production, distribution, and sale of goods take place

SECTION 1 ASSESSMENT

Checking for Understanding

1. **Define** ecology, deforestation, ozone layer, greenhouse effect, acid rain, bioethics, biowarfare, bioterrorism, global economy.
2. **Identify** Rachel Carson, Neil Armstrong, Buzz Aldrin, World Trade Organization.
3. **Locate** Bhopal, Chernobyl, Sudan.
4. **Explain** why many people have become concerned about the environment. Also explain how the technological revolution has created, as well as solved, problems.
5. **List** three countries in which free elections have demonstrated great progress toward democracy. Also list three types of political challenges that remain unsolved and give an example of each.

Critical Thinking

6. **Analyze** What are the individual and global consequences of overpopulation?
7. **Summarizing Information** Create a chart like the one below listing technological advances in transportation, communications, space exploration, health care, agriculture, and weaponry. List the drawback or cost of each technological advance.

Technological Advances	Drawback or Cost
Transportation	
Communications	
Space Exploration	
Health Care	
Agriculture	
Weaponry	

Analyzing Visuals

8. **Compare** the photo on page 753 to the photo of the International Space Station on page 749. Describe the advances and changes in space technology that are reflected in these two photos. How many years have elapsed between the two photos?

Writing About History

9. **Expository Writing** By now, most leaders of major nations have recognized that environmental damage is a significant issue. For this reason, these leaders frequently hold meetings and summits to negotiate solutions. In an essay, discuss why negotiations are needed. What concerns can cause nations or individuals to ignore the environment?

Reteaching Activity

Ask students to list, rank, and describe five important challenges the world faces today. L1

4 CLOSE

Ask students to review the challenges described in this section and select one that causes them the greatest concern. Ask students to explain why this challenge concerns them and ways they can address it. L1 ELL

SECTION 1 ASSESSMENT

1. Key terms are in blue.
2. Rachel Carson *(p. 751)*; Neil Armstrong *(p. 753)*; Buzz Aldrin *(p. 753)*; WTO *(p. 754)*
3. See chapter maps.
4. Human survival is at risk. Technology has created environmental disaters.
5. South Korea, Taiwan, and the Philippines
6. Individual: hunger, poverty; Global: deforestation, loss of plant, animal species, greenhouse effect
7. Transportation: pollution; Communications: constant accessibility; Space Exploration: money from social programs; Health Care: genetic engineering; Agriculture: greater use of fertilizer, pesticides; Weaponry: risk that materials will end in terrorist hands
8. *Apollo 11* was not meant to orbit for long periods, Space Station carries entire crews for extended periods; 31 years
9. Essays will reflect understanding of global environmental issues.

CHAPTER 25
Section 2, 756-758

1 FOCUS

Section Overview

This section discusses the organizations formed to address global concerns and respond to global challenges.

BELLRINGER
Skillbuilder Activity

 Project transparency and have students answer questions.

 Available as a blackline master.

Daily Focus Skills Transparency 25–2

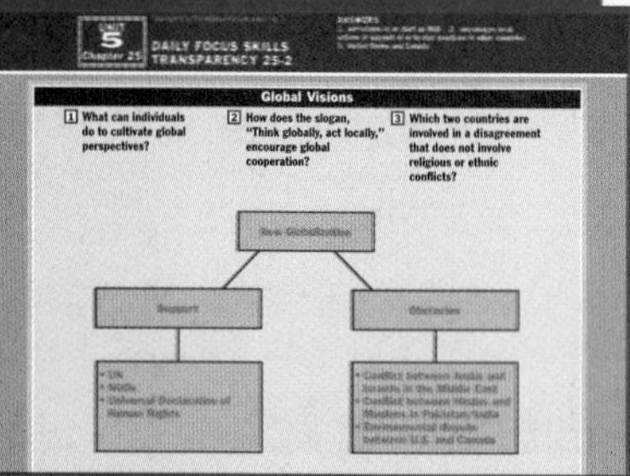

Guide to Reading

Answers to Graphic: Top level: Security Council
Middle level: General Assembly, secretary general
Bottom level: UNESCO, WHO, UNICEF, other agencies

Preteaching Vocabulary: Explain the significance of a *peacekeeping force. (A peacekeeping force is a military unit drawn from neutral member nations to settle conflicts and supervise truces.)* L2

SECTION 2 Global Visions

Guide to Reading

Main Ideas
- Organizations have been established to respond to global challenges.
- Citizens' groups and nongovernmental organizations have also formed to address global concerns.

Key Terms
peacekeeping force, disarmament

People to Identify
Franklin Delano Roosevelt, Hazel Henderson, Elise Boulding

Places to Locate
China, Canada

Preview Questions
1. What international organization arose at the end of World War II to help maintain the peace?
2. How have ordinary citizens worked to address the world's problems?

Reading Strategy
Organizing Information Create a pyramid like the one below that depicts the structure of the United Nations. The Security Council is at the top of the pyramid.

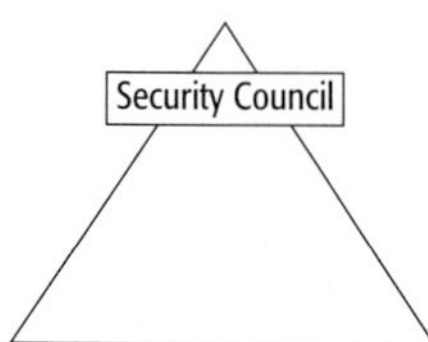

Preview of Events

1945 · 1946 · 1947 · 1948 · 1949

- **1945** United Nations becomes world organization
- **1946** United Nations International Children's Emergency Fund (UNICEF) founded
- **1948** United Nations General Assembly adopts Universal Declaration of Human Rights

Eleanor Roosevelt holds the Universal Declaration of Human Rights.

Voices from the Past

On December 10, 1948, the General Assembly of the United Nations adopted the Universal Declaration of Human Rights:

> ❝All human beings are born free and equal in dignity and rights. . . . Everyone is entitled to all the rights and freedoms set forth in this Declaration, without distinction of any kind, such as race, color, sex, language, religion, political or other opinion, national or social origin, property, birth or other status. . . . Everyone has the right to life, liberty, and security of person. . . . Everyone has the right to freedom of movement. . . . Everyone has the right to freedom of opinion and expression.❞
>
> —***The Universal Declaration of Human Rights,*** **1948**

The United Nations took the lead in affirming the basic human rights of all peoples.

The United Nations

As people have become aware that many problems humans face are global—not national—they have responded to this realization in different ways. The United Nations (UN) has been one of the most visible symbols of the new globalism.

The United Nations was founded in 1945 in San Francisco, when representatives of the Allied forces worked out a plan for a new international organization. U.S. president **Franklin Delano Roosevelt** was especially eager to create such an organization to help maintain the peace after the war. At the Yalta Conference in February 1945, Joseph Stalin of the Soviet Union agreed to join the new organization.

In the original charter, the members pledged "to save succeeding generations from the scourge of war, which twice in our lifetime . . . brought untold sorrow to mankind, and to reaffirm faith in fundamental human rights, in the dignity and

SECTION RESOURCES

Reproducible Masters
- Reproducible Lesson Plan 25–2
- Daily Lecture and Discussion Notes 25–2
- Guided Reading Activity 25–2
- Section Quiz 25–2
- Reading Essentials and Study Guide 25–2

Transparencies
- Daily Focus Skills Transparency 25–2

Multimedia
- Interactive Tutor Self-Assessment CD-ROM
- ExamView® Pro Testmaker CD-ROM
- Presentation Plus! CD-ROM

worth of the human person, in the equal rights of men and women and of nations large and small, and to promote social progress and better standards of life in larger freedom." The United Nations, then, has two chief goals: peace and human dignity.

The General Assembly of the United Nations is comprised of representatives of all member nations. It has the power to discuss any question of importance to the organization and to recommend the action to be taken. The day-to-day administrative business of the United Nations is supervised by the secretary-general, whose offices are located in New York City.

The most important advisory group of the United Nations is the Security Council. It is composed of 5 permanent members—the United States, Russia, Great Britain, France, and **China**—and 10 members chosen by the General Assembly to serve limited terms. The Security Council decides what actions the United Nations should take to settle international disputes. Because each of the permanent members can veto the council's decision, a stalemate has frequently resulted from Security Council deliberations.

A number of specialized agencies function under the direction of the United Nations. These include the United Nations Educational, Scientific, and Cultural Organization (UNESCO), the World Health Organization (WHO), and the United Nations International Children's Emergency Fund (UNICEF). The International Monetary Fund (IMF), an agency of the United Nations, provides funds for developing nations to aid economic development. All these agencies have been successful in helping to address economic and social problems around the world.

The United Nations has on various occasions provided peacekeeping forces, which are military forces drawn from neutral member states to settle conflicts and supervise truces. Missions in Somalia and Bosnia, however, raised questions about the effectiveness of the United Nations in peacekeeping operations.

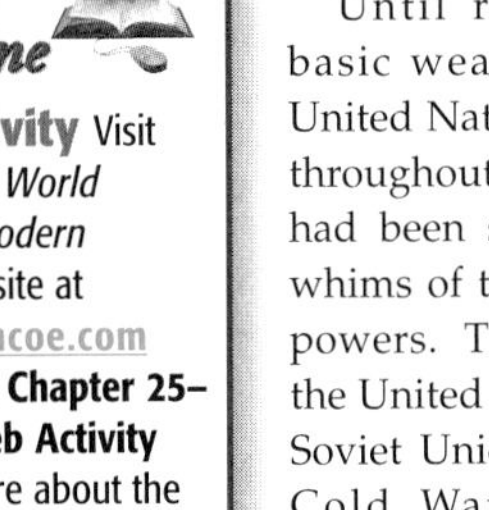

Web Activity Visit the *Glencoe World History—Modern Times* Web site at wh.mt.glencoe.com and click on **Chapter 25–Student Web Activity** to learn more about the United Nations.

Until recently, the basic weakness of the United Nations was that, throughout its history, it had been subject to the whims of the two superpowers. The rivalry of the United States and the Soviet Union during the Cold War was often played out at the expense of the United Nations. The United Nations had little success, for example, in reducing the arms race between the two superpowers. With the end of the Cold War, the United Nations has played a more active role in keeping alive a vision of international order.

United Nations troops give food to starving Bosnian Muslims.

Reading Check **Describing** Outline the history of the United Nations, name its three main divisions, list its specialized agencies, and explain how each unit functions.

New Global Visions

One approach to the global problems we face has been the development of social movements led by ordinary citizens. These movements have addressed issues including environmental problems, women's and men's liberation, human potential, appropriate technology, and nonviolence. "Think globally, act locally" is frequently the slogan of such grassroots groups.

Hazel Henderson, a British-born economist, has been especially active in founding public interest groups. She believes that citizen groups can be an important force for greater global unity and justice.

In *Creating Alternative Futures,* Henderson explained: "These aroused citizens are by no means all mindless young radicals. Well-dressed, clean-shaven, middle-class businessmen and their suburban wives comprise the major forces in California fighting against nuclear power. Hundreds of thousands of middle-class mothers are bringing massive

CHAPTER 25
Section 2, 756-758

2 TEACH

Reading Check

Answer: founded in 1945, goals: peace and human dignity; General Assembly discusses world matters and recommends actions; Security Council resolves international disputes; the secretary-general supervises the UN's day-to-day administration; specialized agencies include UNESCO, WHO, and UNICEF

Daily Lecture and Discussion Notes 25–2

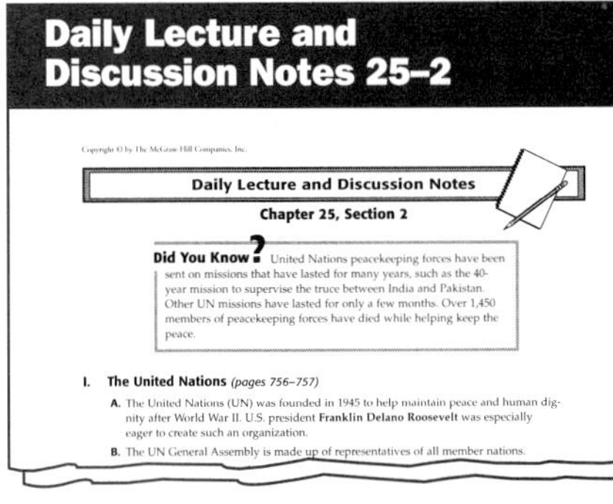

Daily Lecture and Discussion Notes

Chapter 25, Section 2

Did You Know? United Nations peacekeeping forces have been sent on missions that have lasted for many years, such as the 40-year mission to supervise the truce between India and Pakistan. Other UN missions have lasted for only a few months. Over 1,450 members of peacekeeping forces have died while helping keep the peace.

I. **The United Nations** *(pages 756–757)*

A. The United Nations (UN) was founded in 1945 to help maintain peace and human dignity after World War II. U.S. president **Franklin Delano Roosevelt** was especially eager to create such an organization.

B. The UN General Assembly is made up of representatives of all member nations.

Guided Reading Activity 25–2

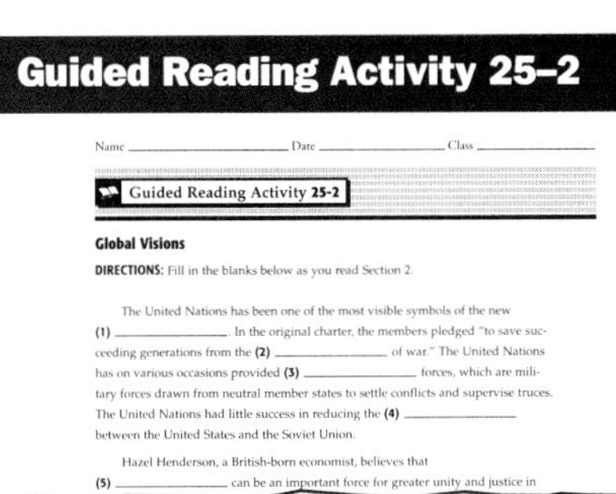

Name ______________ Date ______________ Class ______________

Guided Reading Activity **25-2**

Global Visions

DIRECTIONS: Fill in the blanks below as you read Section 2.

The United Nations has been one of the most visible symbols of the new **(1)** ______________. In the original charter, the members pledged "to save succeeding generations from the **(2)** ______________ of war." The United Nations has on various occasions provided **(3)** ______________ forces, which are military forces drawn from neutral member states to settle conflicts and supervise truces. The United Nations had little success in reducing the **(4)** ______________ between the United States and the Soviet Union.

Hazel Henderson, a British-born economist, believes that **(5)** ______________ can be an important force for greater unity and justice in

3 ASSESS

Assign Section 2 Assessment as homework or as an in-class activity.

Have students use **Interactive Tutor Self-Assessment CD-ROM.**

CRITICAL THINKING ACTIVITY

Researching a Report Have students research a nongovernmental organization on the local, national, or international level. On the local or national levels, students should look for a religious, political, professional, labor, or business organization whose main goal is to stop human rights abuses. On the international level, students might study Amnesty International or the International Committee of the Red Cross. Students should research methods used to further an organization's cause, its membership, and its progress in the past five years. They should write an essay about the selected organization and then state and support their opinions as to whether or not the organization has met its goals. L3

Section Quiz 25–2

Name ______ Date ______ Class ______

Chapter 25 Score

Section Quiz 25-2

DIRECTIONS: Matching Match each item in Column A with an item in Column B. Write the correct letters in the blanks. *(10 points each)*

Column A	Column B
___ 1. certain grassroots social movements led by ordinary citizens	A. New York
___ 2. headquarters of the United Nations	B. Hazel Henderson
___ 3. United Nations specialty agency	C. UNESCO
___ 4. British-born economist active in founding public interest groups	D. Elise Boulding
___ 5. American educator active in encouraging global thinking	E. non-governmental organizations (NGOs)

DIRECTIONS: Multiple Choice In the blank, write the letter of the choice that best completes the statement or answers the question. *(10 points each)*

Reading Check

Answer: citizen groups (or public interest groups) and nongovernmental organizations (NGOs); hindered by political, ethnic, and religious disputes

Reading Essentials and Study Guide 25–2

Name ______ Date ______ Class ______

Reading Essentials and Study Guide

Chapter 25, Section 2

For use with textbook pages 756–758

GLOBAL VISIONS

KEY TERMS

peacekeeping force a military force drawn from neutral states to settle conflicts and supervise truces *(page 757)*

disarmament limiting or reducing armed forces and weapons *(page 758)*

DRAWING FROM EXPERIENCE

Have you heard the slogan "Think globally, act locally"? What do you think this slogan means? How might this slogan be carried out in your community?

In the last section, you read about global challenges at the end of the twentieth century. In this section, you will read about international organizations

Reteaching Activity

Ask students to list and describe five major organizations addressing global challenges. **L2**

4 CLOSE

Guide students in a discussion of the methods used by the United Nations to improve the living conditions of people throughout the world. **L1**

Peace march

pressure to ban commercials and violent programs from children's television."

Related to the emergence of social movements is the growth of nongovernmental organizations (NGOs). NGOs include professional, business, and cooperative organizations; foundations; religious, peace, and disarmament groups, which work to limit or reduce armed forces and weapons; youth and women's organizations; environmental and human rights groups; and research institutes.

According to the American educator **Elise Boulding,** who has been active in encouraging the existence of these groups, NGOs are an important instrument in the cultivation of global perspectives. Boulding states: "Since NGOs by definition are identified with interests that transcend national boundaries, we expect all NGOs to define problems in global terms, to take account of human interests and needs as they are found in all parts of the planet." The number of international NGOs increased from 176 in 1910 to nearly 29,000 in 1995.

Global approaches to global problems, however, have been hindered by political, ethnic, and religious disputes. The Palestinian-Israeli conflict keeps much of the Middle East in constant turmoil. Religious differences between Hindus and Muslims help to inflame relations between India and Pakistan. The United States and **Canada** have argued about the effects of acid rain on Canadian forests.

The collapse of the Soviet Union has led to the emergence of new nations in conflict and a general atmosphere of friction and tension throughout much of Eastern Europe. The bloody conflict in the lands of the former Yugoslavia clearly indicates the dangers in the rise of nationalist sentiment among various ethnic and religious groups in that region. Even as the world becomes more global in culture and as the nations of the world become more interdependent, disruptive forces still exist that can work against efforts to enhance our human destiny.

Many lessons can be learned from the study of world history. One of them is especially clear: a lack of involvement in the affairs of society can easily lead to a sense of powerlessness. An understanding of our world heritage and its lessons might well give us the opportunity to make wise choices in an age that is often crisis laden and chaotic. We are all creators of history. The choices we make in our everyday lives will affect the future of world civilization.

Reading Check **Examining** List two ways people have attempted to resolve global problems and describe the obstacles to solving these problems.

SECTION 2 ASSESSMENT

Checking for Understanding

1. **Define** peacekeeping force, disarmament.
2. **Identify** Franklin Delano Roosevelt, Hazel Henderson, Elise Boulding.
3. **Locate** China, Canada.
4. **Explain** why global approaches to global problems are sometimes difficult to coordinate.
5. **List** the permanent members of the United Nations Security Council. How many members serve limited terms at any one time?

Critical Thinking

6. **Analyze** Why was an international peacekeeping organization created after World War II?
7. **Categorizing Information** Create a chart like the one below listing areas of the world that have political, ethnic, and religious disputes. Place each country in the correct category.

Nature of Dispute	Country
Political	
Ethnic	
Religious	

Analyzing Visuals

8. **Describe** the photo on page 757 in your own words. Then explain why peacekeepers wear military clothing.

Writing About History

9. **Descriptive Writing** Thousands of nongovernmental organizations (NGOs) represent citizens' interests throughout the world. Choose one NGO to examine in detail. Write an essay about the organization's mission, its goals, its accomplishments, and its failures. How has it impacted the world?

SECTION 2 ASSESSMENT

1. Key terms are in blue.
2. Franklin Delano Roosevelt *(p. 756)*; Hazel Henderson *(p. 757)*; Elise Boulding *(p. 758)*
3. See chapter maps.
4. because they are often hindered by political, ethnic, and religious disputes
5. the United States, Great Britain, Russia, France, and China
6. to prevent future wars and to reaffirm faith in fundamental human rights
7. Political: U.S. and Canada, Middle East; Ethnic: former Yugoslavia; Religious: Middle East, India and Pakistan, former Yugoslavia
8. Peacekeeping forces are military forces drawn from neutral member states to settle conflicts. Their clothing signifies their military status.
9. Answers will vary but should be supported by examples and factual details.

Technology
Skillbuilder

Developing Multimedia Presentations

Why Learn This Skill?

You have been assigned a research project about Brazil's rain forest. To vividly present the important issues to your classmates, you would like to show them slides of the endangered animals and plants in the rain forest, along with videos of the region and recordings of native music. This type of presentation is called a multimedia presentation because it uses a variety of media, such as photographs, music, and video, to convey information to others.

Learning the Skill

At its most basic, a multimedia presentation can be as simple as using equipment such as a slide projector, a VCR, a TV, and a portable stereo. You can use pre-recorded materials or make your own videotapes or sound recordings.

With the right tools, you can also develop a multimedia presentation on a computer. Computer presentations can combine text, graphics, audio, animation, and video in an interactive program. To create this kind of presentation, you might use traditional graphic tools and draw programs, animation programs that make still images move, and authoring systems that tie everything together. Your computer manual will tell you which tools your computer can support.

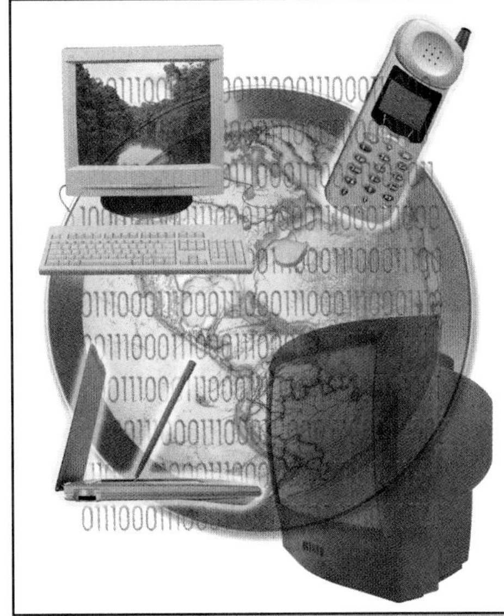

Multimedia equipment

Practicing the Skill

Suppose you want to give a report about the importance of the Brazilian rain forest. Ask yourself the following questions to develop an effective multimedia presentation.

- Which forms of media do I want to include? Video? Sound? Photographs? Graphics? Animation? Anything else?
- What equipment would I need to present the media I want to use?
- If I want to make a computer presentation, which of these media forms does my computer support?
- What kind of software programs or systems do I need? A graphics program? An animation program? A program that allows users to interact with the on-screen presentation? An authoring system that will allow me to change images, sound, and motion?
- Is there a "do-it-all" program I can use to develop the kind of presentation I want?

Applying the Skill

Think of a topic that would be suitable for a multimedia presentation. Keeping in mind the guidelines given above, create a plan that describes the presentation you would like to develop. Indicate what tools you will need and what steps you must take to make the presentation an exciting reality.

759

ANSWERS TO PRACTICING THE SKILL

Answers will vary, but students should conduct the necessary research to answer each question. Research techniques for this project may include interviewing those who work in media-related occupations, visiting local software stores to see what is most current, and speaking to school media specialists.

Applying the Skill: Answers will vary depending on the topic selected.

Technology Skillbuilder

TEACH

Developing Multimedia Presentations This skill helps students develop the ability to create multimedia presentations. This will do more than make for interesting classes. It might prove helpful as students enter the workplace.

Demonstrate some of the technology that is available to students in your school or local library. You might ask staff members in the technology/media department of your school to help with the demonstration.

Additional Practice

Skills Reinforcement Activity 25

Name ______ Date ______ Class ______

Skills Reinforcement Activity 25

Developing Multimedia Presentations

Equipment you may have at home, as well as classroom or library resources, can make it possible for you to develop creative multimedia presentations. Most presentations are more interesting and can be easier to follow if they include diagrams, photographs, videos, or sound recordings.

DIRECTIONS: Plan a multimedia presentation on a topic found in the chapter such as the environment, the technological revolution, political challenges, or social changes. List three or four major ideas you would like to cover. Then think about how multimedia resources could enhance your presentation. Use the technology/media center to do a preliminary survey of materials that may be available and list them on the chart. Use your imagination.

Topic:

GLENCOE TECHNOLOGY

CD-ROM
Glencoe Skillbuilder Interactive Workbook CD-ROM, Level 2

This interactive CD-ROM reinforces student mastery of essential social studies skills.

GLENCOE TECHNOLOGY

MindJogger Videoquiz

Use the **MindJogger Videoquiz** to review Chapter 25 content.

 Available in VHS.

Using Key Terms

1. deforestation **2.** global economy **3.** ecology **4.** disarmament **5.** acid rain

Reviewing Key Facts

6. that the use of pesticides was having deadly, unforeseen results
7. chlorofluorocarbons
8. The greenhouse effect takes place when temperatures on Earth rise because of the buildup of carbon dioxide in the atmosphere. It causes global warming, which could cause sea levels to rise because of melting polar ice, flooding coastal areas.
9. In 1987, representatives from 46 nations met in Montreal to discuss ways to reduce the emission of chlorofluorocarbons. In 1992, an Earth Summit in Rio de Janeiro proposed solutions to environmental challenges.
10. explosive population growth, hunger, poverty, tremendous growth of cities where millions live in slums
11. poor soil, rapidly growing populations, natural catastrophes, and civil war; the Green Revolution — the development of new strains of rice, corn, and other grains that have greater yields — has been promoted as a means of feeding the world's growing population
12. They identify with interests that transcend national boundaries, defining problems in global terms, whereas government agencies would take a limited national approach.
13. has changed traditional roles of women and children; introduced concepts that have led to revolts against existing governments
14. The Security Council is composed of 5 permanent members and 10 members chosen by the General Assembly to serve limited terms. It decides what actions the UN should take to settle international disputes. It is difficult to make decisions because each of the 5 permanent members has veto power.
15. "Think globally, act locally." They deal with issues such as environmental problems, women's and men's liberation, human potential, appropriate technology, and nonviolence. They attract ordinary citizens.

Critical Thinking

16. Industrialized nations import natural resources and expect lower labor costs in developing nations. Developing nations depend upon industrialized nations for capital infusion to develop new industries.
17. The Cold War ended with the disintegration of the Soviet Union, reducing the risk of a major nuclear war. However, nuclear weapons continue to spread, making a regional war possible.

CHAPTER 25 ASSESSMENT and ACTIVITIES

Using Key Terms

1. The destruction of large forests and jungles that affects the world's climate, animals, and plants is called ______.
2. A ______ is based on the interdependency of nations' economic systems.
3. The science of ______ studies the relationship between living things and their environment.
4. Organizations that seek to limit or reduce armed forces and weapons are called ______ groups.
5. When the sulfur produced by factories mixes with moisture in the air the result is ______.

Reviewing Key Facts

6. **History** What environmental message was the theme of *Silent Spring?*
7. **Science and Technology** What chemical is known to be harmful to Earth's ozone layer?
8. **Science and Technology** Explain the greenhouse effect and the problems it could create.
9. **History** When and where did the world's nations meet to discuss environmental issues?
10. **Government** What problems do developing nations face?
11. **Science and Technology** What contributes to the hunger problem in developing nations? What are some of the possible solutions to the hunger problem?
12. **Citizenship** Why are nongovernmental organizations taking greater responsibility for protecting the world's environment?
13. **Culture** How have the introduction of Western ideas and customs had a destabilizing effect in many areas of the world?
14. **Government** What is the United Nations Security Council? Why is it difficult for this council to make decisions?
15. **Citizenship** What is the slogan of grassroots public interest groups? What kind of issues do these groups address, and what kind of members do these groups usually attract?

Critical Thinking

16. **Evaluating** Analyze the interdependency of developing and industrialized nations.
17. **Cause and Effect** Explain the increased potential for regional nuclear wars since the Soviet Union disintegrated.

Chapter Summary

At the beginning of the twenty-first century, the world has become a global society. Nations are politically and economically dependent on each other, and the world's problems are of a global nature, as shown in the chart below.

Cultural Diffusion	Technological Innovation	Cooperation	Conflict
• Jumbo jetliners transport passengers around the world. • Corporations have offices in more than one country. • Advances in communication, such as the Internet, connect people around the globe.	• The science of ecology is born. • American astronauts land on the moon. • Super strains of corn, rice and other grains produce greater crop yields. • Health care advances prolong lives. • Developments in transportation and communication transform the world community.	• The Earth Summit meets in Rio de Janeiro. • Nations enact recycling programs and curb the dumping of toxic materials. • The United Nations forms to promote world peace. • Nongovernmental organizations advocate social and environmental change.	• Massive growth in world population causes overcrowding and hunger in many countries. • Regional, ethnic, and religious differences continue to produce violence around the world. • International terrorists remain a threat to peace and security.

Self-Check Quiz
Visit the *Glencoe World—Modern Times History* Web site at wh.mt.glencoe.com and click on **Chapter 25–Self-Check Quiz** to prepare for the Chapter Test.

Writing About History

18. **Expository Writing** Write an essay comparing the nuclear disaster at Chernobyl with the chemical plant accident in Bhopal and the grounding of the *Exxon Valdez* in Alaska. Which disaster was the most devastating to the environment in your opinion? Why do you have this opinion, and how would you prevent a future disaster?

Analyzing Sources

Rachel Carson cautioned about the dangers of harmful chemicals in her book, *Silent Spring:*

> ❝It is not my contention that chemical pesticides must never be used. I do contend that we have put poisons and biologically potent chemicals into the hands of persons largely or wholly ignorant of their potentials for harm. . . . Future generations are unlikely to condone our lack of prudent concern for the integrity of the natural world that supports all life.❞

19. Summarize the argument that Carson is presenting in this quotation.
20. Who will question the lack of concern shown for the natural world, in Carson's opinion?
21. Why was *Silent Spring* a groundbreaking book? How has it influenced the ways in which people view the relationship between humans and the natural world?

Applying Technology Skills

22. **Using the Internet** The science of ecology has led to a new form of travel known as ecotourism. Use the Internet to research an area of the world where ecotours take place. Select an area to visit as an ecotourist, explain why you have selected this area, and describe what you will see on your travels in your journal.

Making Decisions

23. Grassroots politics have moved the burden of decision making from the politicians to the individual citizen. Having read this chapter, what global issues concern you? What have you done or what would you like to do to help resolve these issues?

NATIONAL GEOGRAPHIC **Radioactive Fallout from Chernobyl, 1986**

Pattern of fallout
0 1,500 miles
0 1,500 kilometers
Orthographic projection
PACIFIC OCEAN, ARCTIC OCEAN, ATLANTIC OCEAN, JAPAN, CHINA, USSR, UNITED STATES, CANADA, NORWAY, SWEDEN, FINLAND, U.K., POLAND, Chernobyl, FRANCE, SPAIN, ITALY, GREECE, TURKEY, ALGERIA, LIBYA, EGYPT

Analyzing Maps and Charts

Use the above map and the text to answer the following questions.

24. Where is the radioactive fallout most concentrated?
25. Where are the furthest traces of radioactive fallout found (using Chernobyl as the point of origin)?
26. What global effects did the explosion at Chernobyl have?

Standardized Test Practice

Directions: Choose the best answer to the following question.

Which of the following statements is *not* true about the United Nations (UN)?

F There are five permanent members of the Security Council.
G Its chief goals are peace and the protection of human rights.
H It is easy to get UN members to agree on a course of action.
J Several UN committees have tackled global poverty and environmental issues.

Test-Taking Tip: If a question contains a key word such as *not* or *except,* slow down. Reread the question to make sure you understand it completely.

Writing About History

18. Students will write an essay. Answers to the rest of the question should be supported by logical arguments.

Analyzing Sources

19. Chemical pesticides can cause long-lasting damage to the environment.
20. future generations
21. It was the first book to draw attention to the problems of pesticides, and it began the modern movement to protect the environment.

Applying Technology Skills

22. Students will create journals.

CHAPTER 25
Assessment and Activities

Have students visit the Web site at wh.mt.glencoe.com to review Chapter 25 and take the Self-Check Quiz.

Making Decisions

23. Answers will vary. Have students use a decision-making process to identify the problem, gather information, list and consider options, consider advantages and disadvantages, and, if possible, choose and implement a solution and then evaluate its effectiveness.

Analyzing Maps and Charts

24. around Greece and Turkey
25. western United States and Canada
26. fallout covered almost two-thirds of the Northern Hemisphere

Standardized Test Practice

Answer: H
Answer Explanation: According to page 757, a stalemate has frequently resulted from Security Council deliberations.

Bonus Question ?

Ask: How can the world's nations eliminate terrorism? *(Answers will vary but may include engaging in international cooperation to locate terrorist cells, eliminate their funding sources, capture their leaders and bring them to trial; impose stricter immigration laws, introduce increased security measures, etc.)* **L1**

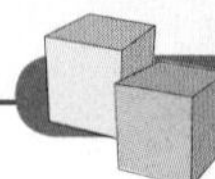

WORLD LITERATURE

Block Schedule

Team Teaching This excerpt from *Civil Peace* from *Girls and War and Other Stories* may be presented in a team-teaching context, in conjunction with English or Language Arts.

Civil Peace by Chinua Achebe

Historical Connection

Civil Peace tells the story of one family during the Nigerian civil war. The war broke out in 1967 when the military governor of eastern Nigeria announced the secession of the region, renaming it the republic of Biafra.

Background Information

Setting The story takes place in the forests of Nigeria in 1970, just after the civil war ended.

Characters Jonathan Iwegbu: a resident of Nigeria, husband of Maria, and father of four
Maria: Jonathan's wife
Army officer: a man who tried to take Jonathan's bicycle

Plot Jonathan and his family are returning to their village. They are thankful for their lives and for two additional "miracles"—Jonathan's bicycle and their family home.

Literary Element *Civil Peace* is a short story that contains elements of a parable.

WORLD LITERATURE

Civil Peace *from* Girls and War and Other Stories

by Chinua Achebe

Chinua Achebe was born in Nigeria and was christened Albert Chinualamogu. He rejected his British name while studying at the University College of Ibadan. Many of his works deal with the impact of Western values and culture on African society. He has done more than almost any other author to spread the understanding and influence of African literature worldwide. "Civil Peace" is one of the stories from *Girls and War and Other Stories* in which Achebe responds to the Nigerian civil war.

Read to Discover

How does Chinua Achebe describe the conditions of the civil war? Do you think this story accurately reflects conditions for African families following civil war?

Reader's Dictionary

commandeer: to seize for military purposes

Biro: a British term for a ballpoint pen

raffia: fiber of a type of palm tree

Jonathan Iwegbu counted himself extraordinarily lucky. "Happy survival!" meant so much more to him than just a current fashion of greeting old friends in the first hazy days of peace. It went deep to his heart. He had come out of the war with five inestimable blessings—his head, his wife Maria's head and the heads of three out of their four children. As a bonus he also had his old bicycle—a miracle too but naturally not to be compared to the safety of five human heads.

The bicycle had a little history of its own. One day at the height of the war it was commandeered "for urgent military action." Hard as its loss would have been to him he would still have let it go without a thought had he not had some doubts about the genuineness of the officer. It wasn't his disreputable rags, nor the toes peeping out of one blue and one brown canvas shoes, nor yet the two stars of his rank done obviously in a hurry in Biro, that troubled Jonathan; many good and heroic soldiers looked the same or worse. It was rather a certain lack of grip and firmness in his manner. So Jonathan, suspecting he might be

ABOUT THE AUTHOR

Chinua Achebe, a Nigerian, is one of Africa's most influential and widely published authors. He has written twenty-one novels, short stories, and collections of poetry. His first, and probably best known novel, *Things Fall Apart,* was published in 1958 and is a remarkable story about post-colonial life in Nigeria. Achebe has received numerous literary awards and is the recipient of the highest award for intellectual achievement in Nigeria. Chinua Achebe was born in Nigeria in 1930 and attended University College in Ibadan before studying at London University, where he received his B.A. The story *Civil Peace* is part of a collection of short stories, *Girls and War and Other Stories*, published in 1973.

amenable to influence, rummaged in his raffia bag and produced the two pounds with which he had been going to buy firewood which his wife, Maria, retailed to camp officials for extra stock-fish and corn meal, and got his bicycle back. That night he buried it in the little clearing in the bush where the dead of the camp, including his own youngest son, were buried. When he dug it up again a year later after the surrender all it needed was a little palm-oil greasing. "Nothing puzzles God," he said in wonder.

He put it to immediate use as a taxi and accumulated a small pile of Biafran money ferrying camp officials and their families across the four-mile stretch to the nearest tarred road. His standard charge per trip was six pounds and those who had the money were only glad to be rid of some of it in this way. At the end of a fortnight he had made a small fortune of one hundred and fifteen pounds.

Then he made the journey to Enugu and found another miracle waiting for him. It was unbelievable. He rubbed his eyes and looked again and it was still standing there before him. But, needless to say, even that monumental blessing must be accounted also totally inferior to the five heads in the family. This newest miracle was his little house in Ogui Overside. Indeed nothing puzzles God! Only two houses away a huge concrete edifice some wealthy contractor had put up just before the war was a mountain of rubble. And here was Jonathan's little zinc house of no regrets built with mud blocks quite intact! Of course the doors and windows were missing and five sheets off the roof. But what was that? And anyhow he had returned to Enugu early enough to pick up bits of old zinc and wood and soggy sheets of cardboard lying around the neighborhood before thousands more came out of their forest holes looking for the same things. He got a destitute carpenter with one old hammer, a blunt plane and a few bent and rusty nails in his tool bag to turn this assortment of wood, paper and metal into door and window shutters for five Nigerian shillings or fifty Biafran pounds. He paid the pounds, and moved in with his overjoyed family carrying five heads on their shoulders.

▲ **Children Dancing, *c. 1948, by Robert Gwathmey***

Interpreting World Literature

1. What does Jonathan's encounter with the false officer reveal about the conditions of the war?
2. Biafra lost the civil war. What clues in the text indicate this outcome?
3. Why was having a bicycle a "miracle"?
4. **CRITICAL THINKING** Do you think it is effective for Achebe to discuss the war through an individual account rather than as a direct discussion of the devastation created? Why or why not?

Applications Activity

Choose a contemporary problem and describe it through the effect it has on an individual or family.

World Literature

Focus

Ask students to research the background of the civil war in Nigeria. Tell students that the research they do will make the story more interesting. Ask students to discover how long the secessionist state of Biafra was in existence. *(from May 1967 to January 1970)* What caused the conflict? *(The Igbo people felt they could not develop or survive in Nigeria.)* Ask students to do research to determine how the international community reacted to the civil war in Nigeria.

TEACH

Analyzing Language

Achebe uses carefully chosen language to describe the supposed military officer who wants to commandeer Jonathan's bicycle. Read aloud the paragraph that describes the officer and then have students look for other carefully constructed, highly illustrative passages.

Interpretation

Achebe emphasizes the importance of family throughout this excerpt. Have students identify and analyze the ways in which Achebe emphasizes the significance of the family.

ANSWERS TO INTERPRETING WORLD LITERATURE

1. The encounter shows there was much confusion in this civil war, that it is difficult to identify who was who. (Answers may vary.)
2. the fact that people who had Biafran money were only too glad to be rid of it
3. It had survived the war, and come back into his hands, allowing him to make a living.
4. Answers will vary. Discussing the war in this way humanizes it; it also provides the reader with a view of how the war affected individuals and their families. It can limit the discussion to a single point of view.

Applications Activity: Students will choose a contemporary problem.

Appendix

Contents

Mini Almanac .765

Primary Sources Library .770

Honoring America: Flag Etiquette,
The Star-Spangled Banner,
The Pledge of Allegiance .782

Glossary .783

Spanish Glossary .790

Index .798

Acknowledgements and Photo Credits .828

Mini Almanac

An almanac is a book or table that contains a variety of statistical, tabular, or general information. The most common almanacs in history have been those that kept astronomical data or that gave weather predictions and related advice to farmers. In agricultural societies it was important to keep accounts of natural phenomena so that farmers would have an idea of when to plant and harvest their crops. Ancient Egyptians carved their almanacs on sticks of wood and called them "fingers of the sun." The first printed almanac was prepared in Europe in 1457. The *Old Farmer's Almanac* has been published continuously since 1792. Because almanacs are compact and concise, they are a popular way of presenting a wide variety of information.

Poor Richard, 1733.

AN

Almanack

For the Year of Chriſt

1733,

Being the Firſt after LEAP YEAR.

	Years
And makes ſince the Creation	7241
By the Account of the Eaſtern *Greeks*	6932
By the Latin Church, when ☉ ent. ♈	5742
By the Computation of *W.W.*	5682
By the *Roman* Chronology	5494
By the *Jewiſh* Rabbies.	

Wherein is contained

The Lunations, Eclipſes, Judgment of the Weather, Spring Tides, Planets Motions & mutual Aſpects, Sun and Moon's Riſing and Setting, Length of Days, Time of High Water, Fairs, Courts, and obſervable Days.

Fitted to the Latitude of Forty Degrees, and a Meridian of Five Hours Weſt from *London*, but may without ſenſible Error, ſerve all the adjacent Places, even from *Newfoundland* to *South-Carolina*.

By *RICHARD SAUNDERS*, Philom.

PHILADELPHIA:
Printed and ſold by *B. FRANKLIN*, at the New Printing-Office near the Market

World Population, A.D. 1–2001

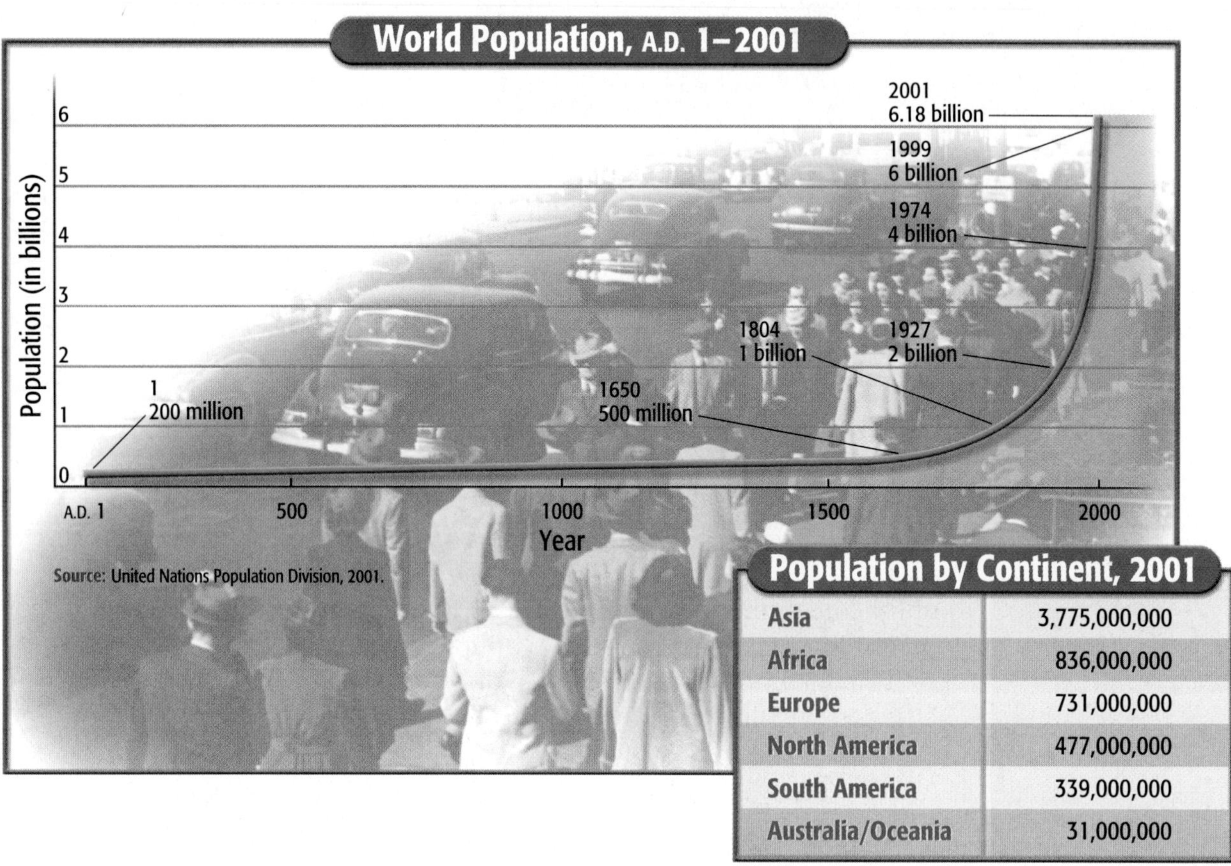

Source: United Nations Population Division, 2001.

Population by Continent, 2001

Asia	3,775,000,000
Africa	836,000,000
Europe	731,000,000
North America	477,000,000
South America	339,000,000
Australia/Oceania	31,000,000

Sources: *World Atlas* and *World Gazeteer*.
Note: Populations are estimates.

Life Expectancy

Country	Years
Andorra	83.47
Japan	80.80
France	78.90
Israel	78.71
New Zealand	77.99
United Kingdom	77.82
United States	77.26
Chile	75.94
China	71.62
Russia	67.34
Egypt	63.69
Brazil	63.24
India	62.86
South Africa	48.09
Mozambique	36.45

Source: U.S. Bureau of the Census, 2001.

Infant Mortality

Country	Infant Deaths per 1,000 Live Births
India	70
South Africa	54
Egypt	41
Brazil	34
China	33
Russia	18
Chile	11
United States	7
Canada	6
United Kingdom	6
France	5
Germany	5
South Korea	5
Japan	4

Source: United Nations, UNICEF, 2001.

Most Populous Countries

Country	Population
China	1,273,111,290
India	1,029,991,145
United States	278,058,881
Indonesia	228,437,870
Brazil	174,468,575
Russia	145,470,197
Pakistan	144,616,639
Bangladesh	131,269,860
Japan	126,771,662
Nigeria	126,635,626

Source: U.S. Bureau of the Census, 2001.

World's Richest Countries

Country	Gross National Product, per Capita (in U.S. dollars)
Luxembourg	45,360
Switzerland	44,355
Japan	41,010
Liechtenstein	40,000
Norway	34,515

Source: World Development Indicators 2000, World Bank.

World's Poorest Countries

Country	Gross National Product, per Capita (in U.S. dollars)
Mozambique	80
Congo, DNC	100
Eritrea	100
Ethiopia	100
Somalia	100

Source: World Development Indicators 2000, World Bank.

Highest Inflation Rates

Country	Rate of Inflation (percent)
Congo, DNC	540
Angola	325
Belarus	200
Iraq	100
Somalia	100
Ecuador	96
Suriname	78
Zimbabwe	60
Cyprus (Turkish)	58
Romania	46

Source: *The World Factbook, 2001.*
Note: Estimates are for 1999 and 2000.

Lowest Inflation Rates

Country	Rate of Inflation (percent)
Argentina	−0.9
Oman	−0.8
Japan	−0.7
Vietnam	−0.6
Fiji	0.0
Lebanon	0.0
Israel	0.1
Cuba	0.3
China	0.4
Saudi Arabia	0.5

Source: *The World Factbook, 2001.*
Note: Estimates are for 1999 and 2000.

World's Ten Largest Companies, 2000

Rank	Company	Revenue (in millions of U.S. dollars)
1.	ExxonMobil (United States)	210,392.0
2.	Wal-Mart Stores (United States)	193,295.0
3.	General Motors (United States)	184,632.0
4.	Ford Motor (United States)	180,598.0
5.	DaimlerChrysler (Germany)	150,069.7
6.	Royal Dutch/Shell Group (Netherlands)	149,146.0
7.	BP (United Kingdom)	148,062.0
8.	General Electric (United States)	129,853.0
9.	Mitsubishi (Japan)	126,579.4
10.	Toyota Motor (Japan)	121,416.2

Source: Fortune 500, 2001.

Most Livable Countries

Rank	Country	Rank	Country	Rank	Country
1.	Norway	10.	Finland	19.	New Zealand
2.	Australia	11.	Switzerland	20.	Italy
3.	Canada	12.	Luxembourg	21.	Spain
4.	Sweden	13.	France	22.	Israel
5.	Belgium	14.	United Kingdom	23.	Greece
6.	United States	15.	Denmark	24.	Cyprus
7.	Iceland	16.	Austria	25.	Singapore
8.	Netherlands	17.	Germany		
9.	Japan	18.	Ireland		

Source: United Nations Human Development Index, 2001.
Note: The criteria include life expectancy, adult literacy, school enrollment, educational attainment, and per capita gross domestic product (GDP).

Highest Adult Literacy Rates

Country	Rate of Literacy (percent)
Andorra	100
Australia	100
Denmark	100
Estonia	100
Finland	100
Latvia	100
Liechtenstein	100
Luxembourg	100
Norway	100
Czech Republic	99.9

Source: *The World Factbook, 2001.*
Note: Literacy is defined by each country.

Lowest Adult Literacy Rates

Country	Rate of Literacy (percent)
Burkina Faso	18
Eritrea	20
Sierra Leone	21
Benin	23
Guinea	24
Somalia	24
Gambia	27
Sudan	27
Ethiopia	28
Niger	28

Source: *The World Factbook, 2001.*
Note: Literacy is defined by each country.

World Adult Illiteracy by Gender

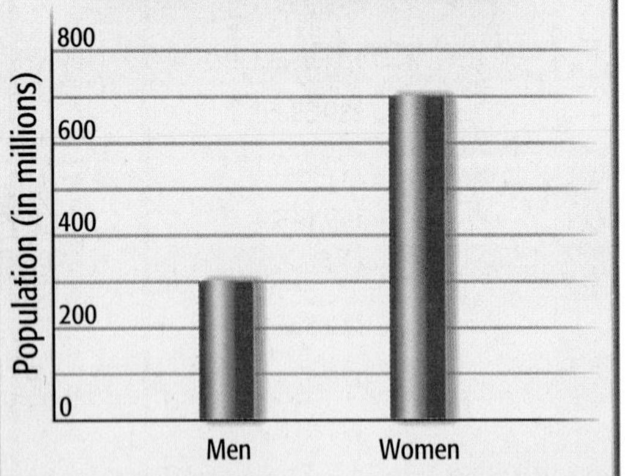

Source: United Nations, 2001.

Years, by Country, in Which Women Gained the Right to Vote

Year	Country	Year	Country
1893	New Zealand	1945	Italy
1902	Australia	1945	Japan
1913	Norway	1947	Argentina
1918	United Kingdom	1947	Mexico
1918	Canada	1950	India
1919	Germany	1952	Greece
1920	United States	1956	Egypt
1930	South Africa	1963	Kenya
1934	Brazil	1971	Switzerland
1944	France	1980	Iraq

Highest Military Expenditures

	Billions of U.S. Dollars per Year	Percentage of Gross Domestic Product (GDP)
United States	276.7	3.2
Japan	43.0	1.0
France	39.8	2.5
United Kingdom	36.9	2.7
Germany	32.8	1.5
Italy	20.7	1.7
Saudi Arabia	18.3	13.0
Brazil	13.4	1.9
India	13.0	2.5
China	12.6	1.2

Source: *The World Factbook, 2001.*

Nuclear Weapons Capability

Country	Date of First Test
United States	1945
Russia (Soviet Union)	1949
United Kingdom	1952
France	1960
China	1964
India	1998
Pakistan	1998

Source: U.S. Department of State and *Time* magazine.

Communication around the World

	Daily newspaper circulation per 1,000 persons	Radios per 1,000 persons	Televisions per 1,000 persons	Telephone main lines per 1,000 persons	Cellular phone subscribers per 1,000 persons	Estimated personal computers per 1,000 persons
Canada	158	1,067	710	677	285	39
China	n/a	335	321	111	66	2
Cuba	118	352	239	44	1	1
France	218	946	595	580	494	30
Germany	311	948	567	601	586	34
Italy	104	880	528	474	737	21
Japan	578	956	686	653	526	32
Mexico	97	329	272	125	142	5
Russia	105	417	410	218	22	4
South Africa	34	355	134	114	12	6
United Kingdom	331	1,443	521	557	670	34
United States	212	2,116	806	700	365	59

Sources: United Nations and International Telecommunications Union, 2001.

0:00 Out of Time?

Selections from the Primary Sources Library are designed to supplement unit study by providing additional first-person accounts. If your teaching time is limited, you may use the selections as part of your quarterly or semester review. You might also use them to condense study of individual chapters into one-day lessons.

Introduction

Request volunteers to read and discuss the introduction to the Primary Sources Library. Then have students complete the activities that follow to familiarize themselves with the types of primary sources.

Work together with an English or language arts teacher to help students collect oral histories. Start by providing students with these guidelines: Interview a relative or friend who is much older than you. Your aim is to find how much their early lives differ from yours. Devise a set of interview questions, such as: How did you and your friends spend your free time? What did you study in school? What was the most pressing world problem when you were my age? What was the biggest discovery or technological change that you witnessed as a young person?

Ask students to provide a transcript or written record of the interview. If a tape recorder is available, you may want students to record the interview. Have students discuss their findings in class.

Primary Sources Library

Contents

An Egyptian Father's Advice to His Son 772
A Woman May Need to Have the Heart of a Man 773
The Buddha's Sermon 773
A Reformation Debate 774
The Silk Industry in China 775
Declaration of the Rights of Woman and the Female Citizen 775
Imperial Decree to Free the Serfs 776
The Unfortunate Situation of Working Women 777
The Impact of British Rule in India 777
Over the Top—World War I 778
Gandhi Takes the Path of Civil Disobedience 779
The Holocaust—The Camp Victims 779
Progress Never Stops 780
An Ideal for Which I Am Prepared to Die 781
China's Gilded Age 781

What Is It and How Do I Use It?

The primary sources as defined here are written testimony or documents from a particular era in history or about an important development. The source may be the writings of a noted historian or political leader, or it may be from the diary of someone who lived at the time and recorded the events of the day.

Reading primary sources is an excellent way to understand how and why people believed and acted as they did in the past. While many people might have written down their stories or beliefs, the sources chosen here are from witnesses who were close to events or especially sensitive to them.

Checking Your Sources

When you read primary or secondary sources, you should analyze them to determine if they are dependable or reliable. Historians usually prefer primary sources to secondary sources, but both can be reliable or unreliable, depending on the following factors.

Time Span

With primary sources, it is important to consider how much time passed from the date the event occurred to the date that the primary source was written. Generally, the longer the time span between the event and the account, the less reliable the account is. As time passes, people often forget details and fill in gaps with events that never took place. Although we like to think we remember things exactly as they happened, the fact is, we often remember them very differently than they occurred.

Reliability

Another factor to consider when evaluating a primary source is the writer's background and reliability. When reading a historical document, try to determine if the statements and information can be proved. If the information can be verified as true by independent sources, then it probably is fact.

TEACHER NOTES

After studying the introduction to the Primary Sources Library, students should be able to meet the following objectives:

- explain the differences between primary sources and secondary sources;
- identify the different types of primary sources;
- understand that primary sources offer a unique view of people and events in a particular era.

Opinions

When evaluating a primary source, you should also decide whether or not the account has been influenced by emotion, opinion, or exaggeration. Writers sometimes distort the truth to suit their personal purposes. Ask yourself: Why did the person write the account? Do any words or expressions reveal the author's emotions or opinions? Again, you may wish to compare the account with another primary source document about the same event. If the two accounts differ, ask yourself why they differ and then conduct your own outside research to determine which account can be verified by other authoritative sources.

Interpreting Primary Sources

To help you analyze a primary source, use the following steps:

- **Examine the origins of the document.**
  You need to determine if it is indeed a primary source.
- **Find the main ideas.**
  Read the document and summarize the main ideas in your own words.
- **Reread the document.**
  Difficult ideas and historical documents are not always easily understood on the first reading.
- **Use a variety of resources.**
  Use a dictionary, an encyclopedia, and maps to further your understanding of the topic. These resources are tools to help you discover new ideas and knowledge and check the validity of sources.

Classifying Primary Sources

Primary sources fall into different categories. While the documents presented here are primarily printed publications, there are other types of primary sources.

Printed Publications

Printed publications include books such as autobiographies. Printed publications also include newspapers and magazines.

Visual Materials

Visual materials include a wide range of forms: original paintings, drawings, sculpture, photographs, film, videos, and maps.

Oral Histories

Oral histories are chronicles, memoirs, myths, and legends that are passed along from one generation to another by word of mouth. Interviews are another form of oral history.

Personal Records

Personal records are accounts of events kept by an individual who is a participant in or witness to these events. Personal records include diaries, journals, and letters.

Artifacts

Artifacts are objects such as tools or ornaments. Artifacts provide archaeologists and historians with information about a particular culture or a stage of technological development.

TEACHER NOTES

Through the study of the selections in the Primary Sources Library and their accompanying questions and activities, students should be able to:

- find the main idea in the selections;
- analyze information in a variety of written texts in order to make inferences and generalizations;
- provide an interpretation of the material in their own words.

Printed Publications

To help students analyze printed publications, instruct them to read the first two paragraphs of the Preamble to the Declaration of Independence (found in the United States history text used in your school). Ask students: What is the subject of these paragraphs? What do they tell you about the beliefs of the people who signed this document?

Personal Records

Tell students that a *journal* is a daily record of events kept by an individual who is a participant or witness to these events. Ask students to keep a journal of the interesting events that they observe or take part in during a week's time. Encourage them to personalize the events by recording their own opinions or interpretations of what they have seen or done.

Songs & Poems

Ask students to write song lyrics or a poem about some important story in the news. Provide samples that students might follow, such as limericks, rhymed and unrhymed lyrics or verses, and so on.

Artifacts

To help students analyze artifacts, provide the following instructions: Find a primary source from your past—a photograph, a report card, an old newspaper clipping, your first CD, or anything else you might have saved. Bring this source into class and explain why you kept it, and what it shows about the time from which the item comes.

FOCUS

Reinforcing Vocabulary

Review the **Reader's Dictionary** with students to be sure they understand any unfamiliar terms.

TEACH

An Egyptian Father's Advice to His Son

Interpreting the Primary Source

Ask students what clues tell them that Vizier Ptah-hotep expected his son to follow his advice. *(Clues appear in the third and fourth paragraphs, in which Vizier Ptah-hotep says that a son should listen to his father's instructions. Otherwise the father can "cast him off" for rebelling.)*

Evaluating the Primary Source

This primary source reveals the authority that an Egyptian father exercised over a household as well as the conduct expected of an upper class son who might one day become "a leader commanding the affairs of the many." The reliability of this source can be judged by reading scholarly accounts of Egyptian families, which prove that children were expected to respect their parents and, in the case of upper class sons, maintain a father's tomb.

A Woman May Need to Have the Heart of a Man

Interpreting the Primary Source

Ask students how the feudal system increased the responsibilities of noblewomen. *(The feudal system required noblemen "to bear arms, to attend the court of his prince, and to travel," leaving their wives to manage and defend their estates.)*

Evaluating the Primary Source

This source shows how, despite limited rights, some noblewomen in the Middle Ages were able to expand their authority and duties during the absences of their husbands. The reliability of this source can be judged by reading historical studies of women during medieval times and determining whether Christine de Pizan was typical or atypical of the period.

The Buddha's Sermon

Interpreting the Primary Source

Ask students to explain how they think the recording of the Buddha's sermons in writing may have increased the influence of his teachings. *(When the sermons were spoken, only those in attendance would have heard the words of Buddha. Once they were written down, many more people could have access to his ideas.)*

For use with Unit 1

The World Before Modern Times

For thousands of years, prehistoric humans were migratory hunters and gatherers. With the development of agriculture, people began to live in settled communities. Throughout the world, these communities emerged into great civilizations with cultures, customs, governments, laws, and written histories.

Reader's Dictionary

fraud: deception

standing: having a good reputation

wretched: bad, poor in quality

manor: a landed estate; a tract of land

diligent: painstaking, steady

lamentation: an expression of mourning

cessation: stop

An Egyptian Father's Advice to His Son

Upper-class Egyptians enjoyed compiling collections of wise sayings to provide guidance for leading an upright and successful life. This excerpt from The Instruction of the Vizier Ptah-hotep *dates from around 2450* B.C.

Then he said to his son:

If you are a leader commanding the affairs of the many, seek out for yourself every good deed, until it may be that your own affairs are without wrong. Justice is great, and it is lasting; it has been disturbed since the time of him who made it, whereas there is punishment for him who passes over its laws. Wrongdoing has never brought its undertaking into port. It may be that it is fraud that gains riches, but the strength of justice is that it lasts. . . .

If you are a man of standing and found a household and produce a son who is pleasing to god, if he is correct and inclines toward your ways and listens to your instruction, while his manners in your house are fitting, and if he takes care of your property as it should be, seek out for him every useful action. He is your son, . . . you should not cut your heart off from him.

If he [the son] goes astray and does not carry out your instruction, so that his manners in your household are wretched, and he rebels against all that you say, while his mouth runs on in the most wretched talk, quite apart from his experience, while he possesses nothing, you should cast him off: he is not your son at all. He was not really born to you. . . . He is one whom god has condemned in the very womb.

This rendition of an Egyptian father teaching his son is on the wall of the Tomb of Sennedjem.

A Woman May Need to Have the Heart of a Man

Christine de Pizan was widowed at age 25. She supported her three children by copying manuscripts, compiling a manual of instructions for knights, and writing books. The following is from her 1405 publication, The Treasure of the City of Ladies.

It is the responsibility of every baron to spend the least possible time at his manors and his own estate, for his duties are to bear arms, to attend the court of his prince and to travel. Now, his lady stays behind and must take his place. . . . Her men should be able to rely on her for all kinds of protection in the absence of their lord. . . . She ought to have the heart of a man, that is, she ought to know how to use weapons and be familiar with everything that pertains to them, so that she may be ready to command her men if the need arises. She should know how to launch an attack or to defend against one.

In addition she will do well to be a very good manager of the estate. . . . She should often take time to visit the fields to see how the men are getting on with the work. . . . She will busy herself around the house; she will find plenty of orders to give. She will have the animals brought in at the right time [and] take care how the shepherd looks after them. . . .

In the winter-time, she will have her men cut her willow groves and make vine props to sell in the season. She will never let them be idle. . . . She will employ her women . . . to attend to the livestock, . . . [and] to weed the courtyards. . . . There is a great need to run an estate well, and the one who is most diligent and careful about it is more than wise and ought to be highly praised for it.

The Buddha's Sermon

Siddhartha Gautama, the Buddha, gave sermons in India, which were written down after 250 B.C. An excerpt from one of these follows.

1. Now this, O monks, is the noble truth of pain: birth is painful, old age is painful, sickness is painful, death is painful, sorrow, lamentation, dejection, and despair are painful. Contact with unpleasant things is painful, not getting what one wishes is painful. In short the five khandhas of grasping are painful.
2. Now this, O monks, is the noble truth of the cause of pain: that craving which leads to rebirth, combined with pleasure and lust, finding pleasure here and there, namely, the craving for passion, the craving for existence, the craving for non-existence.
3. Now this, O monks, is the noble truth of the cessation of pain: the cessation without a remainder of that craving, abandonment, forsaking, release, non-attachment.
4. Now this, O monks, is the noble truth of the way that leads to the cessation of pain: this is the noble Eightfold Path. . . .

Analyzing Primary Sources

1. Does any part of the Egyptian father's advice have value today for sons or daughters? Be specific and support your answer.
2. What are some of the duties and responsibilities of the medieval gentlewoman, according to Christine de Pizan's account?
3. What does de Pizan mean when she says a woman "ought to have the heart of a man"?
4. According to the Buddha, what is the cause of pain?

Evaluating the Primary Source
This primary source reveals the teachings of the Buddha as he expressed them during his lifetime. The reliability of the source can be judged by the accuracy with which the Buddha's words were recorded and later translated into English. If the document was written from memory, it is possible that words were remembered incorrectly or that portions of the sermon were paraphrased.

For other primary source documents related to this time period, see the **World History Primary Source Document Library CD-ROM.**

Analyzing Primary Sources

Answers:

1. Answers will vary, but students should offer statements from the reading that would or would not apply to contemporary families.
2. De Pizan defended and managed the estate in her husband's absence, overseeing work in the house and in the fields.
3. A woman should be familiar with weapons and know how to launch an attack or to defend against one.
4. Answers may include: The craving of pleasure and attachment to things cause pain.

FOCUS

Reinforcing Vocabulary

Review the **Reader's Dictionary** with students to be sure they understand any unfamiliar terms.

TEACH

A Reformation Debate

Interpreting the Primary Source

Ask students to discuss the different ways in which Luther and Zwingli interpret the Bible's description of the Last Supper. *(Luther follows a literal interpretation of the Last Supper—i.e., that God was present in both heaven and in the body of Jesus. Zwingli interprets the passages figuratively, arguing that "one and the same body cannot possibly be in different places.")*

Evaluating the Primary Source

This source illustrates some of the complex issues that split the Protestant Reformation. The reliability of the source can be judged by assessing the objectivity of the person who recorded the debate and whether the positions taken by Luther and Zwingli accurately reflect their beliefs.

The Silk Industry in China

Interpreting the Primary Source

Ask students whether silk was worn by all members of Chinese society or only by some in particular. *(The selection says that people of "lowly station" dressed in "hempen jackets and cotton garments." Students might infer that only members of the aristocracy dressed in silk.)*

For use with Unit 2

The Early Modern World

Beginning with the 1400s, European and Asian nations began exploring the world, learning about new cultures, new peoples, new technologies. Then, between 1600 and the early 1800s, Western civilization was transformed by scientific discoveries and new philosophies. The growing desire for democracy paved the way for political revolution in France and in America.

Reader's Dictionary

Scripture: passage from the Bible

revered: honored or respected

contention: point made in an argument

hemp: a fiber from the mulberry bush

imprescriptible: cannot be taken away by law

▲ *Martin Luther*

Ulrich Zwingli ▶

A Reformation Debate

In 1529, Martin Luther and Ulrich Zwingli debated over the sacrament of the Lord's Supper, or Communion.

LUTHER: Although I have no intention of changing my mind, which is firmly made up, I will nevertheless present the grounds of my belief and show where the others are in error. . . . Your basic contentions are these: In the last analysis you wish to prove that a body cannot be in two places at once, and you produce arguments about the unlimited body which are based on natural reason. I do not question how Christ can be God and man and how the two natures can be joined. For God is more powerful than all our ideas, and we must submit to his word.

Prove that Christ's body is not there where the Scripture says, "This is my body!" God is beyond all mathematics and the words of God are to be revered and carried out in awe. It is God who commands, "Take, eat, this is my body." I request, therefore, valid scriptural proof to the contrary.

ZWINGLI: I insist that the words of the Lord's Supper must be figurative. This is ever apparent, and even required by the article of faith; "taken up into heaven, seated at the right hand of the Father." Otherwise, it would be absurd to look for him in the Lord's Supper at the same time that Christ is telling us that he is in heaven. One and the same body cannot possibly be in different places. . . .

LUTHER: I call upon you as before: your basic contentions are shaky. Give way, and give glory to God!

ZWINGLI: And we call upon you to give glory to God and to quit begging the question! The issue at stake is this: Where is the proof of your position?

LUTHER: It is your point that must be proved, not mine. But let us stop this sort of thing. It serves no purpose.

ZWINGLI: It certainly does! It is for you to prove that the passage in John 6 speaks of a physical meal.

LUTHER: You express yourself poorly. . . . You're going nowhere.

Evaluating the Primary Source

This primary source underscores the importance of the silk industry to Chinese culture in the 1600s. The reliability of this source can be judged by the author's firsthand contact with silk production. If he, like so many Chinese at the time, had not actually seen a silk loom, then his descriptions might be inaccurate. The author's descriptions might also have been affected by his own social class or his intended audience.

The Declaration of the Rights of Woman and the Female Citizen

Interpreting the Primary Source

Ask students to consider why Olympe de Gouges was ahead of her times when she

The Silk Industry in China

During the 1600s Sung Ying-Hsing wrote a book on Chinese industry called the T'ien-kung K'ai-wu *(Chinese Technology in the Seventeenth Century), which included sections on the production of silk.*

. . . Members of the aristocracy are clothed in flowing robes decorated with patterns of magnificent mountain dragons, and they are the rulers of the country. Those of lowly stations would be dressed in hempen jackets and cotton garments to protect themselves from the cold in winter and cover their nakedness in summer, in order to distinguish themselves from the birds and beasts. Therefore Nature has provided the materials for clothing. Of these, the vegetable [plant] ones are cotton, hemp, *meng* hemp, and creeper hemp; those derived from birds, animals, and insects are furs, woolens, silk, and spun silk. . . .

But, although silk looms are to be found in all parts of the country, how many persons have actually seen the remarkable functioning of the draw-loom: Such words as "orderly government" [*chih,* i.e. the word used in silk reeling], "chaos" [*luan,* i.e. when the fibers are entangled], "knowledge or good policy" [*ching-lun,* i.e. the warp thread and the woven pattern] are known by every schoolboy, but is it not regrettable that he should never see the actual things that gave rise to these words? . . .

Emperor's robe, Qing dynasty

Declaration of the Rights of Woman and the Female Citizen

Olympe de Gouges composed her own Declaration of the Rights of Woman and the Female Citizen in 1791. Following are excerpts.

1. Woman is born free and lives equal to man in her rights. Social distinctions can be based only on the common utility.
2. The purpose of any political association is the conservation of the natural and imprescriptible rights of woman and man; these rights are liberty, property, security, and especially resistance to oppression. . . .
4. Liberty and justice consist of restoring all that belongs to others; thus, the only limits on the exercise of the natural rights of woman are perpetual male tyranny; these limits are to be reformed by the laws of nature and reason. . . .
6. The law must be . . . the same for all: male and female citizens. . . .
7. No woman is an exception; she is accused, arrested, and detained in cases determined by law. Women, like men, obey this rigorous law. . . .
11. The free communication of thoughts and opinions is one of the most precious rights of woman, since that liberty assured the recognition of children by their fathers. . . .

Analyzing Primary Sources

1. Was a conclusion reached in the debate presented between Luther and Zwingli?
2. According to Sung Ying-Hsing, from what two sources was all clothing made?
3. What are the rights of women as listed in the excerpts from *Declaration of the Rights of Woman and the Female Citizen*?
4. Olympe de Gouges states that free communication of thoughts is one of the most precious rights of women. Do you agree or disagree?

wrote this document. *(In 1791 women throughout the world enjoyed few political and economic rights. Even the United States denied women the vote.)*

Evaluating the Primary Source

This source provides a look at the seeds of the women's suffrage movement. The reliability of this source can be judged by whether de Gouge stayed true to her stated goal of making the law "the same for . . . male and female citizens" and by examining the legal status of women at the time she wrote this document.

For other primary source documents related to this time period, see the **World History Primary Source Document Library CD-ROM.**

Analyzing Primary Sources

Answers:

1. A conclusion was not reached because neither religious leader would compromise on his stand.
2. The two sources are "vegetable ones" (plants) and those derived from birds, animals, and insects.
3. Rights include: equality with men, liberty, property, security, resistance to oppression, and free communications of thoughts and opinions.
4. Most students will probably agree on the basis of equality and the right to free speech enjoyed by Americans.

FOCUS

Reinforcing Vocabulary

Review the **Reader's Dictionary** with students to be sure they understand any unfamiliar terms.

TEACH

Imperial Decree to Free the Serfs

Interpreting the Primary Source

Ask students to identify the economic condition that peasants had to fulfill to become free peasant-landholders. *(They had to purchase the enclosed land on which they worked to be "free from their obligations towards the proprietors.")*

Evaluating the Primary Source

This source shows that although the serfs attained legal freedom, they received no land individually and remained impoverished. The reliability of this source can be judged by an assessment of the historic conditions that prompted its writing—i.e., efforts by the czar to modernize Russia and to stem the tide of revolution.

The Unfortunate Situation of Working Women

Interpreting the Primary Source

Ask students why a working man's newspaper might publish an article on working women. *(The article uses the plight of women to argue for higher wages for men so that they could "earn enough to support their families.")*

For use with Unit 3

An Era of European Imperialism

During the late 1700s and throughout the 1800s, the nations of Europe and North America began an Industrial Revolution that had far-reaching effects, including the demand for social and political reforms. At the same time, Western nations extended their hold on new lands and on foreign markets.

Reader's Dictionary

autocrat: a monarch who rules with unlimited authority

close: an enclosed area of land

enumerated: counted

abject: existing in a low state or condition

infanticide: killing an infant

regeneration: restoration or renewal

Imperial Decree to Free the Serfs

In 1861, the Russian czar Alexander II issued the Emancipation Manifesto, *an imperial decree to free his country's serfs.*

By the grace of God, we, Alexander II, Emperor and Autocrat of all the Russias, King of Poland, Grand Duke of Finland, etc., to all our faithful subjects, make known:

Examining the condition of classes and professions comprising the state, we became convinced that the present state legislation favors the upper and middle classes, . . . but does not equally favor the serfs. . . . These facts had already attracted the attention of our predecessors, and they had adopted measures aimed at improving the conditions of the peasants. But decrees on free farmers and serfs have been carried out on a limited scale only.

We thus came to the conviction that the work of a serious improvement of the condition of the peasants was a sacred inheritance bequeathed to us by our ancestors, a mission which, in the course of events Divine Providence called upon us to fulfill. . . .

In virtue of the new dispositions above mentioned, the peasants attached to the soil will be invested within a term fixed by the law with all the rights of free cultivators. . . .

At the same time, they are granted the right of purchasing their close, and, with the consent of the proprietors, they may acquire in full property the arable lands and other appurtenances [right of ways] which are allotted to them as a permanent holding. By the acquisition in full property of the quantity of land fixed, the peasants are free from their obligations towards the proprietors for land thus purchased, and they enter definitely into the condition of free peasants-landholders.

Czar Alexander II

Evaluating the Primary Source

This source gives a look at some of the social changes triggered by the Industrial Revolution, especially the working conditions endured by women. The reliability of this source can be judged by comparing it to other accounts of factory work in the 1840s and by determining the goals or biases that may have influenced the author's arguments.

The Impact of British Rule in India

Interpreting the Primary Source

Ask students what changes the author might want the British to make in their colonial policies. *(Changes include greater self-government for Indians, respect of Indian wishes and culture, fairer taxes, lower debts, and so on.)*

The Unfortunate Situation of Working Women

This article was published in L'Atelier, *a Parisian workingman's newspaper, in 1842.*

Although women's work is less productive for society than that of men, it does, nevertheless, have a certain value, and, moreover, there are professions that only women can practice. For these, women are indispensable. . . . It is these very workers in all these necessary trades who earn the least and who are subject to the longest layoffs. Since for so much work they earn only barely enough to live from day to day, it happens that during times of unemployment they sink into abject poverty.

Who has not heard of the women silkworkers' dirty, unhealthy, and badly paid work; of the women in the spinning and weaving factories working fourteen to sixteen hours (except for one hour for both meals); always standing, without a single minute for repose, putting forth an enormous amount of effort. And many of them have to walk a league or more, morning and evening, to get home. Nor should we neglect to mention the danger that exists merely from working in these large factories, surrounded by wheels, gears, enormous leather belts that always threaten to seize you and pound you to pieces.

The existence of women who work as day laborers, and are obliged to abandon . . . the care of their children to indifferent neighbors is no better. . . . We believe that the condition of women will never really improve until workingmen can earn enough to support their families, which is only fair. Woman is so closely linked to man that the position of the one cannot be improved without reference to the position of the other.

The Impact of British Rule in India

In 1871, Dadabhai Naroji commented on the benefits and the problems of British rule in India.

Benefits of British Rule:

In the Cause of Humanity: Abolition of suttee and infanticide. ***Civilization:*** Education, both male and female. . . . Resuscitation of India's own noble literature. ***Politically:*** Peace and order. Freedom of speech and liberty of the press. . . . Improvement of government in the native states. Security of life and property. Freedom from oppression. . . . ***Materially:*** Loans for railways and irrigation. Development of a few valuable products, such as indigo, tea, coffee, silk, etc. Increase of exports. Telegraphs.

The Detriments of British Rule:

In the Cause of Humanity: Nothing. ***Civilization:*** [T]here has been a failure to do as much as might have been done. ***Politically:*** Repeated breach of pledges to give the natives a fair and reasonable share in the higher administration of their own country, . . . an utter disregard of the feelings and views of the natives. ***Financially:*** [N]ew modes of taxation, without any adequate effort to increase the means of the people to pay.

Summary: British rule has been: morally, a great blessing; politically, peace and order on one hand, blunders on the other; materially, impoverishment. . . . Our great misfortune is that you do not know our wants. When you will know our real wishes, I have not the least doubt that you would do justice. The genius and spirit of the British people is fair play and justice.

Analyzing Primary Sources

1. What reason does Czar Alexander II give for freeing the serfs?
2. What physical and economic problems of women workers are described in the Parisian newspaper article? What solution(s) does the author offer?
3. What is the attitude of the *L'Atelier* writer toward women and women's work? Is the author of the article more likely to be a woman or a man? What makes you think so?
4. Summarize the benefits and problems of British rule in India.

Evaluating the Primary Source

This source provides insight into the policies that would eventually lead India to shake off British rule. The reliability of the source can be judged by the author's efforts to weigh the pros and cons of British rule fairly and his knowledge of British colonial policy.

For other primary source documents related to this time period, see the **World History Primary Source Document Library CD-ROM.**

Analyzing Primary Sources

Answers:

1. The czar claimed that "Divine Providence" (God) had called upon him to fulfill a "sacred inheritance" to improve the condition of the peasants.
2. Problems include low pay, long hours, layoffs, dangerous equipment, and fatigue. The solution, says the author, is to pay men enough money to support their families.
3. Students should cite specific opinions or subjective phrases that reveal the author's attitude toward women and women's work as well as give clues to whether the author might be a man or a woman.
4. Encourage students to draw up a balance sheet listing the benefits and detriments named by the author.

FOCUS

Reinforcing Vocabulary

Review the **Reader's Dictionary** with students to be sure they understand any unfamiliar terms.

TEACH

Over the Top

Interpreting the Primary Source

Ask students to suggest what the phrase "over the top" meant to soldiers fighting in World War I. *(It meant climbing out of the trench and heading onto the open battlefield.)*

Evaluating the Primary Source

This source reveals reasons soldiers in World War I called the bombed-out trenches of the battlefront "no-man's-land." The reliability of the source can be judged by studying photographs and other eyewitnesses descriptions of the trenches, including the poem "Dulce et Decorum Est" by English soldier Wilfred Owen.

Gandhi Takes the Path of Civil Disobedience

Interpreting the Primary Source

Ask students why Gandhi considered British rule "a curse." *(He believed British rule had impoverished and exploited millions of Indians, reducing them to political serfdom and robbing them of the strength to resist or defend their culture.)*

Evaluating the Primary Source

This primary source reveals Gandhi's reasons for adopting civil disobedience to British rule. The reliability of the source can be judged by studying other accounts of British policies in India, such as the primary source found on page 997, and by weighing the fairness of Gandhi's condemnations.

The Holocaust—The Camp Victims

Interpreting the Primary Source

Ask students to discuss how Nazi policies violated the human rights of the victims at Auschwitz-Birkenau. *(The Nazis dehumanized the victims by depriving them of the rights that are considered by most societies to belong automatically to everyone, such as the rights to life, liberty, justice, and equality.)*

Evaluating the Primary Source

This source provides an insight into the horrors endured by people sent to the Nazi death camps. The reliability of the account can be

---

Primary Sources Library

For use with Unit 4

The Twentieth-Century Crisis

During the first half of the 1900s, two destructive wars raged throughout the world and brought tremendous political and social change. World War I destroyed the power of European monarchies, while Nazi aggression in Germany eventually led to World War II and the Holocaust.

Reader's Dictionary

parapet: wall of earth piled on top of a trench

snipers: people who shoot at exposed individuals from a concealed location

civil disobedience: refusal to obey governmental demands

exploitation: unfair use for one's own advantage

disarmament: reducing or eliminating weapons

Over the Top—World War I

Arthur Guy Empey reflects upon his experiences during World War I in the trenches in France.

Suddenly, the earth seemed to shake and a thunderclap burst in my ears. I opened my eyes,—I was splashed all over with sticky mud, and men were picking themselves up from the bottom of the trench. The parapet on my left had toppled into the trench, completely blocking it with a wall of tossed-up earth. The man on my left lay still. . . . A German "Minnie" (trench mortar) had exploded in the [trench]. . . . Stretcher-bearers came up the trench on the double. After a few minutes of digging, three still, muddy forms on stretchers were carried down the communication trench to the rear. Soon they would be resting "somewhere in France," with a little wooden cross over their heads. They had done their bit for King and Country, had died without firing a shot. . . . I was dazed and motionless. Suddenly a shovel was pushed into my hands, and a rough but kindly voice said: "Here, my lad, lend a hand clearing the trench, but keep your head down, and look out for snipers. . . ."

Lying on my belly on the bottom of the trench, I filled sandbags with the sticky mud. . . . The harder I worked, the better I felt.

Occasionally a bullet would crack overhead, and a machine gun would kick up the mud on the bashed-in parapet. At each crack I would duck and shield my face with my arm. One of the older men noticed this action of mine, and whispered: "Don't duck at the crack of a bullet, Yank; the danger has passed,—you never hear the one that wings you. Always remember that if you are going to get it, you'll get it, so never worry." . . . [Days later] we received the cheerful news that at four in the morning we were to go over the top and take the German frontline trench. My heart turned to lead.

Battle of the Somme

778

Gandhi Takes the Path of Civil Disobedience

Mohandas Gandhi explains why British rule in India must end.

Before embarking on civil disobedience and taking the risk I have dreaded to take all these years, I would fain approach you and find a way out.

My personal faith is absolutely clear. I cannot intentionally hurt anything that lives, much less fellow human beings, even though they may do the greatest wrong to me and mine. Whilst, therefore, I hold the British rule to be a curse, I do not intend harm to a single Englishman or to any legitimate interest he may have in India.

I must not be misunderstood. Though I hold the British rule in India to be a curse, I do not, therefore, consider Englishmen in general to be worse than any other people on earth. I have the privilege of claiming many Englishmen as dearest friends. Indeed much that I have learned of the evil of British rule is due to the writings of frank and courageous Englishmen who have not hesitated to tell the truth about that rule.

And why do I regard British rule as a curse? It has impoverished the ignorant millions by a system of progressive exploitation and by a ruinously expensive military and civil administration which the country can never afford.

It has reduced us politically to serfdom. It has sapped the foundations of our culture. And, by the policy of cruel disarmament, it has degraded us spiritually. Lacking the inward strength, we have been reduced . . . to a state bordering on cowardly helplessness. . . .

The Holocaust—The Camp Victims

A French doctor describes the victims of one of the crematoriums at Auschwitz-Birkenau during the Holocaust.

It is mid-day, when a long line of women, children, and old people enter the yard. The senior official in charge . . . climbs on a bench to tell them that they are going to have a bath and that afterwards they will get a drink of hot coffee. They all undress in the yard. . . . The doors are opened and an indescribable jostling begins. The first people to enter the gas chamber begin to draw back. They sense the death which awaits them. The SS men put an end to the pushing and shoving with blows from their rifle butts beating the heads of the horrified women who are desperately hugging their children. The massive oak double doors are shut. For two endless minutes one can hear banging on the walls and screams which are no longer human. And then—not a sound. Five minutes later the doors are opened. The corpses, squashed together and distorted, fall out like a waterfall. The bodies which are still warm pass through the hands of the hairdresser who cuts their hair and the dentist who pulls out their gold teeth . . . One more transport has just been processed through No. IV crematorium.

Analyzing Primary Sources

1. How did Arthur Empey feel and act during his time in the trenches of World War I?
2. According to Gandhi, what had British rule done to India?
3. Why do you think Gandhi believed that nonviolent civil disobedience would encourage the British to free India?
4. What is the French doctor's point of view about the events he describes at the Auschwitz-Birkenau death camp?

judged by how well the doctor's descriptions match those given by victims and other eyewitnesses to the Holocaust.

For other primary source documents related to this time period, see the **World History Primary Source Document Library CD-ROM.**

Analyzing Primary Sources

Answers:

1. Feelings might include fear, confusion, or anger (over the loss of life). He acted like a new recruit—ducking the sounds of gunfire, digging in, and eventually facing the terror of going "over the top."
2. Student answers should accurately reflect the effects of British rule cited in the last two paragraphs of the reading.
3. Answers will vary, but Gandhi counted on the support of British citizens who opposed colonial policies, on the British traditions of justice and self-government, on world opinion, and so on.
4. He is detached but some phrases ("two endless minutes") reveal his horror.

FOCUS

Reinforcing Vocabulary

Review the **Reader's Dictionary** with students to be sure they understand any unfamiliar terms.

TEACH

Progress Never Stops

Interpreting the Primary Source

Ask students to identify and describe three of the phenomena experienced by John Glenn during this space flight. (*zero gravity, or weightlessness, little sensation of speed, and viewing four sunsets per day; descriptions will vary*)

Evaluating the Primary Source

The source provides students with historical insight into the very first experiences of Americans in space flight. The reliability of this source can be judged by examining the credentials of the author, John Glenn, who returned to space in 1998, and in corroborating material provided by both American and foreign astronauts. Interested students might wish to examine NASA archives for photographs and other materials about the United States space program.

An Ideal for Which I Am Prepared to Die

Interpreting the Primary Source

Ask students to identify the main cause of Mandela's protest against South Africa's government. *(He opposes laws made by whites to ensure their continued domination and the poverty and misery of black South Africans.)*

Evaluating the Primary Source

This source contains the reasons that Nelson Mandela opposed apartheid. The reliability of this source can be judged by examining the apartheid system as it existed at the time of Mandela's trial, the newspaper accounts of Mandela's trial, and the political policies that Mandela adopted as South Africa's first black president.

China's Gilded Age

Interpreting the Primary Source

Ask students to state the economic reason for the changes the author witnessed on his return to China. *(China had moved away from a centrally planned economy and adopted aspects of a free market.)*

For use with Unit 5

Toward a Global Civilization

Following World War II, the balance of power in the world shifted dramatically. Many nations and peoples came under the political and ideological influence of the United States, which promoted capitalism and individual rights and liberties.

Reader's Dictionary

reserve: a reservation; land set aside for use by a particular group

squatters: those who settle on public land without rights or permission

perturbation: major change or disturbance

Progress Never Stops

In 1962, John J. Glenn, Jr. was commander of the first U.S. crewed spacecraft to orbit the earth. Glenn spoke to a joint meeting of Congress six days after he returned from orbit.

What did we learn from the flight? . . . The Mercury spacecraft and systems design concepts are sound and have now been verified during manned flight. We also proved that man can operate intelligently in space and can adapt rapidly to this new environment.

Zero G or weightlessness appears to be no problem. As a matter of fact, lack of gravity is a rather fascinating thing. Objects within the cockpit can be parked in midair. For example, at one time during the flight, I was using a hand-held camera. Another system needed attention; so it seemed quite natural to let go of the camera, take care of the other chore, then reach out, grasp the camera, and go back about my business.

There seemed to be little sensation of speed although the craft was traveling at about five miles per second—a speed that I too find difficult to comprehend.

The view from that altitude defies description. The horizon colors are brilliant and sunsets are spectacular. It is hard to beat a day in which you are permitted the luxury of seeing four sunsets. . . .

Our efforts today and what we have done so far are but small building blocks in a huge pyramid to come.

But questions are sometimes raised regarding the immediate payoffs from our efforts. Explorations and the pursuit of knowledge have always paid dividends in the long run—usually far greater than anything expected at the outset. Experimenters with common, green mold, little dreamed what effect their discovery of penicillin would have.

We are just probing the surface of the greatest advancements in man's knowledge of his surroundings that has ever been made. . . . Knowledge begets knowledge. Progress never stops.

John Glenn

An Ideal for Which I Am Prepared to Die

Nelson Mandela gave this speech during his trial in South Africa in 1964. Following the trial, he was sentenced to life in prison.

The whites enjoy what may well be the highest standard of living in the world, whilst Africans live in poverty and misery. Forty percent of the Africans live in hopelessly overcrowded and, in some cases, drought-stricken reserves, where soil erosion and the overworking of the soil make it impossible for them to live properly off the land. Thirty percent are labourers, labour tenants, and squatters on white farms. The other thirty percent live in towns where they have developed economic and social habits which bring them closer, in many respects, to white standards. Yet forty-six percent of all African families in Johannesburg do not earn enough to keep them going.

The complaint of Africans, however, is not only that they are poor and whites are rich, but that the laws which are made by the whites are designed to preserve this situation. . . .

During my lifetime I have dedicated my life to this struggle of the African people. I have fought against white domination, and I have fought against black domination. I have cherished the ideal of a democratic and free society in which all persons live together in harmony with equal opportunities. It is an ideal which I hope to live for, and to see realized. But my lord, if needs be, it is an ideal for which I am prepared to die.

China's Gilded Age

Xiao-huang Yin recounts his trip through China in 1994.

Recently I took a six-week journey across China. It was my first trip back since . . . 1985. In the course of my visit I saw—I felt—the perturbations of profound and chaotic social change. China's stunning hurtle from a centrally planned economy to a free market has set off an economic explosion and generated tremendous prosperity. Its economic growth was 13 percent in 1993, and average personal income in urban areas had doubled since 1985. With the state-owned sector accounting for less than 30 percent of total economic output, the socialist system is becoming an empty shell. Across China the lines between the state and private economies are blurring. At the largest national department store in Shanghai, a symbol of Chinese socialist business, customers now bargain for better prices. The counters within the store have been contracted out to shop clerks, who decide the prices. Dual ownership has in essence turned this state enterprise into a private business. . . .

Not everyone gets rich quick, but the economic boom has brought most urban Chinese a huge improvement in their standard of living. Color TV sets, refrigerators, and VCRs, considered luxuries when I lived in China, can be found in almost every working-class urban household—at least in the prosperous coastal cities.

Analyzing Primary Sources

1. What are the immediate and long-term "payoffs" of John Glenn's 1962 space mission, according to his report to Congress?
2. Summarize the demographics of the African population discussed by Nelson Mandela.
3. What ideal does Nelson Mandela discuss?
4. Why does Xiao-huang Yin believe that socialism is becoming an "empty shell" in China?

Evaluating the Primary Source
This source links economic freedom to improved standards of living in China. The reliability of this source can be judged by reviewing journalistic accounts of China since it implemented capitalist-style economic reforms, policies adopted by China toward the free enterprise port of Hong Kong (returned to China by the British in 1997), and the continued control of the Communist party over government.

For other primary source documents related to this time period, see the **World History Primary Source Document Library CD-ROM.**

Analyzing Primary Sources

Answers:

1. Mission proved people can operate in space and adapt to that environment. Long-term benefits are unknown but may include progress and increased knowledge.
2. The demographics should reflect the statistics in the first paragraph of Mandela's speech.
3. Mandela defends the ideal of "a democratic and free society in which all persons live together in harmony with equal opportunity."
4. The author says that the state-owned sector of business accounts for less than 30 percent of China's total economic output.

Honoring America

For Americans, the flag has always had a special meaning. It is a symbol of our nation's freedom and democracy.

Flag Etiquette

Over the years, Americans have developed rules and customs concerning the use and display of the flag. One of the most important things every American should remember is to treat the flag with respect.

- The flag should be raised and lowered by hand and displayed only from sunrise to sunset. On special occasions, the flag may be displayed at night, but it should be illuminated.
- The flag may be displayed on all days, weather permitting, particularly on national and state holidays and on historic and special occasions.
- No flag may be flown above the American flag or to the right of it at the same height.
- The flag should never touch the ground or floor beneath it.
- The flag may be flown at half-staff by order of the president, usually to mourn the death of a public official.
- The flag may be flown upside down only to signal distress.
- The flag should never be carried flat or horizontally, but always carried aloft and free
- When the flag becomes old and tattered, it should be destroyed by burning. According to an approved custom, the Union (stars on blue field) is first cut from the flag; then the two pieces, which no longer form a flag, are burned.

The Star-Spangled Banner

**O! say can you see, by the dawn's early light,
What so proudly we hail'd at the twilight's last gleaming?
Whose broad stripes and bright stars through the perilous fight,
O'er the ramparts we watched, were so gallantly streaming?
And the rockets' red glare, the bombs bursting in air,
Gave proof through the night that our flag was still there;
O! say, does that star-spangled banner yet wave
O'er the land of the free and the home of the brave?**

The Pledge of Allegiance

I pledge allegiance to the Flag of the United States of America and to the Republic for which it stands, one Nation under God, indivisible, with liberty and justice for all.

Glossary

abolitionism a movement to end slavery (p. 384)

absolutism a political system in which a ruler holds total power (p. 223)

acid rain the rainfall that results when sulfur produced by factories mixes with moisture in the air (p. 752)

acropolis in early Greek city-states, a fortified gathering place at the top of a hill which was sometimes the site of temples and public buildings (p. 53)

anarchy political disorder; lawlessness (p. 252)

annex incorporate territory into an existing political unit, such as a city or country (p. 437)

annul declare invalid (p. 179)

apartheid "apartness," the system of racial segregation in South Africa from the 1950s until 1991 (p. 704)

appeasement satisfying demands of dissatisfied powers in an effort to maintain peace and stability (p. 592)

archipelago a chain of islands (p. 110)

armada a fleet of warships (p. 214)

armistice a truce or agreement to end fighting (p. 522)

arms race building up armies and stores of weapons to keep up with an enemy (p. 633)

astrolabe an instrument used by sailors to determine their location by observing the positions of stars (p. 95)

autonomous self-governing (p. 664)

balance of trade the difference in value between what a nation imports and what it exports over time (p. 195)

banner in Qing China, a separate military unit made up of Manchus; the empire's chief fighting force (p. 271)

Bantu a family of languages spoken in central and southern Africa; a member of any group of the African peoples who speak that language (p. 100)

baroque an artistic style of the seventeenth century characterized by complex forms, bold ornamentation, and contrasting elements (p. 231)

bioterrorism the use of biological and chemical weapons in terrorist attacks (p. 754)

biowarfare the use of disease or poison against civilians and soldiers in wartime (p. 754)

blitzkrieg German for "lightning war," a swift and sudden military attack; used by the Germans during World War II (p. 596)

bloc a group of nations with a common purpose (p. 645)

bourgeoisie the middle class, including merchants, industrialists, and professional people (pp. 330, 401)

boyar a Russian noble (p. 228)

Buddhism a religious doctrine introduced in northern India in the sixth century B.C. by Siddhartha Gautama, known as the Buddha, or "Enlightened One" (p. 39)

budget deficit the state that exists when a government spends more than it collects in revenues (p. 669)

bureaucracy an administrative organization that relies on nonelective officials and regular procedures (p. 204)

Bushido "the way of the warrior," the strict code by which Japanese samurai were supposed to live (p. 108)

caliph a successor of Muhammad as spiritual and temporal leader of the Muslims (p. 91)

capital money available for investment (p. 364)

caste system a set of rigid categories in ancient India that determined a person's occupation and economic potential as well as his or her position in society, based partly on skin color (p. 37)

caudillo in postrevolutionary Latin America, a strong leader who ruled chiefly by military force, usually with the support of the landed elite (p. 456)

Christian humanism a movement that developed in northern Europe during the Renaissance combining classical learning (humanism) with the goal of reforming the Catholic Church (p. 172)

Christianity monotheistic religion that emerged during the first century (p. 73)

civil disobedience refusal to obey laws that are considered to be unjust (p. 570)

civilization a complex culture in which large numbers of people share a number of common elements such as social structure, religion, and art (p. 22)

clan a group of related families (p. 275)

clergy church leaders (p. 74)

Cold War the period of political tension following World War II and ending with the fall of communism in the Soviet Union at the end of the 1980s (p. 616)

collaborator a person who assists the enemy (p. 609)

collective bargaining the right of unions to negotiate with employers over wages and hours (p. 537)

collectivization a system in which private farms are eliminated and peasants work land owned by the government (p. 545)

colony a settlement of people living in a new territory, linked with the parent country by trade and direct government control (p. 195)

commercial capitalism economic system in which people invest in trade or goods to make profits (pp. 131, 274)

commodity a marketable product (p. 476)

common law a uniform system of law that developed in England based on court decisions and on customs and usage rather than on written law codes; replaced law codes that varied from place to place (p. 120)

commonwealth a republic (p. 220)

commune in China during the 1950s, a group of collective farms each of which contained more than 30,000 people who lived and worked together (p. 724)

concentration camp a camp where prisoners of war, political prisoners, or members of minority groups are confined, typically under harsh conditions (p. 550)

concession political compromise (p. 480)

Confucianism the system of political and ethical ideas formulated by the Chinese philosopher Confucius toward the end of the Zhou dynasty; it was intended to help restore order to a society that was in a state of confusion (p. 44)

conquistador a Spanish conqueror of the Americas (p. 194)

conscription military draft (p. 500)

conservatism a political philosophy based on tradition and social stability, favoring obedience to political authority and organized religion (p. 372)

consulate government established in France after the overthrow of the Directory in 1799, with Napoleon as first consul in control of the entire government (p. 346)

contras rebels financed by the United States who began a guerrilla war against the Sandinista government in Nicaragua (p. 691)

cooperative a farm organization owned by and operated for the benefit of the farmers (p. 695)

cottage industry a method of production in which tasks are done by individuals in their rural homes (p. 364)

coup d'état a sudden overthrow of the government (p. 343)

creole a person of European descent born in the Americas and living there permanently (p. 454)

Crusade military expedition carried out by European Christians in the Middle Ages to regain the Holy Land from the Muslims (p. 123)

cuneiform "wedge-shaped," a system of writing developed by the Sumerians using a reed stylus to create wedge-shaped impressions on a clay tablet (p. 27)

czar Russian for "caesar," the title used by Russian emperors (p. 227)

D

daimyo "great names," heads of noble families in Japan who controlled vast landed estates and relied on samurai for protection (pp. 108, 278)

Dao "Way," the key to proper behavior under Confucianism (p. 42)

deficit spending when a government pays out more money than it takes in through taxation and other revenues, thus going into debt (p. 538)

deforestation the clearing of forests (p. 752)

deism an eighteenth-century religious philosophy based on reason and natural law (p. 302)

demilitarize eliminate or prohibit weapons, fortifications, and other military installations (p. 592)

democracy "the rule of the many," government by the people, either directly or through their elected representatives (p. 53)

depression a period of low economic activity and rising unemployment (p. 536)

de-Stalinization the process of eliminating Stalin's more ruthless policies (p. 638)

détente a phase of relaxed tensions and improved relations between two adversaries (p. 657)

dictatorship a form of government in which a person or small group has absolute power (p. 401)

direct democracy a system of government in which the people participate directly in government decision making through mass meetings (p. 56)

direct rule colonial government in which local elites are removed from power and replaced by a new set of officials brought from the mother country (p. 433)

disarmament a limit or reduction of armed forces and weapons (p. 758)

discrimination prejudice, usually based on race, religion, class, sex, or age (p. 738)

dissident a person who speaks out against the regime in power (p. 658)

divine right of kings the belief that kings receive their power from God and are responsible only to God (p. 219)

domestication adaptation for human use (p. 21)

domino theory idea that, if one country falls to communism, neighboring countries will also fall (p. 635)

dowry a gift of money or property paid at the time of marriage, either by the bride's parents to her husband or, in Islamic societies, by a husband to his wife (p. 163)

Duma the Russian legislative assembly (p. 414)

dynasty a family of rulers whose right to rule is passed on within the family (p. 27)

E

ecology the study of the relationships between living things and their environment (p. 752)

elector an individual qualified to vote in an election (p. 343)

emancipation the act of setting free (p. 383)

empire a large political unit, usually under a single leader, that controls many peoples or territories (p. 25)

enlightened absolutism a system in which rulers tried to govern by Enlightenment principles while maintaining their full royal powers (p. 311)

entrepreneur a person interested in finding new business opportunities and new ways to make profits (p. 364)

Glossary

epic poem a long poem that tells the deeds of a great hero, such as the *Iliad* and the *Odyssey* of Homer (p. 53)

epidemic an outbreak of disease that spreads rapidly (p. 144)

estate one of the three classes into which French society was divided before the revolution: the clergy (first estate), the nobles (second estate), and the townspeople (third estate) (p. 330)

eta Japan's outcast class, whose way of life was strictly regulated by the Tokugawa (p. 281)

ethnic cleansing a policy of killing or forcibly removing an ethnic group from its lands; used by the Serbs against the Muslim minority in Bosnia (pp. 564, 663)

extraterritoriality living in a section of a country set aside for foreigners but not subject to the host country's laws (p. 467)

faction a dissenting group (p. 338)

fascism a political philosophy that glorifies the state above the individual by emphasizing the need for a strong central government led by a dictatorial ruler (p. 541)

federal system a form of government in which power is shared between the national government and state governments (p. 322)

feminism the movement for women's rights (p. 407)

feudalism political and social system that developed during the Middle Ages, when royal governments were no longer able to defend their subjects; nobles offered protection and land in return for service (p. 118)

fief under feudalism, a grant of land made to a vassal; the vassal held political authority within his fief (p. 119)

filial piety the duty of family members to subordinate their needs and desires to those of the male head of the family, a concept important in Confucianism (p. 43)

fresco a painting done on fresh, wet plaster with water-based paints (p. 166)

genocide the deliberate mass murder of a particular racial, political, or cultural group (pp. 564, 607)

geocentric literally, "earth-centered"; a system of planetary motion that places Earth at the center of the universe, with the Sun, Moon, and other planets revolving around it (p. 295)

global economy an economy in which the production, distribution, and sale of goods take place on a worldwide scale, as in a multinational corporation (p. 754)

grand vizier the Ottoman sultan's chief minister, who led the meetings of the imperial council (p. 243)

greenhouse effect global warming caused by the buildup of carbon dioxide in the atmosphere (p. 752)

guerrilla tactics the use of unexpected maneuvers like sabotage and subterfuge to fight an enemy (p. 577)

guild a business association associated with a particular trade or craft; guilds evolved in the twelfth century and came to play a leading role in the economic life of medieval cities (p. 132)

gunpowder empire an empire formed by outside conquerors who unified the regions that they conquered through their mastery of firearms (p. 242)

han one of the approximately 250 domains into which Japan was divided under the Tokugawa (p. 279)

harem "sacred place," the private domain of an Ottoman sultan, where he and his wives resided (p. 243)

heavy industry the manufacture of machines and equipment for factories and mines (p. 638)

heliocentric literally, "sun-centered"; the system of the universe proposed in 1543 by Nicholas Copernicus, who argued that Earth and the planets revolve around the Sun (p. 295)

heresy the denial of basic church doctrines (p. 134)

hieroglyphics "priest-carvings" or "sacred writings," a complex system of writing that used both pictures and more abstract forms; used by the ancient Egyptians and Mayans (p. 30)

Hijrah the journey of Muhammad and his followers to Madinah in 622, which became year 1 of the official calendar of Islam (p. 90)

Hinduism the major Indian religious system, which had its origins in the religious beliefs of the Aryans who settled India after 1500 B.C. (p. 38)

hominid humans and other humanlike creatures that walk upright (p. 19)

hostage system a system used by the shogunate to control the daimyo in Tokugawa Japan; the family of a daimyo lord was forced to stay at their residence in the capital whenever the lord was absent from it (p. 280)

humanism an intellectual movement of the Renaissance based on the study of the humanities, which included grammar, rhetoric, poetry, moral philosophy, and history (p. 164)

imperator commander in chief; the Latin origin of the word *emperor* (p. 69)

imperialism the extension of a nation's power over other lands (p. 430)

indemnity payment for damages (p. 471)

indigenous native to a region (p. 440)

indirect rule colonial government in which local rulers are allowed to maintain their positions of authority and status (p. 433)

inductive reasoning the doctrine that scientists should proceed from the particular to the general by making systematic observations and carefully organized experiments to test hypotheses or theories, a process that will lead to correct general principles (p. 299)

indulgence a release from all or part of punishment for sin by the Catholic Church, reducing time in purgatory after death (p. 173)

industrial capitalism an economic system based on industrial production or manufacturing (p. 368)

inflation a rapid increase in prices (p. 216)

Inquisition a court established by the Catholic Church in 1232 to discover and try heretics; also called the Holy Office (p. 134)

intifada "uprising," militant movement that arose during the 1980s among supporters of the Palestine Liberation Organization living in Israel (p. 714)

Islam monotheistic religion that emerged in the Arabian Peninsula during the seventh century (p. 90)

J

janissary a soldier in the elite guard of the Ottoman Turks (p. 240)

Judaism monotheistic religion developed among the Israelites (p. 30)

K

kaiser German for "caesar," the title of the emperors of the Second German Empire (p. 381)

kamikaze Japanese for "divine wind," a suicide mission in which young Japanese pilots intentionally flew their airplanes into U.S. fighting ships at sea (p. 614)

khanate one of the several separate territories into which Genghis Khan's empire was split, each under the rule of one of his sons (p. 105)

L

laissez-faire literally, "let [people] do [what they want]," the concept that the state should not impose government regulations but should leave the economy alone (p. 303)

laity regular church members (p. 74)

liberalism a political philosophy originally based largely on Enlightenment principles, holding that people should be as free as possible from government restraint and that civil liberties—the basic rights of all people—should be protected (p. 373)

lineage group an extended family unit that has combined into a larger community (p. 101)

literacy the ability to read (p. 409)

M

magic realism a form of expression unique to Latin American literature; it combines realistic events with dreamlike or fantastic backgrounds (p. 687)

Magna Carta the "Great Charter" of rights, which King John was forced to sign by the English nobles at Runnymeade in 1215 (p. 120)

Mahatma "Great Soul," title given to Mohandas Gandhi by the Indian people (p. 570)

mainland states part of a continent, as distinguished from peninsulas or offshore islands (p. 203)

mandate a nation governed by another nation on behalf of the League of Nations (p. 526)

Mandate of Heaven claim by Chinese kings of the Zhou dynasty that they had direct authority from heaven to rule and to keep order in the universe (p. 41)

Mannerism an artistic movement that emerged in Italy in the 1520s and 1530s; it marked the end of the Renaissance by breaking down the principles of balance, harmony, and moderation (p. 230)

manor in medieval Europe, an agricultural estate run by a lord and worked by peasants (p. 131)

mercantilism a set of principles that dominated economic thought in the seventeenth century; it held that the prosperity of a nation depended on a large supply of gold and silver (p. 195)

mercenary a soldier who sells his services to the highest bidder (p. 159)

Mesoamerica the name used for areas of Mexico and Central America that were civilized before the arrival of the Spanish (p. 141)

mestizo a person of mixed European and native American Indian descent (pp. 319, 454)

Middle Passage the journey of slaves from Africa to the Americas, so called because it was the middle portion of the triangular trade route (p. 198)

militant combative (p. 211)

militarism reliance on military strength (p. 380)

ministerial responsibility the idea that the prime minister is responsible to the popularly elected executive body and not to the executive officer (p. 413)

mobilization the process of assembling troops and supplies and making them ready for war (pp. 502, 612)

modernism a movement in which writers and artists between 1870 and 1914 rebelled against the traditional literary and artistic styles that had dominated European cultural life since the Renaissance (p. 421)

money economy an economic system based on money rather than barter (p. 131)

monk a man who separates himself from ordinary human society in order to dedicate himself to God; monks live in monasteries headed by abbots (p. 117)

monotheistic having one god (p. 32)

Monroe Doctrine the United States policy guaranteeing the independence of Latin American nations and warning against European intervention in the Americas, made by President James Monroe in 1823 (p. 455)

mosque a Muslim house of worship (p. 95)

mulatto a person of mixed African and European descent (p. 319)

multinational corporation a company with divisions in more than two countries (p. 684)

nationalism the unique cultural identity of a people based on common language, religion, and national symbols (p. 350)

natural rights rights with which all humans are supposedly born, including the rights to life, liberty, and property (p. 233)

natural selection the principle set forth by Darwin that some organisms are more adaptable to the environment than others; in popular terms, "survival of the fittest" (p. 390)

Neolithic Revolution the shift from hunting of animals and gathering of food to the keeping of animals and the growing of food on a regular basis that occurred around 8000 B.C. (p. 21)

New Economic Policy (NEP) a modified version of the old capitalist system adopted by Lenin in 1921 to replace war communism in Russia; peasants were allowed to sell their produce, and retail stores and small industries could be privately owned, but heavy industry, banking, and mines remained in the hands of the government (p. 543)

new monarchy in the fifteenth century, government in which power had been centralized under a king or queen, i.e., France, England, and Spain (p. 138)

nomad a person who moves from place to place (p. 20)

occupied held by a foreign power (p. 739)

oligarchy "the rule of the few," a form of government in which a small group of people exercises controls (pp. 53, 583)

organic evolution the principle set forth by Darwin that every plant or animal has evolved, or changed, over a long period of time from earlier, simpler forms of life to more complex forms (p. 390)

orthodoxy traditional beliefs, especially in religion (p. 251)

ozone layer a thin layer of gas in the upper atmosphere that shields Earth from the Sun's ultraviolet rays (p. 752)

Pan-Africanism the unity of all black Africans, regardless of national boundaries (pp. 570, 705)

Pan-Arabism Arab unity, regardless of national boundaries (p. 713)

partisan a resistance fighter in World War II (p. 604)

pasha an appointed official in the Ottoman Empire who collected taxes, maintained law and order, and was directly responsible to the sultan's court (p. 241)

patriarchal dominated by men (p. 27)

patrician great landowners, they formed the ruling class in the Roman Republic (p. 68)

peacekeeping force a military force drawn from neutral members of the United Nations to settle conflicts and supervise truces (p. 757)

peninsulare a person born on the Iberian Peninsula; typically, a Spanish or Portuguese official who resided temporarily in Latin America for political and economic gain and then returned to Europe (p. 454)

per capita per person (p. 725)

perestroika Mikhail Gorbachev's plan to reform the Soviet Union by restructuring its economy (p. 659)

permanent revolution an atmosphere of constant revolutionary fervor favored by Mao Zedong to enable China to overcome the past and achieve the final stage of communism (p. 724)

philosophe French for "philosopher"; applied to all intellectuals—i.e., writers, journalists, economists, and social reformers—during the Enlightenment (p. 301)

photomontage a picture made of a combination of photographs (p. 556)

planned economy an economic system directed by government agencies (p. 508)

plantation a large agricultural estate (p. 198)

plebeian in the Roman Republic, a social class made up of minor landholders, craftspeople, merchants, and small farmers (p. 68)

plebiscite a popular vote (p. 382)

pogrom organized persecution or massacre of a minority group, especially Jews (p. 421)

policy of containment a plan to keep something, such as communism, within its existing geographical boundaries and prevent further aggressive moves (p. 632)

polis the early Greek city-state, consisting of a city or town and its surrounding territory (p. 53)

Politburo a seven-member committee that became the leading policy-making body of the Communist Party in Russia (p. 543)

pop art an artistic movement that emerged in the early 1960s; pop artists took images from popular culture and transformed them into works of fine art (p. 674)

pope the bishop of Rome and head of the Roman Catholic Church (p. 117)

porcelain a ceramic made of fine clay baked at very high temperatures (p. 276)

postmodernism an artistic movement that emerged in the 1980s; it is characterized by a revival of traditional elements and techniques, and includes crafts such as textiles, pottery, and furniture making in addition to traditional artistic media (p. 674)

predestination the belief that God has determined in advance who will be saved (the elect) and who will be damned (the reprobate) (p. 178)

prefecture in the Japanese Meiji Restoration, a territory governed by its former daimyo lord (p. 481)

principle of intervention idea that great powers have the right to send armies into countries where there are revolutions to restore legitimate governments (p. 373)

privatization the sale of government-owned companies to private firms (p. 689)

proletariat the working class (p. 401)

propaganda ideas spread to influence public opinion for or against a cause (p. 503)

protectorate a political unit that depends on another government for its protection (p. 431)

provincial local; of or relating to a province (p. 473)

psychoanalysis a method by which a therapist and patient probe deeply into the patient's memory; by making the patient's conscious mind aware of repressed thoughts, healing can take place (p. 419)

Ptolemaic system the geocentric model of the universe that prevailed in the Middle Ages; named after the astronomer Ptolemy, who lived in Alexandria during the second century (p. 295)

puddling process in which coke derived from coal is used to burn away impurities in crude iron to produce high quality iron (p. 365)

Q

queue the braided pigtail that was traditionally worn by Chinese males (p. 270)

R

rationalism a system of thought expounded by René Descartes based on the belief that reason is the chief source of knowledge (p. 299)

real wages the actual purchasing power of income (p. 645)

realism mid-nineteenth century movement that rejected romanticism and sought to portray lower- and middle-class life as it actually was (p. 390)

redistribution of wealth the shifting of wealth from a rich minority to a poor majority (p. 579)

Reichstag the German parliament (p. 549)

reincarnation the rebirth of an individual's soul in a different form after death (p. 38)

relics of feudalism obligations of peasants to noble landlords that survived into the modern era (p. 330)

reparation payment made to the victors by the vanquished to cover the costs of a war (p. 524)

republic a form of government in which the leader is not a king and certain citizens have the right to vote (p. 67)

revisionist a Marxist who rejected the revolutionary approach, believing instead in evolution by democratic means to achieve the goal of socialism (p. 401)

rococo an artistic style that replaced baroque in the 1730s; it was highly secular, emphasizing grace, charm, and gentle action (p. 309)

romanticism an intellectual movement that emerged at the end of the eighteenth century in reaction to the ideas of the Enlightenment; it stressed feelings, emotion, and imagination as sources of knowing (p. 387)

S

sacrament Christian rite (p. 134)

salon the elegant drawing rooms of great urban houses where, in the eighteenth century, writers, artists, aristocrats, government officials, and wealthy middle-class people gathered to discuss the ideas of the philosophes, helping to spread the ideas of the Enlightenment (p. 306)

salvation the state of being saved (that is, going to heaven) through faith alone or through faith and good works (p. 172)

samurai "those who serve," Japanese warriors similar to the knights of medieval Europe (p. 107)

sanction a restriction intended to enforce international law (p. 595)

sans-culottes "without breeches," members of the Paris Commune who considered themselves ordinary patriots (in other words, they wore long trousers instead of fine knee-length breeches) (p. 335)

satellite state a country that is economically and politically dependent on another country (p. 632)

savanna broad grassland dotted with small trees and shrubs (p. 98)

scientific method a systematic procedure for collecting and analyzing evidence that was crucial to the evolution of science in the modern world (p. 299)

secede withdraw (p. 385)

secular worldly (p. 157)

secularization indifference to or rejection of religion or religious consideration (p. 389)

self-strengthening a policy promoted by reformers toward the end of the Qing dynasty under which China would adopt Western technology while keeping its Confucian values and institutions (p. 468)

separation of powers a form of government in which the executive, legislative, and judicial branches limit and control each other through a system of checks and balances (p. 302)

sepoy an Indian soldier hired by the British East India Company to protect the company's interests in the region (p. 448)

serf in medieval Europe, a peasant legally bound to the land who had to provide labor services, pay rents, and be subject to the lord's control (p. 131)

shah king (used in Persia and Iran) (p. 251)

Shining Path a radical guerrilla group in Peru with ties to Communist China (p. 695)

Shinto "the Sacred Way" or "the Way of the Gods," the Japanese state religion; among its doctrines are the divinity of the emperor and the sacredness of the Japanese nation (p. 108)

Glossary

shogun "general," a powerful military leader in Japan (p. 108)

social contract the concept proposed by Rousseau that an entire society agrees to be governed by its general will, and all individuals should be forced to abide by the general will since it represents what is best for the entire community (p. 304)

socialism a system in which society, usually in the form of the government, owns and controls the means of production (p. 370)

soviet a Russian council composed of representatives from the workers and soldiers (p. 516)

sphere of influence an area in which a foreign power has been granted exclusive rights and privileges, such as trading rights and mining privileges (p. 469)

stalemate the condition that exists when neither of two opposing sides is able to make significant gains (p. 738)

state capitalism an economic system in which the central government plays an active role in the economy, establishing price and wage policies and subsidizing vital industries (p. 740)

sultan "holder of power," the military and political head of state under the Seljuk Turks and the Ottomans (pp. 93, 242)

surrealism artistic movement that seeks to depict the world of the unconscious (p. 556)

suttee the Hindu custom of cremating a widow on her husband's funeral pyre (p. 257)

systematic agriculture the keeping of animals and the growing of food on a regular basis (p. 21)

T

Thatcherism the economic policy of British prime minister Margaret Thatcher, which limited social welfare and restricted union power (p. 668)

theology the study of religion and God (p. 136)

total war a war that involves the complete mobilization of resources and people, affecting the lives of all citizens in the warring countries, even those remote from the battlefields (p. 508)

totalitarian state a government that aims to control the political, economic, social, intellectual, and cultural lives of its citizens (p. 541)

trade embargo a policy prohibiting trade with a particular country (p. 689)

trench warfare fighting from ditches protected by barbed wire, as in World War I (p. 504)

triangular trade a pattern of trade that connected Europe, Africa and Asia, and the American continents; typically, manufactured goods from Europe were sent to Africa, where they were exchanged for slaves, who were sent to the Americas, where they were exchanged for raw materials that were then sent to Europe (p. 198)

ulema a group of religious advisers to the Ottoman sultan; this group administered the legal system and schools for educating Muslims (p. 243)

uncertainty principle the idea put forth by Heisenberg in 1927 that the behavior of subatomic particles is uncertain, suggesting that all of the physical laws governing the universe are based in uncertainty (p. 557)

universal law of gravitation one of the three rules of motion governing the planetary bodies set forth by Sir Isaac Newton in his *Principia;* it explains that planetary bodies do not go off in straight bodies but instead continue in elliptical orbits about the sun because every object in the universe is attracted to every other object by a force called gravity (p. 296)

universal male suffrage the right of all males to vote in elections (p. 374)

urban society a system in which cities are the center of political, economic, and social life (p. 157)

vassal under feudalism, a man who served a lord in a military capacity (p. 118)

viceroy a governor who ruled as a representative of a monarch (p. 449)

war communism in World War I Russia, government control of banks and most industries, the seizing of grain from peasants, and the centralization of state administration under Communist control (p. 519)

war of attrition a war based on wearing the other side down by constant attacks and heavy losses, such as World War I (p. 506)

welfare state a state in which the government takes responsibility for providing citizens with services such as health care (p. 644)

witchcraft the practice of magic by people supposedly in league with the devil (p. 217)

zaibatsu in the Japanese economy, a large financial and industrial corporation (p. 571)

zamindar a local official in Mogul India who received a plot of farmland for temporary use in return for collecting taxes for the central government (p. 256)

Spanish Glossary

A

abolitionism/*abolicionismo* un movimiento para poner fin a la esclavitud (pág. 384)

absolutism/*absolutismo* un sistema político en el cual la autoridad tiene el poder total o absoluto (pág. 223)

acid rain/*lluvia ácida* la lluvia que resulta cuando azufre producido por industrias se mezcla con la humedad en el aire (pág. 752)

acropolis/*acrópolis* en las antiguas ciudades-estados griegas, un lugar de reunión fortificado ubicado en la cima de una colina que a veces era el lugar de templos y edificios públicos (pág. 53)

anarchy/*anarquía* ausencia de autoridad política (pág. 252)

annex/*anexar* unir un territorio a una unidad política, tal como una ciudad o un país (pág. 437)

annul/*anular* declarar inválida una cosa (pág. 179)

apartheid/*segregación racial* "separación," el sistema de segregación racial aplicado en Sudáfrica desde la década de 1950 hasta 1991 (pág. 704)

appeasement/*apaciguamiento* satisfacción de las demandas razonables de poderes insatisfechos en un esfuerzo por mantener la paz y la estabilidad (pág. 592)

archipelago/*archipiélago* una cadena de islas (pág. 110)

armada/*armada* una flota de buques de guerra (pág. 214)

armistice/*armisticio* una tregua o acuerdo para dar fin a una guerra (pág. 522)

arms race/*carrera armamentista* constitución de ejércitos y acopio de armas mantenerse a la par con un enemigo (pág. 633)

astrolabe/*astrolabio* un instrumento utilizado por los navegantes para determinar su ubicación mediante la observación de las estrellas y los planetas (pág. 95)

autonomous/*autónomo* de gobierno propio (pág. 664)

B

balance of trade/*balanza comercial* la diferencia en valor entre lo que una nación importa y lo que exporta en un período de tiempo (pág. 195)

banner/*estandarte* en la China Qing, una unidad militar independiente constituída por Manchúes, y la principal fuerza de combate del imperio (pág. 271)

Bantu/*bantú* una familia de idiomas hablados en el centro y sur de África; un miembro de cualquier grupo de los pueblos africanos que hablan dicho idioma (pág. 100)

baroque/*barroco* un estilo artístico de el siglo XVII y caracterizado por formas complejas, ornamentación audaz, y elementos contrastantes (pág. 231)

bioterrorism/*terrorismo biológico* el uso de armas biológicas y químicas en ataques terroristas (pág. 754)

biowarfare/*guerra biológica* el uso de enfermedades comunicables y agentes tóxicos contra el público y el ejército en tiempo de guerra (pág. 754)

blitzkrieg/*guerra relámpago* término alemán para "guerra relámpago," una táctica utilizada por los alemanes durante la Segunda Guerra Mundial (pág. 596)

bloc/*bloque* un grupo de naciones con un objetivo común (pág. 645)

bourgeoisie/*burguesía* la clase media (pág. 330, 401)

boyar/*boyar* un noble ruso (pág. 228)

Buddhism/*budismo* una doctrina religiosa introducida en el norte de la India en el siglo sexto A.C. por Siddhartha Gautama, conocido como Buda (o "el Iluminado") (pág. 39)

budget deficit/*déficit presupuestario* el estado que existe cuando un gobierno gasta más de lo que cobra en la forma de ingresos (pág. 669)

bureaucracy/*burocracia* una organización administrativa con funcionarios y procedimientos habituales (pág. 204)

Bushido/*bushido* "el código del guerrero," el estricto código según el cual debían vivir los samurai japoneses (pág. 108)

C

caliph/*califa* un sucesor de Mahoma como líder espiritual y temporal de los musulmanes (pág. 91)

capital/*capital* dinero disponible para inversiones (pág. 364)

caste system/*sistema de castas* un conjunto de categorías rígidas en la antigua India que determinaba la ocupación de una persona y su potencial económico, así como también su posición en la sociedad, parcialmente sobre la base del color de la piel (pág. 37)

caudillo/*caudillo* en Latinoamérica post revolucionaria, un líder poderoso que gobernaba principalmente mediante la fuerza militar, a menudo con el respaldo de la elite hacendada (pág. 456)

Christian humanism/*humanismo cristiano* un movimiento que se desarrolló en el norte de Europa durante el Renacimiento que combinaba el aprendizaje clásico (humanismo) con el objetivo de reformar la Iglesia Católica (pág. 172)

Christianity/*cristianismo* religión monoteísta que surgió en el siglo primero (pág. 73)

civil disobedience/*desobediencia civil* rechazo a obedecer leyes que son consideradas injustas (pág. 570)

civilization/*civilización* una compleja cultura en la que grandes números de personas comparten un gran número de elementos tales como la estructura social, la religión, y el arte (pág. 22)

clan/*clan* un grupo de familias relacionadas (pág. 275)

clergy/*clero* líderes de la iglesia (pág. 74)

Cold War/*Guerra fría* el período de tensión política que siguió a la Segunda Guerra Mundial y que culminó con la caída del comunismo en la Unión Soviética a fines de la década de 1980 (pág. 616)

collaborator/*colaborador* una persona que ayuda al enemigo (pág. 609)

collective bargaining/*convenio colectivo* el derecho de los sindicatos a negociar con los empleadores acerca de remuneraciones y horarios (pág. 537)

collectivization/*colectivización* un sistema en el cual se eliminan las fincas privadas y los campesinos trabajan la tierra de propiedad del gobierno (pág. 545)

colony/*colonia* un asentamiento de personas que están viviendo en un nuevo territorio, enlazado a la madre patria por el comercio y el control directo del gobierno (pág. 195)

commercial capitalism/*capitalismo comercial* un sistema económico en el cual la gente invertía en comercio y bienes con el fin de obtener ganancias (pág. 131, 274)

commodity/*mercancía* un producto vendible (pág. 476)

common law/*derecho consuetudinario* sistema de leyes desarrollado en Inglaterra y que era uniforme en todo el país; reemplazó los códigos legales que variaban de lugar en lugar (pág. 120)

commonwealth/*mancomunidad* nación o estado gobernando por el pueblo o representantes del mismo (pág. 220)

commune/*comuna* en China durante la década de los 1950s, un grupo de granjas colectivas cada una de las cuales contenía más de 30.000 personas que vivían y trabajaban juntas (pág. 724)

concentration camp/*campo de concentración* un campo donde se confina a prisioneros de guerra, prisioneros políticos, o miembros de grupos minoritarios, típicamente bajo condiciones duras (pág. 550)

concession/*concesión* acción y efecto de ceder en una posición ideológica para llegar a un acuerdo (político) (pág. 480)

Confucianism/*confucianismo* el sistema de ideas políticas y éticas formuladas por el filósofo chino Confucio hacia fines de la dinastía Zhou; fue concebido para restaurar el orden en una sociedad que estaba en estado de confusión (pág. 44)

conquistador/*conquistador* uno de los conquistadores españoles de las Américas (pág. 194)

conscription/*conscripción* llamado obligatorio al servicio militar (pág. 500)

conservatism/*conservatismo* una filosofía política basada en la tradición y estabilidad social sobre la base de la obediencia a la autoridad política y la religión organizada (pág. 372)

consulate/*consulado* el nuevo gobierno establecido en Francia después del derrocamiento del Directorio en 1799, siendo Napoleón el primer cónsul en control de todo el gobierno (pág. 346)

contras/*contras* rebeldes financiados por los Estados Unidos que empezaron una guerra guerrillera contra el gobierno sandinista en Nicaragua (pág. 691)

cooperative/*cooperativa* una sociedad agrícola perteneciente a, y a menudo administrada para beneficio de los agricultores (pág. 695)

cottage industry/*industria de casa de campo* un método de producción en el que las tareas las realizan las personas en sus hogares (pág. 364)

coup d'état/*golpe de estado* un súbito derrocamiento del gobierno (pág. 343)

creole/*criollo* descendiente de europeos nacido en las Américas (pág. 454)

Crusade/*Cruzada* expediciones militares llevadas a cabo por cristianos europeos para conquistar la Tierra Santa de manos de los musulmanes (pág. 123)

cuneiform/*cuneiforme* "forma de cuña," sistema de escritura desarrollado por los sumerios utilizando un punzón de lengüeta para crear impresiones con forma de cuña en una tableta de arcilla (pág. 27)

czar/*zar* (de "caesar") título adoptado por los gobernantes de Rusia desde finales del siglo XV (pág. 227)

D

daimyo/*daimyo* "grandes nombres," líderes de familias nobles en Japón, quienes controlaban vastas propiedades y confiaban su protección a los samurai (pág. 108, 278)

Dao/*Dao* "Camino," la clave para la conducta apropiada bajo el confucianismo (pág. 42)

deficit spending/*gastos deficitarios* los gastos gubernamentales que exceden a lo que se recibe a través de los impuestos y otros ingresos, por ende entrando en deuda (pág. 538)

deforestation/*deforestación* la tala de bosques (pág. 752)

deism/*deísmo* una filosofía religiosa del siglo XVIII basada en la razón y en la ley natural (pág. 302)

demilitarize/*desmilitarizar* eliminar o prohibir las armas, fortificaciones, y oras instalaciones militares (pág. 592)

democracy/*democracia* literalmente, el gobierno de muchos, bajo el cual los ciudadanos eligen quién los gobernará (pág. 53)

depression/*depresión* un período de baja actividad económica y aumento del desempleo (pág. 536)

de-Stalinization/*de-Stalinización* el proceso de eliminar las políticas más crueles de Stalin (pág. 638)

détente/*disminución* una fase de relajamiento de relaciones o tensiones entre dos adversarios (pág. 657)

dictatorship/*dictadura* una forma de gobierno en la cual una persona o pequeño grupo tiene el poder absoluto (pág. 401)

direct democracy/*democracia directa* un sistema de gobierno en que las personas participan directamente en la toma de decisiones del gobierno a través de asambleas (pág. 56)

direct rule/*dominio directo* gobierno colonial en el que las elites locales son removidos del poder y reemplazadas por un nuevo grupo de oficiales traídos desde la madre patria (pág. 433)

disarmament/*desarme* un límite o reducción de las fuerzas armadas y del armamento (pág. 758)

discrimination/*discriminación* prejuicio, habitualmente sobre la base de la raza, la religión, clase, sexo, o edad (pág. 738)

dissident/*disidente* una persona que critica abiertamente al régimen que tiene el poder (pág. 658)

divine right of kings/*derecho divino de reyes* la creencia de que los reyes reciben su poder de parte de Dios y de que son responsables sólo ante Dios (pág. 219)

domestication/*domesticar* adiestrar animales o adaptar plantas para satisfacer necesidades humanas (pág. 21)

domino theory/*teoría dominó* la idea de que, si un país cae ante el comunismo, los países colindantes también lo harán (pág. 635)

dowry/*dote* dinero o bienes pagados por los padres de una novia a su esposo al casarse ella (pág. 163)

Duma/*Duma* la asamblea legislativa rusa (pág. 414)

dynasty/*dinastía* una familia de gobernantes cuyo derecho a gobernar se transmite dentro de la familia (pág. 27)

E

ecology/*ecología* el estudio de las relaciones entre cosas vivas y su ambiente (pág. 752)

elector/*elector* una persona que tiene derecho para elegir (pág. 343)

emancipation/*emancipación* liberación (pág. 383)

empire/*imperio* una grande unidad política, comúnmente bajo un solo líder, y que controla a muchos pueblos o territorios (pág. 25)

enlightened absolutism/*absolutimo ilustrado* un sistema en el cual los gobernantes trataban de gobernar por medio de principios de Ilustración mientras mantenían sus poderes reales totales (pág. 311)

entrepreneur/*empresario* una persona interesada en hallar nuevas oportunidades de negocios y nuevas formas de obtener ganancias (pág. 364)

epic poem/*poema épico* un extenso poema que cuenta las hazañas de un gran héroe, tales como la *Ilíada* y la *Odisea* de Homero (pág. 53)

epidemic/*epidemia* una infección que esparce rápidamente a través de la población, afectando a muchas personas a la vez (pág. 144)

estate/*estado* una de las tres clases en las que se dividía la sociedad francesa medieval: el clero (primer estado), los nobles (segundo estado), y la plebe (tercer estado) (pág. 330)

eta/*eta* la clase más baja de la sociedad japonesa, cuya forma de vida era estrictamente regulada por el Tokugawa (pág. 281)

ethnic cleansing/*purificación étnica* una política de matar o remover por la fuerza a un grupo étnico desde sus territorios (pág. 564, 663)

extraterritoriality/*extraterritorialidad* vivir en una sección de un país apartada para extranjeros pero no sujeta a las leyes del país anfitrión (pág. 467)

F

faction/*facción* un grupo que está en desacuerdo (pág. 338)

fascism/*fascismo* filosofia política basada en el nacionalismo y en un estado todopoderoso (pág. 541)

federal system/*sistema federal* una forma de gobierno en la cual el poder es compartido entre el gobierno nacional y los gobiernos estatales (pág. 322)

feminism/*feminismo* el movimiento para promover los derechos e intereses de las mujeres (pág. 407)

feudalism/*feudalismo* sistema político y social que se desarrolló durante la Edad Media cuando gobiernos reales ya no podían defender a su pueblo; los nobles ofrecían protección y tierras a cambio de servicio (pág. 118)

fief/*feudo* bajo el feudalismo, una concesión de tierras hecha a un vasallo; el vasallo tenía autoridad política dentro de su feudo (pág. 119)

filial piety/*piedad filial* el deber de los miembros de la familia de subordinar sus necesidades y deseos a aquellos del líder de la familia, un concepto importante en el Confucianismo (pág. 43)

fresco/*fresco* una pintura hecha en yeso fresco y húmedo con pinturas a base de agua (pág. 166)

G

genocide/*genocidio* la matanza masiva de un grupo racial, político o cultural en particular (pág. 564, 607)

geocentric/*geocéntrico* literalmente, "centrado en la tierra"; un sistema de movimiento planetario que ubica a la Tierra como el centro del universo, con el sol, la luna y otros planetas girando en torno a ella (pág. 295)

global economy/*economía global* una economía en la cual la producción, distribución, y venta de bienes se realiza a escala mundial, tipificada por la empresa multinacional (pág. 754)

grand vizier/*gran visir* el ministro jefe del sultán Otomán, quien encabezaba las reuniones del consejo imperial (pág. 243)

greenhouse effect/*efecto invernadero* calentamiento global causado por la acumulación de dióxido de carbono en la atmósfera (pág. 752)

guerilla tactics/*táctica de guerrillas* el uso de maniobras inesperadas tales como el sabotaje y subterfugio para luchar contra un enemigo (pág. 577)

guild/*gremio* una asociación comercial relacionada con un oficio o artesanía en particular; los gremios evolucionaron en el siglo XII y pasaron a tener un papel importante en la vida económica de las ciudades medievales (pág. 132)

gunpowder empire/*imperio de la pólvora* un imperio formado por conquistadores quienes unificaron las regiones conquistadas a través del dominio de las armas de fuego (pág. 242)

H

han/*han* uno de los aproximadamente 250 dominios independientes en los que se dividió Japón bajo Tokugawa (pág. 279)

harem/*harén* "lugar sagrado," el dominio privado de un sultán, en donde residía él y sus esposas (pág. 243)

heavy industry/*industria pesada* la manufactura de máquinas y equipo para fábricas y minas (pág. 638)

heliocentric/*heliocéntrico* literalmente, "centrado en el sol"; el sistema del universo propuesto en 1543 por Nicolás Copérnico, quien sostuvo que la tierra y los planetas giraban en torno al sol (pág. 295)

heresy/*herejía* desacuerdo con las enseñanzas básicas de la iglesia (pág. 134)

hieroglyphics/*jeroglíficos* "grabados sacerdotales" o "escrituras sagradas", un complejo sistema de escritura del antiguo Egipto que utilizaba tanto imágenes como formas más abstractas (pág. 30)

***Hijrah*/Hijrah** el viaje de Mahoma y sus seguidores a Medina en el año 622, que pasó a ser el año 1 del calendario oficial del Islam (pág. 90)

Hinduism/*hinduismo* el mayor sistema religioso de la India, que tuvo sus orígenes en las creencias religiosas de los arios que se establecieron en la India después del año 1500 A.C. (pág. 38)

hominid/*homínido* humanos y otras criaturas humanoides que caminan erectos (pág. 19)

hostage system/*sistema de rehén* un sistema utilizado por el shogunado para controlar el daimyo en Tokugawa Japón; cada daimyo debía mantener dos residencias, una en sus propias tierras y una en Edo, donde se encontraba la corte del shogun; la familia del daimyo era obligada a permanecer en la residencia de Edo cuando él estaba ausente (pág. 280)

humanism/*humanismo* un movimiento intelectual del Renacimiento basado en el estudio de las humanidades, que incluía gramática, retórica, poesía, moral filosofía, e historia (pág. 164)

imperator/*imperator* comandante en jefe; el origen latino de la palabra *emperador* (pág. 69)

imperialism/*imperialismo* la extensión del poder de una nación hacia otras tierras (pág. 430)

indemnity/*indemnización* un pago por daños (pág. 471)

indigenous/*indígena* nativo a una región (pág. 440)

indirect rule/*dominio indirecto* gobierno colonial en el que los gobernantes locales pueden mantener sus posiciones de autoridad y estatus (pág. 433)

inductive reasoning/*razonamiento inductivo* la noción de que los científicos debían proceder desde lo particular a lo general efectuando observaciones sistemáticas y experimentos cuidadosamente organizados para probar hipótesis o teorías, que a su vez conducirían a principios generales correctos (pág. 299)

indulgence/*indulgencia* perdón de todo o parte de un castigo por pecados otorgado por la Iglesia Católica, reduciendo el tiempo en el purgatorio tras la muerte (pág. 173)

industrial capitalism/*capitalismo industrial* un sistema económico basado en la producción industrial o la fabricación (pág. 368)

inflation/*inflación* una situación en la cual los precios suben rápidamente mientras que el valor del dinero disminuye (pág. 216)

Inquisition/*Inquisición* un tribunal establecido por la Iglesia Católica en 1232 para descubrir y someter a juicio a los herejes; llamado además el Santo Oficio (pág. 134)

***intifada*/intifada** "levantamiento," un movimiento que surgió durante la década de 1980 entre quienes respaldaban a la Organización Para la Liberación de Palestina radicada dentro de Israel (pág. 714)

Islam/*Islam* religión monoteísta que surgió en la Península Arábiga en el siglo séptimo (pág. 90)

janissary/*jenízaro* un soldado de la guardia de elite del imperio turco otomano (pág. 240)

Judaism/*judaísmo* religión monoteísta desarrollada por los israelitas (pág. 30)

kaiser/*káiser* término alemán para "césar," el título de los emperadores del Segundo Imperio Alemán (pág. 381)

kamikaze/*kamikaze* término japonés para "viento divino," una misión suicida en la que jóvenes pilotos japoneses intencionalmente estrellaban sus aviones contra buques de guerra de los EE.UU. (pág. 614)

khanate/*kanato* uno de los diversos territorios independientes en los que se dividió el imperio de Genghis Khan, cada uno bajo el gobierno de uno de sus hijos (pág. 105)

laissez-faire/*laissez-faire* literalmente, "dejar [a las personas] hacer [lo que quieran]," el concepto de que el estado no debe imponer regulaciones gubernamentales si no que debe dejar la economía sola (pág. 303)

laity/*laicado* miembros no clericales de la iglesia cristiana (pág. 74)

liberalism/*liberalismo* una filosofía política originalmente basada principalmente en principios de Ilustración, que sostenía que las personas deberían ser lo más libres dentro de lo posible de las restricciones gubernamentales y que las libertades civiles—los derechos básicos de las personas—deberían ser protegidos (pág. 373)

lineage group/*grupo de linaje* una unidad extendida de una familia que se ha combinado en una comunidad mayor (pág. 101)

literacy/*alfabetización* la capacidad de leer y escribir (pág. 409)

magic realism/*realismo mágico* una singular forma de expresión de la literatura latinoamericana; combina eventos realistas con fondos como sueños o fantásticos (pág. 687)

Magna Carta/*Carta Magna* la Gran Cédula de derechos, que el Rey Juan Sin Tierra fue obligado a firmar por los nobles ingleses en Runnymede en 1215 (pág. 120)

Mahatma/*Mahatma* "Gran Alma," un título que los indios utilizaron para referirse a Mohandas Gandhi (pág. 570)

mainland states/*estados continentales* parte de un continente, en contraposición a una península o a unas islas (pág. 203)

mandate/*mandato* una nación gobernada por otra nación en nombre de la Liga de Naciones (pág. 526)

Mandate of Heaven/*Mandato del Cielo* la reclamación por parte de los reyes de la dinastía Zhou de China en el sentido de que ellos tenían la autoridad para gobernar y mantener el universo en orden directamente por derecho celestial (pág. 41)

Mannerism/*manierismo* un movimiento artístico que surgió en Italia en la década de 1520 y 1530; señaló el fin del Renacimiento al desmantelar los principios de balance, armonía, y moderación (pág. 230)

manor/*palacete* en la Europa medieval, una propiedad agrícola administrada por un señor y trabajada por campesinos (pág. 131)

mercantilism/*mercantilismo* un conjunto de principios que dominaban el pensamiento económico en el siglo XVII; sostenía que la prosperidad de una nación dependía de tener grandes cantidades de oro y plata (pág. 195)

mercenary/*mercenario* soldado que sirve a un país extranjero por dinero (pág. 159)

Mesoamerica/*Mesoamérica* término que se refiere a las áreas de México y Centroamérica donde se desarollaron civilizaciones antes de la llegada de los españoles (pág. 141)

mestizo/*mestizo* la progenie de europeos e indígenas americanos (pág. 319, 454)

Middle Passage/*paso central* sección intermedia del comercio triangular, en el cual los africanos esclavizados eran traídos a la América por barco (pág. 198)

militant/*militante* persona que respalda activa y agresivamente una causa (pág. 211)

militarism/*militarismo* política nacional basada en la fuerza militar y la glorificación de la guerra (pág. 380)

ministerial responsibility/*responsabilidad ministerial* la idea de que el primer ministro es responsable ante el ejecutivo popularmente electo y no ante el oficial ejecutivo (pág. 413)

mobilization/*movilización* el proceso de agrupar tropas y suministros y prepararlos para la guerra (pág. 502, 612)

modernism/*modernismo* un movimiento resultante de la rebelión por parte de escritores y artistas entre 1870 y 1914 en contra de los estilos literarios y artísticos tradicionales que habían dominado la vida cultural europea desde el Renacimiento (pág. 421)

money economy/*economía monetaria* un sistema económico basado en el dinero y no en el trueque (pág. 131)

monk/*monje* un hombre que se auto separa de la sociedad humana con el fin de dedicarse a Dios; los monjes vivían en monasterios liderados por abades (pág. 117)

monotheistic/*monoteísta* con un solo dios (pág. 32)

Monroe Doctrine/*Doctrina Monroe* la política de los Estados Unidos que garantiza la independencia de las naciones latinoamericanas y advierte contra la intervención europea en las Américas, promulgada por el presidente James Monroe en 1823 (pág. 455)

mosque/*mezquita* un templo musulmán de adoración (pág. 95)

mulatto/*mulato* la progenie de europeos y africanos (pág. 319)

multinational corporation/*compañía multinacional* una compañía con divisiones en más de dos países (pág. 684)

N

nationalism/*nacionalismo* la singular identidad cultural de un pueblo basada en un idioma, religión, y símbolos nacionales en común (pág. 350)

natural rights/*derechos naturales* derechos con los que todos los humanos supuestamente nacen, incluyendo el derecho a la vida, la libertad y la propiedad (pág. 233)

natural selection/*selección natural* el principio establecido por Darwin en el sentido de que algunos organismos son más adaptables al medio que otros; en términos populares, "supervivencia de los aptos" (pág. 390)

Neolithic Revolution/*Revolución Neolítica* el cambio desde la caza de animales y recolección de alimentos hasta el mantenimiento de animales y el cultivo de alimentos de manera habitual que ocurrió alrededor del 8000 A.C. (pág. 21)

New Economic Policy (NEP)/*Nueva Política Económica* una versión modificada del antiguo sistema capitalista adoptado por Lenin en 1921 para reemplazar el comunismo de guerra en Rusia; se permitió a los campesinos vender sus producto, las tiendas y pequeñas industrias podían ser privadas, pero la gran industria, la banca y las minas permanecieron en manos del gobierno (pág. 543)

new monarchy/*nueva monarquía* en el siglo XV, uno de los gobiernos en los que el poder se había centralizado bajo un rey o reina, particularmente en Francia, Inglaterra y España (pág. 138)

nomad/*nómada* una persona sin residencia fija, que se desplaza de un lugar a otro (pág. 20)

O

occupied/*ocupado* país cuyas tierras son poseídas por un poder extranjero (pág. 739)

oligarchy/*oligarquía* literalmente, el gobierno de unos pocos, en el cual un pequeño grupo de personas controla el gobierno (pág. 53, 583)

organic evolution/*evolución orgánica* el principio establecido por Darwin de que cada planta o animal ha evolucionado, o cambiado, durante un largo periodo desde formas más primitivas y simples de vida hasta formas más complejas (pág. 390)

orthodoxy/*ortodoxia* creencias tradicionales, sobre todo las religiosas (pág. 251)

ozone layer/*capa de ozono* delgada capa de gas en la atmósfera superior que protege a la Tierra de los rayos ultravioleta provenientes del sol (pág. 752)

P

Pan-Africanism/*Panafricanismo* movimiento que promociona la unidad de todos los africanos por todo el mundo (pág. 570, 705)

Pan-Arabism/*Panarabísmo* política que promueve la unidad árabe internacional (pág. 713)

partisan/*partisano* guerreo de resistencia en la Segunda Guerra Mundial (pág. 604)

pasha/*pachá* oficial designado en el Imperio Otomano que cobraba impuestos, mantenía la ley y el orden y era directamente responsable ante la corte del sultán (pág. 241)

patriarchal/*patriarcal* dominado por los hombres (pág. 27)

patrician/*patricio* grandes terratenientes, formaban la clase dominante en la República Romana (pág. 68)

peacekeeping force/*fuerza para mantener la paz* fuerza militar traída de miembros neutrales de las Naciones Unidas para resolver conflictos y supervisar treguas (pág. 757)

***peninsulare*/peninsulare** persona nacida en la Península Ibérica; comúnmente, un oficial español o portugués que residía temporalmente en Latinoamérica para obtener ganancia política y económica y luego regresaba a Europa (pág. 454)

per capita/*per cápita* por persona (pág. 725)

perestroika/*perestroika* plan de Mikhail Gorbachev para reformar la URSS, reestructurando su economía (pág. 659)

permanent revolution/*revolución permanente* una atmósfera constante de fervor revolucionario apoyado por Mao Zedong para permitir que China venza a su pasado y logre la etapa final del comunismo (pág. 724)

philosophe/*filósofo* término francés para "filósofo", se aplica a todos los intelectuales—escritores, periodistas, economistas y reformadores sociales—durante la Ilustración (pág. 301)

photomontage/*fotomontaje* una ilustración compuesta de una combinación de fotografías (pág. 556)

planned economy/*economía planificada* sistema económico dirigido por agencias gubernamentales (pág. 508)

plantation/*plantación* una propiedad agrícola grande (pág. 198)

plebeian/*plebeyo* en la República de Roma, una clase social compuesta de terratenientes menores, artesanos, mercaderes y pequeños granjeros (pág. 68)

plebiscite/*plebiscito* voto popular (pág. 382)

pogrom/*pogrom* persecución organizada de un grupo minoritario, usualmente judíos, en la Rusia de los zares (pág. 421)

policy of containment/*política de contención* plan para mantener algo, como por ejemplo el comunismo, dentro de sus fronteras geográficas existentes e impedir posteriores movimientos agresivos (pág. 632)

polis/*polis* la ciudad-estado de la antigua Grecia, que constaba de una ciudad o pueblo y el territorio de sus alrededores que existe como entidad política (pág. 53)

Politburo/*Politburó* comité de siete miembros que se convirtió en el organismo dominante de determinación de normas del partido comunista en Rusia (pág. 543)

pop art/*arte pop* movimiento artístico que surgió a comienzos de la década del 1960; los artistas de este movimiento tomaban imágenes de la cultura popular y las transformaban en obras de bellas artes (pág. 674)

pope/*papa* el obispo de Roma y líder de la Iglesia Católica Romana (pág. 117)

porcelain/*porcelana* cerámica hecha de arcilla fina horneada a temperaturas muy altas (pág. 276)

postmodernism/*postmodernismo* movimiento artístico que surgió en la década de 1980; está marcado por un renacimiento de elementos y técnicas tradicionales, e incluye trabajos como textiles, cerámica y muebles que se fabrican además de los medios artísticos tradicionales (pág. 674)

predestination/*predestinación* la creencia de que Dios ha determinado anticipadamente quién se salvará (el elegido) y quien se condenará (el réprobo) (pág. 178)

prefecture/*prefectura* en la Restauración Meiji japonesa, un territorio gobernado por su anterior señor daimyo (pág. 481)

principle of intervention/*principio de intervención* la idea de que las grandes potencias tienen el derecho de enviar ejércitos a países donde existen revoluciones a fin de restaurar los gobiernos legítimos (pág. 373)

privatization/*privatización* la venta de compañías del Estado a firmas privadas (pág. 689)

proletariat/*proletariado* la clase trabajadora (pág. 401)

propaganda/*propaganda* ideas que se difunden para influir en la opinión pública a favor de una causa o en contra de ella (pág. 503)

protectorate/*protectorado* unidad política que depende de otro gobierno para su protección (pág. 431)

provincial/*provincial* local; relativo a una provincia (pág. 473)

psychoanalysis/*psicoanálisis* método mediante el cual un terapeuta y un paciente indagan profundamente en la memoria del paciente; haciendo que la mente consciente del paciente tenga consciencia pensamientos reprimidos, podrá ocurrir una cura (pág. 419)

Ptolemaic system/*sístema ptolemaico* el modelo geocéntrico del universo que prevaleció en la Edad Media; nombrado en honor a astrónomo Ptolomeo, que vivió en Alejandría durante el siglo segundo (pág. 295)

puddling/*pudelación* procesos en el cual se utiliza coque derivado del carbón para extraer impurezas por medio del fuego en hierro bruto y producir un hierro de alta calidad (pág. 365)

Q

queue/*coleta* trenza de pelo única en las parte posterior de la cabeza (pág. 270)

R

rationalism/*racionalismo* sistema del pensamiento expuesto por René Descartes basado en la creencia de que la razón es la fuente principal del conocimiento (pág. 299)

real wages/*salario efectivo* el poder adquisitivo de los ingresos (pág. 645)

realism/*realismo* estilo y literatura de mediados del Siglo XIX, que reflejaba las realidades de la vida cotidiana (pág. 390)

redistribution of wealth/*redistribución de la riqueza* el cambio de la riqueza de una minoría rica a una mayoría pobre (pág. 579)

Reichstag/*Reichstag* el parlamento alemán (pág. 549)

reincarnation/*reencarnación* el renacimiento del alma de una persona en una forma diferente después de la muerte (pág. 38)

relics of feudalism/*reliquias del feudalismo* obligaciones de los campesinos hacia sus patrones aristocráticos que sobrevivieron en la época moderna (pág. 330)

reparation/*reparación* pago hecho a los victoriosos por los derrotados para cubrir los costos de una guerra (pág. 524)

republic/*república* forma de gobierno en la cual el líder no es un rey y ciertos ciudadanos tienen derecho a votar (pág. 67)

revisionist/*revisionista* un marxista que rechazó el enfoque revolucionario, creyendo en cambio en una evolución por medio de una democracia para lograr el objetivo del socialismo (pág. 401)

rococo/*rococó* un estilo artístico que reemplazó el estilo barroco en la década de 1730; era muy profano, enfatizando la elegancia, el encanto, y la acción suave (pág. 309)

romanticism/*romanticismo* un movimiento intelectual que surgió e finales del siglo XVIII en reacción a las ideas de la Ilustración, daba énfasis a los sentimientos, la emoción y la imaginación como fuentes del conocimiento (pág. 387)

sacrament/*sacramento* rito cristiano (pág. 134)

salon/*salón* las elegantes salas de las grandes casas urbanas donde, en el siglo VIII, escritores, artistas, aristócratas, funcionarios de gobierno y gente de la clase media se reunían y hablaban de las ideas de los filósofos y ayudaban a difundir las ideas de la Ilustración (pág. 306)

salvation/*salvación* el estado de ser salvado (es decir, ir al cielo) a través de la fe sola o a través de la fe y buenas obras (pág. 172)

samurai/*samurai* "aquellos que sirven," guerreros japoneses similares a los caballeros de la Europa medieval (pág. 107)

sanction/*sanción* restricción para hacer cumplir la ley internacional (pág. 595)

***sans-culottes*/revolucionarios** "sin pantalones," miembros de la Comuna de París, que se consideraban patriotas ordinarios (en otras palabras, usaban pantalones largos en vez de pantalones hasta la rodilla) (pág. 335)

satellite state/*estado satélite* país que depende económica y políticamente de otro país (pág. 632)

savanna/*sabana* amplias tierras de pastoreo dotadas de pequeños árboles y arbustos (pág. 98)

scientific method/*método científico* procedimiento sistemático para recolectar y analizar evidencia que fue crucial para la evolución de la ciencia en el mundo moderno (pág. 299)

secede/*separar* separarse (pág. 385)

secular/*secular* mundano; que no es abiertamente religioso (pág. 157)

secularization/*secularización* viendo el mundo en términos materiales, no espirituales (pág. 389)

self-strengthening/*autofortalecimiento* política promovida por reformadores hacia fines de la dinastía Qing en China bajo la cual China adoptaría la tecnología occidental aunque manteniendo sus valores e instituciones confucianos (pág. 468)

separation of powers/*separación de los poderes* forma de gobierno en la cual las divisiones ejecutiva, legislativa y judicial se limitan y controlan entre sí a través de un sistema de revisiones y balances (pág. 302)

sepoy/*cipayo* soldado indio contratado por la British East India Company para proteger los intereses de la compañía en la región (pág. 448)

serf/*siervo* en la Europa medieval, un campesino confinado legalmente a la tierra que tenía que proporcionar servicios de manos de obra, pagar rentas y estar sujeto al control del señor (pág. 131)

shah/*sha* rey (se usa en Persia e Irán) (pág. 251)

Shining Path/*Sendero Luminoso* grupo de guerrilla radical en Perú con lazos con la China comunista (pág. 695)

Shinto/*sintoísmo* "el Camino Sagrado" o "el Camino de los Dioses," un tipo de religión del estado que se practica en Japón; entre sus doctrinas están la divinidad del emperador y la santidad de la nación japonesa (pág. 108)

shogun/*shogún* "general," líder militar con poder en Japón (pág. 108)

social contract/*contrato social* el concepto propuesto por Rousseau de que una sociedad completa accede a ser gobernada por su voluntad general y que todos los individuos deben ser forzados a soportar por el deseo general, lo que representa qué es lo mejor para la comunidad completa (pág. 304)

socialism/*socialismo* sistema en el cual la sociedad, por lo general en la forma del gobierno, posee y controla el medio de producción (pág. 370)

soviet/*soviet* consejo ruso compuesto de representantes de los trabajadores y los soldados (pág. 516)

sphere of influence/*esfera de influencia* área en la que a un poder extranjero se le ha garantizado derechos y privilegios exclusivos, tales como derechos de comercio y privilegios de minería (pág. 469)

stalemate/*estancamiento* la condición que existe cuando ninguno de los dos lados puede obtener ganancias significativas (pág. 738)

state capitalism/*capitalismo del estado* sistema económico en el cual el gobierno central tiene una función activa en la economía, estableciendo políticas de precios y sueldos y subsidiando industrias vitales (pág. 740)

sultan/*sultán* "poseedor del poder," el líder militar y político del estado bajo los turcos Seljuk y otomanos (pág. 93, 242)

surrealism/*surrealismo* movimiento artístico que trata de representar la vida del inconsciente (pág. 556)

suttee/*sati* la costumbre hindú de quemar viva a una viuda en la pira funeraria de su esposo (pág. 257)

Spanish Glossary

systematic agriculture/*agricultura sistemática* el mantenimiento de animales y la siembra de alimento regularmente (pág. 21)

T

Thatcherism/*thatcherismo* la política económica de la Primera Ministra británica Margaret Thatcher, que limitaba el bienestar social y restringía el poder de sindicatos (pág. 668)

theology/*teología* el estudio de la religión y Dios (pág. 136)

total war/*guerra total* guerra que implica la movilización completa recursos y personas, afecta las vidas de todos los ciudadanos en los países en guerra, incluso aquellos alejados de los campos de batalla (pág. 508)

totalitarian state/*estado totalitario* gobierno que se centra en controlar no sólo el lado político de la vida, sino también la vida económica, social, intelectual y cultural de sus ciudadanos (pág. 541)

trade embargo/*embargo comercial* política que prohibe el comercio con un país en particular (pág. 689)

trench warfare/*guerra de trincheras* pelea desde trincheras protegidas por alambres de púa, como en la Primera Guerra Mundial (pág. 504)

triangular trade/*comercio triangular* ruta de tres direcciones entre Europa, África y América en el Siglo XVII (pág. 198)

U

ulema/*ulema* grupo de consejeros religiosos para el sultán Otomano; este grupo administraba el sistema legal y las escuelas para educar a los musulmanes (pág. 243)

uncertainty principle/*principio de incertidumbre* la idea establecida por Heiseneberg en 1927 de que el comportamiento de las partículas subatómicas no es certero, lo que sugiere que en el fondo de todas las leyes físicas que rigen el universo está la incertidumbre (pág. 557)

universal law of gravitation/*ley universal de gravitación* una de las tres reglas de movimiento que rigen los cuerpos planetarios establecida por Sir Isaac Newton en su *Principia;* explica que los cuerpos planetarios no se mueven en línea recta, más bien continúan en órbitas elípticas alrededor del sol porque cada objeto en el universo se atrae a otro objeto por una fuerza llamada gravedad (pág. 296)

universal male suffrage/*sufragio masculino universal* el derecho de todos los hombres a votar en elecciones (pág. 374)

urban society/*sociedad urbana* sistema social en el cual las ciudades son el centro de la política económica y la vida social (pág. 157)

V

vassal/*vasallo* bajo el feudalismo, un hombre que servía a un señor en calidad de militar (pág. 118)

viceroy/*virrey* gobernanate que representa a un monarca (pag. 449)

W

war communism/*comunismo de guerra* en la Rusia de la Primera Guerra Mundial, el control del gobierno de bancos y la mayoría de las industrias, la confiscación de granos de los campesinos y la centralización de la administración estatal bajo el control comunista (pág. 519)

war of attrition/*guerra de desgaste* guerra que se basa en desgastar al otro bando con constantes ataques y grandes pérdidas, tal como en la Primera Guerra Mundial (pág. 506)

welfare state/*estado benefactor* estado en el cual el gobierno tiene responsabilidad de entregarle a los ciudadanos servicios tales como la atención de salud (pág. 644)

witchcraft/*brujería* la práctica de magia por parte de personas que supuestamente están implicadas con el diablo (pág. 217)

Z

***zaibatsu*/zaibatsu** en la economía japonesa, una gran sociedad financiera e industrial (pág. 571)

zamindar/*zamindar* un oficial a local en la India Mogol que recibía un lote de terreno agrícola para uso temporal a cambio de cobrar impuestos para el gobierno central (pág. 256)

Spanish Glossary

Index

Italicized page numbers refer to illustrations. The following abbreviations are used in the index: m = map, c = chart, p = photograph or picture, g = graph, crt = cartoon, ptg = painting, q = quote

Abbas the Great (Abbas I) (shah of Persia), 250, 251, 252, 253
Abbasid dynasty, 89, 93; Mongol defeat of, 89, 93, 105
Abdulhamid II (sultan of Ottoman Empire), 564
abolitionism, 384
Abraham, 90
absolute monarchy, 425
absolutism, 223–229; in central and eastern Europe, 226–227; defined, 223; enlightened, 310–313
abstract expressionism, 423, 674, 675
abstract impressionism, 556
Abu al-Abbas, 93
Abu Bakr, 89, 91, 92
Achebe, Chinua (Albert Chinualamogu), 701, 709, 762–763
Acheson, Dean, 632
acid rain, 752, 758
acquired immunodeficiency syndrome (AIDS), 706
Acropolis, *p54*
acropolis, 53, 54
Act of Supremacy: of 1534, 179; new, 213
Adams, John, 301, *p301*
Addison, Joseph, 305
Adenauer, Konrad, 643, *p643*
Adoration of the Magi, *p169*
Aegean Sea, 63
Aegospotami, 56
***Aeneid* (Virgil),** 66, 72
Aeschylus, 58
Afghanistan, 60, 238; Soviet Union invades, 658; terrorists in, 673
Africa, *m569*. *See also* Central Africa; East Africa; West Africa; *individual states;* in age of transition, 197–200; Christian missionaries to, 428, 430; colonial rule in, 441–442; culture of, 101, 709; earliest humanlike creatures in, 19; early civilizations in, 97–101; economic problems in, 705–706; Gold Coast and, 191, 199, 568, 703; imperialism in, 436–442, *m437*; independence in, 703–709, *m704*; modern, society and culture in, 708–709; nationalism in, 442, 568–570; new hopes and, 707–708; new leaders in, 705; new nations in, 705–707; political and social structures in, 199–200; political challenges in, 706–707; political movements and revolts in, *c584*; Portuguese explore, seeking gold, 191; religious beliefs in, 81; slave trade and, 197–199, *m198*, 437, 447; society of, 101, 708–709; trade and, 94; women's role in, 708–709
African Americans: equal rights and, 646–647; in military service, 613, 728; racism and, 613, 646–647
African National Congress (ANC), 703, 704, 705, 707
Afrika Korps, 600–601
Afrikaners (Boers), 440–441
Agamemnon, 53
Age of Pericles, 56
Agra, India, 259
agriculture. *See also* farming: collectivization of, 545, 547, 724; expanded food production and, 129–131; Green Revolution and, 753–754; new, in Europe in Middle Ages, 129–131; systematic, 19, 21; of West Africa, *m125*
Aguinaldo, Emilio, 432, *p432*
AIDS (acquired immunodeficiency syndrome), 706
Aix-la-Chapelle, Treaty of, 308, 314
Akbar (emperor of India), 255, 256–257
Akkadians, 25
Alamogordo, New Mexico, 616
Albania: local Communist control in, 639; Warsaw Pact and, 634
Albanians, 526; murder of, 664
Alberti, Leon Battista, 158
Albuquerque, Alfonso de, 192
Aldrin, Buzz, 753
Alexander II (czar of Russia), 361, *p361*, 383–384, 776, *p776*
Alexander III (czar of Russia), 384
Alexander Nevsky (prince of Novgorod), 121
Alexander the Great (king of Macedonia), 34, 51, 59–60; empire of, *m59*
Alexandra (empress of Russia), 515, *p515*, 516
Alexandria, Egypt, 60, 601
Alexis (son of Czar Nicholas II), 515, *p515*
Alexius I (Byzantine emperor), 123
al-Fatah movement, 714
Alfonsín, Raúl, 694
Alfonso I (king of Congo), 199, 200, *p200*
Algeria: French colony in, 375, 438, 564, 643; independence granted to, 643, 704; National Liberation Front (FLN) and, 704; trade and, 400
Allah, 83, 85, 90, 91, 94
Allende, Salvador, 693, 695
Allied Reparations Commission, 534
all-weather roads, 365
alphabet(s). *See also* language(s); writing: Chinese characters and, 288; Greek, 287; Phoenician, 287; Roman, 288, 565
Alps, 132
Alsace, 381, 524
Altamira, Spain, 19
Alvarado, Juan Velasco, 695
American Bowling Congress, 408
American Civil War, 407; aftermath of, 415; Confederate forces surrender, 361, 385; first battle of, 394
American Federation of Labor, 415
American League, 409
American Revolution, 153, 318, 321; French Revolution and, 152, 329
Americas, 140–144. *See also* Central America; Latin America; North America; South America; *individual states;* Columbus reaches (1492), 186, 193, 196, 268; first people in, 140–141; impact of Christopher Columbus on, 192–193; voyages to, 192–194
Amin, Idi, 703, 707
the Amish, 180
Ammann, Jacob, 180
Amritsar, India, 570
Amsterdam, 406
Amur River, 469
Anabaptists, 180–181
Analects, 84
analysis: of political cartoons, 539; of primary and secondary sources, 139
anarchy, 252
Anasazi, 141
Anastasia, 516
Anastasia (daughter of Czar Nicholas II), 516, *p516*
Anatolia, 246, 251
Anatolian Peninsula, 239, 241, 243, 565
ANC (African National Congress), 703, 704, 705, 707
Anderson, Anna, 516, *p516*
Andes, 144
Andrew, Grand Duke, 516
Angkor, 110, 202, 203
Angkor Thom, 110, 111
Angkor Wat, 111, *p111*
Anglican Church (Church of England), 155, 179, 219, 220
Anglican Church in South Africa, 705
Angola, 704
***Animal Farm* (Orwell),** 490
animals: caravans using camels and, 94, 98–99, 105; domestication of, 21; elephant fights as king's entertainment, 261
Annam, 432
Anne (queen of England), 320
annexation, 437
annulment, 179
anschluss, 592
Antichrist, 138
Anti-Comintern Pact, 592
***Antigone* (Sophocles),** 58
Antioch, Syria, 40
anti-Semitism: Hitler and, 549, 553, 604; Holocaust and. *See* Holocaust; Kristallnacht and, 548, 553; Nazi Party and, 549, 553, 567; social Darwinism and, 420; Zionism and, 420–421
Antonius Pius (Roman emperor), 70
Antony, Mark, 69
ANZUS defensive alliance, 744
apartheid, 495, 704
Apollo, 12
***The Apology of Socrates* (Plato),** 13, 58
Appalachian Mountains, 321
appeasement, 591, 592, 593

Appian Way, 49, *p*49, 72
Aqaba, Gulf of, 713
Aquino, Benigno, 738
Aquino, Corazon, 738
Arab Empire: Abbasid dynasty and, 89, 93; creation of, 91–92; economy of, 94; prosperity during, 94; social structure of, 94; success of, 92–93; Umayyad dynasty and, 89, 92, 93
Arabia, Ottoman Turks take control of, 241
Arabian Peninsula, 89, 90, 98, 100, 564
Arabian Sea, 36
Arabian-American oil company (Aramco), 567
Arabic languages, 94, 286, 288
Arab-Israeli dispute, 711, 712, 713–714, 755, 758
Arabs, 89–90; sailing knowledge and, 191
Arafat, Yasir, 711, 714, *p*714
Aramco (Arabian-American oil company), 567
Arandora Star, 610
Archimedes, 294
archipelago, 110
architecture: baroque style and, 230, 231, 309; the Enlightenment and, 308–309; evolution of, in Middle Ages, 136, 137; French classical style of, 309; functionalism and, 423; Gothic style of, 127, 136, 137, 167, 169; Greek classical, 57–58; Islamic, 95; Japanese, 485; Latin American, 687; of medieval castle, *p*119; modernism and, 423; neo-Gothic, 388; Ottoman, 245; Renaissance, 167–168; revolution in, *c*420; rococo style of, 308, 309; Roman, 72; Romanesque style of, 136; romanticism and, 388; Singapore, *p*721
Ardennes Forest, 597
Argentina, 455, 456, 583, 693–694; Falkland Islands war and, 693, 694; Fascist gangs in, 694; Group of United Officers in, 583; oligarchy in, 583; Perón regime in, 583, 680, 693, 694; Radical Party in, 583; repressive military regime in, 684–685; trade and, 400, 459, 581
argument, identifying, 386
Aristotle, 58–59, 94, 293, 294
armada, 214
Armenia: Communists gain control over during Russian civil war, 518; Seljuk Turks in, 93
Armenians, massacre of, by Ottoman Turks, 563, 564–565
Arminius, 68
armistice, 521, 522
arms race, 633, 635, 658
Armstrong, Neil, 753
Arno River, 170
Arouet, François-Marie (Voltaire), 302. *See also* Voltaire
art(s). *See also* architecture; drama; literature; painting; sculpture; theater; music: African, 709; baroque style and, 230, 231; Chinese, 106–107, 276; dadaism and, 554, 556; dadaists and, 554, 556; the Enlightenment and, 308–309; Greek, classical, 57–58; Islamic, 95; Japanese, 281–282, 485–486; Latin American, 687; Ottoman, 245; painting techniques and, 166–167; Persian, 253; photography and, 422; photomontage and, 556; pop, 674–675; postmodernism and, 675; realism and, 390–391; in the Renaissance, 166–169, *m*167; revolution in, *c*420; romanticism and, 388–389; trends in, 674–675
Articles of Confederation, 322
artifacts, 771
Aryans: Hinduism and, 38; in India, 37; migration of, *m*38; Nazi Germany's thinking on, 420, 551, 557, 591, 601, 607, 668
Ashanti, 199
Ashikaga family, 103
Ashurnasirpal (Assyrian king), 34
Asia. *See also* East Asia; Southeast Asia; Southwest Asia; *individual states*: Christian missionaries to, 430, 431; Cold War in, 727–728; early civilizations in, *m*47; nationalism in, 573; new order in, 610–611; revolution in, 573; World War II in, 594–595, 599–600, 602, *m*602, 604, 610–611
Asia Minor, 33, 123
"Asian tigers," 743–744
Asoka (king of India), 36, 40
Assyrian Empire, 33–34
Assyrians, 31, 32, 33–34, 89
astrolabe, 95, 191
astronomy: discoveries in, during Scientific Revolution, 294–297; Islamic scholars and, 94–95; Sumerians and, 27
Atatürk, Kemal, *p*565, 565–566, 571
Athena, *p*48, *p*61
Athens, city-state of, 48, 54–55; Acropolis in, 54, *p*54; Age of Pericles and, 56; Great Peloponnesian War and, 51, 56; Pericles, as leader of, 50, 51, 55–57; war with Sparta and, 50, 56; young people in, 57
Atlantic Ocean, 439
atman, 38
atomic bomb(s), 673; Soviet Union explodes its first, 633, 635; United States drops on Japan, 589, 604, 616
Attica, 54
Attlee, Clement, 644
Augsburg, Peace of, 171, 175, 177, 217
Augustus (Roman emperor) (was Octavian), 66, 69, 71, 72
Aurangzeb, 257
Auschwitz, 609
Austerlitz, battle at, 348
Australia: aborigines in, 81; ANZUS defensive alliance and, 744; British Commonwealth and, 744; German New Guinea seized by, 506; prisoners of war from, as slave laborers for Japan, 611; religion in, 81; SEATO and, 634; trade and, 400; World War I and, 506
australopithecines, 19
Austria, 226, 227, 548; in the age of Enlightenment, 311–313; Austro-Prussian War and, 380, 383; authoritarian regime in, 545–546; becomes independent republic, 523, 525, 545; Concert of Europe and, 372–373; Congress of Vienna and, 371–372; EEC and, 667; Germanic Confederation and, 375; goes to war with France, during French Revolution, 335, 339; Nazi Germany annexes, 591, 592; Nazi Party in, 592; Ottoman Turks advance into, 242; Paris Peace Conference and, 524, 525; Piedmont invaded by, 379; Seven Years' War and, 314–315; uses military to crush revolutions in Spain and Italy, 373; Vienna. *See* Vienna, Austria; War of the Austrian Succession and, 308, 313–314; war with Napoleon, 348; women's voting rights in, 649
Austria-Hungary: anti-Semitism in, 421; assassination of Archduke Francis Ferdinand and, 499, 501; ceases to exist, 523, 525; creation of, 411, 414; democratic movement in, 413, 414; militarism and conscription in, 501; replaced by independent republics, 523; response of, to Archduke Ferdinand's assassination, 501–502; Second Industrial Revolution and, 399; Triple Alliance and, 411, 415, 416, 499, 500, 505; World War I and, 502, 504, 508, 509
Austrian Empire, 227, 311–312; Compromise of 1867 and, 383; as multinational state, 375, 383; revolutions in, 375–376, *m*376; War of the Austrian Succession and, 308, 313–314
Austrian Netherlands, 342
Austro-Prussian War, 380, 383
Autobiography **(Ibn Sina) (Avicenna),** 89
automobile(s), 395, 398, 742; in cities, 742; early, 398; electronic road pricing and, 743; Henry Ford mass produces, 359, 398
autonomous state, 664
Autumn **(Ba Jin),** 478
Avanti (Forward), 542
Avicenna (Ibn Sina), 89, 95
Avignon, France, popes at, 129, 137
Axum, 97, 98
Ayacucho, 455
Ayutthaya, 103, 110
Azerbaijan, 250, 251–252; Communists gain control over during Russian civil war, 518; nationalist movement in, 660
Azikiwe, Nnamdi, 570
the Aztec, 127, 142–143, 585; destruction of, 128, 194

B

B. E. F. Times, 505
Ba Jin, 478, *p*478
Babur (emperor of India), 238, 255–256, 259
Babylon, 25, 34, 60
Babylonians, 31
Bach, Johann Sebastian, 309, 310

Bacon, Francis, 290, *p*290, 299
Bactria. *See also* Afghanistan
Baghdad, Iraq: as capital of Arab Empire, 93; Mongol conquest of, 89, 93, 105; papermaking in, 44; population of, 132
bailey, 118
balance of trade, 195
Balfour, Lord, 567
Balfour Declaration, 560, 567
Balkans, 240, 241, 242; Crimean War and, 378–379; crises in, 416, 500; Eastern Roman Empire in, 123; new territorial arrangements made in, 525; Second Industrial Revolution and, 399; Slavic minorities in, 500, 501; Soviet control over, 639; World War II and, 598
Balkh, 112
Baltic Sea, 121
Baltic states: Jews shipped from, to death camps, 609; Treaty of Brest-Litovsk and, 518; World War II and, 603
Banaras, India, 39
Bangkok, Thailand, 202; cars in, 742
Bangladesh: creation of, 734, 736; cyclone in, 257; as Islamic state, 109; refugees from, 712
banners, 271
Bantu family of languages, 100
Barnard College, 687
Barnes, Harry Elmer, 523
baroque style, 230, 231
Barton, Clara, 407
Basho, Matsuo, 281, *p*281
Basques, 673
Basra, 246
Bastille, fall of, 328, 332, 333
Bataan Peninsula, 599
Batavia, 201, 203. *See also* Djakarta, Indonesia
Batista, Fulgencio, 635, 682, 689
Battle of Britain, 596, 597, 615
Battle of the Somme, *p*497, *p*778
Bay of Bengal, 257
Bay of Naples, 70
Bay of Pigs, 635, 680, 689
Bayezid, 249
bayonet, 218
Beatles, 675
Beauvoir, Simone de, 642, 649, *p*649
Beccaria, Cesare, 304
Becket, Thomas à, 165
Beer Hall Putsch, 549
Beethoven, Ludwig van, 362, 389
Begin, Menachem, *p*701, 714
Beijing, China, 106, 114, 601; *feng shui* and, 730; Gate of Heavenly Peace in, 731–732, 733; Imperial (Forbidden) City in, *p*265, 268, 273, 276, *p*276, 730–731, *p*731, 732; Manchus conquer, 270; Oriental Plaza in, 733; seized by British and French, 462, 464, 468; Summer Palace in, 464, *p*464; Tiananmen Square in. *See* Tiananmen Square; transforming, 730–733
Belarus, 660
Belgian Congo, 703
Belgium, 131, 168–169, 212, 368; Black Death spread to, 137; Brussels. *See* Brussels, Belgium; colonial interests of, 436, 439, 440, 441; EEC and, 645; Jews shipped to, from death camps, 609; NATO and, 633; Nazis invade, 597; rebellion in, 374; Second Industrial Revolution and, 399; Treaty of Locarno and, 535–536; World War I and, 502, 504, 508; World War II and, 597
Belgrade, 242
Belize, 690
Bell, Alexander Graham, 394, 398
Belorussians, 609
Benedict, Saint, 117
Benedictines, 117, 133
Bengal, Bay of, 257
Bengal, India, 258
Bengali, 286
Ben-Gurion, David, 711, *p*711, *q*711
Benin: sculpture from, *p*87, 101, *p*101; slave trade and, 198
Bennett, James Gordon, 444, 446
Benz, Karl, 398
Berbers, 92, 98
Bergen-Belsen, 607
Bering Strait, 140–141
Berkendael Medical Institute, 509
Berlin, 400, 630. *See also* West Berlin; Berlin Wall and. *See* Berlin Wall; Brandenburg Gate and, 656; British attack on, 597; dada show in, 554, 556; postwar division of, 617, 632–633; Soviet troops enter, 603
Berlin Academy, 298
Berlin Air Lift, 631, 633, *m*633
Berlin Conference, 436, 440
Berlin Wall: building of, 629, 631, 635; comes down, 655, *p*655, 656, 661, 663
Bernard of Clairvaux, Saint, 133
Bernhardi, Friedrich von, 420
Bernier, François, 261
Bernini, Gian Lorenzo, 231
Berry, Chuck, 675
Bessemer, Henry, 359
Beveridge, Albert, 432
Bhopal, India, chemical plant disaster in, 751, 752
Biafra, 707
Bialik, Hayyim, 563
Bias, detecting, 417
Bible, 82; Gutenberg's, 154, *p*154, 162; Hebrew, 33, 83; Luther's study of, 173; New Testament of, 74, 180
bibliography, preparation of, 677
Big Ben, *p*388
Bill of Rights: American, 322, 373; English, 221, 332
bin Laden, Osama, 672–673
bioethics, 753
Birth of a Nation, 555
Bishop's Palace at Würzburg, 309
Bismarck, Otto von, 380–381, *p*381, *q*381, 390, 413, 415, 439
Black Death, 127, 129, 136–137
Black Dragon Society, 573
Black Hand, 501
"Black Hole of Calcutta," 258
Black Sea, 64, 121, 137, 240, 312
Black Stone, 90
Blackfriars theater, 232
Blackpool, England, 396
Blair, Eric Arthur (George Orwell), 490–491
Blair, Tony, 668, 750
the blitz, 596, 597, 615
blitzkrieg, 596–597
bloc, 645
***The Body of Civil Law* (Justinian Code),** 14, *p*14, 116, 122
Boer War, 440–441
Boers (Afrikaners), 440–441
Bogotá, Colombia, *p*696
Bohemia, 175, 217, 375, 593
Bohemian kingdom, 121
Boleyn, Anne, 179
Bolívar, Simón, 453, *p*453, *q*453, 455
Bolivia, 194, 455, 681, 690; drug trade and, 686; human rights in, 686; oil industry in, 582
Bologna, Italy, first European university at, 135
Bolsheviks, 514, 516, 520, 543–544, 574; Old, 545; power seized by, 518, 573; renamed themselves Communists, 518. *See also* Communists
Bonaparte, Charles Louis Napoleon. *See* **Napoleon III**
Bonaparte, Jerome (king of Westphalia), 348
Bonaparte, Napoleon. *See* **Napoleon I**
Boniface VIII (pope), 137
***The Book of the City of Ladies* (Christine de Pizan),** 165
***The Book of the Courtier* (Castiglione),** 157, 161–162
Book of Hours (Très Riches Heures), 132
Borgia, Cesare, 157, *p*157
Borodino, Russia, 351
Borte, 113
Bosnia, 240, 244, *p*661; annexed by Austria-Hungary, 416; war in, 663–664, 757
Bosnia-Herzegovina, 240, 661, 663
Bosnian War, 564
Bosporus, 75, 240
Bossuet, Jacques, 223
Botha, P. W., 707
Bouchot, François, 343
Bougainville, 589
Boulding, Elise, 758
bourgeoisie (burghers), 132, 162–163, 330, 368, 401, 402
Boxer Rebellion, 465, 471, 473
Boxers, 471
boyars, 228
Boyle, Robert, 297
Boyle's Law, 297
Brahma the Creator, 39
Brahman, 38
Brahmans, 37
Brandenburg Gate, 656
Brandt, Willy, 643, 667, *p*667; wins Nobel Peace Prize, 666, 667
Brasília, 687
Brazil, 194, 583, 694–695; African slaves shipped to, 198; economic miracle in, 693, 694–695; Getúlio Vargas establishes New State in, 581, 583–584; Great Depression and, 583; independence declared by, 455, 583; plantations in, 198; Portuguese domination in, 318; repressive military regime in, 684–685; slavery abolished in, 437; soccer match with Canada and, *p*143; trade and, 459, 581
Brazzaville, 708
Brest-Litovsk, Treaty of, 514, 518
Brezhnev, Leonid, 658
Brezhnev Doctrine, 658

Briand, Aristide, 535
British East India Company, 448, 449, 466
British North American Act of 1867, 378, 385
British Soccer Cup, 403, 409
Brownshirts (Storm Troops) (SA), 549, 607, 610, 694
Brueghel, Jan (the elder), 127
Brunelleschi, Filippo, 167
Brussels, Belgium, 509; baroque style in, 231
bubonic plague, 137
Buda, 246
Budapest, Hungary, 375, 383
the Buddha, 17, *p*17, 36, *p*39, 39–40, 82; sermon of, 773
Buddhism: the Buddha and, 39–40. *See also* Buddha; followers of, number of, c80; history and beliefs and, 39–40, 82; missionaries to China and, 40; nirvana and, 84; Noble Eightfold Path and, 39–40, 82; in Southeast Asia, 204; Wheel of Law and, 82; worship and celebrations and, 84; Zen, 270
budget deficit, 669
Buenas Aires, Argentina, 585
Bukhara, 112, 114–115
Bulgaria: annexed by Ottomans, 240; authoritarian regime in, 545–546; Paris Peace Conference and, 524, 525; Soviet control over, 639; Warsaw Pact and, 634; World War I and, 505; World War II and, 598, 604
Bulgarians, 121
bureaucracy, 204
burghers (bourgeoisie), 132, 162–163, 330, 368, 401, 402
Burkhan Khaldun, 115
Burma (Pagan) (modern Myanmar), 602; becomes independent, 737; economy of, 433; as emerging mainland state, 201–202, 203; first state formed in eleventh century, 110; Great Britain's control over, 431, 433; prisoners of war from, as slave laborers for Japan, 606, 611; religion in, 204; resistance to colonial rule in, 434; Saya Sang leads uprising in, 429, 434; World War II and, 610, 611
Burton, Richard, 444, 447
Burundi, 707
Bush, George, 669, 682, 691, 715
Bush, George W., 669, 673, 750
Bushido, 108
Byron, Lord, 603
Byzantine Empire, 121, 122–123; Constantinople as capital of, 75, 76; end of, 87, 240; Justinian's reign and, 122; Muslim forces battle with, 122–123; Ottoman Turks conquer, 190, 239, 240–241; Seljuk Turks versus, 123; trade and, 94
Byzantium, 75. *See also* Constantinople

cable television, 753
Cabot, John, 186, 193
Cabral, Pedro, 189, 193
Caesar, Julius, 49, *p*49, 69
Caffa, 137
Cairo, Egypt, 93, 94, 438, 601; becomes center of Islamic civilization, 93; cars in, 742; papermaking in, 44
***Cairo Trilogy* (Mahfouz),** 716
Calcutta, India, 450, 451, 452; "Black Hole of," 258; cyclone in, 257
calendar: Egyptian, 30; Mayan, 142; new, in Revolutionary France, 342
Calicut, India, 191
caliph, 89, 91, 93
Calvin, John, *p*178, 178–179, 182, 212, 219
Calvinism, 178–179, 217; French Wars of Religion and, 209, 211–212; Philip II of Spain opposes, 212–213
Cambodia, 110, 203; Communists in, 738; as French protectorate, 431, 433; Khmer Rouge and, 738; religion in, 204
Cambridge University, 296
Cambyses (king of Persia), 34
camels, caravans using, 94, 98–99, 105
Cameroon, 438
Camp David Accords, 701, 714
Canaan, 31. *See also* Palestine
Canada: acid rain and, 758; after World War II, 648; Amish in, 180; Canada Pension Plan in, 648; as Dominion, 385; as French colony, 195; independence for Quebec and, 666, 670; Liberal Party in, 648, 670; Mennonites in, 180; NAFTA and, 670; as a nation, emergence of, 385; national unity and, 415; NATO and, 633, 648; Official Languages Act and, 670; Parti Québecois in, 670; Quebec. *See* Quebec, Canada; Seven Years' War and, 316, 320, 385; soccer match with Brazil and, *p*143
Canada Pension Plan, 648
Canterbury, archbishop of, 179
Canterbury, England, 165
***The Canterbury Tales* (Chaucer),** 164, 165, 287
Canton (Guangzhou), China, 269, 272, 466, 467, 477
Cape Colony, 440, 441
Cape Horn, 140
Cape of Good Hope, 189, 191
Cape Town, South Africa, 440, 444, 446, *p*706, 708
Capet, Hugh, 121
Capetian dynasty, 121
capital, 364
capitalism: commercial, 131, 194–195, 274; industrial, 368; state, 740
Cárdenas, Lázaro, 584
Caribbean, 193; African slaves shipped to, 198; plantations in, 198
Carlevaris, Luca, 158
Carnegie Steel Company, 415
Carolingian Empire, 117–118; division of, 121
Carpini, John of Plano, 103
***carruca*,** 130
cars. ***See* automobile(s)**
Carson, Rachel, *p*751, *q*751, 751–752
Carter, Jimmy, 658, 669, 691, *p*701, 714
Carthage, destruction of, by Rome, 67
cartogram, reading, 729
cartography, 191
cartoons, political, analyzing, 539
Cartwright, Edmund, 358, 364
Caspian Sea, 115, 251
caste system, 37–38
castes, 37–38
Castiglione, Baldassare, 157, *p*161, 161–162
Castle Church in Wittenberg, Germany, 173
castles of aristocrats, 118–119
Castro, Fidel, *p*629, 635, 680, *p*680, 682, *p*682, 689
Castro, Raúl, 682
Catania, Sicily, 220
Catherine II (Catherine the Great) (Russian ruler), 308, 311, 312, *p*312
Catherine of Aragon, 179
Catholic Church. ***See* Eastern Orthodox Church; Roman Catholic Church**
Catholic Reformation, 182–183
Catholicism. *See also* Eastern Orthodox Church; Roman Catholic Church; Roman Catholic Church: becomes official religion of France, 212; in the Enlightenment, 307; French Wars of Religion and, 209, 211–212; militant, Philip II and, 208, 212–213; versus Protestantism in Northern Ireland, 668
Caucasus, 601
caudillos, 456
cause and effect, 23
Cavaliers, 219
Cavell, Edith, 509, *p*509
Cavendish, Margaret, 297, *p*297
Cavour, Camillo di, 379
CCP. ***See* Chinese Communist Party**
Ceausescu, Elena, 662
Ceausescu, Nicolae, 662
***Celebration of a Marriage*,** 163
cellular telephones, 753
CENTO (Central Treaty Organization), 634
Central Africa, imperialism in, 438–439. *See also individual states*
Central America, 141, 193. *See also individual states*; civilizations in, 128; countries of, 690; deadly games of, 142–143; Spain's colonial empire in, 318–320; states in, independence of, 455; trade and, 459, 582; upheaval in, 690–691
Central Europe. *See also individual states*: absolutism in, 226–227; in High Middle Ages, 121; revolutions of 1848 in, 361, 371, 375–376, *m*376, 378; Slavic people of, 121
Central Powers, in World War I, 506, 521
Central Treaty Organization (CENTO), 634
Cervantes, Miguel de, 230, 232
Cetewayo (Zulu king), *p*356
Ceylon, 203, 735. *See also* Sri Lanka
Chacabuco, Battle of, 455
Chaeronea, Battle of, 59
Chaldeans, 33
Chamberlain, Houston Stewart, 420
Chamberlain, Neville, 593
Chamorro, Violeta Barrios de, 681, 691
Champa, kingdom of, 202
Chang Jiang (Yangtze River), 106, 467, 576
Chang Jiang Valley, *p*579, 730

Index

Chao Phraya River, 110, 202
Charlemagne (king of the Franks), 117–118, 121; Carolingian Empire established by, 118; crowning of, 116, *p*117, 118
Charles I (king of England), 216, 219, 220
Charles I (king of Spain) (also Charles V, Holy Roman emperor), 160, 174, 175, 457
Charles II (king of England), 220
Charles V (Holy Roman emperor) (also Charles I, king of Spain), 160, 174, 175, 457
Charles V (king of Spain), 212–213
Charles VI (Holy Roman emperor), 313
Charles VIII (king of France), 157, 160
Charles X (king of France), 371, 374
Charles the Great (king of the Franks). *See* **Charlemagne**
Charter Oath, 481
Chartres, France, cathedral at, *p*127
Chaucer, Geoffrey, 164, 165, 287
Chechens, 660
Chechnya, nationalist movement in, 660
Cheka (secret police), 519
chemical waste, 752
chemistry, Scientific Revolution and, 297
Cheng, Nien, 723
Chennai (Madras), India, 237, 257, 313, 451
Chernobyl, Ukraine, nuclear disaster in, 749, 752
Chiang Kai-shek, 560, *p*560, 571, 577, *p*579, 723, 743; flees to Taiwan, 579, 723; new Chinese republic founded by, 560, 576, 578–579; "New Life Movement" and, 578; seeks to appease Japan, 594
Chicago School, 423
Chichén Itzá, 142
children: labor performed by, 368–369; as victims of the Holocaust, 609–610
Chile, 144, 455, 582, 583, 695; human rights in, 695; repressive military regime in, 684–685; trade and, 581
China, 103–107, *m*577; arts in, 106–107; attacked by Japan, 594–595; Beijing. *See* Beijing, China; Boxer Rebellion and, 465, 471, 473; British and French take military action against, 464, 468; Buddhist missionaries sent to, 40; cannons produced by, 202; Chinese republic under Sun Yat-sen and, 475–476. *See also* Sun Yat-sen; Ching dynasty of, *m*269; Christian missionaries to, 269, 271, 471; civil service examinations in, 473, 476; civil war in, 475–476, 723–724; Communists in. *See* Chinese Communist Party; Confucius and. *See* Confucianism; Confucius; cultural developments in, 276, 477–478; daily life in, 274–275; early civilizations in, 21, 22, 40–43; earthquake in 1556 and, 220; economy in, 105; English sends trade mission to, 265, 266, 272; extraterritoriality and, 467; family in, 43–44, 274–275, 477; farming in, 18, *p*272; gives Hong Kong to Great Britain, 467; government in, 105; Great Britain returns Hong Kong to, 467, 721, 739, *p*739, 744; Great Depression and, 579; Han dynasty of, 17, 36, 43, 44, 103, 105, 106; imperialism in, 469–470; isolationism and, 266; Japan attacked by Mongol fleet, 88, *p*88, 106, 108; Jin dynasty of, 114; language in, 288; Liao dynasty of, 730; literature in, 106–107, 478; Mandate of Heaven and, 41–42; Marco Polo visits, 105, 189–190, 268; martial arts in, 270–271; Ming dynasty in, 106, 264, 265, 267–270, *m*269, 273, 274; modern-day, trip through, 781; Mongol (Yuan) dynasty in, 103, 105, 106–107, 267, 276; Nationalist Party (Guomindang) in. *See* Chinese Nationalist Party; new Chinese republic under Chiang Kai-shek and, 560, 576, 578–579. *See also* Chiang Kai-shek; New Order in East Asia and, 595; One Hundred Days of Reform and, 465, 470; Open Door policy and, 470–471, 572; Opium Wars and, 465, 466–467, 468; People's Republic of. *See* People's Republic of China; population of, 274, 466; printing in, 106, 162, 273, *p*273; Qin dynasty of, 17, 42–43, 103–104, *m*104, 105; Qing dynasty in. *See* Qing dynasty; redistribution of wealth in, 579; religion in, 55, 106. *See also* Confucianism; Confucius; republic in, 475–476; reunification of, 103–105; Revolution of 1911 in, 463, 475; revolutionary chaos in, 575–579; rulers and gods and, 55; "self-strengthening" and, 468–469; Shang dynasty of, 40–41; silk production in, 275, 775; Silk Road and, 36, 40, 105, 114, 115; society in, 105, 476–477; Song dynasty of, 103, 105, 106; spheres of influence in, *m*469, 469–470; Sui dynasty of, 103, *m*104, 106; Tai Ping Rebellion and, 465, 467–468, 469; Tang dynasty of, 86, 103–104, *m*104, 105, 106, 107, 271; trade and, 70, 94, 273, 466–467, 469–471; Vietnam invaded by, 110; war with Japan over Korea, 470, 484; Westerners in, 266, 267, 268–269, 271–272; White Lotus Rebellion in, 265, 272; World War II and, 594–595, 600; young people in, 476–477; Yuan (Mongol) dynasty of, 105, 106–107, 267, 276; Zhou dynasty of, 41–42
Chinese Communist Party (CCP), 579. *See also* Mao Zedong; People's Republic of China; alliance formed with Chinese Nationalist Party, 575, 576; control Chinese government, 720, 724; founding of, 575, 576; in hiding, 576–577; movement for democracy as threat to, 722, 725–726; war with Chinese Nationalist Party and, 723
Chinese languages, 286, 288
Chinese Nationalist Party, 474, 476, 575, 576, 579; alliance formed with Chinese Communist Party, 575, 576; war with Chinese Communists and, 723
***Chinese Technology in the Seventeenth Century* (Sung Ying-Hsing),** 775
Ching dynasty, *m*269
Chirac, Jacques, 667
Chitambo, 447
chlorofluorocarbons, 752–753
Chongqing, China, 594
Chosu, Japan, 480
Chrétien, Jean, 670
Christian Democratic Union (CDU), 643, 663, 667
Christian humanism (Northern Renaissance humanism), 154, 172
Christian missionary(ies), 200; to Africa, 428, 430; to Asia, 430, 431; to China, 269, 271, 471; David Livingstone as, 428, 444–447; to Japan, 279; in Latin America, 320, 688; in Vietnam, 431
Christianity: Catholic Church and. *See* Roman Catholic Church; Confucianism versus, 45; Constantine proclaims tolerance of, 66, 74; Crusades and, 112, 123. *See also* Crusade(s); dechristianization policy in Revolutionary France and, 341–342; Eastern Orthodox. *See* Eastern Orthodox Church; emergence of, 72–73; in the Enlightenment, 307; followers of, number of, c80; history and beliefs and, 82; Judaism's influence on, 30, 31, 73; missionaries for. *See* Christian missionary(ies); Ptolemy and, 294–295; revival in, 674; during Roman Empire, 72–74; Roman Empire adopts as official religion, 74, 117; Roman persecution and, 74; spread of, 73–74; triumph of, 74; worship and celebrations and, 84
Christina (queen of Sweden), *p*298
Christine de Pizan, 165, *p*165
Chulalongkorn (king of Thailand), 432
Chung Hee Park, 739, 743
Chungara, Dimitila Barrios de, 686
Church of England (Anglican Church), 155, 179, 219, 220
Church of Fourteen Saints, 309
Church of the Holy Wisdom (Hagia Sophia), *p*236, 245
Church of Saint Thomas, 309
Churchill, Winston, 591, *p*591, *q*591, 603, *p*603, *p*631, *q*631, 644; "iron curtain" speech of, 589, 603, 618, 631; Yalta Conference and, 617–618, *p*618
Churma, 446
Ci Xi (Chinese empress dowager), 470, *p*470, 473, 475
Cicero, 165
Cihangir, 249
cinchona tree, 439
Cincinnatus, Lucius Quinctius, 77
Cistercians, 133
city(ies). *See also* city-states: African, 708; around world, population explosion in (1700–1800), 274; bombing of, in war, 615–616; cars in, 742; development of. *See* city(ies), growth of; growth of. *See*

city(ies), growth of; Latin American, with over a million people, 683, 686; medieval, life in, 132
city(ies), growth of: emergence of mass society and, 403–404; during Industrial Revolution, 367–368; during Middle Ages, 131–132; world's population and, 754, *g*754
city-states: defined, 25; Greek, 53. *See also* Athens, city-state of; Sparta, city-state of; Italian, 158–160; Sumerian, 24, 25
Civil Code (Napoleonic Code), 15, 347, 348, 351
civil disobedience: defined, 570; Gandhi and, 562, 570–571, 647; Martin Luther King, Jr. and, 647
***Civil Peace* (Achebe),** 762–763
Civil Rights Act of 1964, 642, 647
civil rights movement, 628, 646–647, 651
civilization: defined, 22; emergence of, 16, 22
clans, 275
***Classified Dictionary of the Sciences, Arts, and Trades (Encyclopedia)* (Diderot),** 291, 303
classless society, 402, 695, 724
Cleisthenes, 54–55
Clemenceau, Georges, 524, *p*524, 534
Clement VII (pope), 175
Cleopatra VII (Egyptian queen), 29
clergy, 74
***Clermont*,** *p*360, 366
Clinton, Bill, 664, 669
Clive, Sir Robert, 258, *p*258
Clovis (king of the Franks), 116, 117
CNN News, 627
***Coalbrookdale by Night*,** *p*361
Code of Hammurabi, 26–27, 35
Colbert, Jean-Baptist, 226
Cold War, 645; in Asia, 727–728; beginning of, 628; conflicts and crises in, 652, *g*668; defined, 616; détente and, 657–658; development of, 631–636; end of, 658, 754; Latin America and, 686; Olympic Games and, 676; political nature of, 658, 676; rivalry in Europe and, 632; spread of, 633–635; superpowers in, confrontation of, 631–633; United Nations and, 757
collaborators, 609
collective bargaining, 401, 537
collectivization, 545, 547, 724
Cologne, Germany, 615
Colombia, 144, 453, 455; American forces sent into, 458; drug trade and, 686, 696; Marxist guerrilla groups in, 696; Panama separates from, 458, 691
colony, 195
Colosseum, *p*71
Columbian Exchange, 194
Columbus, Christopher, 189, *p*189, *q*189, 190, *p*193, *p*196; impact of, on the Americas, 192–193; reaches the Americas (1492), 186, 193, 194, 196, 268; voyages of, 192–193
COMECON (Council for Mutual Assistance), 632
Comintern (Communist International), 573, 576; Anti-Comintern Pact and, 592
commercial capitalism, 131, 194–195, 274
Commercial Revolution, 131, 194–195
Committee of Public Safety: Napoleon made general by, 346; power of reduced, 342; Reign of Terror and, 337, 338, 339–342, 343
commodities, 476
common law, 120
Common Market. *See* **EEC**
commonwealth, 220
communes, 724
communism, 400, 402. *See also entries that begin with Communist*; Anti-Comintern Pact and, 592; expansion of, Truman Doctrine and, 632; Joseph R. McCarthy's "Red Scare" and, 645–646; popularity of, 536; revolts against, 639–640; spread of, 573; war, 519, 543
Communist(s): achieve control of Russia, 514, 518–519; in Asia, 573; Bolsheviks take name of, 518; in Cambodia, 738; Cheka and, 519; control by, patterns of, 639; fall in Eastern Europe, 658, 661–663; in France, 537; in Indonesia, 737; in Laos, 738; in North Korea, 743; in North Vietnam, 635–636; party conference of, initiates reforms in Soviet Union, 657, 659; Politboro of, 543; Red Terror and, 519; revolts against, 639–640; Russian civil war and, 518–519; Soviet Union created by, 543; Vietminh and, 737–738; in Vietnam, 573, 574, 737–738; World War I Allies oppose, 518, 519
Communist China. *See* **People's Republic of China**
Communist International. *See* **Comintern**
***The Communist Manifesto* (Marx and Engels),** 394, 397, 400, 402
Communist Party. *See* **Communist(s)**
Comparisons, making, 61
compass, 191
Compromise of 1867, 383
concentration camps, 550, 589, 608–609
Concert of Europe, 372–373; breakdown of, 378–379; defined, 372; principle of intervention and, 373, 455
concessions, 480
conclusions, drawing, 205
***Concorde*,** 748
Coney Island, New York, 396
Confederation of the Rhine, 348
Confucianism, 36, 44–45, 106, 280, 281, 431, 469, 476, 477, 578, 726. *See also* Confucius; adopted by Vietnam, 110; Christianity versus, 45; followers of, number of, *c*80; history and beliefs and, 82; worship and celebrations and, 84
Confucius, 36, *p*36, 82, 84, 105, 204, 269, 274. *See also* Confucianism; *Analects* and, 84; importance of, 44–45
Congo: Belgian interests in, 439; French interests in, 439; trade and, 200
Congo, Democratic Republic of, 703, 705
Congo River, 100, 439, 447
Congress of People's Deputies, 759
Congress of Vienna, 360, 362, *p*362, 371–372, 373, 375, 376, 415; conservative order and, 372–373; Europe after, *m*372
Congress Party, 735, 736
conquistadors, 194
conscription, 500–501, 568, 573, 592
***Consecration of Emperor Napoleon I and the Coronation of the Empress Josephine*,** *p*346
conservatism, 372–373
Conservative Party, 412, 538, 668
Consistory, 179
Constable, John, 389
Constantine (Roman emperor), 66, 74–76, *p*76
Constantinople, 506. *See also* Istanbul, Turkey; as capital of Eastern Roman Empire, 75, 76; conquered by Ottoman Turks (1453), 236, 239, 240–241, 246; population of, 132; siege of, *p*239
Constitutional Convention, 322
constitutional government, 15, 322, 371, 374, 425
constitutional monarchy, 425
consulate, 346
consumer society, 649
containment, policy of, 632
contras, 688, *p*688, 691
Copenhagen, UN Decade for Women conference in, 686
Copernicus, Nicholas, 294, 295, *p*295; universe of, 290, 295, *c*295, 296
Coral Sea, Battle of, 602
Corday, Charlotte, 338
Córdoba, Spain, 92, 94; Mosque of, 95, *p*95
Cornwallis, Charles, 321, *p*321
Corregidor, 599
Corsica, 345
Cort, Henry, 365
Cortés, Hernán, 128, 140, 143, *p*187, 190, 194
Costa Rica, 455, 690
cottage industry, 364
cotton gin, 384
cotton production, 358, 359, 364, 384
Council for Mutual Assistance (COMECON), 632
Council of People's Commissars, 518
Council of Trent, 155, 182, *p*182, 183
coup d'état, 326, 343, 345, 346
Courbet, Gustave, 387, 391
Cracow, Poland, 674
Cranmer, Thomas, 179
***Creating Alternative Futures* (Henderson),** 758
***The Creation* (Haydn),** 310
Crécy, Battle of, 138, *p*138
Credit-Anstalt, 536
creoles, 454
Crete, 231
Crimea, 601
Crimean War, 361, 378–379, 383, 407
***On Crimes and Punishments* (Beccaria),** 304
Croatia, 227, 240; independence declared by, 661, 663
Croats, 121, 375, 525, 526, 545

Cromwell, Oliver, 219–220, *p*221
crops, growing of. *See also* agriculture; farming
The Crossing of the Beresina, *p*350
Crusade(s), 112, 123; early, 87; First, 87
Cruz, Sor Juana Inés de la, 320, *p*320
Cuba, 193; American forces sent into, 458; Bay of Pigs disaster and, 635, 680, 689; becomes protectorate of the United States, 458; Cuban missile crisis and, 629, 635, 639, 680, 689; revolution and, 689–690; slavery abolished in, 437; Soviet aid to, 689, 690; totalitarian regime in, 635; United States breaks diplomatic relations with, 688, 689
Cuban missile crisis, 629, 635, 639, 680, 689
cubism, 422
culture: Hellenistic, 60; mass, 554–555; popular, 675–676
cuneiform, 27
Curie, Marie, 419, *p*419
Cuzco, Peru, 144
cyclones in India, 257
Cyrus "the Great" (king of Persia), 24, 34
Czech Republic, 227, 665; creation of, 662; NATO and, 660
Czechoslovakia: becomes independent republic, 523, 525, 545, 546; communism falls in, 661, 662; ethnic minorities in, 526, 593; Hitler's demands regarding, 591, 593; Nazi Germany invades, 593; peaceful division of, 662. *See also* Czech Republic; Slovakia; "Prague Spring" and, 629, 640; Soviet army invades, *p*629, 637, 640, *p*640, 662; Soviet control over, 639; Warsaw Pact and, 634; women's voting rights in, 649; World War II and, 593
Czechs, 121, 607; in Austria-Hungary, 414; rebel against Austrian Empire, 375–376

D

dadaism, 554, 556
Daewoo, 743
Dai Viet (Great Viet), 110
***Daily Mail* (London),** 409
Daimler, Gottlieb, 395, 398
daimyo, 103, 278, 279–280, 281, 479, 481
Dakar, 708
Dali, Salvador, 556
Dalldorf, Germany, 516
Damascus, Syria: as capital of Arab Empire, 92, 93; papermaking in, 44
Danse dans un Pavilion, 309
Dante, 164, 165, *p*165
Danton, Georges, 337, 339
Danube River, 76, 121, 242
Danube River Valley, 241
Danzig, Poland, 593
Dao (Way), 42, 45, 106
Daoism, 106
Dardanelles, 63, 64, 240, 379
Darius I (king of Persia), 34
Darjeeling, India, 736
Dark Age, 52–53
Darwin, Charles, 387, 390, 420
database, developing, 697
David, *p*167
David, Jacques-Louis, 327, 346
David (king of Israelites), 31
***David Copperfield* (Dickens),** 390
Dawes Plan, 535
***A Day in the Life of Ivan Denisovich* (Solzhenitsyn),** 637, 638
de Azara, Felix, 323
de Beauvoir, Simone, 642, 649, *p*649
De Fevre, William, 131
de Gaulle, Charles, 643, *p*643, 704
de Klerk, F. W., 707
de Pizan, Christine, 773
death camps, 550, 589, 608–609
Decade for Women, 686
Deccan Plateau, 37, 109, 257
Declaration of Independence (1776), 152, 233, 291, 301, 310, 318, *q*318, 321, 332; signing of, 152, *p*152
Declaration of the Rights of Man and the Citizen (1789), 152, 329, 332–333, 336, *p*336, 340
***Declaration of the Rights of the Negro Peoples of the World* (Garvey),** 568, 570
Declaration of the Rights of Woman and the Female Citizen, 333, 775
Deer Park at Sarnath, 39
Defence of the Realm Act (DORA), 508
deficit spending, 538
deforestation, 752, *m*752
Deir el Bahri, Egypt, 29
deism, 302–303
Dekker, E. Douwes, 429
Delacroix, Eugène, 389
Delhi, India, 256, 261, 449, 450; sacked by Persians, 255, 257
Delhi, Sultanate of, 109
Delphi: oracle at, *p*55; temple at, *p*12–13
democracy: direct, 56, 425; political. *See* political democracy; representative, 425
democratic government. *See* **democracy**
Democratic Party, 668, 669
Deng Xiaoping, *p*725, 725–726, 730, 732
Denmark, 381; EEC and, 667; Jewish population saved in, 609; NATO and, 633; Nazis invade, 597; Thirty Years' War and, 217; World War II and, 597
depression: defined, 536; Great. *See* Great Depression
Descartes, René, 293, *p*298, 298–299
***The Descent of Man* (Darwin),** 390
The Destruction of the Old Order, *p*561
détente, 657–658
deterrence, 635
Devshirme, 242
Dewey, George, 432
Dhahran, Saudi Arabia, oil strike at, 567
***The Diary of Anne Frank* (Frank),** 607
Dias, Bartholomeu, 189, 191
Díaz, Bernal, 128
Díaz, Porfirio, 458
Dickens, Charles, *p*387, *q*387, 390, 477
dictatorship, 401, 425
Diderot, Denis, *p*291, 302, 303, 305, 312
Diocletian (Roman emperor), 74–75, 76
direct democracy, 56, 425
direct rule, 433
the Directory, 326, 342–343
Discobolos, *p*57
***Discourse on Method* (Descartes),** 293, 298
***Discourse on the Origins of the Inequality of Mankind* (Rousseau),** 304
discrimination, 738, 755
dissidents, 658
***Divine Comedy* (Dante),** 164, 165
divine right of kings, 219, 223
Djakarta, Indonesia, 201
Doge, 159
Dome of the Rock, *p*90
Domenico, Ghirlandaio, 163
Domesday Book, 130
domestication of animals, 21
Dominican Republic, 458
Dominicans, 134, 320
domino theory, 635–636, 738
***Don Giovanni* (Mozart),** 310
***Don Quixote* (Cervantes),** 230, 232
Donatello, 164, 167
Donne, John, 603
Donovan, Nancy, 688
dowry, 163
Drake, Francis, 213
drama. *See also* theater: Greek, classical, 58–59; Kabuki, 281, 282
drawing conclusions, 205
The Dream of the Red Chamber, 273, 276
the Dreamtime, 81
Dresden, Germany, bombing of, 615, *p*615
Dreyfus, Alfred, 421
drip paintings, 675
drug trade, 686, 691, 696
Drury, Alice, 513, *p*513
Du Bois, W. E. B., 570
Duarte, José, 690
Dubai, United Arab Emirates, *p*571
Dubček, Alexander, 640
Dublin, 557
Duma, 414, 516
Dunkirk, 597
Dürer, Albrecht, 169, *p*169
Dutch East India Company, 433
Dutch East Indies, 433; invaded by Japan, 599; prisoners of war from, as slave laborers for Japan, 611; World War II and, 610, 611
Dutch Republic, 374; American Revolution and, 321; goes to war with France, during French Revolution, 339
Dylan, Bob, 646–647
dynasty, 27
Dzhugashvili, Joseph (Joseph Stalin), 543. *See also* Stalin, Joseph

E

Early Empire (Roman), 69–70
***Early History of Rome* (Livy),** 77
Earth Summit in Rio de Janeiro, 749, 753
earthquakes, 220
East Africa. *See also individual states*: imperialism in, 439–440; societies in, 100

Index

East Asia, New Order in, 595. *See also individual states*
East Germany. *See also* Germany; West Germany: Christian Democrats in, 663; Communist government falls in, 662–663; creation of, 633; free elections in, 663; refugees from, 712; reunification and, 655, 658, 662–663, 667–668; Soviet control over, 639; Stasi (secret police) in, 662; Warsaw Pact and, 634
East India Company, 187, 195, 258, 259
East Pakistan: becomes Bangladesh, 734, 736. *See also* Bangladesh; created from India, 734–735, 736
Eastern Europe. *See also individual states*: absolutism in, 226–227; authoritarian states in, 545–546; Black Death spread to, 137; Calvinism in, 182; Communist regimes fall in, 658, 661–663; free elections and, 617–618, 632; in High Middle Ages, 121; political upheaval and revolution in, 655, 658, 661–663; population of, 403–404; refugees from, 712; Slavic people of, 121; Soviet occupation of, 639–640
Eastern Orthodox Church: Christian church of Byzantine Empire comes to be known as, 123; schism between Roman Catholic Church and, 129, 137–138
Eastern Roman Empire, 75, 76. *See also* Byzantine Empire
Eastman, George, 395, 422
Ebert, Friedrich, 522
EC (European Community). *See* **EEC; European Union**
Echeverría, Luís, 689
***École de Mars* (School of Mars),** 340
ecology, 752
economy(ies): colonial, 433; global, 754–755; index of economic freedom in 2001, *c*710; money, 131; planned, 508; world, 400; *zaibatsu*, 571–572, 741
Ecuador, 144, 455
Edict of Milan, 74
Edict of Nantes, 211, 212
Edict of Worms, 174
Edison, Thomas, 397, 398
Edo, Japan, 265, 278, 279, 280, 481. *See also* Tokyo, Japan
Edo Bay (Tokyo Bay), 359, 480, 487
education. *See also* university(ies): humanist movement and, 165–166; in India, 450, 451; literacy and, 409–410; in modern Japan, 482–483; in postwar Japan, 741, 745; in the Renaissance, 165–166; in Revolutionary France, 340; student revolts and, 642, 649–650; universal, 408–410
Educational, Scientific, and Cultural Organization (UNESCO), 627, 757
Edward I (king of England), 120
Edward VI (king of England), 179
EEC (European Economic Community) (Common Market), *m*645. *See also* European Union; creation of, 642, 645; expansion of, 667
Egypt, 33, 716, 717; ancient. *See* Egypt, ancient; as British protectorate, 436, 438, 564; Cairo. *See* Cairo, Egypt; Camp David Accords and, 701, 714; Napoleon's plans for, 346; Ottoman Turks take control of, 241; Palestine Liberation Organization (PLO) formed by, 711, 714; Six-Day War and, 700, 713; Suez War of 1956 and, 711, 712–713; United Arab Republic (UAR) and, 712; World War II and, 346
Egypt, ancient: becomes part of Arab Empire, 91, 98; early civilization in, 21, 22, 24; farming in, 18, 98; Fatimid dynasty in, 93, 94; Hellenistic kingdom in, 60; history of, course of, 27–29; Hyksos and, 29; life in, life in Mesopotamia versus, *c*30; Middle Kingdom in, 27, 28–29; New Kingdom in, 27, 29; Nile and, 24, 27, 28–29; Old Kingdom in, 27–28; Persia invades, 34; as province of Roman Empire, 29; pyramids in, 17, 28, 111; rulers and gods and, 55; society in, 29–30; trade and, 70, 94; writing in, 30
The Eighteenth of Brumaire, Napoleon's coup d'état, November 10, 1799, *p*343
***Einsatzgruppen*,** 606, 607–609. *See also* Holocaust
Einstein, Albert, 297, 418, 419, *p*419, 557
Eisenhower, Dwight D., 603, 645
Ekaterinburg, Russia, 518
El Alamein, 601
El Salvador, 400, 455; government in, 690
Elba, Napoleon's exile on, 351
Elbe River, 603
electricity, in Second Industrial Revolution, 398
electronic road pricing, 743
electronic spreadsheet, using, 580
Elgin, Lord, 464
Elizabeth (queen of Belgium), 603
Elizabeth I, (queen of England), 179, 208, *p*208, 213–215, 216, 219, 232; Golden Speech of, 215
Elizabeth Tudor. *See* **Elizabeth I**
Elizabethan Era, 232
e-mail, using, 277
Emancipation Proclamation, 385
***Émile* (Rousseau),** 304
empire, 25
empire building. *See* **imperialism**
Emprey, Arthur Guy, 778
Enabling Act, 548, 550
enclosure movement, 364
***Encyclopedia (Classified Dictionary of the Sciences, Arts, and Trades)* (Diderot),** 291, 303
Engels, Friedrich, 397, 400; classless society and, 402
England. *See also* Great Britain; United Kingdom of Great Britain: Black Death spread to, 137; Church of England (Anglican Church) and, 155, 179, 219, 220; civil war in, 216, 219–220; Commonwealth and, 219–220; under Elizabeth I, 213–214; English Revolution and, 152, 219–221; Glorious Revolution in, 216, 221; Golden Age of Literature in, 230, 231–232; in High Middle Ages, 119–121; Hundred Years' War and, 127, 138; London. *See* London, England; New Model Army in, 219–220; new monarchy in, 138; Normans conquer, 287; Parliament of. *See* Parliament, British; political parties in, 220; Protestant Reformation in, 179–180, 182; restoration of monarchy in, 220–221; Spanish armada defeated by (1588), 211, 213, *p*213, 214, *m*214; Stuart dynasty in, 219, 220, 320; trade and, 159, 194–195, 200, 202, 265, 266, 272; trade mission sent to China by, 265, 266, 272; Tudor dynasty in, 219; united with Scotland, 320
English Channel, 603
English Football Association, 408
English language: in Canada, 670; as international language, 289; old, middle, and modern, 287; speakers of, 286
English Revolution, 152, 219–221
enlightened absolutism, 310–313
the Enlightenment, 300–316, 418; arts and, 308–310; enlightened absolutism and, 310–313; Europe in, *m*306; impact of, 308–316; Later, 304; magazines and, 305, 306; new social science and, 303–304; newspapers and, 300, 306; path to, 300–301; philosophes and. *See* philosophe(s); reading and, 306; religion in, 307; romanticism and, 387–389; social world of, 305–307; women's rights and, 305
***Enola Gay*,** 616
entertainment, elephant fight as, 261. *See also* sports and contests
entrepreneurs, 364
***Entry of Charles VIII into Naples*,** 160
environmental crisis, 751–753; chemical waste and, 752; ecological disasters and, 749, 752–753; population growth and, 752
***The Epic of Gilgamesh*,** 27
epic poem, 53, 66
epidemic(s), 404. *See also* plague(s); AIDS, in Africa, 706; Black Death as, 127, 129, 136–137; in China, 267, 269–270; defined, 144; health care advances and, 753; immunities develop to, 274; smallpox, 144, 299, 389; Spanish flu, 534
Eppler, John, 601
Equal Pay Act, 654, 672
Erasmus, Desiderius, 171, 172
Erhard, Ludwig, 643
Eridu, *p*25
espionage, 601
***Essay Concerning Human Understanding* (Locke),** 301
estates, 161, 330–331
Estates-General, 331
Estonia: becomes new nation-state, 525; nationalist movement in, 660
eta, 281

Ethiopia, 706, 707; defeats Italian attempt to conquer in 1896, 436, 438; Fascist Italy invades, 592; as free state in Africa, 441; religion in, 200

ethnic cleansing, 564, 661, 663

Etruscans, 48, 66, 67

Euphrates River, 24

euro, 655, 667

Europe, *m*120, *m*174, *m*313, *m*412, *m*535. *See also* Central Europe; Eastern Europe; Western Europe; *individual states*; after Congress of Vienna, *m*372; after Peace of Westphalia, *m*219; after World War II, *m*617; in the Age of Enlightenment, *m*306; alliances in (1914), *m*500; artistic Renaissance in, 166–169, *m*167; baroque period in, 231; Black Death in, 127; Concert of. *See* Concert of Europe; discovery of the world from, *c*206; economic and social crises in, 216–217; flu epidemic in, 534; forces of change in, 373–374; Great Depression and, 532; in High Middle Ages, 118–121; imperialism of, height of, *c*430; industrialization of, 366, *m*367, *m*399. *See also* Industrial Revolution; "iron curtain" and, 589, 603, 618, 631; Mannerism movement in, 208, 230–231; map of, after World War I, *m*525, 525–526; Marshall Plan and, 628, 632; Middle Ages in, 118–121, 129–138; missionary activity and, 200; Mongol reconnaissance of, 115; Napoleonic, *m*349; nationalism in, 350, 373–374, 382–384; Neanderthals in, 16, 20; new order in, 606–607; Ottoman Empire expands into, 241–242; politics of in 1930s, *m*541; population of. *See* Europe, population of; reform in, 382–384; revolutions of 1848 in, 361, 371, 374–376, *m*376, 378; rivalry in, 632; Seven Years' War in, 315, *m*315; Spanish conquest's economic impact on, 194; universities in, 129, 135; War of the Austrian Succession and, 308, 313–314; World War I in, *m*507; World War II in, 591–594, 596–598, *m*598, 600–601, 603–604

Europe, population of: doubles during Middle Ages, 129; explodes in 1700–1800, 274; growth and relocation during 1820–1900, *m*404; during Industrial Revolution, 367–368

European Community (EC). *See* **EEC; European Union**

European Economic Community. *See* **EEC**

European Recovery Program (Marshall Plan), 628, 632, 642

European Union, Treaty on, 667

European Union (EU): establishment of, 667; euro established as common currency of, 655, 667; expansion of, *m*667

***Evening News* (London),** 403, 409

Evita, 694

Exclusion Bill, 220

Exploration, Age of, 186–207; European discovery of the world and, *c*206; European explorers in, *c*206; European voyages during, *m*190; line of demarcation and, 193, 194; means to explore and, 189–191; motives to explore and, 189–191; Portuguese trading empire and, 191–192; sea travel in, 191; Spanish empire and, 194; voyages to the Americas during, 192–194

extraterritoriality, 467

***Exxon Valdez* oil spill,** 749, 751, 752

Eylau, battle at, 348

Ezana (king of Axum), 86, 97, 98

***On the Fabric of the Human Body* (Vesalius),** 293, 297, *p*297

***Facing Mount Kenya* (Kenyatta),** 568, 570

fact, opinion and, distinguishing between, 96

factions, 337, 338

Factory Act of 1833, 363, 369

Falkland Islands, 693, 694

Fallingwater, *p*423

family: in China, 43–44, 274–275, 477; marriage and. *See* marriage; in nineteenth century, 406–407; in Renaissance, 163

***Family* (Ba Jin),** 478

Faraday, Michael, 389

farming. *See also* agriculture: in ancient Egypt, 18, 98; carruca and, 130; in China, 18, *p*272; collective, 545, 547, 724; communes and, 724; in India, 18; in Latin America, 319; spread of, to 1B.C., *m*21; watermills and, 130; windmills and, 130

***Fascio di Combattimento* (League of Combat),** 540, 541

fascism: in Argentina, 694; defined, 541; in Germany, 546. *See also* Nazi Germany; in Italy, 540, 541–543, 546. *See also* Fascist Italy; New State in Brazil and, 583; rise of, 541–542; in Spain, 546

Fascist Italy: assists Franco in Spanish Civil War and, 592; expansion by, *m*593; Fascist Party in, 530, 540, 541–543, 546; invades Ethiopia, 592; invades Greece, 598; Munich Conference and, 593; Rome-Berlin Axis and, 591, 592; surrenders in North Africa, 601; World War II and, 601, 603

Fascist Party, 540, 541–543, 546

Fathmy, Hekmath, 601

Fatimid dynasty, 93, 94

Fay, Sidney Bradshaw, 522

Federal Republic of Germany. *See* **West Germany**

federal system, 322

Female Association for the Care of the Poor and Sick in Hamburg, 407

feminism, 407–408, 649

feng shui, 730

Feron, Eloi Firmin, 160

Fertile Crescent, 24

feudal contract, 119

feudalism, 118–119; development of, 87; feudal contract and, 119; Magna Carta (1215) and, 120; manorial system and, 131, 162; relics of, 330, 332

fief, 119

Fielding, Henry, 310

filial piety, 43–44

Fillmore, Millard, 480, 487, *p*487

Finland: becomes new nation-state, 525; EEC and, 667; Treaty of Brest-Litovsk and, 518

fire-lance, 105

Firmont, Henry de, 337

First Continental Congress, 321

First International, 401

Fischer, Fritz, 523

***Five Women Who Loved Love* (Ihara Saikaku),** 281

Five-Year Plans, 540, 544–545

Flanders: northern artistic Renaissance in, 169; trade and, 131

Flaubert, Gustave, 390

flintlock musket, 218, *p*218

flintlock pistol, *p*218

FLN (National Liberation Front), 704

Florence, Italy, 132, 154, 165, 166–167, 170; as city-state, 158–160, 163

Florentine Academy of Design, 231

Florida, transferred to Great Britain by Spain, 316

flu epidemic, 534

food, expanded production of, 130

footbinding, 275

Forbidden (Imperial) City, *p*265, 268, 273, 276, *p*276, 730–731, *p*731, 732

Ford, Henry, 359, 398

Formosa, 470. *See also* Taiwan

Fort William, India, 257, 258. *See also* Calcutta

Fortress of Gwalior in India, 238

Fourteen Saints, Church of, 309

Fox, Vicente, 681, 688, 689

France, 712; anti-Communists in Russia supported by, 518, 519; appeasement of Hitler and, 591, 592, 593; Black Death spread to, 137; Boxer Rebellion and, 471; Chamber of Deputies in, 413; Civil Code (Napoleonic Code) in, 15, 347, 348, 351; colonial interests of. *See* France, colonial interests of; declares war on Germany, 588, 594; education in, 649, 650; EEC and, 645; falls to Nazi Germany, 588, 597; Fifth Republic of, 643; Fourth Republic of, 643; French New Deal and, 537; Great Depression and, 537; Jews shipped from, to death camps, 609; kingdom of. *See* France, kingdom of; Maginot Line and, 597; mandates created by, in Middle East, 566–567; militarism and conscription in, 501; Munich Conference and, 593; under Napoleon III, 382–383; Napoleonic Code (Civil Code) in, 15, 347, 348, 351; NATO and, 633, 643; Open Door policy and, 471; Paris. *See* Paris, France; at Paris Peace Conference, 524; Popular Front government in, 533, 537; population of, 403–404; romantic painting in, 389; SEATO and, 634; Second Empire of, 378, 382–383; Second Industrial Revolution and, 399; second republic of. *See* France, Second Republic of; Senate of, 413; signs armistice with Nazi Germany,

597; socialist policies in, 667; sphere of influence in China established by, 470; Suez War of 1956 and, 711, 712–713; takes military action against China, 464, 468; third republic of. *See* France, Third Republic of; Treaty of Locarno and, 535–536; Triple Entente and, 411, 416, 499, 500, 505; uncertainties in, 667; Union of French Indochina created by, 429, 432; uses military to crush revolutions in Spain and Italy, 373; Vichy France regime in, 597; Vietnam War and, 737; women's voting rights in, 537, 649; World War I and, 498, 502, 504, 505, 506, 508, 522; World War II and, 588, 594, 597

France, colonial interests of: in Africa, 375, 436, 438, 439, 441–442, 564, 569, 643, 703, 704; in Latin America, 153, 454; in Middle East, 526, 565, 567; in Southeast Asia, 427, 431, 432, 434, 435, 737; in West Africa, 438, 564

France, kingdom of: American Revolution and, 321; Bourbon monarchy in, 351, 371–372, 374, 380; Calvinism in, 179, 182; Canada as colony of, 195; Capetian dynasty of, 121; Catholicism becomes official religion of, 212; Concert of Europe and, 372–373; constitutional monarchy established, 371, 374; Crimean War and, 379; establish forts in India, 257; Estates-General as parliament, 331; Franco-Prussian War and, 378, 380, 381, 383; French Revolution and. *See* French Revolution; Revolutionary France; French Wars of Religion and, 209, 211–212; German unification and, 381; Great War for Empire and, 315–316; Hundred Years' War and, 127, 138; Italian wars and, 160; under Louis XIV, 223–226, 308; Louisiana territory transferred to Spain by, 316; new monarchy in, 138; plebiscite in, 382; second revolution in (1848), 374–375, 382; Seven Years' War and, 314, 315–316, 320, 385; Thirty Years' War and, 217; three estates in, before Revolution, *c*330; trade and, 200, 319; War of the Austrian Succession and, 313–314, 316

France, Second Republic of. *See also* Napoleon III: established, 375; fall of, 383, 412; ministerial responsibility and, 413; universal male suffrage in, 374, 375

France, Third Republic of: establishment of, 411, 413; political democracy and, 412–413

Francis I (Austrian emperor), *p*361, 362, *p*362

Francis I (king of France), 175

Francis Ferdinand (archduke of Austria), 496, 499, *p*499, 501

Francis Joseph (emperor of Austria and king of Hungary), 383, 414

Francis of Assisi, Saint, 126, 134, *p*134, *p*208

Franciscans, 126, 134, 320

Franco, Francisco, 546, 592

Franco-Prussian War, 378, 380, 381, 383

Frank, Anne, 607

Frank, Otto, 607

***Frankenstein* (Shelley),** 304, 388

Frankfurt, Germany, 404

Frankfurt Assembly, 375, *p*377, 380

Franklin, Benjamin, 301, *p*301

Franks, kingdom of, 116, 117

Frederick I (emperor of the Romans), 121

Frederick I (king of Prussia), 209, *p*209, 227, *p*227

Frederick II (emperor of the Romans), 121

Frederick II (Frederick the Great) (king of Prussia), 311, *p*311, 312, 313, 315

Frederick II (king of Prussia), 308, *p*308, *q*308

Frederick III (elector of Saxony), 174

Frederick William (the Great Elector) (Prussian ruler), 226–227

Frederick William I (king of Prussia), 311

Freedom and People's Rights Movement, 483

French and Indian War, *m*315

French Indochina. *See* **Indochina, French**

French language, 286, 287, 670

French Republic: established by National Convention, 326, 338; Second. *See* France, Second Republic of; Third. *See* France, Third Republic of; Fourth, 643; Fifth, 643

French Revolution, 153, 328, 329–343, 347, 348, 373, 454; American Revolution and, 152, 329; background to, 329–331; beginning of, 326, 329–335; France during. *See* Revolutionary France; Napoleon's rise and, 345. *See also* Napoleon I; women active in, 341

French Wars of Religion, 209, 211–212

fresco, 166, 169

Freud, Sigmund, 418, 419, *p*419, 421, 557

Friday Mosque, 115

***Friend of the People*,** 338

Fujimori, Alberto, 696

Fujimura-Fanselow, Kumiko, 739

Fujiwara clan, 107

Fulbert of Chartres, Bishop, 116

Fulton, Robert, 360, 366

functionalism, 423

Gabriel (angel), 90

Galen, 297

Galicia, 504, 505

Galilei, Galileo. *See* **Galileo**

Galileo, *p*293, *q*293, 294, *p*296; discoveries of, 153, 293, 296; trial of, 152, 290, 292, *p*292, 293

Gallipoli, 506

Gama, Vasco da, 186, 191

Ganci, Peter, 750

Gandhi, Indira, 720, 734, 735

Gandhi, Maneka, 734

Gandhi, Mohandas, 451–452, *p*562, 779, *p*779; assassination of, 734, 735; referred to as Mahatma, 570; Salt March and, 561, 562, 570–571

Gandhi, Rajiv, 736

Ganges River, 37, 85

Garcia Márquez, Gabriel, 683, 687

Garibaldi, Giuseppe, 378, *p*378, 380

Garvey, Marcus, 568, 570

Gate of Heavenly Peace, 731–732, 733

Gaul. *See also* France

Gautama, Siddhartha. *See* **Buddha**

***General Gordon's Last Stand*,** 438

***General Theory of Employment, Interest, and Money* (Keynes),** 531, 538

generalizations, making, 222

genetic engineering, 753

Geneva, Switzerland, 179, 494

Genghis Khan, 88, 93, 105, *p*112, 112–115, p113, 256, 730; empire of, *m*115

Genoa, Italy, 123, 132

genocide, 564, 607. *See also* Holocaust

Gentileschi, Artemisia, 231

geocentric system, 295

Geoffrin, Marie-Thérèse de, *p*302, 306–307

George, Saint, 164, 167

George I (king of England), 320

George II (king of England), 320

George III (king of England), 265, 266, 272

Georgia: Communists gain control over during Russian civil war, 518; nationalist movement in, 660

German Communist Party, 523

German Democratic Republic. *See* **East Germany**

German Social Democratic Party (SPD), 397, 401, 522, 523, 643, 667

German Southwest Africa (now Namibia), 438

German Worker's Party, 549

Germanic Confederation, Frankfurt Assembly and, 375

Germanic kingdoms, 116–117

Germans, 375; in Czechoslovakia, 526, 593

Germany. *See also* East Germany; West Germany: anti-Semitism in, 421, 553; armistice signed by, 497, 521, 522; Berlin. *See* Berlin; Black Death spread to, 137; Boxer Rebellion and, 471; colonial interests of. *See* Germany, colonial interests of; Communist revolution avoided in, 523; debt restructured, 533, 535; democracy movement blocked in, 413–414; democratic republic created in, 522, 523, 537. *See also* Weimar Republic; dictatorial regime adopted in, 540, 548–553; economic miracle of, 643, 644; female astronomers in, 297–298; first magazine published in, 305; Great Depression and, 532, 536, 537, 549; under Hitler. *See* Nazi Germany; lack of national monarchy in, 138, 175; Lenin shipped to Russia by, 517; R.M.S. *Lusitania* sunk by, 496, 503, 507, 510–513; Lutheranism in, 174–175, 182;

Mennonites in, 180; militarism and conscription in, 501; Nazi. *See* Nazi Germany; Nazi Party in. *See* Nazi Party; Neanderthals first found in, 16, 20; neo-Nazis in, 668; Open Door policy and, 471; Paris Peace Conference and, 524; politics in Protestant Reformation and, 175; population of, 403–404; postwar division of, 617, 632–633, *m*633; racism in, 420; Reichstag in, 413, 549, 550, *p*596; reparations and, 524, 533, 534, 536; response of, to Archduke Ferdinand's assassination, 501–502; reunification of, 655, 658, 662–663, 667–668; Rome-Berlin Axis and, 591, 592; Second Industrial Revolution and, 399; sphere of influence in China established by, 470; Thirty Years' War and, 209, 216, *m*217, 217–218, 226; Treaty of Brest-Litovsk and, 514, 518; Treaty of Locarno and, 535–536; Treaty of Versailles and, 524, 533; Triple Alliance and, 411, 415, 416, 499, 500, 505; unification of, 361, 373, *m*380, 380–381; women's voting rights in, 649; World War I and, 498, 502, 504–505, 506, 507, 508, 509, 510, 511, 512, 522, 564; World War II and. *See* Nazi Germany

Germany, colonial interests of: in Africa, 436, 438, 439–440, 441, 569; in China, 470

Gestapo, 601

Ghana, 97, 98–99, 705; gains independence, 700, 701, 703

Ghazni, Afghanistan, 109, 112

Gibbs, Philip, 498

Gibralter, Strait of, 92, 98, 241

Giovanni Arnolfini and His Bride, 164, 169

***Girls and War and Other Stories* (Achebe),** 762–763

Girondins, 338

Giza, Egypt, 17

Glenn, John J., Jr., 780, *p*780

global economy, 754–755

global visions: new, 757–758; United Nations and, 756–757. *See also* United Nations

global warming, 750, 752

Globe Theater, 230, 232

Glorious Revolution, 216, 221

Goa, India, 192

Gobi, 42, 104–105, 105, 114

Godwin, William, 304

Goebbels, Joseph, 555, 603

Gogh, Vincent van, 422

Golan Heights, 713

Gold Coast, 191, 199, 568, 703. *See also* Ghana; British settlements along, 437

The Golden Lotus, 276

Golden Mask of Agamemnon, *p*53

Golden Pavilion, 109

Gómez, Juan Vicente, 582

Gomulka, Wladyslaw, 639

Good Neighbor policy, 561, 582, 585

Gorbachev, Mikhail, 656, 657, *p*657, *q*657, 658, 659–660, 661

Gordon, Charles, 438, *p*438

Gothic literature, 388

Gothic style of architecture, 127, 136, 137, 167, 169

Gouges, Olympe de, 326, 333, 339, 775

government(s): autonomous, 664; constitutional, 15, 322, 371, 374, 425; democratic. *See* democracy; forms of, 1900, 425; increased powers during war, 508; oligarchy and, 583; parliamentary, 412; representative, 120–121; separation of powers and, 302; totalitarian state as, 541

Government of India Act, 568, 570

Grand Alliance. ***See* Great Britain; Soviet Union; United States**

Grand Canal, 268

The Grand Chatelet seen from the Market Side, 331

grand vizier, 243

graphs, interpreting, 344

gravitation, universal law, 296

Great Britain. *See also* England; United Kingdom of Great Britain: American Revolution and, 321; anti-Communists in Russia supported by, 518, 519; appeasement of Hitler and, 591, 592, 593; Arab nationalists supported by, 566; Battle of Britain and, 596, 597, 615; Boer War and, 440–441; Boxer Rebellion and, 471; CENTO and, 634; China gives Hong Kong to, 467; colonial interests of. *See* Great Britain, colonial interests of; Concert of Europe and, 372–373, 455; Congress of Vienna and, 371–372; conscription and, 500–501; Conservative Party in, 412, 538, 668; Crimean War and, 379; declares war on Germany, 588, 594; decline of, 643–644; domestic servants in, 406; EEC and, 667; establishes control over Burma, 431; Falkland Islands war and, 693, 694; goes to war with France, during French Revolution, 339; Great Depression and, 537, 538; Great War for Empire and, 315–316; Industrial Revolution in, 363–365, *g*366, 382; Labour Party in, 411, 412, 538, 644, 668, 735; Latin American investment by, 582, 584; Liberal Party in, 412; Munich Conference and, 593; nationalism in, 382; NATO and, 633; Open Door policy and, 471; at Paris Peace Conference, 524; Parliament of. *See* Parliament, British; political democracy and, 412; population of, 403–404; Potsdam Conference and, 618; prisoners of war from, as slave laborers for Japan, 611; returns Hong Kong to China, 467, 721, 739, *p*739, 744; SEATO and, 634; Second Industrial Revolution and, 399; Seven Years' War and, 314, 315–316, 320, 321; slave trade declared illegal by, 437; Special Operations Executive and, 601; sphere of influence in China established by, 470; Suez War of 1956 and, 711, 712–713; takes military action against China in 1860, 464, 468; Tehran Conference and, 617; Thatcherism and, 668; trade and, 319, 350, 457, 466–467; trade unions win right to strike in, 394, 401; Triple Entente and, 411, 416, 499, 500, 505; War of 1812 and, 384; War of the Austrian Succession and, 313–314, 316; war with Napoleon, 346, 348, 349–350, 351; welfare state in, 644; women protest American nuclear missiles in, 671, 672; women win right to own property in, 403, 407; women's voting rights in, 649; World War I and, 498, 502, 505, 506, 507, 510; World War II and, 588, 594, 600–601, 603; Yalta Conference and, 617–618

Great Britain, colonial interests of: in Africa, 436, 437–438, 439, 440, 441, 564, 569, 703; in Hong Kong, 462, 467; in India, 237, 257–258, *m*258, 259, 320, 448–452, 562, 777; in Middle East, 526, 565, 567; in North America, 320–321; in Southeast Asia, 426, 431, 737

Great Depression, 530, 532, 537, 538, 572, 579, 582–583, 583, 683; causes of, 536; deficit spending and, 538; responses to, 536

Great Lakes, 316, 366

Great Leap Forward, 723–724, 726

Great Mosque of Samarra, *p*86, *p*94, 95

"Great Peace" in Japan, 265, 279, 280

Great Proletarian Cultural Revolution, 724–725, 726

Great Purge, 545

Great Pyramid, *p*17, 28, 111

Great Schism, 129, 137–138

Great Sphinx, *p*17, 28

Great Wall of China, *p*42, 42–43, 268

Great War. ***See* World War I**

Great War for Empire, 315–316

Greater East-Asia Coprosperity Sphere, 599, 610

Greco, El, 208, 231

Greece, 639; 1400 B.C., *p*52; ancient. *See* Greece, ancient; civil war in, 632; classical. *See* Greece, classical; early civilization in, 51–53; EEC and, 667; Fascist Italy invades, 598; freedom from Ottoman Empire achieved, 416, 564; invades Turkey, 565; Jews shipped from, to death camps, 609; Nazis seize, 598; Truman Doctrine and, 632; World War II and, 598

Greece, ancient, 51–60, 551; 1400 B.C., *m*52; Age of Pericles and, 56; Athens in. *See* Athens, city-state of; colonies of, *m*79; Dark Age of, 52–53; early civilization in, 51–53; Mycenaean civilization and, 48, 51, 52; Persians defeated by, 48, 55; Rome conquered, 67; Sparta in. *See* Sparta, city-state of; young people in, 56–57

Greece, classical, 55–59; architecture of, 57–58; art of, 57–58; culture of, 56–59; defined, 51, 55; drama and, 58–59; Hellenistic Era and, 60; philosophy and, 58–59

Greek language, 288, 294

Green Revolution, 753–754

greenhouse effect, 752

Gregory VII (pope), 129, *p*129, 133

Group of United Officers, 583

Index

Groves, Leslie, 616
Grozny, 660
Guam, 415
Guang Xu (emperor of China), 470, 473, 475
Guangzhou (Canton), China, 269, 272, 466, 467, 477
Guarani Indians, 323
"Guard Squadrons" (SS) *(Schutzstaffeln)* in Nazi Germany, 551–552
Guatemala, 128, 141, 142, 455, 690, 691; American forces sent into, 458
Guernica, 546
Guernica, Spain, 546
guerrilla tactics, 577
Guevara, Ernesto Ché, 681, *p*681, 689–690
guilds, 129, 132, 162–163
guillotine, 339
Gujarat, India, 452
Gulbahar, 248–249
Gulf of Aqaba, 713
Gulf of Mexico, 141, 143
Gulf of Oman, 715
Gulf of Saint Lawrence, 316
Gulf War, 701, 715
gunpowder: Chinese invention and use of, 105, 202, 218; flintlock musket and, 218, *p*218; gunpowder empires and, 202, 242; Spanish explorers and, 144
Gupta Empire, 40, 109
Gustavus Adolphus (king of Sweden), *p*209, 218
Gutenberg, Johannes, 154, 162, *p*162
Gutman, Roy, 661
Guzmán, Dominic de, 134
Gypsies, 609

The Habits of Good Society, 405
Hadrian (Roman emperor), 70, 72
Hagia Sophia (Church of the Holy Wisdom), *p*236, 245
Haiti, 153, 194, 454; American forces and, 458, 582
hajj, 90
Hamburg, Germany, 549; bombing raid on, 612
Hammurabi (Babylonian king), 24, 25; Code of, 26–27, 35
Han dynasty, 17, 36, 43, 44, 103, 105, 106
Han Empire, *m*43
Handel, George Frederick, 309–310
Hangzhou, China, 105, 475
Hankou, China, 594
Hannibal, 67, *p*67
Hanoi, *p*574; seized by French, 431
Hanoverians, 318, 320
hans, 279–280
Hanyang (Seoul), Korea, 282
Hapsburg dynasty, 175, 217, 227, 231, 375, 383, 500
Harappa, 37
harem, 243, 246
Hargreaves, James, 363, 364
Harold II (king of England), 119
Harris, Townsend, 480
Harrow, 408
Harun al-Rashid, 93
Harvey, William, 293, 297
Hastings, Battle of (1066), 116, 119
Hatshepsut (Egyptian pharaoh), 29, *p*29
Havana: seized by Castro, 688, 689; University of, 682
Havel, Václav, 662, 665
Hawaiian Islands, 415, 599
Hay, John, 470
Haydn, Franz Joseph, 310
health care, 753
Heavenly Kingdom of Great Peace, 468
heavy industry, 638
Hebrew Bible, 33, 83
Hebrew language, 288
Hebrew religion. *See* **Judaism**
Hebrew University of Palestine, 563
Heian, Japan, 103, 107–108
Heiji Insurrection, 87
Heisenberg, Werner, 554, 557
heliocentric system, 295
Hellenistic Era, 60
Hellenistic kingdoms, 60
Hellespont, 63
Henan, China, 270
Henderson, Hazel, 757–758, *p*758
Henry II (king of England), 120
Henry IV (king of France) (Henry of Navarre), 212
Henry IV (king of Germany), 133
Henry VIII (king of England), 155, 179, *p*179
Henry the Navigator (prince of Portugal), 191
Herat, 112
heresy, 134, 152, 292
"Hermit Kingdom," 282
Herzegovina, 416
Herzl, Theodor, 418, 421
Hesse, Hermann, 557
Heydrich, Reinhard, 607–608
Hidalgo, Miguel, 454, *p*454
hieroglyphics, 30, 142, 288
High Middle Ages: England in, 119–121; Europe in, 118–121; French kingdom in, 121; nobility during, 118–119; popular religion in, 134–135; women joined religious orders during, 133–134
High Renaissance, masters of, 168, 231
Hildegard of Bingen, *p*133, 133–134
Himalaya, 36, 104
Himmler, Heinrich, 551–552, 607, 610
Hindenburg, Paul von, 537, 550
Hindi, 286, 288
Hindu Kush, 37, 257
Hinduism, 256; followers of, number of, *c*80; history and beliefs and, 38–39, 83; worship and celebrations and, 85
Hindus: cows sacred to, 449; rivalry with Muslims in India, 449, 451, 571, 734, 736, 758
Hindustan Times, 734
Hirohito (emperor of Japan), 573, 604
Hiroshige, A., 486
Hiroshima, Japan: atomic bomb dropped on, 589, 604, 616; children evacuated from, 610
Hispaniola, 193, 196, 454
histories, oral, 771
***The History of the Peloponnesian War* (Thucydides),** 51
***History of the Suffrage Movement* (Pankhurst),** 403
***The History of Tom Jones, a Foundling* (Fielding),** 310
Hitler, Adolf, 349, 530, 541, 542, 543, *p*548, *q*548, *p*549, *q*553, *p*588, *p*592, 596, *p*596, *q*596, 614, 694; art and, 556–557; becomes chancellor, 531, 550; becomes dictator, 550; death of, 604; as *Führer,* 550; German path to war and, 591–594; as mass murderer, 543; with Mussolini and Stalin, *c*552; nonaggression pact with Stalin and, 594, 595; radio used by, 555; Spanish Civil War and, 546, 592; Treaty of Versailles violated by, 588, 592; views of, 548–549
Hitler Youth, 531, 550–551, *p*551, 610
Ho Chi Minh, 573, 574, *p*574, 611, 737–738
Hobbes, Thomas, 230, 233
Höch, Hannah, 556
Hofburg Palace, 362
Hokkaido, Japan, 107
Holland, 348, 350. *See also* Netherlands
Holocaust, 607–610, 712, 778; death camps and, 550, 589, *m*608, 608–609, 779; death toll and, 609; Gypsies and, 609; victims of, *p*779
Holstein, 381
Holtzendorff, Henning von, 507
Holy Land. *See* **Palestine**
Holy League, 212
Holy Roman Empire, 121, 551; end of, 218; Thirty Years' War and, 209, 216, *m*217, 217–218
Homer, 52–53, 62, 63, 66
hominids, 19
Homo erectus, 16
Homo sapiens, 20
Homo sapiens sapiens, 20
Honduras, 193, 455; American forces sent into, 458; government in, 690–691
Honecker, Erich, 656, 662
Hong Kong, 462, *p*468, 733; as "Asian tiger," 744; given to Great Britain by China, 467; New Territories and, 467; returned to China by Great Britain, 467, 721, 739, *p*739, 744
Hong Xiuquan, 468
Honshu, Japan, 107
Hoover, Herbert, 532
Hormuz, Strait of, 715
Hosokawa, Mirohiro, 740
Höss, Rudolph, 606, *q*606, *p*606
hostage system, 280
House of Commons, 121, 219
House of Lords, 121
Houses of Parliament, 388, *p*388. *See also* Parliament, British
Howard, George, 750
Huayna Inca (Incan ruler), 143–144
Hudson River, 195
Hue, Vietnam, 433
Hugh Capet, 121
Huguenots, 224, 226; defined, 212; Edict of Nantes recognizes rights of, 211, 212
Huitzilopochtli, 143
Hülegü, 93
human rights: American Bill of Rights and, 322, 373; in Bolivia, 686; in Chile, 695; English Bill of Rights and, 221, 332
humanism, 164, 294; Christian (Northern Renaissance

humanism), 154, 172; education and, 165–166; Italian Renaissance, 164–165; Northern Renaissance (Christian humanism), 154, 172
Hundred Years' War, 127, 138
Hungarian Revolution: of 1848–1849, 375, 376; of 1956, 375, 640
Hungarians, 121, 241, 526; in Czechoslovakia, 526
Hungary, 175, 227; authoritarian regime in, 545–546; becomes independent republic, 523, 525, 545; Budapest, 375, 383; independence and, 373; Jews shipped from, to death camps, 609; NATO and, 660; Ottoman Turks conquer, 239, 242; Paris Peace Conference and, 524, 525; rebellion in, 640; revolts against Soviet control in, 375, 637; Soviet control over, 639; Warsaw Pact and, 634; women's voting rights in, 649; World War II and, 598, 604
Huns, 40, 76
hunter-gatherers, 20
Husák, Gustav, 640
Hussein (shah of Persia), 251
Hussein, Saddam, 715, *p*715
Hutu, 707
Hyksos, 29
Hyundai, 743

Ibadan, University College of, 762
Ibn Battuta, 97, 102, *p*102
Ibn Saud, *p*566, 567
Ibn Sina (Avicenna), 89, 95
Ibn-Rushd, 94
Ibo society, 200, 706–707
Ibrahim, 248, 249
Ibsen, Henrik, 421
Ice Ages, 20, 21, 140
Iceland, 633
identification of an argument, 386
Ife, 101
iftar, 85
Ignatius of Loyola, 177, *p*177, *q*177, 182, *p*183
***The Ignorant Philosopher* (Voltaire),** 300
Ihara Saikaku, 281
Île-de-France. *See also* Paris
***Iliad* (Homer),** 52, 53, 62, 63
IMF (International Monetary Fund), 757
imperator, 69
Imperial (Forbidden) City, *p*265, 268, 273, 276, *p*276, 730–731, *p*731, 732
Imperial Rule Assistance Association, 573
imperialism: in Africa, 436–442, *m*437; in China, 469–470; defined, 430; European, height of, *c*430; Japanese, 479, 484–485; of the late nineteenth century, 429–431; in Latin America, 457; new, 427, 429–431, 457; racism and, 430; social Darwinism and, 430; in Southeast Asia, 429–434, *m*431
Impressionism, 422
INC. *See* **Indian National Congress**
the Inca, 140, 143–144; conquest of, 127, 144, 194; quipu used by, 145, *p*145
indemnity, 471
Independence Day, 333
India, 34, 60; ancient, society in, 37–38; Aryans in, 37; becomes independent, 720, 735; British colonial interests in, 237, 257–258, *m*258, 259, 320, 448–452, 562; British official's home in, *p*427, 450–451, *p*451; British rule in, 449–451, 562, 777; cannons produced by, 202; caste system in, 37–38; Congress Party in, 735, 736; culture in, 452; cyclones in, 257; early civilization in, 21, 22, 36–38; East and West Pakistan created from, 734–735, 736; education in, 450, 451; farming in, 18; fleet, combined with Turkish ships, destroyed by Portuguese, 191–192, 202; flu epidemic in, 534; French establish forts in, 257; Government of India Act and, 568, 570; Great War for Empire in, 315–316; Gupta Empire and, 40, 109; Hinduism's origins in, 83. *See also* Hinduism; Independence Day in, 333; independence in, move for, 570–571; Indian National Congress in. *See* Indian National Congress; Legislative Council and, 570; literacy in, 450; marriage in, 259; Mauryan Empire and, 40; Mogul dynasty of. *See* Mogul Empire; Muslim League and, 571; Muslim rivalry with Hindus in, 109–110, 449, 451, 571, 734, 736, 758; Napoleon's threat against, 346; nationalism in, 451–452, 570–571; new, 735–736; papermaking in, 44; partition of, 734–735, *m*735; population of, 274, 735; Portuguese trade with, 191–192; relations with Pakistan and, 758; religions in, 109–110; rulers and gods and, 55; Sepoy Mutiny in, 448–449, *p*449; Seven Years' War in, *m*315, 315–316, 320; suttee in, 259; Timur Lenk (Tamerlane) attacks, 103, 109; trade and, 94, 187, 195; Vasco da Gama reaches, 186, 191; viceroy in, 449; World War I and, 506; zamindars in, 450
Indian National Congress (INC), 448, 451, 570–571; renamed Congress Party, 735
Indian Ocean, 89, 109, 110, 191, 202, 268, 712
indigenous people, 440
indirect rule, 432–433, 441
Indochina, French: communism in, 573; creation of, 429, 432; Japan's interest in, 595; World War II and, 611
Indo-Europeans, 551
Indonesia, 110, 602; becomes independent, 734, 737; Communist Party in, 737; Dutch settlers in, 201; Nationalist Party in, 737; World War II and, 611
Indonesian Archipelago, 110, 202, 203, 204
inductive reasoning, 299
indulgence, 173
Indus River, 34, 36, 109
Indus River valley, 37, 109, 255
industrial capitalism, 368
industrial middle class, 368–369
Industrial Revolution, 363–370; capital and, 364; coal and, 365; cotton production and, 358, 359, 364, 384; entrepreneurs and, 364; factories and, 365; in Great Britain, 363–365, *g*366, 382; industrial middle class and, 368–369, 408; industrial working class and, 369–370; iron and, 365; in North America, 366–367, 776; railroads and, 360, 365; Second. *See* Industrial Revolution, Second; social impact in Europe and, 367–370; socialism and, 370; spread of industrialization and, 366–367, *m*367; in United States, *g*366, 366–367; young people in, 368–369
Industrial Revolution, Second, 397–400; new forms of leisure and, 396; new middle classes and, 405; new patterns and, 399; new products and, 398–399; universal education and, 408–410; women's experiences and, 406–408; world economy and, 400
industrial working class(es), 369–370; organization of, 400–401. *See also* political party(ies); trade union(s)
industry, guilds and, 132
INF (Intermediate-range Nuclear Force) Treaty, 654, 658
inferences, making, 205
inflation: defined, 216; in Weimar Germany, 534–535
information: summarizing, 176; synthesizing, 619
Innocent III (pope), 133
Inquisition (Holy Office), 134, 217, 292, *p*292, 293
***Institutes of the Christian Religion* (Calvin),** 178
Institutional Revolutionary Party (PRI), 584, 688–689
The Instruction of the Vizier Ptah-hotep, 772
insulae, 71
Intermediate-range Nuclear Force (INF) Treaty, 654, 658
internal-combustion engine, 398–399
International Children's Emergency Fund (UNICEF), 756, 757
International Monetary Fund (IMF), 757
International Space Station, *p*749
International Women's Year Tribunal, 686
International Wushu (Martial Arts) Association, 271
Internet: in Africa, 627; creation of, 627; defined, 753; Service Provider (ISP) for, 277; use of, in China, 733
interpretation: of graphs, 344; of military movements on maps, 527; of primary sources, 771; of statistics, 710
***The Interpretation of Dreams* (Freud),** 418, 419
intifada, 714
Inuits, 141
IRA (Irish Republican Army), 672
Iran. *See also* Persia: Americans held hostage in, 669, 702, 711, 715; cannons produced by, 202; captured by Ismail, 250, 251; CENTO and, 634; Iraq attacks, 715; modern, begin-

nings of, 566; Nazi Germany and, 566; revolution in, 714–715; Safavid dynasty of. *See* Safavid dynasty of Persia; Safavid Empire; Seljuk Turks in, 93; Shiite Muslims in, 715; terrorist organizations aided by, 672; women in, 716; World War II and, 566

Iranian Plateau, 33

Iraq, 18; attacks Iran, 715; Baghdad. *See* Baghdad, Iraq; British take control of, 526, 567; captured by Ismail, 250, 251; CENTO and, 634; occupies Kuwait, 701, 715; Sunni Muslims in, 715; trade and, 94; women in, 716

Ireland, 214, 736; EEC and, 667

***I...Rigoberta Menchú* (Menchú),** 691

Irigoyen, Hipólito, 583

Irish, 500

Irish Republican Army (IRA), 672

Irnerius, 135

"iron curtain," 589, 603, 618, 631

Iroquois, 141

Irrawaddy River, 110

Isabella of Castile (queen of Spain), 193, *p*193, 194

Isfahan, Iran, 250, *p*250, 251; Royal Academy of, 253, *p*253

Ishmael, 90

Islam, 89–95. *See also* Muslims; Christianity and, 90; Crusades and, 112, 123. *See also* Crusade(s); culture of, 94–95, 716; Five Pillars of, 91; followers of, number of, c80; fundamentalists and, 673; history and beliefs and, 83; in Indian society, 109–110; Islamic society and, 715–716; Judaism's influence on, 90; prophets of Christianity and Judaism and, 83; Ramadam and, 91; spread of, *m*91; worship and celebrations and, 85

Islamic Empire. *See* **Arab Empire**

Islamic militants, 716

Ismail (shah of Persia), 236, 252; Iran and Iraq captured by, 250, 251

ISP (Internet Service Provider), 277

Israel: ancient. *See* Israel, ancient; Arab-Israeli dispute and, 711, 712, 713–714, 755, 758; Camp David Accords and, 701, 714; Six-Day War and, 700, 713; state of, creation of, 31, 700, 711, 712; Suez War of 1956 and, 711, 712–713

Israel, ancient. *See also* Israelites: religion and, 32–33, 72. *See also* Judaism

Israelites, 24, 26, 30–33, 89

Istanbul, Turkey, 241, 242. *See also* Constantinople; Suleimaniye Mosque in, 245; Topkapi Palace in, 243, *p*244, 246

Italian Renaissance, 154, 157–158, *m*159; art and, 166–168; family and marriage in, 163; humanism movement of, 164–165; Italian states during, 158–160; Italian wars and, 160

Italian wars, 160

Italy: baroque movement begins in, 230, 231; Black Death spread to, 137; city-states in, 158–160; colonial interests of, 436, 438, 569; dictatorial regime adopted in, 540, 541–543; EEC and, 645; fascism in, 540, 541–543; Fascist Party in, 540, 541–543, 546. *See also* Fascist Italy; Florence. *See* Florence, Italy; Genoa, 123, 132; Italian wars and, 160; kingdom of. *See* Italy, kingdom of; Mannerism movement in, 208, 230–231; Milan. *See* Milan, Italy; militarism and conscription in, 501; Naples, 132, 160, 175; Napoleon's campaigns in, 346; NATO and, 633; OVRA (secret police) in, 542; at Paris Peace Conference, 524; Pisa, 123, 170; political democracy and, 413; revolution in, 373, 374, 375; Roman conquest of, 67; Rome. *See* Rome; under rule of relative of Napoleon, 348; squadristi (Blackshirts) in, 541; states in, revolts in, 376; Triple Alliance and, 411, 415, 416, 499, 500, 505; unification of, *m*379, 379–380; Venice. *See* Venice, Italy; women's voting rights in, 537, 649; World War I and, 505, 506

Italy, kingdom of: proclamation of, 378, 380; Second Industrial Revolution and, 399

Ito Hirobumi, 481

Iturbide, Agustín de (emperor of Mexico), 455

Ivan III (Russian prince), 138

Ivan IV (Ivan the Terrible) (Russian czar), 227–228

***Ivanhoe* (Scott),** 387, 388

J

Jackson, Andrew, 384

Jacobin club, 338

Jahangir (emperor of India), 257

Jalal, 115

James I (king of England), 219

James II (king of England), 220–221

janissaries, 240, 243, *p*243, 246

Japan: Anti-Comintern Pact signed with Germany and, 592; anti-Communists in Russia supported by, 518, 519; attacks China, 594–595; Black Dragon Society in, 573; Boxer Rebellion and, 471; cannons produced by, 202; Christian missionaries to, 279; Christians persecuted in, 279; Civil Code of 1898 and, 484; class system in, 280–281; conscription in, 568, 573; cooperates with Nazi Germany, 595; culture in, 485–486; early. *See* Japan, early; earthquake in 1703 and, 220; economic miracle of, 644; Europeans in, 279; expansion and, 484, *m*484, *m*572, *m*594; first use of firearms by, 279, 283; German-held islands in Pacific seized by, 506; Great Depression and, 572; Greater East-Asia Co-prosperity Sphere and, 599, 610; Hiroshima. *See* Hiroshima, Japan; homefront during World War II and, 614; Imperial Rule Assistance Association and, 573; imperialism in, 479, 484–485; isolationism and, 266, 479–480; Kamakura shogunate in, 108; *kamikaze* ("divine wind") and, 88, 614; Liberals in, 481; literacy in, 742; martial arts in, 270; Meiji Constitution and, 479, 481, 484; Meiji Restoration and. *See* Meiji Restoration; militarism in, 572–573; modern, rise of, 479–486, *c*482, 571–573; Mongol fleet's attack on, 88, *p*88, 106, 108; Nagasaki. *See* Nagasaki, Japan; new order in, resistance to, 480; New Order in East Asia and, 595; Pearl Harbor attacked by, 589, 599, 600; People's Volunteer Corps and, 616; postwar. *See* Japan, postwar; prefectures in, 481; Progressives in, 481; relations with United States in early 1900s, 485; religion in, 81, 108; Russo-Japanese War and, 416, 479, 484–485; samurai and, 107–108, *p*265, 281, 480; sanctions threatened against, 595; Sat-Cho alliance and, 480, 481; sphere of influence in China established by, 470; surrender of, in World War II, 579, 589, 604; Tokugawa rule in, 265, 279–282, *m*280, 479, 483; trade and, 279, 280, 572; unification of, 265, 278–279; United States drops atomic bombs on, 589, 604, 616; used prisoners of war as slaves, 606, 611; war with China over Korea, 470, 484; women in, 280, 281, 483–484, 614, 742; worker rallies in, 400; World War II and, 594–595, 599–600, 602, 604, 610–611, 614; *zaibatsu* economy in, 571–572, 741

Japan, early: Fujiwara clan in, 107; geography of, 107, *m*107; Heian period in, 103, 107–108; Japanese state rises in, 107–108; life and culture in, 108–109; Nara period in, 107; Yamato clan in, 107

Japan, postwar, 739–742, *m*740; Allied occupation of, 739–740; culture in, 742; education in, 741, 745; foundations of, *c*741; government of, 740–741; "Japanese miracle" and, 740–741; Liberal Democrats in, 740; new constitution and, 739, 740; as occupied country, 739–740; politics in, 740–741; social changes in, 742; Socialists in, 740; state capitalism in, 740; United States restores independence to, 739, 740; *zaibatsu* economy in, 741

Japanese Americans, 613, 614

Japanese language, 286, 288

Japanese Red Army, 673

***Japanese Women* (Fujimura-Fanselow),** 739

Java, 203; Dutch colonial system in, 429; Mongol fleet launched against, 106; religion in, 204; trade and, 400

Jayavarman, 110

Jebe, 114, 115

Jefferson, Thomas, 72, 301, *p*301, *p*318, 321

Jena, battle at, 348

Jenner, Edward, 299, *p*299, 389

Jerusalem, 241; as capital of Israel, 31; during Crusades, 123; Dome of the Rock in, *p*90; Israel occupies, 713; Jesus arrives in, 84; pilgrimages to, by Christians, 134

Index

Jesuits (Society of Jesus), 182, 183, 256, 269, 271, 279, 320, 323
Jesus (Jesus Christ), 72–74, 82, 84, 90. *See also* Christianity; apostles of, 134; death of, 49, 73, 84; followers of, 73; message of, 72–73
jet airliners, 748, 753
Jewish religion. *See* **Judaism.** *See also* Jews
***The Jewish State* (Herzl),** 418, 421
Jews: Holocaust. *See* Holocaust; hostility toward. *See* anti-Semitism; Kristallnacht and, 548, 553; Nazi Germany's persecution of, 550, 567; Nazi's Final Solution and, 606, 607–608, 609. *See also* Holocaust; Palestine as home of, 567, 711, 712; pogroms and, 421; religion of. *See* Judaism; sent to death camps, 550, 589, 608, 609. *See also* Holocaust
Jiangxi Province, China, 576, 577
jihad, 246
Jin dynasty, 114
Jinnah, Muhammad Ali, 571
Joan of Arc, 138
Johannesburg, South Africa, 705, 781
Johansen, John Christian, 526
John (king of England), Magna Carta signed by (1215), 116, 120
John Paul II (pope), 662, 674
John XXIII (pope), 674
Johnson, Lyndon B., *p*646, 646–647; Great Society and, 647; Vietnam War and, 631, 635, 636, 720, 738
Johnston, Audrey Lawson, 513, *p*513
Jordan: achieves self-rule, 711; British take control of, 567; women in, 716
Jordan River, 713
Joseph II (ruler of Austrian Empire), 311–312
Joy, George William, 438
Joyce, James, 554, 557
Juárez, Benito, 456
Judaea: becomes Roman province, 72; Jesus crucified in, 73
Judah, Kingdom of, 31, 32, 72
Judaism, 30, 31, 32–33. *See also* Jews; followers of, number of, c80; history and beliefs and, 83; Torah (the *Pentateuch*) and, 83; worship and celebrations and, 85
Judge, Mychal, 750
Judith Beheading Holofernes, 231
judo, 270
Julius II (pope), 156, 172, *p*172
Jullien, Marc-Antoine, 341
Junkers, 227
Justinian (Byzantine emperor): codified Roman law, 14
Justinian Code *(The Body of Civil Law)*, 14, *p*14, 116, 122
Jutland, battle of, 507

Kaaba, 90
Kabuki, 281, 282
Kabul, Afghanistan, 238
kaiser, 381
Kalahari desert, 98
Kamakura shogunate, 108
kami, 81, 108
***kamikaze* ("divine wind"),** 88, 614
Kanagawa, Treaty of, 462, 479, 480
Kandinsky, Wassily, 423
Kangxi (emperor of China), 265, 267, *p*267, 271
Kanpur (Cawnpore), India, 449
Kant, Immanuel, *q*151
Kara-Khitai, 114
Karakorum, 105, 114
karate, 270
karma, 38, 84
Katte, Hans Hermann von, 311
Kawashima, Yoshiko, 601
keep, 118
Kellogg, Frank B., 535
Kellogg-Briand pact, 535
Kemal, Mustafa. (Kemal Atatürk), 565. *See also* Atatürk, Kemal
Kennan, George, 632
Kennedy, John F., 635, 645, 689
Kent State University, 647, *p*648
Kentucky Fried Chicken, 732, 734
Kenya, 708; reform movement in, 569; Young Kikuyu Association in, 569
Kenyatta, Jomo, 568, *p*568, *q*568, 570, 705
Kepler, Johannes, 294, 295–296
Kerensky, Alexander, 516
Kereyits, 113
Keynes, John Maynard, 531, 538, *p*538
Khadija, 90
Khafre (king of Egypt), 28
Khanbaliq, China, 106. *See also* Beijing
Khartoum, 438
Khmer Empire, 110; disappearance of, 202
Khmer Rouge, 738
Khomeini, Ayatollah Ruhollah, 669, 702, 711, *p*714, 714–715, 716
Khrushchev, Nikita, 375, 635, 637, 638–639, *p*639, 640, 658; de-Stalinization under, 638, 639
Khufu (king of Egypt), 28
Khwarizm empire, 114, 115
Khyber Pass, 256
Kiel, Germany, 522
Kiev, Russia, 121
Kilwa, 100
Kim Il Sung, 743
Kim Young Sam, 743
King, Reverend Martin Luther, Jr., 647, 651
The King and I, 432
Kirch, Gottfried, 298
Kit Kat Club, 601
Kitchener, Lord, 451
Kitty Hawk, North Carolina, 399
knights, 118–119
Knox, John, 179
Kodak camera, 395, 422
Kohl, Helmut, 667–668
kolkhozes (collective farms), 547
Kongfuzi (Confucius), 44. *See also* Confucianism; Confucius
Koran. *See* **Quran**
Korea. *See also* North Korea; South Korea: annexed by Japan, 463, 485, 572, 727; cannons produced by, 202; divided into two zones after World War II, 727; independence of recognized by China, 484; isolationism and, 266; Japan and China go to war over, 470, 484; Japanese invasion of, 282; language in, 288; Manchu army invades, 282; martial arts in, 270; prisoners of war from, as slave laborers for Japan, 611; as "the Hermit Kingdom," 282; Tokugawa relations with, 479; Yi dynasty in, 282
Korean Peninsula, 743
Korean War, 495, 628, 631, 634, 645, 720, *m*727, 727–728, *p*728
Korfmann, Manfred, 64–65
Kosovo: Battle of, 240; war in, 664
Kosovo Liberation Army, 664
Kossuth, Louis, 375
Kosygin, Alexei, 658
Kovác, Michal, 662
Kowloon Peninsula, 467, 468
Kristallnacht, 548, 553
Krupp Armaments works, 509
Kshatriyas, 37
Kublai Khan (emperor of China), 88, *p*88, 93, 103, 106, 108, 190, 730
Kuchlug, 114
kung fu (Shaolin Quan), 270
Kuril Islands, 617
Kursk, Battle of, 601, 603, 605
Kush, 97, 98
Kuwait, Iraq occupies, 701, 715
Kwasniewski, Aleksander, 662
Kyoto, Japan, 103, 107, 279, 280, 481; Golden Pavilion in, 109
Kyushu, Japan, 107

L

La Place Clichy, *p*382
La Rochefoucauld-Liancourt, duc de, 328
labor unions. *See also* trade unions: collective bargaining and, 401, 537; strikes and, 394, 401
Labour Party, 411, 412, 538, 644, 668, 735
Ladies' Mercury, 305
The Lady Fujitsubo Watching Prince Genji Departing in the Moonlight, *p*486
Lagos, 708
laissez-faire, 303
laity, 74
Lake Bangweulu, 447
Lake Tanganyika, 439, 444, 447
Lake Texcoco, 127, 143
Lake Victoria, 444, 447
Lalone, Eugene Galien, 382
language(s), 288, 294. *See also* writing; alphabets and. *See* alphabet(s); Arabic, 94, 286, 288; Bantu family of, 100; Bengali, 286; Chinese, 286, 288; Danish, 288; English. *See* English; French, 287, 670; Greek, 288, 294; Hebrew, 288; Hindi, 286, 288; Indo-Europeans and, 551; Japanese, 286, 288; Korean, 288; Latin, 66, 94, 95, 294, 674; most widely spoken, 286; Persian, 288; Phoenician, 287; Portuguese, 286; Russian, 286, 288; Semitic, 89; Slavic, 416; Spanish, 286, 288; Swahili, 288; Tagalog, 288; Thai, 288; Turkic, 104; Turkish, 288, 565; Urdu, 286; vernacular. *See* vernacular language

Laos: Communists in, 738; as French protectorate, 432, 433; religion in, 204
***Last Supper* (da Vinci),** *p*170
Late Middle Ages: Black Death and, 129, 136–137; Hundred Years' War during, 127, 138; Roman Catholic Church's power declines in, 137–138
***L'Atelier*,** 777
Lateran Accords, 542
Latin America, *m*582, 680–696. *See also* Central America; South America; *individual states*; authoritarianism in, 583–585; colonial empires in, 318–320, *m*319; creoles in, 454; culture in, 585, 687; economic developments in, 683–685; economy of, 457, 459, 581–583; exports from, decrease in, 581, 582; Good Neighbor policy and, 561, 582, 585; Great Depression and, 582–583, 683; main exports of, *m*685; military regimes in, 684–685, *c*690; Monroe Doctrine and, 455; movement toward democracy in, 683, 685; nation building in, 453–459; nationalist revolts in, 453–455; new imperialism in, 457; *peninsulares* in, 454; per capita income in, *m*685; political developments in, 683–685; political movements and revolts in, *c*584; population of, *c*685, 685–686; religion in, 319–320; rule of caudillos in, 456; society in, 685–686; Spain's colonial empire in, 318–320; states in, independence of, 453, 455; terrorists in, 673; trade and, 319, 350, 457, 459, 581–582, 683–684; United States involvement in, 458, 581, 582, 584, *m*684, 686
Latin language, 66, 94, 95, 294, 674
Latins, 66, 67
Latvia: becomes new nation-state, 525; nationalist movement in, 660
Launay, Marquis de, 328
Laurier, Wilfred, 415
***Lavendar Mist*,** 675
Lavoisier, Antoine, 297
law: Code of Hammurabi and, 26–27, 35; common, 120; Roman, 70–71; systems of, 14–15; universal, of gravitation, 296
Law of Nations, 70–71
Lawrence, T. E. (Lawrence of Arabia), 506, 564, *p*564
Lawrence of Arabia (T.E. Lawrence), 506, 564, *p*564
League of Combat *(Fascio di Combattimento)*, 540, 541
League of German Girls, 551
League of Nations, 494, 524, 526; Covenant of, 535–536; Germany joins, 535; Japan withdraws from, 594; Japan's seizure of Manchuria investigated by, 594; mandates supervised by, 566–567, 569; replaced by United Nations, 495; United States Senate refuses to ratify, 534; weaknesses in, 534
Lebanon: France takes control of, 526, 567; gains independence, 711
***Lebensraum*,** 549
Lee Kuan Yew, 744
Leipzig, Germany, 400; Church of Saint Thomas in, 309
leisure: mass, 555; new forms of, 396, 410
Lenin, V. I., *p*518, 520, *p*520, 574; death of, 540, 543, 545; New Economic Policy (NEP) of, 543; rise of, 517, 573; Soviet Union created by, 530, 543; Treaty of Brest-Litovsk signed by, 514, 518
Leningrad, German siege of, 598
Leo X (pope), 173
Leonardo da Vinci, 158, 164, 168, 170, *p*170
Leopold II (king of Belgium), 439
Lepanto, Battle of, 211, 212, 236, 239, 242
Lesseps, Ferdinand de, 438, *p*438
Lévesque, René, 670
***Leviathan* (Hobbes),** 230, 233
Li Bo, 107, 148–149
Li Zicheng, 270
Liao dynasty, 730
Liaodong Peninsula, 470, 484, 512
Liberal Party, 412, 648, 670
liberalism, 371, 373–374
Liberia, 441, 705–706, 707
library: primary sources, 770–781; resources of, using, 254
Libya: seized by French, 438; struggle against Italian rule in, 569; terrorist organizations aided by, 672
Libyans, 29
Liebknecht, Karl, 523
Liliuokalani (queen of the Hawaiian Islands), 415
Lima, Peru, 455
Lincoln, Abraham, 384–385; Emancipation Proclamation of, 385
line of demarcation, 193, 194
lineage groups, 101
Lisbon, Portugal, 220
literacy, 409–410, 450, 742
literature. *See also* poetry; writing: African, 709; Chinese, 106–107, 274, 478; the Enlightenment and, 310; Golden Age of, 230, 231–232; Gothic, 388; Indian, 452; Japanese, 281, 485, 742; Latin American, 687; of the Middle East, 716; modernism and, 421; realism and, 390, 421; revolution in, *c*420; romanticism and, 388; stream of consciousness and, 557, 622; Sumerians and, 27; symbolists and, 421; vernacular, 165
Lithuania: becomes new nation-state, 525; nationalist movement in, 660
***The Little Red Book (Quotations from Chairman Mao Zedong)* (Mao Zedong),** 579
Liverpool, England, 365
***Lives of the Artists* (Vasari),** 170
Livingstone, David, 426, 428, *p*428, 439, *p*444, 444–447
Livingstone, Mary, 444, 446
Livy, 77
Lloyd George, David, 524, 534
Lo Bengula (African king), 436, *p*436, *q*436
Locarno, Treaty of, 533, 535–536
Locke, John, 209, 233, 300, 301, *p*301, 321
Loftus, William, 18
Loire River, 340
Lombards, 122
Lombardy, 371, 376
London, England: Big Ben in, *p*388; the blitz and, 596, 597, 615; first daily newspaper published in, 300, 306; Houses of Parliament in, 388, *p*388. *See also* Parliament, British; language in, 287; population of, 368, 404; theater in, 232
***London Journal*,** 428
London Missionary Society, 428
London *Times*, 329, 378, 535, 592
Long Count (Mayan calendar), 142
López Portillo, José, 689
Lord Chamberlains' Company, 232
Loretto, 408
Lorraine, 381, 524
Los Alamos, New Mexico, 616
Louis XIII (king of France), 217, 224
Louis XIV (king of France) (Sun King), 209, 210, *p*210, *p*223, 223–226, *p*226, *p*291, 308
Louis XV (king of France), 309
Louis XVI (king of France), *p*326, 328, 331, 332, 333–334, 335, *p*337, 341; execution of, 326, 337, 338, 339, 351
Louis XVIII (king of France), 351
Louis Pasteur Institute, 390
Louisbourg, 313, 316
Louisiana territory, transferred to Spain by France, 316
Louis-Napoleon. *See* **Napoleon III**
Louis-Philippe (king of the French), 374, *p*374
Loutherbourg, Philippe Jacques de, 361
Low Countries, 175; artistic Renaissance in, 168–169
Lower Egypt, 27
Lualaba River, 447
Luanda, Angola, 444, 447
Ludendorff, Erich von, 522
Luftwaffe, 597
R.M.S. *Lusitania*, 496, 503, 507, *p*510, 510–513
Luther, Martin, 155, 156, 171, *p*171, *q*171, 172, 173, *p*173, 178, 180, 181–182, 774; advocates break with Catholic Church, 174; excommunicated by Catholic Church, 171, 174; posts Ninety-five Theses, 171, 173, *p*173; rise of Lutheranism and, 174–175
Lutheranism, 174–175
Luxembourg, 168–169; Black Death spread to, 137; EEC and, 645; NATO and, 633; Nazis invade, 597
Luxemburg, Rosa, 523
Lydia, 34
Lyons, France, Reign of Terror in, 340

M

Macao, China, 267
MacArthur, Douglas, 602, 739–740, *p*740
Macartney, Lord George, 266, *p*266, 272
Macaulay, Lord Thomas, 448, *p*448, *q*448, 450
Macdonald, John, 385

Macedonia, 56, 60, 663. *See also* Alexander the Great; as Roman province, 67
Macedonians, 29, 123, 526
Machiavelli, Niccolò, 157, *q*157, 160–161, *p*161
madam-sahib, 450
Madero, Francisco, 458
Madinah, 241; as capital of Arab Empire, 92; Muhammad's journey to *(Hijrah),* 90; pilgrims' visits to, 90, 567
Madras (Chennai), India, 237, 257, 313, 451
Madrid, Spain, 232, 546; baroque style in, 231
Mae Dun, 478
magazines, 305, 306
Magdeburg, Germany, 216
Magellan, Ferdinand, 186, 188, *p*188, 195
Magellan, Strait of, 188
***The Magic Flute* (Mozart),** 310
Maginot Line, 597
Magna Carta (Great Charter) (1215), 116, 120
Magyars, 375; in Austria-Hungary, 414
Mahfouz, Naguib, 716
Mahmud of Ghazni, 109
Main River, 381
mainland states, 201–202, 203
Major, John, 668
making inferences, 205
Makkah, 90, 241, 563, 564; pilgrimage to (hajj), 90, 91, 102, 567
malaria, 439
Malay Peninsula, 110, 192, 202, 203, 204, 431
Malaya: becomes independent, 737; economy of, 433; invaded by Japan, 599; prisoners of war from, as slave laborers for Japan, 611
Malaysia, 744
Mali, Kingdom of, 98, 99, 706
Manchester, England, 365
Manchukuo, Japan, 594
Manchuria, 270, 484, 617; Japanese attack on, 484–485, *p*485, 561, 572, 573, 591, 594; New Order in East Asia and, 595; renamed Manchukuo, Japan, 594
Manchus, 270–271; Korea invaded by, 282; Qing dynasty created by, 270. *See also* Qing dynasty
mandate, 526, 566–567
Mandate of Heaven, 41–42
Mandela, Nelson, 700, 701, *p*701, 703, 704, 705, *p*705, 707–708, 781
Manhattan Project, 616
Manila Bay, Battle of, 432, *p*432
Mannerism, 208, 230–231
manor, 131
manorial system, 131, 162
Mansa Musa (king of Mali), 97, 99
Mantua, Italy, 72
Manzikert, Turkey, 123
Mao Zedong, 575, *p*575, *q*575, 576, *p*578, *p*579, *p*720, 723, 726; death of, 725; establishes the People's Republic of China, 579, 732; Great Leap Forward and, 723–724, 726; Great Proletarian Cultural Revolution and, 724–725, 726; guerrilla tactics used by, 577; Long March of, 575, 577–578, *p*578; mausoleum of, 731, 732; People's Liberation Army (PLA) of, 577–578, 723
map(s): cartography and, 191; military movements on, interpreting, 527; reading cartograms and, 729
Marat, Jean-Paul, 338, *p*338, 340
Marconi, Guglielmo, 395, 397, *p*397, *q*397, 398, 554, 626
Marcos, Ferdinand, 738
Marcus Aurelius (Roman emperor), 70, 74
Maria Theresa (ruler of Austrian Empire), 311, 313, 314, *p*314
Marie Antoinette (queen of King Louis XVI of France), 331, 334, 339, *p*339
Marne: First Battle of, 504; Second Battle of, 522
marriage: annulment and, 179; child, in India, 259; in China, 477; of clergy, 174; dowry and, 163; in Meiji Restoration Japan, 483; in nineteenth century, 406–407; in Renaissance Italy, 163
***The Marriage of Figaro* (Mozart),** 310
Marshall, George C., 632
Marshall Plan (European Recovery Program), 628, 632, 642
martial arts, 270–271
Marx, Karl, 370, *p*394, 397, 571, 573, 689, 690, 691, 695, 726. *See also* Communists; communism; classless society and, 402; theory of, 400–401, 536
Marxist Social Democratic Party, 414
Mary I (queen of England) ("Bloody Mary"), 179–180, 213
Masaccio, 166
mass culture, 554–555
***Mass in B Minor* (Bach),** 309
mass leisure, 555
mass society: emergence of, 403–410; new forms of leisure and, 396, 410; social structure of, 404–406
Massachusetts Bay Colony, 187, 195
Masurian Lakes, Battle of, 504
***Mathematical Principles of Natural Philosophy (Principia)* (Newton),** 290, 296
mathematics: ancient Egyptians and, 30; Arabs and, 94, 191; in the Renaissance, 294; Sumerians and, 27
Matsuo Basho, 281, *p*281
Matthew, Saint, *p*73
Mauryan Empire, 40
May Day, 400
the Maya, 126, 140, 141–142; calendar of, 142
Maybach, Wilhelm, 395, 398
Mazarin, Cardinal, 224
McCarthy, Joseph R., 645–646
McDonald's, 732
McKinley, William, 432
Mecca. *See* **Makkah**
Medes, 33
Medici, Cosimo de', 154, *p*154, 159–160
Medici, Lorenzo de', *p*159, 159–160
Medici family, 154, 159–160, 167
medicine, Scientific Revolution and, 297
Medina. *See* **Madinah**
Mediterranean Sea, 24, 27, 40, 89, 92, 93, 240, 345, 379, 438, 603; Rome becomes master of, 67
Mehmet (son of Süleyman I), 249
Mehmet II (Mehmet the Conqueror) (sultan of Ottoman Empire), 240, 241, 243, 244, 245, 246, 247, 249
Meiji Restoration, 462, 480–484, 740; birth of modern Japan and, *c*482, 571; building modern social structure and, 482–483; daily life and, 483–484; economics of, 481–482; Liberals and, 481; Progressives and, 481; transformation of politics and, 481; women's rights and, 483–484
Mei-ling Soong, 578
***Mein Kampf (My Struggle)* (Hitler),** 530, 549
Mekong delta, 202, 431, 433
Mekong River, 44
Melaka, Sultanate of, 186, 192, 202, 203
memsahib, 450
Menchú, Rigoberta, 691, *p*691
Mendeleev, Dmitri, 387, 389
Menem, Carlos Saúl, 694
Menes (king of Egypt), 24, 27
Mennonites, 180
mercantilism, 195
Mercedes-Benz, 398
mercenaries, 159, *p*159
Merkit, 113
Merv, 112, 115
Mesoamerica: cultures of, *m*141; defined, 141
Mesopotamia, 18, 31, 33, 34, 36, 92, 564; ancient, 24–25, *m*26; city-states of, 24–25; early civilization in, 16, 21, 22; empires in, 25; life in, life in ancient Egypt versus, *c*30; Mongol seizure of, 93; Ottoman Turks take control of, 241; rulers and gods and, 55; Timur Lenk's occupation of, 109
***Messiah* (Handel),** 309
mestizos, 319, 454
Methodism, 307
Metternich, Klemens von (prince of Austrian Empire), *p*371, *q*371, 371–372, 373, *p*373, 375
Mexican Revolution, 458, 584, 585, 688
Mexican War, 456
Mexico, 141, 682, 688–689; American forces sent into, 458; becomes a republic, 455; half of territory lost to United States, 426, 456; Independence Day in, 333, 454; independence declared by, 453, 455; Institutional Revolutionary Party (PRI) in, 584, 688–689; International Women's Year Tribunal in, 686; Mexican War and, 456; NAFTA and, 400, 670; National Strike Council and, 692; oil industry in, 582, 583, 584–585; PEMEX and, 585; revolt in, 453, 454–455; Revolution in, 458, 584, 585, 688; Sánchez Navarro family in, 457; Spanish conquer civilizations in, 128, 186, 189, 194. *See also* Olmec peoples; the Aztec; the Maya
Mexico, Gulf of, 141, 143
Mexico, Valley of, 142–143

Index

Mexico City, 143, 400, 454; student revolt in, 689, 692; UN Decade for Women conference in, 686
Michael Romanov (Russian czar), 228
Michelangelo, 155, *p*155, 156, 167, 168
microprocessor, 627
Middle Ages. *See also* Early Middle Ages; High Middle Ages; Late Middle Ages: Christianity during, 240; Europe in, 129–138; "natural philosophers" during, 293–294; trade revival during, 131
middle class(es): industrial, 368–369; Second Industrial Revolution and, 405
Middle East, *m*565; after World War I, *m*525; Arab-Israeli dispute and, 711, 712, 713–714, 755, 758; British forces destroy Ottoman Empire in, 506; conflict in, 711–716, *m*713, 755, 758; culture in, 716; modern, *m*713; political movements and revolts in, *c*584; society in, 715–716; terrorism and, 673; women's roles in, 716; in World War I, *m*527
Middle Kingdom, 27, 28–29
Middle Passage, 198
Middlebury College, 687
***Midnight* (Mae Dun),** 478
Midway Island, Battle of, 596, 602
migration(s): of Aryans, *m*38; global, 712
Milan, Italy, 132, 175; as city-state, 157, 158–159
militarism: conscription and, 500–501; defined, 380, 501; prior to World war I, 500–501
Milošević, Slobodan, 663, 664
Minamoto Yoritomo, 108
Ming dynasty, 106, 264, 265, 267–270, *m*269, 273, 274
Ming Hong Wu (the Ming Martial Emperor) (emperor of China), 267, 268
ministerial responsibility: defined, 413; political democracy and, 411–413
missionaries, 200
Missionaries of Charity, 736
***Missionary Travels and Researches in South Africa* (Livingstone),** 428, 445
Mississippi River, 321, 366
Mistral, Gabriela (Lucila Godoy Alcayaga), 687, *p*687
Mitsubishi, 571–572
Mitsui, 571–572
Mitterrand, François, 667
mobilization: defined, 502, 612; World War I and, 502; World War II and, 612–616
Mobutu Sese Seko, 705
Modena, 379
Modern Devotion, 173
modernism, 421–423
Mogadishu, 100
Mogul Empire, 238, 253; Akbar's reign in, 255, 256–257; culture in, 259–260; decline of, 257; expansion of, *m*256; grandeur of Moguls and, 255–260; as gunpowder empire, 202; Mogul dynasty India and, 255–256, 448; society and daily life in, 259
Moguls, 109; British defeat in Battle of Plassey, 237, 257, 258; decline of, 257, 448
Mohacs, Battle of, 242
Mohammad Reza Pahlavi (shah of Iran), 566, 702, *p*702, 715
Mohenjo-Daro, 37, *p*37
Moldavia, 379; nationalist movement in, 660
Moluccas (Spice Islands), 188, 192; Portuguese occupy, 202; Portuguese pushed out of, 203
Mombasa, 100
monarchy(ies): absolute, 425; constitutional, 425; new, 138
monastic orders. *See* **religious order(s)**
Moncada, Cuba, 682
Monet, Claude, 422
money economy, 131
Mongkut (king of Thailand), 432
Mongol (Yuan) dynasty, 103, 105, 106–107, 267, 276
Mongol Empire, 105, 112–115, 121
Mongolia, 105, 112, 114, 267
Mongols, 89, 103, 104–105, 112–115, 121, 138, 239, 730
monk(s), 117; orders of. *See* religious order(s)
monotheisim, 32–33, 90
Monroe, James, 455
Monroe, Marilyn, 675
Monroe Doctrine, 455
Montcalm, Louis-Joseph de, 316
Montenegro, 416
Montesquieu, Baron de, 300, 302
Montevideo, Uruguay, *p*459
Montezuma (Aztec ruler), 127, *p*127, 143
Montreal, Canada, 316; international environmental meeting in, 749, 752–753
Moravia, 593
More, Thomas, 179
Morisot, Berthe, 421, *p*421, 422
Morocco, 94, 197, 200; France establishes protectorate in, 438; France grants full independence to, 704; World War I and, 522
Moscow, 138, 598, 659; Napoleon's abandonment of, 351
Moses, 31, 32, 90, 91
Mosque of Córdoba, 95, *p*95
mosques, 95
Mother Teresa (Agnes Gonxha Bojaxhiu), 721, 736, *p*736
Motihari, India, 490
***On the Motion of the Heart and Blood* (Harvey),** 293, 297
motion pictures, 555
motte, 118
Mound Builders, 141
Mount Etna, eruption of, in 1669, 220
Mount Sinai, 32
Mount Vesuvius, 70
the Mountain, 338
Mozambique: Berlin Conference gives Portugal claim on, 440; early European presence in, 199; Portugal surrenders, 704
Mozart, Wolfgang Amadeus, 310, *p*310
MTV, 675
Mu'awiyah, 92
Muhammad, 83, 85, 89, 93, 241, 252; journey of, to Madinah (*Hijrah*), 90; life of, 90; teachings of, 90–91
Muhammad (Khwarizm shah), 114, 115
Muhammad Ahmad (the Mahdi), 438
Muhammad Ali (Egyptian ruler), 438
Muhammad Ture (king of Songhai), 97, 99–100
Mukden, Japan, 594
Mukhtar, Omar, 569
mulatto, 319
Mulroney, Brian, 670
multimedia presentations, developing, 759
multinational corporations, 684, 754
multinational state, 375
Mumbai (Bombay), India, 451
mummification, 28
Mumtaz Mahal, 259
Munich, Germany, 523; Beer Hall Putsch in, 549; Olympic Games in, 676
Munich Conference, 593
Murakami, Haruki, 742
***Mural*,** *p*585
music: African, 101; the Enlightenment and, 309–310; in Japan, 483; modernism and, 423; MTV and, 675; pop, 675; revolution in, *c*420; romanticism and, 389; youth protests and, 646–647
musket, flintlock, 218, *p*218
Muslim League, 571
Muslims, 90. *See also* Islam; pigs taboo to, 449; Ramadam and, 91; rivalry with Hindus in India, 109–110, 449, 451, 571, 734, 758; Shiite, 250–251, 715; Sunni, 243, 250, 251, 715
Mussolini, Benito *(Il Duce)*, 530, 540, *p*540, *q*540, 541–543, *p*592, 598, 603; death of, 604; with Hitler and Stalin, *c*552
Mustafa, 248, 249
Mutsuhito (emperor of Japan), 481, *p*481
Myanmar. *See* **Burma**
Mycenae, 52, 62–63, *p*63, 64
Mycenaean civilization, 48, 51, 52
Mykonos, 65

'N Sync, 675
NAFTA (North American Free Trade Agreement), 400, 670
Nagasaki, Japan, 279, 479, 483; atomic bomb dropped on, 589, 604, 616
Nagy, Imry, 375, 640
Nairobi, 708; UN Decade for Women conference in, 686
Nanjing, China, 268, 467, 468; Chinese republic in, 571, 576, 578; seized by Japan, 591, 594, 611
Nanjing, Treaty of, 467
Nantes, France, Reign of Terror in, 340
Naples, Bay of, 70
Naples, Italy, 132, 160, 175
Naples, kingdom of, 376, 380
***Napoleon Crossing the Great St. Bernard*,** *p*327
Napoleon I (emperor of France), *p*15, 118, 341, *p*343, *p*345, *q*345, *p*346, 371, *p*371, 382; age of, 345–351; coronation of, 327, 345, 346; defeat of, at Waterloo, 327, 345, 351; domestic

Index

policies of, 347–348; Europe under, *m*349; exiles of, 351; fall of, 350–351; Grand Empire of, 348–349; named consul for life, 346; Napoleonic Code and, 15; power seized by, in coup d'état, 326, 343, 345, 346; rise of, 345–346; states at war with, 348–351, 362
Napoleon II, 382
Napoleon III (Louis-Napoleon) (emperor of France), 375, 379, 381, *p*382, 382–383
Napoleonic Code (Civil Code), 15, 347, 348, 351
Napoleonic Wars, 327, 345, 348–351, 362, 440, 454
Nara, Japan, 107
Naroji, Dadabhai, 777
Nasser, Gamal Abdel, 712–713, 717
National Assembly, 442, 667; Declaration of the Rights of Man and the Citizen adopted by (1789), 152, 329, 332–333, 336, *p*336, 340; drafts constitution, 329, 331–332, 334–335, 337, 342
National Convention: called by Legislative Assembly, 337; condemns king, 338; dechristianization policy pursued by, 341–342; factions of, 337, 338; French Republic established by, 326, 338; Reign of Terror and, 337, 338, 339–342, 343
National Geographic Society, 512, 513
National Health Service Act, 644
national holiday, 333
National Insurance Act: of 1911, 412; of 1946, 644
National League, 409
National Liberation Front (FLN), 704
National Socialist German Workers' Party. *See* **Nazi Party**
National Strike Council, 692
nationalism: in Africa, 442, 568–570; alliances prior to World War I and, 499–500, *m*500; Arab, 566–567; in Asia, 573; defined, 350; in Europe, 350, 373–374, 382–384; Hitler and, 549; in India, 451–452, 570–571; in Latin America, 453–459; in Southeast Asia, 434; in Soviet Union's former republics, 660; in the United States, 384–385
nation-state, 333
Native Americans: Catholic missionaries and, 320, 323; Queen Isabella's rules regarding, 194
NATO (North Atlantic Treaty Organization), 643, 648; expansion of, 660; formation of, 628, 633, 644; war in Bosnia and, 664, 757; war in Kosovo and, 664
natural rights, 233
natural selection, 390
Naudet, Thomas, 331
Navajo people, 81
Nazi Germany, 542, 548–553. *See also* Hitler, Adolf; Nazism; Afrika Korps and, 600–601; Anti-Comintern Pact signed with Japan, 592; Austria annexed by, 591, 592; Battle of Britain and, 596, 597, 615; the blitz and, 596, 597, 615; blitzkrieg and, 596–597; collaborators with, 609; conscription and, 592; Czechoslovakia invaded by, 593; divides Poland with Soviet Union, 597; early victories of, 597; economic policies in, 552; *Einsatzgruppen* and, 606, 607–609. *See also* Holocaust; expansion by, *m*593; France falls to, 588, 597; Gestapo and, 601; governing of, after war, 617; Greece seized by, 598; Holocaust and. *See* Holocaust; home front during World War II and, 614; invades Soviet Union, 598, 601, 603, 605, 607; Japan cooperates with, 595; Jews persecuted by, 550, 567; *Kraft durch Freude* ("Strength through Joy"), 555; Luftwaffe and, 597; Munich Conference and, 593; Nazi state in, 551–553; Nazi-Soviet Nonaggression Pact and, 594, 595; Poland invaded by, 594, 596–597; Propaganda Ministry of, 555; Reichstag and, 413, 549, 550, *p*596; resettlement of people by, 606, 607; *Schutzstaffeln* ("Guard Squadrons") (SS) and, 551–552; surrender of, in World War II, 589, 604; surrenders at Stalingrad, 596, 601; surrenders in North Africa, 601; terror and, 551–552; as Third Reich, 551, 592; Treaty of Versailles and, 592; World War II and, 591–594, 596–598, 600–601, 603–604, 605, 614, 663; young people in, 550–551; Yugoslavia seized by, 598
Nazi Party. *See also* Nazi Germany; Nazism: anti-Semitic policies of, 549, 553; Austria controlled by, 592; Hitler expands, 549; Hitler takes control of, 548, 549; Nuremberg laws enacted by, 548, 553; Storm Troops (SA) (Brownshirts) as militia of, 549, 607, 610, 694; takes control of Germany, 550
Nazism. *See also* Nazi Germany; Nazi Party: art and, 556–557; rise of, 549–550; victory of, 550; women and, 552–553, 614
Nazi-Soviet Nonaggression Pact, 594, 595
Neanderthals, 16, 19, 20
Nehru, Jawaharlal, 571, 735
Nehru, Motilal, 571
neo-Gothic architecture, 388
Neolithic Age, 19, 21. *See also* Neolithic Revolution
Neolithic Revolution, 21
neo-Nazis, 668
Nero (Roman emperor), 74
Nerva (Roman emperor), 70
the Netherlands, 348, 350; Austrian, 342; Black Death spread to, 137; Calvinism in, 179, 182, 208, 212–213; colonial interests of. *See* Netherlands, colonial interests of; EEC and, 645; grants independence to Indonesia, 737; Jews shipped from, to death camps, 609; Mennonites in, 180; NATO and, 633; Nazis invade, 597; northern artistic Renaissance in, 168–169; under Philip II of Spain, 212–213; Second Industrial Revolution and, 399; trade and, 159, 187, 195, 200, 202–203, 279, 479; World War II and, 597
the Netherlands, colonial interests of: in Africa, 440; in Indonesia, 201, 429, 737
Neumann, Balthasar, 309
Neva River, 515
Nevsky, Alexander (prince of Novgorod), 121
New Deal, 537, 538, 645
New Economic Policy (NEP), 543, 544
New Granada, 453, 455. *See also* Colombia
New Harmony, Indiana, 370
New Ilium, 64
New Kingdom, 27, 29
New Lanark, Scotland, 370
new leisure, 396, 410
"New Life Movement," 578
New Model Army, 219–220
new monarchies, 138
New Stone Age, 21
New Territories, 467
New Testament, 74, 180
New York, colony of, 195
New York City, 396; cars in, 742; terrorist attacks on World Trade Center in, 657, *p*672, 672–673, 750, *p*750
New York Herald, 439, 444, 446
New York *Morning Post,* 675
New York Times, 535
New Zealand: ANZUS defensive alliance, 744; British Commonwealth and, 744; SEATO and, 634; World War I and, 506
Newcomen, Thomas, 358
Newsday, 661
newspaper(s), *p*410; daily, first, 300, 306; mass, rise of, 409
Newton, Isaac, 290, 294, *p*296, 296–297, 300–301, 301, 302, 418, 557
NGOs (nongovernmental organizations), 758
Nicaragua, 455; American forces sent into, 458; contras in, 688, *p*688, 691; Sandinista National Liberation Front and, 688, 691; Somoza family in, 688, 690–691
Nice, 379
Nicholas I (czar of Russia), 375
Nicholas II (czar of Russia), 411, *p*411, 414, 484, 502, 514–515, *p*515, 516; assassinated, 516, 518; steps down, 514, 516, 518
Nicholas, Saint, 134, 135, *p*135
Niemeyer, Oscar, 687
Niger, 706
Niger River, 100
Niger River valley, 98
Nigeria, 101, 762; civil war in, 703, 706–707; gains independence, 703; Great Britain establishes protectorate in, 437–438; Ibo society in, 200, 706–707; oil industry in, 706; Sokoto in, 441
Nightingale, Florence, 407
Nile Delta, 27, 28
Nile River, 24, 27, 28–29, 30, 444, 447
Nile River valley, 438
***1984* (Orwell),** 490
Ninety-five Theses, 171, 173
Ningxia, China, 114. *See also* Yinchuan
nirvana, 84
Nishapur, 112

Nixon, Richard M., 636, 647, 738; makes state visit to China, 721, 723, 728; resignation of, 666, 669, *p*669; Watergate and, 668–669

Nkrumah, Kwame, 701, 703, 705

Nobel Prize: for literature, 683, 687, 701, 709, 716; for peace, 632, 666, 667, 691, 705, 707, 721, 736

nobility: boyars as, in Russia, 228; castles of, 118–119; in France, 330, 331; Junkers as, in Prussia, 227; in Mogul India, 259; Renaissance, 161–162

Noble Eightfold Path, 39–40, 82

nomads, 20

nongovernmental organizations (NGOs), 758

Noriega, Manuel, 681, *p*681, 691

Normandy, France, Allied forces land at (D-Day), 596, 603

Normans, 287

North Africa, 92; French, British and American forces invade, 601; imperialism in, 438; World War II in, *m*598, 600–601

North America. *See also* Canada; Mexico; United States: civilizations in, 128; Great Britain's colonies in, 320–321; Ice Ages in, 140; industrialization of, 366–367; Seven Years' War in, *m*315, 316; Spain's colonial empire in, 318

North American Free Trade Agreement (NAFTA), 400, 670

North Atlantic Treaty Organization. *See* **NATO**

North China Plain, 730

North German Confederation, 381

North Korea (People's Republic of Korea), 727, 743. *See also* Korea; Korean War; South Korea

North Vietnam, 635–636, 738; Communist regime in, 635–636

Northern Europe, artistic Renaissance in, 168–169

Northern Horizon, 512

Northern Ireland, 668, 671, 672

Northern Renaissance humanism (Christian humanism), 154, 172

Norway, 712; Constitution Day as national holiday in, 333; NATO and, 633; Nazis invade, 597; women's voting rights in, 408; World War II and, 597

Notre Dame cathedral, 126, *p*126, 341

Novotny, Antonin, 640

Novum Organum **(Bacon),** 290

Nubia, 98

Nubians, 29

nuclear proliferation, 750, 754

nuns, 320

Nur Jahan, 257

Nuremberg, Germany, 552, 553, 618

Nuremberg laws, 548, 553

Nyerere, Julius, 705

OAS (Organization of American States), 680, 683, 686

OAU (Organization of African Unity), 700, 703, 705

Observations Upon Experimental Philosophy **(Cavendish),** 297

occupied country, 739–740

Octavian (Augustus), 66, 69. *See also* Augustus

Oda Nobunaga, 279

Odyssey **(Homer),** 53

Official Languages Act, 670

Ohio River valley, 316

oil: in Latin America, 582, 583; in Middle East, 567

Ojukwu, Odumegu, 706–707

Old Bolsheviks, 545

The Old Curiosity Shop **(Dickens),** 477

Old Kingdom, 27–28

Old Stone Age (Paleolithic Age), 16, 20

Oleg, 121

oligarchy, 583

Oliver Twist **(Dickens),** 390

Olmec peoples, 140, 141

Olson, Culbert, 614

Olympic Games: 1968, in Mexico City, 692; 1972, in Munich, 676; 1980, in Moscow, 658, 676; 1984, in Los Angeles, 676; Cold War and, 676; on television, 676

Oman, Gulf of, 715

One Hundred Days of Reform, 465, 470

One Hundred Years of Solitude **(Garcia Márquez),** 687

Onon River, 112

OPEC (Organization of Petroleum Exporting Countries), 714

Open Door policy, 470–471, 572

Opinion, fact and, distinguishing between, 96

Opium War: First, 465, 466–467; Second, 468

Oppenheimer, J. Robert, 616

oracle at Delphi, *p*55

oral histories, 771

Orange Free State, 440

Orange River, 440

Oration on the Dignity of Man **(Pico della Mirandola),** 164

Oresteia **(Aeschylus),** 58

organic evolution, 390

Organization of African Unity (OAU), 700, 703, 705

Organization of American States (OAS), 680, 683, 686

Organization of Petroleum Exporting Countries (OPEC), 714

On the Origin of Species by Means of Natural Selection **(Darwin),** 387, 390

Orozco, José Clement, 561

orthodoxy, 251

Orwell, George (Eric Arthur Blair), 490–491

Osaka, Japan, 279, 280

Osman Turks, 239

Ostia, 70

Otto I (king of Germany), crowned emperor of the Romans, 121

Ottoman Empire, 238, 239–245, 251, *g*252, 253, 421, 438. *See also* Ottoman Turks; art in, 245; Balkan provinces and, 416; British forces destroy in Middle East, 506; collapse of, 526, 560, 565; Crimean War and, 378–379; decline and fall of, 563–565; expansion of, 240–242, *m*241, *c*263; as gunpowder empire, 202, 242; nature of Ottoman rule and, 242–243; problems in, 244–245; religion in, 243–244; society in, 244; World War I and, 506, 564; young people in, 242–243

Ottoman Turks, 175, 190. *See also* Ottoman Empire; Armenians massacred by, 563, 564–565; conquer Constantinople, 236, 239, 240–241, 246; fleet of, defeated by Spain at Battle of Lepanto, 211, 212, 236, 239, 242; join Allies in World War I, 526, 564; rise of, 239–240

outlining, 317

Owen, Robert, 370

Oxford, England, university at, 135

ozone layer, 752–753

P

Pachacuti (Incan ruler), 140, 143–144

Pacific Ocean, 186, 188

Padua, University of, 297

Pagan, kingdom of, 110. *See also* Burma

Paine, Thomas, 153

painting: abstract expressionism and, 423, 674, 675; abstract impressionism and, 556; cubism and, 422; drip, 675; fresco, 166–167; Impressionism and, 422; modernism and, 421–423; Mogul school of, 259–260; pop art, 674–675 and; Postimpressionism and, 422; postmodernism and, 675; revolution in, *c*420; rococo style of, 308, 309; romanticism and, 389; sand, 675; surrealism and, 556

Pakistan, 59; CENTO and, 634; creation of, as independent state, 109, 720, 735, 736; as Islamic state, 571; refugees from, 712; relations with India and, 758; SEATO and, 634; Taliban in, 673

Paleolithic Age (Old Stone Age), 16, 20

Palestine, 33; al-Fatah movement and, 714; Balfour Declaration and, 560, 567; British take control of, 526, *p*560, 567, 712; conflict in, 31, 711, 712, *m*713, 755, 758; during Crusades, 123; Hebrew University of, 563; *intifada* and, 714; Israelites establish control over, 31; Ottoman Empire and, 421; terrorism and, 673, 676; Zionism and, 421, 563, 567, 712

Palestine Liberation Organization (PLO), 31, 700, 714; terrorism and, 673, 676

Palestinian Authority, 714

Pan American flight 103 bombing, 671

Pan-African News Agency, 627

Pan-Africanism, 570, 703, 705

Panama, 690; drug trade and, 691; rebellion in, to separate from Colombia, 458, 691; United States invades, 681, 683, *p*683, 691

Panama Canal: facts regarding, 457; locks of, 457, *p*457; United States involvement with, 457, 458, 691

Panama Canal Zone, *m*456

Pan-Arabism, 712–713

Index

Pankhurst, Emmeline, 407, *p*407
Pankhurst, Sylvia, 403, *p*403, *q*403
Pantheon, *p*72
Papacy. *See also* popes; *individual popes*: Papal monarchy and, 132–133; Papal States and, 132–133, 172; reform of, 182, 183
Papal States, 132–133, 172, 376
papermaking, 44
papyrus, 30
Paraguay, 323, 455
Paris, France, *p*382; Allies liberate, 603; Bastille in. *See* Bastille; capture of, 351; Notre Dame cathedral in, 126, *p*126, 341; rebuilding of, 383
Paris, Treaty of: of 1763, 255, 308, 316, 385; of 1783, 318, 321; of 1856, 379
Paris, University of, 135, 303, 642
Paris Commune, 335, 338
Paris Peace Conference, 523–524, 525
Park Chung Hee, 739, 743
Parliament, British, 382; Acts of Supremacy passed by, 179, 213; Bill of Rights and, 221, 332; British North American Act of 1867 passed by, 378, 385; Defence of the Realm Act (DORA) passed by, 508; East India Company and, 449; emergence of, 120–121; enclosure movement and, 364; Factory Act of 1833 passed by, 363, 369; Government of India Act passed by, 568, 570; Houses of, 120–121, 388, *p*388; National Health Service Act passed by, 644; National Insurance Acts passed by, 412, 644; offer throne to William and Mary, 221; Rump Parliament and, 220; Stamp Act and, 321; Toleration Act of 1689 passed by, 209, 221; while Hanoverians reigned, 320
parliamentary government, 412
Parma, 379
Parthenon, *p*54, 58
Parti Québecois, 670
partisans, 604
passive disobedience. *See* **civil disobedience**
Pasteur, Louis, 389, 390, *p*390
Pastrana, Andres, 696
patriarchal society, 27
patricians, 67, 68, 162, 163
Paul, Saint, 73–74, 134
Paul III (pope), 183, *p*183
***Pax Romana*,** 66, 70
Peace of Augsburg, 171, 175, 177, 217
Peace of Westphalia, 209, 218
peacekeeping forces, 494–495, 757
peanuts, 200
Pearl Harbor attack, 589, 599, 600
Pearson, Lester, 648
peasant(s), 131. *See also* serfs; in France, 330; in Japan, 281; in Renaissance, 162–163; in Russia, *p*383, 383–384
pedagogue, 57
Peloponnesian War, 51, 56
PEMEX, 585
***peninsulares*,** 454
Pennsylvania Dutch, 180
Pentagon, terrorist attack on, 657, 672–673
the *Pentateuch* (Torah), 83
People's Liberation Army (PLA), 577–578, 723
People's Republic of China, 723–728, *m*724. *See also* China; after Mao, 725–726; American relations with resumed, 636; communes in, 724; enter Korean War, 727; establishes diplomatic ties with United States, 721, 723, 728; Great Britain returns Hong Kong to, 467, 721, 739, *p*739, 744; Mao Zedong as creator of, 579, 732; movement for democracy as threat to, 722, 725–726; permanent revolution and, 724–725; President Nixon makes state visit to, 721, 723, 728; Red Guards and, 723, 725, 726; reliance upon Soviet Union and, 728; Shining Path guerrilla group in Chile and, 695, 696; society in, 726
People's Volunteer Corps, 616
Pepsi Foods Ltd., 734
per capita income, *m*685, 725
perestroika, 659
***Perestroika* (Gorbachev),** 657
Pergamum, 60, 67
Pericles, 50, *p*50, 51, 55–56
permanent revolution, 724–725
Perón, Eva (Evita), 694, *p*694
Perón, Juan, 583, 680, *p*680, 693, 694
Perry, Matthew C., 359, 479, 480, *p*480, 487, *p*487
Persia, 92. *See also* Iran; becomes modern state of Iran, 566; earthquake in 1727 and, 220; Mongol attack and seizure of, 93, 105; Qajar dynasty of, 566; Safavid dynasty of. *See* Safavid dynasty of Persia; Safavid Empire
Persian Empire, *m*33, 34; defeated by Alexander the Great, 51, 59; defeated by Arab Empire, 91; war with Greeks and, 48, 55
Persian Gulf, 24, 100, 567, 715
Persian Gulf War, 701, 715
Persians, 29
The Persistence of Memory, *p*556
personal records, 771
Peru, 194, 695–696; drug trade and, 686; Inca in, 194. *See also* Inca; malaria treated by Indians in, 439; oil industry in, 582; Shining Path guerrilla group in, 695, 696
Pétain, Marshal Henri, 597
Peter III (Russian czar), 312, 315
Peter the Great (Russian czar), 223, 227–229, *p*230, 312
Peter, Saint, 73–74, 134
Petrarch, 165
Petrograd, Russia, 515–516, 518. *See also* Saint Petersburg
Philip II (king of Macedonia), 51, 59
Philip II (king of Spain), 188, 212–213, *p*213, 214
Philip II Augustus (king of France), 121, 133
Philip IV (king of France), 137
Philippines, 110, 188, 194, 415; economy of, 433; fall to Japanese, 599; free elections in, 755; government in, 738; language in, 288; religion in, 204; SEATO and, 634; United States acquires, 415, 427, 432; United States authority over, 415, 427, 432, 485; United States grants independence to, 736–737; World War II and, 610, 611
Philistines, 31
philosophe(s): defined, 301; their ideas and, 301–303
philosophy(ies): Arabs and, 94; Greek, 58–59
Phoenicians, 288
photography, 422
photomontage, 556
physics: heroic age of, 557; revolution in, 418–419, *c*420; uncertainty principle and, 554, 557
Picasso, Pablo, 422, 546
Pico della Mirandola, Giovanni, 164, *p*164, *q*164
Piedmont, kingdom of, 375, 376, 379
The Pier and the Ducal Palace, *p*158
Pigs, Bay of, 635, 680, 689
Pilate, Pontius, 73
Piloty, Ferdinand, the Younger, 215
Pinochet, Augusto, 694
Pisa, Italy, 123, 170
Pissarro, Camille, 418, *p*418
Pitt, William (the Elder), 14, 316, 318, 320
Pius VII (pope), *p*346
Pizarro, Francisco, 127, 144, 194
Pizza Hut, 734
plague(s). *See also* epidemic(s): Black Death as, 127, 129, 136–137; bubonic, 137
Plains Amerindians, 141
Plains Indians, 194
Plains of Abraham, 316
planned economies, 508
plantations, 198
Plassey, Battle of, 237, 257, 258
Plato, 49, 58–59, 94, 294
plebeians, 67, 68
plebiscite, 382
PLO. *See* **Palestine Liberation Organization**
Plutarch, 56
Poe, Edgar Allen, 388
poetry: Chinese, 106–107, 148–149; epic, 53, 66; Latin American, 687; romanticism and, 388
pogroms, 421
Pol Pot, 738
Poland, 295; authoritarian regime in, 545–546; becomes new nation-state, 525, 545; Communist rule ended in, 662; death camps in, *m*608, 609; free elections and, 617, 661–662; Germans as ethnic minorities in, 526; Jews shipped from, to death camps, 608; NATO and, 660; Nazi Germany divides with Soviet Union, 597; Nazi Germany invades, 594, 596–597; Nazis' annexation in, 606; Paris Peace Conference and, 524; protests erupt in, 639; revolution attempted in, 374; Russia gains territory of, 312; Solidarity trade union in, 654, 661–662; Soviet control over, 639; Treaty of Brest-Litovsk and, 518; Warsaw Pact and, 634; women's voting rights in, 649; World War II and, 594, 596–597
Poles, 121, 375, 526, 607; in Austria-Hungary, 414;

Index

in Czechoslovakia, 526; in Russia, 500; as slave laborers for Nazi Germany, 609
policy of containment, 632
polis, 53. *See also* city-states
Polish kingdom, 121
political cartoons, analyzing, 539
political democracy: defined, 412; ministerial responsibility and, 411–413; universal male suffrage and, 412; Western Europe and, 411–413
political revolution(s): American Revolution as. *See* American Revolution; French Revolution as. *See* French Revolution; Glorious Revolution as, 216, 221; Mexican Revolution as, 458, 584, 585, 688; Russian Revolution as. *See* Russian Revolution
***Politics* (Aristotle),** 59
Pollock, Jackson, 674, 675, *p*675
Polo, Marco, 105, 189–190, 268, 730
Pompeii, 70
Pompey, 69
Pondicherry, India, 257, 258
Pont du Gard, *p*49
poor nations, rich nations and, gap between, 754–755
pop art, 674–675
popes, 117. *See also* Papacy; *individual popes*; at Avignon, 129, 137
popular culture, 675–676
Popular Front for the Liberation of Palestine, 673
popular sovereignty. *See* **democracy**
population. *See also individual states*: chemical waste and, 752; of China, 274, 466; environmental crisis and, 752; explosion in (1700–1800), 274; of Germany, 403–404; of Great Britain, 403–404; of India, 735; during Industrial Revolution, 367–368; of Latin America, *c*685, 685–686; of London, 368, 404; losses of, in World War II, *g*599; new urban environment and, 403–404; world, 1950–2050, 754, *g*754
Port Arthur, Manchuria, Japanese attack on, 484–485, *p*485
portolani, 191
Portugal: colonial interests of. *See* Portugal, colonial interests of; earthquake in 1755 and, 220; EEC and, 667; goes to war with France, during French Revolution, 339; line of demarcation and, 193, 194; missionary activity and, 200; Muslim fleet destroyed by, 191–192, 202; NATO and, 633; Second Industrial Revolution and, 399; trade and, 109, 191–192, 194, 195, 200, 202–203, 264, 266, 267, 268–269, 279, 283, 319; trading empire of, 191–192
Portugal, colonial interests of: in Africa, 436, 440, 441, 704; in Latin America, 318, 319–320, 454, 455
Portuguese language, 286
Postimpressionism, 422
postmodernism, 675
Potsdam Conference, 618
power loom, 358, 364
Prague, 376, 593; baroque style in, 231
***The Praise of Folly* (Erasmus),** 171, 172
predestination, 178–179
prefectures, 481
Presley, Elvis, 675
Pretoria, South Africa, *p*708
PRI (Institutional Revolutionary Party), 584, 688–689
primary sources: analyzing, 139; checking, 770–771; classifying, 771; defined, 770; interpreting, 771; library of, 770–781; opinions and, 771; reliability of, 770; time span and, 770
***The Prince* (Machiavelli),** 157, 160–161
***The Princess* (Tennyson),** 406
Princip, Gavrilo, 501
***Principia (Mathematical Principles of Natural Philosophy)* (Newton),** 290, 296
principle of intervention, 373
printing: in China, 106, 162, 273, *p*273; of Gutenberg's Bible, 154, 162; moveable type and, 87, 154, 162
privatization, 689
profit, 274
proletariat, 401, 402
propaganda: defined, 503; Fascist, 542; Hitler and, 549, 555; in World War I, 503–504
Propaganda Ministry, 555
protectorate, 431
Protestant Reformation, 156, 171–175. *See also* Protestantism; defined, 171; German politics and, 175; Peace of Augsburg and, 171, 175, 177, 217; reasons for, 172–173; religion on eve of, 172–173; in Switzerland, 177–179
Protestantism: Anabaptists versus, 180–181; Calvinism and, 178–179; versus Catholicism in Northern Ireland, 668; in the Enlightenment, 307; Lutherism as first Protestant faith of, 174–175. *See also* Luther, Martin; Protestant Reformation and. *See* Protestant Reformation; revival in, 674; spread of, Catholic response to, 177–183; women's role and, 181–182
provincial level, 473
Prussia: in the age of Enlightenment, 311, 312–313; army and bureaucracy in, 311; Austro-Prussian War and, 383; Concert of Europe and, 372–373; Congress of Vienna and, 371–372; emergence of, 226–227, *m*227; Franco-Prussian War and, 378, 380, 381, 383; General War Commissariat in, 227; German unification and, 380–381; Germanic Confederation and, 375; goes to war with France, during French Revolution, 335, 339; Junkers and, 227; militarism in, 380; Seven Years' War and, 314–315; uses military to crush revolutions in Spain and Italy, 373; War of the Austrian Succession and, 313–314; war with Napoleon, 348, 351
psycholanalysis, 419
Ptolemaic system, *c*294, 294–295, 296
Ptolemy, 294–295
Pu Yi, Henry ("last emperor" of China), 475
public opinion, manipulation of, 508. *See also* propaganda
puddling, 365
Puerto Rico, 415
Pugachev, Emelyan, 312
Punjab, 736
Puteoli, 70
Putin, Vladimir, 657, 660
pyramid(s): in Egypt, 17, 28, 111; Great, *p*17, 28, 111; Mayan, 141; Toltec, 142
Pyrenees, 117

Q

Qianlong (emperor of China), 266, *p*266, 267, 271–272
Qin dynasty, 17, 42–43, 103–104, *m*104, 105; Revolution of 1911 and, 463, 475
Qin Shihuangdi (emperor of China), 42–43, 45
Qing dynasty, 265, 267, 270–272, 273, 274, *m*466, 775; Boxer Rebellion and, 471, 473; decline of, 465–471; efforts at reform and, 468–469; European imperialism and, 469–470; fall of, 473–475; One Hundred Days of Reform and, 465, 470; Opium War and, 465, 466–467, 468; "self-strengthening" and, 468–469; Tai Ping Rebellion and, 465, 467–468, 469
Quebec, Canada, 291, 316, 385; proposed independence of, 666, 670; siege of, *m*315
Quebrabasa Falls, 446
Quelimane, Mozambique, 444, 447
queue, 270
Quiché Indians, 691
quinine, 439
***quipu*,** 145, *p*145
***Quo Vadis*,** 555
***Quotations from Chairman Mao Zedong (The Little Red Book)* (Mao Zedong),** 579
Quran, 83, 85, 86, 90, 94, 242

R

racism, 420. *See also* social Darwinism; African Americans and, 613, 646–647; defined, 430; Hitler and, 549; imperialism and, 430; internment of Japanese Americans and, 613, 614
Radical Party, 537, 583
radio, 395, 397, 398, 554–555, 626
Raffles, Sir Stamford, 426, *p*426, 431
Rafsanjani, Hashemi, 715
railroads, 360, 365
Rajputs, 109
Ramadam, 91
Ramses the Great (Egyptian pharaoh), 28
Rangoon, University of, 434
Raphael, 161, 168, *p*168, 172
Ras Tanura, Saudi Arabia, 561
Rasputin, Grigori, 514, 515
rationalism, 299
Ravensbruck, 601
Reagan, Ronald, 656, 658, 690, 691, 702; Reagan Revolution and, 669
Reagan Revolution, 669
real wages, 645
realism, 390–391, 421
***realpolitik*,** 380

Red Guards, 723, 725, 726
Red Sea, 29, 93, 98, 438
redistribution of wealth, 579
Reed, John, 514, *p*514, *q*514, 520
Reform Acts of 1867 and 1884, 412
Reichstag, 413, 549, 550, *p*596
Reign of Terror, 337, 338, 339–342, 343, *m*353, 519
reincarnation, 38–39
relics: of feudalism, 330, 332; religious, 134
religion(s). *See also individual religions*: in Africa, 81; in ancient Israel, 32–33. *See also* Judaism; in Australia, 81; in China, 55, 106. *See also* Confucianism; Confucius; deism and, 302–303; in the Enlightenment, 307; Hebrew. *See* Judaism; in India, 109–110; in Japan, 81, 108; in Latin America, 319–320; local, 81; monastic orders and. *See* religious order(s); monotheisim and, 32–33, 90; Navajo, 81; orthodoxy and, 251; in Ottoman world, 243–244; popularity and, 134–135; predestination and, 178–179; relics and, 134; religious orders and. *See* religious order(s); revival and, 674; rulers and gods and, 55; salvation and, 172–173; secularization and, 389; in Southeast Asia, 204
religious order(s): Benedictine, 117, 133; Cistercian, 133; Dominican, 134, 320; Franciscan, 126, 134, 320; Missionaries of Charity as, 736; Society of Jesus (Jesuits) as, 182, 183, 256, 269, 271, 279, 320, 323; women in, 133–134, 736
***Reminiscences* (Schurz),** 377
Renaissance, 157–170; art during, 166–169, *m*167; defined, 157; education in, 165–166; High, masters of, 168, 231; humanism movement of, 164–165, 294; Italian. *See* Italian Renaissance; mathematics during, 294; society of, 161–163
Renoir, Pierre-Auguste, 422
reparations: defined, 524; German, 524, 533, 534, 536
report, writing, 472
representative democracy, 425
representative government, 120–121
republic, 67. *See also individual states*
Republic of Virtue, 340–342
***The Republic* (Plato),** 58
Republican Party, 645, 668, 669
Residence, palace of prince-bishop of Würzburg, 309
revisionists, 401
Revive China Society, 474
Revolution of 1905, 395
Revolutionary Alliance, 474, 475, *p*475
Revolutionary France: Catholic Church during, 334; Committee of Public Safety in. *See* Committee of Public Safety; Constitution of 1795 and, 342–343; Council of 500 and, 342, 343; Council of Elders and, 342–343; dechristianization policy in, 341–342; the Directory and, 326, 342–343; Great Fear and, 332, *m*334; Jacobin club and, 338; Legislative Assembly of, 334, 335, 337; Napoleon and. *See* Napoleon I; as a nation in arms, 342; National Assembly during. *See* National Assembly; National Convention called by Legislative Assembly, 337. *See also* National Convention; new calendar in, 342; old regime in, destruction of, 332–335; radicalism and, 337–343; Reign of Terror in, 337, 338, 339–342, 343, *m*353, 519; Republic of Virtue and, 340–342; slavery abolished in colonies, 341; war with European nations and, 335, 339, 342, 346; young people in, 340–341
***On the Revolutions of the Heavenly Spheres* (Copernicus),** 295
Reza Shah Pahlavi (shah of Iran), 566
Rhee, Syngman, 743
Rhine River, 603
Rhineland, 524, 592
Rhodes, Cecil John, *p*357, *q*357, 440
Rhodesia, 440
Ricci, Matteo, 273
rich nations, poor nations and, gap between, 754–755
***Richard II* (Shakespeare),** 230
Richelieu, Cardinal, 217, 224
Riefenstahl, Leni, 555
Rio de Janeiro, Brazil, *p*681; Earth Summit in, 749, 753
Rist, Johann, 305
***The Rite of Spring* (Stravinsky),** 418, 423
Rivera, Diego, 585
Riza-i-Abbasi, 253
Robespierre, Maximilien, 338, *p*338, 339, 340, 341, 342
***Rocket*,** 365, *p*365
Roman alphabet, 288, 565
Roman Catholic Church: Anabaptists versus, 180–181; Catholic Reformation and, 182–183; elects Polish pope, 662; on eve of Protestant Reformation, 172–173; Fascist regime in Italy supported by, 540, 542; during French Revolution, 334; Gailieo tried by, 290, 292, *p*292, 293; Great Schism of, 129, 137–138; heresy and, 134, 152, 292; indulgences and, 173; Inquisition and, 134, 217; Lateran Accords and, 542; Martin Luther versus. *See* Luther, Martin; Napoleon's agreement with, 347; Papacy and. *See* Papacy; Peace of Augsburg and, 171, 175, 177, 217; popes of, 117. *See also* Papacy; *individual popes*; power of, decline in, 137–138; response of, to spread of Protestantism, 177–183; revival and, 674; role of, 117; sacraments and, 134; schism between Eastern Orthodox Church and, 129, 137–138; Solidarity supported by, 662; Vatican Council II and, 674
Roman Empire, 551; Age of Augustus and, 72; Christianity's development during, 72–74; culture in, 72; daily life in, 71–72; decline of, 74–75; Early, 69–70; Eastern. *See* Byzantine Empire; Egypt as province of, 29; expansion of, *m*69; fall of, 49, 76; "five good emperors" of *Pax Romana* and, 69–70; Holy. *See* Holy Roman Empire; invasions into, *m*75, 76; Late, 74–75; religion in, 72–74, 117. *See also* Christianity; Judaism; Rome in. *See* Rome, ancient; rulers and gods and, 55; slavery in, 71; trade and, *m*69, 70
Roman Republic, 67–68; collapse of, 68–69; establishment of, 48, 67; government of, 68; law in, 70–71; Law of Nations and, 70–71; Senate of, 68, 69; Twelve Tables and, 14, 70
Romanesque style of architecture, 136
Romania: authoritarian regime in, 545–546; communism falls in, 661, 662; following World War I, 525; freedom from Ottoman Empire achieved, 416; Hungarians as ethnic minorities in, 526; revolution in, 662; Soviet control over, 639; Warsaw Pact and, 634; World War II and, 598, 604
Romanians, 375
Romanov dynasty, 223, 228, 516
romanticism, 387–389
Rome: ancient. *See* Rome, ancient; falls to Allies, 603; sack of, by Spanish, 157, 160
Rome, ancient. *See also* Roman Empire; Roman Republic: Colosseum in, *p*71; culture in, 72; daily life in, 71–72; emergence of, 66–67; Etruscans overthrown and, 66, 67; law of, 70–71; Pantheon in, *p*72; Roman state of, 67–68
Rome Treaty, 642, 645
Rome-Berlin Axis, 591, 592
***Romeo and Juliet* (Shakespeare),** 287
Rommel, Erwin, 600–601
Romulus Augustulus (Roman emperor), 76
ronin, 281
***A Room of One's Own* (Woolf),** 622–623
Roosevelt, Eleanor, 495, *p*756
Roosevelt, Franklin Delano, 531, *p*531, *p*561, 597, 599; death of, 604, 618; Good Neighbor policy and, 561, 582, 585; New Deal and, 538, 645; Yalta Conference and, 617–618, *p*618, 756
Roosevelt, Theodore, 485, 511
Rosas, Juan Manual de, 456
Roundheads, 219
Rousseau, Jean-Jacques, 300, 304, *p*304, 305
Roxelana, 248–249
Royal Geographic Society, 444
Royal Road, 34
Royal Standard of Ur, *p*25
Ruhr Valley, 534
Rump Parliament, 220
Runnymeade, England, 120
Russia, 538; in the age of Enlightenment, 311, 312–313; Black Death spread to, 137; "Bloody Sunday" in, 414, *p*414; Bolsheviks in. *See* Bolsheviks; Boxer Rebellion and, 471; boyars, 228 in; under Catherine the Great, 311, 312; civil war in, *m*517, 518–519, 543; colonial interests of, 469; Communists achieve control of, 514, 518–519, 530. *See also* Soviet Union; Concert of

Europe and, 372–373; Congress of Vienna and, 371–372; Crimean War and, 378–379, 383; crushes Hungarian revolution in, 375, 376; the Duma and, 414, 516; emancipation of serfs in, 361, 383–384, 776; expansion of, *m*228; flu epidemic in, 534; goes to war with France, during French Revolution, 339; in High Middle Ages, 121; literacy in, 409; Marxist Social Democratic Party in, 414; Mennonites in, 180; militarism and conscription in, 501; mobilization by, 502; modernization of, 571; Mongols dominate, 121, 138; Napoleon's disaster in, 350–351; new. *See* Russian Republic; Open Door policy and, 471; peasants in, *p*383, 383–384; under Peter the Great, 227–229; Red Terror in, 519; reforms in, 383–384, 413, 414; Revolution of 1905 in, 395, 414; Revolution of 1917 in. *See* Russian Revolution; Romanov dynasty in, 223, 228, 516; Russo-Japanese War and, 416, 479, 484–485; Saint Petersburg is built, 229; Second Industrial Revolution and, 399; Serbia supported by, 501, 502; Social Revolutionaries and, 414; soviets in, 516, 517; sphere of influence in China established by, 470; Treaty of Brest-Litovsk and, 514, 518; Triple Entente and, 411, 416, 499, 500, 505; Turks defeated by, 312; uses military to crush revolutions in Spain and Italy, 373; war with Napoleon, 348, 350–351; withdrawal from World War I, 521; World War I and, 502, 505, 506, 508, 514–515, 516, 521

Russian language, 286, 288
Russian Republic: Boris Yeltsin and, 657, 660; nationalist movement in, 660; uses brutal force against Chechens, 660; Vladimir Putin and, 657, 660
Russian Revolution, 514–519, *m*517, 571, 573, 574; background to, 514–516; beginning of, 497, 515; Bolsheviks and. *See* Bolsheviks; civil war and, 518–519; Council of People's Commissars and, 518; withdrawal of Russia from World War I and, 521
Russo-Japanese War, 416, 479, 484–485
Rustem Pasha, 249
Rutherford, Ernest, 557
Ruzizi River, 447
Rwanda, 707
Ryuku Islands, 484

SA (Brownshirts) (Storm Troops), 549, 607, 610, 694
sacraments, 134, 174
Sadat, Anwar el-, *p*701, 714, 716
Safavid dynasty of Persia, 236, 237, 249. *See also* Safavid Empire; became Shiites, 250–251; culture in, 253; fall of, 237, 250, 251–252; political and social structures in, 252–253; rise of, 250–251
Safavid Empire, 238, 250–253, *m*251, *g*252. *See also* Safavid dynasty of Persia; as gunpowder empire, 202
Safi al-Din, 251
Sahara desert, 81, 98, 200
sahib, 450
Saigon, 431
Saikaku, Ihara, 281
Saint Domingue, slaves rebel against French rule in, 153, 454. *See also* Haiti
Saint Helena, Napoleon's exile on, 351
Saint Lawrence, Gulf of, 316
Saint Lawrence River, 313
Saint Peter's Basilica, 231
Saint Petersburg, Russia, 229, 414, 514. *See also* Petrograd
Saint-Simon, Duc de, 210
Sakhalin, 485
Sakhalin Islands, 617
Saladin (sultan of Egypt and Syria), 123
salon, 302, 306–307
Salon La Tour, 601
salt mine, 102
salvation, 172–173
Salween River, 110
Samarkand, 112, 114, 257
Samarra, Iraq, 86, 94, 95
Samoan Islands, 415
Samsung, 743
samurai, 107–108, *p*265, 281, 480
San Francisco, 617, 756
San Martín, José de, 455
San Salvador, El Salvador, 400
Sánchez Navarro family, 457
sanctions, 495, 595
sand paintings, 675
Sandinista National Liberation Front, 688, 691
Sankore mosque, 99
sans-culottes, 335, *p*335, 337, 339, 340
Sanskrit, 452
Santa Anna, Antonio López de, 456
Santa Claus, 134, 135
Santiago, Chile, 144, 687
Santiago de Compostela, 134
São Paulo, Brazil, 585, 742, 754
Sarajevo, assassination in, 499, 501
Sargon, 25
Sarnath, Deer Park at, 39
satellite dishes, 627
satellite states, 632
satellites, 627, 753
Satsuma, Japan, 480
Saudi Arabia, kingdom of, 672; establishment of, 563, 567; oil discovered in, 561, 567
Saul (king of Israelites), 31
savannas, 98
Savonarola, Girolamo, 160
Savoy, 379, 380
Saya Sang, 429, 434
Scandinavia: Black Death spread to, 137; Lutheranism in, 182; Vikings and, 118
Schanzkowska, Franziska, 516
Schleswig, 381
Schlieffen, Alfred von, 502
Schlieffen Plan, 502, 504
Schliemann, Heinrich, 52, 53, 62, 63–64
***School of Athens*,** 168, *p*168
Schumacher, E. F., 671, *p*671, *q*671
Schurz, Carl, 377, *p*377
***Schutzstaffeln* ("Guard Squadrons") (SS) in Nazi Germany,** 551–552
Schwieger, Walther, *p*510, 510–511
science. *See also* astronomy; mathematics; physics; Scientific Revolution: achievements in, since World War II, 673–674; age of, new, 389–390; in ancient Egypt, 30; ecology as, 752; Islamic scholars, 94–95; new physics and, 418–419; social, new, 303–304
scientific method, 299
Scientific Revolution, 293–299, 300, 418, *c*420; astronomy and, 294–297; background to, 293–294; chemistry and, 297; medicine and, 297; scientific method and, 299; women in, 297–298
Scotland, 214; Calvinism in, 179; united with England, 320
Scott, Walter, 387, 388
sculpture: Benin, *p*87, 101, *p*101; Greek classical, 58; Hellenistic Era, 60; Renaissance, 167–168
Sea of Japan, 480
Sea of Marmara, 240
***The Seasons* (Hayden),** 310
SEATO (Southeast Asia Treaty Organization), 634
secession, 385
Second Continental Congress, 318, 321, 333
Second German Empire, 378, 380, 381, 551
Second Industrial Revolution. *See* **Industrial Revolution, Second**
Second International, 397, 400, 401
***The Second Sex* (de Beauvoir),** 642, 649, *p*649
secondary sources, analyzing, 139. *See also* primary sources
secularism, 157–158
secularization, 389
Sedan, 381
"self-strengthening," 468–469
Selim I (Selim the Grim) (sultan of Ottoman Empire), 241, 247
Selim II (Selim the Drunkard) (sultan of Ottoman Empire), 244, 249
Seljuk Turks, 93, 123, 239
Semitic language, 89
Senegal, 705
Senghor, Léopold, 568, 570, 705
Sennedjem, Tomb of, *p*772
Seoul, South Korea, 400
Seoul (Hanyang), Korea, 282
separation of powers, 302
Sepoy Mutiny (Great Rebellion) (First War of Independence), 448–449, *p*449
sepoys, 448
Serbia, 240, 663; freedom from Ottoman Empire achieved, 416, 501; literacy in, 409; Russian support for, 501, 502; World War I and, 504, 505
Serbians, 375
Serbo-Croatians, 607
Serbs, 121, 525, 526, 545; defeated by Ottomans, 240; ethnic cleansing by, 661, 663, 664
serfs. *See also* peasant(s): defined, 131; emancipation of, in Russia, 361, 383–384, 776; in Renaissance, 162
Seven Years' War, 291, 308, *m*314, 314–316, *m*325, 385, 494
Seville, Spain, 232
Sex Discrimination Act, 654, 672

Sforza, Francesco, 159, *p*159
shah, 251
Shah Jahan (emperor of India), 259
Shaka (Zulu ruler), 440
Shakespeare, William, 230, *p*230, *q*230, 232, 287
shaman, 112–113
Shandong Peninsula, 470
Shang dynasty, 40–41
Shanghai, China, 477, 577, 725; Chinese Communist Party founded in, 575, 576
Shanghai Massacre, 576, *p*576
Shaolin Quan (kung fu), 270
Sharpeville, South Africa, 703, 704
Shelley, Mary Wollstonecraft Godwin, 304, 388
Shiite Muslims, 250–251, 715
Shikoku, Japan, 107
Shimonoseki, Strait of, 480
Shining Path, 695, 696
Shinto, 81, 108
shogun, 108, 280, 281
shogunate, 108, 280
***Shooting an Elephant* (Orwell),** 490–491
Shotoku Taishi (Japanese ruler), 107
Siberia, 469, 518, 613; Japan's interest in, 595
Sicily, 67; Black Death spread to, 137; eruption of Mount Etna in 1669 and, 220; kingdom of, 376, 380; World War II and, 603
Siddhartha Gautama. *See* **Buddha**
***Siddhartha* (Hesse),** 557
Sierra Leone, 437
Sieveking, Amalie, 407
Signing of the Treaty of Versailles, *p*526
Sikhs, 736
***Silent Spring* (Carson),** 748, 751
Silesia, 313, 314, 315
Silk Road, 36, 40, 105, 114, 115
Simons, Menno, 180
Sinai Peninsula, 31, 713
Sinan, 245
Singapore: architecture in, *p*721; as "Asian tiger," 744; British colony founded on, 426, 431; electronic road pricing in, 743
Sinhalese, 735
Sistine Chapel, 155, 156, *p*156, 168
Siva the Destroyer, 39, 83
Six-Day War, 700, 713
Slater, Samuel, 359
slavery: abolished in Cuba and Brazil, 437; abolished in French colonies, 341; abolished in the United States, 415, 437; abolitionism and, 384; Africans brought as slaves to the Americas and, 197, 198; Japanese in World War II and, 606, 611; in Nazi Germany, 591–592, 607, 609; in Ottoman Empire, 242; rebellion against French in Saint Domingue, 153, 454; in Roman Empire, 71; shackled Africans and, *p*186, *p*197; slave revolt in Italy led by Spartacus and, 71; slave trade and, 197–199, *m*198, 437, 447; slaveholders in 1860 and, *m*384; soldiers captured by Mayans and, 141; sources of slaves and, 198–199; as threat to national unity in the United States, 384–385
Slavic language, 416
Slavs, 121; in Austria-Hungary, 414, 416, 500, 501; as slave laborers for Nazi Germany, 591–592, 607, 609
Slovakia, 593; creation of, 662
Slovaks, 375
Slovenes, 375, 525, 526, 545, 607
Slovenia, 227, 240; independence declared by, 661, 663
***Small is Beautiful* (Schumacher),** 671, *p*671, *q*671
smallpox, 144, 299, 389
Smith, Adam, 300, 303
Snowden, Lady, 603
social contract, 304
***The Social Contract* (Rousseau),** 300, 304
social Darwinism. *See also* racism: defined, 420; Hitler and, 549; imperialism and, 430
Social Revolutionaries, 414
Social Security Act, 538, 645
socialism. *See also* communism: "African form of," 705; defined, 370; Industrial Revolution and, 370; Marxist, 400. *See also* Marx, Karl; Second Industrial Revolution and, 400–401
Socialist political parties, 400, 401, 414; in France, 537, 667; in postwar Japan, 740; Second International and, 397, 400, 401
Socialist trade unions, 400, 401, 500
society(ies): classless, 402, 695, 724; consumer, 649; mass. *See* mass society; urban, 157
Society for Revolutionary Republican Women, 341
Society of Harmonious Fists (Boxers), 471
Society of Jesus (Jesuits), 182, 183, 256, 269, 271, 279, 320, 323
Socrates, *p*13, 58, *p*58
Sokoto, 441
Solidarity, 654, 661–662
Solomon (king of Israelites), 31, *p*31
Solomon Islands, 589, 602
Solon, 54
Solzhenitsyn, Alexander, 637, 638
Somalia, 706, 707, 712
Somme, Battle of, *p*497, 498, *p*498
Somme River, 498
Somoza family, 688, 690–691
Song dynasty, 103, 105, 106
Songhai, Kingdom of, 98, 99–100, 197, 200
Sophia (archduchess of Austria), 499, *p*499
Sophocles, 58
Sorbonne, 649
sources: checking, 770–771; primary. *See* primary sources; secondary, analyzing, 139
South Africa: apartheid in, 495, 704; British interests in, 440–441; Cape Town, 440, 444, 446, *p*706, 708; Dutch interests in, 440; European presence in, 199, 200; free elections in, 495, 707; Gandhi in, 451, 452, 570; imperialism in, 440–441; Johannesburg, 705, 781; Nelson Mandela on, 781; racial settlement in, *m*440; sanctions used against, 495; societies in, 100
South African Republic, 440
South America. *See also* Latin America; *individual states*: civilizations in, 128; nationalist revolts in, 455; nations of, 693–696; Spain's colonial empire in, 318–320
South China Sea, 43
South Korea, 400. *See also* Korea; South Korea; as "Asian tiger," 743; free elections in, 755; free market economy of, 743; invaded by North Korea, 634. *See also* Korean War; North Korea invades, 727. *See also* Korean War
South Vietnam, 635–636; United States provides aid to, 720, 738
Southeast Asia. *See also individual states*: in 1200, *m*110; civilization in, 110–111; colonial regimes in, 432–433; colonial rule in, 427, 429–434; cultures of, 110–111; emerging mainland states in, 201–202; in era of spice trade, 201–204; European trade in, *m*203; Europeans arrive in, 202–204; imperialism in, 429–434, *m*431; independent states in, 736–738; Japan seeks raw materials in, 595; political systems in, 204; religion in, 204; societies of, 110–111; trade and, 94; women in, 738
Southeast Asia Treaty Organization (SEATO), 634
Southwest Asia. *See also individual states*: dominated by Muslim empires, 236–261; Neanderthals in, 20
Soviet Georgia. *See* **Georgia**
Soviet Union, *m*544; Afghanistan invaded by, 658; arms race with United States and, 633, 635, 658; Berlin Wall and. *See* Berlin Wall; blockade of West Berlin and, 633; boycotts 1984 Los Angeles Olympic Games, 676; breakup of, 655, *m*659, 659–660; Brezhnev era in, 658; China relies upon, 728; Cold War and. *See* Cold War; collectivization of agriculture in, 545, 547; Congress of People's Deputies established as parliament of, 759; Council for Mutual Assistance (COMECON) and, 632; Cuban missile crisis and, 629, 635, 639, 680, 689; decline of, 657–660; de-Stalinization and, 638, 639; dictatorial regime adopted in, 540, 543–545; end of, 655, *m*659, 659–660; heavy industry in, 638; home front during World War II and, 613; INF (Intermediate-range Nuclear Force) Treaty and, 654, 658; KGB (secret police) and, 657, 658, 660; Khrushchev era and, 638–639. *See also* Khrushchev, Nikita; Nazi Germany divides Poland with, 597; Nazi invasion of, 598, 601, 603, 605, 607; Nazi-Soviet Nonaggression Pact and, 594, 595; new era in, 543–545; plan for Korea after World War II and, 727; Politboro and, 543; Potsdam Conference and, 618; provides aid to Cuba, 689, 690; republics of, nationalist movements in, 660; satellite states and, 632; *Sputnik I* launched by, 626, 628, 635, 638, *p*638, 673; Stalin Era in,

Index

543–545, 637–638. *See also* Stalin, Joseph; Suez War of 1956 and, 711, 712–713; Tehran Conference and, 617; totalitarian control in, 542; upheaval in, 658–660; Warsaw Pact and, 634; World War II and, 591, 598, 600, 601, 603, 605, 613, 630, 637; Yalta Conference and, 617–618, 756

soviets: defined, 516; Lenin on, 517

space exploration, *p*655; American astronauts land on moon, 673, 748, 753; International Space Station and, *p*749; John Glenn and, 780, *p*780; *Sputnik I* launched by Soviet Union, 626, 628, 635, 638, *p*638, 673; X-PRIZE and, 674

Spain: Altamira, 19; American Revolution and, 321; Arab armies occupy, 92; armada defeated by English (1588), 211, 213, *p*213, 214, *m*214; Aztecs destroyed by, 128, 143, 194; Basques in, 673; Black Death spread to, 137; Carthage and, 67; civil war in, 531, 540, 546, 592; colonial interests of. *See* Spain, colonial interests of; Córdoba. *See* Córdoba, Spain; defeats Turkish fleet at Battle of Lepanto, 211, 212, 236, 239, 242; dictatorial regime adopted in, 546; EEC and, 667; exploration in Americas by, 128, 140, 141, 143, 144, 194; fascist regime in, 546; Florida transferred to Great Britain by, 316; goes to war with France, during French Revolution, 339; Golden Age of Literature in, 231, 232; as gunpowder empire, 202; at height of power, *m*213; the Inca conquered by, 127, 144, 194; Italian wars and, 160; line of demarcation and, 193, 194; Madrid. *See* Madrid, Spain; military defeats of, in Latin America, 455; new monarchy in, 138; revolution crushed in, 373; under rule of relative of Napoleon, 348; Second Industrial Revolution and, 399; Spanish-American War and, 415, 427, 432, 458; Thirty Years' War and, 217; trade and, 195, 319; women's voting rights in, 537

Spain, colonial interests of: in Latin America, 128, 186, 189, 194, 318–320, 454–455; in North America, 318

Spanish Civil War, 531, 540, 546, 592

Spanish empire: Age of Exploration and, 194; Catholic missionaries in, 320, 323

Spanish flu epidemic, 534

Spanish language, 286, 288

Spanish-American War, 415, 427, 432, 458

Sparta, city-state of, 54; Great Peloponnesian War and, 51, 56; war with Athens and, 50, 56; young people in, 56–57

Spartacus, 71

SPD (German Social Democratic Party), 397, 401, 522, 523, 643, 667

Spears, Britney, 675

Special Operations Executive, 601

Spectator, 305

Speer, Albert, 614

Speke, John Hanning, 444, 447

Spencer, Herbert, 420

Sphinx, *p*17, 28

Spice Islands. ***See*** **Moluccas**

spice trade, 201–204

spies, 601

spinning jenny, 363, 364

The Spirit of the Laws **(Montesquieu),** 300, 302

sports and contests: deadly games of Central America and, 142–143; elephant fight and, 261; martial arts in China and, 270–271; mass leisure and, 555; new team sports and, 408–409; Olympic games and. *See* Olympic Games

spreadsheet, electronic, using, 580

Spring **(Ba Jin),** 478

Sputnik I, 626, 628, 635, 638, *p*638, 673

Sri Lanka (formerly Ceylon), 203, 673, 712, 735

SS (*Schutzstaffeln*) ("Guard Squadrons") in Nazi Germany, 551–552

Staël, Anne-Louise-Germaine de, 348, *p*348

stalemate, 738

Stalin, Joseph, 530, 542, 543–545, 593, 631, 632, 637–638, 639, 727; Five-Year Plans of, 540, 544–545; Great Purge and, 545; with Hitler and Mussolini, *c*552; as mass murderer, 543; nonaggression pact with Hitler and, 594, 595; Potsdam Conference and, 618; programs of, cost of, 545; rise of, *p*543, 543–544; Yalta Conference and, 617–618, *p*618, 756

Stalingrad: Battle of, 596, 601, 603, 605, *p*605; German surrender at, 596, 601

Stanley, Henry Morton, 439, 444, *p*444, 446, 447, *p*447

The Starry Messenger **(Galileo),** 296

The Starry Night, *p*422

state capitalism, 740

statistics, interpreting, 710

steam engine, *p*395; Newcomen's invention of, 358; Watt's improvement of, 358, *p*358, 363, 364

steamboat, 360, *p*360, 363, 366

steamships, 363

steel: in Industrial Revolution, 359; in Second Industrial Revolution, 398

Steele, Richard, 305

stele, 35, *p*35

Steppenwolf **(Hesse),** 557

Stone Age: New, 21; Old (Paleolithic Age), 16, 20

The Stonebreakers, 387, *p*391

Stonehenge, *p*389

Storm Troops (SA) (Brownshirts), 549, 607, 610, 694

Strait of Gibralter, 92, 98, 241

Strait of Hormuz, 715

Strait of Magellan, 188

Strait of Shimonoseki, 480

Stravinsky, Igor, 418, 423

stream of consciousness, 557, 622

Stresemann, Guatav, 535

strike, 394, 401

Stuart dynasty, 219, 220, 320

student revolts, 642, 646–647, 648, 649–650, 689, 692

stupa, 84

Subedai, 115

Suchodolsky, January, 350

Sudan, 706; British control in, 438; civil war in, 754

Sudetenland, 593

Sudras, 37

Suez Canal, 436, 438, 446, 717

Suez Canal Company, 712, 717

Suez War of 1956, 711, 712–713

suffragists, 407, 408

Sui dynasty, 103, *m*104, 106

Sukarno, Achmed, 737

Süleyman I (Süleyman the Magnificent) (sultan of the Ottoman Empire), 239, 244; world of, 246–249

Süleymaniye Mosque, 245, 246

Sullivan, Louis H., 423

sultan: defined, 93, 242; harem and, 243, 246; janissaries and, 240, 243, *p*243, 246

Sumatra, 203; Mongol fleet launched against, 106

Sumerians, 16, 18; city-states created by, 24, 25; creativity of, 27

Sumitomo, 571–572

summarizing information, 176

Sun Yat-sen, 463, *p*463, 473, *p*473, *q*473, *p*474, 475, 575, 576, 578; death of, 576; honored as founder of modern China, 474; rise of, 474

Sundiata Keita (king of Mali), 97, 98, *p*98, 99

Sung Ying-Hsing, 775

Sunni Ali (king of Songhai), 99, 100

Sunni Muslims, 243, 250, 251, 715

Surat, India, 257

surrealism, 556

Susa, 34

Susi, 446

suttee, 259

Swahili language, 288

Swan, Joseph, 398

Sweden, 229; EEC and, 667; Thirty Years' War and, 209, 217, 218; war with Napoleon, 348; women's voting rights in, 649

Sweig, Stefan, 503

Swiss Republic, 348

Switzerland, 517; Calvinism in, 178–179, 182; Mennonites in, 180; war between Protestant and Catholic states in, 177–178; women's voting rights in, 537; Zwinglian reformation and, 177–178

symbolists, 421

synthesizing information, 619

Syr Darya, 256

Syria, 33, 60, 564; Damascus. *See* Damascus, Syria; France takes control of, 526, 567; gains independence, 711; as part of Arab Empire, 91; terrorist organizations aided by, 672; United Arab Republic (UAR) and, 712

systematic agriculture, 19, 21

Szabo, Violette, 601

Tabriz, Persia, 251; earthquake in 1727 and, 220

tae kwon do, 270

Tagalog, 288

Taghaza, salt mine at, 102

Tagore, Rabindranath, 452
tai chi, 270, 271
Tai Ping Rebellion, 465, 467–468, 469
taille, 330
Taipei, 743
Taiwan, 270; as "Asian tiger," 743–744; Chiang Kai-shek flees to, 579, 723; free elections in, 755; Japan receives from China, 470, 484, 572
Taj Mahal, 237, *p*237, 259, *p*260, 451
Taliban, 673
Tamils, 673, 735
Tang dynasty, 86, 103–104, *m*104, 105, 106, 107, 271
Tannenberg, Battle of, 504
Tanzania, 705
Tatars, 113
Taylor, Humphrey, 703
technology. *See also* Tools: achievements in, since World War II, 673–674; revolution in, 753–754; Sumerian, 27
Tehran, Iran, 566, 702
Tehran Conference, 617
Tel Aviv, Israel, 711; terrorism in, 673
telephone(s): cellular, 753; invention of, 394, 398
television: cable, 753; MTV and, 675; popular culture and, 675, 676; watching, *p*676
Temujin, 105, 112–113. *See also* Genghis Khan
Ten Commandments, 32, *g*32
***Ten Days That Shook the World* (Reed),** 520
Tennis Court Oath, 332
The Tennis Court Oath, 332
Tennyson, Lord, 406
Tenochtitlán, 127, 128, 143
terrorism: attack on Pentagon and, 657, 672–673; attacks on World Trade Center and, 657, *p*672, 672–673, 750; bombing of Pan American flight 103 and, 671; global, 673, 750; growth of, 672–673; at Munich Olympic Games, 676; worldwide response to, 749, 755
Tetzel, Johann, 173
Teutoburg Forest, 68
Texas: independence from Mexico (1836), 456; statehood achieved (1845), 456
Thailand: Angkor capital destroyed by, 110; cannons produced by, 202; as emerging mainland state, 202, 203; maintained as buffer state by British and French agreement, 427, 429, 432; prisoners of war from, as slave laborers for Japan, 611; religion in, 204; SEATO and, 634
Thatcher, Margaret, 668
Thatcherism, 668
theater. *See also* drama: in Japan, 281; in London, 232
Thebes, Egypt, 29
Thebes, Greece, 56, 59
Theodosius the Great (Roman emperor), 74
theology, 136
***Things Fall Apart* (Achebe),** 709
Third Reich, 551, 592
Thirty Years' War, 209, 216, *m*217, 217–218, 226
Thomas, Isaiah, 305
Thrace, 34
Throne of Saint Peter, 231, *p*231
Thucydides, 51, *p*51
Thuku, Harry, 569
Thutmose I (Egyptian pharaoh), 29
Thutmose II (Egyptian pharaoh), 29
Tiananmen Square, 400, *p*722, 731, 732; massacre in, 721, 722, 726, 733
Tianjin, China, 477
Tianjin, Treaty of, 468
Tiber River, 70, 77
Tibet, 104, 469
Tiepolo, Giovanni Battista, 309
Tigris River, 24, 33, 93
Tikal, 141
Timbuktu, Mali, 200; Sankore mosque in, 99
Time, 603
time zones, world, understanding, 641
"The Times They Are a-Changin'" (Dylan), 646–647
Timur Lenk (Tamerlane), 103, 109, 238, 250, 255, 256
Titian, 182
Tito, Josip Broz, 240, 639, 663
Tlatelolco, Mexico, 692
Toghril, 113
Togo, 438
Tojo, Hideki, 573, 595, *p*595, 614
Tokugawa Ieyasu (Japanese ruler), 265, 279–280, 279–282
Tokyo, Japan, 481. *See also* Edo, Japan; earthquake in 1703 and, 220
Tokyo Bay (Edo Bay), 359, 480, 487
Tokyo School of Fine Arts, 484
Toledo, Alejandro, 693, 696
Toleration Act of 1689, 209, 221
Toltec people, 126, 140, 141, 142
Tonkin, 432
tools; in Paleolithic Age, *p*16
Topa Inca (Incan ruler), 143–144
Topkapi Palace, 243, *p*244, 246
Torah (the *Pentateuch*), 83
Tordesillas, Treaty of (1494), 189, 193
Tories, 220
Toronto, Canada, 385
total war, 508–509, 526, 612
totalitarian state, 541
Touré, Sékou, 705
Tours, Battle of, 89, 92
Toussaint-Louverture, François-Dominique, 153, *p*153, 453
townspeople, 162–163
Toyokuni, U., 486
Toyota, 739
Toyotomi Hideyoshi, 279, 282
trade: during Abbasid Dynasty, 93, 94; Africa and, 94; Algeria and, 400; ancient world routes of, *m*41; Argentina and, 400, 459, 581; Australia and, 400; balance of, 195; Black Death causes decline in, 137; Brazil and, 459, 581; Byzantine Empire and, 94; camel caravans and, 94, 98–99, 105; Central America and, 459, 582; Chile and, 581; China and, 70, 94, 273, 466–467, 469–471; commodities and, 476; Congo and, 200; drug, 686, 691, 696; EEC and, 645; embargo on, 689; England and, 159, 194–195, 200, 202, 265, 266, 272; English mission to China and, 265, 266, 272; exploration of the Americas and, 192–193, 194, 195; Flanders and, 131; France and, 319; Great Britain and, 319, 350, 457, 466–467; India and, 94, 187, 195; Italian city-states and, 159, 194; Java and, 400; Latin America and, 319, 350, 457, 459, 581–582, 683–684; Middle East and, 350; the Netherlands and, 159, 187, 195, 200, 202–203, 279, 479; Portugal and, 109, 191–192, 194, 195, 200, 202–203, 264, 266, 267, 268–269, 279, 283, 319; revival of, during Middle Ages, 131; Roman Empire and, *m*69, 70; Safavids and, 252–253; Second Industrial Revolution and, 400; Silk Road and, 36, 40, 105, 114, 115; slave, 197–199, *m*198, 437, 447. *See also* slavery; Southeast Asia and, 94; Spain and, 195, 319; spheres of influence and, 469–470; spice, 201–204; triangular, 198; United States and, 359, 480, 487, 582
trade embargo, 689
trade unions. *See also* labor unions: collective bargaining and, 401, 537; May Day and, 400; Socialist, 400, 401, 500; strikes and, 394, 401
Trafalgar, British defeat of French at, 345, 350
Trajan (Roman emperor), 70
Transvaal, 440
Transylvania, 227
***The Travels of Marco Polo* (Polo),** 190
***The Treasure of the City of Ladies* (de Pizan),** 773
Treatise on Armament Technology, 271
***Treatise on Toleration* (Voltaire),** 300, 302
trench warfare, 504–505; tactics of, 505–506
Tres Riches Heures (Book of Hours), 132
triangular trade, 198
The Tribute Money, *p*166
Triple Alliance, 411, 415, 416, 499, 500, 505
Triple Entente, 411, 416, 499, 500, 505
Tripoli, 438. *See also* Libya
Triumph of Death, *p*127
The Triumph of the Will, 555
Trojan War, 53
Trotsky, Leon, 518, *p*519, 543, 544, 545
Troy, 52, 53, 62, 63–65, *p*64
Trudeau, Pierre, 670
Truman, Harry S, *p*632, 645, *p*727; decides to drop atomic bombs on Japan, 604, 616; Potsdam Conference and, 618; troops sent to Korea by, 727; Truman Doctrine and, 628, 632
Truman Doctrine, 628, 632
Tubingen University, 64
Tudor dynasty, 219
Tunisia: Axis forces surrender in, 603; France grants full independence to, 704; French colony in, 438, 564
Turkey, 62, 246; American missiles in, 635; caliphate abolished in, 563, 566; CENTO and, 634; democratic system put into place, 565; fleet, combined with Indian ships, destroyed by Portuguese,

191–192, 202; Greece invades, 565; join Allies in World War I, 526; modernization of, 565–566, 571; NATO and, 633; Paris Peace Conference and, 524, 525; republic emerges, 560, 565, 566; women in, 716; women's voting rights in, 566
Turkic language, 104
Turkic peoples, 114
Turkish language, 565
Turkish Tripoli, 438. *See also* Libya
Turks: defeat of, in 1687, 227; Holy League against, 212; Ottoman. *See* Ottoman Turks; Russian defeat of, 312; Young, 564
Turner, William, 510, *p*510, 511–512
Tuscany, 379
Tutankhamen (Egyptian pharaoh), 17
Tutsi, 707
Tutu, Archbishop Desmond, 705, *p*705, 707
Twelve Tables, 14, 70
Two Sicilies, kingdom of, 376, 380
***Two Treatises of Government* (Locke),** 233
Tzara, Tristan, 554, *p*554

U 20 (German submarine), 510, 511, 512
UAR (United Arab Republic), 712
Uganda, 703, 707
Uighurs, 104, 114
Ujiji, 447
Ukraine, 518; independence of, 660; Treaty of Brest-Litovsk and, 518; World War II and, 598, 603
Ukrainians, 607; as slave laborers for Nazi Germany, 609
Ulaanbataar, Mongolia, 112
Ulianov, Vladimir Ilyich (Lenin), 517. *See also* Lenin, V. I.
Ulm, battle at, 348
***Ulysses* (Joyce),** 554, 557
Umayyad dynasty, 89, 92, 93
uncertainty principle, 554, 557
UNESCO (Educational, Scientific, and Cultural Organization), 627, 757
UNICEF (International Children's Emergency Fund), 756, 757
union. *See* **labor unions; trade unions**
Union of French Indochina, 429, 432
Union of South Africa, created by British, 441
Union of Soviet Socialist Republics (USSR). *See* **Soviet Union**
United Arab Republic (UAR), 712
United Fruit Company, 582
United Kingdom of Great Britain. *See also* England; Great Britain: birth of, 320; Hanoverians reign in, 318, 320; Parliament of. *See* Parliament, British
United Nations (UN), 648; actions of, to end South African apartheid, 495; conferences celebrating the Decade for Women and, 686; creation of, 495; Educational, Scientific, and Cultural Organization (UNESCO) of, 627, 757; establishment of, 617, 756; General Assembly of, 756, 757; International Children's Emergency Fund (UNICEF) of, 756, 757; International Monetary Fund (IMF) of, 757; Israeli statehood and, 711, 712; Korean War and, 495; League of Nations replaced by, 495; peacekeeping forces and, 495, 757; Security Council of, 757; support prosecution of Korean War, 727, *p*728; Universal Declaration of Human Rights adopted by, 495, 756; World Health Organization (WHO) of, 757; world population projections by, 754
United States: in the 1950s, 645–646; in the 1960s, 646–648; abolitionism and, 384; acid rain and, 758; African Americans and. *See* African Americans; Amish in, 180; anti-Communists in Russia supported by, 518, 519; anti-war protests in, 642, 646–647, 648, 650; ANZUS defensive alliance, 744; arms race with Soviet Union and, 633, 635, 658; authority over Philippines and, 415, 427, 432, 485; Bay of Pigs disaster and, 635, 680, 689; Boxer Rebellion and, 471; boycotts 1980 Moscow Olympic Games, 658, 676; breaks diplomatic relations with Cuba, 688, 689; CENTO and, 634; Civil Rights Act of 1964 and, 642, 647; civil rights movement and, 628, 642, 646–647, 651; Civil War in. *See* American Civil War; Cold War and. *See* Cold War; conscription and, 500–501; constitutional government of, 15, 322. *See also* United States Constitution; Cuba becomes protectorate of, 458; Cuban missile crisis and, 629, 635, 639, 680, 689; Democratic Party in, 668, 669; diplomatic ties with China established, 721, 723, 728; drops atomic bombs on Japan, 589, 604, 616; economy of, 415; Emancipation Proclamation and, 385; Equal Pay Act passed in, 654, 672; expansion abroad and, 415; flu epidemic in, 534; grants independence to the Philippines, 736–737; Great Depression and, 532, 538; Guam acquired by, 415; Hitler declares war on, 600; home front during World War II and, 613–614; House of Representatives of, 322, 669; Independence Day in, 333; Industrial Revolution in, *g*366, 366–367; INF (Intermediate-range Nuclear Force) Treaty and, 654, 658; invades Panama, 681, 683, *p*683, 691; involvement of, in Latin America, 458, *m*684, 686; isolationism policy and, 597; Japanese Americans to internment camps during World War II, 613, *p*613, 614; Latin American investment by, 581, 582, 584; Marshall Plan and, 628, 632; Mennonites in, 180; Mexican War and, 456; NAFTA and, 670; nationalism in, 384–385; NATO and, 633; neutrality acts passed in, 597; New Deal in, 537, 538, 645; Open Door policy and, 470–471; Panama Canal and, 457, 458, 691; at Paris Peace Conference, 523, 524; Pearl Harbor attacked by Japan, 589, 599, 600; plan for Korea after World War II and, 727; policy of containment and, 632; Potsdam Conference and, 618; Puerto Rico acquired by, 415, 458; relations with Japan in early 1900s, 485; Republican Party in, 645, 668, 669; SEATO and, 634; Senate of, 322, 534, 669; Sex Discrimination Act passed in, 654, 672; slavery and, 384–385, 415, 437; Social Security Act and, 538, 645; Spanish-American War and, 415, 427, 432, 458; stock market crash in, 533, 536; Suez War of 1956 and, 711, 712–713; Supreme Court of, 322; Tehran Conference and, 617; terrorist attacks in, 657, 672–673, 749, 750, 755; trade and, 359, 480, 487, 582; Vietnam War and, 629, 631, 635–636, 646–647, 648, 720, 737–738; War of 1812 and, 384; women's voting rights in, 408; Works Progress Administration (WPA) and, 533, 538; World War I and, 508, 509, 521, 522; World War II and, 588, 589, 599–600, 601, 602, 603, 604, 613–614; Yalta Conference and, 617–618, 756; youth protests and, 646–647, 648
United States Constitution, 321, 332; adoption of, 15; amendments following Civil War and, 415; Baron de Montesquieu and, 302; Bill of Rights and, 322, 373; federal system created by, 322; John Locke and, 233; ratification of, 291, 322; separation of powers and, 302
Universal Declaration of Human Rights, 495, 756, *q*756
universal education, 408–410
universal law of gravitation, 296
universal male suffrage: defined, 374; political democracy and, 412; in Second French Republic, 374, 375
university(ies): classroom in, *p*136; curricula at, 135–136; in Europe, first, 135; rise of, during High Middle Ages, 129, 135–136; theology as subject at, 136
Untouchables, 38
Upper Egypt, 27
Ur, 25; Royal Standard of, *p*25
Urals, 518, 613, 638
Urban II (pope), 123
urban society, 157
Urdu, 286
Urgench, 112, 115
Uruguay, 455, *p*459
Uruk, 18, *p*25
USSR (Union of Soviet Socialist Republics). *See* **Soviet Union**
Utica, New York, 366
Uzbekistan, 660

Vaal River, 440
Vaisyas, 37
van Eyck, Jan, 164, 169
van Gogh, Vincent, 422
Vandals, 76
Vanderbilt, Consuelo, 405
Varennes, France, 334
Vargas, Getúlio, 581, *p*581, *q*581, 583–584
Vasari, Giorgio, 170
vassals, 118–119
Vatican City, 540, 542
Vatican Council II, 674
Vedas, 38
Vega, Lope de, 232
Venetia, 376, 379, 380
Venezuela, 455; oil industry in, 582
Venice, Italy, 123, 132; as city-state, 158–159
Veracruz, 140, 141, 143
Verbiest, Ferdinand, 267
Verdun, Battle of, 503, 506
vernacular language: Catholic mass in, 674; literature in, 165
vernacular literature, 165
Versailles: Estates-General meets at, 331; palace at, *p*209, *p*224, 224–225, *p*225, 243, 308, 309, 381; Treaty of. *See* Versailles, Treaty of
Versailles, Treaty of, 522, 525; French demand strict enforcement of, 534, 535; Hitler's violations of, 588, 592; signing of, 497, 521, 524, *p*526; unhappiness with, 533; War Guilt Clause of, 524
Vesalius, Andreas, 293, 297
Vespucci, Amerigo, 186, *p*186, 193
Vesuvius, 70
viceroy, 449
Vichy France, 597
Victor Emmanuel II (king of Italy), 379, 380
Victor Emmanuel III (king of Italy), 542, 603
Victoria (queen of the United Kingdom), 361, *p*361, 382, 436, 445, 466–467; named "Empress of India," 448, 449
Victoria Falls, 426, *p*426, 445
Victorian Age, 382, 405, 407
Vienna, Austria, 383, 419; baroque style in, 231; Congress of. *See* Congress of Vienna; Ottomans defeated at, 236, 239, 242
Vienna Academy of Fine Arts, 548
Vietminh, 737–738
Vietnam, 43; Can Vuong organization in, 434; Chinese invasion of, 110; Chinese reconquer, 267, 268; civil war in, 203; Communists in, 573, 574, 737–738; Confucianism adopted by, 110; as emerging mainland state, 201–202, 203; as French protectorate, 427, 431, 434, 435; kingship in, 204; Mongol armies advance into, 106; religion in, 204; reunification of, under Communist rule, 738; World War II and, 610, 611
Vietnam War, 629, 631, 635–636, *m*737, 737–738; domino theory and, 635–636, 738; stalemate and, 738; youth protests in the United States and, 642, 646–647, 648, 650
Vikings, 118; Swedish, 121
Vinci, Leonardo da. *See* **Leonardo da Vinci**
***The Vindication of the Rights of Women* (Wollstonecraft),** 291, 305
Virgil, 66, *p*66, 72, 165
Virgin Mary, 135
Virginia, University of, *p*72
Visconti family, 157, 159
Vishnu the Preserver, 39, 83
Visigoths, 66, *76*
vizier, grand, 243
Volga River, 121, 518, 601, 605, 613
Voltaire, 300, *p*300, *q*300, 302–303, 311; deism and, 302–303

wabenzi, 706
Walachia, 241, 379
Walesa, Lech, 654, 661–662, *p*662
Walpole, Robert, 318, 320
Wang Tao, *q*475
war communism, 519, 543
war crimes trials, 618
War of 1812, 384
war of attrition, 506
War of the Austrian Succession, 308, 313–314, 316
Warhol, Andy, 674–675
Warren, Earl, 647
Warsaw: Grand Duchy of, 348; Soviet troops occupy, 603
Warsaw Pact, 634
Washington, George, 99, 321, *p*321, 494
Washington, D.C., terrorist attacks and, 657, 672–673
Washington Conference, 572
Watergate, 668–669
Waterloo, Napoleon's defeat at, 327, 345, 351
watermills, 130
Watt, James, 358, 363, 364
Watteau, Antoine, 309
***The Wealth of Nations* (Smith),** 300, 303
weapons: arms race and, 633, 635, 658; atomic bomb and. *See* atomic bomb(s); flintlock, 218, *p*218; gunpowder and. *See* gunpowder; INF (Intermediate-range Nuclear Force) Treaty and, 654, 658; nuclear, 671, 672, 750, 754; women protest against, 671, 672
Web site, evaluation of, 443
Weimar Republic: arts and, 556; creation of, 522, 523, 537; first reparation payment made by, 534; Hitler and, 549–550; inflation in, 534–535; joins League of Nations, 535; problems of, 537; Reichstag and, 413, 549, 550, *p*596
welfare state, 644
Wellington, Duke of, 327, *p*327, 351
Wesley, John, 307, *p*307
West Africa. *See also individual states*: agriculture of, *m*125; Gold Coast of, 191, 199, 437, 568, 703. *See also* Ghana; imperialism in, 436–438; royal kingdoms of, 98–100; slave trade and, 437; trade and, *m*99
The West African Pilot, 570
West Bank, 713
West Berlin: Berlin Air Lift and, 631, 633, *m*633; Soviet blockade of, 633; wall between East Berlin and. *See* Berlin Wall
West Germany. *See also* East Germany; Germany: Christian Democratic Union (CDU) in, 643, 667; creation of, 633; economic miracle of, 643, 644; EEC and, 645; NATO and, 633; reunification and, 655, 658, 662–663, 667–668
West India Company, 195
West Indies, Seven Years' War in, *m*325
West Pakistan: becomes Pakistan, 736. *See also* Pakistan; created from India, 734–735, 736
Western Europe. *See also individual states*: Marshall Plan and, 628, 642; political democracy and, 411–413; recovery of from devastation of World War II, 642–644; unity in, move toward, 644–645; winds of change in, 666–668
Western Roman Empire. *See* **Roman Empire**
Westminster Abbey, 447
Westphalia, Peace of, 209, 218
Wheel of Law, 82
Whigs, 220
Whitestown, New York, 367
Whitney, Eli, 384
WHO (World Health Organization), 757
***A Wild Sheep Chase* (Murakami),** 742
William and Mary (king and queen of England), 221, *p*221
William I (king of Prussia and emperor of the Second German Empire), 378, 380, 381, *p*381
William II (king of Prussia and emperor of Germany), 413, *p*413, 416, 501, *q*501, *p*501, 507, 522, 537
William of Normandy (William I) (king of England), 119–120
William the Silent (prince of Orange), 213
Wilson, Woodrow, 508, 511, 523, 524, 526, 534
windmills, 130
Winkelmann, Maria, 298
Winter Palace, 514, 518
witchcraft, 217
Wittenberg, Germany, 174; Castle Church in, 173
Wittenberg, University of, 173
Wolfe, James, 291, *p*291, 316
Wollstonecraft, Mary, 291, 304, *p*304, 305
women: in African society, 708–709; in China, 275, 477; discrimination and, 738, 755; as domestic servants, 406; experiences of, in nineteenth century, 406–408; in Fascist Italy, 542; feminism and, 407–408, 649; footbinding and, 275; under French Civil Code, 347; in French Revolution, 341; gender gap and, 755; on home front in World War II, 613; in India, 259, 738; in industrial working class, 369–370; international conferences regarding, 686; Islam and, 94; in Japan, 280, 281, 483–484, 614, 742; in Latin America, 686; in the Middle East, 716; in Mogul India, 259;

Nazism and, 552–553, 614; in Ottoman society, 244; pay and, 649, 654, 671, 672, 738, 755; in People's Republic of China, 723, 726; in postwar world, 649; protest American nuclear missiles in Britain, 671, 672; Protestantism's effect on, 181–182; in religious orders, 133–134, 736; rights of. *See* women, rights of; in Scientific Revolution, 297–298; Second Industrial Revolution and, 406; in Southeast Asia, 738; as spies in World War II, 601; in Stalin Era Soviet Union, 545; total war and, 508–509, 612; in Turkey, 566; women's liberation movement and, 649, 672; working, unfortunate situation of, 777

women, rights of: movement for, 305, 407–408, 649, 671–672, 686; voting, 408, 537, 649

Women of Algiers, *p*389

women's liberation movement, 649, 672

Women's Social and Political Union, 403, 407–408

Woods Hole Oceanographic Institution, 512, 513

Woodville, Richard, 497

Woolf, Virginia, 622–623

Worcester Magazine, 305

Wordsworth, William, 388, 389

working class(es): emergence of mass society and, 406; industrial. *See* industrial working class(es)

Works Progress Administration (WPA), 533, 538

world economy, 400

World Health Organization (WHO), 757

world time zones, understanding, 641

World Trade Center attack, 657, *p*672, 672–673, 750, *p*750

World Trade Organization (WTO), 726

World War I (1914–1918), 498, 499–509; in the air, 506; Allied Powers (Allies) in, 497, 505, 506, 507–508, 518, 521, 522, 524, 526, 564. *See also* France; Great Britain; Russia; United States; assassination of Archduke Ferdinand and, 496, 499, 501; beginning of, 395; black Africans fight in, 568, 569; bombing of cities during, 615; Central Powers in, 506, 521. *See also* Austria-Hungary; Germany; Italy; democratic states after, 537–538; on eastern front, 504–505; end of, 521–526; in Europe, *m*507; Europe's map after, *m*525, 525–526; great slaughter and, 505–506; home front and, 508–509; illusions and, 503–504; last year of, 521–523; legacy of, 526, 778; Middle East in, *m*525; naval war in, 507–508; outbreak of, 499, 501–502; peace settlements and, 523–526; rise of dictatorial regimes after, 540–546, 548–553; road to, 499–502; stalemate and, 504–505; timeline and, 494; as total war, 508–509, 526; trench warfare and, 504–506; United States enters, 497, 503, 507–508, 521; as war of attrition, 506; on western front, 504, 521; widening of, 506

World War II (1939–1945), 588–618; Allied offenses in, *m*599, 600–602; Allies in. *See* Great Britain; Soviet Union; United States; in Asia, 594–595, 599–600, 602, *m*602, 604, 610–611; Axis offenses in, *m*599; Axis powers in. *See* Fascist Italy; Japan; Nazi Germany; balance of power after, *m*634; battles in, timeline of, *g*600; bombing of cities during, 615–616; course of, 596–604; D-Day in, 596, 603; in Europe, 591–594, 596–598, *m*598, 600–601, 603–604; Europe after, *m*617; German path to war and, 591–594, 778; Grand Alliance in. *See* Great Britain; Soviet Union; United States; Japanese path to war and, 594–595; last years of, 603–604; mobilization of peoples on home fronts and, 612–616; population losses in, *g*599; timeline and, 494, 591; as total war, 612; war crimes trials following, 618; women as spies in, 601

World Wide Web, 749, 753

Worms, Germany, 171, 174

WPA (Works Progress Administration), 533, 538

Wright, Frank lloyd, 423

Wright, Orville and Wilbur, 397, 399

writing. *See also* language(s); literature: in ancient Egypt, 30; cuneiform system of, 27; Egyptian hieroglyphics and, 30, 288; hieroglyphics and, 30, 142, 288; Mayan hieroglyphics and, 142, 288; in new civilizations, 22; report, 472; Sanskrit and, 452; Sumerians and, 27

Wuhan, China, 477, 576

Würzburg, Bishop's Palace at, 309

Xavier, Francis, 279

Xi Xia, China, 114, 115

Xian Feng (emperor of China), 470

Xiao-huang Yin, 781

Xiongnu, 42

X-PRIZE, 674

Yahweh, 32

Yalta Conference, 617–618, 756

Yamato clan, 107

Yangtze River (Chang Jiang), 106, 467, 576

Yarmuk, 91, 123

Yasuda, 571–572

Yathrib, 90. *See also* Madinah

Yeltsin, Boris, 657, *p*659, 660

Yi dynasty, 282

Yinchuan, China, 114

yoga, 39

Yong Le (emperor of China), 268, 276

Yongan, China, 468

Yorktown, Battle of, 321

Young Kikuyu Association, 569

Young Turks, 564

Yuan (Mongol) dynasty, 103, 105, 106–107, 267, 276

Yuan Shigai, 473, 475–476

Yucatán Peninsula, 126, 141, 142

Yugoslavia: authoritarian regime in, 545–546; becomes independent republic, 523, 525, 545; calls for independence in, 663; Communist Party collapses in, 663; disintegration of, 240, 663; ethnic divisions in, 755, 758; former, *m*663; Nazis seize, 598; Serbs, Croats, Slovenes, Macedonians, and Albanians as ethnic minorities in, 526; Tito's control in, 639, 663; war in Bosnia and, 663–664; war in Kosovo and, 664; World War II and, 598

zaibatsu, 571–572, 741

Zaire, 703

***The Zambezi and Its Tributaries* (Livingstone),** 446

Zambezi River, 100, 445, 446

zamindars, 256, 450

Zanzibar, 444, 447

Zapata, Emiliano, 427, *p*427, 458

Zen Buddhism, 270

Zhang Zhidong, 465, *p*465, *q*465

Zheng He, voyages of, 264, 268, *m*268

Zhongdu, China, 114. *See also* Beijing

Zhou dynasty, 41–42

Zhu Yuanzhang (emperor of China), 106

Zimbabwe, 100, 426, 707

Zionism, 420–421, 563, 567, 712

Zola, Émile, 421

Zulu people, 427, 440

Zürich, Switzerland, 178

Zwingli, Huldrych, 178, 774

Zwinglian reformation, 177–178

Acknowledgements and Photo Credits

Acknowledgements

148 "Taking Leave of a Friend" by Li Po, translated by Ezra Pound, from *Personae*, copyright (c) 1926 by Ezra Pound. Reprinted by permission of New Directions Publishing Corp.
149 "Hard Is the Journey" from Li Po and Tu Fu: *Poems*, translation copyright (c) 1973 by Arthur Cooper. Reprinted by permission of Penguin Books Ltd.
354 Excerpt from *Candide* by Voltaire, translated by Robert M. Adams. Reprinted by permission of W.W. Norton and Company.
490 Excerpt from "Shooting an Elephant" in *Shooting an Elephant and Other Essays* by George Orwell, copyright 1950 by Sonia Brownell Orwell and renewed 1978 by Sonia Pitt-Rivers, reprinted by permission of Harcourt, Inc.
622 Excerpt from Chapter 3 in *A Room of One's Own* by Virginia Woolf, copyright (c) 1929 by Harcourt, Inc. and renewed 1957 by Leonard Woolf, reprinted by permission of the publisher.
646 "The Times They Are A-Changin'" by Bob Dylan. Copyright (c) 1963, 1964 by Warner Bros. Inc. Copyright renewed 1991 by Special Rider Music. All rights reserved. International copyright secured. Reprinted by permission.
762 "Civil Peace" from *Girls at War and Other Stories* by Chinua Achebe. Copyright (c) 1972, 1973 by Chinua Achebe. Reprinted by permission of Doubleday, a division of Random House, Inc.
772 Excerpt from *Ancient Near Eastern Texts: Relating to the Old Testament*, edited by James B. Pritchard. Copyright (c) 1950, 1955, 1969, renewed 1978 by Princeton University Press. Reprinted by permission of Princeton University Press.
773 Excerpt from *The Treasure of the City of Ladies* by Christine de Pizan, translated by Sarah Lawson. Copyright (c) 1985 by Sarah Lawson. Reprinted by permission of Penguin Books Ltd.
779 Excerpt from *Ghandi in India: In His Own Words*. Copyright (c) 1987 Navajivan Trust. Reprinted by permission of the University Press of New England.
779 Excerpt from *Nazism: A History in Documents and Eyewitness Accounts, Volume 2* by J. Noakes and G. Pridham. Copyright (c) 1968, Department of Archaeology, University of Exeter. Reprinted by permission.
781 Excerpt from "China's Gilded Age" by Xiao-huang Yin. *The Atlantic Monthly*, April 1994. Reprinted by permission.

Glencoe would like to acknowledge the artists and agencies who participated in illustrating this program: Morgan-Cain & Associates; Ortelius Design, Inc.; QA Digital.

Photo Credits

v (t)AKG London; (b)SuperStock, Inc.; **vi** The Metropolitan Museum of Art, Gift of Lincoln Kirstein, 1959 (JP 3276), photograph by Otto E. Nelson; **vii** Morris, Christopher/Black Star; **xi** United Nations Photo Library; **xii** The Bodleian Library, Oxford, Ms. Bodl. 264, fol.219R; **xiv** Snark/Art Resource, NY; **xviii** (l)Boltin Picture Library; (c)Museo Archeologico, Chusi, Italy/Canali PhotoBank, Milan/SuperStock, Inc.; (r)Michael Holford; **xv** (l)Bettmann/Corbis; (c)Seidman Collection/Culver Pictures, Inc.; (r)Mary Evans Picture Library; **xix** Bettmann/Corbis; (book) Matt Meadows; **xx** (t Beatles) AP/Wide World Photos; (bl earth)PhotoDisc; (bc shuttle)PhotoDisc; (br circuit board)PhotoDisc; **xxi** Digital Stock; **xxiv** PhotoDisc; **xxv** PhotoDisc; **1** (t)Dallas and John Heaton/Corbis; (c)Papilio/Corbis; (b)Owen Franken/Corbis; **9** AFP/Corbis; **12** Réunion des Musées Nationaux/Art Resource, NY; **16** (c)AP/Wide World Photos; (tl)Michael Holford; **17** (b)Art Resource, NY; (r)Asian Art & Archeology Inc./CORBIS; (t)SuperStock; (l)Erich Lessing/Art Resource, NY; **18** Nik Wheeler/CORBIS; **20** CORBIS/Sygma; **24** Erich Lessing/Art Resource, NY; **25** Michael Holford; **28** (r)O. Louis Mazzatenta; (l)O. Louis Mazzatenta/National Geographic Image Collection; **29** (t)SuperStock; (b)Bettman/CORBIS; **31** (t)Stock Montage/SuperStock; (b)Matthews/Network/SABA; **35** Musee de Louvre, Paris/E.T. Archives/SuperStock; **36** Robert Frerck/Odyssey/Chicago; **37** (l)Robert Harding Picture Library; (r)Borromeo/Art Resource, NY; **39** Christies, London/Bridgeman Art Library/SuperStock; **40** (r)Viren Desai/Dinodia Picture Agency; (l)Ancient Art & Architecture Collection; **42** Keren Su/CORBIS; **44** (l)Ontario Science Centre; (r)Wolfgang Kaehler/CORBIS; **45** Robert Harding Picture Library; **48** (br)Art Resource, NY; (bl)David Lees/CORBIS; (c)Nimatallah/Art Resource, NY; **49** (t)Ric Ergenbright/Stone; (c)Nimatallah/Art Resource, NY; (b)Art Resource, NY; **50** Stock Montage; **51** Erich Lessing/Art Resource, NY; **52** SuperStock International; **53** Nimatallah/Art Resource, NY; **54** Bill Bachmann/Photo Researchers; **55** (t)Erich Lessing/Art Resource, NY; (b)Bridgeman Art Library; **56** Michael Holford; **57** Museo Delle Terme, Rome/E.T. Archives/SuperStock; **58** Scala/Art Resource, NY; **59** Musee de Louvre, Paris/E.T. Archives/SuperStock; **61** Archivo Iconografico, S.A./CORBIS; **62** Kunsthistorisches Museum, Vienna; **64** Robert Frerck/Woodfin Camp/PictureQuest; **65** (b)Mykonos Archaelogical Museum, Mykonos, courtesy of the Hellenic Republic Ministry of Culture; (t)James L. Stanfield; **66** Francis Schroeder/SuperStock; **67** North Wind Picture Archive; **71** Pictor; **72** (l)Sean Sexton Collection/CORBIS; (r)Rob Crandall/Stock Boston; **73** (t)BridgemanArt Library; (b)Scala/Art Resource, NY; **76** Hagia Sophia, Istanbul, Turkey/E.T. Archives, London/SuperStock; **77** North Wind Picture Archives; **81** (cr)Edward Parker/Hutchison Library; (cl)Michael Freeman/CORBIS; (t)Paul Chesley/Stone; (b)L. Clarke/CORBIS; **82** (b)Bibliotheque Nationale, Paris, France/Bridgeman Art Library Int'l. Ltd.; (c)Victoria & Albert Museum, London/Art Resource; (t)The Newark Museum/Art Resource; **83** (c)CORBIS; (b)The Jewish Museum, NY/Art Resource; (t)CORBIS; **84** (t)Bettmann/CORBIS; (b)Ma Wenlin/Sovfoto/Eastfoto/ PictureQuest; (c)Phil Schermeister/CORBIS; **85** (c)Peter Sanders/HAGA /The Image Works/The Image Works, Inc.; (b)Bill Aron/Stone; (t)FPG International; **86** (bl)Dave Bartuff/CORBIS; (cl)Art Resource, NY; (br)Lynn Abercrombie/National Geographic Image Collection; (cr)Ancient Art & Architecture; **87** (c)Erich Lessing/Art Resource, NY; (t)Art Resource, NY; (br)Bridgeman Art Library; (bl)SuperStock; **88** (l)Ancient Art and Architecture; (r)Ancient Art and Architecture; **89** Art Resource, NY; **90** George Chan/Photo Researchers; **94** Lynn Abercrombie; **95** SuperStock; **96** Michael Holford; **97** The British Museum, London/Bridgeman Art Library/Superstock; **98** file photo; **100** (r)Dat's Jazz/CORBIS; (l)Papilio/CORBIS; **101** (r)Werner Forman Archive, British Museum/Art Resource, NY; (l)Courtesy, Detroit Institute of Arts; (c)Bettmann/CORBIS; **102** (l)James L. Stanfield/National Geographic Image Collection; (r)Volkmar Kurt Wentzel/National Geographic Image Collection; **103** National Museum of Taipei; **105** Art Resource, NY; **106** (b)Bridgeman Art Library Int'l. Ltd. (U.S.); (t)Werner Forman Archive/Art Resource; **108** (l)CORBIS; (r)Ancient Art and Architecture; **109** M. Bryan Ginsberg; **111** Hidekaju Nishibata/SuperStock; **112** William H. Bond; **113** (inset)James L. Stanfield; (b)James L. Stanfield; (t)James L. Stanfield; **114** (t)Koji Nakamura; (b)William H. Bond; **116** Stock Montage; **117** Scala/Art Resource, NY; **118** Susan McCartney/Photo Researchers; **121** Giraudon/Art Resource, NY; **122** Scala/Art Resource, NY; **126** Peter Will/Bridgeman Art Library Int'l. Ltd. (U.S.); **127** (t)Adam Woolfitt/ National Geographic Image Collection; (cr)North Wind Picture Archives; (cl)Boltin Picture Library; (b)SuperStock; **128** Charles & Josette Lenars/CORBIS; **129** Mary Evans Picture Library; **130** Ancient Art & Architecture Collection; **132** Art Resource, NY; **133** AKG London; **134** SuperStock; **135** AKG London; **136** Staatliche Museen, Berlin, Photo ©Bildarchiv Preussischer Kulturbesitz; **137** (tr)Art Resource, NY; (tl)SuperStock; **138** Mary Evans Picture Library; **140** Christie's Images/CORBIS; **142** Gianni Dagli Orti/CORBIS; **143** Amwell/Stone; **144** Robert Harding Picture Library; **145** (l)Museum fuer Voelkerkunde, Staaliche Museen, Berlin, Germany/Art Resource; (r)Gianni Dagli Orti/CORBIS; **148** The Metropolitan Museum of Art, Edward Elliott Family Collection. Purchase, The Dillon Fund Gift, 1982. !982.2.2; **149** Bettmann Archive/CORBIS; 154 (l)AKG London/Rabatti – Dominigie; (r)AKG London; **154–155** AKG London/S. Domingie; **155** Stock Montage; **156** Sistine Chapel, Vatican, Rome/SuperStock, Inc.; **157** Scala/Art Resource, NY; **158** Art Resource, NY; **159** (l)Scala/Art Resource, NY; (r)Galleria Degli, Uffizi, Florence/SuperStock, Inc.; **160** AKG London; **161** (t)Archive/Photo Researchers, Inc.; (b)Musée du Louvre, Paris/SuperStock, Inc.; **162** Mary Evans Picture Library; **163** Scala/Art Resource, NY; **164** Scala/Art Resource, NY; **165** (l)Nicolo Orsi Battaglini/Art Resource, NY; (r)Art Resource, NY; **166** Scala/Art Resource, NY; **167** Vatican Museums & Galleries, Rome/Fratelli Alinari/SuperStock, Inc.; **168** (l)AKG London; (r)Vatican Museums & Galleries, Rome/Fratelli Alinari/SuperStock, Inc.; **169** (l)Erich Lessing/Art Resource, NY; (r)Scala/Art Resource, NY; **170** Victor R. Boswell, Jr.; (t)Mary Evans Picture Library; **171** ARCHIV/Photo Researchers, Inc.; **172** Ted Spiegel/Corbis; **173** (t)AKG London; (b)Erich Lessing/Art Resource, NY; **176** Art Resource, NY; **177** Mary Evans Picture Library; **178** Hulton Archive/Getty Images; **179** Scala/Art Resource, NY; **180** SuperStock, Inc.; **182** Giraudon/Art Resource, NY; **183** Scala/Art Resource, NY; **186** (br)Archiv/Photo Researchers, Inc.; (tr)North Wind Picture Archives; (l)Scala/Art Resource, NY; **186–187** Réunion des Musées Nationaux/Art Resource, NY; 405 Bluestone Production/SuperStock, Inc.; **188** (l)North Wind Picture Archives; (r)AKG Berlin/SuperStock, Inc.; **189** The Metropolitan Museum of Art, Gift of J. Pierpont Morgan, 1900(00.18.2); **191** (t)Peabody Essex Museum, Salem, MA; (b)AKG London; **194** AKG London/Ulrich Zillmann; **196** Bettmann/Corbis; **197** North Wind Picture Archives; **199** Art

Resource, NY; **200** Corbis; **201** Réunion des Musées Nationaux/Art Resource, NY; **202** (l)North Wind Picture Archives; (r)Gunshots/Art Archive; **203** AFP/Corbis; **204** Bettmann/Corbis; **205** Adam Woolfit/Corbis; **208** (l)AKG London/Joseph Martin; (r)National Portrait Gallery/SuperStock, Inc.; **208–209** Giraudon/Art Resource, NY; **209** (l)AKG London; (r)Stock Montage/SuperStock, Inc.; **210** (l)Scala/Art Resource, NY; (r)AKG London; **211** Francois Dubois D'Amiens, "The St. Barthlomew's Day Massacre," Musée Cantonal des Beaux-Arts, Lausanne; **212** Giraudon/Art Resource, NY.; **213** Archiv/Photo Researchers Inc.; **214** Bettmann/Corbis; **215** AKG London; **216** AKG London; **218** (pistol) Armee Museum, Ingolstadt, Germany/Bridgeman Art Library; (soldier) AKG London; **220** North Wind Pictures; **221** (l)Ronald Sheridan/Ancient Art & Architecture; (r)Peter Hoadley, William III and Mary Stuart, Rijksmuseum, Amersterdam; **222** (l)Museo Correr, Venice, Italy/Bridgeman Art Library; (r)Brian Wilson/Ancient Art & Architecture; **223** National Museum of American Art, Washington/Art Resource, NY; Réunion des Musées Nationaux/Art Resource, NY; **224** Giraudon/Art Resource, NY; **225** Giraudon/Art Resource, NY; **226** Hyacinthe Rigaud, "Louis XIV," Musée du Louvre, Photo R.M.N.; **227** AKG London; **229** Michael Holford; **230** John Taylor, "William Shakespeare", by courtesy of the National Portrait Gallery, London; **231** Scala/Art Resource, NY; **232** Musée des Beaux-Arts, Pau, France/Bridgeman Art Library; **236** (l)Historical Picture Archive/Corbis; (r)Arte & Immagini srl/Corbis; **236–237** Adam Woolfitt/Corbis; **237** (l)Otis Imboden; (r)Seattle Art Museum/Corbis; **238** Historical Picture Archive/Corbis; **239** Archivo Iconografico, S.A./Corbis; **240** AFP/Corbis; **243** Bettmann/Corbis; **244** Robert Frerck/Stone; **246** James L. Stanfield; **248** (l)James L. Stanfield; (r)James L. Stanfield; **249** (t b)James L. Stanfield; **250** Roger Wood/Corbis; **253** George Holton/Photo Researchers, Inc.; **254** SuperStock, Inc.; **255** Victoria and Albert Museum/Art Resource, NY; **258** Bettmann/Corbis; **260** Stone; **261** North Wind Picture Archives; **264** (l)ChinaStock; (r)Art Trade, Bonhams, London/Bridgeman Art Library; **264–265** Todd Gipstein/Corbis; **265** Fitzwilliam Museum, University of Cambridge, UK/Bridgeman Art Library; **266** (l)Reproduced by courtesy of the Trustees of the British Museum; (r)The Palace Museum, Beijing; **267** The Metropolitan Museum of Art, Rogers Fund, 1942 (42.121.2); **269** Christie's Images/Corbis; **270** Victoria & Albert Museum, London. UK/Bridgeman Art Library; **271** Wolfgang Kaehler/Corbis; **272** Mary Evans Picture Library; **273** 2001 North Wind Pictures; **274** Bridgeman Art Library; **275** (l)Philadelphia Free Library/AKG, Berlin/SuperStock, Inc.; (r)Ronald Sheridan/Ancient Art & Architecture; **276** G. Hunter/SuperStock, Inc.; **277** AFP/Corbis; **278** Michale Maslan Historic Photographs/Corbis; **279** Werner Forman Archive/Art Institute of Chicago/Art Resource, NY; **281** Tenri University, Japan; **282** Reuters NewMedia Inc./Corbis; **283** Michael Holford; **287** (tr)PhotoDisc; (l)Bettmann/Corbis; (br)The Huntington Library, Art Collections and Botanical Gardens/SuperStock, Inc.; **289** (t)Hulton Archive/Getty Images; (b)Robert Holmes/Corbis; **290** (l)Hulton Archive/Getty Images; (r)Archivo Iconographica, S.A./Corbis; **290–291** Giraudon/Art Resource, NY; **291** (t)Erich Lessing/Art Resource, NY; (b)Reproduction of a watercolour by JSC Schaak/Mary Evans Picture Library; **292** Private collection/Bridgeman Art Library; **293** North Wind Picture Archives; **294** Louvre, Paris, France/Bridgeman Art Library; **295** Bettmann/Corbis; **296** (t)Jean-Leon Huens; (b)North Wind Picture Archives; **297** (t)Library of Congress; (b)Hulton Archive/Getty Images; **298** Dumesnil, Queen Christina of Sweden with Descartes, Musée du Louvre, Photo ©R.M.N.; **299** Giraudon/Art Resource, NY; **300** Giraudon/Art Resource, NY; **301** (l)Bettmann/Corbis; (r)Bettmann/Corbis; **302** Erich Lessing/Art Resource, NY; **303** SuperStock, Inc.; **304** (l)Tate Gallery/Art Resource, NY; (r)Giraudon/Art Resource, NY; **305** Pablo Corral V/Corbis; **307** Nathaniel Hone, John Wesley, ca. 1766, courtesy of the National Portrait Gallery, London; **308** Christel Gerstenberg/Corbis; **309** Francis G. Mayer/Corbis; **310** (l)Giraudon/Art Resource, NY; (r)Bettmann/Corbis; **311** Giraudon/Art Resource, NY; **312** (tr)Scala/Art Resource, NY; (l)Hermitage/Bridgeman Art Library; (br)Giraudon/Art Resource, NY; **314** Archivo Iconografico, S.A./Corbis; **315** North Wind Picture Archives; **317** Stock Montage; **318** Giraudon/Art Resource, NY; **320** Mexican, unknown artist, Portrait of Sister Juana Ines de la Cruz [Detail], Philadelphia Museum of Art: The Robert H Lamborn Collection/Philadelphia Museum of Art; **321** Yale University Art Gallery; **323** Corbis; **326** (l)Musée de la Ville de Paris, Musée Carnavalet, Paris, France/Bridgeman Art Library; (r)Réunion des Musées Nationaux/Art Resource, NY; **326–327** Erich Lessing/Art Resource, NY; **327** (l)Chateau de Versailles, France/Bridgeman Giraudon; (r)Bonhams, London, UK/ Bridgeman Art Library; **328** AKG London; **329** Giraudon/Art Resource, NY; **331** Musée Carnavalet, Paris, France/Bridgeman Giraudon; **332** AKG London; **333** Rueters NewMedia Inc./Corbis; **334** (t)Stock Montage; (b)Giraudon/Art Resource, NY; **335** Giraudon/Art Resource, NY; **336** Erich Lessing/Art Resource, NY; **337** AKG London/Jerome da Cunha; **338** (l)Giraudon/Art Resource, NY; (r)Mary Evans Picture Library; **339** (l)Hulton-Deutsch Collection/Corbis; (c)Stock Montage; (r)Giraudon/Art Resource, NY; **340** Musée Carnavalet, Paris, France/Roger-Viollet, Paris/Bridgeman Art Library; **341** Dupelessis-Bertaux, engraved by Malapeau/Mary Evans Picture Library; **343** Réunion des Musées Nationaux/Art Resource, NY; **345** Museum of Art History, Vienna/AKG, Berlin/SuperStock, Inc.; **346** Giraudon/Art Resource, NY; **347** Gianni Dagli Orti/Corbis; **348** Giraudon/Art Resource, NY; **350** AKG London; **354** (l)Giraudon/Art Resource, NY; (r)Christel Gerstenberg/Corbis; **355** Réunion des Musées Nationaux/Art Archive; **356** SuperStock, Inc.; **356–357** Hulton-Deutsch Collection/Corbis; **357** Rhodes Memorial Museum, USA/Bridgeman Art Library; **358** Stock Montage; **359** (t)Library of Congress; (b)Laurie Platt Winfrey; **360** Bettmann/Corbis; **360–361** Science Museum/Science & Society Picture Library; **361** (l)Mary Evans Picture Library; (c)Archivo Iconografico, S.A./Corbis; (r)Mary Evans Picture Library; **362** (l)Stock Montage/SuperStock, Inc.; (r)Bettmann/ Corbis; **363** National Trust/Art Resource, NY; **364** Bettmann/Corbis; **365** Gianni Dagli Orti/Corbis; **368** Library of Congress, Prints and Photographs Division, Detroit Publishing Co. Collection; **369** Culver Pictures, Inc.; **370** Mary Evans Picture Library; **371** Woldemar Friedrich in Die Deutschen Befreiungskriege/Mary Evans Picture Library; **373** Austrian Information Service; **374** (l)Lecomte, Battle in the rue de Rohan, 1830, Giraudon/Art Resource, NY; (r)Giraudon/Art Resource, NY; **375** Hulton-Deutsch Collection/Corbis; **377** (l)Bettmann/Corbis; (r)Mary Evans Picture Library; **378** Museo Civico Modigliana/Dagli Orti/Art Archive; **381** "Proclamation of the German Empire at Versailles", 1871, Anton von Werner, Photo Bildarchiv Preussicher Kulturbesitz, Berlin; **382** (l)Musée du Chateau de Versailles/Dagli Orti/Art Archive; (r)David David Gallery/SuperStock, Inc.; **383** Ullstein Bilderdeinst, Berlin; **384** Bettmann/Corbis; **386** Explorer/SuperStock, Inc.; **387** National Portrait Gallery/SuperStock, Inc.; **388** Eye Ubiquitous/Corbis; **389** The Art Archive/Victoria and Albert Museum London; **390** Erich Lessing/Art Resource, NY; **391** Staatliche Kunstsammlungen, Dresden, Germany/ Bridgeman Art Library, London/SuperStock, Inc.; **394** (l)Culver Pictures Inc.; (r)Underwood & Underwood/Corbis; **394–395** Burstein Collection/ Corbis; **395** (l)AKG London; (r)Private Collection/Barbara Singer/ Bridgeman Art Library; **396** Lake County Museum/Corbis; **397** Hulton Archive/Getty Images; **398** (l)Liaison Agency; (r)Tom Burnside/Photo Researchers, Inc.; **400** AP/Wide World Photos; **402** Verein fur Geschichte der Arbeiterbewegung, Vienna; **403** Hulton Archive/Getty Images; **406** Musée de la Poste, Paris, photo J.L.Charmet; **407** Snark/Art Resource, NY; **408** North Wind Picture Archives; **409** Bettmann/Corbis; **410** Hulton Archive/Getty Images; **411** Mary Evans Picture Library; **413** Bettmann/Corbis; **414** Hulton Archive/Getty Images; **417** SuperStock, Inc.; **418** Musée d'Orsay, Paris/Giraudon, Paris/SuperStock, Inc.; **419** (tl)Hulton Archive/Getty Images; (r)ARCHIV/Photo Researchers, Inc.; (bl)National Portrait Gallery, Smithsonian Institution/Art Resource, NY; **421** Museum of Art, Providence/Lauros-Giraudon, Paris/SuperStock, Inc.; **422** The Starry Night, 1889, Museum of Modern Art, NY; **423** Photo ©E. Louis Lankford; **426** (l)Hulton Archive/Getty Images; **426** (r)Frances Lemmens/Image Bank; **426–427** Hulton Archive/Getty Images; **427** (l)Hulton Deutsch Collection/Corbis; (r)Brown Brothers; **428** (l)Image Select/Art Resource, NY; (r)Hulton Archive/Getty Images; **429** Musée Nat. du Chateau de Malmaison, Rueil Malmaison/Lauros-Giraudon, Paris/North Wind Picture Archives; **432** (t b)North Wind Picture Archives; **433** North Wind Picture Archives; **434** Sipahioglu/Liaison; **435** North Wind Picture Archives; **436** Hulton Archive/Getty Images; **438** (t)Hulton Archive/Getty Images; (b)Leeds Museums and Galleries/Bridgeman Art Library; **439** Hulton-Deutsch Collection/Corbis; **444** North Wind Picture Archives; **445** (falls) Royal Geographical Society, London, UK/Bridgeman Art Library; (journal) From The Last Journals of David Livingstone, in Central Africa, Harper & Brothers, Publishers, 1875; photograph by Mark Thiessen; (map) Royal Geographical Society, London; (sextant) Royal Geographical Society, London; **447** (t)The Picture Desk; (b)Hulton-Deutsch Collection/Corbis; **448** Hulton Archive/Getty Images; **449** North Wind Picture Archives; (tl)Bridgeman Art Library; (tr)The Stapleton Collection/Bridgeman Art Library; **451** (l)Hulton Archive/Getty Images; (r)Werner Forman/Art Resource, NY; **453** Giraudon/Art Resource, NY; **454** Schalkwijk/Art Resource, NY; **455** Museu Nacional de Belas Artes Rio de Janeiro/Dagli Orti/Art Archive; **457** Underwood & Underwood/ Corbis; **458** Bettmann/Corbis; **459** Hulton-Deutsch Collection/Corbis; 680 Peabody Essex Museum, Salem, Mass. Photo by Mark Sexton; **462–463** National Maritime Museum, London; **463** (t)Camera Press/Globe Photos; (b)Asian Art & Archaeology, Inc./Corbis; **464** (l)SuperStock, Inc.; (r)Dean Conger/Corbis; **465** Royal Ontario Museum/Corbis; **467** Christopher Morris/Blackstar/TimePix; **468** (t)Harper's Weekly/Corbis; (inset)Mary Evans Picture Library; (b)M. Setboun/Sygma; **470** Courtesy of the Freer Gallery of Art, Smithsonian Institution, Washington, DC; **471** Bettmann/ Corbis; **472** Michael Newman/PhotoEdit/PictureQuest; **473** Bettmann/ Corbis; **474** (t)Keystone, Paris/Sygma; (b)Hulton-Deutsch Collection/ Corbis; **475** UPI/Bettmann; **476** Bettmann/Corbis; **478** ChinaStock; **479** Michael Maslan Historic Photographs/Corbis; **480** Courtesy of the United States Naval Academy Museum; **481** Bettmann/Corbis; **482** Tom Wagner/Saba; **483** The Metropolitan Museum of Art, Gift of Lincoln

Kirstein, 1959 (JP 3276), photograph by Otto E. Nelson; **485** Culver Pictures, Inc.; **486** Private Collection/Bridgeman Art Library/SuperStock, Inc.; **487** (l)Corbis; (r)AKG London; **490** (t b)Hulton Archive/Getty Images; **491** Mary Evans Picture Library; **492** Ira Nowinski/Corbis; **492–493** Hulton Archive/Getty Images; **493** Hulton Archive/Getty Images; **494** Bettmann/Corbis; **495** (t)United Nations Photo Library; (b)David & Peter Turnley/Corbis; **496** Hulton Archive/Getty Images; **496–497** Bridgeman Art Library; **497** (t b)Bettmann/Corbis; **498** (l)Hulton Archive/Getty Images; (r)Hulton-Deutsch Collection/Corbis; **499** Bettmann Archive; **501** SEF/Art Resource, NY; **503** ©Roger-Viollet, Paris; **504** Collection of Colonel Stuart S. Corning. Photo: Rob Huntley: Lightstream; **505** Hulton Archive/Getty Images; **506** (l)John H. Clark/Corbis; (r)Hulton Archive/Getty Images; **508** Minnesota Historical Society/Corbis; **509** Hulton Archive/Getty Images; **510** (tl)Bettmann/Corbis; (r)Brown Brothers; (bl)Brown Brothers; **511** Titanic Historical Society; **512** Jonathan Blair; **513** (l)Bowman Gray Collection, Rare Book Collection, The University of North Carolina at Chapel Hill; **513** (r)Jonathan Blair; **514** Corbis; **515** Bettmann/Corbis; (inset)Bettmann/Corbis; **516** (l)Rykoff Collection/Corbis; (r)Hulton Archive/Getty Images; **518** Bettmann/Corbis; **519** Bettmann/Corbis; **520** Brown Brothers; **521** Hulton Archive/Getty Images; **524** Réunion des Musées Nationaux/Chateaux de Versailles et deTrianon/Art Resource, NY; **526** National Portrait Gallery, Smithsonian Institution/Art Resource, NY; **530** Hulton Archive/Getty Images; **530–531** Hugo Jaeger/TimePix; **531** (t)National Portrait Gallery, Smithsonian Institute/Art Resource, NY; (b)AKG London; **532** Bettmann Archive; **533** Hulton-Deutsch Collection/Corbis; **534** Culver Pictures Inc.; **536** Bettmann Archive; **537** Bettmann/Corbis; **538** Hulton Archive/Getty Images; **539** David Low/London Evening Standard/Solo Syndication Limited; **540** Hulton Archive/Getty Images; **542** L'Illustration/Sygma; **543** Explorer, Paris/SuperStock, Inc.; **544** Bettmann Archive; **546** Centro de Arte Reina Sofia, Madrid, Spain/Giraudon, Paris/SuperStock, Inc.; **547** ©The Hulton Getty Picture Collection/Stone; **548** Corbis; **549** Hulton-Deutsch Collection/Corbis; **550** Snark/Art Resource, NY; **551** AP/Wide World Photos; **552** (l)Bettmann/Corbis; (c)Seidman Collection/Culver Pictures, Inc.; (r)Mary Evans Picture Library; **553** SuperStock, Inc.; **554** Stefano Bianchetti/Corbis; **555** (l)E.O. Hopp/Corbis; (r)AKG London; **556** Museum of Modern Art, New York, USA/Bridgeman Art Library; **560** (l)Hulton-Deutsch Collection/Corbis; (r)Hulton Archive/Getty Images; **560-561** Schalkwijk/Art Resource, NY; **561** (t)Barry Iverson/TimePix; (b)Stock Montage; **562** Hulton Archive/Getty Images; **563** Hulton-Deutsch Collection/Corbis; **564** (t)Corbis; (b)Hulton Archive/Getty Images; **565** Bridgeman Art Library; **566** Bettmann/Corbis; **568** Black Star; **571** H. Rogers/Art Directors & TRIP Photo Library; **574** (t)Reuters/David Loh/TimePix; (b)Charles Bonnay/TimePix; **575** AFP Worldwide; **576** Hulton Archive/Getty Images; **578** Hulton-Deutsch Collection/Corbis; **579** (l)SIPA Press; (r)AP/Wide World Photos; **580** Life Images; **581** Hulton Archive/Getty Images; **583** Underwood & Underwood/Corbis; **585** Peter Menzel/Stock Boston; **588** Hulton Getty/Tony Stone Images; **588–589** Dallas and John Heaton/Corbis; **589** (tl)AKG London; (tr)Culver Pictures, Inc.; (b)AKG London; **590** (l)AKG London; (r)Hugo Jaeger/TimePix; **591** Bettmann/Corbis; **592** Mary Evans Picture Library; **595** Bettmann/Corbis; **596** National Archives (#306-NT-1222E); **597** Bettmann Archive; **600** TimePix; **601** Hulton Archive/Getty Images; **603** Hultun-Deutsch Collection/Corbis; **605** Hulton Archive/Getty Images; **606** Corbis; **607** AKG London; **608** file photo; **609** file photo; **610** Bettmann/Corbis; **612** Corbis; **613** AKG London; **614** file photo; **615** (l)Bettmann/Corbis; (r)AFP/Corbis; **616** J.R. Eyerman, Life Magazine, ©Time Warner Inc.; **618** E.T. Archive; **619** The Herald & Evening Times Picture Library ©Caledonian Newspapers Ltd.; **622** (l)Bettmann/Corbis; (r)Bridgeman/Art Resource, NY; **623** Bettmann/Corbis; **624** Contemporary African Art Collection Limited/Corbis; **624–625** David & Peter Turnley/Corbis; **625** Eric Bouvet/Liason; **626** UPI/Bettmann/Corbis; **627** (t)Eye Ubiquitous/Corbis; (b)Liu Liqun/Corbis; **628** Moore, Charles/Black Star; **628–629** Sovfoto/Eastfoto; **629** (l)Bettmann/Corbis; (r)Lopinot, John/Black Star; **630** Hulton-Deutsch Collection/Corbis; **631** Woodfin Camp & Associates; **632** AP/Wide World Photos; **636** UPI/Bettmann; **637** Bettmann/Corbis; **638** Sovfoto/Eastfoto; **639** Semyon Raskin/Magnum Photos; **640** ©Prache-Lewin/Sygma; **642** Marc Riboud/Magnum Photos; **643** (l)UPI/Bettmann; (r)Bettmann/Corbis; **644** (l)Hulton-Deutsch Collection/Corbis; (r)Bettmann/Corbis; **646** Bettmann/Corbis; **647** Henry Diltz/Corbis; **648** (t)Ruffner, Howard/Black Star; (bl)Lido/SIPA Press; (r)P. Treanor/Art Directors & TRIP Photo Library; **649** Elliott Erwitt/Magnum Photos; **650** ©C. Raimond-Dityvon/Viva, Woodfin Camp and Associates; **651** AP/Wide World Photos; **654** Werner Wolf/Black Star; **654–655** NASA; **655** (l)Reuters/Bettmann; (r)AP/Wide World Photos; **656** Reuters Bettmann; **657** Novosti/Gamma-Liaison; **659** Reuters/Bettmann; **661** AP/Wide World Photos; **662** AP/Wide World Photos; **664** AFP/Bettmann; **665** Bettmann/Corbis; **666** Mark Simon/Black Star Publishing/PictureQuest; **667** Hulton Archive/Getty Images; **669** Wally McNamee/Corbis; **671** By arrangement with E. F. Schumacher Society, 140 Jug End Road, Great Barrington, MA 01230 www.smallisbeautiful.org, Photo ©Sophie Baker; **672** Matthew McDermott/Corbis Sygma; **675** Hans Namuth Ltd./photo ©Hans Namuth.; **676** Steve McCurry/Magnum/PictureQuest; **677** Tim Wright/Corbis; **680** (l)UPI/Bettmann; (r)AFP/Corbis; **680–681** Stone; **681** (t)Hulton Archive/Getty Images; (b)AFP Worldwide; **682** AFP/Corbis; **683** James Nachtwey/Magnum Photos; **686** Lentz, Vera/Black Star; **687** Bettmann/Corbis; **688** B. Nicklesberg/Woodfin Camp & Associates; Bettmann/Corbis; **689** Bettmann/Corbis; **691** Chip Hires/Gamma Presse; **692** Bettmann/Corbis; **693** Bettmann/Corbis; **694** AFP Worlwide; **696** Emblin, Richard/Black Star; **697** Bettmann/Corbis; **700** The Purcell Team/Corbis; **700–701** Corbis; **701** (t)Hulton Archive/Getty Images; (bl)Corbis; (br)David Turnley/Corbis; **702** (l)Bettmann/Corbis; (r)Adam Woolfit/Woodfin Camp & Associates; **703** Archives Humanité, Diffusion Keystone/Gamma Press; **705** (l)Reuters/Mike Hutchings/Archive Photos; (r)Yousuf Karsh/Woodfin Camp & Associates; **706** Yann Arthus-Bertrand/Corbis; **707** Louis Gubb/JB Pictures; **708** (l)David Keith Jones/Images of Africa Photobank; (r)David Keith Jones/Images of Africa Photobank; **709** Betty Press/Woodfin Camp & Associates; **711** David Rubinger/Woodfin Camp; **712** Betty Press/Woodfin Camp & Associates; **714** (tr)UPPA/Photoreporters; (l)Buu Alain/Gamma; (br)Bettmann/Corbis; **715** (l)David & Peter Turnley/Corbis; (r)Barry Iverson/Woodfin Camp & Associates; **717** Dean Conger/Corbis; **720** (l)Hulton Archive/Getty Images; (r)UPI/Bettmann; **720–721** Bob Krist/Stone; **721** (t)Sygma; (b)Morris, Christopher/Black Star; **722** (l)AP/Wide World Photos; (r)Langevin/Sygma; **723** Bettmann Archive; **724** Marc Riboud/Magnum Photos; **725** Chuck Fishman/Woodfin Camp & Associates; **727** Hulton Archive/Getty Images; **726** US Army Signal Corps/Courtesy of the National Archives/Woodfin Camp & Associates; **730** Stephen Shaver/AFP/Corbis; **731** AP/Wide World Photos; **732** (t b)Stuart Franklin; **733** David and Peter Turnley/Corbis; **734** Chris Brown/SABA/Corbis; **735** Newsmakers/Getty/Liaison Agency; **736** Bettmann/Corbis; **738** file photo; **739** Mike Yamashita/Woodfin Camp & Associates; **740** Library of Congress/Woodfin Camp & Associates; **742** Lindsay Hebberd/Woodfin Camp & Associates; **745** Tom Wagner/Corbis; **748** Hulton Archive/Getty Images; **748–749** NASA; **749** Paul Fusco/Magnum/PictureQuest; **750** AFP/Corbis; **751** Bettmann/Corbis; **753** NASA; **756** Courtesy of the Franklin D. Roosevelt Library; **757** Wesley Bocxe/Photo Researchers, Inc.; **758** Christopher Morris/Black Star/PictureQuest; **759** David Gates/Morgan-Cain & Associates; **760** (t)AP/Wide World Photos; (b)Masterfile; **763** The Butler Institute of American Art; **765** (l)Brown Brothers; (r)Francis G. Mayer/Corbis; **764** PhotoDisc; **772** Anne & Jon Abbott, NYC; **773** (l)Réunion des Musées Nationaux/Art Resource, NY; (r)Ancient Art & Architecture Collection , Ltd.; **774** Scala/Art Resource, NY; **775** Musée d'Orsay/SuperStock, Inc.; **776** (t)Stock Montage; (b)Alinari/Art Resource, NY; **777** The Lowe Art Musuem, The University of Miami/SuperStock, Inc.; **778** Hulton Archive/Getty Images; **780** Bridgeman Art Library; **781** (l)Hulton-Deutsch Collection/Corbis; (r)Hulton-Deutsch Collection/Corbis; **782** Bettmann/Corbis